CW01095251

Proceedings

15th International Conference on Pattern Recognition

ICPR-2000

Volume 4

Applications, Robotics, Systems and Architectures

Proceedings

15th International Conference on Pattern Recognition

Barcelona, Spain

September 3 – 7, 2000

Volume 4

Applications, Robotics, Systems and Architectures

Editors

A. Sanfeliu
J.J. Villanueva
M. Vanrell
R. Alquézar
J. Crowley
Y. Shirai

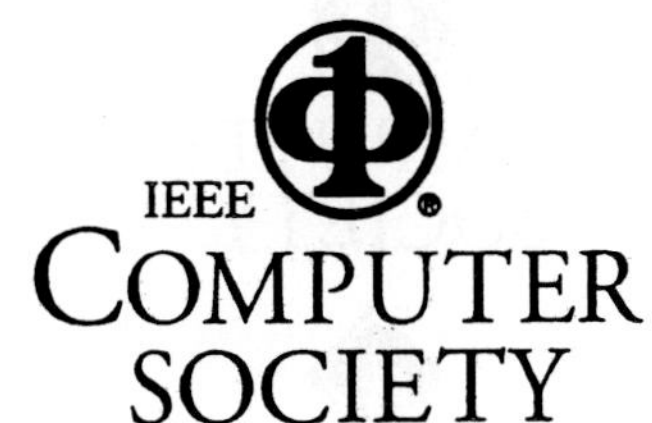

Los Alamitos, California

Washington • Brussels • Tokyo

IEEE Computer Society Order Number PR00750
ISBN 0-7695-0750-6
ISBN 0-7695-0751-4 (case)
ISBN 0-7695-0752-2 (microfiche)
ISSN Number 1051-4651
D. L.: B-36.189-2000

Additional copies may be ordered from:

IEEE Computer Society
Customer Service Center
10662 Los Vaqueros Circle
P.O. Box 3014
Los Alamitos, CA 90720-1314
Tel: + 1-714-821-8380
Fax: + 1-714-821-4641
E-mail: cs.books@computer.org

IEEE Service Center
445 Hoes Lane
P.O. Box 1331
Piscataway, NJ 08855-1331
Tel: + 1-732-981-0060
Fax: + 1-732-981-9667
http://shop.ieee.org/store/
customer-service@ieee.org

IEEE Computer Society
Asia/Pacific Office
Watanabe Bldg., 1-4-2
Minami-Aoyama
Minato-ku, Tokyo 107-0062
JAPAN
Tel: + 81-3-3408-3118
Fax: + 81-3-3408-3553
tokyo.ofc@computer.org

Editorial production by Bob Werner
Cover design by Ernest Estruga
Cover art production by Joe Daigle/Studio Productions

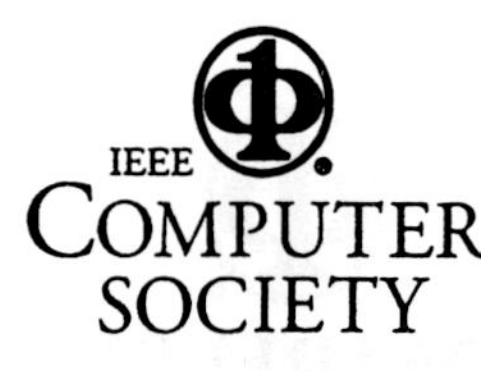

Table of Contents

International Conference on Pattern Recognition — ICPR 2000

Session O4.2A. Image Processing

Session O4.2B. Reconstruction and Synthesis of Images

Session O4.3A. Vision for Robotics

Session O4.3B. Real Time Systems

Session O4.4A. Observation of Humans and Actions I

Session O4.4B. Observation of Humans and Actions II

Poster Presentations

Session P4.1A. Image Database Indexing and Retrieval

Session P4.1A. Remote Sensing

Session P4.1B. Biomedical Imaging and Applications

Session P4.1B. OCR and Document Analysis I

Session P4.2A. OCR and Document Analysis II

Session P4.2A. Virtual Reality and Image Synthesis

Session P4.2B. Automation and Robotics

Session P4.2B. OCR and Document Analysis III

Session P4.3A. Reconstruction and 3D Modeling

Session P4.3A. Surveillance and Monitoring I

Session P4.3B. Mobile Robots

Session P4.3B. Real Time Systems

Session P4.3B. Surveillance and Monitoring II

Session P4.4A. Smart Sensors

Session P4.4A. Visual Inspection

Session P4.4B. Parallel Algorithms and Languages

Session P4.4B. Recognition

Session P5.2B. Contests

Message from the ICPR2000 General Co-Chairs

Welcome to the 15th International Conference on Pattern Recognition and welcome to Barcelona!

Firstly, we would like to thank you all for participating in the ICPR2000. It has been an honour for us to have such a good reception. We never expected so many papers to be sent for submission. It has been a nice surprise.

We received 1438 papers and, we have finally accepted 973 (410 for Track 1; 251 for Track 2; 114 for Track 3; and, 198 for Track 4). From all those received we had to reject some very good papers for logistic reasons, and this large submission delayed the review process for different reasons. We therefore want to offer our apologies for all the changes we have made with the conference dates. We hope we have not caused too many inconveniences to the participants.

In this conference we have incorporated some new issues that we believe makes ICPR more attractive. As well as the combination of four parallel tracks of sessions with their respective Plenary Invited Speakers, we have included Invited Papers and Contests to increase the participation of the congress's people in this event. We have tried to put an Invited Paper for each oral session. We have specially invited 26 well known specialists in order for them to present the state of the art of a topic giving a personal review and outlook in a provocative, entertaining and meaningful way. We have also included several Contests to encourage the participation of research groups to solve specific issues.

We want to thank the help of many people. First of all the help of Edzard Gelsema Ex-president of IAPR, who's death surprised us during the organization of the Congress. We want to give special thanks to the Local Organization Co-Chairs, Maria Vanrell and René Alquézar for their dedication and devotion to ICPR2000, and to Mérida McCarthy for her administrative assistance. We would like to express our appreciation to all the referees for their excellent work and patience, specially considering the unexpected "avalanche" of papers. The work of the Track Chairs for their support at all times, and for maintaining the very high scientific quality of the conference, is also specially recognised. We also want to thank to members of the IAPR, the Centre de Visió per Computador, the Institut de Robòtica e Informàtica Industrial, the ESAII and the OTAC for their valuable help in the organization of the congress. Last but not least, we want to thank specially the collaboration in the organization of the Spanish Association for Pattern Recognition and Image Analysis (AERFAI), the Universitat Politècnica de Catalunya and the Universitat Autònoma de Barcelona.

We hope you all enjoy the conference and your stay in Barcelona!

Alberto Sanfeliu
Juan José Villanueva
ICPR2000 General Co-Chairs

Message from the Acting President of IAPR

It is my great pleasure to welcome you to the 15th International Conferencc on Pattern Recognition. This conference is the main event of the International Association for Pattern Recognition (IAPR). I hope you'll find it rewarding to attend the technical sessions, enjoy meeting colleagues and friends, and have some time for sightseeing in the beautiful city of Barcelona.

This ICPR is special for several reasons. First, it will be the last ICPR in this millenium. Secondly, it received the most papers ever submitted to an ICPR, and the organizers expect the largest number of people ever attending an ICPR. And thirdly, it marks 25 successful years of IAPR activities. Strictly speaking, IAPR was only founded at the 3rd International Conference on Pattern Recognition in Coronado, California, on November 8, 1976. But a sigificant portion of the work to set up the organization was actually done in the year 1975.

The large attendance to this conference is a clear indication of the growing importance of our field. But there are other indicators as well. Since the last ICPR held in Brisbane two years ago, the number of national member societies grew from 32 to 37, with New Zealand, Ireland, France, Turkey, and Cuba joining IAPR as new members. There seems to be even potential for a further increase in the number of member societies, particularly in South America and Africa. IAPR is a very active community. Looking at the previous issues of our Newsletter, I counted nearly 30 IAPR Workshops and Conferences held in 1999 and 2000, in addition to ICPR. All these developments and activities clearly show that our discipline is in very prosperous state.

The year 2000 brought us not only good news. It was with great sadness that we had to accept the deaths of IAPR President E. Gelsema and former IAPR President J.C. Simon. They are missed by all of us. We will remember them always as leading scientists, active promoters of IAPR, and fine individuals.

I would like to take this opportunity to express my appreciation to all our colleagues who were engaged in the organization of this conference, especially to the General Co-Chairs and the Track Co-Chairs. Furthermore, many thanks go to the organizers of various IAPR events and the chairs and members of various committees, particularly the Executive Committee.

It has been very enjoyable and rewarding for me to cooperate with them.

Horst Bunke
University of Bern
Bern, Switzerland
IAPR President

Message from the ICPR2000 Local Organizing Committee Co-Chairs

Welcome to Barcelona and thanks for participating in the 15th International Conference on Pattern Recognition. We thank all the participants and all the people who expressed their interest or will to participate but for any reasons have not finally come.

First of all, we want to thank the opportunity we have had of organizing this event. The organization of a conference like ICPR2000 has been a source of valuable experiences and has given the opportunity to collaborate with many people of our scientific community. Most of the organization has been done using a web-based software which has kept all the data updated and allowed all the people involved in the organization to share all the information at any time. Even though this has brought slight problems, it has been very useful, simplifying all the communications in general. From here, we want to encourage the future organizers to go further in digitalisation and electronic communication in all the stages of the conference organization including the final publication of all the papers.

Due to the large amount of submitted papers, the review process was especially difficult and we would like to thank all the referees for their kind contribution and for their patience, the non-digital shipping of papers introduced the most important delay in the organization. In this respect, we want to express our gratitude to all the track chairs, Yiannis Aloimonos, Jan-Olof Eklundh, Anil K. Jain, Josef Kittler, Tom Huang, Jean Serra, James Crowley and Yoshiaki Shirai, who have been ready to do at any moment all the tasks concerning the technical program. They are responsible of the high technical level of this conference. In this sense, we also want to specially thank to Joan Climent for preparing an excellent tutorial program.

We also appreciate the help of the IAPR Executive Committee, as well as Brian Lovell and Walter Kropatsch as main organizers of previous ICPR conferences, for their guidelines, comments and suggestions, and of Susan and Michael Duff in the dissemination of news regarding this event.

Obviously, this kind of events are not strictly organised by two people, we have always been supported by our colleagues from the Centre de Visió per Computadora of the UAB and the Institut de Robòtica i Informàtica Industrial of the UPC, from them we want to specially thank to Ernest Valveny, Josep Lladós, Albert Pujol, Ramon Baldrich and Xavier Roca.

Finally, we want to thank the help of many people who have taken responsibilities for different parts of the organization. In particular, to Mérida McCarthy for her excellent administrative support and willingness, Pere Quintana for the multiple organization tasks, Imma Valls and Joan Masoliver for their full time assistance on the computer programs and Ernest Estruga for his excellent designs. We also, want to thank to Tom Baldwin, Bob Werner and Lorretta Palagi of the IEEE CS Press for all the facilities in the publication process.

Maria Vanrell
René Alquézar
ICPR2000 Local Organizing Co-Chairs

ICPR2000 Technical Chairs and Referees

Computer Vision and Image Analysis Chairs

Yiannis Aloimonos
Computer Vision Laboratory — Center for Automation Research
University of Maryland, USA

Jan-Olof Eklundh
Computer Science Department
KTH, Royal Institute of Technology, Sweden

Pattern Recognition and Neural Networks Chairs

Anil K. Jain
Computer Science & Engineering Department
Michigan State University, USA

Josef Kittler
Centre for Vision, Speech and Signal Processing
University of Surrey, United Kingdom

Image, Speech and Signal Processing Chairs

Thomas Huang
Beckman Institute
University of Illinois at Urbana-Champaign, USA

Jean Serra
Centre de Morphologie Mathématique
Ecole Supérieure des Mines de Paris, France

Applications, Robotics, Systems and Architectures Chairs

James Crowley
GRAVIR of the Institut IMAG
INRIA Rhône Alpes, France

Yoshiaki Shirai
Dept. of Computer-Controlled Mechanical Systems
Osaka University, Japan

Referees

Track 1: Computer Vision and Image Analysis

Anand, M.N.
Angelopoulou, Elli
Antani, Sameer
Baldrich, Ramon
Basu, Anup
Bhanu, Bir
Bhattacharya, Prabir
Binefa, Xavi
Bischof, Horst
Bobick, Aaron
Bolle, Ruud
Boult, Terry
Branca, Antonella
Burkhardt, Hans
Buxton, Bernard
Caelli, Terry
Charou, Eleni
Chellappa, Rama
Christensen, Henrik
Connell, Jonathan
Coombs, Dave
Cootes, Terry
Crandall, David
Crowley, James
da Fontoura Costa, Luciano
Daniilidis, Kostas
Del Bimbo, Alberto
DeMenthon, Daniel
Deriche, Rachid
Dhome, Michel
Doermann, David
Draper, Bruce
Drew, Mark
Escolano Ruiz, Francisco
Fermueller, Cornelia
Finlayson, Graham
Fisher, Robert
Gandhi, Tarak
Garcia-Sevilla, Pedro
Gargi, Ullas
Haar Romeny, B. M. Ter
Hancock, Edwin
Haralick, Bob
Hassan, Khuram
Heikkilä, Janne
Hlavac, Vaclav
Hoey, Jesse
Hogg, David
Hordley, Steven
Javeed, Omer
Johansen, Peter
Jyrkinen, Lasse
Kaminski, Jeremie
Kanatani, Kenichi
Kanungo, Tapas
Kasturi, Rangachar
Khan, Sohaib
Lavest, Jean-Marc
Leberl, Franz
Lee, Sang
Little, Jim
Lladós, Josep
Lopez, Antonio
Lopez-Krahe, Jaime
Lourakis, Manolis
Lowe, David
Maachi, Waren
Madsen, Claus B.
Marchand-Maillet, Stéphane
Mariano, Vladimir
Martí, Enric
Martínez, Judith
Matsuyama, Takashi
Mau-Tsuen , Yang
Maybank, Stephen
Medioni, Gerard
Milios, Evangelos
Minoh, Michihiko
Mori, Yasuhide
Myles, Zarina
Nayar, Shree
Nelson, Randal
Neumann, Bernd
Neumann, Jan
Nishimura, Takuichi
Oikarinen, Jarkko
Ojala, Timo
Okun, Oleg
Oliensis, John
Oren, Michael
Orphanoudakis, Stelios
Pankanti, Sharath
Park, J.H.
Peleg, Shmuel
Perales, Francisco
Petkovic, Dragutin
Pietikäinen, Matti
Pla, Filiberto
Plamondon, Re'jean
Pujol, Albert
Pun, Thierry
Qiu, Maolin
Radeva, Petia
Rao, Cen
Rasheed, Zeeshan
Reid, Ian
Rigoutsos, Isidore
Roca, Xavi
Röning, Juha
Sakurai, Shigeaki
Saludes, Jordi
Sánchez, Xavier
Scherer, Stephan
Se, Stephen
Segal, Dana
Serrat, Joan
Shah, Mubarak
Sharma, Rajeev
Shavit, Adi
Shirai, Yoshiaki
Shizawa, Masahiko
Siddiqi, Kaleem
Silven, Olli
Smeulders, Arnold
Soini, Antti
Sommer, Gerald
Spetsakis, Minas
Sporring, Jon
Stark, Louise
Stevkovska, Jasmina
Sturm, Peter
Tistarelli, Massimo
Toledo, Ricardo
Triggs, Bill
Valveny, Ernest
Vanrell, Maria
Varona, Xavi
Vemuri, Baba
Venkatesh, S.
Verri, Alessandro
von Seelen, Werner
Walker, Ellen
Weiss, Isaac
Yabe, Hiroaki
Yachida, Masahiko
Yeshurun, Hezy
Yilmaz, Alper
Zomet, Assaf

Track 2: Pattern Recognition and Neural Networks

Abdel-Mottaleb, Mohammed
Abdulghafour, Muhamad
Aladjem, Mayer
Alquezar, Rene
Amin, Adnan
Baldrich, Ramon
Buhmann, Joachim
Chen, Sei-Wang
Climent, Joan
Dawoud, Amer
De Ridder, Dick
Duin, Robert
Farshad, Ramin
Feiguth, Paul
Ferri, Francesc
Flusser, J.
Ghosh, Joydeep
Giles, C. Lee
Grau, Antoni
Grim, J.
Gunsel, Bilge
Gyouten, Keiji
Haindl, M.
Hamamoto, Yoshihiko
Hancock, Edwin
Ho, Tin Kam
Hodge, Lovell
Imaya, Atsushi
Jain, Anil
Jelinek, J.
Jolion, Jean-Michel
Kamel, Mohamed
Kimura, Humitaka
Kropatsch, Walter
Kumazawa, Itsuo
Li, Stan
Llados, Josep
Lopez, Antonio
Lovell, Brian
Lumbreras, Felipe
Marszalec, Elzbieta
Martí, Enric
Martínez, Judit
Matas, Jiri
Mayer, H.
Michalek, J.
Mitani, Yoshihiro
Mizukami, Yoshiki
Murni, Aniati
Murshed, Nabeel
Murty, M. Narasimha
Novovicova, J.
Ogawa, Hidemitsu
Ohmachi, Shinichiro
Oommen, B. John
Paclik, P.
Pekalska, Elzbieta
Pelillo, Marcello
Petrou, Maria
Pudil, Pavel
Pujol, Albert
Roca, Xavi
Roli, Fabio
Saludes, Jordi
Sánchez, Xavier
Serrat, Joan
Sethi, Ishwar
Shihab, Khalil
Shimodaira, Hiroshi
Singh, Samir
Skano, Hitoshi
Skurichina, Marina
Stork, David
Subrahmonia, Jayashree
Tax, David
Taxt, Torfinn
Thomas, Federico
Tombre, Karl
Torras, Carme
Ueda, Naonori
Vanrell, Maria
Varona, Xavi
Vernazza, Gianni
Vidal, Enrique
Visa, Ari
Vitrià, Jordi
Wakabayashi, Tetsuya
Wanas, Nayer
Wilson, Richard
Xu, Lei
Yamashita, Yukihiko
Yeung, Dit-Yan
Ypma, Alexander

Track 3: Image, Speech and Signal Processing

Ablameyko, Sergey
Acton, Scott
Ahuja, Narendra
Albiol, Antonio
Aranda, Joan
Arnold, John
Ayala Gallego, Guillermo
Behara, Sagar
Bertrand, Gilles
Binefa, Xavi
Cetin, A. Enis
Chen, Chang Wen
Chen, Tsuhan
Chin, Roland
Cox, Ingemar
Dubois, Eric
Duncan, James
Efstratiadis, Serafim
Fisher, Bob
Gu, chuang
Hasegawa-Johnson, Mark
Hazen, Timothy
Heijmans, Henk
Howitt, Andrew
Hu, Yu Hen
Kaveh, Mos
Kunt, Murat
Lopez, Antonio
Maitre, Henri
Marqués, Ferran
Memon, Nasir
Mersereau, Russell
Montes, Francisco
Namazi, Nader
Oehler, Karen
Pan, Xiaochuan
Pardàs, Montse
Pavlovic, Vladimir
Pearlman, William
Radeva, Petia
Ramponi, Giovanni
Ramstad, Tor
Rodriguez, Jeffrey J.
Ronse, Christian
Safranek, Robert
Salembier, Philippe
Schlesinger, M.
Sekimoto, Nobuhiro
Sezan, Ibrahim
Sheynin, Stanislav
Siggelkow, Sven
Skodras, Athanassios
Stamon, Georges
Stevenson, Robert L.
Strope, Brian
Tanaka, Naoki
Terol, Ivan
Torres, Luis
Tuzikov, Alexander
Vallmitjana, Santiago
Van Den Boomgaard, Rein
Vannier, Michael
Venetsanopoulos, A.N.
Viergever, Max
Weng, John
Wu, Xiaolin
Yang, Yongyi
Yzuel, Maria
Zerubia, Josiane

Track 4: Applications, Robotics, Systems and Architectures

Abe, Keiichi
Al-Ohali, Y.
Andersen, Claus
Araujo, Helder
Asada, Minoru
Aso, Hirotomo
Ayat, N. E.
Babaguchi, Noboru
Baird, Henry
Belaid, Abdel
Blake, Andrew
Bremond, Francois
Cabrera-Gomez, Jorge
Celaya, Enric
Chen, X.
Cloppet, F.
Cutler, Ross
Dario, Paolo
Davis, Larry
De Souza Britto, Alceu
Del Bimbo, Alberto
Devy, Michel
Etoh, Minoru
Fujisawa, Hiromichi
Goto, Hideaki
Grandidier, F.
Hasegawa, Jun-ichi
Hata, Seiji
Hebert, Martial
Henri, Maitre
Hoshino, Jun'ichi
Hung, Yi-Ping
Impedovo, Sebastiano
Ishii, Akira
Jarvis, Ray
Kato, Nei
Kim, Jinho
Kim, K.K.
Kimura, Fumitaka
Kise, Koichi
Koerich, A.
Konolige, Kurt
Koshimizu, Hiroyasu
Kuno, Yoshinori
Lacey, Gerard
Lam, L.
Lee, Hsi-Jian
Lee, Seong-Whan
Lucas, Simon
Mao, Jianchang
Matthies, Larry
Minoh, Michihiko
Miyatake, Takafumi
Mizutani, Hiroyuki
Nakagawa, Masaki
Nakano, Yasuaki
Nakatani, Hiromasa
Nayar, Shree
Nishida, Hirobumi
Nomura, Yoshihiko
Ohno, Hiroshi
Ohsawa, Yutaka
Ohta, Yuichi
Oka, Ryuichi
Omachi, Shin'ichiro
Oshima, Masaki
Quian, Y.
Sakaue, Katsuhiko
Santos-Victor, José
Sasaki, Shigeru
Sato, Kosuke
Schiele, Bernt
Schomaker, Lambert
Shimada, Yasuhiro
Soriano, Maricor
Srihari, Sargur
Stamon, Georges
Suen, Ching
Sugiyama, Takahiro
Tamura, Shinichi
Thomas, Federico
Thonnat, Monique
Tomita, Fumiaki
Tsotsos, John
Tsuruoka, Shinji
Uchida, Seiichi
Vasanth, Philomin
Vieville, Thierry
Wada, Toshikazu
Wakahara, Toru
Waked, B.
Wu, X.
Xu, Q.
Yagi, Yasushi
Yamada, Hiromi
Yamada, J
Yamamoto, Kazuhiko
Yamamoto, Masanobu
Yamamoto, Shinji
Yardimci, Yasemin
Ye, X.
Yokoya, Naokazu
Zelinsky, Alexander

IAPR Member Societies and Members of the Governing Board

Australia: Australian Association for Pattern Recognition — Dr. Brian C. Lovell
Austria: Austrian Association for Pattern Recognition — Professor W.G. Kropatsch
Belarus: Belarusian Association for Image Analysis & Recognition — Professor S. Ablameyko
Belgium: Pattern Recognition Contact Group of the SOGESCI — Dr. C. Perneel
Bulgaria: Bulgarian Association for Pattern Recognition — Dr. R. Kunchev
Canada: Canadian Image Processing and Pattern Recognition Society — Professor R. Plamondon and Professor D. Laurendeau
China: Pattern Recognition and Machine Intelligence Committee of the Chinese Association of Automation — Professor Qingyun Shi
Cuba: Cuban Association for Pattern Recognition (Asociacion Cubana para el Reconocimiento de Patrones, ACPR) — Dr. Roberto Rodríguez Morales
Czech Republic: Czechoslovak Pattern Recognition Society (CPRS) — Dr. P. Pudil
Denmark: Danish Pattern Recognition Society — Professor K. Conradsen
Finland: Pattern Recognition Society of Finland — Professor E. Oja and Professor M. Pietikainen
France: French Association for Pattern Recognition and Interpretation (AFRIF) — Professor G. Lorette
Germany: Deutsche Arbeitsgemeinschaft fur Mustererkennung (DAGM) — Professor H. Burkhardt and Professor Dr. G. Hartmann
Hong Kong: Hong Kong Society for Multimedia and Image Computing — Professor H.H.S Ip
Hungary: Artificial Intelligence & Pattern Recognition (KEPAF) — Professor T. Sziranyi
India: Indian Unit for Pattern Recognition and Artificial Intelligence (IUPRAI) — Professor D. Dutta Majumder
Ireland: Irish Pattern Recognition and Classification Society (IPRCS) — Dr. Paul F. Whelan
Israel: Israel Association for Computer Vision and Pattern Recognition — Dr. M. Porat
Italy: Italian Association for Pattern Recognition — Professor A. Del Bimbo
Japan: Information Processing Society of Japan — Dr. M. Ejiri and Professor Y. Shirai
Korea (South): Computer Vision and Pattern Recognition Group of Korea Information Science Society – Professor S.-W. Lee and Professor Y.B. Kwon
Netherlands: Nederlandse Vereniging voor Patroonherkenning en Beeldverwerking — Professor A.W.M. Smeulders and Professor M.A. Viergever
New Zealand: Image and Vision Computing New Zealand — Professor R. Klette
Norway: Norwegian Society for Image Processing and Pattern Recognition — Dr. H.C. Palm
Poland: Towarzystwo Przetwarzania Obrazow (TPO) - Association for Image Processing — Dr. L. Chmielewski
Portugal: Associacao Portuguesa de Reconhecimento de Padroes (APRP) Professor F. Muge
Russia: Russian Federation Association for Pattern Recognition and Image Analysis (RAPRIA) — Dr-Eng I. Gourevitch, Professor Y. Zhuravlev, Professor A. Nemirko, and Professor V. Soifer
Slovenia: Slovenian Society for Pattern Recognition — Dr. A. Leonardis
South Africa: Pattern Recognition Association of South Africa — Professor B. Herbst
Spain: Spanish Association of Pattern Recognition and Image Analysis — Professor A. Sanfeliu
Sweden: Swedish Society for Automated Image Analysis — Dr. K. Astrom and Dr. T. Gustavsson
Switzerland: The Swiss Association for Pattern Recognition — Professor Dr. H. Bunke
Taiwan: The Chinese Image Processing & Pattern Recognition Society — Professor Zen Chen and Professor W.H. Tsai
Turkey: Turkish Society for Image Analysis and Pattern Recognition (TOTIAD) — Dr. Aytul Ercil
Ukraine: Ukrainian Association on Information Processing and Pattern Recognition — Professor T.K. Vintsiuk
United Kingdom: British Machine Vision Association and Society for Pattern Recognition (BMVA) – Professor J. Kittler and Professor C.J. Taylor
USA: IEEE Computer Society — Professor J.K. Aggarwal, Professor R.M. Haralick, Professor T. Huang, and Professor K. Price

IAPR Standing Committees

Executive Committee

Professor H. Bunke, Acting President and First Vice President
Professor R. Kasturi, Second Vice President
Professor R.M. Haralick, Past President
Dr. G. Sanniti di Baja, Secretary
Professor W.G. Kropatsch, Treasurer

K.S. Fu Prize Committee

Professor A. Rosenfeld, Chairman
Professor H. Freeman
Professor L. Kanal
Professor T. Kohonen
Professor K. Yamamoto

Conferences & Meetings Committee

Dr. B.C. Lovell, Chairman
Professor A.K. Jain
Professor H.H.S Ip
Professor M. Petrou
Professor I.T. Young

Constitution & Bylaws Committee

Professor M.J.B. Duff, Chairman
Professor J.K. Aggarwal
Professor A.J. Padilha

Education Committee

Professor S.L. Tanimoto, Chairman
Dr. C. Arcelli
Professor V. Krasnoproshin
Professor Y. Ohta
Professor M. Pietikainen
Professor G. Stockman

Fellow Committee

Professor J. Kittler, Chairman
Professor K. Abe
Professor V. Cantoni
Professor B.B. Chaudhuri
Dr. L. O'Gorman

Industrial Liaison Committee

Dr. G. Maderlechner, Chairman
Dr. R.M. Bolle
Dr. A.K. Chhabra
Ms. I. Cox
Dr. M. Ejiri
Dr. B.E. Flinchbaugh
Dr. Tin Kam Ho
Dr. J. Hull
Professor M. Kidode
Mr. M. Kraaijveld
Dr. L. O'Gorman

Membership Committee

Professor G. Borgefors, Chairman
Professor T. Caelli
Professor T. Sziranyi

Nominating Committee

Professor R.M. Haralick Chairman
Dr. T. Gustavsson
Professor S.-W. Lee
Professor A. Sanfeliu
Professor M. Takagi

Publications & Publicity Committee

Dr. M. Haindl, Chairman
Professor S. Ablameyko
Professor J. Bigun
Professor M.J.B. Duff, Newsletter Editor
Dr-Eng I. Gourevitch
Professor E. Oja
Professor K. Tombre, IJDAR Representative

IAPR Technical Committees and Chairs

TC1 Statistical Pattern Recognition Techniques — Dr. P. Pudil

TC2 Structural & Syntactical Pattern Recognition — Dr. A. Amin

TC3 Neural Networks & Machine Learning — Professor A. Visa, Dr. P. Perner

TC4 Computer Vision & Image Understanding — Dr E.R. Hancock

TC5 Benchmarking & Software — Professor I.T. Phillips

TC6 Special-Purpose Architectures — Professor M. Ishikawa

TC7 Remote Sensing and Mapping — Professor M. Petrou

TC8 Applications in Industry — Dr. O. Silven

TC9 Biomedical Pattern Recognition — Professor M.A. Viergever

TC10 Graphics Recognition — Dr. A.K. Chhabra

TC11 Applications in Text Processing — Professor S.-W. Lee

TC12 Multimedia Systems — Professor H.H.S. Ip, Professor A.W.M. Smeulders

TC13 Pattern Recognition in Astronomy & Astrophysics — Dr. A. Bijaoui

TC14 Image Processing — Professor J. Bigun, Dr. L.J. van Vliet

TC15 Graph Based Representations — Professor J.-M. Jolion

TC16 Algebraic & Discrete Mathematical Techniques in PR&IA — Professor Y. Zhuravlev

Handwriting Recognition - The Last Frontiers

Ching Y. Suen[1], Jinho Kim[1,2], Kyekyung Kim[1], Qizhi Xu[1], and Louisa Lam[1,3]

[1] CENPARMI, Concordia University, Suite GM-606, 1455 de Maisonneuve Blvd West
Montreal, Quebec H3G 1M8, Canada
E-mail: {suen, kkkim, qxu}@cenparmi.concordia.ca
[2] Dept. of Electronic Engineering, Kyungil University, Kyungsan, Korea
E-mail: kjinho@bear.kyungil.ac.kr
[3] Dept. of Mathematics, Hong Kong Institute of Education, Taipo, Hong Kong
E-mail: llam@math.ied.edu.hk

Abstract

The last frontiers of handwriting recognition are considered to have started in the last decade of the second millennium. This paper summarizes (a) the nature of the problem of handwriting recognition, (b) the state of the art of handwriting recognition at the turn of the new millennium, and (c) the results of CENPARMI researchers in automatic recognition of handwritten digits, touching numerals, cursive scripts, and dates formed by a mixture of the former 3 categories. Wherever possible, comparable results have been tabulated according to techniques used, databases, and performance. Aspects related to human generation and perception of handwriting are discussed. The extraction and usage of human knowledge, and their incorporation into handwriting recognition systems are presented. Challenges, aims, trends, efforts and possible rewards,, and suggestions for future investigations are also included.

1. Introduction

Apart from printing and electronic media, handwriting is the most common mode of human communication. The sequence we normally follow in our school days is block printing, manuscript writing, and cursive scripts [1]. We still use block printing and manuscript writing to fill in numerous business forms in our daily life, but this mode of writing is 50% slower than cursive writing [1] which is commonly used in personal communications. However, it is well-known that cursive scripts are 2 to 3 times less legible than block printing [1]. Hence it is not surprising to see that cursive script recognition by computer is a very difficult problem even though numerous scientists have been working on this subject for many years [2]. Actually some systems have been developed for on-line recognition (see e.g.[3]). But for off-line recognition, a lot more research has to be done before they can be used economically in practice. Nevertheless, driven by the challenge of developing innovative algorithms to match human performance and by various applications in data processing, plenty of researchers in academic and industrial sectors are still working on this fascinating subject.

During the past 25 years, the field of OCR (Optical Character Recognizer) has made significant advances in handwriting recognition [1, 4-8]. There is also ample evidence in the OCR literature which suggests that the detection and utilization of the distinctive features of characters play a keyrole in high performance [1, 6-7], but they are extremely difficult to define. The same can be said about cursive script recognition. Measurable and visible features such as the density of points, moments, crossing counts, mathematical transforms, loops, end-points, junctions, arcs, concavities and convexities, strokes and their directions, etc. all of which can lead to a good classification of the characters. But the underlying factors which determine the true identity of handwritten words remain to be intractible and it is probably safe to say that no simple scheme is likely to achieve high recognition and reliability rates, not to mention human performance.

The above situation has led to re-newed efforts directed towards more sophisticated systems, not only related to preprocessing, feature extraction and classification stages of their methods; but also approaches such as neural networks, mathematical morphology, and hidden Markov models (HMM). Furthermore, since each classification method has its own strengths and weaknesses, it can be deduced that performance can be improved significantly by combining

1051-4651/00 $10.00

several classifiers, and indeed some real advances have been made [2, 9-10, 53].

Notwithstanding the above achievements, handwriting recognition, especially in totally unconstrained off-line environments, the performance is still inadequate for practical applications. This is compounded by the lack of understanding of the human process in handwriting recognition.

This paper will focus on the state of the art in off-line handwriting recognition and some recent results obtained at CENPARMI on the recognition of handwritten numerals and numeral strings, words, and dates.

1.1. Handwriting Properties and Recognition Problems

Off-line handwriting recognition is performed after the completion of writing. Any handwriting interpretation system must face the high variability of character and word shapes. One can easily think of examples where even the topology of a character or a word written by a person may change from one instance to another. An algorithm for unconstrained handwritten word recognition must be able to successfully recognize the image of any word which can be formed by discrete characters, continuous and discrete cursive forms (group of characters written with a single continuous motion), or a combination of them.

Intensive research on the recognition of isolated digits in the past decade has led to very high recognition rates in the range of 85-99%, and the recent efforts have focussed on methods of achieving high reliability, recognition of touching digits and numeral strings, and cleaning of handwritten data prior to recognition. The recognition of cursive scripts is more difficult and only a recognition rate in the 80-92% range has been obtained. Consequently this paper will address mainly the more difficult situations of numeral string and word recognition. As far as cursive scripts are concerned, they can be performed at the letter level and at the word level. In the former method, it has to face the difficulty of segmenting the words into isolated characters which is a non-trivial task because the boundaries between characters are not always clear. Thus, different interpretations at the letter level are possible which make the recognition process of the whole word ambiguous. The holistic approach of recognizing the words at the global level avoids this segmentation process, but is faced with the ambiguity of many more shapes representing the same word. Also, depending on the vocabulary of the application, different words may have similar global shapes. In any case, the use of linguistic or other information is needed in many situations.

2. Recognition of Unconstrained Handwritten Numerals and Numeral Strings

2.1. A brief overview of the state of the art

2.1.1. Isolated numeral recognition. Many features and classification methods have been proposed in past several decades to recognize handwritten numerals [11-18, 43]. One method includes two categories such as statistical and syntactic methods. The first category includes techniques such as matching, moments, characteristic points and mathematical transforms, while the second one includes essential structural features such as skeletons and contours. The other method includes the use of a single classifier and combined classifiers. Statistical classifiers include nearest-neighbor, Bayesian, polynomial discriminant and neural networks, self-organizing map, and decision tree. Artificial neural networks have been used as a powerful tool for recognizing patterns due to their strong discriminative power. Recently, handwritten numeral recognition using hidden Markov model has emerged because it provides a good probabilistic representation of patterns which have large variations.

Meanwhile, the combined classifiers for recognizing handwritten numerals are divided into homogeneous-classifiers and heterogeneous-classifiers. In the former approach, multiple multi-layer perceptrons have been used in which each classifier is trained independently with particular features or digit groups. This approach attempts to reduce burdens and difficulties in training, implementation of classifiers and training time. In the latter approach, HMM/MLP hybrid classifier has been used to capture the complementary capability of each classifier.

2.1.2. Numeral string recognition. The recognition of numeral strings [16-18, 49-52] has been an intensive research topic in recent years due to many possible application environments such as postal code reading, check processing and tax form processing, etc. The recognition of numeral strings differs from that of isolated digits by including the classification of digit groups and segmentation of touching digits. The segmentation of touching digits is generally difficult when digits overlap or touch each other. Recognition of numeral strings can be classified into segmentation-based and segmentation-free methods. In segmentation-based recognition method [16-17], a numeral string is divided into segments whether by recognition-based or by recognition-free methods. The vertical projection, contour profiles or characteristic points of the thinned image have been used to extract segmentation points.

Both segmentation methods have problem in finding the correct segmentation points and in computing the final segmentation points. Meanwhile, the segmentation-free recognition method [18] recognizes the whole entity of numeral string without segmentation. The objective of this method is to avoid errors caused by incorrect segmentation, but this requires a rather complex classifier and a large memory. Recently, the recognition of numeral strings by a combination of segmentation methods [16] has been studied.

2.2. Summary of CENPARMI results

Many systems have been developed to realize accurate recognition of handwritten numerals and much research has been conducted on CENPARMI, CEDAR and NIST databases. The performances of published reliable systems are summarized in Tables 1 to 3 which are distinguished by databases and recognition results by CENPARMI and other researchers.

The recognition results of isolated handwritten numerals are shown in Tables 1 and 2. Each table shows the recognition results by classification methods using single classifier and combined classifiers. Actually researchers at CENPARMI have been studying the recognition of handwritten numerals for many years on CENPARMI, CEDAR, and NIST databases. High reliability and recognition results by CENPAMI have been achieved on each database as shown in Table 1, reliability and recognition results on NIST database is the highest reported in literature. The recognition system developed at CENPARMI combines neural networks and multiple experts as shown in Table 2.

Table 1. Recognition rates of isolated handwritten numerals.(%)

Authors	Database	Error	Reliability	Recognition
'96 S.W.Lee [12]	CENPARMI	2.90	97.10	97.10
'97 T.M.Ha [11]	CEDAR	0.91	99.09	99.09
'92 IBM [13]	NIST	3.49	96.51	96.51
'92 AT&T [13]	NIST	3.16	96.84	96.84
'97 T.M.Ha [11]	NIST	2.90	97.10	97.10
'98 CENPARMI [14]	NIST	0.93	99.07	99.07

Table 2. Recognition rates of isolated handwritten numerals by combined classification methods.

Authors	Database	Error	Reliability	Recognition
'93 AEG-CENPARMI [45]	CENPARMI	1.50	98.50	98.50
'93 CENPARMI [46]	CENPARMI	0.00	100.00	93.05
'97 S.B.Cho [15]	CENPARMI	3.95	96.05	96.05
'99 CENPARMI [34]	CENPARMI	1.15	98.85	98.85
'93 D.S.Lee [47]	CEDAR	1.13	98.87	98.87
'98 Parascript [48]	CEDAR	0.46	99.54	99.54
'99 CENPARMI [34]	CEDAR	0.23	99.77	99.77

The former method uses pixel distance features and obtained a high reliability of 98.85% by training on big databases and years of intensive investigations. In the latter method, one of most successful applications on achieving high reliability is described. AEG-CENPARMI obtained good recognition result on CENPARMI database by combining six experts which is a collaboration of AEG and CENPARMI.

A new recognizer for handwritten numeral strings has been developed at CENPARMI. A comparison of recognition performances for numeral strings with others in this field is shown in Tables 3 and 4. The recognition of handwritten numeral strings shows recognition rates below 80% because more complicated touching digits are included.

Table 3. The recognition performances of unconstrained handwritten numeral strings.

Authors	Database	Error	Recognition
'98 T.M.Ha [16]	NIST	2.0	86.0
'96 Mitek [29]	Cheques	1.0	55.0
'98 Parascript [48]	5-digit zip code	0.8	64.0
'98 CENPARMI [14]	Cheques	0.0	62.0

Recognition of numerals on numeral strings is a more difficult task when the length of the numeral string is not known.

Recently, prioritized segment-based recognition of unconstrained handwritten two-numeral strings has been developed at CENPARMI. Four kinds of candidate segmentation points, six touching types and prioritized segments are defined to separate touching digits into individual digits. The experiments have been carried out using the touching digit pairs in the NIST database.

Table 4. Recognition performances of touching digit pairs.

Authors	Database	Training samples	Testing samples	Rej. rate	Error Rate	Relia-bility	Rec. rate
'97 Shi [17]	CEDAR	2,819	,089	-	-	-	80.8
'98 Wang [18]	CEDAR	2,819	1,089	-	-	-	83.3
'99 Lu [49]	NIST	53,449	3,355	4.7	7.1	92.5	88.2
'99 CENPARMI	NIST	50,000	3,500	0.0	7.5	92.5	92.5

Table 4 shows the recognition results of touching digit pairs. The recognition, rejection and error rates sum to 100%. It provides the size of training and testing sets as well and "-" indicates that data set or a rate has not been reported. As shown in Table 4, direct comparison is rather difficult due to the use of different databases or different portions of the same database, different numbers of training and testing samples, and also different segmentation methods and recognition algorithms.

The studies based on CEDAR database obtained recognition rates around 80% and those using the NIST database have produced better recognition rates. The CEDAR database contains more unconstrained data than NIST because the writers were requested to write numeral strings in preprinted boxes.

The CENPARMI recognition system of touching digit pairs has produced encouraging results compared with the previous reports based on a relatively large testing data set. On analyzing the experimental results, we have found that the poor recognition results of touching digits have been caused by multi-point touching and overlapping digits. In these cases, the body of touching digits has been divided up incorrectly. More revised segmentation method and combination of holistic method of multi-point touching and overlapping digits are needed to the improve performance.

2.3. Challenges facing the topics and what should be done to reach new height

The recognition methods of unconstrained handwritten numerals and numeral strings have obtained good performance in specific application fields, however a more difficult task remains in real-life applications. The challenge is to cope with complicated writing styles, poor qualities and artifacts introduced during image capture.

To enhance the recognition of patterns, many researchers have suggested that straightforward single methods are inadequate for a complex problem such as handwritten numeral recognition, while combined methods can offer a better recognition performance. Many methods have been proposed using multi-features, multi-classifiers and combined segmentation method to recognize handwritten numerals and numeral strings. A combination system can reinforce the individual methods and suppress their drawbacks, while each method can be combined appropriately depending on its performance. The combination recognition system can take advantage of the complementary capability of each method. Other approaches by researchers have shown the value of postprocessing such as verification and contextual information [42]. Recognition systems by both approaches have shown improved performance.

3. Cursive Script Recognition

3.1. A brief overview of the state of the art

The recognition of cursive script has been studied for several decades, and many interesting results have been reported [19-26,37-41,43]. Unlike handprinted characters, cursive script cannot be segmented into discrete characters accurately for recognition. Two fundamental schemes have been developed to tackle the problem of cursive script recognition such as a holistic approach and an analytical one depending on the feature extraction method. The holistic approach recognizes the word as a complete entity using its global features while the analytical approach segments the word into individual graphemes and extracts features from each grapheme.

Various classifiers for cursive script recognition have also been developed which are strongly related to their feature extraction schemes [44, 50]. Neural networks and matching techniques have also been used. Recently many successful HMMs have also appeared. To improve the performance and reliability, various hybrid schemes of the multiple classifiers have been developed including fusion and combining methods. We can use homogeneous classifiers such as multiple neural networks or heterogeneous classifiers such as neural networks and HMM to implement hybrid classifiers.

In the field of cursive script recognition, the topics related to the efficient preprocessing and segmentation techniques, the more stable feature extraction methods, the more powerful classifier designs and the more efficient hybrid schemes are still considered as challenging tasks.

3.2. Summary of recent CENPARMI results

Cursive script recognition has been studied at various institutions such as NIST, CEDAR and CENPARMI. Cursive script recognition system for cheque processing and mail piece processing have been studied at CENPARMI for more than 10 years. One of the main problems in developing a bank cheque processing system is the need of collecting a database of cheque information. It is a non-trivial task. Fortunately, real cheque samples of Canadian banks have been provided to CENPARMI. A large bank cheque database of CENPARMI has been constructed using real-life cheques as well as cheques written by the staff of Concordia University and local companies.

In the early research at CENPARMI for the recognition of the legal amount, neural networks and k-NN classifiers were used to implement classifiers with 71.8% recognition rate obtained by Guillevic et al[20]. After more intensive study, this system improved to 86.7% for French bank cheques owing to more stable preprocessing techniques, a more robust feature extraction scheme and new classifiers such as an HMM and hybrid models. In this study, they have shown two promising aspects that HMM can be used successfully in cursive script recognition as well as in speech recognition, and HMM can also be used as a co-operative classifier for constructing the hybrid model with conventional classifiers.

The other application of cursive script recognition at CENPARMI has been introduced by Yacoubi et al[21], which shows more than 96% for the recognition of French city names with a lexicon size of 100 by using only HMM classifiers. In this study, HMM was applied quite successfully in cursive script recognition by introducing HMM at the character level.

Recently at CENPARMI, more advanced recognition methods of the legal words and the month words have been developed [19, 50]. In this study, a segmentation based grapheme level HMM has been developed using an analytical feature extraction scheme as shown in Fig. 1. Grapheme is a segmented part of a word that looks like a letter but not necessarily a full letter. One of the main ideas of this study is that if we design a novel architecture and an efficient training scheme of an HMM to solve the over- or under-segmentation problem in the cursive script recognition, the performance should improve.

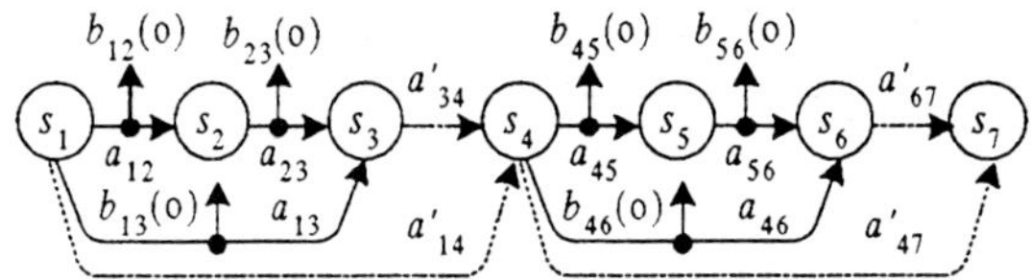

Figure 1. Segmentation based grapheme level hidden Markov model.

In Figure 1, single state transition a_{ij} represents a single grapheme and three cascaded states represent a single letter. During the state transitions, we can observe the output probability $b_{ij}(o_t)$ of the given observation symbol sequence $\mathbf{O}$. Some transitions, a'_{ij}, do not produce any symbol observation outputs to represent skipped letter of the under-segmented word. Each letter has three states s_i and three different state transition paths to represent over-, exact- and under-segmentations. This scheme is less sensitive to the various segment combinations of each grapheme of cursive word.

Another aspect of this study is that a novel hybrid scheme for combining the heterogeneous classifiers has also been studied even though an efficient combining scheme of the conventional classifiers was introduced at CENPARMI back in 1995 [22]. Apart from HMM, several neural network classifiers have been exploited using global feature extraction schemes. A new combining approach has been developed using a multiplication scheme with weighting factor for the heterogeneous classifiers and a fusion scheme for the homogeneous neural networks. At first, two homogeneous MLPs are implemented separately and combined into a new single MLP classifier at the architectural level so called "fusion of two classifiers". Next, HMM is combined with the new MLP as a heterogeneous one. This is based on the idea that classifiers with more different methodologies and different features can better complement each other.

The performance of a cursive recognition system for legal words recently developed at CENPARMI is shown in Table 5.

Table 5. Top 5 performances of the various MLP and HMM combinations for legal word recognition (training 5,223 words and testing 2,482 words with a lexicon size of 32).

Classifier		T1	T2	T3	T4	T5
Single	HMM	82.0	90.5	93.6	95.8	96.7
	MLP	86.0	93.2	95.6	97.5	98.0
Hybrid	Voting	88.1	95.1	97.4	98.3	98.8
	LCA	89.4	95.5	97.3	98.3	98.9
	Multiplication	92.7	97.0	98.3	99.0	99.2

The overall performance of this cursive script recognition system for a legal word database shows a 92.7% recognition rate for 2,482 words with a lexicon size of 32 after training on 5,223 words of CENPARMI's real cheque database. Some of the reported performances of legal word recognition without rejection for real cheque database are shown in Table 6.

Table 6. Performance comparisons of the legal word recognition for real cheque databases.

Classifiers		Class	Train	Test	Rec.	DB
'97 Kim[23]	Dynamic Programming	29	-	-	77.9	English
'98 Han[51]	Pattern Matching	-	-	-	84.9	English
'98 Knerr[24]	NN-HMM	30	130,000	40,000	92.9	French
'98 Guillevic[20]	HMM-Global	30	4,513	1,622	86.7	French
'98 Cote[36]	PERCEPTO Model	32	180	2,929	73.6	English
'98 Bunke[52]	HMM	-	-	-	71.9	Swiss
'99 Soan[26]	HMM-MRF	26	36,829	4,098	82.5	French
Developed	HMM-MLP	32	5,223	2,482	92.7	English

In 1998, Knerr et al introduced an NN-HMM hybrid method that produced 92.9% recognition rate for 30 word classes of French bank cheques. Although they used large quantities of training data, the result seems to be fairly good in the legal word recognition field. Direct comparison of our results with other applications is hard since people used different databases, different number of classes, and different number of training and testing patterns. However we estimate that the recognition rate of more than 92% for 32 cursive word classes with unconstrained real-life database is probably one of the top performers among those ever reported on the recognition of English legal words.

The performance of a cursive recognition system for month words at CENPARMI is shown in Table 7. The performance of this system for month word recognition shows 87.3% recognition rate for 2,152 words with a lexicon size of 21 after training on 4,413 words of CENPARMI's real cheque database. This result can be considered as a milestone in the month word recognition area since it is hard to find the recognition results of month words in the open literature.

Table 7. Top 5 performances of the various MLP and HMM combinations for month word recognition (training 4,413 words and testing 2,152 words with a lexicon size of 21).

Classifier		T1	T2	T3	T4	T5
Single	HMM	76.6	86.2	90.4	93.4	95.3
	MLP	80.0	90.5	94.0	95.5	96.9
Hybrid	Voting	84.1	92.2	95.3	96.9	98.3
	LCA	84.9	92.8	95.4	97.0	98.2
	Multiplication	87.3	94.1	96.3	97.0	97.7

3.3. Challenges facing the topic and what should be done to reach new height

To obtain satisfactory classifiers for real-life cursive script recognition, we have to conduct more intensive studies such as more stable preprocessing and segmentation techniques, adaptive feature extraction schemes which depend on the classifiers, more robust classifier design and more advanced combining schemes. Especially in the designing of hybrid HMM classifiers, mutual interference of classifiers can reduce the performance. Recently at CENPARMI, doubly connected new HMM architecture is under-development which can reduce interference between classifiers by utilizing an architectural level fusion scheme of HMMs.

4. Date Image Processing

Developing an effective automatic date image processing system is very challenging not only because of immense styles of handwriting, but also due to the high degree of variability and uncertainty present in the dates handwritten by users when no format is prescribed, as is the case with North American bank cheques. The *Month* field can be written in either digit or word form before or after *Day*, while punctuations (period ('.'), comma (','), slash ('/') and hyphen ('-')) or a space can be used to identify the end of a field. This means that dates can be represented by a large variety of writing styles, some of which are shown in Figure 2.

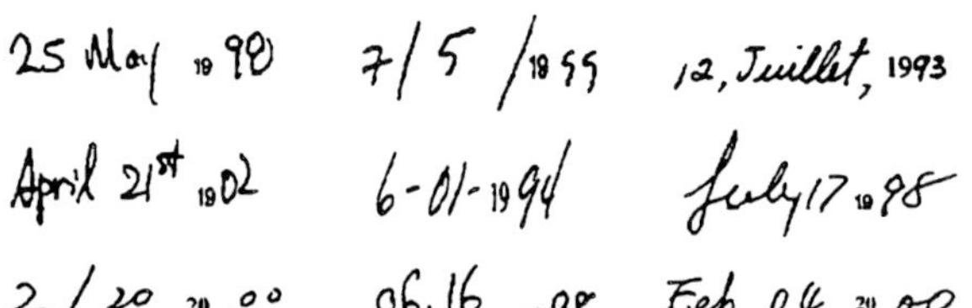

Figure 2. Examples of date images

These variations imply that date processing requires the recognition of both cursive scripts and digits (without knowing a priori the category of the data). It also requires the detection of separators or transitions between the data fields. In addition, in a real industrial application, the cheque images are often composed of complicated backgrounds with a variety of colorful scene images, which give rise to new problems in image preprocessing. The noises introduced by improper binarization has a great impact on the date image analyzer, e.g. it is difficult to distinguish real small punctuation marks from the noise. All these have made date image processing a complicated problem. Perhaps for this reason, there has been no published work on this topic until recently, when work on processing the date image of machine-printed cheques was reported [29]. This reference also considered date processing to be the most difficult target in cheque processing, given that it had the lowest segmentation and recognition performance.

However, the automatic processing of handwritten dates is important in application environments where cheques cannot be cashed prior to the dates shown, while any delay would entail significant financial costs when large numbers of cheques are involved.

4.1. Date Image Segmentation

Since the date image contains fields which may belong to different categories (cursive script or numeric), one approach to process the date image would be to segment it into fields through the detection of the separator or transition between the fields, identify the nature of each field, and apply an appropriate recognizer for each. Given that many recognizers have been developed for words and digits, we wish to concentrate on the segmentation problem by detecting the separators. These separators may be punctuations (period ('.'), comma (','), slash ('/'), hyphen ('-')) or an interword gap, and methods have been designed and implemented to identify them [28].

For the detection of punctuations, two categories of features, shape features and spatial features have been considered [27]. Shape features deal with the geometric aspects of each connected component in an image, particularly its appearance and measurements. Spatial features deal with the contextual aspects of each connected component, and they provide information about the location of the component with respect to the entire image as well as its neighboring components. The shape features used to describe punctuations are *high_density*, *narrow*, *flat*, *slope*, *small*, *simple_curve* and *no_innerloop*; while the spatial features used consist of *exceed_neighbour*, *at_middlezone*, *mid_to_neighbour*, *below_lowerhalf* and *low_to_left* [28]. For the detection of an interword gap, many algorithms can be used to compute the distances between pairs of connected components [31, 33]. We consider the maximum gap to occur where the maximum distance between neighboring components occurs on the largest number of scan lines. This method is completely independent of threshold values, and it has been found to be effective and computationally efficient.

These separator detection methods use shape and spatial features alone, and are simple and efficient, but they have had limited success due to the diverse handwriting styles in real-life environments. Recently some researchers [30, 32] have employed additional information, such as the author's writing style and other cues, in the estimation of interword gaps. We also present here a new date image segmentation method based on contextual analysis, which will be discussed in the following subsection.

4.2. Segmentation with Confirmation

Given that date image segmentation depends heavily on the accurate determination of a separator between the *Day* and *Month* fields, it is important to improve the accuracy in the detection of this separator, which may be a punctuation or an interword gap. This separator can be determined from:

(a) The presence of a significant gap or punctuation, or
(b) A transition between digits and letters.

Consequently, we develop and add a confirmation procedure to our segmentation strategy, so that a two-level strategy is implemented. Using this strategy, more candidates for punctuation and gap are detected than before. However, these candidates are considered to be separators only if they satisfy more stringent conditions than used previously. Otherwise the confirmation procedure is applied at the second level by considering the contextual information or the nature of the subimage on either side of the candidate.

For example, locating the interword gap between *Day* and *Month* can be a difficult task because this gap may not always appear as the widest gap observed when users write the date freely. However, if it can be determined that a gap occurs at a transition between numeric and alphabetic fields, then this can be considered to be the gap between the *Day* and *Month* fields. Similarly, when a candidate for slash is considered, this candidate can be confirmed as slash when subimages on both sides of the candidate show high likelihoods of being numeric, and not confirmed as slash when both subimages are highly unlikely to be numeric. (In the former case, we apply our experimental knowledge that slashes are often used when both *Day* and *Month* are represented numerically, and also the *a priori* condition that each such field should contain at most two digits, so that a slash candidate appearing between two numeric images should be considered a separator rather than digit '1').

For our purpose, the likelihood of a subimage being numeric is determined by a combination of the following information:

(a) the confidence value returned by a connected digit recognizer [34],
(b) the number of digits in the subimage and the value(s) of these digit(s) returned by the connected digit recognizer,
(c) the maximum number of horizontal runs contained in the subimage, and
(d) the number and position of innerloops contained in the subimage.

Based on the above information, a measure can be derived that represents the likelihood of a subimage being numeric, and this measure is used in the confirmation process described above. The effectiveness of this measure $Confid_{numeric}$ in differentiating between alphabetic and numeric images on date images can be seen from results obtained on 4205 samples of month words and 4000 numeric samples extracted from handwritten cheques. These are shown in Figure 3, and it can be seen that there is a strong correlation between very high (low) values of $Confid_{numeric}$ and numeric (alphabetic or word) samples.

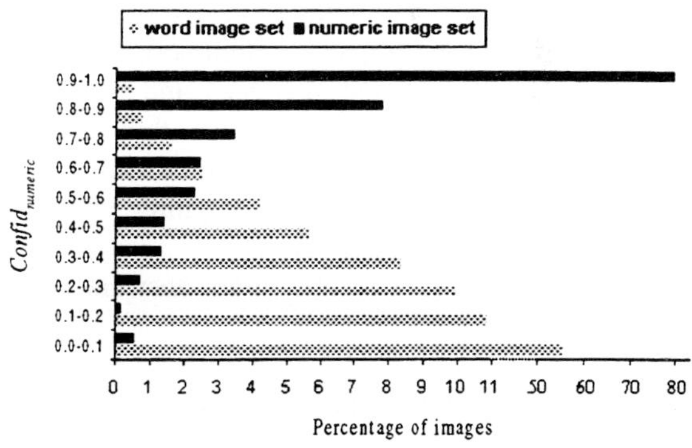

Figure 3. Relationship of $Confid_{numeric}$ to numeric and word images

Using this measure, the two-level strategy is implemented and tested on 1,000 regular bank cheques (written in English), and the results are given in Table 8, for both the previous and two-level methods. For these results, correct segmentation means both the location of the segmentation point and the style of writing the month (in word or numeric form) have been correctly determined.

Table 8. Performance of two methods for segmentation of 1,000 date images(%).

	Correct	Rejection	Error
Two-level strategy	85.80	3.50	10.70
Previous method [28]	72.30	5.50	22.20

From Table 8, it is observed that the new approach has achieved a higher correct segmentation rate and lower error rate than the previous method under the same test conditions.

The performance can be improved by more effective computation of $Confid_{numeric}$, which is the kernel of the confirmation stage. More discriminating features between alphabetic and numeric images, together with results from a cursive month word recognizer are being considered. In addition, the higher correct rate in detecting separator candidates and determining the style of *Month* will help to enhance the segmentation results. In order to eventually produce a successful date reading system, some issues are also being considered. The interaction between the segmentation and recognition stages should be adjusted properly. A verification stage based on the nature of dates can be incorporated to improve the overall reliability. A larger and more comprehensive database should be used to train and test the system.

5. Concluding Remarks - Adding Human Knowledge to the System

Humans start to read and write at the age of about 4-6 years old. From this early age to adulthood, they have practised a lot of writing and also seen and read great varieties of handwritten scripts. Hence they possess ample knowledge in their recognition and such knowledge may be invaluable in designing computer algorithms to recognize cursive scripts.

Hence it is worthwhile to find some answers to the following questions:

- How does the human brain recognize the different characters?
- Is there some way we can extract the character/word recognition and perceptual knowledge and distinctive features from humans who have become such good character recognizers?
- Which parts of the characters/words are crucial to recognition?
- What kinds of features do we get when we see a character or word?
- Can we still recognize characters and words when parts of them are missing?
- How to resolve ambiguous shapes?
- How to reduce the subsitution rate to an absolute minimum?
- How do the above operations transcend across language boundaries?

In an attempt to answer some of the questions raised, we have prepared several psychological experiments aiming at the discovery of the most distinctive parts of handprinted characters [35-36]. The results have already revealed that different parts of a character or word carry different amounts of information for recognition. They have also identified some salient and interesting features. Computer simulation and further experiments are underway. We believe that one way to improve reliability is to focus on the problem of confusions. If confusions between classes can be resolved, most of the substitution errors can be avoided. Imagine a clerk reading the amounts of money on a balance sheet. He/she will read most of them correctly, but some will be ambiguous or illegible. For these cases he/she will probably check with his/her supervisor who has the responsibility of resolving such cases. Hence it seems reasonable to build character recognition systems which work in a similar manner, with a two-tier architecture. The basic recognizer is the 'clerk': it will get most of the cases right but will fail in certain confusing cases. Regardless whether this system may be based on a neural net or algorithmic approach, the only way to resolve the confusing cases will be to pass them onto a second recognizer (the "supervisor") charged with the responsibility of verifying and validating the data. Obviously this is only the beginning, and much more research should be done in this field before we can make computers recognize words and read documents reliably and intelligently.

Also, in the next research cycle of the last frontiers, we believe that a lot can be gained if academic researchers work more closely with the industries. For example, the industries can provide data and real-life testing environments to support academic research. Similarly they can extend their efforts to the recognition of other types of business and financial documents [14]. In an attempt to bridge the gap between the academic and industrial sectors; the authors present the following ideas and pointers to tackle the challenges lying ahead:

a) Extraction of clear data from various backgrounds
b) System which can absorb new knowledge continuously
c) Careful construction of database and selection of useful data
d) Automation of training methodologies
e) Verification and validation schemes to increase the reliability of the system

f) Exchange of novel ideas and new results among academic and industrial researchers

Apart from the use of features to recognize the characters, the context of the characters should be employed to the full extent. For example, the recognition of handwritten zip codes can be greatly facilitated by verifying the digits with the address information; the courtesy amounts on cheques can be verified by the legal amounts [51-52]; the numbers on certain financial statements and forms can be verified by the sum and total; and the letters in words can be verified by a dictionary or spelling check.

Acknowledgements

This work was supported by the Natural Sciences and Engineering Research Council of Canada, the Ministry of Education of Quebec, and the National Networks of Centres of Excellence research program of Canada. The assistance of other members of CENPARMI is gratefully acknowledged.

References

[1] C. Y. Suen, "Handwriting generation, perception and recognition," Acta Psychologica, vol. 54, pp. 295-312, 1983.

[2] A. Yacoubi, M. Gilloux, R. Sabourin, and C. Y. Suen, "Objective evaluation of the discriminant power of features in an HMM-based word recognition system," Proc. 1st Brazilian Symposium on Document Image Analysis, Curitiba, pp. 60-73, Nov., 1997.

[3] C. C. Tappert, C. Y. Suen, and T. Wakahara, "The state of the art in on-line handwriting recognition," IEEE Trans. on Pattern Analysis and Machine Intelligence, vol. 12, pp. 787-808, 1987.

[4] S. Mori, C. Y. Suen, and K. Yamamoto, "Historical Review of OCR Research and Development," Porceedings of the IEEE, vol. 80, pp. 1029-1058, July, 1992.

[5] C. Y. Suen, "Character recognition by computer and applications," T.Y. Young and K.-S. Fu, editors, Handbook of Pattern Recognition and Image Processing, pp. 569-586, Academic Press Inc., Orlando, 1986.

[6] C. Y. Suen, "Distinctive features in the automatic recognition of handprinted characters," Signal Processing, vol. 4, pp. 193-207, 1982.

[7] C. Y. Suen, M. Berthod, and S. Mori, "Automatic recognition of handprinted characters the state of the art," Proceedings of the IEEE , vol. 68, pp. 469-483, 1980.

[8] C. Y. Suen, J. Guo, and Z. C. Li, "Analysis and recognition of alphanumeric handprints by parts," IEEE Trans. on Syst., Man, Cybern., vol. 24, pp. 614-631, 1994.

[9] D. Guillevic and C. Y. Suen, "HMM word recognition engine," Proc. Int. Conf. Document Analysis and Recognition, Ulm, Germany, pp. 544-547, Aug. 1997.

[10] M. Gilloux, "Real-time handwritten word recognition within large lexicons," Proceedings of International Workshop on Frontiers in Handwriting Recognition, Essex, pp. 301-304, Sep. 1996.

[11] T. M. Ha and H. Bunke, "Off-line handwritten numeral recognition by perturbation method," IEEE Trans. on Pattern Analysis and Machine Intelligence, vol. 19, pp. 535-539, May, 1997.

[12] S. W. Lee, "Off-line recognition of totally unconstrained handwritten numerals using multilayer cluster neural network," IEEE Transactions on Pattern Recognition and Machine Intelligence, vol. 18, pp. 648-650,1996.

[13] R. Wilkinson, J. Geist, S. Janet, P. Grother and C. Burges, "The first census optical character recognition system conference," Technical report, National Inst. Of Standards and Technology, Gaithersburg, MD, 1992.

[14] C. Y. Suen, K. Liu, and N. W. Strathy, "Sorting and recognizing cheques and financial documents," In Proc. of the Third Internatinal Association for Pattern Recognition Workshop on Document Analysis Systems, pp. 1-18, 1998.

[15] S. B. Cho, "Neural-network classifiers for recognizing totally unconstrained handwritten numerals," IEEE Transactions on Neural Networks, vol. 8, pp. 43-53, 1997.

[16] T. M. Ha, M. Zimmermann and H. Bunke, "Off-line handwritten numeral string recognition by combining segmentation-based and segmentation-free methods," Pattern Recognition, vol. 31, pp. 257-272, 1998.

[17] Z. Shi and V. Govindaraju, "Segmentation and recognition of connected handwritten numeral strings," Pattern Recognition, vol. 30, pp. 1501-1504, 1997.

[18] X. Wang, V. Govindaraju, and S. Srihari, "Holistic recognition of touching digits," Proceedings of International Workshop on Frontiers in Handwriting Recognition, pp.295-303, 1998.

[19] J. H. Kim, K. K. Kim, and C. Y. Suen, "An HMM-MLP Hybrid Model for Cursive Script Recognition," to be appeared in Pattern Analysis & Applications.

[20] D. Guillevic and C. Y. Suen, "Recognition of Legal Amounts on Bank Cheques," Pattern Analysis & Applications, vol. 1, pp. 28-41, 1998.

[21] A. Yacoubi, M. Gilloux, R. Sabourin, and C. Y. Suen, "An HMM-Based Approach for Off-Line Unconstrained Handwritten Word Modeling and Recognition," IEEE Trans. on Pattern Analysis and Machine Intelligence, vol. 21, pp. 752-760, 1999.

[22] Y. S. Huang and C. Y. Suen, "A Method of Combining Multiple Experts for the Recognition of Unconstrained Handwritten Numerals," IEEE Trans. on Pattern Analysis and Machine Intelligence, vol. 17, pp. 90-94, 1995.

[23] G. Kim and V. Govindaraju, "Bank Check Recognition Using Cross Validation Between Legal and Courtesy Amounts," Automatic Bank check Processing, World Scientific Press, pp. 195- 212, 1997.

[24] S. Knerr and E. Augustin, "A Neural Network-Hidden Markov Model Hybrid for Cursive Word Recognition," Proceedings of the International Conference on Pattern Recognition, Brisbane, Australia, pp. 1518-1520, 1998.

[25] G. Kaufmann and H. Bunke, "A System for the Automated Reading of Check Amounts-Some Key Ideas," Proceedings of the 3rd International Association for Pattern Recognition Workshop on Document Analysis Systems, Nagano, Japan, pp. 302-315, 1998.

[26] G. Soan, "Cursive Word Recognition Using a Random Field Based Hidden Markov Model," International Journal on Document Analysis and Recognition, vol. 1, pp. 199-208, 1999.

[27] E. Cohen, J. J. Hull, and S. N. Srihari, "Control structure for interpreting handwritten addresses," IEEE Trans. Pattern Analysis and Machine Intelligence, vol. 16, pp. 1049-1055, Oct., 1994.

[28] R. Fan, L. Lam, and C. Y. Suen, "Processing of date information on cheques," Progress in Handwriting Recognition, pp. 473-479, eds. A. C. Downton and C Impedovo, World Scientific, 1997.

[29] G. F. Houle, D. B. Aragon, R. W. Smith, M. Shridhar, and D. Kimura, "A multi-layered corroboration based check reader," Document Analysis System II, pp. 137-174, eds. J.J. Hull and S.L. Taylor, World Scientific, 1998.

[30] G. Kim and V. Govindaraju, "Handwritten phrase recognition as applied to street name images," Pattern Recognition, vol. 31, pp. 41-51, 1998.

[31] U. Mahadevan and R.C. Nagabushnam, "Gap metrics for word separation in handwritten lines," In Proc. Of Third Int. Conf. on Document Analysis and Recognition, pp. 124-127, Montreal, Canada, Aug., 1995.

[32] J. Park, V. Govindaraju, and S. N. Srihari, "Efficient word segmentation driven by unconstrained handwritten phrase recognition," In Proc. of Fifth Int. Conf. on Document Analysis and Recognition, pp. 605-608, Bangalore, India, Sep., 1999.

[33] G. Seni and E. Cohen, "External word segmentation of off-line handwritten text lines," Pattern Recognition, vol. 27, pp. 41-52, 1994.

[34] N. W. Strathy, "Handwriting recognition for cheque processing," In Proc. 2nd Int. Conf. on Multimodal Interface, pp. 47-50, Hong Kong, Jan., 1999.

[35] C. Barriere and R. Plamondon, "Human identification of letters in mixed-script handwriting: an upper bound on recognition rates," IEEE Trans. Syst., Man, and Cybern., vol. 28, pp. 78-82, Feb., 1998.

[36] M. Cote, E. Lecolinet, M. Cheriet, and C. Y. Suen, "Automatic reading of cursive scripts using a reading model and perceptual concepts," in press, Inaugural Issue of the new International Journal of Document Analysis and Recognition, Spring 1998.

[37] G. Kaufmann, H. Bunke, and T. M. Ha, "Recognition of cursively handwritten words using a combined normalization perturbation approach," Proc. IWFHR, Essex, pp. 17-22, Sep., 1996.

[38] S. W. Lee (Ed.), "Advances in Handwriting Recognition," World Scientific Publishing Co., Singapore, 1999.

[39] A. C. Downton and S. Impedovo (Eds.), "Progress in Handwriting Recognition," World Scientific Publishing Co., Singapore, 1997.

[40] H. Bunke and P. S. P. Wang (Eds.), "Handbook of Character Recognition and Document Image Analysis," World Scientific Publishing Co., Singapore, 1997.

[41] G. Lorette, "Handwriting recognition or reading? What is the situation at the dawn of the 3rd millennium?," Int. J. of Document Analysis and Recognition, vol. 2, pp. 2-12, 1999.

[42] J. Zhou, Q. Gan, A. Krzyzak, and C. Y. Suen, "Recognition of handwritten numerals by Quantum neural network with fuzzy features," Int. J. of Document Analysis and Recognition, vol. 2, pp. 30-36, 1999.

[43] R. Plamondon and S. N. Srihari, "Online and off-line Handwriting recognition: A comprehensive survey," IEEE Trans. on Pattern Analysis and Machine Intelligence, vol. 22, pp. 63-84, Jan., 2000.

[44] L. Schomaker and E. Segers, "Finding features used in the human reading of cursive handwritting," Int. Journal on Document Analysis and Recognition, vol. 2, pp. 13-18, 1999.

[45] J. Franke, L. Lam, R. Legault, C. Nadal, and C. Y. Suen, "Experiments with the CENPARMI database combining different classification approaches," In proceedings of IWFHR, pp. 305-311, Bufalo, NewYork, May, 1993.

[46] C. Y. Suen, C. Nadal, R. Legault, T. A. Mai, and L. Lam, "Computer recognition of unconstrained handwritten numerals," Proceeding of the IEEE, vl. 80, pp. 1162-1180, 1992.

[47] D. S. Lee and S. N. Srihari, "Handprinted digit recognition: A comparison of algorithms," In Proc. of the third International Workshop on Frontiers in Handwritten Recognition, pp. 153-162, Buffalo, New York, May, 1993.

[48] A. Filatov, V. Nikitin, A. Volgunin, and P. Zelinsky, "The AddressScriptTM recognition system for handwritten envelopes, " In proc. of the Third nternational Association for Pattern Recognition Workshop on Document Analysis Systems, pp. 222-236, Nagano, Japan, Nov., 1998.

[49] Z. Lu, Z. Chi, W. C. Siu, and P. Shi, "A background-thinning-based approach for separating and recognizing connected handwritten digit strings," Pattern Recognition, vol. 32, pp. 921-933, 1999.

[50] J. H. Kim, K. K. Kim, C. P. Nadal, and C. Y. Suen, "A methodology of combining HMM and MLP classifiers for cursive word recognition," to appear, Proc. ICPR-2000, Barcelona, Spain, Sep., 2000.

[51] K. Han and I. Sethi, "An off-Line cursive handwritten word recognition system and its application to legal amount interpretation," Automatic Bankcheck Processing, World Scientific Press, pp. 295-308, 1997.

[52] G. Kaufmann and H. Bunke, "A system for the automated reading of check amounts-some key ideas," Proc. of the 3rd International Association for Pattern Recognition Workshop on Document Analysis Systems, Nagano, Japan, pp. 302-315, 1998.

[53] C. Y. Suen and L. Lam, "Multiple classifier combination methodologies for different output levels," Proc. 1st International Workshop on Multiple Classifier System, Cagliari, Italy, June, 2000.

A Methodology for Special Symbol Recognitions

Jisheng Liang[1] Ihsin T. Phillips[2] Vikram Chalana[1] Robert Haralick[3]

[1] MathSoft, Inc. 1700 Westlake Ave N, Suite 500, Seattle, WA 98109, U.S.A.

[2] Department of Computer Science/Software Engineering, Seattle University Seattle, WA 98122 U.S.A.

[3] Department of Electrical Engineering, University of Washington Seattle, WA 98195 U.S.A.

{jliang, yun, haralick@george.ee.washington.edu}

Abstract

This paper presents a special symbol recognition system that incorporates the result of an OCR to recognize the special symbols those not handled by the current commercial OCR systems. Given a document image and the OCR output, we first refine the character coordinates produced by the OCR. Then, the special symbols are distinguished from the normal characters. Finally, we compute the features from the special symbol sub-images and a supervised classifier is used to assign the sub-images to one of the predefined special symbol categories. The system was tested on 5516 images from the National Library of Medicine. The evaluation results are reported in the paper.

1. Introduction

Optical character recognition (OCR) is a success story among the applications of the field of computer vision and pattern recognition [4]. For example, most of the commercial OCR systems on the market today can produce nearly perfect results on quality printed documents and can yield over 90% accuracy rate on moderately degraded documents. However, when in the domain of special symbols, these same systems can fail in miserably. The reason is simple – these systems were not trained to recognize the special symbols. As a result, when encountering a special symbol, such as a Greek letter or a mathematical symbol, most OCR systems do not know it is a special symbol. It would either recognize it as one or more of its regular symbols with a low confident level or assign it as a "non-recognizable" symbol. The task is left for the operator who is assigned to cleaning-up the OCR errors, manually.

The reason for not developing an OCR system that handles the special symbol is obvious. First of all, there is no commercial market there to support the additional development of an OCR system that handles the special symbols. Second, by including the special symbols into the recognition engine, the speed of the system will be slower. This is not very desirable in the commercial world. As a result, without a special symbol recognition system, the conversion of documents from paper format to electronic format remain costly for those documents that contain a substantial amount of special symbols. This paper presents a special symbol recognition system that incorporates the result of an OCR to recognize the special symbols of those not handled by the current commercial OCR systems.

Our recognition system consists of three major modules: character segmentation, special symbol detection, and special symbol classification modules. The system architecture is shown in Figure 1. The description of these three modules are given in Section 2, 3, and 4 respectively. Our experimental results are given in Section 5.

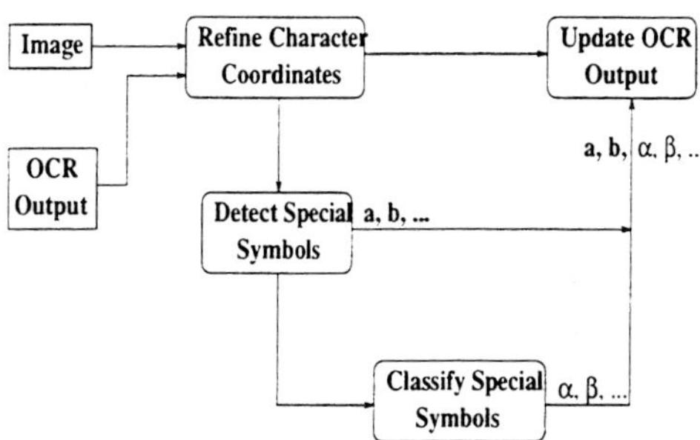

Figure 1. System Architecture.

2. Character Segmentation Refinement

Inputs to the character segmentation module are – a binary document image and the output of a commercial OCR system. The output of the OCR system includes character strings, word boxes, text-line boxes and text-block boxes. First, we compute the set of bounding boxes of the connected components from the input image. Then, we find the correspondences between the computed connected component bounding boxes and the word boxes (of the OCR), and the correspondences between the characters (of the OCR) and the connected components. A character may correspond to one connected component (one-to-one match), or two or more components (one-to-many match). Or, two or more characters may correspond to one connected component (many-to-one match). We use the "relative position" of the characters as a clue for finding the correspondences between the characters and the connected components. The following is the formal definition for the correspondence matching problem.

Problem Statement: Let $A = (a_1, \cdots, a_N)$ be a sequence of characters and let $B = (b_1, \cdots, b_M)$ be a sequence of connected components, the problem is to decompose (split or merge if necessary) the elements of B into a sequence $G = (g_1, \cdots, g_N)$ of glyphs, such that each element of G is associated with a character in A,

$$[(g_1, a_1), (g_2, a_2), \cdots, (g_N, a_N)],$$

that minimizes the criterion function D(F(A), F(G)), where $F(X)$ is a sequence of features of X, and D is the distance measurement between F(A) and F(G). We define $F(X)$ as a transformation that converts each character in X to a character position class. The character position class is defined as the classes follows:

- C 0: within baseline and x-height, e.g. a, c, e, o.
- C 1: that extends above x-height (ascender), e.g. b, A, C, P.
- C 2: character that extends below baseline (descender), e.g., p, g, q
- C 3: character that extends above x-height and below baseline, e.g. {, }.
- C 4: superscript or higher punctuation mark.
- C 5: subscript or lower punctuation mark.

The computation of the character position sequence for a character string is straight forward. However, the computation of the position feature sequence for a sequence of connected components within a word is not trivial. Let a connected component be represented as (x_1, y_1, x_2, y_2), the coordinates of the upper-left and the bottom-right corners of it's bounding box. Taking the bottom-right corners of all the connected component boxes within a text-line, we use a robust line-fitting algorithm [2] to estimate the text line's baseline coordinates. Then, the x-height is estimated from the distance of all the components' upper-left corners to the baseline. The character position class is assigned to each component based on the position of its bounding box with respect to the detected baseline and the x-height of the text-line. Instead of using a global threshold, we build an adaptive classifier for each text-block to determine the character position feature vector for the connected components. A binary tree classifier is adaptively trained given the computed position features and their known position classes. At each node of the classification tree, we search for the best threshold values of the decision rule by minimizing the number of misclassification errors. These feature strings are then matched with each other to decide which connected components correspond to which characters.

3. Special Symbol Detection

A special symbol is usually recognized by an OCR system as a short string of one or more regular characters, where characters within the string, in general, are given low recognition confidence levels by the OCR system. We collect a set of potential special symbol strings among the short strings produced by the OCR. (We consider a string having less than 4 characters long with low character confidence levels as a potential special symbol string.) For each potential special symbol string, we compute the posterior probability of this string being a special symbol, base on the confidence levels of the characters within the string. Using the computed probability, the character on the left and the character on the right of the string, we compute a list of possible special symbol candidates for the string. The actual assignment is done by the classification module (given in Section 4.) Our special symbol detection method is given as follows.

Let the observed character string be $X = x_1 x_2 \cdots x_m$ $m \leq 3$. Each x_i is associate with a pair (a, c), where a is a character and c is the OCR confidence level for the character. The probability that a special symbol $s \in S$ (a known special symbol set) has caused the OCR to produce the string X can be expressed by the use of Bayes' rule as,

$$P(s|X) = \frac{P(X|s)P(s)}{P(X)}. \tag{1}$$

$P(X|s)$ is the probability of observing X under the condition that s is a certain symbol. $P(s)$ is the a priori probability of s, and $P(X)$ is the probability of the character string X.

In the training step, for each given sequence of characters and the confidence levels of the characters, the probability that this sequence of characters is indeed a certain special symbol is calculated. A probability look-up table is constructed for all special symbols $s \in S$.

The context information is also very useful in determining whether a sequence of characters is actually a special symbol. For example, the special symbol "γ" is often recognized as "y" with relatively high confidence. It causes posterior probability $P(s = \gamma | a = y, c)$ to be very low and the symbol "γ" is missed. If we can observe from the data that the probability of "γ" followed by "-" is greater than the probability of the character "y" followed by "-", this context information can be used to update the posterior probability and to detect the symbol "γ".

Let the observed character string before X be $X^- = x_1^- x_2^- \cdots x_n^-$. Let the observed character string after X be $X^+ = x_1^+ x_2^+ \cdots x_p^+$. We use $n = p = 1$. The probability that a special symbol $s \in S$ has caused the OCR to produce X can again be expressed by the use of Bayes' rule as,

$$\begin{aligned} &P(X^-, s, X^+ | X^-, X, X^+) \\ &= \frac{P(X^-, X, X^+ | X^-, s, X^+) P(X^-, s, X^+)}{P(X^-, X, X^+)}. \end{aligned} \tag{2}$$

Based on the assumption of conditional independence among X^-, X, and X^+, then

$$\begin{aligned} &P(X^-, X, X^+ | X^-, s, X^+) \\ &= P(X^- | X^-) P(X|s) P(X^+ | X^+) = C \times P(X|s), \end{aligned} \tag{3}$$

where C is a constant. Therefore, the probability (2) can be approximated as

$$\begin{aligned} &P(X^-, s, X^+|X^-, X, X^+) \\ &\propto \frac{P(X|s)P(X^-, X^+|s)P(s)}{P(X^-, X^+|X)P(X)} \\ &= P(s|X)\frac{P(X^-, X^+|s)}{P(X^-, X^+|X)} \end{aligned} \tag{4}$$

where $P(X^-, X^+|s)$ is the probability when s is a know special symbol, then its left neighbor is X^- and its right neighbor is X^+. And $P(X^-, X^+|X)$ is the probability that, given an observed character sequence X, its left neighbor is X^- and its right neighbor is X^+.

4. Special Symbol Classification

At the end of the special symbol detection module, all potential special symbol strings are given a list of special symbol candidates and the candidates' probabilities. Next step is to determine which symbol to assign to each of these strings. The classification method is as follows.

A sub-image is computed and normalized for each potential special symbol string from the input image. Then, we compute the distance from this sub-image to each of the trained probability maps. (The probability map is computed, off-line, for each special symbol $s \in S$ from the training samples.) Using the probabilities associated with the special symbol candidates as a prior, we use the Bayesian framework to update the probability of each candidate.

To achieve scale and translation uniformity, the regular moments (i.e., m_{pq}) of each image are utilized. An image function $f(x, y)$ can be normalized with respect to scale and translation by transforming it into $g(x, y)$, where

$$g(x, y) = f\left(\frac{x}{a} + \bar{x}, \frac{y}{a} + \bar{y}\right), \tag{5}$$

where $\bar{x} = \frac{m_{10}}{m_{00}}$, $\bar{y} = \frac{m_{01}}{m_{00}}$, and $a = \sqrt{\beta/m_{00}}$ [6]. The normalized image is sampled to an $n \times m$ grid.

Given a set of normalized training samples, we compute the probabilities that a symbol produces foreground value at each pixel, and generate a probability map for each symbol. A probability map is the histogram of a special symbol's normalized images within the training set. Given the image I of a special symbol S_k, its probability map T_k is computed as

$$T_k(i, j) = T_k(i, j) + I(i, j) \tag{6}$$

The values of the probability map is normalized in the range from 0 to 255. Figure 2 shows the computed probability maps for a set of 10 special symbols.

Given a normalized binary (0, 255) sub-image of a given string, we first sample the sub-image into a $n \times m$ grid. Then, we compute the "distance" between the sampled sub-image and each of the trained probability maps. We assign the map with the smallest distance to the sub-image. The

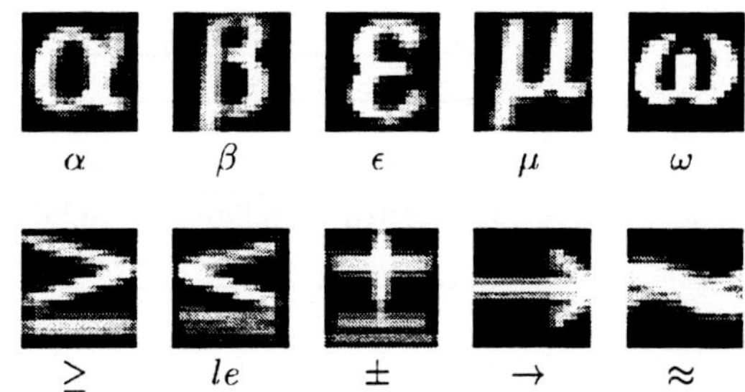

Figure 2. Illustrates the probability maps of some special symbols.

distance d between an image I and a probability map T is defined as the sum of absolute difference:

$$d(I, T) = \sum_i^N \sum_j^M |I(i, j) - T(i, j)|. \tag{7}$$

Let $D = \{d_1, d_2, \cdots, d_i, \cdots, d_N\}$ denotes the distance between an input image I and the trained probability maps $\{T_1, T_2, \cdots, T_N\}$. The likelihood that an input glyph I is indeed a special symbol s_i can be computed as

$$P(I|s_i) = \frac{1/d_i}{\sum_{k=1}^N (1/d_k)} \tag{8}$$

Using the probabilities of the special symbol candidates as the a prior probability, we update the probability of each candidate by observing the image features. Give a sequence of OCR produced character-confidence pairs $X = (X_1, X_2, \cdots, X_N)$, where $X_i = (a_i, c_i)$, we search for the special symbols using the following algorithm.

Algorithm 4.1 *Special symbol recognition*

For $i = 1$ to N, Do

1. For $j = 0$ to 2, Do
   (a) If $i + j > N$, Stop.
   (b) Let $\hat{X} = \bigcup_{k=i}^{i+j} X_k$.
   (c) Determine the left neighbor $X^- = X_{i-1}$ and the right neighbor $X^+ = X_{i+j+1}$.
   (d) Compute the probability that $\hat{X}$ is a special symbol $s \in S$, as the multiplication of the probabilities in Equation 4 and 8,

$$\begin{aligned} &P(X^-, s, X^+|X^-, \hat{X}, X^+) \\ &\propto P(I|s)P(s|\hat{X})\frac{P(X^-, X^+|s)}{P(X^-, X^+|\hat{X})}, \end{aligned} \tag{9}$$

   where I is the image associated with $\hat{X}$.

   End

2. Select $\hat{X}$ that produces the maximum probability. If the probability is larger than a predetermined threshold, replace $\hat{X}$ by the special symbol s.

End

Table 1. Performance of the character segmentation algorithm.

	Total	Correct	Splitting	Merging	Mis-False	Spurious
Ground Truth	36394	36250 (99.61%)	43 (0.12%)	88 (0.24%)	1 (0.00%)	12 (0.03%)
Detected	36396	36250 (99.60%)	90 (0.25%)	42 (0.11%)	1 (0.00%)	13 (0.04%)

Table 2. Performance of the special symbol classification using different features.

Features used	Number of correct detection
Moment invariants	3122 (82.3%)
Zernike moments	3297 (86.9%)
Probability maps	3630 (95.7%)

5. Experimental Results

The data set used in our experiment consists of 5516 pages from the National Library of Medicine.

To evaluate our character segmentation module, we select 32 pages among the 5516 pages and manually groundtruthed the character boxes for the 32 images – a total of 36394 character boxes. The segmentation module was tested on these 32 character-box-groundtruthed images. The evaluation results are shown in Table 1. The evaluation results show that 99.6% (36250) of ground truth character boxes (36394) have been correctly segmented, while 43 boxes are split into total of 90 boxes and 88 boxes are merged into total of 42 detected boxes.

To evaluate our symbol classification module, we selected from the data set 13 special symbols with relatively large number of samples among the special symbols in the data set for training. The selected symbols are: α, β, $\circ$ (Degree), δ, ϵ, γ, $\geq$, κ, $\leq$, μ, $\pm$, $\rightarrow$, $\approx$ (or $\sim$, $\simeq$, $\cong$). The total number of samples is 3794. Three set of features were used in the evaluation: the moment invariants[5], the Zernike moments[6], and the probability map. A decision tree classifier from S-PLUS [3] was used to compute the two moment features and the nearest neighbor classifier was used to compute the probability maps. A 5-fold cross validation method was used to estimate the accuracy of the classification module. The experimental results for the classification modules on the three sets of features are shown in Table 2.

Finally, we evaluated the performance of the combination of the detection and the classification modules. First, we find matches between the special symbols boxes detected by the detection module and the special symbol boxes in the ground truth. The matching results are the numbers of the correct detections, the miss-detections, the false alarms, the splitting and the merging errors. Next, for the special symbols which have been correctly detected (one-to-one match), we determine the rate in which these special symbols are correctly classified. The correct classification rate is used as the performance measure. The miss-detection and the false alarm rates based on different threshold values are plotted in Figure 3(a). The correct classification rate versus the threshold values are shown in Figure 3(b).

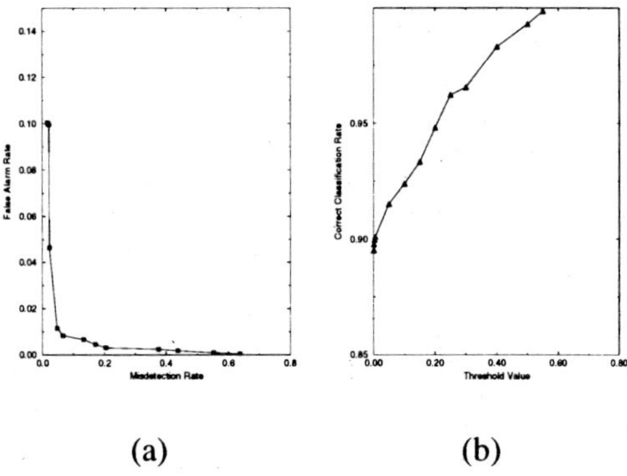

Figure 3. Plots (a) false alarm rate vs. Mis-detection rate; (b) correct classification rate; using different threshold values.

Acknowledge

The authors would like to thank the National Library of Medicine for the support of this work.

References

[1] T.H. Cormen, C.E. Leiserson, and R.L. Rivest. *Introduction to Algorithms*, MIT Press, 1990.

[2] J. Liang *Document Structure Analysis and Performance Evaluation*, Ph.D. thesis, University of Washington, 1999.

[3] MathSoft. *S-PLUS Guide to Statistics*, 1997.

[4] O.D. Trier, A.K. Jain and T. Taxt. Feature extraction methods for character recognition - a survey. *Pattern Recognition*, pp 641-662, Vol. 29, No. 4, 1996.

[5] T. H. Reiss. *Recognizing planar objects using invariant image features*, Lecture notes in computer science 676, Springer-Verlag, 1991.

[6] A. Khotanzad and Y.H. Hong. Invariant image recognition by Zernike moments. *IEEE Transactions on Pattern Recognition and Machines Intelligence*, Vol. 12, No. 5, May 1990.

Automatic Acquisition of Context-based Images Templates for Degraded Character Recognition in Scene Images

Minako Sawaki, Hiroshi Murase and Norihiro Hagita
{minako, murase, hagita}@apollo3.brl.ntt.co.jp
NTT Communication Science Laboratories
3-1, Morinosato-Wakamiya, Atsugi, Kanagawa, 243-0198, Japan

Abstract

This paper proposes a method for adaptively acquiring templates for degraded characters in scene images. Characters in scene images are often degraded because of poor printing and viewing conditions. To cope with the degradation problem, we proposed the idea of "context-based image templates" which include neighboring characters or parts thereof and so represent more contextual information than single-letter templates. However, our previous method manually selects the learning samples to make the context-based image templates and is time-consuming. Therefore, we attempt to make the context-based image templates automatically from single-letter templates and learning text-line images. The context-based image templates are iteratively created using the k-nearest neighbor rule. Experiments with 3,467 alpha-numeric characters in nine bookshelf images show that the high recognition rates for test samples possible with this method asymptotically approach those achieved with manual selection.

1. Introduction

A digital camera is currently one of the most inexpensive and simple tools for gathering image data. It may also become a convenient tool for image-to-text code conversion. As one application, we attempt to recognize characters on the spines of technical journals on bookshelves as recorded in digital camera images. The goal is to construct a personal library/filing database of the journals in the user's vicinity.

Characters in bookshelf images (Fig. 1) are often degraded because of poor printing and viewing conditions. This degradation problem involves problems with computer vision as well as conventional character recognition.

To cope with the degradation problem, conventional methods for character recognition try to construct document-specific character templates using ground truth data or lexical information. Kopec *et al.* extract templates by aligning text-lines and those ground truth data [1]. Nagy *et al.* isolate character templates from word images by word shift algorithm with truth data [2]. Ho [3] recognizes frequently occurring words and extracts templates based on the method in [2].

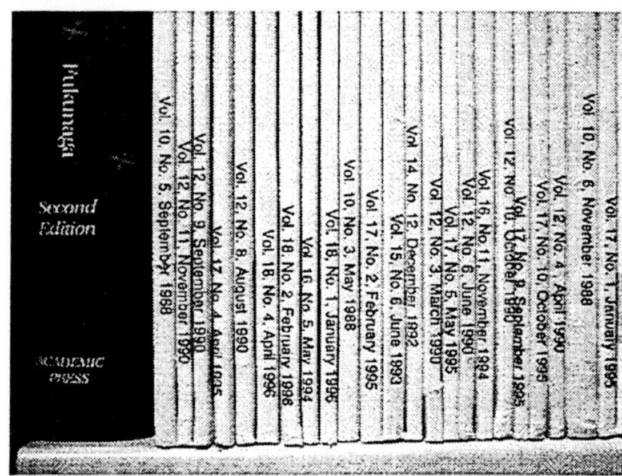

Fig. 1 Example of a bookshelf image.

The authors, on the other hand, proposed templates that include neighboring characters or parts thereof to cope with degraded characters [4, 5]. The templates are referred to as context-based image templates, since they offer more contextual information than single-letter templates. Though they are robust for degraded characters, our previous method manually selects learning samples and so is too heavy a burden.

In this paper, we automatically create the context-based image templates iteratively from single-letter templates in an initial dictionary and learning text-line images. The learning text-line images are recognized with the initial dictionary. The recognized areas in the text-lines are used as learning patterns for context-based image templates. The learning patterns are labeled by the character category decided by the recognition process. Appropriate learning patterns are then automatically selected as context-based image templates using the *k-nearest neighbor* rule. This procedure can also be used to update an existing dictionary. Experiments show the recognition rates with the proposed method asymptotically approach those achieved with manual selection.

1051-4651/00 $10.00 © 2000 IEEE

2. Recognition process

An input color image captured by a digital camera is converted into a gray-scale image and then binarized. Skew detection is needed since journals usually slump on the bookshelf. Journal boundaries are detected using the dark lines caused by shadow. Next, text-line regions between the boundaries are extracted by the transition frequency of pixel colors (white-to-black and black-to-white) during vertical scanning, and the skew of each text-line is then corrected and the size is normalized.

Characters in the text-line region are recognized by displacement matching [4, 5]. An observation window ***F*** moves along the text-line pixel-by-pixel, and ***F*** is matched against stored templates. ***F*** is also shifted along the horizontal-axis to cover text-line misalignment. The complementary similarity measure, which is robust against noise, is employed for matching [4]. If the maximum similarity value exceeds a threshold, the category is selected as the recognition result.

3. Automatic template acquisition

3.1 Approach

To recognize low-quality characters, we proposed the complementary similarity measure S_C [4] and context-based image templates [5]. The complementary similarity measure is robust against additive/deletion noise, however, it is not robust enough against the deformation in scene images arising from poor printing and viewing conditions.

To overcome this problem, we introduced the context-based image templates, which include neighboring characters or parts thereof [5]. Fig. 2 shows examples of learning patterns in a text-line and the context-based image templates. Our previous method [5] used manual operations to screen the learning patterns, label the correct category name, and use them to make the contest-based image templates. However, positioning the characters and typing the correct categories by hand are very tiring activities.

In this paper, we provide a method that automatically acquires context-based image templates from learning images without manual extraction of learning patterns or the transcription process such as ground-truth information. This approach reduces the tiresome work of typing. Also, it enables to a dictionary to be adapted to the input conditions automatically and rapidly without keyboard work. This feature is convenient for a portable recognition system with a digital camera.

Since the adverse effect of mis-classified templates caused by automatic acquisition is a problem, we utilize the *k-nearest neighbor* rule within the learning patterns to eliminate such mis-classified templates. Even with this technique, some mis-classified patterns may remain.

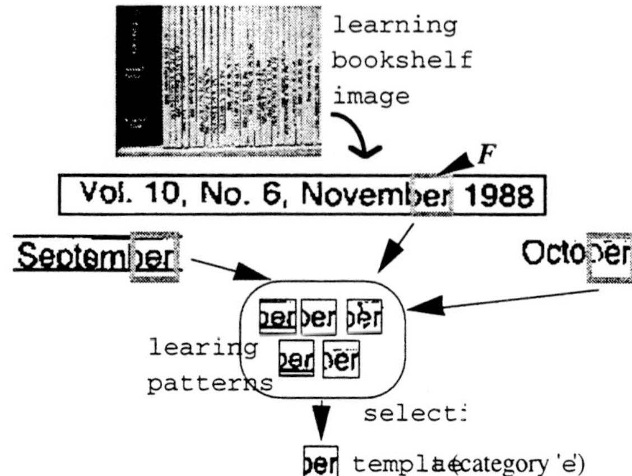

Fig. 2 Context-based image templates.

However, we assume that when the ratio of the number of mis-classified templates to the number of correctly classified templates is low, the mis-classified templates do not decrease the recognition rates significantly.

3.2 Template acquisition for low-quality characters

This section explains the detailed process of the proposed method. The flowchart is shown in Fig. 3.

Step 1) Making the initial dictionary

Initial dictionary is made by manually drawing one single letter image per character category in learning text-line images and registering them as single letter templates. This is the only manual step with the method.

Step 2) Recognition of learning text-lines with the $(t\text{-}1)$th dictionary

The learning text-lines are recognized by the $(t\text{-}1)$th dictionary by displacement matching in the t-th iteration. When the similarity exceeds the threshold, the category is determined as a recognized category. The recognized areas are extracted as learning patterns.

In the first iteration, the initial dictionary is used for recognition. In this case, the dictionary is divided into two in size, and large character group and small character group are recognized alternately one after the other. As each observation window usually includes multiple characters, the recognition with single-letter templates may not achieve high recognition accuracy. In order to avoid mis-classified by the existence of neighboring characters in the observation window, large characters which are relatively robust even with neighboring characters are recognized first and these regions are then whitened out. The small characters are then recognized. Later on, large characters and small characters are recognized alternately one after the other for several times. This recognition method is relatively time-consuming but it's effective in obtaining higher recognition rates with the initial dictionary than using the whole initial dictionary at once.

Step 3) Pattern selection using *k-nearest neighbor* rule

Since the extracted learning patterns may include misclassified patterns, uncertain patterns are eliminated from the dictionary using the *k-nearest neighbor* rule. Patterns whose *k-nearest neighbors* belong to many different categories are assumed to be uncertain templates and are not registered in the updated dictionary.

k-nearest neighbors of a learning pattern are obtained from the learning patterns. When a category achieves a majority, the pattern is registered in the updated dictionary. If the pattern number of the most significant category of *k-nearest neighbor* patterns does not exceed 50% of k, the learning pattern is not registered in the updated dictionary.

Step 4) Stop criterion

When the number of patterns removed becomes small, the iteration of learning is stopped. Otherwise, Steps 2 and 3 are repeated using the updated dictionary.

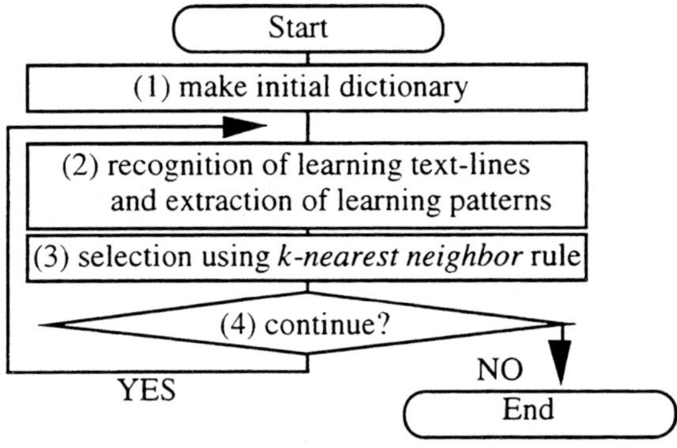

Fig. 3 Template acquisition flow.

4. Recognition experiments

4.1 Experimental conditions

Bookshelf images were captured by using a digital camera (832 x 608 pixels) from a straight view. Journals on the bookshelf were the same kind with different publication dates (journals : *IEEE Trans. Pattern Anal. Machine Intell.*, 1988-1996). Threshold value for binarization was 128 out of 256 gray levels.Thirty seven categories were used consisting of numbers (0-9) and alphabetical categories (*A,D,F,J,M-O,S,V,a-c,e,g-i,l-p,r-v,y*) which are enough for recognizing *No*,

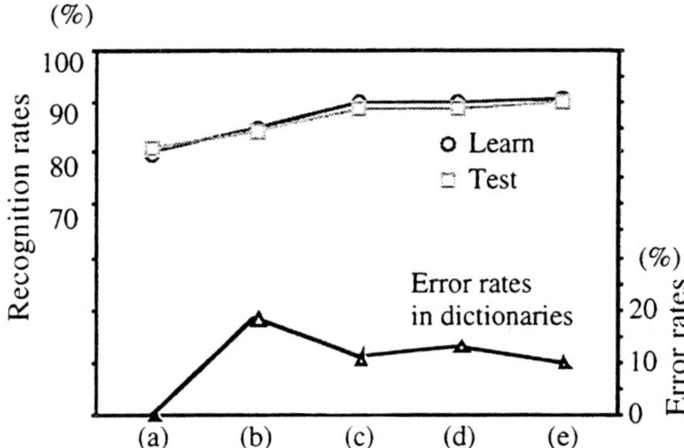

Fig. 4 Recognition rates for bookshelf images and error rates in the dictionaries. (a)initial dictionary, (b)all learning patterns (t=1 iteration), (c)selected dictionary (t=1 iteration), (d) all learning patterns (t=2 iteration), (e) selected dictionary (t=2 iteration).

Vol, *month* and *year*, all of which are often printed on journal spines. Dots (.) and commas (,) were not recognized. 3,860 patterns in 10 bookshelf images and 3,467 patterns in 9 bookshelf images were used as learning and test patterns, respectively (both had 14 words and numbers). The size of F was n = 24 x 24 pixels. In the experiments, the result was regarded as correct when the correct category was determined at the correct position. k of the *k-nearest neighbor* rule was determined as 10 (including own category) from preliminary experiments.

4.2 Experimental results

The recognition rates are shown in Fig 4. The plots correspond to recognition rates with the initial dictionary, all learning patterns (1st iteration), selected dictionary (1st iteration), all learning patterns (2nd iteration), selected dictionary (2nd iteration). We stopped learning after two iterations as the removed pattern number basically saturated at this point. The template numbers in the dictionaries were 37, 3840, 3428, 3906, 3736, respectively. Figure 5 shows examples of templates in the initial and the last dictionary. The recognition rate with the last dictionary was 89.5% for the test patterns. Our previous method achieved 96.3%. Fig. 4 shows that the recognition rates of the proposed method increased with iteration number and approached that achieved with manual template selection.

The error rates, percentage of templates with erroneous category name, were 0.0%, 18.3%, 10.9%, 13.0%, 10.0% for the five dictionaries, respectively (Fig. 4). Error rates in the dictionaries fluctuated during these iteration steps. This is because the error rates increase with pattern extraction and decrease with selection. The values for (c) and (e) compared to (b) and (d) show that error rates were decreased by *k-nearest neighbor* based selection. Throughout learning, the error rates decrease gradually with iteration number. Therefore, our method is effective in automatically acquiring context-based image templates.

All eliminated templates of category '*a*' in the 1st selection step are shown in Fig. 6. Nine patterns of the 13 eliminated patterns (69%) were correctly eliminated.

Fig. 5 Examples of templates (category '*a*') (a)initial dictionary, (b) last dictionary.

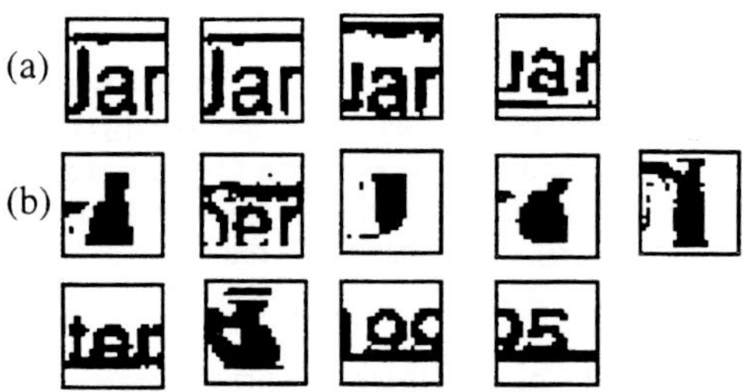

Fig. 6 Templates eliminated by *k-nearest neighbor* rule in the 1st iteration (category '*a*') (a) mis-eliminated patterns, (b) correctly eliminated patterns.

For comparizon, the iteration was continued till t=6 where the recognition rate (test data) started to decrease. The maximum recognition rate (test data) of 90.4% was obtained with the selected dictionary at t=5 while the error rate in the dictionary was 29.7%.

5. Journal volume retrieval system

As an application of the proposed method, a journal volume retrieval system was constructed. This system enables us to locate the desired volume within similar magazines on the bookshelf or to determine if some volumes are missing.

This system consists of a digital camera for image capture and a computer for recognition and retrieval, both commercial products. It recognizes characters in bookshelf images, and search strings are matched against the recognition results. When the desired journal volumes exist, they are displayed on the screen as binary images. Two search strings can be typed at one time, and the system retrieves the volumes using AND search.

The system image is shown in Fig. 7. The recognition results from top to the bottom correspond to the magazines from left to right. In Fig. 7, one journal is retrieved using the search strings of "*96*" and "*Jan*".

6. Conclusions

This paper proposed an automatic method for acquiring templates for degraded character recognition in scene images. To cope with the degradation, we used our

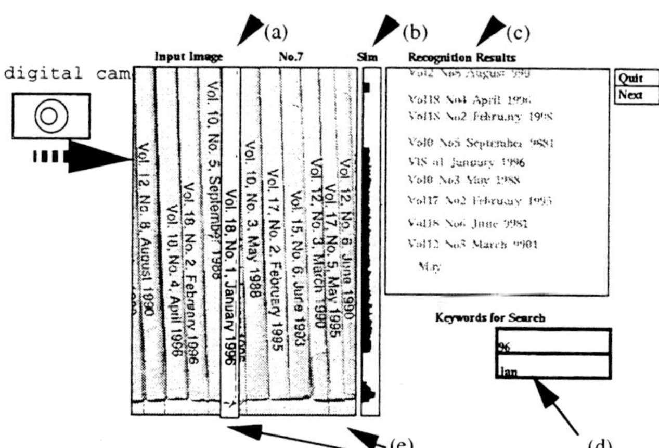

Fig. 7 Journal volume retrieval system (a) input color image, (b) maximum similarity values, (c) recognition results, (d) search strings, (e) retrieved volumes.

context-based image templates, which include neighboring characters or parts thereof. The method creates context-based image templates automatically from single-letter templates and learning text-lines. Learning patterns in the learning text-lines are extracted by the recognition results using an initial dictionary. The learning patterns are then selected by the *k-nearest neighbor* rule for inclusion in an updated version of the original dictionary. These steps are iterated to refine the dictionary. Experiments with 3,467 characters in nine bookshelf images show that the recognition performance of the proposed method asymptotically approached to that achieved with manual extraction.

Our future works include designing an good initial dictionay and applying this method to various kinds of books and observation conditions.

Acknowledgements

We wish to express our gratitude to Dr. K. Ishii for several fruitful discussions. We also thank Mr. T. Iwata for his cooperation.

References

[1]G.E.Kopec and M.Lomelin, "Document-Specific Character Template Estimation", *Proc. of SPIE*, Vol. 2660, pp.14-26 (1996).

[2]G.Nagy and Y.Xu, "Automatic Prototype Extraction for Adaptive OCR", *Proc of ICDAR'97*, pp.278-282 (1997).

[3] T.K.Ho, "Bootstrapping Text Recognition from Stop Words", *Proc. of ICPR'98*, pp.605-609 (1998).

[4] M. Sawaki and N. Hagita, "Text-line Extraction and Character Recognition of Document Headlines with Graphical Designs using Complementary Similarity Measure", *IEEE Trans. Pattern Anal. Machine Intell.*, Vol. 20, No. 20, pp. 1103 - 1109 (1998).

[5] M. Sawaki, H. Murase and N. Hagita, "Character Recognition in Bookshelf Images using Context-based Image Templates", *Proc. of ICDAR99*, pp.79 - 82 (1999).

Crisp and Fuzzy Evaluations and D.P. Algorithms for Dealing with Extra Ink in Cursive Handwriting Recognition*

Carlo Scagliola & Gianluca Nicchiotti
Elsag spa - Via G.Puccini, 2 – 16154 Genoa – Italy
e-mail: {carlo.scagliola , gianluca.nicchiotti}@elsag.it

Abstract

In segmentation-by-recognition methods, words are recognised by searching for the aggregation of basic segments (strokes) that best matches one of the sequences of letters allowed by the lexicon. The presence of spurious strokes ("extra ink") impairs recognition, since they have to be associated anyway with some letter of the word. This paper describes how we solved this problem by properly defining initial crisp evaluations to filter out unambiguous extra ink strokes, and then, for ambiguous strokes, by defining fuzzy measures that evaluate the plausibility with which they can be associated to a class of extra ink instead of to a letter class, and finally by devising search algorithms that allow extra ink strokes to be "consumed" without associating them to letters: it is the matching algorithm that decides if it is less costly to consider a hypothesis as extra ink or to associate it to some letter.

1. Introduction

Segmentation-by-recognition is a general paradigm most frequently and successfully adopted to recognize off-line cursive words [1]: the general idea is that of oversegmenting the image into basic strokes, then of producing a variety of letter hypotheses represented by one stroke or by the aggregation of two or more consecutive strokes and then of looking for the sequence of hypotheses that best matches one of the sequences of letters allowed by the lexicon. The various systems may differ under many respects but, to find the best match, Dynamic Programming is inevitably used and the matching schemes are always such that each letter must be composed of one or more strokes (up to some maximum number) and each stroke must be associated to some letter, alone or aggregated to some nearby strokes.

Now, it often happens, in real-life application, that the image to be recognized may contain also black regions that do not belong to the written word: they may be noise spots or parts of writing belonging to the line above or below in the original image (e.g. an address), or a comma that was not properly segmented out. Those black regions, collectively referred to as "extra ink", may seriously impair word recognition. Since an extra ink stroke has to be necessarily associated to some letter, it may easily cause a correct adjacent letter to receive a poor matching score or a spurious letter to be associated to the extra ink stroke itself. Similar problems may also occur with exaggerated flourishings, especially in the final part of a word, that deform the normal appearance of a letter or that cause hypersegmentation of the final letter (i.e. the final letter is segmented into a number of strokes that exceeds the maximum limit allowed).

This paper describes how we solved this problem by defining initial crisp evaluations to filter out unambiguous extra ink strokes, and by using fuzzy measures to evaluate the plausibility, for ambiguous strokes, of being an extra ink or flourishing. Then a D.P. algorithm finds the best sequence of associations between stroke aggregates and the sequence of letters of a word plus possible extra ink.

2. Dealing with extra ink in word recognition

2.1. Initial "crisp" extra ink filtering

The first step in extra ink processing is done at the preprocessing level, after noise filtering and before skew and slant normalization and reference lines detection [2]. We refer to this step as **crisp** extra ink evaluation.

Initial filtering is very conservative, and only those black regions that clearly do not belong to the word are filtered out. Only two evaluation criteria are used for labeling a black region as extra ink:

- "small" and "far from other regions", i.e. area < th1 and distance from any other region > th2;
- "coming from outside the image" and "narrow", i.e. touching the edge of the image and with a width/height ratio < th3.

1051-4651/00 $10.00

2.2. D.P. equations for dealing with extra ink

The preprocessed image is segmented into basic strokes, then letter hypotheses are constructed either as single strokes or by aggregating two or more strokes and are measured against letter classes [3]. Each hypothesis produces a vector of distances from the 26 letter classes, where the distance from a class is the minimum of the distances from all the codevectors representing the various typical patterns for that class. These distances represent the costs for associating a given letter hypothesis with a given letter class.

The image is finally recognized by matching its characteristics with those expected from the lexicon. The optimal interpretation algorithm considers one lexicon word at a time: for each word, it searches for the sequence of letter hypotheses that attains the minimum cumulative distance from letters. This minimum cost is computed by means of Dynamic Programming; it represents the score for that word, with which the lexicon words are ranked. We describe here first the standard D.P. used in our baseline system, and then the modifications we brought to deal with extra ink during search.

With standard D.P., we define a matrix C(n,j) that stores the minimum partial cumulative cost for associating the first n letters with all the sequences of letter hypotheses that use the first j strokes. The value of C(n,j) is computed recursively by extending the possibly optimal sequences of associations one step shorter, by means of the following standard D.P. equations:

$$C(n,j) = \min_{[k=\text{possible predecessors of } j]} \{C(n-1,k) + d(h_{k,j},u_n)\} \quad (1)$$

where $d(h_{k,j},u_n)$ is the distance between the letter hypothesis joining nodes k and j in the graph (i.e. formed by the strokes k+1, ..., j) and the n-th letter of the lexicon word considered. Eq. (1) is computed up to $j=j_{max}$, number of strokes, and $n=n_{max}$, number of letters in the word.

$C(n_{max}, j_{max})$ is the minimum cumulative cost we are looking for. After normalizing by the number of letters, this cost, that now has the physical meaning of the minimum average cost of associating letter hypotheses with letter classes, can be used as the word's score needed to rank the lexicon. This normalization is absolutely necessary, otherwise shorter words, that cumulate a lower number of distance measures, would be preferred to longer words. This is due to the fact that distance measures are computed with a normalization of the letter hypothesis, to reflect a difference in shape between the hypothesis and letter prototypes, independently of the "amount of image" used by the letter hypothesis [3].

With standard D.P. equations, any stroke **must** be associated with one of the letters of the word under consideration. If a stroke is an extra ink one, this may not cause any harm, especially if it is small and close to true character strokes. However, the distance score for the correct word is certainly increased, and sometimes this results in a recognition error.

Consider the example shown in Fig. 1. The extra comma to the right of the word could not be safely removed by the initial extra ink filtering. When the optimal interpretation algorithm searches for the best match of the strokes with the letters of the true word "Beach", the extra comma is necessarily aggregated with preceding strokes and measured against the letter class "h", resulting in a large distance. When the best match is instead computed against the word "Rancho", the extra comma is associated with the final "o" and, although its distance measure is rather poor, and some other distances are also slightly worse than for the correct letters, the average distance is still better for "Rancho" than for "Beach".

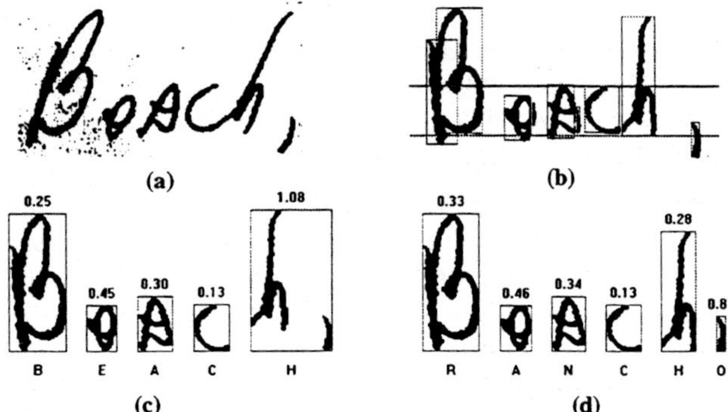

Fig. 1 - Best match for correct and winning words in the presence of extra ink: (a) original image, (b) preprocessed image with superimposed segmentation, (c) optimal hypotheses-letters association for the word "Beach" and (d) for the word "Rancho"

The only way to solve the problem is to allow extra ink strokes to be "consumed" without associating them with any of the letters of the word, thus performing a "horizontal" transition in the cost matrix. The horizontal transitions are attached a cost similar to the one attached to diagonal arcs, i.e. a cost that represents how "distant" the hypothesis is from being considered a piece of extra ink. The computation of this distance term is explained in the next section. It should be noticed, however, that now all the paths that arrive in (n,j) have cumulated a different number of distance terms: every time a horizontal path is taken, one more distance term is added. So, unless the cost function is changed, if extra ink distance terms have approximately the same magnitude as letter classes distance terms, horizontal paths would be penalised: extra ink, although correctly measured, would not be detected by the optimal interpretation algorithm, that would most probably "prefer" to associate the extra ink with a neighbouring letter. The solution is to multiply all the distance measures by a weight term proportional, in some sense, to the "amount of image" consumed in the transitions, so that the minimum global cumulative cost is independent of the number of letters with which the image has been associated [4]. The modified D.P. equations take thus the form shown in Eq. (2):

$$C(n,j)=\min\begin{cases} C(n-1,k) + d(h_{k,j}, u_n) \bullet w_{k,j} \\ C(n,k) + d(h_{k,j}, xi) \bullet w_{k,j} \end{cases} \quad (2)$$

[k=possible predecessors of j]

where $d(h_{k,j}, xi)$ is the distance term between the hypothesis $h_{k,j}$ and the class xi of extra ink, and $w_{k,j}$ is the weight term for the hypothesis $h_{k,j}$.

Clearly, the cumulative weight for any sequence of letter hypotheses that make use of the same strokes must also be the same, in order that all the paths have the same chances of being traversed: whether a path is preferred or not must depend only on the how well the hypotheses that compose that path match with the sequence of letters or extra ink classes. The implied condition is that the weight for an hypothesis that aggregates a number of strokes is the sum of the weights for the hypotheses composed of the same single strokes [4]. We performed preliminary experiments with different weighting functions for a stroke, i.e. proportional to its area, to the square root of its area or simply equal to one, and we found that the simpler weight performed best. The value of $C(n_{max}, j_{max})$ can be divided by the global weight of the image (sum of the weights of the single strokes), that is the same for all interpretations, to obtain again a score with the meaning of a (weighted) average distance.

Comparing eq.(2) with eq.(1), we see that the number of comparisons is now doubled: experimental evaluations confirmed that the computing time of D.P. equations (2) is 2.04 times than before, but this is still only 8.6% of the overall recognition time.

2.3. Computing distance from the extra ink class

The distance between an hypothesis and the general class of extra ink is a measure of how well (or, better to say, how badly) the hypotesis can be considered a member of the extra ink class. By the very definition of extra ink, it is not possible now to "recognize" it by its shape, but rather by its dimensions and especially by its position with respect to the main body of the writing. Therefore it is now impossible to use the same feature extraction and distance measure as used for letter classes. We found that a more sensible approach is that of evaluating the possibility that the hypothesis under measure belongs to the various subclasses of extra ink (i.e. its subclass membership μ [5]), and then transform this possibility into a distance by means of a simple log transformation:

$$f(\mu) = -C_1 \log(\mu) + C_2 \quad (3)$$

where the coefficients C_1 and C_2 are given suitable values in order to obtain, for extra ink hypotheses, distances that cover the same range as the distances obtained by letter hypotheses from the corresponding letter classes.

We defined a small number of subclasses for the general extra ink class, and for each subclass we defined a membership measure based on the theory of fuzzy sets [5]. The subclasses considered are:

- extra ink in the upper part of the image;
- extra ink in the lower part of the image;
- residual comma after the word;
- initial flourishing;
- final flourishing.

The latter two subclasses were defined although they are not strictly extra ink, since exaggerated flourishings may also impair recognition. In any case, a flourishing does not have any linguistic meaning and may be taken out without changing the letter interpretation.

For each of the extra ink subclasses we defined a fuzzy membership function in terms of a linguistic expression whose truth value is evaluated according to standard fuzzy logic composition rules. As an example, we present in Table 1 the linguistic expressions used for computing the membership for the first three subclasses. Italicized expressions refer to fuzzy variables, while non italicized expressions to boolean ones.

Table 1 - Linguistic expressions used to compute the membership of a hypothesis to three extra ink subclasses

Upper extra ink	Entirely above upperline AND (*very far from other strokes* OR (*not connected to any other stroke* AND (*small area* OR *narrow*)))
Lower extra ink	Entirely below baseline AND *not connected to any other stroke* AND (*small area* OR *much below baseline*)
Residual comma	The rightmost hypothesis AND *not connected to any other stroke* AND *mostly below baseline* AND *small area*

The membership functions of Table 1 were defined in a very conservative way, i.e. in such a way that strokes belonging to a letter and contributing to its recognition could not be easily treated as extra ink. For each of the boolean elementary expressions defined above, we simply implemented a function that tested the condition, e.g. that the hypothesis is a single connected region or that it is entirely below the baseline. For each of the fuzzy expressions we instead implemented a function that took some measure and computed a membership value.

For instance, the function "narrow" compares the horizontal dimension of the hypothesis Δx with the average width of all the strokes $\underline{\Delta x}$: if the former is less than 20% of the latter, the membership is 1, while if it exceeds the average width the membership is 0, with intermediate values varying linearly with the ratio $\Delta x/\underline{\Delta x}$:

The computed membership values are finally transformed into distances by applying Eq. (3). The value for C_2 was chosen so that a perfectly plausible extra ink would get anyway a distance equal to the average distance obtained by letter hypotheses from the corresponding class (that in our case was 0.35). The value for C_1 was simply chosen equal to unity, in such a way that a membership of 0.5 would result in approximately a doubled distance.

3. Experimental results

A test set of 696 postal names (city and state names) was selected from the TEST directory of the CEDAR database [6]. From that directory we excluded all the words with less than three letters (basically all the handprinted two letter state abbreviations), and all the images that were clearly out of our input specifications, i.e. those containing exceedingly large portions of writing from the line above or below or even two lines of writing, large underlines or lines crossing the word, etc.

The 696 images included instead many very noisy images and images with extra ink, like descenders coming from the line above, ascenders coming from the line below and commas. The images with extra ink are 186, (26.7% of the total), and other 96 ones (13.7%), although without extra ink, can be defined as "very noisy". Preprocessing removes most of the noise, but sometimes it leaves some spots that can be treated as extra ink.

We ran the word recognition against a dictionary of 1000 postal words. The recognition program computes also, for each recognition, the probability of the correct word to be ranked first in two random subdictionaries of 100 and 10 words, that include the correct one. We ran the test under several conditions, and the results are shown in Table 2.

Table 2 - Recognition results under various conditions

dictionary size	1000	100	10
test condition 1	73.56%	85.65%	93.96%
test condition 2	78.59%	89.58%	96.07%
test condition 3	79.45%	91.20%	97.18%
test condition 4	80.60%	91.89%	97.70%
test condition 5	80.32%	91.49%	97.25%
test condition 6	81.61%	92.17%	97.73%

The conditions are: 1) no extra ink processing at all, 2) no initial "crisp" filtering but extra ink processing during matching, 3) only the initial "crisp" extra ink filtering but no treatment during matching, 4) initial filtering and treatment of only extra ink situations but not flourishings, 5) initial filtering and only flourishing processing during matching, 6) full extra ink processing.

The results in the first column indicate that initial crisp filtering alone (condition 3) improves performance considerably, basically recovering one every five recognition errors, but also that fuzzy evaluation alone (condition 2) achieves almost the same level of performance. The combined processing (condition 6) improves performance by another 2%. Comparing condition 5 and condition 3, we see that also flourishing processing gives a small but non negligible 1% contribution to overall performance.

4. Conclusions

The paper described how we solved the problem of extra ink in off-line handwritten word recognition. Black regions that can be unambiguously labeled as extra ink are removed early. Other, ambiguous, extra ink strokes are instead evaluated by computing a fuzzy membership to the different subclasses of extra ink. The decision whether they can be removed or not is left to the interpretation stage, when the image is matched against the lexicon words: it is the matching algorithm that decides if it is less costly to consider a hypothesis as a piece of extra ink or to associate it to some letter. To this purpose we modified the standard D.P. equations, taking care that no bias exists towards considering a hypothesis as extra ink or not. Experiments indicate a 30% reduction in the recognition error rate.

5. References

[1] R.Plamondon and S.N.Srihari, "On-Line and Off-Line Handwriting Recognition: A Comprehensive Survey", *IEEE Trans. on PAMI*, Vol. 22, No. 1, pp.63-84, Jan. 2000.

[2] G.Nicchiotti and C.Scagliola, "Generalised Projections: a Tool for Cursive Handwriting Normalisation", *Proc. 5-th ICDAR*, pp. 729-732, Bangalore, India, September 1999.

[3] F.Camastra & A.Vinciarelli, "Isolated Cursive Character Recognition based on Neural Nets", *Kuenstliche Intelligenz*, Vol. 2, pp. 17-19, June 1999.

[4] C.Scagliola, "Search Algorithms for the Recognition of Cursive Phrases without Word Segmentation", in S.W.Lee (Ed.), *Advances in Handwriting Recognition*, World Scientific, Singapore, 1999.

[5] L.A.Zadeh, "Fuzzy Sets as a Basis for a Theory of Possibility", *Fuzzy Sets and Systems*, Vol. 1, N. 1, 1978.

[6] J.Hull, "A database for handwriting recognition research", *IEEE Trans. on PAMI*, pp. 550-554, May 1994.

* This work has been funded by the Italian Ministry of University and of Scientific and Technological Research (MURST) under the grant to Parco Scientifico e Tecnologico dell'Elba, Project No. 62413, for the research line "Neural devices for the recognition of cursive handwriting".

IRIS
An Image Recognition and Interpretation System for the Dutch Postbank

I.L. Dijkstra
KPN Research
i.l.dijkstra@kpn.com

N. Smits
Postbank

Abstract

KPN Research has developed an all-purpose check recognition system for the Dutch Postbank. This Image Recognition and Interpretation System (IRIS) is the result of more than thirty years of research and development and contains four major functionalities: (1) determination of the way a check is filled in, (2) recognition of the amount and account fields, (3) recognition of the postcode and (4) signature verification. The IRIS system recognizes a large percentage of amount and account fields on checks without any human intervention. The system has a high yield and a very low substitution error rate. The recognition results are used as direct input for the financial transaction system. In this respect the system is unique in the world. The system has proven itself in operation during the last two years. New developments include signature verification which is in a prototype stage.

1. Introduction

Postbank is a major Dutch bank and part of ING. The bank has more than 8 million customers and uses the concept of home banking. This means that the customer can perform most financial transactions using checks, cash dispensers, telephone (Girofoon), credit cards or the internet (Girotel, I-Pay). Two types of checks are used. (1) Checkbooks can be used at home to transfer money to others. They are sent in using pre-paid envelopes that are provided by Postbank. See Figure 1. (2) Acceptgiros are checks that are usually pre-printed by large companies, such as the telephone companies, and are sent to the recipient by mail as a means of billing.

2. Problem description

The home banking system is very successful and every day one million checks are sent to Postbank. The customer fills in the amount, account number, name and address information and signature and sends the check to the bank. The checks are mainly filled in by hand. Acceptgiros are partly pre-printed. The checks are processed at two locations in The Netherlands.

Before the financial transaction can be performed, all the relevant information on the checks must be available in a digital format. The most labor intensive process is keying all the amounts and account numbers. High reliability is crucial for Postbank. Correcting a wrong transaction is very expensive and errors may result in a loss of customers.

In the early seventies the demanded high reliability was achieved by keying each field twice by different typists. When the data entry results differed, the field was keyed for the third time. The first recognition system that KPN Research developed was accurate enough to replace one of the two data entry typists. The recognition result was compared with the data entry result.

All Postbank checks have a number of elements. The codeline at the bottom of the document contains a code that identifies the type of check. This codeline is partly pre-printed using the standard OCR-B font. The amount and account number are pre-printed or filled in manually. The fields have a red drop-out color that becomes invisible when using a red filter in front of the camera.

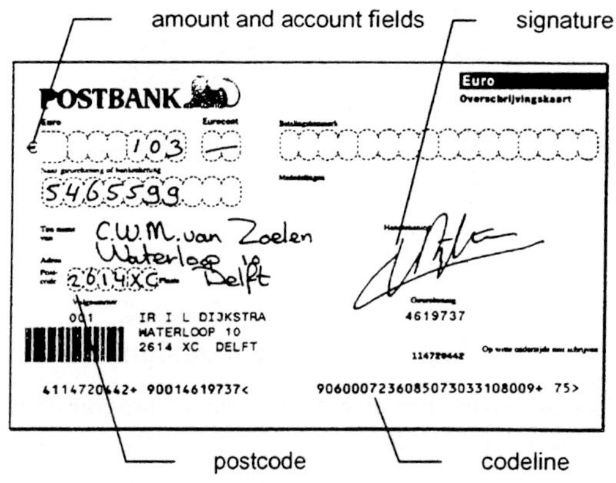

Figure 1 - A check

3. System design

The system can be described as a sequential process with the following steps:

1. image capture
2. codeline recognition
3. landmark detection
4. document verification
5. amount and account recognition
6. postcode recognition
7. signature verification
8. data entry

9. name-number verification
10. transaction
11. image print

KPN Research has developed the image processing and recognitions subsystems 3...7 which are integrated in the image processing infrastructure 1, 2 and 8...11. See Figure 2.

Predecessors of the IRIS system that were developed by KPN Research in the seventies used dedicated hardware. In the late eighties a parallel Transputer architecture was built with 60 processors. The current IRIS system is programmed in Pascal on the OpenVMS operating system and runs on Compaq Alpha workstations with three Alpha processors of 275 MHz.

The IRIS system uses a black box principle: input is an image and the output is the recognition result. Communication is done using TCP/IP and a simple tag-length-value protocol. The images are in TIFF format and are black and white at 200 dpi.

One IRIS system can process 12 checks per second. Multiple pipelines are used to distribute the workload over the three processors. Interprocess communication is done using shared memory. With a total daily workload of one million documents and a total of 8 IRIS systems, there is enough capacity to handle peak volumes. The architecture is scalable by putting in as many IRIS systems in the LAN as needed.

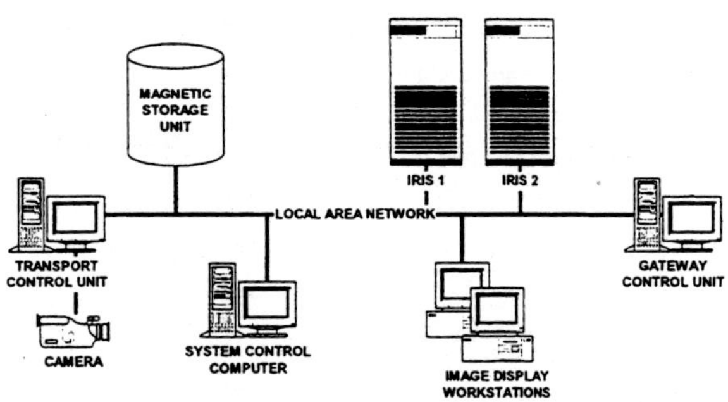

Figure 2 - System design

Pascal is used because of the ease of programming and robustness. KPN Research is currently investigating Windows NT and the object oriented programming language Delphi Pascal as the platform for the next generation IRIS systems that will be developed at the beginning of the next millennium.

4. System performance

4.1. Document verification

Landmark detection is done by a simple XOR operation of a mask against a subimage at a predefined position of the check. All coordinates of the system are relative to this landmark. This is done because the begin-of-document detection and end-of-document detection are not completely reliable. The skew is within 1.5 degrees and is therefore not a real problem and is ignored. Local transformations of the image, caused by fluctuations in the speed of the transport belt, are minimal and therefore also ignored.

The verification system determines how the check is filled in. The home banking concept is very flexible and there are a lot of special categories, such as transactions to savings accounts, urgent transactions, transactions to foreign accounts, invalid documents. About 15% of all checks has a special category. The verification system looks at a large number of fields on the check and determines several features of each field. An expert system determines on the basis of all these features if the check belongs to a certain special category or is a normally filled in check. The system determines categories with an accuracy of more than 95%. The system has been operational since 1997.

4.2. Amount and account recognition

The most important aspect of IRIS is the recognition of the amount and the account fields on checks. The following steps are used:

1. noise filtering
2. writing style recognition
3. character segmentation
4. character recognition
5. heuristic rejection
6. reliability rejection
7. quality monitoring

Figure 3 - Amount and account field

Noise filtering is the first and relatively simple step. Noise is not a big problem because the checks are relatively clean. The fields are designed by Postbank especially for optimal OCR and ICR using borders with a red drop-out color. See Figure 3 (in this case imaged without a red filter).

After noise filtering, the writing style is determined: handwriting, typewriter print or dot matrix print. Each writing style will be processed by different segmentation and recognition modules.

The next step is segmenting the amount and account fields into separated digits. Segmentation is a very difficult process, with problems such as touching digits and digits that are broken into several segments.

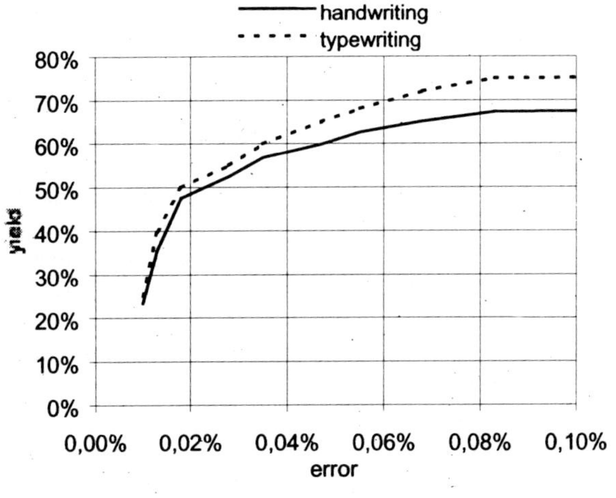

$$\text{yield} = \frac{\#\,\text{high confidence fields}}{\#\,\text{fields}}$$

$$\text{error} = \frac{\#\,\text{high confidence fields wrongly recognized}}{\#\,\text{high confidence fields}}$$

Figure 4 - Yield and error on a field basis

The next step is the recognition of the separated characters. This is done using the HYCR which stands for High Yield Character Recognizer. The HYCR is a feature based neural network recognition system with a very high yield on handwritten characters. The HYCR is better at recognizing isolated handwritten digits than a human. However, a human is not trained to recognize isolated handwritten digits, but is much better at recognizing handwritten fields, thereby using context information that the HYCR doesn't use. The HYCR is trained using a large set of live images with groundtruth values of all relevant fields. See [1] for a benchmark of the HYCR on the well known NIST database.

See Figure 4. The relatively high yield at very low error rates makes it very suited for bank applications. Note that the account numbers have no checksum and the checks are loose - not batched - so the sum of all the amounts is not available. Furthermore, there is no legal amount - courtesy amount redundancy. As a final step some heuristics are used, such as a simple check if for example, the account number has leading zeros or a cents field has only one digit. Such very unusual fields are rejected. Rejected fields are keyed and the keying result is compared with the recognition result.

Quality monitoring is very important for this bank application. During normal production hours 2% of all amount and account fields are keyed manually, even if recognition was done with high confidence. This process gives a continuous and realistic estimation of the error rate. It works better than counting the number of customer complaints. When the error rate is not within a certain predefined interval a warning signal is given to the field engineer.

The system can recognize a high percentage of handwritten amount and account fields so accurately, that the financial transaction can be performed fully automatically. In this respect it is the first system of its kind in the world. Primarily because it deals with handwriting and Postbank account numbers have no check digits and a legal amount as in [3] is not available. The system has been operational since 1997.

4.3. Postcode recognition

At the moment, each check is manually processed to guarantee that the account number matches the name and address information which is also filled in manually on the check. This process is called name-number verification and is done completely manually on a terminal.

Automating this process is difficult because it means the handwritten name-address fields have to be recognized automatically. Because the fields contain cursive script, this is not (yet) feasible.

As a first step the postcode on the check is read and it is verified if this postcode matches the account number using a database with customer information. See Figure 5. The system will be operational in the year 2000.

The expected yield of the system is 88% on a mix of handwritten and machine printed postcodes. The error is not so important because mismatches are sent to a manual verification process.

Figure 5 - Postcode - number verification

As mentioned before, acceptgiros are usually sent by large companies to their clients as a means of billing. Most companies use window envelopes, so the address on the acceptgiro becomes the address of the envelope. By printing the postcode and house number as a bar-code, the so called KIX®, companies can claim reductions from PTT Post. PTT Post uses the KIX to sort mail very efficiently. The KIX is available as a font and is based on the BPO four state code as specified in [2]. See Figure 6. Because the KIX is much easier to read than the postcode the IRIS system will be enhanced with a KIX-reader. The KIX-reader has a yield of more than 99%.

Figure 6 - A KIX

5. Future extensions

KPN Research is currently working on signature verification. This is an option that is currently considered as one of the future extensions of the IRIS system.

5.1. Signature verification

KPN Research has built a prototype for off-line signature verification. Currently signature verification at Postbank is done using two images: an image of the live signature and an image of the reference signature(s). Manually verifying the signature of each check is very expensive.

When a new customer applies for a Postbank account, a signature reference card has to be filled in. These signature reference cards have all been imaged and are now available as an image database.

The signature verification prototype uses some of the technology of the character recognizer but in a very different way. A feature vector is determined for the reference signature(s) and the live signature. It is possible that more than one reference signature will be used for an optimal yield.

Both feature vectors are compared using an optimized distance measure. Signatures with a large distance are rejected and are sent to a manual signature verification process. See Figure 7.

The threshold distance will probably be different for each Postbank customer. Some customers have very regular signatures, while other customers have signatures that vary very much over time.

The number of times a signature is successfully used as a reference will be counted during production. Signatures that are never used as a reference will be removed from the signature reference database.

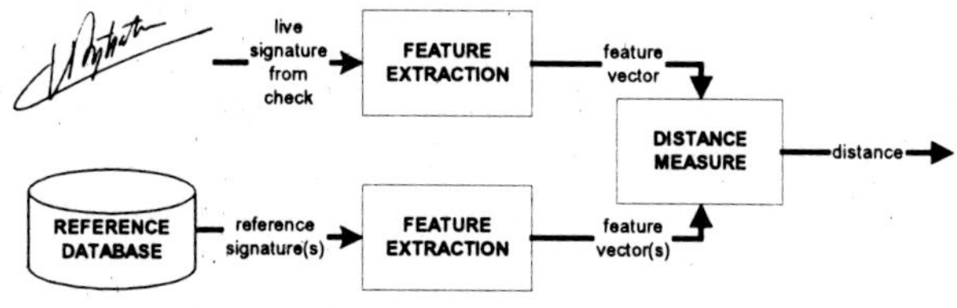

Figure 7 - Signature verification

6. Conclusions

The IRIS system recognizes a high percentage of amount and account fields on checks without any human intervention. The system has a high yield and a very low substitution error rate on fields without any checksum or redundancy. The recognition results are directly used as input for the financial transaction system. The high yield makes the system unique in the world. The system has proven itself in operation during the last two years as a very efficient and reliable component of the transaction processing system of Postbank. New developments include signature verification which is in a prototype stage.

References

[1] I.L. Dijkstra and R. Wilcke, "The performance of the HYCR on the NIST database", KPN Research, Proceedings Mail Systems 2000, 1994, pp. 133-136.

[2] "BPO 4 state code specification for customer coding trials", Royal British Post, Postal Technology, Issue 3.

[3] N. Gorski, V. Anisimov, E. Augustin, O. Baret, D. Price and J.-C. Simon, "A2iA Check Reader: A Family of Bank Check Recognition Systems", Proceedings ICDAR 1999, pp. 523-526.

[4] S. Impedovo, P.S.P. Wang and H. Bunke, eds., "Automatic Bankcheck Processing", World Scientific, 1997.

[5] C.Y. Suen, M. Berthod and S. Mori, "Computer recognition of handprinted characters: the state of the art", Proceedings of IEEE 68, 1980, pp. 469-483.

[6] J.V. Moreau, B. Plessis, O. Bougeois and J.L. Plagnaud, "A Postal check reading system", Proceedings 1st International Conference on Document Analysis and Recognition, ICDAR '91, Saint-Malo, France, 1991, pp. 758-766.

[7] R. Plamondon and G. Lorette, "Automatic signature verification and writer identification: the state of the art", Pattern Recognition 22, 1989, pp. 107-131.

OCR with No Shape Training

Tin Kam Ho
Bell Labs, Lucent Technologies
700 Mountain Avenue, 2C425
Murray Hill, NJ 07974, USA
tkh@bell-labs.com

George Nagy
Dept of ECSE
Rensselaer Polytechnic Institute
Troy, NY 12180-3590, USA
nagy@ecse.rpi.edu

Abstract

We present a document-specific OCR system and apply it to a corpus of faxed business letters. Unsupervised classification of the segmented character bitmaps on each page, using a "clump" metric, typically yields several hundred clusters with highly skewed populations. Letter identities are assigned to each cluster by maximizing matches with a lexicon of English words. We found that for 2/3 of the pages, we can identify almost 80% of the words included in the lexicon, without any shape training. Residual errors are caused by mis-segmentation including missed lines and punctuation. This research differs from earlier attempts to apply cipher decoding to OCR in (1) using real data (2) a more appropriate clustering algorithm, and (3) decoding a many-to-many instead of a one-to-one mapping between clusters and letters.

1. Introduction

In today's pixelated environment, any Tom, Dick and Jane can design or download the font that best conveys his or her message or personality. It is therefore of more than academic interest to liberate OCR from the stereotypic prototypes of predetermined character shapes. Document-specific OCR can learn the peculiarities of the dominant font much the way that we interpret a scrawled postcard by exploiting the similarity of letters or groups of letters in obscure words with those that appear in easily-read words.

Although there have been many earlier studies [1], [3], [4], [5], [8], [9], [10], [11], [19], [20], [21], [22] that exploited language context to decode character or word bitmaps, we believe that this is the first application of such techniques to a large collection of short, dirty documents. Our fax data, from the ISRI corpus, contains letterheads, addresses, signatures, upper and lower case, punctuation, underscores, and averages less than twenty lines of body type per document [25].

Neither the methods cited above, nor those developed expressly for substitution ciphers [6], [7], [13], [17], [18], [24], [26], [27], are robust enough to unscramble the many-to-many mappings encountered in the OCR application. Such mappings arise because impure clusters correspond to more than one alphabetic class of letters, and bitmaps corresponding to the same alphabetic class may appear in several clusters. We have developed a simple deciphering algorithm that is more effective for OCR than the classical methods.

Our work has benefited from renewed interest in symbol-based compression for the forthcoming JBIG2 standard [2], [12], [15]. Symbol-based text-image compression is typically twice as efficient as JBIG1 compression, which in turn is nearly twice as good as CCITT-G4. We therefore designed our OCR in the expectation of rapid adoption of the symbol-based text-image compression standards. Building OCR on top of symbol-based compression offers the benefit of dual-mode representation of documents [23] that allows search on the character-coded version and preserves the original page-image for viewing.

A critical advance in symbol-image compression has been the development of cluster-distance metrics that weight groups of adjacent difference pixels more heavily than an equal number of scattered difference pixels [16]. A further improvement that we introduce is the separation of difference clumps consisting of foreground pixels from clumps of background pixels. This metric, combined with a standard nearest-center clustering algorithm, improves significantly the purity of the resulting clusters.

The next section describes our data, preprocessing, clustering algorithm, decoding procedure, and evaluation. In the third section we present our results. In the conclusions we speculate on what is ahead in the direction that we have taken.

1051-4651/00 $10.00 © 2000 IEEE

2. Data And Methodology

2.1. Data

The data consists of 200 English-language business letters transmitted locally in 204x196 dpi fine mode facsimile from a Xerox 7024 fax machine to a fax modem. The sample includes typewritten and poorly copied letters, some with handwritten annotations. The average number of words per letter is 257, and the average number of characters is 1600. 87% of the words could be found in our 21,466-word lexicon compiled from the Brown corpus.

According to [25], the average character accuracy of the tested commercial OCR systems barely topped 97%, in contrast with the nearly 99% obtained without facsimile transmission on the same documents scanned at 300 dpi. A character-level accuracy of 97% corresponds to a word accuracy of only about 85%.

2.2. Preprocessing

For layout analysis we follow [14]. We find the connected foreground components using 4-connectivity and merge some adjacent components like the dots on i's and j's. Text-line and word boundaries are determined using thresholds based on the average height of the connected components. At the end of this stage most of the character images are isolated, but some are conjoined and some are fragmented.

2.3. Unsupervised Classification

The first cluster is seeded by the first character-bitmap on the page. New clusters are created whenever a character bitmap cannot be assigned to one of the existing clusters. A character bitmap is assigned to the cluster to which its bitmap distance is least (distance is calculated only to the first bitmap of each cluster). The symmetric distance metric is computed by aligning two bitmaps to be compared according to their horizontal and vertical pixel medians, then shifting one relative to the other in a 3x3 neighborhood to find the best match. Because most of the bitmap pairs are highly dissimilar, the clustering algorithm has various bailout rules that allow it to abandon unpromising pairings quickly.

The symmetric distance between two aligned bitmaps A and B is defined as the asymmetric distance between A and B plus the asymmetric distance between B and A. The asymmetric distance between A and B is the count of the number of pixels that are black in A and white in B, with each black difference pixel in A weighted by the number of its black 4-neighbors in A. The asymmetric distance between B and A is the converse.

At the end of the initial clustering pass, similar clusters are merged if the ratio of their average intra-cluster to inter-cluster distance is larger than 0.5. The two averages are based on all pairs of bitmaps within the same cluster, and on all pairs in different clusters, respectively. The ratio is retained for further use.

Any singleton cluster is merged into the nearest larger cluster if its distance to any one of the members of that cluster is less than an arbitrary threshold value.

2.4. Context Analysis

Context analysis is done by iterative applications of several simple modules each attempting to assign labels to the clusters by different rules. Every tentative assignment is evaluated using a v/p ratio which is the number of valid words from the lexicon over the number of word-patterns containing them. A word-pattern may contain a mixture of elements from labeled and unlabeled clusters. Only one match will be counted even if there are multiple matches for the same word-pattern from the lexicon. Word interpretations are built up progressively from the accepted assignments. The most useful modules are as follows.

- JointAssign: We take the three largest clusters and try to assign to them every triplet of eight most common letters (observed in the Brown corpus) {a,e,i,o,n,r,s,t}, from which we select the triplet that maximizes the number of matching lexicon entries among all those words which contain at least two occurrences of these three clusters. For instance, by assigning e,i,o to clusters 1,2,3 respectively, the following strings (x standing for any other clusters) can be interpreted as the patterns below them and matched with words from lexicon in the third line:

  ```
  clusters>  x3x13xx1x xxx3x2xx23x 1xx2x3
  patterns>  _o_eo__e_ ___o_i__io_ e__i_o
  matches >  homeowner association ??????
  ```

  The v/p ratio in this case is 2/3. If the best triplet makes a v/p ratio above 0.75, we accept the assignment. Otherwise, we try clusters 2,3,4, and 3,4,5 in turn.

- UniqueMatch: Next, every word-pattern containing at least one unlabeled cluster is checked to see if some assignment yields a unique lexicon match. For instance, the unlabeled cluster "_" in the pattern "w_ic_" will be tentatively labeled with "h" since it produces a unique match "which". The one in "_low" will not be assigned since the pattern matches both "flow" and "glow". The tentative assignment will be checked to make sure v/p is at least 0.25. The search is iterated with the updated patterns until no more new unique matches are found.

- MostMatch: If there are still unlabeled clusters, then the algorithm assigns every letter in turn to one of the unlabeled clusters and checks which assignments results in the highest v/p ratio. If the best ratio is at least 0.75, and the second best is not too close (at least 0.1 below), then this assignment is ratified. For example, if cluster 9 appears in only four words, "9low," "9ierce," "a99air," and "lu99a," then f is assigned to 9 because it yields 3 lexicon words out of 4 (v/p = 0.75), whereas p results in only two matches (v/p = 0.5), and g in only one (v/p = 0.25) (if "luffa" appeared in the lexicon, then the match would be even safer).

- VerifyAssign: Finally, every assignment is verified by trying to replace it with each of the other 25 letters. If the v/p ratio can be improved, and either more than one word contains this cluster or the single word that contains it has at least two letters, then the label is replaced, and the verification is continued. Precaution is taken to guard clusters that appear only once as a single-letter word from receiving assignment of "a" or "i" unless context from other words would also justify it.

Other modules exploit the most frequent short words (1-4 letters) and the most frequent bigrams, or try to assign an unlabeled cluster to its nearest labeled neighbor determined by intra/inter-cluster distance ratio.

These modules make cumulative contributions in the interpretation process. Jointly, they are able to handle split clusters of the same symbol. Loose requirements (v/p less than 1) on the simultaneous assignment of all bitmaps in the same cluster give some tolerance for clustering errors that yield impure clusters.

2.5. Evaluation

The evaluation considers both the (partially) labeled sample and the ground-truth as a sequence of words without regard to line breaks. The two sequences are matched with the words as the basic units (two words have to be identical to be counted as a match) and the length of the longest common subsequence (LCS) is calculated (raw score 1). Then the interpretation is spell-corrected using the same lexicon for calculating another LCS score (raw score 2). To compare across different pages, we normalize raw scores 1 and 2 by the number of words in the truth file (called true words) to obtain final scores 1 and 2.

Business letters contain, of course, many proper nouns and digit sequences that can be identified only when their constituent letters share a cluster with bitmaps of lexical words. Errors in such assignments cannot be corrected by the spell checker. So we also count the true words appearing in the lexicon and normalize the raw scores with it to obtain final scores 3 and 4.

3. Results

The median proportion of characters per sample that are assigned alphabetic labels is 93% - the remainder are in clusters that cannot be matched to the lexicon. These include mis-segmented patterns, special symbols (e.g., $), digits, and punctuation. The median number of clusters per sample is 244; typically 55% of these are singletons.

Figure 1 shows a plot of the ratio of percent true words that are correctly interpreted (score 4). From the plot, we see that there are two clusters of results: most of the pages show up in a group with the scores above 50% and average near 80%, while the rest are below 50% and average near 20%. Table 1 lists the averages of all four scores broken down by these two groups. For pages in the first group, good knowledge of the letter content can be obtained from the word interpretations (see example in Figure 2). Pages in the second group suffered from catastrophic failures in the interpretation process so that no meaningful contents can be extracted. Recalling that shape based recognition of these pages achieved a word-level accuracy of only about 85% (before spell check), we believe that our method deserves further pursuit.

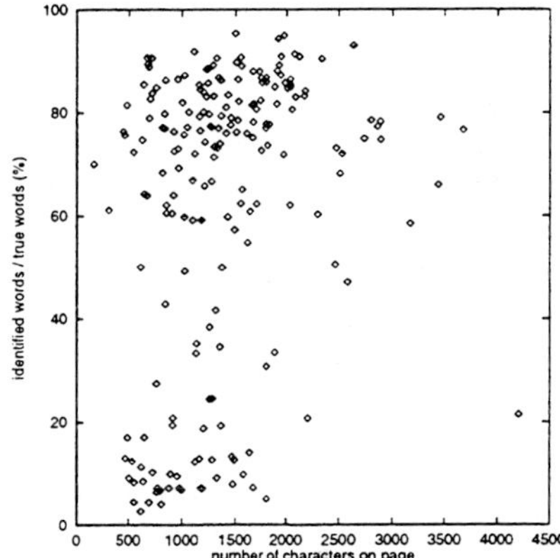

Figure 1. Percent true words (contained in our lexicon) identified versus number of characters on the page.

```
dear homeowners a an accordance with article add
of the bypass of the mess pillage homeowners
association a and paragraph a of the declaration
of a covenant a conditions a and restrictions for
the property a notice is hereby given that the
annual meeting of the mess pillage home owners
will be held at a a a a am on steady remember la
a saga at the recreation room located at ...
```

Figure 2. An example interpretation sequence after spell check.

4. Conclusions

We are convinced that adaptive, document-specific character recognition algorithms are necessary to improve OCR beyond its current plateau. Although commercial software performs very well on clean pages and on common fonts,

Table 1. Average scores by performance group. avg: average of scores 1 to 4.

group	#pages	score 1	score 2	score 3	score 4
avg $\geq$ 50	137	64.2	68.7	73.4	78.5
avg $<$ 50	63	11.4	16.2	13.7	19.4
all	200	47.6	52.2	54.6	59.9

its error rate increases abruptly on low-quality pages and unusual typefaces that are easily read (in context) by humans. Context recognition based on the homogeneity of type shapes and image distortion within the same document is, of course, only one of the possible remedies. In this research, we explore how far linguistic context alone can take us. We expect that future systems will integrate contextual methods with shape based classifiers instead of restricting the use of context to post-processing.

The method that we have described can be readily applied to text images compressed with symbol-matching. Widespread acceptance of the standard will stimulate the development of special-purpose hardware. With methods such as those advocated here, the resulting volume of compressed text images can be efficiently converted to character-coded form without resorting to further pixel-level manipulation. Access to a standard file format for sequences of compressed character bitmaps will also greatly facilitate the development of OCR algorithms for specific applications.

The major weakness of our method is its inability to cope with digits, special symbols, and punctuation. Not only are these glyphs not recognized, but punctuation appended to a word precludes matching it correctly to the lexicon. Although it is clear that context is insufficient to recognize unconstrained, poorly digitized text, it is surprising that it comes fairly close to what has been achieved with shape-based methods.

However, contextual methods are also applicable to non-alphabetic symbols. We are currently attempting to extend contextual bitmap identification to this set. Since digits, special symbols and punctuation are seldom combined with letters or with each other in unique configurations, we expect that will have to rely more on statistical morphology than on strictly lexical methods. Fortunately, the availability of large corpora in coded form allows us to compile the necessary information.

Acknowledgements

Tin Ho thanks Jim Reeds for helpful discussions.

References

[1] R. Casey, G. Nagy, Autonomous reading machine, *IEEE Trans. Comput.*, **C-17**, 5, May 1968, 492-503.

[2] L. Bottou, P. Haffner, P.G. Howard, P. Simard, Y. Bengio, Y. LeCun, High quality document image compression with DjVu, *J. of Electronic Imaging*, **7**, 3, 1998, 410-425.

[3] R. Casey, G. Nagy, Advances in pattern recognition, *Scientific American*, 224, April 1971, 56-71.

[4] R. Casey, Text OCR by solving a cryptogram, *Proc. ICPR 8*, Paris, 1986, 349-351.

[5] C. Fang, J.J. Hull, A word-level deciphering algorithm for degraded document recognition, *Procs. SDAIR-5*, Las Vegas 1995, 191-202.

[6] A. Goshtasby, R.W. Ehrich, Contextual word recognition using probabilistic relaxation labeling, *Pattern Recognition*, **21**, 5, 1988, 455-462.

[7] G. Hart, To decode short cryptograms, *Commun. ACM*, **37**, 9, Sept. 1994, 102-108.

[8] T.K. Ho, J.J. Hull, S.N. Srihari, A word shape analysis approach to lexicon based word recognition, *Pattern Recognition Letters*, **13**, 1992, 821-826.

[9] T.K. Ho, Bootstrapping text recognition from stop words, *Procs. ICPR-14*, Brisbane 1998, 605-609.

[10] T.K. Ho, Fast identification of stop words for font learning and keyword spotting, *Procs. ICDAR-5*, Bangalore 1999, 333-336.

[11] T. Hong, J.J. Hull, Improving OCR performance with word image equivalence, *Procs. SDAIR-5*, Las Vegas 1995, 177-190.

[12] P. Howard, F. Kossentini, B. Martins, S. Forchhammer, W.J. Rucklidge, The emerging JBIG2 Standard, *IEEE Trans. Circuits and Systems for Video Technology*, **9**, 7, November 1998, 838-848.

[13] D.G.N. Hunter and A.R. McKenzie, Experiments with relaxation algorithms breaking simple substitution ciphers, *Computer Journal*, **26**, 1, 1983, 68-71.

[14] D. Ittner, H.S. Baird, Language-free layout analysis, *Procs. ICDAR-2*, Tsukuba Science City 1993, 336-340.

[15] Joint Bilevel Document Image Experts Group, Progressive bi-level image compression, ITU recommendation T.82, ISO-IEC International Standard 11544, 1993.

[16] O. Johnsen, J. Segen, G.L. Cash, Coding of two-level pictures by pattern matching and substitution, *BSTJ*, **62**, 8, Oct. 1983, 2513-2545.

[17] S. Khoubyari, J.J. Hull, Font and Function Word Identification in Document Recognition, *Computer Vision and Image Understanding*, **63**, 1, January 1996, 66-74.

[18] A. Konheim, *Cryptography, a primer*, Wiley, New York 1981.

[19] D.S. Lee, J.J. Hull, Information extraction from symbolically compressed images, *Procs. SDIUT*, Annapolis 1999, 176-182.

[20] D.S. Lee, J.J. Hull, Duplicate detection for symbolically compressed documents, *Procs. ICDAR-5*, Bangalore 1999, 305-308.

[21] G. Nagy, S. Seth, K. Einspahr, T. Meyer, Efficient algorithms to decode substitution ciphers with application to OCR, *Procs. ICPR 8*, Paris, 1986, 352-354.

[22] G. Nagy, S. Seth, K. Einspahr, Decoding substitution ciphers by means of word matching with application to OCR, *IEEE-Trans. PAMI-9*, 5, Sept. 1987, 710-715.

[23] G. Nagy, S. Seth, M. Viswanathan, DIA, OCR, and the WWW, in *Handbook of Character Recognition and Document Image Analysis* (H. Bunke and P.S.P. Wang, editors), World Scientific 1097, 729-754.

[24] S. Peleg and A. Rosenfeld, Breaking substitution ciphers using relaxation algorithm, *Commun. ACM*, **22**, Nov. 1979, 598-605.

[25] S.V. Rice, F.R. Jenkins, T.A. Nartker, The fifth annual test of OCR accuracy, TR 96-01, Information Science Research Institute, University of Nevada - Las Vegas, April 1996.

[26] C. Shannon, Communication theory of secrecy systems, *Bell System Technical J.*, **28**, 1949, 636-715.

[27] E.A. Williams, *An invitation to cryptograms*, Simon and Schuster, New York 1959.

ISSUES AND DIRECTIONS IN VISUAL INFORMATION RETRIEVAL

A. Del Bimbo
University of Florence - Dipartimento di Sistemi e Informatica
Via S.Marta 3, 50139 Firenze, Italy
delbimbo@dsi.unifi.it

Abstract

Visual Information retrieval is attracting an increasing number of researchers from disparate fields, like image nalysys, computer vision, databases, knowledge representation, artificial intelligence, man-machine interaction. Although a number of prototype systems have been made available, recently, nevertheless this discipline has not yet reached a mature stage, and overall has not yet been credited as of concrete use in practical applications. Among the very many different lines of development we focus particularly on the importance of bridging the semantic gap between the user and visual information retrieval systems. We focus on usage of semiotics as a framework for extraction of semantics, graphs and graph matching as the representation model and retrieval engine and visualization spaces to capture sematics during the interaction.

1 Introduction

Visual information retrieval is a new subject of research in Information Technology. Its purpose is to retrieve, from a database, images or image sequences that are relevant to a query. It is an extension of traditional information retrieval so to include visual media. The need for visual information retrieval has become apparent recently, as more and more visual information has become available in digital archives. The emergence of Multimedia as the "new" technology and the possibility of sharing and distributing image/video data through large-bandwidth computer networks have further emphasize the importance and need of tools for retrieving visual information.

Interactivity with visual content is essential to visual information retrieval. Visual elements such as perceptual properties - color, texture, shape, spatial relationships, motion -, impressions, emotions - associated with the combination of perceptual features -, semantic primitives corresponding to abstractions - like objects, roles and scenes - or concepts, stories - associated with the discourse which is developed by the visual message -, are used as clues for retrieving images with similar content from a database.

In first generation retrieval systems, these attributes were extracted manually. Cost of annotation was typically very high and the whole process suffered from the subjectivity of descriptions, in that the annotator is a different person from the one who issues the query. However, since the early 90's, researchers working in the image interpretation field have introduced an integrated feature-extraction object-recognition subsystem. Exploiting achievements in pattern recognition and computer vision, it supported automatic extraction of perceptive features like color and texture, or of semantic primitives like shape and spatial relations. Objective measurements of perceptual properties have permitted to overcome the substantial inadequacy of text - used in first generation retrieval system - in modeling perceptual aspects and saved time in the annotation of visual data. Virtually all the systems proposed so far use only low-level perceptively meaningful representations of pictorial data, which have limited semantics.

The feature vector model was naturally employed to organize color and texture features as well as - to a certain extent - shape descriptors. The great advantage of the adoption of this model is that it permits to exploit indexing methods already available for multidimensional spaces and to use metric similarity distances for measuring feature similarity. As a result, most second-generation retrieval systems have concentrated on color and texture, few on shape and very few include spatial relations. In particular, spatial relationship representation, in that they are intrinsecally relational, are not suited with the vector model. Re-

1051-4651/00 $10.00 © 2000 IEEE

lations between spatial entities are generally checked after that entities have been matched on the basis of their individual features.

Queries by content of single images are naturally expressed through visual examples. Examples can either be authored by the user or extracted from image samples. To initiate a query, the user selects which features and ranges of model parameters are important and chooses a similarity measure. The system checks the similarity between the visual content of the user's query and database images.

Relevance feedback has been employed as the euristic mechanism to close the loop of interaction between the user and the system. Despite of the availability of very many prototype systems performing retrieval based on perceptual properties, many issues are still open. They basically address:

- New models for representation of perceptual content and tools for their automatic extraction.
- Effective indexing of visual descriptors.
- Similarity models to decide similarity of perceptual features.
- New visual interfaces and interaction mechanisms for database access.

However, the most critical point is that similarity of perceptual properties is generally of little use in most practical cases of retrieval by content, if not combined with similarity of higher level information. In general, when searching for visual data the user refers to the scene, the story (including the characters, their roles, actions and their logical relations), as well as the feeling (which depends on the combination of perceptual facts). In the absence of high-level representations of the visual content, relevance feedback is generally credited to informally account for semantics in the retrieval process. In any case, there is no formal proof that the recursive querying mechanisms converges to the desired solution, neither that the user's intent is captured, since the interaction relies in the modification of a limited number of "best examples".

Retrieval by content of video has followed a different evolution. Unlike still images, video conveys informative messages through multiple planes of communication. These include the way in which frames are linked together by using *editing effects* (cuts, fades, dissolves, mattes...), and what is in the frames (the characters, the story content, the story message). Changes in color, texture, shape and motion (of both camera and characters/objects) observed in multiple frames, are more important than information embedded in a single frame. Techniques employed to obtain video (shot angles, camera movements...) are also very important and contribute to the information content of the video stream. Segmentation into shots and feature extraction from shots is only a step to derive information aggregates useful for retrieval.

Much more than single images, retrieval of video is generally meaningful only if performed at high-levels of representation.In fact, the human memory is much more concerned with the narrative and discourse structure of the video content than merely with individual perceptual elements of the video. Individual frames are not perceived as such, nor the spectator realizes the segmentation into shots and the editing performed by the director. Instead he perceives the rythm of the sequence (which is induced by the editing), the scenes (which are obtained from shots), the story (including the characters, their roles, actions and their logical relations), as well as the feeling (which depends on the combination of perceptual facts, like colors, objects, music..., and, for example in movies, from the meaning of the story). An additional characteristic of video retrieval is that it is not possible to define video content univocally. Each type of video (commercials, news, movies, sports...) has its own peculiar characteristics. These are reflected in the way in which video units are extracted, organized in knowledge structures, indexed and accessed by users.

Researchers working in the image interpretation field have provided well established tools for automatic segmentation of video streams. Clustering of video based on perceptual properties - aimed to perform video content classification - as well automatic annotation based on audio and text content have been proposed in some prototype systems, especially for news and advertising. Browsing and navigation are common modalities of viewing video content. Retrieval based on key-frame similarity - reusing results of single image retrieval - which has been suggested in some prototype systems, has shown to be generally useless in practice. Audio has been exploited in particular types of video - notably news and sports - to extract meaningful high-level information useful for retrieval. Full automatic annotation of video content remains still far from being possible.

Based on the above discussion, the very problem with second-generation retrieval systems remains bridging the semantic gap between the system and users. This has to do with image classification based on semantically-meaningful categories of information and automatic extraction of high-level concepts from visual data to save cost of annotation. Although the problem seems to face only the level of representation that can be obtained automatically, indeed the user interface and feature organization play equally essential roles in obtaining effective retrieval systems. Feature organization and interactivity are to-day substantially designed to support the perceptual adjustment of retrieval results to the user's requests. Very little research has also been done on new models of interaction suited to focus on semantics of image data.

In the following sections we will discuss shortly three lines of research which are credited to represent true challenges of the field - among the others - in the next few years:

- Semiotics - as the science that studies the relationships between signs and their meanings - is potentially able to provide a sound scientific support where to cast results of computer vision and image analysis to extract high-level information from image data.
- Graph-based representations are suited to model relations between entities, and therefore semantics of images; they need integration with presently used data representation and index structures based on feature vectors.
- Visualization spaces have storng potential for the extraction of semantic attributes through the interaction with the user; they should relax the need of intelligence within the system, and underline the essential role of interfaces in the retrieval process.

2 The role of Semiotics in Visual Information Retrieval

The perspective of semiotics includes "the objects of sense", which are implemented as texts, or logotypes, images, sounds, films, behaviors... The "communication context", that is the context where objects of sense are inserted is also considered as an object of sense [11] [21] . According to semiotics the world of sense can be understood. The objective of the discipline remains the description of conditions for the production of sense and of the way in which it is received. Starting from signs, semiotics defines the system of relations which is formed by invariants of production and reception of sense. It suggests that signs relate to their meaning according to the specific cultural background. Meaning is obtained through a dynamic process, so that it is possible to distinguish between different levels of communication invariants. Semioticians usually identify two distinct steps for the production of meaning: - an abstract level formed by *narrative* structures, that is, structures including all those basic signs that create meaning and those values determined by sign combinations, and - a concrete level formed by *discorse* structures, describing the way in which the author uses narrative elements to create a story.

In that semiotics deals with meaning of signs with reference to the context of fruition, it appears as a formally sound framework for retrieval of visual data based on semantic information. According to semiotics, semantics of visual data can be defined at different levels starting from perceptual features. Perceptual features represent the evidence upon which to build the interpretation of visual data. Semantics can be extracted at different levels of signification through a suitable set of rules. Construction rules depend on the specific data domain to which they refer (such as movies, commercials, and TV news - for videos - paintings, photographs, and trademarks for still images), as well as from the cultural background of the user.

2.1 The Narrative Level

At the narrative level meaning can be directly obtained from perceptual facts using a process of syntactic construction called *compositional semantics.* Compositional semantics has been introduced in [1] . Two distinct steps of the signification hierarchy, the *expressive* and the *emotional* level, can be obtained from compositional semantics and represent plausible intermediate steps in the construction of meaning of a visual message.

Without loss of generality, the perceptual properties of a visual message can be represented through a set of scores $P = \phi_i$, $i = 1, ..., n$. Each score $\phi \in [0, 1]$ represents the extent to which the i-th feature appears in the message. At the expressive level, perceptual data are organized into a group of new features, the expressive features, obtained as a combination of distributions of perceptual features. Combination rules are modeled as functions F acting over the perceptual feature set P and returning a score expressing the degree of truth by which the rule F holds. Hence, a rule F, can be defined as $F_i : [0, l]^n \rightarrow [0, 1]$. The set $F = F_1, ..., F_n$ defines semantics of the visual message at the expressive level. Operators of logical composition between rules can extend the signification of the representation. Plausible definitions of these operators are: $F_1 F_2 = min(F_1, F_2)$ $F_1 v F_2 = max(F_1, F_2)$

The emotional level can be built from the perceptual and espressive levels, as a second level in the signification hierarchy. Rules at the emotional level can be represented through functions G acting over the set of perceptual and expressive features $P \times F$ and returning a score that espresses the degree of truth by which the rule G holds. Hence, a rule G, can be defined as $G_k : [0,1]^{n+m} \rightarrow [0,1]$. The set $G = G_k$ qualifies the content of the visual message at the emotional level. Operators of logical composition between rules can extend the representation's semantics.

The espressive level generally depends on collective cultural backgrounds. On the other hand, the emotional level relies on collective cultural backgrounds but also depends on subjective elements such as individual culture and psychological moods. Expressive and emotional levels are discussed below for still art images and video commercials with reference to results described in [8] [1] [22] [23] . A further example of expressive level detection in movies can be found in [15] , where semantically meaningful content categories of movies like violence and sex have been distinguished.

2.1.1 Still Art Images

Expression in art images. Among the many authors who recently addressed the psychology of art images, Arnheim [29] discussed the relationships between artistic form and perceptive processes. Kandinsky and Itten [30] formulated theories about use of color in art and about the semantics it induces. Itten observed that color combinations can be classified in terms of contrast and harmonic accordance. Contrast is defined between pure, light-dark, warm-cold, and saturated-unsaturated colors. Contrast is generally used to emphasize color properties and psychological effects. Contrasting properties can be identified as those which occupies opposite locations in the Itten's color space representation. The absence of contrasting hues and the presence of a single dominant color region inspire a sense of uneasiness strengthened by the presence of dark yellow and purple colors. For example, since in the western culture, red-orange colors induce a sense of warmth (yellow through red-purple are warm colors) and green-blue conveys a sensation of cold (yellow-green through purple are cold colors,), cold sensations can be emphasized by the contrast of a large cold region with a smaller warm color region or dampened by its coupling with a highly cold tint. Lightness contrast determine a sense of plasticity and the perception of rent planes of depth. Harmonic accordance combines hues and tones to generate a stability effect onto the human eye. Harmonic accordance is obtained as the combination of colors which are connected by a regular polygon (with n sides, in general) in the Itten's color space representation. Retrieval by content of art images based on expression is reported in [8] [1] .

Emotion in art images. The mapping of low-level color primitives into emotions must consider theories about the use of colors and cognitive models, and involve cultural and anthropological backgrounds. However, within a certain homogeneous cultural context artists use color combinations unconsciously and consciously to produce optical and psychological sensations [1] . In the western culture, red communicates happiness, dynamism, and power. Orange, the warmest color, resembles the color of fire and thus communicates glory. Green communicates calmness and relaxation, and is the color of hope. Blue, a cold color, improves the dynamism of warm colors, suggesting gentleness, fairness, faithfulness, and virtue. Purple communicates melancholy and sometimes fear. Brown generally serves as the background color of relaxing scenes. Complementary colors convey calmness and quiet in the observer. In the presence of two noncomplementary colors, the human eye looks for the complementary of the observed color. This results into a sense of anguish. The presence of regions in harmonic accordance communicates a sense calmness and joy. Line primitives also contribute to create emotions in art images. For example, slanted lines communicates dynamism and action, while a flat lines communicate calmness and relaxation.

2.1.2 Video Commercials

Expression in commercials. Main narrative signs of commercials are colors, editing effects, rhythm, shot angles, and lines. Semiotics classifies expressiveness of commercials into four different categories [11] . Practical commercials emphasize the qualities of a product according to a common set of values. They describe the product in a familiar environment so that the observer perceives it as useful. Characterizing features are frontal camera takes, smooth shot transitions and prevalence of horizontal and vertical lines. Critical commercials introduce a hierarchy of reference values. The product is the central subject of the story, which emphasizes the product's qualities through an apparently objective description of its features. Although critical commercials are better recognized at the discourse level, nevertheless they are characterized by a small number of camera breaks, smooth camera motions and ever-changing colors in the background, so as to enhance the realism of the film and draw the audience's attention to the color of the product, which remains constant. Utopic commercials provide evidence that the product can succeed in criticai tests. Situations appear as in a dream. The number of dominant colors is small, so as to define a closed-chromatic world; all editing effects are usually represented. Playful commercials emphasize the accordance between,users' needs and product qualities. The commercial clearly states to the audience that they're watching advertising material. Situations differ from everyday life and are deformed in a caricatural and grotesque fashion. All possible camera effects are used to stimulate the active participation of the audience. Unnatural colors, improbable camera takes are often present. Retrieval according to semiotic categories is discussed in [22] .

Emotion in commercials. The choice of a given combination of narrative signs affects both the espressive and emotional levels of signification [1] , [23] . Emotions are associated with the appropriate use of editing effects, which generate the rythm of the sequence, combined with sound and motion. Usually, sound and motion reinforce the message provided by the rythm. For example, if the video consists of a few long shots, the effect is that of calmness and relaxation. Alternatively, videos with many short shots separated by cuts induce a sense of action and dynamism in the audience.

2.2 The Discourse Level

At the discourse level extraction of sense is much more difficult due to the higher complexity in the definition of rules which organize visual features into meaningful stories. The discourse level requires the recognition of objects and the understanding of the scene in which objects are located. Recognition is performed through classification of multiple instances of the same object under uncertainty. Uncertainty is due to geometrical transformations, illumination changes, partial occlusions... For the purpose of the discussion, we can distinguish two categories of still image databases: - the first is concerned with heterogeneous images. Metadata are not based on ground truth and interpretation of content is mainly subjective. Generally the user is not an expert and retrieval is based on perceptive similarity. - the second deals with images having homogeneous semantic content. Metadata are based on a ground truth defined by domain experts. Interpretation of content is objective and based on a-priori knowledge. The semantics at the discourse level can be extracted automatically with images in the second category. The object geometry and object invariants can be used for classification. Typical applications are professional-specific applications like face retrieval in criminal investigation, evidence of patology in medical image retrieval... In unconstrained domains, perceptual organization of features into meaningful objects and obtaining semantic descriptions of scenes through model matching is still an unsolved problem. Therefore, for images in the first category only narrative structures are reliably extracted.

For video, visual features, per-se, are not sufficient for the definition of sense at the discourse level. In general cross-media analysis is necessary to the derivation of meaning at this level. Text, audio, music are important correlated components of the discourse structure. However, different categories of video have different possibilities of extracting discourse structures automatically. In news, images have an ancillary function with respect to speech. The structure is well defined and clearly defines and limits the different services. Recognition of anchorman shots from services permits the reconstruction of the news structure. Speech understanding in the anchorman shots can be used to extract discourse semantics [25] [17] . Sports video are basically organized around key events. Different sports are distinguished at the narrative level by different combinations of visual signs. Speech, crowd cheering are cues that add sense to the visual message and used to derive the structure of discourse [18] . Movies follow basic rules of filming that can be exploited to derive, in certain cases, boundaries of scenes (for example the shot-reverse-shot technique is widely used to film dialogue scenes) [16] . The story is however complex to extract and generally speaking, determined by the background context, the roles and presence of characters, their speech and sounds [24] . Commercials are basically concerned with the narrative level of semantics. Stories however are present in critical- and utopic-type commercials and generally complex to detect.

3 Graphs for the Organization of Semantically Meaningful Representations

Data models and knowledge structures provide a formal support for organizing indexes of visual content at different levels of abstraction [9] . Point access methods are commonly employed to index visual attributes that are modeled through feature vectors. Performance of PAMs depends on the number of features actually used to represent properties and the distance measure which is adopted. For most PAMs performance diminishes if the number of features exceeds ten. High dimensional data are usually mapped onto a lower dimensional space, before indexing. Feature vectors are however not suited to model semantic information. Joint representation of properties of image entities and of their mutual relationships can be accomplished by an attributed relational graph:

$$
\begin{array}{ll}
image\ model \stackrel{def}{=} & < \ E, a, w \ > \\
& E = set\ of\ spatial\ entities \\
& a : E \rightarrow A \cup \{\mathtt{any_a}\} \\
& w : E \times E \rightarrow W \cup \{\mathtt{any_s}\}
\end{array}
\quad (1)
$$

where entities are represented by vertices in E and their qualifying features are captured by the attribute label a taking values in the feature space A. Relationships are labeled by a descriptor w which weights its relevance. Graphs have been used for representing semantic information in several prototype visual information retrieval systems [5] [19] [3] [2]. The representation of image contents as an attributed relational graph, rather than as a set of independent entity vectors, basically changes the complexity of matching algorithms and feasibility of indexing schemes. The distance between two sets of independent vectors can be computed in polynomial time, while the distance between two attributed relational graphs requires the identification of an optimal error-correcting sub-graph isomorphism.

The problem of comparing a query graph against a set of model graphs has been addressed with different approaches.

- One solution is to reduce a graph to a vectorial representation, under the assumption that all graphs contain a set of pre-defined entities and relationships. This enables the use of PAMs also for indexing semantic information. However, this approach is not suited in the case in which entities in images are identified by numeric features, densely changing and there is not a structural relationship between entities. In these cases, graphs cannot be represented with vectors with a predefined dimensionality [27] .

- The graph decomposition approach requests that at archiving time model graphs are repeatedly decomposed in subgraphs, organized within a hierarchical index. Matching is accomplished by comparing the input graph against the index subgraphs bottom-up. This approach turns out to be efficient when different images include common subgraphs [26] .

- Metric indexing is an alternative solution where entities are organized according to their mutual distances, whithout casting them into a vectorial representation [28] . The database is partitioned in a hierarchical set of clusters. Each cluster is represented by a reference entity and a radius which provides an upper bound for its maximum distance to any entity in the cluster. Since the distance used is metric, triangular inequality can be used to reduce search complexity. Graph matching is still necessary to evaluate the distance between the query and database entities in the index.

Graph matching can be solved either through state-space search or look-ahead strategies. The former derive the optimal distance by exhaustive checking of all the possible assignments of the entities of the query to those of the description. Look-ahead strategies compute a partial interpretation and perform a forecast of the future cost that will be spent if the match is completed. This allows a more informed direction of search and permits to discard partial matches that cannot lead to acceptable similarity matches [2] .

No comprehensive solution has been yet proposed supporting the application of attributed relational graphs for content-based retrieval in image databases.

4 The Need for Visualization Spaces

Most of the work on content-based retrieval assume that the user has a concrete idea of what he/she is searching. Indeed this is hard in single image retrieval and almost impossible to achieve for video retrieval. Retrieval of single images is therefore commonly obtained through an interactive session. Images obtained are fed back to the system with annotations to improve the quality of the result. This process is hopefully expected to converge to a satisfactory solution, although there is no assurance of it. Keeping memory of user's interaction allows to understand the user's objective better. A bias is learned and updated during the interactive session so as to adapt to the user's subjectivity and needs. Although items are retrieved based on low-level features, the user bias implicitely introduces semantics in the retrieval loop. However, users do not accept long periods of query refinements. Moreover, usually they only go through the first few retrieved images, thus eventually loosing the possibility to feed back useful examples. For video databases, browsing must face with the long presentation time of video data. Users, instead need efficient ways to access collections based on conceptual criteria which are related to their task.

Visualization space can improve retrieval at the semantic level. Generally speaking, in visualization spaces, displays present both visual information and structural relationships between visual elements that concur in the definition of semantics.

Display of narrative structures can be performed by visualizing clusters that are formed in the data space according to narrative attributes. Few examples of visualization spaces have been proposed so far. In [7] the visualization space has a number of interest points (POI) corresponding to meaningful colour and shapes. The position of retrieved images in the display depends on their similarity according to POI's features. In [14] images are instead clustered in a three-dimensional user-defined feature space. Explicit representation of how much individual images include of each semantic primitive or combination of semantic primitives can be obtained using information display spaces [6]. Information display spaces represent attibutes as points (POI, points of interest) in the display. Queries can be represented as n-tip stars, each tip corresponding to a POI, located in the center of the IDS, with tip leghts proportional to the relevance of the attribute. Retrieved images can be represented, in turn, as stars. Positions of retrieved stars in the IDS indicate the correspondence between image content and semantic primitives.

An example of display of narrative structures for video has been reported in [22] where commercials are clustered according to the four semiotic categories of reference: practical, critical, utopic and playful.

Display of discourse structures must provide visual summaries of stories and meaningful events or episodes. A visual summary of video information - the scene transition graph - which displays both visual content and temporal flow of a video, has been suggested in [19] . Nodes of the graph are collections of similar shots. Arcs between nodes indicate temporal interrelationships between shots and the flow of the story. Story elements are visualized by clicking on graphs. Video posters - which include images having size and location which represent their relative importance - have been used in [20] to separate important images from non-important ones according to heuristics. Graph-based conceptual schemas of movie structures, which clusters the structural elements - shots, episodes, scenes - of a movie are presented in [16] .

5 Conclusions

Semantics is concerned with relationships between entities and the domain that is represented in the images. Automatic extraction of semantic information is the needed step to make visual information retrieval systems effective in practical applications. Extraction of semantics is related to the context of operation and the user's cultural profile. On the other hand this step is strictly associated with the definition of suited knowledge structures and visualization tools for indexing and accessing visual information effectively. Semiotics, which is concerned with the description of conditions for the production of sense and of the way in which it is received appears as the formal background to casting the development of retrieval by semantic information.According to semiotics it is possible to distinguish between different levels of communication invariants which are readable to specific user categories.

References

[1] C.Colombo, A.Del Bimbo, P.Pala, "Semantics in Visual Information Retrieval", IEEE Multimedia, vol. 6, n. 3, July-September 1999

[2] S.Berretti, A.Del Bimbo, E.Vicario, "The Computational Aspect of Retrieval by Spatial Arrangement", IEEE ICPR, Int. Conference on Pattern Recognition, Barcelona, 2000

[3] S.Berretti, A.Del Bimbo, E.Vicario, "Weighting Spatial Arrangement of Colors in Content-based Image Retrieval", Proc. IEEE ICMCS99, Int. Conf. On Multimedia Computing and Systems, Florence, June 1999.

[4] A. Del Bimbo, "Visual Information Retrieval" Morgan Khaufman, San Francisco,1999

[5] I.M.Walter, R.Sturm,P.C.Lockemann,H.H.Nagel, "A Semantic Network-based Deductive Database System for Image Sequence Evaluation", in Visual Database Systems II, E.Knuth, L.M.Wegner eds Elsevier Science Pubs, 1992

[6] A.Del Bimbo, P.Pala, "Image Retrieval by Multiple Feature Combination", in .... M.Lew Ed, in press.

[7] L. Cinque, S. Levialdi, K. Olsen, "A Multidimensional Image Browser", Journal of Visual Languages and Computers, 1998

[8] J.M.Corridoni, A.Del Bimbo, P.Pala, "Image Retrieval by Color Semantics", ACM Multimedia Journal, 1999

[9] R.Hull, R.King, "Semantic Database Modelling: Survey, Applications and Research Issues, ACM Computing Surveys Vol. 19, n.3, September 1987

[10] P.Aigrain, H.Zhang, D. Petkovic, "Content-based Representation and Retrieval of Visual Media: a State of the Art", Multimedia Tools and Applications, Vol.3, 1996

[11] J.M.Floch, "Semiotica Marketing e Comunicazione" F.Angeli Ed. 1997

[12] S.K.Chang, A.Hsu, "Image Information Systems: Where do we go from here?", IEEE Trans. on Knowledge and Data Engineering, Vol.4, n.5, 1992

[13] F.Idris and S.Panchanathan, "Review of Image and Video Indexing Techniques", Journal of Communication and Imagr representation, Vol.8, n.2, 1997

[14] S. Santini, R. Jain, "Image Databases are not databases with images", Proc. ICIAP97, firenze, Italy, 1997

[15] N.Vasconcelos, A.Lippmann, "Towards Semantically Meaningful Feature Spaces for the Characterization of Video Content" Proc. ICIP97, Int. Conf. On Image Processing, S.Barbara, October 1997

[16] J.M.Corridoni, A.Del Bimbo, "Structured Representation and Automatic Indexing of Movie Information Content", Pattern Recognition Vol.31, n.12, 1998

[17] M.Bertini, A.Del Bimbo, P.Pala, "Content-based Indexing and Retrieval of News Video", Proc. Int. Symposium on Image/Video Communications over Fixed and Mobile Networks, Rabat, Marocco, April 2000

[18] D.Yow, B.L.Yeo, M.Teung, B.Liu, "Analysis and Presentation of Soccer Higlight from Digital Video"" Proc. 2nd Asian Conference on Computer Vision, 1995

[19] M.Yeung, B.L.Yeo, B.Liu "Extracting Story Units from Long Programs for Video Browsing and Navigation" Proc. IEEE Int. Conf. On Multimedia Computing and Systems, Hiroshima, Japan, 1996

[20] M.Yeung, B.L.Yeo, "Video Visualization for Compact Presentation and Fast Browsing of Pictorial Content", IEEE Trans. on Circuits and Systems for Video Technolofy, Aug. 1997

[21] A.J.Greimas, "Semiotique Figurative et Semiotique Plastique", in Actes Semiotiques - Documents, VI, 60, Paris 1984

[22] M.Caliani, C.Colombo, A.Del Bimbo, P.Pala, "Commercial Video Retrieval by Induced Semantics", IEEE CBAIVD98, Int. Workshop on Content-Based Access of Image and Video Databases, Bombay, India, 1998.

[23] J.M.Sanchez, X.Binefa, J.Vitria, P. Radeva, "Linking Visual Cues and Semantic Terms under Specific Digital Video Domains", Journal of Visual Languages and Computing, Vol. 11, 2000

[24] S.Pfeiffer, R.Lienhart, S.Fischer, W.Effelsberg, "Abstracting Digital Movies Automatically", Journal of Visual Communication and Image Representation, Vol.7,n.4, Dec.1996

[25] M.A.Smith, T.Kanade, "Video Skimming and Characterization through the Combination of Image and Language Understanding", IEEE CBAIVD98, Int. Workshop on Content-Based Access of Image and Video Databases, Bombay, India, 1998.

[26] B.Messmer, H.Bunke, "A new Algorithm for Error Tolerant Subgraph Isomorphism Detection", IEEE trans. on Pattern Analysis and Machine Intelligence, Vol. 20, n.5, May 1998

[27] E.Petrakis, C.Faloutsos,K-I,Lin, "Similarity Searching in Medical Image Databases", IEEE Trans. on Knowledge and Data Engineering, Vol.9, n.3, May 1997

[28] P.Ciaccia, M.Patella, P.Zezula, "M-tree: an Efficient Access Method for Similarity Search in Metric Spaces", Proc. Int. Conf. On Very Large Image Databases, 1997

[29] R.Arnheim, "Art and Visual Perception: a Psychology of the Creative Eye", Regents of Univ. of California, 1954

[30] J.Itten, "Art of Color, Otto Maier Verlag, Germany, 1961

Automatic Video Scene Extraction by Shot Grouping

Tong Lin[1]

National Laboratory on Machine Perception
Peking University
Beijing 100071, China
Tonysc007@263.net

Hong-Jiang Zhang

Microsoft Research, China
No.5 Zhichun Road
Beijing 100084, China
hjzhang@microsoft.com

Abstract

For more efficient organizing, browsing, and retrieving digital video content, it is important to extract video structure information at both scene and shot levels. This paper presents an effective approach to video scene segmentation based on a pseudo-object-based shot correlation analysis. A new measure of the semantic correlation of consecutive shots based on dominant color grouping and tracking is proposed. A new shot grouping method named expanding window is designed to cluster correlated consecutive shots into one scene. Evaluations based on real-world sports video programs validate the efficiency and effectiveness of our shot correlation measure and scene structure construction.

1. Introduction

Efficient and automatic content organization and management of digital video is a key to the success of future video libraries, and various video applications on Internet has highlighted the need for smart content filtering and selective content delivery. Video structure parsing is the process to extract construction units of video programs. The structural information resulted from video parsing, especially semantically defined structures which appear to be more meaningful to human perception, is essential to automatic and content-based organization and retrieval of video,

There are usually two layers of construction units in video: shots and scenes (also often referred as story units). A shot consists of a sequence of frames recorded contiguously and representing a continuous action in time or space. A video scene consists of a sequence of semantically correlated shots. Earlier work in video structure analysis mostly focused on shot boundary detection, and numerous techniques have been proposed for parsing video streams into individual shots. After detecting shot boundaries, corresponding key frames can then be extracted to perform image analysis techniques for understanding shot content. While shot-based video analysis approaches provide users with better access than unstructured raw video stream, they are still not sufficient for meaningful video browsing and retrieval. Extracting scene structure information of videos will also facilitate hierarchical video abstraction, indexing and browsing.

There are a number of algorithms developed to detect scene boundaries in video sequences. Following the idea of examining boundary heterogeneities used in edge detection, an approach to scene boundary detection was proposed that determines a shot boundary being a scene boundary if color, motion and audio change simultaneously [1]. However, this approach does not consider a shot as a whole, and the beginning and ending frames contribute more to scene segmentation.

Most of others approaches attempt to merge similar and consecutive shots into scenes [2][3][4][5][6]. These approaches explore the internal homogeneity of a scene. Different shot similarity measures have been proposed, such as matching blocks between key frames [2], comparing color histograms between key frames [3] or mean color histogram [4], and comparing color histograms between any frame in two shot [6]. In other words, these approaches rely heavily on similarities between frames, either key-frames or individual frames in video shots. However, shot similarities defined by key-frames do not represent the temporal information completely. Also, comparing every pair of frames in two shots is very expensive computationally. More importantly, it is often because they are semantically correlated rather than visually similar when a sequence of shots is considered a scene. Therefore, scene detection approaches based on visual similarity of frames between two shots often do not produce good results, and what needed is a quantitative measure of semantic correlations between shots.

In this paper, we present an effective approach to video scene extraction, which consists of two significant new features. First, in contrast to previous works, we use shot correlation rather than similarity in grouping shots into scenes. For this, we have developed a new scheme to measure the semantic correlation of consecutive shots using dominant color grouping and tracking. The

[1] The work presented in this paper was performed while this author was working as a summer intern at Microsoft Research, China.

1051-4651/00 $10.00 © 2000 IEEE

correlation measure depends not only on dominant colors of individual frames, but also their temporal variation. Therefore, this measure meets the nature of video as a temporal media. Also, a new shot grouping method named expanding window is designed to group correlated consecutive shots into scenes.

The rest of this paper is organized as follows. In Section 2, we first describe focus of our work, together with the definition of semantic correlation and considerations. Then, we present the new framework for measuring shot correlation, and the approach for scene structure construction using expanding window shot grouping method. In Section 3, we present experimental evaluation of the proposed approaches based on a data set real world sports programs. Concluding remarks are given in Section 4.

2. The Proposed Approach

A scene is defined as one or more consecutive shots that they are semantically correlated [1], or they all share the same "content" in terms of action, place and time [3]. While shots are marked by physical boundaries, scenes are marked by semantic boundaries, so scene boundary detection is a far more difficult task compared with shot boundary detection. **Figure 1** shows two examples of video scenes, each consists of a sequence of shots taken from the same place and in a successive order of time, and present an event.

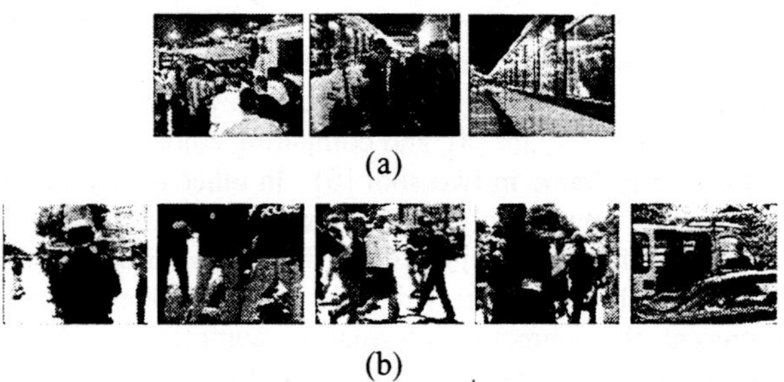

Figure 1: Two examples of video scenes, each consists of a sequence of shots taken from the same place and in a successive order of time, and present an event.

In this paper, we define a scene as a sequence of consecutive shots that they are semantically correlated, or they share the same semantics in terms of time, place, objects or events. However, our task is to detect scene boundaries rather than semantic contents of scenes; thus, the key problem in scene segmentation is to determine if two shots are semantically correlated.

To solve this problem, we have focused on developing a measure of shot correlation without solving the difficult image understanding problems, such as object segmentation, recognition and tracking. In general, we can classify shots into two types: focusing on the environment, such as a street, without dominant foreground objects; or focusing on static or moving objects, such as a car or person. When a scene is composed by either one of these types of shots, or a combination of the two with a transition, there will be at least one aspect (dominant objects or background) in common between the shots. We define such a common aspect between two shots as their correlation. We find that color is an effective yet computational inexpensive feature to be used in representing such a correlation. As described in detail in the following, we have designed a measure based on dominant color grouping and tracking in a shot. The correlation measure depends not only on dominant colors of individual frames, but also their temporal variation. Therefore, this measure meets the nature of video as a temporal media. This new measure is distinctive from that proposed in previous works and is one of the two significant contributions presented in this paper.

2.1 Shot Correlation Measure

The color-based correlation measure between two shots, *a* and *b*, denoted as *cor (a, b)*, is calculated by dominant color object comparison and tracking between the two shots as following. This is achieve by first calculate the color histogram of each frame, from which dominant colors of the frame are identified, as described in the following.

We use the *HSV* color space in calculating color histograms since the *HSV* color space is natural and approximately perceptually uniform. Also, we can define a quantization of *HSV* to produce a collection of colors that is compact and complete. In our method, the HSV color space is quantized by a 3D Cartesian coordinate system with 10 values for X and Y, 5 values for Z (the lightness), respectively, as shown in **Figure 2**. This is because the *HSV* space is cylindrical, and the similarity between two colors given by indices *(h1,s1,v1)* and *(h2,s2,v2)* is given by the Euclidean distance between the color points *(x1,y1,z1)* and *(x2,y2,z2), respectively,* in the cylindrical *HSV* color space. The fineness of the color quantization will influent the extraction of dominant objects. A fine quantification will be able to discriminate more objects, while it may also cause the extraction of dominant objects being sensitive to lighting dominant objects between frames, which may result in loss of tracking of dominant objects.

To determine dominant colors of a video shots, pixels of each frame, or DC blocks in I frames when MPEG1/2 video are used, of the shot are projected into the quantized HSV color space. The normalized distribution of these pixels in the 3-D color space thus forms a normalized 3D color histograms of the frame. All dominant local maximum points in the 3-D color histogram are identified; and a sphere surrounding each local maximum point within a small neighborhood (with diameter of 3 quatization units) in the color space is defined as a color object. These colors objects (top 20 in our implementation) with the largest numbers of pixels are identified as dominant objects. These dominant objects capture the most significant color information of a frame and are more resilient to noise. We then form a 3-D *dominant color histogram*, $hist_d(k, x, y, z)$, for each frame by counting only pixels included in dominant color objects, where k denotes the frame number, and (x, y, z) denotes a color bin. It is worth noticing that we do not perform object segmentation in the spatial domain though the segmentation in *HSV* color space could be mapped back to a frame image, leading to a spatial segmentation; rather, we consider pixels falling into a dominant regions in the color space an object, which may (often) not represent a spatial object in a frame.

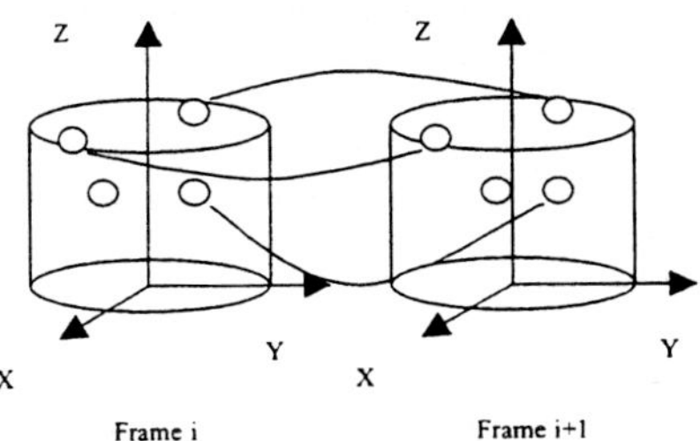

Figure 2: Color object segmentation and tracking.

Then, color objects defined as above in consecutive frames are tracked in the HSV color space to identify dominant objects of a shot. If the centers of two color objects in two consecutive frames are sufficient close, these two color objects are recognized as the same color object. Such a color tracking process will continue until all frames in the shot are tracked. After tracking, only the color objects that have longer duration in a shot are retained as dominant objects. In the words, we form an overall dominant color histogram for each shot, $hist_d^a(x, y, z)$ (a denotes a shot), consisting of only dominant color objects that are not only dominant in a frame, but also dominant across the entire shot. To give more weight to color objects with longer duration in a shot since they are more dominant, the histogram bins, corresponding to each dominant objects are weighted by its relative duration in a shot as,

$$hist_d^A(x, y, z) = hist_d^a(x, y, z) \times d_l / d_0 \qquad (1)$$

where d_0 is the duration of the shot, and d_l is duration of the dominant color object with color (x, y, z). Also, $hist_d^A(x, y, z)$ is normalized by normalizing the mean size of each dominant color object within the shot. Therefore, the dominant color histogram of a shot represents both structural content in a frame and temporal content in a shot. Also, these dominant color objects often represent dominant objects or background in a shot and the correlation between these color objects in two shots is a good representation of correlations between the two shots. The correlation score between two shots, a and b, is calculated by performing the histogram intersection between two dominant color histograms of the two shots. That is,

$$\mathrm{Cor}(a, b) = \Sigma_x \Sigma_y \Sigma_z min[hist_d^A(x, y, z), hist_d^B(x, y, z)] \qquad (2)$$

This correlation score has the following properties:

1) $0 <= cor(a, b) <= 1$, $cor(a, a) = 1$
2) $cor(a,b) = cor(b,a)$

2.2 Shot Grouping

A new method named expanding window is designed to group correlated consecutive shots into one scene based on the correlation scores as defined above. With this method, there is no need to compare many shot pairs and constructing complex links, as in [2, 6].

Considering the temporal constraints, i.e. shots that are closer to each other in time is more likely to belong to the same scene, the correlation score between two shots is weighted by temporal attraction factor:

$$w = 1/(1+d/C) \qquad (3)$$

where d is the minimum distance between the two shots (from the ending frame of the previous shot to the beginning frame of the current shot) and C is a constant, determined by the average shot length.

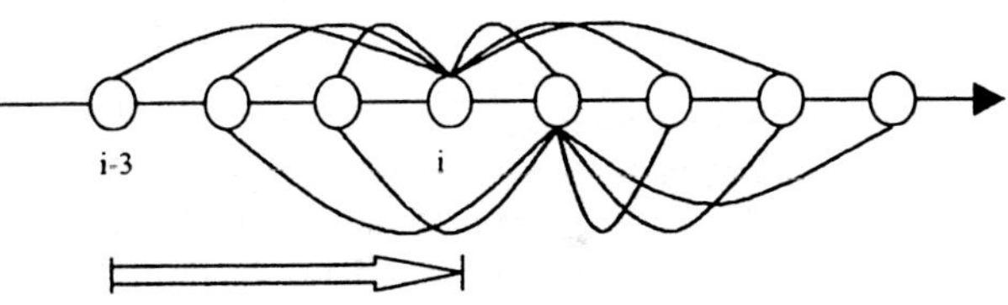

Figure 3. Expanding window shot grouping method, where shot i is the current new shot.

Assume every scene should contain at least 3 shots. Initially, the first 3 shots form a new scene, i.e. the size of expanding window is set to 3. Every time a new shot comes in, its correlation scores with the last 3 shots in the window is calculated and the maximum v, among the three correlation scores, is determined. Then, if

$$v > mean\text{-}var \qquad (4)$$

this shot is absorbed by the expanding window into the current scene. In (4), *mean* and *var* are the mean and variation of maximum correlation scores between shots contained in the current expanding window, respectively. Otherwise, we consider a few more subsequent shots for more confidence, as shown in **Figure 3**, because it is often that a scene may contain a shot that is uncorrelated with either previous or next shot. That is, we define an attraction ratio of the current shot i toward a new scene as

$$R(i) = (right(i)+right(i+1))/(left(i)+left(i+1)) \quad (5)$$

where

$$left(i)=max\{cor(i,i-1), cor(i,i-2), cor(i,i-3)\}$$
$$left(i+1)=max\{cor(i+1,i-1), cor(i+1,i-2)\}$$
$$right(i)=max\{cor(i,i+1), cor(i,i+2), cor(i,i+3)\}$$
$$right(i+1)=max\{cor(i+1,i+2), cor(i+1,i+3), cor(i+1,i+4)\}$$

If

$$R(i) > T \text{ and } R(i) > R(i-1) \text{ and } R(i) > R(i+1) \quad (6)$$

(where T is a threshold and we set T=1.5), then, the attraction to shot i from right side is greater than from left side, thus, the current shot i starts a new scene. Otherwise, the current scene absorbs this shot.

3. Experimental Results

We first tested the performance of the proposed correlation measure (SCM) in grouping similar shots, in comparison with those using mean color histogram (MCH) and keyframe color histogram (KCH). A shot database is used for comparing the proposed shot grouping method based the shot correlation measure, There are 419 shots from forty minutes TV sports news, including track and field events, swimming, soccer, basketball, etc. We pick out 8 shots each belongs to a scene as benchmark queries, and find k ground-truth correlated shots for each test. Also choose k as cut-off value, so recall is equal to precision. From Table 1, we could see that our solution outperforms the other commonly used ones.

To test the proposed shot grouping approach, we use 52 minutes soccer sequence from France98 World Cup to recognize different soccer matches. Here a scene is defined as all the consecutive shots in one match. There are 471 shots, and 40 different soccer matches, thus, there are 39 scene boundaries. Using the proposed algorithm, 61 scene boundaries are found, of which 30 are true boundaries, 9 missed, and 31 false alarms. Misses are caused by very similar grass color and lighting, which can only be recognized by even human viewer with very careful watching and with information from speech and close tracking of player' s uniform colors. Alternating long shots and close-ups causes most of falsies, which are often reasonable for human visual perception. Figure 4 shows one example of corrected detected scene boundaries. It is also found that though that the proposed shot grouping method outperform other shot grouping methods, the performance will be increased significantly if audio information is integrated into the scene detection process, which is our next in developing the video scene segmentation system.

4. Conclusions

In this paper, we have presented a new measure for shot correlation and a method for applying this measure in grouping shots into scenes. The proposed method outperforms other key-frame or average color histogram based methods, though the performance needs further improvement. Since scene extraction requires more semantic information than just colors and their temporal variations, information from audio content analysis and segmentation will be helpful. How to integrate audio classification and segmentation with shot correlation analysis is our next step in developing a more robust scene extraction system.

5. References

[1] J. Huang, Z. Liu and Y. Wang, "Integration of Audio and Visual Information for Content-based Video Segmentation", *Proc. ICIP'98*, Chicago, Oct. 1998.

[2] A. Hanjalic, R. L. Lagendijk, and J. Biemond, "Automated high-level movie segmentation for advanced video-retrieval systems", *IEEE Transactions on Circuits and Systems For Video Technology*, Vol. 9, No. 4, pp. 580-588, June 1999.

[3] J. M. Corridoni and A. Del Bimbo, "Structured representation and automatic indexing of movie information content", *Pattern Recognition*, Vol. 31, No. 12, pp. 2027-2045, 1998.

[4] B. Gunsel, Y. Fu, and A. M. Tekalp, "Hierarchical temporal video segmentation and content characterization", in *Multimedia Storage and Archiving Systems II*, Proc. SPIE Vol. 3229, pp. 46-56, 1997.

[5] Y. Rui, T. S. Huang, and S. Mehrotra, "Exploring video structure beyond the shots", *Proc. IEEE Conf. on Multimedia Computing and Systems*, pp. 237-240, 1998.

[6] J. R. Kender and B. L. Yeo, "Video scene segmentation via continuous video coherence", *Proc. IEEE Int. Conf. on Computer Vision and Pattern Recognition*, pp. 367-373, 1998.

	k	n(SCM)	n(MCH)	n(KCH)
Soccer	8	5	6	2
Basketball	10	6	5	4
Marathon	5	3	2	1
Boat Race	4	2	1	3
Broad Jump	2	2	1	1
Swimming	9	9	9	9
Chess	9	6	6	5
Beach Volleyball	6	5	5	2
Total	53	38	35	27

Table 1. Comparison on different shot correlation queries

Figure 4; Detected scene boundary in a shot sequence caused by focus changing from long shots to close-ups. Each image is the first frame of one shot.

Locale-based Visual Object Retrieval under Illumination Change

Zinovi Tauber, Ze-Nian Li, and Mark S. Drew
School of Computing Science, Simon Fraser University,
Vancouver, B.C. Canada V5A 1S6 *

Abstract

Providing a user with an effective image search engine has been a very active research area. A search by an object model is considered to be one of the most desirable and yet difficult tasks. An added difficulty is that objects can be photographed under different lighting conditions. We have developed a feature localization scheme that finds a set of locales *in an image. We make use of a diagonal model for illumination change and obtain a candidate set of lighting transformation coefficients in chromaticity space. For each pair of coefficients,* Elastic Correlation *is performed, which is a form of correlation of locale colors. A Least Square (LS) minimization for pose estimation is then applied, followed by a process of texture support and shape verification. Tests on a database of over 1,400 images and video clips show promising image retrieval results. Moreover, it has been shown that the method is capable of recovering lighting changes.*

Keywords: Color, Elastic Correlation, Illumination Invariance, Locales, Object Recognition, Search by Object Model

1. Introduction

The World-Wide Web (WWW) is being increasingly populated with images and videos. There is a growing need for effective indexing and retrieval of large amounts of such media data. Most common image content indexing techniques use global image features [1, 2]. Arguably, one of the most useful searching methods is by object model. Global image features do not lend themselves well to object retrieval. Background objects can heavily affect the global feature vectors. Recently, attempts have been made to use image segmentation for object indexing [3] with some success. There is no system however that retrieves objects based on visual contents or models with high speed and accuracy.

In our C-BIRD (Content-Based Image Retrieval from Digital libraries) system [4], we use a technique for coarse localization of image features into *locales*. Locales can be overlapped and/or non-connected, and the set of all locales does not have to include all image pixels.

A major problem with both color histogram search and color object search is that the same object in different photographs may have different colors if the illumination changed. In [5] we used a diagonal color shift model to normalize an image. We use the same diagonal model to recover illuminant change here.

The retrieval task performs localization of the user selected model on the fly and matches the model locales to the image locales stored in the database. In [6] we matched model locales to image locales using Least Square (LS) minimization for both illuminant chromaticity shift and pose estimation. Although we had a closed-form solution for the minimization we still had to enumerate every possible assignment of model locales to image locales which was computationally prohibitive. In this paper we propose first obtaining a set of estimates for a chromaticity shift (or *chroma shift* for short) from an image to a model using voting for each locale correspondence, and then applying a form of correlation called elastic correlation. Since very few matches pass this strict pre-selection step and go on to pose estimation, the search speed is improved by two orders of magnitude!

Given a set of assignments of model locales to image locales we use LS minimization for pose estimation, histogram intersection on the locale texture, and finally the Generalized Hough Transform (GHT) [7] on the database image according to the estimated pose. In this paper, we also demonstrate the recovery of chromaticity change between pairs of various illuminants.

The remainder of this paper is as follows. Section 2 describes the process of image feature localization. Section 3 describes our search method. Section 4 shows results of object retrieval from the C-BIRD database and the recovery of lighting change, and Section 5 concludes the paper.

2. Feature Localization

We argue [4] that a more useful and attainable process than image segmentation is a coarse localization of image features based on proximity and compactness. A localization of a feature is defined as *locale*. A locale $\mathcal{L}_f$ uses squares of pixels (tiles) as its positioning units, and has the following descriptors: (1) envelope L_f–a set of tiles representing the locality of $\mathcal{L}_f$; (2) geometric parameters–mass $M(\mathcal{L}_f)$, centroid $C(\mathcal{L}_f)$, eccentricity $E(\mathcal{L}_f)$; and (3) other features of the locale, e.g., locale texture histogram.

Although the envelope L_f of a locale $\mathcal{L}_f$ is being defined in tile units, the geometric statistics and the texture histogram are measured in pixels. A tile has feature x if

*Email: {zinovi,li,mark}@cs.sfu.ca http://www.cs.sfu.ca

1051-4651/00 $10.00 © 2000 IEEE

enough pixels in it have feature x. As a consequence, after a feature localization process the following is often true: (1) $\exists x : \mathcal{L}_x$ is *not connected*; (2) $\exists x \exists y : \mathcal{L}_x \cap \mathcal{L}_y \neq \phi,\ x \neq y$: *non-disjointness*; and (3) $\cup_x \mathcal{L}_x \neq I$, the entire image: *non-completeness*.

The localization process on color feature proceeds as follows. In order to remove illumination effects, here we actually use chromaticity. First, the image is reduced resolution and converted from RGB color space to a chromaticity-luminosity color space. For a pixel with color (R, G, B), we define $I = R+G+B$ (which is closely related to gray-level intensity) and chromaticity values $r = R/I$ and $g = G/I$.

After enhancing the edge colors the image is partitioned into tiles of size 16×16. Geometrical statistics are gathered for each tile.

To generate locales we use a method similar to "pyramid-linking" for merging tiles into locales. In terms of parent-child relation, the overlapped pyramid is used. In our implementation we used a 4×4 overlapped pyramid structure. Working bottom-up, tile parent nodes compete for links to child nodes in a fair competition. Tiles are allowed to merge to a parent node if the merged locale will have $E(\mathcal{L}_f) < \tau$, where τ is a threshold normalized against $M(\mathcal{L}_f)$. The competition criterion is to merge the geometrically closest allowable tile centroid to the parent locale centroid. After a competition cycle, $M(\mathcal{L}_f)$, $\mathbf{C}(\mathcal{L}_f)$, and $E(\mathcal{L}_f)$ are updated accordingly.

3. Object Retrieval under Illumination Change

All images in the digital repository are preprocessed offline to generate locales which are stored in the database. Once a user submits an object search query by providing an object sample image, it is treated as a model and processed to generate the model locales. For each image in the database we attempt to match its locales to the model locales, taking into account the possible illumination changes. The matching process consists of the following steps: (a) chroma shift estimate, (b) elastic correlation, (c) pose estimation, and (d) texture support and shape verification.

3.1. Chroma Shift Estimation

As illustrated in [5], a practical working model of illumination change is the *diagonal model*. Given color (R', G', B') under model illumination and color (R, G, B) under image illumination we have

$$R' = \alpha R\,,\ G' = \beta G\,,\ B' = \gamma B \qquad (1)$$

Adapting the diagonal model for chromaticity values is more complex. Dividing by γ, we define

$$\tilde{\alpha} = \alpha/\gamma = \frac{R'B}{RB'} = \frac{r'b}{rb'}\,,\quad \tilde{\beta} = \beta/\gamma = \frac{G'B}{GB'} = \frac{g'b}{gb'}\,, \qquad (2)$$

then

$$r' = \frac{\alpha R}{\alpha R + \beta G + \gamma B} = \frac{\tilde{\alpha} r}{(\tilde{\alpha}-1)r + (\tilde{\beta}-1)g + 1}\,, \qquad (3)$$

and similarly g'. It follows that we only need to recover the two *chroma shift* parameters $\tilde{\alpha}$ and $\tilde{\beta}$ in order to derive r' and g' from r and g.

It's necessary to obtain a minimal set of shift parameters for locale matching to be efficient. Every pair of shift parameters in the candidate set will have to be tested until a match is found. Although we have considered a few fast ways to get such a candidate set, we believe the one presented below to be the best compromise in speed and accuracy.

We use a voting scheme to find the best $\tilde{\alpha}, \tilde{\beta}$ pair. The 2D voting space $\Phi\{\tilde{\alpha}, \tilde{\beta}\}$ is discretized into 50×50 bins. The range of the correct $\tilde{\alpha}, \tilde{\beta}$ values is restricted to 0.1–10.0. Hence,

$$\Phi = \{\tilde{\alpha}, \tilde{\beta} \mid 0.1 \leq \tilde{\alpha}, \tilde{\beta} \leq 10.0\}. \qquad (4)$$

A logarithmic scale for the voting space axis is employed. Using base 10 we define the voting array dimensions as -1.0-1.0.

Each image locale is being matched with each model locale to calculate an $\tilde{\alpha}, \tilde{\beta}$ pair. Since the diagonal model is an approximation and a locale color can be affected by noise, complete confidence cannot be put in the calculated $\tilde{\alpha}, \tilde{\beta}$ even for the two matched locales. Therefore a Gaussian voting is utilized, where every $\tilde{\alpha}, \tilde{\beta}$ pair will add its normalized Gaussian probability to cells around its cell.

Another complicating factor is that, as noted, the locale color values can possibly vary, making the calculated $\tilde{\alpha}, \tilde{\beta}$ unstable for small color values. That necessitates the formulation of a 2D Gaussian function with a larger variance as the color value reduces on either dimension. The standard deviation values we used range from 1.0 to 5.0, and the Gaussian mask size is 5×5.

The position of $\phi(\tilde{\alpha_p}, \tilde{\beta_p})$ that has a high score yields the set of candidate chroma shift values $(\tilde{\alpha_p}, \tilde{\beta_p})$. Typically the highest score corresponds to the best $\tilde{\alpha}, \tilde{\beta}$ estimate for the model object and the image object. In case there are more than one candidate $(\tilde{\alpha_p}, \tilde{\beta_p})$, they will all be forwarded to the next step for further examination.

3.2. Elastic Correlation

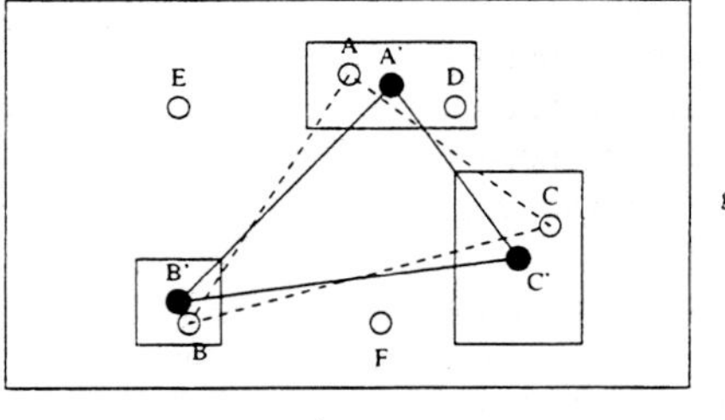

Figure 1. Elastic correlation in $\Omega\{r', g'\}$.

Elastic correlation is a process for verifying good matches between model locales and image locales for each $(\tilde{\alpha_p}, \tilde{\beta_p})$. As shown in Fig. 1, the model image has three locale colors located at A', B' and C'. All the image locale colors, A, B, C, D, E and F, are being shifted to the model illuminant using eq. 3 and the current $(\tilde{\alpha_p}, \tilde{\beta_p})$ values. Although the locales (A', B', C') and (A, B, C) are supposed to be matching entities, they do not appear exactly at the same location. Instead of a rigid template matching (or correlation) method, we employ the elastic correlation technique in which the nodes A, B, C are allowed to be located at the vicinity of A', B', C', respectively. In the model chromaticity space $\Omega\{r', g'\}$, we define a window around each model locale and then check whether any image locale chromaticity is inside the window. If a sufficient percentage of the model locales find matching image locales and the associated masses exceed a chosen threshold, we accept the hypothesized $(\tilde{\alpha_p}, \tilde{\beta_p})$.

The correlation process used here is made even more *elastic* by allowing non-fixed window size. Much like in the previous voting in Φ space, the window size in $\Omega\{r', g'\}$ is larger on either dimension when r' and/or g' values are small to compensate the increased uncertainty/error with small color values. This of course implies that the shape of the window is often not square.

Having a set of possible image locales associated with each model locale, it's necessary to establish a set of plausible assignments of image locales to model locales for pose estimation. Since the number of possible pairs is typically less than 100, the computation is fast.

3.3. Pose Estimation

Having an assignment of image locales to model locales, and using the MSE criterion, we define an objective function

$$obj = \sum_{i=1}^{n} w_i ||\mathbf{x}_i - s\mathbf{R}\mathbf{x}'_i - \mathbf{x}_0||^2 \tag{5}$$

where $\mathbf{x}_i$ is the centroid of image locale i, $\mathbf{x}'_i$ is the centroid of the corresponding model locale i, $\mathbf{x}_0$ is the translation, s is the scale, $\mathbf{R}$ is the rotation matrix, w_i are the weights associated with each pair of corresponding locales, and n is the number of assigned locales. This objective function models a rigid-body transformation. When it is minimized we obtain the best pose parameters for the locale assignment as well as a measure of error for those parameters. For details, see [8, 6].

Having the best pose parameters estimated, all that is left is to calculate the objective value in eq. 5. If the error is within a small threshold, then the pose estimate is considered a "color hypothesis," and is passed to further screening processes described later.

3.4. Texture Support and Shape Verification

The details of the two final steps for Search by Object Model are described in [4]. Each locale has an associated texture histogram. As for color histogram intersection [1], so can texture histogram intersection be calculated in a very fast manner. We adjust the directionality mapping based on the estimated rotation, and the granularity mapping based on the estimated scale. If all the model locale texture histograms have high intersection values with their corresponding image locale texture histograms then we consider the assignment to have "texture support."

The final match verification process is "shape verification" by the Generalized Hough Transform (GHT). It uses estimated pose parameters, so a full search of all possible scales and rotations is not required, only a verification of a match at a particular location, scale and orientation is needed. The GHT is very robust with respect to noise and in our tests it always produces a single sharp peak. If the GHT procedure returns a peak we then report the current image as a match.

4. Experimental Results

4.1 Search by Object Model

Our database consists of over 1,400 images and video clips taken from various sources. We performed a search of the full database with 4 model objects which we know exist in the database, but under different illuminations. E.g., Fig. 2(a) shows a sample result for a pink book model search before the step of checking texture. It shows an 80% recovery of all pink book images, plus three false positives. For all test runs, the searches produce a mean Recall of 83%. Although using color alone could produce many false positive matches, most of the false ones are eliminated in the subsequent stages of texture checking and shape verification by GHT. Fig. 2(b) illustrates the result after checking texture, which yields a precision of 90%. Typical speed of a search on the entire database is about 15 to 20 seconds on a modest PIII-500 MHz server, with over 90% time spent on accessing data in the database.

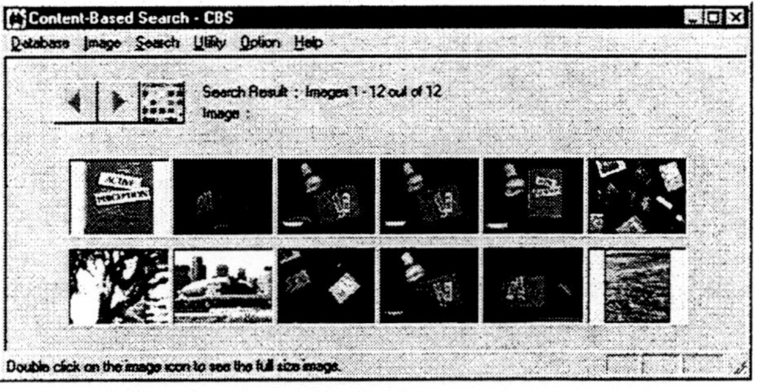

(a)

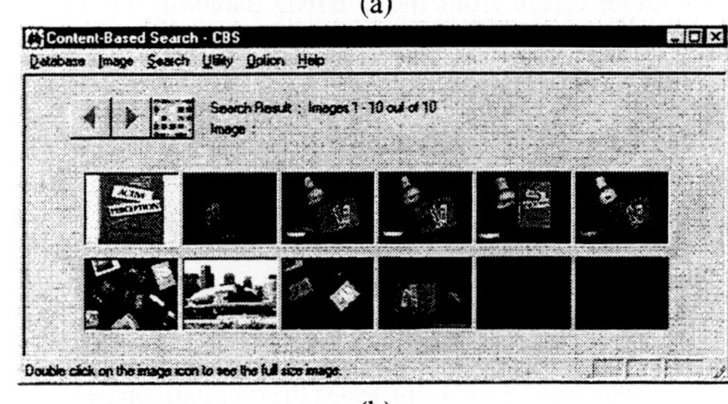

(b)

Figure 2. Search Result for a Pink Book.

4.2 Recovery of Lighting Change

We used several database objects from [9], for example, one of them is "beach-ball". The ball is under 5 different illuminations respectively, hence it provides the first five test images. Since explicit lighting for images in the database is known [9], if we compare a source image with a target image that is taken under another light, we can explicitly calculate values for $\tilde{\alpha}$, $\tilde{\beta}$ for the actual lighting change, and this is viewed as "ground truth".

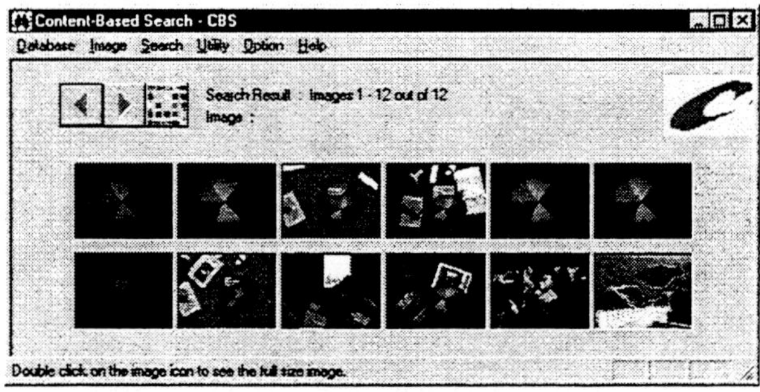

Figure 3. Search Using a Beach-ball as Model.

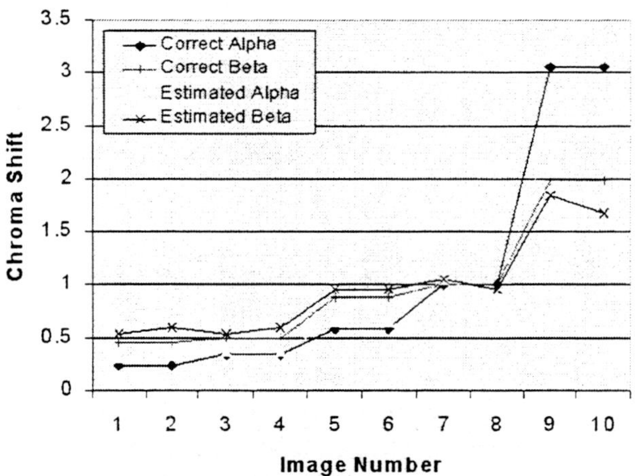

Figure 4. Correct and Recovered $\tilde{\alpha}$s and $\tilde{\beta}$s.

We also formed five new beach-ball images by selecting some target image from the C-BIRD database, randomly, and placing a copy of one of the five beach-balls into the target image, thus forming a composite image. Here, the ball is placed into a random image, with known rotation (e.g., 33°), scaling (e.g., 0.58) and translation. Now the 10 beach-ball images are inserted into the C-BIRD database. Each time we use one of the first five beach-ball images as model image to test whether we can find the correct match with the right rotation and scale, and lighting change ($\tilde{\alpha}$, $\tilde{\beta}$). Fig. 3 shows one of the search results in which all 10 beach-ball images are retrieved together with 2 false targets from the C-BIRD database. Fig. 4 illustrates the comparison between the correct ("ground truth") $\tilde{\alpha}$, $\tilde{\beta}$ and the recovered values. It is apparent that when $\tilde{\alpha}$, $\tilde{\beta}$ are close to one, namely, when the chromaticity change of the illuminants is moderate, the estimation errors are small (less that 10%); otherwise, the errors increase, however they are still satisfactory.

Table 1 summarizes the quality of the 5 beach-ball searches in which a ball under a particular light is used as a model image each time. $\Delta\theta$ is the estimation error of rotation angles, and ΔS the estimation error of scaling factors.

Table 1. Quality of the 5 Beach-ball Searches

Light for model image	Precision	Recall	$\Delta\theta$ (degree)	ΔS
Sylvania Cool White	73%	80%	0.50	0.021
Macbeth 5000K	83%	100%	0.40	0.019
Macbeth 5000K+3202	62%	80%	0.83	0.017
Philips Ultralume	78%	70%	0.30	0.018
Halogen	64%	70%	0.65	0.035

5. Conclusions

The search method we suggested in this paper starts with the chroma shift voting scheme and the elastic correlation. It offers a fast and accurate solution to the assignment problem under illumination change. In essence, by performing the chromaticity voting we eliminate the illumination change problem, and reduce the combinatorics of the problem dramatically. Then we have a series of fast checks in terms of pose estimation, texture and shape that leads to high reliability of the retrieved images. Moreover, we have explicitly combined search under a combination of difficult conditions, viz., displacement as well as lighting change. By actually recovering lighting change, we yield a partial solution for a very vexing problem — that of color constancy.

A main limitation in the current approach is that it relies on the diagonal model for color shifts. The diagonal model is only approximate, and seems to be more accurate when the illumination change is smaller. The system currently only handles 2D object models, an extension to retrieval of 3D objects will be a major future work.

References

[1] M. J. Swain and D. H. Ballard. Color indexing. *Int. J. Comput. Vision*, 7(1):11–13, 1991.

[2] M. Flickner, H. Sawhney, and W. Niblack. Query by image and video content: The QBIC system. *IEEE Comput.*, pages 23–32, Sept. 1995.

[3] P. Salembier and F. Marques. Region-based representations of image and video: segmentation tools for multimedia services. *IEEE Trans. on Circuits and Systems for Video Technology*, 9(8):1147–1169, 1999.

[4] Z.N. Li, O.R. Zaïane, and Z. Tauber. Illumination invariace and object model in content-based image and video retrieval. *J. Vis. Comm. and Image Rep.*, 10:219–244, 1999.

[5] M.S. Drew, J. Wei, and Z.N. Li. Illumination–invariant color object recognition via compressed chromaticity histograms of color–channel–normalized images. In *Proc. ICCV98*, pages 533–540, 1998.

[6] M.S. Drew, Z. Tauber, and Z.N. Li. Feature localization and search by object model under illumination change. In *Proc. IS&T/SPIE Symp. on Electronic Imaging, Storage and Retrieval for Media Databases*, pages 399–410, 2000.

[7] D. Ballard. Generalizing the hough transform to detect arbitrary shapes. *Pattern Recognition*, 13(2):111–122, 1981.

[8] B. K. P. Horn. Closed-form solution of absolute orientation using orthogonal matrices. *J. Opt. Soc. Am.*, 5:1127–1135, 1988.

[9] B.V. Funt, K. Barnard, and L. Martin. Is machine colour constancy good enough? In *Proc. ECCV98*, 1998. http://www.cs.sfu.ca/ colour/Images/eccv-98-db.html.

Optimal Color Composition Matching of Images

Jianying Hu
Lucent Technologies Bell labs, 600 Mountain Avenue, Murray Hill, NY 07974
Aleksandra Mojsilovic
IBM TJ Watson Research Center, 30 Saw Mill River Road, H4 B31, Hawthorne, NY 10532

Abstract

Color features are among the most important features used in image database retrieval, especially in cases where no additional semantic information is available. Due to its compact representation and low complexity, direct histogram comparison is the most commonly used technique in comparing color similarity of images. However, it has many serious drawbacks, including a high degree of dependency on color codebook design, sensitivity to quantization boundaries, and inefficiency in representing images with few dominant colors. In this paper we present a new algorithm for color matching. We describe a statistical technique to extract perceptually relevant colors. We propose a new color distance measure that guaranties optimality in matching different color components of two images. Finally, experimental results are presented comparing this new algorithm to some existing techniques.

1. Introduction

Color features have been extensively used in image database retrieval, especially in cases where no additional semantic information is available. Color features are usually very robust to noise, image degradation, changes in size, resolution or orientation. Color histogram, representing the joint probability of the intensities of the three color-channels, is the simplest and the most often used color feature. It is often employed in combination with the Euclidean distance as the color metric, providing undemanding yet efficient retrieval method. As an improvement of a basic histogram search, numerous more sophisticated representations and metrics have been developed. For example, Swain and Ballard proposed histogram intersection, a L_1 metric, as similarity measure for histogram comparison [1]. To measure similarity between close but not identical colors Ioka and Niblac introduced an L_2-based metric [2][3]. However, although the histogram representation is simple to compute, it lacks discriminatory power in retrieval of large image databases. Another disadvantage of the traditional histogram approach is huge amount of data needed for representation, which furthermore increases complexity of the retrieval process. To facilitate fast search of large image databases and better measurements of image similarity in terms of color composition, different research groups proposed more compact and flexible representations [4][5][6]. However, these algorithms still do not match human perception very well.

In this paper we propose a new algorithm for color matching, which includes a new technique for the extraction of perceptually relevant colors and a new color distance measure that has guaranteed optimality in matching different color components of two images. We present experimental results comparing this new algorithm to some existing methods.

2. Color feature extraction

The goal of feature extraction is to obtain compact, perceptually relevant representation of the color content of an image. So far, features based on the image histogram have been widely used in image retrieval. However a feature set based solely on that information does not adequately model the way humans perceive color appearance of an image. It has been shown that in the early perception stage human visual system performs identification of dominant colors by eliminating fine details and averaging colors within small areas [6]. Consequently, on the global level, humans perceive images only as a combination of few most prominent colors, even though the color histogram of the observed image might be very "busy".

Based on these findings, we perform extraction of perceived colors through the following steps. First a color image is transformed from the *RGB* space into the *Lab* color space. This step is crucial, since our metric relies on the perceptual uniformity of the *Lab* space where fixed Euclidean distance represents a fixed perceptual distance regardless of the position in the space [7]. The set of all possible colors is then reduced to a subset defined by a compact color codebook. The codebook is independent of the particular image database and is generated by first sampling the luminance axis into N_L levels and then quantizing the (a, b) plan at each level using a hexagonal

1051-4651/00 $10.00 © 2000 IEEE

spiral lattice [8].

The next step is to extract visually dominant colors. We developed a statistical method to identify colors of speckle noise and remap them to the surrounding dominant color. The method is based on the observation that human beings tend to ignore isolated spots of a different color that are randomly distributed among a dominant color. We first partition each image into non-overlapping $N \times N$ (N is typically 20) windows and then proceed independently in each window. For each window, we compute an $m \times m$ *neighborhood color histogram matrix*, H, where m is the number of colors found in the region. $H[i,j]$ is the number of times a pixel having color j appears in the $D \times D$ (D is a small number, typically 3-5) neighborhood of a pixel having color i, divided by the total number of pixels in the $D \times D$ neighborhoods of pixels having color i. Note that unlike the commonly used color co-occurrence matrix, the neighborhood color histogram matrix is not symmetric. Each row i in H represents the color histogram in the collection of neighborhoods of pixels having color i.

Based on this histogram matrix, speckle colors are detected and remapped in the following manner. For each color i, we examine row i and find the entry $H[i,k]$ that has the maximum value. If k equals i, then i is determined to be a dominant color, and no remapping is done. Otherwise, i is determined to be a speckle color, occurring mostly in the neighborhood of color k. Therefore all pixels of color i in the window are remapped to color k.

3. Optimal color composition distance

This section introduces a new method for measuring the distance between two images in terms of color composition. We first define a color component of an image as a pair $CC_i(I_i, P_i)$, where I_i is the index to a color in a particular color codebook and P_i is the area percentage occupied by that color. A color component CC_i is considered to be dominant if I_i represents perceptually relevant color. Hence, the color composition of an image is represented by the set of dominant color components (DCC) found in the image. Based on human perception, for two images to be considered similar in terms of color composition, two conditions need to be satisfied [6]. First, the colors of dominant color components of the two images need to be similar. Second, the color components with similar colors need to have similar area percentage. Therefore, the distance between two images in terms of color composition should be a measure of the optimal match between the color components of the two images.

Previously proposed color metrics all fail to capture both factors. The most naive metric, the Euclidean distance between the color histograms, captures the second factor well. However it is too rigid with regard to the first factor: the area percentages are only compared for color components with exactly the same color. The same problem occurs in the histogram intersection method proposed by Swain and Ballard [1]. Pei and Cheng proposed a method which allowed more flexible color matching using a dynamic programming approach [5]. However they disregard the area percentage factor completely. In [4], Ma, Deng and Manjunath proposed a more balanced metric (referred to as MDM metric henceforth). They define the distance between two color components to be the product of the difference in area percentage and the difference in color space. In [6] Mojsilovic, Hu *et al.* proposed a modified version of this metric, where the distance between two color components is defined to be the sum of the difference in percentage area and the difference in color space. Both MDM and modified MDM methods are early attempts at providing a distance measure that takes into account both color and area percentage factors. Unfortunately, in both cases neither the metric itself nor the distance computation is well defined. This drawback often offsets the advantage brought by considering both factors and eventually leads to unsatisfactory results.

To overcome these problems we define a new metric called optimal color composition distance (OCCD). The OCCD metric measures the difference between two images in terms of color composition based on the optimal mapping between the two corresponding sets of color components. First, the set of color components of each image is quantized into a set of n color units, each with the same area percentage p, where $n \times p = 100$ (we chose n=20). We call this set the *quantized color component* (QCC) set. Apparently, different color units in the QCC set may have the same color and the number of color units labeled with a particular color I_i is proportional to the corresponding area percentage P_i. Since every unit now has the same area percentage, it suffices to label each by the color index along. Thus the color composition of an image is now represented as a set of n labeled color units. Suppose we have two images A and B, having QCC sets $\{C_A | U_A^1, U_A^2, \ldots, U_A^n\}$ and $\{C_B | U_B^1, U_B^2, \ldots, U_B^n\}$. Let $I(U_x^k), x = A, B$; $k = 1, \ldots, n$, denotes the color index of unit U_x^k, and let $\{M_{AB} | m_{AB} : C_A \to C_B\}$ be the set of one-to-one mapping functions from set C_A to set C_B. Each mapping function defines a mapping distance between the two sets:

$$MD(C_A, C_B) = \sum_{i=1}^{n} W(I(U_A^i), I(m_{AB}(U_A^i))),$$

where $W(i, j)$ is the distance between color i and color j in a given color codebook. Our goal is to find the optimal mapping function that minimizes the overall mapping distance. The distance between the images A and B is then defined to be the minimal mapping distance.

To solve this optimization problem, we create a graph, G_{AB}. It contains $2n$ nodes, one for each color unit in C_A or C_B, and n^2 edges, one between each node in C_A and each node in C_B. The cost for an edge is defined to be the distance between the two corresponding colors. The resulting graph is an undirected, bipartite graph. The problem of finding the optimal mapping between color units in A and those in B can now be cast as the problem of minimum cost graph matching. The latter is a well-studied problem and there are well-known solutions with $O(n^3)$ complexity, where n is the number of nodes in the graph. We used Rothberg's implementation [9] of Gabow's algorithm [10].

Given the set of color components, the color units for each image are filled in the following fashion. For each color component we compute the number of bins it occupies as: $n_i = ceiling(P_i/p)$. Then, we sort the dominant color components according to the area they occupy, and start assigning the color units beginning with the "most dominant color", until all twenty units have been assigned.

4. Experimental results

In this section we illustrate the performance of the new algorithm (OCCD) by comparing it to several previously proposed methods. These previous methods include: 1) the simplest scheme based on the Euclidean distance between the target and query histograms; 2) Swain's histogram intersection method [1]; 3) MDM metric [4]; and 4) Modified MDM metric [6].

For the comparison we used an interior design database, consisting of 335 color patterns. This database was chosen because there is little meaning attached to it - in that way we were able to test our scheme and compare it to other methods without too much bias of semantic information. In the examples shown below, all retrieval results are displayed with the query image at the upper-left corner, and the 5 retrieved images arranged from left to right and top to bottom in order of decreasing similarity.

Fig. 1 illustrates the performances of traditional histogram method (Fig. 1a) and histogram intersection (Fig. 1b) compared to that of OCCD (Fig. 1c). In this example, both histogram based methods fail to pull some of the very similar images, because they ignore colors that are close to each other and yet happen to fall into different quantization bins. OCCD succeeds to retrieve these images by allowing flexibility in comparing both the colors and the area percentages they occupy. Fig. 2 shows a comparison of the performances of the MDM method (Fig. 2a), the modified MDM method (Fig. 2b), and the OCCD method (Fig. 2c). In this case both MDM and modified MDM methods perform poorly, with the former biased toward the background and the latter biased toward the foreground. Such unpredictable behavior is likely caused by the fact that the metric is ill defined in both methods. OCCD provides a well-defined metric and guaranteed optimality in distance computation, thus achieving much better results.

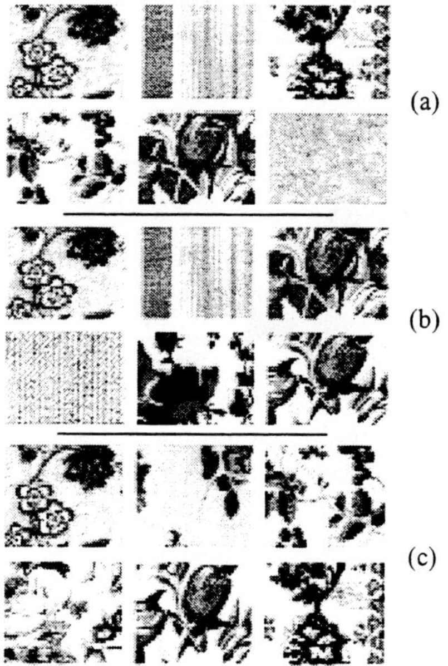

Fig. 1. Retrieval results using: a) traditional histogram, b) histogram intersection, and c) OCCD methods.

A subjective experiment was carried out to definitively compare the different methods. The traditional histogram method was not included in this experiment because its problems are well established. Also, including too many schemes in comparison tends to get the subjects more confused. Fifteen representative patterns were chosen from the interior design database as query images. For each query image, four different retrieval results were generated using the histogram intersection method, MDM method, modified MDM method and the OCCD method, respectively. Each query result contained the top 5 matching images retrieved from our database, displayed in the same manner as the examples in Figs. 1 and 2. Thirteen subjects (7 men, 6 women) were asked to evaluate these results. Each subject was presented the four retrieval results for each query image, arranged in random order on one page, and asked to rank order them based on how they matched their own judgement. A ranking of 1 was given to the best retrieval result, 2 to the second best result, etc.

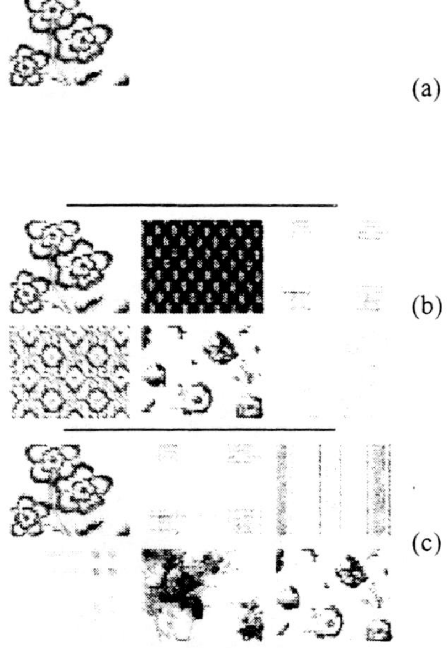

Fig. 2. Retrieval results using: a) MDM, b) modified MDM, and c) OCCD methods.

We expected large variations in the evaluation results due to the difficulties reported by the subjects in comparing different rankings, as well as in separating color from other factors such as pattern or spatial arrangement. However, despite these difficulties, the evaluation results showed significant amount of consistency among different subjects for most images. Ten of fifteen images used yielded majority votes (*e.g.*, >6) for a single scheme as the best, indicating that the corresponding rankings were reasonably consistent. The remaining five images were then discarded. Of the ten query images yielding consistent rankings, the results produced by OCCD method had majority votes as the best method for eight images, and the results produced by histogram intersection were voted best for two. Table 1 gives the average rank for each scheme computed from these ten query images. OCCD clearly has the best ranking. These results demonstrate that the OCCD method indeed best matches human perception overall.

Table 1. Average rankings for the tested methods.

Histogram Intersection	MDM	Modified MDM	OCCD
2.3	2.8	3.3	1.6

5. Conclusions

Due to very compact representation and low complexity, direct histogram comparison is the most often used technique in color based image database retrieval. However, there are serious drawbacks to this approach. First, discrimination ability of the color histogram largely depends on the selection of the color quantization method, as well as on the size of the color codebook. Second, for most natural images histogram representation is very sparse, and therefore histogram representation is not efficient. Furthermore, histogram comparison is highly sensitive to quantization boundaries. This paper describes a new method for extracting visually dominant colors from images, and a new color distance measure that overcomes the above drawbacks and better matches human perception in judging image color similarity.

References

[1] M. Swain, and D. Ballard, "Color indexing", *International Journal of Computer Vision*, vol. 7, no. 1, 1991, pp. 11-32.

[2] M. Ioka, "A method of defining the similarity of images on the basis of color information", *Technical Report RT-0030*, IBM Research, Tokyo Research Laboratory, Nov. 1989.

[3] W. Niblack, R. Berber, W. Equitz, M. Flickner, E. Glasman, D. Petkovic, and P.Yanker, "The QBIC project: Quering images by content using color, texture and shape". in *Proc. SPIE Storage and Retrieval for Image and Video Databases*, 1994, pp. 172-187.

[4] W. Y. Ma, Y. Deng, and B. S. Manjunath, "Tools for texture/color base search of images", In *Proc. of SPIE*, vol. 3016, 1997, pp. 496-505.

[5] S.C. Pei, C.M. Cheng, "Extracting color features and dynamic matching for image data-base retrieval", *IEEE Trans. On Circuits and Systems for Video Technology*, Vol. 9, No. 3, April 1999, pp. 501-512.

[6] A. Mojsilovic, J. Kovacevic, J. Hu, R. J. Safranek and K. Ganapathy, "Matching and retrieval based on the vocabulary and grammar of color patterns", *IEEE Trans. Image Processing*, Jan. 2000.

[7] G. Wyszecki and W. S. Stiles, *Color science: Concepts and methods, quantitative data and formulae*, John Wiley and Sons, New York, 1982.

[8] A. Mojsilovic, and E. Soljanin, "Quantization of color spaces and processing of color quantized images by Fibonacci lattices", *IEEE Trans. Image Processing*, (submitted).

[9] ftp://dimacs.rutgers.edu/pub/netflow/matching/weighted/solver-1.

[10] H. Gabow, "Implementation of algorithms for maximum matching on nonbipartite graphs", *Ph.D. Thesis,* Stanford University, 1973.

Processing Pictorial Queries with Multiple Instances using Isomorphic Subgraphs*

Andre Folkers and Hanan Samet
Computer Science Department and
Center for Automation Research and
Institute for Advanced Computer Science
University of Maryland at College Park
College Park, Maryland 20742
E-mail: {folkers, hjs}@umiacs.umd.edu

Aya Soffer
IBM Research Laboratory
Matam, Haifa 31905
Israel
E-mail: ayas@il.ibm.com

Abstract

An algorithm is given for processing pictorial query specifications that consist of a query image and a similarity level that must hold between the query image and database images. The similarity level specifies the contextual similarity *(how well the content of one image matches that of another) as well as the* spatial similarity *(the relative locations of the matching symbols in the two images). The algorithm differs from previous approaches in its ability to handle multiple instances of each object in both the query and database images by searching for isomorphic subgraphs. The running time of the algorithm is* $O(m\ 2^m)$ *in the worst case where all symbols in both the query and database image are from the same class, but falls far below this bound in the presence of spatial constraints.*

1. Introduction

A basic requirement of an image database is the ability to query the database pictorially. One of the main issues is whether the similarity criteria used by the database system match those of the user. In [10] we presented a pictorial query specification tool for spatially referenced image databases. Using this tool, a user can specify which objects should or could appear in a target image as well as the number of occurrences of each object. Moreover, it is possible to impose spatial constraints on the distance and relative direction between objects. We also described an algorithm for finding database images that satisfy such pictorial queries. In [11] we expanded this algorithm to handle multiple instances of symbols. This algorithm finds all images that contain the desired symbols and then checks the spatial constraints for all possible matchings of query and database symbols.

Most existing image database research has dealt with global image matching based on color and texture features [5, 8]. There has also been some work on the specification of topological and directional relations among query objects [1–3, 7, 9]. The focus of this work has been on defining spatial relations between objects and efficiently computing them. The issue of multiple instances of objects and the complexity arising from it is at best mentioned as a problem, and usually ignored.

In this paper we describe a method for processing such pictorial queries using isomorphic subgraphs. Both the query image and the database images can be viewed as graphs. The vertices represent symbols and the edges represent the relation between these symbols. There can be several subgraphs in the database image that match a given query graph since each image may have several instances of each symbol. Examining and matching each such subgraph is a very costly operation. This algorithm uses a bottom-up strategy to find all possible subgraphs of a database image that are isomorphic to a query image. The idea is that many potential subgraphs can be eliminated early on by the bottom-up process and thus do not need to be fully matched.

In [6] another strategy for solving this matching problem has been presented using *Error-Tolerant Subgraph Isomorphism Detection*. In the rest of this paper we review pictorial query specification, and present our algorithm and an example of its usage.

2. Notation and Definitions

Let V be the set of all symbols in the database images and in the query image. Let $D = (V_D, E_D)$, $V_D = \{d_1, d_2, \ldots, d_m\} \subseteq V$ be the graph of the symbols in one database image D. Let $Q = (V_Q, E_Q)$, $V_Q = \{q_1, q_2, \ldots, q_n\} \subseteq V$ be the graph of the symbols in the query image Q. We define three functions to denote the

*The support of the National Science Foundation under Grants IRI-97-12715 and CDA-950-3994 is gratefully acknowledged.

1051-4651/00 $10.00 © 2000 IEEE

basic properties of symbols in V:

$$\mathrm{cl}: V \to C, v \mapsto \mathrm{cl}(v), \tag{1}$$

$$\mathrm{loc}: V \to \mathbf{R}^2, v \mapsto \mathrm{loc}(v) = (x,y)^T, \tag{2}$$

$$\mathrm{cert}: V \to [0,1], v \mapsto \mathrm{cert}(v) = \Pr[\mathrm{cl}(v) \text{ is the correct classification of } v]. \tag{3}$$

Function cl assigns a class name to every symbol in V. It can also be applied on sets of symbols. The result is the set of classes that occur in the respective set of symbols. Using the function cl we define the numbers

$$m_c = |\{ d \in V_D \mid \mathrm{cl}(d) = c \}| \quad \text{and} \tag{4}$$

$$n_c = |\{ q \in V_Q \mid \mathrm{cl}(q) = c \}| \tag{5}$$

for each $c \in \mathrm{cl}(V)$. Function loc returns the location of a symbol in the 2-dimensional plane, and function cert returns the probability that the classification of a symbol is correct.

3. Pictorial Query Specification

3.1. Matching Similarity

The *matching similarity level* is a value between 0 and 1. It specifies how certain the classification of a symbol in the database image must be, so that we take it into account. If $\mathrm{cert}(v) \geq msl$, then v is considered similar with respect to the matching similarity level.

3.2. Contextual Similarity

We distinguish between four different *contextual similarity levels* that a database image D can satisfy. Their formal definition is

1. $\forall c \in \mathrm{cl}(V_Q): m_c \geq n_c$, and $\mathrm{cl}(V_D) = \mathrm{cl}(V_Q)$
2. $\forall c \in \mathrm{cl}(V_Q): m_c \geq n_c$
3. $\mathrm{cl}(V_D) \subseteq \mathrm{cl}(V_Q)$
4. $\exists c \in \mathrm{cl}(V_D): c \in \mathrm{cl}(V_Q)$.

Let $R_l = \{D_1, D_2, \ldots\}$ denote the set of images that satisfy *csl*=*l* for a certain query Q. For *csl*=1 and *csl*=2, multiple symbols from the same class act with an AND semantic, while for *csl*=3 and *csl*=4 they act with an OR semantic. This means that different numbers of instances of a certain class do not alter the sets R_3 and R_4, but they do alter R_1 and R_2. The query graph is always a subgraph of the graphs in database images in R_1 and R_2. Images in R_3 and R_4 can also be subgraphs of the query image.

3.3. Spatial Similarity

The *spatial similarity level* specifies how close the database image D and the query image Q are with respect to distance and directional relation between the symbols in the query. We distinguish between five different levels which are defined as

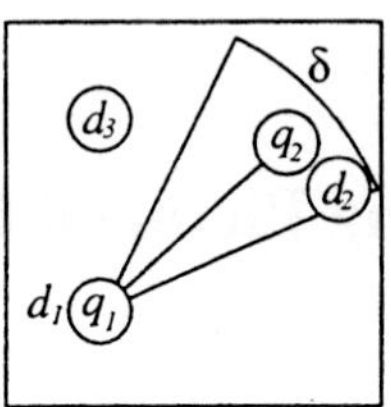

Figure 1. Similar directional relation

1. exact same location
2. same relation, bounded distance
3. same relation, any distance
4. any relation, bounded distance
5. any relation, any distance.

The case *ssl*=1 is ignored in the rest of this paper because there is a more effective algorithm to check this spatial constraint than the one we propose in Section 4.2.

We use the Euclidean distance between the symbols which is denoted by the function dist:

$$\mathrm{dist}: V \times V \to \mathbf{R}, (v_1, v_2) \mapsto \mathrm{dist}(v_1, v_2) \tag{6}$$

To compare two directed egdes $(q_1, q_2) \in E_Q$ and $(d_1, d_2) \in E_D$ with respect to their directional relation we relocate the vertices q_1 and q_2 so that $\mathrm{loc}(q_1) = \mathrm{loc}(d_1)$. The directional relation between (q_1, q_2) and (d_1, d_2) is similar with respect to a threshold angle $\delta \in [0, 2\pi]$, denoted by $(q_1, q_2) \sim_\delta (d_1, d_2)$, if the vertex d_2 is located within a sector with arc length δ. The center of this sector is at $\mathrm{loc}(q_1)$ and it is symmetric to the axis, which is defined by the edge (q_1, q_2). In Figure 1 we see an example where $(d_1, d_2) \sim_\delta (q_1, q_2)$ and $(d_1, d_3) \not\sim_\delta (q_1, q_2)$ holds.

4. Pictorial Query Processing

4.1. Generate the Set of Candidates Images

The function *genCandidates* computes the set R_Q of database images that satisfy the matching similarity level and the contextual similarity level indicated by *msl* and *csl*. The set R denotes all images in the database. At the beginning, for each class c, the database images that contain symbols of class c are stored in sets R_c. If *csl*=1 or *csl*=2, then we have to intersect these sets to get all images that contain at least one symbol of each class in Q. Otherwise, we compute the union of the sets R_c and get a set R_Q of images, where each image D contains at least one of the symbols in Q. Note, that we have to eliminate duplicates in R_c during union or intersection of these sets.

```
funct genCandidates(Q, msl, csl) : R_Q ≡
  foreach c ∈ cl(V_Q) do
    R_c = {D ∈ R | ∃v ∈ V_D : cl(v) = c ∧
           cert(v) ≥ msl}
  end
```

```
    if csl = 1 ∨ csl = 2 then R_Q = ⋂_c R_c fi
    if csl = 3 ∨ csl = 4 then R_Q = ⋃_c R_c fi
    R_E = ∅                    /* set of invalid candidates */
    foreach D ∈ R_Q do
      if csl = 1 ∨ csl = 3
        then if cl(D) ⊈ cl(Q) then R_E = R_E ∪ D fi fi
      if csl = 1 ∨ csl = 2
        then if ∃c ∈ cl(V_Q) : m_c < n_c
                then R_E = R_E ∪ D fi fi
    end
    R_Q = R_Q \ R_E.
```

4.2. Check Spatial Constraints

The algorithm given by function *getIsoSubgraphs* uses a bottom-up strategy to find all possible subgraphs in D that are isomorphic to Q with respect to the parameters of edges and vertices. It is an adaptation of a more general algorithm described in [4].

```
1  funct getIsoSubgraphs(Q, D, ssl) : S ≡
2    choose q_1 ∈ V_Q
3    S^(1) = ∅
4    foreach d ∈ { d ∈ V_D | cl(d) = cl(q_1) }
5      S^(1) = S^(1) ∪̇ (⟨q_1⟩, ⟨d⟩)
6    end
7    i = 1
8    foreach q_e ∈ V_Q \ {q_1}
9      S^(i+1) = ∅
10     foreach G = (⟨q_1, ..., q_i⟩, ⟨d_1, ..., d_i⟩) ∈ S^(i)
11       foreach (q_e, d_e) ∈ validExt(G, Q, D, q_e, ssl)
12         S^(i+1) = S^(i+1) ∪̇
13             (⟨q_1, ..., q_i, q_e⟩, ⟨d_1, ..., d_i, d_e⟩)
14       end
15     end
16     i = i + 1
17   end
18   S = S^(i).
19 funct validExt(G, Q, D, q_e, ssl) : P ≡
20   /* G is a set of pairs of isomorphic graphs G_1, G_2 */
21   V_G2 = { d ∈ V_D | d is element of G_2 }
22   V_E_D = { d ∈ V_D | cl(d) = cl(q_e) } \ V_G2
23   P = ∅
24   foreach d_e ∈ V_E_D
25     if isValid(G, Q, D, q_e, d_e, ssl)
26       then P = P ∪̇ (q_e, d_e) fi
27   end.
```

getIsoSubgraphs returns a set S of pairs of isomorphic subgraphs for the parameter graph Q in D that satisfy the spatial constraints indicated by *ssl*. It computes only solutions where the whole graph Q is mapped onto a subgraph of D. As a consequence, *getIsoSubgraphs* works only for queries where *csl*=1 and *csl*=2. Two isomorphic subgraphs are denoted by a pair of sequences of vertices, e.g., the pair $(\langle q_1, \ldots, q_i\rangle, \langle d_1, \ldots, d_i\rangle)$ denotes that vertex q_k is mapped onto vertex d_k $(k = 1, \ldots, i)$.

First, an initial set $S^{(1)}$ of all isomorphic subgraphs with length 1 is created. It consists of pairs $(\langle q_1\rangle, \langle d\rangle)$ where each $d \in V_D$ belongs to the same class as q_1. Starting with this set, the main loop of the algorithm searches for isomorphic subgraphs of size 2 and based on this, it looks for some of size 3 and so on.

The function *validExt* returns extensions of form (q_e, d_e) where q_e is fixed as it is given as a parameter. The subgraphs that we want to extend are given in $G = (G_1, G_2)$. G_1 is the sequence of vertices of the current subgraph of Q, while G_2 is the sequence of vertices of the current subgraph of D. By construction, q_e is always a new vertex that does not occur in G_1. We compute the set V_{E_D} of remaining vertices which could be used as extensions to the sequence in G_2 (line 22) because we do not want a vertex of V_D to occur twice in sequence G_2.

Every possible extension pair is tested by function *isValid* to determine if it satisfies the spatial constraints. If yes, then it is added to the set *P*. Depending on the *ssl* value, the function *isValid* checks for $k = 1, \ldots, i$, if $\mathrm{dist}(d_k, d_e) \leq \mathrm{dist}(q_k, q_e)$, or if $(d_k, d_e) \sim_\delta (q_k, q_e)$, or if both hold, and returns the result. It just returns true if *ssl*=5.

The function *getIsoSubgraphs* returns the complete result only for *csl*=1 and *csl*=2. If *csl*=3 or *csl*=4, then we also have to return the mappings of all subgraphs of Q onto subgraphs of D. The brute force approach to compute these mappings is to call *getIsoSubgraphs* for each subgraph of Q and to take a union of all of the results. Since Q is usually a small graph we can use this brute force approach

4.3. Execution Time

First, we derive the worst case complexity of function *getIsoSubgraphs*, assuming that Q has n and D has m vertices, which are all from the same class. We count how often the union operations in lines 5 and 12 are executed. During initialization, we have m union operations. The main loop has $n-1$ iterations and in the i-th iteration, $i = 1, \ldots, n-1$, we get $\binom{m}{i}(m-i)$ union operations. This is because the maximal number of elements in $S^{(i)}$ is $\binom{m}{i}$ and *validExt* returns at most $m-i$ extension pairs, which actually occurs if *ssl*=5. Therefore, after some transformations and exploiting that $n \leq m$, we get an upper bound on the number of union operations:

$$m + \sum_{i=1}^{n-1} \binom{m}{i}(m-i) \leq m(2^m - 1). \quad (7)$$

This implies a worst case complexity in $O(m\,2^m)$ for *csl*=1 or *csl*=2. For *csl*=3 and *csl*=4, we get an additional factor of 2^n since we invoke *getIsoSubgraphs* this many times. The worst case complexity is $O(m\,2^{n+m})$.

Once we add spatial constraints, the order in which the vertices of Q are processed can affect the running time significantly. Choosing a vertex q_i so that its edges with the vertices $\{q_1, \ldots, q_{i-1}\}$ are the most restrictive ones with respect to the spatial constraints leads to a shorter running time for *getIsoSubgraphs* (see the example in Section 4.4).

4.4. Finding the Isomorphic Subgraphs

We want to show how function *getIsoSubgraphs* finds the possible mappings. In Figure 2 we see a query graph $Q = (\{a, b, c\}, E_Q)$ and a result graph $D = (\{\alpha, \beta, \gamma, \sigma\}, E_D)$. The distance between the vertices is indicated by the number next to the respective edge. In this example, all vertices are members of the same class. Therefore, each vertex in Q can be mapped onto each vertex in D.

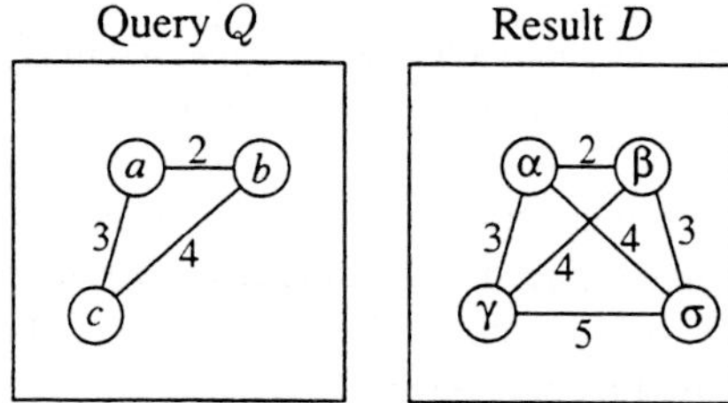

Figure 2. Sample Query and Result

We want to find all subgraphs in D that satisfy query Q, when *ssl*=4. First, we describe a short run of function *getIsoSubgraphs*. We choose $q_1 = a$ as the starting vertex and build the initial set $S^{(1)} = \{ (\langle a \rangle, \langle d \rangle) \mid d = \alpha, \beta, \gamma, \sigma \}$. Then we choose $q_e = b$ in the main loop. For both isomorphic subgraphs $G = (\langle a \rangle, \langle \alpha \rangle)$ and $G = (\langle a \rangle, \langle \beta \rangle)$, *validExt* returns only one extension pair. The remaining two values for G, i.e., $(\langle a \rangle, \langle \gamma \rangle)$ and $(\langle a \rangle, \langle \sigma \rangle)$, do not lead to any more extension pairs and are excluded from further processing. Therefore, $S^{(2)}$ contains only two elements, when we reach the third iteration where q_e is set to c. Each pair in $S^{(2)}$ also has only one extension pair and so we get two elements in $S^{(3)}$, which is returned as the result.

This is a short run of *getIsoSubgraphs* because many subgraphs are excluded early in the process; e.g., all subgraphs where a is mapped onto γ or σ are excluded in the first iteration. The reason for these early exclusions is that we chose a, whose outgoing edges are the most restrictive ones, as the first vertex.

If we start with $q_1 = c$ and continue with $q_e = b$ in the main loop, the running time of *getIsoSubgraphs* is longer. For both pairs $(\langle c \rangle, \langle \alpha \rangle)$ and $(\langle c \rangle, \langle \beta \rangle)$ the function *validExt* returns three valid extensions, while for the pairs $(\langle c \rangle, \langle \gamma \rangle)$ and $(\langle c \rangle, \langle \sigma \rangle)$ it returns two valid extensions, respectively. All together we get ten elements in $S^{(2)}$ and only two possible subgraphs are excluded, because $\text{dist}(\gamma, \sigma) > \text{dist}(c, b)$. So, in the third iteration where q_e is set to a, we get ten calls to *validExt* compared with only two in the short run. We call this a long run, because most of the invalid subgraphs are excluded in the last iteration.

5. Concluding Remarks and Future Work

The computation of subgraph isomorphism is known to be NP-complete [4]. Therefore, we cannot expect to find an efficient algorithm that solves our problem fast in all cases. Future work consists of exploiting the spatial constraints and finding more strategies to reduce the search space in addition to the ones we described.

References

[1] S. K. Chang, Q. Y. Shi, and C. Y. Yan. Iconic indexing by 2-D strings. *IEEE PAMI*, 9(3):413–428, May 1987.

[2] A. Del Bimbo and P. Pala. Visual image retrieval by elastic matching of user sketches. *IEEE PAMI*, 19(2):121–132, Feb. 1997.

[3] M. J. Egenhofer. Query processing in spatial-query-by-sketch. *Journal of Visual Languages and Computing*, 8(4):403–424, Aug. 1997.

[4] R. Englert and J. Seelmann-Eggebert. P-subgraph isomorphism computation and upper bound complexity estimation. Technical Report IAI-TR-97-2, Institute of Computer Science III, University of Bonn, Jan. 1997.

[5] C. Faloutsos, R. Barber, W. Equitz, M. Flickner, W. Niblack, and D. Petkovic. Efficient and effective querying by image content. *Journal of Intelligent Information Systems*, pages 231–62, 1994.

[6] B. T. Messmer and H. Bunke. A new algorithm for error-tolerant subgraph isomorphism detection. *IEEE PAMI*, 20(5):493–504, May 1998.

[7] D. Papadias and T. K. Sellis. A pictorial query-by-example language. *Journal of Visual Languages and Computing*, 6(1):53–72, Mar. 1995.

[8] A. Pentland, R. W. Picard, and S. Sclaroff. Photobook: Content-based manipulation of image databases. In *Proceedings of the SPIE, Storage and Retrieval of Image and Video Databases II*, volume 2185, pages 34–47, San Jose, CA, Feb. 1994.

[9] A. P. Sistla, C. Yu, and R. Haddad. Reasoning about spatial relationships in picture retrieval systems. In J. Bocca, M. Jarke, and C. Zaniolo, editors, *20th Intern. Conf. on Very Large Data Bases*, pages 570–581, Santiago, Chile, Sept. 1994.

[10] A. Soffer and H. Samet. Pictorial query specification for browsing through spatially referenced images databases. *Journal of Visual Languages and Computing*, 9(6):567–596, Dec. 1998.

[11] A. Soffer and H. Samet. Query processing and optimization for pictorial query trees. In D. P. Huijsmans and A. Smeulders, editors, *3rd Intern. Conf. on Visual Information Systems*, pages 60–67, Amsterdam, The Netherlands, June 1999. (Also Springer-Verlag Lecture Notes in Computer Science 1614).

Texture Similarity Queries and Relevance Feedback for Image Retrieval

Blancho Patrice
Laboratoire LIGIV - Saint–Étienne - FRANCE
blancho@vision.univ-st-etienne.fr

Hubert Konik
Laboratoire LIGIV - Saint–Étienne - FRANCE
konik@vision.univ-st-etienne.fr

Abstract

The measurement of perceptual similarities between textures is a difficult problem in applications such as image classification and image retrieval in large databases. Among the various texture analysis methods or models developped over the years, those based on a multi-scale multi-orientation paradigm seem to give more reliable results with respect to human visual judgement.
This work[1] introduces new texture features extracted from an oriented multi-scale pyramid structure called a "steerable pyramid". These texture features are then used in the search through an image database to find the most "similar" textures to a selected one. We have also introduced a relevance feedback to improve the retrieval quality.

1. Introduction

Speaking about texture is always a problem in computer vision. In fact, "texture is an apparently paradoxical notion. On the one hand, it is commonly used in the early processing of visual information (...); on the other hand, no one has succeded in producing a commonly accepted definition of texture" [10]. Since it is all the more difficult to appreciate texture similarity for such a high subjective notion, we decided to address texture representations as described in psychophysic models, to extract a few textures descriptors wich will be used for image retrieval by texture similarity in a texture database. Then, we have chosen to evaluate the efficiency of our query system with two different approaches: a qualitative and a quantitative study of our results. The last section will show how the user's judgment can be taken into account in a *relevance feedback* process.

2. Related Work on Texture Perception Model

Studies in psychophysic have permitted to improve our understanding of human visual perception. The most accepted theory is that the brain performs a *multi-channels, frequencies* and *orientations* analysis of the visual stimulus (image) formed on the retina. These studies on human texture perception have led to various models in image processing, often based on a *multi-resolution* paradigm, performed with a *pyramidal or wavelet-based decomposition*[9, 8].

Heeger and Bergen [1] have recently used such a decomposition for the purpose of texture image synthesis. Their results, and their synthesized images, indicate that many textures can be characterized by moments of distributions of each sub-band.

We will show in the following sections that simple statistics parameters from the distribution set of responses of filters applied to texture images, in a particular oriented, multi-scale image representation called *the steerable pyramid*, can be used to represent textures.

3. The Steerable Pyramid Model

The **Steerable Pyramid** [6, 7] is an overcomplete wavelet transform which uses *steerable filters* to decompose an image onto a set of sub-band images localized in scale and orientation at the same time.

As with all other pyramid decompositions (the Laplacian pyramid for example), this transform divides an image into several spatial frequency bands which are re-divided into a set of orientation bands.

The figure 1 depicts the principle of the image decomposition in a steerable pyramid (only the first level is shown). This is a recursive system which implies two different operations: a filtering process, represented by the convolution kernels and a sub-sampling operation: the $\downarrow 2$ box. This decomposition uses a low-pass, a band pass and oriented band-pass filters respectively tuned at 0, 45 ,90 and 135^0 (I_{B_i} boxes are the first-level sub-band images for the input image I, and I_{L_1} is the sub-sampled low-pass filtered image which will be decomposed at the following level).

An example of a such a decomposition is shown in the figure 2.

The input image is decomposed with the four basis filters presented previously in a 3-level pyramid. The fourth

[1]work supported by the Région Rhône-Alpes grant ACTIV

1051-4651/00 $10.00 © 2000 IEEE

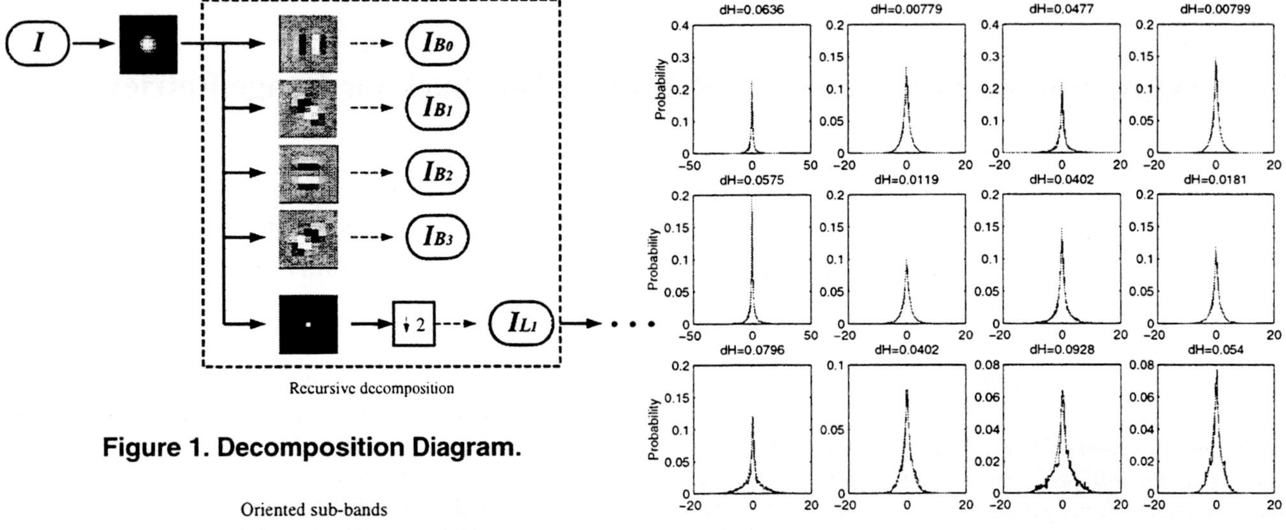

Figure 1. Decomposition Diagram.

Oriented sub-bands

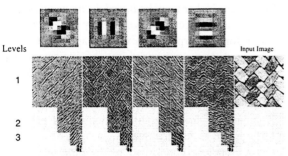

Levels

Input Image

1

2

3

Figure 2. Decomposition of an image in a Steerable Pyramid.

Figure 3. Fit and the relative entropy of the model.

shared image in each sub-band is the last remaining low-pass filtered image.

This pyramid decomposition also presents some very interesting properties for image retrieval tasks in database containing the same image at different orientation: the representation is approximately *invariant by translation* and, by the steerability principle, this decomposition is *rotation invariant* too [6].

4. Texture Signature

Heeger and Bergen results show that a given class of textures images could be characterized by a set of response distribution of each oriented band-pass filters; figure 3 is an example of the coefficients intensity distributions for each sub-band image of a texture decomposition. We will present in this section two different texture features set extracted from these distributions and then how these features are used to find "similar" images in a textures database. Moreover, using only these distributions implies a lack of spatial information and then, we introduce a *spatial density feature*.

4.1. Moment-based features

The first texture signature is composed by the four first statistical moments of each coefficient distribution:

mean	μ	$=$	$\sum_{i=0}^{m-1} c_i.P(c_i)$
variance	σ^2	$=$	$\sum_{i=0}^{m-1} (c_i - \mu)^2.P(c_i)$
skewness	S	$=$	$1/\sigma^3.\sum_{i=0}^{m-1} (c_i - \mu)^3.P(c_i)$
kurtosis	K	$=$	$1/\sigma^4.\sum_{i=0}^{m-1} (c_i - \mu)^4.P(c_i)$

where coefficient c_i is discretized with m levels; $M(c_i)$ is the number of coefficients c_i in the sub-band and N is the number of pixels in the sub-band. The probability is then: $P(c_i) = M(c_i)/N$.

The texture signature for each image is then composed of 48 parameters (4 parameters for each sub-band in a 3-levels, 4 orientations decomposition).

4.2. Parametric Density Function

The second set of descriptors is created from a parametric density function model fitted on each sub-band intensity distribution [3]. The density function can be expressed as $p(i) \propto exp(-|\frac{i}{\alpha}|^{\beta})$ and the density parameters (α, β) are estimated by minimizing the relative Entropy (Kullback-Liebler divergence) between the model and the coefficient histogram. The figure 3 presents the distributions fits and the resulting relative entropy of each model.

4.3. Density of Coefficients Local Extrema (CLE)

To complete these two energetic features, we used a spatial descriptor [2], based on the density of emergent points in an image. More precisely, an emergent point $I(r_0, c_0)$ verifies these properties:

$$\begin{cases} I(r_0, c_0 - 1) < I(r_0, c_0) \text{ and } I(r_0, c_0) > I(r_0, c_0 + 1) \\ I(r_0 - 1, c_0) < I(r_0, c_0) \text{ and } I(r_0, c_0) > I(r_0 + 1, c_0) \end{cases}$$

A map of these *coefficients local extrema* is constructed for each sub-band. Finally, the *mean density* η of local extrema on a V_{24} neighbourhood is computed for each map. The figure 4 gives examples of CLE mean density feature for two different sub-band images. We then supplement each of the two previously described parameter sets with the 12 mean density parameters, to create the final texture signatures.

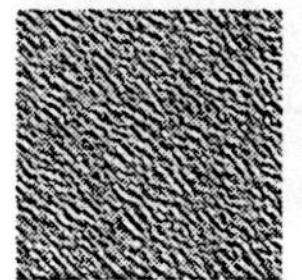
Fabric18-1 sub-band 1

CLE map $\eta = 0.115$

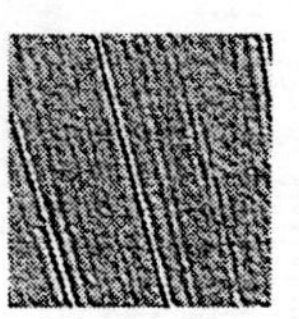
Leaves2-1 sub-band 2

CLE map $\eta = 0.049$

Figure 4. CLE values for 2 different texture images.

5. Query Processing

We apply these texture features to the search through an image database to find the most "similar" textures to a selected one. The Density of CLE (see section 4.3) is used as a database pre-filtering. We define two different *dissimilarity functions* $\mathcal{D}(f, g)$ between 2 textures f (the query image) and g (in the subset of images selected by the pre-filtering), according to the feature set used:

- Moment-based feature set.
  ➥ $\mathcal{D}(f, g)$ is the weighted L^2 norm between the 2 feature sets:

$$\mathcal{D}(f,g) = \sum_{i=1}^{4} \mathcal{W}_f^i \cdot \sum_{b=0}^{\text{Nband-1}} (\mathcal{M}_f^i(b) - \mathcal{M}_g^i(b))^2$$

with $\mathcal{W}_f^i$: weight updated in feedback
$\mathcal{M}_f^i(b)$: i^{th} moment of texture f, sub-band b

- Parametric density function feature set.
  ➥ $\mathcal{D}(f, g)$: Symmetrized version of the Kullback-Liebler divergence:
  f_b: discretized distribution model of the subband b, characterized by the density parameters (α, β) (see section 4.2);

$$\mathcal{D}(f,g) = \sum_{b=0}^{\text{Nband-1}} (I_{KL}(f_b, g_b) + I_{KL}(g_b, f_b))$$

with $I_{KL}(f_b, g_b) = \sum_{i=0}^{\text{Nsamples-1}} f_b(i) \log \frac{f_b(i)}{g_b(i)}$

6. Relevance Feedback

We implemented a *relevance feedback* process with the moment-based feature set so the user can put forward a quality judgement upon the results of the query, and then adjust the following results towards what he is looking for. The $\mathcal{W}_f^i$ update is performed via this algorithm:

1. Initialization of the $\mathcal{W}_f^i$ (*Normalization*).
2. Select the *Query Image*: f.
3. Find and Rank the M closer images according to $\mathcal{D}(f, g)$.
4. User marks *Relevant Textures*.
5. Update the $\mathcal{W}_f^i$: $\mathcal{W}_f^i \longleftarrow \mathcal{W}_f^i + \epsilon_i, \quad 1 \le i \le 4$ by minimizing :

$$Q = \frac{\sum_x^{\text{Nrel}} \mathcal{D}(f, x)}{\sum_y^{\text{Nnotrel}} \mathcal{D}(f, y)}$$

6. New Query with the new $\{\mathcal{W}_f^i\}$ set.

The step 5 tries to minimize the dissimilarity measures between the marked textures and, on the contrary, to maximize the dissimilarity of the irrelevant ones.

7. system description

Our texture database was created from the MIT Media Lab VisTex Database [2] [5]; we extracted 668 texture images by splitting the 167 larger Vistex textured images in 4 new images (see figure 5 for examples). We created a *query-by-example system* where the user selects an image from the database, and the system gives as a result the 7 closest images according to the feature subset the user can choose.

Figure 5. Images from VisTex Database.

8. Experimental Results

The performance of the feature sets can be evaluated according to two criteria:

1. Quantitative. The 'closest' images from the selected texture should be the three other images extracted from

[2] http://www-white.media.mit.edu/vismod/imagery/VisionTexture

the same larger Vistex texture. The quality of the results depends a lot on the considered texture class.

2. Qualitative. The Vistex database contains many "perceptualy similar textures", allowing the user to judge the final ordering subjectively.

8.1. Quantitative Results

Objectively, it is easier to evaluate quantitative results, thanks to the construction of our reference database. In fact, each original mono-textured image is divided onto four equal size ones. Then, the query must return these similar images first.

We compute the *overall efficiency of retrieval* coefficient [4]: For a database of size K (here $K = 668$), with M_i images similar to image i, in the N_q first images retrieved, the system retrieves n_q similar images to the query image q; the coefficient is then defined by:

$$\eta_R = \frac{\sum_{q=0}^{K} n_q}{\sum_{q=0}^{K} N_q}; \quad \begin{array}{l} \eta_R = 87.5\%\text{(Moment-based features set.)} \\ \eta_R = 81.3\%\text{(Density-parameters features.)} \end{array}$$

8.2. Qualitative Results

Some textures are similar in a perceptual sense, even though they were issued from different original samples.

The question of texture similarity is problematic because of the subjectivity of human texture perception. The problem is to define precisely what kind of similarity we query. Must our method be robust to illuminant, to the scale, to the angle of view ? For example, the texture of a brick wall is clearly different according to the distance we observe it. Our aim is finally to evaluate similarity with equivalent scaling and equivalent contrast. No single image can capture reality anyway...

8.3. Relevance Feedback results

The figure 6 illustrates how the user's quality judgement can be taken into account in a relevance feedback process as described in section 6. Texture 0 (upper left) is the query; textures 4 and 6 are not marked as relevant by the user after the first query (top figure). The following query (bottom figure) gives a much more relevant result.

9. Conclusion

We have presented new feature sets for achieving a robust texture database retrieval tool, and the experiments presented indicate these sets describe mono-textured images quite accurately. This is still an early stage towards the creation of a whole image indexation system, and the next step will be to adapt those descriptors to multitextured images.

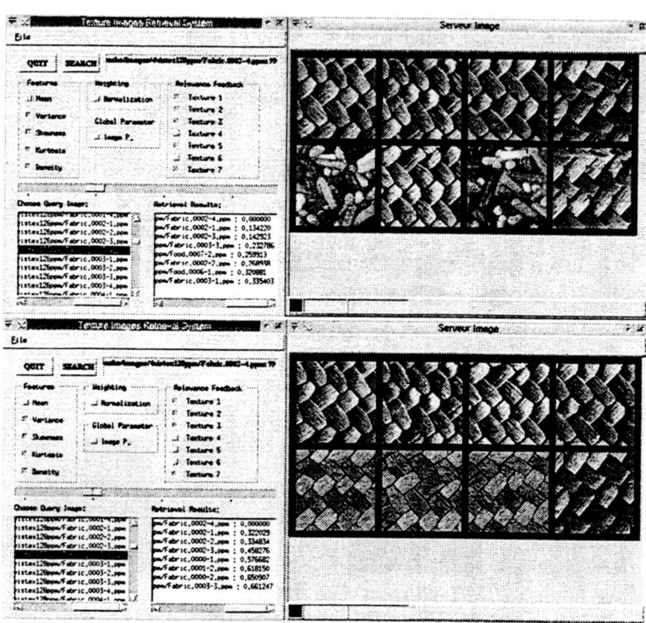

Figure 6. Relevance Feedback.

References

[1] D. J. Heeger and J. R. Bergen. Pyramid-based texture analysis/synthesis. In *Proc. ACM SIGGRAPH*, Aug. 1995.

[2] K. Karu, A. Jain, and R. Bolle. Is there any texture in the image? *Pattern Recognition*, 29:1437–1446, 1996.

[3] S. G. Mallat. A theory for multiresolution signal decomposition: The wavelet representation. *IEEE transactions on Pattern Analysis and Machine Intelligence*, 11(7):674–693, July 1989.

[4] M. K. Mandal, T. Aboulnasr, and S. Panchanathan. Illumination invariant image indexing using moments and wavelets. *Journal of Electronic Imaging*, 7(2):282–293, Apr. 1998.

[5] R. W. Picard and T. Kabir. Finding similar patterns in large image databases. In *IEEE Trans. Acoustics, Speech, and Signal Processing*, volume 5, pages 161–164, Minneapolis, MN, Apr. 1993. MIT Media Laboratory Perceptual Computing Section TR205.

[6] E. P. Simoncelli and W. T. Freeman. The steerable pyramid: A flexible architecture for multi-scale derivative computation. In *IEEE Second International Conference in Image Processings*, Oct. 1995.

[7] E. P. Simoncelli, W. T. Freeman, E. H. Adelson, and D. J. Heeger. Shiftable multi-scale transforms. *IEEE Transaction on Information Theory, Special Issue on Wavelets*, 38(2):587–607, 1992.

[8] B. A. Wandell. *Foundations of Vision*. Sinauer Associates, Sunderland, Massachusetts, 1995.

[9] A. B. Watson. The cortex transform: Rapid computation of simulated neural images. In *Computer Vision, Graphics and Image Processing*, volume 39, pages 311–327, 1987.

[10] S. Zucker and K. Kant. Multiple-level representation for texture discrimination. *Proc. Conf. Pattern Recognition and Image Processing*, pages 609–614, 1981.

On ridges and valleys

Juan Serrat, A. López and D. Lloret
Computer Vision Center & Dept. Informàtica
Edifici O, Universitat Autonoma de Barcelona
08193 Cerdanyola, Spain
e–mail joans@cvc.uab.es

Abstract

Ridges and valleys are earth's relief structures. They can have an imaging counterpart provided we model a digital image as a landscape by considering grey level values as height. These two dual entities have received comparatively little attention from the computer vision community with regard to others like edges or corners. In this paper we first propose a taxonomy or classification of the several definitions of ridge and valley lines and review their implementation on discrete images. Then, we illustrate the application of one type of characterization, a creaseness measure, to solve several problems of image registration, where ridge and valley lines are taken as landmarks.

1. Introduction

Common operators in image analysis and computer vision such us the gradient, curvature, laplacian etc. lie on the implicit modeling of images as the discretization of a graphic surface. A particular case within this general model is to think of grey–level images as the sampling of a topographic relief or landscape. This conception gives rise to build new operators or algorithms which approximate, in the discrete, geomorphological entities like ridge and valley lines, watersheds, basins or drainage patterns. Despite an image does not actually represent height measurements in a landscape's array of sites, as would be the case of digital elevation model (DEM) images, those entities can be of great value. Often, they closely correspond to structures of interest for analysis purposes. In general, ridge and valley lines have been applied mostly for 1) computation of medial axes or skeletons, 2) segmentation and, of course, 3) extraction of drainage networks from DEM images.

A medialness measure essentially assigns to each point within an object the distance to its boundary according to a given metric. The farthest points are those in the middle of the object. Therefore, we can view the medial axis as the ridges of the medialness, which is in turn the degree of symmetry around each point. Although this is one approach to define the medial axis or skeleton of binary objects, it is desirable to extend this concept to grey–level objects, that is, those whose boundaries are unknown. The intensity axis of symmetry proposed by Gauch and Pizer [6] goes in this way. But also creases (that is, ridges for bright objects and valleys for dark ones) and creaseness measures like the level curves curvature have been proposed as a reliable approximation to the medial axis and medialness, respectively. Figure 1 shows an example. This is the approach taken in a number of applications like fingerprint analysis [9, 18], road delineation in aerial images [20, 28], hand–written OCR [32, 12] and medical image analysis [1, 26, 19].

Figure 1. (a) black fringes of the zebra are valleys, white fringes are ridges; (b) Gaussian smoothing of a); (c) 'valleys' from the zebra, which have been extracted simply by thresholding the level curves curvature and discarding short segments; (d) c) over a).

Segmentation has also been approached through crest lines, though it is no wonder given the huge number of proposed methods along the years. Contours can be assimilated to ridges of the (regularized) gradient. One of the main concerns of segmentation techniques is to assure closed contours, in order to avoid any edge linking postprocess. For this reason, most often they resort to a type of ridges which

1051-4651/00 $10.00 © 2000 IEEE

we will name 'separatrices' (section 2). In particular, the watershed transform created by the mathematical morphology school [34]. This, an other separatrix schemes partition the image into basins and hills, which are the sought regions. Their main drawback is the image oversegmentation due to irrelevant critical points to which these methods are very sensitive. Hence, computation of separatrices is often preceded by a filtering phase in order to get rid of such points, considered a kind of noise. Figure 2 shows an example, in which a ridge and a valley line are taken as markers of a watershed transform, being markers another strategy to avoid fragmentation.

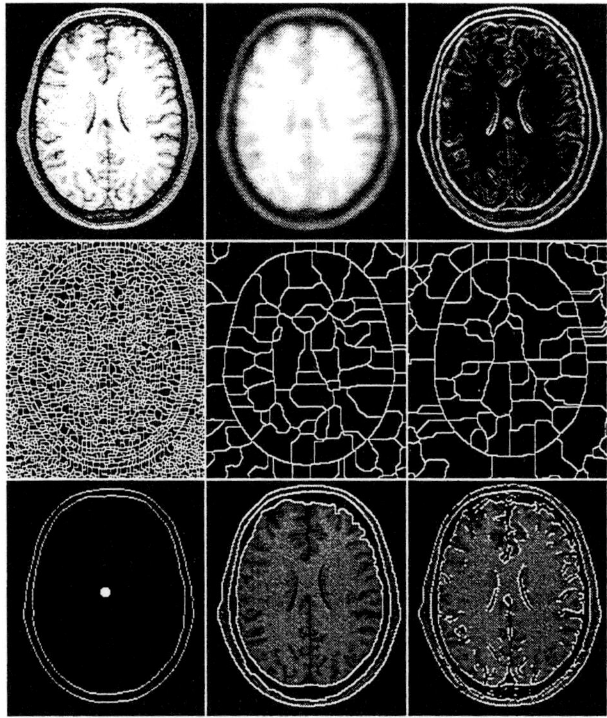

Figure 2. (a) MR slice; (b) Gaussian smoothing; (c) gradient magnitude of b); (d) watersheds of the gradient magnitude; (e) watersheds of the smoothed image; (f) watercourses of the smoothed image; (g) markers: largest creases by thresholding κ plus an interior point of the brain, and the image border; (h) boundaries found by the watershed transform using the markers; (i) creases obtained by thresholding κ of c).

We can not forget the application domain the closest to the adopted landscape image model, namely, the analysis of DEMs. It usually means the extraction of the drainage pattern (figure 3). Many studies in geomorphology and hydrology require the delineation of stream channels and divide line networks. For instance, the shape of the drainage pattern gives a clue on the type of soil composing the terrain, as it determines the way erosion acts. Methods for drainage pattern delineation consists in the simulation of rain water fall, that is, to compute the accumulation of water at each point if we suppose it follows the steepest descent path.

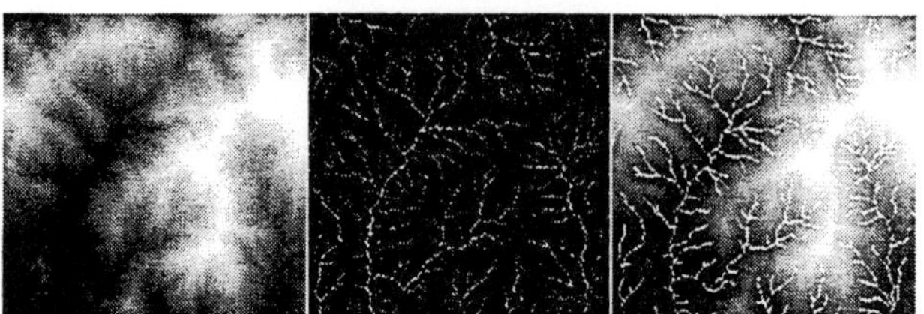

Figure 3. (a) sampled DEM; (b) logarithmic display of its accumulation array; (c) main drainage channels.

In this paper we focus on ridge and valley lines in two-dimensional images, and their extension to three dimensions. These two dual geometric entities have comparatively received little attention from the computer vision community with regard other ones like contours or, to a lesser extent, corners and junctions. And in spite of its proven utility. We believe this is due to several reasons.

Firstly, the concepts of ridge and valley are not simple, clearly distinct and unambiguous. We can loosely say that valley lines are the places where rain water in a terrain gathers to run downhill, and ridge lines are the valley lines of the relief turned upside–down. But then, could we distinguish them from the profusion of terms in English (alike in French and Spanish) to refer to similar but not identical concepts, like 'crease', 'crest', 'divide line' or 'watershed' for ridge, and 'watercourse', 'creek', 'groove', 'ravine', 'trough' or 'thalweg' for valley ?

Secondly, in an attempt to precisely define what ridge and valley lines are, a number of mathematical characterizations have been proposed since mid XIX century, and most of them are not completely equivalent. Some of them are even clearly distinct.

Finally, several of these definitions have been approximated by different operators or algorithms in order to be applied to digital images. Thus, for instance, we can find in the literature several attempts to compute the extrema of curvature of the relief's level curves, a characterization that we will call the vertex condition.

This article aims at reviewing and establish a coherent taxonomy of ridge and valley mathematical characterizations (section 2). In particular, we intend to express each one in a common notation, thus stressing their differences and similarities. Section 3 shows the application of a creaseness measure based on the vertex condition in three problems on image registration, the domain in which we have been working in the last few years. Finally, we summarize the conclusions in section 4.

2. A taxonomy

In hydrology, the word *runoff* refers to the flow of water over the Earth's surface. The flowing water seeks the easiest downhill route, which is the one that follows the *steepest slope*. These routes of steepest slope are called *slopelines* or *flowlines*, and constitute the integral curves of the relief's gradient vector field. Therefore, the family of slopelines is perpendicular to that of *level curves*, which are the lines of points at equal height that appear in cartographic maps.

Since water goes downhill following the steepest descent paths, each channel can be represented by the special slopeline along which the water coming from other slopelines gathers. The set of all these special slopelines constitutes the drainage pattern.

The historical attempts to mathematically characterize the drainage pattern of a landscape gave rise to other interesting geometric entities that later have been adopted and generalized in computer vision. We have classified them as *local, multilocal* and *global*, according to the region of influence induced by the nature of each definition. Given the function $L : \Omega \subset \mathbf{R}^d \rightarrow \Gamma \subset \mathbf{R}$ we have:

- **Local definitions.** At each point $\mathbf{x} \in \Omega$, they make a local test based on the local jet $J_n[L](\mathbf{x}) = \{\partial^j L/\partial\alpha_1 \cdots \partial\alpha_j\}_{j=0}^{n}$, that tries to identify the local anisotropy of the relief. We will use the term *creases* for both the ridge and valley structures defined by such a local test. Some of these tests provide a degree of ridgeness or valleyness (creaseness) instead of classifying the point as lying on a crease or not.

- **Multilocal definitions.** At each point $\mathbf{x} \in \Omega$, these methods depend not only on $J_n[L](\mathbf{x})$ but also on the jets at points in a region of influence. This region can be a fixed neighborhood for each $\mathbf{x}$, or be determined by the image geometry. This last case includes drainage patterns since the runoff in a zone does not depends on the runoff of zones arbitrarily far away.

- **Global definitions.** When the classification of a point $\mathbf{x} \in \Omega$ as ridge/valley depends on image features at an arbitrary distance from $\mathbf{x}$, we consider the method to be global. In this class we include algorithms that divide the space Ω into districts by special lines called *separatrices*. The well known watershed transform produces a type of separatrices.

2.1. Creases

2.1.1 The Saint-Venant/Haralick's Condition

One of the first works on the characterization of drainage lines dates back to 1852 and is credited to Saint-Venant[1] who classified a point as being on a *faîte* (ridge) or on a *talweg* (valley) if it was a locus of minimum slope along a level curve of the relief. Saint-Venant's definition can be tested locally and it can be written [29, 2] in compact tensorial form as:

$$L_{\mathbf{vw}} = 0 \text{ and } \mid L_{\mathbf{ww}} \mid < \mid L_{\mathbf{vv}} \mid , \tag{1}$$

where $L_{\mathbf{vv}} < 0$ means ridge and $L_{\mathbf{vv}} > 0$ valley. According to the tensorial notation used in [30], $\mathbf{w}$ denotes the gradient direction, $\mathbf{v}$ the orthogonal direction to the gradient and $L_{\mathbf{u}}$ the derivative of L in the direction of vector $\mathbf{u}$.

Saint-Venant's condition fails to detect the special slopelines that form the landscape's drainage pattern. The curvature of the slopelines can be defined as:

$$\mu = -L_{\mathbf{vw}}/L_{\mathbf{w}} , \tag{2}$$

Therefore, $L_{\mathbf{vw}} = 0$ along a slopeline would imply that it is a straight line, which means that valley lines should be planar curves confined in vertical planes, clearly in conflict with reality.

As it is noted in [10], Saint-Venant's condition has been later reformulated by Haralick [8] as loci of extremal height of L in the direction along which L reaches the greatest magnitude of its second order directional derivative. Let λ_1 and λ_2 be the eigenvalues of $\nabla\nabla L$, with $\mid \lambda_1 \mid \geq \mid \lambda_2 \mid$, and $\mathbf{v}_1$ and $\mathbf{v}_2$ their corresponding eigenvectors. Then, $\mathbf{v}_1$ and $\mathbf{v}_2$ are the directions in which the second directional derivative of L is extremized and λ_1, λ_2 being the values of each extremum. Therefore, following Haralick, an equivalent definition is :

$$L_{\mathbf{wv}_1} = 0 , \tag{3}$$

where $\lambda_1 < 0$ means ridge and $\lambda_1 > 0$ valley. When the Haralick condition (3) holds, we obviously have $\mathbf{v}_1 = \mathbf{v}$ and $\lambda_1 = L_{\mathbf{vv}}$.

2.1.2 The vertex condition

Another typical local crease detector that has been claimed to delineate the drainage patterns [11] looks for extrema of the curvature of the relief's level curves. The curvature of the level curves can be defined in terms of the landscape derivatives as:

$$\kappa = -L_{\mathbf{vv}}/L_{\mathbf{w}} , \tag{4}$$

[1] References to historical papers by Saint-Venant, Cayley, Maxwell, Rothe and others can be found in [16]

where, the sign of κ classifies the surface as convex ($\kappa > 0$) or concave ($\kappa < 0$) with respect to the vertical axis. In [6, 4, 31] the crease condition for a 2D image is formulated as:

$$\nabla\kappa \cdot \mathbf{v} = 0 \ , \tag{5}$$

where $\mathbf{v}^t \cdot \nabla\nabla\kappa \cdot \mathbf{v} < 0$ and $\kappa > 0$ means ridge, and $\mathbf{v}^t \cdot \nabla\nabla\kappa \cdot \mathbf{v} > 0$ and $\kappa < 0$ means valley. These maxima in magnitude of the curvature are connected from one level to the next, forming a subset of the so-called *vertex curves* [6] or *extremal curvature curves* [31].

Looking at the level curves of a map, it seems intuitively a reasonable assumption that valley vertex curves are the loci where water gathers. However, intuition drive us to an erroneous conclusion since vertex curves are not necessarily slopelines and, therefore, there exist non-generic situations where water does not accumulate along a valley vertex curve. Examples are the oblique gutter and the curved gutter in [10].

2.1.3 Mean curvature

Related to the principal curvatures of a surface we have the mean curvature κ_m, which is the arithmetic mean of all the principal curvatures. In [22] maxima of $\mid \kappa_m \mid$ in any direction were classified as crease points in the context of range images. In [4], 1D crease points were identified as local extrema of the mean curvature κ_m of a hypersurface, that is, points where $\nabla\kappa_m = 0$.

2.1.4 Creaseness measures

For some applications we may be more interested in a creaseness measure rather than in a ridge/valley classification of the pixels. If the Haralick condition (3) holds then $\lambda_1 = L_{\mathbf{vv}}$. Therefore, $\mid L_{\mathbf{vv}} \mid$ can be taken as a creaseness measure under the rationale that if $L_{\mathbf{vv}}$ is high, then there are more chances that the second directional derivative along the direction $\mathbf{v}$ is the highest in magnitude. The vertex condition 'maxima in magnitude of the relief's level curve curvature' is thus converted into 'high values in magnitude of the relief's level curve curvature'. According to (4) $L_{\mathbf{vv}}$ can be considered as the measure κ weighted by the gradient magnitude in order to nullify its response at isotropic regions. However, this is a trade-off since along anisotropic structures $L_{\mathbf{w}}$ is also lower on the center of a ridge/valley region than it is on its boundary. In [33, 17], the family of operators $L_{\mathbf{vv}}L_{\mathbf{w}}^{\alpha}, -1 \leq \alpha \leq 0$ was defined, where α controls the trade-off between $L_{\mathbf{vv}}$ and κ.

The same authors went to 3D not by a direct tensorial extension of $L_{\mathbf{vv}}$ or κ, but by means of the operators $L_{\mathbf{pp}}$ and $L_{\mathbf{qq}}$. If $S_{L(\mathbf{x})}$ is the level surface passing through the point $\mathbf{x}$ and $TS_{L(\mathbf{x})}$ is its tangent plane, then we denote by $\mathbf{p}, \mathbf{q} \in TS_{L(\mathbf{x})}$ the principal directions of $S_{L(\mathbf{x})}$, $\mathbf{q}$ being the direction corresponding to the maximum principal curvature and $\mathbf{p}$ corresponding to the minimum principal curvature.

2.2. Separatrices

After Saint-Venant, other attempts at characterizing drainage lines were based in the work of Cayley dated in 1859. He considered local elevation maxima, minima and saddle points: *summits*, *immits* and *knots*, respectively, in his terminology. Cayley observed that in general the level curves around a knot consist of a family of concentric hyperbolas and stated that there are only two slopelines 'crossing' the knot, those intersecting each other at right angles. He termed these slopelines *ridge* and *course lines*. For the ridge line the knot is a point of minimum elevation, for the course line it is a point of maximum elevation. The ridges are considered to end in a summit. Thus, a ridge line is a slopeline going from one summit to another through a single knot. Similarly, course lines are considered slopelines going from an immit to another through a single knot or reaching the sea level instead of an immit.

In 1870 Maxwell continued the work of Cayley. He stated that through each point passes a slopeline which ends at a certain maximum and begins at a certain minimum. Then, he defined the *basins* or *dales*, as districts whose slopelines come from the same minimum, and *hills* as districts whose slopelines run to the same maximum. In this way the landscape may be independently divided into basins and hills. Watersheds were then defined as slopelines separating basins, and watercourses as slopelines separating hills. In this way watersheds are the only slopelines which do not reach a minimum, watercourses the only slopelines that do not reach a maximum.

Nackman [21] formulated the work of Maxwell in terms of the so-called *slope districts*. A slope district is defined as the overlapping region between a basin and a hill. Rosin [25] approximates a discrete image by piecewise continuous patches. This was done by interpolating an extra point in the center of every four neighbor pixels, having as grey value the average of them. The original and interpolated pixels were then triangulated to obtain a continuous surface. Next, maxima, minima and saddles are found. After, slopelines are grown uphill and downhill from saddles to terminate at maxima and minima, respectively. A similar approach was presented by Griffin [7] who directly triangulated the pixels without interpolating a middle center point. In both cases, due to the discrete nature of images, rare situations appear making difficult the partition of the image into the slope districts of Nackman. The mathematical morphology school has proposed several algorithmic definitions of watersheds [34] in digital spaces. The most efficient algorithm is based on an immersion process analogy, in which the flooding of water in the image is efficiently simulated by using hierarchical queues.

2.3. Drainage patterns

According to Koenderink and van Doorn [10] the proper mathematical characterization of the drainage pattern of a terrain goes back to 1915 and is due to R. Rothe. He stated that the lines sketching the drainage pattern of a surface must be slopelines, a restriction that cannot be guaranteed by local conditions. Rothe identified valleys as (parts of) slopelines where other slopelines converge and eventually join them in a minimum (maybe at infinity) to form a stream.

Mathematically, these special slopelines are singular solutions of the ordinary differential equation defining the slopeline family $\varphi = \mathbf{v} \cdot d\mathbf{x} = 0$ where $d\mathbf{x} = (dx, dy)$. It is well-known that it is not an exact form since it is not closed. This in turn means that we can express it as $\varphi = \theta d\omega$, where θ and ω are not uniquely defined functions. After a rather non-trivial geometric reasoning [10] the condition to identify the special slopelines was found to be:

$$\theta L_{\mathbf{vw}} = 0 \ , \qquad (6)$$

where $L_{\mathbf{vw}} = 0$ is the Saint-Venant's condition, which is a wrong one, and $\theta = 0$ is Rothe's proposal. However, somehow the discussion about which is the right characterization of these special slopelines still remains [24].

Researchers working with real topographic data (DEMs) extract drainage patterns not through literal implementation of Rothe's characterization but by a simulation process. The runoff simulation basically consists of measuring the number of drops of water arriving to each pixel. A drop of water starts at a pixel an goes downhill by following the gradient orientation until a minimum or the image border is reached. The drop increases the count of the pixels that visits along its way. Rothe's special slopelines in the continuous domain are thus found (maybe unconsciously) as those segments which exhibit a higher overlapping of discrete slopelines.

The automatic procedures that extract drainage patterns from square sampled DEMs can be divided in two main groups attending to the routing strategy they use, that is, how water is propagated from a given pixel to simulate the runoff :

- single flow algorithms: the water in a given pixel is drained to only one of its neighbors [5, 27].
- multiple flow algorithms: the water in a given pixel is distributed among several of its neighbors [23, 3].

Both types of algorithms have as main problem the presence of pits and flat areas since runoff stops at these landscape features. The main disadvantage of single flow algorithms is their inability to accommodate divergent flow, which can produce errors in convex hills. On the other hand, they are able to accommodate quite well convergent flow. The main disadvantage of multiple flow algorithms is precisely that they spread the water even in convergent areas and hence the concentration along the channels is less salient.

3. Three image registration applications

In this section we try to illustrate the usefulness of ridge and valley lines in the context of a class of applications, namely, image registration. More specifically, we have developed a new creaseness operator to detect these structures, which is based on the vertex condition, that is, the curvature of the level curves (in general, $d-1$ sets for d–dimensional images) [16, 15]. This operator, called ST-MLSEC for "structure tensor multilocal level set extrinsic curvature", is employed to detect ridge and valley lines. They are later input as landmarks into a hierarchical search process whose output is the value of the rigid transform parameters that best align the two sets of landmarks in the sense of maximize correlation. ST-MLSEC overcomes two problems which suffer other crease measures based on the curvature like $L_{\mathbf{vv}}$ or direct estimations of curvature κ : discontinuities around extrema and saddle points, and unbounded response. Besides, it yields a clean and robust response, its degree of sensitivity can be adjusted and the localization is quite precise. For these reasons, we have found it to be very suitable in the following registration problems.

3.1. CT and MRI volumes

The registration of CT and MRI brain volumes of a same subject allows to combine partially complementary information. While CT depicts the bone accurately, MRI differentiates soft tissues much better. The problem of fusing these two types of images appears because the patient head is not exactly in the same position and orientation with respect to the CT and MRI scanners, hence a geometric transform or mapping must be found that aligns the two volumes.Since the skull does not deform, we can assume that the transform relating the two coordinate systems is rigid, that is, a 3D translation, scaling and rotation. While scaling parameters can be deduced from the image resolution, the rest can not. To do so, the skull is taken as anatomical landmark for registration. We observe that the skull forms a 3D ridge in the CT and a valley in the MRI images. Our method is quite similarly to that of van den Elsen [33], except that they employ $L_{\mathbf{pp}}, L_{\mathbf{qq}}$ and their search strategy is different and much slower than ours. Figure 4 and 5 show two examples. Reference [13] has the details and provides quantitative assessment. It is interesting to note that results are comparable and better in some situations than those of registration by maximization of the mutual information, a kind of method of reference in the medical image registration field.

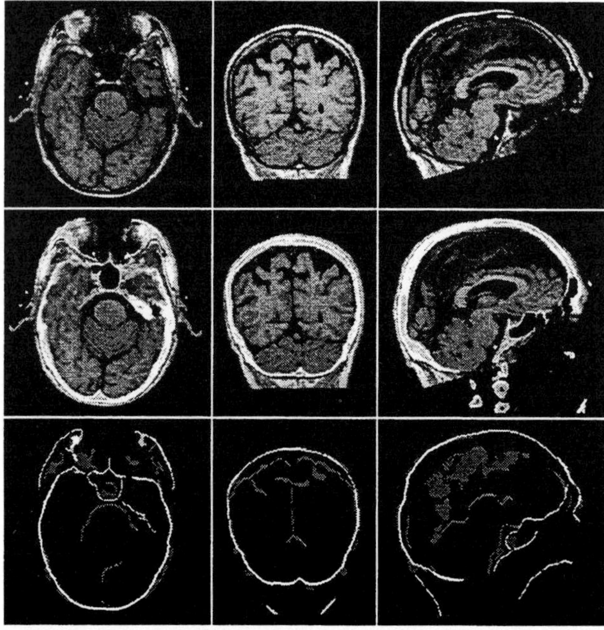

Figure 4. Top row: MRI registered to CT. Middle: CT bone overlapped to registered MRI. Bottom: CT ridges (white) over MRI valleys (grey)

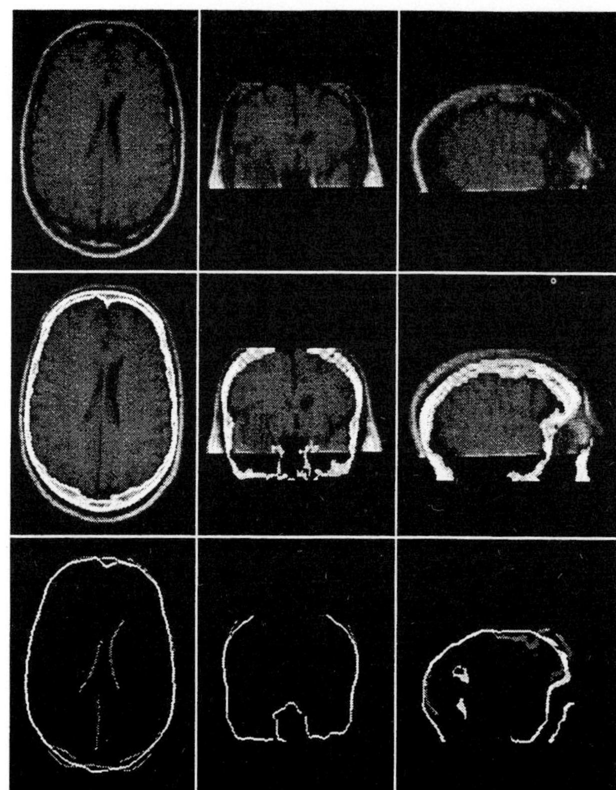

Figure 5. same as fig. 4 for a T1 weighted and lower resolution MRI

3.2. Retinographies

Retinal images, which show the vascular tree of the eye, are an important mean to assess the condition of the retina. For a number of diseases, it is convenient to track the evolution of vessels through the years in temporal series. Also, studies are performed to quantify blood flow velocity along vessels from an animated sequence. In all cases, it is necessary to register the images before performing a point–wise comparison, because the position and orientation of the eye can change. There are several retinal imaging modalities. Retinographies taken by an ophtalmoscope under natural light are called "green images", as a green filter is put in front of the lens to enhance the visibility of vessels. Fluoresceinic angiographies sense the fluorescence emitted from vessels after the injection of a contrast dye. SLO stands for scanning laser ophtalmoscopy and is a novel angiographic technique which registers how vessels are filled by the blood flow in order to compute the time delay at points of interest. The central idea is that vessels can be taken as landmarks. Moreover, they are thin and elongated bright objects over a darker background. Thus, they can be thought as creases (ridges) and reliably delineated by the creaseness measure we propose. Figure 6 shows the registration of a pair of SLO frames. Details on the mapping parameters and the search method are explained in [14].

3.3. Mosaicing

This last example deals with the registration of pictures for mosaicing. Concretely, they are images of the famous Michelangelo's statue "La Pietá". Conventional pictures of many small patches of the surface are taken to be later superimposed to a three–dimensional model of the statue (texture mapping). The shadowing due to lighting conditions creates ridge and valley lines that, even though they do not correspond to the actual ridges and valleys of the 3D model, can be used as landmarks for registration. Figure 7 shows the result for two adjacent patches.

4. Summary

The attempt of mathematically characterize the drainage pattern gave rise to several proposals, some of them clearly wrong. During the second half of the XIX century there was debate about what was the correct characterization. Computer vision seems to have continued this controversy, at least in the sense of a variety of algorithms and operators

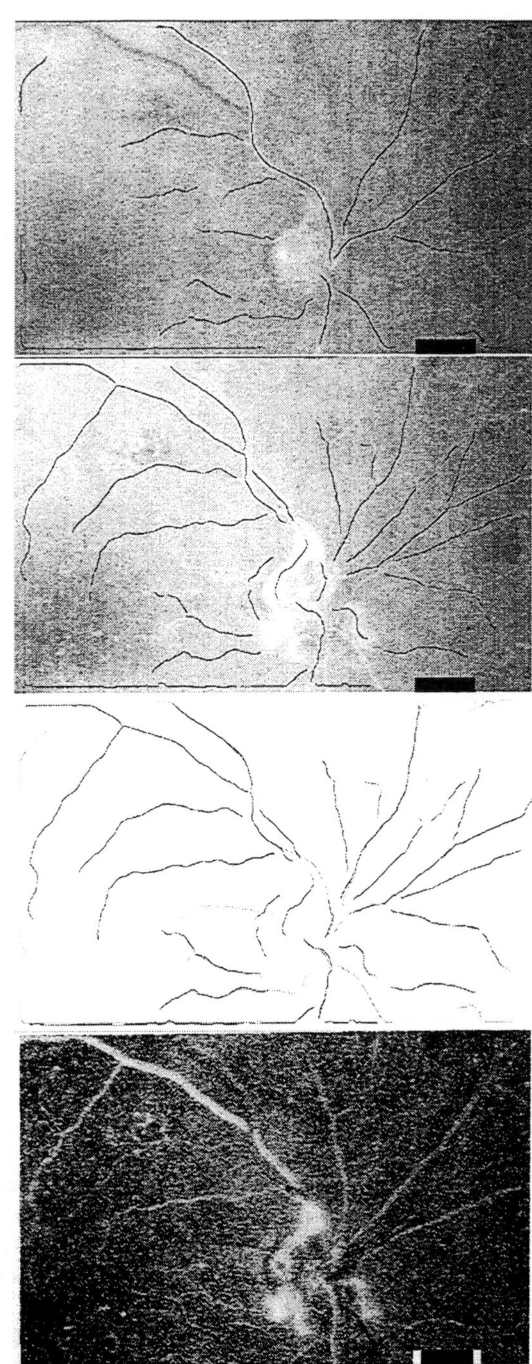

Figure 6. (a) and (b) : two SLO frames several seconds apart and their ridges; (c) ridge registration; (d) frame difference

to extract ridge and valley lines. Our point is that whether a definition fails to find the actual drainage pattern or not, it really does not matter since most of the times we merely want to sketch the medial lines in images other than DEMs. Therefore, we can choose between the hydrologic and the morphologic viewpoint attending to their own merits with regard to the specific application at hand.

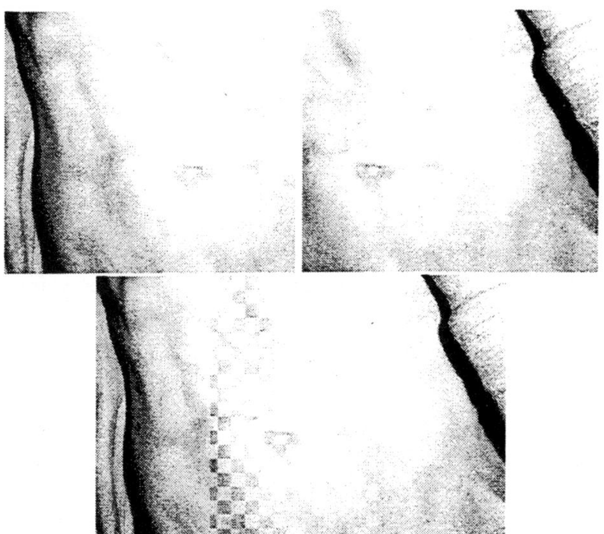

Figure 7. (a) two patches (b) fusion of the registered patches, the checkerboard appears because we visualize a small square of each image alternatively. Original images courtesy of IBM Corp.

Also, we have shown that crease lines, a characterization of ridge and valley lines based on the curvature of level sets, are suitable to register very different types of images. The three examples have in common that the landmarks used to register the images are precisely lines of ridge and valley, which we are able to detect quite reliably. This can be so even for non–medical images, like in the statue pictures or remote sensing images.

Acknowledgments

This research has been funded by CICYT grants TIC97–1134–C02–02 and TAP98–0618. CT and MRI volumes were kindly provided by Dr. van den Elsen from Utrecht University and Dr. J.M. Fitzpatrick from Vanderbilt University. Thanks also to Cástor Perez Mariño from Universidade da Coruña for providing the SLO example.

References

[1] N. Armande, O. Monga, and P. Montesinos. Thin nets extraction in medical images. In Y. Bizais, editor, *Proc. Int. Conf. on Information Processing in Medical Imaging*, Lecture Notes in Computer Science, pages 383–384. Springer-Verlag, 1995.

[2] S. Chinveeraphan, R. Takamatsu, and M. Sato. Understanding of ridge-valley lines on image-intensity surfaces in scale-space. In Hlavac and Sara, editors, *Proc. Int. Conf. on Computer Analysis of Images and Patterns*, volume 970 of *Lec-*

ture Notes in Computer Science, pages 661–667. Springer-Verlag, 1995.

[3] J. Desmet and G. Govers. Comparison of routing algorithms for digital elevation models and their implications for predicting ephemeral ggullies. *Inter. Journal of Geographical Information Systems*, 10:311–331, 1996.

[4] D. Eberly, R. Gardner, B. Morse, S. Pizer, and C. Scharlach. Ridges for image analysis. *Journal of Mathematical Imaging and Vision*, 4:353–373, 1994.

[5] J. Fairfield and P. Leymarie. Drainage networks from grid digital elevation models. *Water Resources Research*, 27:709–717, 1991.

[6] J. Gauch and S. Pizer. Multiresolution analysis of ridges and valleys in grey-scale images. *IEEE Trans. on Pattern Analysis and Machine Intelligence*, 15:635–646, 1993.

[7] L. Griffin, A. Colchester, and G. Robinson. Scale and segmentation of grey-level images using maximum gradient paths. *Image and Vision Computing*, 10:389–402, 1992.

[8] R. Haralick. Ridges and valleys on digital images. *Computer Vision Graphics and Image Processing*, 22:28–38, 1983.

[9] A. Jain, L. Hong, and R. Bolle. On-line fingerprint verification. *IEEE Trans. Pattern Analysis and Machine Intelligence*, 19:302–313, 1997.

[10] J. Koenderink and A. van Doorn. Local features of smooth shapes: ridges and courses. In *Geometric Methods in Computer Vision II*, volume 2031, pages 2–13. SPIE, 1993.

[11] I. Kweon and T. Kanade. Extracting topographic terrain features from elevation maps. *CVGIP: Image Understanding*, 59:171–182, 1994.

[12] S. Lee and Y. Joon. Direct extraction of features for gray scale character recognition. *IEEE Trans. Pattern Analysis and Machine Intelligence*, 17:724–729, 1995.

[13] D. Lloret, A. López, J. Serrat, and J. Villanueva. Creaseness-based CT and MR registration: comparison with the mutual information method. *Journal of Electronic Imaging*, 8(3):255–262, 1999.

[14] D. Lloret, J. Serrat, A. López, and J. Villanueva. Retinal image registration using creases as anatomical landmarks. In J. V. A. Sanfeliu, editor, *Proc. Int. Conf. on Pattern Recongition*. IAPR, IEEE Computer Society, September 2000.

[15] A. López, D. Lloret, J. Serrat, and J. Villanueva. Multilocal creaseness based on the level set extrinsic curvature. *Computer Vision and Image Understanding*, 2(77):111–144, 2000.

[16] A. López, F. Lumbreras, J. Serrat, and J. Villanueva. Evaluation of methods for ridge and valley detection. *IEEE Pattern Analysis and Machine Intelligence*, 21(4):327–335, 1999.

[17] J. Maintz, P. van den Elsen, and M. Viergever. Evaluation of ridge seeking operators for multimodality medical image matching. *IEEE Trans. on Pattern Analysis and Machine Intelligence*, 18:353–365, 1996.

[18] D. Maio and D. Maltoni. Direct gray-scale minutiae detection in fingerprints. *IEEE Trans. Pattern Analysis and Machine Intelligence*, 19:27–39, 1997.

[19] A. Manceaux-Demiau, J. Mangin, J. Regis, O. Pizzato, and V. Frouin. Differential features of cortical folds. In J. Troccaz, E. Grimson, and R. Mosges, editors, *Proc. 1st Joint Conf. on Computer Vision, Virtual Reality and Robotics in Medicine and Medical Robotics and Computed-Assisted Surgery*, volume 1205 of *Lecture Notes in Computer Science*, pages 439–448. Springer-Verlag, 1997.

[20] O. Monga, N. Armande, and P. Montesinos. Thin nets and crest lines: Application to satellite data and medical images. In *Proc. IEEE Inter. Conf. on Image Processing*, pages 468–471. IEEE Computer Society Press, 1995.

[21] L. Nackman. Two-dimensional critical point configuration graphs. *IEEE Trans. on Pattern Analysis and Machine Intelligence*, 6:442–450, 1984.

[22] S. Pankanti, C. Dorai, and A. Jain. Robust feature detection for 3D object recognition and matching. In *Geometric Methods in Computer Vision II*, volume 2031, pages 366–377. SPIE, 1993.

[23] P. Quinn, K. Beven, P. Chevalier, and O. Planchon. The prediction of hillslope flow paths for distributed hydrological modelling using digital terrain models. *Hydrological Processes*, 5:59–79, 1991.

[24] J. Rieger. Topographical properties of generic images. *International Journal of Computer Vision*, 23:79–92, 1997.

[25] P. Rosin, A. Colchester, and D. Hawkes. Early image representation using regions defined by maximum gradient paths between singular points. *Pattern Recognition*, 25:695–711, 1992.

[26] Y. Sato, S. Nakajima, N. Shiraga, H. Atsumi, S. Yoshida, T. Koller, G. Gerig, and R. Kikinis. Three-dimensional multi-scale line filter for segmentation and visualization of curvilinear structures in medical images. *Medical Image Analysis*, 2:143–168, 1998.

[27] P. Soille and M. Ansoult. Automated basin delineation from digital elevation models using mathematical morphology. *Signal Processing*, 20:171–182, 1990.

[28] C. Steger. Extracting curvilinear structures: a differential geometric approach. In B. Buxton and R. Cipolla, editors, *Proc. 4th Euro. Conf. on Computer Vision*, volume 1064 of *Lecture Notes in Computer Science*, pages 630–641. Springer-Verlag, 1996.

[29] B. Ter Haar Romeny, editor. *Geometry-Driven Diffusion in Computer Vision*. Kluwer Academic Publishers, 1994.

[30] B. ter Haar Romeny and L. Florack. A multiscale geometric model of human vision. In W. Hendee and P. Well, editors, *The Perception of Visual Information*, pages 73–114. Springer-Verlag, 1993.

[31] J. Thirion and A. Gourdon. Computing the differential characteristics of isointensity surfaces. *Computer Vision and Image Understanding*, 61:190–202, 1995.

[32] O. Trier, T. Taxt, and A. Jain. Recognition of digits in hydrographic maps: Binary versus topographic analysis. *IEEE Trans. on Pattern Analysis and Machine Intelligence*, 19:399–404, 1997.

[33] P. van den Elsen, J. Maintz, E.-J. Pol, and M. Viergever. Automatic registration of CT and MR brain images using correlation of geometrical features. *IEEE Trans. on Medical Imaging*, 14:384–396, 1995.

[34] L. Vincent and P. Soille. Watersheds in digital spaces: An efficient algorithm based on immersion simulations. *IEEE Trans. Pattern Analysis and Machine Intelligence*, 13:583–598, 1991.

Efficient Retrieval of Deformed and Occluded Shapes

Zusheng Rao[1] Euripides G.M. Petrakis[2] Evangelos Milios[1] *
[1] Dept. of Computer Science
York University, Toronto Canada, M3J 1P3
[2] Dept. of Electronic and Comp. Engineering
Technical University of Crete, Chania, Crete, Greece
e-mail: zrao@cs.yorku.ca, petrakis@ced.tuc.gr, eem@cs.dal.ca

Abstract

We propose an approach for matching deformed and occluded shapes using Dynamic Programming (DP). Our algorithms handle noise and shape distortions by allowing matching of merged sequences of consecutive small segments in a shape, with larger segments of another shape, while being invariant to translation, scale and orientation transformations of shapes. We illustrate the effectiveness of our algorithms in retrieval of shapes on two different two-dimensional datasets, one of static hand gesture shapes and another of marine life shapes.

1. Introduction

The increasing amounts of image data in many application domains has generated additional interest for real-time management and image database retrieval by shape content. For example, [2] reports experiments with traditional shape representation and matching methods (e.g., Fourier, moments) on 500 trademark images. More recently, the effectiveness of such methods in conjunction with color features is investigated in [1] using 1,100 trademark images. SQUID [5] supports retrievals on a dataset of 1,100 marine life species. In [4] we demonstrate the superiority of a multi-scale DP matching method over Fourier and moment-based methods on 980 static hand gesture shapes and on the dataset of SQUID. A promising method, but untested in shape retrieval, defines a shape distance and association of shape parts on the basis of area features (shape skeleton) [7], by reducing shape matching to a largest subgraph isomorphism problem.

*This work was carried-out while E. Petrakis was visiting York University. Current address of E. Milios is Faculty of Computer Science, Dalhousie University, eem@cs.dal.ca. This work was supported by a grant from the Natural Sciences and Engineering Research Council of Canada.

In this work, we propose shape matching algorithms for deformed and occluded shapes based on dynamic programming. The methods referred to above do not focus on occlusion and, as noted in [6], earlier DP shape matching methods (e.g., [8, 4]) are not optimal, that is, they may miss the optimal match. Our algorithms are optimal, in that they always find the least cost match [6]. We tested our algorithms on a dataset of 980 two-dimensional hand gesture shapes and on a marine life database with 1,500 shapes.

The rest of this work is organized as follows: The main idea behind our approach is given in Section 2. The DP table and the definition of the cost functions are discussed in Section 3. Our shape matching algorithm is presented in Section 4. Finally, experimental results are presented in Section 5 followed by conclusions and issues for future research in Section 6.

2. Main idea

The shape matching algorithm that lies at the core of our methodology takes in two shapes and computes: (a) Their distance; the more similar the shapes are, the lower the value of the distance function and (b) The correspondences between similar parts of the two shapes.

In matching two shapes A and B, the algorithm builts a DP table, where rows and columns correspond to segments of A and B respectively. Starting at the lower left corner and proceeding upwards and to the right, the table is filled with the cost of the partial match containing the segments (rows and columns) swept so far. Because convex segments cannot match concave ones, only about half the cells are assigned cost values, in a checkerboard pattern. Merges, where a segment sequence of one shape matches a single segment of the other shape can occur. Merges introduce "jumps" in the traversal of the DP table. Reaching the top row implies a complete match, where all segments of shape A has been swept. Additional information is stored in each cell to allow the tracing of a path starting from that cell and working backwards. The tracing of a path reveals segment associations between the two shapes.

2.1. Matching cases

We distinguish among the following three cases of matching:

Both shapes are open: The algorithm will find the *best* association of all segments of A to all or to a subsequence of segments of B (i.e., part of B may be left unmatched) or vice versa. Because we cannot know in advance which shape is included within the other one, we run the algorithm twice (i.e., once for each possibility) and we take the matching with the minimum cost.

Shape A is open and shape B is closed: The algorithm will find the best association of all segments of A to all or to a subsequence of segments of B. Shape A may be contained within shape B, but not the other way around; this is the only possibility (i.e., part of B may be left unmatched).

Both shapes are closed: The algorithm will find the *best* mapping between A and B so that, no segments remain unassociated in either shape.

We have addressed the third case in [4]. That algorithm is not optimal (i.e., may miss the least cost match). In this paper, we handle the case with A and B closed by pretending that A is open, repeating the algorithm for open and closed shape matching M times (once for each possible starting point on A) and by taking the least cost match as the cost of matching. In the following, we focus on the first two cases.

3. Definitions and methodology

Let A and B be the two shapes to be matched. Let $A = a_1, a_2, \ldots a_M$ and $B = b_1, b_2, \ldots b_N$ be the sequence of N and M convex (C) and concave (V) segments of the two shapes respectively, with a_i being the segment between inflection points p_i and p_{i+1} and b_j the segment between inflection points q_j and q_{j+1}. Henceforth, $a(i-m|i)$, $m \geq 0$, denotes the sequence of segments $a_{i-m}, a_{i-m+1}, \ldots, a_i$; similarly for $b(j-n|j)$, $n \geq 0$.

3.1. Dynamic Programming (DP) table

The DP table has $\mathcal{M}$ rows and $\mathcal{N}$ columns, where $\mathcal{M}$ and $\mathcal{N}$ are defined as follows:

Both shapes are open: $\mathcal{M} = M + 1$ and $\mathcal{N} = N + 1$.

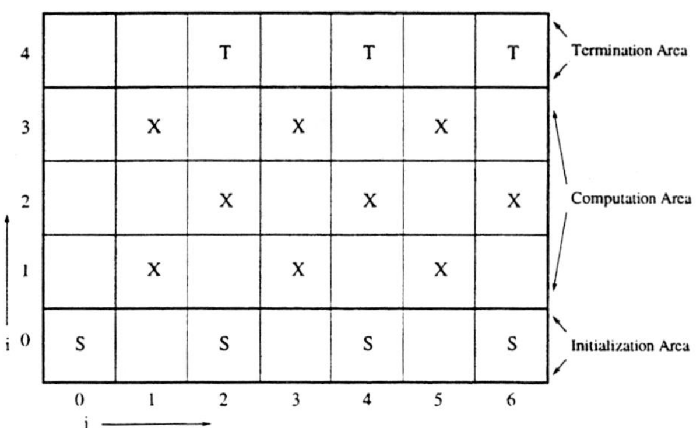

Figure 1. Example of a DP table with $\mathcal{M} = 4$ (shape A) and $\mathcal{N} = 6$ (shape B). S, X and T denote cells in the initialization, computation and termination areas respectively.

Shape A is open and shape B is closed: $\mathcal{M} = M + 1$ and $\mathcal{N} = 2N$. Shape B is repeated twice to force the algorithm consider all possible starting points on B. If B is closed, its indices are taken modulo N. If A is closed and B is open, we switch the roles of A and B.

Both shapes are closed: This case reduces to the previous one.

The rows of a DP table are indexed by i, $0 \leq i \leq \mathcal{M}$ and its columns are indexed by j, $0 \leq j \leq \mathcal{N}$ where, i, j are indices to segments of A and B respectively. The first row ($i = 0$) and the first column ($j = 0$) do not correspond to segments of A and B respectively, but they are placeholders for initializing the filling of the DP table.

The cell at the intersection of row i and column j is referred to as $cell(i, j)$. A link between cells (i_{w-1}, j_{w-1}) and (i_w, j_w) denotes the matching of the merged sequence of segments $a(i_{w-1} + 1|i_w)$ with $b(j_{w-1} + 1|j_w)$. $cell(i_{w-1}, j_{w-1})$ is called *parent* of $cell(i_w, j_w)$. A *path* is a linked sequence of cells $((i_0, j_0), (i_1, j_1), \ldots (i_t, j_t))$, not necessarily adjacent, indicating a partial match, where $i_0 < i_1 < \ldots < i_t$ and $j_0 < j_1 < \ldots < j_t$. This path associates segment sequences $a(i_{w-1} + 1|i_w)$ of A with sequences $b(j_{w-1} + 1|j_w)$ of B for $w = 1, 2, \ldots t$.

Each $cell(i_w, j_w)$ contains the following values: w, $g(i_w, j_w)$, m_w, n_w, u_w, v_w and ρ_w where, w is the number of matched sequences of segments, $g(i_w, j_w)$ is the partially accumulated match cost up to that cell, u_w and v_w denote number of unmatched segments of A and B respectively, m_w and n_w are the indices of the parent cell of $cell(i_w, j_w)$ (i.e., $m_w = i_{w-1}$ and $n_w = j_{w-1}$) and are used to trace back a path. Finally, ρ_w denotes the scale factor corresponding to the parts of A and B which have been matched up to $cell(i_w, j_w)$ and it is defined in Section 3.3.

Fig. 1 illustrates an example of a DP table. The DP table consists of three distinct areas:

Initialization area: It is first row of the DP table. If a_1 and b_j, $1 \leq j \leq \mathcal{M}$, have the same polarity, then $w, g(0,j), m_w, n_w, u_w, v_w, \rho_w$ of $cell(0,j)$ are $0, 0, 0, 0, M, N, 1$ respectively. If a_1 and b_j have different polarity, we set $g(0,j) = \infty$.

Computation area: It is the area after the first column and between the first and last row of the DP table. Cells in this area correspond to incomplete paths.

Termination area: It is the last row of the DP table. All complete paths end at cells in this area. The best match corresponds to the path with the least cost.

3.2. Cost of matching

A *complete match* is a correspondence between sequences of segments in order, such that no segments are left unassociated in shape A and there are no crossovers or omissions. A complete match is characterized by a *complete path* $((i_0, j_0), (i_1, j_1), \ldots, (i_W, j_W))$, a path that starts at the initialization and ends at the termination area. The cost $D(A, B)$ of matching shape A with shape B is defined as

$$D(A,B) = \min_{(i_w, j_w)} \sum_{w=1}^{W} \psi\left(a(i_{w-1}+1|i_w), b(j_{w-1}+1|j_w)\right). \tag{1}$$

Function $\psi\left(a(i_{w-1}+1|i_w), b(j_{w-1}+1|j_w)\right)$ represents the dissimilarity cost of its two arguments and consists of three additive components:

$$\begin{aligned} \psi\left(a(i_{w-1}+1|i_w), b(j_{w-1}+1|j_w)\right) = \\ MergingCost\left(a(i_{w-1}+1|i_w)\right) + \\ MergingCost\left(b(j_{w-1}+1|j_w)\right) + \\ \lambda\ DissimCost\left(a(i_{w-1}+1|i_w), b(j_{w-1}+1|j_w)\right). \end{aligned} \tag{2}$$

The first two terms in Eq. 2 represent the cost of merging segments $a(i_{w-1}+1|i_w)$ in shape A and segments $b(j_{w-1}+1|j_w)$ in shape B respectively while, the last term is the cost of associating the merged sequence $a(i_{w-1}+1|i_w)$ with the merged sequence $b(j_{w-1}+1|j_w)$. The role of merging cost is to restrict non promising merges. Constant λ represents the relative importance of the merging and dissimilarity costs. In this work λ was set to 1. Each allowable merging should be a recursive application of the grammar rules $CVC \Rightarrow C$ and $VCV \Rightarrow V$) [3]. This is enforced by the DP algorithm.

Next, we define geometric quantities (features) required in the definition of the cost functions as illustrated in Fig. 2.

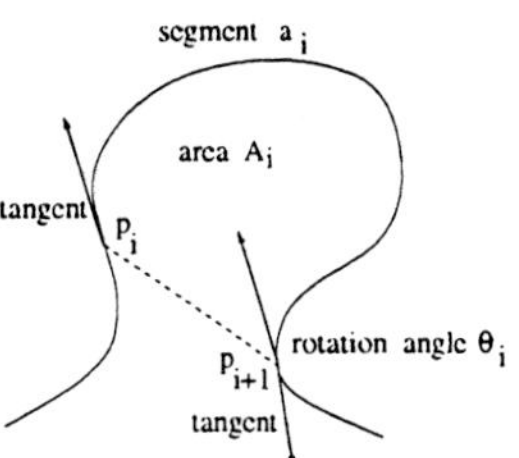

Figure 2. Geometric quantities for defining the importance of a segment

Rotation Angle θ_i is the angle traversed by the tangent to the segment from inflection point p_i to inflection point p_{i+1} and shows how strongly a segment is curved.

Length l_i is the length of segment a_i.

Area A_i is the area enclosed between the chord and the arc between the inflection points p_i and p_{i+1}.

3.3. Scale factor

If one of the two shapes is scaled with respect to the other, then the length of one of the two shapes (i.e., shape B) has to be multiplied by an appropriate *scale factor*. Although we know that the matched part of shape A will be the whole shape A, the length of the matched part of shape B is unknown before the algorithm is completed. To handle this problem, we compute a scale factor ρ_t for each partial match $((i_0, j_0), (i_1, j_1), \ldots, (i_t, j_t))$:

$$\rho_t = \frac{\sum_{w=1}^{t} \sum_{i=i_{w-1}}^{i_w} l_i(A)}{\sum_{w=1}^{t} \sum_{j=j_{w-1}}^{j_w} l_j(B)}, \tag{3}$$

where $1 \leq t \leq W$ and $l_i(A)$ and $l_j(B)$ are the lengths of a_i and b_j respectively. This value is an approximation of the actual scale factor of a complete match. Notice that ρ_0 is undefined since the total matched length is 0 for both shapes. In this work ρ_0 is set to 1.

3.4. Dissimilarity cost

The cost of associating a group of segments from shape A with a group of segments from shape B is computed as

$$DissimCost = W \max_{all\ features\ f} \{d_f\}. \tag{4}$$

The term d_f is the cost associated with the difference in feature f (i.e., length, area or angle). The intuition behind the use of max is that it tends to emphasize large differences on any feature. W is a weight term associated with the importance of this partial match. Specifically, the proportion of the matched shape length with respect to the total length is used to define W:

$$W = \max \left\{ \frac{\sum_{i=i_{w-1}+1}^{i_w} l_i(A)}{length\ of\ A}, \frac{\sum_{j=j_{w-1}+1}^{j_w} l_j(B)}{length\ of\ B} \right\}. \tag{5}$$

The term d_f is defined as

$$d_f = \frac{|F_A - S_w(f)F_B|}{F_A + S_w(f)F_B}, \tag{6}$$

where, $F_A = \sum_{i=i_{w-1}+1}^{i_w} |f_i|$, $F_B = \sum_{j=j_{w-1}+1}^{j_w} |f_j|$ and $S_w(f)$ is a parameter depending on the feature f. Specifically, $S_w(f) = \rho_{w-1}$ for f being length and ρ_{w-1}^2 for f being area. For f being rotation angle, $S_w(f) = 1$ since, angle measurements do not depend on the scale factor.

3.5. Merging cost

Let the types of the segments being merged be $CVC\ldots C$. In the following, the opposite case is obtained by switching C and V in the formulaes. The merging cost is defined as follows:

$$MergingCost = \max_{all\ features\ f} \{W_f C_f\}, \tag{7}$$

where subscript f refers to a feature (length, area or rotation angle). For all features:

$$C_f = \frac{\sum_{V\ segs\ of\ group} |f|}{\sum_{all\ segs\ of\ group} |f|}. \tag{8}$$

The intuition behind these formulaes is that they measure the importance of the absorbed segments (of type V) relative to the whole matched consecutive segments of the group. For f being any feature (length, area, rotation angle) the weight term of the merging cost is defined as

$$W_f = \frac{\sum_{V\ segs\ of\ group} |f|}{\sum_{V\ segs\ of\ shape} |f|}. \tag{9}$$

The intuition behind this weight term is to measure the importance of the absorbed segments within the shape as a whole.

4. Algorithm

Fig. 3 outlines the algorithm. The *for* loop for j_w does not run over all the indicated values, as convex to concave matches are not possible. In fact, only half of the cells are used. At each cell, the algorithm computes the optimum cost of the incomplete path ending at this cell:

$$g(i_w, j_w) = \min\{ g(i_{w-1}, j_{w-1}) + \psi\left(a(i_{w-1}+1|i_w), b(j_{w-1}+1|j_w)\right)\}. \tag{10}$$

```
// Initialization: Fill the first row
for j_w = 0, 1, ..., N do
    fill cell(0, j_w)
end for
// Fill from the 2nd to the M-th row
for i_w = 1, 2, ..., M do
    for j_w = 1, 2, ..., N do
        fill cell(i_w, j_w) using ρ_{w-1}, Eq. 2 and Eq. 10;
        compute ρ_w using Eq. 3;
    end for
end for
// Select the least cost complete path
    select the least cost path from the M-th row;
    retrace path using m_w, n_w cell values;
```

Figure 3. Outline of the algorithm.

Merging always involves an odd number of segments that is, $(i_{w-1}, j_{w-1}) = (i_w - 2m_w - 1, j_w - 2n_w - 1)$, where $m_w \geq 0$ and $n_w \geq 0$. Eq. 10 determines the minimum cost transition from cell $cell(i_{w-1}, j_{w-1})$ to $cell(i_w, j_w)$ for all possible values of m_w and n_w. Indices m_w and n_w are stored at $cell(i_w, j_w)$ and can be used to retrace the path from $cell(i_w, j_w)$ back to its starting point.

4.1. Matching examples

Fig. 4 illustrates segment correspondences (indicated by consecutive lines connecting the starting and ending points of the associated segments) obtained by matching hand silhouettes (left) and fish silhouettes (right). One of the two shapes has been shrunk and rotated properly to illustrate the associations between matched parts of the two shapes.

5. Shape retrieval

In our experiments we used the following datasets:

- GESTURES[1]: Consists of 980 open shapes which are generated from a dataset of 980 closed shapes by editing.
- MARINE[2]: Consists of 1,500 open shapes of marine species which we generated from the 1,100 closed shapes of SQUID[3].

To evaluate our algorithm we carefully created 34 queries (17 closed and 17 open shapes) for each dataset. We used

[1] `http://www.cs.yorku.ca/~eem/gesturesDB.`

[2] `http://www.cs.yorku.ca/~eem/marineDB.`

[3] `http://www.ee.surrey.ac.uk/Research/VSSP/imagedb/demo.html.`

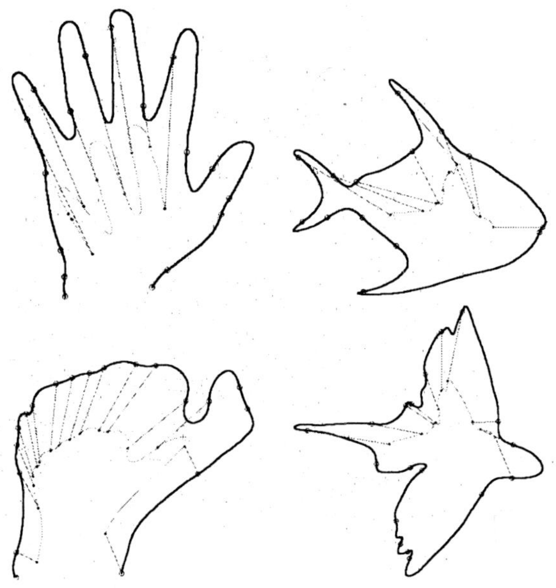

Figure 4. Segment associations reported by the matching algorithm on representative matches from the gestures and the marine life datasets.

human relevance judgements to compute the effectiveness of our method. Two shapes (i.e., a query and a stored shape) are considered similar if a human judges that they represent the same figure or that the one is contained within the other. To measure effectiveness, we computed *precision*, that is the percentage of similar shapes retrieved with respect to the number of retrieved shapes.

Retrieved shapes	1	5	10	15	20
GESTURES	0.91	0.80	0.75	0.70	0.65
MARINE	0.80	0.52	0.45	0.40	0.38

Table 1. Average values of precision for the gestures and the matine life datasets.

Table 1 illustrates the average values of precision for the above two datasets and for answers containing between 1 up to 20 shapes. This result demonstrates that our method is best suited for applications where one is interested in retrieving a few best matches. Notice that the algorithm achieves always at least 10% better precision on the GESTURES dataset than on the MARINE dataset. Presumably, this is because the shapes in the MARINE dataset have much more shape detail and noise and are much more difficult to handle than the shapes in the GESTURES dataset. The algorithm requires less than 1 second per shape match on the average on a Pentium PC, 200MHz.

6. Conclusions

We propose a shape matching algorithm for handling shape similarity retrievals in image databases. Our algorithm is based on dynamic programming, performs implicitly at multiple scales by allowing the matching of merged sequences of segments and handles noisy, deformed and occluded shapes. Future work includes the experimentation with more datasets and methods, the handling of combined queries involving more than one feature (e.g., shape, color, text), the development of indexing methods that could speed-up retrievals and the development of a graphical user interface on the World Wide Web.

Acknowledgements

We are grateful to Aristidis Diplaros for his help in the experiments and Prof. Mokhtarian of the Centre for Vision, Speech and Signal Processing laboratory at the University of Surrey, UK, for providing us the marine dataset.

References

[1] A. Jain and A. Vailaya. Shape-Based Retrieval: A Case Study With Trademark Image Databases. *Pattern Recognition*, 31(9):1369–13990, 1998.

[2] B. Mehtre, M. Kankanhalli, and W. Lee. Shape Measures for Content Based Image Retrieval: A Comparison. *Information Processing and Management*, 33(3):319–337, 1997.

[3] E. Milios. Shape Matching using Curvature Processes. *Computer Vision, Graphics and Image Processing*, 47:203–226, 1989.

[4] E. Milios and E. Petrakis. Shape Retrieval Based on Dynamic Programming. *IEEE Trans. on Image Processing*, 9(1):141–147, 2000.

[5] F. Mokhtarian, S. Abbasi, and J. Kittler. Efficient and Robust Retrieval by Shape Content through Curvature Scale Space. In *Proceedings of Int. Workshop on Image DataBases and MultiMedia Search*, pages 35–42, Amsterdam, The Netherlands, 1996.

[6] Z. Rao, E. Milios, and E. Petrakis. Retrieval of Deformed and Occluded Shapes using Dynamic Programming. TR CS-1999-06, Department of Computer Science, York University, Toronto, 1999. http://www.cs.yorku.ca/techreports/1999/CS-1999-06.html.

[7] K. Siddiqi, A. Shokoufandeh, S. Dickinson, and S. Zucker. Shock Graphs and Shape Matching. *Int. Journal of Computer Vision*, 35(1):13–32, 1999.

[8] N. Ueda and S. Suzuki. Learning Visual Models from Shape Contours Using Multiscale Convex/Concave Structure Matching. *IEEE PAMI*, 15(4):337–352, April 1993.

Fast Tracking of Ellipses using Edge-Projected Integration of Cues

Markus Vincze, Minu Ayromlou, Michael Zillich
Institute of Flexible Automation, Vienna University of Technology
Gusshausstr. 27-29/361, 1040 Vienna, Austria
{vm, ma, mz}@infa.tuwien.ac.at, www.infa.tuwien.ac.at*

Abstract

Commercial applications of ellipse tracking require robustness and real-time capability. The method presented tracks ellipses at field rate using a Pentium PC. Robustness is obtained by integrating gradient and intensity values for the detection of contour edgels and by using a RANSAC-like method to find the most likely ellipse. The method adapts to the appearance along the ellipse circumference and effectively separates object from background. Experiments document the capabilities of the approach with real-world examples.

1. Introduction

Finding and following objects is needed for applications ranging from surveillance over air vehicle guidance to robotics. The objective is to control or follow the motion of an object or mechanism. Commonly the pose of an object is determined from image features such as points, lines and contours. A feature of particular interest is the circle as it provides 5 DOF (degrees of freedom) in one feature (compared to 2 DOF for a line or point feature). This is exploited in applications such as automated landing approaches, part grasping or map building [3, 5, 13].

Any method that tracks a circle or ellipse has to deal with two major problems, robustness and performance. Robust tracking is needed to operate in unconstrained or only slightly constrained environments that are common in industry and service. An example is approaching and grasping objects in a natural, cluttered surrounding. The second requirement on a tracking algorithm is good performance, that is efficient computational execution. The applications impose a stringent time constraint: vision should supply the control signal for the servoing loop as fast as possible to reduce latency. The present limit in data acquisition is field rate, which should be achieved for tracking to obtain best dynamic performance when controlling motion (both egomotion and external motion) [12].

* This work is partly supported by the Austrian Science Foundation (FWF) under grant P13167, EU-project RobVision EP28867 and EU-project FlexPaint GRD1-1999-10693.

In summary, it is necessary to develop an algorithm that robustly detects and tracks an ellipse and that operates at field rate (see review in 1.1). A method is proposed that tracks an ellipse using a bundle of tracker lines that are configured to find the contour of the ellipse relatively to the previous tracking step. Section 2 introduces the concept of the model-based ellipse tracker. Utilising the ellipse model to place the line trackers reduces search time and renders the approach suitable for field time. Robustness is tackled by edge-projected integration of cues (EPIC) to separate the object from the background and by using a RANSAC-like voting scheme. Section 3 demonstrates the capability and the limitation of the approach with real-world experiments.

1.1. Related Work

The most common technique to detect ellipses is the Hough Transform (HT). The HT is fairly robust but needs a five parameter space and is therefore computationally very expensive. Variations of the basic method use multi-step approaches to reduce calculation time, e.g., a modified HT using a 2-dimensional accumulator array [14], the Randomised Hough Transform [10], or selecting only the parameters needed for the application [1]. However, frame rate cannot be obtained with these methods.

Another approach uses the geometric symmetry of ellipses from an edge image [9]. This approach first locates candidates of ellipse and circle centres. In a second step, the geometric symmetry is exploited to extract ellipses. The algorithm works very fast but lacks robustness if ellipses of different sizes are to be detected. The most promising approach for a real-time application is the k-RANSAC algorithm for ellipse detection [2] (based on the RANSAC idea [4]) though presently execution at frame rate is not feasible.

During recent years contour tracking has been demonstrated including a Kalman filter [11], conditional densities [8], or temporal information [6]. These trackers have not been used to track an ellipse. Using these technique shows problems to obtain real-time, a difficulty to assure that an ellipse and not another contour is found, and slow tracking speeds of only a few pixel per image.

1051-4651/00 $10.00 © 2000 IEEE

2. Model-based Ellipse Tracker

The basic idea of the tracking algorithm is the combination of low level one-dimensional image analysis performed on strategically distributed tracker lines with the model of the geometry of ellipses to re-find the contour edge quickly and reliably. Finding edge pixels along a tracker line can be performed at very high rates. Placing a set of tracker lines strategically around the contour of the ellipse requires a fraction of the processing power of area based methods without loosing robustness. To further increase robustness of re-finding the correct ellipse the following two measures are proposed.

- The contour of the ellipse is detected by edge-projected integration of cues (EPIC) to find candidate edgels (edge pixels). EPIC integrates edgels with mode values such as intensity or color.
- A model of the ellipse is utilised to find a probabilistic best fit to the candidate edgels.

The use of different cues for contour detection aids in effectively distinguishing the object from varying background. The model assures that an ellipse shaped object is actually found. With this combination of measures the chance of following a distracting contour is highly reduced. The two measures have been found effective both in terms of robustness and computational costs.

At each tracking cycle the states of the ellipse tracker and the tracker lines are updated. The following processing steps are executed:

```
Place tracker lines along contour        (2.1)
Find edgels on each tracker line         (2.2)
Repeat for the number of trials          (2.3)
  Select 5 edgels & construct an ellipse
  For all edgels
    Determine distance to this ellipse
    If the distance is below a threshold
      Each edgel contributes one vote
  End for
  Store number of votes for this ellipse
End repeat
Select ellipse with highest number of votes
```

The numbers to the right refer to the section that outlines the procedure in more detail. The states of the tracker lines encompass position, orientation, and mode values. The states of the ellipse are the ellipse parameters and the averaged mode values from the tracker lines. An ellipse is determined by five independent parameters in the image, the ellipse centre x and y, the angle of the main axis relative to the image x-axis θ, and the length of the two semi-axes, a and b. Using these parameters the five components of the pose of the circle can be calculated (e.g. [3, 5]).

2.1. Placement of Tracker Lines

The prediction of the expected location of the ellipse in the image can utilise any scheme of prediction, e.g., a Kalman filter. All five ellipse parameters can be predicted as well as the mode values. The primary goal of prediction is to keep track of a fast moving ellipse. The principal configuration of placing lines is depicted in Fig. 1. The number of tracker lines must be larger than 5.

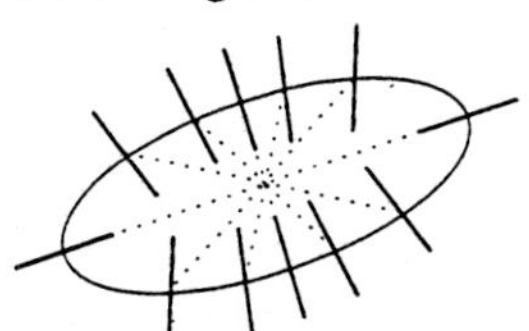

Figure 1. Placing tracker lines with an orientation orthogonal to the contour.

2.2. Robust Edge Detection - EPIC

After placing the tracker lines, edgels on each tracker line are searched for. The likelihood l_j that an edgel is the correct edgel of the ellipse contour is evaluated to

$$l_j = \frac{1}{W} \sum_{i=1}^{n} w_i C_i \quad \text{with } i = 1, 2, 3, 4, \text{ and } W = \sum_{i=1}^{n} w_i, \tag{1}$$

where the w_i are weights for the cues C_i. In the final implementation the following four cues have been found to be most significant. Other cues can be integrated easily, such as strength of gradient (which is not useful since it is likely to find strong background edgels), color or motion.

$$C_1 = \begin{cases} 1 : x_{Mj} > 8 \text{ [pixel values]} \\ 0 : \text{otherwise} \end{cases} \tag{2}$$

$$C_2 = \begin{cases} 1 : max(x_{Mj}) \\ 0 : \text{otherwise} \end{cases} \tag{3}$$

$$C_3 = 1 - (m^t_{left} - m^{t-1}_{left})/255 \tag{4}$$

$$C_4 = 1 - (m^t_{right} - m^{t-1}_{right})/255 \tag{5}$$

The superscripts t and $t-1$ refer to the mode values of the present and previous cycle, respectively. x_{Mj} is the magnitude of the gradient at the location of the edgel.

The functionality of the cues is as follows. C_1 (weight $w_1 = 1$) selects practically all edges above a small threshold. C_3 and C_4 select edgels with similar mode values as the previous edgels. It can be easily seen that identical and similar mode values at cycles t and $t-1$ result in a high contribution to the likelihood.

Cues 1, 3, and 4 select all edgels with good mode values. However, C_1 uses a low threshold to find all edgels. The result is that edgels inside the object are selected, too, as these edgels also have the correct mode values assuming the entire surface of the object has one mode value. An effective means to bias the likelihood of detecting the correct contour edge is cue C_2. C_2 slightly emphasizes the selected of the strongest edge (the weight w_2 is 0.3 compared to 1 for the other weights). The rationale is that the contour edge is likely to be stronger than a hypothetical edge inside the object.

Finally, the edgels with a likelihood higher than a threshold indicate the new location of the ellipse and they are the input to the subsequent voting scheme.

The mode values of the previous tracking cycle m^{t-1} have been determined depending on the success of finding the correct edgel. If the tracker line found a valid edgel, the mode values are inherited from the previous cycle. Otherwise the edgel that lies on the final contour of the ellipse is determined and the mode values for this edgel are calculated and used in the next cycle.

2.3. Voting for Best Ellipse

In the last step of ellipse tracking a model-based voting algorithm is used to find the ellipse from the edgels of the tracker lines (see the repeat loop in the basic description in Section 2). The idea is adopted from the RANSAC methodology introduced by [4]. The principle to find ellipses is given in Section 2.

To assure the robustness of this approach it is necessary to investigate the likelihood of finding the correct ellipse. The basic requirement is to find $n = 5$ "good" edgels, that is, edgels within the error tolerance. The likelihood that an edgel is within the error tolerance is denoted by g. Then the likelihood of selecting five good edgels is g^n. If the procedure of selecting n edgels is repeated k times, the probability to find the correct ellipse, e, is denoted by

$$e = 1 - (1 - g^n)^k. \quad (6)$$

Fig. 2 plots e over k for five values of g. The Figure shows that the likelihood to find the correct ellipse depends most strongly on the likelihood to find good edgels, g. If good points are found in less than 50 or 60% of the edgels, the number of trials required to obtain a 90% likelihood of finding the correct ellipse increases substantially.

This strong dependence on the likelihood to find good edgels is the rationale to employ the elaborate scheme of combining cues in eq. (1). Using gradient information alone would require a very high number of trials k to obtain a similar likelihood to find the correct ellipse. Using EPIC highly increases the likelihood of finding good edgels. In most of our experiments 60, 70, sometimes up to 90 percent of edgels have been found correctly.

The consequence of this analysis is that searching for edgels with EPIC is the prerequisite to effectively apply the probabilistic ellipse finding scheme. The two techniques are designed to be forgiving to outliers. The combination of the two techniques renders a robust technique of ellipse tracking in real-time, that is field time.

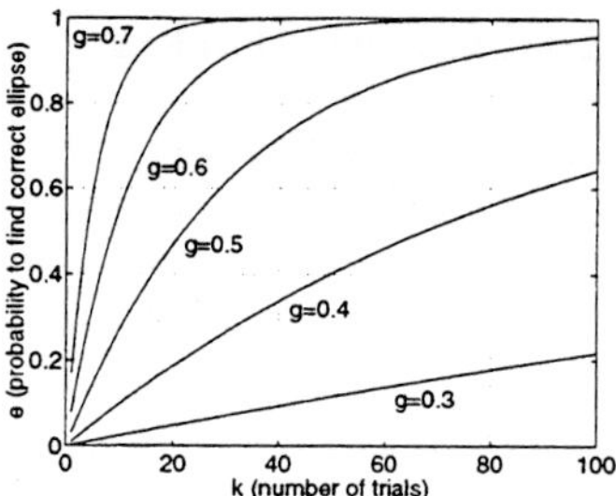

Figure 2. Probability e to find the correct ellipse depending on the number of trials k and the likelihood to find edgels within the error tolerance g.

3. Experiments and Results

The ellipse tracker has been implemented exploiting the efficient vision software *XVision* [7] of the *Vision and Robotics Group* at Yale University. XVision enables the user to access the parts of the image that are needed for the ellipse tracking. This renders the approach faster than obtainig the entire image. Classes have been added for edge finding using cue integration as in eq. (1) and for the ellipse tracker.

The experiments have been performed on a Pentium 350 MHz PC running a Linux operating system. The vision system consists of a Sony EVI-331T camera and an ITI ICPCI AM-CLR frame grabber. In the experiments the fields have been used giving a cycle rate of 50 Hz. The camera is equipped with an auto-focus and an auto-iris. Changes in iris cause a slight sudden change of intensity values. However tracking is robust to these changes.

The time t to track one ellipse is linear in the parameters: the number of tracker lines n placed along the contour of the ellipse, the length of every tracker line l, and the number of trials k. For $k = 30$ trials, using $n = 30$ tracker lines of length $l = 40$ the PC requires $6.2ms$. This allows to track three ellipses at field rate and leaves the time that is needed to calculate the pose from the ellipse parameters.

The capability of the ellipse tracker is now evaluated with real-world experiments. The first experiment compares the new method of finding edgels to common gradient based methods. Fig. 3 shows two images of a sequence of 48 images. Using strength of the gradient edge only, the ellipse tracker is immediately distracted by the floor to wall edge, which has a similar gradient. Fig. 4 shows the same sequence using this time with the cue-integrating scheme to find edgels. Tracking succeeds through the entire sequence.

The second experiment in Fig. 5 shows the adaptation of the tracker lines to the mode values along the ellipse circumference. The reflective material of the ladle changes

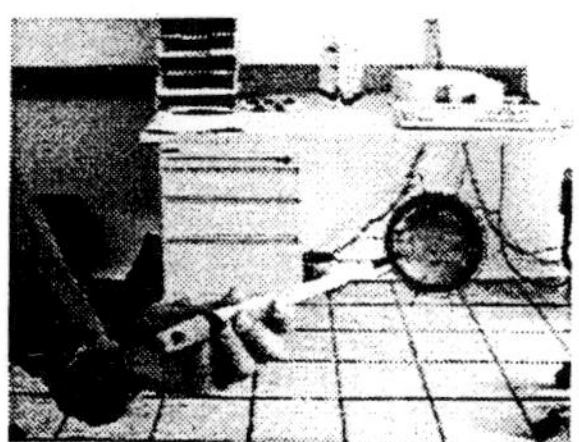
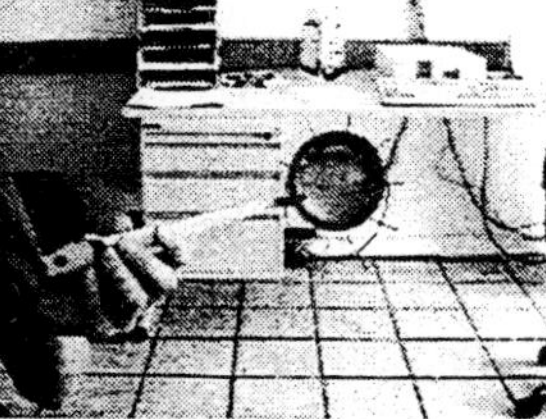

Figure 3. Tracking a ladle in front of an office scene using gradient information alone.

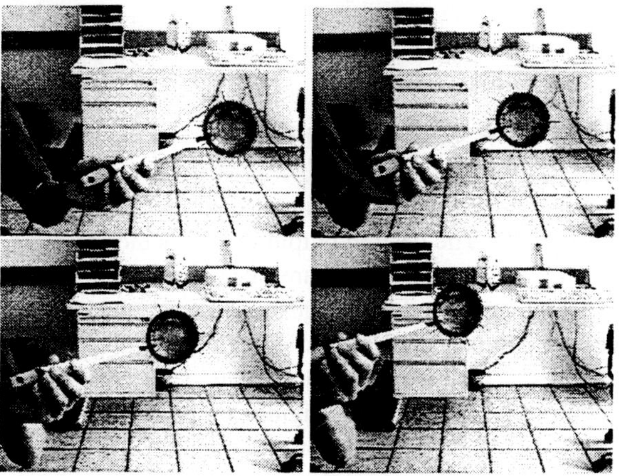

Figure 4. The same sequence as in Fig. 3 using the scheme to integrate gradient and mode cues.

from dark to bright in some areas when moving over the plate. Some of the tracker lines show little contrast between ladle and background. However, tracking continues to find the ellipse.

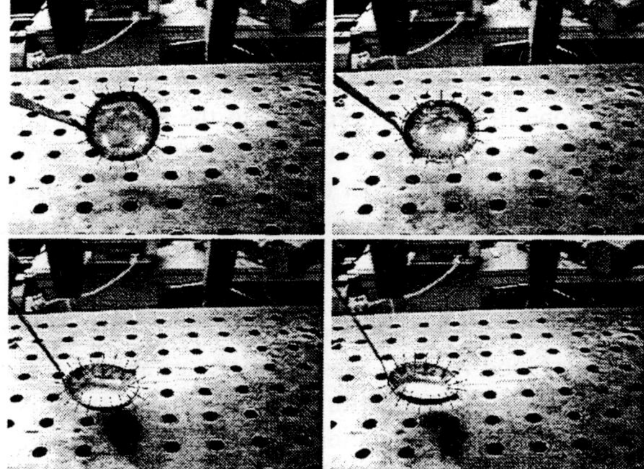

Figure 5. Tracking of a metallic ladle over a metallic plate containing circles.

4. Conclusion

A new concept of rapid and robust ellipse tracking has been introduced. EPIC successfully integrates visual cues to robustly and reliably find the most likely contour edgels of the ellipse. A probabilistic RANSAC-like algorithm then selects the most likely ellipse. With one setting of parameters the method works robust when background varies, when the ellipse surface changes orientation and the reflected intensity varies along the contour, and when size and illumination change the appearance. Besides robustness the algorithm also attains real-time execution on a Pentium PC (6.2 ms). The tracker presented here is capable of following an elliptic object that moves with relatively high speed, compared to using contour trackers based on gradient or energy functions. In each cycle the ellipse can move half the distance of the tracker lines (10 to 20 pixels), which can be nearly as large as the smaller of two semi-axis of the ellipse.

References

[1] Bennett, N., Burridge, R., Saito,N., *A Method to Detect and Characterize Ellipses Using the Hough Transform*, IEEE Transactions on Pattern Analysis and Machine Intelligence 21(7), pp. 652-657, 1999.

[2] Cheng, Y.S., Lee, S.C.: *A new method for quadrative curve detection using K-RANSAC with accelereration techniques*, Pattern Recognition 28(5), pp. 663-682, 1995.

[3] Ferri, M., Mangili, F., Viano, G.: *Projective Pose Estimation of Linear and Quadratic Primitives in Monocular Computer Vision;* CVGIP: Image Understanding 58(1), pp. 66-84, 1993.

[4] Fischler, M.A., Bolles, R.C.: *Random Sample Consensus: A Paradigm for Model Fitting with Applications to Image Analysis and Automated Cartography;* Communications of the ACM 24(6), pp. 381-395, 1981.

[5] Forsyth, D., Mundy, J.L., Zisserman, A., Coelho, C., Heller, A., Rothwell, C.: *Invariant Descriptors for 3-D Object Recognition and Pose;* IEEE PAMI 13(10), pp. 971-991, 1991.

[6] Gee, A.H., Cipolla, R.: *Fast Visual Tracking by Temporal Consensus;* Image and Vision Computing 14(2), pp. 105-114, 1996.

[7] Hager, G., Toyama, K.: *The XVision-System: A Portable Substrate for Real-Time Vision Applications*, Computer Vision and Image Understanding 69(1), pp. 23-37, 1998.

[8] Isard, M., Blake, A.: *Contour tracking by stochastic propagation of conditional density*, Proc. European Conf. Computer Vision, pp. 343-356, 1996.

[9] Lei, Y., Wong, K.C., *Ellipse detection based on symmetry*, Pattern Recognition Letters 20(1), pp. 41-47, 1999.

[10] McLaughlin, R.A., *Randomized Hough transform - improved ellipse detection with comparison*, Pattern Recognition Letters 19(3-4), pp. 299-305, 1998.

[11] Terzopoulous, D., Szeliski, R.: *Tracking with Kalman snakes*, in: A. Blake, A.Yuille, eds., Active Vision, MIT Press, Cambridge, 1992.

[12] Vincze, M., Weiman, C.: *On Optimal Tracking Performance of Visual Servoing*, IEEE ICRA, pp. 2856-2861, 1997.

[13] Wunsch, P., Hirzinger, G.: *Real-Time Visual Tracking of 3D-Objects with Dynamic Handling of Occlusion*, IEEE ICRA, 1997.

[14] Yip, R.K.K., Tam, P.K.S., Leung, D.N.K.: *Modification of Hough transform for circles and ellipse detection using a 2-dimensional array*, Pattern Recognition 25(9), pp. 1007-1022, 1992.

Features detection and navigation on neurovascular trees

Anna Puig
Software Department
Universitat Politècnica de Catalunya
anna@lsi.upc.es

Dani Tost

Isabel Navazo

Abstract

The 3D Reconstruction of the cerebral vascular anatomy can greatly improve the diagnosis of vascular pathologies such as embolysms and haemorrhages. This paper presents a new method for the automatic extraction of the blood vessels surface and the labelling of its features, specifically branching, aneurysms and stenoses. The method works with segmented Magnetic Resonance Angiography images. It extracts a discrete medial axis transform from the stacked images and it vectorizes it. During the vectorization process, the features are detected and labelled automatically. The final output is a labelled continuous medial axis transform representation of the vascular tree suitable for interactive visualizations and navigations, along with 3D geometrical and topological queries.

1. Introduction

MRA (Magnetic Resonance Angiography) is one of the medical imaging techniques most used for the diagnosis of vascular pathologies. It obtains a stack of 2D parallel gray images such that the points corresponding to blood flow are marked with higher intensity values. The analysis of MRA data can be improved by providing a 3D reconstruction of the vascular structure which allows navigations through the vessels and 3D geometrical queries.

Previous attempts to perform this reconstruction are limited to normal vessels: single segments extractions [1] or branching detections [14], [5]. The automatic identification of anomalies of the vascular structure has not been addressed in the bibliography. Specifically, vascular structures present two main anomalies: local diameter growth called aneurysms, and diameter narrowing called stenoses. This paper addresses the automatic detection of these features. It proposes a method for the automatic extraction of the vascular center line and its associated diameters, that identifies and labels regular vessel segments, branching, stenoses and aneuryms.

2. Overview of the method

As mentioned above, the input data are a stack of 2D MRA images. The desired output of the method is a graph model of the vascular structure such that the nodes represent branching and the edges are vessels. Nodes and edges are composed of labeled segments (regular, stenoses or aneurysms) and they are represented by a medial line and the contour cross sections at significant points. This model can be easily polygonalized for visualization purposes.

The method proceeds in three steps:

- Segmentation of the MRA images to obtain a 3D binary voxel model
- Extraction of the Discrete Medial Axis Transform (DMAT) of the 3D discrete model
- Vectorization of the DMAT and automatic identification of the features.

MRA images present low error signal and heterogeneity in the intensity. Therefore, the former step, segmentation, must be done in a process previous to the reconstruction. In [3] the Phase-Contrast segmentation is performed during the acquisition stage in order to isolate the vascular structure from the stationary tissue. In most cases however, the segmentation is performed on the images, after their capture.

Several authors have developed segmentation algorithms suitable for blood vessels. These methods are able to detect narrow tubular structures with low contrast and small objects causing signal attenuation. They manage low noise signals and heterogeneity in the intensity taking into account the photometric properties of the data ([3]), the shape of the blood vessels ([5]) and the continuity of the vascular map ([12]). Any of these methods is suitable for the proposed strategy.

The main contribution of this work are the two latter steps. They can be performed simultaneously in a single pass using a seed strategy. However, for clarity, they are next exposed separately.

1051-4651/00 $10.00

3. Medial Axis Transform extraction

There are three main approaches for discrete objects skeletonization:

- Thinning [6]
- Morphological methods [7]
- Distance-Map based methods [4]

The two former methods compute medial lines that are connected but which do not always reflect the topological features of the objects. The latter approach extends to the discrete case the definition of the Medial Axis Transform (MAT) of analogical objects [2]. It defines the skeleton of a discrete object as the set of pixels which are centers of maximum-sized discrete disks fitted into the object. This skeleton shares with the continuous one the property of being a complete representation scheme of the object, i.e. it reflects all its features. It is therefore the most suitable approach for the purpose of features identification.

A major drawback of the Discrete Medial Axis Transform (DMAT) is that, by opposite to the continuous MAT, which is path-connected for path-connected objects, the DMAT is not connected in general. The preservation of the connectivity is essential to keep up the characteristics of the object boundary. In addition, it allows to apply pattern recognition algorithms directly on the skeleton rather than on the object. Several extensions of the basic definition have been proposed in 2D [11], [8] in order to grant the connectivity of the DMAT by adding to the maximum disk centers a suitable set of connecting pixels. These approaches try to identify saddle points, i.e. pixels whose neighborhood contains alternative humps and valleys. These saddle pixels conveniently linked with neighbours constitute the set of connecting pixels. These methods require at least two pass in the images.

In this work, a different method has been followed: the connecting pixels have been defined on the basis of specific tangency properties which guarantee that the reconstruction error is kept under a given threshold. Specifically, the computed DMAT must fulfill that, if the object is vectorized according to a given metrics and its MAT is computed, then the discretization of this MAT is the same set of pixels as the original DMAT. This requirement grants the reversibility of the method and its provides control on the reconstruction error. It is based on the Euclidean metrics.

A complete description of this DMAT and the demonstration of its properties can be found in [10]. It is next described in a more intuitive way. Figure 1.a shows the MAT of a key-shaped 2D object. Figure 1.b depicts its discretization with black pixels and the set of maximal disks centers with white pixels inside the object. This set is disconnected. Comparing the two pictures, it becomes clear that this is because the discretization of the radii and of the disk centers produces disjoint maximal continuous disks to be rasterized as non-maximal disks, i.e. disks included into other ones. The new definition of the DMAT is based on the characterization of these non-maximal disks centers.

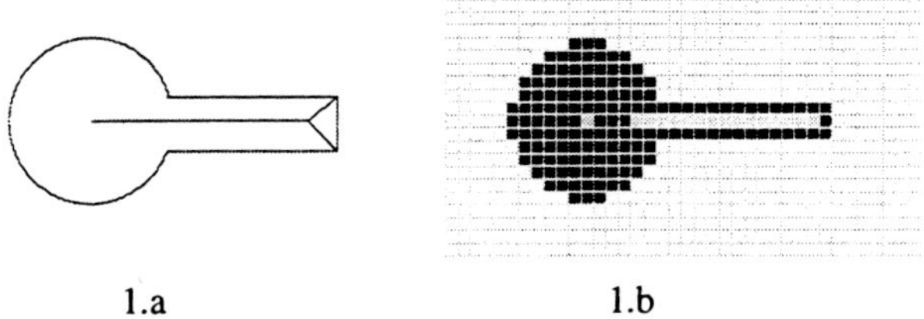

Figure 1. MAT and DMAT of a key-shaped 2D object.

Let define the *Door Set* of a disk D_{ij} fitted into an object O, the set of pixels which are inside the object and outside the disk but which have an 8-neighbour inside the disk. Figure 2 shows in the key-shaped example a maximal disk that occupies all the left part of the key. The white pixels at the right boundary of the disk are its door set. As its name indicates, the door set constitutes a "door" from the disk to the remaining of the object. End-points have only one door set, whereas, in general, normal maximal disks have two opposite door sets. Given a maximal disk, the door sets of any of its subdisk are mostly pixels internal to it. However, some subdisks may have door pixels in the door set of the disk. Figure 3 shows an example of this case: the door set of a subdisk of the maximal disk depicted in Figure 2 is outlined with white pixels. The left part of this door set belongs to the maximal disk, whereas its right part shares pixels of the maximal disk's door.

The non-maximal disks that share their door set with the maximal disk to which they belong are precisely the disks which would maximal in a continuous object. Therefore, the centers of these subdisks constitute the set of connecting pixels between maximal disks centers. It is proved in [10] that this set is connected and that it fulfills the reversibility property mentioned above.

An advantage of this definition is that the characterization of the connecting pixels is local, similarly to the maximal disks centers detection. Therefore, thanks to the connectivity of the set, a seed strategy can be used to compute the complete DMAT.

This method has been implemented and tested both in 2D and 3D with sets of synthetic images of different sizes and with different objects. Results show that the occupancy of the objects in the images strongly determines the time processing. The run time is linear in relation to the size of the axis (complexity of the object). Therefore, it works bet-

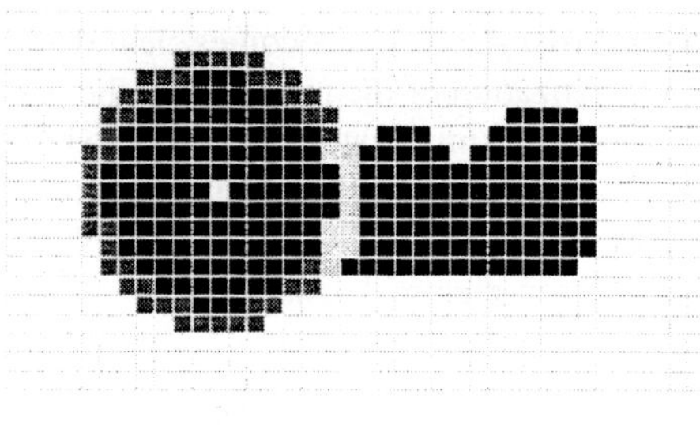

Figure 2. Door Set of a maximal disk.

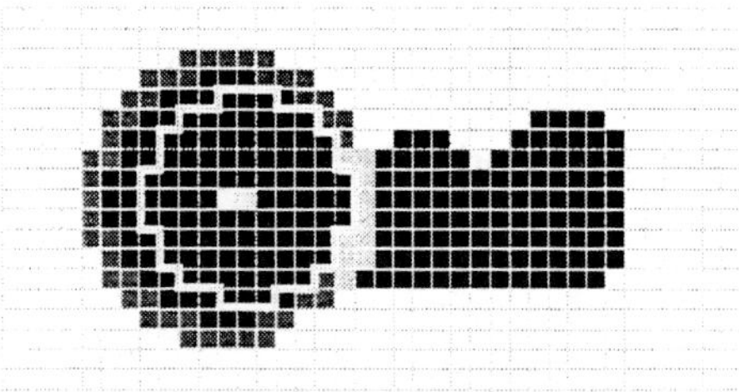

Figure 3. A maximal disk and a non-maximal disk that share their door sets.

ter on thinned objects or on objects whose radius is low in relation to the image/volume size. In particular, the DMAT extraction cost of a MRA data set of $128 \times 128 \times 60$ is about 16 minutes.

4. Features detection

Following the formulation of [13] and extending it to the discrete case, the pixels/voxels of the DMAT are classified into six different sets. These sets can be related with the labelling of the vascular features.

Specifically, the DMAT set can be decomposed into sets of *waves*, i.e. connected sets of voxels that are either *linear*, *surface-shaped* or *volume-shaped* depending on their width along the axis direction. In regular cylindrical sections, the DMAT is linear. Surface and volume waves indicate branching and vascular accidents.

The taxonomy of the DMAT voxels depends on the wave to which they belong and the adjacency with other waves. Concretely,

- CI voxels belong to inner waves of linear sets
- SI voxels belong to inner waves of surface sets
- VI voxels belong to inner waves of volume sets
- CII voxels correspond to end-lines: they belong to linear waves and are adjacent to voxels belonging to waves of different direction.
- SII voxels correspond to end surface: they belong to a surface wave adjacent to a wave of a different set
- Accordingly, VII voxels are end volumes: they belong to a volume wave adjacent to a wave of a different set.

Figure 4 shows an example of this taxonomy. The medial axis is the set of represented segments and surface components. The vertices are labeled as CII, PII or SII voxels depending on if they are at the junction of curves, curves and surfaces or surfaces. CI and SI refers to the voxels on curves and surfaces respectively. The formal definition of this taxonomy can be found in [9] The labelling algorithm is based on this classification. It is based on a seed strategy that begins with a voxel of the DMAT and a main direction associated to this voxel. The algorithm analyzes the projections of the voxel wave onto the coordinate planes, and from this it classifies the voxel into one of the six sets. The wave is taken as an input for next step of the algorithm.

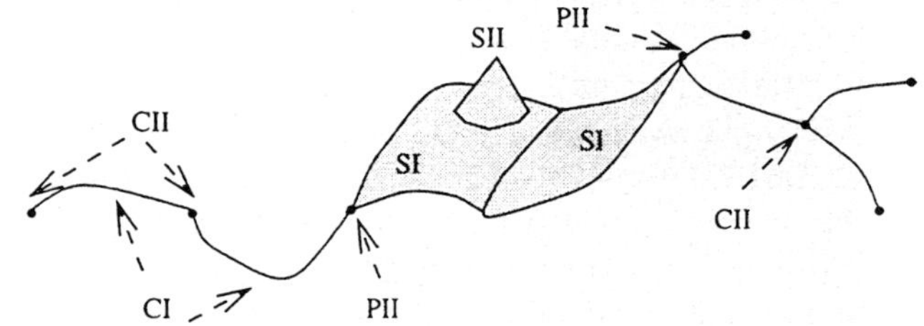

Figure 4. Taxonomy of the medial axis sets.

This classification splits the DMAT into CI (linear), SI (surface) and VI (volume) segments ended with voxels typified as CII, SII and VII. Linear sets correspond to regular segments. Surface sets appear in branching of the medial axis, i.e. real branching of the vessels or vascular accidents. Finally, volume sets correspond to complex real branching between more than two vessels. Concretely, these segments are labelled as follows:

- Normal features are CI sets connected with CII or SII voxels. A connection between CI sets indicates a change of direction of the axis. This connection is normally done by CII sets but double rasterizations can also produce SII voxels at the junction.
- Real branching of the vessels between two or more vessels are a set of connected CII, SII and SI voxels that join more than two linear sets of the DMAT as well as SII, VII and VI voxels that join a surface set with two or more other sets.
- A non-normal segment is a set of SI voxels connected by SII or VII voxels. These non-normal segments are aneurysms and stenoses. They are distinguished one from another depending on the diameters relation.

This labelling strategy is fast and, in general, accurate. However, it should be noted that small branches can be confused with aneurysms, as the two features give CI voxels joined by SI and SII sets. The distinction between the two cases is based on a metrics provided by physicians which can be tunned on demand. Similarly, symmetrical aneuryms or stenoses would not be directly detected as they would not produce a branching in the axis. However, according to physicians, this symmetric cases are very rare.

The feature identification of a MRA data set of $128 \times 128 \times 60$ adds an overhead of 2-3 minutes to the DMAT algorithm. Figure 5 shows an MRA 3D volume set. Each feature is drawn with a different color. The boxes that enclose the features of the model are drawn with the same colors.

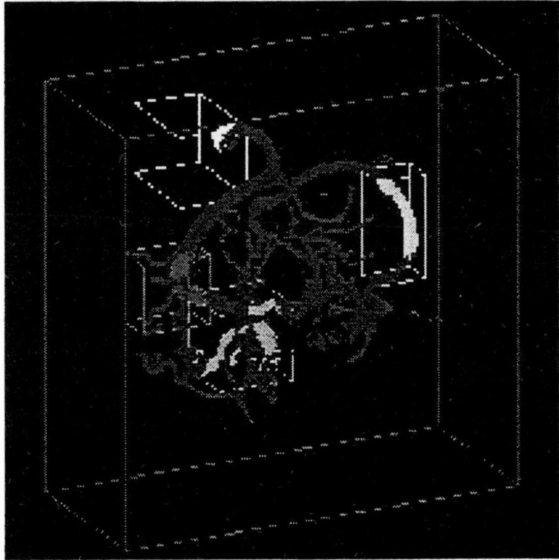

Figure 5. Vessels identification of a MRA data set.

5. Conclusion

A new method for the extraction and automatic labelling of the cerebral vascular structure has been presented. It works on MRA segmented images and it computes a connected discrete medial axis transform of the vessels. The voxels of the medial axis are classified into several sets according to their neighbourhood and to the type of surface element that they represent. This taxonomy provides a natural way to characterize the segments of the medial axis as normal segments, branching, aneurysms and stenoses. Comparing to previous methods, this classification is wider and it allows identifying the vascular accidents. The characterization and the vectorization of the axis, provide the desired representation. The strategy has been tested with real and phantom data. It has proved to be suitable for blood vessels, giving accurate results at a reasonable cost because of the low occupancy and the elongated nature of the vessels. Other possible applications of the method are the extraction and labelling of other objects with similar shape, such as intestines from medical images and rivers or roads from digital pictures.

References

[1] C. Barillot, B. Gibaud, J. Scarabin, and J. Coatrieux. 3d reconstruction of cerebral blood vessels. *IEEE Computer Graphics and Applications*, 5(12):13–19, December 1985.

[2] H. Blum. A transformation for extracting new descriptors of shape. *Models for the Perception of Speech and Visual Form. MIT Press, Cambridge, Mass.*, pages 362–380, 1967.

[3] H. Cline, W. Lorensen, R. Kikinis, and F. Jolesz. Three-dimensional segmentation of mr images of the head using probability and connectivity. *Journal of Computer Assisted Tomography*, 14(6):1037–1045, November/December 1990.

[4] P. Danielsson. Euclidean distance mapping. *Computer Graphics and Image Processing*, 14:227–248, 1980.

[5] H. Ehricke, K. Donner, W. Koller, and W. Straber. Visualization of vasculature from volume data. *Computer and Graphics*, 18(3):395–406, 1994.

[6] T. Lee, R. Kashyap, and C. Chu. Building skeleton models via 3-d medial surface/axis thinning algorithms. *CVGIP: Graphical Models and Image Processing*, 56(6):462–478, November 1994.

[7] Y. Masutani, K. Masamune, and T. Dohi. Region-growing based feature extraction algorithm for tree-like objects. *Proceedings of 4th International Conference Visualization in Biomedical Computing, Hamburg, Germany*, pages 161–171, September 1996.

[8] C. Niblack, P. Gibbons, and D. Capson. Generating skeletons and centerlines from the distance transform. *CVGIP: Graphical Models and Image Processing*, 5:420–437, September 1992.

[9] A. Puig. *Contribution to Volume Modeling and to Volume Visualization.* PhD thesis, Software Department, Universitat Politecnica de Catalunya, Barcelona, Spain, October 1998.

[10] A. Puig. Discrete medial axis transform for discrete thin objects and elongated objects. *Report LSI-99-48-R, Polytechnical University of Catalunya, Spain*, 1999.

[11] G. Sanniti and E. Thiel. Skeletonization algorithms on path-based distance maps. *Image and Vision Computing*, 14:47–57, 1996.

[12] R. Verbeeck, D. Vandermeulen, J. Michiels, P. Suetens, G. Marchal, J. Gybels, and B. Nuttin. Computer assited stereotactic neurosurgery. *Image and Vision Computing Volume*, pages 468–485, October 1993.

[13] P. Vermeer. Medial axis transform to boundary representation conversion. *PhD Thesis, Purdue University*, May 1994.

[14] C. Zahlten, H. Jurgens, and H. Peitgen. Reconstruction of branching blood vessels from ct-data. *Proceedins of Rostock*, 1994.

Segmentation of bone tumor in MR perfusion images using neural networks and multiscale pharmacokinetic features

M. Egmont-Petersen, A.F. Frangi , W.J. Niessen,
P.C.W. Hogendoorn, J.L. Bloem, M.A. Viergever J.H.C. Reiber*

Abstract

The decrease in the volume of viable tumor is an indicator for the effect preoperative chemotherapy has on bone tumors. We develop an approach for segmenting dynamic perfusion MR-images into viable tumor, nonviable tumor and healthy tissue. Two cascaded feed-forward neural networks are trained to perform the pixel-based segmentation. As features, we use parameters obtained from a pharmacokinetic model of the tissue perfusion (parametric images). Additional multiscale features that incorporate contextual information are included. Experiments indicate that multiscale blurred versions of the parametric images together with a multiscale formulation of the local image entropy are the most discriminative features.

1. Introduction

Segmentation of bone tumor leading to a distinction between viable and non-viable tumor tissue is required for the ongoing assessment of chemotherapy. In general, malignant tumors are highly vascularized tissues because of a high density of small blood vessels. Therefore, a distinction between viable and non-viable tumor can only be performed by dynamic Magnetic Resonance (MR) perfusion imaging using an intravenous contrast tracer [9]. We present a feature-based neural network approach for segmentation of dynamic MR-images. Dynamic features are obtained from parametric images that are generated with a pharmacokinetic model of the tissue perfusion. Furthermore, we use concepts of the linear scale-space [5] to incorporate contextual (spatial) information at several scales into the neural classifier. The true class label of each pixel in the training and test sets is obtained from post-operative histological studies (our gold standard).

*M. Egmont-Petersen, J.L. Bloem and J.H.C. Reiber are with the Department of Radiology, (P.C.W. Hogendoorn, Dept. of Pathology), Leiden University Medical Center, Leiden, The Netherlands; A.F. Frangi, W.J. Niessen and M.A. Viergever are with the Image Sciences Institute, University Medical Center Utrecht, Utrecht, The Netherlands.
Corresponding author: M. Egmont-Petersen (michael@lkeb.azl.nl)

2. Features

Our starting point is an MR-image sequence, $s(x, y; t)$, that characterizes the perfusion properties of each pixel, i.e., the up-take and secretion of a blood tracer over time.

2.1. Pharmacokinetic features

The exchange of tracer (blood) between the blood compartment (vessels) and the extracellular water compartment can be characterized by a two-compartment pharmacokinetic model with three basic parameters: wash-in rate m_1, wash-out rate m_2, and the maximal enhancement a. The concentrations of tracer in the blood and extracellular compartments, C_b and C_e, are given by the following differential equations:

$$V_b \frac{dC_b}{dt} = -k_1(C_b - C_e) - k_2 C_b \quad (1)$$

$$V_e \frac{dC_e}{dt} = k_1(C_b - C_e) \quad (2)$$

For the extracellular (tumor) compartment, these differential equations have the following solution [3, 8].

$$C_e \propto s_0(x, y) + a\left(e^{-m_2 t} - e^{-m_1 t}\right) + \epsilon(x, y) \quad (3)$$

with a the maximal signal amplitude and $s_0(x, y) = s(x, y; 0)$ the signal intensity before tracer has arrived. The model parameters can be fitted to the dynamic MR-signal of each pixel (x, y) by minimizing the residual error, $\epsilon(x, y)$, using non-linear regression (Levenberg Marquardt algorithm). A *parametric image*, e.g. $m_1(\mathbf{x})$, is defined as the set of values of a particular perfusion parameter (m_1) corresponding to each pixel in an MR-section.

2.2. Multi-scale spatial features

The parametric images are computed on a pixel-by-pixel basis. To incorporate spatial relations into the segmentation, we suggest to look at the parametric images at multiple scales within the framework of the Gaussian scale-space [4, 5]. Let $I(\mathbf{x})$ represent the intensity function in a certain neighborhood of a point $\mathbf{x}_o$ by means of its Taylor expansion (a second-order approximation)

1051-4651/00 $10.00 © 2000 IEEE

$$\mathcal{I}_\sigma(\mathbf{x}_o + \delta\mathbf{x}) \approx \mathcal{I}_\sigma(\mathbf{x}_o) + \delta\mathbf{x}^T \nabla\mathcal{I}_\sigma(\mathbf{x}_o) + \delta\mathbf{x}^T \mathcal{H}_\sigma(\mathbf{x}_o)\,\delta\mathbf{x} \quad (4)$$

where $\mathcal{I}_\sigma(\mathbf{x})$, $\nabla\mathcal{I}_\sigma(\mathbf{x})$, and $\mathcal{H}_\sigma(\mathbf{x})$ are the blurred versions of $I(\mathbf{x})$, its gradient vector and the Hessian matrix. Blurring is performed using an n-D Gaussian kernel

$$\mathcal{I}_\sigma(\mathbf{x}) = I(\mathbf{x}) * G(\mathbf{x};\sigma) \quad (5)$$

$$G(\mathbf{x};\sigma) = \frac{1}{\sqrt{2\pi\sigma^2}^{\,n}}\, e^{-\frac{\|\mathbf{x}\|^2}{2\sigma^2}} \quad (6)$$

The first- and second-order derivatives of $I(\mathbf{x})$, can be obtained by a convolution with the first- or second-order derivative of the Gaussian kernel (regularized operators). The maximal enhancement parametric image, $a(\mathbf{x})$, is the one providing the richest anatomical information. Consequently, a second-order expansion is used to represent this image. To obtain an invariant measure of first- and second-order structure, we consider the norm of the gradient (edgeness) and the eigenvalues of the Hessian matrix (curvature). A zero-th order expansion (solely blurring the images) is used for the wash-in and wash-out images.

In order to incorporate *textural* information from the maximal enhancement parametric image, we computed the entropy of the local image histogram as follows

$$H_a(\mathbf{x},\sigma) = -\sum_{k=0}^{G-1} P(k)\log_2[P(k)]|_{\mathcal{N}(\mathbf{x},\sigma)} \quad (7)$$

with $P(k)$ the probability that a pixel value occurs in the k-th histogram bin. The local histogram (discretized into 64 bins) is computed at a given scale σ, using a version of the image that is blurred with a Gaussian kernel of that scale. The window size from which the entropy is computed, is coupled to the scale parameter by $\mathtt{width}(\mathcal{N}(\mathbf{x},\sigma)) = \lceil 2\sigma \rceil + 1$, where $\lceil\cdot\rceil$ denotes the integer ceiling operation.

In summary, our feature vector includes seven components at each scale σ:

$$\vec{\mathbf{f}}_\sigma = [a_\sigma, m_{1,\sigma}, m_{2,\sigma}, g_\sigma, \lambda_\sigma^0, \lambda_\sigma^1, h_\sigma] \quad (8)$$

where a_σ, $m_{1,\sigma}$, and $m_{2,\sigma}$ are the intensities of the blurred parametric images, g_σ, is the norm of the gradient of a_σ, and $|\lambda_\sigma^0| \leq |\lambda_\sigma^1|$ are the two eigenvalues of the Hessian matrix of a_σ, and h_σ is the entropy of a_σ.

3. Tissue classification using neural networks

3.1. Choice of classifier

A large variety of statistical classifiers such as the linear discriminant, k-nearest neighbor and neural networks could be trained to segment the dynamic MR-images. A theoretical comparison of statistical classifiers along several criteria in [2] indicated that when a nonlinear classifier is required that has a small error rate and is fast in application, a feed-forward neural network is a good choice (for a discussion see [2]).

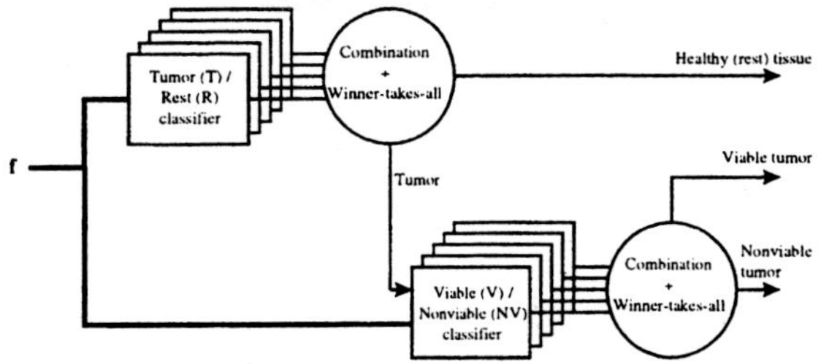

Figure 1. Overview of the cascade classifier with five combined classifiers for each stage. After the parallel classifiers are combined with the mean rule, a winner-takes-all decision is made at each stage.

To obtain a good performance in spite of the uneven prior (class) distribution, we developed a cascaded classifier scheme. The segmentation of the dynamic MR-images is performed by two cascaded feed-forward neural networks. The first stage (TR classifier) has been trained to classify individual pixels into healthy tissue (+background) or tumor; a subsequent stage (VNV classifier) classifies pixels labeled as tumor into viable and non-viable.

3.2. Feature selection

One way of getting some insight into the properties of a (black-box) neural network is by feature selection [2]. The goal we pursued was to study the decrease in performance when computing (all) features at particular scales, and when *groups* of features are removed from the classifier. We divided the features into three categories: dynamic features ($A = \{a_\sigma, m_{1,\sigma}, m_{2,\sigma}\}$), differential features ($D = \{g_\sigma, \lambda_\sigma^0, \lambda_\sigma^1\}$), and entropy ($E = \{h_\sigma\}$).

It has been experimentally shown that neural networks are insensitive to peaking [6] so including less informative features should not deteriorate their performance. Consequently, we may perform feature selection according to a backward search by removing groups of features.

4. Experiments

4.1. Performance assessment

Performance assessment is based on the quality measures correctness, ρ, and the kappa statistic, κ [1] (both computed from a contingency table).

4.2. Image material

Each patient had been treated with chemotherapy and underwent surgery a few days after performing the MR perfu-

Figure 2. Segmentation results. *Up*) **pre-contrast image,** *center*) **histological mask, and** *bottom*) **neural network segmentation.**

sion study (Gd-DTPA was used as contrast tracer). For each MR-section, 47 to 60 dynamic images were acquired with a temporal resolution of 3.3 sec.

Histological analysis resulted in a so-called macro-slice of which the position and orientation corresponded with that of the MR-section. The histologic macro slice is the gold standard (mask) that indicates the correct class label of all pixels in the image section under study (Fig. 2, center).

4.3. Image preprocessing

After the computation of the parametric images and the scale-space features, all features had to be normalized. The amplitude of MR-signals has no absolute value so a robust normalization scheme is required. We experimented with the 95-th percentile of the histogram computed from the amplitude parametric images $a(\mathbf{x})$ (The wash-in and wash-out parameters are independent of intensity rescalings). For each feature, f_i, the mean, $\overline{f}_i$, and standard deviation, SD_{f_i}, of that feature was computed for the tumor class (viable and non-viable tumor were pooled together) in the training set. Each feature, $\mathbf{f}$, was normalized according to: $f_i^n = (f_i - \overline{f}_i)/SD_{f_i}$.

In our experiments, we have used four scales σ: 1 mm, 2 mm, 4 mm and 6 mm (resulting in 28 features). The smallest scale is of the order of the *inner scale* or pixel size in the original images.

4.4. Training feed-forward neural network classifiers for scale selection

Images corresponding to five patients were used to generate independent training and test sets. A total of 10000 patterns (pixels) were selected randomly from the five patients, another 10000 patterns were kept for testing purposes.

After random initialization of the weights, the training of all neural networks was performed by the Scaled Conjugate Gradient algorithm. Each network was trained until either the relative change of the MSE was smaller than 0.1% over the last 100 epochs, or 5000 epochs was reached.

In a pilot experiment, we experimented with all 28 features and network topologies ranging from 1 to 96 nodes in the hidden layer. On a test set, the TR networks with 8 hidden nodes gave a good trade-off between complexity and performance. For the VNV networks, a topology with 48 hidden nodes was chosen. *Bagging* [7] was used to rule out the influence of different initial weight configurations. The output vector of the five classifiers was combined according to the mean rule. Final decision on the class label is made by applying the winner-takes-all rule on the combined output vector.

We investigated the effect of computing the spatial features at different scales on classifier performance. Different subsets of features were composed by varying the scale in $\vec{\mathbf{f}}_\sigma$. For each stage of the cascade (TR and VNV classifiers), five neural networks with equal topology were trained per experiment (Both were trained independently using each subset of scaled features).

The results from the experiment indicate that the first classifier (TR) reaches the best performance when features at the scales 2+4 mm are used (evaluated using the kappa statistic, see Table 1). The second classifier (VNV) gave the best results on the test set when all scales were included.

4.5. Assessing the contribution of different feature groups

In order to obtain a better understanding of the discriminative power of our features, we experimented with removing groups of features from the classifiers. We subdivided the features in three groups: dynamic A, differential D and entropy E (see Section 3.2). Neural networks were trained with combinations of these subsets.

Table 2 shows the results of the experiments with subsets of features. For both stages (TR and VNV), most of the discriminative power is provided by the sub-set A (pharmacokinetic parameters at multiple scales). In the TR stage, addition of textural information (E) improves the classification. Therefore, the optimal classifier will contain a first stage using the sets A and E, and a second stage with only dynamic features (A).

5. Conclusion

In this paper, we have presented a multi-scale feature-based neural network classifier for automatic segmentation of MR perfusion images of bone tumor. It classifies each

Table 1. Multi-scale versus single-scale features for the TR and VNV classifiers.

		Scales							
		1 mm	2 mm	4 mm	6 mm	1+2 mm	1+4 mm	2+4 mm	All
TR	κ	0.859	0.909	0.929	0.907	0.914	0.941	0.956	**0.935**
	ρ	0.947	0.966	0.973	0.965	0.968	0.978	0.984	**0.975**
VNV	κ	0.403	0.530	0.531	0.493	0.554	0.594	0.563	**0.612**
	ρ	0.864	0.891	0.897	0.888	0.898	0.905	0.901	**0.911**

Table 2. Discriminative power of different feature groups: blurred amplitude of maximal enhancement, and wash-in/out parametric images (A), norm of gradient and Hessian eigenvalues of maximal enhancement image (D), and entropy of maximal enhancement image (E).

		Groups of Features						
		A	D	E	A+D	A+E	D+E	A+D+E
TR-Mean	κ	0.934	0.757	0.664	0.938	**0.953**	0.842	0.935
	ρ	0.975	0.911	0.876	0.977	**0.982**	0.940	0.975
VNV-Mean	κ	**0.648**	0.465	0.189	0.574	0.599	0.520	0.612
	ρ	**0.916**	0.877	0.832	0.904	0.907	0.891	0.911

pixel as either viable, non-viable or "rest" (healthy + background) tissue.

The experimental results indicate that neural networks are suitable for combining several types of information, in our case dynamic and spatial properties of tissue perfusion. Using feature selection, one is able to:

- investigate at which scales the features have the highest discriminative power
- identify the best (sub)set of features for a particular application at hand

However, feature selection is impeded by the peaking phenomenon, which was observed in our backward search selection procedure. Consequently, earlier results indicating that feed-forward neural networks should be insensitive to peaking [6] could not be confirmed. Comparable experiments with other nonparametric classifiers (e.g. support vector machines) should be performed.

A thorough clinical evaluation is still required to establish the accuracy of the viable tumor area estimates, the parameter of clinical relevance. Inclusion of more patients will allow us to assess the imprecision of the estimated tumor area.

6. Acknowledgments

This project was financially supported by the Dutch Cancer Foundation (KWF), Grant RUL 97-1509 and by the Dutch Ministry of Economic Affairs, IOP Beeldverwerking Grant IBV-97009.

References

[1] Egmont-Petersen M, Talmon J, Brender J and McNair. P, On the quality of neural net classifiers, *Artif Intel Med* 6(5) (1994) 359–381.

[2] Egmont-Petersen M and Pelikan E, Detection of bone tumours in radiographic images using neural networks, *Pattern Anal & Appl* 2(2) (1999) 172–183.

[3] Egmont-Petersen M, Hogendoorn P C W, van der Geest R, Vrooman H A, van der Woude H-J, Janssen J P, Bloem J L and Reiber J H C, Detection of areas with viable remnant tumor in postchemotherapy patients with Ewing's sarcoma by dynamic contrast-enhanced MRI using pharmacokinetic modeling, *Mag Res Img* (2000, in press).

[4] Florack L M J, ter Haar Romeny B M, Koenderink J J and Viergever M A, Scale and the differential structure of images, *Imag Vis Comp* 10(6) (1992) 376–388.

[5] Florack L M J, ter Haar Romeny B M, Koenderink J J and Viergever M A, Linear scale-space, *Journal of Mathematical Imaging and Vision* 4(4) (1994) 325–351.

[6] Hamamoto Y, Uchimura S and Tomita S, On the Behavior of Artificial Neural Network Classifiers in High-Dimensional Spaces, *IEEE Trans Pattern Anal and Machine Intell*, 18(5) (1996), 571–574.

[7] Kittler J, Hatef M, Duin R and Matas J, On combining classifiers, *IEEE Trans Pattern Anal Machine Intell* 20(3) (1998) 226–239.

[8] Tofts P S and Kermode A G, Measurement of the blood-brain barrier permeability and leakage space using dynamic MR imaging. 1. Fundamental concepts, *Magn Res Med* 17(2) (1991) 357–367.

[9] van der Woude H, Bloem J, Verstraete K, Taminiau A, Nooy M and Hogendoorn P, Osteosarcoma and ewing's sarcoma after neoadjuvant chemotherapy: value of dynamic mr imaging in detecting viable tumor before surgery, *Am J Roentgenol* 165(3) (1995) 593–598.

Segmenting at higher scales to classify at lower scales. A mathematical morphology based methodology applied to forest cover remote sensing images

Teresa Barata, Pedro Pina, Isabel Granado
CVRM / Centro de Geo-Sistemas, Instituto Superior Técnico
Av. Rovisco Pais, 1049-001 Lisboa, Portugal
{tbarata, ppina, igranado}@alfa.ist.utl.pt

Abstract

A methodology based on mathematical morphology to classify forest cover types in remote sensing images is presented. The information automatically extracted at higher scales (aerial photographs) by morphological segmentation approaches is afterwards used to classify different forest cover types at lower scales (satellite images). In this methodology the spectral process is guided by the spatial process, once the previous segmentation of the different textural elements is then used in the classification procedure, where the geometrical modelling of the shape of the training sets of points is also performed. Tests were done in a region of centre Portugal using aerial photographs and Landsat TM images for olive, corkoak, pine and eucalyptus trees.

1. Introduction

The objective of the segmentation/classification procedures is the discrimination of the different classes by assigning each spatial elementary unit to the most appropriated class, according to some criteria of similarity (classification) or by the definition of homogeneous zones also according to some criteria (segmentation). However, most of the methods fail to model the geometry of the training sets when they present irregular and complex shapes [6], being the imposition of regular patterns to the training classes a not always good strategy. Mathematical morphology [11], the theory mainly concerned with the analysis of images that appeals to topological and geometrical concepts and functionals, seems well adequate to be used in this context. But paradoxically, although well suited, not only to deal with irregular and complex shapes but also to segment complex images, its application in multivariate images has been quite rare ([12] [13] are the main exceptions). Moreover, forest resources are an application field where the need of improvements is as demanding as appealing, particularly in automatic cartographic updating.

2. Proposed methodology: the spatial process guides the spectral process

The key idea under the developed methodology is to perform an automatic segmentation of the several forest cover types at a higher scale (aerial photographs or orthophotomaps) where the detail allows to identify, among others, the trees individually, and then to use these markers at lower scales like the satellite one, to automatically constitute the training sets of points to the classification procedures. Moreover, at the characteristics or features space, the modelling of irregular and complex shapes of these training sets is also envisaged. The scheme of the proposed methodology is presented in figure 1.

2.1. Segmentation at higher scales

Each vegetation or forest cover type must be previously selected to be segmented. Due to the high textural variety presented by each forest cover type individual approaches are developed. In the following, the approaches used for olive, corkoak and pine+eucalyptus trees are presented.

The olive tree areas are characterised by presenting darker regular patterns on a whiter background (figure 1a). The segmentation of this forest type starts with a kind of isotropic top-hat to segment only small, dark and isotropic objects (the olive trees) leaving outside this set, the dark and thin structures (roads, water lines, etc.). This transform was originally used to segment small black spots in human retina [4]. Once the olive trees exhibit a regular pattern, the filtering of non-olive trees can be done by grouping the olive trees by a closing with a size corresponding to the distance between the trees in the pattern, creating strong clusters that resist to erosion-reconstruction filters, being the final result of the segmented olive trees obtained by the intersection of this image with the one resulting from the top-hat (figure 2b).

1051-4651/00 $10.00

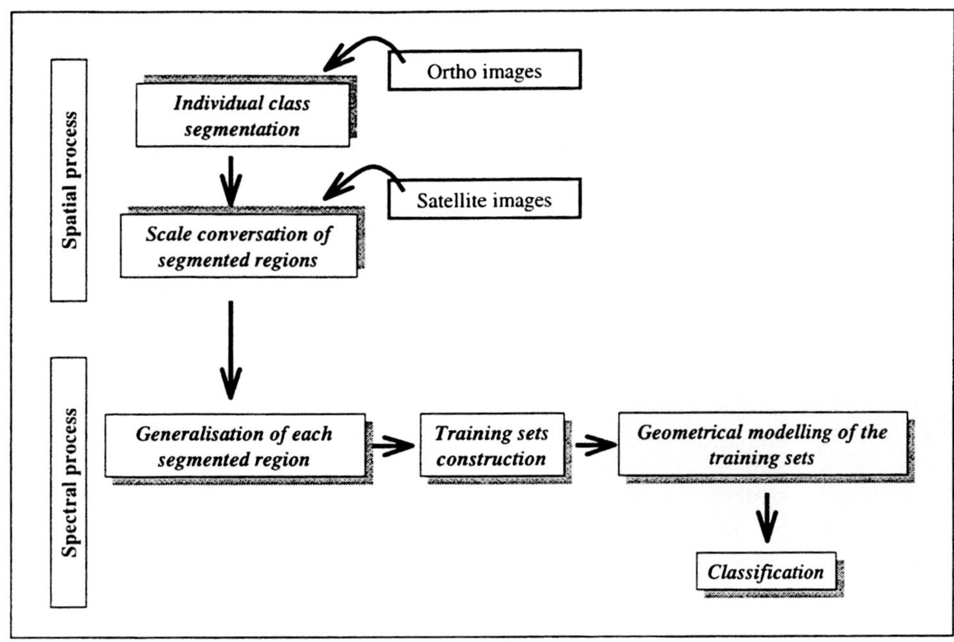

Figure 1. Scheme of the proposed methodology

Corkoak trees have, in general, bigger cupolas in comparison to the olive trees, and do not present a spatial regular pattern (figure 2c), like the one exhibited by the olive trees. To obtain corkoak trees points location, a similar procedure to the olive trees was used, applying an isotropic top-hat transform to obtain the small, dark and circular structures. In the following, the filtering by erosion-reconstruction suppresses the small darker spots that are not considered as trees. In figure 2d are presented the centres of each segmented tree.

The pine and eucalyptus trees areas appear often mixed with very similar intensity levels in any spectral band or channel. The cupola shapes and the spatial pattern presented by the trees are not also very discriminating features. This way, pine and eucalyptus trees kept together in the same class, are characterised as great dark regions with irregular contours with infinite shapes (figure 2e). Thus, the developed segmentation algorithm is based on the watershed transform with its most recent improvements (modification of the homotopy with imposition of internal and external markers on the gradient image [1]). The details of the sequence developed can be consulted in [3], being an example of the segmentation of this joint class presented in figure 2f.

2.2. Classification at lower scales

In order to update, for cartographic purposes, the information concerning the different classes at a lower scale (satellite images), using the extracted information with the details exhibited at a higher scale (aerial photographs), the classification must be performed, considering each segmented region as the unitary element to be classified. The novel sequence here presented for the classification guided by the information extracted spatially at a higher scale is based on a previous work [8] and is constituted by three main phases:

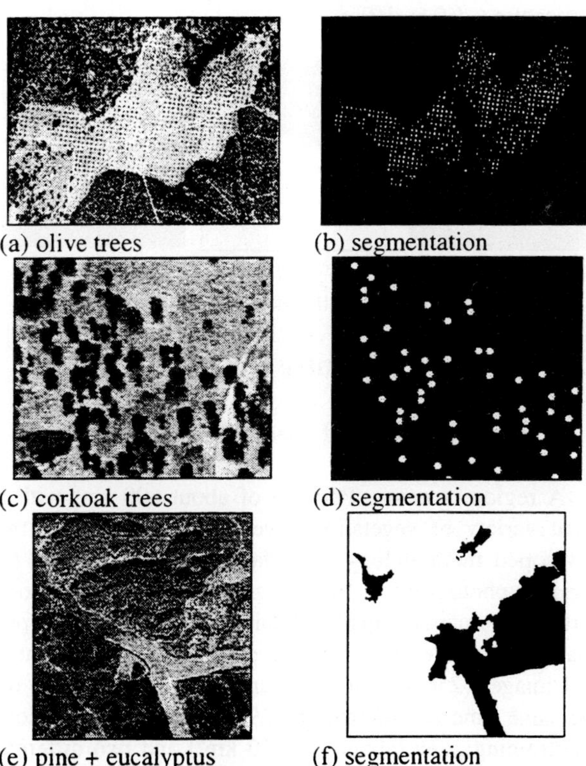

(a) olive trees (b) segmentation
(c) corkoak trees (d) segmentation
(e) pine + eucalyptus (f) segmentation

Figure 2. Forest cover types segmentation

1. *Generalisation of each segmented region*: it consists on considering each segmented region as the unitary element to be classified. Therefore, each unitary element (watershed basin) should be represented by a minimum number of features (ideally a single one).
2. *Modelling the clusters of the training samples in the features space*: it consists on applying alternating or alternating sequential filters for connecting closer points and for eliminating smaller or unconnected regions or points. In figure 3 is presented an alternating filter of type opening-closing.

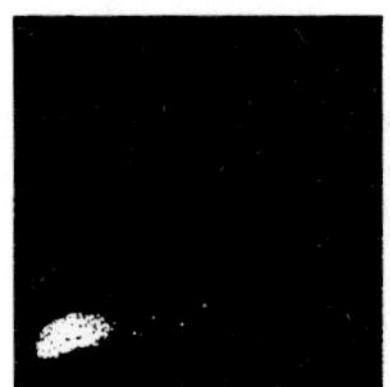

(a) training points (b) open-close
Figure 3. Training sets modelling (2)

3. *Definition of the decision regions*: it consists on suppressing the overlapping regions and by assigning each point of these regions to the closest class (computation of the geodesical SKIZ), and also by computing internal and external distance functions (respectively, $d_i(f)$ and $d_e(f)$) for each decision region, to quantify the distance of each classified unit to its centre ($d(f) = d_i(f) + d_e(f)$).

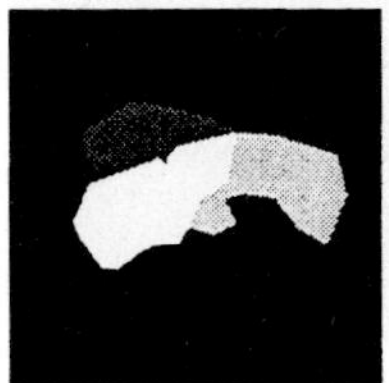

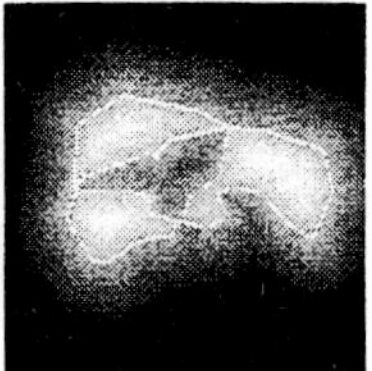

(a) overlapping (b) partition (c) dist.functions
Figure 4 . Training sets modelling (3)

3. Case study in a centre region of Portugal

3.1. Data available and spectral features used

A region in centre Portugal of about 600 km^2 with a great variety of vegetation covers was used to test the developed methodology. The data available consists on aerial photographs with geometrical corrections (orthophotomaps) in the RGB colour system (256 grey per channel, 1 metre/pixel) and the corresponding Landsat 5 TM images (256 grey levels/channel, 30 metres/pixel) on the same time period (autumn 1997). Within this region, one training zone (about 12 x 10 km^2) and two different zones of the same dimension were selected to perform the classification tests. All these three regions were photointerpreted by an expert, *i.e.*, the pine+eucalyptus regions were delimited with contours and each olive and corkoak tree was marked with a point.

In this process, the basins detected by the watershed transform are going to be used as the points of the clouds of the training sets for the classification procedure [9]. Being the elementary units and its borders defined at higher scale (orthophotomaps) and converted in the following to the satellite scale, it is needed to investigate which are the better spectral features to use in the classification of the different forest cover types at the higher scale. The satellite Landsat 5 TM has a spectral resolution of 6 different wavelengths (red, green, blue, near-, mid- and far-infrared with a spatial resolution of 30 metres/pixel). Preliminary tests have shown a high degree of overlapping between the training sets of points of the three different classes using directly the 6 spectral characteristics of the Landsat 5 TM satellite. Although not used in this case study, an automatic search of the best characteristics can be envisaged using genetic algorithms (Ramos, 1998). It was then decided to use other more discriminant features, as the ones given by the tasselled cap transform. This transform [2][5][7] permits to obtain a new co-ordinate axis having a more precise physical meaning. The new axis system gives origin to three new components or images: brightness (B), greenness (G) and wetness (W). Thus, the training sets of points of the three vegetation classes (olive, corkoak and pine+eucalyptus trees) were constructed 2 by 2 with the B, G and W images, being the watershed basins in each one of the three images substituted by the mean grey level of the points that constitute it: B vs. G, B vs. W and G vs. W. This way, for each pair, three training sets were constructed: olive trees, corkoak trees and pine+eucalyptus trees.

The training sets were processed using the previous algorithm, in order to create the nuclei for each class, leading to the definition of decision regions. Each point of the watershed lines in the geographical image was assigned to the most frequented class in its neighbourhood.

3.2. Classification results

Once defined the elementary units to classify, having chosen the characteristics to use and having created the decision regions for each class, the classification procedure can now be performed. There were performed a total of 15 classifications using the 3 characteristics computed with the tasselled cap transform (B, G and W) and using different sizes of the alternating filter AF (opening-closing type) to model the training sets: combinations of the characteristics B-G, B-W and G-W using sizes from 1 to 5 of the hexagonal structuring element.

The best result obtained was the one given by using the B-V pair of features and whose partition was obtained with an alternating filter by opening-closing of size 5. To have a classification rate through the computation of the confusion matrix, the images constructed by the expert were used as patterns or ground truth images. Moreover, in order to better evaluate the proposed methodology to classify vegetation cover types, the results obtained were compared to the results obtained with other three classification methods: minimum distance, maximum likelihood and mahalanobis distance. The main diagonal of the confusion matrix are presented in table 1, where the values presented correspond to the percentage of area that were misclassified, *i.e.*, that should have been correctly classified in a given class but were wrongly classified in another one. In the same table are also plotted the values of a global index k (kappa index of agreement-KIA) [5]. In what concerns the results obtained, it can be said that globally the pine+eucalyptus present the best classification results (errors varying between 5.33 % and 12.78 % and that olive and corkoak trees present higher errors for all the methods tested from (26.67 % to 73.14 %). This was somehow already anticipated, because in every scatter-plot, no matter what characteristics were used, there was always noticed a great overlapping between the olive and corkoak trees classes, and a much smaller overlapping between these two classes and the other one (pine+eucalyptus). Anyhow, the proposed morphological approach improves the classification rates in this difficult application area.

Table 1. Confusion matrix results (% of error) (MD – minimum distance, ML – maximum likelihood, MAH – Mahalanobis distance, MOR – morphological)

	MD	ML	MAH	MOR
Olive	36.57	26.61	26.67	37.42
Pine+euc	09.38	07.11	12.78	05.33
Corkoak	61.01	73.14	72.69	48.38
KIA	0.5537	0.5537	0.5033	0.6398

4. Conclusions

In this paper is presented a complete methodology to classify images at a lower scale using features extracted at a higher scale. The methodology developed appeals mainly to mathematical morphology operators, that are used to segment different vegetation cover types in orthophotomaps and to model the training sets of points in the characteristics space in order to create the decision regions for each class involved, permitting then to classify the elementary units that can have different size and shape. The classification results obtained show that there is an increase in the classification rate in comparison to other traditional methods.

Presently, this methodology is under improvement by automatically defining the type of filter to be used when modelling the shape of the training samples, by automatically creating the decision regions borders with different weighted distances and by introducing more classes.

References

[1] BEUCHER S., MEYER F., 1993, The morphological approach to segmentation: The watershed transformation, in *Dougherty E. (ed.), Mathematical Morphology in Image Processing*, 433-482, Marcel Dekker, New York.

[2] CHUVIECO E., 1996, *Fundamentos de teledetección espacial*, 3ª edición, Ediciones RIALP, Madrid.

[3] GRANADO I., MENGUCCI M., BARATA T., MUGE F., 1999, Automatic classification of forest landuse on ortho-images, using mathematical morphology, *in Shulcloper J.R., Martinez Trinidad J.F., Sanchéz Diaz G., Carrasco Ochoa J.A., Muñoz Gutierrez S., Mayol Cuevas W. (eds.), Memorias SIARP'99*, 389-398, Havana, Cuba.

[4] LAY B., 1983, *Analyse automatique des images angiofluorographiques*, PhD thesis, École des Mines de Paris.

[5] LILLESAND T., KIEFER R., 1994, *Remote sensing and image interpretation*, 3rd edition, John Wiley & Sons, NY.

[6] MADIER J.P., FLOUZAT G., JOURLIN M., 1986, A non-parametric supervised multispectral classification method using binary morphological operators, *Proceedings of IGARSS'86*, ESA-SP-254, vol.1, 547-552.

[7] MATHER P.M., 1981, *Computer processing of remotely-sensed images*, 2nd edition, John Wiley & Sons.

[8] MUGE F., PINA P., 1994, Applications of morphological operators to supervised multidimensional data classification, in *Serra J. & Soille P. (eds.), Mathematical Morphology and its Applications to Image Processing*, 361-368, Kluwer Academic Publishers, Dordrecht.

[9] PINA P., 1999, *Characterisation, modeling and simulation of structures by mathematical morphology* (in portuguese), PhD Thesis, Instituto Superior Técnico, Lisboa.

[10] RAMOS V., *Evolution and cognition in image analysis* (in portuguese), MSc Thesis, Instituto Superior Técnico, Lisboa.

[11] SERRA J., 1982, *Image analysis and mathematical morphology*, Academic Press, London.

[12] SOILLE P., 1992, *Morphologie Mathématique: Du relief à la dimensionalité. Algorithmes et méthodes*, PhD thesis, Université Catholique de Louvain.

[13] SOILLE P., 1999, *Morphological image analysis*, Springer-Verlag, Berlin.

Dynamic Recognition and Reconstruction of the Human Heart

Antoni Susín, Isabel Navazo, Àlvar Vinacua and Pere Brunet
Institut de Robòtica i Informàtica (I.R.I.)
c. Gran Capità 2–4
E08034
Barcelona, Spain
susin@ma1.upc.es {isabel,alvar,pere}@lsi.upc.es

Abstract

Medical imaging is constantly advancing due to technological improvements in both data gathering devices and data processing of their output. In this progress the heart presents special demands because of its incessant and brisk movement, and intrinsic characteristics. In this paper we briefly survey techniques that can be used to construct a tree-dimensional model of a heart and discuss our approach within an ongoing effort to produce accurate models of a patient's beating heart for both diagnosis and medical training.

1. Introduction

The field of medical imaging has significantly changed over the years, becoming both an integral part of health care and an increasingly important area of research spanning many disciplines.

A major problem in cardiac imaging is identifying regions of damaged heart muscle (myocardium) especially in the left ventricle (LV). One of the main causes of damage is the process of narrowing of the coronary arteries. If the blockages are severe enough to restrict the blood flow to the heart, then the heart muscle suffers from a lack of oxygen (an infarction). If the artery gets occluded completely, blood flow to the muscle stops entirely and the muscle locally dies, forming an area of scar tissue on the heart. This process is commonly named a Heart Attack.

Cardiologists assume that one identifying characteristic of these affected regions is reduced contraction during the systolic (contraction) phase of the cardiac cycle. Magnetic resonance tagged images (tagg-MRI) have shown great potential for noninvasively measuring the motion of a beating heart. Tagged images appear with a spatially encoded pattern that moves with the tissue and can be analyzed to reveal the motion of the myocardium and to extract measures of local contractile performance such as strain. Unfortunately, this medical imaging technique is not extended to the practical clinic uses yet.

Other medical imaging techniques to provide information about the heart are classical Magnetic Resonance Images (MRI) which describe the anatomy of the heart and Single-Photon Emission Computed Tomography (SPECT) acquisitions which are designed to measure the myocardial perfusion (blood flow) distribution, particularly in the LV myocardium. Many techniques have been proposed to track the LV motion from this kind of images, most of them using dynamic deformable models as will be introduced in section 2. But due to the complexity of the modeling, the topic of tracking the LV motion remains an open problem. Two of our main objectives are the reconstruction of a 3D model of the heart and its motion simulation [9].

In fact, the most extended routine clinical test is the use of SPECT images. The information resulting from this image procedure —the spatial myocardial perfusion distribution— allows to detect and localize infarction (dead tissue) as well as ischemia (viable tissue that is at risk of infarction). In practice, two types of acquisitions are done and compared for the same patient corresponding to images during "stress" (immediately after patient exercises) and during "rest" (after the patient has rested). Although some quantification techniques exist, the physicians diagnose based on looking at the 2D images obtained and integrating the information into a mental picture of the 3D-myocardial perfusion distribution.

One of the open problems in cardiology medical imaging is the reconstruction of a complete volumetric heart model that allows the visualization of its morphology, and provides information about its perfusion, comparing the stress and rest models and simulating its motion. The use of SPECT acquisition images introduces some extra difficulties to obtain the heart's left ventricle reconstruction because they have a low-resolution (64x64), are relatively noisy and possibly misleading (there is no data in dead zones). The most widely used techniques for the reconstruction are based on deformable models due to their ability to segment (identify), match and track the contour of the anatomical structures by jointly considering constrains derived from the images together with knowledge about the location and approximate shape of these structures [10].

The paper is organized as follows: In section 2, we briefly outline previous work in dynamic deformable models. Section 3 presents details of our proposed method to obtain a 3D-model of the heart from SPECT images. Finally, we present some results and we state our conclusions and briefly describe future work.

2. Deformable models

Here we review previous work on deformable models from the point of view of two medical applications. The first one is related with the automatic segmentation of the images obtained using medical diagnostic equipment such as Computed Tomography (CT) or Magnetic Resonance Imagery (MRI), and the second is related with interaction between the user and the model on surgery simulations. We will give a short description of the different approaches that can be found in the literature today for both situations.

To avoid the manual process of segmentation which needs a lot of experience, medical knowledge and is too time consuming, an automatic model is required. This also helps by eradicating the influence of the operator on the test results, standardizing them. The first deformable model used in this context was presented by Kass, Witkin and Terzopolous [11]. They introduce the notion of *Snake* or *active contour* as a segmentation method of an ill-defined contour in a 2D image. An active contour is an energy-minimizing spline which is attracted toward features (lines and edges) of the image. In its first version a snake was 1D, consisting of a parametrized curve $\mathbf{x}(s) = (x(s), y(s))$. This idea was extended by Tsumiyama *et al.* [21] introducing the *Active Net*, which is an active surface (2 parameters) used for extracting a 2D region. There also exist an *3D Active Net* [19] (2 parameters) used for extracting the surface covering a 3D volume data, and also an *Active Cubes* (3 parameters) [4] for extracting a 3D volume region.

All the above active models move towards a minimum of an energy functional $E(\mathbf{x}) = \int (E_{int}(\mathbf{x}) + E_{ext}(\mathbf{x}))\, ds$, with separated internal and external terms. The way of modeling these terms gives the different approaches to construct the deformable model. The internal energy term can be expressed as [11]

$$E_{int} = \alpha \left| \frac{\partial \mathbf{x}}{\partial s} \right|^2 + \beta \left| \frac{\partial^2 \mathbf{x}}{\partial s^2} \right|^2 \qquad (1)$$

where α and β are weighting parameters that control the tension and rigidity respectively. A classical approach [15],[16],[22],[18], is to solve the Euler-Lagrange equation corresponding to the energy minimum

$$-\frac{\partial}{\partial s}\left(\alpha \frac{\partial \mathbf{x}}{\partial s}\right) + \frac{\partial^2}{\partial s^2}\left(\beta \frac{\partial^2 \mathbf{x}}{\partial s^2}\right) + \nabla E_{ext} = 0 \qquad (2)$$

This can be viewed as a force balance equation $\mathbf{F}_{int} + \mathbf{F}_{ext} = 0$ using the relation $\mathbf{F} = \nabla E$. Equation 2 is a static problem but a potent approach is to construct a dynamical system with an equilibrium at the energy minimum. This leads to dynamic deformable models that unify the description of shape and motion. The Lagrange equations of a dynamic deformable model can be stated as

$$\mu(s) \frac{\partial^2 \mathbf{x}}{\partial t^2} + \gamma(s) \frac{\partial \mathbf{x}}{\partial t} + \mathbf{F}_{int} + \mathbf{F}_{ext} = 0, \qquad (3)$$

where $\mu(s)$ and $\gamma(s)$ are the mass and damping density respectively and the first two terms represent inertial and damping forces. The equilibrium is achieved when the internal and external forces balance and the contour comes to rest, that is $\frac{\partial^2 \mathbf{x}}{\partial t^2} = \frac{\partial \mathbf{x}}{\partial t} = 0$.

In order to numerically compute a minimum energy solution one approach is to discretize equation 3 using finite differences [11],[20],[22],[18] or using finite element methods [12],[14].

The second application of deformable models that we focus in concerns itself with surgery simulations. These models ([6], [7], [3], [5], [8]) can be volumetric or surface models [17], [12], [13], with applications for example to liver, face skin or laparoscopic gall-bladder surgery simulations.

In this context visual-realism and real-time interactions are the most important requisite. Real-time interaction means that any action of the operator generates an instantaneous response from the model, despite the complexity of its geometry. Moreover, the non-rigidity of most of the human organs means that their shape will change during an operation and the realism of the deformations is another key point in surgery simulations. The most widely used representations are based on mass-spring [3], [13], [8] and finite element methods [6], [12], [17]. Mass-spring models are faster from a computational point of view, but the behavior of the model can be very related with the spring connections. This representation simplifies also another difficult point which is the changes in the topology of the model when a cut is simulated [3]. The finite element methods are based on the elasticity theory (mainly linear elasticity) to compute the reaction of the model. Due to their high computational cost some strategies of preprocessing or an hybrid mass-spring/ finite elements model [5] can be used. In the virtual heart project we aim at using a hybrid model that allows us to extend the surface model obtained from the SPECT data of the LV to a volumetric model that can be mixed with an mass-spring model in the areas where the operator is acting. We do not yet have finished results in this area.

3. Left ventricle reconstruction: The proposed approach

Our goal here is the construction of a closed, 3D polygonal model of the left ventricle of the human heart. This model will afterwards be enhanced to support the representation of volume information (blood perfusion) and physically-based deformations. It will result in practical tools and solutions useful in the diagnosis of cardiac diseases.

The model construction is based on SPECT images for the analysis of heart perfusion and MRI (Magnetic Resonance) for the acquisition of the shape of the ventricle. The first step (segmentation) is the identification of the regions in the images that correspond to the anatomic structure of the heart. Segmentation requires a high degree of interaction and a priori anatomic knowledge. Then, a polygonal mesh is automatically adapted to the segmented data using a snake-like approach [11]. More specifically, our algorithm works in the following three steps:

- SPECT data are processed using local filters and interactive segmentation in order to separate the image zones with left ventricle information from other possible organs that can appear in the SPECT image —liver, bowels, ...—. This is repeated for the different cuts and for the different temporal images along a heart cycle. The segmentation module includes specific tools for image processing in order to remove noise and enhance the relevant data of the ventricle.
- A generic triangular 3D mesh is automatically adapted to the SPECT segmented data in order to reconstruct both the internal and external surfaces of the left ventricle at a given instant t_k.
- Using gated-SPECT data, a model for the surface mesh deformation between systole and diastole is obtained. The same algorithm of the previous step can be used, taking into account that the final 3D mesh for t_k is a good starting mesh for the adaptation to the t_{k+1} data.

The rest of this section details the algorithm for adapting the generic triangular 3D mesh to the segmented data at a given instant in time. The mesh is dynamically adapted to the data by simulating a particle system with external and internal forces that push the mesh to the data while guaranteeing a certain mesh elasticity. As the goal is to model the left ventricle, we use two different initial meshes that will be pushed to the internal and external boundaries of the SPECT data of the ventricle.

The algorithm to fit the 3D mesh to the heart SPECT data is based on a modification of Baraff's algorithm [2] which was proposed for cloth deformation applications. The surface is modeled by a 3D triangular mesh, with particles at the vertices. From the mesh initial location, the particles at the mesh vertices start to move because of forces acting on them. The mesh shape consequently changes, and the forces push the mesh to the boundary of the data. Every particle is affected by two kinds of forces: internal and external.

Internal forces control triangle deformation and model the elasticity of the mesh. We have three different internal forces: stretch, shear and bend. Forces are the gradients of local energy functions. To force stability, a damping force is also included, depending on the temporal derivative of the energy. The stretch force tries to avoid deformation of the triangle edges, while shear tends to keep internal angles from diverging too much from right angles. Finally, bend forces try to avoid bending of adjacent mesh triangles.

External forces act on the mesh vertices and push them towards the data. They must be computed from a gradient vector field derived from the volume data. We have observed, nevertheless, that local gradient estimations do not work. Local gradient estimations are unable to push the mesh to the data when the mesh is far from the final shape and location, and fail to adapt it to data concavities. Instead of this, we build a global gradient vector field (GVF) computing its vector value for every voxel in the segmented volume data model. The GVF is computed through the minimization of the functional proposed by Xu and Prince [23],[22],

$$\Psi = \int\int\int \mu\Delta\mathbf{V} + |\nabla I|^2|\mathbf{V} - \nabla I|^2 dxdydz. \quad (4)$$

Where I is the data intensity value at every voxel of the volume model. The functional includes two terms. The first one is a diffusion term that spatially propagates the field in a smooth way, while the second one depends on the local changes of the intensity I. Both terms are averaged with a parameter that controls the relative importance of both aspects. In regions where the intensity I is almost constant the diffusion term dominates, while the gradient produced by I changes is the relevant term in regions with strong intensity changes.

The minimization problem to obtain the GVF is solved through the associated Euler equations, using finite differences and iteratively finding the stationary state of the vector field. For a detailed description, see [1].

The dynamics of the particles at the mesh vertices are driven by the standard Newton equation. A state vector $(\mathbf{x},\mathbf{v})$ is defined for each particle. The dynamics of the whole mesh is modeled by a system of 6n First-Order Ordinary Differential Equations (for a mesh with n vertices). They relate the time derivatives of the state vectors to the same state vectors and to the external and internal forces. For the ODE integration we use an implicit Euler scheme. We use a time discretization so that $t_{k+1} = t_k + h$. At each integration step t_k,

- the total forces (external force plus stretch, shear and bend) are computed for each mesh vertex, together with their partial derivatives with respect to $\mathbf{x}$ and $\mathbf{v}$
- a linear system of dimension 3n is solved to compute the n. incremental vectors $\Delta\mathbf{v}$ so that $\mathbf{v}_{k+1} = \mathbf{v}_k + \Delta\mathbf{v}$ for each mesh vertex [1].
- the new locations of the mesh vertices are computed using the first-order approximations $\mathbf{x}_{k+1} = \mathbf{x}_k + \Delta\mathbf{x}$ where $\Delta\mathbf{x} = h * (\mathbf{v}_k + \Delta\mathbf{v})$ for each vertex.

The advantage of using an implicit integration method is that larger integration steps —h— can be used. The counterpart is that a linear system must be solved at each step. However, the corresponding matrix is sparse (due to the local behavior of the energy) and fast iterative methods can be used for solving the system. We have experimentally observed that the iterative Euler integration is performing well in the practical cases we have analyzed.

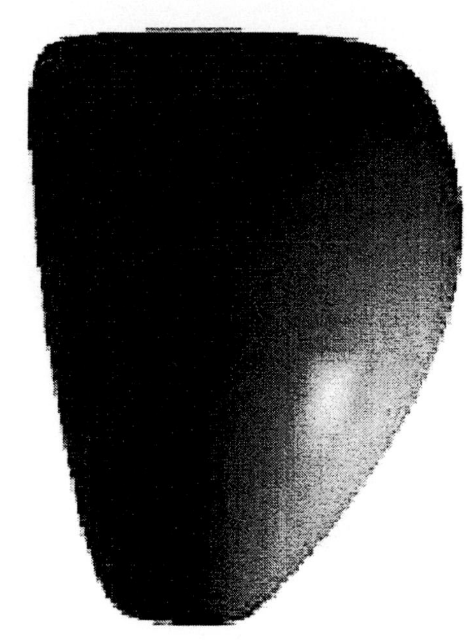

Figure 1. Initial surface for the segmentation process.

4. Results

We would like to conclude showing the actual data and results one obtains through this approach. Here we present images of the model reconstructed from data of a normal (healthy) patient. Generally speaking, severely injured hearts present a higher demand on the system as portions of them are completely missing in the data because of the nature of the data-gathering techniques used (SPECT).

Figure 1 shows the initial model that our application uses. It has of course been chosen as an idealized model of a heart, in order to reduce the algorithm's cost to detect the muscle's boundary. This initial, smooth mesh is placed surrounding the actual data from the patient (Figure 2), and the vertices' positions are adjusted according to the algorithm described, to obtain a three-dimensional mesh adapted to the exterior surface of the myocardium (Figure 3). By construction this surface corresponds to the theoretical definition of where the boundary of the muscle lies used in nuclear medicine (doctors estimate that this is where the gradient of the perceived perfusion is maximal).

Finally, here is a picture (Figure 4) showing a two-dimensional section of the vector field generated by the GVF algorithm from the original SPECT data. The lower left window displays a representation of the original voxel data for the slice, whereas the top left window shows the computed gradient vector field. The two top windows at the right represent the magnitudes of the gradient vectors along the vertical line seen on the left windows. Notice how the walls of the myocardium correspond to points of greatest slope (and zero module) for this vector field. Notice how this vector field captures both the internal and the external surfaces of the ventricle's wall, from distinct starting meshes.

5. Conclusions and future work

The problems that arise from processing data of the heart's perfusion are challenging and relevant, as they test the limits of our abilities to automatically manipulate this data in a useful way and impact directly on some of the ailments with high impact on the populations' health and life expectancy.

We have presented here some results from our ongoing project to build a dynamic model of a patient's beating heart. From the segmentation of the internal and external surfaces of the myocardium, we are now proceeding to the construction of efficient volume models that allow physicians to assess accurately certain localized measures of the heart's function (like muscle elasticity and wall thickness),

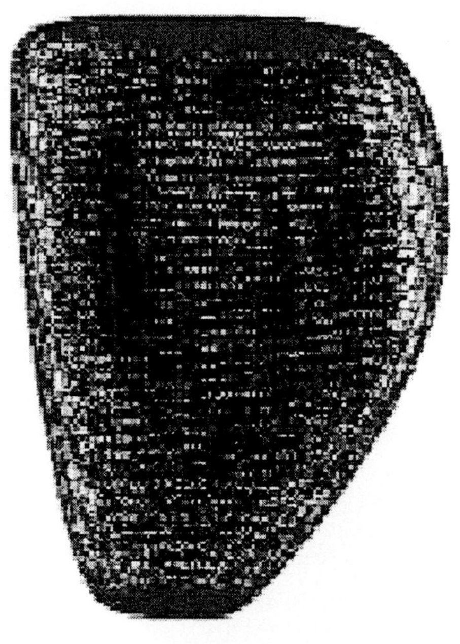

Figure 2. The initial surface and the vector field obtained from actual patient SPECT data

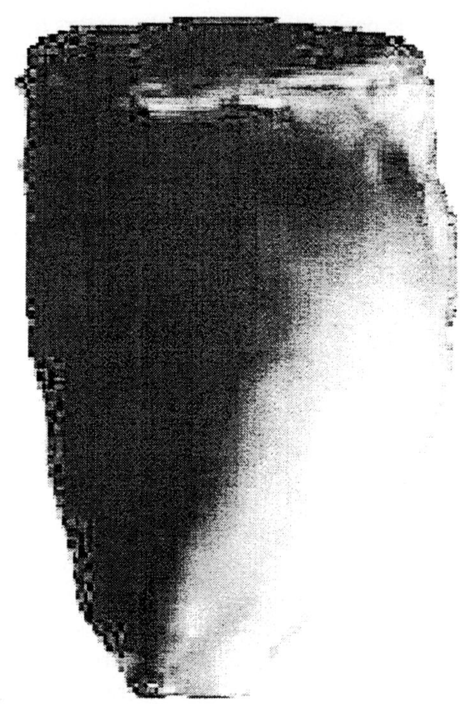

Figure 3. The external surface constructed by the algorithm

and to interact with it in advanced environments (for example a Workbench).

6. Acknowledgements

We want to thank Dr. Jaume Candell and Dr. Santiago Aguadé of the Vall d'Hebron Hospitals in Barcelona, who provided medical guidance and the SPECT data, and our co-workers Josep Oriol Esteve, Óscar García, Eva Monclús and Lyudmila Rodríguez who are helping the Virtual Heart project advance.

References

[1] J. Amatller, O. Garcia, and A. Susin. Modelo dinámico para la segmentación automática de imágenes 3d. *Proc. CEIG2000 (accepted for publication)*, 2000.

[2] D. Baraff and A. Witkin. Large steps in cloth simulation. In M. Cohen, editor, *SIGGRAPH 98 Conference Proceedings*, Annual Conference Series, pages 43–54. ACM SIGGRAPH, Addison Wesley, July 1998. ISBN 0-89791-999-8.

[3] D. Bielser, V. Maiwald, and M. Gross. Interactive cuts through 3-dimensional soft tissue. Technical Report CSTR-309, ETH Zurich, 1998.

[4] M. Bro-Nielsen. Active nets and cubes. Technical report, IMM-Image Analysis Group, 1994.

[5] M. Bro-Nielsen and S. Cotin. Real time volumetric deformable models for surgery simulation using finite elements and condensation. *Eurographics'96*, pages 57–66, 1996.

[6] S. Cotin, H. Delingette, and N. Ayache. Real time elastic deformations of soft tissues for surgery simulation. *IEEE transactions on Visualization and Computer Graphics*, 5:62–72, January-March 1999.

[7] S. Cotin, H. Delingette, and N. AyacHelo. Efficient linear elastic models of soft tissues for real time surgery simulation. Technical Report 3510, INRIA, 1998.

[8] S. Cover, N. Ezquerra, and J. O'Brien. Interactively deformable models for surgery simulation. *IEEE Computer Grafics and Applications*, 13(no. 6):68–75, 1993.

[9] J. Dereck, J. Feldmar, M. L. Goris, and F. Betting. Automatic registration and alignment on a template of cardiac stressand rest spect images. In *Mathematical Methods in Biomedical Image Analysis*, pages 212–221, 1996. També disponible com rapport de l'INRIA, numero 2770.

[10] N. Ezquerra, L. de Braal, E. García, C. Cooke, and E. Krawczynska. Interactive, knowledge-guided visualiza-

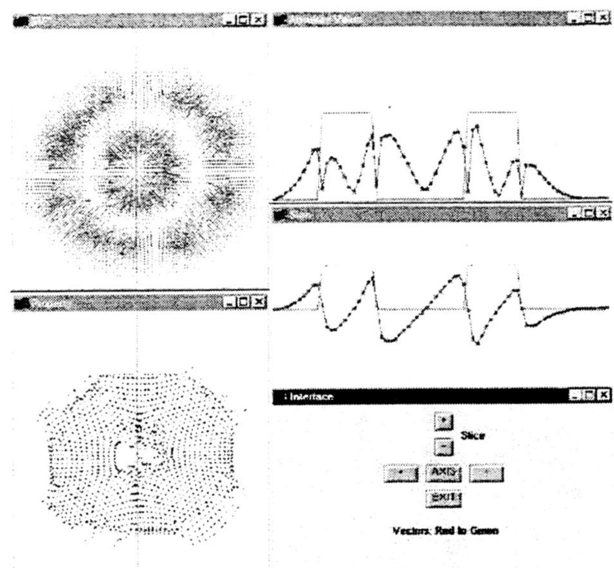

Figure 4. A planar section of the vector field constructed from the input data

tion of 3d medical imagery. *Future Generation Computer Systems*, 15:59–73, 1999.

[11] M. Kass, A. Witkin, and D. Terzopoulos. Snakes: Active contour models. *International Journal of Computer Vision*, 1(num. 4):321–331, 1988.

[12] R. M. Koch, M. H. Gross, F. R. Carls, D. F. von Büren, G. Fankhauser, and Y. I. H. Parish. Simulating facial surgery using finite element models. In H. Rushmeier, editor, *Proceedings of the SIGGRAPH '96 conference*, Annual Conference Series, pages 421–428. ACM SIGGRAPH, Addison Wesley, Aug. 1996. held in New Orleans, Louisiana, 04-09 August 1996.

[13] Y. Lee, D. Terzopoulos, and K. Waters. Realistic modeling for facial animation. *Proc. SIGGRAPH'95*, pages 55–62, 1995.

[14] T. McInerney and D. Terzopoulos. A dynamic finite element surface model for segmentation and tracking in multidimensional medical images with application to cardiac 4d image analysis. *Journal of Computarized Medical Imaging and Graphics*, pages 1–25, 1994.

[15] T. McInerney and D. Terzopoulos. Topologically adaptable snakes. *Proc. ICCV'95*, pages 840–845, 1995.

[16] T. McInerney and D. Terzopoulos. Deformable models in medical image analysis: A survey. *Medical Image Analysis*, 1:91–108, 1996.

[17] M. Roth, M. Gross, S. Turello, and F. Carls. A Berstein-Bezier based approach to soft tissue simulation. *Proc. Eurographics'98*, 17:1–10, 1998.

[18] I. Takanashi, S. Muraki, A. Doi, and A. Kaufman. 3d active net for volume extraction. pages 1–13, 1997.

[19] I. Takanashi, S. Muraki, A. Doi, and A. Kaufman. 3d active net for volume extraction. In *Proc. SPIE*, number 3298, pages 184–193. SPIE, 1998.

[20] D. Terzopoulos and K. Fleisher. Deformable models. *Visual Computer*, 4:306–331, 1988. Snakes en varies dimensions. Model hibrid solid-deformable.

[21] Y. Tsumiyama, K. Sakaue, and K. Yamamoto. Active net: Active net model for region extraction. *IPSJ SIG notes CV 63-2,*, 89(no. 96):1–8, 1989.

[22] C. Xu and J. Prince. Gradient vector flow: A new external force for snakes. *IEEE Proc. Conf. on Computer Visualization and Pattern Recognition CVPR'97*, pages 66–71, 1997.

[23] C. Xu and J. Prince. Snakes, shapes and gradient vector flow. *IEEE Transactions on Image Processing*, pages 359–369, March 1998.

3D Fundus Pattern Reconstruction and Display from Multiple Fundus Images

Koichiro DEGUCHI[†,‡] Junko NOAMI[‡] Hidekata HONTANI[‡]

† Graduate School of Information Sciences, Tohoku University, Aoba-campus 01, Sendai 980-8579 JAPAN

‡ Faculty of Engineering, University of Tokyo, 7-3-1 Hongo, Bunkyo-ku, Tokyo, 113-8656 JAPAN

Abstract

This paper proposes a method to reconstruct and display 3D fundus (inner bottom of eye-ball) pattern from a set of multiple partial images of fundus. They were taken from several different view angles by shifting fundus camera. Because they are distorted by eye lens, a simple stereo technique does not work for the 3D reconstruction from any pair of images. Moreover, every fundus image's distortions differ from each other. In this method, we utilize the fact that a fundus has a spherical shape and that the image of sphere by the eye lens results in a quadratic surface. First, we determine each camera's viewing position and pose relative to the eye-ball and the shape of the quadratic surface by matching feature points in every fundus image on the quadratic image surface. Then, we identify the eye lens parameters so that the quadratic surface should be originated from a spherical fundus surface. As the final result, we obtain a wide area 3D fundus pattern reconstructed from the set of fundus images. This result will be helpful for medical diagnoses.

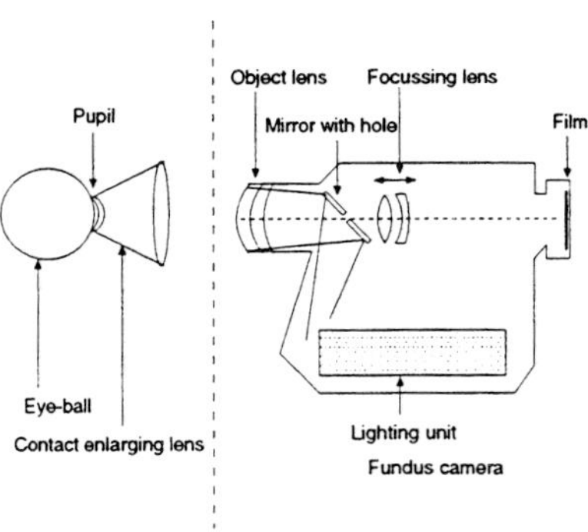

Fig. 1: Optical system of fundus camera and human eye

1 Introduction

In this paper, we propose a new method for reconstruction and display of 3D fundus pattern, a pattern on inner bottom of an eye-ball, from its multiple images.

Fundus is only a part where human internal blood vessels and nerves can be observed directly from outside of the body. The observation of the fundus is useful not only for diagnosis of eye diseases but also for checking whole body conditions. But, a fundus area covered by a single fundus image is not wide and the image is planer while the real fundus is spherical. So, it will be very useful if multiple fundus images taken from some different view angles can be integrated in 3D form and displayed. It also be useful to show 3D position of the region of interest for orientations between doctors and for laser therapy.

For any pair of the multiple images, however, a simple stereo technique does not work for the 3D reconstruction, not only because the viewing direction of the fundus camera relative to the eye-ball is not accurately identified, but also because the fundus is observed through eye lens and, sometimes, a contact wide-angle lens for enlarging the viewing field[1], as shown in Fig.1. The optical system of the fundus camera employs a specialized mechanism to observe wide fundus area through pupil, and produces high distortion of image. But, this distortion can be corrected once the camera optical system has been calibrated. However, the optical properties of human eyes are different from one to one, individually, and also from time to time, and hard to be calibrated. The relative camera positions and viewing directions for the multiple images can also not be calibrated beforehand. This means that viewing directions of the multiple images cannot be assumed to be known.

Our new method considers the skew of the lines of sight by those incidental lenses and calibrates all of optical parameters, then, gives reconstruction of the 3D fundus shape and display of its pattern in 3D form.

First, the combination of the eye lens and the enlarging contact lens is modeled with a single simple lens. Then, taking into account of the fact that the fundus shape (shape of the inner bottom of eye-ball) can be considered spherical, we identify the optical parameters of the modeled single lens. At the same time, we reconstruct the 3D fundus shape applying these identified optical parameters for the multiple view images.

2 Principles of the Reconstruction

Figure 1 shows the optical arrangements of the fundus camera, the contact enlarging lens and the eye lens. Viewing field of fundus images with respect to pupil center is usually less than 50[degree]. The enlarging contact lens is not always used.

In our system, the optical system of the fundus camera has been calibrated beforehand by the two-plane method proposed by the authors[2]. The description of this calibration method is skipped in this paper.

Actual eye-ball shapes have a small skew from a sphere, but the fundus, the bottom part of the eye, can be considered as a part of a sphere. If the combination of the eye lens and the contact enlarging lens can be modeled with a single simple lens, the spherical shaped surface of the fundus is mapped onto a quadratic surface as its real image.

The multiple fundus images are taken by changing the viewing direction of fundus camera to have common areas partially between neighbour images. We had 9 images in the experiments. These 9 images have their own respective skews by optical system of human eye lens.

Here, we assume that the combination of the optical systems of eye lens and the enlarging contact lens can be modeled by a single lens. By the single lens, the spherical shaped surface of the fundus is mapped onto a quadratic surface as its real image. This means that the surface we observe from fundus camera through the eye lens with/without enlarging contact lens is just this quadratic image surfaces, as shown in Fig.2.

In our method, first, we extract feature points from the 9 fundus images and find the correspondences between them. Then, those corresponding pairs are registered on a quadratic surface. We find the parameters of the quadratic surface on which the registrations will be achieved best. At the same

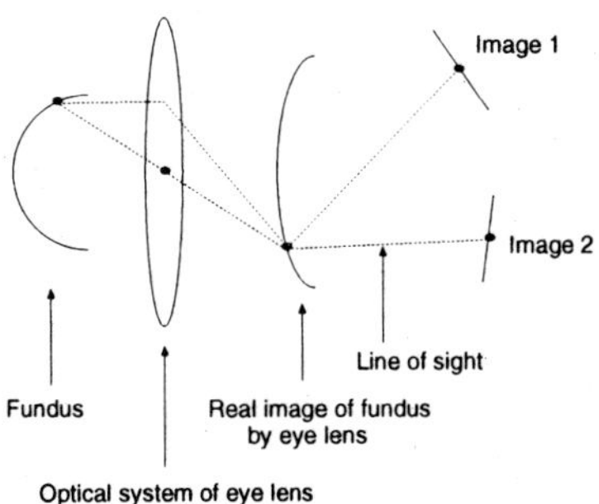

Fig. 2: Optical model for multiple fundus images

time, the positions and viewing directions of fundus camera to take the individual images are identified to produce best fits of the corresponding point pairs.

From the surface parameters, we can reconstruct the optical system of the modeled single lens and the fundus sphere. Finally, the fundus patterns are back projected from the multiple images onto the reconstructed fundus sphere.

3 Geometry of the optical system

We denote the focal length of the modeled single lens on the side to fundus with F, on the side of image with $\frac{G}{F}$. Then, the lens forms an image of a point (X, Y, Z) on the fundus sphere at (a, b, c) according to (1), where the origins of those coordinate systems were set at above respective focal points. The relation of the coordinate systems are shown in Fig.3.

$$\begin{cases} a = F\frac{X}{Z} \\ b = F\frac{Y}{Z} \\ c = \frac{G}{Z} \end{cases} \quad (1)$$

Denoting the center of the fundus sphere by (C_x, C_y, C_z), and its radius by R, (X, Y, Z) holds

$$(X - C_x)^2 + (Y - C_y)^2 + (Z - C_z)^2 - R^2 = 0 \quad (2)$$

Then, by (1) and (2), the image of this point will be shown to lie on the next quadratic surface;

$$\alpha_1(a^2 + b^2) + \alpha_2 c^2 + \alpha_3 ac + \alpha_4 bc + \alpha_5 c + 1 = 0 \quad (3)$$

where,

$$\begin{cases} \alpha_1 = 1/F^2 \\ \alpha_2 = ({C_x}^2 + {C_y}^2 + {C_z}^2 - R^2)/G^2 \\ \alpha_3 = -2C_x/FG \\ \alpha_4 = -2C_y/FG \\ \alpha_5 = -2C_z/G \end{cases} \quad (4)$$

We can interpret that every one of the multiple fundus images was the image of this quadratic surface of (3) taken from unknown viewing point. The camera coordinate system *s-t-u* can be related to the *a-b-c* system with unknown rotation matrix R and unknown translation vector $\boldsymbol{t}$ as

$$\begin{bmatrix} s \\ t \\ u \end{bmatrix} = R \begin{bmatrix} a \\ b \\ c \end{bmatrix} + \boldsymbol{t} \quad (5)$$

Here, we assume the mapping of a point in *s-t-u* system onto the image (x, y) is the orthogonal projection.

Now, we have 2 unknown parameters of the focal lengths F and G, 5 of the quadratic surface, and N sets of unknown camera pose and position parameters $\boldsymbol{t}$, R for N images.

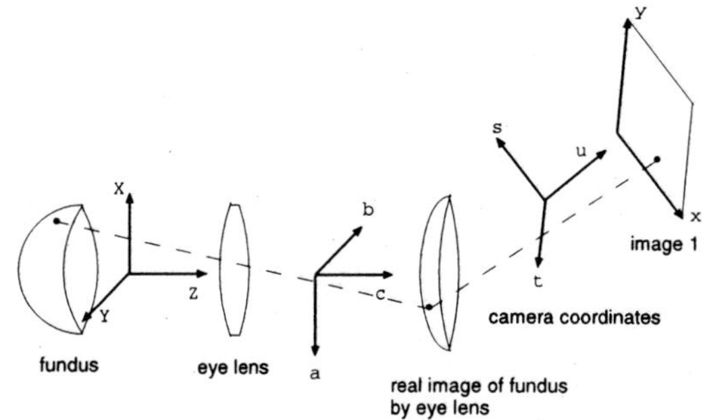

Fig. 3: Fundus sphere forms its real image through eye lens. The multiple fundus images are its images taken from several view directions.

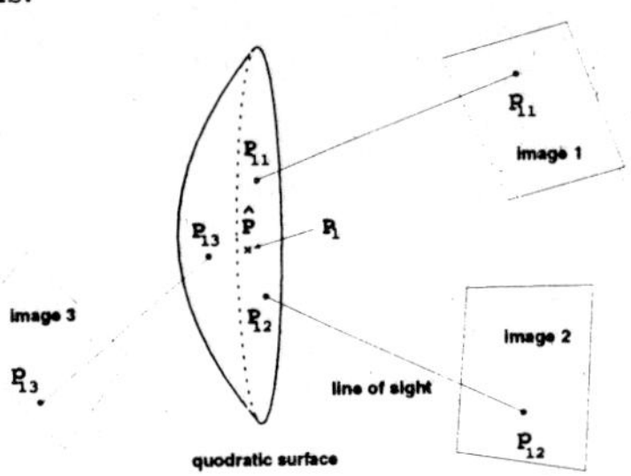

Fig. 4: The form of the quadratic surface are determined so that the deviations of each respective feature point back-projected from multiple images will be minimized

4 Reconstruction of fundus pattern

First, feature points on every fundus images are extracted. In our method, we selected branching or bending points of blood vessels. Then, correspondences of those features between neighbor images are found.

Those feature points can be considered to lie on the quadratic surface. If the form of the quadratic surface and every camera poses and positions are given, the positions of the feature points on the quadratic surface are determined.

Now, we denote the feature points on the quadratic surface with $\boldsymbol{P}_i$ $(1 \leq i \leq M)$, the number of camera views with N, and the set of camera views which take the feature point $\boldsymbol{P}_i$ with D_i. That is, the point $\boldsymbol{P}_i$ is observed by the j-th camera and $j \in D_i$. For this point of $\boldsymbol{P}_i$, its image position in the j-th image is denoted with $\boldsymbol{p}_{ij}$. Every image point $\boldsymbol{p}_{ij}$ has its respective line of sight in the space as shown in Fig.4. This line of sight can be determined using (5). We denote the back-projected point on the quadratic surface from $\boldsymbol{p}_{ij}$ along with this line of sight with $\boldsymbol{P}_{ij}$.

In this paper, as described before, we assumed the image projections are orthogonal, and the degree of freedom for pose and position of each camera is 5. By giving 5 those parameters for the j-th camera and 5 parameters for the quadratic surface, the position of a point $\boldsymbol{P}_{ij}$ is determined as the crossing point on the line of sight and the quadratic surface. This position $\boldsymbol{P}_{ij}$ does not necessarily coincide with its true position $\boldsymbol{P}_i$ because of the estimation errors of above parameters and also of its observation error in the images.

By giving tentative parameters for the quadratic surface and every camera poses and positions, we calculate tentative point positions $\boldsymbol{P}_{ij}$ from the corresponding image points $\boldsymbol{p}_{ij}$ $(j \in D_i)$. Then, we derive their gravity point on the surface $\hat{\boldsymbol{P}}_i$ and consider this point as the estimation of $\boldsymbol{P}_i$. If the quadratic surface and the camera pose and position parameters are correctly estimated, for i, every $\boldsymbol{P}_{ij}$ coincides at this point. So, we employ next criterion for the estimations of the parameters of the quadratic surface and the camera

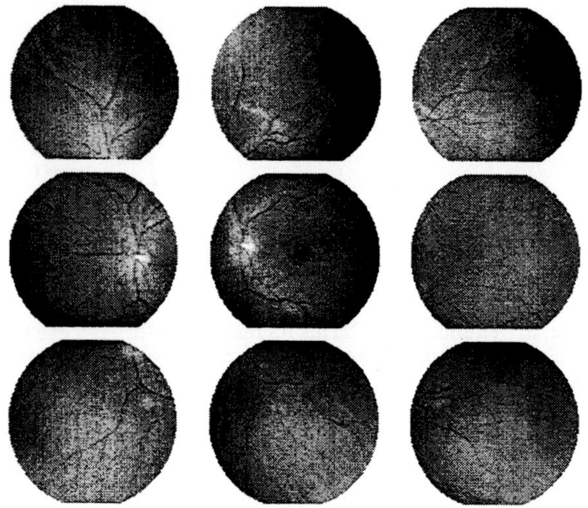

Fig. 5: Original st of 9 fundus images taken from different view angle and used in the Experiment.

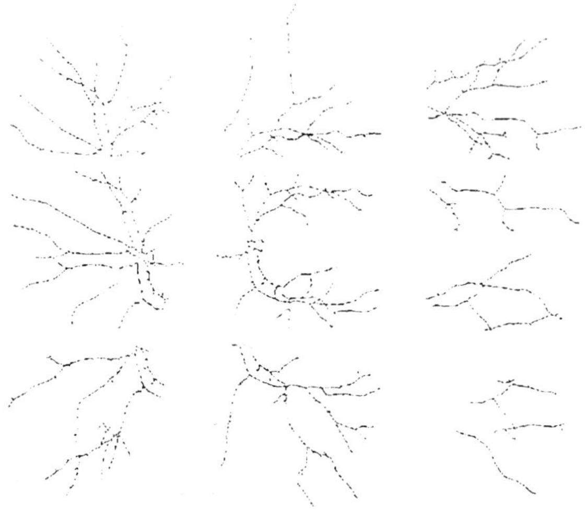

Fig. 6: Extracted blood vessel pattern from the images of Fig.5

poses and positions,

$$E = \sum_{i=1}^{M} \left[\frac{1}{N_i - 1} \sum_{j \in D_i} \left| \boldsymbol{P}_{ij} - \hat{\boldsymbol{P}}_i \right|^2 \right] \qquad (6)$$

where N_i is the number of the elements in D_i. We minimize this criterion by the Powell method. The number of parameters to be adjusted is $5N + 5$.

When the positions of the feature points on the quadratic surface, which is the real image of the fundus by the eye lens, are determined, their original positions on the fundus sphere can be derived by inverse mapping of (1). The value of F for this mapping is given as $F = \frac{1}{\sqrt{\alpha_1}}$ from (3). The value of G can be set arbitrarily, because it only determines total scale of X-Y-Z coordinates.

This reconstruction is based only on the fact that the shape of the fundus is considered to be spherical, and all the parameters of the camera positions and poses and the feature point positions are optimized simultaneously. After this reconstruction, the fundus patterns in the multiple images are back-projected on the fundus and displayed.

5 Experiments

Here, we show the experimental results using 9 real fundus images taken from different unknown view points of fundus camera. Those original images are shown in Fig.5.

From every image, first, we extracted blood vessels based on color analysis, then, applied thinning process on them. The results are shown in Fig.6. Next, we picked up their branching points and bending points. From the image shown in Fig.6, total 177 points were selected as the feature points. We found correspondences for these feature points between neighboring images by a graph matching algorithm [3]. Finally, 78 sets of correspondences were extracted. A part of correspondences are shown in Fig.7. This figure shows the center and its upper images in Fig.6, with labels of the feature points. The points having same labels correspond each other between these images.

Among the 9 images, two points had their correspondences on four images, 16 points on three images, and the rest 60 points on two images. When $N = 9$, the total number of unknowns was 50.

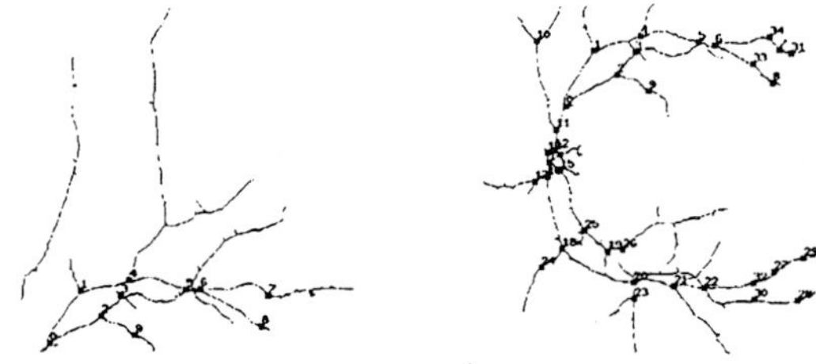

Fig. 7: Examples of the image correspondences in two neighboring images in Fig.5. After thinning the images of blood vessels, their branching and bending points were extracted. Then correspondences were found. The points having same label correspond each other

Using these correspondences, and minimizing E of (6) by the Powell method, the parameters were adjusted. The initial values for all the parameters were set to zero except $\alpha_5 = 1$. This means that all the cameras were assumed to locate at the origin with the same pose and the quadratic surface is plane ($z = -1$). At this initial stage, the extracted feature points distributed as shown in Fig.8 (upper).

Direct application of the Powell method on these image set was not efficient and sometimes the process was trapped into local minimums. To avoid this inefficiency, we employed two step approach. In the first step, parameters of the quadratic surface and camera poses were fixed and only camera positions were adjusted to minimize the criterion E. This is the rough registration of images within the image plane. Fig.8 (middle) shows the feature point distribution resulted at the end of the first step.

Then, starting from the result of the first step, we adjusted all the parameters of the camera positions and poses and those of the quadratic surface. Throughout of these minimization processes, position and pose of the central image of the 9 images were kept to remain at the origin.

Final result of the feature point distribution on the resulted quadratic surface is shown in Fig.8(lower). Each corresponding point overlaid respectively on a curved quadratic surface. Pose and position parameters of the 9 cameras were obtained at this stage.

Trajectories of each camera position while adjustments by

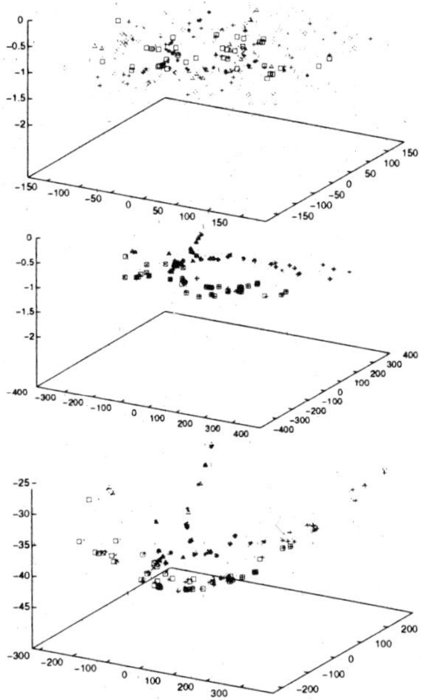

Fig. 8: The estimation process of the quadratic surface by corresponding image feature points in 9 images. Upper: initial positions of every feature points in 9 images all of which were within a plane of $z = -1$. Middle: the point distributions after only camera positions were adjusted. Lower: finale converged distributions after also camera poses were adjusted

the Powell method are shown in Fig.10. At the beginning, all the cameras located at the origin, and, in the first step, they moved within the plane of $z = 0$. Then, they reached at their final respective positions in 3D space in the second step.

From the coefficients of the second order terms of the resulted quadratic surface, we identified the focal length F of the modeled eye lens. Giving an arbitrary value to G, we have the feature point distribution on fundus sphere by (1). This distribution is shown in Fig.9.

Using the camera poses and positions and the form of the quadratic surface, we back-projected fundus images onto the fundus sphere. The result is shown in Fig.11. This figure shows wide area fundus pattern covered by the original multiple images. The patterns of blood vessels and nerves are continuously shown across the areas of different original images. This final result is in 3D form, and we display it as is viewed from arbitrarily view angle. In Fig.11, we show three displays viewed from different view angles.

6 Conclusions

We proposed a method for 3D reconstruction and display of fundus pattern from multiple fundus images. This method utilizes only the fact that real fundus shape is almost spherical. By this fact and modeling the combination of eye lens and an enlarging lens as a single lens, we identify all the optical parameters of eye and fundus camera, and positions and poses of the camera of the multiple images. Then, by back-projecting all the image onto the reconstructed fundus surface, we have 3D display of the fundus pattern.

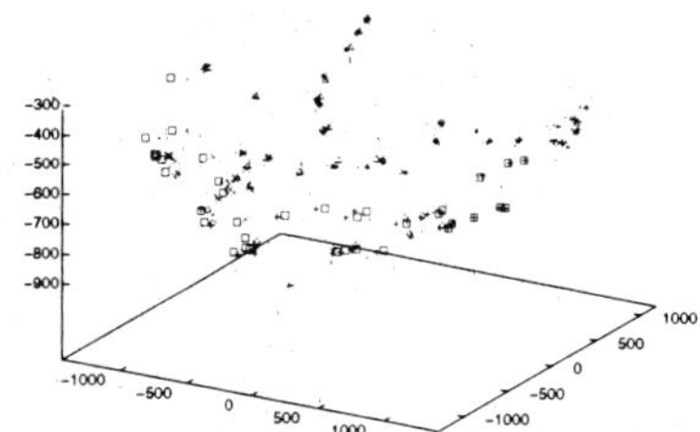

Fig. 9: Final feature point distribution on the estimated fundus sphere

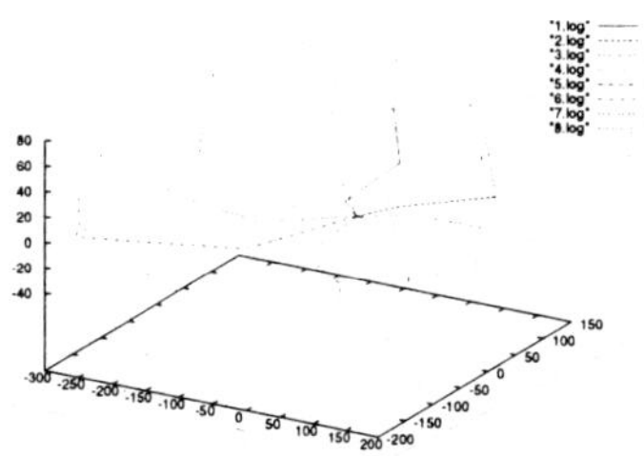

Fig. 10: Trajectories of each camera position while adjustments by the Powell method

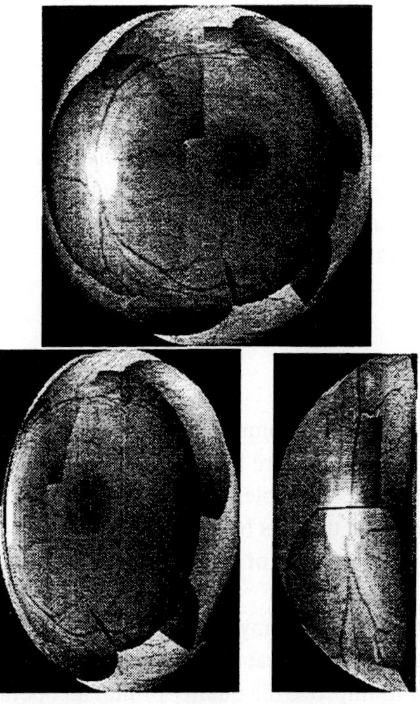

Fig. 11: Reconstruction result of 3D fundus pattern. Three displays from different view angles are shown

References

[1] K. Deguchi *et al.*: 3D Fundus Shape Reconstruction and Display from Stereo Fundus Images, IEICE Trans. Inf. & Syst., *to appear*

[2] K. Deguchi and I. Morishita : A Unified Linear Camera Calibration Method Using Two Parallel Calibration Planes, *Trans. of the Society of Instrument and Control Engineers*, Vol. 29, No. 9, pp. 1023-1032 (1993).

[3] Y. Amit and A. Kong : Graphical templates for model registration, *IEEE Trans.*, PAMI-18, pp. 225-236 (1996)

A Surveillance System Integrating Visual Telepresence *

P. Peixoto, J. Gonçalves, H. Antunes, J. Batista and H. Araújo
ISR - Institute of Systems and Robotics
Dept. of Electrical Engineering - University of Coimbra
3030 Coimbra - PORTUGAL
peixoto@isr.uc.pt

Abstract

In this paper we describe an indoor surveillance system who enables the control of a binocular active vision system by a remote operator wearing a head mounted display. Visual feedback to the head mounted display is obtained using the images captured by the active vision system. To maximize the 3D perception of the operator the system is able to adjust the vergence angle of the active vision system in order to maintain fixation on the objects in the center of the image. A wide-angle lens static camera located on the surveillance area is also used to enable the detection and tracking of intruders. In case of an intrusion a map with the location of the detected targets is displayed on top of the images being shown on the head mounted display. This information allows the remote operator to redirect his attention to where the target is.

1. Introduction

Currently available commercial surveillance systems are not automated and require human attention to make an interpretation of the available data (typically video data). Despite all the effort that has been put on research in this area, automatic interpretation of the data is still a very arduous task.

While there is not any system capable of fully autonomous operation, visual telepresence seems to be a satisfactory way to improve the quality of human operated commercial surveillance systems. If the human operator could be given the illusion of immersion within the remote environment then his task could be simplified, giving him a totally different degree of perception, as he would get by watching video images on a monitor. The advent of low cost head mounted displays already equipped with head tracking devices and the increase in the computational power make this kind of systems possible today.

One of the fundamental characteristics of an active telepresence sensor or sensors should be the ability of obtain the necessary views of the scene in response to the state of the operators head. A special effort should be put in the process of image generation. It should be done in real time (potentially with one view for each eye) to provide the operator with the illusion of immersion within the remote environment. Several approaches have been proposed ranging from model-based remote environment generation [1, 9] to the reconstruction of the remote environment using a set of images captured by an array of fixed cameras [3, 7].

Another possible solution consists on giving the sensors the ability to mimic the operators head movements. The main handicap of this approach is related to the ability of the mechanical system, in which the sensor is mounted, to have nearly the same range of motion as a normal human operator. Active vision systems have been previously used to achieve this active sensing [5]. The motion of the active vision system should be done in a very smooth way in order to induce on the user a comfortable perception of the remote environment. Another aspect to take into account is the fact that active vision systems tend to exhibit positioning latency problems. These latencies caused by delays inherent to the rotation of the degrees of freedom involved are often below the rates that operators exhibit when changing their position and especially their gaze. These delays in the updating the display, although initially distracting, can ultimately induce nausea on the operator. The use of predictive techniques such as the Kalman filter may reduce this latency up to an acceptable level.

In this paper we describe an approach to visual telepresence that uses a head mounted display and a binocular active vision system that could be applied in a surveillance context. The idea is to combine previous work in the automatic detection of intrusion [8] using a static camera equipped with a wide-angle lens with a system where a human operator wearing a head-mounted display, could look around

*The authors gratefully acknowledge the support of the project PRAXIS/2/2.1/TPAR/2074/95, funded by the Portuguese Foundation for Science and Technology.

1051-4651/00 $10.00 © 2000 IEEE

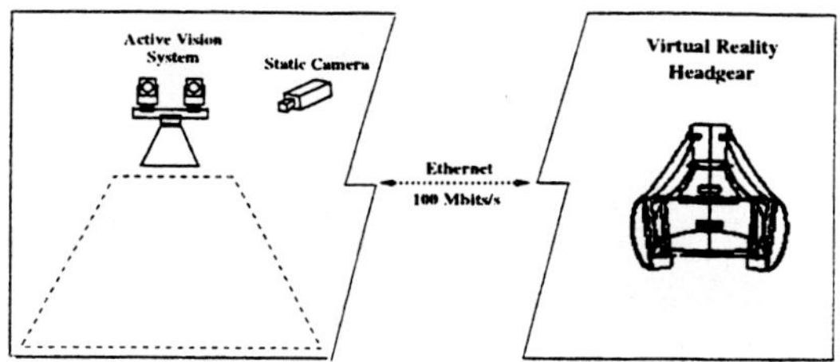

Figure 1. Overall system components

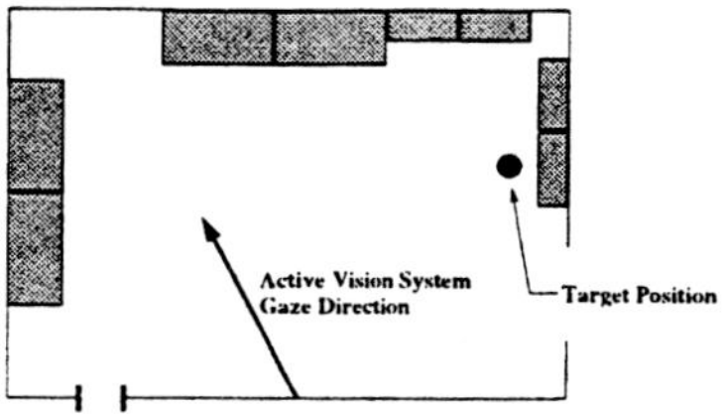

Figure 2. A map of the room is overlapped on the images displayed on the helmet showing the gaze direction of the active vision system.

an actual, but physically remote, environment where an intrusion was detected.

2. System Description

Figure 1 shows the system configuration composed of a local unit integrating an active vision system and a static camera and a remote unit integrating a head mounted display. Both subsystems are connected by an Ethernet network.

The static camera is responsible for the early detection and tracking of possible intruders along the surveillance area. Upon the detection of an intruder an alarm is issued and the remote operator can use the head mounted display to track the target. An on-screen map is displayed showing to the operator the exact location of the target on the scene (see figure 2). The target detection and tracking using the static camera is based on an optical flow segmentation. A Kalman filter is attached to each detected target and the information returned by the filter is used to predict the location of the target in the next frame. Assuming that all target points considered in the static camera image lie on the ground plane then any point on this plane can be mapped to a point in the image plane of the static camera using an homography. In this way, using an inverse mapping, we can have the position of each target on the ground plane and then project the target position on the map of the surveyed area [8].

The binocular active vision system used in this work, built in our laboratory [2], was developed with the purpose of simulating the performance of the human visual system taking into account the appropriate requirements for this kind of task.

The head mounted display used was the VFX1 Virtual Reality HMD from Interactive Imaging Systems Inc. The VFX1 has the possibility of displaying stereo images on two 0.7" color LCDs with a resolution of 263x230. It also includes a head movement tracker that can give information about pitch, roll and yaw. The sensor information from the head tracker is available at a frequency of 60Hz.

The fact that the tracking device is integrated on the head mounted display enables a very good degree of autonomy of the system because there is no external reference needed for the sensors. That means that no special setup or calibration is needed every time the user changes his location giving the operator more freedom of movements during the telepresence process.

The head mounted display and the active vision system are connected by a 100 MBit/s Ethernet local network used to exchange both images and sensor information. This connection gives sufficient bandwidth for displaying the two 263x230 images at a constant rate of 25 images per second.

The head tracking information (pitch, yaw and roll), after being filtered is used to send velocity commands to the motors of the active vision system (pan, tilt, swing). This control in velocity mode enables a smooth motion of the active vision system. This feature is essentially important for the quality of the visual feedback to the operator.

3 Motion Model development

As stated before, the use of predictive techniques can attenuate the effects of the active vision system latency. Kalman filtering using a predefined model of motion copes with the delays and low sampling rate of the sensorial information of the head tracking device and also bounds the effect of measurement errors in the sensors and enables a smooth tracking motion.

If we assume that the operator's head position coordinates are sampled at an uniform interval time T and that during that interval the head is assumed to be moving with a constant acceleration then we can assume the motion model expressed in the following equations:

$$\begin{aligned} \ddot{x}_{k+1} &= \ddot{x}_k + T w_k \\ \dot{x}_{k+1} &= \dot{x}_k + T\ddot{x}_k + \frac{T^2}{2} w_k \\ x_{k+1} &= x_k + T\dot{x}_k + \frac{T^2}{2}\ddot{x}_k + \frac{T^3}{6} w_k \end{aligned} \quad (1)$$

Where x_k, $\dot{x}_k$, $\ddot{x}_k$ are the head position, velocity and acceleration at time kT respectively, ω_k is the rate of change of acceleration which is modeled as a white noise process.

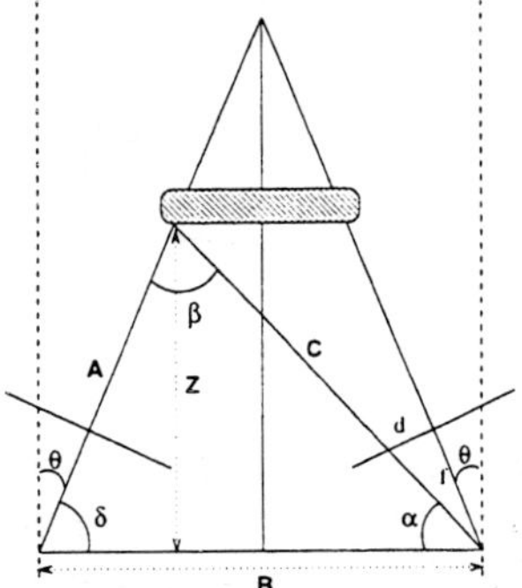

Figure 3. Geometric configuration assumed to compute the vergence angles.

This model can be expressed in matrix form as

$$\begin{bmatrix} x_{k+1} \\ \dot{x}_{k+1} \\ \ddot{x}_{k+1} \end{bmatrix} = \begin{bmatrix} 1 & T & \frac{T^2}{2} \\ 0 & 1 & T \\ 0 & 0 & 1 \end{bmatrix} \begin{bmatrix} x_k \\ \dot{x}_k \\ \ddot{x}_k \end{bmatrix} + \begin{bmatrix} \frac{T^3}{6} \\ \frac{T^2}{2} \\ T \end{bmatrix} \omega_k \tag{2}$$

and

$$y_k = \begin{bmatrix} 1 & 0 & 0 \end{bmatrix} \begin{bmatrix} x_k \\ \dot{x}_k \\ \ddot{x}_k \end{bmatrix} + v_k \tag{3}$$

or $X_{k+1} = FX_k + Gw_k$ and $y_k = CX_k + v_k$ where F is the state transition matrix, X_k is the state vector, G is the noise vector, C is the measurement vector, y_k is the noisy measurement.

In order to improve the performance of the filter for a wider range of head dynamics an algorithm that automatically adjusts the variance of the system noise as a function of the prediction error can be used [4]. The method we implemented was proposed by Kiruluta et al. [6] and consists on the assumption that the acceleration is represented as a stochastic process whose mean value switches whenever a step discontinuity in acceleration is encountered. It consists on adding an input term to the acceleration process. The modified acceleration process becomes

$$\ddot{x}_{k+1} = \ddot{x}_k + u_k + Tw_k \tag{4}$$

where u_k represents the acceleration bias term, i.e. the effect of a head maneuver is to introduce a step change in the acceleration process of magnitude u_k (see [6] for details about the computation of u_k).

4 Vergence Control

To maximize the 3D perception of the operator the system is able to adjust the vergence angle of the active vision system in order to maintain fixation on the objects presented in the center of the image.

Figure 4. Three images taken from the system cameras to illustrate the behavior of the vergence control. Both images are presented interlaced in order to evidence the disparity.

The configuration we adopted is shown in figure 3. We are assuming that the vergence angle on both cameras is the same. The goal is to maintain fixation in the object present at the center of the image. This is done using a grey level correlation on both images. We try to find a match between a block on the center of one of the images with an equivalent block on the other image. The disparity (d) between both blocks is present due to the fact that the target has moved to a different position (changing its depth), or that a new target has appeared on the scene. In this case the vergence angle θ on both cameras must be updated in order to keep fixation on the target.

The computation of the new vergence angle is the following: we start by computing the new target depth (Z). From figure 3we can see that

$$Z = C \cdot \sin \alpha \tag{5}$$

On the triangle $[ABC]$ we can apply the law of Sines,

$$\frac{A}{\sin \alpha} = \frac{B}{\sin \beta} = \frac{C}{\sin \delta} \tag{6}$$

with $\delta = (\frac{\pi}{2} - \theta)$ and $\beta = (\frac{\pi}{2} - \alpha + \theta)$.
Combining the two previous equations we obtain

$$Z = B \frac{\sin \alpha \cos \theta}{\cos \alpha \cos \theta + \sin \alpha \sin \theta} \tag{7}$$

Since $\sin \alpha$ and $\cos \theta$ can't be zero in the assumed configuration then the previous equation becomes

$$Z = \frac{B}{\cot \alpha + \tan \theta} \tag{8}$$

Finally the new vergence angle θ_N can be computed as

$$\theta_N = \arctan \frac{\frac{B}{2}}{\frac{B}{\cot \alpha + \tan \theta}} = \arctan \frac{\cot \alpha + \tan \theta}{2} \tag{9}$$

with $\alpha = \frac{\pi}{2} - \theta - \arctan\frac{d}{f}$, d is the computed disparity measured in the image plane and f the focal length used.

The new vergence angle is used to update the position of the motors that control the vergence angle of both cameras. The entire process (correlation and vergence update) is performed at 25 frames per second.

Figure 4 illustrates three frames captured by the active vision system. The images from both cameras are here shown interlaced in order to allow us to better see the disparity present. In the first image the system was verged on a certain subject. When another one comes in front of the cameras the system adjusts its vergence in order to fixate on the new subject.

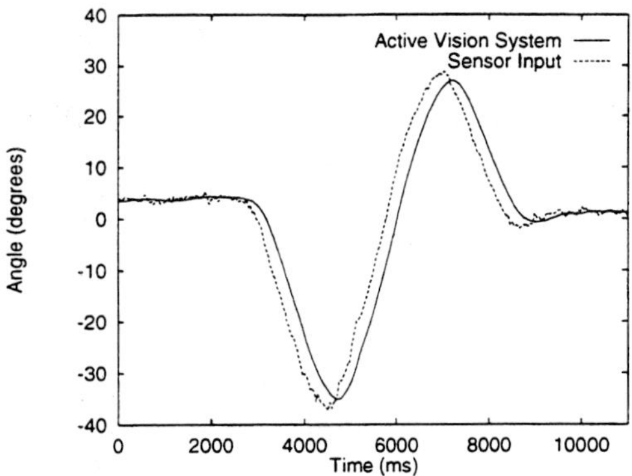

Figure 5. Test showing actual sensor information and motor response of the active vision system for pan angle

5. Results and Conclusions

The entire system runs in real-time without the use of any kind of special hardware. Both the active vision system and the head mounted display are controlled by two computers equipped with Pentium II 300 Mhz processors.

Figure 5 shows an example of the information obtained by the head mounted display sensors compared to the actual response of the active vision system for the pan degree of freedom.

In this paper we described a system aimed at visual telepresence by remote control of an active vision system for surveillance purposes. The use of a static camera improves the functionality of the system since it allows the autonomous detection and tracking of intrusions. A related advantage is the possibility of having the remote user warned about the intruder whereabouts. A future development of this project could be the integration of multiple vision units in order to expand the surveyed area. Upon an alarm condition the remote operator could then be shown the remote environment related to the area where the alarm was originated.

The use of remote dynamic sensors can provide a relatively inexpensive solution while providing a good level of functionality in a dynamic environment. We tried to envision a solution that could employ low-cost hardware without compromising performance. Special care put on the design of the active vision system led to mechanical performances in the same range as usual normal human head movements (velocities up to 360 $\deg/s$). Three degrees of freedom were controlled giving the user more freedom of motion. Usual latencies in this kind of systems were reduced by using predictive models. The kinematics model was implemented in a Kalman filter and used to generate one-step-ahead prediction estimates for a number of head trajectories. Results suggest that the system is capable of dealing with normal human movements. Both smooth and abrupt head movement were mimicked by the active vision system. The motors are controlled in velocity mode which enables a smooth motion of the active vision system which is essentially important for the quality of the visual feedback to the operator.

References

[1] A. Azarbayejani, T. Starner, B. Horowitz, and A. P. Pentland. Visually controled graphics. *IEEE Transactions on Pattern Analysis and Machine Intelligence*, 15:602–605, 1993.

[2] J. Batista, P. Peixoto, and H. Araujo. Visual behaviors for real-time control of a binocular active vision system. *Control Engineering Practice*, 5(10):1451–1461, October 1997.

[3] H. Fuchs, G. Bishop, K. Arthur, L. McMillan, R. Bajcsy, S. W. Lee, H. Farid, and T. Kanade. Virtual space teleconferencing using a see of cameras. In *First International Symposium on Medical Robotics and Computer Assisted Surgery*, pages 161–167, Pittsburgh, USA, 1994.

[4] P. O. Gutman and M. Velger. Tracking targets using adaptative kalman filtering. *IEEE Transactions on Aerospace Electronic Systems*, 26:691–698, September 1988.

[5] J. J. Heuring and D. W. Murray. Visual head tracking and slaving for visual telepresence. In *Proc. IEEE Int Conf. on Robotics and Automation*, Minneapolis, USA, May 1996.

[6] A. Kiruluta, M. Eizenman, and S. Pasupathy. Predictive head movement tracking using a kalman filter. *IEEE Transactions on Systems, Man, and Cybernetics*, 27(2), April 1997.

[7] B. C. Madden and H. Farid. Active vision and virtual reality. In M. S. Landy, L. T. Maloney, and M. Pavel, editors, *Exploratory Vision: The Active Eye*, pages 301–339, New York, 1995. Springer-Verlag.

[8] P. Peixoto, J. Batista, H. Araujo, and A. T. de Almeida. Combination of several vision sensors for interpretation of human actions. In P. Corke and J. Trevelyan, editors, *Experimental Robotics VI*, volume 250 of *Lecture Notes in Control and Information Sciences*, pages 519–528. Springer-Verlag, 2000.

[9] D. Terzopoulos and K. Waters. Analysis and synthesis of fatial image sequences using physical and anatomical models. *IEEE Transactions on Pattern Analysis and Machine Intelligence*, 15(6):569–579, 1993.

Production of Video Images by Computer Controlled Camera Operation Based on Distribution of Spatiotemporal Mutual Information

Masaki Onishi, Masao Izumi and Kunio Fukunaga
Department of Computer and Systems Sciences, College of Engineering,
Osaka Prefecture University, 1-1 Gakuen-cho, Sakai, Osaka, 599-8531 Japan
onishi@com.cs.osakafu-u.ac.jp, {izumi,fukunaga}@cs.osakafu-u.ac.jp

Abstract

This paper define a spatiotemporal mutual information on the pixels of a given video image on the basis of information theory (Shannon's communication theory), which can be interpreted as the theoretical estimation of interested spots for human being. As an application of this spatiotemporal mutual information, we propose a method of producing a vivid video image of the distance learning by using the computer controlled camera operation and switching of plural camera images on the basis of the video image processing. The results of questionnaire survey for the produced video image confirm the effectiveness of our approach.

1. Introduction

Recent years, high-speed digital data transmission becomes possible accompanied with development of network technique, and a distant learning system, which uses communications satellite or ISDN network, is developed not only at universities but other kind of school and companies [1] [2]. One of the representative methods takes video image of distant learning by a fixed camera. On the other hand, there is a method taking video image using plural cameras and switch the images by a director. Problems encountered in the former method are easy to be a monotone video image and lack of real atmosphere of classroom. Many operators such as cameramen and directors are necessary in the latter method.

In this paper, we propose a method of producing the most suitable video image for members at a virtual classroom by controlling camera direction and zooming, and switching of plural camera images. In the first, we define a spatiotemporal information for each pixel of the video image taken by fixed camera using the Shannon's communication theory. This information reflects a degree of interest in the pixels of the video image for the members of the virtual classroom. In the next, we examine the distribution of spatiotemporal information on the video image, then control the camera point of view to focus on a spot with large distribution. And, by choosing the most suitable video image among plural camera images under the switching rule, which was decided beforehand, the automated camera controlled system and switching system produces a vivid video image, which includes necessary information for the members of the distant learning class.

2. Distribution of spatiotemporal information

2.1. Probability density function of color parameter

We define an appearance probability of a color parameter of a given pixel $\boldsymbol{P}_i = [\, x_i \; y_i \,]^T$ in the form of a probability density function based on distribution of color parameters of the neighborhood pixels, and suppose that the probability function of color parameter $\boldsymbol{X}_i = [\, R_i \; G_i \; B_i \,]^T$ of the pixel $\boldsymbol{P}_i$ follows a 3-dimensional normal distribution function.

$$p(\boldsymbol{X}_i) = \frac{1}{(2\pi)^{\frac{3}{2}} |\Sigma|^{\frac{1}{2}}} \exp\{-\frac{1}{2}(\boldsymbol{X}_i - \boldsymbol{\mu})^T \Sigma^{-1} (\boldsymbol{X}_i - \boldsymbol{\mu})\} \tag{1}$$

Here, $\boldsymbol{\mu}$, Σ denote a mean value and a covariance matrix of the color parameter $\boldsymbol{X}_i$ at the neighborhood pixels and are given by following equations.

$$\boldsymbol{\mu} = \frac{1}{n} \sum_{k=1}^{n} \boldsymbol{X}_k \tag{2}$$

$$\Sigma = \frac{1}{n} \sum_{k=1}^{n} (\boldsymbol{X}_k - \boldsymbol{\mu})(\boldsymbol{X}_k - \boldsymbol{\mu})^T \tag{3}$$

As the probability $p(\boldsymbol{X}_i)$ is defined by the distribution of the color parameter of the pixel at the neighbor region, this value can be interpreted to be a degree of appearance of the color parameter $\boldsymbol{X}_i$ at the pixel $\boldsymbol{P}_i$.

2.2. Spatial information and temporal information

Here let us define generating information of the pixel of an image. The information $H(\boldsymbol{X}_i)$ of pixel $\boldsymbol{X}_i$ is given by the following equation (1). This definition of the information of the pixel is based on the definition of information, which is given by the Shannon's communication theory.

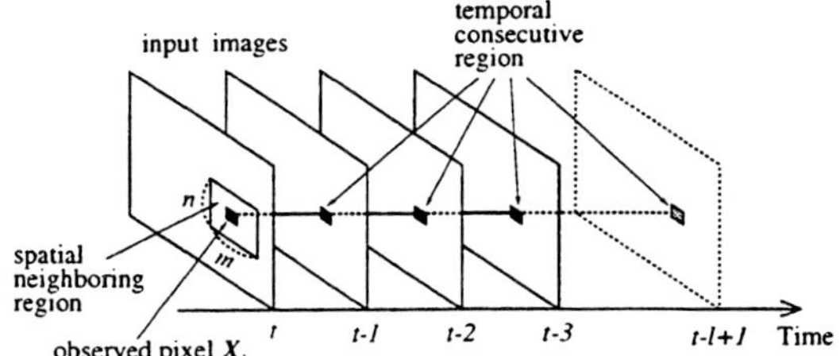

Figure 1. Neighboring and consecutive region.

$$H(\boldsymbol{X}_i) = -\log_2 p(\boldsymbol{X}_i) \tag{4}$$

This information $H(\boldsymbol{X}_i)$ is getting large as the value of $p(\boldsymbol{X}_i)$ decreases. We can examine the distribution of the generating information of an image by calculating the information of each pixel of the image.

In this paper, we discuss two kind of information, one is originated in a spatial variation of the color parameter of the pixels of an image and the other is temporal variation of the color parameter at a fixed pixel. The spatial information is given by the variation of color parameters on an image at the time t, and is getting large in general in the case when the pattern of an image becomes complicated. On the other hand, the temporal information is defined by the variation of the color parameters along the time axis at the fixed pixel $\boldsymbol{X}_i$.

To show the relationship of the spatial and temporal information, let us examine Figure 1. The figure shows $m \times n$ pixels along the spatial direction on one frame image and l pixels along the temporal direction, namely last l frame images. Taking the $m \times n$ neighbor pixels on a frame image into account, the information $H_s(\boldsymbol{X}_i)$ represents the spatial information. In the case when the l pixels along the time axis at $\boldsymbol{X}_i$, the temporal information is given by $H_t(\boldsymbol{X}_i)$. Figure 2 (a) shows an input gray image at time t, (b) shows the distribution of spatial information and (c) gives the temporal information respectively.

2.3. Mutual information between spatial and temporal information

It is necessary that the video image of the lecture include the spot, which is focused by members at the virtual classroom as much as possible when taking a video image. The necessary spot of the scene for the persons at the virtual classroom is a region composed by pixels with both spatial and temporal information, such as the region of a lecturing person (lecturer) with a motion or letters just written by the lecturer.

On the other hand, the degree of interest in a region of the letters written on the blackboard at a long time ago has been reduced even if the spatial information is still large. There is also no interest in the erased region on the blackboard

(a) Input video image.

(b) Distribution of spatial information.

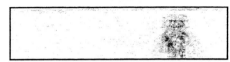

(c) Distribution of temporal information.

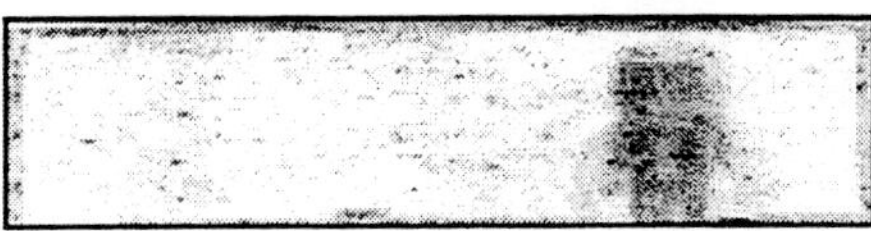

(d) Distribution of spatiotemporal information.

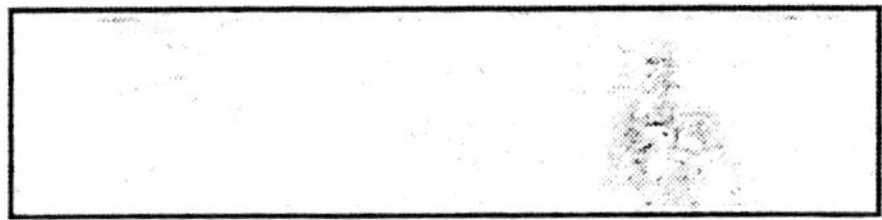

(e) Distribution of mutual information.

Figure 2. Distribution of mutual information.

even if enough temporal information is large. By applying a way of thinking of mutual information between spatial and temporal information, we define mutual information $I(\boldsymbol{X}_i)$ of the region to which the members at virtual classroom pay attention by the following equation.

$$\begin{aligned} I(\boldsymbol{X}_i) &= \log_2 \frac{p_{st}(\boldsymbol{X}_i)}{p_s(\boldsymbol{X}_i) \cdot p_t(\boldsymbol{X}_i)} \\ &= H_s(\boldsymbol{X}_i) + H_t(\boldsymbol{X}_i) - H_{st}(\boldsymbol{X}_i) \end{aligned} \tag{5}$$

Here, $H_{st}(\boldsymbol{X}_i)$ denotes the spatiotemporal information of the pixel $\boldsymbol{X}_i$ on the domain of the neighbor $l \times m \times n$ pixels where $m \times n$ pixels to the spatial direction and l frame images to the time direction as shown in Figure 1. Figure 2 (d) shows a distribution of the spatiotemporal information for the input image shown in (a), and (e) shows the mutual information.

3. Computer controlled operation based on the distribution of mutual information

As a natural consequence, the person at the virtual classroom concentrates the region with large information. A video image including necessary information for the person present produces so as to control the camera to focus the region with the distribution of large degree of information which is calculated for the video image taken by the fixed monitor camera.

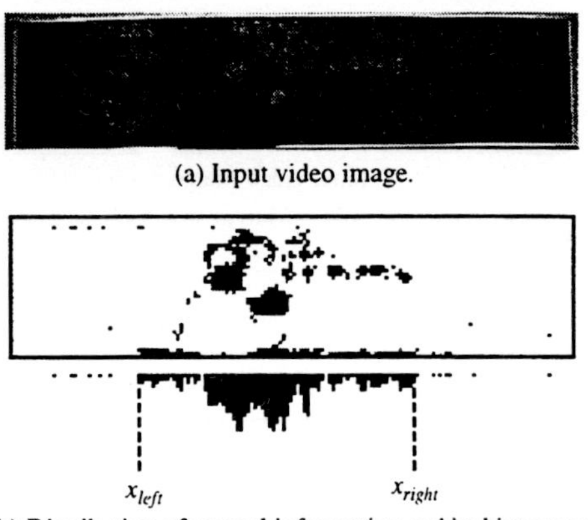

(a) Input video image.

(b) Distribution of mutual information and its histogram.

Figure 3. Distribution of mutual information and its histogram.

In the first, we examine the histogram of the binary mutual information to the direction of horizontal axis as shown in Figure 3 (b). The camera controller sets the line of camera sight to be $(x_{right} + x_{left})/2$ and the zooming range (angleview) to be in proportion to $(x_{right} - x_{left})^{-1}$ so as to be able to catch the interested region for the person present the virtual classroom.

4. Switching of plural video images

Section 3 discusses how to control one camera to take a spot with the necessary information at the video image for the person at the virtual classroom. Suppose that we take a video image by only one camera, there sometimes occurs occlusions of the written letters on the blackboard covered by the lecturer. As this kind of problem could not be solved by one camera, it is necessary to consider switching of the plural camera images so as to obtain the most effective video image. There are several kinds of standards for choosing the best camera angle image. The representative conditions are as follows.

1. The letters written on the blackboard can be always seen without occlusion.
2. The camera line of sight coincides the lecturer's eyes.

Considering the above conditions and experiences through the video image of real distance learning lecture, we prepare lists of switching conditions. In our experiment, the placement of the two shooting cameras and the fixed monitoring camera is shown in Figure 4.

Concrete control conditions are as follows.

1. In the case of zooming out, the blackboard in the video picture may have a distortion when the camera placed in the left hand side of the classroom takes the scene. In this case, the image is taken by the center camera (*CameraI*).

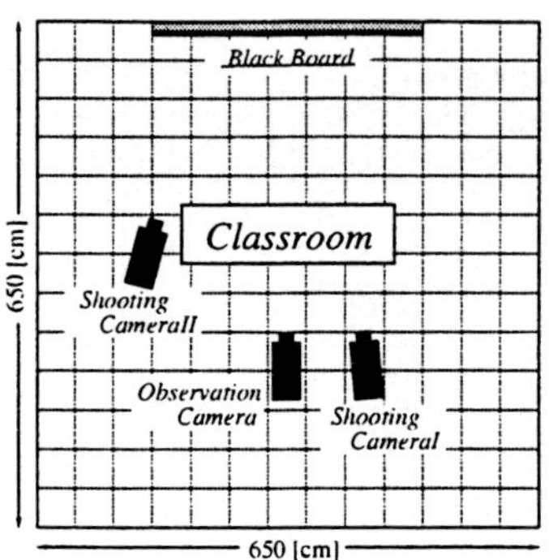

Figure 4. Camera layout in the classroom.

2. In the case when the information is distributed at the right hand side of the blackboard, the image of the center camera (*CameraI*) should be chosen. Conversely, the image of the left camera (*CameraII*) should be chosen on the condition that the information is distributed at the left hand side of blackboard.

These two conditions intend to avoid the distortion of the image, especially the image of the blackboard.

The lecturer is standing at the left hand side of a block of the distribution of information in the case when the point (x_{right}) does not move and the point (x_{left}) moves to the left. Under this condition, the scene is taken by the *CameraI* to avoid the increase of the dead angle caused by the occlusion of the lecturer. Conversely, the scene is taken by the *CameraII* under the condition when the point x_{left} does not move and the point x_{right} moves to the right. Table 1 shows these rules of camera switching. Under the other conditions except above, there is no necessary to switch the video image. Initial camera is set to be *CameraI.*

5. Experiments and Discussions

5.1. Experiments

Controlling the operations of pan, tilt and zooming of the two shooting cameras placed as shown in Figure 4 on the

Table 1. Rules of camera switching.

Taking the video image by *CameraI*
$(x_{right} - x_{left})^{-1}$: sufficient small
$(x_{right} + x_{left})/2$: around the right edge of the blackboard
x_{right} : no change $\cap$ x_{left} : move to left on a large scale
Taking the video image by *CameraII*
$(x_{right} + x_{left})/2$: around the left edge of the blackboard
x_{left} : no change $\cap$ x_{right} : move to right on a large scale

Figure 5. Some examples of video images of the experiment.

basis of the distribution of information using the fixed monitor camera, the lecture scene was taken by the two shooting cameras in real time. Image size of the fixed observation camera is set to be 640×160 pixels on the observation camera and the camera are placed so as to keep the both edges of the blackboard within the field of camera vision. Real image processing was performed with a reduced resolution (160×40 pixels) of the original image considering the processing time.

In this experiment, calculation of the distribution of mutual information on the observation camera image, the control of the shooting cameras and switching of the camera images are done by one personal computer (Pentium 400MHz, memory 128 Mbytes). Every 3 frames of the video image of the observation camera can be processed on this computer.

The duration time of the generating information on the pixels on the observation camera image was set to be 15 seconds, and the parameters of spatiotemporal information are set to be $l = m = n = 3$ taking the processing time into account in the experiments. Figure 5 shows some examples of our video images [1].

5.2. Evaluation of video images by a questionnaire survey

We have examined the effectiveness of the proposed method of the computer controlled camera operations and switching by the visual test. A lecture on explanation of our proposed method is chosen as the sample video image of a lecture (video image was about 20 minute long), and we conduct a questionnaire on 35 persons on the points of camera operation and switching of the images. The questionnaire was set out on the following three case of camera

[1] See: http://www.com.cs.osakafu-u.ac.jp/~onishi/research-e.html

Table 2. Results of questionnaires.

Question item	Man	Com	F
Easy to recognize the lecturer's expression	4.36	4.23	0.58
Easy to read written letters on the blackboard	4.47	4.23	2.85
Easy to understand the lecturer's gestures	3.86	3.80	0.06
Easy to look at interested points	4.23	3.91	3.23
Atmosphere of the lecture	3.87	3.72	0.51

In this table, "Man" shows manual operation image, and "Com" shows computer operation image.

operations.

1. Video image taken by fixed observation camera
2. Video image by experts (Manual operation image)
3. Video image taken by our propose method (Computer operation image)

The video image by experts was taken by 2 cameramen and 1 director who switch the two video images. The placement of video cameras used by the above three cases is shown in Figure 4. The suitability of the camera shooting was evaluated with 5-step estimation method. The level 3 estimation (middle level) was set to be the case of the video image by the fixed observation camera. The result of the questionnaire survey is shown in Table 2 where the value F was defined by a ratio of the mean square and the mean square of error of the shooting methods. The value F is getting large as the difference among the methods increases.

6. Conclusions

In this paper, we have defined the spatiotemporal mutual information on the pixels of a given video image on the basis of information theory (Shannon's communication theory). This can be interpreted as the theoretical estimation of interested spots for human being. As an application of this spatiotemporal mutual information, this paper has proposed a method of producing a vivid video image of the distance learning by using the computer controlled camera operation and switching of plural camera images on the basis of the video image processing. The results of questionnaire survey confirm the effectiveness of our approach.

References

[1] S. C. Brofferio, "A University Distance Lesson System: Experiments, Services, and Future Developments," *IEEE Trans. on Education*, vol.41, no.1, pp.17–24, Feb. 1998.

[2] M. Minoh and Y. Kameda, "Distance Learning Environment based on the Interpretation of Dynamic Situation of Lecture Room," *Proc. of 3rd Int. Workshop on Cooperative Distributed Vision*, pp.283–301, Nov. 1999.

Surface Recovery from Planar Sectional Contours

G. Cong and B. Parvin *

Computing Sciences
Lawrence Berkeley National Laboratory
Berkeley, CA 94720
http://vision.lbl.gov

Abstract

In this paper, we propose a new approach for surface recovery from planar sectional contours. The surface is reconstructed based on the so-called "Equal Importance Criterion," which suggests that every point in the region contributes equally to the reconstruction process. The problem is then formulated in terms of a partial differeXntial equation, and the solution is efficiently calculated from distance transformation. To make the algorithm valid for different application purposes, both the isosurface and the primitive representations of the object surface are derived. The isosurface is constructed by PDE (Partial Differential Equation), which can be solved iteratively. The traditional distance interpolating method, which was used by several researchers for surface reconstruction, is an approximate solution of the PDE. The primitive representations are approximated by Voronoi Diagram transformation of the surface space. Isosurfaces have the advantage that subsequent geometric analysis of the object can be easily carried out while primitive representation is easy to visualize. The proposed technique allows for surface recovery at any desired resolution, thus avoiding the inherent problems of correspondence, tiling, and branching.

1 Introduction

Surface reconstruction from a set of planar sectional contours has been an important problem in diverse scientific fields. These contours define the intersections of the object surface with a set of parallel planes along a desired orientation. For example, CT and MRI techniques can provide dense serial sectional representation of electron density and water molecule concentration at different locations along a particular axis. Similarly, in confocal microscopy, cross sections are obtained by focusing the optical system at specific locations along the z axis. The propose of our work is to utilize these cross sections to recover the three-dimensional surfaces of the object for visualization as well as geometric analysis.

Most of the existing techniques treat the "surface from contours" as a primitive reconstruction problem. The primitives are calculated from the adjacent planar contours according to their geometrical relationship. The approaches lead to three sources of ambiguities [7, 12, 16, 17, 18, 21, 32, 33]: (1) correspondence, (2) tiling, and (3) branching problems. A few techniques aim to represent the surface as the zero-set of an implicit function [15, 20, 25] which can be visualized by, *e.g.,* the matching cubes algorithm. A field function is computed in each slice, and the volume data is constructed by spline interpolation of the slice images. These approaches also lead to some ambiguities: (1) field function, (2) artificial surface and (3) efficiency.

*This work is supported by the Director, Office of Science, Office of Advanced Scientific Computing Research, Mathematical, Information, and Computational Sciences Division of the U. S. Department of Energy under Contract No. DE-AC03-76SF00098 with the University of California. The publication number is LBNL-45799.

In this paper, we treat the problem in a new way. We derive both the isosurface-based and primitive-based representations of the target object so that the reconstructed surface is efficient for visualization as well as geometric analysis. This approach is based on representing the problem as a partial differential equation (PDE), which can be solved iteratively [10]. The isosurface is calculated by linear interpolation between the distance transformation of adjacent contours while the primitives are computed from the Voronoi Diagram (VD). Although the distance interpolation is used by Jones and Chen [20], it is only an approximation of the solution of the PDE. Our solution naturally avoids the correspondence, tiling, and branching problems in favor of a more robust and efficient solution. The underlying constraint is based on the Equal Importance Criterion (EIC), which suggests that all points contribute equally to the shape-reconstruction process. Formally, the constraint states that surface height decreases linearly along the trajectory of its gradient. As a result, the problem reduces to solving a PDE. Experimental results on both synthetic data and real contours are included.

2 Equal Importance Criterion

The proposed reconstruction problem is underconstrained and ill-posed. To constrain the problem, we impose a smoothness measure based on the Equal Importance Criterion (EIC). Consider a pair of contours $\mathcal{C}_1$ and $\mathcal{C}_2$. Let $\mathcal{O}_i(x,y), i = 1,2$ be the binary "object function" such that $\mathcal{O}_i(x,y) = 1$ if the point (x,y) belongs to the object (inside), $\mathcal{O}_i(x,y) = 0$ if (x,y) is on the curve, and $\mathcal{O}_i(x,y) = -1$, otherwise. The surface space $R(\mathcal{C}_1,\mathcal{C}_2)$ is defined by:

$$R(\mathcal{C}_1,\mathcal{C}_2) = \{(x,y)|\mathcal{O}_1(x,y)\mathcal{O}_2(x,y) \leq 0\} \quad (1)$$

In $R(\mathcal{C}_1,\mathcal{C}_2)$, we want to construct a surface $f(x,y)$ such that $f(\mathcal{C}_1) = 1, f(\mathcal{C}_2) = 2$. Obviously, in the absence of no constraints, infinitely many solutions exist. To constrain the problem, we assert that *every point in $R(\mathcal{C}_1,\mathcal{C}_2)$ is equally important and contributes similarly to the reconstruction process. Any other assumption means that we know something about the surface.* We call this the *Equal*

Importance Criterion. This constraint is formalized by requiring that the change in the gradient-magnitude along the gradient direction should be zero, that is: $\mathcal{J}_1(f) = \nabla(|\nabla f|) \cdot \frac{\nabla f}{|\nabla f|} = 0$ where ∇f indicates the gradient of f, $|\ |$ the norm and $\cdot$ the inner product. The above PDE implies that along each trajectory of the gradient of the surface, the magnitude of the gradient is a constant. In another words, the height decreases linearly from 2 to 1. The level curves of the surface are equally distributed along the gradient direction. Thus, in view of height, which is our only evidence about surface, all points are equally important to us. $\mathcal{J}_1$ can be reduced to the "Infinity Laplacian" $\mathcal{J}_2(f) = f_x^2 f_{xx} + 2f_x f_y f_{xy} + f_y^2 f_{yy} = 0$ which has been studied in the literature [1, 2, 3, 14]. Thus,

$$\begin{aligned} \mathcal{J}_2(f) = 0, \quad (x, y) \in R(\mathcal{C}_1, \mathcal{C}_2) \\ s.t. \quad f(\mathcal{C}_1) = 1, \quad f(\mathcal{C}_2) = 2. \end{aligned} \tag{2}$$

3 Isosurface reconstruction

In our PDE-based approach, the correspondence, tiling, and branching problems have been eliminated and the distance between $\mathcal{C}_1$ and $\mathcal{C}_2$ in the z direction is no longer important because it only changes the solution by a scale. We now develop an efficient solution for the above equation.

3.1 Solving the PDE

Let's define $\mathcal{D}_i(x, y), i = 1, 2$ as the *Distance Transformation* of curve $\mathcal{C}_i$, where $\mathcal{D}_i(x, y)$ has the same sign of $\mathcal{O}_i(x, y)$. For each point p (shown in Figure 1), there should be a gradient trajectory γ passing through it such that it intersects $\mathcal{C}_1$ and $\mathcal{C}_2$ at p_1 and p_2, respectively. Since $\mathcal{C}_1$ and $\mathcal{C}_2$ are equal height contours, it is easy to show that the normal of these two contours and the gradient of surface are in the same direction. Thus, $\gamma \perp \mathcal{C}_1$ at p_1 and $\gamma \perp \mathcal{C}_2$ at p_2. We can approximate the curve γ, passing through p, by drawing two line segments $pp'_1 \perp \mathcal{C}_1, pp'_2 \perp \mathcal{C}_2$, to create $p'_1 p p'_2$. Let l denote the length of γ from p_1 to p_2. Hence, $l \approx |p'_1 p| + |p'_2 p|$. The preceding formulation indicates that $|p'_1 p| = -\mathcal{D}_1(p)$, $|p'_2 p| = \mathcal{D}_2(p)$. Since the height decreases linearly, f can be approximated by:

$$f(x, y) = \frac{2|p'_1 p| + |p'_2 p|}{|p'_1 p| + |p'_2 p|} = \frac{\mathcal{D}_2(x, y) - 2\mathcal{D}_1(x, y)}{\mathcal{D}_2(x, y) - \mathcal{D}_1(x, y)} \tag{3}$$

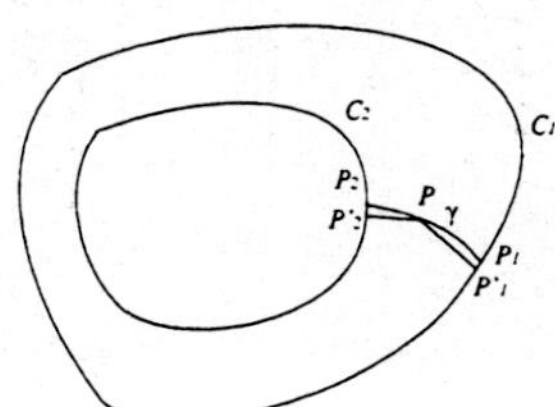

Figure 1: Approximation solution of the PDE.

3.2 Isosurface construction

The three-dimensional isosurface representation, $\phi(x, y, z), 1 \le z \le 2$, can now be expressed as:

$$\phi(x, y, z) = (z - 1)\mathcal{D}_2(x, y) + (2 - z)\mathcal{D}_1(x, y) \tag{4}$$

This (zero value) isosurface $\phi(x, y, z) = 0$ is:

$$z(x, y) = \frac{\mathcal{D}_2(x, y) - 2\mathcal{D}_1(x, y)}{\mathcal{D}_2(x, y) - \mathcal{D}_1(x, y)} \tag{5}$$

which is exactly the surface that we reconstructed in Equation (3). Note that Equation (4) is exactly the distance interpolation as used in [20]. Equation (4) is better than Equation (3) because it works for any adjacent $\mathcal{C}_1$ and $\mathcal{C}_2$ even if $\mathcal{C}_1 = \mathcal{C}_2$. Thus, our algorithm treats any contour and topological changes naturally and cannot fail. From Equation (5), since $1 \le z \le 2$ if and only if $\mathcal{D}_2(x, y)\mathcal{D}_1(x, y) \le 0$, thus $\phi(x, y, z) = 0$ occurs only in the region $R(\mathcal{C}_1, \mathcal{C}_2)$. Thus, we cannot get an artificial isosurface.

The proposed method can be applied iteratively to every pair of adjacent contours $\mathcal{C}_i, \mathcal{C}_{i+1}, i = 1, ..., m-1$ for constructing a series of subsurfaces $\mathcal{S}_i$. These subsurfaces, $\mathcal{S}_i : i = 1, ..., m-1$, form the whole surface, namely $\mathcal{S} = \bigcup_i \mathcal{S}_i$. The final output of the algorithm is a three-dimensional data with new slices inserted between every $\mathcal{C}_i$ and $\mathcal{C}_{i+1}$. If we want a resolution of $\sigma < 1$, say 0.1, along the z direction, reconstruction should include between each pair of adjacent contours $Z - 1$ new slices with $Z = \frac{1}{\sigma}$(an integer Z is expected).

In most cases, the contours are close to one another, thus, the smoothness of the union surface is not a problem. When the contours are considerably apart, the surface may be not smooth at the contour locations. The simplest way to smooth the surface is to convolve $\phi(x, y, z)$ with a small scale three-dimensional Gaussian filter, which is well known as equivalent to move every point on the surface along its normal direction at a speed of its mean curvature [22]. Those points or regions with high curvatures will be smoothed.

4 Primitive representation

A three-dimensional triangle is the basic surface patch used in most visualization systems. In this section, we show how to approximate the surface defined by Equation (3) as an assembly of triangles. The basic idea is to partition $R(\mathcal{C}_1, \mathcal{C}_2)$ into two-dimensional triangles and then project them to three-dimensional space.

4.1 Partitioning $R(\mathcal{C}_1, \mathcal{C}_2)$

Partitioning is based on the Voronoi Diagram (VD), one of the most fundamental data structures in computational geometry and computer vision [4, 24, 23, 35]. Like most of the previous works [5, 11, 28, 37], we assume that $\mathcal{C}_1, \mathcal{C}_2$ are polygonal curves. The vertices and segments linking them are called elements. The VD is a set of points inside $R(\mathcal{C}_1, \mathcal{C}_2)$, where each of them has at least two closest elements equidistant to it. $R(\mathcal{C}_1, \mathcal{C}_2)$ is divided by its VD into singly-connected regions, called Voronoi Regions (VR), according to the nearest-neighbor-rule. Each point in $R(\mathcal{C}_1, \mathcal{C}_2)$ is associated with the element closest to it, and all the points in one VR have the same closest element. See Figure 2. The "net-like" VD consists of line segments and parabola that are fitted by polygon curves [19, 34, 36]. Thus, each VR becomes a polygon.

An iterative approach then partitions each VR into triangles. The approach begins by randomly finding two non-sequential vertices in one VR so that when linked by a segment, the segment is totally inside the VR. This segment

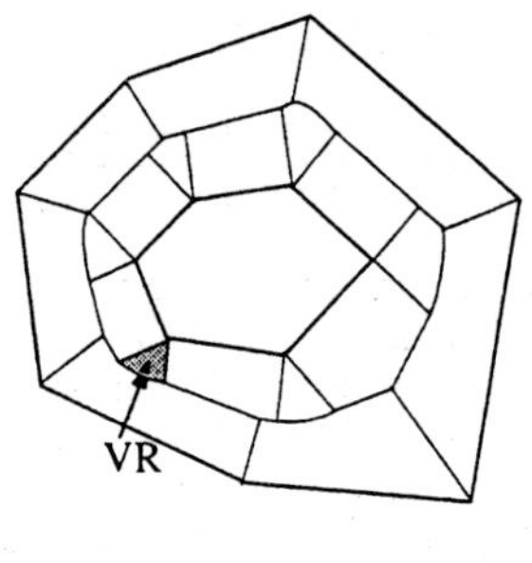

Figure 2: Voronoi diagram.

divides the VR into two parts. The algorithm returns for each part that is a triangle. Otherwise, this part is set as a new polygon, and the process continues recursively.

4.2 Reconstructing three-dimensional triangles

The computed two-dimensional triangles are then projected into three-dimensional space, and the corresponding z-values of the vertices (of the triangles) are calculated by Equation (3). An example is shown in Figure 3.

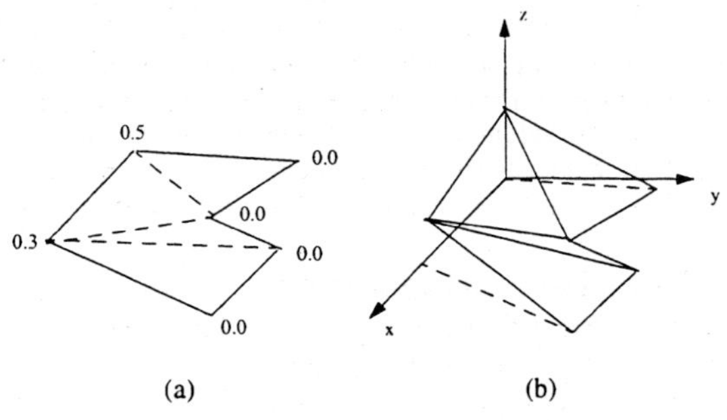

Figure 3: 3D triangle reconstruction. (a) Two-dimensional triangles; and (b) three-dimensional patches.

Two specific situations need more careful treatment. First, if C_1 and C_2 intersect at point p, then the z-value of p can be either 1 or 2, as shown in Figure 4. In 2D, let $p = (x, y)$. In 3D, p is denoted by $p_1 = (x, y, 1)$ on C_1 and $p_2 = (x, y, 2)$ on C_2. In this case, an additional triangle $b-p_1-p_2$ besides triangles $a-b-p_2$ and $b-c-p_1$ must be constructed to preserve the continuity of the surface. Second, if C_1 and C_2 share a common segment, as shown in Figure 4, the z-value of that segment can also be either 1 or 2. In 2D, let $a = (x_1, y_1)$, $b = (x_2, y_2)$. In 3D, a and b are denoted by $a_1 = (x_1, y_1, 1), a_2 = (x_1, y_1, 2), b_1 = (x_2, y_2, 1), b_2 = (x_2, y_2, 2)$, respectively. Hence, a rectangle $a_1 - a_2 - b_2 - b_1$ must be constructed.

5 Experimental results

The proposed protocol has been tested on real medical images for both the isosurface representation (Figures 5) and the primitive representations (Figure 6).

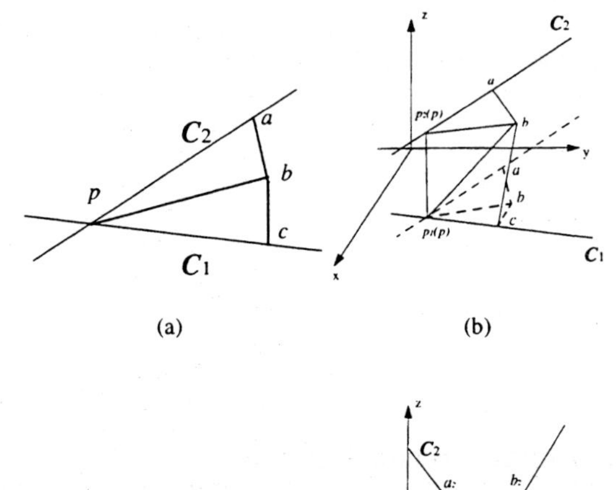

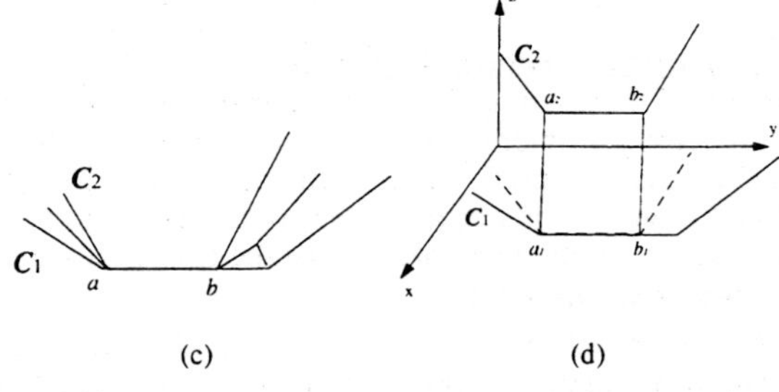

Figure 4: C_1, C_2 intersect at point p. (a)Two-dimensional partition; (b)three-dimensional triangles; (c)Two-dimensional partition; and (d) three-dimensional rectangle.

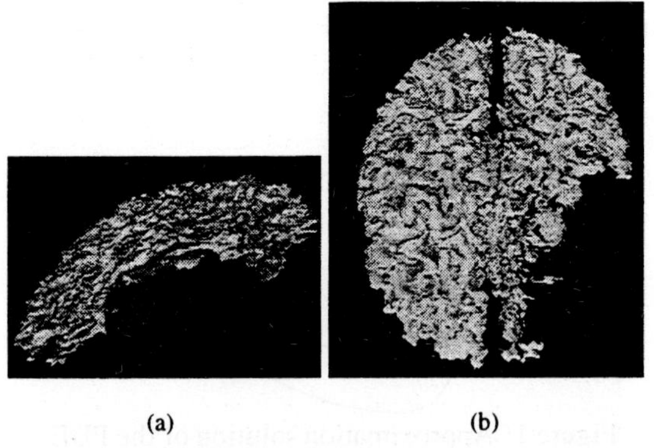

Figure 5: Reconstruction results of white matter in cortex and region due to edema.

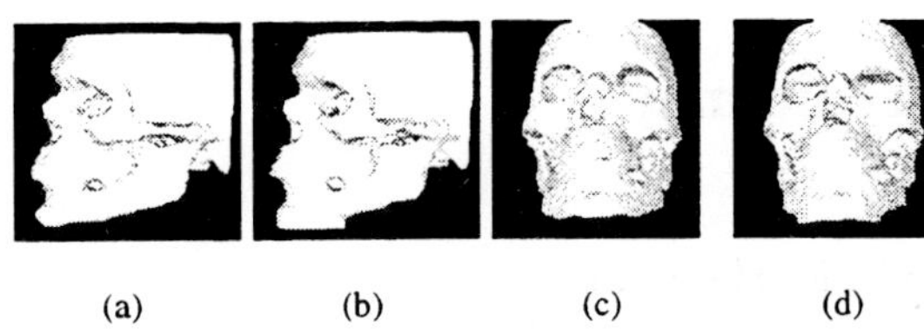

(a) (b) (c) (d)

Figure 6: Surface reconstructed from CT data. (a)(c) surface reconstructed from 22 contours; (b)(d) surface reconstructed from 16 contours;

6 Conclusion

Shape from cross-sectional contours is an important problem in diverse fields of science and has been studied extensively. However, some of these methods suffer from correspondence, tiling, and branching problems. The novelty of the proposed method is in its unique smoothness measure, the corresponding PDE, and its simple solution based on distance transformation. We showed that a linear solution provides an adequate representation of the isosurface. In the case of primitive representation, VD gives us a natural segmentation of the surface space and enables us to construct small surface patches more easily for any shape. We have tested and verified our approach on data with different degrees of complexities, ranging from simple geometric features to complex and convoluted structures of cortex.

References

[1] G. Aronsson. Extension of function satisfying lipschitz conditions. *Arikv för Matematik*, 6:551–561, 1966.

[2] G. Aronsson. On the partial differential equation $u_x^2 u_{xx} + 2u_x u_y u_{xy} + u_y^2 u_{yy} = 0$. *Arikv för Matematik*, 7:133–151, 1967.

[3] G. Aronsson. On certain singular solutions of the partial differential equation $u_x^2 u_{xx} + 2u_x u_y u_{xy} + u_y^2 u_{yy} = 0$. *Manuscripta Math*, 41:133–151, 1981.

[4] F. Aurenhammer. Voronoi diagrams - a survey of a fundamental geometric data structure. *ACM Computing Surveys*, 23:343 – 405, 1991.

[5] C. Bajaj, E. Coyle, and K. Lin. Arbitrary topology shape reconstruction from planar cross sections. *Graphical Models and Image Processing*, 58(6):524–543, 1996.

[6] J. Boissannat. Shape reconstruction from planar cross sections. *Computer Vision, Graphics, and Image Processing*, 44(1):1–29, 1988.

[7] J. Boissannat and B. Geiger. Three dimensional reconstruction of complex shape based on the delaunay triangulation. *INRIA, Tech. Rep.*, 1992.

[8] G. Borgefors. Distance transformations in arbitrary dimensions. *Computer Vision, Graphics, and Image Processing*, 27:321–345, 1984.

[9] Y. Bresler, J. Fessler, and A. Macovski. A bayesian approach to reconstruction from incomplete projections of a multiple object 3d domain. *IEEE Transactions on Pattern Analysis and Machine Intelligence*, 11(8):840–858, 1988.

[10] G. Cong and B. Parvin. An algebraic solution to surface recovery from cross-sectional contours. *Graphical Models and Image Processing*, 61(4):222–243, 1999.

[11] R. Durikovic, T. Yauchi, K. Kaneda, and H. Yamashita. Shape-based calculation and visualization of general cross-section through biological data. In *Proceedings of International Conference on Information Visualization*, 1997.

[12] A. Ekoule, F. Peyrin, and C. Odet. A triangulation algorithm from arbitrary shaped multiple planar contours. *ACM transactions on graphics*, 10(2):182–199, 1991.

[13] T. Elvins. A survey of algorithm for volume visualization. *Computer Graphics*, 26:194–201, 1992.

[14] L. Evans. Estimates for smooth absolutely minimizing lipschitz extensions. *Electronic Journal of Differential Equations, http://ejde.math.swt.edu/Volumes/1993/03-Evans/abstr.html*, 1993(3):1–9, 1993.

[15] M. Floater and G. Westgaard. Smooth surface reconstruction from cross-sections using implicit methods. *SINTEF Rep.*, 1996.

[16] H. Fuchs, Z. Kedem, and S. Uselton. Optimal surface reconstruction from planar contours. *Communications of the ACM*, 20(10):693–702, 1977.

[17] B. Geiger. Three dimensional modeling of human organs and its application to diagnosis and surgical planning. *INRIA, Tech. Rep.*, 1993.

[18] G. Gitlin, J. O'Rourke, and V. De Pigueiredo. On reconstruting polyhedra from parallel slices. *International Journal of Computational Geometry and Application*, 6(1):103–122, 1996.

[19] R. Gonzalez and R. Woods. *Digital Image Processing*. Addison-Wesley, Reading, MA, 1992.

[20] M. Jones and M. Chen. A new approach to the construction of surfaces from contours data. *Computer Graphics Forum*, 13:75–84, 1994.

[21] E. Keppel. Approximating complex surfaces by triangulation of contour lines. *IBM Journal of Research and Development*, 19:2–11, 1975.

[22] B. Kimia, A. Tannenbaum, and S. Zucker. On the evolution of curves via a function of curvature, i: The classic case. *JMAA*, 163(2), 1992.

[23] D. Lee. Media axis transformation of a planar shape. *IEEE Transactions on Pattern Analysis and Machine Intelligence*, 4:363–369, 1981.

[24] D. Lee and R. Drysdale. Generation of voronoi diagrams in the plane. *SIAM J. Comput.*, 10:73–87, 1981.

[25] D. Levin. Multidimensional reconstruction by set-valued approximation. *IMA J. Numerical Analysis*, 6:173–184, 1986.

[26] W. Lin and S. Chen. A new surface interpolation technuque for reconstructing 3d objects from serial cross-sections. *Computer Vision, Graphics, and Image Processing*, 48:124–143, 1989.

[27] W. Lorensen and H. Cline. Match cubes: a high resolution 3d surface reconstruction algorithm. *Computer Graphics*, 21:163–169, 1987.

[28] D. Meyers, S. Skinner, and K. Sloan. Surface from contours. *ACM transactions on graphics*, 11(3):228–258, 1992.

[29] J. Miller, D. Brean, W. Lorensen, R. O'Bara, and M. Wozny. Geomotrically deformed models: a method for extracting closed geometric models from volume data. *Computer Graphics*, 25:217–226, 1991.

[30] O. Monga, N. Ayache, and P. Sander. From voxel to intrinsic surface features. *Image and Vision Computing*, 10(6), 1992.

[31] O. Monga, S. Benayoun, and O. Faugeras. From partial derivatives of 3d density images to ridge lines. In *Proceedings of the Conference on Computer Vision and Pattern Recognition*, pages 354–359, 1992.

[32] J. Oliva, M. Perrin, and S. Coquillart. 3d reconstruction of complex polyhedral shapes from contours using simplified generalized voronoi diagram. *Proceedings of Eurographics*, 15:397–408, 1996.

[33] Y. Shinagawa and T. Kunii. The homotopy model: A generalized model for smooth surface generation from cross sectional data. *The Visual Computer*, 7(2-3):72–86, 1991.

[34] M. Sonka, V. Hlavac, and R. Boyle. *Image Processing analysis and Machine Vision*. Chapman & Hall, 1995.

[35] V. SriniVasan and L. Nackman. Voronoi diagram for multiply-connected polygonal domains i : Algorithm. *IBM Journal of Research and Development*, 31:361–381, 1987.

[36] W. Wang. Banary image segmentation of aggregates based on polygonal approximation and classification of concavities. *Pattern Recognition*, 31(10):1502–1524, 1998.

[37] Y. Wang and J. Aggarwal. Surface reconstruction and representation of 3-d scenes. *Pattern Recognition*, 19(3):197–207, 1986.

View Synthesis from Needle-maps

Philip L. Worthington and Edwin R. Hancock,
Department of Computer Science, University of York, York Y01 5DD, UK.

Abstract

This paper investigates the use of shape-from-shading for view synthesis. The aim of our study is to determine whether needle-maps delivered by a new shape-from-shading (SFS) algorithm can be used as a compact object-representation. Specifically, we aim to show that the needle-maps can be used to generate novel object views. To this end we conduct two sets of experiments. Firstly, we use the recovered needle maps to re-illuminate objects under varying lighting directions. Here we show that a single input image can be used to construct faithful re-illuminations under radical illumination changes. Secondly, we investigate how the needle map can be used to generate new object poses. Here we show that needle maps can be used for both view interpolation and view extrapolation.

1 Introduction

Appearance-based object recognition has recently attracted considerable interest in the computer vision literature [3, 4]. Although there are various realizations of the idea, the unifying principal is to compute a compact representation of the 2D appearance of 3D objects under multiple viewing and illumination conditions. One of the criticisms of appearance-based object recognition is the demands it places on data collection. Sufficient image data must be accumulated so that accurate object representations can be constructed. For each representative object pose (or characteristic view) there must be sufficient image data to span the range of different lighting directions that are likely to be encountered. The data collection process is not only time-consuming, but also requires that the lighting conditions be carefully controlled. This means that object appearance may only be learned under highly controlled conditions. As a result the method is of limited use for autonomously learning object appearance in an uncontrolled environment.

A more efficient strategy is to collect a small sample of object images. From this sample a set of images is generated so as to span the appearance space for a particular object. In other words, we replace data collection under controlled lighting conditions with view synthesis from a set of representative images. The observation underpinning this paper is that Shape-from-Shading, and by extension other Shape-from-X modules such as Shape-from-Texture, provides an obvious yet hitherto unexplored route to view synthesis. Shape-from-shading has long been a subject of active research within the vision community [1]. Its role has been to deliver a dense map of local surface orientation information from shading patterns. SFS aims to recover the required orientation information by solving the image irradiance equation. However, there are few reported attempts to use SFS for any practical object recognition or shape analysis tasks [8]. Many of the difficulties encountered by existing shape-from-shading schemes can be attributed to the fact that they over-smooth the recovered needle map. We have recently developed a new framework for shape from shading [6, 7] which addressees this problem. The novel contribution in the current paper is to investigate how our improved needle-maps can be used for object re-illumination and view synthesis.

2 Object Re-illumination using SFS

The needle-map returned by shape-form-shading may be re-illuminated by a new light source from any chosen direction. This provides an estimate of the appearance of the object under the new lighting conditions. The input information required is a single image and a single application of the SFS algorithm. Of course, re-illuminating in this fashion ignores the possibility of self-occlusion. However, occlusion effects may be taken into account by integrating the needle-map and performing hidden-surface calculations. This adds considerable computational expense, and takes the scheme into the realm of model-based recognition. Here, we consider the simple case only, and assume that self-occlusion effects are relatively small. This is the case for objects that are predominantly convex.

A sequence of images may be generated by re-illumination using different light sources. The idea underpinning this paper is that the set of images generated in this way can be used in an appearance-based object recognition scheme. This process of view synthesis replaces that of gathering many images under varying and controlled lighting conditions. Indeed, it may be possible to calculate sufficiently good estimates of the appearance under all illuminations from a single image. This should be contrasted with

1051-4651/00 $10.00 © 2000 IEEE

the need for three or more images to calculate the illumination cone [2].

3 Novel View Generation using SFS

The generation of novel views using SFS information is significantly more complex than re-illumination, and here involves a hybrid approach between appearance-based and model-based recognition. We consider both extrapolation from a single view, and interpolation using two views. However, both operate in much the same manner. The needle-map is crudely integrated by simply summing the needle-map components in the x and y directions to generate two surfaces, which are then averaged to reduce noise artifacts. This rough surface approximation may then be rotated by the desired angle about an arbitrary axis. However, the boundary of the surface, where regions may appear or disappear from view, requires special treatment. In this paper, we simply reflect the surface across the image plane to produce a closed object prior to rotation. An alternative approach would be to extrapolate the surface where it meets the image plane, using either the tangent to the surface at the boundary points, or a spline approximation. Such approaches may well yield improved results. This follows intuitively from the assumption that most real-world surfaces are piecewise smooth and that most objects are predominantly convex. Hence, the probability that the current occluding boundary is coincident with a surface discontinuity is assumed small relative to the probability that it continues smoothly, and the surface extrapolated accordingly.

We take the following computational approach. The rotation of the object, Θ, is split into three components: $\delta\Theta_1, \Theta', \delta\Theta_2$, where $\Theta = \delta\Theta_1 + \Theta' + \delta\Theta_2$ and $\{\delta\Theta_1, \delta\Theta_2\} \ll \Theta'$. The small rotation, $\delta\Theta_1$, is used to estimate the initial direction of motion, $\{\mathbf{v}_1\}$, of each initial point, $\{P_1\}$. Similarly, the final small rotation, $\delta\Theta_2$, is used to calculate the final trajectories, $\{\mathbf{v}_2\}$, as each point $\{P_1\}$ maps to a new location, $\{P_2\}$. The transformation which maps the unit vector $\mathbf{v}_1$ to $\mathbf{v}_2$ is then applied to the surface normal at P_1 to yield the estimated surface normal at the corresponding point P_2.

Essentially, each initial vector $\{\mathbf{v}_1\}$ is taken to be an estimate of the tangent to the vector connecting the surface point $\{P_1\}$ to the centre of rotation of the object, and similarly for $\{\mathbf{v}_2\}$ at $\{P_2\}$. Therefore, we assume that the surface normals remain rigid with respect to these vectors, and apply the transformation $\{\mathbf{v}_1\} \rightarrow \{\mathbf{v}_2\}$ to obtain a new needle-map for the rotated object.

4 Experiments

We have investigated using SFS information for both re-illumination and novel-view generation, using the USC range image database of busts of famous composers. For each range image we have generated illuminated intensity images using a Lambertian lighting model.

Our experiments have focused upon using the images generated from SFS to approximate the manifolds of objects in the parametric eigenspace [3]. The eigenspace approach is an elegant and accurate approach to object recognition, but requires large numbers of model images to construct a manifold which describes the appearance of an object under a wide range of viewing conditions. Any reduction in this number which does not adversely impact upon recognition accuracy is clearly important in reducing the time and expense of collecting model data.

4.1 Re-illumination

In the first instance, we consider the possibility of using SFS information to significantly reduce the number of model images which must be obtained in order to capture the appearance of an object under variable lighting conditions. Figure 1 shows the results of re-illuminating the needle-map of the Bach bust obtained by applying the SFS scheme of Section 2. From top to bottom, the rows compare the illuminations and re-illuminations as the light source swings from left to right across the bust. In each case the left hand image is the ground-truth illumination while the right-hand image is the re-illumination generated from the needle-map. For each of the re-illuminations the needle is computed from the ground-truth image in which the light-source direction is $\mathbf{s} = (0, 0, 1)$. The corresponding pair of images are shown in the middle row. Here there is perfect agreement between the two images since our recovered surface normals are constrained to satisfy the image irradiance equation as a hard constraint. The re-illuminations preserve most of the gross image structure even when the light source is moved through a large angle from the image plane normal. The range images contain a lot of fine surface detail. As the re-illumination angle is increased then this is lost. This is largely attributable to our relatively crude image reconstruction method, which does not allow for hidden surface removal at small light grazing angles. However, the regions of light and shadow roughly agree throughout, and much of the large-scale image structure is preserved.

In our next set of experiments we visualise the parametric eigenspace for two different views of a bust. Figure 2 shows the first three components of the image eigenvectors as the lighting direction is varied. The light source direction swings from $\mathbf{s} = (0, 0, 1)$ (i.e. the image plane normal to $\mathbf{s} = (1, 0, 0)$ as the points move from the bottom left-hand corner of the eigenspace to the top right-hand corner. For each view we compare the trajectory in the eigenspace for the ground-truth illumination and the needle-map re-illumination. The divergence between the trajectories is not significant until the light source direction has moved by 60 degrees. This would suggest that re-illumination can result in a a significant reduction in the amount of training data required. It is interesting to bear in mind that the eigenspace is generated from a small and homogeneous set of images.

Moreover, there are only 4, largely similar objects (Bach, Beethoven, Brahms and Chopin). There are 3 views of Bach, 2 each of Beethoven and Brahms, and a single view of Chopin. 10 illuminations of each view were generated in the range $0° - 90°$. Hence, the eigenspace will be extremely sensitive to small differences in appearance.

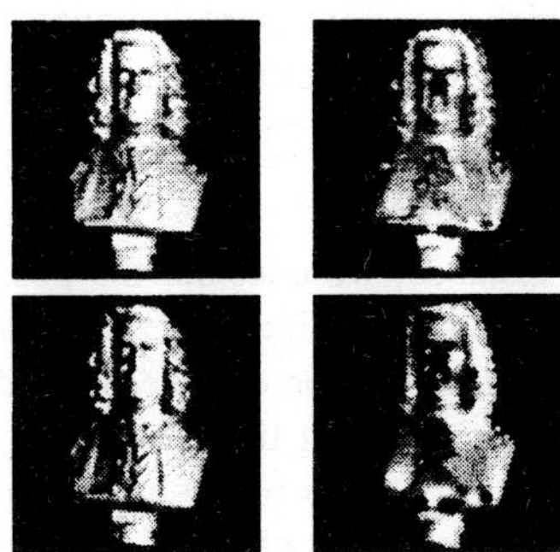

Figure 1. The frontal image of the Bach bust, illuminated by a light source in direction $(0, 0, 1)$, is used as input to our SFS scheme. Th recovered needle-map is then re-illuminated. The left-hand column shows how the bust should look for light-source directions of (top to bottom) $20^{\circ} and, 40^{\circ}$ to vertical in the x direction. The right-hand column shows the corresponding re-illumination results.

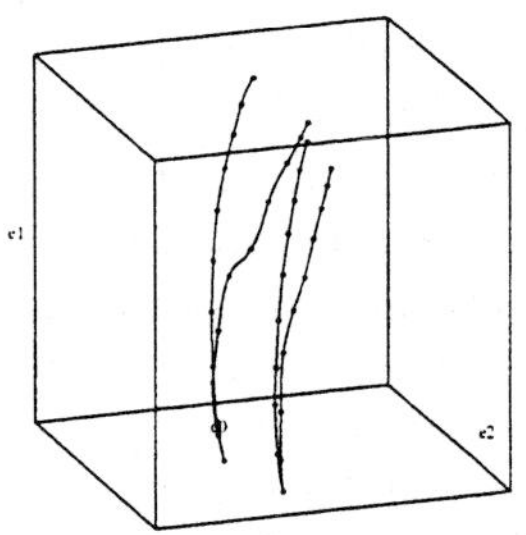

Figure 2. The two views of the Beethoven bust are treated as in Figure 1. The trajectories of the true images and the re-illuminated images are plotted for light source directions $0° - 90°$ to vertical in the x direction. The smoother curve of each pair corresponds to the true images, whilst the re-illumination curve diverges from this as the light source is rotated away from the vertical.

In Figure 3 we show the more complex, 3-D manifolds which can be generated using 3 or more view of an object, in this case the Bach bust. The inner manifold corresponds to the re-illumination of the 3 initial views for the range $0° - 90°$. For re-illumination angles of around $0° - 60°$, the correlation between the manifolds is fairly good, although the true manifold has greater extent.

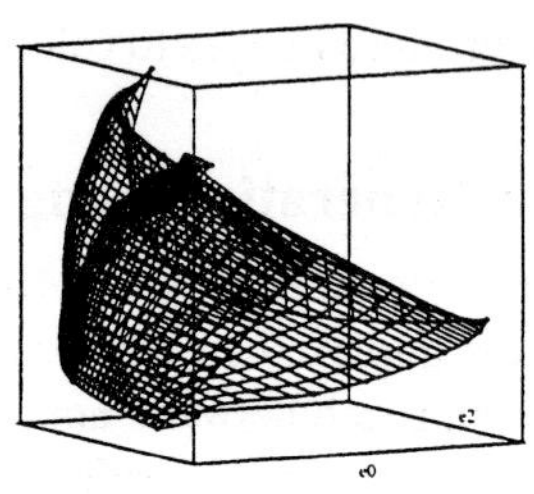

Figure 3. There are 3 range images of the Bach bust, allowing the generating of a 3-D manifold in eigenspace. The 3 views are each illuminated over the range $0° - 90°$ to produce the manifold. The smaller manifold enclosed by the larger one is the result of re-illumination from SFS data.

4.2 Novel View Generation

Generating novel views from SFS data may be accomplished either by extrapolating from a single view, or by interpolating between two or more views. In the first instance, we consider the extrapolation scheme described in Section 3. Figure 4 demonstrates the results obtained using the Beethoven bust. We generate two re-illumination curves, one from each extrapolated needle-map. Both trajectories are have approximately the anticipated location and direction.

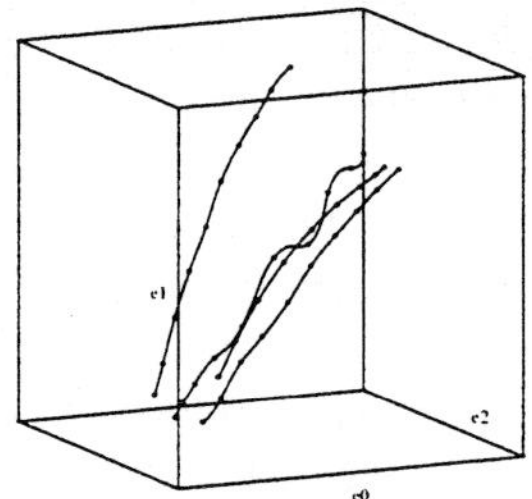

Figure 4. Taking the 2 views of the Beethoven bust, we apply our SFS view-extrapolation scheme to generate two intermediate needle-maps, one from each image. Using each of these, we repeat the re-illumination process over the light source direction range $0° - 90°$. The two outer curves represent the true illumination trajectories for the two busts, whilst the middle curves are the re-illumination trajectories from the extrapolated needle-maps.

Using the simple view-interpolation method described above, we can generate novel views from two model images. Figure 5 shows the re-illuminated images generated from the interpolated needle-map, and compared against the true illumination images. The top row shows the images used for the interpolation and the image generated by re-illuminating the interpolated needle-map with a light source in direction $(0, 0, 1)$. The interpolation process is applied only once; the middle column of subsequent rows shows the results of re-illuminating the interpolated needle-map, with the true illumination images shown for comparison. Given the simplicity of the interpolation scheme employed, these results appear extremely promising. In Figure 6 we plot the re-illumination trajectory of the interpolated needle-map in comparison to the true illumination trajectories of the two views.

Figure 5. The two views of the Beethoven bust are shown illuminated over the range of light source directions $0° - 30°$ (left- and right-hand columns). The middle column shows the results of view-interpolation using SFS, followed by re-illumination over the same range. Although this early attempt at view-interpolation introduces many distorting artifacts, particularly at the boundary of the object, considerable surface detail is retained towards the centre of the object. This detail is relatively stable and accurate under the re-illumination process.

5 Conclusions and Outlook

The results presented here for view-extrapolation and view-interpolation are much more preliminary in nature, and considerable experimentation and refinement remains to be undertaken. Nonetheless, the use of a fast, model/appearance-based hybrid approach as described here has significant potential, as demonstrated by the well-behaved trajectory obtained by re-illuminating the interpolated needle-map.

The view-interpolation results may be significantly improved through establishing correspondence between the two model views to be interpolated. Moreover, an interesting prospect is to adapt the linear combination of views method of Ullman [5] to the combination of needle-maps, thus obviating the need for constructing a 3-D model at any point.

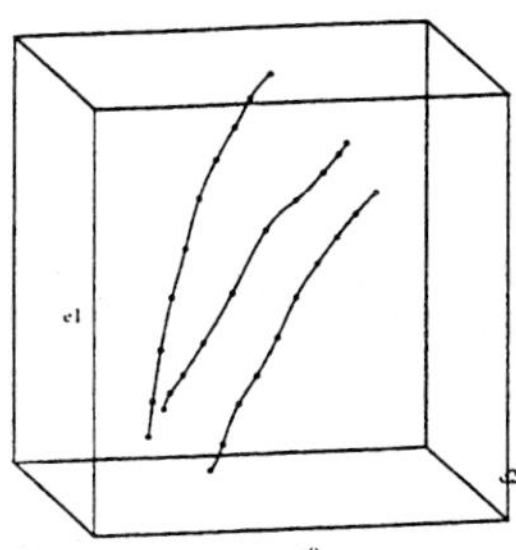

Figure 6. Taking the 2 views of the Beethoven bust, we apply our SFS view-interpolation scheme to generate an intermediate needle-map. From this, we repeat the re-illumination process over the light source direction range $0° - 90°$. The two outer curves represent the true illumination trajectories for the two busts, whilst the middle curve is the re-illumination trajectory from the interpolated needle-map.

References

[1] B.K.P. Horn, "Obtaining Shape from Shading Information." In Winston, P.H. (ed.), *The Psychology of Computer Vision*, McGraw Hill, pp.115-155, 1975

[2] A.S. Georghiades, D.J. Kriegman and P.N. Belhumeur, "Illumination Cones for Recognition Under Variable Illumination: Faces," *Proc. CVPR*, pp. 52-58, 1998.

[3] H. Murase and S.K. Nayar, "Learning Object Models from Appearance," *Proc. AAAI.*, 1993.

[4] S. Ullman and R. Basri, "Recognition by Linear Combinations of Models," *IEEE PAMI*, Vol. 13, No. 10, pp. 992-1006, 1991.

[5] S. Ullman, *High-level Vision*, MIT Press, 1996.

[6] P.L. Worthington and E.R. Hancock, "New Constraints on Deta-closeness and Curvature Consistency for Shape-from-shading," *IEEE PAMI*, Vol 21, pp. 1250–1267, 1999.

[7] P.L. Worthington and E.R. Hancock, "3D Surface Topography from Intensity Images," *Proc. ICCV99*, pp. 911–917. .

[8] P.L. Worthington, B. Huet and E.R. Hancock, "Appearance based object recognition using shape-from-shading", *Proc. ICPR*, pp. 412–416, 1998.

Practical Visual Inspection Techniques
-- Optics, Micro-electronics and Advanced Software Technology --

Seiji HATA
Faculty of Engineering, Kagawa University
hata@eng.kagawa-u.ac.jp

Abstract

Visual Inspection technologies are widely applied in the modern production lines and proved their efficiency. They have wide successful application fields from the precise electronics devices inspection to the huge power plants monitoring, from the modern industrial products inspection to the fruits and vegetable classification. To meet with these wide fields of applications, many progresses have been introduced into the practical visual inspection technologies. The wide dynamic range TV cameras have been introduced to observe the specular objects. Also, sophisticated optical-electronical LSI has been introduced to get the 3-D shapes of electronics components. Also, new kinds of image processing systems have been introduced in the visual inspection field. High performance image processing LSIs are continuously designed and applied to many visual inspection systems and other applications. New software technologies have been also introduced to the visual inspection applications. The field of visual inspection was established in early 70s, and now is expanding its effective fields and technologies. Here, a part of these expansions is discussed

1. Introduction

To introduce the new trend of technology of practical visual inspection techniques, the three aspects of the technologies are introduced in this paper. They are the optical devices, the LSIs and Software technologies. They are brief introductions, but they will shows the active and vivid activities in the visual inspection field.

2. Optical Devices

In the visual inspection systems, to get the clear original images of the inspection objects is the most important problem. Some of the problems of the imaging devices are as follows;

1) The dynamic range of human eyes is 10^4, but that of the CCD camera is 10^2. To apply the image processing technologies to the various applications, this great difference of the dynamic range should be eliminated.
2) To execute the accurate visual inspection, precise and wide range 3-D data of the objects should be extracted in real time.

To meet with these requirements, following developments have been introduced.

2.1 Wide Dynamic Range CCD Camera

To inspect the solder joints or specular objects such as metal surfaces, wide dynamic range imaging devices should be introduced. To meet with the requirement, Naotoh, et. al. developed a wide dynamic range CCD camera described in fig.1. The camera generates the combined image of two cameras. One camera extracts long shutter speed image and another camera extracts short shutter speed image of optically dark image. The combination of two images described below generates more than 10^4 level wide dynamic range image.

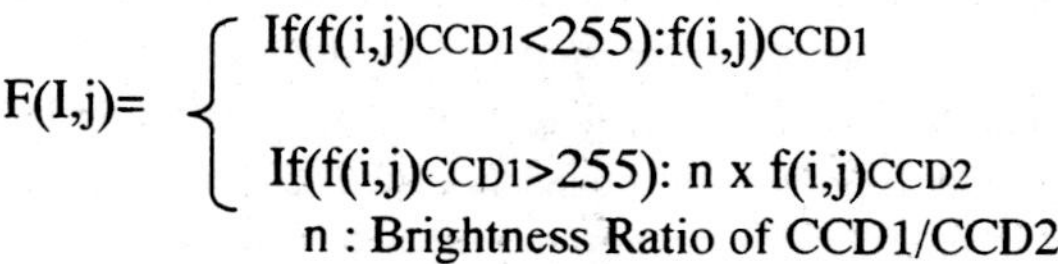

$$F(I,j)= \begin{cases} If(f(i,j)_{CCD1}<255):f(i,j)_{CCD1} \\ If(f(i,j)_{CCD1}>255):\ n \times f(i,j)_{CCD2} \end{cases}$$

n : Brightness Ratio of CCD1/CCD2

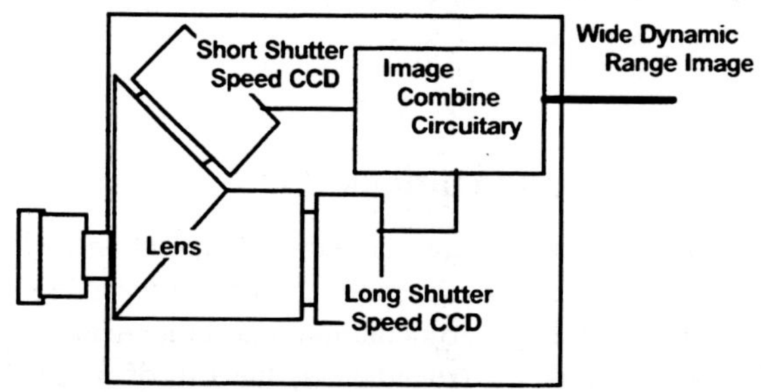

Fig.1 Wide Dynamic Range Camera

2.2 Optical-Electronical Range Imaging Device

1051-4651/00 $10.00 © 2000 IEEE

Confocal optical system can measure the height of the object. But it can extract only one point at one time. So, when the system is applied to a 3-D shape extraction system, it takes long time to extract the 3-D shape of wide object surfaces. To solve the problem, Wakai, et. al. developed Optical-Electrical range imaging LSI. Many confocal micro optical systems are arranged in 2-D array. Photo sensors are also arranged as the same way. Their combination form a range imaging LSI and it can extract a 3-D shape of the surface of electronics components to inspect the components.

2.3 Other Input Devices

There are many progresses in the image input devices. Some of them are the 4M pixels high resolution CCD with zoom and wide image output capability and low cost CCD camera on printed circuit board and retina camera with preliminary image processing functions. They have many capabilities and will have more successful 'application fields in the visual inspection.

3. Image Processing Systems

Recent high performance microcomputers are changing the configuration of image processing systems. Many software oriented image processors have been introduced and proved their efficiency. But, the new algorithms such as optical flow analysis, motion picture analysis and stereo image processing require much higher perfor-mance of image processors.

Kobayashi, et. al. have been developed high performance image processing LSIs since beginning of 80's. Fig.2 shows the history and performance of their LSIs.

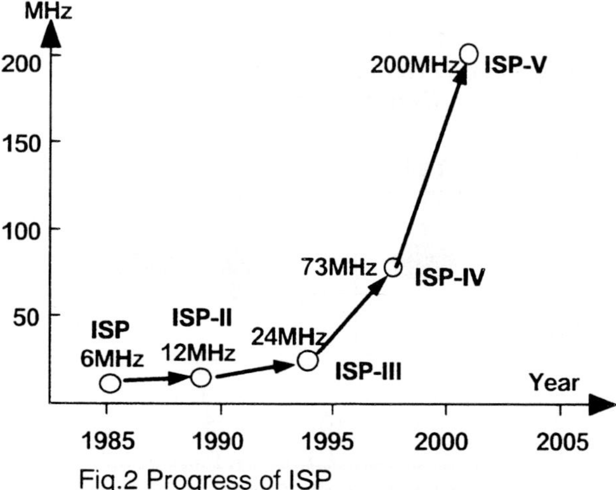

Fig.2 Progress of ISP (Image Signal Processor) Series

Fig.3 ISP-IV

Fig.4 Vision Sensor with ISP

The LSI series has been including many image processing function from the basic filtering operations to current motion picture analysis functions.

Many image processing systems have been developed using the ISP series. Currently, the vision sensor with ISP has been introduced, which has rich image processing functions and personal computer functions in a CCD camera body. The system should be the next generation of intelligent sensors which can be used easily in the production lines.

4. Advanced Software Technology

Today, many advanced software technologies has been introduced into practical production lines. In the visual inspection field, also, many advanced technologies are practically used. KE, NN, Fuzzy networks, GA, etc. are some of them. The aims of these applications are followings;

1) To get the more detailed classification of defects to combine the visual inspection functions and quality control functions of the production line. It means the real-time quality control using visual inspection.
2) To introduce the easy operation to enable the operators on the production lines justify the visual inspection system.

The second point is very important point to apply the visual inspection systems to the wide variety of production lines where the many kinds of products are produced and the production process are changed frequently.

One of other important software technologies currently introduced into production lines is the "KANSEI" processing, the processing of human impression.

Here, an attempt to introduce a fuzzy neural network and an application of KANSEI processing are introduced.

4.1 A Fuzzy Neural Network for Easy Operation

A fuzzy neural network had been introduced to construct easy configurable a printed pattern visual inspection system. The inspection system detects the defects on the printed materials and classifies the defects into several categories such as ink spatter, stain, doctor line, foreign object, etc. The unique points of the system are the followings;

1) The operator can identify the defects by simple descriptions using natural language.
2) From the operator's description, the system defines the structure of its fuzzy networks. Through the learning process using real images, the system adjust the system with high reliability.

Fig. 5 shows a part of a description of the defects by the operators. From the description, the system generates the configuration of its fuzzy neural network. The weighting parameters of the network are adjusted using the example images with defects and without defects.

The system was experimentally applied to several visual inspection systems and proved its efficiency.

4.2 "KANSEI" Image Processing of CDT Grading

There are two kinds of visual inspection. One is the visual inspection for production quality control. At that time, the final goal of the inspection is to eliminate the defect loss of the production and increase the reliability of products.

The other kind of inspection is the final quality inspection of products. For the display and printing devices, the final quality of displayed or printed images is evaluated by their users. So, the inspection should be evaluate the method reflecting the human sensitivities.

One of such inspection systems is the CDT white purity inspection.

For the color display tube(CDT), the quality of white became very important. The evaluation of the quality of CDT is executed by human operators. They watch the CDT displaying white, and judge the grade from 0 to 20(fig.7) according to his experiences. If only the vague yellow zone appears on the CDT, the grade of the CDT is very high, 6 or 7. If the strong red zone and purple zone appear on the CDT, the grade of the CDT is low, more than 15. At that time, the CDT cannot be shipped.

How many defects do you want to identify?: 6
Plaese assign the defect name.
Defect(0) : Doctor
Defect(1) : Foreign Material
Defect(2) : Stain

Names are OK?(y/n) : y

Please describe the (Foreign Material)

How about the AREA?
0: Not Specified
1: Small
2: Rather Small
3: Mediam
4: Rather Big
5: Big
Please input the number: 3

How about the ROUNDNESS?
0: NOt Specified
1: Round

AAA: User Input

Fig.5 Defects Description by Operators

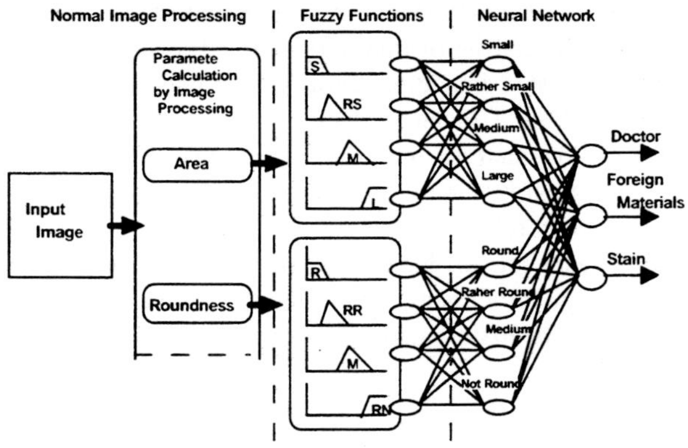

Fig.6 Fuggy Neural Network
Generated from Description

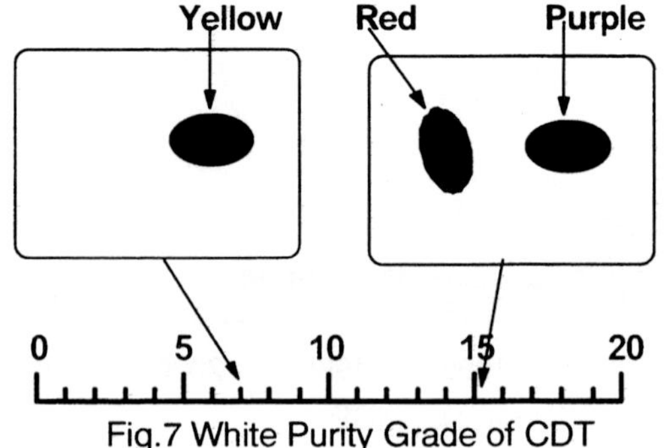

Fig.7 White Purity Grade of CDT

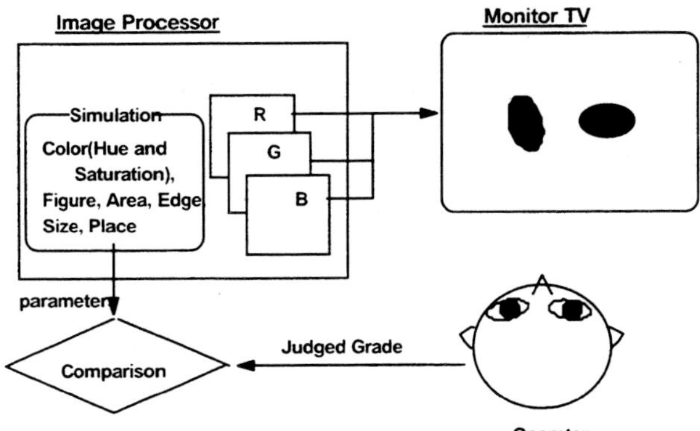

Fig,8 Experiment from Cognitive Science

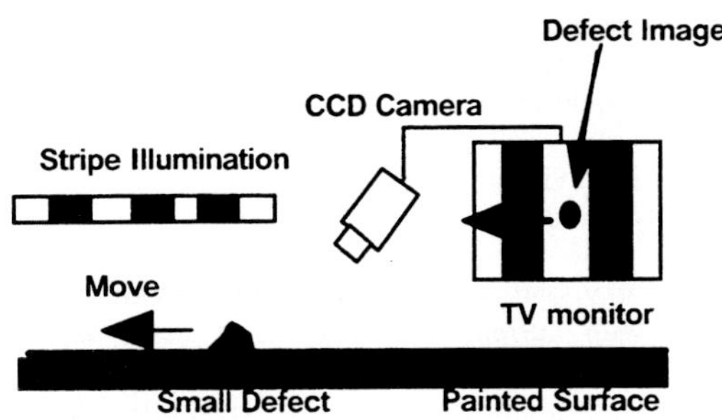

Fig.9 Reliable Small Defects Detection

But this kind of grading is very human oriented, and engineers did not know how they decide the grade. To understand the algorithm that the inspectors judge the CDT grade and to develop the evaluation machine of CDT white grade, the experiment from the cognitive science was introduced.

Fig.8 shows the experience. Many possible parameters those describe the white purity defects are listed. Changing these possible parameters, the purity defects are simulated by a image processor and displayed on a high grade monitor TV. The skillful operator evaluates the grade of the simulated white purity defects. Comparing the operators judges and the simulated parameters of the simulated defects, the judging algorithm of the operator was estimated.

From the experience, the followings are resulted.

1) The color difference from the white is the principal parameter to decide the grade. The color hue is also affects the evaluation. The effect of the hue is similar to the MacAdam Ellipse of color difference recognition.
2) Additional parameters of grading are the area of defects and the strength of edges of defects. These effects can be added to the color difference grade.

Using these results, the grade evaluation system of CDT was developed. The system was successful and proved its higher stability than the human operators.

The system means that the color hue affects the sensitivity of visual defects of display devices and printings. The effect of the color and brightness to inspect the visual defects was widely evaluated by the successive research[1].

4.3 Reliable Small Defects Detection Using Motion Picture Analysis Method

Today's powerful image processor enables to introduce many advanced algorithms into practical visual inspection field. The motion picture analysis method is one of them.

The system inspects the paints defects on automobile bodies. The method of the inspection is as follows;

1) The CCD camera observes the reflected image of the stripe illumination as is shown in fig.9.
2) The small defects reflect the illumination by illegal way. So, the defect point is observed as a dark or bright spot. But when the defect is small, the brightness change cannot be detected, stably.
3) According to the automobile body movement, the defect spot moves in the monitor TV. The next position of the defect in the image can be calculated. So, a image sequence detection of small defects results the reliable small defects detection.

5. Conclusion

It is a quarter of a century after the first successful industrial applications of image processing was introduced into real production lines. During the period, the visual inspection system has been the biggest application field of industrial image processing. Many applications were introduced and proved their effectiveness.

But, as are shown in this short paper, currently, many powerful and effective devices, image processing systems, advanced algorithms and the application themselves are just under development. The field is very active and promising, just now and it will be, also, in the next century.

6. References

Most of the researches introduced here are reported in Japanese.

[1] S.Hata, Y.Miyashita, H.Hanafusa, Human Sensitivbity of Color Defects Inspection, IECON'96, pp.713-718

Visual Attention Control for Nuclear Power Plant Inspection

Nobuyuki Kita
Electrotechnical Laboratory
nkita@etl.go.jp *http://www.etl.go.jp/~nkita/*

Abstract

Industrial inspection robots, which are to move around a nuclear power plant and carry out inspection tasks, must follow a given route while observing static and dynamic features of the environment. To fulfill the visual sensing requirements of such a robot for both a wide field of view to ensure safe motion and high resolution to enable precise observation, we have developed a stereo active vision system equipped with foveated wide-field image acquisition and mounted it on a mobile robot.

With this or other types of active sensors, only the foveated center of the field of view can extract precise information, so the camera pose must be controlled to fixate the target area for execution of a particular visual task. The activities of inspection robots lead to multiple visual tasks, requiring both reactive and premeditated types of attention, and therefore the robot must apply its sensing resources sequentially among multiple possibilities. In this paper, we propose a new framework for visual attention control for a mobile robot, describe the implementation of the proposed framework and show some examples in which the camera pose is controlled to achieve multiple visual tasks.

1. Introduction

Since the early discovery of any defects or problems is crucial to the safe operation of a nuclear power plant, highly-trained inspectors must currently make daily tours. The disadvantages of this situation are clear: humans cannot enter areas of high radiation, and will accumulate radiation even in low radiance areas.

There have been many efforts to substitute machines for human inspectors. One typical approach, in use in commercial plants, involves multiple pan-tilt cameras mounted throughout a plant. Sensing systems mounted on platforms moving along fixed routes, for example on rails, have also been introduced. Nuclear power plants, however, have a very complicated structure mainly consisting of pipes. This makes visual sensing very difficult, because occlusions are common. Cameras at static locations or moving on limited trajectories cannot cover every point crucial for the safe operation of the plant.

A more powerful approach is clearly inspection by mobile robots equipped with various sensors. While remote operation of such mobile robots by human operators is feasible and will be realized in the near future [1], it is desirable for them to be autonomous to as large a degree as possible to decrease the human operators' effort and error. A vision system for such autonomous robots needs to execute multiple visual tasks and the following attributes are desirable:

(1) High-resolution images for inspection

(2) A wide field of view for obstacle-avoidance during motion

(3) Real-time visual information feedback to enable reaction to dynamic situations

A practical vision system which can provide these capabilities with current technology is a stereo active vision system equipped with foveated wide-field image acquisition, as implemented in the ESCHeR active head shown in Fig.1 [2]. The key feature of ESCHeR is the special lenses that project a very wide field of view onto a normal CCD. The images obtained using these lenses provide high resolution at the center of the image and low resolution in its periphery as shown in Fig.2. This enables both precise inspection of features imaged in the small central area (the fovea) and coarse observation of a wide area of the environment.

Figure: 1 ESCHeR: ETL Stereo Compact Head for Robots Vision.

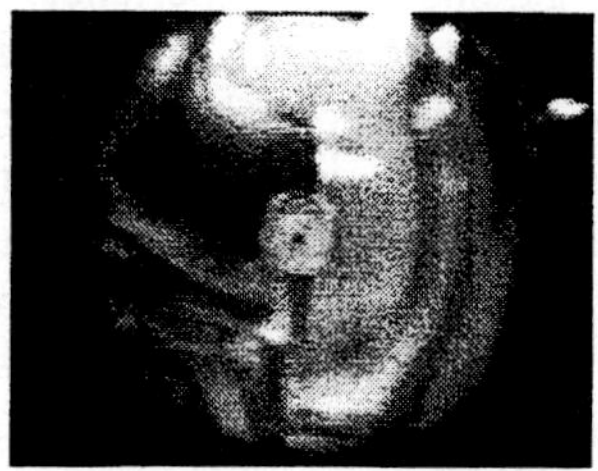

Figure: 2 An example of the input image.

With this or other types of active sensors, only the foveated center of the field of view can extract precise information, so the camera pose must be controlled to fixate the target area for execution of a particular visual

1051-4651/00 $10.00 © 2000 IEEE

task. When multiple visual tasks are given to the robot, the procedure for deciding the next fixation location is very important not only for the efficient execution of the visual tasks but also for the safety behavior control. This process is called "visual attention" and has been well investigated, but previous authors have not considered the case of multiple tasks being tackled by mobile robots. In this paper, we propose a new visual attention framework for mobile robots to deal with multiple visual tasks, which need both reactive and premeditated types of attention. In the next section, the background of visual attention research in machine vision is briefly reviewed. Our new framework is explained in Section 3, followed by the details of the implementation and some examples, which show image sequences obtained from an active camera whose pose is controlled by the proposed method.

2. Attention control for machine vision

Depending on the task at hand, the way of controlling a sensor will follow many different patterns[3]. Many attention control methods corresponding to particular tasks have been proposed[4][5][6][7]. These methods detected limited types of bottom-up features and selected one as the next fixation target according to the criteria defined for the particular tasks. Milanese proposed a more flexible method for object recognition tasks[8] based on the "feature integration model" of psychological visual attention[9]. In this work, various types of features were extracted from an input image in parallel, and the priorities of attention were derived from knowledge about the relationship between known objects in the scene and the extracted features.

While the above methods selected fixation targets from the set of extracted "bottom-up" features, and can be referred to as "***reactive attention control***", there has also been research into the case where fixation targets are derived from other knowledge about the scene which is not related to these features[10][11][12][13][14]. Mavar et. al. decided "from where to look next" for 3D reconstruction according to knowledge about how to avoid occlusions[15]. Westin et. al. used a 3D simulator of a real environment to control attention, where for example, in order for attention not to be attracted to known moving objects, they synthesized the predicted view of the object and used it as a mask for bottom-up motion cues[16]. We call these types of approaches "***premeditated attention control***".

3. Attention control for industrial plant inspection robot

In the case of industrial plant inspection, an outline of the inspection tour, such as the route to follow, locations needing particular observation and so on, can be defined a priori and given as prior knowledge. The robots are the required to achieve these primary goals reliably and efficiently while maintaining safety. Achieving these goals requires the execution of various sub-tasks, which will depend many details of the robot system and environment. It is the performance of these tasks which must be scheduled by an attention control system.

3.1. Multiple visual tasks

In our inspection setup, a vision robot is potentially accompanied by a blind assistant robot which carries extra equipment adapted for different operations (for instance a lighting system or audio sensors). The tasks which must be dealt with by the robot's vision sensor are as follows: (Fig.3):

Task 1. Visual inspection of specified parts of the plant
Task 2. Visual navigation
Task 3. Surveillance of the accompanying blind robot
Task 4. Obstacle avoidance
Task 5. Unpredicted abnormality or incident detection

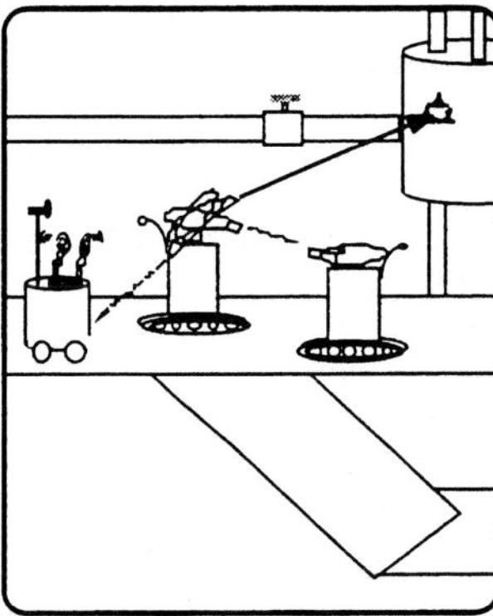

Figure: 3 Visual tasks during a robotic inspection.

Each of these tasks establishes a contrasting set of target areas of the scene from which it is required to extract visual data, and which can be thought of as trying to "attract" the attention of the visual sensor. In Task 1, inspection, the attention targets are clearly defined as those requiring visual observation, and their locations can be given a priori as 3D positions in the world coordinate system. Landmarks for visual navigation in Task 2 can also be defined in advance as 3D positions in the world coordinate system, or in a map-building framework can be the positions of landmarks detected by the robot itself in earlier operation. Task 3, surveillance of the assistant robot, is required because this second robot does not carry navigation sensors of its own and requires external assistance to estimate its position accurately. The position of this robot is continually estimated from odometry and thus the target area for its visual surveillance can be defined in the robot coordinate system. In Task 4, obstacle avoidance, attention should be drawn to unknown objects in the robot's path, which are detected as bottom-up features from the input images. Finally, for Task 5, abnormality detection, region whose appearance are fairly different from what would be expected need attention and can be extracted as 2D regions from input images. Summarising, Tasks 1, 2 and 3 need premeditated types of attention and Tasks 4 and 5 require reactive attention.

3.2. The framework for attention control

When presented with multiple visual tasks, a robot must make a decision about where to look next using two steps[17]. First, tentative foci of attention for each task are identified according to specific selection rules for each process. Second, an actual attention point is selected from all of these candidates. The problem is that attention candidates derived for different tasks have different forms, such as 3D world coordinates or 2D image coordinates, and it makes the definition of criteria for the second step of selection difficult. We propose a new framework in which the second selection step can be made in uniform coordinates: all possible target points will be considered in image space.

For an inspection robot in a nuclear power plant of which a world model is known, as can be reasonably expected in an industrial environment and is the case in our implementation, the robot is able to synthesize a virtual view from the world model based on the current estimated robot position and the camera directions. If we insert salient markers at possible target locations for premeditated types of attention into the world model, for example by placing a marker at a position on the blind assistant robot, or on parts of the fixed scene which are landmarks for navigation, these markers appear as salient 2D features when projected into a virtual view. Since the virtual view is based on the same coordinate system as the actual input view from which salient features for reactive attention control tasks are extracted, the integration of the salient features for both types of attention is straightforward. We use this integrated 2D view space as a uniform space for the second step selection. The model proposed by Westin[16] is similar to this framework, but in our framework we can use the virtual view not only for deterring but also attracting the robot's attention.

4. Implementation and demonstration

4.1. Environment server

In order to realize the proposed framework, we must consider the following issues:

1. Devising and maintaining markers for regions requiring premeditated attention in the virtual environment.
2. It should be possible to influence the location of these markers with respect to the wishes of an operator or plant controller.
3. Simulating temporal changes in the environment, including the motion of the robots in real-time.
4. Synthesizing images from the robot's point of view.

We have developed a view simulator, primarily aiming to facilitate evaluation of the visual sensors and algorithms used by a humanoid robot [18]. This kind of detailed simulation provides great advantages in research, since methods can really be tested in realistic circumstances before facing the real world. Using this simulator, we are able to satisfy 3 and 4, but only perspective projection is supported for image synthesizing. We are extending the view simulator so as to satisfy the rest of the above issues. We call this extended system an ***environment server***.

4.2. Active guideline

We coin the term "*Active Guidelines*" (AG) to describe a specific type of marker which can be inserted into the scene model to represent the candidates of premeditated types of attention process. An AG is a sphere emitting light and located anywhere in the virtual environment including on moving objects. The strength of light emitted by an AG can be controlled by several parameters. The properties of each AG can be set initially with using the GUI of the environment server (Fig.4) and also dynamically changed by other processes during the execution of an inspection tour. Figure 5 shows an example of a synthesized view, where several AGs appear as bright dots.

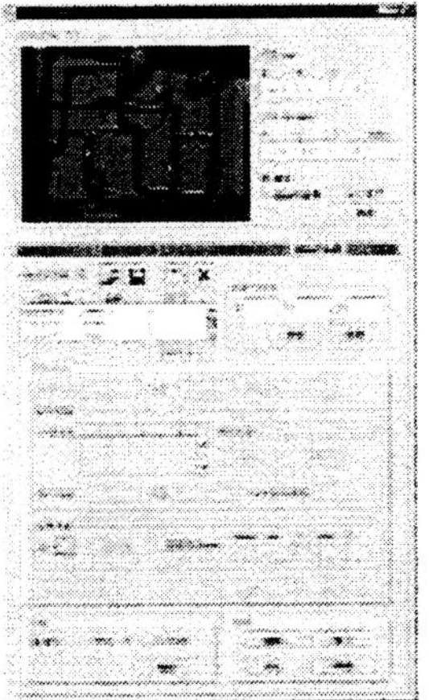

Figure: 4 GUI of environment server.

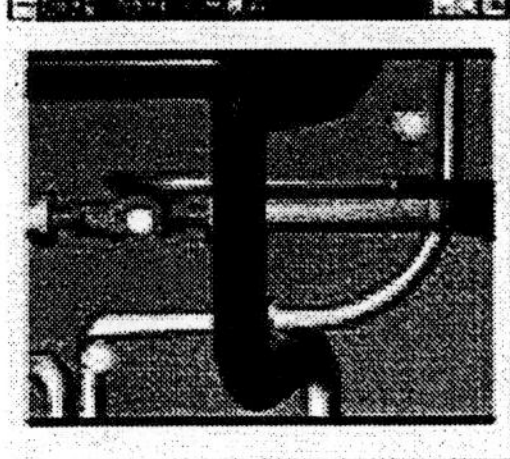

Figure: 5 An example of robot view.

Using Active Guidelines, various kinds of premeditated attention control can be implemented. For visual inspection, AGs are located on inspection targets like valves and pipes. Their intensity functions are set as shown in Fig. 6(a) in order to attract the attention from the start of the inspection tour and not to attract once the target has been inspected. For visual navigation, AGs are put on the landmarks and their intensity functions are set as shown in Fig. 6(b) so that their saliency increases monotonically while the robot moves without observing any landmarks and falls when successful landmark measurements are made. A similar function is set for an AG attached to the blind rob ot, which needs to be occasionally observed in the same way as landmarks. Furthermore, an AG can be used to represent inhibition of attention to a particular part of the scene. For example, in order to ignore a mobile obstacle while it is moving as predicted, a negative saliency can be set at the obstacle's predicted position, compensating the positive output from the obstacle detection process. Finally, AGs can be placed to draw attention to unpredicted motion.

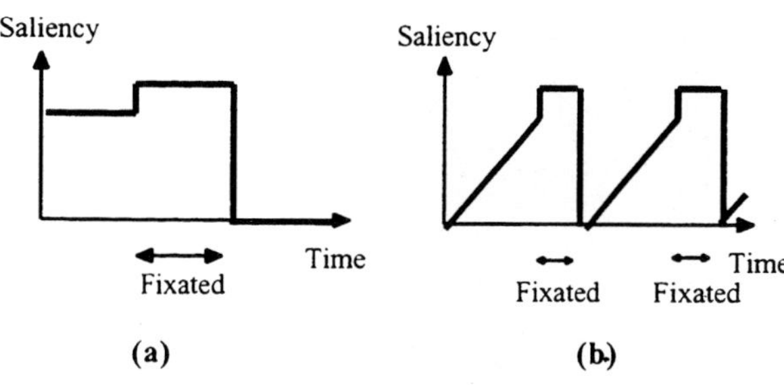

Figure: 6 An example of AG's action.

4.3. The system architecture

Figure 7 shows the overall architecture of the proposed attention control mechanism. The system is based on perspective projection because of the lack of current ability to synthesize the foveated images produced by our active head's cameras. Candidates are extracted from real images for reactive types of attention control and from synthesized images for premeditated types. The robot integrates all candidates into the 2D view space and selects only one candidate as the next fixation location.

4.4. Demonstration of visual attention control

Figure 8 shows the results of a very simple experiment, supported under our current implementation. Only one-type of bottom-up feature extraction, a temporal difference filter, was applied to real views. The images in the upper row are virtual views generated from the environment server, and those in the lower row are real views from the left camera. These views were sampled when the robot is about to finish a task given at the current fixation poi. nt. Then fixation locations for the next steps were chosen from the candidates derived from

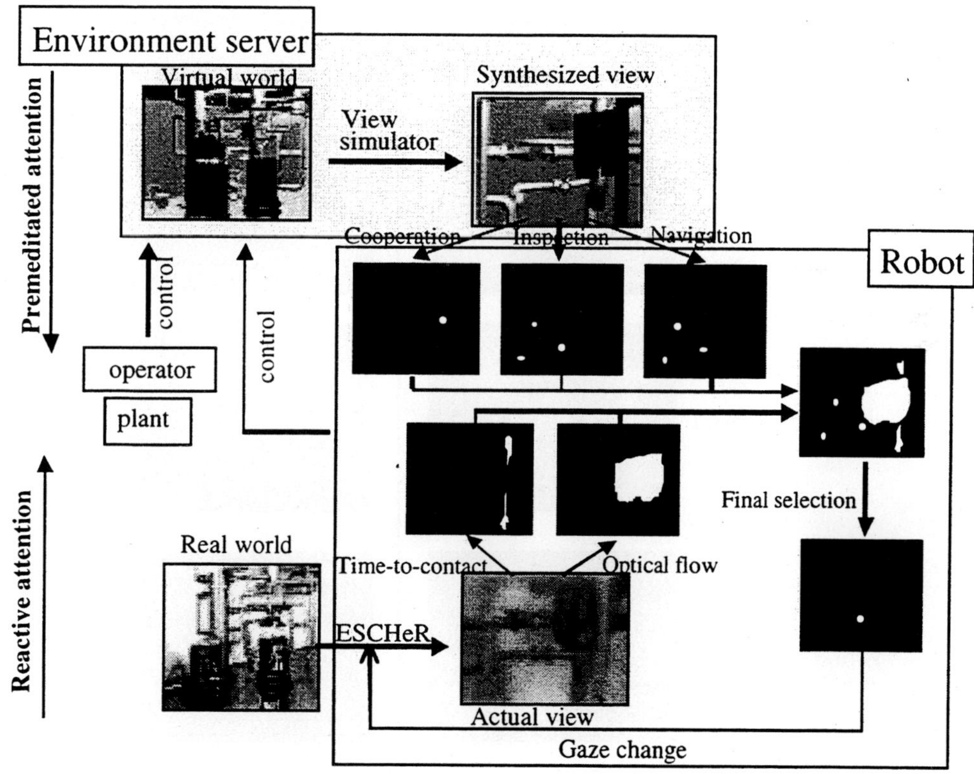

Figure: 7 Overall architecture of the proposed attention control.

both virtual and real views. For example, in the step 1, the visual task at the current fixation point, a thermometer, was finished, and four bright regions were derived from the virtual view and no bottom-up features from the real view as candidates for the next fixation. A simple criteria, the brightness and the closeness of the 2D distance to the current fixation location, was applied and the camera poses were controlled to the next fixation. Once an AG is fixated, the brightness of the AG was strengthens so as to keep the fixation during the visual task execution and it is turned down when finishing the task. In steps 2 and 3, the AG located on the blind robot appeared in the virtual views, and it was selected as the next fixation target at step 3 because its brightness increased enough. In step 4, after a measurement of the relative position of the blind robot, the temporal difference filter output one region with high intensity in the integrated 2D view and it was selected as the next fixation target for step 5.

5. Summary

We have proposed a new visual attention control framework for robot vision systems which have multiple

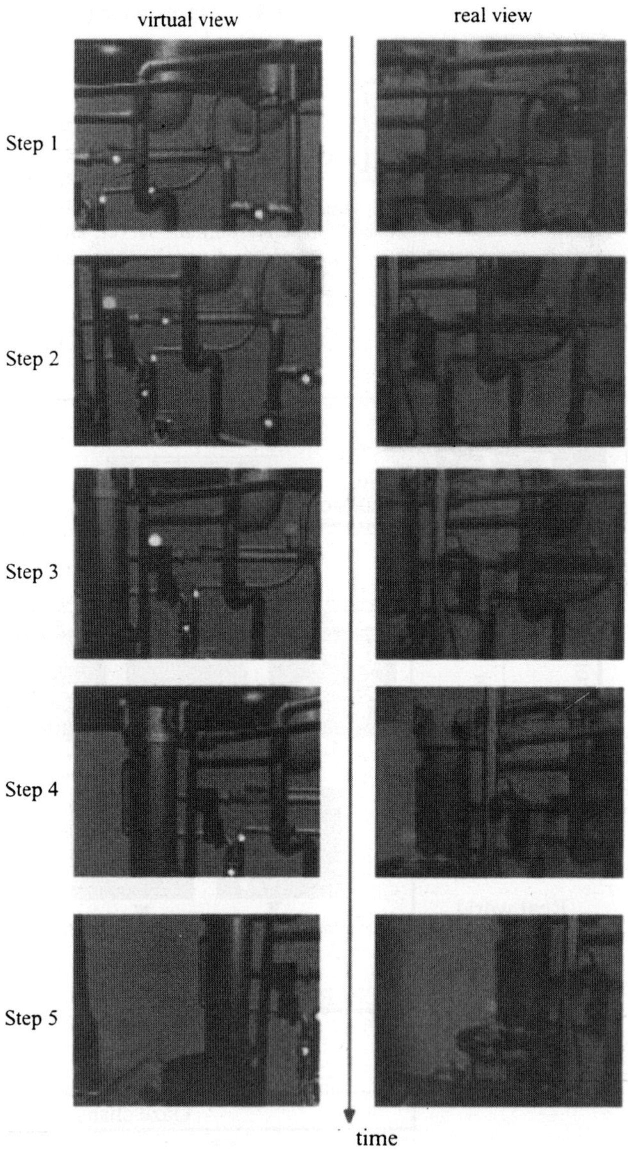

Figure: 8 Experimental example of attention control.

inspection robots in a nuclear power plant in mind. We tasks requiring both reactive and premeditated types of attention, with the particular application of mobile have proposed the use of an environment server and active guidelines as implementation tools for the framework. The experimental example described showed that the proposed framework be applied usefully to a real robot system.

Under the current implementation, a perspective view is used instead of a foveated view when images are generated from the environment server. This means that a small region. To take advantage of our robot's special cameras which have a wide but foveated field of view, and enlarge the possible region of the next fixation, we will soon extend the server that foveated views of the virtual world can be generated.

Acknowledgements

The author would like to thank Dr. Andrew Davison for help with building the overall system, and Dr. Hirukawa, Mr.Kohara and Mr.Tanaka for help with building the environment server.

References

[1] H. Asama et. al.: "Demonstration of Mobile Robot Teleoperation for Plant Inspection", Proc. of Int. Symp. on Artificial Intelligence, Robotics and Intellectual Human Activity Support for Nuclear Applications, pp. 251-254 (1997).

[2] Y. Kuniyoshi, N. Kita, S. Rougeaux & T. Suehiro: "Active Stereo Vision System with Foveated Wide Angle Lenses", *Asian Conf. on Computer Vision*, 359-363 (1995).

[3] A. Yarbus: "Eye movements and vision", Plenum press (1967).

[4] J. J. Clark, N. J. Ferrier: "Control of Visual Attention in Mobile Robots", Int. Conf. On Robotics and Automation, 826-831 (1989).

[5] M. J. Swain, R. E. Kahn and D. H. Ballard: "Low Resolution Cues for Guiding Saccadic Eye Movements", Proc. of CVPR'92, 737-740 (1992).

[6] L. Birnbaum, M. Brand and P. Cooper: "Looking for Trouble: Using Causal Semantics to Direct Focus of Attention", Proc. of 4th ICCV, 49-56 (1993).

[7] F. Ennesser and G. Medioni: "Finding Waldo, or Focus of Attention Using Local Color Information", Proc. of CVPR'93, 711-712 (1993).

[8] R. Milanese et. al.: "Integration of Bottom-Up and Top-Down Cues for Visual Attention Using Non-Linear Relaxation", Proc. of CVPR'94, 781-785 (1994).

[9] A. M. Treisman and G. Gelade: "A Feature-Integration Theory of Attention", *Cognitive Psychology*, 12, 97-136 (1980).

[10] R. D. Rimey and C. M. Brown: "Where to Look Next Using a Bayes Net: Incorporation Geometric Relations", Proc. of 2nd ECCV, 542-550 (1992).

[11] K. Brunnstrom, J. O. Eklundh and T. Uhlin: "Active Fixation for Scene Exploration", Int. Journal of Computer Vision, 17(2), 137-162 (1996).

[12] E. Marchand and F. Chaumette: "Controlled Camera Motions for Scene Reconstruction and Exploration", Proc. of CVPR'96, 169-176 (1996).

[13] P. Whaite and F. P. Ferrie: "Autonomous Exploration: Driven by Uncertainty", Tran, on PAMI, 19, 3, 193-205 (1997).

[14] A. J. Davisn and D. W. Murray: "Mobile Robot Navigation Using Active Vision", D. Phil Thesis, Univ. of Oxford (1998).

[15] J. Maver and R. Bajcsy: "Occlusions as a Guide for Planning the Next View", Tran. On PAMI, 15, 5, 417-433 (1993).

[16] C. F. Westin et. al.: "Attention Control for Robot Vision", Proc. of CVPR'96, 726-733 (1996).

[17] N. Kita: "Intelligent Plant Inspection by Using Foveated Active Vision Sensor", Proc. of Human-Computer Interaction, 1177-1181 (1999).

[18] H. Hirukawa et. al.: "View Simulator of HRP virtual plathome", The 17th Annual Conf. Of the Robotics Society of Japan, 1217-1218 (1999) [In Japanese]

Gabor Filters for Object Localization and Robot Grasping

Jörg Walter · Bert Arnrich
Department of Computer Science · University of Bielefeld
D-33501 Bielefeld · Email: walter@techfak.uni-bielefeld.de

Abstract

We present a system for learning the 3 DOF fine-positioning task of a robot manipulator (Puma 260) using a gripper mounted camera. Small lateral gripper-target misalignments are corrected in one step. Larger ones employ a previous coarse adjustment move in order to bound the parallax effects of the close camera focus. We build object-specialized, neural network-based pose estimators with a rather small set of Gabor filters. Gabor filters perform a spatially localized frequency analysis and resemble the spatial response profile of receptive fields found in visual cortex neurons. The system demonstrates efficiency w.r.t. speed and accuracy, as well as robustness against changing illumination and object conditions.

1. Introduction

Neural networks were evolved by nature to enable perception and action. Therefore, artificial neural networks seem as an appropriate choice for learning one of the most demanding sensor-based manipulation skills – grasping. One of the main obstacles for industrial applications is the availability of robust and inexpensive sensor–action systems. As the price and size of reasonable vision systems is decreasing, camera sensors become a popular expansion to robot systems. Traditional robot vision research focuses on the use of explicit world models and their construction from raw sensor data. Scene reconstruction is undoubtedly useful but expensive and often too complex in a changing real-world environment. We think that locally operating learning schemes are the best candidates to advance intelligent robot systems. This leads to the question what are the best feature extraction approaches for feeding a learning network. Previous work [6] employed line segment Hough Transforms (e.g. [2]) and [7] used principal component analysis (PCA) and appearance-based eigenimages [5] for same task. We will briefly compare their results with our Gabor-filter-based approach.

Gabor wavelets proved advantageous for object and face recognition [4], there acknowledged for their pose invariance. Here, we examine the reverse task. Knowing the object, how well can we estimate the pose? And, can we build a robust and efficient sub-system?

System Overview: The overall aim of our system is the structure assembling demonstrated using a set of wooden pieces including nuts, screws, ledges, and cubes, see Fig. 1. This task can be divided into several smaller ones: a single piece has to be identified, the gripper is brought in a suitable pre-grasp position, the target is firmly enclosed and gets finally transfered to the desired mating/assembly position with other parts. The robot system consists of a 6 DOF manipulator with a camera attached to the parallel yaw gripper with a tilted viewing angle.

Grasping without any alignment help requires that the objects are picked with certain precision. Failures include the risk of *(i)* object–gripper collisions, *(ii)* pushing/displacing something before yaw closure, and *(iii)* bad object-in-gripper alignment (creating trouble for part mating later).

Here we discuss the critical pre-grasp phase, i.e. the 3 DOF fine-positioning of the manipulator after an initial coarse positioning has been completed. This implies that the resting object is visible inside the viewing angle of the hand camera and its type and vertical position is known. Now the system has to deal with significantly changing appearance of the target objects with respect to *(i)* the lo-

Figure 1. The end-effector over the target: *(a)* **the gripper and the hand camera. A "cube" viewed by the hand camera before** *(b)* **– and after the fine positioning** *(c)*. **Note the tool tips in the upper rim of** *(b,c)*.

cal lighting situation (occlusion of lamps by the robot itself, interfering humans, etc.), *(ii)* image contrast and color (several possible object colors), *(iii)* parallax effects by the camera viewing from a close and tilted position.

2. Object Representation With Gabor Filters

In order to efficiently employ a learning neural network for pose estimation we need a suitable object representation gained from the sensory input, in our case a camera image. "Suitable" means here, that the feature set is of minimal size – providing the desired accuracy and, as a consequence, more rapid learning with fewer input neurons.

Biology gave us inspiration: 1987, Jones and Palmer [3] showed by cat visual cortex experiments, that receptive fields of simple cells fit well to a profile model, previously suggested by Daugman 1980 [1]. This model describes the spatial sensitivity by a 2D extention of Gabor's work (1946, originally in the time domain). By a local formulation of the frequency content he created a "localized" Fourier analysis, here written as a complex kernel function:

$$\Psi_{\lambda\sigma\alpha}(x,y) = \exp\left(-\frac{x^2+\alpha^2y^2}{2\sigma^2}\right)\exp\left(-2\pi i\frac{x}{\lambda}\right) \quad (1)$$

Eq. 1 describes a Gaussian bell function – modulating a planar wave. The wave has the period length λ in x-direction; the elliptical Gaussian has a longitudinal width σ and σ/α transversal (aspect ratio α).

Equation 1 can be called *mother wavelet* and a complete family of self-similar *daughter* wavelets (sometimes called *jet*) can be constructed by the generating function

$$\begin{aligned} \Psi_{pqm\theta\lambda\sigma\alpha}(x,y) &= 2^{-2m}\Psi_{\lambda\sigma\alpha}(x',y') \\ x' &= 2^{-m}[+x\cos\theta + y\sin\theta] - p \quad (2) \\ y' &= 2^{-m}[-x\sin\theta + y\cos\theta] - q. \end{aligned}$$

Here the substituted variables incorporate dilations of the wavelet in size 2^{-m}, translations in position (p,q), and rotations through the angle θ.

Each cell's receptive field can be modeled by a Gabor wavelet function, parameterized by the center (p,q), the wavelength $\lambda/2^m$ in direction θ with Gaussian elliptic envelope (with width $\sigma/2^m$ and $\sigma/2^m\alpha$) and a complex phase angle ψ (projecting a mixture of the real and imaginary part).

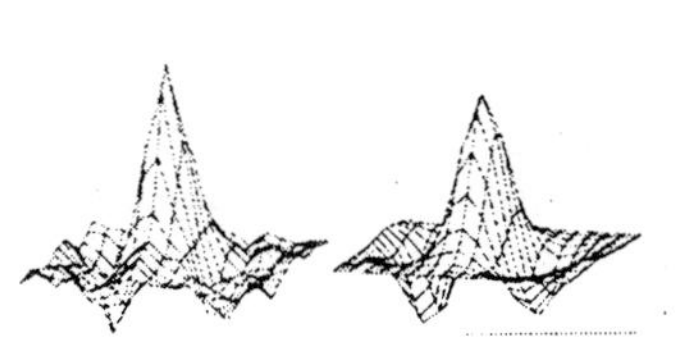

Figure 2. The 2D Gabor filter *(right)* fits simple cell spatial response profile *(left)* of receptive fields in cat striate cortex neurons [3]. See also Fig. 4.

Our system uses a collection of n those artificial neurons, all looking at the same image but each with a different receptive field. Thus the seen object gets represented by n values, i.e. the scalar product of the image by the appropriate Gabor filter mask. For a larger group of neurons, which differ only in their center position (p,q), the procedure can be speeded up by performing a convolution and implementing it as a product in the 2D-Fourier space.

3. Experimental Setup

The "Cubical" Challenge: In the following, we focus on one target object, the cubical wooden piece already shown in Fig. 1. Its size is little smaller than the open gripper and therefore calls for grasping tolerance of about 2 mm and 5-8°. The wooden "cube" is challenging for machine vision: *(i)* due to the widely rounded corners its facial surfaces are actually ring shaped; *(ii)* the three axial screw holes cause peculiar shadows. *(iii)* the contour, seen from an tilted viewing angle, resembles an egg with moving bumps when rotating the "cube". One way to avoid latter problem, is to turn the end-effector such, that for image grabbing the camera is looking vertically downwards. The price is a robot transfer delay (decrease of operation speed) and extra kinematic restrictions within the robot's workspace.

Pre-Grasp Procedure: In order to allow vivid and accurate operation we keep the gripper vertical and subdivide the fine positioning in two parts: *(i)* a fast and coarse – pure translational part and *(ii)* a rotational/translational fine part. Fig. 3 displays the simplified procedure in an UML-activity diagram. The grabbed image is preprocessed and the object's center of gravity in image coordinates (u,v) mapped by the first neural network (MLP) to the Cartesian translational command $(\Delta x, \Delta y)$ required to move the robot over the target object. If the displacement is too large – therefore the parallax effects are too disturbing – the robot moves first and looks again (top loop, $r_{fine} = 4\,mm$). The rotational adjustments are determined from an (u,v)-centered region of interest (ROI with size 50×50 pixel). A small set of features $\mathbf{f}$ is extracted and a second neural network (also MLP) maps to the shortest rotational approach command $\Delta\phi$. Executing the robot move command prepares the system for the next step, which is usually the force-torque guarded grasping of the object. Alternatively, the procedure can be repeated (by closing the loop) for testing or in case of poor image conditions.

Preprocessing: The grabbed color image of size 192×144 pixels is reduced to one channel by a pixel-wise maximum selection in the R,G, and B channel. Then the mean and standard deviation of all pixel values is computed and a global linear pixel intensity transformation is applied which normalizes the image to the training standard conditions

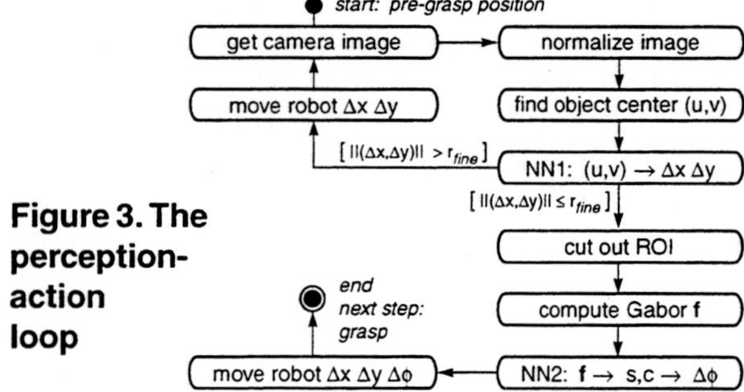

Figure 3. The perception-action loop

(i.e. the same intensity average and variance).

Object Localization: The normalized image is binarized and a standard blob detection algorithm selects the object center. If the image is not cluttered, a fast row and columnwise histogramming is sufficient. The first neural network NN1, a 2-3-2 resilient backprop accelerated MLP, maps to the desired translational correction $(\Delta x, \Delta y)$, which is used in the Cartesian transfer command and send to the robot.

Object Rotation and Angle Wrapping: The second neural network (NN2) has to code for the shortest rotational correction $\Delta\phi$. Here occurs the problem of angle wrapping ($\phi = \phi \pm 360°$) and the rotation object symmetry count κ, e.g., for the cube $\kappa = 4$ (i.e. same appearance for $\Delta\phi = 0°$, $90°$, $180°$, $270°$). We solve this with an angular sine/cosine pair encoding for the MLP-output layer

$$s = \sin(\kappa\Delta\phi), \quad c = \cos(\kappa\Delta\phi), \tag{3}$$

and the back-transformation

$$\Delta\phi = \frac{1}{\kappa}\,\text{atan}\left(\frac{s}{c}\right). \tag{4}$$

Selecting the Training Data Set: The desired nominal grasping position is *"demonstrated"* to the system by guiding the robot *once* (e.g. via a 3D-mouse) in the correct pose and defining the approach distance. Starting from there, a set of images is automatically aquired. An image gets grabbed from the hand camera after displacing the robot by the value $-(\Delta x, \Delta y, \Delta\phi) \in [-a, a] \times [-a, a] \times [-b, b]$ (for NN1 $a = 25\,mm$ and NN2 $a = 5\,mm$, $b = 180°/\kappa$; the training set is sampled from a 3×3×7-grid, while the test set is randomly sampled). The image processing results in association with the desired robot command $(\Delta x, \Delta y)$ for NN1, and $\Delta\phi$ for NN2, providing the training data for the supervised learning phase of the neural networks.

Selecting the Gabor Filter Set: Since the optimal feature set for our task was unknown, we carried out some systematic simulation tests with varying Gabor filter combinations. The RMS positioning accuracy of the entire system was evaluated on 10 training and test cycles with randomized starting conditions for NN2.

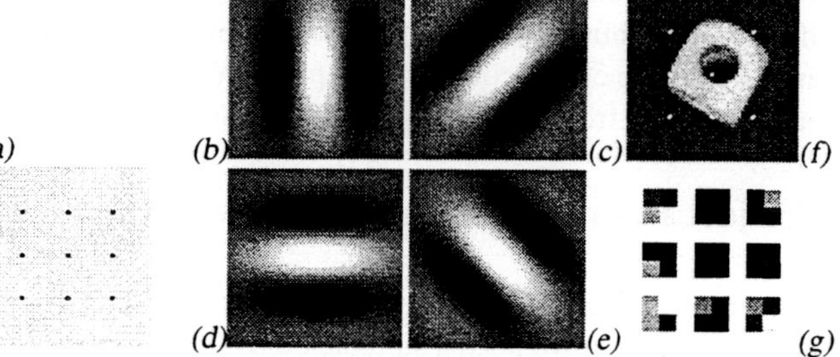

Figure 4. *(a)* Locations of the receptive fields centers (p, q) in the ROI-image. *(b-e)* Gabor filter set with 4 orientations, shown only for the middle location. The other 32 filters are shifted versions. *(f)* The ROI image with (a) superimposed. *(g)* The resulting 36 features visualized as gray image.

The winning filter set configuration was a surprise: it consists of only nine different center positions on a 3×3 grid centered in the $(50 \times 50\,pix)$ image ($p, q \in \{13, 25, 27\}\,pix$). At each position we centered four even Gabor filters with $\lambda = 30\,pix$, $\sigma = 12.5\,pix$, and $\theta \in \{0°, 45°, 90°, 135°\}$ as depicted in Fig. 4. The first surprise was, that already 36 image features are sufficient for the rotation estimation task. The second was, that the system does not prefer higher Gabor frequencies which would be more sensitive to the edge positions.

4. Experimental Results

Accuracy: We achieved an asymptotic RMS positioning accuracy of $0.08\,mm$, $0.2\,mm$ (in x, y direction) and $0.8°$ (in ϕ) after a couple of iterations in the fine-positioning loop in Fig. 3. This is far more than required. For reasonably good illumination conditions one short – pure translational (termed "half" loop) – and one full positioning loops is sufficient (half+full="$1\frac{1}{2}$"), see Tab. 1.

Robustness – Illumination: Changing local lighting conditions are a real threat to many vision based control algorithms. The described preprocessing method proved quite efficient: with stepwise dimmed lights and furthermore changing to a single sideward lamp (producing bad cast-shadows), we found that the performance degraded only in the speed of convergence. The basic operation was stable up to extremely poor illumination conditions.

Different Object Colors and Background: The training object (yellow cubical) shows very good contrast to the gray table surface. But the fine-positioning system works without modifications also for comparable objects, for other colors, and under bad conditions, e.g. poor brightness contrast and dim light. As Fig. 5 displays, partly covered objects or even textured background did not bring the grasping system to tumble.

Table 1	Gabor System	PCA System in [7]	Hough System in [6]
Accuracy with *Good* Illumination	(0.5, 0.7, 6.6°) after $1\frac{1}{2}$ loops		(4 DOF: x, y, z, ϕ)
($x/mm, y/mm, \phi/°$)	(0.1, 0.3, 1.2°) after $2\frac{1}{2}$ loops	(0.4, 0.7, 0.6°)	(0.5, 0.8, 1, 1.4°)
Save Grasp requires	$1\frac{1}{2}$ loops	5 loops	$2\frac{1}{2}$ loops
Accuracy with *Poor* Illumination	(0.2, 0.2, 1°) after $6\frac{1}{2}$ loops	(3.1, 1.0, 6.1°)	—
Save Grasp requires	$3\frac{1}{2} - 5\frac{1}{2}$ loops	20 loops	*[miracle]*
Controller	2 × MLP	4 × Neuro-Fuzzy	PSOM + Model
ϕ Feature Generation by	36 general filter masks	3 eigenimages	line HT
Total Time per Loop Iteration	1–2 sec	1–2 sec	1–2 sec
Training Time	< 1 min	3 hours	< 1 min

5. Discussion and Conclusion

We presented a pre-grasp fine positioning scheme for a robot camera-in-hand system. It employs a small set of only 36 Gabor masks probing the image for spacial frequency content at nine locations and four orientations. The feature set is universal for a family of similar objects and can be easily adapted and/or enriched for a broader spectrum of shapes. The preprocessing stage performs an image intensity adaptation and guidance of the rotational sensor (ROI). The overall system is robust with respect to the image condition, e.g. changes in illumination and some amount of occlusions and clutter.

Comparison With PCA-System: The PCA and neuro-fuzzy controlled approach [7] was implemented in the same lab, pursuing the same goal – but applying different techniques. Based on the appearance of the object, the *eigen-images* are computed and the image is encoded in an only three-dimensional *eigenspace* (for the rotational part). The small number is mainly a compromise to balance between the exponentially growing training time and the information gained. Of course, as more useful information the system can extract, as fewer iterations it needs for precise grasping. As Tab. 1 lists, the main disadvantage of the PCA-FC system is the limited training and performance speed. On the other hand, the PCA-system displays reliability and robustness.

Comparision With Hough-Transform (Line-HT): [6] employs classical image processing techniques. The image is taken from a vertical viewing angle, since the contour (more precise, the binarized edge-processing output) must be polygonal. The method delivers good results if (and only if) the conditions are highly normalized (good illumination, good background contrast, no clutter, etc.). The main reason for the poor robustness is the focus on differential image information (edges), the associated noise sensitivity, and the information loss in the binarization step. The countermeasures are expensive (e.g. contour following, region growing, etc.) and do not fundamentally solve the problem.

Summarizing, the Gabor-filter based system uses very favorably image processing techniques, working also in visual cortex neurons. Employing only 36 "simple cells" we built a technical system which was *(i) calibration free* (e.g. no camera calibration required), *(ii) direct* (no expensive image processing like segmentation, region growing, etc.), and *(iii) fast* (Gabor feature detection and ANN mappings could be implemented in real-time). It demonstrated *(iv)* the *robustness* real-world capable system require.

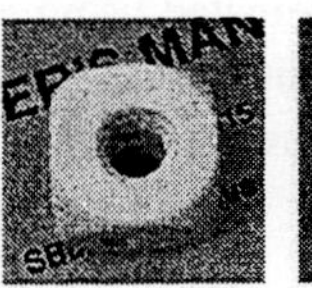
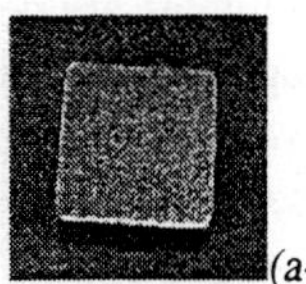
(a-d)

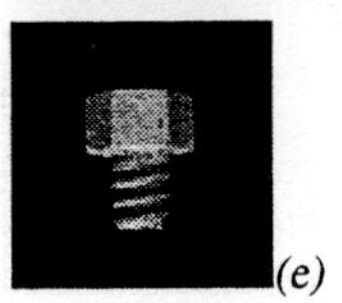
(e)

Figure 5. *(a-c)* Poor image conditions – successfully mastered. *(d-e)* other target objects (block *(d)* used the same NN2, the screw *(e)* a different).

References

[1] J. Daugman. Two-dimensional spectral analysis of cortical receptive field profiles. *Vision Research*, 20:847–856, 1980.

[2] J. Illingworth and J. Kittler. A survey of the Hough transform. *Computer Vision, Graphics, Image Processing*, 44:87–116, 1988.

[3] J. Jones and L. Palmer. An evaluation of the two-dimensional gabor filter model of simple receptive fields in cat striate cortex. *Journal of Neurophysiology*, 58:1233–1258, 1987.

[4] M. Lades, J. C. Vorbrüggen, J. Buhmann, J. Lange, C. von der Malsburg, R. P. Würtz, and W. Konen. Distortion invariant object recognition in the dynamic link architecture. *IEEE Trans. Computers*, 42:300–311, 1993.

[5] H. Murase and S. Nayar. Visual learning and recognition of 3-d objects from appearance. *Int. Journal of Computer Vision*, 14:5–24, 1995.

[6] D. Schwammkrug, J. Walter, and H. Ritter. Rapid learning of robot grasping positions. In *Proc. 7th Int. Symp. Intelligent Robotic Sys (SIRS)*, pages 149–155, July 1999.

[7] J. Zhang, R. Schmidt, and A. Knoll. Appearance-based visual learning in a neuro-fuzzy model for fine-positioning of manipulators. In *Proc. IEEE ICRA*, 1999.

Landmark Identification Based on Projective and Permutation Invariant Vectors *

Christos I. Colios† and Panos E. Trahanias†‡
†Institute of Computer Science
Foundation for Research and Technology – Hellas
P.O. Box 1385, Heraklion, 711 10 Crete, Greece
‡Department of Computer Science
University of Crete
P.O. Box 2208, Heraklion, 714 09 Crete, Greece
{colios,trahania}@ics.forth.gr

Abstract

In this paper we address the issue of environment representation for navigational tasks by using reference scene patterns, the so-called landmarks, to adequately describe the robot's workspace. Mathematical tools from projective geometry are employed for landmark identification. A complete framework is presented for landmark extraction and recognition based on projective and point-permutation invariant vectors.

1 Introduction

Vision-based navigation in indoor environments is a difficult task due to the cognitive workspace representation it involves. We address this problem by using as workspace representation images of distinct objects, the so-called *landmarks*, to unambiguously characterize the environment [2, 7]. With respect to the use of a detected landmark, automatic identification of landmarks involves two different aspects: (a) landmark learning, and (b) landmark recognition. Of major importance to both issues is the landmark representation. A 5-D, projective and point-permutation invariant vector [5] is employed as a *non-iconic* landmark representation. The invariance of this vector facilitates landmark matching under different vantage points. The only assumption made regards the existence of planar surfaces (valid in most indoor workspaces), which is a prerequisite for the computation of the invariant vector. Additional constraints provided by the invariant vector are used to further strengthen the landmark learning and recognition procedures.

*This work was partly supported by EC Contract No. ERBFMRX-CT96-0049 (VIRGO http://www.ics.forth.gr/virgo) under the TMR Programme and EC Contract No. IST-1999-12643 (TOURBOT http://www.ics.forth.gr/tourbot) under the IST Programme.

2 Landmark Representation

Visual landmarks constitute in the proposed framework non-iconic patterns that contain quintuples of points. Each quintuple is formed by coplanar points, with no three of them being collinear, and is regarded as a *sub-landmark* ($\mathcal{SL}$). A set of sub-landmarks in an image frame forms a *Visual Landmark* ($\mathcal{VL}$).

Each sub-landmark, besides the actual coordinates of its constituent points, is internally represented using a projective and point-permutation invariant vector [5]:

$$\mathcal{PPIV} = \left(\mathcal{J}_{14}(m_0), \mathcal{J}_{14}(m_1), \mathcal{J}_{14}\left(\frac{m_0}{m_1}\right),\right. \left.\mathcal{J}_{14}\left(\frac{m_1-1}{m_0-1}\right), \mathcal{J}_{14}\left(\frac{m_0(m_1-1)}{m_1(m_0-1)}\right)\right) \quad (1)$$

In eq. (1), m_0, m_1 are the two independent projective invariants on the projective plane $\mathcal{P}^2$ and $\mathcal{J}_{14}$ the used point-permutation invariant (derived in [5]). An important characteristic of $\mathcal{PPIV}$ stems from the fact that each of the vector components is directly related to one of the five points in the quintuple used for its computation. By ordering the components of $\mathcal{PPIV}$, direct point to point correspondences between two quintuples can be deduced.

3 Learning Phase

During training, potential landmarks are extracted, examined and, if appropriate, committed to memory. $\mathcal{SL}$ candidates are detected using a set of *salient points* on the image. Such points are extracted purely bottom-up (data-driven) as prominent corners in the image frame that reside in salient areas.

3.1 Extraction of Salient Points

There are two issues concerning the extraction of salient points: (a) detection of salient areas and (b) extraction of distinct points, in our case corners, in these areas. The attention mechanism we employ to detect areas of interest is the *saliency map*, developed by Trahanias et al. [7].

Having detected a salient area, corners within it should next be extracted. Since we are interested in robust and consistent detection of a fairly small number of corners in a salient area, a criterion of *goodness* is particularly important for each extracted corner. The KLT-corner detector (KLT-CD) [6] operates based on such a criterion; consequently it has been employed in our approach. The set of corners extracted by KLT-CD is additionally examined in order to detect and reject spurious corners, i.e. corners that do not appear consistently over successive image frames.

3.2 Selection of Sub-landmarks

The next step in the learning phase is the formulation of *legal* quintuples, i.e. quintuples of coplanar points, with no three of them being collinear.

A. Point Collinearity: Although collinearity is preserved under perspective transformations, quasi-collinearity is not. Let three points $\mathbf{x}_0$, $\mathbf{x}_1$, $\mathbf{x}_2$ in $\mathcal{P}^2$. A robust criterion for testing against (quasi)collinearity can be formulated by employing the *Grim Matrix* $\mathcal{M}_{012} = \sum_{i=0}^{2} \mathbf{x}_i \mathbf{x}_i^T$ [4]. The smallest eigenvalue of $\mathcal{M}_{012}$ is also the smallest eigenvalue of $\mathcal{X}_{012} = (\mathbf{x}_0 \mathbf{x}_1 \mathbf{x}_2)$ [1]. The closeness to rank deficiency of $\mathcal{X}_{012}$ is a robust measure of the collinearity of the three points. In practice, it is required that the smallest eigenvalue of $\mathcal{M}_{012}$ is less than a threshold t_{cl}.

B. Point Coplanarity: Quintuples passing the collinearity test are then examined to verify their coplanarity. This is achieved through the invariance of $\mathcal{PPIV}$. Unfortunately, the invariance criterion is only a strong indication and not necessarily a proof of coplanarity. Moreover, $\mathcal{PPIV}$ suffers from numerical instabilities and cannot be used alone as a robust criterion for coplanarity. In the proposed framework it is augmented with two additional criteria: the *convex hull test* and the *projectivity test*. Both are robust criteria and safeguard against erroneous tests of $\mathcal{PPIV}$ invariance in non-corresponding quintuples.

$\mathcal{PPIV}$ Invariance: A quintuple of coplanar points, observed in two different frames $\mathcal{F}$ and $\mathcal{F}'$, results in the same value of $\mathcal{PPIV}$ (eq. (1)). This can be used as a test for coplanarity, by examining the condition

$$|\mathcal{PPIV} - \mathcal{PPIV}'| \leq t_{PPIV} \quad (2)$$

where t_{PPIV} a predefined threshold value.

Convex Hull Test: The convex hull of a point set is preserved under projective transformations [3]. This, combined with the fact that a pair of matched quintuples in two different frames puts also their constituent five points in correspondence (through eq. (1)), provides the ability to use the *convex hull invariance* as an additional matching criterion. This invariance is expressed with the following conditions:

- preservation of the number of points on the convex hull,
- corresponding points lie either on or inside the convex hull, and
- for points lying on the convex hull, neighboring relations are preserved.

Let a quintuple in frame $\mathcal{F}$ with convex hull $\mathcal{CH}$, and n quintuples in frame $\mathcal{F}'$ with convex hulls $\mathcal{CH}'_j$, $0 \leq j \leq n-1$. We assume that vectors $\mathcal{PPIV}$ and $\mathcal{PPIV}'_j$ satisfy eq (2) $\forall j \in [0, n)$. In other words there are more than one matching candidates in $\mathcal{F}'$ for the quintuple in $\mathcal{F}$.

The fact that the five components of $\mathcal{PPIV}$ suffer from numerical instabilities may also introduce mismatches in providing point to point correspondences. Therefore, we employ the convex hull test as a criterion to prune false matching candidates, and also to detect and correct erroneous point correspondences. That is, when two false point to point correspondences are detected between the quintuple in $\mathcal{F}$ and a matching candidate with index j in $\mathcal{F}'$ then we assume that these mismatches could be possibly due to numerical instabilities in the calculation of $\mathcal{PPIV}$ and $\mathcal{PPIV}'_j$. The *convex hull test* may detect that two point pairs are false. Then quintuple j will not be excluded; on the contrary it will be temporarily assumed that these point pairs have been mismatched due to inaccuracies in the calculation of $\mathcal{PPIV}$ and $\mathcal{PPIV}'_j$ and they will be mutually exchanged. If more than two false point pairs are detected, then the quintuple in $\mathcal{F}'$ is rejected.

The application of the convex hull test, therefore, has a twofold result: (a) false matching quintuples in $\mathcal{F}'$ are detected and rejected and, (b) erroneous point correspondences across quintuples in $\mathcal{F}$ and $\mathcal{F}'$ are temporarily inverted (corrected), and the corresponding quintuples in $\mathcal{F}'$ are retained.

Projectivity Test: This test is applied in order to detect the quintuple, if one exists, in $\mathcal{F}'$, among all retained quintuples, for which the best point correspondences between $\mathcal{F}$ and $\mathcal{F}'$ exist. The formulation of the projectivity test is best described through the *homography matrix* [4]. Four known point correspondences can be used to estimate this matrix and additionally verify the estimated position of the fifth. The distance of the estimated point position from the actual position of the fifth point is used to quantify the accuracy of the point correspondences. These steps are repeated for all possible projective bases. The mean average of the five calculated distances is taken as the result of the projectivity test. The quintuple in $\mathcal{F}'$ with the lowest projectivity test-value is identified as the correct matching quintuple, provided that this value is below a predefined threshold t_p.

3.3 Visual Landmark Construction

In the proposed framework, a visual landmark ($\mathcal{VL}$) consists of a set of sub-landmarks ($\mathcal{SL}_s$). In order to minimize the effect of numerical instabilities at recognition time, we select, from all detected, legal $\mathcal{SL}_s$, as most promising candidates the *vector outliers*. For n quintuples identified as $\mathcal{SL}$ candidates, this is formulated as $d_i = \sqrt{\sum_{j=0}^{4}\left(\mathcal{PPIV}_i^j - \mathcal{PPIV}_{mean}^j\right)^2}$, where $\mathcal{PPIV}_i$ is the vector of the ith $\mathcal{SL}$ candidate and $\mathcal{PPIV}_{mean}$ the mean of $\mathcal{PPIV}_i$s.

4 Recognition Phase

In this phase, a process, similar to that used in the learning phase, is employed to trace legal quintuples. Next we attempt to match each detected coplanar quintuple to one sub-landmark of a stored visual landmark, i.e. we try to build a visual landmark hypothesis.

In order to find the most promising stored candidate for each quintuple we calculate the euclidean distance of the latter's invariant vector from the vectors of every stored sub-landmark. Starting from the most promising stored sub-landmarks, we search for matching candidates that stand the convex hull and the projectivity constraints. The matched sub-landmark is used thereon as a guide for the detection of other sub-landmarks that will strengthen our landmark hypothesis. Once the hypothesis is verified to a certain extend, the landmark is considered recognized.

5 Experimental Results

The proposed framework has been implemented and experimentally verified. Here we present sample results from our experiments; an illustrative result is first given to demonstrate the learning and recognition phases. Quantitative results are then presented for evaluation purposes.

5.1 Illustrative Result

In this section we present a sample result that refers to the workspace scene, observed when the mobile platform reaches the end of a corridor, which forms a "T" junction with another corridor (Fig. 1a).

Learning Phase: KLT-CD has resulted in a set of 27 corners. By consulting the saliency map an area of interest has been identified (the poster area) and the corner points in it have been isolated; 17 salient corners were identified, shown in Fig. 1a. From the 6188 possible quintuples that can be formed using the 17 corners, the application of the collinearity test has resulted in 478 quintuples. This set is further pruned by accepting only quintuples with 4 or 5 points on their convex hull, resulting in 100 quintuples.

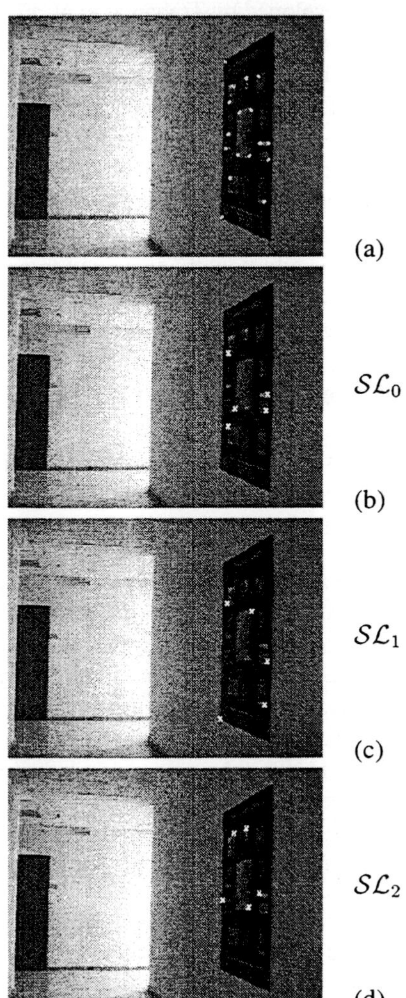

Figure 1. (a) imaged scene; the detected corners are superimposed on the image, (b),(c),(d) identified outlier sub-landmarks.

After these steps the retained 100 quintuples were tested for coplanarity by verifying constancy of the invariant vectors. To further strengthen our hypothesis we applied the convex hull and the projectivity test as described in section 3.2. In this example we were able to identify as coplanar 17 quintuples that satisfied the above mentioned criteria. Thus, these quintuples represent the strongest features in the salient area under consideration. From the set of 17 quintuples, the three most outliers were finally selected as sub-landmarks, with invariant vectors:

$\mathcal{SL}_0 : \mathcal{PPIV}_0 = (2.0196, 2.1090, 2.2187, 2.2901, 2.4340)$,
$\mathcal{SL}_1 : \mathcal{PPIV}_1 = (2.1863, 2.2871, 2.5833, 2.7217, 2.7966)$
$\mathcal{SL}_2 : \mathcal{PPIV}_2 = (2.0152, 2.0888, 2.1765, 2.2857, 2.4168)$.

The three sub-landmarks, $\mathcal{SL}_0$, $\mathcal{SL}_1$, and $\mathcal{SL}_2$, shown in Figs 1b,c,d, respectively, constitute a visual landmark.

Recognition Phase: During navigation the same scene is viewed from a different vantage-point (Fig 2). Under a similar procedure coplanar quintuples are extracted and successful matches with stored patterns are examined.

From the detected coplanar quintuples we were able to successfully match 3 of them, namely $\mathcal{SL}'_0$, $\mathcal{SL}'_1$ and $\mathcal{SL}'_2$, with the 3 stored sub-landmark patterns $\mathcal{SL}_0$, $\mathcal{SL}_1$ and $\mathcal{SL}_2$, respectively. These quintuples constitute the recognized sub-landmarks, and are shown in Fig. 2. The calculated invariant vectors for the recognized sub-landmarks are:

$$\mathcal{SL}'_0 : \mathcal{PPIV}'_0 = (2.0230, 2.1391, 2.2632, 2.2705, 2.4227),$$
$$\mathcal{SL}'_1 : \mathcal{PPIV}'_1 = (2.2319, 2.4213, 2.4835, 2.7966, 2.7999)$$
$$\mathcal{SL}'_2 : \mathcal{PPIV}'_2 = (2.0134, 2.0902, 2.1724, 2.2552, 2.3747).$$

An interesting observation regards the recognition of $\mathcal{SL}'_0$, where two erroneous point correspondences have resulted. However, the application of the convex-hull test has detected and appropriately corrected this mismatch. The mentioned points are the ones depicted with the arrows in Fig. 2a. In the other two cases the invariant vector provided the correct point to point correspondences. The projectivity test resulted in the values 3.65, 10.24 and 1.73 for the three sub-landmarks $\mathcal{SL}'_0$, $\mathcal{SL}'_1$ and $\mathcal{SL}'_2$, respectively.

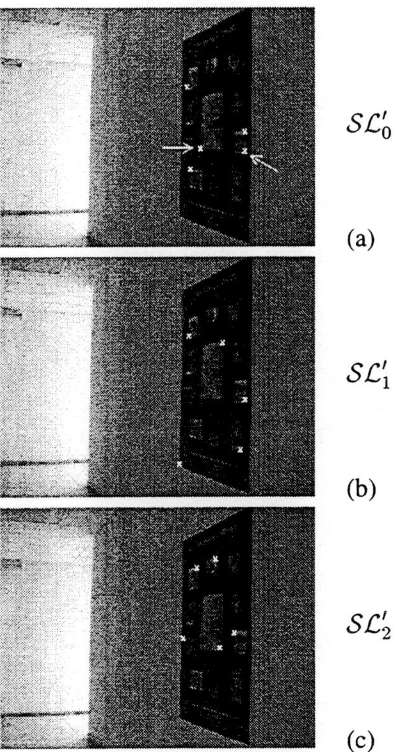

Figure 2. Recognized sub-landmarks.

5.2 Quantitative Results

In order to quantitatively evaluate the proposed framework, we have performed an experiment in the same workspace as above. The evaluation scenario we considered consisted in fifty navigation trials; each time sub-landmark recognition events have been reported. The results obtained from this experiment are summarized in Table 1. Each row in the table indicates, for each sub-landmark, the number and percentage of: (a) **C**orrect **R**ecognitions (CR), (b) **M**is-**R**ecognitions (MR), (c) **F**alse **P**ositives (FP), and (d) **F**alse **N**egatives (FN).

Table 1. Landmark recognition results.

	CR		MR		FP		FN	
$\mathcal{SL}$	#	%	#	%	#	%	#	%
$\mathcal{SL}_0$	47	94	1	2	0	0	2	4
$\mathcal{SL}_1$	44	88	1	2	3	6	2	4
$\mathcal{SL}_2$	49	98	0	0	1	2	0	0
Total	46.7	93.3	0.7	1.4	1.3	2.7	1.3	2.7

As can be observed a 93.3% correct recognition rate has been achieved. By investigating the cases where errors have occurred, we concluded that these were mainly due to (a) inaccuracies in the detection of the position of the corners, (b) extreme placement of the camera towards the wall containing the sub-landmarks, and (c) small variations of the salient areas. The above manifest themselves as either errors in the calculation of various parameters involved, distortions in the landmark patterns, and false positive/negative alarms with respect to the presence of a (sub)landmark. The obtained recognition accuracy of 93.3% is a promising result that may be further improved by considering previous (sub)landmark recognition events during the current recognition task.

References

[1] E. Biglieri and K. Yao. Some properties of singular value decomposition and their applications in to digital signal processing. *Signal Processing*, 18:277–289, 1989.

[2] R. Greiner and R. Isukapalli. Learning to select useful landmarks. *IEEE Tr. Syst. Man Cybern., Part B: Cybernetics*, 26(3):437–449, 1996.

[3] R. Hartley. Cheirality invariants. In *DAPRA Image Understanding Workshop*, pp.745–753, Washington DC, 1993.

[4] K. Kanatani. Computational projective geometry. *CVGIP: Image Understanding*, 54:333–348, 1991.

[5] R. Lenz and P. Meer. Efficient invariant representations. *Intl. J. Computer Vision*, 2(26):137–152, 1998.

[6] J. Shi and C. Tomasi. Good features to track. In *IEEE Conf. Comp. Vision Pattern Rec.*, pp.593–600, Seattle, 1994.

[7] P. E. Trahanias, S. Velissaris, and S. C. Orphanoudakis. Visual recognition of workspace landmarks for topological navigation. *Autonomous Robots*, (7):143–158, 1999.

Optical Transformations in Visual Navigation

Didi Sazbon, Ehud Rivlin
Faculty of Computer Science
Technion, Israel Institute of Technology
Haifa, Israel

Zeev Zalevsky, David Mendelovic
Faculty of Engineering
Tel-Aviv University
Tel-Aviv, Israel

Abstract

The navigational tasks of computing time-to-impact and controlling movements within specific range are addressed here. By using specially designed lenses various components of these procedures, consisting of mathematical transformations, can be provided at image acquisition time, and therefore, speed up execution time. This study discusses the optical implementation of different correlators based on the Fourier transform and Mellin transform. In addition, the fractional versions of these correlators are defined and analyzed here. Based on the experimental results it can be concluded that the optical implementation of transformations can indeed play a significant role in speeding up execution time in respect to the above mentioned navigational tasks.

1. Introduction

Algorithms concerning visual navigation aspects are usually known to be computationally heavy and considered as time consuming. Therefore, physical sensors that provide as much information as possible directly at acquisition time have an utmost importance. Sensors performing special operations can considerably save processing time. An example to such a sensor can be a retina-like sensor performing the log-polar mapping, which has many applications in motion estimation [1-8]. Constructing such special purpose sensors can be a very complicated task from an engineering point of view, because it usually involves a special geometrical positioning of known sensors. Moreover, the use of many sensors and the supporting algorithms enlarges significantly the overall cost of the system.

Here, a different approach is taken, which suggest the common use of cameras, but with optically implemented functions. This means that the functions we wish to obtain directly at acquisition time, will be implemented within the camera, by using special purpose lenses. In addition to the high speed in which relevant data can be supplied, lenses are usually cost effective. Thus, this solution is optimal in both senses, speed and cost.

The special lenses are formed by different combinations of regular Fourier lenses and special purpose designed filters [9-11]. This paper concentrates on two designs: (a) Fourier and Mellin based correlators, and (b) Fractional Fourier and Fractional Mellin based correlators, which concept is first introduced here. Each design answers a specific problem in visual navigation. The first design serves in the computation of time-to-impact, and the later in controlling and estimating specific ranges.

2. Optical Transformations and Visual Navigation

In what follows we present two optical transformations and their possible implementation to visual navigation. First, correlators, optical correlators, and their possible application to time-to-impact calculation are discussed. Then, the concept of fractional correlators is introduced, and its possible application to selective range estimation is explained.

2.1 Correlators and Their Application to Time-to-Impact Estimation

The 2D Mellin Transform is given by:

$$M(u,v) = \int_{-\infty}^{\infty}\int_{-\infty}^{\infty} f(x,y) \cdot \frac{\exp\left\{-2\pi i\left(u\ln\sqrt{x^2+y^2} + v\tan^{-1}\frac{y}{x}\right)\right\}}{x^2+y^2}\,dxdy \qquad (1)$$

1051-4651/00 $10.00 © 2000 IEEE

Therefore, the Mellin Transform of an image is in fact its Fourier Transform in a log-polar representation. Replacing x and y with the log-polar coordinates (ρ,θ), the Fourier Transform of the image in its log-polar coordinates is obtained. The log-polar mapping is defined by:

$$\rho = \ln\sqrt{x^2+y^2} \qquad \theta = \tan^{-1}\frac{y}{x} \tag{2}$$

and therefore,

$$M(u,v) = \int_0^{2\pi}\int_{-\infty}^{\infty} f(\rho,\theta)\exp\{-2\pi i(u\rho+v\theta)\}d\rho d\theta = FT(f(\rho,\theta)) \tag{3}$$

where FT denotes the Fourier Transform.

Thus, if the tested pattern is a rotated and scaled version of the reference pattern, the correlation image using the Mellin Transform instead of the Fourier Transform will produce a translated correlation-peak in the ρ and θ plane. Clearly, a translation in the ρ coordinate is actually a scaling in the *x-y* plane, and a translation in the θ coordinate is actually a rotation in the *x-y* plane. Therefore, the resulted transform is invariant both to scaling and rotation.

An interesting application of the correlators is the calculation of time-to-impact. In this case the motion is restricted to rotation and scaling, without allowing any other form of translation. It is known that under perspective projection of a camera with focal length F, the length, l, of an object in the image plane is given by

$$l = F\frac{L}{R} \tag{4}$$

where L is its physical length, and R is its distance from the center of projection of the camera. If the natural logarithm of l is taken, then

$$\ln l = \ln L + \ln F - \ln R \tag{5}$$

and by taking its derivative, we obtain

$$\frac{d\ln l}{dt} = \frac{d(\ln L + \ln F - \ln R)}{dt} = -\frac{1}{R}\frac{dR}{dt} = -\frac{1}{R}v = -\frac{v}{R} \tag{6}$$

where v is the velocity of the imaged object. Note that L and F are constants, and thus the derivatives of their components are zero. On the other hand, the distance of the camera from the object is given by

$$\frac{1}{TTI} = \frac{v}{R} \tag{7}$$

where TTI denotes the time-to-impact. Combining the last two equations yields

$$TTI = \left(-\frac{d\ln l}{dt}\right)^{-1} \tag{8}$$

meaning, that the time-to-impact can be extracted from the change in the temporal variations of the logarithm of the object in the image plane.

Therefore, if two images of the object are taken Δt time apart, the derivative of $\ln l$ can be calculated from these images, and the time-to-impact can be obtained directly. If the object has length L_1 in the first image and length L_2 in the second image then

$$TTI = \left(-\frac{\ln L_1 - \ln L_2}{\Delta t}\right)^{-1} \tag{9}$$

Both L and L_2 can be given directly in pixels, because any other representation is equivalent to summation and subtraction of the same constant.

Note that by using the Mellin based correlators, the time-to-impact computation of the imaged object is straight forward. Let L_2 be a scaled version of L, meaning $L_2 = sL$, then:

$$TTI = \left(-\frac{\ln L_1 - \ln L_2}{\Delta t}\right)^{-1} = \left(-\frac{\ln L_1 - \ln sL_1}{\Delta t}\right)^{-1} = \left(-\frac{\ln\frac{L_1}{sL_1}}{\Delta t}\right)^{-1} = \left(\frac{\ln s}{\Delta t}\right)^{-1} \tag{10}$$

Thus, one needs to know only the scaling factor, s, which is calculated directly from the shift of the correlation peak.

2.2 Fractional Correlators and Their Application to Range Control

The common correlators provide information regarding the translation of a certain object or about its scaling and rotation. In some visual systems there is no need to know every type of motion, and the only interesting movements are limited to a specific range. For example, if a robot is moving around in a room consisting of known obstacles, it should not come near an obstacle if it is at a certain distance away. We would like to be able to detect only the nearby obstacles and ignore the others. A variant of this example would be a stationary robot sorting objects from the same type, that should ignore objects bigger or smaller than a desired range of sizes. In this case, we would like to recognize only the objects that are in the desired range and ignore all others. Another example would be an helicopter that should fly over a target in a specific range.

Here, a new type of correlators, that can recognize movements in a specific range, are introduced. The correlators are based on the concepts of fractional transformations, i.e. the Fractional Fourier Transform (FRT) and the Fractional Mellin Transform. The optical implementation of the FRT in optics is well documented [9-15], and is done by changing the distances and the focal length of the lenses performing the Fourier Transform and its inverse.

The 2D Fractional Fourier Transform of order (p_1, p_2) is given by:

$$F^{(p_1,p_2)}(u,v) = C \cdot \int_{-\infty}^{\infty}\int_{-\infty}^{\infty} f(x,y) \cdot \exp\left\{ \begin{matrix} -2\pi i\left(\frac{ux}{\sin\phi_1} + \frac{vy}{\sin\phi_2}\right) \\ +\pi i\left(\frac{u^2+x^2}{\tan\phi_1} + \frac{v^2+y^2}{\tan\phi_2}\right) \end{matrix} \right\} dxdy \quad (11)$$

where C is a constant, and

$$\phi_1 = \frac{p_1\pi}{2} \quad \text{and} \quad \phi_2 = \frac{p_2\pi}{2} \quad (12)$$

Note that $F^{(0,0)}(u,v) = f(x,y)$, which is the image itself, and $F^{(1,1)}(u,v) = F(u,v)$, which is the Fourier Transform of the image.

We define the 2D Fractional Mellin Transform of order (p_1, p_2) by:

$$M^{(p_1,p_2)}(u,v) = \int_{-\infty}^{\infty}\int_{-\infty}^{\infty} f(x,y) \cdot x^{-\frac{2\pi}{in\phi_1}u-1} \cdot \exp\left\{\frac{\pi i}{\tan\phi_1}\left(u^2 + \ln^2 x\right)\right\} \cdot x^{-\frac{2\pi}{\sin\phi_2}v-1} \cdot \exp\left\{\frac{\pi i}{\tan\phi_2}\left(v^2 + \ln^2 y\right)\right\} dxdy \quad (13)$$

where ϕ_1 and ϕ are the same as in the FRT case. Note that $M^{(0,0)}(u,v) = f(\rho,\theta)$, which is the image itself in log-polar representation, and $M^{(1,1)}(u,v) = M(u,v)$, which is the Mellin Transform of the image. In the general case $M^{(p_1,p_2)}(u,v) = FRT^{(p_1,p_2)}(f(\rho,\theta))$, which is the Fractional Fourier Transform of order (p_1, p_2) of the image in its log-polar representation.

How does the correlation pattern change when we apply the fractional correlators instead of the conventional correlators? The fractional transformations of order (1,1) are actually the 2D Fourier or Mellin transforms of the image, and the correlation pattern has a peak at the positions corresponding to those of the conventional correlators. As the order decreases, enlarging the movement results in a lower magnitude of the principal peak and increase of the side lobes (additional peaks). If the order is only slightly decreased, then the location of the principal peak still corresponds to the position of the peak in the regular correlators, otherwise it may not correspond. Therefore, in order to limit the range of the desired movement, we should pre-determine the order of the fractional transformation used and the threshold level, in such a way, that the resulted peak would still be in a position corresponding to the correct movement. An object moving outside the range that was pre-determined will produce a correlation-peak which falls below the threshold level.

3. Experimental Results and Discussion

The images of the computer depicted in Figure 1a and Figure 1b are taken one time unit apart, which we will assume to be equal to one second. The first image is taken approximately 2.85 meters away from the computer and the second image is taken approximately 2.6 meters away from the computer. A rough approximation of the time-to-impact can be logically deduced by assuming a constant velocity of 0.25 meters per second, which turns out to be ~10.4 seconds.

Now, we will assume that we do not know the actual location of the computer in the room, and we would like to estimate the time-to-impact using only the two images. The scaling factor using the Mellin correlator on these two images resulted in a 1.1 scaling, and the resulted time-to-impact is:

$$TTI = \left(\frac{\ln 1.1}{\Delta t}\right)^{-1} = \frac{1}{\ln 1.1} = 10.492 \text{ seconds}$$

This result agrees with the rough approximation done by calculating the real distances and velocities.

Hence, the computation of time-to-impact can be deduced straight forward by using the Mellin based correlators. The location of the correlation peak corresponds to the scaling of the object in the second image in respect to the object in the first image. This technique can be implemented optically to give a correlation image at acquisition time, and therefore, can be used as a real-time technique.

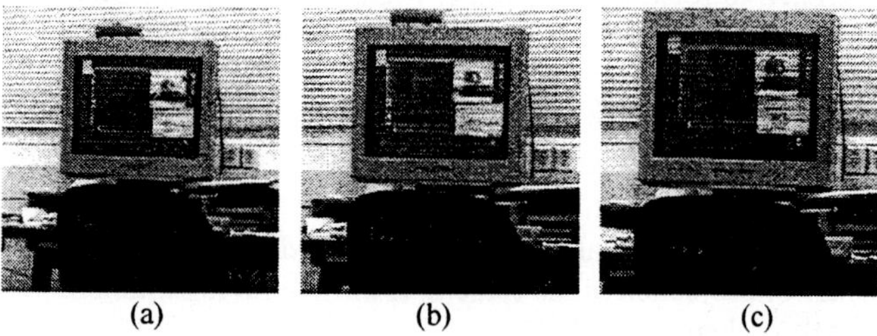

(a) (b) (c)

Figure 1: A sequence of images with a scaling factor of 1.1.

The sequence of the three images depicted in Figure 1 can be used also in order to demonstrate the specific range estimation capability of the fractional correlators. Images 1a, 1b, and 1c, are taken in such a way that each is a scaled version of the previous with a scaling factor of 1.1. Image 1a was correlated using the fractional Mellin correlator with itself and with the other two images, and the correlation peaks were measured. A variety of fractional orders, *p*, were used, and the table presented in Figure 2 indicates the locations of the correlation peaks measured for each fractional order. All the fractional orders used had values in the range [0.95,1], which implies that regular Mellin properties are strongly dominant. In other words, where shifts in specific ranges are concerned, the locations of the correlation peaks in these ranges should be around the locations of the correlation peaks resulted from using the Mellin transform.

The table shows that a fractional order of 0.995 allows scaling of 1.1 but does not allow scaling of 1.21. This means that when using p=0.995, an object that is located away from the camera a distance corresponding to a scale of 1.1 will be detected. On the other hand, positioning the object in a distance corresponding to a scale of 1.21 will not produce a detection indication. Note that the auto-correlation peaks of the image with itself are located at the center of the image for any choice of p, as is expected.

p	correlation peak image 1a (scaling=1)	correlation peak image 1b (scaling=1.1)	correlation peak image 1c (scaling=1.21)
1	121,121 31.9345	127,121 28.9544	132,121 26.9186
0.999	121,121 31.9326	127,121 28.9530	132,121 26.9071
0.998	121,121 31.9269	127,121 28.9491	132,121 26.8752
0.997	121,121 31.9176	127,121 28.9426	132,121 26.8556
0.996	121,121 31.9052	127,121 28.9359	125,121 26.8332
0.995	121,121 31.8900	126,121 28.9327	122,121 26.8193
0.994	121,121 31.8727	126,121 28.9312	122,121 26.8121
0.99	121,121 31.7952	122,121 28.9273	122,121 26.7971
0.95	121,121 31.5852	121,121 28.8348	121,121 26.7478

Figure 2: Using the Fractional Mellin correlator on the images from Figure 1 produced the correlation peaks (locations in pixels and values) given in the table. It can be seen that a choice of fractional order p=0.995 allows scaling of 1.1 but not of 1.21. This implies that ranges up to a scaling of 1.1 can be detected, and ranges larger that 1.21 can not be detected.

The conclusion that can be drawn out of such experiments is that movements with specific ranges can be controlled via the fractional correlators, by a proper choice of the fractional order that fits the desired ranges. This technique can be implemented optically to give a correlation image at acquisition time, and therefore, can be a real-time technique.

References

1. R. Jain, *Direct Computation of the Focus of Expansion*, IEEE Transactions on Pattern Analysis and Machine Intelligence, Vol. 5, No. 1, pp. 58-64, 1983.
2. M. Tistarelli, and G. Sandini, *Estimation of Depth from Motion Using an Anthropomorphic Visual Sensor*, Image and Vision Computing, Vol. 8, No. 4, pp. 271-278, 1990.
3. M. Tistarelli, and G. Sandini, *On the Advantages of Polar and Log-Polar Mapping for Direct Estimation of Time-to-Impact from Optical Flow*, IEEE Transactions on Pattern Analysis and Machine Intelligence, Vol. 15, No. 4, pp. 401-410, 1993.
4. H. Tunley, and D. Young, *First Order Optic Flow from Log-Polar Sampled Images*, ECCV, vol. A, pp. 132-137, 1994.
5. P. Questa, and G. Sandini, *Time to Contact Computation with a Space-Variant Retina-Like C-mos Sensor*, Proc. IROS, pp. 1622-1629, 1996.
6. F.L. Lim, G.A.W. West, and S. Venkatesh, *Use of Log Polar Space for Foveation and Feature Recognition*, IEE Proceedings of Vision, Image, and Signal Processing, Vol. 144, No. 6, pp. 323-331, 1997.
7. C. Silva, and J. Santos-Victor, *Egomotion Estimation Using Log-Polar Images*, ICCV, pp. 967-972, 1998.
8. I. Ahrns, and H. Neumann, *Real-Time Monocular Fixation Control Using the Log-Polar Transformation and Confidence-Based Similarity measure*, ICPR, pp. 310-315, 1998.
9. D. Mendlovic, and H.M. Ozaktas, *Fractional Fourier Transformations and Their Optical Implementation: Part I*, JOSA A10, pp. 1875-1881, 1993.
10. H.M. Ozaktas, and D. Mendlovic, *Fractional Fourier Transformations and Their Optical Implementation: Part II*, JOSA A10, pp. 2522-2531, 1993.
11. H.M. Ozaktas, and D. Mendlovic, *Fourier Transforms of Fractional Orders and Their Optical Interpretation*, Opt. Commun., Vol. 101, pp. 163-165, 1993.
12. A.W. Lohmann, *Image Rotation, Wigner Rotation and the Fractional Fourier Transform*, JOSA A10, pp. 2181-2186, 1993.
13. D. Mendlovic, H.M. Ozaktas, and A.W. Lohmann, *Graded Index Fibers, Wigner Distribution Functions and the Fractional Fourier Transform*, Applied Optics, Vol. 33, pp. 6188-6193, 1994.
14. J. Garcia, D. Mendlovic, Z. Zalevsky, and A.W. Lohmann, *Space Variant Simultaneous Detection of Several Objects Using Multiple Anamorphic Fractional Fourier Transform Filters*, Applied Optics, Vol. 35, pp. 3945-3952, 1996.
15. J.H. Caulfield, D. Mendlovic, and Z. Zalevsky, *Fractional Correlator With Real Time Control of the Space-Invariance Property*, Applied Optics, Vol. 36, pp. 2370-2375, 1997.

Robust Localization Using Panoramic View-Based Recognition *

Matjaž Jogan and Aleš Leonardis
Faculty of Computer and Information Science, University of Ljubljana
Tržaška 25, 1001 Ljubljana, Slovenia
{matjaz.jogan,alesl}@fri.uni-lj.si

Abstract

The results of recent studies on the possibility of spatial localization from panoramic images have shown good prospects for view-based methods. The major advantages of these methods are a wide field-of-view, capability of modelling cluttered environments, and flexibility in the learning phase. The redundant information captured in similar views is efficiently handled by the eigenspace approach. However, the standard approaches are sensitive to noise and occlusion. In this paper, we present a method of view-based localization in a robust framework that solves these problems to a large degree. Experimental results on a large set of real panoramic images demonstrate the effectiveness of the approach and the level of achieved robustness.

1. Introduction and motivation

When dealing with autonomous systems that freely move in space, an important problem to solve is the estimation of the instantaneous position. In the case of autonomous robot navigation, localization is necessary for motion planning. In augmented reality applications, localization of the observer is crucial for registration that allows a combination of virtual and real environments.

In our work we define the problem of localization as the task of recognizing a panoramic view (see Fig. 1 for an example of cylindrical panoramic images) from a set of panoramic views acquired in the learning phase. In the last decade many researchers have shown that feasible models of the world can be constructed without using precise geometrical information [2, 6, 7]. Namely, a model of the world can be constructed as a memory map, built from adequately compressed sets of images. Such methods have been successfuly tested in the areas of object [5, 7] recognition. The main motivation for applying such an approach to the problem of localization is the analogy between recognizing an object in the scene and recognizing the environment. In contrast to object recognition, the target to be recognized in the case of localization is not only a part of the image (on a cluttered background), but rather the complete image. If we use panoramic images as representations of positions, we can expect that views taken from nearby positions and oriented in the same way tend to be strongly correlated as it is in the case of looking at an object from two nearby viewpoints (Fig. 1). This allows us not only to design an efficient strategy based on correlation, but also to build a compact representation that eliminates redundancy.

Figure 1. Two cylindrical panoramic images (labeled 50 and 53 in the path set) taken from viewpoints 60 cm apart.

Another motivation comes from the discoveries on navigation strategies of insects, that are, although limited in the brain size, capable of amazingly confident navigation and of self-localization. In fact, some studies (see [4] and the references therein) imply, that wood ants may use a representation of the environment that is built from wide-angle snapshots of the scene. Localization is then performed by comparing the instantaneous view with the stored snapshots. According to this and some other studies the patterns are processed retinotopically, i.e, the snapshot is not segmented, but interpreted as a whole.

For building a compact model from a set of images, the *eigenspace* approach proved itself as a viable one [3]. A similar work was done by Aihara et al. [1] who used

*This work was supported by the Ministry of Science and Technology of Republic of Slovenia (Project J2-0414 and SI-CZ Intergovernmental S&T Cooperation Programme).

1051-4651/00 $10.00 © 2000 IEEE

row-autocorrelated transforms of cylindrical panoramic images in order to achieve invariance to rotation of the sensor around the optical axis. The approach suffers from less accurate results on novel positions, since by correlating the images some of the information is lost. An alternative approach was proposed by Pajdla and Hlaváč [8] who used an appearance-preserving rotational invariant representation, i.e, the *Zero Phase Representation (ZPR)*.

The major limitation of these approaches is the sensitivity of the matching stage to noise and occlusion. It is clear that one has to cope with occlusions in the scene, such as, for example, people walking by, other objects being moved around the environment etc. In this paper, we propose a method for robust localization by applying a robust procedure for recovery of parameters from the eigenspace [5].

The paper is organized as follows. In section 2 we first discuss the major properties of panoramic images and the distribution of their correlation over the sensed environment. In section 3 we describe the procedure for building the environment model from panoramic views and give an overview of the robust recognition of views. In section 4 we present the results on non occluded and occluded data. We conclude with a summary and an outline of future work.

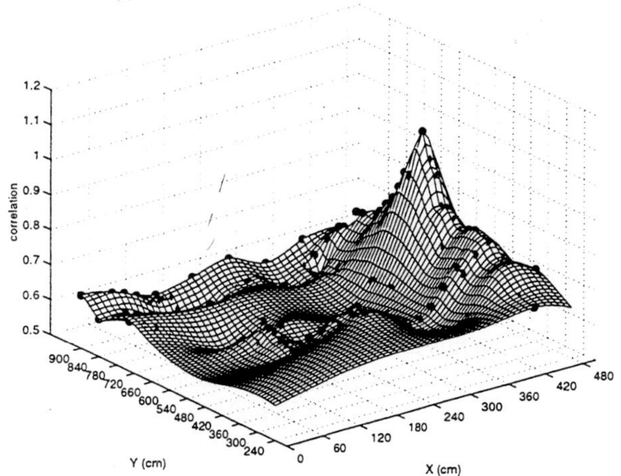

Figure 2. Correlation of panoramic images in space. XY plane represents the coordinates of the experimental environment. Measured and then interpolated is the correlation with image at X=440, Y=660.

2. Correlation of panoramic images

We have already emphasized the analogy between localization and object recognition. When looking at an object from two nearby viewpoints, there is a high probability that the two views are very similar to each other. If the panoramic sensor has a fixed orientation, as if using an external compass, two images taken at nearby positions also tend to be strongly correlated. As it can be seen in Fig. 2, the distribution of correlation is far from a simply characterized function, however, it gives a good indication of the current location.

Of course, we cannot expect that an external compass is always available. In such a case, one has to employ a transformation that maps cylindrical panoramic images into a representation that is invariant to the rotation of the sensor and also preserves the properties of the correlation distribution. As it was shown in [3], this can be achieved by using a transformation that preserves appearance, such as the ZPR transform, proposed in [8].

3. Panoramic eigenspace

As already stated we represent the environment by a set of panoramic images $\mathcal{I} = \{\mathbf{x}_1 \ldots \mathbf{x}_N\}$, taken in the learning phase at arbitrary positions. We transform the images so that they are all oriented the same way. This enables us to efficiently compress them by the eigenspace method. The eigenspace method consists of solving the *Singular Value Decomposition* on the covariance matrix of the (normalized) images in $\mathcal{I}$, to obtain an orthogonal set of vectors $\mathbf{e}_1, \mathbf{e}_2 \ldots, \mathbf{e}_n$, usually referred to as *eigenimages.* If we then choose a subset of p eigenimages with the largest *eigenvalues*, we can approximate in the least squares sense each image parametrically as a linear combination of that subset to a desirable degree of accuracy. Namely, every model image $\mathbf{x}_i$ therefore projects into some point $\mathbf{q}_i$ in the *eigenspace*, spanned by the selected eigenimages [7].

The major advantage of the eigenspace method is that the correlation in the image space is related to the Euclidean distance in the eigenspace, i.e., the stronger are the two images correlated, the closer will their projections lie in the eigenspace. It is therefore possible to densely interpolate the set of points to obtain a spline that represents an approximation of an arbitrarily dense set of real-world images [7]. Panoramic views from intermediate positions are in that way approximated by a spline.

3.1. Robust recognition

Once the model is built, recognition of a view is performed by recovering the coefficient vector $\mathbf{q}$ of the instantaneous image $\mathbf{y}$, or searching for the point on the spline which is the nearest to the projected point. As every point $\mathbf{q}$ is associated with the position parameters, we can make an estimation of the current position. The standard method to recover the parameters is to project the image vector onto the eigenspace [7]:

$$q_j(\mathbf{y}) = < \mathbf{y}, \mathbf{e}_j >; \; j = 1 \ldots p \; . \tag{1}$$

However, this way of calculation of parameters is non-robust and thus not accurate in the case of noisy or occluded data. If we imagine a mobile robot roaming around with a model acquired under a set of stable conditions, every change in the environment, such as displaced objects, people walking around etc., can result in severe occlusions with respect to the original stored images.

To overcome this problem, we propose to use the robust approach [5], that, instead of using the whole image vectors, generates and evaluates a set of hypotheses $\mathbf{r}$ as subsets of image points $\mathbf{r} = (r_1, r_2, \ldots, r_k)$. In fact, the coefficients can be retrieved by solving a set of linear equations on $k = n$ points:

$$x_{r_i} = \sum_{j=1}^{n} q_j(\mathbf{x}) e_{jr_i} \;\; 1 \leq i \leq n \; . \tag{2}$$

The principle of such computation is illustrated in Fig. 3.

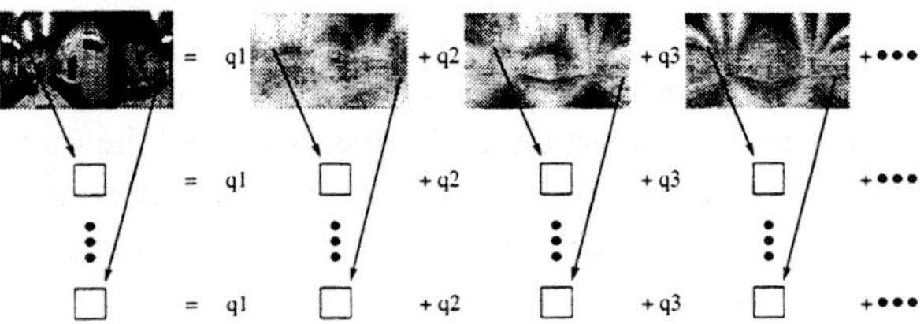

Figure 3. Calculating the coefficients from a set of linear equations.

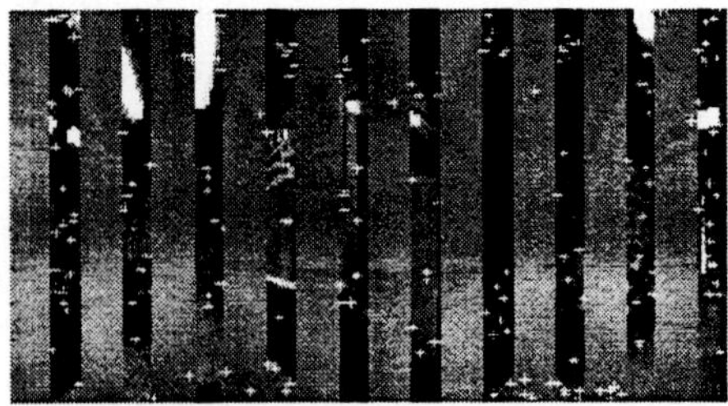

Figure 4. Image at 60% occlusion. Crosses denote the points that contribute to the generation of a hypothesis.

By selecting only p, $p \leq n$ eigenimages as our basis, we cannot use the previous set of equations, but we rather try to solve an over-constrained system in a robust way, so that the solution set of parameters minimizes

$$E(\mathbf{r}) = \sum_{i=1}^{k} (x_{r_i} - \sum_{j=1}^{p} q_j(\mathbf{x}) e_{jr_i})^2 \; . \tag{3}$$

We solve the system on $k, k > p$ points, where k is significantly smaller than the total number of image points. The set of points is randomly selected and due to the robust solving of the equation, only the points on which the error is arbitrary small contribute to the computation of the parameters. As we can see in Fig. 4, at this stage most of the points in the occluded regions are excluded from the computation.

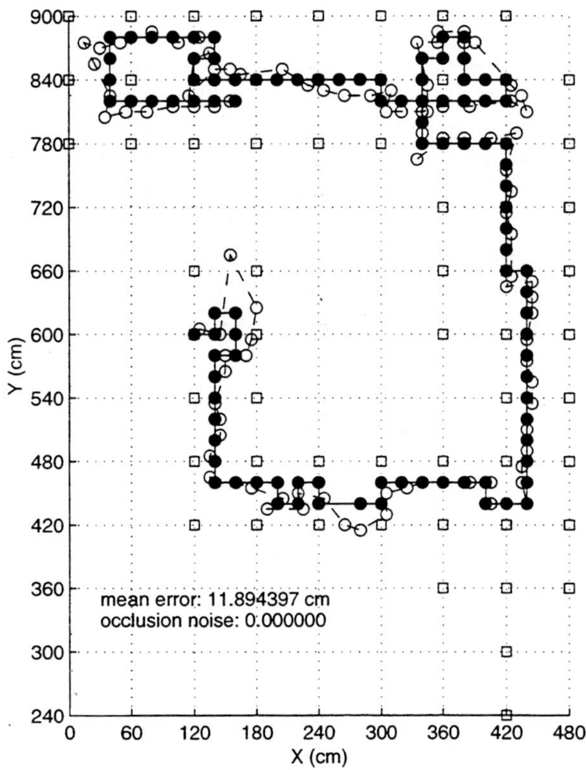

Figure 5. Localization on an imaginary path of 100 images.

To increase the probability of avoiding points that are noise or represent occlusion, several different hypotheses are generated. A hypothesis consists of a set of parameters, an error vector ϵ calculated as the squared difference between the data and the reconstruction, and the domain of compatible points that satisfy an error margin constraint. These hypotheses are then subject to a selection procedure, based on the *Minimal Description Length* principle, as described in [5].

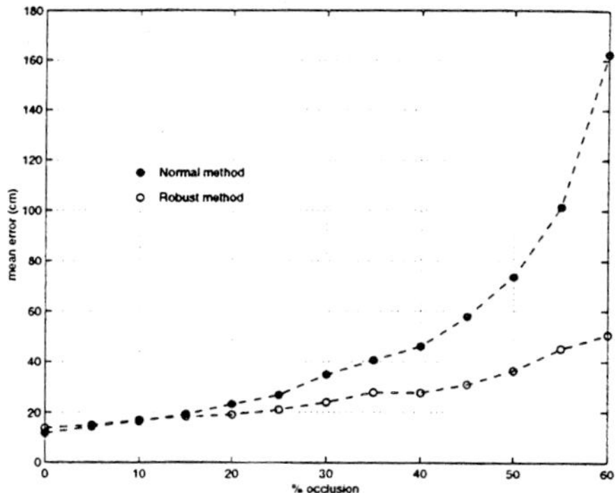

Figure 6. Mean error of localization for the standard and for the robust method.

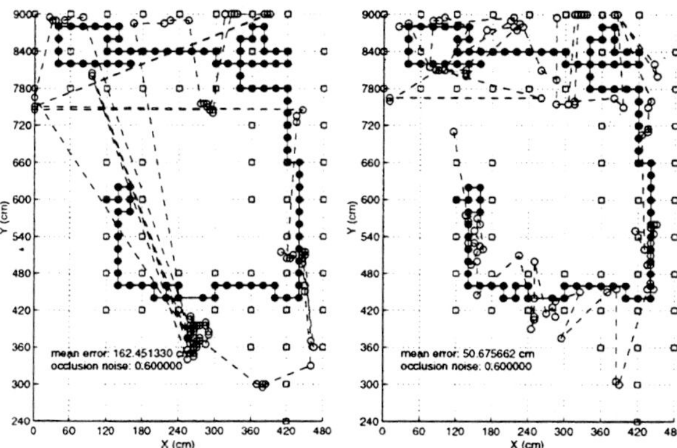

Figure 7. Localization on an imaginary path of 100 images at 60% occlusion. Left: standard method; right: robust method.

4. Experimental results

To perform the experiments we used a training set of 62 cylindrical panoramic images taken indoors in a laboratory with lots of occlusion and artificial lighting. The images were taken using a spherical mirror camera and warped to form cylindrical images. The images were taken at positions 60 cm apart. The experimental layout is depicted in Fig. 5, with squares denoting the positions where training images were taken. As a testing set we used 100 images taken at measured positions, depicted in Fig. 5 as full circles.

From the training set of images we constructed a 10 dimensional eigenspace. The empty circles in Fig. 5 denote the recovered path after projecting all 100 original test images. The spline used for projection was interpolated at 5 cm resolution. Since there is no significant occlusion (besides some change in the illumination of the windows area), the standard and the robust method of coefficient retrieval perform almost equally well regarding precision. In fact, as it can be seen from the graph in Fig. 6, the mean error of the localization is between 11 cm and 13 cm for 0% occlusion. The performance of the robust estimator may vary slightly since the hypothesis generation includes a stochastic step.

The performance of both methods at higher levels of occlusion noise is compared in Fig. 6. We can see a significant improvement in precision as a result of applying the robust method. Even in situations of severe occlusion when more than half of the surrounding is invisible, the robust method retrieves positions that are reasonably close to the correct ones. This can be clearly seen in Fig. 7. On the left we can see that the standard method breaks under ambiguity of the data while the results of the robust estimator on the right show quite regular localization results with mean error under 60 cm.

5. Conclusion

In this paper we presented a method for robust view-based localization using panoramic images. As our experiments show, we can perform relatively accurate localization by using a pure view-based model of a pre-learned environment. By applying a robust framework to the recognition phase we can also achieve a significant improvement of performance when occlusions or noise are present in the input images. If we consider a scenario of a mobile robot in an office environment, the expected levels of noise seem acceptable for the algorithm.

We are currently exploring the problem of robustness in the learning phase and incremental on-line building of models of the environment.

References

[1] H. Aihara, N. Iwasa, N. Yokoya, and H. Takemura. Memory-based self-localisation using omnidirectional images. In *14th ICPR*, pages 297–299, 1998.

[2] H. Ishiguro and S. Tsuji. Image-based memory of environment. In *Proc. IEEE/RSJ Int. Conf. Intelligent Robots and Systems*, pages 634–639, 1996.

[3] M. Jogan and A. Leonardis. Panoramic eigenimages for spatial localisation. In *8th CAIP*, pages 558–567, 1999.

[4] S. Judd and T. Collett. Multiple stored views and landmark guidance in ants. *Nature*, 392:710–714, 16 April 1998.

[5] A. Leonardis and H. Bischof. Robust recognition using eigenimages. *CVIU*, 78(1):99–118, 2000.

[6] S. Nayar and T. Poggio, editors. *Early visual learning*. Oxford University Press, 1996.

[7] S. K. Nayar, S. A. Nene, and H. Murase. Subspace methods for robot vision. *IEEE Trans. on RA*, 12(5):750–758, 1996.

[8] T. Pajdla and V. Hlaváč. Zero phase representation of panoramic images for image based localization. In *8th CAIP*, pages 550–557, 1999.

Needs and Seeds in Character Recognition

Yasuaki Nakano
Dept. of Information Engineering
Shinshu University
4-17-1 Wakasato, Nagano 380–8553 JAPAN
nakano@cs.shinshu-u.ac.jp

Abstract

This paper discusses the relation between technical seeds in character recognition and market needs. The seeds can meet the market needs in condition that the seeds are at the level high enough. The character recognition techniques used so far, however, have not been matured but owed much to many constraints. In other words, human beings have made many artificial limitations so as to put premature OCR techniques into the practical use. The technical progress and competition are making these constraints unnecessary. In this context, the unconstrained OCR techniques will be explained.

1. Introduction

Character recognition may seem as a very matured technology. Many new ideas and applications, however, are emerging from new and old viewpoints.

If the needs meet seeds suitably, a huge market can grow in very rapid speed.

In this paper, I will search many seeds and needs in character recognition area.

Character recognition has been utilized for about fifty years. OCR (Optical Character Recognition) was put into practice for the recognition of computer-printed numerals first in 1950's.

In late 1960's, hand-printed character recognition was put into the practical use in United States and Japan. In Japan, there were two kind of main application, i.e. the handwritten ZIP code readers developed by Toshiba and NEC and the business form readers developed by the main computer producers in Japan.

As for the handwritten ZIP code reader in Japan, I want to point out that many advantageous conditions existed. In the specification proposed from Japan Postal Office, the substituted error rate was 1% and the rejection error rate was 10%, both per letter. Of course, the target was very severe for the techniques of the days. Considering that the ZIP codes in Japan had three to five digits, the allowable substitution error rate was 0.3% and the rejection error rate was 3%, per character. Though the target was very tough, it was very favorable that some errors could be allowed, since the errors only made the mail be delivered for a few days lately.

On the other hand, the another target, business form readers were under very difficult condition that the substitution errors were not allowed, because these readers were used to read financial datas mainly. In Japan, however, the hand-printed character recognition has been very prosperous and the total sales may exceed several ten million U. S. dollars. Was the reason of OCR prosperity in Japan the excellency of recognition techniques? Perhaps, the answer will be "No."

To meet the condition of zero (or very close to zero) substitution errors, two constraints were introduced.

The first limitation was usage of the colored ink to make it easier to detect the written characters. Fig. 1 illustrates a fictional form, in which the preprinted information such as guidances or frames are printed in colored ink. So, using the appropriate illumination, the preprinted information is unvisible to OCR and only the necessary datas to be recognized are seen. In the figure, plural characters are hand-printed in a frame, but in the early period only one character was printed separately in a box. The latter condition made it very easy to detect and segment a character. This situation was (and partially is) same in the ZIP code readers.

The second limitation was the adoption of the hand-printing font.

In Japan, the hand-printing fonts for numerals, alphabetics, kana syllabaries and kanji were settled and used for OCR. It is not true that the characters not obeying the limitation are misrecognized nor rejected, and many OCR companies have struggled to expand the range of font variation. But, this limitation helped OCR companies very much in the infant era of OCR in Japan.

In Europe and U. S., it is doubtful that the usage of the recommended hand-printing font might have been accepted. They write words in the cursive style, so the character sepa-

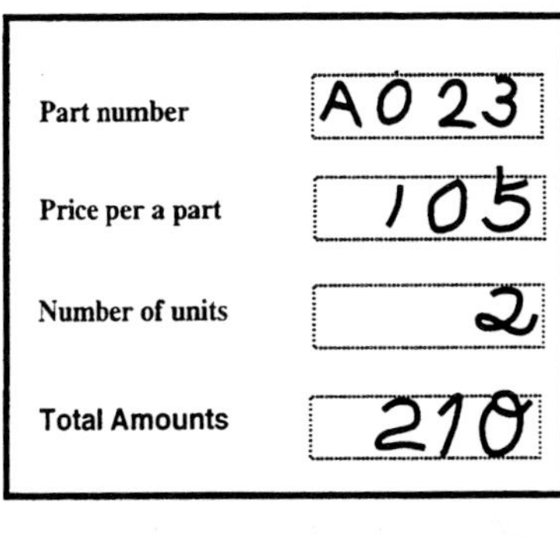

Figure 1. Elimination of the background by colored ink
Top: Image visible to human beings
Bottom: Image visible to OCR

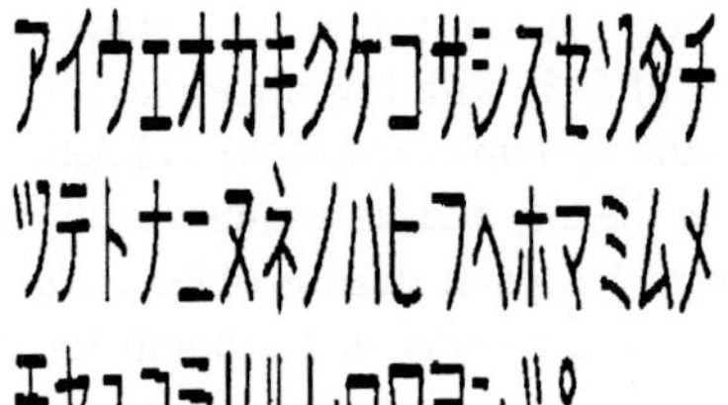

アイウエオカキクケコサシスセソタチ
ツテトナニヌネノハヒフヘホマミムメ
モヤユヨラリルレロワヲン゛゜ー

Figure 2. Recommended handprinted fonts for katakana

ration by character frames or the adoption of the font might have been considered as the violation to the culture. In Japan, fortunately the alphabet or katakana has been used as the symbols and not as the constituents of words. So, the limitation was easily accepted.

As the result, in Europe and U. S., the very difficult targets such as handwritten address recognition in the mail or the handwritten numerals and alphabets on bank checks remained as the challenge to character recognition. As illustrated in the following section, the progress at these fields in Europe and U. S. have been very remarkable.

On the other hand, the favorite limitation for OCR is vanishing even in Japan. The main target is the address recognition on the mail and OCR should recognize the address written in kanji as well as the seven-digit ZIP.

2. Recognition of Cursive English Words

As explained in the previous section, there are two major needs for the cursive English (or European) word recognition.

One is the recognition of handwritten addresses on the mails. The project promoted by U. S. Post Office and researches mainly done at CEDAR [1], SUNY, contributed much to the project.

CEDAR supplies the CD–ROM database of the real address datas written on the envelopes recorded at post offices. This CD–ROM accelerates the research of the cursive English word recognition remarkably.

In this section, our research of address recognition using the database will be explained.

In the cursive word recognition, the so-called "oversegmentation" may be one of the standard technique.

This approach was first introduced to numeral recognition by Fujisawa et al. [3], in the handprinted character recognition, though for the printed character recognition similar approaches had been known. The principle is explained in Fig. 3.

In this figure, the candidates of the touching points are extracted at more points than the expected numbers (so, the name "oversegmentation" is used.)

All combination of the segmented parts is tested if they compose a character by the recognition unit. When the hypothesis that the combination of the components may be a character, the hypothesis is accepted.

For the numerals, the test of the hypotheses by a recognition unit may be appropriate, because the recognition ability can be high enough. For the English cursive words, however, the recognition rate may not be so high as to confirm the properness of the hypotheses.

So, the confirmation by the word recognition unit becomes feasible. In the address recognition, the matching of

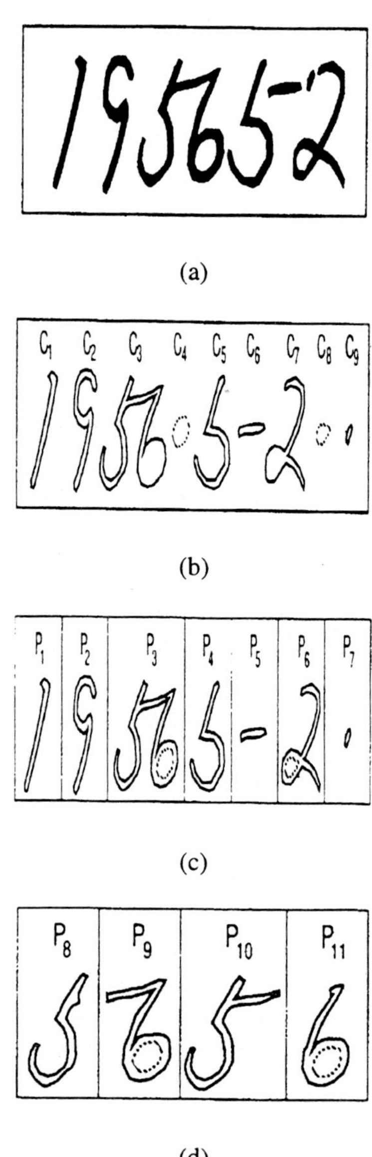

Figure 3. Principle of Oversegmentation (b) Assign Each Outer Contour to a Virtual Frame (c) Make multiple Hypotheses (d) For the Possible Touching, Separation is Tested

the recognition result of the ZIP code to the state, city and street will be very powerful.

But in our experiments, only the city names are available and the recognition results were matched with a city name dictionary.

The process of the recognition is shown in Fig. 4.

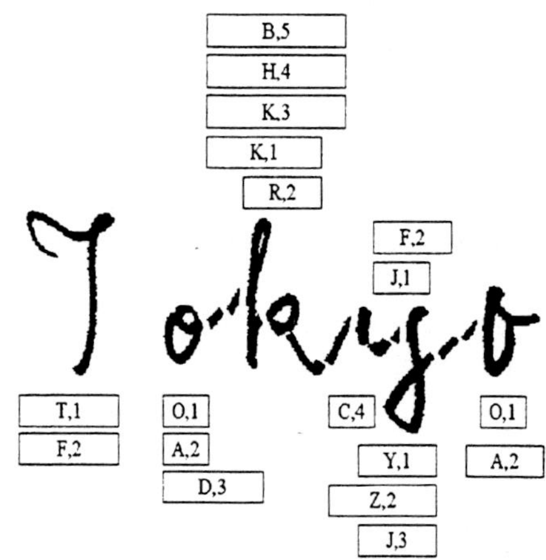

Figure 4. Example of Cursive Word Recognition "T, 1" means "T" was the top candidate in OCR "Tokyo" gets the best score in lexical matching.

Applying the method to the state/city names included in the CEDAR database, the word recognition rate was 79.8% and the cumulative recognition rate until the fifth order was 91.7%. The value is far from the satisfaction and we are working to improve the results.

Recently a Russian company ParaScript^{TM} has developed address recognition system and obtained very high finalization rate of 64% with low error rate [4]. This system and other similar systems exploit the validation method by cross-checking the city and state names with zip datas.

Judging from the demonstration of Parascript [5], the performance may be a wonder and a bomb for the OCR researchers.

Another needs for the cursive word recognition is bankcheck recognition. In Europe and U. S. many bankchecks are used and a very large portion of them are handwritten in cursive style. In Japan, however, personal bankchecks are seldomly used and the needs for bankcheck recognition does not exist actually.

In the bankcheck recognition, the characters are written on the complex background, so the extraction and segmentation is very important for the recognition performance.

Many researchers exploit the cross-checking technique

by comparing the recognition results of legal amounts and courtesy amounts.

3. Segmentation in Address Recognition

As is explained in the previous section, handwritten character recognition in the postal system is and will be a very large market. In Japan the situation is the same and the address recognition on mails has been used for several years.

The problem of the mails in Japan is that the addresses are written in the free format both in vertical or horizontal direction.

So, the problems in the address recognition become very complicated, because Japanese addresses can be written even in a mixed fashion of vertical and horizontal direction.

The most difficult may be to separate and detect each character in a line. After the direction of the writing is decided, a height (in the vertical written format) of a character is estimated and used to separate a character. Usually the height estimation can be done using the width information of a line. However, there are many characters from many sources and the height is different in the sources. For example, numerics may be smaller than kanji. Besides a kanji can include many subpatterns (radicals) and these subpatterns might have as almost same size as numerals or kana syllabaries.

So, it is difficult to segment characters only by the heights or widths. The "oversegmentation technique" incorporating language processing will be indispensable as well as the cursive English address recognition.

In the hand-printed Japanese address recognition, the oversegmentation is applied even when no character touches. In the case of kanji, radicals forming kanji are processed in the same manner as Figure 4, where each radical plays the same role as character fragments of a cursive word. And in kanji, oversegmentation verified only by the recognition unit can not be complete.

In the example of Figure 5, the combination of two radicals can be seen as a character (as an ordinary Japanese reads so), while each radical can also be seen as a character. So, even if the recognition is complete, the recognition unit cannot determine the optimum candidate. The linguistic processing (lexical matching) can only determine the candidate.

Sometimes, a character touches to another one. So, the technique to segment touching characters are needed. After determining the candidate touching points, the processing is same as the case in which no touching is allowed. Recently, touching addresses become to be recognized using the oversegmentation technique [8].

Currently, the recognizable addresses are mainly handprinted in the block style. But some older people write characters in the cursive fashion. The cursive Japanese address recognition will be very tough.

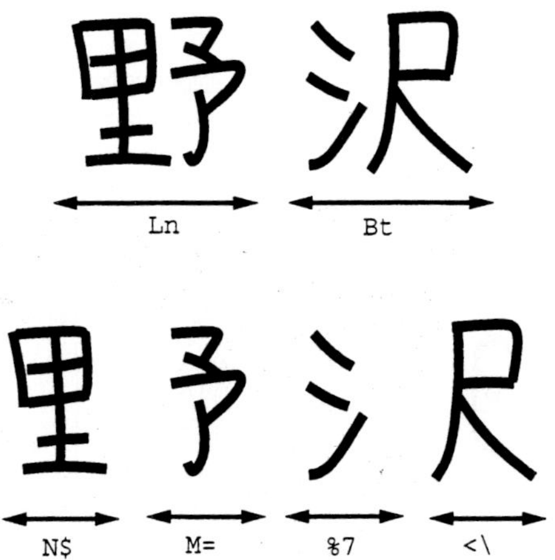

Figure 5. In this word, each radical can be recognized as a character as well as its combination. So, the recognition part can not determine a sole candidate.

The techniques explained in this section will be developed also in China, Korea and other Asian countries for the post office automation.

4. Neural Networks

In recent years, it is claimed that Neural Networks will solve many problems in the pattern recognition. This paper will point out the limit of Neural Network (NN in short) approaches in the pattern recognition,

It is true that NN seems to have solved many problems in the pattern recognition. The handprinted numeral recognition is not the exception.

In Figure 6 a typical configuration of a Neural Network for characrter recognition.

For the handprinted numeral recognition, NN showed very high recognition rate for the "Training Set." The problem has been that the recognition rate for the "Test Set" was far from the satisfaction compared to that of the "Training Set." The situation can be seen in the first column of Table 1.

This problem might have been resolved by Yamada et al. [6] by increasing the size of the training set. Many researchers had been working to improve the recognition rate by increasing the training times at the learning processes fixing the training set in vain, while Yamada showed that increasing the learning set can serve for the improvement of the recognition rate as shown in the second column of Table 1.

The phenomenon may be illustrated by Figure 7. Gener-

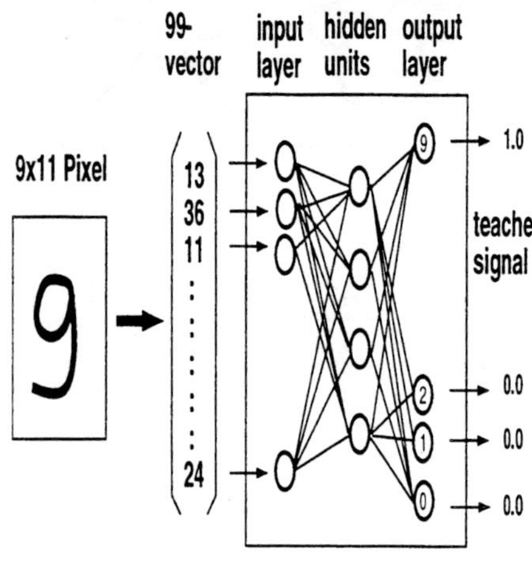

Figure 6. A typical configuration of a Neural Network for character recognition.

Table 1. Recognition Rates of Handprinted Characters using NN

Year	Configuration (Neurons of Layers)	Amount of Training (Sample ×times)	Recognition rate	
			Test	Train
	99-40-40-10	100×250	94.2%	99.4%
1988	99-80-10	100×250	95.8%	99.6%
	99-192-10	100×?	96.2%	100.0%
1989	99-80-10	500×20	98.1%	100.0%

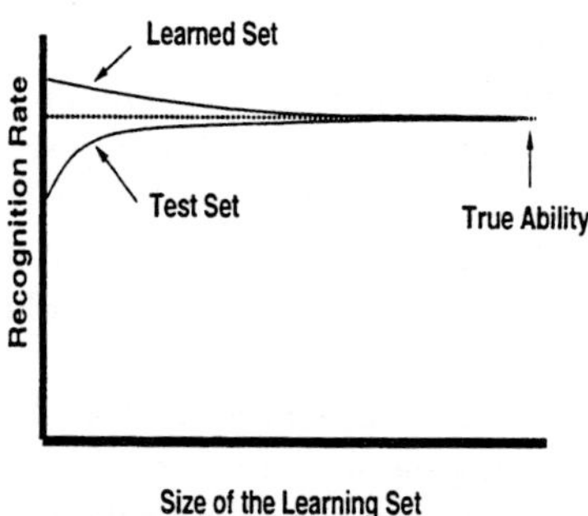

Figure 7. Tendency of the Recognition Rate vs Sample Size

ally speaking, the recognition rate for the training set will be decreasing if the amount of the training set increases, while that for the test set will increase. The reason will be understood easily.

As the result, to increase the amount of the training set is the only way to improve the recognition ability of NN. This conclusion may be very tiresome and against the dream for the NN, but this is the fact.

5. Majority Logics

In the printed character OCR's, it is well admitted that the majority logic contributes to get the very high recognition rates [7]. The reason may be explained that different algorithms of the different companies do behave differently in th recognition. So, by taking the majority in the recognition results among the different machines, an accurate result might be obtained.

This idea was confirmed recently in the recognition of the Japanese handwritten numeral OCR as well as the English printed OCR.

However, the idea has not been verified for the printed Japanese character recognition, so an experiment to certify the idea has been done.

In the experiment, six commercial OCR's for the printed Japanese documents were tested. A virtual OCR which outputs the majority of the OCR results was constructed and compared to six OCR's. The majority calculation is not so easy as supposed, because insertion and deletion of characters make it difficult simple comparison of the candidate outputs in the different machine. Seventeen test documents were selected from the document image database, JEIDA'93.

Total number of characters included in seventeen documents was 9,775. The results of recognition by six OCR's are tabulated in Table majorityOCR. From the table, the recognition rate ranges from 91.30% to 98.10%. This table shows also the result of the virtual OCR using majority logic, which is very high and 99.33%. It must be noted that insertion and deletion errors decrease drastically. The reason will be in that the segmentation algorithm in each OCR differs from each other, so insertion and deletion may occur at the different places.

The history of the idea of the majority is very old, and a patent of this idea was filed in 1960's in Japan. But, in the period when an OCR algorithm was implemented by wired logics, it is too difficult to use several algorithms in a machine from the economic viewpoint. The recent progress of microprocessors and memories, both in speed and cost, are making it real to install plural algorithms in a system. This tendency will be same in the future, so it is not fictional but realistic to use the majority logic in a commercial system.

Table 2. Effect of Majority Logic
"M" means a virtual OCR outputting the majority.
Subst., Ins. and Del. denote Substition, Insertion and Deletion errors, respectively.

OCR	Subst.	Ins.	Del.	Rate (%)
a	285	28	2	96.78
b	472	357	21	91.30
c	189	10	8	97.88
d	214	23	6	97.51
e	175	6	5	98.10
f	156	51	11	97.77
M	60	6	0	99.33

Actually, the Parascript^{TM}'s paper [4] explains that it integrates several character recognition algorithms.

6. HMM

HMM (Hidden Markov Model has been widely used in the speech recognition. Recent achievements in on-line character recognition also use HMM, because ink datas in on-line character recognition are also one-dimensional as well as speech.

In several years, HMM was introduced to two-dimensional character recognition. Essentially, for the two-dimensional characters, two-dimensional models should be used and some researches discusses two-dimensional HMM [11], [12].

However, two-dimensional models require very long learning time and a huge database for the learning. By the reason, one-dimensional HMM may be useful if it can realize the comparable performance as the two-dimensional HMM. So, the applicability of one-dimensional HMM for the recognition of off-line characters was examined.

Figure 8 shows a typical diagram of Left-to-Right type one-dimensional HMM.

In the Left-to-Right type HMM, the state transition probability $a_{i,i}$ and $a_{i,i+1}$ determine the occurrence probability of the output sequence.

A HMM for each character class is constructed by the learning. In our experiments, the target classes are upper–case alphabet characters and the number of the constructed HMM is twenty six.

Character recognition is done by calculating the likelihood of an unknown character for each class HMM to output the feature sequence of the inputted character.

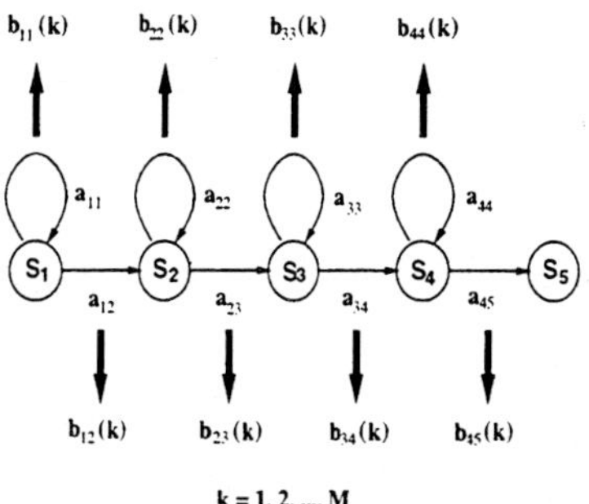

Figure 8. Left-to-Right type HMM

The feature sequence of a character is extracted by segmenting the character into vertical (or horizontal) slices and calculating some features for the slices. The feature vector for each slice is quantized to a symbol using the vector quantizing technique. So, the feature sequence of a character is a symbol string whose length is the number of the slices. Figure 9 shows an example of the feature.

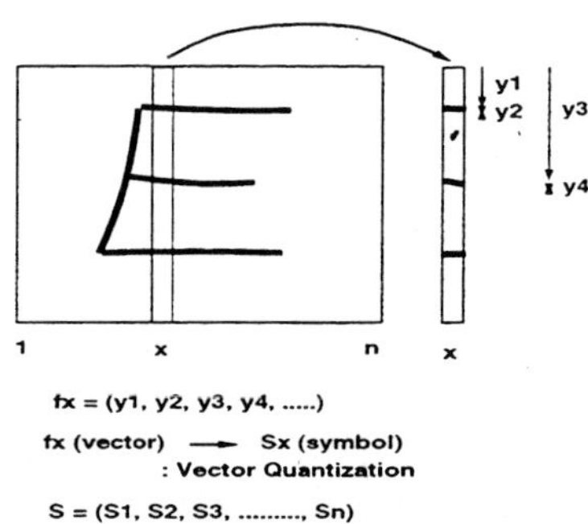

Figure 9. Feature Extraction in One-dimensional HMM

In order to obtain high recognition rate by one-dimensional HMM comparable to two-dimensional HMM, the Multidirectional HMM (MD-HMM in short) was proposed. In this HMM, several one-dimensional HMM's are constructed in many directions. (In our experiment, only two directions are used, but theoretically more than two directions can be used.) In each HMM, the different feature sequences extracted in each direction were used in learning and recognition.

By integrating of the outputs of the MD-HMM, a character pattern is recognized. Table 3 shows an experimental result for the Handprinted Alphabet Pattern database, ETL-6.

From the result, MD-HMM has better performance than the one-dimensional HMM and the improvement is obvious. Though MD-HMM has worse performance at the first rank

Table 3. Recognition Rates by Multidirectional HMM

Method	Cumulative Recognition Rate		
	1	2	3
1D-HMM	94.3%	96.2%	96.6%
MD-HMM	95.3%	98.3%	99.4%
2D-HMM	96.5%	98.6%	99.1%

recognition rate than two-dimensional HMM, it outperforms two-dimensional HMM in the second and third rank recognition rate. Thus, it can be concluded that MD-HMM has almost same performance as two-dimensional HMM with much more simplicity.

7. Concluding Remarks

In the lecture at ICDAR'97 [9] Nagy gave a report of the fictional conference ICDAR 2007, i.e. he prophesied the status quo of OCR and related techniques in the next decade. In his lecture (not appeared in the proceedings) he prophesied that few researches on handwritten character recognition will be done, because schools will not teach handwriting but typewriting.

The rapid expansion of the computer network represented by WWW will also threaten the future of OCR for the machine printed or handwritten characters.

In this paper, however, we explained many promising methods as the technical seeds, and if there are needs matching to the seeds, the prosperity of OCR business will be enlarged far beyond of our imagination. For example, even in the WWW, the content retrieval from web sources may use pattern recognition as a tool and the OCR may play a role.

To be too pessimistic on the future of the character recognition will not the correct attitude.

References

[1] J.J.Hull et al.,Combination of Segmentation-based and Wholistic Handwritten Word Recognition Algorithms, Proc. of Int. Workshop on Frontiers in Handwriting Recognition, pp.447–452 (1991)

[2] H. Yamada and Y. Nakano, Cursive Handwritten Word Recognition Using Multiple Segmentation Determined by Contour Analysis, IEICE Trans. Inf. and Syst., Vol.E79-D, pp.464-470 (1996)

[3] H.Fujisawa, Y. Nakano and K. Kurino, Segmentation Methods for Character Recognition; From Segmentation to Document Structure Analysis, Proc. of the IEEE, Vol.80, pp.1079-1092 (1992)

[4] A. Filatov et al: The AddresScript^{TM} Recognition System for Handwritten Envelopes, Proc. of 3rd IAPR Workshop on Document Analysis Systems, pp.185-188 (1998)

[5] ParaScript, `http://www.us.paragraph.com/`

[6] K. Yamada et al.: Handwritten Numeral Recognition by Multilayered Neural network with Improved Learning Algorithm, Proc. of Int. Joint Conf. on Neural Network, pp.259-266 (1989)

[7] S. V. Rice et al.: A Report on the Accuracy of OCR Devices, ISRI Technical Report, pp.1-6, Information Science Research Institute, University of Nevada, Las Vegas (1992)

[8] H. Ikeda et al.: A Recognition Method for Touching Japanese Handwritten Characters, Proc. of 5th International Conference on Document Analysis and Recognition, pp.641–644 (1999)

[9] G. Nagy: Conference Report: ICDAR'07, Proc. of 4th International Conference on Document Analysis and Recognition, pp.1112–1112 (1997)

[10] L. R. Rabiner: A Tutorial on Hidden Markov Models and Selected Applications in Speech Recognition, Proc. IEEE, pp. 257–286 (1989)

[11] G. E. Kopec and P. A. Chou: Document Image Decoding Using Markov Source Models, IEEE Trans. on Pattern Analysis and Machine Intelligence, Vol. 16, pp. 602–617 (1994) pp. 257–286 (1989)

[12] H. S. Park and S. W. Lee: A Truly 2-D Hidden Markov Model for Off-Line Handwritten Character Recognition, Pattern Recognition, Vol. 31, pp. 1849–1864 (1998) pp. 257–286 (1989)

A Stereo Vision-based Augmented Reality System with a Wide Range of Registration

Masayuki Kanbara†, Hidehiko Iwasa‡, Haruo Takemura† and Naokazu Yokoya†
†Graduate School of Information Science, Nara Institute of Science and Technology
8916-5 Takayama-cho, Ikoma-shi, Nara 630-0101, JAPAN
{masay-ka, takemura, yokoya } @is.aist-nara.ac.jp
‡ Netsystems, Inc.
3-2-2 Marunouchi Chiyoda-ku, Tokyo 100-0005, JAPAN
iwasa@netsystems.co.jp

Abstract

This paper proposes a vision-based augmented reality system with a wide range of registration. To realize an augmented reality system, it is required to geometrically register real and virtual worlds. In the case of a vision-based augmented reality with marker tracking, its measurement range is usually limited because markers placed in the real world should be captured by cameras. The proposed method realizes a stereo vision-based augmented reality system with a wide range of registration by automatically detecting and tracking new markers that come into sight. The feasibility of the system has been successfully demonstrated through experiments.

1 Introduction

Augmented reality produces an environment in which virtual objects are superimposed on user's view of the real environment. Augmented reality has received a great deal of attention as a new method for displaying information or increasing the reality of virtual environments. A number of applications have already been proposed and demonstrated [1, 2, 3, 4]. To implement an augmented reality system, we must solve some problems. A geometric registration is especially the most important problem because virtual objects should be superimposed on the right place as if they really exist in the real world. The geometrical registration is achieved by determining the user's viewpoint and viewing direction in the world coordinate defined in the real world.

One of solutions for the registration problem is to use 3-D trackers such as electromagnetic, ultrasound or mechanical trackers [5, 6]. By using these devices, it is possible to acquire three dimensional position and orientation of user's viewpoint. However, because of the physical limitation of devices, the measurement range of these trackers is limited. The limitation is fatal for some kind of applications in which users of the system move on a large scale.

To overcome the limitation, we have proposed a registration method in which three markers of unknown three dimensional positions are used[7]. The position of user's viewpoint and the viewing direction are estimated by using the image sequences which include the three markers taken by a pair of stereo cameras on a head mounted display (HMD) [7]. Although the method removes the limitation in the sensc that the measurement range is not restricted by the measurement device, it still has a problem that three markers should always be captured by cameras.

The method proposed in this paper extends the our previous work by introducing the new functionality of detection and tracking of additional markers. The method registers the real and virtual worlds using images captured by stereo cameras which are fixed near user's viewpoint. We use three blue markers of known positions and red markers of unknown positions. Three blue markers are used to define a world coordinate system in the real world and to register the real and virtual worlds. Once the world coordinate system is defined, the method starts to detect red markers using color information and estimate their positions in the world coordinate. These captured red markers are used to make new coordinate systems when some or all of the initial three blue markers disappear from the images during the change of user's viewpoint. By using newly generated coordinate systems, the method continuously registers the real and virtual worlds. The range of registration is consequently unlimited.

The following part of the paper is structured as follows. Section 2 describes detailed algorithms of the wide range registration with two kinds of markers. In Section 3, the experimental results with the proposed method and discussion about the prototype system are described. Finally, Section 4 summarizes the present work.

2. Algorithms for Registration with Two Kinds of Markers

2.1. Marker tracking and estimation of 3-D positions of markers.

To define a fixed world coordinate system in a real world captured by stereo cameras, at least three points whose positions in the real world are known should be included in the images. It is also needed that their positions in the camera coordinate system must be obtained to superimpose virtual objects in the right place in the images of the real world. In our method, we use three blue markers to represent such reference points.

These blue markers are detected based on their color information. To reduce the computational cost, only the first images of stereo pair are scanned entirely to find blue regions. Next, the center of gravity of each blue region is treated as the image coordinate of the marker. When three markers are found in both left and right images, stereo matching is performed based on the epipolar constraint and all markers are then labeled (Labels: 1,2,3).

When the processing speed is fast enough, the markers' positions in adjacent frames can be assumed to be close to each other. A search area for each marker is determined on the current frame based on the position of the marker in the previous frame. The center of gravity for all blue pixels in the search area is calculated and is treated as the image coordinate of the marker.

The relationship between two cameras and a marker is illustrated in Figure 1. The origin of the camera coordinate system is placed at the middle between the centers of projection of two cameras. The X-axis is set along the baseline of the cameras. The Z-axis is set to the direction parallel to the optical axes of the cameras. A marker at $P(X,Y,Z)$ in 3-D space is projected onto the left and right images at $P_l(x_l, y_l)$ and $P_r(x_r, y_r)$ in the image coordinates, respectively. Then the following equations stand:

$$X = \frac{B(x_l + x_r)}{2(x_l - x_r)}, \quad (1)$$

$$Y = \frac{B(y_l + y_r)}{2(x_l - x_r)}, \quad (2)$$

$$Z = \frac{fB}{x_l - x_r}, \quad (3)$$

where f is the focal length and B is the baseline length. Note that $y_l = y_r$. Thus when f and B are known, $P(X,Y,Z)$ is calculated from the coordinates $P_l(x_l, y_l)$ and $P_r(x_r, y_r)$.

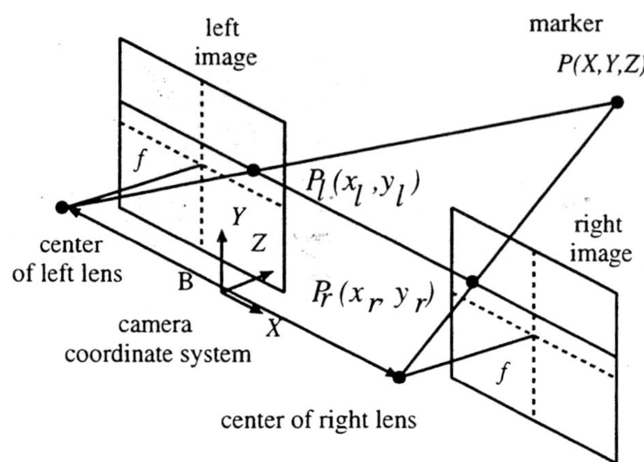

Figure 1. Geometry of stereoscopic projection of a marker.

2.2. Calculation of model-view matrix.

After the positions of three blue markers in the camera coordinate system are acquired, it becomes possible to calculate a model-view matrix which represents the spatial relationship between two coordinate systems. Figure 2 illustrates the relationship among the world coordinate system, the camera coordinates system, and markers. Among a model-view matrix - $\mathbf{M}$, a position of a point in the world coordinate system - $\mathbf{w}$, and its position in the camera coordinate system - $\mathbf{c}$, the following equation stands:

$$\mathbf{c} = \mathbf{M}\mathbf{w}. \quad (4)$$

The matrix $\mathbf{M}$ can be decomposed into the rotation $\mathbf{R}$ and the translation $\mathbf{T}$ as follows:

$$\mathbf{M} = \left[\begin{array}{ccc|c} & \mathbf{R} & & \mathbf{T} \\ \hline 0 & 0 & 0 & 1 \end{array}\right]. \quad (5)$$

In the proposed method, the world coordinate system is simply defined as follows:

- The origin is set at the marker labeled as No. 1 (m1 in Figure 2),
- The x-axis is set on the line that connects the markers labeled as No. 1 and No. 2 (m2 in Figure 2),
- The $x - y$ plane is set on the plane on which three markers reside.

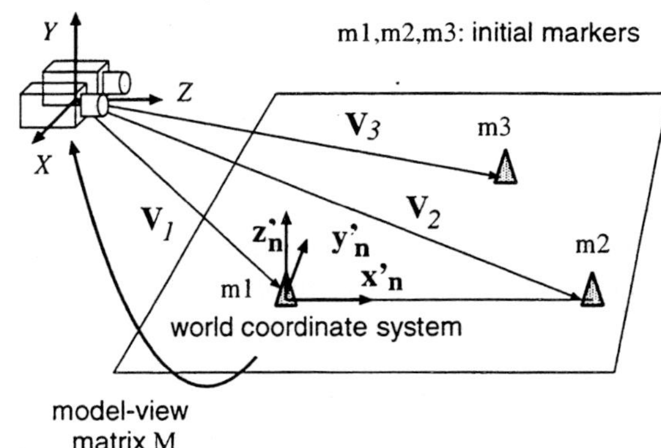

Figure 2. Relationship between the world and camera coordinates.

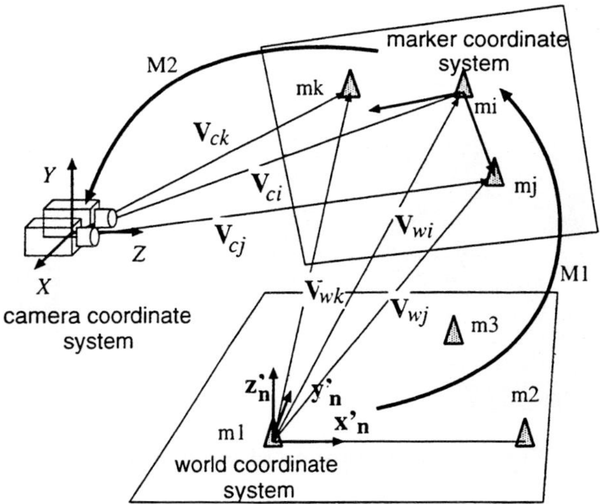

Figure 3. Relationship between the marker and camera coordinates.

According to the definition above, the translation component $\mathbf{T}$ can be given by the camera coordinate position of the marker No. 1. The rotation component $\mathbf{R}$ can be calculated with the following steps.

1. When the 3-D positions of the markers Nos. 1, 2, and 3 are given as $\mathbf{V_1}$, $\mathbf{V_2}$, and $\mathbf{V_3}$, respectively, the direction of the vector of each axis of the world coordinate $(\mathbf{x_n}, \mathbf{y_n}, \mathbf{z_n})$ can be defined as follows:

$$\begin{aligned} \mathbf{x_n} &= \mathbf{V_2} - \mathbf{V_1}, \\ \mathbf{y_n} &= (\mathbf{V_3} - \mathbf{V_1}) - \frac{\mathbf{x_n} \cdot (\mathbf{V_3} - \mathbf{V_1})}{\mathbf{x_n} \cdot \mathbf{x_n}} \mathbf{x_n}, \\ \mathbf{z_n} &= \mathbf{x_n} \times \mathbf{y_n}. \end{aligned} \quad (6)$$

2. Normalize $\mathbf{x_n}, \mathbf{y_n}$, and $\mathbf{z_n}$ into $\mathbf{x'_n}, \mathbf{y'_n}$, and $\mathbf{z'_n}$, respectively:

$$\mathbf{x'_n} = \frac{\mathbf{x_n}}{||\mathbf{x_n}||}, \quad \mathbf{y'_n} = \frac{\mathbf{y_n}}{||\mathbf{y_n}||}, \quad \mathbf{z'_n} = \frac{\mathbf{z_n}}{||\mathbf{z_n}||}. \quad (7)$$

3. The rotation $\mathbf{R}$ can be represented by using $\mathbf{x'_n}, \mathbf{y'_n}$, and $\mathbf{z'_n}$ as follows:

$$\mathbf{R} = [\mathbf{x'_n}\ \mathbf{y'_n}\ \mathbf{z'_n}]. \quad (8)$$

By using $\mathbf{T}$ and $\mathbf{R}$, the model-view matrix $\mathbf{M}$ can be uniquely determined. Now it should be noted that the geometric alignment of the real and virtual world coordinates is achieved by the model-view matrix.

2.3. Registration using additional markers

To continuously calculate a model-view matrix even when initial three blue markers disappear from captured images during the change of viewpoint, we introduce additional red markers of unknown positions. Figure 3 illustrates the relationship among the initial markers (m_1, m_2, and m_3) and the additional markers (m_i, m_j, and m_k) captured by stereo cameras. $\mathbf{V_{ci}}, \mathbf{V_{cj}}$, and $\mathbf{V_{ck}}$ are the 3-D positions of the additional markers in the camera coordinate system that are currently captured by stereo cameras. $\mathbf{V_{wi}}, \mathbf{V_{wj}}$, and $\mathbf{V_{wk}}$ are the positions of the additional markers in the world coordinate system which are estimated by using the method described in Section 2.4.

The relation between positions of a point in the two different coordinate systems can be represented as follow:

$$\mathrm{c} = \mathbf{M_2 M_1 w}, \quad (9)$$

where $\mathbf{w}$ is a position of a point in the world coordinate system that is defined by the initial markers, and $\mathbf{c}$ is its position in the camera coordinate system. $\mathbf{M_1}$ is a matrix that represents the transformation from the world coordinate system to the marker coordinate system. $\mathbf{M_2}$ is a matrix that represents the transformation from the marker coordinate system which is defined by using m_i, m_j, and m_k as same as the world coordinate system to the camera coordinate system. These matrices can be decomposed as follows:

$$\mathbf{M_1} = \left[\begin{array}{ccc|c} & \mathbf{R_1^{-1}} & & -\mathbf{V_{wi}} \\ \hline 0 & 0 & 0 & 1 \end{array}\right], \quad (10)$$

Figure 4. Appearance of the experiment.

$$\mathbf{M_2} = \left[\begin{array}{ccc|c} & \mathbf{R_2} & & \mathbf{V_{ci}} \\ \hline 0 & 0 & 0 & 1 \end{array}\right], \quad (11)$$

where the rotations $\mathbf{R_1}$ and $\mathbf{R_2}$ are estimated by using the equations in Section 2.2. $\mathbf{R_1}$ can be estimated by replacing $\mathbf{V_1}$, $\mathbf{V_2}$ and $\mathbf{V_3}$ in equation (6) with $\mathbf{V_{wi}}$, $\mathbf{V_{wj}}$ and $\mathbf{V_{wk}}$. $\mathbf{R_2}$ can be estimated in the same manner.

2.4. Detecting and tracking additional markers coming into sight

Detection of red regions is accomplished in the same manner as in the detection of blue markers. When red markers are detected in stereo images, the positions of these markers in the camera coordinate system are estimated by triangulation and the positions in the world coordinate system are obtained by using the current model-view matrix. The position $\mathbf{V_w}$ of the marker in the world coordinate system is determined by its camera coordinate $\mathbf{V_c}$ as follows:

$$\mathbf{V_w} = \mathbf{M_1^{-1}} \mathbf{M_2^{-1}} \mathbf{V_c}, \quad (12)$$

where $\mathbf{M_1}$ and $\mathbf{M_2}$ are the matrices calculated by using currently captured three markers whose positions have already been known.

3. Implementation and Experiments

We have constructed a prototype of video see-through augmented reality system by using two small CCD cameras (Toshiba IK-UM42) mounted on a HMD (Olympus Media Mask) for demonstrating the proposed geometrical registration algorithm. The baseline length between two cameras is set to 6.5 cm. The optical axes of the cameras are set to be parallel to the viewer's gaze direction (actually the head direction). The images captured by the cameras are fed into a graphic workstation (SGI Onyx2 IR: 16CPU MIPS R10000 195MHz) through the digital video interface (DIVO). The input real world images are merged with the image of virtual objects and output from the DIVO interface to the HMD. As mentioned in the previous section, three blue markers with position information are used to define the world coordinate system in the real environment and red markers are used as additional markers to define marker coordinate systems. Figure 4 shows an appearance of experiment using the prototype system.

Figure 5 shows the image sequences of experimental results. Figure 5(a) shows the result of registration between real lines (black lines) in the real world and virtual objects (white lines). The positions of the virtual lines are located at be the same positions as the real lines in 3-D space. Black rectangles denote the tracked markers. As shown in Figure 5(a), markers in each image are tracked successfully. Even when the initial markers exit from the frame due to the movement of the user's viewpoint, the registration between the real and virtual lines is still maintained. Figure 5(b) shows the composition of a small virtual tree into a real desktop scene by using the initial and additional markers. It should be noted that the stereoscopic image composition is achieved in real time though only monocular image sequences are given in Figure 5. The average frame rate of the system is 10 frames per second, when the virtual object shown in Figure 5(b) (about 3200 polygons) is synthesized.

As confirmed in these experiments, the proposed method can continuously register real and virtual worlds even when initial markers disappear from user's view by detecting additional markers and estimating their relative positions to initial markers. As a result, users can change their viewing direction on a large scale in contrast with the case of augmented reality system with only three markers.

4. Conclusion

This paper has proposed a stereo vision-based augmented reality system with a wide rang of registration. The proposed method realizes a wide rang of registration by automatically detecting and tracking additional markers during the change of user's viewpoint. The feasibility of the system has been successfully demonstrated through experiments. We will further investigate a more accurate position estimation method of continuously tracking all markers to remove the an overhead for detecting appearing markers. Our future work will also include an extension of the method to automatically find natural features in a real environment as markers.

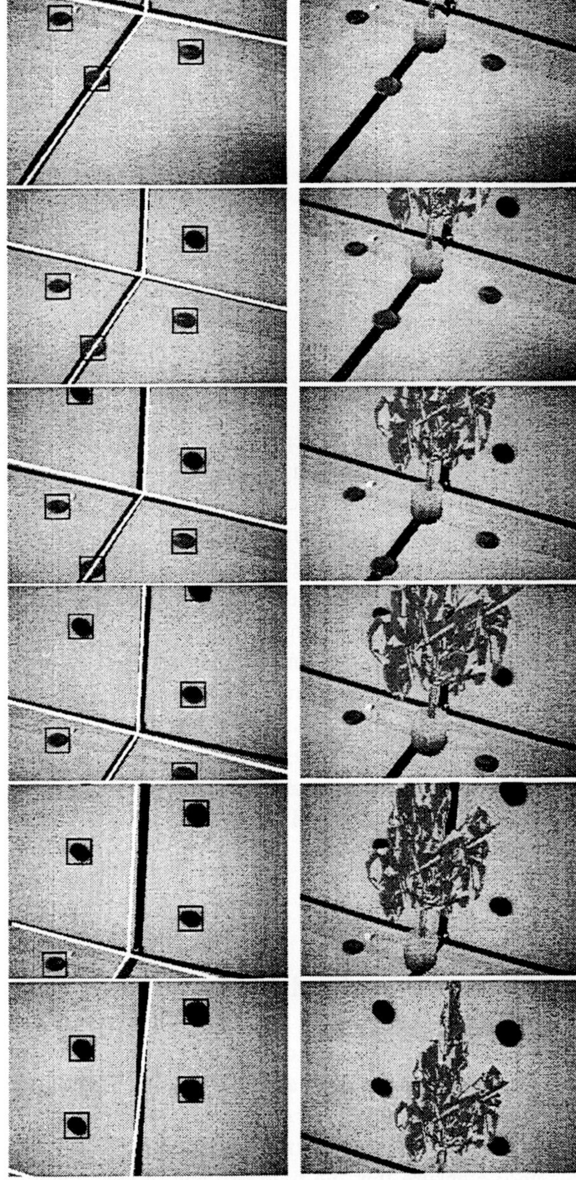

(a) Result of registration. (b) Composition of a virtual object.

Figure 5. Experimental results: Registration and virtual object composition.

References

[1] R. T. Azuma: "A Survey of Augmented Reality," Presence, Vol. 6, No. 4, pp. 355–385, 1997.

[2] T. Okuma, K. Kiyokawa, H. Takemura and N. Yokoya: "An Augmented Reality System Using a Real-time Vision Based Registration," Proc. ICPR'98, Vol. 2, pp. 1226–1229, 1998.

[3] M. Uenohara and T. Kanade: "Vision-Based Object Registration for Real-time Image Overlay," Proc. CVRMed'95, pp. 13–22, 1995.

[4] J. Rekimoto: "Matrix: A Realitime Object Identification and Registration Method for Augmented Reality," Proc. APCHI, pp. 63–68, 1998.

[5] S. Feiner, B. MacIntyre and D. Seligmann: "Knowledge-based Augmented Reality," Commun. of the ACM, Vol. 36, No. 7, pp. 52–62, 1993.

[6] M. Bajura, H. Fuchs and R. Ohbuchi: "Merging Virtual Objects with the Real World: Seeing Ultrasound Imagery within the Patient," Proc. SIGGRAPH'92, pp. 203–210, 1992.

[7] M. Kanbara, T. Okuma, H. Takemura and N. Yokoya: "A Stereoscopic Video See-through Augmented Reality System Based on Real-time Vision-based Registration," Proc. IEEE Virtual Reality 2000, pp. 255–262, 2000.

Ball Tracking and Virtual Replays for Innovative Tennis Broadcasts

Gopal Pingali, Agata Opalach, Yves Jean
Visual Communications Research
Bell Laboratories, Lucent Technologies
Murray Hill, NJ 07974
email: {gsp,agata,yvesjean}@lucent.com

Abstract

This paper presents a real-time computer vision system that tracks the motion of a tennis ball in 3D using multiple cameras. Ball tracking enables virtual replays, new game statistics, and other visualizations which result in very new ways of experiencing and analyzing tennis matches. The system has been used in international television broadcasts and webcasts of more than 15 matches. Six cameras around a stadium, divided into four pairs, are currently used to track the ball on serves which sometimes exceed speeds of 225 kmph. A multi-threaded approach is taken to tracking where each thread tracks the ball in a pair of cameras based on motion, intensity and shape, performs stereo matching to obtain the 3D trajectory, detects when a ball goes out of view of its camera pair, and initializes and triggers a subsequent thread. This efficient approach is scalable to many more cameras tracking multiple objects. The ready acceptance of the system indicates the growing potential for multi-camera based real-time tracking in broadcast applications.

1. Introduction

Computer vision has rich potential for enabling a new class of applications involving broadcasting, viewing of remote events and telepresence. While the research community has recognized the importance of video analysis and multi-camera based systems for interactivity, immersion, and search (see, for instance [5, 4, 1, 3, 6]), there have been few reports of successful deployment of such systems in real-world applications. Over the last two years, we have developed and deployed a multi-camera based real-time tracking and visualization system which is being regarded as introducing a new paradigm into sports broadcasting.

The system tracks the players and the ball in tennis matches in real time to introduce a number of innovations in live television broadcasts and webcasts of international tournaments. While the player tracking system has been described before [2], this paper focuses on the recently introduced multi-camera ball tracking system. Ball tracking is challenging because of the small size of the ball (67 mm in diameter), the relatively long distances it travels (over 26 m in length), the high speeds at which it travels (the fastest serves are over 225 kmph), changing lighting conditions, especially in outdoor events, and varying contrast between the ball and the background across the scene.

The configuration of the ball tracking system and the tracking approach are described in section 2. Section 3 presents new visualizations enabled by ball tracking which have been readily accepted and extensively used by broadcasters.

2. Ball Tracking

2.1. System design and configuration

The system consists of six monochrome progressive scan (60 Hz) cameras connected to a quad-pentium workstation with dual PCI bus. The number of cameras was chosen to be sufficient to cover the volume over which the ball typically travels and to ensure that the field of view of each camera is not too large. Progressive scan cameras which operate at 60 Hz are needed to capture images with temporal resolution good enough for ball tracking and so that the ball appears big enough in the image to be tracked. While cameras with an even higher speed and resolution could be used, we have chosen these based on the constraint of real-time processing and to stay within cost bounds. A general purpose computer has been used to ensure ease in developing the system, integrating it with other systems, and upgrading. Monochrome, rather than color cameras, have been chosen so that the bandwidth of a dual PCI bus is sufficient for full-frame capture at 60 Hz from all six cameras. Thus, color which is a strong cue for ball tracking, had to be sacrificed to meet the other system constraints. This has made ball segmentation a more challenging problem.

The six cameras are placed around a stadium with four cameras on the side and two at the ends of the court. Each of the four side cameras is paired with one of the end cameras to form a set of four stereo pairs that track the ball in 3D. Auto-iris lenses are used with the cameras to cope with large changes in lighting in the course of a day. Additionally, tracking parameters are dynamically updated, as explained in section 2.3.

2.2. Multi-threaded tracking

A multi-threaded approach is taken to tracking to achieve an efficient (real-time) solution that is scalable and works with distributed computing resources. A processing thread is associated with each camera pair. Figure 1 gives an overview of the processing steps in each thread. Each thread waits for a trigger signal to start frame capture and processing. Each thread has the following set of parameters: a trigger to start processing, a pair of associated cameras, calibration parameters of each camera, difference image thresholds for each camera, ball size parameters, expected intensity range for the ball, expected ball position in each camera image, size of the search window in each camera image, a trigger signal for the subsequent processing thread, and a pointer to the parameters of the subsequent thread. Camera calibration parameters are obtained beforehand using the algorithm in [7], taking advantage of the calibration grid provided by the court itself.

On receiving its trigger, a thread executes a loop of capturing frames from the camera pair, detecting the ball in the captured frames, stereo matching, and updating the 3D trajectory and tracking parameters, until the ball goes out of view of any one of its associated cameras. At this time, the current thread initializes the parameters for the thread corresponding to the subsequent camera pair and triggers that thread.

This multi-threaded approach scales in a straightforward manner to any number of cameras tracking an object over a large area. With a few modifications, the approach also scales to multiple objects being tracked by multiple cameras. In this case, a thread associated with a camera pair (or set of cameras) has triggers associated with each object to be tracked. The thread tracks an object when it receives a trigger signal corresponding to the object. Different tracking schemes can be used by a thread for different types of objects. For instance, different sets of parameters and tracking schemes are used for tracking the players and the ball in the tennis application.

2.3. Ball segmentation and detection

Ball segmentation/detection in any camera image is achieved by frame differencing the current and previous images and thresholding the result, finding the regions in the current image that lie in the expected intensity range for the ball, performing a logical AND operation of the regions obtained from the preceding two steps, subjecting the resulting regions to size and shape (aspect ratio) checks, and choosing the detection closest to the expected position in the (rare) case of multiple detections. All these operations are performed only in a window defined by the expected ball position and search size parameters. Most parameters, such as the range of intensity values, expected size, size of the search window, and the differencing threshold, are dynamically updated during the course of tracking. The expected position of the ball is continually updated based on the current velocity of the ball.

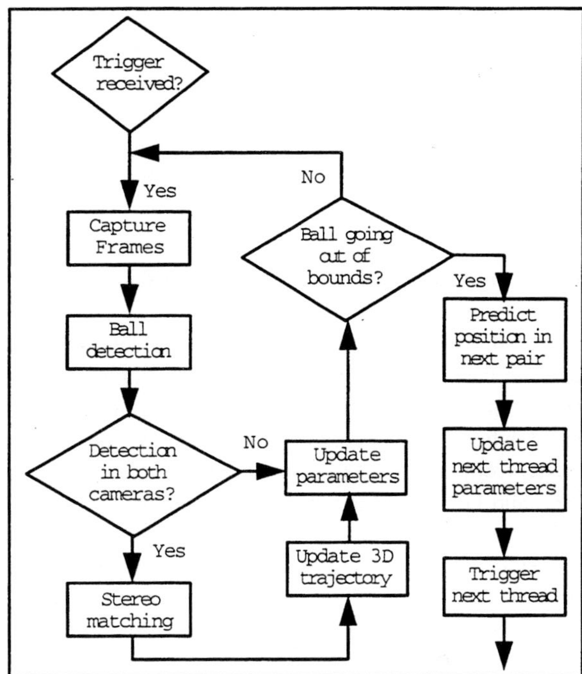

Figure 1. Overview of processing in each thread associated with a camera pair

Parameters such as the search size and range of intensity values are initially set to conservative values. The first thread to be triggered is determined based on the direction of the serve. This thread initially has no expected ball position but a relatively large search window. The search for the ball is performed in only one of the two cameras to ensure efficiency. Once the ball is detected in one camera, the search region in the other camera is based on epipolar constraints. Once tracking commences, the search regions are tightly defined and ball detection is performed in parallel in images from both cameras. When the current velocity of the ball indicates that the ball will be out of bounds of the current camera pair by the next frame, the positions of the ball in the next camera pair are determined based on the current 3D velocity of the ball and 3D to image mapping using camera calibration parameters. Thus, once the initial thread starts tracking, subsequent threads look for the ball in well-defined search windows. The dynamic update of segmentation and tracking parameters has been key to the success of this system.

2.4. Landing spot determination

The ball landing spot for each serve is determined by analyzing the 3D trajectory obtained from tracking and performing an appropriate interpolation. Interpolation is peformed where the z (height) component of the velocity changes from negative to positive, indicating the ball stops falling and begins rising. If the 3D trajectory of length n has time samples $(t_1, t_2, ..., t_n)$, and the time sample t_c represents the last sample with a negative z velocity (computed from time t_{c-1} to t_c), then the landing spot is at a time t_l which is either between t_c and t_{c+1} or between t_{c-1} and t_c. In the first case, the 3D velocity and acceleration parameters at time t_c are projected forward to determine when the ball would reach the ground. In the second case, the velocity and acceleration parameters at time t_{c+1} are projected backwards to determine the landing spot and landing time. The choice between the two is made based on how well the new velocity resulting from the interpolation blends with the known velocities. Our experiments have shown that the choice is unambiguous.

Figure 2. Example of tracking the ball in a pair of cameras

2.5. Results and Accuracy Issues

Ball tracking has been successfully performed on hundreds of serves in more than 15 matches at the 1999 World Championship in Hannover and the 1999 Paris Open. Figure 2 shows an example of ball tracking in one pair of cameras. We have achieved real-time tracking and have verified that the hand-off between cameras or threads is smooth. The 3D trajectories are stored in a database along with a host of other information related to the match as explained in section 3.1. The visualizations and statistics obtained from the ball trajectories have been eagerly used in numerous international live television broadcasts and webcasts. Some of the results are presented in section 3.

We have verified the accuracy of the system by several means: a) determining the accuracy of ball tracking in the image plane by careful analysis on a number of recorded sequences – these have shown ball tracking accuracy to be within a pixel; b) determining the accuracy of image to 3D mapping based on test points – these have shown object space errors under 15mm; c) careful comparison of trajectories and landing spots obtained by tracking with video sequences from different broadcast cameras; and d) comparison of speed of serve at racket obtained from ball tracking with that obtained by a radar gun – the difference has been within 10 kmph and has been partly due to a lack of precise match in the times at which the two speeds are measured. All these experiments indicate positional accuracy to be within a few millimeters and typically within 20 mm. However, it would be useful to further determine accuracy using an independent high speed modality for capturing ground truth data.

3. Virtual Replays and Visualizations

Ball tracking has enabled an exciting set of visualizations of a tennis match, immersive for a viewer. Users decide which part of the game is interesting to them and which visualization they wish to explore.

3.1. Data selection

The database contains a description of both dynamic and static aspects of the real-world environment. Ball trajectories are one example of dynamic data, together with player motion trajectories [2] and the changing game score. Tennis court geometry and player and tournament related information are examples of static data.

A powerful selection mechanism allows the user to choose any subset of this voluminous data. In the context of tennis, this selection includes **score-based queries** (e.g. *All serves won by a player*), **statistics-based queries** (e.g. *All serves at a speed above 200kmph*) or **space-based queries** (e.g. *All serves directed to the right corner of the left service box*). Each query can be further narrowed down using a **time constraint**, for example limiting it to one set, one game, or even any particular match period (e.g. *All serves in the first half hour of the match*). In addition, the system supports **historical queries**, allowing data selection across several matches (e.g. *All aces by Sampras against Agassi in 1999*).

3.2. Virtual mixing console

Having selected a data subset, the user is presented with a set of tools for viewing and analysis. The concept of a *virtual mixing console* is used to facilitate visualization selection, smooth transition between different visualizations, and combination of several visualizations. Selected visualizations share space in a visualization window. Currently, three types of visualizations are offered: virtual replays, service landing positions, and serve statistics, described in more detail in the following sections. A new type of visualization can be easily plugged into this scheme.

3.3. Virtual replays

Any particular serve can be viewed from any point of view at any speed. For instance, a spectator can become the receiver of a serve and appreciate the dynamics of the game from this position. A large variety of statistics can be offered for each serve, including the ball's speed at the racket, its speed after bounce, and the height at which it passed above the net or at which it reached the receiver.

Figure 3 shows a match-point ace, served by Sampras in the final against Agassi during the 1999 ATP World Championships. Figure 4 presents the serve by Agassi which reached the greatest height at the receiver, in the same match. Comparing even these two examples shows how wide a variety of serves one can expect in a tennis match.

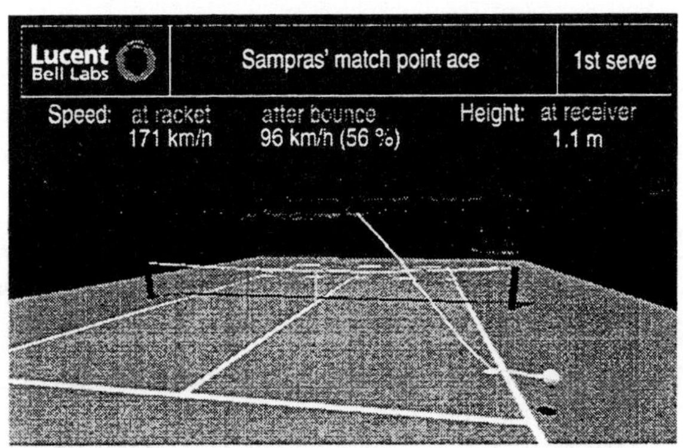

Figure 3. Virtual replay of a first serve

3.4. Multiple serve visualizations

A sequence of serves can be selected and shown as consecutive virtual replays to reveal the serving style of a player or to compare the styles of different players. Figure 5 shows superimposed trajectories from virtual replays of all aces served by Pete Sampras during the final of 1999 ATP World Championships against Andre Agassi. The density of aces in the central part of the court indicates Sampras' preference for this down-the-middle style of serve.

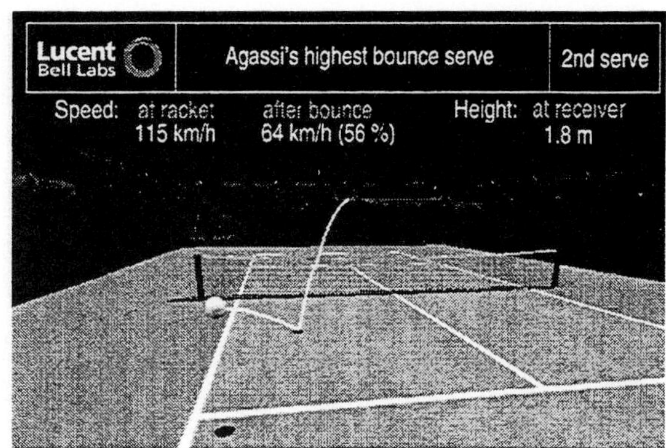

Figure 4. Virtual replay of a second serve

Figure 5. Consecutive virtual replays of a sequence of serves

Another way of analyzing multiple serves is a *Service landing position map* which gathers spots on the court where the players direct their serves. Figure 6 shows landing position maps for the 1999 Paris Open finalists, Andre Agassi and Marat Safin. Agassi serves very precisely and consistently into the corners of the serving box while Safin's serves are more spread out with all his second serves going into the center.

If a more detailed query is used for data selection, the service patterns can be analyzed in more detail. For instance, Figure 7 shows two maps for Safin, showing his serves won and lost. A careful viewer will notice that he often lost points when serving into the center of the serving box and far from the service line.

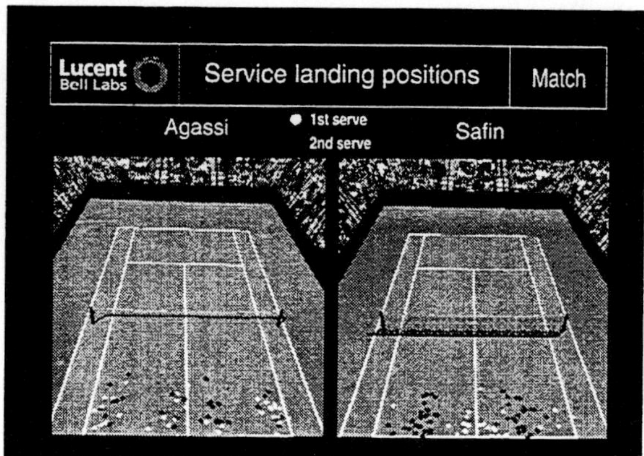

Figure 6. Maps showing serve landing spots of two players in a match

4. Conclusions

This paper presented a multi-camera real-time ball tracking system that has been used in live broadcasts by more than 20 television networks broadcasting in more than 70 countries, in addition to webcasts from an official tennis website (atptour.com). The approach taken here exemplifies several aspects of designing a successful visual tracking system. These include: a judicious choice of cameras – their number, placement, type, and speed; use of tight constraints provided by the environment and the application; highly efficient processing for real-time operation; dynamic update of parameters to cope with environmental changes; scalability of the solution to increased number of tracked objects, increase in covered area, increased number of cameras, and increased computational and bandwidth resources; and integration of tracking with a larger system to make it relevant to the application at hand.

Future work includes dealing with player-ball interactions and occlusion of the ball due to players, tracking the ball through out a game rather than just on serves, extension of the multi-threaded tracking approach to other applications, and experiments for better determination of accuracy using an independent high speed modality as ground truth.

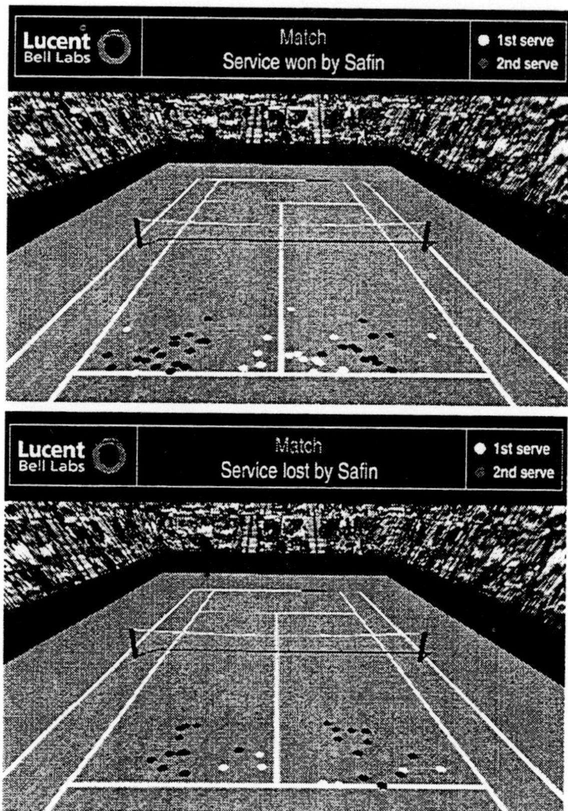

Figure 7. Service landing positions maps for service points won and lost

References

[1] Q. Cai and J.K. Aggarwal. Tracking human motion using multiple cameras. In *International Conference on Pattern Recognition*, pages 68–72, 1996.

[2] G.Pingali, Y. Jean, and I. Carlbom. Real-time tracking for enhanced sports broadcasts. In *Proceedings of CVPR98*, pages 260–265, 1998.

[3] I. Haritaoglu, D. Harwood, and L. Davis. W4 - a real time system for detecting and tracking people and their parts. In *Proceedings of the European Conference on Computer Vision*, 1998.

[4] S. Intille and A. Bobick. Visual tracking using closed worlds. In *Proceedings of the Fifth International Conference on Computer Vision*, pages 672–678, 1995.

[5] T. Kanade, P.J. Narayanan, and P. Rander. Virtualized reality: Concepts and early results. In *Proceedings of IEEE Workshop on Representation of Visual Scenes*, 1995.

[6] G. Sudhir, J.C.M. Lee, and A.K. Jain. Automatic classification of tennis video for high-level content-based retrieval. In *Procedings of IEEE Workshop on Content-Based Access of Image and Video Databases (CAIVD'98)*, 1998.

[7] R.Y. Tsai. An efficient and accurate camera calibration technique for 3d machine vision. In *Proceedings of the IEEE Conference on Computer Vision and Pattern Recognition*, pages 364–374, 1986.

Cooperative Agents for Object Recognition

Ulrich Büker
Heinz Nixdorf Institute
University of Paderborn
email: bueker@get.uni-paderborn.de

Abstract

In this paper an agent-based object recognition system is described. It is used to observe, recognize, and localize objects with multiple cameras. Each camera is controlled by an agent, performing a recognition process, while communicating hypotheses and results with the other agents. Thus, they form a group of cooperative and collaborating agents, making the recognition results more robust. In addition, they are designed to immediately react on incoming information to speed up the recognition process.

1. Cooperative Systems

In the field of artificial intelligence, much research has been done on agent based technologies during the past years. Up to now, there is no common definition on what exactly an agent is. However, there are some characteristics that an agent should show, like autonomy, intelligence, cooperation, and communication capability. According to their role, agents are classified as collaborative agents, interface agents, mobile agents, information agents, or reactive agents [10]. Thus, a setup of several computer vision systems, which are sharing information to jointly search for an object belongs to the class of *cooperative multi-agent systems*.

1.1. State of the Art

There are only a few systems known in the field of cooperative or agent based object recognition, which can be seen as a subfield of *distributed computer vision (DCV)*. Most work in DCV is done on low-level or intermediate-level processing, while research on distributed high-level recognition can hardly be found. Hempel and Büker propose a parallel object recognition system based on symbolic object models in form of semantic networks, which is implemented on standard SMP-architectures [7]. Oswald and Levi present a cooperative recognition system, which uses an appearance-based object representation and a non-parametric statistical classifier. A bayesian belief network is used to integrate the recognition results of two such recognition systems, which are viewing a scene from different viewpoints [9]. Yiming and Tsotsos describe a formulation of a multi-agent environment, in which each agent is supposed to be a mobile platform, equipped with an active camera. The task of the team is to find a target in its environment [11]. Therefore, the team members have to collaborate. However, Yiming and Tsotsos concentrate on learning and modifying various cooperation styles based on the search results.

In our paper, we want to concentrate on the aspect of recognizing objects with a set of distributed agents, each of them equipped with its own camera. Instead of only integrating the several recognition results, the agents are designed for an immediate information exchange. They are able to react on information received from another agent and thus, they can change their own recognition plan.

1.2. Structure of the Paper

The recognition process for each of the agents is based on a view-based object representation, as described in section 2. The design of the agents is presented in section 3.1, while their environment is explained in section 3.2. Communication among the agents is based on a blackboard architecture (sect. 3.3). A description of the reactive manner of the agents is given in section 3.4. Results are presented in section 4.

2. View-based Object Representation

2.1. Tolerant Contour Representations

In our system, we use a view-based object representation, which shows several similarities to the response activities of so-called *simple* and *complex cortical neurons* of the human visual system. Therefore, we derive two different contour maps from the response of a Gabor filter set [4].

We apply the Gabor filters to the grey-valued input image of size N to obtain *orientation columns* $g_n := (g_{n1},...g_{nR})$ at each image position n. An element g_{nr}, therefore, represents the value of the Gabor filter response at each pixel position $n \in \{1,... N\}$ with orientation $r \in \{1,... R\}$. Combining all response vectors at different positions results in a new vector $g := (g_1,... g_N)$. By changing the order of indexing, we can also obtain the alternative notation with $g'_r := (g_{1r},... g_{Nr})$ and $g' := (g'_1,... g'_R)$. A simple example of an image with an oriented edge after filtering is given in Fig. 1b, where g'_r shows optimal filter response at corresponding orientation r.

By skeletonizing and thresholding the filter responses as shown in Fig. 1c, we obtain our so-called *simple representation* k'_r which is insensitive against changes in lighting since its elements are binary valued. Further note that at each position n only one k_{nr} for all $r \in \{1,...,R\}$ may be set. Contrary to the spatially and orientationally confined activity of the *simple representation*, our *complex* or *tolerant representation* elements t_{nr} exhibit broader response activity patterns, as can be

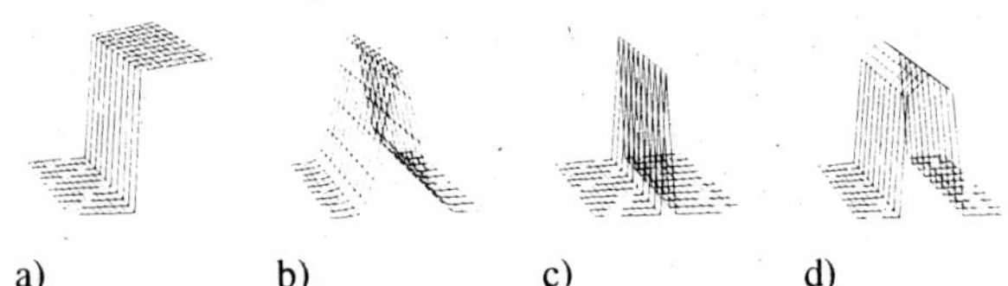

a) b) c) d)

Figure 1. a) oriented image edge, b) absolut value of gabor filter response g'_r, c) simple representation k'_r and d) tolerant representation t'_r (only corresponding orientations r are shown)

seen in Fig. 1d. An element t_{nr} therefore is still active even if the underlying edge is slightly displaced or rotated, although this minor correspondence results in lower activity to indicate suboptimal cover.

Both representations are utilized in our system for recognition by exploiting the aforementioned spatial and rotational tolerances. The prototype of an object of interest is captured in the simple representation, while the camera image, in which the prototype is to be detected, is transformed into the tolerant representation. Matching a prototype $\boldsymbol{k}'_r$ with a transformed camera image $\boldsymbol{t}'_r$ is done by evaluating their normalized scalar product:

$$\frac{\langle k, t\rangle}{\langle k, k\rangle} = \frac{\langle k_1, t_1\rangle + \ldots + \langle k_r, t_r\rangle + \ldots + \langle k_R, t_R\rangle}{\langle k_1, k_1\rangle + \ldots + \langle k_r, k_r\rangle + \ldots + \langle k_R, k_R\rangle} \quad (1)$$

Note that comparing a prototype with an image of the same object yields a maximum match of one, and that slightly displacing or rotating the object in front of the camera reduces the match by only a small amount due to the inherent tolerance in the complex representation. Furthermore, additional background clutter in the camera view does not reduce the match-value itself since the match is normalized by the prototype's constant number of contour-elements. Yet, the possibility of a mismatch due to high scene clutter is low because of the sparse coding property of our representations.

In order to make recognition invariant against changes in position, rotation and scaling, every valid combination of those parameters must be iteratively applied to either the prototype(s) or the transformed camera image during the matching process. A standard matching algorithm, which is very efficient on sparsely coded data with only a fraction of all image elements being non-zero, is the widely used General-Hough Transform [1]. The result is a 4-dimensional accumulator array, in which the highest entry above some threshold corresponds to the best matching position, orientation and scale of the prototype in the camera image. Other recognition-schemes without a tolerant representation encounter difficulties when trying to recognize real-world objects, since slight distortions or slight changes in viewpoint result in scattered accumulator entries ([1], [5], [8]). Our unique tolerant representation on the other hand already includes the averaging in the representational space, thus avoiding a clustering step in the accumulator space. Furthermore, at each position only the best matching orientation and scale parameters need to be stored. This means that our tolerant representation reduces the accumulator array dimension from 4 to 2 in the Hough transform.

2.2. Object Recognition in 6 DoF

In the last section, it was already mentioned that our representations $\boldsymbol{t}$ not only tolerate foveation and normalization errors but also minor perspective distortions. This is very convenient for the extension of our system to 3D applications by a view based approach. View based strategies assume that 3D objects are represented by a set of learned views, and that additional views from other directions may be recognized by interpolation between neighboring learned views. In our system the set of learned views is a set of tolerant representations $\boldsymbol{t}^l$ which are also reliably recognized from slightly different directions. So we need no special module for interpolation between neighboring views.

We only have to find a strategy how to cover the view sphere with a minimum number of learned views. Generally spoken, the relative position of the camera with respect to the object can be changed in six degrees of freedom. By foveation of the object we already remove two degrees of freedom and we can describe the situation by four variables $(r, \alpha, \vartheta, \varphi)$. We need not learn different views from different distances r due to distance invariance of our system. Finally, orientation invariance makes recognition independent of rotation α of the camera around its axis. We only have to learn views from different positions (ϑ, φ) on the sphere. The strategies how to find a minimum number of views covering the sphere is given in detail in [3]. Obviously, we need only one prototypical view for a ball, and typically the number is between 20 and 60.

The approach of learning prototypical sets of tolerant views has proved to be very powerful. Successful applications are described in [2].

3. Cooperative Agents

The general concept of using active agents for object recognition is based on the observation that robust recognition of complex 3D objects is often impossible when evaluating only a single 2D image of a scene. This is mainly due to three reasons:

- ❒ 3D objects may share some common aspects, thus they cannot be distinguished when seen from certain viewpoints;
- ❒ 3D objects may look very similar except of some small details on which recognition has to focus;
- ❒ some views of an object in an arbitrary scene may be disturbed i.e. by occlusions or bad illumination.

In these cases it is necessary for the recognition system to react on data already gathered from the environment and to be able to change the external parameters of the sensors as described by the paradigm of *active vision*.

3.1. Design of an Agent for Recognition

Instead of using one camera with a very flexible but complex behavioral scheme, we propose using a set of small agents, each of them equipped with its own camera (Fig. 2).

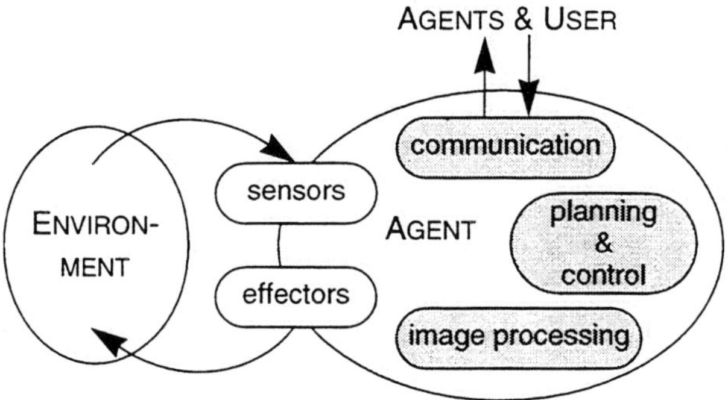

Figure 2. Design of an active recognition agent

Each agent is equipped with a set of operators for image processing and recognition. A planning module is used to control the recognition process and to react on incoming information.

3.2. Scenario

Figure 3 shows a setup of four agents detecting and observing an object in a scene. Each of the agents is able to recognize its view of the object. In addition the agents can estimate the position (x, y, z) and the orientation $(\alpha, \vartheta, \varphi)$ of the object in the scene. By communicating the recognition results, the agents can react on first hypotheses and can try to verify them, by concentrating on the estimated position in the scene.

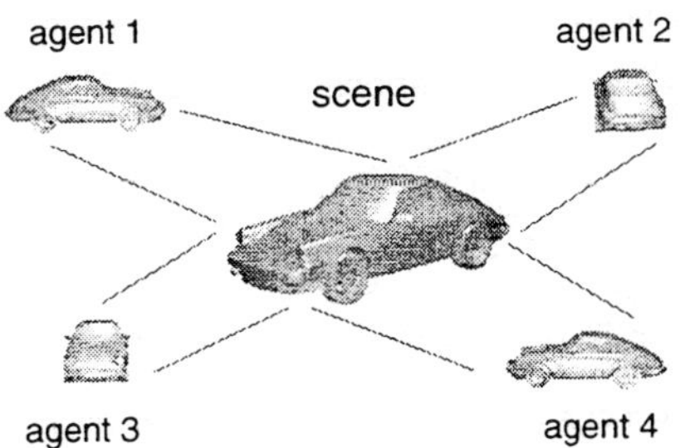

Figure 3. Four agents observing an object

Therefore, it is necessary that every agent is able to transform image coordinates to world coordinates and vice verse. In a first step, an agent transforms the image coordinates of a recognized object into the camera coordinate system, which has its origin in the image center. The x- and y-axis correspond to the image plane, while the z-axis is perpendicular to the plane and corresponds to the viewing direction.

The main point of this transformation is that the recognition process explicitly delivers a scaling factor s between learned prototype and presented image. Since it is well known for every prototype, from which distance r_l it has been learned, we get an estimated object distance $r_p = s\, r_l$. Using r_p and a pinhole model of the camera, we get the object coordinates $(x, y, z)_{camera}$. The coordinates of the object within a world coordinate system common to all the agents are calculated by the affine transformation

$$(x, y, z)^T{}_{world} = \boldsymbol{R}\,(x, y, z)^T{}_{camera} + \boldsymbol{T}. \qquad (2)$$

The orientation of the object within this coordinate system is then given by

$$(\alpha, \vartheta, \varphi)^T{}_{world} = (\alpha, \vartheta, \varphi)^T{}_{camera} + (\Delta\alpha, \Delta\vartheta, \Delta\varphi)^T \qquad (3)$$

where $(\Delta\alpha, \Delta\vartheta, \Delta\varphi)$ are the parameters which form the matrix $\boldsymbol{R}$.

Obviously, these transformations can be used to calculate the objects location within the coordinate systems of the other agents, when used in a reversed order. Thus, every agent is able to estimate the position of an once recognized object and it can estimate the viewing angles.

Although, position estimation during the recognition process is rather accurate, it is not exact. Thus, an agent which is trying to verify the recognition result of another agent, has to consider a region of interest, rather than a single image point. This region is defined by a tolerance vector.

3.3. Communication between Agents

In our system we propose a blackboard agent for communication among the agents. Thus, instead of using direct point-to-point communication among the vision agents, information is written to a blackboard that actively distributes the information to other agents (Fig. 4). This blackboard agent also groups the agents according to their special purposes.

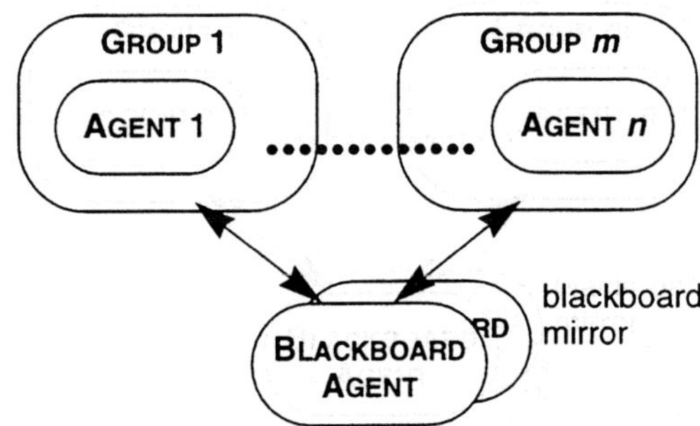

Figure 4. Communication among the agents via a blackboard agent

Hereby, it is easier to design a fault tolerant system, since only the blackboard agent has to notice, when one of the agents breaks down. In addition, new agents can dynamically join the system by notifying the blackboard agent. Of course, we rely on a stable central blackboard agent, when using such a system design. Thus, the blackboard agent is mirrored to enhance fault tolerance. However, we think, that the agents itself are more stable then the communication paths, especially in the case of a wireless lan as its medium. Fig. 5 shows a snapshot of a part of the *xpvm* user interface, visualizing communication between the different agents. It can be seen, that hypotheses are first send to the blackboard and are then distributed to the other agents.

3.4. Cooperation between Agents

Among the few existing agent-based vision systems, most of them do communication after image analysis is completed. In these cases, the recognition results of each agent are com-

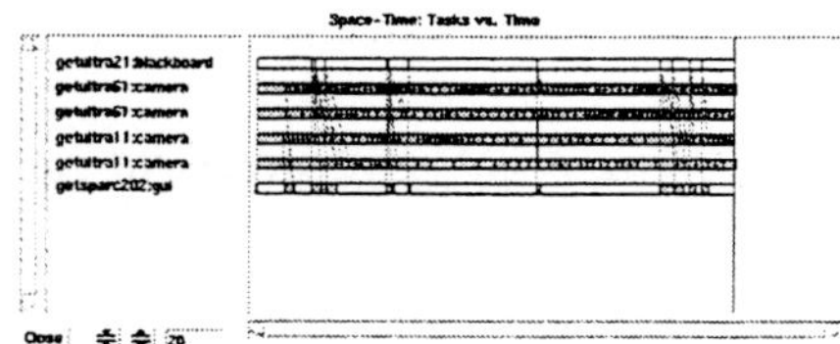

Figure 5. Communication between the agents

bined to get a more robust result. Belief networks are one of the tools used for this step. In our system, we do not only combine results, we directly interfere with the recognition process. This means that as soon as an agent recognizes an object, this result is sent to the blackboard. After storing it on the blackboard, it is distributed to those groups of agents, which are interested in this information.

Within an agent, the information is received by its communication module, which then interrupts the control module. Thus, the planning module can directly react on the recognition result of another agent and can focus its work on a certain region of interest, knowing which kind of object to be expected there.

Hence, an agent is working in different states:

- it is joining the distributed system;
- it is searching for objects in the scene;
- it is verifying a hypotheses, proposed by another agent.

The planning module uses a set of rules to switch between different states, due to internal and external information. The two main rules are:

1. IF state=searching AND hypothesis is given THEN state=verifiying
2. IF state=verifying AND no more hypotheses are given THEN state=searching

4. Results

The system is implemented in C++ using *PVM (parallel virtual machine)*. Experiments were made with a scenario of several objects placed on a table, which was observed by four cameras. These experiments showed that recognition was significantly improved and mainly two sources of errors were eliminated:

- misclassifications, due to ambiguous views of objects could be dissolved
- misclassifications, due to wrong distance estimations could be removed (Fig. 6).

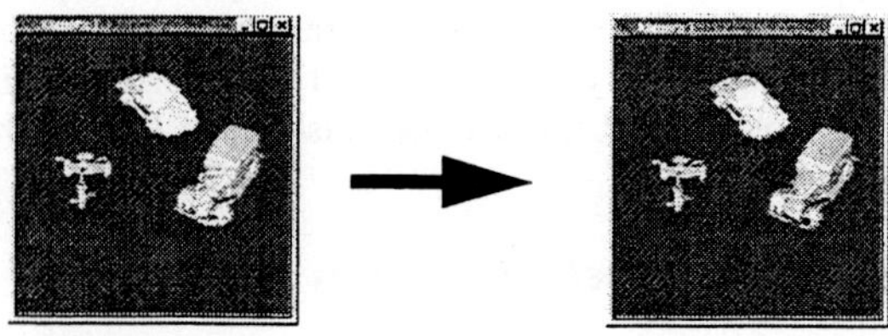

Figure 6. Rejection of a false hypothesis, verification of a correct one

The first kind of errors appeared when similar objects were used in the experiments, e.g. a sedan and a station wagon of the same brand could not be distinguished when viewed from the front. The second kind of errors appeared, when for example highlights on the object surface were classified as separate objects in a large distance. In this case, the other agents could not verify the classification result at the estimated position. Thus, they correctly rejected the hypotheses.

5. References

[1] Ballard, D.H.: „Generalizing the Hough transform to detect arbitrary shapes.“ Pattern Recognition, vol. 13, no. 2, 1981, pp. 111-122.

[2] Büker, U.; Götze, N.; Hartmann, G.; Kalkreuter, R. Stemmer, R.; Trapp, R.: An Active Object Recognition System for Disassembly Task. In: Proceedings of the 7th IEEE International Conference on Emerging Technologies and Factory Automation. ETFA ‘99, Piscataway (IEEE), 1999, pp. 79 - 88.

[3] Dunker, J.; Hartmann, G.; Stöhr, M: Single view recognition and pose estimation of 3D-objects using sets of prototypical views and spatially tolerant contour representations. In: Proceedings of 13th Conference on Pattern Recognition (ICPR'96 Wien). Los Alamitos (IEEE Computer Society Press) 1996, Vol. IV, pp. 14-18.

[4] Gabor, D.: Theory of communication. J. IEE, Vol. 93, 1946, pp. 429-457

[5] Grimson, W.E.L., Huttenlocher, D.P.: „On the sensitivity of the Hough transform for object recognition“. IEEE Transactions on Pattern Analysis and Machine Intelligence, vol. 12, no. 3, 1990, pp. 255-274.

[6] Hartmann, G.; Büker, U.; Drüe, S.: A Hybrid Neuro-AI-Architecture. In: Jähne, B. et al. (Eds.): Handbook on Computer Vision and Applications, vol. 3, San Diego, CA. (Academic Press), 1999, pp. 153-196.

[7] Hempel, O.; Büker, U.: A Parallel Control Algorithm for Hybrid Image Recognition. In: Yi Pan; Selim G. Akl; Keqin Li: Parallel and Distributed Computing and Systems. Proceedings of the 10th IASTED International Conference. Anaheim (IASTED/ACTA Press) 1998, pp. 206 - 209.

[8] Olson, C.F., Huttenlocher, D.P.: „Automatic Target Recognition by Matching Oriented Edge Pixels.“ IEEE Transactions on Image Processing, vol. 6, no. 1, 1997, pp. 103-113.

[9] Oswald, N.; Levi, P.: Cooperative vision in a multi-agent architecture. In: Del Bimbo, A. (Ed.): 9th Int. Conf. on Image Analysis and Processing. ICIAP'97, vol. 1, Berlin (Springer), pp.709-716.

[10] Müller, J.; Wooldridge, M.; Jennings, N.: Intelligent Agents III - Agent Theories, Architectures, and Languages, Proceedings of the ECAI/ATAL, Budapest, 1996.

[11] Yiming, Ye; Tsotsos, J.K.: On the collaborative object search team: a formulation. In: Weiss, G. (Ed.): Distributed Artificial Intelligence Meets Machine Learning. Berlin (Springer), pp. 94-116.

Real-Time Obstacle Avoidance Using an MPEG-Processor-based Optic Flow Sensor

Norbert O. Stöffler, Tim Burkert, and Georg Färber
Institute for Real-Time Computer Systems
Technische Universität München
D-80333 München, Germany
stoffler@rcs.ei.tum.de, www.rcs.ei.tum.de/~stoffler/

Abstract

This paper describes a vision system for obstacle detection in mobile robot navigation. The system uses an image processing board equipped with an MPEG motion estimation processor that calculates a robust optic-flow-like vector field in real-time. This field is then evaluated by algorithms running in software on the host PC. As the solutions to the general problem of structure and motion from optic flow are too instable for the use in this application, the typical constraints of mobile robotics are exploited, i.e. a reduced set of motion parameters and a known ground plane. Ego-motion can then be reconstructed with robust one dimensional methods. A new criterion for obstacles that copes well with the noise properties of the motion field is introduced. For vectors belonging to obstacles the 3D information is reconstructed allowing not only qualitative detection of obstacles but quantitative path planning.

1. Introduction

The work presented in this paper is part of a research project toward the development of autonomous, vision guided, mobile robots. Such robots must robustly sense and avoid obstacles while driving through unknown environments. One possible approach that is not impaired by, but even exploits the movement of the camera is to use the *optic flow*. 3D motion of the camera is projected onto this 2D velocity field (or displacement field in the case of isochronous sampling using standard video cameras) on the image plane (x, y) (see Fig. 1).

If the displacement vectors are regarded to be equivalent to the velocity vectors (an acceptable assumption for realistic frame rates and velocities [1]) and the focal length of the camera is normalized to 1 (a mathematical convenience that does not restrict generality), the optic flow can be expressed

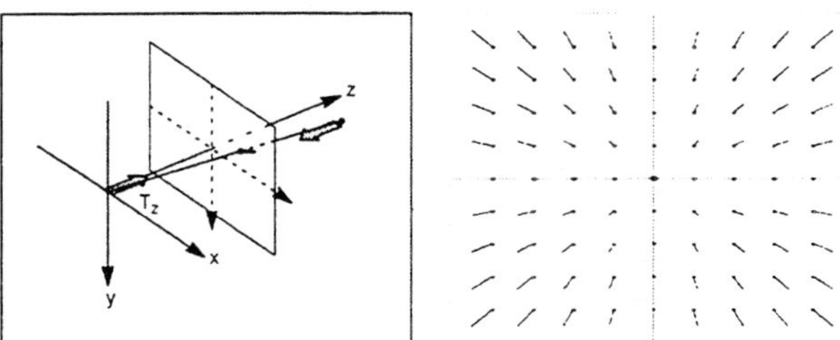

Figure 1. Coordinate system and optic flow

by the following well known equation:

$$\begin{bmatrix}\Delta x\\ \Delta y\end{bmatrix} = \frac{1}{Z}\begin{bmatrix}T_z x - T_x\\ T_z y - T_y\end{bmatrix} + \omega_x \begin{bmatrix}xy\\ y^2+1\end{bmatrix} - \omega_y \begin{bmatrix}x^2+1\\ xy\end{bmatrix} - \omega_z \begin{bmatrix}-y\\ x\end{bmatrix} \quad (1)$$

Before reconstructing the 3D parameters, this 2D vector field has to be estimated from the variation of brightness patterns in an image sequence I_t. The classical solutions to this problem include the evaluation of spatio-temporal derivatives, the tracking of single feature points and the correlation of small patches. The real-time optic flow calculation technique presented in section 2 is inspired by the similarity of those correlation techniques to the block-wise MPEG-1/2 motion compensation.

Many papers in the optic flow literature address the problem of the reconstruction of motion and depth parameters by solving Eqn. (1) for a set of vectors, some even perform segmentation of independently moving objects [1, 9, 10, 16]. Unfortunately, those complete solutions are computationally expensive and numerically instable. Graphically, this instability results from the similarity of optic flow fields generated by rotation and lateral translation [15]. The difference between those two field contributions is often hardly the magnitude of noise.

Common approaches used by robotic researchers [3, 4, 5, 12] include the assumption of constraints to the motion parameters, for example to mere translation. Also qualitative detection without 3D reconstruction is proposed, avoiding the need of exact knowledge of the ego-motion.

The method for obstacle detection presented in section 3 exploits the constraints of the mobile robot application too, but works in presence of rotation, estimates the ego-motion, and recovers the 3D information of objects. It uses robust methods to cope with quantization noise and faulty vectors which are occasionally produced during the optic flow calculation.

Section 4 explains some important implementation details and section 5 shows the results of the obstacle detection and exemplary navigation.

2. Real-time optic flow sensor

According to the MPEG-1/2 standards, reduction of the temporal redundancy in an image sequence I_t is achieved by replacing pixel information by reference vectors to other images. For real-time encoding, specialized processors, so called *MEPs* (*Motion Estimation Processors*) have been developed, which calculate these reference vectors by block-matching. A reference block (*RB*, 16×16 pel) from image I_{rb} is compared with a search window (*SW*, 32×32 pel) in the image I_{sw}. For all possible offsets $\mu, \nu \in \{-8 \ldots 7\}$, a correlation-like value called *SAD* (*Sum of Absolute Differences*) is calculated; the minimum designates the best match, and its position defines the reference vector:

$$\begin{aligned} SAD(\mu,\nu) &= \textstyle\sum_{\kappa=-8}^{7} \sum_{\iota=-8}^{7} |SW(\mu+\iota, \nu+\kappa) - RB(\iota,\kappa)| \\ SAD(\Delta x_{pel}, \Delta y_{pel}) &= \min_{\mu,\nu \in \{-8\ldots7\}} SAD(\mu,\nu) \end{aligned} \quad (2)$$

If consecutive images are compared (i.e. $sw - rb = 1$), the resulting set of vectors

$$\mathcal{F} = \{\boldsymbol{f}_i : \boldsymbol{f} = \begin{bmatrix} \Delta x \\ \Delta y \end{bmatrix}, i \in \{1 \ldots n\}\}$$

can be regarded as optic flow.

The idea to use one of those extremely optimized MEPs for the generation of optic flow is not new. In particular Inoue et al. describe the integration of a MEP into their image processing transputer network [8]. Resulting from their work, a commercial version is available, and meanwhile is used in various research projects [2, 7].

A problem that several researchers report is that the optic flow generated by such a correlation processor can become very noisy. This happens when the image structure inside the *RB*s or *SW*s is ambiguous or completely missing. Then the detection of a significant minimum according to Eqn. (2) fails and faulty vectors are calculated. Fig. 2a illustrates the problem. The flow was generated by a linear forward movement of the camera, so all vectors should intersect in a single point, the *FOE* (*Focus Of Expansion*). Due to local lack of structure, many vectors point to completely different directions. Unfortunately, this effect dominates in most indoor environments. Further evaluation of such a flow field is virtually impossible.

Figure 2. Optic flow, generated by a MEP: a) complete, b) sifted.

To solve this problem, we augmented the MEP with external circuitry that calculates an additional confidence value for each vector. In the simplest case, this confidence value can be tested against a fixed threshold to sift out the faulty flow vectors Fig. 2b.

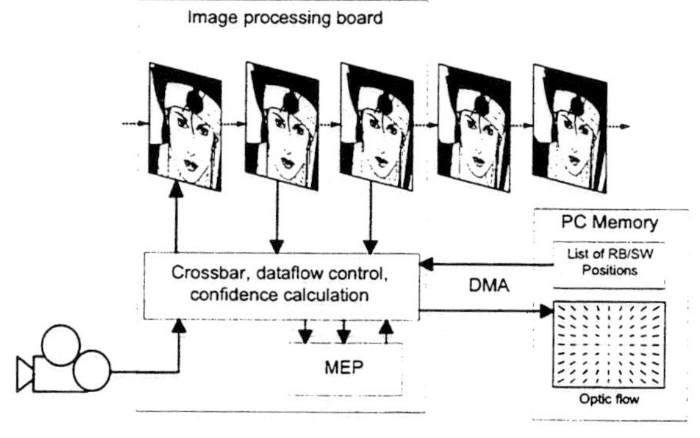

Figure 3. System structure

Our prototype system consists of an ISA image processing board containing the MEP, and a LINUX host PC (see Fig. 3). A ring-buffer of three frame memories allows the comparison of two images and simultaneous acquisition of the next image into the third memory. Depending on the utilization of the MEP internal pipeline, up to 525 vectors can be calculated per frame (PAL, 25 Hz). To achieve the highest possible flexibility, the coordinates of *RBs* and *SWs* can be randomly set by the software running on the PC for each single matching operation. This feature is exploited by the implementation described in section 4. For a more detailed description of the hardware see [13].

3. Reconstruction of motion parameters and depth

The approach pursued in this work is to simplify the problem by allowing only two degrees of freedom for the camera motion. In this case Eqn. (1) can be solved for each vector individually, and robust one dimensional techniques can be used for the determination of the ego-motion. This simplification is possible in several applications, for example fixed pan-tilt surveillance cameras. When the camera is mounted on a mobile robot with non-holonomic kinematics the motion can also be decomposed into a translation T along the trajectory of the vehicle and a rotation ω around the vertical axis. To keep the formulas simple, it is also assumed that the camera is mounted with its x-axis horizontally and the y-z-plane in parallel to the heading of the vehicle. Describing the pitch-angle ρ of the camera by the two trigonometric shorthands $\alpha = cos(\rho)$ and $\beta = sin(\rho)$ Eqn. (1) is reduced to

$$\boldsymbol{f} = \frac{T}{Z}\boldsymbol{e} + \omega\boldsymbol{h} \tag{3}$$

with $\boldsymbol{e}$ representing the "expansive" part of the field contributed by translation and $\boldsymbol{h}$ representing the hyperbolic part contributed by rotation:

$$\boldsymbol{e} = \begin{bmatrix} \alpha x \\ \alpha y + \beta \end{bmatrix}, \boldsymbol{h} = \begin{bmatrix} \alpha(x^2+1) - \beta y \\ \alpha x y + \beta x \end{bmatrix}$$

This equation can be solved for each vector:

$$\omega = \frac{\alpha x \Delta y - (\alpha y + \beta)\Delta x}{\alpha\beta y^2 - \alpha^2 y + \beta^2 y - \alpha\beta} \tag{4}$$

$$\frac{T}{Z} = \frac{\Delta x - \omega(\alpha(x^2+1) - \beta y)}{\alpha x} \tag{5}$$

The first result ω should correspond to the rotational velocity of the vehicle and therefore be identical for each vector. Thus, the rotation could be estimated by a simple least square fit over all ω_i as proposed e.g. in [4]. As even the sifted flow field sometimes contains faulty vectors (for example due to cyclic patterns in the images), this can yield poor results in practice. Better performance is achieved by using robust mode estimators with high breakdown points. The *shortest half window* mode estimator (*shorth*, [11]) can tolerate up to 50 % outliers and performs very well in the experiments. Also it is computationally inexpensive:

$$\begin{aligned} \xi_j &: \xi_j \leq \xi_{j+1}, j \in \{1 \dots n-1\} \\ \delta_j &= (\xi_{j+\lfloor \frac{n}{2} \rfloor} - \xi_j) \\ \delta_m &= \min_{j \in \{1 \dots n - \lfloor \frac{n}{2} \rfloor\}} \delta_j \\ \text{shorth}(\xi_j) &= \frac{1}{2}(\xi_m + \xi_{m+\lfloor \frac{n}{2} \rfloor}) \quad (6) \\ \hat{\omega} &= \text{shorth}(\omega_i) \quad (7) \end{aligned}$$

A foreground/background separation technique that can be used to get an estimate for ω even in the presence of large moving objects (larger than 50% of the field) has already been published in [14].

The second solution to Eqn. (3), $\frac{T}{Z}$, still depends on the depth of the corresponding 3D point and thus has an individual value for each vector (it is the reciprocal value of the so called *Time To Collision, TTC*). To get also an estimate for the translation T, additional assumptions have to be made. In the case of a camera mounted on a mobile robot, beside the pitch angle also the height h of the camera above the ground plane is known. If the robot moves on an infinite ground plane without any obstacles, the Z coordinate can be calculated for each point in the image plane:

$$Z = \frac{h}{\alpha y + \beta} \tag{8}$$

Of course this postulate cannot be made for a system which is intended to detect obstacles. But as a vehicle always has a minimum braking distance, it is reasonable to assume the absence of obstacles in the area directly in front of the robot. This area is called *ground window* in the following and the set of vectors inside this window is $\mathcal{G}$.

By inserting Eqn. (8) into Eqn. (5) one could get a value T for each vector. But, using this method, the influence of the pixel quantization would vary over the image plane. Also remaining faulty vectors pollute the estimation. Therefore, we propose a different technique: First, the optic flow field is derotated using $\hat{\omega}$:

$$\boldsymbol{d} = \boldsymbol{f} - \hat{\omega}\boldsymbol{h} \tag{9}$$

Each derotated vector $\boldsymbol{d}$ should then coincide with an epipolar line through the *FOE* and thus be collinear with $\boldsymbol{e}$. In practice it deviates a little from this epipolar line due to the quantization error, or completely in case of a faulty vector. The first category of errors should be corrected as good as possible, the second category should be detected and eliminated from $\mathcal{F}$. For the first purpose, the projection of each vector $\boldsymbol{d}$ on its epipolar line is used for the calculation of $\frac{T}{Z}$:

$$\frac{T}{Z} = \frac{\boldsymbol{e}^{\top}\boldsymbol{d}}{||\boldsymbol{e}||^2} \tag{10}$$

For the detection and elimination of faulty vectors the distance of the vector from the epipolar line can be calculated and thresholded:

$$\mathcal{F}^* = \{\boldsymbol{f}_i : |\frac{\boldsymbol{e}^{\top}\begin{bmatrix} 0 & 1 \\ -1 & 0 \end{bmatrix}\boldsymbol{d}}{||\boldsymbol{e}||}| < \lambda \wedge \frac{T}{Z} > 0\} \tag{11}$$

Then $\hat{T}$ is determined using the *shorth* estimator again, which allows up to 50% obstacles even inside the ground window:

$$\hat{T} = \text{shorth}(\frac{e_i^\top d_i}{||e_i||^2} Z_i), d_i \in \mathcal{G} \cap \mathcal{F}^* \quad (12)$$

Now Z could be calculated for each vector and the distance from the ground plane could be used to detect obstacles. Another criterion would be the ratio between the vector length and the length of a predicted ground vector, as proposed in [5]. Both approaches have the drawback, that the impact of pixel quantization is stronger for short vectors. Again, a better criterion for obstacles is

$$\mathcal{O} = \{f_i : \frac{e_i{}^\top d_i}{||e_i||} - \frac{\hat{T}}{Z_i}||e_i|| > \tau\} \quad (13)$$

Both criteria according to Eqn. (11) and Eqn. (13) calculate *distances in image coordinates*, which can be compared to fixed thresholds λ and τ in the magnitude of the pixel quantization.

To get rid of single bogus detections which have passed sifting and elimination, we also apply a simple morphological operation to $\mathcal{O}$. For the remaining vectors $f \in \mathcal{O}$ finally the Z-coordinate is calculated to get a 3D obstacle point.

4. Implementation

As a standard video camera is used, only fields (not frames) can be evaluated due to the interlacing problem. Additional considerations have to be made when implementing an algorithm according to section 3 using the optic flow sensor presented in section 2.

4.1. Placement

Placing the *RB*s along a regular grid in the image plane would result in detailed surveillance of the area close in front, but only few information in the distance. Besides, the calculation of $\frac{T}{Z}$ according to Eqn. (10) becomes instable for small values of $||e||$. Thus, *RB*s should not be placed inside an area below a threshold for $||e||$, which results in a practically blind spot in the upper middle of the image plane (that graphically can be considered the intersection of a cone around the *FOE* with the image plane). Fig. 4 shows the chosen optimized placement of the vectors and the position of the ground window. Unfortunately this non-regular placement of the *RB*s prevents the optimal use of the MEPs internal pipeline, reducing the number of possible vector calculations to 350 (and even a little less in practice due to the latencies of the LINUX operating system). Also morphological operations become more complicated but can be accelerated by a precalculated lookup table containing neighborhood information.

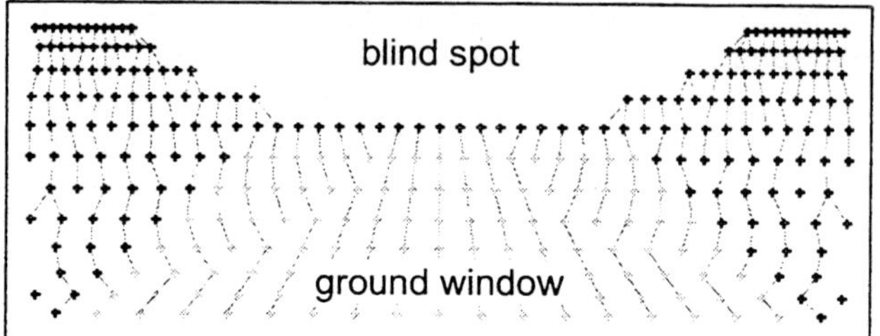

Figure 4. Optimized placement of the vectors

4.2. Biasing

As the vector length generated by realistic motion of the robot significantly exceeds the maximal vector length that can be calculated by the MEP, the positions of the *SW*s have to be biased against the positions of the *RB*s. This is achieved by using the current motion estimates $(\hat{\omega}, \hat{T})$ to predict the field for the next operation cycle using Eqn. (3). Each *SW* is then centered around the center of the corresponding *RB* plus a bias vector $b = f(\hat{\omega}, \hat{T})$ (see Fig. 5). This biasing technique transforms the limitations on the velocities to limitations on the accelerations.

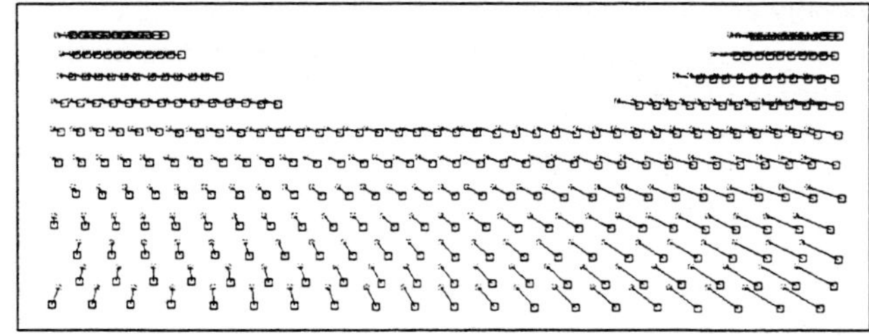

Figure 5. Search window bias

4.3. Rate control

Another problem is, that at realistic velocities the translational component $\frac{T}{Z}e$ of most of the vectors is too short to significantly exceed the pixel quantization error. Unfortunately it is not possible to just skip $(r-1)$ images in order to reduce the frame rate to $\frac{1}{r}$, which would increase the vector length. The reason is, that the field is dominated by the rotational component ωh, which has to be estimated at maximal rate.

Our solution is to vary the length l of the hardware ringbuffer (Fig. 3): I_{rb} is repeatedly "frozen" and compared to the next r images according to Fig. 6. Using this method, no image is lost and it is possible to estimate $\hat{\omega}$ with every frame, but determine $\hat{T}$ and obstacles at a randomly chosen lower rate.

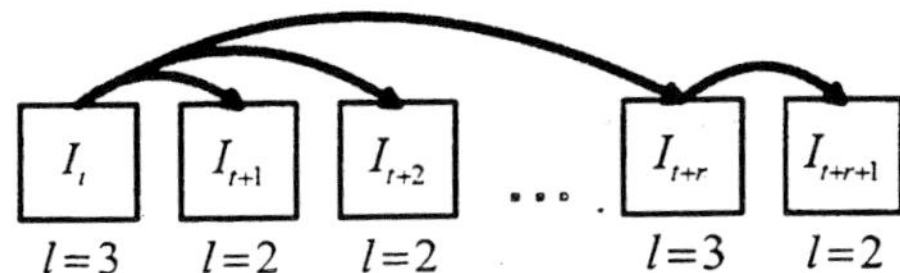

Figure 6. Rate control

5. Obstacle avoidance

Fig. 7 shows some snapshots from the experiments. Vectors corresponding to the detected obstacle points are marked with black squares, the image in the middle shows a rotation $\omega \approx 30°/\mathrm{s}$.

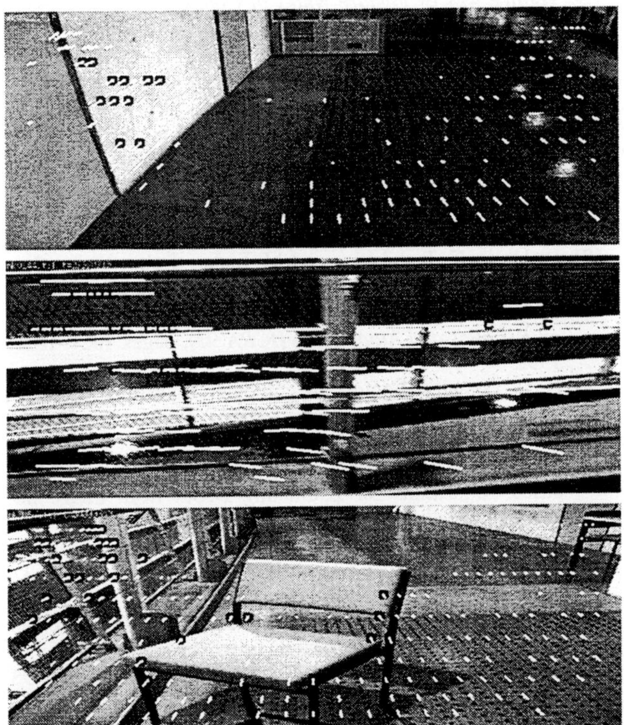

Figure 7. Obstacle detection examples

To generate a local 2D obstacle map for robot navigation, the 3D points are transformed into the robot coordinate system. Fig. 8 corresponds to the bottom image of Fig. 7; obstacle points belonging to the chair and the railing can be seen. The magnitude of the accuracy of 3D reconstruction is 10 cm, which is by far sufficient for obstacle avoidance.

Also a short history of obstacle sets is fused to increase accuracy and robustness. This is achieved by transforming older sets of obstacle points into the current robot coordinate system. The parameters $\Delta x_{robot}, \Delta y_{robot}, \Delta\varphi_{robot}$ for this transformation are calculated from the optic flow by integrating the estimated motion parameters $\hat{\omega}, \hat{T}$. Obstacles

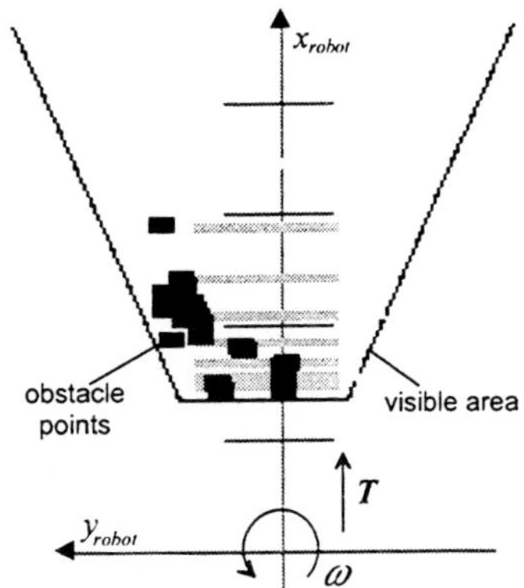

Figure 8. Obstacle map in 2D robot coordinates

are then fused by increasing probabilities in an occupancy grid.

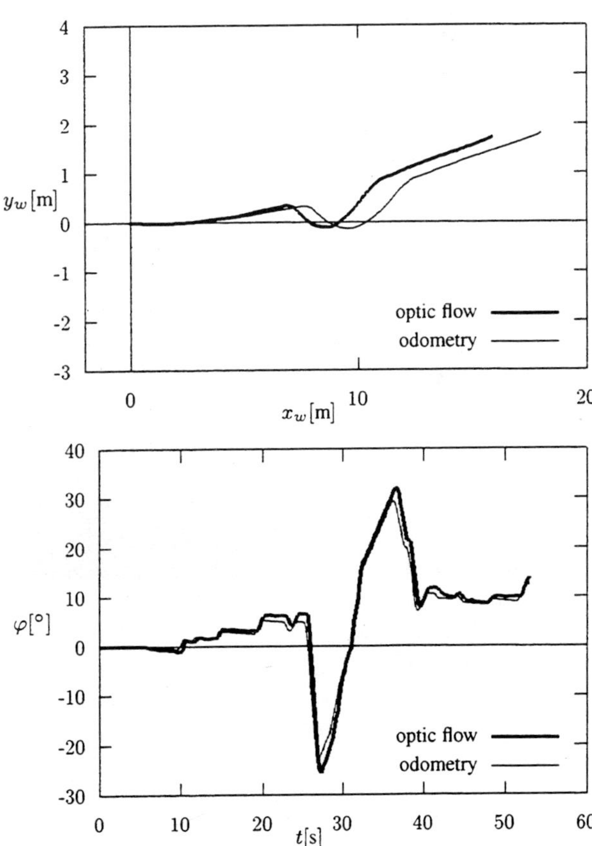

Figure 9. Trajectory and heading of the robot

Robot control is currently performed by a very simple navigation algorithm inspired by the dynamic window approach [6], which periodically (typically every 200 ms) chooses the best trajectory in terms of distance to obstacles and closeness to the next way point. For fast evaluation the set of possible trajectories (circular lanes of the robots width) is precalculated for each possible turn radius $R = \frac{T}{\omega}$ and the set of corresponding map elements is stored in lookup tables. Fig. 9 depicts the result of the navigation experiment, from which the bottom snapshot of Fig. 7 was taken. The "way point" was fixed at $x_{robot} = 5\,\text{m}$ and $y_{robot} = 2\,\text{m}$, providing an "unreachable goal" on the left side. Together with the obstacles in the occupancy grid this results in the behavior to follow a wall on the left.

At the beginning of this experiment, the robot followed the bow of the railing. After approximately 7 m it detected the chair, rounded it, and then returned to the railing again. The figures show the absolute position of the robot in the world coordinate system as well as the heading φ over time. Both plots compare values calculated by the odometry with values calculated by integrating the motion parameters from optic flow. The drift is small enough to use the optic flow values for local calculations like the history fusion.

6. Conclusion

We have presented a real-time vision system consisting of a MEP-based optic flow sensor and a set of robust evaluation techniques to do obstacle detection for a mobile robot. The robot MARVIN (Mobile Autonomous Robot with Vision-based Navigation, see Fig. 10) currently uses the system for navigating through the corridors of our laboratory at speeds of $T = 0.4\,\text{m/s}$ and $\omega_{max} = 30°/\text{s}$. The typical pitch-angle of 25° delivers obstacles from a minimal distance of 1.5 m to a maximal distance of 3.5 m in the central area and 8 m in the peripheral areas.

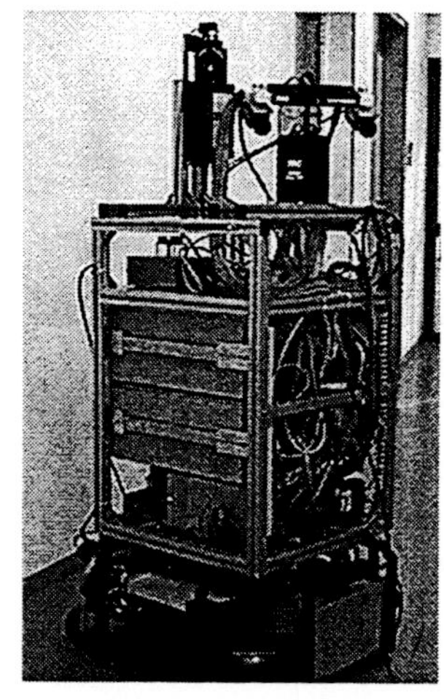

Figure 10. MARVIN

In similar robotic systems, only qualitative scene descriptions are derived from optic flow, which allow only qualitative navigation approaches [2, 3, 4, 12]. Since the result of our obstacle detection approach is a local occupancy grid, standard robot navigation techniques can be implemented.

References

[1] G. Adiv. Determining Three-Dimensional Motion and Structure from Optical Flow Generated by Several Moving Objects. *IEEE Trans. on Pattern Analysis and Machine Intelligence*, 7(4):319–336, July 1985.

[2] G. Cheng and A. Zelinsky. Real-Time Visual Behaviours for Navigating a Mobile Robot. In *Proc. IEEE/RSJ Int. Conf. on Intelligent Robots and Systems (IROS'96)*, pages 973–980, Osaka, J, Nov. 1996.

[3] D. Coombs, M. Herman, T. Hong, and M. Nashman. Real-time obstacle avoidance using central flow divergence and peripheral flow. In *Proc. 5th Int. Conf. on Computer Vision*, pages 276–283, Cambridge, MA, USA, June 1995.

[4] A. Dev, B. J. A. Kröse, and F. C. A. Groen. Navigation of a mobile robot on the temporal development of the optic flow. In *Proc. IEEE/RSJ Int. Conf. on Intelligent Robots and Systems (IROS'97)*, pages 558–563, 1997.

[5] W. Enkelmann. Obstacle detection by evaluation of optical flow fields from image sequences. In O. Faugeras, editor, *Proc. 1st European Conf. on Computer Vision (ECCV'90)*, volume 427 of *Lecture Notes in Computer Science*, pages 134–138, Antibes, F, Apr. 1990. Springer-Verlag.

[6] D. Fox, W. Burgard, and S. Thrun. The Dynamic Window Approach to Collision Avoidance. *IEEE Trans. on Robotics and Automation*, 4(1), Mar. 1997.

[7] M. Inaba, K. Nagasaka, F. Kanehiro, S. Kagami, and H. Inoue. Real-Time Vision-Based Control of Swing Motion by Human-form Robot using the Remote-Brained Approach. In *Proc. IEEE/RSJ Int. Conf. on Intelligent Robots and Systems (IROS'96)*, pages 15–22, Osaka, J, Nov. 1996.

[8] H. Inoue, T. Tachikawa, and M. Inaba. Robot Vision System with a Correlation Chip for Real-time Tracking, Optical Flow and Depth Map Generation. In *Proc. IEEE Int. Conf. on Robotics and Automation (ICRA'92)*, pages 1621–1626, 1992.

[9] H. C. Longuet-Higgins. A computer algorithm for reconstructing a scene from two projections. *Nature*, 293(5):133–135, 1981.

[10] L. Matthies, R. Szeliski, and T. Kanade. Kalman Filter-based Algorithms for Estimating Depth from Image Sequences. *Int. J. Computer Vision*, 3(3):209–236, 1989.

[11] P. Meer. Robust Techniques for Computer Vision. Tutorial at the 14th Int. Conf. on Pattern Recognition, Brisbane, QLD, AU, Aug. 1998.

[12] J. Santos-Victor and G. Sandini. Visual-Based Obstacle Detection: A purposive approach using the normal flow. In U. R. et al., editor, *Intelligent Autonomous Systems*. IOS Press, 1995.

[13] N. O. Stöffler and G. Färber. An Image Processing Board with an MPEG Processor and Additional Confidence Calculation for Fast and Robust Optic Flow Generation in Real Environments. In *Proc. Int. Conf. on Advanced Robotics (ICAR'97)*, pages 845–850, Monterey, California, USA, July 1997.

[14] N. O. Stöffler and Z. Schnepf. An MPEG-Processor-based Robot Vision System for Real-Time Detection of Moving Objects by a Moving Observer. In *Proc. 14th Int. Conf. on Pattern Recognition*, pages 477–481, Brisbane, Australia, Aug. 1998.

[15] J. Weng, N. Ahuja, and T. S. Huang. Optimal Motion and Structure Estimation. *IEEE Trans. on Pattern Analysis and Machine Intelligence*, 15(9):864–884, Sept. 1993.

[16] J. Weng, T. S. Huang, and N. Ahudja. Motion and Structure from Two Perspective Views: Algorithms, Error Analysis, and Error Estimation. *IEEE Trans. on Pattern Analysis and Machine Intelligence*, 11(5):451–476, May 1989.

Tools and Techniques for Video Performance Evaluation

David Doermann and David Mihalcik
Laboratory for Language and Media Processing
University of Maryland, College Park, Maryland 20742

Abstract

In this work we outline a reconfigurable VIdeo Performance Evaluation Resource (ViPER), which provides an interface for ground truth generation, metrics for evaluation and tools for visualization of video analysis results. A key component is that the approach provides the basic infrastructure, and allows users to configure data generation and evaluation. Although ViPER can be used for any type of data, we focus on applications which require video content.

1 Introduction

An important requirement of any system that tries to automate content based analysis is a method to evaluate performance. Such evaluation is often carried out by comparing *Results* obtained from a given algorithm against *Ground Truth* — a set of results determined a priori to be correct. In video, the combination of spatial and temporal dimensions makes applying traditional evaluation methodologies difficult since we need to localize in both time and space. Although much work has been in computer vision evaluation, the evaluation work in video has focused primarily on evaluation of specific tasks such as motion estimation, or on segmentation [1, 2, 3], rather then on more general tasks of object detection, localization and classification.

The first goal of ViPER is the creation of a flexible ground truth format which facilitates the representation of both static and dynamic descriptors of the video. ViPER provides a segment-based view of the video, where attributes of descriptors are recorded for arbitrary sets of consecutive frames. The instances of descriptors and attributes are identified by the user developing the ground truth, and groups which develop ground truth for a specific class of problems are encouraged to develop guidelines for representation.

The second goal is to provide tools to easily create and share ground truth data. The process of creating ground truth can be tedious, especially in the video domain, since it can involve substantially similar content from frame to frame and require repeatedly scanning sequences of frames. We have developed a GUI that can be used to record the requisite information in a single scan of the video content. The system operates using the configuration files and data formats described below, with the configuration file being the only information that is provided a priori.

Finally, the third goal is to provide metrics which can be used to evaluate both the temporal and spatial aspects of video. We provide a core set of metrics for each of the datatypes currently implemented, as well as detection and precision and recall computation.

2 Representation and Interface

In ViPER, the ground truth (and subsequent results) are stored in files as sets of *descriptor* records. Each descriptor annotates an associated range of frames by instantiating a set of attributes for that range. So that applications can interpret the descriptors and render attributes appropriately, users provide a *configuration* which serves as a comprehensive baseline of what can appear in each record. For each valid descriptor type, there is a single *configuration record* in the GT formatted as follows:

```
descriptor-type descriptor-name
     attribute1 : attribute-type [default value]
     attribute2 : attribute-type [default value]
     ...
     attributeN : attribute-type [default value]
```

where the descriptor-type is either CONTENT (general properties about a range of frames) or OBJECT (instances components in the scene). Current attribute-types are shown in Table 1.

Each instance of a record is then formatted as:

```
descriptor-type descriptor-name id sframe:eframe
     attribute1 : attribute-value
     attribute2 : attribute-value
     ...
     attributeN : attribute-value
```

The ViPER interface is shown in Figure 1. Individual frames are controlled with the use of step-increment and

Table 1. ViPER Attribute Types

TYPE	DESC/REP	MEASURE	RNG
bvalue	boolean	bool equal	[0,1]
dvalue	integer	abs diff	[0-∞]
fvalue	float	abs diff	[0-∞]
svalue	string	Levenstein	[0-∞]
		equality	[0,1]
point	(x, y)	Eucl dist	[0-∞]
circle	(x, y, r)	OC/DC/ED	[0,1]
bbox	(ulx, uly, h, w)	OC/DC/ED	[0,1]
obox	(ulx, uly, h, w, o)	OC/DC/ED	[0,1]
lvalue	enumerated list	set equality	[0,1]
relation	obj IDs		

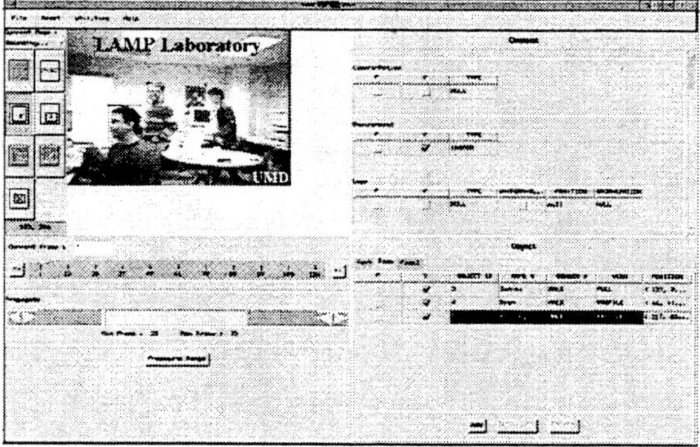

Figure 1. Layout of the ViPER-GT GUI.

step-decrement arrows, a slider or by entering a frame number directly. When the video is moved to a given frame, changes in the objects and their attributes are reflected in tables linked back to the frame. For a given frame, users can select a cell representing a spatial attribute (point, bbox, obox or circle) in the content or object panels and a drawing panel is provided to view individual frames and to edit spatial attributes. Lists are entered via pull-downs, booleans via toggles and other attributes can be manually entered for each object as text. Each object instance can also be propagated attribute across multiple frames which is especially helpful for spatial attributes that do not change much across frames.

3 Evaluation

The problem of performance evaluation of video is a difficult and often subjective task. Since we are not necessarily dealing with a strict classification problem, we need to consider whether two descriptions are "close enough" to satisfy a particular set of constraints. This may include, for example, constraints on the temporal range over which the description is valid, on the spatial location of objects detected in scene or on other properties of the scene or objects extracted by the system. In continuing with our record-based philosophy, we provide a mechanism through which we can match *candidate* records from the results with *target* records from the ground truth.

Target: An object or content record delineated temporally in the Ground Truth along with a set of attributes (possibly spatial).

Candidate: An object or content record delineated temporally in the Results along with a set of attributes (possibly spatial).

Our evaluation is based on a hierarchy of matching in both time and space and is split into two interdependent concepts: detection and localization. Ultimately, constraints on the localization will form a basis for "correct" detection. We will first consider detection based on the range of frames over which a pair of records is valid, then use localization constraints on both the temporal range and on attributes to judge the correctness of detection.

3.1 Detection

> ... a decision as to whether a particular object or content descriptor is adequately identified, either temporally, spatially or both.

A target record is said to be *minimally detected* if there exists at least one matching record in the candidate set. At the lowest level, we can ignore any localization constraints and say that a candidate minimally *matches* a target if the temporal range of the candidate and the temporal range of the target correspond on at least one frame. Localization constraints, both temporal and spatial, can then be used to constrain the definition of a match.

3.2 Localization

> ... a measure of how well a given target is identified.

As part of the detection process, each target has associated with it a set candidate matches, which we can then constrain. In general there are two ways we can constrain the initial set, with temporal localization on the range or with attribute localization - constraints on the individual attributes.

For example, the temporal correspondence may be required meets a certain tolerance with respect to the number or percentage of frames in common. At a frame level, we may require the difference between the attributes of corresponding frames be within a given tolerance (e.g. the face overlap >= X). At an attribute level, we can even introduce attribute localization constraints by requiring that the overall deviation of a candidates attribute from the target over the entire range be within some tolerance (The average overlap is at least 75%).

3.2.1 Temporal Localization

When matching objects temporally, we consider only metrics on the range of frames over which the target is valid. Although we can have a match mode as one-to-one, many-to-one, one-to-many, many-to-many between targets and candidates, it suffices to consider only the one-to-one case for now.

For a given pair of ranges (one from the target and one from the candidate), we will define three range metrics[1], but users can define additional metrics:

OVERLAP_COEF - the fraction of frames in the target range which are also in the candidate range.

$$OC = \frac{|Range_{target} \cap Range_{candidate}|}{|Range_{target}|}$$

Note this measure is not symmetric and does not in any way penalize for excessively large candidate. Nevertheless, if your only goal is to make sure the target is detected, it is a simple and effective metric.

DICE_COEF - a normalized measure of the number of frames in common, providing a similarity measure between [0,1]:

$$DC = \frac{2 * |Range_{target} \cap Range_{candidate}|}{|Range_{target}| + |Range_{candidate}|}$$

This coefficient rewards ranges which not only have a large number of frames in common, but also have minimal extra frames which are not in common. It is computed as twice the intersection divided by the sum of the candidate and target ranges.

EXTENT_COEF - the difference in start and end point correspondence between the target range and the candidate range.

$$\begin{aligned} \alpha &= |End_{target} - End_{candidate}| \\ &\quad + |Start_{target} - Start_{candidate}| \\ EC &= 1 - e^{-\alpha} \end{aligned}$$

This measure is useful for example, when it is necessary to precisely specify the start and end of a descriptor as it considers only the deviation of the endpoints and not how much of the candidate or target where correctly detected. It is simply the difference in end range positions.

[1] These 1D metrics are later extended to 2D as spatial metrics

Given a target/candidate pair whose ranges overlap we define a "correct" detection based only on the temporal range as one whose range metric meets a given tolerance. All correct detections, again, will be reported as a single or set of matched candidates.

3.2.2 Attribute Localization

Attribute localization, like temporal localization, may be computed by considering one-to-one, many-to-one, one-to-many or many-to-many correspondences. Each data-type will have associated with it a distance measure or set of distance measures which can be applied between corresponding attributes of a descriptor (Table 1).

On a frame by frame basis, *attribute localization* can be defined by a distance (or dis-similarity) measure as a function of the instances of attributes. A tolerance can be set on this distance to define a "close enough" attribute localization and subsequent correct detection. For 2D spatial attributes including bounding boxes (bboxes), oriented boxes (oboxes) and circles, the OVERLAP and DICE coefficients are extended from the definitions above by simply considering the overlap in the 2D plane which is easily computed geometrically.

3.3 Correctness

When evaluating performance, there we must be able to subject the measures defined above to various constraints. For each descriptor, we will allow the specification of a tolerance (and where appropriate a metric) both on the range metric and on individual attribute metrics. Furthermore, we will provide a number of fundamental "levels" of matching between a candidate and a target to define correct detection. We note that each of these levels is subsequently more restrictive, not in magnitude but in the types of features and metrics it considers. Our software will explicitly implement each of these levels.

Level 0: any candidate/target combination which has at least one frame in common is a level 0 *temporal correspondence*.

Level 1: any candidate/target combination for which the number and distribution of **corresponding** frames meets a specified tolerance is a level 1 *temporal match*. A temporal tolerance and metric (defined above) used to compute the match is specified on a per descriptor basis.

Level 2: any candidate/target combination for which the number and distribution of **valid** corresponding frames meet a given tolerance is a level 2 *frame-constrained temporal match*. A pair of corresponding frames in a temporal match is valid if all instances of attributes at that frame meet their respective tolerances. Level 2 extends level 1 by considering the effect of frame by frame tolerances of the attributes on the temporal or range tolerance.

Level 3: any candidate/target combination for which all attributes are valid is considered a level 3 *attribute-constrained temporal match*. An attribute is considered valid iff either the 1) average, 2) minimum or 3) median computed over all pairs of corresponding frames in a temporal match meets a given tolerance. The type of metric (average, minimum or median) as well as the tolerance is specified by the user.

Level 0 is useful for simple detection of a descriptor, level 1 requires a minimal temporal overlap, level 2 further constrains the attributes in individual frames and level 3 constrains the attributes across time.

4 Implementation

We have implemented all parts of the system in Java. The evaluation software is configurable so that different metrics can be used, both the ground truth and results data can be filtered by object type and by range of attributes. In this way, we can cycle through the parameter space and compare performance for a single algorithm with different metrics or different subsets of the data or multiple algorithms on the same data.

We have used for a number of tasks including detection of scene changes, detection of text is scene images and tracking of faces in video. The back end of our system processes raw detections and provides explicit associations as well as precision and recall summaries based on thresholds at a descriptor and/or attribute level. Graphical summaries of the detections and localizations are also produced from the raw results.

For evaluating our system for the detection and tracking of text in video sequences[4], the ground truth contains information such as the position of text blocks, the type of motion, the text blocks content, and the quality. Runs will evaluate both detection and recognition results for either different algorithms on the same parameters or the same algorithm as a function of text quality. Figure 2a shows the overall detection results as a function of quality, Figure 2b shows the precision and recall, while Figure 2c shows the localization for the same case. In this case quality was based only on text clarity, it appears our detection algorithms are not dependent on text quality.

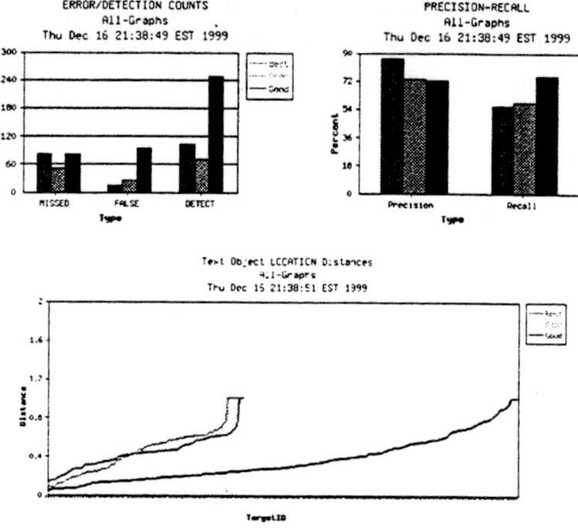

Figure 2. Examples of Bar Chart Summaries and Distance Graphs

5 Discussion

We have presented a framework for performance evaluation which combines both temporal and spatial aspects of detection. The approach is reconfigurable with respect to both the evaluation and performance criteria, and can easily be extended to incorporate new temporal, spatial and attribute metrics. The system is being adapted to provide XML I/O, enhanced graphical capabilities and ranked retrieval metrics. Although the system was originally developed for video, it is also being used successfully for still images and document images. The software system is available for research use and can be down-loaded from http://lamp.cfar.umd.edu/.

References

[1] G. Ahanger and T. Little. A survey of technologies for parsing and indexing digital video. *JVCIR, Special Issue on Digitial Libraries*, 7(1):28–43, 1996.

[2] J. Boreczky and L. Rowe. Comparison of video shot boundary detection techniques. In *SPIE 2670*, pages 170–179, 1996.

[3] U. Gargi, R. Kasturi, and S. Antani. Performance characterization and comparison of video indexing algorithms. In *CVPR*, pages 559–565, 1998.

[4] H. Li, D. Doermann, and O. Kia. Automatic text detection and tracking in digital video. *IEEE Transactions on Image Processing - Special Issue on Image and Video Processing for Digital Libraries*, pages 147–155, 1999.

Tracking humans from a moving platform

Larry Davis, Vasanth Philomin and Ramani Duraiswami
Computer Vision Laboratory
Institute for Advanced Computer Studies
University of Maryland, College Park, MD 20742, USA
{lsd, vasi, ramani}@cs.umd.edu

Abstract

Research at the Computer Vision Laboratory at the University of Maryland has focussed on developing algorithms and systems that can look at humans and recognize their activities in near real-time. Our earlier implementation (the W^4 system) while quite successful, was restricted to applications with a fixed camera. In this paper we present some recent work that removes this restriction. Such systems are required for machine vision from moving platforms such as robots, intelligent vehicles, and unattended large field of regard cameras with a small field of view. Our approach is based on the use of a deformable shape model for humans coupled with a novel variant of the Condensation algorithm that uses quasi-random sampling for efficiency. This allows the use of simple motion models which results in algorithm robustness, enabling us to handle unknown camera/human motion with unrestricted camera viewing angles. We present the details of our human tracking algorithms and some examples from pedestrian tracking and automated surveillance.

1 Introduction

The Computer Vision Laboratory at the University of Maryland has been investigating problems related to detection, tracking and analysis of human activities for almost ten years. Our earliest work focused on tracking of facial features in the context of recognizing human facial expressions from motion [11, 2]. The system described in [2], which involved robust flow estimation, image stabilization, and tracking of several facial features, required more than one minute of what then passed for CPU time per frame. Clearly, the system was far from real time, which limited both experimentation during development as well as performance evaluation over large data sets. Just seven years later at SIGGRAPH 2000 we demonstrated in collaboration with IBM Almaden a real time system for detection of faces and facial features, recognition of facial expressions and online mimicry of those facial expression on an electromechanical face.

Another early project was described in [5]. Here, multi-perspective videos of humans in action were analyzed and 3D volumetric models with many degrees of freedom were fit to these images as the body was tracked through the sequence. This system, which was implemented using Khoros and ran on a rather underpowered UNIX workstation, took many minutes per frame to analyze. But at SIGGRAPH 1998 we were able to demonstrate, in collaboration with the M.I.T. Media Laboratory and the ATR Media and Communications Laboratory, a 3D motion capture system that utilized six cameras, eight PCs and was able to recover coarse body shape data at rates of 28 frames per second. That system used many of the processing elements integrated into our W^4 visual surveillance system, a PC based system that could detect and track people and their body parts at speeds of more than thirty frames per second [7]. The W^4 system, however, was designed with a stationary camera in mind (as shown by its heavy dependency on background subtraction techniques) and so takes a "Stop and Look" approach when dealing with moving camera platforms. More recently, in collaboration with Daimler-Chrysler Research, we addressed the problem of detection of humans from moving vehicles [4] using an efficient variant of a multi-feature distance transform algorithm. The system described in [4] was able to achieve near real-time performance in natural environments as a result of an efficient organization of shape templates into a hierarchical data structure for matching (resulting in a matching strategy with logarithmic complexity rather than linear), a coarse-to-fine search over the transformation parameters and a SIMD (Single Instruction Multiple Data) implementation of the time-consuming steps of the algorithm.

We have been able to achieve these several order of magnitude increases in computational capability through a combination of better algorithm and data structure design, relentless increases in processing power of commodity computing, and advances in both communication hardware and software for multiprocessor systems. In this paper we discuss recent research in our laboratory that addresses the related problem of tracking humans from moving camera platforms. In particular, we describe how efficient random sampling techniques can be employed in the Condensation algorithm [8] to improve its asymptotic complexity and robustness, especially for problems that involve high-dimensional state spaces.

This paper is organized as follows: Section 2 gives a brief introduction to the shape model used to model humans and explains how to learn the model automatically from segmented pedestrian contours. This gives a set of deformation parameters which along with the Euclidean parameters (translation, rotation and scaling) constitute the state space. Section 3 describes the tracking algorithm that addresses the issues of an unknown motion model, robustness to outliers, and use of quasi-random points for efficiency. In Section 4 we successfully apply this algorithm to real video sequences of pedestrians as well as automated surveillance sequences. Section 5 concludes the paper.

2 Learning a linear human model

The Point Distribution Model (PDM) [3] has proven to be a useful method for building a compact linear shape model from training examples of a class of shapes. The conventional PDM requires manual labelling of a set of points called the "landmark" points in each training image. These points are concatenated to form a shape vector and the shape vectors resulting from all the training images are aligned using Procrustes analysis [6]. A mean shape and a set of modes of variation are then generated using Principal Component Analysis (PCA). A method for automatically extracting the human silhouettes from a training set of images and building a linear shape model is described in [1]. First, the silhouettes are extracted using background subtraction followed by morphological operations and then tracing the boundary points of the resulting foreground regions to form edge chains. A uniform B-spline with the control points placed at approximately uniformly spaced intervals along the contour is produced efficiently from each of these silhouettes. The control points of the B-spline are then used as the landmark points in the PDM.

We use techniques similar to that described in [1] and [3] with some improvements to build a linear human model. One improvement is in the parameterization of the B-spline curve that is fitted to each extracted contour. Suppose that the set of points in a single human contour is $\{Q_k\}, k = 0,\ldots,m$, and we want to approximate these points with a pth degree B-spline. Suppose that the values for the parameters $\bar{u}_k$ and the knot vector $U = u_0, \ldots, u_r$ are precomputed and known. We then set up and solve the (unique) linear least squares problem for the unknown control points P_i. Assume that $p \geq 1$, $m > n$ and $n \geq p$. We seek a pth degree nonrational curve

$$C(u) = \sum_{i=0}^{n} N_{i,p}(u)P_i \quad u \in [0,1]$$

satisfying:

- $Q_0 = C(0)$ and $Q_m = C(1)$;
- the remaining Q_k are approximated in the least squares sense, i.e.

$$\sum_{k=1}^{m-1} |Q_k - C(\bar{u}_k)|^2$$

  is a minimum with respect to the $n+1$ variables, P_i; the $\{\bar{u}_k\}$ are the precomputed parameter values and $N_{i,p}$ are the pth degree B-spline basis functions. The resulting curve generally does not pass precisely through Q_k, and $C(\bar{u}_k)$ is not the closest point on $C(u)$ to Q_k.

The choice of $\bar{u}_k$ and U affects the shape and parameterization of the curve. The most common method for choosing $\bar{u}_k$ is the chord length parameterization, which is the one used in [1]. Here, if d is the total chord length given by

$$d = \sum_{k=1}^{m} |Q_k - Q_{k-1}|$$

then $\bar{u}_0 = 0$, $\bar{u}_m = 1$ and

$$\bar{u}_k = \bar{u}_{k-1} + \frac{|Q_k - Q_{k-1}|}{d} \qquad k = 1,\ldots,m-1$$

This gives a good parameterization of the curve in the sense that it approximates a uniform parameterization. However, when the data takes very sharp turns such as in the case of human shapes, the chord length method does not perform well. We use the centripetal method ([9]) that gives better results with such data, where if

$$d = \sum_{k=1}^{m} \sqrt{|Q_k - Q_{k-1}|}$$

then $\bar{u}_0 = 0$, $\bar{u}_m = 1$ and

$$\bar{u}_k = \bar{u}_{k-1} + \frac{\sqrt{|Q_k - Q_{k-1}|}}{d} \qquad k = 1,\ldots,m-1$$

The placement of the knots should reflect the distribution of the $\{\bar{u}_k\}$ and we choose the knot vector U as follows. Let $c = \frac{m+1}{n-p+1}$, then the internal knots are given by

$$i = \lfloor jc \rfloor \qquad \alpha = jc - i$$
$$u_{p+j} = (1-\alpha)\bar{u}_{i-1} + \alpha\bar{u}_i \quad j = 1,\ldots,n-p \qquad (1)$$

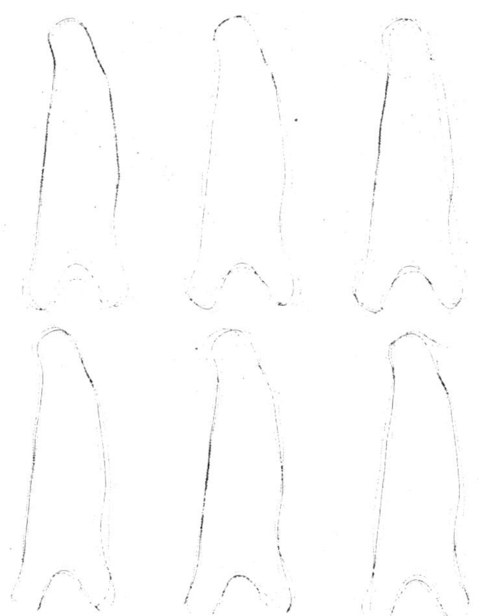

Figure 1. Modes of variation of pedestrian shapes

Equation (1) guarantees that every knot span contains at least one $\bar{u}_k$, and under this condition the matrix in the least squares formulation is positive definite and well-conditioned.

We also use a weighted least squares method to align two shapes in the Procrustes analysis, where the weights are chosen so that more significance is given to the more stable landmark points i.e. the points which vary their position the least over the entire training set. As a result, emphasis is given to aligning the stable parts of the object rather than the unstable parts during shape alignment. Figure 1 shows some of the significant modes of variation of the human shapes in the training set of pedestrian contours.

3 Tracking algorithm

The Condensation algorithm [8] has attracted much interest in the active vision area as it offers a framework for dynamic state estimation where the underlying probability density functions (pdfs) need not be Gaussian. The algorithm is based on a Monte Carlo or sampling approach, where the pdf is represented by a set of random samples. As new information becomes available, the posterior distribution of the state variables is updated by recursively propagating these samples (using a motion model as a predictor) and resampling. An accurate dynamical model is essential for robust tracking and for achieving real-time performance. This is due to the fact that the process noise of the model has to be made artificially high in order to track objects that deviate significantly from the learned dynamics, thereby increasing the extent of each predicted cluster in state space. One would then have to increase the sample size to populate these large clusters with enough samples. A high-dimensional state space (required for tracking complex shapes such as pedestrians) only makes matters worse. Even when one uses a "perfect" pseudo-random sequence for generating N sample points, the sampling error will only decrease as $O(N^{-1/2})$ as opposed to $O(N^{-1})$ for another class of sequences known as quasi-random sequences which have low discrepancy. We introduced quasi-random sampling in the context of the Condensation algorithm in [10] and showed that even in low dimensions, a significantly fewer amount of sample points were needed to achieve the same sampling error when compared to pseudo-random sampling. For reasons of brevity, the details are not discussed here; the readers are referred to [10]. In typical implementations of the Condensation algorithm, a "perfect" pseudo-random number generator is almost never used and a linear congruential generator (such as the system supplied `rand()` function) is used instead. These generators, although very fast, have an additional inherent weakness that they are not free of sequential correlation on successive calls, i.e. if k random numbers at a time are used to generate points in k-dimensional space, the points will lie on $(k-1)$-dimensional planes and will not fill up the k-dimensional space.

Since we do not want to make any assumptions about how the vehicle and the pedestrian are moving or about the viewing angle, we propose using a zero-order motion model with large process noise high enough to account for the greatest expected change in shape and motion. In other words, we need to concentrate our samples in large regions around highly probable locations from the previous time step. These high-dimensional regions which correspond to the large process noise can now be efficiently sampled using quasi-random sampling as described below.

Given the sample set $\{(\mathbf{s}_{t-1}^{(n)}, \pi_{t-1}^{(n)})\}$ at the previous time step, $\pi_{t-1}^{(n)}$ being the associated probabilities, we first choose a base sample $\mathbf{s}_{t-1}^{(i)}$ with probability $\pi_{t-1}^{(i)}$. This yields a small number of highly probable locations, say M, the neighborhoods of which we must sample more densely. If there were just one region requiring a dense concentration, an invertible mapping from a uniform space to the space of equal importance could be constructed, as given below in Equation (3) for the case of a multi-dimensional Gaussian. Since we have M regions, the importance function cannot be constructed in closed form. One therefore needs an alternative strategy for generating from the quasi-random distribution, a set of points that samples important regions densely.

We have devised a simple yet effective strategy that achieves these objectives. Let the M locations have centers $\mu^{(j)}$ and variances $\sigma^{(j)}$ based on the process noise, where these quantities are k-dimensional vectors. We then overlay $M+1$ distributions of quasi-random points over the space, with the first M distributions made Gaussian, centered at $\mu^{(j)}$ and with diagonal variance $\sigma^{(j)}$ (3). Finally, we also overlay a $(M+1)$th distribution that is spread uniformly over the entire state space. This provides robustness against sudden changes in shape and motion. The total number of points used is N, where

$$N = N_1 + N_2 + \ldots + N_{M+1}, \tag{2}$$

the sample size in the Condensation algorithm. We have in effect chosen $\mathbf{s}_t^{(n)}$ by sampling from $p(\mathbf{X}_t/\mathbf{X}_{t-1} = \mathbf{s}_{t-1}^{(i)})$.

The conversion from a uniform quasi-random distribution to a Gaussian quasi-random distribution is achieved using the mapping along the lth dimension

$$y_{jl} = \mu_l^{(j)} + \sqrt{2}\sigma_l^{(j)} \operatorname{erf}^{-1}\left((2\xi_l - 1)\right), \tag{3}$$

where erf^{-1} is the inverse of the error function given by

$$\operatorname{erf}(z) = \frac{2}{\sqrt{\pi}} \int_0^z e^{-t^2} dt,$$

and ξ_l represents the quasi-randomly distributed points in $[0, 1]$.

Finally, we measure and compute the probabilities $\pi_t^{(n)} = p(\mathbf{Z}_t/\mathbf{X}_t = \mathbf{s}_t^{(n)})$ for these new sample positions in terms of the image data $\mathbf{Z}_t$. We use a measurement density based on the multi-feature distance transform algorithm (see [4] for details) that has been successfully used for detecting pedestrians from static images. Therefore

$$\log p(\mathbf{Z}_t/\mathbf{X}_t) = \log p\left(\mathbf{Z}/\mathbf{X}\right) \propto \left\{ -\frac{1}{M} \sum_{i=1}^{M} d_{typed}^2(z_i, I) \right\},$$

where the z_i's are measurement points along the contour, I is the image data, and $d_{typed}(z_i, I)$ denotes the distance between z_i and the closest feature of the same type in I. We use oriented edges discretized into eight bins as the features in all our experiments.

4 Results

We now present some results on tracking pedestrians from a moving vehicle (Figure 2) and humans from an overhead surveillance camera that pans from side to side (Figures 3 and 4). First, a linear shape model was built from automatically segmented human contours using the techniques described in Section 2 and the dimensionality was reduced using PCA to find an eight-dimensional space of deformations. We used $N = 2000$ samples in the Condensation algorithm and introduced 10% of random samples at every iteration to account for sudden changes in shape and motion. Figures 2, 3 and 4 show the tracker output as contours corresponding to the modal (highest probability) state and the mean state. The tracker was able to recover very quickly from failures due to sudden changes in shape or motion and track people through partial occlusion. Figure 3 shows a specific example where the person being tracked is temporarily occluded by a pole between Frames 38 and 50.

5 Conclusions

In this paper, we have developed a framework for tracking humans from moving camera platforms. Our approach used the Condensation tracker and extended it to high-dimensional problems by incorporating quasi-Monte Carlo methods into the conventional algorithm. Specifically, we overlaid layers of quasi-random Gaussian grids over the state space which allowed for efficient sampling. As a result, we could handle general situations where there are no restrictions on the dynamics of the camera or the human being tracked and there are no assumptions on the viewing angle.

Acknowledgements

We gratefully acknowledge the partial support of ONR contract N000149510521 and Department of Justice contract JUST1999LTVXK019.

References

[1] A. Baumberg and D. C. Hogg. Learning flexible models from image sequences. In *Proc. European Conference on Computer Vision*, 1994.

[2] M. J. Black and Y. Yacoob. Recognizing facial expressions in image sequences using local parameterized models of image motion. *International Journal of Computer Vision*, 25(1):23–48, 1997.

[3] T. F. Cootes, C. J. Taylor, A. Lanitis, D. H. Cooper, and J. Graham. Building and using flexible models incorporating grey-level information. In *Proc. IEEE International Conference on Computer Vision*, pages 242–246, 1993.

[4] D. Gavrila and V. Philomin. Real-time object detection for "smart" vehicles. In *Proc. IEEE International Conference on Computer Vision*, volume 1, pages 87–93, Kerkyra, Greece, 1999.

[5] D. M. Gavrila and L. Davis. Towards 3-D model-based tracking and recognition of human movement: a multi-view approach. In *Int. Workshop on Face and Gesture Recognition*, Zurich, Switzerland, 1995.

Figure 2. Tracking results for Daimler-Chrysler pedestrian sequence using quasi-random sampling. Dark - Modal state estimate; Light - Mean state estimate.

Figure 3. Tracking results for a surveillance sequence with occlusion using quasi-random sampling. Dark - Modal state estimate; Light - Mean state estimate.

Figure 4. Tracking results for a surveillance sequence with occlusion using quasi-random sampling (cont'd from Figure 3). Dark - Modal state estimate; Light - Mean state estimate.

[6] C. Goodall. Procrustes methods in the statistical analysis of shape. *Journal of the Royal Statistical Society B*, 53(2):285–339, 1991.

[7] I. Haritaoglu, D. Harwood, and L. Davis. W4: Who, when, where, what: A real time system for detecting and tracking people. In *Face and Gesture Recognition Conference*, pages 222–227, Japan, 1998.

[8] M. Isard and A. Blake. Contour tracking by stochastic propagation of conditional density. In *Proc. European Conference on Computer Vision*, pages 343–356, Freiburg, Germany, 1996.

[9] E. T. Y. Lee. Choosing nodes in parametric curve interpolation. In *CAD*, volume 21, pages 363–370, 1989.

[10] V. Philomin, R. Duraiswami, and L. S. Davis. Quasi-random sampling for condensation. In *Proc. European Conference on Computer Vision*, 2000.

[11] Y. Yacoob and L. S. Davis. Recognizing human facial expressions from long image sequences using optical flow. *IEEE Transactions on Pattern Analysis and Machine Intelligence*, 18(6):636–642, 1996.

A Fast Background Scene Modeling and Maintenance for Outdoor Surveillance

Ismail Haritaoglu[1], David Harwood[2] and Larry S. Davis[2]
[1]IBM Almaden Research, San Jose, CA 95120
[2]Computer Vision Laboratory University of Maryland, College Park, MD 20742
(ismailh@almaden.ibm.com, harwood,lsd@umiacs.umd.edu)

Abstract

We described fast background scene modeling and maintenance techniques for real time visual surveillance system for tracking people in an outdoor environment. It operates on monocular grayscale video imagery, or on video imagery from an infrared camera. The system learns and models background scene statistically to detect foreground objects, even when the background is not completely stationary (e.g. motion of tree branches) using shape and motion cues. Also a background maintenance model is proposed for preventing false positives, such as, illumination changes (the sun being blocked by clouds causing changes in brightness), or false negative, such as, physical changes (person detection while he is getting out of the parked car). Experimental results demonstrate robustness and real-time performance of the algorithm.

1 Introduction

The primary objective of this paper is to present set of techniques for continuous detection of people and objects using shape cues for a real time outdoor surveillance system for monitoring people activities which is going to be used by police department at University of Maryland, College Park for surveillance. To be able to develop real time surveillance system which is running 24 hour day, you not only concentrate on solving detection problem, but also you should consider on high level techniques interpretation of changes in the scene for long term operation. For example, if you detect a car while is being parked on lot, you no not need to detect it for hours while it is staying there without any motion. Therefore we describe computational models that

- build an initial statistical model for a background scene that allows us to detect foreground regions even when the background scene is not completely stationary

Figure 1. Examples of detection tracking two people playing freezebee.

- maintenance background model to adapt the changes in the scene

The system has been designed to work with only monochromatic stationary video sources, either visible or infrared for outdoor surveillance where color will not be available, and people need to be detected and tracked based on weaker appearance and motion cues. As the surveillance area does not stay the same for a long period of time, the system updates the background model parameters adaptively to decrease the number of false positives due to illumination changes, such as, the sun being blocked by clouds causing changes in brightness, or physical changes, such as a deposited object. Additionally, any foreground object detected for a long time without any motion (a parked car) can cause false negatives (a person cannot be detected while he is getting out of the car). The maintenance method allows us to handle that type of false negative cases.

The reminder of this paper is organized as follows. Section 2 describes brief related work and our statistical background model. Section 3 focuses on obtain initial background parameters at presence of moving people in the scene. Section 4 explains how we maintain background parameter for long term or short term changes in the scene.

1051-4651/00 $10.00 © 2000 IEEE

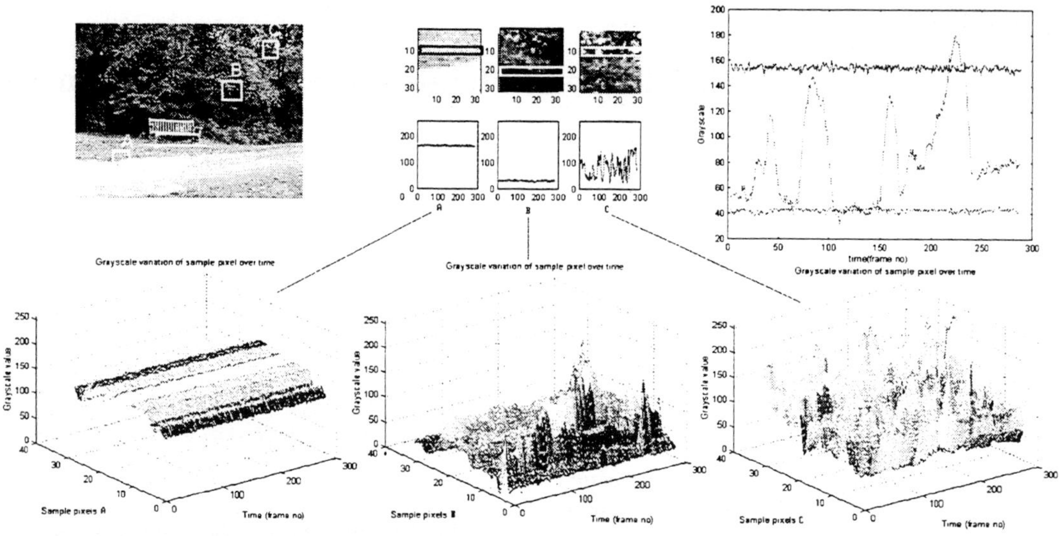

Figure 2. Three sample region selected in background where there is no background motion (A), small portion has background motion (B), and large portion has background motion (C). Top middle graphs shows the intensity variation over time for sample pixel in regions A, B and C. Bottom graphs show the intensity variation at pixels in regions A,B,C over time

2 Background Scene Modeling

A simple and common background modeling method involves subtracting each new image from a model of the background scene and thresholding the resulting difference image to determine foreground pixels. The pixel intensity of a completely stationary background can be reasonably modeled with a normal distribution[9, 6], and it can adapt to slow changes in the scene by recursively updating the model. However, those approaches have difficulty in modeling backgrounds in outdoor scenes. because they cannot handle the small motions of background objects such as vegetation (swaying tree branches). In Figure 2 we look at three sample regions chosen from the strong wind video: one where the wind did not cause background motion (region A), a second where the wind caused background motion only in a small portion of the region (region B), and a third in which the wind made the tree branches sway significantly (region C).The intensity variation of pixels in region A is low; however the intensity variation of pixels in region C is very high. Those observations reflect the fact that more than one process may be observed over time at a single pixel. Figure 2(b) shows the observed intensity distribution over time at a pixel where there is a tree leaf motion, and the maximum interframe difference distribution of the sequence. In this case, more than one process may be observed over time at a single pixel. In [2] a mixture of three Normal distributions was used to model the pixel value for traffic surveillance applications to model road, shadow, and vehicle. In [3], pixel intensity is modeled by a mixture of K Gaussian distributions (typically K is 3 to 5). [1] uses a non-parametric background model by estimating the probability of observing pixel intensity values based on a sample of intensity values for each pixel. [8] uses directional-consistent flow information to handle periodic motion of background scene. We used a model of background variation that is computationally efficient. We assume each pixel intensity distribution is *bimodal*. The background scene is then modeled by representing each pixel by three values; its minimum $m(x)$ and maximum $n(x)$ intensity values and the maximum intensity difference $d(x)$ between consecutive frames observed during this training period (Figure3 (a)). Other methods developed in our laboratory [5, 1] have more sensitivity in detecting foreground regions; but are computationally more intensive.

3 Learning Initial Background Parameters

We obtain the background model even if there are moving foreground objects in the field of view, such as walking people, moving cars, etc. It uses a two stage method based on excluding moving pixels from initial background model computation. In the first stage a pixelwise *median filter* over time is applied to several seconds of video (typically 10-60 second) to distinguish moving pixels from stationary pixels. In the second stage, only those stationary pixels are

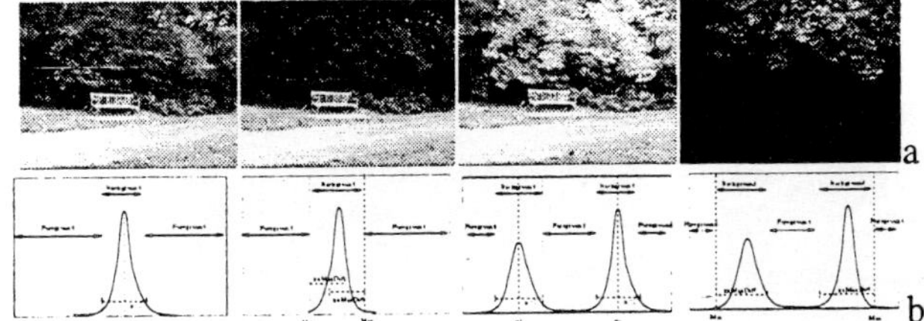

Figure 3. a:An original image, minimum, maximum and maximum interframe difference images obtained by using 300 background frames (top row, left to right), b: the foreground/ background region classification used in W^4

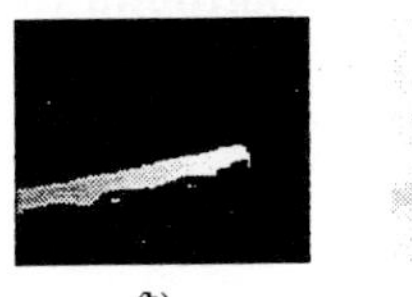

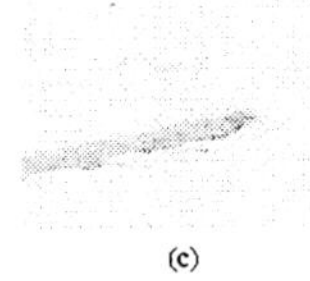

(a) (b) (c)

Figure 4. An example of change-map used in background model computation: (a) input sequnce, (b) motion history map, (c) detection map

processed to construct the initial background model.

Let V be an array containing N consecutive images, $V^i(x)$ is the intensity of a pixel location x in the ith image of V. $\sigma(x)$ and $\lambda(x)$ are the standard deviation and median value of intensities at pixel location x in all images in V. The initial background model for a pixel location x, $[m(x), n(x), d(x)]$, is obtained as follows:

$$\begin{bmatrix} m(x) \\ n(x) \\ d(x) \end{bmatrix} = \begin{bmatrix} min_z\{V^z(x)\} \\ max_z\{V^z(x)\} \\ max_z\{|V^z(x) - V^{z-1}(x)|\} \end{bmatrix} \quad (1)$$

where $|V^z(x) - \lambda(x)| > 2 * \sigma(x)$. Here, $V^z(x)$ is classified as moving pixels.

4 Maintenance Background Model

The surveillance area does not stay the same for a long period of time. There could be illumination changes, such as the sun being blocked by clouds causing changes in brightness, or physical changes, such as a deposited object. As we use an intensity-based background model, any changes in illumination can cause false positives. Additionally, any foreground object detected for a long time without any motion (a parked car) can cause false negatives (a person cannot be detected while he is getting out of the car). [7] is a good reference that explain the problems of background scene maintenance for surveillance systems. In these cases, we use two different methods to update the background.

- A **pixel-based update** method updates the background model *periodically* to adapt to illumination changes in the background scene.
- An **object-based update** method updates the background model to adapt to physical changes in the background scene. A deposited/removed object, or a parked car would be added into the background scene if it does not move for a long period of time.

We use the following method to update the background model: during tracking, a change map is dynamically constructed to determine whether a pixel-based or an object based update method applies. The change map consists of three main components:

- a *detection support map* (gS) which represents the number of times a pixel location is classified as a background pixel in the last N frames.

$$gS(x,t) = \begin{cases} gS(x,t-1)+1 & \text{if } x \text{ is background} \\ gS(x,t-1) & \text{if } x \text{ is foreground} \end{cases} \quad (2)$$

- a *motion support map* (mS) which represents the number of times a pixel location is classified as a moving pixel.A pixel is classified as a moving pixel by subtracting three consecutive images.

$$mS(x,t) = \begin{cases} mS(x,t-1)+1 & \text{if } M(x,t)=1 \\ mS(x,t-1) & \text{if } M(x,t)=0 \end{cases} \quad (3)$$

where

$$M(x,t) = \begin{cases} 1 & \text{if } (|I(x,t) - I(x,t+1)| > 2*\sigma) \\ & \wedge (|I(x,t-1) - I(x,t)| > 2*\sigma) \\ 0 & \text{otherwise} \end{cases} \quad (4)$$

- a *change history map* (hS) which represents the elapsed time (in frames) since the last time that the pixel was classified as foreground pixel.

$$hS(x,t) = \begin{cases} 255 & \text{if } x \text{ is foreground} \\ hS(x,t-1) - \frac{255}{N} & \text{otherwise} \end{cases} \quad (5)$$

We use gS to determine the parts of the background which are updated by the pixel-based method, and mS,gS and hS to determine the parts of the background which are updated by the object-based method. The change-maps are set to zero after the background model is updated. In Figure 4,

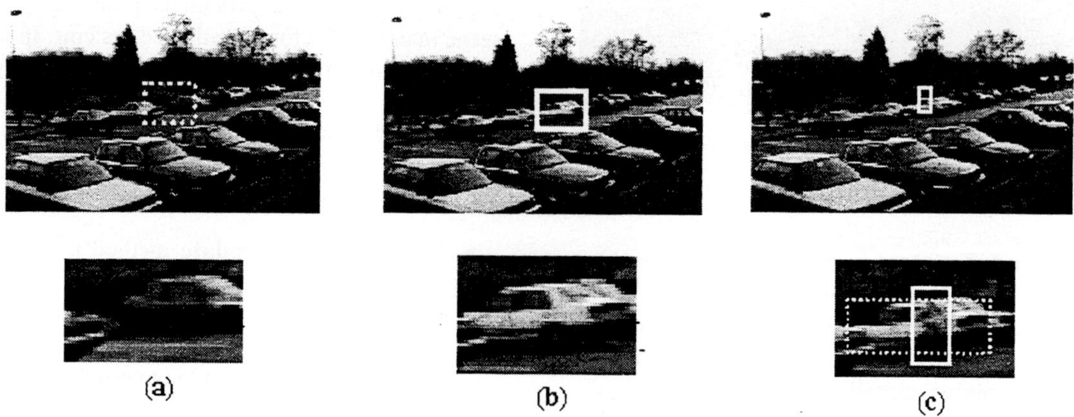

Figure 5. A car which has been parked for a long time is added to background model (a) (b), so the person getting off the car is detected (c).

an example of a change map used in the background update method is shown.

During tracking the background model is computed separately for all pixels which are classified as foreground pixels $(m^f(x), n^f(x), d^f(x))$, and for all pixels which are classified as background pixels $(b^b(x), n^b(x), d^b(x))$. Let $m^c(x)$, $n^c(x)$, $d^c(x)$ be the background model parameters currently being used; the new background model parameters $m(x)$, $n(x)$, $d(x)$ are determined as follows:

$$[m(x), n(x), d(x)] = \begin{cases} [m^b(x), m^b(x), d^b(x)] \\ \quad \text{if } (gS(x) > k * N) \text{ (pixel-based)} \\ [m^f(x), n^f(x), d^f(x)] \\ \quad \text{if } (gS(x) < k * N \wedge mS(x) < r * N) \\ [m^c(x), n^c(x), d^c(x)] \\ \quad \text{otherwise} \end{cases} \tag{6}$$

where k and r are typically 0.8 and 0.1 respectively. Figure 5 shows an example of a car which has been parked for a long time is added to background model, so the person getting out of the car is detected and tracked successfully.

5 Foreground Region Detection

Foreground objects are segmented from the background in each frame of the video sequence by a four stage process: thresholding, noise cleaning, morphological filtering and object detection. Each pixel is first classified as either a background or a foreground pixel using the background model. Giving the minimum $m(x)$, maximum $n(x)$ and the median of the largest interframe absolute difference d_μ images over the entire image that represent the background scene model $B(x)$, pixel x from image I^t is a foreground pixel if:

$$B(x) = \begin{cases} 0 \text{ background} & \begin{cases} (I^t(x) - m(x)) < kd_\mu \\ \vee I^t(x) - n(x)) < kd_\mu \end{cases} \\ 1 \text{ foreground} & \text{otherwise} \end{cases} \tag{7}$$

We ran a series of experiments to determine the best threshold constant k using different background scenes while the background intensity variation is at different levels. For image sequences where there is high intensity variation of background pixels (sequence 4 and sequence 5 in Figure 6), our method yields large number of false positives when $k < 2$. For other sequences, the false positive rate is very low. We generated the ground truth for foreground pixel and compare it with the detected foreground pixel. Table 1 shows the true positive rates for different k. Our experiments show that $k = 2$ gives the highest true positive rates with the lowest false positives rates, we consistently use $k = 2$ in our system.

We tested performance of detection by using 12 hour of data. And our systems has 98.8% correct detection rate on the number of people on the scene, with 3.2% false positive rate which is acceptable for real time outdoor surveillance systems. Most of the false positives are due to wind causing clouds moving very fast and reflection of clouds on the car windshields, and shadows.

6 Conclusion and Discussion

We described fast background scene modeling and maintenance techniques for real real time visual surveillance system for tracking people in an outdoor environment. The system learns and models background scene statistically to detect foreground objects, even when the background is not

Figure 6. An example of foreground region detection while background has different intensity variation

	k=2	k=3	k=4	k=6	k=8
seq 1	0.89	0.80	0.72	0.51	0.32
seq 2	0.52	0.40	0.29	0.03	0.02
seq 3	0.81	0.70	0.59	0.41	0.28
seq 4	0.85	0.77	0.70	0.50	0.40
seq 5	0.85	0.77	0.71	0.59	0.46
seq 6	0.87	0.77	0.72	0.60	0.48

Table 1. True pixel-based detection rate for different background scenes which have different intensity variations are shown in Figure 6(seq 1 is left most, seq 6 is right most)

Examples	(a)	(b)	(c)	(d)
Thresholding	3.69	3.73	3.79	3.85
Connected components	2.01	2.40	2.98	2.72
Noise removing	3.08	3.67	4.48	4.15
Morphological op.	1.25	1.70	2.47	2.26

Table 2. Execution times in ms for sample image sequences where there are one (a), two (b), (d) three (c) people in the current scene interacting with each other

completely stationary (e.g. motion of tree branches) and distinguishes people from other objects (e.g. cars) using shape and motion cues. Our background model is an adaptive model for preventing false positives, such as, illumination changes (the sun being blocked by clouds causing changes in brightness), or false negative, such as, physical changes (person detection while he is getting out of the parked car).

It has been implemented in C++ and runs under the Windows NT operating system. Currently, for 320x240 resolution gray scale images, It runs at 30 Hz on a PC which has 400 Mhz Pentium processors depending on the number of people in its field of view. Table 2 gives the average execution times of each component of detection for four different image sequence where there are different number of people in the scene.

References

[1] A. Elgammal, D. Harwood and L. Davis Non-parametric model for background subtraction In *IEEE Frame rate workshop*, 1999

[2] N. Friedman and S. Russell, Image segmentation in Video sequences: a probabilistic approach. In *Uncertainty in Artificial Intelligent*, 1997

[3] E. Grimson and C.Stauffer and R. Romano and L. Lee Using adaptive tracking to classfy and monitoring activities in a site In *Computer Vision and Pattern Recognition Conference*, pages 22–29, 1998.

[4] I. Haritaoglu, W4: A real time system for detecting and tracking people and Monitoring their activities In *Ph.D. Thesis*, Computer Science Dept. University of Maryland,

[5] T. Horprasert, D. Harwood, and L.S. Davis. A Statistical Approach for Real-time Robust Background Subtraction and Shadow Detection Proc. IEEE ICCV'99 FRAME-RATE Workshop, Kerkyra, Greece, 1999.

[6] T. Olson and F. Brill. Moving object detection and event recognition algorithms for smart cameras. *Proc. DARPA Image Understanding Workshop*, pages 159–175, 1997.

[7] K. Toyama, J. Krumm, B. Brumitt and B. Meyers WallFlower: Principle and Practice of Background Maintenance Proc. Internationa conference of Computer Vision, 1999

[8] L. Wixson and M. Hansen Detecting salient motion by accumulating directional-consistent flow Proc. International Conference of Computer Vision, 1999

[9] C. Wren, A. Azarbayejani, T. Darrell, and A. Pentland. Pfinder: Real-time tracking of the human body. Technical Report 353, MIT Media Lab Perceptual Computer Section, 1995.

An Appearance-based Body Model for Multiple People Tracking

Ismail Haritaoglu[1], David Harwood[2] and Larry S. Davis[2]
[1]IBM Almaden Research, San Jose, CA 95120
[2]Computer Vision Laboratory University of Maryland, College Park, MD 20742
(ismailh@almaden.ibm.com, harwood,lsd@umiacs.umd.edu)

Abstract

We describe an appearance-based human body model for tracking multiple people when they are interaction with others causing significant occlusion amongst them, or when they reenter the scene. The proposed model allows real time surveillance systems understand "who is who" after multiple people interactions, partial or total occlusions, or when a person "reappear" in the scene. It combines the grayscale textural appearance *and* expected shape *information together in a 2D dynamic template. Experimental results demonstrates robustness and real time performance of the proposed model.*

1 Introduction

Visual interpretation of people and their movements is an important issue in many applications, such as surveillance systems and virtual reality interfaces. The ability to find and track people is therefore an important visual problem. The problem is more difficult when there are small groups of people moving together, or interacting with each other as shown in Figure 1. In these cases individual people are not visually isolated, but are partially or total occluded by other people. In these difficult cases, tracking people and understanding "who is who" is a difficult problem. In a crowded environment, such as airport, where people shows most of time unpredictable direction of motion and enormous amount of interaction with others makes motion-based tracking systems fails. Other information about each individual, such as, their face, their clothes, their body shape, might be useful for distinguish those people from each other. The problem that we focused in this work is to find a method to extract enough information about each person in the scene to be able identify them after they reappear by either reentering the scene or after totally occlusion. Appearance model we proposed allows our system [5] to handle occlusion and to identify people after occlusion and understand "Who is Who".

With increasing processor power, more attention has been given to intelligent real-time surveillance system which detect and track people, and recognize their interactions. Most previous systems assume that there is only one person in the scene [3, 8]; other systems can track detected multiple foreground regions by assuming that each region contains only one person [1, 7]. However, a foreground region could contain multiple people, such as when two or more people move together or when two people who are being tracked individually come together. In these cases, people are typically not visually isolated but are partially or totally occluded.

None of these previous system can track people individually in such cases; they only track the blob corresponding to the group. Recently CMU's VSAM system [7] has been extended to classify a foreground blob as containing multiple people or a single person using simple size attributes; but they do not attempt to track each person. Previous systems do not model the appearance of the people being tracked, so they do not know "who is who" before or after interactions or occlusions or after the people "reappear" the scene, they do not know any information about it. Understanding relative identity of the people is an important information for high level interpretation of human activities. Our system is only system that are using appearance-based human model to be able to identify people after the occlusion event is complete and people separate, or "reappear" in the scene.

For example, if you want to get information about a person who was seen by other, you might ask: What type and color of his/her clothes? What is her/his age, gender, height, his/her body?, etc. Intuitively, what types of information might be used to identify people?

- Global shape information: height, width of their torso, legs, head, etc.
- Appearance information: texture of the region of their lower part of body, torso, etc.

In our system, we combined these two information together in a 2D dynamic template -called a -called a Textural

1051-4651/00 $10.00 © 2000 IEEE

Figure 1. An example of multiple people instructions

Temporal Template. It has two components that can be used for subsequent identification: a *textural* component which represents the *grayscale textural appearance* of the person and a *shape component* which represents expected shape information of the person. It is created for each person when they are detected first time and updated as long as people is not totally occluded. If there is a drastic change in their shape (for example, a person who was standing posture could be in bending posture), a new template is created and assigned to the same person. Therefore a single person could be multiple textural temporal template, one for each main posture (standing, sitting, bending, lying down). A body posture analysis is applied to the silhouette to compute estimated posture of respective person and only the corresponding template are updated for respective person. When a person is appear in the scene, his/her 2D grayscale template are compare with textural temporal templates of each person who were in occlusion or who left the scene.

2 Appearance Model

Our tracking system determine when a new person enters the system's field of view, and initialize motion models for tracking that person. It compute the correspondence between the foreground regions detected by the background subtraction and the people currently being tracked. Details of multiple people tracking could be found in [5].

When two people meet they are segmented as one foreground region by the background subtraction algorithm. Our system recognizes that this occurs based on a simple analysis of the predicted bounding boxes of the tracked objects and the bounding box of the detected (merged) foreground region. The merged region is tracked until it splits back into its constituent objects. A problem that arises when a merged region splits, and the people "re- appear", is determining the correspondence between the people that were tracked before the interaction and the people that emerge from the interaction. To accomplish this, we combine the *grayscale textural appearance* and *shape* information of respective person together in a 2D dynamic template -called a *textural temporal template*.

The temporal texture template for an object is defined by:

$$\Psi^t(x,y) = \frac{I(x,y) + w^{t-1}(x,y) \times \Psi^{t-1}(x,y)}{w^{t-1}(x,y) + 1} \quad (1)$$

Here, $I(x)$ refers to the intensity of pixel(x) which is classified as foreground pixel, and all coordinates are represented relative to the *median* coordinate of the person. The w^t are the number of times that a pixel in Ψ_y is classified as a foreground pixelfor last N frame. The initial $w^t(x)$ of Ψ_y are zero and are incremented each time that the corresponding location (relative to the median template coordinate) is detected as a foreground pixel in the input image. Note that a temporal textural templates has two components that can be used for subsequent identification: a *textural* component which represents the *grayscale textural appearance* of the person (second row in Figure 2; and a *shape component* (w^t) which represents probabilistic shape information (third row in Figure 2) of the human body for last N frame. $w^t(x,y)$ is then normalized to probability map $w^t_n(x,y)$. After normalization, $w^t_n(x,y)$ is the probability of the pixel location (x,y) belongs to person in last N time frames. Figure 3 showns an example of probability map for person body shape. For example, while a person is walking, due to articulated motion of their arm and leg, the locations near arms and legs has lower probability than the locations near to his torso (which has more rigid than the legs or arms). In Figure 2 third row, darker locations has higher shape probability (high $w^t_n(x,y)$ makes more contribution to correlations).

After separation or reappearance, each constituent object is matched with the separating people by correlating their temporal templates with detected silhouettes over a small neighborhood search window. We compute the weighted correlation $C(p,r)$ between each detected separating person p and tracked person r at time t. Let $\mathbf{S^t}$ be the grayscale silhouette of a separating person and Ψ^t be template of a person who has been tracked but it disappear for a while

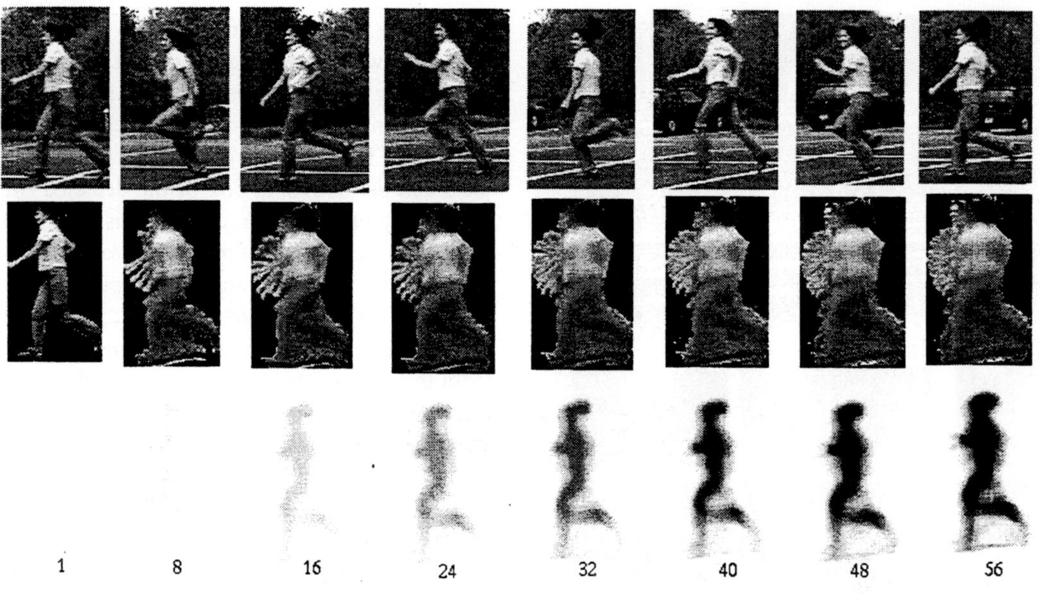

Figure 2. An example of how textural(second row) and shape (third row) components of temporal texture templates are updated over time.

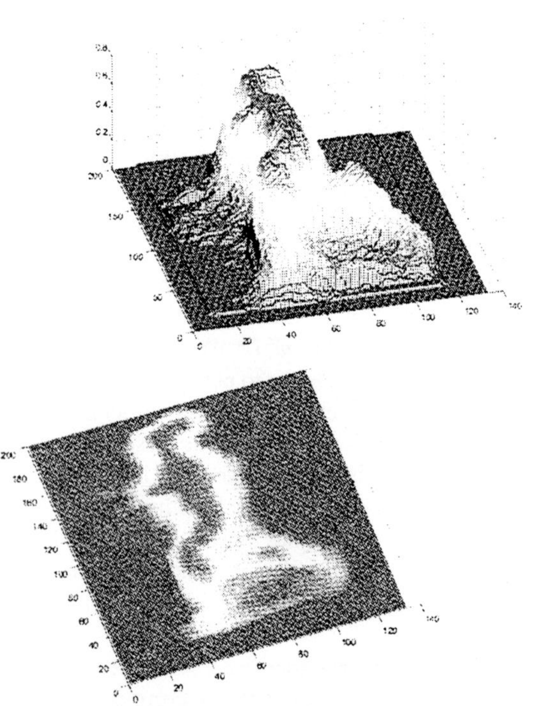

Figure 3. An example of shape probability map for person shown in Figure 2

(due to either occlusion or leaving the scene).

$$C(p,r) = \frac{\sum_{(x,y)\in S^p} |S_p^t(x,y) - Psi^t(x,y)| \times w^t(x,y)}{\sum w^t(x,y)} \quad (2)$$

Those correlation values are normalized. If those normalized correlation are lower than pre-determined threshold , detected person could be matched with tracked person after they reappear. The lowest $C(p,r)$ which is higher than a pre-determined threshold indicated a new person enters the system's field of view, so the system gives it to a new label to it initialize motion models for tracking that person.

Since the temporal texture template is view-based, it could fail to match if there were a large change in the pose of the object during tracking. Therefore, instead of one template per person, we construct one template per person for a given body posture. People can be in many different postures while they are performing actions. Each posture has different appearances, varying with the point of view. We observed that four different main postures (standing, sitting, crawling/bending and lying down) have large differences in body shape. The order in other postures is typically a variation of one of the main postures. Any body posture is classified into one of the four *main postures* (standing, sitting, crawling/bending, lying).

A body posture is represented by the normalized horizontal and vertical projection histograms, the median coordinate, and the major axis of its silhouette. Average normalized horizontal and vertical projection templates for each main posture (and for each view-based appearance of each main posture) were computed experimentally using 4500 silhouettes of seven different people in three different views. These features are used to determine the similarity of the given posture to one of the four main postures. We compare the observed silhouette with the projection templates of the four main postures using the sum of absolute difference method to estimate the most similar main posture. Let S^i be the similarity between the detected silhouette and the ith main posture, H^i and V^i the horizontal and vertical projections of the ith main posture, and P and R the horizontal and vertical projections of the detected silhouette. S_i is calculated as

$$S_i = -log(\sum_{h}^{128}\sum_{v}^{128}(H_h^i - P_h)^2 + (V_v^i - R_v)^2 \quad (3)$$

We determine the most similar main posture by using the highest Score [6] The different view-based appearance of the people in the same posture does not cause problem because probabilistic shape map can handle these kind of variation. As long as the people reappear in the scene in a posture that its corresponding the template for that posture has already been created, our methods works well.

3 Experimental Results and Discussion

We run serious experiments to test our proposed method comparing other 2D template based alternative methods. Alternative methods used in this experiment are keeping last N 2D grayscale silhouette of each person and compare those templates when a person reappears in the scene. When $N = 1$, only last detected silhouette for respective person kept in memory which requires less memory and computational inexpensive, however it does not identify people as good as our proposed method, When $N = t$, all the detected silhouettes kept in memory which requires much more memory than our methods, and it is computational expensive that is not appropriate for a real-time application. For 2 hours test video where there are 230 time multiple people interactions (at least one person is totally occluded or reappear on the scene), our method successfully identify people in 204 case which yields 89% success rate. The other methods only successfully identify people in 87 cases (37% success rate) when $N = 1$ and in 186 cases (81% success rate) when $N = 60$. Our methods failed to identify people correctly 26 cases. Most of the time where our method failed while people were wearing very similar things, such as uniform, and similar body shape. Also our method failed couple of times while people is carrying some object in their body (hands, back or in front) changes the location of the object in their body (or left object) after they reappear. (People loading truck).

We implemented proposed method in C++ and runs under the Windows NT operating system. Currently, for 320x240 resolution gray scale images, it runs at 30 Hz on a PC which has 400 Mhz Pentium II processor depending on the number of people in its field of view. Table 1 gives the average execution times in millisecond of each template computation and updating four different image sequence where there are different number of people in the scene.

	(a)	(b)	(c)	(d)
Posture Analysis	1.77	2.77	1.54	3.42
T3 Update	1.17	1.20	2.56	1.6
T3 Matching	3.98	1.61	2.49	4.72

Table 1. Execution times in ms for sample image sequences where there are one (a), two (b), (d) three (c) people in the current scene interacting with each other

References

[1] D. Beymer and K. Konolige Real Time Person Tracking Using Stereo Proc. IEEE ICCV'99 FRAME-RATE Workshop, Kerkyra, 1999.

[2] A. Bobick, J. D. S., Intille, F. Baird, L. Cambell, Y. Irinov, C. Pinhanez, and A. Wilson. Kidsroom: Action recognition in an interactive story environment. Technical Report 398, M.I.T Perceptual Computing, 1996.

[3] T. Boult Frame-rate omnidirectional surveillance and tracking of camouflaged and occlude targets. In *Second Workshop of Visual Surveillance at CVPR*, pages 48-58, 1999

[4] E. Grimson and C. Stauffer and R. Romano and L. Lee. Using adaptive tracking to classify and monitoring activities in a site In *Computer Vision and Pattern Recognition Conference*, pages 22-29, 1998.

[5] I. Haritaoglu W4:Areal time system for detection and tracking of people and monitoring their activities *Ph.D. Thesis*, University of Maryland, Computer science Dept, 1999

[6] I. Haritaoglu, D. Harwood, and L. Davis. Ghost: A Human Body Part Labeling System Using Silhouettes. In *International Conference on Pattern Recognition*, 1998.

[7] A. Lipton, H. Fujiyoshi, and R. Patil. Moving target detection and classification from real-time video In *Proceedings of IEEE Workshop on Application of Computer Vision*, 1998.

[8] C. Wren, A. Azarbayejani, T. Darrell, and A. Pentland. Pfinder: Real-time tracking of the human body. IEEE Transaction on Pattern Analysis and Machine Intelligence, 19(7), pges 780-785,1997

Human body posture measurement by matching foot pressure distribution to video images

Satoshi SHIMADA[*], Kazufumi ISHIDA[**] and Sakuichi OHTSUKA[*]
[*]NTT Cyber Space Laboratories [**]NTT-AT Image Processing Technology Department
E-mail:shimada@nttcvg.hil.ntt.co.jp

Abstract

We present a posture measurement method that uses foot pressure distribution and video camera images. The method first estimates the position, posture and size of subject in the real world from his or her foot pressure distribution. These estimates are represented by a stick model. The position of the skeleton in the camera image is then detected by using the estimated skeleton obtained by projecting the stick model onto the camera image as initial value. We tested this method on 80 walking patterns of eight women. The results show that the detected skeleton lies at the center of the leg.

1. Introduction

Posture measurement of the human body is important for motion analysis in medical rehabilitation and sports. The accurate measurement of joint position and joint angle is used to analyze the walking pattern of a patient or to refine and enhance the characteristic motions of an athlete in his or her sport.

Most current posture measurement methods used in the fields of rehabilitation and sport attach angle sensors or markers to the subject. These methods have limited practicality because they tend to bother the subject and because installation takes too long. In addition, the results these methods produce are not very reliable because the attachments can disturb the subject. A better method that does not disturb the user involves detecting joint position from video images with manual joint identification. This method is obviously very labor.

Thus, it would be desirable to have a method that could both accurately measure posture from a camera image without fixing markers or sensors to the subject and reduce the workload of the measurement staff. One idea is to use a stick model of the subject's skeleton to measure joint position and joint angle from a camera image.

Although methods for detecting the skeleton in a video camera image have been examined, they have not reached a sufficient level of reliability for practical use. In the published research, the image region containing the person is extracted from the overall image as the first step in detecting the skeleton. The region extraction methods that have been examined include detection of the moving object region by thresholding an image taken with a specific background [1, 2], background differencing [3, 4], tracking [5-7], and thermal imaging [8]. It is difficult to apply these methods to the fields of medical treatment and sports, because the backgrounds tend to change and people other than the subject can intrude into the camera's field of view.

We have already developed a gait analysis system that uses foot pressure distribution [9]. The measurement procedure is practical and accurate, because the foot pressure sensor does not disturb the subject. We believed that by analyzing foot pressure distribution and posture simultaneously, we could create a synthetic motion analysis system.

Our new skeleton detection method involves the integrated processing of a video camera image and foot pressure distribution; no region extraction is used. While it is difficult to obtain the position, size and posture of a person in the real world from just a video camera image, these parameters can be easily estimated by using foot pressure distribution.

2. Method

Figure 1 illustrates the measurement procedure. The system first estimates the position, posture, and size of the subject in the real world from his or her foot pressure distribution. Second, these estimates are used to create a 3-D stick model of the subject's skeleton. Third, the 3-D stick model is projected onto the camera image. This yields the initial estimation of the skeleton in the camera image. Fourth, the estimated skeleton is corrected by matching it to the edge images of the subject.

Our method is applicable to complicated scenes in which conventional methods that analyze only the image have problems because the subject's motion can be estimated from the foot pressure distribution, which does not depend on information contained in the image.

3. Sensor calibration

Calibration is necessary to determine the proper relation between foot pressure sensor coordinates and camera view. The coordinate system O-XYZ, defined from the base of the foot pressure sensor is used as the world coordinate system. The coordinate system O-$X_cY_cZ_c$ is defined from the lens center of the camera. The

1051-4651/00 $10.00 © 2000 IEEE

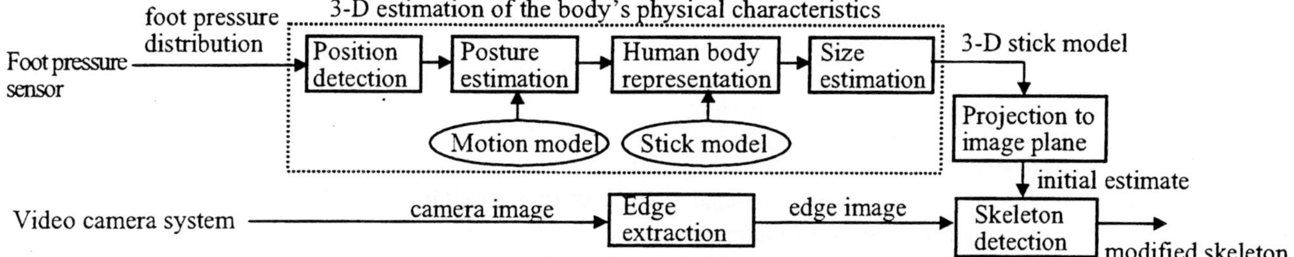

Figure 1: Proposed posture measurement system.

relationship between the two coordinate systems is given by the following equation.

$$[X_c\ Y_c\ Z_c]^T = \mathbf{R}\ [X\ Y\ Z]^T + \mathbf{t}, \quad (1)$$

where **R** and **t** are a 3×3 rotation matrix and translation vector respectively. The camera image can be expressed in the (u,v) plane to which the $X_cY_cZ_c$ space projects, and the relation is given by the following set of equations.

$$\begin{cases} u = (X_c/Z_c)\, f \\ v = (Y_c/Z_c)\, f, \end{cases} \quad (2)$$

where f is the focal distance of the camera. The rotation matrix can be calculated from the vanishing line detected from the rectangular outline of the foot pressure sensor in the camera image (see [10] for examples). The translation vector can be calculated from the position of the foot pressure sensor in the camera image.

4. Estimation of body characteristics

4.1 Position detection

The foot pressure distribution is expressed in the X-Y plane of the world coordinate system. Therefore, when the foot touches the ground, the position of the foot in the foot pressure distribution yields the position in world coordinates.

4.2 Posture estimation

There is no direct correspondence between foot pressure distribution and posture. In order to establish correspondence, we introduce the motion model. The posture change in walking and sport can be described using a state transition model because these motion are standardized movements. The motion model links the posture at each state to the state transition model. The posture is determined by distinguishing which state it is in motion model from the foot pressure distribution and by referring to the motion model.

For example, walking motion can be represented by the transition order of the following five states.

Heel contact: The heel touches the ground for the first time.

Heel strike: The heel is fully loaded.

Heel off: The heel lifts off the ground.

Kick up: The tip of the toe is fully loaded.

Toe off: The tip of the toe lifts off from the ground.

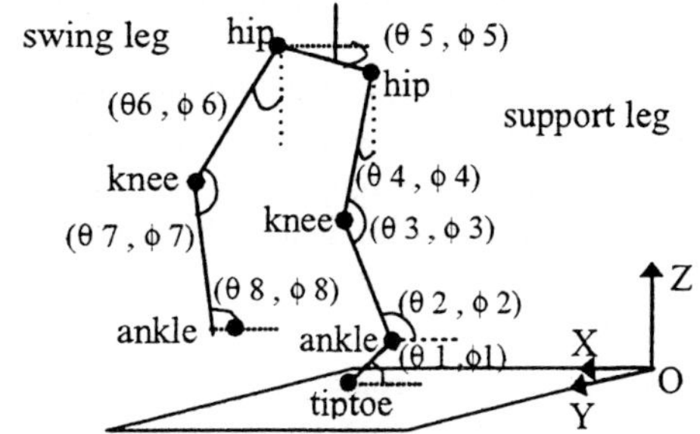

Figure2: Standard stick model and joint angles.

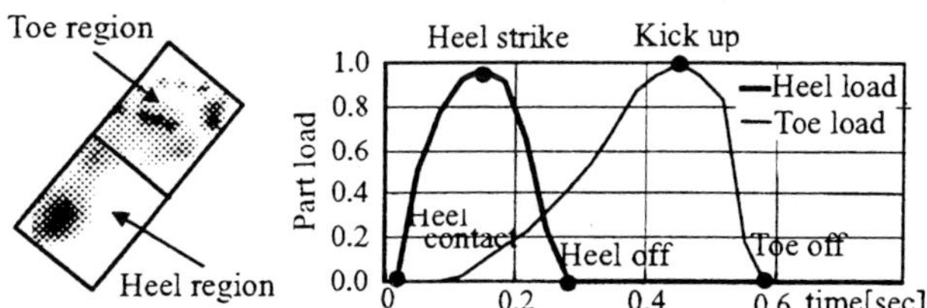

Figure 3: Relation between load and motion state.

Joint angles in each state are stored in a lookup table. The joint angles are θ_n and ϕ_n in Fig. 2. These angles can be previously measured values or the average of measured values of similar movements.

The state of motion at any time is distinguished from the foot pressure distribution. The footprint is extracted from the foot pressure distribution. The rectangle inscribing the foot region is detected and divided into 2 equal parts, the heel and toe regions as shown in Fig. 3. The total of the foot pressure values in each region is taken as the load carried by that particular region. The change in the load of each region distinguishes each state. Figure 3 shows an example of the data recorded for walking. The black marks in this figure show the load of the heel and toe regions in each state defined in walking motion model. It shows that each state of walking motion model can be distinguished by changes in the load of each region.

The times at which the motion states switch are detected using the relationship between motion state and the load of each region, and the posture at each time is estimated by referring to the motion model. Linear interpolation is used to determine the posture over the measurement period.

4.3 Stick model representation

The 3-D stick model is based on the estimated position and posture. The standard stick model shown in Fig. 2 is configured to match the estimated position and posture. The transformation starts with the leg supporting the load (support leg). The foot of the stick model is moved to the estimated position of the foot in the world coordinate system. Next, the knee and hip are moved to match the estimated joint angle. At heel off, the foot joint is added and the ankle is moved to match the foot joint angle from the position of the tip of the toe.

Next, the leg not supporting the load (swing leg) is transformed. The position of the swing leg hip joint is first determined from that of the support leg. The swing knee and ankle are then moved to match the estimated joint angle.

4.4 Size estimation

When both legs touch the ground, each leg can be independently positioned. Therefore, the position of the hip joint is determined from both legs. The scale of the stick model is chosen so that the angles between the right hip joint and left hip joint, θ_5 and ϕ_5 in Fig. 2, match the registered values.

5. Skeleton detection

The initial estimation of the skeleton is modified by referring to the edges in the camera image because the contours of the subject are directly visible in the edge image. The stick model in the world coordinates is projected onto the image plane by Eqs. 1 and 2. This yields the initial estimation of the skeleton. The estimate is then matched to the edges and modified. The matching process is as follows.

The system searches for points on an edge in the direction orthogonal to the estimated skeleton for point S_i (i=1, 2, ..., L) on the skeleton. In Fig. 4, P_1, P_2, P_3 and P_4 are detected. The pairs (P_j, P_k) that satisfy the next conditions are selected from detected edge points.

$$\begin{cases} | S_i - P_j | < W_{max} \\ | S_i - P_k | < W_{max} \\ W_{min} < | P_j - P_k | < W_{max} , \end{cases} \quad (3)$$

where | | represents the distance between two points in the image. W_{max} and W_{min} are the maximum and minimum widths of the body parts in the image respectively. The center point of selected pair is taken as a candidate point. All candidate points selected from S_i are plotted in the image. The straight line that best fits the candidate points for all S_i (i=1, 2,...,L) is detected by Hough Transformation. The initial skeletal position is modified to fit the straight line.

Occlusion is a problem for processing the rear leg in the image. It is possible to distinguish whether a skeleton part has been hidden by projecting the stick model onto

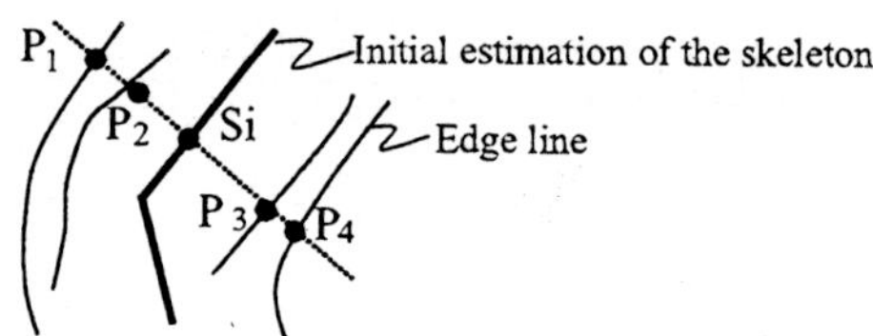

Figure 4: Skeleton detection using edge images.

the camera image. First, skeleton detection processing is carried out for the front part of the skeleton. Next, processing for the occluded part is carried out. This process uses the edge left after the edge of the front leg and its vicinity are removed (within region W_{max}).

6. Experimental results

We measured the posture of the lower human body in walking to evaluate the performance of our method.

6.1 Joint angles of walking motion model

The joint angles were for the walking motion model. Eight 20 year-old subjects conducted 11 trials each in which they walked naturally. Four video cameras were synchronized to a foot pressure sensor. The foot pressure sensor was 240 cm long and 44 cm wide and could record pressure at 5mm intervals (both directions) at 30 times per second. The five states of the walking motion model were distinguished from the foot pressure distribution, and the joint angles in each state were obtained from the stereo images captured by the 4 cameras. The average joint angles (averaged over the 88 trials) in each state were then stored in the walking motion model.

6.2 Results of skeletal position estimation

Data for ten trials was collected for each subject. Figure 5 shows an example of the initial estimation of the skeleton. Most of the estimate is located inside the legs. The accuracy of this estimation was evaluated by using the results of manual joint position identification. The results for the thigh and shin bones are shown in Fig.6. The results can be summarized as follows. The highest accuracy is for the shinbone of the support leg. An angle error of 7 degrees covers 90% of these cases. The lowest accuracy is for the shinbone of the swing leg. An angle error of 23 degrees covers 90% of these cases. This error is due to the wide latitude possible in foot movement after toe off. The accuracy for the thighbone doesn't change for either leg; an angle error of 10 degrees covers 90% of the cases. It should be noted that this high level of accuracy was only possible by starting with the foot pressure distribution, which does not depend on information contained in the images

6.3 Results of skeleton detection

Skeleton detection was carried out. Figure 7(a) shows an example of an edge image. Figure 7(b) shows the distribution of skeleton candidate points detected from

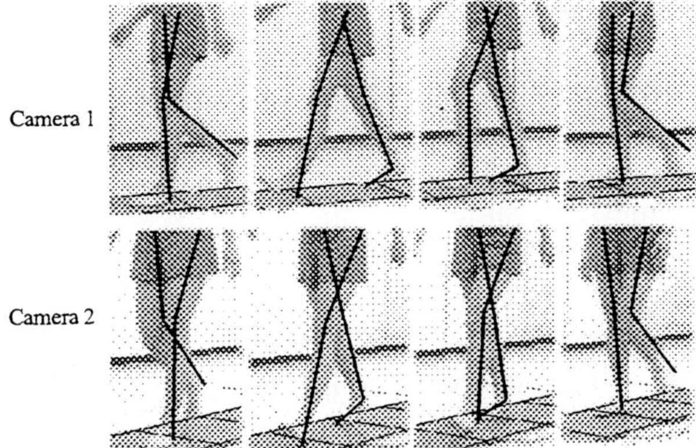

Figure 5: Initial estimation. The black lines show the initial estimate produced by the foot pressure distribution.

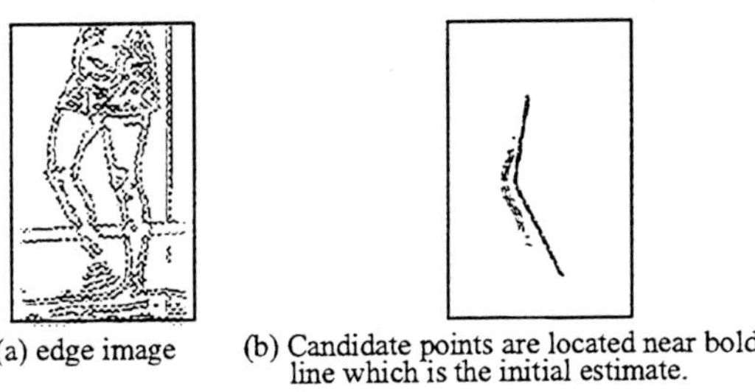

(a) edge image (b) Candidate points are located near bold line which is the initial estimate.

Figure 7: Example of edge image and candidate points.

this edge image and estimated skeleton. In this figure, the line on the right is the initially estimated skeletal position, and the plotted points show the candidate points. Fitting a straight line to the candidate points yields the correct skeleton. The result is shown in Fig. 8. We confirmed that the corrected skeleton lies at the center of the leg.

7. CONCLUSION

We developed an automatic posture measurement method that uses foot pressure distribution and video camera images. The position, posture and size of the human body in the real world are first estimated from his or her foot pressure distribution and then the skeleton is detected by matching the estimated results to the camera image. We described how to estimate posture from foot pressure distribution and how to modify the estimated skeletal position by using edge image.

Good results were confirmed in experiments on walking motion. We showed that posture could be estimated from the foot pressure distribution. Note that our method can accurately estimate spatial characteristics of the human body without using information contained in an image. This means that we can obtain an estimate of the skeleton's position without worrying about image noise in complicated scenes that may include multiple human bodies and/or background changes.

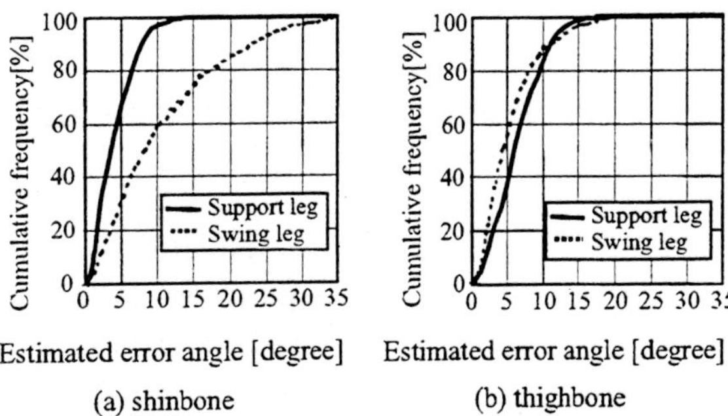

Figure 6: Estimated error angle for various joints.

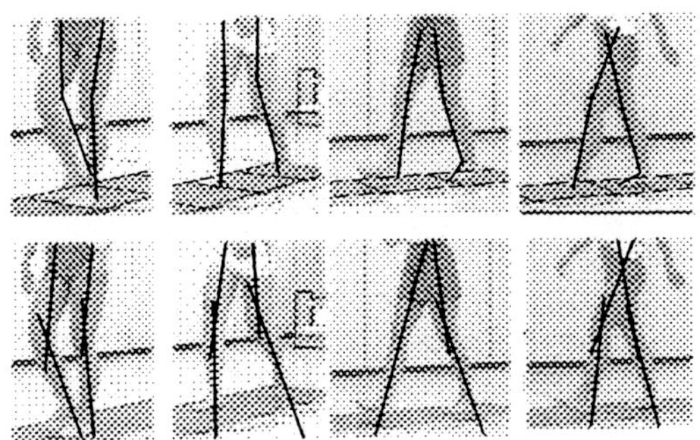

Upper: Initial stick figure skeleton, Lower: Modified skeleton.

Figure 8: Modified skeleton after matching to edge image.

References

[1] J. O'rourke and N. I. Badler. Model-based image analysis of human motion using constraint propagation. IEEE trans. PAMI, Vol. 2, No. 6, pp. 522-536, 1980.

[2] K. Akita. Image sequence analysis of real world human motion. Pattern Recognition. Vol. 17, No. 1, pp. 73-83, 1984.

[3] W. Long and Y. Yang. Stationary background generation: an alternative to the difference of two images. Pattern Recognition. Vol. 23, No. 23, pp. 1351-1359, 1990.

[4] J. Ohya and F. Kishino. Human posture estimation from multiple images using genetic algorithm. Proc. of ICPR, pp. 750-753, 1994.

[5] M. K. Leung and Y. yang. First Sight: A human body outline labeling system. IEEE trans. PAMI, Vol. 17, No. 4, pp. 359-377, 1995.

[6] M. Yamamoto, A. Sato and S. Kawada. Incremental tracking of human actions from multiple views. Proc. of CVPR, pp. 2-7, 1998.

[7] C.Bregler and J.Malik. Tracking people with twists and exponential maps. Proc. of CVPR, pp. 8-15, 1998.

[8] S. Iwasawa, K. Ebihara, J. Ohya and S. Morishima. Real-time estimation of human body posture from monocular thermal images. Proc. ICPR, pp. 15-20, 1997.

[9] S.Shimada, S.Ohtsuka, A.Tomono and M. Arai. A study on gait analysis system using large area tactile sensor. Technical Report of IEICE, MBE96-139, 1997 (in Japanese)

[10] R. O. Duda and P. E. Hart. Pattern classification and scene analysis. John Wiley & Sons, 1973.

Incremental Observable-Area Modeling for Cooperative Tracking

Norimichi Ukita Takashi Matsuyama
Department of Intelligence Science and Technology
Graduate School of Informatics, Kyoto University
Yoshidahonmachi, Sakyo, Kyoto, 606-8501 JAPAN
souhaku@vision.kuee.kyoto-u.ac.jp tm@i.kyoto-u.ac.jp

Abstract

In this paper, we propose an observable-area model of the scene for real-time cooperative object tracking by multiple cameras. The knowledge of partners' abilities is necessary for cooperative action whatever task is defined. In particular, for the tracking a moving object in the scene, every Active Vision Agent (AVA), a rational model of the network-connected computer with an active camera, should therefore know the area in the scene that is observable by each AVA. Each AVA should then decide its target object and gazing direction taking into account other AVAs' actions. To realize such a cooperative gazing, the system gathers all the observable-area information to incrementally generate the observable-area model at each frame during the tracking. Hence, the system cooperatively tracks the object by utilizing both the observable-area model and the object's motion estimated at each frame. Experimental results demonstrate the effectiveness of the cooperation among the AVAs with the help of the proposed observable-area model.

1. Introduction

This paper presents a real-time cooperative distributed vision (CDV, in short) system with multiple communicating *Active Vision Agents* (AVAs, in short)[1]. AVA is a rational model of the network-connected computer with an active camera. CDV system has many advantages (e.g. wide area observation, robustness by integrating multilateral information, flexibility of the system-organization, and compensation for troubles). In recent years, a number of related researches are, therefore, reported (see [2], for example). Various vision systems can be realized by employing CDV system. Above all, a object tracking system is one of the important basic technics for realizing applied systems (for example, autonomous surveillance and monitoring systems, ITS(Intelligent Transport System)).

In this paper, we put our focus upon the sharing knowledge of all the AVAs' abilities (i.e. observable area in the scene) for the efficient object tracking and scene observation. Our system incrementally acquire the observable-area information of each AVA, and enables AVAs to dynamically and appropriately changing their roles by taking into account all the AVAs' observable areas.

Experimental results demonstrate the effectiveness of the cooperation among AVAs with the proposed model.

2. Cooperative Tracking

2.1. Design of AVAs' behaviors while tracking

In our previous system(Sec. 5 in [1]), a group (we call an *agency*) of communicating AVAs cooperatively tracks a single object without being interfered by obstacles, where 1. each AVA possesses a Fixed-Viewpoint Pan-Tilt-Zoom (FV-PTZ, in short) camera, and 2. the external camera parameters (i.e. the 3D position of each camera) are calibrated.

The FV-PTZ camera allows us to generate background images taken with arbitrary combinations of the pan-tilt-zoom parameters from several images taken beforehand (Sec. 3 in [1]). An AVA can, therefore, detect an anomalous region by the background subtraction during widely observing the scene and adjusting the zoom. Thus the tracking by a single AVA is achievable by changing the gazing direction to the detected region in the image (Sec. 4 in [1])[1] .

With these resources, we designed the system as follows:

1. All AVAs search around for an object autonomously (Fig.1, 1.).
2. An AVA (denoted by AVA_m) detects an object, it regards this object as the target object and broadcasts the 3D view line (denoted by L_m) from the camera to the object. An agency is then formed(Fig.1, 2.).
3. Each AVA searches for the object along L_m after it receives the broadcasted message. If an AVA (denoted by AVA_w) detects an anomalous region, it replies to AVA_m the 3D view line (denoted by L_w) from the camera to the object (Fig.1, 3.).

[1] In order to apply this tracking method to the real-world system, the background subtraction method, that is robust for the illumination changes, the flicker of leaves and so on, is required. A lot of researches about this problem are reported (see [3], for example).

1051-4651/00 $10.00 © 2000 IEEE

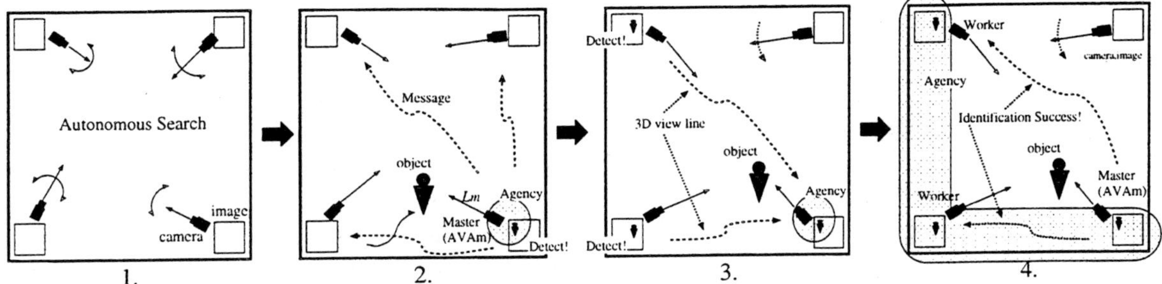

Figure 1. Object tracking system by multiple AVAs

4. AVA_m computes the distance between L_m and L_w. If the distance is less than the threshold, 1. the objects detected by AVA_m and AVA_w are considered as the same object, 2. the middle point between L_m and L_w is considered as the 3D position of the object. AVA_w is then joined into the agency, and engage in tracking the identified object.
5. AVA_m broadcasts the 3D position so that all AVAs gaze the identified object (Fig.1, 4.). The image-capturing timings are almost synchronized among all AVAs in one agency because the image-capturings are activated by the message from AVA_m.
6. Repetition of the object identification and the gaze navigation allows all AVAs to track the target object.
7. When all AVAs fail in tracking the object, they start searching for an object again.

AVA_m is called the master AVA and the other AVAs in the same agency are called the worker AVAs. The master authority is dynamically transfered to the worker AVA whose detected region of the target object is most reliable[2].

In accordance with the AVA's behavior mentioned above, all AVAs cooperatively keep gazing the object even if the 3D geometric configurations of the scene is not known *a priori*.

2.2. Problem of Gaze Navigation

In our previous system, all AVAs can keep tracking an object of interest through the compulsory gaze navigation by the master AVA. All the AVA, therefore, keep obeying the gaze navigation even if the AVA cannot observe the target object due to obstacles. This problem is caused by lack of the information on the 3D geometric configurations of the scene. The AVA cannot, therefore, know whether the target object is interfered by the obstacle or the object detection is a failure when no anomalous region is detected in the observed image. The AVA that cannot observe the target object due to obstacles, however, should change its role for increasing the efficiency of the whole system. For example, the following functions can be considered for such an AVA.

[2] The reliability is determined by 1. the size of the detected region in the image, 2. the distance from the image center to the detected region in the image, and 3. the distance from the object to the camera in the scene.

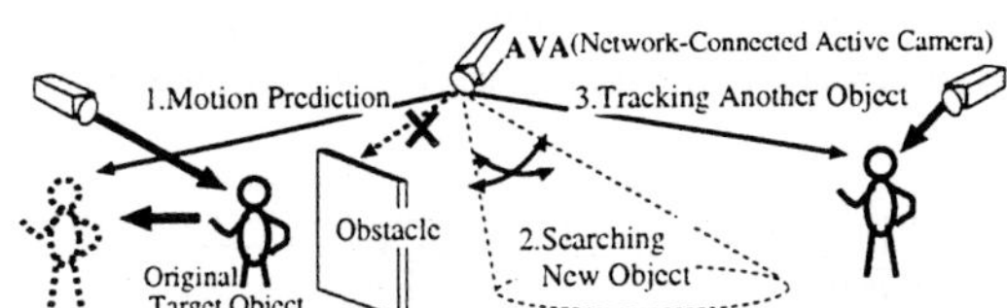

Figure 2. Dynamic role assignment to AVA

- The AVA predicts the position where the target object will appear within its observable area, then changes its gazing direction to ambush the object(Fig.2, 1.).
- The AVA gazes the area where none of the other AVAs observes to find another object(Fig.2, 2.).
- If the AVA can observe the target object of another agency[3], it joins this agency(Fig.2, 3.).

To solve the gaze navigation problem, we expand our previous system to identify each AVA's visible/invisible area in the scene and employs this information for the gaze navigation. In the proposed system, all the visible/invisible information is gathered as the *observable-area model* of the scene, and the master AVA assigns the appropriate role to each AVA by referring the observable-area model.

3. Observable-Area Model

3.1. Data Structure of Observable-Area Model

We adopt the octree representation[4] for the data structure of the observable-area model. We have the following advantages in employing the octree representation:

- The octree representation allows us to reduce the amount of data, since the visible/invisible area usually masses in the scene.
- Easiness of resizing cubes in the octree allows us to localize the resolution of the observable-area model.

In each cube in the octree, three kinds of the visible/invisible labels are attached to each AVA.

UNDEFINE The system has not identified whether or not the AVA can observe the area.

VISIBLE The AVA can observe the area.

INVISIBLE The AVA cannot observe the area.

[3] In the multiple object tracking system, one agency is formed for each tracking target.

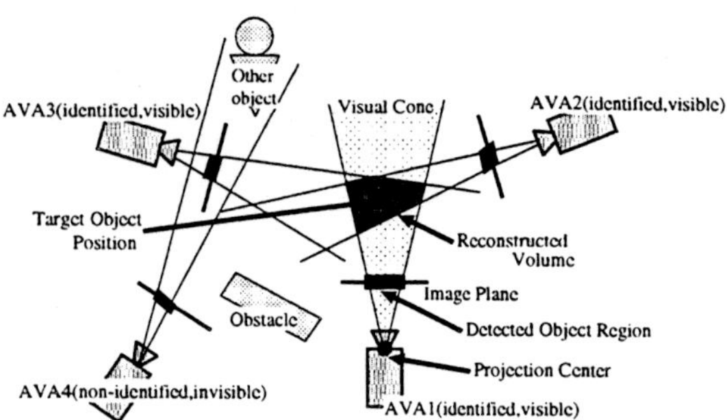

Figure 3. Reconstruction of the volume and generating the visible/invisible information

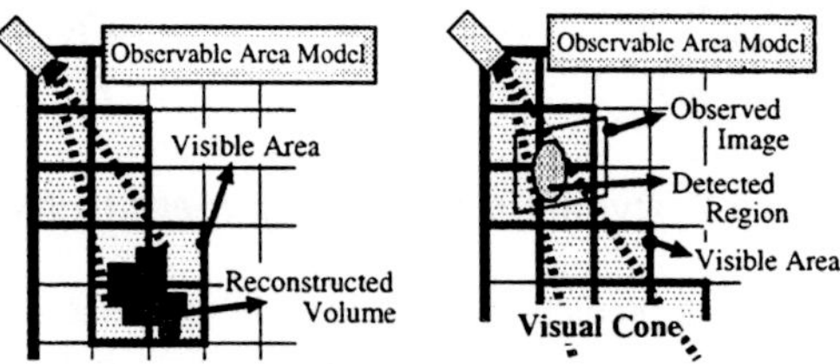

Figure 4. Visible area propagation (Left: CaseA, Right: Case B)

3.2. Generating Visible/Invisible Information

In our previous system[1], the object identification and 3D position reconstruction are realized by incorporating 3D view lines. In the proposed system, however, the master AVA computes the intersection of the visual cones, each of which is determined by the projection center of a camera and the detected region in the observed image. If the intersection exists, all the detected regions are considered as the same object. Moreover, the 3D position of the object can be obtained for the gaze navigation, since the computed intersection corresponds to the volume of the object.

If the image observed by AVA_w is actually used for the volume reconstruction, the system can then identify the area where the detected object exists to be visible from AVA_w. Otherwise, the area is identified to be invisible from AVA_w (Fig.3). The master AVA can, therefore, generate the visible/invisible information while tracking.

3.3. Generating Observable-Area Model

After a new visible/invisible information is obtained as mentioned in Sec.3.2, all the visible/invisible labels in the new information are respectively compared with those in the observable-area model to update the observable-area model. If the label in the new information is different from that in the cube whose position corresponds to the new information in the observable-area model, this cube is decomposed into octants. This decomposition is executed as long as the following two conditions are both satisfied.

1. The label in the new information and that in the observable-area model are different.
2. $\frac{distance}{focallength} < \frac{\text{constant}}{2^{depth}}$ ($distance$ is the length from the camera to the area, $focallength$ is the focal length of the camera and $depth$ is the depth of the octree.)

Since the resolution of the reconstructed volume of the object depends on $focallength$ and $distance$, the number of decomposition is defined by the above inequality.

After the decomposition, each cube is given the visible/invisible label. To the three kinds of labels, the following order of priority is applied in case of substituting the label for the cube.

$$\text{INVISIBLE} > \text{VISIBLE} > \text{UNDEFINE}$$

For example, VISIBLE and UNDEFINE are not recorded in the cube that has been identified as INVISIBLE. If all the labels of eight suboctants are the same, the suboctants are unified.

Moreover the visible information is propagated to facilitate generating the observable-area model. Two cases exist for the propagation of the visible area (Fig.4).

Case A The volume has been reconstructed.

Case B The volume has not been reconstructed.

In the case A, each cube corresponding to the reconstructed volume is identified to be visible. We can then identify the area between the object and the camera to be also visible from this camera if it can observe the object. The cubes between the object and the camera are ,therefore, updated as the visible area.

In the case B, the whole area included in the visual cone is updated as the temporary visible area except the area that has been already identified to be visible or invisible. Due to this function, there is a possibility of falsely attaching the temporary visible label to the area that is not yet estimated but actually invisible. To correct the observable-area model by the subsequent observation, the temporary visible label is updated when the area is identified as visible or invisible.

3.4. Control of Observable-Area Model

Since the observable-area model is made from the visible/invisible information which is generated by the master AVA, the master AVA can obtain the model by itself. Accordingly, the master AVA can refer the model immediately without increasing the load of the network. The master AVA, however, dynamically exchanges inside the agency for stabilizing the tracking. Thus, in proposed system, the master AVA delegates the following tasks to a model-control module, *observable-area model controller.*

- Keeping and updating of the observable-area model.
- Planning the appropriate roles of AVAs by referring the observable-area model.

This controller receives all the information from the master AVA at each frame to have the observable-area model.

The observable-area model controller assists the master AVA in improving the performance of the system.

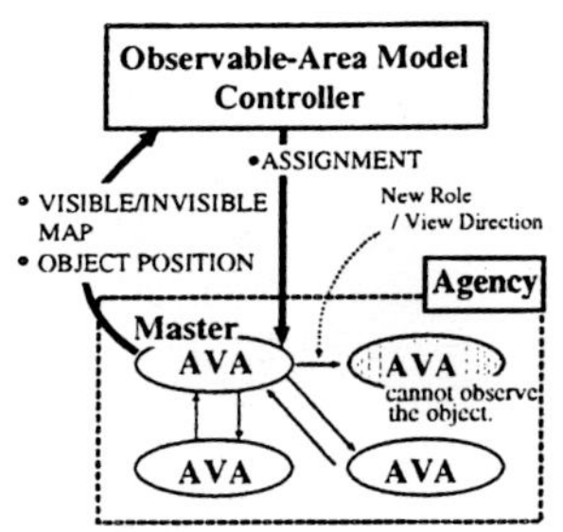

Figure 5. Message Flow

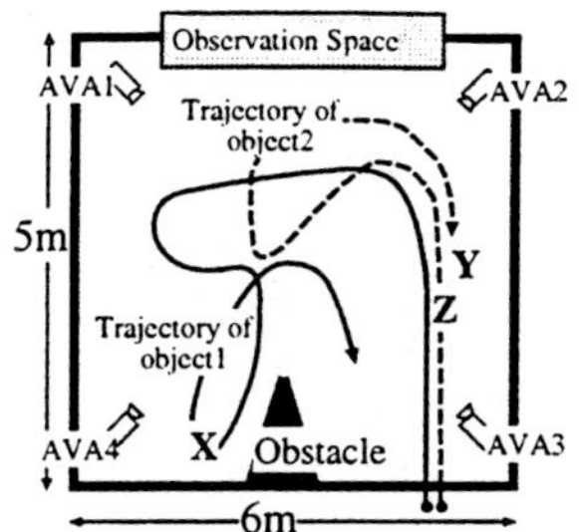

Figure 6. Experimental Environment

4. Cooperation with Observable-Area Model

This section addresses the communication protocol for 1. the updating of the observable-area model controller and 2. the role assignment to the AVA (Fig.5).

I. From AVA to Observable-Area Model Controller

At each frame, the master AVA transmits the following two messages to the observable-area model controller.

- **VISIBLE/INVISIBLE MAP** : The transmitted visible/invisible information for each AVA allows the observable-area model controller to update the observable-area model.
- **OBJECT POSITION** : The transmitted 3D position of the object allows the observable-area model controller to keep the object's motion trajectory.

II. From Observable-Area Model Controller to AVA

The observable-area model controller decides the role assignment to each AVA every after the updating of the model. If the model decides a new role assignment, the following message is transmitted to the master AVA.

- **ASSIGNMENT** : 1. The ID of the AVA that is assigned a new role, and 2. the details of the role, are included in the message.

The message is broadcasted because the master AVA dynamically exchanges, and accepted by only the master AVA. If master AVA receives ASSIGNMENT message and approve the effectiveness of the role assignment, the master AVA assigns the role to the AVA.

Since only the master AVA is allowed to order the worker AVAs, the system can avoid sending the different roles to one worker AVA at the same time.

5. Experimental Results

We experimented to verify the effectiveness of the proposed model for cooperative tracking. Our experimental results demonstrated the improvement in cooperation of the AVAs while tracking.

We conducted our experiments in the environment shown in Fig.6. Each AVA consists of a PC(PentiumIII 600MHz) and a FV-PTZ camera(SONY EVI-G20). In addition, all the PCs are connected by the Ethernet. Each camera is placed about 2.5m above the floor.

In this environment, object1 came into the observation space, and stayed for a while at the location X after moving along the trajectory. Note that AVA3 could not observe object1 when it was at the location X. Next, object2 moved along the trajectory and stopped at the location Y. After that, object1 started moving again.

Fig.7 shows an example of image sequences observed by AVA2 and AVA3. The size of each image is 320×240 $[pixel]$. The images from A1 to A14 and the images from B1 to B14 are respectively captured by AVA2 and AVA3 in the tracking without the observable-area model. The images from a1 to a14 and the images from b1 to b14, on the other hand, are respectively captured by AVA2 and AVA3 with the observable-area model. The enclosed regions with the white and black lines in the images indicate respectively the detected regions of object1 and object2. Each AVA captures the images at about 0.5 sec intervals on average.

Without the observable-area model, after searching (A1, A2 and B1, B2), AVAs detected object1 and regarded it as the target object, and then began to cooperatively track object1 (A3, A4 and B3, B4). However, AVA3 kept gazing at the direction of the 3D position of object1 transmitted from the master AVA, though AVA3 could not observe it due to the obstacle (from B5 to B13). The other AVAs, on the other hand, kept tracking object1 (from A5 to A14).

With the observable-area model, each AVA behaved in the same way as the cooperative tracking without the observable-area model (from a1 to a4 and from b1 to b4). AVA3 started, however, searching for another object (b7, b8) after AVA3 could not observe object1 (b5, b6). AVA3 then detected object2 at the location Z and started tracking it independently (b9, b10, b11, b12). Note that AVA2 modified the zoom parameter to acquire high resolution object images because each AVA could know that object1 stayed at the same place for a while through the message from the observable-area model controller (a9, a10). Note also that the gaze of AVA2 was directed toward object1 that was regarded as the target object even if AVA2 could also observe object2 (a11, a12). After that, when object1 started walking and became close to the area where AVA3 could observe, the observable-area model controller instructed the master AVA to change its gazing direction to object1 (b13). As a result, AVA3 changed its role, from independent tracking to cooperative tracking, and started again tracking object1 (b14). The visible/invisible area information for AVA3 is shown in Fig.8 where the two different views are illustrated. P and Q respectively indicate the visible and invisible area. Note that we see the obstacle area at R[4] .

[4] We can also estimate the 3D geometric information of the scene by integrating the observable-area information of each AVA.

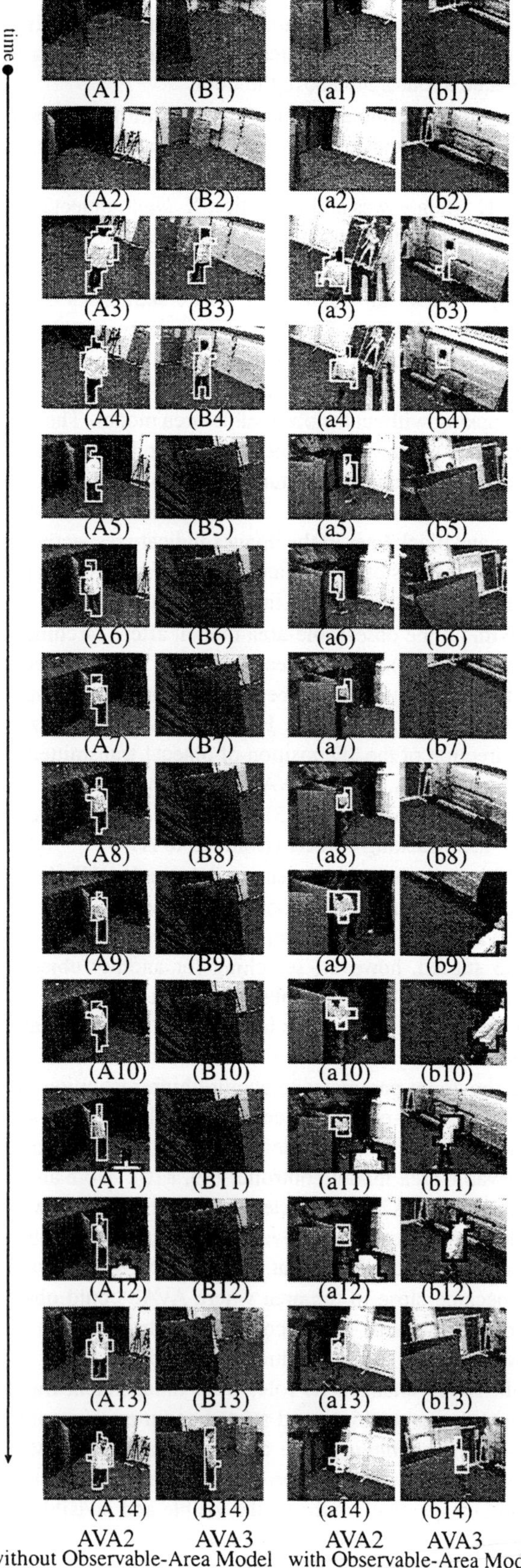

Figure 7. Partial Image sequences

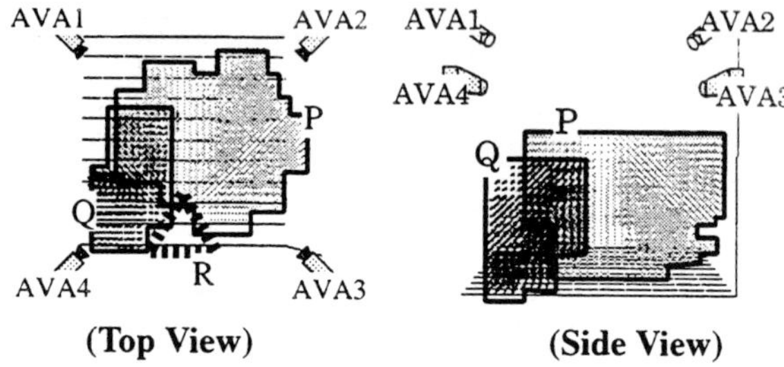

Figure 8. Acquired observable-area model

Comparing the experimental results of the two cases, we may conclude that the proposed model improves the effectiveness of cooperation in tracking.

6. Concluding Remarks

We proposed the incremental observable-area model for cooperative tracking. Our model allows a tracking system to assign the appropriate role to each AVA. We should note that the proposed model is evaluated by multi-agent systems with visual perception, however, the basic idea, i.e. the knowledge of partners' abilities are necessary for cooperation, is applicable to various types of multi-agent systems.

The proposed system is the expansion of our previous system[1] that tracks a single object. Thus the target object that is cooperatively tracked by multi-AVAs is a single, even if the AVA that is assigned a new role tracks another object independently. The flexible real-world system requires, however, the ability to track multi-target[5]. We are, therefore, now developing our system into multi-target tracking system by multi-agencies.

This work was supported by the Research for the Future Program of the Japan Society for the Promotion of Science (JSPS-RFTF96P00501).

References

[1] T. Matsuyama, "Cooperative Distributed Vision - Dynamic Integration of Visual Perception, Action and Communication -", Proc. of Image Understanding Workshop, pp. 365-384, 1998.

[2] T. Kanade, *et al.*, "Cooperative Multisensor Video Surveillance", Proc. of Image Understanding Workshop, pp. 3-10, 1997.

[3] C. Stauffer, E. Grimson, "Adaptive background mixture models for real-time tracking", Proc. of CVPR99, Vol.II, pp.246-252, 1999.

[4] N. Ahuja, J. Veenstra, "Generating Octrees from Object Silhouettes in Orthographic Views", IEEE Trans. on PAMI, Vol2, No.2, pp. 137-149, 1989.

[5] A. Nakazawa, H. Kato, S. Inokuchi., "Human Tracking Using Distributed Vision Systems", Proc. of 14th ICPR, pp.593-596, 1998.

Realtime 3D Depth Flow Generation and its Application to Track to Walking Human Being

Satoshi KAGAMI Kei OKADA Masayuki INABA Hirochika INOUE

Dept. of Mechano-Informatics, Univ. of Tokyo.
7-3-1, Hongo, Bunkyo-ku, Tokyo, 113-8656, Japan.
Email: {kagami, k-okada, inaba, inoue}@jsk.t.u-tokyo.ac.jp

Abstract

This paper proposes a 3D Depth Flow Generation method which measures 3D motion vector of every pixels between two time sequential images. First, definition of 3D Depth Flow, and simple method in order to generate 3D Depth Flow are denoted. Then implementation of realtime 3D Depth Flow Generation system using only PC, and experimental results are denoted. Finally, as an application, walking human tracking task using mobile robot is denoted.

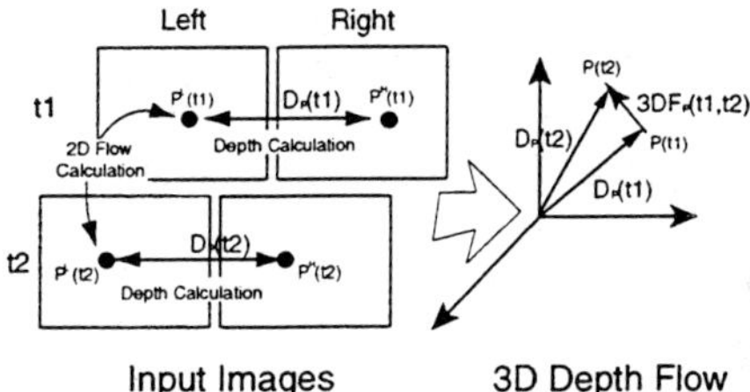

Figure 1. 3D Flow Vector Generation Method

1. Introduction

Real-time 3D Vision functions are fundamentally important for a robot that behaves in real-world. Recently, remarkable fast 3D depth map generation systems have been proposed in computer vision field (ex. [7,8]). However, computing the non rigid 3D motion of a scene is not so popular so far. For example, observing a walking human from a moving camera requires non rigid 3D motion reconstruction. There are several researches which solves this problem by taking non rigid 3D motion approach (ex. [6, 11] or with an assumption of the target (ex. [1, 10]). .

In order to solve this problem with no assumption of the target, the 3D Depth Flow is defined as 3D motion vector of every pixels within two image sequences. Each 3D vector contains not only motion component but also 3D position component. This 3D Flow is also a problem of search the corresponding points between two range images. However, range images does not contain much information for obtaining a correspondence.

Therefore, simple 3D flow generation method by combining depth map generation and 2D optical flow generation is proposed. The 2D optical flow is utilized as a correspondence calculation of every pixel of time sequential two images.

Then realtime 2D optical flow generation method by enhancing recursive correlation calculation method [3] and online consistency checking method by enhancing left-to-right right-to-left consistency checking method [2, 4] are denoted.

Finally as an application, realtime human tracking task using mobile robot by combining with 3D flow generation, realtime depth map generation and sonar system are denoted.

2. 3D Depth Flow

Following this paper, we assume that epipolar line along stereo cameras are horizontal. In this situation, a moving point $P(t)$ in time t is projected to the camera screen as $P^R(t), P^L(t)$ respectively (Fig.1), and $P^R(t)$ is denoted as $(x_P^R(t), y_P^R(t))$. In this situation, diparity D of designated point P is represented as follows, $D_P(t) = x_P^L(t) - x_P^R(t)$.

Then 3D Depth Flow is represented as follows:

$$D_P(t1) = x_P^L(t1) - x_P^R(t1)$$
$$3DF_P(t1, t2) = \begin{pmatrix} x_P^L(t2) - x_P^R(t1) \\ y_P^L(t2) - y_P^R(t1) \\ D_P(t2) - D_P(t1) \end{pmatrix} \quad (1)$$

1051-4651/00 $10.00 © 2000 IEEE

2.1. Simple 3D Depth Flow Generation Method

Simple 3D Depth Flow generation method is proposed by combining two time sequential depth image and optical flow between these images, since the first two elements of $3DF_P(t1, t2)$ of Equation.1 is same as 2D optical flow. Optical flow is used as for a correspondence each pixels of two images (Fig.1). Therefore simple 3D Depth Flow can be calculated as follows:

1. Search correspoding to $x_P^L(t1)$ in right image as $x_P^R(t1)$, and calculate $D_P(t1)$.
2. Search correspoding to $x_P^L(t2)$ in next left image as $x_P^L(t2)$.
3. Search correspoding to $x_P^L(t2)$ in right image as $x_P^R(t2)$, and calculate $D_P(t2)$.
4. 3D Depth Flow can be calculated from above four points as a set of $D_P(t1)$ and $3DF_P(t1, t2)$.

2.2. Real-time 3D Flow Generation System

In order to develop a real-time onbody 3D Flow generation system, four key issues are adopted : 1) 1D & 2D recursive correlation calculation method, 2) cache optimization, 3) applying MMX multimedia instruction set, and 4) online consistency checking method. Then system evaluation and experiments are denoted in section 5. Finally, application for walking human tracking are denoted in section 6.

3. 1D & 2D Recursive Correlation Calculation

3.1. 1D Recursive Correlation Calculation

Correspondence calculation of every pixel from one image to another is required to generate depth map. In this paper, we assume that epipolar line is horizontal, thus no horizontal disparity occurs for a correspondent two image region. To calculate a correspondence, correlation technique is applied for example as shown in Equation.2.

$$
\begin{aligned}
O(x, y) &= \min_d\{C_1(x, y, d)\} \\
C_1(x, y, d) &= \sum_{i,j}\{|I_1(x+i, y+j) - I_2(x+d+i, y+j)|\}
\end{aligned}
\tag{2}
$$

In Equation.2, $I(x, y)$ shows intensity of pixel (x, y), $\{x, y|0 \le x, y < N\}$. Window size of correlation is $W \times W$, and $\{i, j|0 \le i, j < W\}$. Furthermore, disparity d is $\{d|0 \le d < D\}$. Introducing recursive correlation technique [3], total computational order is known to be changed from $O(N^2W^2D)$ to $O(N^2D)$ by reducing a redundancy. Set disparity of each pixel $O(x, y)$ and SAD (Sum of Absolute Difference) value of disparity d is set to $C_1(x, y, d)$. Set $P(x, y, d)$ as a difference of two pixels with disparity d. $C_1(x, y, d)$ is calculated recursively as follows:

$$
\begin{aligned}
P(x, y, d) &= |I_1(x, y) - I_2(x+d, y)| \\
Q(x, 0, d) &= \textstyle\sum_j P(x, j, d) \\
Q(x, y+1, d) &= Q(x, y, d) \\
&\quad + P(x, y+W, d) - P(x, y, d) \\
C_1(0, y, d) &= \textstyle\sum_i Q(i, y, d) \\
C_1(x+1, y, d) &= C_1(x, y, d) \\
&\quad + Q(x+W, y, d) - Q(x, y, d)
\end{aligned}
\tag{3}
$$

3.2. 2D Recursive Correlation Calculation

So far, since 2D optical flow generation requires high computation performance, hardware approach have been proposed to generate 2D optical flow [5,9]. These hardwares enable to calculate fast 2D optical flow. However, we enhanced one dimensional recursive correlation algorithm to two dimensions in order to calculate optical flow. This approach has two advantages, one is no special hardware required, and the second is consistency checking method or other method can be easily adopted in order to omit occluded or mismatched region. In this time, total computational order is changed from $O(N^2W^2D^2)$ to $O(N^2D^2)$ by reducing a redundancy.

$$
\begin{aligned}
O(x, y) &= \min_{k,l}\{N(x, y, k, l)\} \\
C_2(x, y, k, l) &= \sum_{i,j}\{|I_1(x+i, y+j) - I_2(x+i+k, y+j+l)|\}
\end{aligned}
\tag{4}
$$

In Equation.4, search area l, k is $\{l, k|0 \le l, k < D\}$. As shown above, set flow vector of each pixel as $O(x, y)$ and set SAD value of disparity l, k as $C_2(x, y, l, k)$. Same as one dimensional recursive correlation, $P, Q1, Q2, C_2$ is shown as below.

$$
\begin{aligned}
P(x, y, k, l) &= |I_1(x, y) - I_2(x+k, y+l)| \\
Q1(x, 0, k, l) &= \textstyle\sum_j P(x, j, k, l) \\
Q1(x, y+1, k, l) &= Q1(x, y, k, l) \\
&\quad + P(x, y+W, k, l) - P(x, y, k, l) \\
Q2(0, y, k, l) &= \textstyle\sum_i P(i, y, k, l) \\
Q2(x+1, y, k, l) &= Q2(x, y, k, l) \\
&\quad + P(x+W, y, k, l) - P(x, y, k, l) \\
C_2(0, y, k, l) &= \textstyle\sum_i Q1(i, y, k, l) \\
C_2(x, 0, k, l) &= \textstyle\sum_j Q2(x, j, k, l) \\
C_2(x+1, y+1, k, l) &= C_2(x, y, k, l) \\
&\quad + Q1(x+W, y, k, l) - Q1(x, y, k, l) \\
&\quad + Q2(x, y+W, k, l) - Q2(x, y, k, l) \\
&\quad + P(x, y, k, l) + P(x+W, y+W, k, l) \\
&\quad - P(x+W, y, k, l) - P(x, y+W, k, l)
\end{aligned}
\tag{5}
$$

Table 1. Calculation Time : a) Correlation, b) Recursive Correlation Method, c) Cache Optimal Correlation, d) Adopt MMX Instructions

	PentiumIII-500MHz			
	Depth map Generation		2D Flow Generation	
	WithCC	WithoutCC	WithCC	WithoutCC
a)	5,332.7	2,594.5	1,928.7	903.5
b)	66.5	51.2	78.3	63.6
c)	41.9	34.0	40.9	31.5
d)	32.6	23.6	25.4	18.6

(msec)

(N=128, W=15, D=20 in Depth map Generation, and N=64, W=16, D=8 in 2D Optical Flow Generation)

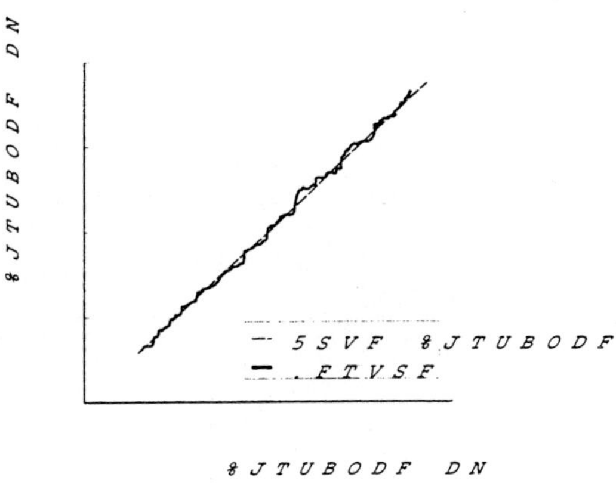

Figure 2. Measurement Experiment in Depth Direction

4. Avoiding an Occluded or Mismatched Region

Stereo matching and optical flow matching have an occlusion problem from its principle. From an correlation calculation, the best matching region is obtained according to each small region, but there exists no matching region is found in case of occlusion or no features exists. Therefore, unreliable matching can be obtained using only from correlation calculation. There are many methods are proposed to obtain reliable matching. In this paper, consistency checking method [2, 4] are adopted.

4.1. Online Consistency Check inside Recursive Correlation Loop

The consistency checking method can be implemented inside loop of recursive correlation calculation, so that no additional memory consumption is needed. Once $C_1(x, y, d)$ of Equation.2 is calculated locally, first two steps of consistency checking can be calculated simultaneously, then the third step calculates O(x,y). Therefore, consistency checking can be implemented inside "x" loop of and computational time augments only about 20–30%.

5. Experiments

All experiments are executed on PentiumIII-500MHz with 100MHz external bus clock, with Linux 2.2.10. All programs are written in C and in inline assembler, and are compiled using GCC-2.7.2.3. Calculation time is measured by using RDTSC instruction. Frame grabber is BT848 based PCI board, and it transmits every image into main memory by DMA transfer, and program can obtain the input image after one frame latency.

5.1. Accuracy and Resolution

Fig.2 shows the true and measured distance in depth direction with N = 128, and with viewing angle is 53.8deg. In this case, accuracy is about 1cm in 1m. In order to fit vertical resolution along with depth resolution, N = 64 for 2D optical flow is adopted.

5.2. Execution Time

Table 1 shows calculation time of Equation.2 and Equation.4 with and without consistency checking. Both depth map generation and 2D optical flow generation with consistency checking satisfy frame rate. Thus, dual-PentiumIII-500MHz can generate 3D Flow of 64 × 64 in real-time.

5.3. 3D Flow Generation

Fig.3 shows original images in upper row, depth images in middle row and 2D/3D flow images in lower row. Obtained 3D Flow shows that the right person moves toward front right direction.

6. Walking Human Tracking Application

Given 3D Depth Flow, walking human tracking task is implemented on a mobile robot. The robot is controlled from the obtained relative 3D Depth Flow, which can be calculated by canceling its own motion. Then the robot can smoothly track the target by avoiding an obstacle in the environment without lose track of the target. In case of the target turn back, a detected target motion vector attains robot future position which is estimated from the current position and current motion vector, robot starts avoiding to not disturb the human motion.

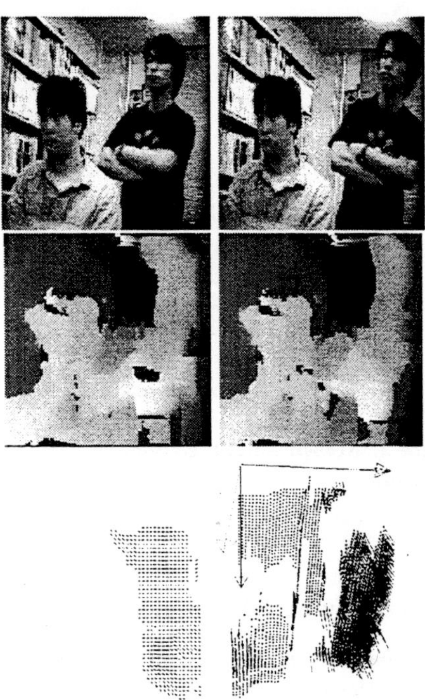

Figure 3. Experiment : i) Original image(t0), ii) Original image(t1), iii) Depth image(t0), iv) Depth image(t1), v) 2D optical flow(t1-t0), vi) 3D Depth Flow image(t1-t0)

7. Conclusion

In this paper, 3D Depth Flow definition and simple 3D flow generation method based on the combination of depth map generation and 2D optical flow generation, are denoted. The 3D Depth Flow enables camera to detect moving object while camera is also moving. This function will be fundamentally important for a robot which moves in human world.

In order to achieve real-time onboard system, four key issues are adopted : 1) 1D & 2D recursive correlation calculation method, 2) cache optimization, 3) applying MMX multimedia instruction set, and 4) online consistency checking. The real-time 3D Flow implementation and its experiments are also denoted.

As an application of 3D flow could be 1) for a robot which "runs" in human walking environment, 2) for a robot which "physically contacts" to the moving humans, 3) for a legged robot of which views are vibrating while it is walking, and so on. We believe this 3D flow will open a new world for a vision based mobile robot.

Acknowledgments

This research has been supported by Grant-in-Aid for Research for the Future Program of the Japan Society for the Promotion of Science, "Research on Micro and Soft-Mechanics Integration for Bio-mimetic Machines (JSPS-RFTF96P00801)" project and several grants of Grant-in-Aid for Scientific Research.

References

[1] D. Beymer and K. Konolige. Detection and Tracking of People using Stereo and Correlation . In *Proceedings of IEEE International Conference on Computer Vision*, 1999.

[2] R. Bolles and J. Woodfill. Spatiotemporal Consistency Checking of Passive Range Data. In T. Kanade and R. Paul, editors, *Robotics Research: The Sixth International Symposium*, pages 165–183. International Foundation for Robotics Research, 1993.

[3] O. Faugeras, B. Hots, H. Mathieu, T. Viéville, Z. Zhang, P. Fua, E. Théron, L. Moll, G. Berry, J. Vuillemin, P. Bertin, and C. Proy. Real time correlation-based stereo: algorithm, implementations and applications. Technical Report N°2013, INRIA, 1993.

[4] P. Fua. A Parallel Stereo Algorithm that Produces Dense Depth Maps And Preserves Images Features. In *Machine Vision and Applications*, pages 35–49, 1991.

[5] H. Inoue, T. Tachikawa, and M. Inaba. Robot Vision System with a Correlation Chip for Real-time Tracking, Optical Flow and Depth Map Generation. In *Proc. IEEE International Conference on Robotics and Automation*, pages 1621–1626, 1992.

[6] S. KAGAMI, K. OKADA, M. INABA, and H. INOUE. Real-time 3d optical flow generation system. In *Proc. of International Conference on Multisensor Fusion and Integration for Intelligent Systems (MFI'99)*, pages 237–242, 1999.

[7] T. Kanade, A. Yoshida, K. Oda, H. Kano, and M. Tanaka. A Stereo Machine for Video-rate Dense Depth Mapping and Its New Applications. In *Proc. of the 1996 International Conference on Computer Vision and Pattern Recognition*, pages 196–202, Jun 1996.

[8] K. Konolige. Small Vision Systems: Hardware and Implementation. In Y. Shirai and S. Hirose, editors, *Robotics Research: The Eighth International Symposium*, pages 203–212. Springer, 1997.

[9] T. Morita, N. Sawasaki, T. Uchiyama, and M. Sato. Color Tracking Vision System. In *Proc. of 14th Annual Conference of Robotics Society of Japan*, volume 1, pages 279–280, 1996.

[10] R. Okada, Y. Shirai, J. Miura, and Y. Kuno. Tracking a Person with 3-D Motion by Integrating Optical Flow and Depth (In Japanese). *Trans. of the Institute of Electronics, Information and Communication Engineers*, J82-D-II(8):1252–1261, Aug. 1999.

[11] S. Vedula, S. Baker, P. Rander, R. Collins, and T. Kanade. Three-Dimensional Scene Flow. In *Proc. IEEE International Conference on Computer Vision*, pages 722–729, 1999.

A Calibration-Free Gaze Tracking Technique*

Sheng-Wen Shih and Yu-Te Wu
Department of Computer Science
and Information Engineering
National Chi Nan University, 545, Taiwan
(stone and ytw)@csie.ncnu.edu.tw

Jin Liu
Heinrich-Hertz Institute Berlin,
10587 Berlin, Germany
liu@hhi.de

Abstract

We propose a novel method to estimate and track the 3-D line of sight of a person based on 3-D computer vision techniques. Most of the existing nonintrusive gaze tracking methods share a common drawback: users have to perform certain experiments in calibrating the user-dependent parameters before using the gaze tracking systems. These parameters are functions of the radius of the cornea, the position of the pupil, the position of user's head, etc.. Our approach, in contrast, employs multiple cameras and multiple point light sources to estimate the light of sight without using any of the user-dependent parameters. As a consequence, the users can avoid the inconvenient calibration process which may produce possible calibration errors. Computer simulations have been performed to confirm the proposed method.

1. Introduction

When we stare at a 3-D point, our oculomotor mechanism controls our eyes such that the image of the point appears at the fovea region of our eyes. The 3-D LoS (*Line of Sight*) of the eye is a straight line which passes through the 3D point, the fovea spot and the optical center of the eye. The problem of 3-D gaze tracking is to determine and track the 3-D LoS of a person from the appearance of his eyes and has numerous applications in the area of human computer interaction. For example, we can use the gaze point of a man to develop a more efficient interface in controlling computers than the traditional mouse. There are basically three types of gaze tracking techniques: (1) techniques based on reflected light [1] [2] [3], (2) techniques based on electric skin potential [4], and (3) techniques based on contact lenses [5]. Techniques of the first type is nonintrusive including limbus tracker, pupil tracker, pupil and cornea reflection tracker, and Purkinje image tracker. The techniques of the second and the third types are intrusive and will not be discussed in this paper. Most of the existing nonintrusive gaze tracking methods using light reflected by different portion of the eye (such as the cornea, the lens, the iris, and the retina) share the common drawback: the users are asked to perform tedious calibration of user-dependent parameters before using the gaze tracking systems. Moreover, most of the methods focused on monocular (2-D) vision techniques and imposed stringent constraints to simplify the 3-D gaze tracking problem into a 2-D problem. These constraints require the user to hold their head quite still or the apparatus to be fixed relative to the user's head.

In this paper, we propose a novel method to resolve the user-dependent calibration problem and estimate the 3-D line of sight based on 3-D computer vision techniques. The estimation theory developed in this work is based on the simplified eye model proposed by Le Grand [6]. We show that the line of sight of a user can be directly measured by using multiple cameras and point light sources without using any user-dependent parameters. Therefore, the proposed system is *calibration-free to the users.*

Our method first uses the first Purkinje images of point light sources to determine the location of the eye by using multiple cameras (refer to section 2). The estimated 3-D position of the eye and the observed centers of the pupil images are then used to compute the gaze direction of the eye (refer to section 3).

2. Computing Cornea Center From the First Purkinje Image

It is well known that when a beam of light enters a surface that separates two media, part of the light is reflected by the surface and part of the light is refracted after traveling through the surface. The light which is reflected by the exterior cornea surface is called the first Purkinje image (See Figure 1(a)). Note that, since the first Purkinje image is the result of specular reflection, observers at different direction

*This work is supported in part by the National Science Council of Taiwan under Grants NSC 87-2218-E-260-003.

1051-4651/00 $10.00 © 2000 IEEE

will observe different images. Figure 1(b) shows the first Purkinje image of an infrared LED (Light Emitting Diode). LEDs are commonly used as the point light sources in gaze tracking systems since it is safe and cost effective.

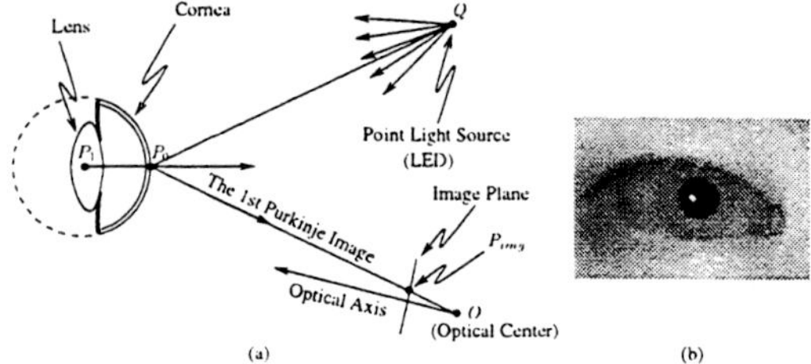

Figure 1. The first Purkinje image of an LED.

Let O denote the optical center of a camera and Q denote the position of a point light source. Let us assume that the camera parameters and the position of point light source relative to the camera reference frame, denoted by $\overrightarrow{OQ}$, have been accurately calibrated (the calibration process is irrelevant to the users). Given the 2-D point of the first Purkinje image in the retinal plane, denoted by P_{img}, and the calibrated optical center of the camera, O, we can compute the 3-D vector $\overrightarrow{OP_{img}}$ (see Figure 1).

According to the law of reflection, the location of the point light source, the beams of incident and the reflected light and the normal vector of the reflected surface are coplanar. That is, both the normal vector, $\overrightarrow{P_1P_0}$, and the cornea center, P_1, are on the plane QP_0O

Based on the location of the point light source and its first Purkinje image recorded by a camera, a linear constraint for computing the location of the cornea center can be formulated by the following plane equation in the camera coordinate system:

$$s \cdot k_c = 0, \tag{1}$$

where the normal vector s of the planar surface P_0OQ is the cross-product of $\overrightarrow{OP_{img}}$ and $\overrightarrow{OQ}$ and $k_c = \overrightarrow{OP_1}$ is the vector representing cornea center. If there are N point light sources, $Q_i, i =, 1, 2, ..., N$ and N identified Purkinje images for every point light sources, we will have N plane equations with the form of equation (1). However, the solution of these plane equations is not unique. The following proposition summarize this property.

Proposition 1. *If the optical center of a camera, O, and a set of the point light sources, Q_i's, are not collinear, then the solutions to the plane equations in the form of equation (1) is a 3-D line.*

Proof. It is obvious that the plane equations is not of full rank because all the planes contains both the optical center of the camera, O, and the cornea center, k_c. Furthermore, if there exists two point light sources, Q_i and Q_j, such that $\overrightarrow{OQ_i}$ and $\overrightarrow{OQ_j}$ are not collinear, then $s_i = \overrightarrow{OP_{img,i}} \times \overrightarrow{OQ_i}$ and $s_j = \overrightarrow{OP_{img,j}} \times \overrightarrow{OQ_j}$ are not collinear; hence, the rank of the plane equations is two. □

It follows from Proposition 1 that if the cornea radius, ρ, of the user is unknown, gaze tracking systems using one camera can only determine the 3-D direction instead of the 3-D position of the cornea center with respect to the camera reference coordinates. The condition for obtaining a unique solution for the cornea center when the cornea radius is unknown is summarized in the following proposition:

Proposition 2. *If the cornea radius, ρ, is unknown, then one will have to use at least two cameras and at least two point light sources to recover the 3-D position of the cornea center. Furthermore, in order to provide unique solution for the 3-D cornea center, any of the optical centers of the cameras and the point light sources should not be collinear.*

Proof. According to Proposition 1, a 3-D line which contains the optical center of the camera and the cornea center in the camera reference frame can be determined by using a camera and at least two point light sources, where the optical center of the camera and the point light sources are not collinear. When we have two cameras and two point light sources satisfying the non-collinear conditions, we obtain two 3-D line equations; one line passes through the optical center of one camera and through the cornea center and the other line passes through the optical center of the other camera and through the cornea center. If the optical centers of the two cameras do not coincide with each other, these two lines intersect at one point, i.e., the location of the cornea center. □

3. Orientation of the 3-D Line of Sight

3.1. Virtual Image of the 3-D Pupil

Our pupil is located inside a convex lens composed of the cornea and the aqueous humor. Due to the refraction of the convex lens, any object point, P, inside the cornea has a virtual image, P', when it is viewed from an outside camera. For example, it is the virtual image of a pupil, not the pupil itself, that is observed from a camera.

To derive the relation between the location of the real object point and the location of its virtual image, we define an auxiliary 3-D coordinate system with origin at the cornea center, x-axis is parallel to $-k_c$, and its x-y plane contains the optical axis of the eye (see Figure 2). Note that the optical axis of the eye is unknown at this moment. The estimation method for the optical axis of the eye, which does not involve the definition of the auxiliary 3-D coordinate system, will be discussed in the next subsection.

Suppose that the angle between the pupil normal and the x-axis is ϕ, that the radius of the pupil is r_p, and that distance between the cornea center and the pupil center is d.

The 3-D coordinates of the pupil circular edges can be defined as follows:

$$\begin{pmatrix} p_x \\ p_y \\ p_z \end{pmatrix} = \begin{pmatrix} d\cos(\phi) - r_p\cos(\theta)\sin(\phi) \\ d\sin(\phi) + r_p\cos(\theta)\cos(\phi) \\ r_p\sin(\theta) \end{pmatrix}, \quad (2)$$

where $\theta \in [0,\ 2\pi]$. The coordinates of the virtual pupil image can be computed based on basic geometric optics, and the derived coordinates of the virtual pupil image are given by

$$P_{vp} = \left[\rho - \frac{n'l}{R \cdot l + n} \quad m \cdot p_y \quad m \cdot p_z\right]^t, \quad (3)$$

where $l = \rho - p_x$, $R = \left|\frac{n'-n}{\rho}\right|$, $m = \frac{n}{R \cdot l+n}$, n is the refraction index of the cornea, and $n' \approx 1$ is the refraction index of the air.

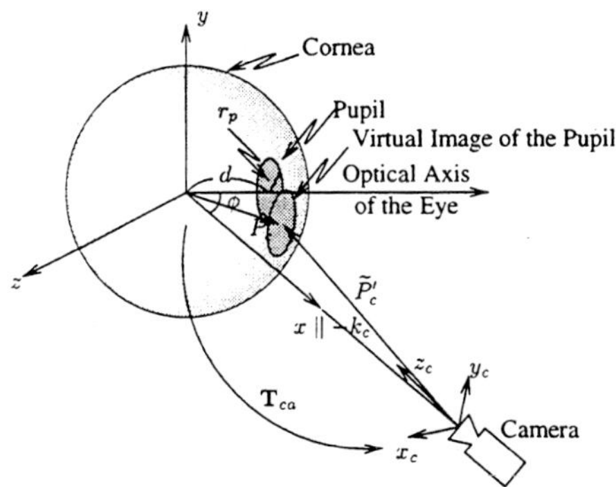

Figure 2. The auxiliary 3-D coordinate system located at the cornea center.

It can be shown that the virtual image of the pupil is still a planar object, and the center of the virtual pupil can be determined by setting r_p to zero in P_{vp}

$$P'_c = \lim_{r_p \to 0} P_{vp} \quad (4)$$

Likewise, when r_p is set to zero in equation (2), we obtain the center of the real pupil, $P_c = [d\cos(\phi)\ d\sin(\phi)\ 0]^t$, which is on the x-y plane of the auxiliary 3-D coordinate system, and the center of the virtual pupil image shown in equation (4) is also on the x-y plane (because $\lim_{r_p \to 0} m \cdot p_z = 0$). It follows that P_c, P'_c *and the x-axis of the auxiliary 3-D coordinate system are coplanar.*

Suppose that the 3-D virtual image of the pupil is recorded on a 2-D image by a camera and that from the recorded image, the edge points of the 2-D pupil image are found to be p_i, $i = 1, 2, ..., N$. Because the center of the 3-D virtual pupil image is invisible, its 2-D image location, denoted by p'_c, can only be inferred by using p_i's. Estimation of p'_c using p_i is a difficulty problem because of the nonlinearity of the perspective projection. However, since the radius of the virtual pupil image is very small compared with the distance between the eye and the gaze tracking cameras, affine projection can be used to accurately describe the relationship between the 3-D virtual pupil image and its projected 2-D pupil image. The image location of the virtual pupil image center, p'_c, can be determined by $\hat{p}'_c = \frac{1}{N}\sum_{i=1}^{N} p_i$ owing to the linearity of affine projection. After the image location of the virtual pupil image center is determined, we shall discuss the estimation of the orientation of the LoS in the following subsections.

3.2. Linear Constraint for the Direction of LoS

Because each camera can record only one pupil image, to determine the 3-D position of P_c without knowing the values of n and d, we will have to use at least two cameras and will need the following proposition.

Proposition 3. *Suppose that a gaze tracking system equipped with at least two cameras has been calibrated so that the transformation matrices between any two reference frames of the cameras are known. If the cornea center, k_c, is estimated by using the method described in section 2, the 3-D coordinates of k_c with respect to the ith camera reference frame coordinates, denoted by k_{ci}, can be computed with the calibrated transformation matrices. Let the direction of the center of the virtual pupil image in the ith camera reference frame be denoted by $\widetilde{P}'_{ci}$ which can be estimated by back-projecting $\hat{p}'_{ci}$ into the 3-D space. Given two pairs of $\widetilde{P}'_{ci}$'s and k_{ci}'s, for $i \in \{i_1,\ i_2\}$, where $\widetilde{P}'_{ci}$ and k_{ci} are not collinear, the gaze direction, defined by the vector pointing from the cornea center toward the real pupil center, can be determined by solving linear equations.*

Proof. Recall that k_{ci}, $\widetilde{P}'_{ci}$ and $\widetilde{P}_{ci}$ are coplanar, where $\widetilde{P}_{ci}$ is the 3-D vector of the gaze direction in the ith camera reference frame. If $\widetilde{P}'_{ci}$ and k_{ci} are not collinear for $i \in \{i_1,\ i_2\}$, then we can define two planar equations: $\left(k_{ci_1} \times \widetilde{P}'_{ci_1}\right)^t \widetilde{P}_{ci_1} = 0$, and $\left(k_{ci_2} \times \widetilde{P}'_{ci_2}\right)^t \mathbf{R}_{i_2,i_1} \widetilde{P}_{ci_1} = 0$, where $\mathbf{R}_{i_2,i_1}$ is the relative orientation matrix between camera reference frames i_1 and i_2. These two equations are linear dependent when $\mathbf{R}_{i_2,i_1}\widetilde{P}'_{ci_1}$, $k_{ci_2} = \mathbf{R}_{i_2,i_1} k_{ci_1}$, and $\widetilde{P}'_{ci_2}$ are coplanar. In this singular case, $\widetilde{P}_{ci_1}$ is coplanar with both $\mathbf{R}^{-1}_{i_2,i_1} \widetilde{P}'_{ci_2}$ and $\widetilde{P}'_{ci_1}$, i.e., the user is fixating at a point of the line connecting the optical centers of the two cameras. Otherwise, the direction of $\widetilde{P}_{ci_1}$ can be determined by solving the above two planar equations. □

4. Simulation Results

In the computer simulation, we assumed that a pair of stereo cameras were used for gaze tracking. The focal lengths of the lenses of both the cameras are 75mm, and the vertical and horizontal pixel spacing are all 0.01mm. These two simulated cameras were placed at the lower-left and lower-right corners of a simulated 17-inch monitor, respectively. Two point light sources were used in the simulation. One is placed at the middle location of the stereo cameras, and the other one is placed at 150mm above the left camera. The synthesized spherical cornea is located at 450mm in front of the monitor and of the same height as the top edge of the monitor. Radius of the cornea sphere was set to 8mm. Refraction index of the cornea, i.e., n, was set to 1.336. The distance between the real pupil center and the cornea center was set to 5mm. The radius of the pupil circle, r_p, is set to 3mm. Images were generated by using true parameters and 2-D noise was added for simulating measurement error.

To simulate the head movement of users, the 3-D position of the eye is generated by a 3-D random vector whose length varies with a standard deviation of about 17.32mm. The camera parameters are generated by a procedure simulating camera calibration with 200 calibration points and a 2-D measurement white Gaussian noise with a standard deviation of 0.1 pixels. The positions of the point light sources used for LoS estimation are generated by adding random unit vectors multiplied by 0.3mm.

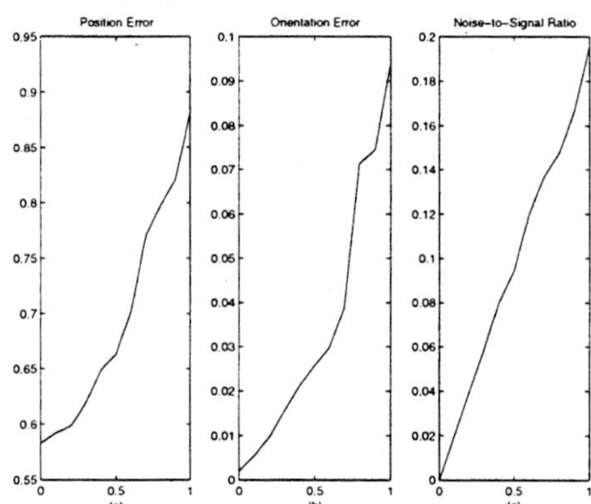

Figure 3. The estimation error.

Figure 3(a) and (b) show the RMSE (Root-Mean-Square Error) of the estimated cornea position and the estimated gaze direction, respectively. When 2-D measurement noise is absent, the estimation error is due to the calibration error. Cornea center error is about 0.58mm and gaze direction error is about 0.002 radians. As the amount of image measurement noise increased from 0 to 1.0 pixels, the position error increased gradually to about 0.88mm. However, the gaze direction error increased more rapidly than the position estimation error does. This is because that the position of the cornea center is estimated by using stereo vision technique which is very robust, whereas estimation of the gaze direction is related to the 2-D line segment connecting the center of the 2-D pupil image, p'_c and the image location of cornea center, i.e., the 2-D projection of k_c. The length of this line segment is only about several pixels. Figure 3(c) shows the mean ratio of the 2-D noise and the length of this line segment. When the amount of 2-D noise is 1 pixel, the noise-to-signal ratio is 0.2; therefore, estimation of the gaze direction is sensitive to noise. Nevertheless, since the 2-D noise is at the order of about ± 0.5 pixels which is equivalent to have 0.026 radians of gaze direction error, the estimation error of the fixation point measured on the monitor screen is about 11mm. It is possible to reduce the fixation point error to some extent if the user stares at the point of interest for a while and multiple measurements are performed.

5. Conclusions and Future Work

We have proposed a novel method to estimate the 3-D line of sight. Our method employs multiple cameras to determine the cornea center and the gaze direction using linear solutions. We have also shown that the sufficient condition for solving the 3-D gaze tracking problem using the proposed linear solutions is to use at least two cameras and at least two point light sources. The advantage of using the proposed method is that the user is independent of the calibration process. Simulation results show that the proposed method is promising. Our future work is to develop a method for estimating the positions of multiple point light sources and to implement the gaze tracking system based on the proposed method.

References

[1] T. Cornweet and H. Crane, "Accurate two-dimensional eye tracker using first and fourth purkinje images," *Journal of Optical Society America*, vol. 63, no. 8, 1973.

[2] J. K. P. White, T. E. Hutchinson, and J. M. Carley, "Spatially dynamic calibration of an eye-tracking system," *IEEE Transactions on Systems, Man and Cybernetics*, vol. 23, no. 4, pp. 1162–1168, 1993.

[3] S. Pastoor, J. Liu, and S. Renault, "An experimental multimedia system allowing 3-d visualization and eye-controlled interaction without user-worn devices," *IEEE Transactions on Multimedia*, vol. 1, no. 1, pp. 41–52, 1999.

[4] J. Gips, P. Olivieri, and J. Tecce, "Direct control of the computer through electrodes placed around the eyes," in *in the Proceedings of the Fifth International Conference on Human-Computer Interaction*, (Elsevier, Orlando, Florida), pp. 630–635, 1993.

[5] L. Bour, "Dmi-search scleral coil," Tech. Rep. H2-214, Dept. of Neurology, Clinical Neurophysiology, Academic Medical Centre, AZUA, Meibergdreef 9, 1105AZ Amsterdam, Netherlands, 1997.

[6] Y. L. Grand, *Light, Color and Vision*. Wiley, 1957.

Fingerprint-based User-friendly Interface and Pocket-PID for Mobile Authentication

Kaoru Uchida
Computer and Communication Media Research, NEC Corporation
k-uchida@bc.jp.nec.com

Abstract

This paper presents an enhanced user interface, "Fingerprint User Interface (FpUI)," that exploits fingerprint identification technology, and discusses its application to information systems, specifically to a mobile authentication terminal for networked services and digital appliances. FpUI utilizes information regarding not only who put a finger on its sensor but which specific finger it was. A user can assign commands, data objects, status, or personalized settings to individual fingers for user-friendly direct manipulation. A mobile terminal, "Pocket-PID," with fast, accurate fingerprint identification capability is proposed which features (1) an easy-to-use FpUI, (2) high security (the identification function is totally enclosed within the unit, which authenticates a user's identity without the possibility of actual fingerprint data being disclosed), and (3) secure and usable non-contact communication capability which facilitates implementation of networked services based on biometric user identification.

1. Introduction

Personal identification using biometrics, i.e. personal physiological or behavioral traits, is one of the most promising "real" applications of pattern recognition; it is becoming evident that this technology has the potential to meet the increasing demand for automated user verification, and to contribute to the security of future information systems and networked services, including electronic commerce.

Fingerprint identification, the most mature biometrics technology, uses algorithms and software with proven reliability and was first used in law enforcement and later in physical access control applications. It is now also used for personal purposes, mainly for logins to stand-alone computers and network services [1]. In these applications, however, fingerprints have only been used as a means of personal verification, based on the fact that they are invariant with time and unique among people, and system designers have only exploited this single aspect of their potential.

We focus on the fact that a person's fingerprints are different from finger to finger as well, and propose what we call the "Fingerprint User Interface" (FpUI), which allows a user to assign commands and data objects to individual fingers to augment man-machine interactions.

In this paper, I first discuss the concept, implementation and possible applications of FpUI. Then, as a useful application for FpUI, I propose a mobile terminal, "Pocket-PID," and discuss it in detail. Finally I describe my experimental implementation of Pocket-PID.

2. Fingerprint-based user interface: FpUI

2.1. FpUI as multimodal human interface

When we interact with computer systems by, for example, hitting keys, all that the system knows is which key has been hit and when. If the keys were equipped with fingerprint sensors and software were utilized that could distinguish differences among fingerprints, a system would be able to take actions determined not only by whose but also by which finger activated a given sensor. This is the concept behind the "Fingerprint User Interface" (FpUI) for enhancing man-machine interactions [2].

An FpUI can be categorized as a multimodal user interface [3]; it introduces an individual's ten fingers as a set of new communication modalities.

Let us consider the situation in which the FpUI is applied to a single-sensor man-machine system. A table is first prepared, describing the relationship between a fingerprint and an FpUI action (i.e. what action to be taken when a person X presents his N-th finger to the sensor).

Figure 1 illustrates how FpUI works. When a user touches the sensor with a certain finger, it obtains an image of the fingerprint. Note that a good automated image capture mechanism ought to be employed so that the system will be able to obtain an image of sufficient quality when the user puts his finger naturally on the sensor. Fingerprint identification is executed on the acquired image to locate a matching fingerprint in the prepared table, and the action associated with the result is carried out in response.

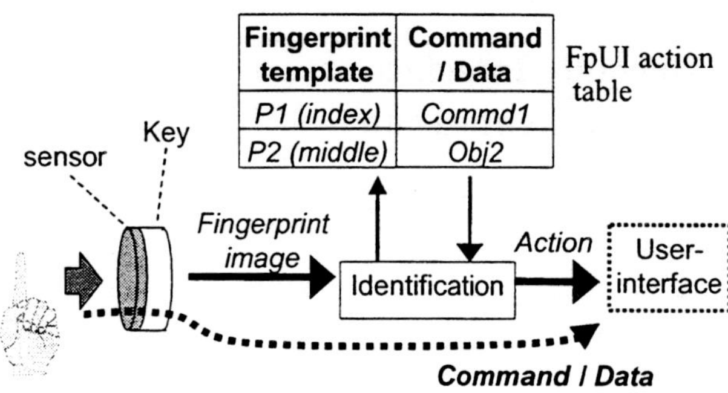

Figure 1. Fingerprint User Interface

2.2. FpUI with 1-to-N matching

To implement FpUI, we need both a small, thin fingerprint sensor and a fast, accurate fingerprint identification algorithm that can perform "1-to-N" matching.

Several solid-state fingerprint sensing chips are currently available for the fabrication of sensors that are smaller and thinner than conventional optical ones. With respect to identification, what we need is software that can search an entire fingerprint database for a match of the input image and execute the action associated with the data. This "1-to-N" matching is in contrast to the "1-to-1" matching used in most existing fingerprint-based personal verification systems, in which a user is required to claim his identity first, after which the system checks to see if the input fingerprint matches the data it holds for that identity.

2.3. Examples of FpUI applications

The FpUI concept itself is simple and straightforward, and it proves very effective in a number of ways. Below are some example of applications, that might broaden the use of biometrics technology.

2.3.1. Fingertip commands. Different commands can be assigned to different fingers. While the conventional "hitting the key" action only provides an execution trigger, this UI enables execution of specific actions tied to specific fingers. Using such "fingertip commands," an interface designer can reduce the number of required keys and avoid the use of mode keys (such as control and alt keys), which often confuse computer novices. It also facilitates the use of "blind operations," which may be needed, for example, when a car-driver operates a stereo, or when a user tries to operate appliances in darkness.

2.3.2. Fingertip saver. At the time of login, a fingerprint can be used not only for user verification but also for system customization (e.g. desktop design, shortcuts, etc.) based on user preference; a user can also choose among multiple sets of working environments by the choice of finger used. In addition to static setups, the dynamic status of a pending session can be saved and later restored just by presenting a fingertip, so that a user can continue his work more easily.

Metaphorically, this FpUI represents "saving" a state in each finger, and its significance increases dramatically when used on a small terminal, as opposed to on a computer with a large keyboard. It is also particularly well-suited to digital appliances for children or for elderly people who are not familiar with conventional user interfaces. For example, when a group of children share a video game or an electronic picture book in home or at school, each user could make a finger "remember" how far he had gone, and could resume later with just a touch of that finger. Such "fingertip bookmarking" is a good example of the potential user-friendliness of FpUI for non-experts.

It would be particularly useful for a user to be able to resume his work, with a fingertip, at any terminal whatever among multiple client terminals connected in a network. Such a networked-FpUI could be implemented by customizing the client where the input was made according to the result of fingerprint identification carried out on the server.

2.3.3. Fingertip memo. The concept of "state memorization" suggests the idea of a user interface utilizing fingers virtually as data storage for various data objects. For example, keeping an URL in each finger would help us browse Web sites just by changing fingers. Creating documents might also be facilitated by allocating frequently used text segments (such as signatures or greetings) to fingers, so as to be able to insert them instantly. By using a "memorize then retrieve" sequence dynamically, we might copy-and-paste via multiple fingertip copy buffers (clipboards).

This application could also be used over a network, with one object that has been virtually copied to a finger on one PC being pasted on another by the touch of that finger. Figure 2 shows how this might be done. Such direct manipulation might be viewed as an extension of Pick-and-Drop [4].

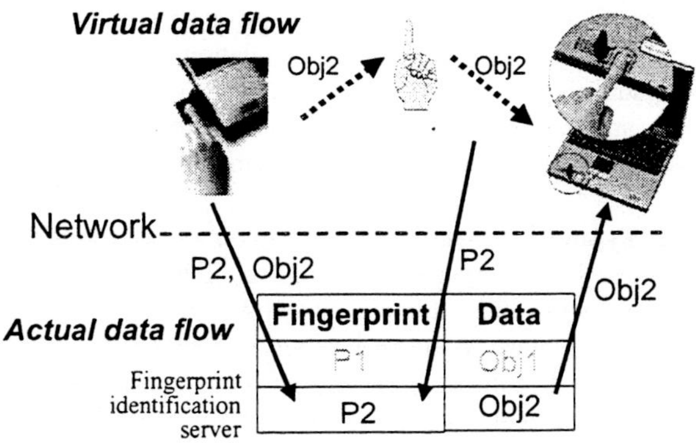

Figure 2. Fingertip memo

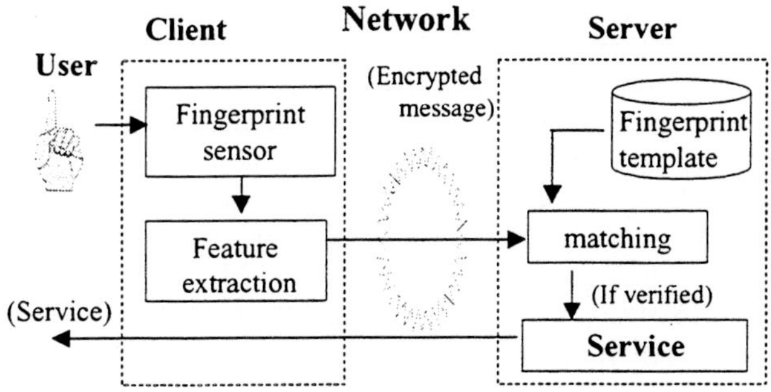

Figure 3. Server-based authentication

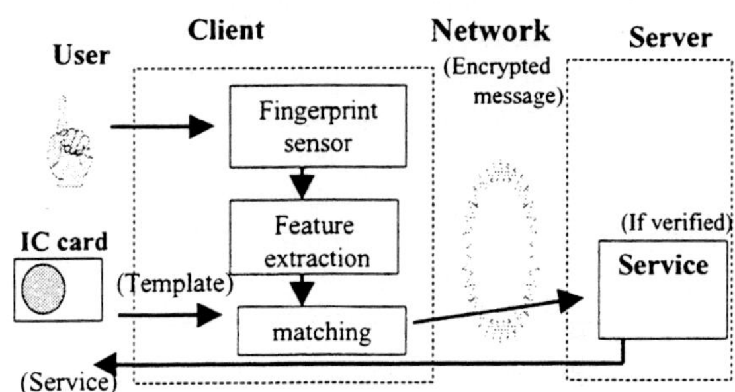

Figure 4. Authentication using an IC card

3. Pocket-PID for security and usability

3.1. Fingerprint identification on a mobile unit

As previously noted, FpUI shows more of its advantages on smaller terminals. The system I propose here consists of a PDA-like unit with fingerprint identification capability, "Pocket-PID" (Personal Identificator), which a user would carry, and a service terminal, typically a PC with an IrDA port, connected to a network. The Pocket-PID could be used to prove the owner's identity so that a service though the terminal could be authorized. Such a system would have the following characteristics, each of which I will discuss in the following subsections:

1. Authentication process security enclosed in the unit
2. IrDA communication for enhanced usability
3. Incorporation of FpUI

3.2. Secure management of fingerprint data

In conventional network-based services using fingerprint user verification, an authorized user's fingerprint template is stored typically either (1) in the server (as in Figure 3), or (2) in the user's IC card (as in Figure 4).

The former configuration may be sufficiently secure for intranet-based closed systems, but if we were to extend this framework to an open-network-based service, users would be likely to feel uncomfortable about the management and handling of their biometric data at the server and in the open network.

The latter design, on the other hand, provides a better solution, but even this would not be secure enough if the client machine were run by a dishonest administrator, in which case the user's fingerprint data could be secretly copied at the client terminal, and could be used for malicious purposes afterwards.

In the system I propose, on the other hand, as shown in Figure 5, the Pocket-PID unit stores the user's fingerprint template within it, has a fingerprint sensor on it, and executes verification by itself, thus avoiding the possibility of the disclosure of fingerprint information.

This all-in-one identification on a mobile unit has been achieved with the use of a thin fingerprint sensor having solid-state imaging capability and an accurate and fast identification software which runs on a low power CPU.

3.3. Usability by non-contact communication

To augment usability of the Pocket-PID, we have designed it so that it can be simply used by pointing it at a PC. It is not necessary to connect it physically by cable, the Pocket-PID communicates with PCs via a non-contact communication channel, such as IrDA or bluetooth.

But because IrDA messages can easily be intercepted and recorded, and other machines could pretend to be the user's Pocket-PID by using recorded messages to forge an illegal session, we have implemented a special protocol to prevent any such "replay attacks." In this protocol, the two parties first mutually verify that their counterpart is genuine and trustable, agree on a one-time key for encryption with a secret algorithm, and then exchange encrypted and digitally-signed messages, including fingerprint identification results.

This IrDA-based configuration also provides a solution to another possible difficulty that could hinder the wide-ranged use of fingerprints in net-based services: the cost of building and running systems. To make fingerprint-based authentication universally available (using a framework as in Figure 3 or 4) without a tool like Pocket-PID, numerous fingerprint sensors would have to be installed at various service points, including homes, retail stores, and on public service terminals. Also, the need to perform identification and to exchange fingerprint data over networks securely without the fear of jeopardizing privacy would greatly increase the software and operating costs of the whole complex system.

With the Pocket-PID configuration, on the other hand, all that a service client terminal would need is a communication port, such as an IrDA port, and communication software for transmitting the authentication interchange. Because the user's Pocket-PID unit exchanges the encrypted authentication results directly with the server, client installation and operational costs would be minimal.

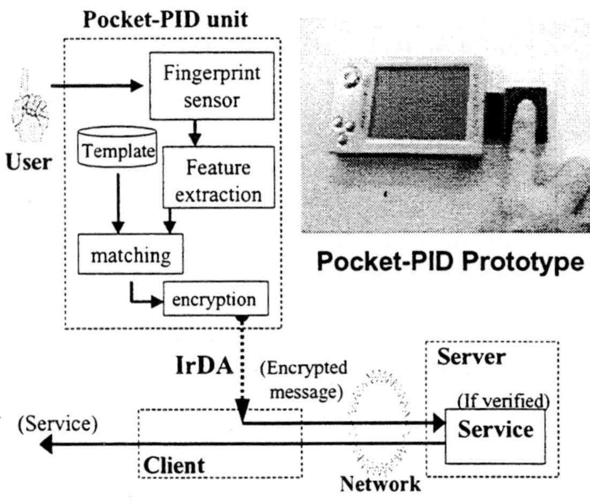

Figure 5. Authentication using Pocket-PID

3.5. FpUI on a Pocket-PID used as a digital assistant

A user of a Pocket-PID as a digital assistant would further benefit from the FpUI as well with its fingerprint identification capability.

3.5.1. Fingertip remote control. The combination of "fingertip commands" and IrDA (or bluetooth) communication makes possible "fingertip remote control," for controlling PCs or digital appliances by changing fingers. The user could register in advance relationships between individual fingers and specific infrared (or wireless) messages, and the Pocket-PID would transmit the appropriate message when a given finger was presented.

3.5.2. Typing assistant. Text writing on a PDA might be facilitated by taking advantage of the "fingertip memo" function, with, for example, inserting frequently used phrases or a signature being inserted in response to a finger touch. In editing, a user might copy-and-paste text segments or objects by means of a fingertip clipboard.

3.5.3. Virtual data carrier. Since a fingerprint is universally unique, a public information system might be designed so that "fingertip memos" were available over the Internet. When a user wanted to take home a copy of data he had found on a public information terminal, for example, he could point his Pocket-PID at that terminal and virtually copy the data into his fingertip. He could later retrieve the data at home from a PC connected to the Internet, since the Pocket-PID holds a pointer to the actual data associated with a given finger.

3.5.4. User specific personalization. Though all these examples of FpUI usage take advantage of the differences among the fingers of a single user, naturally they all are executable only by that user since fingers are universally unique as well. This contributes greatly to privacy management and to unit personalization, and facts regarding what actions are to be taken on what kind of data will be securely protected.

4. Prototype implementation of Pocket-PID

4.1. Experimental implementation

I have designed and implemented a prototype system, based on the proposed concept, consisting of a palm-size PC as the Pocket-PID unit and a PC used as a client terminal (Figure 5).

Fingerprint identification software based on a minutia-relation algorithm [5] is run on this unit. The algorithm is basically the same one that NEC has used in a number of their systems, including AFISs (Automated Fingerprint Identification Systems) for law enforcement applications, and the software attains highly accurate 1-to-N identification at a considerable speed even on the relatively slow CPU in the unit. I have also engineered a small, thin input scanner using a capacitive fingerprint sensor chip (FPS110 from Veridicom [6]) that works on a palm-size PC.

In the prototype, fingerprint feature extraction from a 1.5x1.5 mm image takes about 2 seconds and feature matching with an enrolled template takes about 0.03 seconds, with acceptable FRR (False Rejection Rate) and FAR (False Acceptance Rate). An identification out of N fingers thus can be carried out on average in $(2+0.03*N/2)$ seconds.

4.2. Sample applications

As an example application for mobile authentication, I have implemented a "pocket encryption unit." For encryption of data on a PC, the user puts his finger on the unit, which then generates a random key associated with the fingerprint and sends it to the PC via IrDA. The PC service program receives the message and uses the key to encrypt the data. Decryption is possible only when the user's finger is presented to the same unit, at which time a decryption key is sent from the unit to the PC. The IrDA communication itself is encrypted, and total security is guaranteed.

Another FpUI application I implemented is "fingertip remote browsing." By pointing the unit at a PC and changing fingers, the unit can be used to remotely control the browser on the PC by sending predefined URLs, and a user can enjoy easy net-surfing. Such a system of Web bookmarks indexed by fingers would be usable on any PC provided that the PC is running appropriate service software. Thus a user could metaphorically carry his favorite set of Web bookmarks in his Pocket-PID.

My evaluation of the implemented example applications on the prototype has confirmed that FpUI represents a significantly improved interface for palm-size PCs.

5. Conclusion

An enhanced user interface that takes advantage of a fingerprint identification technology, "FpUI," has been proposed and discussed. A mobile terminal with FpUI offers users both security with respect to fingerprint data and ease of use, a convenient man-machine interface utilized with just the touch of fingers.

FpUI is expected to be of increasing significance in the future when ever greater numbers of computer non-experts daily use digital appliances and intelligent mobile terminals for such Internet services as net-banking and electronic commerce. We hope to create a Pocket-PID, now the size of a palm-size PC, in the form of a card-size unit and also to implement it on such portable net-terminals as cellular phones and watches, so as to be literally pockettable.

Acknowledgments

I would like to thank Masanori Mizoguchi, Atsushi Sugiura and Jun Tsukumo for their very valuable comments and advice.

6. References

[1] L. O'Gorman, "Fingerprint Verification," in *Biometrics: Personal Identification in Networked Society*, Kluwer Academic Publishers, 1999, pp. 43-64.

[2] A. Sugiura and Y. Koseki, "A User Interface Using Fingerprint Recognition," *UIST98*, San Francisco, 1998.

[3] Maybury, "Intelligent Multimedia Interfaces," *AAAI-Press/MIT-Press*, 1993.

[4] Rekimoto, "Pick-and-Drop: A Direct Manipulation Technique for Multiple Computer Environments," *UIST97*, pp.31-39.

[5] K. Asai, et al, "Automatic Fingerprint Identification," *Proc. Society of Photo-Optical Instrumentation Engineers*, **182**, 1979, 49-56,.

[6] Ingris, et al, "A Robust, 1.8V, 250μW, Direct Contact 500 dpi Fingerprint Sensor," *ISSCC98, SA 17.7*, 1998, p. 285.

Invariant Face Detection with Support Vector Machines

† Jean-Christophe Terrillon, ‡ Mahdad N. Shirazi, † Mohamed Sadek,
† Hideo Fukamachi and † Shigeru Akamatsu
† ATR Human Information Processing Research Laboratories
2-2 Hikaridai, Seika-cho, Soraku-gun, Kyoto 619-0288, Japan
‡ Kansai Advanced Research Center, Communications Research Laboratory
588-2 Iwaoka, Iwaoka-cho, Nishi-ku, Kobe 651-24, Japan
terril@hip.atr.co.jp

Abstract

This paper present an analysis of the performance of Support Vector Machines (SVMs) for the automatic detection of human faces in static color images of complex scenes. SVMs are a new interesting type of binary classifier based on a novel statistical learning technique that has been developed in recent years by V. Vapnik et al. at AT&T Bell Labs [2] [4] [6] [22]. Skin color-based image segmentation is initially performed for several different chrominance spaces by use of the single Gaussian chrominance model and of a Gaussian mixture density model, as described in [17]. Feature extraction in the segmented images is then implemented by use of invariant Orthogonal Fourier-Mellin Moments (OFMMs) [16] [20]. For all chrominance spaces, the application of SVMs to the invariant moments obtained from a set of 100 test images yields a higher face detection performance than when applying a 3-layer perceptron Neural Network (NN), depending on a suitable selection of the kernel function used to train the SVM and of the value of its associated parameter(s). The training of SVMs is easier and faster than that of a NN, always finds a global minimum, and SVMs have a better generalization ability [5].

1. Introduction

Support Vector Machines (SVMs) are a new type of classifier which provides a novel approach to the problem of pattern recognition and is a generalization of a large class of Neural Networks (NNs), Radial Basis Functions (RBFs) and polynomial classifiers for solving binary classification problems. SVMs are based on a new statistical learning technique developed by Vapnik *et al.* at AT&T Bell Labs [2] [4] [6] [22]. Although the theory underlying SVMs has been developed in the last 20 years [21], their application to real-life pattern recognition problems is very recent [5] [11] and is receiving increasing attention.

In the specific task of automatic face detection in complex scene images, different approaches have been used in the last several years. They include feature-based approaches, such as the detection of facial features and use of geometrical constraints [23] and labeled graphs [7], and learning-based approaches such as density estimation of the training data [9], clustering and distribution-based modeling [18], and NNs [14] [15] [3]. In contradistinction to the above-mentioned approaches, the application of SVMs to face detection uses no prior information in order to obtain the decision surface between faces and "non-faces".

To our knowledge, the only work published until now on face detection by use of SVMs is that of Osuna *et al.* [12]. They trained a SVM on overlapping sub-images of an original grey-level image which is scanned exhaustively at many possible scales, and obtained very good face detection results on a set of over 300 test images. Finally, Oren *et al.* [10] applied SVMs to pedestrian detection, where a subset of wavelet coefficients of a window in an image is used as the feature vector to be classified.

In this paper, we propose a new approach to face detection by which we combine a skin color-based image segmentation with the application of SVMs to fully translation-, scale- and in-plane rotation-invariant orthogonal moments that are derived from a generalization of the circular Fourier and radial Mellin transform (OFMMs) [16] [20]. A number of low radial-order OFMMs are selected and calculated for each cluster (face candidate) remaining in the segmented images after a connected-component analysis, and form the feature vectors with which to train and to test the SVMs for face detection. Initial color segmentation is performed for several different chrominance spaces. The single Gaussian model and a Gaussian mixture density model are used alter-

1051-4651/00 $10.00 © 2000 IEEE

natively to describe the chrominance distribution of human skin in each space.
The paper is organized as follows : in section 2, we briefly describe SVMs and explain why the underlying statistical learning theory is more general and powerful than the techniques that are usually applied to train NNs, RBFs or polynomial classifiers. In section 3, we first briefly examine the distribution of human skin in the following chrominance spaces : normalized r-g and CIE-xy, a normalized perceptually plausible tint-saturation-luminance space TSL, CIE-DSH, HSV, and the perceptually uniform CIE-L*u*v* and CIE-L*a*b* spaces. For both the single Gaussian and Gaussian mixture density models, we then describe the calibration method used to find a suitable threshold for skin color-based image segmentation in each chrominance space. Section 4 summarizes the shape analysis performed on the segmented images, that includes the initial connected-component analysis and the feature extraction of the remaining face candidates by use of the OFMMs. Experimental results of face detection with the SVMs for the different chrominance spaces are presented and discussed in section 5. A comparison is made with the corresponding results obtained with a 3-layer perceptron NN and that we present in [20]. Conclusions are drawn in section 6.

2. Support Vector Machines

In a binary classification problem where feature extraction is initially performed, we assume that we have a set of l feature vectors $\mathbf{x}_i \in R^n$, $i = 1, ..., l$ with which are associated class labels $y_i \in \{-1, 1\}$ such that we obtain a training data set $D = \{(\mathbf{x}_i, y_i)\}_{i=1}^{l}$. In the simplest case where the two classes are linearly separable in R^n, we wish to determine, among the infinite number of possible hyperplanes that separate the data, which one will yield the smallest generalization error. As is shown in [5], such an optimal hyperplane is the one with the maximum margin of separation between the two classes, where the margin is the sum of the distances from the hyperplane to the closest data point (or points) of each of the two classes. Such points lying on the same margin hyperplane, and whose removal would change the solution found, are called support vectors. They are shown in Figure 1, which illustrates the two-dimensional case ($n = 2$). Considering that y_i labels one class as $+1$ and the other class as -1, all the training data must satisfy the following constraints :

$$\begin{aligned} \mathbf{x}_i \cdot \mathbf{w} + b &\geq +1 \quad \text{for } y_i = +1 \\ \mathbf{x}_i \cdot \mathbf{w} + b &\leq -1 \quad \text{for } y_i = -1 \end{aligned} \tag{1}$$

which can be combined into one set of inequalities :

$$y_i(\mathbf{x}_i \cdot \mathbf{w} + b) - 1 \geq 0 \tag{2}$$

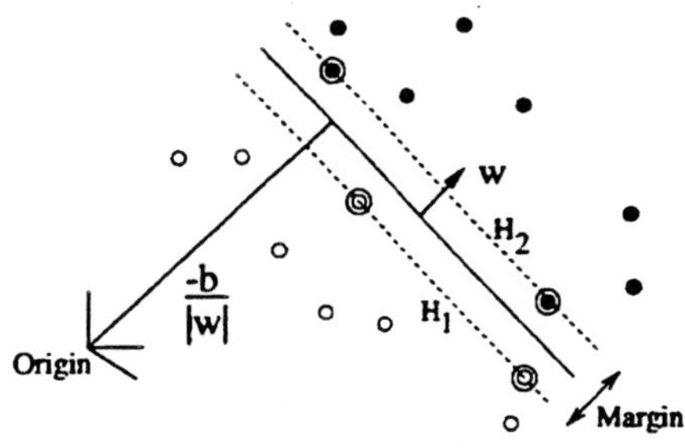

Figure 1. Hyperplanes separating two linearly separable classes in R^2, with the maximum margin of separation between the two classes. The support vectors are circled (taken from [5]).

which holds for all i. Since the margin is $2/||\mathbf{w}||$, the support vector classifier constructs the optimum hyperplane by minimizing $||\mathbf{w}||^2/2$ subject to the constraint of Eq. 2 [5]. In practical applications, the two classes are not completely separable, and a hyperplane that maximizes the margin while minimizing a quantity proportional to the misclassification errors can still be determined : one minimizes the quantity

$$\| \mathbf{w} \|^2/2 + C\sum_{i=1}^{l} \xi_i \tag{3}$$

subject to the constraints $\xi_i \geq 0 \; \forall i$ and

$$\begin{aligned} \mathbf{x}_i \cdot \mathbf{w} + b &\geq 1 - \xi_i \quad \text{for } y_i = +1 \\ \mathbf{x}_i \cdot \mathbf{w} + b &\leq -1 + \xi_i \quad \text{for } y_i = -1 \end{aligned} \tag{4}$$

where C is a parameter chosen by the user that controls the tradeoff between the margin and the misclassification errors. Just as for the separable case, this is a Quadratic Programming (QP) problem, that is, maximize the Lagrangian

$$L = \sum_{i=1}^{l} \lambda_i - \frac{1}{2} \sum_{i,j=1}^{l} \lambda_i \lambda_j y_i y_j \mathbf{x}_i \cdot \mathbf{x}_j \tag{5}$$

where the λ_i are the Lagrange multipliers, subject to the constraints $0 \leq \lambda_i \leq C$ and $\sum_{i=1}^{l} \lambda_i y_i = 0$. The solution is given by ([5])

$$\mathbf{w} = \sum_{i=1}^{N_s} \lambda_i y_i \mathbf{x}_i \tag{6}$$

where N_s is the number of support vectors. In the solution, the support vectors have their Lagrange multiplier $\lambda_i > 0$. All other training points have $\lambda_i = 0$. N_s is usually small, and is proportional to the generalization error of the classifier. The non-separable case is illustrated in Figure 2. Once trained, the SVM assigns to a test vector $\mathbf{x}_j \in R^n$ the label

$$sgn(\mathbf{x}_j \cdot \mathbf{w} + b) = sgn(\sum_{i=1}^{N_s} \lambda_i y_i \mathbf{s}_i \cdot \mathbf{x}_j + b) \tag{7}$$

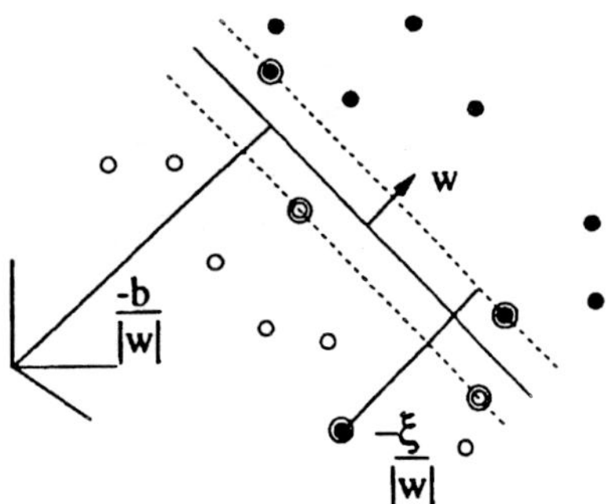

Figure 2. Separating hyperplanes when the two classes are not linearly separable in R^2 (taken from [5]).

where $\mathbf{s}_i$ are the support vectors.

We note that the data in the training problem (Eq. 7) always appear as a dot product $\mathbf{x}_i \cdot \mathbf{x}_j$.

It is also unlikely that real-life classification problems can be solved by a linear classifier, so that an extension to non-linear decision functions (or surfaces) is necessary. In order to accomplish this, an initial mapping Φ of the data into a (usually significantly higher dimensional) Euclidean space H is performed as $\Phi : R^n \to H$, and the linear classification problem is formulated in the new space with dimension d. The training algorithm then only depends on the data through dot products in H of the form $\Phi(\mathbf{x}_i) \cdot \Phi(\mathbf{x}_j)$. Since the computation of the dot products is prohibitive if the number l of training vectors $\Phi(\mathbf{x}_i)$ is very large, and since Φ is not known a priori, the Mercer-Hilbert-Schmidt theorem ([5]) for positive definite functions allows to replace $\Phi(\mathbf{x}_i) \cdot \Phi(\mathbf{x}_j)$ by a positive definite symmetric kernel function $K(\mathbf{x}_i, \mathbf{x}_j)$, that is, $K(\mathbf{x}_i, \mathbf{x}_j) = \Phi(\mathbf{x}_i) \cdot \Phi(\mathbf{x}_j)$. Only K is needed in the training algorithm and we do not need to know Φ explicitly. The QP problem to be solved is exactly the same as before and $\mathbf{s}_i \cdot \mathbf{x}_j$ is replaced by $K(\mathbf{s}_i, \mathbf{x}_j)$. Some examples of possible $K(\mathbf{x}_i, \mathbf{x}_j)$, that lead to well-known classifiers, are:

$$K(\mathbf{x}_i, \mathbf{x}_j) = \left(\frac{\mathbf{x}_i \cdot \mathbf{x}_j}{a} + b\right)^p, \quad (8)$$

a full polynomial of degree p with real parameters a and b. The dimension d of H is $(n + p + 1)!/[p!(n + 1)!]$. A particular case of the full polynomial is the simple polynomial with $a = b = 1$;

$$K(\mathbf{x}_i, \mathbf{x}_j) = \exp(-\gamma ||\mathbf{x}_i - \mathbf{x}_j||^2), \quad (9)$$

a Gaussian RBF with real parameter γ, and with $d \to \infty$;

$$K(\mathbf{x}_i, \mathbf{x}_j) = \tanh(\kappa \mathbf{x}_i \cdot \mathbf{x}_j - \delta), \quad (10)$$

a multilayer perceptron NN with real parameters κ and δ;

$$K(\mathbf{x}_i, \mathbf{x}_j) = \frac{1}{1 - \mathbf{x}_i \cdot \mathbf{x}_j} \quad (11)$$

Vovk's real infinite polynomial.

A great advantage of the SVMs over other classifiers such as a multilayer perceptron NN is that they use structural risk minimization which minimizes a bound on the generalization error (which depends on both the empirical risk and the capacity of the function class implemented by the machine), and therefore they should perform better on novel test data [5], whereas the other classifiers use empirical risk minimization and only guarantee a minimum error over the training data set. The solution found by the SVM classifier is always global, because it originates from a convex QP problem [5]. The mapping to a higher dimensional space significantly increases the discriminative power of the classifier. The requirement of maximum margin hyperplanes in H obviates the "curse of dimensionality ", and thus ensures the generalization performance of the SVM [5]. Finally, the SVM approach is better founded theoretically than that for the other classifiers, so that less training (and testing) trials are needed to achieve good results. Two limitations of SVMs are the selection of a suitable kernel and of the associated parameter(s) to solve a given problem, and the size of the training datasets (above several thousand sample data, the training becomes very difficult to implement, although a problem decomposition has been used successfully in [12] on 50,000 samples). Also, the SVMs have been used until now only for binary classification problems, and the design for multiclass SVMs remains to be done. A detailed analysis of the theoretical foundations of SVMs is presented in [5].

3. Skin Color-based Image Segmentation

3.1. Skin Chrominance Distribution in Different Color Spaces

In our experiments, images of 11 Asian and 19 Caucasian subjects were recorded under slowly varying illumination conditions in an office environment with a single video camera mounted on an SGI computer. 110 skin sample images were manually selected to calculate the cumulative skin pixel histogram in each of the chrominance spaces mentioned in the introduction of the paper and to calibrate the camera for color segmentation. The histograms for each space are shown in Figure 3. The normalized chrominance-luminance space TSL is defined as

$$T = \begin{cases} arctan(r'/g')/2\pi + 1/4, & g' > 0 \\ arctan(r'/g')/2\pi + 3/4, & g' < 0 \\ 0 & g' = 0 \end{cases}$$
$$S = [9/5(r'^2 + g'^2)]^{1/2}$$
$$L = 0.299R + 0.587G + 0.114B \quad (12)$$

where $r\prime = (r - 1/3)$ and $g\prime = (g - 1/3)$, $r = R/(R+G+B)$ and $g = G/(R+G+B)$, T is the tint, S is the saturation and where L is the luminance (for Gamma-corrected RGB values). The values of T, S and L are normalized in the range [0.; 1.0].

Visually, the skin distribution in the normalized chrominance spaces (T-S, r-g and CIE-xy) fits well to the single Gaussian model whereas in the un-normalized spaces, it is complex-shaped and cannot be described well by a simple model.

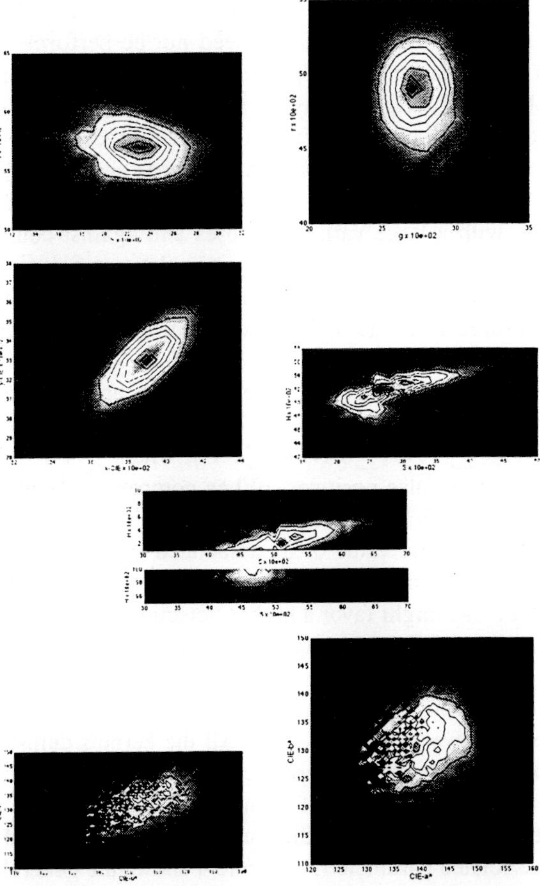

Figure 3. 2-D top view of the cumulative histograms in different chrominance spaces of 110 skin sample images (1.5 x $10E+05$ skin pixels) of 11 Asian and 19 Caucasian subjects used for calibrating the SGI camera. From top to bottom and left to right : normalized T-S, r-g and CIE-xy spaces, CIE-SH, H-S, CIE-u*v* and CIE-a*b* spaces (appropriately shifted or corrected for discontinuities, except H-S space). Total histogram dimensions are 100 x 100 bins in all spaces except in CIE-u*v* and CIE-a*b* spaces where the dimensions are 200 x 200 bins.

3.2. Skin Color Calibration

In the simplest case, it is assumed that the skin chrominance distribution for both Asians and Caucasians may be modeled by an elliptical Gaussian joint probability density function (pdf) with mean vector μ_{sk} and with covariance matrix $\mathbf{\Sigma}_{sk}$. The Mahalanobis metric is inherent to the single Gaussian pdf model and determines the probability that a given pixel belongs to the class representing human skin. It is used for skin color calibration and for thresholding of test images. The color calibration requires finding a "standard" threshold value of the Mahalanobis metric for each chrominance space such that the proportion of true positives TP over the ensemble of skin pixels in the 110 skin sample images is equal to the proportion of true negatives TN over an ensemble of "non-skin" pixels in 5 large images not containing skin [19]. This is assumed to be a suitable tradeoff to efficiently discriminate between human skin pixels and "non-skin" pixels, and for color segmentation in each space. The single Gaussian model is a particular case of a Gaussian mixture density model. The latter model is flexible enough to describe complex-shaped distributions. The corresponding pdf is a weighted sum of normalized Gaussian components, with a number of Gaussian components c_{sk}. The parameters to estimate for each component j are the mixture coefficient π^j_{sk}, the mean vector μ^j_{sk} and the covariance matrix $\mathbf{\Sigma}^j_{sk}$. The mixture coefficients satisfy the normalization constraint $\sum_{j=1}^{c_{sk}} \pi^j_{sk} = 1$. The estimation of the skin distribution in each chrominance space can be performed by maximizing the likelihood function through an iterative procedure known as the Expectation-Maximization (EM) algorithm [13]. The number of components c_{sk} is assumed to be known. In order to determine c_{sk}, one needs to use information criteria such as the Akaike Information Criterion (AIC) [1]. For each chrominance space, we chose to use 8 clusters, which yield visually plausible estimates even for complex-shaped distributions. Such a number of components represents a good tradeoff between the accuracy of estimation of the true distributions and the computational load for thresholding. The color calibration and the thresholding of the original images are based on the same method as for the single Gaussian model, but use the likelihood. A detailed analysis of the calibration and segmentation can be found in [19] and [17].

The result of thresholding is a binary image that is subjected to the shape analysis by use of the OFMMs after a connected-component analysis.

Finally, we note that the support vector classification algorithm could also have been used for skin pixel detection, but the number of data points involved (1.5 x $10E+05$ pixels for the 110 skin sample images and 7.85 x $10E+05$ pixels for the non-skin sample images) would have required a difficult decomposition problem, and lowering the number of samples significantly in order to use the SVMs would adversely affect the quality of the segmentation.

4. Shape Analysis

A local median filter with a window of 3 x 3 pixels is applied to the thresholded images and a connected-component analysis is performed in order to obtain clusters of connected pixels. The clusters of area less than 0.5% of the area of the image in number of pixels are discarded so that only a small number of main clusters (face candidates) are used for further analysis.

For feature extraction, we use Orthogonal Fourier-Mellin moments (OFMMs), whose theoretical foundations are presented in details in [16] and in [20]. After a transformation from polar to cartesian coordinates, the translation- and scale-invariant OFMMs are given by

$$\Phi_{nm} = \exp(im\alpha)\frac{n+1}{\pi}\sum_{s=0}^{n}\frac{\alpha_{ns}}{M'^{s/2+1}_{0,0}}\int\int_{-\infty}^{\infty}(x+iy)^{\frac{s-m}{2}}$$

$$\times\,(x-iy)^{\frac{s+m}{2}}f(x,y)dxdy \qquad (13)$$

where $\alpha_{ns} = (-1)^{n+s}(n+s+1)!/[(n-s)!s!(s+1)!]$, $n = 0, 1, 2, \ldots$ is the radial order, $m = 0, \pm 1, \pm 2, \ldots$ is the circular harmonic order, $M'_{0,0}$ is the zero-order geometric moment of the object to be analyzed $f(x, y)$ (the area of the object in a binary image), α is an arbitrary angle, and where $i^2 = -1$. The modulus of the OFMMs, $|\Phi_{nm}|$, is rotation invariant, and the OFMMs are orthogonal over the interior of the unit circle. In addition to the same invariant properties as Hu's moments generalized by Li [8] that are derived directly from the Fourier-Mellin integral (FMMs) and that we applied to face detection with a 3-layer perceptron NN in [19], and in [17] for nine different chrominance spaces, the OFMMs, owing to their orthogonality, have the advantages of non-redundancy of information, robustness with respect to noise and the ability to reconstruct the original object, with a relatively small number of orders, in particular objects of small size, as was shown in [16]. In this sense, the OFMMs are highly condensed image features. In [20], we apply the OFMMs to face detection also with a 3-layer perceptron NN, with 11 moments as the input vector, 6 nodes in the hidden layer and with one output unit to discriminate between faces and "non-faces". The selection of appropriate combinations of (low radial order) moments is based on object reconstruction experiments (of faces and non-faces) and on a theoretical analysis of the OFMMs for a pure ellipse, since we assume that well-segmented frontal views of faces are approximately elliptical, with holes at the location of the eyes and of the mouth. The following combination of OFMMs was selected ([20]): $|\Phi_{0,1}|$, $|\Phi_{0,3}|$, $|\Phi_{0,4}|$, $|\Phi_{0,6}|$, $|\Phi_{1,0}|$, $|\Phi_{1,1}|$, $|\Phi_{1,3}|$, $|\Phi_{1,4}|$, $|\Phi_{2,0}|$, $|\Phi_{2,1}|$ and $|\Phi_{2,6}|$. We use the same combination in this paper for comparison purposes. When a face is detected (either by the SVM or by the NN), it is marked by an ellipse using the first and second-order geometric moments of the cluster representing the face, as described in [19].

5. Experimental Results of Face Detection

The face detection system is implemented on an SGI Indigo 2 Impact 10000 computer. As when we applied a NN, the training file consists here of a total of 227 vectors (or clusters), obtained from 108 segmented images of 9 Asian and 20 Caucasian subjects. The segmentation was performed with the normalized T-S chrominance space in both cases. The T-S space produces the best results in the chrominance analysis and the color calibration when using the single Gaussian chrominance model [17]. Considering then that the faces in the training set are well segmented, it is reasoned that the training need not be performed for each chrominance space separately, so that the same trained SVM (or NN weights) may be applied to test images segmented by use of the other chrominance spaces. The test file consists of 100 images with 144 faces and 65 subjects (30 Asians, 34 Caucasians and one subject of African descent), with a large variety of poses and against complex backgrounds. 77% of the images in the test file are not part of the training set. The face detection performance is measured in terms of the rate of correct face detection CD, defined as $CD = \sum TP/(\sum TP + \sum FN)$, where $\sum FN$ is the proportion of false negatives, and in terms of the rate of correct rejection of distractors CR, computed as $CR = \sum TN/(\sum TN + \sum FP)$, where $\sum FP$ is the proportion of false positives. When comparing the performance of the SVMs with that of the NN, the selection of the kernel and of the value of its associated parameter(s) that are used to train the SVM can be based on two different criteria : one might favor a higher detection rate CD to the detriment of CR (assuming that a suitable post-processing after the detection of face candidates reduces the proportion of false positives FP) or one might try to find the best tradeoff between CD and CR. All the kernels defined in Section 2, as well as a kernel consisting of linear splines with an infinite number of points, were used to train and test the SVM, and several different values were selected for the associated parameter(s). Figure 4 shows the general results of face detection with both the SVMs and the NN for the single Gaussian model and for five chrominance spaces, while Figure 5 shows the results for the Gaussian mixture density model and for the CIE-L*u*v* and CIE-L*a*b* spaces. The total number of blobs is the cumulative number of clusters (face candidates) in the test file remaining after the connected-component analysis, which depends on the chrominance space and model that are used for segmentation. The shaded areas emphasize the best comparative results. Here the results reflect the best tradeoff between CD and CR. In the case of the single Gaussian model, the kernel yielding the best performance was found to be the Gaussian RBF for all five chrominance spaces, and generally with intermediate values of γ ($0.5 < \gamma < 2.0$) (it is interesting to note that in both [12] and [10], a simple polynomial of degree $p = 2$ was used and produced very good results). CD is significantly higher for almost all chrominance spaces when using the SVM, while CR is slightly higher for most spaces. Independently of the type of classifier that is used, the face detection performance is generally reduced for most of the un-normalized spaces (such as HSV), owing to a lower goodness of fit of the corresponding skin chrominance distributions to the single Gaussian model and also to a higher overlap between the skin and non-skin distributions in those spaces. A more detailed analysis of the effects of these two criteria on the quality of segmentation and subsequently, on the face detection performance, is presented in [17]. However, the SVMs partially compensate the detrimental effects of a lower quality of segmentation because they always find a global solution to a binary classification problem.

Figure 6 shows two examples of the simultaneous detection of the faces of two Caucasian subjects for the normalized T-S space and of two Asian subjects for the r-g space. As those examples show, the general performance in terms of CR is good considering the complexity of the scene images, but is not very high due to the higher tolerance of the invariant moments to false positives.

As Figure 5 shows, in the case of the Gaussian mixture density model, three different types of kernels have been found to yield a suitable tradeoff between CD and CR, as compared to the performance of the NN : They are, once again, a Gaussian RBF (with $\gamma = 1.0$ for both the CIE-L*u*v* and CIE-L*a*b* color spaces), a simple polynomial with degree $p = 3$ (for both spaces) and linear splines with an infinite number of points. CD is less significantly higher than when applying a NN, because the overlap between the skin and non-skin chrominance distributions in both spaces, which ultimately determines the face detection performance, is larger than in the other spaces [17].

Overall, whatever the skin chrominance model that is used, the performance of the SVMs is superior to that of the NN. Figures 7 and 8 show the variation of CD and of CR as a function of the parameter γ when applying a Gaussian RBF kernel for the single Gaussian model (in the CIE-xy, DSH and HSV spaces) and for the mixture Gaussian model (in the CIE-L*a*b* space) respectively. The CD and CR obtained with the NN are shown for comparison. A strong negative correlation between CD and CR is observed in all cases. If one favors CD to the detriment of CR, a value of $CD = 84.8\%$ is obtained for the CIE-xy space for $\gamma = 0.5$ (against 55.2% with the NN), compared to 75.2% if a tradeoff between CD and CR is favored (as shown in Figure 4, with $\gamma = 2.0$), but the value of CR is then low ($CR = 53.5\%$, against $CR = 75.6\%$ with the NN). The same significantly higher value of CD than with the NN is produced for the HSV space, which is again strongly detrimental to CR. The best tradeoff between CD and CR produces values of CD and CR that are both higher than the

Single Gaussian Model, OFMMs

		SVM		NN	
color space	Total # Blobs	CD(%)	CR(%)	CD(%)	CR(%)
TSL	294	93.1	72.8	91.3	81.1
r-g	369	82.4	73.3	73.5	72.7
CIE-xy	430	75.2	70.4	55.2	75.6
CIE-DSH	352	74.4	74.3	68.3	69.0
HSV	525	65.6	74.7	52.5	71.9

Figure 4. General results of face detection with the SVM (left) and with a 3-layer perceptron NN (right) for the single Gaussian skin chrominance model and for five different chrominance spaces. The kernel used to train the SVM is a Gaussian Radial Basis Function (RBF) with parameter $\gamma = 0.5, 1.0, 2.0, 1.0$ and 10.0 respectively.

Mixture Gaussian Model, OFMMs

		SVM						NN	
		RBF, $\gamma = 1.0$		SP, p = 3		Linear Splines			
color space	Total # Blobs	CD(%)	CR(%)	CD(%)	CR(%)	CD(%)	CR(%)	CD(%)	CR(%)
CIE-L*u*v*	422	65.8	74.1	70.8	68.3	70.8	72.7	65.2	76.2
CIE-L*a*b*	421	63.2	74.4	71.2	66.9	68.0	70.7	60.2	70.3

Figure 5. General results of face detection with the SVM (left) and with a 3-layer perceptron NN (right) for the Gaussian mixture density model and for the CIE-L*u*v* and CIE-L*a*b* color spaces. The kernels used to train the SVM are a Gaussian RBF (with parameter $\gamma = 1.0$ for both spaces), a simple polynomial (with degree $p = 3$ for both spaces) and linear splines with an infinite number of points.

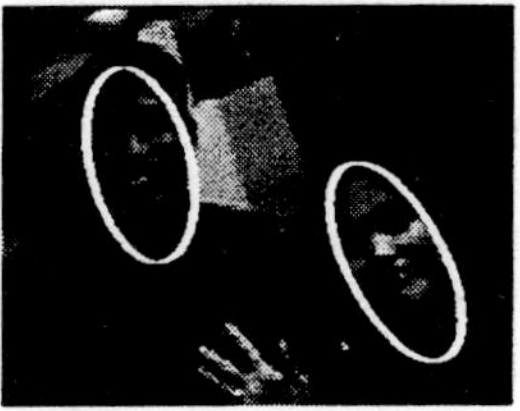

Figure 6. Examples of the simultaneous detection of the faces of two Caucasians (left) and of two Asians (right).

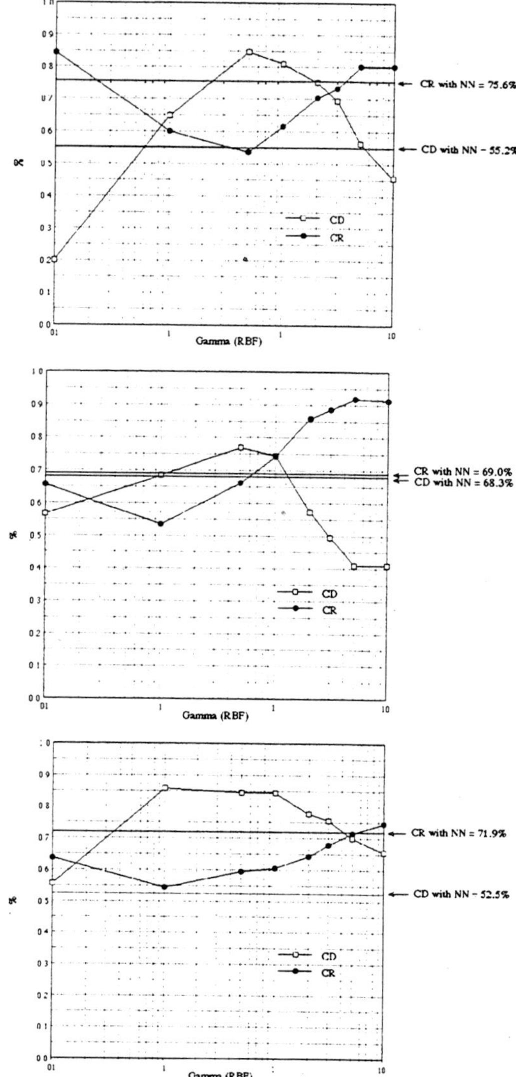

Figure 7. Graphs of CD and of CR as a function of the parameter γ when applying a Gaussian RBF kernel to train an SVM for face detection in binary images segmented by use of the single Gaussian chrominance model in the CIE-xy (top), CIE-DSH (middle) and HSV (bottom) color spaces. The CD and CR obtained with the NN are shown for comparison in each graph.

corresponding values obtained with the NN for the CIE-DSH and HSV spaces (Figure 7), and for the CIE-L*a*b* space (Figure 8), but this is clearly not the case for the CIE-xy space (top graph of Figure 7). In the latter case, it is therefore not easy to find a suitable tradeoff, which then depends on the relative weights that are given to CD and CR. Given the novelty of the application of SVMs to real-life pattern recognition problems, the results presented in this paper for the specific task of automatic face detection

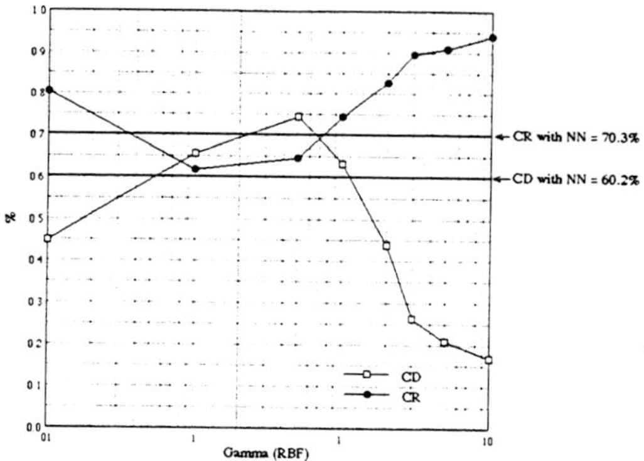

Figure 8. Graphs of CD and of CR as a function of the parameter γ when applying a Gaussian RBF kernel to train an SVM for face detection in binary images segmented by use of the mixture Gaussian chrominance model in the CIE-L*a*b* color space. The CD and CR obtained with the NN are shown for comparison.

suggest that the selection of a suitable kernel and of a suitable value of the associated parameter(s) is an important task that requires further research.

6. Conclusions

In conclusion, For all chrominance spaces and for both skin chrominance models that were used, the most robust face detection system when applying SVMs to invariant OFMMs for binary face/non face classification in segmented images is obtained by use of a Gaussian RBF kernel and generally for intermediate values of the associated parameter γ. Two other kernels, a simple polynomial with degree $p = 3$ and linear splines with an infinite number of points, also produce good results with the mixture Gaussian chrominance model. One might favor the face detection rate CD to the detriment of the rate of correct rejection of distractors CR if a suitable post-processing after the detection of face candidates, using the luminance for example, reduces the proportion of false positives FP. Overall, the performance of the SVMs is superior to that of a 3-layer perceptron NN, provided that a suitable selection of the kernel and of the value of the associated parameter is made. However, as stated in [5], one weakness of the SVMs is that the best choice of kernel for a given problem is still a research issue.

Acknowledgements

The authors would like to thank the SVM groups at Royal Holloway, AT & T and GMD which provided the code for the implementation of the SVMs for public use on the World Wide Web at the URL address : http://svm.first.gmd.de/.

References

[1] H. Akaike. Information theory and an extension of the maximum likelihood principle. In *Proceedings of the Second International Symposium on Information Theory*, Budapest, 1973. pp. 267-281.

[2] B. E. Boser, I. M. Guyon, and V. N. Vapnik. A training algorithm for optimal margin classifier. In *Proceedings of the Fifth Annual ACM Workshop on Computational Learning Theory*, Pittsburgh, PA, 1992. pp. 144-152.

[3] G. Burel and D. Carel. Detection and localization of faces on digital images. *Pattern Recognition Letters*, 15:963–967, 1994.

[4] C. J. C. Burges. Simplified support vector decision rules. In *Proceedings of the International Conference on Machine Learning*, 1996. pp. 71-77.

[5] C. J. C. Burges. A tutorial on support vector machines for pattern recognition. *Data Mining and Knowledge Discovery*, 2(2):121–167, 1998.

[6] C. Cortes and V. Vapnik. Support vector networks. *Machine Learning*, 20:1–25, 1995.

[7] N. Krueger, M. Poetzsch, and C. v.d. Malsburg. Determination of face position and pose with learned representation based on labeled graphs. Technical Report Technical Report 96-03, Ruhr-Universitaet, January 1996.

[8] Y. Li. Reforming the theory of invariant moments for pattern recognition. *Pattern Recognition*, 25(7):723–730, 1992.

[9] B. Moghaddam and A. Pentland. Probabilistic visual learning for object detection. Technical Report 326, MIT Media Laboratory, June 1995.

[10] M. Oren, C. Papageorgiou, and P. Sinha. Pedestrian detection using wavelet templates. In *Proceedings of the Conference on Computer Vision and Pattern Recognition*, Puerto Rico, 1997. pp. 193-199.

[11] E. Osuna, R. Freund, and F. Girosi. Support vector machines : Training and applications. Technical Report A. I. Memo 1602, MIT A. I. Lab., 1997.

[12] E. Osuna, R. freund, and F. Girosi. Training support vector machines : an application to face detection. In *Proceedings of the Conference on Computer Vision and Pattern Recognition*, Puerto Rico, 1997. pp. 130-136.

[13] R. Redner and H. Walker. Mixture densities, maximum likelihood, and the em algorithm. *SIAM Review*, 26:195–239, 1994.

[14] H. Rowley, S. Baluja, and T. Kanade. Neural network-based face detection. In *Proceedings of the Conference on Computer Vision and Pattern Recognition*, San Francisco, California, 1996. pp. 203-208.

[15] H. Rowley, S. Baluja, and T. Kanade. Rotation invariant neural network-based face detection. In *Proceedings of the Conference on Computer Vision and Pattern Recognition*, Santa Barbara, California, 1998. pp. 38-44.

[16] Y. Sheng and L. Shen. Orthogonal fourier-mellin moments for invariant pattern recognition. *J. Opt. Soc. Am. A*, 11(6):1748–1757, 1994.

[17] M. N. Shirazi, J.-C. Terrillon, H. Fukamachi, and S. Akamatsu. Comparative performance of different skin chrominance models and chrominance spaces for the automatic detection of human faces in color images. In *Proceedings of the 4th International Conference on Face and Gesture Recognition*, Grenoble, France, March 2000. pp. 54-61.

[18] K. Sung and T. Poggio. Example-based learning for view-based human face detection. Technical Report A.I. Memo 1521, MIT A.I. Laboratory, December 1994.

[19] J.-C. Terrillon, M. David, and S. Akamatsu. Detection of human faces in complex scene images by use of a skin color model and of invariant fourier-mellin moments. In *Proceedings of the 14th International Conference on Pattern Recognition*, Brisbane, Australia, 1998. pp. 1350-1355.

[20] J.-C. Terrillon, D. McReynolds, M. Sadek, Y. Sheng, and S. Akamatsu. Invariant neural network-based face detection with orthogonal fourier-mellin moments. September 2000. This conference.

[21] V. Vapnik. *Estimation of Dependences Based on Empirical Data [in Russian]*. Nauka, Moscow, 1979. (English translation : Springer Verlag, New York, 1982).

[22] V. Vapnik. *The Nature of Statistical Learning Theory*. Springer Verlag, New York, 1995.

[23] J. Yang and T. Huang. Human face detection in a complex background. *Pattern Recognition*, 27:53–63, 1994.

SmartCar: Detecting Driver Stress

Jennifer Healey and Rosalind Picard
Massachusetts Institute of Technology
Media Laboratory
20 Ames St, Cambridge MA, USA
fenn, picard@media.mit.edu

Abstract

Smart physiological sensors embedded in an automobile afford a novel opportunity to capture naturally occurring episodes of driver stress. In a series of ten ninety minute drives on public roads and highways, electrocardiogram, electromyogram, respiration and skin conductance sensors were used to measure autonomic nervous system activation. The signals were digitized in real time and stored on the SmartCar's pentium class computer. Each drive followed a pre-specified route through fifteen different events, from which four stress level categories were created according to the results of the subjects self report questionnaires. In total, 545 one minute segments were classified. A linear discriminant function was used to rank each feature individually based on recognition performance and a sequential forward floating selection (SFFS) algorithm was used to find an optimal set of features for recognizing patterns of driver stress (88.6%). Using multiple features improved performance significantly over the best single feature performance (62.2%).

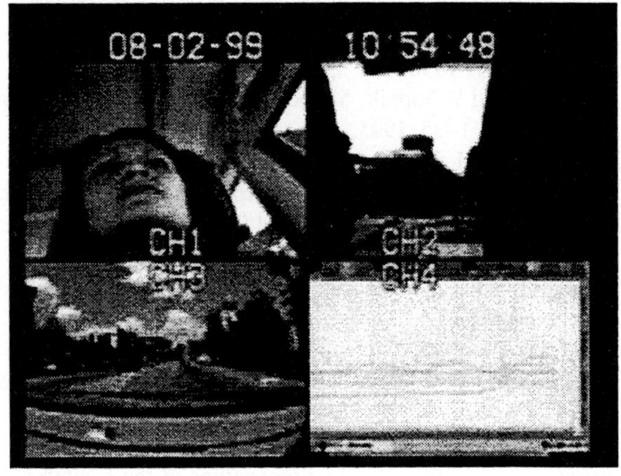

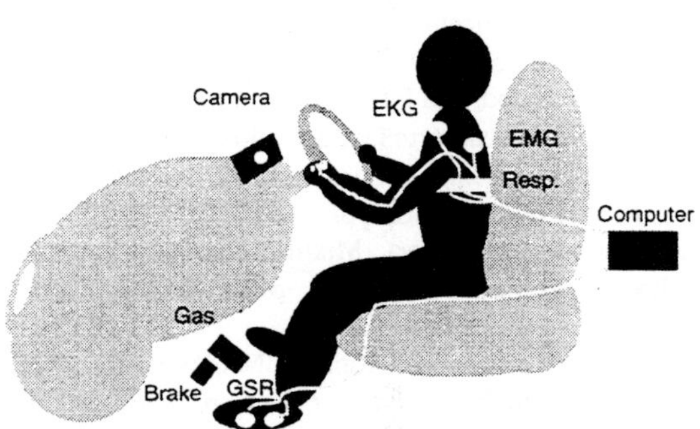

Figure 1. Above: a sample frame from the video collected during the experiment showing driver facial expression and road conditions schynchronized to the real-time physiological responses. Below: a diagram showing sensor placement. GSR sensors are placed on both the hand and the foot.

1. Introduction

Stress has been identified as an important health risk, contributing adversely to chronic problems such as back pain and migrane headaches and to life threatening conditions such as cardiac arrest and cancer, yet the problem of accurately detecting, recording and quantifying the salient features of stress remains a challenge to health professionals and researchers. Many features of physiological signals have been proposed as indicators of stress by cardiologists and psychophysiologists, but these are usually evaluated individually and their performance for recognition is seldom tested. This paper shows how pattern recognition techniques can be applied to identify the best combinations of features to detect stress in automobile drivers derived from four physiological sensor signals: electromyogram (EMG - $\mathcal{E}$), elec-

1051-4651/00 $10.00

trocardiogram (EKG), galvanic skin response (GSR - $\mathcal{G}$) and respiration through chest cavity expansion ($\mathcal{R}$). These signals were chosen because previous studies have found them useful for assessing arousal and stress[ELF83]. GSR has been noted as being particularly useful in studying driver stress[Hel78]. For this analysis, a SmartCar system was developed to collect physiological data from natural driving situations along with multiple video recordings to provide ground truth for validation. Four stress categories were defined by a questionnaire analysis of perceived stress ratings. Twelve features characterized each of 545 one minute data segments taken from the ten days of driving records. Each of these segments was labeled as belonging to one of four stress categories: low, neutral, high or very high stress.

2. Data Collection

A SmartCar system was developed for this experiment by augmenting a car with an on-board Pentium computer with video cameras a microphone and four physiological sensors. Figure 1 shows the placement of the sensors on the subject and the composite image record of the video cameras plus the video feed from the computer monitoring the sensors. The driving route was designed to simulate a commute to work. Table 1 shows a sequential list of the driving events as they were encountered and the median stress rating given to that event by the median of the questionnaires scores which ranged from "1" to "7." From these ratings four stress categories were created: very high (events 7,10), high (events 3, 12, 13), neutral (events 4,5,6,8,9) and low stress (events 1,2 14,15). The toll events and the garage exit were excluded from analysis due to excessive motion artifacts and inconsistencies in the experimental protocol.

3. Feature Extraction

Ten complete records of physiological data were collected from this experiment. Each record consists of approximately ninety minutes of data, however, the length of time for the experiment and for each of the fifteen driving driving events varied from day to day due to traffic conditions. From the records 545 one minute segments were extracted which belonged to one of the fifteen driving categories in Table 1.

From each of the one minute segments the following features were extracted: the mean and variance of the signals $\mathcal{E}$, $\mathcal{G}$, and $\mathcal{R}$, represented respectively by the symbols: $\mu_{\mathcal{E}}$, $\sigma_{\mathcal{E}}$; $\mu_{\mathcal{G}}$, $\sigma_{\mathcal{G}}$; and $\mu_{\mathcal{R}}$, $\sigma_{\mathcal{R}}$; features of the GSR orienting response, including the frequency of occurrence S_F, the sum of durations ΣS_D, the sum of magnitudes ΣS_M and the sum of the estimated areas ΣS_A. Two features were derived from the EKG signal, the heart rate (HR) and autonomic

Event Num.	Event Description	Stress Rating
1.	Beginning stationary period (rest1)	1
2.	Garage Exit	2
3.	City Road (city1)	4
4.	Toll Booth (toll1)	3
5.	Highway driving period (hwy1)	3
6.	Toll Booth (toll2)	3
7.	Exit Ramp Turnaround (exit)	5
8.	Toll Booth (toll3)	3
9.	Highway driving period (hwy2)	3
10.	Two Lane Merge (merge)	5
11.	Toll Booth (toll4)	3
12.	Bridge crossing (bridge)	4
13.	City Road (city2)	4
14.	Enter Garage	1
15.	End stationary period (rest2)	1

Table 1. A summary of driving events and the median stress rating from the ten questionnaires

balance (AB) from short term power spectrum heart rate variability.

Four features of the GSR response are derived from an algorithm which detects the onset and peak of individual responses, as shown in Figure 2. The detection algorithm first smoothes the segment using a digital elliptical filter with a cutoff at 4Hz. Next the derivative of the signal was calculated using the first forward difference ($\delta_{\mathcal{G}}$ [n] = $\mathcal{G}$[n] - $\mathcal{G}$ [n-1]) and a threshold was applied (0.093 μS per sec was found to yield good performance in practise). Responses occurring less than one second after a previous response were counted as a continuation of that response. Once the response was detected, the zero-crossings of the derivative preceding and following the response were identified as the onset and peak of the response respectively. The features for the magnitude S_M and duration S_D of each response are derived as:

$$S_M = t_{peak} - t_{onset} \quad (1)$$

$$S_D = \mathcal{G}_{peak} - \mathcal{G}_{onset} \quad (2)$$

From these measurements the area of the response is estimated by $S_A = \frac{1}{2} * S_M * S_D$. For each one minute segment, the sum of response magnitudes (ΣS_M), durations (ΣS_D), areas (ΣS_A) and the frequency of responses (S_F) are calculated.

The AB feature is calculated by finding the ratio of low frequency energy to high frequency energy in the spectrum

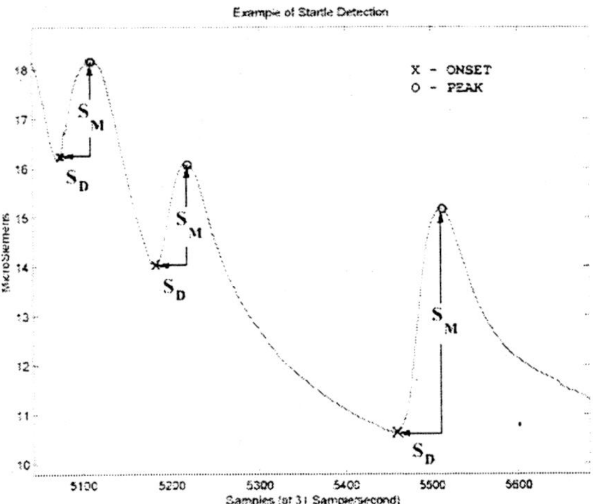

Figure 2. An example of GSR responses occurring in a one minute segment and the results of the algorithm showing onset "X" and peak "O" detection. The features S_M and S_D are derived as shown.

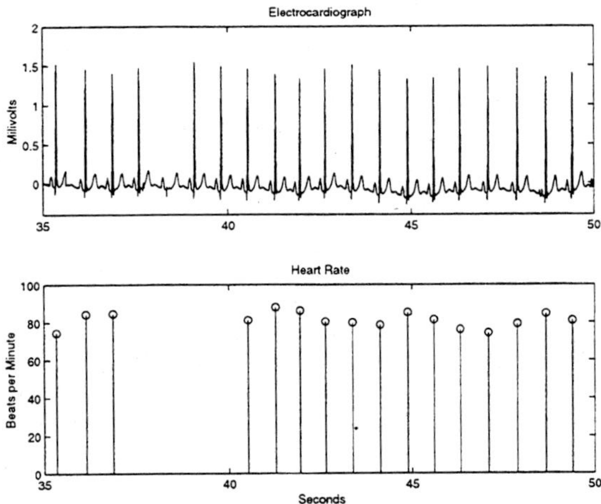

Figure 3. Above: The peaks or the "R" waves in the electrocardiograph signal are first detected using the WAVE software[Moo93]. Outliers in the heart rate time series, caused by missed beats are ignored rather than estimated. A Lomb-Scargill periodogram is then calculated on this time series.

of the heart rate (HR) signal. This feature used a five minute window of the heart rate time series centered on the midpoint of the minute segment used for the other features. To calculate AB, the heart rate time series was first derived from the EKG signal by detecting the amount of time between successive "R" wave peaks in the EKG. These peaks were detected using the WAVE software program developed by George Moody (available at http://ecg.mit.edu). This program was used to reject outliers as shown in Figure 3 and use a least-squares spectrum estimation (Lomb-Scargill) method to determine heart rate variability[Moo93] [Lom76]. Autonomic balance is a measure of the variability of the time series of the heart rate derived from the EKG. The low frequency (LF) variations in the heart rate (0.01-0.08 Hz) are influenced by both sympathetic and parasympathetic activity, while the high frequency (HF) variations (0.15-0.5 Hz) are almost exclusively due to parasympathetic activity[SSea93]. The ratio of low to high frequency energy and reflects the sympathovagal balance, a measure that increases in stressful situations and decrease with relaxation[MAea95]. The ratio of the sum of the energy in the LF band of this spectrum to the HF band is then calculated as the AB feature:

$$AB = \frac{LF}{HF} = \frac{\sum_{0Hz}^{0.08Hz} lombPSD(HR)}{\sum_{0.15Hz}^{0.5Hz} lombPSD(HR)} \quad (3)$$

For the AB feature, outliers could be eliminated to create a better estimate, however to calculate the heart rate variable (HR) a a uniformly sampled and smoothed instantaneous heart rate signal was created using the function "tach" from the WAVE software.

4. Analysis

Each of the individual features was tested to see how well it performed in a recognition task using a linear classifier. Using this classifier each class $k = 1, 2, 3, 4$ was modeled as a gaussian with μ_k equal to the sample mean for that class and σ^2 equal to the pooled variance. The classification was implemented by assigning the feature to the class k for which g_k was maximum[The89] where:

$$g_k(\hat{y}) = \frac{2m_k}{\sigma^2}\hat{y} - \frac{\mu_k^2}{\sigma^2} + 2ln(Pr[w_k]); \quad (4)$$

and the a priori probability of belonging to class k, $Pr[w_k] = \frac{1}{n_k}$ (where n_k is the number of members in class k). For the results in Table 2 leave one out and test cross-validation was used where first μ_k and σ^2 were calculated using all but the feature for one minute, then classifying the excluded feature according to the maximum g_k.

A second analysis was performed using features selected from Jain and Zongker's sequential forward floating selection (SFFS) algorithm [JZ97]. This algorithm used a k-nearest neighbor classifier and the leave one out and test

Feature	Rank	Correct	Feature	Rank	Correct
$\mu_{\mathcal{R}}$	1	62.2%	$\sigma_{\mathcal{E}}$	6	53.5 %
$\mu_{\mathcal{G}}$	2	62.0%	ΣS_A	7	53.0 %
ΣS_D	3	58.5%	HR	8	52.6 %
$\mu_{\mathcal{E}}$	4	58.3%	AB	9	52.5 %
S_F	5	57.6%	$\sigma_{\mathcal{R}}$	10	50.2 %
ΣS_M	5	57.6%	$\sigma_{\mathcal{R}}$	11	48.3 %

Table 2. A ranking of each individual feature

Optimal Selected Feature Set	SFFS kNN
AB, HR, ΣS_D, ΣS_M, $\mu_{\mathcal{E}}$, $\mu_{\mathcal{R}}$, $\sigma_{\mathcal{R}}$	88.6 %
AB, HR, ΣS_D, ΣS_M, S_F, $\mu_{\mathcal{G}}$, $\sigma_{\mathcal{G}}$	88.4 %

Table 3. Recognition rates achieved using Jain and Zongker's FS-SFFS algorithm with a k nearest neighbor classifier. No significant drop in performance occurs when $\mathcal{E}$ and $\mathcal{R}$ are eliminated from the initial pool.

method and shows that by combining multiple physiological features, the recognition of driver stress can be significantly improved as shown in Table 3. A further feature selection and classification analysis was done eliminating signals which might primarily depend on physical motion, $\mathcal{E}$ and $\mathcal{R}$, from the initial pool. The result shows no significant decrease in performance indicating both that the stress detected is more likely to be mental and emotional and that high recognition rates can be achieved with few sensors using multiple features.

5. Conclusions

This research shows the application of pattern recognition techniques to the problem of emotional stress detection using features from multiple physiological signals. The results show that by detecting patterns across combinations of features, performance for recognizing stress in drivers improves significantly from at best 62.2% to 88.6%. This performance was shown not to depend mainly on motion artifacts. Perfect performance is not expected due to ambiguities in labeling the stress level, however, the recognition rates from this research suggest that stress information could be used by a computer to control non-critical driving applications, such as as music selection and managing on-board information appliances such as cell phones and navigation aids. In the broader picture, a regular commute offers the opportunity to record daily stress signals for analysis. Records of these stress patterns over time could provide an indicator of changes in life stress, giving a quantified feedback to the individual about how life choices could be affecting their stress level and providing a new metric with which to make informed choices about their health and behavior.

6. Acknowledgments

The authors would like to acknowledge Kelly Koskelin coding the AB variables, Susan Mosher for data collection, Tom Minka for help with the pattern recognition code and Tanzeem Choudhury for proof-reading. We would also like to thank George Moody and Pr. Roger Mark for the EKG software and Doug Jain and Anil Zongker for the SFFS code. This work was supported by the MIT Media Lab's Digital Life and Things That Think consortia.

References

[ELF83] Paul Ekman, Robert W. Levenson, and Wallace V. Friesen. Autonomic nervous system activity distinguishes among emotions. *Science*, 221:1208–1210, Sep. 1983.

[Hel78] M. Helander. Applicability of drivers' electrodermal response to the design of the traffic environment. *Journal of Applied Psychology*, 63(4):481–488, 1978.

[JZ97] A. Jain and D. Zongker. Feature-selection: Evaluation, application, and small sample performance. *PAMI*, 19(2):153–158, February 1997.

[Lom76] N. R. Lomb. Least-squares frequency analysis of unequally spaced data. *Astrophysics and Space Science*, 39:447–462, 1976.

[MAea95] Rollin McCraty, Mike Atkinsom, and William Tiller et al. The effects of emotions on short-term power spectrum analysis of heart rate variability. *American Journal of Cardiology*, 76:1089–1093, 1995.

[Moo93] George B. Moody. Spectral analysis of heart rate without resampling. In *Computers in Cardiology*, pages 715–718, Los Alamitos, CA, 1993. IEEE Computer Society Press.

[SSea93] J. Paul Spiers, Bernard Silke, and Ultan McDermott et al. Time and frequency domain assessment of heart rate variability: A theoretical and clinical appreciation. *Clinical and Autonomic Research*, 3:145–158, 1993.

[The89] C. W. Therrien. *Decision Estimation and Classification*. John Wiley and Sons, Inc., New York, 1989.

Structuring Personal Activity Records based on Attention — Analyzing Videos from Head-mounted Camera

Yuichi NAKAMURA † ‡ Jun'ya Ohde † Yuichi OHTA †
† Institute of Engineering Mechanics and Systems
University of Tsukuba
1-1-1 Tennodai, Tsukuba, 305-8573, JAPAN
‡ PRESTO, Japan Science and Technology Corporation (JST)

Abstract

This paper introduces a novel method for analyzing video records which contain personal activities captured by a head mounted camera. This aims to support the user to retrieve the most important or relevant portions from the videos. For this purpose, we use the user's behaviors which appear when he/she pays attention to something. We define two types of those behaviors, one of which is "gaze at something in a short period" and the other is "staying and continuously see something". These behaviors and the focused object can be detected by estimating camera and object motion. We describe, in this paper, the details of the method and experiments in which the method was applied to ordinary events.

1 Introduction

We often need a help for recording or memorizing our activities. Although we can usually remember impressive events, it is hard to recall things in detail, *e.g.*, in which order we did something or what was there. We hope devices for augmenting our memory by visual information processing. Fortunately, in the near future, we will certainly get wearable hardware with enough computational power to deal with real-time image processing and large amount of videos.

One of the leading works is DyPERS which gives appropriate information to the users according to what the user sees[1]. The system retrieves pre-recorded information when a pre-registered object appears in the user's view. However, we still need considerable efforts to realize a system that can record our activities and provides an appropriate memory.

One of the most important topics is data structuring, summarization, and retrieval from enormous video records. Videos taken as personal experiences can be long and redundant, and the user needs to take great pains in searching for the right portion. This disadvantage may spoil the merit of video records.

For this purpose, we propose a new method for structural analysis and summarization of the video data. First, we define two types of behaviors that occurs when the user pays attention. Next, we describe a method for detecting those behaviors by separating the camera motions and object motions. Then, we describe that structuring videos based on these behaviors effectively reduces the user's efforts to recall or retrieve the information he/she wants.

2 Attention and Apparent Motion

2.1 Views from Head Mounted Camera

The system needs to capture the views around the user at anytime he wants. One of the best locations of a camera is on the user's head, since the view from the camera can be similar to what the user sees. The user can easily recall what happened by checking the view.

To deal with videos taken from a head mounted camera, however, we have to solve the following problems.

- Views can be shaky. The user may sometimes feel pains in watching those videos.
- Videos are usually long and redundant. It requires considerable time to look through them.

For this purpose, we propose a new method for structurally summarizing those videos:

- It picks up scenes that the user tends to remember, and that can be anchors of his/her memory.
- It presents a comprehensible overview and to enable quick access to the video contents by providing the above scenes to the user.

It first applies motion estimation to an image sequence, and detects two kinds of scene in which the user intentionally looks at something. Figure 1 shows the brief overview of our idea. By presenting those scenes, the system enables us to browse our activity records.

1051-4651/00 $10.00 © 2000 IEEE

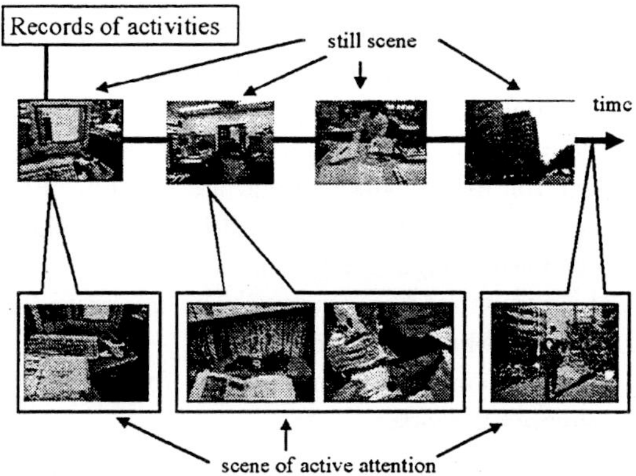

Figure 1. Overview: The upper row shows where the user was and what the user continuously saw; the lower row shows what user gazed.

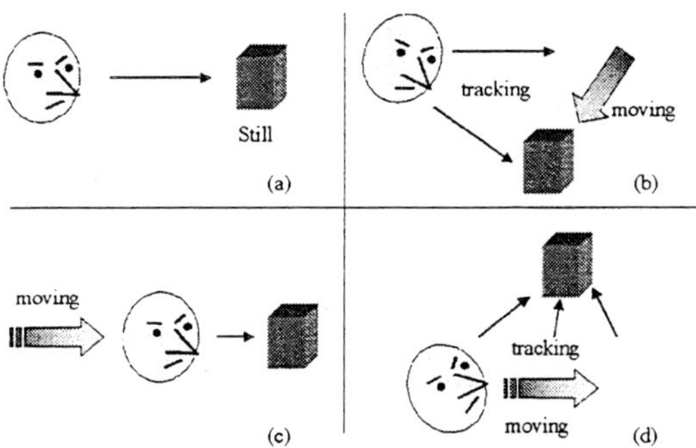

Figure 2. Head motion in paying attention

2.2 Attention and Behaviors

When a person is paying attention to visual objects or events, head movements shown in Figure 2 occur.

For these behaviors, we first define two types of attention.

Active Attention: We often gaze at something and track it when it attracts our interest. If the target stays still, head motion will be Figure 2(a) or (b). If the person is moving, they will be Figure 2(c) or (d). This type of behavior lasts relatively short time, *e.g.*, a few seconds.

Passive Attention: We often look vaguely and continuously at something around ourselves during desk works, conversations, or rests. This type of behavior does not always express a person's attention. However, this kind of scene can be a very good cue to remember where the person was. Head motions tend to be still as shown in Figure 2(a), often with small movements such as nodding. The duration of those scenes is usually long, for example, 10 minutes.

We consider both of the above as important keys which effectively represent the video contents. Hereafter, we call the video frames in which those behaviors occur as *scene(s) of attention*.

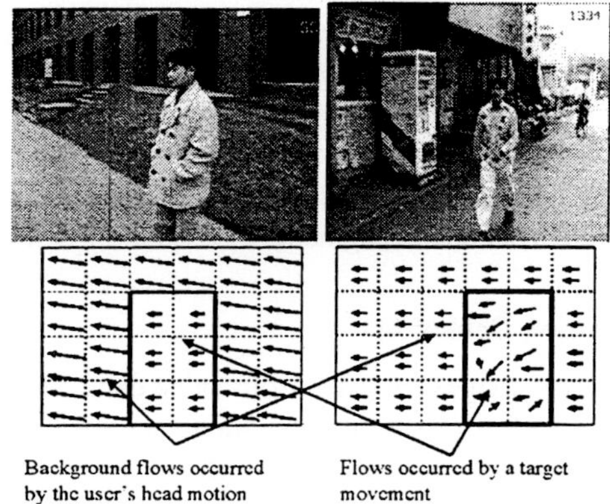

Figure 3. Apparent motion vectors on active attention

2.3 Image Features

Head motions cause the apparent motion of the background in an image, while the region of a target is likely to stay around the image center. In most case, therefore, we have at most two important image regions which have different apparent motions.

background motion: Apparent motions caused by the camera motion, *e.g.*, the head motion.

target motion: We assume that the biggest region which has motions different from that of the background draws the user's attention. If the region is staying almost at the same position of our view, it has high possibility of being the target at which the user is gazing.

In the case of passive attention, we have to consider Figure 2(a) with small movements or slow movements for looking around. The view does not change much, and the images taken during those periods largely overlap each other. Consequently, we can detect passive attention by detecting the background motion.

In the case of active attention, we track an object of interest. The apparent motion vectors on the object are relatively small compared to those on background as shown in the left column in Figure 3. If an object is rotating or deforming, a region with complicated motion vectors appears as shown in the right column of Figure 3. If a region of the above types stays in the view, we can assume it draws the user's attention. Although this is not always true, we anyway tend to remember the biggest target moving in front of us. Thus the scene or the object could be a good cue to recall our activities.

3 Scene Detection

The flow of our scene detection process is as follows:

1. Find the correspondence and motion parameters between two consecutive images, which are apart by one to several frames. We apply a motion estimation method based on the central projection model.

2. Detect still scenes which correspond to passive attention, by finding portions with small background motion and by merging them.
3. Detect a target which is possibly gazed and tracked, by using the correspondence obtained by 1. If a target is detected, label the segment as a scene of active attention.

3.1 Motion Detection

First, two images are taken from video data. They are the images apart from each other by one to several frames. We applied a motion estimation method based on the central projection model. Although not a few methods with simpler models have been proposed for video mosaicing (for example, [3]), most of them assume conditions which do not hold in our environment. Indoor objects can be close to the camera, and the depth range in the view widely varies.

In central projection model, the apparent motion $u(\mathbf{x})$ of an image point $\mathbf{x}$ can be calculated by using the camera motion $\mathbf{t} = (t_1, t_2, t_3)^T$ and the camera rotation $\boldsymbol{\omega} = (\omega_1, \omega_2, \omega_3)^T$.

$$u(\mathbf{x}) = \frac{1}{Z(\mathbf{x})}\mathbf{A}\mathbf{t} + \mathbf{B}\omega \qquad (1)$$

where,

$$\mathbf{A} = \begin{bmatrix} -f & 0 & x \\ 0 & -f & y \end{bmatrix},$$

$$\mathbf{B} = \begin{bmatrix} (xy)/f & -(f^2+x^2)/f & y \\ -(f^2+x^2)/f & -(xy)/f & -x \end{bmatrix}$$

f is the focal length, $Z(\mathbf{x})$ is the depth at the position $\mathbf{x}$ on the image plane.

We denote the intensity $I(\mathbf{x}, T)$ at point $\mathbf{x}$ at time T. If the above camera motion and rotation occurred during $[T - \delta t, T]$, the following relationship ideally holds.

$$I(\mathbf{x}, T) = I(\mathbf{x} - \mathbf{u}, T - \delta t)$$

Thus we can expect to get the motion parameters by minimizing the following error E.

$$E = \sum_{x,y}\{I(\mathbf{x}, T) - I(\mathbf{x} - \mathbf{u}, T - \delta t)\}^2 \qquad (2)$$

To make this calculation possible, we assume the depth is uniform within each small block, *e.g.*, a block of 5x5 pixels.

We need a new method for applying the above calculation to shaky videos from a head-mounted camera, though the above idea is based on Bergen's method [4]. Note that the objective of this calculation is the correspondence between two images, and the above central projection model is used mainly as the constraints. In this sense, the accuracy of the obtain motion parameters, especially for the depth, is not important if the correspondence is correctly obtained.

The process is as follows:

1. By dyadic down-sampling, for example, 1/2, 1/4, and 1/8, multi-resolution images are created.
2. The initial motion parameters are given to the system. For the most coarse image, the motion parameters obtained for the previous frame are given[1]. For finer images, the parameters obtained by the calculation for more coarse images are given.
3. The error defined in equation 2 is minimized by the Levenberg-Marquardt method.
4. The above operations are applied for all resolutions throughout the video.

The above method does not work well when the camera motion is small, since the method needs to determine the depth. To prevent this, we first check the apparent motion by simply checking the differences of the two images. The two images are blurred, and one of these is subtracted from the other. If the sum of the differences is smaller than the threshold, we think that the camera motion is too small to calculate the above motion parameters.

In this case, we just skip the motion estimation step and the images are gathered into a group with no motions (hereafter abbreviated as *no-motion-group*).

3.2 Still Scene Detection

A still scene is detected by combining the above obtained no-motion-groups. For this purpose, we check the apparent motions of the image center between two still no-motion-groups. If the total motion is smaller than the predetermined threshold, we regard those groups belong to the same scene. Thus we merged them, and label the group as a scene of passive attention.

3.3 Active Attention and Target

Active attention of the user is detected by separating egomotion, *i.e.*, apparent motion by the camera movement, and object motions.

1. The image at the previous frame is transformed so that the viewing position and the camera orientation is equal to those of the current image. By using the motion parameters, $(\boldsymbol{t}, \boldsymbol{\omega}, Z(\mathbf{x}))$, transform the image $I_{T-\delta t}$ at the frame $T - \delta t$ to the view $I^T_{T-\delta t}$ at time T.
2. The similarity between the image I_T and $I^T_{T-\delta t}$ are evaluated. We consider a window around each pixel, *e.g.*, a window of 5x5 pixels. Correlation of the two windows from different images at the same position is calculated.
3. The candidate region is detected. The image plane is divided into small blocks B_k, and the number N_k of pixels which correlation value is smaller than the threshold th_d is counted in each block. If N_k is larger than the threshold th_c, the block is labeled as a candidate region. If two or more such candidate blocks are touching each

[1] For the first (initial) frame of a sequence, the initial motion parameters are all set to zero, *i.e.*, no motion.

other, they are merged into one region. Then, the largest region is detected as a candidate at the current frame.

4. The score $P_k(t)$ for each candidate block at time t is determined.

$$P_k(t) = \begin{cases} P_k(t-1) + p & \text{if candidate} \\ P_k(t-1) - q & \text{otherwise} \end{cases}$$

where p is the score obtained from one frame, and q is the forgetting factor. At any time when the score is greater than threshold th_e, we consider the block is the target of attention.

4 Experiments

We applied our method to several videos, any of which is around 10 minutes in length.

Apparent motion is estimated at every four frames. The results are usually satisfactory for our purpose. Since the accuracy of motion estimation throughout the sequences is hard to measure, we evaluated the results by the number serious errors. If the number of the pixels which have no correspondence pixels in the other image exceed 30% of the total number of pixels, we regard the case as a serious error. In our experiments, the rate of those serious errors is less than 1%, though the rate is slightly different among videos.

Here we show one example in detail. The video is 12 minute (22,000 frames) in length, and recorded during cooking in the user's home. The detected scenes are shown in Figure 4. In each column, the vertical direction expresses the pseudo time axis. The leftmost images are detected scenes of passive attention (still scenes) and the images on the right side are scenes of active attention.

For each scene of passive attention, the representative frames are the frames at the first or the last of the duration, and their sizes are determined by the scene duration. Seven scenes are reasonably grouped except that Scene3 and Scene4 are separated. Motion estimation failed at some frames between them because of the rapid head movement which caused blurred images.

Scenes of active attention are connected to the corresponding scene of passive attention. If it has no corresponding scene, it is directly connected to the vertical line. The red rectangle in each scene expresses a candidate of the target to which paid attention.

The detected scenes are satisfactory for the summarization of the video. Most of the detected targets are the objects at which the user gazed. The detection result includes not a few false positives, in this case, 4 scenes (d, e, g, and o) out of 23 detected scenes. We need further investigation to eliminate false detection, though this is not a serious problem.

5 Conclusion

In this paper, we briefly presented the overview of our video structuring scheme. We first showed how the user's

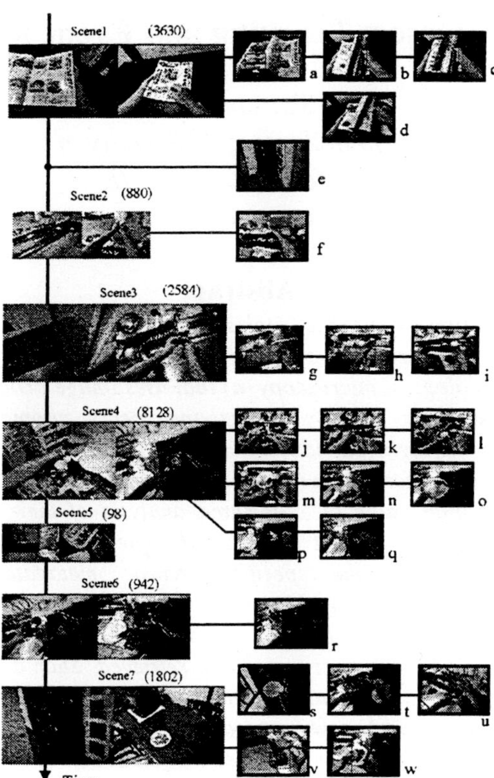

Figure 4. Detection Result : In each column, the vertical direction expresses time passing. The leftmost images are the still scenes and the images on the right side are the scenes of active attention. Each rectangle in the images expresses a candidate of the target to which paid attention.

attention can be estimated from videos taken by head-mounted cameras. Then, we described the method for detecting scenes of attention by motion estimation between frames. Although our experiments are simple, our method showed enough potential for realizing augmented memory. This research is still at the beginning stage. We need further investigation such as improvement toward real-time processing, evaluation, combination with other image analyses, and so on.

References

[1] Jebara,T., Schiele,B., Oliver,N., Pentland,A., "DyPERS: Dynamic Personal Enhanced Reality System", MIT Media Laboratory, Perceptual Computing Technical Report ♯463

[2] Kawashima, T., et.al., "Situation-based Selective Video-Recording System for Memory Aid", Proc. ICIP, III, 835-838, 1996

[3] Szeliski,R. and Shum,H.: "Creating Full View Panoramic Image Mosaics and Environment Maps", Proc. SIGRAPH, pp.251-258, 1997.

[4] Bergen,J., Anandan,P., and Hanna,K.: "Hierarchical model-based motion estimation" Proc. ECCV, pp.237-252, 1997.

Object Tracking and Event Recognition in Biological Microscopy Videos

Shotton, D.M.
Department of Zoology University of Oxford, Oxford OX1 3PS, UK
david.shotton@zoo.ox.ac.uk

Rodríguez, A.; Guil, N.; and Trelles O.
Computer Architecture Department, University of Malaga, 29017 Malaga, Spain
{andresr;nico;ots}@ac.uma.es

Abstract

We present a video analysis and content-based video query and retrieval system for research videos arising from biological microscopy (a) that uses image processing procedures to identify objects and events automatically within the digitized videos, thus leading to the generation of content information (specific intrinsic metadata) of high information value by automated analysis of their visual content, and (b) that permits subsequent queries to be performed on the specific intrinsic metadata thus generated, allowing important factual and analytical information to be obtained and selected video sequences matching the query criteria to be retrieved. Such a system requires the novel use of image and video processing techniques, and new approaches to the organization, accessing and querying of video metadata databases.

1. Introduction

Moving image data (videos, movies, animations and four-dimensional (4D) confocal microscopy images, having the spatio-temporal dimensions of x, y (and, for 4D confocal data, also z) and ***time***, represent the most complex and demanding image type to be stored in scientific digital image databases such as the BioImage Database [1, 2]. This is both because digitized video files are typically two or three orders of magnitude larger that those for other forms of multidimensional image data such as three-dimensional (3D; x, y, z) volume images or multispectral satellite images, and also because their subsequent viewing by a database user has a time-critical component.

In this work, we have developed an analysis and annotation system for a specific type of scientific video recordings. This system allows the generation of information (metadata) of high intrinsic value from moving image data that are recorded digitally or on videotape, by intelligent analysis of their visual content, information that it is impossible to query by traditional query methods that rely upon separately recorded ancillary textual metadata. The extracted metadata are stored and organised in a database over which a content-based query and retrieval prototype has been built. The system is being used to extract knowledge in an automated manner from research video recordings arising from cell biological microscopy, but the system developed is easily extendable to other types of moving image data (e.g. soccer game videos). Such a system requires the use of image and video processing techniques, and new approaches to the organization, accessing and querying of video metadata databases.

2. System and Methods

The proposed strategy for video analysis and content-based querying can be formulated in the following steps:

Object detection: Image processing is required initially to identify the discrete objects in each image sequence, and to track the movement of these objects along the space/time axes. To this end, various visual feature extraction algorithms have been combined and improved, in the light of detailed biological knowledge of the systems.

Image understanding and event analysis: Using the data from the trajectories of the individual objects, we address a particular issue of image understanding, namely the automatic detection of events. After event detection, an automatic event annotation procedure is used to produce the video metadata database.

Query formulation: The spatio-temporal attributes of the objects and events detected or defined in the previous steps are subsequently used for the video query and retrieval system.

Video selection: The result of a successful query is the identification of a particular video sequence or a set of video clips from among those stored in the database.

2.1. Metadata definition and data model

We define and distinguish three classes of metadata relating to images and video recordings [3]:

Ancillary metadata is simple text-based information concerning the image or video filename, title, format, subject, author, and technical details of the image or video preparation, but which does *not* relate specifically and directly to the visual content of the image or video frames.

Generic intrinsic metadata relate to attributes of images and video frames such as colour, size, shape, and texture, reducible to numerical image primitives than, once extracted, may be employed to locate images using the simple paradigm "*Find me any image or video frame that looks like this one*", or that can be used to produce a storyboard for a video or to create the foundation for a frame-accurate index that provides non-linear access to the video [4].

Specific intrinsic metadata, resulting from intelligent manual or automated analysis of the images or video frames, describe the spatial positions of specific objects within images, and the spatio-temporal locations of objects and events within videos. Of the three metadata types, we have focused our work on this latter one, which is the most rewarding in terms of information content, since it relates directly to the spatio-temporal features within a video that are of most immediate importance to our human understand of video content, namely "*Where, when and why is what happening to whom?*" Subsequent query by content on this kind of metadata extends the query domain from the conventional one of textual keyword or image matching techniques, to include direct interrogation of the spatio-temporal attributes of the objects of real interest within the video and of their associated event information.

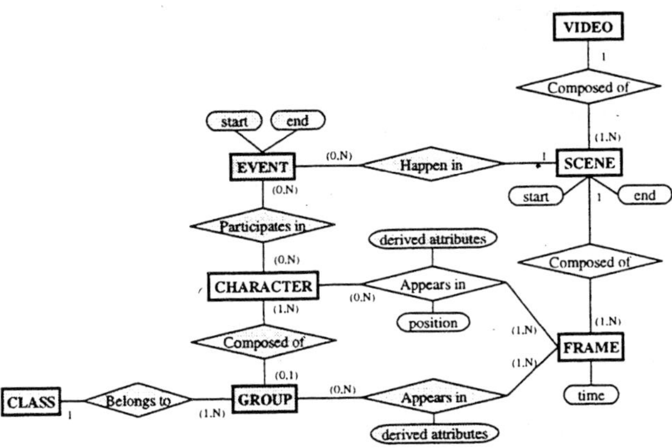

Figure 1. Metadata E-R model

The specific intrinsic metadata describing the video content is stored using the data model outlined in Figure 1. With this model we can register the **characters** that appears in the video, group them in significant **groups** and follow the spatio-temporal position and behavioural evolution of the individuals and groups through the **frames** that compose the **scenes** in the **video**. The model also registers special happenings in the scenes (**events**) that can involve characters, and stores specific parameters defining what, where, when... happened to whom in these events.

The metadata required for different types of video item vary. However, the metadata model described above is designed to be inclusive, and to permit metadata relating to novel video items to be added easily, so that the same database system can be used for different types of videos [3].

The application domain chosen for our demonstration of query by content of videos using such specific intrinsic metadata involves the analysis of scientific videos of biological specimens. Initially, two sets of cell biological videos have been used as the model subjects for this work, both derived from studies of living cells under the light microscope.

2.2. Analysis of Wound healing videos

The first, *wound healing videos*, were made using time-lapse microscopy to record the closure of *in vitro* wounds made in confluent monolayers of cultured epithelial cells under a variety of experimental conditions, for example transient perfusion exposure of the cells to drugs that effect cytoskeletal polymerization [5, 6]. For this type of video, questions of interest relate to the rates of wound healing, as measured by reduction of cell-free areas, as healing proceeds under different drug regimes, in contrast, for example, to the *in vitro* motility of the same type of cells at the free margins of unwounded colonies.

The automatic feature extraction procedure for this type of videos is designed to measure the rate of wound healing by the progressive loss of open wound area. To this end, we have used computer image processing techniques to distinguish the uniform character of the cell-free open wound in each frame from those regions of cellular monolayer on either side, where the image texture is quite different, being characterized by high frequency modulations of the image intensity.

Segmentation of the uniform wound region from the rest of the image has been undertaken by using a differential operator that calculates the changes in the first spatial derivative of the image [8]. Further histogram equalization and image thresholding allows us to exclude high contrast zones. The resultant threshold closely follows the margins of the ruffling wound edge cells.

Once the image processing has been completed, an internal bounding box is used to compute the wound area per unit length of wound, and the edge lengths, for each video frame. This internal bounding box, which is used as a safeguard to exclude end effects, is defined as a rectangle oriented parallel with the axis of the linear wound (computed by principal components), which lies fully within the video frame, and which is wider than the maximum wound width. The size and position of this bounding box (see Figure 2) is kept constant for all the frames of the video that are to be analysed.

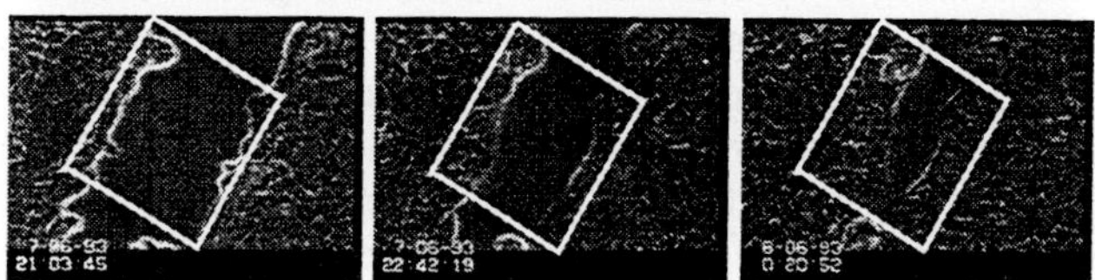

Figure 2. Feature extraction in a wound healing video

The loss of wound area per unit length of wound per minute within this bounding box permits the rate of wound closure, and hence the effectiveness of the healing process, to be calculated. Significant changes in this healing rate may be related to changes in the external environment of the cells.

2.3. Analysis of Moving Bacterial Cell Videos

The second, *bacterial rotation videos*, are recordings in real time of the movements of free-swimming bacteria, and of the rotations of bacteria tethered to glass coverslips using an anti-flagellin antibody, as their flagellar rotations change velocity or direction in response to environmental stimuli [7]. For this type of video, questions of interest relate to the determination of individual and population statistics concerning run lengths and velocities, and the frequencies, durations and patterns of tumbles of free-swimming bacteria, and concerning the rotational directions and speeds of tethered bacteria, and the frequencies and their patterns of stops and reversals, correlated with changes of environmental conditions.

The real time bacterial motility video recordings that we have analysed were made in the laboratory of Professor Judy Armitage. The commercial system presently in use in that laboratory for the analysis of bacterial motility [9] has severe limitations in the number of bacteria that can be simultaneously tracked, and extent of the data that is analysed and stored, both problems related to the fact that it is designed to work with limited hardware resources in real time direct from a video camera or a videotape.

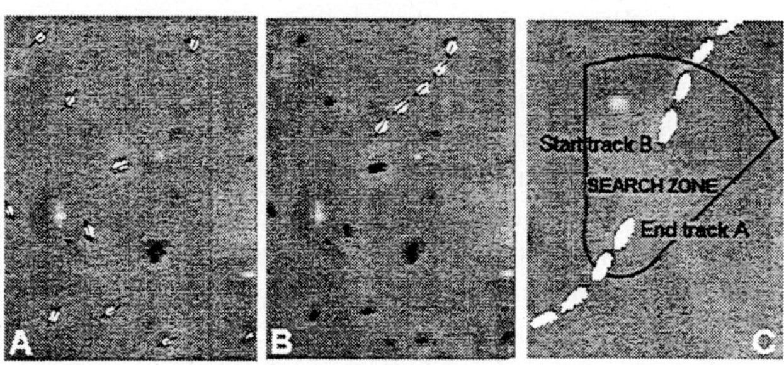

Figure 3. Automated identification and tracking of mobile bacteria

These bacterial motility videos contain large numbers of 'characters' (the bacteria), presenting a high level of complexity for the analysis and metadata extraction. In a first stage of the analysis, an initial segmentation of the frame images is undertaken with due regard for the variations in background illumination between frames, using a dynamic thresholding procedure [8,10]. Subsequently, individual bacteria are identified using a growing region algorithm, where bacterial "objects" are built from an initial seed point inside each bacterium. For each cell, we can then calculate its initial position, area and orientation in space (Figure 3a).

The next step is to track the movements of the cells (Figure 3b). The tracking problem can be defined as one of recognising the same object in consecutive frames of the video. The initial algorithm used to solve this problem is simple, and relies on the fact that any bacterium is likely to show a similar area and orientation on adjacent frames of the video, and that its position in any frame is likely to be close to that in the preceding frame. Application of this algorithm results in bacterial trajectories from which features such as speed, direction and curvature can be extracted. However, since in the space between the microscope slide and the overlying coverslip the individual bacteria are swimming unrestricted in three dimensions, they may stray from the narrow focal plane of the microscope objective lens and become temporarily lost from view, and hence lost to the initial segmentation and cell recognition algorithms, causing fragmentation of their trajectories. Since for the scientific analysis of bacterial movement is important to have trajectories as long as possible, there is a need to link partial or broken trajectories into longer and continuous ones. This is achieved by a post-processing algorithm that checks, for every partial trajectory that ends, whether there is another partial trajectory which is spatially adjacent and which starts within an appropriate time interval (a few frames later), that matches the first one in features such as speed and direction, and the shape and size of the bacterium. If these conditions are fulfilled, the two trajectories may be linked to form a longer one (see Figure 3c).

For the rotating tethered bacteria, the task of identifying the same cell in successive video frames is obviously more straightforward, and the salient features to record from such videos are the instantaneous speed, handedness and duration of each rotation, accelerations and decelerations, the frequency of reversals, and the duration of stops.

3. Results

The spatio-temporal attributes of the objects and events detected in the previous steps must be properly organized in a searchable database, to allow subsequent queries to locate particular cells, events or behaviours, correlated with changes of environmental conditions.

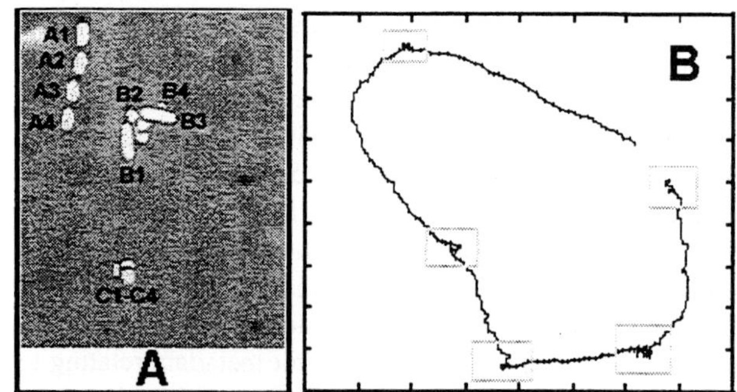

Figure 4. Event detection for assigning behaviour state

For example, for free swimming bacteria, the important events to detect are changes between behavioural states, namely **forward swimming** (Figure 4Aa), with all the flagella rotating counter-clockwise, **tumbling** (Figure 4Ab), with the flagella rotating clockwise, and **stationary** (Figure 4Ac). For each bacterium, the system determines and stores specific intrinsic metadata relating to such states (see Figure 4B for an example of typical bacterium tracking where five tumbling states are detected, marked with boxes). The instantaneous velocity, the duration, direction and curvature of individual trajectories, and the frequency, duration and patterns of tumbles and stops, together with spatio-temporal information form the metadata that locates these events or actions within the video as a whole, and that can be used to correlate them with details about the environmental conditions pertaining at the time. In addition, summary statistical metadata may be produced describing the motility of the whole bacterial population in the video.

Once the metadata database has been built, the system allows the following types of query to be made concerning such videos. For *wound healing videos*: determination of the rate of wound healing at particular times; or changes in the rate in response to drug treatment. The first query can be answered by directly looking at the appropriate register in the spatio-temporal position table, where we can find the wound area for each frame in the video (results for wound area are displayed in Figure 5), with its associated derived metadata, the instantaneous wound healing rate. It can be seen that there is very good agreement between the automated results (this study) and those obtained manually [5]. Changes in this rate due to drug administration can be found by searching the database for differences in the healing rate before and after administration of the drug.

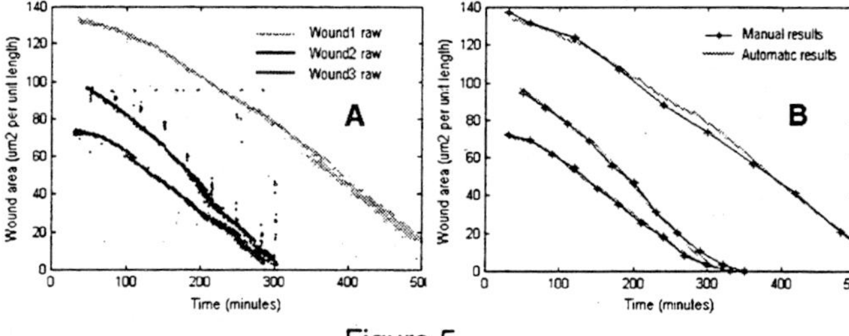

Figure 5.
A: Wound area evolution for three healing experiments;
B: Comparison with experimental results after area filtering

Examples of queries for videos of *swimming bacteria* are: "Identify all the video clips showing bacteria that swim at a velocity of at least x µm per second", and "Find me all video sequences where, after the administration of drug A, the average tumble frequency decreases by more than 30%". For the first query, a simple selection permits identification of the video frames containing all bacteria with a speed, averaged over the preceding 25 frames (1 second), above x µm per second (recorded as derived metadata in the spatio-temporal position table). The second question requires a calculation of the average tumble frequency in the scenes before and after the drug administration, determined from the temporal information recorded for all tumbles.

As result of a successful query, a list of pointers to video files together with a set or ranges of frame numbers is returned by the system, allowing the video clips matching the query to be recovered.

4. Discussion

The system developed allows the automated analysis of the content of scientific videos, producing meaningful specific intrinsic metadata that support subsequent queries to obtain important factual and analytical information, and to retrieve selected video sequences matching the query criteria. In all cases we have observed a significant increase in both accuracy and efficiency when undertaking such analyses using the algorithms developed, rather than by hand.

Moreover, the metadata stored in the database can be subjected to further analysis and mined to produce more elaborate knowledge, for example, the discovery of common patterns in the behaviour of the characters (the bacteria), or their classification into two classes (e.g. normal and non-tumbling mutants). Due to the modular nature of the system, this resulting new knowledge can also be stored in the database as further derived specific intrinsic metadata, which can then be subjected to further queries.

It is clear that this system could have widespread usefulness for the analysis of other types of moving image data.

5. References

[1] J.M. Carazo and E.H.K. Stelzer, "The BioImage Database Project: Organizing multi-dimensional biological images in an object-relational database", J. Structural Biology 155 (1999), pp. 97-102 (http://www.bioimage.org).

[2] T. Boudier and D.M. Shotton, "Video on the Internet: an introduction to the digital encoding, compression and transmission of moving image data", J. Structural Biology 125 (1999), pp. 133-155.

[3] A. Rodríguez, N. Guil, O. Trelles and D.M. Shotton, "Metadata extraction and organization for the automated content analysis of biological videos" (2000) (manuscript in preparation).

[4] A. Gupta, "Visual Information Retrieval Technology - A Virage Perspective", Virage Inc. White Paper. (1997) (available at http://www.virage.com).

[5] J.W. Lewis, "The effects of colchicine and brefeldin A on the rate of experimental *in vitro* epithelial wound healing", Undergraduate research project dissertation, Univ. Oxford. (1994).

[6] J.W. Lewis and D. M. Shotton, "Time-lapse video microscopy of wound healing in epithelial cell monolayers: effects of drugs that induce microtubule depolymerization and Golgi disruption", Proc. Roy. Microscop. Soc. 30 (1995), pp. 134-135.

[7] M. Manson, J. Armitage, J. Hoch and R. Macnab, "Bacterial locomotion and signal transduction", J. Bacteriology 180 (1998), pp. 1009-1022.

[8] N. Guil, J.M. Gonzalez and E.L. Zapata, "Bidimensional shape detection using an invariant approach", J.Pattern Recognition 32 (1999), pp. 1025-1038.

[9] G. Hobson, "Hobson Tracker User Manual", Hobson Tracking Systems Ltd., 697 Abbey Lane, Sheffield S11 9ND, UK (1996).

[10] D.H. Ballard and C.M. Brown, "Computer Vision", (1982) Prentice Hall, pp. 143-146.

Automatic Genre Identification for Content-Based Video Categorization

Ba Tu Truong
Svetha Venkatesh
Department of Computer Science
Curtin University of Technology
GPO Box U1987, Perth, 6845, W. Australia
{truongbt, svetha}@cs.curtin.edu.au

Chitra Dorai
IBM T.J. Watson Research Center
P.O. Box 704, Yorktown Heights
New York 10598, USA
dorai@watson.ibm.com

Abstract

This paper presents a set of computational features originating from our study of editing effects, motion, and color used in videos, for the task of automatic video categorization. These features besides representing human understanding of typical attributes of different video genres, are also inspired by the techniques and rules used by many directors to endow specific characteristics to a genre-program which lead to certain emotional impact on viewers. We propose new features whilst also employing traditionally used ones for classification. This research, goes beyond the existing work with a systematic analysis of trends exhibited by each of our features in genres such as cartoons, commercials, music, news, and sports, and it enables an understanding of the similarities, dissimilarities, and also likely confusion between genres. Classification results from our experiments on several hours of video establish the usefulness of this feature set. We also explore the issue of video clip duration required to achieve reliable genre identification and demonstrate its impact on classification accuracy.

1. Introduction

Automatic classification of digital video into various genres, or categories such as sports, news, commercials, music, cartoons, documentaries, and movies is an important task, and enables efficient cataloging and retrieval with large video collections. At the highest hierarchy level, film and video collections can be categorized into different program genres. Video classification into TV genres is discussed in [2, 6, 5]. Approaches such as [3, 11] classify movie trailers using film genre labels. At the next level of the hierarchy, domain videos such as sports can be classified into different sub-categories [1, 8]. At a much finer level of resolution, a video sequence itself can be segmented and each segment can then be classified according to its semantic content. Events in a baseball telecast [4] or newscasts [12] can be indexed in this manner.

Our work addresses the problem of video classification at the highest level of abstraction: Genres. In particular, we examine a set of features that would be useful in distinguishing between sports videos, music, news, cartoons, and commercials. In contrast to [2, 6] we concentrate on features that can be extracted only from the visual content of a video. Rather than learning features from video data sets, we use human perception and discernment of video genre characteristics as a starting point, and extract computational features that would reflect those visual characteristics such as editing, motion, and color. Some of our features are similar to those proposed in [2] and some are *new*, but we also go beyond [2] to show classification results on several hours of video. In addition, we address the important related issue of the length of a clip required to be processed for reliable genre identification and its impact on the classification performance using proposed features, since this issue has not been studied elsewhere.

2. Proposed Feature Set and Trends

Consider a video clip, V, a contiguous sequence of $n+1$ frames, $V = \{f_1, f_2, ..f_{n+1}\}$. A frame transition vector, $T = \{t_1, t_2, \ldots, t_n\}$ is first computed from V, where each t_i is a feature set, $\{t_i^\mu, t_i^v\}$ computed jointly from frames f_i and f_{i+1}. Specifically, $t_i^\mu = |f_{i+1}^\mu - f_i^\mu|$ and $t_i^v = |f_{i+1}^v - f_i^v|$, where f_i^μ and f_i^v denote the mean and variance of luminance values of pixels in frame f_i, respectively.

2.1. Shot Processing

The video sequence is automatically segmented into shots using the method detailed in [10] which performs segmentation by detecting effects such as cuts, fades, and dissolves in the video. After this step, each member t_i of T receives a label, x from the set, $\mathcal{L} = \{shot, cut, fade, dissolve\}$ depending on whether f_i and f_{i+1} are part of a pure shot, cut, fade or dissolve transition respectively. The transition vector T is then grouped into k segments, $\{S_1, S_2, \ldots, S_k\}$, where S_i is a set of consecutive elements, $\{t_j, t_{j+1}, \cdots\}$ that have the same label. Each S_i is also assigned a label from $\mathcal{L}$ according to the label type of frames it contains. Let Γ^x and Ω^x denote sets containing segments S_i and t_i of label type x, respectively. Let Δ^{shot} denote the set of pure shot frames in the video sequence.

2.2. Feature Extraction

We now extract a set of features that capture distinctive cinematic aspects of a video genre such as editing (features

1051-4651/00 $10.00 © 2000 IEEE

1 and 2), motion (features, 3 to 6), and color (features, 7 through 10). The precise definitions of these features together with their intuitive meanings follow. Accompanying each feature is a plot of the values of the feature computed for 50 video samples (60sec each) randomly selected from each genre (c.f. Section 3), after sorting the values in ascending order.

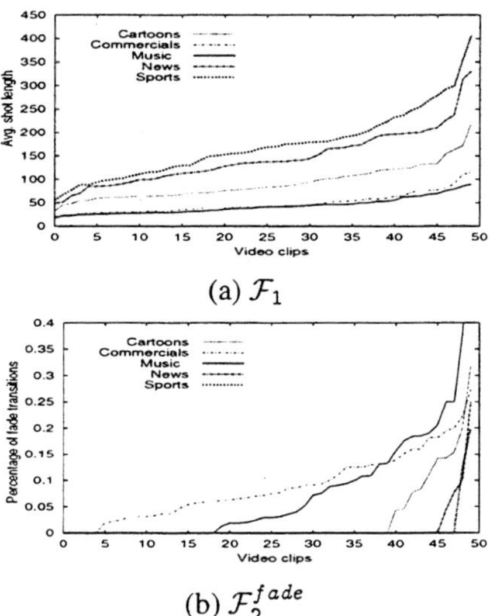

(a) $\mathcal{F}_1$

(b) $\mathcal{F}_2^{fade}$

Figure 1. Editing feature values in ascending order for 50 video samples from each genre.

Average shot length $\mathcal{F}_1$ is a useful feature in video characterization, since it is fundamental to our perception of scene pace and content. Therefore, short-duration shots are often used in commercials and music videos with fast music. In contrast, longer shots are used in sports to maintain the continuity of actions (see Figure 1a). Shot length is measured as the number of frames between the last frame of the preceding transition and the first frame of the succeeding transition. So if a shot contributes to the existence of a segment S_i then its length would be $|S_i| + 1$. The average shot length computed from the whole clip, V, is used as a classification feature:

$$\mathcal{F}_1 = \frac{\sum_{i=1}^{k} \theta_i}{|\Gamma^{shot}|}, \text{ where } \theta_i = \begin{cases} |S_i| + 1 & \text{if } S_i \in \Gamma^{shot} \\ 0 & \text{otherwise.} \end{cases}$$

The percentage of each type of transition used for editing can also identify a video genre. For example, while $fade$ transitions are common in commercials and sometimes in music, they are rarely used in sports and news (see Figure 1b). We compute the percentage of each type of transitions x, $x \in \{cut, fade, dissolve\}$ as:

$$\mathcal{F}_2^x = \frac{|\Gamma^x|}{|\Gamma^{cut}| + |\Gamma^{fade}| + |\Gamma^{dissolve}|}.$$

Camera movement influences the narration of scene content. In sports such as soccer and rugby fixed cameras are positioned around the field, and since the ball changes its position continuously, a lot of camera movement is needed to track the ball continuously. In contrast, in newscasts, the object of interest such as an anchor person or a reporter remains relatively static (see Figure 2a). Camera motion magnitude of a frame, f_i is computed using two consecutive frames, f_i and f_{i+1} with the method proposed in [9], and the overall amount of camera movement of a video segment is computed using frame tilt and pan:

$$\mathcal{F}_3 = \frac{\sum_{i=1}^{n} \theta_i}{|\Delta^{shot}|}, \text{ where } \theta_i = \begin{cases} |f_i^{\text{tilt}}| + |f_i^{\text{pan}}| & \text{if } f_i \in \Delta^{shot} \\ 0 & \text{otherwise.} \end{cases}$$

In music videos, there are often special effects such as quick changes of lighting and flash lights causing a large change in the variance of pixel luminance between two consecutive frames. We measure the prevalence of these effects as the number of shot features, t_i whose pixel luminance variance is above a certain threshold:

$$\mathcal{F}_4 = \frac{|\Omega_1|}{|\Omega^{shot}|}, \text{ where } \Omega_1 = \{t_i \in \Omega^{shot} \mid t_i^v > T_1\}.$$

Figure 2b shows $\mathcal{F}_4$ as being distinctly higher for music videos than news.

The rate of "quiet" visual scenes, where both camera and object motion are very little, varies between different video categories. We expect music videos to be rather dynamic, while anchor shots in newscasts are rather static (see Figure 2c). The prevalence of static scenes in videos is measured using the number of frame transitions t_i whose mean and variance in pixel luminance are both less than certain thresholds.

$$\mathcal{F}_5 = \frac{|\Omega_2|}{|\Omega^{shot}|}, \Omega_2 = \{t_i \in \Omega^{shot} \mid t_i^\mu < T_2 \text{ and } t_i^v < T_3\}.$$

A new feature proposed based on motion is the average length of *motion runs*. A motion run R_i is defined an unbroken sequence of those frames, f_i whose sum of absolute pixel-wise luminance differences between f_i and f_{i+1} exceeds a certain threshold, T_4. Let $|R_i|$ be the length of this run. Let R denote the set of all motion runs in the video clip. Then

$$\mathcal{F}_6 = \frac{\sum_i |R_i|}{|R|}.$$

Figure 2d shows $\mathcal{F}_6$ for the five genres. $\mathcal{F}_6$ is consistently high for sports when compared against cartoons. The main reason for this is that motion in sports tends to occur continuously in time, while in the normal production process of a cartoon a single drawing may be exposed a number of times resulting in a lower pixel-wise difference between consecutive frames.

There are also the distinctions in the distribution of color histograms between different video genres. Let $f_i^{\mathcal{H}}$ denote the luminance histogram of frame f_i and $f_i^{\mathcal{H}_k}$ denote the histogram of k largest bins in the color histogram, i.e., the

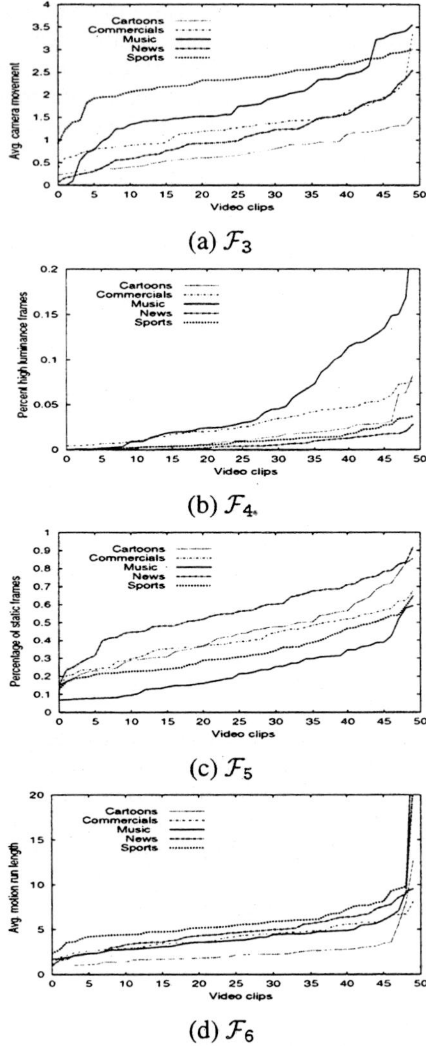

Figure 2. Motion features for 50 video samples from each genre.

set of k most prevalent luminance levels. We measure the coherence of these k bins based on δ, the standard deviation of indices of $f_i^{\mathcal{H}_k}$ as a new feature. Thus:

$$\mathcal{F}_7 = \frac{\sum_{i=1}^{n+1} \theta_i}{|\Delta^{shot}|}, \text{ where } \theta_i = \begin{cases} \delta(f_i^{\mathcal{H}_k}) & \text{if } f_i \in \Delta^{shot} \\ 0 & \text{otherwise.} \end{cases}$$

Figure 3a shows that sports have the lowest value of $\mathcal{F}_7$, since the color of the playing field tends to be highly homogeneous, while music videos tend to have high values of $\mathcal{F}_7$ indicating high color variability.

The HSV color space provides two other interesting features. For example, the average brightness for cartoons is much higher than other video genres (see Figure 3b). We compute $\mathcal{F}_8$ based on $f_i^{\mathcal{V}}$, the percentage of pixels having brightness above a certain threshold T_5.

$$\mathcal{F}_8 = \frac{\sum_{i=1}^{n+1} \theta_i}{|\Delta^{shot}|}, \text{ where } \theta_i = \begin{cases} f_i^{\mathcal{V}} & \text{if } f_i \in \Delta^{shot} \\ 0 & \text{otherwise.} \end{cases}$$

We compute $\mathcal{F}_9$ based on $f_i^{\mathcal{S}}$, the percentage of pixels having saturation above a certain threshold T_6.

$$\mathcal{F}_9 = \frac{\sum_{i=1}^{n+1} \theta_i}{|\Delta^{shot}|}, \text{ where } \theta_i = \begin{cases} f_i^{\mathcal{S}} & \text{if } f_i \in \Delta^{shot} \\ 0 & \text{otherwise.} \end{cases}$$

Figure 3c shows that the average saturation for cartoons and sports is much higher when compared against commercials and music videos.

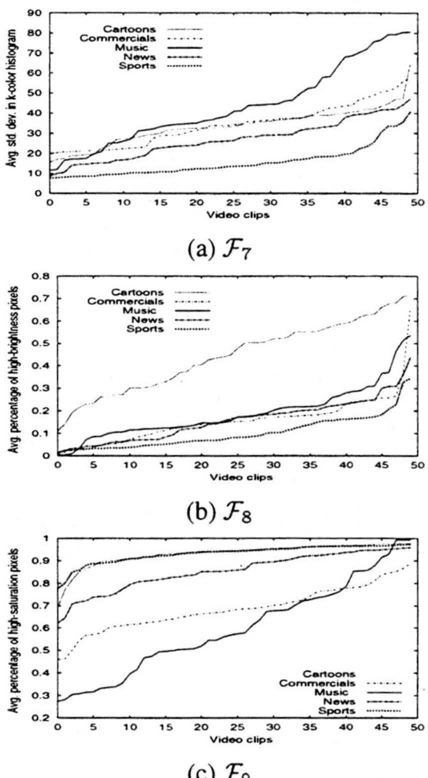

Figure 3. Color statistics for 50 samples from each genre.

3. Experimental Results

We collected about 8 hours of TV material and digitized and encoded it in the MPEG-1 format. To ensure the variety of data, news and commercials from different channels on different days and at different times of the day were used. Some clips were in fact recorded more than 5 years ago. Sports clips came from different sub categories such as soccer, Australian football, rugby, and motor racing. Music clips were extracted from different dance music videos.

The C4.5 decision tree [7] is used to build the classifier for genre labeling. All the video material is first divided into units of approximately equal duration. The system was tested with features computed for different basic clip durations of 40sec, 60sec, and 80sec. During feature extraction, all the six thresholds were determined empirically and used stably and consistently across all clips for all durations. During each classification experiment for a clip duration d, 60% of all the clips obtained by segmenting the eight-hour material into d-long units were randomly selected for training while the remaining 40% of the clips were used for testing. For each duration, 100 such sets were randomly derived and used for classification, and the overall classification results are presented in Table 1. We measure in percentage the best, worst, average classification across 100 runs and the standard deviation for each duration, as we expect that slightly different decision trees would be built with different data combinations.

Stats.	Dur. d	*All*	-Ca.	-Co.	-Mu.	-Ne.	-Sp.
Best %	40'	84.6	88.4	87.2	85.4	89.2	85.3
	60'	86.2	88.3	**92.3**	90.3	**91.5**	**89.2**
	80'	**89.7**	**91.4**	90.0	**90.4**	91.2	89.0
Worst %	40'	78.4	83.4	83.1	81.1	83.5	80.3
	60'	**81.0**	83.1	**85.3**	**85.5**	**85.2**	**82.7**
	80'	79.5	**83.6**	83.1	83.7	82.3	80.5
Avg. %	40'	80.0	84.8	84.5	82.2	.85.2	82.0
	60'	**83.1**	85.3	**86.8**	**87.2**	**87.4**	84.8
	80'	81.7	**85.7**	85.0	86.1	85.2	**87.4**
Stdv.	40'	**1.41**	**1.21**	**1.05**	**1.07**	**1.40**	**1.45**
	60'	1.66	1.54	1.46	1.28	1.90	1.81
	80'	1.91	1.56	1.73	1.80	2.17	2.09

Table 1. Genre classification results.

The *All* category in the table represents the classification results when samples from all genres were used in training and testing, while others such as -{*Ca*} represent classification results obtained omitting samples from one given genre, say *Ca*, cartoons during training (-{*Co*} is for omitting commercials, -{*Mu*}, music, -{*Ne*}, news, and -{*Sp*} for sports). The best result in each group are typeset in bold. In the best case for *All*, the classification rates are 86% (60sec) and 90% (80sec). The average classification for *All* is between 80 % and 83%. Examination of the standard deviation of the results implies that using video clips of 60 sec duration is the most appropriate strategy, as it offers the best trade off in terms of high classification and low standard deviation.

The best classification rate rises when one genre is omitted to around 92% due to patterns that exist in the genre confusion matrix. It is useful to analyze Figs. 1, 2, and 3. The average shot length, ($\mathcal{F}_1$) and its trends across samples are similar for ⟨commercials & music⟩, and also for ⟨sports & news⟩. Cartoons fall somewhere in between, but can be confused with either of the four genres. The motion feature, ($\mathcal{F}_3$) is similar for ⟨news & commercials⟩ and is close to but lower than music. However, all three categories are close. Further, cartoon features are close to those of news. Feature, $\mathcal{F}_4$ is high for music, but is still close to commercials. However, $\mathcal{F}_4$ well separates out news from ⟨commercials & music⟩. $\mathcal{F}_5$ clearly separates out ⟨news, commercials, & music⟩ and thus complements motion features $\mathcal{F}_3$ and $\mathcal{F}_4$. Features, $\mathcal{F}_6$, $\mathcal{F}_8$, and $\mathcal{F}_9$ separate out cartoons from all other categories. $\mathcal{F}_7$ separates out sports from music. A high degree of confusion can exist for news and sports since they are close in all features other than motion. Similarly, music and commercials have almost identical shot length and similar motion, and can lead to a mix-up.

4. Conclusion

We have presented a set of features that embody the visual characteristics of a video sequence for video genre identification. The experimental results on several hours of videos indicate that these features perform well in classifying videos into sports, news, commercials, cartoons, and music, thus enabling automatic genre-based filtering during categorization and search. Our study on the length of a clip needed to recognize its genre indicates that 60sec can serve as the most appropriate video duration to achieve reliable classification accuracy. Future work will investigate temporal sequencing of shots and their semantics to further improve the performance of our system.

References

[1] Y. Ariki, A. Shibutani, and Y. Sugiyama. Classification and retrieval of TV Sports News by DCT features. In *IPSJ International Symposium on Information System and Technologies for Network Society*, pages 269–272, Sept. 1997.

[2] W. Effelsberg, S. Fischer, and R. Lienhart. Automatic recognition of film genres. In *The Third ACM International Multimedia Conference and Exhibition (MULTIMEDIA '95)*, pages 367–368, New York, Nov. 1995. ACM Press.

[3] G. Iyengar and A. B. Lippman. Models for automatic classification of video sequences. In *Storage and Retrieval VI*, San Jose, Jan. 1998.

[4] T. Kawashima, K. Tateyama, T. Iijima, and Y. Aoki. Indexing of baseball telecast for content-based video retrieval. In *IEEE 1998 International Conference on Image Processing ICIP'98*, pages 871–874, Chicago, Oct. 1998.

[5] V. Kobla, D. DeMenthon, and D. Doermann. Detection of slow-motion replay sequences for identifying sports videos. In *IEEE 1999 International Workshop on Multimedia Signal Processing*, Copenhagen, Denmark, Sept. 1999.

[6] Z. Liu, J. Huang, and Y. Wang. Classification of TV programs based on audio information using hidden Markov model. In *IEEE Signal Processing Society 1998 Workshop on Multimedia Signal Processing*, pages 27–32, Dec. 1998.

[7] J. R. Quinlan. *C4.5: Programs for machine learning*. Morgan Kaufmann Publishers, San Mateo, California, 1993.

[8] E. Sahouria and A. Zakhor. Content analysis of video using principal components. In *IEEE 1998 International Conference on Image Processing ICIP'98*, volume 3, pages 541–545, Chicago, Oct. 1998.

[9] M. Srinivasan, S. Venkatesh, and R. Hosie. Qualitative extraction of camera parameters. *Pattern Recognition*, 30(4):593–606, 1997.

[10] B. T. Truong, C. Dorai, and S. Venkatesh. New enhancements to cut, fade, and dissolve detection processes in video segmentation. In *ACM Multimedia (Submitted)*, 2000.

[11] N. Vasconcelos and A. Lippman. Towards semantically meaningful feature space for the characterization of video content. In *International Conference on Image Processing ICPR'97*, volume 1, pages 25–28, Santa Barbara, California, June 1997.

[12] H. Zhang, S. Y. Tan, S. W. Smoliar, and G. Yihong. Automatic parsing and indexing of news video. *Multimedia Systems*, 2(6):256–266, 1995.

Content based Image Retrieval using Interest Points and Texture Features

Christian Wolf[1], Jean-Michel Jolion[2], Walter Kropatsch[1], Horst Bischof[1]

[1]Vienna University of Technology, Pattern Recognition and Image Processing Group
Favoritenstraße 9/1832, 1040 Wien, Austria
[2]INSA de Lyon, Laboratoire Reconnaissance de Formes et Vision
3, Avenue Albert Einstein, 69626 Villeurbanne cedex, France

Abstract

Content based image retrieval is the task of searching images from a database, which are visually similar to a given example image. In this work we present methods for content based image retrieval based on texture similarity using interest points and Gabor features. Interest point detectors are used in computer vision to detect image points with special properties, which can be geometric (corners) or non-geometric (contrast etc.). Gabor functions and Gabor filters are regarded as excellent tools for feature extraction and texture segmentation. This article combines these methods and generates a textural description of images. Special emphasis is devoted to distance measures on texture descriptions. Experimental results of a query system are given.

1. Introduction

Content[1] based image retrieval systems use the contents of a query image provided by the user to search for similar images in a possibly large database. All of the known methods for pre-attentive search emphasize the need for descriptions of images and powerful metrics to compare these descriptions. Most common approaches are based on colour [13], structure [5], textures [9] or combinations [11]. In this paper we describe a texture based method using a Gabor filter bank to extract local texture features on interest points.

Interest points should deliver pre-attentively "interesting" points in an image. For man-made objectives, corners provide valuable information about the scene, therefore the first developed interest operators for robotics have been mainly corner detectors [10, 3, 12]. However, more recently it was discovered that their ability to reduce the amount of information necessary to describe images makes them a nice vehicle for image indexation. Other detectors gathering points more suitable to indexation purposes have been developed [2, 8, 1]. The methods described in this paper do not rely on a specific detector. Similar results are obtained by the interest operators of Jolion [2], Loupias et al. [8] and Harris and Stephens [3].

The paper is outlined as follows: Section 2 gives a short overview of Gabor filters and features. Section 3 explains two different representations based on these features. Section 4 describes our experimental results and finally Section 5 finishes with a conclusion.

[1]This work was supported in part by the Austrian Science Foundation (FWF) under grant S-7002-MAT

2. Gabor Filters and Gabor Features

A common definition of texture is the repetition of basic texture elements. Therefore, widely used properties are frequency, direction, phase etc. However, these properties depend on the scale the image is analysed. For this reason Gabor filters are a suitable tool to extract texture features. They have already been used for texture based image retrieval [9]. The filters of a Gabor filter bank are designed to detect different frequencies and orientations. In our paper we use them to extract features at key points detected by interest operators. The basic idea is to extract a fixed number of interest points e.g. $N = 200$ in the image and to select regions of fixed size e.g. $R = 32$ pixels around each point, referred to as *interest regions*. Each interest region is input to a Gabor filter bank of $S \times K (3 \times 8)$ filters, K being the number of orientations and S the number of scales. This will give us $N \cdot K \cdot S = 4800$ filter responses to process.

3. Combining Responses

The most important description of the filter response is the maximum amplitude, from now on referred to as *amplitude* only. It tells how strong this interest region responds

1051-4651/00 $10.00 © 2000 IEEE

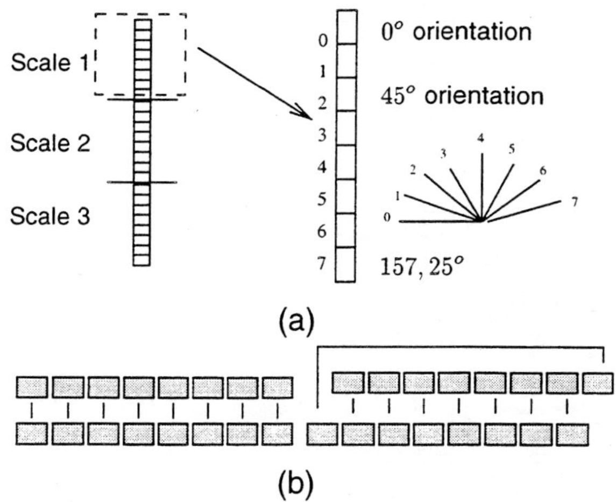

Figure 1. Feature vector storing amplitudes (a) Cyclic permutation of the subvectors (b)

to the filter applied to it. Literally spoken it specifies how much structure of the given orientation in the given scale is present in the region.

The Gabor filter responses can be used in different ways to characterize images. We will introduce two different methods in this paper. The first, will represent images as sets of feature vectors, the second describes images by sets of histograms.

3.1. Feature vectors

A characterization of images by sets of feature vectors collected on interest points was developed by Schmidt and Mohr [11]. They used invariant features. Our method is based on texture feature vectors built from the output of the Gabor filter bank, each feature vector corresponding to one interest point. The 3×8 elements of a vector represent the responses of the 3×8 sized filter bank, where each element holds the maximum amplitude of a filter response. We compare two vectors in feature space. We split the vector into 3 parts, one for each scale. The subvectors contain 8 entries, one for each orientation (Figure 1). They can be interpreted as points in a 8 dimensional feature space in which similarity is expressed by the Euclidean distance $d_E(\mu, \nu) = \sqrt{\sum_i (\mu_i - \nu_i)^2}$ (μ and ν denote two subvectors). We introduce a cyclic permutation to compensate for rotation. So the distance between two feature subvectors μ and ν is actually the minimum of 3 distances: [2]

$$dist(\mu, \nu) = \min\{d_E(\mu, \nu),\ d_E(per(\mu), \nu),\ d_E(\mu, per(\nu))\}$$

[2]Classic image indexation applications like video indexing, are not interested in a complete rotational invariance but must take into account small variations of orientations ($\pm 22^o$ in our implementation).

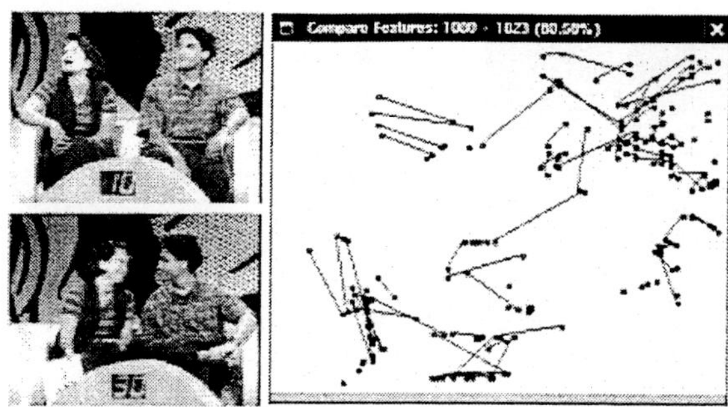

Figure 2. Two images and their corresponding points

where $per(x)$ is a cyclic permutation of the vector x one element clockwise (Figure 1.b). The distance of the entire vectors, *i.e.* all 3 scales, is calculated as mean of the subvectors for each scale.

With the suitable distance between two feature vectors, we now define a distance between two images. Schmidt and Mohr used a voting algorithm: Each vector V_i of the query image is compared to all vectors V_j in the database, which are linked to their images M_k. If the distance between V_i and V_j is below a threshold t then the respective image M_k gets a vote. The images having maximum votes are returned to the user.

Our modification explicitely searches for corresponding points in both images. The means to qualify two points as being a pair is the minimum distance in feature space. A matrix stores the distances of all possible feature pairs, the lines i denoting the key points of the query image, the columns j the key points of the compared image, and the elements $E_{i,j}$ the distance between point i of the query image and point j of the compared image. We search the minimum element of the matrix and assign $N(A, B) := 1$. Both column and line of this minimum are deleted from the matrix, since these two points are not available for other pairs. Then we repeat the search for the minimum element of the remaining matrix and increment $N(A, B)$ each time until the minimum distance does not exceed a given threshold. The distance between the two images is calculated using the number of corresponding points found:

$$d(A, B) = \frac{2 * N(A, B)}{N(A) + N(B)}$$

where $N(A)$ denotes the number of interest points of the image A. The highest cost of the algorithm is the cost for calculating the distance matrix, which is $O(N(A)N(B))$

Figure 2 shows two example images and their maps of interest points superimposed in a single image. Corresponding interest points are connected with a straight line.

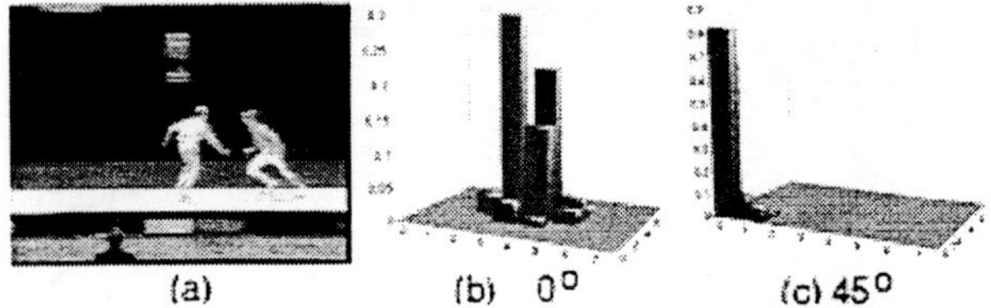

Figure 3. Image (a) and histograms for 0° (b) and 45° (c)

3.2. Histograms

Motivated by the drawback of the computational expensive distance method presented in the last chapter we developed a histogram based representation and comparison technique, which uses the same output of the Gabor filter bank. In the feature vector representation our data is ordered by interest points. We now re-order the data by scales and orientations of the filter bank, and get for each combination of scale and orientation a distribution of maximum amplitudes — the responses for all interest regions to the filter for this scale and orientation.

This information, which represents one image, can be stored in a set of 24 histograms ordered by filter index. The responses of one filter are embedded in a single two dimensional histogram. To fill one histogram all interest points are taken. For each point the n-nearest neighbour search (using spatial distance) is performed. The result of this search are n pairs of interest points, whose amplitudes we insert into the histogram. The maximum amplitude of the first point is used to calculate the bin index of the first dimension, and the maximum amplitude of the respective neighbour for the bin index of the second dimension.

Figure 3 shows an example image and two 2D histograms out of its 24 histograms. The images' fourier spectrum contains frequencies mainly in the horizontal orientation (orientation 0). Therefore the histogram for orientation 0 shows strong responses, *i.e.* high bins from indices 4 to 6. The histogram for orientation index 2, which corresponds to structures in orientations around 45 degrees, shows only one high bin at index $(0,0)$, *i.e.* almost no response.

The comparison of two images is based on already known distance measurements of histograms and their means. For the single histogram distances we used the Battacharrya distance, which performed slightly better than the L_2 distance, thus confirmed results of Huet and Hancock [5]. We included some compensation for rotation by comparing each histogram not only with its corresponding histogram but as well with the immediate neighbours of the same scale, similar to the feature vector approach (Figure 1.b). We can represent our ordered set of 3×8 histograms as a set of 3 vectors, each containing 8 histograms. By cyclic permutation of each of these vectors and taking the minimum of comparison and comparison with one rotated vector, we get the final distance.

Figure 4. Examples of the image database

4. Experimental Results

Our test database contains 609 images grabbed from a French television channel. The images are all of the same format (384x288 pixels) and coded in JPEG with 75% quality. The contents differs from outdoor activities (reports of sports) to talk shows, full scope shots of people, weather forecasts, logos and advertisements. To be able to measure a query performance a clustering of the image set was necessary. The clusters contain images of successive sequences. In fact, the pictures of one cluster mostly are taken from the same program and sometimes even from the same scene (Figure 4). One column of the matrix contains images of the same cluster. Although all images of the database are compared during a query not all of them are grouped into clusters and used as query images. The reason is to avoid too small groups, which would degrade the query performance curves without justification. Eliminating all clusters with less than 10 images, the remaining 568 images are grouped into 11 clusters with the following (increasing) sizes:

1	2	3	4	5	6	7	8	9	10	11
10	11	14	15	15	19	32	36	86	156	174

Since there is no general definition for visual similarity between images, measuring retrieval performance is a difficult task and depends on the purpose. A single query uses one image out of a cluster C, which contains d images. The system answers with c images of which r are from the original cluster C. We use a measure which is widely used for indexation systems: precision.

$$P = \frac{r}{c}$$

As the name suggests, the precision of the result of a single query denotes how precise the result set responds to the desires of the user. By changing the size of the result set we get a performance curve for this query. We calculate the final curve for a retrieval method by averaging the curves for all single queries using different query images.

Figure 5 displays curves for both retrieval methods. The first method performs slightly better than the histogram based method . However, it takes 37 seconds to compare one query image against the database of 609 images (standard PC, 300 MHz), whereas the second method finishes within 5.1 seconds.

The curves are displayed together with the theoretical limits of query performance. A logical lower bound is the performance of a method selecting random images. The upper boundary shows the performance of a query that picks all similar images if possible. This curve depends on the clustering of the database. A constant performance of 100% is only possible, if all clusters contain at least as many images as we retrieve in our result sets.

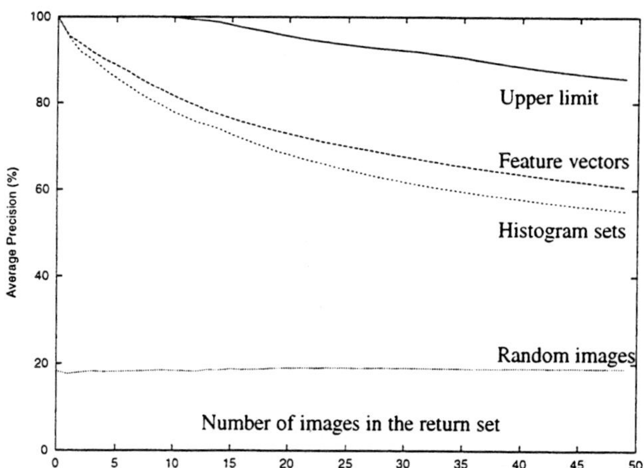

Figure 5. Precision using different methods

5. Conclusion and Outlook

In this paper we presented two methods to use interest point detectors and a Gabor filter bank to create texture based descriptions for image indexing. Both methods give good results according to our test image database. For indexation purposes the histogram based statistical method needs much less computational efforts, whereas the performance decrease is statistically not significant.

The image representation introduced in this paper holds a rough texture description of images. The similarity measure is able to distinguish groups of images of the same type, i.e. images having similar content without considering many details. Typical applications could be e.g. databases of television broadcast stations, which need to find screenshots of similar scenes or shots of the same telecast.

Future work will integrate a structural component by combining the feature vector approach with attributed graph pyramids [6, 7]. Another task currently pursued is to join this texture based approach with methods based on colour, structure and shape into one weighted indexation system, which uses feedback of the user to recalculate the weights of the system [4].

References

[1] S. Bhattacharjee. Image retrieval based on structural content. Technical Report SSC/1999/004, Dept. of Electrical Eng., E.P.F.L, CH-1015, Lausanne, 1999.

[2] S. Bres and J. Jolion. Detection of interest points for image indexing. In *3rd Int. Conf. on Visual Inf. Systems, Visual 99*, pages 427–434. Springer, Lecture Notes in Computer Science, 1614, June 1999.

[3] C. Harris and M. Stephens. A combined corner and edge detector. In *Proceedings 4th Alvey Visual Conference*. Plessey Research Roke Manor, UK, 1988.

[4] A. Heinrichs, D. Koubaroulis, B. Levienaise-Obadia, P. Rovida, and J. Jolion. Robust image retrieval in a statistical framework. Technical Report RR-99-04, Laboratoire Reconnaissance de Formes et Vision, Lyon, May 1999.

[5] B. Huet and E. Hancock. Cartographic indexing into a database of remotely sensed images. In *Third IEEE Workshop on Applications of Computer Vision (WACV96)*, pages 8–14, Sarasota, Dec 1996.

[6] J. Jolion and A. Montanvert. The adaptive pyramid, a framework for 2d image analysis. In *Computer Vision, Graphics and Image Processing: Image Understanding*, pages 55(3):339–348, May 1992.

[7] W. Kropatsch. Building irregular pyramids by dual-graph contraction. *IEE Proc.-Vis Image Signal Process.*, 142(6):366–374, December 1995.

[8] E. Loupias, N. S. S. Bres, and J. Jolion. Wavelet-based salient points for image retrieval. In *International Conference on Image Processing, Vancouver, Canada*, 2000.

[9] B. Manjunath and W. Ma. Texture features for browsing and retrieval of image data. *IEEE Transactions on Pattern Analysis and Machine Intelligence*, 18(8), August 1996.

[10] H. Moravec. Towards automatic visual obstacle avoidance. In *Proc. of 5th International Joint Conference on Artifical Intelligence, 584*, page p. 587, 1977.

[11] C. Schmidt and R. Mohr. Local gray value invariants for image retrieval. *IEEE Transactions on Pattern Analysis and Machine Intelligence*, 19(5), May 1997.

[12] S. Smith and J. Brady. Susan - a new approach to low level image processing. *Int. Journal of Computer Vision*, 23(1):45–78, May 1997.

[13] M. Swain and D. Ballard. Color indexing. *International Journal of Computer Vision*, 7(1):11–32, 1991.

Content-Based Watermarking Model †

Ruizhen Liu and Tieniu Tan
National Laboratory of Pattern Recognition
Institute of Automation, Chinese Academy of Sciences
P. O. Box 2728, Beijing 100080, P. R. China
{liurz, tnt}@nlpr.ia.ac.cn

Abstract

In this paper, we propose a new general additive watermarking model based on the content of digital images, called as CBWM (Content-Based Watermarking Model). It provides a common basis to study many existing watermarking algorithms that are based on unitary transforms and to evaluate their performance and characteristics. CBWM is designed to address two important issues of digital watermarking. One is the requirement of robustness. In order to improve robustness and security, the embedded watermark is designed to be orthogonal to the feature vector of the original image, which means that watermarking casting is image content dependent. The second issue is watermark detection. CBWM presents a statistical approach to watermark detection based on the Neyman-Pearson criterion and describes a method for computing the probability of false alarm and missing rejection during watermark detection. In experimental tests, CBWM is applied to the popular discrete cosine transform and promising results are obtained.

1. Introduction

Digital watermarking has been proposed as a solution to the problem of copyright protection of multimedia documents in networked environments [1,2,3].

An effective watermarking scheme should be robust. Robustness of watermarking algorithms requires that watermarks should be bound with the significant components of the original image. This means the watermark should be embedded into an image's perceptual components [3]. In general we can regard the image's perceptual components which represent the main feature of the image as its feature sets or feature vectors. Although most current existing watermarking methods embed watermarks into the image's perceptual components, the watermarks and the perceptual components (representing image contents) are typically independent of each other. Thus these methods are in principle weak in robustness and security, as it is possible for malicious attackers to remove or destroy watermarks without degrading the image's quality.

In this paper, we describe a general content-based watermarking model (CBWM) to present possible solutions to the above problems. The basic idea of CBWM is that watermarks embedded should be coupled with the feature vectors of the original image. From the optimal viewpoint in pattern classification and signal detection, they should be orthogonal to the feature vector. CBWM also presents a statistical approach to watermark detection based on the Neyman-Pearson criterion and gives a general algorithm for computing the probability of false alarm and missing rejection. To the best of our knowledge, such studies, although important, are rare in the open literature.

The rest of this paper is organized as follows. Section 2 describes the basic principles of CBWM. Section 3 gives complete statistical analysis about watermark detection. Section 4 shows the experimental results of our model against the benchmark software (Stirmark) for robustness test and compares the new model with the Cox method [3]. Section 5 concludes the paper.

2. Watermarking Algorithm

In this section, we will describe the watermarking scheme of CBWM. It is a general model for transform-domain watermarking algorithms. If we take a linear algebra viewpoint, we can observe that a discrete image is an array of non-negative scalars which may be regarded as a matrix. Let an M-by-N image be designated as $A=\{a_{ij}\}\in \mathbf{F}^{M\times N}$, $i=1,2,..,M$, $j=1,2,...,N$, where $\mathbf{F}$ can be either the real number domain $\mathbf{R}$ or the complex number domain $\mathbf{C}$. $\widetilde{A}=\{\widetilde{a}_{ij}\}\in \mathbf{F}^{M\times N}$ is the transform coefficient matrix of A. That is for a mapping operator T we get $T: A\rightarrow \widetilde{A}$. Most current digital watermarking schemes use unitary transforms, i.e. T is a unitary operator. Let vector $C=\{c_k\}\in \mathbf{F}^K$ be a subset of the transform coefficients of the original image (i.e., $\{c_k\}\in \{\widetilde{a}_{ij}\}$, where $k=1,2,...,K$) which represent the

† This work is supported by the Chinese NSF (Grant No. 59825105) and the Chinese Academy of Sciences.

1051-4651/00 $10.00 © 2000 IEEE

perceptually significant components of the original image. Generally watermarks are embedded into these perceptual components of an image due to the requirement of robustness, so $\{c_k\}$ is selected to represent the feature of the image. Thus it can be considered as the feature vector of A. We insert the watermark $W=\{w_k\}\in \mathbf{F}^K$ into the feature vector $\{c_k\}$. Then we have the following general watermarking framework.

2.1. Watermark embedding algorithm

Most current watermarking methods are based on the spread-spectrum communication theory [3,4,5,6], in which the original documents or images are assumed to be ergodic, zero-mean, and wide-sense stationary. This assumption is not always valid and may result in wrong conclusions in many cases. We will describe CBWM based watermark casting and detection methods, which do not make such assumptions. One key issue of CBWM lies in the fact that it is an additive watermarking model and the watermark space is orthogonal to the feature vector of the original image.

If we embed the watermark $\{w_k\}$ in the feature vector $\{c_k\}$, a new feature vector $\widetilde{C}=\{\widetilde{c}_k\}\in \mathbf{F}^K$ is obtained as follows:

$$\widetilde{c}_k = c_k + a w_k, \qquad k=1,2,\ldots,K \tag{1}$$

where scale factor a is a constant used to control the watermark energy to be inserted. We call the watermark casting scheme described in Eq.(1) as additive watermarking model.

We use the new feature vector $\{\widetilde{c}_k\}$ to substitute the original vector $\{c_k\}$ and get a new transform matrix $\widetilde{B}$ from $\widetilde{A}$. Then we reconstruct the watermarked image B using the modified transform matrix $\widetilde{B}$, i.e. $T^{-1}:\widetilde{B}\rightarrow B$. Here we assume T is a bijective operator and its inverse operator T^{-1} exists.

2.2. Watermark Detection

Given the original image A, the watermarked image B and the watermark $W=\{w_k\}$, we can obtain the feature vector $\widetilde{C}=\{\widetilde{c}_k\}\in \widetilde{B}$ (Note that for some cases, we can only use the watermarked image B to extract $\widetilde{C}$). Then we compute the scalar Z as follows:

$$Z=\sum_k \widetilde{c}_k w_k \tag{2}$$

Given threshold Z_T, we have binary decision that just yields a 'yes' or 'no' to answer whether the watermarked image B contains the watermark W. The hypothesis test is

$$\begin{aligned} H_1 &: Z > Z_T \\ H_0 &: Z < Z_T \end{aligned} \tag{3}$$

where hypothesis H_1 means the watermark exists and H_0 means the watermark does not exist.

2.3. Watermark selection

Intuitively, the watermarks should be closely related to the contents of the images for robustness and security. For the image feature vector $C=\{c_k\}$, we could find a watermark space, denoted as $F_W\subset \mathbf{F}^K$, which is orthogonal to vector C:

$$F_W=\{W\in \mathbf{F}^K : \sum_k c_k w_k = 0, k=1,2,\ldots,K\} \tag{4}$$

That is, for any vector belonging to watermark vector space $W=\{w_k\}\in \mathbf{F}_W$, we have:

$$C^H W = 0 \tag{5}$$

Then Eq.(2) becomes

$$Z=\sum_k \widetilde{c}_k w_k = a\sum_k w_k^2 = aE \tag{6}$$

where variable E can be regarded as the energy of the inserted watermark.

By choosing the watermark in the way as discussed above, we can ensure that the watermark selected depends on the content of the original image. It can be seen that watermark space $\mathbf{F}_W$ is a subspace of vector space $\mathbf{F}^K$. There are an infinite number of vectors that satisfy Eq. (4), and the selection of a suitable watermark is in practice a constrained optimization process formulated as:

$$W=\arg\min_{W\in \mathbf{F}^K} O(C,W) \tag{7}$$

where the object function $O(C,W)$ is defined as:

$$O(C,W)=|C^H W| = |\sum_{i=1}^{K} c_i^H w_i| \tag{8}$$

and C is the feature vector of the original image. The terminating condition of the optimization process is:

$$O(C,W)<\delta \tag{9}$$

where the positive constant $\delta>0$ is a pre-defined threshold for optimization.

If we consider the case of using meaningful watermarks (i.e. watermarks are texts, images, company logos, or user-defined passwords etc.), the optimization problem becomes:

$$k_{ev}=\arg\min_{k_n\in \mathbf{R}} \widetilde{O}(C,\widetilde{W}) = \arg\min_{k_n\in \mathbf{R}} \left|C^H \widetilde{W}\right| \tag{10}$$

where the key k_{ev} to be found is used to randomize or encrypt the meaningful watermark W in the consideration of security and robustness. The new watermark $\widetilde{W}$ is defined as follows:

$$\widetilde{W}=f(A,W,k_{ev}) \tag{11}$$

In general $f(\cdot)$ should be a one-way, non-symmetric encoding function in order to be secure enough [7,8].

3. Statistical Analysis

3.1. Statistical Model

Given the watermarking scheme described in Section 2, we can make a framework of statistical models for watermark detection. Contrary to most current watermarking schemes, CBWM makes no assumption about the nature of the original image or the watermark.

The watermarking algorithm described in Section 2 can be called watermark detection instead of watermark encoding, because it only makes a binary decision – whether the image has particular watermark or not. If the feature vector C and the watermark W satisfy Eq.(5) upto a given small positive number δ, we can compute the value of scalar variable Z according to Eq. (2). If the given image contains the watermark, Eq. (2) yields:

$$Z = \sum_k \tilde{c}_k w_k = \sum_k c_k w_k + \sum_k a w_k^2 \le \delta + m \cong m \quad (12)$$

otherwise we have

$$Z = \sum_k \tilde{c}_k w_k = \sum_k c_k w_k \le \delta \quad (13)$$

In Eq. (12) and (13), δ is a very small scalar and can be neglected. So watermark detection is in fact the following hypothesis test:

$$H_1: \ Z = m + e(t)$$
$$H_0: \ Z = e(t) \quad (14)$$

where m is a constant and $e(t)$ is the error term due to image distortions. Here we consider image distortions (such as image filtering, adding noise, geometric transform etc.) as noise, and suppose it is Gaussian, i.e. $e(t) \sim N(0, \sigma^2)$.

3.2. Neyman-Pearson Criterion

In the case of watermark detection for still images described in Eq. (3), we do not know if the watermark exists or not. That means the *a priori* probability of watermark existence is unknown. So we hope if the probability of false alarm P_F (watermark is detected but actually does not exist) is fixed, the probability of missing detection P_M (watermark exists but is not detected) should be minimized.

Given P_F, we compute the estimation threshold Z_T in the sense of minimizing P_M according to the Neyman-Pearson criterion. According to the detection model described in Eq. (14), probability density functions of the model can be defined as:

$$f(Z \mid H_1) = \frac{1}{\sqrt{2\pi\sigma}} \exp[\frac{-(Z-m)^2}{2\sigma^2}]$$
$$f(Z \mid H_0) = \frac{1}{\sqrt{2\pi\sigma}} \exp(\frac{-Z^2}{2\sigma^2}) \quad (15)$$

and the decision criterion is defined as Eq. (3).

The value of threshold Z_T can be obtained from the probability of false alarm P_F:

$$P_F = \int_{Z_T}^{\infty} f(Z \mid H_0) dZ = \int_{Z_T}^{\infty} \frac{1}{\sqrt{2\pi\sigma}} \exp(\frac{-Z^2}{2\sigma^2}) dZ \quad (16)$$

Then the binary decision of whether the image B contains watermark W or not can be made according to Eq. (13).

The probability of missing rejection P_M can be computed as follows:

$$P_M = 1 - erfc^*(\frac{Z_T - m}{\sigma}) \quad (17)$$

where $erfc^*(\cdot)$ is error function

4. Experimental Results

CBWM is a general model, so it can be applied to any watermarking methods which are based on transforms. There are two key issues in using this algorithm. One is how to select the feature vector of the original image. Different selections result in different watermarking algorithms. Another is the selection of the suitable watermark. Because watermark selection is in practice a constrained optimization problem, and the objective function is non-glossy and non-continuous, the optimization algorithms should be chosen carefully. Traditional ones such as gradient methods are not suitable.

We apply our model to DCT, which means CBWM selects the feature vector of the original image in DCT transform domain, just like that of the Cox method [3]. We use the watermark-attacking tool "StirMark" designed and proposed by Petitcolas *et al.* [9] to perform the robustness experiments.

The algorithm is tested with a variety of images, but for the sake of space, here we only give the results of using the 256-by-256 gray image Lena. The feature vector $C = \{c_i\}$ is the first 256 highest DCT coefficients (excluding the DC component). The scale factor $a = 0.2$. Similar to the Cox method, the watermark used is a 256-by-1 binary vector which is required to satisfy Eq. (9). We can see that watermark space is a linear subspace of $\mathbf{F}^K$, so the suitable watermark is not hard to find. Here we simply adopt Monte Carlo random searching algorithms. If we embed meaningful watermarks, more complex optimal algorithms should be used (such as genetic algorithms, simulated annealing etc.)

Stirmark3.1 is used to simulate 88 types of image distortions to perform robustness test and the Neyman-

Pearson criterion is employed to examine the existence of the embedded watermark. Threshold Z_T is computed according to Eq. (17), given the probability of false alarm P_F=0.01. Note that watermark detection needs the original image to extract the feature vector. In order to compare our result, we also apply Stirmark to the Cox method to perform the same robustness test (see Table 1).

From the results of Table 1, we can see that CBWM can not detect the inserted watermark successfully for two kinds of image distortions: centered cropping and rotation. If the watermarked image is cropped for more than 10 percent or is rotated for more than 15^0, the watermark can not be detected safely. For other cases, the watermark can be detected completely. Table 1 also shows that the Cox method fails to detect the embedded watermark in many cases. In addition to cropping and rotation, median filtering (with the filter's size being 4-by-4), geometric transformation and shearing in x-y direction can also fail the Cox method in detecting the watermark's existence. If we compute the total rate of correct detection, the Cox method is 68.18% (60/88), which is lower than CBWM's result: 84.09% (74/88).

Table 1: Comparison results of the Cox method and the CBWM method

Test method	No. of Test Cases	Successful Detection	
		Cox method	CBWM
Symmetric and asymmetric line and column removal	5	5	5
Filtering(median, Gaussian, FMLR, sharpening)	6	5	6
JPEG compression	12	12	12
Centered Cropping	9	2	3
General linear geometric transformation	3	2	3
Change aspect ratio, scaling x-y axis	8	8	8
Rotation with cropping and without scaling	16	8	12
Rotation with cropping and scaling	16	8	12
Scaling	6	6	6
Shearing in x – y direction (%)	6	3	6
Strimark random bend	1	1	1
Total	88	60	74

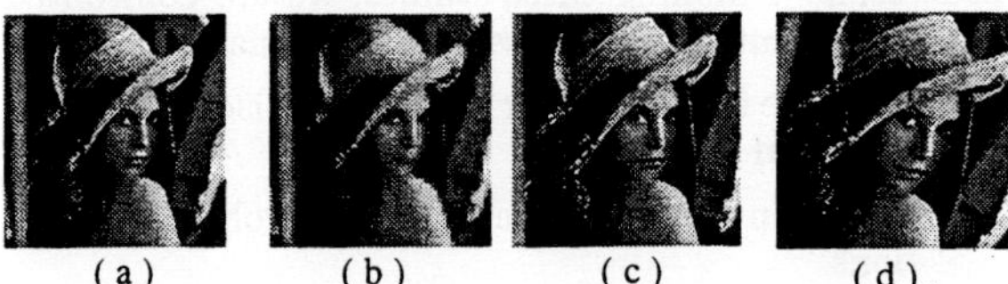

(a) (b) (c) (d)

Figure 1. Some experimental results of CBWM

Figure 1 shows some experimental results of CBWM and some images from which the embedded watermark can not be detected after StirMark's attack. (a) is the original image Lena; (b) is the watermarked image; (c) is the watermarked image after centered cropping for 10 percent; (d) shows the watermarked image rotated for 15^0.

5. Conclusion

A general content-based watermarking model CBWM for digital images has been presented in this paper. Compared with most existing watermarking schemes, CBWM has two advantages: (1) The watermark embedded is orthogonal to the feature vector of the original image to ensure a high level of security and robustness; (2) CBWM adopts the Neyman-Pearson decision theory and gives a general statistical approach to watermark detection under the case of unknown the *a priori* probability. We use Stirmark as the benchmark to test the model's robustness. Experimental results show that CBWM can improve the performance (e.g. robustness) of transform domain watermarking methods considerably.

6. References

[1] Swanson M. D., Kobayashi M. and Tewfik A. H., "Multimedia data-embedding and watermarking technologies", *Proceedings of the IEEE*, 1998, Vol.86, No.6, pages 1064-1087.

[2] Acken J. M., "How watermarking adds value to digital content", *Communications of the ACM*, 1998, Vol.41, No.7, pages 74-77.

[3] Cox I. J., Kilian J., Leighton F. T. and Shamoon T., "Secure Spread Spectrum Watermarking for Multimedia", *IEEE Trans. on Image Processing*, 1997, Vol.6, No.12, pages 1673-1687.

[4] D.Kundur and D.Hatzinakos, A robust digital image watermarking method using wavelet-based fusion, *Proceedings of ICIP'97*, 1997, Vol.1, pages 544-547.

[5] Hsu C. T. and Wu J. L., "Hidden digital watermarks in images", *IEEE Trans. on Image Processing*, 1999, Vol.8, No.1, pages 58-68.

[6] Hsu C. T. and Wu J. L., "Multiresolution watermarking for digital images", *IEEE Trans. on Circuits and Systems II-Analog and Digital Signal Processing*, 1998, Vol.45, No.8, pages1097-1101.

[7] Craver S., Memon N., Yeo B. L. and Yeung M. M., "Resolving rightful ownerships with invisible watermarking techniques: Limitations, attacks, and implications", *IEEE Journal on Selected Areas in Communications*, 1998, Vol.16, No.4, pages573-586.

[8] Qiao L. T. and Nahrstedt K., "Watermarking schemes and protocols for protecting rightful ownership and customer's rights", *Journal of Visual Communication and Image Representation*, 1998, Vol.9, No.3, pages 194-210.

[9] Petitcolas F., Anderson R. J. and Kuhn M. G., "Attacks on Copyright Marking Systems", *Proceedings of Infomation Hiding'98*, 1998, pages 218-238.

Discourse Structure Analysis for News Video by Checking Surface Information in the Transcript

Yasuhiko Watanabe† Yoshihiro Okada† Sadao Kurohashi‡ Eiichi Iwanari†
† Dept. of Electronics and Informatics, Ryukoku University, Seta, Otsu, Shiga, Japan
‡ Graduate School of Informatics, Kyoto University, Yoshida-Honmachi, Sakyo, Kyoto, Japan
watanabe@rins.ryukoku.ac.jp

Abstract

Various kinds of video recordings have discourse structures. Therefore, it is important to determine how video segments are combined and what kind of coherence relations they are connected with. In this paper, we propose a method for estimating the discourse structure of video news reports.

1 Introduction

A large number of studies have been made on video analysis, especially segmentation, feature extraction, indexing, and classification. On the other hand, little attention has been given to the discourse structure (DS) of video data.

Various kinds of video recordings, such as dramas, documentaries, news reports, and sports castings, have discourse structures. In other words, each video segment of these video recordings is related to previous ones by some kind of relation (coherence relation) which determines the role of the video segments in discourse. For this reason, it is important to determine how video segments are combined and what kind of coherence relations they are connected with.

In this paper, we propose a new method for estimating the discourse structure of video news reports by using three kinds of clues in the transcript: (1) clue expressions indicating some relations, (2) occurrence of identical/synonymous words/phrases in topic chaining or topic-dominant chaining relation, and (3) similarity between two sentences in list or contrast relation. We applied our method to NHK[1] News. This method is aimed to make the process of retrieval, summarization, and information extraction more efficient.

2 Discourse Structure and Video

Discourse structure is the subject of a large number of studies in natural language processing. So several methods for estimating the discourse structure of a text have been explored(Sumita 92) (Kurohashi 94). In addition, some researchers showed that the information of discourse structure is useful for extracting significant sentences and summarizing a text (Miike 94) (Marcu 97). As a result, it is likely that information of video discourse structure is utilized for extracting significant video segments and skimming. Therefore, methods for estimating the discourse structure of videos should be investigated.

As shown, video skimming and extraction of significant segments are closely related to the discourse structure estimation. For this reason, it may be useful to look at them before we discuss some points about discourse structure analysis.

One of the simple ways to skim a video is by using the pair of the first frame/image of the first shot and the first sentence in the transcript. However, this representative pair of image and language is often a poor topic explanation. To solve this problem, Zhang, et.al, proposed a method for key-frame selection by using several image features such as colors, textures, and temporal features including camera operations (Zhang 95). Also, Smith and Kanade proposed video skimming by selecting video segments based on TFIDF, camera motion, human face, captions on video, and so on (Smith 97). These techniques are broadly applicable, however, still have problems. One is the semantic classification of each segment. To solve this problem, Nakamura and Kanade proposed the spotting by association method which detects relevant video segments by associating image data and language data (Nakamura 97). Also, Watanabe, et.al, proposed a method for analyzing telops (captions) in video news reports by using layout and language information (Watanabe 96). However, these studies did not deal with coherence relations between video segments.

In contrast to this, several works on discourse structure have been made by researchers in natural language processing. Pursuing these studies, we are confronted with two points of discourse structure analysis:

- available knowledge for estimating discourse structure, and
- definition for discourse units and coherence relations.

First, we shall discuss the available knowledge for es-

[1] Nippon Hoso Kyokai (Japan Broadcasting Corporation)

timating discourse structure. Most studies on discourse structure have focused on such questions as what kind of knowledge should be employed, and how inference may be performed based on such knowledge (e.g., (Grosz 86), (Hobbs 85), (Zadrozny 91)). In contrast to this, Kurohashi and Nagao pointed out that a detailed knowledge base with broad coverage is unlikely to be constructed in the near future, and that we should analyze discourses using presently available knowledge. For these reasons, they proposed a method for estimating discourse structure by using surface information in sentences (Kurohashi 94). In video analysis, the same problems occurred. Therefore, we propose here a method for estimating the discourse structure in a news report by using surface information in the transcript.

Next, we shall discuss the definition for discourse unit and coherence relation. As mentioned, discourses are composed of segments (discourse units), and these are connected to previous ones by coherence relations. However, there has been a variety of definitions for discourse unit and coherence relation. For example, a discourse unit can be a frame, a shot, or a group of several consecutive shots. In this study, we consider one shot or more than one shots as a discourse unit. We will explain how to extract the discourse units in Section 3.1. In contrast to this, coherence relations strongly depend on the genre of video data: dramas, documentaries, news reports, sports castings, and so on. From the number of coherence relations suggested so far, we selected the following relations for our target, news reports:

List: S_i and S_j involve the same or similar events or states, or the same or similar important constituents

Contrast: S_i and S_j have distinct events or states, or contrasting important constituents

Topic chaining: S_i and S_j have distinct predications about the same topic

Topic-dominant chaining: A dominant constituent apart from a given topic in S_i becomes a topic in S_j

Elaboration: S_j gives details about a constituent introduced in S_i

Reason: S_j is the reason for S_i

Cause: S_j occurs as a result of S_i

Example: S_j is an example of S_i

where S_i denotes the former segment and S_j the latter.

3 Estimation of Discourse Structure

Our determination of how video segments are combined and what kind of coherence relations are involved is made in the next way:

1. extract discourse units from a news report,
2. extract three kinds of clue information from transcripts, and then, transform them into reliable scores for some relations, and
3. choose the connected sentence and the relation having the maximum reliable score. If two or more connected sentences have the same maximum score, the chronological nearest segment is selected.

3.1 Extraction of Discourse Units

A shot is generally regarded as a basic unit in video analysis. In this study, however, not only a shot but also more consecutive ones are considered a basic unit (discourse unit). This is because there are some cases where several consecutive shots correspond with one sentences in a transcript. In this case, these consecutive shots should be regarded as a discourse unit. In contrast to this, one shot should be regarded as a discourse unit when it correspond with one or more sentences in a transcript. In both cases, the start/end point of a discourse unit often lies in the pause because the announcer needs to take breath at the end of a sentence. As a result, discourse units are extracted in the next way:

1. Detect scene cuts in a video by using DCT components (Iwanari 94). In this study, sound data was collected on a sampling condition, 11kHz, 8bit (-127 $\sim$ +128), and monoral.
2. Detect speech pauses in the video. If amplitudes in an analysis frame are less than the threshold, the frame is determined as a speech pause. We set an analysis frame to 1.25 sec, and the threshold to ± 6. This determination is processed every 4 ms.
3. extract the start/end points of discourse units by detecting the cuts in the pause.

For evaluating this method, we used 50 news reports of NHK News. The recall and precision of discourse unit detection were 80% and 77%, respectively, while those of scene change detection were 92% and 78%. We modified the extracted discourse units by hand and used them in the discourse structure analysis described in Section 3.2. In addition, each discourse unit was associated with the corresponding sentences in a transcript by hands. This is because NHK news reports do not have closed captions.

3.2 Detection of Coherence Relations

In order to extract discourse structure, we use three kinds of clue information in transcripts:

- clue expressions indicating some relations,
- occurrence of identical/synonymous words/phrases in topic chaining or topic-dominant chaining relation, and
- similarity between two sentences in list or contrast relation.

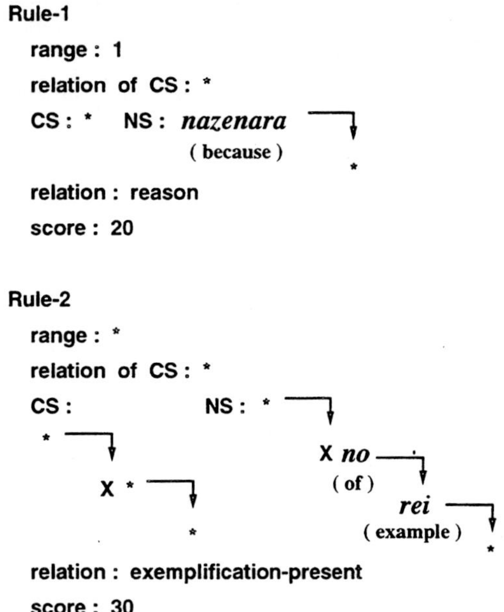

Figure 1: Examples of heuristic rules for clue expressions

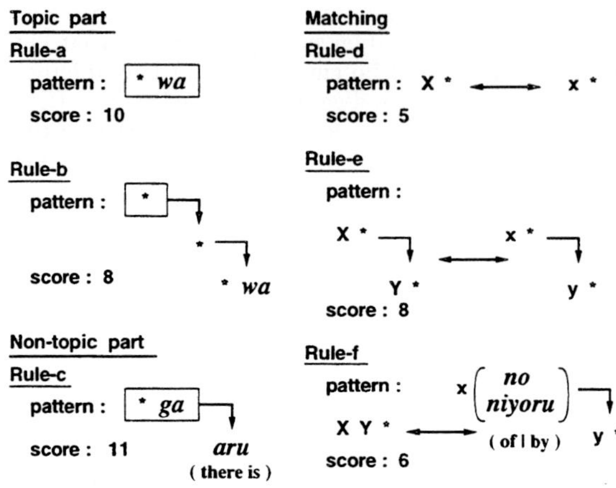

Figure 2: Examples of rules for topic/non-topic parts

Then they are transformed into reliable scores for some relations. In other words, as a new sentence (NS) comes in, reliable scores for all possible connected sentences and relations are calculated by using above three types of clues. As a final result, we choose the connected sentence (CS) and the relation having the maximum reliable score.

3.2.1 Detection of Clue Expressions

In this study, we use 41 heuristic rules for finding clue expressions by pattern matching and relating them to proper relations with reliable scores. A rule consists of two parts: (1) conditions for rule application and (2) corresponding relation and reliable score. Conditions for rule application consist of four parts: (i) rule applicable range, (ii) relation of CS to its previous DS, (iii) dependency structure pattern for CS, and (iv) dependency structure pattern for NS. Pattern for CS and NS are matched not for word sequences but for dependency structures of both sentences. We apply each rule for the pairs of a CS and NS. If the condition of the rule is satisfied, the specified reliable score is given to the corresponding relation between the CS and the NS.

For example, Rule-1 in Figure 1 gives a score (20 points) to the reason relation between two adjoining sentences if the NS starts with the expression "*nazenara* (because)". Rule-2 in Figure 1 is applied not only for the neighboring CS but also for farther CSs, by specifying the occurrence of identical words "X" in the condition.

3.2.2 Detection of Word/Phase Chain

In general, a sentence can be divided into two parts: a topic part and a non-topic part. When two sentences are in a topic chaining relation, the same topic is maintained through them. Therefore, the occurrence of identical/synonymous word/phrase (the word/phrase chain) in topic parts of two sentences supports this relation. On the other hand, in the case of topic-dominant chaining relation, a dominant constituent introduced in a non-topic part of a prior sentence becomes a topic in a succeeding sentence. As shown, the word/phrase chain from a non-topic part of a prior sentence to a topic part of a succeeding sentence supports this relation.

For these reasons, we detect word/phrase chains and calculate reliable scores in the next way:

1. give scores to words/phrases in topic and non-topic parts according to the degree of their importance in sentences,
2. give scores to the matching of identical/synonymous words/phrases according to the degree of their agreement, and
3. give these relations the sum of the scores of two chained words/phrases and the score of their matching.

For example, by Rule-a and Rule-b in Figure 2, words in a phrase whose head word is followed by a topic marking postposition "*wa*" are given some scores as topic parts. Also, a word in a non-topic part in the sentential style, "*ga aru* (there is ...)" is given a large score (11 points) by Rule-c in Figure 2 because this word is an important new information in this sentence and topic-dominant chaining relation involving it often occur. Matching of phrases like "A of B" is given a larger score (8 points) by Rule-e than that of word like "A" alone by Rule-d (5 points) in Figure 2.

Table 1: Analysis results

Relation	Success	Failure
List	0	1
Contrast	1	0
Topic chaining	9	3
Topic-dominant c.	11	1
Elaboration	0	3
Reason	0	0
Cause	2	0
Example	0	0
Total	23	8

3.2.3 Calculation of Similarity between Sentences in a Transcript

When two sentences have list or contrast relation, they have a certain similarity. As a result, we measure such a similarity for finding list or contrast relation in the next way. First, the similarity value between two words are calculated according to exact matching, matching of their parts of speech, and their closeness in a thesaurus dictionary. Second, the similarity value between two word-strings is calculated roughly by combining the similarity values between words in the two word-strings with the dynamic programming method for analyzing conjunctive structures (Kurohashi 94). Then, we give the normalized similarity score between a CS and an NS to their list and contrast relations as a reliable score.

4 Experiments and Discussion

For evaluating this method, we used 10 news reports of NHK News. Each report was a few minutes in length. As mentioned, news reports of NHK News do not have closed captions. For this reason, each video segment (discourse unit) was associated with the corresponding sentences in a transcript by hands. The experimental results are shown in Table 1.

In this experiment, three topic chaining and one topic-dominant chaining relations could not be extracted. The reasons were (1) the topic words of the following sentences were omitted [2] and (2) the topic word was changed (e.g., driver → man who drove the car). Also, 3 elaboration relations could not be extracted. This was because there were no clue expressions for the elaboration relation in the sentences. On the contrary, we could extract clue expressions for list and contrast relations. However, it was difficult to find the connected sentence because the similarity between NS and CSs can get rather low.

In this study, we introduce a reliable score for determining only one CS and relation. However, in some cases (e.g., a compound sentence), there are many clues for an NS supporting various relations to several CSs. In these cases, we should have extract more CSs and relation than one.

In this study, we assumed that image and language data correspond to the same portion of a news report. For this reason, it is likely that the relation between images slightly differs from the analysis result when image and language are taken form different portions (correspondence problem between image and language).

[2]There are many ellipses in Japanese sentences.

5 Conclusion

In this study, we have proposed a method for estimating discourse structure of video news reports by using surface information of sentences in transcripts: clue expressions, word/phrase chains, and similarity between sentences. We intend to investigate a method for applying discourse structure information to information retrieval, summarization, and information extraction.

References

Grosz and Sidner: Attention, Intentions, and the Structures of Discourse, Computational Linguistics, 12-3, (1986).

Hobbs: On the Coherence and Structure of Discourse, Technical Report No. CSLI-85-37, (1985).

Iwanari and Ariki: Scene Clustering and Cut Detection in Moving Images by DCT components, (in Japanese), technical report of IEICE, PRU-93-119, (1994).

Kurohashi and Nagao: Dynamic Programming Method for Analyzing Conjunctive Structures in Japanese, COLING-92, (1992).

Kurohashi and Nagao: Automatic Detection of Discourse Structure by Checking Surface Information in Sentences, COLING-94, (1994).

Marcu: From Discourse Structures to Text Summaries, ACL workshop on Intelligent Scalable Text Summarization, (1997).

Miike, Itoh, Ono, and Sumita: A Full-Text Retrieval System with a Dynamic Abstract Generation Function, SIGIR-94, (1994).

Nakamura and Kanade: Semantic Analysis for Video Contents Extraction - Spotting by Association in News Video, ACM Multimedia 97, (1997).

Smith and Kanade: Video Skimming and Characterization through the Combination of Image and Language Understanding Techniques, IEEE CVPR, (1997).

Sumita, Ono, Chino, Ukita, and Amano: A Discourse Structure Analyzer for Japanese Text, International Conference of Fifth Generation Computer Systems, (1992).

Watanabe, Okada, and Nagao: Semantic Analysis of Telops in TV Newscasts, (in Japanese), technical report of Information Processing Society of Japan, NL-116-16, (1996).

Zadrozny and Jensen: Semantics of Paragraphs, Computational Linguistics, 17-2, (1991).

Zhang, Low, Smoliar, and Wu: Video Parsing, Retrieval and Browsing: An Integrated and Content-Based Solution, ACM Multimedia 95, (1995).

Discrete Angle Watermark Encoding and Recovery

Imants Svalbe[+], Andrew Tirkel[*] and Ron van Schyndel[+]
[+]*Department of Physics, Monash University, Australia*
[*]*Scientific Technology, East Brighton, Australia*
imants.svalbe@sci.monash.edu.au

Abstract

Angles derived from sets of image pixel values present an effective medium for embedding "invisible" watermarks. The derived angles can be dithered by the addition of small offset angles. The watermark is a pseudo-noise sequence of dither angles. The watermark embedding is followed by re-quantisation for image storage or transmission. Watermark recovery is achieved by performing a complex correlation between the watermarked image and the reference pseudo-noise sequence. This occurs without recourse to the original image.

This paper analyses the form of the observed de-correlation as the watermark to image ratio is decreased. The dependence of sequence recovery on 1) the magnitude of the added dithered angle 2) the angle derivation scheme used and 3) on the level of quantisation in the original data is discussed.

The novel spatially distributed embedding method used here also offers potential robust data encryption advantages.

1. Introduction

Traditional watermarking schemes modulate the amplitude of pixel values to embed a message, copyright or descriptors into images or other data [1].

This paper describes results for an angle based embedding scheme that exploits discrete Cartesian to discrete polar conversions to watermark arbitrary image data types. The method described in this paper can be applied to pixel values in any transform domain of the image, as well as to the original image values.

This research follows an investigation of encoding watermarks in the hue angle of colour image data [2]. Chae et al [3] adopt a related pixel dithering strategy to that used here for the embedding of grey or colour images into the Y channel of YUV coded colour images, [5] also adopts a similar "constellation" embedding approach. Watermarking in colour image data is also reported for example in [4], where the blue channel is encrypted to minimise perceptual changes in the watermarked image.

Related angle encoding [8] aimed to detect the digital delay times for the fundamental and overtones in discrete phase-angle encrypted carrier wave signals. The objective there was to characterise the properties of non-linear transmission channels rather than watermark.

The angles used here are not hue related, but are obtained, for example, as the inverse tangent derived from pairs of pixel values found at a pre-determined pattern of image locations.

The set of angles thus derived from the image is dithered by adding perturbing angles. The set of derived angles is pre-quantised, to permit the addition of dither to the derived angle vectors without overlap between adjacent angle bins.

The perturbing angles are typically downscaled values from some selected alphabet of angles, usually comprised of equal subdivisions over the range 0-2π. The pattern of perturbing angles is chosen to be isomorphic to a pseudo-noise sequence or array of angles with near optimal auto-correlation properties [6, 7]. This helps maximise the watermark recovery process after estimation of the sequence of encoded dither angles.

Further work is required to make this scheme more robust. The effects of JPEG image compression and small spatial distortions such as local warping and image cropping may be addressed as in [3], by encoding images after mapping to an appropriate transform domain using, for example, wavelets.

Section 2 outlines several schemes to derive angles from quantised pixel data and comments on the distribution of angles produced. Quantisation of these derived angles and the subsequent dither encoding mechanism is presented in Section 3. Section 4 briefly describes the auto- and cross-correlation properties of the pseudo-noise sequences used to select the dither angles. A typical "s-shaped" form for the decrease in correlative recovery results as the size of the embedded angles is decreased to make the watermark less perceptible. Section 5 analyses the contributing effects that cause the s-shaped loss of angle watermark recovery.

1051-4651/00 $10.00 © 2000 IEEE

2. Obtaining angles from pixel values

Angles can be assigned to directly correspond to a range of pixel grey levels, but such mappings mirror the more traditional 1D amplitude encoding.

By selecting, for example, pairs i and j of pixels, with values v_i and v_j, an angle can be obtained from the ratio of their values as $artan[v_i / v_j]$. Adding a dither angle to the derived angle and then re-quantising the resulting total angle components, as v_i' and v_j', perturbs each pair of original pixel values in a distributed, less perceptible, non-linear fashion. This process effectively associates pairs of pixel values as projections onto an orthonormal basis.

The stored value of either or both selected pixels may change (at the least significant bit level) with respect to the original values, for each encoded pixel entry. This reduces the dependence on and interaction with image content and greatly extends the available encoding space. It maintains, however, the same level of perceptible differences between original and watermarked images.

A correlative approach is used to recover the set of dither angles, as outlined in section 5. This guards against sensitivity to individual erasures of the watermark dither angles caused by quantisation.

The relative position of the selected pixel pair can be chosen arbitrarily. We chose to use a raster scan pattern that maintains a large distance between selected pixels, such as pairing pixels from opposite ends of the image. This randomizes the derived angle distribution more effectively. Each image pixel can only be dithered once when embedding a single watermark

This strategy has proven to be adequate for a range of natural images and for random test images with Gaussian or uniform distributions. Correlation effects between the chosen pixels appear to be negligible, but this still warrants further investigation.

Taking the *artan* of integer ratios does place restrictions on the possible angles and all angles are not equally probable [9]. Some angles, such as 45°, occur frequently and are also difficult to dither because of the large gaps to the next available angles with integer ratios.

The addition of a small dither to a vector needs to survive the re-quantisation of the pixel derived angle components from v_i to v_i', so length of the vectors associated with each pixel value pair also affects the dither encoding ability. The selected pixel pairs can also be filtered to ensure the vector length exceeds some minimum value. For images with a small number of quantisation levels, $0 \leq v \leq V$, the shorter maximum length of these vectors also restricts the available angle space for encoding.

A ratio of positive integers produces angles over the range 0 to 90 degrees, with an angle distribution symmetric around 45 degrees. Pixel values can be negatively offset, or interpreted as two's complement values, to produce a (related) 360° set, with 8-fold symmetry in the derived angles.

3. Angle quantisation and dither encoding

The set of derived angles is quantised to provide a fixed, minimum interval, of size $d\theta = 2\pi/s$, between all derived angle members. The gaps between the allowed quantised angle values are used to store the added dither angles, ensuring separability of the image values and the embedded watermark. The scale parameter s can range from 1 to 400 before dithered angles fail to be encoded and recovered sufficiently for 8-bit pixel data.

The quantisation method provides superior isolation of watermark from image content. Other schemes use the mean or median of the local angle distribution to estimate the angle onto which the dither is added [2]. Here the local angle associated with any pixel is largely unrelated to the angle associated with the adjoining pixels, because of the use of a spatially disjoint pixel pair selection mechanism. This angle-encoded method is immune to local angle estimation techniques.

The dither angle to be embedded for each pixel pair corresponds to that of a unit vector with angles $2\pi/n$, where n is an integer. For binary sequences, the dither angle is effectively $\pm\ \pi/2$. When adding a binary dither angle to the derived angle, the unit dither angle vector is added in a direction perpendicular to the derived angle, to maximise the separability of the watermark signal from the image derived angle.

4. Pseudo-random dither angle sequences

The sequence of dither angles to be embedded is chosen to be a 1D "complexified" Legendre sequence (or a related 2D Legendre array) [6, 7, 10].

Binary Legendre sequences, of (prime) length p, have optimal auto-correlation values of $p(p-1)$ or -1 and a cross-correlation magnitude of order $\sqrt{p}$ [6]. The strong Legendre correlation properties enable extremely robust extraction of the watermark signal. Recovery is possible even when the encoding losses are significant due to the smallness of the added dither signal or because of perturbation of the image due to noise added in the transmission channel.

Legendre sequences have a second favorable property, in being invariant to Fourier transformation [11]. Without requiring knowledge other than the length of the encoding sequence, a strong cross correlation will be obtained between the encoded sequence and its Fourier transform. The message can thus be determined as being watermarked, without needing to disclose the watermark content, although the encoded data capacity will be low.

5. Mechanisms affecting angle recovery

This section presents some of the results obtained for the dithered angle-watermarking scheme.

Figure 1 shows the characteristic "s-shaped" loss of correlative recovery that occurs as the size of the scaling parameter s increases, making the added dither angles smaller. For 8-bit uniformly distributed data, the watermark can still be recovered for s = 400, where the added dither angle is about 0.2°, for the case of binary sequence encoding. The image signal to watermark ratio is about 50 dB in this case for a 251*251 watermark.

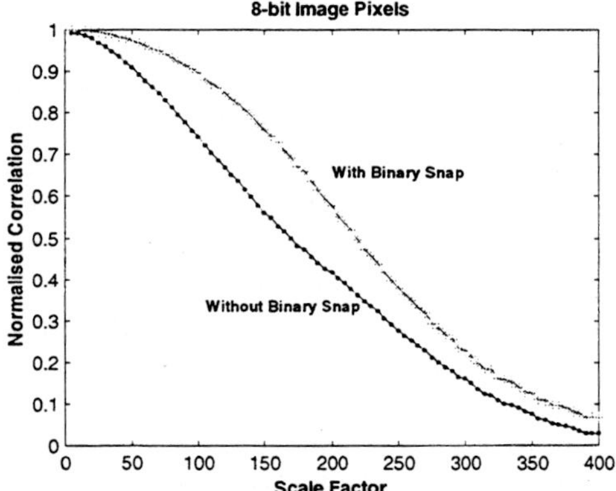

Figure 1. Relation between encoding scale-factor and degree of correlative recovery for a uniformly distributed 8-bit noise image with and without snapping the recovered angles (see text).

Figure 2 shows that the maximum value of s required to secure a fixed fraction (here 90%) of the possible peak correlation value scales linearly with the number of quantisation bits, V, used to represent the original image data. The Legendre sequence correlation value also drops linearly with the number of sequence entries that are incorrectly encoded or recovered.

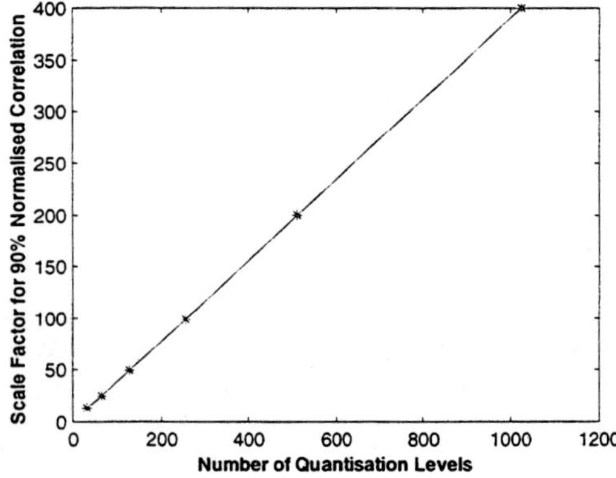

Figure 2. Dependence of degree of correlative recovery with image bit depth (expressed as number of quantisation levels).

Figure 3 shows a histogram of the recovered dither angles, again for the case of uniformly distributed 8-bit image data and a binary Legendre sequence. As the value of s increases, the two peaks in the recovered angles, centered on $\pm \pi/2$, spread and eventually merge so that the dither vectors are miss-classified. In Fig. 1, the curve marked "With binary Snap" is obtained by rounding the estimated dither angles to either $\pi/2$ or $-\pi/2$ before correlation with the reference Legendre sequence. Using the "snapped" recovered angles increases the resulting complex correlation, as the estimated vectors all lie parallel or anti-parallel to the reference set. The same snapping approach can be used in the recovery of an arbitrary number of dither angles.

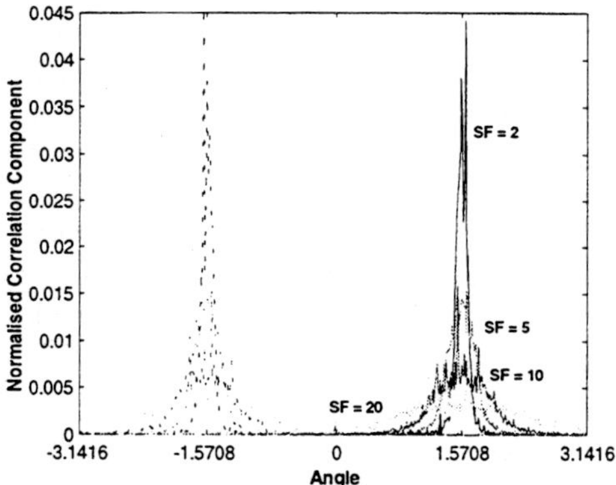

Figure 3. Histogram of recovered angles for a binary watermark. Curves for scale factors, SF, of 2,5,10,20 are shown.

Figure 4 confirms that the degree of misalignment of the estimated dither vector angles accounts for the loss of correlation. The cosine of the estimated angle for each unit vector gives the useful component that adds constructively to the correlation. The sum of the cosine weighted unit vectors reproduces the s-shaped curve of Figure 1, with excellent precision. The sum of the sines of the recovered vector angles converges to zero.

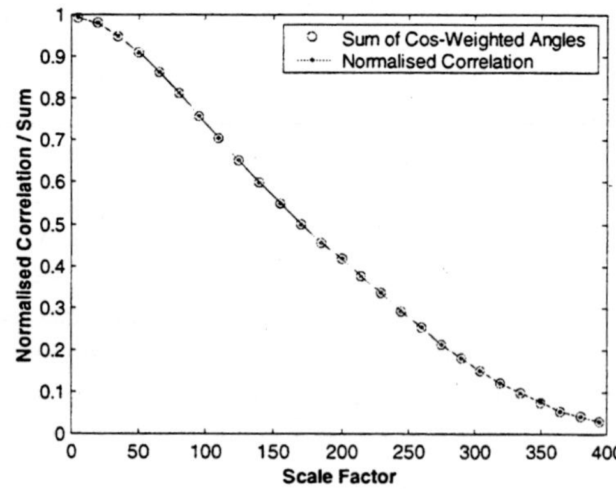

Figure 4. The sum of the recovered angles, weighted by the cosine of the distance to the template angle. This yields a distribution identical to the correlation curve of Fig. 1.

Figure 5 shows the number of true and false classifications for the recovered angles of the unit vectors as a function of the scaling parameter *s*. The true and false curves converge when the dither angle estimation becomes random.

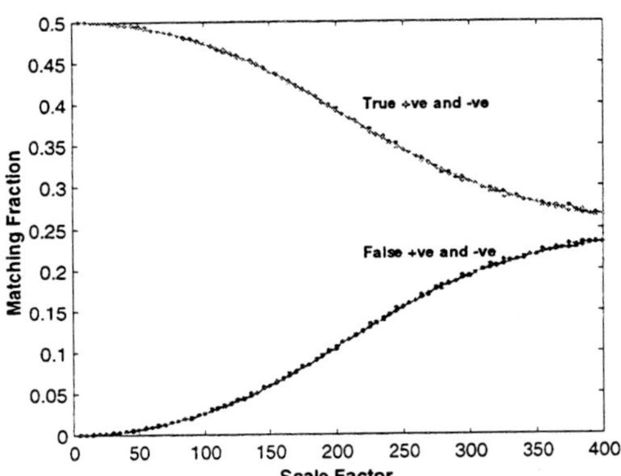

Figure 5. The fraction of recovered angles classified as true and false matches to the watermark template as a function of scale factor

6. Conclusions

An angle-encoding scheme has been described to embed watermarks in arbitrary image data. The angle-encoding scheme uses pairs of pixel values to derive an angle, onto which a dither angle is added as the watermark content. The sequence or array of added dither values is derived from complexified Legendre sequences [6] to maximise the correlative recovery of the watermark.

We have measured the decrease in correlation as the image to watermark signal ratio increases and have outlined the relative effect of contributing factors determining the decline in watermark recovery.

The inclusion of a transform based embedding step is required to provide some resistance to compression losses. Future work would also include provision of an adaptive mechanism to adjust the scaling parameter *s* to better suit the individual pixel pair values for each discrete derived angle. This will increase the coding density and the recoverability of the watermark.

A watermark can also be embedded in arbitrary images in higher dimensions by associating more than 2 pixels to form a vector . For example, using a triplet of pixel values (x, y, z) allows two dither angles to be added (as $d\theta$ and $d\phi$) to a 3D (r, θ, ϕ) vector. This extension should offer further enhancements to the coding advantages already described in this paper. We aim to investigate the generation of pseudo-random sequences or arrays for double angles.

7. Acknowledgments

RvS is supported an Australian Postgraduate Award, provided through the Australian Research Council. Thanks are also due to Professors Charles Osborne and Tom Hall from Monash for useful discussions.

8. References

[1] N. Nikolaidis, I. Pitas, "Digital Image Watermarking: an Overview", ICMCS 99, Volume 1, Florence, Italy, pp 1 – 6.

[2] R. van Schyndel, A. Z. Tirkel, I. D. Svalbe, "A Multiplicative Color Watermark", IEEE-EURASIP Workshop on Non-Linear Signal and Imaging Processing, Antalya, Turkey, 1999, pp. 336-340.

[3] J. J. Chae and B. S. Majunath, "A Technique for Image Data Hiding and Reconstruction without Host Image", SPIE Conference on Security and Watermarking of Multimedia Contents, San Jose, California, USA, January, 1999, pp. 386 - 396.

[4] M. Kutter, "Digital Signature of Color Images using Amplitude Modulation", SPIE, vol. 3022, San Jose, Feb., 1997, pp. 518-525.

[5] B. Tao and M. Orchard, "Coding and Modulation in Watermarking and Data Hiding", SPIE Conference on Security and Watermarking of Multimedia Contents, San Jose, California, USA, January, 1999, pp. 503 – 510.

[6] R. M. Schroeder, *Number Theory in Science and Communications*, 2nd Edn. 1997, Springer-Verlag.

[7] A. Z. Tirkel, R. van Schyndel, T. E. Hall, C. F. Osborne, "Secure Arrays for Digital Watermarking", IEEE International Conference on Pattern Recognition, Brisbane, Australia, August 1998, pp. 1643-1645.

[8] R. van Schyndel, A. Z. Tirkel, I. D. Svalbe, "Delay Recovery from a Non-Linear Polynomial Response System", IEEE International Workshop on Intelligent Signal Processing and Communication Systems, Melbourne, November 1998, Vol. 1, pp. 294-298.

[9] I. D. Svalbe, "Natural Representations for the Hough Transform", IEEE Transactions on Pattern Analysis and Machine Intelligence", vol. 12, no. 2, 1991, pp. 336-342.

[10] R. G. van Schyndel, A. Z. Tirkel, I. D. Svalbe, T. E. Hall and C. F. Osborne, "Algebraic Construction of a new class of Quasi-orthogonal Arrays in Steganography", SPIE Electronic Imaging 1999, San Jose, USA, January, 1999, pp. 354 - 364.

[11] R. van Schyndel, A. Z. Tirkel, I. D. Svalbe, "Key Independent Watermark Detection", IEEE International Conference on Multimedia Computing and Systems, Florence, Italy, Vol. 1, June 1999, pp. 580-585.

Feature Relevance Learning with Query Shifting for Content-Based Image Retrieval

Douglas R. Heisterkamp
doug@cs.okstate.edu

Jing Peng
jpeng@cs.okstate.edu

H. K. Dai
dai@cs.okstate.edu

Department of Computer Science
Oklahoma State University
Stillwater, OK 74078

Abstract

Probabilistic feature relevance learning (PFRL) is an effective technique for adaptively computing local feature relevance for content-based image retrieval. It however becomes less attractive in situations where all the input variables have the same local relevance, and yet retrieval performance might still be improved by simple query shifting. We propose a retrieval method that combines feature relevance learning and query shifting to try to achieve the best of both worlds. We use a linear discriminant analysis to compute the new query and exploit the local neighborhood structure centered at the new query by invoking PFRL. As a result, the modified neighborhoods at the new query tend to contain sample images that are more relevant to the input query. The efficacy of our method is validated using both synthetic and real world data.

1. Introduction

Probabilistic feature relevance learning for content-based image retrieval [8] computes flexible metrics for producing retrieval neighborhoods that are elongated along less relevant feature dimensions and constricted along most influential ones. The technique has shown promise in a number of image database applications. It, however, becomes less appealing in situations where all the input variables have the same local relevance, and yet retrieval performance might still be improved by simple query shifting.

On the other hand, MARS [9] is a simple query shifting mechanism that attempts to improve retrieval performance by adaptively moving the input query toward relevant retrievals and, at the same time, away from irrelevant ones. Similarity computation remains fixed throughout the retrieval process. While MARS has been shown to improve retrieval performance in simple tasks, it is clear that in many problems the mere shifting of the query is insufficient to achieve desired goals, as we shall see later.

In this paper, we propose a novel, principled approach that combines probabilistic feature relevance learning, as in [8], and query shifting, as in [9], to try to achieve the best of both worlds for content-based image retrieval [1, 6, 8, 9]. We use a linear discriminant analysis to compute the new query and exploit the local neighborhood structure centered at the new query by invoking PFRL. As a result, the modified neighborhoods at the new query tend to contain sample images that are more relevant to the input query.

2. Feature Relevance Learning with Query Shifting

We begin this section by briefly introducing the basic ideas behind PFRL and query shifting. We then describe in detail our method that combines PFRL and query shifting in a principled way.

2.1. PFRL

In PFRL [8], retrieved images with relevance feedback are used to compute local feature relevance. Let $\mathcal{R}_{\text{KNN}} = \{\mathbf{x}_j, y_j\}_1^K$ be the set of K retrievals, where $\mathbf{x}_j$ denotes the feature vector representing the jth retrieved image, and y_j is either 1 (relevant image) or 0 (irrelevant image) marked by the user as the class label associated with $\mathbf{x}_j$. If we let the class label $y \in \{0, 1\}$ at query $\mathbf{x}$ be treated as a random variable from a distribution with the probabilities $\{\Pr(1|\mathbf{x}), \Pr(0|\mathbf{x})\}$, we have

$$f(\mathbf{x}) \doteq \Pr(y = 1|\mathbf{x}) = E(y|\mathbf{x}).$$

In the absence of any variable assignments, the least-squares estimate for $f(\mathbf{x})$ is $E[f] = \int f(\mathbf{x})p(\mathbf{x})d\mathbf{x}$, where $p(\mathbf{x})$ is the joint density. Now given only that $\mathbf{x}$ is known at dimension $x_i = z_i$. The least-squares estimate becomes $E[f|x_i = z_i] = \int f(\mathbf{x})p(\mathbf{x}|x_i = z_i)d\mathbf{x}$. Here $p(\mathbf{x}|x_i = z_i)$ is the conditional density of the other input variables.

In image retrieval, $f(\mathbf{z}) = 1$, where $\mathbf{z}$ is the query. Then $[(f(\mathbf{z}) - 0) - (f(\mathbf{z}) - E[f|x_i = z_i])] = E[f|x_i = z_i]$ represents a reduction in error between the two predictions. Thus, a measure of feature relevance at query $\mathbf{z}$ can be defined as

$$r_i(\mathbf{z}) = E[f|x_i = z_i].$$

The relative relevance can be used as a weighting scheme for a weighted K-nearest neighbor search (KNN):

$$w_i(\mathbf{z}) = \exp(Tr_i(\mathbf{z}))/\sum_{l=1}^{q} \exp(Tr_l(\mathbf{z})).$$

Here T is a parameter that can be chosen to maximize (minimize) the influence of r_i on w_i. For further details, see [8].

2.2. Query Shifting

The *Standard Rocchio* equation is commonly used in the information retrieval field to determine the next query location based on relevance feedback [10]. The Standard Rocchio is

$$\mathbf{z}' = \alpha\mathbf{z} + \beta\frac{1}{n_r}\sum_{\mathbf{x}\in\mathcal{R}_r}\mathbf{x} - \gamma\frac{1}{n_i}\sum_{\mathbf{x}\in\mathcal{R}_i}\mathbf{x},$$

where $\mathbf{z}'$ is the new query location, $\mathbf{z}$ is the initial query location, $\mathcal{R}_r$ is the set of relevant retrievals, $\mathcal{R}_i$ is the set of irrelevant retrievals, n_r is the number of relevant retrievals, n_i is the number of irrelevant retrievals. The second term is equivalent to $\beta\boldsymbol{\mu}_r$ where $\boldsymbol{\mu}_r$ is the mean of the relevant retrievals. The third term is equivalent to $\gamma\boldsymbol{\mu}_i$ where $\boldsymbol{\mu}_i$ is the mean of the irrelevant retrievals. The Standard Rocchio expressed in terms of the retrieval means is $\mathbf{z}' = \alpha\mathbf{z} + \beta\boldsymbol{\mu}_r + \gamma.\boldsymbol{\mu}_i$ The values for the parameters α, β, and γ are determined by experimental runs over the database. The settings of $\alpha = 1.0, \beta = 0.75, \gamma = 0.25$ were reported in [10] to perform well in many cases. A common alternative is to ignore the influence of irrelevant retrievals ($\gamma = 0$) [3]. Another approach takes this theme further by setting $\alpha = 0$, $\beta = 1$, $\gamma = 0$, *i.e.*, the new query is $\boldsymbol{\mu}_r$. Moving to $\boldsymbol{\mu}_r$ has been claimed to be the optimal new query location [4]. It is easy to see that it is not since it ignores the effect of irrelevant retrievals [1]. See Figure 1, where moving to the positive mean also moves closer to the negative mean.

[1]It is optimal based on their criterion of minimum distance to relevant retrievals, but the criterion really should be a multiple criterion optimization of minimizing distance to relevant retrievals and maximizing distance to irrelevant retrievals.

2.3. Combining PFRL with Query Shifting

We present a hybrid system for learning feature relevance that seeks to draw upon the exploitation feature of PFRL and the exploration feature of query shifting.

For a given query image $\mathbf{z}$ in a q-dimensional feature space, we explore a new query $\mathbf{z}'$ in the q-dimensional feature space for more relevant retrievals, if necessary, as follows. The computation of $\mathbf{z}'$ is aided by a feature extraction that transforms from the q-dimensional feature space to a one-dimensional space, which retains sufficient information of the retrieval images.

Classical discriminant analysis (see, for example, [11]) attempts to project patterns into a space with lower dimensionality than the original pattern space. The discriminant analysis projection maximizes the inter-class scatter while keeping the intra-class scatter constant. When the number of pattern classes is two, like in our case, the discriminant analysis projection can be realized by the one-dimensional Fisher linear discriminant projection, which requires to calculate the intra-class and inter-class scatter matrices.

To determine the exact location of $\mathbf{z}'$ without computing the scatter matrices, we consider the projections of all K retrieved images onto the line L passing through the two sample means $\boldsymbol{\mu}_r$ and $\boldsymbol{\mu}_i$. Parameterize the points on L as $L(\lambda) = \lambda\boldsymbol{\mu}_r + (1-\lambda)\boldsymbol{\mu}_i$ with real λ. We will let $\mathbf{z}' = L(\lambda^*)$ for some suitably chosen λ^*.

Our objective is to find λ^* such that in the vicinity of $L(\lambda^*)$, the frequency of retrieving relevant class-1 images is high. This suggests to select λ^* that maximizes the conditional expectation of an image pattern $\mathbf{x}$ given that the component of $\mathbf{x}$ in the direction of L is $L(\lambda^*)$. That is,

$$\lambda^* = \arg\max_{\lambda} E[f(\mathbf{x}) \mid \text{proj}_L(\mathbf{x}) = L(\lambda^*)].$$

After computing $\mathbf{z}'$, we exploit the neighborhood structure centered at the next query $\mathbf{z}'$ by invoking PFRL on all previous (cumulative) retrieval images to generate the relative relevance weights used to determine the KNN in the next iteration.

An estimate for the conditional expectation for a point on L can be determined by projecting the KNN retrievals onto L and using the following equation [2, 8]

$$\hat{E}[f(\mathbf{x})|\text{proj}_L(\mathbf{x}) = L(\lambda)] = \frac{\sum_{\mathbf{x}\in\mathcal{R}_r^+} y(\mathbf{x})1(|\text{proj}_L(\mathbf{x}) - L(\lambda)| \leq \Omega)}{\sum_{\mathbf{x}\in\mathcal{R}_{\text{KNN}}^+} 1(|\text{proj}_L(\mathbf{x}) - L(\lambda)| \leq \Omega)},$$

where $1(\cdot)$ is an indicator function for its predicate argument, $y(\mathbf{x})$ is the label of a retrieved image $\mathbf{x}$, and $\mathcal{R}_{\text{KNN}}^+$ and $\mathcal{R}_r^+$ are the sets of cumulated retrieved images and retrieved relevant images respectively. The retrieved images are cumulated for each individual query sequence. When the user initiates a query with a new image, the accumulations are reset.

The value of Ω is chosen such that

$$\sum_{\mathbf{x}\in\mathcal{R}_{\text{kNN}}} 1(|\text{proj}_L(\mathbf{x}) - L(\lambda)| \leq \Omega) = C.$$

Due to the discrete nature of the estimate, a segment of L will maximize $\hat{E}$, (possibly multiple segments, in which case we choose the largest segment). Any of the points on the segment maximizing $\hat{E}$ can be chosen for the next query location. We chose the mean of the relevant samples that contributed to the estimate, $\hat{E}$. With this choice, moving to the relevant mean (i.e., $\lambda = 1$) is obtained as a special case by letting $C = K$. The α, β, γ parameters are determined from λ by setting $\alpha = 0$, $\beta = \lambda$, and $\gamma = \lambda - 1$.

3. Experimental Results

In the following we compare the retrieval methods of query shifting, PFRL, and PFRL combined with query shifting on synthetic and real data. We also compare μ_r and $L(\lambda^*)$ for the query shift location. In all the experiments in this section, the data is normalized along each feature dimension of each entire data set.

First an example query using synthetic data is presented. Then the average retrieval precision of the different methods on real data is presented.

The synthetic data used is the 2D example data that was provided with the *Multivariate Data Generation Software* [5] from the ICPR 2000 Algorithm Performance Contest. A query (represent as $\star$) at location (-83.5, -97.2) is presented in Figure 1 with both the shift to μ_r ($\oplus$ in figure) and the shift to $L(\lambda^*)$ ($\otimes$ in figure). Just query shifting is used in this example. The shift to μ_r also moves closer to μ_i ($\ominus$ in figure) with the resulting effect on the KNN of replacing three relevant images with two relevant and one irrelevant. The shift to $L(\lambda^*)$ moves away from μ_i with the resulting effect on the KNN by replacing three relevant and seven irrelevant images with ten relevant images.

The retrieval methods of PFRL, shifting to μ_r, shifting to $L(\lambda^*)$, PFRL+μ_r, and PFRL+$L(\lambda^*)$ was applied to each of the following four databases. For all of the retrieval methods, each image in the database was selected as a query. For each iteration, upto five iterations, the 20 nearest neighbors were returned with relevance feedback. The average retrieval precision for each method and each database is presented in Figure 3.

Database 1. The data (Texture Data) was obtained from MIT Media Lab at: whitechapel.media.mit.edu/pub/VisTex. There are a total of 640 images of 128×128 in the database with 15 classes. The images in this database are represented by 8 Gabor filters (2 scales and 4 orientations). Examples of the textures are presented in Figure 2.

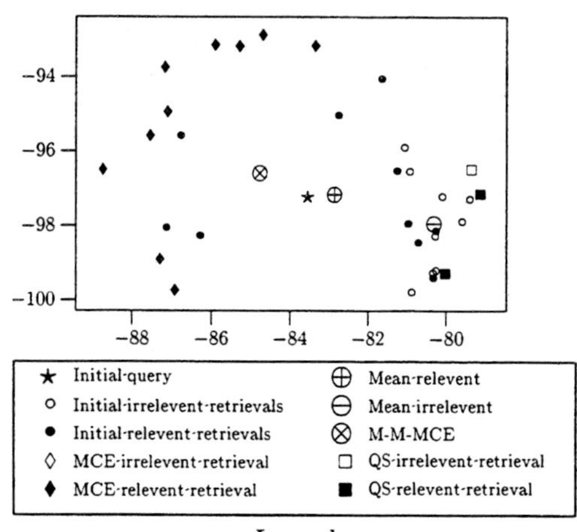

Figure 1. Synthetic 2D data: example query

Figure 2. Example images from texture data

Database 2. This is a set (Sonar Data), also taken from [7], of 208 data points having two classes (Mines and Rocks) with equal number of instances in each class. The data are represented by 60 features. For details, see [7].

Database 3. This data set (Vowel Data) has $q = 10$ measurements and 11 classes. There are a total of $N = 528$ samples in this database. This set is also taken from [7].

Database 4. The data set (Segmentation Data), taken from the UCI repository [7], consists of images that were drawn randomly from a database of 7 outdoor images. The images were hand-segmented by the creators of the database to classify each pixel. Each image is a region. There are 7 classes, each of which has 330 instances. Thus, there are a total of 2310 images in the database. These images are represented by 19 real valued attributes.

The retrieval precision of PFRL combined with query shifting consistently outperformed just query shifting and PFRL individually. Shifting to $L(\lambda^*)$ outperformed shifting to μ_r both individually and when combined with PFRL, though the magnitude of improvement is much less than the magnitude of improvement of either combined method over the individual methods.

The close performance of shifting to $L(\lambda^*)$ and shifting to μ_r can be explained by noting that often $L(\lambda^*)$ is at or very close to μ_r. For example using the texture data, 84% of the time the maximum condition expectation is very close to μ_r (within 0.01 of the mean-mean distance). Only 3% of the time is it far away (greater than 0.3 of the mean-

mean distance). Thus shifting to $L(\lambda^*)$ performs the same as shifting to $\mu_r$in the common case and in the infrequent case that μ_r is a bad location, it performs much better.

4. Summary

This paper presents a novel method that combines probabilistic feature relevance learning and query shifting to try to achieve the best of both worlds. This method uses a linear discriminant analysis to compute the new query upon which to estimate local retrieval neighborhood using PFRL. As a result, the modified neighborhood at the new query tends to contain data samples that are more relevant to the input query. The experimental results using both synthetic and real data show convincingly that feature relevance learning coupled with query shifting outperformed either PFRL or query shifting alone.

A potential extension to the technique described in this paper is to consider additional derived variables (features) for local relevance estimate and query shifting, thereby contributing to the overall retrieval performance. The challenge is to be able to have a mechanism that computes such informative derived features efficiently.

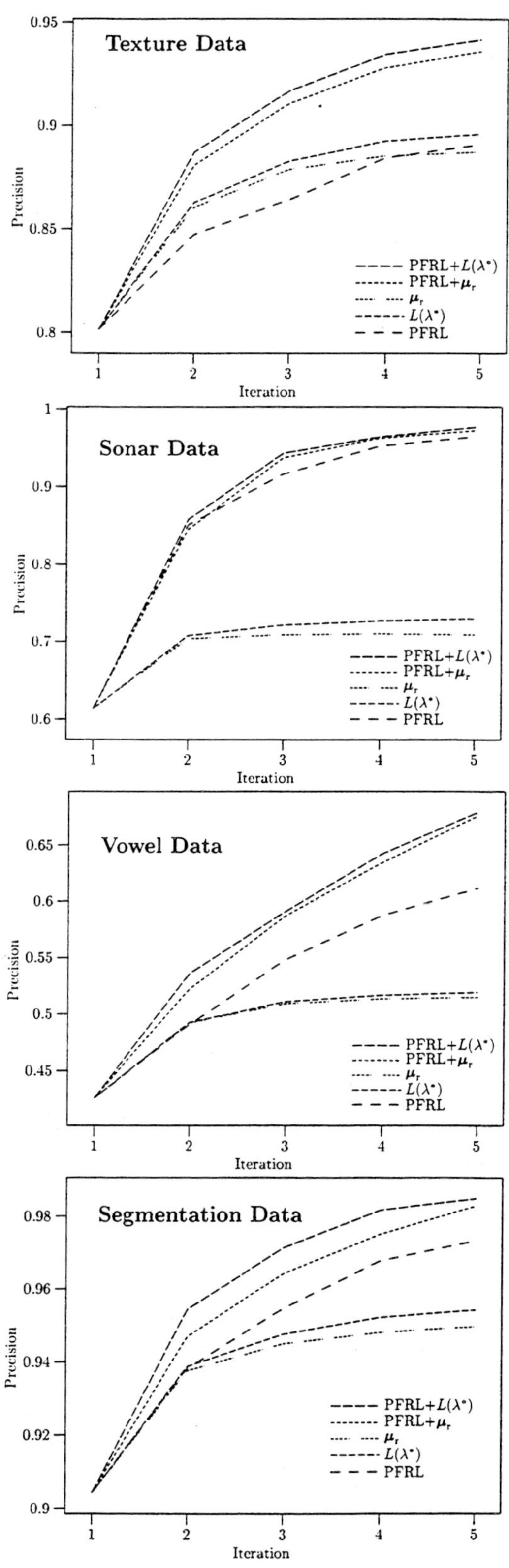

Figure 3. Precision graphs

References

[1] M. F. *et al.* Query by image and video content: The qbic system. *IEEE Computer*, pages 23–31, September 1995.

[2] J. H. Friedman. Flexible metric nearest neighbor classification. Technical report, Department of Statistics, Stanford University, 1994.

[3] D. A. Grossman and O. Frieder. *Information Retrieval: Alogithms and Heuristics*. Kluwer, 1999.

[4] Y. Ishikawa, R. Subramanya, and C. Faloutsos. Mindreader: Querying databases through multiple examples. Technical Report CMU-CS-98-119, Carnegie Mellon University, 1998.

[5] J. Liang. Multivariate data generate software. http://isl.ee.washington.edu/IAPR/ICPR00/gendata/packages/gendata.tar.gz.

[6] T. Minka and R. Picard. Interactive learning with a 'society of models. *Pattern Recognition*, 30(4):565–81, April 1997.

[7] P. Murphy and D. Aha. Uci repository of machine learning databases. www.cs.uci.edu/~mlearn/MLRepository.html.

[8] J. Peng, B. Bhanu, and S. Qing. Probabilistic feature relevance learning for content-based image retrieval. *Computer Vision and Image Understanding*, 75(1/2):150–164, 1999.

[9] Y. Rui, T. Huang, and S. Mehrotra. Content-based image retrieval with relevance feedback in mars. In *Proceedings of IEEE International Conference on Image Processing*, pages 815–818, October 1997.

[10] P. Schauble. *Multimedia Information Retrieval: Content-Based Information Retrieval from Large Text and Audio Databases*. Kluwer, Boston, 1997.

[11] S. S. Wilks. *Mathematical Statistics*. John Wiley & Sons, Inc., New York, 1963.

From Video Shot Clustering to Sequence Segmentation

Emmanuel Veneau, Rémi Ronfard
Institut National de l'Audiovisuel
4, avenue de l'Europe
94366 Bry-sur-Marne cedex, France
{eveneau,rronfard}@ina.fr

Patrick Bouthemy
IRISA/INRIA
Campus Universitaire de Beaulieu
35042 Rennes cedex, France
bouthemy@irisa.fr

Abstract

Segmenting video documents into sequences from elementary shots to supply an appropriate higher level description of the video is a challenging task. This paper presents a two-stage method. First, we build a binary agglomerative hierarchical time-constrained shot clustering. Second, based on the cophenetic criterion, *a* breaking distance *between shots is computed to detect sequence changes. Various options are implemented and compared. Real experiments have proved that the proposed criterion can be efficiently used to achieve appropriate segmentation into sequences.*

1 Introduction

Browsing and querying data in video documents requires to first extract and organize information from the audio and video tracks. The first step in building a structured description is to segment the video document into elementary shots which are usually defined as the smallest continuous units of a video document. Numerous methods for shot segmentation have been proposed (e.g., see [3]). Nevertheless, shots are often not the relevant level to describe pertinent events, and are too numerous to enable efficient indexing or browsing.

The grouping of shots into higher-level segments has been investigated through various methods which can be gathered into three main families. The first one is based on the principle of the Scene Transition Graph (STG) [9], which can be formulated in a continuous way [7], or according to alternate versions [4]. Methods of the second family [1, 2] use explicit models of video documents or rules related to editing techniques and film theory. In the third family [5, 8], emphasis is put on the joint use of features extracted from audio, video and textual information. These methods achieve shot grouping more or less through a combination of the segmentations performed for each track.

We present a method based on a so-called *cophenetic criterion* which belongs to the first family. The sequel is organized as follows. Section 2 describes our method involving an agglomerative binary hierarchy and the use of the cophenetic matrix. Section 3 specifies the various options we have implemented with respect to extracted features, distance between features, hierarchy updating, and temporal constraints. Experimental results are reported in Section 4, and Section 5 contains concluding remarks.

2 Binary hierarchy for describing shot similarity

We assume that a segmentation of the video into shots is available, where each shot is represented by one or more extracted keyframes. The information representing a shot (except its duration) is given by the (average) signature computed from the corresponding keyframes. We build a spatio-temporal evaluation of shot similarity through a binary agglomerative hierarchical time-constrained clustering.

2.1 Binary agglomerative hierarchical time-constrained clustering

To build a hierarchy following usual methods [10], we need to define a similarity measure s between shots, and a distance between shot clusters, called index of dissimilarity δ. The temporal constraint, as defined in [9], involves a temporal distance d_t. We introduce a temporal weighting function W accounting for a general model for the temporal constraint. The formal definitions of all these functions will be given in Section 3. The time-constrained distance $\tilde{d}$ between shots is defined (assuming that similarity is normalized between 0 and 100) by :

$$\tilde{d}(i,j) = \begin{cases} 100 - s(i,j) \times W(i,j) & \text{if } d_t(i,j) \leq \Delta T \\ \infty & \text{otherwise} \end{cases} \quad (1)$$

where i and j designate two shots and ΔT is the maximal temporal interval for considering any interaction between shots.

At the beginning of the process, each shot forms a cluster, and the time-constrained dissimilarity index $\tilde{\delta}$ between clusters is then the time-constrained distance $\tilde{d}$ between shots. A symmetric time-constrained $N \times N$ proximity matrix $\tilde{\mathcal{D}} = [\tilde{d}(i,j)]$ is considered [6], using $\tilde{\delta}$ to evaluate the dissimilarity between clusters. The hierarchy is built by merging the two closest clusters at each step. The matrix $\tilde{\mathcal{D}}$ is updated according to the index of dissimilarity $\tilde{\delta}$ to take into account each newly created cluster. This is iterated until the proximity matrix contains only infinite values. The resulting binary time-constrained hierarchy supplies a description of the spatio-temporal proximity of the extracted shots.

2.2 Cophenetic dissimilarity criterion

In [6], another proximity matrix $\mathcal{D}_c$, called *cophenetic* matrix, is proposed to capture the structure of the hierarchy. We will use the time-constrained version $\tilde{\mathcal{D}}_c$ of this matrix to define a criterion for the segmentation of the video into sequences. The *cophenetic* matrix is expressed as $\tilde{\mathcal{D}}_c = [\tilde{d}_c(i,j)]$, where $\tilde{d}_c$ is the so-called *clustering distance* defined by :

$$\tilde{d}_c(i,j) = \max_{p \neq q / (i,j) \in C_p \times C_q} \{\tilde{\delta}(C_p, C_q)\}$$

where $\tilde{\delta}$ is the index of dissimilarity constructed from $\tilde{d}$, and C_p and C_q are two clusters. Assuming that the shot indices follow a temporal order, the *cophenetic* matrix leads to the definition of our criterion for sequence segmentation, called *breaking distance*, calculated between two consecutive shots as : $\tilde{d}_b(i, i+1) = \min_{k \leq i < l} \{\tilde{\mathcal{D}}_c(k,l)\}$.

2.3 Segmentation using the breaking distance

If the breaking distance $\tilde{d}_b$ between consecutive shots exceeds a given threshold τ_c, then a sequence boundary is inserted between these two shots. An example is presented on Fig 1 where two different thresholds to perform segmentation into sequences $\tau_1 = 20$ and $\tau_2 = 45$ are considered. Fig. 2 displays results corresponding to thersholds τ_1 and τ_2.

2.4 Comparison with the STG method

We have formally proved that our method delivers the same segmentation into sequences as the STG method described in [9]. Considering that STG method considers in a binary way inter-shot spacing and implies non-obvious setting of parameters [7], the advantage of our formulation is to smooth the effects of time, in the time-constrained distance, using continuous temporal weighting functions, and to consider a threshold parameter related to sequence segmentation and not to shot clustering. As a consequence, our approach allows one to visualize what the segmentation results are according to the selected threshold value which can then be appropriately tuned by the user. There is no need to rebuild the STG whenever the threshold is changed.

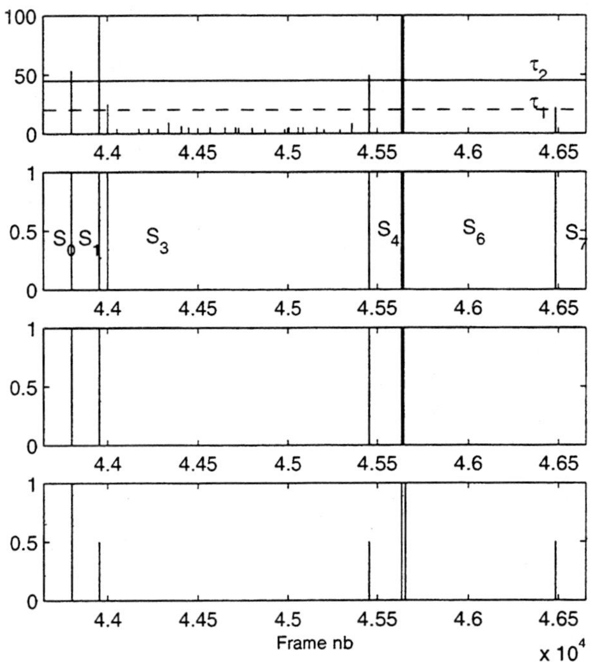

Figure 1. Thresholding the breaking distance values on excerpt 1 of *Avengers* movie (upper row), detected sequence boundaries for τ_1 (upper middle row) and τ_2 (lower middle row), and manual segmentation (lower row)

3 Description of implemented options

3.1 Signatures for shots

We have considered in pratrice three kinds of signatures : shot duration, color and region-based color histograms. Color and region-based color histograms are defined in the (Y, C_b, C_r) space with respectively 16, 4, and 4 levels, and 12 image blocks are considered for region-based histograms. The shot duration gives a relevant information on the rhythm of the action and on the editing work.

3.2 Distances between signatures

Various distances between signatures have been tested. Comparison between histograms can be achieved using histogram intersection, euclidian distance, χ_2-distance. The distance chosen between shot durations is the Manhattan distance.

3.3 Updating of the agglomerative binary hierarchy

In order to update the classification hierarchy, two algorithms are available [10] :

- the *Complete Link* method. The index of dissimilarity between clusters is defined by :

$$\tilde{\delta}(C_p, C_q) = \max_{(i,j) \in C_p \times C_q} \{\tilde{d}(i,j)\}$$

- the *Ward's* method. The index of dissimilarity between clusters is given by :

$$\tilde{\delta}(C_p, C_q) = \frac{n_{C_p}.n_{C_q}}{n_{C_p} + n_{C_q}} \tilde{d}(G_{C_p}, G_{C_q})$$

where G_{C_i} is the gravity centre of cluster C_i, n_{C_i} represents either $Cardinal(C_i)$ or $Duration(C_i)$.

In both cases, the Lance and William formula, given by $\tilde{\delta}(A \cup B, C) = a_1\tilde{\delta}(A, C) + a_2\tilde{\delta}(B, C) + a_3\tilde{\delta}(A, B) + a_4|\tilde{\delta}(A, C) - \tilde{\delta}(B, C)|$, is used to update the proximity matrix. We have $a_1 = a_2 = a_4 = \frac{1}{2}$, $a_3 = 0$ for the *Complete Link* method, and $a_1 = \frac{n_A + n_C}{n_{A \cup B} + n_C}$, $a_2 = \frac{n_B + n_C}{n_{A \cup B} + n_C}$, $a_3 = 0$, $a_4 = \frac{n_C}{n_{A \cup B} + n_C}$ for the *Ward's* method.

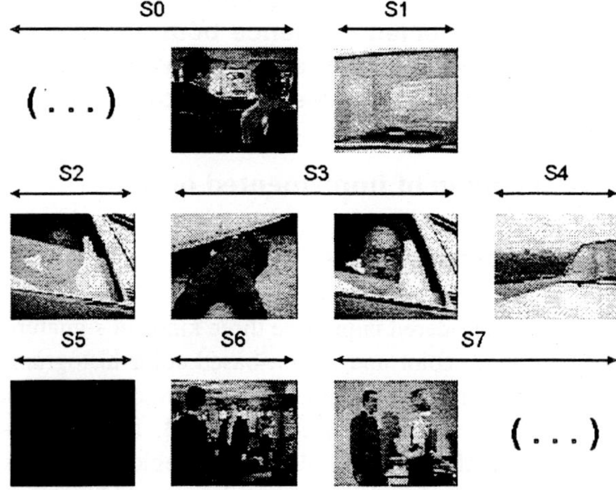

Figure 2. Obtained sequence segmentation on excerpt 1 of *Avengers* movie for threshold τ_1. S_3 is an angle / reverse angle sequence. S_5 is a fade out / fade in effect.

3.4 Temporal weighting function

The temporal weighting function is used to constrain the distance and the index of dissimilarity as introduced in equation 1. In [9], only one type of temporal weighting function was proposed, i.e. rectangular function which is not smooth. We have tested three smooth functions : linear, parabolic, and sinusoidal.

4 Experimental results

We have evaluated our method on a three hour video corpus. We report here results on four excerpts of two minutes. Three excerpts are taken from *Avengers* movies to evaluate the segmentation into sequences in different contexts. The first one comprises an angle / reverse angle editing effect and a transition with a dissolve effect. The second one includes a set change, and the third one involves color and rhythm changes. Obtained segmentations can be compared with a hand segmentation acting as ground truth. In plots displayed in Figures 1, 3 and 4, main sequence changes are represented by a value of 1 and secondary changes by a value of 0.5. The last excerpt is extracted from a news program to test the relevance of the built hierarchy.

Among the implemented options, three sets of descriptors and functions are selected : (O_1) color histograms intersection, rectangular temporal weighting function, and Complete Link method, (O_2) color histograms intersection, parabolic temporal weighting function, and Ward's method based on cluster duration, (O_3) Manhattan distance on shots duration, parabolic weighting function, and Ward's method based on cluster duration.

Results obtained on the news program excerpt show that the clustering distance $\tilde{d}_c$ provides a correct description of the similarity between shots at different levels, even if the information distribution is not homogeneous in the various levels of the hierarchy. An adaptive thresholding applied to breaking distance values would be nevertheless necessary to avoid heterogeneous results. Tests have shown that the best video segmentation into sequences is found using option set O_2.

In the processed excerpts, most of the sequence changes were correctly detected, when the proper options were selected. On Fig.1, we can point out that, using τ_1 and option O_1, all changes are detected with only one false alarm, the angle / reverse angle effect is recognized. Selecting the threshold value is nevertheless a rather critical issue. On excerpt 2, with a relevant threshold, we extract all the correct boundaries with option O_1, with only one false alarm (Fig. 3). Using option O_2 false alarms and missed detections increase on excerpt 2. The color and rhythm changes in excerpt 3 (Fig. 4) have been better detected using option

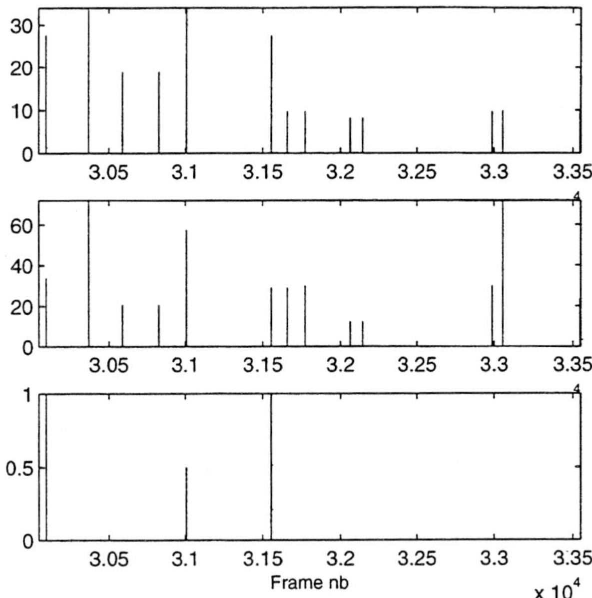

Figure 3. Breaking distance values on excerpt 2 of *Avengers* movie using option O_1 (upper row), option O_3 (middle row), and manual segmentation (lower row)

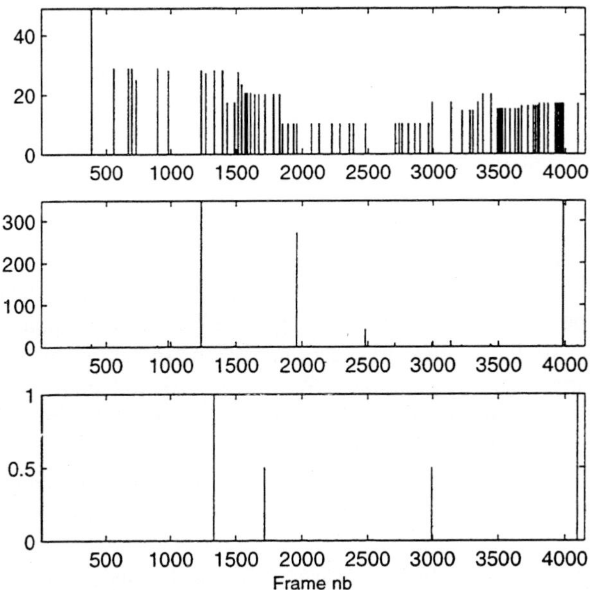

Figure 4. Breaking distance values on excerpt 3 of *Avengers* movie using option O_1 (upper row), option O_3 (middle row), and manual segmentation (lower row)

O_3, rather than O_1. Consequently, how to automatically select the proper option remains an open issue.

5 Conclusion

The method described in this paper, based on the cophenetic matrix, enables to accurately and efficiently segment video documents into sequences by building a binary agglomerative time-constrained hierarchy. We have implemented several versions. Selecting the most appropriate one improved results and gave a better description of the similarity of the shots through the hierarchy. Experiments on a larger base will be conducted in future work for selecting the best parameter set and evaluating alternative thresholding stategies.

References

[1] P. Aigrain, P. Joly, and V. Longueville. Medium knowledge-based macro-segmentation of video into sequences. In M. T. Maybury, editor, *Intelligent Multimedia Information Retrieval*, pages 159–173. AAAI/MIT Press, 1997.

[2] J. Carrive, F. Pachet, and R. Ronfard. Using description logics for indexing audiovisual documents. In ITC-IRST, editor, *Int. Workshop on Description Logics (DL'98)*, pages 116–120, Trento, 1998.

[3] A. Dailianas, R. B. Allen, and P. England. Comparison of automatic video segmentation algorithms. In *SPIE Photonics West*, volume 2615, pages 2–16, Philadelphia, 1995.

[4] A. Hanjalic, R. L. Lagendijk, and J. Biemond. Automatically segmenting movies into logical story units. In *Third Int. Conf. on Visual Information Systems (VISUAL'99)*, volume LNCS 1614, pages 229–236, Amsterdam, 1999.

[5] A. G. Hauptmann and M. A. Smith. Text, speech, and vision for video segmentation : The informedia project. In *AAAI Fall Symposium, Computational Models for Integrating Language and Vision*, Boston, 1995.

[6] A. K. Jain and R. C. Dubes. *Algorithms for Clustering Data*. Prentice Hall, 1988.

[7] J. R. Kender and B.-L. Yeo. Video scene segmentation via continuous video coherence. Technical report, IBM Research Division, 1997.

[8] R. Lienhart, S. Pfeiffer, and W. Effelsberg. Scene determination based on video and audio features. Technical report, University of Mannheim, November 1998.

[9] M. Yeung, B.-L. Yeo, and B. Liu. Extracting story units from long programs for video browsing and navigation. In *Proc. of IEEE Int. Conf. on Multimedia Computing and Systems*, Tokyo, 1996.

[10] J. Zupan. *Clustering of Large Data Sets*. Chemometrics Research Studies Series. John Wiley & Sons Ltd., 1982.

Acknowledgements Images from the *Avenger* movie, part of the AIM corpus, were reproduced thanks to INA, Department Innovation.

Haruspex: an image database system for query-by-examples *

Alessandra Lumini, Dario Maio
DEIS - CSITE-CNR - Università di Bologna, viale Risorgimento 2, 40136 Bologna - Italy.
[alumini,dmaio]@deis.unibo.it

Abstract

This paper describes a color-based approach to effectively resolve query-by-examples in an image database. We present a prototype database system designed to store and query a collection of ceramics. Our case study is a database of images representing ceramics from the International Museum of Ceramics in Faenza. We consider statistical features on color distribution, not requiring a strong segmentation procedure to detect the object from the background. Results on a collection of about 2000 images are reported providing a validation of the approach.

1. Introduction

There is a growing interest in Image Database Systems in various application fields, such as medical imaging, electronic catalogues, remote sensing and so on. A basic requirement of an image database is querying by an example image. The goal is to effectively identify images that are similar to the example, according to a similarity criterion, possibly responding to human perception.

Several general purpose systems already exist: QBIC [1], VisualSeek [2], PhotoBook [3], Virage [4], Chabot [5] are designed to manage, store and retrieve images from different sources. A large research effort is currently being made for the definition of similarity measures and features to provide a compact representation of the image: colors, shapes, and textures are the most studied properties [6]. Nevertheless, due to complexity and variety of the images it is a very arduous task to design a system able to manage and query any class of images.

In this work we present a prototype database system designed to store and query a collection of ceramics. Our case study is a database of images representing ceramics from the International Museum of Ceramics in Faenza. The collection, acquired by digitally scanning part of the photographic archives of the museum, consists of color images representing objects (plates, bowls, vases).

The presence of dark shadows and the lack of contrast are some of the factors that make the segmentation of the object from the background and the edge extraction somewhat difficult. Moreover, the photographs are taken from different points of view, with various conditions of brightness. The system here presented overcomes these problems by adopting a color based-approach, without requiring a fine segmentation of the object. An area of interest is extracted by finding an object bounding ellipse, then the ellipse is partitioned into 7 regions and statistical color measures are extracted from each of them for indexing purpose. The invariance with respect to translation, to scaling and to a restricted set of large angle rotations, results from the feature similarity function which exploits the spatial arrangement of the regions.

The paper is organized as follows: in section 2 an overview of the system is given, outlining the single steps discussed in the next sections. Section 3 describes the image segmentation procedure; in section 4 the feature extraction process is explained, in section 5 the adopted similarity measure is presented. Finally, in section 6 some experimental results are reported and section 7 draws some concluding remarks.

2. System overview

HaruspeX[1] is an Image Database System which can handle collection of images stored in a PostgreSQL database. HaruspeX has an open architecture: new data type and shared libraries can be added to include features and similarity measures that improve the search of images using query-by-examples. We developed and employed this system to create image tables in our collection of ceramics and test new algorithms for perceptual searches.

An image retrieval system based on the comparison of automatically extracted features requires a loading phase and a retrieval phase.

The loading phase consists of the following steps (for each image to be stored):

- image processing for object segmentation
- image partitioning and color space transformation
- feature extraction

* The present work was funded by the Italian National Research Council (CNR) in the framework of the Project on Cultural Heritage (Progetto Finalizzato Beni Culturali).

[1] HaruspeX is OpenSource (free download at http://bias_o2.csr.unibo.it/haruspex). A demo is also available.

1051-4651/00 $10.00 © 2000 IEEE

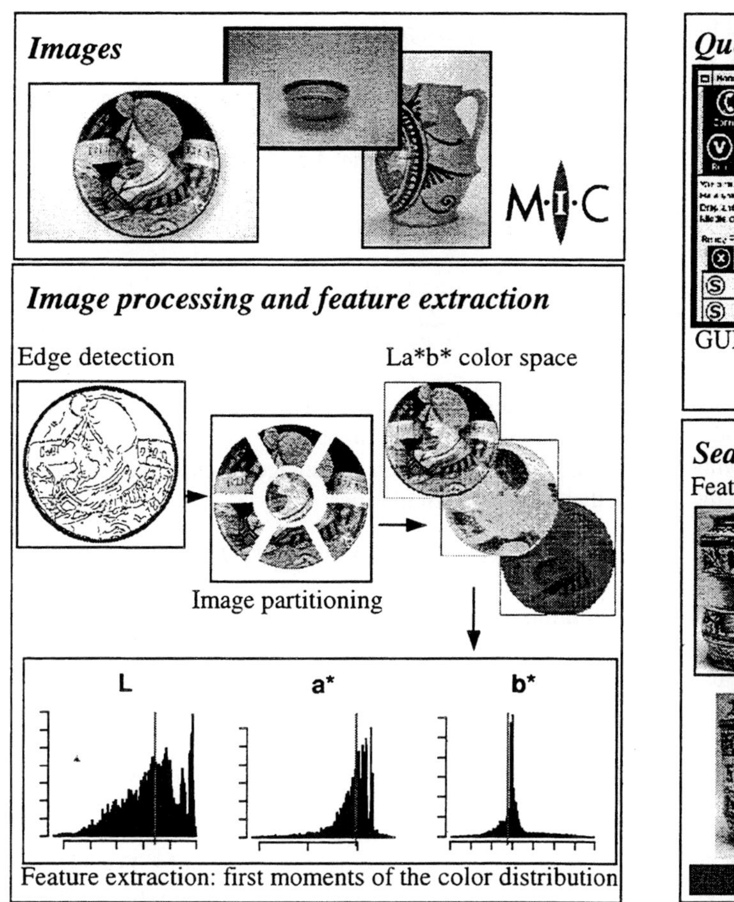

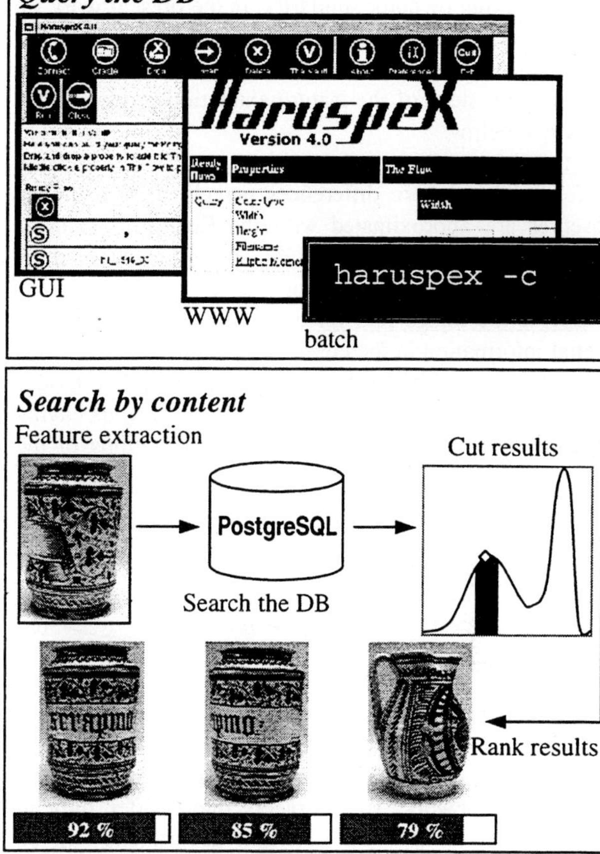

Figure 1. An operative schema of the Haruspex system: loading phase (left) and retrieval phase (right).

The retrieval phase consists of the following steps:

- processing the example image to compute a feature representation;
- searching the database for the images most similar to the example with respect to the similarity measure adopted.
- presenting results ranked by similarity

In figure 1 a schema of the system is shown.

3. Image segmentation

The automatic segmentation of the area of interest from the background is one of most crucial tasks of the system. Unfortunately, some technical factors such as the presence of shadows and of various lighting sources make this task very difficult. Several methods proposed in the literature [7][8], are very expensive and require ad hoc parameterization to deal with different lighting conditions.

In this application domain, no perfect pixel wise segmentation is required, but instead a stable and unsupervised extraction of the salient area is needed. Since ceramics typically have regular shapes, we opted for a parametric estimation of the outer boundaries of the objects, also considering the saving of computational time. Among the alternatives shown in figure 2, we chose the elliptical boundary, which provides a better description of the objects.

The main steps of the segmentation algorithm are: the edge detection, performed by means of the LoG operator [9] and the ellipse fitting, performed by simply extracting the major and minor axes from the edge-image.

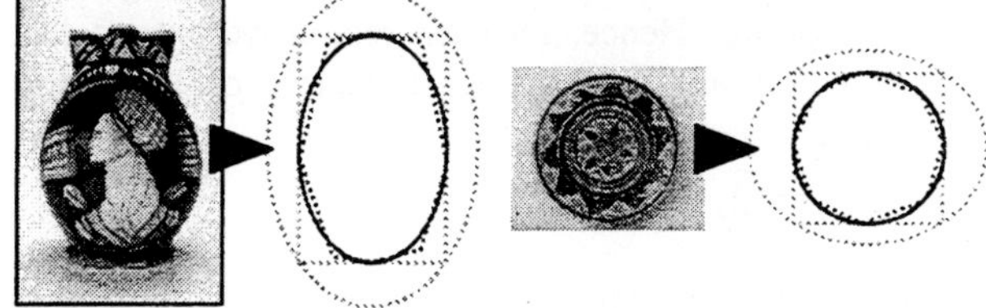

Figure 2. Outer boundary extraction.

4. Feature Extraction

Color features are strictly connected with human perception, and, compared with texture and shape information, they are easier to extract. Moreover, color patterns play a significant role in the ceramic field, where they are studied in order to localize and date objects.

According to these requirements we propose a method for image indexing by color similarity. In the present work we extend and improve the use of spectral covariance and image partitioning [10] for the retrieval of ceramics.

The main steps of the feature extraction procedure are described below.

1. Map the image into the color space. A perceptually uniform color, where differences perceived by a human observer are approximated with the Euclidean distance between two points in the color space, is obtained by transforming the RGB images into La*b* images.

2. Divide the image into fixed regions. In order to store spatial information in the color index we divide the image into sub-images. Unlike the approach in [10], that divides an image into 5 partially overlapping fuzzy regions having different areas, we studied several segmentations of the bounding ellipse in radial regions having equal area (figure 3).

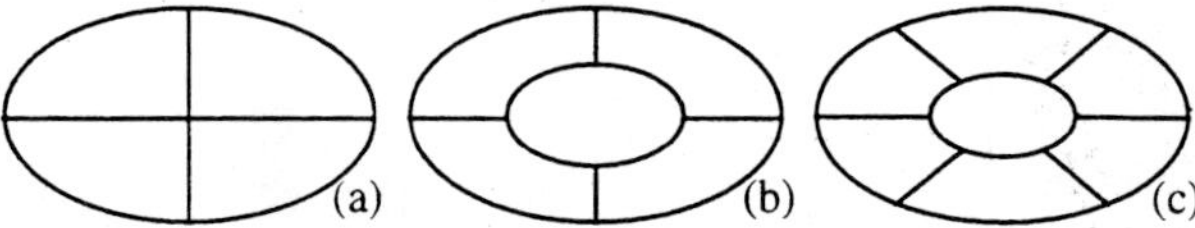

Figure 3. Some segmentations of the interesting area.

Experimental results on these three partition methods with several percentages of overlap prove that the presence of a central region has great importance in the ceramics framework, since objects often differ only in their internal motif, while external decorations can be quite similar. Moreover, overlap has demonstrated to be useless for our purpose, and, finally, the segmentation in 7 regions (figure 3c) has proved to be more resistant to rotations than others. The importance of having equal area regions will be made clearer in the discussion of rotation invariance, in the next section.

3. Extract measures based on the first moments of the color distribution. In [13] it has been proved that characterizing color distributions with the statistical moments gives better performance than working with color histograms. Hence, for each region we extract the average color and the covariance matrix of the color channels. The average color is:

$$\mu_{r,s} = \frac{1}{\#R_r} \sum_{j \in R_r} p_{sj}$$

where $s \in [L, a^*, b^*]$ is the color component, R_r is the region with index $r \in [0, \ldots, 6]$ and p_{sj} is the value of the jth pixel of the channel s. The covariance matrix is given by:

$$c_{r,s,t} = \frac{1}{\#R_r} \sum_{j \in R_r} (p_{sj} - \mu_{s,r})(p_{tj} - \mu_{t,r})$$

where $s,t \in [L, a^*, b^*]$ and $r \in [0,..,6]$.

Since the covariance matrix is symmetric the total number of features extracted from an image is 63. No pre-normalization is required.

5. Similarity measure

We define a dissimilarity value between regions as the sum of differences between features weighed by their variance over the database. Let I and H be two objects, and let $\{I_0,..,I_6\}$ and $\{H_0,..,H_6\}$ be their regions, respectively. The distance between two regions is defined as:

$$d_R(I_j, H_l) = \sum_{s \in \{L, a^*, b^*\}} \frac{\mu_{s,j} - \mu_{s,l}}{\sigma(\mu_s)} + \sum_{s,t \in \{L, a^*, b^*\}} \frac{c_{s,t,j} - c_{s,t,l}}{\sigma(c_{s,t})}$$

where $\sigma()$ denotes the standard deviation of the respective features over the entire database.

The distance between two images is expressed in terms of their region dissimilarities:

$$d(I,H) = d_R(I_0, H_0) + \min_{f \in F} \sum_{j=1}^{6} d_R(I_j, H_{f(j)})$$

A minimization over a set F of permutations of the region ordering is required in order to get rotation and mirroring invariance. As stated before, equal area regions are useful in distance calculation, in order to avoid normalization.

It should be noted that in our case study, the color analysis is not sufficient to discriminate objects in similarity searches; for this reason we include a shape measure able to distinguish circular objects from elongated ones. A cutting method that can be disabled by the user has been introduced, based on the ratio between the major and minor axes of the bounding ellipse. In figure 4 the axes-ratio distribution, related to the objects stored in the database, is shown: the two peaks of the bimodal distribution represent plates and vases, respectively. The confidence interval is estimated by imposing a fixed percentage of retrieved objects (fixing the area of the region highlighted in figure 4). Only objects belonging to that region are evaluated and ranked for the solution.

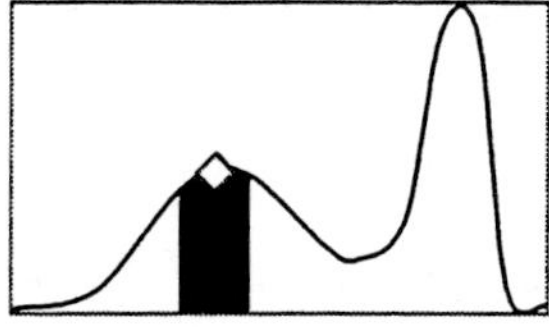

Figure 4. Axes-ratio distribution.

6. Experiments

The simulations have been effected on a database containing 1968 color images, taken from different points of view. A first experiment consists in evaluating the validity of the features, by calculating their covariance matrix. The results, reported in figure 5, prove that the features are totally uncorrelated.

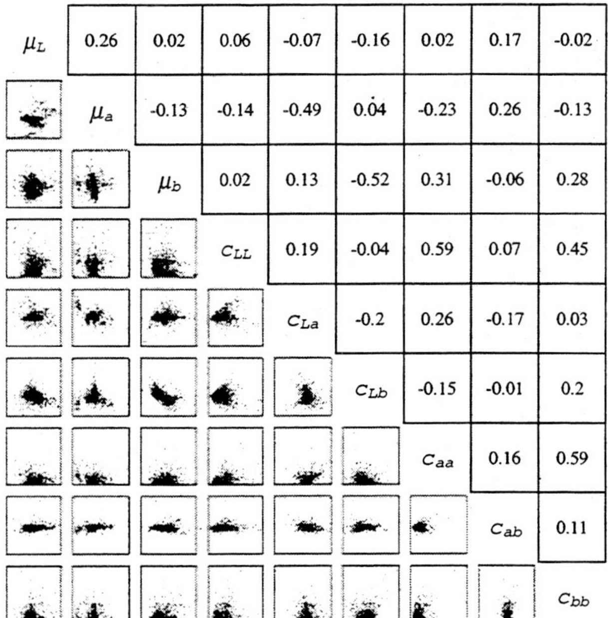

μ_L 0.26 0.02 0.06 -0.07 -0.16 0.02 0.17 -0.02
μ_a -0.13 -0.14 -0.49 0.04 -0.23 0.26 -0.13
μ_b 0.02 0.13 -0.52 0.31 -0.06 0.28
c_{LL} 0.19 -0.04 0.59 0.07 0.45
c_{La} -0.2 0.26 -0.17 0.03
c_{Lb} -0.15 -0.01 0.2
c_{aa} 0.16 0.59
c_{ab} 0.11
c_{bb}

Figure 5. Covariance matrix (top-right) and scattering diagram (bottom-left) of the features extracted from the test images.

A second experiment evaluates scaling and rotation invariance by measuring the similarity between an object and a scaled/rotated version of the same. The two graphs in figure 6 show that the similarity value depends on the amount of scaling/rotation, but it is high enough to put the searched image in the first or the second place of the retrieval ranking.

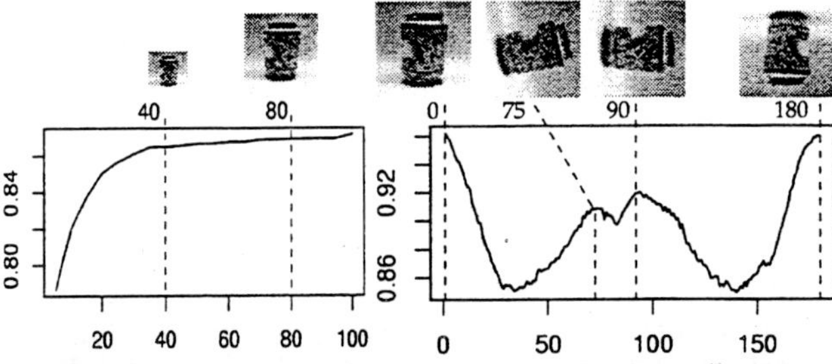

Figure 6. Similarity value as a function of scaling percentage and rotation angle.

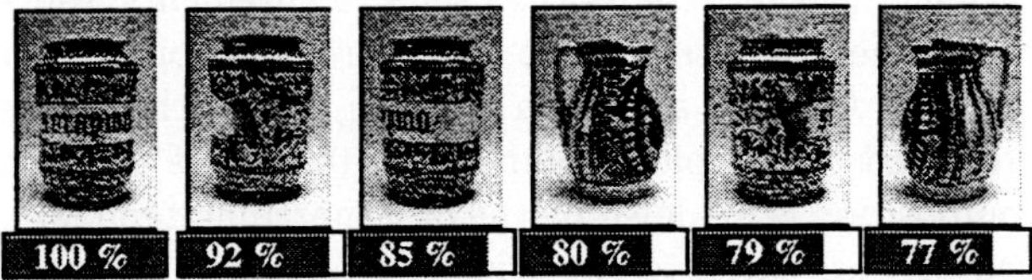

Figure 7. A query result ranked by similarity. The first image is the query object.

Finally retrieval results are reported (figure 7). The presence, in the first positions of the query result, of images of the same object, taken from different points of view demonstrates the efficacy of the retrieval method. In particular the cutting method allows the objects having a very different shape from the searched one to be left out of the solution. In fact for the same query object shown in figure 6, there was a plate having similarity measure equal to 83%, if the cutting option is disabled.

7. Concluding remarks

We have presented a color-based approach to effectively resolve query-by-examples in an image database. We have shown, in simple experiments carried out on a database of ceramics, that the use of spectral covariance and image partitioning allows the user to gain results which respect human perceptual canons.

Acknowledgments

The authors thank Alessandro Baldoni for developing the system software and designing the user interface.

References

[1] Niblack W. et al., "The QBIC project : Querying images by content using color, texture and shape", Int. Symp. on Electronic Imaging, SPIE 1993.

[2] Smith J.R., Chang SF "VisualSEEk: a fully automated content-based image query system", *Proc. of ACM Multimedia*, Boston, 1996.

[3] Pentland A., Picard R.W., Sclaroff S. "Photobook: content-based manipulation of image databases", *Multimedia Tools and Applications*, Kluwer Academic Pub., Boston, pp. 43-80, 1996.

[4] Bach JR et al. "Virage image search engine: an open framework for image management", *Stor. and Retr. for Image and Video DB IV*, San Jose, CA, pp. 76-87, SPIE 1996.

[5] Ogle VE, Stonebraker M, "Chabot: Retrieval from a Relational Database of Images", *IEEE Computer*, v. 28, no. 9, 1995

[6] Del Bimbo A., *Visual Information Retrieval*, Morgan Kaufmann Publishers, San Francisco, 1999.

[7] Tang Y., et al. "Modified fractal signature (mfs): a new approach to document analysis for automatic knowledge acquisition". *IEEE tKDE*, v. 9, no. 5: pp. 747–762, 1997.

[8] Najman L., and Schmitt M., "Geodesic saliency of watershed contours and hierarchical segmentation". *IEEE Transactions on pattern analysis and machine intelligence*, v. 18, no. 12: pp. 1163–1173, 1996.

[9] Sotak G.E., and Boyer K. L., "The Laplacian–of–Gaussian kernel: a formal analysis and design procedure for fast, accurate convolution and full–frame output". *Computer Vision, Graphics, and Image processing*, no. 48: pp. 147–189, 1989.

[10] Stricker M.A. and Dimai A., "Spectral covariance and fuzzy regions for image indexing". In *SPIE Proceedings*, 1997.

Image Retrieval Based on Compositional Features and Interactive Query Specification

Kozaburo Hachimura Akira Tojima*

Faculty of Science and Engineering, Ritsumeikan University

Kusatsu, Shiga 525-8577, Japan

{hachi, tojima}@img.cs.ritsumei.ac.jp

Abstract

Content-based image retrieval by specifying composition of images has been studied. Compositional parameters are extracted from images by image segmentation and object extraction procedures. Query is specified through an interactive procedure controlled by a genetic algorithm: First, a user selects one of seven composition templates, each of which represents the typical composition. The system then successively generates patterns of "composition models" according to the templates selected. These composition models describe the pattern of object distribution within an image. A user iteratively selects composition models which properly describe the composition he/she wants. As a result of this interactive and iterative process the system obtains parameter values for an evaluation function. The function are used for judging conformity of images to the query. This method reduces the user's burden of properly specifying the query corresponding to the composition and reflecting user's preference. Experiments proved the effectiveness of the method.

1. Introduction

The function of content-based retrieval is very essential for image databases. There are several approaches for content retrieval of images, but one which may be attractive is retrieval based on impressions. The basic idea of this approach is to retrieve images judging similarity of images according to visual impression we get from images.

We get impressions of an image from various factors, such as objects depicted, textures, the colors and the composition. Although it is difficult to extract all of the features by image processing and pattern recognition, color distribution and compositional features may be dealt with algorithmically to a certain extent.

We have already examined impression-based retrieval using color information, and have obtained satisfactory results [1]. This paper presents another approach of impression-based retrieval in which compositional information of images is used.

Since similar compositions will give us similar visual impressions, we can use composition as key information in image retrieval. Principal problems in this approach are how to represent compositional information of images, and how to specify query for retrieval.

In the succeeding chapters we will first review query specification for retrieval by composition, and then describe methods of representing compositional features and interactive query specification.

2. Query Specification for Retrieval Based on Composition

Some works on image retrieval using compositional information may be found. In [2], a query is expressed by a region-based sketch, and when retrieving, the sketch is matched to images stored in the database. However, it is not necessarily easy to properly depict a sketch which represents the user's requirements, especially when the user has no concrete idea about target images. Another approach is in [3], in which images are fitted to 4 typical composition templates and the composition is modeled by the best matching template. Features are extracted by using this template, and used for retrieval. However, these templates are too simple to deal with images in general, and it is difficult to incorporate user's preference.

Since the concept of "composition" is not necessarily well-defined, it is neither easy nor realistic to try to extract exact information about the composition of an image. We employ a much more natural way of

*Currently with Sharp Corp. (tojima@isl.nara.sharp.co.jp)

thinking: We extract and use information about how objects are arranged in the image as the approximation for composition.

Even in this case, because user's requirement for composition is generally not definite but ambiguous, specification of queries by explicitly expressing the object arrangement does not work well.

The paper [4] showed that an interactive algorithm is useful for incorporating human personal cognitive properties in the image retrieval process, especially when the user has no concrete target image before retrieval. In this case, the system presents candidate pictures successively according to the user's previous selection.

There is also a study where an interactive genetic algorithm (GA) was used for deciding proper lighting conditions for CG-generated 3D objects [5]. In this case, candidate lighting conditions to be selected by the user are successively generated by GA. It is shown that this algorithm is effective when the user has less experience in this task domain.

Taking these earlier research results into account, we employ an interactive GA for specifying a query which incorporates the user's preference in the query and reduces user's burden of specifying the query.

Figure 1 illustrates the overall framework. At the query specification stage a user first selects one of the composition templates which represent categories of composition. Then, GA successively produces candidates of "composition model", namely pattern of object arrangement, and the user iteratively selects models which the user thinks suit the composition required. By observing the user's selection during the iteration, the parameters to be used in the image retrieval process are derived.

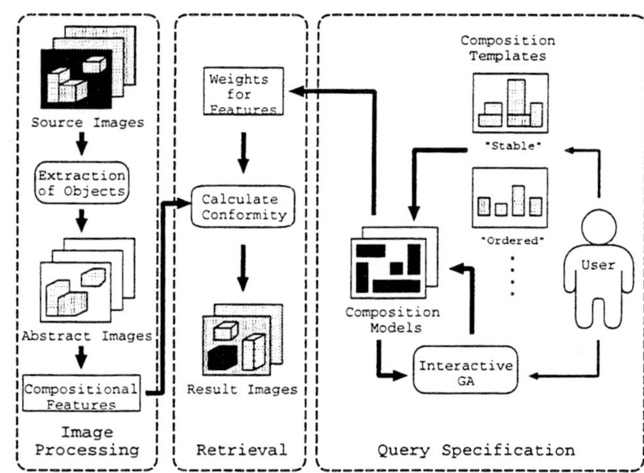

Figure 1. Image retrieval using composition model

3. Extraction of Compositional Information

In a data registration stage, every image goes through the following image processing steps:

1. Image segmentation based on colors.
2. Extraction of background and object regions.
3. Extraction of compositional parameters from object regions.

In the image segmentation, a new processing technique which considers the presence of edge is implemented, and even the background region with gradual color/shade change is not over-segmented [6].

A region with a color of maximum occurrence and regions contacting with border of a image is extracted as background region. Each of the regions remaining after removal of background regions is considered to be an object region.

Object regions are dealt with from two different points of view: First, all of the regions left after the extraction of background regions are regarded as object regions, and these regions are referred to as "micro objects". Furthermore, a group of micro objects connected each other is considered to form one larger object region, which is called a "macro object". Figure 2 illustrates the concept of micro objects and macro objects: Regions numbered 1 through 6 are micro objects, and composite regions labeled A through C are macro objects.

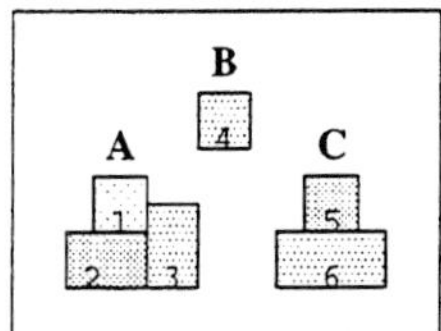

Figure 2. Micro objects and macro objects

Twenty four feature values concerning composition are extracted from an image containing micro and macro objects. Although we have to cut the detail for lack of space, features are described below being classified into four categories. Numbers in parentheses are numbers of features in each category.

Basic features(4): Numbers of micro and macro objects, Average and standard deviation of size of macro objects.

Distribution of objects(9): Total size of objects,

Size of the largest macro object, Concentricity of objects, Symmetry of object distribution, etc.

Location of objects(6): Deviation of centroids of macro objects, Deviation of Y coordinates of macro object's bottom end, Deviation of X coordinates of macro object's centroid, etc.

Others(5): Distribution of directions of principal moment axis of macro object, Deviation of minimum distance between macro object's centroids, Average value of unevenness in macro object's contour, etc.

All of these extracted features are stored in the database together with the image data at the data registration stage.

4. Query Specification Incorporating User's Intention and Preference

4.1. Overall Procedure

We use the following iterative method for generating queries properly incorporating the user's intentions and preferences:

1. User selects one of the composition templates.
2. System generates and displays 9 initial composition models.
3. User selects composition models from those displayed.
4. By using GA, system generates composition models which are similar to the previously selected ones.
5. Repeat steps 3 and 4 for appropriate number of times.
6. When iteration terminates, the system determines conformity function which will be used in retrieval.

The composition templates are shown in Figure 3. Each of them represents typical pattern of object distribution, and is named according to the impression caused by the composition.

4.2. Generating Composition Models by Using GA

GA successively generates the composition models, i.e. patterns of object distribution. The composition model is illustrated in Figure 4. Four kinds of rectangle corresponding to micro objects are depicted on the canvas. Macro objects are modeled by the presence of small "glue" rectangles between micro objects.

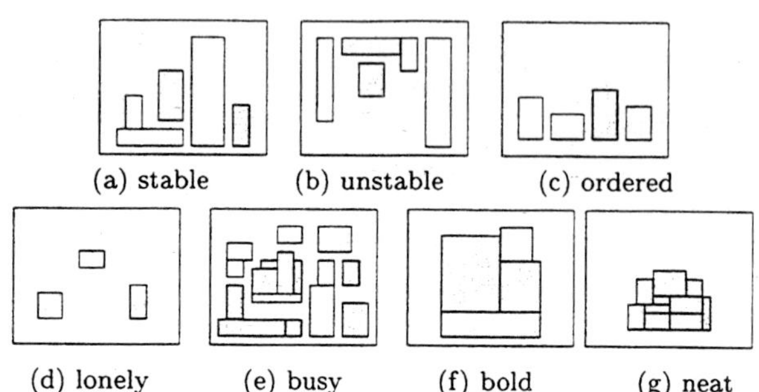

Figure 3. Composition templates

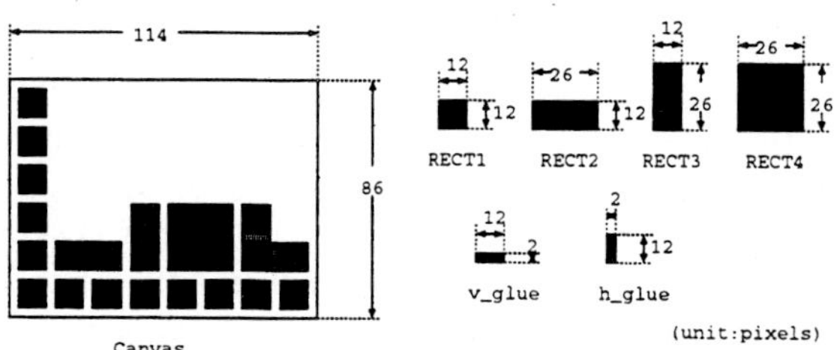

Figure 4. Composition model

The system generates 9 initial composition models by using parameters prepared for every composition template. On and after the second iteration, the GA generates composition models which are similar to the ones selected by the user at preceding iterations. Each rectangle in the model acts as an "individual" in the GA, and its "gene" is coded as 10 bits of data containing information about type of rectangles, presence of glue and position of rectangles.

The fitness value used for deciding the possibility for an individual to survive at the n-th iteration is defined as

$$F_n(x, y) = \sum_{k=1}^{n-1} R(k, x, y) + (n-1)R(n, x, y),$$

where $R(k, x, y)$ represents occurrence of a rectangle at the coordinate (x, y) in k-th iteration: When a rectangle occurs in the coordinate, R is 1, otherwise R is 0. Individuals with larger fitness values have a higher possibility of survival. The GA is programmed so that about as many individuals as selected in the previous iteration will survive.

Mutation at the probability of 0.5% and a simple crossover method are used for producing succeeding generations.

4.3. Conformity Function for Retrieval

Retrieval of images is made by using a function judging the conformity of images to the query. The generic form of the function is:

$$C = \frac{\sum_{i=1}^{N} w_i P_i}{\sum_{i=1}^{N} w_i},$$

where N is a number of features, P_i's and w_i's are normalized values derived from corresponding raw feature values obtained from images and weights for them, respectively.

By changing weight values of the function we can form different queries for various compositional patterns. The simplest way is to use built-in fixed weight values according to each of 7 composition templates. However, of course, this method lacks flexibility, and cannot take difference in preference of each user into account.

In our iterative query specification process, a user selects composition models which the user think well represent compositional pattern of target images. During the process, the system observes the change of feature values obtained from composition models, and classifies patterns of change into several types. Weights w_i's and methods of normalizing feature values are determined according to this classification of the corresponding feature value.

The basic idea is as follows: If a feature value fluctuates, this feature has presumably nothing to do with the user's intention. The weight value for this feature may, therefore, be set zero. On the other hand, if a feature value is increasing or almost constant, this feature has undoubtedly some relation with the user's intention. In this case, the weight is given some appropriate value depending on magnitude of the feature value. Actually, patterns of change are classified into 8 types, and weight w_i and method of calculating normalized P_i are determined according to the classification.

In this way, a query representing user's intention and preference for retrieval is, eventually, expressed as a set of weight values for features in the conformity function. The resulting conformity function with weights and methods of normalization are passed to the retrieval process.

Although all of the images are, in principle, subject to conformity calculation, a by-passing mechanism is also implemented. For example, when a certain feature is found to be constant at a high level in the query specification process, and if there are images whose corresponding feature value is less than the threshold, calculation of conformity will be by-passed for these images at the retrieval time.

5. Image Retrieval and Evaluation

5.1. Image Retrieval

Figure 5 shows user interface of the retrieval system. The selected composition template is depicted in the left-top corner of the window, and 9 composition models produced by GA at the right-hand side.

Experiments of retrieval were made on about 150 paintings, most of which were Western still-life oil paintings. This is because composition plays a very important role in still-life paintings.

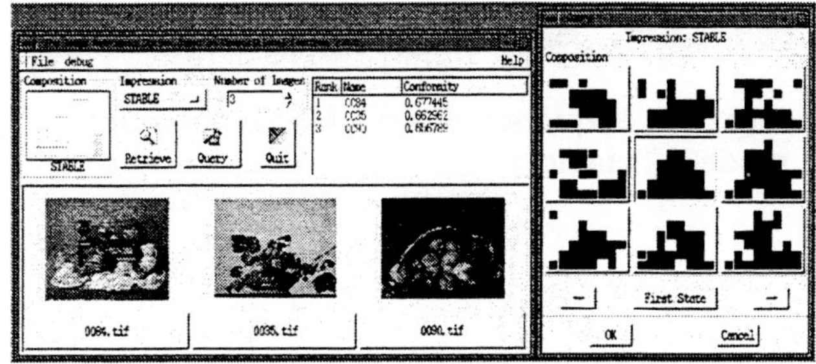

Figure 5. User interface

Figure 6 shows one example of retrieval. In this case, the composition template of "busy" was selected, and after that, the model selection process was iterated 9 times. A sequence of selected composition models during iteration is shown in Figure 7. Values of conformity of the resulting images in Figure 6 were 0.902, 0.824 and 0.807, from left to right, respectively.

Figure 6. Result of image retrieval ("busy")

Figure 7. Sequence of selected composition models ("busy")

Figure 8 shows another example of retrieval. This time, the composition template "stable" was chosen by the user, and a sequence of composition models selected by the user is shown in Figure 9. Values of conformity of the resulting images in Figure 8 were 0.794, 0.781 and 0.768, from left to right, respectively.

Figure 8. Result of image retrieval ("stable")

Figure 9. Sequence of selected composition models ("stable")

5.2. Evaluation Experiment

To verify the validity of the method of query specification, a simple evaluation experiment was first carried out. Several artificial images made by copying certain composition models were mixed in the database, and retrieval was tried by the query specified by iteratively selecting composition models which look like the artificial images. Consequently, most of these artificial images were successfully retrieved. This proves that the conformity function are properly adjusted by the interactive GA process.

Another evaluation experiment was made concerning whether images which satisfy the user's requirement were retrieved in top ranks. Experiments were made by 5 persons. Each of them did 35 trials, i.e. 5 for each of 7 composition templates. Result of experiments is summarized in Table 1. The table shows the percentage of success, namely the cases where images that met user's requirement were retrieved in the highest 3 ranks. The results are summarized according to the composition templates selected.

The reason why results of using templates "bold" and "neat" are not as good as others may be that few images with these compositions are originally included in the database.

It is difficult to make strictly objective and quantitative evaluation, because the result of retrieval will be judged on the user's perception and subjectivity. It is also difficult to exactly indicate which images in a database are relevant for the given query. However, the result of the evaluation experiment shows that the method works well in specifying queries based on composition of images.

Table 1. Result of evaluation experiment

Template	%
Stable	92
Unstable	88
Ordered	88
Lonely	88
Busy	100
Bold	80
Neat	80
Average	88

6. Conclusions

A method of retrieving images, which is based on compositional features, has been proposed. Query specification by the interactive GA has been used, and it has been proved that this method works well for properly incorporating user's intention and preference in the retrieval requests.

References

[1] K. Hachimura, Retrieval of Paintings Using Principal Color Information, *Proc. 13th ICPR*, III, 130-134, 1996.

[2] H. Nishiyama and Y. Matsushita, An Image Retrieval System Considering Image Composition, *Trans. Inf. Proc. Soc. Japan*, 37(1):101-109, 1996.

[3] H. Kobayashi, Y. Okouchi and S. Ota, Image Retrieval System using the Combination with KANSEI Features, *Tech. Rep. IEICE*, PRMU97(261):75-80, 1998.

[4] M. Oda, An Image Retrieval System that Uses Human Cognitive Properties on Image Concept Formation, *Trans. Inf. Proc. Soc. Japan*, 35(7):1449-1456, 1994.

[5] K. Aoki and H. Takagi, Interactive GA-Based Design Support System for Lighting Design in 3-D Computer Graphics, *Trans. Inst. Elec. Inf. Comm. Eng. D-II*, J81-D-II(7):1601-1608, 1998.

[6] A. Tojima and K. Hachimura, Extraction of Compositional Features from Paintings and Application for Retrieval, *Trans. Inf. Proc. Soc. Japan*, 40(3):912-920, 1999.

Image Retrieval by Positive and Negative Examples

J. Assfalg, A. Del Bimbo, P. Pala University of Florence
Dipartimento di Sistemi e Informatica
Via S.Marta 3, 50139 Firenze, Italy
{assfalg,delbimbo,pala}@dsi.unifi.it

Abstract

Systems for content based image retrieval typically support access to database images through the query-by-example paradigm. This includes query-by-image and query-by-sketch. Since query-by-sketch can be difficult in some cases —lack of sketching abilities, difficulty to detect distinguishing image features— generally querying is performed through the query-by-image paradigm. A limiting factor of this paradigm is that a single sample image rarely includes all *and* only *the characterizing elements the user is looking for.*

In this paper a system is presented that supports query-by-image using multiple image examples. Examples can be positive *and* negative *and can be edited in order to disregard unrelevant image features.*

1 Introduction

Content Based Image Retrieval (CBIR) is an extension to traditional information retrieval that supports querying of images through a visual specification, thus addressing perceptual content of visual information [1]. Typically, queries are performed through the query-by-example paradigm which requires the user to provide a representation of the *visual concept* characterizing the searched image.

In modern CBIR systems, querying-by-example mainly takes place in two different forms: query-by-image and query-by-sketch. Query-by-image allows the user to take a sample image —either from a sample image set or from the answer to a previous query— and use it as a prototype to retrieve images with similar content. This paradigm supports retrieval by global image similarity addressing global color/texture distribution, and the overall image structure. Query-by-sketch allows the user to sketch contours of salient regions on a white-board. Regions can be manually authored or traced from an image, following the objects' contours. Once they have been sketched, regions can be characterized by color, texture, shape, position, and area. This paradigm supports retrieval based on local properties of images.

Although it is widely employed in current systems for content-based retrieval, query-by-sketch has several drawbacks. The main drawback being that users find it difficult to create by scratch suitable images embodying the visual concept to be searched for. This is usually due to the lack of visual memory of most users, lack of sketching abilities, and difficulty of detecting those distinguishing salient features that actually characterize that concept. Due to this, examples are built —in most cases— according to the query-by-image paradigm. Existing images, either retrieved with a previous query or selected from a random subset of the database, are used as examples. A limiting factor, in this case, is that a single sample image rarely includes all and only the characterizing elements of a visual concept. On the one hand, a sole example typically includes a subset of the characterizing features. On the other hand, some features included in the example may not contribute to the definition of the visual concept. The former issue can be addressed by querying through multiple sample images. The latter requires that content editing of each example be supported by the system.

Furthermore, specification of a visual concept can be achieved by submitting several examples, providing positive as well as negative instances of that concept. Usage of positive and negative examples has been exploited for interactive learning of image classification ([6], [7], [9]). Examples are used to associate low-level features with high-level concepts to be used at query time.

Positive and negative examples have also been used to support relevance-feedback interaction ([4], [5], [10]) which allows the user to score the relevance of retrieved images. Relevance scores are used to change the system similarity measure so as to converge to a result that

1051-4651/00 $10.00 © 2000 IEEE

matches user's expectations. This prevents the use of any indexing structure that develops on a predefined similarity measure.

In this paper a system is presented that supports efficient querying by *Positive* and *Negative* examples. The system features a color-based retrieval engine. Histograms encode color content and an M-tree structure is used for indexing. Querying is performed through a visual interface which lets the user specify positive and negative examples.

The paper is organized as follows: Section 2 provides insight on content representation through histograms, and related properties; then, Section 3 expounds our solution for retrieval by positive and negative examples; Finally, in section 4 experimental results are reported and conclusions are drawn.

2 Histograms Properties

A generic histogram H with n bins is an element of the histogram space $\mathcal{H}^n \subset \mathbb{R}^n$.

Given an image and a discretization of a feature space, histogram bins count the number of occurences of points of that feature space in the image. Histograms provide a synthetic representation for content, and have been used for different features, such as color and shape ([2] [11]).

Histograms also support a multi-resolution description of image features. Given a partitioning of an image into n fine-grained regions, histograms provide a representation for the content of each of these regions. The representation of wider regions, at a less fine-grained level can be computed by merging the histograms of each region $\mathcal{R}_k^i$ at level i that contributes to the region $\mathcal{R}^{i+1}$ at level $i+1$ ($\mathcal{R}^{i+1} = \cup_{k=1}^m \mathcal{R}_k^i$). Each j-th bin h_j^{i+1} at level $i+1$ is computed as follows:

$$h_j^{i+1} = \sum_{k=1}^{m} h_{j,k}^i \qquad \forall j = 1, \ldots, n \tag{1}$$

It is also possible to provide lower resolution descriptions based on a coarser discretization of the feature space, with dimension $\bar{n} < n$.

In order to compute the similarity between two histograms, a norm must be defined in the histogram space. This is accomplished through the introduction of a positive definite, symmetric *distance matrix* $A \in \mathbb{R}^{n \times n}$ that allows the distance between two histograms H and H' to be computed as:

$$\begin{aligned} \mathcal{D}(H, H') &= (H - H')^T A (H - H') = \\ &= \sum_{i=1}^{n} \sum_{j=1}^{n} (h_i - h'_i)(h_j - h'_j) a_{ij} \end{aligned} \tag{2}$$

being h_i (h'_i) the i-th element of H (H').

This expression evidences that elements a_{ij} weight the extent to which the difference between the i-th and j-th bins contributes to $\mathcal{D}$. If the distance matrix A is a diagonal one, only differences between corresponding bins contribute to the computation of $\mathcal{D}$. However, if A isn't a diagonal matrix, elements a_{ij} ($i \neq j$) can be used to model the cross-distance between non-corresponding elements. This is particularly useful in order to partly recover from the loss of information associated with the discrete nature of content representation through histograms.

For the implementation of the system presented in this paper, 39 reference colors were selected to discretize the color space, and histograms with 39 bins are used to encode color information for each of the tiles images are partitioned into. Histograms are normalized with respect to the image size so as to provide scale invariance of the representation.

A distance matrix A_C has been defined for the computation of the distance between color histograms and structure histograms, respectively. The color distance matrix A_C is a 39×39 symmetric matrix whose elements a_{ij} encode the perceptual similarity between i-th and j-th reference color.

3 Using Positive and Negative Examples

The basic idea underlying our approach for querying by positive and negative examples is illustrated in Figure 1.

Let $\{P^i\}_{i=1}^n$ be the set of positive sample histograms and $\{N^i\}_{i=1}^m$ be the set of negative sample histograms. We want to represent the query requirements expressed through the positive and negative samples using a single composite query histogram H. The composite query histogram H must be close to all the elements of $\{P^i\}_{i=1}^n$ and far from all the elements of $\{N^i\}_{i=1}^m$. Hence H can be found as the histogram which minimizes the following functional:

$$\mathcal{F} = \sum_{i=1}^{n} \mathcal{D}(H, P^i) - \sum_{j=1}^{m} \mathcal{D}(H, N^j) \tag{3}$$

being $\mathcal{D}(\cdot, \cdot)$ the histogram distance function. That is:

$$\mathcal{D}(H, P^i) = \sum_r \sum_s (H_r - P_r^i)(H_s - P_s^i) a_{rs} \tag{4}$$

$$\mathcal{D}(H, N^j) = \sum_r \sum_s (H_r - N_r^j)(H_s - N_s^j) a_{rs} \tag{5}$$

Since the solution to Eq.(3) must be a regular histogram, Eq.(3) must be minimized subject to two dis-

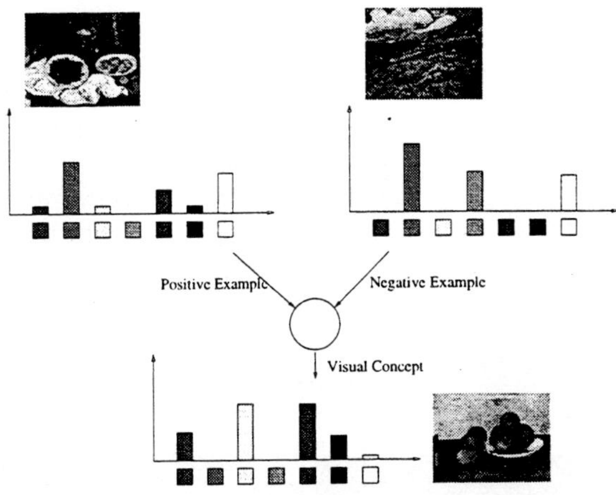

Figure 1. Some examples, both positive and negative, are used to describe the visual concept. The system combines histograms of the examples to derive a single composite query histogram representing the visual concept. An image embodying the visual concept is also shown.

tinct constraints. These are related to the norm of the solution (the histogram must be a normalized vector) and to the positiveness of individual histogram components.

Thus, the composite query histogram $H = (H_1, \ldots, H_r)$ is the solution of an optimization problem with bilateral and unilateral constraints:

$$\begin{cases} \min\limits_{H} \mathcal{F} \\ \sum\limits_{i=1}^{r} H_i = 1 \\ H_i \geq 0 \qquad \forall i = 1, \ldots, r \end{cases} \tag{6}$$

The resulting histogram summarizes the positive and negative examples, and could be thought of as the histogram of a query image featuring the visual concept that is the object of the user's query.

4 Experimental Results

The user interface is shown in Figure 2. The interface is composed of two main parts. The lower part includes the output image viewer. This displays images that are either randomly selected (obtained through the *Randomize* button) or retrieved as the result of a query session. The upper part of the interface includes two panels on the left and on the right —used to collect positive and negative examples, respectively—, and one editing area in the middle.

Images can be selected from the output viewer and added either to the positive or negative sample sets (through the *Add Positive* and *Add Negative* buttons, respectively).

A simple query with one positive sample image is shown in Figure 2[1]. Retrieved images are displayed in the lower part of the interface. Similarly to the query image, all retrieved images feature bright and saturated red, cyan and green colors.

In Figure 3 a query refinement is shown. The query has been edited so as to keep regions featuring blue color patches. According to this choice, some of the pictures retrieved in the previous example non longer appear in the result set. In particular, most of the pictures in the last row have been replaced by other ones, featuring more blue color patches.

Figure 4 shows a further refinement including a negative example. The regions with white color patches in the upper corners have been selected by the user as relevant in describing a negative example. As a consequence of this new query, the pictures featuring the white arches have been discarded.

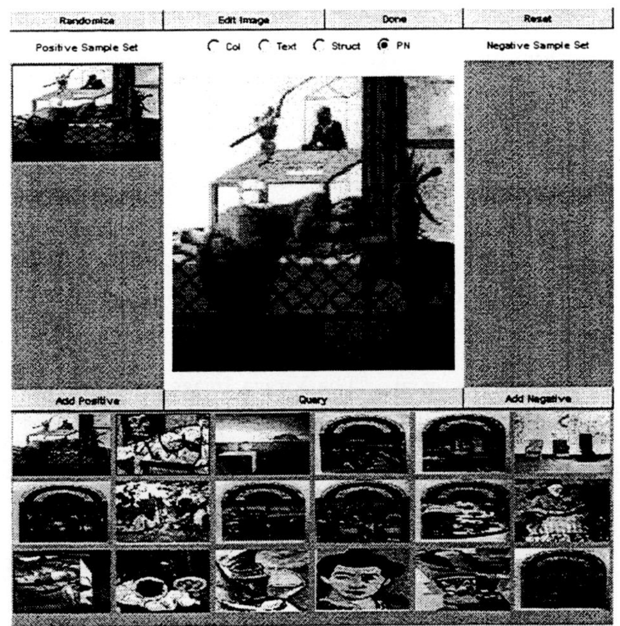

Figure 2. An image selected from a random set is used to run a query. Similar retrieved images are shown in the bottom panel.

[1]Color pictures for this paper can be found at `http://viplab.dsi.unifi.it/PN/`

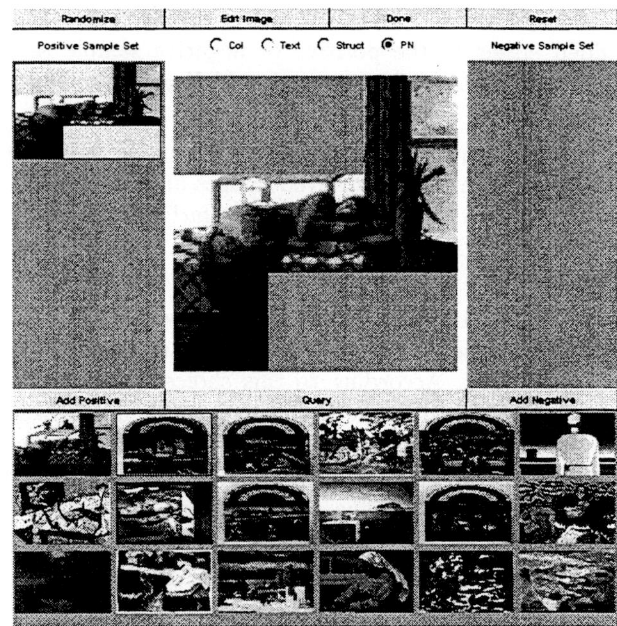

Figure 3. The query is refined by discarding not relevant regions in the sample image.

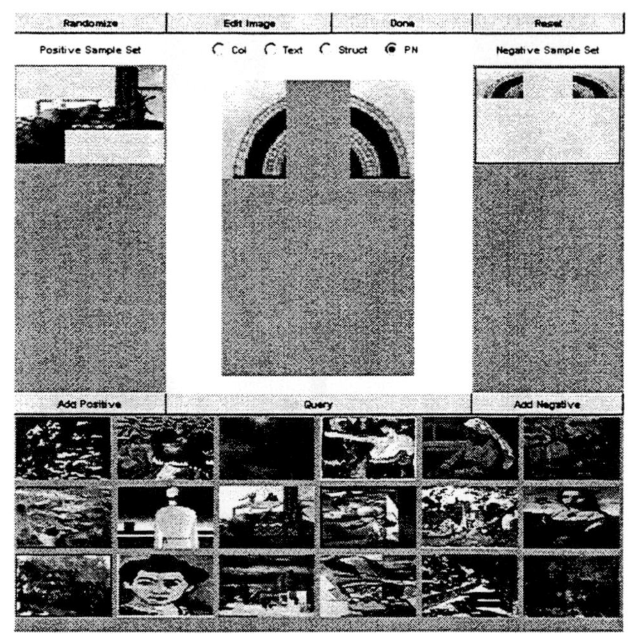

Figure 4. A negative example is added to the query. Compare the result set with the one in Figure 3.

References

[1] A. Del Bimbo, "Visual Information Retrieval", Academic Press, London 1999.

[2] M. Flickner, et al., "Query by Image and Video Content: the QBIC System", *IEEE Computer*, Vol. 28, n. 9, pp. 310-315, Sept. 1995.

[3] J.R. Bach, et al., "The Virage Image Search Engine: an Open Framework for Image Management", *Proc. SPIE Storage and Retrieval for Still Image and Video Databases*, vol. 2760, 1996, pp. 76-87.

[4] L. Taycher, M. La Cascia and S. Sclaroff, "Image Digestion and Relevance Feedback in the ImageRover WWW Search Engine", *Proc. Visual '97*, San Diego, CA, Dec. 1997.

[5] Y. Rui, T.S. Huang, M. Ortega, S. Mehrotra, "Relevance Feedback: A Power Tool for Interactive Content-Based Image Retrieval", *IEEE Transactions on Circuits and Systems for Video Technology*, Vol. 8, n. 5, September 1998.

[6] P. Lipson, E. Grimson, P. Sinha, "Configuration Based Scene Classification and Image Indexing", *Proceedings of the IEEE Conference on Computer Vision and Pattern Recognition (CVPR'97)*, 1997.

[7] T.P. Minka, R.W. Picard, "Interactive Learning Using a 'Society of Models' ", *Pattern Recognition*, 30(4), 1997.

[8] A. Nagasaka, Y. Tanaka: "Automatic video indexing and full video search for object appearances", *IFIP Trans., Visual Database Systems II*, pp. 113-127, Knuth, Wegner (Eds.), Elsevier, 1992.

[9] A.L. Ratan, O. Maron, W.E.L. Grimson, T. Lozano-Pérez, "A Frameork for Learning Query Concepts in Image Classification", *Proccedings of the IEEE Conference on Computer Vision and Pattern Recognition (CVPR'99)*, Fort Collins (CO), June 1999.

[10] S. Santini, R. Jain, "Beyond Query by Example", *Proceedings of the Sixth ACM International Multimedia Conference, ACM Multimedia '98*, Bristol, England, September 1998.

[11] A. K. Jain and A. Vailaya. Image retrieval using color and shape. *Pattern Recognition*, 29(8):1233–1244, Aug. 1996.

Object Image Retrieval with Image Compactness Vectors

Catherine Achard
Laboratoire des Instruments et Systèmes, Paris, France
achard@ccr.jussieu.fr

Jean Devars
Laboratoire des Instruments et Systèmes, Paris, France
devars@ccr.jussieu.fr

Lionel Lacassagne
Laboratoire des Instruments et Systèmes, Paris, France
lionel@lis.jussieu.fr

Abstract

We present in this paper a new global measure to characterise an image: the compactness vector. This measure considers both object shape and grey level distribution function and does not require any preliminary segmentation. It presents many invariants as rotation, translation, scale and luminance and is then a powerful tool for image retrieval from a query image. We present here some object retrieval examples from large database images.

1. Introduction

Due to the low cost of scanners and storage devices, large images databases have been created. They are used in many applications as archives of criminal faces, archives of radiography with some pathology, and so one. These databases increase every day and a procedure is required for automatically indexing and retrieving images.

Previously, features as filenames or keywords have been used to characterise images. But when the base is very large, it is really painful for a human to determine keywords. Moreover, for complex images, it is difficult to find all keywords that characterise them.

So, we search for automatically indexing images. That's why we must use characteristics as color, texture, luminance or shape. Currently, methods use a single attribute.

For example, Swain and Ballard [1] use as index color histograms. To compare indexes, they employ a histogram intersection measure. Schiele and Crowley [2] introduce different distances between histograms and different local characteristics to compute histograms. They compare results and obtain an insensitive method according to scale and signal intensity variations (for grey level images). Other works, as [3] or [4], lead to a color indexing insensitive to changes in incident illumination. Kankanhalli et al. [5] or Gong et al. [6] use methods based on a clustering algorithm in a 3D-color space to obtain a faster indexing system.

We can too use shape indexes as [7], [8], [9], [10], [11] or [12]. A major inconvenient for these methods is that they need generally a preliminary segmentation. Quality of indexing technique is then dependent of quality of segmentation.

However, a single attribute is too restrictive for describing an image. Without color information, or with two images having the same color, if becomes essential to use shape information. On the over hand, with two objects having similar shape, it is attractive to employ color to distinguish between them. Thus, Jain and al. [13] use color histogram and edge direction histogram for indexing images. In [14], a color adjacency graph is proposed. Each node represents a single chromatic component defined as a set of pixels forming a unimodal cluster in the chromatic scattergram. Edges encode information about of colour components and their reflectance ratio. This method needs a preliminary clustering algorithm. Nastar [15] proposes the image shape spectrum witch is a shape index of the intensity surface. Good results are obtained but the method is not insensitive to change in intensity.

In this article, we propose a new features vector (the compactness vector) based on grey level distribution and shape, for object image retrieval in large databases. It is very easy to compute and does not need a preliminary segmentation. This vector is, by definition, insensitive to rotation, translation and scale. We discuss later a method to incorporate invariance to change in signal intensity.

2. The compactness vector

The main idea is to use level sets for characterising an object. The level set "*n*" for a grey level image I(x,y) is defined by:

$$E\{n\} = \{I(x,y) \,/\, I(x,y) > n\} \tag{1}$$

An image defined with 256 grey levels leads to 256 level sets, each one correlated with the participation the grey levels in the object. We have now to characterise these level sets, which are binary images. For this, we have chosen the compactness defined by:

$$C = \frac{2\pi \ Area}{Perimeter^2} \quad (2)$$

The area and the perimeter are, of course, those of object in the binary image. Compactness is an interesting tool since it has several advantages as implicit invariance to rotation, translation and scale. Computing compactness for each level set leads to the Compactness Vector (CV). It will be used as index for image retrieval.

Remark: for all images, this vector has some similarities:

- its first component is the compactness of the image frame.
- the last component is always zero.

The discriminative part of the vector is then its evolution between these limits.

3. Implementation details

Directly implemented the CV is very expensive in computation time. However, using mathematical morphology, it can be expressed very simply.

To obtain the area of each level set, it suffices to compute the reverse cumulate histogram (cumulate from high to low levels). To reach the perimeter, a multi-level morphological dilatation is required. Perimeter of the level set "*n*" is then obtained by subtracting the cumulate histogram of the dilated image and the cumulate histogram of the original image, and this, for the level "*n*". So, the CV computation can be decomposed in tree steps for an original image I:

- Compute the multi-level morphological dilatation D.
- Compute the reverse cumulate histogram (from right to left) of I and D : HI and HD
- The area of the level set "*n*" is given by HI(n) while his perimeter is given by HD(n)-HI(n).

Remark: the morphological dilatation can be realised with several structuring elements (with unitary radius) without really influence results. We use, for results presented in this article, the extremal filter:
$\begin{matrix} 0 & 1 & 0 \\ 1 & 0 & 1 \\ 0 & 1 & 0 \end{matrix}$

4. Measure between two CV

Several distances can be used for quantifying the similarity between two CV. Among them, we can cite:

- the L1 distance:

$$d1(V1,V2) = \sum_i \left| V1(i) - V2(i) \right| \quad (3)$$

- the L2 distance:

$$d2(V1,V2) = \sum_i [V1(i) - V2(i)]^2 \quad (4)$$

- the normalised L1 distance:

$$d1N(V1,V2) = \sum_i \frac{\left| V1(i) - V2(i) \right|}{\max(V1(i),V2(i))} \quad (5)$$

- the normalised L2 distance:

$$d2N(V1,V2) = \sum_i \frac{[V1(i) - V2(i)]^2}{\max^2(V1(i),V2(i))} \quad (6)$$

5. Invariance

5.1. Invariance to rotation and translation

In order to test rotation and translation invariance, we have built a base of four objects. For each one, we have taken six images in different configurations of position. The base is then composed of 24 images. A retrieval example for a multimeter is given figure 1 where the eight more similar images with the L1 distance are presented. This result shows the capacity of the CV to be a significant signature and to be insensitive to rotation.

Figure 1 - Retrieval of the top left image

5.2. Invariance to lighting

Using distances presented in section 4 does not allow the illumination invariance. Indeed, signal intensity change leads to translations combined with contraction or dilatation on the CV. An example is given figure 2 where two images with different lighting and their CV are presented. For these images, we can see on the CV a translation and a contraction.

So, if we want to be insensitive to signal change, we have to introduce a distance which authorise displacements along the grey level axe. It is the "edition distance" that has been defined for computing distance between chains. Let us consider two chains $x=a_1a_2...a_n$ and $y=b_1b_2...b_m$. We note $x(i)=a_1a_2...a_i$ and $y(j)=b_1b_2...b_j$. By convention, we put $x(0)=y(0)=\lambda$ where λ is the neutral element. We compute then the distance D(i,j)=d(x(i),y(j)) by recurrence to obtain the searched measure D(x(n),y(m))=d(x,y). Initialisation is realised by D(0,0)=0. Then, we compute by iteration:

$$D(i,j) = \min\begin{cases} D(i-1,j-1) + C(a_i,b_j), \\ D(i-1,j) + C(a_i,\lambda), \\ D(i,j-1) + C(\lambda,b_j) \end{cases} \quad (7)$$

- $C(a_i,b_j)$ is the substitution cost of a_i by b_j,
- $C(a_i, \lambda)$ is the removing cost of a_i,
- $C(\lambda,b_j)$ is the insertion cost of b_j.

Here, we have chosen $C(a_i, b_j) = C(a_i,\lambda) = C(\lambda,b_j) =$ *dist*(ai,bj) where *dist* is one of the four distances presented chapter 4.

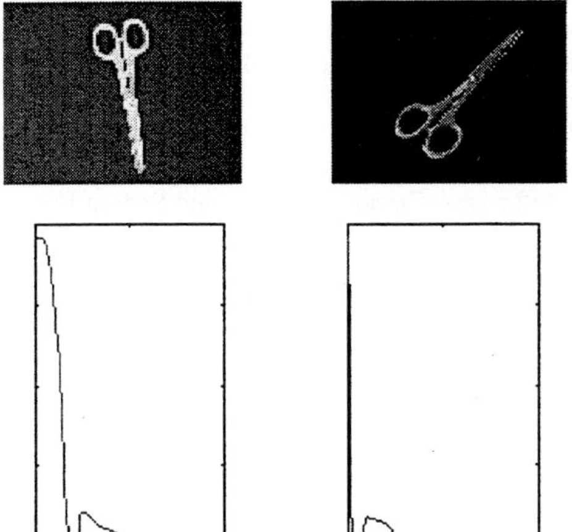

Figure 2- Top : Original images with different illumination. Bottom : their CV.

To test this new measure, we add to the preceding base four images per object taken with different illuminations (the base is now composed by 40 images). A retrieval result where *dist* is the L1 normalised distance is presented in figure 3. Note that we have also introduced a change in scale.

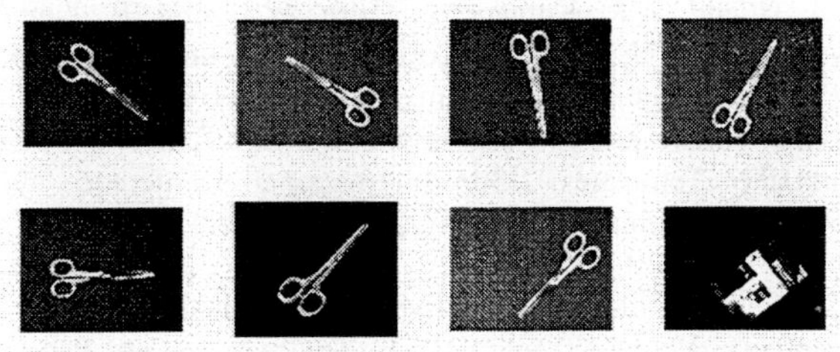

Figure 3 - Retrieval of the top left image

The CV seems to be insensitive to the usual desired transformations, but we have now to prove its discriminatory power. Then, we have to work on larger databases.

6. Experimental results

Results on two bases are presented.

The first one is the Olivetti Research Laboratory Face database that contains 400 images (40 persons and 10 images per person). Images are taken with varying lighting, pose, facial expressions and facial details.

The second one is the Columbia database that contains 1440 images of 20 3D objects. There are 72 images per object taken with 5 degrees increments direction.

It is important to keeping mind that we have none priori knowledge about the number of classes present in the base. The goal is not to recognise objects but to retrieve similar images to the query image.

In order to show some databases images, we present in figure 3 and 4 two retrieval examples, one for each base. We see on these results that the CV seems to be a good index since it can find similar images from a query image.

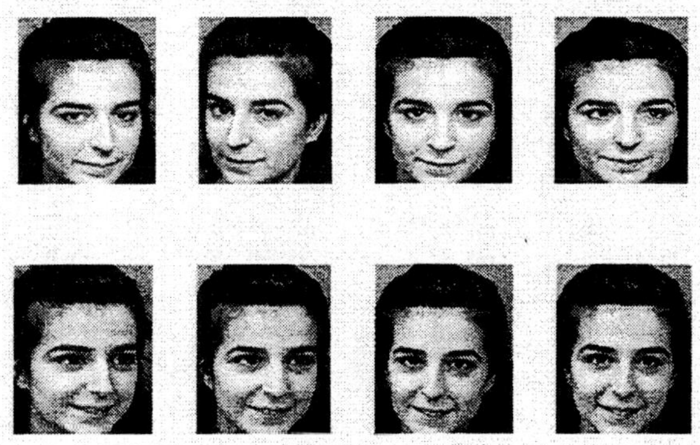

Figure 3- Retrieval of the top left image. Olivetti database

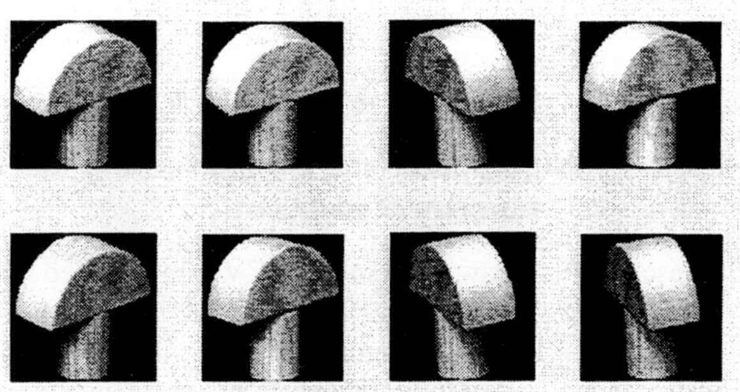

Figure 4- Retrieval of the top left image. Columbia database.

To present quantified results on these bases, we use a nearest neighbour rule: if the nearest image was of the same object, a correct score is given. We tabulate below summaries results obtained from the different distances.

	Olivetti	Columbia
L1	97.25 %	99.51 %
L2	96.75 %	99.17 %
normalised L1	97.50 %	99.31 %
normalised L2	97.25 %	98.19 %
Edition and L1	81.50 %	98.40 %
Edition and L2	75.00 %	96.11 %
Edition and normalised L1	78.75 %	98.47 %
Edition and normalised L2	78.75 %	97.57 %

Table 1 - Recognition rate with different distances

The distance witch leads to the best results is the "L1 distance". Recognition rate better than 95 % are obtained for both bases. When the lighting invariance is desired, scores decrease to 81 % for the first base and 98 % for the second. This consequence is expected as we have added an invariant. Also we can remark that results are better for the second base. Actually, it is because it possesses a bigger number of similar images than the first base.

The CV was defined with all grey levels but we can compute it with a smaller number of grey levels. So, we have studied the behaviour of the CV when it is reduced. Results of recognition are presented in table 2. Differences between CV have been obtained with the L1distance.

Number of level set	Olivetti	Columbia
256	97.25	99.51
128	97.25	99.51
64	97.25	99.58
32	97.5	99.65
16	96.25	99.17
8	87	98.47
4	61.75	91.87

Table 2 - Recognition rate by decreasing the number of level sets.

These results show that smaller CV can be used for indexing database images. For both studied bases, 32 grey levels lead to best (or similar) results. On Columbia database, with only four numbers to characterise an image, we obtain a recognition rate of 91.87 %. Naturally, for complex images and large databases, 256 grey levels can be required.

7. Conclusion

We present in this article a new index for object indexing and retrieval. It considers both grey level distribution and shape and is then a discriminative tool. This index is a vector called the Compactness Vector witch is defined with one component per grey level. We show that it can be summarise at 32 components without decreasing results quality. The CV has many advantages in the indexing context: it is insensitive to rotation, translation, scale and changes in signal intensity. To establish its discriminatory power, we test it on large databases images. Good recognition rates have been obtained.

8. References

[1] M.J. Swain and A.H. Ballard. Color Indexing. International Journal of Computer Vision, 1991, vol. 7, n° 1, pp 11-32.

[2] B. Schiele and J.L. Crowley. Object Recognition Using Multidimensional Receptive Field Histograms. Fourth European Conference on Computer Vision, Cambridge, England, April 1996, pp. 610-619

[3] G. Healey and A. Jain. Using Physics-based Invariant Representations for the Recognition of Regions in Multispectral Satellite Images. Computer Vision and Pattern Recognition, San Francisco, June 1996, pp. 750-755.

[4] Funt and Finlayson. Color Constant Color Indexing. IEEE Transactions on Pattern Recognition and Machine Intelligence, 1995, vol. 17, n° 5, pp. 520-529.

[5] M.S. Kankanhalli, B.M. Mehtre and J.K. Wu. Cluster-based Color Matching for Image Retrieval. Pattern Recognition, 1996, vol. 29, n° 4, pp. 701-708.

[6] Y. Gong, G. Proietti and C. Faloutsos. Image Indexing and Retrieval Based on Human Perceptual Color Clustering, Computer Vision and Pattern Recognition, Santa Barbara, June 1998, pp. 578-583.

[7] B. Günsel and A.M. Tekalp. Similarity Analysis for Shape Retrieval by Example. 13th International Conference On Pattern Recognition, Vienna, Austria, 1996, pp. 330-334.

[8] S. Sclaroff. Deformable prototypes for encoding shape categories in image databases. Pattern Recognition, 1997, vol. 30, n° 4, pp. 627-641.

[9] J. Bigun, S.K. Bhattacharjee, S. Michel. Orientaion Radiograms for Image Retrieval: An Alternative to Segmentation. 13th International Conference On Pattern Recognition, Vienna, Austria, 1996, vol. C, pp. 346-350.

[10] J. Huand, A.R. Kumar, M. Mitra, W.J. Zhu, R. Zabih. Image Indexing Using Color Correlograms. Computer Vision and Pattern Recognition, San Jaun, June 1997, pp. 762-768.

[11] A.D. Bimbo and P. Pala. Effective Image Retrieval Using Deformable Templates, 13th International Conference On Pattern Recognition, Vienna, Austria, 1996, vol. C, pp. 120-124.

[12] A. Califano and R. Mohan. Multidimensional Indexing for Recognizing Visual Shapes. IEEE Transactions on Pattern Recognition and Machine Intelligence, 1994, vol. 16, n° 4, pp. 373-390.

[13] A.K. Jain and A. Vailaya. Image Retrieval using Color and Shape. Pattern Recognition, 1996, vol. 29, n° 8, pp. 1233-1244.

[14] J. Matas, R. Marik, J. Kittler. On Representation and Matching of Multi-Coloured Objects. 5th International Conference on Computer Vision, Cambridge, MA, USA, 1995, pp. 726-732.

[15] C. Nastar, The image shape spectrum for image retrieval, Research Report INRIA n° 3206, july 1997.

Performance Analysis in Content-based Retrieval with Textures*

Kun Xu(1), Bogdan Georgescu(2), Dorin Comaniciu(3), Peter Meer(1)
(1)Electrical and Computer Engineering Department
(2)Department of Computer Science
Rutgers University, Piscataway, NJ, 08855-0909, USA
(3)Imaging & Visualization Department, Siemens Corproate Research
755 College Road East, Princeton, NJ 08540, USA
kunx, georgesc, comaniciu, meer@caip.rutgers.edu

Abstract

The features employed in content-based retrieval are most often simple low-level representations, while a human observer judges similarity between images based on high-level semantic properties. Using textures as an example, we show that a more accurate description of the underlying distribution of low-level features does not improve the retrieval performance. We also introduce the simplified multiresolution symmetric autoregressive model for textures, and the Bhattacharyya distance based similarity measure. Experiments are performed with four texture representations and four similarity measures over the Brodatz and VisTex databases.

Keywords: content-based retrieval, texture description, similarity measure.

1. Introduction

Retrieval from a database of images (video sequences) by finding semantic similarities with the visual information contained in the query, is a task of great practical interest today. Numerous systems were built and some are even enjoying commercial success. See [1] for a comprehensive review.

The similarity measure between a query image and the images in the database is usually computed employing low-level features associated with salient regions: color, texture, shape etc. These features provide only a crude representation of the image and most of the semantic information, the very content which distinguishes an image from other types of information, is lost.

In this paper we investigate performance bounds in content-based image retrieval due to the inadequacy of the employed feature representation. We chose *texture* as a case study since two standard (partially overlapping) databases are available [12, 13], and the problem of texture modeling while relative simple and well defined, still exhibits the pitfalls of inadequate representations.

2. Images and Texture Homogeneity

The Brodatz [12] and VisTex [13] databases are frequently employed in texture studies. The latter contains a subset of the former. Brodatz has 112 while VisTex contains 132, 512x512 gray level images.

*The research was supported by the NSF under the grants IRI 95-30546 and IRI 96-18854.

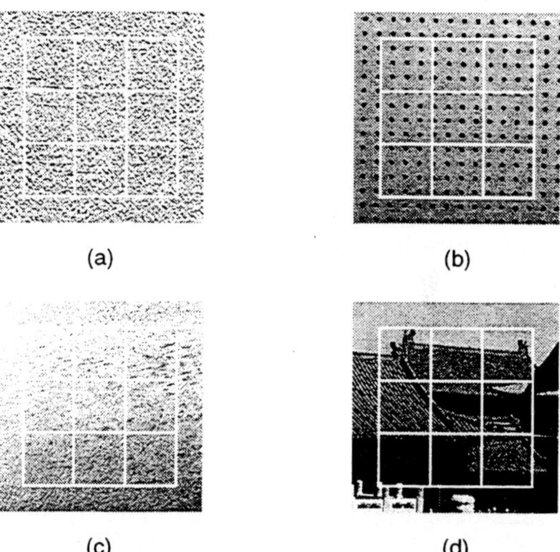

Figure 1. Examples of classes. (a) D57 Handmade Paper (Brodatz). (b) Tile.0007 (VisTex). (c) D38 Water (Brodatz). (d) Tile.0005 (VisTex).

A class is defined by dividing the 384x384 central part of each image into nine nonoverlapping 128x128 images [5]. Thus the Brodatz database contains 1008 and the VisTex database 1188 images.

The three main perceptual properties of textures: periodicity, directionality and randomness [5] are easy to recognize by humans but elusive when to be described quantitatively by a machine. For example, the resolution of the analysis is a crucial parameter since the periodicity of a texture is directly related to the size of the texture element (texel). While it is possible to have an approximate estimate of the texel size [4], in Section 3 only texture representation methods which use the same window sizes for the entire database: the multiresolution simultaneous autoregressive (MRSAR) model [6], and the Gabor filter bank [3], are considered.

Let examine the nine 128x128 images associated with the same class. Since the original 512x512 images included into the texture databases *were classified as texture by a human observer*, it is not unexpected to find significant differences between separate regions of the same image. In Figure 1 examples of decreasing class homogeneity are shown. The nine images in Figure 1a are very similar, while it will be difficult to retrieve using as query the image in the upper left cor-

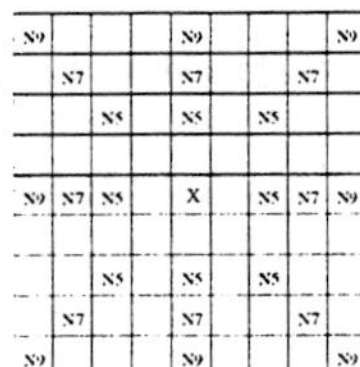

Figure 2. Neighborhood definitions for the three resolutions of the MRSAR model.

ner of Figure 1d the other eight images belonging to the same class.

3. Feature Extraction Methods

In the spatial domain textures are characterized by a two step procedure. First, a window is slided across the image and at each location the local structure is represented by a vector. Next, the mean and the covariance of these vectors is used as the texture representation of the entire image. To reduce the artifacts due to the difference between the size of the window and the texel, the procedure is repeated for several window dimensions. The final representation is the concatenation of the outputs of individual procedures.

3.1. Gabor Filters

In the spatial domain the 2D Gabor functions are complex sinusoidal gratings modulated by 2D Gaussian functions. In the spatial frequency domain they correspond to 2D bandpass filters. A typical Gabor filter bank design is described in [3]. The frequency domain filtering is equivalent to applying 24 spatial filters of increasing sizes, and thus a 24-dimensional feature vector is associated with every pixel in the image.

3.2. MRSAR Method

The MRSAR method models the texture as a second-order noncausal Markov random field. In [6] the four parameters of the underlying autoregressive model are estimated independently at three resolutions using windows of size 5x5, 7x7 and 9x9 [2]. For each resolution k the model is defined as

$$g(i,j) = \sum_{(m,n)\in\mathcal{N}_k} a_k(m,n)g(i-m,j-n)+n_k(i,j) \quad (1)$$

where $\mathcal{N}_k$ is the employed neighborhood of pixel (i,j) at resolution k, see Figure 2, $g(\cdot,\cdot)$ the gray level values in the image and $n_k(i,j)$ the error term associated with the model. A symmetric model is assumed with $a_k(n,m) = a_k(-n,-m)$ for all k. Together with the standard deviation σ_k of the error term, at each resolution five parameters are estimated and after concatenation a 15-dimensional feature vector is obtained.

The least squares estimations are carried out in a large 21x21 window slided across the image with two pixel steps. Careful analysis of the MRSAR procedure reveals that

- At each resolution the estimation process in the 21x21 window integrates together representations of widely different local structures.
- The noise process driving the AR model is independent of the resolution.
- The noise standard deviation σ_k is one to two orders of magnitude larger than the autoregressive coefficients $a_k(n,m)$.

Based on the above observations the original MRSAR procedure can be simplified. The texture in the 21x21 region is represented by a single, 12-dimensional symmetric autoregressive model,

$$g(i,j) = \sum_{(m,n)\in\mathcal{N}} a(m,n)g(i-m,j-n)+n(i,j) \quad (2)$$

where now $\mathcal{N}$ includes all the locations marked in Figure 2. Together with the standard deviation of the noise σ, thus the texture is represented by a 13-dimensional vector. This representation will be called ORSAR (one resolution SAR). As will be shown, the retrieval performance is not significantly affected by using the ORSAR representation.

4. Similarity Measures and Performance Assessment

The ensemble of locally defined texture representations (feature vectors) is traditionally characterized by mean $\boldsymbol{\mu}$ and covariance $\boldsymbol{C}$. Employing only the first two moments of the ensemble, the distribution is implicitly assumed of being unimodal and normal.

Given the query image, described as $(\boldsymbol{\mu}_q, \boldsymbol{C}_q)$, an often used similarity measure is its Mahalanobis distance from the entries in the database $(\boldsymbol{\mu}_d, \boldsymbol{C}_d)$

$$m = (\boldsymbol{\mu}_q - \boldsymbol{\mu}_d)^T \boldsymbol{C}^{-1}(\boldsymbol{\mu}_q - \boldsymbol{\mu}_d) \;. \quad (3)$$

The covariance of the query $\boldsymbol{C} = \boldsymbol{C}_q$ is used to define the underlying metric. However, the Mahalanobis distance fails when the two distributions differ only by their second order statistics. The Bhattacharyya distance [7, p.99]

$$b = \frac{1}{4}(\boldsymbol{\mu}_q - \boldsymbol{\mu}_d)^T(\boldsymbol{C}_q + \boldsymbol{C}_d)^{-1}(\boldsymbol{\mu}_q - \boldsymbol{\mu}_d) + \frac{1}{2}\ln\frac{\left|\frac{\boldsymbol{C}_q+\boldsymbol{C}_d}{2}\right|}{\sqrt{|\boldsymbol{C}_q||\boldsymbol{C}_d|}} \quad (4)$$

on the other hand, takes all the available information into account. Recently, we have shown an efficient way to compute the Bhattacharyya distance exploring the special structure of most feature spaces [9].

To compare the performance of the three feature representation (Gabor, MRSAR, ORSAR) and two similarity measures (Mahalanobis, Bhattacharyya), in Figure 3 the average recognition rate is plotted against the number of retrievals for two databases (Brodatz, VisTex). The databases have over 1000 entries, but in practical situations only the quality of the first few (say) 40 retrievals is of interest.

The Bhattacharyya based similarity measure always outperformed the traditional Mahalanobis based measure. The Gabor filter has slightly better performance

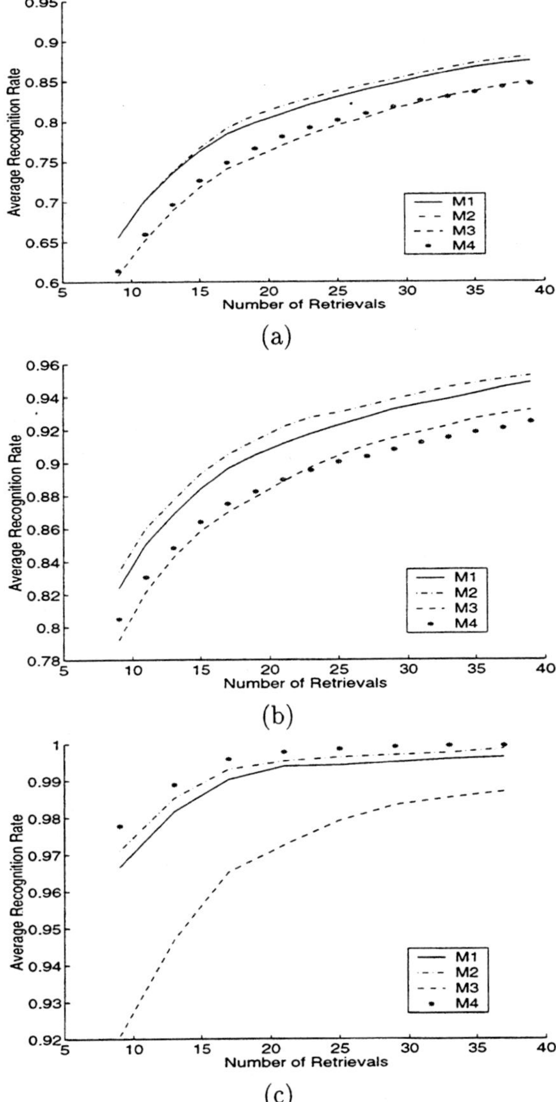

Figure 3. The retrieval performance. (a) VisTex database. (b) Brodatz database. (c) hBrodatz database. Employed representation/similarity measure (feature space dim). M1:ORSAR/Bhatt(13). M2:MRSAR/Bhatt(15). M3:MRSAR/Maha(15). M4:Gabor/Bhatt(24).

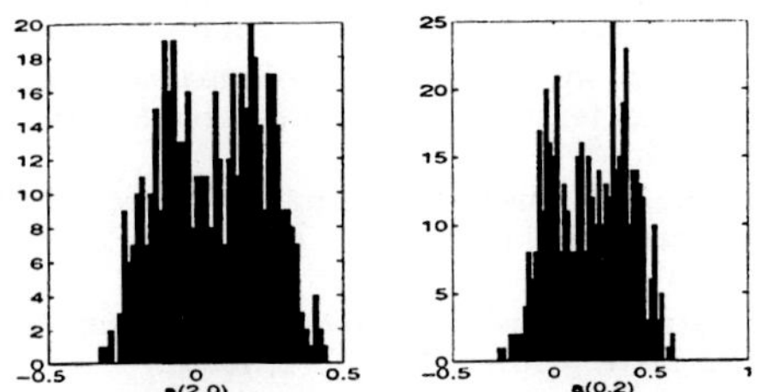

Figure 4. Marginal histograms of two autoregressive coefficients.

than the MRSAR (with Mahalanobis similarity measure) as was also reported in [3]. The VisTex database with less homogeneous classes yielded a lower retrieval rate.

The effect of class inhomogeneity on the retrieval performance can be seen by defining the homogeneous hBrodatz database. For this database 50 images were selected from the original Brodatz set. The example in Figure 1a is typical for hBrodatz. The retrieval performance shown in Figure 3c. In comparison to Figure 3a the recognition rates are shifted upward with at least 0.1, except the method M4 (Gabor/Bhatt) which became the best. This change in performance ranking may explain why often texture segmentation studies cannot find a universally optimal feature representation method [10, 11].

In the sequel will focus on the ORSAR representation with Bhattacharyya similarity measure to show the intrinsic limitations of nonsemantical, exclusively low-level features based retrievals.

5. Semiparametric and Nonparametric Similarity Measures

The feature vector distribution derived from an image is not necessarily unimodal, especially if the texel and the window of analysis have comparable sizes. A 13-dimensional distribution is difficult to visualize, and in Figure 4 two marginal distributions are shown for an image of the class in Figure 1b. Note the strong bimodality. We can ask the question: will a more accurate description of the feature distribution improve the retrieval performance?

To investigate this issue the Bhattacharyya distance between two *arbitrary* distributions $q(\boldsymbol{x})$ and $d(\boldsymbol{x})$ will be employed [7, p.99]

$$B(\boldsymbol{q}, \boldsymbol{d}) = -\ln \int \sqrt{q(\boldsymbol{x})d(\boldsymbol{x})}d\boldsymbol{x} \ . \tag{5}$$

5.1. Semiparametric Representation

The feature vector distribution is represented as the mixture of M multivariate normals. For computational considerations M was kept small, M = 4 in our experiments. Using a simple ISODATA procedure [8, p.98] the feature space is first clustered into M clusters, which are approximated by a mean vector and a covariance matrix. Then

$$\begin{aligned} B(\boldsymbol{q}, \boldsymbol{d}) &= -\ln \int \sqrt{\left(\sum_{i=1}^{M} \frac{n_i}{N} q_i(\boldsymbol{x})\right)\left(\sum_{j=1}^{M} \frac{n_j}{N} d_j(\boldsymbol{x})\right)}\, d\boldsymbol{x} \\ &\approx -\ln \sum_{i=1}^{M} \frac{\sqrt{n_i n_{j_i}}}{N} \int \sqrt{q_i(\boldsymbol{x}) d_{j_i}(\boldsymbol{x})}d\boldsymbol{x} \\ &\approx -\ln \sum_{i=1}^{M} \frac{\sqrt{n_i n_{j_i}}}{N} e^{-b(\boldsymbol{q}_i, \boldsymbol{d}_{j_i})} \end{aligned} \tag{6}$$

where n_i is the number of points belonging to the i-th multivariate normal, and $j_i = \arg\min_j b(\boldsymbol{q}_i, \boldsymbol{d}_j)$, with b computed as in (4).

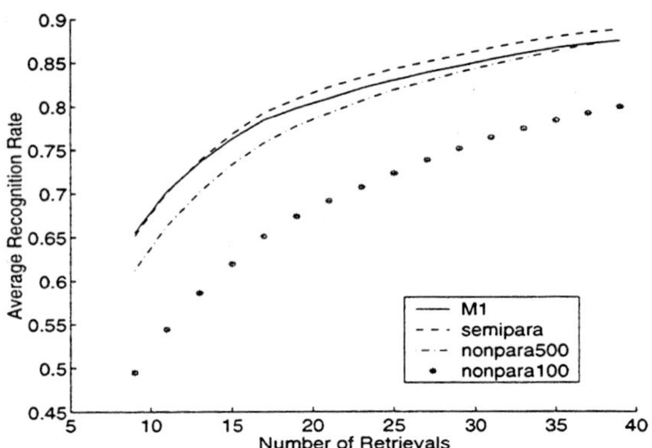

Figure 5. The retrieval performance for the VisTex database using different methods.

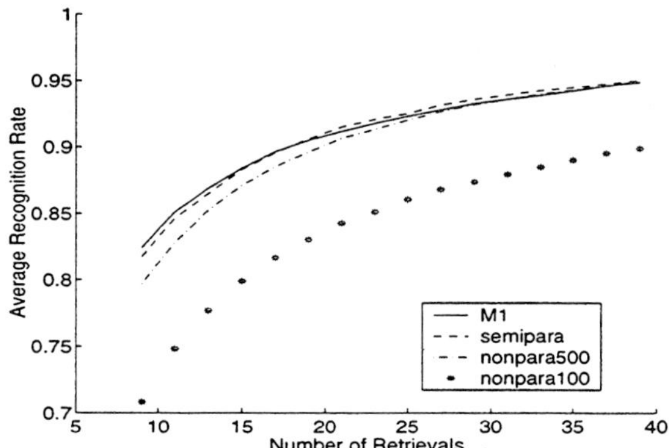

Figure 6. The retrieval performance for the Brodatz database using different methods.

In Figures 5 and 6 the retrieval performance using the semiparametric representation are shown. The performance does not change significantly.

5.2. Nonparametric Representation

To avoid the artifacts introduced by the mixture of Gaussians, the distance (5) can be evaluated directly. First however, the feature space has to be reduced to N data points. We used N = 100 and 500 in the experiments. The retained points correspond to the N densest regions, each containing the same number of points in the original set. These regions are delineated by analysing the nearest neighbor distances.

Next, the retained point sets are scaled to be within the unit 13-dimensional hypercube using as scaling factors the largest value in the database along each dimension. The terms $q(\boldsymbol{x}) \cdot d(\boldsymbol{x})$ are computed by centering a $h < 1$ size hypercube on the two points of a pair of nearest neighbors in the *combined* $\boldsymbol{q}, \boldsymbol{d}$ point sets, and finding the volume of the intersection. The optimal h was determined by Bayesian inference from the histograms of nearest neighbor distances for nine representative classes from the database. For example, for $N = 500$ and the Brodatz database, $h = 0.22$. The nonparametric similarity measure is then defined as

$$B(\boldsymbol{q}, \boldsymbol{d}) = 1 - \frac{1}{N} \sum_{i \in \boldsymbol{q}, j_i \in \boldsymbol{d}} V_{i,j_i} \tag{7}$$

where V_{i,j_i} is the volume of overlap between the h-sized hypercubes centered on the points i in point set $\boldsymbol{q}$ and j_i its nearest neighbor in $\boldsymbol{d}$. Note that V_{i,j_i} can be zero.

The retrieval performance (Figures 5 and 6) improves with N, however never reaches that of the parametric ORSAR approach. The sensitivity of nonparametric representations in such high dimensional spaces is probably more detrimental than the simple, unimodal description by ORSAR.

6. Conclusion

We conclude based on the experiments presented that the main factor in limiting texture retrieval performance is not the inaccurate description of the feature distribution, but the nonhomogeneity of the images within a class. Extrapolating this observation to the general content-based retrieval problem, our findings suggest the importance of including semantic descriptions, however simplistic they are. These descriptions should attempt to capture more global invariant characteristics than those represented by the low-level features.

References

[1] S. Antani, R. Kasturi, R. Jain, "Pattern recognition methods in image and video databases: past, present and future", *Advances in Pattern Recognition, Lecture Notes in Comp. Science*, Springer, Vol. 1451, 31–53, 1998.

[2] R.W. Picard, T. Kabir, F. Liu, "Real-time recognition with the entire Brodatz texture database", *IEEE Conf. on CVPR*, New York, 1993, 638–639.

[3] B.S. Manjunath, W.Y. Ma, "Texture features for browsing and retrieval of image data", *IEEE Trans. on PAMI*, Vol. 18, 837–842, 1996.

[4] A. Khotanzad, J.-Y. Chen, "Unsupervised segmentation of textured images by edge detection in multidimensional features", *IEEE Trans. on PAMI*, Vol. 11, 414–420, 1989.

[5] F. Liu, R.W. Picard, "Periodicity, directionality, and randomness: Wold features for image modeling and retrieval", *IEEE Trans. on PAMI*, Vol. 18, 722–733, 1996.

[6] J. Mao, A.K. Jain, "Texture classification and segmentation using multiresolution simultaneous autoregressive models", *Pattern Recognition*, Vol. 25, 173–188, 1992.

[7] K. Fukunaga, "*Introduction to Statistical Pattern Recognition*", Second Edition, Academic Press, 1990.

[8] A.K. Jain, R.C. Dubes, "*Algorithms for Clustering Data*", Prentice Hall, 1988.

[9] D. Comaniciu, P. Meer, K. Xu, D. Tyler, "Retrieval performance improvement through low rank corrections", *Proc. IEEE Workshop on Content-based Access of Image and Video Libraries*, Fort Collins CO, June 1999, 50–54.

[10] P.P. Ohanian, R. C. Dubes, "Performance evaluation for four classes of textural features", *Pattern Recognition*, Vol. 25, 819–833, 1992.

[11] T. Randen, J.H. Husøy, "Filtering for texture classification: A comparative study", *IEEE. Trans. on PAMI*, Vol. 21, 291–310, 1999.

[12] P. Brodatz, "*Textures: A Photographic Album for Artists and Designers*", Dover, New York, 1966.

[13] Vision Texture Database, MIT Media Lab, www-white.media.mit.edu/vismod/imagery/VisionTexture/vistex.html

Query simplification and strategy selection for image retrieval

R. Brunelli and O. Mich
ITC-irst
38050 Povo, Trento, ITALY
brunelli,mich@itc.it

Abstract

While many systems are currently available supporting the query-by-example paradigm for image retrieval, some key issues, such as the effective introduction of relevance feedback and the automatic selection of an optimal search strategy, need further investigation. This paper discusses query splitting as a way to improve the effectiveness of relevance feedback techniques based on feature weighting. The possibility of selecting among a set of image retrieval strategies the one which optimizes speed and quality on each given query is also presented and discussed.

1. Introduction

The current ever growing amount of multimedia data has motivated the development of image retrieval systems based on the automatic description of their visual characteristics. These retrieval systems focus on the *query-by-example* paradigm: the user formulates a query by providing examples of objects similar to the one he/she wishes to retrieve. The system converts them into an internal representation used for assessing their similarity to the items stored in the database to be searched. The main advantage of *query by example* is that the user is not required to provide an explicit description of the items which is instead computed by the system. In order for this paradigm to be effective, good content descriptions must be computed automatically by the system and ways to compare them obtaining results in accordance with human judgments should also be available. This paper focuses on the use of *relevance feedback* as a way to improve image retrieval effectiveness for this class of systems.

2. Image retrieval with relevance feedback

Let a generic image $\mathcal{I}$ be characterized as a triple $(\boldsymbol{I}, \boldsymbol{F}, \boldsymbol{M})$ whose elements represent a complete description of the image pixels $\boldsymbol{I}$, a derived feature description $\boldsymbol{F} = \{\boldsymbol{F}_i\}$, automatically computed by the system, and associated meta data $\boldsymbol{M}$ providing information on image contents. A query by example $\boldsymbol{Q}$ is defined by giving a set $\boldsymbol{E}$ of images and, possibly, by selecting a subset $\boldsymbol{f}$ of $\boldsymbol{F}$ and a comparison strategy $\boldsymbol{S}$

$$\boldsymbol{Q} = (\boldsymbol{E}, \boldsymbol{f}, \boldsymbol{S}) \tag{1}$$

In order to answer a query, the images in the query set $\boldsymbol{E}$ must be compared to those stored in a database using the strategy $\boldsymbol{S}$, obtaining a *dissimilarity* score for each of them. Derived descriptors are often represented as numerical vectors while meta data are usually in textual form. The analysis presented in this paper will be limited to the use of derived descriptors represented as numerical vectors, leaving out any available meta data in the computation of image similarity. These vectors represent the histograms of several image features, such as luminance, saturation, gradient, stored as numerical vectors [1]. The distance between an image I and an image set $\boldsymbol{E}$ (the query) can be computed using the following formula:

$$D(\mathcal{I}, \boldsymbol{E}) = \min_{\mathcal{I}' \in \boldsymbol{E}} d(\mathcal{I}, \mathcal{I}') \tag{2}$$

where d represent the distance defined in the metric space associated to the Cartesian product of the image descriptors. Following the results reported in [1] the distance used in the metric space is the L_1 norm.

Relevance feedback is a fundamental mechanism by which system response can be improved by using information fed by the user [2, 7, 6]. Whenever the system presents to the user a set of images considered to be similar to the provided examples, the user can pick among them the images he/she considers most *relevant* to the submitted query and add them to the original query. The resulting extended set $\boldsymbol{E}_R$ can be used to improve system response in a variety of ways [6]. In this paper we discuss relevance feedback using a feature weighting approach.

The image derived descriptors $\boldsymbol{F} = \{\boldsymbol{F}_i\}$ are obtained by binning, with the same number of bins, the density estimates of the corresponding image characteristics (e.g. lu-

1051-4651/00 $10.00 © 2000 IEEE

minance, hue, etc.). Exploiting the homogeneity of descriptors normalization and dimensionality, the dissimilarity of two images can be computed by:

$$d(\mathcal{I}, \mathcal{I}') = \sum_{ij} w_{ij} |F_{ij} - F'_{ij}| \quad (3)$$

where i represents the i-th descriptor and j the value of the j-th bin of the descriptor. This distance introduces a metric structure in the derived descriptors space and can be used to compute the distance of the query set $\boldsymbol{E}_R$ from each database item using the formula reported in Eq. 2. The set $\{w_{ij}\}$ is computed by the system and is used to incorporate relevance feedback into the comparison metric. Relevant images should be similar to each other for some of the components of their descriptors F_{ij}. This means that the standard deviations σ_{ij} computed over set $\boldsymbol{E}_R$ should be small for the components capturing the similarity of the images and larger for the components which are *not relevant*. A parametrized family of weighting schemes can then be introduced

$$w_{ij} = k_\beta \sigma_{ij}^{-1} \quad (4)$$

where $k_\beta = \left(\sum_{lm} \sigma_{lm}^{-\beta}\right)^{-1}$ is a normalizing factor, while β is a parameter which modulates the weighting effect and can be varied to optimize image comparison results. There are some major drawbacks related to the use of Equation 4:

- the use of σ_{ij} implicitly assumes that the images in the query represent a compact set with ellipsoidal shape;
- the comparison metric is modified in the same way over the complete descriptor space;
- the time necessary for the computation of D depends on the number of images in the query set $\boldsymbol{E}$.

Furthermore, the amount of weighting specified by β is expected to be query dependent and should be optimized on a case-by-case basis.

3. Query Optimization

The effect of the drawbacks associated to the use of Equation 4 on the effectiveness and efficiency of relevance feedback can be minimized by

- determining whether the specified query set $\boldsymbol{Q}$ while not being compact itself, is composed by two or more compact sets: the query could then be split into simpler sub-queries, each of them better suited to the use of Equation 4;
- condensing the query set using fewer images while preserving the effectiveness of the original set;

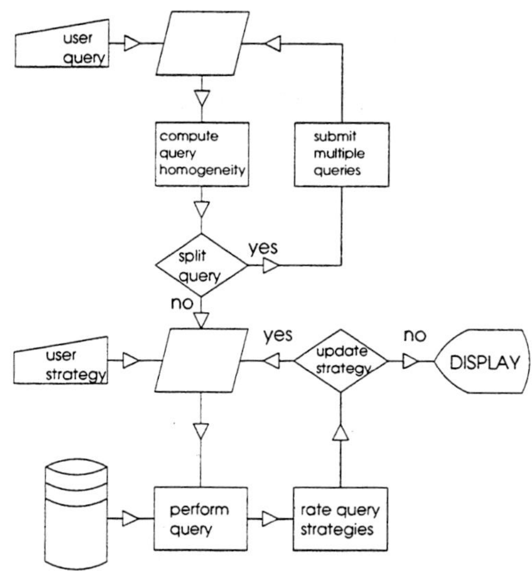

Figure 1. The figure reports the flow chart of the proposed query supervisor agent.

- adaptively choosing the value β, the parameter modulating the amount of metric change.

A block structure of the resulting query optimization module is reported in Figure 1.

3.1. Query subdivision

The cloud of points representing the query images in the descriptor space may exhibit local grouping, i.e. clusters, suggesting the splitting of the original query set into multiple subsets. The main issue is whether the structure of the point distribution supports the presence of multiple clusters or not. There are no completely satisfactory methods to determine the number of clusters for any type of cluster analysis [5]. Furthermore, due to the small number of images used to define the query, no asymptotic results can be used, and methods relying on density estimates (over the query set) can not be applied. The chosen strategy is based on two steps: establish whether the original query should be split or not, and, if the original query should be split, determine the number of clusters into which it should be split.

The first step is based on the use of a statistic originally proposed by Duda and Hart [3]. Let us denote with $d(\mathcal{I}, \mathcal{I}')$ the distance between the descriptors of two images $\mathcal{I}, \mathcal{I}'$ and with $J(c)$ the clustering criterion function for c clusters $C_1, \ldots, C_c$ computed for n samples:

$$J(c) = \sum_{i=1}^{c} \sum_{\mathcal{I} \in C_i} d(\mathcal{I}, \boldsymbol{m}_i) \quad (5)$$

where $\boldsymbol{m}_i$ is the *central* image of the i-th cluster. The quantity $J(c)$ is a random variable whose average value decreases monotonically with c. If data are organized into $\hat{c}$ well separated clusters, the value of $J(c)$ is expected to decrease rapidly until $\hat{c} = c$, and more slowly thereafter. Knowledge of the distribution of $\mathcal{J} = J(2)/J(1)$ under the null hypothesis that all samples belong to a single cluster forms the basis for a test to reject or accept the null hypothesis. A Monte Carlo approach was chosen to obtain the distributions of $\mathcal{J}$ for different sample sizes n (from 6 to 16). The resulting distributions are reported in Figure 2. The distributions for different values of n are markedly different, n being too small to ensure an asymptotic regime.

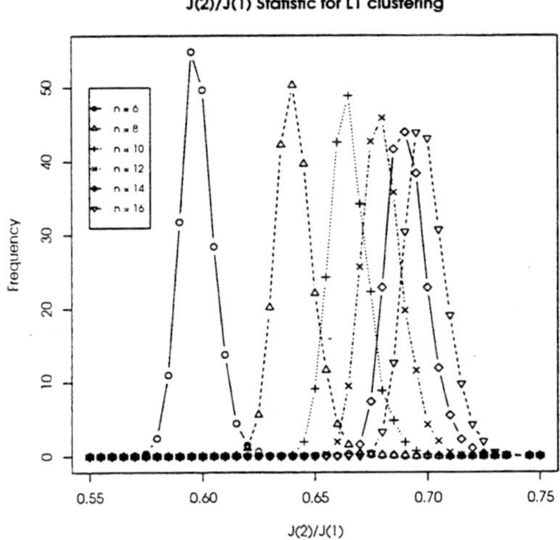

Figure 2. The plot reports the distribution of the $J(2)/J(1)$ statistic for L_1 clustering for randomly generated sample points.

Given a set of n query images the value of $\mathcal{J}$ is computed: if the null hypothesis of a single cluster can be rejected with the prescribed confidence, the appropriate number of clusters should then be determined. The most appropriate number of sub-queries into which the original query should be split is determined by the so called *silhouette* coefficient $\mathcal{S}(c)$ introduced in [4] to quantify how distinctly each sample point is assigned to its cluster. The value of $\mathcal{S}(c)$ is bound to the closed interval $[-1, 1]$: the higher the value the better the overall classification of data for the given clustering. The appropriate number of clusters can then be determined by maximizing $\mathcal{S}(c)$ over a set of possible cluster numbers.

The original query images can then be split into several, simpler queries, each of which is better conditioned for the application of relevance feedback mechanisms (see Figure 3). The resulting simplified queries are then submitted to the image databases. For each simplified query a new

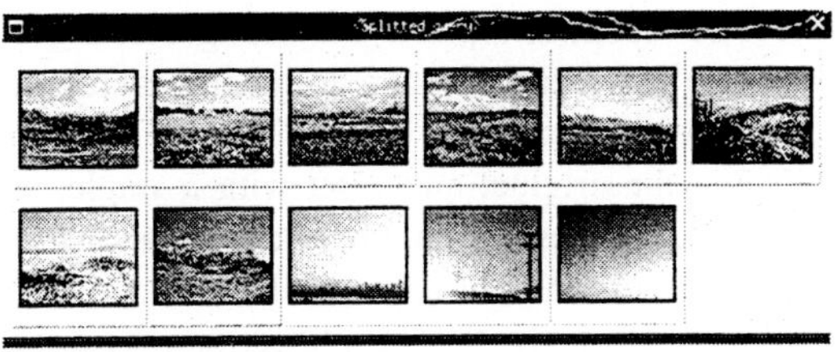

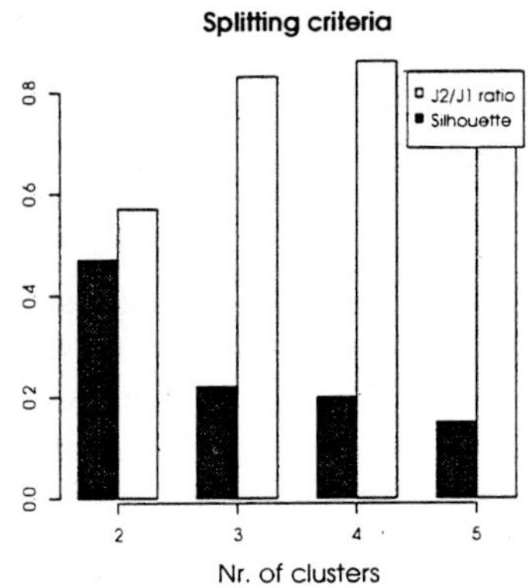

Figure 3. The upper figure shows the images of a complex query and the way it would be split by the system into two simpler queries (whose images are identified with a different shading of the frames). The value of the $J2/J1$ ratio supports the presence of clusters while the silhouette coefficient suggests that the optimal number of clusters is 2.

comparison metric is computed according to Eq. 4. The metric used for image comparison is no longer a uniform modification of the unweighted distance: each sub-query locally modifies the comparison metric, overcoming one of the limitations of the original feature weighting approach.

3.2. Strategy optimization

Splitting the original query into smaller ones does not impact directly on the complexity of the computation of D and does not provide any hint on the optimal value of β. However, the system, upon receiving user feedback, can automatically compare different query strategies by looking at the ranking of the images selected by the user as relevant in the corresponding answers: the lower the average rank, the better the strategy. Two aspects characterize the choice of the optimal search strategy: the determination of the best query representation and the selection of the optimal β value. In the following analysis two representations for the query set are considered: the original set $\boldsymbol{E}_R$ and a condensed set obtained replacing the images in E_R with a *virtual* image represented by the arithmetic average of the descriptors in set.

Replacing the original query set with a single, *virtual* average image reduces the amount of computation required to estimate the distance of each database image from the query images. However, this simplification may not be always appropriate. As an example, if the original query set is not compact, the results may be meaningless, as the average image could be located in a region of feature space which is not representative of the original set. It is therefore necessary to verify that the condensed representation results be strongly correlated to those obtained using the full representation.

At each interaction, an image retrieval system returns an image set $\boldsymbol{A}$ with the N database images most similar to the submitted query. Using this restricted number of images, it is possible to decide which representation of the query set is most efficient for the given query. This can be done by simulating system response using the restricted set $\boldsymbol{A}$ as image database. If the responses using the full and condensed representations are strongly correlated, the condensed representation is to be preferred being faster. The amount of correlation of the two answers can be quantified by their Spearman rank correlation coefficient. Given a confidence level, it is possible to decide whether the two query representations results are sufficiently correlated or not using a non-parametric test based on the value of the Spearman coefficient.

The next step in choosing the optimal strategy is the selection of β. Let us restrict to a discrete set $\{\beta_j\}$ of possible values. For each value β_j a query can be performed on $\boldsymbol{A}$: the optimal value of β is chosen by minimizing the average rank of the relevant images added by the user (see Figure 4). It is important to note the increase in correlation between the full and condensed queries with increasing β and the shape of the average rank curve which exhibits well defined minima. The condensed query representation is then employed using the value of β identified by the lowest average rank for which the rank correlation of the condensed and complete representation results satisfy the required confidence level.

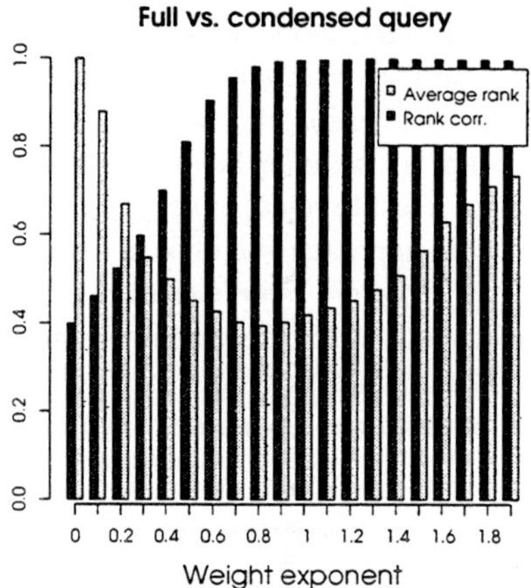

Figure 4. The average rank of the query images for a condensed search with different weights. The rank correlation with the results obtained using all the images in the query bag is also reported. In this particular case, the value $\beta = 0.8$ would be chosen.

4. Conclusions

In this paper the possibility of tuning search strategies and comparison metrics to varying user behavior was investigated and novel solutions presented using pattern analysis techniques. The resulting image retrieval system is able to optimize retrieval speed by reducing the number of query images while preserving retrieval effectiveness. The use of local modification of the image comparison metric further enhances the ability of the system at modeling user needs on a per query basis. While preliminary results look promising, more work is needed to assess the advantages of the proposed approach. Future research will address the problem of quantifying the improvements related to the proposed strategy over the more traditional approaches.

References

[1] R. Brunelli and O. Mich. On the Use of Histograms for Image Retrieval. In *Proceedings of ICMCS'99*, Florence, June 1999.

[2] I. Cox, M. Miller, S. Omohundro, and P. Yianilos. PicHunter: Bayesian Relevance Feedback for Image Retrieval. In *Proc. of Int. Conf. on Pattern Recognition*, Austria, 1996.

[3] R. O. Duda and P. E. Hart. *Pattern Classification and Scene Analysis*. Wiley, New York, 1973.

[4] L. Kaufman and P. J. Rousseeuw. *Finding Groups in Data. An Introduction to Cluster Analysis*. John Wiley & Sons, New York, 1990.

[5] G. W. Milligan and M. C. Cooper. An examination of procedures for determining the number of clusters in a data set. *Psychometrika*, 50:159–179, 1985.

[6] K. Porkaew, K. Chakrabarti, and S. Mehrotra. Query Refinement for Multimedia Similarity Retrieval in MARS. In *Proceedings of the ACM International Multimedia Conference*, Orlando, Florida, US, November 1999.

[7] Y. Rui, T. Huang, and S. Mehrotra. Content-based Image Retrieval with Relevance Feedback in Mars. In *Proc. of IEEE Int. Conf. on Image Processing '97*, pages 815–818, October 1997.

Region-based Image Retrieval System Using Efficient Feature Description

ByoungChul Ko, Hae-Sung Lee, Hyeran Byun
Dept. of Computer Science, Yonsei University, Korea, 120-749
{soccer1, geneel, hrbyun}@aipiri.yonsei.ac.kr

Abstract

In this paper, we introduce a region-based image retrieval system, FRIP. This system includes a robust image segmentation scheme using scaled & shifted color and shape description scheme using Modified Radius-based Signature. For image segmentation, by using our proposed circular filter, we can keep the boundary of object naturally and merge small senseless regions of object into a whole body. For efficient shape description, we extract 5 features from each region: color, texture, scale, location, and shape. From these features, we calculate the similarity distance between the query and database regions and it returns the top K-nearest neighbor regions.

1. Introduction

As the use of digital video information grew rapidly in recent years, it became more important to manage multimedia databases efficiently. Furthermore, the dramatic improvements in the hardware technology have made it possible in the last few years to process, store and retrieve huge amounts of data in multimedia format [1].

Many researchers and institutions are currently involved in providing tools and methods to efficiently manage pictorial digital libraries. Query-by-image is perhaps the most popular way in the content-based image retrieval (CBIR) system. But, if the CBIR system only use the global properties of image, it may be easy to miss many similar images. So, most recent CBIR systems have been focused on object or region based image retrieval.

Several systems have been developed recently to search object or region through image database using color, texture, and shape attributes (e.g. QBIC [2], Netra [3], VisualSEEk [4], Blobworld [5]).

Most of these systems, basically, work in the same way: (1) images are segmented into several regions, (2) some feature vectors are extracted from each region in the database and (3) the set of all feature vectors is organized into a database index. At the query time, features are extracted from the query image, a user-provided sketch or a region from a segmented image and is matched against the feature vectors in the index.

In this paper, we present FRIP(Finding Region In the Pictures), a retrieval system based on region. FRIP uses color for region segmentation and uses color, texture, location, and shape information for indexing regions in the database.

This paper is organized as follows. In the next section, we describe the image segmentation process. In section 3, the feature extraction techniques are introduced. Section 4 is dedicated to similarity matching algorithm. The experimental results and evaluations are explained in section 5.

2. Image segmentation process

Image segmentation refers to partitioning an image into different regions that are homogeneous or similar in image characteristics. In this work, we segment an image into regions using scaled and shifted color coordinate and our circular filter.

2.1. Scaling and shifting color coordinate

The human visual system can be modeled as using three perceptual attributes; hue, saturation, and luminance. Here, the hue is usually preserved to not disturb the natural coloring of the image. So, to enhance an image quality, we need to modify not the hue component but the saturation and luminance component. Normally, color image is transformed from RGB to YIQ color to modify the saturation and luminance. After transformation, modified color coordinates are converted back to RGB color space again. But, this process is computationally not efficient. So, in this system, we use a hybrid technique for image enhancement [6].

$$\begin{bmatrix} R' \\ G' \\ B' \end{bmatrix} = k\frac{L'}{L}\begin{bmatrix} R \\ G \\ B \end{bmatrix} + (1-k)\left(\begin{bmatrix} R \\ G \\ B \end{bmatrix} + \begin{bmatrix} L'-L \\ L'-L \\ L'-L \end{bmatrix}\right) \quad (1)$$

where ,

R', G', B' : *transformed RGB color*

L' : *Contrast stretched luminance from L*

k : *scaling and shifting factor*

1051-4651/00 $10.00 © 2000 IEEE

The luminance is defined from LHS color system: $L=0.299R+0.587G+0.114B$. Here, we define desired luminance L' as the contrast-stretched luminance. The contrast of a luminance is the distribution of light and dark pixels of image. Images with good contrast exhibit a wide range of pixel values. So, we apply this method to L value in order to expand the image histogram to cover all ranges of pixels. If k=0.5, then $(R'G'B')$ is the average of the processed vectors of scaling and shifting in the RGB cube. But, through experiment, we found out that the scaling of saturation is more important than the shifting of luminance. So, we decided 0.7 as the value for k. This hybrid method alleviates the over-saturation and under-saturation problem in the scaling and shifting techniques. By avoiding the conversion of RGB color space to any other color space, we reduce the computation time in addition to obtaining enhanced color image.

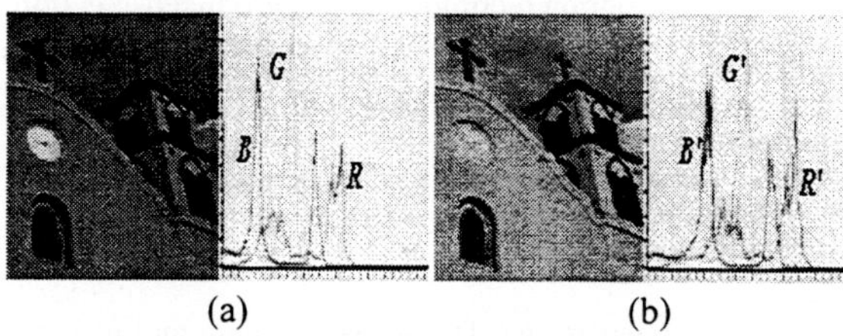

(a) (b)

Figure 1. (a) Original image (b) scaled and shifted image

2.2. Region segmentation by the proposed method

In this paper, image segmentation is divided into two parts: (1) first-level segmentation step using circular filter and region merging, and (2) iterative step using region labeling and iterative region merging.

2.2.1. First-level segmentation. First, modified colors in the image are coarsely quantized with significant color values. For example, if the quantization interval is 10 and the color values of $R'G'B'$ are 18, 32, and 251, these values are quantized with the middle value of the interval, 15, 35, and 255. By this step, the number of color bins are reduced from 256 to 25. Secondly, median filtering is applied to eliminate noise. Thirdly, image averaging is applied. By averaging filter, peak spots or small different color regions in the whole body region are converted to blurred appearance which makes it easer to merge into a neighboring big region.

After image averaging, we apply our proposed circular filter. This circular filtering step is essential to merging some senseless regions which cannot be merged to whole region by normal region merging algorithm. In our algorithm, we use two kinds of different sized filter. The big one is an 11×11 window, as shown in Figure. 2-(b), and the small one is a 7×7 window. Here, the window of big one is useful for determining a set of small initial areas by removing the senseless regions for region merging, in the first level segmentation step and the window of small one is useful for removing the remaining small senseless regions, in the iterative merging step.

From Figure 2-(b), if the number of pixel value, '245', is more than the number of any other pixel values and satisfy the equation (2), the center point, '65', is changed into '245'. Here, we use $T_1=200$ as a threshold for color.

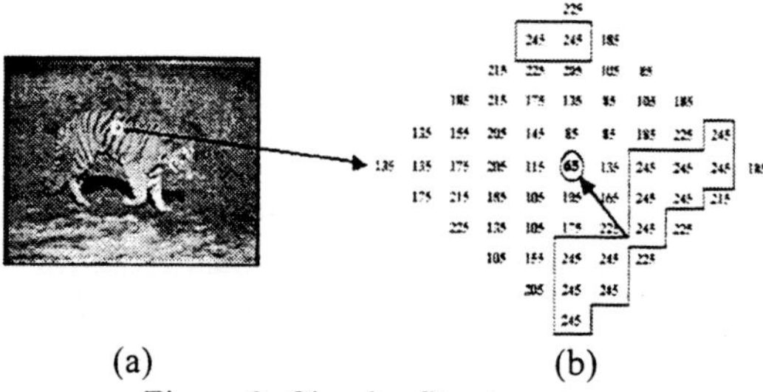

(a) (b)

Figure 2. Circular filtering step

For a given color image, above processes are computed in each of the three color bands.

$$|C(a,b)-M_c| \le T_1 \tag{2}$$

where,

$C(a,b)$: *Color value of center point*

M_c : *Color value with maximum number of pixels in the color region*

By using circular filter, we can keep the boundary of object naturally and merge stripes or spots of objects into body region.

Finally, we use region merging algorithm to merge small regions into adjacent regions which have the most similar color property based on the mean of the region, R'_m and homogeneity function (3).

$$\sum_i^N \left| R_{R'G'B'} - R^i_{m\,R'G'B'} \right| \le T_2 \tag{3}$$

where, N : *Number of neighbor regions*

2.2.2. Region labeling and iterative merging. At the iterative step, we use connected-component algorithm to label regions. By using region-labeling, we can protect over-segmentation problem. This process can be obtained by combining the three color channel as $I=(3*R'+4*G'+2*B')/9$. Each region which has the same color value is projected to buffer as a value of 255. This binary image is raster scanned from left to right and from top to bottom. In this step, each region is labeled by a different region number. In addition, regions that are N (30) pixels or less in size are considered to be non-significant region like noises and are not labeled.

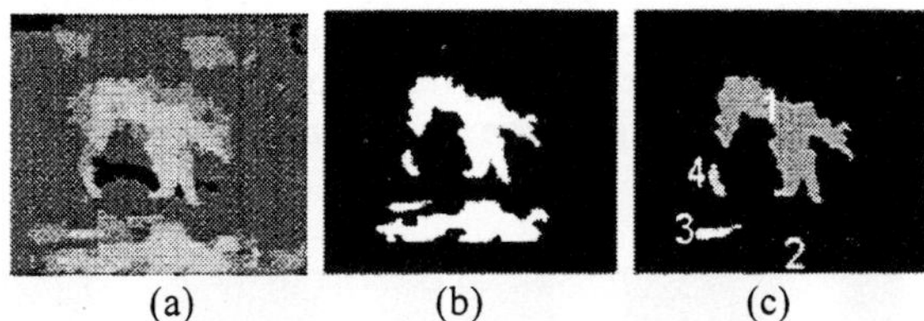

Figure 3. Region labeling (a) segmented regions by first-step (b) projected same color regions to buffer (c) labeled regions as a different number by connected component.

After the region labeling, if the number of region is over 30 and the threshold ***T2*** for region merge is below 100, we repeat the circular filtering with a 7×7 window and region merging step with increased ***T2*** until the two con conditions are satisfied. Here, to the save storage space of shape description for region-based image retrieval application, we restrict the maximum region number to 30.

2.3. Segmentation results

Experiments have been carried out with this method on a set of four color spaces, RGB, HSI, CIE-XYZ and R′G′B′ and database consists of dynamic kinds of images described in chapter 5. The average segmentation time requires approximately 35 second per one image using a Pentium PC, 450 MHz. Here, we found that the scaled and shifted color system, R′G′B′ provides the best segmentation results than others, even though the image intensity is small or partially changed by shadow and surface curvature.

3. Feature extraction

From segmented image, we need to extract features of each region. That is, the semantics of image should be extracted and stored as index.

Features (color, texture, scale, location, shape) of each region are used to describe the content of image. These five features are:

*1. **Color*** : We extract average color of ***RGB*** color space from each region.
*2. **Texture*** : We choose the Biorthogonal Wavelet Frame(BWF). By BWF, we can obtain a fast and precise directional feature compared with multi-resolution method.
*3. **Scale*** : We describe a scale as the size of the region; that is, scale is the number of pixels in the region.
*4. **Location*** : After region segmentation process, the centroid is calculated from each region. Location of each region is defined by this centroid.

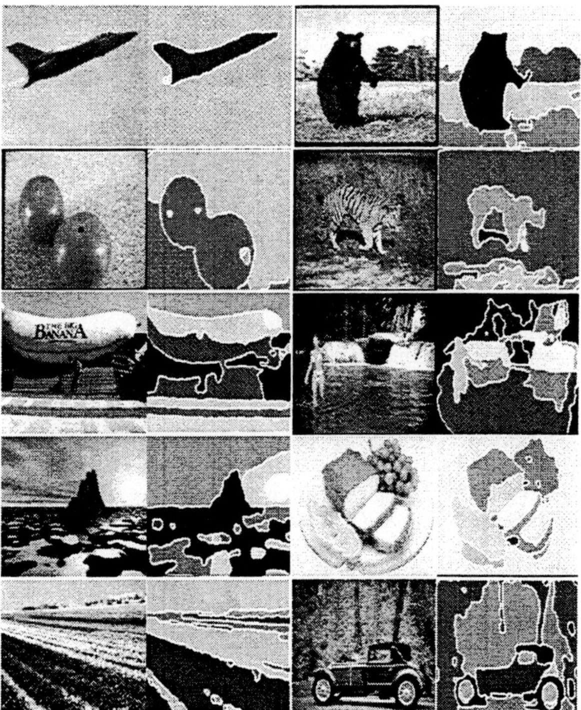
Figure 4. The results of the segmentation by our algorithm

*5. **Shape*** : For efficient shape matching, we use two properties. One is the eccentricity of region and the other is our Modified Radius-based Signature (MRS). At the first step, if the eccentricity is quite different between query and database region, these database regions are removed. So, at the second step, we can significantly reduce comparison time for shape matching. At the second step, with major-axis and centroid of region, we estimate the same starting point and radii of region regardless of rotation and scale change. By our MRS, we can get the invariant results about small distortion as well as rotation and scale changes of region because it provides local information of shape in addition to global information. Here, to reduce index size, we extract 12 radius distance values per 30 degrees and add these to the index for the region.

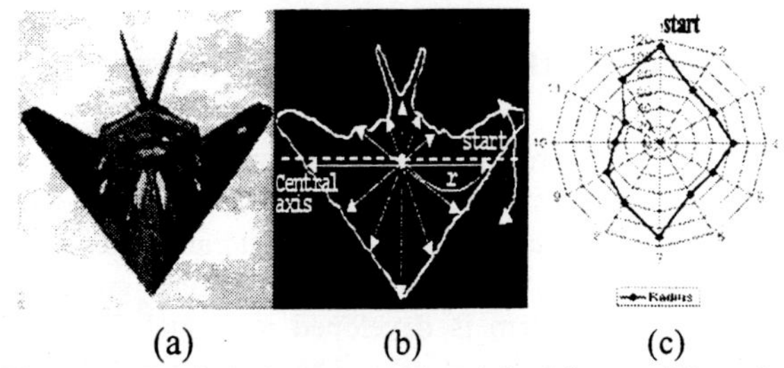

Figure 5. Region signature: (a) original image (b) region boundary (c) polygon by our signature

Finally, we save 12 statistical properties of each region of the image as an index to database.
The properties are shown in below:

```
Image
  keys : imageNo
  {
  attribute int RegionNo;
  attribute int AverRed(AR);
  attribute int AverGreen(AG);
  attribute int AverageBlue(AB);
  attribute int NumberOfPixels(NP);
  attribute int CenterOfX(Cx);
  attribute int CenterOfY(Cy);
  attribute int MajorLength(Rmax);
  attribute int MinorLength(Rmin);
  attribute Array<int> Signature[12];
  attribute float AmplOfYDirect(Yd);
  attribute float AmplOfXDirect(Xd);
  }
```

4. Stepwise matching strategy for region comparison

The actual matching process is to search for the *k* elements in the stored region set closest to the query region. After regions are segmented, the user selects a region that he/she wants to search. Finally, by the user specified constraints, such as (1) scale-care/don't care, (2) shape-care/don't care, (3) location-care/don't care, the overall matching score is calculated by linear combination of each features.

In order to determine the 5 weights $(a_1 \sim a_5)$, we normalize all the feature vectors to 0 ~ 1 value, and their associated weightings are adjusted to *1/f*, where *f* is the number of feature vectors selected by user. The system carries out image retrieval using K-nearest neighbor search, based on current weightings to compute the similarity between the query region and database regions, and finally, it returns the top K-nearest images.

During the matching, linear combination of five distances is used to carry out final score according to the user constraints.

5. Experimental results and evaluation

We have performed a variety of queries using a set of 2,600 images from the *WWW* and Corel photo-CD, containing various categories such as natural images (e.g. landscape, animals) and synthetic images (e.g. graphics, drawing). This system is developed in Visual C++ 6.0 language as an off-line system. The retrieval results are accessible at *http://vip.yonsei.ac.kr/Frip*. Since there is no standard criterion for the performance, we performed tests only on some specific domain data such as, sunset, eagle, and tiger. The users can choose color, texture, scale, shape, and location in order to search regions more precisely. Figure 6 shows the retrieval results of sunset region. We obtained an average retrieval rate of 78% on these 3 domains.

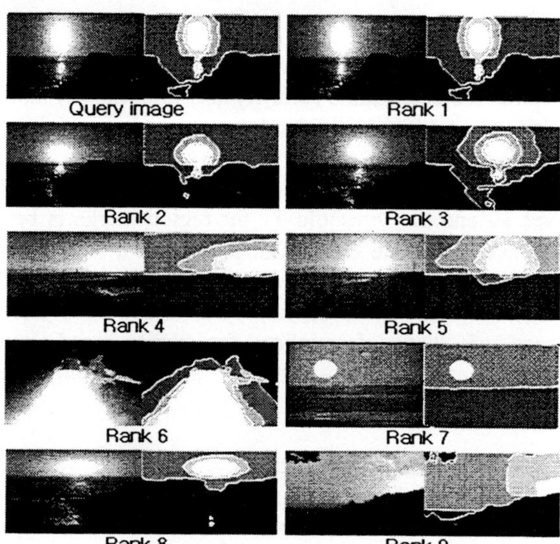

Figure 6. Retrieval results of sunset (left: original image, right: segmented image)

6. References

[1] L. Cinque, S. Levial, K.A. Olsen, and A. Pélicano, "Color-Based Image Retrieval Using Spatial-Chromatic Histograms", *Int. Conf. on Multimedia computing and Systems,* June 7-11, 1999, Florence, Italy

[2] Faloutsos, M. Flickner, W.Niblack, D. Petkovic, W. Equitz, R. Barber. "Efficient and Effective Querying by Image Content", *Research Report #RJ 9203 (81511),* IBM Almanden Research Center, San Jose, Aug.

[3] W.Y.Ma, B.S. Manjunath. "Netra: A toolbox for navigating large image database", *IEEE International Conference on Image Processing,* 1997.

[4] J.R. Smith and S.F. Chang. "VisualSEEk: A Fully Automated Content-Based Image Query System", *ACM Multimedia* , Boston MA, 1996.

[5] Carson, M.Thomas, S. Belongie, J.M. Hellerstein, and J. Malik. "Blobworld: A system for region-based image indexing and retrieval", *In Proc. Int. Conf. Visual Inf. Sys,* 1999.

[6] Christopher C. Yang, Jeffrey J. Rodriguez, "Efficient Luminance and Saturation Processing Techniques for Color Images", *Journal of visual communication and image representation,* vol. 8, pp. 263-277, 1997.

Statistical motion-based object indexing using optic flow field

R. Fablet[1] P. Bouthemy[2]
[1]IRISA/CNRS [2]IRISA/INRIA
Campus universitaire de Beaulieu, 35042 Rennes Cedex, France
e-mail: {rfablet,bouthemy}@irisa.fr

Abstract

In this paper, we propose an original approach for content-based video indexing and retrieval. It relies on the tracking of entities of interest and the analysis of their apparent motion. To characterize the dynamic information attached to these objects, we consider a probabilistic modeling of the spatio-temporal distribution of the optic flow field computed within the tracked area after canceling the estimated dominant motion due to camera movement. This leads to a general statistical framework for motion-based video classification and retrieval. We have obtained promising results on a set of various real image sequences.

1 Introduction and problem statement

In order to cope with the increasing development of digital video libraries, new methods are to be defined to access and manipulate this tremendous amount of information, which implies a content-based analysis of these visual documents [1]. The first step consists in extracting the elementary temporal units (shots) which compose the video. Then, the content of each extracted shot is characterized based on key-frame selection [4], mosaic image construction [7], extraction and tracking of entities of interest, [2, 5]. The description of the motion content attached to entities of interest usually consists in determining the trajectory of these objects exploiting 2D parametric motion models and in extracting qualitative pertinent features such as the direction of the displacement [5]. However, in case of complex motion (fluid motion, crowds, sport events), motion information cannot be easily handled in such a way. Therefore, we aim at deteriminning a new characterization of the motion distribution attached to the considered entities of interest. We compute the residual optic flow field within the tracked area after canceling the estimated dominant motion due to camera movement. Exploiting a statistical framework, we consider a hierarchical motion-based classification stage, and we define a statistical retrieval scheme with query by example.

This paper is organized as follows. Section 2 describes how we interactively extract entities of interest and automatically track them in a video shot. In Section 3, the statistical modeling of the motion distribution based on the estimation of residual optic flow fields is presented. We introduce the statistical framework for motion-based classification and retrieval in Section 4. Finally, Section 5 contains experimental results and concluding remarks.

2 Tracking entities of interest

The first step of our indexing scheme consists in extracting entities of interest in the video shots. To this end, we consider the semi-automatic tracking technique presented in [6]. A region is specified by the user through an interactive interface by pointing the vertices of the bounding polygon. Then, at each instant, the dominant motion, represented by a 2D affine motion model, is estimated over this region using a robust estimator (see subsection 3.1) and used to project the polygon in the next image which constitutes the new position of the tracked entity and the new support to compute again the dominant motion at the next instant.

Figure 1. *Results of tracking of a hockey player (a-b-c) and of a specified area of a rugby playing field (d-e-f). The bounding polygon encompassing the tracked area is displayed in white.*

This tracking technique can cope with a variety of challenging situations such as complex motions, changes in illumination or partial occlusions [6]. In Fig. 1, we display two examples of tracking. The first one involves a hockey player and the second one a specific area of a rugby playing field in a video shot acquired with a mobile camera. Whereas the first case could also be processed using a motion detection module even if it represents a not so easy situation, the second one cannot be addressed with usual techniques developed for motion segmentation. This tracking module offers new functionalities in the context of video indexing, especially considering the formulation of video queries. In many situations such as sport events, the information of interest can be not only a single player but also a group of players or more generally a given zone of the scene.

3 Motion distribution characterization

We aim at adapting statistical tools presented in [3] to cope with motion characterization within a tracked area in the video shot. In [3], our approach relies on the analysis of the spatio-temporal distribution of local motion-related measurements directly computed from the spatio-temporal derivatives of the image intensity function. When focusing on an area of interest, the use of dense optic flow field becomes reasonable w.r.t. required computational load, while providing complete motion information in terms of direction and magnitude. Besides, we want to evaluate the actual motion of the tracked object. To this end, we compute the residual optic flow field after canceling the estimated dominant image motion assumed to be due to camera movement.

3.1 Dominant motion estimation

We model the dominant motion between two successive images as a 2D affine motion model. The estimation of the six affine motion parameters is achieved with the robust gradient-based estimation method described in [10]. The use of a robust estimator ensures the motion estimation not to be sensitive to secondary motions due to mobile objects in the scene. The minimization is performed by means of an iterative reweighted least-square technique embedded in a multiresolution framework.

3.2 Residual optic flow estimation

To estimate the residual optic flow field, we exploit the technique described in [8]. The problem is stated as the global minimization of an energy function which involves robust estimators both in the regularization energy term to preserve motion discontinuities and in the data-driven energy term to discard the optic flow constraint when not valid. This minimization is efficiently performed through a multigrid algorithm which exploits different levels of local parameterization of the flow field.

In practice, when considering two successive images of a video, we first compute the dominant image motion. Then, focusing on the area of interest, the flow field resulting from the estimated 2D affine motion model is used as an initialization for the dense optic flow field estimation in this area. Finally, the residual optic flow field to be used in the motion characterization stage is the difference between the computed dense optic flow field and the dominant motion field.

3.3 Statistical motion distribution modeling

The characterization of motion information within the area of interest relies on a statistical modeling of the distribution of the occurrences of the computed residual optic flow field. Such a statistical representation will be denoted as model V. The conditional likelihood $P_V(o)$ of sequence of residual optic flow fields o computed within the tracked area over the shot is given by:

$$P_V(o) = \prod_{k=1}^{k=K} \prod_{r \in \mathcal{R}_k} P_V\left(o_k(r)\right) \quad (1)$$

where K is the length of the shot, $\mathcal{R}_k$ the tracked region in image k of the shot, $o_k(r)$ the residual velocity at point r in image k and $P_V\left(o_k(r)\right)$ the conditional likelihood of the occurrence of velocity $o_k(r)$ w.r.t model V.

To estimate model $\widehat{V}$ for a given tracked area over a shot, we exploit a Parzen window density estimator. Since we consider a simple kernel estimate, it comes to compute the histogram H^o of the occurrences of a quantized version of residual optic flow fields o within the tracked area. Let us note Λ the range of quantized residual velocities (in practice, the horizontal and vertical components of the residual optic flow vectors are quantized over sixteen levels within $[-8, 8]$). Model estimate $\widehat{V}$ is then defined by the set of model components $\left\{P_{\widehat{V}}(\lambda)\right\}_{\lambda \in \Lambda}$ given by:

$$\forall \lambda \in \Lambda, \ P_{\widehat{V}}(\lambda) = H^o(\lambda) / \left[\sum_{\lambda' \in \Lambda} H^o(\lambda')\right] \quad (2)$$

In addition, given a model V and a sequence of residual optic flow fields o, the conditional log-likelihood, $LF_V(o) = \ln P_V(o)$ issued from relation (1), can be simply expressed as a dot product between histogram H^o and the set of model potentials V $\{\ln P_V(\lambda)\}_{\lambda \in \Lambda}$:

$$LF_V(o) = \sum_{\lambda \in \Lambda} H^o(\lambda) \cdot \ln P_V(\lambda) \quad (3)$$

4 Statistical motion-based object classification and retrieval

The statistical representation of the spatio-temporal motion distribution within the tracked region can be exploited for motion-based video indexing and retrieval using partial query. Considering a set of video sequences, the associated stored set of extracted regions of interest and their associated motion distributions, we aim at retrieving, from this database, examples similar to a video query in terms of motion content. The general idea is to define an appropriate similarity measure between shots and to determine the closest matches according to this measure.

As far as query formulation is concerned, we can also supply the user with an interactive interface to express the video query. Using the tracking module presented in Section 2, the user can specify an area of interest in the first image of the query shot and this region is automatically tracked along the shot. Then, the residual optic flow fields within the tracked region are computed at the successive instants of the shot. We will consider this tracked area as the video query in the sequel. This scheme allows the user to formulate a wide range of partial video queries such as tracking specific entities (objects, characters) or focusing on a particular area of the scene involving different entities.

4.1 Bayesian retrieval

Similarly to [3], we formulate the retrieval process as a Bayesian inference issue. In fact, considering a query q and a stored set of videos $(n)_{n \in \mathcal{N}}$, we determine the best matches n^* according to a MAP criterion expressed using the Bayes rule as follows: $n^* = \arg\max_n P(q|n)P(n)$

The distribution $P(n)$ represents the a priori knowledge on the processed database. In our case, we will introduce no a priori, which implies an uniform distribution $P(n)$. Knowing the statistical model V^n attached to an element n of the video base and computed as described in Section 3, $P(q|n)$ is expressed as the conditional likelihood $P_{V^n}(o_q)$ of the quantized residual optic flow fields o_q estimated for query q, *w.r.t.* model V^n:

$$n^* = \arg\max_n P_{V^n}(o_q) \tag{4}$$

4.2 Hierarchical classification and retrieval

To handle large video databases, it is generally required to build a hierarchical structure of the database related to content similarity. To this end, we consider an ascendant hierarchical classification scheme [3]. It consists in iteratively forming new clusters in the hierarchy of entities of interest within video shots of the processed base by merging in turn pairs of elements which minimize a given similarity measure. This process results in a binary tree.

Considering two elements of the database n_1 and n_2, their associated models V_{n_1} and V_{n_2} and the quantized residual optic flow fields o_{n_1} and o_{n_2}, the similarity measure $D(n_1, n_2)$ is a symmetric version of the Kullback-Leibler divergence $KL(n_1 \| n_2)$:

$$D(n_1, n_2) = \frac{1}{2}\left(KL(n_1 \| n_2) + KL(n_2 \| n_1)\right) \tag{5}$$

$KL(n_1 \| n_2)$ is approximated using an empirical average of the ratios of log-likelihood for the distributions attached to models V_{n_1} and V_{n_2} (see [3] for details). It indeed comes to approximate $KL(n_1 \| n_2)$ by the following ratio:

$$KL(n_1 \| n_2) \approx \ln\left(P_{V_{n_1}}(o_{n_1}) / P_{V_{n_2}}(o_{n_1})\right) \tag{6}$$

When evaluating the similarity measure between two clusters C^1 and C^2, we exploit the following definition of D:

$$D(C^1, C^2) = \max_{(n_1, n_2) \in C^1 \times C^2} D(n_1, n_2) \tag{7}$$

In the ascendant classification procedure, the creation of a new cluster in the hierarchy requires to attach to the corresponding node a statistical model in order to perform later the retrieval process through this indexing structure. Since the occurrence histogram of the quantized residual optic flow vectors for the regions of interest of a group of video shots is the merge of individual occurrence histograms, the associated model can be easily estimated using relation (2).

When performing retrieval operations over a given video base, its hierarchical representation is efficiently used to satisfy a video query. First, the node of the highest level of the tree which verifies the MAP criterion is chosen. Then, at each step, we select the child node of the current selected node, still using the MAP criterion, until a given number of answers or a given precision is reached.

5 Results and concluding remarks

We have carried out experiments on a set of real image sequences. We have paid a particular attention to choose a video set representative of various motion situations : sport videos (basket, rugby, hockey,...), rigid motion situations (cars, train, ...), and low motion activity examples. Finally, we consider a database of 50 video sequences.

For each element of this database, we have selected entities of interest over which we have performed the estimation of their residual optic flow fields. Then, we have computed the associated occurrence histograms and ML statistical models. Afterwards, we have applied the hierarchical motion-based classification scheme. In Fig. 2, we report three examples of retrieval operations. For each query, four answers are sought. The first example involves a news program where the entity of interest is the anchor. It presents a very weak motion activity. The four retrieved answers belong also to this class of video. The second example is a shot of a hockey game with a close-up on a player. The proposed answers involve also video with important motion activity and a focus on a particular player. The last query is concerned with a specific part of the playing field in a hockey game. The system again delivers correct examples similar to the query in terms of motion content, since they also correspond to a wide-angle shot of the playing field.

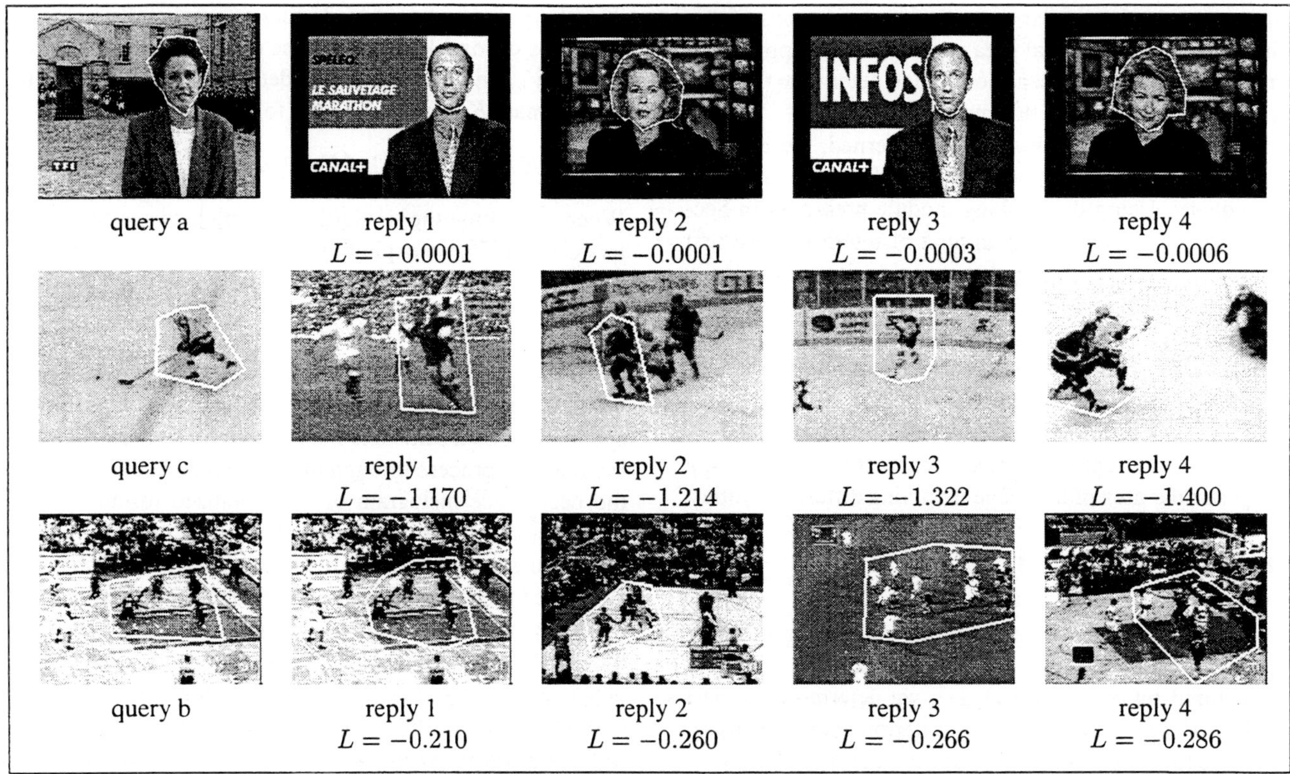

Figure 2. *Examples of motion-based retrieval operations. For each query shot and for each retrieved shot, we display the first image, and the entity of interest is delimited by a white polygon. Besides, for each reply, we report the value of log-likelihood L of the query w.r.t. statistical motion model V attached to this reply.*

We have described in this paper an original approach for motion-based video indexing and retrieval. It relies on the statistical analysis of the motion distribution of the residual optic flow fields computed within a tracked region of interest in the video shot. Exploiting a probabilistic modeling, we have established a general statistical framework for hierarchical video object classification and retrieval with query by example based on motion content. We have obtained promising results on a set of real videos. In future work, we will evaluate this approach on a larger database. We are also investigating other means of designating the region of interest involving automatic motion detection module.

Acknowledgments: The authors would like to thank E. Mémin for providing the code for optic flow estimation, and INA (Institut National de l'Audiovisuel) for supplying the MPEG-1 news sequences.

References

[1] P. Aigrain, H-J. Zhang, and D. Petkovic. Content-based representation and retrieval of visual media : A state-of-the-art review. *Multimedia Tools and Applications*, 3(3):179–202, September 1996.

[2] J.D. Courtney. Automatic video indexing via object motion analysis. *Pattern Recognition*, 30(4):607–625, April 1997.

[3] R. Fablet, P. Bouthemy, and P. Pérez. Statistical motion-based video indexing and retrieval. In *Proc. 6th Conf. on Content-Based Multimedia Information Access, RIAO'2000*, pp 602–619, Paris, April 2000.

[4] A. Muffit Ferman and A. Murat Tekalp. Efficient filtering and clustering methods for temporal video segmentation and visual summarization. *Jal of Visual Communication and Image Representation*, 9(4):336–351, December 1998.

[5] M. Gelgon and P. Bouthemy. Determining a structured spatio-temporal representation of video content for efficient visualization and indexing. In *Proc. 5th Eur. Conf. on Computer Vision, ECCV'98*, Freiburg, June 1998, LNCS Vol 1406, pp 595–609, Springer.

[6] M. Gelgon, P. Bouthemy, and T. Dubois. A region tracking technique with failure detection for an interactive video indexing environment. In *Proc. 3rd Int. Conf. on Visual Information Systems, VISUAL'99*, Amsterdam, June 1999. LNCS Vol 1614, pp 261–268, Springer.

[7] M. Irani and P. Anandan. Video indexing based on mosaic representation. *Proc. of the IEEE*, 86(5):905–921, May 1998.

[8] E. Mémin and P. Pérez. A multigrid approach for hierarchical motion estimation. In *Proc. 6th IEEE Int. Conf. on Computer Vision, ICCV'98*, pages 933–938, Bombay, January 1998.

[9] R. Mohan. Video sequence matching. In *Proc. Int. Conf. on Acoustics, Speech, and Signal Processing, ICASSP'98*, pp 3697–3700, Seattle, May 1998.

[10] J.M. Odobez and P. Bouthemy. Robust multiresolution estimation of parametric motion models. *Jal of Visual Communication and Image Representation*, 6(4):348–365, December 1995.

Detection and Reconstruction of Human Scale Features from High Resolution Interferometric SAR Data

Regine Bolter and Franz Leberl
Computer Graphics and Vision
Graz University of Technology
Inffeldgasse 16/E/2, A-8010 Graz, Austria
bolter,leberl@icg.tu-graz.ac.at

Abstract

In contrast to opical imagery, modern high resolution IFSAR sensors deliver intensity images and corresponding interferometric height and coherence data from a single flight path at pixel sizes of 30cm to 10cm. Due to the all-weather, day-night applicability of SAR sensors, multiple views over a short time can be easily obtained. However, many image users find it difficult to "read" radar images. They differ from the natural human visual impression and the familiar analogy communicated by optical imagery. The goal of our work is to convert radar data into models of the terrain and render those models in analogy to the optical sensing approach that the human visual system represents. Therefore intelligent combinations of multiple views and measurements from all IFSAR data sources available are necessary to help to overcome problems inherent in the SAR data as e.g., blur, speckle, layover, and shadow. Using basic image analysis methods we present in this paper our first fully automated approach to separate buildings from other objects in an IFSAR dataset. The building shapes are reconstructed using a simple building model and the results are compared to measurements made from optical imagery.

1. Introduction

High resolution SAR imagery has begun to get consideration as a source for detection and reconstruction of human scale features [2]. Airborne sensors deliver high resolutions at pixel sizes of 30cm to 10cm and single pass interferometry supports the geometric reconstruction of various human scale features. Interferometrically derived digital elevation models are usually less detailed than the basic magnitude images and suffer from effects of image blur, speckle, layover, and shadows. However, due to the all-weather, day-night capability of SAR sensors it is possible to image any region multiple times over a short period.

Extraction of man-made objects from optical imagery is a lively topic in the remote sensing community, e.g., [4] and [6]. Previous demonstrations of such measurements from SAR data were based on manual work, some limited automated methods can be found. In [7] fusion of IFSAR and multispectral optical image data results in boundary boxes of buildings. [5] describes an automated region growing approach to localize buildings starting from the shadows they cast. The reconstruction of building shapes of urban tower blocks from IFSAR data by applying a range segmentation algorithm is presented in [3]. Another approach to enhance the quality of IFSAR imagery is described in [2]. In contrast to these previous demonstrations, which are performed on a single data source we want to employ the best source for each single measurement and combine the results in an intelligent way.

2. Test Data

In this paper we focus on the detection and reconstruction of buildings at the McKenna MOUT site, Ft.Benning, GA. The buildings on this site are clustered in a compact group resembling a northern European village, surrounded by undeveloped land. Figure 1 shows an optical image of the test site. From an airborne Sandia Spotlight IFSAR sensor the testsite was imaged from four cardinal azimuth directions. Each pass was processed into four channels: magnitude, correlation, height and bin number, and converted to UTM coordinates with a resolution of 0.4m. The original slant range magnitude images are also available. An ARC/INFO data set of the Fort Benning MOUT site is used as the ground truth to evaluate the building extraction results. This data set contains the UTM coordinates of building corners, building areas, perimeters as well as building heights, etc., shaded view can be seen from Figure 2

1051-4651/00 $10.00 © 2000 IEEE

Figure 1. Optical image of the Ft. Benning MOUT testiste

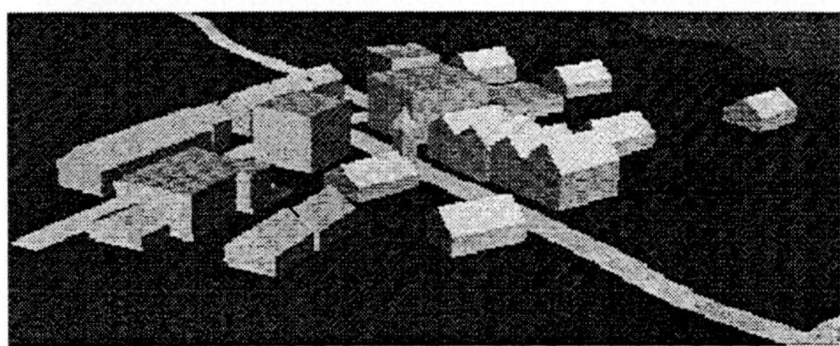

Figure 2. Shaded view of ground truth. Building elevations are typically 6 to 12 m.

3. Methods

To simplify the radar interpretation process, our first goal is to separate the buildings from the other objects in the imaged scene, e.g. trees, bushes, streets, grassland. As stated previously, each single data source is disturbed by speckle noise and in case of the steep slopes of buildings and trees especially by layover and shadow effects. These effects depend directly on the illumination direction, therefore a combination of the information gained from the four cardinal azimuth directions might help.

For the interferometric height data, shadow results in an area of no values facing away from the backslope of an object, and layover results in the so called "front porch" anomaly [2]. This effect appears as an extended region on the near-range side of an object that is characterized by altitudes in between the values on the ground and the values at the objects top.

Figure 3 shows from left to right four independents views of interferometric height data of two individual buildings from our testsite. The view dependence of layover and shadow effects can be seen. For the combination of these four independent views we used a simple maximum decision strategy as described in [1]. For each pixel in the scene, the maximum height value over all four measurements was chosen. Although due to the front porch effect this may result in larger building areas than actually given, this strategy makes the detection of even small buildings possible. The resulting fused height image of these two buildings can be seen from the right hand side of figure 3. These combined height measurements are still noisy, therefore a 3-by-3 median filter was applied after the maximum combination step.

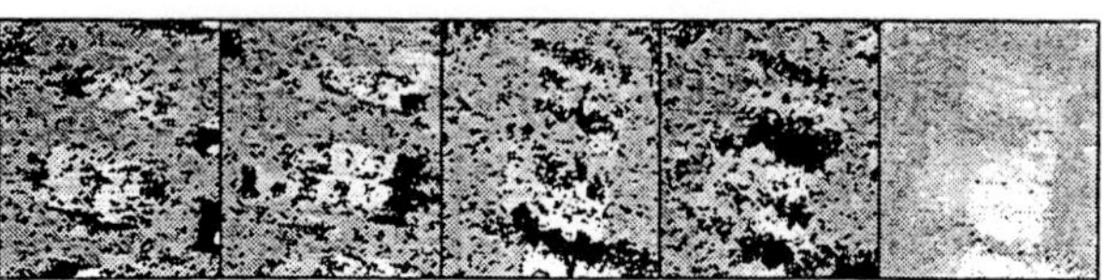

Figure 3. From left to right: interferometric height data for two buildings from four independent views and maximum combination of these four views. The area covers approximately 50 x 58 m^2.

From this enhanced height image a decision between bare earth and objects rising up from the bare earth can be drawn easily. A large area minimum filter was applied to extract the bare earth. The window width of the filter was larger than the largest object in the scene, in our case this was 15 by 15 pixels. Every pixel in the filtered image was assigned the minimum value from the surrounding window. Subtracting the resulting bare earth from the original height measures and applying a single threshold delivered a binary mask, where all objects rising up from the bare earth by more than the threshold were selected.

From these binary masks it is possible to calculate startpoints for regions of interest where buildings are supposed to be. Therefore several morphological erosions were applied to the binary mask. The resulting regions were labeled, and all regions exceeding a certain number of pixels were considered for further exploitation. The next step was to blow up these start regions to their original size and shape. Therefore the same number of morphological operations as before was performed on the start region, but this time the dilation operator was used and the resulting region was intersected with the original mask. Because in this first approach, we just want to fit simple building models, minimum bounding rectangles over the selected regions were calculated.

The differentiation between buildings and other objects rising up from the bare earth, e.g. trees, bushes, can not be drawn from the height measurements alone. Therefore during the height measurement combination step a corresponding combined coherency map was computed. For each position in the map, the coherency value corresponding to the selected height value was chosen. Texture measures were calculated in the selected region from the coherency and height information. Mean and standard deviation of the

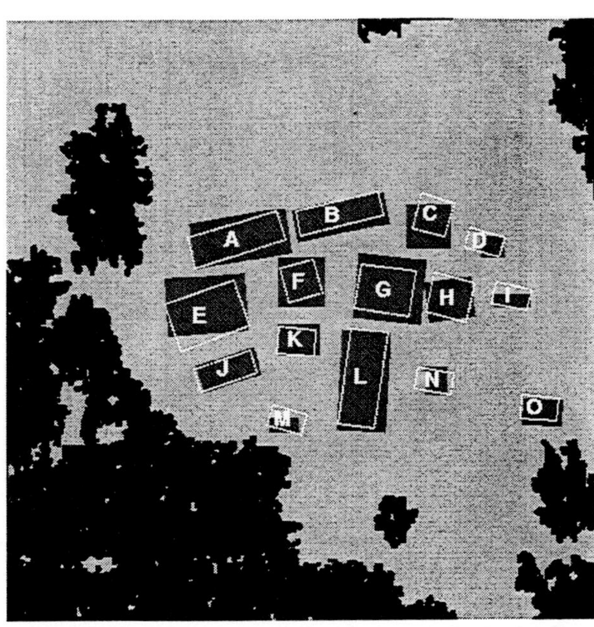

Figure 4. IFSAR segmentation result with overlaid building's footprints corresponding to the ground truth data. The area covers approximately 220 x 220 m^2.

coherency and height data first among the selected points and than over the whole minimum bounding rectangle were calculated. From these measurements a decision between buildings and other objects was possible. The mean coherency for buildings is usually superior to the vegetation mean coherency, the standard deviation of the height values is usually lower than for the vegetation, if calculated just on the segmented points. Due to the steep slopes of buildings the standard deviation of the height values for buildings increases significantly if calculated over the whole minimum bounding rectangle, compared to vegetation. Figure 4 shows the result of this simple segmentation process into three classes, bare earth, trees and buildings.

To improve the visual impression for the IFSAR image user we tried to fit simple building models over the segmented building areas. Two basic building models are flat roofed and symmetric gable roofed. Using all points within the minimum bounding rectangle we calculated a least squares plane fit. Then the rectangle was split up in the middle and planes were fit to each half, for both directions of the rectangle. The quadratic errors between actual height data and fitted plane were calculated for all planes, and the model with the overall minimum error was chosen. Figure 5 shows a shaded view of the resulting buildings.

Figure 5. Shaded view of extracted buildings.

4. Results

Ground truth data for the building models is available for the testsite. The footprints of the buildings extracted manually from the optical imagery are overlaid to the corresponding footprints of the buildings extracted automatically with our method from the IFSAR data as can be seen from the segmented image in Figure 4. In Table 1 the resulting centroid values of the buildings in offsets to UTM coordinates are compared to the ground truth measurements. Table 2 gives the resulting area and height measurements of our method and the corresponding ground truth data and resulting errors.

5. Discussion

The described segmentation method works quite well for the given dataset, although discrimination in just three classes will be not sufficient for some applications. The extracted building centers correspond quite well to the ground truth data, as can be seen from Table 1. The R.M.S. error of the shift vector is $\pm$ 2.18 m. The extracted areas, on the other hand, differ significantly from the actual buildings areas, as can be seen from Table 2. Small buildings are underestimated, larger buildings are overestimated. This is obviously a problem of the segmentation procedure of the noisy height measurements. Enhancements should be possible, by incorporating not just the height and coherence measurements but also the original slant range magnitude SAR images of the four independent views. Therefore the information from the slant range images has to be transformed to UTM coordinates.

The model fitting procedure delivered satisfactory results, too, as can be seen from the shaded view of the extracted buildings from Figure 5. The R.M.S. error for the maximum height of the extracted buildings lies below 1 meter, if the maximum error for the church (k) is excluded. The steeple of the church can not be covered by our simple models, the resulting gable roof for the church is tilted towards the steeple, as can be seen from the shaded view in Fig-

Bldg.	Cent. X		Cent. Y		
	optical	IFSAR	optical	IFSAR	error
A	489.983	491.681	621.318	621.290	1.70
B	526.127	526.834	629.862	628.605	1.44
C	559.093	557.518	629.054	625.121	4.24
D	577.152	580.073	619.899	618.242	3.36
E	479.750	479.692	595.179	598.735	3.56
F	512.775	513.017	606.923	606.457	0.53
G	542.010	543.903	603.641	603.815	1.90
H	565.001	565.239	601.150	600.157	1.02
I	586.376	586.778	601.554	599.751	1.85
J	486.183	487.617	576.224	576.383	1.44
K	510.991	512.204	586.255	586.746	1.31
L	534.218	534.759	573.632	572.319	1.42
M	507.844	506.921	559.444	557.485	2.16
N	559.497	560.362	572.521	572.319	0.89
O	596.087	597.345	563.282	561.549	2.14
RMS					2.18

Table 1. Extracted buildings center coordinates in offsets to UTM and the corresponding error in meters.

ure 5. One other building (L) corresponds not to our simple models, apart from these two exceptions just one building (F) was assigned a wrong model, a gable roof instead of a flat roof. So within the limits of the available three simple building models (flat roofed, gable roofed in two directions) the results are quite promising, especially because no manual interaction was needed during the extraction procedure.

6. Summary and Outlook

In this paper we have presented our first fully automated approach to building extraction from multiple view interferometric SAR datasets. By an intelligent combination of the different measurements available and applications of standard image analysis methods, a coarse segmentation into three classes was possible. To split this classification into more classes, the incorporation of original slant range magnitude images will be necessary.

The extracted building models fit quite well to the actual buildings, apart from the estimated building areas. Incorporation of original slant range magnitude images should help in this case as well. The building's back walls are defined in the slant range images by the shadows they cast, combining the shadow-edges from four independent views should give a better hint of the actual building dimensions. More complex building models should be incorporated by splitting the selected building areas into further planes.

Bldg.		Area			Hgt.	
	optical	SAR	error	opt.	SAR	err.
A	349.9	541.1	+191.1	8.8	7.9	-0.9
B	259.1	370.0	+110.9	8.9	10.0	+1.1
C	149.4	244.8	+95.4	7.4	7.0	-0.4
D	88.4	59.5	-28.9	6.2	6.9	+0.7
E	439.3	558.6	+119.3	7.0	6.0	-1.0
F	147.4	277.5	+130.1	7.4	7.6	+0.2
G	297.1	535.8	+238.7	11.0	9.2	-1.8
H	201.9	230.0	+28.1	3.7	4.3	+0.6
I	90.4	56.3	-34.1	6.2	6.4	+0.2
J	166.1	206.1	+40.0	6.1	4.1	-2.0
K	117.6	160.5	+42.9	12.1	7.5	-4.6
L	426.9	589.5	+162.6	9.4	10.2	+0.8
M	92.9	55.8	-37.1	6.1	5.2	-0.9
N	94.1	75.3	-18.8	6.1	5.1	-1.0
O	102.5	123.4	+20.9	6.1	4.8	-1.3
RMS			±109.6			±1.6

Table 2. Extracted buildings area and height measurements compared to ground truth data. The building areas are given in square meters, the height data in meters.

Acknowledgements

We wish to thank SANDIA for the IFSAR data and Bob Wilson from Vexcel Corporation, Boulder, for the ground truth data.

References

[1] R. Bolter and F. Leberl. Phenomenology-Based and Interferometry-Guided Building Reconstruction from Multiple SAR Images. In *Proceedings of EUSAR*, 2000.

[2] G. Burkhart, Z. Bergen, and R. Carande. Elevation Correction and Building Extraction from Interferometric SAR Imagery. In *Proceedings of IGARSS'96*, pages 659–661, 1996.

[3] P. Gamba, B. Houshmand, and M. Saccani. Detection and Extraction of Buildings from Interferometric SAR Data. *IEEE T-GRS*, 38(1):611–618, January 2000.

[4] A. Gruen, O. Kuebler, and P. Agouris, editors. *Automatic Extraction of Man-Made Objects from Aerial and Space Images*. Birkhäuser Verlag, 1995.

[5] K. Hoepfner, A. Hanson, and E. Riseman. Recovery of Building Structure from SAR and IFSAR Images. In *ARPA Image Understanding Workshop*, pages 559–563, 1998.

[6] F. Leberl, R. Kalliany, and M. Gruber, editors. *Mapping Buildings, Roads and other Man-Made Structures from Images*. Proceedings of the IAPR TC-7 Workshop "Remote Sensing and Mapping", R. Oldenburg, Wien, 1997.

[7] R. Xiao, C. Lesher, and B. Wilson. Building Detection and Localization Using a Fusion of Interferometric Synthetic Aperture Radar and Multispectral image. In *ARPA Image Understanding Workshop*, pages 583–588, 1998.

Fusing 3D information for crop / weeds classification*

A.J. Sáchez and J.A. Marchant
Universidad Politénica de Valencia ; Silsoe Research Institute
asanchez@aii.upv.es ; john.marchant@bbsrc.ac.uk

Abstract

The main goal of this work is to construct a 3D-world map to help to distinguish between crop and weeds and finally to permit the location of crop and weeds to apply a variable treatment. To solve the problem of recovering a 3D-local map, we use a motion technique with the possibility of changing zoom. Every independent local map will be fused into the world map.

The crop/weeds classification will eventually be performed using the height of the plants among other features like position, texture, shape, etc.

Keywords: *3D reconstruction, active vision, motion, zoom, data fusion, classification.*

1. Introduction

Perception is not a goal in itself, but a means to obtain certain behaviour by an agent. In order to plan and execute actions, an agent must have a description of the environment. Perception is the process of maintaining an internal description of the external environment.

The external environment is that part of the universe which is accessible to the sensors of an agent at an instant in time. In theory, it would seem possible to use the environment itself as the internal model. In practice, this requires an extremely complete and rapid sensing ability.

The main goal of this work is to construct a 3D-world map, which helps the crop and weeds classification using the height like a feature and permits to easily get a 3D-world map of crop and weeds to apply a variable spraying treatment.

1.1. Problem description

The main problem consists of recovering 3D information from a sequence of images acquired with one monochrome camera mounted on an autonomous guided vehicle [9, 3]. To solve this problem of 3D recovery, we use a motion technique with the possibility of changing zoom. Finally, every local map is fused into the 3D-world map.

An error function for depth recovery is derived to perform fusion. This error function permits us to estimate the uncertainty of depth recovery.

Another important problem is to find stable features in the agricultural environment where we are working, due to the natural objects and the natural light conditions.

1.2. Previous work

A considerable amount of work has been aimed at combining a few methods to make a flexible and robust depth recovery system. Abbott & Ahuja [1], designed and implemented a system integrating depth from camera vergence, stereo and focus. Das & Ahuja [5], constructed a system integrating stereo and focus. Grosso et. al. [6], integrated motion and stereo.

The advances in sensor fusion from within the vision community have largely applied via the robotics community. Some review works of the problem of data fusion are [4], [7] and [2].

2. Framework for 3D recovery

This section begins with a description of the framework for 3D-world modelling before classification.

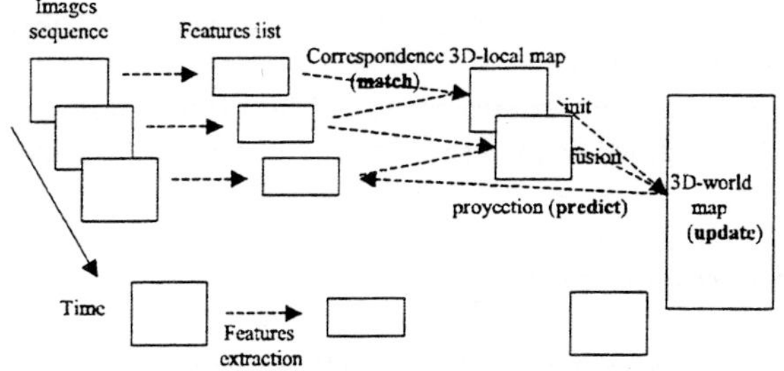

Figure 2.1. Framework for 3D recovery.

In this framework (Fig. 2.1), every image in the sequence undergoes a feature extraction process, which

* This work has been sponsored by FEDER TAP Spanish programme, project n° 1FD97-2158-C04-03.

generates a list of features. After that, the correspondence process will return a local map using a pair of features from the list and the 3D-world map.

To solve the problem of 3D recovery in a local map, we will use a motion technique with the possibility of changing zoom.

Every local map is an independent observation of the world. They are transformed into a common coordinate space and are fused into the 3D-world map by a cyclic process composed of three phases: **Predict**, **Match** and **Update**.

3. Feature extraction with natural objects

In the environment where we are working it is difficult to find stable features due to: discrete images; natural light conditions; natural objects with smooth surfaces, where the edges depend on the camera point of view; and object motion because of the wind.

The adopted solution consists of defining the features like pixels on the image with a Gauss-filtered gradient (Fig. 3.1) with a finite size in the camera direction. So, the gradient decreases the effect of changing illumination conditions and the Gauss-filter decreases the effect of the discrete images.

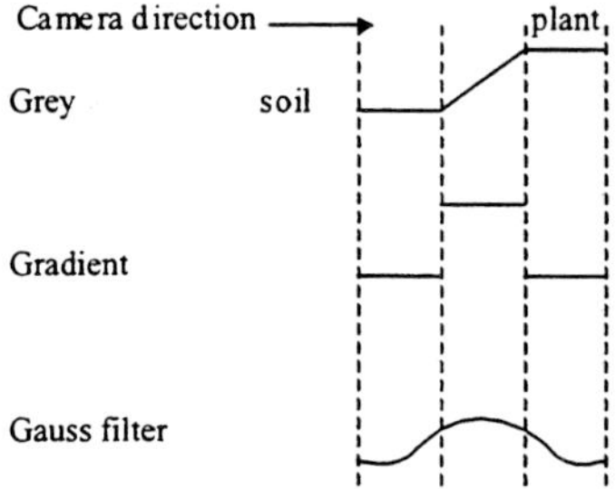

Figure 3.1. Gauss-filtered gradient function.

The third and fourth problems are avoided by increasing the image acquisition frequency and rejecting the correspondences which do not accord with the epipolar restriction.

All the image features are stored in a list of features $(x_b, y_b)^t$ defined with respect to the camera coordinate system.

4. Correspondence

If you use a high acquisition image frequency to get more stable features, you will recover a worse depth estimation because of a smaller disparity (Δr). So, it is convenient to calculate the depth estimation between images far apart. One solution to this compromise point, is feature tracking on high acquisition frequency and depth estimation with a lower frequency. Another solution is zooming that causes a disparity increase.

If the feature we want to correspond has a high uncertainty, we search for the corresponding feature taking into account the epipolar and geometrical restrictions. But, if this feature has a lower uncertainty, we search for the corresponding feature near the projection of the 3D estimation stored in the 3D world-map (**prediction**).

In the former case, for each feature in the list $(xu_b, yu_b)^t$ we search for the correspondence in a subset of the feature list $(xu_n, yu_n)^t$ which accomplishes:

1.- The geometrical restriction:

$$\Delta r_{min} \leq \Delta r \leq \Delta r_{max}$$

2.- And the epipolar restriction:

$$\left\{ \begin{array}{ll} xu_n \approx \dfrac{xu_b}{yu_b}\left(yu_n + \dfrac{ty_2}{tz_2} f_2 \right); & tz_2 \neq 0.0 \\ xu_n \approx xu_b; & tz_2 = 0.0 \end{array} \right\}$$

In the subset of features, we choose the $(xu_n, yu_n)^t$ which maximises the correlation of a neighbourhood window between the gauss-filter gradient images [$g_b(x,y)$, $g_n(x,y)$] and the original images [$o_b(x,y)$, $o_n(x,y)$] (**matching**).

The correspondence uncertainty is measured using the first maximum correlation and the difference with the second maximum correlation (Fig. 4.1).

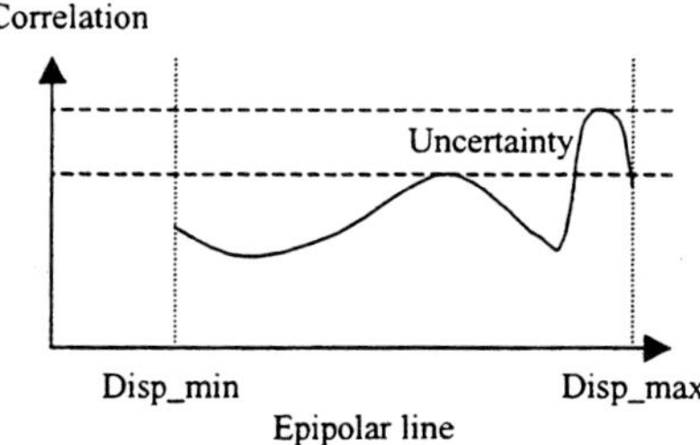

Figure 4.1. Correlation function on the epipolar line.

5. Depth estimation

The images are acquired with one monochrome camera with a variable zoom objective mounted on an autonomous guided vehicle. The camera motion on a "static" scene produces a disparity map, which depends on the camera motion and the scene geometry. So, if we know the camera motion, we can use the disparity map to calculate the scene geometry.

The next figure (Fig. 5.1) shows the 3D-reconstruction problem, where we take into account the possibility of a zoom change ($f_1 \neq f_2$) in motion.

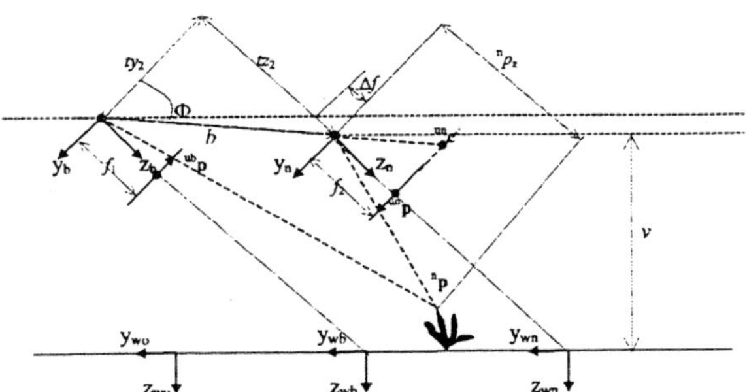

Figure 5.1. 3D reconstruction problem.

The disparity (Δr) is defined as:

$$m = \frac{f_1}{f_2}\,;\ \Delta r = (m \cdot yu_n - yu_b)$$

where $xu_b = {}^{ub}p_x;\ yu_b = {}^{ub}p_y;\ xu_n = {}^{un}p_x;\ yu_n = {}^{un}p_y$

The camera motion is defined by the translations:

$$tx_2 = 0.0\,;\ ty_2 = b \cdot \cos(\phi)\,;\ tz_2 = b \cdot \sin(\phi)\,;$$

So, the depth estimation can be calculated:

$$\left\{\begin{matrix} {}^{n}p_z = \dfrac{(tz_2 \cdot yu_b) + (ty_2 \cdot f_1)}{\Delta r}; & \Delta r \neq 0.0 \\ {}^{n}p_z = {}^{n}T_{wn} \cdot v; & \Delta r = 0.0 \end{matrix}\right\}$$

The depth estimation uncertainty E_z can be estimated:

$$E_z \approx |\partial Z_b| + |\partial Z_{f_1}| + |\partial Z_{\Delta r}|$$

Assuming Φ is known and the disparity $\Delta r = (m \cdot yu_n - yu_b)$ is an independent variable.

$$\partial Z_b = \frac{\partial b}{b} z\,;\quad \partial Z_{f_1} = \frac{\left(1 - \dfrac{tz_2 \cdot yu_b}{z\Delta r}\right)\partial f_1}{f_1} z\,;\quad \partial Z_{\Delta r} = -\frac{\partial \Delta r}{\Delta r} z\,;$$

where $z = {}^{n}p_z$

$$E_z \approx \left(\left|\frac{\partial b}{b}\right| + \left|\frac{\left(1 - \dfrac{tz_2 \cdot yu_b}{z\Delta r}\right)\partial f_1}{f_1}\right| + \left|\frac{\partial \Delta r}{\Delta r}\right| \right) \cdot z$$

6. Fusion

If a feature can find a correspondence in the next image, the information of the depth estimation is stored in the next feature list. The first estimation will be (${}^{b}p_z$, ${}^{b}E_z$) = (0,∞) and after it will be updated fusing the new estimation (${}^{n}p_z$, ${}^{n}E_z$) with the previous one (${}^{b}p_z$, ${}^{b}E_z$) using probabilistic analysis:

$${}^{b}p_z = z_1\,;\ {}^{b}E_z = \sigma_1\,;\ {}^{n}p_z = z_2\,;\ {}^{n}E_z = \sigma_2\,;$$

$$p_{joint}(z) = \frac{k}{2.0 \cdot \Pi \cdot \sigma_1 \cdot \sigma_2} \cdot e^{\left(\frac{-(z-z_1)^2}{2.0\sigma_1^2}\right)} \cdot e^{\left(\frac{-(z-z_2)^2}{2.0\sigma_2^2}\right)}$$

The maximum likelihood estimation is:

$${}^{b}p_z = \frac{z_1\sigma_2^2 + z_2\sigma_1^2}{\sigma_1^2 + \sigma_2^2}\,;\ {}^{b}E_z = {}^{b}p_z \frac{\sigma_1\sigma_2}{\sqrt{z_1^2\sigma_2^2 + z_2^2\sigma_1^2}}\,;$$

When a feature cannot find a correspondence, we generate a new point in the 3D-world map, storing (${}^{wo}p_x$, ${}^{wo}E_x$, ${}^{wo}p_y$, ${}^{wo}E_y$, ${}^{wo}p_z$, ${}^{wo}E_z$) with respect to 3d-world coordinate system.

$${}^{b}p_x = \frac{{}^{b}p_z \cdot xu_b}{f_1}\,;\ {}^{b}p_y = \frac{{}^{b}p_z \cdot yu_b}{f_1}$$

The uncertainty E_x y E_y, will be:

$$E_x \approx |\partial X_z| + |\partial X_{xub}| + |\partial X_{f_1}|\,;\ E_y \approx |\partial Y_z| + |\partial Y_{yub}| + |\partial Y_{f_1}|$$

$$\delta X_z = \frac{\partial z}{z} x\,;\ \delta X_{xu_b} = \frac{\partial xu_b}{xu_b} x\,;\ \delta X_{f_1} = \frac{\partial f_1}{f_1} x$$

$$\delta Y_z = \frac{\partial z}{z} y\,;\ \delta Y_{yu_b} = \frac{\partial yu_b}{yu_b} y\,;\ \delta Y_{f_1} = \frac{\partial f_1}{f_1} y$$

$$E_x = \left(\left|\frac{\partial z}{z}\right| + \left|\frac{\partial xu_b}{xu_b}\right| + \left|\frac{\delta f_1}{f_1}\right| \right) \cdot x\,;\ E_y = \left(\left|\frac{\partial z}{z}\right| + \left|\frac{\partial yu_b}{yu_b}\right| + \left|\frac{\delta f_1}{f_1}\right| \right) \cdot y$$

${}^{wo}\mathbf{p} = {}^{wo}\mathbf{T}_o\,{}^{o}\mathbf{T}_b\,{}^{b}\mathbf{p}$; with respect the 3D-world (**Update**)

7. Crop/weed classification

The crop is usually higher than weeds in the spraying season. This fact permits us to use the height of the plants as one of the features in crop/weeds classification (Fig. 7.1). Other possible features are position, texture, shape, etc [3, 8].

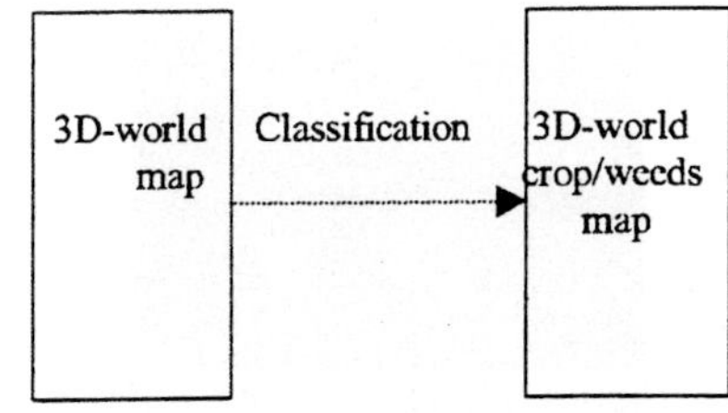

Figure 7.1. Crop/weeds classification.

8. Experiments and results

Figure 8.1 shows an image sequence acquired in lab conditions. The process results in a 3D local map for every image pair and fuses the 3D information on a 3D-world map using the uncertainty information. The height information is coded by grey intensity on the image maps.

The image 8.1 (b) shows only the plants higher than 150 mm.

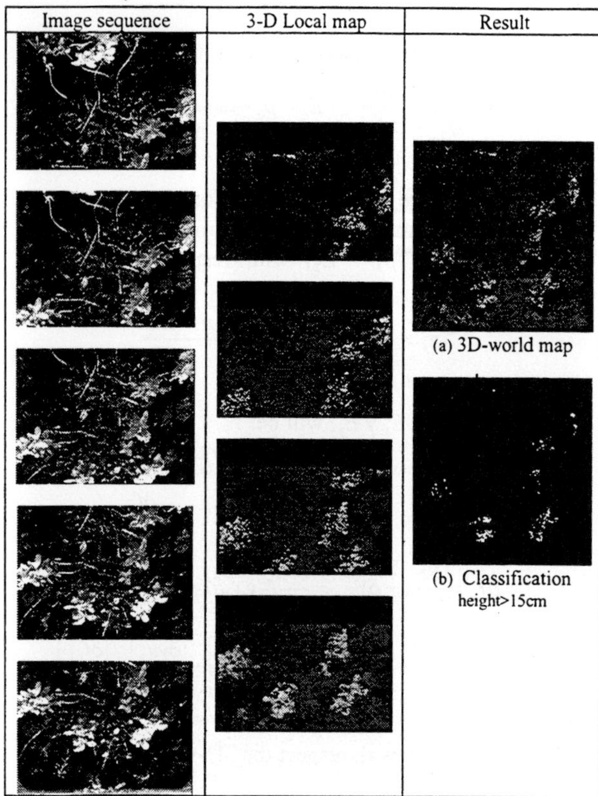

Figure 8.1. Result.

Figure 8.2 shows the maximum plant height in millimeters on the 3D-world map.

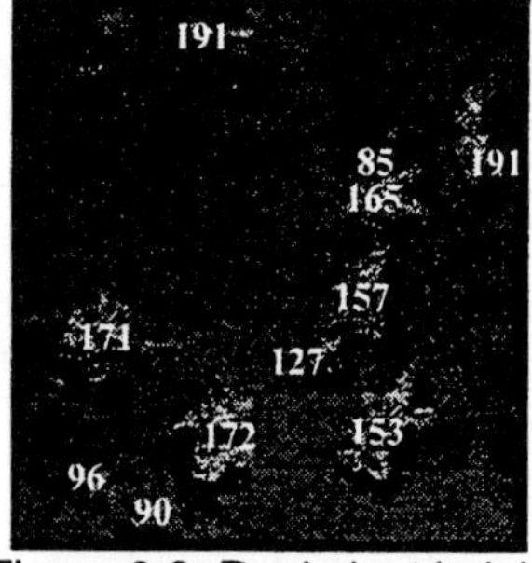

Figure 8.2. Real plant height.

Conclusions

1. It is difficult to select stable features in our environment. We can smooth the image to eliminate the discrete effect or we can use features like edges in the camera direction to reduce the effect of changing light conditions.

2. One problem in object recognition is the resolution of the object in the picture. To solve this problem, it is very interesting to permit the possibility to change zoom. Another reason to introduce variable zoom is because the depth estimation uncertainty depends on it. We have implemented a method to estimate 3D information from motion taking into account zoom.

3. Data fusion is important to reduce the depth estimation uncertainty. We have estimated uncertainty of depth estimation to permit fusion of local 3D maps.

4. It is possible to extract 3D information from a camera in motion to help crop/weeds classification.

References

[1] A. L. Abbott and N. Ahuja. *"Surface reconstruction by dynamic integration of focus, camera vergence, and stero"*. Proc. on Second International Conference on Computer Vision, IEEE Computer Press, pp. 532-543, (1988).

[2] I. Bloch. *"Information combination operators for data fusion: A comparative review with classification"*. IEEE Transaction on systems, Man and Cybernetics 26-1 (1996) pp 52-67.

[3] R. Brivot and J.A. Marchant. *"Segmentation of plants and weeds for a precision crop protection robot using infrared images"*. Proc. I.E.E, Vision, Image, and Signal Processing 143-2 (1996) pp118-124

[4] J. L. Crowley and Y. Demazeau. *"Principles and techniques for sensor data fusion"*. Signal Processing Elsevier 32 (1993) 5-27 pp 5-27.

[5] S. Das and N. Ahuja. *"Integrating multiresolution image acquisition and cooarse-to-fine surface reconstructuion from stereo"*. Proc. on Workshop on Interpretation of 3D Scenes, IEEE ComputerSociety Press, pp. 9-15, (1989).

[6] E. Grosso, G. Sandini and M. Tistarelli. *"3-D object recognition using stereo and motion"*. IEEE Transaction on systems, Man and Cybernetics 19-6 (1989) pp 1465-1476.

[7] M. Kokar and K. Kim. *"Preface to the special section on data fusion: architectures and issues"*. Control Eng. Practice 2-5 (1994) pp 803-809.

[8] E. Molto, J. Blasco, N. Aleixos, J. Carrion and F. Juste. *"Machine vision discrimination of weeds in horticultural* Paper No. 96G-037, AgEng96, European Society of Agricultural Engineers, 23rd-26th Sept 1998 Madrid.

[9] N.D Tillett, T. Hague, and J.A. Marchant. *"A robotic system for plant scale husbandry"*. J. agric. Engng Res 69-2 (1998) pp169-178.

Pattern Recognition of Radar Echoes for Short-range Rainfall Forecast

Edwin S.T. Lai, P.W. Li
Hong Kong Observatory, 134A Nathan Road, Kowloon, Hong Kong
stlai@hko.gcn.gov.hk
C.M. Chan, M.C. Chu, W.H. Wong
Department of Physics, The Chinese University of Hong Kong, Shatin, Hong Kong

Abstract

A four-layer feed-forward back-propagation Artificial Neural Network (ANN) is applied to weather radar echo maps of reflectivity data for the prediction of heavy rainfall events in the short-range of 1 to 2 hours. Inputs for the ANN are the cross correlations of statistical measures of a sequence of radar images. The ANN is trained to capture increasingly organized echo patterns that often are preludes to localized heavy rain. Results show that the ANN is able to achieve a success rate of 89% against a false alarm rate of 33%.

In parallel, a separate module utilizing Hough transform is developed to depict the lining up of echoes on the reflectivity maps. The module provides an objective analysis tool for forecasters to test the hypothesis that crossing or merging of echo lines, the so-called "X" patterns, would lead to enhanced convection at preferred locations.

Working in tandem, the ANN helps to isolate specific sectors on the radar maps where organization is taking place so that the Hough Transform Module (HTM) can be meaningfully applied in the appropriate target areas. In turn, parameters derived from the HTM, along with the standard statistical measures, can be fed back into the ANN for further training and system enhancement in the identification of "X" patterns.

1. Introduction

At the Hong Kong Observatory, automated radar image analysis is a crucial component in the development of a short range forecasting system for the prediction of rainstorms (i.e. SWIRLS – Short-range Warning of Intense Rainstorms in Localized Systems). By far, weather radar is still the most practical and reliable observational platform for monitoring rain clouds that have spatial resolution of several kilometres and a life span in the order of minutes. Data from the radar scan are processed and displayed for forecasters' reference every six minutes.

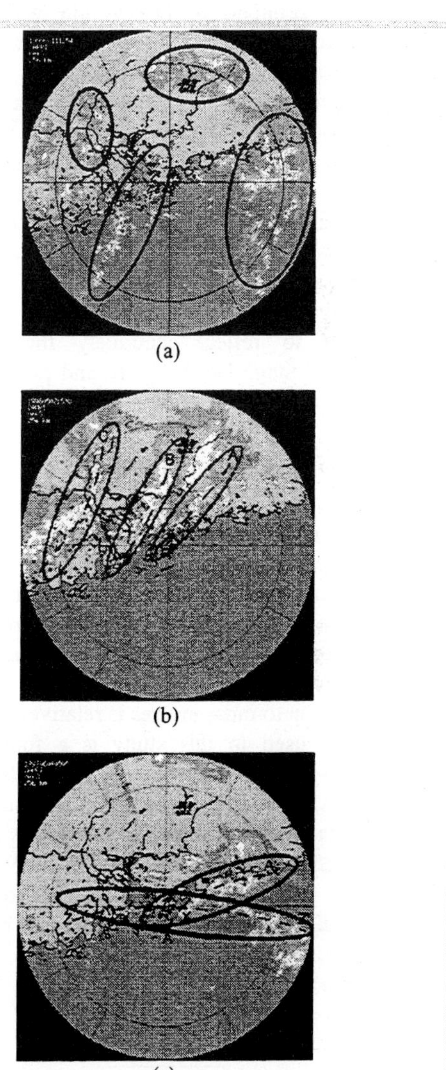

(a)

(b)

(c)

Figure 1 - Schematics of rainstorm evolutionary process: (a) Stage I - scattered and disjointed echoes; (b) Stage II - organized echo bands; (c) Stage III - crossing or merging of echo lines.

1051-4651/00 $10.00 © 2000 IEEE

As intense convection tends to develop explosively, the forecasters have to keep a close watch on the radar monitors while at the same time assimilating weather information from other sources and attending to forecast formulation and warning procedures. If what transpires on the radar screen can be automatically and objectively analyzed, the forecasters will be in a better position to assess accurately and respond quickly as the rainstorm event unfolds. From forecasters' experience, isolated, scattered, unconnected and disjointed radar echoes (Stage I in Figure 1) that move along nicely with the prevailing flow will not pose a serious threat in terms of excessive rain. The likelihood of heavy rain will increase if convective activity persists or re-generates at preferred locations, or is lined up and advected along a corridor of sustained development. The detailed patterns may differ from case to case in a variety of ways; but in general the trend of increasing organization is unmistakable (Stage II of Figure 1). Occasionally, the forecasters may recognize the emergence of the "X" pattern signature in which lines of echoes cross or merge and convection becomes enhanced near the intersecting point (Stage III in Figure 1). The challenge for any automated pattern recognition algorithm is to reflect accurately the evolutionary processes from Stage I to Stage II, and possibly to Stage III as well, before degenerating back to Stage I.

2. The Artificial Neural Network

Artificial neural networks (ANNs) are known to be useful in pattern recognition. The application of ANN in operational meteorology has met with some degree of success in the classification of cloud systems on satellite images, for examples [1, 2, 3, 4]. Similar approaches have been attempted in Hong Kong [5] but experience in ANN application to radar images is relatively limited.

The ANN used in this study is a four-layer feed-forward back-propagation type. There are altogether four input neurons, two hidden layers and one output neuron. The output status of the ANN is either positive or negative in terms of echo organization. Following Weszka et al. [6], we use the lowest four moments of the radar reflectivity distribution to characterize a radar image. They are the mean m, standard deviation s, skewness s, and kurtosis k:

$$m \equiv \frac{1}{N}\sum_{i=1}^{N} z_i,$$

$$d \equiv \sqrt{\frac{1}{N}\sum_{i=1}^{N}(z_i - m)^2},$$

$$s \equiv \frac{1}{N}\sum_{i=1}^{N}\left(\frac{z_i - m}{d}\right)^3,$$

$$k \equiv \frac{1}{N}\sum_{i=1}^{N}\left(\frac{z_i - m}{d}\right)^4,$$

where z_i is the radar reflectivity at the ith pixel, and N is the total number of pixels in the image. The size of the radar images used in this study is $N = 480 \times 480$ pixels.

The above moments characterize the spatial distribution of radar reflectivity on a given radar map at a given moment. The mean and standard deviation indicate echo intensity and the degree of concentration respectively. The skewness and kurtosis characterize the deviations from a Gaussian distribution, reflecting to some degree the organization of radar echoes. In Figure 2, the four moments in a typical rainstorm development scenario are plotted as functions of time. As the echoes become organized, the mean and standard deviation generally rise while the skewness and kurtosis drop. Armed with this knowledge, we compute the temporal correlations among the four moments. As input identifiers for the ANN, four cross-correlations out of the six possible combinations formed from the set $\{m, d, s, k\}$ are used, namely:

$$C_{md} \equiv \frac{1}{N_t \sigma_m \sigma_d}\sum_{j=1}^{N_t}(m_j - \bar{m})(d_j - \bar{d}),$$

$$C_{ds} \equiv \frac{1}{N_t \sigma_d \sigma_s}\sum_{j=1}^{N_t}(d_j - \bar{d})(s_j - \bar{s}),$$

$$C_{sk} \equiv \frac{1}{N_t \sigma_s \sigma_k}\sum_{j=1}^{N_t}(s_j - \bar{s})(k_j - \bar{k}),$$

$$C_{km} \equiv \frac{1}{N_t \sigma_k \sigma_m}\sum_{j=1}^{N_t}(k_j - \bar{k})(m_j - \bar{m}).$$

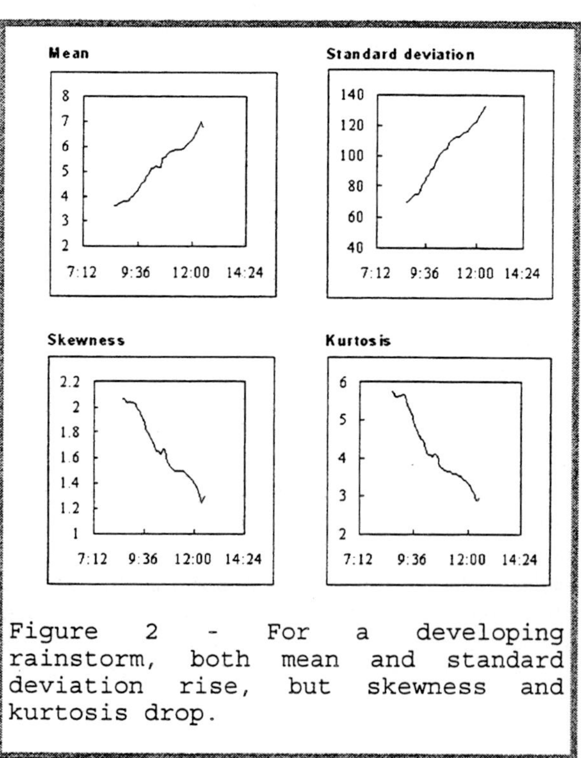

Figure 2 - For a developing rainstorm, both mean and standard deviation rise, but skewness and kurtosis drop.

Here, j labels the time-ordered radar maps, running from 1 to N_t, the number of consecutive radar images used (with radar images coming in every six minutes, we take $N_t = 5$ to look for half-hourly trend); $\overline{m}$, $\overline{d}$, $\overline{s}$, $\overline{k}$ are respectively the means of m, d, s, k over N_t images; and σ_i is the standard deviation of the moment $i = m, d, s, k$, e.g.

$$\sigma_m = \sqrt{\frac{1}{N_t}\sum_{j=1}^{N_t}(m_j - \overline{m})^2}\ .$$

Note that the cross-correlations $\{C_{md}, C_{ds}, C_{sk}, C_{km}\}$ as defined above take on values ranging from −1 to 1.

In practice, a z_i threshold of $30dBZ$ is imposed to isolate and highlight the significant pattern. Radar pixels with $z_i < 30dBZ$ are discarded. To gain more spatial information, the radar image is divided into 25 (5 x 5) equal-sized boxes. Input identifiers computed for each box will be fed to the ANN except for boxes with m not rising monotonically throughout the 5-image radar sequence.

The output neuron produces a number A between 0 and 1. In the present study, we take $A \geq 0.75$ as positive and $A \leq 0.25$ as negative. In the training set, there are altogether 20 rain events from the rainy seasons of 1997 and 1998, in which 12 show increasing organization and lead to heavy rain, and the remaining 8 weakening and bringing only light to moderate rain. For each event, a sequence of five consecutive radar images is extracted for ANN training. Starting from a set of random network parameters, the ANN is updated repeatedly according to the error back-propagation algorithm until the total error for the 20 cases drop below 0.2. All cases in the training set are correctly classified as either positive or negative by the ANN. The ANN is tested using six 5-image radar sequences taken from the same rainy seasons but outside the training set.

The test results are tabulated in Table 1. On the first column are the dates and times of the last radar image in each sequence indicated as "yymmddhhmm" (year/month/day/hour/minute). ANN outputs for all 25 boxes are displayed in the second column. Boxes failing to meet the pre-condition and hence receiving no ANN output are marked with an "X". "P" means positive, i.e. $A \geq 0.75$; "N" means negative, i.e. $A \leq 0.25$. On the third column, verifications by human subjective judgment are represented by similar notations of "P" and "N" for positive and negative classifications respectively. The notations in the fourth column have the following meanings:

PP = positive in both ANN and human assessment;
PN = positive in ANN but negative by human;
NP = negative in ANN but positive by human;
NN = negative in both ANN and human assessment.

Table 1 - Test results of the ANN on six rainstorm cases.

yymmddhhmm	ANN outputs	Human judgment	PP	PN	NP	NN
9704301330	X X P X X	X X N X X		1		
	N N X X X	N N X X X				2
	X X P X X	X X P X X	1			
	X P X X X	X P X X X	1			
	X X X X X	X X X X X				
9704301406	X X X X X	X X X X X				
	X P P X X	X N P X X	1	1		
	X X X X X	X X X X X				
	X P X X X	X P X X X	1			
	X X X X X	X X X X X				
9706140306	X X X N X	X X X N X				1
	X X X X X	X X X X X				
	X X N N X	X X N N X				2
	P N N N P	N N N N N		2		3
	X X X X X	X X X X X				
9706140230	X X X N X	X X X N X				1
	X X X X X	X X X X X				
	X N X P X	X N X P X	1			1
	X P N N X	X P N N X	1			2
	X X X X X	X X X X X				
9805021506	X X X X X	X X X X X				
	N X X N X	N X X N X				2
	N X P X X	N X P X X	1			1
	X X X X X	X X X X X				
	X X X X X	X X X X X				
9805021542	X N X N X	X N X N X				2
	X P X N X	X P X N X	1			1
	N X N X X	N X N X X				2
	X X X X X	X X X X X				
	X X X X X	X X X X X				
		Total:	8	4	0	20

From Table 1, skill scores in terms of NAP (No Alarm Probability), FAR (False Alarm Rate), CSI (Critical Success Index) and HSI (Heidke Skill Index) are computed:

NAP = NP / (PP+NP) = 0
FAR = PN / (PP+PN) = 0.33
CSI = PP / (PP+PN+NP) = 0.67
HSI = [(PP+NN)-R] / [(PP+PN+NP+NN)-R] = 0.71;

where R, random forecast, is given by

R = [(PP+PN)x(PP+NP)+(NP+NN)x(PN+NN)] / S; and
S = PP+PN+NP+NN.

Good performance is characterized by low NAP and FAR but high CSI and HSI. For the test cases, NAP is found to be very good as no significant events have been missed. FAR is not bad but can be better. Both CSI and HSI are considered to be reasonable, with positive values in the latter meaning that ANN out-performs the low-skill random forecast.

3. The Hough Transform Module

By Stage III, the radar echoes are organized in such ways that they tend to congregate into rainbands. Convective patterns associated with many severe weather systems, such as tropical cyclones, warm or cold fronts, and squall lines, all have banding features that on the scale of the radar images can be approximated into straight lines. Hough transform has been recognized as one of the more efficient algorithms for identifying linear patterns on 2-dimensional images [7]. It has nice properties such as: (i) fast – computation time increases only linearly instead of quadratically with the number of pixels; (ii) high degree of tolerance – the line width, angular resolution and brokenness can be specified arbitrarily; (iii) flexible – the region of interest can be specified at any location inside the image.

In this study, the Hough transform module (HTM) is so designed to facilitate operational and research development. To highlight the prominent features on the radar images, echoes on the transformed space are multiplied by a weighting factor which is proportional to the respective pixel intensity value, i.e., z_i^{α}, and α is arbitrarily set to be 3. The region of interest is movable rather than fixed at the centre of the radar image. Once the centre and range are specified, the HTM will search for echo lines within the specified region of interest and ignores pixels outside. This serves to overcome the scaling problem and users can then zoom in on specific rain systems, be it local scale features of tens of kilometres in length or mesoscale features stretching to hundreds of kilometres. In fact, through a graphical user interface, users can adjust the parameters to optimize the line identification processes.

4. Concluding Remarks

Both ANN and HTM have shown initial promises in depicting the evolution of rainstorms, the former in terms of echo organization and the latter in the lining up of echoes. Training of the ANN will be a continuous process, and in time the system should become even more robust and resilient. HTM's application in operational forecasting will require further parameter-tuning, e.g. threshold setting, line attributes, etc., for optimization and customization purposes.

An effective way of combining ANN and HTM in rainstorm detection will be further explored. Figure 3 is an example of what can be done: through ANN, an area of positive echo organization is highlighted; and HTM is then applied to the highlighted area for identification of linear patterns. A more focussed approach is not simply a matter of saving computation time; it also draws forecasters' attention to the main area of activity and keeps track of the evolving pattern between successive images.

But ultimately, we hope to make better use of ANN and HTM for short-term prediction of enhanced convection in association with the notorious "X" pattern. Echo growth and decay for the purpose of quantitative precipitation forecast is still an area of active research in the SWIRLS development programme. By integrating ANN and HTM into a reliable objective tool in "X" pattern identification, rainfall enhancement with respect to the signature pattern can then be systematically analyzed and studied. If the popular hypotheses nominally linked with the so-called "X" pattern can be confirmed and suitably quantified, a positive impact on the rainfall forecast algorithm would logically follow.

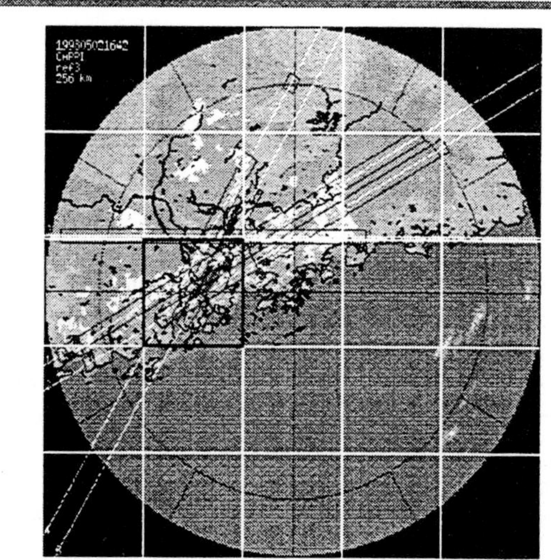

Figure 3 - Typical output from the combined ANN and HTM. Radar echoes appear to be merging within the highlighted section to the left of the central box.

5. References

[1] Kay, J., J.A. Maslanik and A.J. Schweiger, "Classification of merged AVHRR and SMMR Arctic data with neural networks", *Photogramm. Eng. Remote Sens.*, **55**, 1989, pp. 1331-1338.

[2] Lee, J., R.C. Weger, S.K. Sengupta and R.M. Welch, "A neural network approach to cloud classification", *IEEE Trans. on Geosci. and Remote Sensing*, **28**, 1990, pp.846-855.

[3] Lee, V.C.S., S.L. Hung, A.Y.S. Cheng, C.Y. Lam and C.M.Tam, "An operational cloud classifier for satellite images", *Proceedings of the 2nd International Conference on East Asia and Western Pacific Meteorology and Climate*, 1992, pp.480-487.

[4] Welch, R.M., S.K. Sengupta, A.K.P. Rabindra, N. Rangaraj and M.S. Xvar, "Polar cloud and surface classification using AVHRR imagery: and intercomparison of methods", *J. Appl. Meteorol.*, **31**, 1992, pp.405-420.

[5] Pankiewicz, G.S., "Pattern recognition techniques for the identification of cloud and cloud systems," *Meteorol. Application*, **2**, 1995, pp.257-271.

[6] Weszka, J.S., C.R. Dyer and A. Rosenfeld, *IEEE Trans. Syst. Man. Cybern.* SMC-6, 1976, pp.269-285.

[7] Duda, R.O. and P.E. Hart, "Use of Hough transform to detect lines and curves in pictures", *Comm. of ACM*, **15**, 1972, pp.11-15.

Registration of highly-oblique and zoomed in aerial video to reference imagery

Rakesh Kumar, Supun Samarasekera, Steve Hsu, Keith Hanna
Sarnoff Corporation, 201 Washington Road, Princeton, NJ-08543
Email: rkumar@sarnoff.com

Abstract

In this paper, we present methods for estimating precise geo-coordinates of objects observed in highly oblique video from an airborne camera in real time. High precision is achieved by registering observed video frames in real time to rendered views of the scene using stored reference imagery. The reference imagery includes previously collected satellite images and terrain maps that have been precisely aligned to geo-coordinates. We present methods that work for both nadir and highly oblique video imagery and under a variety of conditions where any one frame may not have enough information for accurate geo-registration.

1. Introduction

Aerial video is rapidly emerging as a low cost, widely used source of imagery for surveillance, monitoring and targeting applications. However, there remains a key technical problem in the use of video from moving vehicles: determining how the locations of objects in a video display relate to the geographic locations of these objects on the real world [Kanade98]. This mapping between camera coordinates and ground coordinates, called geo-spatial registration, depends both on the location and orientation of the camera and on the distance and topography of the ground. Camera location continuously changes as the airborne camera moves. Rough geo-spatial registration can be derived from camera telemetry data (GPS location of the aircraft and orientation of the camera) and digital terrain map data (from a database). Higher precision is achieved by registering observed video frames in real time to stored reference imagery. Applications of geo-spatial registration include aerial mapping, target location and tracking, and enhanced visualization. We perform re-projection of video and the overlay of textual/ graphical annotations of objects of interest in the current video using the stored annotations in the reference database.

In previous work [Kumar98], we presented algorithms for geo-registration which work well mainly with wide field of view, nadir video imagery. In this paper, we extend that work in two significant ways: (1) we extend the system to handle zoomed in video, where any one video frame may not have enough information for accurate geo-registration and (2) we extend the system to handle highly oblique video.

In section 2, we review the components of a geo-registration scheme. Section 3 presents the new bundle block method for aligning oblique video frames. Finally, results are presented in Section 4.

2. Components of a Geo-registration System

Figure 1 shows the main components of a video based geo-registration system. We create a reference image database in geo-coordinates along with the associated DEM (digital elevation maps) and annotations [GLMX, Mckeown96,Heller98]. The visual features available in the reference imagery database are correlated with those in video imagery to achieve an order of magnitude improvement in alignment in comparison to purely ESD (engineering support data: GPS, camera look angle etc.) based alignment. To achieve this, a section of the reference image is first warped to the perspective of the Unmanned Aerial Vehicles (UAV) sensor based on the ESD alone. Subsequently, precise sub-pixel alignment between the video frame and reference imagery corresponding to the relevant locale is used for the accurate geo-location of the video frame. The process of precise alignment of video to reference imagery is itself divided into the following steps:

Frame-to-frame alignment: Video frames at typically 30 frames a second contain significant frame-to-frame overlap. In order to meet the real time constraints for the geo-registration system, as a first step in the front-end processing, we exploit this redundancy by identifying *key* video frames based on computing frame to frame motion. The frame to frame motion is modeled with low order parametric transformations like translation, affine and projective transformations [Bergen'92]. The frame-to-frame alignment parameters can also enable the creation of a single extended view mosaic image that authentically represents all the information contained in the aligned input frames in a compact image.

ESD, Database and Rendering Engine: The ESD supplied with the video is decoded to define the initial estimate of the camera model (position and attitude) with respect to the reference database. The camera model is used to apply an image perspective transformation to reference imagery obtained from the database to render a set of synthetic reference images [PowerScene] from the perspective of the sensor, which are subsequently used for coarse search and fine geo-registration.

In our previous system, we would match the video frames to reference imagery in the form of an orthophoto. However in the case of oblique video, the appearance between the orthophoto and the video images can be quite different and it is difficult to find matching features.

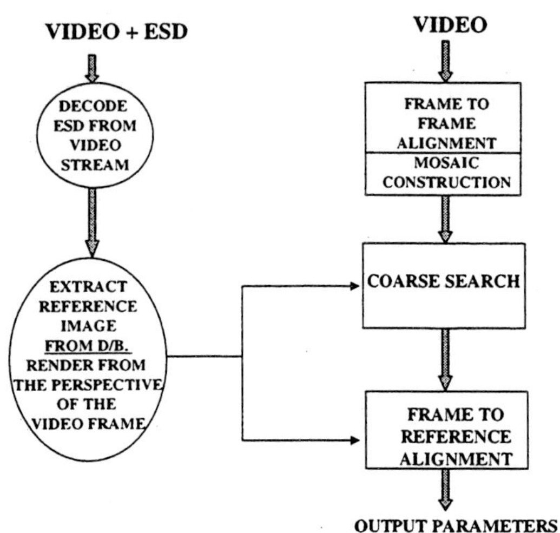

Figure 1: Geo-registration System

Instead we match the video to rendered reference images which have approximately the same perspective as the video image. This also minimizes occlusion effects, since the rendering process naturally does hidden surface removal.

Coarse Search: A coarse indexing module then locates the video imagery more precisely in the rendered reference image. An individual video frame may not contain sufficient information to perform robust matching and therefore results are combined across multiple frames using the results of frame to frame alignment

In our current real-time implementation, local appearance matching is performed using normalized correlation of multiple image patches in the image. These individual correlation surfaces often have multiple peaks. Disambiguation is obtained by imposing global consistency by combining the frame-to-frame motion information with the correlation surfaces. Specifically, we are looking for a number of potentially poor local matches that exhibit global consistency as the UAV flies along. This is currently implemented by multiplying the correlation surfaces after they have been warped or shifted by the frame-to-frame motion parameters. The correlation-based search is done across a range of rotation, translation and zoom motion parameters. The net result is that the sequence of frames is located to within a few pixels in the reference frame. The final correlation score is used as a measure of accuracy in the coarse search step.

Frame to Reference Registration: A fine geo-registration module then refines this estimate further using the relative information between frames to constrain the solution. In general, the transformation between two views of a scene can be modeled by: (i) an external coordinate transformation that specifies the 3D alignment parameters between the reference and the camera coordinate systems, and (ii) an internal camera coordinate system to image transformation that typically involves a linear (affine) transformation and non-linear lens distortion parameters. Our approach to the precise alignment problem combines the external coordinate transformation and the linear internal transformation into a single 3D projective view transformation. Twelve parameters (a_1 to a_{12}) are used to specify the transformation. The reference image coordinates (X_r,Y_r) together with the depth $k(X_r,Y_r)$ are mapped to the ideal video coordinates (X_I,Y_I) by:

$$X_I = \frac{a_1 * X_r + a_2 * Y_r + a_3 * k(X_r,Y_r) + a_{10}}{a_7 * X_r + a_8 * Y_r + a_9 * k(X_r,Y_r) + a_{12}}$$
$$Y_I = \frac{a_4 * X_r + a_5 * Y_r + a_6 * k(X_r,Y_r) + a_{11}}{a_7 * X_r + a_8 * Y_r + a_9 * k(X_r,Y_r) + a_{12}} \quad \textbf{(1)}$$

This transformation together with the DEM data and any non-linear lens distortion parameters completely specifies the mapping between the video pixels and those in the reference imagery. One major advantage of our approach is that camera calibration need not be known. This increases the applicability of our proposed system to arbitrary video camera platforms. Note in many aerial imaging instances, equation (1) can be reduced to be a planar projective transform (where the terms $a_3 = a_6 = a_9 = 0$). This approximation is valid when there is only a small view-point difference between the rendered reference image and the video frame and the distance between camera to ground is large as compared to the height of objects in the scene.

In the previous approach [Kumar '98], we would do fine alignment of each frame separately. The alignment parameters would be estimated by minimizing SSD using a multi-resolution coarse-to-fine estimation scheme and warping with Gaussian/ Laplacian pyramids [Bergen92,Kumar94]:

$$E(\{A\}) = \sum_x ((I(x, ref) - I(Ax, video))^2 \quad \textbf{(2)}$$

In equation (2) a point x in the reference image is transformed into the video coordinate system by the Matrix A. Two problems occur using this approach. (1) The individual video frames may be quite different from the reference imagery. This can be due to multiple reasons such as changes in the world, different image acquisition times, different imaging sensors used, etc. (2) Due to an aperture effect, certain video frames may not have sufficient distinguishing information to match them to the reference imagery. For instance, images of runways do not have distinguishing features for reliable matches along the runway direction. To mitigate against these effects, we would like to match a block of frames simultaneously to the reference imagery. The block of frames would provide a larger context for robust matching. Note, the frame to frame alignment within the block can be stable because of local features.

3. Block Alignment of Video Frames

In the block based approach, we use the results from the frame-to-frame processing to constrain the simultaneous alignment of several sets of frames to a set of rendered reference images. As noted earlier, we match the video frames to rendered reference images whose perspective is close to the video frame. In the block alignment scheme for an oblique video sequence, different video frames will be matched to different rendered reference images (see Figure 2). However since we have rendered the reference images, the relationship between them is completely known. We establish tie-points between the reference frames and video frames and between the video frames themselves. We solve for the frame to reference parameters by minimizing the error term:

$$E = \sum_{i=1}^{k} E_{f2f}(i,i+1) + \sum_{j=1}^{m}\sum_{i=1}^{k} E_{r2f}(j,i) \qquad (3)$$

E is the sum of the frame to frame matching errors (E_{f2f}) and rendered reference frame to video frame matching errors (E_{r2f}). These errors are a function of the frame to reference motion parameters (equation 1). In Figure 2, we show 3 rendered reference images with video frames tied to each of them. In practice the number of rendered reference frames depends on the motion of the video in the bundle set. The number of video frames used in a bundle depends on there being enough multi-directional features present at the two ends of the bundle to be able to tie them robustly to the reference imagery.

The following bundle estimation scheme [Sawhney98] is used to establish matches and compute alignment parameters between the reference imagery and the video frames:

1) Divide the video into blocks based on parallax and the extent of overlap in the computed frame-to-frame motion.
2) Render a reference frame for each block using a central viewpoint for the block.
3) Compute initial frame-to-reference parameters for each frame using either the coarse search and ESD results or the predicted motion based on the frame to frame motion computation.
4) Find robust matches between significant points in the video frames and the rendered reference images. Computing optic flow between the respective two images can be used to do this [Bergen'92].
5) Define a matrix bundle of correspondences where both correspondences between reference frames and video frames and correspondences between one video frame to the next are established. Common tie points are used to link both neighboring video frames to each other and to neighboring reference frames.
6) Refine frame to reference parameters by minimizing the pixel correspondence error (equation 3) using the bundle set of equations set up in step 5. Calculate the point matching error using the estimated parameters.
7) Iterate steps 4 to 6, until there is convergence in the minimization of the error term E. The estimated motion parameters are used to find better matches and these are in turn used to refine the frame to reference motion parameters.

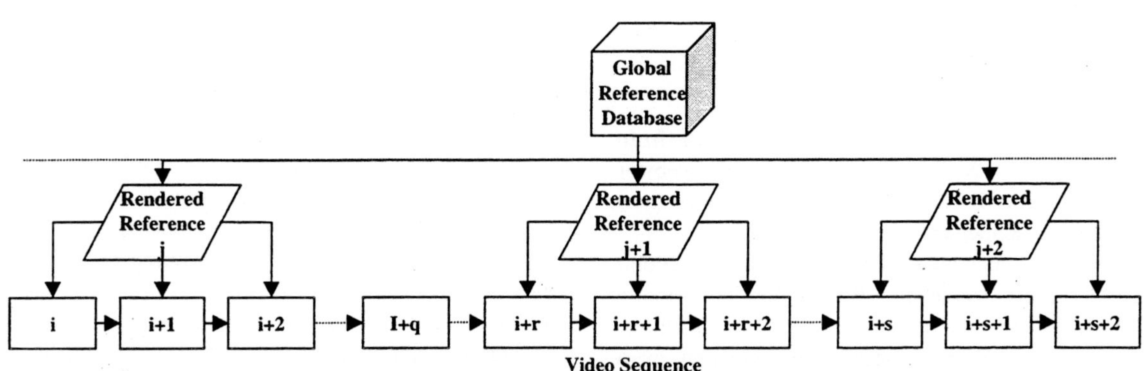

Figure 2: Scheme for multi-block alignment of oblique video imagery

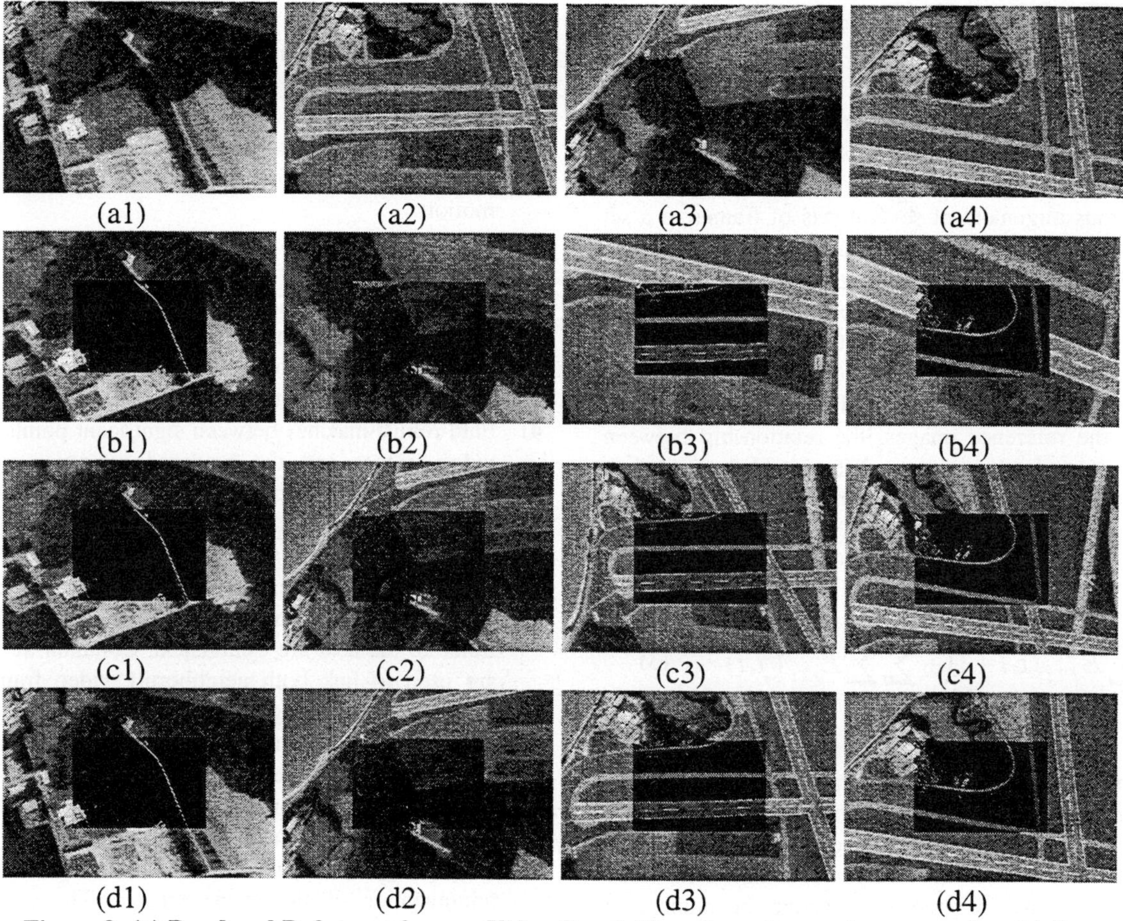

Figure 3: (a) Rendered Reference frames. Video Overlaid on the reference imagery using (b) Frame to frame motion (c) Successive geo-registration of individual frames (d) Multi-frame bundle

Note we used the bundle adjustment scheme to refine both the matches (step 4) and the motion parameters (step 6). For real time applications, we use a sliding sub-block scheme, where a new sub-block of frames is added at each time instant and a earlier sub-block of frames is removed from the block estimation. Finally, in the case of nadir imagery, we need not have multiple rendered reference images and all the video frames can be matched to one reference frame.

4. Results

The results that are presented were obtained from video captured from a X-drone UAV flying over Webster Field, Maryland. Key frames obtained at 3 Hz were used to geo-register the sequences.

Figure 3 show the results of processing a 25-second nadir aerial video sequence. We show progressive improvements that are made with the different algorithms. Row (a) shows the reference imagery approximately from the viewpoint of the video at some sampled time instances across the sequence. Row (b) shows how the video is overlaid on the reference imagery based on concatenating the frame-to-frame motion computation with the geo-registration results of the first video frame. Small errors in the frame-to-frame alignment cause the frame to reference alignment to drift.

Row (c) shows how this result can be improved by geo-registering every frame to the reference imagery using the frame-to-frame motion as a prediction. However, as any given frame may be locally ambiguous the results may stray away from the true solution easily. Image (c3) shows how the registration begins to fail along the runway due to lack of features in the vertical direction (aperture effects). In image (c4) the system is unable to recover from the errors that occurred before.

Row (d) shows the result of the bundle adjustment. A sliding block of ten key frames is used in the bundle adjustment step. The results from the previous block of frame and the frame-to-frame parameters are used to initialize the next block. We are able to obtain good geo-localization across the whole sequence.

Figure 4 shows how the method is extended to work with a 15-second oblique video sequence across rapidly varying viewpoints. Images (a), (b) and (c) are obtained by geo-registering local blocks of frames to a rendered reference of a close by view. Subsequently all these

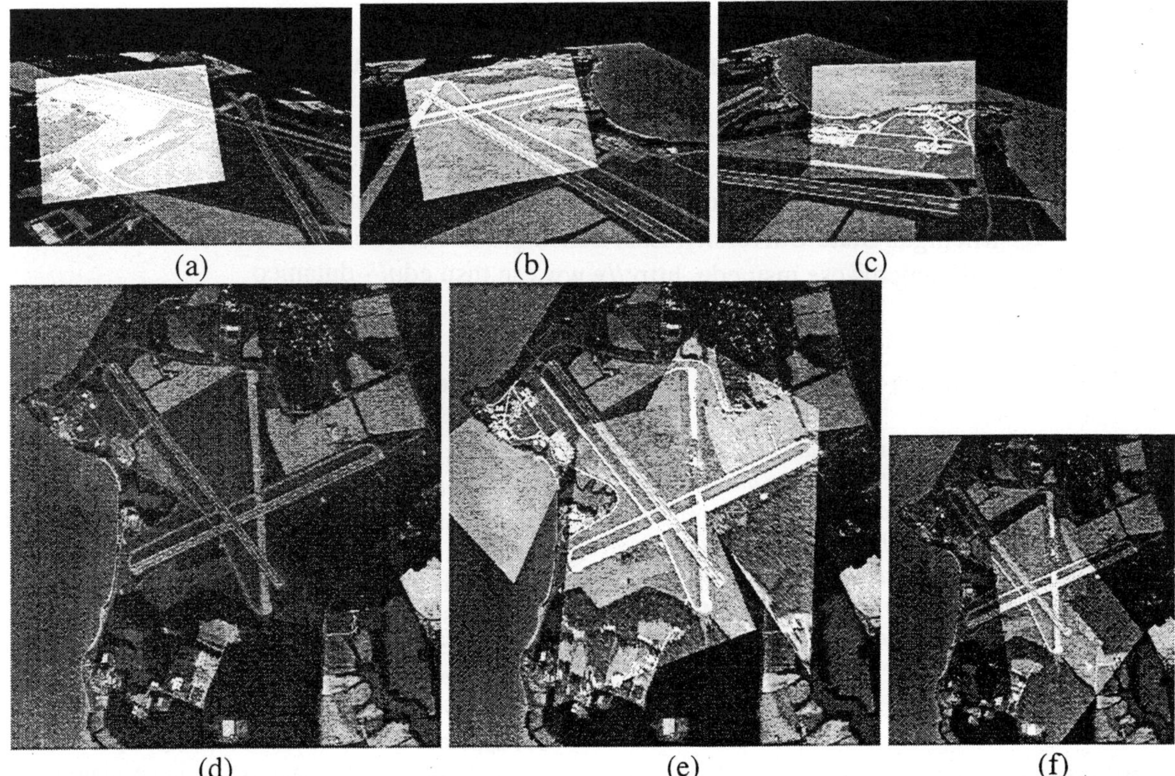

Figure 4: (a), (b) and (c) Independent bundles using different reference images (d) Original ortho-photo reference (e) After bundle adjustment of a, b and c. (f) Prediction of a frame not in a, b or c after global adjustment

blocks are bundle adjusted together to obtain a globally consistent result. Image (e) shows the same images as seen on (a), (b) and (c) placed over orthographic view of the reference imagery after the global bundle adjustment. Image (f) show an image that was not in any of the original bundles. In the global bundle adjustment this frame was included only as a frame-to-frame constraint. Although as seen in Figure 3 (b) frame-to-frame alone is ineffective in providing good geo-registration, as a part of the bundle adjustment process it provides good geo-localization.

The current system can be improved further by adding robust methods for detecting failures of the individual bundle adjustments and subsequently recovering from it. Match measures between the video and reference can also be improved for better alignment results.

5. References

[Bergen92] J. R. Bergen, P. Anandan, K. J. Hanna, and R. Hingorani, "Hiearchical model-based motion estimation," ECCV, pp. 237-252, 1992.

[Kumar94] R. Kumar, P. Anandan and K. Hanna, "Direct Recovery of Shape from Multiple Views: A Parallax based Approach", ICPR'94, Jerusalem, Israel, pp. 685-688, 1994.

[GLMX] General Dynamic Information Systems GLMX system, See also "Rapid Generation and Use of 3D Site Models to Aid Imagery Analysts/Systems Performing Image Exploitation", Proceeding of the SPIE, Volume 1944, Conference on Integrating Photogrammetric Techniques with Scene Analysis and Machine Vision, April 1993.

[PowerScene] Cambridge Research Associates PowerScene System: http://www.cambridge.com/

[Mckeown96] David M. McKeown, Jr., Stephen J. Gifford, Michael F. Polis, Jeff McMahill and Christian D. Hoffman, "Progress in Automated Virtual World Construction," Proceedings 1996 ARPA Image Understanding Workshop, pp. 325-335.

[Heller98] A.J.Heller, M.A. Fischler, R.C. Bolles, C.I. Connolly, R.Wilson and J. Pearson, "An integrated feasibility demonstration for automatic population of geo-spatial databases," 1998 Image Understanding Workshop, Monterey, California, Nov.20th-23rd, 1998.

[Kanade98] T. Kanade, R.T. Collins, A.J.Lipton, P. Burt and L.Wixson, "Advances in Cooperative Mulit-Sensor Video Surelliance", 1998 Image Understanding Workshop, Monterey, California, Nov.20th-23rd, 1998.

[Kumar98] R. Kumar, H.S. Sawhney, J.C.Asmuth, A. Pope and S. Hsu, "Registration of video to geo-referenced imagery," ICPR'98, Brisbane, Australia, Aug. 16th-20th, 1998.

[Sawhney98] Harpreet S. Sawhney and S. Hsu and R. Kumar, "Robust Video Mosaicing through Topology Inference and Local to Global Alignment", ECCV'98, Germany, 1998

Road Detection in Panchromatic SPOT Satellite Images

Nicolae Duta
Department of Computer Science and Engineering
Michigan State University, East Lansing, MI 48824-1226, USA
dutanico@cse.msu.edu, http://www.cse.msu.edu/~dutanico

Abstract

The goal of this study is to detect the main road network in high resolution, panchromatic SPOT satellite images. We describe an automatic procedure for road detection which has the following advantages over the previous approaches: (i) it does not require manual initialization, (ii) it is able to detect some of the secondary roads in addition to the main highways, and (iii) the detection time is small (~ 3 min) even on large images.

1 Introduction

The goal of this study is to detect the main road network in high resolution, panchromatic SPOT satellite images, with possible applications to automated cartography. For about twenty years there has been an intensive effort to produce fully automatic software for road extraction from satellite images [1, 2, 4, 6] but, despite this effort, there is no software sufficiently reliable for practical use. Among the well known methods for road detection we mention those based on finding the path with minimal cost between two specified nodes in a graph using dynamic programming (Fischler *et al.* [1], Merlet and Zerubia [4]), and the *active testing* approach of Geman and Jedynak [2]. All these methods emphasize the fact that road detection is a *global problem* (a road can only be defined at the scale of the whole image) and, due to computational limitations, are faced with a trade-off between the size of the images that can actually be processed and the intervention of a human (manual selection of the road ends [4] or of a point on the road along with the road direction at that point [2]). Though we agree that determining if an image structure represents a road is a global problem, we also believe that deciding where to start constructing the structure can be solved more locally. This paper describes an automatic procedure for road detection/tracking in SPOT images which is based on two stages: (i) a *partial detection* stage finds several salient pieces of road (subsequently called *"road seeds"*) in the input image, and (ii) a *full tracking* stage constructs a *"road tree"* for each seed and selects the best path in the tree as corresponding to a road.

2 Method description

A road can be modeled as a continuous line, nearly linear on small pieces, that differs somehow in contrast from the adjacent terrain [2]. One can notice that in small images (256×256) a road generally begins at a border of the image and ends at another border, and this remains true only for a few highways in a large image (1024×1024) (see Fig.2). Therefore, the properties considered to define a road are: (i) *piecewise linearity*, (ii) *connectivity*, (iii) *homogeneity*, (iv) *separability from the nearby background* and (v) *length*.

Our approach consists of the following steps:

1. *Preprocessing*. The histogram of the input image is equalized in order to enhance the contrast and make possible that a set of fixed threshold values have similar outcomes on different images.
2. *Construction of a partial road structure composed of several road segments/arcs ("road seeds")*. A road seed is defined as a parallelogram shaped region of the image, 2-4 pixels wide, 10-15 pixels long, which is visually homogeneous and well separated from the nearby background. We attempt to detect road seeds by finding their cross-sections parallel to the image axes; horizontal cross-sections are used for constructing road regions which are rather vertically oriented (e.g., the road seed in Fig.1(a) is composed of the horizontal cross-sections A_1B_1 through $A_{10}B_{10}$, and although all seeds contain the same number of cross-sections, 10, their actual lengths vary depending on the orientation with respect to the image axes), while vertical cross-sections are employed for rather horizontal road pieces.

Since we assume that a road seed is separable from the background, it follows that each cross-section through the road seed should be separable from its $1D$ background. Therefore, one can detect road cross-sections by clustering adjacent pixels on each row/column of the input image, such that the clusters obtained are visually homogeneous and separated. We employed a version of the agglomerative hierarchical class of clustering algorithms [3] (with inter-cluster similarity given by group-average distance) that takes into account the fact that the points of interest have a $1D$ spatial structure. Bidimensional pieces of road can subsequently be constructed by connecting clusters ($1D$ pixel segments)

1051-4651/00 $10.00 © 2000 IEEE

on consecutive rows/columns. Since roads are usually 2-3 pixels wide, the only subjects considered for connecting are segments at most four pixels long whose corresponding endpoints are no more than two pixels shifted one from the other (in order to enforce piece-wise linearity). Such segments are connected if their average gray values differ by no more than a small threshold ϵ (typically 15 for a 256 gray-level image). The connection is actually a pointer from a cross-section to its "predecessor" on the row right above it (see for example the pointer from A_3B_3 to A_2B_2 in Fig.1(a)). If each cross-section is considered to be a vertex, we obtain a tree, because there may be more segments on a row which may continue the same segment on the previous row. However, it is also possible that a given segment may succeed to more than one segment on the previous row; and since it is more difficult to handle arbitrary graph structures, we chose to assign it to the longest already constructed tree. Most of the time, this heuristic produces the desired outcome, although occasionally, the real road at a given location is not represented by the longest tree, and the resulted tree structure does not correspond to a road. After the entire image has been processed, we are left with a partial road structure composed of several trees of different depths and widths. Due to the conservative value of ϵ, the trees are relatively short. However, they are homogeneous and can be well separated from the nearby background. This incomplete road structure serves for defining the *road seeds*: disjoint sets of 10 consecutive road profiles (schematically shown in Fig.1(a)) are extracted from the longest path of each tree. Empirical statistics show that most such regions in a SPOT image are actually part of the road structure (see Fig.2(a)).

3. *Full road tracking*. Each *road seed* found in Step 2 is used as the first arc of a *road tree* whose remaining arcs are constructed based on the assumption that roads are piece-wise linear (see Fig.1(c) and Fig.2(b)). Finally, the best path in each road tree is reported as corresponding to a road.

Let Y and Z be two pixels in the input image. The line segment YZ is defined as the set S(YZ) formed by the pixels which immediately surround segment YZ (e.g., $A_1, ..., A10, B_1, ...B10$ in Fig. 1(a)). We define the probability P(YZ) of a segment YZ corresponding to a road region based on a local filtering of four pixel cliques along YZ. An elementary clique is a pattern of four pixels (p, r, p', r') in S(YZ) arranged like in Fig.1(b). To each clique (p, r, p', r'), we associated a filter (an extension of the qualitative filter introduced by Geman and Jedynak [2]) based on two pairs of close parallel profiles (pa, $p'b'$, rb and $r'a'$ in Fig.1(b)) approximately perpendicular to YZ. The profiles are intended to be two pixels long, as well as the distance between the farthest pairs (e.g., pa and rb), but due to digitization, the actual lengths can vary slightly depending on the orientation of YZ. The image response to this filter models the fact that *two pixels located in close proximity and both belonging to a road are expected to have a smaller*

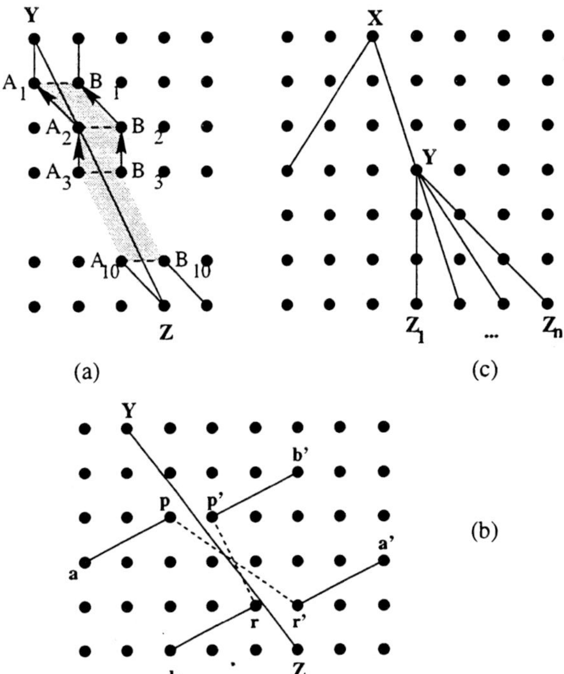

Figure 1. The definition of a ***road seed*** **(the dashed region $A_1, A_2, .., A_{10}, B_{10}, ..., B_1$) (a), schematic drawing of a clique (b), and a road tree in the full tracking stage (c). Each arc represents a piece of road of length approximately equal to that of the starting seed.**

intensity difference than two pixels belonging to different structures (road and background). Let $I(t)$ denote the image intensity at pixel t. We define the output of the filter associated with the clique (p, r, p', r') as $c(p, r, p', r') = c_1(p, r, p', r') + c_2(p, r, p', r')$ where $c_1(p, p', r, r') = 1$ if $|I(p) - I(r')| < \min(|I(p) - I(a)|, |I(r') - I(a')|)$, and 0 otherwise; and $c_2(p, p', r, r') = 1$ if $|I(r) - I(p')| < \min(|I(r) - I(b)|, |I(p') - I(b')|)$ and 0 otherwise. The overall filter response for a line segment in the image is the sum of the individual responses of all elementary cliques along that segment. The probability P(YZ) of YZ corresponding to a road segment is defined as the normalized (by the number of cliques along YZ) filter response:

$$P(Y, Z) = (\sum_{(p,r,p',r')\text{clique along } YZ} (c1(p, r, p', r') + c2(p, r, p', r')))/$$
$$(2 \times \#\text{ of cliques along } YZ).$$

The following tracking procedure is applied to each *road seed* X_0Y_0 constructed in Step 2:

Algorithm 1 (Road tracking)
Input: A *road seed* X_0Y_0.
A0. Initialize a tree queue $Q = \{X_0Y_0\}$.
While $Q \neq \emptyset$, execute *Steps A1* and *A2*.
A1. Set the current arc XY equal to the top of the queue:

$XY = Top(Q)$.

A2. Prolong the current arc XY with almost collinear segments $YZ_1,...,YZ_n$ of lengths approximately equal to $||XY||$ (Fig.1(c)). The number of possible prolongations reflects the prior knowledge one has about the road curvature. For this study, we chose $n = 11$ covering a road curvature of $[-45^o, +45^o]$. Append to Q all arcs $YZ_i, i \in \{1...n\}$ which may continue the tree path ending in XY. A candidate arc YZ_i can be a continuation of the path ending in XY if it satisfies the following two conditions :

C1. *Gray value homogeneity*. Most (66%) pixel values along YZ_i do not differ from the gray level average of the path ending in Y by more than a threshold $T1$.

C2. *Separability from the background*. The probability $P(YZ_i)$ associated to the segment YZ_i exceeds a threshold $T2$.

B. Execute *Steps A1,A2* with the tree queue initialized to Y_0X_0. In this way, the road containing the seed X_0Y_0 is tracked in both directions.

C. After the two trees rooted in X_0Y_0 and Y_0X_0 are constructed in Steps A and B, determine the path of maximum probability in the combined tree. If this probability exceeds a threshold T_3 and at least one of the two trees ends at an image border, report a road corresponding to this path.

In order to make the implementation fast, the *road seeds* which are sufficiently close to an already detected road are discarded.

3 Experimental results

The method presented above has been used to implement an automatic road tracking system. In order to determine the values of the required parameters we performed the following experiments:

1. Determine the average gray level difference beyond which two adjacent $1D$ pixel clusters can be visually separated. For being effective, these measurements have to be done on SPOT images; they give different results on other type of images and, in our case, they do not seem to obey Weber's law [5].

2. Statistical analysis of the gray level homogeneity of the pixels which belong to the same road, in order to find the thresholds ϵ and $T1$ used for connecting two adjacent cross-sections (Step 2) or road arcs (Step 3).

3. Statistical analysis of road pixels in order to find the best filter arrangement and the maximum response to different types of roads.

The data set we have used for testing the algorithm consists of 12 SPOT images with dimensions between 256×256 and 1088×1088. The results have been compared to the map of manually tracked roads in the following way: an image line segment was considered to be well labeled as a road segment if it was at most 3 pixels away from a manually tracked road. We defined the accuracy of the method as the ratio between the number of well labeled segments and the total number of classified segments.

Some of the detection results are presented in Fig.2. Figs.2(a-b) show the road seeds and the road tree constructed from one (the uppermost) of these seeds. Fig.2(c) shows the road structure detected in two images of size 1024×1024 (shown only partially). Each road is tracked independently, we currently do not explicitly integrate the results of multiple trackings. Both highways, as well as the longest secondary roads, were detected, despite the fact that they do not have the same width. There may be some road portions which are not easily separable from the background; they are shown using black arcs in Fig.2. The time required to track the road network present in a 1024×1024 image using our method is about 3 minutes (on a Sun UltraSparc 10), slightly more if many roads are present. The average accuracy of our method (computed as described above) over the 12 test images has been found to be about 90%.

4 Conclusions

An automatic procedure for road detection in SPOT satellite images has been presented. The method appears to be reliable and robust provided the images are of relatively good quality. The results exhibit a 90% accuracy over a 12 image test set and might be improved by adding more sophisticated criteria to decide if a path in a tree is a road.

Acknowledgements

The author would like to thank Andre Gagalowicz, Don Geman, Bruno Jedynak and Milan Sonka for providing the data and for helpful discussions and feedback.

References

[1] M. A. Fischler, J. M. Tenenbaum, and H. C. Wolf. Detection of roads and linear structures in low-resolution aerial imagery using a multisource knowledge integration technique. *Comp. Vision, Graphics, and Image Proc.*, 15:201–223, 1981.

[2] D. Geman and B. Jedynak. An active testing model for tracking roads in satellite images. *IEEE Trans. Pattern Anal. and Machine Intelligence*, 18(1):1–14, 1996.

[3] A. K. Jain and R. C. Dubes. *Algorithms for Clustering Data*. Prentice Hall, New York, 1988.

[4] N. Merlet and J. Zerubia. New prospects in line detection by dynamic programming. *IEEE Trans. Pattern Anal. and Machine Intelligence*, 18(4):426–431, 1996.

[5] W. K. Pratt. *Digital Image Processing*. John Wiley and Sons, New York, 2nd edition, 1991.

[6] A. Yuille and J. Coughlan. Fundamental limits of Bayesian inference: Order parameters and phase transitions for road tracking. *IEEE Trans. Pattern Anal. and Machine Intelligence*, 22(2):160–173, 2000.

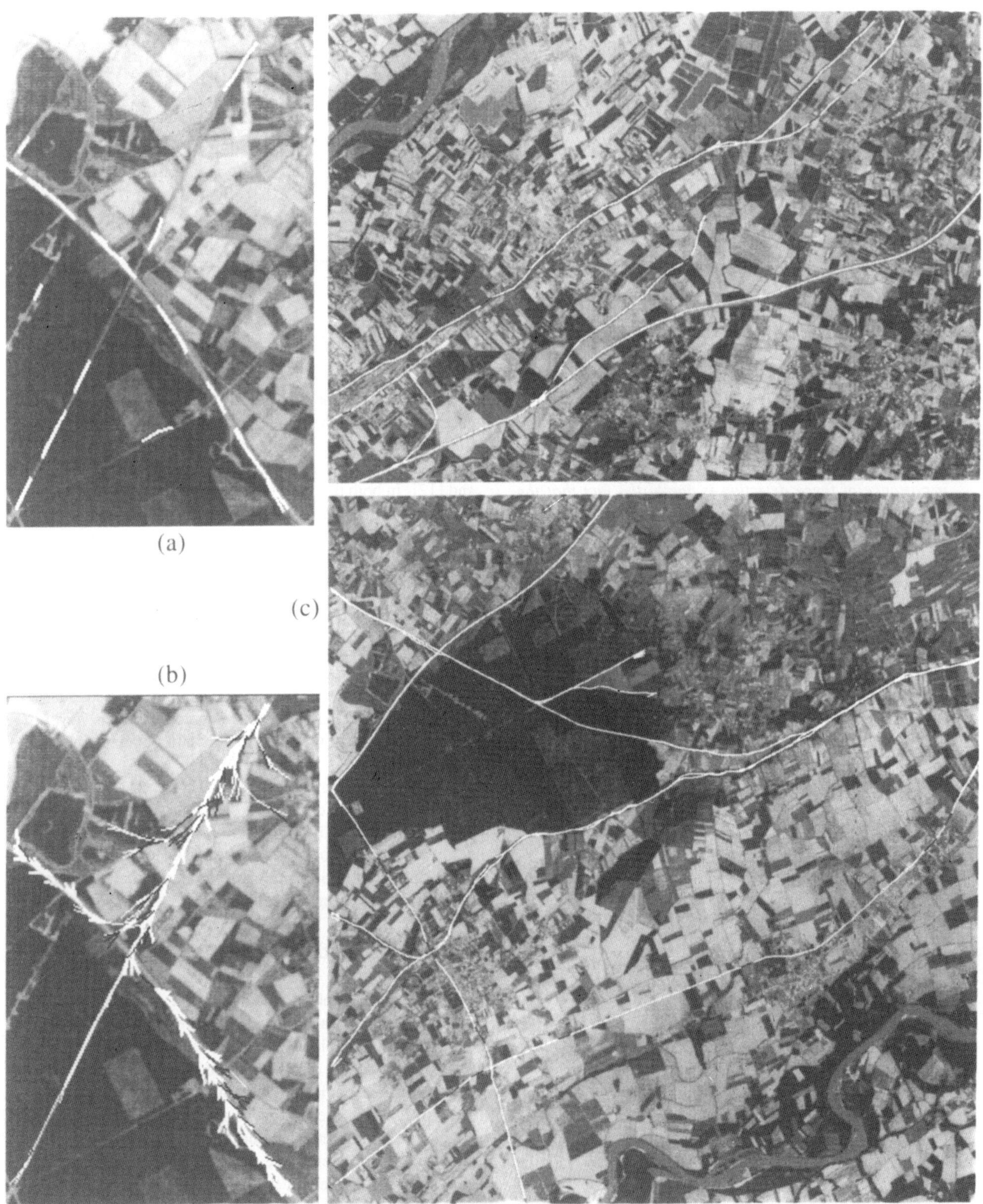

Figure 2. Results produced by our road network detection method on two SPOT images of Toulouse region (France). (a) Road seeds used as starting points for road tracking. (b) Road tree constructed from the uppermost seed in (a). (c) Detection results on two 1024×1024 images. The road portions which are not well separated from the background are shown using black arcs.

An Active Contour Model for the Automatic Detection of the Fovea in Fluorescein Angiographies

J. Gutiérrez I. Epifanio E. De Ves F. J. Ferri
Universitat de València.
Departament d'Informàtica.
Avda. Vicent Andreés Estellés s/n. 46100 Burjassot (València)

Juan.Gutierrez@uv.es

Abstract

Fovea segmentation in fluorescein angiographies is a fundamental first task in any study of ocular diseases. The importance of fovea detection is due to the fact that the nearer the centre of the fovea a lesion is, the graver this lesion is. The proposed method is based on B-snakes and uses a greedy algorithm to minimise an appropriate energy which accurately leads to a convenient characterisation of the boundary of the foveal zone. A first initialisation step which consists of finding the most appropriate local minimum along with a procedure to construct an initial contour involving a region growing algorithm, lead to a convenient and robust initialisation of the proposed active contour model. [1]

1. Introduction

Fluorescein angiography is a common practice to visualise the ocular fundus. In this technique, photographs of the ocular fundus are taken after intravenous injection of sodium fluorescein as it circulates in the vessels of the retina and the choroid.

The detection of the fovea is a very important task for ocular diagnosis systems. The fovea is a small, slightly concave area without retinal capillaries. As a consequence, it appears as a dark area, in contrast to the rest of the retina where retinal vessels are enhanced by the fluorescent liquid. The fovea is so important because some specialised cells that provide central vision lie in it. Therefore, the severity of a lesion depends on its distance to the fovea.

As the fovea has no precise definition in terms of its appearance, the so-called FAZ (Foveal Avascular Zone) will be used in this work to refer to the dark area around the fovea.

Although the image segmentation problem has been broadly treated at the Computer Vision literature its applications to the ophthalmic context are not very abundant. Some general works related to the assisted diagnosis of ocular diseases by analysing fluorescein angiographies are [3] and [12]. In both theses, a wide description of the problem and some specific algorithms to segment images in their relevant anatomical structures are presented. Other works ([4], [9], [8], [10]) present different procedures to segment retinal images.

With regard to the fovea segmentation, Zana [13] used mathematical morphology and proposed an algorithm based on region merging. Ibáñez and Simó [6] applied Bayesian methodology to detect the fovea contour.

In this paper, we propose an algorithm to segment automatically the FAZ based on active contours models, devoting especial attention to the procedure to obtain the initial contour.

The paper is organised as follows. In the next section we describe the approach used to detect the FAZ. In section 3 the mathematical details of the proposed approach will be presented. Section 4 shows the results of applying our methodology to digital angiographies, and finally, several conclusions are given in Section 5.

2. Approach and Motivation

Ocular angiographies contain a global view of the ocular fundus where some anatomical structures such as the fovea, the optic disc and blood vessels as well as other elements related with specific diseases can be observed.

In a typical ocular angiography, the FAZ appears as a relatively dark area which is not completely homogeneous. Another relevant feature of this zone is that capillaries end in it, therefore the surrounding area has a higher grey level as the effect of the fluorescein liquid. However, FAZ boundaries are not well-defined since there are not clear edges delimiting this area.

For these reasons, classical segmentation algorithms based exclusively on edge detection are not appropriate for our particular segmentation problem. Therefore, we have

[1] This paper has been partially supported by Spanish projects GV98-14-12, TIC98-677-C02-02 and 1FD97-279

1051-4651/00 $10.00 © 2000 IEEE

explored a segmentation technique introduced by Kass et al. [7] which presented the concept of an *active contour model*, commonly called *snake*. Snakes can be represented as energy minimising contours guided by external constraints forces and image forces such as lines, edges, subjective contours and region homogeneities found in the image. Furthermore, internal energy forces impose smoothness constraints on the modelled contours. This approach permits using the ends of little capillaries as a subjective contour that may be detected by an appropriate active contour model.

A critical step in active contour models is the estimation of an initial curve. In this kind of images, where there is no clear feature that may attract the snake, this task is even more relevant. The proposed initialisation consists of two steps. Firstly, a zone of interest is identified and characterised using a point inside the FAZ. Secondly, an initial contour is constructed around this point. Prior to this contour initialisation procedure, images will be normalised through histogram equalisation.

3. Modelling FAZ Boundary by means of Active Contours

3.1. Obtaining an Initial Point inside the FAZ

The whole process of FAZ boundary detection is extremely influenced by the initial location of the FAZ zone. Due to the high variability both in structure and in lighting conditions, a robust procedure to look for the FAZ zone is needed prior to adjusting (finely) an active contour model to its boundary.

Starting from the fact that the FAZ is a relatively large and dark zone in which there are no borders (because of absence of vessels), the first step is to look for local minima of the brightness function across an appropriately smoothed image. In particular, images are convolved with a Gaussian kernel based on a large standard deviation.

Local minima can now be obtained by thresholding. If this procedure gets more than one minimum, the one with the largest absolute difference between its grey value and the average grey value of pixels at a distance R is selected. That is, let M be the set of these local minima. Among points belonging to this set M, the best candidate will be the one satisfying,

$$(x_f, y_f) = \arg \max_{(x_0,y_0)\in M} \left| I(x_0, y_0) - \frac{\sum_{\mathcal{N}(x_0,y_0)} I(x,y)}{\sharp\mathcal{N}(x_0, y_0)} \right|$$

where

$$\mathcal{N}(x_0, y_0) = \{(x, y) : (x - x_0)^2 + (y - y_0)^2 = R^2\}$$

and $I(x, y)$ is the grey level of the image at point (x, y).

3.2. Active Contour Initialisation

Finding a point inside the FAZ is not a very complex task, as it has been shown. However, the process of constructing an initial contour is rather difficult because, a priori, the shape and size of the FAZ are unknown. This is the reason why a procedure to obtain a first estimation of the contour is needed. This contour has to be close enough to the final desired FAZ boundary but smooth enough to allow a good convergence of the active contour model which will be applied afterwards.

A region growing algorithm [5] has been applied starting from the selected minimum. The goal is to obtain a first approximation of the FAZ using information from the borders induced by vessels. To characterise both the borders and near regions around them, the chamfer distance [1] is computed from the edges in the equalised image. The criterion applied to aggregate a new point takes into account both the mean and the standard deviation of chamfer distance values in a convenient neighbourhood of the point. In particular, the inverse of chamfer distance values in a 3×3 neighbourhood is considered.

The contour obtained through region growing is characterised by using the second order moments to avoid irregularities. In this way, its shape is approximated by an ellipse oriented in the direction of principal axes. The parameters of this ellipse can be computed efficiently as the region growing algorithm iterates.

An undersampled version of this ellipse will be used as the initial control points in the active contour model proposed in next section.

3.3. Obtaining the Final FAZ Boundary

The active contour model used to deform the ellipse in such a way that it fits the FAZ, is presented in this part. Particularly, the model is a B-Snake that will be minimised by a greedy algorithm.

A B-Snake is a set of points (control points) approximated by means of a piecewise cubic polynomial (a B-spline curve). An energy to be minimised is defined over this approximated curve. Let $(x_0, y_0), \cdots, (x_{n-1}, y_{n-1})$ be the control points. The curve is obtained using the B-Spline basis as follows

$$Q(t) = (x(t), y(t)) = \left(\sum_{i=0}^{n-1} x_i B_{i,3}(t), \sum_{i=0}^{n-1} y_i B_{i,3}(t) \right)$$

where each basis function is defined according to the following recursive rule [2]

$$B_{i,0}(t) = \begin{cases} 1, & \text{if} \quad u_i \leq t < u_{i+1} \\ 0, & \text{elsewhere.} \end{cases}$$

$$B_{i,k}(t) = \frac{t - u_i}{u_{i+k} - u_i} B_{i,k-1}(t) + \\ + \frac{u_{i+k+1} - t}{u_{i+k+1} - u_{i+1}} B_{i+1,k-1}(t)$$

where $u_0, u_1, ...$ is the set of knots. If they are evenly spaced it is easy to obtain a parametric polynomial representation for each basis function:

$$B_{0,3}(t) = \begin{cases} \frac{t^3}{6} & \text{if} \quad 0 \leq t < 1 \\ \frac{1}{6}(-3t^3 + 12t^2 - 12t + 4) & \text{if} \quad 1 \leq t < 2 \\ \frac{1}{6}(3t^3 - 24t^2 + 60t - 44) & \text{if} \quad 2 \leq t < 3 \\ \frac{(4-t)^3}{6} & \text{if} \quad 3 \leq t < 4 \\ 0 & \text{elsewhere.} \end{cases}$$

The other basis functions are simply translated copies of $B_{0,3}(t)$.

An internal energy depending on the physical properties of the object, i.e. elasticity and bending, and an external energy derived from the image data are defined over the curve. This model is put on the image by the action of external forces which move and deform it from its initial position to stick it for the best to the desired attributes in the image.

If $Q'(t)$ and $Q''(t)$ are the first and second derivatives of the curve respectively, the B-snake equation can be stated as follows,

$$E_{B-Snake}(Q(t)) = \int_{\Omega} E_{int}(Q(t)) + E_{ext}(Q(t))dt \quad (1)$$

where

$$E_{int}(Q(t)) = \alpha|Q'(t)|^2 + \beta|Q''(t)|^2$$

and

$$E_{ext}(Q(t)) = \gamma C(Q(t))$$

C denotes the chamfer distance [1] computed by using the edges of the equalised image.

The basis functions are of compact support, therefore a discrete version of equation (1) can be minimised using a greedy algorithm. This procedure has been successfully used to minimise the snake equation [11]. At each control point a neighbourhood is considered and the control point is updated to the minimum energy position. This is performed for every control point until a termination criterion is satisfied. In this work the considered neighbourhood is a segment of the line passing through the current point and the centre of mass of the whole curve (in the case of smooth circular contours this is an approximation to the normal in that point).

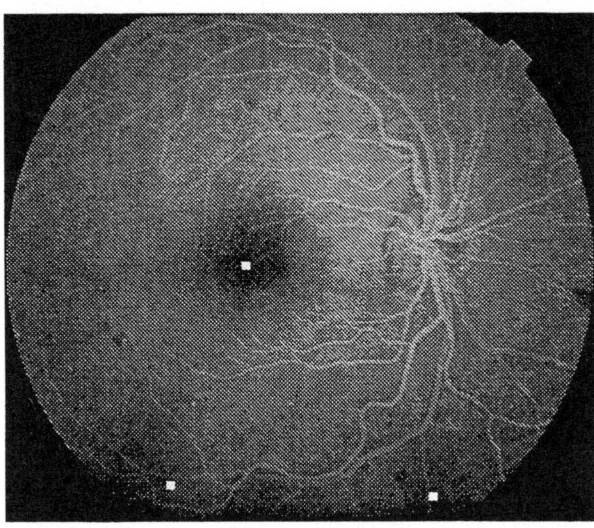

Figure 1. Typical angiography image with the obtained local minima

4. Experimental Results

The previous method has been applied to a set of 30 ocular fundus images which are representative of different kinds of diseases such as diabetic retinopathy and vascular occlusions. All these images have been taken by a Canon CF-60U and Nikon NFC 50 fundus cameras, transformed into video signal with a photo video camera PHV-A7E Sony, and digitised with a Matrox MVP-AT card with 576×768 pixels.

The values of the parameters α, β and γ in the B-Snake equation (1) have been ajusted empirically. In particular, the setting $\alpha = 1.0$, $\beta = 100.0$ and $\gamma = 100.0$ has been fixed for the whole set of images under study.

Figure 1 shows an image where several dark areas appear in the retina. Landmarks in the figure represent local minima that belong to the set M. After selecting the minimum which correctly represents the FAZ, the region growing procedure gets the result shown in figure 2. Figure 3 shows the ellipse computed from the initial region in figure 2.

Starting from the elliptical contours obtained as explained in previous sections, the proposed method is able to efficiently compute FAZ contours which dramatically resemble the subjective FAZ contour as usually (and manually) marked by physicians for most ocular diagnosis applications. Figure 4 shows the resulting FAZ contours for two of the considered images.

5. Conclusions

This paper proposes a new algorithm to segment the fovea in fluorescein angiographies. The suggested method

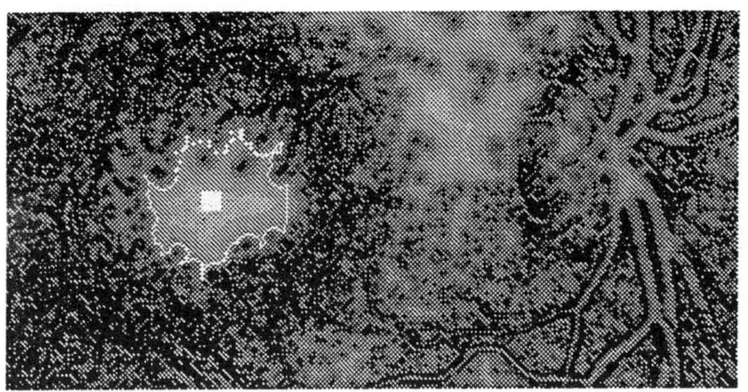

Figure 2. Chamfer distance image with the contour of the grown region and its starting point

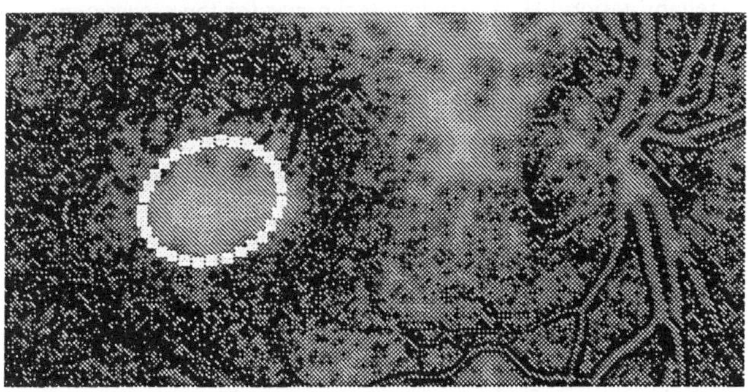

Figure 3. Chamfer distance image with the computed ellipse

is based on active contours and permits the detection of the fovea in a fully automatic way.

The final results obtained by applying this method to a numerous set of images demonstrate that it could be a very useful tool for detecting the fovea and, therefore, for clinical studies and for aiding to decision making in an ophthalmic context.

Acknowledgments

The authors would like to thank Dr. Lucía Martínez-Costa and Dr. Pilar Marco for providing the images.

References

[1] G. Borgefors. Hierarchical chamfer matching: A parametric edge matching algorithm. *IEEE Transactions on Pattern Analysis and Machine Intelligence*, 10(6):849–865, 1988.

[2] D. de Boor. *A Practical Guide to Splines*. Springer, 1978.

[3] E. de Ves. *Técnicas para la correspondencia y reconocimiento de estructuras de imágenes digitales. Aplicación al diagnóstico asistido de enfermedades oculares mediante análisis de angiografías*. PhD thesis, Universitat de València, 1999.

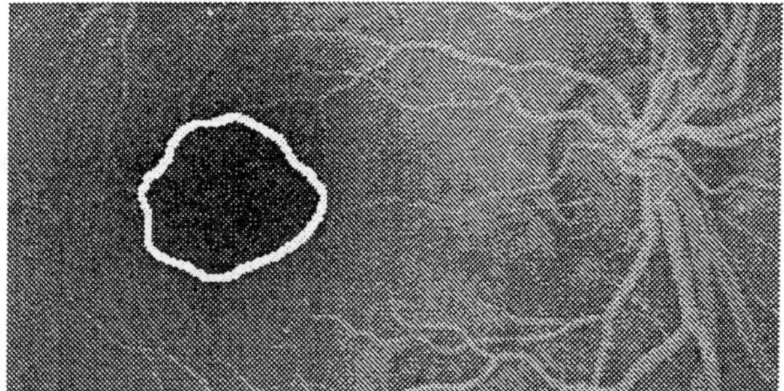

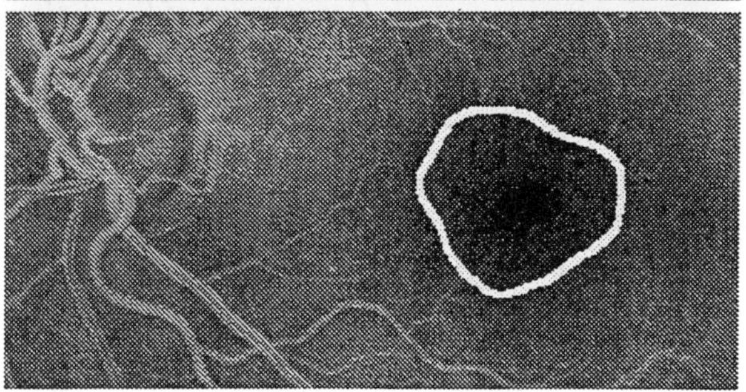

Figure 4. Final contours after appliyng the active contour model

[4] M. H. Goldbaum, N. Katz, S. Chaudhuri, and M. Nelson. Image understanding for automated retinal diagnosis. In K. L, editor, *Proceedings of the IEEE for the 13TH Annual Symposium for Computer Application in Clinical Medicine. Computer Soc Press*, pages 756–760, 1989.

[5] R. Gonzalez and P. Wintz. *Digital Image Processing*. Addison-Wesley Publishing Company, 1987.

[6] M. Ibáñez and A. Simó. Bayesian detection of the fovea in eye fundus angiographies. *Pattern Recognition Letters*, 20:229–240, 1999.

[7] M. Kass, A. Witkin, and D. Terzopoulos. Snakes: Active contours models. *International Journal of Computer Vision*, 1(4):321–331, 1988.

[8] R. Kutka and S. Stier. Extraction of line properties based on direction fields. *IEEE Transactions on Medical Imaging*, 15(1):51–58, 1996.

[9] I. Liu and Y. Sun. Recursive tracking of vascular networks in angiograms based on the detection-deletion scheme. *IEEE Transactions on Medical Imaging*, 12(2), 1993.

[10] Y. A. Tolias and S. M. Panas. A fuzzy vessel tracking algorithm for retinal images based on fuzzy clustering. *IEEE Transactions on Medical Imaging*, 17(2), 1998.

[11] D. Williams and M. Shah. A fast algorithm for active contours and curvature estimation. *GVGIP Image Understanding*, 55(1):14–26, 1992.

[12] F. Zana. *Une approche bayesienne pour le recalge d'images multimodales: application aux images retiniennes*. PhD thesis, Ecole Nationale Superieure des Mines de Paris, 1999.

[13] F. Zana, I. Meunier, and K. J.C. A region merging algorithm using mathematical morphology: application to macula detection. In *ISMM98*, pages 423–430, 1998.

Analysing constructional aspects of figure completion for the diagnosis of visuospatial neglect

R.M. Guest, M.C. Fairhurst, J.M. Potter[+], N. Donnelly[*]
Electronic Engineering Laboratory, University of Kent, UK
[+]*Nunnery Fields Hospital, Canterbury, UK*
[*]*Department of Psychology, University of Southampton, UK*
Email: {r.m.guest, m.c.fairhurst}@ukc.ac.uk

Abstract

Visuospatial neglect (VSN) is a condition following a stroke or head injury whereby a patient fails to respond to stimuli on one side of the visual field. A standard clinical assessment technique for analysis of VSN is a pencil-and-paper based figure drawing task. Traditional static analysis of this task involves assessing the presence of the major components of the drawing. Marking of drawings is subjective, relying on assessors' own judgement and experience, and therefore no standardisation exists between assessors. Using a computer-based test capture system, this paper establishes a standardised performance assessment for a drawing task including a series of novel dynamic performance features pertaining to the timing and constructional aspects of test performance. A case study of two patients demonstrates the ability to detect VSN from a response which would have traditionally been assessed as normal and hence improve the sensitivity of the task.

1. Introduction

This paper investigates the computer-based analysis of a simple figure completion drawing task for the diagnosis of visuospatial neglect (VSN) [1] within a population of stroke patients. It is shown that by extracting novel constructional features describing the task execution, VSN performance can be detected from responses that would appear normal by conventional static (visual inspection) assessment.

VSN causes a patient to fail to react to stimuli positioned within the side of the visual field opposite to the location of the lesion [2]. This can lead to problems in performing everyday tasks such as washing, dressing and eating [3]. The effects are more prevalent in patients with a lesion in the right hemisphere of the brain (Right cerebral vascular accident - RCVA) leading to a deficit in the left of the visual field. VSN is recognised as a barrier to recovery following a stroke and therefore accurate assessment of the condition is critical to the selection of effective schemes of rehabilitation [4]. A standard technique for the assessment of VSN is the use of a series of pencil and paper based tests that can be used to *quantify* performance [5]. One of these tests involves the completion or drawing of a task printed on a sheet of paper which is placed directly in front of the patient. Test responses are evaluated by therapists or trained assessors.

Conventional assessment of drawing tasks relies upon the subjective application of a set of marking criteria, based on the individual assessor's judgement of the quality of the response, usually based on the presence of specific components of the target drawing. This subjective assessment often leads to inconsistencies in application of the marking rules [6]. This deficiency can be overcome through the use of a computer-based capture and assessment system. The system enables the analysis of both *static data,* pertaining to the outcome of the drawing task and *dynamic data* that details the constructional and sequencing aspects of task performance. The algorithmic application of static assessments enables accurate and consistent feature extraction from patient responses. While conventional assessments rely on the subjective judgement of the drawn response, computer-extracted static features uniformly and consistently quantify the visual image and hence the subjectivity in assessment across multiple subjects and test attempts is removed.

More importantly, the sensitivity to the detection of VSN is improved by analysis of the dynamic features. Assessment of drawings that appear normal to direct visual inspection applying a static analysis (i.e. containing the correct number of sides and positioning to form a 'perfect' visual response) often reveals dynamic feature deficiencies which are characteristic of a VSN-based population, thereby improving the ability of a simple drawing task to detect the condition.

2. Methodology

The results documented in this paper are extracted from *test overlays* each containing half of a simple diamond shape of height 95mm and half-width of 50mm, located so that the vertical split of the shape is positioned at the horizontal centre of each overlay. The test subject has to draw the vertical mirror image of the shape within the right visual field (i.e. presented with the left side components of the shape) in the first overlay. This is reversed in the second overlay when completion to the left side of the visual field is required. Test overlays are positioned individually on a Wacom WD1212 graphics digitisation tablet (spatial accuracy of 6.25 lines/mm) connected to a portable computer. As the test subject moves the pen and marks the overlay, the positional data are sampled at a rate of 100Hz by the computer. The data is stored sequentially and timestamped as received. Performance related features can be extracted from this stored data stream.

In the case of the diamond, each side of the drawn image constitutes a component and therefore two components were expected within the patient's response. This 'component-based' approach to drawing assessment is used within the Rivermead Behavioural Inattention Test (BIT) [7] (an existing standard for VSN detection) and is therefore a clinical standard for drawing evaluation. The feature provides an initial performance indication.

The features extracted from the test responses are categorised as either *static* (the outcome of the drawing) or *dynamic* (constructional/timing aspects of the execution of the drawing). Many of the static features can be defined with reference to Figure 1.

i) Drawing image height and *width.*

ii) Positional displacement - calculated at three reference points (*top, junction and bottom*). Each displacement is calculated independently using the Euclidean distance between the ideal and actual drawn position. In the case of the actual junction reference point, this position is defined as the point where the two sides intersect. If no intersection occurs, then an extrapolated position is calculated.

iii) Total length drawn - the total travel distance of the pen in mm. Perseveration (multiple drawing of a particular image side) is usually represented by an increased travel distance.

iv) Junction distance error - as the sides of the diamond do not need to intersect, this feature provides a Euclidean distance accuracy measure for the junction of the two components.

The dynamic data extracted from the test responses contain information concerning timing and ordering aspects of test performance. Nine features are defined:

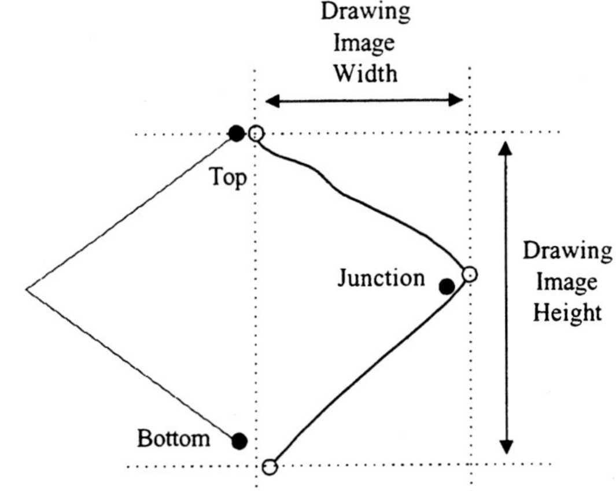

Figure 1. Static feature definitions

i) Drawing time (s) - the time period when the pen is drawing on the surface of the tablet.

ii) Movement time (s) - the time during which the pen is removed from the surface *during the drawing process.* In this way movement times are ignored a) before the pen initially marks the overlay and b) when the pen is finally removed from the tablet surface at the end of the drawing process.

iii) Component pre-movement time (s) [8] - the time during which the pen is stationary on the tablet surface between the drawing of individual components (sides of the diamond). This indicates a hesitation in drawing associated with a planning phase for the next drawing movement.

iv) Component movement time (s) - the time during which the pen is removed from the tablet surface between the drawing of individual components. If the pen is not removed then this feature returns a zero value.

v) Starting position - Using the *Top, Junction and Bottom* position identifiers to denote the starting position of the drawing sequence.

vi) Drawing sequence - Table 1 defines the eight possible component-based drawing sequences using the three reference points (as shown in Figure 1) defined for the starting position feature.

vii) Pen lifts - The number of times the pen is removed from the tablet *during* the drawing time (not including the final pen lift at the end of the drawing). Quantifies the number of movement segments within the drawing.

viii) Mean velocity (mm/s) - Pen velocity across the surface of the tablet is calculated by taking the first derivative of the coordinate pair displacement against time. Third order, four coefficient polynomial modelling is used to obtain a derivative of displacement at each coordinate point [9]. A mean pen velocity is calculated over the test response only *when the pen is on the tablet.*

Table 1. Drawing Sequence Specification

ID	Sequence
1	Top - Junction, Bottom - Junction
2	Top - Junction, Junction - Bottom
3	Junction - Top, Junction - Bottom
4	Junction - Top, Bottom - Junction
5	Junction - Bottom, Top - Junction
6	Junction - Bottom, Junction - Top
7	Bottom - Junction, Junction - Top
8	Bottom - Junction, Top - Junction

ix) Mean acceleration (mm/s^2) - Pen acceleration is the second derivative of the coordinate displacement. Calculated in a similar way to the Mean Velocity, pen acceleration is calculated between pairs of samples when the pen is drawing on the tablet surface. A mean is obtained across individual drawing responses.

3. Results based on a Case Study

To demonstrate the ability of computer-extracted features to detect the differences between a stroke control and a VSN subject, a case study comparing two subjects can be used to illustrate a range of static and dynamic results that show a clear performance differential. The responses from a stroke control (SC) subject - an RCVA stroke subject without neglect - (age 78, Male) and a VSN subject - diagnosed using the BIT and clinical evaluation (age 75, Female) are shown in Figures 2*a* and 2*b* respectively. Both subjects produce responses that contain the correct number of sides for the two completion overlays and hence using conventional 'component-present' assessment criteria, the VSN subject response would be considered normal.

Table 2 shows a range of dynamic and static features extracted from the responses. It can be clearly observed that the *drawing and movement times* are slower for the VSN response, with the pen being removed repeatedly from the drawing surface during the drawing process. The VSN subject draws with small rapid movements rather than using a continuous drawing stroke. This is reflected in both the *mean velocity* and *acceleration* results and the number of *pen lifts* within the drawing.

The VSN subject also spends an increased time in a planning (non drawing or movement) phase between components (*component pre-movement time*), again indicating that the drawing is treated as separate components requiring individual planning and execution phases rather than as a global image. It is also interesting to note that the VSN subject modified the drawing order of the components between visual fields (as defined in Table 1) whereas the *drawing sequence* is consistent for the stroke control subject.

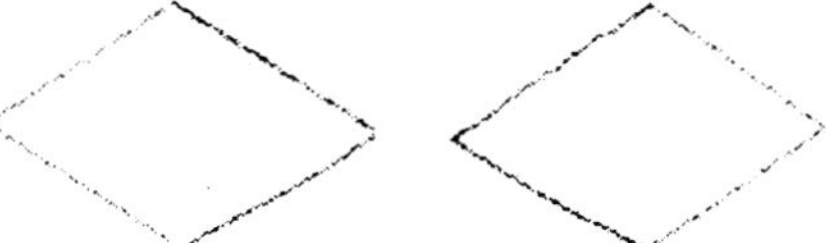

Figure 2a. Stroke control responses

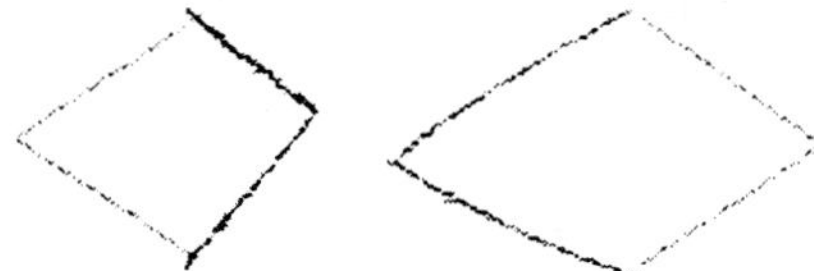

Figure 2b. VSN subject responses

The VSN subject compresses the *drawing width* when copying from the inattentive visual field (overlay 1) and expands when drawing into this field (overlay 2). The VSN subject also draws less (in terms of *total length drawn*) on overlay 1. The width compression/expansion contained within the VSN subject drawings is also represented in the *junction positional error*.

4. Summary

This paper has presented a case study demonstrating the ability of novel dynamic constructional/timing based measurements to identify a VSN test response even when the response appears normal to conventional component-based visual assessment. By algorithmically applying static measurements, the accuracy and consistency of the obtained results also show performance deficits by the VSN group which may not have contributed to a conventional assessment of the drawing response.

The figure completion task is part of a wider computer-assessed battery of neuropsychological tests for neglect which have been used in a clinically based trial. By comparing the results from the computer-based task to the findings of a range of standardised clinical assessments indicates that the accuracy and test sensitivity of the diagnosis of visuo-spatial neglect is improved. The combination of accurate and objective assessment of static features and the novel dynamic measurements both aid the diagnosis of neglect and also further the understanding of the condition with respect to constructional and timing aspects of test performance. This produces a clearer indication of rehabilitation progress and an enhanced tool to aid clinical assessment.

The authors acknowledge the support of the South Thames NHS R&D Project Fund

5. References

[1] Heilman, K.M., Watson, R.T., Valenstein, E., "Neglect and related disorders", In: *Clinical Neuropsychology* (eds. Heilman, K.M., Valenstein, E), Oxford University Press, Oxford, UK. 1993, pp. 279-336.

[2] Halligan, P.W., Marshall, J.C., Wade, D.T., "Visuospatial neglect : Underlying factors and test sensitivity", *The Lancet*, ii, 1989, pp. 908-910.

[3] Edmans, J.A., Lincoln, N., "The relationship between perceptual deficits after stroke and independence in activities of daily living", *British Journal of Occupational Therapy*, 53, 1993, pp. 139-142.

[4] Robertson, I.H., "The rehabilitation of attentional and hemi-attentional disorders", In: *Cognitive Neuropsychology and Cognitive Rehabilitation* (eds. Riddoch, M.J., Humphreys, G.W.), Lawrence Erlbaum Associates, Hove, UK, 1994, pp. 173-186.

[5] Halligan P.W., Robertson I.H., "The assessment of unilateral neglect." In: *A Handbook of Neuropsychological Assessment* (eds. Crawford, J.R., Parker, D.M., McKinlay, W.W), Lawrence Erlbaum Associates, Hove, UK, 1992, pp. 151-175.

[6] J. Sword, J. Potter, A. Deighton, R. Guest, N. Donnelly, M. Fairhurst., "Inter-rater reliability in the Rivermead Behavioural Inattention Test", *In: Proc. British Geriatric Society Scientific Meeting*, Cork, 1999.

[7] Wilson, B., Cockburn, J., Halligan, P., *The Behavioural Inattention Test*, Thames Valley Test Company, Fareham, Hampshire, 1987.

[8] Donnelly, N., Guest, R., Fairhurst, M., Potter, J., Deighton, A., Patel, M., "Developing algorithms to enhance the sensitivity of cancellation tests of visuospatial neglect", *Behavior Research Methods, Instruments and Computers*, 31 (4), 1999, pp. 668-673

[9] Willams, C.S., *Designing Digital Filters*, Prentice Hall, New Jersey, 1986.

Table 2. Dynamic and static features extracted from example responses

	Overlay 1		Overlay 2	
Subject	**VSN**	**SC**	**VSN**	**SC**
Dynamic Features				
Pen Lifts	22	0	15	0
Movement Time (s)	6.30	3.03	5.46	1.21
Drawing Time (s)	7.74	4.06	5.35	6.62
Drawing Sequence ID	1	2	3	2
Starting Position	1	1	2	1
Mean Velocity (mm/s)	10.74	5.32	11.66	4.22
Mean Acceleration (mm/s^2)	0.41	0.23	0.34	0.19
Comp. Pre-movement Time (s)	3.13	0.07	4.04	0.15
Comp. Movement Time (s)	1.14	no pen lift	2.89	no pen lift
Static Features				
Drawing Image Width (mm)	25.23	50.32	62.23	50.41
Drawing Image Height (mm)	82.55	91.24	96.21	88.76
Total Length Drawn (mm)	83.66	126.11	148.13	124.33
Top Positional Error (mm)	2.79	1.80	8.08	1.43
Junction Positional Error (mm)	20.82	5.68	19.68	3.60
Bottom Positional Error (mm)	2.20	2.71	5.46	1.44
Junction Error Distance (mm)	2.95	1.41	1.73	1.99

Automatic Left Ventricular Endocardium Detection in Echocardiograms Based on Ternary Thresholding Method

Wataru Ohyama*, Tetsushi Wakabayashi*, Fumitaka Kimura*,
Shinji Tsuruoka*, Kiyotsugu Sekioka**
*Faculty of Engineering, Mie University, Tsu, Mie, 514-8507, Japan
**School of Medicine, Mie University, Tsu Mie, 514-0001, Japan
ohyama@hi.info.mie-u.ac.jp

Abstract

Methods for automatic detection of left ventricular endocardium in echocardiograms are required to quantitatively evaluate the functional performance of the left ventricle. This study proposes a new automatic detection method based on ternary thresholding method for echocardiograms. Two thresholds are determined by the discriminant analysis for the gray level histogram so that the input image is segmented into three regions, i.e. cardiac cavity (black region), near epicardium (white region) , and the rest (gray region). Then the input echocardiogram is binarized with the lower threshold (between black and gray) to detect the cardiac cavity. The binary images are contracted n times to remove small regions and to disconnect the region of cardiac cavity from the other false regions. Among the obtained regions which corresponds to the cardiac cavity is selected and dilated 2n times to create a mask which restricts the region of the second thresholding operation. The masked image of each frame is binarized with another threshold determined by the discriminant analysis in the restricted area. Results of the evaluation test showed that the accuracy of the extracted contours was favorably compared with the accuracy of manually traced contours.

1. Introduction

The ultrasound systems are widely used for functional evaluation of heart because of the portability and the non-invasive real time visualization capability of internal structure. Several methods for automatic extraction of left ventricular endocardium in echocardiograms have been proposed, which are required to quantitatively evaluate the functional performance of the left ventricle[1, 2, 3, 4, 5, 8]. Although the ultrasound systems with real time endocardium detection function are commercially available [6], there is still a room for further improvement in
(1) automatic control of some parameters such as gain and threshold,
(2) detection of the endocardium behind the inner wall structure such as papillary muscle, and
(3) detection of endocardium as closed continuous curve.

In principle, the simplest way for the endocardium detection is to binarize the echocardiograms to detect the cardiac cavity. However, considerable image processing techniques have to be preformed before and after the binarization to correctly detect the endocardiums because the SN ratio of echocardiograms are generally low [5]. The authors proposed a double thresholding method and experimentally showed the effectiveness [8]. The method consists of two thresholding operations, one for restricting the location of the cardiac cavity, and the other for final endocardium detection in the restricted region. This paper proposes a new double thresholding method that employs the discriminant analysis based ternary thresholding method to determine the first threshold.

2. Ternary Double Thresholding Method (TDTM)

Fig.1 shows the flowchart of the automatic endocardium detection. The process consists of the three parts:
(1) noise suppression by mean filtering across frames of ultrasound image sequence,
(2) ternary thresholding and mask generation for restricting the location of cardiac cavity, and
(3) binarization of the ultrasound image in the restricted region.
Each part is described in the following subsection.

2.1. Noise suppression

The echocardiograms contain considerable speckle noise, which is harmful for the endocardium detection. To suppress the noise, the mean of two adjacent frames is repeatedly taken four times:

$$f_k^{(m)}(i,j) = \frac{1}{2}\left\{f_{k+1}^{(m-1)}(i,j) + f_k^{(m-1)}(i,j)\right\} \qquad (1)$$

where k is the number of frame, m is the number of repetition, and $f_k^{(0)}(i,j)$ is the value of (i,j) pixel of the

1051-4651/00 $10.00 © 2000 IEEE

input image. Hereafter the noise-suppressed image is simply denoted by $F_k = \{f_k(i,j)\}$ omitting the superscript.

2.3. Ternary thresholding for ultrasound image

Fig.2 (a), (b) show an example of typical ultrasound image and its gray scale histogram, respectively. Fig. 3 and Fig.4 show the results of binary and ternary quantization based on the discriminant analysis for the gray scale histogram respectively [7].

Two thresholds t_1 and t_2 which maximize the between-class gray scale variance

$$\sigma_B^2(t_1,t_2) = \sum_{j=1}^{3} \omega_j(\mu_j - \mu_T)^2 \quad (2)$$

are used for the ternary quantization, where ω_j, μ_j and μ_T are *a priori* probability of class *j*, the average gray scale of class *j*, and the total average gray scale, respectively.

Since the echocardiograms generally contain three regions, i.e. the cardiac cavity (black region), rear epicardium (white region), and the rest (gray region), the ternary quantization is more reasonable than binarization, and it generates a quantized image which reflects the physical structures of input image adequately. The result of ternary quantization can be utilized to detect a part of epicardium as well as the endocardium.

2.4. Mask generation for region restriction

Two thresholds $t_1, t_2 (t_1 < t_2)$ are determined so that the noise-suppressed image F_k is segmented into three regions. To detect the region corresponding to the cardiac cavity the image is binarized by the lower threshold t_1.

$$b_k(i,j) = \begin{cases} 0 & (f_k(i,j) > t_1) \\ 1 & (f_k(i,j) \le t_1) \end{cases} \quad (3)$$

Then the binary image $B_k = \{b_k(i,j)\}$ is contracted *n* times to remove small regions, and to disconnect the region of cardiac cavity from other false regions, i.e.

$$B_k^- = \underbrace{(\cdots((B_k \ominus H) \ominus H) \cdots \ominus H)}_{n \text{ times}} \quad (4)$$

where (-) denotes morphological contraction, and

$$H = \begin{bmatrix} 1 & 1 & 1 \\ 1 & 1 & 1 \\ 1 & 1 & 1 \end{bmatrix} \quad (5)$$

is the structuring element.

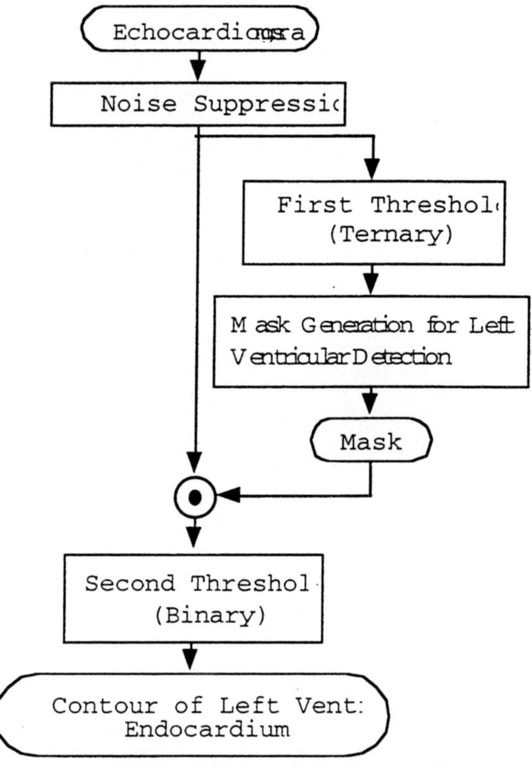

Fig1 Flowchart of Extraction of Left

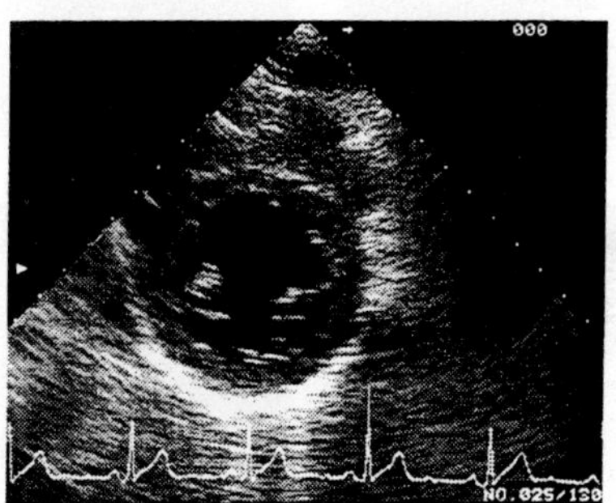

(a) Ultrasound image

blac ⟷ whit

(b) Gray scale histogram of ultrasound image

Fig.2 Example of typical ultrasound image and its gray scale histogram

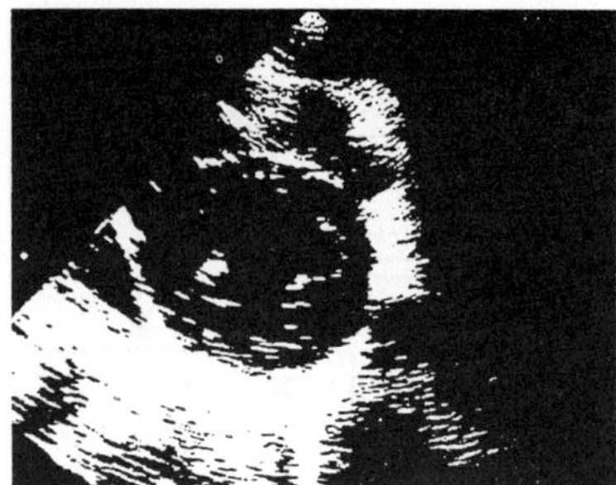

Fig. 3 Binary image of Fig.2(a)

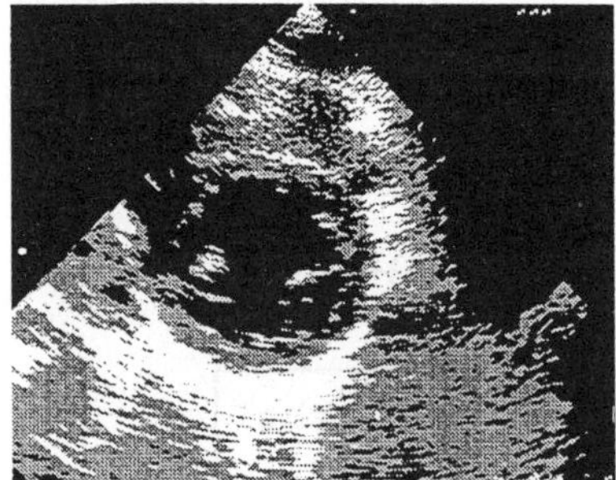

Fig. 4 Ternary image of Fig.2(a)

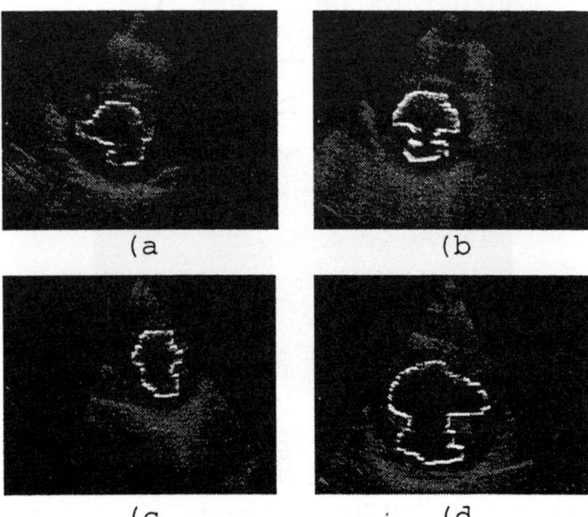

Fig. 5 Left ventricular image imposed with mask

Among the multiple regions in the B_k^- the one which corresponds to the cardiac cavity is selected and dilated $2n$ times to create a mask M_k which restricts the region of the second thresholding operation. The size and the location of the cardiac cavity in the preceding frame are utilized to select the corresponding region. The sequence of masks is contracted and dilated in time domain to correct abrupt deformation of the masks due to inappropriate threshold selection.

Fig.5 shows examples of the images imposed with the masks. The region of low contrast in each figure is the masked region.

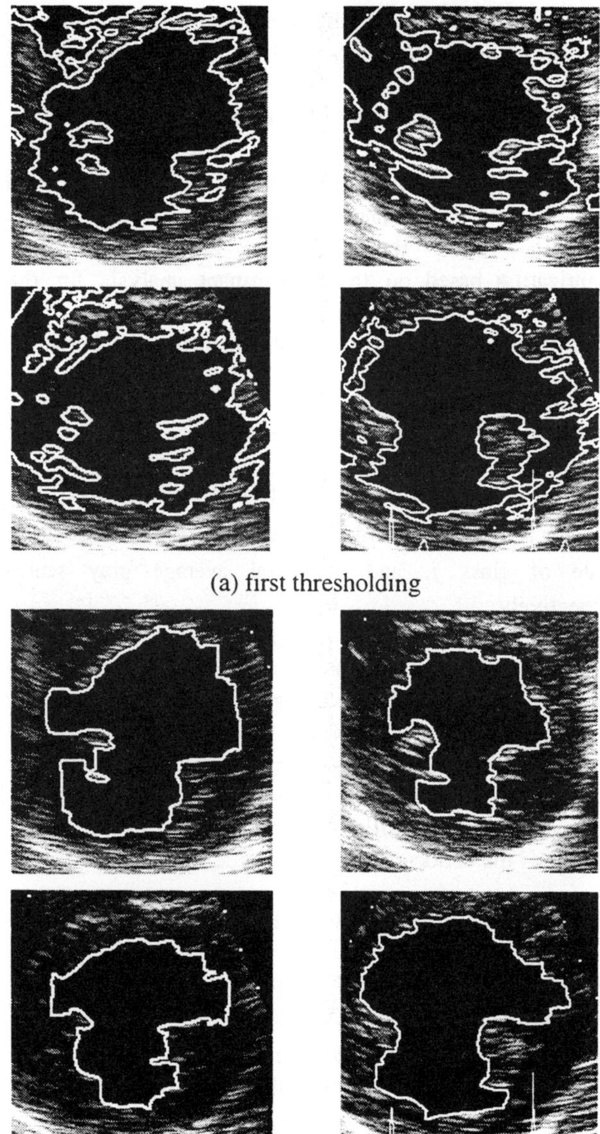

(b) second thresholding

Fig. 6 By first and second thresholding extracted endocardial contour

The masked image of each frame is binarized again in the same way as in the first thresholding operation.

3. Evaluation test

Total of 867 left ventricle short-axis echocardiographic images (for 15 cases) acquired with an ultrasound system (Hitachi Medical Corporation EUB565A) were used to evaluate the accuracy of the automatic endocardium detection. The parameter n for contraction/dilation operations was set to 5 in the experiment.

Fig.6(a) and (b) show the example of extracted endocardial borders by the first and the second thresholding operation, respectively. While the tangential contours to the ultrasound beam are not correctly extracted by the first thresholding operation due to the reduced signal amplitude, they are correctly extracted by the second thresholding operation in the restricted area.

The automatically detected endocardium was compared with the manually traced one in the same echocardium to evaluate the accuracy of the proposed method. The correlation coefficients of two distances from the centroid of the cardiac cavity to each endocardium was used as the measure of the accuracy evaluation (Fig.7). The correlation coefficients for the cases:

(1) manual trace by the same person A
(2) manual trace by two person A, B
(3) automatic detection and manual trace by person A
(4) automatic detection and manual trace by person B

were (1) 0.983(±0.011), (2) 0.967(±0.022), (3) 0.962(±0.018), and (4) 0.942(±0.028) . Fig.8 (a),(b) show the scatter diagrams of the case (1) and (3) respectively. This result shows that the accuracy of the automatic extraction is favorably compared with the accuracy of the manual trace.

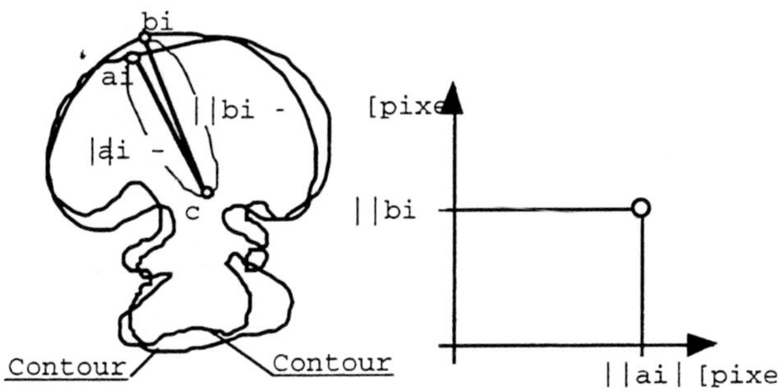

Fig.7 Generation of the scatter diagram for two contours

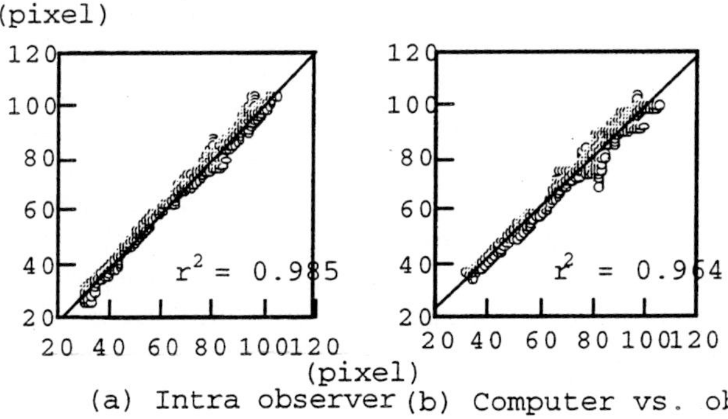

Fig.8 Scatter diagrams

4.Conclusion

We proposed a new method of automatic endocardium detection by ternary double thresholding operation. The result of evaluation test showed that

(1) the tangential contours to the ultrasound beam were correctly extracted by the double thresholding operation, and that
(2) the accuracy of the automatic detection was favorably compared with the accuracy of the manually trace.

The proposed method has characteristics such that

(1) it is less dependent on the intensity and the contrast of the input images since it employs the threshold determination method based on the discriminant analysis of the gray scale histogram,
(2) it is suitable to high speed parallel processing and hardware implementation since it is mainly composed of simple local operations for thresholding and contraction/dilation.

Further studies on

(1) performance evaluation using more images,
(2) improvement of success rate of automatic extraction,
(3) application to the quantitative evaluation of the left ventricle functional performance, and
(4) application of the ternary thresholding to the epicardium detection

are remaining as future research topics.

References

[1] H. Yamada, and K. Yamamoto, "Recognition of Echocardiogram by Dynamic Programming Matching Method", Trans. of IEICE, Vol. J71-D No.4, Apr. 1988, pp.678-684

[2] K. Fujimura, N. Yokoya, and K. Yamamoto, "Recognition of Echocardiographic Images by Active Contour Method", Technical report of IEICE, PRU92-97, Dec. 1992, pp.63-68

[3] G. Ohashi, A. Ohya, M. Natori, and M. Nakajima, "Edge Extraction Method Using Neural Network for Three Dimensional Display of Ultrasonic Echo Image", Trans. of IEICE, Vol. J76-D-II No.2, Feb. 1993, pp.368-373

[4] M. Okada, F. Kimura, S. Tsuruoka, Y. Miyake, S. Umaoka, K. Sekioka, "Local Spatial Phase Analysis of Left Ventricular Wall Motion Using Hilbert Transform", Trans. of IEICE, Vol. J69-D No.10, Oct. 1986, pp.1490-1499

[5] Joseph W. Kilingler, Jr, Clifton L. Vaughan, Theodore D. Fraker, Jr, "Segmentation of Echocardiographic Images Using Mathematical Morphology.", IEEE Trans. Biomedical Engineering, Vol.35 No.11, Nov. 1988, pp. 925-934

[6] Byron F. Vandenberg, Linda S. Rath, Patricia Stuhlmuller, et al, "Estimation of Left Ventricular Cavity Area With an On-line, Semiautomaticed Echocardiographic Edge Detection System.", Circulation, Vol 86 No.1, Jul. 1992, pp159-166

[7] N.Otsu, "A Threshold Selection Method from Gray Level Histograms", IEEE Trans. Syst., Man. and Cybern., Vol.SMC-9, No.l, Jan. 1979, pp. 62-66

[8] W.Ohyama, F.Kimura, T.Wakabayashi, et al, "An Automatic Extraction of Left Ventricular Endocardium in Echocardiogram", Proc. of the 4th APCMBE, Sep. 1999, p.425

Combining Experts with Different Features for Classifying Clustered Microcalcifications in Mammograms

L.P. Cordella°, F. Tortorella*, M. Vento°

(°) Dipartimento di Informatica e Sistemistica
Università degli Studi di Napoli "Federico II"
via Claudio, 21 80125 Napoli – Italy
E-mail: {cordel,vento}@unina.it

(*) Dipartimento di Automazione, Elettromagnetismo, Ingegneria dell'Informazione e Matematica Industriale
Università degli Studi di Cassino
via G. di Biasio, 43 03043 Cassino - Italy
E-mail: tortorella@unicas.it

Abstract

At present, mammography is the only not invasive diagnostic technique allowing the diagnosis of a breast cancer at a very early stage. A visual clue of such disease particularly significant is the presence of clusters of microcalcifications. Reliable methods for an automatic recognition of malignant clusters are very difficult to accomplish because of the small size of the microcalcifications and of the poor quality of the mammographic images. In this paper we propose a novel approach for automating the recognition of malignant clusters, based on the adoption of a Multiple Expert System (MES). The approach has been successfully tested on a standard database of 40 mammographic images, publicly available.

1. Introduction

Mammography is today the only not invasive diagnostic technique which allows the diagnosis of a breast cancer at a very early stage [1], when the cancerous mass cannot be yet detected by other means (e.g. physical examination). Unfortunately, the low quality of mammographic images and the intrinsic complicacy in detecting likely cancer signs make the analysis particularly difficult and fatiguing for the radiologist (specially during mass screenings) with a consequent decreasing quality of the diagnosis. In this case, a computer aided analisys could be very useful to the radiologist both for prompting suspect cases and for helping in the diagnostic decision [2].

A visual clue of breast cancer particularly significant is the presence of microcalcifications. These are tiny granule-like deposits of calcium with size ranging from about 0.1 mm to 0.7 mm and shape sometimes irregular. Microcalcifications can appear spread all over the breast or grouped in clusters. In these cases the cluster also can assume peculiar forms. It has been experimentally proved that some kinds of microcalcifications are associated to an high probability of cancer [3], and many studies have concerned the correlation between the shape of single and clustered microcalcifications and the presence of a breast cancer [4]. In the recent past, many methods have been presented in the litearature mostly devoted to the automatic detection of microcalcifications (e.g. see [5]) while few proposals have regarded the problem of the automatic recognition of malignant clusters. Moreover, these approaches are mainly focused on the analysis of the single microcalcification, without taking into account that the cluster, considered as a whole, can also provide useful information for the classification regarding the distribution of the microcalcifications within the breast tissue.

In this paper we propose a novel approach, based on the adoption of a Multiple Expert System (MES), for the recognition of malignant clusters. Such a system aggregates several experts, each made of a classifier working on a different feature set. The outputs of the experts are combined to provide the final classification decision. The rationale of this approach, in the recent past widely investigated in other application domains, is that the combination of a set of experts could take advantage of the strength of the single experts without be affected by their weaknesses. In the case of the recognition of malignant clusters, this approach revealed to be particularly appropriate because it allowed the decision about the malignancy of a cluster to be taken on the basis of the evidences coming from both the microcalcifications and the entire cluster. The approach has been experimented with a standard database of mammographies, obtaining encouraging results which confirmed its effectiveness.

2. The system architecture

The recognition system we propose is a MES composed of two different experts: the first one (**μC-Expert**) is devised for the classification of the single microcalcifications, while the second one (**Cluster Expert**) considers the entire cluster. To decide about the malignancy of a cluster containing N microcalcifications,

1051-4651/00 $10.00 © 2000 IEEE

each microcalcification is classified by using the μC-Expert, while the cluster, considered as a whole, is classified by the Cluster Expert. The final response is given by combining the N+1 classification decisions.

Shape Features	Compactness of the microcalcification
	Roughness of the border
	Average contrast microcalcification/background
	Average local density
Texture Features	Energy in the Area of Interest
	Energy in the background
	Average luminance
	Standard deviation of the luminance
	Entropy of the 1st order histogram
	Energy of the 2nd order histogram
	Contrast of the 2nd order histogram
	Entropy of the 2nd order histogram

Tab. 1: The features for the microcalcifications.

The classifiers adopted to build both the μC-Expert and the Cluster Expert are Multi-Layer Perceptrons (MLPs), trained with the Back Propagation algorithm, with 25 hidden neurons and 2 output neurons, associated to the benign and the malignant class.

Ellipticity of the cluster
Mass density of the cluster
Average mass of the microcalcifications
Standard deviation of the masses of microcalcifications
Average distance between microcalcifications and the center of mass of the cluster
Standard deviation of distance between microcalcifications and center of mass

Tab. 2: The cluster features.

The description used by the μC-Expert employs mostly features already proposed in the literature. They refer both to shape properties of the microcalcifications and to the global texture in the area of interest containing the microcalcification (see table 1). For a detailed definition of the adopted features, see [6].

As regards the features describing the cluster they take into account the shape of the cluster and the distribution of the mass within the cluster (see table 2). To this aim, it is worth noting that the mass of a microcalcification can be estimated by considering the luminance of its pixels, which is correlated with the density of total mass crossed by the X-ray beam.

3. The combination scheme

One of the main points in the implementation of a MES is the definition of the combining rule most suitable for the application at hand. Many rules have been proposed in literature [6,7], based on statistical methods, evidence theory or heuristic approaches. The most suitable combining scheme for the case we are considering is the "Weighted Voting" rule, according to which the "vote" (i.e. the output) of each expert is weighted by the estimated reliability associated to the expert; all the votes are finally collected and the input sample is assigned to the class for which the sum of the votes is the highest. The reason for this choice is that this rule allows the outputs coming from the μC Experts and those coming from the Cluster Expert to be weighted in a different way, so as to take into greater account the expert most reliable. The combination is accomplished with a two-stage scheme (see fig. 1) to avoid any bias due to the number of microcalcifications in the clusters, which is highly variable. In the first stage (μC aggregation) the results coming from the μC Experts are aggregated and weighted, thus obtaining two confidence degrees about the malignancy (M_m) or benignancy (M_b) of the cluster, which are combined in the second stage with the analogous confidence degrees (C_m and C_b) coming from the Cluster Expert. The aggregation is accomplished in two ways, which have different behaviors as the number of microcalcifications varies. With the first one, the confidence degrees about the malignancy (O_m) and the benignancy (O_b), are evaluated by averaging the outputs of the μC Experts, while the second solution evaluates two analogous confidence degrees (N_m, N_b) by simply counting the number of the microcalcifications classified as malignant (benign) and normalizing these values with respect to the total number N of microcalcifications in the cluster. Experiments have shown that N_m and N_b work better when N is high while the contrary happens for (O_m, O_b). As a consequence, the values for (M_m, M_b) are evaluated by a weighted sum of (O_m, O_b) and (N_m, N_b), with weights dinamically varying with N. The resulting analytical expression for the combination rule is:

$$V_m = \alpha(N)\cdot O_m + \beta(N)\cdot N_m + \gamma\cdot C_m$$

$$V_b = \alpha(N)\cdot O_b + \beta(N)\cdot N_b + \gamma\cdot C_b$$

where V_m (V_b) is the final confidence degree for the malignancy (benignancy) of the cluster, while $\alpha(N)$ and $\beta(N)$ are the weight functions for the μC aggregation and

γ is a costant weight. Both the weight functions are linear; $\alpha(N)$ is increasing with N, while $\beta(N)$ is decreasing. The parameters of the weight functions and γ are evaluated by means of an optimization phase performed by using a set of clusters representative of the particular domain. As a result, two particular values of N are determined such that the highest weight is given to the pair (O_m, O_b) for $N < N_0$ and to the pair (N_m, N_b) for $N > N_1$; thus, in these two intervals, the contribution coming from the for μC-Experts is prevailing with respect to the Cluster Experts. This is consistent with the experimental evidence that the cluster features are not very reliable with a low number of microcalcifications, while, for clusters with many microcalcifications, the outputs of the μC-Experts are more accurate.

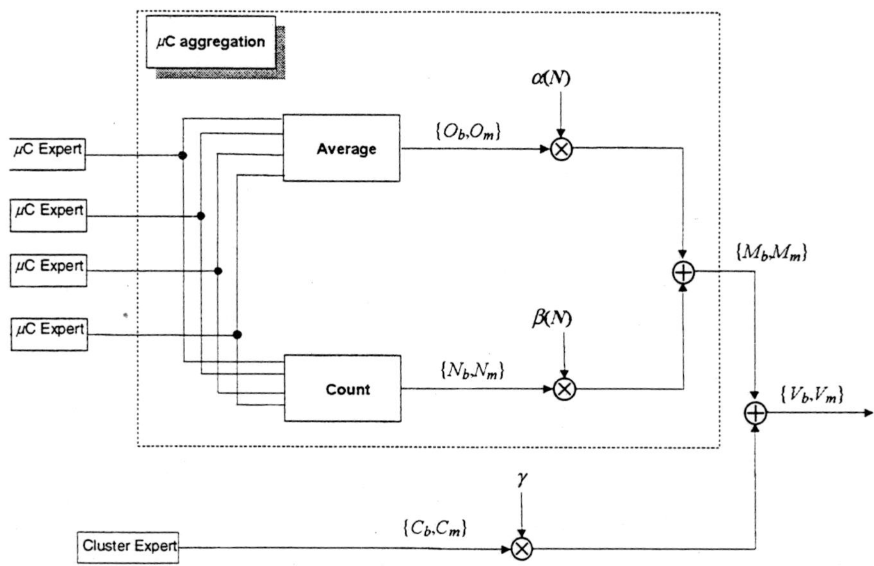

Fig. 1: The two-stage combining scheme.

4. Experimental results

For testing our approach we have used a public database (available at the site http://figment.csee.usf.edu/) of 40 mammographies containing 102 clusters (72 malignant clusters and 30 benign ones), with 1792 malignant and 331 benign microcalcifications. Images were provided by courtesy of the National Expert and Training Centre for Breast Cancer Screening and the Department of Radiology at the University of Nijmegen, the Netherlands. All images have size 2048 by 2048 and use 12 bits (2 bytes) per pixel of gray level information. Some preprocessing was performed to convert the images to a 8 bit/pixel format using an adaptive noise equalisation described in [8]. This database represents a severe test bed, since the size of the microcalcifications is typically very small. Moreover, the low number of clusters (specially of benign clusters) makes very difficult training experts based on neural networks. For this reason, we have adopted a leave-one-out approach: for each cluster in the database, we employ the remaining clusters to constitute the training sets for learning the μC-Expert and the Cluster Expert. A successive optimization phase provides the parameters of the weight functions. The classification is finally performed on the cluster extracted.

A first analysis of the performance obtained with our approach has been carried out by assigning the cluster to the class with the highest vote between V_m and V_b. The relative results are shown in table 3: the first column provides the recognition rate (in percentage) obtained by considering only the Cluster Expert; the successive two columns report the results obtained by the μC-Expert with the two possible aggregations, while the last column contains the results given by the whole MES.

	Cluster Expert	μC-Expert (O_b,O_m)	μC-Expert (N_b,N_m)	MES
Malignant	60.00 %	75.74 %	75.37 %	75.37 %
Benign	70.00 %	67.5 %	60.00 %	73.50 %

Tab. 3: The recognition rates of each expert and of the MES.

It is worth noting that the recognition rate exhibited by the MES on the malignant clusters is lightly smaller than the best result obtained by the experts, while there is a significant improvement in the recognition of benign clusters and thus a significant decrease of false positives.

Another goal of our experiments was to measure the performance of the MES in terms of sensitivity and specificity. For this purpose, we have evaluated the *Receiver Operating Characteristic* (*ROC*) graph of the MES, which is extensively used for visualizing and analyzing the accuracy of diagnostic systems [9]. ROC graph reports, as a threshold imposed on the output of the MES varies in the range [0,1], the *True Positive* (*TP*) rate on the Y axis and the *False Positive* (*FP*) rate on the X axis. Informally, the nearer the curve to the upper right point of the diagram, the better the performance obtained (higher *TP* and/or lower *FP*). Fig. 2 shows the ROC curves evaluated for each single expert and for the whole MES. It is possible to note that the MES performs better both for low and for high values of *FP*, while it has quite the same performance of the single experts for medium values of *FP*.

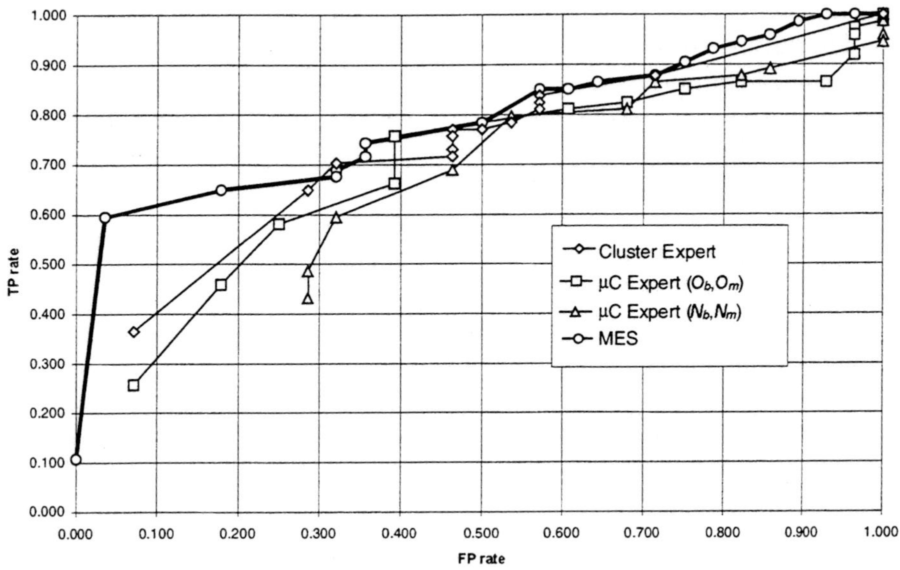

Fig. 2: The ROC curves of the single experts and of the whole MES.

An immediate way to globally compare the MES with respect the single experts is to measure the area under the respective ROC curves. In the ideal case (expert with *TP*=1 for each *FP*∈[0,1]), this measure is 1; in real situations, the more the area approaches 1, the better the diagnostic system. Table 4 shows the results obtained.

	Cluster Expert	μC-Expert (O_b,O_m)	μC-Expert (N_b,N_m)	**MES**
Area under ROC curve	0.709	0.671	0.565	0.786

Tab. 4: The area under the ROC curve obtained by each expert and by the whole MES.

Also in this case it is possible to note that the performances exhibited by the MES are better than each single expert.

References

[1] R. Mc Clelland "Screening for Breast Cancer: Opportunities, status and challenges" in *Recent Results in Cancer Research*, vol. 119, S. Brunner and B. Langfeldt eds., Springer-Verlag, Berlin, pp. 29-38, 1990.

[2] E.D. Pisano, F. Shtern "Image processing and Computer Aided Diagnosis in digital mammography: A clinical perspective", *Int. Journal of Pattern Recognition and Artificial Intelligence*, vol. 7, no. 6, pp. 1493-1503, 1993.

[3] M. Lanyi, *Diagnosis and differential diagnosis of breast calcifications*, Springer-Verlag, New York, 1986.

[4] B. Zheng, W. Qian, and L. P. Clarke, "Digital Mammography: Mixed Feature Neural Network with Spectral Entropy Decision for Detection of Microcalcifications", *IEEE Trans. on Medical Imaging*, vol. 15, no. 5, pp. 589-597, 1996.

[5] A.P. Dhawan, Y. Chitre, C. Kaiser-Bonasso, M. Moskowitz, "Analysis of Mammographic Microcalcifications Using Gray-Level Image Structure Features", *IEEE Trans. on Medical Imaging*, vol. 15, no. 3, pp. 246-259, 1996.

[6] L. Xu, A. Krzyzak, C.Y. Suen, "Method of Combining Multiple Classifier Systems and Their Application to Handwritten Numeral Recognition", *IEEE Trans. on Systems, Man and Cybernetics*, vol. 22, no. 3, pp 418-435, 1992.

[7] B. Ackermann, H. Bunke, "Combination of Classifiers on the Decision Level for Face Recognition", Technical Report IAM-96-002, Institut für Informatik und angewandte Mathematik, Universität Bern, 1996.

[8] N. Karssemeijer, "Adaptive Noise Equalization and Recognition of Microcalcification Clusters in Mammograms", *Int. Journal of Pattern Recognition and Artificial Intelligence*, vol. 7, no. 6, pp. 1357-1376, 1993.

[9] J. Swets, "Measuring the Accuracy of Diagnostic Systems", *Science*, vol. 240, pp. 1285-1293, 1988.

Compound Extraction and Fitting Method for Detecting Cardiac Ventricle in SPECT Data

Timothy S. Newman
Department of Computer Science
University of Alabama in Huntsville
Huntsville, AL 35899 USA

Hong Yi
Department of Computer Science
University of Alabama in Huntsville
Huntsville, AL 35899 USA

Abstract

A new method for automatic extraction of the left ventricle of the heart from Single Photo Emission Computed Tomography (SPECT) data is presented. The method involves extracting and fitting compound analytical (quadric) surfaces which well-approximate the shape of the left ventricle (LV). The approach exploits geometric shape constraints and utilizes Hough-based processing, hierarchical clustering, and least-squares fitting. Through extraction of the left ventricle, shape and size change analysis can be aided—which is useful for determination of cardiac health.

1. Introduction

Study of the behavior and shape of the cardiac left ventricle over the systolic cycle provides insight into the functioning of the heart. For example, LV wall motion, wall thickening, and the fractional volume of blood ejected (ejection fraction (EF)) [8] are useful functional assessment measures. A number of semi-automatic or automatic LV extraction techniques have been presented for use in perfusion SPECT imaging, CT, or tagged MR data (e.g., [2, 7]).

In this paper, a method for automatically extracting the LV in a sequence of tomographic gated blood pool (GBP) SPECT images is presented. Gating ties the data collection to the beating of the heart and allows an image sequence to be collected over an idealized heart beat. *Planar* determination of the cardiac ejection fraction is considered the current SPECT clinical gold standard, however at least one recent study has demonstrated that the tomographic GBP SPECT images allow more accurate estimation of the EF [1]. Typically, the planar determination has been made based on manual or semi-automatic estimation of the LV boundary in a single planar slice image through the center of the LV. Such methods suffer from high variability in estimation [8] and cannot consider the full 3D extent of the LV.

1.1. LV Shape Models

One common paradigm for determining LV shape and volume uses variations on Simpson's Rule; the LV contours are manually traced on each planar slice in a dataset and EF is computed using the sum of the volumes of all the traced contours. Some methods have "fit" an ellipsoidal surface to the collection of manually traced contours, although usually just one or two of the cross-sections are used for the fitting [4, 5]. (These cross-sections are used to estimate the ellipsoid's axis lengths.) In perfusion data, methods for LV shape recovery that utilize superquadrics ([2]), compound surfaces, and other shape models have also been utilized. The compound fitting methods typically have fit an ellipsoid to central and basal regions and a hemispherical or conical surface to apical regions of the LV (e.g.,[5]).

Previously, one of us has developed a method—that builds on our prevous work in fitting quadric surfaces in range data [9]—for automatic extraction of the LV in tomographic GBP SPECT data [10]. The method uses an ellipsoidal model that is fit using all of the LV data (i.e., not just one or two slices of the dataset). However, that method suffers from fitting inaccuracies in the apical region of the LV. In this paper, we introduce a method that allows accurate extraction of the entire LV. The method involves ellipsoidal extraction and fitting for the basal and central regions and paraboloid extraction and fitting for the LV apex.

2. Quadric Fitting

A quadric surface in arbitrary position in space can be described by the equation:

$$k_1x^2 + k_2y^2 + k_3z^2 + k_4xy + k_5xz + k_6yz + k_7x + k_8y + k_9z + k_{10} = 0. \quad (1)$$

Although fitting such a quadric might seem to require a non-linear approach, Hall et al. [6] have described a least-squares-based approach to fitting *centered* quadrics. Hall's

1051-4651/00 $10.00 © 2000 IEEE

approach can hence be applied for ellipsoidal surface parameter recovery. Whenever $k_{10} \neq 0$, the Equation 1 can be formulated as a set of m linear equations in the form

$$C\,\mathbf{a} = \mathbf{b}, \tag{2}$$

where the coordinate matrix C is

$$C = \begin{bmatrix} {x_1}^2 & {y_1}^2 & {z_1}^2 & x_1y_1 & x_1z_1 & y_1z_1 & x_1 & y_1 & z_1 \\ {x_2}^2 & {y_2}^2 & {z_2}^2 & x_2y_2 & x_2z_2 & y_2z_2 & x_2 & y_2 & z_2 \\ \vdots & \vdots & \vdots & \vdots & \vdots & \vdots & \vdots & \vdots & \vdots \\ {x_n}^2 & {y_n}^2 & {z_n}^2 & x_ny_n & x_nz_n & y_nz_n & x_n & y_n & z_n \end{bmatrix}, \tag{3}$$

the vector of unknowns $\mathbf{a}$ is

$$\mathbf{a} = \begin{bmatrix} a_1 & a_2 & a_3 & a_4 & a_5 & a_6 & a_7 & a_8 & a_9 \end{bmatrix}^T,$$

and $\mathbf{b}$ is a column vector of 1's. Given n data points, the over-constrained least-squares solution to the system defines the unknowns a_i. In this section, we will demonstrate how the least squares fitting of Hall et al. can be utilized for recovery of ellipsoid pose and extended for recovery of paraboloid pose.

2.1. Ellipsoid Fitting

An ellipsoid in standard position can be represented as the implicit equation

$$f(x, y, z) = \frac{x^2}{a^2} + \frac{y^2}{b^2} + \frac{z^2}{c^2} - 1 = 0, \tag{4}$$

where a, b, and c are the half-lengths of the principal axes. Eqn. 4 can be expressed as

$$\hat{\mathbf{x}}^T G \hat{\mathbf{x}} + \mathbf{p}\hat{\mathbf{x}} = d, \tag{5}$$

where $\hat{\mathbf{x}} = [x\ y\ z]^T$, $\mathbf{p} = [0\ \ 0\ \ 0]$, $d = 1$, and

$$G = \begin{bmatrix} \frac{1}{a^2} & 0 & 0 \\ 0 & \frac{1}{b^2} & 0 \\ 0 & 0 & \frac{1}{c^2} \end{bmatrix}. \tag{6}$$

Rigid movement of the ellipsoid from its standard position by a translation vector $\mathbf{t} = [x_0\ y_0\ z_0]$ and by a rotational transformation $R(\alpha, \beta, \gamma)$, where R is a 3×3 special orthogonal rotation matrix, can be viewed as modifying Eqn. 5 to become:

$$\mathbf{x}^T G_1 \mathbf{x} + \mathbf{p_1}\mathbf{x} = d, \tag{7}$$

with $\mathbf{x} = [x - x_0\ \ y - y_0\ \ z - z_0]^T$, $\mathbf{p_1} = \mathbf{p}R$, and $G_1 = R^T G R$ (G_1 is symmetric). Eqn. 7 is equivalent to the original Eqn. 2, although terms have been reorganized. Solution of Eqn. 2 yields the a_i, which define the positional parameters x_0, y_0, z_0, and the entries g_{ij} of G_1, as well as a term d'. For example, the positional parameters can be found by simultaneous solution of the three equations:

$$-2a_1x_0 - a_4y_0 - a_5z_0 - \frac{p_{31}}{d'} = a_7\,, \tag{8}$$

$$-a_4x_0 - 2a_2y_0 - a_6z_0 - \frac{p_{32}}{d'} = a_8\,, \tag{9}$$

$$-a_5x_0 - a_6y_0 - 2a_3z_0 - \frac{p_{33}}{d'} = a_9\,, \tag{10}$$

where the p_{3j} are entries of the matrix $\mathbf{p_1}$ (for ellipsoids, the $p_{3j} = 0\ \forall j$). The d' term is

$$d' = \frac{d - p_{31}x_0 - p_{32}y_0 - p_{33}z_0}{1 + a_4x_0y_0 + a_5x_0z_0 + a_6y_0z_0 + e}, \tag{11}$$

where $e = a_1{x_0}^2 + a_2{y_0}^2 + a_3{z_0}^2$, $p_{31} = p_{32} = p_{33} = 0$ for ellipsoids, and the entries of G_1 are $g_{ii} = a_i d'$ and for $i \neq j$, $g_{ij} = \frac{a_{i+j+1}d'}{2}$.

The eigenvalues of G_1 are the three diagonal entries of G in Eqn. 6 and the corresponding eigenvectors define R [6], thus enabling recovery of shape and axis orientation parameters for an ellipsoid.

2.2. Paraboloid Fitting

Hall et al. [6]'s method is restricted to recovery of centered quadrics. However, we have extended it to support recovery of paraboloid parameters from scattered point data [11]. Since a paraboloid in the standard position is

$$f(x, y, z) = \frac{x^2}{a^2} + \frac{y^2}{b^2} - z = 0, \tag{12}$$

Eqn. 7 defines a paraboloid when $d = 0$, $\mathbf{p} = [0\ \ 0\ \ -1]$,

$$G = \begin{bmatrix} \frac{1}{a^2} & 0 & 0 \\ 0 & \frac{1}{b^2} & 0 \\ 0 & 0 & 0 \end{bmatrix}. \tag{13}$$

However, least squares solution of the a_i can not directly yield the positional parameters. We have shown [11] that if a variable $v = \frac{1}{d'}$ is introduced, then

$$G_2 = vG_1 = \begin{bmatrix} a_1 & \frac{a_4}{2} & \frac{a_5}{2} \\ \frac{a_4}{2} & a_2 & \frac{a_6}{2} \\ \frac{a_5}{2} & \frac{a_6}{2} & a_3 \end{bmatrix}, \tag{14}$$

which can be diagonalized, yielding $G_2 = R^T(vG)R$. (Since this matrix R is a standard orthogonal matrix, it must be the same as the rotation matrix R.) In Eqn. 8 through 10, the p_{3j} entries are non-zero for paraboloids, and the positional parameters can be represented as functions of v. By re-organizing terms and substituting the functional expressions for x_0, y_0, z_0, Eqn. 11 can be expressed as a quadratic $pv^2 + qv + s = 0$, where $q = 0$ and other terms' coefficients are functions of a_i and p_{3j} terms [11]. The p and s terms are invariants of a paraboloid so they exist and v has a real solution [11]. Solution of v yields the positional parameters x_0, y_0, z_0 and shape parameters a and b, completing recovery of paraboloid pose and size.

3. LV Extraction

Our extraction approach involves first accumulating evidence of the LV from each slice image of the dataset. The evidences are then grouped to support compound fitting of surfaces that closely estimate the LV endocardial wall.

3.1. Initial Processing

In GBP SPECT data, the voxels of highest intensity are those that are in the pool of blood in the heart's chambers. The GBP SPECT data is noisy, however, thus automatic extraction of reasonable LV boundaries is somewhat challenging. A typical slice image is shown in Figure 1. As an initial estimate of blood boundaries, Marr-Hildreth edge detection is applied to slices. The edge detection is applied in all three directions to reduce edge loss. Isovalue thresholding is used to eliminate weak edges. A collection of 3D edge contours extracted from one dataset is shown in Figure 2.

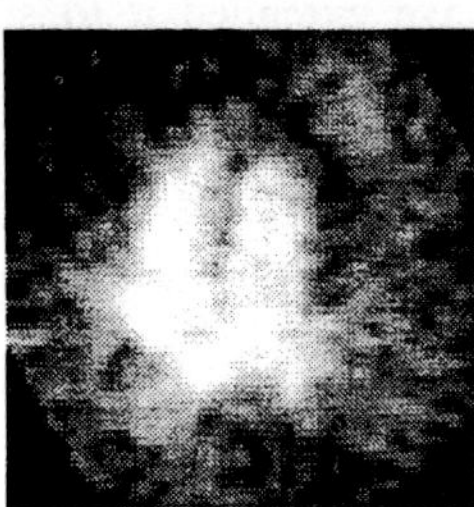

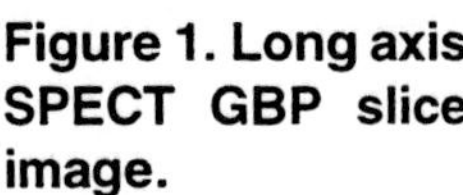

Figure 1. Long axis SPECT GBP slice image.

Figure 2. 3D Rendering of thresholded edge contours.

3.2. Forming Elliptic Cross-Sections

Next, the LV region of the data needs to be determined. To support that, the set of edge points is processed. Hough-based processing [3] is used in each slice to detect ellipses. Since the surface representing the center and base of LV is ellipsoidal, planar intersections with the ellipsoid are elliptic. (Moreover, planar intersections along the symmetry axis of the paraboloid are elliptic.) The Hough accumulation is in a six-dimensional space on parameters $(x_0, y_0, z_0, a, b, \theta)$ (the center, axis lengths, and relative orientation of major axis).

3.3. Clustering

Ellipse cross-sections are then automatically grouped into classes (some of which could represent ellipsoids in the data). The grouping mechanism is the agglomerative hierarchical (single-link) clustering [3]. The primary goal in the clustering is to locate the basal and central regions of the LV, which can be well-modeled as an ellipsoid [5]. It can be shown that the intersections of an ellipsoid with a series of parallel planes are ellipses whose center positions are linearly arranged with a shared orientation angle θ and shared axial length ratio $\frac{a}{b}$. Hence, our single-link clustering uses a distance function that considers these factors.

3.4. Ellipsoidal Recovery of LV

Following formation of clusters, ellipsoids are fit to each cluster's collection of ellipse bounding points. The ellipsoid-fitting procedure described in Section 2 is used to perform the fitting. Ellipsoids are fit to every cluster, although we have empirically observed that among the largest five clusters, the one with reasonable shape and smallest RMS fitting error corresponds to the LV. This fitting results in excellent fits to the basal and central region, as we have demonstrated in [10]. However, fitting is not as good in the apical region. Therefore, we utilize a compound fitting approach to achieve a reasonable recovery of the entire LV.

3.5. Compound Surface Fitting

The compound fitting involves truncation of the ellipsoid in the apical region and recovery of a paraboloid that well-fits the region. The apex is located at the lower LV pole along its long axis, so paraboloid fitting is desirous in that polar region. Since the apical region is approximately the lower third of the LV [4, 5], the edge contours located in that part of the LV are determined and a paraboloid is fit to them. However, in certain cases, this strategy fails to utilize the most apical regions of the LV (since the ellipsoid does not well-fit that region of the LV, portions of the apex may not be within the cluster, moreover, the original clustering is not perfect so some edge contours near the apex can be members of other clusters).

To ensure that the entire apical region is the basis for paraboloid fitting, edge contours lying within slices adjacent to the bottomost portion of the cluster are examined in a volume that extends along the ellipsoid long axis. Edge contours falling within the region are examined up to a distance of one-third of the ellipsoidal axis length from the bottom pole of the LV ellipsoid, and each successive slice that has an edge contour bounding box smaller than the extent of the preceeding slice is added to the set of considered slices. The process terminates once the bounding extent reaches a minimal size. From that low point, the edge contours from the lowest $L/3$ slices of the LV are used for paraboloid fitting. Typically, there are an insufficient number of edge contour points at the apex, thus the paraboloid fitting is performed on points sampled from idealized ellipses fit (using least-squares fitting) to each slice's edge contour points.

4. Results

Our method has been applied to eight tomographic GBP SPECT datasets. The compound fitting process results in an accurate analytic fit of LV shape in all regions of the LV. A sample fitting result is illustrated in Fig. 3, which shows overlay of the slice plane of Fig. 1 and the compound surfaces on an isosurface. The boundary of the original truncated ellipsoid in this slice is shown in Fig. 4, and the boundary of the compound surface is shown in Fig. 5. Comparison with the Figs. 1 and 4 demonstrates the improvement offered by the compound fitting approach.

For this dataset, the recovered ellipsoid and paraboloid centroids are (35.6, 32.2, 26.7) and (34.5, 31.4, 16.7). The ellipsoid's original axis lengths are 6.3, 6.0, and 5.4, and the shape parameters for the paraboloid are 1.75 and 1.6. The RMS error for the ellipsoid region is 0.67 and for the paraboloid region is 0.65.

Figure 3. 3D Geometry.

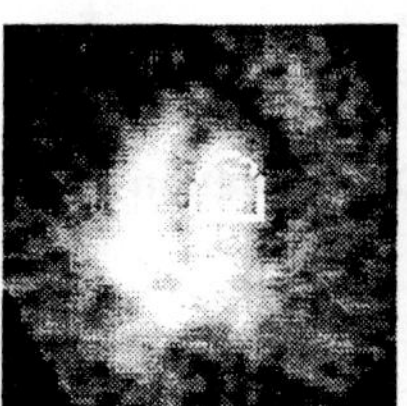

Figure 4. Fit Ellipsoid.

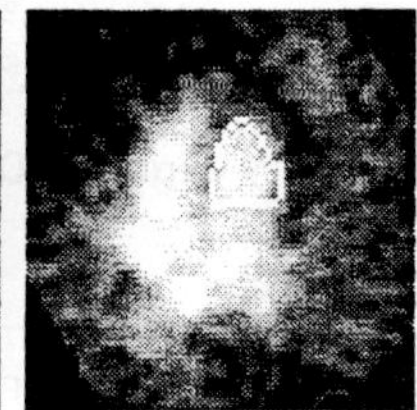

Figure 5. Compound fit.

5. Conclusion

We have presented a new technique for automatic extraction of the LV in GBP SPECT data. Through compound fitting of ellipsoidal and paraboloid surfaces, accurate determination of the LV can be possible.

Acknowledgments

We thank the National Institutes of Health for supplying the SPECT data. Partial support for this project was provided by the National Science Foundation under grant ASC 9702401, the Space Grant Consortium, and the ALVIS Center.

References

[1] M. Bartlett, G. Srinivasan, W. C. Barker, A. Kitsiou, V. Dilsizian, and S. L. Bacharach, "Left Ventricular Ejection Fraction: Comparison of Results from Planar and SPECT Gated Blood-Pool Studies," *J. Nuc. Med.*, **37**, 1996, pp. 1795-1799.

[2] C. Chen and T. Huang, "On the Integration of Image Segmentation and Shape Analysis with its Application to Left Ventricle Motion Analysis," *Proc., Bio. Image Processing and Bio. Vis.*, San Jose, 1993, pp. 218-229.

[3] R. O. Duda and P. E. Hart, *Pattern Classification and Scene Analysis*, John Wiley & Sons: New York, 1973.

[4] M. Dulce, G. Mostbeck, K. Friese, G. Caputo, and C. Higgins, "Quantification of the Left Ventricular Volumes and Function with Cine MR Imaging: Comparison of Geometric Models with Three-Dimensional Data," *Radiology*, **188**, 1993, pp. 371-376.

[5] T. Force, E. Folland, N. Aebischer, S. Sharma, and A. Parisi, "Echocardiographic Assessment of Ventricular Function," from *Cardiac Imaging: A Companion to Braunwald's Heart Disease*, ed. by M. Marcus, H. Schelbert, D. Skortor, and G. Wolf, W. R. Saunders: Phila., 1991, pp. 374-401.

[6] E. Hall, J. Tio, C. McPherson, and F. Sadjadi, "Measuring Curved Surfaces for Robot Vision," *IEEE Computer*, **15**, 1982, pp. 42-54.

[7] J. Park, D. Metaxas, and L. Axel, "Volumetric Deformable Models with Parameter Functions: A New Approach to the 3D Motion Analysis of the LV from MRI-SPAMM," *Proc., Fifth Int'l Conf. on Computer Vision*, Cambridge, MA, June 1995, pp. 700-705.

[8] F. H. Sheehan, "Cardiac Angiography," in *Cardiac Imaging: A Companion to Braunwald's Heart Disease*, ed. by M. Marcus, H. Schelbert, D. Skortor, and G. Wolf, W. R. Saunders: Phila., 1991, pp. 109-148.

[9] T. Newman, P. Flynn, and A. Jain, "Model-Based Classification of Quadric Surfaces," *Comp. Vision, Graphics, and Image Proc.: Image Understanding*, **58(2)**, 1993, pp. 235-249.

[10] T. Newman, S. Raynaud, and W. C. Barker, "A New Method for the Visualization of the LV in Gated Blood Pool SPECT Images," *Proc., Medical Imaging '98 Conf. on Image Display*, San Diego, Feb. 1998, pp. 40-47.

[11] M. Dai and T. Newman, "Accurate Reference Surface Recovery and Defect Detection for Hyperboloid and Paraboloid Surfaces," *Proc., Fifth Int'l Conf. on Quality Control by Artificial Vision*, Trois-Rivieres, Canada, May 1999, pp. 165-170.

Computerized Analysis of Pulmonary Nodules in Topological and Histogram Feature Spaces

Y. Kawata[1], N. Niki[1], H. Ohmatsu[2], M. Kusumoto[3], R. Kakinuma[2], K. Mori[4], H. Nishiyama[5], K. Eguchi[6], M. Kaneko[3], N. Moriyama[3]
[1]*Dept. of Optical Science, Univ. of Tokushima,* [2]*National Cancer Center East,*
[3]*National Cancer Center,* [4]*Tochigi Cancer Center,*
[5]*The Social Health Medical Center,* [6]*National Shikoku Cancer Center*
{kawata, niki}@opt.tokushima-u.ac.jp

Abstract

This paper focuses on an approach for characterizing the internal structure which is one of important clues for differentiating between malignant and benign nodules in three-dimensional (3-D) thoracic images. In this approach, each voxel was described in terms of shape index derived from curvatures on the voxel. The voxels inside the nodule were aggregated via shape histogram to quantify how much shape category was present in the nodule. Topological features were introduced to characterize the morphology of the cluster constructed from a set of voxels with the same shape category. In the classification step, a hybrid unsupervised/supervised structure was performed to improve the classifier performance. It combined the k-means clustering procedure and the linear discriminate classifier. Receiver operating characteristics analysis was used to evaluate the accuracy of the classifiers. Our results demonstrate the feasibility of the hybrid classifier based on the topological and histogram features to assist physicians in making diagnostic decisions.

1. Introduction

There has been a considerable amount of interest in the use of thin-section CT images to observe small pulmonary nodules for differential diagnosis without invasive operation [1]. In assessing the malignant potential of small pulmonary nodules in thin-section CT images, it is important to examine the condition of nodule interface, the nodule internal intensity, and the relationships between nodules and surrounding structures such as vessels, bronchi, and spiculation [1]. A number of investigators have developed a feature extraction and a classification methods for characterizing pulmonary nodules. [2]-[10]. Although the performances of the computer algorithms are expected to depend strongly on data set, they indicate the potential of using computer aided diagnosis techniques to improve the diagnostic accuracy of differentiating malignant and benign nodules.

This paper focuses on the analysis of the internal structure in the 3-D pulmonary nodules. In previous study [10] we found that curvature indexes such as shape index and curvedness were promising quantifies for characterizing the internal structure of nodules. However, there were several distribution patterns of CT density inside the nodule, such as solid or infiltative types. Therefore, it might be desirable to decompose input samples into classes with different properties to improve classification performance. In the present study, we combine an unsupervised and a supervised model and apply them to classification of malignant and benign nodules. The unsupervised model is based on k-means clustering (KMC) procedure [16] which clustered the nodules into a number of classes by using CT density distribution. A supervised linear discriminate (LD) classifier [16] is designed for each classes by using topological and histogram measures based on curvature indexes. We demonstrate the feasibility of the hybrid classifier based on the histogram and topological features for classification of malignancy from other lesions. We also compare the performance of the hybrid classifier with that of the experienced physicians.

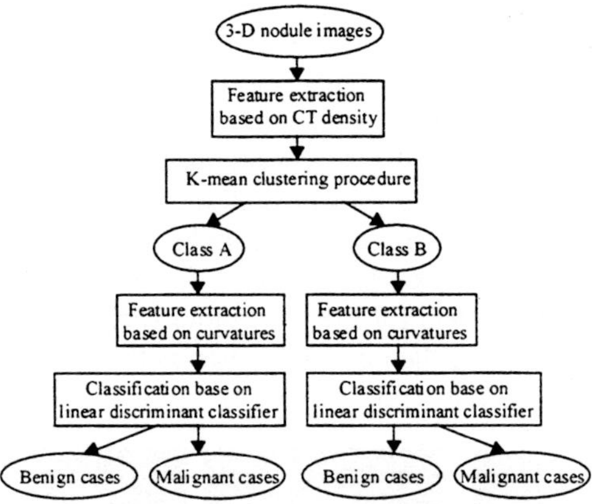

Figure 1 Classification procedure.

2. Methods

2.1. Overview

In order to improve the accuracy of a classifier, we propose to design a hybrid classifier that combines the unsupervised KMC procedure with a supervised LD classifier. The classification procedure of the pulmonary nodules is shown in Fig.1. The KMC analyzes the similarity of the sample data and classify subclasses that may be separated from the sample data. This may improve the performance of the second-stage LD classifier if the subclass causes the sample data to deviate from

1051-4651/00 $10.00 © 2000 IEEE

multivariate normal distributions for which the LD classifier is an optimal classifier.

2.2. Nodule segmentation

The segmentation of the 3D pulmonary nodule image consists of three steps [10] ;1)extraction of lung area, 2) selection of the region of interest (ROI) including the nodule region, 3) nodule segmentation based on a geometric approach. This lung area extraction step plays an essential role when the part of a nodule in the peripheral lung area touches the chest wall. The ROI including the nodule was selected interactively. A pulmonary nodule was segmented from the selected ROI image by the geometric approach proposed by Caselles [11]. The deformation process of the 3-D deformable surface model can automatically stop when the deforming surfaces reach the object's boundary to be detected. In our application we added a stopping condition to exclude vessels and bronchi which were in contact with the nodule [6].

2.3. Curvature based representation

Each voxel in the region of interest (ROI) including the pulmonary nodule was locally represented by a vector description which relied on the CT value and two curvature indexes that represented the shape attribute and the curvature magnitude. By assuming that each voxel in the ROI lies on the surface which has the normal corresponding to the 3-D gradient at the voxel, we computed directly the curvatures on each voxel from the first and the second derivatives of the gray level image of the ROI [12]. To compute the partial derivatives of the ROI images, the ROI images were blurred by convolving with a 3-D Gaussian function of width σ. In order to take only nonnegative values, we modified the of the shape index [13].

2.4. Histogram features

In order to characterize the pulmonary nodule through the local description, we used the shape spectrum which was introduced for object recognition by Dorai and Jain [13]. Using the shape spectrum, we measured the amount of the voxel which had a particular shape index value h. The augment shape spectrum with scale σ is given by

$$H(h;\sigma) = \frac{1}{V}\iiint_O \delta(S_I(x;\sigma) - h)dO \qquad (1)$$

where $S_I(x;\ \sigma)$ was the shape index at the voxel x, V is the total volume of the specified region O, dO is a small region around $\boldsymbol{x}$ and δ is the Dirac delta function. The discrete version of Eq.(1) is derived by dividing the shape index range into B bins and counting the number of voxels falling in each bin k and normalizing it by the total number N of discrete voxels in the specified region. The discrete version is expressed by

$$H(h = \frac{k}{B}) = \frac{1}{N}\sum_{i=1}^{N} \chi_k(S_I(x_i;\sigma)) \qquad (2)$$

with

$$\chi_k = \begin{cases} 1 & \frac{k-1}{B} \le x < \frac{k}{B} \\ 0 & otherwise \end{cases} \qquad (3)$$

Here, the segmented 3-D pulmonary nodule image is utilized as the specified region O. The shape index value one is included in the B-th bin. The discrete version of the shape spectrum was called shape histogram. The number of voxel falling in each bin represented the value of the histogram feature. For computational purposes, such as comparing spectra of different nodules, the shape histogram was normalized with respect to the volume of nodule. The normalized number of voxel falling in each bin represents the value of the shape histogram feature. In this study the number of bin B was given the value 100. The similar equations for the curvedness and CT density are obtained in the same manner. The domains of curvedness and CT density were specified to [0,1] and [-1500, 500], respectively. A voxel in which the curvedness value was larger than 1 was considered as a voxel with curvedness value 1. For the CT density the similar process was performed. To classify malignant and benign nodules, we combined a set of histogram features, such as shape, curvedenss, and CT density histogram.

2.5. Topological features

The distribution morphology of the shape category can characterize the internal structure of the nodule. Therefore, we divided the inside of the nodule into four shape categories by the shape index value and then, computed the topological features of each 3-D cluster which constructed from a set of voxels with the same shape category. The four shape categories were peak, saddle ridge, saddle valley, and pit surface types and the interval of the shape index for each shape categories were set [0, 0.25), [0.25, 0.5), [0.5, 0.75), [0.75, 1], respectively. The topological features used here were the Euler number, the number of connected components, cavities, and holes of a 26-connected object [14]. The Euler number of a 3-D digital figure is defined as the following equation,

$$E = b_0 - b_1 + b_2 \qquad (4)$$

where E is the Euler number and b_0, b_1, and b_2 respectively represent the number of connected components, holes, and cavities. These valuables, b_0, b_1, and b_2 are called the first, second, an third Betti-number, respectively. Yonekura et al. [14] provided computation schemes for the basic topological properties such as the connected component and the Euler number of 3-D digital object. The Euler number, the number of connected components, cavities, and holes were obtained by their schemes [14]. In addition, we quantified how each shape category distribute inside the nodule by using a method computing exact Euclidean distance transforms [15]. Using the Euclidean distance in the nodule, we measured the amount of the voxel which had a particular distance

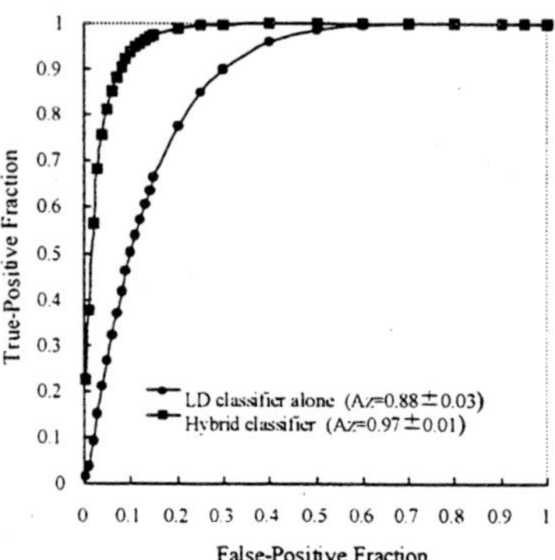

Figure 2 ROC curves of the hybrid classifier and the LD classifier alone.

value d in the i-th shape category. The distance spectrum with shape category is given by

$$DH(d; i) = \frac{1}{V}\iiint \delta(D(x; i) - d)dO \quad (5)$$

where $D(x; i)$ is the distance value at the voxel x with i-th shape category. The discrete version was derived by the similar manner as the histogram features. In this study the number of bin was given the value 25. The normalized number of voxel falling in each bin represents the value of the shape distribution feature. This feature was included in the topological features.

2.6. Classification

We first classified the sample nodules into two classes by using the mean CT density values for three different region. These different considered regions are as follows: (i)core region shrinking to T_1% of the maximum distance value of the 3-D nodule image, denoted as R1, (ii) complement of the core region in the 3-D nodule image, denoted as R2, (iii) marginal region extended to T_2% of the maximum distance value of the 3-D nodule image, denoted as R3. In this study T_1 and T_2 values were assigned to 60 and 26, respectively. For each class a LD classifier was designed by using the topological and histogram features. In order to reduce the number of the features and to obtain the best feature set to design a good classifier, feature selection with forward stepwise selection procedure was applied. In this study the minimization of Wilks' lambda was used as an optimization criterion to select the effective features. A leave-one-out procedure was performed to provide a less biased estimation of the linear discriminate classifier's performance. The discriminant scores were analyzed using receiver operating characteristic (ROC) method [17]. The discriminant scores of the malignant and the benign nodules were used as the decision variable in the ROCKIT program developed by Metz which fits the ROC curve based on maximum likelihood estimation. This program was also used to test the statistical significance of the difference between pairs of ROC curves. The two-tailed p values were reported in the comparison procedure described in the next section.

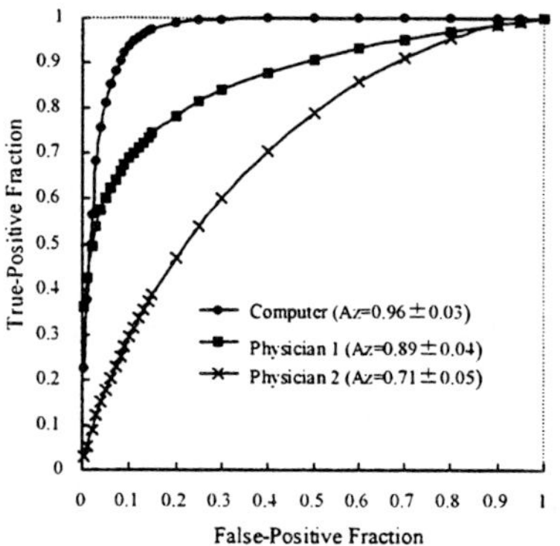

Figure 3 Comparison of ROC curves obtained by using the physicians malignancy rating and the hybrid classifier's discriminate score.

3. Experimental Results

Thin-section CT images were obtained by the helical CT scanner (Toshiba TCT900S Superhelix and Xvigor). Per patient, thin-section CT slices at 1mm intervals were obtained to observe whole nodule region and its surroundings. The range of pixel size in each square slice of 512 pixels was between 0.3x0.3 mm^2 and 0.4x0.4 mm^2. The 3D thoracic image was reconstructed by a linear interpolation technique to make each voxel isotropic. The data set in this study included 210 3-D thoracic images provided by National Cancer Center Hospital East and Tochigi Cancer Center. Among the 210 cases, 141 contained malignant nodules, and 69 contained benign nodules. Whole malignant nodules were cytologically or histologically diagnosed. In benign cases, lesions showed no change or decreased in size over a 2-year period were considered as the benign nodules. The size of nodules was less than 20 mm in diameter.

We compared the hybrid classifier with the LD classifier alone. In the hybrid classifier, the KMC procedure classified input samples into two classes denoted as class A and class B. The class A contained 50 cases (13 benign cases and 37 malignant cases) and the class B contained 160 cases (56 benign cases and 104 malignant cases). In comparison with the class B, the nodule of the class A had ill-defined surface and the region with lower CT density value occupied the inside of the nodule. The histogram feature used here was combined with three histogram features such as shape, curvedness, and CT density histograms. The topological features were yield for four clusters. The LD classifiers were designed from the combined topological and histogram features. For the class A and B, the number of the selected features was 9 and 21, respectively. In the LD classifier alone, the number of the selected features was 15. The ROC curves of the hybrid and the LD classifiers were plotted in Fig. 2. The classification accuracy in the hybrid classifier was significantly higher than those in the LD classifier alone ($p<0.01$).

In order to compare the performance of physicians with that of the hybrid classifier, the probability of malignancy of each pulmonary nodule in thin-section CT images which were printed on films, was ranked by eleven physicians on a scale of 1 to 10, where a ranking of 1 corresponded to the nodules with the most benign cases. The number of nodules used in this comparison was 119 cases provided by the National Cancer Center East. Based on the ranking, the ROC curves using three physicians malignancy rating and the computer's discriminate score output in the combined feature space were plotted in Fig. 3. The physicians 1 and 2 respectively have 15 years, and one year of experience in the chest radiology. The difference between the ROC curves of the hybrid classifier and those of two physicians was statistical significance ($p < 0.05$). These results show that the classification performance of the hybrid classification approach achieved the experienced physician results.

4. Conclusion

In this study, the topological and histogram measures based on curvature information were introduced to characterize the internal structure of 3-D nodule images. A hybrid classifier combining an unsupervised k-means clustering algorithm with a supervised LD classifier has been designed and applied to the classification of malignant and benign nodules. The *Az* value under the ROC curve for our data set was higher for the hybrid classifier compared to that of the LD classifier alone. A greater improvement was obtained by introducing the k-means clustering procedure. The performance of the hybrid classifier was also compared with those of the experience physicians. The classification performance of the hybrid classifier reached the performance of the experienced physicians. These results indicate that the hybrid classifier is a promising approach for improving the accuracy of classifiers for CAD applications.

Acknowledgements

The authors are grateful to physicians cooperating to the reading test. The authors would like to thank Prof. Charles E. Metz for the ROCKIT program.

References

[1] K. Mori, Y. Saitou, K. Tominaga, K. Yokoi, N. Miyazawa, A .Okuyama, M. Sasagawa, "Small nodular legions in the lung periphery: new approach to diagnosis with CT," *Radiology*, vol.177, pp.843-849, 1990.

[2] S.S. Siegelman, E.A. Zerhouni, F.P. Leo, N.F. Khouri, F.P. Stitik, "CT of the solitary pulmonary nodule," *AJR*, vol.135, pp.1-13, 1980.

[3] D. Cavouras, P. Prassopoulos and N. Pantelidis, "Image analysis methods for solitary pulmonary nodule characterization by computed tomography, " *European Journal of Radiology*, vol.14, pp.169-172, 1992.

[4] M.F. McNitt-Gray, E.M.Hart, J. Goldin, C.-W, Yao, and D.R. Aberle, "A pattern classification approach to characterizing solitary pulmonary nodules imaged on high resolution computed tomography," *Proc. SPIE*, vol. 2710, pp.1024-1034, 1996.

[5] Y.Kawata, N.Niki, H.Ohmatsu, R.Kakinuma, K.Eguchi, M.Kaneko, N.Moriyama, "Shape analysis of pulmonary nodules based on thin-section CT images," Proc.SPIE,vol.3034,pp.967-974, 1997.

[6] Y. Kawata, N. Niki, H. Ohmatsu, R. Kakinuma, K. Eguchi, M. Kaneko, N. Moriyama, "Quantitative surface characterization of pulmonary nodules based on thin-section CT images", *IEEE Trans. Nuclear Science*, vol. 45, pp.2132-2138, 1998.

[7] Y. Hirano, Y. Mekada, J. Hasegawa, J. Toriwaki, H.Ohmatsu, and K.Eguchi, "Quantification of vessels convergence in three-dimensional chest X-ray CT images with three-dimensional concentration index," *Medical Imaging Technology*, vol.15, pp.228-236, 1997.

[8] T. Tozaki, Y. Kawata, N. Niki, H. Ohmatsu, R. Kakinuma, K. Eguchi, N. Moriyama, "Pulmonary organs analysis for differential diagnosis based on thoracic thin-section CT images," *IEEE Trans. Nuclear Science*, vol.45, pp.3075-3082, 1998.

[9] H. Kitaoka and R. Takaki, "Simulations of bronchial displacement owing to solitary pulmonary nodules, "*Nippon Acta Radiologica*,vol.59,pp.318-324, 1999.

[10] Y. Kawata, N.Niki, H.Ohmatsu, "Curvature based internal structure analysis of pulmonary nodules using thoracic 3-D CT images," *IEICE Trans*., vol.J-83-D-II, no.1, 2000.

[11] V. Caselles, R. Kimmel, G. Sapiro, and C. Sbert, "Minimal surfaces based object segmentation," *IEEE Trans. Pattern Analysis Machine Intelligence*, vol.19,pp.394-398, 1997.

[12] J.-P, Thirion and A. Gourdon, "Computing the differential characteristics of isointensity surfaces," *Comput. Vision and Image Understanding*, vol.61, pp.190-202, 1995.

[13] C. Dorai and A.K. Jain, " COSMOS-A representation scheme for 3D free-form objects", *IEEE Trans. Pattern Analysis Machine Intelligence*, vol.19, pp.1115-1130,1997.

[14] T. Yonekura, S. Yokoi, J. Toriwaki, T. Fukumura, "Connectivity and euler number of figures in the digitized three-dimensional space", *Trans. IECE*, vol. J65-D, pp.80-87,1982.

[15] T. Saito and J. Toriwaki, "Euclidean dstance transformation for three dimensional digital images, " *Trans IEICE*, vol. J76-D-II, pp.445-453, 1993.

[16] R.O. Duda and P.E. Hart, "Pattern classification and scene analysis", John Wiley, Sons, 1973.

[17] C.E. Metz, "ROC methodology in radiologic imaging," *Investigative Radiology*, vol.21, pp.720-733, 1986.

Discriminant snakes for 3D reconstruction in medical images*

X.M. Pardo
Dept. Electrónica e Computación
Universidade de Santiago de Compostela
15706 Santiago, Spain. pardo@dec.usc.es

P. Radeva
Computer Vision Centre
Universitat Autònoma de Barcelona
089193 Bellaterra, Spain. petia@cvc.uab.es

Abstract

In this work we propose a new statistic deformable model that we call discriminant snake for 3D reconstruction in volumetric images. Our discriminant snake generalises the classical snake attracted by edge points, it deforms due to a generalised contour representation. The snake selects and classifies image features by a parametric classifier and each snaxel deforms to minimise the dissimilarity between the learned and found image features inside the feature space. We apply our statistic snake to segment anatomical organs and the results are very encouraging.
Keywords: *statistic snake, principal component analysis, Fisher linear discriminant analysis, supervised learning, 3D reconstruction.*

1. Introduction

The 3D reconstruction of objects from volume images is incresingly used in medicine and industrial applications. Manual delineation of the region of interest on volume images is, at least, fatigous and very time consuming, which has motivated the search for optimal computational techniques. Among the wide variety of image segmentation techniques, deformable models are receiving an special attention, mainly in medical imagery, due to their ability to interpret sparse set of features (e.g. edge points) and link them to obtain object contours applying general assumptions about the contour shape [12, 9, 11].

The classical snake is an image feature technique that uses energy terms defined from gradient features of global interest to find the desired contour [7]. In most real applications such assumption is too strong. Different authors suggest to combine the gradient-based potential with valley and crest maps [16, 3]. However, on one hand, the best way of integrating different features remains to be an open problem and in the other hand, these features are not selective enough yet. This leads to heuristical combinations that enhance too many feature points that do not belong to the object of interest, meanwhile others go unnoticed.

Constraints on shape have been proposed to compensate this lack of selectivity. *Hand-crafted* parameterized templates, with few degrees of freedom have been used, for example, for modeling features of faces [16]. More general methods, as Fourier descriptors, have been used for representing shapes in medical images [14]. Alternative approaches based on modal analysis have also been proposed to constraint the model to deform only in ways implied by the training set of shapes [4, 3].

Although shape models convey important information, they are not the panacea; high accuracy techniques must make the most of grey level information too. In line with this idea, shape models and appearance models are combined in face recognition [8].

Our approach based on the statistics ot the image features (texture) offers an alternative to those approaches based on shape statistics. We propose to use a bank of Gaussian derivative filters of different scales as the generalization of edge, crest and valley detectors, whose goal is to increase the selectivity on the description of the target object. At this point, the description of target image features is still too general. It is neccessary to locally decide (learn) the best way of combinig derivative degrees and scales in the description of each contour part by means of a classification vector. A supervised learning in conjunction with discriminant analysis is carried out to characterize each contour patch. Then a classifier is assigned to each snake patch and the external energy is represented by the distance of each snake point to the cluster of its target contour in the corresponding feature space.

Our statistic snake approach is particularly of interest for segmentation and tracking of objects in temporal or spatial image sequences. The snake is able to learn the changes in contour features inside each image as well as along the image sequence in an adaptive way.

The paper is organized as follows: in section 2 we give

*This work is supported by CICYT and EU grants TIC98-1100 and 2FD97-0220, and Xunta de Galicia grant PGIDT99PXI20606B.

a formulation of the snake as an energy-minimization technique, in section 3 we introduce our statistic snake based on principal component and Fisher linear discriminant analysis. In section 4 we give the results of applying our snake model to the problem of segmentation in medical images and finish the article by conclusions.

2. Snake formulation

A snake is an elastic curve ($u(s)$) that evolves from its initial shape and position as a result of the combined action of external and internal forces [7]. The internal forces model the elasticity of the curve, whereas external forces push the snake towards features of the image [7]. The external energy is generally defined from a potential field P:

$$E_{ext}(u) = \int P(u(s))ds.$$

A typical potential for a snake attracted to image edge points is given by [7]:

$$P(u(s)) \propto -|G_\sigma * \nabla I(u(s))| \quad (1)$$

where $I(u)$ represents the intentisity value, and G_σ is a Gaussian smoothing function of size σ.

The potential must define a contour which minima correspond, as accurately as posible, to the image features of interest. The total energy of the snake is the sum of the external and internal energies. The smallest energy correspond to the desired contour. The minimization of the energy function is generally performed using variational principles and finite difference techniques [7, 1]. Practical computations demand discretization over time and space. In finite difference approximations, the curve $u(s)$ is sampled at certain points where computations are done. Methods like finite elements and B-splines produce curves of high degree of continuity and the features of each curve vertex are now evaluated in its corresponding curve patch.

In the classical implementation, the external energy defines global coarse features of interest which rest especificity. Next, we describe the formulation of the new generalized and locally defined external energy.

3. Supervised feature learning

The feature spaces must be capable of representing any image features of interest and each snaxel must be able to distinguish between its corresponding contour target and other structures (in particular, other parts of the contour or contours of near objects). To that aim, the features are extracted by applying a bank of filters to the image and then a learning process yields the relevant features to characterize each contour configurations and discriminate between them. The different steps involved in the learning process are described in the following sections.

3.1. Feature extraction and potential field

We use a bank of Gaussian derivative filters to characterize the objects of interest, that contains derivatives up to degree three (variance of higher-order filters tends to be highly correlated to the outputs of lower order filters [13]). Additionally, we consider different scales to a number sufficient of characterizing all possible configurations, and of allowing the snake to follow the traslation of the object of interest in image sequences.

In general, it is useful to determine the response of filters at arbitrary orientations. As the directional derivative operator is steerable, we use a set of basis filters $\{G^d(x, y, \sigma, \theta_k)\}_{k=1}^{d}$ for defining the derivative of Gaussian of degree d at arbitrary angle ϕ, $G^d(x, y, \sigma, \phi)$. Derivative of degree d can be obtained by the interpolation of $d+1$ equiangular orientations. Given the basis functions for each filter degree, filters at arbitrary orientations can be synthesized by means of interpolant functions [6].

We define $\mathcal{G}_{\mathcal{D}_\Sigma}$ as the filter bank with derivatives until $\mathcal{D}$ degree and N_Σ scales $\sigma \in \{2^0, 2^1, \ldots, 2^{N_\Sigma - 1}\}$. The dimension of the bank of filters is:

$$d_\mathcal{G} = dim(\mathcal{G}_{\mathcal{D}_\Sigma}) = N_\Sigma \sum_{d=0}^{\mathcal{D}} (d+1). \quad (2)$$

Note, for example, that if $\mathcal{D} = 1$ we have an edge detector.

Due to the high dimension of the feature space generated by the bank of filters is necessary to reduce the dimensionality by eliminating non discriminat filter responses and to weight the contribution of the remaining filter responses to the classifier, as described below.

The relative importance of derivative features depends on the task domain. It seems natural to perform a self-training for reduction of the space and weighting the features. We apply a technique commonly used for dimensionality reduction based on PCA [15].

Given the problem of segmentation, a set of N sample image feature vectors on object-contour and non object-contour $\{s_1, s_2, \ldots, s_N\}$ are chosen, taking values in an $d_\mathcal{G}$-dimensional space, where $d_\mathcal{G}$ is the dimension of the bank of filters applied to the original image. Each component of s_i corresponds to the response of a filter (image convolution by a Gaussian derivative). Looking for a certain contour k, each image feature j can be classified to one of two clases $\{C_k, \bar{C_k}\}$, representing the pixels belonging to the contour k and the complementary class (complementary contour parts and remainder scene). Our goal is to obtain an optimal linear transformation that maps the original $d_\mathcal{G}$-dimensional space into an 1-dimensional feature space where the classification of image features is applied by measuring the distance to the class center of the corresponding learned configuration.

3.2. External forces by statistic classifiers

To map the original $d_{\mathcal{G}}$-dimensional space into an 1-dimensional feature space we use Fisher linear discriminant functions [5]. Applying FLDA the new scalar feature r_j is defined by the following linear transformation:

$$\mathcal{F}_k : (p_{j1}, \ldots, p_{jd_{\mathcal{G}}}) \in \mathcal{P} \longrightarrow r_j = V_k^T \mathcal{P}_j \in \mathbf{R}$$

where $V_k \in \mathbf{R}^{d_{\mathcal{G}}}$ is a vector that projects the features of pixel j in $\mathbf{R}$ to give the similarity to the contour class k. In order to find an optimal projection into a reduced feature space where the distance between samples of class C_k and the remainder samples is maximized, we have to obtain the best discriminant function.

PCA is used to reduce the dimension of the feature spaces (one per patch) from $\mathbf{R}^{d_{\mathcal{G}}}$ to $\mathbf{R}^m$. After PCA, we only maintain the m eigenvectors with largest eigenvalues that retain the 95% of the sample variance.

The optimal projection V_{k_opt} is defined as the vector which maximizes the ratio of the determinant of the between-class scatter matrix of the projected samples to the within-class scatter matrix of the projected samples [2, 5], which can be obtained by means of a FLDA. As a result, we obtain for each contour part C_k:

$$V_{k\_opt}^T = V_{k\_fld}^T V_{pca}^T$$

where:

$$V_{pca} = \arg\max_{V_k} |V_k^T S_T V_k|$$

$$V_{k\_fld} = \arg\max_{V_k} \frac{|V_k^T V_{pca}^T S_{bc} V_{pca} V_k|}{|V_k^T V_{pca}^T S_{wc} V_{pca} V_k|},$$

where S_{bc}, S_{wc} and S_T are the between class, within class and total scatter matrices, respectively.

Each patch k of the snake curve has its own classifier $\mathcal{V}_{C_k}$ that defines the image features it is looking for. The scalar product of the mean feature vector μ_{C_k} of the patch and the classifier vector gives the center of the class $\mathcal{C}_{C_k}$ of points in the feature space that corresponds to the contour patch of interest:

$$\mathcal{V}_{C_k} = V_{k\_opt}$$
$$\mathcal{C}_{C_k} = \mathcal{V}_{C_k}^T \mu_{C_k}.$$

We define the local external energy of the snake by measuring the similarity of the actual image features $\mathcal{P}_f$, in the current location of the snake, to the desired contour configuration in terms of the distance from the projection of the image feature vectors $\mathcal{P}_f$ to the class center:

$$D_{C_k} = \left(\mathcal{V}_{C_k}^T(\mathcal{P}_f - \mu_{C_k})\right)^2 = \left(\mathcal{V}_{C_k}^T \mathcal{P}_f - \mathcal{C}_{C_k}\right)^2.$$

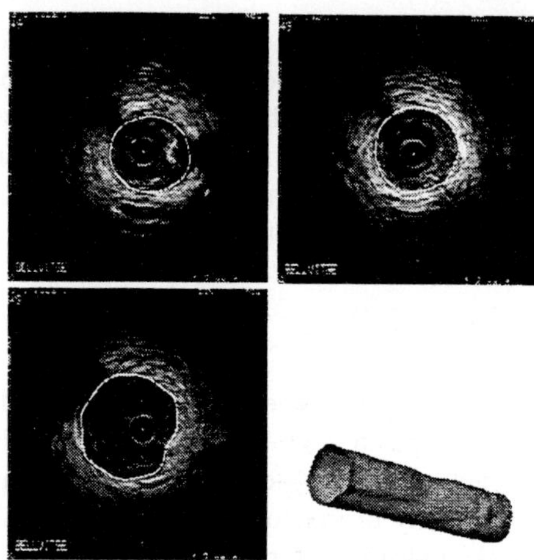

Figure 1. Samples of the segmentation of coronary vessels in a IVUS image sequence.

As a result each snaxel interprets in different way the image filter responses depending of the goal it carries (the contour type it has learned in its previous stage).

Given the problem of the 3D reconstruction, when the contour is delineated for a slice, its features are learned and the curve and the classifiers are moved to the next slice. In this way, the features of each class are updated and each patch searches for specific features discriminating between different objects and contour patches.

4. Results

In order to validate our approach we test our statistic snake on IVUS images. As an illustrative example, Fig. 1 shows the segmentation in intermediate slices of a sequence of 400 IVUS images of a coronary vessel. In these images, some contour parts of the blood vessel are very difficult of delineating even for a human operator. In that case we use a model shape information that avoids severe changes between contours of adjacent slices when there are not cues about the location of some contour parts.

To quantitatively evaluate the new approach, 5 experts $(e_1, e_2, e_3, e_4, e_5)$ manually segmented images from two different sequences of IVUS images. Model contours (M) were computed as the average hand-crafted contours and used as the ground truth segmentation. For each test image (j), we computed the distance between each pair of contours (e_i^j, M^j) and (S^j, M^j), where S^j represents the contour fitted by the snake approach in image j. The distance is characterized by its mean and variance $(\bar{d}, s^2)$ in pixels. The average distance given but the snake is similar to the ones given by manual segmentations (see Table 1). To objec-

Table 1. t-test between the segmentations provided by several experts and the snake.

e_1	e_2	e_3	e_4	e_5	S
d, s^2	d, s^2	d, s^2	d, s^2	d, s^2	d, s^2
IVUS 1					
1.77, 1.92	1.49, 1.28	1.51, 1.28	1.71, 1.43	1.43, 1.21	2.29, 2.59
IVUS 2					
1.36, 0.96	0.97, 0.56	1.22, 0.69	1.22, 0.69	1.14, 0.69	1.63, 1.17

IVUS 1					
	e_1/S	e_2/S	e_3/S	e_4/S	e_5/S
t	0.495	0.832	0.817	0.598	0.907
P-value	> 0.2	> 0.2	> 0.2	> 0.2	> 0.2
H_0	true	true	true	true	true

IVUS 2					
	e_1/S	e_2/S	e_3/S	e_4/S	e_5/S
t	0.576	1.594	0.956	0.948	1.335
P-value	> 0.2	> 0.1	> 0.2	> 0.2	0.2
H_0	true	true	true	true	true

tively compare the segmentations of our approach with the manual ones, we perform a statistical test. The hypothesis to be tested, the null hypotesis (H_0), is that there is non significative difference between the manual and the automatic segmentations. We use the Student's t test [10].

The average distance and variance from each contour point to the model contour were computed in each image sequence and compared to the results provided by the snake. We obtain the P-values from tabulated values [10] and decide on the hypotesis truthfulness using the usual significance level $\alpha = 0.05$. In all the cases, the null hypotesis was true, so there are not significant differences between expert and snake segmentations (see Table 1). The average distance from the final contours, given by the experts and our approach, to the ground truth segmentation and its variance are very similar. The same discrepances found between *ideal* and the automatic segmentation, are also found between the different manual segmentations.

5. Conclusions

The goal of this work is the generalization of the classical feature-based snake technique to reconstruct anatomical organs in images of different modality. Given the fact that object contour is rarely well defined by high gradient magnitude location we integrate gradient and texture image features chracterizing the contour obtained by a set of derivtive filters with different scales (multivalued potential). As a result, our model is a natural generalization of contour-, valley- and crest-based snakes.

The presented snake applies statistic methods to learn different contour configurations. The snake selects and self-trains the image features that are locally best representing the object contour. A parametric external energy of the snake is designed according to the fact that different patches of the snake are looking for different parts of the contour. As a result, the snake is more selective and robust and avoids ambiguities in case of two or more, even similar, objects close each other. We apply our snake to segment medical images obtaining better results than original snakes even in case of presence of near anatomical structures and changes in the morphology.

References

[1] A. A. Amini, T. E. Weymouth, and R. C. Jain. Using dynamic programming for solving variational problems in vision. *IEEE Trans. Patt. Anal. Machine. Intell.*, 12(9):855–867, 1990.

[2] P. Belhumeur, J. Hespanha, and D. Kriegman. Eigenfaces vs. fisherfaces: recognition using class specific linear projection. *IEEE Trans. Patt. Anal. Machine. Intell.*, 7:711–720, 1997.

[3] A. Blake and Isard. *Active contours.* Springer-Verlag, 1998.

[4] T. F. Cootes, C. J. Taylor, D. H. Cooper, and J. Graham. Active shape models–their training and application. *Computer Vision and Image Understanding*, 61(1):38–59, 1995.

[5] R. O. Duda and P. E. Hurt. *Pattern Clasification and Scene Analysis.* Wiley-Interscience, New York, 1973.

[6] W. Freeman and E. Adelson. The design and use of steerable filters. *IEEE Trans. Patt. Anal. Machine. Intell.*, 13(9):891–906, 1991.

[7] M. Kass, A. Witkin, and D. Terzopoulos. Snakes: active contour models. *International Journal of Computer Vision*, 1:321–331, 1988.

[8] A. Lanitis, C. J. Taylor, and T. F. Cootes. Automatic face identification system using flexible appearance models. *Image and Vision Computing*, 13(5):393–401, 1995.

[9] T. McInerney and D. Terzopoulos. Deformable models in medical image analysis: a survey. *Medical Image Analysis*, 1(2):91–108, 1996.

[10] W. Mendenhall and R. J. Beaver. *Introduction to probability and statistics.* PWS-KENT Publishing Company, Boston, 1991.

[11] J. Pardo, D. Cabello, and J. Heras. A snake for model-based segmentation of biomedical images. *Pattern Recognition Letters*, 18(14):1529–1538, 1997.

[12] P. Radeva, J. Serrat, and E. Marti. A snake for model–based segmentation. In *Proceedings of International Conference on Computer Vision (ICCV'95)*, MIT, USA, 1995.

[13] R. Rao and D. Ballard. Natural basis functions and topographic memory for face recognition. In *Proc. International Joint Conf. on Artificial Intelligence*, pages 10–17, 1995.

[14] L. H. Staib and J. S. Duncan. Boundary finding with parametrically deformable models. *IEEE Trans. Patt. Anal. Machine. Intell.*, 14(11):1061–1075, 1992.

[15] M. Turk and A. Pentland. Eigenfaces for recognition. *J. Cognitive Neuroscience*, 3(1), 1991.

[16] A. Yuille, P. Hallinan, and D. Cohen. Feature extraction from faces using deformable templates. *IJCV*, 8(2), 1992.

Eigensnakes for vessel segmentation in angiography

Ricardo Toledo, Xavier Orriols, Petia Radeva, Xavier Binefa, Jordi Vitrià, Cristina Cañero and J.J. Villanueva *
Computer Vision Center and Dpt. d'Informàtica
Universitat Autònoma de Barcelona
Edifici O, 08193, Bellaterra, SPAIN
{ricardo, xevi, xavierb, petia, jordi, juanjo}@cvc.uab.es

Abstract

In this paper we introduce a new deformable model, called eigensnake, for segmentation of elongated structures in a probabilistic framework. Instead of snake attraction by specific image features extracted independently of the snake, our eigensnake learns an optimal object description and searches for such image feature in the target image. This is achieved applying principal component analysis on image responses of a bank of gaussian derivative filters. Therefore, attraction by eigensnakes is defined in terms of classification of image features. The potential energy for the snake is defined in terms of likelihood in the feature space and incorporated into a new energy minimising scheme. Hence, the snake deforms to minimise the mahalanobis distance in the feature space. A real application of segmenting and tracking coronary vessels in angiography is considered and the results are very encouraging.

Keywords. Snakes, Principal Component Analysis, Statistical Learning, Segmentation, Angiography.

1. Introduction

The main areas of research in computer applications for angiography during the past 15 years have been devoted to geometric and densitometric methods to automate quantitative analysis of coronary arteriograms. The first steps include assessment of coronary lesion severity [10] in individual segments followed by a growing interest in automated identification and analysis of entire coronary tree. Over the last few years, attention has been directed to research towards 3D reconstruction from biplane projection [2, 9], to improve measurements of small vessels [11] to mix data coming from different imaging devices [7] and to obtain 3D dynamic models [13]. On the other hand, computer and communication technologies are growing at incredible speed, increasing performance with parallel decreasing in prices. Such phenomena open new research fields with clear application feasibility that few years ago should have been only of theoretical scope. Correct vessel segmentation is a key issue in any automatic analysis task. To extract and use the information present in the coronary image, many conventional methods have been proposed, although ambiguities and artifacts make the segmentation process highly dependent on heuristics (parameter tuning). Despite the increasing quality of the imaging equipment, the computer analysis task still remains non-trivial. Hence, the impact of any improvement of the segmentation step is important. Two main strategies to segment the coronary tree have been reported:

- *Scanning* consists of edge or ridge extraction usually by a mask convolution. The second step implies recognition of the vascular structure by chaining the centerline points while excluding heuristically noise points. Most of the reported image feature detectors are conventional ones: Laplacian of a Gaussian [6], hat transform [15], ridge detector based on level-set theory [4], etc.
- *Tracking* begins at an a-priori known position of the vessel in the image. In a single pass operation, feature extraction and vessel structure recognition are performed. By its own nature, a tracking strategy is computationally more efficient than scanning. In [12], given a starting point and direction, a line profile extracted some pixels ahead in that direction is used to compute the centerline of a vessel and a new forward direction for the tracking. In [1], a curve sampling profile is extracted and used for tracking the whole tree.

Conventional image feature detectors used in scanning are too general for the purpose of vessel detection in angiography bringing too many false responses. On the other hand, tracking strategy relies on simple densitometric features that are not enough to discriminate the vessel appearance. Moreover, the tracking strategy needs a continuous set of image features; too strong constraint for angiographies.

*This work was supported by CICYT and EU grants TAP98-0631, TEL99-1206-C02-02, TIC98-1100 and 2FD97-0220.

To cope with these shortcomings we define a new statistic model called eigensnake that integrates snake technique as a global segmentation and interpolation method combined with statistic image feature learning. Segmentation using snakes is a well-known technique that comprises two steps; feature detection using a scanning method to construct a potential map followed by an energy minimisation of the snake curve towards minima of the potential (the image features of interest). The object recognition step is built in the curve shape deformation. Taking advantage of this property, our proposal is to reduce the method to only one step. The idea is to specify the feature detector depending of the target object avoiding the map construction of the conventional snakes. The eigensnake has defined its external energy as a function of the Mahalanobis distance of the image features located in the snaxel position to a learned statistical vessel description. The vessel description is obtained from object responses of gaussian derivative filters over different scales. To obtain filter response invariant to the vessel orientation, we project the filter output along the direction of grey-level variance [14]. Given that each point of the vessel is represented by a set of filter responses, a dimensional reduction is carried out by means of Principal Component Analysis to define a reduced feature space. A likelihood map is constructed to illustrate the separability of vessel and no vessel representations. The snake deforms using as external energy the Mahalanobis distance between the image features in the pixels under analysis and the learned feature projecting them into the reduced space. This process guides the snake towards the vessel centrelines. The paper is organised as follows: section two is a summary of snake principles, section three explain the learning process, section four focuses on the external energy building process, section five presents the results and finally, conclusions are given.

2. Snakes

Snakes are physics-based models, defined in Newton mechanics that deform under external and internal forces. These models are represented as elastic curves with associated energy. External energy is defined as a function of the curve distance to the image features of interest. Internal energy depends on the smoothness and continuity of the model shape. The segmentation by snakes is defined as an energy- minimisation problem. The snake deforms as close as possible to the image features of interest minimising its external energy, while keeping its shape as smooth as possible minimising its internal energy. Representing parametrically the position of the snake as $\mathbf{v}(s) = (x(s), y(s))$, the energy functional of the snake is written as follows:

$$E_{snake} = \int_0^1 E_{int}(\mathbf{v}(s)) + E_{ext}(\mathbf{v}(s))ds \qquad (1)$$

where $E_{int}(\mathbf{v}(s))$ is the internal energy and $E_{ext}(\mathbf{v}(s))$ is the external energy. Snake energy 1 is minimised by Euler-Lagrange equation yielding:

$$-\frac{\delta}{\delta s}(\alpha \mathbf{v}_s) + \frac{\delta^2}{\delta s^2}(\beta \mathbf{v}_{ss}) + \nabla E_{ext}(\mathbf{v}(s)) = 0 \qquad (2)$$

The external force ∇E_{ex} makes the snake to approach and lock on image features (minimising the external energy). To define the external energy a detector of image features is applied and a potential map as a function of the distance to the extracted image features is built [8, 3]. Our aim is to define a new statistical external energy so that the snake is attracted only by image features matching statistically constructed vessel description.

3 Learning the feature

To define the statistical external energy, a learning process is carried out invariant to vessel orientation applying the structure tensor. A set of generalized filters projected on the first eigenvector of the structure tensor is used to construct the probabilistic model of the vessel.

3.1 Extraction of structure orientation

A structure tensor [14] is used to learn vessel appearance in the direction of maximal grey-level variation (perpendicular to the vessel). A tensor J_ρ is obtained by a tensor product of the image gradient ∇u_σ smoothed by a gaussian kernel: $k_\rho(x,y) = \frac{1}{2\pi\rho^2} exp(-\frac{|x|^2+|y|^2}{2\rho^2})$. The expressions for the smoothed image and the structure tensor are as follows:
$u_\sigma(x,t) = (K_\sigma * u(.,t))(x)$
$j_\tau(\nabla u_\sigma) = K_\tau * (\nabla u_\sigma \nabla u_\sigma^T) \quad (\tau \geq 0)$
The eigenvalues of the tensor describe the contrast variation in the eigendirections $\mathbf{e}_1$ and $\mathbf{e}_2$. The eigenvector $\mathbf{e}_2$ associated to the lower eigenvalue gives the orientation of the lowest fluctuation, detecting the vessel flow, while the first eigenvector describes the normal direction used in the learning process (fig. 1(a)).

3.2 Derivative projections

A bank of Gaussian derivative filters $\frac{\delta^k K_\rho}{\delta x^{k1} \delta y^{k2}}$ at different scales ρ is used to obtain a statistic vessel description. Note that different scales are necessary to cope with the vessel diameter variability while using different derivatives allows us to generalise edge- crest- and valley detectors. We use the coherence direction of the vessel structure to orient the filters. We define a mapping of the image pixels to the space of filter responses as follows:
$F : I \rightarrow \mathbf{R}^n$

$(x, y) \to \mathbf{f} = (f_1, \dots, f_n)$
Each sample f_i is a filter output $u_{k\rho}$ in a vessel pixel oriented by the eigenvector $\mathbf{e}_1$:
$u_{k\rho}(x, y) = \frac{\delta^k K_\rho}{\delta x^{k1} \delta y^{k2}} * u(x, y) \quad k = k_1 + k_2$
$f_l = u_{k\rho}(x, y) \cdot \mathbf{e}_1, l = 1 \dots n$. A matrix is built where each row is a sample along the vessel. Given a set of training points (fig. 1(b)) we get their filter responses $f_l, l = 1, \dots, n$ and construct the training data matrix $\mathbf{D}m$. In fig. 2(a) first derivative projection with $\rho = 9$ is showed. Figure 2(b) depicts a training data matrix.

3.3 Dimensional reduction

Using Principal Component Analysis [5] a dimensional reduction is carried out as follows: $W : R^n \to R^l \quad (l < n) : \quad \mathbf{f} \to y$. To obtain the principal components, we compute the eigenvectors of the covariance matrix Σ of $\mathbf{D}m_{mxn}$. The eigenvectors are sorted according to their associated eigenvalues (variances) and form the columns of matrix W. Such reduced space is used to measure the distance of an image feature to the learned ones. The measure can be regarded as a likelihood function giving the probability of each pixel belonging to a vessel category. Figure 3(a) shows the training data projected onto the first two eigenvectors. Fig. 3(b) shows all image features projected onto the first two eigenvectors, the center of the cluster contains the learned data of fig. 3(a). Figure 3(c) shows the learned data projected onto the principal component coordinate system.

4 A probabilistic energy-minimizing scheme

Our aim is to make the snake to be attracted by image features corresponding to the statistical description of the object. To this purpose, we define the external energy of the snake as a function of the Mahalanobis distance of the projected image features x to the centre μ of the learned cluster. The Mahalanobis distance [5] is computed in the reduced feature space, defined as follows:

$$E_{ext}(\mathbf{v}) = D_I^2(\mathbf{v}, \mu) = (WFI(\mathbf{v}) - \mu)^T \Lambda^{-1} (WFI(\mathbf{v}) - \mu) \quad (3)$$

where Λ is a diagonal matrix containing the eigenvalues of the training covariance matrix and $I(\mathbf{v})$ is a vector representation of the image neighbourhood around the snake pixels. Using 2 and the gradient of the probabilistic external energy in 3, we get a new energy minimising scheme for the snake:

$$-\frac{\delta}{\delta s}(\alpha \mathbf{v}_s) + \frac{\delta^2}{\delta s^2}(\beta \mathbf{v}_{ss}) + (cos\varphi, sin\varphi)\frac{\delta D}{\delta \mathbf{e}_1} = 0 \quad (4)$$

where $\frac{\delta D}{\delta \mathbf{e}_1} = (WFI(\mathbf{v}) - \mu)^T \Lambda^{-1} (W \frac{\delta F}{\delta \mathbf{e}_1} I(\mathbf{v}))$ and $\mathbf{e}_1 = (cos\varphi, sin\varphi)$ is the first eigenvector.

5 Results

To illustrate the viability of our eigensnakes, we consider a real application of detecting coronary vessels in angiographies. We tested our approach on 23 images and 5 different vessels. Using five scales for the filters with parameter $\rho = 9 \dots 13$ and derivatives up to third degree, we learned 130 points, and constructed a data matrix $D_{m \times n}, m = 130, n = 26$. Ought to the high number of pixels (samples) in any image, a dimensional space reduction by means of PCA is carried out from $n = 26$ to $l = 4$. In our case, the first four principal axes (eigenvectors) explain up to 99% of the variances, (fig. 3)(c).

For illustrative purposes a mahalanobis distance map is built projecting all image features onto the reduced space and measuring the distance to the training vessel cluster. The Mahalanobis distance map shows the snake convergence to a vessel. Due to the statistic learning, Mahalanobis distance is small mainly in vessel positions. As a result, false responses of vessel appearance are diminished and the snake does not suffer from local energy minima shortcoming. On the other hand, approaching the vessel, the Mahalanobis distance exponentially decreases driving the snake to lock on the vessel features. Figure 4(a) shows the probabilistic external energy map as a function of the Mahalanobis distance. In fig.4(b) a snake is used to segment a vessel. The snake has converged to the vessel in 30 iterations using the energy showed in figure 4(a). One can notice that in a real application the built-in map approach (4) is preferable to obtain faster energy-minimisation scheme avoiding explicit construction of likelihood map for the whole image.

6 Conclusions

In this paper we have proposed a new formulation of the energy-minimising scheme that allows statistically learning and detecting image features characterising different appearances of non-rigid elongated objects. Incorporating the statistical framework, the approach can be extended to the labelling task and to obtain the whole coronary tree using a likelihood matching.

References

[1] K. Barth, B. Eicker, and J. Seissl. Automated biplane vessel recognition in digital coronary angiograms. *Proceedings SPIE. Medical Imaging IV. Image Processing*, 1233:266–274, 1990.

[2] A. C. M. Dumay. *Image Reconstruction from Biplane Angiographic Projections*. PhD thesis, Technische Universiteit Delft. Netherlands, 1992.

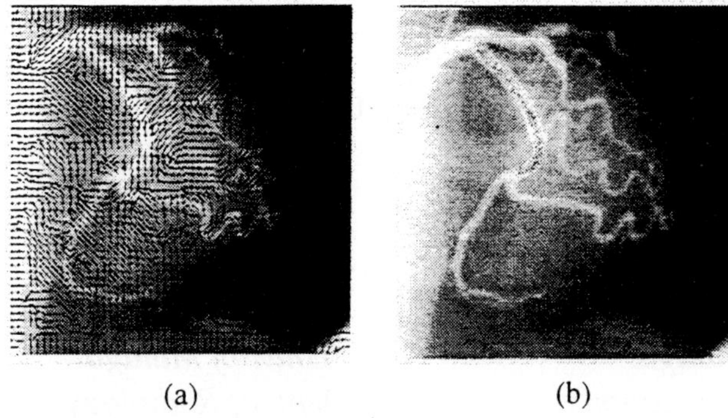

Figure 1. (a) First eigenvector, (b) Training image samples

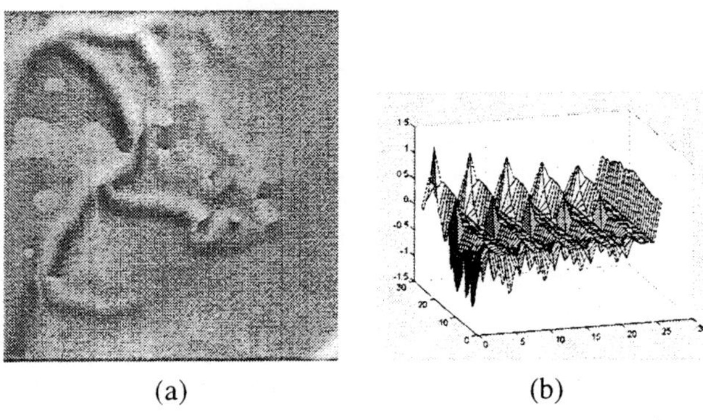

Figure 2. (a) First derivative, (b) Learned data matrix

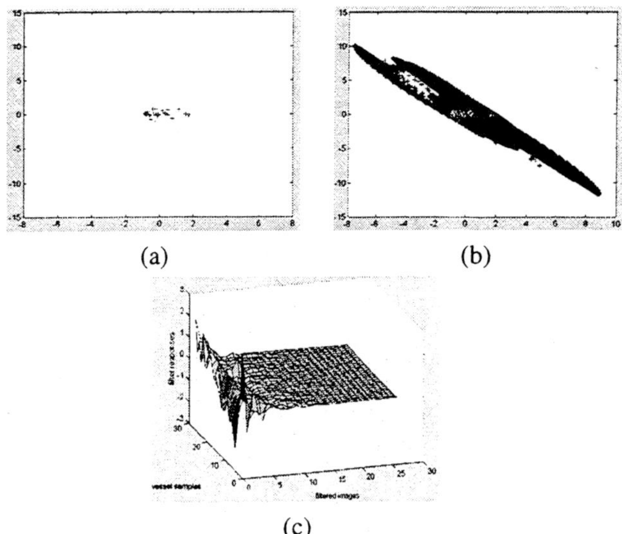

Figure 3. (a) Learned cluster, (b) Image projection, (c) Representation of training image feature in the feature space determined by principal axes

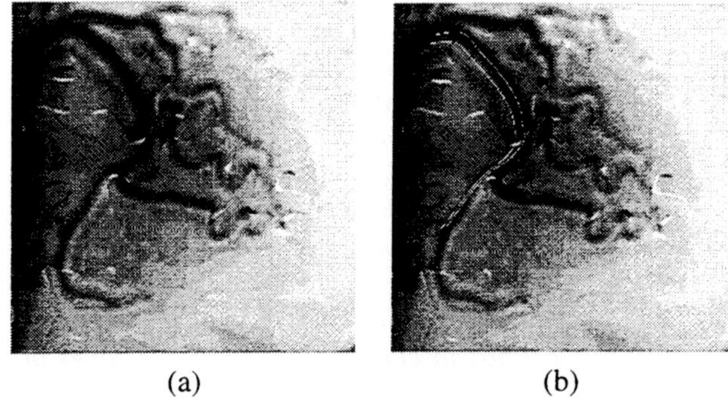

Figure 4. (a) Probabilistic external energy, (b) Snake segmentation

[3] M. Kass, A. Witkin, and D. Terzopoulus. Snakes : Active contour models. In *ICCV*, pages 259–268, 1987.

[4] A. Lopez, R. Toledo, J. Serrat, and J. Villanueva. Extraction of vessel centerlines from 2D coronary angiographies. In *Eighth Spanish Conference on Pattern Recognition and Image Analysis*, volume 1, pages 489–496, 1999.

[5] K. V. Mardia, J. T. Kent, and J. M. Bibby, editors. *Multivariate Analysis*. Academic Press. Harcourt Brace & Company Publishers, 1995.

[6] R. Poli, G. Coppini, M. Demi, and G. Valli. An artificial vision system for coronary angiography. *Proc. Computers in Cardiology*, pages 17–20, 1991.

[7] G. Prause, X. Zhang, S. DeJong, C. R. McKay, and M. Sonka. Semi-automated segmentation and 3d reconstruction of coronary trees: Biplane angiography and intravascular ultrasound data fusion. physiology and function from multidimensional images. *Proceedings SPIE*, 2709, 1996.

[8] P. Radeva, J. Serrat, and E. Martí. A snake model-based segmentation. In *ICCV*, pages 816–821, 1995.

[9] P. Radeva, R. Toledo, C. V. Land, and J. Villanueva. 3d vessel reconstruction from biplane angiograms using snakes. *Proc. Computers in Cardiology*, pages 773–776, 1998.

[10] J. Reiber and P. Serruys, editors. *Progress In Quantitative Coronary Arteriography*. Kluwer Academic Publishers, 1994.

[11] M. Sonka, G. Reddy, and S. Collins. Adaptive approach to accurate analysis of small diameter vessels in cineangiograms. *IEEE Transactions on Medical Images*, 16:87–95, 1997.

[12] Y. Sun. Automated identification of vessel contours in coronary arteriograms by an adaptive tracking algorithm. *IEEE Transactions on Medical Images*, 8:78–88, 1989.

[13] R. Toledo, P. Radeva, C. von Land, and J. Villanueva. 3D dynamic model of the coronary tree. In *Computers in Cardiology*, pages 777–780, 1998.

[14] J. Weickert. Coherence-enhancing diffusion of colour images. In *Image and Vision Computing*, volume 17, 1999.

[15] X. Zhang, S. M. Collins, and M. Sonka. Tree pruning strategy in automated detection of coronary trees in cineangiograms. l_1. *Proceedings of International Conference on Image Processing ICIP'95 IEEE*, 17:656–659, 1995.

Microcalcifications Detection Using Multiresolution Methods

Raul Mata.
Univ. of Jaen.
Dept. of Electronic.
raul@ujaen.es

Enrique Nava.
Univ. of Malaga.
Dept. of Communications.

Francisco Sendra.
Univ. of Malaga.
Dept. of Radiology.

Abstract.

The detection of clustered microcalcifications can aid radiologist to detect early breast cancer. Microcalcifications exhibit some important characteristics, like its small size and high luminosity. So, a CAD method can be useful to avoid them being overlooked. In this paper a multiresolution analysis is proposed by decomposing the image through a band-pass filter bank, so that in each sub-band image become visible only the details at the given scale. Thereafter all the images will be combined in a final one in order to obtain an image that contains all the interest details at the scale where microcalcifications tend to appear. Once the image is obtained, it is necessary to determine which details correspond with microcalcifications. Statistical analysis of the histogram permits to classify the susceptible zones of containing microcalcifications. Applying these statistics techniques over the whole image and representing the results in a 2-D map, clustered microcalcifications regions appear clearly distinguishable.

1. Introduction.

The detection of clustered microcalcifications can aid radiologist to detect early breast cancer, though its location is difficult due to their small size (0.05 to 1 mm of diameter [1]). If we add the convenience of detecting these anomalies when microcalcifications present a small size, a CAD method can be useful to avoid them being overlooked. Microcalcifications exhibit some important characteristics: small size and high luminosity. We adopt the detection criteria proposed by Karssemeijer [2], namely that a cluster is considered detected if two or more microcalcifications are found in the region identified by the radiologist. These characteristics have allowed that several recognition techniques of microcalcifications attempt to find small high luminosity details. Nevertheless, problems are encountered due to the similarity with background.

Some techniques have been developed for detection of clusters based on textures analysis [3], spatial filtering of the mammography [4], [5] and wavelet transform [6], all of them with the objective of showing detail information, that is, sharply and located variations in luminosity.

In this paper a multiresolution analysis is proposed by decomposing the image through a band-pass filter bank, so that in each sub-band image become visible only the details at the given scale. Thereafter all the images will be combined in a final one in order to obtain an image that contains all the interest details at the scale where microcalcifications tend to appear. Statistical analysis of the histogram [7] permits to classify the susceptible zones of containing microcalcifications.

In Section 2 an image pre-processing is performed to facilitate subsequent analysis. In Section 3 multiresolution decomposition for the obtaining of detail images at each level is accomplished. Posterior combination of them conduces to the generation of a final image with all the details. In Section 4 a statistical analysis of the image is accomplished due to its classification. Finally, in Section 5 results obtained applying the methods analysed in the previous sections and the conclusions are shown.

2. Pre-processing of the image.

Clustered microcalcifications appear as small white highly luminous spots groups that appear generally with irregular forms on a variable luminosity and fibrous texture background. Microcalcifications that appear on dark backgrounds are easier of detecting, by the notable difference in luminosity. However, the detection on clear background is more difficult, so it is convenient to enhance the mammography before its decomposition were achieved. This pre-processing of the image implies the linear expansion of the luminosity ranges and non-linear modification of the luminosity, so that high luminosity

1051-4651/00 $10.00 © 2000 IEEE

zones are expanded in contrast (differences between clear background and clusters will be emphasised), in detriment of the dark zones (where differences were clearly visible). Modifications in mammography can be observed in Figure 1 when initial enhancement is applied to the image.

Original Mammogram

Linear expansion

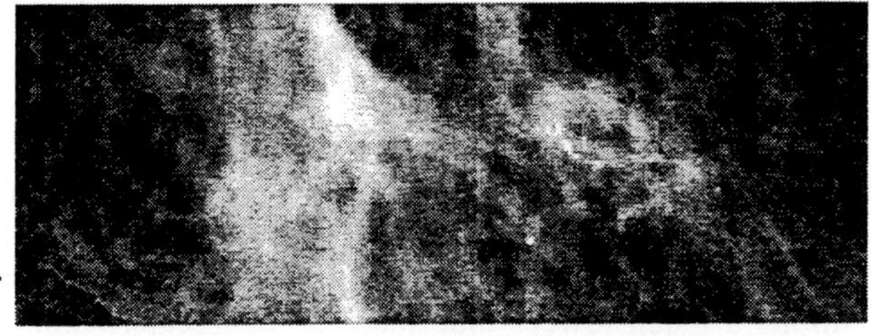

Non-linear contrast enhancement

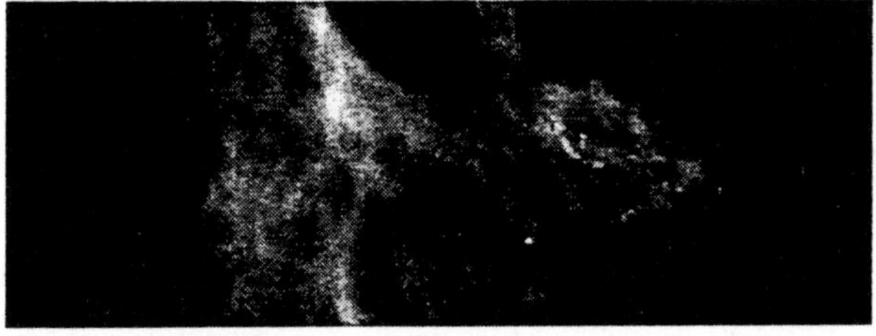

Figure 1: Original mammogram and enhanced images. Pre-processing phase.

3. Multiresolution representation.

To achieve the detection of clusters, the different microcalcifications must be located. Nevertheless, they exhibit several sizes, so that the searching at a given scale implies the disregarding of other microcalcifications with different size. Other components that appear in mammography are elongated forms (due to breast tissue characteristics). These elements can be mistaken for a clustered microcalcifications with linear appearance. Next, methods used for detection of small details that will permit to differentiate between microcalcification and linear structures are presented.

3.1. Multiscale decomposition.

Localisation of elements within a definite size will be accomplished through a band-pass filter bank processing. The frequency bands, where it is possible to locate microcalcifications, are found between 0.25 to 0.55 on a normalised frequency. Smaller frequencies locate elements with excessively large dimensions, while greater frequencies locate elements that corresponded with the small luminosity variations of the mammography texture.

Values used for the band-pass of the filters (around 0.025 on a normalised frequency) try to obtain a quite selective frequency response. Thus, pre-processed image is filtered by rows (horizontal), columns (vertical) and diagonal (vertical and horizontal consecutive), in a similar way to the undecimated wavelet transform [8].

In this way, a low-high (LH), high-low (HL) and high-high (HH) sub-bands at full size are obtained, which correspond with horizontal, vertical and diagonal details. Preserving the size is a very important feature for combination of the images obtained. A final image containing details at given scale, by combining the vertical, horizontal and diagonal detail bands (or images) is obtained.

In [6], sum of all the detail bands gives an image containing small elements detected in each direction. But this assembling has the problem of locating as small details (consequently, as microcalcifications) objects that have a small size in only one direction, as could be linear structures. A product-based method generates an image in which appear detail elements in two directions at least.

Global details image

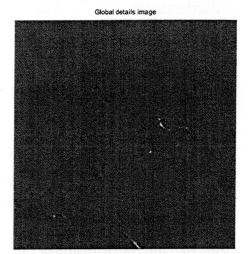

Figure 2: Final image containing all the details at different scales.

3.2. A multiscale details image obtaining.

Individual images containing details at a specific scale must be combined in order to obtain a new all sizes details image.

Since clusters present a set of microcalcifications with different sizes, only sections in mammography containing small detail elements at different scales simultaneously should be considered as real clustered microcalcifications. Isolated microcalcifications do not present clinical interest and provide no information of interest in the detection of breast cancer.

Before accomplishing the combination of the images, a non-linear contrast modification is performed at each scale with a double objective:

a) Weight equalisations of the details at different scales, because of the small size details appear with lower amplitude than greater size elements.
b) Bright and differentiated microcalcifications would hide badly distinguishable ones from background. So, the amplitude increase of the lower weighted areas will be accomplished, emphasising thus the lowly luminosity details that could have been masked.

Once the magnitude comparable detail images are obtained at the different scales, a weighted sum is accomplished, so that the resulting image contains not only the contribution of all the details elements at different scales, but zones with similar size detail objects will be reinforce. In Figure 2 the image containing all details at different scales is shown.

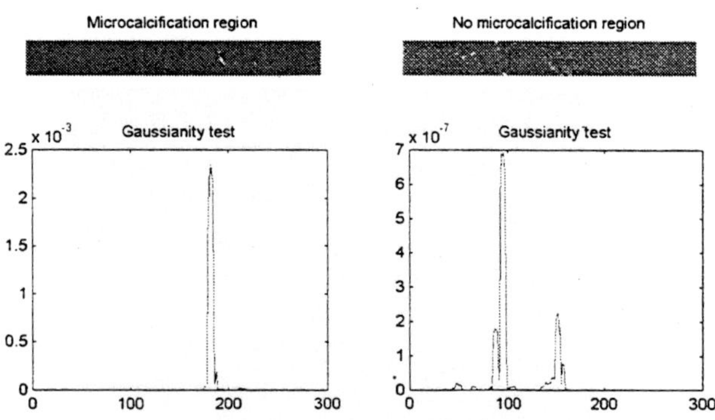

Figure 3: Two regions of the global detail image and the result of the gaussianity test.

4. Clustered microcalcifications detection using statistical analysis.

Studies accomplished by Gürcan [7] on histograms characterisation on images with or without microcalcifications carries out the conclusion of an asymmetry existence in zones with clusters, while no asymmetry could be detected when no microcalcifications are present. Moreover, a Gaussian distribution could approximate regions within microcalcifications, due a gaussianity test indicates regions of the mammography susceptible of containing clusters. Gaussianity test used [9], estimates the first three moments, so that closely values to zero indicate a Gaussian distributed sequence. The gaussianity test is performed as follows:

$$\left.\begin{aligned} I_1 &= \frac{1}{N\times M}\sum_{i=1}^{M}\sum_{j=1}^{N} e[i,j] \\ I_2 &= \frac{1}{N\times M}\sum_{i=1}^{M}\sum_{j=1}^{N} e^2[i,j] \\ I_3 &= \frac{1}{N\times M}\sum_{i=1}^{M}\sum_{j=1}^{N} e^3[i,j] \end{aligned}\right\} \Rightarrow h(I_1, I_2, I_3) = I_3 - 3I_1(I_2 - I_1^2) - I_1^3$$

where e[i, j] are values at locations (i,j) in detail images of the total of NxM pixels, and h is the value that indicates how much nearby the sequence from a gaussian distribution is.

In Figure 3 two regions of the global detail image (for regions with and without microcalcifications) and the gaussianity test obtained for each one are presented. It can be observed how the no microcalcifications region exhibits a much lower value than the microcalcifications contained region. Applying this gaussianity test over the whole image and representing the results in a 2-D map clustered microcalcifications regions appear clearly distinguishable.

5. Results and conclusions.

In Figure 4 the graphical summary of the results obtained in the work is presented. Taking a mammography represented in the Figure 4(a), it is submitted at the multiscale analysis processes, and a final image is obtained as result (Figure 4(b)) containing all the details at different scales, which probably correspond to a clustered microcalcification. In Figure 4(c) the original image with the details image, so that emphasise susceptible clustered region, are superposed. Finally, applying the gaussianity test, the microcalcifications detection process is automated, being the zones within microcalcification represented in the Figure 4(d)

6. References.

[1] L.W. Bassett, "Mammographic analysis of calcifications", *Radiol. Clin. No. Amer.* Vol 30, pp 93-105, 1992.

[2] N. Karssemeijer, "A stochastic model for automated detection of calcification in digital mammograms", *Proc. 12th Int. Conf Inform. Processing Med. Imag*, Wye , UK pp 333-337, 1988.

[3] Dirk Meersman, Paul Scheunders and Dirk van Dyck. "Classification of microcalcification using texture-based features", *Computational Imaging and Vision. Digital Mammography*, Vol 13. Pp 233-236.Nijmegen, 1998

[4] W. Qian, L.P. Clarke, M. Kallergi, R. A. Clark, "Tree-structured nonlinear filters in digital mammography ", *IEEE. Transactions on Medical Imaging*, vol 13, n° 1, March 1994

[5] P.A. French, J.R. Zeidler, W. H. Ku, "Enhanced Detectability of Small Objects in Correlated Cluster Using and Improved 2-D Adaptive Lattice Algorithm", *IEEE Transactions on Medical Imaging*, vol 6, n° 3, pp. 383-397 March 1997

[6] Robin N. Strickland, "Wavelet Transforms for Detecting Microcalcification in Mammograms", *IEEE Transactions on Medical Imaging*, Vol 15, No.2 pp 218-229. April 1996

[7] M. Nafi Gürcan, Yasemín Yardimci and A. Enis Cetin, "Microcalcification detections using adaptative filtering and gaussianity tests", *Computational Imaging and Vision. Digital Mammography*,Vol 13. pp 157-164. Nijmegen, 1998

[8] Stephane G. Mallat, "A Theory for Multiresolution Signal Decomposition: The wavelet representation", *IEEE Transactions on Pattern Analysis and Machine Intelligence*, Vol. 11 No. 7. pp 674-693. July 1989.

[9] And. Moulines, K. Choukri, "Time-Domain Procedures for Testing that a Stationary Times-Series is Gaussian ", *IEEE Transactions on Signal Processing*, vol. 44, n° 8, pp.2010-2025, August 1996.

(a)

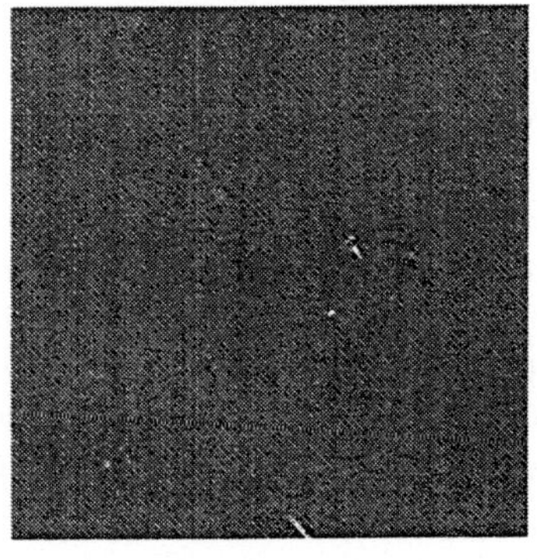

(b)

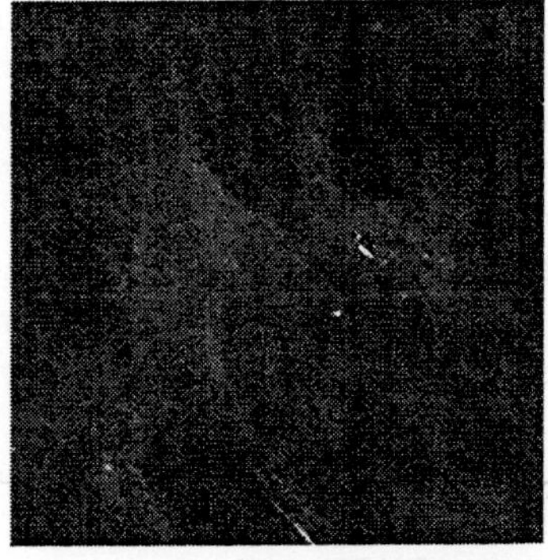

(c)

Gaussianity map

(d)

Figure 4: Graphical summary of the results. The original mammogram (a) and global details image, containing the microcalcifications at all the scales considered (b). A new image (the original and detail images superposed) is shown in (c). Finally, a gaussianity map shows clusters detected (d).

Optical Signatures of Small, Deeply Embedded, Tumor-Like Inclusions in Tissue-Like Turbid Media Based on a Random-Walk Theory of Photon Migration

David Hattery
National Institutes of Heath and George Washington University
hattery@ieee.org

Murray Loew
George Washington University
loew@seas.gwu.edu

Victor Chernomordik and Amir Gandjbakhche
National Institutes of Health
vchern@helix.nih.gov and amir@helix.nih.gov

Abstract

Optical methods for detecting tumors in tissue are desirable in part because optical photons are non-ionizing. The highly scattering nature of tissue makes traditional, and even time-gated, optical imaging impractical for sites deeper than a few millimeters. Scattering in tissue causes dispersion in the path lengths of traversing photons which blurs images. With a theoretical description of path length dispersion, however, the perturbation caused by a localized anomaly may be identified from time-resolved intensity data.

Random walk theory has used to show a quantitative, closed-form relationship between the perturbation and the inclusion size and scattering properties relative to the background. Using Monte Carlo data, we show a method for analyzing the sensitivity of the relationship to signatures of small, deeply embedded, abnormally scattering inclusions.

1. Introduction

The optical characteristics of tissue contain clues that may aid a physician seeking a diagnosis. Further, probing tissue with visible and near infrared light is considered relatively safe since these photons are non-ionizing. Recent advances in the theory of photon migration have made it possible for researchers to detect and quantify the scattering and absorption properties of deeply embedded inclusions. Before this capability will be clinically useful to physicians, the sources of errors must be identified and quantified. This work builds on a physically-based theory of photon migration and uses Monte Carlo simulations to locate and quantify the sources of error. These error estimates may be used to bound the values of optical parameters measured *in vivo* and thus form the basis of a clinically useful optical medical device.

The optical signature of a deeply embedded inclusion, however, is generally obscured by the scattering of photons traveling to and from the site of the inclusion. To increase the resolution of an image, only photons with ballistic or nearly ballistic paths (small scattering angles) may be used. These photons are exceedingly rare after penetrating less than one centimeter of tissue. The inverse exponential relationship between resolution and intensity has no solution that is clinically useful [1]. In such an attempt at imaging, however, most of the penetrating photons are discarded. Although these photons, especially the later arriving photons, have had a tortuous traversal of the tissue, in aggregate they contain much useful information on the presence of, and properties of abnormal inclusions in the tissue. To extract this information, a statistical model of photon motion in highly turbid media is required.

One such theory is the diffusion approximation to photon transport theory which is used in finite element models to reconstruct scattering and absorption properties in tissue [2,3]. This model predicts that the scattering perturbation will scale in proportion to the volume of the inclusion for very small inclusions.

Random walk theory (RWT) may be used to derive an analytical solution for the distribution of photon path-lengths in turbid media such as tissue [4]. Using RWT, an expression may be derived for the probability of a photon arriving at any point and time given a specific starting point and time.

From these probabilities, one may derive an expression for the contrast that results from a small, localized site with greater scattering than the background. The contrast is a function of time and depends on the scattering perturbation and is proportional to the area of the inclusion. Monte Carlo data support the RWT result that the perturbation is proportional to area and not volume for inclusions larger than two mean scattering distances in diameter.

Given a set of time-resolved data, we will show how one may determine the sensitivity of the resulting predictions of the inclusion's scattering perturbation and size. This will provide an estimate of the validity of the RWT results.

1051-4651/00 $10.00 © 2000 IEEE

2. Theory

Tissue may be modeled as a 3D cubic lattice containing a finite inclusion, or region of interest as shown in Figure 1. The lattice has an absorbing boundary corresponding to the tissue surface and the lattice spacing is proportional to the transport-corrected mean photon scattering distance, $1/\mu_s'$. The behavior of photons in the RWT model is described by four dimensionless parameters, L, ρ, n, μ: respectively the thickness of the slab in number of lattice points; the offset of the detector in number of lattice points; the number of steps taken by a photon; and the probability of absorption per lattice step. In the RWT model, photons may move to one of the six nearest neighboring lattice points with probability 1/6. If we know the number of steps, n, taken by a photon traveling between two points on the lattice, then we also know the length of the photon's path.

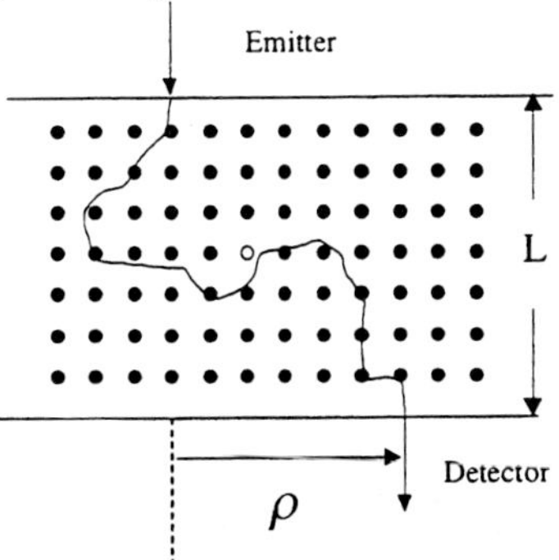

Figure 1. Cubic Lattice model of tissue with RWT parameters

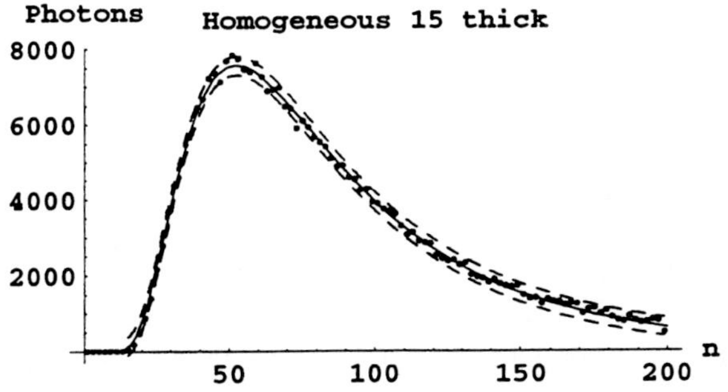

Figure 2. Photon time of arrival from a Monte Carlo simulation with parametric fit and 95 percent CI (dashed line).

The dimensionless RWT parameters, L, ρ, n, μ, described above, may be expressed in terms of actual parameters: time, t, the speed of light in tissue, c, the thickness of the tissue, T, offset, r, and the scattering and absorption properties of the tissue, μ_s', and μ_a, as follows:

$$L = \frac{\mu_s' T}{\sqrt{2}} + 1, \quad \rho = \frac{\bar{r}\mu_s'}{\sqrt{2}}, \quad n = \mu_s' ct, \quad \mu = \frac{\mu_a}{\mu_s'} \quad (1)$$

RWT is useful in predicting the probability distribution of photon path-lengths over distances of at least five mean-photon scattering distances. The derivation of these probability distributions has been previously described [4]. For simplicity in this derivation, the tissue-air interface is considered to be perfectly absorbing; a photon arriving at this interface is counted as arriving at a detector on the tissue surface. The derivation uses the Central Limit Theorem and a Gaussian distribution around lattice points to obtain a closed-form solution independent of the lattice structure.

For a homogeneous slab into which a photon has been inserted, the probability of a photon arriving at a point, r after n steps is [4]:

$$\Gamma(n,r) = \frac{\sqrt{3}\mu_s^{\,2}}{2}\left[\frac{1}{2\pi(n\mu_s - 2)}\right]^{\frac{3}{2}} e^{\frac{-3r^2\mu_s}{4(n-2/\mu_s)}} \sum_{k=-\infty}^{\infty}\left[e^{\frac{-3\left[(2k+1)L-2\sqrt{2}/\mu_s\right]^2}{4(n-2/\mu_s)}} - e^{\frac{-3\left[(2k+1)L\right]^2}{4(n-2/\mu_s)}}\right] e^{-n\mu_a} \quad (2)$$

Equation (2) is used soley for denoising both the homgeneous and inclusion containing data. Plotting Eq. (2) for r=0 yields a photon arrival curve as shown in Figure 2 with Monte Carlo simulation data overlaid.

Assuming homogeneous tissue, except for a compact region containing an abnormal site in which the scattering coefficients are greater than that of the background, we may model the scattering perturbation as a delay caused by the increased time spent by photons at the site of the inclusion. Quantitatively, we start with time-resolved intensity data where $I(x,\Delta t)$ is recorded at position x for many different Δt, where $\Delta t=0$ is defined as the point where a non-scattered photon has had just enough time to arrive at the detector; $I(x,0)$ is the intensity from ballistic photons. To obtain contrast, one must have a reference which, in theory, is the intensity measured when no inclusion exists. In practice, it can be a spatially averaged intensity, or the intensity at a point, x_0, far from any expected inclusions. In the latter case, we use $I(x_0,\Delta t)$ as a reference to calculate time-dependent contrast functions from intensity data:

$$C(x,\Delta t) = \frac{I(x,\Delta t) - I(x_0,\Delta t)}{I(x_0,\Delta t)} = C_a + C_{sc} \quad (3)$$

which shows that the contribution to contrast can come from either a change in absorption, or a change in scattering within the inclusion. In the RWT construct, it has been shown that the two contributions have different dependencies and may, therefore, be separated. Without loss of generality, we may consider an inclusion with no contrast from absorption.

Increased scattering inside an inclusion results in an additional time delay for photons [5]. So, for a purely scattering inclusion the contrast is given by:

$$C_{sc}(x,\Delta t) \approx \frac{d_i^2 \Delta\mu_{sc}' \mu_s'}{2} \frac{1}{p(\Delta t)} \frac{dW(x,\Delta t)}{dt} \quad (4)$$

where $\Delta\mu_s' = \mu_s' - \mu_s^{(0)'}$ is the perturbation of the scattering coefficient in the inclusion, and $W(x,\Delta t)$ is the probability that a photon arriving at the detector has also passed through the inclusion. This function has been shown to behave like a point-spread function (PSF) of an imaging system and we will refer to it as the PSF.

$C_{sc}(x,\Delta t)$ depends on the *slope* of the time derivative of the PSF which is largest at small times. Hence, the largest $C_{sc}(x,\Delta t)$ corresponds to the smallest available time delays, Δt, as can be seen in Figures 3 and 4. On the other hand, for large Δt the contribution from $C_{sc}(x,\Delta t)$ is negligible. Thus, we will focus on short times when the scattering coefficient is largest. It can be shown [5] that at large Δt, perturbations are primarily due to a change in absorption. So, we may use the different dependencies on the time delay to separate scattering from absorption perturbations.

From Eq. (4) it can be seen that, for a purely scattering inclusion, if one plots contrast as a function of the derivative of the PSF normalized by the probability of photon arrival in the absence of an inclusion, the result is linear. Furthermore, the slope depends only on the size and scattering perturbation of the inclusion as shown in Figure 5.

This theory has been applied to phantom data. Using time-resolved data, the size and scattering perturbation of the inclusion were predicted. The resulting errors were less than 10 percent. We would like to identify the sources of those errors and provide a means to bound the errors.

3. Analysis

Monte Carlo simulation data of photon transport in tissue provides noisy data that is a good model for the data collected from phantoms and tissue. We are interested in determining the signal-to-noise ratio (SNR) which will determine the minimum detectable signal threshold where we define the signal as the slope. The slope is the first term in Eq. (4) and is shown in Figure 5. Moving from raw data to the slopes in Figure 5 involves four steps: parametric fit of data to Eq. (2); computing the contrast as a function of time using Eq. (3); plotting the contrast as a function of the PSF normalized by $1/p(\Delta t)$; and finally, using linear regression to obtain the slope.

In the first step, we parametrically fit the data to Eq. (2) and compute the 95 percent confidence interval of the fit. To evaluate the distribution of the data, we observe that variability in the number of photons arriving at a particular time occurs when arriving photons experience slight path length perturbations that move their arrival to earlier or later times. Since these perturbations occur during scattering events, and each photon experiences many such scatterings, by the Central Limit Theorem it is safe to assume that this data is Gaussian.

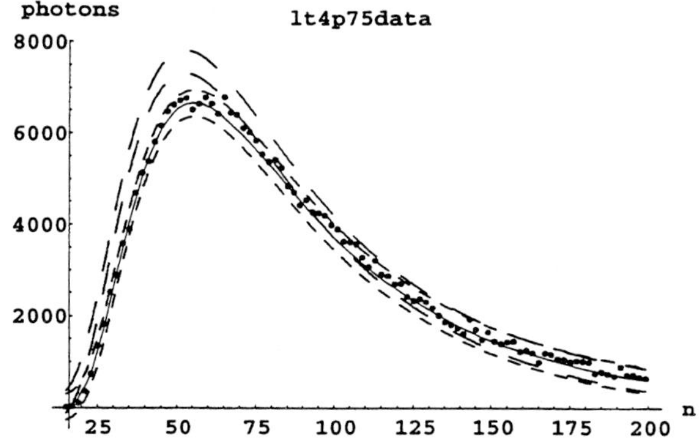

Figure 3. Scattering Perturbation from 4x4x4 cubic inclusion at center of slab with scattering coefficient 175% of the background (long dashes are 95%CI for reference data, short dashes are 95%CI for perturbed data the points of which are plotted along with the parametric fit) 100M simulation photons.

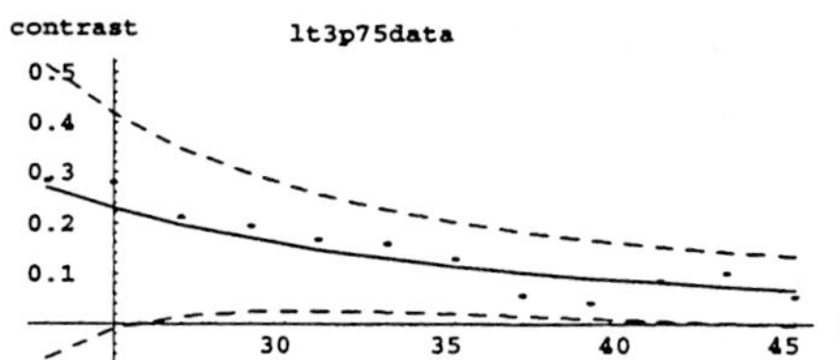

Figure 4. Scattering contrast as a function of step, n, computed from raw data, parametrically fit data, and with 95 percent confidence interval for fit data (dashed lines).

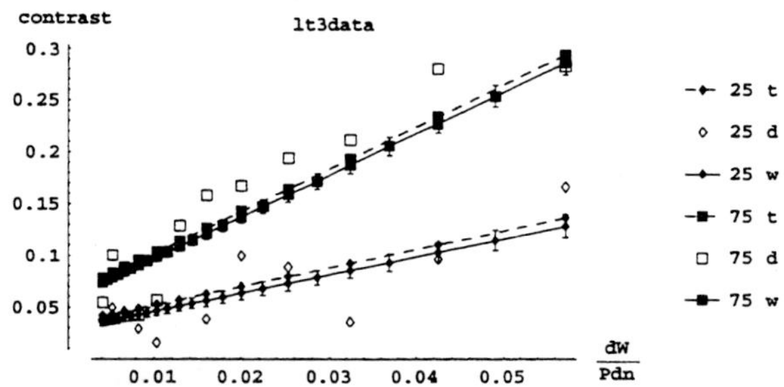

Figure 5. Increased scattering inclusions showing contrast from theory, t, raw data, d, and weighted method, w, for two inclusions with increase in scattering from the background of 25, and 75 percent.

Contrast is normally computed from the parametric fit which uses all of the time of arrival data. As a result, noise in the computed contrast is very low and this a fundamental reason for the technique's excellent sensitivity on experimental data [5]. The contrast function's distribution, however, is not known. So, to determine the effect of data variability on the end result, we generate 50 samples of intensity at a given point in time for both reference and perturbed data and compute the contrast from each sample pair. This is done for approximately 15 different points in time that are on the rising slope shown in Figure 3. Thus, the actual contrast data distribution is retained in these samples.

The 50 samples for each of the 15 times are then transformed into the $1/p(\Delta t)\, dW/dn$ space. Again, we do not know the form of the distribution, but when we perform a linear regression on the sampled data, the error in the slope due to the input data will be obtained as indicated by the error bars in Figure 5.

Table A shows the predicted slope from the theory, along with slopes computed using raw data, parametrically fit data, the weighted technique described above and the regression error for the weighted slope. The values computed from the raw data are included for comparison, but are generally a poor predictor of the slope. The parametric and weighted techniques are better and more consistent. This is due to the reduction in noise during the parametric fitting of the data. As can be seen, the regression error is independent of inclusion size and relative scattering. Thus, it provides an estimate of the noise from which a SNR can be computed. For the cases in the table, SNR ranges from 10 to 50.

Table A. Four slope calculations and error for a 15mm thick slab with scattering 1/mm containing three different sizes of inclusions with greater scattering than the rest of the slab.

Inclusion		Slope				Error
size mm	Scatter-ing (%)	Theory Prediction	Raw data	Para-metric	Weight-ed	Weight-ed σ
2	125	0.50	0.36	0.49	0.23	0.140
2	150	1.00	1.57	1.75	1.64	0.136
2	175	1.50	1.17	1.73	1.73	0.123
3	125	1.13	2.07	1.42	1.18	0.129
3	150	2.25	2.75	3.01	2.89	0.123
3	175	3.38	4.74	3.89	3.71	0.132
4	125	2.00	2.98	3.80	3.60	0.127
4	150	4.00	5.10	6.28	6.24	0.113
4	175	6.00	5.39	6.72	6.57	0.137

From Table A, we can see that the regression error, and hence the noise in the intensity data, is not a good predictor of the error in the quantification of the perturbation from a small inclusion. From Eq. (4), the perturbation is made up of two factors: a component that quantifies the number of photons that have visited the site and were subsequently collected and a component that quantifies how long the photons spent in the inclusion. We suspect that the error will be proportional to the product of the two. We plan to run Monte Carlo simulations to check the results against predicted values. We expect that for a given number of photons in a Monte Carlo simulation, smaller inclusions will be visited less, and the time spent in the inclusions will be less. Thus, the perturbation from a small inclusion will have a larger error than better visited larger inclusions. From this, we should see that large inclusions are more accurately quantified than small ones. Further, there appears to be a small bias error that results in consistent under-prediction of the slope. The perturbations do not scale with volume as would be expected from the diffusion approximation to transport theory. This indicates that the RWT approach is superior, but a correction to the theory is still warranted.

4. Conclusion

The quantitative technique described above is a powerful tool that may prove valuable to physicians. Before such a technique is ready for clinical use, the sources of errors must be identified and quantified. We have shown a method for determining the SNR which affects signal detectability. The system noise, however, does not fully explain the quantification errors of the inclusion properties. Using Monte Carlo simulations, we plan to take a detailed look at the errors in each component of the perturbation. The errors in those components will provide the basis for an accurate assessment of theerrors in the signal from small, deeply embedded inclusions in tissue. We expect that the signal error will be proportional to the number of photons in the simulation and the ratio of the inclusion volume to the slab volume. We believe the existing results show that this technique has potential as a valuable clinical tool.

5. References

[1] A.H. Gandjbakhche, R. Nossal, and R.F. Bonner, "Resolution limits for optical transillumination of abnormalities deeply embedded in tissues," Med. Phys, 21, pp185-191, 1994.

[2] S.R. Arridge, and J.C. Hebden, "Optical imaging in medicine: II. Modelling and reconstruction," *Phys. Med. Biol.*, **42**, pp. 841-853, 1997.

[3] J Chang, R. Aronson, H.L. Graber, R.L. Barbour, "Imaging diffusive media using time-independent and time-harmonic sources: dependence of image quality on imaging algorithms, target volume, weight matrix, and view angles," *Proc. of SPIE*, **2389**, pp.448-464, 1995.

[4] A.H. Gandjbakhche, G.H. Weiss, R.F. Bonner, and R. Nossal, "Photon path-length distributions for transmission through optically turbid slabs," *Phys. Rev. E*, **48**, pp. 810-818, 1993.

[5] A. H. Gandjbakhche, V. Chernomordik, J. C. Hebden and R. Nossal, "Time-dependent contrast functions for quantitative imaging in time-resolved transillumination experiments," *Applied Optics*, **37**, pp. 1937-1981, 1998.

Segmentation of artery wall in coronary IVUS images: A Probabilistic Approach

Debora Gil, Petia Radeva, Jordi Saludes *
Computer Vision Center and Dpt. d'Informàtica
Universitat Autònoma de Barcelona
Edifici O, 08193, Bellaterra, SPAIN
{ debora, petia, saludes}@cvc.uab.es

Abstract

Intravascular ultrasound images represent a unique tool to analyze the morphology of arteries and vessels (plaques, etc). The poor quality of these images makes traditional segmentation algorithms (such as edge detection) fail to achieve the expected results. In this paper we present a probabilistic flexible template to separate different regions in the image. In particular, we use elliptic templates to model and detect the shape of the vessel inner wall in IVUS images. The use of elliptic templates forces a global probabilistic approach, that makes use of image statistics inside regions. We present the results of successful segmentation obtained from 12 patients undergoing stent treatment. A physician team has validated these results.

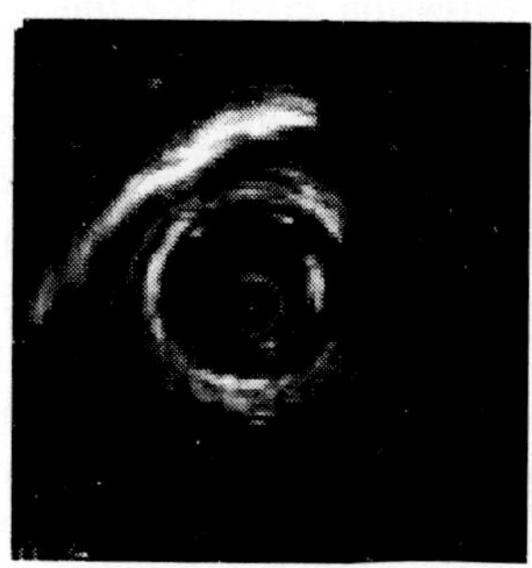

Figure 1. Slice of artery obtained by intravascular ultrasound

1. Introduction

1.1. Intravascular Ultrasound Sequences

Intravascular Ultrasound (IVUS) imaging is a relatively new medical tool which consists of placing a catheter, with a sensor on its tip, inside the artery. This sensor rotates as it emits pulses of ultrasound. When it receives the echoes the tissues return, it generates an image like the one shown in figure 1. Dark zones correspond to the artery lumen, light zones to the artery wall and the brightest parts with a dark shadow behind, to calcium plaque.

1.2. Previous Research

Due to the amount of information they carry ([5], [4]), IVUS images are increasing their role in the diagnosis of several diseases. Consequently, segmentation and tracking from IVUS images of the vessel inner wall has been approached in several recent works ([2], [7]). The poor quality of the images suggests the use of techniques such as probabilities [1] or fuzzy logic [2] guiding an active contour to adjust the inner wall. In the case of coronary images one has the additional problem of the dark shadows that the calcium plaque produces. That makes probabilistic approaches taking into account only the statistics in a neighborhood of the model border [1] fail to obtain good results. F. Escolano proposed in [2] the use of circular deformable models guided by a function which had an added term to cope with noise. The rigidity of the shape prevented the template from being mislead by dark shadows.

In this paper, we suggest the use of elliptic templates guided by the global statistics of the image. On one hand, the use of probabilities is a good way of reducing the impact of noise. On the other, using such a restricted deformable shape makes the model more stable under the presence of artifacts such as shadows due to calcium plaque and the sensor. We use an elliptic shape instead of a circle to better adjust the model to the inner wall and because this shape also gives a direct estimation of the maximum and minimum diameters of the lumen. The only assumption made is that lumen and tissue appear in the image as gray-level pixels generated by two distinct normal distributions.

*This work was supported by TIC98-1100 .

1051-4651/00 $10.00 © 2000 IEEE

2. Description of the method

The image will be always thought of as a function, $i(x, y)$, of two variables. The origin of our coordinate system will be supposed to be at the center of the image.

The first step is to select the region of interest in the image. Notice that since the outer part of any IVUS is completely dark, dealing with the whole of the image may induce some errors, specially during the selection of the threshold α (see next paragraph). Denote by $\mathbb{D}_r$ the disk of radius r centered at the origin and by P the probability of having a dark gray-level inside $\mathbb{D}_r$. Let us consider the function $g(r) = P(i(x, y) < 0.2)$. Notice that if one takes disks of increasing radius, the global minimum of g indicates the point we stop having significant echoes. From now on, whenever we talk about the image we will be thinking of this selected part.

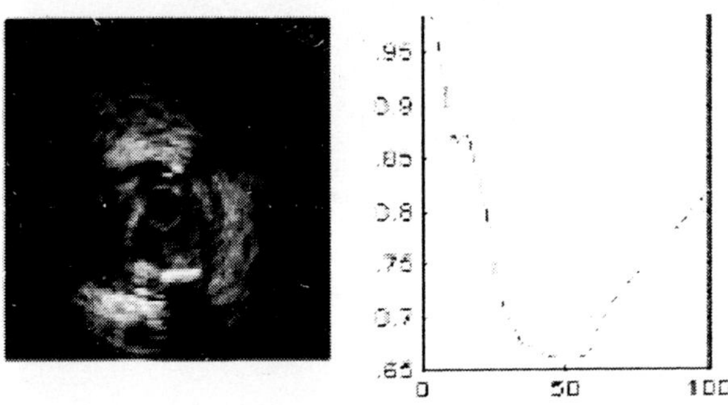

Figure 2. Right: original image. Left: graphic of the function g(r)

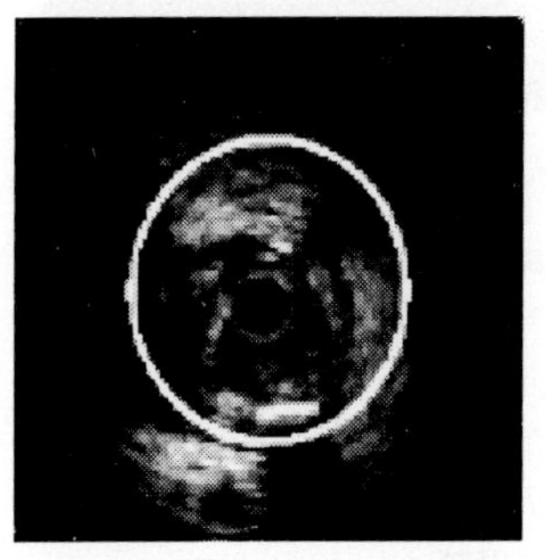

Figure 3. Right: area of interest. Left: pixels under threshold $\alpha = 0.26$

The method we propose is based on the assumption that lumen and tissue appear in the image as gray-level pixels generated by two distinct normal distributions. Let α be the value that separates both distributions. We compute it automatically by means of the method described in [6]. The threshold is obtained taking into account the histogram of the area of interest. Once this parameter α has been fixed, we proceed to the deformation of the ellipse as follows.

Let $\mathcal{E}_{int}$ denote the interior of the deformable ellipse and $\mathcal{E}_{ext}$ its complement in the image. Then, to segment the lumen we search for the ellipse that maximizes the following function:

$$F = \frac{\int_{\mathcal{E}_{int}} I(x, y)dxdy}{Area\ of\ \mathcal{E}_{int}} + (1 - \frac{\int_{\mathcal{E}_{ext}} I(x, y)dxdy}{Area\ of\ \mathcal{E}_{ext}}) \quad (1)$$

where

$$I(x, y) = \begin{cases} 1 & ; if\ i(x, y) \leq \alpha \\ 0 & ; otherwise \end{cases}$$

The first term represents the probability that the gray level of the inner points of the ellipse belong to the probabilistic distribution corresponding to the lumen. The second one represents the probability of having an outside gray level belonging to the distribution which corresponds to the tissue.

Notice that an ellipse is defined by five parameters (a, b, σ, x_0, y_0). The pair (x_0, y_0) are the coordinates of the center, σ is the angle of rotation and the parameters a and b are the lengths of the principal axes [see figure below].

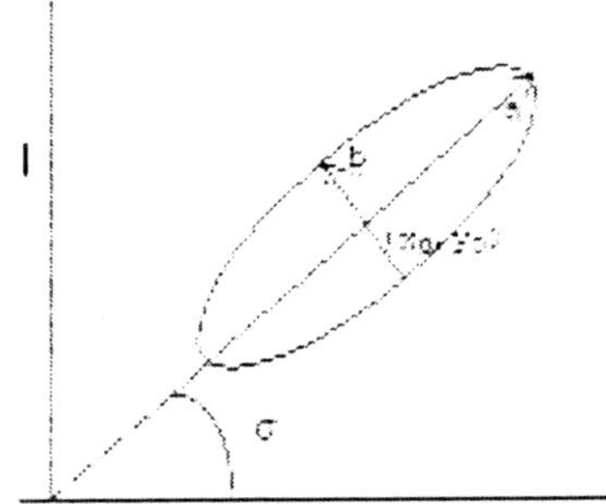

Figure 4. representation of the five parameters of an ellipse

The problem, then, reduces to maximize a function, $F = F(a, b, \sigma, x_0, y_0)$, of 5 variables. Its maximum is obtained by the steepest descent method [3].

Consider the following change of variables

$$\begin{pmatrix} \tilde{u} \\ \tilde{v} \end{pmatrix} = \begin{pmatrix} a\cos\sigma & b\sin\sigma \\ -a\sin\sigma & b\cos\sigma \end{pmatrix} \begin{pmatrix} u \\ v \end{pmatrix} + \begin{pmatrix} x_0 \\ y_0 \end{pmatrix}$$

In these new variables $(\tilde{u}, \tilde{v})$, the function in (1) can be written as

$$F(a,b,\sigma,x_0,y_0) = \frac{\int_{\mathbb{D}} abI(\tilde{u},\tilde{v})dudv}{Area\ of\ \mathcal{E}_{int}} + \\ + (1 - \frac{\int_{\mathbb{D}^c} abI(\tilde{u},\tilde{v})dudv}{Area\ of\ \mathcal{E}_{ext}})$$

where $\mathbb{D}$ is the disk of radius one centered at the origin and $\mathbb{D}^c$ is its complement.

2.1. Dynamics of the parameters

Following the steepest descent method, the dynamics of the parameters are obtained by means of the partial derivatives of F.

The iterative procedure needs an initialization of the ellipse. As initial ellipse for the first frame, we take a circle centered at the origin of a radius close to the one of the sensor. Indeed, any ellipse contained in the inner wall would do. Since the sensor always lies inside the lumen, this is the initial shape we consider. Sometimes, though, when the center of the lumen is far away from the origin, it is highly recommended to start with a circle centered at the lumen. If one wanted the method to be completely automatic, a global minimization method (such as simulated annealing) for the first frame should be used. At each new frame, we take as initial ellipse the one segmenting the lumen of the former image.

Sometimes, the method fails to converge to the inner wall. We detect these failures by comparing two consecutive ellipses. If the Euclidean norm between the two sets of parameters is high, we reject the segmentation result.

3. Results

The method has been used to segment and track the inner wall of coronary arteries in short sequences (up to 30 frames at a rate of 12 frames per second) extracted from IVUS made to patients undergoing stent treatment. We have tested the method on a set of 270 frames from twelve different patients. The results obtained have been validated by a medical team. According to experts the method detects the inner wall in 80% of the cases if the lumen is not completely obstructed by proliferation. Some of the ellipses obtained are shown in the figures below. They illustrate four different kinds of IVUS images.

Images in figure 5 have got shadows due to the sensor. The one on the left, at the right inferior quadrant. The other, at the left inferior quadrant. Figure 6 (left) presents a shadow due to calcium plaque that occupies most of its right side. While figure 6 (right) shows a stent, which appears as bright spots around the lumen. A typical binary image we work with is the one of figure 7 (left). The white area inside the lumen corresponds to the sensor.

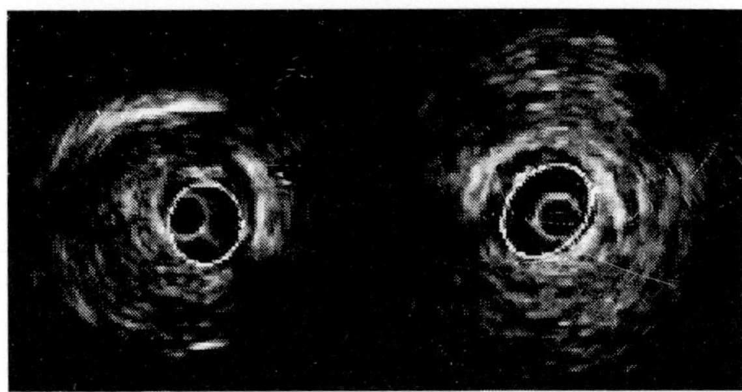

Figure 5.

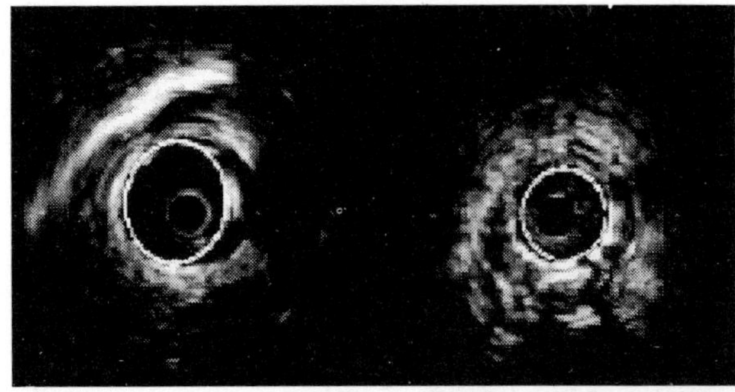

Figure 6.

Figure 7. Right:original image. Left:pixels above threshold α

Results obtained using other methods are shown in figure 8. The use of probabilities only in a neighborhood around the border of the template kept the ellipse in figure 8 (left) from absorbing the sensor. The ellipse on the right was guided taking into account the total number of inner points with gray level under α and the total number of outer points with gray level above this threshold. The dark echoes due to the small upper plaque mislead the template.

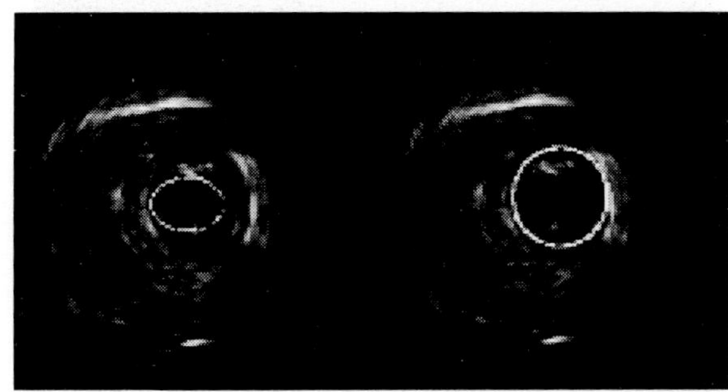

Figure 8. ellipses obtained using other methods

4. Conclusions and Future Developments

The method presented in this paper introduces a simple global probabilistic model which behaves well in low quality images. The method detects the inner wall in 80% of the frames when severe restenosis is not observed. We are studying if the problem can be overcome considering gray-level pixels generated by three normal distributions instead of two and taking into account other features such as spatial and temporal coherence in the sequence.

The tracking of the inner wall in IVUS sequences is one of the first steps to obtain a faithful 3-D reconstruction of the coronary tree. This is vital to decide whether a patient can go under stent treatment or not. It can also help to estimate the heart dynamics. There is the hypothesis that heart and artery dynamics may be a way of evaluating heart tissue damage after a coronary stroke. Our future work will focus on both 3-D artery reconstruction and estimation of heart dynamics.

References

[1] Song Chun Zhu, Alan Yuille, *Region Competition:Unifying Snakes, Region Growing, and Bayes/MDL for Multiband Image Segmentation.* IEEE Trans. Pattern An. Mach. Intelligence, **Vol. 18, No 9** , (September 1996).

[2] F. Escolano, M. Cazorla, D. Gallardo and R. Rizo *Deformable Templates for Plaque Thickness Estimation of Intravascular Ultrasound Sequences* Pattern Recognition and Image Analysis. Preprints of the VII National Symp. on Patt. Recog. and Im. An.Vol 1 (April 1997)

[3] R. Fletcher *Practical Methods of Optimization* John Wiley and Sons

[4] D. Hausmann, Andre J.S. Lundkvist, Guy Friedrich, Krishnankutty Sudhir, Peter J. Fitzgerald and Paul G. Yock *Lumen and Plaque Shape in Atherosclerotic Coronary Arteries Assesed by In Vivo Intracoronary Ultrasound* Beyond Angiography. Intravascular Ultrasound: State-Of-The-Art **XX Congres of the ESC, Vol 1** (August 1998)

[5] F. De Man, I. De Scheerder, M.C. Herregods, J. Piessens and H. De Geest *Role of Intravascular Ultrasound in Coronary Artery Disease: A new gold standart?* Beyond Angiography. Intravascular Ultrasound: State-Of-The-Art **XX Congres of the ESC, Vol 1** (August 1998)

[6] Nobuyuki Otsu *A Threshold Selection Method from Gray-Level Histograms.* IEEE Trans. on Sys. Man and Cybernetics, **Vol. SMC-9,No 1**, pp 62-65, (January 1979)

[7] B. Solaiman, R. Debon, F. Pipelier, J.-M. Cauvin and C. Roux *Information Fusion:Application to Data and Model Fusion for Ultrasound Image Segmentation.* IEEE Trans. on Bio. Eng., **Vol. 46, No 10**, pp 1171-1175 (October 1999)

Spotting approaches for biochip arrays

T. Kaifel, C. Schiekel, T. Kämpke
Research Institute for Applied Knowledge Processing (FAW)
Helmholtzstr. 16, D-89010 Ulm, Germany
{kaifel,schiekel,kaempke}@faw.uni-ulm.de

Abstract

This paper presents a technique for segmenting spot-objects of possibly different sizes in images of biochip arrays. As these images are taken after the biochips underwent a complex chemical process, they are subject to blur effects, distortions, and local intensity shifts. Image segmentation is reduced to quantisation which in turn is reduced to function approximation. The approximation requires neither parametric assumptions nor parametric input and it iteratively optimizes an n-step histogram function by coarser step functions. Thus, a discrete "scale space" is created. The notion of so-called stable minima is used for finding good binarisation thresholds. Stability issues are combined with heuristic criteria tailored to segmenting biochip images. Finally, the complete approach is applied to a series of real biochip images.

Key words: image segmentation, quantisation, bioinformatics

1. Introduction

Biochip technology attracts growing interest world wide. Biochips are miniaturized function elements consisting of biological and technical components. They are used for biological analysis such as expression profiling and for medical diagnosis such as mutation detection. Biochips contain so-called spots whose number ranges from a few dozens to several thousands depending on the particular chip type. The spots are typically arranged in an array. In contrast to electronic chips, there is no "wiring" or any other interconnection between the spots. Each spot gives rise to a biological or medical experiment during a hybridisation process. During this process, the substance of each spot reacts to some degree with a liquid under investigation. The intensities of the reactions serve as indicators for the similarity between the spot substances and the probe liquid. Reaction intensity is detectable after the reaction according to the amount of the probe liquid which "aligned" to the spots. CCD imaging or laser scanning results in images such as shown in fig.1.

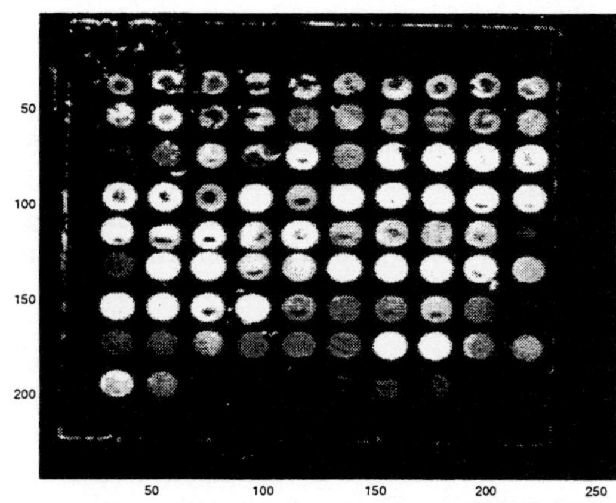

Figure 1. Image of typical biochip

Manual spot evaluation appears to be infeasible in case of large spot numbers. Automated or semi-automated biochip evaluation is thus required. This consists of precisely locating the spots by positioning a grid and of segmenting each spot from its background. We focus on the segmentation issue in the sequel.

A thresholding operation is used to convert gray level images into regions of two types. These region types correspond to foreground and background. If there are two clear peaks in the gray level histogram of the image and if the peaks are separated by a clear "valley", then this valley may serve as bi-level threshold. However, in most cases the histograms are not bi-modal. There exist segmentation algorithms for these cases, but most of them need input parameters and achieve poor results in use with few data [7]. Kämpke et al. [1, 6, 2] proposed a concept for robust image segmentation which does not require any parametric input except the number of region types. The approximation approach in its pure form did not always result in the "best" or in an acceptable segmentation of a biochip image. The approach was improved and adapted by analyzing the underlying scale space leading to several threshold candidates. A criterion to choose the best is established. The complete approach is described in the next section.

Section 3 illustrates the approach on various examples of biochips with different arrays and different physical sizes and proportions. We conclude with an empirical assessment of the approach.

2 Methods

The algorithm [1], which works directly on the data of the histogram, is used as basis for the segmentation of each spot of a biochip. The histogram is approximated by step functions with fewer steps. This optimisation is done by minimizing the 2-norm of the histogram and the n-step function. Approximating step functions are then checked for minima, which are rated in a score matrix. The criterion for rating a minimum involves the width and the depth of the surrounding minimum region. The scores of the minima are aggregated. A set of stable minima with scores above a given threshold is then used to compute the best threshold.

While generating the histogram, gaps between adjacent bins are eliminated when these gaps are "small". More precisely, the number of bins in the histogram is set to $1.5 \cdot \sqrt{q}$, where q is the number of pixels in the spot image. To avoid sparsity effects, the modified image histogram should satisfy $1.5 \cdot \sqrt{q} \geq 12$.

Quantisation is done by finding the best step-function s_n with n breakpoints. Approximation is in the sense of the 2-norm so that the distance between the histogram f and s_n is

$$\| f - s_n \| = \sqrt{\int_a^b (f(x) - s_n(x))^2 \, dx}$$

The distance is the quantisation error of s_n for f.

The algorithm quantitizes the histogram into $N - 3$ different step functions, where $2 < n < N$ and N is the number of breakpoints in the histogram.

The set of all coarsening step functions is considered as scale-space with respect to the histogram. Stable minima in the scale-space serve as thresholds. Let T_m be the set of these minima. The scores of these minima are computed by the sum of the width and the depth of the minimum-region over all step functions.

$$h(t_m) = \sum_{n=3}^{N} \alpha(n) \cdot w_n(t_m) + (1 - \alpha(n)) \cdot d_n(t_m)$$

with $t_m \in T_m$, $w_n(t_m)$ is the relative width of the minima t_m of the n-step function, d_n is the relative height of the minima t_m of the n-step function, and

$$\alpha(n) = \frac{N - n}{N - 1}.$$

It is sufficient to consider only those minima whose score is above 30% of the high-score. These stable minima are combined in set T_s.

The candidate set T_s is reduced by deleting all stable minima that appear to be caused by noise within (not "between") background and foreground. Therefore, we first set the background area to 20% of the width of the histogram. All stable minima in this area are deleted. This is also done for the spot area in the upper part of the histogram.

To have the spot fully segmented, the edge pixels of the spot should be included. Using the minima with the best score as threshold, as proposed by [6], does not ensure that the edge pixels are part of the segmented image. To guarantee that the edge pixel are included, we choose the best threshold t as

$$t = \min_{t_s \in T_s} \{h(t_s)\}.$$

3. Experiments

The complete algorithm was tested on four different types of biochip arrays, namely XNA-on-gold-Chip, serum-Chip, protein-Chip and DNA-Chip. The images of these biochips differ in resolution and the arrays themselves differ in physical size and proportions. For example, the maximum number of spots was 20, while all chips combined contain 60 spots.

Because there is no optimal spot segmentation, which could be used as a reference, the reference was made by segmenting the images manually. For segmenting the spots, there is the criterion that most of the pixels at the edge of the spot should be included in the segmentation. But this method does not give best results as well because the placement of the threshold is subjective. Even different image-processing-specialists may deviate in finding the best threshold. In a test, 30 pictures were segmented manually by two persons. The test-persons did not see the segmentation by the algorithm, so, they were not biased

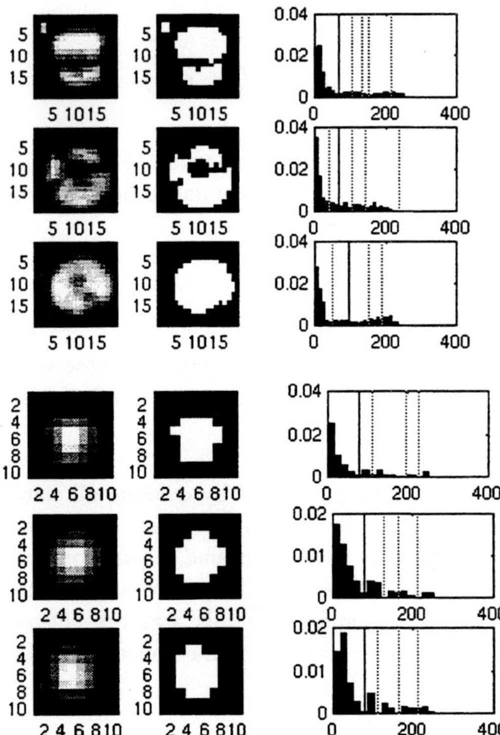

Figure 2. The results of three examples of spots from the DNA-Chip and the serum-Chip are shown. In the first column the original gray value image is shown. In the second column the binarised image is shown. In the third column the histogram with the stable minima are shown. The chosen threshold is represented by a solid line, while the dashed lines are the other good stable minima.

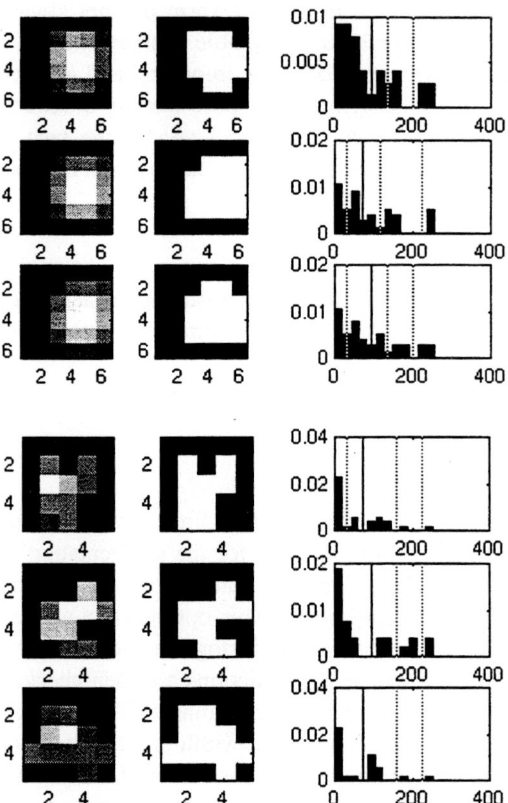

Figure 3. The results of three examples of spots the Protein-Chip and the XNA-on-gold-Chip are shown. In the first column the original gray value image is shown. In the second column the binarised image is shown. In the third column the histogram with the stable minima are shown. The chosen threshold is represented by a solid line, while the dashed lines are the other good stable minima.

by any proposed image segmentation. As a value for the spots, the sum of the gray values of all segmented pixels is used. This is motivated by assessment procedures from molecular biology. The average value deviated by 5% to the average value from the other person.

The evaluation of the experiments were done by a deviation value between the segmented pixels of the spots by the algorithm presented in this paper and the manual segmentation. The deviation value d is computed as follows:

$$d = \left| \frac{I_h - I_a}{I_h} \right|$$

where I_h is the sum value of the pixels segmented by hand, and I_a is the sum value segmented by the algorithm computed as:

$$I = \sum_{(x,y)\in N_p} g(x,y)$$

where $g(x,y)$ is the gray value of the pixel (x,y) and N_p is the set of all segmented pixels of one spot image. We summarize the experiment in the following table.

Biochip-type	number of spot	spot size in pixel	deviation in %
XNA-Chip	10	5x5	10.07
Serum-Chip	20	10x10	10.47
Protein-Chip	20	6x6	6.39
DNA-Chip	10	19x19	5.34

In the first column the names of the type of biochip arrays are listed. In the second column the number of spot images evaluated in this experiment are shown. In the third column the resolutions of the spots are given in terms of pixels. The fourth column shows the average deviation of the spot images. The overall deviation amounts 8.1 %.

4 Conclusion

The test series reveals that the average deviation between manual and algorithmic segmentation is above 8%. Though this does not look promising at first sight, the results are considered to be informative by physicians and biologists with respect to classifying the hybridisations as "weak", "medium", or "intense".

An itemised account of the test series reveals that large deviations such as the 10.47% for the serum-chip, occured in only about 10% of all cases. The average deviation without the outliers is about 3.87% which renders the approach to be practically feasible from a quantitative viewpoint.

Another strength of the proposed procedure is its robustness towards varying spot sizes. Small spots (6x6 pixels) were evaluated with the same algorithmic settings as large spots (19x19 pixels) and results were of the same quality, even for small spots. Most algorithm here have problems with few data.

References

[1] T. Kämpke and R. Kober. Nonparametric image segmentation. *Pattern Analysis and Applications*, 1:145–154, 1998.

[2] T. Kämpke and R. Kober. Nonparametric optimal binarization. *ICPR 14th International Conference on Pattern Recognition*, 1:27–29, August 1998.

[3] J. Kittler and J. Illingworth. Threshold selection based on simple image statistic. *Computer Vision, Graphics and Image Processing*, 30:125–147, 1985.

[4] Y. Liu and S. N. Srihari. Document image binarization based on texture features. *IEEE Transactions on pattern analysis and machine intelligence*, 19(5):540–544, May 1997.

[5] N. Otsu. A threshold selection method from grayscale histograms. *IEEE Transactions on Systems, Man and Cybernetics*, pages 62–66, August 1978.

[6] M. Schuster, T. Kämpke, and C. Schiekel. Nonparametric multilevel thresholding. *IAESTED Signal and Image Processing*, October 1998.

[7] J. Zhang, J. W. Modestino, and D. A. Langan. Maximum-likelihood parameter estimation for unsupervised stochastic model-based image segmentation. *IEEE Transactions on Image Processingl*, 3(4):404–419, July 1994.

Thyroid Cancer Cells Boundary Location by a Fuzzy Edge Detection Method

C.C. Leung, F.H.Y. Chan, and K.Y. Lam
The University of Hong Kong
Pokfulam, Hong Kong.
ccleung@eee.hku.hk
fhychan@eee.hku.hk
akylam@hkucc.hku.hk

P.C.K. Kwok
The Open University of Hong Kong
Hon Min Tin, Hong Kong.
ckkwok@ouhk.edu.hk

W.F. Chen
First Military Medical University
Guangzhou, China.
chenwf@fimmu.edu.cn

Abstract

Morphometric assessment of tumor cells is important in the prediction of biological behavior of thyroid cancer. In order to automate the process, the computer-based system has to recognize the boundary of the cells. Many methods for the boundary detection have appeared in the literature and some of them applied to microscopic slice analysis. However, there is no reliable method since the gray-levels in the nuclei are uneven and are similar to the background. In this paper, a Fuzzy Edge Detection Method is used and is based on an improved Generalized Fuzzy Operator. The method enhances the nuclei and effectively separates the cells from the background.

1. Introduction

Morphometric assessment of the different parameters of tumor cells is important in the study of thyroid cancer. However, objective measurement is not possible without the help of reliable computer software. The objective assessment includes some algorithms [1-5] to detect the boundary of the cells based on the gradient method. However, these conventional edge detection methods cannot detect the boundary with reasonable accuracy. The reasons are (1) for the incomplete cancer cells, the gray-level of its nucleus is lighter than the complete cancer cells; (2) the nucleus and the background have similar gray levels; (3) in some cells, the nucleus and the cell membrane are very distinct that they may be separated into two concentric rings and double counted. These problems are evident in a conventional thresholding algorithm such as the Yanowitz et al [8] method. Adaptive thresholding proposed by Chan et al [7] shows some improvement. It is a region based heuristic algorithm with the following steps.

1. Image smoothing using average filtering.
2. Obtain the gray-level gradient magnitude.
3. Derive the threshold surface by deforming the original image gray-level surface.
4. The threshold surface interpolation.
5. Segmentation based on the threshold surface.

However, incomplete cells are still not detected reliably with this method. Double counting is sometimes occurred.

In this paper, a Fuzzy Edge Detection Method is proposed. It is based on the Generalized Fuzzy Operator (GFO) [6]. It enhances those cells whose gray-level is similar to the background and produces complete boundary of the cells.

2. Definitions of GFO

Definition 1. Denote the Generalized Fuzzy Set (GFS) S in the region R as

$$S = \int \frac{\mu_S(x)}{x}, x \in R \qquad \text{(2-1)}$$

Where $\mu_S(x) \in [-1,1]$ is called the Generalized Membership Function (GMF) of S on R. Since $\mu_S(x) \in [-1,0)$. The GMF of x in S is not a subordinate on R, for $\mu_S(x) \in [0,1]$. The GFM of x in S is subordinate on R; and $\mu_S(x) = 0$. The fuzzy bound point function (FBF) in S is on R.

According to the definition in [6], we can write,

$\mu_T(x) = \mathrm{GFO}[\mu_S(x)] =$

1051-4651/00 $10.00 © 2000 IEEE

$$\begin{cases} \sqrt[\beta]{1-[1+\mu_s(x)]^\beta}, & -1 \le \mu_s < 0 \\ [\mu_s(x)]^\beta, & 0 \le \mu_s < r \\ \sqrt[\beta]{1-\alpha[1-\mu_s(x)]^\beta}, & r \le \mu_s(x) \le 1 \end{cases} \quad (2\text{-}2)$$

From (2-2), we can deduce the following properties:

Property 1. When $\beta \to \infty$,

$$\mu_T(x) = \begin{cases} 1, & -1 \le \mu_s(x) < 0 \\ 0, & 0 \le \mu_s(x) < r \\ 1, & r \le \mu_s(x) \le 1 \end{cases} \quad (2\text{-}3)$$

Property 2. When $\beta > 1$,

$$\begin{cases} \mu_T(x) > \mu_S(x), if -1 \le \mu_S(x) < 0, \\ \qquad r < \mu_S(x) \le 1 \\ \mu_T(x) < \mu_S(x), \ if 0 < \mu_S(x) \le r \end{cases} \quad (2\text{-}4)$$

Then the generalized fuzzy set S becomes a normal fuzzy set T, such that

$$T = \text{GFO}[S] \quad (2\text{-}5)$$

3. Enhancement and Edge detection

From Section 2, we use the GFO to map all the pixels in the original image into the GFS. For an image $X(i,j)$, where i=1,2,...,N and j=1,2,...,M.

We use a Sine function to map $X(i,j)$ into a fuzzy set $P(i,j)$:

$$P(i,j) = \sin\left\{\frac{\pi}{2}\left(1 - \frac{X(i,j) - X_{min}}{D}\right)\right\} \quad (3\text{-}1)$$

where $\dfrac{X_{max} - X_{min}}{2} \le D$.

Then, $P \in [-1,1]$ is mapped to the new fuzzy set P' as shown in the following equation,

$$P'(i,j) = \begin{cases} \sqrt[\beta]{(1-(1+P(i,j))^\beta}, & -1 \le P < \gamma - \Delta \\ P^2(i,j), & \gamma - \Delta \le P \le \gamma + \Delta \\ \sqrt[\beta]{(1-\alpha(1-P(i,j))^\beta}, & \gamma + \Delta < P \le 1 \end{cases} \quad (3\text{-}2)$$

By setting β=2, and the newer image $X'(i,j)$ is

$$X'(i,j) = X_{min} + D\left\{1 - \left[\frac{\sin^{-1}(P'(i,j))}{\frac{\pi}{2}}\right]\right\} \quad (3\text{-}3)$$

In the present application, the objective of Morphometric assessment is to locate the boundary of the thyroid cancer cell. We used the improved GFO to put the boundary gray level be mapped to a distinctly different gray levels. Now, the membrane's boundary has a gray level distribution in the range [γ-Δ γ+Δ]. In equation (3-2), this range is mapped to a minimum value in P'. Above or below this range, it is mapped to progressively higher values as shown in Figure 1. The characteristics of the improved GFO is a "V" shaped curve located in [-1 1] of P. This function resembles a band-pass function so that the edge pixels are mapped to a range of values distinct from the others. The parameter "γ" can be adjusted to shift the "V" type function along the $P(i,j)$ axis, depending on the actual gray levels of the boundary of interest. α can affect the right arm of the "V" shaped function.

4. Results and Discussions

We implemented our method in a Pentium PC. The algorithm was programmed in the MATLAB. The original image of the thyroid cancer cell is shown in figure 2. Point "A" is an incomplete cell with a hollow-looking nucleus. Point "B" shows another incomplete cell, so that the gray-level of this cell is almost the same as the background. Moreover, some cells overlap and merge together. Figure 3 is a binary image that is the result of using the Adaptive Thresholding Method [7]. In using this method, an area with solid interior is counted as a cell. However, in point "A", the hollow ring will not be counted as a cell since certain tissue boundary is also processed as the hollow ring in the same slice shown in point "A^1". In point "B", an irregular pattern shows up in the result and it will not be counted as a cell. It is caused by no function to enhance the incomplete cell in this method. Figure 4 is the result based on the new proposed method. The boundaries show up distinctly in both points "A" and "B". In another case, when two cells appeared to be merged together, they are separated after processing.

In the example, γ, α, Δ and D are chosen as –0.9946,

0.1, 0.01 and 79.406 respectively for the present example. The characteristics of the fuzzy set are shown in Figure 5. The relationship between the original and the new pixel values is shown in Figure 6. At an original gray level of around 160, the pixels are mapped to a minimum value. The other pixels will be mapped to other distinctly different gray levels. In this example, the thyroid cancer cells have boundary pixels with gray levels of around 160. For the incomplete cells, the boundaries are enhanced.

5. Conclusion

The proposed Fuzzy algorithm is a simple, effective and efficient method for edge detection and enhancement. We have demonstrated that it is very suitable for application in the counting of thyroid cancer cells captured from a microscopic slice. It solves the problems better than the Adaptive Thresholding Method.

6. References

[1] Nevatia, R., "A color edge detection and its use in scene segmentation". IEEE Trans. Syst. Man and Cybern., SMC-7, vol.11, pp.820-825, 1977.

[2] Shen, J., "An optimal linear operator for edge detection". Proc. of IEEE Computer Vision and Pattern Recognition Conference, pp.109-114, 1986.

[3] Rosin, P.L. and West, G.A.W., "Segmentation of Edges into Lines and Arcs". Image Vision Computing, vol.7, pp.109-114, 1989.

[4] R.F. Wagner, M.F. Insana, and S.W. Smith, "Fundamental correction lengths of coherent speckle in medical ultrasonic images". IEEE Trans. Ultrason., Ferroelect., Freq. Contr., vol. 35, pp.34-44, 1988.

[5] A.C. Bovik, "On detecting edges in speckle imagery". IEEE Trans. Signal Processing, vol. 36, pp.1618-1627, 1988.

[6] Chen, W.F., Lu, X.Q., Chen, J.J., and Wu, G.X., "A new algorithm of edge detection for color image: Generalized fuzzy operator". Science in China (Series A), vol.38, No.10, pp.1272-1280, 1995.

[7] Chan, F.H.Y., Lam, F.K., and Zhu, H., "Adaptive Thresholding by Variational Method". IEEE Trans. Image Processing, Vol.7, No.3, pp.468-473, 1998.

[8] Yanowitz, S.D, and Bruckstein A.M., "A new method for image segmentation". Comput. Vision, Graph., Image Process., Vol.46, pp.82-95, 1989.

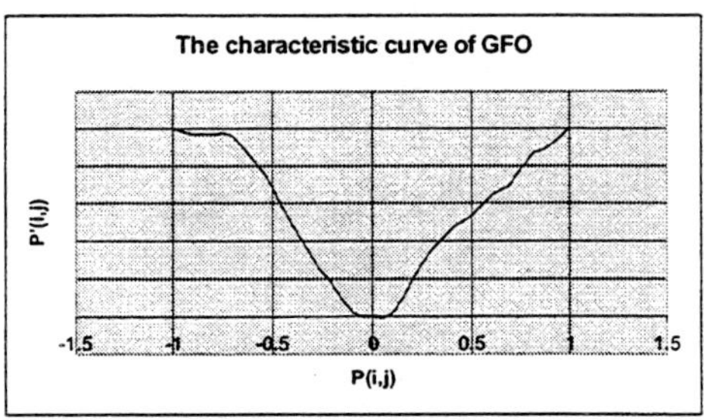

Figure 1. The characteristics of the GFO ($\gamma = 0$), α and γ can change the shape based on the "V" shaped curve.

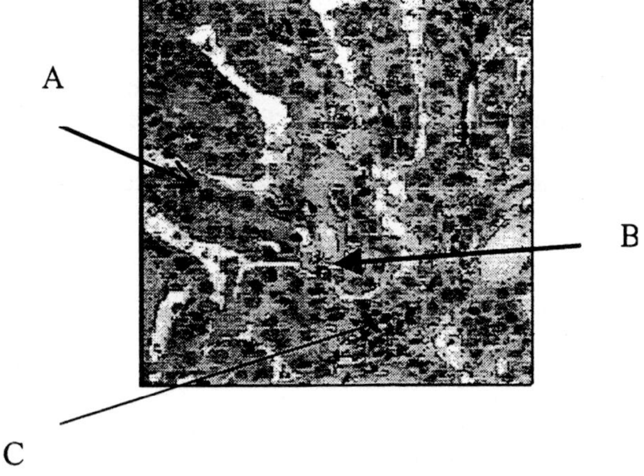

Figure 2 The microscopic slice contains two types of thyroid cancer cells, one is in growing so that it's nuclei is not in rigid (point A). However, some cells its nucleus is rigid but lighter (point B). The other is the completed growth cell (point C), the nucleus is rigid and color is black.

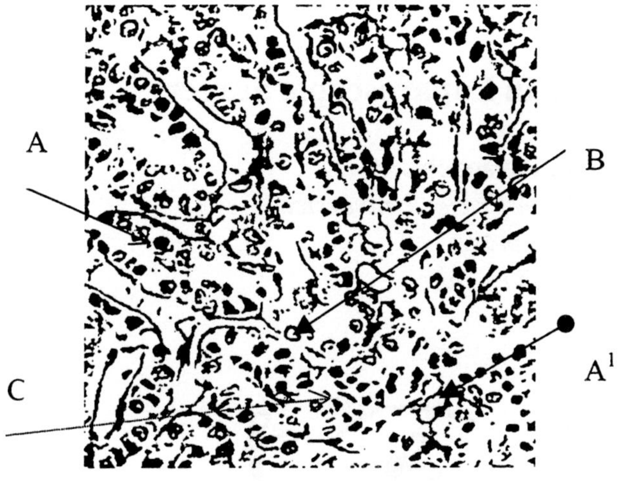

Figure 3. Using the Adaptive thresholding method to detect the thyroid cancer cells. Some of the cells cannot be counted.

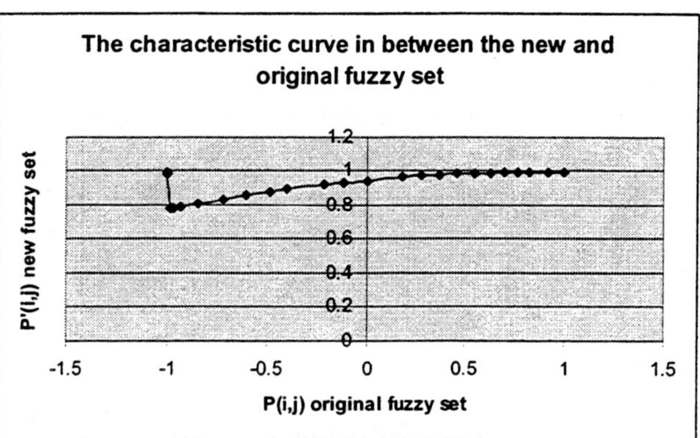

Figure 5. The characteristics of the GFO are used in the microscopic slice. γ is set on –0.9946.

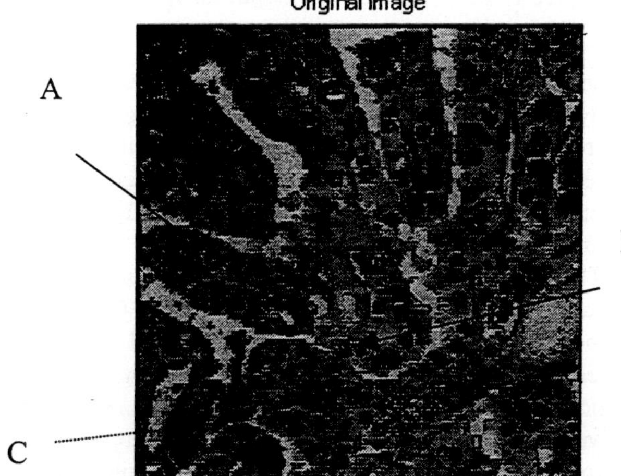

Figure 4. Using the improved GFO to process the image, most of the cells can be detected. The problem occurs in the result of Adaptive Thresholding method can be solved.

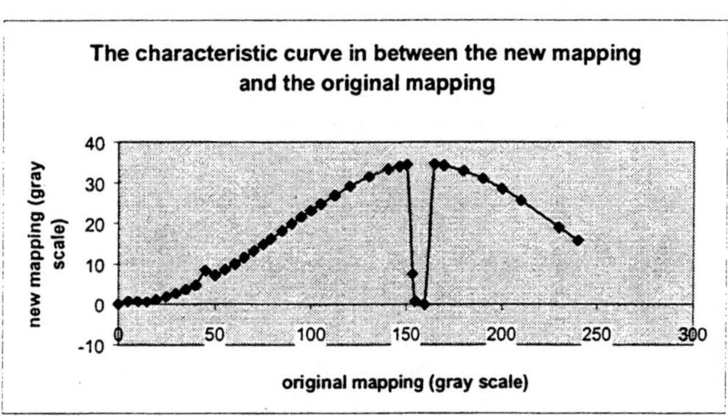

Figure 6. The relationship of the original image and the GFO image. The gray scale nearly 160 can be enhanced in the new image.

Toward Application of Image Tracking in Laparoscopic Surgery

Xiaoli Zhang and Shahram Payandeh
Experiment Robotics Laboratory, Simon Fraser University
Burnaby, BC, V5A 1S6, Canada
xzhanga@cs.sfu.ca, shahram@cs.sfu.ca

Abstract

In the past few years, the application of image tracking in laparoscopic surgery has gained popularity. In such an approach, the robot controls the movement of the laparoscope (endoscope) in surgery by following the feedback of the image tracking information. The calibration of the distorted endoscopic images is an important first step toward realizing such an approach. However, there exist very few methods for such calibration. In this paper, a new method of calibration and measurement of the endoscopic images is proposed. The high distortion of the endoscopic images makes the calibration difficult. Endoscopic images have typical barrel distortion. That is, the distortion increases as the observation becomes more and more eccentric. We propose a new idea that only concentrates on the center area of the image. Within this area, we can ignore the complex and time-consuming distortion-correction step. A simple method for finding the intrinsic calibration parameters is then proposed. Design of a marker for the tracking task is also described. Some experimental results are presented to show the feasibility of the proposed method.

1. Introduction

With the development of techniques, the endoscopic surgery (e.g. laparoscopic surgery) becomes more and more popular. It is mainly because the minimal invasive nature of endoscopic surgery allows operation to be performed on patients through small incisions. Hence, compare to the traditional surgery, it can greatly reduce the pain and provide a more rapid recovery for patients [1].

As shown in Fig 1. an endoscope is used to transmit images from the surgical site to the surgeon on a video monitor. In general, the surgeon requires the operating site to be always centered in the endoscope field of view. Generally speaking, the surgeon's two hands are used for performing the operation. As a result, an assistant surgeon is needed to hold and move the endoscope.

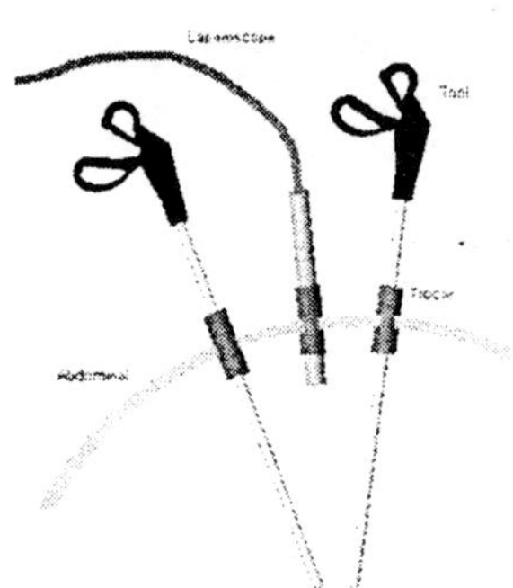

Figure 1. Tools needed for Laparoscope Surgery

However, if a person is used to control the movement of the camera, during lengthy procedures, accurately and timely adjustment of the view can not be guaranteed. Whereas using robot to control the camera will result in less erroneous camera motion and accidental contacts of the endoscopic lens with the internal organ [2], and can off-load routine tasks.

There have already existed voice-controlled robot in the market, e.g. AESOP[2](Computer motion, CA, USA) for positioning the endoscope. But it would waist the surgeon's time and distract his concentration from the surgical procedure in "speaking to" the robot. It can be shown that to realize the automatic control approach of the robot, the image tracking technique for getting the 3D position of the tools is one alternative approach. We propose to design a marker and attach the marker to the tools. When needed, the image tracking technique can be used to track the marker as the tool moves. Hence to realize the automatic control of the laparoscope. However, there are many difficulties associate with such an approach. First, images taken from the endoscope are distorted and it is difficult to get the correct measurement of the images. Second, tools may enter the endoscope field of view from any direction and with any angle. These make the tracking task difficult.

2. Calibration Method

Camera calibration techniques have been investigated

for many years, there are many papers talked about camera calibration [3], [4]. But camera calibration using rigid endoscopic has not been addressed before. In general, endoscopic images have particular characteristics.

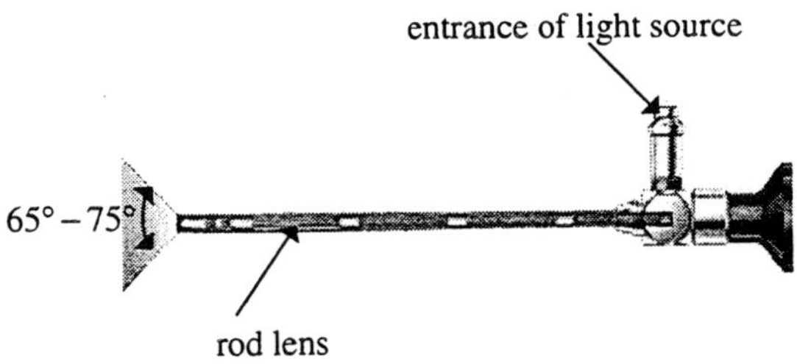

Figure 2. Rod Lens endoscope

The endoscope filed of view, typically between $65^o - 75^o$, as shown in Fig 2., is narrow compare to the wide filed of view of human eyes. So one can only see a small section of the viewing place within a circle through the endoscope. In addition, various forms of distortion are present. Transformation of straight line into curves (barrel and pincushion distortion) is common. So the necessary measurement for the calibration directly from endoscopic images is difficult. Some researchers have investigated the distortion-correction of endoscope images [5], [6]. But it is complex and time-consuming to correct the endoscopic images for image tracking problems. As in barrel distortion, image areas are compressed in inverse ratio to the distance from the image center, so image areas farther away from the center appear significantly smaller. One simplified approach is only investigating the image within small center area without distortion-correction. But now the question is can this distortion in this area be negligible? Experiment results show that the answer is positive.

Typical parameters used for calibration can be classified into two classes: extrinsic parameters and intrinsic parameters. In order to get meaningful measurement results from endoscope images, our approach focus on getting intrinsic parameters: the effective focal length, the real image center and the scale factor.

Fig 3. Illustrates the basic geometry of the camera model. $O - XYZ$ is the camera coordinate system, (X,Y,Z) is the 3D coordinates of the object P in the camera coordinate system, with the Z axis the same as the optical axis. (x_d, y_d) is the image coordinates of (X,Y,Z) if a perfect pinhole model assumption is used. (x_f, y_f) which is not show in the image is the coordinates used in the image buffer. Its unit is in pixel, additional parameters (scale factors) need to be specified that relates the image coordinate in the front image plane to the computer image coordinate system. f, the focal length,

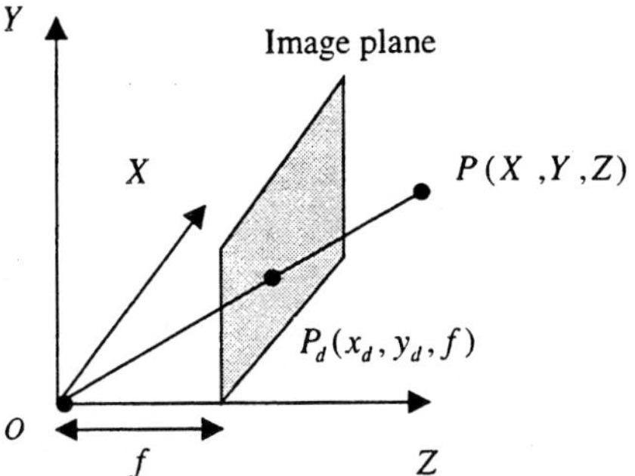

Figure 3. Camera geometry with perspective projection

is the distance between front image plane and the optical center. Here we define the image center as the optical axis passing through the image plane. In theory, the image center is the center of the image plane. But in real situation, especially the endoscope, the real image center is distorted. In the following, first we propose a simple and fast method to get the real image center, then use the proposed method to get other calibration parameters such as: the effective focal length and the scale factor.

The first problem is how to get the real image center. Since abdominal cavity is dark, an external light source is needed. As shown in Fig 2. a fiber optic cable transmits the light to the side of the endoscope. The light source is evenly distributed through the rod lens. As shown in Fig 4. (a), light source forms a white circle in the image. The simplest method of getting the real image center is letting the endoscope point to a white background and record the image. Then choosing the center of the white circle in the image as the real image center. The result is shown in Fig 4. (b).

The second parameter to be calibrated is the real focal length. As shown in Fig 3. Transformation from 3D camera coordinate (X,Y,Z) to image coordinate (x_d, y_d) using perspective projection with pinhole camera geometry, we can get the following equation:

$$x_d = f \times X / Z , y_d = f \times Y / Z \qquad (1)$$

when x_d, y_d, X and Z are known parameters. From equation (1), we can get the effective focal length. Also, when f, x_d, y_d and X are known parameters, we can get the depth information of the object.

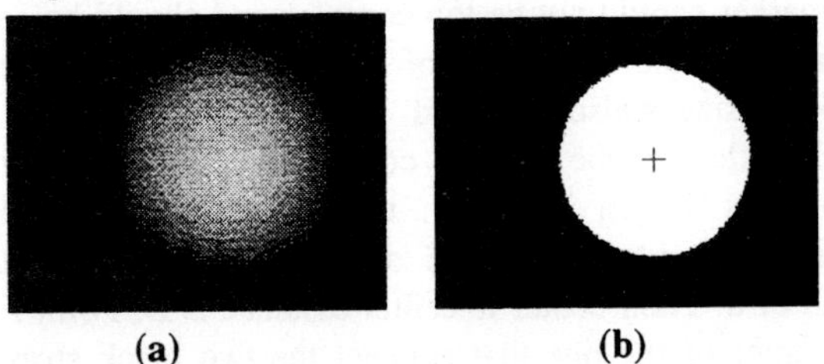

Figure 4. Endoscopic image (a) original gray scale image, (b) binary image (the image center has been marked)

To map the real image coordinate (x_d, y_d) to computer image coordinate (x_f, y_f), we need to add scale factors: S_x, S_y.

$$x_f = S_x x_d, y_f = S_y y_d \quad (2)$$

Normally, manufacturers of CCD cameras supply the information of center to center distance between adjacent sensor elements in the Y direction (i.e. scale factor S_y) as a fixed value: $S_y = N_{fY} / d_y$, where N_{fY}: number of pixels in the Y direction; d_Y: dimension of CCD in the Y direction.

Scale factor is an uncertain value due to various reasons, such as slight hardware timing mismatch between image acquisition hardware and camera scanning hardware, or the imprecision of the timing of TV scanning itself. Here we propose a simple and fast method to get S_x.

We use the endoscope to get an image of known dimension (e.g. square grids), then get the squares' center to center distances of pixel unit in the X and Y direction D_x, D_y. We can get the equation: $S_x / S_y = D_x / D_y$.

So

$$S_x = S_y \times D_x / D_y \quad (3)$$

In actual implementation, we can get several squares' center to center distances and use their mean values to reduce the possible error that may bring by the image processing method.

3. Toward Design of Markers

Image tracking is an active area of research. Some researchers have proposed many techniques for different tracking tasks [7], [8]. In our application, the marker is attached to the tip of the tools, then identified for the tracking task.

In general, the tracking task includes recognizing markers and calculating its relative position with the camera. As mentioned before, the tool may enter the field of view from different positions and different angles which would make the tracking task more complex. However, a good marker design will minimize the influence of this factor. For the real-time image tracking, the marker should not be too complex and should be easy to find. As the restriction of the size of the tools, the marker's size is also restricted.

Considering the above constrains, we design the marker as shown in Fig 5. two black stripes are the designed markers. They are of the same size with the width of d. Their center to center distance is D. Point P is the center of the line that connect the two black stripes' centers. Designing the marker in this shape has several advantages. For one thing, the shape of the marker is simple and its contrast with the tools is great, so it is easy

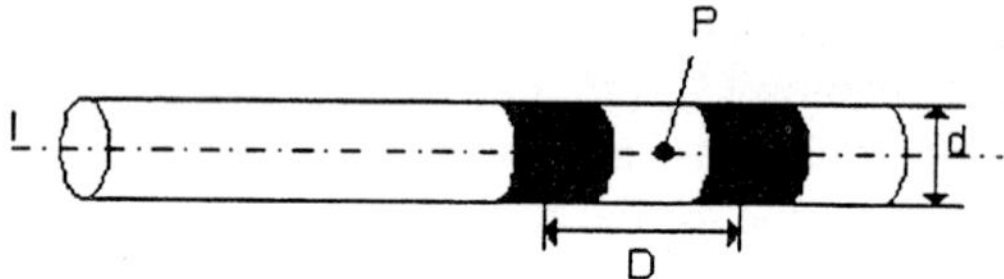

Figure 5. A design of marker

to identify the marker. For the other, we only care about the center to center distance of the two black stripes when we want to get the depth information, while the length D will not being influenced by rotations along the axis l.

To simplify the problem, here we assume that the tool is almost perpendicular to the camera. The two stripes appear as two squares in this position. The tracking task is keeping the markers on the tool at the center area of the field of view and also keeping the distance of the camera to the tool at a fixed value.

For D is a known value, using its pixel value in the image plane, we can get the real length that one pixel represents. So from the pixel change of point P (the center of the two markers, as shown in Fig 5.) in the x and y direction in the image plane, we can calculate the real world value of the displacement that the endoscope should move. And from the pixel change of the length D in the image plane, we can calculate the displacement of distance between the endoscope and the tools, then can adjust their relative distance accordingly. Using this method, we can realize the 3D marker-tracking task.

4. Experiment Results

A testing grid containing a rectangular array of squares of 4mm side length, separate by 4mm in the horizontal and vertical direction, was used to validate the proposed calibration method.

The calibration parameters are estimated as follows:

Step 1. Find the real image center. Using the method described above, we can easily find the real image center.

Step 2. Get scale factors. In this step, first we will test if our assumption that the distortion in the center area is negligible is valid. As we know the closer the endoscope to the object the more distorted the image appears. So after getting the real image center, the test grid was placed perpendicularly 50mm away from the endoscope (the typical range for endoscope surgery is 40mm-100mm) and one square's center is the same as the real image center. Fig 6. Shows the original gray scale endoscope image and the image after threshold and marking the center of each blob. We only use 9 center squares for calculation. From the center coordinates of the 9 squares, we found that to the blobs along a line in the x or y direction of the image plane, their corresponding centers' x or y coordinates are only at most 1 pixel difference. To our task that does not need precise calculation, this difference is negligible, namely, we can skip the distortion-correction step. Using mean values of the center to center distance between neighbor squares along x and y axis to get scale factors:

(a)

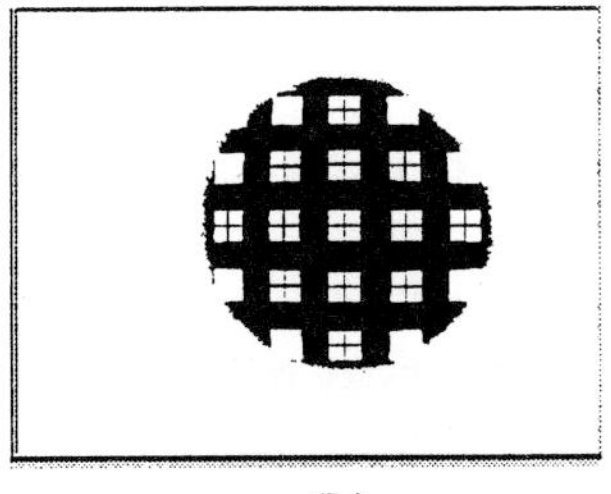

(b)

Figure 6. (a) original gray scale image, (b) binarised image and the blob center have been marked

$$S_x/S_y = D_x/D_y = 66.67/65.83 \approx 1$$

Step 3. Get the focal length, from step 2 we can see that the scale factors in the x and y direction are almost the same. In this task, we do not need to get the real value in the unit cm of the focal length, so we map the camera coordinate directly to the computer image coordinate. Using the equation:

$$f = x_f \times Z / X = 66.67 \times 50 / 0.8 = 4167 \text{ (pixel)}$$

Step 4. Using the focal length and equation (1) to get the depth information. Image of the markers were record at various distances from the endoscope (40, 60, 70, 80 and 90 mm). The experimental data are shown in Table 1.

Table 1. Experimental data via the proposed algorithm

No.	Measured distance (mm)	Calculated distance (mm)	Errors (mm)
1	40	42.5	2.5
2	60	60.5	0.5
3	70	69.4	0.6
4	80	78.1	1.9
5	90	88.2	1.8

As to the tracking task, the size of the marker is known. Using the method described in section 3, the movement of the endoscope in the x and y direction of the camera coordinate can be calculated using the following equation, here we define the real image center as $o(a,b)$, a, b are in pixel value. And we assume that at the beginning of the tracking, Point P (as shown in Fig. 5) is at the image center:

$$D / d_{img} = \Delta X_t /(x_t - a) = \Delta Y_t /(y_t - b) \quad (4)$$

where D is the real size of the marker's center to center distance, d_{img} is the number of pixels of D in the image plane, x_t and y_t are the coordinates of point P in pixel units, while ΔX_t and ΔY_t are the value of the displacement the endoscope should follow. Since we have got the focal length, using the equation (1) mentioned above, we could also get the depth information. This information can be used to control the endoscope so to keep a fixed distance between the endoscope and the tools.

5. Conclusion

In this paper, a novel idea to realize the endoscope automation is proposed. Two critical points in this technique: endoscope calibration and marker design are discussed and the solution is proposed.

There are several good features of the proposed method. First, the new technique for finding the real image center is simple and reliable. Second, the proposed endoscope camera calibration attempts a new calibration field. Third, the marker design considers many constrains and tries to minimize the influence of unknown factors in the image tracking task. Finally, here we mainly use the blob feature analysis (e.g. the blob center). Using this feature to get the information is simple, robust and can save much image processing time.

However, as the tool may enter the camera field of view in different angles. Though the designed marker can overcome the rotation along the axis of the tools. If the tool is not perpendicular to the camera, the foreshortening factor will reduce the precision of the result. Further research is still needed to solve this problem. E.g. using an alternative feature of the marker that is uninfluenced by different angles and positions of the tool.

References

[1] A. Faraz and S. Payandeh, "A robotics case study: Optimal design for laparoscopic positioning stands", *International Journal of Robotics Research*, Vol. 17, No. 9, Sept. 98, pp. 986-995.

[2] L.Mettler, M. Ibrahim and W. Jonat, " One Year of Experience Working with the Aid of a Robotic Assistant the Voice-controlled optic holder AESOP in Gynaecological Endoscopic Surgery", *Human Reproduction*, Vol. 13, No. 10, 1998, pp. 2748-2750.

[3] C. Chen, S. Stitt and Y. F. Zheng, "Robotic Eye-in-Hand Calibration by Calibrating Optical Axis and Target Pattern", *Journal of Intelligent and Robotic System*, 12, 1995,pp.155-173.

[4] R. Y. Tasi, "A Versatile Camera Calibration Technique for High-Accuracy 3D Machine Vision Metrology Using Off-the-Shelf TV Cameras and Lenses", *IEEE Journal of Robotics and Automation*, VolRA-3, No.4, 1987, pp. 323-344.

[5] K. V. Asari, S. Kumar, and D. Radhakrishnan, "A New Approach for Nonlinear Distortion Correction in Endoscopic Images Based on Least Squares Estimation", *IEEE Transaction on Medical Imaging*, Vol. 18, No. 4, April 1999, pp. 345-354.

[6] E. J. Doolin and L. Strande, "Calibration of Endoscopic Images", *Ann Otol Rhinol Laryngol 104*, 1995, pp. 19-22.

[7] N. P. Papanikolopulos, P.K. Khosla, and T. Kanade. " Visual Tracking of a Moving Target by a Camera Mounted on a Robot: A Combination of Control and Vision", *IEEE Transactions on Robotics and Automation*, Vol. 9, No. 1, Feb. 1993, pp. 14-20.

[8] S. Reddi and G. Loizou, " Analysis of Camera Behavior During Tracking", *IEEE Transaction on Pattern Analysis and Machine Intelligence*, N0.8, August 1995, pp. 127-134.

A Model of Stroke Extraction from Chinese Character Images

Ruini Cao, Chew Lim Tan
School of Computing, National University of Singapore
Email: caoruini, tancl@comp.nus.edu.sg

Abstract

Given the large number and complexity of Chinese characters, pattern matching based on structural decomposition and analysis is believed to be necessary and essential to off-line character recognition. This paper proposes a new model of stroke extraction for Chinese characters. One problem for stroke extraction is how to extract primary strokes. Another major problem is to solve the segmentation ambiguities at intersection points. We use the degree information and the stroke continuation property to tackle these two problems. The proposed model can be used to extract strokes from both printed and handwritten character images.

1. Introduction

Extracting the stroke information is important in off-line character recognition. Given the large number and complexity of Chinese characters, pattern matching based on structural decomposition and analysis is believed to be necessary and essential. [1-4] Recently, there is a growing interest in obtaining temporal information from static line images to improve the overall performance of the recognition system. [5-6] This approach is considered as a bridge from the off-line handwriting character recognition problem to the on-line one that is generally agreed to have better performance. Stroke segmentation is however one of the prerequisites of extracting dynamic writing information.

There are two major problems for stroke extraction. One is how to extract primary strokes. Another problem is to solve the segmentation ambiguities at intersection points. Most existing methods for stroke extraction use thinning process. [3-7] These approaches have an intrinsic problem of spurious branches or pattern distortion, which may lead to unreliable extraction of strokes. Algorithms without thinning process exploit other kinds of stroke information, such as stroke width variations, curvature changes or stroke continuation property. [1,8-10]

In this paper, we propose a new model that combines the stroke continuation property with the component connectivity information. The proposed model is entirely based on thick-line images. Compared with the model in [10], the proposed model exhibits better performance in solving the ambiguities and grouping broken strokes. We propose a different way to estimate the line tangent orientation. This way proves to be more discriminating. We also come up with a general way to group non-smooth zigzag strokes.

The remainder of the paper is organized as follows: In section 2 to section 4, we explain how to extract primary strokes, how to separate overlapped strokes, and how to extract complete strokes. In section 5, we present some experiment results and discussions. Section 6 gives the conclusion.

2. Extraction of primary strokes

We define the primary stroke in terms of the degree. The degree of a pixel is the number of the branches incident on it. According to the degree information, a line image can be divided into three regions: end point regions, regular regions and singular regions. A pixel belongs to an end point region if its degree is equal to 1. If the degree of a pixel is equal to 2, it belongs to a regular region. Singular regions are made up of pixels whose degree is 3 or more. (See Figure 1) The primary stroke is the connected end point regions and regular regions.

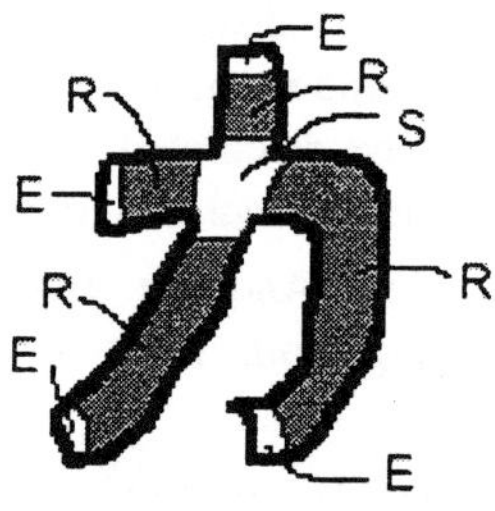

Figure 1. Decomposition of a line picture into regular regions (R), end point regions (E), and a singular region (S)

We use the direction contribution of the segments to estimate the degree for each pixel on the thick-line image. Given a binary image, for each black pixel $p(r,c)$, let $D_k(r,c)$ denote the orientation distance between the pixel and the boundary point along the kth quantized orientation, where $k = 1, 2, \ldots, M$, and M is an integer that denotes the quantization number from 0° to 360°. The orientation distance is called point-to-boundary orientation distance (PBOD).

The distribution of the PBODs contains information about the degree of each pixel. We can easily tell that the PBODs along the quantized orientations of the branches are much larger than that along other quantized orientation. So, to estimate the degree of each pixel, we need only calculate the number of the crests of the distribution of all the PBODs of the pixel. Figure 2 shows some cases of the distribution. The resolution of quantization is 3°.

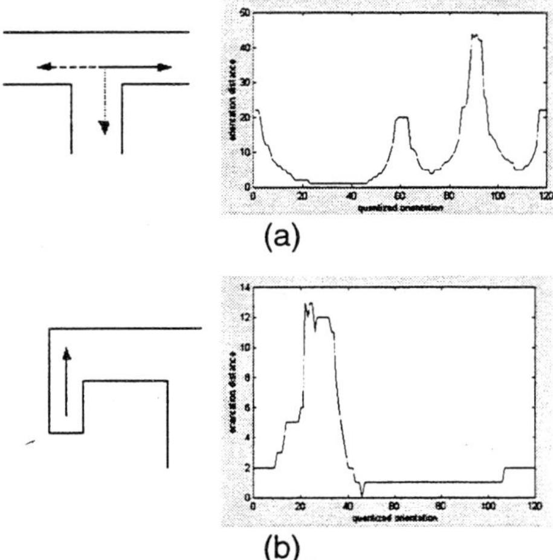

Figure 2. Distribution of PBODs: (a) Pixel at the singular region; (b) Pixel at the end point region

3. Separation of overlapped strokes

To separate overlapped strokes, we need to interpret the singular region in a correct way. We construct a 3-D ρ-space to tackle this problem.

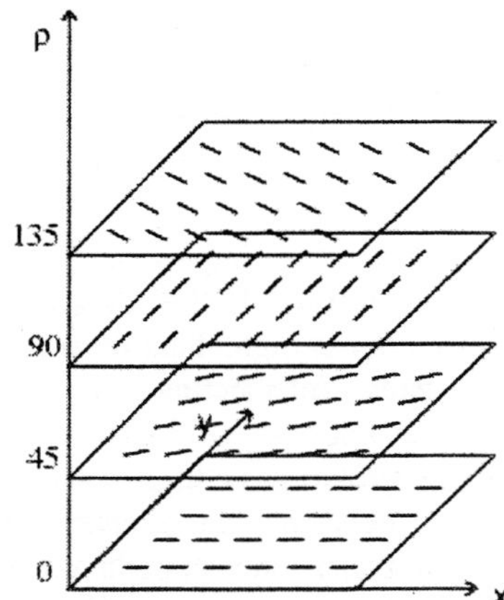

Figure 3. Illustration of the ρ-space

The ρ-space is a 3-D space where the first 2 dimensions are the spatial image dimensions, and the third dimension is the orientation dimension (See Figure 3). Each element *(i, j, m)* in the ρ-space is set to be 1 if and only if the tangent orientation of the line passing the pixel *(i, j)* is *m*; otherwise, it is set to be 0. We can imagine that there are *N* orientation planes in the ρ-space and the 2-D image is mapped to the ρ-space by putting each pixel on some of the planes depending on the tangent orientations of the lines passing the pixel.

The ρ-space helps extract smooth stroke segments. Consider a pixel *p(i, j, k)*. It has 24 neighbors, counting the points on the plane *(k-1)* and the plane *(k+1)*. (Note that the first plane and the last plane are contiguous.) A transition between adjacent planes does not violate the smoothness of a curve since the tangent orientation changes only a little. Hence, finding the connected components in the ρ-space extracts the smooth strokes.

The ρ-space has the advantage of being able to represent more than a single orientation at a single point. For a pixel in the end point region and the regular region, there is only one line passing it, so the pixel is mapped only onto one plane in the ρ-space. Whereas, for a pixel located at the singular region, there are at least two lines passing it. Obviously, the tangent orientations of the two lines are different. So, the pixel will be mapped onto two different planes in the ρ-space. The two overlapped lines passing the pixel will then be separate from each other. (See Figure 4)

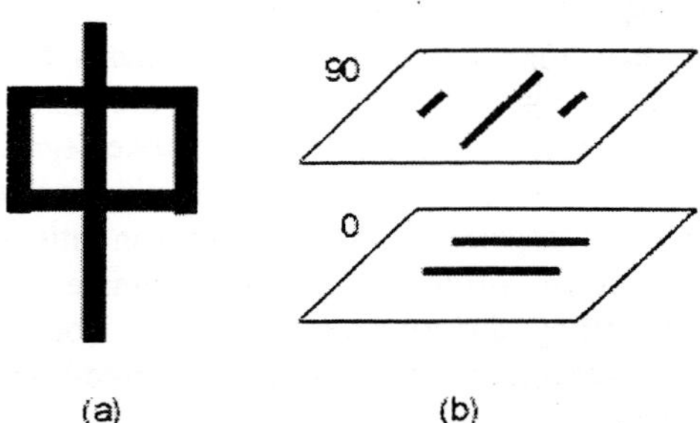

Figure 4. Segmentation in the ρ-space: (a) A character image; (b) Overlapped strokes are mapped into different planes and are separated

Now, the key problem is how to find the tangent orientations of the lines passing each pixel. We also exploit the direction contribution of the segments.

Given a binary image, for each black pixel *p(r,c)*, let $D_k'(r,c)$ denote the orientation distance between two boundary points along the *k*th quantized orientation, where $k = 1, 2, \ldots, N$, and *N* is an integer that denotes the quantization number from 0° to 180°. The orientation distance is called boundary-to-boundary orientation distance (BBOD).

We find all the crests of the distribution of the BBODs of one pixel and take the quantized orientations corresponding to the crests as the tangent orientations of the lines passing this pixel. This is based on the observation that the BBOD along the line tangent orientation is often much larger than the BBODs along other orientations.

The tangent orientation obtained in this way is more discriminating than that obtained in [10] where the tangent orientation (called OLLS there) is obtained by binarizing the BBODs using a threshold defined as the mean of all the BBODs of the pixel. First, the latter way may miss some short strokes joining with long strokes since the BBOD along the orientation of the short stroke may be less than the mean value. Secondly, binarization of BBOD may cause confusion at two branches when the trough between them is larger than the mean value that usually occurs near junctions.

4. Extraction of complete strokes

We summarize the proposed model in the following.

Stage 1. According to the line tangent orientation, we first map the 2-D line image into the 3-D ρ-space. Then we perform connected components labeling in the ρ-space. After projecting each 3-D connected component onto a 2-D plane, we get the smooth stroke segments. One assumption here is that overlapped strokes are smooth at the intersections.

Stage 2. The strokes obtained so far are usually over-segmented due to L-type connection or bad line smoothness. We further group the segments by linking them at the pixels where primary strokes are broken.

In this paper, we only address the stroke segmentation problem. As for obtaining dynamic writing information, after we get segmented strokes, we can utilize some popular human writing rules to determine the most possible writing direction of strokes. [6] For example, Chinese characters usually follow the top-to-bottom and left-to-right rules.

5. Experiments and discussions

The proposed model was tested using a set of printed Chinese characters that are selected randomly. The number of the characters in the testing set is 111. There are about 849 strokes in total. The model segmented 806 strokes correctly. The accuracy is 93%. There are about 98 characters whose strokes are all segmented correctly. The correct rate is 88%. Among the correctly segmented characters, the complexity is about 7 strokes per character on the average.

Some of the typical cases are shown in Figure 5 to Figure 7. The results by the model in [10] are also shown to give some comparison. We can easily see that the proposed model performs better in separating overlapped strokes (Figure 6) and preserving the connectivity of primary strokes (Figure 6 and 7). The strokes extracted by the proposed model are closer to the correct way of segmenting Chinese character strokes. Figure 8 shows an example of extracting strokes from handwritten character images. We can see that so long as the overlapped strokes are smooth at intersections, the proposed model can separate them successfully.

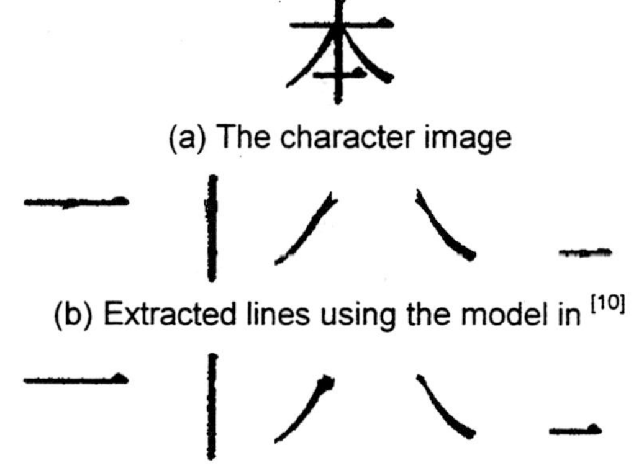

(a) The character image

(b) Extracted lines using the model in [10]

(c) Extracted strokes by the proposed model

Figure 5. Segmentation example: the two models produce the same results

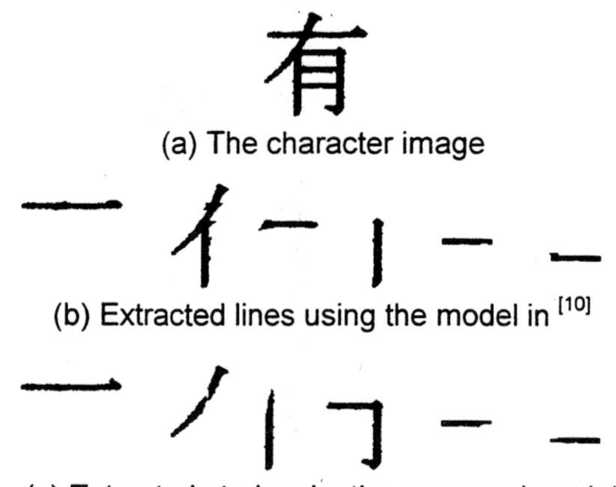

(a) The character image

(b) Extracted lines using the model in [10]

(c) Extracted strokes by the proposed model

Figure 6. Segmentation example: the proposed model is more discriminating

During the test, one important parameter is the resolution of quantization. If the resolution is high, the orientation selectivity is high. That means it can separate overlapped strokes intersecting at smaller angles. However, if the resolution is too high, in the case that one of the overlapped strokes has a high degree of curvature at the intersection, the estimated orientations will be not continuous. That means the smoothness information is lost. Therefore, there is a tradeoff in selecting the resolution of quantization. When we did the experiments, the resolution of quantization was selected at 3°.

It is necessary to mention here that the strokes are not completely equivalent to the strokes defined as the path between pen-up and pen-down in the on-line character recognition system. This is one intrinsic difference between off-line and on-line system. Namely, on-line system traces pen-up and pen-down, whereas off-line system finds two ends of one line. When two strokes are linked end to end, they cannot be segmented from each other in the off-line case (See the first connected component in Figure 7c).

6. Conclusion

A new model of stroke extraction is proposed in this paper. First we extract the primary strokes according to the degree information of each pixel on the thick-line image. Then we construct a 3-D ρ-space to solve the segmentation ambiguities at intersection points.

The proposed model is performed entirely on thick-line character images, so no distortions are introduced. It also exhibits better performance in separating overlapped strokes and preserving connectivity of primary strokes. This model can be used to extract strokes from both printed and handwritten character images.

7. References

[1] F. Chang, Y. Chen, H. Don, W. Hsu and C. Kao, Stroke segmentation as a basis for structural matching of Chinese characters, *Proceedings of 2nd International Conference on Document Analysis and Recognition,* Japan, 1993

[2] W. Ip, K. Chung and D. Yeung, Offline handwritten Chinese character recognition via radical extraction and recognition, *Proceedings of 4th International Conference on Document Analysis and Recognition*, Germany, 1997

[3] K. Liu, Y. S. Huang and C. Y. Suen, Robust stroke segmentation method for handwritten Chinese character recognition, *Proceedings of 4th International Conference on, Document Analysis and Recognition*, Germany, 1997

[4] H. Chiu and D. Tseng, A novel stroke-based feature extraction for handwritten Chinese character recognition, *Pattern Recognition,* **32**, 1999, pp. 1947-1959

[5] Y. Kato and M. Yasuhara, Recovery of drawing order from scanned images of multi-stroke handwriting, *Proceedings of 5th International Conference on Document Analysis and Recognition,* India, 1999

[6] J. Zou and H. Yan, Extracting strokes from static line images based on selective searching, *Pattern Recognition,* **32**, 1999, pp. 935-946

[7] Y. Nakajima, S. Mori, S. Takegami and S. Sato, Global methods for stroke segmentation, *International Journal on Document Analysis and Recognition* **2**, 1999, pp. 19-23

[8] L. Y. Tseng, C. T. Chuang, An efficient knowledge-based stroke extraction method for multi-font Chinese charaters, *Pattern Recognition* **25**, 1992, pp. 1445-1458

[9] C. M. Privitera, R. Plamondon, A system for scanning and segmenting cursive handwritten works into basic strokes, *Proceeding of 3rd International Conference on Document Analysis and Recognition*, Canada, 1995

[10] Y. S. Chen and W. H. Hsu, An interpretive model of line continuation in human visual perception, *Pattern Recognition* **22**, 1989, pp. 619-639

[11] S. Liang, M. Ahmadi and M. Shridhar, Segmentation of handwritten interference marks using multiple directional stroke planes and reformalized morphological approach, *Transactions on Image Processing* **6**, No. 8, 1997, pp.1195-1202

(a) The character image

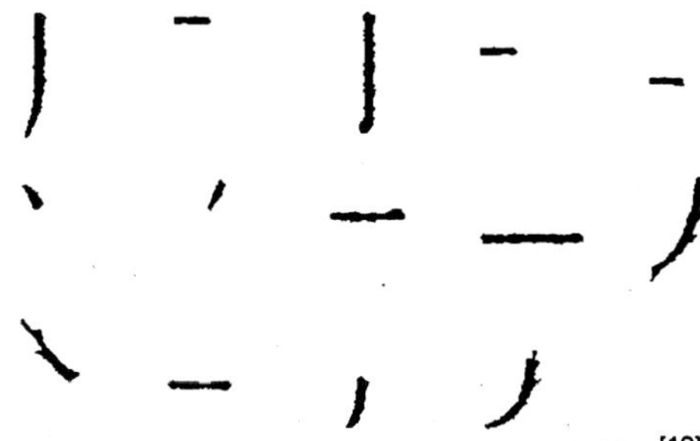

(b) Extracted lines using the model in [10]

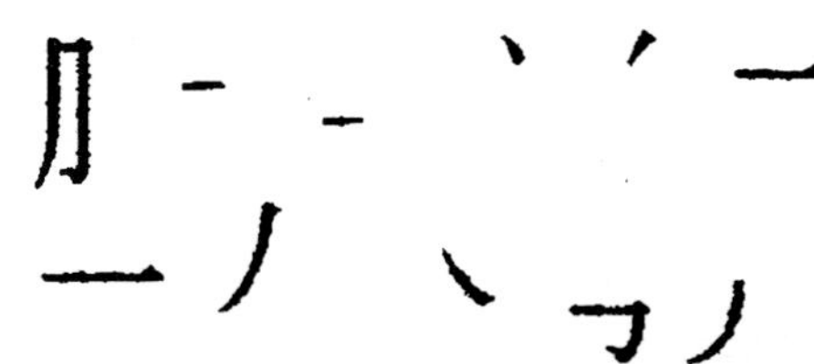

(c) Extracted strokes by the proposed model

Figure 7. Segmentation example: the proposed model groups zigzag strokes

(a) The character image

(b) Extracted strokes

Figure 8. Segmentation results for handwritten characters

A pen-based Japanese character input system for the blind person

Nobuo Ezaki
Toba National College of Maritime Technology
Mie 517-8501 Japan
ezaki@toba-cmt.ac.jp

Toru Hikichi
Toyohashi University of Technology
Aichi 441-8580 Japan
hikichi@parl.tutkie.tut.ac.jp

Kimiyasu Kiyota
Kumamoto National College of Technology
Kumamoto 861-1102 Japan
kkiyota@tc.knct.ac.jp

Shinji Yamamoto
Toyohashi University of Technology
Aichi 441-8580 Japan
yamamoto@parl.tutkie.tut.ac.jp

Abstract

We have developed a pen-based Japanese character input system for the blind person (particularly acquired blind person). This system is composed of a personal computer and a control board with an electric tablet. The blind person is able to get the screen information by using a voice synthesizer. We have investigated the various problems when the blind person edits the document by using this system and solved those problems. Therefore this pen-based system makes easy to input Japanese characters for the novice blind user without the training. We apply to the electronic mail system for the blind person by utilizing this system.

1. Introduction

In recent years, the personal computer support applications of the blind person are one of a serious problem, because blind persons have been increasing due to eye diseases and traffic accidents today. The Braille word processors with the Braille keyboard or JIS keyboard are commercialized as the Japanese word processor system of the blind person. There are various types of Japanese characters, such as Kanji, Kana and Katakana. They have to learn the operation of the Kana to Kanji translate software by using the keyboard. This software has to be able to select a correct Kanji character from various characters of the same Kana sound (these are called homonym). Therefore, the operation of a Japanese character input using a keyboard is quite cumbersome for novice users. In these problems, we have studied the pen-based Japanese character input system as the Japanese word processor of the blind person [1]-[4]. This system is able to input Japanese character directly without using the keyboard. Although the selection of the candidate character is necessary for our proposed system, the burden of the user is able to reduce by the development of a high accuracy character recognition algorithm. This paper describes that the basic concept of the pen- based Japanese character input system for the blind person. Next, it is shown that the recognition algorithm for the distorted Japanese character written by the blind person. Furthermore we describe regarding the operational performance of the command control board for the blind person and we apply to the electronic mailing system by using this system.

2. Outline of the system for the blind person

2.1. System configuration

A Figure 1 is a block diagram of the proposed pen-based Japanese character input system for the blind person. This system is composed of the personal computer and a control board with an electric tablet. The control board is used to command all operation in the system. The personal computer has a voice synthesizer that notifies the display screen information for the blind person. This system is also composed of many kinds of the software such as a character recognition processing, an editing processing, an error correction processing, a file management processing and a mailing processing.

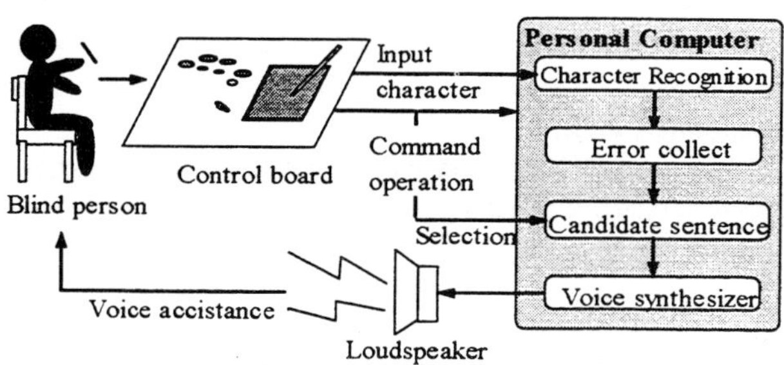

Figure 1. Block diagram of the proposed system

2.2. Character recognition algorithm

A structural analysis method is very useful for the handwritten character recognition. However, as the stroke positions become unstable for the character written by blind person as shown in Fig. 2, the above method is no longer useful. We have investigated characteristics of Japanese Kanji characters written by many blind persons. From analysis result, we found the following some stable features [1].

(1) The same blind person can write almost the same stroke shape, stroke number and stroke writing order.

(2) The relative position of the stroke representative points in the partial pattern is stable.

Two kinds of character recognition algorithm; namely, the RDS method and the LSDS method have been proposed for this system by using the above features. The RDS method is based on the relative direction between two strokes in a writing order. We represent each stroke of the Kanji by three typical points (a starting point, a middle point and an ending point). The solid and broken lines in Fig. 3 (a) and (b) show the real and imaginary strokes (an imaginary stroke means an imaginary line between a pen-up point of the stroke and a pen-down point of the following stroke), respectively. We extract only the vector components between the starting point in a certain stroke and the starting point in the next stroke, or between the middle points of the two strokes, etc., as shown in Fig. 3 (a). These vector directions are finally simplified to eight directional numbers (a vector length is not considered) in Fig. 3 (c). The classification process is as follows. Let N represent the stroke number of the characters, D i, j denotes the eight directional codes between the i th stroke and the (i+1) th stroke in the template pattern, and X i, j denotes it in the input pattern where j means a representative point as follows;

$$j = \begin{cases} 1 & \textit{Starting point of a real stroke} \\ 2 & \textit{Middle point of a real stroke} \\ 3 & \textit{Ending point of a real stroke} \\ 4 & \textit{Middle point of an imaginary stroke} \end{cases} \quad (1)$$

Function Pi,j then gives an evaluation value based on the relation between Xi,j and Di,j as follows;

$$P_{i,j} = \begin{cases} 2 & \textit{if } X_{i,j} = D_{i,j} \\ 1 & \textit{if } X_{i,j} = D_{i,j} \pm 1 \\ 0 & \textit{Others} \end{cases} \quad (2)$$

The corresponding sum of Pi,j;

$$T_{RDS} = \frac{\sum_{i=1}^{N-1}\sum_{j=1}^{3} P_{i,j} + \sum_{i=1}^{N-2} P_{i,4}}{2 \cdot \{3 \cdot (N-1) + (N-2)\}} \quad (3)$$

is calculated for all template patterns. The character of the largest T_{RDS} is outputted as the candidate character. The RDS method is available to character having many strokes, but recognition error increases for character having less than 5 strokes. It is because stroke shapes are not considered. To improve the above problem, we extracted more precise information about each stroke. This recognition method is called the LSDS method (the method based on the line segment directions in a stroke) in this paper. A stroke is divided into several line segments by the same segment length as shown in Fig. 4. A feature parameter set is expressed as a set of eight direction codes that correspond to each line segment. Here, let Ri,j and Fi,j denote the direction of the j th line segment in the i th stroke on a template and gives an evaluation value as follows;

$$Q_{i,j} = \begin{cases} 2 & \textit{if } F_{i,j} = R_{i,j} \\ 1 & \textit{if } F_{i,j} = R_{i,j} \pm 1 \\ 0 & \textit{Others} \end{cases} \quad (4)$$

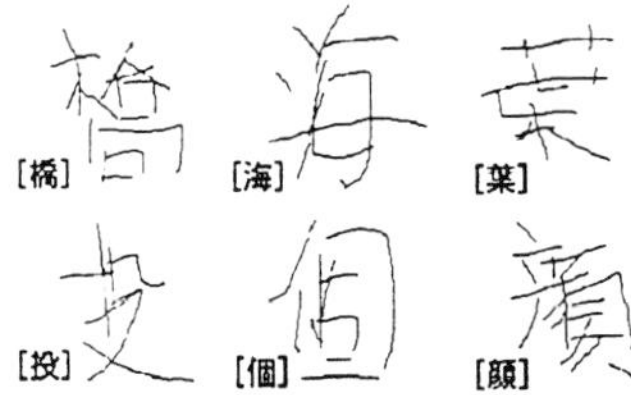

Figure 2. An example of the character written by the blind person

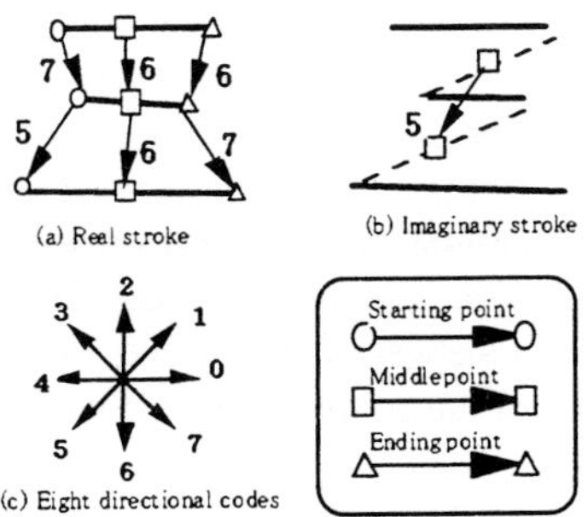

Figure 3. The RDS method

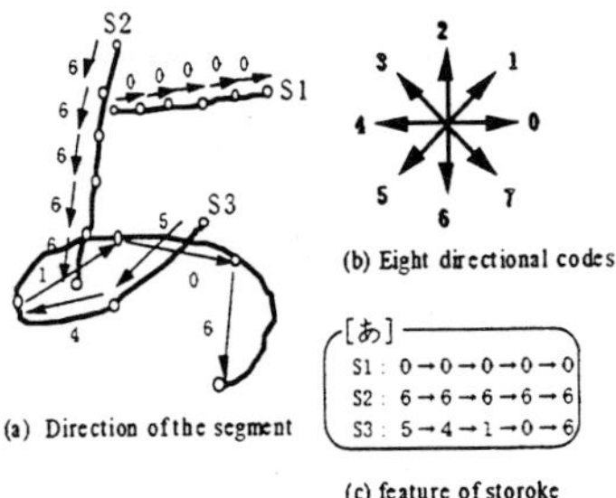

Figure 4. The LSDS method

The corresponding sum of the Qi,j ,

$$T_{LSDS} = \frac{\sum_{i=1}^{N}\sum_{j=1}^{n} Q_{i,j}}{2 \cdot n \cdot N} \tag{5}$$

is calculated where n means a segment number on a certain stroke. The combination of the two methods is desirable to recognize all type of Japanese character written by the blind person. This method is named the fusion method in this paper. The sum of the T_{RDS} and T_{LSDS} is used as recognition in the fusion method [4]. Adding weight ratios (w_1 and w_2) of the T_{RDS} and T_{LSDS} are 50:50 in the case of the character having more than three strokes, 20:80 in the case of the character having two strokes and 0:100 in the case of one stroke character in the following formula.

$$T_F = w_1 * T_{RDS} + w_2 * T_{LSDS} \tag{7}$$

2.3. Error correction method

It was difficult to distinguish similar characters to use the fusion method that is the recognition algorithm for the one character order. Therefore we adapt the error correction method by using a tree search algorithm that uses word dictionary and Japanese grammar; namely, Japanese phrase search algorithm based on the Japanese linguistic information. The tree search algorithm is applied to best-first search method. A Japanese phrase is estimated by evaluations of each character of the phrase.

We examined the recognition test for 6 subjects. The character samples for the recognition are 1,048 characters of the illustrative sentence of a letter per one person. From the experimental results, the total average recognition rate was an 83.9% in the fusion method. However the error correction method corrected an 83.5% of miss-recognized Japanese characters (Kanji, Hiragana, Katakana, numerals and symbols). Therefore, the recognition accuracy was improved to a 97.3% for the testing 1,048 characters.

3. Basic function of the control board

The blind person uses tactile sense information effectively. To enable the smooth input for the blind person, the user's both hands should be fixed in the regular position on the control board. Therefore the control board is designed that the command button is operated by the left hand, and the electric tablet is operated by the right hand, respectively as shown in Fig. 5. For the easy description of the blind person, there is a step in a character input area. The command buttons of the control board consist of 7 push-type buttons and 1 dial-type button. The push-type button is used for the character input control and the command mode change. As these buttons are different size, the user is able to distinguish the option buttons by the size. The dial-type button is used for the cursor movement and the selection of menu options.

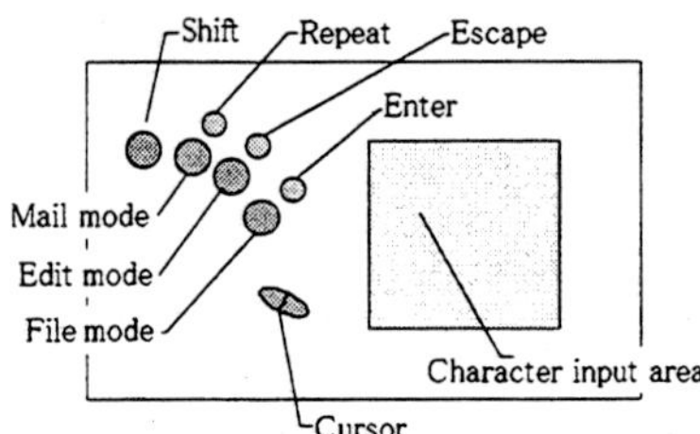

Figure 5. The control board for the blind person

4. Basic operation of this system

A figure 6 shows flow chart of the basic operation for the proposed system. At the beginning, this system is in the character input mode automatically after the starting of the computer. Using the push-type buttons, this system is switched to another operation mode such as the file control mode, the editing mode and the mailing mode, from the character input mode. The voice guide is always announced by using the voice synthesizer when the screen information changes.

4.1.Character write mode

The blind person writes one character by using the electric tablet. He pushes the [enter] button on the control board. Then, the system begins to recognize the character by using the fusion method. Next the system changes to the character write mode again. The user writes a next character by the repeating this procedure. After the one phrase input, the [enter] button is pushed again. Then error correction method begins automatically, and then the voice synthesizer announces the first candidate phrase. If a correct answer is announced, the user pushes the [enter] button of the control board. If wrong answer is

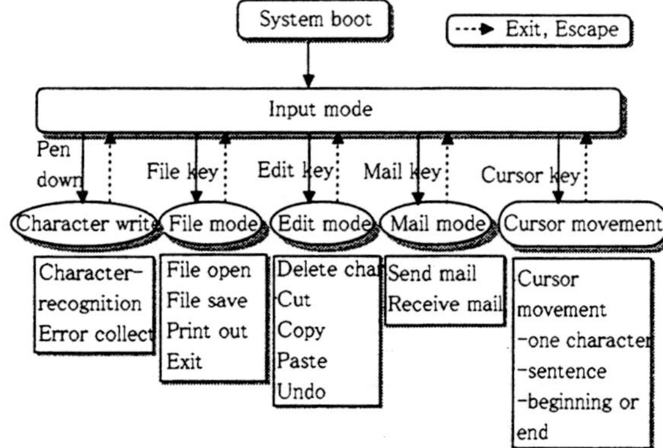

Figure 6. The basic operation of system

announced, the user pushes the [cursor] button. The system then announces the next candidate phrase. When there is no correct phase in the candidate phrases, the system returns automatically to the re-writing mode.

The cursor movement is a serious problem for the blind person who can not to see the screen information. So, we regard a Japanese sentence as the character sequence of one dimension. Here the [cursor] button is used for one character movement. It is a basic cursor movement in this proposed system. Furthermore we prepare two option of the cursor movement. The cursor movement of one phrase is implemented by push the [cursor] button with the [shift] button. To move the cursor position to the beginning/ending of the sentence, the user pushes the [cursor] button and the [escape] button with the [shift] button. Then the system announces the cursor position by the voice synthesizer. Therefore the blind person can move the cursor positions by above procedure.

4.2.Voice support

The voice support is the most suitable information communication method to the blind person. This system announces all information of the display screen by the voice synthesizer. However the user often fails to catch voice announcements. Therefore we add the [repeat] button. This button is used when the user wants to listen to the voice announcement repeatedly. The voice synthesizer has some kinds of the timbre such as the male/female voice sound. We distinguished it by the situation. The male voice sound is used to announce the system information. And sentence information with the cursor movement is announced by the female voice sound. Furthermore, we add the voice guide function for the novice user. Then the voice output speed is able to change it easily by the user.

4.3.Edit mode

In the document editing such as a cut and a copy, the user has to select the object area at the beginning in the normally commercial word processor. However the blind person chooses the command option at the beginning in our proposed system. This procedure prevents that the blind person delete the sentence by his mistake. In addition the undo function becomes effective when the sentence/mode is changed. It can return easily to the previous system condition.

4.4.File mode

The user has to input a file name when the document is saved to the holder. Though a file name can be inputted directly by the pen, our proposed system has the file naming function that makes the file name from the first sentence of the document automatically.

In order that the user is able to grasp the contents of the file easily, the system announces the first phrase with the file name when the user choices the file loading mode.

4.5.Electoric mailing system

We apply to the electric mailing system for the blind person by using the proposed pen-based Japanese input system. The mailing system that is connected by the Internet gives the opportunity of the participation of the society for the handicapped person. We expect that the blind person is able to communicate with the various persons by using this system. The current system has the mailing list and the user is able to send the electric mail to the person who is registered in the list. If new electric mail arrived in this system, the system announces the arrival message for the blind person.

5. Conclusion

We have proposed the pen-based Japanese character input system for the blind person. This system works to the information devices as the simple Japanese input system for the novice blind person. The advantage of the system is not only applied easy character input method without the training, but also the blind person is given a pleasure to write the Japanese character by his hand.

At present, the prototype is experimentally produced based on the proposed basic concept. Future work is the evaluation experiment by utilizing this system on the school for the blind and the social welfare organization.

References

[1] K.Kiyota, T.Sakurai, and S.Yamamoto, "Deformation analysis and classification of on-line handwritten Chinese character for the visually disabled persons." , Trans. IPS Japan, Vol.36, No.3, 1995, pp.636-644.

[2] K.Kiyota, N.Ezaki, T.Yanai, and S.Yamamoto, "A basic design of on-line Japanese input interface for visually disabled person",Vol.J79-A, No.2, 1996, pp.310-317.

[3] K.Kiyota, T.Sakurai, and S.Yamamoto, "On-line character recognition for the visually disabled person based on the relative position of stroke representative points.", IEICE Trans. Inf. & Syst, Vol.J80-D-II, No.3, 1997, pp.715-723.

[4] K.Kiyota, T.Yanai, N.Ezaki, and S.Yamamoto, "An improvement of on-line Japanese character recognition system for visually disabled persons", Proc. of the 14th International Conference on Pattern Recognition, 1998, pp.1752-1754.

Automatic Ground-Truth Generation for Skew-Tolerance Evaluation of Document Layout Analysis Methods

Oleg Okun and Matti Pietikäinen
Machine Vision and Media Processing Unit, Infotech Oulu and Department of EE
P.O.Box 4500, FIN-90014 University of Oulu, Finland
{oleg,mkp}@ee.oulu.fi

Abstract

Generation of ground-truths is of great importance for unbiased performance evaluation of document layout analysis methods. This is especially necessary because many methods are claimed to be skew-tolerant. However, experimental evaluation of this fact is often based only on human subjective judgement and restricted to a few experiments. The main obstacle for obtaining human-independent and more automated performance evaluation is that usually there are only ground-truths for upright images, i.e., images with no skew of text lines, because currently available ground-truthing techniques are too time-consuming. In this paper, we propose a new methodology of automatic generation of ground-truths for skewed images by using the ground-truths available for upright images. This methodology is simple and quite fast because processing is done at the level of small square blocks, but not at pixel level.

1. Introduction

Performance evaluation of document layout analysis methods is of great importance for document image processing applications. A fair and unbiased evaluation of obtained results is useful, both for the developers and the end users of such applications, because it allows them to compare different methods and improve their performance.

One typical approach to this problem is to use ground-truths for each image. The ground-truth is a special file containing description of image regions, for example, as polygons or rectangles with their labels such as text, graphics, or picture. This description is considered to be ideal which one should obtain as a result of layout analysis, despite the fact that it is sometimes difficult to define exact criteria for perfect image partitioning into regions. That is, the aim of using ground-truths is to match them to the results obtained after applying a particular layout analysis method to the image in question in order to have qualitative and quatitative estimations on the efficiency of that method.

In recent years, a large number of document layout analysis methods have been proposed (see [4] for a review), and many of them are claimed to be tolerant to a certain degree of skew [2, 3] that is associated with the orientation of text lines. However, this claim is not supported by extensive experiments (usually a test set consists of a few to 100–200 images), because ground-truthing is usually a time consuming procedure [1, 5], making generation of many ground-truths difficult. This is the main reason for the popularity of visual evaluation of layout analysis results, and this is why in many cases ground-truths, if available, are only for upright images (with no skew).

One solution to skew-tolerance evaluation could be skew correction before layout analysis. In this case, one could use the ground-truths for the upright images. But this can only help if a given method *does* skew correction and yet, skew estimation may be inaccurate by nullifying correction. Also there are methods doing layout analysis on skewed images without prior skew estimation and correction [2, 3].

We propose another solution to automatically generate ground-truths for skewed images using the ground truths available for upright images. It is also assumed that it is unnecessary to scan the skewed images to do this. Our methodology is based on the following principles: 1) block partitioning of both the upright and skewed images (it is supposed that each block on the upright image has a specific class label), 2) skew simulation for the upright image, and 3) block labelling of the skewed image based on the skew-compensating rotation of a representative square of every block, followed by matching the rotated square to the blocks of the upright image.

2. Image partitioning into blocks

Image partitioning into blocks means that the image is implicitly divided into small non-overlapping square blocks in horizontal and vertical directions. Let us assume that the block size is NxN pixels. To minimise inclusion of data from different classes, such as text, graphics or picture, in the same block, N is set from 8 to 24, depending on image resolution so that an area of NxN pixels in an image corresponds to an area not larger than 2x2 mm^2 in a paper document.

Why did we choose this representation? The reasons were twofold. First, it allows one to have a common representation for different layouts (rectangular, constrained polygons with horizontal and vertical edges, and unconstrained polygons with arbitrarily oriented edges). Second, this representation is widely used in texture-based document segmentation and image compression, and it may be equally suitable for binary, grey-scale, or colour images. Besides, it provides easy access to data and this allows flexible data manipulation. Also it is quite straightforward to obtain image partitioning into blocks from bitmaps.

For our task, it is necessary to obtain the block partitioning for ground-truths of the upright images as well. In many cases, the ground-truths are available in simple text formats and we assume that it is not difficult to derive block-based ground-truths from them. The new ground-truth, based on block partitioning may be presented with a 2D array GT, where each element is the class label (digit or character) for a particular block and dimensions of this array are equal to the number of blocks in horizontal and vertical directions.

3. Brief description of our methodology

Given a skew angle α and the ground-truth GT for an upright image partitioned into NxN pixel blocks, our methodology consists of the following steps:

1. Rotate corner points of the upright image by α about the image centre (we assume that positive (negative) angles correspond to clockwise (counter-clockwise) rotation) and compute the positions of corner points of the skewed image.
2. Partition the skewed image into NxN pixel blocks (N is the same as it is for the upright image).
3. For each block in the skewed image,:
    (a) Find coordinates of corner points of its representative square (we will show in the next section why it can be used instead of the block itself) rotated by α and with the points located on the sides of a given block.
    (b) Rotate the representative square by $-\alpha$ for skew compensation.
    (c) Determine which blocks in the upright image contain or intersect the rotated square.
    (d) Use their class labels and a set of predefined rules to assign a label to the block in question corresponding to the given representative square.

As a result, we obtain a 2D array which is similar to the GT and whose elements are class labels for blocks containing text, background, graphics, pictures, or mixture of several classes.

4. Implementation details

Coordinates of the corner points of the skewed image can be found as presented in Fig. 1. $A_0B_0C_0D_0$ represents the bounding box of the original image. When it is rotated (skewed) by an angle α, it is transformed into the rectangle $A_1B_1C_1D_1$ so that A_2, B_2, C_2, and D_2 become corner points of the skewed image. The coordinates of these corner points can be easily computed based on those of A_1, B_1, C_1, D_1, and α. After this, it is easy to partition the skewed image into NxN pixel blocks, where N has the same value as in the upright image partition.

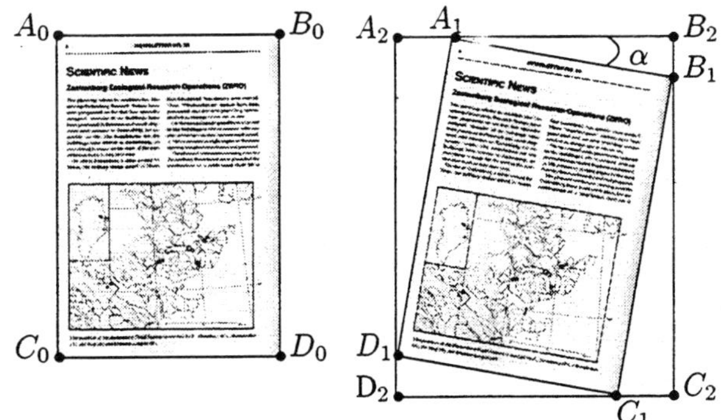

Figure 1. Rectangles $A_0B_0C_0D_0$ and $A_2B_2C_2D_2$ represent bounding boxes of the upright and skewed images, respectively. The rectangle $A_1B_1C_1D_1$ is a rotated bounding box of the upright image by the angle α.

All that remains is to label the blocks in the skewed image. Our idea is to apply a rotation transformation in order to find correspondence between the blocks in the upright and skewed images. In this case, unlabelled blocks will obtain class labels of their labelled counterparts.

It is easy to see that the areas outside $A_1B_1C_1D_1$ in Fig. 1 belong to the background because they do not have a match within $A_0B_0C_0D_0$ if $A_1B_1C_1D_1$ is rotated by $-\alpha$. It will be simpler first to detect such areas and to assign them to the background before processing other regions. To do this, it is sufficient to rotate the upper-left and lower-right corner points of each block in the skewed image around the image centre by $-\alpha$ and check if the positions of *both* rotated points are outside $A_0B_0C_0D_0$. If this is the case, the block is labelled as background.

At the first look, a straightforward solution to labeling blocks within $A_1B_1C_1D_1$ would be to rotate two other corner points (upper-right and lower-left) of a block by $-\alpha$ in order to find which blocks in the upright image intersect that block. However, this approach has several disadvantages. First, one will need to match a rotated block against the blocks with a normal orientation (see Fig. 2). This operation does not seem to be simple. Second, it may be desirable to relate a block label to the intersection area of blocks from the upright and skewed images. However, this is not easy in the case shown in Fig. 2, where intersection areas are not rectangles but polygons.

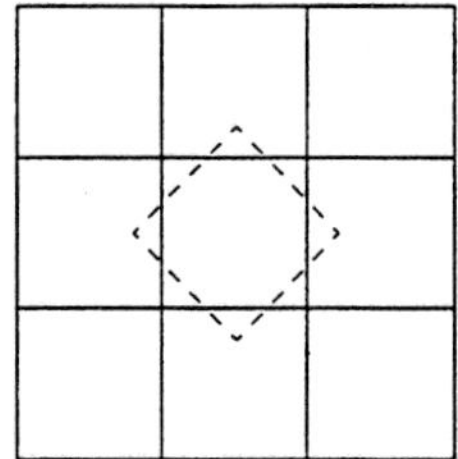

Figure 2. A difficult case for labelling a rotated (dashed) block from the skewed image, which is laid on the upright image.

Therefore we propose a simpler method for dealing with block labelling inside $A_1B_1C_1D_1$. Our solution is based on the following property.

Property. Let $P_1P_2P_3P_4$ and $R_1R_2R_3R_4$ be a block in the skewed image and a block rotated by an angle α and having corner points located on its sides as shown in Fig. 3, respectively. In this case, $R_1R_2R_3R_4$ is a (representative) square of $P_1P_2P_3P_4$ and the ratio $r = \frac{S_R}{S_P} \geq 0.5$, where S_R and S_P are the areas of $R_1R_2R_3R_4$ and $P_1P_2P_3P_4$, respectively (see proof in Appendix).

This means that $R_1R_2R_3R_4$ always occupies at least half the area of a block in the skewed image. Since maximal sizes of this block on paper are very small (2x2 mm^2 at maximum), we can use $R_1R_2R_3R_4$ instead of $P_1P_2P_3P_4$ for *every* block to label it (that is why it is called 'representative') because this will not lead to significant error. In this case, when we rotate $R_1R_2R_3R_4$ by $-\alpha$, we get a block without slant and it is now very easy to determine its intersection with blocks in the upright image. There are only four possibilities (see Fig. 4) because $|R_1R_2| \leq |P_1P_2|$. In order to find the intersections, we can, in fact, rotate only two points – R_1 and R_4 – and after that we need to determine which block contains each of these points. The

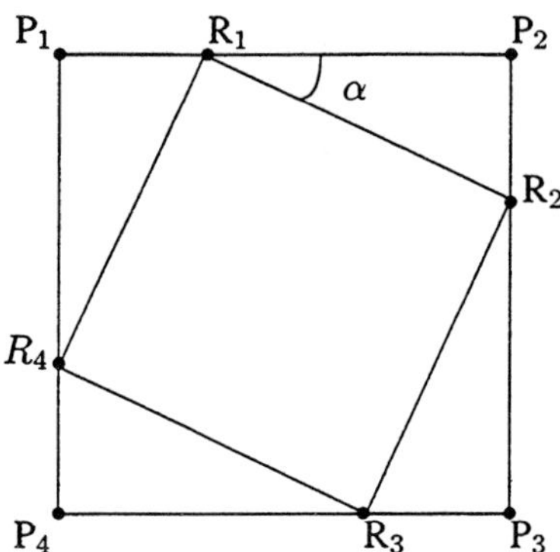

Figure 3. Illustration to Property.

last task is simple because it is necessary to divide x- and y-coordinates of the points by N in order to get the corresponding block label in a 2D array GT.

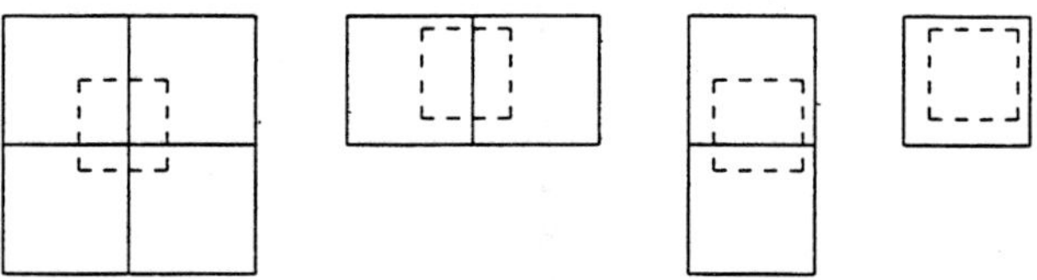

Figure 4. Four cases of intersection of blocks in the upright image and a block in question (shown dashed) from the skewed image.

We assume that there are only four original classes (backgound, text, graphics, and picture) that can be in the image. As a result, there are only 15 possible class labels for the blocks, including four pure and eleven mixed, for example, text+background+picture, when data of several classes are inside the same block. Allowing mixed classification is not a significant flaw of our methodology because block sizes are quite small so they do not include large areas of objects.

5. Experiments

In order to evaluate the usefulness of our methodology, we conducted several experiments using a special tool implemented in MATLAB under Windows.

First, we chose various colour images of advertisements with an image resolution of 300 dpi, containing complex-shaped, non-rectangular regions. For each image, we manually extracted regions either as polygons or rectangles, depending on a region's shape. After that, all polygons were automatically partitioned into rectangles followed by a block-based (N=24) ground-truth generation for each upright image from its set of rectangles. We chose rectangles as an intermediate data representation, because they facilitate the derivation of ground-truths at block level. By having a block-based ground-truth for every upright image, we generated ground-truths for skewed images according to the described methodology, with skew angles varying from $-90°$ to $+90°$.

To verify the accuracy of the ground-truth generation, we automatically created a separate ideal block-based ground-truth for every skew angle. The aim was to match ideal and obtained ground-truths for each angle and to derive quantitative estimations on the accuracy. The ideal ground-truth was created by rotating rectangles, obtained after region extraction and polygon partitioning, by a skew angle. All blocks in the skewed image crossing or being within a given rotated rectangle were given the label of this rectangle (crossing blocks were usually given extra labels, too, because they lie on the borders between different classes of regions). Ideal ground-truth generation is rather brute force-like but the purpose is to obtain as accurate a region description at block level as possible.

Matching ideal and generated ground-truths was done by using a look-up table consisting of 15x15 entries (the number of different labels resulting from 4 original data classes is 15). Each entry has a specific number corresponding to one of 11 different cases when matching block labels of two ground-truths. Among them, there are completely accurate and completely erroneous classifications as well as 9 cases when *some* (not all!) labels were missed, added or misclassified in the obtained ground-truth.

The rate of correct classification was about 90 per cent or higher, depending on how accurately regions were manually extracted. When, after polygon partitioning into rectangles, there were no overlapping rectangles, this rate was higher than when overlaps were present. The number of completely erroneous classifications was very small (less than 1 per cent or even zero). Among other cases, 'one label missed' and 'one label added' dominated, with more cases of the second type because we tried to minimise the loss of information. The total occurrence of cases than those mentioned was about 1 per cent. The blocks with missed or added labels were typically located on borders of the regions and the 'background' label was usually missed or added. Because the background does not contain any useful information in many cases, we consider the influence of this factor on the ground-truth accuracy as minor. In combination with the rare occurrence of actual errors and other cases, we conclude that our methodology provides appropriately accurate ground-truths to be used in practice.

The time for ground-truth generation with our methodology was 4.5-5.5 s (Pentium-III, 500 MHz), excluding the time for region extraction (user- and document-dependent) and for polygon partitioning into rectangles (up to 5-8 s per polygon). It was 50-60 times less than the time for ideal ground-truth generation.

6. Conclusions

In this paper, we propose a new methodology for generating ground-truths for skew-tolerance evaluation of document layout analysis methods. A large number of accurate ground-truths for skewed images can be easily and quickly obtained. In order to generate ground-truths, the only parameter to be set is N, whose value depends on image resolution. Future research should concentrate on fully automatic region extraction and on conversion of ground-truths from other formats to our representation.

7. Acknowledgements

Financial support of TEKES (Finland) is gratefully acknowledged. We also thank the anonymous reviewers for their comments and Dr. Ari Vesanen for implementing our ideas in MATLAB.

8. Appendix

Let us assume that $h = |R_1R_4| = |R_2R_3|$ and $w = |R_1R_2| = |R_3R_4|$. In this case, we have that

$$|P_1P_2| = |P_1R_1| + |R_1P_2| = h\sin\alpha + w\cos\alpha = N,$$
$$|P_2P_3| = |P_2R_2| + |R_2P_3| = h\cos\alpha + w\sin\alpha = N.$$

By solving these two equations, we obtain $h = w = \frac{N}{\cos\alpha+\sin\alpha}$, that is, $R_1R_2R_3R_4$ is a square and $r = \frac{1}{(\cos\alpha+\sin\alpha)^2} = \frac{1}{1+\sin 2\alpha}$. As $\sin 2\alpha \in [0,1]$ (negative values are excluded to avoid different results when rotating by $+\alpha$ and $-\alpha$), $r \in [0.5, 1]$ and $r_{min} = 0.5$.

References

[1] A. Antonacopoulos and A. Brough. Methodology for flexible and efficient analysis of the performance of page segmentation algorithms. In *Proc. of the 5th Int'l Conf. on Document Analysis and Recognition*, pages 451–454, 1999.

[2] A. Antonacopoulos. Page segmentation using the description of the background. *Computer Vision and Image Understanding*, 70(3):350–369, 1998.

[3] K. Etemad, D. Doermann, and R. Chellappa. Multiscale segmentation of unstructured document pages using soft decision integration. *IEEE Trans. on PAMI*, 19(1):92–96, 1997.

[4] O. Okun, D. Doermann, and M. Pietikäinen. Page segmentation and zone classification: the state of the art. Technical Report LAMP-TR-036, Laboratory for Language and Media Processing, University of Maryland, MD, USA, 1999.

[5] B. Yanikoglu and L. Vincent. Pink panther: a complete environment for ground-truthing and benchmarking document page segmentation. *Pattern Recognition*, 31(9):1191–1204, 1998.

Backgrounds as Information Carriers for Printed Documents *

Koichi Kise, Yasuo Miki, Keinosuke Matsumoto
Dept. of Computer and Systems Sciences, College of Eng., Osaka Prefecture University
1-1 Gakuencho, Sakai, Osaka 599-8531, Japan
kise@cs.osakafu-u.ac.jp

Abstract

This paper presents a method of embedding and recovery of a large amount of data on printed documents. The proposed method is characterized by the following points: (1) As the medium for recording the data, backgrounds (white space) of pages are utilized. Since white space is dominant in ordinary pages, this enables us to record a large amount of data. (2) As the representation of data, an arbitrary figure (such as a logo mark of a company) is stippled to obtain a set of points, each of which is superimposed on a page image. This allows us to prevent the appearance of a page from deteriorating, since stippled figures play a role of background patterns on printed documents. The experimental results show that the method is capable of both recording 7.8KB of data and reading the embedded data with the accuracy of 99%.

1. Introduction

In recent years, a large amount of documents are made using computers and delivered through networks. Thus, most of the original forms of documents are electronic data, which are useful for retrieval, reproduction and modification. Nevertheless we continue to print electronic documents on paper. This would be because the paper medium is still superior to the electronic media in point of readability and portability, etc. for us.

Once an electronic document is printed out, it is generally difficult to retrieve the original from the printed one. In addition, if an electronic document is modified or abandoned after printing, we face the problem that no original exists. The information recorded in printed documents, therefore, needs to be recycled into the electronic information flow. The research on OCR and document image analysis has been devoted to realize the recycle. An ultimate goal is the error-free conversion from printed documents to electronic ones. Although we have commercial OCR systems with high accuracy in these days, 100% recognition rate cannot be expected in many cases.

In this paper, we propose a different approach for the conversion. In contrast with OCR which is an approach of "a machine reads what a human reads", the proposed method is an approach of "a machine reads what a human doesn't read". This approach itself is not new; we have already had bar-codes[4] and RFID tags[5]. These methods, however, have the following shortcomings when they are applied to printed documents. It is difficult for bar-codes to record a large amount of data such as full-text data without spoiling visual appearance of a page. This is mainly because bar-codes are totally meaningless to us. RFID tags would be advantageous to solve this problem, but it requires a special device to read the data.

Our method is designed to attain a large capacity without deterioration of the page appearance and special devices. The large capacity is realized by using the *backgrounds* (white space) of pages as a medium of record. The preservation of the appearance is achieved by using as the representation of data an *arbitrary figure* which is also meaningful for us. This paper presents the method of recording and recovery of data to/from stippled arbitrary figures, only with ordinary devices: a computer, a scanner and a printer.

2. Proposed method

2.1. Overview

Figure 1 shows a printed page generated by the proposed method. This page includes 7.8 K Bytes of data embedded in the 12 stippled figures of our university logo: each bit of the embedded data is represented by either printing or erasing a small dot. The method is both to generate such a printed page and to recover embedded data from it.

The scenario of making use of the method is as follows. (1) Defining and sharing a model — Prior to print documents with embedded data, it is required to determine a figure to be stippled to convey data. A figure is arbitrary for

*This research was supported by Grand-in-Aid for Scientific Research from Japan Society for the Promotion of Science.

1051-4651/00 $10.00 © 2000 IEEE

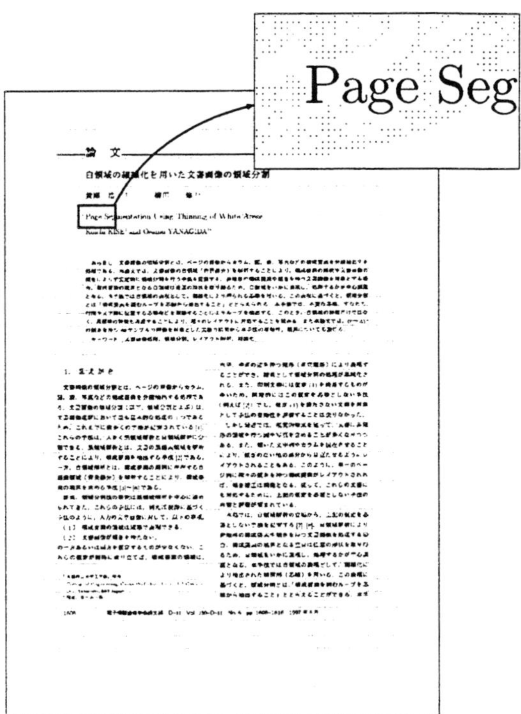

Figure 1. A page image with embedded data.

the method but should be felt natural by users when it is printed as background patterns on a paper. A company logo would be a good choice for company users. The stippled version of a figure is called a *model* in this paper. A model should be shared by users who print and/or recover data on the documents.
(2) Printing documents — The method is intended to act as a wrapper of a word processor. When a user prints his/her document, its data are embedded on the background of its printout.
(3) Recovering data — When a user recovers embedded data, a printed page with embedded data is first scanned to convert it to a page image. Then the data are recovered from the image by matching dots on the image to the model.

2.2. Processing

Figure 2 shows the three phases of processing of our method: model generation, embedding of data on a page and recovery of data from a page.

2.2.1 Model generation

This phase is to generate a model that acts as *key* for printing and recovery of data. The input is a binary image of an arbitrary figure. As shown in Fig. 3, a model is easily generated by representing a figure by grid points.

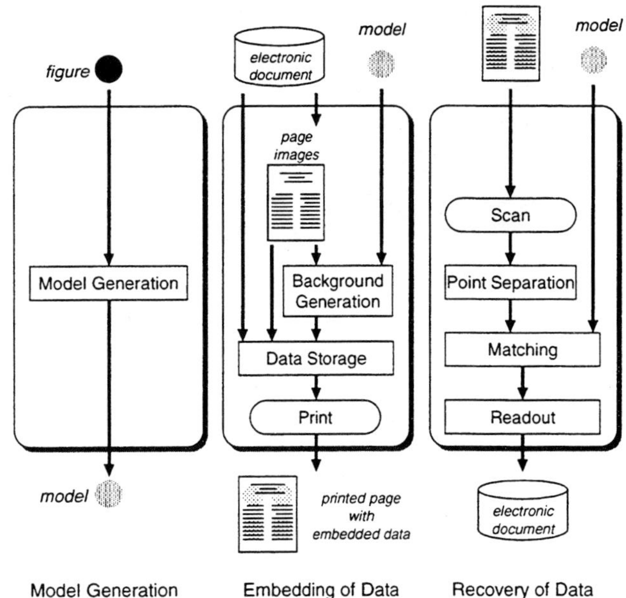

Figure 2. Three phases of processing.

Let $f(x, y)$ be a binary image of an input figure where $f(x, y) = 1(0)$ if a pixel at (x, y) is black (white). Then, the model $m(x, y)$ for f is defined as

$$m(x, y) = \begin{cases} f(x, y) & \text{if } x = iI \text{ and } y = jI, \\ 0 & \text{otherwise,} \end{cases}$$

where i and j are integers and I is the interval of the grid.

Points in a model are classified into the following two types: *contour* and *internal*. A contour point is a black point ($m(iI, jI) = 1$) at least one of whose four neighbors $m((i-1)I, jI)$, $m((i+1)I, jI)$, $m(iI, (j-1)I)$, $m(iI, (j+1)I)$ is white (0). An internal point is a black point which is not a contour point. In order to make pages look natural, it is required for users to be able to recognize the shape of an original figure on the background. Since contour points of a model play an important role for this purpose, we utilize internal points solely for recording data.

Note that this process is required only once when a new figure is utilized to store data. We assume that the model is shared by all users who print and/or recover data. Since the same model can be utilized for embedding different data, we consider that this assumption is acceptable.

2.2.2 Embedding of data

The input to this phase is data (i.e., an electronic document) and a model. After converting each page of an electronic document to a page binary image, the data are embedded on pages by the following two steps: background generation and data storage. In the following, the processing for a single page is described.

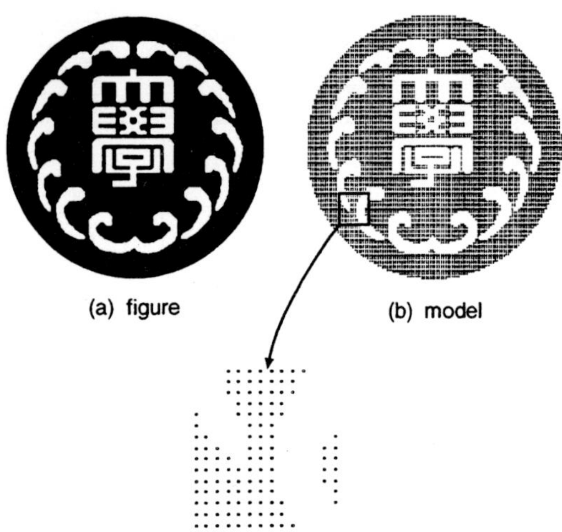

Figure 3. A figure and a model.

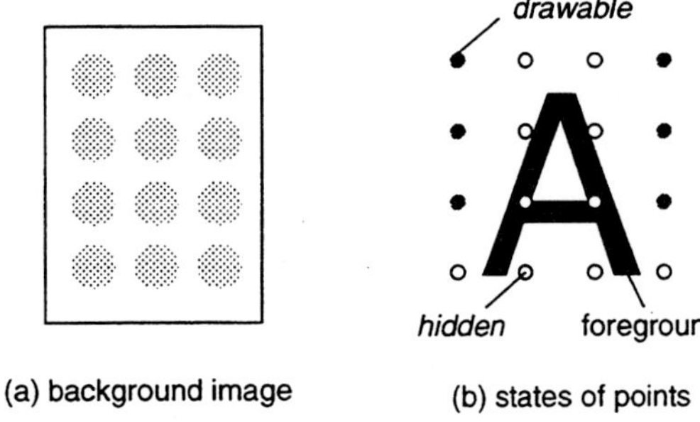

Figure 4. Embedding of data.

[step 2-1] background generation

As shown in Fig. 4(a), multiple models are arranged on a grid to produce a binary image $b(x, y)$ called a background image whose size is equal to an original page image. For the purpose of stable extraction of points at the steps of "recovery of data", a point in a model is represented as $L \times L$ black pixels.

[step 2-2] data storage

The background image $b(x, y)$ is modified according to the data, and then superimposed on an original page image to produce a page image with embedded data. The processing is as follows:

(1) Determine a state of each point

Since a page image has its own black pixels (foreground), some of the black points on the background image are hidden by the foreground as shown in Fig. 4(b). As a result, these points cannot be utilized for recording data. In addition, it is safe not to utilize points that are too close to the foreground, since they would be merged to the foreground when the page is printed or scanned.

If the Euclidean distance between a black pixel in the background image and that in the foreground is less than

Table 1. Points on the background image.

type	*state*	
	hidden	drawable
contour	0	1
internal	0	0 or 1

$I \cdot T_1$, the point on the background image is called a *hidden* point, where I is the interval of the grid in the model, and T_1 is a threshold. The rest of points are called *drawable* points.

(2) Erase points on the background image

Points on the background image are classified as shown in Table 1. In this table, 0 and 1 indicate "erased from the background image", and "drawn". In these points, drawable internal points are solely utilized to represent the data. After compressing the data, we encode it by an error correcting code so as to acquire tolerance to errors. Then some of the drawable internal points are erased from the background image according to the encoded data.

(3) Superimpose

The modified background image is superimposed on original page image by taking logical OR of each pixel.

2.2.3 Recovery of data

When a user intends to recover embedded data from printed pages, each page is scanned to convert it to a page binary image. Then the three steps of processing shown in Fig. 2 are applied.

[step 3-1] point separation

The first step is to separate points on the background from the scanned page image. This is easily achieved by selecting small connected components from the page image. Figure 5 illustrates an example of separated points at this step: the wide blanks at the upper left part are due to overlap with the foreground. As a result, the page image is separated into a point image and a foreground image.

[step 3-2] matching

In order to read the data from the point image, it is necessary to identify drawable internal points. For this purpose, the model is matched to the point image and the number, the positions, the rotation and the scale of embedded models are estimated.

First, vertical and horizontal projection is applied as shown in Fig. 6 while rotating the point image. As a result, we have $S_\theta(k)$, i.e., a projection profile[1] of the point image at θ. Then, using the technique of skew estimation[3], the

[1] It should be smoothed with a window function.

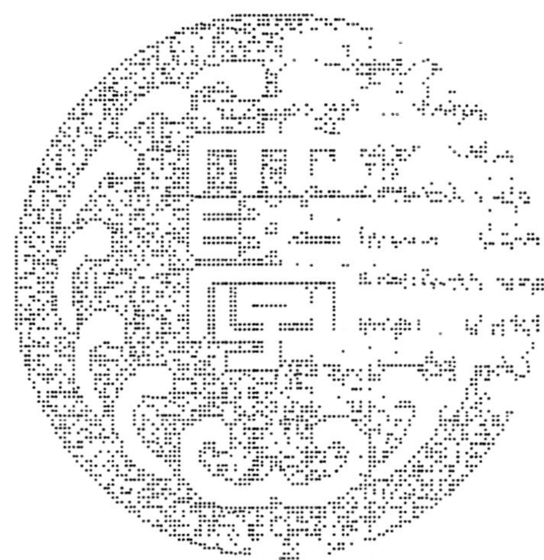

Figure 5. Examples of separated points.

estimated rotation angle $\hat{\theta}$ is obtained as

$$\hat{\theta} = \arg\max_{\theta} \sum_{k} S_{\theta}^{2}(k).$$

In addition, the dot-dash lines in Fig. 6 called the grid lines, which define the location of each point, are obtained by finding the peaks of $S_{\hat{\theta}}$. The number of models embedded and the scale are simultaneously obtained from the grid lines. In the following, the interval of the grid on the point image is denoted as $\hat{I}$.

According to the estimated number of embedded models, multiple models are placed on the grid defined by the grid lines in Fig. 6. This indicates that the locations of all points in each model are determined as a part of the intersection points of the grid lines.

[step 3-3] readout

The final step is readout of the embedded data. For this purpose, it is necessary to identify drawable internal points.

The internal points have already been identified by matching with the model at the previous step, all we have to do at this step are (1) to distinguish drawable and hidden internal points, and (2) to identify the state (0 or 1) of each drawable internal point. The former is done by measuring the minimum distance d_f of each internal point to the black pixels in the foreground image which has already been obtained at the step 3-1. If the following condition

$$d_f \geq \hat{I} \cdot T_2$$

is satisfied, the internal point is determined as drawable. Next, the minimum distance d_p of each drawable internal point to the centroids of connected components in the point image is measured. If the condition

$$d_p \leq \hat{I} \cdot T_3$$

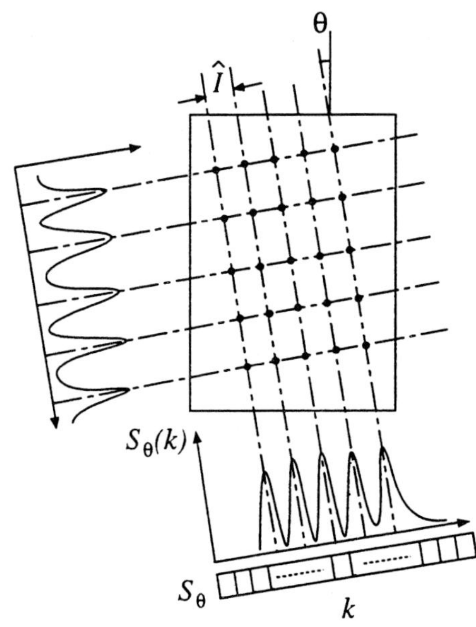

Figure 6. Parameter estimation by projection.

is fulfilled, the internal point is determined as drawn (1 in Table 1).

Finally, the recovered data are decoded to obtain the embedded data.

3. Preliminary experiments

3.1. Conditions

We tested potential applicability of the method by preliminary experiments for a front page of a Japanese technical paper.

In the phase of model generation, the logo of our university shown in Fig. 3(a) was utilized as the figure. The size of the image was 1224 × 1224. The model was generated with the interval $I = 10$.

In the phase of embedding of data, *random* data were embedded without encoding instead of the encoded data of the electronic document. The original page image was generated from the LaTeX file at 600dpi. The size was 4967 × 7025. Next, we prepared two background images B1 and B2. B1 was generated using the point size 2 × 2, and B2 was generated using 1 × 1, both of which were at 600dpi. In both images, the number of embedded models was 12 as shown in Fig. 4(a). The parameter T_1 was set to 1. The total number of drawable internal points was 62191 for B1, and 61514 for B2. Thus about 62 K bits (7.8KB) of data were embedded on a page. The page images with B1 and B2 were printed at 600dpi.

Table 2. Page images and their results.

image	recall	precision	T_2	T_3
#1 (B1 / orig. / 0°)	99.63%	99.72%	0.820	0.195
#2 (B1 / orig. / 3°)	99.49%	99.74%	0.830	0.230
#3 (B1 / copy / 0°)	99.45%	99.52%	0.850	0.520
#4 (B2 / orig. / 0°)	98.21%	98.70%	0.735	0.235

In the phase of recovery of data, the printed pages were scanned at 1200dpi. We obtained four page images listed in Table 2 by changing conditions. In this table, "orig." means that the printout was directly scanned, while "copy" indicates that the printout was first copied on recycle paper and then scanned. 0° and 3° indicate approximate skew angles of scanned page images. The parameters T_2 and T_3 were varied to find the best values.

3.2. Results

The results were evaluated based on the *recall* R and the *precision* P of the drawable internal points defined as $R = N_c/N_e$, $P = N_c/N_i$, where N_e is the number of drawable internal points embedded in a printed page, N_i is the number of drawable internal points identified from the point image, and N_c is the number of correctly identified drawable internal points. In the experiments, the values of parameters T_2 and T_3 which maximized the product $R \times P$ were determined to be the best.

Recall and precision obtained with the best parameters are shown in Table 2. Except for the image #4, recall and precision of more than 99% were obtained. Although the small size of points lowered the result for the image #4, its recall and precision were still more than 98%. The values of parameters were not so sensitive to recall and precision. The recall and precision with the parameters fixed to be the best for all images were 99.13% and 99.31%, respectively.

3.3. Discussion

From the preliminary experiments, we confirmed that the method was capable of storing a large amount of data on a printed page, as well as recovering the embedded data accurately. In order to put the method to practical use, however, a number of problems should be solved. Some of them are listed below.

(1) Test using encoded data : Experiments using encoded data of electronic documents are required to verify the error-free conversion from printed documents to electronic ones.
(2) Test for pages with figures and photos : There exist original small dots in figures and photos. Thus the influence of these original dots should be verified.
(3) Disuse of a model : Since the assumption that users share a model would limit the applicability of the method, it should be modified not to rely on a model.
(4) Expansion of the capacity : Although the current capacity of embedded data seems enough for recording encoded full-text of a page, it is obviously insufficient for recording a whole electronic description of a page such as a PDF file. In order to expand the capacity, we are planning to utilize colors.

4. Related work

(1) Digital watermarking[2] : Although digital watermarking can be utilized to record data on images, it is quite different from our method in the following points. While most of the technologies of digital watermarking are to *hide* the data in *electronic* media, our method is not to hide the data and for *printed* pages.
(2) DataGlyphs[1] : DataGlyphs are sophisticated codes invented at Xerox to record a large amount of data on printed pages. It also preserves the page appearance, since the printed data are perceived as uniform gray texture in a page. Although DataGlyphs are superior to our method in many points, it does not provide recording data on *designed* patterns like a figure in our method.

5. Conclusion

We have proposed a method of embedding and recovery of a large amount of data on printed documents. The key of the method is to utilize both a background as a medium of record and an arbitrary figure as a representation of data. From the preliminary experiments, it is clarified that the method records 7.8KB of data on a single black-on-white page and recovers 99% of recorded data. We plan to extend our method to be more reliable, more attractive for users and to have larger capacity.

References

[1] D.L.Hecht. Embedded data glyph technology for hardcopy digital documents. In *Proc. of SPIE*, volume 2171, pages 341–352, 1994.

[2] H.Berghel. Watermarking cyberspace. *Comm. of the ACM*, 40(11):19–24, 1997.

[3] H.S.Baird. The skew angle of printed documents. In *Proc. of SPSE's 40th Annual Conf. and Sympo. on Hybrid Imaging Systems*, pages 21–24, 1987.

[4] ⟨ URL:http://www.adams1.com/ ⟩.

[5] R. Want, K. P. Fishkin, A. Gujar, and B. L. Harrison. Bridging physical and virtual worlds with electronic tags. In *Proc. of ACM Conf. on Human Factors in Computing Systems*, pages 370–377, 1999.

Extraction of Relevant Information from Document Images Using Measures of Visual Attention

Gerd Maderlechner, Angela Schreyer and Peter Suda

Siemens AG, Corporate Technology
Otto-Hahn-Ring 6, D-81730 Munich, Germany
Tel. +49-89-63653389, Fax.+49-89-63640153
email: gerd.maderlechner@mchp.siemens.de

Abstract

This paper describes an approach to attention based layout segmentation using general principles of the human visual perception to achieve this goal. The text is considered as texture in different resolution levels. A new measure of attractiveness is introduced. The segmentation is generic and not limited to specific document classes and models. The resulting regions of interest may be used for further interpretation. The overall speed of browsing and searching large volumes of scanned documents can be increased considerably.

1. Introduction

The attention of a human reader and the reading speed strongly depends on the layout of a document The term layout is used for the geometrical arrangement of document components (i.e. text, graphics and figures) on the page as well as for the typographic features of the text (i.e. font type, style, size, alignment and line spacing).

Although the human visual and cognitive perception of documents is not exactly known, there are interesting results from psychophysical experiments [1, 2, 3] which can be used in document layout segmentation.

Under the assumption, that the authors and publishers make use of the layout to emphasize the relevant content, a fast extraction of this information should be possible by reverse determination of the emphasis from the layout.

2. Stream Model

According to the communication theoretical model, a sender (author) forms a one-dimensional stream of information (message string M with emphasis and structural tags), and the writing or printing process generates a two-dimensional document. The emphasis and structure is represented by the layout features. The communication channel corresponds to all processes between the ideal document image and the scanned image, like printer and scanner distortions, paper and ink quality and manipulations. The receiver (reader) converts the 2-dim image back to a 1-dim message M' including the emphasis and structural tags (hopefully M = M', which requires e.g. that the reader understands the language, meaning, layout etc. from common sense). In document image analysis the message and emphasis has to be reconstructed from the 2-dimensional image. In this work the main effort is to recognize the emphasized parts from the layout features.
Recently Doerman et. al. [4] introduced the term *function* of a document to describe the efficiency with which a document transfers its information to the reader. A similar messaging model between author and reader is proposed independent on the class of document.

3. Attention measures

An attention value (*attractiveness*) is given to every word or graphics part contained in a document. Each of these

Table 1: Results of questionaire on ranking of layout features (1 = highest ranking)

Question:	block type	layout feature	additional features
Mean deviation:	0.4	0.9	0.8
Ranking:			
1	• halftone	• white space	• color
2		• font size	• ruler/frame
3	• line graphics	• bold	
4		• bullets	• underline
5	• text	• indentation	
6		• all capital	
7		• italics	

Den beiden Anredeformen ***„schïr fü"*** *(für A stungsbereichs) und* ***„tóng dschïr"*** *(Genos ge, Kollegin), die bis vor kurzem allgemein jetzt nur noch gelegentlich begegnen.*

mein Mann.	wǒ hsiān sch
meine Frau.	wǒ tài tài.
mein Sohn.	wǒ ér dsir.
meine Tochter.	wǒ nǚ ér.
mein älterer Bruder.	wǒ gē ge.
mein jüngerer Bruder.	wǒ dì di.
meine ältere Schwe-	wǒ djiě djie.

Figure 1: Examples of texture pattern used by Julesz to study the pre-attentive vision, and to develop the texton theory [2]. For comparison an example from a real document showing similar pre-attentive features for the text blocks and the bold words.

objects displays layout features with a significance value which is normalized to [0,1]. The measure of attention is calculated for each object by weighted summation of the significance values.
The weights were derived from a survey. 46 persons were asked about their perception of document layout, in order to establish a set of relevant layout features and their ranking with respect to attractiveness. Table 1 shows the main questions and the results of the survey, where weight ≈ 1/ranking of respective layout feature.

The determination of the attention measure is performed in three steps:

1. Segmentation into text and graphics blocks according to texton theory and texture model (see below)
2. Determination of the following layout features:
   - for text blocks and words: surrounding white space, font size, indentation, bullets, and font styles bold italics and all-capitals,
   - for graphic blocks: surrounding white space, black intensity, and area.

   (In the survey the persons suggested further layout features like color, rulers, frames, and columns which could be considered in an extended version of the system.)
3. Calculation of attractiveness by normalization and

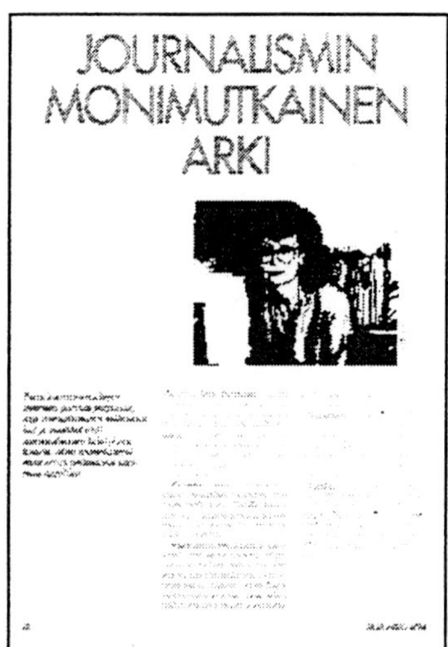

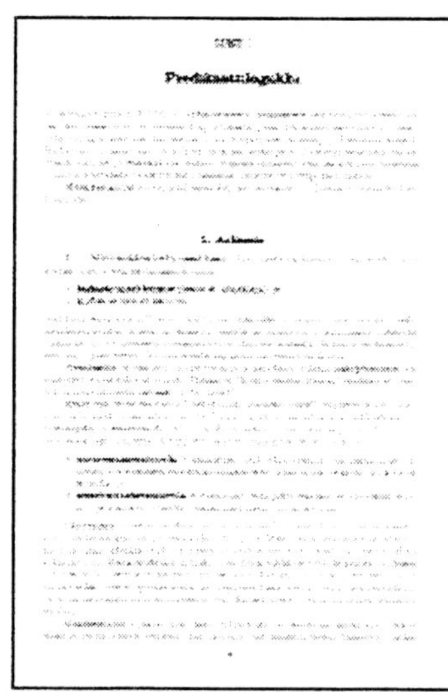

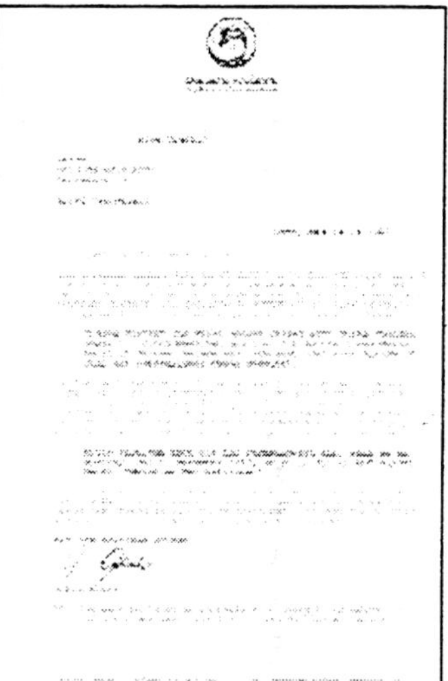

Figure 2: Results of the attention based segmentation. The measure of attractiveness is indicated with increasing gray scale values (from light to dark). The results are plausible for journals, reports and business letters.

summation for words and graphic blocks.

4. Segmentation and layout features

We start with binary images scanned at 300dpi in run-length representation, and perform the texture analysis and segmentation steps on results of connected component analysis, in contrast to [6]. The segmentation is based on the assumption that text consists of texture regions with *textures* at different resolution levels. In [3] text is also treated as texture in four characteristic spatial scales corresponding to the text block, text lines, words and letter levels. The letter level is dominated by small vertical strokes. By psychophysical experiments using synthetic textures made from regularly arranged letters or other simple strokes (see Figure 1), Julesz could discriminate a global and fast pre-attentive visual perception of textures from a slower focal attention which uses local search [2]. In his texton theory he explained this phenomenon by the visual stimulus caused by texture elements (*textons*), which are defined as elongated blobs (strokes) with orientation, width, length and density. We adopted this concept and developed a hierarchical bottom up segmentation starting from strokes (as parts of connected components), letters, words, lines to blocks. Details are given in [5] which also describes a texture-based font style classifier.

In addition to the hierarchical extension of the texton theory we applied the Gestalt principles proximity and continuation to the grouping process of the basic document objects.

As a side effect of the implementation of psychophysical principles we get an understanding of proven layout rules (e.g. the alignment of text lines or blocks).

An alternative approach to attention based segmentation is described in [6], which mainly relies on physiological principles of human vision, like eye movement fixations, analysis of gazing points and space-variant receptive fields (log-polar mapping). It is applicable to arbitrary images using features of similarity, salient angles, etc., whereas our approach is more specific to document images and document layout structures.

5. Results and discussion

Figure 2 shows three examples for the classification of attractiveness on scanned document. The Finnish journals were chosen because the test persons (not Finnish speaking) should not be influenced by the meaning of the text, but the visual appearance is like other Latin languages. Note, that the values of attractiveness are normalized to the highest value on the respective document.

A second survey with interactive display of these results has indicated very reasonable behavior of the measures of attention (Fig. 3).

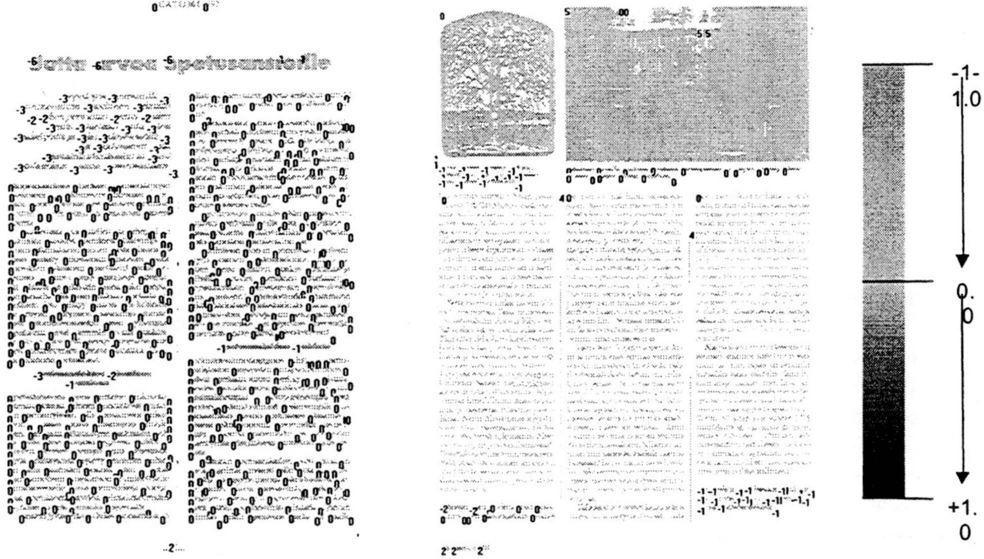

Figure3: Numerical comparison between the computed attractiveness A and the human ranking H measured as the difference A-H. Darker values correspond to higher A than human ranking. Figures and graphics are slightly more emphasized and font styles are less emphasized by the algorithm.

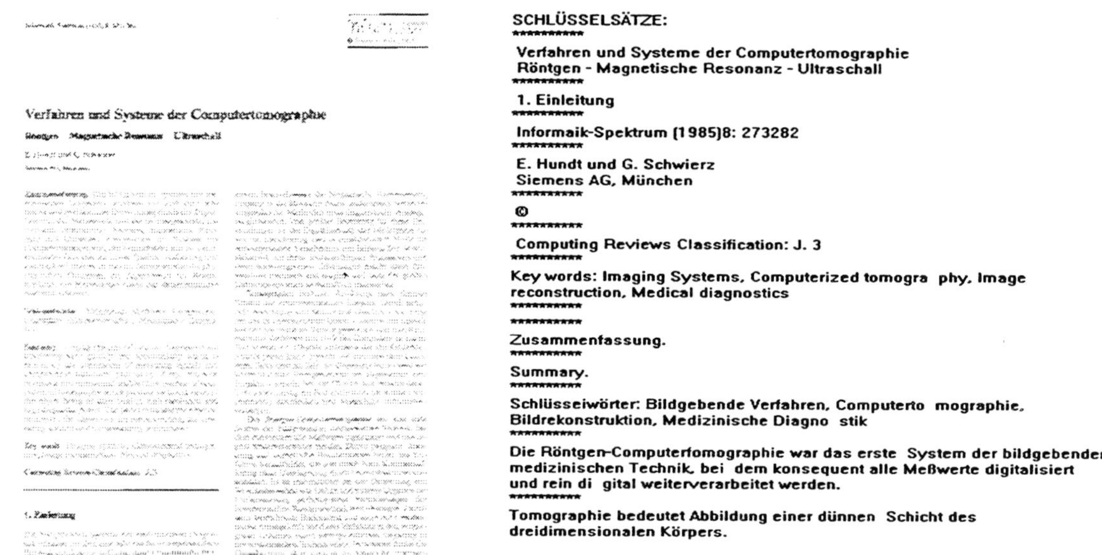

Figure 4: Example of an extracted summary in text form after character recognition in the text blocks with the highest measures of attractiveness $A > A_{thr}$ ($A_{thr} = 0.5$ with $0 < A < 1.0$ and $A_{median} = 0.36$

The textual segments (blocks and words) with high attractiveness have been processed by OCR and arranged in a list of keywords and sentences, sorted in decreasing attractiveness values (Fig. 4). The text between two delimiters (***) corresponds to a text block or a relevant keyword which is followed by the sentence in which it is included.

The performance of the whole extraction process, including connected component analysis, segmentation, layout feature extraction, font classification, and calculation of attractiveness is less than 1 sec per page on a 200 MHz Pentium PC. The accuracy of the attractiveness measures is within the variance of the human evaluation.

6. Conclusion and future work

The layout of a document was successfully used to extract relevant text and non-text information from a document image according to a communication theoretical stream model. Texture analysis using a hierarchy of textons was applied to layout segmentation. Measures of attractiveness are based on psychophysical experiments and were adapted and proven in several surveys.

The most attractive document parts can be extracted as rectangular regions of interest according to their ranking, thus enabling a more efficient interactive browsing through large document archives. Further automatic processing using OCR, document type information and application specific knowledge is in progress. First results have been shown. The attention based layout segmentation and information extraction can be used in browsing, searching and abstracting tools.

12. References

[1] J. R. Anderson: *Cognitive Psychology and its Implications*, W. H. Freeman and Company, San Francisco, 1947

[2] B. Julesz, J. R. Bergen: "Textons: The Fundamental Elements in Pre-attentive Vision and Perception of Textures", *The Bell System Technical Journal*, Vol. 62, No. 6, 1983, pp. 1619 - 1645

[3] R. Watt: "The Visual Analysis of Pages of Text" in R. Sassoon: *Computers and Typography*, Intellect Books, Oxford, 1993, pp. 179 – 201

[4] D. Doermann, E. Revlin , A. Rosenfeld: "The Function of Documents", *Image and Vision Computing*, 16, 1998, pp. 799 - 814

[5] A. Schreyer, P. Suda, G. Maderlechner: "Font Style Detection Using Textons", *Proc. DAS*, Nov. 1988 in Nagano, pp. 99 - 108

[6] V. Eglin, H. Emptoz: "Logarithmic Spiral Grid and Gaze Control for the Development of Strategies of Visual Segmentation on a Document", *Proc. ICDAR*, Aug. 1997 in Ulm, Germany, 1997, pp. 689 – 692

Hough transform for rotation invariant matching of line-drawing images

Pasi Fränti[1], Alexey Mednonogov[2] and Heikki Kälviäinen[2]

[1] Department of Computer Science
University of Joensuu
P.O. Box 111, FIN-80101 Joensuu, FINLAND
Email: franti@cs.joensuu.fi

[2] Department of Information Technology,
Lappeenranta University of Technology
P.O. Box 20, FIN-53851 Lappeenranta, FINLAND
Email: Heikki.Kalviainen,Alexey.Mednonogov@lut.fi

Abstract

Hough transform can be used for indexing of line-drawing images for content-based image retrieval. Angular information is used for generating the feature vector (index) as it gives global description of the image, allows compact indexing, fast retrieval and scale, translation and rotation invariant matching. In the case of very large images, however, the angular information is not always sufficient to differentiate images from each other.

To alleviate this problem, we extend the idea by including also positional information of the lines in the feature vector. This gives more representative description of the images and therefore allows more accurate image matching. The main problems of this approach are: (1) to keep the feature vector compact, and (2) to preserve the property of the matching being translation and rotation invariant. We give solutions to both of these problems and introduce a new indexing scheme, which has better matching accuracy but at the cost of slower retrieval time.

Keywords: content-based retrieval, document image processing, indexing, Hough transform, line-drawings.

1. Introduction

We consider database of complex engineering drawings, e.g., electrical circuits, cartographic maps, architectural and urban plans. We assume that the images are binary (black-and-white) images, and that they consist mainly of lines; this is a reasonable assumption for a variety of engineering drawings. Non-linear components such as symbols and complex curves are not taken into consideration in the assessment of the similarities.

In content-based image retrieval [1], the images are indexed by generating a *feature vector* describing the content of the image. Given the sample image, the task is to find all database images similar to the query image. Image retrieval is performed by measuring the similarity of the feature vectors of the query image and the database images.

The selection of the features is the key part of the indexing scheme. The size of the feature vector should be small enough to be stored compactly and processed efficiently, but it should also representative so that then images can be differentiated from each other on the basis of their feature vectors.

Hough transform [2-5] is well suited for this task because it gives a global description of the spatial image content. It makes no assumptions on the image type and, in principle, it should be applicable to any type of bi-level images. In a recent study [6], we have studied the use of angular information of Hough transform for the indexing. This solution allows compact indexing, fast retrieval and scale, translation and rotation invariant matching. Unfortunately the angular information is not always sufficient to differentiate images.

In the present paper, we extend the previous idea and include positional information of the lines in the feature vector. We utilize the full accumulator matrix, which is thresholded and binarized in order to keep the feature vector compact. The matching is revised in order to preserve scale, translation and rotation invariant matching.

2. Hough transform

In Hough Transform, global features are sought as sets of individual points over the whole image. In the simplest case the features are straight line segments. In the case of binary images, the line detection algorithm can be described as follows:

1. Create the set D of the black pixels in the image.
2. Transform each pixel in D into a parameteric curve in the parameter space.
3. Increment the cells in the accumulator matrix A determined by the parametric curve.
4. Detect local maxima in the accumulator array. Each local maximum may correspond to a parametric curve in the image space.
5. Extract the curve segments using the knowledge of the maximum positions.

In Step 2, the transformation can be $\rho = x \cdot \cos\theta + y \cdot \sin\theta$ where (x, y) are the coordinates of the pixel to be transformed, and ρ and θ are the parameters of the corresponding line. Thus, every pixel (x, y) can be seen as a curve in the (ρ, θ) parameter space where θ varies from the minimum to the maximum value, giving the corresponding ρ values. By transforming every point (x, y) in the image into the parameter space, the line parameters can be found in the intersections of the parameterized curves in the accumulator matrix.

3. Indexing using angular information

We denote the accumulator matrix by A, where each row in corresponds to one value of ρ, and each column to one value of θ. The procedure for generating the feature vector from the accumulator matrix is described in Fig. 1. First we extract only the most significant information by thresholding the matrix using a threshold value T (Step 1). Next, we shrink the thresholded accumulator matrix to one-dimensional θ-vector by summing up the remaining coefficients in each column (Step 2). Finally, we normalize the feature vectors according to the mean value of the components of the vector (Steps 3 and 4).

1. Threshold the matrix:

$$A'_{ij} = \begin{cases} A_{ij}, & \text{if } A_{ij} > T \\ 0, & \text{if } A_{ij} \le T \end{cases} \quad \forall\ i = 1..M,\ j = 1..N$$

2. Calculate preliminary feature vector:

$$F_j^0 = \sum_{i=1}^{M} A'_{ij} \quad \forall\ j = 1..N$$

3. Calculate vector mean:

$$m = \frac{1}{N}\sum_{j=1}^{N} F_j^0$$

4. Normalize the feature vector:

$$F_j = \frac{F_j^0}{m} \quad \forall\ j = 1..N$$

Figure 1: Algorithm for generating feature vector.

The use of only angular information (θ-vector) has the advantage that the matching is independent of the spatial location of the lines and therefore the method is translation and scaling invariant by its nature.

We approximate the dissimilarity of the images by calculating the distance of their feature vectors. Let us assume that we got feature vector D for database image and feature vector S for sample query image (both of size N). The distance is calculated as:

$$d = \sum_{j=1}^{N} (D_j - S_j)^2 \tag{1}$$

where d=0 coincides to absolutely similar images and d=d_{max} coincides to images with no similarities found.

Rotation invariant matching of the method can be obtained if we consider the matching as a histogram matching problem. The best match can be found by rotating the feature vector of the sample query image, and calculating the distance in all positions. The distance of the feature vectors is thus defined as the minimum distance of all possible fittings:

$$d = \min_{k=1,2,\ldots,N} \sum_{j=1}^{N} (D_j - S_j^{(k)})^2 \tag{2}$$

where $S^{(k)}$ is a vector obtained by cyclic rotation of the feature vector S by k steps to the right. Thus, we use exhaustive search for finding the minimum distance. This requires $O(N^2)$ time, where N is the size of the feature vector.

4. Indexing using full matrix

The angular information can be sufficient for differentiating images with clearly different types. For example, drawing of buildings consists mainly of 45° and 90° angles. However, large and more complex images can result in practically uniform distribution of θ-values and in this case, the use of angular information is not sufficient to differentiate such images.

We propose to use the full matrix and in this way, utilize also the spatial location of the lines in respect to each other. The main problem of this approach is that the matrix can be quite large even after thresholding. This is because the lines are recognized not only by their orientation (θ) but also by their location (ρ). This will distribute the observations wider in the feature space. At the same time, the storage and retrieval constraints forces us to keep the size of the feature vector relatively small.

We reduce the amount of information in two ways. Firstly, we extract only the K most significant information by thresholding the matrix. This was done also in the θ-based approach. In addition to that, we perform binarization of the thresholded values.

Secondly, we optimize the size of the accumulator array by normalizing the coordinate space. This is done by calculating the centroid (μ_x,μ_y), i.e. the arithmetic average of the location of the object pixels:

$$\mu_x = \frac{1}{NM}\sum_{i=1}^{NM} x_i \qquad \mu_y = \frac{1}{NM}\sum_{i=1}^{NM} y_i \tag{3}$$

The purpose of the normalization is to utilize the accuracy of the array more effectively by eliminating empty space from the matrix. We can now obtain a proper range for ρ by calculating the standard deviation of the spatial location of the object pixels in respect to their centroid:

$$\sigma = \sqrt{\frac{1}{NM}\sum_{i=1}^{NM}\left\{(x_i - \mu_x)^2 + (y_i - \mu_y)^2\right\}} \tag{4}$$

The range can then be defined as:

$$[\rho_{\min}, \rho_{\max}] = [0, 2.5 \cdot \sigma] \tag{5}$$

where 2.5 is a constant so that approximately 99% of the pixels belong to the range, assuming that the pixels are scattered around the centroid with Gaussian distribution.

Denote the binary matrix value of the database image as D_{ij}, and of the query image as S_{ij}. Scaling and translation invariant matching can be obtained by calculating their distance as:

$$d_{TS} = \sum_{S_{ij}\neq 0}^{NM} \min_{D_{kl}\neq 0}\left\{(i-k)^2 + (j-l)^2\right\} \tag{6}$$

Using this equation we define rotation invariant matching by rotating the feature matrix along the θ-axis, and calculating the distance in all positions. The distance is defined as the minimum distance of all possible fittings:

$$d_{RTS} = \min_{m} \sum_{S^{(m)}\neq 0} d_{TS} \tag{7}$$

In the database, the feature matrix is stored as a list of the preserved values: $\{(\theta_1,\rho_1), (\theta_2,\rho_2), \ldots, (\theta_K,\rho_K)\}$. In this way, the feature vector can be stored compactly, and the space requirement (in bits) is:

$$K \cdot \log_2(\rho_{\max} - \rho_{\min}) + K \cdot \log_2 360 \tag{8}$$

5. Experiments

We test the retrieval accuracy of the proposed method using a small image database of 10 images shown in Fig. 2.

The database is generated by taking two different vector objects as the starting point. The objects were rotated by 5, 10, 15, 20 and 25 degrees around the *y*-axis and the corresponding images were stored in the database. The idea is that the rotation is performed in 3-D vector space and not in the 2-D image plane. The original images are denoted as image *A* and *B*, and their rotated versions as images *A1*, *A2*, *A3*, *A4*, *A5*, *B1*, *B2*, *B3*, *B4*, *B5*.

Next we generate four query images from the two original images, as shown in Fig. 3. The first query image (*a1s*) is a scaled version of the image *A*, and the second one (*a1sr*) is a scaled and rotated version of the same image. The third (*b1s*) and fourth (*b1sr*) images are generated from the image *B* respectively. The hypothesis is that the first two query images should match the database image *A1* since only scaling and 2-D rotation were performed. Slightly weaker matching should be made to the images *A2*, *A3*, *A4* and *A5*. Moreover, the images *a1s* and *a1sr* should not match to *B1*, *B2*, *B3*, *B4* and *B5*.

The results of the matching of images *a1s* and *a1sr* are show in Fig. 4 as the distance between the query image and the database image. The results verify the hypothesis as the image *A1* is the closest to both *a1s* and *a1sr*. The results also show that the images *A2* and *A3* are rather close according to the measured distance values of both approaches. The images *A4* and *A5*, however, do not match as well in the case of θ-based approaches as their distance is already as far as that of the best matched images *B4* and *B5* in the wrong test set. The full matrix approach, on the other hand, is clearly capable of differentiating the two image sets in the case of all five images. The results (not shown here) for *b1s* and *b1sr* are similar for the θ-based approach and even better for the full matrix approach.

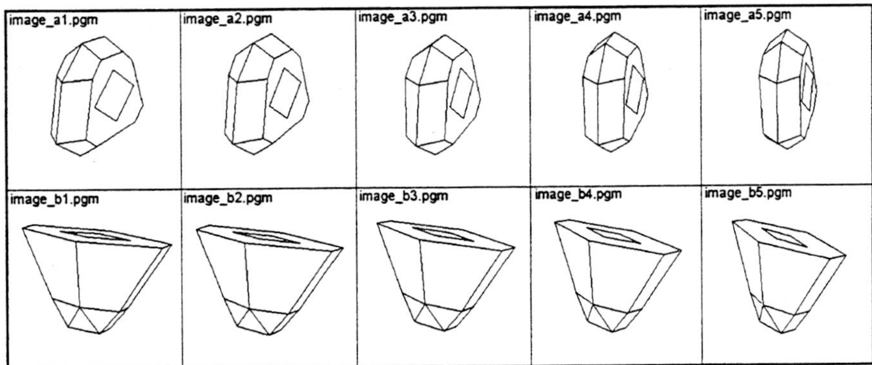

Figure 2: Test database of 10 images. The images have been generated by performing 3-D rotation for the two original images (*Image A* and *Image B*).

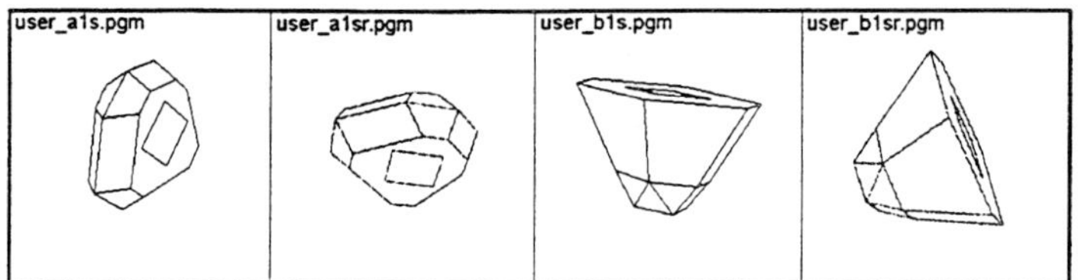

Figure 3: Four query images from left to right: scaled version of *Image A*, scaled and 2-D rotated version of *Image A*, scaled version of *Image B*, scaled and 2-D rotated version of *Image B*.

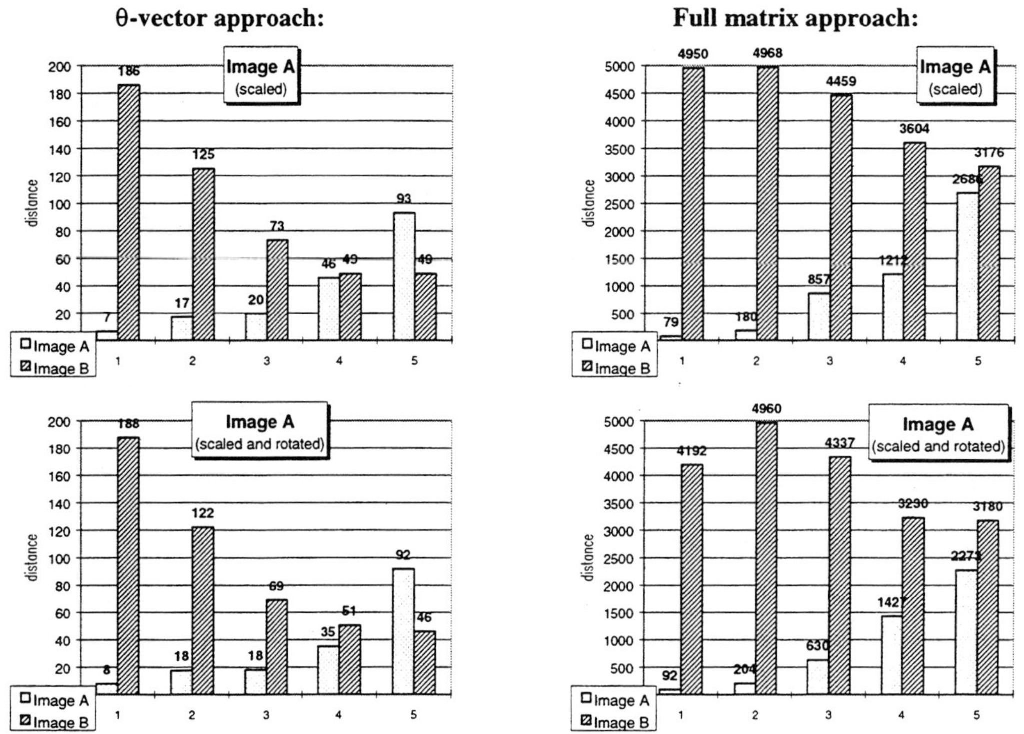

Figure 4: Matching results of the query image *A* (scaled=*a1s*, scaled and rotated=*a1sr*). The left colum shows the results for the θ-based approach according to (2), and the right column for the full matrix approach according to (7).

6. Conclusions

We introduced a novel method for indexing of line-drawing images using Hough transform. The index was generated as the list of *K* most significant values of the Hough matrix. The proposed indexing scheme works well for content-based image retrieval where the aim is to find images that are similar to a given query image. The method is invariant of scaling, translation and rotation. Extension to gray-scale and color image seems to be straightforward, too.

References

1. W.-Y. Ma, H.J. Zhang, "Content-based image indexing and retrieval", in *Handbook of Multimedia Computing*, pp.227-254, CRC Press, 1999
2. P.C.V. Hough, Methods and means for recognizing complex patterns. U.S. Patent 3,069,654, 1962
3. J.R. Parker, *Algorithms for image processing and computer vision*. John Willey & Sons, 1996
4. V.F. Leavers, Survey: Which Hough Transform. *CVGIP Image Understanding* 58 (2): 250-264, 1993.
5. H. Kälviäinen, P. Hirvonen, L. Xu, E. Oja, Probabililistic, non-probabilistic Hough transforms: overview and comparisons. *Image, Vision Computing* 13 (4), 239-251, May 1995.
6. P. Fränti, A. Mednonogov, V. Kyrki and H. Kälviäinen, "Content-based retrieval of line-drawing images using Hough transform", Res. Report 71, Dept. of IT, Lappeenranta Univ. of Technology, May 2000.

Image-based Document Vectors for Text Retrieval

Zhaohui Yu, Chew Lim Tan
School of Computing, National University of Singapore
Email: yuzhaohu, tancl@comp.nus.edu.sg

Abstract

We propose a method for constructing a vector for a document image to represent its content to facilitate text retrieval. The method is based on an N-Gram algorithm for text similarity measure based on the frequency of occurrence of n-character strings appearing in the electronic text. Instead of using ASCII values, the present study investigates the use of character images to obtain the document vector and has found promising results for use in our news article retrieval project.

Keywords: *Document Image, Text Retrieval, Similarity Measure, N-Gram Algorithm*

1 Introduction

This paper describes a novel approach to construct a document vector as a similarity measure using N-Gram algorithm without the recognition of the characters. The application we have in mind is the text retrieval from newspaper microfilm images [1].

Figure 1 outlines the steps in constructing vectors of document images based on contents. To identify the features, character objects in the predominant font are extracted from image documents and then character object equivalent classes are identified based on shape similarity. From several sets of classes, one unified class set can be estimated. The objects, which belong to the same class, are assumed to represent the same term. Layout analysis is performed to determine the reading order of character objects. An object sequence can be obtained from each image document to construct a vector using N-Gram algorithm. These document vectors are used to calculate the similarity between image-based document.

The remainder of this paper is organized as follows. Section 2 presents the stages to construct document vector and similarity measure. Section 3 describes experimental results that demonstrate the effect of these techniques. Finally, conclusions and future work are given in Section 4.

2 Document Vector Construction

We will discuss how character features are extracted for vector construction and how vectors are used for similarity measure.

2.1 Character Object Class

In document image, there are three kinds of character object. The first is isolated character, which has only one connected component. The second is also isolated character, but it has more than one connected component,

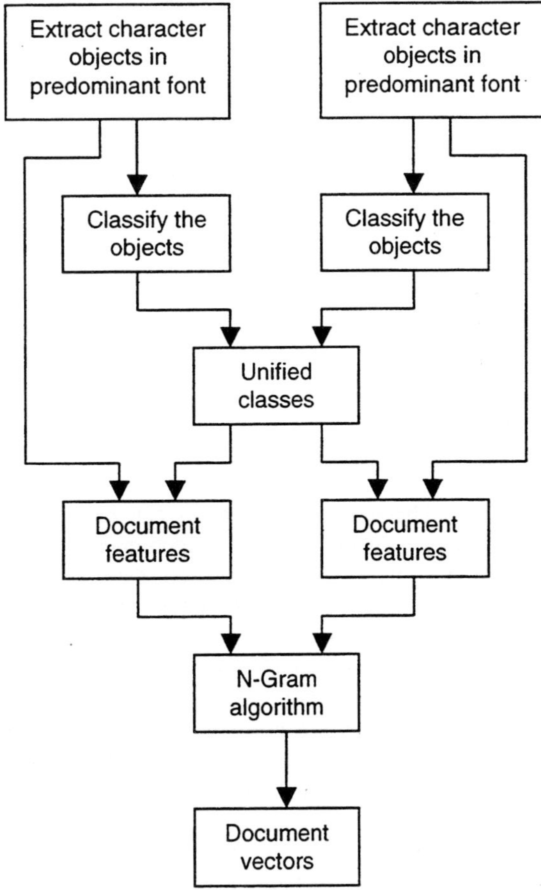

Figure 1. Construction of document vectors

such as lower character “i” and “j”. The third is several characters that are connected to each other.

Character object can be extracted by measuring the connected components of image and comparing the relative positions of adjacent components. One object includes only one connected component or several connected components, which have unambiguous relative positions.

In newspapers, the main body of text is usually printed in the one font, which is generally the predominant font, whereas headings and captions may appear in a variety of fonts. For construction of document vectors, only text in the predominant fonts is considered. To identify character object corresponding to the same term, an unsupervised classifier is used to place each character object into a set of classes. Each class is regarded as representing one unique term.

For each character object, we can create a vertical traverse density (VTD) vector and a horizontal traverse density (HTD) vector. For the character object m and n in image document, they will belong to same class, if

$$diff(VTD_m, VTD_n) \le Threshold * \min(w_m, w_n)$$

and

$$diff(HTD_m, HTD_n) \le Threshold * \min(h_m, h_n)$$

Where, $diff(V_1, V_2)$ is a function to calculate the difference between the vector V_1 and V_2, w_i and h_i is the width and height of object i. Otherwise, the character object m and n belong to different classes.

The result of classification is shown in Figure 2. Item (a) is the original image and item (b) show the extracted character objects. In item (c), each rectangle outlines a character object extracted and the number expresses the sequence number of class that the object belongs to. The objects that have same number represent same term. Item (d) list the total class set created from this image.

2.2 Unifying Character Object Class

One set of character object classes can be obtained from each image document. The predominant fonts of different images may have different font sizes. And the numbers of different sets of classes maybe also different. To find a unified way to express the feature of image documents, we must build a unified object classes.

Firstly, the VTD vector and HTD vector of all character object classes are normalised. The number of permitted dimension of vectors is set sufficiently large. All the features of VTD and HTD will be preserved. The normalised classes are then classified again to create a set of unified classes. Finally, a look-up table from the original class set to the unified class set is built for each image document. Using these tables, all character objects in these image documents can be mapped to the unified character object classes. The objects corresponding to the same class will be regarded as representing the same term.

After all character objects have been expressed by a set of classes, the layout analysis is performed to determine the reading order of character objects and the space

DILI — The young men with the long hair and the camouflage jackets were back on duty yesterday in their east Dili neighbourhood, taking no chances against a return of the feared pro-Indonesian militia.

(a)

DILI — The young men with the long hair and the camouflage jackets were back on duty yesterday in their east Dili neighbourhood, taking no chances against a return of the feared pro-Indonesian militia.

(b)

DILI — The young men with the long hair and the camouflage jackets were back on duty yesterday in their east Dili neighbourhood, taking no chances against a return of the feared pro-Indonesian militia.

(c)

0 D 1 I 2 L 3 T 4 h 5 e 6 y 7 o 8 u 9 n 10 g 11 m 12 wi 13 t 14 l 15 a 16 i 17 r 18 d 19 c 20 fl 21 j 22 k 23 s 24 w 25 b 26 ty 27 as 28 f 29 p

(d)

Figure 2. Character objects and classification

between two adjacent objects. One list is built for each document. The item of list is the sequence number of class that the character object belongs to. This list will be used to construct the document vector.

2.3 Similarity between Vectors

The use of N-Gram algorithm in various text processing has been reported in [2,3,4]. On the other hand, instead of text processing, the use of character images has been attempted by researchers [5-9] for summary extraction, similarity measurement and document retrieval. The present method attempted to use image-processing approach to the text-based N-Gram method. The algorithm is adapted for image-based similarity measure.

First, the class number list is converted to a set of n-gram slices. An n-gram is an n-item slice of a stream. N-grams, which are sequences of n consecutive items, are copied out of the list using a window of n-item length, which is moved over the list one item forward at a time.

Secondly, every possible n-gram is given a number, so called hash key. How the n-grams are numbered is not important, as long as each instance of a certain n-gram is always given the same number, and that two different n-grams are always assigned different numbers.

Then, a hash table is created to keep track of how many times each n-gram has been found in the list being studied. Every time an n-gram is picked, the element of the hash table given to the n-gram is increased by one. When all n-grams have been put into a hash table, the occurrence numbers of the hash table is divided by total number of extracted n-grams. This means that the absolute number of occurrence will be replaced with the relative frequencies of corresponding n-grams. The reason for doing this is that similar texts of different lengths after this normalisation will have similar hash tables.

Lastly, the hash tables are used to calculate the similarity. The hash tables can be treated as document vectors. Document vectors from the similar text point in almost the same direction. The similarity score between two texts is defined as their scalar product divided by their lengths. A scalar product is calculated through summing up the products of the corresponding elements. This is the same thing as the cosine of the angle between two documents seen from the origin. So, the similarity between image document *m* and *n* will be

$$Similarity(X_m, X_n) = \frac{\sum_{j=1}^{J} x_{mj} x_{nj}}{\sqrt{\sum_{j=1}^{J} x_{mj}^2 \sum_{j=1}^{J} x_{nj}^2}}$$

Where, X_m and X_n are the document vector of image *m* and *n*, *J* is the dimension number of document vector, and $X_i = x_{i1} x_{i2} \cdots x_{iJ}$.

3 Experimental results

To verify the validity of our method, the corpus was selected from recent international news in *The Strait Times*, a major local newspaper. In this corpus, four articles talk about Indonesia. And the other four talk about the news in Japan, Kampuchea, Thailand and Russia respectively. The paper articles were scanned at 600 pixels/inch (ppi). To make the process simple, some preprocessing is done. First, the images are de-skewed. Then, noise such as small dirty spots is removed from the image. Next, headings and captions are removed from the imaged documents. As a standard of evaluating, ASCII version articles of original documents are created. An OCR system is used to extract the text in the documents and the text was then hand-corrected.

The processed images are used as the input to our method. As a comparison, the ASCII version of articles is used to extract the n-gram slices and build the document vectors. From the document vectors, we also can obtain a group result of the similarity of each pair documents. The two group results are shown in Table 1, in which *n* of N-Gram algorithm is equal to six.

From the result, we can see that the similarities of documents measured from both methods share some resemblance though not entirely equivalent to each other. The result of ASCII version of documents provides more distinguishable similarity measure. This is because that the character objects we extracted are not equivalent to characters and the objects corresponding to same character may be classified into different object classes.

But the two results exhibit similar trend. When two ASCII version documents have large similarity, their corresponding image documents also have large similarity. Figure 3 shows the comparison of the similarities between news N04 to the other news. Where, the square points show the result of image documents, and the diamond points show the result of ASCII version documents.

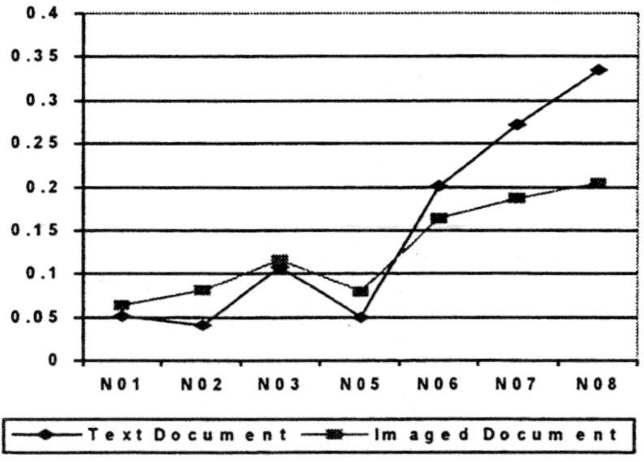

Figure 3. The similarity between news N04 and the other news

4 Conclusion and Future Work

We proposed a document vector construction process based on an N-Gram algorithm without the use of OCR. We extract the features of document images by obtaining and classifying the character objects. Then, N-Grams algorithm is used to measure their similarity. This method is suited for gauging the similarity of image documents that have the same font style. It is our future research direction to examine for those documents of different font styles. The final objective of our method is to be used for microfilm images in a news retrieval project. Microfilm images are noisier than the images studied in the present project. So, how to deal with noise will also be another future research.

References

[1] C.L. Tan, S.Y. Sung, D. Shi, B. Yuan, Y.T. Lim, Y. Xu, "News articles retrieval from microfilm images" , IJCAI'99 Workshop:Text Mining: Foundations, Techniques and Application, Stockholm, Sweden, August 2, 1999, pages 110-116

[2] Marc Damashek, "Gauging similarity via n-grams: Language-independent sorting, categorization, and retrieval of text", Science, 267, 1995, pages 843-848

[3] Cavnar, William B., and Trenkle, John M., "N-Gram-Based text categorization", Proceedings of the 1994 Symposium On Document Analysis and Information Retrieval, University of Nevada, Las Vegas, April 1994.

[4] C.Y. Suen, "N-gram statistics for natural language understanding and text processing" IEEE Trans. on Pattern Analysis & Machine Intelligence. Vol. PAMI-1, No. 2, April 1979, pages 164-172

[5] F.R. Chen and D.S. Bloomberg, "Extraction of thematically relevant text from images", Proceeding of the Symposium on Document Analysis and Information Retrieval, 1996, pages 163-178

[6] F.R. Chen, D.S. Bloomberg, "Extraction of indicative summary sentences from imaged documents", Proceedings of the Fourth International Conference on Document Analysis and Recognition (ICDAR'97), Volume 1, 1997, pages 227-232

[7] J.J. Hull; J.F. Cullen, "Document image similarity and equivalence detection", Proceedings of the Fourth International Conference on Document Analysis and Recognition (ICDAR'97), Volume 1, 1997, pages 308-312

[8] D. Doermann, Li Huiping, O. Kia, "The detection of duplicates in document image databases", Proceedings of the Fourth International Conference on Document Analysis and Recognition (ICDAR'97), Volume 1, 1997, pages 314-318

[9] Yaodong He; Zao Jiang; Bing Liu; Hong Zhao, "Content-based indexing and retrieval method of Chinese document images", Proceedings of the Fifth International Conference on Document Analysis and Recognition (ICDAR'99), 1999, pages 685-688

[10]A.F. Smeaton, A.L. Spitz, "Using character shape coding for information retrieval", Proceeding of the Fourth International Conference on Document Analysis and Recognition (ICDAR'97), Volume 2, 1997, pages 974-978

Table 1. Comparison of document similarity between N-Gram algorithm (text mode) and our method

		N01	N02	N03	N04	N05	N06	N07	N08	News Title
N01	*	1.000	0.067	0.060	0.051	0.049	0.050	0.038	0.057	Wanted A Japanese Bill Gates
	**	1.000	0.089	0.070	0.064	0.093	0.100	0.093	0.103	
N02	*	0.067	1.000	0.117	0.041	0.058	0.087	0.027	0.066	Bangkok wants thais to holiday at home
	**	0.089	1.000	0.113	0.081	0.090	0.111	0.097	0.105	
N03	*	0.060	0.117	1.000	0.108	0.187	0.107	0.064	0.070	Hun Sen set to meet Annan over tribunal
	**	0.070	0.113	1.000	0.117	0.161	0.135	0.116	0.120	
N04	*	0.051	0.041	0.108	1.000	0.050	0.201	0.271	0.335	Plan to send more police to Dili
	**	0.064	0.081	0.117	1.000	0.080	0.164	0.187	0.205	
N05	*	0.049	0.058	0.187	0.050	1.000	0.113	0.058	0.075	Russian graft probe moves to Switzerland
	**	0.093	0.090	0.161	0.080	1.000	0.156	0.140	0.117	
N06	*	0.050	0.087	0.107	0.201	0.113	1.000	0.252	0.370	Tensions rise after vote in East Timer
	**	0.100	0.111	0.135	0.164	0.156	1.000	0.213	0.278	
N07	*	0.038	0.027	0.064	0.271	0.058	0.252	1.000	0.347	Vigilantes taking no chances
	**	0.093	0.097	0.116	0.187	0.140	0.213	1.000	0.256	
N08	*	0.057	0.066	0.070	0.335	0.075	0.370	0.347	1.000	Jakarta rushes troops to E. Timor
	**	0.103	0.105	0.120	0.205	0.117	0.278	0.256	1.000	

Notes:

*: The result of N-Gram algorithm based on text-mode documents.

**: The result of out method.

Parameter-independent Geometric Document Layout Analysis *

Dae-Seok Ryu[1], Sun-Mee Kang[2], and Seong-Whan Lee[1]
[1]Center for Artificial Vision Research, Korea University
Anam-dong, Seongbuk-ku, Seoul 136-701, Korea
{dsryu, swlee}@image.korea.ac.kr
[2] Dept. of Computer Science, Seokyeong University
Chongnung-dong, Seongbuk-ku, Seoul 136-704, Korea
smkang@bukak.seokyeong.ac.kr

Abstract

We propose a new method independent of parameters for segmenting the document images into maximal homogeneous regions and identifying them as texts, images, tables and lines. A pyramidal quadtree structure is constructed for multiscale analysis and top-down approach, and a periodicity measure is suggested to find a periodical attribute of text regions. To obtain robust page segmentation results, a confirmation procedure using texture analysis is applied to only ambiguous regions. Experimental results with the document database from the University of Washington show that the proposed method works better than the previous ones.

1. Introduction

With the advance in information technology and the increased need for information, the volume of documents containing information has increased more and more. In spite of the use of electronic documents, the amount of paper documents has never decreased, because the publication of newspapers, periodicals, reports, books, etc. has increased continuously, and most human beings prefer paper documents for reading and archiving.

However, it is very difficult and cumbersome to store and retrieve the ever increasing number of paper documents. On the contrary, electronic documents have several advantages in storage, retrieval and updating. If paper documents could be converted to electronic documents automatically, it would be possible to search for the contents of the documents in seconds, and to retrieve and update them efficiently. However, it is not trivial to automatically transform paper documents into electronic format. To achieve this transformation, geometric document layout analysis should be performed first of all. Geometric document layout analysis involves specifying the geometry of the maximal homogeneous regions and classifying them into text, image, table, drawing, etc.

A number of approaches have been proposed in various ways for page segmentation and geometric document layout analysis. One major problem associated with previous methods is the dependence on thresholds and parameters, so adaptively setting the various thresholds and parameters has been unavoidable [3].

In this paper, we present a new method, with which we are able to segment a document image, independent of parameters, even though various character font sizes and text spacings may exist.

2. Proposed geometric document layout analysis method

The proposed method for page segmentation and region identification is described as follows: Given a binary document image,

1. Construct a pyramidal quadtree structure, and get multiscale images of the input document image (section 2.1).
2. Extract bounding boxes of connected components for the top-level image.
3. Estimate the periodicity of each region along the horizontal and vertical directions at each level except the top level, and get the periodical attribute of a region (section 2.2).
4. If a region is not a single periodical region, find a position for splitting and split it into two regions (section 2.3).
5. Repeat steps 3-4 until the region becomes a single periodical region.
6. Confirm the segmentation results (section 2.4).
7. Identify each maximal homogeneous region as text, image, table and line (section 2.5).

*This research was supported by Creative Research Initiatives of the Ministry of Science and Technology, Korea.

2.1. Construction of pyramidal quadtree structure

Human beings at first glance see an object in a low resolution and gradually see it closer in a higher resolution. In order to simulate this, the pyramidal quadtree structure is employedas shown in Figure 1.

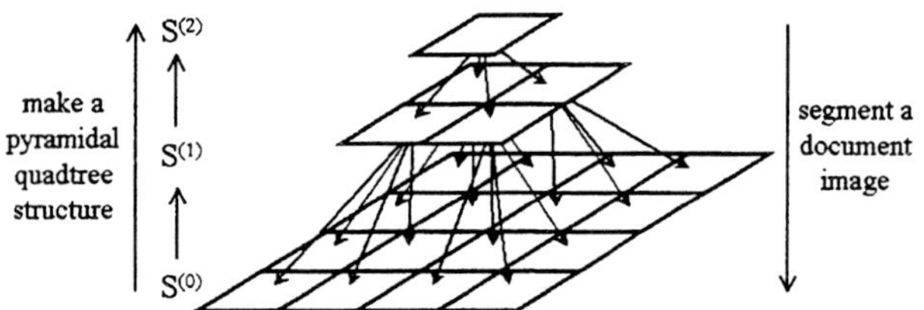

Figure 1. The pyramidal quadtree structure in the case of 3 levels

2.2. Periodicity estimation

Text regions can be easily distinguished from the other regions by the property that text lines of a paragraph are aligned horizontally or vertically and have almost the same line spacing. If we apply this property of text regions to page segmentation, we could easily segment not only text regions but also the other regions into each homogeneous region. For this purpose, we concentrate on extracting the periodical attribute of a text region and we call it a periodicity. The sequence of finding the periodicity of a region is shown in Figure 2.

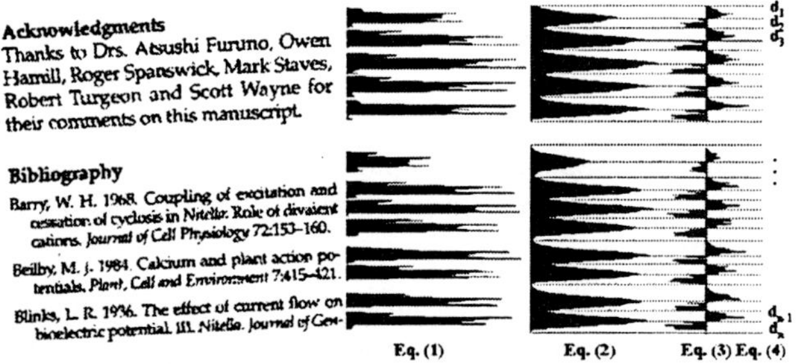

Figure 2. The sequence of finding a periodicity of a region (left to right)

First, we find the page skew angle (θ) by a skew detection algorithm [1], and then get the horizontal (or vertical) projection profile according to the page skew angle (θ), as shown in Eq.(1). In this equation, $I(x, y)$ is the intensity value in a $width \times height$ image, and $P_H^{(n)}$ is the horizontal projection profile at the nth level.

$$P_H^{(n)} = \{p_y \mid p_y = \sum_{x=0}^{width-1} I(x, y + x\tan\theta),\ 0 \leq y < height\} \quad (1)$$

At the second step, smoothing is applied to control the amount of details in the projection profile, as shown in Eq.(2), where s is the kernel size and m_y is integer value.

$$\begin{aligned} M_H^{(n)} &= \{m_y \mid m_y = \lfloor \frac{1}{s} \sum_{i=y-s/2}^{y+s/2} p_i \rfloor, \\ &\qquad 0 \leq y < height,\ p_i \in P_H^{(n)}\} \end{aligned} \quad (2)$$

At the third step, we find the first derivative of the smoothed projection profile, or get the gradients of neighbored elements in the smoothed projection profile, as described in Eq.(3).

$$F_H^{(n)} = \{f_y \mid f_y = \frac{dm_y}{dx},\ 0 \leq y < height,\ m_y \in M_H^{(n)}\} \quad (3)$$

At the fourth step, using Eq.(4) we find the zero crossing points which are correspond to local maxima or minima points of the smoothed projection profile.

$$\begin{aligned} Z^{(n)} &= \{z \mid (f_z < 0\ and\ f_{z+1} \geq 0)\ or \\ &\qquad (f_z > 0\ and\ f_{z+1} \leq 0), f_z \in F_H^{(n)}\} \end{aligned} \quad (4)$$

Therefore, the variation in the distances between neighboring zero crossing points, calculated by Eq.(5), indicates the frequency distribution of the region. That the variation of a region is low means that the frequency distribution of text lines of the region is almost the same, that is, the region is composed of a homogeneous region. On the other hand, that the variation of a region is high means that the frequency distribution of text lines of the region is jagged, so the region needs to be segmented further.

$$V = \frac{\sum_{i=1}^{n}(d_i - m)^2}{n}, \quad \begin{cases} d_i = z_{i+1} - z_i,\ z_i \in Z^{(n)} \\ m = \frac{\sum_{i=1}^{n} d_i}{n} \end{cases} \quad (5)$$

In the same way, we can compute vertical projection profile, its variance, and the periodicity of a region in the vertical direction.

2.3. Determination of splitting position

When a region is determined that it requires further splitting because it is not a homogeneous region, there are two cases in the horizontal direction, as shown in Figure 3. The case (a) of Figure 3 needs to be split more because one white space is larger than the other white spaces, and the case (b) of Figure 3 needs to be split more because one black space is larger than the other black spaces. In these two cases, we find a suitable position for splitting using the method given in the following, and split it into two regions.

Let W denote the set of white spaces of a region, w_i
Let B denote the set of black spaces of a region, b_i
Sort the set W(or B) in the increasing order of the magnitude of w_i(or b_i)
$w_{med} \leftarrow$ the median element of W
$b_{med} \leftarrow$ the median element of B
$w_{max} \leftarrow$ the last element of W
$b_{max} \leftarrow$ the last element of B

if $w_i > w_{med}$ and $w_i = w_{max}$, split w_i
if $b_i > b_{med}$ and $b_i = b_{max}$, split w_{i-1}

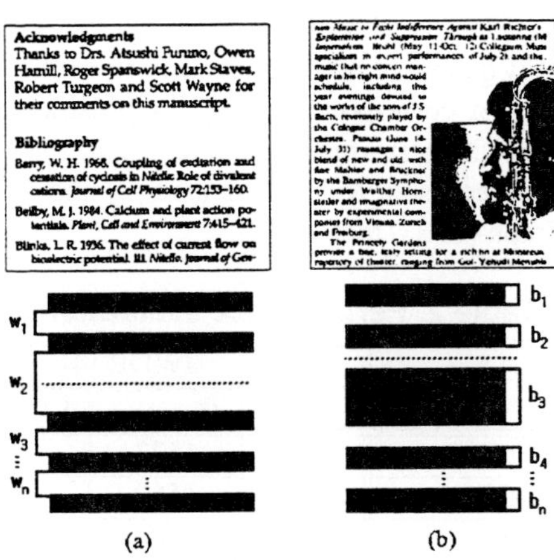

Figure 3. Two cases requiring further horizontal splitting

The processes described in section 2.2 and 2.3 are repeated for each region until no further splitting is required.

2.4. Confirmation of segmentation results

By repeating the processes described in section 2.2 and 2.3, we segmented a document image into maximal homogeneous regions. However, there are three types of segmentation or identification errors with only the periodicity estimation, as shown in Figure 4.

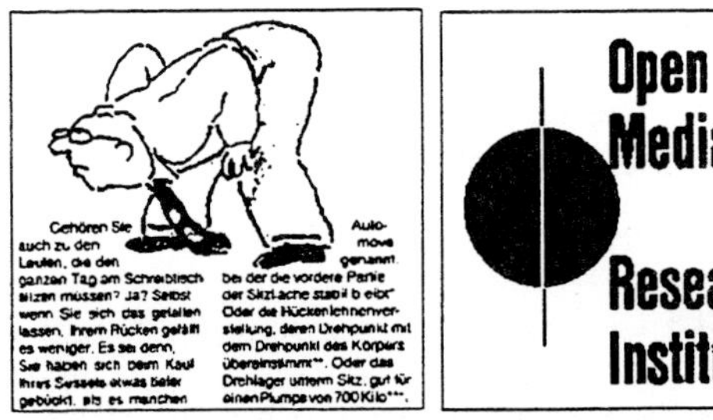

(a) Touching or overlapping regions

(b) A region beginning with a very large character

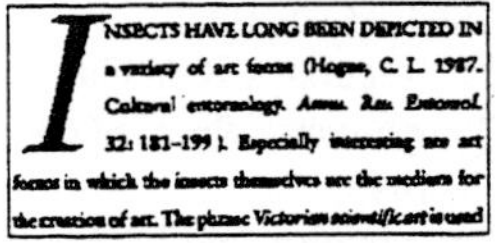

Ministry of Defence

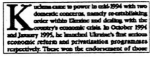

(c) A region composed of a few words and a single text line

Figure 4. Examples of error causing images

If a region is composed of a single period and has just one peak in the smoothed horizontal projection profile, we can not be confident with only the result of the periodicity estimation. Therefore, in this case, we confirm whether it is a homogeneous region or not by its texture analysis. In this paper, 2D Harr wavelet transform is adopted for texture analysis, since it is the simplest and fastest transform among the wavelet transforms and can be applied to binary images.

By 2D Harr wavelet transform, a document image can be transformed into four sub-images: LL, LH, HL, and HH sub-images [5]. And it can be computed repeatedly from level 1 to level N with a pyramidal algorithm by using Eq.(6).

$$LL^{(n)} = LL^{(n-1)} + LH^{(n-1)} + HL^{(n-1)} + HH^{(n-1)} \quad (6)$$

In order to classify the transform coefficients into images, texts, horizontal lines, and vertical lines, we first assign the coefficients $c, c \in \{I, T, H, V\}$, to the corresponding classes (image, text, horizontal line, or vertical line) according to Table 1, at each level. If the coefficient is high in the LH sub-image and low in the HL sub-image, it means that there are only horizontal components, therefore, we assign it to horizontal line(H). On the other hand, if the coefficient is low in the LH sub-image and high in the HL sub-image, it means that there are only vertical components, and we therefore assign it to vertical line(V). If the coefficient is high in both LH and HL sub-images, it means that there are both horizontal and vertical components, and it is therefore assigned to text(T). If the coefficient is low in both LH and HL sub-images, it would be an image or background which has neither horizontal nor vertical components. In that case, we reference the corresponding coefficients of the LL sub-image. So, if its corresponding coefficient is low in the LL sub-image, it is assigned to image(I), and if its corresponding coefficient is high in the LL sub-image, it is assigned to background(X).

Table 1. Assigning the coefficients to the corresponding classes at each level

		LH	
		low (0)	high (1)
HL	low (0)	I / X	H
	high (1)	V	T

At the second step, the assigned coefficients are weighted by their neighbors, which are also assigned by Table 1. Weight matrices corresponding to each class are given in Figure 5. The assigned coefficients are weighted with neighboring coefficients of equal class type, as shown in Eq.(7). In this equation, m_i^c is the ith element of the weight matrix of the corresponding class, and b_i is 1, if the assigned class of b_i is equal to class $c, c \in \{I, T, H, V\}$, otherwise, b_i is 0. $V_{x,y}^n(c)$ is the weighted value of the corresponding coefficient at point (x, y) of the nth level. At the following step, we accumulate the weighted value $V_{x,y}^n(c)$ of each level as shown in Eq.(8). By applying this equation from the top level (level N) to the bottom level (level 1), we can obtain the final accumulated value of corresponding coefficient c, which is equal to $A^1_{x,y}(c)$. At the final step, we decide the classes of the corresponding coefficients with images, texts, horizontal lines, or vertical lines at level 1. As shown in Eq.(9), we decide the class of the corresponding coefficient c by its maximal value among the accumulated values of I, T, H, and V.

$$V^n_{x,y}(c) = \sum_{i=1}^{9} m^c_i \cdot b_i \tag{7}$$

$$A^n_{x,y}(c) = V^n_{x,y}(c) + A^{n+1}_{\lfloor x/2 \rfloor, \lfloor y/2 \rfloor}(c), \quad n = N-1, \cdots, 1 \tag{8}$$

$$D(x,y) = \arg \max_c A^1_{x,y}(c), \qquad c \in \{I, T, H, V\} \tag{9}$$

After removing the non-text regions (image, horizontal line, and vertical line) and small connected components of the text region, we apply the processes described in section 2.2 and 2.3 once again. Through this procedure, better segmentation results are obtained.

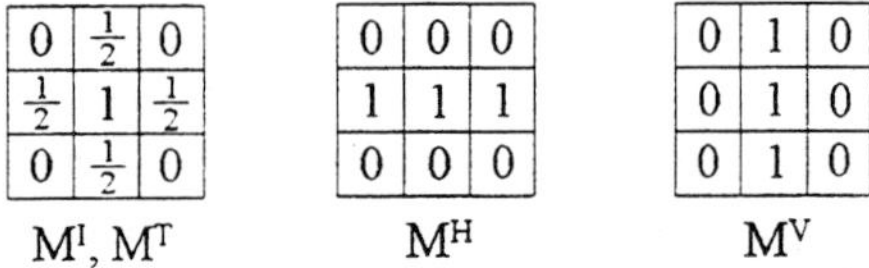

Figure 5. Weight matrices of each class

2.5. Homogeneous region identification

In this section, we identify the segmented maximal homogeneous regions as texts, images, tables and lines at the base image, level 0. The method for the region identification proceeds as follows:

- **Text identification :** If a region has a horizontal periodicity and it is composed of one or more peaks in the smoothed horizontal projection profile, it is classified as a paragraph. If a region has a vertical periodicity and is composed of just one peak in the smoothed horizontal projection profile, it is classified as a single text line, such as title, sub-title, legend and caption.
- **Line :** After applying the Run Length Smoothing Algorithm (RLSA), if a region is composed of one connected component and its ratio of width to height or height to width is larger than 5, it is classified as a line.
- **Table :** For the remaining regions, we extract any existing horizontal lines. The top and bottom lines, which should be similar in length with the width of the region, are detected. Furthermore, there should be more than one horizontal line in the region other than the top and bottom lines.
- **Image :** The rest of the regions are regarded as image regions.

3. Experimental results and analysis

Our proposed method has been tested on 150 images from the document database available from the University of Washington (UWDB) [4].The performance with UWDB[4] is quantitatively evaluated as shown in Table 2. In addition, the corresponding graph is illustrated in Figure 6 to show the performance comparison of the proposed method with recursive X-Y cut method [2] and Block Adjacency Graph (BAG) method [3].

Table 2. Performance evaluation

	UWDB [4]		
	N_{total}	$N_{correct}$	Correct(%)
Region location	1559	1523	97.7
Text identification	1473	1469	99.7
Image identification	139	135	97.1
Table identification	4	4	100
Ruler location	101	101	100

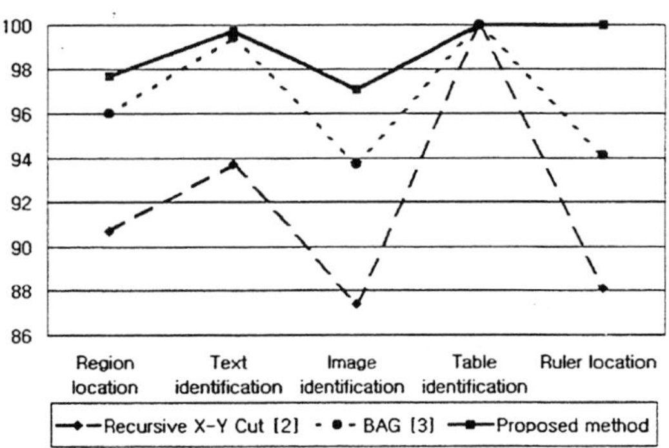

Figure 6. The comparison of previous methods and the proposed method

References

[1] B. Gatos, N. Papamarkos, and C. Chamzas. Skew Detection and Text Line Position Determination in Digitized Documents. *Pattern Recognition*, 30:1505–1519, 1997.

[2] J. Ha, R. Haralick, and I. Phillips. Recursive X-Y Cut using Bounding Boxes of Connected Components. *Proc. of the 3rd ICDAR, Montreal*, pages 952–955, 1995.

[3] A. Jain and B. Yu. Document Representation and Its Application to Page Decomposition. *IEEE Trans. on PAMI*, 20:294–308, 1998.

[4] I. Phillips, S. Chen, and R. Haralick. CD-ROM Document Database Standard. *Proc. of the 2nd ICDAR, Tsukuba*, 30:478–483, 1993.

[5] Y. Y. Tang, H. Ma, J. Liu, B. F. Li, and D. Xi. Multiresolution Analysis in Extraction of Reference Lines from Documents with Gray Level Background. *IEEE Trans. on PAMI*, 19:921–926, 1997.

Simultaneous Highlighting of Paper and Electronic Documents

Jonathan J. Hull and Dar-Shyang Lee
Ricoh California Research Center
Menlo Park, CA
{dsl, hull}@rsv.ricoh.com

Abstract

The ability to automatically record the marks applied to paper documents on their electronic originals would preserve the information represented by those annotations. Users could even lose the original paper document. The marked-up version could be re-generated by merely re-printing it.

We describe a solution that saves an electronic representation for the highlights users commonly apply over the top of machine-printed text. A unique combination of algorithms is presented that maps the image captured from a pen scanner affixed to a highlighting pen onto text strings in electronic documents. Documents are automatically located in a large database using characteristics of the highlighted text. We describe here the system components, including the image recognition algorithms, and discuss their performance in finding a unique mapping from an image of text onto a sequence of words in an electronic document within a large database.

1. Introduction

Electronic documents are becoming increasingly prevalent in our lives. URL's for World Wide Web documents are widely advertised and every day, more content, such as scientific papers, is made available on the Internet. However, users often still prefer to read paper documents. The advantages of paper include its high resolution, persistence, portability, lack of a power requirement, easy re-generation by printing, and easy modification by addition of written annotations.

Highlights are one kind of written annotation that are very popular [6]. These are colored markings that are applied over the top of machine-printed text. They represent information added to a document at some cost in cognitive effort. As such, they are worthy of preserving in an electronic form that could be retrieved later. Ideally, this would even allow users to lose the original paper document and still be confident they could locate the annotated electronic version. This would be a significant advantage for users who have difficulty finding old documents.

We propose a method for capturing highlights as they are applied to paper documents and recording them on the electronic originals from which they were produced. This is suitable for paper documents for which the corresponding electronic original *exists* and is *accessible*. This is often a practical problem because it implies users must take some explicit action to prepare the electronic document for later access. That is, they must anticipate that at some future time they will highlight the document.

We provide access to electronic originals for most paper documents in an office with a document management system, known as the Infinite Memory Multifunction Machine (IM^3) [5], that saves an electronic version of every printed, copied or faxed document as a side-effect of processing them. Users make no explicit decision about whether any particular document is captured. Instead, *every* document is captured without asking the users.

Highlights are captured from a pen scanner attached to a highlighting marker. We use a commercially available pen scanner. Ideally, the scanning electronics would be embedded in the highlighting pen or in cartridges that would hold highlighting markers. Highlights are mapped onto the correct electronic document by combining the recognition results from one or more highlighted sequences of words (phrases).

There are several existing approaches that provide an interface between paper and electronic documents. They typically record the path followed by a pen when users write. Examples include video cameras focused on desktops or sheets of paper [2]. Another solution embeds small gyroscopes in a pen [8]. In both cases, the motion of a pen is transformed to a raster image. However, no means are provided for identifying the page being written on. While some solutions are obvious, such as scanning pre-printed bar codes before writing, this requires that bar codes be printed on a page before the user writes on it. This makes it difficult to use either of these methods for writing on an existing document and having that ink trace be registered with the electronic original. One solution to

1051-4651/00 $10.00 © 2000 IEEE

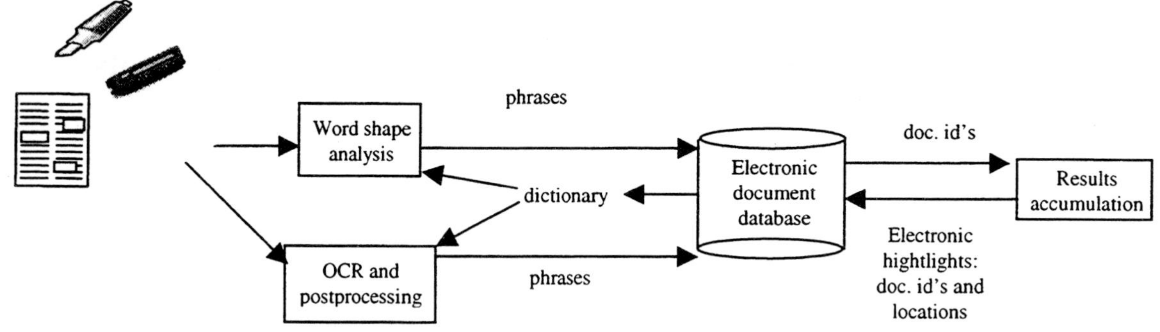

Figure 1. System design for simultaneous paper and electronic document highlighting.

this problem is to use specially prepared paper [3] that distributes an identification mark across its surface.

Another paper-electronic document interface uses a small video camera focused on the tip of a pen [1]. Highlights were captured by the camera. Users could manually indicate electronic actions that would be taken the next time the highlighted text was seen. However, no methodology was provided for automatically mapping highlighted text onto a collection of documents.

2. System Design

The design for the simultaneous annotation system is shown in Figure 1. A marker is combined with a pen scanner. Users can highlight documents as they normally do. Images of the highlighted words are transferred to a word shape analysis technique and an OCR process. Their results form queries to an electronic document database. Identifiers for documents that match the queries are accumulated across different annotations. When the document being processed is identified, electronic versions of the highlights are passed to the document database. They identify a document and the position of each annotation within the document.

The objective of the word shape analysis routine is to identify rough characteristics such as the number of characters in each word, whether they contain holes, and whether they are capitalized or lower case [4, 7]. Given a set of connected component features, a rule–based system calculates a set of candidate identifications for each character. These are composed into a regular expression that is used to query the dictionary. This returns a list of words that match the given constraints. A dynamic programming solution for phrase lookup is then applied independently to the lists of word candidates returned by word shape analysis and the OCR module. See Figure 2 for an example.

The electronic document database used in our experiments is the IM^3 system mentioned earlier. It has been in daily use at our laboratory for more than four years and during that time has captured over 70,000 documents containing more than 300,000 pages. About 20 users contributed data to this system, on average, over this period.

ASCII text is extracted from every document entered in the IM^3 and a full text index is constructed. This allows us to pose word-based conjunctive, disjunctive, and phrase queries. They return identifiers (id's) for the IM^3 documents that match the query.

The results accumulation module receives the list of IM^3 document id's found in the full text index. It identifies a unique document that contains a given set of images. Its underlying principle of operation is that while one image may map onto many documents, a number of images from the same document are highly likely to map onto that document and only that document. The major unknown factors are the number of images and the number of words needed in each image to obtain high accuracy.

3. Experimental Results

There are several factors that are important for technical success. One is the accuracy in recognition processing. It should produce sets of candidates for each word that contain the correct choice. The other key factor for success is the performance of results accumulation. It should need only a small number of short phrases to locate unique documents in a large database. This would provide an easy-to-use index for a document that is encoded directly in short sequences of words. I.e., it is a steganographic key that everyone can see but which does not modify the appearance of the document.

High-scoring Segment Pairs

(a)

[ABCDEGHJKLMNOQRUVWXZbdh]ig[ABCDEGHJKLMNOQRUVWXZbdh]
[rsxz][ce][amouvw][rsxz]ing [SFIPTYflt][ce]g[amouvw][ce]n[SFIPTYflt] [SFIPTYflt][amouvw]i[rsxz][rsxz]

(b)

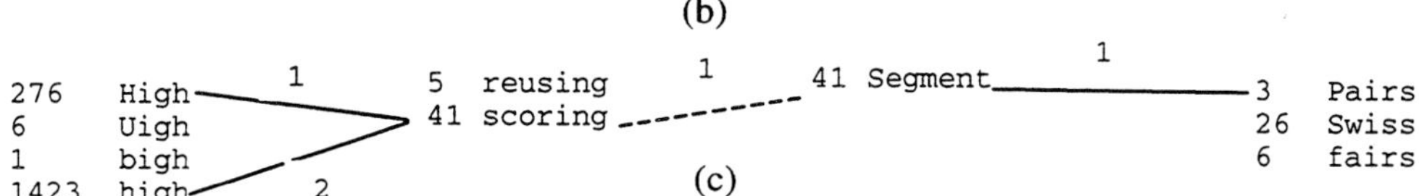

(c)

Figure 2. An example image from the pen scanner (a), regular expressions that locate words with the same shape (b), and word alternatives and their frequencies (c). Links between words show successful pair-wise dictionary lookups and their frequencies. The correct choice is determined at the "scoring Segment" lookup.

Recognition processing comprises word shape analysis and OCR plus post-processing. Others have investigated the performance of word shape in detail and reported better than 90% word accuracy [7]. We expect similar performance. The commercial OCR package we're using (from IRIS) is tuned for pen scanners. It typically produces better than 95% correct character recognition performance. The addition of custom dictionaries and post-processing should improve this.

The performance of the results accumulation module was investigated in two phases. First the number of documents that contain one or more phrases was determined. Phrases were randomly selected from each document in a subset of the IM^3 database. These were used as queries to the text index and the number of documents returned by each query, individually and in common, were calculated. This estimates the number of annotations needed to identify a unique document.

The document collection used in these experiments was derived from one user's IM^3 database. These were gathered from late 1995 through the end of 1999 and contain every document printed or photocopied by that user. Altogether, this comprises 9967 documents with 34,564 pages.

The second phase of the experiments estimated the effect of duplicates on the performance observed in the first phase. Duplicates were a significant consideration because the test collection contained many form letters and versions of documents that were printed several times during their lifetime.

3.1. Phrase matching

The ability of one or more phrases to identify a unique document was investigated by randomly selecting phrases of those lengths from each document in the test set. Numbers of phrases (N) from 1 to 4 were considered as well as a range of phrase lengths (PL) from 3 to 6. For

	Number of words per phrase			
Number of phrases	3	4	5	6
1	29% 65	35% 52	38% 28	39% 27
2	42% 21	45% 16	45% 10	46% 9
3	47% 9	48% 8	49% 6	49% 6
4	50% 6	50% 6	52% 5	52% 4

Table 1. Performance of phrase matching. The percentage of documents uniquely specified and the average number of documents are shown.

each document in the database, N lines were randomly chosen that contained at least PL words. A starting position within each line was also randomly chosen and PL words beginning at this position were used as a query.

The results of this experiment are shown in Table 1. The percentage of documents uniquely identified by the chosen test phrase are indicated as well as the average number of documents found. This characterizes the number of alternatives the results accumulation module receives for any combination of phrase queries. The results show that performance improves significantly as more phrases with longer words are used. Performance peaks with about 50% of the queries returning only the correct choice. The average peaks at 4.

3.2. Duplicate Documents

The presence of duplicate documents is an obvious concern. The test database was taken from live data and was not preprocessed in any way. It contains many drafts of the same document as well as large numbers of form letters that differ only in the destination address. The prevalence of duplicates and their effect on performance was estimated by examining the results for 4 six-word queries. Each of the approximately 10,000 documents was compared to the files returned by multiple phrase matching. The percentage of unique vocabulary in the test document that occurred in each matching document was determined. This gives a rough approximation of whether they are the same document. If the percent unique vocabulary in common exceeds a threshold, we say they are the same (i.e., *duplicates*).

The results of the duplicate detection experiment are shown in Table 2. It is seen that when exact duplicates (100% vocabulary in common) are considered equivalent to the query document, the percent uniquely specified increases to 73%. This improves to 90% when 90% common vocabulary is the threshold and 98% when 75% common vocabulary is the threshold. The average number of returned documents decreases to 1. Examination of several cases shows that most of them are instances of the same two-paragraph form letter. This leads to the conclusion that when the percent unique peaks at around 50% in Table 1, an exact match is in fact being located. If more than one document is present, it is most likely a duplicate of the original.

Duplicate detection threshold					
75%	80%	85%	90%	95%	100%
98% 1	96% 2	94% 2	90% 3	85% 3	73% 3

Table 2. Effect of duplicates on matching highlights to electronic documents.

Duplicates are thus not a significant issue. They are an obvious concern, but we expect to compensate for them in the design of the user interface on the highlighting scanner or at retrieval time.

4. Conclusions

We presented a novel combination of components that allow users to highlight text in a paper document and have those highlights simultaneously recorded on the original electronic version. This preserves the highlights and guarantees that they can be re-generated if the paper document is lost. When used in combination with a document management system that retains electronic originals for every printed, copied, or faxed document, users could pick up almost any document, highlight it, and be confident those highlights would be recorded. No special preparation of the paper or electronic original would be required. Experimental results on a real-world collection of almost 10,000 documents captured over 4 years showed that a small number of short highlights can often uniquely specify a document. This demonstrates the feasibility of simultaneous paper-electronic document highlighting. Future work will consider issues that must be addressed before making this capability available to the public.

5. References

[1] T. Arai, D. Aust, and S.E. Hudson, "PaperLink: A technique for hyperlinking from real paper to electronic content," Proceedings of the ACM 1997 SIGCHI Conference, Atlanta, GA, March 22-27, 1997, 327-334.

[2] H. Bunke, T.V. Siebenthal, T. Yamasaki, and M. Schenkel, "Online handwriting data acquisition using a video camera," Fifth International Conference on Document Analysis and Recognition, Bangalore, India, September 20-22, 1999, 573-576.

[3] M. Dyteman and M. Cooperman, "Intelligent paper," Electronic Publishing, Artistic Imaging, and Digital Typography, R. Hersch, J. Andre, and H. Brown (eds), Springer Verlag, April, 1998, 392-406.

[4] J.J. Hull, "Hypothesis generation in a computational model for visual word recognition," IEEE Expert, v. 1, no. 3, Fall 1986, 63-70.

[5] J.J. Hull and P.E. Hart, "The infinite memory multifunction machine (IM^3)," DAS98: Pre-proceedings of the Third IAPR Workshop on Document Analysis Systems, Nagano, Japan, November 4-6, 1998, 49-58.

[6] C. Marshall, "Toward an ecology of hypertext annotation," Proceedings of ACM Hypertext'98, Pittsburgh, PA, June 20-24, 1998, 40-49.

[7] A.L. Spitz, "Shape-based word recognition," International Journal of Document Analysis and Recognition, v. 1, no. 4, May, 1999, 178-190.

[8] C. Verplaetse, "Inertial proprioceptive devices: self-motion-sensing toys and tools," IBM Systems Journal, v. 35, nos. 3 and 4, 1996, 639-650.

Stochastic Error-Correcting Parsing for OCR Post-processing.

Juan C. Perez-Cortes Juan C. Amengual Joaquim Arlandis
Rafael Llobet
Instituto Tecnológico de Informática (ITI)
Universidad Politécnica, Camino de Vera s/n
46071, Valencia, Spain
jcperez@disca.upv.es

Abstract

In this paper, stochastic error-correcting parsing is proposed as a powerful and flexible method to post-process the results of an optical character recognizer (OCR). Deterministic and non-deterministic approaches are possible under the proposed setting. The basic units of the model can be words or complete sentences, and the lexicons or the language databases can be simple enumerations or may convey probabilistic information from the application domain.

1 Introduction

The result of automatic optical recognition of printed or handwritten text is often affected by a considerable amount of error and uncertainty, and it is therefore essential the application of a correction algorithm. A significant portion of the ability of humans to read a handwritten text is due to their extraordinary error recovery power, thanks to the lexical, syntactic, semantic, pragmatic and discursive language constraints they apply.

Among the different levels at which language can be modeled [2], the lowest one is the word level, involving lexical constraints on the sequential relations of characters inside each word. The next one is the sentence level, which takes into account syntactic and semantic constraints on the sequence of words or word categories inside a sentence (or a field, for instance, in a forms-processing application). The higher levels consider a wider context and require specific *a priori* knowledge of the application domain.

Word and sentence level models typically apply dictionary search methods, n-grams, Edit Distance-based techniques, Hidden Markov Models, and other character or word category transition models.

A common goal of OCR post-processing methods is to guarantee (or, at least, maximize the probability) that the words or sentences generated by corrections to the OCR output are correct in the sense that they belong to the language of the task. This language can be as simple as a small set of valid words (e.g. the possible values of the *country* field in a form) or as complex as an unconstrained sentence in a natural language. Correspondingly, several approaches exist to the problem, which can be categorized into two main groups: deterministic and non-deterministic.

The deterministic approach is often applied to uncomplicated languages and requires, in its simplest form, the compilation of a complete lexicon (a finite list of tokens, which can be words, sentences, etc.). In this case, a token t, output by an OCR algorithm and referred to as the *recognized string*, will be said to belong to the language with a certain likelihood when its difference, according to a suitable similarity measure, to the most similar token c in the lexicon is lower than a given threshold. Token c will be returned as the *corrected string* in response to t. When it is not feasible to build a list with all possible valid strings, a non-enumerative representation of the language can be used, like a formal grammar or a set of prefixes, word roots, suffixes, etc.

In a non-deterministic model, the corrected string is not forced to belong *necessarily* to an explicit or implicitly enumerated list of tokens. Instead, the recognized (input) string is analyzed, and a corrected string is built by maximizing the probability that every symbol or sub-sequence of symbols belongs to the language. In other words, the corrected string is a version of the recognized string that conforms more closely to the constraints of the language model.

In forms-processing applications, it is often useful a deterministic model for fields like *name, city, state,* etc., but a non-deterministic model is preferred for more complex inputs as *address, occupation,* etc. In the latter case, however, the sequential application of a deterministic model for each word, followed by a non-deterministic model, with symbols corresponding to words or syntactic word categories, can provide better results. Similar combinations, or

1051-4651/00 $10.00 © 2000 IEEE

non-deterministic models alone, can be also useful in other, more general, document processing tasks.

2 Previous work

A large number of data structures have been proposed to efficiently perform approximate search in a lexicon, an essential part for deterministic correction models. The simplest one is an alphabetically sorted list of words. Unfortunately, specific techniques and indices are needed to carry out approximate search in them. The same can be said about other generic data structures like hash tables, search trees, etc. In [6], an excellent survey of approximate string search methods is presented.

Other more specific techniques exist, like the methods that try to benefit from the high performance of exact search algorithms, by generating a number of neighboring strings to the one sought for, and searching all of them [11]. Unfortunately, that neighborhood can grow exponentially with the number of symbols of the string, and thus heuristic and probabilistic constraints have to be imposed.

In other cases, the lexicon is subdivided according to different criteria, like the length of the words, the first symbols, etc., reducing the search time by only a constant factor. Another interesting group of techniques is based on fast metric-space nearest neighbor search techniques, considering the strings as points in a dissimilarity space and performing dimensionality reduction techniques, tree search, or fast search based on the properties of the metrics.

On the other hand, the *n*-gram models constitute a simple but widely used family of non-deterministic techniques. Their high potential can be illustrated by some results reported in [2], where an *n*-gram model was applied to a 10,000 English word lexicon, finding only 68% of the 676 possible digrams, 20% of the 17576 trigrams and 2% of the 456976 *4*-grams.

The general concept used by the technique proposed in this work was first applied to text correction in [9]. The idea is to build a finite-state machine (or a Markov model) that accepts (or generates with a certain probability) the strings in the lexicon or language sample. When the model is applied to a candidate word, if it is accepted, no correction is performed, and if not, the smallest set of transitions that could not be traversed shows which is the most similar string in the model. When this concept is applied to a formal grammar, it is called Error-Correcting Parsing (ECP). The classical algorithm, widely used in different fields, to find the maximum likelihood path on a Markov model and to perform ECP on a regular grammar is the Viterbi Algorithm, based on the Dynamic Programming paradigm. Their applications were recognized through the work of Forney [4], and it was used for the first time in [10] for text correction. In [12] and [7], improvements and new concepts were applied to the method, including the contribution of the confusion matrix to the error model. In [13], further refinements were introduced.

In [3], a related approach to the problem of finding the most similar strings is presented. In that method, no error-correcting parsing is needed, but the construction of the automaton allows an efficient conventional parsing, directly yielding the required results. A high spatial cost is, however, the main problem of the approach.

Many recent works on language modeling have been carried out in the field of continuous speech recognition [8]. Although the requirements are very different (for example, deterministic language models are seldom applied to speech), many basic techniques used in that discipline can be applied to OCR tasks with little modification.

3 Stochastic Error Correcting Parsing for OCR Post-processing

In recent years, mainly due to important achievements in parsing efficiency, the Viterbi Algorithm has been used for stochastic error correcting parsing with excellent results in complex pattern recognition and speech-oriented language modeling tasks [1].

Here, we propose the application of a grammatical inference algorithm to build a stochastic finite-state machine that accepts the smallest *k*-Testable Language in the Strict Sense (*k*-TS language) [5] consistent with a task-representative language sample. The set of strings accepted by such an automaton is equivalent to the language model obtained using *n*-grams, for $n=k$. The stochastic extension of the basic *k*-TS language is performed through a maximum likelihood estimation of the probabilities associated to the grammar rules, evaluated according to their frequency of utilization by the input strings. This computation is carried out incrementally and simultaneously with the inference process.

A major advantage of the chosen setting resides in its flexibility. The language sample can be a simple lexicon (with each word appearing only once), a list of words extracted from a real instance of the task (with each word appearing as many times as in the sample), a list of sentences with the characters, words or word categories as the symbols of the grammar, etc. Only in the first case, when using a classical lexicon, the automaton is not required to be stochastic, since a lexicon is not a representative language sample (as will be seen, this gives rise to clearly poorer results in the experiments presented in section 4). In the other cases, if the sample is representative of the task, the model will take advantage of the probabilistic information present in the data.

The value of k can also be used to define the behavior of the model. In a lexical model, if k is made equal to the length of the longest word in the database, a deterministic

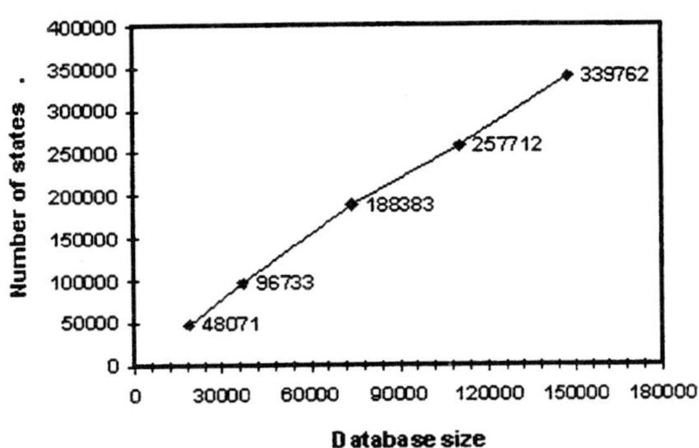

Figure 1. Number of states of the model, plotted against the number of words in the lexicon.

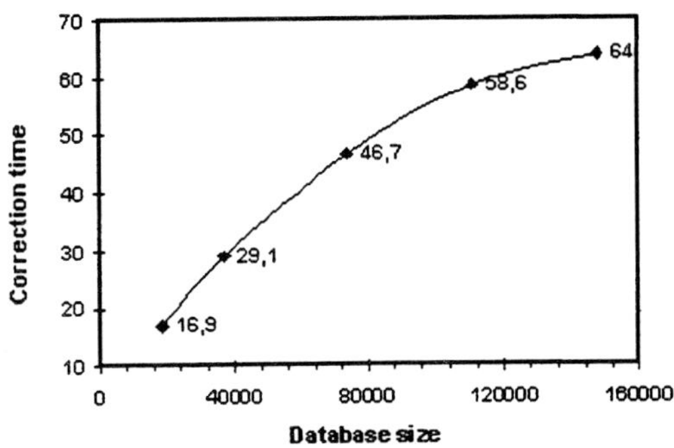

Figure 2. Times (in ms) in a 450Mhz Pentium.

post-processing method is obtained (only words that exist in the database can be generated), but if k is set to a lower value, a non-deterministic model will result, where the corrected words can belong, or not, to the reference database. Note that the stochastic nature of the underlying grammar (i.e. its ability to take into account the relative frequencies of the different symbol sequences) does not depend on the choice of k, and that, therefore, for instance, a deterministic model can be based on a stochastic grammar, when the database is a language sample and k is large, and a non-deterministic model could make use of a regular grammar, when the database is a simple lexicon and k is small.

The worst case spatial cost of a straightforward implementation of the model is linear with the size of the database but, in practice, it is usually slightly sub-linear. In figure 1, the number of states of a model composed by words derived from a lexicon of 18450 Spanish names, artificially enlarged by randomly exchanging some of the letters, is shown. The average length of the strings was 6.66.

Once the language model has been built, a number of issues regarding the parsing procedure remain to be discussed. The most important one is the error model and dissimilarity measures that will allow the system to generate a correct word or sentence from an incorrect input string (in the non-deterministic case, substrings instead of the string as a whole are considered). The efficiency of the procedure is another important aspect to address.

We have used an Stochastic Error-Correcting Parsing algorithm based on an extension of the Viterbi Algorithm [1]. Formally, our problem is to find a minimal cost path through a multistage directed graph (trellis) associated to the finite automaton (model) and to the input string a. In this graph, each node q_{jk} corresponds to a state q_j of the automaton in the kth stage of the parsing process, corresponding to the kth symbol of a, and each arc $t_k = (q_{ik}, q_{j\,k+1})$ represents a transition from state q_i in stage k and state q_j (which can be the same) in stage $k+1$ (next symbol of a). All the details, diagrams and algorithms can be found in [1].

The extension for error correction implies the addition of new arcs to the graph, according to the error rules of the dissimilarity function chosen [1]. The most widely used error model is based on the insertion-deletion-substitution editing operations. We can use a different cost for each of the three operations. The cost of substitution is usually the lowest one, since it is often the only directly imputable to an OCR error. In many applications, insertions and deletions are rare, being caused by writer's mistakes or document segmentation problems. If the cost of these operations are high, they will be included only in otherwise high probability paths.

As for the cost of substitutions, it can be estimated from two sources of information: the confusion matrix of the classifier and the *a posteriori* class-conditional probabilities provided by the classifier output. The first one provides a very consistent estimation (since it can be derived from a very large sample) of the *a priori* probability of a given character being mixed up with another one by the classifier. The second one can be considered less reliable, but it takes into account the features of the character under analysis, and therefore conveys a more dynamic information, compared to the static nature of the confusion matrix. In the results presented here, only the confusion matrix has been used. Ongoing work is being carried out on the integration of the *a posteriori* class-conditional probabilities into the parsing method, and not only in the cost of the substitution operations.

The computational cost of the parsing procedure can be very low if techniques like beam-search are used to improve the efficiency of the algorithm [1]. In figure 2, the time to correct an input string with an average length of 5.95 symbols is plotted against the size of the lexicon. A beam width of $\alpha = 30$ was used.

Table 1. Percentages of incorrect names and characters at 0% rejection rate.

	Word errors	Char. errors
OCR	6842 (**32.54%**)	9294 (**6.36%**)
Non-stochastic model	1006 (**4.78%**)	1888 (**1.29%**)
Stochastic model	303 (**1.74%**)	659 (**0.45%**)

Table 2. Examples of processed strings.

Corrected names		Incorrectly "corrected" names		
OCR output	**Corrected**	**OCR output**	**"Corrected"**	**Correct**
HDRTD	MARTA	SANA	JANA	SARA
ROSDN?	ROSANA	NHRJH	NURIA	MARIA
HONICB	MONICA	IUAN	JUAN	IVAN
EOGENLO	EUGENIO	HARTA	MARTA	MARIA
?DRID	MARIA	ANTONI?	ANTONIO	ANTONIA
JE?OMIYO	JERONIMO	JIZID	JULIA	MARTA
OOLORES	DOLORES	SOAUA	JOANA	SONIA

4 Experiments

A deterministic correction model for the *name* field in a handwritten form processing application has been chosen to perform some tests. A commercial neural network-based OCR system in use by a document processing company was applied to a real handwritten form-processing task, taking the OCR output as the input to our method. The data provided by the OCR did not include a reliability index for each character, but the special symbol "?" was output when the quality of the recognition was below a certain threshold, which was fixed by the company operators using standard criteria. The confusion matrix was computed using a validation set of 777080 characters from a different set of forms.

The number of strings tested was 21028, totalizing 146060 characters, and the training language sample consisted of 27125 (mostly Spanish) first names, 8088 of which were unique. Several tests were conducted: the first without correction of the OCR output, the second using the 8088-word conventional lexicon to build a non-stochastic k-TS automaton, and in the last one, the full list of 27125 names was used to build a stochastic model. Since a fairly complete list of Spanish names was available, all the models tested were deterministic (the value of k was set to the length of the longest name). The results are shown in table 1. The ECP postprocessing does improve the results of single character recognition as it could be expected [1], but it is remarkable the decrease achieved in word error rate. This is explained by the (combined) effect of both language and error models, which also appears in Speech Recognition when independently trained stochastic acoustic and language models are tightly integrated [8]. Some examples of both corrections and miscorrections are shown in table 2

5 Conclusions

A post-processing method for the correction of OCR results has been proposed. A stochastic finite-state automaton accepting a k-Testable Language in the Strict Sense is learned from a language sample extracted from the application domain. Then, a modified version of the Viterbi Algorithm is used to perform a stochastic error correcting parsing of the strings provided by the OCR module, and the resulting string is given as the corrected output. Excellent time and space efficiency as well as very good correction results have been obtained. Moreover, the flexibility of the method allows the designer to define very precisely the conditions of the correction procedure for different tasks with widely variable requirements.

References

[1] J. Amengual and E. Vidal. Efficient error-correcting viterbi parsing. *IEEE Trans. on PAMI*, 20(10):1109, Oct. 1998.

[2] H. L. Berghel. A logical framework for the correction of spelling errors in electronic documents. *Information Processing and Management*, 23(5):477–494, Sept. 1987.

[3] H. Bunke. Fast approximate matching of words against a dictionary. *Computing*, 55(1):75–89, 1995.

[4] G. Forney. The viterbi algorithm. *Proceedings of IEEE*, 61(3):268–277, March 1973.

[5] P. Garcia and E. Vidal. Inference of k-testable languages in the strict sense and application to syntactic pattern recognition. *IEEE Trans. on PAMI*, 12(9):920–925, sep 1990.

[6] P. Hall and G. Dowling. Approximate string matching. *ACM Surveys*, 12(4):381–402, December 1980.

[7] J. Hull and S. Srihari. Experiments in text recognition with binary n-gram and viterbi algorithms. *IEEE Trans. on PAMI*, 4(5):520–530, sep 1982.

[8] F. Jelinek. *Statistical Methods for Speech Recognition, in Language, Speech and Communication.* MIT Press, 1997.

[9] H. Morgan. Spelling correction in system programs. *Communications of the ACM*, 13:90–94, 1970.

[10] D. Neuhoff. The viterbi algorithm as an aid in text recognition. *IEEE Trans. Information Theory*, 21:222–226, 1975.

[11] E. Riseman and A. Hanson. A contextual postprocessing system for error correction using binary n-grams. *IEEE Trans. Computer*, 23:480–493, 1974.

[12] R. Shinghal and G. Toussaint. Experiments in text recognition with the modified viterbi algorithm. *IEEE Trans. on PAMI*, 1(2):184–192, April 1979.

[13] R. C. S.N. Srihari, J.J. Hull. Integrating diverse knowledge sources in text recognition. *ACM Trans. Off. Inform. Sys.*, 1(1):68–87, 1983.

Text Extraction in MPEG Compressed Video for Content-based Indexing*

Young-Kyu Lim, Song-Ha Choi and Seong-Whan Lee
Center for Artificial Vision Research, Korea University
Anam-dong, Seongbuk-ku, Seoul 136-701, Korea
{yklim, shchoi, swlee}@image.korea.ac.kr

Abstract

Video text extraction is a core technique for multimedia applications such as News-On-Demand(NOD) and digital libraries, and research about video text extraction have been conducted vigorously.

In this paper, we propose an efficient method for extracting texts in MPEG compressed videos for content-based indexing. The proposed method makes the best use of 2-level DCT coefficients and macroblock type information in MPEG compressed video, and this method can be organized into three stages to increase overall performance : text frame detection, text region extraction, and character extraction. The main advantage of the proposed method is that it can avoid the overhead of decompressing video into individual frames in the pixel domain. We evaluated this method using various types of news video data.

1. Introduction

Video text has drawn considerable attention for content-based video retrieval because it contains meaningful information about video contents, when text is superimposed in the video sequence. A great deal of video data will be kept in a compressed form for the purpose of saving storage space. So, an algorithm which can operate on a compressed form is highly desirable.

In this paper, we present an efficient text extraction method which makes the best use of 2-level DCT coefficients and macroblock type information in MPEG compressed video. The purpose of this research is to detect text frames in real time, to extract text regions included in those frames and to extract individual characters for OCR input. We are most concerned with text region extraction. We first detect text frames in the reduced images using intensity and neighboring pixel differences. The detected frames are verified and text regions included in those frames are extracted. Finally, individual characters are extracted by local thresholding and connected component analysis.

*This research was supported by Creative Research Initiatives of the Ministry of Science and Technology, Korea.

2. Related works

Recently, many researchers have studied about the methods of video text and superimposed caption extraction from video frames.

Smith and Kanade[5], Kurakake *et al.*[2], and Li and Doermann[3] proposed an indexing method for content-based image retrieval by using textual information in video. Lienhart and Stuber[4] employed a modified spilt and merge to perform segmentation. Gargi *et al.*[1] proposed a four-stage approach - detection, localization, segmentation, and recognition. The detection stage is performed in a compressed domain, but the compressed video data were fully decompressed in the remaining stages. Yeo[6] proposed a scheme for detecting embedded captions using pixel-wise difference in video sequences. This method operates on reduced image sequences that are directly reconstructed from compressed video.

Most of the previous methods work on an uncompressed domain and depend greatly on heuristics concerning size, color, etc. Our approach will try to overcome these limitations.

3. The proposed text extraction method

Our proposed method consists of three stages - text frame detection, text region extraction, and character extraction from MPEG compressed video.

3.1. Text frame detection

Generally, there are two kinds of text in video[4]. One is artificial text superimposed by a video titling machine. The other is scene text showing naturally in scenes like text on a cloth. In the remainder of this paper, text or character will be considered as artificial text.

From observation of TV news data, text remains stationary for some time when it contains an important message and is constant on numerous subsequent frames. The basic characteristic of text frame which was shown in TV news video are summarized in Fig. 1.

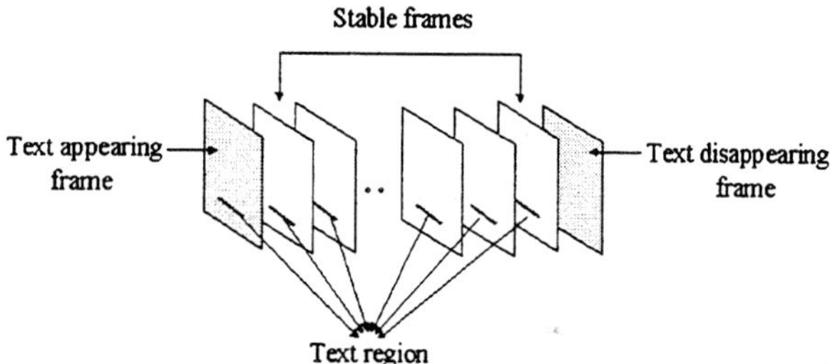

Figure 1. The basic structure of the text frame

We first construct a spatially reduced image, called the DC image, directly from I frame. The DC image is formed from block wise averaging of the original image. In general, locations in which text can appear in the image are somewhat restricted. We called these locations by the region of interest. Since typically text does not appear in the boundary of the image, we can define this region set A, as shown in Eq. (1). Using this assumption, the text frame detection process was performed over the region of interest.

We extract the pixel satisfying two conditions: the intensity is higher than the threshold(TH_1) and the neighboring pixel difference is greater than the threshold(TH_2) for the region of interest.

$$\begin{aligned} A &= \{\forall(x,y) \mid W*k \le x \le W*(1-k), \\ &\quad H*k \le y \le H*(1-k)\}, \ (0 \le k \le 1) \end{aligned} \tag{1}$$

where (x, y), k, W and H represent the pixel location in image, the constant for adjusting the region of interest, the width and the height of the image, respectively.

$$TF_i = \begin{cases} 1, & if \ \ I(P_i) > TH_1 \ \ and \\ & \quad |Diff(P_i)| > TH_2 \\ 0, & otherwise \end{cases}, \tag{2}$$

where $I(P_i)$ and $Diff(P_i)$ represent intensity and neighboring pixel difference of DC image, respectively.

The number of pixels that satisfy the above conditions is used for identification of a text frame:

$$Total_{TF} = \sum_{i \in A} TF_i, \tag{3}$$

where A means the region of interest.

If $Total_{TF}$ is greater than the threshold, we regard the corresponding frame as a text frame.

3.2. Text region extraction

Since the sign of 2-level AC coefficients depend on the edge direction, the strength sum is required. The 5 AC coefficients arranged in a zig-zag scan order are defined as the set S.

We first the use edge strength to extract a candidate of text block, macroblock with the properties of text. The edge strength is defined as Eq. (4).

$$ES(S) = \sum_i s_i^2, \quad i = 1, ..., 5 \tag{4}$$

where $ES(S)$ means the summation of edge strength and s_i means each element of the given set S.

We define the macroblock as a text block, if it satisfies the Eq. (5).

$$TH_{min} \le ES(S) \le TH_{max} \tag{5}$$

Text region extraction was performed on the resultant image of a candidate of text block extraction like Fig. 2.

As this image has not only the text region but also the background region, the histogram in horizontal orientation is applied to remove the background region. This satisfies the text characteristic of horizontal alignment. The horizontal histogram is defined by projecting the white pixels(WP) of the skeleton into the y-axis and accumulating the number of white pixels in each point of the y-axis:

$$TH_h \le Horizontal[i], \ Horizontal[i] = \sum_{j=0}^{H-1} N_{ij} \tag{6}$$

$$N_{ij} = \begin{cases} 1, & if \ \ (i,j) = WP \\ 0, & otherwise \end{cases}, \tag{7}$$

where $Horizontal[i]$ represents i-th horizontal histogram, H is the height of an image and i is the line number.

Figure 2. The examples of extracting a candidate of text block

The candidate of text region is verified using macroblock type information, as it also contains a non-text region. The example of macroblock type in the two different frames are shown in Fig. 3.

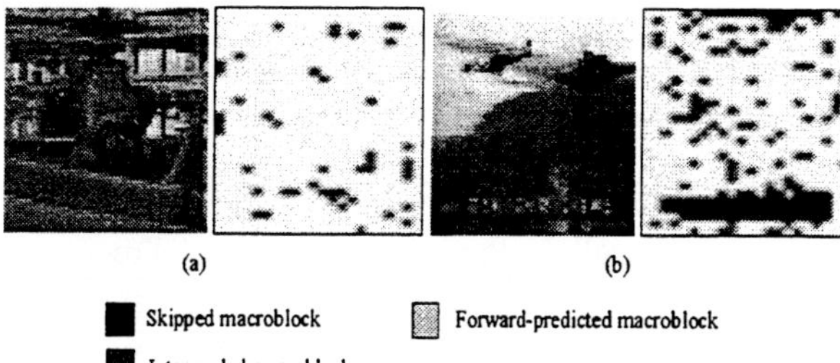

Figure 3. The example of macroblock types (a) The case that the frame does not have a text region (b) The case that the frame has a text region

To discriminate the text region from the background in the extracted region, the number of skipped macroblocks within its region is used. The macroblock type information is identified in the text frame detection stage. Its type and position are stored in advance. We first examine the macroblock type in the extracted text region using Eq. (8) and the number of skipped macroblocks(N_{SM}) in Eq. (9).

$$M_s[i] = \begin{cases} 1, & if \;\; i \in R \; and \; f(MB_i) = SM \\ 0, & otherwise \end{cases} , \quad (8)$$

where $f(MB_i)$ returns the type of macroblock in the current P frame, SM is the skipped macroblock and R is the extracted text region.

$$N_{SM} = \sum_i M_s[i], \qquad N_{other} = Total_{mb} - N_{SM}, \quad (9)$$

where $Total_{mb}$ is the number of all the macroblocks included in the extracted region.

We define another feature, the number of skipped macroblock to the number of other macroblock types as ratio.

$$Ratio_{MB} = \frac{N_{SM}}{N_{other}} \quad (10)$$

If N_{SM} or $Ratio_{MB}$ is greater than threshold, this is identified as a text region. The rectangular box circumscribes the extracted region.

Fig. 4(a) is a selected image identified as text frame and Fig. 4(b) shows the generated text block map for text region extraction. We can see the text region is highlighted correctly, but there are some isolated areas. These areas are connected by dilation in Fig. 4(c). Fig. 4(d) shows the processing step of text region extraction.

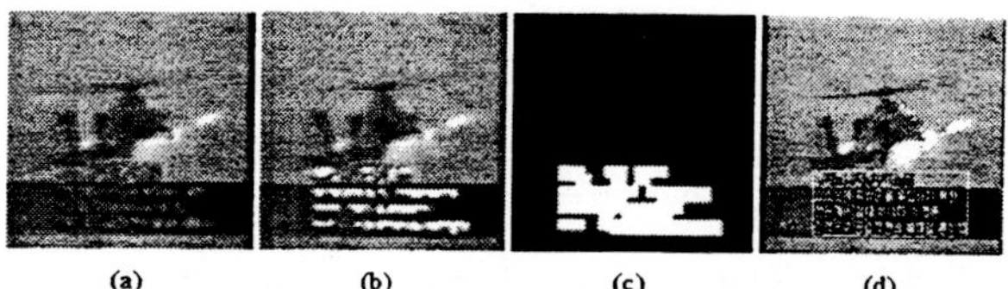

Figure 4. The processing step of text region extraction (a) A selected text frame (b) The text block label map (c) After dilation (d) Extracted text region and bounding box generation

3.3. Character extraction

It is difficult to directly extract characters in a DC image, so minimal decompression processing is required. The decompression is done only on the extracted text region. This helps to reduce processing time in comparison with full decompression. Text has relatively strong contrast with its background, which is a necessary condition for character extraction. The adjusting operation for dynamic range has the effect of increasing contrast in comparison with the background. This operation also makes the boundary between character and its background clearer. The expression for this operation is given in Eq. (11).

$$P(x,y) = C(1 + \log(G(x,y)) \quad (11)$$

where $P(x,y)$, $G(x,y)$ and C mean the pixel value applied by dynamic range adjustment, the gray-level at pixel point (x,y) and the constant, respectively.

After adjustment, median filtering is carried out to remove noise in the image and thresholding technique is used for coarse extraction.

In order to extract information from a binarized image, connected components should be generated.

4. Experimental results and analysis

Table 1. The results of text frame detection

Type	N_T	NT_C	NT_{FN}	NT_{FP}
News1	58	57	1	2
News2	50	47	3	2
News3	54	42	2	3

We used various news video data which were collected by the Optibase MPEG Fusion MPEG-2 encoder from KBS/MBC broadcasting station.

Table 1 and 2 represent the results of text frame detection and text region extraction using the proposed technique, respectively. In Table 1 - 3, N_T, N_C, N_{FN}, and N_{FP} mean the number of total frames or characters, the number of correct, the number of missed, and the number of false positive, respectively.

Table 2. The results of text region extraction

Type	N_T	N_C	N_{FN}	N_{FP}
News1	63	62	1	5
News2	58	53	5	2
News3	55	53	2	3

Table 3 represents the character extraction results. These three results present that overall system performance will still be good in spite of using compressed video data.

Table 4 shows the average processing time for this proposed method. The most time consuming process is DC image construction and text frame detection because most of the necessary features are extracted from MPEG compressed video stream.

Table 3. The results of character extraction

Type	N_T	N_C	N_{FN}	N_{FP}
News1	1615	1512	103	121
News2	963	881	82	42
News3	1225	1127	98	71

Table 4. The processing time of the proposed method

Operation	Time(s)
DC image const. + text frame detection	1.114
Text region extraction	0.325
Character segmentation	0.057

We compared the proposed method with the previous one[1]. Table 5 and Table 6 are the results of efficiency comparisons. The evaluation criteria for two methods are precision and recall.

The results show that the proposed method produces results better than the previous method.

Table 5. The comparison of the results in text region extraction

Type	Gargi *et al.*'s method		Proposed method	
	Recall	Precision	Recall	Precision
News1	92.1%	90.6%	92.5%	92.4%
News2	86.2%	92.6%	91.4%	96.4%
News3	87.2%	92.3%	96.4%	94.6%

Table 6. The comparison of the results in character extraction

Type	Gargi *et al.*'s method		Proposed method	
	Recall	Precision	Recall	Precision
News1	90.5%	90.7%	93.8%	92.6%
News2	88.7%	91.6%	91.5%	95.4%
News3	88.1%	91.4%	92.0%	94.1%

5. Conclusion and further research

In this paper, we proposed a new text extraction method in MPEG compressed video for efficient content-based video retrieval and browsing. The proposed text extraction method makes the best use of DCT coefficients and macroblock type information in MPEG compressed video. The experimental results show that the proposed method is far more accurate in text extraction than the compared traditional approaches. But, our approach was restricted to the extraction of artificial text inserted by a video titling machine and was carried out on news video data.

Additional research is required to extract scene text which is often shown in TV sports news video data, documentary video data, etc. We plan to develop a more efficient and robust text extraction and recognition algorithm without any limitation.

References

[1] U. Gargi, S. Antani, and R. Kasturi. Indexing test events in digital video databases. *Proc. of 14th Int. Conf. on Pattern Recognition, Brisbane, Australia*, pages 1481–1483, 1998.

[2] S. Kurakake, H. Kuwano, and K. Odaka. Recognition of visual feature matching of text region in video for conceptual indexing. *Proc. of SPIE'97 - Storage and Retrieval for Image and Video Databases V, San Jose*, 3022:368–379, 1997.

[3] H. Li and D. Doermann. Automatic identification of text in digital key frames. *Proc. of 14th Int. Conf. on Pattern Recognition, Brisbane, Australia*, pages 618–620, 1998.

[4] R. Lienhart and F. Stuber. Automatic text recognition in digital video. *Proc. of SPIE'97 - Image and Video Processing, San Jose*, 2666:180–188, 1997.

[5] M. A. Smith and T. Kanade. Video skimming for quick browsing based on audio and image characterization. Technical Report CMU-CS-95-186, Carnegie Mellon University, 1995.

[6] B. L. Yeo. Visual content highlighting via automatic extraction of embedded captions on mpeg compressed video. *Proc. of SPIE'96 - Digital Video Compression: Algorithms and Technologies, San Jose*, 2128:142–149, 1996.

A Method of Analyzing the Handling of Paper Documents in Motion Images

Keiji Yamada, Koji Ishikawa, and Noboru Nakajima
C&C Media Research Laboratories, NEC Corporation
{yamada, koji, noboru}@ccm.cl.nec.co.jp

Abstract

In this paper, we describe a new system for analyzing the motions involved in handling documents on a desk. Video images are captured by a camera mounted above the desk and the motion which occurs when someone handles the document is classified as movement of the document, turning of the pages, or finger pointing. Furthermore, the system can detect the appearance of fresh regions as a result of movement of the document and the turning of its pages and it can also detect the positions of fingers in the image to realize a natural pointing function. We evaluated implementations of some components of the system and found that they provide sufficient performance to act as parts of a user interface for an interactive document management system.

1. Introduction

A huge number of paper documents are still processed in offices, although almost all are now electronically produced and management systems for them have been gaining in popularity. If management of the paper documents that are piled up on desks can be integrated to these systems to some extent, we will be able to make better use of the huge amount of knowledge that is still stored on paper.

OCR (Optical Character Recognition) can be applied to turn paper documents into electronic documents. To implement this approach, however, someone has to spend a great deal of time by the scanner digitizing all of the paper documents. The need to carry out such a boring operation is a factor against the OCR approach.

In order to address this problem, we need to develop a document management system as follows:

1. It should allow users to scan documents without placing a noticeably heavy work load on them.
2. Placing the documents on the system should also offer definite advantages.

We have designed a real world document management system that we call RDocMan. RDocMan scans paper documents interactively in real time by using a combination of a typical video camera and a pan-tilt camera.

This paper describes a new method of analyzing video images which are captured by a typical video camera that is set above a desk. The method can recognize document handling activities such as movement of the document, turning of its pages, and finger pointing as well as detect newly appearing document regions and indicated points. The results of this analysis are used in automatic document scanning by means of the pan-tilt camera and other interactive information services in RDocMan.

This application of dual video cameras is one of the main differences between the RDocMan system and a conventional Digital Desk system[1, 2].

2. RDocMan: A real world document management system

We have developed RDocMan in order to satisfy the demands outlined in the introduction. In RDocMan,

1. newly appearing documents can be detected and automatically scanned without being turned over,
2. information related to the detected document or the part at which the user's finger is pointing is immediately presented to the user. This doesn't interrupt, but rather assists in, the user's intellectual work.

In order to achieve the goals outlined in the introduction, RDocMan consists of three subsystems as shown in Fig.1.

In the capture subsystem two cameras are placed above the desk. A fixed video camera captures scenes over the whole desk. The user's activities on the desk are analyzed as reflected in images from this camera. A pan-tilt camera with a magnifying lens is used to scan documents at a high resolution. This is achieved by the combination of high resolution images with an image mosaic technique and a super resolution technique that are based on the structure as reflected in the document layout[3]. The high resolution images that are generated are passed through OCR and the results are transferred to the document management subsystem.

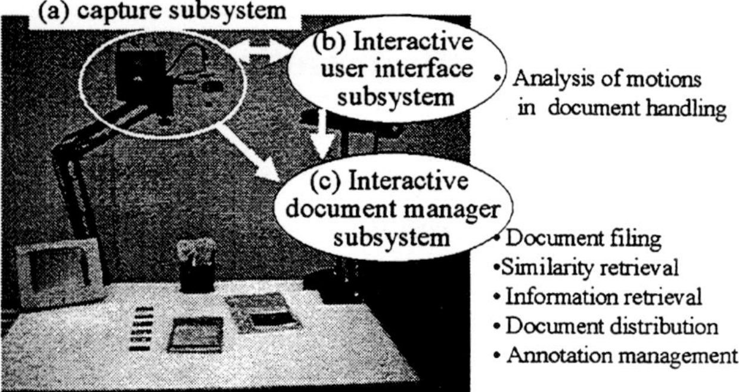

Figure 1. The proposed real world document management system RDocMan

The second part of RDocMan is the interactive user interface that is based on the analysis of the motions involved in document handling, and is the main topic of this paper. Documents which have not previously appeared on the desk top can be detected. The user interface can find the point in a document at which the user's finger is pointing. Pointing of the finger is thus used as a pointing device, in the computer-user interface sense, for the document management subsystem.

The third subsystem is an interactive document manager that files the high resolution images of the document with their OCRed texts and provides information related to the parts of the document. It can show the meaning of a word at which the user points and retrieve relevant articles from the Internet[3].

The document manager also implements document retrieval based on similarity of document layout, photographs, tables, and text[3, 4]. Furthermore, it manages hyperlinks between annotations put on paper documents and electronic documents corresponding to the paper documents[5]. Document handling such as movement of the document and finger pointing activity is detected and used to control these functions.

3. Analysis of motion involved in document handling and document detection

3.1. Considerations in the analysis

Motions involved in document handling are analyzed to automatically detect both finger pointing and the appearance of new documents. This is used to provide a user interface for the document management system.

We will briefly consider the properties of objects such as documents, and hands on a desk.

1. Document surfaces might consist of many colorful regions, but almost all of them in fact consist of white background regions and black letters.
2. Similar documents will overlap on the desk.
3. The background is not stable because a document under the one being moved will often be moved slightly.
4. The color of skin is useful for the detection of fingers. Similar colors are, however, often used in printed documents.
5. Objects move relatively quickly. While working at a desk, we will sometimes move documents at speeds of more than 100 cm per second.
6. The shape of documents will also change while they are in motion. When turning a page, both its appearance and its three dimensional shape are altered.

The general similarity of documents and instability of the background on a desk make it difficult to accurately segment documents from each other and from the surface of the desk. Document borders may be too ambiguous to detect in an image frame. We also need information beyond color to distinguish real fingers from those in photographs. Images of motion on the desk thus need to be analyzed to determine the motion of the document and of the user's hands. Considerations of speed and the shapes of objects in motion make objects hard to track. They make the correct estimation of optical flow difficult.

Fortunately, our purpose is not to obtain a detailed description of the objects in motion, but to determine the regions of newly appearing pages and of the user's finger when the motion stops. The analysis system is a kind of pattern classification. For its design, we assume that

1. Document handling activity includes document motion and hand motion.
2. Document motion consists of
   (a) **document movement**: the document being moved by the user's left or right hand in any direction,
   (b) **page turning**: pages being turned from left to right or from right to left.
3. While the user is indicating part of the document by pointing, the document will be still and only hands will move. We call this **finger pointing**.

3.2. Analysis of motions in document handling

When the document comes to rest after a period of motion, the kind of motion that occurred since the preceding time at which the document was stationary can be analyzed. Feature values are extracted from each video frame while the document is in motion. The kind of motion is assessed and the regions of the document subsequent to the period of motion are detected. The analysis is described in some detail in the following paragraphs.

(1) The process of each video frame

a) Frame differences and detection of hand regions

Moving parts are indicated by the binary difference image $D_t(x,y)$ for two consecutive frames, $I_{t-1}(x,y)$ and $I_t(x,y)$. Regions with a color that is similar to the range of skin colors are selected from the frame and are represented by $\hat{H}_t(x,y)$. Then the hand regions $H_t(x,y)$ for the t-th frame is generated by

$$H_t(x,y) = \hat{H}_t(x,y) \cdot D_t(x,y) \qquad \text{for all } x, y. \quad (1)$$

In $H_t(x,y)$ and $D_t(x,y)$, pixel values are 1's and 0's at the pixels which belong to and don't belong to the objective regions, respectively.

b) Detection of document regions

Subtraction of the hand regions from the difference image produces the document region $B_t(x,y)$.

c) Extraction of motion features

The motion features are (i) the vector from the center of the hand region of the current frame to the center of the hand region in the previous frame, (ii) a similar vector related to the document regions, (iii) the difference $A_d(t)$ between the current area $A_c(t)$ of the document region and its average area $A_a(t)$, where $A_a(t) = \frac{1}{t}\sum_{j=1}^{t} A_c(j)$ and $A_d(t) = (A_c(t) - A_a(t))/A_a(t)$, and so on. Totally, sixteen features are extracted in each frame.

d) Generation of accumulated document regions

The document region $B_t(x,y)$ is added to the accumulated document image $P_t(x,y)$ under the assumption that the motion is the turning of pages.

$$P_t(x,y) = P_{t-1}(x,y) + B_t(x,y) \qquad \text{for all } x, y. \quad (2)$$

Examples are shown in Fig.2(c) and Fig.3 (c). The document region is shifted so that the center (x_p, y_p) of the document region in the $(t-1)$-th frame is located at the center (x_c, y_c) of the current document region. Then, the accumulated document image $M_t(x,y)$ is updated by

$$M_t(x,y) = M_{t-1}(x - x_c + x_p, y - y_c + y_p) + B_t(x,y) \ . \quad (3)$$

Examples are shown in Fig.2(b) and Fig.3 (b).

(2) The process of the final decision

a) Decision on the motion

At pauses in the motion, a discriminant score for each kind of motion is calculated from the feature vector which consists of feature values generated during the movement. We used a three-layer perceptron with three output scores which correspond to document movement, page turning , and finger pointing. Actually, the period of the motion is segmented into seven sections equally spaced in time. The feature values for each kind of motion feature are averaged

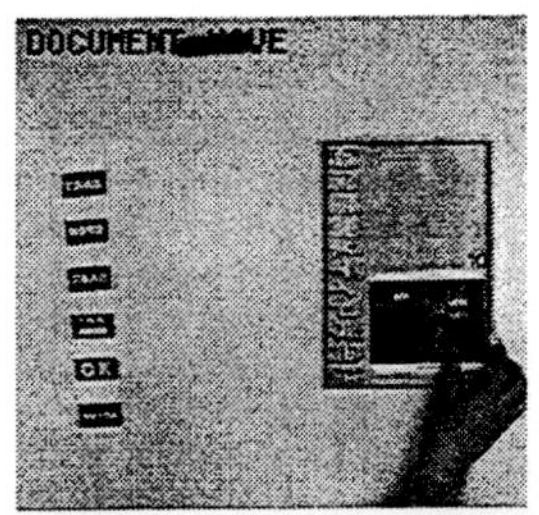

(a) detected document region after document movement

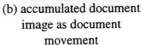

(b) accumulated document image as document movement

(c) accumulated document image as page turning

Figure 2. Accumulated document images after a document movement

in each section. Totally, 112 (16×7) feature values are used as input into the three layer perceptron with fifty hidden units.

b) Generation of candidate document regions

When pages are turned, a document region candidate is generated as the minimum bounding rectangle of a detected object in the accumulated document image as page turning. A region is generated in a similar way subsequent to document movement.

c) Scoring the candidate document regions

The sizes of the candidate document regions are compared with the sizes of previously detected documents. If the size of the candidate document region as page turning is different from those of the documents that were previously detected at the same position, a cost value is subtracted from the discriminant score for page turning in the above process (2)-a). The discriminant score of the document movement is also modified in the same way.

d) Final decision

The kind of motion which has the maximum score is selected and the resulting document region is selected as the detected document. If the discriminant score of finger pointing is the largest, the top of the hand region is determined to be the position indicated by the finger.

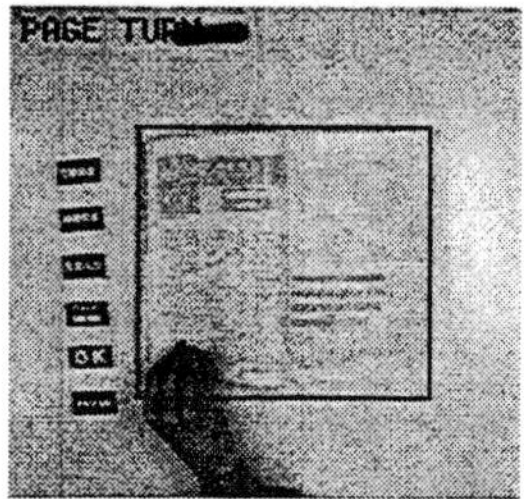

(a) detected document region after page turning

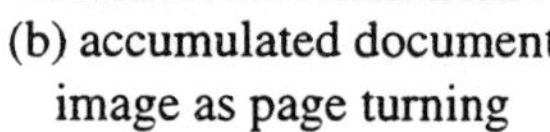

(b) accumulated document image as page turning

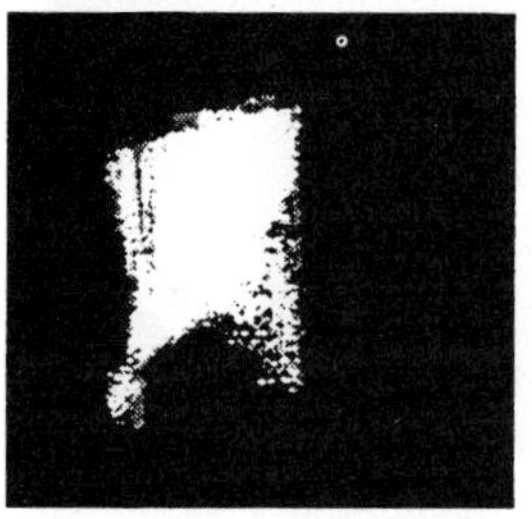

(c) accumulated document image as document movement

Figure 3. Accumulated document images after page turning

4. Evaluation of the proposed method

In order to examine the proposed method, we evaluated the classification accuracy and measured the precision of the detected document region and that of the detected position at which a finger pointed.

(1) We evaluated the accuracy with which the turning of pages was discriminated from movement of the document. Ten subjects randomly moved the documents, turned the pages, moved only the hands for a total of 1727 times. Examples of the decisions are shown in Fig.2(a) and Fig.3(a). The total error rate was 5.6%. The classification rates are listed in Table 1. It shows that motions of page turning were often mis-classified as document movements. This will be improved by verifying resultant document regions in detail.

Table 1. Total error rates

		Detected classes		
		Document movement	Page turning	Finger pointing
Correct classes	Document movement	96.0%	2.7%	1.1%
	Page turning	8.2%	91.2%	0.6%
	Finger pointing	2.6%	0.4%	97.0%

(2) We evaluated the precision with which regions were detected as the difference between the top left-hand corner of the detected region and the top left-hand corner of the corresponding real region, and the corresponding difference for the bottom right-hand corner. For the measurement a subject randomly moved the document and turned the pages one thousand times. For document movements, almost all differences were within 1.0 cm. The maximum difference was 1.5 cm. For page turning, the differences were larger than those arising from document movements and were mainly within 1.5 cm.

(3) We evaluated the machine-estimated precision of the positions of finger tips in the same way. In this case, a subject moved his finger at a thousand times. The precision was measured. The differences between the detected positions and the actual positions were almost all within 6mm. If the gap between lines in the text is wider than 6mm, the finger tip can be used to indicate words that are wider than 6 mm. on the page.

5. Concluding remarks

In this paper, we have outlined a new method of analysis for the motions involved in the handling of a document on a desk in the real world. We have demonstrated the accuracy of the method by experimental evaluation. The results indicated that the methods can be used in a sophisticated electronic document scanning and OCR system that is easy to use. Pointing of fingers and detection of motion are the main inputs to the user interface. In the proposed method, the rotations of documents are not allowed. Turning pages in the direction other than the horizontal direction cannot be dealt with, either. We need to deal with these activities. Furthermore, we will improve the accuracy of the system by recording motions to obtain a corrective feedback.

References

[1] P. Wellner, Interacting with Paper on the DigitalDesk. Communications of the ACM, Vol. 36, no. 7, pp. 86-96, 1993.

[2] Stuart Taylor, Chris Dance, William Newman, et al., Augmented paper: using a video camera to support selective scanning from paper to screen, Xerox XRCE Cambridge Technical Report, EPC-1998-105, 1998.

[3] N.Nakajima, N. Tanaka, K. Yamada, Document Reconstruction and Recognition from an Image Sequence, the proc. of ICPR'98, pp.922-925, Aug. 1998

[4] T.Kamiya, H. Daimon, K. Ishida, N. Nakajima, M. Namiuchi, T. Segawa, the Development of a Document Digitizing System: The "Information Factory", Int. Symp. on Digital Media Information Base, Nov. 1997

[5] N. Ito, N. Fujita, H. Shimazu, N. Nakajima, and Keiji Yamada, TransWorld: paper world as avatar of electronic world, CHI, Extended Abstracts, pp.206-207, 1999.

Affine-Invariant Gray-Scale Character Recognition Using GAT Correlation

Toru Wakahara and Yoshimasa Kimura

NTT Cyber Solutions Laboratories
1-1 Hikari-no-oka, Yokosuka-shi, Kanagawa, 239-0847 Japan
E-mail: waka@marsh.hil.ntt.co.jp

Abstract

This paper describes a new technique of gray-scale character recognition that offers both noise-tolerance and affine-invariance. The key ideas are twofold. First is the use of normalized cross-correlation to realize noise-tolerance. Second is the application of global affine transformation (GAT) to the input image so as to achieve affine-invariant correlation with the target image. In particular, optimal GAT is efficiently determined by the successive iteration method. We demonstrate the high matching ability of the proposed method using gray-scale images of numerals subjected to random Gaussian noise and a wide range of affine transformation. The achieved recognition rate of 92.1% against rotation within 30 degrees, scale change within 30%, and translation within 20% of the character width is sufficiently high compared to the 42.0% offered by simple correlation.

1. Introduction

Most current OCR systems binarize the input image as preprocessing. However, input images often suffer from gray-scale degradation or image distortion and have complex backgrounds with color or textures. In such cases, the conventional binarization process loses a significant amount of information. This is a real problem because demand is increasing for the direct recognition of text in video frames and WWW images.

Regarding the direct recognition of gray-scale characters, there are two major approaches. The first approach is using topographic features [1]. This approach is effective in segmenting touching characters, but is sensitive to image defects and noise. The second approach is correlation-based matching [2]. However, correlation in itself is weak against geometrical distortion like affine transformation. On the other hand, the "perturbation method" [3] and "tangent-distance" [4] were proposed with the aim of distortion-tolerant image matching. However, both of these techniques can deal with only a limited range of affine transformation.

In our former paper [5], we introduced the concept of global affine transformation as a general deformation model to realize distortion-tolerant shape matching as applied to binary images of characters. By extending the concept of GAT as applied to the matching of gray-scale images, we proposed the promising technique of affine-invariant correlation of gray-scale characters using GAT iteration [6]. Conventional correlation-based matching was greatly reinforced in two ways. First is the use of normalized cross-correlation as a noise-tolerant matching measure. Second is the application of global affine transformation (GAT) to the input gray-scale image so as to realize affine-invariant correlation with the target gray-scale image.

This paper demonstrates the high matching ability of the proposed method using gray-scale images of numerals subjected to random Gaussian noise and a wide range of affine transformation including rotation, scale change, shearing, and translation. Moreover, extensive recognition experiments show that the proposed GAT correlation method achieves far superior recognition rates to the normalized cross-correlation without GAT and the conventional normalized inner product of the two images.

2. GAT correlation method

This paper deals with the matching of two gray-scale images. We denote the two images as **F**, the input gray-scale image, and **G**, the target gray-scale image, and represent **F** and **G** by gray level functions $f(\boldsymbol{r})$ and $g(\boldsymbol{r})$, respectively, as follows:

$$\mathbf{F} = \{ f(\boldsymbol{r}) \},\quad \mathbf{G} = \{ g(\boldsymbol{r}) \},\quad \boldsymbol{r} \in K \tag{1}$$

where $\boldsymbol{r}$ denotes a 2D loci vector defined in the bounded 2D domain of K. Of course, gray level functions $f(\boldsymbol{r})$ and $g(\boldsymbol{r})$ take on non-negative values.

1051-4651/00 $10.00 © 2000 IEEE

2.1. Normalized cross-correlation

The conventional and most popular matching measure for the two images is the normalized inner product or "simple similarity measure" $S(f, g)$ defined by

$$S(f, g) \equiv (f, g) / \|f\| \cdot \|g\|$$
$$= \int_K f(\boldsymbol{r})\, g(\boldsymbol{r})\, d\boldsymbol{r} \,/\, [\, \int_K f(\boldsymbol{r})^2 d\boldsymbol{r} \int_K g(\boldsymbol{r})^2 d\boldsymbol{r}\,]^{1/2}, \quad (2)$$

where (f, g) denotes the inner product of f and g. However, the discrimination ability of the simple similarity measure $S(f, g)$ deteriorates considerably in the presence of image defects and noise [2].

As Iijima [7] proved theoretically, the normalized cross-correlation, defined by

$$C(f, g) = \int_K (f(\boldsymbol{r}) - \mu)\,(g(\boldsymbol{r}) - \nu)\, d\boldsymbol{r} \,/$$
$$[\, \int_K (f(\boldsymbol{r}) - \mu)^2 d\boldsymbol{r} \int_K (g(\boldsymbol{r}) - \nu)^2 d\boldsymbol{r}\,]^{1/2}, \quad (3)$$

where μ and ν are the mean gray levels of $f(\boldsymbol{r})$ and $g(\boldsymbol{r})$, respectively, remains unchanged under image blurring or image degradation.

Therefore, we adopt the normalized cross-correlation to realize noise-tolerance. Moreover, we transform $f(\boldsymbol{r})$ and $g(\boldsymbol{r})$ so that they have zero mean and unit norm, and, finally, obtain the matching measure given by

$$C(f, g) = \int_K f(\boldsymbol{r})\, g(\boldsymbol{r})\, d\boldsymbol{r}. \quad (4)$$

However, we still have the problem that the correlation in itself cannot compensate for geometrical distortion such as affine transformation.

2.2. Affine-invariant correlation by GAT

This subsection introduces affine-invariant correlation by GAT and a simple computational model of determining optimal GAT using the successive iteration method [6].

First, we define global affine transformation (GAT). GAT is uniform affine transformation as applied to input gray-scale image **F** to generate GAT-superimposed input gray-scale image **F*** as follows

$$\mathbf{F}^* = \{ f^*(\boldsymbol{r}) \}, \quad \boldsymbol{r} \in K$$
$$\boldsymbol{r}^* = \mathrm{A}\boldsymbol{r} + \boldsymbol{b},$$
$$f^*(\boldsymbol{r}^*) = f^*(\mathrm{A}\boldsymbol{r} + \boldsymbol{b}) = f(\boldsymbol{r}), \quad (5)$$

where $\mathrm{A} = (\, \boldsymbol{a}_1\ \boldsymbol{a}_2\,)$ is a 2×2 matrix representing rotation, scale change, and shearing; and $\boldsymbol{b} = (\, b_x, b_y\,)^T$ is a 2D translation vector. Here, $\boldsymbol{a}_1$ and $\boldsymbol{a}_2$ represent two basis vectors of the affine-transformed space.

Second, we define a fundamental objective function Φ of optimal GAT for affine-invariant correlation by

$$\Phi = \int_K f^*(\boldsymbol{r})\, g(\boldsymbol{r})\, d\boldsymbol{r} = \int_K f(\boldsymbol{r})\, g(\mathrm{A}\boldsymbol{r} + \boldsymbol{b})\, d\boldsymbol{r}$$
$$\rightarrow \ \max \text{ for A}, \boldsymbol{b}, \quad (6)$$

which, however, requires exhaustive trial and error to determine optimal A and $\boldsymbol{b}$ because A and $\boldsymbol{b}$ are directly embedded in the general gray-level function g. Therefore, we adopt an equivalent objective function Ψ by introducing a Gaussian kernel of A and $\boldsymbol{b}$ into Φ as

$$\Psi = \iint_K f(\boldsymbol{r})\, g(\boldsymbol{r}')\, \exp(-\|\mathrm{A}\boldsymbol{r} + \boldsymbol{b} - \boldsymbol{r}'\|^2 / D)\, d\boldsymbol{r} d\boldsymbol{r}'$$
$$\rightarrow \ \max \text{ for A}, \boldsymbol{b}, \quad (7)$$

where D specifies the spread of the Gaussian kernel. Also, it is to be noted that (7) is equivalent to (6) as $D \rightarrow 0$. Here, we give the D value in a deterministic way as

$$D = 1/2\ \{ \text{Mean of} [\, \min_{\boldsymbol{r}'} \|\boldsymbol{r} - \boldsymbol{r}'\|^2 ;$$
$$f(\boldsymbol{r}) = g(\boldsymbol{r}') \ \text{ for } \forall \boldsymbol{r} \in K\,]$$
$$+ \text{Mean of} [\, \min_{\boldsymbol{r}} \|\boldsymbol{r}' - \boldsymbol{r}\|^2 ;$$
$$g(\boldsymbol{r}') = f(\boldsymbol{r}) \ \text{ for } \forall \boldsymbol{r}' \in K\,]\, \}. \quad (8)$$

Third, by setting the differentials of Ψ with respect to A and $\boldsymbol{b}$ equal to zero and linearizing the obtained equations, we obtain the following set of linear equations:

$$\mathrm{O} = \iint_K \gamma(\boldsymbol{r}, \boldsymbol{r}')\, f(\boldsymbol{r})\, g(\boldsymbol{r}')\, \boldsymbol{r}\, (\mathrm{A}\boldsymbol{r} + \boldsymbol{b} - \boldsymbol{r}')^T$$
$$\times \exp(-\|\boldsymbol{r} - \boldsymbol{r}'\|^2 / D)\, d\boldsymbol{r} d\boldsymbol{r}',$$
$$\boldsymbol{0} = \iint_K \gamma(\boldsymbol{r}, \boldsymbol{r}')\, f(\boldsymbol{r})\, g(\boldsymbol{r}')\, (\mathrm{A}\boldsymbol{r} + \boldsymbol{b} - \boldsymbol{r}')$$
$$\times \exp(-\|\boldsymbol{r} - \boldsymbol{r}'\|^2 / D)\, d\boldsymbol{r} d\boldsymbol{r}', \quad (9)$$

where $\gamma(\boldsymbol{r}, \boldsymbol{r}')$ is introduced as a matching stabilizing constraint based on topographic features as

$$\gamma(\boldsymbol{r}, \boldsymbol{r}') = \max\ \{ (\nabla f(\boldsymbol{r}), \nabla g(\boldsymbol{r}')), 0 \}. \quad (10)$$

It is to be noted that $\gamma(\boldsymbol{r}, \boldsymbol{r}')$ equals zero when the angle between two gradient vectors, $\nabla f(\boldsymbol{r})$ and $\nabla g(\boldsymbol{r}')$, is more than 90°. On the other hand, when the angle between the two gradient vectors is less than 90°, the greater the norms of $\nabla f(\boldsymbol{r})$ and $\nabla g(\boldsymbol{r}')$ are, the greater the value of $\gamma(\boldsymbol{r}, \boldsymbol{r}')$ is. This can have the desired effect in that $\gamma(\boldsymbol{r}, \boldsymbol{r}')$ reinforces the contribution of edges to correlation matching, while suppressing the contribution of grounds.

2.3. Successive iteration method for GAT

Start : Calculate the initial value of $C_0 = C(f, g)$ of (4) between the original input and target gray-scale images, **F** and **G**.

Loop : Determine the GAT components of A and $\boldsymbol{b}$ by solving the simultaneous linear equations of (9) by conventional techniques like Gaussian elimination [8]. Next, generate the GAT-superimposed input gray-scale image $\mathbf{F}^* = \{ f^*(\boldsymbol{r}) \}$ by (5) and substitute $\mathbf{F}^*$ for **F**. Update the value of D of (8) and $\gamma(\boldsymbol{r}, \boldsymbol{r}')$ of (10).

Pause : Calculate the updated value of $C_1 = C(f, g)$ of (4). If $C_1 > C_0$, substitute C_1 for C_0, and go to *Loop* ; otherwise, output the maximal value of C_0 as the final result of affine-invariant correlation, and then stop.

3. Experimental results

We conducted matching and recognition experiments using gray-scale images of numerals subjected to random Gaussian noise and a wide range of affine transformation.

Figure 1 shows all target gray-scale images $g(\boldsymbol{r})$ with zero mean and unit norm, where each point is denoted by black circle, double circle, white circle, dot, and blank according to temporary quantization into 5 discrete levels. The spatial resolution was 32×32. These images were free of noise, and served as clean templates.

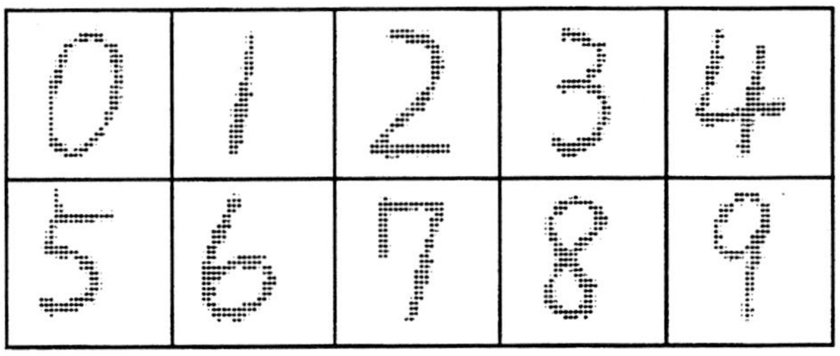

Figure 1. Target images of numerals.

On the other hand, each input gray-scale image $f(\boldsymbol{r})$ was artificially generated by applying arbitrary affine transformation A and $\boldsymbol{b}$ and, then, adding random Gaussian noise $n(\boldsymbol{r})$ with zero mean and unit variance to one of the target images $g(\boldsymbol{r})$ as follows:

$$f(\boldsymbol{r}) = g(\mathrm{A}^{-1}(\boldsymbol{r} - \boldsymbol{b})) + \kappa \cdot \delta \cdot n(\boldsymbol{r}), \quad \kappa \in (0, 1] \qquad (11)$$

where κ controls the magnitude of added random Gaussian noise, and δ denotes the dynamic range of $g(\boldsymbol{r})$. Finally, $f(\boldsymbol{r})$ was transformed to have zero mean and unit norm so that we calculate the normalized-cross correlation by (4).

Incidentally, when applying the GAT correlation method to these examples of digital images, we replaced the integral with the sum in (9) and calculated gray-scale gradients by the Roberts operator [9] in (10).

Figure 2 shows an example of the matching process using GAT iteration between the target image of "four" and the input image generated by the following affine parameters: $\|\boldsymbol{a}_1\| = 1.20$, $\|\boldsymbol{a}_2\| = 1.10$, $\angle \boldsymbol{a}_1 = -20°$, $\angle \boldsymbol{a}_2 = 60°$, $b_x = 2$, $b_y = -2$, and random Gaussian noise of $\kappa = 0.7$. Fig. 2 (a) shows the initial overlapped image of the target and input images, the correlation value is low at 0.282, where the points of the target image are denoted by asterisks. Fig. 2 (b)-(d) show GAT matching results at iterations of 3, 9, and 19, respectively, where the obtained correlation values were 0.394, 0.795, and 0.827 in this order. The estimated affine parameters for the result of Fig. 2 (d) were as follows: $\|\boldsymbol{a}'_1\| = 1.27$, $\|\boldsymbol{a}'_2\| = 1.30$, $\angle \boldsymbol{a}'_1 = -18.8°$, $\angle \boldsymbol{a}'_2 = 57.1°$, $b'_x = 2.48$, $b'_y = -1.48$, which were satisfactory compared to the correct ones.

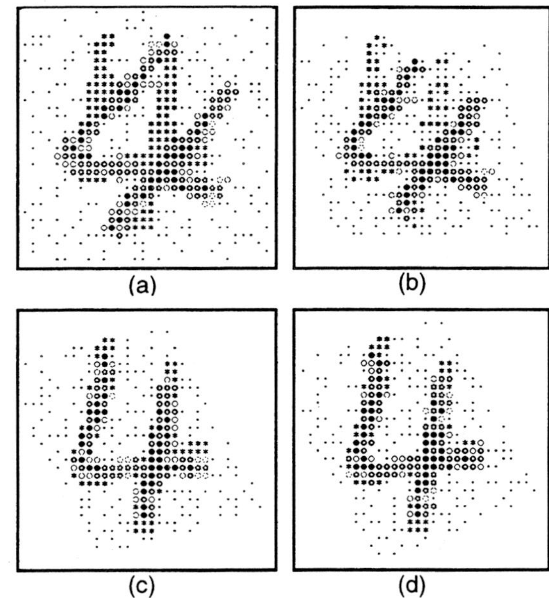

Figure 2. Example of GAT iteration.

Next, we show three kinds of quantitative results gained by applying the proposed GAT correlation method to the matching of input images artificially generated by either pure rotation or pure scale change or pure translation against their correct target images. Random Gaussian noise of $\kappa = 0.7$ was added to each input image.

First, Figure 3 shows the relation between the mean of normalized cross-correlation values and the rotation angle which was varied from −45° to +45° in 5 degree steps. Hence, the total number of input images was 10 digits times 19 rotation angles.

From Fig. 3, it is found that the converged correlation achieved a high value, more than 0.7, even if the original correlation value without GAT iteration was around 0.2.

Secondly, Figure 4 shows the relation between the mean of normalized cross-correlation values and the scale change which was varied from 0.5 to 1.5 in 0.1 steps. Here, the total number of input images was 10 digits times 11 scale changes.

From Fig. 4, it is found that the GAT correlation method is more robust against image expansion than against image shrinking. This asymmetry is due to blurring effect of the Gaussian kernel in (7) which is apt to bring about image contraction by GAT.

Thirdly, Figure 5 shows the relation between the mean of normalized cross-correlation values and the norm of translation, Δ, defined by $\Delta = \max(|b_x|, |b_y|)$, where b_x and b_y took integer values $\in [-5, +5]$. Hence, the total number of input images was 10 digits times 121 translations.

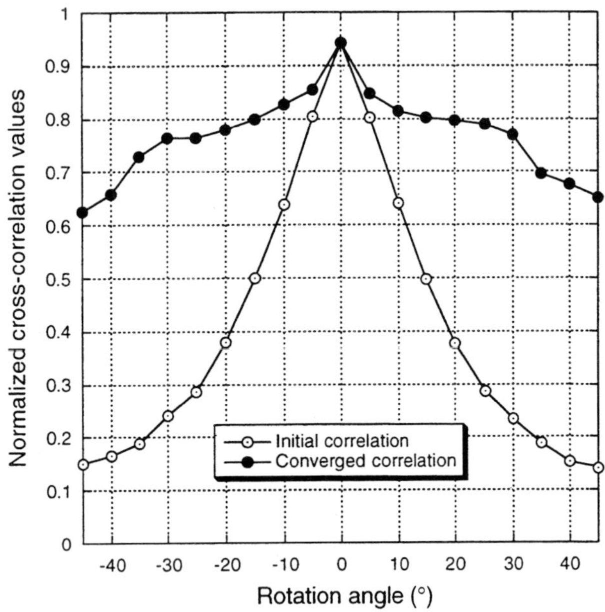

Figure 3. Relation between correlation values and rotation angle along with noise.

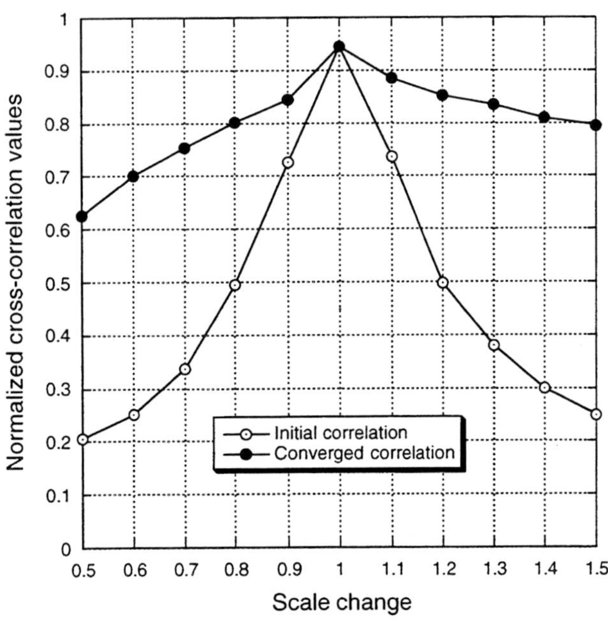

Figure 4. Relation between correlation values and scale change along with noise.

Figure 5 shows that the proposed method achieved a high correlation value, more than 0.8, even if the original correlation value without GAT iteration was less than 0.2.

From Fig. 3, Fig. 4, and Fig. 5, it is found that the proposed method is more robust against translation than against rotation or scale change. This is because the matching stabilizing factor $\gamma(\boldsymbol{r}, \boldsymbol{r}')$ of (10) requires high similarity in gray-scale gradients of matched points.

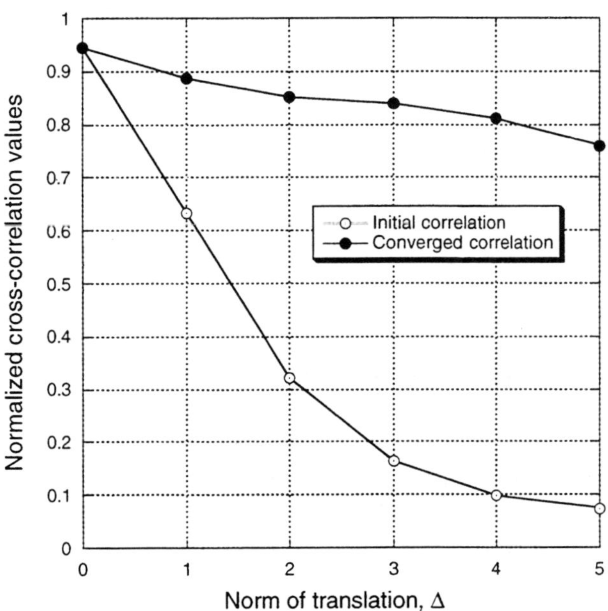

Figure 5. Relation between correlation values and norm of translation along with noise.

Finally, we show the results of extensive recognition experiments conducted using artificial input images subjected to combinations of rotation, scale change, and translation along with random Gaussian noise.

Figure 6 shows the relation between the recognition rates and the norm of translation, Δ, under various combinations of rotation and scale change. The range of rotation was set at within 30 degrees in 5 degree steps. Also, the range of scale change was set at between 0.7 and 1.3 in 0.1 steps. Hence, the number of artificially generated input images per digit for each translation vector $\boldsymbol{b}$ was 13 times 7. Finally, random Gaussian noise of $\kappa = 0.7$ was added to each input image.

In Fig. 6, the corresponding recognition rates obtained by using the normalized cross-correlation without GAT and the normalized inner product are also plotted. Here, we call these two conventional methods "simple correlation" in contrast to GAT correlation.

Figure 6 shows clearly that the discrimination ability of GAT correlation is far superior to that of simple correlation. Actually, the achieved recognition rate of 92.1% against rotation within 30 degrees, scale change within 30%, and translation of $\Delta \leq 3$ or within 20% of the character width is quite high compared to the 42.0% offered by simple correlation.

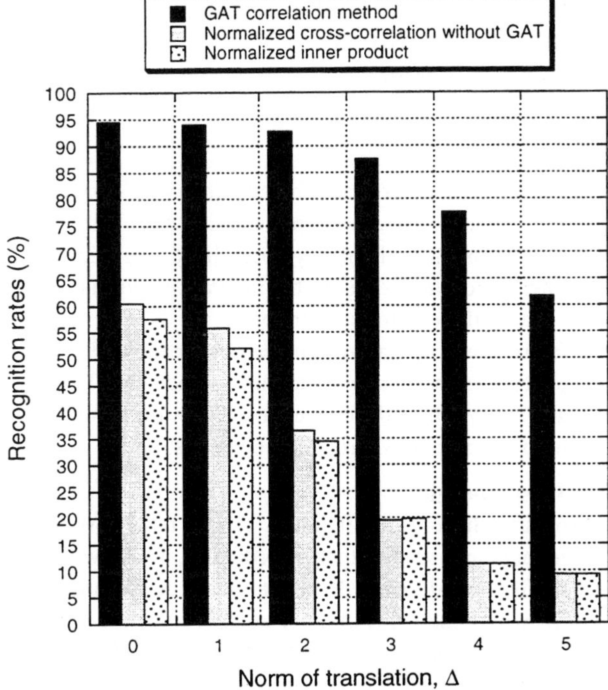

Figure 6. Relation between recognition rates and norm of translation under rotation, scale change, and noise.

A failure in GAT correlation can be attributed to any one of the following factors: 1) the "local optimum" problem in iteratively determining optimal GAT, 2) the excessive image contraction that occurs when the values of D of (8) are too large, and 3) the limit of topographic constraints using gray-scale gradients in $\gamma(\boldsymbol{r}, \boldsymbol{r}')$ of (10).

Finally, we discuss the trade-off between recognition time and recognition ability within GAT correlation.

If we adopt simple correlation by preparing multiple templates against rotation within 30 degrees in 5 degree steps, scale change between 0.7 and 1.3 in 0.1 steps, and translation of $\Delta \leq 3$ in integer steps, the total number of templates is 4,459=13×7×49. On the other hand, the present recognition time of GAT correlation is about 10^4 times larger than that of simple correlation using a single template. In this situation, simple correlation using 4,459 templates per digit is only about two times faster than GAT correlation. However, as is clear, if we prepare multiple templates against a wider range of affine transformation, including shearing, the recognition time of simple correlation would be much larger than that of GAT correlation. From this consideration, we can say that GAT correlation provides a very powerful and useful solution to the problem of affine-invariant gray-scale character recognition under both heavy image degradation and geometrical distortion.

4. Conclusion

We have demonstrated successful experiments in which the GAT correlation method was applied to the matching and recognition of gray-scale images of numerals subjected to random Gaussian noise and a wide variety of affine transformation. Future work is to apply our method to gray-scale character recognition not only in real-life paper documents but also in video frames and WWW images.

References

[1] L. Wang and T. Pavlidis, "Direct gray-scale extraction of features for character recognition," *IEEE Trans. Pattern Anal. Machine Intell.*, vol. 15, pp. 1053-1067, 1993.

[2] M. Sawaki and N. Hagita, "Recognition of degraded machine-printed characters using a complementary similarity measure and error-correction learning," *IEICE Trans. Inf. & Syst.*, vol. E79-D, pp. 491-497, 1996.

[3] T. M. Ha and H. Bunke, "Off-line, handwritten numeral recognition by perturbation method," *IEEE Trans. Pattern Anal. Machine Intell.*, vol. 19, pp. 535-539, 1997.

[4] P. Simard, Y. LeCun, and J. Denker, "Efficient pattern recognition using a new transformation distance," *Advances in Neural Information Processing Systems,* vol. 5, pp. 50-58, Morgan Kaufmann, 1993.

[5] T. Wakahara and K. Odaka, "Adaptive normalization of handwritten characters using global/local affine transformation," *IEEE Trans. Pattern Anal. Machine Intell.*, vol. 20, pp. 1332-1341, 1998.

[6] T. Wakahara and Y. Kimura, "Affine-invariant correlation of gray-scale characters using GAT iteration," *Proc. of 5th Int. Conf. Document Analysis and Recognition,* Sept. 1999, pp. 613-616.

[7] T. Iijima, *Pattern Recognition.* Tokyo: Corona, 1973, Chap. 6 (in Japanese).

[8] Mathematical Society of Japan, *Encyclopedic Dictionary of Mathematics.* Cambridge, MA: MIT Press, 1977.

[9] A. Rosenfeld and A. C. Kak, *Digital Picture Processing.* Second Edition. San Diego, CA: Academic Press, 1982.

Automatic Generation of Structured Hyperdocuments from Multi-Column Document Images *

Ji-Yeon Lee, Song-Ha Choi and Seong-Whan Lee
Center for Artificial Vision Research, Korea University
Anam-dong, Seongbuk-ku, Seoul 136-701, Korea
{jylee, shchoi, swlee}@image.korea.ac.kr

Abstract

In this paper, we propose two methods for converting complex multi-column document images into HTML documents, and a method for generating a structured table of contents(ToC) page based on the logical structure analysis of the document image.

Experiments with various kinds of multi-column document images show that HTML documents corresponding to the paper documents can be generated in a visual layout, and that their structured table of contents page, with the hierarchically ordered section titles hyperlinked to the contents, can be also produced by the proposed methods.

1. Introduction

The popular use of the internet, in these days, demands a type of documents accessible through the Web, for the purpose of sharing the documents. However, only a few works have been done on the conversion of paper documents into hyperdocuments. Most of the studies were about the conversion of single column document images that include text and image objects only [4, 5].

In this paper, we propose a system that converts multi-column document images into HTML documents, and also generates a table of contents page for the converted HTML documents. For the system, two methods are presented; one is implemented using the table structure and the other using their layer structure. We also suggest a method of generating a ToC page through a logical structure analysis [2].

2. HTML conversion of multi-column document images

2.1. An approach based on table structure

As a result of the geometrical structure analysis, a document image is divided into objects, each of which is classified as text, image, or table object. It is very easy to represent text and image objects by inserting simple tags in an HTML document without any specialized operations. On the other hand, table objects, having various formats, need some manipulations for conversion.

We propose a new algorithm for converting table objects in a paper document image into table objects in HTML format and apply this to the conversion of a multi-column document image into a hyperdocument as it is.

(1) Object merging

To have the objects fit into a virtual table format, we merge them and modify their coordinates, as shown in Figure 1. First, we divide a document image horizontally into regions where the value of a horizontal projection profile is zero. Second, for each of the horizontally divided regions, we divide it vertically where the value of a vertical projection profile is zero. Finally, from left to right and from top to bottom, object merging takes place in each region.

(2) Object ordering

By regarding each of the merged objects as a cell in a table, we construct a virtual table and arrange the objects in the same order that the cells of a table are created in an HTML document. The criteria for the arrangement order of the objects are as follows:

Let O_i and O_j be the *i*th and *j*th objects, respectively. Let x_i^{TL} and y_i^{TL} be the top and leftmost *x* and *y* coordinates of the O_i.

(1) If $|y_i^{TL} - y_j^{TL}| < th$ and $x_i^{TL} < x_j^{TL}$, $i, j = 1,..,n$, then O_i and O_j have the following properties:

- O_i and O_j exist in the same row.
- O_i has priority over O_j.

(2) If $|y_i^{TL} - y_j^{TL}| > th$ and $y_i^{TL} < y_j^{TL}$, $i, j = 1,..,n$, then O_i and O_j have the following properties:

- O_i and O_j exist in different rows.
- O_i has priority over O_j.

Figure 2 shows the result images of each stage of the approach based on the table structure.

*This research was supported by Creative Research Initiatives of the Ministry of Science and Technology, Korea.

1051-4651/00 $10.00 © 2000 IEEE

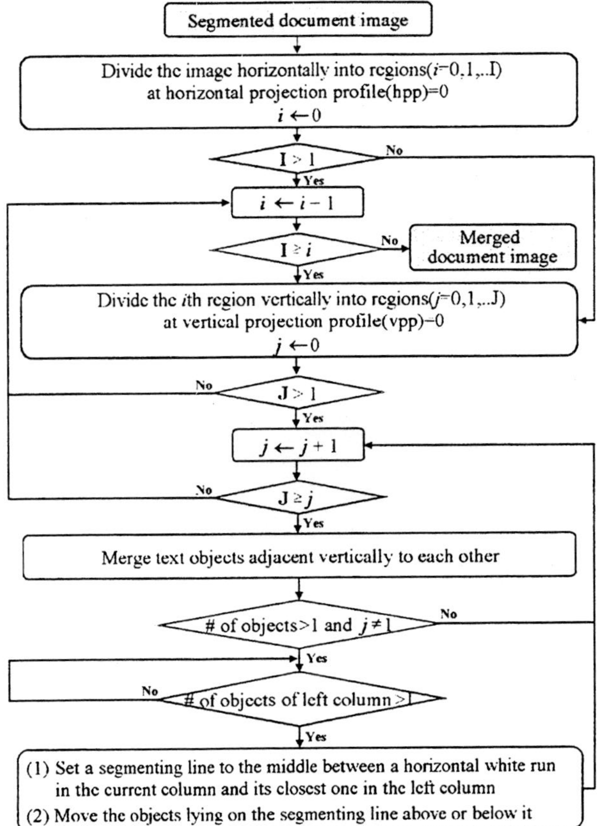

Segmented document image
Divide the image horizontally into regions(i=0,1,..I)
at horizontal projection profile(hpp)=0
i ←0
I > 1
No
Yes
i ← i - 1
I ≥ i
No
Merged
document image
Yes
Divide the ith region vertically into regions(j=0,1,..J)
at vertical projection profile(vpp)=0
j ←0
No
J > 1
Yes
j ← j + 1
No
J ≥ j
Yes
Merge text objects adjacent vertically to each other
# of objects>1 and j≠1
No
Yes
No
# of objects of left column>1
Yes
(1) Set a segmenting line to the middle between a horizontal white run
in the current column and its closest one in the left column
(2) Move the objects lying on the segmenting line above or below it

Figure 1. Flowchart of merging text objects

(3) Table-to-HTML algorithm

In this section, we present a Table-to-HTML algorithm as follows. The algorithm converts not only a table object in a document image into that of its HTML document but also a multi-column document image into its corresponding HTML document by considering it as a table object as a whole.

Initialize: $Colspan = Rowspan = 1, i = j = 0$;

If $Cell[i][j]_T$ and $Cell[i][j]_L == 1$, then {

(1) while ($Cell[i][j]_R == 1$)
Increase $Colspan$ and j values by one,

(2) while ($Cell[i][j]_B == 1$)
Increase $Rowspan$ and i values by one

}

Else move to next cell

$Cell[i][j]_T$, $Cell[i][j]_B$, $Cell[i][j]_L$ and $Cell[i][j]_R$ are the top, bottom, left and right lines of the cell, located in the ith row and the jth column of a table, respectively. While each cell is checked from left to right and from top to bottom, tagging is performed. And if a new row starts, we insert <TR><TD> tags; otherwise, we insert only a <TD> tag.

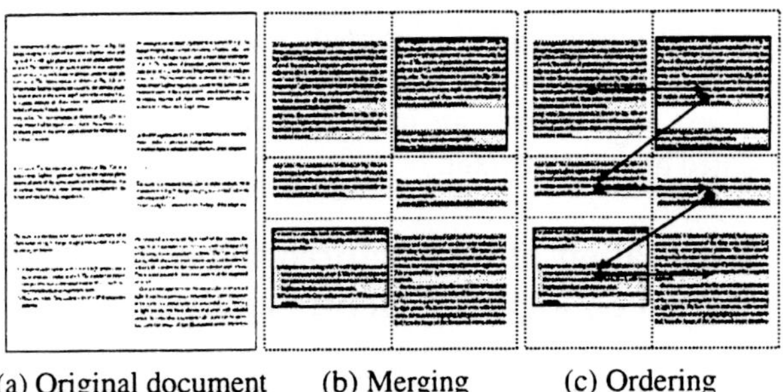

(a) Original document (b) Merging (c) Ordering

Figure 2. Result images of each conversion stage based on table structure

2.2. An approach based on layer structure

In this section, we use the layer structure for the conversion of multi-column document images.

(1) Object resizing

In order to have the converted HTML document fit into the screen's size regardless of the size of the input document, the objects in the image need to be resized in a constant rate before conversion. The conversion rate($CR = P_w/S_w$) for resizing is defined as the ratio of the width of the input image(P_w) to the width resolution of the user's screen(S_w).

This rate is also applied to the conversion of font size and line space as follows.

- $\tilde{O}_{fs} = O_{fs} \times CR$
  where O_{fs} and $\tilde{O}_{fs}$ are the font sizes of a text object and its converted object, respectively.
- $\tilde{O}_{ls} = (\tilde{O}_h - \tilde{O}_{fs} \times TL_n)/(TL_n\text{-}1)$
  where $\tilde{O}_{ls}$, $\tilde{O}_h$, and TL_n are the converted line space, the height of a text object, and the number of the lines in the text object, respectively.

(2) The structural properties of a text object

For more exact conversion, we must know concrete properties of the objects. In the discussion on the properties of text objects, text lines can be largely classified into 4 types under the following conditions.

Let $O_{sx(ex)}$ be the starting(ending) x coordinate of an object and $TL_{sx(ex)}$ be the starting(ending) x coordinate of a text line. Then,

- ***Indented Line(IL)***, if $(\Delta sx>th) \wedge (\Delta ex<th)$
- ***Entered Line(EL)***, if $(\Delta sx<th) \wedge (\Delta ex>th)$
- ***New Line(NeL)***, if $(\Delta sx>th) \wedge (\Delta ex>th)$
- ***Normal Line(NoL)***, if $(\Delta sx<th) \wedge (\Delta ex<th)$

where Δsx and Δex represent $|O_{sx}\text{-}TL_{sx}|$ and $|O_{ex}\text{-}TL_{ex}|$, respectively.

According to the line types defined above, proper tags are inserted to the HTML document. When a TL is of IL

type, "text-indent:Npx;" is inserted. When it is of EL type, "<BR>" is inserted. When it is of NeL type, "<BR>" and "text-indent:Npx;" are inserted. Here, N represents an indented distance in pixel.

3. Generation of a structured hyperdocument based on logical structure analysis

In this section, we take many related papers as input, and automatically generate a ToC page by extracting section titles and arranging them with respect to their hierarchical relation. A ToC page generated based on the logical structure analysis provides us with a clear overview of the logical flow of the entire input documents and its hyperlinks to the contents makes feasible the retrieval by section title or page number.

3.1. Section title extraction

We convert a technical paper that includes various objects and has well-formatted structure. For generation of a ToC page, we extract only section titles from the objects by referring to text line types defined in Section 2.2. When the current text line is of any type and starts with a special pattern and the previous line is of *EL* type, we regard the current line as a section title candidate. What is meant by the ***special pattern*** is the pattern in the form of [(number or text)+symbol(including space)]. Figure 3(a) shows an example of section title candidates extracted from a page of a technical paper.

3.2. Section number sorting and verification

We modify the pattern of a section title candidate as shown in Figure 3(b) and, starting at the highest level, sort all section title candidates by section number in ascending order at each level. We construct a hierarchical tree of the sorted section numbers. To verify their suitability, the section numbers at each level of the tree are searched for any missing or inappropriate section numbers.

Special pattern

(a)	❶		❷			❸ Section level				
7.11 Ordering	7	.	1	1		0	-1	-1	-1	-1
7.10 Classification	7	.	1	0		0	-1	-1	-1	-1
7.11.2 About texts	7	.	1	1	.	2	-1	-1	-1	-1
8 Experiments	8	.	0	0		0	-1	-1	-1	-1

(a) Original pattern (b) Modified pattern for sorting

Figure 3. Section title candidates

4. Experimental results and analysis

Experiments were carried out with various kinds of the document images taken from magazines, newspapers, books, scientific and technical journals, manuals, UWDB(the database of University of Washington) [3], *etc.*

Figure 4(b) and Figure 4(c) show an example of the converted images using the table and layer structure, respectively. As a result of using these two approaches, HTML documents are generated very similar to the original document images both in appearance and logic.

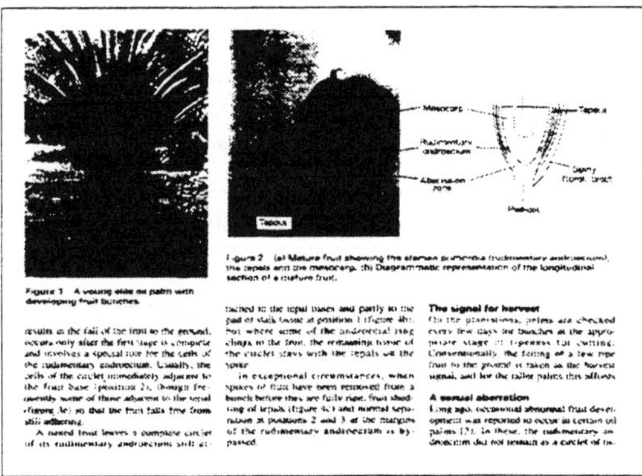

(a) Original document image

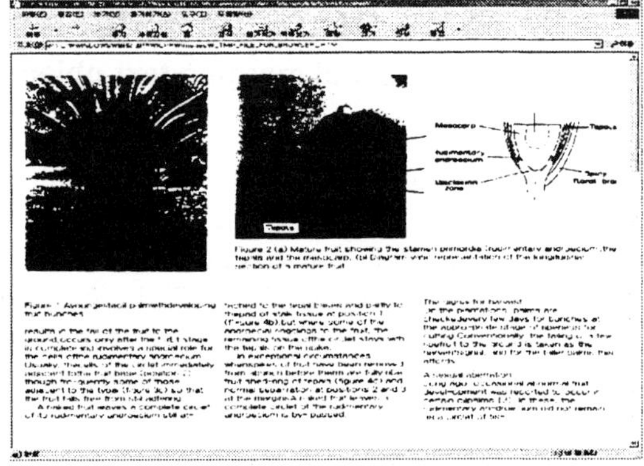

(b) Hyperdocument generated using table structure

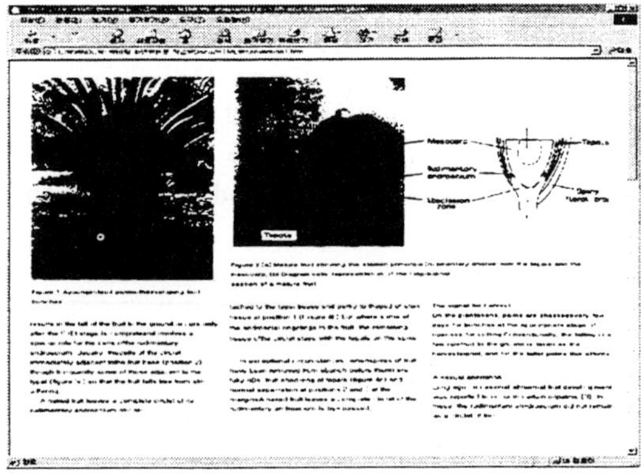

(c) Hyperdocument generated using layer structure

Figure 4. Example of the converted images

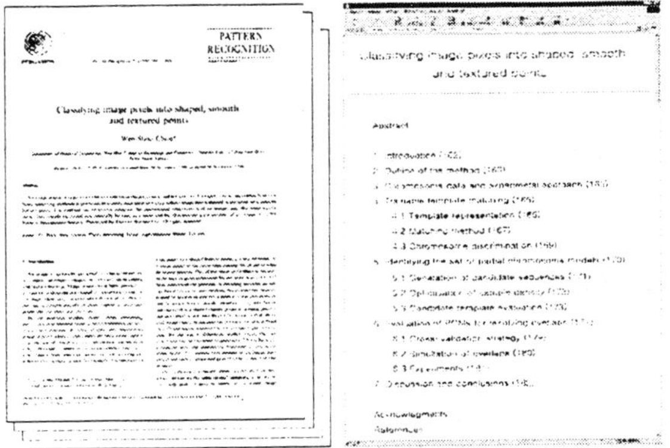

(a) Input document images (b) Table of contents page

Figure 5. Structured ToC generation

In case of the conversion based on the table structure, the sizes of spaces between the objects in an HTML document may be considerably different from one another. This is because the objects are merged for arrangement in a table format convertible into an HTML document. Besides, an object lying across columns cannot be represented, although a partial overlap of objects in a column can be avoided. Therefore, the conversion based on the table structure is adequate for conversion of formatted document images like general books and technical papers. On the other hand, in the case of using the layer structure, the conversion of complex and unformatted multi-column document images, *i.e.*, documents without regular shape or structure, like magazines, advertisements, *etc.*, is performed well. However, several objects may overlap when the font size or line space of a text object is not correctly calculated, and the spaces between the objects may become larger or smaller than those of the objects in the original image.

Figure 5(b) shows a ToC page generated from input document images, Figure 5(a). Each section title is arranged hierarchically and has the page number of the beginning of the section and is hyperlinked to it.

Table 1 shows the experiment result of extracting section titles from different kinds of papers. N_c, N_{fn} and N_{fp} denote the number of section titles correctly extracted, false negatives, and false positives, respectively. In X/Y representation of N_c, X and Y denote the number of the correctly extracted section titles and the total number of the section titles in the input documents, respectively. As shown in Table 1, a ToC was generated with accuracy of about 90%.

[1]Pattern Recognition, Vol. 31, No. 4, April 1998.

[2]IEEE Trans. on PAMI, Vol. 20, No. 12, Dec. 1998.

[3]Proc. of Int. Conf. on Pattern Recognition, 1998, pp. 949-984.

[4]Proc. of Int. Conf. on Document Anal. and Recog., 1997, pp. 1-50.

Table 1. Results of section title extraction

Papers		Section title extraction		
		N_{fn}	N_{fp}	N_c
Journal	PR [1]	20	13	116/137 (85%)
	PAMI [2]	19	11	142/158 (90%)
Conference	ICPR [3]	8	7	75/81 (92%)
	ICDAR [4]	7	8	102/115 (89%)

5. Conclusions and further research

In this paper, we proposed two methods for converting multi-column document images into HTML documents using the table and layer structures and also proposed a method for generating a structured ToC page by extracting the section titles from input document images.

For the conversion of each paper image into its hyperdocument, the proposed conversion methods were tested on various kinds of complex multi-column document images. Experimental results revealed that the proposed methods performed well for various kinds of multi-column document images. However, they showed different performance on different types of document images. Hence, a scheme is needed to determine which one of the conversion methods to be applied for better performance when document images are given.

For the generation of a structured ToC page, experiments were carried out on technical papers. Experimental results showed that, using the proposed ToC generation method, we could create it by extracting the section titles from input document images without regard to the accuracy of character recognition.

References

[1] T. G. Kieninger and A. Dengel. A paper-to-html table converting system. *Proc. of the 3rd IAPR Workshop on Document Analysis Systems, Nagano, Japan*, pages 356–365, Nov. 4-6, 1998.

[2] C. Lin, Y. Niwa, and S. Narita. Logical structure analysis of book document images using contents information. *Proc. of the 4th ICDAR, Ulm, Germany*, pages 1048–1054, Aug. 18-20, 1997.

[3] I. Phillips, S. Chen, and R. Haralick. Cd-rom document database standard. *Proc. of the 2nd ICDAR, Tsukuba, Japan*, pages 478–483, Oct. 20-22, 1993.

[4] T. Tanaka and S. Tsuruoka. Table form document understanding using node classification method and html document generation. *Proc. of the 3rd IAPR Workshop on Document Analysis Systems, Nagano, Japan*, pages 157–158, Nov. 4-6, 1998.

[5] M. Worring and A. W. M. Smeulders. Content based internet access to paper documents. *International Journal on Document Analysis and Recognition*, 1(4):209–220, 1999.

Automatic Quality Measurement of Gray-Scale Handwriting Based on Extended Average Entropy*

Jeong-Seon Park, Hee-Joong Kang and Seong-Whan Lee
Center for Artificial Vision Research, Korea University,
Anam-dong, Seongbuk-ku, Seoul 136-701, Korea
{jspark, hjkang, swlee}@image.korea.ac.kr

Abstract

With a surge of interest in OCR in 1990s, a large number of handwriting or handprinting databases have been built one after another around the world. One problem that researches encounter today is that all the databases differ in various ways including the script qualities.

This paper proposes a method for measuring handwriting qualities that can be used for comparison of databases and objective test for character recognizers. The key idea involved is classifying character samples into a number of groups each characterizing a set of qualities.

In order to evaluate the proposed method, we carried out experiments on KU-1 database. The result we achieve is meaningful and the method is helpful for the target tasks.

1. Introduction

There are several handwritten character databases[5], covering a variety of writing styles and shape distortions, which have been frequently used to test the performance of various recognition systems. In order to evaluate and compare objectively the performance of those systems, it is necessary to carry out the task on common databases. However, this is often not possible, because of the unique properties of character databases each of which is used for and adapted to training and testing each specific recognition method. It is, therefore, desirable to estimate the level of recognition difficulty of a given database by some automatic quality measurement which is independent of the characteristics of recognition methods.

To date, several methods have been reported by concerning the evaluation of handwriting qualities[1, 2, 3, 4]. In the human perception based method[3], however, the use of the evaluation measures which are computed by subjective factors to determine the weight coefficient of the quality evaluation measure did not guarantee an objective evaluation of handwriting qualities. In the recognition based method[1], the sorted quality of each character is strongly affected by the features of the specified recognition system, also the simple, iterative method could not set the evaluation reference correctly. Finally, entropy based methods[2, 4] only evaluated the degree of variation among the data of the same character.

In this paper, we propose an *extended average entropy(EAE)* measure which has been stemmed from the *average entropy(AE)* in binary-scale[2], to directly measure the handwriting variations in gray-scale databases without adopting any error-causing binarization. Then, we use the EAE measure to evaluate the quality of handwriting and to classify all samples within a class into several groups according to their handwriting qualities.

*This research was supported by Creative Research Initiatives of the Ministry of Science and Technology, Korea.

2. Variation measures

In this section, we introduce the *average entropy(AE)* measure in binary-scale and extended the AE measure to gray-scale. The *extended average entropy(EAE)* will be used in next section, to measure the handwriting qualities of each group.

2.1. Average entropy in binary-scale

Given a collection of M binary images of $X \times Y$ pixels for a class, let $f(x,y)$ be the number of black pixels at position (x,y) for the collection. Then we can estimate the probability of black pixel occurring at position (x,y) as follows:

$$p(x,y) = \frac{f(x,y)}{M}, \quad \begin{cases} x = 1,\, 2,\, \cdots,\, X \\ y = 1,\, 2,\, \cdots,\, Y \end{cases} \tag{1}$$

where X, Y are the horizontal/vertical dimension respectively, and M is the number of sample images in a class.

Then, the entropy at position (x,y) is calculated by the following equation[2]:

$$\begin{aligned} h(x,y) &= -p(x,y)\log_2 p(x,y) \\ &\quad -(1-p(x,y))\log_2(1-p(x,y)), \end{aligned} \tag{2}$$

where $(1 - p(x,y))$ denotes the probability of a white pixel occurring at position (x,y) in the set of binary-scale images. The entropy has a value of $0 \leq h(x,y) \leq 1$. Using Eq. (2), we defined the *average entropy(AE)* of the collection of class images, e^a, as follows:

$$e^a = \frac{1}{X \cdot Y} \sum_{x=1}^{X} \sum_{y=1}^{Y} h(x,y), \tag{3}$$

where the *AE* has a value of $0 \leq e^a \leq 1$. $e^a = 0$ when all images in a class are the same, and $e^a = 1$ when the probability of a black pixel occurring at every position is exactly $\frac{1}{2}$.

2.2. Extended average entropy in gray-scale

Given M images of size $X \times Y$ with L gray levels $l = \{0, 1, 2, \cdots, L-1\}$, let the gray level of a pixel (x,y) be denoted by $I(x,y)$. Then, we define the frequency of the gray level l at position (x,y) as follows:

$$F(x,y;l) = \sum_{m=1}^{M} C_m(x,y;l), \tag{4}$$

where $C_m(x,y;l) = 1$ when $I(x,y) = l$, i.e., the gray level at position (x,y) is equal to l. Therefore, the frequency has a value of $0 \leq F(x,y;l) \leq M$.

The probability of the gray level l at position (x,y) can be easily calculated by

$$P(x,y;l) = \frac{F(x,y;l)}{M}, \quad \begin{cases} x = 1,\ 2,\ \cdots,\ X \\ y = 1,\ 2,\ \cdots,\ Y \\ l = 0,\ 1,\ \cdots,\ L-1 \end{cases} \tag{5}$$

with the following stochastic constraint:

$$0 \leq P(x,y;l) \leq 1, \quad \sum_{l=0}^{L-1} P(x,y;l) = 1.$$

We define the entropy at position (x,y) in gray-scale images of a class as follows:

$$H(x,y) = -\sum_{l=0}^{L-1} P(x,y;l) \log_L P(x,y;l). \tag{6}$$

Note that the base of the logarithm differs from that of the entropy in binary-scale.

Using Eq. (6), we define the *extended average entropy (EAE)* in gray-scale, E^A, as follows:

$$E^A = \frac{1}{X \cdot Y} \sum_{x=1}^{X} \sum_{y=1}^{Y} H(x,y), \tag{7}$$

where the EAE has a value of $0 \leq E^A \leq 1$ with the equalities in order when all images in a class are the same and when the probabilities $P(x,y;l)$ for all l at each position are the same.

3. Automatic handwriting quality measurements

An overview of the proposed method is shown in Figure 1. As can be seen from the figure, no preprocessing and feature extraction is used because our intention is to measure the handwriting variation of original data only.

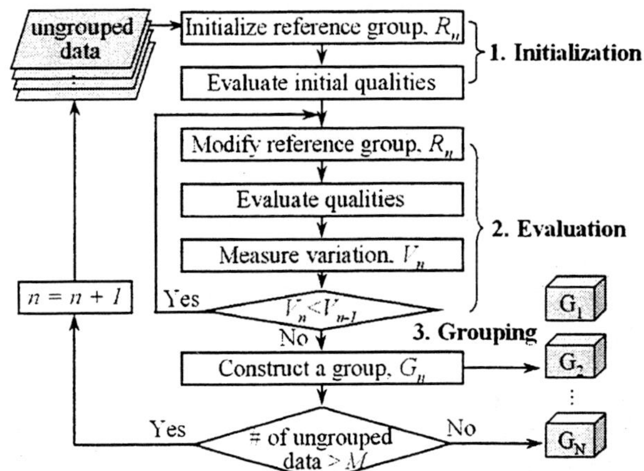

Figure 1. Overview of the proposed method

3.1. Initialization step

There are many types of variations in handwritten characters, including different writing styles, obviously it is helpful to start with a good reference group for a successful grouping of character samples.

In this phase, for making the n-th group G_n, the temporary reference group is set and all data are sorted according to the results of initial quality evaluation.

- **Initialize a reference group, R_n** : Select a set of M arbitrary samples from the ungrouped set, and assign it to the temporary reference group R_n. Then, the corresponding reference template is created by the average behavior of the samples in the reference group as follows:

$$A_n(x,y) = \frac{1}{M} \sum_{m=1}^{M} I_m(x,y), \tag{8}$$

where M is the number of gray-scale images in the reference group. Then, the average image has the value of $0 \leq A_n(x,y) \leq L-1$ for all (x,y).

- **Evaluate initial quality** : The qualities of all samples in the ungrouped set are evaluated and sorted according to their distance from the reference template.

Let I_i be the i-th gray-scale image in the ungrouped set and A_n is the average image of gray-scale images of a current reference group as defined in Eq. (8). Then, $D_i = ||I_i - A_n||, (i = 1, 2, \cdots, M)$ is the distance of the i-th image to the reference template.

3.2. Evaluation step

Since the initialization of the the reference group by the previous method[1] is too simple, there may be unnecessary computation and the good reference group might not be set. Therefore, the proposed method examines the variation within the reference group, to confirm its suitability. In this phase, the reference group is modified and the quality of each sample is evaluated and the variation measure of the group is examined to guarantee that the reference group is properly set.

- **Modify reference group, $\mathbf{R}_n$** : The reference group R_n is replaced by the first M samples of the sorted data, and a reference template is made by the average image using Eq. (8).
- **Evaluate qualities** : The quality of each sample is evaluated and sorted according to its distance from the reference template the same as in the initialization step.
- **Measure variation, V_n** : In order to ensure that the reference group is good, the EAE in gray-scale is calculated as $V_n = E^A$. If the variation is less than the previous variation value, V_{n-1}, the reference group is regarded as good group but still have the possibility to be improved by the reference group modification.

3.3. Grouping step

Each group is constructed by assigning a different number of samples according to their EAE measure, i.e. the greater the EAE, the smaller the number of samples in the group; and the smaller the EAE, the larger the number of samples. Based on this concept, we construct the group G_n using the following procedure:

while $(V_n < V_T)$ {
add the next similar image to the current group, G_n
calculate the handwriting variation, V_n
}
remove the grouped data from the ungrouped data

By applying this procedure, we expect that the handwriting samples are grouped with a different number of data according to their handwriting variations.

Figure 2 shows an example of the process constructing the fourth group of Hangul character '완'. In the figure, upper images are the reference templates made by averaging samples of the reference group, and lower images are some samples of constructed to the fourth group G_4, while n denotes the iteration count and V_n denotes the variation value. As the iteration count increases, the reference template has better shape and the variation values are reduced and both are converged after 6 times of iteration.

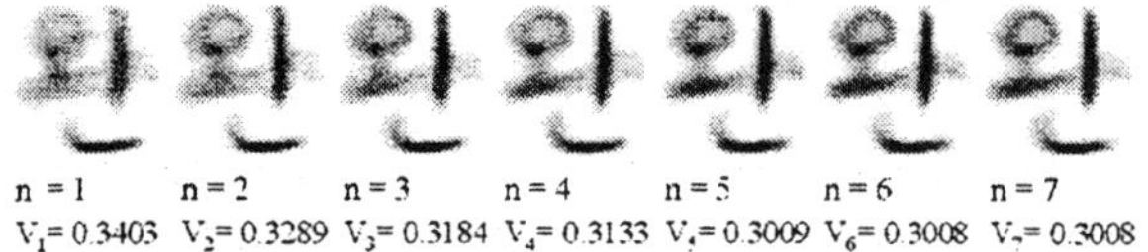

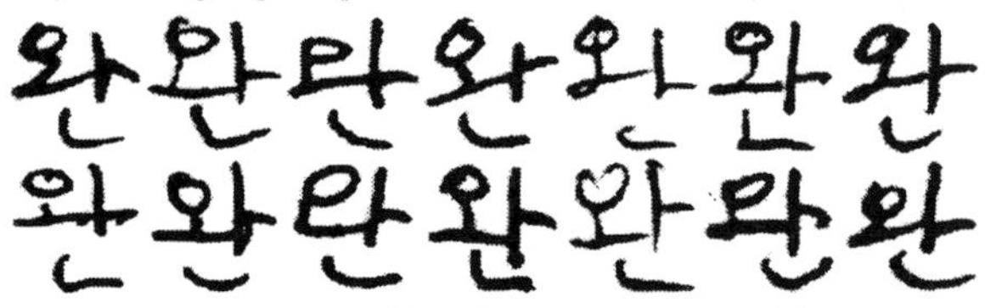

Figure 2. An example sequence of constructing the fourth group of character '완'

4. Experimental results and analysis

4.1. The KU-1 database

As detailed in previous research[5], KU-1 is a large-set off-line handwritten Hangul character database. It consists of 1,000 sets of the 1,500 most frequently used Hangul hand-written characters among the KS C 2,350 Hangul character set. They were generated by more than 1,000 different writers of different social environments, occupations, and geographical distributions. Each character, written in a 9×9 mm box, has been scanned with a resolution of 300 DPI. Samples of the KU-1 database can be seen at the site: *http://image.korea.ac.kr/database/KU-1*.

4.2. Preliminary experiment

In order to examine the effect of the proposed evaluation method, we have chosen some character samples and let them evaluated by human subjects.

In the preliminary experiments of subjective evaluation, human subjects were presented about 500 samples for each character class to give their evaluation : G1) very good, G2) good, G3) normal(+), G4) normal(-), G5) poor, or G6) very poor. Then, we took the average of the value overall subjects.

Figure 3 shows the two evaluation results which were carried out by human subjects and the proposed evaluation method, respectively. In the figure most samples are classified to the same group by both methods, so we can find out that the proposed evaluation method achieves similar results to the human subjective evaluation.

4.3. Experimental results

In order to verify the performance of the proposed method, the test set has been divided into six data groups,

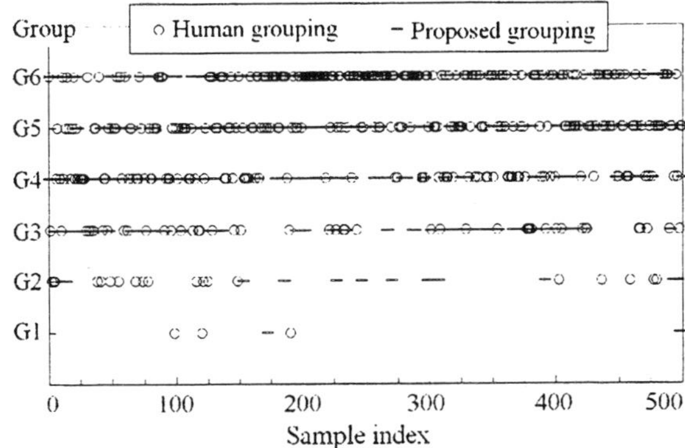

Figure 3. Human subjective evaluation vs. proposed objective evaluation

and then variation have been analyzed. Figure 4 shows the results for each data group.

The results show that the variation increases at linearly from the first group, $G1$ and that the proposed method classifies samples into several groups properly and the measurement of quality is done correctly, using the *extended average entropy(EAE)* in gray-scale. However, the nearly constant rate of variation for each Hangul type is a little different and depends on the complexity of character structure. This means that a character with a complex structure has more variants in shapes than a character with a simple structure. In other words, a complex character has a large variety of strokes, whereas a simple character has a small variety of strokes. From the above observations, we can conclude that the structure of a character is closely related to the variations in its shape.

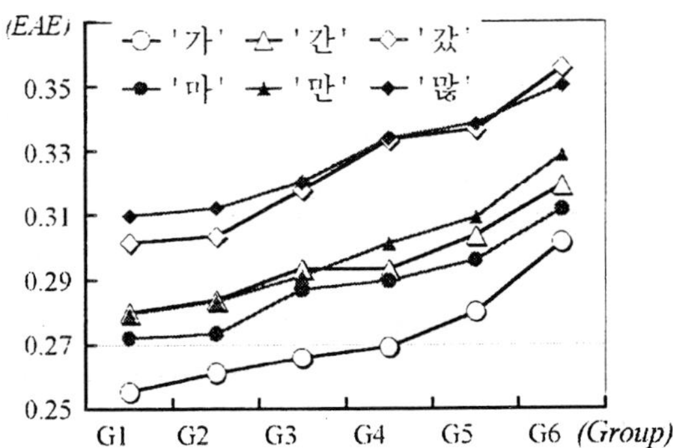

Figure 4. The EAE of each quality group

Figure 5 shows the first 20 samples of each data group organized through the handwriting quality measurement. From this figure, we can verify that the connectivity among strokes and the variety of strokes are more conspicuous, and the separation of phonemes is weaker, as the data differ more from the first group. Thus, it is evident that the proposed method measures the handwriting qualities in accordance with the human criteria.

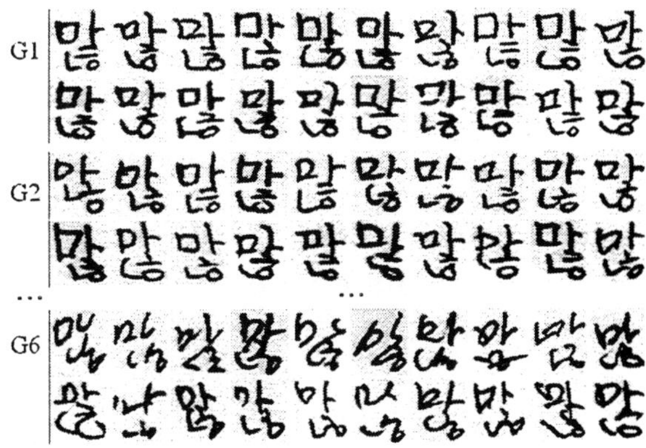

Figure 5. First 20 samples of each data group

5. Concluding remarks

In this paper, we proposed an automatic quality measurement method of gray-scale handwriting data, to offer a means by which different databases can be compared objectively. First, we defined an *extended average entropy(EAE)*, an extension of the *average entropy(AE)* in binary-scale, to directly measure the handwriting qualities in a given gray-scale character database. Second, we measured the quality of each sample in a class, and classified all data within a class into several groups according to their handwriting qualities.

The experimental results confirmed that the proposed method was useful for measuring the qualities of handwritten Hangul characters objectively and automatically. We also showed that the proposed method evaluated the handwriting qualities in accordance with the human criteria, through the preliminary experiment.

References

[1] S. L. Chou and S. S. Yu. Sorting qualities of handwritten Chinese characters for setting up a research database. *Proc. of 2nd ICDAR*, Tsukuba, Japan, 1993, pp. 474–477.

[2] H. Hase, M. Yoneda, and M. Sakai. Evaluation of handprinting variation of characters using variation entropy. *IEICE Transactions D*, J71-D(6):1048–1056, 1988.

[3] T. Kato. Evaluation system for hand-written characters. *Proc. of SPIE/IS&T Conf. on Machine Vision Application in Character Recognition and Industrial Inspection*, San Jose, 1992, pp. 73–82.

[4] D.-H. Kim, E.-J. Kim, and S.-Y. Bang. A variation measure for handwritten character image data using entropy difference. *Pattern Recognition*, 30(1):19–29, 1997.

[5] D.-I. Kim, S.-Y. Kim, and S.-W. Lee. Design and construction of a large-set off-line handwritten Hangul character image database ku-1. *Proc. of National Conf. on Korean Language Information Processing*, Pusan, Korea 1997, pp. 152–159. (in Korean).

Character Pattern Extraction Based on Local Multilevel Thresholding and Region Growing

Hideaki Goto
Education Center for Information Processing,
Tohoku University,
Kawauchi, Aoba, Sendai-shi 980–8576, Japan
hgot@ecip.tohoku.ac.jp

Hirotomo Aso
Graduate School of Engineering,
Tohoku University,
Aramaki, Aoba, Sendai-shi 980–8578, Japan
aso@ecei.tohoku.ac.jp

Abstract

Recent remarkable progress in computer systems and printing devices makes it easier to produce printed documents with various designs. Text characters are often printed on colored backgrounds, and sometimes on complex backgrounds. Some methods have been developed for character extraction from document images and scene images with complex backgrounds. However, those methods are designed to extract rather large characters, and often fails to extract small characters. This paper proposes a new method by which character patterns can be extracted from document images with complex background. The method is based on the local multilevel thresholding and pixel labeling, and the region growing. This framework is very useful for extracting character patterns from badly illuminated document images. The performance of extracting small character patterns has also been improved by suppressing the influence of mixed-color pixels around character edges.

1. Introduction

With the recent remarkable progress in computer systems and printing devices, we have a number of documents in which text characters are printed on colored backgrounds, and on complex background images. Systems for document analysis and recognition require a process which separates text characters from such colored and/or complex backgrounds so that the optical character recognition stage can recognize the texts. Even if a document has a white, uniform background and consists of black texts, the document image inputted by a image scanner or a camera often has uneven brightness due to the uneven illumination. In order to design robust document recognition systems, the character extraction process have to be tolerant of such an uneven brightness of the document image as well.

The intensity gradient based thresholding is very useful for badly illuminated document images [5], however, it cannot segment text characters in the documents with complex backgrounds. Some methods have been developed for the character extraction from color document images. The methods based on isochromatic line analysis cannot handle small characters, because the strokes of small characters are often unclear. The methods based on the color clustering can handle smaller characters, however, they still fail to extract very small characters [3]. The robustness of the process for badly illuminated documents has not been well considered yet.

This paper proposes a new method by which small character patterns can be extracted from document images with complex background. The method is based on the local multilevel thresholding and pixel labeling, and the region growing. This framework is very useful for extracting character patterns from badly illuminated document images.

2. Character pattern extraction based on local multilevel thresholding and region growing

2.1. Detection of local representative gray levels and pixel labeling

The character pattern extraction method proposed in this paper consists of the following four major stages.

1. Local multilevel thresholding and initial pixel labeling.
2. Edge compensation in labeled images.

1051-4651/00 $10.00 © 2000 IEEE

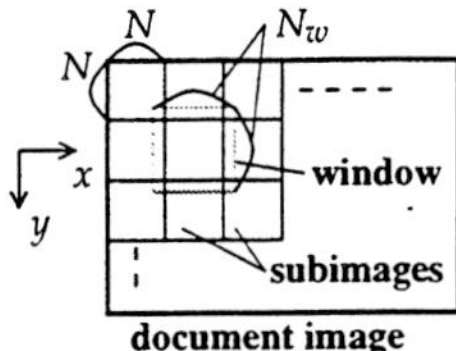

Figure 1. Partitioning of the input image

3. Region growing based on label merging between neighboring subimages.
4. Creation of decomposed images.

At the beginning, the input document image is partitioned into square subimages as shown in Figure 1. Let $P(x,y)$ denote the pixel at the coordinate (x,y), and let $f(x,y)$ denote the intensity of the pixel. Let R^i denote the i-th subimage. The input image is assumed to be a 400dpi, 8bit grayscale image. We used $N = 50$ (3.2mm on the document) as the subimage size, and $N_w = 60$ as the window size, since they seemed to be appropriate in our preliminary experiments.

The weighted histogram of the pixel intensity is calculated in every window co-centered by each subimage. For the pixel at (x,y), the weight is defined as $w(x,y) = \max(1 - \alpha E(x,y), 0)$, where $E(x,y)$ denotes the intensity component of the Sobel's edge detection operator, and α denotes a positive coefficient. We had verified that the process is not so sensitive to α, and used $\alpha = 1/32$. The weighted histogram is expected to be useful for the extraction of small characters. The reason is as described below.

The character patterns in the document image are slightly or strongly blurred in general. There are a lot of mixed-color pixels whose gray level (or color) is the mixture of the background's and the character's. Due to the mixed-color pixels, the normal histogram has some spurious peaks between the character's gray level (about 60) and the background's gray level (about 230) as shown by the broken line in Figure 2. If we apply the multilevel thresholding using the peaks in the histogram, the spurious peaks will split thin strokes of characters into several gray levels, and make it difficult to extract the character strokes correctly. If the document image is blurred more, the valley between the two gray levels will be filled, and consequently, it will be impossible to discriminate the characters and the background. The weighted histogram will help making the valley clear, because it suppresses the counts of the mixed-color edge pixels (Figure 2).

The calculated histogram is smoothed by the moving average and the hysteresis smoothing. The width of the moving average is 7. The half width of the cursor in hysteresis smoothing is 20% of the height of the histogram. Then, the peaks in smoothed histogram are

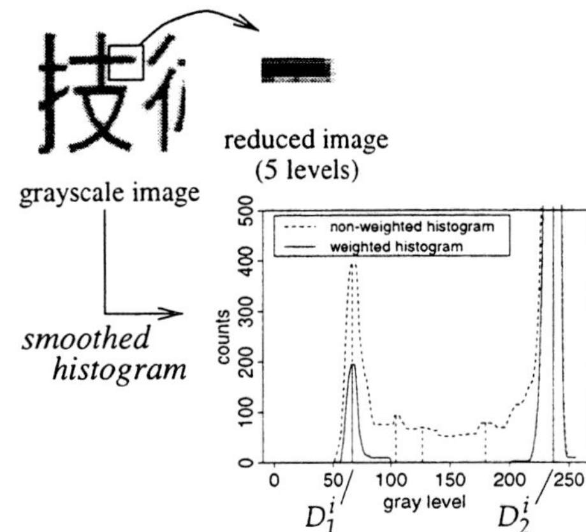

Figure 2. Detection of representative gray levels at each subimage

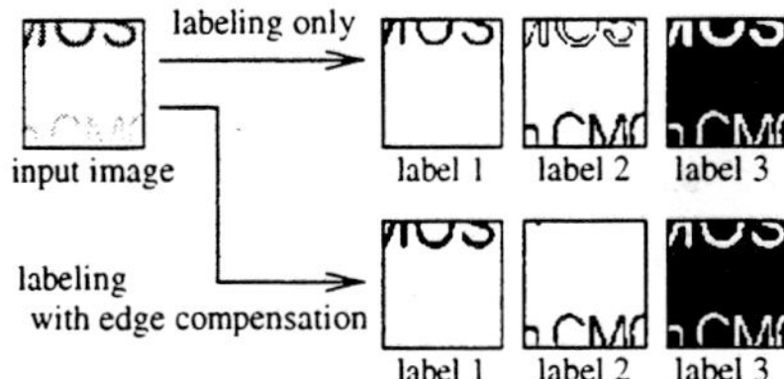

Figure 3. The effect of edge compensation

found and the peak positions are regarded as the representative gray levels. Let D_j^i denote the gray level of the j-th peak in the i-th subimage. For each pixel $P(x,y)$, the number j which minimize $|f(x,y) - D_j^i|$ is found, and the pixel is tagged with the label (i,j). The gray level of the pixel is turned into $f'(x,y) = D_j^i$.

2.2. Edge compensation in labeled images

If more than one foreground image coexist in the same subimage and if their gray levels differ, the result of the multilevel thresholding often shows undesirable split of the foreground images. In Figure 3, note that the character stokes above are split into two labels; the skeletons and the edges. We cannot avoid such a result only tuning up the multilevel thresholding, because the spatial information is not taken into account in the thresholding.

In order to reduce the splits of the strokes, the edge compensation process is applied to the initially labeled subimages. Each labeled subimage is scanned in horizontal and vertical ways, and the edge compensation is performed on every scan line (Figure 4). The pixels on the edge are relabeled using two gray levels adjacent to the edge. The "edge" here is such that the length is less than $T_{sp} = 7$ and the length of every step is less than $T_{st} = 3$. The splits of the strokes will be suppressed by the edge compensation as shown in Figure 3.

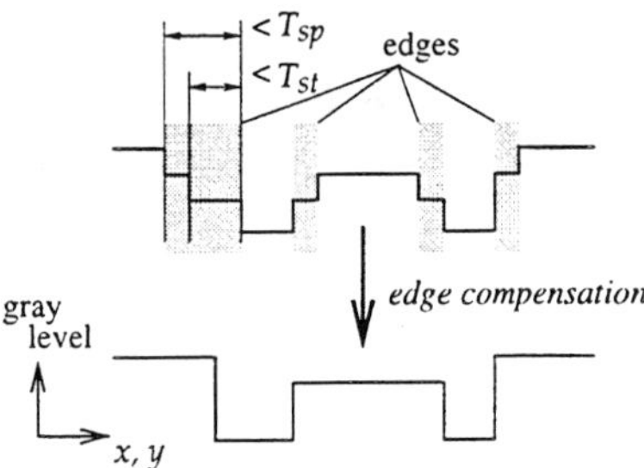

Figure 4. Edge compensation on a scan line

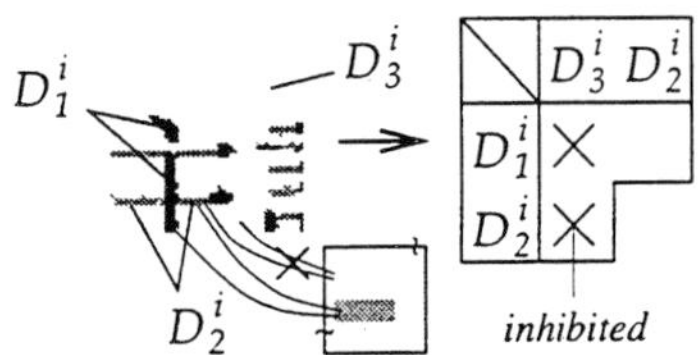

Figure 5. Creation of merging inhibition table

2.3. Region growing

Considering computers pick up text information in the document image easily, the whole character patterns in the same line should appear in a single binary image. We need the merge process of the local labels among neighboring subimages, suppressing the undesirable merging between the character patterns and the background images. The merge process can be regarded as the "region growing" of the connected components found in the labeled images.

The similar method based on the local labeling and the region growing was proposed by Beveridge *et al.* [1] for the segmentation of natural scene images. However, the method is not suitable for the character pattern extraction from document images, because it often fails picking up thin objects. The gray level (or color) of thin strokes is not so stable. Therefore, we have to design some special algorithms for the character extraction.

Let R^i, R^k denote the pair of subimages adjoining each other in the 8-neighborhood manner. Let D^i_j, D^k_l denote the representative gray levels in the subimages respectively. First, each label (x, y) is put into the individual set of label. Let $R(i, j)$ denote the set of label which contains the label (i, j). For every pair of D^i_j and D^k_l, the following condition and the additional condition described later are checked, and the set $R(i, j)$ and $R(k, l)$ are merged together if both condition is satisfied.

$$|D^i_j - D^k_l| \le \theta \quad (1)$$

The parameter θ denotes the threshold of gray level difference.

The results of our preliminary experments shows it is impossible to obtain good results using only the condition (1). The text lines are easily split as θ decreases, while the strokes and the backgrounds are easily merged as θ increases. No optimum value exists for θ. To overcome this difficulty, we use the following additional condition.

In every subimage, the merging inhibition table is created. In Figure 5, there are three representative gray scales, D^i_1, D^i_2 and D^i_3, in the subimage. If the label set $R(i, 2)$ were merged with $R(i, 3)$ indirectly via another label in the neighboring subimage, the character strokes would be lost. So, the merging between the gray level D^i_2 and D^i_3 should be inhibited. The inhibition flag between D^i_j and $D^i_{j'}$ is turned on if a connected component in D^i_j adjoins another connected component in $D^i_{j'}$ with the border line longer than 1/4 of the total edge length of the former component. The merging between the label set $R(i, j)$ and $R(k, l)$ is permitted only when no inhibited merging will occur for any pair of the labels in $R(i, j)$ and $R(k, l)$.

A small value is used for θ at the beginning, and θ is gradually increased as the region growing proceeds. We used the series $\theta = 4, 8, 16, 24, 32, 48, 64$.

2.4. Creation of decomposed images

The label sets obtained by the region merging are tagged with the serial numbers $0, 1, ..., M$. The sets of pixels, $L_0, L_1, ..., L_M$, corresponding to the label sets are created. A binary image is created for each pixel set, L_m, turning the pixel $P(x, y) \in L_m$ to black and turning other pixels to white. We call the M binary images "decomposed images."

We omit the explanation of the text line extraction from the decomposed images because we can use some of the previously proposed methods for text line extraction from binary images [2].

2.5. Experimental results

The ability of the proposed method was evaluated using various types of document images. The size of the documents was A4 or B5. All documents were scanned by a flatbed image scanner at 400dpi.

The rates of text line extraction are shown in Table 1. Note that the extraction rates are improved for "Tech. paper" which contains rather thin character strokes. The difference of the rates is not very large in general, however, the extracted character patterns are far more patchy in the non-weighted mode than in the weighted mode.

Table 1. The rates of text line extraction

	pages (lines)	extracted text lines (rate)	
		non-weighted	weighted
Magazine cover	12 (169)	139 (82.2%)	138 (81.7%)
Magazine	8 (1017)	1003 (98.6%)	1002 (98.5%)
Tech. paper	2 (218)	210 (96.3%)	218 (100%)

The document set "Magazine cover [1]" consists of the documents in which text characters are printed on complex background. Each document contains not only large characters but also a text line which consists of about 50 characters of size 6pt. Figure 6 shows a result out of the document set. The result image is the composition of three decomposed images which contain character patterns. Note that the small character patterns are extracted correctly.

The document set "Magazine[2]" consists of English documents, and the document set "Tech. paper[3]" consists of Japanese technical papers. The size of the characters used in the main texts of these documents is around 7pt to 9pt. The previous methods designed for the character extraction from document/scene images with complex backgrounds are not capable of extracting such small characters. All characters in the main texts were extracted correctly by the proposed method, if we used the weighted histogram. Most failure were found in the text lines which contains the characters of various gray levels.

The documents in the set "Tech. paper" are badly illuminated. Figure 7 shows the proposed method is tolerant of the uneven brightness of the document image. We can expect the method works well as far as the brightness in the image changes gradually compared to the size of subimage.

We also examined the performance of the local adaptive binarization used in Ohya's method [4]. The binarization works very good for text regions with plain background. However, the text line extraction rates for the document set "Magazine cover" were very low: 21% for the subblock size 16×16, and 50% for 128×128.

2.6. Conclusions

We have proposed a new method for character extraction from document images with complex background. The method is based on the local multilevel thresholding and pixel labeling, and the region growing. The experimental results ensured the framework is very useful for extracting character patterns from badly

[1]UNIX MAGAZINE, Jan.-Dec., 1998, ASCII CORP.

[2]TIME (ASIA), JANUARY 18, pp.38–45, 1999.

[3]IEICE Trans. D-I, Vol.J80-D-I, No.11, pp.881–885, 1997.

input image

extracted character patterns (weighted)

Figure 6. Character pattern extraction from a document image with complex background

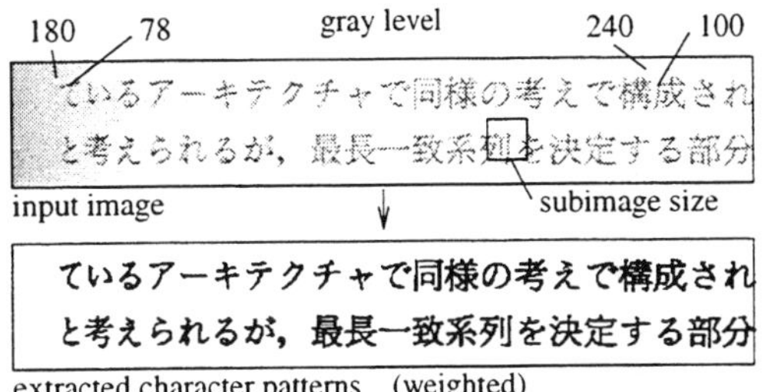

Figure 7. Character pattern extraction from a badly illuminated document image

illuminated document images. The weighted histogram and the edge compensation process are useful for improving the performance of extracting small character patterns. Character strokes can be extracted as far as their thickness is more than about 1.5 pixels.

It is one of our future work to enhance the method so it can handle color document images.

References

[1] J. R. Beveridge, J. Griffith, R. R. Kohler, A. R. Hanson, and E. M. Riseman. Segmenting images using localized histograms and region merging. *International Journal of Computer Vision*, 2:311–347, 1989.

[2] H. Goto and H. Aso. Robust and fast text-line extraction using local linearity of the text-line. *Systems and Computers in Japan*, 26(13):21–31, Nov. 1995.

[3] A. K. Jain and B. Yu. Automatic text location in images and video frames. In *Proceedings of 14th International Conference on Pattern Recognition*, pages 1497–1499, 1998.

[4] J. Ohya, A. Shio, and S. Akamatsu. Recognizing characters in scene images. *IEEE Trans. on PAMI*, 16(2):214–220, Feb. 1994.

[5] J. R. Parker. Gray level thresholding in badly illuminated images. *IEEE Trans. on PAMI*, 13(8):813–819, Aug. 1991.

Efficient best-first dictionary search given graph-based input

Simon Lucas
Department of Electronic Systems Engineering
University of Essex
Colchester CO4 3SQ, UK
sml@essex.ac.uk

Abstract

This paper describes a novel method for applying dictionary knowledge to optimally interpret the confidence-rated hypothesis sets produced by lower-level pattern classifiers. The problem is cast as enumerating the paths in a graph in best-first order given the constraint that each complete path is a word in some specified dictionary. The solution described here is of particular interest due to its generality, flexibility and because the time to retrieve each path is independent of the size of the dictionary. Results are presented for searching dictionaries of up to 1 million UK postcodes given graphs that correspond to insertion, deletion and substitution errors.

A. Introduction

Contextual knowledge is of critical importance in most pattern recognition applications. Examples of the type of knowledge that can be applied to improve recognition accuracy include dictionary, grammatical, arithmetic, logical or database type knowledge. See [8] for discussion of the importance of context in document image analysis. Note that where applicable, dictionary type knowledge is an extremely tight form of constraint. The work described here was funded by The Post Office (UK) in order to develop more robust and efficient mail address and form reading software, but should also have applications in many related areas, such as optimal retrieval of vehicle registration numbers from video images for example.

This paper describes a graph-based version of a dictionary search system originally reported in [6] and subsequently extended to cope with other kinds of contextual information [5]. The original system [6] showed that best-first retrieval could be done in a way that did not get slower as the size of the dictionary grew. This should be contrasted with conventional approaches that either get slower linearly with respect to the size of a flat dictionary [7] or with respect to the size of a Trie structured dictionary [3].

The input to our system is a directed graph where each arc in the graph corresponds to the probability of a particular pattern class being present in a particular portion of the input space. This allows the system to cope naturally with substitution, insertion and deletion errors, and any number of alternative segmentations of the input, as would naturally arise in cursive script or due to touching printed characters. Importantly, the retrieval time can still be made independent of dictionary size.

B. Input Graph

The system takes its input from a graph, a simple example of which is shown in Figure 1. Note that input graphs can have any structure, and are not limited to the structure depicted here. The requirement is to produce the n best paths through the graph that are words[1] in some specified dictionary. Note that it is not sufficient to produce the single best word since any given word field in a document or image may have to be cross-referenced with other information. For example, postcode or zipcode should match the address block on a mail piece, vehicle registration number should match the car details.

The arcs are grouped into sets (each set shown in a rectangular box), where each member of the set connects the same two nodes but with different labels. Each arc label has two parts: a character hypothesis and a probability or confidence value. There is an implied order in that the graph should be traversed from left-to-right.

B.1. Searching the Graph

The object of the search is to provide a best-first enumeration of paths through the graph such that each complete path corresponds to a dictionary entry. Note that while

[1] The system is equally well-suited to enumerating all paths that are sub-strings of dictionary words.

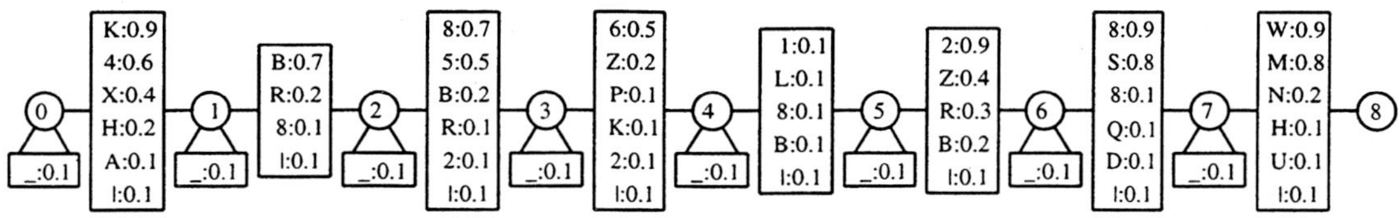

Figure 1. A simple example input graph.

Thompson[9] used a chart parser to perform the task of enumerating all paths through a lattice, the requirement of producing only paths that are substrings of dictionary words produces a fresh set of challenges, especially when the dictionaries in question are massive e.g. in excess of a million entries. If the numbers on each label are independent probabilities, then we find the probability that a word connects two nodes by a particular sequence of arc traverals by multiplying together the probability on each arc. Note that the true probability that a word connects two nodes should be found by summing over all possible arc traversal sequences that support it. This is difficult to compute, however, so we settle for the former estimate. In HMM terminology this is analogous to Viterbi rather than forward/backward estimation.

If all paths were legal, then finding the best path between any two nodes of the graph [2] may be done using Dijkstra's algorithm [4], which has worst-case time-complexity of $O(n^2)$ given n nodes in the graph. This is a simple algorithm that can be coded up in a few lines of any high-level language. Note that this algorithm is a kind of dynamic programming algorithm [1].

There are two requirements that complicate matters. Firstly, we are only interested in paths whose labels, when concatenated, form a valid string in the dictionary. Secondly, we are interested not only in the best path, but the n-best paths.

C. Path Algebras

Searching a dictionary given a directed graph as input is equivalent to finding all paths through the graph such that the concatenated arc labels for a given path form a valid word in the dictionary. An elegant way to describe this, and a host of related problems is to use a path algebra [2]. In the path algebra formulation, the problem reduces to specifing the general form of an element of the algebra, the join and product operators and the zero and unit elements.

Having done this, standard matrix methods can then be used to find solutions to the problem at hand, where these methods are independent of the choice of algebra.

Note that for fast dictionary retrieval the use of such general methods does not directly lead to a computationally efficient solution. The process of finding paths through a directed graph using a path algebra works as follows. The arcs produced by the OCR engine (the primitive arcs) are used to construct the initial matrix, A^1. All paths in this matrix consist of a single arc. Note, however, that there are three important concepts of length: span in image space, length in string space (number of string characters in a path) and length in graph space (number of primitive arcs in path). Deletion errors (deletions in the sense that the writer omitted to write something that he should have written) are modelled as arcs from a node to itself. These have zero extent in image space but typically a length of 1 in string space. Insertion errors (which could be caused by a writer erroneously inserting an extra character, or by poor segmentation of the input) are modelled by arcs labelled with the empty string denoted by `|' in Figure 1. These have a non-zero extent in image space, but a length of zero in string space.

Given A^1 we can then (in theory) find paths of graph-length n by computing $(A^1)^n$. This is a simple and elegant way of viewing the problem. The approach adopted here to computing this efficiently involves two strategies: use lazy evaluation and only extend paths that are substrings of words in the dictionary. The lazy evaluation procedure is based on two operators - for the path algebra we define lazy join and lazy product. When applied to the input matrix, these operators set up a network of lazy computing elements where all paths of a given length connecting the same two nodes are retrieved by a single lazy join module. Once this network is set up, we then create a root node as the lazy join of all the possible graph spans that we suspect a complete word might cover. Having done this, the root node then delivers paths consisting of legal whole words or legal substrings in the dictionary, in strictly best-first order.

As an example, consider the part of the network that finds paths between nodes zero and two in the graph of Figure 1. Suppose we are using a trie data structure for substring checking. This leads us to compute A^n by post-multiplying by the adjacency matrix A^1 i.e. $A^n = A^{n-1}A^1$

[2] or alternatively, in equal worst case time, the best path from a given node to all other nodes

due to the fact that we traverse the trie character by character from the beginning of a word. Hence, if we denote the element connecting nodes i and j with paths of length n as a^n_{ij} then paths between zero and two of length two can only be computed in one way:

$$a^2_{02} = a^1_{01}a^1_{12}$$

On the other hand, paths of length three between these two nodes may be formed by the join of two product terms:

$$a^3_{02} = a^2_{02}a^1_{22} \vee a^2_{01}a^1_{12}$$

but note that a^2_{01} can be formed in two ways:

$$a^2_{01} = a^1_{01}a^1_{11} \vee a^1_{00}a^1_{01}$$

The system uses matrix multiplication in this way to build up a network of lazy join and lazy product nodes. The lazy product node always has two inputs, and expands the product of its two input sets as necessary. As it combines input pairs it multiplies the confidence values and extends the path label if this would make a valid sub-word, otherwise it discards this pair and gets the next one until it either finds a valid one, or until one of the input sets is empty. The lazy join operator may have any number of inputs - each of which is an ordered lazy set. An ordered lazy set is an object that implements three methods: *value* returns the belief value of the first element in the set; *isEmpty* returns true if the set is empty; *pop* returns the next element of the set.

The lazy join works by keeping all its elements ordered in a priority queue. On initialisation, it determines the value of each element and sorts them into order. This can be done in $N \log N$ time for sets with N elements in.

When *pop()* is called on a LazyJoin it pops its priority queue to get the ordered lazy set with the best element. It then calls *pop* on this set to return the next best element. If this set is now *empty* then it is discarded, otherwise is it re-inserted into the priority queue, an operation that scales logarithmically with the size of the queue. Unfortunately space restrictions prevent a full explanation of the system's operation, but note that the output of a lazy join may act as the input to many other lazy joins and lazy products. Therefore, the outputs have to be stored in an array to ensure that no work is replicated. The size of the output arrays can be seen as analogous to a beam-width, since they correspond to the maximum search depth at any node. We start with output arrays of size 200, but grow them dynamically by doubling the array size at any node whenever an overflow would occur. Interestingly, for the results in Table 2 this size occasionally grows as large as 3,200 — this would be equivalent to an exteremely wide beam if using a beam search.

To check substring legality there are many possible data structures we could use, some of which are mentioned in the discussion below. Here we use a special form of compressed trie, where links are encoded in two arrays of integers. Time to find a successor link in this structure grows $O(\log N)$ where N is the number of successors of a node in the trie, but note that N is bounded by the size of the alphabet. This structure is more compact than having an array of successors for each node, and more importantly it can be saved to and loaded from disk more quickly. For example, loading a pre-compiled trie dictionary of 200,000 UK postcodes takes about 100ms[3]. The use of this structure explains why the retrievals in Table 2 become slower in some cases as the dictionary size increases.

Words	setTime (ms)	meanRetrievalTime (ms)
10k	128 (136)	0.78 (0.7)
50k	116 (18)	0.98 (0.6)
100k	165 (5)	0.56 (0.5)
500k	166 (5)	0.86 (0.4)
1000k	164 (5)	1.10 (0.1)

Table 1. Performance on graph of Fig. 1.

Words	setTime (ms)	meanRetrievalTime (ms)
10k	1286 (316)	3.0 (0.6)
50k	4667 (918)	3.2 (0.9)
100k	4493 (898)	4.9 (3.3)
500k	3500 (823)	6.8 (4.8)
1000k	3444 (748)	8.7 (5.6)
∞	121 (153)	0.3 (0.5)

Table 2. Performance on random graphs.

D. Initial Results

As an initial test the set of arcs shown in Figure 1 were fed into the system to retrieve the fifty best paths in the dictionary of the (alphabetically) first 100,000 UK postcodes.

Note that the system is extremly flexible. We can either get the best words in the dictionary that span the entire graph, or the best words in the dictionary that span any two nodes of the graph. The output shown below is for paths that span zero to eight in the graph.

```
27993600 length 8 paths from 0 to 8
Set graph in 280 ms elapsed
0  8  AB56_2SW  0.00011340
0  8  AB56_2SN  0.00002520
0  8  B26_2SW   0.00002268
0  8  AB56_2QW  0.00001417
     << 40 deleted >>
0  8  B8_1SN    0.00000078
```

[3]All timing results reported here are for a Java implementation running on a 450Mhz PIII.

```
0  8  AB56_1BN  0.00000070
0  8  B26_2DN   0.00000063
0  8  B26_2QN   0.00000063
0  8  B26_1SN   0.00000056
0  8  AB2_6SN   0.00000056
50 retrievals in 50 ms elapsed
```

Next, we list the output when doing retrieval over all spans of the graph.

```
Added 52 Arcs
27993600 length 8 paths from 0 to 8
Set graph in 330 ms elapsed
1  6  B5_6BR    0.00052500
1  6  B5_6BB    0.00035000
1  6  B5_6LB    0.00035000
1  7  B5_6BS    0.00028000
1  8  B26_2SW   0.00022680
    << 40 deleted >>
0  6  B8_2BR    0.00001470
2  8  B8_2SH    0.00001440
2  8  B8_2SU    0.00001440
0  8  AB56_2QW  0.00001417
0  6  AB2_6BZ   0.00001400
50 retrievals in 60 ms elapsed
```

The timings indicate that setting up the initial network for a particular graph takes a few hundred milliseconds, but that once this is done each retrieval generally takes about one millisecond. Note that this retrieval time is independent of the dictionary size. The timing results for using this graph to search various dictionary sizes are shown in Table 1 (averaged over 10 trials, standard deviations in parentheses).

Next we constructed random graphs of the same topology as Figure 1 but with all possible 38 labels (i.e. 36 alphanumeric plus skip plus space) connecting successive nodes and also looping back to each node (i.e. each non-final had an out-degree of 76), but with the confidence values chosen from a uniform random distribution in the range zero to one. For these random graphs there are now 2.2×10^{15} possible paths of arc-length 8 between the start and end node. For this graph, we also did retrieval where all possible strings were allowed (i.e. the dictionary size is infinite – the free monoid Σ^*). This demonstrates emphatically that as dictionary size is increased given a fixed alphabet there must come a point where the time per retrieval decreases.

E. Discussion and Conclusions

The need to search a dictionary given graph-based input is a requirement of most high-accuracy OCR systems. The system reported here is interesting because of its fast operation (potentially independent of the size of the dictionary) and its flexibility. For example, it is not necessary to know where a word begins and ends - the system does not require that a word connect the start and end nodes of the graph, though of course this constraint can be enforced if desired. It should be emphasised that the system is noise-free in the sense that it only returns strings that are both paths in the graph and words in the dictionary, and that if a word is in the graph, it is guaranteed to be returned in the correct order (unlike a beam-search method which could miss it).

The results above provide some empirical evidence that the system does indeed perform best-first enumeration of words in a graph independent of the size of the dictionary, and that the system works well for large dictionaries. It would be useful to prove this theoretically, but there are more urgent things to be addressed. One of these is how the choice of data structure for valid substring checking (during the product operation) affects system performance. Potential future candidates include constant-time trie suffix-trie, directed acyclic word graphs and strictly hierarchical context-free grammars.

We also need to research how this system can best be applied to practical problems. Viewed as a black box, the system simply enumerates the best n dictionary words that are paths in the input graph. The question is how we can best set up the input graph in order to cope with the errors that naturally occur in a particular application.

References

[1] R. Bellman. *Dynamic Programming*. Princeton University Press, (1957).

[2] B. Carré. *Graphs and Networks*. Oxford University Press, (1979).

[3] D. Chen, J. Mao, and K. Mohiuddin. An efficient algorithm for matching a lexicon with a segmentation graph. In W. Lea, editor, *Proceedings of the Fifth International Conference on Document Analysis and Recognition*, pages 543 – 546. IEEE, (1999).

[4] E. Dijkstra. A note on two problems in connection with graphs. *Numerishe Mathematik*, 1:269–271, 1959.

[5] A. Downton, L. Du, S. Lucas, and A. Badr. Generalized contextual recognition of hand-printed documents using semantic trees with lazy evaluation. In *Proceedings of the Fourth International Conference on Document Analysis and Recognition*, pages 238 – 242. IEEE, Ulm, Germany, (1997).

[6] S. Lucas. Rapid best-first retrieval from massive dictionaries. *Pattern Recognition Letters*, 17:1507 – 1512, (1996).

[7] M. Mohamed and P. Gader. Handwritten word recognition using segmentation-free hidden markov modeling and segmentation-based dynamic programming. *IEEE Transations on Pattern Analysis and Machine Intelligence*, 5:548 – 554, (1996).

[8] J. Schurmann, N. Bartneck, T. Bayer, J. Franke, E. Mandler, and M. Oberlander. Document analysis - from pixels to content. *Proceedings of the IEEE*, 80:1101 – 1119, (1992).

[9] H. Thompson. A chart-parsing realisation of dynamic programming: best-first enumeration of paths in a lattice. In *Proceedings of the European Conference on Speech Communication and Technology.*, Brussels, 1989.

Improved Degraded Document Recognition with Hybrid Modeling Techniques and Character N-Grams

Anja Brakensiek, Daniel Willett, Gerhard Rigoll
Dept. of Computer Science, Faculty of Electrical Engineering
Gerhard-Mercator-University Duisburg
47057 Duisburg, Germany
{anja, willett, rigoll}@fb9-ti.uni-duisburg.de

Abstract

In this paper a robust multifont character recognition system for degraded documents such as photocopy or fax is described. The system is based on Hidden Markov Models (HMMs) using discrete and hybrid modeling techniques, where the latter makes use of an information theory-based neural network. The presented recognition results refer to the SEDAL-database of English documents using no dictionary. It is also demonstrated that the usage of a language model, that consists of character n-grams yields significantly better recognition results. Our resulting system clearly outperforms commercial systems and leads to further error rate reductions compared to previous results reached on this database.

1. Introduction

During the last years, Hidden Markov Models (HMMs, see [7]) have been used not only for speech recognition but also for on- and off-line handwriting recognition (for example [2, 8]). However, the greatest advantage of HMM-technologies, the possibility of segmentation-free recognition, is also useful for machine-printed documents of poor quality and low resolution (see also [1, 4, 9]).

Such degraded multifont documents consist of noise and blurred characters, which are connected or split, so that a separate character-segmentation would become difficult. One possibility to handle such documents is to improve the image quality (see [5]) or to recognize the actual font first (like in [10]), another possibility, which we prefer, is to handle these problems using robust modeling techniques, and to perform a unified segmentation and recognition procedure.

In the following sections a robust optical character recognition (OCR) system for machine-printed degraded documents is described. For our recognition experiments we use the SEDAL-database[1], which contains several English documents (see also [9]). This database consists of real and self-printed documents of different fonts, which are faxed, copied and scanned at a resolution of 200 dpi.

In [9], it has been shown that the recognition performance of commercial products degrades significantly due to a reduction in resolution or in case of light or dark (connected characters) documents. Some examples of this database, which are used for testing (six real-world documents), are shown in Fig. 1.

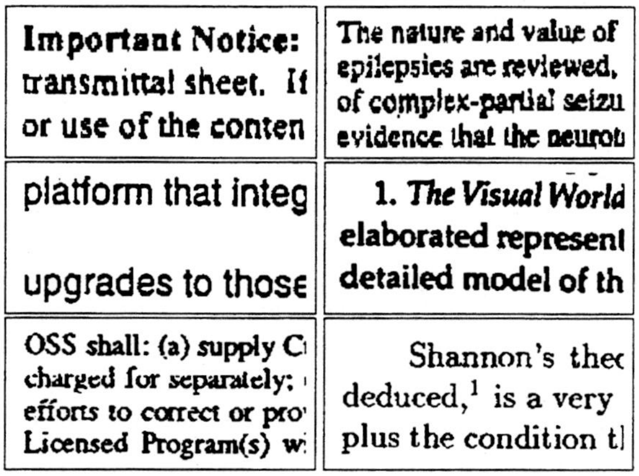

Important Notice: transmittal sheet. If or use of the conten	The nature and value of epilepsies are reviewed, of complex-partial seizu evidence that the neurou
platform that integ upgrades to those	1. The Visual World elaborated represent detailed model of th
OSS shall: (a) supply C charged for separately; efforts to correct or pro Licensed Program(s) w	Shannon's thec deduced,[1] is a very plus the condition t

Figure 1. Examples of the SEDAL-database (top: intel, neurofax; middle: precept, vision; bottom: maintenance, james)

This paper deals with the recognition of (and training on) some binary documents of this database using the description of labels and word-segmentation. So errors, which can occur in row- or word-segmentation (symbols in document-headers, noise, underlining), are eliminated. The next section (Section 2) presents the baseline recognition system for degraded documents, including feature extraction and two

[1] System Design and Automation Laboratory at the University of Sydney, Australia, http://www.sedal.usyd.edu.au

1051-4651/00 $10.00 © 2000 IEEE

different HMM modeling techniques. In Section 3, the use of contextual knowledge for language models (character n-grams) is described. The recognition experiments and results are given in Section 4. Finally, Section 5 summarizes the presented work and gives an outlook on additional tasks in the future.

2. Basic OCR System

Our OCR system consists of about 80 different linear HMMs, one for each character (upper- and lower-case letters, numbers and special characters like ' ' , : (! '). There are mostly 7 states per HMM used for numbers and upper-case characters and 5 states for lower-case characters depending on the character width (compare also [1, 9]).

For training we use about 63000 characters from several documents of the SEDAL-database. The test-set (see Fig.1) consists of some disjoint documents of the same database containing about 12600 characters (2200 words) altogether. Both, the training- and the test-set are based on word units whose positions within the document are known. So the presented recognition results refer to a character error rate, which depends only on substitutions, insertions and deletions of characters and which is independent of space counting or word segmentation errors. One reason for using the character- instead of the word-recognition rate is the unknown and unlimited vocabulary in real-world documents (for example reports on special topics or actual news), another reason is to allow a comparison with commercial software and the SEDAL-results presented in [9].

After preprocessing, which includes skew correction and normalization of character height, the text part is divided into thin vertical frames for feature extraction. A detailed description follows in Section 2.1. For recognition, these features are used to find that character sequence by a Viterbi algorithm, which is the most probable for the detected state-probabilities. The HMM modeling techniques used in our system (discrete and hybrid) are described in Section 2.2 in greater detail. An improvement of recognition results without any lexicon can be achieved using language models. This option means that the recognized character sequence is depending on the feature model as well as the language model (see Section 3).

2.1. Feature extraction

Fig.2 illustrates the most important aspects of feature extraction. After skew correction the baseline and coreheight (height of small characters such as a,e,n) of the word have to be estimated. This is done by interpreting the histogram (horizontal projection of the word), which depends on the number of black pixels (script) and black-white transitions in a horizontal line. The (approximately) correct detection of these lines is crucial for the following feature extraction, because the normalization of character height as well as the position of the sliding feature frame is based on them. The length of this frame will be set to the double coreheight (independent of top and bottom of the word or line) and is centered on this core-segment to be independent of ascenders and descenders. The following features are derived from the segmented and preprocessed word image:

- DCT (Discrete Cosine Transform) coefficients of a thin window slid along the horizontal direction (10-dimensional vector)
- some complementary features such as number of black pixels, height over baseline and length of descenders (3-dimensional vector) of this sliding frame

These feature vectors $\underline{x}$ are quantized by two separate codebooks (size 400 and 200) using multiple frame input in order to take the neighboring feature vectors into account.

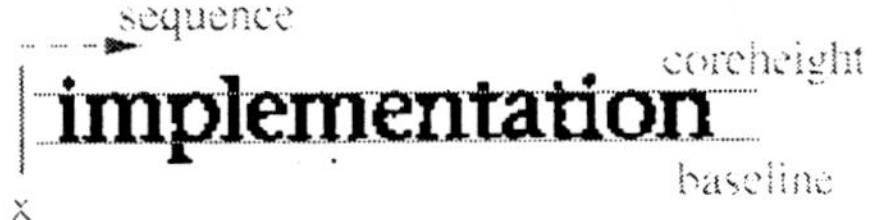

Figure 2. Feature extraction

When using hybrid HMMs instead of discrete ones, the k-means vector quantizer is replaced by a codebook obtained by a neural network as described in Sec.2.2.

2.2. HMM modeling techniques

In general, there are three different modeling techniques used for HMMs: continuous, discrete or hybrid (see [7, 8]). In this paper recognition experiments using a discrete and a hybrid approach are compared, because continuous modeling provided only poor performance as is shown in [2].

Using discrete HMMs the feature vector $\underline{x}$ is first processed by a vector quantizer (VQ), which leads to the generation of a VQ label y_n according to:

$$\underline{x} \overset{VQ}{\rightarrow} y_n \tag{1}$$

By using this k-means VQ the probability of vector $\underline{x}$ in state s is approximated by the probability of the label y_n as:

$$p(\underline{x}|s) = p(y_n|s) \tag{2}$$

Using the hybrid approach as described in [8], a winner-takes-all neural network replaces the k-means VQ. It can be shown, that the continuous state-conditioned probabilities can be reconstructed from the discrete probabilities. This neural VQ is trained according to the MMI (Maximum Mutual Information) criterion:

$$I(Y,W) = H(Y) - H(Y|W) = H(W) - H(W|Y) \quad (3)$$

where Y is the neural firing sequence, W the string of classes (characters) corresponding to the training vector sequence X and H the entropy.

Due to the structure of these hybrid HMMs, the recognition is as fast as using discrete HMMs.

3. Contextual Knowledge

Our OCR system works without any dictionary. So, to improve recognition performance we use language models (backoff n-grams), which are well known in speech recognition, on the character level. This model influences the transition probabilities between the trained character HMMs. Using Bayes rule the solution for our character recognition problem can be described as follows:

$$W^* = \underset{W}{\operatorname{argmax}}\ p(W|X) = \frac{\underset{W}{\operatorname{argmax}}\ p(W) \cdot p(X|W)}{p(X)} \quad (4)$$

with $p(X|W)$ presenting the feature model (see Sec.2.1) and $p(W)$ the grammar or language model (see also [1, 11]). The probability of the features $p(X)$ is nonrelevant, because it is the same for all classes W. This language model is described by a backoff n-gram of characters (not words) with n=2, 3 or 5. It takes into account that, for example, the character sequence 'qu' is much more probable than 'qo'. The formula for estimating a backoff bigram is the following

$$P(w_2|w_1) = \begin{cases} (N(w_1,w_2) \cdot d)/N(w_1) & : N(w_1,w_2) > t \\ p(w_2) \cdot b(w_1) & : else \end{cases} \quad (5)$$

with $N(w_1, w_2)$ the number of times character w_2 follows w_1. The discounting coefficient d and the backoff factor $b(w_1)$ are necessary to correct the probabilities for observed and unseen events (see [3]). Examples for applications of language models are the use of bi- or trigrams of characters (compare also [1]) for word recognition, as described in this paper or n-grams of words in order to enhance sentence-recognition or document classification (for example [6]).

We generate the n-gram model (including also special characters) by using the statistical character-sequences of about 3.8 millions of words from English documents (several HTML-pages), which leads to 110342 (26129 or 3711) different 5-gram (3- or 2-gram) sequences. It should be noticed, that this database is quite easy to create, because only the ASCII-text (and no image) is necessary.

The language model is trained with the CMU toolkit (see [3]) and a more detailed description of the decoding procedure using this kind of language model can be found in [11].

4. Experimental Results

We tested the influence of two different factors on the character recognition rate: first, the modeling technique, which compares discrete with hybrid HMMs and second, the inclusion of language models consisting of n-grams.

The test set, we use, is similar to that used in [9], in which an average character recognition rate of about 86.3% is presented (using HMMs combined with a neural network and a test-set of 11655 characters). For comparison, the recognition rate of commercial products is about 75%, as described in [9].

Here, a character recognition rate of 86.1% is achieved based on the discrete modeling technique. As can be seen in Tab.1 (compare examples in Fig.1), the relative error rate is reduced by about 28% in average using hybrid (character recognition rate: 90.0%) instead of discrete HMMs. A comparable effect of error reduction depending on the modeling technique could be observed for on- and off-line handwriting experiments, too (see results described in [2, 8]). If we take into account, that some different characters of different fonts look equal (for example 'I', 'l' (small 'L') and '1' (one) or '0' and 'O') or very similar (blurred '.' and ',') and cannot be distinguished by humans without word-context or font information, the recognition rate increases by about 1.5% ignoring such substitutions (compare Tab.1 last column). Most substitution errors, which occur, are confusions between 'l', 'I' and 'i' and confusions between 'e' and 'c', which can be explained by a similar shape in noisy dark and light documents. Most insertions belong to very small characters, like 'j', 'r', ',' and ''' (apostrophe), several deletions to the character 'i'. The greatest quota of the character error rate however consists of the number of substitutions, so that the recognition rate increases only to 90.6% (using hybrid HMMs) when ignoring insertions and deletions.

Table 1. Character recognition results (in %) using different modeling techniques without language model

document	no. of chars	recog. discrete	recog. hybrid	I=l=1,O=0,.=, hybrid
intel	396	91.4	95.5	96.5
neurofax	2061	75.9	83.3	84.8
precept	1923	87.2	90.2	93.1
vision	2643	92.6	95.5	96.4
maintenance	2979	81.2	85.7	87.7
james	2592	91.6	93.9	94.1
total	12594	86.1	90.0	91.5

Another kind of error occurs, whenever the estimation of baseline and coreheight is wrong. This results in a substitution of character sequences (the whole word), in which no visual similarity between original and recognition can be seen. These errors are very seldom (within the test documents), but can occur, if a word (and the corresponding row) only consists of small characters (without ascenders) or only consists of upper-case characters and the font size is unknown. A further problem are superscript characters or indices (as in Fig.1: james), which have to be handled separately, as well as underlined words.

The second test series investigates the effect of using language models on character recognition. Using n-grams for character recognition, the accuracy increases significantly (see Tab.2), so that in average a character recognition rate of about 97.1% (using 5-grams) can be obtained. This means a relative error reduction of about 70% compared to the results without language model in Tab.1. The number of substitutions concerning similar characters in different fonts as described above, is very small (e.g. 5-gram: recognition rate of 97.2% instead of 97.1%). Most errors, which occur now, are substitutions between 'e' and 'a' or 'o' and confusions between single (apostrophe) and double quotation marks. Comparing the recognition results using different character n-grams, the error rate decreases with increasing context depth. This tendency is terminated using 7-grams (recognition rate of 97.1%), which can be explained by the average word-length of about 5.7 characters.

Table 2. Character recognition results (in %) with hybrid HMMs using language models

document	2-gram hybrid	3-gram hybrid	5-gram hybrid	word recog. 5-gram, hyb.
intel	97.5	97.7	98.7	96.2
neurofax	92.0	93.6	95.5	84.7
precept	95.3	96.4	97.1	89.2
vision	96.7	97.5	97.9	93.5
maintenance	92.1	93.6	96.5	91.9
james	95.9	96.3	97.9	94.6
total	94.5	95.5	97.1	91.6

Another fact, which is described in Tab.2, is that a character recognition rate of 97.1% implies a word recognition rate (based on characters, without lexicon) of only 91.6% (testset: 12594 characters = 2218 words in total). This must be taken into account, using such a character based recognizer in (word) retrieval systems, for example.

5. Summary and Outlook

We presented in this paper a HMM based OCR system for degraded English documents of low resolution. For evaluation of our recognition methods we use the SEDAL-database [9] that consists of multifont real world documents. The above experiments of this segmentation-free approach show the better performance of a hybrid modeling technique for HMMs, which depends on a neural vector quantizer, compared to discrete HMMs. The relative error rate for character recognition can be reduced by about 28%.

Additionally, we describe the influence on recognition accuracy (character recognition without dictionary) obtained by the use of a language model based on character n-grams. Here the relative error rate decreases by about 70% using 5-grams. Future work will imply a robust word segmentation of variable documents including images, symbols or tables (for example newspapers) and research on confidence measures for document retrieval.

References

[1] I. Bazzi, R. Schwartz, and J. Makhoul. An Omnifont Open-Vocabulary OCR System for English and Arabic. *IEEE Transactions on Pattern Analysis and Machine Intelligence*, 21(6):495–504, June 1999.

[2] A. Brakensiek, A. Kosmala, D. Willett, W. Wang, and G. Rigoll. Performance Evaluation of a New Hybrid Modeling Technique for Handwriting Recognition Using Identical On-Line and Off-Line Data. In *5th International Conference on Document Analysis and Recognition (ICDAR)*, pages 446–449, Bangalore, India, Sept. 1999.

[3] P. Clarkson and R. Rosenfeld. Statistical Language Modeling Using the CMU-Cambridge Toolkit. In *Proc. Eurospeech '97*, pages 2707–2710, Rhodes, Greece, Sept. 1997.

[4] A. Elms, S. Procter, and J. Illingworth. The advantage of using an HMM-based approach for faxed word recognition. *Int. Journal on Document Analysis and Recognition (IJDAR)*, 1:18–38, 1998.

[5] J. Hobby and T. Ho. Enhancing Degraded Document Images via Bitmap Clustering and Averaging. In *Proc. Int. Conference on Document Analysis and Recognition (ICDAR)*, volume 1, pages 394–400, Ulm, Germany, Aug. 1997.

[6] M. Junker and R. Hoch. An experimental evaluation of OCR text representations for learning document classifiers. *Int. Journal on Document Analysis and Recognition (IJDAR)*, 1:116–122, 1998.

[7] L. Rabiner and B. Juang. An Introduction to Hidden Markov Models. *IEEE ASSP Magazine*, pages 4–16, 1986.

[8] G. Rigoll, A. Kosmala, and D. Willett. A New Hybrid Approach to Large Vocabulary Cursive Handwriting Recognition. In *International Conference on Pattern Recognition (ICPR)*, pages 1512–1514, Brisbane, Aug. 1998.

[9] M. Schenkel and M. Jabri. Low resolution, degraded document recognition using neural networks and hidden Markov models. *Pattern Recognition Letters*, 19:365–371, 1998.

[10] H. Shi and T. Pavlidis. Font Recognition and Contextual Processing for More Accurate Text Recognition. In *Proc. Int. Conference on Document Analysis and Recognition (ICDAR)*, pages 39–44, Ulm, Germany, Aug. 1997.

[11] D. Willett, C. Neukirchen, and G. Rigoll. DUCODER-The Duisburg University LVSCR Stackdecoder. In *Proc. IEEE Int. Conf. on Acoustics, Speech, and Signal Processing (ICASSP)*, Istanbul, June 2000.

JKanji: Wavelet-based Interactive Kanji Completion

Robert Stockton[1*]
rgs@justresearch.com

[1]Just Research
4616 Henry Street
Pittsburgh, PA 15213
U.S.A.

Rahul Sukthankar[1,2 †]
rahuls@cs.cmu.edu

[2]The Robotics Institute
Carnegie Mellon University
Pittsburgh, PA 15213
U.S.A.

Abstract

JKanji is an interactive character completion system that provides stroke-order-independent recognition of complex hand-written glyphs such as Japanese kanji or Chinese hanzi. As the user enters each stroke, JKanji offers a menu of likely completions, generated from a robust multi-scale matching algorithm augmented with a statistical language model. Drawbacks of traditional wavelet-based approaches are addressed by a redundant, phase-shifted basis that is insensitive to variations of the input character across quadrant boundaries. Unlike many existing systems, JKanji can incrementally incorporate new training examples, either to adapt to the idiosyncrasies of a particular user, or to increase its vocabulary. On a kanji input task with a vocabulary of 6369 kanji and English characters, JKanji has demonstrated 93%–96% recognition accuracy and up to 80% reduction in the number of input strokes. JKanji is computationally efficient, processing images at 5–10Hz on an inexpensive portable computer, and is well-suited for integration into personal digital assistants (PDAs) as an input method. JKanji's recognition system also processes low-quality digital camera images and has been integrated into a prototype tourist's guide *that interprets unfamiliar kanji in the environment.*

1. Introduction

Traditional computer input devices, such as keyboards, are ill-suited for languages with large vocabularies of complex glyphs (e.g., Japanese kanji or Chinese hanzi). Research has therefore focused on alternative input methods such as optical character recognition [6] or stroke-based handwriting recognition [3]. The former has proved successful in processing scanned documents, while the latter has become increasingly common in interactive applications.

Kanji completion is an interactive task that combines certain aspects of both character recognition and handwriting recognition. However, kanji completion differs from these tasks in two important respects: (1) a kanji completion system must endeavor to match a user's partially-drawn glyphs against the (complete) glyphs in the training set as early as possible; (2) a kanji completion system can rely on the user to select the correct glyph from a small menu of likely completion candidates at each stage of the process. We present JKanji, an approach to the task of interactive glyph input that addresses common problems with existing input methods by employing techniques inspired by work in sketch-based image retrieval [2]. Our system has three main goals: (1) increasing the speed of stroke-independent[1] glyph input; (2) incrementally incorporating additional training data (either new characters in the vocabulary or idiosyncratic examples of known glyphs); (3) providing a solution suitable for handheld devices (low requirements on computing power and memory usage).

JKanji has been integrated into a text-editor targeted for non-native kanji users (see Figure 1) and is also a component in a prototype *tourist's guide*. The latter is a device equipped with a digital camera, capable of interpreting common kanji signs from images (see Section 3).

*Robert Stockton (**rstock@whizbang.com**) is now with WhizBang! Labs–Research, 4616 Henry Street, Pittsburgh, PA 15213, U.S.A.

†Rahul Sukthankar (**rahuls@cs.cmu.edu**) is now with Carnegie Mellon University and Compaq Computer Corporation (Cambridge Research Lab), One Cambridge Center, Cambridge, MA 02142, U.S.A.

[1]While native speakers are taught to use a canonical stroke order when entering characters, non-native speakers (who may benefit most from a character completion system) typically do not. JKanji can also be used to enter user-defined characters that have no canonical stroke order.

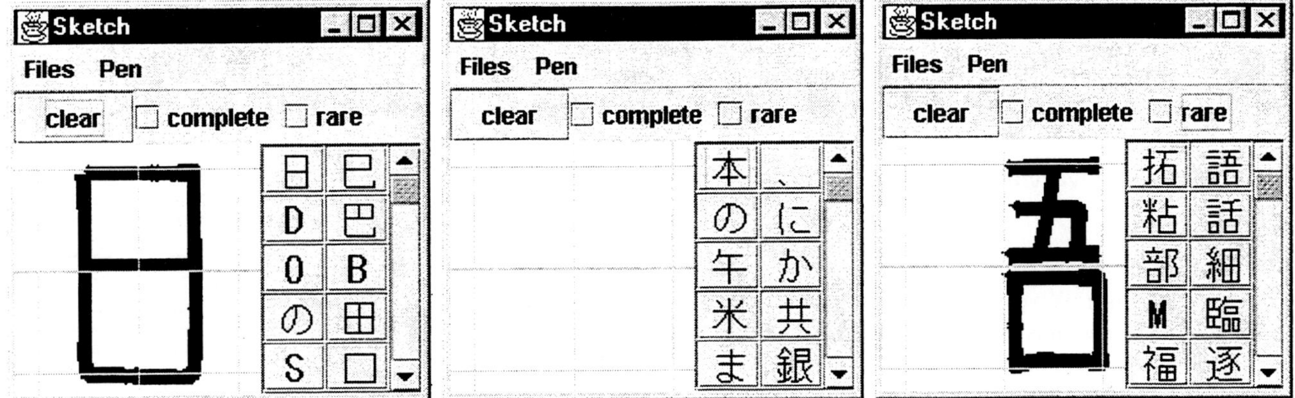

Figure 1. JKanji significantly facilitates interactive kanji input. Here, the user is entering the phrase "Japanese language". Upon confirmation that the first glyph is "sun", JKanji's language model immediately suggests "book" (the combination means "Japan"). The third glyph, recognized after the first few strokes, demonstrates partial matching. JKanji is not stroke-order dependent.

2. System Architecture

JKanji consists of several components, shown in Figure 2. The input to the system consists of a sequence of images: snapshots of a sketchpad window[2], captured at the conclusion of each glyph stroke (up to 10Hz). These images are first preprocessed to ensure consistency in line thickness, and scaled appropriately. Next, a feature vector is extracted from each pre-processed image using a set of redundant wavelet decompositions. These feature vectors are matched against stored feature vectors corresponding to the training images, and the best matches (weighted by several language models) are presented to the user. This asymmetric matching process is designed so that a partial glyph in the input image correctly matches the respective complete glyph in the training data. As the user adds strokes to the glyph in the input area, JKanji recomputes the wavelet features and updates the candidate list; this process repeats until the desired glyph appears and is selected by the user. At this point, dynamic language model parameters are updated and JKanji clears the input area in preparation for a new character. JKanji's language model enables it to frequently predict likely glyphs before the user enters *any* strokes (see Figure 1), thus drastically reducing the input effort. The major components are detailed below.

2.1. Training set preparation

JKanji can incorporate training data from a variety of sources. In the experiments described in this paper, one image for each of 6369 kanji was synthesized from the *MS Gothic* font and processed as described below to create a single training example per glyph in the vocabulary[3]. The user may easily augment the training set, either when difficulties in matching a known glyph are experienced (adapting to user idiosyncrasies), or when he/she wishes to add a new glyph; the wavelet features for the current input image (assumed to be a complete glyph) are simply appended to the vocabulary of known kanji characters. The language models (described in Section 2.5) are initialized from a corpus of Japanese natural language text.

2.2. Image pre-processing

Unlike traditional handwriting input systems, JKanji does not extract features from a time-series of the user's gestures. Rather, the snapshot of each successive version of the sketched glyph is processed independently. This lack of temporal information results in two important benefits: (1) JKanji is insensitive to stroke-order; (2) JKanji can easily be applied to noisy input from scanned text or photographs (see Section 3).

Each image is first processed to ensure that strokes are of uniform width using a heuristic algorithm adapted from [6]: *shrink* or *grow* filters are successively applied until the *thickness metric* for the input image matches that of the images used during training.

JKanji creates two copies of the input image: one to test the hypothesis that the image is a complete glyph, and the other to attempt partial matches. The former is centered and then robustly scaled so that 75% of the dark pixels lie within a specified "central region"; the latter is scaled with-

[2]Glyphs are entered using a mouse-driven sketchpad with physics-based smoothing (inspired by *DynaDraw* [1]).

[3]Training and input images are treated identically in JKanji except during the asymmetric matching process.

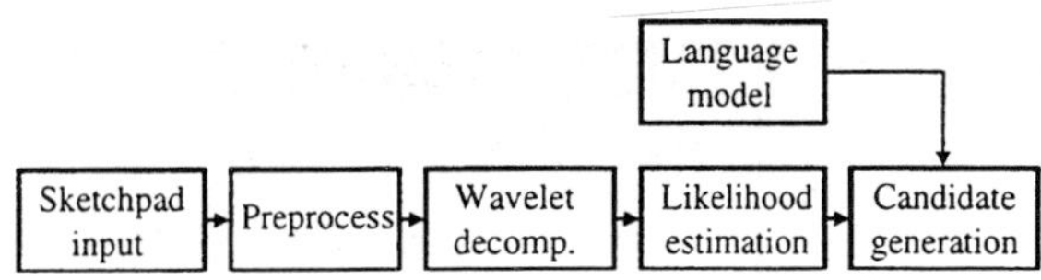

Figure 2. Overview of JKanji system.

out centering (centering would destroy information about subfeature location). Wavelet features for each of these two images are independently computed, and matched against candidate glyphs in the training set as described below.

2.3. Wavelet decomposition

Wavelet-based approaches are becoming increasingly popular in pattern recognition, and have recently been applied to character recognition [4]. However, JKanji's wavelet decomposition is unrelated to prior research in this area; it was inspired by work in sketch-based image retrieval [2]. For background material on wavelets, see [5, 7].

A serious drawback with employing a wavelet-based approach in this domain is that the decomposition is overly sensitive to small variations in the neighborhood of quadrant boundaries. Kanji characters are particularly prone to this problem since they commonly contain centered vertical and horizontal strokes. Slight shifts in such a stroke's position can cause significant changes in the wavelet coefficients. To alleviate this problem, JKanji employs a novel redundant basis: (1) three copies of the input image are made, with the pixels in each "barrel shifted" (toroidal translation) up and to the left by 0, $1/5$, and $1/3$ of the image width; (2) 128×128 wavelet decompositions are independently performed on each of the three images; (3) the most important coefficients (see below) from each of these decompositions are retained. Since the barrel shift multiples share no common factors, a particular stroke in the original input image will lie on a critical region in at most one of the three decompositions (see Figure 3).

The images are filtered (both horizontally and vertically) using a simple variant of the Haar wavelet[4]. Although the Haar basis is rarely the best choice for filtering natural images, our experiments have shown that it outperforms Daubechies and cubic spline bases in the kanji completion domain. We hypothesize that this is because the binary images created by the sketchpad application consist of crisply separated black and white regions (see Figure 1) whose sharp discontinuities are effectively expressed by the Haar basis.

[4]Identical to the Haar wavelet except: (1) scaling constants are omitted; (2) averages are replaced by sums. This integer variant is more efficient than the standard Haar. The scaling constants for coefficients in different frequency bands is partially subsumed in the w_{ij} weights (see Section 2.4).

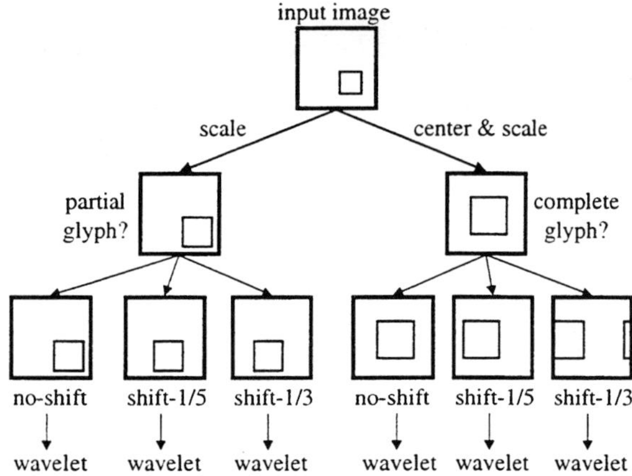

Figure 3. JKanji considers two independent hypotheses: that the input glyph will partially or completely match glyphs in the training set. To overcome quadrant effects present in standard wavelet decompositions, three redundant wavelet coefficients are extracted by barrel shifting each scaled input image.

From the 128×128 wavelet coefficients in each of three images, the signs and coordinates of the 40 coefficients with the greatest magnitude are retained as features. Each glyph can be compactly expressed as a list of 120 signed integers (2 bytes each). Therefore, the 6369 kanji in JKanji's training set consume only $6369 \times 40 \times 3 \times 2 \approx 1.5$ MB of storage space (small enough to comfortably fit into a handheld computer's RAM).

2.4. Likelihood estimation

In this step, the 120 features of the input image (probe) are compared against the stored features of every kanji (target) in the training set. JKanji employs an asymmetric weighted comparison metric in order to reward similarity between probe and target without overly penalizing missing strokes in the probe kanji. Specifically, the score for a target kanji is increased whenever a coefficient in the probe appears in the target (with the same sign). The increment $w_{i,j}$ is a function of the coefficient's coordinates:

$$w_{i,j} = b^{\lfloor \log_2 \max(i,j) \rfloor}$$

where $b = 1.2$ (determined empirically). Since two versions of the wavelet decomposition are performed per kanji (for partial and complete matches), each kanji is assigned a final score that is the maximum of its two scores. This score is used to determine an ordering of the training set kanji (in response to the given input glyph).

The final step of this stage is to convert the ranking into likelihood estimates. The target kanji are assumed to follow Zipf's law [8] and accordingly, each kanji is assigned a likelihood proportional to the inverse of its rank.

2.5. Language models

The likelihood estimates implicitly assume a uniform prior distribution on every kanji in the training set. This is almost certainly violated when the input stream consists of a coherent sequence of well-formed, meaningful text. JKanji therefore considers three additional priors: (1) a unigram model based upon a large corpus of Japanese text; (2) a bigram model based upon the same corpus[5]; (3) a unigram model based solely upon the user's input to the kanji editor. Note that (2) and (3) are dynamically updated as the user enters text.

The user may selectively enable or disable particular language models. For instance, a user using JKanji simply for dictionary lookup could disable the bigram model, or could restrict JKanji to the uniform prior.

2.6. Candidate merging

The goal of this stage is to generate a single list of kanji candidates, to be displayed to the user. JKanji uses an unorthodox scheme that has produced excellent empirical results: the rankings according the each language model is independently computed by multiplying the likelihoods for each kanji by its respective prior generated from the model. These ordered rankings are now interleaved (with duplicates removed) to create a menu of candidates (see Figures 1 and 4).

3. Tourist's Guide

Tourists who are unable to read kanji could benefit substantially from a handheld device that recognized glyphs in their environment (e.g., shop signs or posters). We have developed a prototype application that enables users to snap a picture with a handheld digital camera and select an unfamiliar glyph in the image. JKanji processes this low-quality image and presents a menu of likely matches. The user may move a cursor over each match to obtain a translation. For instance, in Figure 4, JKanji correctly recognizes the glyph for "son" from a blurred and noisy image. This task is substantially more difficult than the text editor application since: (1) creating a good binary input image from the noisy greyscale photograph is non-trivial; (2) JKanji is unable to derive benefits from its bigram language model; (3) the appearance of the glyph may differ substantially from its single prototype in the training set (*MS-Gothic*). Nevertheless, as discussed in Section 4, JKanji's performance is surprisingly promising.

[5] Such a model can give the probability $P(x|y)$ of seeing a particular kanji, x, given that the previous kanji was y.

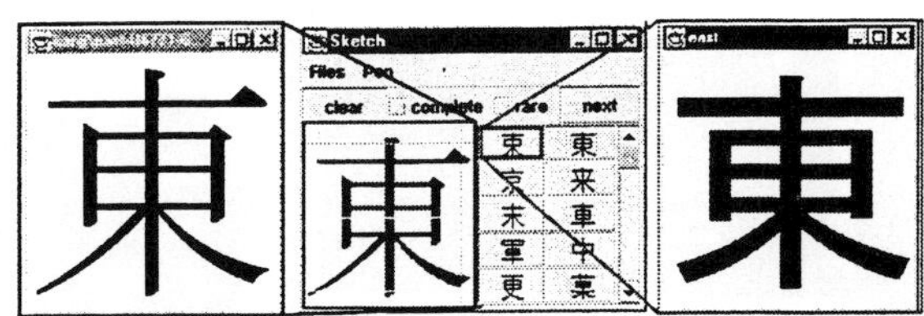

Figure 5. JKanji correctly recognizes 93% of 6369 glyphs from *MS-Mincho* even though it was trained on glyphs from the *MS-Gothic* font.

4. Results

We first present baseline results that demonstrate the competency of JKanji's glyph recognition system. In this experiment, JKanji was trained on *MS-Gothic* glyphs and tested on each of the glyphs in the *MS-Mincho* font. Although the glyphs differ in appearance (see Figure 5), JKanji achieved a 96.2% accuracy on the 2521 common glyphs and 93.0% on the complete set. In this experiment, JKanji received no benefit from its language models since the unigram and bigram frequency statistics of the test glyphs were not consistent with the natural language corpus for initialization.

An instrumented version of the kanji text editor was tested by several users (both native Japanese speakers and novices). Since recognition accuracy is not meaningful in this interactive context (users modify the glyph until JKanji offers the correct completion), we present statistics on kanji completion: JKanji reduced the number of input strokes required to enter Japanese text by 50%-80% (greater benefits were achieved when the input was consistent with the bigram language model). Novice users who were unfamiliar with canonical kanji stroke order reported the greatest benefits.

Finally, the tourist's guide prototype was tested on a set of low-quality images captured using a handheld digital camera. JKanji performed surprisingly well on this challenging task (see Figure 4), correctly recognizing 76% of the glyphs (in the absence of a bigram language model).

5. Conclusion

JKanji demonstrates that an interactive kanji completion system can significantly reduce the effort required to enter complex glyphs. JKanji has been successfully integrated

Figure 4. JKanji can also recognize kanji characters in photographs or scanned documents. A glyph extracted from a low-quality image of a poster (left) is shown enlarged (center). The correct identification is also shown (right).

into two prototype applications: a kanji text editor, and a tourist's guide.

6. Acknowledgments

Thanks to Justsystem Corporation for the Japanese document training data, researchers at Just Research for evaluating JKanji text editor, and Gita Sukthankar for valuable feedback on this paper.

References

[1] P. Haeberli. Dynadraw: A dynamic drawing technique, 1989. <http://www-europe.sgi.com/grafica/dyna/>.

[2] C. Jacobs, A. Finkelstein, and D. Salesin. Fast multiresolution image querying. In *Proceedings of SIGGRAPH*, 1995.

[3] H. Kim, J. Jung, and S. Kim. Online chinese character-recognition using art-based stroke classification. *Pattern Recognition Letters*, 17(12), 1996.

[4] T. Shioyama, H. Wu, and T. Nojima. Recognition algorithm based on wavelet transform for handprinted chinese characters. In *Proceedings of ICPR98*, 1998.

[5] G. Strang and T. Nguyen. *Wavelets and Filter Banks*. Wellesley Cambridge, 1997.

[6] R. Suchenwirth. *Optical recognition of Chinese characters*. Braunschweig, 1989.

[7] W. Sweldens. The wavelet home page. <http://www.wavelet.org/>.

[8] G. Zipf. *Psycho-Biology of Languages*. Houghton-Mifflin, 1935.

Layout Analysis of Complex Documents

Toyohide Watanabe and Tsuneo Sobue
Department of Information Engineering, Nagoya University
Furo-cho, Chikusa-ku, Nagoya 464-8603, JAPAN
E-mail: watanabe@nuie.nagoya-u.ac.jp

Abstract

Many methods/approaches for understanding document images have been investigated to extract/classify meaningful information from paper-based documents. These methods/approaches focused on the same types/classes of documents, whose layout structures can be represented by single specification. However, widely used documents are not always simple, but composed of different types/classes of simple ones: these documents cannot be represented by a simple document model. In this paper, we address the layout analysis of complex documents. In particular, the knowledge representation of layout structure is discussed. Although the representation means are divided into structure-description and operator-specification, our representation means is based on operator-specification.

1. Introduction

In the model-driven approach, the document model takes an important role to specify layout structures. Many methods about document models do not make use of logical information such as neighboring relationships, connective relationships and so on[1], but apply the physical information such as the lengths, sizes, positions, etc. of data items directly. Of course, the adaptability of model and flexibility of interpretation mechanism grow up if the logical information could be applied. The subjects about how to specify the model, what to specify as a description level and which specification is applicable are important in the basic framework. Different types/classes of documents are associated individually with different layout/logical structures, and cannot be analyzed under one unified document model[1]. In many investigations the application ranges are limited to the recognition/analysis of only one document class or similar kinds of documents: only simple documents were investigated. Here, the simple document is defined as a document which can be composed of single document class. Also, the complex document is defined as a document which is systematically composed of several document classes.

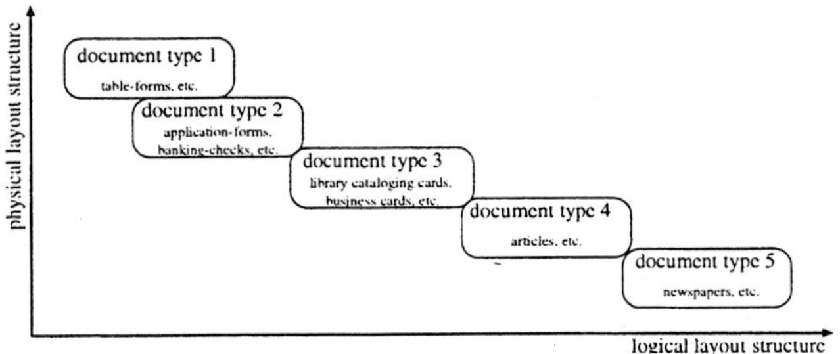

Figure 1. Classification of document

In this paper, we address the layout analysis of complex document: in particular, we discuss the representation method of document model in order to specify the layout knowledge for various kinds of documents.

2. Framework

2.1. Document Model

In Figure 1, individual document types are categorized with regard to two feature axes such as physical and logical layout structures[1]. The physical layout structure indicates the assignment of individual data items for the corresponding areas predefined on sheets, while the logical layout structure points out dynamically the locations among several data items within the pre-assigned regions, under the mutual relationships.

On the other hand, the document classes are collections of documents with the same or similar layout patterns in document types. Thus, the simple document is also defined as a document which can be directly derived from a single document class. While, the complex document is regarded as a document which is composed integratedly of two or more different document classes. Since documents are organized under the configuration, features of data items and relationships among data items, the document models may be represented by only one document class or by two or more document classes. The design of document models depend on how to grasp document structures.

2.2. Approach

The document model was mainly organized from two views: operator-specification and structure-description. The operator-specification focuses on the constructive and neighboring relationships among item data and the document model represents the adaptation sequence of operators[3,4]. While, the structure-description concentrates on the physical features of item data such as the positions, lengths, directions, sizes, etc. and the document model includes the declarative representation of physical features[5,6]. The structure-descriptions have been often used because the representation can reflect directly the constructive view of corresponding document structure and the constructive view is intuitive for model designers/composers. For example, the method of Q.Luo, et al. for library cataloging cards[3] and the method of A.Dengel, et al. for office letters[4] are examples in the former, while the method of T.Watanabe, et al. for table-form documents[2,7], the method of J.Higashino, et al. for application-forms[5] and the method of K.Kise, et al. for business cards[6] are examples in the latter. We assume that complex documents which we discuss in this paper should be composed of two or more simple documents of document types 1-4.

Our representation method of layout knowledge is based on the operator-specification because the means make the meanings of individual item data clear stepwisely and the interpretation mechanism is flexibly organized by means of the adaptation of operators. The basic strategy is to transform the layout knowledge of structure-description to that of operator-specification. For example, the structure-description tree, which was composed by the method in [7], can be easily transformed to the operator-specification tree, which can be organized by the method in [3]: though in [7] the upper-left corners of each field are corresponded to the fields, table-form documents can be represented by the method in [3], if the vertical and horizontal line segments divide individual areas into smaller rectangular sub-areas stepwisely and partitioning positions are looked upon as locations of line segments.

In Figure 2(a), item fields "A", "B" and "C" are surrounded with the vertical and horizontal line segments. In this case, the method in [7] makes each field correspond to the upper-left corners (e.g. upper-left corners "a", "b" and "c" in place of "A", "B" and "C" in Figure 2(b)), and transforms them into the structure-description tree under the connective relationships among upper-left corners. This transformation is shown in Figure 2(b). While, Figure 2(c) shows a result of layout structure on the basis of the method in [3]: individual data item fields are looked upon as areas partitioned on the neighboring relationships for vertical and horizontal line segments. In the operator-specification tree, the root node indicates the whole area and the vertical partitioning operator "1" divides this area into two vertically connected areas: common areas of fields "A" and "B"; and a field "C". Also, the horizontal partitioning operator "2" divides into horizontally connected fields "A" and "B".

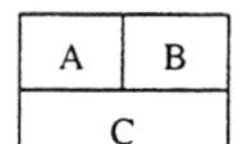

(a) Fragment of table-form document

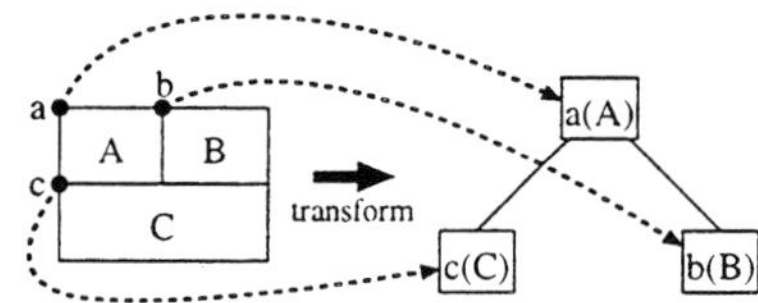

(b) Representation of layout knowledge in [11]

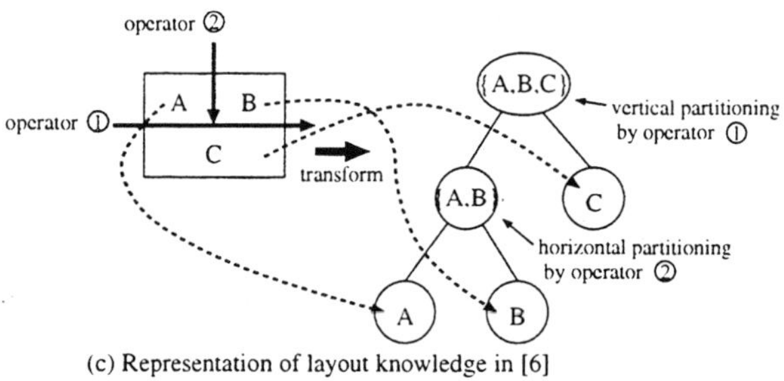

(c) Representation of layout knowledge in [6]

Figure 2. Structure-description and operator-specification

This compatibility between structure-description and operator-specification makes it possible to integrate various representation methods of layout knowledge for different document types. Figure 3 is an example of complex document, which we apply as the explanation. We can observe various features for complex documents in Figure 3. It is impossible to specify this layout structure as a document model, using the traditionally proposed representation means. Our approach assumes that these partial structures are organized under the hierarchically nested structure.

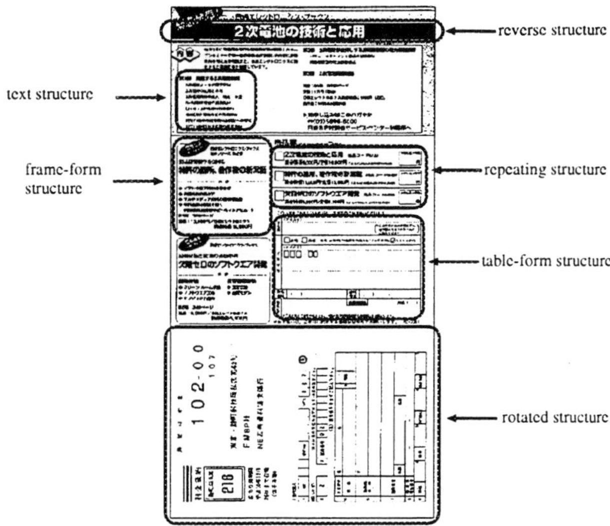

Figure 3. Example of complex document

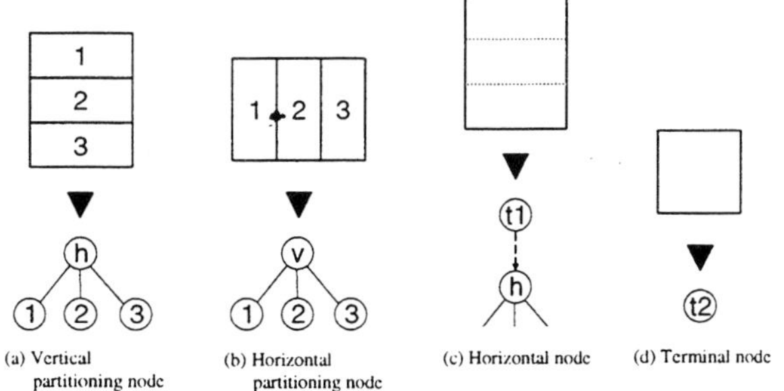

Figure 4. Types of nodes

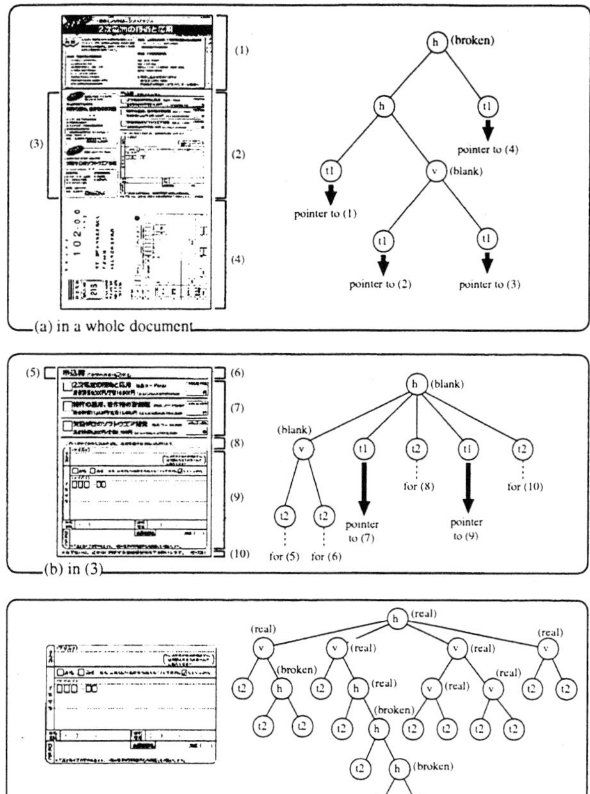

Figure 5. Operation-specification tree of document in Figure 3

3. Representation of Layout Knowledge

The document structure is looked upon as a configuration whose item data are hierarchically organized. The upper-level item data can be partitioned into several lower-level item data with regard to the consistent neighboring relationships. In this case, the partitioning sequence can be indicated, using the tree structure, and is called the operator-specification tree. Each node corresponds to item data block/field and each edge does to the relationship between the parent node for item data block/field to be partitioned and child nodes for partitioned item data blocks/fields. In addition, operators are attached with the corresponding nodes. 4 kinds of operators are prepared as shown in Figure 4.

1) Vertical partitioning ("v") node: This indicates that one item data block should be divided into two or more vertically neighboring blocks.

2) Horizontal partitioning ("h") node: This indicates that one item data block should be divided into several horizontally neighboring blocks.

3) Hierarchical ("t1") node: This indicates that one item data block contains a partial structure or several item data blocks. Thus, this holds pointers to operator-specification sub-trees for the partial structure or item data blocks.

4) Terminal ("t2") node: This indicates directly an item data field.

Figure 5(a) illustrates the main operator-specification tree for the document in Figure 3. Figures 5(b) and (c) represent the operator-specification sub-tree for sub-structure blocks (3) and (9), respectively. Moreover, Figure 5(c) corresponds to the final specification in hierarchically partitioned structure. In Figure 5, the dividers (e.g. real, broken, blank, etc.) are attached with "h" and "v" nodes.

4. Layout Analysis

The partitioning operation is applicable directly to the previously partitioned block because these are effective for blocks whose surrounding outer regions are blank. The divider partitions a processing block into two or more sub-blocks.

1) Blank divider: This partitions a processing block into two or more sub-blocks. The horizontal histogram in "h" and vertical histogram in "v" take basic roles to determine the partitioning locations. The number of divisions depends on the number of child nodes pointed from current parent node.

2) Character indent-up/down dividers: In text structure, the indentation of characters often indicates the start of paragraph. These partition individual item data blocks/segments on the basis of the constructive features.

3) Real/broken line dividers: These are available in table-form structures and indicate that item data blocks are separated by real/broken line segments.

5. Experiment

We evaluated not only complex documents, but also simple documents. Simple documents were selected by 10 journal-paper pages, 10 table-form documents, 10 business cards and 10 library description sheets: the total number is 40. While, 50 complex documents were used. Individual documents were scanned in 400 dpi, sampled in 256 levels and binarized.

Table 1 shows the experimental result. 76 documents were completely distinguished with respect to all item data in each document: the ratio is 84.4%. Also, in complex documents, 42 samples for 50 documents are successfully recognized: the ratio is 84%. For about 15% failed documents, the failure causes are (1) to be yet insufficient in knowledge representation for some layout structures, (2) to be not separated as independent rectangular areas because several data item fileds are overlayed, and so on. These errors depend on that (1) our binarization as the preprocessing was not sufficient to judge whether line segments are real or broken, and also (2) our binarization attached with noises because the original document images were printed by color. Moreover, the recognition ratio of individual item data for all documents is almost 96% in average. The result was successful.

Table 1. Experimental result

Input images		A	B	C	D	C/D
Complex document		50	42	1878	1810	96.4
Simple document	d_1	10	8	121	112	92.6
	d_2	10	10	247	247	100
	d_3	10	8	77	72	93.5
	d_4	10	8	312	301	96.5
total		90	76	2635	2542	96.5

A: No. of documents
B: No. of correctly analyzed documents
C: No. of total item data
D: No. of correctly analyzed item data
C/D: Recognition ratio of item data(%)
d_1: Journal paper
d_2: Table-form document
d_3: Business card
d_4: Library description sheet

6. Conclusion

In this paper, we discussed the recognition of complex document from viewpoints of knowledge representation of layout structure and layout analysis with document model. Also, in our experiment we showed that our approach is very successful. As our future work, the following subjects are important in order to make our method powerful: improvement/investigation of knowledge representation means for layout structure; and extension of layout analysis method.

References

[1] H.Masai and T.Watanabe: "Document Categorization for Document Image Understanding", *Proc.of ACCV'98*, Vol.2, pp.108-112.

[2] T.Watanabe and Q.Luo: "A Multi-layer Recognition Method for Understanding Table-form Documents", *Int'l J.of Imag. Syst.&Tech.*, Vol.7, pp.279-288(1996).

[3] Q.Luo, etc.: "Recognition of Document Structure on the Basis of Spatial and Geometric Relationships between Document Items", *Proc.of MVA '90*, pp.461-464.

[4] A.Dengel and G.Barth: "High Level Document Analysis Guided by Geometric Aspects", *Int'l J.of PR and AI*, Vol.2, No.4, pp.641-655(1988).

[5] J.Higashino, etc.: "A Knowledge-based Segmentation Method for Document Understanding", *Proc.of ICPR'86*, pp.745-748.

[6] K.Kise, etc.: "Model Based Understanding of Document Images", *Proc.of MVA '90*, pp.471-474.

[7] T.Watanabe, etc.: "Structure Analysis of Table-form Documents on the Basis of the Recognition of Vertical and Horizontal Line Segments", *Proc.of ICDAR'91*, pp.638-646.

Part-of-Speech Tagging for Table of Contents Recognition

A. Belaïd[1], L. Pierron[2] and N. Valverde[3]
[1]LORIA-CNRS, [2]LORIA-INRIA, [3]LORIA-ITESOFT
Campus Scientifique B.P. 239
54506 Vandoeuvre-Lès-Nancy France
{abelaid,pierron,valverde}@loria.fr

Abstract

A labeling approach to automatic recognition of tables of contents (TOC)s is described. A prototype is used for consulting electronically scientific papers in a digital library system named Calliope. This method operates on an a roughly structured ASCII file, produced with OCR.. Labeling is based on a part of speech (POS) tagging. Tagging is initiated by a primary labeling of text component using some specific dictionaries. Significant tags are then grouped in title and author strings and reduced in canonical forms according to contextual rules. Non labeled tokens are integrated in one or another field per either applying contextual correction rules or using a structure model generated from well detected articles. The designed prototype operates with a great satisfaction on different TOC layouts and character recognition qualities. Without manual intervention, 95.41% rate of correct segmentation was obtained on 38 journals including 2703 articles *and 81.74% rate of correct field extraction.*

1. Introduction

Document analysis is often based on the detection of some regularities on a document structure and content. There are two methodologies for regularity detection: 1) by using an *a priori* model summarizing different regularity schemes. This imposes to assure a certain generality in the model writing in order to cover the maximum of possible cases; 2) by discovering progressively the regularity from some indices directly extracted from the content, related to linguistic, typographical or contextual aspects. This avoids the use of an a priori model and leads to discover an adapted model for each circumstance.

POS tagging [1] takes a key place for this modeling approach essentially when document is produced by OCR, containing some corrupted characters and structure defaults. The interest of POS tagging is to restore the content syntax and also the document structure. It can help to identify keywords and to associate them to specific fields.

The application related in this paper concerns the recognition of TOCs by identifying their articles. Articles have a relatively simple structure composed of three essential fields: *title*, *authors* and *page number*. In spite of the simplicity of this structure, two factors may handicap the straightforward extraction of fields: order unstable and bad separation. These two factors may be accentuated by OCR errors such as the suppression of the separation between two fields and the introduction of errors in field words which can corrupt their identification. The POS tagging may help marking out a field from the identification of some keywords as proper nouns for author fields and nominal groups for the title.

A few TOC recognizers appear in the literature. On one hand, Takasu and al. [4,5] propose a system named CyberMagazine, based on image segmentation into blocks and syntactic analysis of their contents. The article recognition combines the use of decision tree classification and a syntactic analysis using a matrix grammar. On the other hand, Story and O'Gorman [2,3] propose a method combining OCR techniques and image processing. Blocks are first located by the image processing ``docstrum". Then, the TOC layout and relationships between the different article references are found according to an *a priori* model given manually for each kind of journal. These relationships are used, for example, to determine automatically the page number when the user clicks on one article title, or to give specific information concerning one article.

Contrary to these systems, ours works directly on a text file produced by OCR without any text preprocessing. The article structure is discovered progressively by a recursive and adapted labeling of the text components and its extension to the nearest context according to the article reference properties. Then the model generated from some reliable articles is used to complete the structure of the unachieved articles.

2. TOC Analysis

The TOC analysis follows three major steps. First, a primary labeling of lines and text components is performed. Second, based on these labels more syntactic forms are constructed to represent each article reference. At last, the final structure of the TOC articles is built and used to improve the structure of the bad structured articles.

2.1. Primary Labeling

The text file is examined line by line and each line, space or token within a line is labeled according to labels given in Table 1. A tabulation is a regular long space, occurring at the same position in several lines. A dotted line is a consecutive list of dots. Common nouns correspond to words belonging to a common dictionary, revealing the possible presence of a title in the area examined. Proper nouns are extracted from an author dictionary indicating the possible presence of authors. Initials correspond to first name abbreviations (i.e. capital letter followed by a dot) , revealing the possible presence of an author. The connectors "and" and "by" are important indices revealing the possible presence of authors in an area containing initials and proper nouns. NL is reserved for unknown tokens because they are not found in the dictionaries or because they are bad recognized by OCR.

SL	Space Line
SP	Long Space
TB	Tabulation
DL	Dotted Line
CN	Common Noun
PN	Proper Noun
IT	Initial for first name
NS	Numerical String
PT	Punctuation
PU	PT starting an article
CR	Connector like AND
NL	Not Labeled

Table 1 : Token Labels

2.2. Article Location

A TOC is rarely written in a distinctive manner in the page. Textual zones accompanies the TOC as headers in the top, footnotes in the bottom, or sometimes as editorial zones at different places. So, in order to make the method location independent, we have based the search for the TOC location, on the detection of page numbers.

2.2.1. Page Number Extraction. In our method, only references accompanied by their page numbers are considered. So, as the numerical strings are easy to extract, the first step for the reference location is the NS location. Knowing that these NSs are regular, all the NSs are first extracted and then only those presenting some location regularities are considered. The regularities correspond to 1) position at the beginning, at the end or within the reference, 2) vertical alignment, 3) after a specific punctuation like dotted line, 4) after or before a space line. A weight between 0 and 100 is assigned to each regularity. Then, for each NS, a total weight is performed by adding regularity weights. Those presenting a high amount greater than a given threshold are retained.

2.1.3. Article Delimitation. Some logical rules are used to mark up the obvious beginning or ending lines of TOC references. Let CL, PL, NL, BL, EL be respectively the current line, the previous line, the next line, the beginning line and the ending line. Rules used for reference location are :

CL = BL iff:
✓ CL begins by PU or by NS
✓ CL contains NS and PL=SL
✓ CL contains NS and PL = EL
CL = EL iff:
✓ CL contains NS and NL=SL
✓ CL contains NS and NL = BL

Then, knowing the beginning or the end of an article, the systems tries to delimit it by deducing the missing label. This is done either at this level if the context is rich enough or later by using more information from labeling and article modeling.

3. Authors and Title Extraction

Reduction rules are applied recursively on the initial tags, grouping progressively in different steps the authors (Aut) and title (Tit) components.

3.1. Gathering Rules

The first step deals with author and title field initialization by gathering some obvious consecutive labels. Table 2 outlines these gathering rules. "+" means a succession.

AUTHOR (Aut)	TITLE (Tit)
IT + PN ⇒ Aut	CN + CN ⇒ Tit
PN + IT ⇒ Aut	CN + CR ⇒ Tit
IT + IT + PN ⇒ Aut	
PN + IT + IT ⇒ Aut	
PN + PN ⇒ Aut	
PN + PN + IT ⇒ Aut	
PN + PN + PN ⇒ Aut	

Table 2 : Gathering Rules.

3.2. Reduction Rules

In the second step, the sub-fields are assembled by grouping either similar elements or by assimilating embedded terms representing punctuation or connectors. Table 3 shows some of these different rules.

AUTHOR	TITLE
IT + Aut ⇒ Aut	Tit + Tit ⇒ Tit
Aut + IT ⇒ Aut	CN + Tit ⇒ Tit
Aut + CR + Aut ⇒ Aut	Tit + CN ⇒ Tit
BY + Aut ⇒ Aut	Tit + CR + Tit ⇒ Tit
	Tit + CR + Tit ⇒ Tit

Table 3 : Grouping Rules

3.3 Contextual Cleaning Rules

At the issue of the sub-field grouping some typographic elements remain non classified. This is always the case for the punctuation, spaces or tabulations situated at the end lines (EL) or at the beginning of lines when an article is written on several lines. With the help of the context, it is possible to know if these indices can be considered as field delimiters or simply if they belong to one of the surrounding fields. Table 4 gives some of these cleaning rules.

AUTHOR	TITLE
Aut + SP/PT+Aut ⇒ Aut	Tit+SP/PT+Tit ⇒ Tit
Aut + EL+TB+Aut ⇒ Aut	Tit+EL+TB+Tit ⇒ Tit

Tableau 4 : Contextual Cleaning Rules

3.4. NL Contextual Assimilation

Due to current OCR errors and to the existence of unknown proper nouns in the author fields, a great number of tokens remain non labeled. The use of part of speech tagging will allow us to find contextual situations where it is possible to rectify these bad marks. This is made in three different phases.

3.4.1. Contextual Correction. Some contextual situations can promote the identification of missing fields. Table 5 lists some of that situations. In fact, it is easy to observe that for author, for example, the presence of the first or last name accompanied with an NL before an ending mark or before a title, can be interpreted as an author. Similar situations can be examined for the title.

AUTHOR
IT/PN+NL+EL+ TB ⇒ Aut+EL+TB
IT/PN + NL + DL ⇒ Aut + DL
IT/PN + NL + IT EL+ Tit ⇒ Aut + EL + Tit
Tit + EL+ TB + NL/CN/PN/ ⇒ Tit+EL+TB+Aut
NL/CN/PN/IT + EL + TB + Aut ⇒ Tit+EL+TB+Aut
TITLE
CN+NL + EL+ TB ⇒ Tit
CN+NL + DL ⇒ Tit + DL
CN+NL + EL+ Aut ⇒ Tit + EL + Aut
Aut+EL+TB + NL/CN/PN/IT ⇒ Aut+EL+TB+Tit
NL/CN/PN/IT + EL+TB+Tit ⇒ Aut+EL+TB+Tit

Table 5: Contextual Assimilation Rules

3.4.2. POS Tagging. A contextual assimilation is tried when the NL tags are surrounded by two similar sub-fields. The POS examines the favorable cases for this assimilation by studying the "meaning" of tokens placed at the end and at the beginning of respectively the left and the right sub-fields. For example, for authors, the intermediate non labeled term can be a connector if the two surroundings authors are complete, i.e. composed each one by two first names and one last name. It can be an initial if the author at the right contains only one first name, etc. For the title, The POS examines the grammatical categories of the surrounding tokens. For example, if the left token is an article or a subject, there is a chance to assimilate the non labeled term as a verb or a noun. Table 6 summarizes these different contextual situations.

AUTHOR	TITLE
Aut+NL+Aut ⇒ Aut	Tit+NL+Tit ⇒ Tit
Aut+NL+EL+Aut ⇒ Aut	Tit+NL+EL+Tit ⇒ Tit
Aut+EL+NL+Aut ⇒ Aut	Tit+EL+NL+Tit ⇒ Tit
Aut+NL+EL+NL+Aut ⇒ Aut	Tit+NL+EL+NL+Tit ⇒ Tit

Table 6 : POS Rules.

3.4.3. Reference Model Generation. Once the labeling reduction phase is finished, we try to determine the most repeated form articles which we regard as model to go to rectify the non well labeled articles. Thus, for each article, we determine some structure indices related to : the number of columns, the position of the page numbers, the apparition order of the articles references, etc. Then, we determine for all the articles extracted the most regular structure.

Two cases can occur:

- Authors and title are located in two different columns. It is the easiest case because one can decide to assign directly the non labeled tokens to more pertaining field in each column Let x and y be tokens representing respectively a title and an author in article lines. Let $_i = x_j$ TAB y_k the lines representing an article (assuming that the model have given title and author in this order). Than, the tokens are modified as follows:

$\forall$i If $x_i \cong$ Tit $\Rightarrow x_i$ = Tit ; $\forall$j If $y_j \cong$ Aut $\Rightarrow y_j$ = Aut

- Authors and title are located in the same column, separated or not by a tabulation or a punctuation. It is the most frequent case (> 80%) for periodic. In this case we consider the article as a sequence: 1)$\{$ = $\{x_i\}$ TAB|PN$\{y_j\}$ or :2) $\{$ = $\{x_i\}$. If the model proposes a title in the beginning, then:

> - in 1) : $\forall$i If $x_i \cong$ Tit $\Rightarrow x_i$ = Tit ; $\forall$j If $y_j \cong$ Aut $\Rightarrow y_j$ = Aut
> - in 2) : $\forall$i<k If $x_i \cong$ Tit $\Rightarrow x_i$ = Tit . ; $\forall$j>k If $y_j \cong$ Aut $\Rightarrow y_j$ = Aut

where k is the indice of the last title in $\{$.

Table 7 gives a complete labeling example. In the final labeling, articles are surrounded by "<" and ">" and ignored lines are preceded by "-".

4. Experiments and results

We tested this prototype on 38 reviews, including 2703 articles and 1486 fields author. The rate of localization of articles is 95.43% and the rate of recognition of fields is 95.43% for the numbers of page and 81.74% for the separation of the titles and the authors. For the delimitation of articles, the difficulties come, on one hand, from the suppression by the OCR of the blank lines due to the presence bordering on particular fonts, and on the other hand from the proximity between the titles of headings and articles. This introduces ambiguities on the article limits (starting and ending points), due to the merger between the heading and the article line. The consequence might that we dont get enough of well recognized articles to validate a meaningful model. Another concern is the ambiguity within the identification of all the items making of an article line.

This is due to either a weak field separation or not significant token identification. The identification of fields works well if separation is honest between authors and titles of articles: fields in different columns, authors on a line with share.

5. Conclusion and prospects

We presented in this paper a system of TOC analysis of a homogeneous type (textual). The TOCs are digitized and converted into text with OCR. The recognition method uses a syntactical approach. It is based on linguistic labeling of words and syntactic reduction. The method works by field sweep line by line, by separating the articles between them initially, then article by article by separating the fields inside articles. The system operates without any a priori model. It adapts the extraction process on each new TOC by only taking into account somc general and logical knowledge on the article structure. In this version, only one OCR (TextBridge) was used without any parameterization. In the future, we will extend this prototype by 1) combining many OCRs in order to improve the data quality, 2) reinforcing the POS rules for improving the incorporation of more linguistic rules, 3) enlarging the use of more complicated TOCs within magazines having complex layout.

6. References

[1] E. Brill, A simple Rule-Bases Part of SpeechTagger, In Proceedings of ANLP, 1992

[2] L. O'GORMAN, " Image and Document Processing Techniques for the Right Pages Electronic Library System ", ICPR, Vol. 2, pp. 260-263, 1992.

[3] G. A. STORY, L. O'GORMAN, D. FOX, L. LEVY SCHAPER, H. V. JAGADISH, " The Right Pages Image-Based Electronic Library for Alerting and Browsing ", Computer, September 1992.

[4] A. TAKASU, S. SATOH, E. ATSURA, " A Document Understanding Method for Database Construction of an Electronic Library ", ICPR, pp. 463-466, 1994.

[5] A. TAKASU, S. SATOH, E. KATSURA, " A Rule Learning Method for Academic Document Image Processing ", ICDAR'95, Vol. I, pp. 239-242.

a) TOC Text			b) Primary Labeling	b) Final labeling
Contents			CN	-
			SL	-
			SL	-
Articles			CN	-
			SL	-
Spatial Representation for	Tony J. Prescon	85	CN CN CN TB PN IT PN TB NS	<Tit TB Aut TB NS
Navigation in Animats			CN CN NL	>Tit
			SL	-
Monitoring Strategies for	Marc S. Adkin and I'aul R. Cohen	125	CN CN CN TB PN IT NL CR NL IT PN TB NS	<Tit TB Aut TB NS
Embedded Agents: Experiments			CN CN PT CN	= Tit
and Analysis			CR CN	> Tit
			SL	-
Discovring the competitors	Luc Steels	173	CN CN CN TB PN PN TB NS	#Tit TB Aut TB NS
			SL	-
Rovlows			NL	-
			SL	-
Biological Adaptations and	James H. Fetzer	201	CN CN CN TB PN IT NL TB NS	< Tit TB Aut TB NS
Evolutionary Epistemology			CN CN	> Tit

Table 7 : Example of TOC Labeling

Structure Extraction from Various Kinds of Decorated Characters Using Multi-Scale Images

Shin'ichiro Omachi[1], Masaki Inoue[2], and Hirotomo Aso[1]

[1] Graduate School of Engineering, Tohoku University
Aoba 05, Aramaki, Aoba-ku, Sendai-shi,
980-8579 Japan
{machi,aso}@ecei.tohoku.ac.jp

[2] Hitachi Software Engineering Co., Ltd.
6-81, Onoe-cho, Naka-ku, Yokohama-shi,
231-0015 Japan
m-inoue@cap.hitachi-sk.co.jp

Abstract

Decorated characters are widely used in various documents. Practical optical character reader is required to deal with not only common fonts but also complex designed fonts. However, since appearances of decorated characters are complicated, most general character recognition systems cannot give good performances on decorated characters. In this paper, an algorithm that can extract character's essential structure from a decorated character is proposed. This algorithm is applied in preprocessing of character recognition. The proposed algorithm consists of three parts: global structure extraction, interpolation of structure, and smoothing. By using multi-scale images, topographical features such as ridges and ravines are detected for structure extraction. Ridges are used for extracting global structure, and ravines are used for interpolation. Experimental results show clear character structures are extracted from very complex decorated characters.

1. Introduction

Decorated characters are widely used in various documents. Practical optical character reader (OCR) is required to deal with not only common fonts but also complex designed fonts.

A lot of approaches of character recognition have been developed [5, 8]. The approaches can be classified into two categories: structural analysis and pattern matching. In both categories, features of character images are extracted based on the information of connected components of black pixels. However, appearances of decorated characters are so complicated and strange that there is no guarantee that the connected components of black pixels represent the essential structure of the character. Moreover, it is difficult to construct standard patterns for decorated characters, since there are various kinds of fonts that are specially designed. Therefore, most general character recognition systems cannot give good performances on decorated characters.

Some special methods that deal with decorated characters used in headlines are proposed [6, 9, 10]. However, all of these methods only cope with special case that characters represented by texture images or characters with textured background. Broken or degraded character recognition [1, 3] sometimes requires the same kinds of techniques as the recognition of decorated characters since the broken or degraded parts of a character may be regarded as decorations. However, obviously decorated character recognition is much more difficult and complex.

Usually, decorated characters are constructed by one or combination of the following four procedures: (1) using texture images, (2) transforming the structure of the original character, (3) adding some decorations, (4) deleting some parts of a character. Therefore, it is necessary for character structure extraction to erase the texture, to delete the additional decoration, and to interpolate the deleted parts.

By investigating the peculiarities of decorated characters, in this paper, an algorithm that can extract character's essential structure from a decorated character is proposed. This algorithm is applied in preprocessing of character recognition. The algorithm consists of three parts: global structure extraction, interpolation of structure, and smoothing. In the proposed algorithm, topographical features such as ridges and ravines obtained from *intensity surface* [2, 4] are extracted from multi-scale images. Ridges are used for global structure extraction, and ravines are used for interpolation. Experimental results show clear character structures are extracted from very complex decorated characters. Moreover, the effectiveness of the algorithm is shown by recognition experiments with decorated characters.

(a) Logotype. (b) Character A.

Figure 1. Examples of decorated characters.

2. Structure extraction from decorated characters

2.1. Structure of decorated characters

Fig. 1 gives some kinds of decorated characters. In the figure, (a) shows a logotype, and (b) shows four different fonts of character A. These A's are some examples of decorated characters discussed in [11]. Investigating these characters, it is easy to know that global structures represent the outward forms of the characters, while local structures are decorations. The characters' essential structures can be obtained by extracting the global structure.

One possible method for extracting global structure of an image is blurring and binarization. However, appropriate degree of blur and threshold of binarization depend on individual decorated character. Moreover, blurring will change the character structure in unexpected way in some cases. Therefore, it is difficult to extract character structure from decorated character using simple blurring technique without human operations.

In the proposed algorithm, images are blurred with various values of parameter to get multi-scale images. Furthermore, from the multi-scale images, the necessary information of topographical features for extracting global and local character structures are obtained.

2.2. Multi-scale images

In the proposed algorithm, the intensity surfaces of multi-scale images are used to extract the character's structure. If an image is blurred by Gaussian filter, brightness of each pixel is changed according to *scale*. Here, scale means the variance of the Gaussian filter. Scale-space describes the information of the thickness of each part of an image at each scale [7]. Scale-space $L(x, y; t)$ of an image $f(x, y)$ is the convolution of $f(x, y)$ and Gaussian function $g(x, y; t)$ with scale t, and it is given by the following function.

$$L(x, y; t) = g(x, y; t) * f(x, y). \quad (1)$$

By blurring the original image at various scales, multi-scale images are obtained. Multi-scale images of character N in Fig. 1(a) are displayed in Fig. 2. In this figure, (a) is the original image, and (b)~(d) are the images that are blurred at various scales. Fig. 3 shows the intensity surface of each

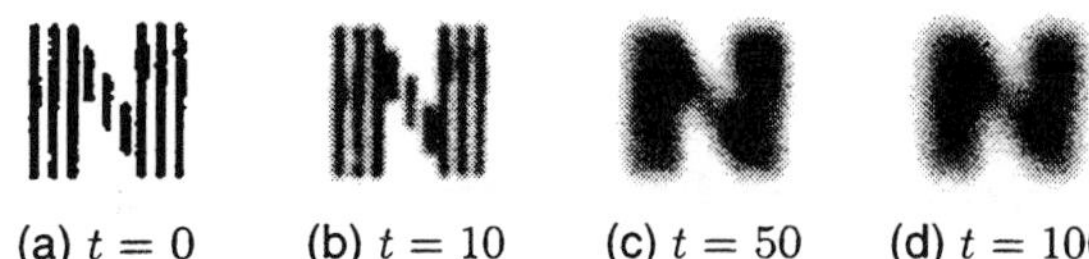

(a) $t = 0$ (b) $t = 10$ (c) $t = 50$ (d) $t = 100$

Figure 2. Multi-scale images.

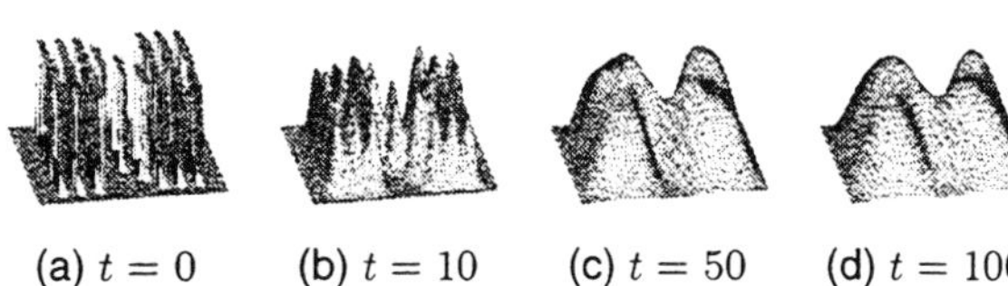

(a) $t = 0$ (b) $t = 10$ (c) $t = 50$ (d) $t = 100$

Figure 3. Intensity surfaces.

case in Fig. 2. Global and local structure are extracted based on these intensity surfaces of the multi-scale images.

2.3. Global structure extraction

Using the intensity surfaces, a method of extracting global structure by detecting ridges is proposed. By observing Fig. 3, it is thought if the ridges of the intensity surface of image blurred at a certain scale represent the global structure, the global structure can be extracted by detecting ridges at that scale. For each pixel of the image, denote the direction that the absolute value of quadratic differential is maximum as p, and its orthogonal direction as q. The condition that (x, y) is a pixel on the ridge at scale t is,

$$\frac{\partial L(x, y; t)}{\partial p} = 0, \quad \frac{\partial^2 L(x, y; t)}{\partial p^2} < 0. \quad (2)$$

For simplicity, p and q are quantized to one of the eight kinds of directions ($45° \times n, 0 \leq n \leq 7$).

For structure extraction, appropriate pixels that represent the structure of character need to be selected among the points that satisfy Eq. (2). In this paper, ridge strength is defined as Eq. (3) and the ridge pixels are selected by choosing the scale t at which the strength is the local maximum.

$$S(x, y; t) = \left\{ \frac{\partial^2 L(x, y; t)}{\partial p^2} - \frac{\partial^2 L(x, y; t)}{\partial q^2} \right\}^2. \quad (3)$$

If the following conditions are satisfied, the ridge strength will be the local maximum at (x, y).

$$\frac{\partial S(x, y; t)}{\partial t} = 0, \quad \frac{\partial^2 S(x, y; t)}{\partial t^2} < 0. \quad (4)$$

However, if the above processing is applied directly to decorated character images, local structures are extracted simultaneously, and it makes the essential structure extraction impossible. An example of this problem is shown in

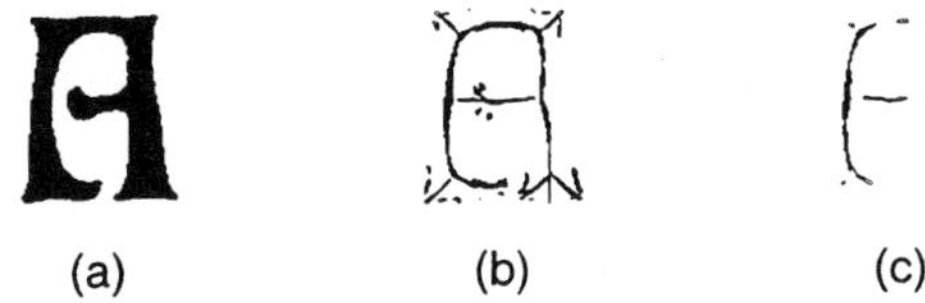

(a) (b) (c)

Figure 4. Ridge detection. (a) Original image. (b) All the ridges are detected. (c) Only strong ridges are extracted.

Fig. 4. Fig. 4(a) is the original image, and Fig.4(b) shows all the black pixels of Fig. 4(a) that satisfy Eqs. (2) and (4). Fig.4(b) shows that although the global structure of character A is extracted, the local structures of decorations are also extracted simultaneously. It is obviously that how to avoid extracting local structures is a big problem. Here, to choose the ridges that represent the global structure, the pixels with large value of ridge strength (Eq. (3)) are used.

Global structure extraction processing is summarized as follows. First, multi-scale images are obtained by blurring the original image by changing the scale from $t = 1$ to $t = 100$. Then the pixels that satisfy Eqs. (2) and (4) are extracted. Denote the number of extracted pixels be N, and among these pixels, θN pixels whose ridge strength calculated by Eq. (3) are large are chosen. Here, θ is a constant that satisfies $0 < \theta \leq 1$.

Fig. 4(c) shows the result of extracting global structure from Fig. 4(a). Here, $\theta = 0.4$. This figure shows that the local structures are removed while the global structure of the original image is extracted successfully.

However, Fig. 4(c) is not a connected structure. To enable the recognition of the decorated character, it is necessary to extract the connected structure that represents the character's essential structure. In the next section, a method for acquisition of the connected structure by interpolating discontinuous line segments is presented.

2.4. Interpolation of structure by recursive ravine detection

For interpolation, a method of interpolating gaps between lines by detecting ravines recursively is proposed. The condition that (x, y) is a pixel on ravine at scale t is,

$$\frac{\partial L(x,y;t)}{\partial p} = 0, \quad \frac{\partial^2 L(x,y;t)}{\partial p^2} > 0. \qquad (5)$$

If larger scale t is adopted, wider gap between lines can be interpolated. Interpolation algorithm by recursive ravine detection is as follows.

1. Initial value of scale t_1 is given. $t \leftarrow t_1$.
2. Detect ravines at scale t. Detected ravines are added to the image.
3. $t \leftarrow t/2$.
4. 2. and 3. are repeated for k times.
5. Blur the image at a small scale.

Here, $t_1 = 30$ and $k = 5$.

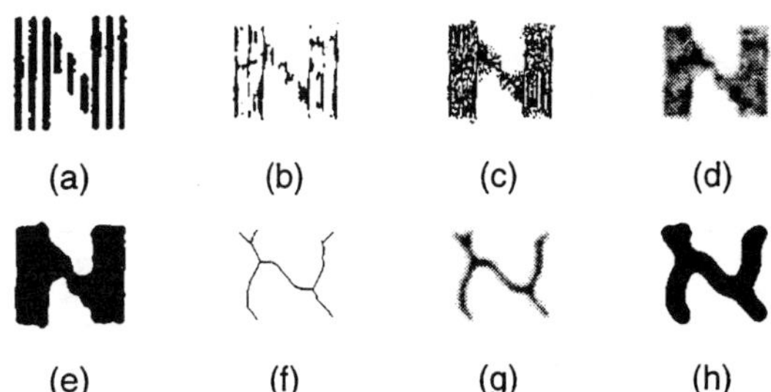

(a) (b) (c) (d)

(e) (f) (g) (h)

Figure 5. Structure extraction of a decorated character. (a) Original image. (b) Detected ridges. (c) Ravines are detected recursively and are added to the image of (b). (d) Blurred. (e) Binarized. (f) Skeletonized. (g) Blurred. (h) Result.

2.5. Smoothing by thinning

The line widths of images obtained by the method described in the previous sections are not uniform. Moreover there are unevenness on the contours since the decorated structures are partially left. In order to resolve these problems, smoothing is needed. Smoothing is done by thinning, blurring at a small scale, and binarization.

Fig. 5 displays the process of character structure extraction of decorated character N.

3. Experiments

In order to verify the effect of our method, the proposed algorithm is applied for character structure extraction. Furthermore, recognition experiments are carried out. Three different characters segmented from the logotype in Fig. 1(a) and four kinds of character A in Fig. 1(b) are used for evaluation. For recognition, an existing OCR is adopted. The original images and the results are shown in Table 1. In the table, the results below the original images are the results of recognizing the original images using the OCR, while the results below the extracted images are the recognition results of the extracted character structures by the same OCR.

Although totally different kinds of decorated character images are tested, the extracted images in Table 1 show that character structure is clearly obtained in every case. These

Table 1. Results of structure extraction and recognition.

	(a)	(b)	(c)	(d)	(e)	(f)	(g)
Original image							
Result	I ',Jt		I Iljll'	j˜	˜	A	El
Extracted image							
Result	N	E	W	A	A	A	R

results clarify the effectiveness of the proposed algorithm. Original character images are recognized incorrectly except (f). For the cases of (a) and (c), texture images are regarded as a combination of many characters, since decorations are extracted as the important features of characters. Compared with these results, most of the images extracted by the proposed algorithm are correctly recognized. The only failed case is (g) that A is recognized as R. Since the topological features of A and R are similar, it is thought to be necessary to use the knowledge of natural languages for distinguishing them.

For comparison, experiments without ridge detection are also carried out. In this case, (a) and (g) are not recognized correctly. In addition, although (f) is recognized correctly, extracted image is far from that of character A.

4. Conclusions

Decorated characters are widely used in various documents. Practical OCR is required to cope with not only common fonts but also complex designed characters. In the case of recognizing decorated characters, the most important point is to separate character's essential structures from decorated parts.

In this paper, an algorithm for extracting character structures from various kinds of decorated character images was proposed. This algorithm is applied in preprocessing of character recognition. The proposed algorithm consists of three parts: global structure extraction, interpolation of structure, and smoothing. First, global structure is obtained by detecting strong ridges using multi-scale images. Next, gaps are interpolated by recursive ravine detection. Finally, character structure that is appropriate for recognition is made by smoothing.

A logotype and several different designed characters of A were used to investigate the effectiveness of our algorithm. The results have shown that structures of decorated characters are extracted successfully. These clear structures make the recognition possible. The recognition results have proved that although the original decorated characters are unrecognizable, after applying our algorithm in the preprocessing, almost all the decorated characters can be recognized correctly.

Although the complex designed characters tested in this paper are almost recognized successfully, it dose not mean our method can deal with any kind of decorated character. In order to improve our method, much more kinds of decorated characters should be tested. Moreover, in this paper, optimal character recognition method has not been considered. Recognition method which is suitable for the images obtained by the proposed algorithm is needed to be developed. Applying the algorithm for decorated digits is also a future work.

References

[1] T. R. Chou and F. Chang. Optical Chinese character recognition for low-quality document images. *Proc. Fourth Int'l Conf. Document Analysis and Recognition (ICDAR'97)*, pages 608–611, August 1997.

[2] R. M. Haralick, L. T. Watson, and T. J. Laffey. The topographic primal sketch. *International Journal of Robotics Research*, 2(1):50–72, 1983.

[3] J. D. Hobby and T. K. Ho. Enhancing degraded document images via bitmap clustering and averaging. *Proc. Fourth Int'l Conf. Document Analysis and Recognition (ICDAR'97)*, pages 394–400, August 1997.

[4] H. Hontani and K. Deguchi. Multi-scale image analysis for detection of characteristic component figure shapes and sizes. *Proc. 14th Int'l Conf. Pattern Recognition (ICPR'98)*, pages 1470–1472, August 1998.

[5] S. Impedovo, L. Ottaviano, and S. Occhinegro. Optical character recognition — a survey. *International Journal of Pattern Recognition and Artificial Intelligence*, 5(1&2):1–24, 1991.

[6] S. Liang, M. Ahmadi, and M. Shridhar. A morphological approach to text string extraction from regular periodic overlapping text/background images. *CVGIP; Graphical Models and Image Processing*, 56(5):402–413, September 1994.

[7] T. Lindeberg. *Scale-Space Theory in Computer Vision.* Kluwer Academic Publishers, 1994.

[8] S. Mori, K. Yamamoto, and M. Yasuda. Research on machine recognition of handprinted characters. *IEEE Trans. Pattern Analysis and Machine Intelligence*, 6(4):386–405, July 1984.

[9] H. Ozawa and T. Nakagawa. A character image enhancement method from characters with various background images. *Proc. Second Int'l Conf. Document Analysis and Recognition (ICDAR'93)*, pages 58–61, October 1993.

[10] M. Sawaki and N. Hagita. Text-line extraction and character recognition of document headlines with graphical designs using complementary similarity measure. *IEEE Trans. Pattern Analysis and Machine Intelligence*, 20(10):1103–1109, October 1998.

[11] J. Schürmann. *Pattern Classification.* John Wiley & Sons, Inc., 1996.

Automatic generation of woodblocks for virtual printing

Shinji Mizuno*, Tsuyoshi Kasaura*, Shinji Yamamoto*, Minoru Okada**, and Jun-ichiro Toriwaki***
* Toyohashi University of Technology, 1-1 Hibarigaoka Tenpaku-cho Toyohashi 441-8580, Japan
mizuno@cc.tut.ac.jp
** Chubu University, Kasugai, Japan, *** Nagoya University, Nagoya, Japan

Abstract

We present a method to generate virtual woodblocks for virtual printing from a gray value image or a full-color image. In this method, a virtual board is carved automatically by the virtual sculpting system extracting features or colors of the given image. A printing image is synthesized using the woodblocks in the virtual printing system. Using a gray value image as a draft, the sculpting system generates one virtual woodblock that expresses gray values with carving marks, and we can transform the draft image into another one like a woodblock print by using it in the printing system. Using a full-color image, several virtual woodblocks for each color of ink are generated, and we can synthesize a multicolored woodblock print by printing a virtual paper sheet with virtual woodblocks for each color one after another.

The methods we propose here are useful in synthesizing non-photorealistic images with computer graphics.

1. Introduction

In the field of computer graphics (CG), studies of synthesizing photorealistic images have been progressed remarkably and they are often used in many fields. On the other side, non-photorealistic images are also used in the actual world such as illustrations or art images. Synthesizing non-photorealistic images with CG is useful and increasing attention is paid recently. Many methods to synthesize such images have been reported. For example, the method in which a photo image is transformed into a painting[1][2], a 3D model is rendered into an image like a painting[3][4], and a painting is synthesized with interactive operations using drawing patterns such as a pen or a writing brush[5].

As one of the methods to synthesize non-photorealistic images with CG, authors have developed an interactive virtual designing system based on virtual sculpting and printing[6][7] (**Figure 1**). In this system, a virtual print is synthesized by simulating actual woodblock printing. A user generates virtual woodblocks with virtual sculpting system by oneself, and synthesizes a monocolored or multicolored image using the woodblock(s).

In this paper, we propose methods to generate virtual woodblocks automatically. When a gray value image is given to the virtual sculpting system as a draft, a virtual woodboard is carved to a woodblock. One side of a virtual woodboard corresponds to the gray value image, and elements of each carving operation are decided by extracting features of the image. When a full-color image is given to the system, several virtual woodblocks are generated automatically. The full-color image is separated into several images with an approximate color, and woodblocks for each color are generated. Using them in printing system in succession, a virtual multicolored print is synthesized.

2. Summary of virtual woodblock printing

A virtual woodblock print is synthesized from a printing woodblock, a paper sheet, a printing blush and ink prepared

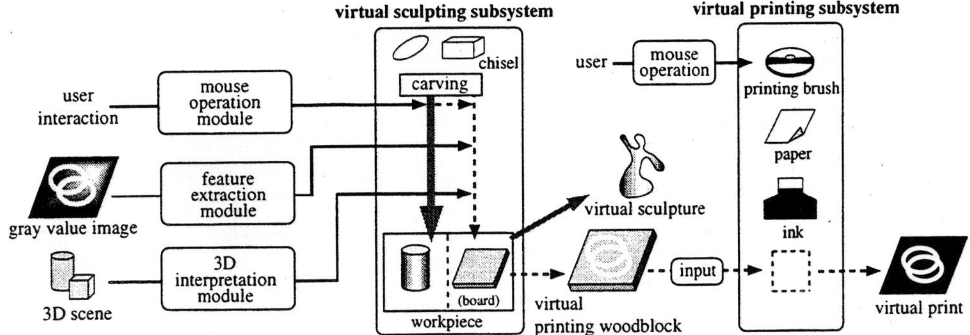

Figure 1. Interactive designing system based on virtual sculpting and virtual printing.

in a virtual 3D space, and it is similar to the actual woodblock printing.

The virtual printing woodblock is generated by the virtual sculpting system interactively. This system uses ellipsoidal ,cubic or cylindrical chisels and carves a virtual woodboard to produce a virtual printing woodblock. A surface of the virtual woodblock is similar to that of a actual woodblock. The virtual paper sheet is expressed as a set of 2D lattice points and is placed on the virtual woodblock. Each lattice point can move only in the direction of perpendicular line of the woodblock, under a few constraints in the angle of the paper sheet surface at the point. The movement is controlled by the user with the virtual printing brush. Virtual ink consists of two factors: a moisture value and a color. A synthesized woodblock print is a digital image, and its value is decided at each point based on ink and the distance between the paper sheet and the woodblock. Fundamentally, the black value increases as the distance decreases.

A multicolored woodblock print is synthesized by using several woodblocks. Each virtual ink is used for each virtual woodblock, and multicolored and multiwoodblock printing is realized by mixing printing images synthesized by each woodblock. A moisture value controls the mixing.

3. Generating a virtual printing woodblock using a gray value image

3.1. Outline

In this chapter, we present a method to generate a virtual printing woodblock by using a gray value image as a draft. At first, a gray value image is prepared as a draft. The system isolates carving areas from the gray value image and selects carving methods for each carving area. The system decides carving elements and carves the corresponding area of a virtual woodboard automatically based on features of gray values such as the average or the gradient vector of values in the area. A virtual printing block is generated by repeating this procedure. Using this woodblock, the input gray value image can be transformed into another one looks like a woodblock print.

3.2. Isolating the carving area

The area of carving $V = \{v_{mn}\}$ in the gray value image is isolated automatically. For isolation of carving areas, several filters are prepared for a given gray value image $f(v_{mn})$.

1) Edge filter :

This filter isolates edge areas for carving by using a gradient vector $g(v_{mn})$ of each point of the image.

$$V = \{v_{mn} \mid |g(v_{mn})| > t_g\}, \quad t_g : \text{threshold}.$$

2) Gray value filter :

This filter isolates carving areas by using a gray value $f(v_{mn})$ of each point of the image.

$$V = \{v_{mn} \mid l_f < f(v_{mn}) < u_f\}, \quad l_f, u_f : \text{thresholds}.$$

It is usually used to isolate the area with upper or lower gray values than a specific value. When l_f and u_f are close, this filter isolates the areas with a specific gray value.

There are some rooms for a user in carving area isolation by changing thresholds, area limitation to filter, logical operations for optional two areas, and so on. Besides, pointing out a arbitrary pixel of the image, the user can isolate a connected area with close gray value of the pixel.

3.3. Carving method

Automatic carving is based on features of the draft gray value image. Focusing points are sampled at proper intervals on the draft image. Each focusing point corresponds to a point on the surface of the woodblock. Several features of gray values in a small square area around each focusing point, such as an average or a gradient vector of gray values, are used to decide carving elements at the corresponding point on the woodblock. For example, an average of gray values can decide carving depth or carving frequency, and a gradient vector can decide a carving direction (**Figure 2**). A small gray value (white) usually makes carving depth and carving frequency increased.

In generating a printing woodblock in the actual world, an artist changes a chisel, a direction and a way of carving according to the carving area or the printing style. In this system, it is controlled with carving parameters for each carving area. Following are primary parameters:

1) Carving mode : area's edge carving, gray value carving, or pattern carving based on a pattern image.

2) Chisel size : varied automatically according to the gradient of gray values in the area, or fixed.

3) Expression for densities of gray values : carving depth, carving frequency, or fixed.

4) Carving direction : varied automatically according to

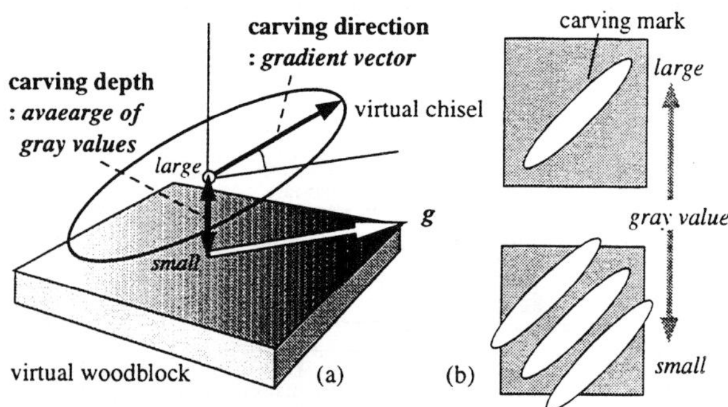

Figure 2. An example of decision of the position of a virtual chisel (a), and representation of the gray value by carving frequency (b).

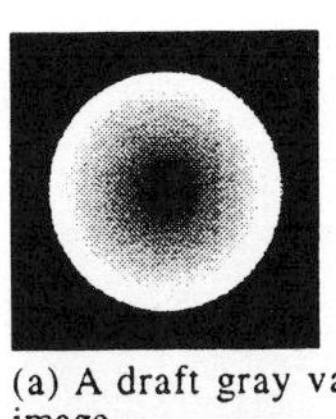

(a) A draft gray value image.

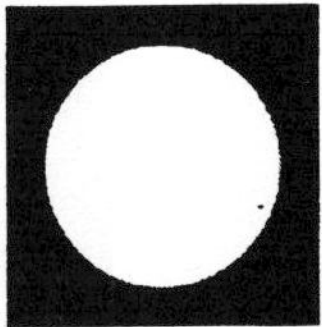

(b) An isolated carving area by filtering (white).

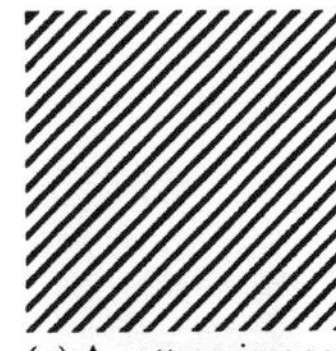

(c) A pattern image.

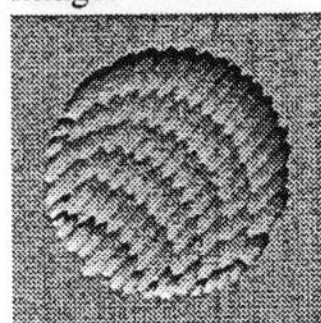

(d) Gray value carving (direction: fixed).

(e) Gray value carving (by carving frequency).

(f) Pattern carving based on the image (c).

Figure 3. Automatic carving method.

gradient vectors, or fixed.

5) Vagueness of carving : changes the probability of carving, and gives aberrations to directions of carving.

Figure 3 shows examples of carving. The system decides carving elements and carves a virtual woodboard automatically according to carving parameters. In default of appointment of parameters, the edge area of a woodboard is carved deep and completely, and the gray value area is carved as the carving marks express the density of the gray value with carving depth. The user can decide these carving parameters for each isolated area, and can change the printing style. Repeating the procedure of an area isolation and carving in the area, a virtual printing woodblock is completed.

4. Virtual printing woodblocks from a full-color image

4.1. Virtual multicolored woodblock printing

We present a method to generate several virtual printing woodblocks from a full-color image for multicolored printing. In virtual multicolored woodblock printing, several woodblocks are used, and it is similar to the actual multicolored printing (**Figure 4**). We introduce virtual ink[7] which consists of two factors: a color and a moisture value. Each woodblock uses each color of ink, and usually occupies each area in a print. However, printing areas of several woodblocks may overlap each other in case an additional printing area is small or a black color of ink is used to shade an area printed already. A moisture value of ink is used to control transparency of the ink used to print additionally.

4.2. Generating virtual woodblocks

Formerly, woodblocks for multicolored printing were generated by the user, or automatically with the user's selection of carving areas. In this paper, we develop a method to generate several woodblocks automatically from a full-color image of a draft.

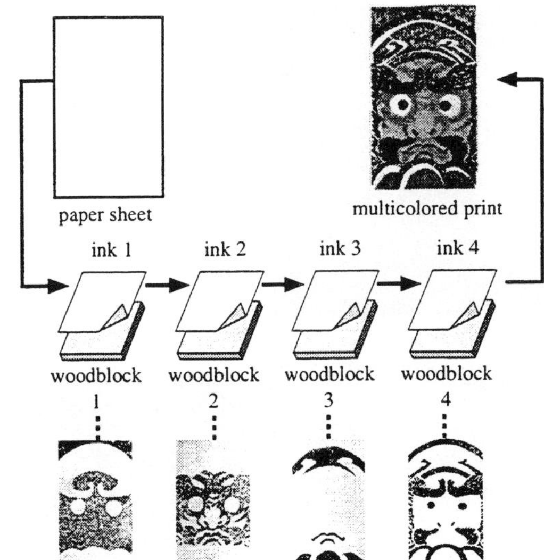

Figure 4. Multicolored printing.

In Japanese traditional multicolored printing called "UKIYO-E", no more than about ten woodblocks are used for each color of a print, and there are not so many kinds of ink. In our study, we select sixteen key colors which are often used in actual Japanese traditional multicolored prints.

A draft full-color image is given to the sculpting system. A color of each pixel of the image is changed to one of key colors which is nearest to the original color in the L*u*v* color system, that is one of uniform spacing of colors[8], and the draft image is separated into several regions each of which is composed with the key color. The region with low luminance in each region is also extracted for shading. Small components of each region are removed by researching a neighborhood. For each region, a gray value image, with black value inside the region and white value outside the region, is synthesized.

The sculpting system generates virtual woodblocks by using these gray value images for each region. The method to generate each woodblock is similar to the one mentioned in Chapter 3.

A virtual paper sheet is printed by using these woodblocks in succession with each ink. At last, the woodblock for shading is used additionally with black ink of an appropriate moisture value, and a multicolored print is completed.

5. Experiment

Figure 5 is an example of a virtual printing block generated from a gray value image. Figure 5(a) is a gray value image of a draft, and the system isolates the edge area and the gray value area by using some filters. Each carving method is selected for each carving area and the virtual

(a) A draft gray value image.

(b) A woodblocks generated from the draft image (a).

(c) A synthesized monocolored print.

Figure 5. A virtual woodblock from a gray value image.

woodblock is completed (Figure 5(b)) In this example, the gray value area is carved to express the densities with carving frequency and carving directions are the same as those of gradient vectors. A synthesized printing image is shown in Figure 5(c).

Figure 6 shows an example of multicolored virtual woodcut printing. Figure 6(a) is a full-color image of a draft, and (b) and (c) are some of virtual woodblocks generated by the system extracting regions of the draft full-color image with key colors. In this experiment, the draft image is separated five regions by the system, four gray value images except for the white region are synthesized, and using these images as new drafts, four woodblocks are generated automatically. A multicolored print is synthesized by using these woodblocks with each ink in succession (Figure 6(d)).

6. Conclusion

In this paper, we proposed methods to generate woodblocks for virtual woodblock printing by using a gray value and a full-color image as drafts. They are useful to synthesize non-photorealistic computer graphics.

In a gray value image method, the sculpting system generates a virtual printing woodblock automatically by extracting features of the draft image. In a full-color image method, the system separates the full-color image into several regions with approximate colors, and generates virtual woodblocks for each region.

We are going to develop a method to automatic generation of virtual woodblocks using understanding of the draft image. For example, we would like to transform a draft image of a human face into a Japanese woodblock print "UKIYO-E" with deformation of the face.

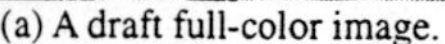

(a) A draft full-color image.

(b) One of virtual woodblocks from the draft image (a) (for gray).

(c) One of virtual woodblocks from the draft image (a) (for blue).

(d) A synthesized multicolored print (using four woodblocks).

Figure 6. Virtual woodblocks from a color image.

Reference

[1] M. Salisbury, C. Anderson, D. Lischinski, and D. H. Salesin, "Scale-dependent reproduction of pen-and-ink illustration", *ACM Computer Graphics (Proc. SIGGRAPH '96)*, 461-468, 1996.

[2] S. Saito, and M. Nakajima, "Automatic production of the hand writing type image from a natural image with FFT", *IPS.Japan SIG Notes*, 95-CG-74-3, 11-16, 1995 (in Japanese).

[3] J. Hamel, and T. Strothotte, "Capturing and Re-Using Rendition Styles for Non-Photorealistic Rendering", *Computer Graphics Forum (EUROGRAPHICS '99)*, 18(3), 174-182, 1999.

[4] B. J. Meier, "Painterly rendering for animation", *ACM Computer Graphics (SIGGRAPH '96)*, 477-484, 1996.

[5] M. P. Salisbury, S. E. Anderson, R. Barzel, and D. H. Salesin, "Interactive pen-and-ink illustration", *ACM Computer Graphics (Proc. SIGGRAPH '94)*, 101-108, 1994.

[6] S. Mizuno, M. Okada, and J. Toriwaki, "Virtual sculpting and virtual woodcut printing", *The Visual Computer*, 14(2), 39-51, 1998.

[7] S. Mizuno, T. Okouchi, M. Okada, and J. Toriwaki, "Multiworkpiece and Multicolor Virtual Woodcut Printing", *Proc. International Conference on Virtual System and MultiMedia '99*, 523-530, 1999.

[8] A. K. Jain, "Fundamental of Digital Image Processing", Prentice-Hall, 1989.

Construction and Presentation of a Virtual Environment Using Panoramic Stereo Images of a Real Scene and Computer Graphics Models

Jun Shimamura
Cyber Space Laboratories
NTT (Nippon Telegraph and Telephone Corporation)
1-1 Hikarino-oka, Yokosuka, Kanagawa 239-0847, Japan
jun@marsh.hil.ntt.co.jp

Haruo Takemura, Naokazu Yokoya and Kazumasa Yamazawa
Graduate School of Information Science
Nara Institute of Science and Technology
8916-5 Takayama, Ikoma, Nara 630-0101, Japan
{takemura, yokoya, yamazawa}@is.aist-nara.ac.jp

Abstract

The recent progress in computer graphics has made it possible to construct various virtual environments such as urban or natural scenes. This paper proposes a hybrid method to construct a realistic virtual environment containing an existing real scene. The proposed method combines two different types of 3-D models. 3-D geometric model is used to represent virtual objects in user's vicinity, enabling a user to handle virtual objects. Texture mapped cylindrical 2.5-D model of a real scene is used to render the background of the environment, maintaining real-time rendering and increasing realistic sensation. Cylindrical 2.5-D model is generated from cylindrical stereo images captured by an omnidirectional stereo imaging sensor. A prototype mixed reality system has been developed to confirm the feasibility of the method, in which panoramic binocular stereo images are projected on a cylindrical immersive projective display depending on user's viewpoint in real time.

1. Introduction

The recent progress in computer graphics has made it possible to construct various virtual environments such as urban or natural scenes. Moreover, the mixed reality technology which merges the real and virtual worlds seamlessly has recently become popular [6, 7].

The construction methods for virtual environments, such as large scale urban or natural scenes, are generally classified into two categories: polygon based and image based. The polygon based method which constructs an environment using polygonal representation of objects has the advantage of easily realizing interaction between a user and virtual objects, however the image synthesis time is dependent on the complexity of the constructed scene. This problem is particularly critical in simulation and virtual reality applications because of the demand for real-time feedback. A number of approaches have been proposed to overcome this problem [8], however the problem still exists, since scene complexity is potentially unbounded. On the other hand, the image based method constructs the environment using multiple real images [2, 5] or deforming real images [1] and requires less rendering time because the number of polygons is independent of the scene complexity. In addition, real images can present highly realistic sensations to a user with ease. However, such an approach has several drawbacks. Firstly, the implementation that enables a user to arbitrarily change his/her viewpoint and viewing orientation in a large environment is essentially impossible because of memory limitation. Secondly, the representation of depth and occlusion is difficult when the texture images are mapped to a planar or cylindrical surface. Finally, the realization of interaction between a user and virtual objects is difficult.

This paper proposes a hybrid method to construct a realistic virtual environment containing an existing real scene and computer graphics (CG) models. Our approach is based on acquiring full panoramic 2.5-D models of dynamic real worlds using a video-rate omnidirectional stereo imaging sensor [4]. CG objects are merged into the full panoramic 2.5-D model of real scene maintaining consistent occlusion between real and virtual objects. Thus it is possible to

1051-4651/00 $10.00

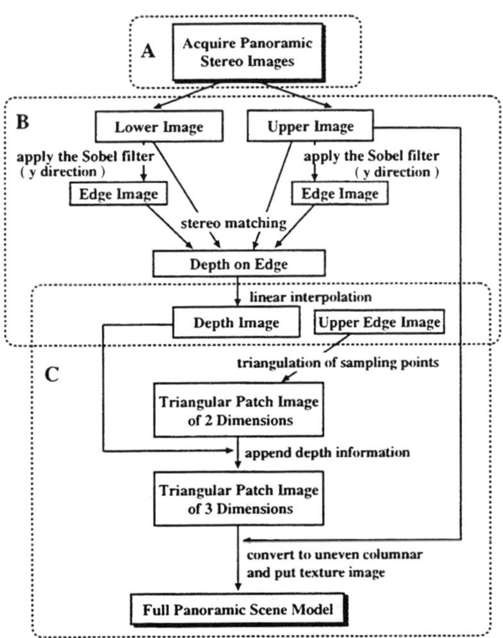

Figure 1. Flow diagram of constructing a full panoramic 2.5-D model.

yield rich 3-D sensation with binocular and motion parallax. Moreover, CG objects can be manipulated in the virtual environment. We have developed a prototype of immersive mixed reality system using a projective display with a large cylindrical screen, in which a user can walk through the virtual environment and can manipulate CG objects in real time.

2. Construction of full panoramic 2.5-D models of dynamic real scenes

To increase realistic sensation for a user, real images often would be used in virtual environment. Traditionally, the real images are mapped onto a planar or cylindrical surface. However, the drawbacks of the method are that operationality and reality are decreasing because the user can not sense binocular nor motion parallax in constructed environment. In this section, we describe a novel method to construct a full panoramic 2.5-D models of dynamic real scenes that provides realistic sensation in mixed reality applications.

Figure 1 shows a flowchart for the construction of full panoramic 2.5-D models. First, a pair of panoramic stereo images are captured by an omnidirectional stereo imaging sensor at video rate (Figure 1 A). Next, a depth map of the real scene is estimated from these stereo images (Figure 1 B). Finally, the full panoramic 2.5-D models are constructed from these depth images and then the texture images are mapped on the model (Figure 1 C).

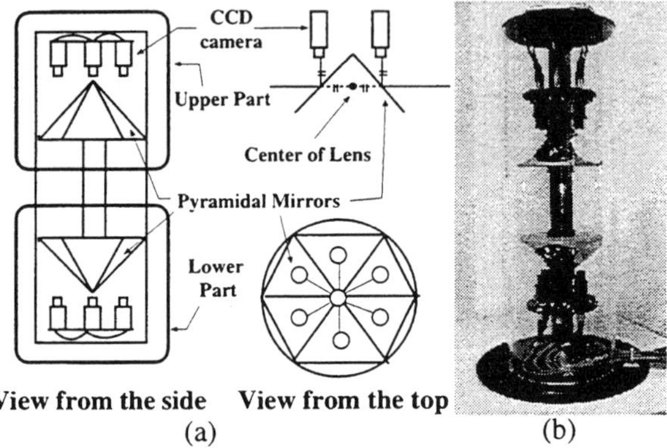

Figure 2. Geometry (a) and exterior (b) of omnidirectional stereo imaging sensor.

2.1. Capturing panoramic stereo images of a real dynamic scene

Omnidirectional stereo imaging

We use an omnidirectional stereo imaging sensor [4] that is composed of twelve cameras and two hexagonal pyramidal mirrors. The sensor component is designed so that the virtual lens centers of six cameras are located at a fixed point as shown in Figure 2 (a). It can take an omnidirectional image satisfying the single viewpoint constraint. In the system, two symmetrical sets of the component are used for omnidirectional stereo imaging. Each camera is a standard NTSC CCD camera with a wide-angle lens. The figure of the mirror is an equilateral hexagonal pyramid. The top of the mirror faces the six cameras and the base plane of the mirror is placed to be perpendicular to the line of sight of the cameras. The sensor, properly arranged, captures images of a real dynamic scene through the reflection on the pyramidal mirror. Figure 2 (b) shows an appearance of the sensor.

The omnidirectional stereo image sensor produces synchronized twelve video streams. The image captured by each camera is distorted because of using a wide-angle lens. The Tsai's calibration method [9] is applied to eliminate the distortion. The color difference among different camera images caused by the inequality of multiple cameras is resolved by linearly transforming each color component of images imposing the continuity constraint on the boundaries of adjacent camera images. Finally, by projecting each image generated from upper and lower cameras onto a cylindrical surface, twelve sheets of images are combined into a pair of full panoramic stereo images; upper and lower panoramic images. Consequently, a pair of panoramic stereo images which satisfy the vertical epipolar constraint is generated [4]. It should be noted that the stereo images here have vertical disparities, in contrast with familiar binocular stereo images with horizontal disparities.

Representation of dynamic scene

In our approach, a dynamic scene is represented by decomposing the scene into a static scene and dynamic events (moving objects) from panoramic stereo images. The static scene image and moving object regions are extracted from panoramic images using existing techniques as follows.

1. Static scene image generation:

   A panoramic image of a static scene is generated by applying a temporal mode filter to a panoramic image sequence in a time interval. A stereo pair of panoramic static scene is obtained by applying this filter to both upper and lower images of omnidirectional stereo images.

2. Moving object extraction:

   Moving objects are extracted by subtracting consecutive image frames in time sequence.

2.2. Depth estimation from panoramic stereo images

In this section, the depth estimation from panoramic stereo images is described. The depth of an existing real scene is the principal factor in representing depth relationship between virtual and real objects correctly. We acquire panoramic depth based on stereo matching. However, there is high possibility of false matching caused by noises in performing stereo matching on the whole image. In order to acquire an accurate depth map, many stereo algorithms have been proposed in computer vision. But, we note that the precise depth information is not necessarily required in VR-related applications. Thus, we estimate depth values only on edges, where the matching is thought to be reliable. Thereafter, intermediate data are approximated by linear interpolation. The following steps describe the method in more detail.

1. By adopting the Sobel filter, non-vertical edges are detected in the upper and lower images.
2. Stereo matching is performed and the depth values are computed. Note that only pixels on detected edges in the upper image are matched to those in the lower image, matching window size is 9×9 pixels, and similarity measure is the normalized cross-correlation having a high threshold. In the same way, the lower image as a reference image is matched to the upper image.
3. Matching errors are excluded by considering the consistency between upper-to-lower and lower-to-upper matchings above.
4. To eliminate remaining noises and interpolate empty depth values on edges, the median filter (5×3) is applied to the upper depth map.
5. The depth values at the pixels between the edges are linearly interpolated to complete a dense depth map.

2.3. Generation of cylindrical model

By using a panoramic depth map estimated in Section 2.2, a cylindrical 2.5-D model of a real scene is constructed using the following steps.

1. Edges are detected from the upper image and then points on edges with reliable depth are sampled at a fixed interval (3 pixels). Non-edge points are sampled at a fixed interval (31 pixels) over an entire region.
2. By applying the Delaunay's triangulation [3] to points extracted in Step.1, 2-D triangle patches are generated.
3. A 2.5-D triangular patch model is generated by assigning 3-D data of the depth image created in Section 2.2 to the vertices of 2-D triangles obtained in Step 2.
4. Finally, the upper panoramic texture image is mapped onto the constructed 2.5-D cylindrical model.

3. Presentation of a mixed environment

In order to confirm the feasibility of the proposed method, we have developed a prototype system for presenting a mixed environment of a real scene and CG objects. The cylindrical 2.5-D model is constructed on a graphics workstation, SGI Onyx2 (Infinite Reality2×2, 8CPUs MIPS R10000, 250MHz). Virtual objects are created by using a computer graphics software (Alias/WaveFront), and are easily merged into a real scene model maintaining correct occlusion among real and virtual objects because the real scene model has depth information. For presenting the mixed environment to a user in our system, 3-D images are projected on a large cylindrical screen with the size of 6m in diameter and 2.4m in height of the CYLINDRA[1] system, which actually has a 330-degree view covered by six projectors. Note that the projected images are a pair of panoramic stereo images with horizontal disparities. In the system, a user is able to change viewing position and orientation by a joystick device (SideWinder Precision Pro/Microsoft Inc.) and is able to experience stereoscopic vision as well as motion parallax through liquid crystal shutter-glasses (SB300/Solidray Inc.). The hardware configuration of the system is illustrated in Figure 3.

Here we demonstrate an application to sight simulation. Figure 4 shows a pair of panoramic stereo images (3006×330 pixels) of "Heijo-kyo" (historical site in Nara) which contains the reconstructed "Suzaku-mon" gate captured by the omnidirectional stereo imaging sensor. In the experiment, the baseline of omnidirectional stereo imaging sensor is set to 25.0mm, and each focal length of CCD camera is set to 4.0mm. Figure 5 shows panoramic stereo images of a static scene generated from a sequence of dynamic stereo images including Figure 4. It can be clearly

[1]CYLINDRA is an abbreviation for Cylindrical Yard with Large, Immersive and Novel Display for Reality Applications.

observed in Figure 5 that moving objects are eliminated from Figure 4 (moving object regions in Figure 4 are highlighted at white boxes in Figure 5). Depth map computed from panoramic stereo images in Figure 5 is shown in Figure 6 in which depth values are coded in intensities. A brighter pixel is closer and a darker pixel is farther. Black pixels show pixels where depth values are not computed from stereo images. The resolution of depth is about 1.0m at the distance of 10.0m. Computation time of generating the panoramic depth image is about 40 minutes with 8 CPUs.

Figure 7 illustrates a bird's-eye view of texture-mapped full panoramic 2.5-D model constructed by applying the algorithm described in Section 2.3 to the depth image. The whole cylindrical model in Figure 7 consists of 13400 polygons. Figure 8 shows a mixed environment consisting of a static real scene and 3-D virtual objects (Four trees: 41340 polygons). From three different viewpoint images, it is clearly seen that motion parallax is presented in the system. Figure 9 shows examples of superimposing dynamic event layers onto the static scene, in which images of two time instances are rendered assuming two different viewpoints. A walking person is rendered as a dynamic event in this scene. Figure 10 shows a user performing the walk-through in the mixed environment using the CYLINDRA system. In the present system with this example, image updating rate is about 13 frames/sec, when 2 CPUs are used to compute stereoscopic images of 6144×768 pixels.

It has been found that a user can feel real-time feedback and deep realistic sensation in the mixed environment constructed by the proposed method. In addition, we have confirmed that a user can handle virtual objects by using depth relationships among objects, and can sense binocular and motion parallax in the panoramic environment.

On the other hand, a user of the system have to stay relatively close to the center of cylindrical 2.5-D model in order to have better realistic sensation. When a user moves far away from the center, occluded areas which are not observed from the panoramic image sensor appear in the scene and cause a sense of incompatibility. To solve this problem, a method of preparing multiple cylindrical 2.5-D models with different sensor positions and switching among those models based on a user's position would be effective.

4. Conclusion and future directions

In this paper, we have proposed a novel method of constructing a large scale virtual environment. The constructed environment consists of cylindrical 2.5-D model of a real scene and polygonal CG objects. In order to represent approximate depth relationship among objects, depth values are appended to the cylindrical panoramic image. Consequently, the proposed method maintains real time rendering because of constructing an approximate scene using real images and increases realistic sensation. Applying the proposed method, a user can virtually walk to arbitrary directions in real time in the mixed world of real and virtual objects as same as in the real world, and can handle virtual objects by using depth relationships among objects. In the environment, a user can also feel deep realistic sensation of a mixed world.

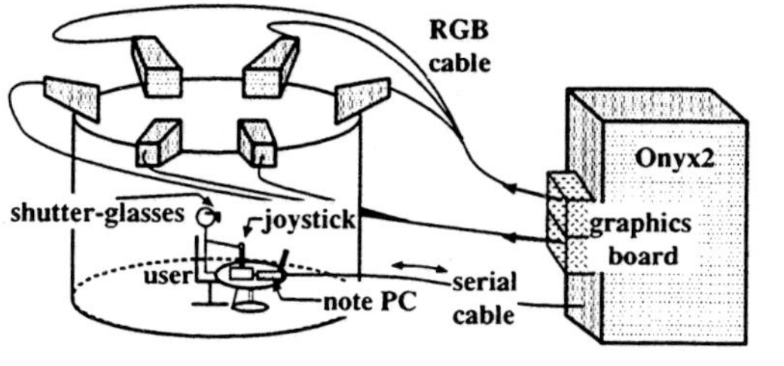

Figure 3. Hardware configuration of prototype system.

As the future work, we will extend the model far larger by using multiple panoramic stereo images. We will also implement an algorithm that smoothly switches constructed models when user's viewpoint changes.

Acknowledgments

This work was supported in part by the Telecommunications Advancement Organization of Japan.

References

[1] G. U. Carraro, T. Edmark, and J. R. Ensor. Techniques for handling video in virtual environment. *Proc. SIGGRAPH98*, pages 353–360, 1998.

[2] S. E. Chen. QuickTime VR – An image-based approach to virtual environment navigation. *Proc. SIGGRAPH95*, pages 29–38, 1995.

[3] P. Heckbert, Eds. *Graphics Gems IV*. Academic Press Professional, Boston, 1994.

[4] T. Kawanishi, K. Yamazawa, H. Iwasa, T. Takemura, and N. Yokoya. Generation of high-resolution stereo panoramic images by omnidirectional imaging sensor using hexagonal pyramidal mirrors. *Proc. 14th IAPR Int. Conf. on Pattern Recognition (14ICPR)*, I:485–489, August 1998.

[5] A. Lippman. Movie-Maps: An application of the optical videodisc to computer graphics. *Computer Graphics*, 14(3):32–42, 1980.

[6] P. Milgram and F. Kishino. A taxonomy of mixed reality visual display. *IEICE Trans. on Information and Systems*, E77-D(12):1321–1329, December 1994.

[7] Y. Ohta and H. Tamura, Eds. *Mixed Reality –Merging Real and Virtual Worlds*. Ohmsha & Springer-Verlag, Tokyo, 1999.

[8] F. Sillion, G. Drettakis, and B. Bodelet. Efficient impostor manipulation for real-time visualization of urban scenery. *Computer Graphics Forum*, 16(3):207–218, 1997.

[9] R. Y. Tsai. A versatile camera calibration technique for high-accuracy 3D machine vision metrology using off-the-shelf tv cameras and lenses. *IEEE Journal of Robotics and Automation*, RA-3(4):323–344, August 1987.

Figure 4. A pair of computed panoramic stereo images.

Figure 5. A pair of panoramic stereo images of a static scene without moving objects.

Figure 6. Panoramic depth map generated from stereo images.

Figure 7. Bird's-eye view of full panoramic 2.5-D scene model.

Figure 8. Mixed environment observed from different viewpoints(center: original viewpoint of sensor).

Figure 9. Superimposing dynamic event layers onto a static scene layer with virtual objects (top: original viewpoint; bottom: new higher viewpoint).

Figure 10. User's appearance in mixed environment using CYLINDRA system.

Expanding Possible view point of Virtual Environment Using Panoramic Images

Takuji Takahashi   Hiroshi Kawasaki   Katsushi Ikeuchi   Masao Sakauchi
Institute of Industrial Science
University of Tokyo
7-22-1 Roppongi, Minato-ku, Tokyo JAPAN 106
E-mail : takuji@cvl.iis.u-tokyo.ac.jp

Abstract

This paper presents a new method for creating a 3D virtual broad city environment with walk-through systems based on Image-Based Rendering(IBR). In that virtual city, people can move rather freely and look at arbitrary views. The strength of our method is that we are able to easily render any view from an arbitrary point to an arbitrary direction on the ground in a virtual environment; previous methods, on the other hand, have strong restraints concerning their re-constructable areas.

One of the other applications of our method is a driving simulator in the ITS domain. We can generate any view on any lane on the road from images taken by running along just one lane. Our method first captures panoramic images running along a straight line, indexing the capturing position of each image. The rendering process consists of selecting some suitable slits divided vertically from stored images, and reassembling them to create an image from a novel observation point.

1 Introduction

The computer graphics community has expended much effort to creating large-scale virtual environments from real scenes. Generally speaking, 3-D geometrical models and surface attributes of the objects in the environment are used to create virtual environments, for example, a town or city. This method is called Image-Based Modeling (IBM). However, the ability of IBM is limited when it comes to creating images of relatively complex or small objects such as trees in city scenes; IBM also requires a huge amount of polygons for preparation.

Generating a 3-D virtual world directly from real scene images without using an explicit 3-D model and surface attributes of the objects is a promising technique. This method, referred to as Image-Based Rendering (IBR), creates new views by re-sampling those prerecorded pixels in a timely manner. This method can generate a highly photo-realistic virtual world.

"Aspen Movie Map"[6] was the pioneering work of this IBR technology. This system consists of a computer-controlled laser disc, which records the images along streets in the town of Aspen, CO.. The user can walk along the street where images have been captured. However, in this environment, the user can view the images only from the original viewpoint of the camera. In "QuickTime VR"[7] a series of captured environment images pasted on a cylindrical environment can generate a virtual world in which users can look around a scene from fixed points. This system, however, does not allow users to walk around in the environment.

One of the key concepts developed in the IBR is the plenoptic function. Three approaches have been described, that of "Lumigraph"[11] and "Lightfield"[10] and "Ray-space method"[12]. All of these approaches use a clever 4D parameterization of viewing position and direction. "Rendering with Concentric Mosaics"[13] is the 3D plenoptic function which, as its name says, creates concentric mosaics. In spite of the merits of the previously proposed plenoptic functions, the primary disadvantage of these plenoptic functions is that the range of field of view using these approaches is relatively small. It is not clear if these methods are feasible for viewing a wide real scene. One of the works most closely related to ours, rendering large-scale scenes, is Hirose and MR Systems's[14]. Using a vehicle-mounted image capturing system, they constructed a photo-realistic virtual world; in that virtual environment, the users had the impression of actually walking in the environment. However, this method can show only images captured near a path.

This paper proposes a new plenoptic function resolving those issues. Namely, the strength of our method is that we can create any view from any position to an any direction on the ground, in a wide area of a city. Thus, when synthesizing a large-scale virtual environment such as a city, our method has a great advantage.

2 Rendering Arbitrary View

2.1 Capturing Panoramic Images

For preparation, we store a sequence of panoramic images with a record of the capturing position of each image. One application of our system is creating a virtual whole city; another application is to build a driving simulator for which it is natural and simple for us to run on a road to capture prerecorded images of a city. Here, we are mainly concerned with the case where a camera runs along a straight line. As shown in Fig.1, by moving from C_0 to C_n, we capture images along with recording their positional information given by GPS sensor. Here we denote the ground plane as the $x-y$ plane and a panoramic image captured at (x_i, y_j) as C_k (x_i, y_j). We can pick up arbitrary slits from each panoramic image for reconstruction purposes.

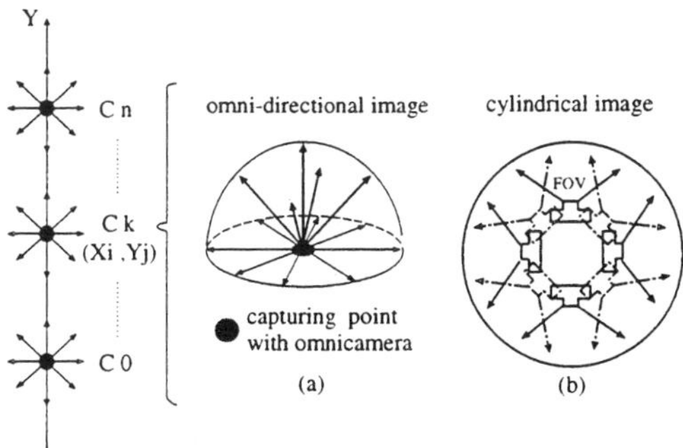

Figure 1: Capturing panoramic images

At each location, we construct a panoramic image. The simplest and easiest method for capturing panoramic images is to use an omni-directional camera. This type of camera has an orthographic lens that has a single effective viewpoint (see Fig.1-(a)). From the sensed omni-directional image, we can generate pure perspective images, and, thus can make panoramic images from the omni-directional image. Using one omni-camera, we can take images of 360 degrees in a horizontal direction; those images cover the northern hemisphere of a viewing sphere. Another method for capturing panoramic images is to arrange some cameras cylindrically as shown in Fig.1-(b). These cameras' optical axes intersect at one point with rays around the center of cameras. Projecting these perspective images to cylindrical coordinates, we store cylindrical images at each location. Hereafter, 'panoramic image' means both of these images.

2.2 Reconstruction of Novel Views

Given a series of panoramic images on a straight line, we can construct a novel view from any arbitrary region. Consider the case of rendering the novel image at the point P, as illustrated in Fig.2. For constructing the view from P, we need rays around P from R_s to R_e as shown in the figure. By finding the slits corresponding to the rays from stored panoramic images and then collecting those slits, we can synthesize a new view. For example, the ray of R_s is substituted for the θ_i ray in the $C1$ panoramic image.

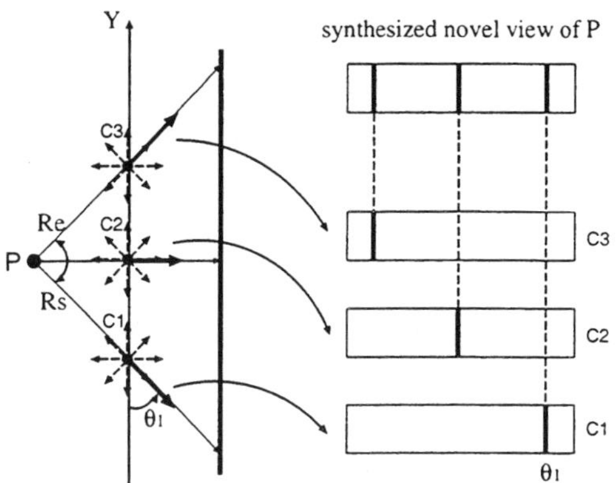

Figure 2: Reconstructing a novel view

3 Features

3.1 Region of Re-construct

In this section, we discuss the areas where it is possible to reconstruct novel views. First, consider an $x - y$ plane on the ground. Let us assume that the camera moves in a straight line for the interval from the position,C_0 to the position,C_n, see Fig.3. On or about the running line, we can render any rotation direction images. On the other hand, as the location of the viewing point is further away from the camera running line, the limit of rotation angle is more restricted. In the Fig.3, the novel images from point P can be rendered in the range as within arrows shown in the figure. Finally, upon rendering the view from the position P, we can render a novel view at only one rotation angle. Although there is a difference concerning the flexibility of the rotation angle, the re-constructable region on the plane is combining two sectors as FOV is the angle at the circumference. The area is shaded shown in Fig.3.

More importantly, we can enlarge the shaded area of the re-constructable region. By running for a longer distance, the boundary curve of the region is enlarged, i.e., the radius of the curve is lengthened. Additionally, rendering a view from the same point, the flexibility of rotation angle is increased. So, running in a straight line for an infinitely long distance, we can render a novel view of any angle and at any point on the ground plane.

3.2 Singular Direction

With respect to reconstruction, we can classify a novel view into two cases: with or without a singular direction. Here we define the singular direction along the direction

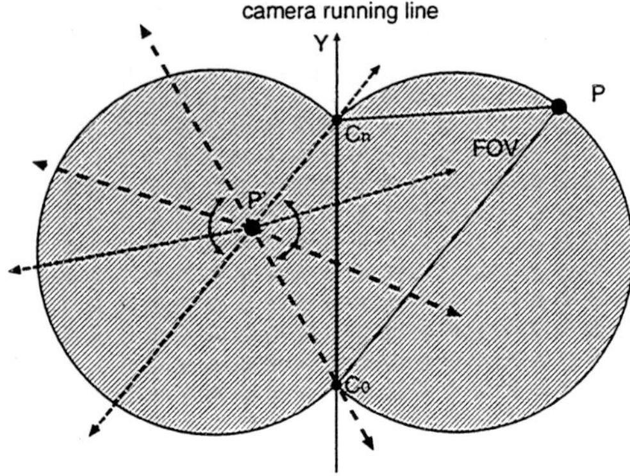

Figure 3: Reconstructable area on the ground

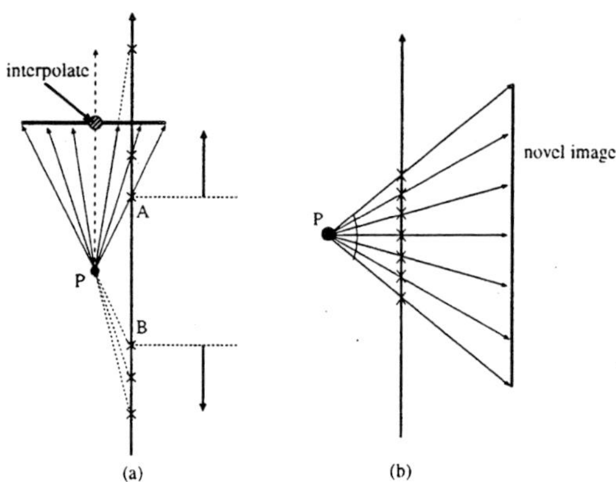

Figure 4: (a):With a singular direction (b):Without a singular direction

parallel to the running direction. Namely, the first case includes the ray parallel to the singular direction, while the second case does not. When reconstructing a view toward the moving direction from the driver's seat, we have to consider the first case, while for a side view, we consider the second case.

First, we will discuss the case with a singular direction. As shown in Fig.4-(a), a ray parallel along the singular direction does not exist except moving for an infinite distance. We have to interpolate this ray by using a morphing or other technique. However, usually along the singular direction, no object or very distant objects exist in the ITS applications. Thus, the distortion of any far objects is relatively small, or we could substitute this ray for the singular direction ray of stored images.

In the none singular case, a view to be rendered does not include the ray parallel to the singular direction. As shown Fig.4-(b), in this case, all necessary rays are contained in the series of panoramic images.

3.3 Vertical Distortion

Just as with the concentric mosaics, this system has the effect of the vertical distortion. We can devise several methods to reduce this distortion. If we know the distances between the camera optical center and the points in the scene, full perspective correction based on distances can be done. This method, however, requires acknowledge of geometry in the real scenes.

In many real scenes in the ITS application domain, it is a reasonable to approximate that pixels along a vertical line have the same depth such as walls of buildings. To estimate the depth value of each vertical lines, we employ the method called the "dynamic EPI" analysis [15]. Usually EPI analysis is done by static image analysis, but this method use the motion vector on the EPI plane. And as a result of this method, we can retrieve the depth value robustly and easily. Using this estimated value, we can scale the whole line uniformly.

4 Experimental Results

We have implemented this system and created many novel views from captured images in real scenes, both of an indoor area and a landscape of the city.

First, we describe experimental results for indoor scenes. Using a HyperOmni camera[16], and moving along a straight line, we captured a sequence of omni-directional images of our laboratory scene. From this camera's characteristics, we can easily generate a perspective image from omni-directional image.

Using these prerecorded images, novel views from position A, B, and C, as depicted in Fig.5, are rendered. And Fig.6$-(a)$, Fig.6$-(b)$, and Fig.6$-(c)$ are viewed from position A, B, C, respectively. These positions are depicted in Fig.5, close to the blackboard and the bookshelf in order. Note that the relation between the left edge of the blackboard and the right edge of the bookshelf behind the blackboard differs in those images. More precisely, in Fig.6$-(a)$, the right edge of the bookshelf and the left edge of the blackboard are not overlapped; in Fig.6$-(b)$, where the view point is closer to the objects than that in Fig.6$-(a)$, the left edge of the blackboard is lapped over the right edge of the bookshelf. In the Fig.6$-(c)$, the right edge of the bookshelf is completely occluded by the blackboard. Eventually, these three rendered images show occlusion correctly corresponding to their viewing positions, which are not on the image capturing line.

Next we present results for an outdoor scene, located in the landscape of the town YOKOHAMA. This experiment uses cylindrical images which are captured by some cameras positioned cylindrically as shown in Fig.1$-(b)$ on the car. The car runs on a public road in YOKOHAMA, capturing images and recording positions of those images by GPS. Then, we project them to cylindrical coordinates and store cylindrical images of each capturing point.

Our method rendered novel images viewing from a virtual running line, shown in Fig.8. Notice that these images are not viewed from the image capturing point, that is, these sequence of rendered images are viewed from another driving line on the road.

5 Conclusion and Future Work

This paper describes a new method for creating a 3-D large-scale virtual environment, for example, cities or towns. Mosaicing panoramic images captured by an omnidirectional camera or a measuring device of a similar type, our rendering system can create any view from an arbitrary point to an arbitrary direction on the ground in a virtual environment.

First, we capture panoramic images running along a straight line, and index the capturing position of each image. The rendering process is very simple and easy to compute. We need only select some suitable slits from stored panoramic images, and reassemble them to generate an image from a novel observation point. In other words, once images are recorded along a straight path, an arbitrary view around the path can be constructed.

Compared with similar methods of IBR, such as other plenoptic functions, this system has a great advantages. The main contribution of our method is that we can generate any view to any direction at any position on the ground; the disadvantage of similar approaches is that the range of field of view is relatively small. Thus, because it produces a large scale space, such as a virtual city, our system is outstanding. This method can also correctly render occluded objects, and where they are located. We plan to develop a driving simulator of the entire city of Tokyo using this method for the ITS purpose.

References

[1] S. B. Kang and R. Szeliski, 3-D scene data recovery using omnidirectional multibaseline stereo, in *Proc. of Computer Vision and Pattern Recognition Conf.*, pages 364-370, 1996

[2] S. Peleg and M. Ben-Ezra, Stereo panorama with a single camera, in *Proc. of Computer Vision and Pattern Recognition Conf.*, pages 395-401, 1999

[3] Y. Yu, P. Debevec, J. Malik and T. Hawkins, Inverse Global Illumination Recovering Reflectance Models of Real Scenes from Photographs, in *Proc. of ACM SIGGRAPH 99*, pages 215-224, 1999

[4] P. E. Debevec, C. J. Taylar, and J. Malik, Modeling and Rendering Architecture from Photographs: A hybrid geometry-and image-based aproach, in *Proc. of ACM SIGGRAPH 96*, pages 189-198. 1996

[5] S. K. Nayar, Omnidirectional Video Camera, in *Proc. of Computer Vision and Pattern Recognition '97*, page 482 - 488, 1997

[6] A. Lippman, Movie-Maps. An Application of the Optical Videodisc to Computer Graphics, in *Proc. of ACM SIGGRAPH '80*, pages 32-43, 1990

[7] S. E. Chen, QuickTime VR - An image-based approach to virtual enviroment navigation, in *Proc. of ACM SIGGRAPH'95*,pages 29-38, 1995

[8] E. H. Adelson and J. Bergen, The Plenoptic function and the elements of early vision, in *Computional Models of Visual Processing*,pages 3-20,MIT Press,Cambridge,MA,1991

[9] L. McMillan and G. Bishop, Plenoptic modeling: An image-based rendering system, in *Proc. of ACM SIGGRAPH'95*,pages 39-46, 1995

[10] M. Levoy and P. Hanrahan, Light field rendering, in *Proc. of ACM SIGGRAPH '96*,pages 31-42, 1996

[11] S. J. Gorther, R. Grzeszczuk, R. Szeliski, and M. F. Cohon, The lumigraph, in *Proc. of ACM SIGGRAPH*,pages 43-54, 1996

[12] T. Naemura, H. Harashima et al., Ray-Based Creation of Photo-Realistic Virtual World, *VSMM'97*, pages 59-68, 1997

[13] Heung-Yeung Shum and Li-Wei-He, Rendering with Concentric Mosaics, in *Proc. of ACM SIGGRAPH*, pages 299-306, 1999.

[14] M. Hirose, T. Endo, et al., Building a Virtual World from the Real World, in *Proc. of International Symposium on Mixed Reality*. (1999-3). 183-197

[15] H. Kawasaki, T. Yatabe, K. Ikeuchi and M. Sakauchi, Construction of a 3d city map using epi analysis and dp matching , Asian Conference on Computer Vision2000 (2000).

[16] Y. Onoe, K. Yamazawa, H. Takemura, and N. Yokoya, Telepresence by real-time view-dependent image generation from omnidirectional video streams, in *Computer Vision and Image Understanding, Vol.71, No.2*, pages 154-165, 1998.

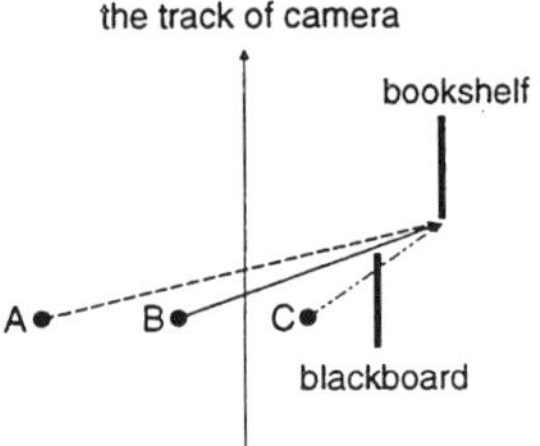

Figure 5: Rendered viewing positions (a),(b), and (c); synthesized images shown in Fig.8 are viewed from those points, respectively.

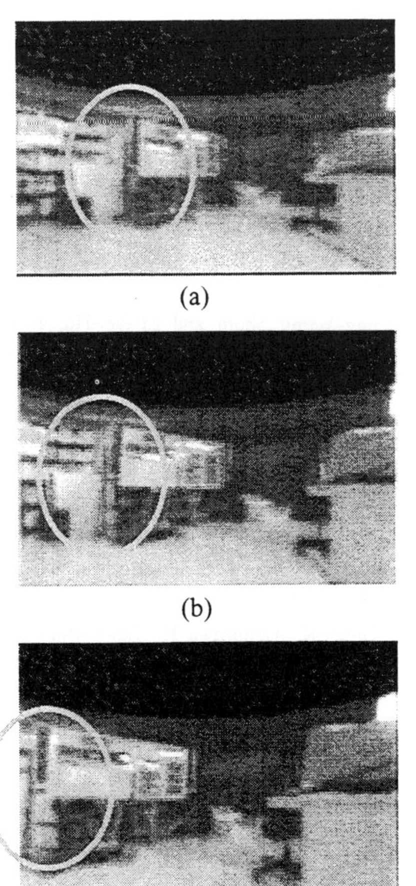

Figure 6: Rendered images; In (a), the left edge of the blackboard and the right edge of the bookshelf are separated. In (b), the left edge of the blackboard is lapped over the right edge of the bookshelf. in (c), the right edge of the bookshelf is occluded by the blackboard.

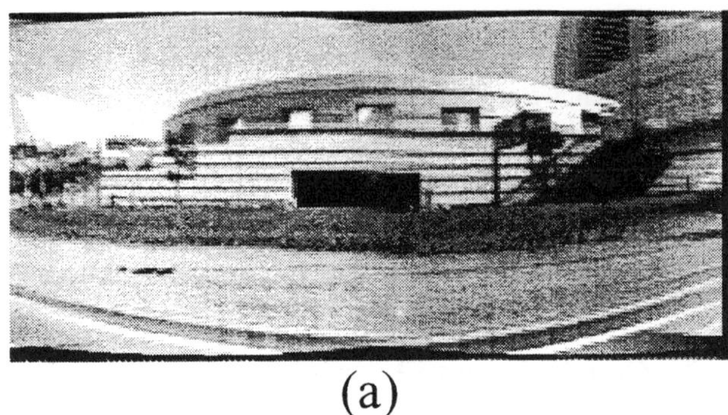

(a)

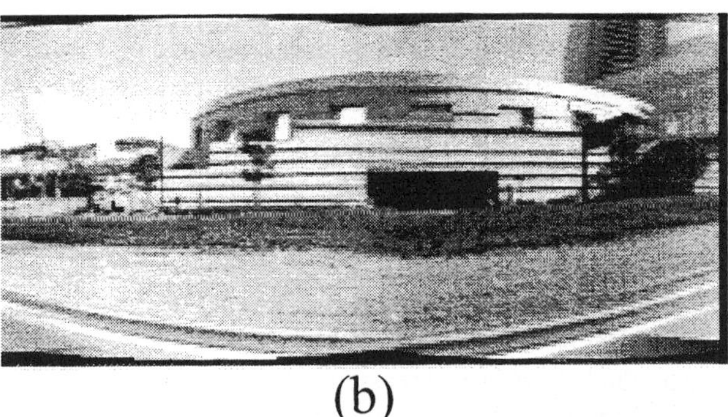

(b)

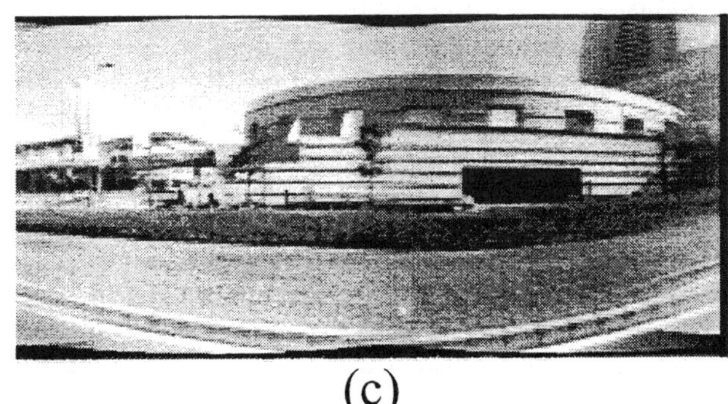

(c)

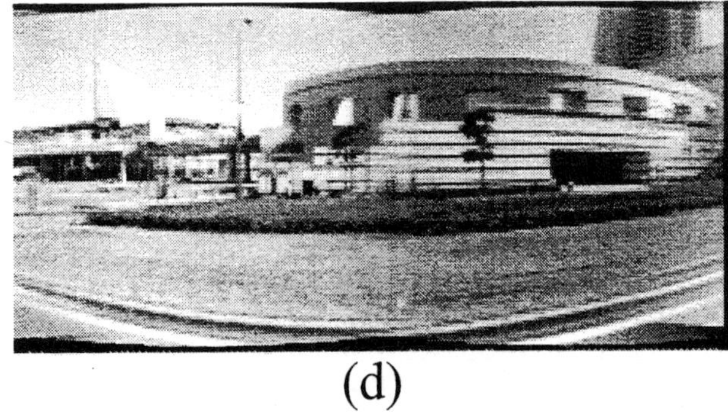

(d)

Figure 7: Rendered novel images viewed from virtual running line. These are views on another driving line.

Generating Images with Interactive Manipulation and its Model Capture

Toshihiro Masaki, Toyoki Yamauchi, Yoshifumi Kitamura, and Fumio Kishino
Department of Electronic and Information Systems Engineering
Graduate School of Engineering, Osaka University
2-1, Yamada-Oka, Suita, Osaka 565-0871, JAPAN
{masaki, toyoki, kitamura, kishino}@eie.eng.osaka-u.ac.jp

Abstract

In this paper, the methods of interactive new image generation using processed video contents, and its 3D model capture are proposed; we mainly stress the key technique of the system and the implementation of moving 3D object extraction. In order to reflect a user's intention for generating new multimedia contents, we discuss the methods of storage, retrieval, and presentation. This system is an example of the novel creation of multimedia contents by using the technologies of computer vision and virtual reality. The user is able to generate novel multimedia contents without shape modeling by a human. The proposed low-cost extraction and interaction algorithm can track objects at 8 frames/sec with sufficient accuracy.

1. Introduction

The technology of three-dimensional (3D) shape reconstruction from multiple view images has recently been studied, mainly because of advances in computation power and data handling. Research on 3D shape modeling has conventionally been applied to a recognition of a a real scene structure or an object shape. However, most of these models use algorithms to build static models. Conventional systems to create a model of time-varying real-world events from image sequences require a large-scale system and enormous computational costs [1, 2, 3].

On the other hand, the database system of multimedia contents has also been one of the most attractive research themes, for example, the automatic indexing of video images [4], classification of video images [5], description of video contents [6], and retrieval continuous media [7]. However, interactive and intuitive retrieval methods have not been discussed very much.

In this paper, we propose the computer assisted generation of new multimedia contents with interactive manipulation with the use of computer vision and multimedia databases. We implement simplified real time 3D modeling methods for the proposed system. With this scheme, the moving objects in the real world are integrated into various virtual/mixed reality worlds [8, 9] in real time. Time-varying 3D objects in the these world are easily manipulated according to the user's intention. This system is an example of a novel creation of multimedia contents by using the technologies of computer vision and virtual reality.

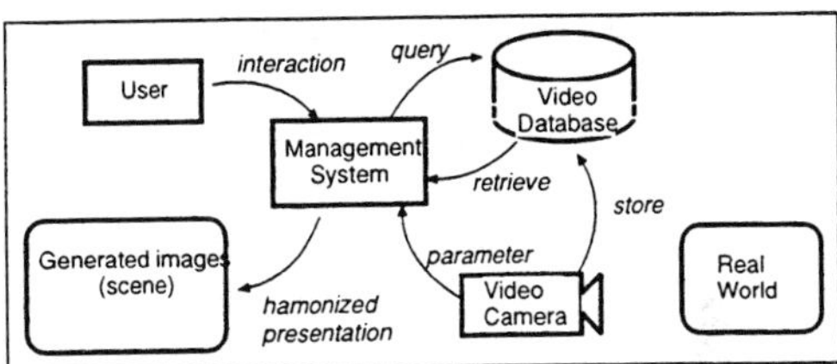

Figure 1. System overview.

2. Generating images with interactive manipulation

This section describes the proposed method of generating new video images with interactive manipulation. The applications making use of this method enable the objects in the real world to be present in the virtual world just as users intend them to be. The proposed method has the possibility to apply various remarkable studies of pattern recognition. Figure 1 shows an overview of the system. In order to create interactive virtual/mixed reality with the use of real objects, we discuss three key techniques: storage of the parameters of real objects, content retrieval with interaction, and harmonized presentation with scene and retrieved contents.

2.1 Storage of the parameters of real objects

The objects in the real world must be stored in the video database or presented directly to users in this application. Conventionally, the model of form and motion must be implemented in a virtual world in order to express realistic moving objects [10]. However, this implementation is very hard or takes a long time to model complicated shapes or motions.

On the other hand, the proposed technique allows interaction with various objects (contents) in the video, and only the video is inputted into the system. Robust algorithms for the extraction of video contents must be developed to capture real objects. In particular, each object contained in a video sequence must be extracted with reasonable speed, and a moving object must be tracked with sufficient accuracy. Then, extracted objects are converted into the data set that is usually applied in the virtual environment, i.e. polygons and textures. In order to manipulate real objects using a consolidated interaction method for real and virtual objects and to create many multimedia contents from one video scene, we must extract various parameters from real objects, such as form, color, texture, position, speed, direction, and so on.

Once these parameters are extracted in real time, they can be used as the model of motion capture. The motion capture usually tracks the motion of real objects, and this is then applied to the CG (Computer Graphics) or virtual objects that are modeled by a human. On the other hand, real objects captured by the system have the possibility to be the target of motion capture. The motion of these virtualized real objects can be obtained from either captured data or stored parameters.

2.2 Content retrieval with interaction

In the proposed application, we utilize various user interactions for the retrieval from the video database to generate a virtual environment. Conventionally, preselected keywords or sample images are the inputs for an image retrieval system using a video database [4, 5, 6, 7], but these inputs are not suitable for an interactive system concerned with intuitiveness. Multimodal interfaces, such as gesture and voice, involve the most intuitive approach to obtaining user's intentions. This system provides an interactive interface on which the user may draw, write, speak, or move.

The main focus of research on user modeling is how to generate the most appropriate interpretation for incoming streams of multimodal input. Not only is the multimodal interface applied as the input, but also the situations of the virtual world or conditions of the objects are used as the inputs of content retrieval to construct a more sophisticated interaction. With the use of this method, the retrieved object or scene from the video database will vary, even if the user interaction is completely the same.

2.3 Harmonized presentation with scene and retrieved contents

Most studies on image retrieval or video databases concentrate on taking an appropriate picture from a mass of data. Moreover, the user simply browses the results of retrieved images. In the generation of new video images with interactive manipulation, the retrieved contents are not image frames but parameters such as form, color, texture, position, speed, direction, and so on. There is no serious problem if a user only intends to add retrieved contents to the scene. However, when the user wants to replace the contents in the scene with to the retrieved ones, the system must switch them smoothly, i.e. it must harmonize the scene presentation with the retrieved contents. Various techniques are required to do this, such as selecting the appropriate start frame of retrieved contents, complementating of parameter, and 3D morphing.

3. Simplified 3D modeling in real time

In this section, we introduce simplified 3D modeling to store parameters of real objects or present directly to users in real time. Many methods for obtaining the 3D shape modeling of real objects have been studied recently. One of the applications of 3D shape reconstruction is an arbitrary view generation from limited multiple view images. These studies can be mainly broken down into two groups. In the first group, new view images are generated from 3D structure models that are reconstructed from range images obtained by range-scanning hardware [11]. In the second group, image based modeling has also seen significant development, in which a set of real images implicitly represent the object scene [12, 13]. However, most of these models have used algorithms to build static models. Virtualized reality [1, 2] and 3D rooms [3], which create a model of time-varying real-world events from image sequences, are based on multi-baseline stereo (MBS) [14]. MBS usually requires calibrations, model refinement, and enormous computational costs. The virtualized reality system uses a silhouette to directly carve out free space from volumetric model as a post processing for the stereo algorithm.

In this paper, we also present real-time 3D shape modeling for the storage of the parameters of real object for proposed interactive image generation system; the modeling only uses an exact counter of objects from multiple images. Special hardware like a turn table is not used. This system can obtain time-varying 3D representation, since it extract silhouettes frame by frame.

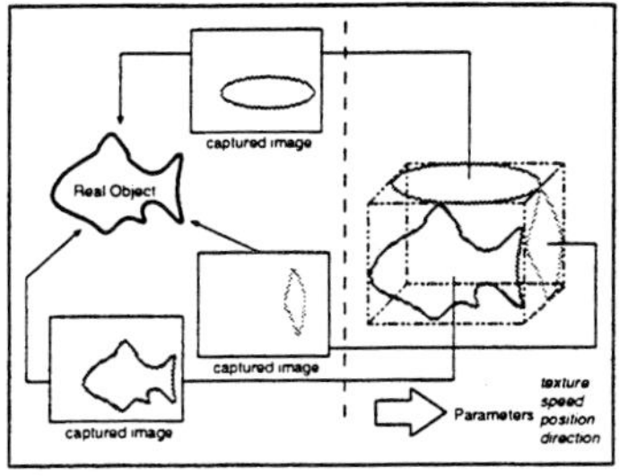

Figure 2. Proposed method of real-time 3D reconstruction.

3.1 Silhouette-based simple 3D reconstruction

Figure 2 shows the outline of proposed real-time 3D reconstruction. The texture, 3D shape, position, and moving vector of real objects are simultaneously obtained in real time, and these parameters are used as presentation to the user as well as storage in the database.

We have developed an extraction algorithm for finding the boundaries of objects with a low computational complexity [15]. This process can be mainly divided into the two steps shown in Fig. 3. In the first step, coarse areas (block-based) of moving objects are extracted by using the differences among three video frames. Then in the second step, a pixel sequence of the boundary of an accurate object is determined based on the edge detection. The texture of object can be extracted simultaneously. Here, the extracted objects can be manipulated in a manner similar to virtual objects, which usually consist of textures and polygons.

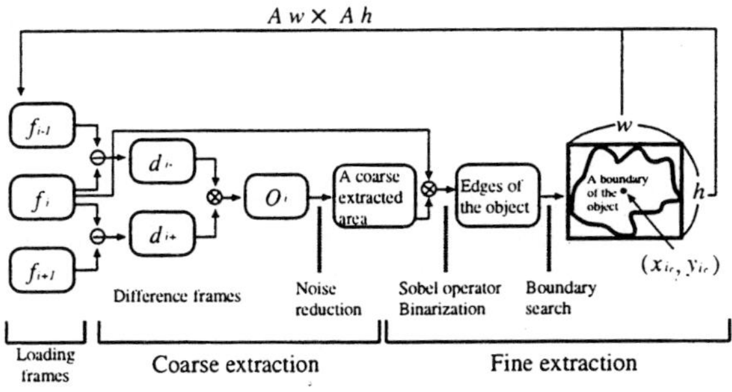

Figure 3. Flow chart of extraction algorithm.

In order to introduce the simple 3D reconstruction of real objects, we assume that the objects are convex, and the maximum number of cameras which capture the real object is three at most. The prism (pillar) with the base as the silhouette of the object is first constructed. The intersection nodes of each prism are detected. In this method, a 3D shape polygon model of an object is obtained in real time because of its low computational cost. The accuracy of the model depends on the preciseness of the silhouettes, teh accuracy is not influenced by texture of the object, since the proposed method does not employ a stereo matching algorithm.

4. Implementation

The simple 3D reconstruction algorithm in our approach is implemented on a SGI OCTANE (two CPUs :MIPS R10000, 195MHz) using OpenGL. This algorithm enables users to make desirable scenes from video sequences with other parts of the approach. The algorithm is evaluated based on video scenes featuring a swimming goldfish in a real fishtank. Three cameras are settled as they cross at a right angle to each glass in order to reduce the influence of the refractive index. The scene consists of 100 frames, and the size of each video frame is 320 dots × 240 dots (Fig. 4).

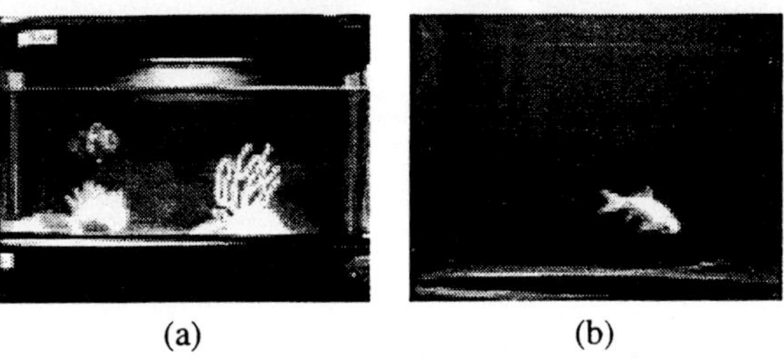

(a) (b)

Figure 4. Original source images.

4.1 3D reconstruction

Figures 5 (a) and (b) show the intersection model and simplified 3D shape model with texture, respectively. The average processing time for modeling is 41.6 msec/frame, and the average frame rate of modeling is 24.0 frame/sec.

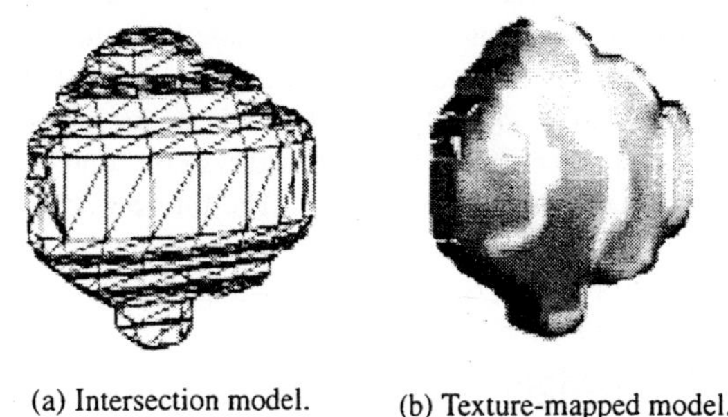

(a) Intersection model. (b) Texture-mapped model.

Figure 5. Processes of proposed 3D modeling.

4.2 Interaction with reconstructed 3D model

The interactive manipulations of moving real objects in video sequences are achieved by using the image data of the extracted area, since the system converts the extracted video image into a 3D model which consists of polygons and textures. Manipulations like movements, changes in color/size/direction/background, and feeding are implemented as combinations of cutting, copying, pasting, and changing attributes of parameters. The user can interact with the moving real objects by using a mouse and a function menu as the simple method for content retrieval. Figure 6 shows example frames of 2D and 3D interactive systems, respectively. All frames are generated from an original source images (see Fig. 4). They show that a user can create various fishtanks from video sequences.

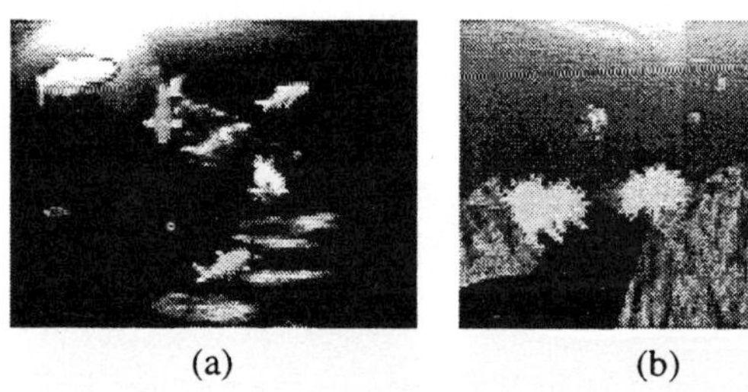

(a) (b)

Figure 6. Snapshots of proposed system.

5. Conclusion

This paper has described a new interactive image generation using processed video contents. We have mainly stressed the key technique of the system and the implementation of moving 3D object extraction. The proposed low-cost extraction and interaction algorithm can track objects at 8 frames/sec with sufficient accuracy. The user is able to generate novel multimedia contents without shape modeling by a human. This system is an example of the novel creation of multimedia contents by using the technologies of computer vision and virtual reality. In the future, we plan to implement other parts of the proposed system; content retrieval and harmonized presentation. The future work also includes reducing the processing time and making the algorithm more robust in extracting moving objects.

6. Acknowledgments

This research was supported by "Research for the Futures" Program of Japan Society for the Promotion of Science under the Project "Advanced Multimedia Content Processing" (Project No. JSPS-RFTF97P00501).

References

[1] P. Rander, P. J. Nakayanan, and T. Kanade: "Virtualized Reality: Constructing time-varying virtual worlds from real world events", in Proc. IEEE Visualization, pp. 277–283, (1997).

[2] S. Vedula, P. Rander, H. Saito, and T. Kanade: "Modeling, combining, and rendering dynamic real-world events from image sequences", in Proc. International Conference on Virtual Systems and Multimedia (1998).

[3] H. Saito, S. Baba, M. Kimura, S. Vedula, and T. Kanade: "Appearence-based virtual view generation of temporally-varying events from multi-camera images in the 3D room", in Proc. International Conference on 3-D Digital Imaging and Modeling (1999).

[4] H. D. Wactlar, T. Kanade, M. A. Smith, and S. M. Stevens: "Intelligent access to digital video: Informedia project", IEEE computer vol. 29, no. 5 (1996).

[5] Y. Ariki and Y. Sugiyama: "Classification of TV sports news by DCT features using multiple subspae method", in Proc. International Conference on Pattern Recognition, pp. 1488–1491 (1998).

[6] K. Zettsu, K. Uehara, K. Tanaka, and N. Kimura: "A time-stamped authoring graph for video databases", in Proc. International Conference on Database and Expert Systems Applications, pp. 192–201 (1997).

[7] Y. Prie, A. Mille, and J. M. Pinon: "AI-STRATA: A user-centered model for content-based description and retrieval of audiovisual sequences", in Lecture Notes in Computer Science 1554, Springer, pp.328–343 (1999)

[8] P. Milgram and F. Kishino: "A taxonomy of mixed reality visual displays", IEICE Transactions on Information and System, vol. E77-D, no. 9, pp.1321–1329 (1994).

[9] R. T. Azuma: "A survey of augmented reality", MIT Press, PRESENCE, vol. 6, no. 4, pp.355–385 (1997).

[10] X. Tu and D. Terzopoulos: "Artificail fishes: Physics,locomotion, perception, behavior", in Computer Graphics, Annual Conference Series (Proc. SIGGRAPH), pp.43–50 (1994).

[11] G. Curless and M. Levoy: "A volumetric method for building complex models from range images", in Computer Graphics, Annual Conference Series (Proc. SIGGRAPH), pp. 303–312 (1996).

[12] P. Debevec, C. Taylor, and J. Malik: "Modeling and rendering architecture from photographs: A hybrid geometry- and image-based approach", in Computer Graphics, Annual Conference Series (Proc. SIGGRAPH), pp. 11–20 (1996).

[13] S. J. Gortler, R. Grzeszczuk, R. Szeliski, and M. F. Cohen: "The lumigraph", in Computer Graphics, Annual Conference Series (Proc. SIGGRAPH) pp.43–54 (1996).

[14] M. Okutomi and T. kanade: "A Multiple-Baseline Stereo", IEEE Trans. on PAMI, vol. 15, no. 4, pp. 353-363 (1993).

[15] T. Masaki, T. Yamaguchi, and Y. Kitamura: "An Interactive digital fishtank based on live video images", in Lecture Notes in Computer Science 1554, Springer, pp. 386–396, (1999).

Generating the Human Piano Performance in Virtual Space

Hiroyuki Sekiguchi, Shigeru Eiho
Department of Systems Science
Graduate School of Informatics, Kyoto University
Gokasyo, Uji City, Kyoto, JAPAN 611-0011
seki@image.kuass.kyoto-u.ac.jp

Abstract

Piano performance requires dynamic hand-finger movements. Since the movements are constrained due to the anatomical components, such as tendons and skeletons, the movements in piano performance are quite complicated, and that makes it difficult to master this instrument.

It is clear that to observe good examples of performance is helpful for learning. For this purpose, we have tried to develop a system that shows us the most appropriate example of performance for any given scores.

In this article, we discuss several algorithms used in our system, which generate a kind of optimal movements of hands and fingers at the piano performance.

1. Introduction

It is quite easy for us to sound the piano. We can draw out a wide interval sound with correct pitch by just pushing a key. On the other hand, we are also aware that the piano is one of the most difficult instruments to master. As piano performance requires acrobatic hand-finger movements, it is no doubt that it is necessary for us to improve finger's agility. But that is not enough to overcome our physical limitations. That is, it is also essential to optimize the hand-finger movements in piano performance.

However, hand-finger movements in performance are quite complicated because of the complex anatomical structures of our hand, and that makes it difficult to learn how to play the piano. It is obvious that the most helpful and effective method is to observe good performance.

Recently, a new piano instruction system, which shows us video-recorded performance with its score sheet, has been developed. However, this kind of system has several defects as follows:

1. High cost for making video materials.
2. Unchangeable viewpoint, tempo, and playing style.

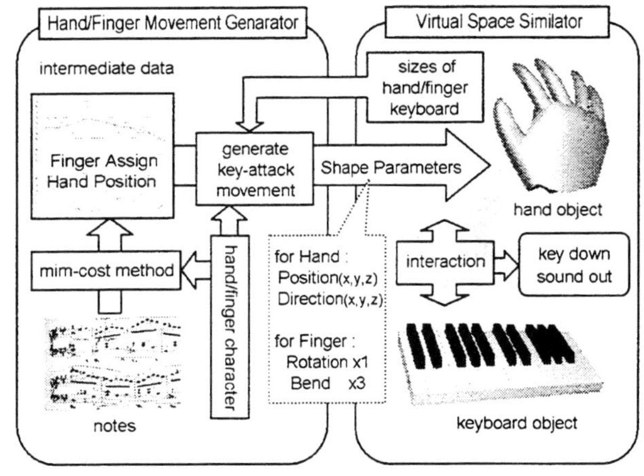

Figure 1. Structure of the system

Those problems will be solved by a kind of system, which generates the appropriate hand-finger movements from a given piano score and displays them by 3-D animation. Moreover, this kind of system will be able to produce the most suitable way for each student by applying one's finger size and agility to the hand object in the 3-D scene.

2. System structure

Fig.1 shows the structure of our system. This system consists of two software modules. The virtual space simulator (the right part of Fig.1) manipulates two hand objects and a keyboard object in the virtual space. These objects are designed to act like those in the real world. For example, a key sinks by finger's attack, and the moment it reaches the bottom, a sound comes out. Its loudness also depends on the speed of key movement.

The shape of hand and fingers is determined by 26 parameters: six of them represent 3-D position and direction of a hand, and the rest represent a rotation angle and three bend angles of each finger. These parameters are generated by the hand movement generator (the left part of Fig.1), and updated at quite a short interval (less than 10ms) to generate natural piano performance.

3. Generating movements of hand and fingers

3.1. The actions of piano performance

Those 26 parameters at every moment are to be fixed so that the hand object acts as a pianist's one. But geometric information we can get from the notes written on a score sheet is very little: only fingertip position at the moment a finger is pushing a key. In order to fix all parameters, we make use of some knowledge and information. They are, for example, how hand and fingers move in performance, how far each finger can bend or rotate, and so on.

For this reason, first, we examined the actual hand-finger movement in piano performance. A video camera, a 3-D position sensor, and a keyboard with digital interface are used to gather the performance data. Consequently, we found the following knowledge from this observation:

- The movement in performance consists of two different actions: 'Adjusting' and 'Attacking'.
- 'Attacking' is to push a key at the desired moment and it is performed by the following actions.

  In case of the thumb : Increase its rotation angle.

  The other fingers : Increase bending angles.
- 'Adjusting' is to rotate a finger left or right, and it is performed before 'Attacking' by the following actions.
  1. Assigning a finger [number] to each note.
  2. Moving a hand to the appropriate position.
  3. Adjusting finger-rotation angles.

'Attacking' is simple and momentary movement and it is not difficult to create it. On the other hand, 'Adjusting' is rather complicated movement. Therefore, in this article, we mainly explain how to fix the parameters in 'Adjusting'.

3.2. The order to fix parameters

As we stated above, there are three essential parameters in 'Adjusting': (1) finger assignment, (2) hand positioning and (3) finger rotation angle. Since it is impossible to fix these three at a time, we evaluate the priority of each parameter, then fix them one to one in its priority order.

Among these parameters, the most important parameter is the finger assignment, for it deeply affects the difficulty in playing. We set the second priority on the hand positioning, which is important to generate smooth and economical movements. The rotation angle of each finger is to be calculated at the last stage.

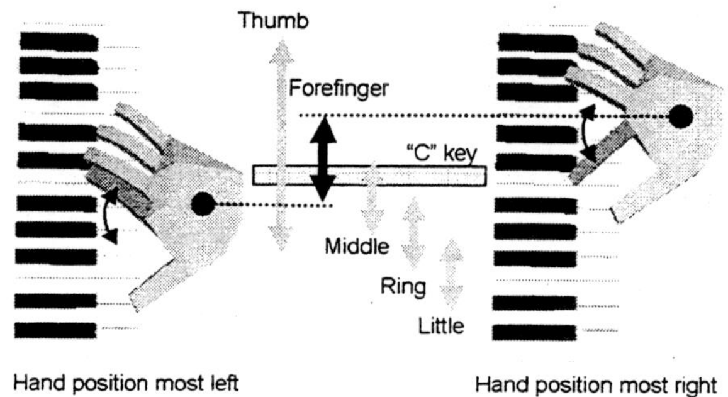

Figure 2. Assignable hand position

3.3 Finger assignment

Several studies have been made on the finger assignment algorithms [1], [2], [3]. However, they apply to a series of monophonic notes, but not to chords (polyphonic notes) or break (note-off time). Here, we would like to show our finger assignment algorithm, which notable feature is its good practicability in spite of its simplicity.

We see from Fig.2 that the hand position is restricted by the combination of an attacking key and a using finger. For example, assuming that the forefinger is attacking the key "C", a hand must be placed between the two hand sketches, where, the forefinger in the left sketch is stretched to the right limit and one in the right is to the left limit.

In this case, the assignable hand position is showed by black vertical arrow. The other grayed arrows are the positions applied to the other fingers. Here, the arrows possibly seem to be located in reverse, note that each arrow represents the hand position, To put it plainly, when a right-positioned finger (e.g. the little finger) is used, a hand has to be shifted to the left to push the same key.

Now, let us consider the case that a couple of notes are played in succession. In Fig.3 (a), the vertical axis indicates the sideways position of the keyboard (from left to right), and the horizontal axis indicates the elapsed time. Region-I means an assignable hand position while the middle finger

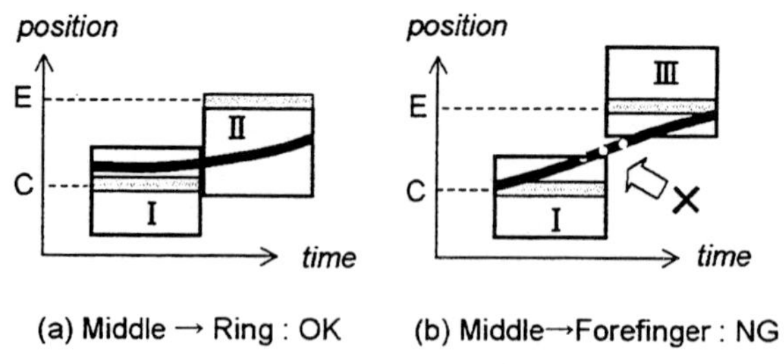

Figure 3. Playing two successive notes

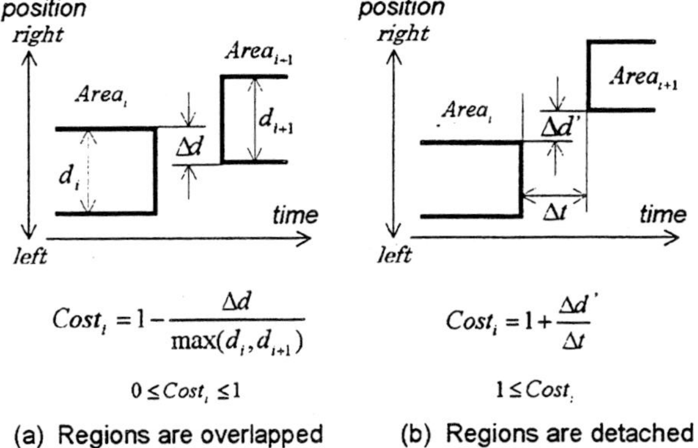

Figure 4. Fingering cost calculation

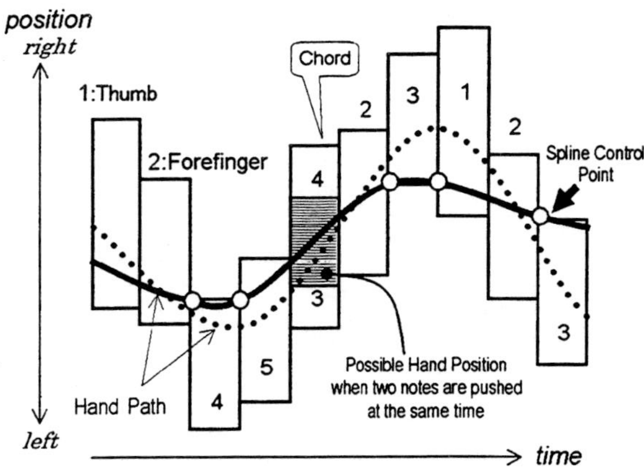

Figure 5. Hand-movement path

is pressing the key "C". Similarly, Region-II stands for the ring finger on the key "E". A thick line from Region-I to Region-II represents one of the hand movement paths. In this case, as Region-I connects to Region-II, a hand movement path that passes through both regions is in existence. This means that it is possible to play these two notes successively by using the above finger assignment.

Next, let us assume that the latter note is played by the forefinger. In this case, as shown in Fig.3 (b), the two regions are detached each other, so the hand has to pass through non-assignable region. That is, the diagram tells us that this finger assignment is an impractical one.

On the basis of this idea, we introduce a cost function, which evaluates the difficulty of playing two successive notes in detail. The cost is calculated by the geometrical factors of these two regions: overlapped length Δd in an overlapped case (a) in Fig.4, detached length $\Delta d'$ and break time length Δt in a detached case (b) in Fig.4.

In the case (a), the longer overlap are shared, the smaller cost is to be assigned. Because a longer overlap has more possibility that a finger is placed at a relax position. With normalization by the length of the region, the cost in the case (a) is given by next equation:

$$Cost_i = 1 - \Delta d / max(d_i, d_i + 1)$$

In this case, the cost is between 0 and 1.

If the two regions do not connect spatially each other, as we pointed out above, a practical hand movement path does not exist. But if there exists any break (note-off) time between them, it becomes possible to move a hand and play two notes. We may say the difficulty of this movement largely depends on the speed, which is required between the two regions. As a result, the cost in the case (b) is given by the next equation:

$$Cost_i = 1 + \Delta d' / \Delta t$$

In this case, the cost is always larger than 1.

In addition to the cost, we need to take some characteristic differences among fingers into account. Especially, as the difference between the thumb and other fingers is quite obvious, we added 1.5(on black key) or 0.1(on white key) to the original cost on every time the thumb is used. That helps to prevent the frequent use of the thumb. These additional values are defined by trial and error approach, by comparing our finger assignment with the reference one.

A total cost for each fingering (a sequence of the finger assignment) is given by summing up these costs thus calculated. Finally, the fingering with the minimum cost is selected as the most appropriate one. Since the cost calculation for all fingerings needs enormous computation time, we perform this calculation locally. To be concrete, a finger assignment is performed for each note respectively, using the following six notes for its calculation.

3.4. Solution of the hand position

As we said earlier, a hand must be located inside all of the hand-assignable regions. As a result, the hand movement path is determined as a line that passes throughout all of the regions. Fig.5 shows two examples of hand movement paths. Both lines are true because they satisfy the above condition, and yet, the thick line is considered to be better than the dotted line, for the former requires less hand movement than the latter.

The shortest path is obtainable as a connected straight lines. In this case, however, the hand movement becomes quite a mechanical one. Of course, it is not suitable as human hand movement, so, then we change the series of straight lines into one smooth curved line by applying cubic-natural-spline function.

In case that two or more notes are played simultaneously, it just needs to let the line pass through common regions. (See the shading in the center of Fig.5)

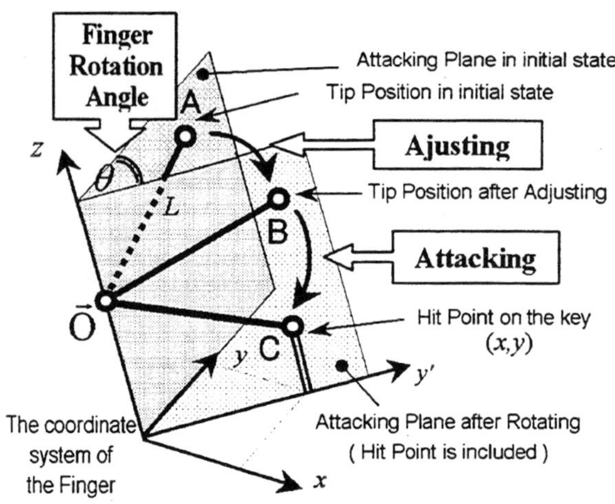

Figure 6. Movement path of the fingertip

3.5. Solution of finger rotation angles

After finger assignment and hand positioning process, a finger rotation angle is calculated. Fig.6 illustrates how a fingertip moves during an attacking sequence.

Point 'A' is the initial position of the fingertip. During an attacking sequence, the fingertip moves on the attacking plane which includes 'A'. While this attacking plane does not include the hit point 'C', the place has to be rotated so that it includes 'C' before attacking.

The rotation angle θ is defined as an angle between the two planes, and it is calculated geometrically under the following assumptions.

1. The hand position and the finger shape are stable during attacking sequence.
2. A hit point is located somewhere on the center line of the key surface.

Under these conditions, the coordinates of the hit point 'C' in the global system are solved from O, the finger base position, L, the distance between O and the fingertip, and a location of the key to hit on.

The values x, y of point 'C' are acquired by converting the coordinate system, from the global to the hand, and from the hand to the finger. Then the rotation angle is obtained simply $\theta = \arctan(x/y)$. Note that this explanation applies to the fingers but the thumb. In case of the thumb, the solution is quite different from the above, and yet, we omit it for being brief.

4. Discussion

In this section, we will evaluate the hand and finger movements generated by the method we have stated above.

4.1 Evaluation of Finger Assignment

First, let us examine the result of the finger assignments. In general, there are several acceptable finger assignments for one passage (a series of notes). Since that is inconvenient for evaluation, we used a piano piece with only a few appropriate finger assignments.

Table 1 shows a sample score, the beginning of Chopin's "Fantasie Impromptu" (Op.66). As this passage has several difficulties in playing (e.g., attacking on black and white alternately, a rapid running up in 6th measure, and an irregular and complicated movement in 7th measure), its appropriate finger assignment is almost limited to one reference fingering. Here, our result can be evaluated by examining the coincidence with the reference.

A figure sequence in 'Reference' row is the finger assignment written on the score, and the below two 'Algorithm' rows are our results. Each figure corresponds to each finger, e.g., "1" stands for the thumb. 'Algorithm-1' uses the cost function stated in 3.3, and yet, additional 'thumb-use' cost is not counted here. Consequently, the assignment generated 'Algorithm-1' considerably differs from the reference one.

'Algorithm-2', including these costs on its calculation, gives us quite a close assignment to the reference one. The remaining differences are two assignments of the Ring(4) finger instead of the Middle(3), and one assignment sequence 3-4-3 instead of 2-3-2 in the 5th measure. Since these differences are practically trivial, we may say that 'Algorithm-2', the improved finger assignment method, can produce a good result from the practical point of view.

4.2 Evaluation of Hand and Finger Movement

Fig.7 shows the sequential images of hand-finger movement which corresponds to the first four notes in the 6th measure of the above score. The movement is generated by the method stated in 3.4 and 3.5.

Since the hand movement path is formed by the cubic-natural-spline curve, the hand moves quite smoothly. However, we found several problems remained as for hand movement.

1. The movement seems somewhat unnatural because of its excessive smoothness.
2. A quick hand action often causes vibrations or unnecessary large movements.

These problems are mainly due to the characteristics of natural-spline function. We may partially fix it by placing additional spline nodes on appropriate positions, however basically, we need to seek for more appropriate functions for describing hand movements.

Table 1. Results of the finger assignment

measure #	5	6	7	
		8		Same ratio
Reference	●○● ○●●○ ●●●● ○●○● 232 1235 4232 1235	○●● ●○●● ○○●● ○●●● 123 4123 5432 1352	○●○● ●○○● ●●○● ○●○○ 1413 2413 5214 1243	Ref
Algorithm 1	121 2124 3232 1235	121 2121 5432 1242	1312 1213 4213 1243	59%
Algorithm 2	232 1245 4343 1235	123 4123 5432 1352	1413 2413 5213 1243	85%

*1 ○ : white key, ● : black key *2 white number in black-box : assignment different from reference

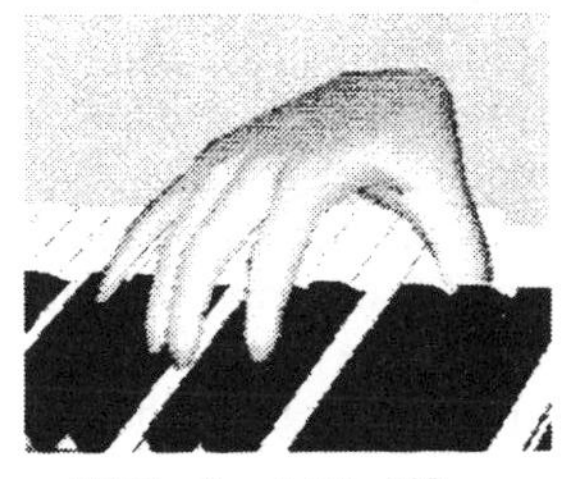

(1) The thumb hits "A"

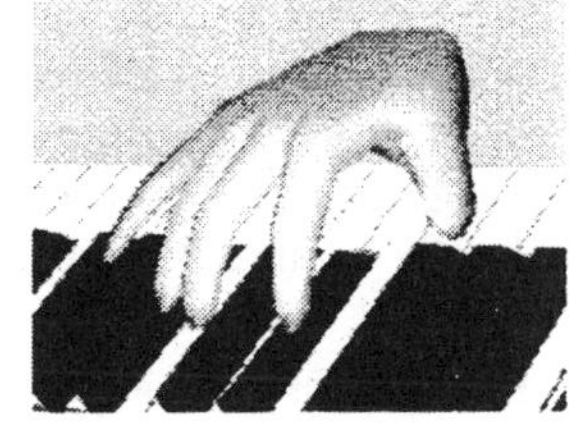

(2) The forefinger hits "C#"

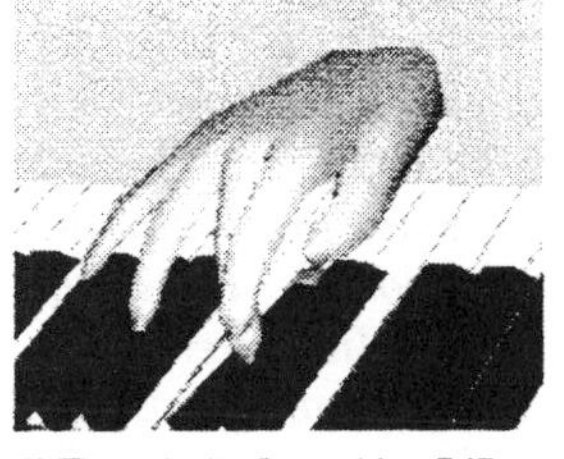

(3) The middle finger hits "D#"

(4) The ring finger hits "F#"

Figure 7. A series of the produced images during the performance

As for the calculation of finger rotation angles, there also remain some problems. Since fingertip position can not be fixed when it is above the key surface, we have to presume its position in that case. We currently use linear interpolation function for this purpose. But it is inevitable that finger movement becomes somewhat mechanical, because each fingers is moving individually with its constant speed. To fix the defect, we should incorporate the following factors into our algorithm: (1) start and stop timing of finger movement, (2) more suitable non-linear functions to describe the movement, and (3) mutual dependency among fingers.

5 Conclusion

We have developed an algorithm that generates hand-finger movement in piano performance. The algorithm consists of three parts: (1) finding the most appropriate finger assignment based on assignable hand positions, (2) setting the most smooth and shortest path of the hand movement, and (3) calculating the rotation angle of each finger. Then we evaluated the result on our simulation system with the hand and the keyboard objects in a virtual 3-D space.

Since this algorithm is designed to produces the smoothest and minimum movement, it offers us a kind of suitable way of piano performance. However, in order to make the performance more realistic, some unnecessary movements, i.e., swinging arms and body, vertical hand movement at the excitement and so on, seem to be required. It calls for further investigations.

In future, an ideal performance model that fits for each person, regardless of child or adult, will be produced on this kind of system. That feature will be quite helpful for students or people who become interested in piano performance.

References

[1] JA.Sloboda. Determinants of finger choice in piano sight-reading. *Journal of Experimental Psychology: Human Perception and Performance*, 24(1):185–203, 1998.

[2] R.Parncutt. An ergonomic model of keyboard fingering for melodic fragments. *Music Perception*, 14(4):341–382, 1997.

[3] R.Parncutt. Modeling piano performance: Physics and cognition of a virtual pianist. *Proceedings ICMC97*, 15–18, 1997.

Real-Time Camera Parameter Estimation from Images for a Mixed Reality System

Takashi Okuma and Katsuhiko Sakaue
Electrotechnical Laboratory
1-1-4 Umezono, Tsukuba,
Ibaraki 305-8568, JAPAN
E-mail:{okuma,sakaue}@etl.go.jp

Haruo Takemura and Naokazu Yokoya
Nara Institute of Science and Technology
8916-5 Takayama, Ikoma,
Nara 630-0101, JAPAN
E-mail:{takemura, yokoya}@is.aist-nara.ac.jp

Abstract

This paper describes a method of estimating position and orientation of a camera for constructing a mixed reality (MR) system. In an MR system, three-dimensional (3-D) virtual objects should be merged into a 3-D real environment at right position in real time. To acquire the user's viewing position and orientation is the main technical problem of constructing an MR system. The user's viewpoint can be determined by estimating position and orientation of a camera using images taken at the viewpoint. Our method estimates the camera pose using screen coordinates of captured color fiducial markers whose 3-D positions are known. The method consists of three algorithms for Perspective n-Points (PnP) problems and uses each algorithm selectively. The method also estimates the screen coordinates of untracked markers that are occluded or are out of the view. It has been found that an experimental MR system that is based on the proposed method can seamlessly merge 3-D virtual objects into a 3-D real environment at right position in real-time and allows users to look around an area in which markers are placed.

1. Introduction

Mixed reality (MR) environment can be defined as an environment in which the virtual and real environments are composed in real-time [1]. It attracts much attention, because it enables us to add information on the real environment [2][3]. Some applications of MR, such as an automatic instruction system for maintenance, require precise registration between virtual objects and real environments. In order to realize this geometric registration, three-dimensional (3-D) coordinates of the real and virtual environments should be aligned properly with respect to each other. For this purpose the user's viewing position and orientation must be precisely measured.

In general, there exist the following two major methods to acquire the position and orientation of user's eyes.

- A method that uses 3-D position sensors, such as magnetic, ultra sonic and mechanical sensors[4][5].
- A method that estimates the user's viewpoint by analyzing camera images taken at the viewpoint. This type of method is sometimes referred to as vision-based tracking or registration[6][7][8].

The hybrid of above two is also used to improve the accuracy and the stability of geometric registration.[9][10]

3-D position sensors used in the former methods can directly acquire 3-D position and orientation information. However, the drawbacks are that the system requires a special equipment and its measuring area is rather limited to a relatively narrow space.

On the other hand, the latter estimates the viewing position from the 2-D positions on the image plane (the screen coordinates) of known feature points. There is potentially no limitation in its measuring area. However, it is difficult to acquire the screen coordinates of the known feature points accurately because of noise, change of lighting condition and so on. It is also difficult to track the feature points stably because they are often occluded or go out of the view.

In this paper, we propose a method that consists of three algorithms for calculation of camera pose and that uses each algorithm selectively. The method estimates the camera pose using the screen coordinates of captured color fiducial markers whose 3-D positions are known. The method also estimates the screen coordinates of untracked markers that are temporarily occluded or are out of the view, so that it can track the markers stably.

2. Related work

Since it is difficult to estimate camera parameters only from input images, a hybrid method consisting of vision based registration and magnetic, ultra sonic, and/or mechanical sensors has often been used. Bajura et al. proposed a method of revising the position and orientation using captured one marker[9]. State et al. suggested a method of registration using three known points captured by a pair of stereo cameras with 3-D sensors[10]. These hybrid methods are stable and accurate, but the drawbacks are that the system requires a special equipment and its measuring area is rather limited to a relatively narrow space.

Neumann et al. showed a prototype augmented reality system using only vision-based registration[5]. This system estimates the position and orientation of the camera using the screen coordinates of known three markers captured by the camera. Kanbara et al. built a prototype augmented reality system using vision-based registration based on stereo matching algorithm[11]. This system calculates the camera pose from three fiducial markers whose physical relationships are unknown. This system also calculates the depth of the user's hand to show the composed image in which the real hand correctly occludes virtual objects.

3. Camera pose estimation algorithms

Our method estimates the camera parameters by the following four steps:

Step 1. [Preparation of a marker information list] A list that has sets of marker information is prepared. A set of marker information contains the color information and the 3-D position in the world coordinate system.

Step 2. [Tracking of markers] Fiducial markers of known positions are extracted and tracked based on their color information.

Step 3. [Calculation of the model-view matrix] A calculation method for a PnP (Perspective n-Points) is selected according to the number of tracked fiducial markers. Then the selected algorithm calculates a model-view matrix that represents the relationship between the camera and world coordinates.

Step 4. [Estimation of the screen coordinate of untracked markers] The camera coordinates of the untracked markers are calculated using the computed model-view matrix. Then the screen coordinates of the markers are calculated using perspective projection of the camera coordinates.

The following sections describe these processes in more detail.

3.1. Tracking of markers

The screen coordinates of the markers in the input images are acquired in order to estimate camera parameters. At the first frame, all of the pixels in the frame buffer are scanned to extract marker pixels of a predefined color. Then, the center of gravity of each marker area is calculated in the screen coordinate. Then, tracking windows are set around the extracted marker positions.

In the second and subsequent frames, pixels in each tracking window are processed to track the gravity of the marker area. Then, screen coordinates of the markers are updated. When pixels that have the marker color are not extracted in the tracking window, the marker is judged to be occluded or go out of view. Then, the screen coordinates of these markers are estimated later, using the model-view matrix that is calculated at the following process.

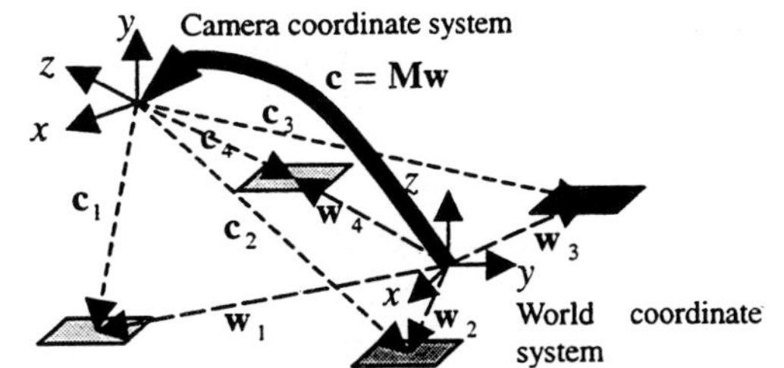

Figure 1. Coordinate systems and a model-view matrix.

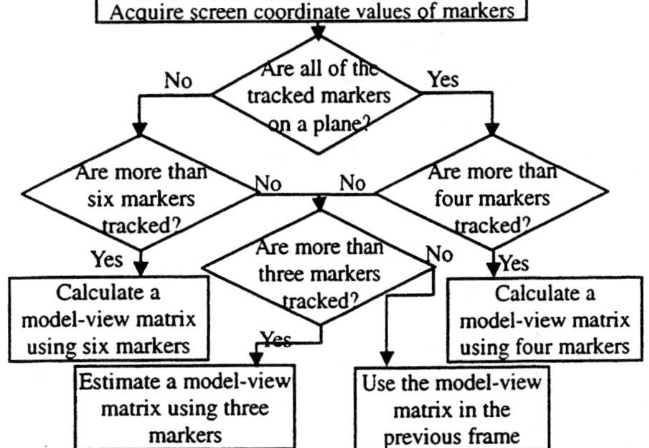

Figure 2. A process of model-view matrix calculation.

All of the markers' positions and colors are predefined. At the first frame, the markers must be identified with the color information. In the second and subsequent frames, markers can be identified with their screen coordinates, because the screen coordinates can be calculated using the model-view matrix and the known 3-D positions. Therefore, all of the markers' colors, except that used to identify the markers at the first frame, can be the same colors.

3.2. Calculation of the model-view matrix

The camera pose is expressed by a 4×4 transformation matrix that converts the world coordinate system to the camera coordinate system as shown in the Figure 1. This matrix is called a model-view matrix. Among a model-view matrix (M), a position of a point in world coordinate (w) and its position in the camera coordinate (c), the following equation stands.

$$\mathbf{c} = \mathbf{M}\mathbf{w} . \quad (1)$$

Our method estimates the camera pose using screen coordinates of captured color fiducial markers of known 3-D positions. It employs a combination of three calculation methods of PnP problems: The first is based on known six points, the second is based on known four points on a plane and the third is based on known three points as shown in Figure 2.

Step 3-1. If all of the tracked markers are not on a plane, the process moves to Step 3-2, or else the process moves to Step 3-3.

Step 3-2. If more than five markers are tracked, the process moves to Step 3-5, or else the process moves on to step 3-4.

Step 3-3. If four markers on a plane are tracked, the process moves to Step 3-6, or else the process moves to Step 3-4.

Step 3-4. If more than two markers are tracked, the process moves to Step 3-7, or else the process moves to Step 3-8.

Step 3-5. The model-view matrix is calculated using any six of the tracked markers (see Sec. 3.2.1.).

Step 3-6. The model-view matrix is calculated using the four markers (see Sec. 3.2.2.).

Step 3-7. Candidates of the model-view matrix are calculated using the three markers, and then the model-view matrix is selected from them (see Sec. 3.2.3.).

Step 3-8. The model-view matrix is set as thc model-view matrix of the previous frame

3.2.1. Camera pose from known six points. When i-th marker, whose world coordinate $\mathbf{w}_i = (w_{ix}, w_{iy}, w_{iz}, 1)^T$ is known, is projected onto the image plane with screen coordinate $\mathbf{s}_i = (s_{ix}, s_{iy})^T$, the following equation stands.

$$\mathbf{s}_i = \begin{pmatrix} c_{ix}/c_{iz} \\ c_{iy}/c_{iz} \end{pmatrix} = \begin{pmatrix} \dfrac{m_{11}w_{ix} + m_{12}w_{iy} + m_{13}w_{iz} + m_{14}}{m_{31}w_{ix} + m_{32}w_{iy} + m_{33}w_{iz} + m_{34}} \\ \dfrac{m_{21}w_{ix} + m_{22}w_{iy} + m_{23}w_{iz} + m_{24}}{m_{31}w_{ix} + m_{32}w_{iy} + m_{33}w_{iz} + m_{34}} \end{pmatrix} \tag{2}$$

where

$$\mathbf{M} = \begin{pmatrix} m_{11} & m_{12} & m_{13} & m_{14} \\ m_{21} & m_{22} & m_{23} & m_{24} \\ m_{31} & m_{32} & m_{33} & m_{34} \\ 0 & 0 & 0 & 1 \end{pmatrix} \tag{3}$$

Therefore, **M** can be acquired by solving simultaneous equations of Eq. (2) [12].

$$\begin{pmatrix} \mathbf{w}_1 & \mathbf{0} & -s_{1x}\mathbf{w}_1 \\ \mathbf{w}_2 & \mathbf{0} & -s_{2x}\mathbf{w}_2 \\ \vdots & \vdots & \vdots \\ \mathbf{w}_n & \mathbf{0} & -s_{nx}\mathbf{w}_n \\ \mathbf{0} & \mathbf{w}_1 & -s_{1y}\mathbf{w}_1 \\ \mathbf{0} & \mathbf{w}_2 & -s_{2y}\mathbf{w}_2 \\ \vdots & \vdots & \vdots \\ \mathbf{0} & \mathbf{w}_n & -s_{ny}\mathbf{w}_n \end{pmatrix} \begin{pmatrix} m_{11} \\ m_{12} \\ m_{13} \\ m_{14} \\ m_{21} \\ m_{22} \\ m_{23} \\ m_{24} \\ m_{31} \\ m_{32} \\ m_{33} \\ m_{34} \end{pmatrix} = \mathbf{0}. \tag{4}$$

When the rank of this $2n \times 12$ matrix is 11, Eq. (4) can be solved. The smallest n is 6 if the rank of the matrix is 11. Therefore, when screen coordinates of known six points are acquired, the model-view matrix can be uniquely determined except a constant factor as follows. From Eq. (4), when $n = 6$ and $m'_{ij} = m_{ij}/m_{34}$, the following equation stands.

$$\begin{pmatrix} \mathbf{w}_1 & \mathbf{0} & -s_{1x}w_{1x} & -s_{1x}w_{1y} & -s_{1x}w_{1z} \\ \mathbf{w}_2 & \mathbf{0} & -s_{2x}w_{2x} & -s_{2x}w_{2y} & -s_{2x}w_{2z} \\ \vdots & \vdots & \vdots & \vdots & \vdots \\ \mathbf{w}_6 & \mathbf{0} & -s_{6x}w_{6x} & -s_{6x}w_{6y} & -s_{6x}w_{6z} \\ \mathbf{0} & \mathbf{w}_1 & -s_{1y}w_{1x} & -s_{1y}w_{1y} & -s_{1y}w_{1z} \\ \mathbf{0} & \mathbf{w}_2 & -s_{2y}w_{2x} & -s_{2y}w_{2y} & -s_{2y}w_{2z} \\ \vdots & \vdots & \vdots & \vdots & \vdots \\ \mathbf{0} & \mathbf{w}_6 & -s_{6y}w_{6x} & -s_{6y}w_{6y} & -s_{6y}w_{6z} \end{pmatrix} \begin{pmatrix} m'_{11} \\ m'_{12} \\ m'_{13} \\ m'_{14} \\ m'_{21} \\ m'_{22} \\ m'_{23} \\ m'_{24} \\ m'_{31} \\ m'_{32} \\ m'_{33} \end{pmatrix} = \begin{pmatrix} s_{1x} \\ s_{2x} \\ \vdots \\ s_{6x} \\ s_{1y} \\ s_{2y} \\ \vdots \\ s_{6y} \end{pmatrix} \tag{5}$$

Since the model-view matrix should be composed only of translation matrix and rotation matrix, the following equations stand.

$$\mathbf{m}_x = (m_{34}m'_{11}, m_{34}m'_{21}, m_{34}m'_{31})^T \tag{6}$$

$$\mathbf{m}_y = (m_{34}m'_{12}, m_{34}m'_{22}, m_{34}m'_{32})^T \tag{7}$$

$$\mathbf{m}_z = (m_{34}m'_{13}, m_{34}m'_{23}, m_{34}m'_{33})^T \tag{8}$$

$$\mathbf{m}_t = (m_{34}m'_{14}, m_{34}m'_{24}, m_{34})^T \tag{9}$$

$$|\mathbf{m}_x| = |\mathbf{m}_y| = |\mathbf{m}_z| = 1 \tag{10}$$

$$\mathbf{m}_x \times \mathbf{m}_y = \mathbf{m}_z \tag{11}$$

From Eqs. (6) and (10), m_{34} can be calculated as:

$$m_{34} = \frac{1}{\sqrt{m'^2_{11} + m'^2_{21} + m'^2_{31}}} \tag{12}$$

Eqs. (5) and (12) derive the m_{ij} ($i = 1,2,3; j = 1,2,3,4$), all elements of the model-view matrix. Practically, all elements are calculated without Eq. (11), therefore a linearization is occurred.

3.2.2. Camera pose from known four points on a plane. Since there exists a transformation matrix that moves four points on a plane onto the z=0 plane, we can assume that the world coordinates of known four points are on the z=0 plane without lack of generality. When the world coordinates $p_i = (p_{ix}, p_{iy}, 0, 1)^T$ ($i = 1,2,3,4$), Eq. (4) derives the following equation:

$$\begin{pmatrix} \mathbf{p}'_1 & \mathbf{0} & -s_{1x}\mathbf{p}'_1 \\ \mathbf{p}'_2 & \mathbf{0} & -s_{2x}\mathbf{p}'_2 \\ \mathbf{p}'_3 & \mathbf{0} & -s_{3x}\mathbf{p}'_3 \\ \mathbf{p}'_4 & \mathbf{0} & -s_{4x}\mathbf{p}'_4 \\ \mathbf{0} & \mathbf{p}'_1 & -s_{1y}\mathbf{p}'_1 \\ \mathbf{0} & \mathbf{p}'_2 & -s_{2y}\mathbf{p}'_2 \\ \mathbf{0} & \mathbf{p}'_3 & -s_{3y}\mathbf{p}'_3 \\ \mathbf{0} & \mathbf{p}'_4 & -s_{4y}\mathbf{p}'_4 \end{pmatrix} \begin{pmatrix} m_{11} \\ m_{12} \\ m_{14} \\ m_{21} \\ m_{22} \\ m_{24} \\ m_{31} \\ m_{32} \\ m_{34} \end{pmatrix} = \mathbf{0} \tag{13}$$

where $\mathbf{p}'_i = (p_{ix}, p_{iy}, 1)$.

In the same way as the method with known six points, the m_{ij} ($i = 1,2,3; j = 1,2,4$) can be calculated[8][13]. The elements m_{i3} can be calculated from Eq. (11) [8].

3.2.3. Camera pose from known three points. When the screen coordinates of only the three known points are acquired, plural candidates of the camera coordinates of the points can be obtained. The maximum number of candidates is four[14]. Therefore, when only three markers are tracked, our method calculates the candidates of the camera coordinates of them. Then, candidates of the model-view matrix are calculated using each candidate of the camera coordinates. Finally, one of the candidates of the matrix is selected as the model-view matrix.

We employ the Finsterwalder's method[14] for calculation of the camera coordinates. The method calculates the candidates of the camera coordinates $\mathbf{c}_{ij}$ ($i=1,2,3$; $1 \leq j \leq 4$) using the world coordinates and screen coordinates of them.

In order to calculate the candidates of the model-view matrix from the candidates of camera coordinates and the world coordinates, the object coordinate system is defined as follows:

- origin : $\mathbf{w}_1$
- the direction of x-axis : $\mathbf{w}_2 - \mathbf{w}_1$
- the direction of y-axis : $(\mathbf{w}_3 - \mathbf{w}_1) \times (\mathbf{w}_2 - \mathbf{w}_1)$
- the direction of z-axis : the vector product of the x-axis and the y-axis

A transformation matrix $\mathbf{M}_{w \to o}$ that transforms the world coordinate to the object coordinate can be obtained as follows:

$$\mathbf{M}_{w \to o} = \begin{pmatrix} \mathbf{a}_x & \mathbf{a}_y & \mathbf{a}_z & \mathbf{w}_1 \\ 0 & 0 & 0 & 1 \end{pmatrix}^{-1}, \quad (14)$$

where

$$\mathbf{a}_x = \frac{\mathbf{w}_2 - \mathbf{w}_1}{|\mathbf{w}_2 - \mathbf{w}_1|}, \quad (15)$$

$$\mathbf{a}_y = \frac{(\mathbf{w}_3 - \mathbf{w}_1) \times \mathbf{a}_x}{|(\mathbf{w}_3 - \mathbf{w}_1) \times \mathbf{a}_x|}, \quad (16)$$

$$\mathbf{a}_z = \mathbf{a}_x \times \mathbf{a}_y . \quad (17)$$

In the same way, a transformation matrix $\mathbf{M}_{c_j \to o}$ that transforms the camera coordinate to the object coordinate can be obtained as follows:

$$\mathbf{M}_{c_j \to o} = \begin{pmatrix} \mathbf{c}_x & \mathbf{c}_y & \mathbf{c}_z & \mathbf{c}_{j1} \\ 0 & 0 & 0 & 1 \end{pmatrix}^{-1}, \quad (18)$$

where

$$\mathbf{c}_x = \frac{\mathbf{c}_{j2} - \mathbf{c}_{j1}}{|\mathbf{c}_{j2} - \mathbf{c}_{j1}|}, \quad (19)$$

$$\mathbf{c}_y = \frac{(\mathbf{c}_{j3} - \mathbf{c}_{j1}) \times \mathbf{c}_x}{|(\mathbf{c}_{j3} - \mathbf{c}_{j1}) \times \mathbf{c}_x|}, \quad (20)$$

$$\mathbf{c}_z = \mathbf{c}_x \times \mathbf{c}_y . \quad (21)$$

From the definitions of transformation matrices, the following equations stand:

$$\mathbf{o}_i = \mathbf{M}_{w \to o} \mathbf{w}_i , \quad (22)$$

$$\mathbf{o}_i = \mathbf{M}_{c_j \to o} \mathbf{c}_{ji} . \quad (23)$$

Therefore, the candidates of the model-view matrix are given as follows:

$$\mathbf{M}_j = \mathbf{M}_{c_j \to o}{}^{-1} \mathbf{M}_{w \to o} \quad (24)$$

When more than three markers (not on a plane) are tracked, all of the screen coordinates of tracked markers are compared with the calculated screen coordinates with each $\mathbf{M}_j$. The matrix, which yields the screen coordinates nearest to the tracked screen coordinates, is selected as the model-view matrix. When only the three markers are tracked, the model-view matrix that indicates the camera position nearest to the position in the previous frame is selected.

3.3. Estimation of the screen coordinate of untracked markers.

After the model-view matrix is calculated, the screen coordinates of untracked markers are calculated. First, the camera coordinates of untracked markers are calculated with Eq. (1). The screen coordinates are then calculated using perspective projection of the camera coordinates onto the image plane. Note that the screen coordinates may be out of view. Finally, the tracking windows are set around the calculated screen coordinates.

This process makes it possible to start/restart tracking the markers that has been out of the view and has been occluded.

4. Experiment and Discussion

The proposed algorithms are implemented on a PC (SGI VW540 Pentium III Xeon 500Hz 4CPUs). A small CCD camera is mounted on a HMD. A video see-through function using the proposed algorithm is realized in the following experiment. Each digitized image consists of 720×486 pixels.

Figure 3 shows the sample outputs of the experimental system: a MR VRML browser. In this system, 3-D models described in VRML by a user are composed in a real scene. Therefore, the user wearing the HMD can confirm the rendering result of editing VRML file in the real scale. Users can see the keyboard, an editor window on the display, and the virtual objects described by them at the same time. In Figure 3, a flower and butterflies are virtual objects that are described by the user, and the vase is the real object.

In this experiment, five different colors are used as the fiducial marker colors. Four colors are used in order to identify each marker from others at the first frame. Therefore, the marker that has one of the four colors must be a unique in a real scene, and must be placed on a plane in order to calculate the model-view matrix at the first frame. Figure 3(a) shows an example of the output image at the first frame. The rest of markers have the fifth color. Figure 3(b) shows some markers that are not captured at the first frame are tracked. The total number of markers is nine. This experimental system can synthesize virtual and

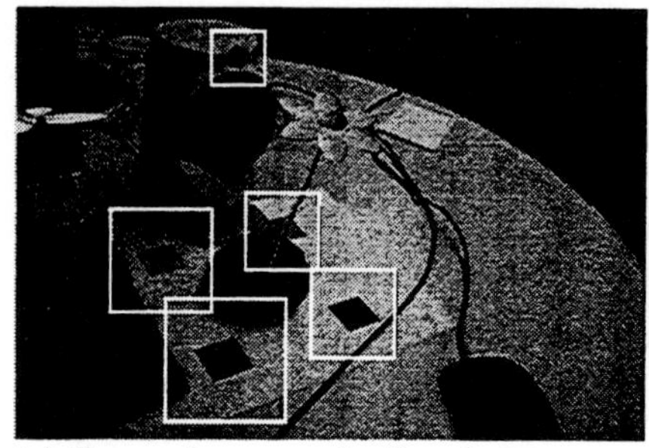

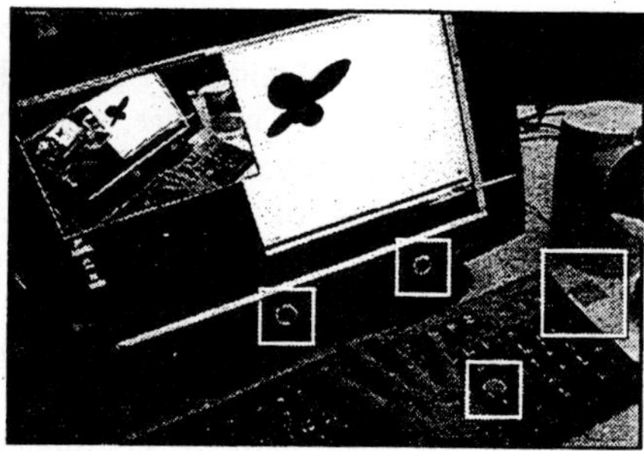

(a) Output image at the first frame (b) Examples of tracking markers that are not captured at the first frame

Figure 3. Execution example of the MR VRML browser.

real images at 15 frames per second.

Currently, needs color markers of known positions to obtain camera parameters. Therefore, user's motion is rather limited to an area from which markers can be observed. We should further investigate a method of automatically detecting and tracking natural feature points.

5. Conclusion

In this paper, we have proposed a method of estimating camera parameters for MR systems. The proposed method consists of three algorithms for PnP problems and uses each algorithm selectively. The method also estimates the screen coordinates of untracked markers that are occluded or are out of the view, so that the method allows users to look around an area in which markers are placed. The experimental system using the proposed method works at 15 frames per second.

In the future work, we will investigate a method of automatically detecting and tracking natural feature points, in order to expand the range of user's looking-around area. We should also make error analyses of the proposed method in the future work.

Acknowledgments

This work was supported in part by Grant-in-Aid for Scientific Research under Grant No. 09480068 from the Ministry of Education, Science, Sports, and Culture, and also by the Real World Computing (RWC) Program.

References

[1] P. Milgram and F. Kishino, "A taxonomy of mixed reality visual display," IEICE Trans. on Information and Systems, vol.E77-D, No.12, pp.1321-1329, 1994.

[2] Y. Ohta and H. Tamura Eds. , *Mixed Reality – Merging Real and Virtual Worlds,* Ohmsha & Springer-Verlag, 1999.

[3] R.T. Azuma, "A survey of augmented reality," *Presence*, vol.6, No.4, pp.355-385, 1997.

[4] S. Feiner, B. MacIntyre and D. Seligmann, "Knowledge-based augmented reality," Communications of the ACM, Vol.36, No.7, pp.53-61, 1993.

[5] A. State, M.A. Livingston, W.F. Garrett, G. Hirota, M.C. Whitton, E.D. Pisano and H. Fuchs, "Technologies for augmented reality systems: Realizing ultrasound-guided needle biopsies," *Proc. SIGGRAPH 96*, pp.439-446, 1996.

[6] U. Neumann and Y. Cho, "A self-tracking augmented reality system," *Proc. VRST 96*, pp. 109-115, 1996.

[7] K.N. Kutulakos and J.R. Vallino, "Calibration-free augmented reality," *IEEE Trans. Visualization and Computer Graphics*, Vol.4, No.1, pp.1-20, 1998.

[8] T. Okuma, K. Kiyokawa, H. Takemura and N. Yokoya, "An augmented reality system using a real-time vision based registration," *Proc. ICPR 98*, pp.1226-1229, 1998.

[9] M. Bajura and U. Neumann, "Dynamic registration correction in video-based augmented reality systems," *IEEE Computer Graphics and Applications*, Vol.15, No.5, pp.52-60, 1995.

[10] A. State, G. Hirota, D.T. Chen, W.F. Garrett and M.A. Livingston, "Superior augmented reality registration by integrating landmark tracking and magnetic tracking," *Proc. SIGGRAPH 96*, pp.429-438, 1996.

[11] M. Kanbara, T. Okuma, H. Takemura and N. Yokoya, "Real-time composition of stereo images for video see-through augmented reality," *IEEE International Conference on Multimedia Computing and Systems (ICMCS'99)*, Vol. I, pp.213-219, June, 1999.

[12] K. Deguchi, "A unified approach to PnP camera calibration problem by projective geometry," Proc. IPSJ Symposium, Vol.90, No. 20, pp.41-50, 1990. (in Japanese.)

[13] Y. Nakazawa, S. Nakano, T. Komatsu and T. Saitou, "A system for composition of real moving images and CG images based on image feature points," The Journal of the institute of image information and television engineers, Vol.51, No.7, pp.1086-1095, 1997. (in Japanese.)

[14] R.M. Haralick, C.-N. Lee and K. Ottenberg, "Analysis and solutions of the three point perspective pose estimation problem," *Proc. CVPR '91*, pp.592-598, 1991.

Real-Time Micro Environmental Observation with Virtual Reality

Kohtaro Ohba, Jesus Carlos Pedraza Ortega, Kazuo Tanie,
Mechanical Engineering Lab., MITI.,
{kohba, mv267, tanie}@mel.go.jp

Gakuyoshi Rin,
DHT Corporation
rin@dht.co.jp

Ryoichi Dangi,
Kawasaki Steel Techno-Research Corporation
dangi@ktec.co.jp

Yoshinori Takei,
Tokyo Institute of Technology
ytakei@noc.titech.ac.jp

Takeshi Kaneko and Nobuaki Kawahara
Denso Corp., Research Laboratories
{tkaneko, nkawaha}@rlab.denso.co.jp

Abstract

In this paper, the observation technique on the micro environments with a real-time virtual reality camera system, whitch is constructed with a dynamic focusing lens and a smart vision sensor using the "depth from focus" criteria, has been discussed

In the operation with a microscope, such as the micro-surgery, DNA operation and etc., the small depth of a focus makes bad controllability to actuate 3D micro objects with actuators. For example, if the focus is on the object, the actuator could not be seen in the microscope. On the other hand, if the focus is on the actuator, the object could not be observed. In this sense, the image, which includes all image informations at each focus values, i.e. "all-in-focus image" is useful to actuate objects in micro environments. However, one drawback on the all-in-focus image is that there is no information about the depth of objects. Then, it is also important to reconstruct a micro 3D environment in real-time to actuate objects in the micro virtual environments.

Important factors to realize real-time system with the "depth from focus" criteria, which can obtain the all-in-focus image and micro 3D reconstruction, simultaneously, had been discussed. Finally, the real-time system is constructed by a dynamic focusing lens, which can change the focus in high frequency, and a smart vision system, which is capable in capturing and processing the image data in high speed with SIMD architecture.

1. Introduction

So called "shape from X" problem, 3D modeling criteria, could be categorized into;

- Shape from Triangular Surveying,
- Shape from Focus [1][2][3][4],
- Shape from Coherence,
- Shape from Time of Flight,
- Shape from Diffraction,
- and Shape from Polarization.

Each method has particular characteristics with the algorithm, real-time applications, the range and the resolution of measurements. For example, the triangular surveying is mainly used for the robotics environments with the simpleness to use. But it needs more than two set of camera or laser equipments to measure. Calibration for the stereo system and correlation of each images are also required.

On the other hand, the vision system in the micro environments to actuate objects in the micro world becomes necessary in many fields, such as mechanical and medical usages, with the micro actuator improvement. However the microscope view is quite limited due to the fact that the microscope equipments has objection in the small field of a focus. This problem doesn't allow us to see the overview of the micro environments in the process of micro actuation as shown in Figure 1. In these figures, we are trying to construct micro 3D object with the $4\mu m$ grass balls. Figure (a) shows

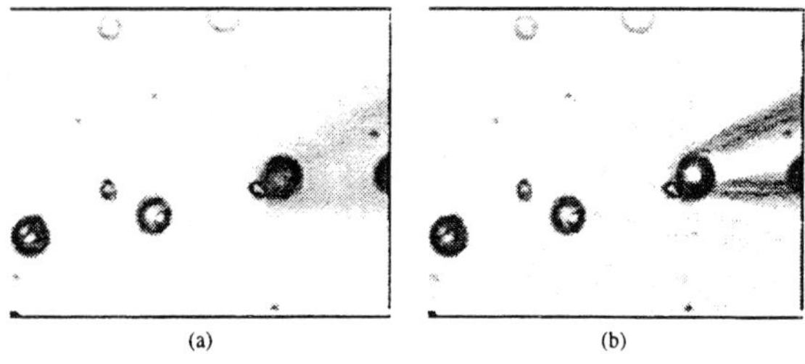

Figure 1. Typical Microscope Images with Micro Actuation.

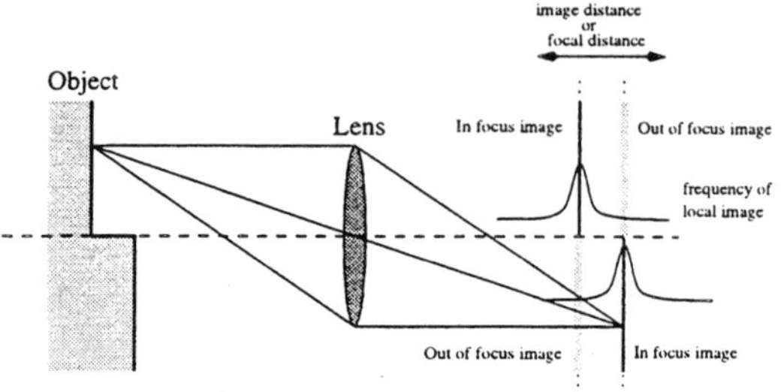

Figure 2. Concept of the "Depth from Focus".

the in-focus image for the first ball, besides the second ball and actuator are almost in the same location but different depth. And figure (b) shows the second ball and gripper in focused. Therefore, the operator should be a professional to operate the microscope and the micro-actuator. If there is real-time micro 3D modeling system, one can see the overview of the micro environments, and can change the view point wherever he wants. Further more, the texture of the objects is quite important to operate in the process of micro-surgery.

Generally speaking, for the vision system in the micro environments, the "small depth of a focus" is a drawback for the micro operation with the microscope, but, as the matter of fact, it is a big benefit on the "shape from X" problem.

In this study, a real-time micro VR camera system is developed to achieve the micro 3D modeling and the all-in-focus texture of objects, simultaneously, with the "depth from focus (defocus)" criteria, a dynamic focusing lens and a smart vision sensor system.

2. Depth from Focus Criteria

The "all-in-focus" image coule be basically obtained with the Depth from Focus criteria discussed as shown in several papers [1]-[4]. The idea is that the all-in-focus image coule be obtained with the mixture of in-focus images in the different image distance with the evaluation of the Image Quality Measure (IQM) values. And, the 3D construction could be obtained with a function of "image distance" or "focal distance" value at each pixel. The IQM is defined with the equation; $IQM = \frac{1}{|D|}\sum_{x=x_i}^{x_f}\sum_{y=y_i}^{y_f}\left(\sum_{p=-L_c}^{L_c}\sum_{q=-L_r}^{L_r}|I(x,y)-I(x+p,y+q)|\right)$, where $I(x,y)$ depicts the image intensity at the image pixel (x,y). And $(-L_c,L_c)-(-L_r,L_r)$ and $(x_i,x_f)-(y_i,y_f)$ are the area for the evaluation of frequency and the smoothing, respectively[9]. And D is the total pixel number to make standard the image quality measure value with the number of pixels in the area $(-L_c,L_c)-(-L_r,L_r)$ and $(x_i,x_f)-(y_i,y_f)$.

3. Problems on Real-Tims System

To realize the real-time micro VR camera with the criteria mentioned before, there are two big issues to solve. One is "the quick-response dynamic focusing lens system", which could change the focus in high frequency with the dynamics on the optical construction. And the other problem is "the high performance image processing system" to process and show the final VR output in real-time, ex. within less than frame rate, $33msec.$, with several number of image data. Ordinal image processing system takes one frame with $33msec.$, even though the processsing time is less than $33msec.$.

4. Dynamic Focusing Lens

Changing the focus with the optical configuration is quite difficult to actuate because of its dynamics. Fortunately, Kaneko et.al., developed a compact and quick-response dynamic focusing lens, which is including the PZT bimorph actuator and the glass diaphragm [5] shown in Figure 3.

This lens is capable to be a convex lens or concave lens with the voltage to drive the PZT bimorph, and was evaluated the robustness with more than $150Hz$ high frequency shown in the papers [5].

We applied this lens with the combination of the usual micro zoom lens.

5. High Speed Image Processing System

The usual image processing system is based on the frame rate, $30 frame/sec$. But to capture and process with the previous criteria in real-time, high speed image processing system should be required.

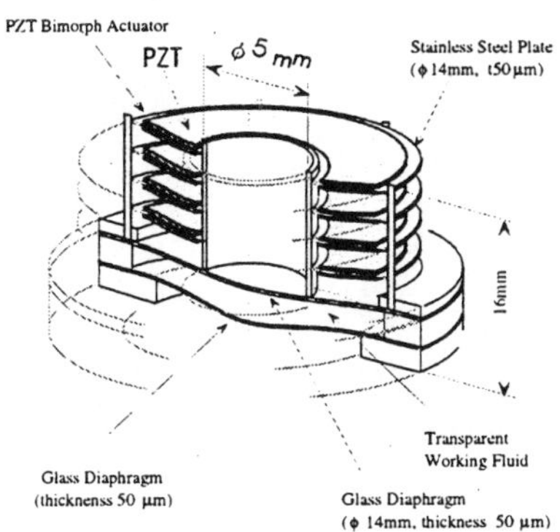

Figure 3. Shematic View of Dynamic Focusing Lens.

Figure 4. System Overview.

In these days, vision chip had been proposed by several researchers to process the image signal on the C-MOS vision device [6][7]. And several architectures are developed;

1. Single ADC Architecture,
2. Column Parallel ADC Architecture,
3. and Pixel Parallel ADC Architecture.

The single ADC architecture is the usual PC based vision system, and has big traffic on the data transportation from sensor module to PC. And the second and third system have merit to be able to capture and process the image signal in parallel, and the traffic is quite low. But the pixel parallel ADC architecture has the drawback of the low resolution, up to now.

Then, we apply to use the IVP C-MOS vision chip (MAPP2200), which has the resolution of $256 * 256 pixel$, a column parallel ADC architecture and a column parallel DSP processing[8]. We can make assembling program for DSP on MS Visual C++ on WindowsNT, and also the C library is supported. To realize the image quality measure in real-time, the parallel processing subroutine was assembled.

6. System

An micro zoom lens (Asahi co. MZ-30) with the dynamic focusing lens is attached on the smart camera (MAPP2200) in Figure 4. The dynamic focusing lens is controlled by PC through DAC, and the images are captured and processed in the column of image.

The spatial resolution is depending on the optical setting, but in this case, the view area is almost $16mm$ square, then the resolution is $62.5\mu m$. The depth resolution is based on the number of frame in the range of variable focusing, $1.67mm$ at this time (21 frames with $35mm$ depth range, the input voltage from $-30V$ to $+30V$ to charge the PZT).

The all-in-focus image and the micro VR environments from one image sequence, Figure 5, are obtained in Figure 6 and 7, respectively. The resolution of the depth is still not enough, but the all-in-focus image is quite reasonable to observe.

Up to now, the processing time is $2sec.$ for final VR output. This is caused by not enough processing capacity for the gray level processing in the DSP on the vision chip MAPP2200. We are now under construction of a vision chip, which is including a more powerful DSP.

7. Conclusion

In this paper, a real-time micro VR camera system was developed to achieve the micro 3D model and all-in-focus images with the criteria of "depth from focus". This system is constructed with the dynamic focusing lens and smart camera systems.

In the future work, the resolution for this real-time micro VR system will be evaluated, and the processing system will be improved and realize the thirty frame par second as the final output for the real-time use.

Acknowledgments

This research was done as the cooperative research between the Mechanical Engineering Lab., DHT Cor-

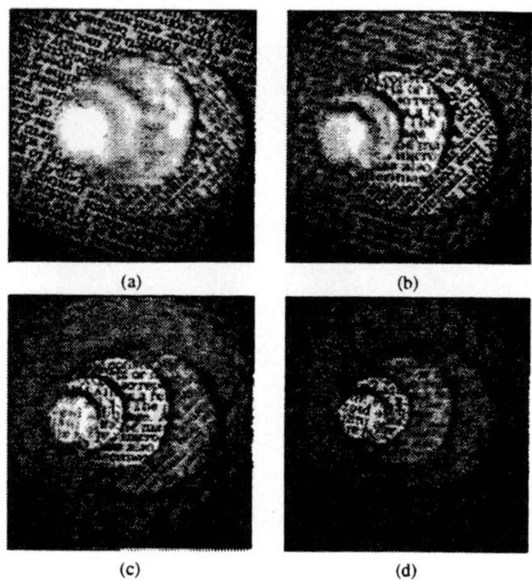
(a) (b) (c) (d)

Figure 5. Samples of the Single Focus Image.

Figure 6. A Sample of the All-in-Focus Image.

poration, Kawasaki Steel Techno-Research Corporation and DENSO Corporation.

And, a part of this work for the dynamic focusing lens was performed under the management of the Micromachine Center as the Industrial Science and Technology Frontier Program, "Research and Development of Micromachine Technology", of MITI supported by New Energy and Industrial Technology Development Organization.

References

[1] Kazuya Kodama, Kiyoharru Aizawa, and Mitsutoshi Hatori, "Acquisition of an All-Focused Image by the Use of Multiple Differently Focused Images", The Trans. of the Institute of Electronics, Information and Communication Engineering

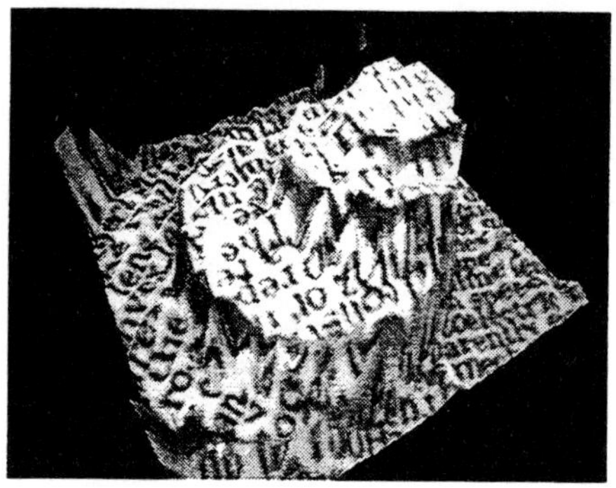

Figure 7. A Sample of the Micro VR Environments.

Engineers, D-II, Vol.J80-D-II, No.9, pp.2298-2307, 1997.

[2] Masahiro Watanabe and Shree K. Nayer, "Minimal Operator Set for Passive Depth from Defocus", CVPR'96, pp.431-438, 1996.

[3] Shree K. Nayer, Masahiro Watanabe, and Minoru Noguchi, "Real-Time Focus Range Sensor", ICCV'95, pp.995-1001, 1995.

[4] Shree K. Nayer, and Yasuo Nakagawa, "Shape from Focus", IEEE Trans. on PAMI, Vol.16, No.8, pp.824-831, 1994.

[5] Takashi Kaneko, Takahiro Ohmi, Nobuyuki Ohya, Nobuaki Kawahara, and Tadashi Hattori, "A New, Compact and Quick-Response Dynamic Focusing Lens", Transducers'97, 1997.

[6] Bladimir Brajovic and Takeo Kanade, "Sensory Attention: Computational Sensor Paradigm for Low-Latency Adaptive Vision", DARPA Image Understanding Workshop 1997.

[7] Alireza Moini, "Vision Chips or Seeing Silicon", http://www.eleceng.adelaide.edu.au/ Groups/GAAS/Bugeye/visionchips/index.html, March 1997.

[8] "User Documentation MAPP2200 PCI System", IVP, 1997.

[9] Sridhar R. Kundur and Daniel Raviv, "Novel Active-Vision-Based Visual-Threat-Cue for Autonomus Navigation Tasks", Proc. CVPR'96, pp.606-612, 1996.

A Control Model for Vergence Movement on a Stereo Robotic Head Using Disparity Flux*

Hee-Jeong Kim, Myung-Hyun Yoo and Seong-Whan Lee
Center for Artificial Vision Research, Korea University
Anam-dong, Seongbuk-ku, Seoul 136-701, Korea
{hjkim, mhyoo, swlee}@image.korea.ac.kr

Abstract

Vergence movement enables human and vertebrates, having stereo vision, to perceive the depth of an interesting visual target fixated by both left and right eyes. To simulate this on a binocular robotic camera head, we propose a new control model for vergence movement using disparity flux. Experimental results showed that this model is efficient in controlling vergence movement in various environments. When the perception-action cycle is short enough to approach to the real-time frame rate, the precision of disparity flux increases, and then a more accurate control of vergence movements on the stereo robotic head is possible.

1. Introduction

Human and many vertebrates, having stereo vison, can perform eye movements consisting of saccade, pursuit, tremor and vergence movement. The critical ecological reason for the existence of eye movements is the necessity to shift the high-resolution foveal area onto the most interesting, important and informative parts of a visual scene, that is, stable fixation on the visual target. Among four basic eye movements, the vergence movement plays a significant role in fulfilling this necessity, directly related to the perception of depth using stereoscopic information.

In the view of machine vision research, vergence movement is defined as the motion of turning both cameras of a stereo head-eye system symmetrically so that their image centers display the same point or feature in the real world within a limited number of perception-action cycles. The binocular geometry of vergence is illustrated in Figure 1. The left and right optical center points and fixation point are the vertices of a triangle inscribed in the geometrical horopter circle. Here the angle between the left and right optical axes on its intersection with the horopter, that is, the fixation point, is called a vergence angle θ_{verge}. The angle parameters including the vergence angle θ_{verge} of the camera axes for controlling the vergence movement can be obtained using disparities estimated from correspondence matching in stereo image pairs. To estimate disparities for the control of vergence movement, vision researchers have developed ideas and techniques such as the correlation method, phase analysis method, and so on [1, 2, 3]. Here, we choose the phase analysis method to estimate disparities in stereo image pairs [2, 3]. With these disparity maps we propose a new control model for vergence movement on a binocular robotic head using disparity flux.

*This research was supported by Creative Research Initiatives of the Ministry of Science and Technology, Korea.

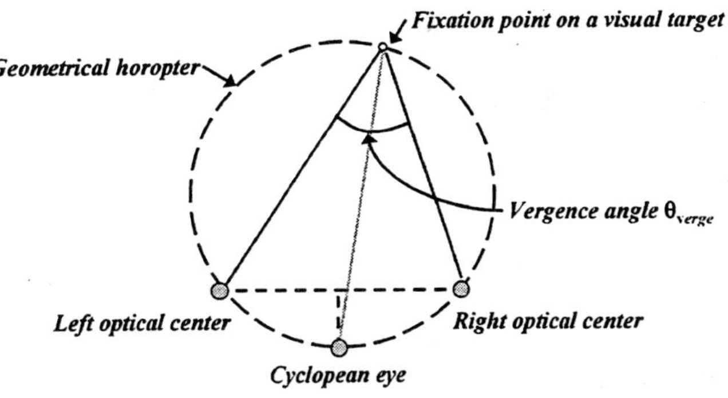

Figure 1. Binocular geometry of vergence

2. The proposed architecture for vergence control

2.1. Disparity estimation

The basic idea of the phase-based algorithm for estimating disparities is conceptualized to compute a local disparity as a spatial shift from a local phase difference observed in the frequency domain, obtained by convolving both left and right spatial images with a complex filter such as the Gabor filter. Many researchers in stereo vision laboratories, for example, the Computer Science Institute at the University of Kiel and the CVAP Laboratory at the Royal Institute of Technology, have used the phase-based method to estimate disparities and to construct disparity map [2, 3]. These ideas are formulated as:

$$V_l(x,y) \cong e^{j\omega D(x,y)} \cdot V_r(x,y) \qquad (1)$$

$$D(x,y) \cong (argV_l - argV_r)/\omega, \qquad (2)$$

where $V_l(x,y)$ and $V_r(x,y)$ are the left and right images convolved with the Gabor filter respectively. $D(x,y)$ is a disparity value at (x,y) in a spatial image. And ω is the central filter frequency(radian/pixel). Also, in order to improve the performance of this method we adopt the coarse-to-fine strategy as in [2, 3].

2.2. Disparity flow

To utilize disparity maps obtained from the phase-based disparity estimation process, we propose a simple concept of disparity flow. The *disparity flow* is defined as the signed quantity of change of the disparity value D at a given spatial location (x,y) for one perception-action cycle Δt. This simple concept is illustrated in Figure 2. And the disparity flow F_D is formulated as follows:

$$F_D = \frac{dD(x,y)}{dt} = D_{t-\Delta t}(x,y) - D_t(x,y). \qquad (3)$$

Here, the shorter the perception-action cycle is, the higher the precision of disparity flow is. That is, a small change in a disparity value is reflected to the control mechanism of vergence when the perception-action cycle approaches to the real-time frame rate.

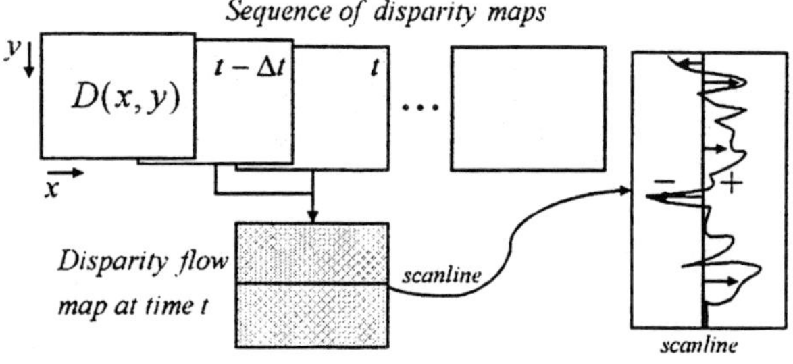

Figure 2. The concept of disparity flow

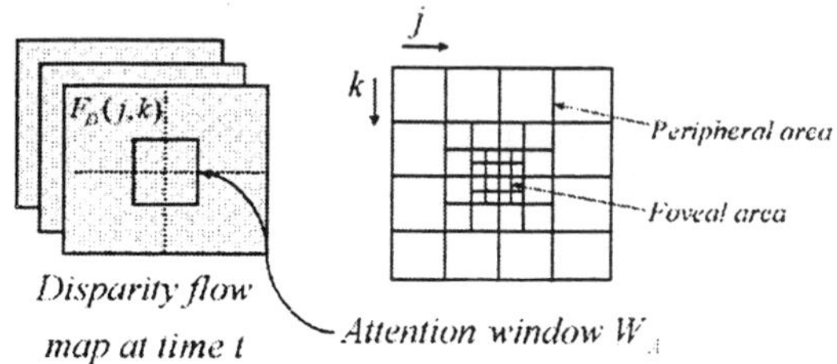

Figure 3. Flux of disparity flows passing through a multi-level attention window

2.3. Disparity flux

After the process of computing disparity flow maps we use the *flux of disparity flows* to reflect them to our control mechanism of vergence. The flux of disparity flows is defined as the total volume of disparity flows F_D, passing through an *attention window* W_A, per perception-action cycle Δt. This can be expressed as the mathematical formula given below:

$$\Phi_{F_D} = \int_{W_A} F_D dW_A \cong \sum_{j,k=0}^{n} F_D(j,k), \qquad (4)$$

where n is the total number of squares, as j times k, in the attention window W_A. An attention window[1] [4] is a pick-up box which is made by a logarithmic subdivision toward the center point of the window as shown in Figure 3. To compute the flux of disparity flows at a given time we simply pick up one disparity flow value in every square of the attention window whose center point coincides with the center of the disparity flow map and all the disparity flow values picked up in this manner are then summed. This is illustrated in Figure 3.

It can be easily noticed that the computed flux using the attention window at a specific time will flow out of the window or flow into the window or remain unchanged. Namely, the total sum of the disparity flow values in the attention window at a specific time may indicate the direction of the flow, the sign (+) or (-) or zero. This signed property of the sum can be utilized to control the vergence axes on a binocular robotic head at any specific moment.

2.4. Vergence-adjustment mapping process

When motion occurs with a change of depth on the fixation point in a visual scene, disparity flows in the attention window are generated. If the flux at any given time

[1] As we see in Figure 3, the attention window consists of logarithmic subdivided squares, similar to the fovea-peripheral log-polar map in space-variant sensing. In Figure 3 the total number of the levels of the window is 3.

is a small value near to zero or exactly equal to zero, then it is said that the current state of vergence is very *stable*. Instantly, when disparity flows are detected in the attention window, or the current flux value is not in the stable range close to zero, the left and right vergence axes are controlled to converge or diverge symmetrically as the vergence-adjustment angle through the mapping process *until* the flux value is included in the range of stable vergence. The mapping process consists of two steps: one step to quantize the flux value into 7-levels and the other step to link that level with an appropriate adjustment angle in the table[2]. For selecting the action of vergence, convergence or divergence, the signed property of the summed disparity flows is used. The overall flow chart of the proposed control architecture for vergence movement is illustrated in Figure 4. In this figure the control flow forms a closed-loop, a compact perception-action cycle.

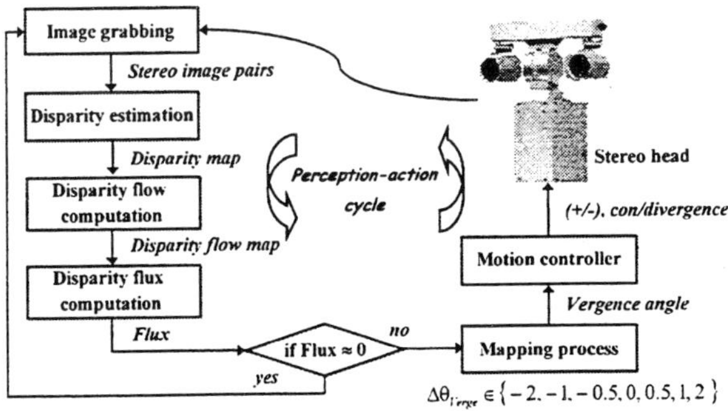

Figure 4. Overview of the proposed control architecture

3. Experimental results

3.1. Experimental environment

Experiments were carried out to test the performance of the proposed control model for vergence movement on our 4-DOF binocular head-eye robot.[3] To capture stereo image pairs for estimating disparities, two image grabbers[4] connected with CCD cameras were used. And a motion controller[5] was used to control the left and right axes of our head-eye robot.

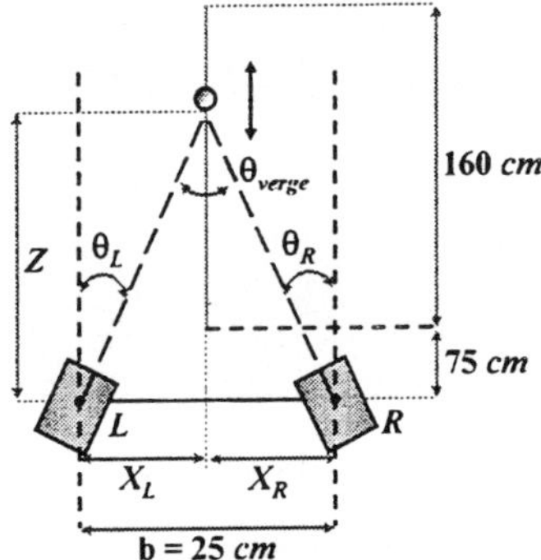

Figure 5. Set up used for experiments: The cameras are verging on a pole object on the extended line from the center of the baseline.

In order to be able to accurately quantify the performance of the proposed vergence system, the experimental set-up[6] shown in Figure 5 was used to create controlled vergence stimuli in a realistic environment, similar to the one used in [1]. This set-up is composed of a pole object on the extended line from the center of the baseline b of our binocular camera head, as shown in Figure 5. The length of the baseline b of our head-eye robot is a constant value(25 cm). θ_L and θ_R are the left and right vergence motor angles, respectively. From this simple figure, we can develop a relationship between a vergence angle θ_{verge} and a relative depth Z of a verged object. First, the vergence angle is defined as the angle between the optical axes of the two cameras, that is equivalent to the sum of θ_L and θ_R. This is expressed as follows:

$$\theta_{verge} = |\theta_L| + |\theta_R|. \tag{5}$$

In this set-up, the left and right vergence motor angles are equal, *i.e.*, the horizontal distances X_L and X_R from the center of the baseline[7] b are the same as half of the baseline length. Thus, the depth Z of the fixation point on the verged object from the center of the baseline can be obtained by:

$$\theta = |\theta_L| = |\theta_R| = \frac{\theta_{verge}}{2}, X = X_L = X_R = b/2 \tag{6}$$

$$Z = \frac{X}{tan\theta} = \frac{b}{2tan\theta} = \frac{b}{2tan(\theta_{verge}/2)}. \tag{7}$$

[2]The vergence-adjustment table can be seen like {-2, -1, -0.5, 0, 0.5, 1, 2}. An element of this table represents how many degrees of the relative angle between the left and right vergence axes the vergence is to be adjusted.

[3]This head-eye robot is a commercial component made by Helpmate Robotics Inc. It is a BiSight system, mounted on a UniSight system, equipped with FUJINON H10x11E-X41 lenses connected to PULNiX TMC-7 series color CCD cameras on each vergence axis of the robot.

[4]Matrox Meteor-II image grabber made by Matrox Electronic Systems Ltd.

[5]A PMAC(Programmable Multi-Axes Controller, IBM PC-ISA bus version) made by DELTA TAU data systems Inc. is used for our head-eye system. This PMAC board is connected to a PC-based host computer(Pentium III MMX 500Mhz) via ISA bus.

[6]In this setup the tilt angle is exactly zero, that is, the head-eye robot looks straight ahead.

[7]*i.e.*, the distance between the rotation centers of two cameras

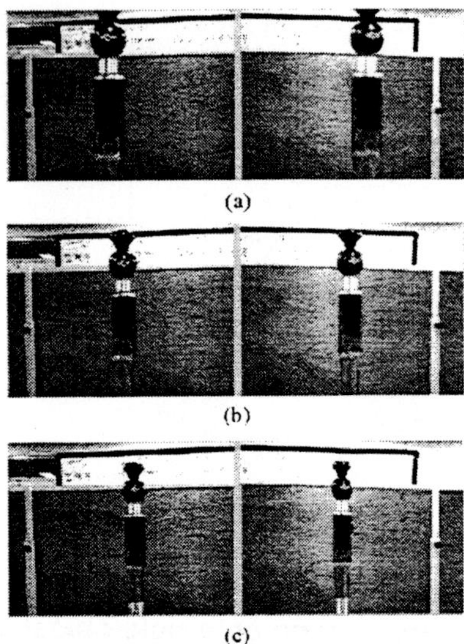

Figure 6. Constant vergence angle(open-loop) experiment: (a) object: 75 cm, fixation: 95 cm, flux = -780 (b) object: 95 cm, fixation: 95 cm, flux ≈ 0(verged) (c) object: 115 cm, fixation: 95 cm, flux = 832

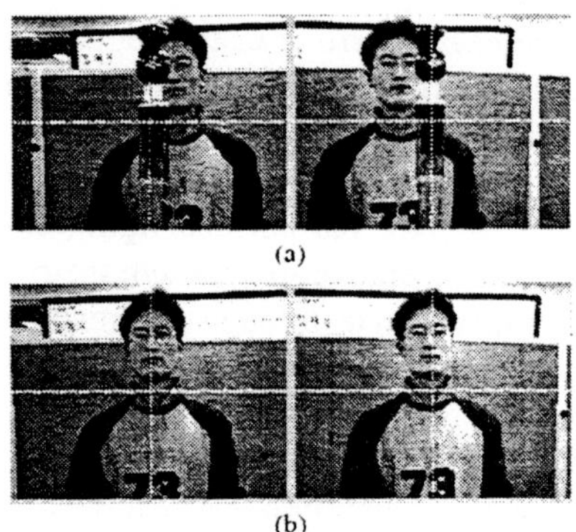

Figure 7. Saccadic vergence experiment: (a) object: 95 cm, fixation: 95 cm (b) object: 135 cm, fixation: 135 cm

3.2. Results and analysis

In order to measure the performance of the proposed control system in different situations, some experiments were conducted as described below.

- **constant vergence angle experiment**

The objective of this experiment was to test the open-loop response of the vergence system to change of the flux and direction of motion. The vergence angle was fixed so that the left and right optical axes were verging midway along the extended line from the center of the baseline(95 cm). Figure 6 was obtained by moving the pole object back and forth(by constant step off 20 cm) in a range 75∼115 cm from the center of the baseline. In Figure 6 (b) the disparity flux is almost zero at the 95 cm from the baseline. It shows that the flux reaches its minimum value, which indicates stable verging, when the visual target crosses the fixation point(at 95 cm from the baseline in this experiment).

- **saccadic vergence experiment**

To measure the response of the proposed control system on unexpected depth changes with large vergence errors in the visual scene, the saccadic vergence experiment was conducted at indoor environment ranging approximately from 95 cm to 135 cm. In Figure 7 (a), the fixation point was initially located at the pole object at 95 cm with stable vergence. When the pole object disappears in the visual field, the flux abruptly changes and vergence movement of the head-eye robot is issued. When the flux value approached to zero, vergence movements are turned off and the flux is in the stable vergence range in Figure 7 (b).

4. Conclusions and further research

We proposed a control model for dynamic vergence eye movement of stereo head-eye system using disparity flux. Experiments under various conditions show that this model makes it possible a precise control of vergence movement. Also, this model can be applied to the control of vergence tracking.

The perception-action cycle close to the real-time frame rate as well as a more efficient disparity estimation method robust to the variation of illumination and the noise would contribute to the more accurate control of dynamic vergence. This control model will be further studied to include smooth pursuit movement.

References

[1] C. Capurro, F. Panerai, and G. Sandini. Dynamic vergence using log-polar images. *International Journal of Computer Vision*, 24:79–94, 1997.

[2] M. Hansen and G. Sommer. Real-time vergence control using local phase differences. *Machine Graphics and Vision*, 5:51–63, 1996.

[3] A. Maki, T. Uhlin, and J. O. Eklundh. Disparity selection in binocular pursuit. *In Proc. of IAPR Workshop on Machine Vision Applications, Kawasaki, Japan*, pages 182–185, 1994.

[4] J. H. Piater, R. A. Grupen, and K. Ramamritham. Learning real-time stereo vergence control. *In Proc. of the 1999 IEEE International Symposium on Intelligent Control, Cambridge, MA*, 1999.

Camera Calibration with a Motorized Zoom Lens

Yong-Sheng Chen†‡ Sheng-Wen Shih∗ Yi-Ping Hung†‡ Chiou-Shann Fuh‡

†Institute of Information Science, Academia Sinica, Taipei, Taiwan
‡Dept. of Computer Science and Information Engineering, National Taiwan University, Taipei, Taiwan
∗Dept. of Computer Science and Information Engineering, National Chi Nan University, Nantou, Taiwan
Email: hung@iis.sinica.edu.tw

Abstract

This paper presents a simple and efficient method of calibrating the intrinsic camera parameters for all the lens settings of a motorized zoom lens. We fix the aperture setting and perform the camera calibration, adaptively, over the ranges of the zoom and focus settings. Bilinear interpolation is used to provide the values of the intrinsic camera parameters for those lens settings where no observations are taken. Our experiments show that the proposed method can provide accurate intrinsic camera parameters for all the lens settings, even though camera calibration is performed only for a small number of sampled lens settings. A calibration object suitable for zoom lens calibration is also presented.

1. Introduction

Motorized zoom lenses have great potential in the applications of active vision [3], 3-D reconstruction [2], and tracking [1]. In such applications, the aperture, zoom, and focus of the lens can be controlled to adapt to different lighting conditions or to obtain the desired field of view, depth of field, spatial resolution, or focused distance. Although a motorized zoom lens is more flexible and useful than a monofocal lens, it is not an easy job, in general, to calibrate a motorized zoom lens. The goal of motorized zoom lens calibration is to determine the relationship between the lens settings (control parameters for the driving motors) and the intrinsic camera parameters (ICPs). Unfortunately, a motorized zoom lens usually consists of some compound lens groups and various mechanical assembly. The relationship between the lens settings and the ICPs is quite complicated [6]. One way to determine this relationship is to treat each configuration of lens settings as a monofocal lens and to perform camera calibration [5] for each configuration. However, this method is extremely inefficient because a motorized zoom lens usually has many configurations.

In the past, Tarabanis et al. [4] proposed techniques for zoom lens calibration by using a special optical bench. They constructed a sparse table storing the camera parameters (CPs) calibrated for sampled lens settings. CPs for other lens settings can be obtained via interpolation. Willson and Shafer [6] also have developed zoom lens calibration technique. They used an autocollimated laser for locating the image center and calibrated the eleven CPs for regularly sampled lens settings. For each CP, they approximately modeled the relationship between the CP and the lens settings (zoom and focus) with a bivariate polynomial function. The calibrated CPs of the sampled lens settings were then used to determine the coefficients of the polynomial functions. These polynomial functions can provide accurate CPs for a continuous range of lens setting. Average prediction error of less than 0.14 pixels was achieved.

In this paper, we present a simple and efficient method of calibrating a motorized zoom lens. A small number of sampled lens settings are adaptively chosen for performing camera calibration. The calibrated ICPs are stored in a table. For those lens settings where the table entries are empty, the desired ICPs can be obtained via interpolation. This table can be used to provide accurate ICPs of any lens setting for many applications.

2. Camera Model

Given a 3-D point in the world coordinate system, the camera model and the associated CPs can predict its projected image coordinates. For a monofocal lens, here, the pinhole camera model with radial distortion is considered. Totally, there are twelve CPs in this camera model: the image coordinates, (u_0, v_0), of the piercing point where the optical axis pierces the image plane; the horizontal and vertical pixel width, s_u and s_v; the effective focal length, f; the first coefficient of radial distortion, κ; the X-Y-Z Euler angles, α, β, and γ; and the translation vector between the origins of the world and the camera coordinate systems, t_x,

t_y, and t_z. Among these CPs, the vertical pixel width, s_v, can be obtained from the specification of the CCD camera. The remaining eleven CPs can be estimated by using Weng et al.'s method [5], provided that a set of known calibration points are observed in the image. In the following, the 3-D world coordinates of the calibration points and their corresponding image measurements will be referred to as the *calibration data*.

Since the influence of the aperture setting is negligible, as shown in Section 4, we only consider the zoom and focus settings. For each combination of the zoom and focus settings, the zoom lens can be treated as a monofocal lens and its CPs can be calibrated individually. When we adjust the zoom or the focus setting, some of the CPs remain unchanged during the adjustment. For example, the pixel width, s_u and s_v, and the extrinsic CPs, α, β, γ, t_x, t_y, and t_z, are not supposed to vary. Hence, once these CPs arc determined in the initial stage, they can be fixed during the remaining procedure of zoom lens calibration. When adjusting the zoom or the focus setting, the ICPs, u_0, v_0, f, κ, and Δt_z, will change accordingly, where Δt_z is the displacement of the perspective center in the Z axis. We should estimate these ICPs for each combination of the zoom and the focus settings.

3. Zoom Lens Calibration

The calibration object we used is a plate mounted on a computer-controlled translation stage, as shown in Figure 1. This plate can be moved along the direction of the stage such that the calibration data of different distances from the lens can be obtained. On the calibration plate, there are many circles used as the calibration patterns. Each circle projected in the image plane will be "symmetrically" blurred if the circle is out of focus. This defocusing problem can be avoid by measuring the centroids of the circles in the image as the image coordinates of the calibration data.

To remedy the problem of varying field of view and spatial resolution during the adjustment of the zoom and focus, circles of two different sizes were used. When the zoom of the lens is set to be wide-angle, many larger circles as well as the smaller circles in the middle of the calibration plate appear in the image, as shown in Figure 1(b). These larger circles can provide more accurate centroid positions estimated in the image. When the zoom of the lens, on the other hand, is set to be telephoto, only a few smaller circles in the middle of the calibration plate appear in the image, as shown in Figure 1(c). These smaller circles still can provide accurate centroid positions due to larger magnification.

Image coordinates of the calibration data, i.e., the center of the circles, can be estimated by using simple image processing techniques. Considering the varying field of view, the calibration plate may partially appear in the image. We need to identify the circles appearing in the image in order to obtain their corresponding 3-D world coordinates. For easy identification, the larger circle in the middle surrounding by twenty-four smaller circles is chosen to be the fiducial circle. The origin of the world coordinate system is set to the center of the fiducial circle. The 3-D coordinates of the other circles are measured in advance according to this origin. If the lens is properly aligned such that the fiducial circle always appear in the image for all the zoom settings, it will be easy to locate the fiducial circle by utilizing the sizes of the circles. Each circle appearing in the image can then be identified and its 3-D world coordinates can be obtained.

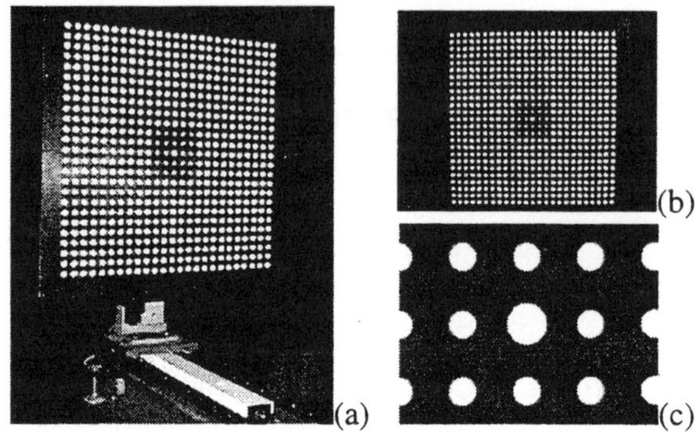

Figure 1. (a) The calibration object we used and its images acquired with (b) wide-angle and (c) telephoto zoom settings.

In our work, there are three thousand steps for both the zoom and focus motors and totally nine million lens settings in combination. To reduce the frequency of camera calibration performed and the storage required to store the ICPs, sampling and interpolation over the range of the lens settings should be used. Therefore, our goal is to create a two-dimensional table indexed by the values of the lens settings to store the ICPs estimated at the sampled lens settings. The ICPs of the other lens settings where the actual camera calibration is not performed can be approximated via bilinear interpolation between the four neighboring lens settings in the table.

Since the ICPs vary nonlinearly with respect to the lens setting, an uniformly sampled table might not represent their relationship very well. A better sampling policy is the "calibration on demand" that allows adaptive sampling positions and variable sampling rate. Therefore, the table will be adaptively created by trial and error to store the ICPs estimated at sampled lens settings. Our decision criterion is based on the residual error, which is the difference between the predicted and measured image coordinates of the calibration data.

Figure 2 gives an example of how we determine the sampled positions. At first, we adjust the aperture stop for suitable lighting condition and then fix the aperture stop.

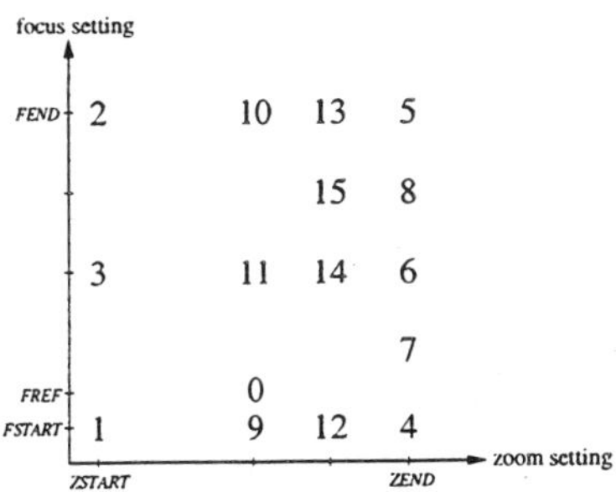

Figure 2. An example of sampled positions.

Then, we set the zoom setting to be the middle of its range, $[ZSTART, ZEND]$. Next, the calibration plate is moved to the middle of its range and the focus setting is adjusted in its range, $[FSTART, FEND]$, until the image of the calibration plate is sharpest. This focus setting is referred to as $FREF$. Camera calibration is then performed (step 0 shown in Figure 2) to obtain all the CPs. During the following zoom lens calibration procedure, the CPs, s_u, s_v, α, β, γ, t_x, t_y, and t_z are fixed and the remaining ICPs, u_0, v_0, f, κ, Δt_z, are calibrated.

For each zoom setting to be calibrated, camera calibration is first performed at the start and end of the focus setting, for example, steps 1 and 2 shown in Figure 2. The obtained ICPs and residual errors are stored in the table. Then the focus setting is set to the middle of its range. The ICPs and the residual error, $perror$, at this focus setting can be interpolated by using the ICPs and residual errors previously obtained at the start and end of the focus setting. Next, the images of the calibration plate are acquired and the 2-D image coordinates of the calibration data are estimated. Then, we compute the residual error, $ferror$, between the estimated image coordinates and the predicted positions calculated from the interpolated ICPs. Large $ferror$ means the interpolated ICPs are not accurate and the camera calibration has to be performed (step 3 shown in Figure 2). This procedure is recursively repeated for each middle focus setting between two calibrated focus settings (for example, steps 4 to 8 in Figure 2) until the interpolated ICPs are accurate, i.e., $ferror$ is small enough. Because the residual errors of camera calibration are not the same for all lens settings, the decision that $ferror$ is small enough or not is adaptively determined by the criterion: $ferror < (1 + FRATIO) * perror$.

We can adaptively calibrate for the zoom setting in the same way as for the focus setting. The start and end of the zoom setting are first calibrated by using the previously mentioned procedure, which is illustrated by the steps of the first and the last columns shown in Figure 2. Then, the zoom setting is set to be the middle of its range and the focus setting is set to $FREF$. Next, the images of the calibration plate are acquired and the 2-D image coordinates of the calibration data are estimated. Then, we calculate the residual error, $zerror$, between the estimated image coordinates and the predicted positions calculated by using the interpolated ICPs among the first and last columns in the table. If $zerror$ is small, i.e., $zerror < (1 + ZRATIO) * perror$, the interpolated ICPs is accurate. Otherwise, camera calibration has to be performed to obtain accurate ICPs (the middle column shown in Figure 2). Again, this procedure is repeated recursively for each middle zoom setting between two calibrated zoom settings until the interpolated ICPs are accurate, i.e., $zerror$ is small enough.

Two parameters, $FRATIO$ and $ZRATIO$, determine the sampling rate and the sampling positions of the constructed table. They control the maximum difference of the residual errors between the ICPs calculated via actual camera calibration and bilinear interpolation.

Figure 3. Our motorized zoom lens.

4. Experimental Results

In this work, we constructed a motorized zoom lens by using a Fujinon TV zoom lens H6 $\times$ 12.5R, as shown in Figure 3. Three servo motors were used for driving the aperture, zoom, and focus of the lens through pushrod links. We adopted servo motor because of its faster response, despite of the disadvantage of poor repeatability due to the large dead zone.

To avoid the hysteresis problem [6] due to the backlash, we set the motor to the desired setting in always the same direction. That is, the motor is first set to the setting a little before the desired one and then set to the desired setting.

The aperture experiment was conducted to explore the relationship between the aperture setting and the CPs. The zoom setting was set to the middle of its range and the focus was adjusted to obtain the sharpest image of the calibration plate. Then, we estimated the CPs at a specific aperture setting (1500). For other six aperture settings, images of the calibration plate were taken and the image coordinates of the calibration data was measured. The image coordinates can be predicted by using the previously estimated CPs and the residual error from the measured image coordinates was found relatively small, as depicted in Figure 4. The average

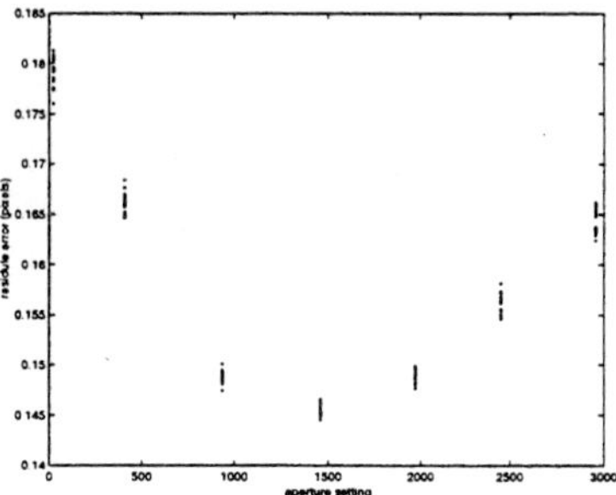

Figure 4. Residual for aperture settings.

amount of the increased residual error is 0.0125 pixels. We conclude that the influence of the aperture setting on the CPs is negligible and the aperture setting were then fixed during the proposed calibration procedure.

In another experiment, we performed the proposed zoom lens calibration method for our motorized zoom lens. The parameters $FRATIO$ and $ZRATIO$ were set to 0.5 and 1, respectively. A table with 120 entries was created and the stored ICPs are depicted in Figure 5, where t_{z0} is the value of the fixed CP t_z obtained in the initial camera calibration. The mean residual error in the table is 0.19 pixels. To evaluate the repeatability of the motorized zoom lens, the sampled lens settings in the table were set again and the images of the calibration palate were taken. We then calculated the residual errors between the measured image coordinates in these images and the predicted positions by using the fixed CPs and the ICPs provided by the table. Mean residual error in this repeatability experiment is 0.44 pixels. Also, four hundred trials of residual error evaluation with random lens settings were performed and the mean residual error obtained is 0.475 pixels, which is only 8% increase of the repeatability error.

Another experiment was conducted with different values of the parameters $FRATIO$ and $ZRATIO$, which were set to 1 and 2 respectively. Since the amount of increasing residual error allowed was larger, a table with smaller size (52 entries) was created at the expense of higher interpolation error, which was 0.54 pixels (22.7% increase) in this experiment.

5. Conclusions

In this paper, we have proposed a motorized zoom lens calibration procedure for determining the relationship between the lens settings and the camera parameters. The major advantage of the proposed method is to reduce, in an adaptive manner, the amount of image acquisition and camera calibration, which is a time-consuming task, while maintaining the required calibration accuracy. In our experiments, the average residual error of the camera parameters given by the table (with only 120 entries) is less than half pixel. Another contribution of this work is the proposed calibration object suitable for zoom lens calibration.

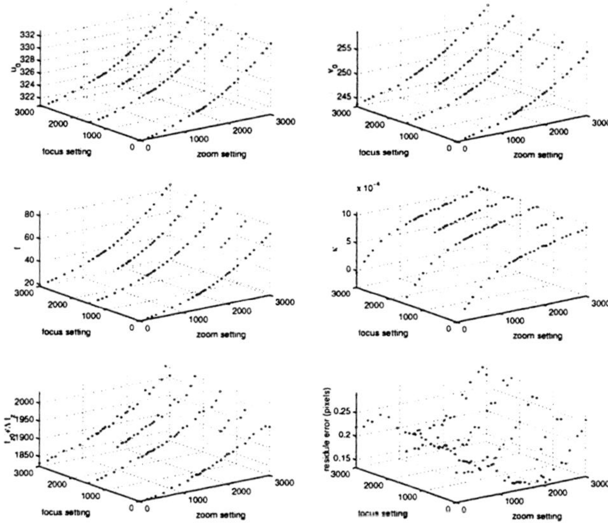

Figure 5. The ICPs stored in the table.

Acknowledgments

Dr. Shih would like to thank Academia Sinica for the support of his summer visit. This work was also supported in part by the National Science Council of Taiwan, under Grants NSC 88-2213-E-001-010. The authors would like to thank the reviewers for their helpful comments.

References

[1] J. A. Fayman, O. Sudarsky, and E. Rivlin. Zoom tracking. In *Proceedings of International Conference on Robotics and Automation*, pages 2783–2788, Leuven, Belgium, May 1998.

[2] J.-M. Lavest, G. Rives, and M. Dhome. Three-dimensional reconstruction by zooming. *IEEE Transactions on Robotics and Automation*, 9(2):196–207, 1993.

[3] S.-W. Shih, Y.-P. Hung, and W.-S. Lin. Calibration of an active binocular head. *IEEE Transactions on Systems, Man, and Cybernetics*, 28(4):426–442, 1998.

[4] K. Tarabanis, R. Y. Tsai, and D. S. Goodman. Calibration of a computer controlled robotic vision sensor with a zoom lens. *CVGIP: Image Understanding*, 59(2):226–241, 1994.

[5] J. Weng, P. Cohen, and M. Herniou. Camera calibration with distortion models and accuracy evaluation. *IEEE Transactions on Pattern Analysis and Machine Intelligence*, 14(10):965–980, 1992.

[6] R. G. Willson. *Modeling and Calibration of Automated Zoom Lenses*. PhD thesis, Carnegie Mellon University, Pittsburgh, Pennsylvania, Jan. 1994.

Mirror-Based Trinocular Systems in Robot-Vision

Brian Kirstein Ramsgaard, Ivar Balslev, and Jens Arnspang

Maersk Mc-Kinney Möller Institute for Production Technology,
SDU - Odense University, Campusvej 55, DK 5230 Odense M, Denmark

Abstract

A new variant of multi ocular stereo vision has been developed. The system involves a single camera and two orthogonal planar mirrors. The resulting device is a low-cost, compact sensor, particularly suitable for depth determination in robot vision applications. The motivation for the work is the need for a sensor determining spatial coordinates of a robot's tool and the object to be processed. The system inherently posses fewer calibration parameters and provides a higher accuracy in the depth determination than traditional two-camera stereo systems. A prototype of the new device has been built, and test results are presented.

ICPR Topics: Applications, Robotics and Architecture (automation and robotics, smart sensors, range imaging), Computer Vision and Image Analysis (early vision, scene understanding).

1 Introduction

In automated production in partially structured environments there is a great need for touch free sensors determining spatial coordinates. In this field the sensors used are often computer vision systems. Overviews of general computer vision techniques, suitable for implementation in a robot task context are given in Refs. [1-3], describing the major techniques such as depth from stereo, depth and structure from motion, depth from structured light and various other range finding techniques. In the present paper we develop further the stereo-related techniques. The classic version of machine stereo vision requires two cameras and includes: a) Calibration of two sets of internal and external camera parameters; b) Establishing epipolar lines; c) Finding and matching candidates along these lines; d) Estimating scene depth from the established correspondences. In order to make step c) easier and enhance the results of d), it has been suggested to use more cameras, see for example [4-6]. This however adds complication to step a), yielding both more internal and external sets of camera parameters to be determined in the calibration. A simple and fruitful alternative is to use mirrors to produce virtual cameras, as for example suggested in [7-9]. Then step a) will be concerned with calibration of only one set of internal camera parameters, extended with a few mirror parameters. Furthermore some mirror techniques allow for easier matching procedures, due to the over-determined situation [7]. In the present work two planar mirrors are placed perpendicular to each and aligned so that their intersection is parallel to the optical axis of the camera. As will be discussed later, this arrangement has two fundamental advantages in the above step c). First, the presence of more than one pair of corresponding points gives a safer identification of these points. Secondly, the problem in conventional systems in case of lines, edges or contours parallel to the base line is absent.

In the present work we are particularly interested in computer vision systems to be used after the robot tool is already close to the objects to be processed, but where the further guiding of the robot requires precise data on the relevant spatial coordinates. For human size robots, the desired range of a 3D-sensor is of the order 100-200 mm. In the development of a prototype, the following additional requirements have been in our focus: 1) low cost, 2) compact structure allowing the sensor to be mounted on the robot arm carrying the tool as well, and 3) real-time capability of the image analysis and interpretation.

Fig. 1 shows the system considered. Two rectangular mirrors are perpendicular to each other, and their intersection line L0 is parallel to the camera axis. An object can be imaged in the camera via zero, one, or two mirror reflections. The resulting camera image is shown in Fig. 2. The far edges of the mirrors are imaged as lines, assumed to be parallel to the image edges. The image formed without reflection falls in the first 'quadrant'. Images formed via one reflection fall in the second and fourth quadrant. The latter images can

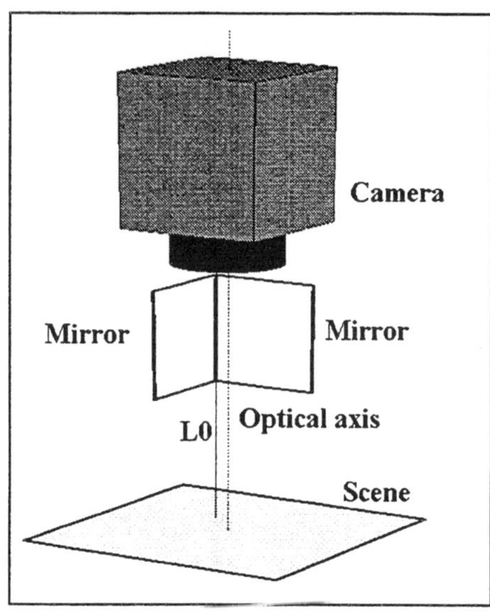

Figure 1. - Overview of the system

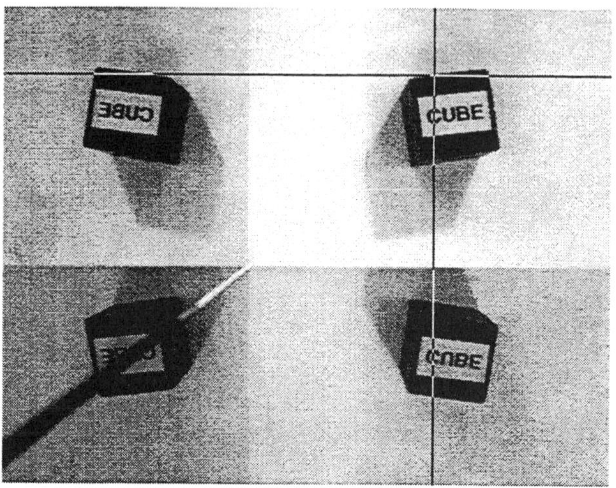

Figure 2. - Camera image of the device viewing a one-inch cube on a white background. Upper right is the direct view, upper left and lower right are images formed via one reflection. The enhanced lines drawn through an edge point in the direct image are epipolar lines discussed in Sect. 2. The intensity along these lines is shown in Fig. 3.

be considered as taken by two virtual cameras. In the present paper we shall not consider the imaging via two reflections (falling in the third 'quadrant') since the quality of this image depends critically on a perfect alignment. The two virtual and the real camera is equivalent to a trinocular arrangement. This system can also be considered as two binocular systems, each composed of a virtual and a real camera.

We shall discuss the following properties of the system: Aspects of the search for corresponding points (Sect. 2), the effective viewing volume in which an object is imaged by all three cameras (Sect. 3), and the accuracy of the depth estimation (Sect. 4)

2 The search for corresponding points

There are epipolar lines for each of the two camera pairs. In an ideal alignment these two classes of epipolar lines are mutually orthogonal and parallel with the image edges. Fig. 3 shows the gray tone intensity along two epipolar lines through a particular edge point in the primary image. Dots indicate corresponding points. Note that for the chosen edge direction, the vertical epipolar line gives a much better determination of corresponding points than the horizontal one. In fact, the singularity encountered in binocular stereo vision in case of edges and contours along the epipolar lines is absent in the present device. In general, both matching results are well defined, and in this case they provide a valuable crosscheck. In a non-ideal alignment the epipolar lines must be derived from camera-matrices, obtained by independent calibration af all three cameras.

3 The viewing volume

Consider first the imaging involving one of the mirrors. Fig. 4 shows important rays in a plane through the camera pin hole, perpendicular to one of the active mirrors. The system parameters of a particular camera pair are 1) the relevant viewing angle α of the camera, 2) the pinhole to mirror edge distance d, and 3) the distance b between the camera axis and the relevant mirror. Thus $2b$ is the base line of the camera pair. Fig. 4 shows the projection of the planes limiting the viewing volume. The angle between these planes is given by

$$\tfrac{1}{2}\alpha - \beta, \qquad \text{where } \beta = \arctan(\frac{b}{d}) \qquad (1)$$

Considering both camera pairs, the viewing volume is a pyramid with top angles $\frac{1}{2}\alpha_h - \beta_h$ and $\frac{1}{2}\alpha_v - \beta_v$ between opposite faces. Subscripts h and v on the parameters α, β, and b refer to the horizontal and vertical camera pair, respectively.

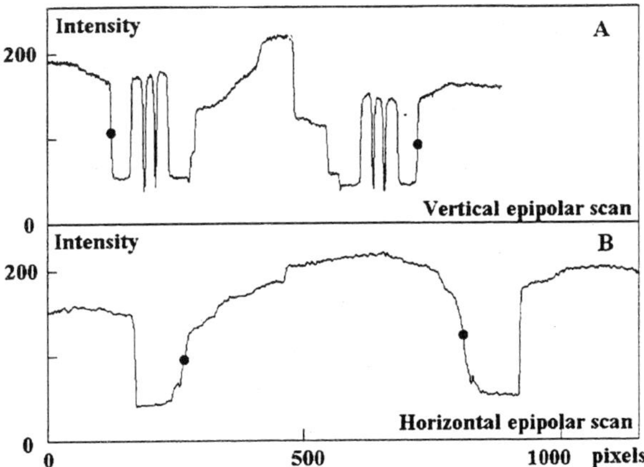

Figure 3. - Vertical (A) and horizontal (B) scans along epipolar lines through an edge point in the direct image (see Fig. 2). Dots indicate corresponding points.

Note that the trinocular viewing pyramid is rather narrow. The angles in the viewing pyramid can be enhanced by using wide-angle optics, large mirrors and small values of b_h and b_v. However, as discussed below a reduction of the base lines $2b_h$ and $2b_v$ is harmful for the precision of the depth estimation. Using standard optics, typical values of the parameters are:

$$\alpha_h = 40^o, \; b_h = 10 \text{ mm}, \; d = 100 \text{ mm}$$

This gives a horizontal top angle of the trinocular viewing pyramid of 14°. The vertical top angle becomes somewhat less according to the aspect ratio of the CCD plate.

4 The accuracy of the depth estimation

Let Z be the depth coordinate of an object (see Fig. 4). This can be determined if all three cameras are fully calibrated. However, in the present analysis, we shall use the relation [2]:

$$Z - Z_o = b_h f/(x - x_o) \quad (2)$$

where f is the focal length, Z_o is the Z coordinate of the pin hole (Z_o is zero in Fig. 4), x is the horizontal position of the midpoint between the relevant corresponding image points, and x_o is the x value for objects with $Z = \infty$. Consequently the uncertainty ΔZ of Z is given by

$$\Delta Z = -(Z - Z_o)^2 \Delta x/(b_h f) \quad (3)$$

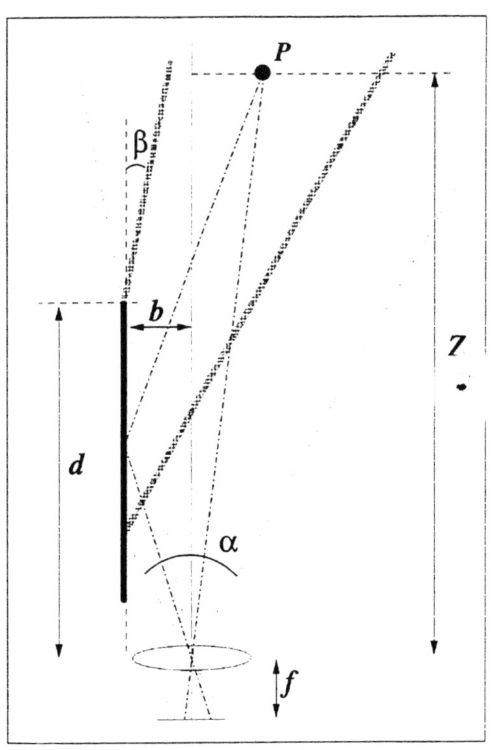

Figure 4. - Construction rays in a plane through the camera pin hole, perpendicular to one of the active mirrors. The vertical condensed line is the active mirror, and the thick gray lines show the viewing area. P is an object point. The quantities d, b, f, Z, α, and β are discussed in the text.

where Δx is the uncertainty determining the horizontal position x of the midpoint between corresponding points. Assuming a CCD camera producing images with a horizontal dimension of 1000 pixels, the sensitivity parameter $|\Delta Z/\Delta x|$ attains values shown in the following table.

Optics	Standard	Wide angle
α_h	40°	55°
d	100 mm	100 mm
b_h	10 mm	20 mm
$\frac{1}{2}\alpha_h - \beta_h$	14°	16°
$\|\Delta Z/\Delta x\| \, (Z = d)$	0.7 mm/pixel	0.5 mm/pixel
$\|\Delta Z/\Delta x\| \, (Z = 2d)$	2.8 mm/pixel	2.1 mm/pixel

These results emphasize that the depth estimation is effective on short ranges only.

In a setup using standard optics and $d = 100$ mm, we determined $(b_h f)$, Z_o, and x_o of Eq. (2) by calibration measuring a point object at three known depth values in the range 1 - 3 d. Subsequent determination of the depth of a cube surface (see Fig. 2) with $Z - Z_o \approx 2d$ yielded an uncertainty in agreement with the above table. It is important to note that digital removal of radial distortion is necessay for achieving the calculated depth uncertainties.

5 Conclusion

A new variant of mirror-based multi ocular vision systems has been proposed and illustrated by simple tests. At close range the technique offers significant benefits, compared to traditional binocular stereo systems. A bench mark test involving detailed exploration of the depth accuracy and efficient ways of calibration in a specified production domain, would be a natural choice for further application oriented research.

Acknowledgements

The authors are indebted to René Dencker Eriksen, John Immerkær and Henning Hørslev Hansen for fruitful discussions. The project has been supported by the A. P. Møller and Chastine Mc-Kinney Møller Foundation.

References

[1] D. H. Ballard and C. M. Brown, *Computer Vision*, Prentice Hall, 1982.

[2] B. K. P. Horn, *Robot Vision*, MIT Press, 1986.

[3] M. Sonka, V. Havel, R. Boyle, *Image Processing, Analysis and Machine Vision*, Brooks/Cole Publishing Company, 1999.

[4] T. Kanade, *Development of a Video-Rate Stereo Machine.* In Proceedings of the 94th ARPA Image Understanding Workshop, 1984, Monterey, California, pp. 549-558.

[5] J. Arnspang, *Local Differential Kinematics of Multi Ocular Surface Vision,* Ph.D. dissertation, University of Copenhagen, DIKU Tech. Report 88/1-3, 88/6, 1988.

[6] S. B. Kang, J. A. Webb, C. L. Zitnick, T. Kanade, *An Active Multibaseline Stereo System with Real-Time Acquisition*, Carnegie-Mellon University Tech. Report CMU-CS-94-167, 1997.

[7] S. K. Nayar, *Determining Depth, using Two Specular Spheres and a Single Camera.* Cambridge Symposium on Advances in Intelligent Robotics Systems, 1988.

[8] J. Arnspang et. al., *Using Mirror Cameras for Estimating Depth.* CAIP 95, Prague, 1995.

[9] B. Barnes (ed.), *Alternative Camera Technology,* The ALCATECH Workshop at Ruzengaard, Denmark, July 1996. Official Report at ONR, Washington, DC.

Remote Robot Execution through WWW Simulation

S.T. Puente, F. Torres, F. Ortiz, F.A. Candelas
Automatics and Computer Vision Group (http://www.disc.ua.es/gava)
Dept. of Physics, Systems Engineering and Signal Theory.
University of Alicante (Spain)
spuente@disc.ua.es

Abstract

Nowadays, every industry's goal is to improve their manufacturing processes and to increase their cadence of production, in order to be competitive. This goal usually implies a higher automation level (i.e. an increase on the number of robots used in the production chain) and also a more efficient use of the existing robots.

This paper shows the state of art on teleoperation and simulation systems and proposes some possible network architectures devoted to the development of such systems. A method for the optimization of robot tasks is also suggested. The application proposed can teleoperate a robot arm with five degrees of freedom through Internet by using a previous simulation system and visual feedback. This simulation can be accessed simultaneously by different workers. As a result, the number of robots required can be reduced on new applications or dangerous environments.

1. Introduction

Nowadays several virtual systems exist in Internet that allow to manage or to learn disciplines like robotics, artificial vision, etc [1][2][3]. Most of these systems permit the use of physical system without a previous simulation, what makes the workers to be proceeded sequentially, lacking of an important factor at time of being used for a group.

This publication presents a system for the use of a robot arm that permits its concurrent utilization without causing problems to the system.

In the next point a state of art in simulation and teleoperation systems are presented. The possible system architectures are shown in the thirtd point. The proposed system is described in the fourth section. The conclusions are exposed in the fifth point.

2. State of art

There are many ways to achieve environments that emulate the reality. The most traditional method is to reproduce physically, at different or equal scale, the original system; other way is through the use of a visual feedback, the original system is recorded [4][5][6] and this feedback reproduces the system for us. Currently the most interesting way of doing it is through virtual environments, generated by computer simulations. [7][8]

Virtual environments are used to get real system simulations, reducing costs on test measurements as well as providing a better a way to learn for the worker.

These environments also permit the immersion of the worker in the simulation, through stereoscopic glasses.

The use of robots in dangerous places for people, radioactive materials handling, explosives detonation, as well as to carry out various types of tasks in the space, submarine exploration, microassembly, mining,... [9] are different advantages of robots versus humans. Initially the telemanipulator is used for these tasks; it permits to carry out the orders of the worker by a set of simple controls without the physical necessity of having a direct control.

In the master/slave systems, a robot arm (master) of equal form, although it can have different size, is manipulated by the worker by reproducing the movements of this in the remote robot (slave). [10][11][12]

A new system could be gotten by mixing simulated environments and teleoperated systems where the user has a real simulation system which is reproduced by the real one. [3]

This last type of systems could offer in addition to simulation a feedback to the worker through images. [3][7]

Remark that in teleoperated systems through virtual environments this could be remote control. The physical presence of the worker near the system is not necessary as telemanipulators or traditional master/slave systems. System operation could be remote control through Internet by using VRML and Java. The first one allows to simulate virtual systems easily and Java language lets the worker to interact with the environment and the real system at same time. [8][13][14][15][16][17]

3. General architecture

Teleoperation systems using simulation permits diverse architectures in their design.

The first option consists of carrying out the simulation and the teleoperation, on the same computer, the worker computer, so the computer where is executed the simulation is the same that is connected to the robot controller in order to send orders to it. In this system the worker must be close to the controller; the maximum distance to connect the computer to the controller, usually by a serial port, what implies a maximum distance of 15m according to the RS232 norm.

Another way consists of setting the simulation and teleoperation systems separated. The simulation takes part into the worker computer. This system permits the worker be further than the previous one because it can be interconnected by a local network.

A last possibility could be to have the systems completely separated. The worker works from a computer and in other one the calculus of simulation is made. A third computer is connected with the robot controller in order to send it orders. This system, as the previous one, let the worker works at greater distance thanks to the computers distribution in a local network but also has the advantage of doing a distribution task saving resources due to each computer makes a specific task, optimizing the response time of the system.

3.1. Internet architecture

Architectures proposed previously could be implemented in Internet, although one must keep in mind certain restrictions as the limited bandwidth of the connection, the safety using the robot, etc. [17]

The most standardized way of connecting the system to Internet would be through a HTML page. This possibility is restricted due to the limitations of this language, so the architectures based on Java are proposed by creating an applet that allows to manage the system where Java3D, VRML could be use to carry out the simulation. [3][8]

An option to carry out the simulation is to use the web server as the same computer connected to the robot controller, with will operate all the necessary calculations. [1]

Another possibility is to carry out the calculations from a different computer.

For teleoperation the computer that is connected to the robot controller could be connected to the web server through a local network. So the worker could carry out all operations through the web server, and as a result the robot remains protected from a direct access. Also the bandwidth required for this is minimum because one must only transmit the teleoperation orders. [7]

4. Application purpose

The description of the application is shown in two parts, a general structure and an operation mode.

The system is based on the last architecture described in 3.1. The teleoperation is separated from the system and the simulation is performed into the worker computer.

The system is operational at http://www.disclab.ua.es/gava/proyectos/teleoperacion/tele.html

4.1. General structure

The architecture of the system is based on a client/server structure through Internet (fig. 1), following the layout of the previous section. VRML has been use for the simulation. [7][8][17]

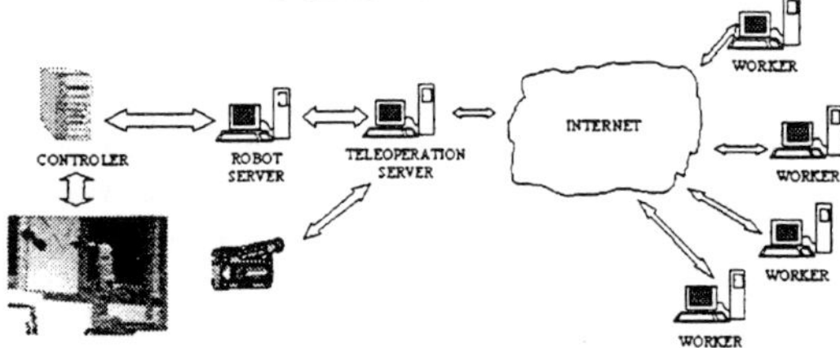

Figure 1. System architecture

The robot that has been applied to the system is the SCORBOT ER-IX of ESHED ROBOTEC with five degrees of freedom.

Its controller is the CONTROLER B of ESHED ROBOTEC, that allows to manage until twelve motors.

The robot controller is communicated by a serial port RS-232 to the robot server.

To the general architecture proposed a camera CDC SONY XC-75CE of ½ inch with an objective CANON TV LENS JF7.5mm 1:1.4 has been added. The camera is connected to the web server to transmit a video to the worker applet.

4.2. Operation mode

The operation scheme is based on a web page, with an applet in Java [14][15] where one or more workers could be connect to the simulation. This allows the workers to carry out various simulation movements of the robot arm as well as example exercises to learn the basic use of it, all of them through simulation.

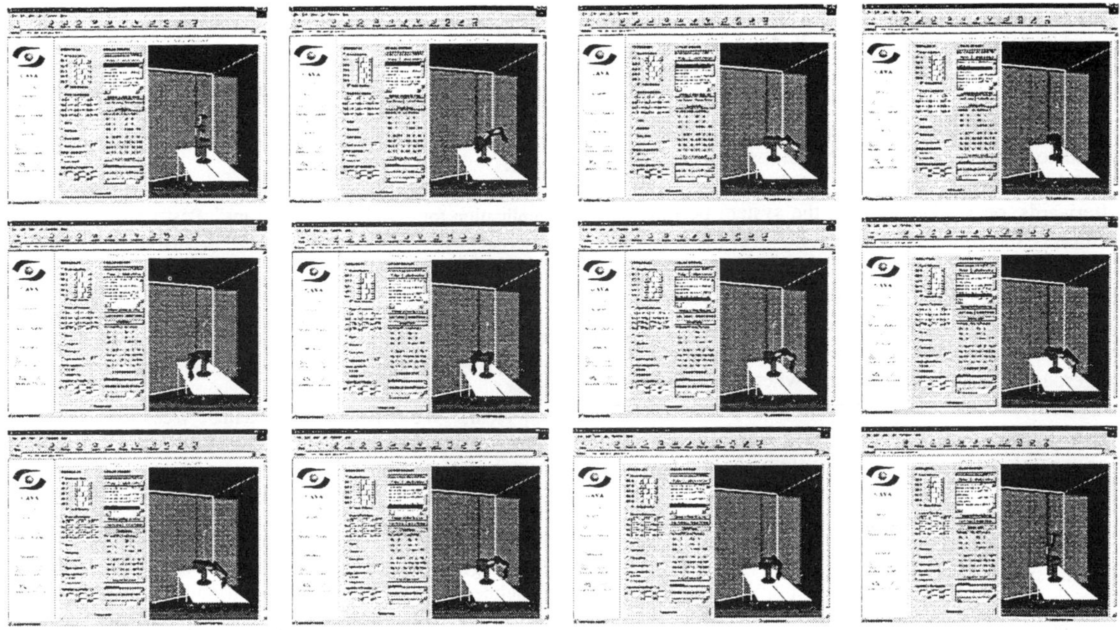

Figure 2. System simulation

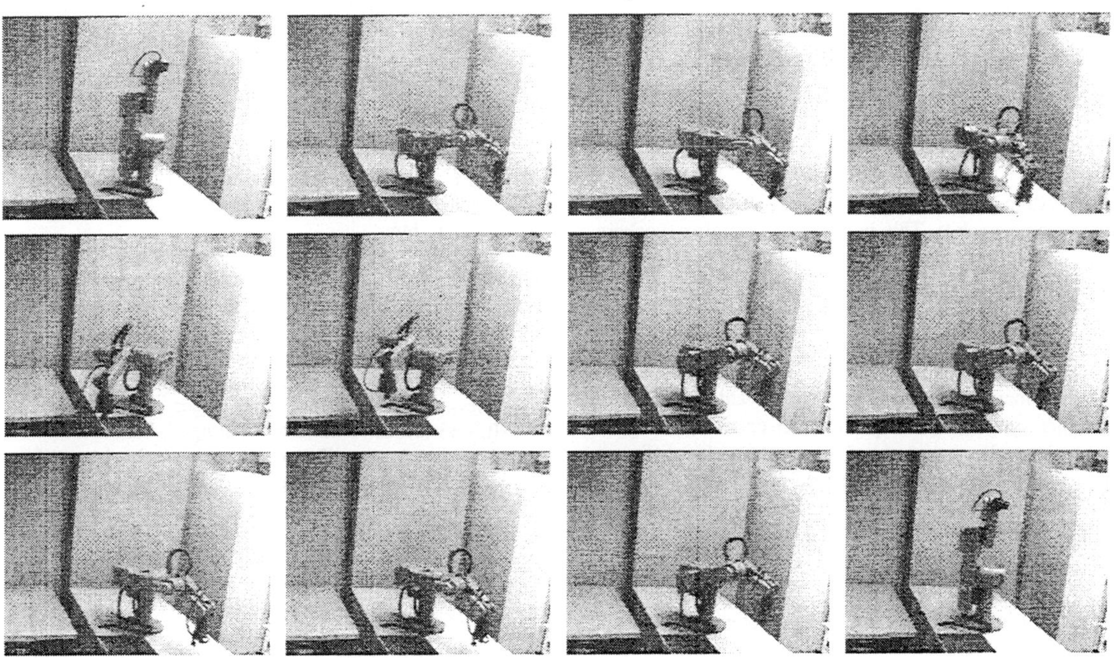

Figure 3. Video of real execution

This is visualized in VRML [13][14][16], together with applet that gives the worker all the possibilities of simulation and visualization from different perspectives (fig.2).

Due to the system multiples workers design are permitted to simulate concurrently getting the maximum profit of the available resources.

Afterwards, on worker request, the system permits the realization of the simulated movements over the real arm; for this purpose the robot server is designed (fig. 1). The worker must authorized to do it. Parallel the worker could simulate another movements in order to carry out a different task, as it would occur in disassembly systems or in dangerous substance management where the task are or in dangerous substance management where the task are always different.

The requests for using the real system are managed by a FIFO queue.

The server will indicate to the worker the time left to do the request operations on the real arm according to the state of the system.

The execution access is administrated through requests in the teleoperation server. Also the server keeps a full report about all the accesses of each worker and what they have done.

When the worker is allowed to carry out the execution over the robot, the server notifies to the camera that will produce an AVI video of the arm movements, and will transmit it to the applet so that the worker could see the results (fig. 3). [4][5][6]

5. Conclusions

This system permits an easy way of learning the basic movements of a robot. This is useful for training workers in managing industrial robots, in the redesign of industrial applications, etc.

Besides carrying out a simulation, it permits the use of a real robot to see the results, what implies a consequent added learning.

On the other hand it has the great advantage of being an Internet system, which permits an easier and bigger diffusion as well as the use of a robot arm for different workers, that involves a greater profit in the expenditure done.

Others advantages of the system are: it shows a distributed philosophy. The simulation could operate independently of the execution of the robot arm. This could be useful, for instance, in non-predetermined tasks.

6. References

[1] J.M. Sebastián, D. García, D. Santos, P. Campoy, "Proyecto Titere. Realización de Prácticas de Laboratorio en Puestos de Trabajo Remotos mediante la Transmisión de Imágenes por Red Telefónica Conmutada" XIX Jornadas de Automática, 1998, pp 21-26.

[2] Ambientes virtuales en Internet: una propuesta orientada a teleoperación. http://www.mox.uniandes.edu.co/proyectos.html

[3] Teleoperation projects and virtual environments http://www.mox.uniandes.edu.co/proyectos/1998/ambientes_virtuales

[4] Heiner Wolf, Konrad Froitzheim, "Inline Video – A new application for Standard Mechanisms", Poster proc. of the Third International World-Wide Web Conference, Darmstadt, April'95

[5] Klaus H. Wolf, Konrad Froitzheim, Michnel Weber, "Interactive Video and Remote Control via the World Wide Web", Lecture Notes in Computer Science 1045, Interactive Distributed Multimedia Systems and Services, Berlin, March 1996

[6] Heiner Wolf, Konrad Frotzheim, "WebVideo a Tool for WWW-based Teleoperation", Proc. IEEE ISIE'97, Grimaraes, July 7, 1997.

[7] F. Torres, S.T. Puente, I. Damas, C. Puerto, F.A. Candelas. "ASTRO: Aprendizaje mediante Simulación y Teleoperación de Robots". Proc. XX Jornadas de Automática. 1999. pp. 209-213

[8] Holger Bönisch, Stefan Fiedler, Konrad Froitzheim, Peter Schulthess, "A VRML-based Visualization of User-Vicinities in the WWW", Proc. of the ATMSA 6th International Conference on Telecommunications, Nashville, Mar. 1998.

[9] Some background on teleoperation and haptic interfaces. http://www.ee.ebc.ca/home/staff/faculty/tims/etc/www/bg_tel.html

[10] Antonio Burriertos, Luis Felipe Peñín, Carlos Balaguer, Rafael Aracil, Fundamentos de Robótica, Mc Graw Hill. 1997. pp.8-130.

[11] K.S. Fu, R.C. Gonzalez, C.S.G. Lee. Robótica Control, Detección, Visión e Inteligencia. Mc Graw Hill. 1988. pp. 1-84.

[12] J.M. Azorín, R. Saltaren, J.M. Sabater, R. Puerto, "Simulador de un Sistema de control Maestro-esclavo de N GDL", proc. XX Jornadas de Automática. 1999. pp. 505-508

[13] Standard specification of VRML. http://www.vrml.org/fs_specifications.htm

[14] EAI (External Authoring Interface). API to connect Java and VRML. http://www.web3d.org/WorkingGroups/vrml-eai/.

[15] Java 1.2. API User's Guide. Sun's Microsystems, Inc. http://www.javasoft.com.

[16] Bibliography reference for VRML. http://www.sgi.com.

[17] Holger Bönish, Stefan Fiedler, Konrad Froitzheim, Peter Schulthess, "Visualizing the User Space of the WWW with VRML", Virtual Environments 98, Stutgart, Jun 1998.

[18] Issues in Internet Telerobotics. http://telerobot.mech.uwa.edu.au/ROBOT/anupaper.htm

Robot-arm Pick and Place Behavior Programming System Using Visual Perception*

Antonio J. Sánchez and José M. Martínez
Universidad Politénica de Valencia (P.O. Box 22012, E-46071 Valencia, Spain)
asanchez@isa.upv.es ; jomarsa@master.ivia.es

Abstract

The main goal of this paper is to present a programming robot-arm system for carrying out flexible pick and place behavior using visual perception. Object manipulation from visual data involves determining the pose of the object with respect to the manipulator. Taking into account visual positioning is an ill-posed problem due to the perspective projection, this system uses a camera and a sensor distance, and both of them mounted on a robot-arm tool adapter, for locating (positioning and orienting) objects.

On the other hand, this programming system is modular, composed by different dynamic link libraries to be independent with the hardware and offers a friendly graphic interface, where the user can define pick and place object locations on the image space.

1. Introduction

Nowadays, robots are merely powerful manipulators, rapid and precise. Blind and deaf, generally enclosed in solid cages, they live in extraordinarily ordered worlds where imagination is often synonymous with breakdown, and sometimes with accident.

There are a lot of industrial applications that require the use of robot-arms in order to move objects (pick and place behavior). In these applications, robot-arms have to be programmed in a well-known environment, to avoid possible collisions between tools and objects.

In previous work, a programming robot tool with graphical CAD systems has been implemented [4] within the research line in robot programming in the Robotic Systems and Robot Programming Laboratory of the Department of System Engineering (DISA) in the Polytechnics University of Valencia (UPV).

Recently however, new mutations have appeared with eyes, ears, etc. To give robots more autonomy, and to permit them to act efficiently in our diverse, cluttered, and changing environment, they must be equipped with powerful tools for perception and intelligence [1].

Now, a programming robot-arm system for carrying out flexible "pick and place" behavior using visual perception has been developed. This system uses certain visual techniques for locating objects. After, the camera is calibrated [5], the user can define pick and place object locations, and finally, the robot-arm runs the pick and place behavior defined on the image space.

2. Hardware description

The Robotics Systems Laboratory has a flexible manufacturing system with two ABB industrial robots programmed in ARLA language, a conveyor and different auxiliary devices for research and training purposes.

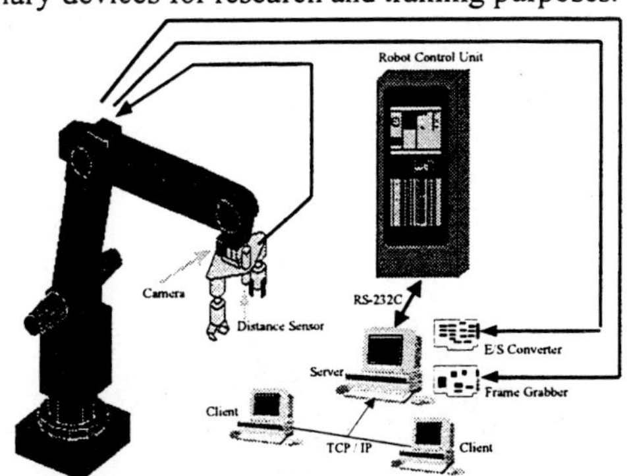

Figure 2.1. Hardware description.

The experimental hardware used in this work (Fig. 2.1) is composed by local computer network system, robot-arm system, vision system and distance sensor system.

The computer system consists of a local network (Ethernet) of PCs. The robot server PC is the central unit, who receives information from the sensors and sends the pick and place program to the robot-arm control unit. The rest of PCs can communicate with the robot server PC via TCP/IP. This client/server application offers a tele-

* This work has been sponsored by FEDER TAP Spanish programme, project n°1FD97-2158-C04-03.

programming robot-arm system, which could be used on the network.

The robot-arm adopted for the experimental purposes is a 5 DOF ABB industrial robot (IRB-L6) equipped with a special tool adapter designed and implemented in the Laboratory (Fig. 2.2).

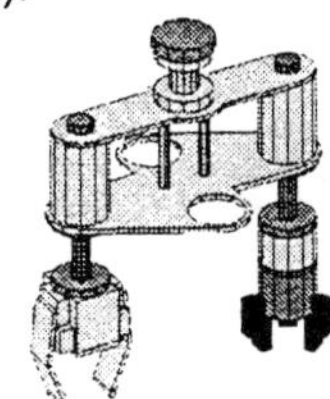

Figure 2.2. Tool adapter.

This tool adapter has two hands to manipulate objects and two holes to transports the sensors (distance and vision) to perceive the robot environment.

The communication between the robot server computer and robot-arm control unit is via RS-232C, using a library named "ComTools" which offers functions to read the robot tool center point (TCP0) pose or move the TCP0 to a desired pose.

Position with respect to the robot base coordinate system and orientation (in quaternions) with respect to the coordinate system linked to the first robot element (S1) define a pose. So, it is necessary to include an orientation change due to the first joint to get ${}^{base}T_{TCP0}$ from the values returned by the robot control unit and apply the inverse transformation to move the robot to a desired pose knowing ${}^{base}T_{TCP0}$. The application uses RPY orientation notation, so the orientation must be converted to quaternions.

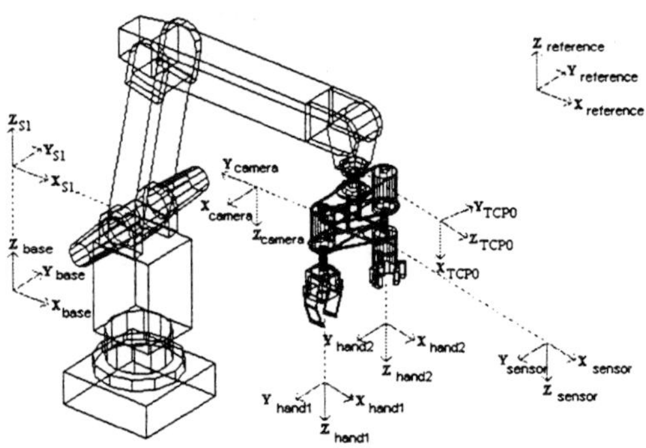

Figure 2.3. Robot-arm coordinate systems.

The relations between the robot tool center point (TCP0) and the others tools must be defined using homogeneous transformation matrix. The user must define ${}^{TCP0}T_{hand1}$, ${}^{TCP0}T_{hand2}$, and ${}^{TCP0}T_{sensor}$, but ${}^{TCP0}T_{camera}$ can be calibrated using the application (Fig. 2.3).

The vision system consists of a small CCD monochrome camera (Pulnix TM-526A) fixed on the robot tool adapter and a frame grabber (μTech MV-200) plug in the server computer.

The distance sensor consists of an ultrasonic sensor (Honeywell 940-A4) fixed on the robot tool adapter and an A/D converter plug in the server computer.

3. Camera model calibration

The camera must be calibrated with high precision to get good object location accuracy.

The camera model used here is Tsai's model. Tsai's model is based on the pinhole model of 3D-2D perspective projection with 1st order radial lens distortion. The model ${}^{camera}T_{reference}$ has 11 parameters, five intrinsic and six extrinsic parameters.

This application uses Tsai's coplanar algorithm, modified for Visual C++ compiler.

3.1. Calibration

The model calibration consists of solving ${}^{camera}T_{reference}$ using the n-equations system:

$$i_n(u,v) = {}^{camera}T_{reference}\, p_n(x,y,z),$$

knowing the 3D $p_n(x,y,z)$ reference world coordinates of the feature points and the corresponding coordinates $i_n(u,v)$ of the feature points in the image.

The calibration accuracy depends on the amount of features used to solve the n-equations system. The features used to calibrate the model are corners in a template with twenty rectangles (Fig. 3.1). It is used rectangles instead of circles because it is possible to draw more rectangle corners than circle centers in the same area, although circle centers are easier detectable in the image than rectangle corners.

Tsai's coplanar algorithm returns ${}^{camera}T_{reference}$ from $p_n(x,y,z)$, $i_n(u,v)$ and other intrinsic camera constants.

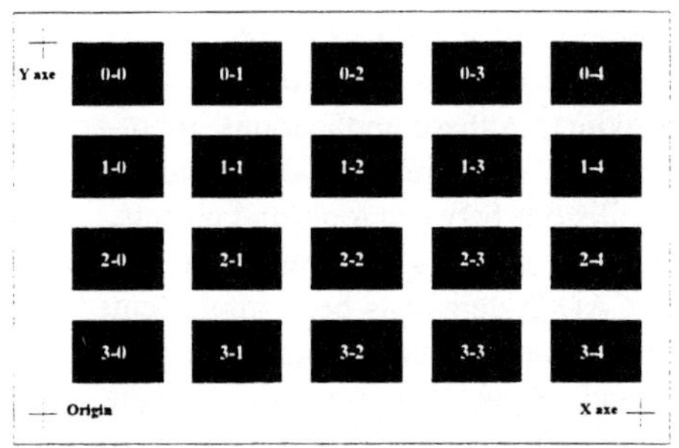

Figure 3.1. Calibration template.

3.1.1. Reference world corners position. Initially, it is known the corners position with respect to reference world system defined by the centres of the three crosses (Y axe, Origin and X axe), which appear in the calibration template. They define the robot work plane on the XY reference world plane.

These three points are located with respect the robot base coordinate system moving the robot until a special pointing tool, mounted on a hand, touches the points and reading these poses from the robot control unit. The user must define ${}^{TCP0}T_{pointer}$ transformation matrix. Then we can calculate the ${}^{base}T_{reference}$ transformation matrix depending on:

$$
\begin{aligned}
{}^{base}T_{Yaxe} &= {}^{base}T_{TCP0}\,{}^{TCP0}T_{pointer},\\
{}^{base}T_{Origin} &= {}^{base}T_{TCP0}\,{}^{TCP0}T_{pointer},\\
{}^{base}T_{Xaxe} &= {}^{base}T_{TCP0}\,{}^{TCP0}T_{pointer},
\end{aligned}
$$

where ${}^{base}T_{TCP0}$ can be read from the robot control unit on each point.

3.1.2. Image corners detection. The positions of the image corners are calculated automatically analyzing locally the rectangles in the image calibration template.

The user must point on the centers of the three crosses (Y axe, Origin, X axe) and select local windows around all the rectangles in the template. The order of this selection (0-0, 0-1... 0-4, 1-0 ... 3-4) is important to perform the correspondence between image and world reference corners.

First of all, the edges are detected on every local window in the image template searching zero crossing after applying Gaussian Laplacian filter. These edges are considered features on the image to detect the lines using the Hough Transform technique [2].

After that, the corners can be calculated like the intersections of the detected lines. In the example on the Fig. 3.2, it can be seen results of this method.

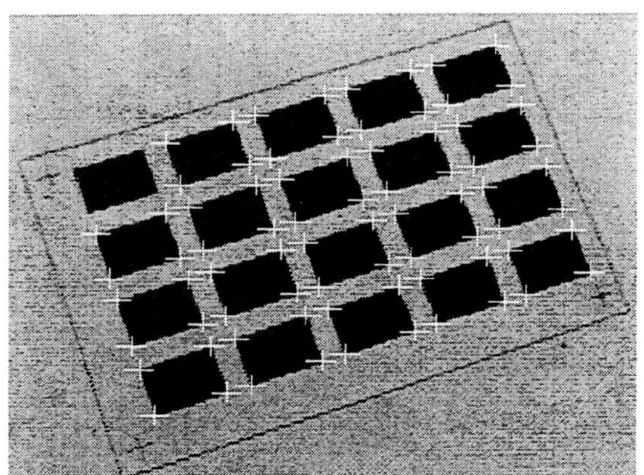

Figure 3.2. Image corners detection.

3.1.3. Corners correspondence. The correspondence between image and reference world corners is performed using the order of the local windows selected by the user, but if a corner from a rectangle is missed, the others detected corners are discarded. In Fig. 3.2, you can see an example on the first rectangle, which is discarded.

It is possible to discard some of the features because Tsai's coplanar calibration algorithm requires eleven features and the calibration template has eighty corners.

4. Pick and place Behavior

The flexible programming system permits to select the pick and place object locations on the image space, to calculate the locations with respect the robot base coordinates system and move the robot-arm to pick and place the object using the active tool.

4.1. Coordinate systems relations

Once ${}^{camera}T_{reference}$ and ${}^{base}T_{reference}$ are estimated, it is possible to calculate ${}^{TCP0}T_{camera}$, using ${}^{base}T_{TCP0}$. Then ${}^{TCP0}T_{camera} = {}^{TCP0}T_{base}\,{}^{base}T_{reference}\,{}^{reference}T_{camera}$.

The problem of calculates ${}^{camera}T_{object}$ is ill posed, due to the projection on the image plane. It is used a distance sensor to solve this problem. Others kinds to solve this problem are depth from focus, depth from zoom, depth from motion stereo, depth from binocular stereo [3], etc.

4.2. Pick and place object selection

The pick and place object selection is performed clicking the mouse on a live image displayed on the PC screen. The user must click on the centre of the object in the robot work plane and drag the mouse to define the orientation (Fig. 4.1) to pick the object with the active robot hand. The pick and place object selection operation is easier if the camera is perpendicular to the robot work plane.

This operation defines three points, (${}^{camera}\boldsymbol{o}$, ${}^{camera}\boldsymbol{x}$, ${}^{camera}\boldsymbol{y}$), on the image plane.

The actual robot configuration, ${}^{base}T_{TCP0}$, must be read from the control unit, to recalculate the actual extrinsic camera parameters.

4.3. Pick and place object location

The ${}^{base}T_{WpObject}$ transformation matrix is calculated from the object selection information, knowing the object coordinate XY plane is the robot work plane, that is, ${}^{reference}o_Z=0$. So it can get the object center on the work plane with respect to the base ${}^{base}T_{WpObject}=[\,({}^{base}\boldsymbol{x}\ 0)^t\ ({}^{base}\boldsymbol{y}\ 0)^t\ ({}^{base}\boldsymbol{z}\ 0)^t\ ({}^{base}\boldsymbol{o}\ 1)^t]$ applying:

$$
\begin{aligned}
{}^{base}\boldsymbol{o} &= {}^{base}T_{TCP0}\,{}^{TCP0}T_{camera}\,{}^{camera}\boldsymbol{o},\\
{}^{base}\boldsymbol{x} &= (\,{}^{base}T_{TCP0}\,{}^{TCP0}T_{camera}\,{}^{camera}\boldsymbol{x}) - {}^{base}\boldsymbol{o},\\
{}^{base}\boldsymbol{y} &= (\,{}^{base}T_{TCP0}\,{}^{TCP0}T_{camera}\,{}^{camera}\boldsymbol{y}) - {}^{base}\boldsymbol{o},\\
{}^{base}\boldsymbol{z} &= {}^{base}\boldsymbol{x} * {}^{base}\boldsymbol{y}.
\end{aligned}
$$

Now, it must be measured the object height from the robot work plane. Then the distance sensor is moved above the ${}^{base}\boldsymbol{T}_{WpObject}$ pose. To perform this movement it is needed the transformation matrix ${}^{base}\boldsymbol{T}_{TCP0}= {}^{base}\boldsymbol{T}_{WpObject}\, \boldsymbol{T}_{tz\text{-}s}\, {}^{sensor}\boldsymbol{T}_{TCP0}$, where $\boldsymbol{T}_{tz\text{-}s}$ is a secure translation on $Z_{0Object}$ axis direction. To filter noise in the distance between object and sensor it is performed the mean ($\boldsymbol{m}$) of some measures. The object height is $h = |\, {}^{base}\boldsymbol{T}_{sensor}\,(0\ 0\ \boldsymbol{m}\ 1)^t - {}^{base}\boldsymbol{o}\, |$. The translation due to the object height is H = max(h/2, h-th, sd), where th is the tool height and sd is a security distance from the work plane.

Then ${}^{base}\boldsymbol{T}_{object}={}^{base}\boldsymbol{T}_{WpObject}\boldsymbol{T}_{tz\text{-}H}$, where $\boldsymbol{T}_{tz\text{-}H}$ is an -H translation on $Z_{WpObject}$ axis direction due to object height.

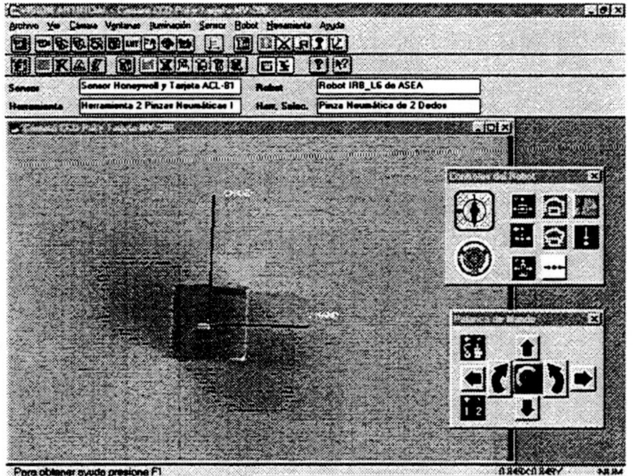

Figure 4.1. Pick object selection.

4.4. Object grasping

Once the object is located, we can send to the robot-arm control unit a command sequence to pick the object. First of all, the active tool must be moved to an approximation point, defined by an offset in the normal work plane direction, after that the tool will be moved to the pick position and finally the tool will come back to the approximation point.

The pick position is calculated making ${}^{base}\boldsymbol{T}_{tool}= {}^{base}\boldsymbol{T}_{object}$, so the ${}^{base}\boldsymbol{T}_{TCP0} = {}^{base}\boldsymbol{T}_{object}\, {}^{tool}\boldsymbol{T}_{TCP0}$.

The robot control unit needs the object pose (position and orientation), to grasp the object. The position is defined with respect to the base coordinate system, but the orientation is defined in quarternions with respect the coordinate system associated to the first element, which compose the robot arm. So, ${}^{base}\boldsymbol{T}_{TCP0} = {}^{base}\boldsymbol{T}_{object}\, {}^{tool}\boldsymbol{T}_{TCP0}$ must be recalculated taking into account the first robot link.

The problem of place the object is symmetric to the pick problem.

5. Software description

The application has been developed using OOP with Visual C++ compiler for Windows.

The main advantage of this application is its modular design. The application is discomposed in a vision module, a robot-arm module, a tool module and a sensor module. All of these modules are implemented in different dynamic link library, so the application is independent of the vision system, robot, tool and sensor system. That is, it is possible to change the hardware just implementing the new library without changing the main application.

The behavior parameters like security distances, speeds, etc. can be defined by the user.

6. Results and conclusions

This modular robot-arm system has a friendly user interface. First of all, the camera is calibrated with high precision. Then, the user can define pick and place object positions on the image space. And finally, the robot-arm performs the pick and place task defined on the image space.

The location error increases when the object position is far of the calibration area template.

This system will be improved with implementing an automatic pick and place object selection depending on the robot task. Other improvement is to add new robot behaviors like search or track objects.

References

[1] Ayache, "Artificial Vision for Mobile Robots: Stereo Vision & Multisensory Perception", The MIT Press, 1991.

[2] Davies, "Machine Vision: Theory, Algorithms & Practicalities", Academic press, 1997.

[3] Subbarao, Murali; "Parallel Depth Recovery by changing camera parameters", Proc. on Second Int. Conf. on Computer Vision, IEEE Computer Society Press, 1988.

[4] Sánchez, Mellado, & Vendrell, "Integrated System for Computer Aided Robot Programming", Advanced Manufacturing Processes, Systems & Technologies, 1996.

[5] Tsai, "An efficient & accurate camera calibration technique for 3D machine vision", In Proc. *IEEE* Computer Soc. Conf. Computer Vision & Pattern Recognition, June 1986.

Vision Guided Homing for Humanoid Service Robot

Yi Jin and Ming Xie
School of MPE, Nanyang Technological University
P145597232@ntu.edu.sg

Abstract

Human beings can easily use eyes to guide arms and hands to reach any particular pose. We have been trying to make robot imitate such intelligent hand-eye coordination behavior. In this paper we report our research work on vision guided homing for humanoid service robot HARO-1 which has active stereo vision and two modular arms. The work is based on the 3D vision reconstruction and geometric kinematics analysis. This intelligent behavior of HARO-1 significantly improves its performance by automatically rectifying its original home position and implementing self-homing guided by stereo vision system. The implementation and experimental studies are also presented in the paper.

1. Introduction

Nowadays it is commonly believed that robotics reaches the stage of looking into the aspect of intelligence that will be the key issue to make robots more user-friendly and more useful [1]. Here we believe that one possible way of developing intelligent robot is to make robot imitate intelligent behaviors of human beings such as hand-eye coordination and head-eye coordination.

In recent years, a perceivable trend of robotics technology is moving towards the direction of service robot [1,2]. Service robot is a semi or fully autonomous machine working in everyday environment. It performs service for both human beings and machine themselves.

In NTU, we have designed and developed a human-like service robot named HARO-1 [3], as is shown in Figure 1. It is composed of several subsystems, including an active stereo head on modular neck, two modular arms with active links, mobile body, mobile base with three wheels, dextrous hands and the computing system.

In order to perform a large variety of tasks, service robot must possess both software and hardware flexibility. The re-programmability nature of software systems has made software flexibility easily attainable. While hardware flexibility can be achieved by adopting reconfigurability and modularity in the design for the robot's arms, neck, and so on.

Vision guided homing (VGH) is an interesting research topic [4]. In our opinion, VGH has two meanings. Broadly speaking, it means how to send robot arm to desired pose in task space by stereo vision. And in particular, for HARO-1, VGH means how to use stereo vision to guide robot arm return to nominal home position without using homing sensors. In this paper we report our research work focused on the latter.

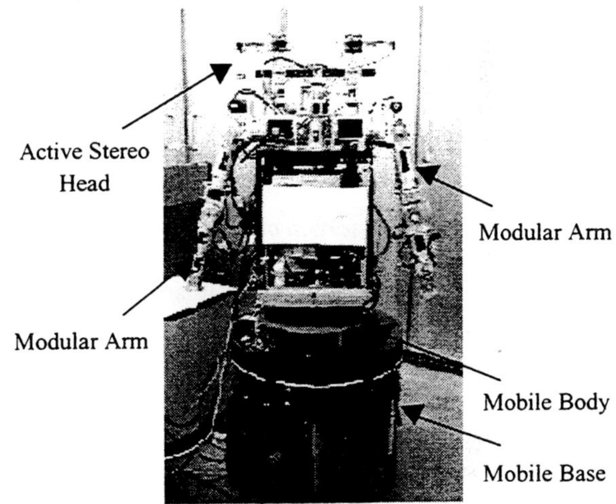

Figure 1 Humanoid Service Robot HARO-1

We present our proposed VGH algorithm in this paper. This algorithm is based on the 3D vision reconstruction and kinematics analysis of the modular arms. By doing so there is no need of adding homing sensors to the hardware at all. We have performed preliminary experiments that demonstrate efficiency of the algorithm.

This paper is organized as follows. Section 2 presents our work on the kinematics modeling of modular arms for HARO-1 humanoid service robot. Section 3 presents the vision guided homing algorithm. Section 4 reports some implementation issues and experimental studies on vision guided homing. Finally, section 5 concludes this paper.

2. Kinematics modeling of modular arms

2.1. Configuration of modular arms

With the advent of new requirements on manipulator modularity and reconfigurability, researchers have started to re-think the design solutions of robot arm [5].

For our HARO-1 humanoid service robot, we have designed and developed a unique entity - Active Link that integrates link and joint, as basic building block for the modular robot arm [6]. Each arm has 3 serially connected active links with 6 DOF. If an application requires higher flexibility and mobility, additional modules can be added to provide more DOF; conversely, DOF of the arm can be scaled down when the application is simple.

Geometrically, an active link can be represented as a set of 3 frames illustrated in Figure 2:

$$L_i = \{\theta_i^a, \theta_i^p, l_i\} \quad (1)$$

Where θ_i^a, θ_i^p and l_i represent the axial rotation, pivoting rotation and translation of link i.

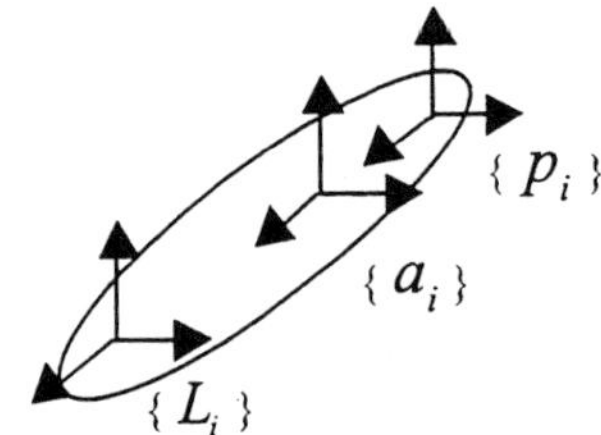

Figure 2: Illustration of An Active Link

The forward kinematics of modular arm is given as follows:

$$^{W}M_E = {}^{W}M_{L_0}\,{}^{L_0}M_{a_0}\,{}^{a_0}M_{P_0}\,{}^{P_0}M_{L_1}\,{}^{L_1}M_{a_1}\,{}^{a_1}M_{P_1}\,{}^{P_1}M_{L_2}\,{}^{L_2}M_{a_2}\,{}^{a_2}M_{P_2}\,{}^{P_2}M_E \quad (2)$$

Where:

{W} represents the world coordinate frame.

{E } represents the frame attached to the wrist.

2.2. Inverse kinematics of modular arms

Due to the unique feature of active links, we can derive a new closed form geometric inverse kinematics solution for modular arm. The essence is that it is always possible to find a constraint plane, in which we can derive the solution to the inverse kinematics of the modular arm.

The basic idea of our solution is shown in Figure 3. Figure 3 (a) shows the home position of the modular arm and notations used to describe the desired position and orientation of the modular arm. Where inputs of inverse kinematics are the desired position and orientation of the wrist: $\vec{P}$ and $\vec{X}$, $\vec{Y}$, $\vec{Z}$. And outputs are the link's parameters: $\{\theta_i^a, \theta_i^p\}$ (i = 0, 1, 2).

This method can be extended to the modular arm with N (N > 3) active links. In this case, additional algorithm is proposed to optimize the posture of the arm [7].

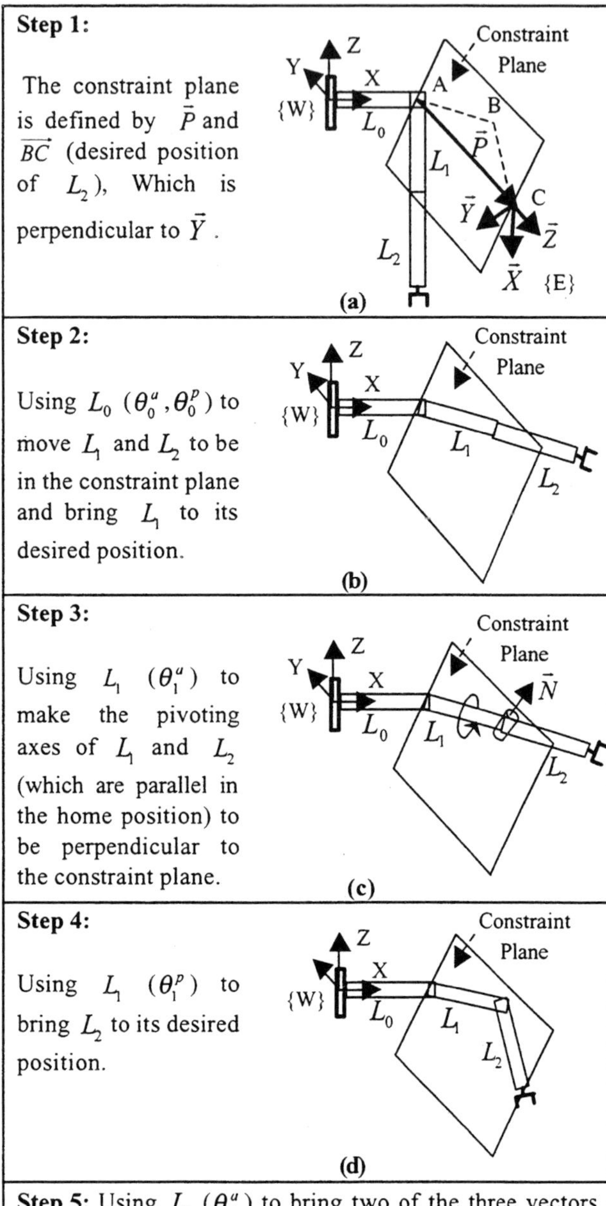

Step 1:
The constraint plane is defined by $\vec{P}$ and $\vec{BC}$ (desired position of L_2), Which is perpendicular to $\vec{Y}$.
Constraint Plane
Z
Y
X
{W}
L_0
L_1
L_2
A
B
C
$\vec{P}$
$\vec{Y}$
$\vec{Z}$
$\vec{X}$ {E}
(a)
Step 2:
Using L_0 (θ_0^a, θ_0^p) to move L_1 and L_2 to be in the constraint plane and bring L_1 to its desired position.
(b)
Step 3:
Using L_1 (θ_1^a) to make the pivoting axes of L_1 and L_2 (which are parallel in the home position) to be perpendicular to the constraint plane.
$\vec{N}$
(c)
Step 4:
Using L_1 (θ_1^p) to bring L_2 to its desired position.
(d)
Step 5: Using L_2 (θ_2^a) to bring two of the three vectors representing the orientation of the wrist to their desired orientation $\vec{Y}$ and $\vec{Z}$.
Step 6: Using L_2 (θ_2^p) to bring the third vector representing the orientation of the wrist to its desired orientation $\vec{X}$.

Figure 3: Solution of Inverse Kinematics

3. Vision guided homing of modular arms

3.1. Problem statement

Home position is very important to motion control of manipulator. Positioning accuracy is directly dependent on accuracy of home position. Now we are facing the problem that how to make robot accurately know the nominal home position and do homing. Of course we can resort to those conventional methods by adding sensors. But this will make robot's design and implementation more complicated. Inspired by our study on robotic hand-eye coordination [1,8], we try to use vision to guide arm to do homing. Some works have been done toward this direction. The proposed solution is based on vision reconstruction and kinematics analysis. By doing so, there is no need of adding extra sensors to the hardware at all.

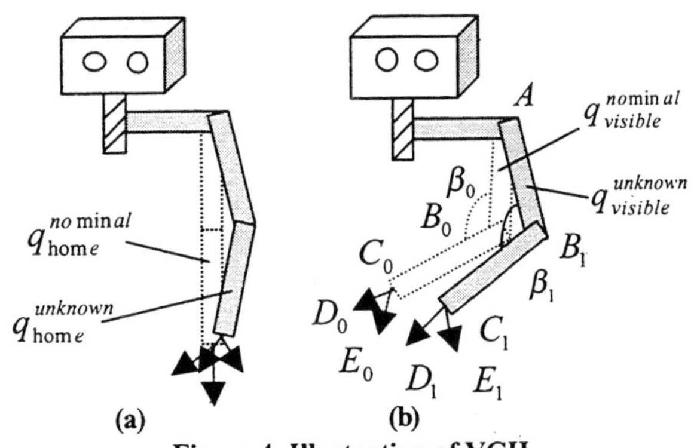

Figure 4: Illustration of VGH

The problem of VGH can be expressed as follows. According to Figure 4 (a), in the kinematics modeling, we have a nominal home position $q^{nominal}_{home}$ for the modular arm. When the robot is powered on, we can not assume that the arm is in its nominal home position. We define this unknown position as $q^{unknown}_{home}$. So the problem is how to use vision to guide the arm from current home position $q^{unknown}_{home}$ to go back to ominal home position $q^{nominal}_{home}$.

3.2. Proposed solution

According to Figure 4 (a), our aim is to use stereo vision to move arm from $q^{unknown}_{home}$ to $q^{nominal}_{home}$, but the two positions $q^{nominal}_{home}$ and $q^{unknown}_{home}$ are both invisible to robot's eyes. Therefore, the arm should be moved to a visible position $q^{unknown}_{visible}$ as is shown in Figure 4 (b).

According to Figure 4, our solution deals with four positions. Figure 5 shows the relationship of these positions. Here we use Q_q and Q_q^{-1} to represent joint rotational angles from one position to another position:

$$Q_q = (\Delta q_0^a, \Delta q_0^p, \Delta q_1^a, \Delta q_1^p, \Delta q_2^a, \Delta q_2^p) \quad (3)$$

$$Q_q^{-1} = (-\Delta q_0^a, -\Delta q_0^p, -\Delta q_1^a, -\Delta q_1^p, -\Delta q_2^a, -\Delta q_2^p) \quad (4)$$

According to Figure 5, our solution can be separated into three stages. In the first stage, we move the arm from $q^{unknown}_{home}$ to $q^{unknown}_{visible}$ by joint rotational angles Q_q. In the second stage, vision is used to guide arm from $q^{unknown}_{visible}$ to $q^{nominal}_{visible}$ step by step. Then in the third stage, the arm goes back to $q^{nominal}_{home}$ by joint rotational angles Q_q^{-1}.

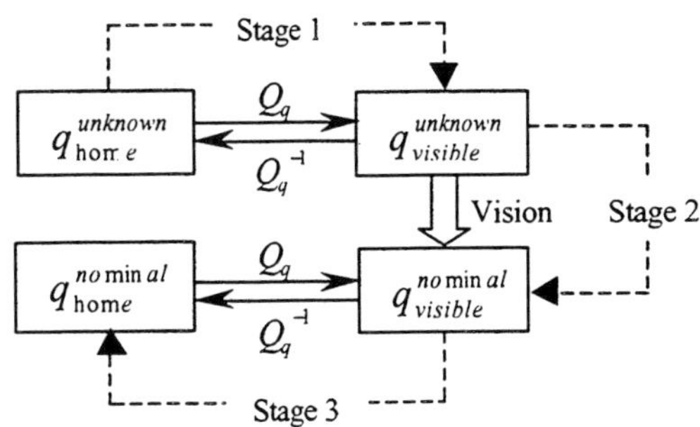

Figure 5: Solution of VGH

4. Implementation & experimental studies

4.1. System description

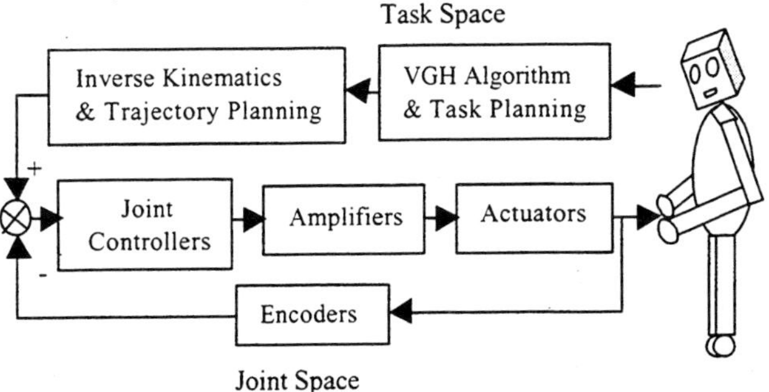

Figure 6: Illustration of VGH System

The VGH system is shown in Figure 6. We consider VGH as a kind of hand-eye coordination. The core algorithm of VGH is a kind of look and move strategy, which is implemented iteratively until the arm arrives at its desired pose $q^{nominal}_{visible}$. According to Figure 6, in the joint space joint controllers are used to stabilize the control loop, fulfilling tasks given by task planner and making arms move to desired pose. Inverse kinematics is a bridge between task space and joint space.

4.2. Role of vision system

During the look and move process of VGH, vision system plays the role of the online motion planner. We use vision to perceive points of interest on the modular arm. After image feature extraction pose estimation is used to compute the control input of the next step.

According to Figure 7, we use perspective projection camera model. Where (X, Y, Z) represents 3D coordinates of a point in task space, and (u, v) represents its projection on image plane. The mapping relationship can be described by 3D camera calibration matrix $M_{3\times4}$, which contains intrinsic and extrinsic parameters of the camera. It can be computed from six or more mapping pairs through least square method.

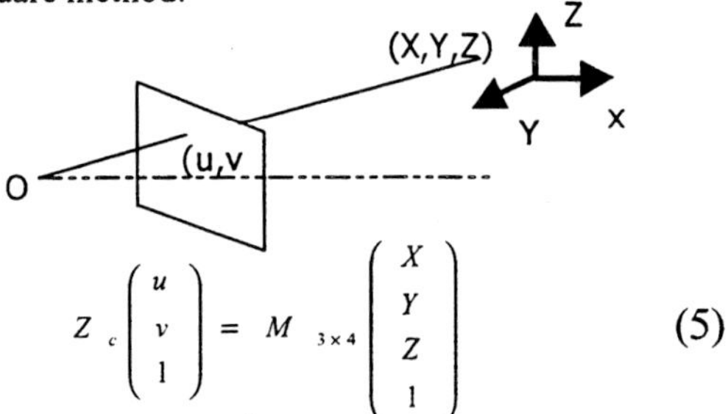

$$Z_c \begin{pmatrix} u \\ v \\ 1 \end{pmatrix} = M_{3\times4} \begin{pmatrix} X \\ Y \\ Z \\ 1 \end{pmatrix} \quad (5)$$

Figure 7: Perspective Projection Camera Model

After calibration for cameras, we can compute 3D coordinates of a point from its corresponding projections in left and right images using least square estimation.

4.3. Implementation issues and studies

For real implementation of VGH for HARO-1, an important issue is that we cannot directly observe certain points on the modular arm as is shown in Figure 4 (b). Take point C_1 as an example. It is the centre point of the wrist and can not be found directly. To solve the problem, we select another two points M and N attached on the modular arm that can be observed directly as is shown in Figure 8. Considering vector $\overline{MN}$ is parallel to vector $\overline{B1C1}$, we can compute 3D coordinates of point C_1 if given 3D coordinates of points M, N and B_1.

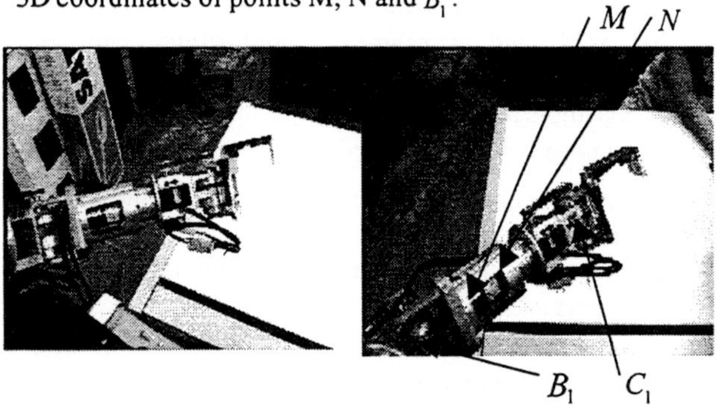

Figure 8: A Modular Arm from View of Robot's Eyes

According to Figure 4 (a), in current experimental studies, the starting position $q_{home}^{unknown}$ is not very far from $q_{home}^{nominal}$. While in fact for VGH algorithm, this starting position is not constrained according to Figure 5. That is, the VGH algorithm can guide arm from an arbitrary pose to go back to nominal home position.

Preliminary experimental result shows the efficiency of VGH algorithm. Although the result has some errors, it can be improved by increasing the accuracy of robot kinematics, camera calibration and vision reconstruction.

5. Conclusion

We have presented in this paper the new idea of vision guided homing for a humanoid service robot. A new geometric inverse kinematics method with full rank is presented for modular arm. The proposed VGH algorithm is based on this kinematics modeling and 3D vision reconstruction. This intelligent behavior of HARO-1 significantly improves its performance by automatically rectifying its original home position and implementing self-homing. In the future more work will be done to increase the positioning accuracy by improving robot kinematics, camera calibration and vision reconstruction.

12. References

[1] M. Xie, "Towards visual Intelligence of Service Robot", *Proc., 4th ICCARV*, Singapore, Dec 1996, pp. 2217-2221.

[2] S. Yuta, "Towards Useful Autonomous Robotic Systems for Field and Service Applications", *Proc., 1st Int. Conf. Field and Service Robotics*, Canberra, Australia, Dec. 1997, pp.10-13.

[3] W.T. Ang and M. Xie, "Mobile Robotic Hand-Eye Co-ordination Platform: Design and Modelling", *Proc., Int. Conf. Field and Service Robotics*, Australia, Dec 1997, pp.319-326.

[4] R. Basri, E. Rivlin and I. Shimshoni, "Visual homing: Surfing on the epipoles", *IEEE Int. Conference on Computer Vision, ICCV'98*, Bombay, India, Jan 1998, pp. 863-869.

[5] T. Matsumaru, "Design and Control of the Modular Robot System: TOMMS", *IEEE ICRA*, 1995, pp. 2125-2131.

[6] W.T. Ang and M. Xie, "Design of Active Links for Modular Robot", *Proc. ICCIM*, Singapore, Oct. 1997, pp.1295-1303.

[7] J. Foret, W. T. Ang, M. Xie and J. G. Fontaine, "Configuration Control of a Modular Arm with N Active Links", *SPIE ISAM* Boston, USA, Nov 1998, pp. 299-310.

[8] W. Xiong, Y. Jin and M. Xie, "Effective and Efficient 3D Object Location Using Automatic Camera Calibration", *Proc. Int. Conf. FSR.*, Pittsburg, USA, Aug 1999 pp. 139-143.

A New System for the Real-time Recognition of Handwritten Mathematical Formulas

Takahiro Suzuki
Graduate School of Eng., Nagoya Univ.
Nagoya 464-8603 Japan
tsuzuki@suenaga.cse.nagoya-u.ac.jp

Shiro Aoshima
NTT Information Sharing Platform Laboratories
Tokyo 180-8585 Japan
aoshima.shirou@lab.ntt.co.jp

Kensaku Mori
Faculty of Eng., Nagoya Univ.
Nagoya 464-8603 Japan
mori@cse.nagoya-u.ac.jp

Yasuhito Suenaga
Faculty of Eng., Nagoya Univ.
Nagoya 464-8603 Japan
suenaga@cse.nagoya-u.ac.jp

Abstract

This paper presents a new system for the on-line and real-time recognition of handwritten mathematical formulas. Mathematical formulas are inputted into the system as hand drawings on a computer screen using a data tablet. The system analyzes the inputted data stroke by stroke in order to recognize the structure of the formula based on the relationship of bounding boxes that include components of the formula. A recognized result is obtained as a source code from the "LaTeX" type setting system. Our system can recognize arbitrary combinations of superscripts, subscripts, square roots, overlines, underlines, and fractions. The input of the math formula is independent of stroke order. In several experiments, the system proved to be very effective for inputting various math formulas in real-time.

1. Introduction

Techniques of real-time handwritten character recognition have been widely used on various electronic equipments, such as PDAs (personal digital assistants) or personal computers. Although most methods can recognize typical handwritten characters including alphanumerics and kanji, it is still impossible to handle the kind of mathematical formulas that are indispensable in technical documents. LaTeX and MathType (Design Science Inc.) are examples of systems that support the creation of documents including mathematical formulas. However, the user often feels difficulty in inserting LaTeX commands to the document, since LaTeX has a lot of tag commands for the typesetting of mathematical formulas. MathType is a representative system that enables the user to insert mathematical formulas by using the WYSIWYG environment. Users can choose desired formulas from the program's menus or buttons, but they must do a lot of mouse operations.

There are few research papers on mathematical formula recognition, and many of them only deal with methods for printed documents with mathematical formulas [1]. Wang and Faure reported a hand-written formula recognition method as an off-line procedure [2]. The on-line character recognition systems reported in [3],[4],[5],[6] cannot handle mathematical formulas.

This paper describes an on-line mathematical formula recognition method that is usable as an input system for technical documents. In the next section, we describe our proposed system. Section 3 explains our recognition methods. Section 4 explains functions of our system. Section 5 shows the evaluation experiments and results. Finally, Section 6 summarizes this paper.

2. Proposed System

Figure 1 shows the processing flow of the proposed system.

The user directly writes a mathematical formula on the computer screen and the system recognizes it. The system also enables the user to delete arbitrary characters, and the input of formulas is independent of stroke orders.

The mathematical formula structure differs from typical text structures where characters in the same line are located on the baseline. Mathematical formulas have special structures, called "*two-dimensional structures*" in this paper, where characters and mathematical symbols are located on different lines, such as overlines, underlines, and fractions. The *two-dimensional structure* is formed by a

1051-4651/00 $10.00 © 2000 IEEE

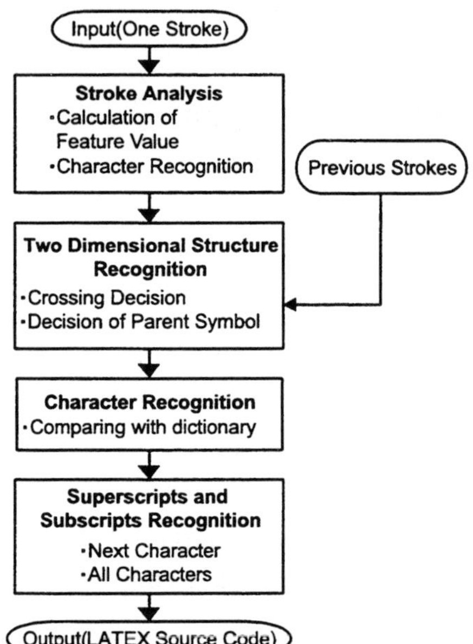

Figure 1. System flow

limited number of mathematical symbols except for superscripts and subscripts. Moreover, this structure depends on the mathematical symbols.

In handwriting, we write characters stroke by stroke, and form each character using a combination of multiple strokes.

The system uses these characteristics for achieving automated and real time recognition of mathematical formulas.

3. Recognition Procedure

3.1. Stroke Analysis

Here, the system calculates the features of an input stroke to select a single stroke character that has the most similar features to the input stroke.

As the user writes a mathematical formula on a data tablet, stroke information is transferred to the host computer as a time sequence of coordinates. The system encodes this stroke as a sequence of Freeman's chain codes and calculates three kinds of features: *chain code histogram*, *sub-vector sequence*, and *region information*.

[Features for stroke analysis]

a. chain code histogram
A histogram of chain codes for each stroke is calculated.

b. sub-vector sequence
Each stroke is divided into n ($n \leq L$) subsections of equal length, where L is the length of a stroke. Each divided stroke is represented by a vector (sub-vector) that connects a starting point and an ending point of each subsection. If $n > L$, the system does not divide a stroke and recognizes the stroke as "dot".

c. region information
The information includes the height and width of the bounding box of a stroke, and the position of the starting point of a stroke in the bounding box.

The system selects the most appropriate character corresponding to the input stroke by consulting the stroke dictionary, which is prepared by inputting stroke and character pairs beforehand.

3.2. Two-dimensional structure Recognition

We should determine the vertical position of an input stroke for recognizing a mathematical *two-dimensional structure*. Characters or mathematical symbols exist under or over some particular symbols (i.e., $\frac{b}{a}$, $\sqrt{c+d}$). We call these characters and mathematical symbols *"child blocks"* (i.e., a, b, $c+d$ in the previous examples), and the particular symbols *"parent symbols"*(i.e., —, $\sqrt{\ }$). Currently, the system can treat only six mathematical symbols as *parent symbols*, ($\sum$, $\prod$, $\_$, $\overline{\ }$, —, and $\sqrt{\ }$).

As described in 3.1, an input stroke is assigned to a single stroke character. When a character or a character with cross-sections from the previous character exists around the six predetermined symbols, the system executes the process described below.

In the case of $\sum$, $\prod$, $\_$, $\overline{\ }$, or —, the system determines the vertical relationship of crossing characters by comparing vertical coordinates. In the case of $\sqrt{\ }$, the system determines it by containing the relationship between the bounding box of the square root and that of crossing character.

This process finds the positional relationship of the *parent symbols* and their *child blocks*. It is iterated for the entire mathematical formula, since there may be multiple and nested *two-dimensional structures* in one mathematical formula.

3.3. Character Recognition

Features for single stroke characters were defined in Section 3.1. We need to obtain features for multiple stroke characters by connecting features of each stroke in the order of writing. They are obtained as shown below.

[Features for character recognition]

a. Connected chain code histogram
Directly connect chain code histograms of all strokes.

b. Connected sub-vector sequence
Connect two sub-vector sequences with the vector between the ending point of the previous sequence and the starting point of the next sequence.

c. Connected region information
Calculate the vertical and horizontal distances between the upper/lower/left/right edges of the two bounding boxes.

According to the number of strokes, the system searches for an appropriate character that has the same number of strokes in the prepared dictionary. This selection is performed by finding a character that maximizes correlation R between an input stroke and a character in the dictionary.

3.4. Superscripts and Subscripts Recognition

Superscripts and subscripts are detected by comparing the vertical positions of two adjacent characters. The right character is determined as a superscript if it is vertically higher than the left character. In the opposite case, a subscript is selected. If neither conditions are satisfied, the two characters are determined to be on the same line.

3.5. Other functions

(a) Deletion For a pleasant input environment, this system enables the user to delete any character that he/she selects at any time. The system then re-recognizes the structure of a mathematical formula and updates the recognition result.

(b) Adding a symbol When we write mathematical symbols (i.e.$\sqrt{}$, $\underline{}$, $\overline{}$, —) before writing characters, the length of mathematical symbols may often be shorter for covering all characters. In this case, we extend the length of mathematical symbols by adding extra lines, such as an upper line, a lower line, or a line of a fraction. The system will also accept these extensions of the symbol.

When the user inputs an extended part, it is recognized as a subtraction sign in the first stage. If the above stated starting point of the subtraction sign is near the end of four symbols, the system recognizes the subtraction sign as extension of the symbol.

4. Experiment

Table 1 shows a list of characters that the proposed system is currently able to recognize. Figure 2 shows a screen shot of the proposed system. The user uses a data tablet to directly write a mathematical formula on the window. The operation window is divided into two parts; the upper side is a window for writing a mathematical formula, while the lower side is an output area. As the user adds a stroke on the input window, the system executes the recognition procedure stated in Section 3 and promptly updates the LaTeX source code. Two hundred milli-seconds is required for each update.

Table 1. Recognizable characters

Alphabet	a,b,c,d,e,f,g,h,i,j,k,l,m,n, o,p,q,r,s,t,u,v,w,x,y,z A,B,C,D,E,F,G,H,I,J,K,L, M,N,P,Q,R,S,T,U,V,W,Y,Z
Greek Alphabet	α,β,σ,δ,ε,ω,π
Numeral	0,1,2,3,4,5,6,7,8,9
Mathematical Symbol	-,+,<,>, ≤,≥,≠,√,∫,Σ,Π,∞ (),{},sin,cos,tan,lim,log

We have validated recognition rates by writing four kinds of mathematical formulas on the screen. Three kinds of recognition rates were measured: character, superscript and subscript, and *two-dimensional structure* recognition. In this measurement, twenty-four users tried to input the four kinds of mathematical formulas shown in Figure 3. Each user tried to write each mathematical formula five times. Table 2 shows the recognition rates of those formulas. Figure 4 displays an example of input and output of mathematical formula from our system.

The recognition rate of a mathematical structure (superscript, subscript, and *two-dimensional structure*) was about 90%. The system could accurately recognize combinations of structures within typical mathematical formulas. The system could process a stroke within a quarter of a second. The user can input mathematical formulas fairly freely, without any significant stress.

The character recognition rate was about 80%. A low recognition rate was caused by the loss of important feature points in the stroke analysis. This process divides a

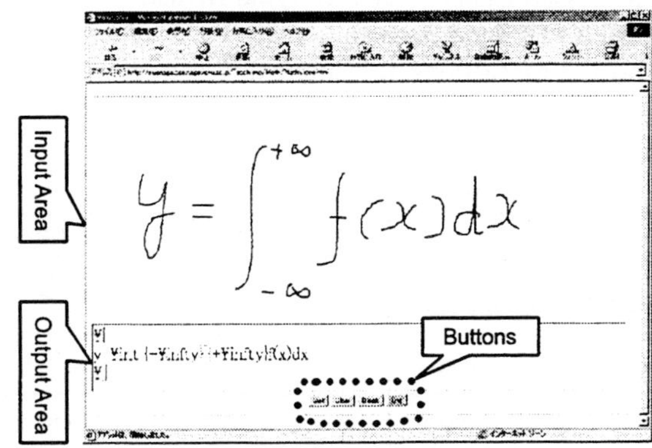

Figure 2. Window screen from system

(1) $y = \int_{-\infty}^{+\infty} f(x)dx$ (2) $g = \frac{2q}{1+\sqrt{1+p^2+q^2}}$

(3) $f(x) = \frac{1}{\sqrt{2\pi}\sigma} e^{-\frac{(x-m)^2}{\sigma^2}}$ (4) $a = c_0^2 + \sum_{n=0}^{\infty} \frac{c_n^2}{2}$

Figure 3. Four mathematical formulas used the experiment

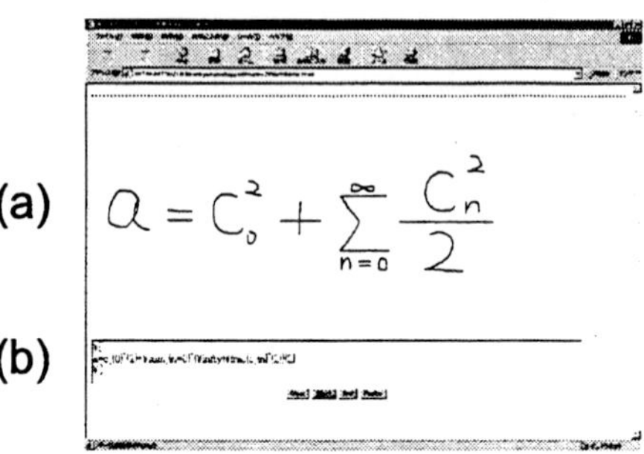

(c) $a = c_0^2 + \sum_{n=0}^{\infty} \frac{c_n^2}{2}$

Figure 4. An example result. ; (a) input, (b) recognition result (LaTeX source code), (c) output

stroke into n-divisions in order to obtain features for the stroke analysis. Important feature points such as bending points may disappear in this dividing process. Since many excellent methods of character recognition except for mathematical formulas have been reported by researchers, the employment of these methods should improve the character recognition rate and lead to better performance for our system.

5. Conclusions

In this paper, we have proposed an on-line and real-time recognition system of handwritten mathematical formulas that is implemented on a personal computer. The experimental recognition rates of this system were about 80% in character recognition and about 90% in structure recognition. The average processing time required for the processing was 200 milli-seconds per stroke. In the future work, we plan to develop new features that can express stroke forms more accurately, improve the dictionary and character recognition process, and develop a new method that can recognize other mathematical formula structures such as matrices.

References

[1] Masayuki Okamoto and Hiroyuki Higashi, "Mathematical Expression Recognition by the Layout of Symbols," Transactions of Institute of Electronics, Information and Communication Engineers (D-II), **J78-D-II**, 3, pp. 474-482 (March, 1995).

[2] Zi-Xiong Wang and Claudie Faure, "Structural Analysis of Handwritten Mathematical Expressions," Proc. ICPR, pp. 32-34 (1988).

[3] Yasushi Yamazaki and Naohisa Komatsu, "An Extraction Indicidual Characteristics Based on Categorized Handwritting Information," Transactions of Institute of Electronics, Information and Communication Engineers (D-II), **J79-D-II**, 8, pp. 1335-1346 (August, 1993).

[4] Kimiyasu Kiyota, Toshihiko Ssakurai and Shinji Yamamoto, "On-line Character Recognition for the Visually Disabled Person Based on the Relative Position of Stroke Representative Points," Transactions of Institute of Electronics, Information and Communication Engineers (D-II), **J80-D-II**, 3, pp. 715-723 (March, 1997).

[5] Yannis A. Dimitriadis and Juan Lopez Coronado, "Towards an Art Based Mathematical Editor That Uses On-line Handwritten Symbol Recognition," Pattern Recognition, **28**, 6, pp. 807-822 (June, 1995).

[6] Andreas Kosmala and Gerhard Rigoll, "On-Line Handwritten Formula Recognition Using Statistical Methods," In Proc. Int. Conference on Pattern Recognition (ICPR), pp. 1306-1308 (August, 1998).

Table 2. Experimental results

	Character Recognition	Superscripts and Subscripts Recognition	Two-Dimensional Structure Recognition
Formula(1)	74% (1158/1560)	94% (1352/1440)	
Formula(2)	86% (1551/1800)	93% (1230/1320)	75% (186/240)
Formula(3)	81% (2130/2640)	94% (1810/1920)	89% (527/600)
Formula(4)	76% (1468/1920)	93% (1221/1320)	88% (422/480)
Sum	80% (6307/7920)	94% (5613/6000)	86% (1135/1320)

A Robust Document Processing System Combining Image Segmentation with Content-based Document Compression

Yibing Yang†and Hong Yan†‡
†School of Electrical and Information Engineering
University of Sydney, NSW 2006, Australia
‡Department of Electronic Engineering
City University of Hong Kong, Kowloon, Hong Kong
E-mail: {ybyang, yan}@ee.usyd.edu.au

Abstract

A new document processing system combining image segmentation with content-based document compression is proposed in this paper. Firstly, a grayscale document image is divided into small blocks and analyzed. Then, a modified logical thresholding method based on local structure analysis and the adaptive logical level technique is used to transform the grayscale document into a binary image. We extract all patterns from the binary document and use a multistage matching method to extract representative patterns. A decomposition method is used to deal with relatively large patterns. Finally, high ratio compression is achieved by coding the relative positions of symbols, extracted representative patterns and other decomposed patterns using the adaptive arithmetic coder and Q-Coder respectively.

1. INTRODUCTION

A large number of paper-based documents exist, and are continuously produced every day even though many of new printed documents have corresponding electronic versions produced by computers. Never before have we had so many documents to process, analyse, store and transmit as we have today. Computers provide the most efficient and convenient means of analysing and processing various information. The conversion of paper documents into suitable and flexable electronic forms has high economic potential. Accordingly, how to use computers to facilitate automatic processing, analysis and efficient storage and transmission of paper-based documents is an important subject in our information and computer era [1-3]. A practical document processing and compression system needs to process and compress a large number of documents every day. Thus, the system should be able to complete the whole processing procedure automatically, adaptively and effciently without the need for prior knowledge and pre-provided parameters, not only for normal quality documents, but for poor quality ones.

It is still difficult to deal with, and efficiently compress documents of very low quality. In this paper, we propose a new scheme for document image processing combining image segmentation with content-based document compression. Our system targets segmentation and compression of a wide range of documents with either good or bad quality, as well as with various styles and backgrounds. Firstly, we analyse the feature information (Section 2) of a scanned grayscale document and segment it into a binary image by using a modified adaptive logical level method (Section 3). Next, a multistage pattern matching method is proposed to match, decompose and synthesize small pattern set and large pattern set, which are extracted from the document, in order to reduce redundancies at the pattern level and at the decomposed component level (Section 4). Finally, high ratio compression is achieved by coding the relative positions of symbols, extracted representative patterns and other patterns decomposed using the adaptive arithmetic coder [4] with different orders and Q-Coder respectively (Section 5). Experimental results (Section 6) show that our system can process, analyse and compress various scanned documents efficiently and achieve better processing results and higher compression ratios than most other alternative systems.

2. DOCUMENT FEATURE ANALYSIS

2.1. Selection of Analysis Region

Document images may contain many variations in background and styles and some images may be degraded by noise. In most situations, we may not have prior knowledge of the documents to be processed. The thresholded image may appear with nonuniform stroke width or possibly even with lost strokes or over-connected characters if we use general thresholding methods [5] to process the images with variable or inhomogeneous background intensity and noise. Generally, most documents contain many printed or handwritten characters and line-drawings. The average stroke width of the characters and the line width of the line objects (drawings, tables, diagrams and graphics) provide an important feature which distinguishes the objects in the documents from the background.

Firstly, the document image is divided into $N \times N$, $(N = 4, ..., 16)$ blocks to select an analysis region, which is a block selected for feature analysis in the next step. The local statistical analysis is used for every other region in the diagonal, horizontal and vertical directions in Fig. 1(a). Some regions may contain both background and objects, and other regions may contain only background. A region is selected as an analysis region, if (1) the pixel numbers with near zero level along the horizontal scan direction in the selected region is more than 1/3 of the total pixel num-

1051-4651/00 $10.00 © 2000 IEEE

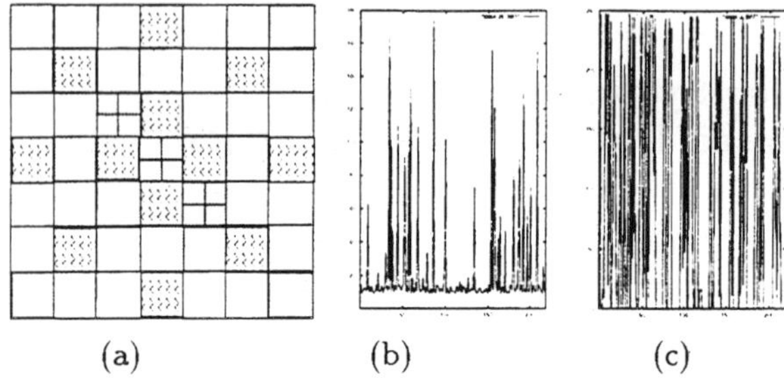

Figure 1: (a) Local region analysis and selection in the diagonal, horizontal and vertical directions. (b) and (c) Grayscale distributions of the document background and object with bad illumination and signal-dependent noise, respectively.

bers in this direction, (2) all local minimum gray levels are zero, and (3) all local differences between neighbouring local minimum and maximum gray levels are more than 10 and (4) all intervals/distances between neighbouring local minimum and maximum gray levels are more than 2 pixels. The number of local regions or the direction of analysis can be gradually increased until $N = 16$, if no local region is selected with $N < 16$.

2.2. Feature Analysis

The stroke widths of the characters and the line widths of the line-objects can be regarded as one of the features of the documents, because highly structured-stroke units and line units frequently appear in most documents. This structured-stroke information provides an effective means to distinguish objects from complex backgrounds and noise. We can obtain the structured-stroke information by using a local run-length histogram analysis for the selected regions. Figures 1(b) and (c) illustrate the grayscale distributions from the local regions with the background and objects from a degraded document image respectively. Here, we only consider black runs which are relevant to the characters or line objects. We denote a run-length histogram as a one dimensional array $R(i)$, $i \in I$, $I = \{1, 2, ..., L\}$, where L is the longest run to be counted. $R(i)$ is the frequency of the run of length i. Black run-length can be counted from the one-dimensional gray level distributions across the selected regions in horizontal and vertical directions, as shown in Fig. 1(c).

The line width of the line-objects and the character stroke width (SW) can be defined as the run-length with the highest frequency in the run-length histogram excluding the unit run-length. That is, $SW = i$, if $R_{max}(i) = \max_{i \in I} R(i)$, $i \neq 1$. It actually reflects the average width of strokes in a document image. If an image contains some complex background patterns or noise, the highest peak may be formed by these factors instead of the characters. In this case, selected region analysis and only black run analysis become necessary to prevent producing the wrong stroke widths. Statistical study shows that the mean stroke width is usually one pixel, and accordingly, all unit-runs should be removed as background in the resulting binary

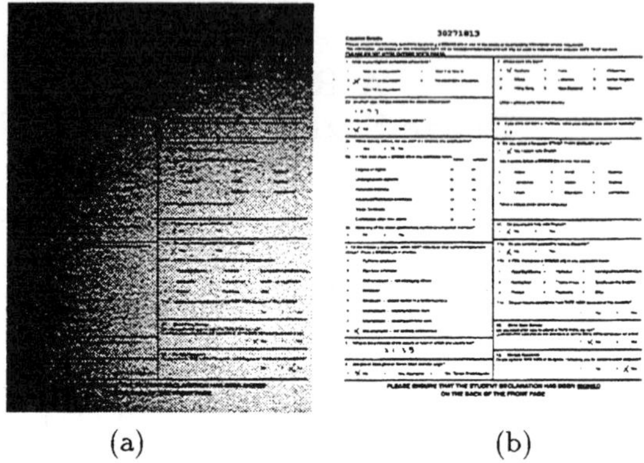

Figure 2: (a) Original document image with poor quality. (b) Segmentation result using our modified logical thresholding method.

image, whether it is produced by noise or other background changes.

3. ADAPTIVE THRESHOLDING

A logical level technique proposed by Kamel and Zhao [6] is developed on the basis of a comparison of the gray level of the processed pixel or its smoothed gray level with some local averages in the neighborhoods around a few other neighbouring pixels. This technique can generally determine the thresholds of various document images, but it needs to predetermine the character stroke width and a global parameter T. For some images with bad illumination, variable background intensity and noise, the predetermined character stroke width and global parameter T may cause an uneven thresholding effect and therefore a false thresholding result. Our modification [7] automatically and adaptively selects the stroke width information and the local parameter T, instead of using predetermined global parameters to overcome unstable thresholding effects from documents to documents.

We obtain the average maximal stroke width SW using above analysis. Here, we use a local statistical analysis to adaptively and automatically determine the local parameter T. Local T can be determined as follows: (1) Calculate local maximum $g_{max}(x,y)$, minimum $g_{min}(x,y)$, and average $g_{ave}(x,y)$ in a square window of (2SW+1); (2) $T = 2/3(2/3 g_{min}(x,y) + 1/3 g_{ave}(x,y)$, if $| g_{max}(x,y) - g_{ave}(x,y) | > | g_{min}(x,y) - g_{ave}(x,y) |$; (3) $T = 2/3\ (1/3\ g_{min}(x,y) + 2/3\ g_{ave}(x,y)$, if $| g_{min}(x,y) - g_{ave}(x,y) | > | g_{max}(x,y) - g_{ave}(x,y) |$; (4) Expand the window size to repeat the calculation, if $| g_{min}(x,y) - g_{ave}(x,y) | = | g_{max}(x,y) - g_{ave}(x,y) |$. Our method can determine the thresholds for various document images containing signal-dependent noise, complex and variable background and very low local contrast, without obvious loss of useful information (as shown in Fig. 2).

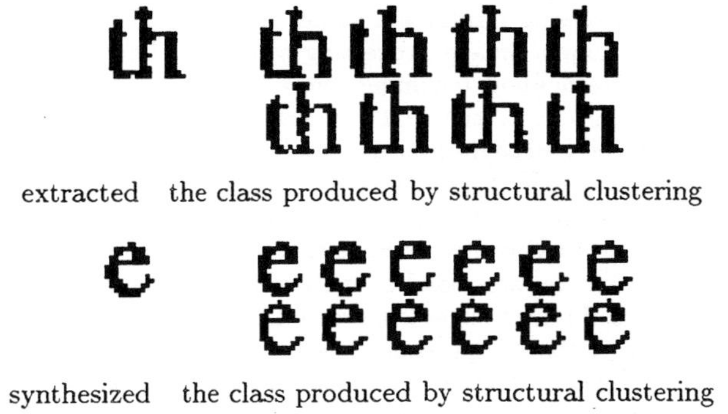

extracted the class produced by structural clustering

synthesized the class produced by structural clustering

Figure 3: The extracted and synthesized representative patterns, where, the left-most patterns are the extracted and synthesized representative patterns from all others, in a class on the right.

Figure 4: The segmentation and matching of the connected character string.

Figure 5: The large frame pattern (left) and the decomposed and matched result (right).

4. PATTERN MATCHING

4.1. Multistage Pattern Matching and Synthesizing

We propose a multistage pattern matching, decomposition and synthesizing technique [8] to achieve high compression for document images. The goal of the method is to remove redundancy as far as possible at the pattern level and at the decomposed component level. The pattern matching process is performed in two steps in this paper, direction-based error matching and structural clustering. We exploit some strict and low tolerance matching criteria based on the individual accumulated error numbers ($AEN(m,n), m = 1,2; n = 1,2,..,4$), which is defined as the sum of errors along four directions, the diagonal, cross-diagonal, horizontal and vertical directions of two error maps at the first stage of matching. An error number is defined as the number of errors successively appearing in the error-maps. The match is rejected if any one $AEN(m,n) > k_n$, where k_n is defined as $(pattern\_size)/4$ in direction n. In structural clustering, multi-stage matching [8] is performed based on pattern structure and shape, stroke width, direction and position distribution, as well as boundary information. We cluster those patterns with the same shape, stroke width and position distribution into the same class. In order to achieve accurate matching, we choose the best pattern from a class as the representative pattern of this class, which will produce minimum accumulated errors for all other replaced patterns in this class. Also we can synthesize a new pattern to replace all patterns in a class when the average size of the patterns is large in one of the directions, or the number of the patterns is small in a class. The synthesized new pattern is produced according to the *major rules* applying to pattern size, stroke or line width and position, as well as pixel levels in boundaries. Figure 3 gives an example of the matching and clustering results by using the proposed method.

4.2. Large Pattern Decomposition and Matching

Document images may contain some large connected patterns, such as connected character strings and the frames of tables and diagrams. These large patterns take up a large space in documents and the same large pattern does not in general appear very frequently. The direct compression of these large connected patterns may result in low compression efficiency. Accordingly, we decompose these large patterns into small and basic components which may appear in documents frequently, and then match the basic components to reduce the redundancy at the component level.

Our decomposition method is performed in two steps. The large patterns are firstly divided into two types – connected pattern strings and large frame patterns according to their size and structure. For the former, the average height and frequency of the black runs in horizontal and vertical directions should be similar to those in the small patterns in the same documents. A large pattern is regarded as a large frame pattern if; (1) the average pattern size, at least in one direction, is much larger than that of the small patterns in the same document, (2) the standard deviation of the black runs is small, (3) similar black runs appear regularly in one or two directions and the black run-lengths are much smaller than the white run-lengths within the large pattern; or if it is the long and narrow large patterns. The connected character strings can be decomposed and matched by using partial structural matching and feature matching which are performed from the starting and ending sides of the connected patterns. A partial structure alignment is performed first based on the width of the smaller pattern and then on the height within a one-pixel difference. Figure 4 shows an example of the connected pattern string decomposition and partial matching. The large frame patterns can be decomposed and matched by using pattern segmentation. A large frame pattern can be segmented into line segments and connected or crossed line segments whose height and width can be defined as the average height and width of small patterns in the document, so that more matches can be produced, and the redundancy can be removed as much as possible at the decomposed component level. It is worth noting that the increase in the pattern position parameters, due to pattern decomposition, will not reduce compression efficiency, because the position parameters of the decomposed components have a rather high correlation with the decrease of the pattern's space. Figure 5 shows a large frame pattern and its segmented results.

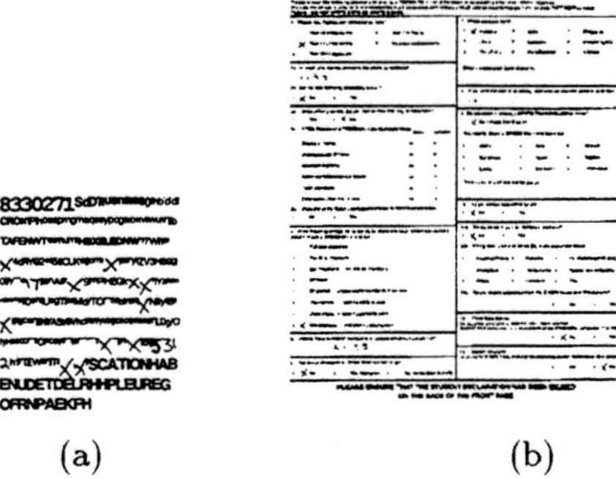

(a) (b)

Figure 6: (a) The representative pattern subimage extracted from the processed bilevel image in Fig. 1(b). (b) Reconstructed image from (a), Fig. 5 (b) and index data.

5. DOCUMENT COMPRESSION

After pattern matching and decomposition, we are left with two types of data sets. One is the index data with pattern position and matching information. The other includes two sub-images, one is the sub-image with all extracted and synthesized small patterns, and the other consists of the decomposed and segmented large patterns. Here, the context-based adaptive arithmetic coder [4] is used to carry out index data compression. We use the entire index data to make probability estimation, that is, dynamically estimating and updating the probability of each symbol occurring, based on all symbols that precede it, while considering the structure of the data. In order to decrease the cost of updating the model, we rearrange the index data structure, in the order which has a high correlation with local data, thereby achieving efficient coding. For the sub-images with representative small patterns and decomposed large frame patterns, we use the arithmetic coding based on pixel-by-pixel context modeling such as that used in JBIG [9] to compress image type data. The order of the patterns in the representative pattern sub-image is rearranged in order to fully use two dimensional correction between the scan lines of the bilevel image and provide more efficient compression. High compression can be achieved by compressing the matched small patterns and the components which are the results decomposed from the narrow, long, and large frame patterns. Figure 6 shows an example of compression and uncompression using our method. Our image segmentation and compression methods can be useful for implementation of the future JBIG2 standard [10].

6. EXPERIMENTS AND DISCUSSIONS

We have tested our system on a large range of document images with different resolutions (150, 200, 300, 400 dpi) and various types of styles, fonts and page layout. Experimental results show that our system can process, segment and compress poor quality grayscale document images as well as normal quality bilevel document images efficiently, without the need for any prior knowledge of the document image and manual fine-tuning of parameters, and achieves better processing results and higher compression than most other document image processing systems. The modified logical thresholding technique more accurately keeps useful information in the text regions of document images, without the overconnected and broken strokes of the characters (shown in Fig. 2). Our compression is content-lossless and its multi-page processing capability allows it to have a much higher compression ratio than other currently available lossy/lossless methods because the number of processed image pages is increased. For one-page images, on average, the compression ratios of our method are 4.55 times as high as Group 3; 3.45 times as high as the Group 4; 2.77 times as high as JBIG. For multi-page images, the compression ratios of our method are on average higher than for one page images. The increase in the compression ratio will be obvious, if all image pages are from one source, such as the same book or document. On average, for two-page images from similar sources, the compression ratios of our method are about 5.73 times as high as Group 3, 4.41 times as high as Group 4 and 3.46 times as high as JBIG; for five-page images from similar sources, the compression ratios of our method are about 6.91 times as high as Group 3, 5.37 times as high as Group 4 and 4.10 times as high as JBIG.

References

[1] A. L. Spitz and A. Dengel (eds.), *Document Analysis Systems*, World Scientific, Singapore, 1995.

[2] Y. Y. Tang, S. W. Lee and C. Y. Suen, Automatic Document Processing: A Survey, *Pattern Recognition*, **29**(12):1931-1952, 1996.

[3] J. D. Gibson, T. Berger, T. Lookabaugh, D. Lindbergh and R. L. Baker, *Digital Compression for Multimedia*, Morgan Kaufmann publishers, Inc. San Francisco, California, 1998.

[4] P. G. Howard and J. S. Vitter, Arithmetic coding for data compression, *Proc. IEEE*, **82**(6):857-895, 1994.

[5] H. Yan, Unified formulation of a class of optimal image thresholding techniques, *Pattern Recognition*, **29**(12):2025-2032, 1996.

[6] M. Kamel and A. Zhao, Extraction of binary character/graphics images from grayscale document images, *CVGIP: Graphical Models and Image Processing*, **55**(3):203-217, 1993.

[7] Y. Yang and H. Yan, An adaptive logical method for binarization of degraded document images, *Pattern Recognition*, in press.

[8] Y. Yang and H. Yan, Content-lossless document image compression based on structural analysis and pattern matching, *Pattern Recognition*, in press.

[9] ISO/IEC International Standard 11544 (JBIG), *Progressive Bi-level Image Compression*, ITU-T Recommendation T.82", March, 1993.

[10] B. Martins and Forchhammer, Lossless, near-lossless, and refinement coding of bilevel images, *IEEE Trans. Image Processing*, **8**(5):601-613, 1999.

A Syntactic Approach for Processing Mathematical Expressions in Printed Documents

U. Garain and B. B. Chaudhuri
Computer Vision & Pattern Recognition Unit
Indian Statistical Institute, Calcutta
INDIA
E-Mail: {utpal,bbc}@isical.ac.in

Abstract

In this paper, we propose an approach for understanding mathematical expressions in printed document. The overall approach is divided into three main steps: (i) detection of mathematical expressions in a document, (ii) recognition of the symbols present in the expression and (iii) arrangement of the recognized symbols. The detection of mathematical expressions is done through recognition of a few most common symbols and exploiting some structural features of the expressions. A hybrid of feature based and a template-based technique is used for the recognition of symbols. A two-pass approach is used for arrangement of the symbols. The first pass (Scanning or Lexical Analysis) performs a micro-level examination of the symbols in order to identify the symbol groups occurring in them and to determine their categories or descriptors. The second pass (Parsing or Syntax Analysis) processes the descriptors synthesized in the first pass, to determine the syntactic structure of the expression. A set of predefined rules guides the activities in both the passes. Experiments conducted using this approach on a large number of documents show high accuracy.

1. Introduction

The existing OCR systems show high accuracy in processing the text portions but fail to process other document elements like figures, logos, table, mathematical formulas and equations properly. This is one of the main stumbling blocks for automatic processing of technical documents since this type of documents generally contain a large number of Mathematical Expressions (MEs). The inability of the existing OCR systems to handle MEs is partly because they involve a large set of symbols that are not standardized and show wide variations in font size and style. Moreover, mathematical notations convey meaning through subtle use of spatial relationships among the symbols while it is very difficult to capture all such relationships and faithfully convert them into electronic form.

A naive approach for handling documents that contain MEs is to manually key in the expressions into the computer. This approach is not acceptable when a huge number of such technical documents should be processed on-line. Hence, an automatic approach for processing of MEs in the documents is called for.

This paper concentrates on understanding MEs contained in printed documents. Processing of such documents involves three main operations: identification of MEs in the document, symbol recognition, and symbol arrangement. The problem has attracted the attention of several earlier workers. Blostein and Grbavec [1] presented an interesting, systematic review on mathematical notation recognition. The existing techniques for recognition of MEs fall in one of the four types: syntax-directed [2, 3], projection-profile cutting [4, 5], graph rewriting [6, 7], and procedurally coded math syntax [8, 9].

Most of these studies start their processings with the pre-segmented MEs. Some of the studies [2, 3, 6] even avoid the symbol recognition step where error-free recognition results were assumed.

Earlier we reported our initial work in [10]. The present work is an extention and improvement of the earlier work. Functionally, the system is divided into three parts, namely (i) detection of ME areas, (ii) recognition of the symbols present in the ME, and (iii) arrangement of the recognized symbols. We modified our earlier techniques for detection of MEs and for arrangement of the symbols. We achieved much better results because of this new approach.

This paper is organized as follows. Section-2 describes the procedure for detection of ME areas whereas section-3 deals with symbol recognition. Techniques for the re-composition of the MEs are described in section-4. Section-5 presents the test results.

2. Detection of ME areas

Our approach for processing MEs is based on a statistical survey where we manually scanned more than 10,000 document pages drawn from various engineering and scientific books, technical journals, proceedings, etc. Details of this survey could be found in [10]. In a nutshell, the survey helps to gather knowledge about the structure of MEs in printed document and the different symbols that may occur in MEs.

During the statistical survey, we encountered more than 11,000 MEs that are of two types: either (i) printed in a separate line or block, with white spaces above and below or (ii) embedded directly into the text line. Hence, the first step in ME recognition is to detect the location of the ME in the document. Among earlier works, Lee and Wang [11] presented a method of extracting MEs where they exploited some basic expression forms. More recently, Kacem et al presented their approach for separation of mathematical formulas from standard text in [12].

In our approach, the detection of separately printed MEs is done without any character recognition. The following two important features are used: (i) Separately printed MEs are surrounded by wide white spacing. (ii) The left lower-most black pixels of the ME symbols are generally scattered over the ME area whereas such pixels of the symbols of a text line generally lie on a straight line. So, if we calculate standard deviation (SD) among the left lower-most black pixels of the ME symbols, we get a value much larger than the SD-value when it is calculated among the lower most black pixels of the symbols of a text line.

Detection of embedded MEs is done through recognition of some frequently occurring ME symbols. In our statistical survey we found that in more than 90% cases the equal to symbol ('=') or one of the plus ('+'), minus ('-') or division ('/') symbols occurs in MEs. Other symbols that occur frequently are shown in section-3.

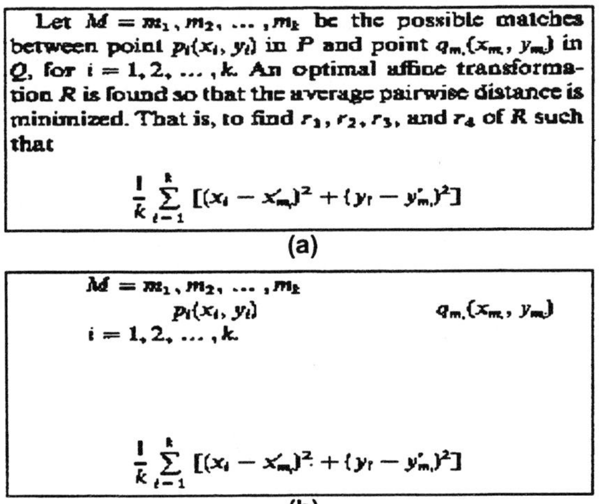

Let $M = m_1, m_2, \ldots, m_k$ be the possible matches between point $p_i(x_i, y_i)$ in P and point $q_{m_i}(x_{m_i}, y_{m_i})$ in Q, for $i = 1, 2, \ldots, k$. An optimal affine transformation R is found so that the average pairwise distance is minimized. That is, to find r_1, r_2, r_3, and r_4 of R such that

$$\frac{1}{k}\sum_{i=1}^{k}[(x_i - x'_{m_i})^2 + (y_i - y'_{m_i})^2]$$

(a)

$$M = m_1, m_2, \ldots, m_k$$

$p_i(x_i, y_i)$ $q_{m_i}(x_{m_i}, y_{m_i})$

$i = 1, 2, \ldots, k.$

$$\frac{1}{k}\sum_{i=1}^{k}[(x_i - x'_{m_i})^2 + (y_i - y'_{m_i})^2]$$

(b)

Figure 1. Extraction of Mathematical Expressions.

At first we check each text line to decide whether they contain one of the 25 frequently occurring mathematical symbols (detected in our statistical study). Once the presence of some symbols is confirmed in a text line say, T, it is decided that T contains an ME. Next, the ME area is detected and then extracted from T. Let W_1 be the first word from the left-hand side that contain one or more mathematical symbols in T. Construction of ME area is started by including W_1. Next the ME area grows towards both left and right side following certain rules. Two such rules are given below:

- If W_1 contains only a binary operator then both the immediate left and right side words are included in the ME area.
- Words adjacent to W_1 (on immediate left and right) are included in the ME area provided they contain:
  - One or more mathematical symbols (including brackets),
  - Superscript or subscripts,
  - Single or a series of dots,
  - Numerals.

Applying these rules each word included in an ME area is checked. Figure 1(a) shows a document containing both embedded and separate MEs. Figure 1(b) shows the extracted ME areas.

3. Symbol recognition

Recognition of mathematical symbols is a difficult task because it has to deal with a large character set. The set consists of Roman and Greek letters, operator symbols with a variety of typefaces (normal, bold or italic), brackets and abbreviation symbols (e.g. symbols for *for all, there exist*). Different font sizes are used to designate superscripts, subscripts and limit expressions.

We divide the character set into two groups. The first group, *group-1* includes 26 symbols of which 25 symbols are as follows.

"=" "+" "–" "/" "(" ")" "[" "]" "{" "}" "<" ">" "Σ" "∫" "–" "∪" "∩" "⊂" "⊃" "Π" "√" "×" "∀" "∈" "Δ"

The 26th symbol is the fraction or division line that exists between the numerator and the denominator. *Group-1* symbols have very high rate of occurrence, so error in recognizing the symbols of this group not only affects the overall symbol recognition rate but also the efficiency of the module that detects the ME areas (as embedded MEs are detected through character recognition). Hence, *group-1* symbols are recognized through a feature-based approach that is more flexible to size and style variation of the character font than the template based one. Moreover, these symbols have relatively simple shapes and hence recognition through stroke/feature analysis is more efficient.

Group-2 mostly includes the Roman and Greek letters (e.g. α, β, δ, λ, etc.) which have more complex stroke patterns. For the recognition of such symbols we combine the positive aspects of feature based and template based approaches. A run number based normalized template matching technique [13] is used for recognizing the *group-2* symbols.

Our run number based template matching technique is more or less invariant to scaling and insensitive to character style variations except for the italic style. We find that in 47% of the cases the MEs are printed in italic style. So, we apply an approach for the detection of italic characters [14], de-italicize them, and then use our template matching technique on the slant-corrected characters.

In MEs, there are some symbols that have more than one meaning. For example, a dot represents a full-stop sign, a decimal sign, a multiplication symbol, etc. Our symbol recognition procedure tries to resolve such ambiguities by using some contextual information. The notational conventions for writing MEs define this contextual processing.

4. Arrangement of symbols

At the end of character recognition stage a ME is represented by a list of symbols (L) in random order. At first, L is sorted according to the bounding-box co-ordinates of the symbols. Next, the symbols are arranged into a character string satisfying the notational conventions of the 2-D language for mathematical expression. This is done by two functions: (i) Scanning (Lexical Analysis) and (ii) Parsing (Syntax Analysis).

4.1. Scanning (Lexical Analysis)

The scanner performs a micro-level examination of the symbols of L in order to identify symbol groups (e.g. $x^y, a_i, etc.$) occurring in it and to determine their syntax categories. Formation of symbol groups is important to recognize an ME because same set of symbols conveys different meaning depending upon the spatial relationships among the symbols. For example, "x^y" and "$x\ y$" both involve same set of symbols (i.e. 'x' and 'y'), but present different meanings.

The formation of symbol groups takes help of the spatial relationships among the symbols. Spatial relationships among the symbols are determined by identifying the physical structure of the ME. For this purpose, we use the bounding-box coordinates, coordinates of the centroids and the size information of the symbols. On finding the end of a symbol group, a *semantic routine* is called, which further processes the group and provides a syntax category or descriptor (e.g. variable, integer, operator, etc.) for that group. This leads to the detection and indication of certain recognition errors.

4.2. Parsing (Syntax Analysis)

Parsing attempts to develop a syntax tree for the expression. Elementary subtrees in the tree are built around the operators and each of these subtrees must correspond to a predefined rule that reflects the logical relationships among different symbol groups. The rules define whether an expression involving an operator is valid or not. The rules are made as general as possible. For example, our system covers 20 forms of integrals, including single integrals, line integrals, double (surface) integrals, and triple (volume) integrals, all with various combinations of limits. Similarly, 5 different types of summation with various combinations of limits are covered by the rules.

We use bottom up parse to develop the syntax tree for L through a sequence of reductions. If L can be reduced to a single expression then we assume that the proper arrangement of the symbols is achieved. Attempts for reduction start with the first symbol group of L and proceed to the right. At each stage, n symbols to the left of the current position are matched with all RHS alternatives of the rules that are n symbols in length. If a match is found, these n-symbols are replaced with LHS of the rule. The building of the syntax tree is guided by the precedence among the operators that prevents the generation of multiple trees for a single expression. Fig. 2(a) and 2(b) show an expression and the generated parse tree, respectively. Each symbol in Fig. 2(b) is marked with its category or descriptor (V: variable, O: operator, C: constant, E: expression, etc.). The rules that are applied during reduction are indicated at the root of the subtrees.

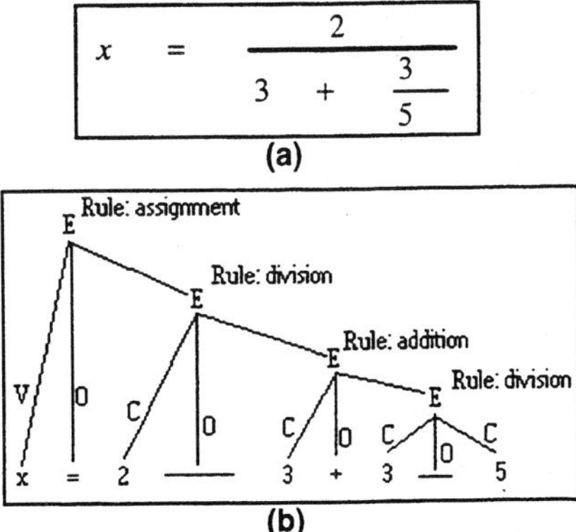

Figure 2. Syntax tree for a Mathematical Expression.

4.3. Coding of expressions

Finally, the *ME* is encoded in an HTML like code. Options are there to encode the MEs into other standard format like Latex, etc. Figure 3(b) shows the codified version of the expression in Figure 3(a).

$$R(C) = \int_0^L \sqrt{(x(s)-P_x)^2 + (y(s)-P_y)^2}\, ds \qquad (2)$$

(a)

R(C) = <INTEGRATION> <UPLIM> L </UPLIM> <LOWLIM> 0 </LOWLIM> <SQRT> (x(s) - P _x) ² + (y(s) - P _y) ² </SQRT> ds </INTEGRATION> <EQU NO> (2) </EQU NO>

(b)

Figure 3. Coding of Mathematical Expressions.

5. Test results

Algorithms for detection of ME areas, recognition and arrangement of symbols have been tested on 150 technical documents (average size: 3000X2000 pixels) containing 168 MEs. Among these documents 30% is noise-free (computer generated laser print) and the rest was taken from real life documents (noise affected) like technical journals, books, etc.

Our system is implemented in C-language on a 166 MHz Pentium PC with 32 MB RAM. Documents are scanned at 300 dpi. On an average, the system takes only 66 seconds to process a document including the time required for binarizing a gray-level image.

Test result shows that 162 MEs (both separate and embedded) are properly detected. This shows more than 95% accuracy. Among the six unidentified MEs, four are embedded MEs. The rest two are missed because of the complicated document structure. In these cases, our algorithm fails to analyze the document structure itself. On the other hand, a part of normal text line is misidentified as embedded MEs for 3 cases. In such cases, some text symbols are wrongly recognized as mathematical symbols.

The character recognition module shows high accuracy of about 98.3%. Since group-1 symbols have relatively simpler shapes than those of group-2 symbols, stroke feature based technique shows better accuracy than the template matching technique.

Arrangement of symbols is somewhat more difficult. Wrong arrangement of one or two symbols may drastically change the meaning of the expression even after all other symbols are arranged properly. An example where our system fails to analyze the ME properly is $\prod_i a_i$. Here the system misinterprets a_i as superscript of i of the product sign and codes the ME as the product over i^{ai} . But actually it is the product over a_i. Recognition error also plays significant role in symbol arrangement stage. Mis-recognized symbols prevent the lexical analyzer from forming meaningful symbol groups. However, warning or error messages can be issued in such cases.

6. Conclusions and Future Directions

In this paper, we presented a system for processing mathematical expressions in printed documents. The method of finding expressions in a document offers the option of creating a database of mathematical expressions after scanning a large volume of technical documents. Proper arrangement of the symbols along with their size and style information helps in re-composing the MEs more faithfully.

At present, our system produces some HTML like code for the MEs but it does not solve the problem of presenting a technical document in the WWW as HTML is unable to format mathematics with their specialized notations. Now we are modifying the system to encode the recognized MEs into a suitable format like in MathML (Mathematical Markup Language released the WWW Consortium in April 1998, see http://www.w3.org/math/ for details).

Our future plan is to integrate a speech output to our current system. This may be helpful for the visually impaired persons to realize a mathematical formula. Finally, we feel needs for some kind of benchmarking as well as groundtruthing policy for such systems. This will help in evaluating different systems proposed for processing MEs.

Acknowledgement

The authors would like to thank Dr. U. Pal for some useful discussions on this work.

References

[1] D. Blostein and A. Grbavec, "Recognition of Mathematical Notation", Handbook of Character Recognition and Document Image Analysis, World Scientific Publishing Company, Eds: H. Bunke, P. S. P. Wang, 1997, pp 557-582.

[2] R. H. Anderson, "Syntax-directed recognition of handprinted 2-D mathematics", Ph.D. Dissertation, Harvard University, Cambridge, M. A., 1968.

[3] S. K. Chang, "A method for the structural analysis of 2-D mathematical expressions", Information Sciences, 2 (3), 1970, pp. 253–272.

[4] M. Okamoto and H. Twaakyondo, "Structure Analysis and Recognition of Mathematical Expressions", IEEE Computer Society Press, 1995, pp 430-437.

[5] M. Okamoto and H. Miyazawa, "An experimental implementation of a document recognition system for papers containing mathematical expressions", Structured Document Image Analysis. Springer, 1992, pp. 36-53.

[6] A. Grbavec and D. Blostein, "Mathematics recognition using graph rewriting", ICDAR, 1995, pp. 417-421.

[7] A. Kosmala, G. Rigoll, S. Lavirotte, and L. Pottier, "On-line Handwritten Formula Recognition using Hidden Markov Model and Context Dependent Graph Grammar", ICDAR, 1999, pp. 107-110.

[8] H. Lee and M. Lee, "Understanding mathematical expressions using procedure-oriented transformation", Pattern Recognition, 27(3), 1994, pp. 447–457.

[9] P. Chou, "Recognition of equations using a two-dimensional context-free grammar", In Proceedings of SPIE Visual Communication and Image Processing IV, 1989, pp. 852-863.

[10] B. B. Chaudhuri and U. Garain, "An approach for processing Mathematical Expressions in printed document", Lecture Notes in Computer Science (LNCS-1655), Springer, Eds: Seong-Whan Lee and Y. Nakano, 1998, pp. 310-321.

[11] H. Lee and J. Wang, "Design of a mathematical expression recognition system", ICDAR, 1995, pp. 1084-1087.

[12] A. Kacem, A. Belaid, and M. B. Ahmed, "EXTRAFOR: automatic EXTRAction of mathematical FORmulas", ICADR, 1999, pp. 527-530.

[13] U. Garain and B. B. Chaudhuri, "Compound character recognition by a run number based metric distance", SPIE, Vol. 3305. 1998, pp. 90-97.

[14] B. B. Chaudhuri and U. Garain, "Automatic detection of italic, bold and all-capital words from documents", ICPR, 1998, pp. 610-612.

Accuracy Improvement of Slant Estimation for Handwritten Words

Yimei Ding[†], Fumitaka Kimura[†], Yasuji Miyake[†], Malayappan Shridhar[††]

[†]Faculty of Engineering, Mie University, 1515 Kamihama, Tsu 514-8507, JAPAN
[††]ECE Dept., University of Michigan-Dearborn, Dearborn, MI 48128-1491, USA
tei@hi.info.mie-u.ac.jp

Abstract

Handwritten words are usually slant or Italicized due to the mechanism of handwriting and the personality. In order to improve the accuracy of character segmentation and recognition, the authors proposed a chain code method for the slant estimation and correction[1]. However the method is very simple and usually gives good estimate of the word slant, there was a problem such that the slant tends to be underestimated when the absolute of the slant is close or greater than 45°. To solve the problem, we proposed an iterative chain code method[6]. In this paper, we introduce a new non-iterative method using 8-directional chain code for improving the linearity and the accuracy of the slant estimation. The experimental results show that the proposed method improves the linearity and the accuracy of the slant estimation efficiently without sacrificing the processing speed and the simplicity.

1. Introduction

Handwritten words are usually slant or Italicized due to the mechanism of hand writing and the personality. In order to simplify the character segmentation task and to improve the accuracy of the character segmentation and recognition, several techniques for estimating word slant have been proposed, e.g. the run-length based technique[2], the projection method [3], the extrema analysis method[4], and the generalized chain code estimator[5].

The authors proposed a chain code method for slant estimation and correction[1]. However the method is very simple and usually gives good estimate of the word slant, there was a problem such that the relationship between the actual slant and the estimated slant is not linear, and the slant tends to be under estimated when the absolute of the slant is close or greater than 45°.

To solve the problem, the authors proposed an iterative chain code method[6] which repeats the slant estimation and the correction until the slant reduces to sufficiently small. Although the linearity and the accuracy were improved, the required processing time was increased and the slant corrected image got jagged as the number of iteration increases.

Refering to [5], we tested generalized chain code estimators which have an enhancement parameter to compensate the under estimation of the slant. Although the enhancement could improve the under estimation, the accuracy and the linearity were not sufficiently improved.

In this paper we introduce a new non-iterative method using 8-directional chain code for improving the linearity and the accuracy of the slant estimation.

2. Slant estimation and correction by chain code method

Average slant of an English word is easily estimated using the chain code histogram of entire border pixels[1]. The estimator is given by

$$\theta = \tan^{-1}\left(\frac{n_1 - n_3}{n_1 + n_2 + n_3}\right) \tag{1}$$

where n_i is the number of chain elements at an angle of i x 45° (/ or | or \). Shear transformation is then applied to correct the slant.

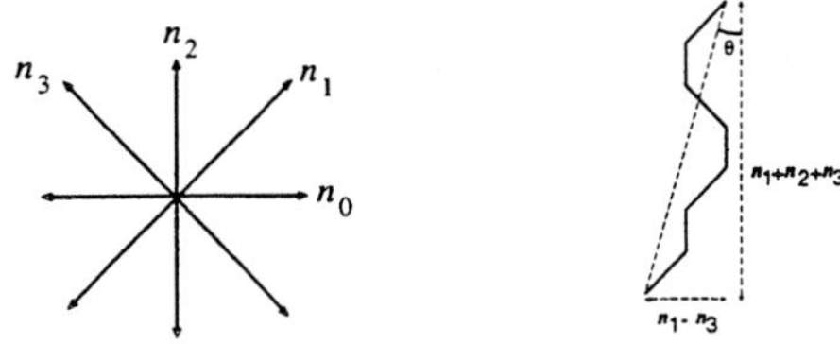

Figure 1. Average slant of a chain code sequence

1051-4651/00 $10.00

2.1. Evaluation of estimation accuracy

In order to evaluate the estimation accuracy for an input pattern, we shear it by every 5° from −60° to 60° and estimate the slant of each sheared word image.

Fig.2 shows the relationship between the angle of shearing and the estimated slant for a test pattern sheared by every 5° from −60° to 60°.

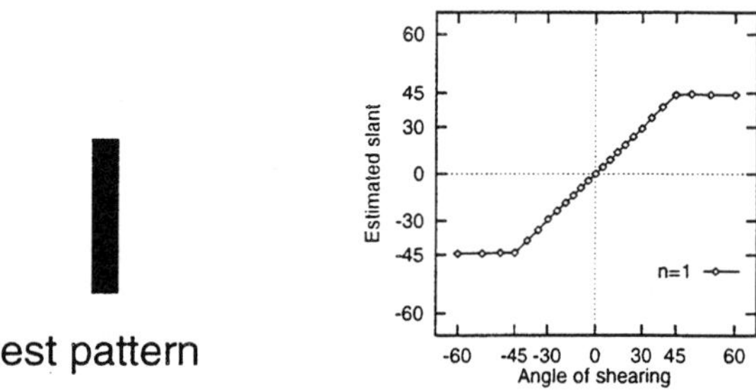

Figure 2. Evaluation of estimation accuracy for a test pattern

In the range of [−45°, 45°], the estimated slant is almost linear and close to the actual slant of the input pattern. However, if the absolute of the slant exceeds 45°, the estimate is no more correct and valid. This phenomenon is attributed to the inequalities $n_1 - n_3 \leq n_1 + n_2 + n_3$ or $|\tan\theta| \leq 1$.

2.2. Generalized chain code methods

In [5], a generalized chain code estimator (3) was proposed which has an enhancement parameter $k \in [0, 1]$.

$$\theta = \tan^{-1}\left(\frac{n_1 - n_3 + kn_2}{n_1 + n_2 + n_3}\right) \quad (2)$$

Fig.3 shows characteristic curve of slant estimator(3) for the test pattern. With the increase of the parameter k, not only the linearity is not improved beyond [−45°,45°], but also it is deteriorated in [−45°,45°].

We modified the generalized chain code estimator to obtain an alternate generalized chain code estimator(4) utilizing $k^{'}n_0$ instead of kn_2 as the enhancement term.

$$\theta = \tan^{-1}\left(\frac{n_1 - n_3 + k^{'}n_0}{n_1 + n_2 + n_3}\right) \quad (3)$$

where n_0 is the number of horizonal chain elements, and $k^{'}$ is given by

$$\begin{cases} k^{'} = k & (n_1 - n_3 \geq 0) \\ k^{'} = -k & (n_1 - n_3 < 0) \end{cases} \quad (4)$$

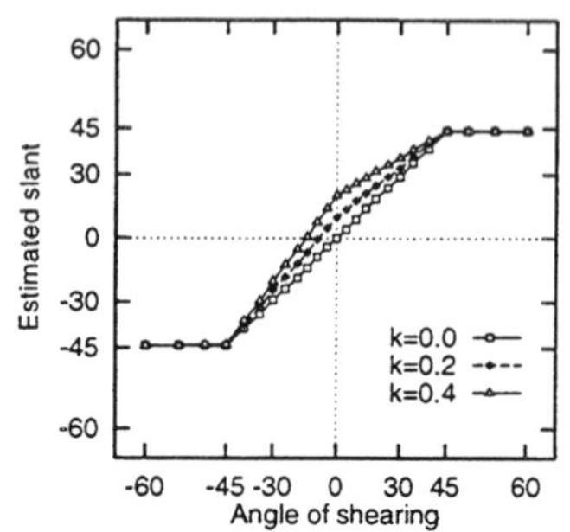

Figure 3. Evaluation of slant estimation by generalized chain code method

Fig.4 shows characteristic curves of the alternate generalized chain code method for the test pattern and a real world data. With the increase of the parameter k, the linearity and the under estimation can be improved to some extent.

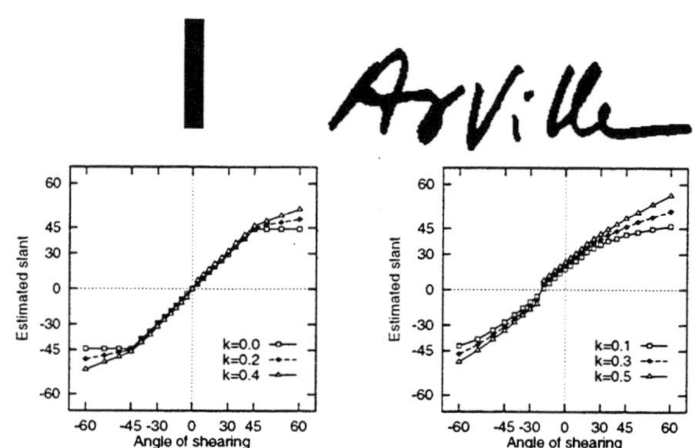

Figure 4. Estimation accuracy by generalized chain code method

The problem of this generalized chain code method is the dependency between k and n_0. If an input word image contains smaller (larger) number of horizontal chain code elements, the value of k has to be larger (smaller). Because of the dependency, it is difficult to achieve maximum linearity as long as the value of k is fixed to a predetermined value.

3. Accuracy improvement by 8 directional chain code method

To extend the range in which the linearity is preserved, we propose an 8-directional chain code method described below.

Instead of tracing the boder pixels one by one with 8-neighborhood, we trace the every two pixels. Obtained chain code is then quantized to 8 directions as shown in Fig.5. Each direction is numbered 0 to 7 in counter clockwise, and n_i denotes the number of chain code elements in direction i.

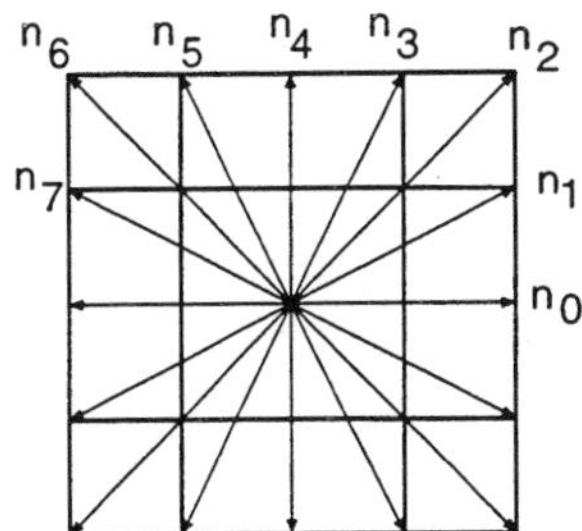

Figure 5. 8-directional quantization of chain code

The slant estimator of the 8-direction chain code method is given by

$$\tan\theta = \frac{(2n_1 + 2n_2 + n_3) - (n_5 + 2n_6 + 2n_7)}{(n_1 + 2n_2 + 2n_3) + 2n_4 + (2n_5 + 2n_6 + n_7)} \quad (5)$$

where $(2n_1 + 2n_2 + n_3)$ is the sum of horizontal projection of the element 1, 2, 3, $(n_5 + 2n_6 + 2n_7)$ is the sum of horizontal projection of the element 5, 6, 7, and the denominator is the sum of vertical projection of the element 1 to 7.

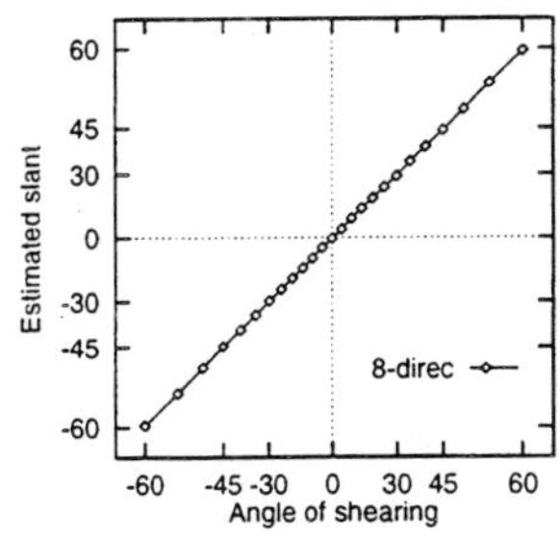

Figure 6. Evaluation of estimation accuracy of 8-directional method for the test pattern

Fig.6 shows the characteristic curve of the 8-directional method for the test pattern. This result shows that the lineartity is preserved in wider range, which is potentially [-arctan(2), arctan(2)].

4. Evaluation and comparison of estimation accuracy

4.1. Comparison with 4-directional method

Fig.7 shows characteristic curves of 4-directional method, the simple iterative method[6] and 8-directional method. In the iterative method, the 4-directional method was applied twice successively. Fig.7(a) is for the test pattern and Fig.7(b) for the real world data. Those results show that the linearity of the 8-directional method as well as the iterative method is better than that of 4-directional method. Fig.4 also shows the regression lines and the correlation coefficients. Both the correlation coefficients and the slope of the regression line of the 8-directional method approach to 1.

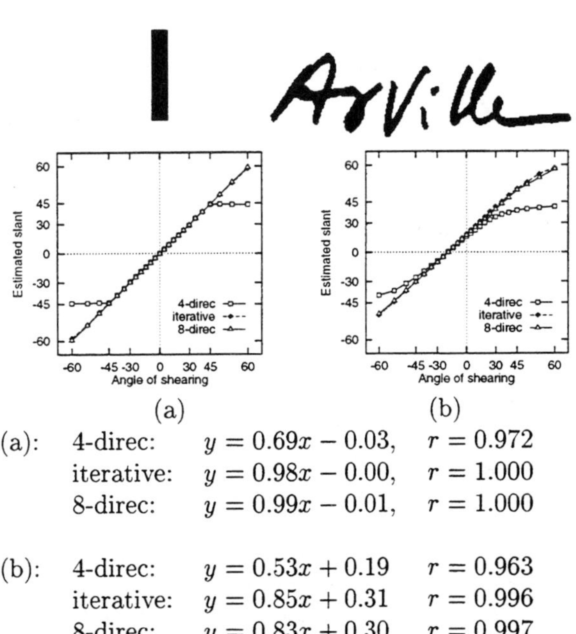

(a): 4-direc: $y = 0.69x - 0.03$, $r = 0.972$
iterative: $y = 0.98x - 0.00$, $r = 1.000$
8-direc: $y = 0.99x - 0.01$, $r = 1.000$

(b): 4-direc: $y = 0.53x + 0.19$ $r = 0.963$
iterative: $y = 0.85x + 0.31$ $r = 0.996$
8-direc: $y = 0.83x + 0.30$ $r = 0.997$

Figure 7. (a)Accuracy improvement by 8-directional method (b)Estimation accuracy for real world data

Table 1 shows the average slope of the regression lines and the average correlation coefficients of the 4-directional method, the iterative method and the 8-directional method for 1000 handwritten words.

Fig.8 shows examples of slant corrected word images. The upper row shows input images, the sencond row to the bottom row show the slant corrected images by the 4-directional method, the iterative method and the 8-directional method respectively. The slant corrected images by the 8-directional method are better

Table 1: Average slope and average correlation coefficients

Range	Average of	Slant estimation method		
		4-dire	iterative	8-dire
[−45°,45°]	slope	0.63	0.87	0.83
	co-co	0.991	0.999	0.999
[−60°,60°]	slope	0.53	0.81	0.79
	co-co	0.971	0.994	0.996

than those by the 4-directional method because they tend to be underestimated. The results by the 8-directional method are also better than those by the iterative method, because the shear transformation is applied only once in the 8-directional method, while it is applied twice in the iterative method.

Figure 8. Examples of slant corrected images

4.2. Evaluation and comparison of processing speed

Table 2 shows average processing time of slant estimation for 100 handwritten English words by each method. Used CPU is a hyper SPARC 125MHz. While the processing time of the iterative method increases proportional to the number of iteration, the processing time of 8-directional method is almost the same as the one of the 4-directional method.

Table 2 Average processing time for slant estimation

	4-direc	iterative	8-direc
time(sec)	0.44	0.90	0.45

4.3. Comparison with manually measured word slant

Table 3 shows the slant of ten handwritten English words estimated by the 4-directional method, the iterative method and the 8-directional method together with the average slant manually measured with a protractor by 20 persons. The 8-directional method and the iterative method give good estimates of the manually measured average slant.

Table 3: Comparision with manually measured word slant

Word	Estimated Slant(degree)			
	4-dir	iterative	8-dir	Manual
im01	13.81	16.53	16.87	15.87
im02	19.28	27.44	27.02	29.12
im03	29.27	36.89	36.62	35.25
im04	18.31	22.60	23.47	24.25
im05	-12.88	-16.53	-15.93	-15.12
im06	-22.17	-28.96	-27.72	-29.50
im07	33.25	43.25	42.57	40.25
im08	32.67	45.27	44.95	43.00
im09	33.08	46.24	45.62	44.62
im10	37.75	46.77	45.66	45.05

5. Conclusion

The result of experimental comparison showed that the 8-directional method improved the linearity and the accuracy of the slant estimation without sacrificing the processing speed and the simplicity.

Further comparative studies with more image data and slant estimators, estimation of local slant, and slant estimation of oriental character strings are remained as future research topics.

References

[1] F.Kimura, M.Shridhar and Z.Chen, "Improvements of a Lexicon Directed Algorithm for Recognition of Unconstrained Handwritten Words", Proc. of the 2th ICDAR, pp. 18-22,1993.

[2] R.M. Bozinovic and S.N. Srihari, "Off-line Cursive Script Word Recognition", IEEE Transactions on PAMI, vol. II, No. 1, pp. 68-83, Jan. 1989.

[3] Didier Guillevic, Ching Y. Suen, "Cursive Script Recognition: A Sentence Level Recognition Scheme", Proc. of 4th IWFHR, pp. 216-223, Dec. 1994.

[4] Atul Negi, K.S.Swaroop, Arun Agarwal,"A Correspondence Based Approach to Segmentation of Cursive Words", Proc. of 3th ICDAR, vol. II, pp. 1034-1037, Aug.1995.

[5] L.Simoncini, Zs.M.Kovacs-V, "A System for Reading USA Census'90 Hand-Written Fields", Proc. of 3th ICDAR, Vol. II, pp. 86-91, Aug. 1995.

[6] Yimei Ding, Fumitaka Kimura, Yasuji Miyake, Malayappan Shridhar, "Evaluation and Improvement of Slant Estimation for Handwritten Words", Proc. of 5th ICDAR, pp. 753-756, Sep. 1999.

Automatic Training of Page Segmentation Algorithms: An Optimization Approach

Song Mao and Tapas Kanungo
Language and Media Processing Laboratory
Center for Automation Research
University of Maryland, College Park, MD 20742

Abstract

Most page segmentation algorithms have user-specifiable free parameters. However, algorithm designers typically do not provide a quantitative/rigorous method for choosing values for these parameters. The free parameter values can affect the segmentation result quite drastically and are very dependent on the particular dataset that the algorithm is being used on. In this paper, we present an automatic training method for choosing free parameters of page segmentation algorithms. The automatic training problem is posed as a multivariate non-smooth function optimization problem. An efficient direct search method — simplex method — is used to solve this optimization problem. This training method is then applied to the training of Kise's page segmentation algorithm. It is found that a set of optimal parameter values and their corresponding performance index can be found using relatively few function evaluations. The UW III dataset was used for conducting our experiments.

1 Introduction

Page segmentation is a crucial preprocessing step in OCR system. In many cases, OCR accuracy heavily depends on page segmentation accuracy. While numerous segmentation algorithms have been proposed in the literature [12, 6, 14, 11, 9, 1], relatively little research effort has been devoted to automatic training of algorithms with user-specifiable free parameters.

Some research algorithms [6, 11, 5] specify default parameter values. In performance evaluation literature, Hoover *et al.* [4] manually selected the algorithm parameters. A common aspect of these training methods is that a set of "optimal parameter values" are *manually* selected based on some assumption regarding the training dataset. To objectively optimize a segmentation algorithm on a given training dataset, a set of optimal parameter values should be *automatically* found by a training procedure.

In this article, we pose the automatic algorithm training problem as an optimization problem. We set-theoretically define a textline based performance metric, which is used to construct an object function. The objective function is a function of the algorithm parameters and the training dataset. This average performance metric on the training data set is used as the objective function value. The simplex search technique introduced by Nelder and Mead [10], which belongs to the class of direct search method [2], is used to find the optimal solution. This method is applied to Kise's Voronoi-diagram-based segmentation algorithm on the University of Washington III dataset [13].

This paper is organized as follows. In Section 2, we define page segmentation and error metrics. In Section 3, we pose the automatic training problem as an optimization problem. In Section 4, we specify the experimental protocol. In Section 5, we report experimental results and provide discussions. Finally, in Section 6, we give our conclusions.

2 The Page Segmentation Problem and Error Metrics

In this section we define page segmentation and the error metrics used. These definitions are based on set theory and mathematical morphology [3].

2.1 Page Segmentation Definition

Let I be a document image, and let G be the groundtruth of I. Let $Z(G) = \{Z_q^G, q = 1, 2, \ldots, \#Z(G)\}$ be a set of groundtruth zones of document image I where $\#$ denotes the cardinality of a set. Let $L(Z_q^G) = \{l_{qj}^G, j = 1, 2, \ldots, \#L(Z_q^G)\}$ be the set of groundtruth textlines in groundtruth zone Z_q^G. Let the set of all groundtruth textlines in document image I be $\mathcal{L} = \cup_{q=1}^{\#Z(G)} L(Z_q^G)$. Let A be a given segmentation algorithm, $Seg_A(\cdot, \cdot)$ be the segmentation function corresponding to the algorithm A. Let R be the segmentation result of algorithm A such that $R = Seg_A(I, \mathbf{p}^A)$ where $Z(R) = \{Z_k^R | k = 1, 2, \ldots, \#Z(R)\}$.

Let $D(\cdot) \subseteq \mathcal{Z}^2$ be the domain of its argument, the groundtruth zones and textlines have the following properties: 1) $D(Z_q^G) \cap D(Z_{q'}^G) = \phi$ for $Z_q^G, Z_{q'}^G \in Z(G)$ and $q \neq q'$, and 2) $D(l_i^G) \cap D(l_{i'}^G) = \phi$ for $l_i^G, l_{i'}^G \in \mathcal{L}$ and $i \neq i'$.

2.2 Error Measurements and Metric Definitions

While a performance metric is typically not unique, researchers can select a particular performance metric to study certain aspects of page segmentation algorithms, a set of error measurements is necessary. Let $T_X, T_Y \in Z^+ \cup \{0\}$ be two length thresholds (number of pixels) that determine if the overlap is significant or not. Let $E(T_X, T_Y) = \{e \in Z^2 | -T_X \leq X(e) \leq T_X, -T_Y \leq Y(e) \leq T_Y\}$ be a region of a rectangle centered at $(0,0)$ with a width of $2T_X + 1$ pixels and a height of $2T_Y + 1$ pixels where $X(\cdot)$ and $Y(\cdot)$ denote the X and Y coordinates of the argument respectively. We now define two morphological operations: dilation and erosion [3]. Let $A, B \subseteq Z^2$. Morphological *dilation* of A by B is denoted by $A \oplus B$ and is defined as:
$A \oplus B = \{c \in Z^2 | c = a + b \text{ for some } a \in A, b \in B\}$.
Morphological *erosion* of A by B is denoted by $A \ominus B$ and is defined as:
$A \ominus B = \{c \in Z^2 | c + b \in A \text{ for every } b \in B\}$.

Now, we define three types of textline based error measurements:

1) Groundtruth textlines that are missed:
$$C_L = \{l^G \in \mathcal{L} | D(l^G) \ominus E(T_X, T_Y) \subseteq (\cup_{Z^R \in Z(R)} D(Z^R))^c\},$$

2) Groundtruth textlines whose bounding box is split:
$$S_L = \{l^G \in \mathcal{L} | (D(l^G) \ominus E(T_X, T_Y)) \cap D(Z^R) \neq \phi, (D(l^G) \ominus E(T_X, T_Y)) \cap (D(Z^R))^c \neq \phi, \text{ for some } Z^R \in Z(R)\},$$

3) Groundtruth textlines that are horizontally merged:
$$M_L = \{l_{qj}^G \in \mathcal{L} | \exists l_{q'j'}^G \in \mathcal{L}, Z^R \in Z(R), q \neq q', Z_q^G, Z_{q'}^G \in Z(G) \text{ such that } (D(l_{qj}^G) \ominus E(T_X, T_Y)) \cap D(Z^R) \neq \phi, (D(l_{q'j'}^G) \ominus E(T_X, T_Y)) \cap D(Z^R) \neq \phi, ((D(l_{qj}^G) \ominus E(0, T_Y)) \oplus E(\infty, 0)) \cap D(Z_{q'}^G) \neq \phi, ((D(l_{q'j'}^G) \ominus E(0, T_Y)) \oplus E(\infty, 0)) \cap D(Z_q^G) \neq \phi\}.$$

Let the number of groundtruth error textlines be $\#\{C_L \cup S_L \cup M_L\}$ (miss-detected, split or horizontally merged), and the total number of groundtruth textlines is $\#\mathcal{L}$. We define the performance metric $\rho(I, G, R)$ as textline accuracy:

$$\rho(I, G, R) = \frac{\#\mathcal{L} - \#\{C_L \cup S_L \cup M_L\}}{\#\mathcal{L}}. \quad (1)$$

We only consider three types of textline errors — split, missed and horizontally merged. Our textline-based performance metric has the following features: 1) it is based on set theory and mathematical morphology, 2) it is independent of shape of zones, 3) it is independent of OCR recognition error, 4) it ignores the background information (white space, salt and pepper noise etc.), 5) segmentation errors can be localized, and 6) quantitative evaluations on lower level (e.g. textline, word and character) segmentation algorithms can be readily achieved with little modifications. However, this performance metric needs textline level groundtruth. In general, $\rho(I, G, R)$ can be any user-specified function.

3 Automatic Algorithm Training: The Optimization Problem

We pose the automatic segmentation algorithm training problem as an optimization problem. An optimization problem has three components, the objective function that gives a quantitative measure of goodness, a set of parameters that the objective function is dependent on, and a parameter subspace that defines acceptable or reasonable parameter values. The acceptable or reasonable parameter subspace is typically termed as the constraints of the optimization problem. The purpose of an optimization procedure is to find a set of parameter values for which the objective function gives the "best" (minimum or maximum) measure values. In this section, we first define the objective function for our page segmentation algorithm training problem, then we introduce a direct search algorithm to optimize the defined objective function, and finally we discuss the starting point selection in our optimization problem.

3.1 The Objective Function

Let $\mathbf{p}^A$ be the parameter vector for the segmentation algorithm A, let $\mathcal{T}$ be a training dataset, and let $\rho(I, G, Seg_A(I, \mathbf{p}^A))$ where $(I, G) \in \mathcal{T}$ be a performance metric. We define the objective function $f(\mathbf{p}^A; \mathcal{T}, A, \rho)$ to be minimized as the average textline error rate on the training dataset:

$$f(\mathbf{p}^A; \mathcal{T}, A, \rho) = \frac{1}{\#\mathcal{T}} \left[\sum_{(I,G) \in \mathcal{T}} 1 - \rho(G, Seg_A(I, \mathbf{p}^A)) \right].$$

where $\rho(G, Seg_A(I, \mathbf{p}^A))$ is given by Equation 1. This objective function has the following properties: 1) The function has no explicit mathematical form and is non-differentiable, 2) Only function evaluations are possible, 3) Obtaining a function value requires nontrivial computation. This objective function can be classified as a *multivariate non-smooth function*. In the following section, we describe an optimization algorithm to minimize this objective function.

3.2 The Simplex Search Method

Direct search methods are typically used to solve the optimization problem described in Section 4.1. We choose the simplex search method proposed by Nelder and Mead [10] to minimize our objective function.

We give the notation used to describe the simplex method: Let $\mathbf{q}_0$ be a starting point in segmentation algorithm parameter space, and let $\lambda_i, i = 1, \ldots, n$ be a set of scales. Let $\mathbf{e}_i, i = 1, \ldots, n$ be n orthogonal unit vectors in n-dimensional parameter space, let $\mathbf{p}_0, \ldots, \mathbf{p}_n$ be $(n+1)$ ordered points in n-dimensional parameter space such that their corresponding function values satisfy $f_0 \leq f_1 \leq, \ldots, \leq f_n$, let $\bar{\mathbf{p}} = \sum_{i=0}^{n-1} \mathbf{p}_i/n$ be the centroid of the n best (smallest) points, let $[\mathbf{p}_i\mathbf{p}_j]$ be the n-dimensional Euclidean distance from $\mathbf{p}_i$ to $\mathbf{p}_j$, let α, β, γ and σ be the *reflection, contraction, expansion and shrinkage coefficient,* respectively, and let T be the threshold for the stopping criterion. For a segmentation algorithm with n parameters, the Nelder-Mead algorithm works as follows:

1 Given $\mathbf{q}_0$ and the λ_i, form the initial simplex as
$\mathbf{q}_i = \mathbf{q}_0 + \lambda_i \mathbf{e}_i, i = 1, \ldots, n.$,
2 Relabel the $n+1$ vertices as $\mathbf{p}_0, \ldots, \mathbf{p}_n$ with
$f(\mathbf{p}_0) \leq f(\mathbf{p}_1) \cdots \leq f(\mathbf{p}_n)$,
3 Get a reflection point $\mathbf{p}_r$ of $\mathbf{p}_n$ by $\mathbf{p}_r = (1+\alpha)\bar{\mathbf{p}} - \alpha\mathbf{p}_n$
where $\alpha = [\mathbf{p}_r\bar{\mathbf{p}}]/[\mathbf{p}_n\bar{\mathbf{p}}]$.
4.1 If $f(\mathbf{p}_r) \leq f(\mathbf{p}_0)$, replace $\mathbf{p}_n$ by $\mathbf{p}_r$ and $f(\mathbf{p}_n)$ by $f(\mathbf{p}_r)$, get an expansion point $\mathbf{p}_e$ of $\mathbf{p}_n$ by
$\mathbf{p}_e = (1-\gamma)\bar{\mathbf{p}} + \gamma\mathbf{p}_n$ where $\gamma = [\mathbf{p}_e\bar{\mathbf{p}}]/[\mathbf{p}_n\bar{\mathbf{p}}] > 1$.
If $f(\mathbf{p}_e) < f(\mathbf{p}_n)$, replace $\mathbf{p}_n$ by $\mathbf{p}_e$ and $f(\mathbf{p}_n)$ by $f(\mathbf{p}_e)$.
Go to step 5.
4.2 Else if $f(\mathbf{p}_r) \geq f(\mathbf{p}_{n-1})$, if $f(\mathbf{p}_r) < f(\mathbf{p}_n)$ replace $\mathbf{p}_n$ by $\mathbf{p}_r$ and $f(\mathbf{p}_n)$ by $f(\mathbf{p}_r)$, get a contraction point $\mathbf{p}_c$ of $\mathbf{p}_n$ by $\mathbf{p}_c = (1-\beta)\bar{\mathbf{p}} + \beta\mathbf{p}_n$, $\beta = [\mathbf{p}_c\bar{\mathbf{p}}]/[\mathbf{p}_n\bar{\mathbf{p}}] < 1$.
If $f(\mathbf{p}_c) \geq f(\mathbf{p}_n)$, shrink the simplex around the best vertex $\mathbf{p}_0$ by $\mathbf{p}_i = (\mathbf{p}_i + \mathbf{p}_0)\sigma$, $i \neq 0$, else replace $\mathbf{p}_n$ by $\mathbf{p}_c$ and $f(\mathbf{p}_n)$ by $f(\mathbf{p}_c)$, go to step 5.
4.3 Else, replace $\mathbf{p}_n$ by $\mathbf{p}_r$ and $f(\mathbf{p}_n)$ by $f(\mathbf{p}_r)$.
5 If $\sqrt{\sum_{i=0}^{n}(f(\mathbf{p}_i) - f(\bar{\mathbf{p}}))^2/n} < T$, stop else go to step 2.

3.3 Multiple Starting Point Selection

The objective function corresponding to each segmentation algorithm need not have a unique minimum. Furthermore, direct search optimization algorithms are *local* optimization algorithm. Thus, for each (different) starting point, the optimization algorithm could converge to a different optimal solution. We constrain the parameter values to lie within a reasonable range and randomly choose six starting locations within this range. The optimal solution corresponding to the lowest optimal value is chosen as the best optimal parameter vector.

4 Experimental Protocol

We select the University of Washington Dataset [13] for the algorithm training task. A training dataset of 100 document pages was randomly sampled from the selected 978 documents in the UW III dataset. The dataset contains geometric textline and zone groundtruth for each page. We compute a performance metric only on text regions.

Kise's algorithm [6] works as follows: 1) label connected components, 2) remove noise connected components, 3) generate the Voronoi diagram for each connected component using the sample points on its border, 4) delete superfluous Voronoi edges according to a area-spacing criterion to generate zone boundaries, 5) remove noisy zones.

Kise's algorithm has eleven free parameters and is insensitive to seven of them. We fix the seven parameters as follows: maximum height and width thresholds of a connected component, $C_h = 500$ pixels and $C_w = 500$ pixels, maximum connected component aspect ratio threshold, $C_r = 5$, minimum area threshold of a zone, $A_z = 50$ pixels^2 for all zones, and minimum area threshold, $A_l = 40000$ pixels, and maximum aspect ratio threshold, $B_r = 4$ for the zones that are vertical and elongated. The last parameter is the size of the smoothing window, which is fixed at $sw = 2$. The optimal values for the other four parameters are searched from the following ranges recommended by Kise:
1) sampling rate sr: {4-7}, 2) maximum size threshold of noise connected component nm: {10-40}, 3) margin control factor for Td2 fr: {0.01-0.5}, 4) area ratio threshold ta: {40-200}.

The machines we use are Ultra 1,2 and 5 Sun workstations running Solaris 2.6 operating system. After the training step, a set of optimal parameter values are found for each research algorithm.

5 Experimental Results and Discussions

From Figure 1 and Table 1, we can make the following observations [1]:

1) The error rates for all starting points converge in the range of 4.74% to 5.52%, 2) The convergence rate before first 30 function evaluations is much faster than that beyond 30
function evaluations, 3) The value parameter nm for most (five) starting points converges to 11 pixels, 4) There is relatively small variance in the convergence values of parameter sr, nm and ta, 5) There is relatively large variance of the convergence values of parameter fr, 6) There is a relatively large variance of the number of function evaluations corresponding to six starting points.

[1] Note that some numbers reported in this paper differ from those reported in our technical report [7]. In [7] we used Numerical Recipes version of Nelder-Mead algorithm whereas in this paper we use the original [10] algorithm.

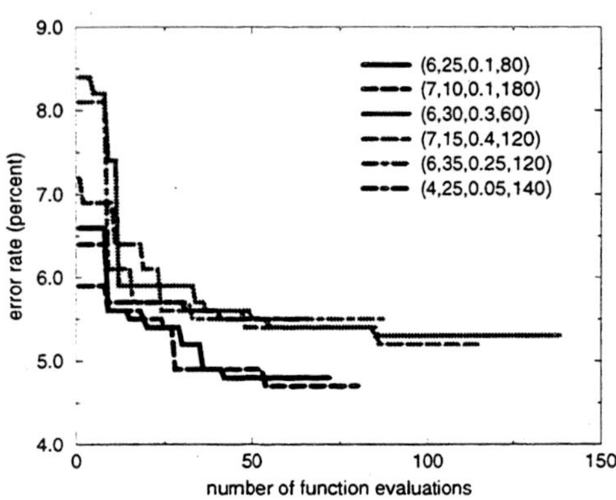

Figure 1. Convergence curves corresponding to six randomly selected starting points in the training of the Voronoi algorithm.

Table 1. Optimization results of Voronoi algorithm for six randomly selected starting points within a reasonable working parameter subspace.

start parameter values (sr, nm, fr, ta)	optimal parameter values (sr, nm, fr, ta)	error rate (percent)	number of function evaluations	timing (hours)
(6, 25, 0.1, 80)	(6, 15, 0.079, 106)	4.80	72	14.06
(7, 10, 0.1, 180)	(6, 11, 0.083, 199)	4.74	80	14.97
(6, 30, 0.3, 60)	(6, 11, 0.147, 148)	5.31	138	39.30
(7, 15, 0.4, 120)	(8, 11, 0.098, 190)	5.18	116	31.52
(6, 35, 0.25, 120)	(6, 11, 0.246, 193)	5.52	95	32.78
(4, 25, 0.05, 140)	(4, 11, 0.138, 160)	5.49	66	15.80

From the above observations, we can see that the Voronoi algorithm objective function has multiple local minima, but the performance at these local minima is stable. The algorithm only needs about 30 function evaluations to reach a stable performance. The optimal algorithm performance is insensitive to the value of parameter fr. The fact that the optimal value of parameter ta is big implies that the text and non-text connected components are well separated. The fact that the values of parameter fr are generally small indicate we should choose a conservative (large) interline spacing threshold. This training methodology is very general and has been applied to many page segmentation algorithms [8, 7].

6 Conclusions

We posed the automatic segmentation algorithm training problem as a multivariate non-smooth function optimization problem. A textline based performance metric was defined using set theory and mathematical morphology. This textline based metric was used to construct the objective function to be minimized. Nelder-Mead simplex method was then used to solve the optimization problem. An empirical analysis of the effect of initial parameter values and scales on optimization results was performed. From the experimental results, we found that a set of "optimal" parameter values and their corresponding "optimal" objective function value can be quickly found with relatively less computation.

References

[1] H. S. Baird, S. E. Jones, and S. J. Fortune. Image segmentation by shape-directed covers. In *Proceedings of International Conference on Pattern Recognition*, pages 820–825, Atlantic City, NJ, June 1990.

[2] P. E. Gill, W. Murray, and M. H. Wright. *Practical Optimization*, chapter 4. Academic Press, London and New York, 1993.

[3] R. M. Haralick and L. G. Shapiro. *Computer and Robot Vision*. Addison-Wesley Publishing Company, Reading, MA, 1992.

[4] A. Hoover, G. Jean-Baptiste, X. Jiang, P. J. Flynn, H. Bunke, D. B. Goldof, K. W. Bowyer, D. W. Eggert, A. Fitzgibbon, and R. B. Fisher. An experimental comparison of range image segmentation algorithms. *IEEE Transactions on Pattern Analysis and Machine Intelligence*, 18:673–689, 1996.

[5] A. K. Jain and B. Yu. Document representation and its application to page decomposition. *IEEE Transactions on Pattern Analysis and Machine Intelligence*, 20:294–308, 1998.

[6] K. Kise, A. Sato, and M. Iwata. Segmentation of page images using the area Voronoi diagram. *Computer Vision and Image Understanding*, 70:370–382, 1998.

[7] S. Mao and T. Kanungo. A methodology for empirical performance evaluation of page segmentation algorithms. Technical Report CAR-TR-933, University of Maryland, College Park, MD, 1999. http://www.cfar.umd.edu/~kanungo/pubs/trsegeval.ps.

[8] S. Mao and T. Kanungo. Empirical performance evaluation of page segmentation algorithms. In *Proceedings of SPIE Conference on Document Recognition*, San Jose, CA, January 2000.

[9] G. Nagy and S. Seth. Hierarchical representation of optically scanned documents. In *Proceedings of International Conference on Pattern Recognition*, volume 1, pages 347–349, Montreal, Canada, July 1984.

[10] J. Nelder and R. Mead. A simplex method for function minimization. *Computer Journal*, 7:308–313, 1965.

[11] L. O'Gorman. The document spectrum for page layout analysis. *IEEE Transactions on Pattern Analysis and Machine Intelligence*, 15:1162–1173, 1993.

[12] L. O'Gorman and R. Kasturi. *Document Image Analysis*. IEEE Computer Society Press, Los Alamitos, CA, 1995.

[13] I. Phillips. *User's Reference Manual*. CD-ROM, UW-III Document Image Database-III.

[14] F. Wahl, K. Wong, and R. Casey. Block segmentation and text extraction in mixed text/image documents. *Computer Vision, Graphics, and Image Processing*, 20:375–390, 1982.

Fast Discrete HMM Algorithm for On-line Handwriting Recognition

T.Hasegawa, H.Yasuda, and T.Matsumoto
Department of Electrical, Electronics, and Computer Engineering
Waseda University
takashi@mse.waseda.ac.jp

Abstract

A fast Discrete HMM algorithm is proposed for on-line hand written character recognition. After preprocessing input stroke are discretized so that a discrete HMM is used. This particular discretization naturally leads to a simple procedure for assigning initial state and state transition probabilities. In the training phase, complete marginelization with respect to state is not performed.

A criterion based on normalized maximum likelihood ratio is given for deciding when to create a new model for the same character in the learning phase, in order to cope with stroke order variations and large shape variations.

Experiments are done on the Kuchibue database from TUAT. The algorithm appears to be very robust against stroke number variations and have reasonable robustness against stroke order variations and large shape variations.

A drawback of the proposed algorithm is its memory requirement when the number of character classes and their associated models becomes large.

1. Introduction

Recent developments in pen input devices including PDA are calling for good on-line handwriting recognition algorithms.

This is due to the fact that as machines get smaller, keyboards become more difficult to use. Pen input interface is also preferred by those who are not familiar with keyboards.

An important distinction between on-line and off-line handwriting recognition problems is the fact that spatio-temporal information is available in the former, while only spatial information is available in the latter. There are two great challenges in on-line hand writing recognition problems;

i) Stroke number variations, stroke connections and shape variations.

A Kanji character is composed of up to 30 strokes. However, for casual writing characters, many writers tend to connect and abbreviate the strokes of a Kanji. The examples in Fig 1 illustrate this problem. Fig.1 (a) shows Kanji "愛" ("love") which consists of 13 strokes when written in a proper manner. The examples from Fig.1 (b)-(d) show the same character written in a casual manner.

ii) Stroke order variations.

Fig.2 shows Kanji character "飛" ("flight") written in three different stroke orders The left most column data

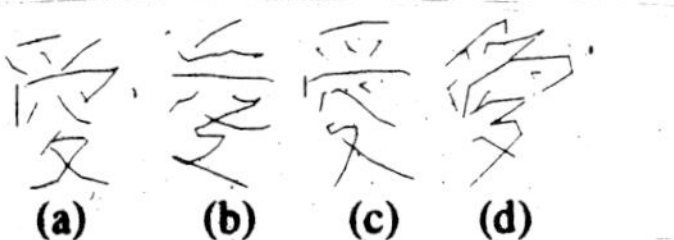

Fig.1 Examples of Kanji characters

shows the first stroke, the second column shows the second stroke. Up to this point, the three data sets have the same stroke orders. Significant stroke order variations emerge in the third column on. The final completed "飛" is shown in the right most columns.

Requirements for overcoming i) and ii) are often

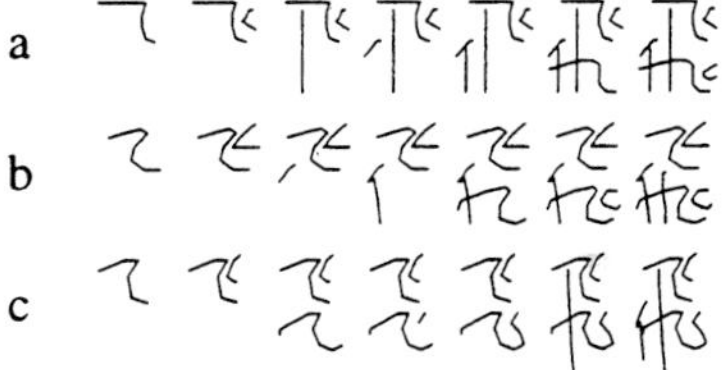

Fig.2 Examples of different stroke orders

contradictory. For instance, if one discards temporal information, then one may be able to overcome stroke order variation problem.

However, such an algorithm often suffers from its inability to cope with stroke number variations. On the other hand, an algorithm, which copes with stroke number variations often, performs unsatisfactory on stroke order variations.

This paper proposes a fast learning / recognition algorithm using a class of Discrete HMM tailored for on-line handwritten character recognition. Then, reports several preliminary recognition experiments against several data sets containing Japanese Kanji characters (JIS first category), Katakana and Hiragana from the Kuchibue database [1]. Many of the characters are written in an extremely casual manner. The average recognition rate

1051-4651/00 $10.00 © 2000 IEEE

was 87.80% while the top fifth recognition rate was 98.19%.

2. Preprocessing

2.1. Quantization

Typical raw data taken from digitizer, is

$$(x_1(t_i), x_2(t_i), p(t_i)) \in \mathbf{R}^2 \times \{0,1\}, i = 0,1,\ldots,M \tag{1}$$

where $(x_1(t_i), x_2(t_i))$ is the pen position whereas is pen up / down information. The sampling rate is approximately 10 points/sec.

In order to formulate the problem in terms of discrete HMM, we quantize the data. Consider

$$V_1(t) := v_{1k} \in \{1,2\}, k = 1,2 \tag{2}$$

$$V_2(t) := v_{1l} \in \{1,2,\ldots,L\}, l = 1,2,\ldots,L \tag{3}$$

where $V_1(t)$ represents the pen up / pen down information which is already quantized, and $V_2(t)$ represents the quantized angle information which results from the following scheme. Let

$$\theta := \tan^{-1} \frac{x_2(t) - x_2(t-1)}{x_1(t) - x_1(t-1)}, -\frac{\pi}{2} < \theta < \frac{\pi}{2} \tag{4}$$

i) If $x_1(t) - x_1(t-1) \geq 0$, then $V_2(t) = \theta$

ii) If $x_1(t) - x_1(t-1) < 0$, then

$$V_2(t) := \begin{cases} \pi - \theta, x_2(t) - x_2(t-1) \geq 0 \\ \theta - \pi, x_2(t) - x_2(t-1) < 0 \end{cases} \tag{5}$$

Simplified notation t is used instead of t_i. Therefore, at each time t, there are two symbols that $V_1(t)$ can take, whereas there are L symbols that $V_2(t)$ can take.

3. The Discrete HMM

HMM is a general probabilistic structure which is applicable to a broad class of problems where time evolution is important.

Every general discipline must be tailored before being applied to a specific type of problem, which is a basic engineering function, and HMM is no exception. The general framework of HMM must be carefully tuned to the on-line handwritten character recognition problem. This section gives the complete details of the proposed Discrete HMM structure.

3.1. Discrete HMM Structure for Online Handwriting Recognition

In order to make an HMM precise, let us first recall the output symbols $(v_{1k}, v_{2l}), k = 1,2, l = 1,\ldots,L$ defined in the previous section, and let

$$O(t) := (V_1(t), V_2(t)), t = 1,\ldots,T \tag{6}$$

be observed output sequence.

An HMM of a character

$$\mathsf{H} = \mathsf{H}\left(\{a_{ij}\}\{b_{ik}^1\}\{b_{il}^2\}\pi, N\right) \tag{7}$$

is defined by the joint distribution of $\{Q(t), O(t)\}_{t=1}^T$ given H;

$$P(\{Q(t), O(t)\}_{t=1}^T \mid \mathsf{H}) = \pi Q(1) \prod_{t=1}^{T-1} a_{Q(t+1)Q(t)} \prod_{t=1}^{T} b_{Q(t)V_1(t)}^1 b_{Q(t)V_2(t)}^2 \tag{8}$$

Where $\{Q(t)\}$ stands for hidden state at time t, $\{a_{ij}\}$ state transition probability, b_{ik}^1, b_{il}^2 output emission probabilities, and π initial state probability.

Learning in HMM amounts to an estimation of parameters $\{a_{ij}\}\{b_{ik}^1\}\{b_{il}^2\}\{\pi_i\}$ and N, whereas *recognition* is deciding from which character $\{O(t)\}_{t=1}^T$ comes.

In order to tune HMM to our current type of problem, we will use **the left to right model** so we put the following constraints on $\{a_{ij}\}$ and π_i:

i) a. $a_{ij} = 0$ unless $i = j$ or $i = j+1, a_{NN} = 1$

b. $a_{NN} = 1$, i.e., the $\{a_{ij}\}$ matrix is restricted to the one in the form

$$\{a_{ij}\} = \begin{bmatrix} a_{11} & & & & \\ a_{21} & a_{22} & & 0 & \\ & \ddots & \ddots & & \\ & & a_{N-1,N-2} & a_{N-1,N-1} & \\ & 0 & & a_{N,N-1} & 0 \end{bmatrix} \tag{9}$$

ii) $\pi = (1,0,\ldots,0)$ (10)

Note that i)-a indicates that the last state, q_N, cannot become any other state and ii) demands that the initial state $Q(1)$ must be always q_1. Observe that constraint i)-a demands that state q_i cannot jump to $q_{j+k}, k \geq 2$, which corresponds to the causality of a trajectory associated with H. The reasons for these constraints demands will become clear when the learning and recognition algorithms are explained.

3.2 Recognition

Learning and *recognition* are closely related in HMM. We will explain our recognition algorithm first. The proposed recognition scheme decides that

$$\arg\max_{\mathsf{H}} P\left(O(t)_{t=1}^T, Q(T) = q_N \mid \mathsf{H}\right) \tag{11}$$

is the most probable character. To explain the reason for using the constraint $Q(T)=q_N$ instead of maximizing marginalized likelihood $P(O(t)_{t=1}^{T} \mid H)$ let us consider the two Kanji characters "品"("object") and "口"("mouth"). Suppose that a writer meant "口", from which $O("口")(t)_{t=1}^{T}$ is obtained. Since "口" is a subset of "品", one of

$$P(\{O("口")(t)\}_{t=1}^{T}, Q(T)=q_i \mid H("品")) \quad (12)$$

can be large so that the marginalization

$$P(O\{("口")(t)\}_{t=1}^{T} \mid H("品"))= \quad (13)$$

$$\sum_{i=1}^{N} P(O\{("口")(t)\}_{t=1}^{T}, Q(T)=q_i \mid H("品"))$$

can be large which can often cause erroneous recognition results.

Equation (11) forces $Q(T)$ to be the final state q_N of H("品"), which significantly reduces erroneous recognition. Similar reasoning applies to other cases including "林" and "森".

3.3 Learning

The well-known Baum-Welch learning algorithm uses a gradient search to compute

$$\arg\max_{H} P(O(t)_{t=1}^{T}, Q(T)=q_N \mid H) \quad (14)$$

with N fixed. The efficiency of this method naturally depends on each problem. In the current on-line character recognition problem,there are two major hurdles -

i) The likelihood (14) is typically non-convex with respect to the parameters, and the serious problems are created by the local minima.

ii) The dimensions of the parameter space are determined by the sum of the non-zero parameters of $\{a_{ij}\},\{b_{ik}^{1}\},\{b_{il}^{2}\}$ and, $\{\pi_i\}$ which amounts to $2(N-1)+N(L+2)+N$; the computational effort is significant.

Our learning algorithm given below is fast because it is non-iterative and simple, and, most importantly, works well. Given training data sets $\{O_c(t)\}_{t=1}^{T_c}, c=1,\ldots,C$, our algorithm starts with generating first model from $\{O_1(t)\}_{t=1}^{T_1}$.

3.3.1. Generation of the First Model When the first data set is given for learning, our proposed algorithm first attempts to associate a clear meaning to the states, so that they naturally leads to our learning algorithm. The algorithm, however, is still HMM in that it has nontrivial $\{b_{ik}^{1}\},\{b_{il}^{2}\}$.

Let the first data set $\{O_1(t)\}_{t=1}^{T_1}$ be given,

3.3.2. Multiple Training Data Set. Let $\{O_c(t)\}_{t=2}^{T_c}, c=2,\ldots,C$ be the rest of the data sets for training.

Step 1 State Clarification
Given the first data set

$$\{O_c(t)\}, 1\le c\le C, 1\le t\le T_c \quad (15)$$

make a division between $O_1(t)$ and $O_1(t+1)$ if

1. $V_1(t)\ne V_1(t+1)$, i.e., if the pen up / down information changes; or
2. $|V_2(t)-V_2(t+1)|>\theta_0$, i.e., if the angle variation exceeds threshold, where $\theta_0>0$ is an empirical value;

and then associate the state q_i between the two successive observations

This data also assign the state. Suppose that the first data is as shown in Fig.3-a and the new data is as in Fig.3-b. Because of the stroke connection in Fig.3-b which is not present in Fig.3-a, the two data sets result is different number of states, which gives rise to a difficulty in learning. Our next step in the learning scheme is to use the Viterbi algorithm to make appropriate correspondence between models with different number of state.

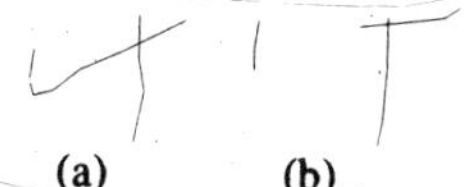

Fig.3 Examples of training data with different stroke numbers.

3.3.3. Model Generation So far, our algorithm has presumed that the number of H coincides with the

Step 2 Most Probable State Transition $\{Q_c(t)\}$

For $\{O_c(t)\}_{t=2}^{T_c}, c=2,\ldots,C$ let

$$Q_c(T_c):=\arg\max_{q_i} P(O_c(\tau)_{\tau=1}^{T_c}, q(T_c)=q_i \mid H)$$

(16)

$$Q_c(t-1):=\arg\max_{q_i} P(\{O_c(\tau)\}_{\tau=1}^{T}, q(t-1)=q_i, q_t=Q_c(t) \mid H)$$

(17)

and compute $n(O_c,q_i)$, $n(O_c,q_i,v_{ik})$ and $n(O_c,q_i,v_{2l})$, $c=2,\ldots,C$ as in Step 1.2

number of different characters. This must be modified for the following reasons:

i) A character may be written in different stroke orders;

ii. A character may have significantly different shape variations.

This calls for a model generation procedure. It is important that the model generation procedure be automatic. In the following step, we propose a new model generation criterion, normalized likelihood ratio which works well.

> Step 3 Model Generation
>
> Let $\mathrm{H}\left(\{a_{ij}\},\{b_{ik}{}^1\},\{b_{il}{}^2\},\{\pi_i\},N\right)$ be the HMM obtained by the previous steps. Let $\{O_c(t)\}_{t=1}^{T_c}$ be another training set for the same character. If the normalized log likelihood ration exceeds a threshold;
>
> $$\frac{-\log P\left(\{O_1(t)\}_{t=1}^{T_1}, Q(T_1)=q_N(\mathrm{H}_1) \mid \mathrm{H}\right) / T_1}{-\log P\left(\{O_c(t)\}_{t=1}^{T_c}, Q(T_c)=q_N(\mathrm{H}_c) \mid \mathrm{H}\right) / T_c} > r_{th} \qquad (18)$$
>
> then create a new model H_2 based on $\{O_c(t)\}_{t=1}^{T_c}$, using the previous steps, where $r_{th} > 0$ is an empirical value.

4. Experiment

Database Kuchibue [1] contains Kanji, Hiragana, Katakana, Western alphabets, numerals and symbols. In our experiment, we used 2965 Kanji classes (JIS First Level), 46 Hiragana classes, and 46 Katakana classes. Each data set consists of 10502 characters where 5643 are Kanji, 4372 are Hiragana, and 487 are Katakana. Of the 120 data sets, Kuchibue 21 to 120 (100 data sets) were used for learning with the following parameter (see (18)): $r_{th} = 0.65$.

Our algorithm described in the previous section created 5224 models (Kanji 5059, Hiragana 72, Katakana 93). Recognition experiment was performed against Kuchibue 1 - Kuchibue 20 (20 data sets). Table (1) shows average recognition rates. Table (2) shows the numbers of the models created. The average recognition time was 0.20 sec/characters (Pentium2 400MHz, WindowsNT4).

Fig.4-a shows several examples of Kanji characters that were correctly recognized and Fig4-b gives examples of erroneously classified characters.

Table (1) Recognition Rate

Data	Recognition rate [%]	Top five recognition rate [%]
Kanji	91.53	97.61
Hiragana	84.04	98.76
Katakana	76.38	98.70
Overall	87.80	98.19

Table (2) Generated Models

Character category	Number of classes	Number of generated models
Kanji	2898	5059
Hiragana	66	72
Katakana	67	96
Overall	3105	5224

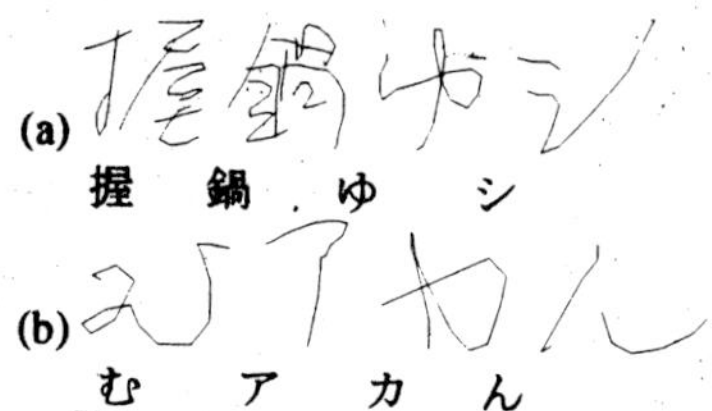

Fig.4 Examples of characters which were correctly / not correctly recognized

5. Discussion

There are significant variations of recognition rates among the individual Kuchibue data sets (Table (1)). This appears to be attributable to the fact that this database contains great varieties of casualness in writing those characters.

When Kanji, Hiragana, Katakana and others are all contained, some of the casually written characters are difficult to classify, e.g., Katakana "エ" and Kanji "工". The proposed algorithm appears to be extremely robust against stroke number variations while maintaining reasonable robustness against stroke order variations.

Since the top fifth recognition rate is 98.19%, a significant improvement recognition performance may be possible by exploiting grammatical structure associated with character sequence instead of individual characters. This is one of the challenging future projects.

Another future project will be adaptation of the algorithm to small portable devices where computational power and memory size are severely limited.

[1] N.Nakagawa (1996). "TUAT Nakagawa Lab. HANDS-kuchibue_d-97-06," Tokyo University of Agriculture and Technology.

[2] L.R.Rabiner. (1996). "A Tutorial on Hidden Markov Models and Selected Application in Speech Recognition,", Proc. IEEE, vol. 77, pp.257-285.

[3] Waseda University. (1996). "A Fast HMM Method for On-Line Handwriting Recognition." Japanese Patent, no.319496

[4] K.Takahashi, H.Yasuda and T.Matsumoto. (1997). "A Fast HMM Algorithm for On-line Handwritten Character Recognition.," 4th ICDAR97, Proceedings Vol.1, pp.369-375.

[5] R.Koehle, T.Matsumoto. (1997). "Pruning Algorithms for HMM On-line Handwriting Recognition," Technical Report of the IEICE, PRMU97-5, pp33-39.

Locating Uniform-Colored Text in Video Frames

Vladimir Y. Mariano Rangachar Kasturi
Department of Computer Science and Engineering
Pennsylvania State University, University Park, PA 16802, USA
{mariano,kasturi}@cse.psu.edu

Abstract

In this paper a method is proposed for locating horizontal, uniform-colored text in video frames. It was observed that when a row of pixels across such a text region is clustered in perceptually uniform $L^*a^*b^*$ color space, the pixels of one of these clusters would belong to the text strokes. These pixels would appear as a line of short streaks on the row since a typical text region has many vertical and diagonal strokes. The proposed method examines every third row of the image and checks whether this row passes through a horizontal text region. For a given row R, the pixels of R are hierarchically clustered in $L^*a^*b^*$ space and each cluster is tested whether similar-colored pixels in R's vicinity are possibly part of a text region. Candidate text blocks are marked by heuristics using information about the cluster's line of short streaks. The detected text blocks are fused to come up with the text regions. The method was tested on key frames of several video sequences and was able to locate a wide variety of text.

1. Introduction

Large amount of stored video data has motivated much research in content-based video retrieval for several years. Detecting text in digital video has been an active area of research with the goal of identifying keywords [3, 5] for video characterization.

Different methods were used in recent work for detecting text. Kanade et. al. [3] combined interpolation, multi-frame integration, character extraction and recognition for text segmentation. Li, Doermann and Kia [4] used a hybrid wavelet/neural network segmenter to segment text regions. Zhong et. al. [6] used intensity variation information encoded in the DCT domain to locate caption text regions.

A few methods have used color information for detecting text in video frames. Jain and Yu [2] used multi-valued image decomposition on video frames to obtain subimages with different colors. Connected component analysis is used to find text regions. A method by Gargi, Antani and Kasturi [1] first creates a "slats" image where a slat is a segment of a scan line between two color edges of minimum height. Slats on consecutive scan lines that are similar in color and are aligned are merged to form stroke segments which correspond to character strokes.

In this paper we present a method for locating text based on color uniformity of text pixels and horizontal alignment. An image is searched for rows that pass through vertical and diagonal strokes of text.

2. Observations

Caption text is embedded in video as a horizontal group of characters with the same color. Degradation due to digitization (ex. MPEG encoding) would still retain color uniformity among the text characters. An experiment was made by taking a row of pixels that goes through the middle of caption text on a non-uniform background. These pixels were clustered in $L^*a^*b^*$ space and each cluster was marked back on the row. One of the clusters clearly marked the pixels belonging to the text and appeared as short streaks. When other pixels in the image having the same range of color values as this cluster were marked, we observed that the top pixels of the characters are included in this group. Furthermore, these top pixels were aligned horizontally with deviation of at most a few pixels. The same is observed with the bottom pixels. Using these observations, heuristics were formed for detection of horizontal text.

3 Proposed Method

The algorithm visits every $Interval$ rows in the image. $Interval$ is set small enough to be able to detect very small text and large enough so as not to consume too much time. In our experiment we set $Interval = 3$. Given a row R on the image, we want to find out whether or not R passes through the middle of a text region.

3.1 Clustering in $L^*a^*b^*$ space

The pixels of R are transformed and clustered in the perceptually uniform $L^*a^*b^*$ color space using hierarchical clustering. The algorithm first assigns each pixel as a cluster and the distance of pairs of clusters are stored in an array. Two clusters A and B are merged if $||\mu_A - \mu_B||$ is minimum and for each pixel p in $A \cup B$, $||p - \mu_{A \cup B}|| < MaxClusterRadius$, where μ_Z is the mean $L^*a^*b^*$ vector of cluster Z and $|| \cdot ||$ is the weighted Euclidean norm. The weighted norm was used to achieve a slight invariance to lightness (weights: $L^* = 0.8, a^* = 1.1, b^* = 1.1$). In our experiments, we set $MaxClusterRadius = 10$ (ranges: $L^* = 0\ldots100$, $a^* = -97\ldots88$, $b^* = -100\ldots88$). Merging continues until no two clusters can be merged.

3.2 Determining bounding rows

Each cluster C is tested to see if it contains pixels belonging to text. Locating the bounding rows (top and bottom rows of text) is the first step (Fig. 1). The cluster points are marked back on row R to create streaks $S_i, i = 1\ldots N_s(numberofstreaks)$ of pixels in the row R. Then all pixels in the entire image are examined and each pixel with a value within the range of values represented in the cluster are colored with a value of T. All other pixels are marked T'.

We now try to find out if there are bounding rows above and below R which may contain horizontal text. Given a pair of adjacent streaks S_i and S_{i+1}, we find R_a – the first row above R in which the segment covering S_i and S_{i+1} is colored T'. We also find R_b – the first row below R in which the segment covering under S_i and S_{i+1} is colored T'. The R_a of each pair of adjacent streaks is computed and collected in an alignment histogram H_a, where the bins are the rows of the image. H_b is computed in the same way by taking all the R_b's. We declare the existence of a bounding row B_a if at least 60% of the elements in H_a are contained in three or fewer adjacent histogram bins. B_b's existence is computed in the same way from H_b. If B_a and B_b exists, *height* is defined as their difference.

If the cluster C contains text pixels, then B_a and B_b would mark the text block's upper and lower row boundaries , and *height* would define its vertical dimension. Figure 1 illustrates the computation of B_a, B_b and *height*.

3.3 Finding text blocks

We look for text blocks using heuristics on *height* and the short streaks' lengths and gaps. Streaks longer than *height* are discarded and added to the gaps. Gaps longer than *height* are considered not part of a text block. The remaining regions are now smaller blocks with short streaks.

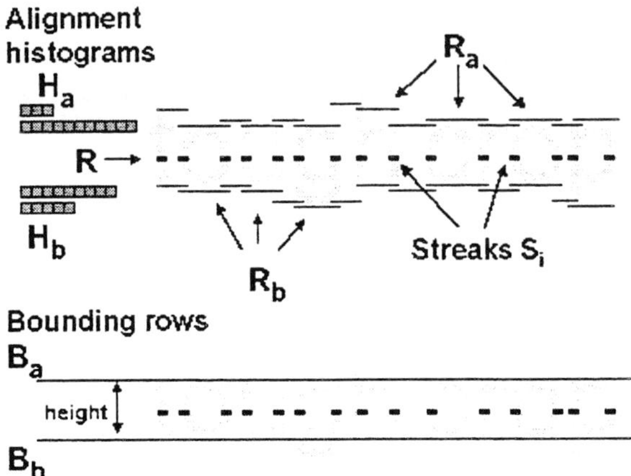

Figure 1. Computing the bounding rows. One of the color clusters in row R are marked as short streaks and pixels of the text "tough crop" lie within the range of values of the cluster. Each segment of the bounding top (R_a) and bottom (R_b) rows are shown separated for clarity even when they are actually on the same row.

If a block's width is greater than $1.5*height$ and the number of short streaks inside is greater than 3, then it is considered a text block, otherwise it is discarded. Finally, the text block is expanded a few pixels to the left and right to ensure full coverage of the characters at the ends.

Figure 2 shows how the text block "For generations" is detected. The pixels of row R (passing through the middle of text) are clustered in color space. One of the color clusters is marked black. Pixels in the image having similar color as the black ones are marked white. On the left side of the image, the two alignment histograms H_a (above R) and H_b (below R) are used to mark the bright bounding rows B_a and B_b. The short streaks marked black and the *height* between the bounding rows are used to find the text block. The two black streaks on the right were not included in the text block because their gap from the other streaks is greater than *height*. Figure 3 shows the text block binarized according to the color cluster.

3.4 Fusing the detected text blocks

It was observed that other color clusters were caused by the presence of text. The characters' color "shadows" and the pixels in the transition from text foreground to background result in other detected text blocks which largely overlap with the foreground text block. All the detected text blocks are fused (set union) to come up with the final regions of text.

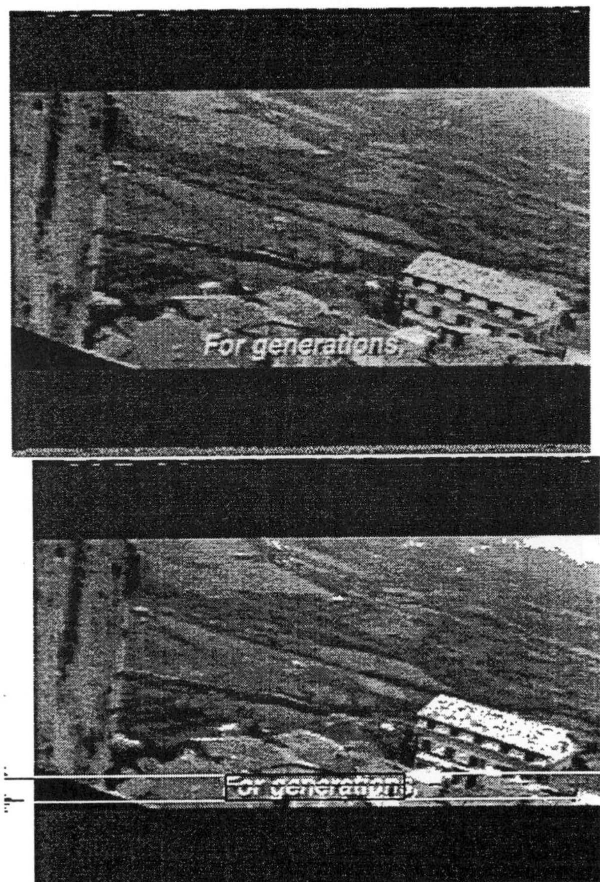

Figure 2. Analysis of a video frame and detected text block.

4. Experiments and Results

The method was tested on a variety of video frames from news clips, sports reviews, commercials and movie previews. Several video sequences totalling 14 minutes were manually segmented and 213 key frames were extracted. The algorithm was able to find captions (Fig. 4), text on uniform and non-uniform background (Fig. 5) , text with different sizes and colors (Fig. 7), and low contrast text (Fig. 8). Figure 6 shows typical false alarms which include fences and vertical stripes. The overall detection rate was 94% while the false alarm rate was 39%.

5. Conclusion and Future Work

This paper introduced a new method for locating horizontal, uniform-colored text in video frames. Every third row is tested to determine whether it passes through text by analyzing color clusters in $L^*a^*b^*$ space. The method is able to identify regions of text of different sizes, in uniform and non-uniform backgrounds. We are currently working on modifying the method to detect non-horizontal text.

6. Acknowledgement

The support of the Philippine Department of Science and Technology is gratefully acknowledged.

Figure 3. Pixels in text block belonging to color cluster in Fig. 2

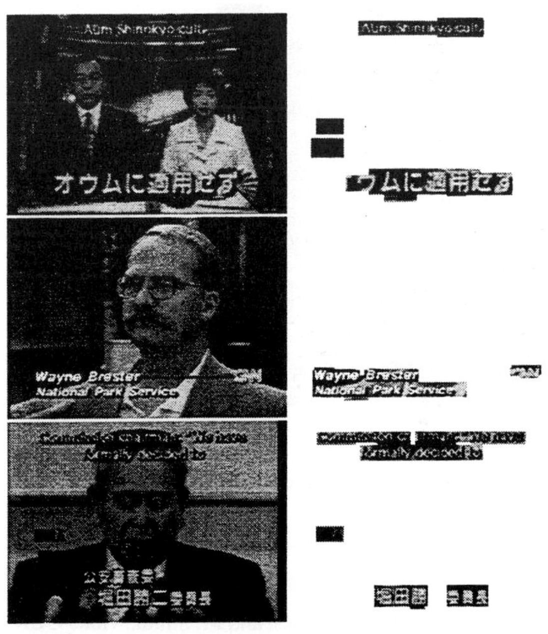

Figure 4. Caption text on non-uniform background. The two small boxes in the first image are faint text watermarks.

References

[1] U. Gargi, S. Antani, and R. Kasturi. Indexing text events in digital video databases. In *Proc. International Conference on Pattern Recognition*, pages 916–918, 1998.

[2] A. K. Jain and B. Yu. Automatic text location in images and video frames. *Pattern Recognition*, pages 2055–2076, December 1998.

Figure 5. Text on uniform and non-uniform background.

Figure 6. Examples of detected text with false alarm.

[3] T. Kanade, T. Sato, E. Hughes, and M. Smith. Video OCR for digital news archive. In *Proc. IEEE Workshop on Content-Based Access of Image and Video Databases*, pages 52–60, January 1998.

[4] H. Li, D. Doermann, and O. Kia. Automatic text detection and tracking in digital video. *IEEE Transactions on Image Processing*, 9(1):147–156, January 2000.

[5] J.-C. Shim, C. Dorai, and R. Bolle. Automatic text extraction from video for content-based annotation and retrieval. In *Proc. International Conference on Pattern Recognition*, volume 1, pages 618–620, August 1998.

[6] Y. Zhong, H. Zhang, and A. K. Jain. Automatic caption localization in compressed video. In *Proc. International Conference on Image Processing*, volume 2, pages 96–100, 1999.

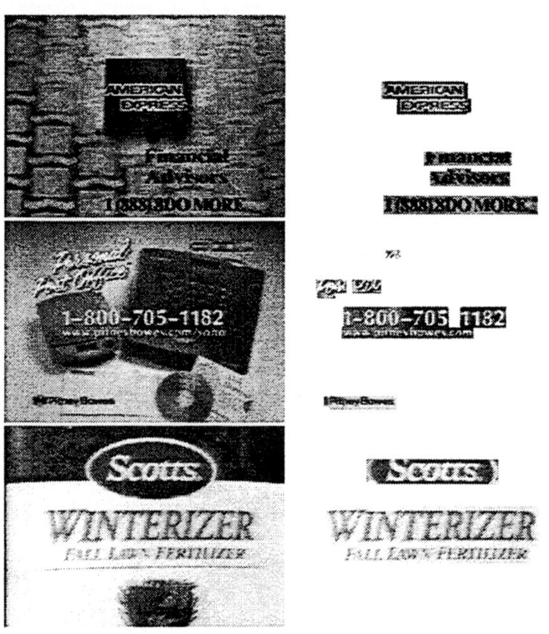

Figure 7. Text with different sizes and colors.

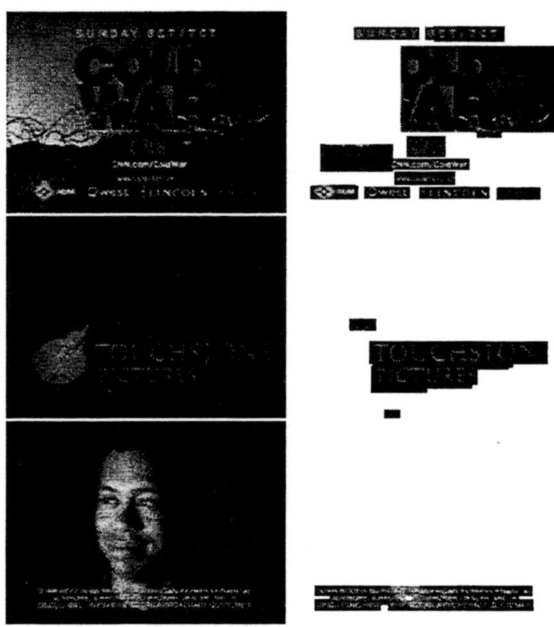

Figure 8. Big and small low contrast text.

Multi-Font Arabic Word Recognition Using Spectral Features

Mohammad S Khorsheed and William F Clocksin
Computer Laboratory, University of Cambridge
New Museums Site, Pembroke Street
Cambridge CB2 3QG, England
e-mail: msmk2@cl.cam.ac.uk

Abstract

In this paper we present a new technique for recognising Arabic cursive words from scanned images of text. The approach is segmentation-free, and is applied to four different Arabic typefaces, where ligatures and overlaps pose challenges to segmentation-based methods. We transform each word into a normalised polar image, then we apply a two dimensional Fourier transform to the polar image. The resultant spectrum tolerates variations in size, rotation or displacement. Each word is represented by a template that includes a set of Fourier coefficients. The recognition is based on a normalised Euclidean distance from those templates.

1. Introduction

The Arabic alphabet is used by several widespread languages such as Arabic, Persian and Urdu. Arabic script presents challenges because all orthography is cursive and letter shape is context sensitive. Previous research on script recognition has used an optical character recognition approach that depends on segmentation of words. The word is first segmented into either primitives [7] or characters [2], then features are extracted from the segments, then the word is classified by comparing the features with a model. Another technique [5, 6] is to decompose the word skeleton into small strokes (pieces of the character) which then are transformed into a sequence of observations that is fed to a hidden Markov model [9]. The Viterbi algorithm [3] is used to find the best path through the model which represents the word to be recognised. However, these studies have demonstrated the difficulties in attempting to segment Arabic words into individual characters [1] owing to context sensitivity, co-articulation effects, and stylistic features such as overlaps.

A global approach, which has been applied to English [8] script but not to Arabic, treats the word as a whole. Features are extracted from the unsegmented word and compared to a model. While [8] used word shape profile as a feature, we required a model which is invariant to rotation, translation and dilation. In this paper we implement a global approach to recognising cursive Arabic words. Each word is represented by a set of Fourier coefficients extracted from the word image. The recognition of an unknown word is based on a normalised Euclidean distance between the coefficient set and a model.

2. Feature Extraction

Given a scanned image in the form of a bitmap, our system first isolates each Arabic word (separated by white space), then finds a feature set for the word which is invariant to the Poincare group of transformations: dilation, translations and rotations. A normalisation process uses a log-polar transform to transform rotation into translation (Figure 1).

Complex numbers are used to represent 2D coordinates. Let $g(x, y)$ be a word image with Y rows and X columns. Each dark (inked) pixel in the image may be represented using a complex number Z:

$$\begin{aligned} Z &= x + jy \qquad (1) \\ & \quad 0 \le x < X, 0 \le y < Y \end{aligned}$$

Let $O = (O_x, O_y)$ be the centroid of all dark pixels in the word image and D_{max} be the maximum Euclidean distance between O and all pixels

$$\begin{aligned} D_{max} &= \max_{x,y}(\|Z - O\|) \\ &= \max_{x,y}(\sqrt{(x - O_x)^2 + (y - O_y)^2}) \qquad (2) \end{aligned}$$

A coordinate transform, U, for each pixel exists which transforms the object to normalised polar coordinates with

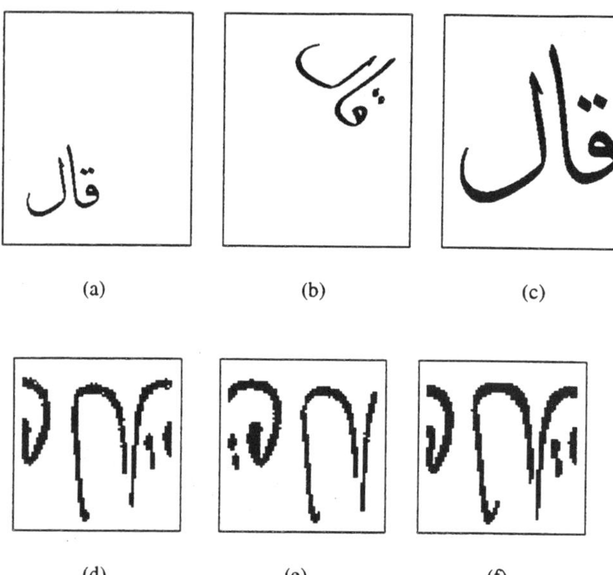

Figure 1. Three images (a), (b), and (c) of the word (قال *qāl*, 'say'), and below each one is the normalised polar equivalent.

origin O.

$$\begin{aligned} \mathbf{U}(Z) &= r + j\theta \\ &= \frac{\sqrt{(x-O_x)^2+(y-O_y)^2}}{D_{max}} + j\tan^{-1}\left(\frac{y-O_y}{x-O_x}\right) \\ & \qquad 0 \le r \le 1, -\pi \le \theta \le \pi \end{aligned} \quad (3)$$

This results in a normalised polar image $f(x, y)$ which has $N \times N$ pixels (here $N = 64$). The application of the Fourier transform to $f(x, y)$ can be represented as

$$\mathbf{F}(w_x, w_y) = \sum_{x=0}^{N-1}\sum_{y=0}^{N-1} f(x,y)e^{-j\frac{2\pi}{N}(xw_x+yw_y)} \qquad 0 \le w_x, w_y < N \quad (4)$$

Any rotation in the word image is transformed into translation in the normalised polar image so we need to consider the translation property of the Fourier transform which is represented as

$$f(x-x_0, y-y_0) \xrightarrow{\mathcal{F}} \mathbf{F}(w_x, w_y)e^{-j\frac{2\pi}{N}(x_0w_x+y0w_y)}$$

This shows that a shift in the origin of the function $f(x, y)$ results in multiplying $F(w_x, w_y)$ by the indicated exponential term. Take the magnitude

$$\begin{aligned} |\mathbf{F}(w_x, w_y)||e^{-j\theta}| &= |\mathbf{F}(w_x, w_y)||\cos\theta - j\sin\theta| \\ &= |\mathbf{F}(w_x, w_y)|[\cos^2\theta + \sin^2\theta]^{\frac{1}{2}} \\ &= |\mathbf{F}(w_x, w_y)| \end{aligned} \quad (5)$$

so a shift in $f(x, y)$ does not affect the magnitude of its Fourier transform.

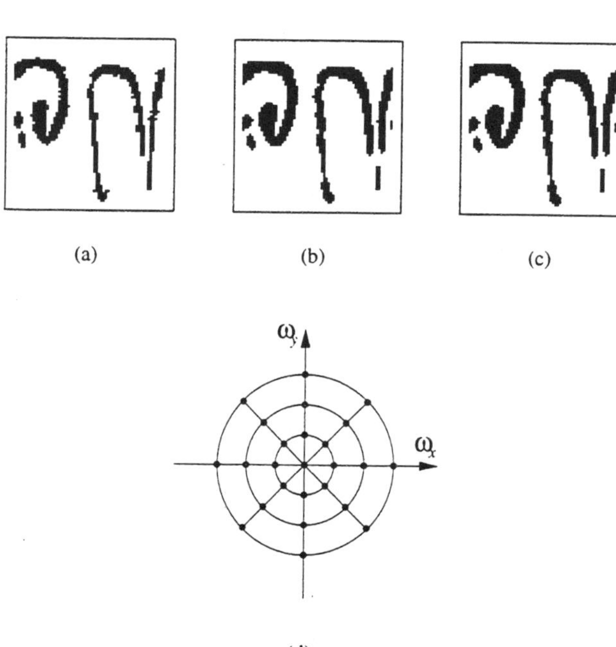

Figure 2. Three reconstructed polar images for the polar image shown in Fig 1-e, using: (a) half the Fourier spectrum, (b) the lower 16 frequency band, (c) the lower 8 frequency band, (d) polar raster of samples in the Fourier domain.

Jain [4] shows how Fourier descriptors can be used for image reconstruction and shape matching. Since the word image is a real signal, half the Fourier spectrum is sufficient to reconstruct the word image completely. Moreover, a selection of lower frequencies is sufficient for modelling words. Fig 2 shows three reconstructed polar images for that shown in Fig 1-e.

3. Results

More than 1700 sample words were used to assess the performance of the proposed method. The samples were printed using four different fonts: Simplified Arabic, Thuluth, Andalus, and Arabic Traditional, illustrated in Fig 3.

The samples were rendered at random angles ranging $0 \rightarrow 2\pi$, at random sizes ranging between $18 \rightarrow 48pt$, and at random translations up to twice the size of the sampled word.

Images of the text were captured using a scanner with a resolution of 300 dpi. Each word image was transformed using Eq. 3 into a normalised polar image. Next, the fast Fourier transform was applied to the polar image, and a set of the Fourier coefficients was extracted to be the feature vector representing that image word.

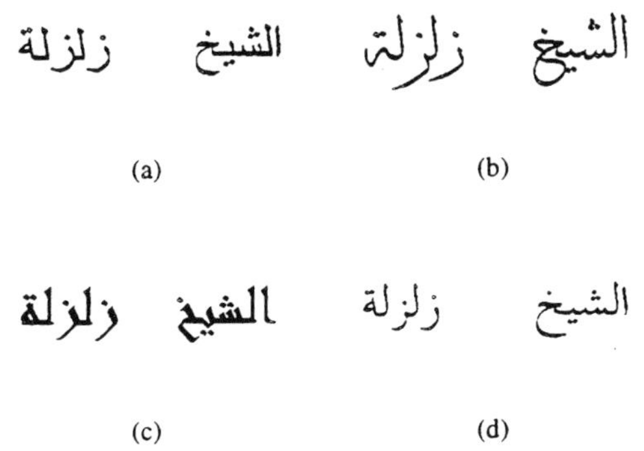

الشيخ زلزلة (a)

الشيخ زلزلة (b)

الشيخ زلزلة (c)

الشيخ زلزلة (d)

Figure 3. Four different Arabic fonts: (a) Simplified Arabic, (b) Thuluth, (c) Andalus, and (d) Arabic Transparent. Each displays the words (ألشيخ *alšīḫ*, **'Sheik') and (ألزلزلة** *alzlzlt*, **'Earth tremor').**

Each word in the lexicon was represented by a template formed from the average coefficient values of a sample of training words.

$$\mu_i = \frac{1}{N_i} \sum_{\mathbf{x} \in \omega_i} \mathbf{x} \qquad i = 1, 2, ..., M \tag{6}$$

where M is the number of words, N_i is the number of word images representing word ω_i and used to calculate this template. Here the template is formed from one sample of each of the four fonts.

To perform recognition of sampled words, four samples at different sizes, rotations and translations of each word were compared with each template using one of two comparison functions. Fig 4 summarises the error rates when the Euclidean distance is used to compare a sample word with every template. Two graphs are shown: one in which the lower 8 frequency bands that includes 106 coefficients were used to construct the templates, and one where lower 16 frequency bands that include 402 coefficients were used. The error rate is the number of misrecognised words divided by the total number of comparisons.

One observation from Fig 4 is that the templates formed using the lower 16 frequency bands had a lower error rate than those formed using the lower 8 frequency bands. Using more features increases the computational burder while it can also lower the recognition rate due to the so-called *peaking phenomenon.* Here using 16 frequency band gives a higher recognition rate.

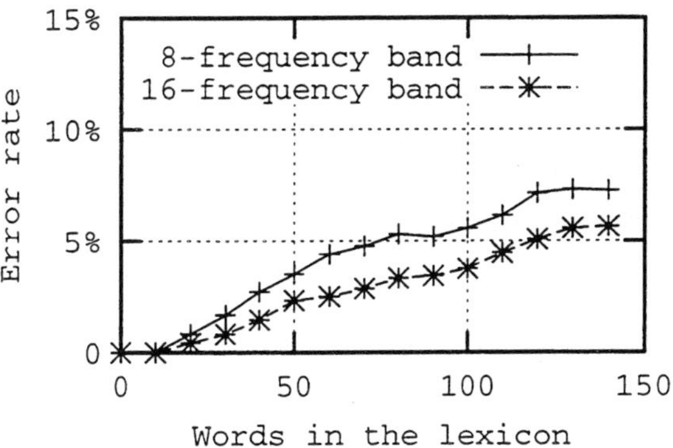

Figure 4. Error rate against lexicon size using Euclidean distance measure.

In an attempt to improve recognition rate, a more sophisticated comparison function, the Standard measure, can be obtained by normalising by the sample variance. Let μ_i be the average word vector calculated in equation (6), and σ_i is the standard deviation vector computed below

$$\sigma_i = \frac{1}{N_i}[\sum_{\substack{i=1 \\ \mathbf{x} \in \omega_i}}^{N_i} (\mathbf{x} - \mu_i)^2]^{\frac{1}{2}} \quad i = 1, 2, ..., M \tag{7}$$

then the Standard distance is calculated as follows

$$\begin{aligned} \mathbf{SD}_i(\mathbf{x}) &= \frac{\mathbf{x} - \mu_i}{\sigma_i} \qquad i = 1, 2, ..., M \\ &= \sum_{j=1}^{L} \frac{|x_j - \mu_{ij}|}{\sigma_{ij}} \end{aligned} \tag{8}$$

Fig 5 summarises the recognition error rates based on the Standard distance measure. One observation is that the templates formed using the lower 16 frequency bands showed *lower* performance than those formed using the lower 8 frequency bands. It is likely that this is an example of the peaking phenomenon, where increasing the dimensionality of the feature space leads to lower recognition rates due probably to over-fitting. This observation concurs with general experience that some classification functions seem much more sensitive to the feature dimensionality than others. It should also be noted that because templates are formed from

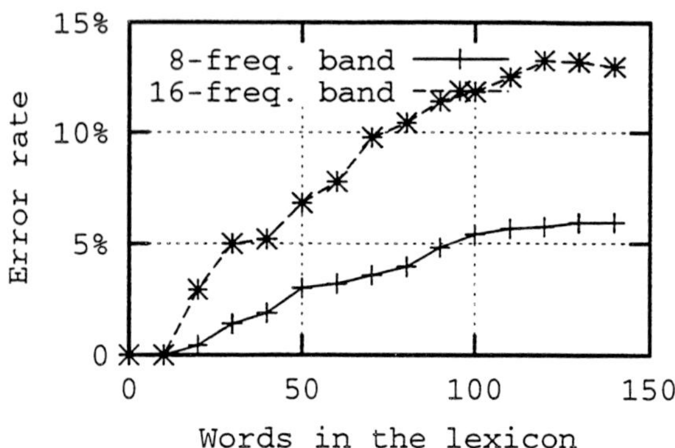

Figure 5. Error rate against lexicon size using Standard distance measure.

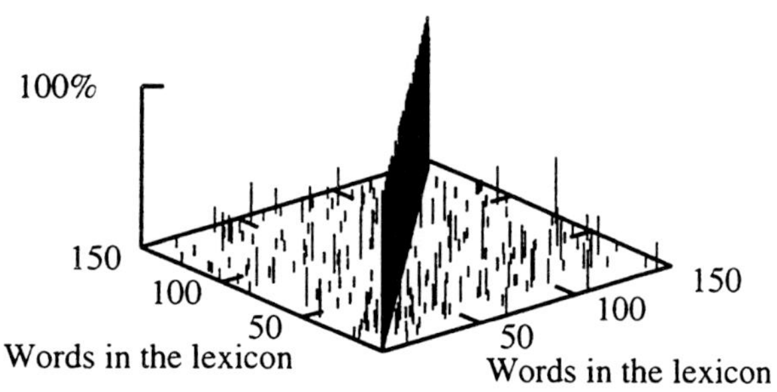

(a)

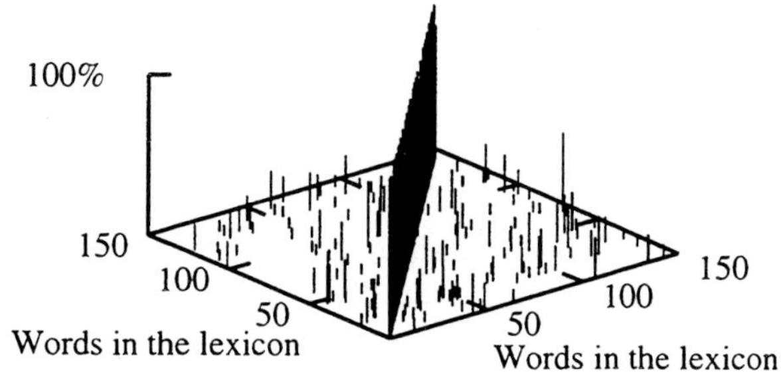

(b)

Figure 6. Three dimensional depictions of confusion matrices for the 145 words subjected to 252300 recognition tests: (a) lower 8 frequency bands and (b) lower 16 frequency bands.

samples written in multiple fonts, that σ will be large, having a dominant effect on **SD**.

Fig 6 shows the confusion matrices for all the 145 words in the lexicon. The templates were formed using the lower 8 and 16 frequency bands, respectively.

4. Conclusion

A new method for recognising cursive Arabic words has been presented. This method is based on transforming a word image into a 'thumbnail' pattern which is invariant to dilation, translation, and rotation. The method showed recognition rates of over 90% while demonstrating the variation in sensitivity to feature dimensionality depending on the comparison function used.

This method may not be as suitable if many more fonts are used, particularly if handwriting samples are used. In these situations it is likely that the Hidden Markov Model technique can improve the recognition rate [5].

References

[1] B. Al-Badr and S. Mahmoud. Survey and bibliography of arabic optical text recognition. *Signal Processing*, 41:49–77, 1995.

[2] A. Amin and J. Mari. Machine recognition and correction of printed arabic text. *IEEE Trans. on Systems, Man, and Cybernetics*, 19(5):1300–1306, 1989.

[3] G. Forney. The viterbi algorithm. *Proceedings Of The IEEE*, 61(3):268–278, 1973.

[4] A. Jain. *Fundamentals Of Digital Image Processing*. Prentice Hall, 1989.

[5] M. S. Khorsheed and W. F. Clocksin. Off-line arabic word recognition using a hidden markov model. In *Statistical Methods For Image Processing - A Satellite Conference Of The 52nd ISI Session In Helsinki*, Uppsala, Sweden, 1999.

[6] M. S. Khorsheed and W. F. Clocksin. Structural features of cursive arabic script. In *Proceeding of The Tenth British Machine Vision Conference*, volume 2, pages 422–431, University Of Nottingham, UK, 1999.

[7] B. Parhami and M. Taraghi. Automatic recognition of printed farsi texts. *Pattern Recognition*, 14(6):395–403, 1981.

[8] C. Parisse. Global word shape processing in off-line recognition of handwriting. *IEEE Trans. on Pattern Analysis and Machine Intelligence*, 18(4):460–464, 1996.

[9] L. Rabiner. A tutorial on hmm and selected applications in speech recognition. *Proceedings of The IEEE*, 77(2):257–286, Feb. 1989.

On-line Signature Verification using Pen-Position, Pen-Pressure and Pen-Inclination Trajectories

T.Ohishi, Y.Komiya, T.Matsumoto
Department of Electrical, Electronics and Computer Engineering Waseda University
3-4-1 Ohkubo, Shinjuku-ku, Tokyo, Japan, 169-8555
ohishi@matsumoto.elec.waseda.ac.jp

Abstract

A new algorithm is proposed for pen-input on-line signature verification incorporating pen-position, pen-pressure and pen-inclinations trajectories. Preliminary experimental result looks encouraging.

1. Introduction

1.1. Propose

Personal identity verification has a great variety of applications including access to computer terminals, buildings, credit card verification, to name a few[1]. Algorithms for personal identity verification can be roughly classified into four categories depending on static/dynamic and biometric/physical or knowledge-based as shown in Fig1.1. (This figure has been partly inspired by a brochure from Cadix Corp, Tokyo.) Fingerprints, iris, retina, DNA, face, blood vessels, for instance, are static and biometric. Algorithms which are biometric and dynamic include lip movements, body movements and on-line signature. Schemes which use passwords are static and knowledge-based, whereas methods using magnetic cards and IC cards are physical.
Each scheme naturally has its own advantages and disadvantages. While magnetic cards and IC cards are simple, they suffer from susceptibility to theft and loss. Although good passwords are fairly secure, there are already many incidents where passwords are broken. In addition, complicated passwords tend to be forgotten by individuals.

Of the many possible biometric schemes, voice is a good candidate, but its dependency on individual's physical condition, e.g., having a cold, may degrade verification quality. Fingerprint is another good candidate. However, fingerprint image can be degraded when an individual perspires. In order to obtain a good iris image, individual's eyes must be wide open and he/she must not wear glasses. Very strong light needs to be injected onto retina to obtain its image.

This paper proposes a new algorithm PPI (pen-position/pen-pressure/pen-inclination) for *on-line pen input signature verification*. The algorithm considers writer's signature as a trajectory of pen-position, pen-pressure and pen-inclination which evolves over time, so that it is dynamic and biometric. Since the algorithm uses pen-trajectory information, it naturally needs to incorporate stroke number (number of pen-ups/pen-downs) variations as well as shape variations. The proposed scheme first generates "templates" from several authentic signatures of individuals. In the verification phase, the scheme computes a distance between the template and a input trajectory. Care needs to be taken in computing the distance function because; (i) length of a pen input trajectory may be different from that of template even if the signature is genuine; (ii) number of strokes of a pen input trajectory may be different from that of template, i.e., the number of pen-ups/pen-downs obtained may differ from that of template even for an authentic signature.

If the computed distance dose not exceed a threshold value, the input signature is predicted to be genuine, otherwise it is predicted to be forgery.

A preliminary experiment is performed on a database consisting of 293 genuine writings and 540 forgery writings, from 8 individuals. Average correct verification rate was 97.6 % whereas average forgery rejection rate was 98.7 %. Since no fine tuning was done, this preliminary result looks very promising.

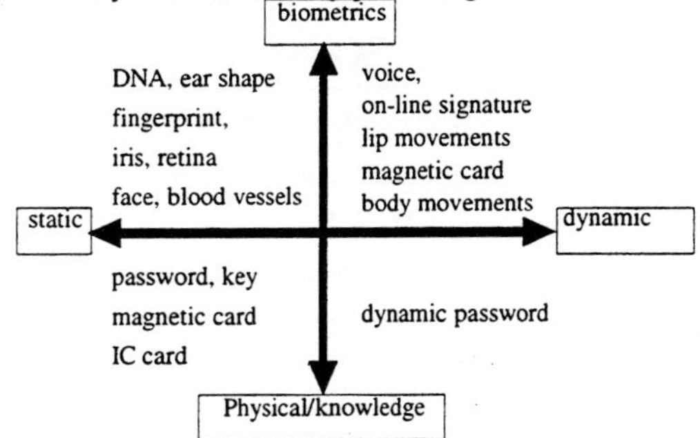

Fig1.1 Authentication Methods

1.2. Related works

Kato et. al. [2] use pen position and pen pressure for on-line signature verification while Taguchi et. al. [3] use pen inclination. The algorithm proposed in [4] computes distances between input and templates for each stroke so that there are difficulties when stroke number varies.

Yoshimura et. al.[5] use the direction of pen movement for on-line signature verification. One of the main distinctions between the previous works and our algorithm PPI given below lies in the fact that the latter uses the trajectory of pen-position, pen-pressure and pen-inclinations in a combined manner.

2. The algorithm

2.1. Overall algorithm

Figure 2.1 describes an overall algorithm of PPI.

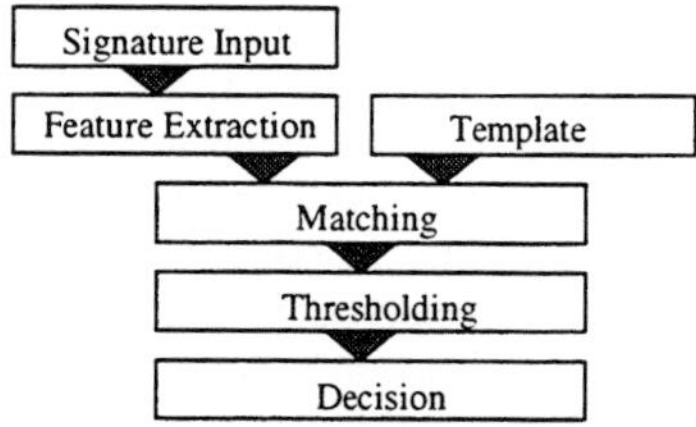

Fig 2.1 Overall algorithm

2.2. Feature extraction

The raw data available from our tablet (WACOM Art Pad 2 pro Serial) consists of five dimensional time series data:

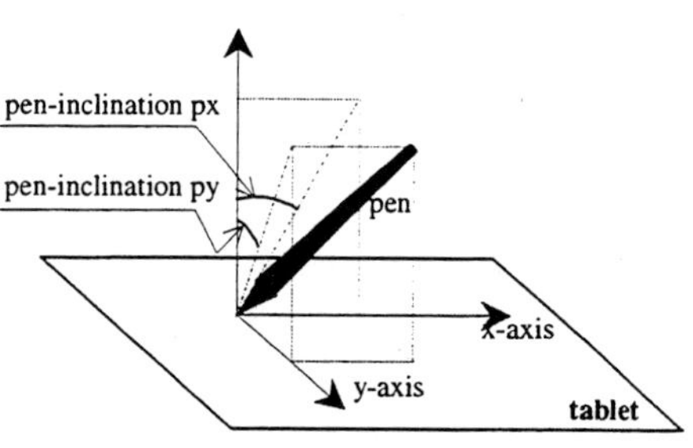

Fig2.2 Raw data from tablet

$$(x(t_i), y(t_i), p(t_i), px(t_i), py(t_i)) \in R^2 \times \{0,1,...,255\} \times R^2 \quad i = 1,2,...,I \qquad (2.1)$$

where $(x(t_i), y(t_i)) \in R^2$ is the pen position at time t_i, $p(t_i) \in \{0,1,...,255\}$ represents the pen pressure, $px(t_i)$ and $py(t_i)$ are pen inclinations with respect to the x- and y-axis as shown in Fig 2.2. Usually, $t_i - t_{i-1} \approx 5ms$ so that there are too many points which is not appropriate. Uniform resampling often

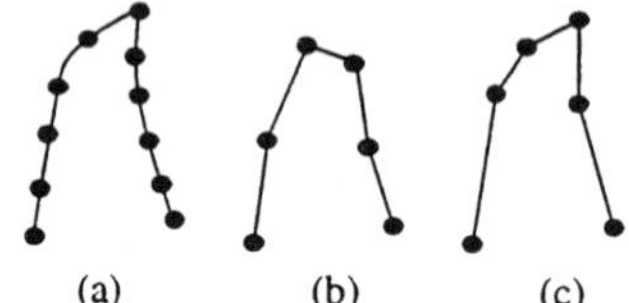

(a) (b) (c)

Fig2.3 Our resampling algorithm preserves sharp

results in a loss of important features. Consider, for instance, the raw data given in Fig 2.3(a). If one resamples the data uniformly then the sharp corner may be lost as is shown in Fig 2.3(b). Our resampling procedure checks if

$$\theta_i := \tan^{-1} \frac{y(t_i) - y(t_{i-1})}{x(t_i) - x(t_{i-1})} \leq \theta^* \qquad (2.2)$$

where θ^* is a threshold value. If (2.2) holds, then $(x(t_i), y(t_i))$ is eliminated, otherwise it is kept. This typically gives Fig 2.3(c) which retains a sharp corner while portions of pen trajectory without sharp corners retain information with smaller number of points. This is a preprocessing done in our pen-input on-line character recognizers which worked very well . Details are omitted.

Let

$$\Delta f_i := \sqrt{(x(t_i) - (x(t_{i-1}))^2 + (y(t_i) - (y(t_{i-1}))^2} \qquad (2.3)$$

then our feature consists of the following five dimensional data

$$(\theta_j, \Delta f_j, p_j, px(t_i), py(t_i)) \in R^2 \times \{0,1,...,N\} \times R^2 \quad i = 1,2,...,I \quad j = 1,2,...,J \qquad (2.4)$$

Our verification algorithm described below computes a weighted sum of three different distance measures between an input data and stored templates.

2.3. Angle distance measure

Let

$$(\eta_l, \Delta g_l, q_l, qx(t_k), qy(t_k)) \in R^2 \times \{0,1,...,N'\} \times R^2 \quad k = 1,2,...,K \quad l = 1,2,...,L \qquad (2.5)$$

be the resampled feature trajectory of a template and consider

$$|\theta_j - \eta_l| d(p_j, q_l) \rho(\Delta f_j, \Delta g_l) \qquad (2.6)$$

where

$d(p_i, q_j) := |p_i - q_j| + 1$

incorporates pen-pressure information. The last term "1" is to avoid zero value of a $d(p_i, q_j)$. Function ρ is defined by

$$\rho(\Delta f_j, \Delta g_l) := \sqrt{\Delta f_j^{\,2} + \Delta g_l^{\,2}} \qquad (2.7)$$

which is to take into account local arc length of the trajectories. Generally $K \neq I, L \neq J$ even when signatures are written by the same person so that time-warping is necessary to compute (2.6) over the whole trajectories. The following is our angle distance measure

$$D1 := \min_{\substack{j_s \le j_{s+1} \le j_s + 1 \\ l_s \le l_{s+1} \le l_s + 1}} \sum_{s=1}^{S} \left|\theta_{j_s} - \eta_{l_s}\right| d(p_{j_s}, q_{l_s}) \rho(\Delta f_{j_s}, \Delta g_{l_s}) \qquad (2.8)$$

where

$$j_1 = l_1 = 1, j_s = J, l_s = L$$

are fixed.

Because of the sequential nature of the distance function Dynamic Programming is a feasible means of the computation:

$$D1(0,0) = 0$$

$$D1(j_s, l_s) = \min \begin{cases} D1(j_s - 1, l_s - 1) + \left|\theta_{j_s} - \eta_{l_s}\right| \\ \quad \times d(p_{j_s}, q_{l_s}) \rho(\Delta f_{j_s}, \Delta g_{l_s}) \\ D1(j_s - 1, l_s) + \left|\theta_{j_s} - \eta_{l_s}\right| \\ \quad \times d(p_{j_s}, q_{l_s}) \rho(\Delta f_{j_s}, 0) \\ D1(j_s, l_s - 1) + \left|\theta_{j_s} - \eta_{l_s}\right| \\ \quad \times d(p_{j_s}, q_{l_s}) \rho(0, \Delta g_{l_s}) \end{cases}$$

$$d(p,q) = |p - q| + 1$$

$$\rho(\Delta f, \Delta g) = \sqrt{\Delta f^2 + \Delta g^2}$$

2.4. Pen inclination distances

Define pen-inclination distances

$$D2 := \min_{\substack{i_{s'} \le i_{s'+1} \le i_{s'} + 1 \\ k_{s'} \le k_{s'+1} \le k_{s'} + 1}} \sum_{s'=1}^{S'} \left|px_{i_{s'}} - qx_{k_{s'}}\right| \qquad (2.9)$$

$$D3 := \min_{\substack{i_{s''} \le i_{s''+1} \le i_{s''} + 1 \\ k_{s''} \le k_{s''+1} \le k_{s''} + 1}} \sum_{s''=1}^{S''} \left|py_{i_{s''}} - qy_{k_{s''}}\right| \qquad (2.10)$$

which are computable via DP also.

2.5. Distance measure

Our total distance measure between input trajectory and template trajectory is given by

$$D = \lambda_1 \cdot D1 + \lambda_2 \cdot D2 + \lambda_3 \cdot D3$$

where $\lambda_i, i = 1,2,3$ are empirical values so that $\lambda_i \cdot Di$ are of the same order.

2.6. Template generation

In order to explain our template generation procedure, recall two types of errors in signature verification:

a) Type I Error (False Rejection Error)

b) Type II Error (False Acceptance Error)

Given m_0 authentic signature trajectories, divide them into two group S_1 and S_2 consisting of m_1 and m_2 trajectories, respectively, where the former is to generate templates while the latter is for verification test. Compute the total distance measure D between each of the signatures in S_1 and sort them according to their distances. Choose three signatures with the smallest D. These will be used as templates.

2.7. Threshold value

In order to select the threshold value for distance between input and template, compute the $3 \times (m_1 - 3)$ distances between the chosen three and the remaining $m_1 - 3$ signatures and let the threshold value Th be the average of five largest distances.

2.8. Signature verification

Note that three template signatures are generated for each individual. Given an input signature, compute the distance measure between it and the three templates and let $D_{\min}$ be the smallest. We introduce a parameter $c \in [0.5, 2.0]$ to be selected and the input is predicted to be authentic if

$$D_{\min} \le c \cdot Th$$

while the input is estimated as a forgery if

$$D_{\min} > c \cdot Th.$$

3. Experiment

This section reports our preliminary experiment using the algorithm described above. Eight individuals participated the experiment. The data were taken for the period of three months. There are 293 authentic signatures, 540 forgery signatures and 69 signatures for template generation. Table3.1 shows the details. Figure 3.1 shows average verification error as a function of parameter c described above, where the intersection between Type I Error and Type II Error curves gives 1.9%. Figure 3.2 shows the error curves of individual "E" where zero error is achieved at $c = 1.4$.

Figure 3.4(a) is an unsuccessful attempt of a forgery rejected by our algorithm while Fig. 3.4(b) is an authentic signature accepted by the PPI.

The second experiment was done using Hirakana signatures instead of Kanji signatures. Collected date consist of 517 authentic signature, 880 forgery signature and 30 signatures for template generation from three individuals. Only angle distance measure (D1) was used in this particular experiment. Fig 3.3 shows average verification error, where the intersection between Type I Error and Type II Error curves gives 2.4%.

Fig 3.5(a) is an unsuccessful attempt of a forgery rejected by our algorithm while Figure 3.5(b) is an authentic signature accepted by the PPI.

Table 3.1 Data for Experiment

individuals	authentic		forgery	total
	test	Templates	test	
A	40	10	117	167
B	40	10	81	131
C	31	7	79	117
D	32	8	58	98
E	47	11	77	135
F	31	7	39	77
G	32	7	39	78
H	40	9	50	99
total	293	69	540	902

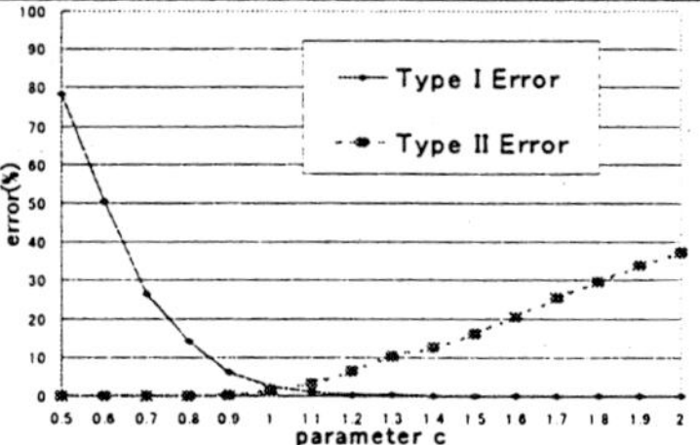

Fig 3.1 Average verification errors

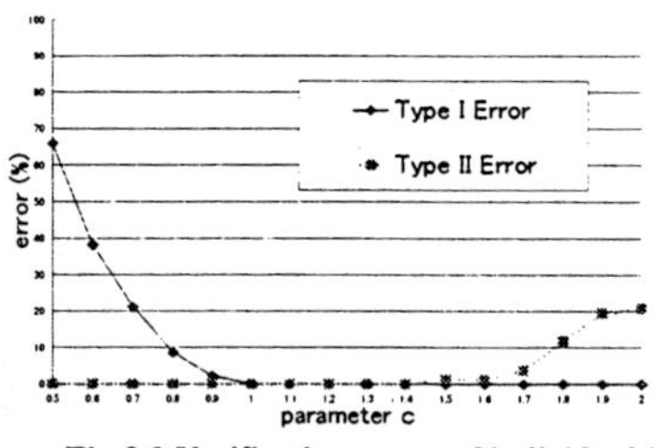

Fig 3.2 Verification errors of individual "E"

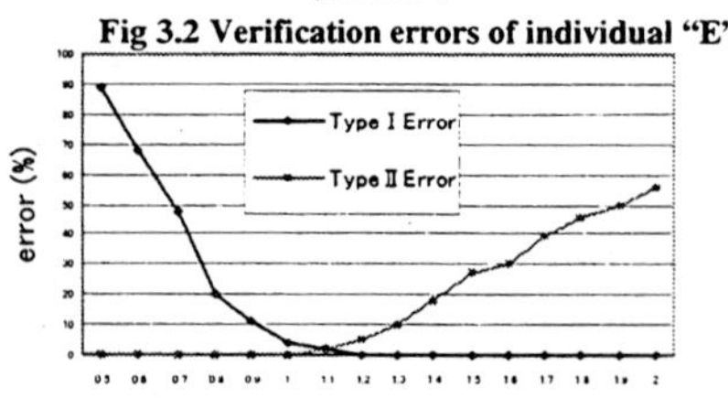

Fig 3.3 Average verification errors with Hirakana signatures

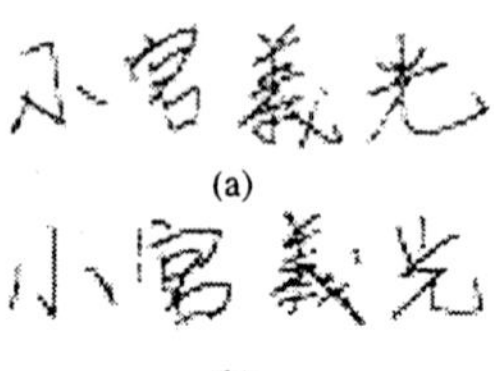

(a)

(b)

Fig 3.4 (a) Forgery rejected by the PPI algorithm. (b) Genuine signature accepted by the PPI.

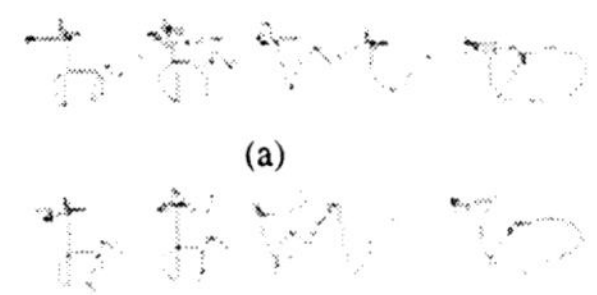

(a)

Fig 3.5 (a) Forgery rejected by the PPI algorithm. (b) Genuine signature accepted by the PPI.

4. Summary

A new algorithm was proposed for pen input signature verifier which incorporates trajectory of pen-position, pen-pressure and pen-inclinations. Preliminary experimental results look promising.

Hirakana signatures contain many smooth curve elements instead of line segments and sharp angle elements. It appears that important information about individuals' biometric features is contained in Hirakana signatures.

5. References

[1] T. Tabuki, "Personal Identification by Signature, Proc. Seminar on Sensing Technology and Applications, Osaka, Japan, 1997.

[2] Masami KATO, Yoshihiro KAWASHIMA, "Signature Verification Using Online Data such as Pen Pressure and Velocity", IPSJ, pp.2-199, 1993.

[3] Hideo TAGUCHI, Koichi KIRIYAMA, Eiji TANAKA and Katsuhiko FUJII, "On-Line Recognition of Handwritten Signatures by Feature Extraction of the Pen Movement",IEICE, D Vol.J71-D No.5 pp.830-840, 1988.

[4] Chang Ji JIN, Masaharu WATANABE, Toshio KAWASHIMA and Yoshinao AOKI "On-Line Signature Verification by Non-public Parameters", IEICE, D-II Vol.J75-D-II No.1 pp.121-127, 1992.

[5] I Yoshimura, and M Yoshimura, "On-line Signature Verification Incorporating the Direction of Pen Movement", Trans.IEICE Jpn., E74, pp.2803-2092, 1991.

Script-Independent, HMM-based Text Line Finding for OCR

Zhidong Lu, Richard Schwartz

BBN Technologies, GTE Corp.,
Cambridge, MA, USA
{zlu, schwartz}@bbn.com

Christopher Raphael

Department of Mathematics and Statistics,
University of Massachusetts,
Amherst, MA, USA

Abstract

In this paper we present a new, script-independent, HMM-based technique to locate text lines on images containing one or more paragraphs of single-column text. The parameters of the HMMs are trained on-line on each image using an unsupervised training procedure. We present results of line finding experiments in Arabic, Chinese and English to demonstrate the performance as well as the script-independent nature of the technique. Comparison of HMM-based line finding with manual line finding shows that the use of HMM-based technique does not lead to a significant increase in the recognition error rate.

1. Introduction

Text line finding is the task of locating lines of text in a text image. The line finding procedure we present in this paper is part of the BBN Byblos OCR System [1-3]. The basic modeling paradigm we employ, both, for line finding as well as for the actual recognition, is that of hidden Markov models (HMM). HMMs allow us to model the variability of a feature vector as a function of one independent variable. In speech [4], there is a natural independent variable: time. In OCR, there are two independent variables since text images are two-dimensional (2-D), so 1-D HMMs cannot be used directly. Fortunately, standard text documents consist of pages that contain characters lined up in straight text lines but not characters placed in arbitrary locations on a page. By exploiting this regularity of text lines, it is possible to formulate the fundamentally 2-D OCR problem as two, independent, 1-D pattern recognition tasks. The first task is to locate the lines of text on a page, also called line finding, and the second task is to recognize the sequence of characters in each line of text. This paper is concerned with the first task, that of line-finding.

In our line finding program, each row of pixels is represented by a numerical feature vector. The fact that the feature vector we extract does not depend on the script being recognized is one reason that our approach is script-independent. Another reason is that the HMM modeling approach itself does not change with the script being recognized. In particular, the fact that there is no separate character segmentation component, neither in training nor in recognition, allows the same system to recognize text lines in different scripts. Finally our unsupervised on-line training approach does not confine the system to any pre-trained script. To demonstrate the script-independence of our approach, we present line-finding results in three different scripts: Arabic, English, and Chinese.

In Section 2, we present the HMM-based approach for line finding. Experimental results are discussed in Section 3 with comparison to manual line finding.

2. Hidden Markov model approach

2.1 Description of the problem

We assume that a zone of text contains one or more paragraphs of single-column text with no image or diagram figures. Additionally, we assume that the zone has been properly preprocessed so as to ensure that text lines are horizontal. The line finding problem is that of locating the pixel locations of the top and bottom of each line of text in the zone.

2.2 Feature extraction

A single feature is computed for each row of pixels. The feature extraction procedure is as follows:

1) The image is downsampled to 120 dpi . This step is performed to reduce computation.
2) A sliding window of 20 pixel in width, which is about 2 character widths in a 12pt font, is applied to each row of pixels in the image. The sliding window moves in 1-pixel increments. For each

1051-4651/00 $10.00 © 2000 IEEE

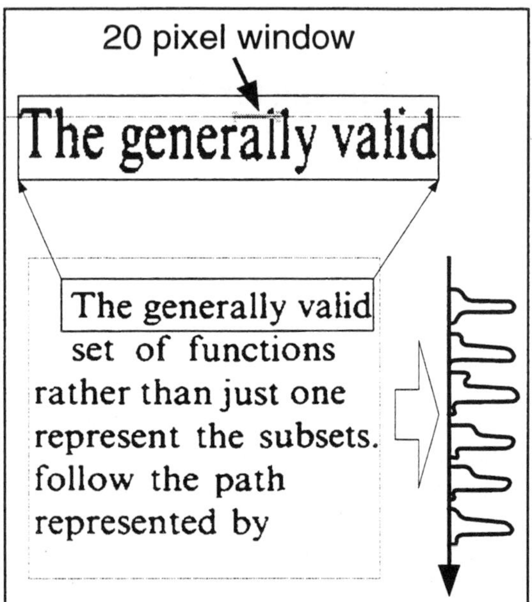

Figure 1. Raw feature of pixel rows, shown on the right, is the maximum sum of blackness in a 20-pixel window sliding across the pixel row of a binary image, shown on the left.

location of the window, the number of black pixels is counted.

3) A maximal horizontal projection is performed to get the maximum of the values counted in the previous step for each row of pixels. This is the raw feature value for a row of pixels. This procedure makes the feature insensitive to the length of a text line.
4) The raw feature is then quantized down to 10 bins such that the feature histogram is equalized over the whole image. The quantized value is used as the feature for that row of pixels.

The feature sequence for a zone is a 1-D sequence where the vertical position in the zone is the independent variable. Figure 1 shows how the raw feature is extracted from an image of English text.

2.3 Hidden Markov models for lines

The line finding program uses three different types of HMMs to model three kinds of vertical regions: a text line, white space between two text lines, and a horizontal rule. As shown in Figure 2, we regulate the transitions among the models with a grammar such that a zone starts with a white space and ends with a white space. The transitions are ergodic among the three types of models except that a white space cannot go to another white space. The text line models, labeled as TL1, TL2, ..., TLn in Figure 2, are models for text lines of different line height. There is only one white space model as shown in Figure 2. The horizontal rule models, labeled as HR1, HR2, ..., HRn in Figure 2, are models for horizontal rules of different thickness.

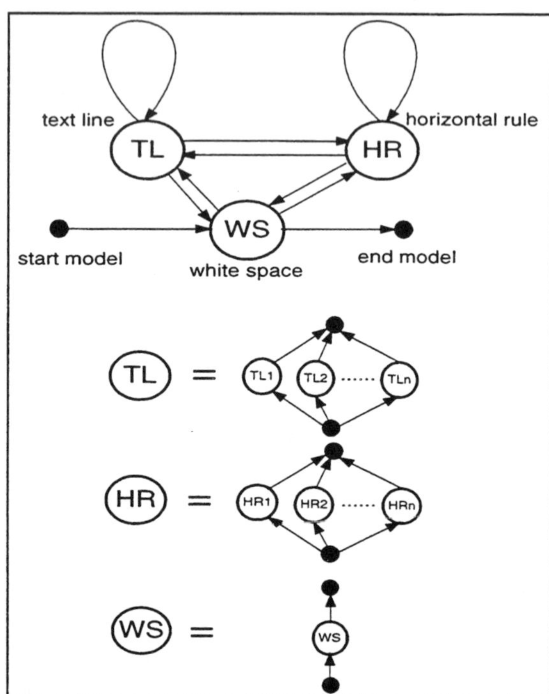

Figure 2. The transitions among the three types of models.

Five different output probabilities are used model the observed data of the single feature. They are labeled as white state, edge state, low black state, medium black state, and high black state.

The HMMs are all left-to-right models made up of a different number of the above states. Figure 3 shows some examples of the hidden Markov models. The HMM for a TEXT LINE has a core of 2 high black states in the center and on each side there is a number of states arranged in the way of a ladder. The ladders on each side of the HMM are of the same length which ranges from 4 to 24 states. The ladder consists of two strings of states, one of white states and the other of non-white states (edge states or black states). The edge states are only at the outside ends of the non-white strings of the ladder. The black states in the ladders are arranged such that the black states change from low black to medium black and to high black as the state goes from the outside of the ladder towards the center of the hidden Markov model. A model of a length of 9 states is shown in Figure 3a) to demonstrate the transition topology in the HMM.

There is only one HMM for WHITE SPACE which is a string of 30 white states. It allows a self-transition loop

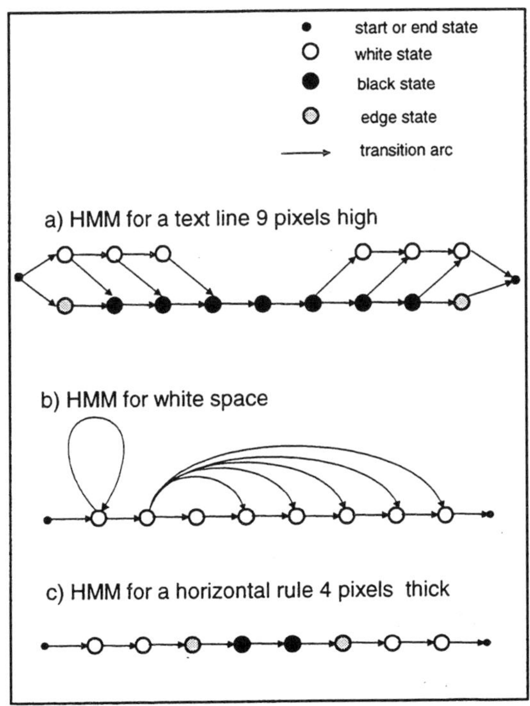

Figure 3. Examples of hidden Markov models for text line, white space, and horizontal rule.

at the 1st state and can skip from the 2nd state to the 4th state and beyond. Figure 3b) shows an 8-state version of white space model.

The HMMs for HORIZONTAL RULE have a string of states with a core of 2 to 5 high black states. On each end of the core there is an edge state. Outside the edge states, there is a string of white states on each side of the model. The strings of white states have the same length of 10 states. Figure 3c) shows a short version of horizontal rule model to demonstrate the transition topology.

2.4 Training and finding lines(recognition)

The transition probabilities of the models are initialized such that each state transits to any of the next possible states with equal probability. The output probabilities (probability mass functions) for the different states are initialized as follows:

1) For the white state, the probability of the feature value being 0 is set to 0.95; the remaining 0.05 probability is equally distributed among the other nine possible output values.
2) The low, medium, and high black states are initialized to the same probability mass function where the probability mass increases linearly with the feature value.
3) The probability mass function for the edge state *decreases* linearly with the increase in feature value (in fact, it is a flipped version of the probability mass function of the black states).

Having the models constructed and initialized, we used the expectation-maximization (EM) algorithm to train the model on the zone to be recognized. We calculate the forward and backward probabilities from the current transition probabilities and output probabilities. From the forward and backward probabilities, we compute the expected transition probabilities and the expected output probabilities (E-step) and use them as the new set of transition probabilities and output probabilities (M-step). Then we go back to calculate the forward and backward probabilities again if needed. Usually 4 iterations are used for this EM training procedure.

The Viterbi algorithm is used to find the most likely

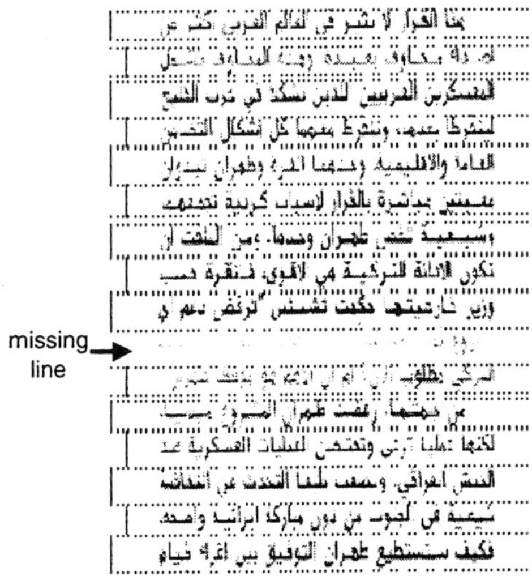

Figure 3: Example of line finding error in Arabic. The error is due to faded text. The vertical bars in front of the text line indicate the text lines found.

line sequence. From the line sequence we can obtain the top and bottom locations of the text lines, white spaces between text lines, and horizontal rules.

3. Experiments and results

To show the script-independent nature of our line finding technique, we have carried out line finding experiments on three different languages, Arabic, Chinese, and English. Then the results of the line finding technique were used for our OCR system that can recognize the above three languages [3]. The Arabic corpus is the DARPA Arabic OCR Corpus [5]. The English corpus is the University of Washington English Document Image Database I [6]. The Chinese corpus is a newspaper corpus collected in house. The line finding error can be measured in two ways: 1) whether the correct number of lines is found in a zone and the lines are roughly in the right locations; 2) whether it is comparable with the manual line finding in terms of the OCR error rate.

We have tested our HMM-based line finder on 345 Arabic zones with about 15,000 text lines, 153 Chinese zones of about 3,300 text lines, and 208 English zones of about 1,900 text lines. In the English experiment, all the text lines were found correctly. In the Chinese experiments, there is only one line finding error—a missing line. In the Arabic experiments, 17 zones had either missed one text line or had one extra text line (see Figure 3 for an example of missing line in Arabic).

While our line finding program has worked well in finding the correct number of lines in a zone, there remained some doubt as to whether the line finding program computes the "correct" location of the lines. We use "correct" in the sense that the uncertainty in the line locations should not contribute significantly to the total character error rate in OCR.

In order to verify the accuracy of the line finding program, we carried out an English OCR experiment to compare the recognition results obtained by using manual line finding with the results by using the HMM-based line finding program.

We manually marked the line locations and heights of about 1,900 lines in 208 English text zones with varying number of lines. Then using the manual line finding results, we trained the OCR system with half of the zones and tested on the other half. Also we performed HMM-based line finding and trained the OCR system with half of the zones and tested on the other half. The character error rate (CER) results are listed in Table 1.

Table 1. CER for manual line finding and HMM line finding

# of lines in zone	CER of HMM line finding	CER of manual line finding
1-4	3.9%	3.1%
5-9	2.2%	2.0%
10-14	2.3%	2.0%
15 or more	1.8%	1.7%
Average CER	2.24%	2.06%

The zones containing a smaller number of lines exhibit higher CER in both cases because of the larger variety of fonts (such as bold/italic) and sizes in these zones. On average, the CER with manual line finding is only 10% less than the CER with HMM-based line finding. This implies that the HMM-based line finding program is quite accurate in finding the "correct" line locations. The biggest difference, of 25%, occurs in the zones of less than 5 lines. This is predictable since our algorithm uses unsupervised training which performs better on zones with more lines.

4. Conclusion

In this paper, we have presented a novel, HMM-based approach for locating lines of text on a simple text image. The HMM-based approach uses unsupervised training on each zone and is script-independent. This approach is shown to work well on different languages such as Arabic, Chinese, and English. The accuracy and consistency of this line finding program have been shown to be comparable with manual line finding.

5. Acknowledgement

The authors would like to thank John Makhoul and Premkumar Natarajan for their help in preparing this paper.

6. References

[1] I. Bazzi, R. Schwartz, and J. Makhoul, "An Omnifont Open-vocabulary OCR System for English and Arabic," *IEEE Trans. Pattern Analysis and Machine Intelligence*, Vol. 21, No. 6, 495-504, 1285-1294, 1999.

[2] Z. Lu, R. Schwartz, P. Natarajan, I. Bazzi, and J. Makhoul, "Advances in the BBN BYBLOS OCR System", Proc. Int. Conf. Document Analysis and Recognition, Bangalore, India, pp. 337-340, Sept. 1999.

[3] R. Schwartz, C. LePre, J. Makhoul, C. Raphael, and Y. Zhao, "Language-independent OCR Using a Continuous Speech Recognition System," Proc. Int. Conf. on Pattern Recognition, Vienna, pp. 842-845, Aug. 1996.

[4] L.R. Rabiner, "A tutorial on hidden Markov models and selected applications in speech recognition", Proceedings of the IEEE 77, 257, 1989.

[5] R.B. Davidson and R.L. Hopley, "Arabic and Persian OCR training and test data sets," Proc. Symp. Document Image Understanding Technology (SDIUT97), Annapolis, MD, 303-307, 1997.

[6] I.T. Phillips, S. Chen, and R.M. Haralick, "CD-ROM document database standard," Proc. Int. Conf. Document Analysis and Recognition, Tsukuba City, Japan, pp. 478-483, Oct. 1993.

Statistical-based Approach to Word Segmentation

Yalin Wang[†] Ihsin T. Phillips[‡] Robert Haralick[†]

[†] Department of Electrical Engineering
University of Washington Seattle, WA 98195 U.S.A.

[‡] Department of Computer Science/Software Engineering
Seattle University Seattle, WA 98122 U.S.A.

{ylwang, yun, haralick@george.ee.washington.edu}

Abstract

This paper presents a text word extraction algorithm that takes a set of bounding boxes of glyphs and their associated text lines of a given document and partitions the glyphs into a set of text words, using only the geometric information of the input glyphs. The algorithm is probability based. An iterative, relaxation-like method is used to find the partitioning solution that maximizes the joint probability. To evaluate the performance of our text word extraction algorithm, we used a 3-fold validation method and developed a quantitative performance measure. The algorithm was evaluated on the UW-III database of some 1600 scanned document image pages. An area-overlap measure was used to find the correspondence between the detected entities and the ground-truth. For a total of $827,433$ *ground truth words, the algorithm identified and segmented* $806,149$ *words correctly, an accuracy of* 97.43%.

1. Introduction

A document structure analysis system converts a scanned document page or a document encoded by a Page Description Language (PDL), such as PostScript and Portable Document Format (PDF), into a well partitioned hierarchical representation that reliably identifies the basic document components – text words, text lines, and text blocks. Thus, extracting words (word segmentation) from a scanned document page or a PDF is an important and basic step in document structure analysis and understanding systems, but the task is not trivial. Incorrect word segmentation could lead to OCR errors and could also lead to errors in information retrieval and in understanding of the input document. This paper presents a text word extraction algorithm that takes a set of bounding boxes of glyphs and their associated text lines of a given document and partitions the glyphs into a set of text words, using only the geometric information of the input glyphs.

There are many document layout analysis algorithms in the literature; however, only several word segmentation methods can be found. Baird et al.'s word segmentation method [3] assumed that the distribution of the inter-symbol distances parallel to the text-line orientation is bimodal and segmented the words by finding an appropriate threshold. No performance evaluation of their text word segmentation was reported. Chen et al.'s method ([2]) used the recursive morphological closing transform to segment the words. He reported a 95% accuracy using hundreds of test images. Bapst et al.([1]) used typographic information to improve the existing word segmentation method and has shown good result. However, no quantitative performance evaluation was reported in this paper.

Our algorithm takes a set of glyph bounding boxes and their associated text lines of a given document. It partitions the glyphs into a set of text words. We adopt an engineering approach to systematically characterizing the text word based on a large document image database, and use the statistical methods developed in [4] to extract the text words from the image. All the probabilities are estimated from an extensive training set of various kinds of measurements among the glyphs and among the text words in the training data set. The off-line probabilities estimated in the training then drive all decisions in the on-line text word extraction. An iterative, relaxation-like method is used to find the partitioning solution that maximizes the joint probability. The algorithm was tested on 1600 document pages within the UW III document database. The evaluation result is reported in this paper.

The remainder of this paper is organized as follows: In Section 2, we present the abstract problem formulation. In Section 3, we describe the detail of our word segmentation algorithm. Our experimental protocol and results are given in Section 4. Our conclusions and statements of future work are discussed in Section 5.

2. The Word Segmentation Problem Statement

Given a set of bounding boxes of glyphs and their associated text lines, the word segmentation problem is to partition the input glyphs into a set of text words that maximizes the probability of glyphs to word assignment.

Let $\mathcal{A}$ be the set of input glyphs. Let Π be a partition of $\mathcal{A}$ where each element of the partition is a word. Let L be a set of labels. The function $f : \Pi \to L$ associates each element of Π with a label. $V : \wp(\Pi) \to \Lambda$ specifies the measurement made on the subset of Π, where Λ is the measurement space. Let $A = (A_1, A_2, \cdots, A_M)$ be a linearly ordered set (chain in $\mathcal{A}$) of input entities. Let $\mathcal{R} = \{Y, N\}$ be the set of grouping labels. Let A^P denote a set of element pairs, such that $A^P \subset A \times A$ and $A^P = \{(A_i, A_j)|A_i, A_j \in A \text{ and } j = i+1\}$. The function $r : A^P \to \mathcal{R}$, associates each pair of adjacent elements of A with a grouping label, and $r(i) = r(A_i, A_{i+1})$.

The consistent partition and labeling problem can be formulated as follows([4]): *Given an initial set $\mathcal{A}$, find a partition Π of $\mathcal{A}$, and a labeling function $f : \Pi \to L$, that maximizes the probability:*

$$\begin{aligned} &P(V(\tau) : \tau \in \Pi, f, \Pi|\mathcal{A}) \\ &= P(V(\tau) : \tau \in \Pi|\mathcal{A}, \Pi, f)P(\Pi, f|\mathcal{A}) \\ &= P(V(\tau) : \tau \in \Pi|\mathcal{A}, \Pi, f)P(f|\Pi, \mathcal{A})P(\Pi|\mathcal{A}) \end{aligned} \quad (1)$$

We make an assumption of conditional independence: when the label $f(\tau)$ is known, no knowledge of other labels will alter the probability of $V(\tau)$. We use $P(\Pi|\mathcal{A}) = P(r|A)$ and let N be the number of elements in $\mathcal{A}$. We can decompose the probability (1) as follows:

$$\begin{aligned} &P(V(\tau) : \tau \in \Pi, f, \Pi|\mathcal{A}) \\ &= \prod_{\tau \in \Pi} P(V(\tau)|f(\tau))P(f|\Pi, \mathcal{A}) \times \prod_{i=1}^{N-1} P(r(i)|A_i, A_{i+1}) \end{aligned} \quad (2)$$

The search space for the above equation is 2^{N-1}, where N is the number of input glyphs. Fortunately, the glyphs within words follows a particular sequential order, Thus, with the ordering constraint, the partitioning problem can be done iteratively. The next section describes an iterative search method of order $O(N)$ that finds the consistent partition labeling by monotonically maximizing the joint probability in equation (2).

3. Text Word Segmentation Algorithm

An iterative searching method can find the consistent partition and labeling that maximizes the joint probability (2). First, the grouping probability $P(r(i)|A_i, A_{i+1})$ between each pair of adjacent input entities is computed by observing the spatial relationship between the two input entities. An initial partition is determined based on the grouping probabilities. Then, we adjust the partition and assign labels to the members of the partition by optimizing the joint probability. At each iteration, the adjustment that produces the maximum improvement of the joint probability is selected. The iteration stops when there is no improvement on the joint probability.

The overview of our word segmentation algorithm is shown in Figure 1. The detailed description of the consistent partition and labeling algorithm can be found at [4]. We describe how we compute the three conditional probabilities in (2) in the subsections below.

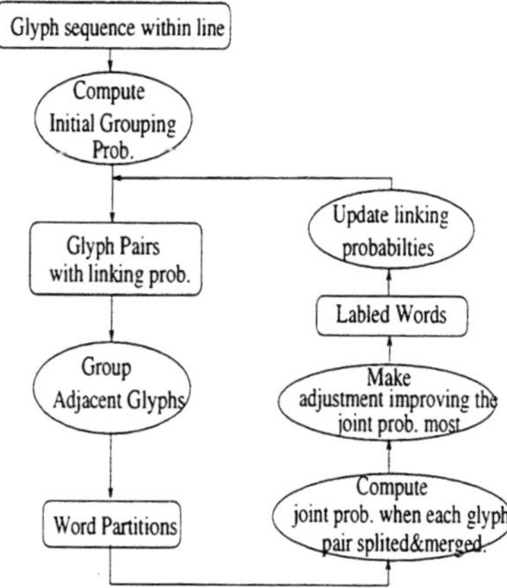

Figure 1. Overview of the word segmentation algorithm

3.1. Initial Grouping Probability

Without loss of generality, we assume that the reading direction of the text words in the given line is left-right. The text word segmentation algorithm starts with a set of the bounding boxes of the text glyphs within the given text line.

We first construct the reading order of the input glyphs. For each pair of adjacent glyphs within the same text line, g_i and g_{i+1}, we compute the probability that they are within the same text word:

$$P(r|g_i, g_{i+1}) = P(SameWord(g_i, g_{i+1})|g_i, g_{i+1})$$

For each pair of horizontally adjacent glyphs g_i and g_{i+1}, the glyph is represented by a bounding box (x, y, w, h). Given the line l, where the line is represented by a bounding box (x_l, y_l, w_l, h_l), we make the following measurements:

- inter-glyph distance: $d(i, i+1) = x_{i+1} - x_i - w_i$
- left-top offset: $e_{lt} = y_i - y_l$
- left-bottom offset: $e_{lb} = y_i + h_i - y_l$

- right-top offset: $e_{rt} = y_{i+1} - y_l$
- right-bottom offset: $e_{rb} = y_{i+1} + h_{i+1} - y_l$

The inter-glyph distance $d(i, i+1)$ is normalized by the threshold, $thre_{otsu}$, which is calculated from the distance set for the given line using Otsu's algorithm([5]).

$$d_i = \frac{d(i, i+1)}{thre_{otsu}}$$

The other four measurements are all normalized by the given line height.

$$lt_i = \frac{e_{lt}}{h_l}, \quad lb_i = \frac{e_{lb}}{h_l}, \quad rt_i = \frac{e_{rt}}{h_l}, \quad rb_i = \frac{e_{rb}}{h_l}$$

Given the above measurements, we compute the probability that g_i and g_{i+1} belong to the same word,

$$P(SameWord(i, i+1)|d_i, lt_i, lb_i, rt_i, rb_i)$$

3.2. Labeling Checking Probability

Given the initial word segmentation result, we have two sets of different types of horizontal distance. Let D_{iw} be the set of distances between the horizontally adjacent words and D_{ig} be the set of distances between the horizontally adjacent glyphs which belong to the same word. We have:

$$D_{iw} = \{d_{iw}(i, i+1)|w_i, w_{i+1} \text{are horizontally adjacent words}\}$$
$$D_{ig}(j) = \{d_{ig}(i, i+1)|g_i, g_{i+1} \text{are horizontally adjacent glyphs and belong to the same word } j\ \}$$

A text word usually has homogeneous inter-glyph distance and the inter-word distance is usually larger than the maximum inter-glyph distance of its adjacent words. Given one detected word W, we compute the conditional probability that W has homogeneous inter-glyph distance and appropriate inter-word distance. Assuming their conditional independence, we have

$$\begin{aligned} &P(V(W)|TextWord(W)) \\ &= P(V(W)|IntG(W), IntW(W)) \\ &= P(V_1(W)|IntG(W))P(V_2(W)|IntW(W)) \end{aligned}$$

Assuming that W is the jth segmented text word and it has m glyphs, we can estimate the conditional probability of it having homogeneous inter-glyph distance by:

$$P(V_1(W)|IntG(W)) = P(\sum_{i=1}^{m-1}(|d_{ig}(i, i+1) - Median(D_{ig}(j))|)|IntG(W))$$

In a line, one inter-word distance should be larger than the maximum inter-glyph distance in its two adjacent words. Assuming that W is not the last glyph in the given line, we can estimate the conditional probability on its following inter-word distance by:

$$P(V_2(W)|IntW(W)) = P(d_{iw}(j, j+1) - Max(D_{ig}(j) \cup D_{ig}(j+1))|IntW(W))$$

3.3. Context Checking Probability

Given a line and its segmented words, we can expect the minimum inter-word distance should be larger than the maximum inter-glyph distance. Let $\mathcal{G}$ be the set of the glyphs in the given line, $\mathcal{W}$ be the set of the segmented words. Assuming that there are S words in the line, we can do the context checking by computing:

$$P(TextWord|\mathcal{W}, \mathcal{G}) = P(Min(D_{iw}) - Max(\bigcup_{j=1}^{S} D_{ig}(j))|\mathcal{W}, \mathcal{G})$$

4. Experimental Result

We use discrete contingency tables to represent the joint and conditional probabilities used in the algorithm. A tree structure quantization is used to partition the value of each variable into bins. At each node of the tree, we search through all possible threshold candidates on each variable, and select the one that gives minimum value of entropy of the resulting distribution. The total number of terminal nodes, which is equivalent to the total number of cells, is predetermined. For each joint or conditional probability distribution, a cell count is computed from the groundtruthed document images in the UW-III Document Image Database([6]). The cell count is simply the number of units in the sample whose quantized measurement vector falls in the given cell. The joint probability can be computed directly from the cell count. For the performance evaluation, we use an area-overlap measure to find the correspondence between the detected entities and the ground-truth([2]). We applied our word segmentation algorithm to the total of 1600 images from the UW-III Document Image Database using the cross validation method. Of $827,433$ ground truth words , the numbers and percentages of miss, false, correct, splitting, merging and spurious detections are shown in Table 1. Figure 2 shows one example page of the segmented word entities.

5. Conclusion and Future Work

This paper presents a statistical-based word segmentation algorithm based on the methods developed in [4]. The algorithm uses only the geometric information of the bounding boxes input glyphs. The algorithm was tested on the 1600 pages within UW-III Document Image Database and achieved a 97.43% accuracy rate. Figure 3 give a few

Table 1. Performance of the statistical-based word segmentation algorithm.

	Total	Correct	Splitting	Merging	Mis-False	Spurious
Ground Truth	827433	806149 (97.43%)	7602 (0.92%)	12193 (1.47%)	630 (0.08%)	859 (0.10%)
Detected	834048	806149 (96.65%)	21715 (2.60%)	4911 (0.59%)	367 (0.04%)	906 (0.11%)

INTRODUCTION

(a)

W Weight

E_p Activation energy of permeation

(b)

Autoconversion of cloud droplets

(c)

and Reinhardt (1974)

(d)

Figure 3. Illustrates examples that the word segmentation algorithm failed.

examples at which our algorithm failed. Our algorithm finds the global optimization by searching for the local optimization. When they do not match, glyphs may be segment as word individually, as shown in Figure 3(a). Our current context checking favors large inter-word distance, which gives us the kind of error shown in Figure 3(b). Other errors are due to the Italic fonts(Figure 3(c)) and the thin characters(Figure 3(d)). So our future work will include using a polygon instead of a rectangle as the entity enclosing box, doing the context checking in a larger region, and dealing with the small width characters and the various inter-word distances within one line.

References

[1] F. Bapst and R. Ingold. Using typography in document image analysis. *Electronic Publishing, Artistic Imaging, and Digital Typography. EP'98 & RIDT'98 Proceedings.*, pages 240–251, Mar./Apr. 1998.

[2] S. Chen, R. M. Haralick, and I. Phillips. Simultaneous word segmentation from document images using recursive morphological closing transform. *Proceedings of the 3rd ICDAR*, pages 761–764, Aug. 1995.

[3] D. J. Ittner and H. S. Baird. Language-free layout analysis. *Proceedings of the 2nd ICDAR*, pages 336–340, Oct. 1993.

[4] J. Liang. *Document Structure Analysis and Performance Evaluation.* Ph.D thesis, Univ. of Washington, Seattle, WA, 1999.

[5] N. Otsu. A threshold selection method from gray-level histograms. *IEEE Transactions on SMC, Vol. SMC-9*, pages 62–66, 1979.

[6] I. Phillips. Users' reference manual. *CD-ROM, UW-III Document Image Database-III*, 1995.

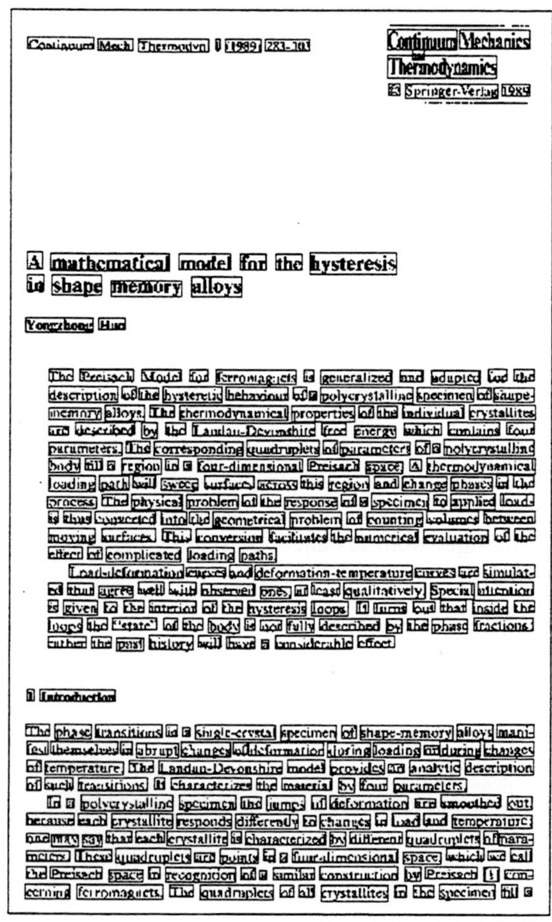

Figure 2. Example of the word segmentation result

3-D Face Modeling with Multiple Range Images

Pujitha Gunaratne, Hisanari Shogo, and Yukio Sato
Nagoya Institute of Technology, Gokiso-Cho, Showa-Ku, Nagoya 466-8555, Japan.
{pujitha,shogo}@hilbert.elcom.nitech.ac.jp, sato@elcom.nitech.ac.jp

Abstract

A method of constructing 3-D model of a human face by integrating multiple range images that were measured at different view directions is presented in this paper. The images were obtained by a high-speed rangefinder system, which is capable of measuring the frontal face and capturing a texture image in approximately one second. A complete face model construction is thus performed by measuring the face in different orientations and integrating corresponding range maps using a least squares estimator. Range image integration is carried out in two ways. First by direct application of the least squares estimator to range values and next by applying it to corresponding texture index values. A Sobel filter is applied to the intensity images to extract feature boundaries for the estimator. Both methods prove high accuracy returns and the average error of integration has been estimated to be below 1.3 mm.

1. Introduction

Computer generated 3-D facial models of humans have been studied over the past with diverse attention. Computer animation, game industry, virtual environments and teleconferencing, are some of the fields that demand for accurate 3-D facial models.

With the evolution of range sensing technology, rangefinder systems that produce dense range maps and color intensity images have been designed and presented [1], [2]. The high-speed face measurement system we used here is one of such, which is capable of measuring the face and producing a dense range map, together with its corresponding color texture image, in one second [2]. Since the measured face is essentially a frontal model, multiple viewpoint based image acquisition technique is sought to generate a complete 3-D face model. The strategy we adapt here is to measure the face in different poses, implicating different view locations, and then integrating the multiple range images to form the complete model.

Multiple range image integration has been studied in the past with different magnitude [3], [4], [5]. Kawai et al. [3] presented a method of range data integration based on region segmentation and extraction of feature parameters. Although they have modeled some arbitrary complex objects, such a method is not suitable for objects with curved surface, which are difficult to segment. Registration methods presented in [4] and [5] employ iterated closest point (ICP) algorithms. An obvious limitation with such algorithms is the requirement of enough structural complexity for robustness. Hence those methods would not be suitable for face modeling. In this work, we present a simple, yet robust technique of multiple range image integration. It takes the advantage of known physical characteristics and features of the subject, the human face, and utilizes the information in color texture data for the integration task.

The initial transformation parameters of translation and rotation matrices are evaluated from manual selection of three feature points on the corresponding intensity images. The integration task is twofold. Direct integration, which is based on selecting match points on the overlapping range boundaries, and the Feature extraction, from texture images. A Sobel filter is applied to the intensity images of two merging range images, and edges are extracted. Then the edge matching is performed in two intensity images. Resulting transformations are then applied to the corresponding range images. We apply a least squares estimator for the integration tasks in both cases. Finally the integration results are shown with accuracy of 1.3mm.

2. Face model construction

The face measuring system we use, equips with two laser range scanners and a CCD camera that captures range and color texture images in one-second [2].

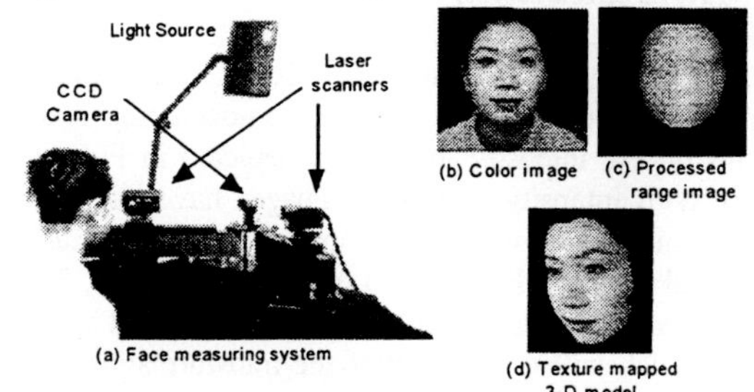

Figure 1. 3-D Frontal face model construction

Fig. 1(a) shows the face measuring system. During a single complete operation, two laser scanners measure each half of the face complementarily, and produce a frontal face model by integrating both range images on a weighted average. (Fig. 1(c)). At the same time, the CCD camera captures the frontal texture image of the face. Succeeding texture mapping process produces the textured 3-D frontal face model as depicted in Fig. 1(d). The measurement error is estimated as 1mm [2].

Thus, in order to construct a complete face model, which covers the entire face area, up to ears, we measure the face with different orientations and capture the unmeasured lateral areas of the initial passes.

3. Multiple image integration

The image integration process can be described as follows:

a) Measure the face from multiple viewpoints. – Three additional range and texture images are taken from left, right and head-up positions.

b) Determine three arbitrary points within the face area, which are visible in both front and lateral views of the texture images.

c) Calculate the 3-D translation (**T**) and rotation (**R**) matrices from the spatial data, correspond to the selected points, fetched by corresponding range images.

d) Using the calculated **R** and **T** matrices, transform the range images, so as to align with each other. Apply a least squares estimator to merge both range images smoothly. Fig. 2 shows images obtained from multiple view directions used for integration.

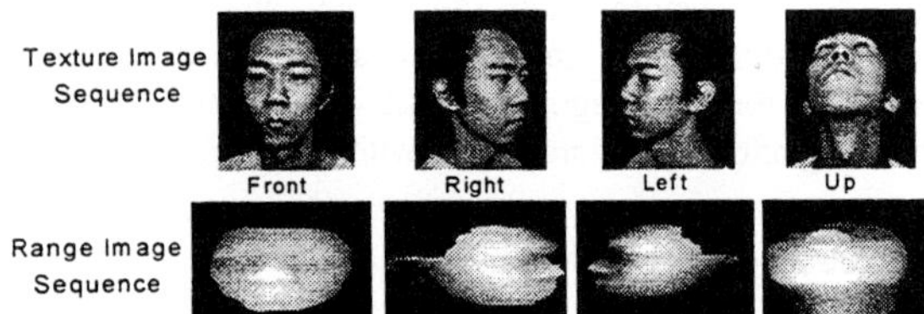

Figure 2. Images from multiple viewpoints

4. Matrix calculation

In order to generate translation and rotation parameters, we manually select 3 non-occluding feature points on the intensity images, as depicted in Fig. 3(a). Since both intensity and range images have one-to-one correspondence between them, spatial coordinates can be extracted directly (Fig. 3(b)). Let u_i and v_i {i=1, 2, 3} be selected vertex points on intensity images U and V (Fig. 3(c)), which will coincide after the transformation. Thus the matrix transformation is performed as follows;

a) Calculate the Center of the Gravity of each triangle, G_1 and G_2, correspond to images U and V respectively.

b) Calculate the normal vectors $\mathbf{N_1}$ and $\mathbf{N_2}$ of each triangle from corresponding range images *U* and *V*.

c) Translate G_1 and G_2 to the origin *O*, so as to coincide with each other (Fig. 3(c1)).

d) Align the normal vectors $\mathbf{N_1}$ and $\mathbf{N_2}$ along the Z-axis, so as to make the triangles are co-planer with XY plane (Fig. 3(c2)).

e) Calculate the direction vectors $\mathbf{r}_1$ and $\mathbf{r}_2$ of any vertex, drawn from the center of the gravity.

f) Rotate the triangles in XY plane; in order to coincide $\mathbf{r}_1$ with $\mathbf{r}_2$ (Fig. 3(c3)). Thus, we can derive the composite transformation as follows.

$$V' = R_V^{-1} R_{UV} R_U (U' - T_U) + T_V$$

Where, *U'* and *V'* represent the total number of points in each range image. R_u, R_v, T_u, and T_v are intermediate transformation matrices as shown in fig. 3(c). Generation of transformation matrices is illustrated in Fig. 3. Hence, the correct orientation of the two range images can be defined. Then employing a least-square algorithm we carry out the integration process of the two range images.

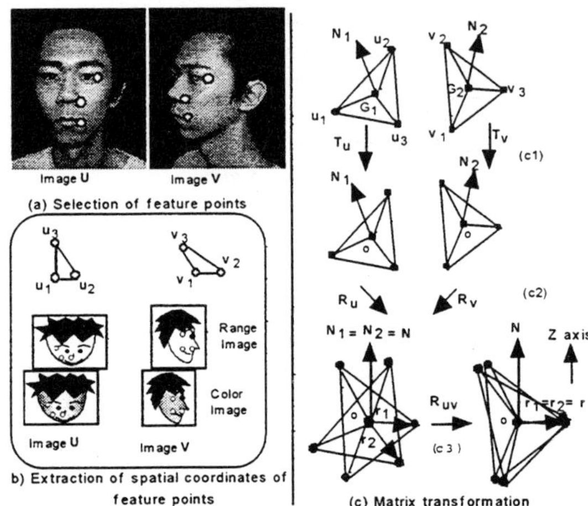

Figure 3. Feature point selection and matrix transformation

Once the transformation parameters are known, range image integration is done with two approaches. One is using range values and the other is with texture index values. In each case, least squares estimator with simplex method is applied for merging data sets.

5. Adaptation with range values

Merging is carried out for each match point appears in both range images. Any two points are defined to be the match points, if their range depth is the closest than their neighbors. Thus the least-square estimation function is defined as the average of squared summation of distance between the match points, and given as:

$$\frac{1}{N}\sum_{i=0}^{N}\left\|\mathbf{P}_{Ui}-\mathbf{P}_{Vi}\right\|^2$$

Where, $\mathbf{P}_{Ui}$ and $\mathbf{P}_{Vi}$ are the distances of match point $\mathbf{P}_i$ in both images. N is the total number of match points.

6. Adaptation with texture values

Use of texture index values is somewhat similar to the previous method with range values, in that, the index values replace the range values of the least squares estimator. The intensity values show a significant variation in locations where there is high feature density. Thus we apply a Sobel filter to the intensity images and extract the index values of those prominent feature boundaries (Fig. 4). Then, for all range values in each image, we extract the corresponding index values of the intensity image and set a threshold value.

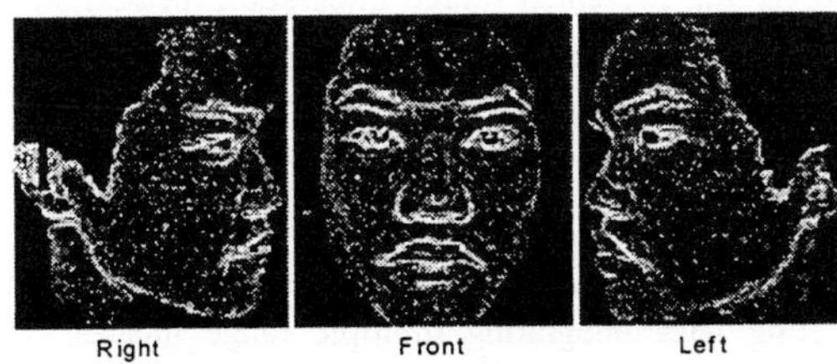

Figure 4. Sobel filtered images

According to this threshold value, we can categorize texture index values which lie above and below.

a) Points above the threshold (feature boundaries) – if the intensity images of the merging range images have texture index values which are greater than the threshold, the match points of those index values are determined only if their corresponding range values are the closest to each other than the neighbors.
b) Points below the threshold (other area) – the match points of such index values are defined as the ones who have the closest spatial values in their corresponding range counterparts. This phenomenon is illustrated in the following Fig. 5.

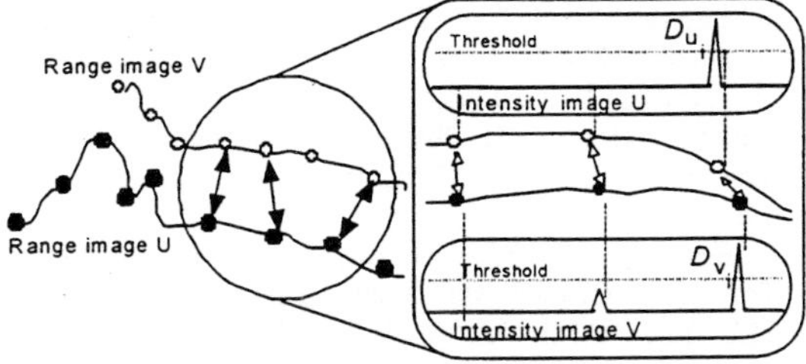

Figure 5. Extraction of spatial values of match points

The space of match points is further refined by discarding those ones, which do not converge sufficiently in the integration process. The estimation function in this case is defined as the average of the square summation of the distance between match points, and given as:

$$\frac{1}{N}\sum_{i=0}^{N}\alpha\left\|\mathbf{P}_{Ui}-\mathbf{P}_{Vi}\right\|^2$$

Where,

$$\alpha=\begin{cases}1 & \text{color index val.} < \text{threshold}\\ 1+\dfrac{(D_{Ui}+D_{Vi})}{2D_{\max}} & \text{color index val.} > \text{threshold}\end{cases}$$

Values $\mathbf{P}_{Ui}$ and $\mathbf{P}_{Vi}$ represent the match points. N is the total number of match points. D_{Ui} and D_{Vi} represent the index values of pixel i in the intensity images U and V, respectively. They take values from 0 to 255 and D_{max} is the maximum index value 255. The weights that applied when the index values become greater than the threshold is calculated experimentally.

7. Improvement measures

a) To speed up the convergence process of the least-squares algorithm, the resolution of the color images is increased, so that prominent edges appear in Sobel filtered feature boundaries.
b) Once a match point is detected, search space of other match points is pruned by defining a reasonable neighborhood of the previous match point.
c) Applying a median filter along the common pixels after the integration alleviates possible texture boundaries due to multiple image integration. For those pixels that belong to both images, filtered value is taken as the final texture value. The texture mapping process is sequenced through, always mapping the frontal image over the two lateral ones to avoid significant texture variations along the mapping boundaries of the frontal image, which has a high feature density.

8. Experimental evaluation

In the experiment, first we construct the frontal face model as described in section 2. Then the lateral images are taken from both sides by varying the rotation angle.

Since the accuracy of the measurement depends on the head-posing angle against the projected laser stripes of the rangefinder, we calculate the average error of integration for a polystyrene head model with varying vertical rotation angle. This also addresses the issue of non-uniformity in integration results due to the variation in rotation angles. This mainly depends on the shape of the measuring object and the scope of the laser beam projection. If the surface is oriented slanted to the laser projection angle, the resultant measurement is proved to be highly noisy. Therefore the measuring angle of the face is also a determining factor for robust matching results. In this experiment, we performed the matching at different view angles.

The error term of integration can thus be defined as the average error of the range value of the closest point with regard to the depth of the range data, and is given by the following error estimator.

$$\frac{1}{N}\sum_{i=0}^{N}\left\|\mathbf{P}_{Ui}-\mathbf{P}_{Vi}\right\|$$

$\mathbf{P}_{Ui}$ and $\mathbf{P}_{Vi}$ are match points and N is the total number of match points. For the experimental point of view, we have also performed a manual adaptation to compare the variation against the algorithm driven approach as shown in Fig. 6.

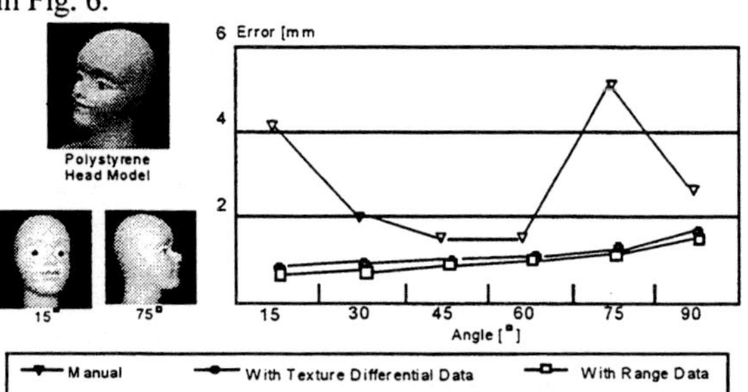

Figure 6. Estimated integration error due to the change in rotation angle

Analyzing the results depicted in Fig. 6, we can state that the integration process with range values have more precision than using texture index values, although there is not much of a significance. However it can be clearly seen that the head rotation angle is a predominant and sensitive factor for the integration.

Once the most suitable angle is determined, face is measured in that angle. The integration is then applied with both methods discussed in section 5 and 6. The threshold value used in texture index based integration is set to 20 with trial-and-error. The integration result of the images that showed in Fig. 2 is given in Fig. 7.

(a) Left and Front integreation (b) Right and Front integreation

Figure 7. Views of image integration

We performed the integration for 10 human samples. Those results are given in Table 1.

Table 1. Average integration error of 10 human samples

		Error [mm]
Left	Manual	2.761
	Range	1.188
	Differential	1.203
Right	Manual	2.772
	Range	1.294
	Differential	1.248

The results of two methods we carried out, namely the spatial method and the texture index differential method, do not deviate much, hence, both can be accepted as stable. Furthermore, the error margin with the method that used range data is approximately 1.20 mm. When using the texture index information, the error approximated to 1.25mm. Observing the results it is clear that the integration error is not only depend on convergence algorithms, but also other physical factors such as, head pose (Table 1 – differences in left and right integration), orientation (rotation angle in Fig. 6), lighting conditions (sensitivity to texture index driven approach) etc. However the presented image integration method shows stable results. It can be noted that the error of integration is below 1.3 mm, thus, reflecting high mode of precession.

9. Conclusion

In this research we presented a technique for 3-D face modeling with integrating multiple range images. This technique uses match points derived from both range and texture data, for the integration. A least squares estimator is applied on range and texture images separately during the merge. It also determines a suitable rotation angle for most stable results by evaluating an error function. According to the results, we can predict that the range value based integration technique is less sensitive to the head orientation angle than the texture index based method. Finally the presented method integrates multiple range images with 1.3mm accuracy to claim its stability.

10. References

[1] K. Hattori, Y. Sato, "Accurate Rangefinder with Laser Pattern Shifting", Proc. of ICPR, vol.c, pp.849-853, 1996.

[2] K. Hasegawa, K. Hattori and Y. Sato, "A High Speed Face Measurement System", Vision Interface '99, Trois-Rivieres, Canada, pp. 196-202, 1999.

[3] Y. Kawai, T. Ueshiba, T. Yoshimi, and M. Oshima, "Reconstruction of 3D Objects by Integration of Multiple Range Data", Proc. 11th ICPR, the Hague, Vol. I, pp. 154-157, 1992.

[4] R. Bergevin, M. Soucy, H. Gagnon, and D. Laurendeau, "Towards a General Muli-View Registration Technique", IEEE Trans. PAMI, Vol. 18, No. 5, pp. 540-547, 1996.

[5].T. Masuda, N. Yokoya, "A Robust Method for Registration and Segmentation of Multiple Range Images", Comp. Vision and Image Under., Vol. 61, NO. 3, pp. 295-307, 1995.

3D Curve Reconstruction by Biplane Snakes

C. Cañero, P. Radeva, R. Toledo, J.J. Villanueva
Computer Vision Center and Dept. Informàtica
Universitat Autònoma de Barcelona
08193 Bellaterra (Barcelona), Spain
cristina@cvc.uab.es

J. Mauri
Cardiac Catheterization Laboratory
Hospital Universitari Germans Trias i Pujol
08916 Badalona (Barcelona), Spain
jmauri@ns.hugtip.scs.es

Abstract

Stent implantation for coronary disease treatment is a highly important minimally invasive technique that avoids surgery interventions. In order to assure the success of such an intervention, it is very important to determine the real length of the lesion as exactly as possible. Currently, lesion measures are performed directly from the angiography without considering the system projective parameters or, alternatively, from the 3D reconstruction obtained from a correspondence of points defined by the physicians. In this paper, we present a method for 3D vessel reconstruction from biplane images by means of deformable models. In particular, we study the known shortcoming of point-based 3D vessel reconstruction (no intersection of projective beams) and illustrate that using snakes the reconstruction error is minimal. We validate our method by a computer-generated phantom, a real phantom and coronary vessels.

1. Introduction

Nowadays, medical imaging techniques are supposed not only to give qualitative information, but also quantitative measurements about the objects to be analyzed. Whereas the technique of angiography has been developed in order to obtain images from the coronary vessels from different views, measurements of the vessels have become necessary very soon. This is the case of the determination of the stent size. When the selected stent is too large, the vessel comes too rigid, otherwise, the lesion is not treated. Obtaining the length of a stenosis is of vital importance for the success of this kind of intervention. In order to obtain these measurements, a view of the affected vessel is taken and the length of the lesion is infered. The imprecision in the system calibration, as well as the foreshortening due to the view, make these measurements inexact and unreliable. To cope with it we adress a three-dimensional reconstruction of the vessel from two views.

There are two main approaches to reconstruct a curve in space: computing the curve which interpolates the corresponding points marked by the user (usually with imprecision) or obtaining the curve whose projections approximate the vessel in the images as well as possible.

There are different works following the bottom-up strategy: Dumay et al. in [1] describe a method for the reconstruction of a point using two views. Wahle et al. in [5] address three dimensional reconstruction of skeletons of the coronary tree from biplane views. Wunderlich et al. in [6] present a procedure in order to obtain the length of a lesion after reconstructing from biplane angiograms. The bottom-up approach has three shortcomings: first, in many cases it is difficult to determine corresponding points. Second, even when the user is helped by the epipolar line [1] to match points in different views, measurement error in the calibration parameters makes fail the epipolarity constraint. Third, the curve is directly interpolated among marked points.

Instead, we consider the second approach proposing a top-down strategy: an elastic curve in the space deforms in order to adapt its projections to the vessels in the images. Therefore, the user initializes the curve by few points in the zone of the vessel to be reconstructed. Then, the curve deforms until its complete adaptation to the vessels in the images. This new kind of deformable curves is called *biplane snake*. Preliminary results of this aproach were presented in [4] for orthogonal views. The aim of this paper is to extend the technique and validate it by phantoms and experts; we show the results improvement compared to the bottom-up approach.

The remaining of this paper is organized as follows: section 2 discusses the problem of the 3D reconstruction of a single point and proposes a measure of the reconstruction error. Section 3 extends the technique to the reconstruction of curves introducing the *biplane snakes*. Section 4 presents tests on computer-generated phantoms, mechanic phantoms and also shows its application in a real case. Finally, section 5 states some conclusions and propose several future guidelines.

1051-4651/00 $10.00 © 2000 IEEE

2. Single point 3D-reconstruction

Let F_1, F_2 be the focus position of the X-ray beams in two views, and D_1, D_2 be the projections φ_1, φ_2 of the point D to be reconstructed. Theoretically, the 3D reconstruction of D is the intersection of the projective lines F_1D_1 and F_2D_2 (see figure 1). In practice, projective lines fail to intersect. Dumay et al. in [1] propose as the aproximated 3D reconstructed point the point D' which minimises the distance to both projective lines. This point is situated upon a segment perpendicular to both projective lines. The vectorial representation of this segment is as follows:

$$\overrightarrow{S_1S_2} = (\overrightarrow{OF_2} + \sigma\overrightarrow{F_2D_2}) - (\overrightarrow{OF_1} + \tau\overrightarrow{F_1D_1}) \quad (1)$$

where τ, σ are determined from the perpendicular constraints:

$$\overrightarrow{S_1S_2} \cdot \overrightarrow{F_1D_1} = \overrightarrow{S_1S_2} \cdot \overrightarrow{F_2D_2} = 0$$

The *backprojection* φ^{-1} of D_1, D_2 is expressed as follows [1]:

$$D' = \varphi^{-1}(D_1, D_2) = \overrightarrow{OF_1} + \tau\overrightarrow{F_1D_1} + \frac{1}{2}\overrightarrow{S_1S_2}$$

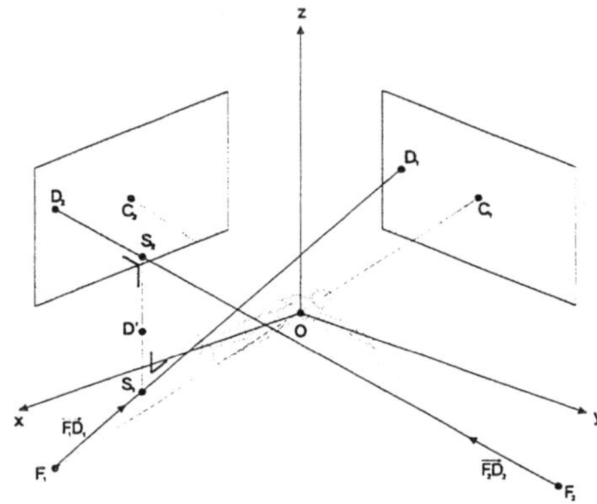

Figure 1. The minimum distance reconstruction of corresponding points D_1 and D_2.

The distance between projective lines calculated from (1) defines a measure of the reconstruction error as follows:

$$\varepsilon_1(D_1, D_2) = ||\overrightarrow{S_1S_2}|| \quad (2)$$

Alternatively, considering D_1', D_2' as the projections of D' in both planes, we define the reconstruction error as:

$$\varepsilon_2(D_1, D_2) = ||\overrightarrow{D_1D_1'}|| + ||\overrightarrow{D_2D_2'}|| \quad (3)$$

It is easy to see that by reducing (3) we reduce (2). On the other hand, error (3) is in the image plane units, and this fact gives numerical stability to our error minimization procedure.

3 3D-reconstruction of a curve

Let us consider a target curve $T(v)$ projected in image planes and a curve $Q(u)$ that is used to reconstruct $T(v)$. Let $Q_i(u), T_i(v)$ be the projections of $Q(u)$ and $T(u)$ in image plane i, respectively. We are interested in the curve which minimizes the following error:

$$\varepsilon(Q(u)) = \sum_{i=1}^{2} \int \min_{v} (||Q_i(u) - T_i(v)||)\, du \quad (4)$$

Several issues should be discussed. First, it could happen that more than one curve minimizes expression (4). An example of this fact is shown in figure 2. Two pairs of views (fig. 2(a) and 2(c)) with Anterior-Posterior (AP) and Left Lateral (LAT) projections of target curve (dashed lines) and deforming curve (continuous line). In fig 2(b) the reconstructed curve from the pair 2(a) (thick) coincides with the generating (thin) curve. In fig 2(d) (reconstruction from 2(c)) both curves differ in space. To solve this problem an expert's initialization is introduced. Second, feature extraction in real images is not perfect; several vessels will appear in the same image, so a selective and robust method for 3D reconstruction is necessary. To treat all these issues, we develop a model based on the technique of *snakes*[2]. First, it is able to take into account the expert's initialization. Second, it deforms towards image features under general constraints on model shape. Third, the B-Snakes implementation of Menet et al. in [3] allows to define the curve with only a few control points, which simplifies the initialization but also accelerates the minimization procedure.

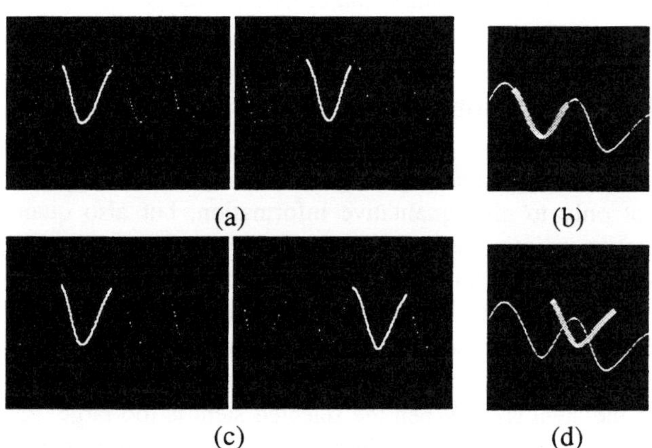

Figure 2. 3D reconstruction could present ambiguity.

The *snake* deforms by minimizing its energy, which is defined as follows:

$$E_{total}(Q(u)) = \int E_{internal}(Q(u)) + E_{external}(Q(u))du$$

Internal forces reduce internal energy preserving the smoothness, and external forces attract the *snake* to the features in the image. In our case, our aim is the 3D reconstruction of the curve so that its projections coincide with the vessels. For this purpose, we define the external energy of the spatial snake as a function of distance of the projected snake to the image features. The 3D snake deforms to adjust its projections to the image vessels. Note that this external energy stems from two images; giving the name of *biplane snakes* to our deformable models. Applying the Euler-Lagrange equation we get [2]:

$$-\frac{\partial}{\partial u}(\alpha Q_u(u)) + \frac{\partial^2}{\partial u^2}(\beta Q_{uu}(u)) + \nabla E_{ext}(Q(u)) = 0$$

We redefine the external force ($\nabla E_{ext}(Q(u))$) of the *biplane snakes* as follows (figure 3):

$$F_{ext}(Q(u)) = \varphi^{-1}[Q_1(u) + \nabla V_1(Q_1(u)), Q_2(u) + \nabla V_2(Q_2(u))] - Q(u) \quad (5)$$

Figure 4 shows an example of the evolution of reconstruction error during deformation of the *biplane snake*. The external energy decreases reducing the real reconstruction error (mean distance of $Q(u)$ to the target curve $T(v)$).

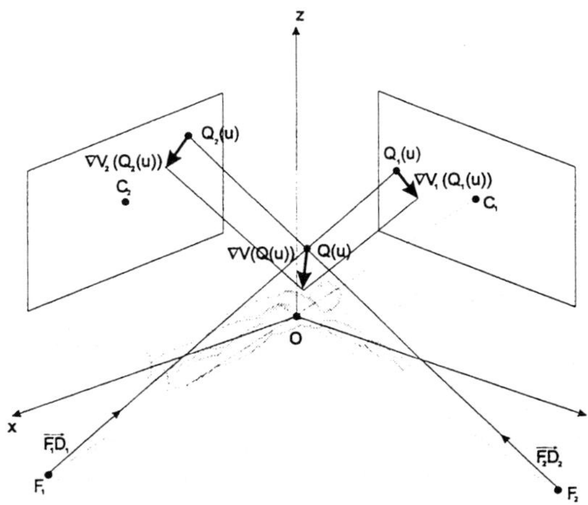

Figure 3. The external force from both projections is backprojected in space.

4 Results

In order to validate the *biplane snake* technique, we do several experiments: tests with computational phantoms, tests with a mechanical phantom and tests with real images of angiography.

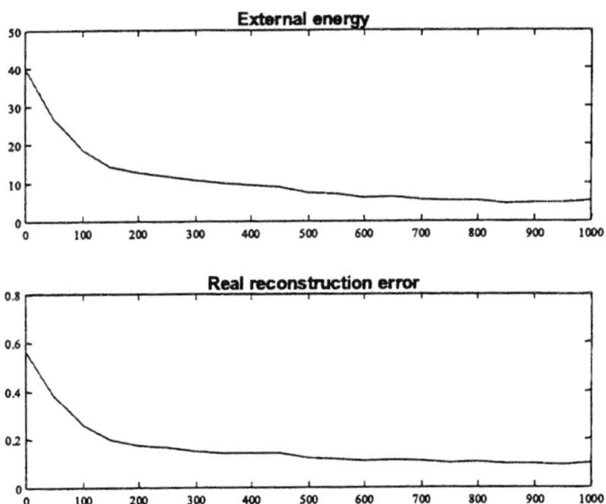

Figure 4. Evolution of the *biplane snake*.

4.1 Tests on computational phantom

The first experiment consists of generating two images with projections of a curve. A user is asked to mark corresponding points of the curve as exactly as possible in order to achieve a manual reconstruction. The epipolar line [1] helps the user on determining the point correspondence. The curve generated by the user is used as initial snake. The deformation of the *snake* is performed until 500 iterations. We do this with 5 different generator curves and 4 experts ($obs1 \ldots obs4$). We repeat the experiment, but now introducing random error in the parameters used to generate the images. Results are shown in figure 5. The mean relative improvement of error was of 9% for the first case (fig. 5(a)) and 12% for the second (fig. 5(b)).

4.2 Tests on physical phantom

In order to demonstrate that real length measurements obtained by biplane snakes are correct, we constructed a wire phantom simulating a vessel. Then, we took images of the phantom from different points of view with the angiography acquisition system in clinical conditions. Finally, we reconstructed the same wire segment from several projections and, marking on the beginning and the end of the segment of the obtained curve, we computed its length. We repeated this procedure ten times for each pair of projections using different snake initialisations. Figure 6 shows the statistics of the error done when measuring the length of a segment of 32mm (for an explanation of the abbreviations see [1]). Note that the mean error is $< 0.6mm$, which met the requirement in the clinic.

4.3 Tests on real vessels in angiography

Finally, we have tested our technique in order to reconstruct coronary vessels in different real angiography cases.

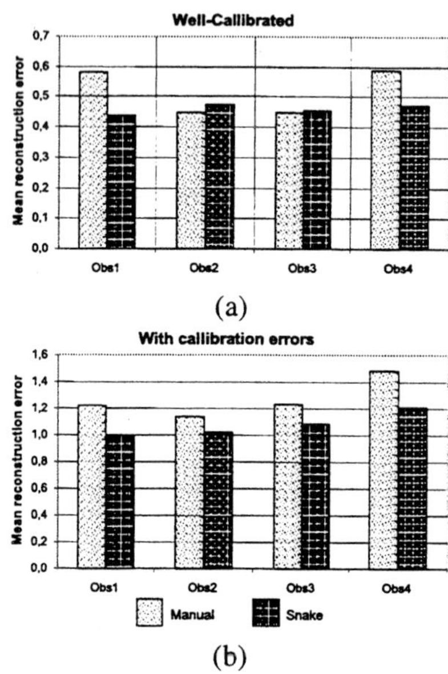

Figure 5. Mean reconstruction error for computational phantom.

Error [mm]	AP-LAT	RAO30-LAT	RAO30-LAO60
Mean	0.59	0.59	0.55
Max	2.20	1.50	1.40
Variance	0.34	0.19	0.14

Figure 6. Mean length measurement error for physical phantom.

Figure 7 shows a reconstruction of the left coronary of a patient from their projections AP and RAO30 (see figure 7(a)) and 7(b)). Three curves are reconstructed adapting its projections to the images as shown in figures 7(c) and 7(d). The user can then interact with the point of view of the 3D reconstruction (see figure 7(e) and figure 7(f)) and get absolute length of the vessel segments.

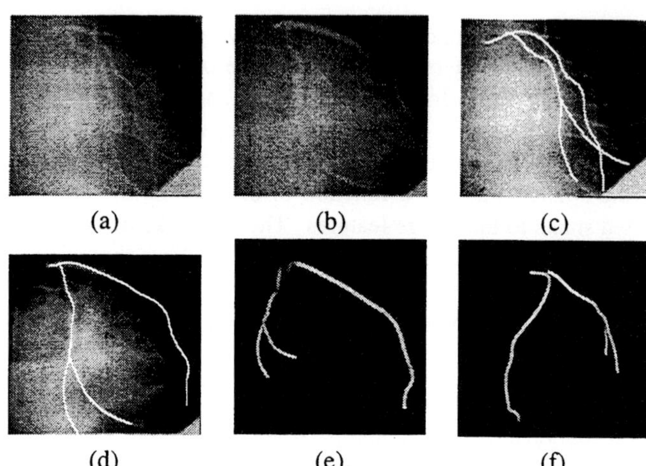

Figure 7. Reconstruction of left coronary main vessels of a patient.

5 Conclusions

In this paper, we address the problem of the 3D reconstruction of coronary vessels by biplane snakes. To this purpose we rest on biplane snakes to deform in space adjusting its projections to the vessels in the angiography. We show that gain of 3D reconstruction by biplane snakes is obtained in precision of measurements as well as time of computation due to the reduced user interaction. Tests on 3D reconstruction of computer-generated phantoms show that the biplane snake meaningfully reduces the reconstruction error in case of uncalibrated acquiring system. Tests on a wire phantom show that average error of length measurements is in the permissible clinical limits. Finally, different tests on 3D reconstruction of real vessels are carried on and validated by a physician team.

6 Acknowledgements

This work was partly supported by a grant from the Generalitat de Catalunya (Spain), with expedient number 1999FI 00753 APTIND CVC and research project of Ministerio de Educación y Ciencia (Spain) with number TIC98-1100.

References

[1] A. C. M. Dumay, J. H. C. Reiber, and J. J. Gerbrands. Determination of optimal angiographic viewing angles: Basic principles and evaluation study. *IEEE Transactions on Medical Imaging*, 13(1), March 1994.

[2] M. Kass, A. Witkin, and D. Terzopoulos. Snakes: Active contours using finite elements to control local shape. In *ICCV*, pages 259–268, 1987.

[3] S. Menet, P. Saint-Marc, and G. Medioni. B-snakes: Implementation and application to stereo. In *DARPA Image Understanding Workshop*, pages 720–726, September 1990.

[4] C. Molina, G. P. Prause, P. Radeva, and M. Sonka. Catheter path reconstruction from biplane angiography using 3d snakes. *SPIE - Medical Imaging*, February 1998.

[5] W. Wahle, H. Oswald, G. Schulze, J. Beier, and E. Fleck. 3-d reconstruction, modelling and viewing of coronary vessels. In *CAR'91*, pages 669–676, 1991.

[6] W. Wunderlich, F. Fischer, H.-R. Arntz, H.-P. Schultheiss, and A. Morguet. Development and clinical evaluation of an online procedure for lesion length measurement in coronary intervention. In *CIC'99*, September 1999.

3D Model Based Pose Determination in Real-Time: Strategies, Convergence, Accuracy

Martin Berger, Thomas Auer,
Gernot Bachler, Stefan Scherer
Computer Graphics and Vision
Graz University of Technology
Inffeldgasse 16, 8010 Graz, Austria

Axel Pinz
Institute of Electrical Measurement
and Measurement Signal Processing
Graz University of Technology
Kopernikusgasse 24, 8010 Graz, Austria

E-mail: berger@icg.tu-graz.ac.at

Abstract

In this paper a new real-time model based pose determination system based on the Gauss-Newton method is described. Various model fitting strategies, which use gradient search, are discussed and compared. A novel strategy, the adaptive perpendicular search, is proposed for both, matching ambiguity avoidance and convergence enforcement. It is shown to be highly effective in practice, while keeping the computational cost low. A sufficient initial pose estimate as an input for the Gauss-Newton based methods is obtained from the Parametric Eigenspace. With certain restrictions, the overall pose determination system performs in real-time, as required in industrial applications.

1. Introduction

Many approaches for model based pose determination have been proposed over the last ten years [2], [10], [9], [1], [4], [5], [7]. Some of them [10], [9], [7] are based on optimization methods which perform well if a reasonable initial estimate is given. This is always the case for tracking applications (e.g. [11]), where the pose of an object in the preceeding frame can be used (in combination with prediction) to calculate the pose of the same object in the actual frame. If the problem of single images without prior knowlegde is considered, this becomes much harder. In this paper we present a novel approach for an industrial pose determination system. It combines appearance based pose determination with classical optimization methods. The combination of these methods yields more accurate and robust results than appearance based approaches alone. Note that the appearance based methods need a reasonable segmentation module in the training phase as well as in the recognition step, whereas more robust methods [3], [6] can deal with cluttered background. Nevertheless our approach is justified because:

- In many industrial applications the background problem is well-defined.
- Robust methods are computationally too expensive in order to achieve real-time performance as required in industrial applications.

In the following we will compare some fitting strategies based on the Gauss-Newton optimization scheme (Sect. 2) and propose a computationally inexpensive but effective adaptive perpendicular search strategy. Then we will describe how to obtain a pose estimate as input for the optimization step, while keeping the computational cost low (Sect. 3). Sect. 4 will compare the strategies on models of varying complexity, analyze their convergence behaviour and prove the real-time applicability of the overall system.

2. Model Fitting Strategies

As stated above, our approach combines an appearance based method and a fully perspective optimization technique. This enables the avoidance of local minima which may destabilize the solution. This occurs very likely if features (such as lines and edges) are visible in the image, but are hidden in the model projected with the estimated pose parameters (or vice versa). Moreover, it is not always possible to provide an initial set of parameters in order to avoid local minima of the objective function. Since in our application a flat workplace is considered, the whole problem can be reduced from 6 degrees of freedom to 3. This restriction is known as 'ground plane constraint' (GPC, cf. [5]).

We will now briefly review the Gauss-Newton method, the Levenberg-Marquardt extension, the gradient weighting method and motivate the introduction of the adaptive perpendicular search strategy.

2.1. Gauss-Newton Method

Suppose $\mathbf{p}$ to be a vector of (generally non-linear) unknown pose parameters, which is iteratively refined by subtracting a vector of corrections $\mathbf{x}$ in each iteration step i. Given a vector of errors $\mathbf{e}$ in the image, the Gauss-Newton method solves for $\mathbf{x}$ which would eliminate the error.

$$\mathbf{p}^{(i+1)} = \mathbf{p}^{(i)} - \mathbf{x}^{(i)} \qquad \mathbf{Jx} = \mathbf{e} \qquad J_{ij} = \frac{\partial e_i}{\partial x_j} \tag{1}$$

where $\mathbf{J}$ is the Jacobian of the objective error function $\mathbf{e}$. Lowe [7] proposed to measure the pose error $\mathbf{e}$ perpendicular to image line features. The overdetermined system is solved by minimizing the term $\|\mathbf{Jx} - \mathbf{e}\|^2$ in a least squares sense. This may cause instabilities, but compared to other numerical methods it represents the most efficient (and thus fastest) way to compute a solution.

2.2. Levenberg-Marquardt Method

Lowe [7] showed that the Levenberg-Marquardt method is well suited to stabilize the solution. An additional parameter λ is introduced together with a weighting matrix $\mathbf{W}$ (which accounts for parameter standard deviations). This leads to the minimization of

$$\|\mathbf{Jx} - \mathbf{e}\|^2 + \lambda^2 \|\mathbf{W}(\mathbf{x} - \mathbf{d})\|^2 \tag{2}$$

where $\mathbf{d}$ represents a vector of default pose parameters. The strategy of varying the parameter λ according to the progression of the residual error, allows to control the behaviour of the method between pure gradient descent (large value of λ) and the Gauss-Newton method (small value of λ).

2.3. Gradient Weighting Method

For the majority of applications, neither a parameter set estimation nor their standard deviations are known a-priori. Pece and Worrall [9] presented a weighting of the gradients along a search line perpendicular to a projected model line by using a Gaussian windowing function

$$e_i = \sum_{\nu} |\Delta I(\nu)| \cdot \exp\left(-\frac{(\nu - \mu_i)^2}{2\sigma^2}\right) \tag{3}$$

where e_i is the ith row of the error vector $\mathbf{e}$; ν denotes the distance along the search line; $\Delta I(\nu)$ is the discrete derivative at position ν along the search line; μ_i is the center of the gaussian windowing function (the location of the projected model line); σ represents a scaling factor. This goodness-of-fit measure is independent to the direction of contrast between object and background, and, to some extent also to the type of image feature. Therefore it tends to avoid false matches. Despite the improved convergence behaviour, errors in minimizing the error perpendicular to projected model lines still occur. This happens frequently with models consisting of thin structures delimited by two edges and is a major drawback of the above method as these edges are very likely to occur in industrial parts (see object in Fig. 5(b)).

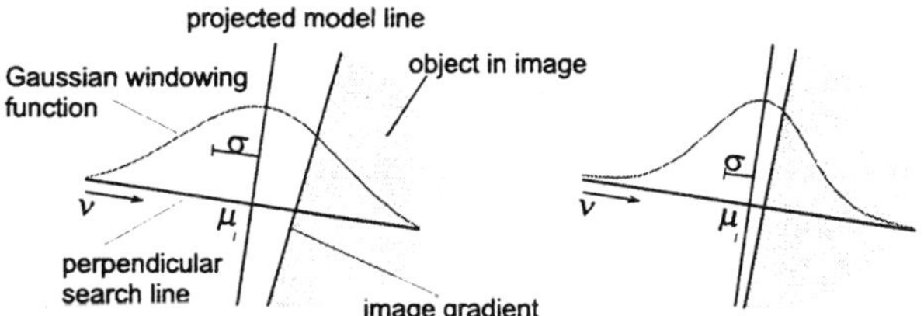

Figure 1. The adaptive perpendicular search strategy: as the norm of the pose corrections $\|\mathbf{x}\|$ decreases, the parameter σ is decreased together with the maximum allowed search distance.

2.4. Performance Improvement - the Adaptive Perpendicular Search Strategy

Due to the described false matches, some oscillations occur, as can be seen from a residual error plot in Fig. 2. Nevertheless, the described methods are very fast and therefore suitable for real-time applications. Using a computationally inexpensive, but in practice very effective strategy, forces faster convergence and avoids oscillations around the minimum. The maximum allowed perpendicular distance for gradient search is decreased by one as the length of the correction vector $\mathbf{x}$ decreases. Provided the starting pose was close (i.e. $\pm 10^o$, ± 10mm in x and y) to the solution, this strategy showed an excellent behaviour in both forcing convergence and decreasing the number of iterations required to reach the minimum (see Sect. 4).

3. How to Obtain an Initial Estimate

For fast iterative pose computation and a low number of iterations it is necessary to avoid local minima. This strongly depends on the quality of the starting pose estimate. Several methods from the field of object recognition, which implicitly deliver a pose estimate, can theoretically be considered as modules for providing the input for an iterative alignment. Most of them are robust but time consuming. Since for the presented system it is crucial to have a *good guess* in a *short time*, we chose the Eigenspace approach [8]. Based on the Principal Component Analysis (PCA), eigenimages are calculated and stored together with the transformed sample image vectors. The major advantage of this approach is the fast retrieval of an object class and a pose estimate in the database. A major drawback of

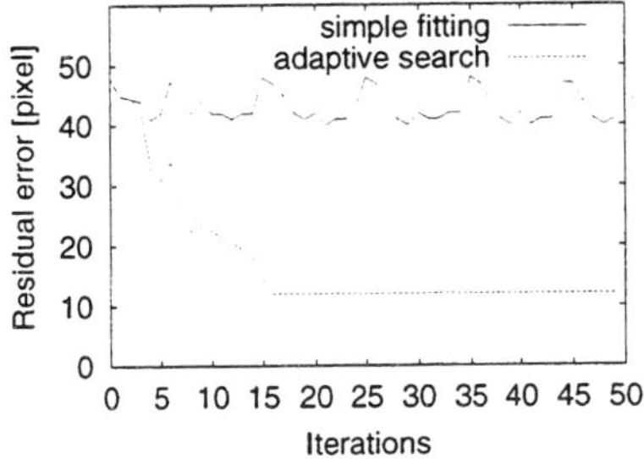

Figure 2. Progress of the residual error without (solid line) and with (dashed line) adaptive perpendicular search. Note the oscillations which occur due to false matches.

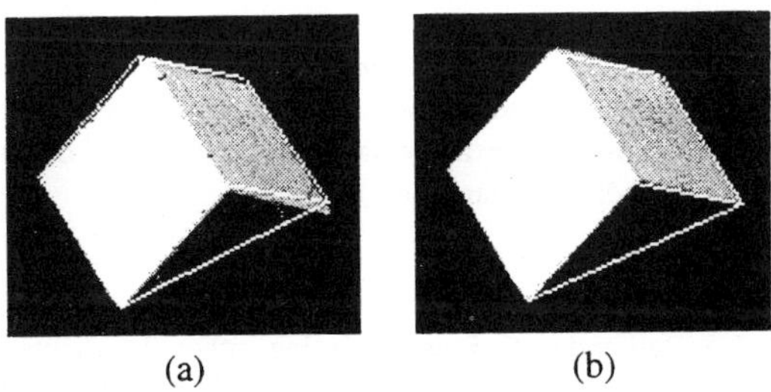

(a) (b)

Figure 3. Model fits without (a) and with (b) adaptive perpendicular search. Note the error residuals in the left image.

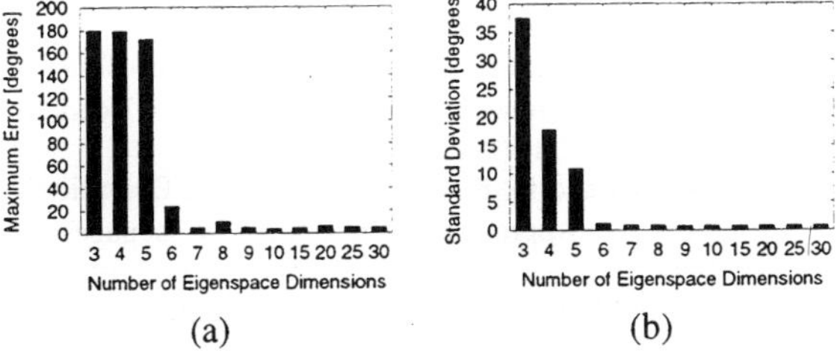

(a) (b)

Figure 4. Error graph of the Eigenspace method: the maximum absolute value (a) and the standard deviation (b) of pose error.

the classical approach is that an object must be separable from its background. Extensions [6], [3] were made for the retrieval of eigenimages even on cluttered background or in the presence of occlusion. Again, these methods are very robust, but time consuming. However, background segmentation is in general not crucial in industrial applications. Fig. 4(a) shows the maximum, Fig. 4(b) the standard deviations of pose error with respect to the number of eigenspace dimensions used. It can be seen that the pose error does not decrease significantly for more than 9 dimensions. Hence, 10 was chosen for the experiments described below. The PCA-approach is suitable for obtaining a rotation angle through the estimation of the nearest appearance present in the database. The translational parameters (i.e. the shifts on the ground plane) are estimated by translating the bounding rectangle of the projected model on the bounding rectangle of the object in the image.

4. Experiments

All experiments were carried out with two classes of test objects. The first class consists of simple wooden toy parts having a small number of faces and edges. The second class is built of more complex industrial plastic parts with more than 100 faces and edges in the model. One object of each class is shown in Fig. 5.

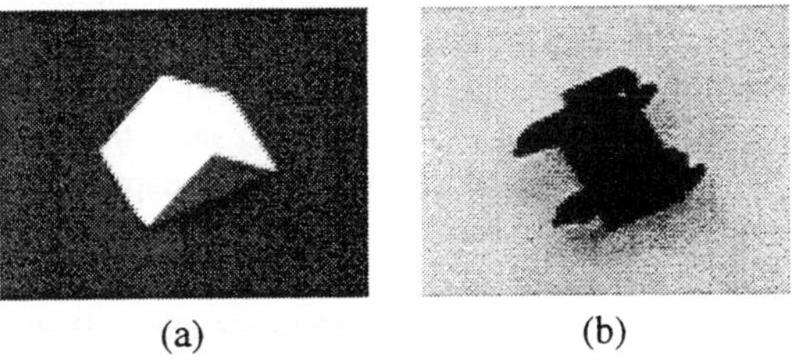

(a) (b)

Figure 5. Two objects representing different topological types (a) convex, without holes (b) non-convex, with holes.

4.1. Convergence and Speed

It can be observed that the *convergence* of the methods based on the classical Gauss-Newton approach is rather slow, even if the pose estimate was close to the correct pose parameters. This is mainly due to matching errors which tend to keep the system oscillating, when search areas are wide enough. Here the proposed adaptive search algorithm shows an excellent behaviour: oscillations are attenuated and the number of iterations is decreased significantly, which is essential for the overall performance.

Table 1 shows the convergence behaviour and typical time consumption of the outlined methods. The test object used was the plastic part shown in Fig. 5(b). The iteration was aborted if the norm of the correction vector $\mathbf{x}$ fell short of a bound of 0.005 or the number of iterations exceeded 50. All experiments were performed on a standard PC, Pentium II, 333 MHz, 256MB RAM.

Method	iter.	$\|\|x\|\|$	time [ms]
Gauss-Newton	50	0.111	190
Levenberg-Marquardt	50	0.132	230
Gradient Weighting	50	0.139	491
Adaptive Perp. Search	17	< 0.005	< 150

Table 1. Comparison of various fitting strategies: avg. number of iterations necessary, avg. norms of the correction vector (at iteration abort) and avg. time consumptions.

4.2. Accuracy

In Sect. 4.1 the real-time applicability of the proposed method was shown. In the following its accuracy is investigated. The camera used has a resolution of 348 by 288 pixels, a focal length of 25 mm and a distance to the object of approximately 1.5 m. As outlined in Sect. 4.1, the adaptive perpendicular search strategy allows to decrease the number of iterations drastically. Fig. 6(a - b) show the achieved accuracy with the wooden toy part and the adaptive perpendicular search strategy. Fig. 6(c - f) show the accuracy for the industrial part with and without adaptive perpendicular search. It can be observed that the pose error does not change significantly or is even better. The peaks in the graphs 6(c - f) at 120 and 300 degrees are due to shape ambiguities, which cause match errors and consequently pose errors. Apart from these peaks, the shift error is below 1 mm and the rotation error is below 2 degrees. Note that the principle of fitting projected 3D models to images is less error-prone for translation than for rotation.

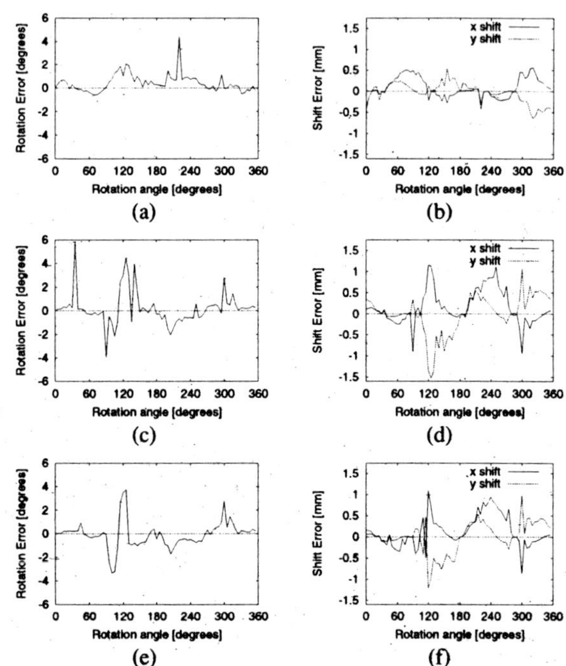

Figure 6. Rotational and translational error plots for 360 views of the wooden toy part with adaptive perpendicular search (a, b), for the industrial object without (c, d) and with perpendicular search (e, f).

5. Conclusions and Outlook

This paper discussed the industrial application of Gauss-Newton based pose refinement algorithms. A computationally inexpensive strategy, the adaptive perpendicular search, was introduced in order to improve the performance of known strategies. This new strategy turned out to be useful for both accuracy and speed improvement, since false matches could be avoided. The Parametric Eigenspace was shown to be a suitable initial pose estimation module. Further research will deal with more cluttered background and partially occluded objects.

References

[1] H. Araújo, R. L. Carceroni, and C. M. Brown. A Fully Perspective Formulation to Improve the Accuracy of Lowe's Pose-Estimation Algorithm. *CVIU*, 70(2):227–238, 1998.

[2] J. S. Beis and D. G. Lowe. Indexing without Invariants in 3D Object Recognition. *IEEE Trans. on Pattern Analysis and Machine Intelligence*, 21(10):1000–1015, October 1999.

[3] H. Bischof and A. Leonardis. Robust Recognition of Scaled Eigenimages Through a Hierarchical Approach. In *Proc. of CVPR'98*, pages 664–670, 1998.

[4] D. F. DeMenthon and L. S. Davis. Model Based Object Pose in 25 Lines of Code. *IJCV*, 15:123–141, 1995.

[5] D. Koller, K. Daniilidis, and H.-H. Nagel. Model-Based Object Tracking in Monocular Image Sequences of Road Traffic Scenes. *IJCV*, 10(3):257–281, 1993.

[6] A. Leonardis and H. Bischof. Dealing with Occlusions in the Eigenspace Approach. In *Proc. of CVPR'96*, pages 453–458, 1996.

[7] D. G. Lowe. Fitting parameterized three-dimensional models to images. *IEEE Trans. on Pattern Analysis and Machine Intelligence*, 13(5):441–450, May 1991.

[8] H. Murase and S. K. Nayar. Visual Learning and Recognition of 3-D Objects from Appearance. *IJCV*, 14:5–24, 1995.

[9] A. Pece and A. Worrall. A Newton method for pose refinement of 3D models. In *Proc. of the 6th Int. Symposium on Intelligent Robotic Systems*, Edinburgh, UK, July 1998.

[10] T. N. Tan, G. D. Sullivan, and K. D. Baker. Model-Based Localisation and Recognition of Road Vehicles. *IJCV*, 27(1):5–25, 1998.

[11] M. Uenohara and T. Kanade. Real-Time Vision Based Object Registration for Image Overlay. In *CVRMed'95, Nice, France*, 1995.

3D Objects Coding and Recognition Using Surface Signatures

Sameh Yamany
Computer Science Dept.
Old Dominion Univ., Virginia, USA
Norfolk, VA23529
yamany@cs.odu.edu

Aly Farag
Electrical and Computer Eng. Dept.
University of Louisville, USA
Louisville, KY 40292
farag@cvip.uofl.edu

Abstract

This paper presents a new concept for 3D coding of free-form surfaces. The proposed coding technique uses the surface signature representation scheme [1]. This representation scheme captures the 3-D curvature information of any free-form surface and encodes it into a 2-D image corresponding to a certain point on the surface. This image is unique for this point and is independent of the object translation or orientation in space. For this reason this image is called "Surface Point Signature" (SPS). Using SPS in 3D coding has many applications in 3D compression, 3D pose estimation and in 3D object recognition.

1. Introduction

3D object recognition has become an integral part in many computer and robot vision systems and still presents a topic of high interest in these fields [2, 3, ?].

In order for any 3D object recognition algorithm to perform accurately and efficiently, appropriate representation scheme for the surface is needed. Most of the surface representation schemes found in literature have adopted some form of shape parameterization especially for the purpose of object recognition. One benefit of the parametric representation is that the shape of the object is defined everywhere which enables high level tasks such as visualization, segmentation and shape analysis to be performed. Moreover, such representation allows stable computation of geometric entities such as curvatures and normal directions. However, parametric representation are not suitable to present general shapes especially if the object is not of planar, cylindrical or toroidal topology. Free-form surfaces, in general, may not have simple volumetric shapes that can be expressed in terms of parametric primitives. Discontinuities in the surface normal or curvature, and consequently in the surface depth, may be present anywhere in a free-form surface.

We introduced a new free-from surface representation scheme that matches and estimates the pose of free-form objects in cluttered 3D scenes [1]. This representation scheme captures the surface curvature information, seen from certain points and produces images, called surface point signatures (SPS), at these points. Matching signatures of different surfaces enables the recovery of the transformation parameters between these surfaces. Furthermore, we applied a selection process to select feature points on the surface to be used in the matching process. This reduction process solves the long registration time reported in the literature, especially for large surfaces.

The proposed coding idea in this paper starts by generating SPS images for specific points on the 3D object surface. These images are then segmented into corresponding curvature clusters. These curvature clusters and their relations uniquely describe the structure of the 3D object and can be used to synthesize the 3D object.

2 Surface Point Signature (SPS) Generation

Rather than just depending on the 3-D coordinates of the point on a free-form surface, the SPS framework obtains a "signature" image at each surface point. The signature, computed at each important point, encodes the surface curvature seen from this point, thus giving it more discriminating power than the "splash" [4] and the "point signature" [5]. Also using the curvature as a measure of matching is more discriminating than the point density used in the "spin image" [6].

As shown in Figure 1, for a specific point P defined by its 3-D coordinates and the normal U_P at the patch where P is the center of gravity, each other point P_i on the surface can be related to P by two parameters:
1- the distance $d_i = ||P - P_i||$ and
2- the angle $\alpha_i = cos^{-1}\left(\frac{U_P.(P-P_i)}{||P-P_i||}\right)$.

This is a polar implementation of the SPS image and it can be easily converted into Cartesian form. Also we can notice that there is a missing degree of freedom in this rep-

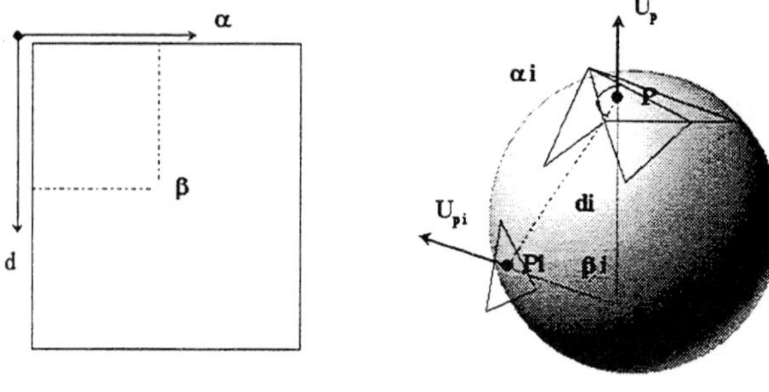

Figure 1. *For each important point P we generate an SPS image where the image axis are the distance d between P and each other point on the surface and the angle α between the normal at P, U_P and the vector from P to each other point. The image encodes the angle β which represents the change in the normal at these points from U_P.*

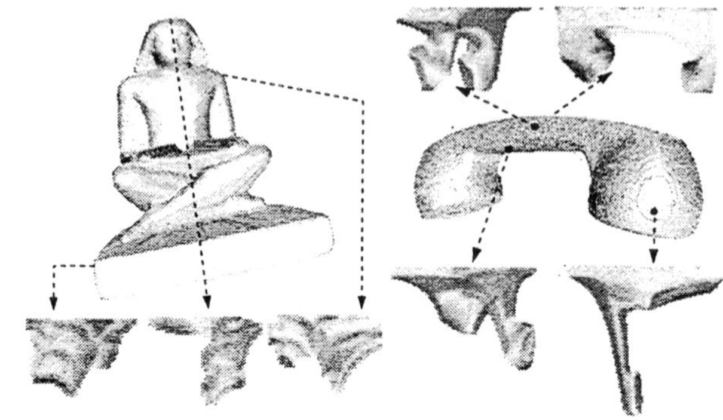

Figure 2. *Examples of SPS images taken at different important points locations. Notice how the image features the curvature information. The dark intensity in the image represents a high curvature seen from the point while the light intensity represents a low curvature. Also notice how different is the image corresponding to a location from images of other locations.*

resentation which is the cylindrical angular parameter. This parameter depends on the surface orientation which defies the purpose of having an orientation independent representation scheme. The size of the SPS image depends on the object size. However, in order to perform matching, normalizing the images is important. We chose to normalize each object to its maximum length, yet while doing matching and recognition we re-normalize the scene image to the maximum length of object in study, thus enabling scale independent matching. At each location in the image we encode the angle $\beta_i = cos^{-1}(U_P.U_{P_i})$. This represents the change in the normal at the surface point P_i relative to the normal at P.

Due to the fact that we are ignoring the cylindrical angular degree, the same pixel in the SPS image can represent more than one 3-D point on the surface. We take the average of their angles β_i and encode it in the SPS corresponding pixel location. Figure 2 shows some SPS images taken at different important points on the statue and a phone handset.

3 Using SPS in 3D coding

The idea is to use the generated SPS images to code the 3D object. This is done by segmenting the SPS images into homogeneous curvature clusters. The relation between these clusters will define a unique 3D code for the point location and the object in study.

The segmentation was performed using fuzzy thresholding where each pixel is assigned to a curvature cluster according to its membership value. Each signature image is segmented as follows,

$$t'_s(i,j) = \arg\max_k(V_k(t(i,j/s))), \quad k \in [1,c] \quad (1)$$

Where $t'_s()$ is the segmented output at scale factor s, $V_k(x)$ is the fuzzy decision function and c is the number of curvature clusters. The fuzzy decision function assigns the pixel to belong to a certain curvature cluster if its fuzzy membership is larger than a certain value (a value of 0.7 is used in our experiments), otherwise the value is computed from the average membership values of its neighboring pixels. This produces homogeneous segmented regions and reduces the effect of noisy pixels. Fuzzy membership functions were a-priori defined to the segmentation procedure. Figure 3 shows the result of segmenting signature images at different scale sizes.

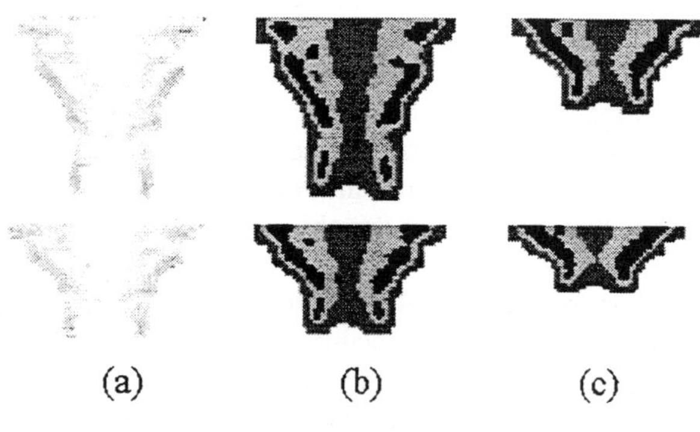

Figure 3. *(a) Two signature images at two different sizes. (b) The corresponding segmented images of the signatures in (a). (c) Another two examples of the same segmented signatures a two smaller sizes.*

4 Object Recognition using SPS Coding

The signature representation was used in matching objects in a 3D scene with their corresponding models in a library. The proximity of the objects in the scene creates large amounts of clutter and occlusion. These contribute to extra and/or missing parts in the signature images. In [1] it was shown that using the signature polar representation, the effect of clutter, for many points, is only found in the third and/or fourth quadrant of the image. Since the size of the object is one variable in the matching, we normalize the signature images generated with the largest distance in the scanned scene. Matching is then performed between the scene signature images and the model signature images at different scale factors. Point correspondences are established once the correct scale is determined and the scene and object images are normalized to same scale factor.

Figure 4 shows different 3D objects with their different SPS coding images. Notice how different each code for each object. Using these SPS image codes for each 3D object, the object can be localized in a 3D image and identified uniquely. Figure 5 shows an example of matching a model object with two 3D scenes each containing a different size of the object. Using the SPS codes the object is identified and localized in both scenes. Also, such a scheme could be used to compress 3D object libraries to include only the different coding images for each object, hence reducing the size of the library.

Figure 6 shows more examples. Using the signature matching criterion, all of the models in the scene are simultaneously matched and localized in their correct scene positions. The models in the library and the 3D scenes are scanned using a Cyberware 3030 laser scanner with a resolution of 1mm. Some models (e.g. the duck, bell and cup) were obtained from a CAD/CAM library.

Figure 4. *Examples of different 3D objects and their corresponding SPS coding at specific point locations.*

References

[1] S. M. Yamany and A. A. Farag, "Free-form surface registration using surface signatures," *IEEE Int. Conf. Computer Vision (ICCV'99),Kerkyra,Greece* , Sept 1999.

[2] C. Dorai and A. K. Jain, "Cosmos-a representation scheme for 3d free-form objects," *IEEE Transactions on Pattern Analysis and Machine Intelligence* **19**, pp. 1115–1130, October 1997.

[3] C. S. Chua and R. Jarvis, "3d free-form surface registration and object recognition," *International Journal of Computer Vision* **17**, pp. 77–99, 1996.

[4] F. Stein and G. Medioni, "Structural indexing: Efficient 3-d object recognition," *IEEE Trans. Patt. Anal. Machine Intell.* **14**(2), pp. 125–145, 1992.

[5] C. S. Chua and R. Jarvis, "Point signatures: A new representation for 3d object recognition," *Internation Journal of Computer Vision* **25**(1), pp. 63–85, 1997.

[6] A. Johnson and M. Helbert, "Efficient multiple model recognition in cluttered 3-d scenes," *IEEE Proc. Computer Vision and Pattern Recognition (CVPR'98)* , pp. 671–678, 1998.

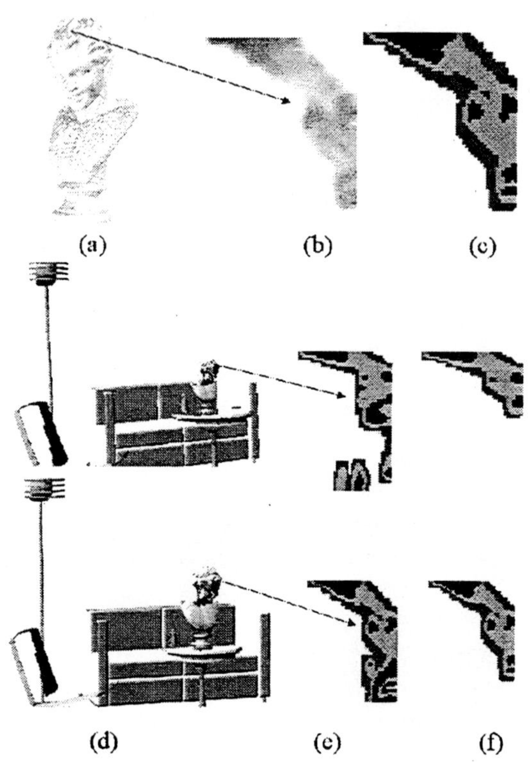

Figure 5. *(a) Library object (b) One signature image from the library (c) The Corresponding segmented signature (d) Two 3D scenes with the object at different sizes (e) Corresponding segmented Scene signatures (f) Matched object segmented signature at the exact scale.*

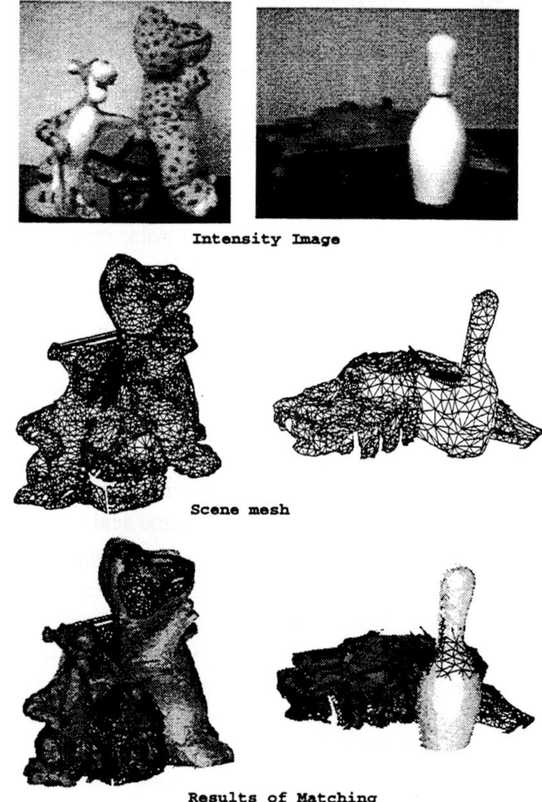

Figure 6. *Examples of using the signature representation in object matching. A library of 10 objects is used. Some of these objects were scanned using a Cyberware 3030 laser scanner with a resolution of 1mm. Others are obtained from CAD libraries.*

3D Reconstruction of Book Surface Taken from Image Sequence with Handy Camera

Kenji Nakamura, Hideo Saito, Shinji Ozawa
Department of Electrical Engineering, Keio University
3-14-1 Hiyoshi Kouhoku-ku
Yokohama 223-8522, Japan
{kenji,saito,ozawa}@ozawa.ics.keio.ac.jp

Abstract

In this paper, we propose a method for reconstruction of 3D shape of book surface by integrating shape that is recovered from an image sequence taken with moving camera. The image sequence is divided into a number of blocks. The factorization method is applied to each block for obtaining a part of 3D shape of the object. The 3D shapes reconstructed from the block of the sequence are merged into one integrated 3D Model. For the merging, position and pose of each 3D shape is adjusted based on the surface normal of the overlapped area. The merged 3D model of all region of the book surface is shown for demonstrating the effectiveness of the proposed method.

1. Introduction

Recently computer technology has been advanced quickly. This leads us to use an application in the cyberspace, where we can freely handle virtual objects in the computers for virtual shopping, virtual education, virtual library, etc. For such kind of applications, it is very important to digitize the information of various objects. One of the digitization method of books and paperworks is use of scanning paper devices. Although it is widely used, there are some problems, such as limitation of scanning resolution and distortion caused by various shape of the object. Furthermore huge region cannot easily be scanned at one time.

Recent document scanner can be categorized into two groups. One group is contact type, i.e., office photocopier and the fax machine. The other group is non-contact type. Contact type may damage the document because the document surface must be pressed onto scanner surface. Furthermore, the scanning region limits the range of document, therefore huge area like a page of newspaper cannot be digitized in one scan.

Non-contact methods basically rely on cameras for digitization of the object. However the resolution of the camera image is limited, so many methods are proposed for integrating images (mosaic) and generating integrated high-resolution images. Since most of those methods use 2D image information for mosaicing images, alignment is not perfect if there is shape variation on the surface of the object [1, 2, 3].

In this paper, we propose to apply the factorization [5] for 3D shape reconstruction from image sequence and integrating the reconstructed shape into one huge 3D model based on 3D information of the object. In this method, we assume that image sequence of book surface is taken by a hand-held camera. The image sequence is divided into some blocks for applying factorization. The 3D shape recovered from every block's image sequence is merged for generating wider range of shape model.

2. Outline of our method

The image sequence taken with a handy camera is divided into some blocks of image sequence. Blocks overlap each other as shown in Figure 1. One block consists of 30 frames and overlaps 20 frames between neighboring blocks. It is important to make blocks overlap each other for registration of 3D shapes recovered from the blocks.

Figure 1 shows the flow chart of the proposed method. For applying the factorization method, we suppose camera can be modeled by orthographic projection. Feature points are extracted [4] in the first frame in each block, and then tracked in the block image sequence. A measurement matrix is constructed from those tracked feature points [5]. The matrix

1051-4651/00 $10.00

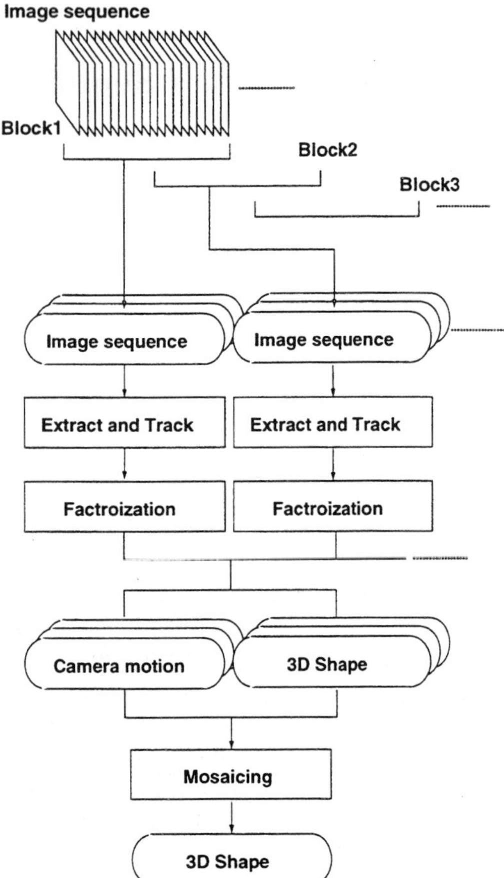

Figure 1. Outline of our method.

is factorized into two matrices which represent object 3D position of the feature points and camera motion respectively [4, 5, 6]. After the factorization, all the blocks are merged into an integrated 3D shape model according to the estimated 3D position of the feature points and camera motion for each block. The integrated 3D shape and texture provide a textured 3D model for all the part of the object surface.

3. Mosaic and integration

As described above, we can obtain a part of 3D shape. For each block, a set of 3D points and camera motion parameters are obtained from the factorization. For each set of 3D points, 3D surface model represented by triangular patches is generated by the Delaunay triangulation[7, 8].

The 3D surface models of all the blocks are initially registered based on the camera motion parameters that are obtained from the factorization. However, more

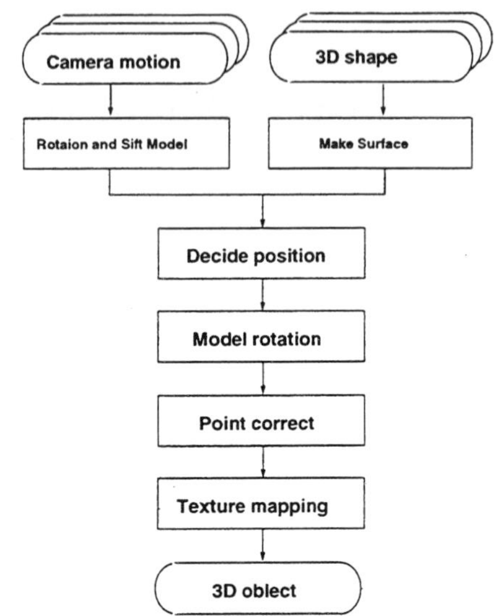

Figure 2. Mosaic Flowchart.

accurate adjustment of registration is required because of some errors in shape recovery by the factorization.

The overlap region between neighboring blocks of neighboring models is used for accurate adjustment of the 3D surface models recovered from all the block image sequence. The average surface normal of the overlapped region is calculated from normal of feature points in overlapped region. The normal of each feature point is provided by the average value of the normal of surrounding triangle meshes of the feature point. In Figure 3, the one of model is rotated around the center of gravity for making the normal correspond to another model's normal using angle difference.

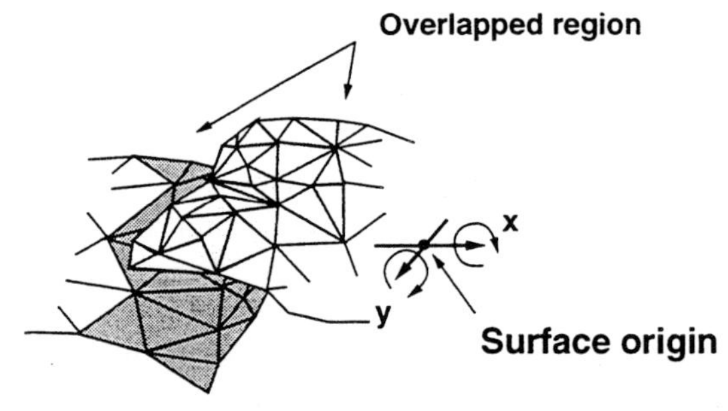

Figure 3. Rotational adjustment of model.

After the rotational adjustment, translation registration is adjusted according to the correspondence of the feature points between the neighboring block-

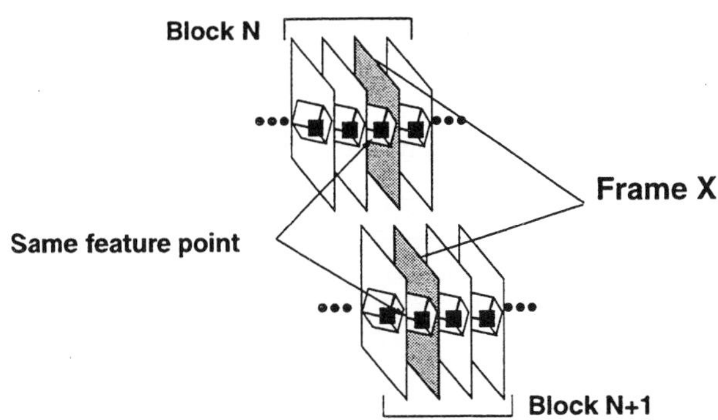

Figure 4. Coressponding feature point.

s. Some specific feature points are extracted in both neighboring blocks, because there are overlapped frames between the blocks as shown in Figure 4. However, such feature points that are extracted in the both blocks are not initially identified, since extraction of feature points is independent in the blocks.

For finding such feature points, the 3D position of the feature points are compared between the blocks, and then the distances between them are calculated. If the distance is smaller than a threshold, the feature points are regarded as the same point on the object surface.

In such a way, some feature points, which can be regarded as the same points between the neighboring blocks, are selected from all of the feature points. Finally, the average translation vector between the selected feature points determines the final adjustment translation between the recovered 3D shapes of neighboring blocks.

4. Experiments

4.1. Experiments Arrangement

The system arrangement is shown in Figure 5. We trace over the object with handy camera. We take image sequence 1/30 interval. The size of taken image 256×240 pixels and 8bit intensity resolution.

4.2. Shape recovery results

Figure 6 shows the result of 3D shape recovery of one block by factorization. Figure 6 (a) shows the feature points that are extracted at the first frame. Figure 6(b) shows recovered 3D feature points using factorization method and 3D surface model for the points.

Figure 7 shows experimental object, which is a dictionary. Figure 8 shows integrated shape model of wire frame that is recovered using our method. Figure 9 shows integrated 3D shape model with texture that is recovered using our method.

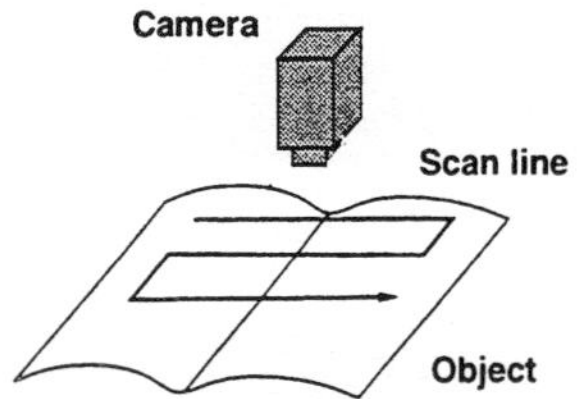

Figure 5. System arrangement.

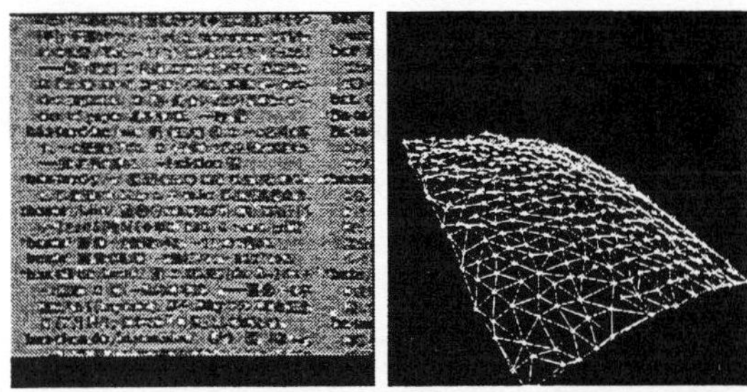

(a)Extract feature point (b)3D surface model

Figure 6. Recovered 3D feature points.

Figure 7. The object.

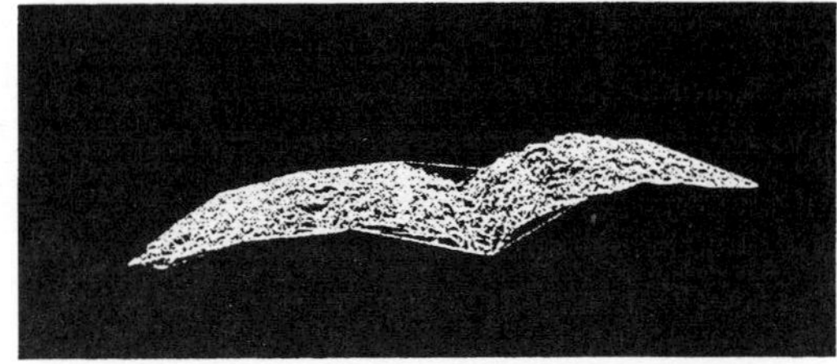

Figure 8. Recovered 3D model.

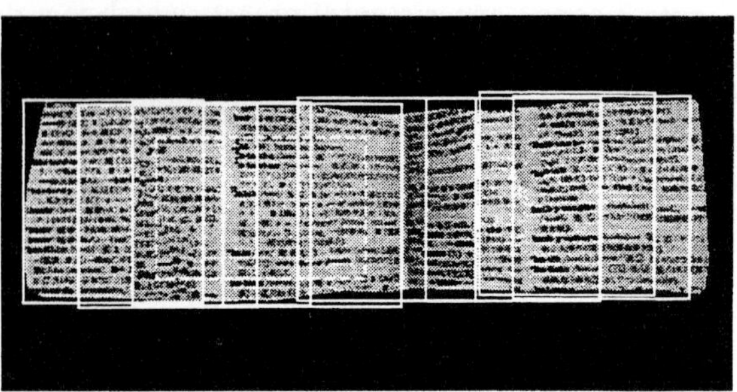

Figure 9. Textured 3D model.

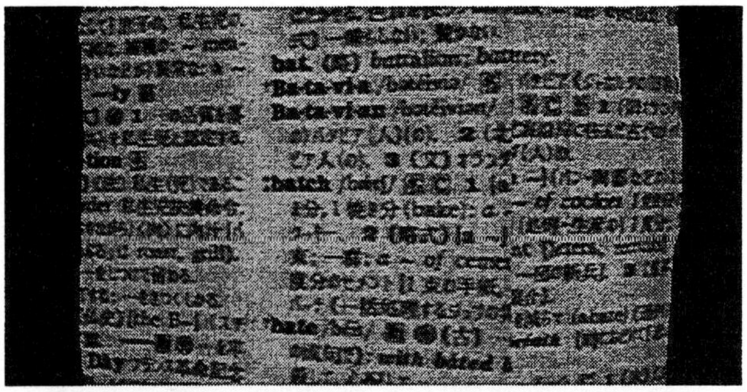

Figure 10. Merged texture without adjustment.

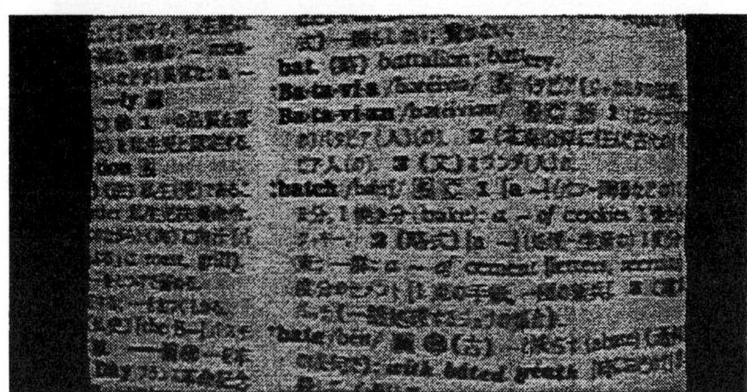

Figure 11. Merged texture with adjustment.

The squares of solid line in Figure 9 represent region of blocks. This model consists of 8 models. Figure 10 and Figure 11 shows merged texture image in the region indicated by the dotted line in Figure 9. Figure 10 is textured 3D model that is reconstructed and integrated using factorization without adjustment. Figure 11 is textured 3D model that is reconstructed and integrated using factorization and our method. The seam observed in Figure 10 is removed in Figure 11, that demonstrates effectiveness for registration in our method.

Table 1 shows average distance of same feature points between models. The distance without adjustment using only factorization method is reduced by using adjustment of the registration of the proposed method.

Table 1. Average of point distance

coordinate	no adjustment	adjustmen
x	8.735	1.131
y	3.455	0.196
z	12.144	0.041

5. Conclusions

In this paper, we propose a method for mosaic and integration of a 3D shape of book surface, which is recovered from a image sequence taken with unknown camera motion. We generated integrated 3D model using 3D shape and estimated camera motion derived using the factorization. We demonstrated that the adjustment of registration in the proposed method reduce the registration error, so that we can obtain seamless integrated 3D model of book surface.

As a future work, we are planning to generate super-resolved texture map by using multiple images projected onto the same book surface.

References

[1] A.Zappala,A. Gee and M.Taylor: "Document Mosaicing," BMVC 8-11 Sep. 1997.

[2] S.Mann and R.W.Picard: "Video orbits of the projective group:A new perspective on image mosaicing," Technical Report No.388, MIT Media Laboratory,1995.

[3] R.Szeliski: "Video mosaicing for virtual enviroments," IEEE Computer Graphics and Applications,March 1996.

[4] C.Tomasi and T.Kanade: "Detection and Tracking of Point Features," Technical Report in CMU,CMU-CS-91-132(1991).

[5] C.Tomasi and T.Kanade : "Shape and Motion from Image Stream : a Factorization Method," Technical Report in CMU,CMU-CS-92-104(1992).

[6] W.H.Press, B.P.Flannery, S.A.Teukolsky and W.T.Vetterling: "Numerical recipes in C :the art of scientific computing," Cambridge Univercity Press 1998.

[7] J.R.Shewchuk: "Delaunay Refinment Mesh Generation," Technical Report in CMU-CS-97-137,May. 18 1997.

[8] J.Ruppert: "A new and simple Algorithm for Quality 2-Dimensional Mesh Generation," Proceeding of the Fourth Annual Symposium on Discrete Algorithms,page 83-92,January. 1993.

Integrating Aspects of Active Vision into a Knowledge-Based System

U. Ahlrichs, D. Paulus, H. Niemann
Lehrstuhl für Mustererkennung (Informatik 5)
Universität Erlangen-Nürnberg, Martensstraße 3, 91058 Erlangen, Germany
ahlrichs@informatik.uni-erlangen.de

Abstract

While the strategy of active vision is well established in early vision, it is not widespread in high-level vision. In this paper we suggest an approach for integrating aspects of active vision into a knowledge-based system. One aspect is the selection of optimal *camera actions which are chosen to make the recognition process more reliable and efficient. We integrated such camera actions into our knowledge base. In addition, we describe the extensions of the control algorithm which is needed to use the information represented in the knowledge base, closing the loop between acting and sensing. Experiments show the efficiency and flexibility of the system. As an example, the task of locating objects in an office room is evaluated.*

1 Introduction

Active perception [1, 2] which has become more and more popular during the last years, deals with modeling and control strategies for perception [2]. In contrast to the Marr paradigm, a camera controls the image acquisition process as an *active* observer to get *optimal* images concerning subsequent image processing steps. This includes, for example, the adjustment of zoom if the image contains objects which cannot reliably be recognized in wide-angle images. In addition, modeling of sensors and the environment including the involved objects is essential. We use semantic networks for knowledge representation. In order to integrate the ideas of active perception, not only the information about objects is required in the knowledge base, but also the knowledge about the adjustment of camera parameters.

In order to use a-priori knowledge represented in the knowledge base during the data-interpretation process, control strategies are needed, which include the control of the interaction between the individual modules like image acquisition and object recognition. Furthermore, a feedback between modules has to be performed by the control algorithm. Strategies for decision making are also needed to guide the data interpretation; we use utility-based judgments for decision making where the functions for the computation of the judgments are integrated into the knowledge base. The control algorithm which is based on an A*-search uses these judgments to select an appropriate camera action depending on the state of the data interpretation process.

In classical image analysis, of course, many systems like SIGMA [6] are known which use information represented in a knowledge base. None of these systems include an active camera control component. Related work to our system can be found, for example, in [5, 8]. A review concerning selective perception can be found in [3].

The knowledge base for the application domain is introduced next (section 2). Afterwards, we outline the control algorithm (section 3). Finally, we demonstrate the feasibility and efficiency of our approach by experiments with a system for exploration of office scenes. (section 4).

2 Knowledge Base

The application domain chosen here is the exploration of arbitrary office scenes. Since the main contribution of the paper is the conceptional work regarding the integration of *camera actions*, i.e. the adjustment of camera parameters, into a semantic network and regarding the extensions of the control algorithm, the object-recognition task of the system is simplified in this context: At the moment only red objects are considered, i.e. the task of the system is to find three predefined red objects, a punch, a gluestick, and an adhesive tape dispenser which need not be visible in an image taken with the initial camera set-up. The 2-d object models used at the moment can easily be substituted by more sophisticated ones in a later stage. Additionally, the knowledge base can be easily extended due to the modularity of the concept-centered representation.

[1]This work was partially funded by the German Research Foundation (DFG) under grant number Ni 191/12-1.

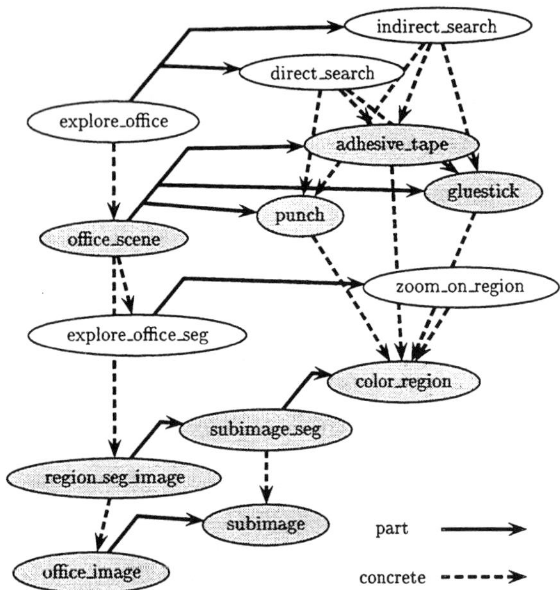

Figure 1. Semantic network for our domain.

2.1 Declarative Knowledge

The structure of the knowledge base for our application domain is shown in Figure 1. We use our semantic network formalism ERNEST for knowledge representation [7]. The knowledge base which was specified manually unifies the representation of objects and their relations and the representation of camera actions on different levels of abstraction. The knowledge base consists of so-called *concepts* which are depicted as ovals in Figure 1. The gray ovals contain, for example, the *objects* of the application domain, e.g. the concepts "punch", "gluestick" or "adhesive_tape". These three concepts are *parts of* the concept "office_scene" and they are connected with the concept "color_region" by a *concrete* link, which was introduced in [7] for relating concepts of different conceptual systems to each other.[1]

Concepts for *camera actions* are also integrated into the knowledge base. On the highest level of abstraction one can find camera actions which are equivalent to search procedures and which are used to find objects in a scene. The first example is the concept "direct_search". Each computation of this concept calculates a new pan angle for the camera in such a way, that overview images (images captured with a small focal length) are obtained. The second example is the concept "indirect_search". This concept represents an indirect search [10], i.e. the search for an object using an intermediate object, e.g. in order to find a punch we first find a table and then search for the punch on it.

On the intermediate level of abstraction in Figure 1, the camera action "zoom_on_region" can be found. The effect of this action is the fovealization of regions which are hypotheses for the objects. If an object in a hypothesis is too small to be reliably recognized, i.e. the height and width of the dedicated object cannot be determined reliably (cf. section 2.2), we use the fovealization to get more detailed information about it. We refer to images captured after fovealization as *close-up views*.

The *computation* of a camera action concept leads to the selection of new camera parameters or the *performance* of a camera action. So, only one camera action concept can be computed at once. In order to represent competing camera actions, i.e. actions which cannot be performed at the same time, we make use of *modalities* [7]. Modalities have been introduced to represent different concurrent realizations of a concept, such as a chair with or without arm rests or with varying number of legs. For example, the concept "explore_office" has as parts the concepts "direct_search" and "indirect_search", each of them is represented in one modality of "explore_office". The same holds for the concept "office_scene" which contains two modalities, one for "explore_office_seg" and one for "region_seg_image".

During analysis these ambiguities arising from modalities are resolved and so-called *instances* are computed for each concept. The *instantiation* of a concept includes the computation of its components, i.e. the *attributes* and the *relations*, as well as of its judgment. The judgments indicate the match between image data and a-priori knowledge. Additionally, they specify the *utility* of camera actions (section 2.2). Based on these judgments the camera action which is optimal with respect to the criterion defined by the judgment functions can be selected by the control algorithm.

2.2 Procedural Knowledge

The functions for the computation of the attributes and relations of a concept and the judgment of the corresponding instance build up the *procedural* knowledge of the network which includes the functions for attribute calculation and the judgment functions.

The task of our system - considered from the image processing view - splits into several subtasks. First hypotheses for the object location have to be determined. This is done by histogram-backprojection [9] where histograms of the interesting objects are learned before analysis. Using the resulting hypotheses, subimages can be built on which a color-region segmentation is performed. The subimages are represented by the concept "subimage", whereas the segmented color regions are an attribute of "subimage_seg". Usually, the objects in the overview images are too small to be reliably verified. In this case the color region segmentation is performed using close-up views which are captured

[1] In the following the "_seg" part of the concept names stands for segmentation.

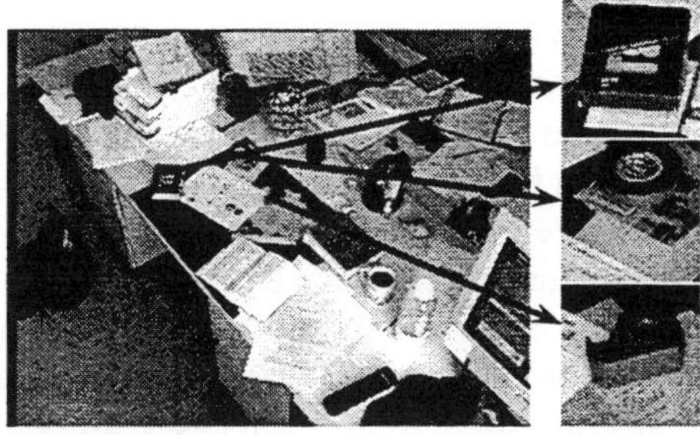

Figure 2. Typical office scene and close-up views for hypotheses.

after a camera move such that the optical axis points to the center of the hypothesized area resulting from backprojection. In addition to the region representation, the concept "color_region" contains attributes for the region's height and width as well as for the region's color. The objects are recognized by their height and width. Judgments are required to guide the instantiation of concepts and to select the sequence of camera actions.

A management of uncertainty is provided by the control algorithm based on the judgment functions. Probabilities are used to rate the instances of the scene concepts "punch", "gluestick" and "adhesive_tape". The judgment of the instance $I(C_k)$ related to the concept C_k subsume the judgments of the concepts' components $comp^k$. Therefore, the judgment of an instance is defined as $p(I(C_k)|comp^k) = \alpha p(I(C_k)) \prod_{l=1}^{n} p(comp_l^k|I(C_k))$. The constant α denotes the normalization factor. We assume that the individual distributions are pairwise independent and $p(I(C_k))$ is uniformly distributed. In order to rate the individual attributes, parameters of a normal distribution for each attribute are estimated using 40 images for each object. During interpretation values for the attributes are calculated and judged according to the corresponding distribution.

Camera actions are performed in order to provide more information about the scene and reduce the uncertainty of intermediate results. The control algorithm has to decide whether new information is needed and which camera action yields the information with lowest cost. Therefore, *utilities* are used to judge the camera actions [4]. The utility measure relies on the intermediate results of the interpretation, i.e. the evidence if all searched objects have been found. The judgment of an instance which corresponds to an object reflects this information. For each instance we have a hypothesis with states *object found* and *object not found*. Depending on these states the optimal camera action is chosen. The utilities are calculated using a utility table which contains the utility of an action a provided that the hypothesis is in state h, where a belongs to the set of executable actions and h is a state of the random variable H. In general, just the distribution of H is known. Therefore, we can only compute the mean utility $EU(a|e) = \sum_{h \in H} U(a,h)p(h|e)$. The variable e denotes the evidence which arises from the intermediate results of analysis. The control algorithm chooses the action which maximizes the mean utility.

To give an example: Recall the two camera actions "indirect_search" and "direct_search", which form an action set. We define the vector $\boldsymbol{v} = (I(L), I(A), I(K)) \in \{0,1\}^3$ as hypothesis H. Hence, the states of H are all configurations of this vector which describe if instances of the punch $I(L)$, the adhesive tape $I(A)$ and the gluestick $I(K)$ are available. Within this vector, 1 denotes "object found", and 0 denotes "object not found". For example, if $\boldsymbol{v} = (1,1,1)$ the punch, the adhesive tape and the gluestick have been found. At the moment we use 0 and 1 as utilities. For example, if we have found a well-rated instance of the intermediate object, the indirect search is more useful than the direct search. For the action "zoom_on_region" we use a hand-crafted utility function based on the region's size and the current zoom setting.

3 Using Knowledge - the Control Algorithm

During analysis, the observed image data and the knowledge stored in the semantic network are matched with each other. The task of the control algorithm is to find the best rated instance of the *goal concept* and the *optimal* sequence of camera actions with respect to the criterion defined by the judgment functions. The goal concept corresponds to the goal of the interpretation process which is "explore_office" in Figure 1. Matching is done by expanding the network and instantiating its concepts. During the expansion and instantiation, so-called *search tree nodes* are built which contain the intermediate results of analysis. Competing segmentation results or competing instances, which are modality-dependent, are assigned to competing search tree nodes. For example, one search tree node contains the instance of "direct_search" and another the instance of "indirect_search" depending on the modality of the instance of "expl_office".

These search tree nodes form the search space of the A*-search algorithm, where the judgment of each node corresponds to the judgment of the goal concept's instance. Therefore, the judgments of the camera actions which influence the judgment of this instance as explained in section 2.2 are the basis for the control algorithm's decision which action should be performed.

The structure of the network determines how to calculate instances and propagate restrictions. It does not impose a sequence of instantiations on the network. Specifically, no performance of a closed loop of camera actions and image processing routines is possible directly. Therefore, we apply so-called *local analysis strategies*. They define the sequence of expansions and instantiations within the search

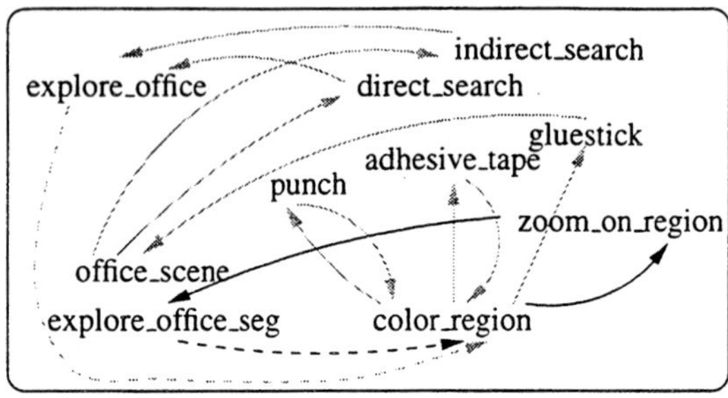

Figure 3. Sequence of concept instantiations

tree node and allow for closed loops of acting and sensing. The sequences specify that after the instantiation of a camera action concept a new image has to be taken and analyzed. Additionally, local strategies provide a means to define the direction of analysis, i.e. if the analysis is performed data-driven or model-driven. In Figure 3 the sequence of concept computations is shown for an excerpt of the knowledge base depicted in Figure 1. The control algorithm starts with the concept "color_region" which can be instantiated. Afterwards, depending on the modality of the instance of "office_scene" the objects are instantiated or a new zoom and a new pan value are calculated. During the instantiation of "explore_office_seg", a camera action is performed and therefore, the control algorithm decides to instantiate the concept "color_region" again using the close-up views.

4 Experiments

The knowledge-based system was tested in two different office environments using two similar cameras and actors. The first one, office1, is shown in Figure 2. In order to test the suitability of the whole approach, an active system which corresponds to the knowledge base depicted in Figure 1 was compared to a *passive system*, i.e. a system which does not perform any camera action, but analyses the scene based on the originally provided image data. All the objects which the system had to search for were therefore positioned in the first overview image and neither a direct nor an indirect search was performed. The task of the control algorithm was, besides the search for the best matching regions, to decide if a fovealization would be necessary. 20 experiments were performed in each office with both systems. In each experiment the position of the objects were changed. As the experiments revealed, the active system outperforms the passive system in both office scenes. In office 2 a recognition rate of 80 % was achieved by the active system, in comparison to 66 % using the passive system. The highest recognition rate, 93 %, was achieved in office1 by the active system whereas the passive system achieved 90 %.

In office1 zoom actions were performed if segmentation errors due to reflections occurred. In office2 all objects except the punch were too small to be verified realibly. The judgment function for "zoom_on_region" reflects these observations. However, there are still some problems. If an object hypothesis in office2 which is not fovealized gets a very high rating, a zoom action is not performed even if the object is very small. Furthermore, the judgments after performing a camera actions are in some cases not optimistic and therefore, the A*-search yields a wrong result. These problems need further research and will be solved in the future.

5 Conclusions

In this article we have proposed an approach for active knowledge-based scene exploration. As the experiments revealed, the approach is suitable to solve the proposed task. In future, we want to integrate more sophisticated object models. Additionally, the we will learn local analysis strategies during the exploration of a scene. Instead of the discrete utility values continuous variables will be used.

References

[1] J. Aloimonos, I. Weiss, and A. Bandyopadhyay. Active vision. *International Journal of Computer Vision*, 2(3):333–356, 1988.

[2] R. Bajcsy. Active perception. *Proceedings of the IEEE*, 76(8):996–1005, 1988.

[3] C. Brown. Issues in Selective Perception. In *Proceedings of the International Conference on Pattern Recognition*, volume A, pages 21–30, Los Alamitos, California, 1992. IEEE Computer Society.

[4] F. V. Jensen. *An Introduction to Bayesian Networks*. UCL Press, London, 1996.

[5] B. Krebs, B. Korn, and F. Wahl. A task driven 3d object recognition system using bayesian networks. In *International Conference on Computer Vision*, pages 527–532, Bombay, India, 1998.

[6] T. Matsuyama and V. Hwang. *SIGMA. A Knowledge-Based Aerial Image Understanding System*, Plenum Press, New York and London, 1990.

[7] H. Niemann, G. Sagerer, S. Schröder, and F. Kummert. ERNEST: A Semantic Network System for Pattern Understanding. *IEEE Transactions on Pattern Analysis and Machine Intelligence (PAMI)*, 12(9):883–905, 1990.

[8] R. Rimey and C. Brown. Task–oriented Vision with Multiple Bayes Nets. In A. Blake and A. Yuille, editors, *Active Vision*, pages 217–236, Cambridge, Massachusetts, 1992.

[9] M. J. Swain and D. H. Ballard. Color indexing. *International Journal of Computer Vision*, 7(1):11–32, November 1991.

[10] L. Wixson. Gaze Selection for Visual Search. Technical report, Department of Computer Science, College of Arts and Science, University of Rochester, Rochester, New York, 1994.

Multi-directional Camera 3-D Vision System for Micro-operation

Seiji Hata, Daisuke Torigoe, Shuxiang Guo, Kohichi Sugimoto,
Faculty of Engineering, Kagawa University
hata@eng.kagawa-u.ac.jp

Abstract

Handling of micro-objects about 0.1 mm square is essential in the fields of bio-technology and micro-machine production. These operations have some difficulty because it requires the unnatural hands manipulations under the microscopic images. So the productivity of those operations is not high. To solve these problems, a 3-D software camera system has been introduced. The system consists of two subsystems those are the 3-D entire shape model with texture extraction system and the stereo image generation system. Here, the method of 3-D model extraction system using multi-directional camera is introduced, then the attempt to generate the stereo image from the 3-D model is described.

1. Introduction

Handling of micro-objects about 0.1 mm square is essential in the fields of bio-technology and micro-machine production. These operations have some kind of difficulty because they require the unnatural hands manipulations under the microscopic images and the productivity of those operations is not high.

Fig.1 is an example of such operations. It shows a bio-operation of clone seedlings production. There are following problems in such operations;

1) The operator is hard to recognize the entire shape of the objects, because he can see only the one directional image under the microscope

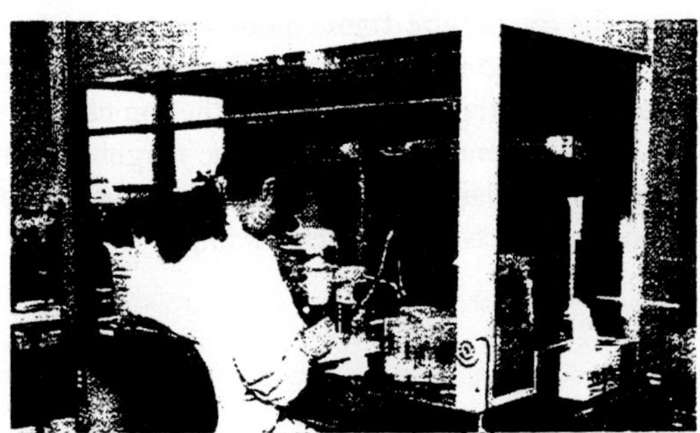

Fig.1 Micro-operation under Microscope

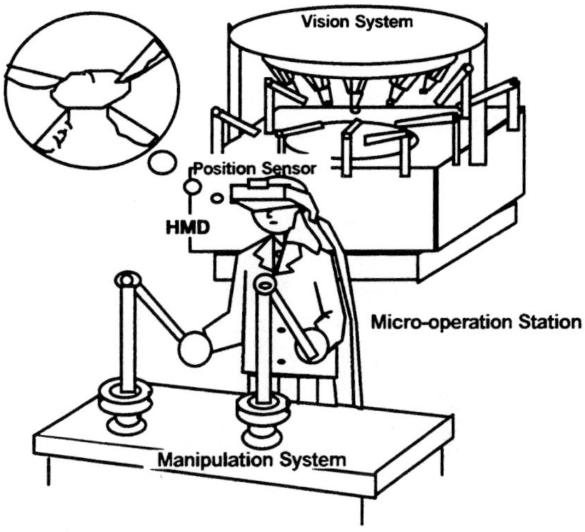

Fig.2 Micro-operation Assist System

2) The lack of 3-D recognition of the objects causes the difficulty of operations such as cutting and handling.
3) The mismatches of enlarged images by the microscope and the micro-operation of hands causes the unnatural feeling of operators.

In this paper, a concept of micro-operation assist system is introduced. Then, the details of vision systems to construct the 3-D entire model with texture and an attempt to generate stereo image are explained.

2. Micro-Operation Assist System

To increase the productivity of such a micro-operation shown in fig.1, a concept of micro-operation assist system has been introduced. The structure of the system is shown in fig.2. The aims of this system are as followings;

1) It enables the operator to handle the micro objects as if they have the ordinary sizes he treats in his ordinary life.
2) To achieve the aim described in 1), the system enables the operator to observe the objects enlarged in their size to about 100 mm. The operator can observe the stereo images of the objects, and the images are generated according to the operator's head position and orientation to give the natural stereo images to the operator. It helps

1051-4651/00 $10.00 © 2000 IEEE

the operator to recognize the 3-D shapes of the objects,

3) The Manipulation system, also, enables the operator to handle the object in its enlarged sizes. To meet with the requirement, the manipulator motion is reduced according to the enlarged ratio of the vision system.
4) The micro-force feedback system also enlarges the feedback force to the operator hands.

In this paper, the vision system of the micro-operation system is mainly discussed. The vision system employs the idea of the software camera introduced by Kanade, et. Al[1].

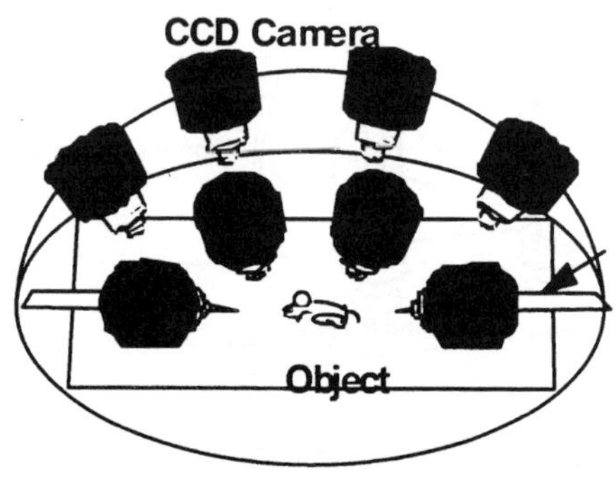

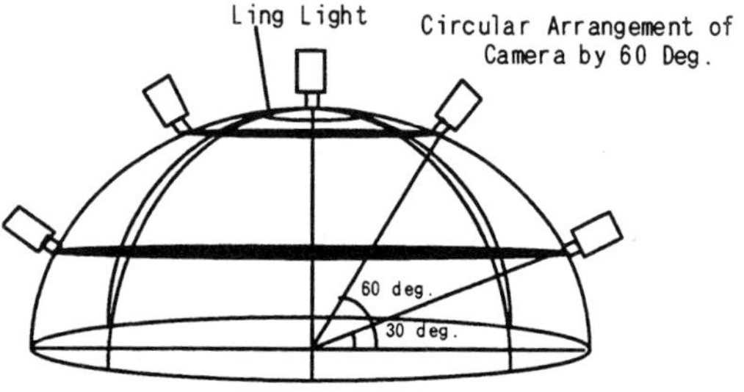

Fig.3 Optical Structure of Multi-directional Vision System

3.Multi-directional Vision Sensor For Micro-operation

As is described in chap.2, the vision system should generate the multi-directional images according to the operator's head position and orientation. So, it should generate the continuously changing enlarged stereo images according to the observing direction of the operator. But the limited directional microscope images cannot meet this kind of requirements. So, the idea of soft-camera is introduced.

The flow of the vision system is as follows;

1) The entire 3-D shape model of the object is extracted using the multi-camera stereo processing method. The model includes the texture on the object surface.
2) From the entire 3-D shape model, the system generates the stereo images on the HMD according to the operator's head position and orientation. At that time, the real time image generation is required.

To extract the entire shape model of the object, the optical system should observe the object from many directions. It is required to get the images of least shading parts of the object. Fig.3 shows the structure of the multi-directional vision system designed to get the entire model. 17 cameras are mounted into the system. So, to meet with the real-time stereo image generation, high-speed multi-camera stereo image processing and stereo image generation is required. The accuracy of the model is also required to generate the precise and realistic stereo images for HMD.

4. High Speed Multi-Camera Stereo Image Processing

The multi-directional vision system observes 17 images from the 17 cameras to get the least shading models of the object. To get the model, the multi-camera stereo image processing method is employed. But to execute the multi-camera stereo image processing requires long processing time to get many corresponding points from the many combinations of 17 cameras mounted in the vision system.

To meet with the real-time and accurate multi-camera stereo image processing, the method shown in fig.4 has been introduced.

The model is described as a wire-frame model of triangular patches. Every triangle is attached its surface texture on the object.

As is shown in fig.4, to construct the accurate 3-D shape model of the object in real-time, the method to select the camera combination has been developed.

First, the rough wire-frame model (initial model) of the object is extracted using two cameras. In many cases, one camera of the initial two cameras is the top camera shown in fig. 3 and the another camera is the neighbor camera to the top camera. Using these two cameras, stereo-matching processing extracts the corresponding

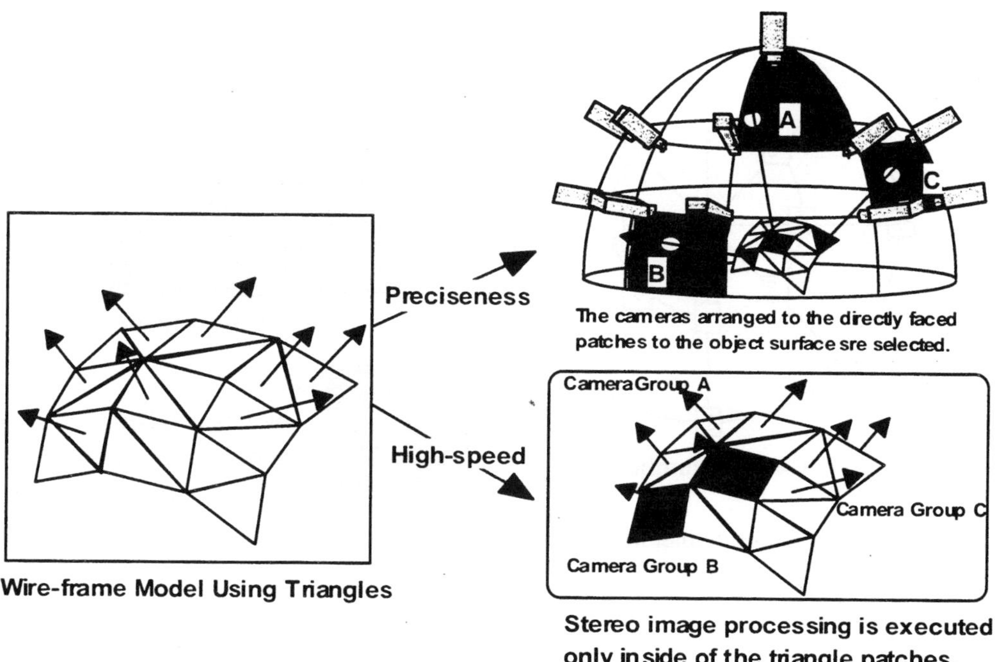
Preciseness
High-speed
Wire-frame Model Using Triangles
The cameras arranged to the directly faced patches to the object surface sre selected.
A
B
C
CameraGroup A
Camera Group C
Camera Group B
Stereo image processing is executed only inside of the triangle patches.
Fig.5 Accurate and High-Speed Multi-Camera Stereo Image Processing

points between two cameras and concludes the 3-D positions of the corresponding points.

Including all these corresponding points, a rough model of the object is constructed. The process is as follows;

1) The contour line include all the measured corresponding points is defined in the top image, then, the 2-D coordinates of the vertices of the contour line are changed to their 3-D coordinates.
2) The highest or the lowest point in the measured corresponding points is selected. It is called a top point.
3) Between the top point and all the vertices are connected by lines. These areas parted by the contour line and the connected line become triangles.
4) In the every parted triangle, the distances between the corresponding points and the triangle plane are evaluated. If all the distances of the corresponding points included in the triangle remains in some threshold distance, the triangle is fixed. Otherwise, the corresponding point of longest distance is selected and the triangle separation is continued to the new triangles.The process continues until all the distances between the corresponding points and the triangle plane is under the pre-defined threshold distance
5) Then, the refine process begins. At every triangle defined by 3) and 4), the normal vector is calculated. The object is assumed to be very small. The half Gaussian sphere is introduced. The 17 cameras are arranged on the sphere and the camera mounted points separates the sphere into 16 patches as is shown in fig.3. When the normal vector of a triangle calculated, the vector is placed center of the sphere, and the pointed patch by the normal vector of the triangle is selected.
6) The camera combination to form the patch is used to precise 3-D position detection. The 3-D coordinates of the corresponding points included in the triangle are measured, again, using the selected camera combination. Also, the distances between the corresponding points and the triangle plane are evaluated, again. If some distances exceed the predefined threshold, the triangle separation process will be executed. All these re-calculation are executed using selected camera combination for every triangle, the execution time is minimized.
7) After the re-construction of the triangles model, the texture for every triangle is extracted from one of the selected cameras.

After these procedures, the system can construct the precise wire-frame model with texture.

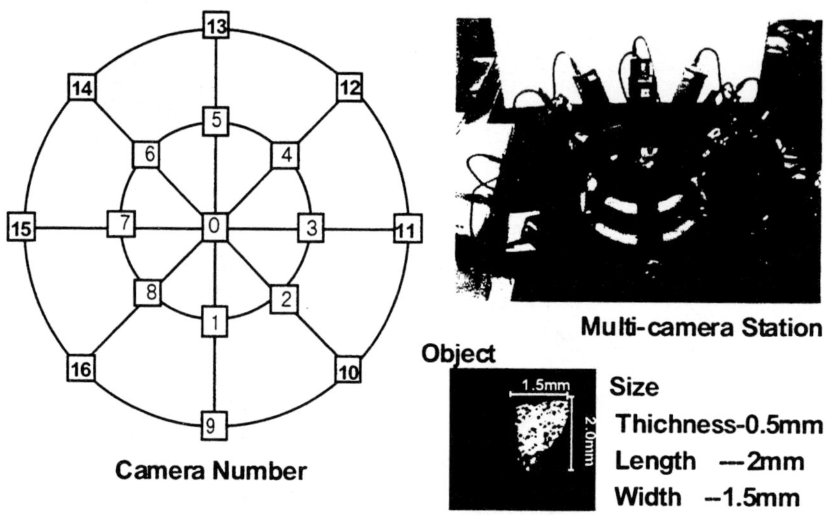

Fig.5 Experimental Multi-directional Vision System and Object

5. Experimental Result

Fig.5 shows the experimentally developed multi-directional vision system and the object observed. The camera number of the top camera is 0, and the other numbers are as are shown in the figure.

Fig.6 shows the images of the object observed by the 17 cameras shown in fig.5.

Fig.7 shows the result of the initial model construction. The selected corresponding points are measured their 3-D coordinates. The right-up picture of fig.7 shows the result. Then, the wire-frame model is initially constructed using the procedure described in chapter 4.

Fig.8 shows the result of re-construction of precise wire-frame model using camera combination. A triangle is selected, and the 3-D positions of the corresponding points in the triangle are re-calculated. Then, the distances between the corresponding points and the triangle plane are evaluated. In this case, some distances exceed the predefined threshold, some new triangles are introduced in the right picture.

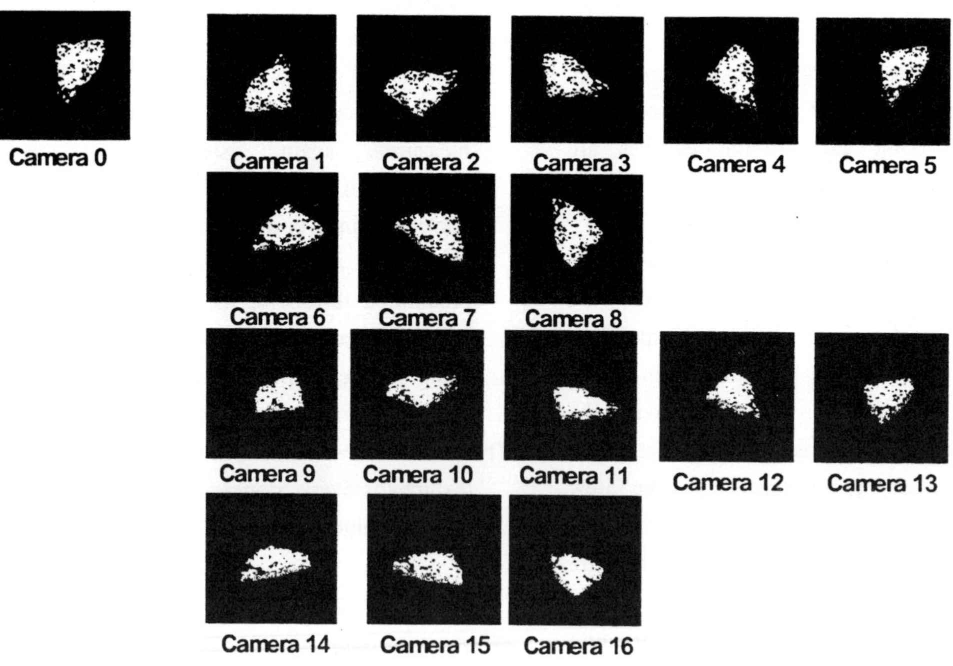

Fig. 6 Observed Images Observed by Multi-Directional Vision System

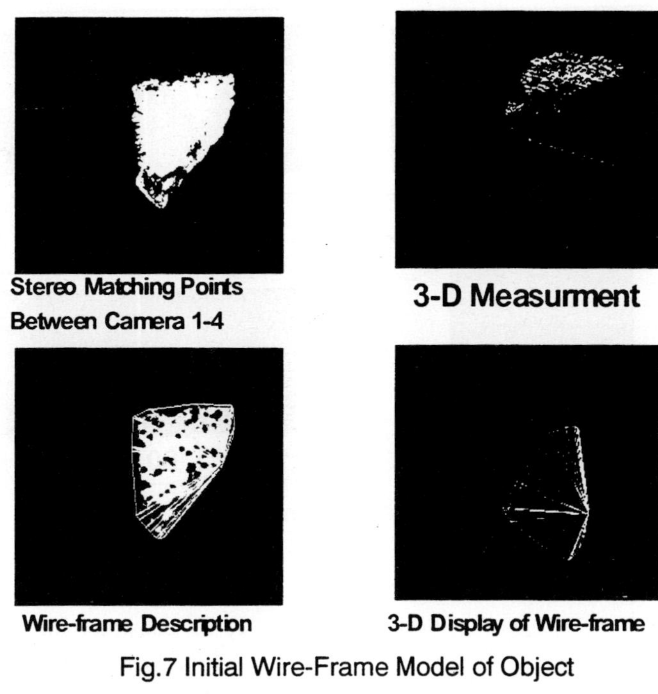

Fig.7 Initial Wire-Frame Model of Object

Fig.8 Precise Model Reconstruction

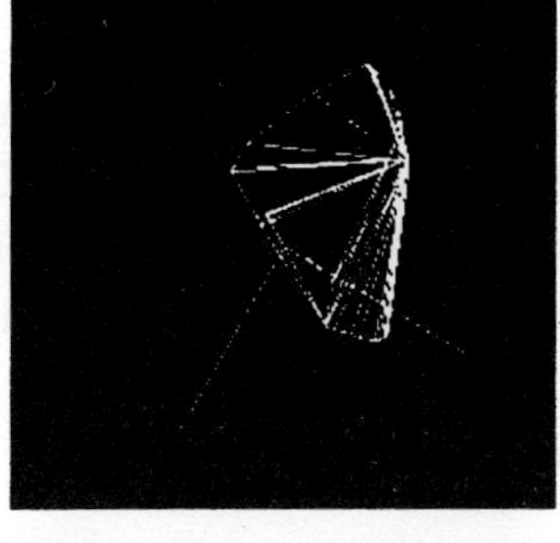

Wire-Frame Model Texture Mapping

Fig.9 Generated Wire-Frame Model with Texture

Fig.9 shows the generated wire-frame model of the object. The texture on the every triangle is extracted. The result of the texture mapping on the triangle is shown in right picture of fig.9.

Using the wire-frame model with the texture, the system can generate every directional images of the object. Using the technique, the system can generates the stereo images to be displayed in the HMD introduced in fig.2. Fig. 10 shows the generated stereo images from the extracted model. A combined images shows a left eye image and right eye image for HMD. The images are enlarged 100 times from it original size.

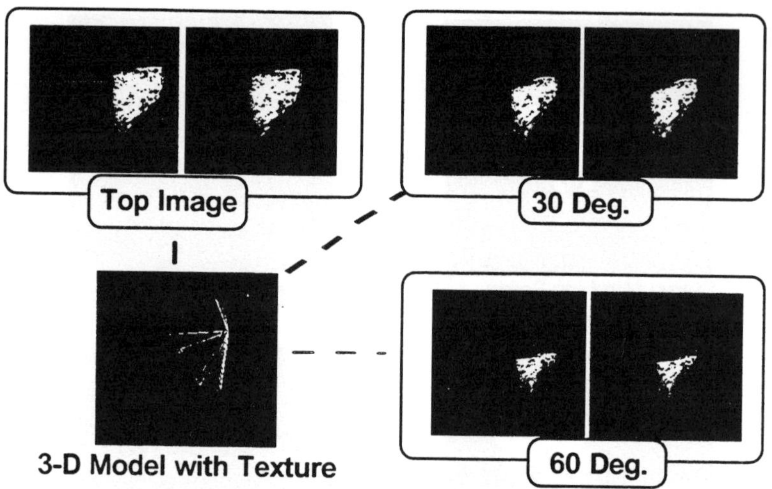

Fig.10 Stereo Images Generated for HMD

As is shown in fig.2, operators can see enlarged stereo image of the object as if it is on the operation desk.

6. Conclusion

Handling of micro-objects less than 1 mm is essential in the fields of biotechnology and micro-machine production. These operations have some kind of difficulty because it requires the unnatural hands operations under the microscopic images and the productivity of those operations is not high. To solve these problems, a 3-D software camera system has been introduced. The system consists of two subsystems those are the 3-D entire shape model with texture extraction system and the stereo image generation system from the model.

To construct the 3-D entire shape model, a multi-directional vision system has been introduced. It has 17 cameras to observe objects from many directions to get the least shading images of the object. The 17 images from the 17 camera are processed using the multi-camera stereo image processing method. First, the system extracts the rough model of the object. The model is described as the wire-frame model with many triangles. Then, the camera combination which directly faces to the selected triangle is defined. Using the camera combination, the precise model is re-constructed. The triangles of the model are attached with textures on their surfaces.

Using the model, the system generates the any directional images.

The remained problems are as follows;

1) To construct the real-time multi-camera image processing and graphic display system to enables the smooth operation of the object.
2) To generate real-time stereo images for HMD according to the operators head position and orientation. The images should be seen natural and it should including the surroundings of the operation stage.
3) To connect the vision system with the micro-operation and manipulation system as is shown in fig.2.

7. Acknowledgements

This study is done under the support of many companies, i.e., TADANO, HITACHI, SHIKOKU MEASUREMENT, RYUSHO, FUTEC and AOI KIKOU. We thank to these companies for their kind cooperation.

8. References

[1] T.Kanade, et.al.: Virtualized Reality: Concepts and Early Results, presented at the IEEE Workshop on the Representation of Visual Scenes (in conjunction with ICCV'95), Boston, MA, June 1995

Real-time Generation and Presentation of View-dependent Binocular Stereo Images Using a Sequence of Omnidirectional Images

Koichiro Yamaguchi
R&D Center
NTT DoCoMo
3-5 Hikarino-oka, Yokosuka, Kanagawa 239-8536, Japan
yamaguchi@mlab.yrp.nttdocomo.co.jp

Haruo Takemura, Kazumasa Yamazawa, and Naokazu Yokoya
Graduate School of Information Science
Nara Institute of Science and Technology
8916-5 Takayama, Ikoma, Nara 630-0101, Japan
{takemura, yamazawa, yokoya}@is.aist-nara.ac.jp

Abstract

This paper presents a new method to generate and present arbitrarily directional binocular stereo images from a sequence of omnidirectional images. A sequence of omnidirectional images is taken by moving an omnidirectional image sensor in a static real environment. The motion of the omnidirectional image sensor is constrained to a plane. The sensor's route and speed are known. In the proposed method, a fixed length of the sequence is buffered in a computer to generate arbitrarily directional binocular stereo images by combining captured rays. Using the method a user can look around a scene in the distance with rich 3D sensation without significant time delay. This paper describes the principle of real-time generation of binocular stereo images. In addition, we introduce a prototype telepresence system of view-dependent stereo image generation and presentation.

1. Introduction

In recent years, the acquisition of a remote scene for telepresence or surveillance has become of great interest [1]. The important issue in telepresence is to produce the wide field of view and a stereoscopic effect. A telepresence system that expands the field of view has been developed by Onoe et al. [8, 9]. This system uses an omnidirectional image sensor, and generates view-dependent images without significant time delay. However the generated images are monoscopic. One of approaches to produce both the wide field of view and a stereoscopic effect is to use rotating stereo cameras. But this approach has a problem in terms of time delay from the change of viewing direction to the change of displayed image caused by rotating remote stereo cameras.

Recently, image-based rendering techniques have been proposed to generate a virtual environment from a set of photographs. QuickTime VR [3] is a system that uses these techniques. The user can alter viewing direction, while the viewpoint is fixed. A typical approach to relax this fixed viewpoint problem is to use the plenoptic function [2, 6]. The Lightfield [5] and the Lumigraph [4] defined as 4D plenoptic functions make it possible to render images of a scene from any arbitrary viewpoints in a bounding box without finding scene depth. Using the plenoptic functions an arbitrarily directional binocular stereo images can be obtained. However, such methods require a lot of images to render arbitrary views.

In this paper we propose a new method to generate arbitrarily directional binocular stereo images from a sequence of omnidirectional images in real time by combining captured rays. A sequence of omnidirectional images is taken by moving an omnidirectional image sensor in a static real environment. We constrain the motion of the omnidirectional image sensor to a plane and the sensor's route and speed are known. Compared with the Lightfield and the Lumigraph, the proposed method has smaller data size, as we constrain the viewpoint to the proximity of the sensor's route.

This paper is structured as follows. We first briefly describe the video-rate omnidirectional image sensor in Section 2. Real-time generation of arbitrarily directional binocular stereo images is then discussed in Section 3. We de-

1051-4651/00 $10.00 © 2000 IEEE

scribe a prototype telepresence system of view-dependent stereo images generation and presentation, as well as experimental results in Section 4. We finally summarize the present work in Section 5.

2. Omnidirectional Image Sensor

We employ HyperOmni Vision [11] as an omnidirectional image sensor in our study. HyperOmni Vision uses a hyperboloidal mirror and a standard CCD video camera as shown in Figure 1(a). The geometry of HyperOmni Vision is illustrated in Figure 1(b). The hyperboloidal mirror has two focal points O_M and O_C. The optical center of the camera lens is placed at O_C. Given a world coordinate (X, Y, Z) as shown Figure 1(b), the hyperboloidal mirror surface is represented as follows:

$$\frac{X^2+Y^2}{a^2} - \frac{Z^2}{b^2} = -1 \ (Z > 0). \quad (1)$$

The inner focal point O_M of the mirror is at $(0, 0, c)$ and the outer focal point O_C is at $(0, 0, -c)$ in the world coordinate, where $c = \sqrt{a^2+b^2}$.

A ray going toward the point O_M is reflected by the mirror and is focused on the point O_C. Thus, we can get a central projection of 360-degree filed of view at the point O_M onto the hyperboloidal surface by the CCD camera. This single viewpoint constraint guarantees that common planar perspective images can be computed from a captured omnidirectional image [11], as shown in Figure 2. A point $P(X, Y, Z)$ in world coordinate is projected to a point $p(x, y)$ on an image plane. This projection is represented as:

$$x = \frac{Xf(b^2-c^2)}{(b^2+c^2)(Z-c) - 2bc\sqrt{X^2+Y^2+(Z-c)^2}},$$
$$y = \frac{Yf(b^2-c^2)}{(b^2+c^2)(Z-c) - 2bc\sqrt{X^2+Y^2+(Z-c)^2}}. \quad (2)$$

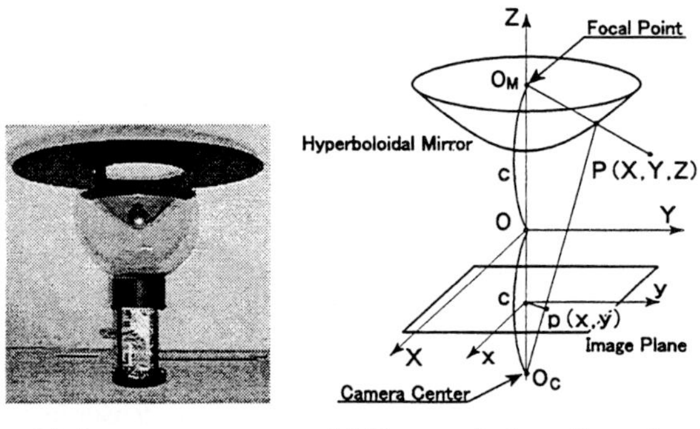

(a) Appearance (b) Geometrical configuration

Figure 1. HyperOmni Vision ver.2A.

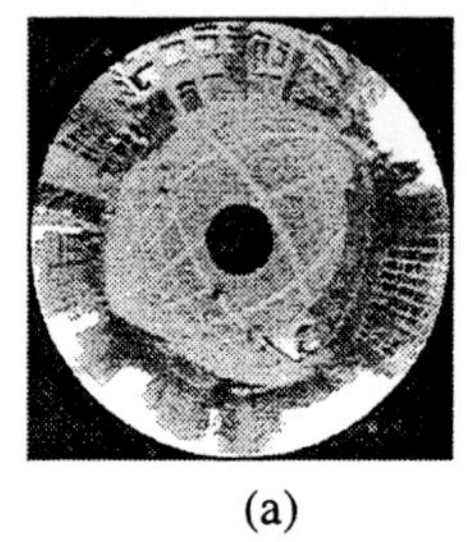

(a) (b)

Figure 2. Omnidirectional image (a) and perspective image (b).

3. Real-time Generation of Novel Binocular Views

3.1. Rendering a Novel View

A sequence of omnidirectional images taken by HyperOmni Vision moving straight in a static scene is used. Route and speed with which HyperOmni Vision moves on a straight line are known. Given a sequence of omnidirectional images, we can render a novel view at an arbitrary point located in the plane on which a sequence of omnidirectional images is taken.

The basic idea of novel view generation is illustrated in Figure 3. HyperOmni Vision moving from the point X to the point Y takes a sequence of omnidirectional images. Let us describe how to generate a perspective image of W by H pixels from the viewpoint A. The generation is done by computing all pixels on the image plane. For example, when computing pixels on the vertical line that includes the point P, pixels are taken from the omnidirectional image captured at the point Q where the line $\overline{PA}$ and the line $\overline{XY}$ intersect, because the ray AP is the same as the ray QP captured at the point Q [4, 5]. The vertical line that includes the point P is rendered by generating a perspective image of 1 by H' pixels from the omnidirectional image captured at the point Q and scaling the resulting image to H pixels. It should be noted

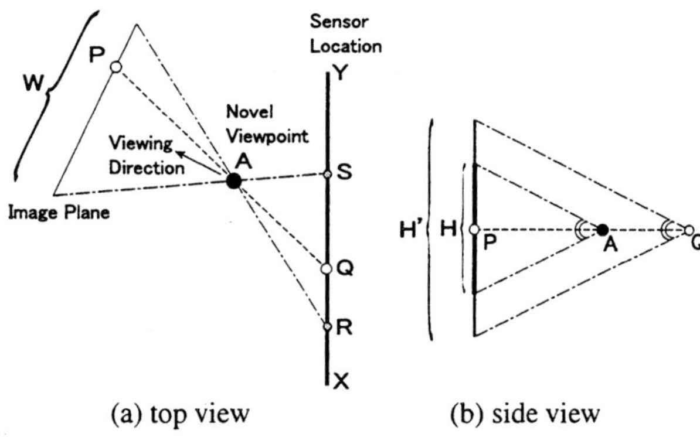

(a) top view (b) side view

Figure 3. Illustration of generating a novel view.

in this case that the focal length is |QP| and the vertical field of view is the same as the vertical field of view with which the vertical line of H pixels is generated from the point A. Similarly, we compute the entire image of viewpoint A by using omnidirectional images obtained from the point R to the point S.

This method causes some vertical distortions in the image generated. If the distances between the image sensor and objects in a scene are known, we can reduce the vertical distortion. However, we actually do not know the distance and cannot correct the distortion. The vertical distortion decreases as the distance between the objects in a scene and the sensor increases [10].

A sequence of omnidirectional images is captured at video rate. This means that the omnidirectional images on the line $\overline{XY}$ are obtained at discrete points. Thus, there is a case that the omnidirectional image required to generate a novel view does not exists. In such a case, we generate the novel view by using the omnidirectional image of the nearest neighbor. Consequently the entire novel view is created by concatenating perspective images computed from omnidirectional imges at different locations.

3.2. Generation of Stereo Images

We generate arbitrarily directional binocular stereo images from a sequence of omnidirectional images by using the method described in the previous section. Here, we assume that both left and right eyes are located on the plane where the sequence of images is taken. Images for left and right eyes can be computed by specifying two different viewpoints with a certain distance.

3.3. Reduction of Correspondence Calculation

In order to generate binocular stereo images by using the proposed method, we must calculate the correspondence between stereo images and omnidirectional images. Such a computation is time consuming and is difficult to be performed in real time. We have developed the following method to achieve real-time generation of stereo images.

Omnidirectional images exist at discrete points on the route of HyperOmni Vision, say T_1 to T_5 in Figure 4. An image to be generated can be vertically divided into a number of regions according to omnidirectional images used for rendering the regions. In Figure 4, a perspective image is generated from three omnidirectional images captured at T_2, T_3 and T_4 and can be vertically divided into three regions. We space a grid in every region as shown in Figure 4 and compute the exact transformation only for grid points. Entire images are efficiently computed from clipped omnidirectional images and grid points by using an image warping technique with bi-linear interpolation [7].

The flow of an efficient stereo image generation algorithm is as follows.

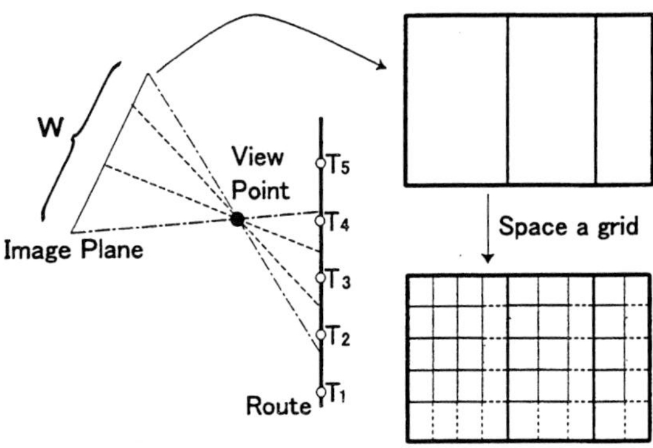

Figure 4. Division of an image plane and spacing a grid.

1. The destination stereo images are vertically divided according to the number of omnidirectional images required.
2. A $m \times n$ grid is spaced in every divided region, where $m = \lceil \frac{w}{W} \times 16 \rceil, n = 12$.
   (w is a width of region, and W is a width of computed image.)
3. The exact transformation is computed for every grid point.
4. Hardware texture mapping generates the rectangular region in stereo images.

We can efficiently generate a pair of binocular stereo images of viewing direction by using this algorithm.

4. Prototype System for Immersive Telepresence

We have implemented the proposed method and constructed a prototype system of stereo images generation and presentation. The prototype system generates binocular stereo images from a sequence of temporarily recorded omnidirectional images in real time and continuously presents binocular stereo images of user's arbitrary viewing direction.

4.1. System Overview

The prototype system configuration is illustrated in Figure 5. In the system we have used a graphics workstation (SGI Onyx2 IR2 (MIPS R10000 195MHz, 16CPU)) with a video board (DIVO), HyperOmni Vision ver.2A, a mobile robot platform (Nomad-200), a 3D magnetic tracker (POLHEMUS 3SPACE FASTRAK) and a head mounted display (HMD) (OLYMPUS Mediamask).

The flow of process in the system is as follows.

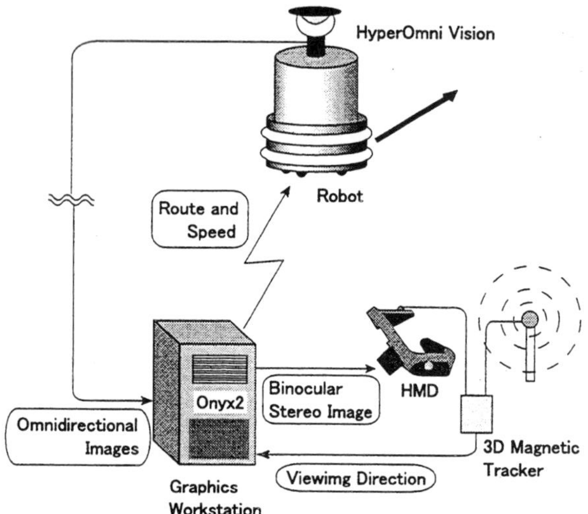

Figure 5. Hardware cofiguration of prototype system.

1. The robot with HyperOmni Vision is moved straight at a constant speed by the workstation. The latest sequence of omnidirectional images is buffered in the workstation.
2. Viewing direction of a user is sent to the workstation from a 3D magnetic tracker attached to the HMD.
3. Binocular stereo images of user's viewing direction are generated in real time and are displayed on the HMD.

The process of generating binocular stereo images is executed using a single CPU of the workstation.

4.2. Experiments

In our experiment of binocular stereo image generation and presentation, the robot with HyperOmni Vision is moved straight at the constant speed of 17.5cm per second. A sequence of omnidirectional images for the latest two seconds is buffered in the workstation memory. The system generates binocular stereo images that the center of eyes is located at the point of acquiring the central omnidirectional image among buffered images in the workstation. Therefore, a user looks around a scene from the viewpoint at the point that the robot passed one second ago.

The distance between two eyes for binocular stereo images is set to 7cm. The horizontal field of view of the image is 60 degree. The computed images are of 640 × 480 pixels.

Figure 6 shows a sampled input sequence of omnidirectional images in the period of 35 second. Generated binocular stereo images are shown in Figure 7. In Figure 7, the binocular parallax can be clearly observed between left and right images of stereo pair. The parallax is easily recognized by watching a chair, which is closer to the sensor,

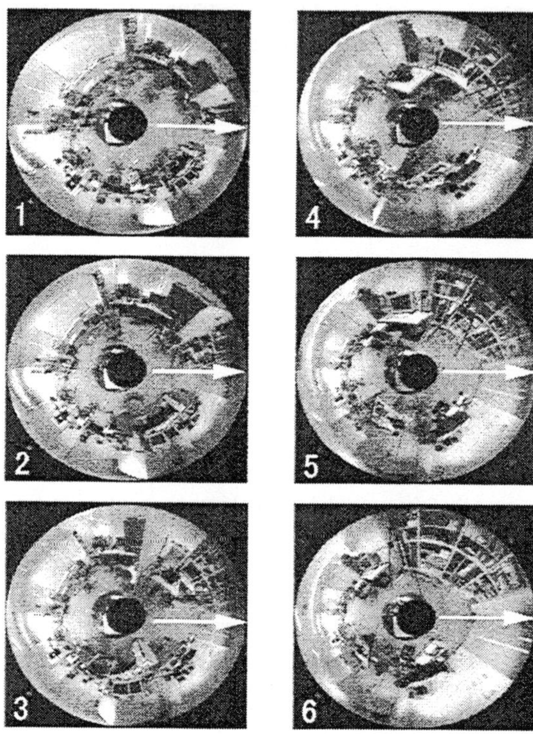

Figure 6. An input sequence of omnidirectional images (arrows show moving direction of sensor).

in stereo images (a), (b) and (c) of Figure 7. Vertical distortions in stereo images are also observed. However it has been proven that a user can look around the scene with rich 3D sensation without any sense of incompatibility. Experiments have shown that users do not perceive discontinuities caused by concatenating perspective images computed from omnidirectional images at different locations.

A pair of stereo images is computed in 0.017 second. Images displayed on HMD are updated every 0.033 second (video-rate). In the present setup, we can generate stereo images when a user looks around the scene with the viewing angle of from 40 to 140 degree and from –40 to –140 degree against the direction towards which the robot is moving. It should be noted that the shortage of omnidirectional images buffered in the workstation causes the fact that we cannot generate stereo images when viewing direction is close to the robot's moving direction. The number of omnidirectional images with respect to viewing direction is illustrated in Figure 8. The vertical axis in Figure 8 shows the number of omnidirectional images required for generating each of stereo pair. The number of omnidirectional images used for viewing direction from –40 to –140 degree is same as that for the direction from 40 to 140 degree.

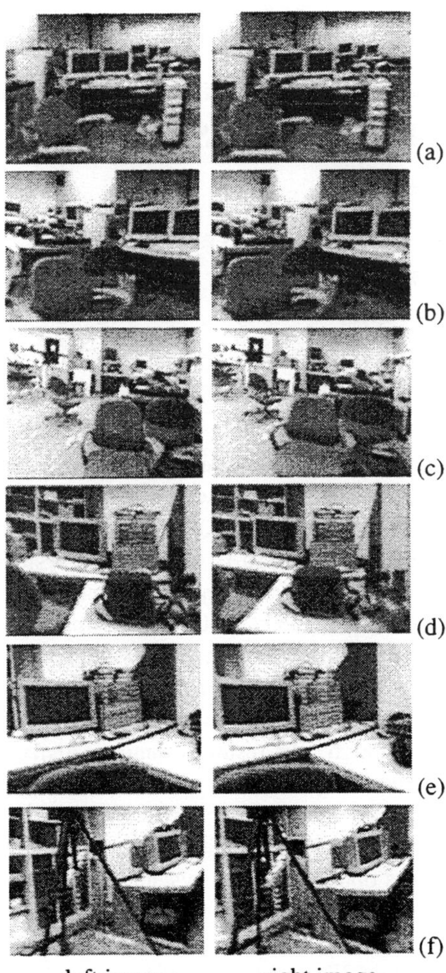

Figure 7. A sequence of generated binocular stereo images in the period of 35 sec. (viewing directions are (a) 52, (b) 96, (c) 122, (d) −56, (e) −81, (f) −118 degree from the moving direction, respectively).

5. Conclusions

In this paper we have proposed a new method to generate novel binocular stereo views in arbitrary direction from a sequence of omnidirectional images in real time. We have constructed the prototype of immersive telepresence system based on the proposed method. In our experiments, a user could look around a real scene in the distance and well perceive parallax in generated binocular stereo images.

The future work is to generate stereo images in all directions using multiple sequences of omnidirectional images. Sequences of omnidirectional images are taken along different paths. We also would like to compensate vertical distortions.

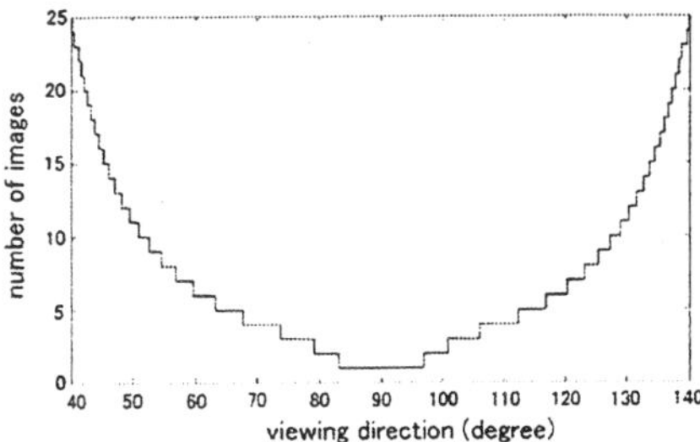

Figure 8. The number of omnidirectional images with respect to viewing direction.

Acknowledgments

This work was supported in part by the Real World Computing Partnership, Telecommunications Advancement Organization of Japan and Grant-in-Aid for Scientific Research under Grant No.11780307 from the Ministry of Education, Science, Sports and Culture.

References

[1] S. Moezzi, Ed.. Special issue on immersive telepresence. *IEEE MultiMedia*, 4(1):17–56, 1997.

[2] E. H. Adelson and J. Bergen. The plenoptic function and the elements of early vision. *Computational Models of Visual Processing*, M. Landy and J. A. Movshon, Ed., pages 3–20, MIT Press, 1991.

[3] S. E. Chen. QuickTime VR - An image-based approach to virtual environment navigation. *Proc. SIGGRAPH 95*, pages 29–38, August 1995.

[4] S. J. Gortler, R. Grzeszczuk, R. Szeliski, and M. F. Cohen. The lumigraph. *Proc. SIGGRAPH 96*, pages 43–54, August 1996.

[5] M. Levoy and P. Hanrahan. Light field rendering. *Proc. SIGGRAPH 96*, pages 31–42, August 1996.

[6] L. McMillan and G. Bishop. Plenoptic modeling: An image-based rendering system. *Proc. SIGGRAPH 95*, pages 39–46, August 1995.

[7] J. Neider, T. Davis, and M. Woo. *OpenGL Programming Guide*. Addison-Wesley Publishing Company, 1993.

[8] Y. Onoe, K. Yamazawa, H. Takemura, and N. Yokoya. Telepresence by real-time viewdependent image generation from omnidirectional video streams. *Computer Vision and Image Understanding*, 71(2):154–165, August 1998.

[9] Y. Onoe, K. Yamazawa, H. Takemura, and N. Yokoya. Visual surveillance and monitoring system using an omnidirectional video camera. *Proc. 14th IAPR Int. Conf. on Pettern Recognition(14ICPR)*, I:588–592, August 1998.

[10] K. Yamaguchi, K. Yamazawa, H. Takemura, and N. Yokoya. Realtime generation and presentation of arbitrarily directional binocular stereo images using a sequence of omnidirectional images. *IEICE Tech. Report, PRMU99-159*, pages 67–72, November 1999. (in Japanese).

[11] K. Yamazawa, Y. Yagi, and M. Yachida. Obstacle detection with omnidirectional image sensor hyperomni vision. *Proc. 1995 IEEE Int. Conf. on Robotics and Automation*, pages 1062–1067, May 1995.

Reconstruction of Realistic 3D Surface Model and 3D Animation from Range Images Obtained by Real Time 3D Measurement System

Takeo MIYASAKA, Kazuhiro KURODA, Makoto HIROSE and Kazuo ARAKI
School of Computer and Cognitive Sciences,
Chukyo University, Toyota, Japan
araki@sccs.chukyo-u.ac.jp

Abstract

We have developed a new type of 3D measurement system which enabled us to obtain successive 3D range data at video rate with an error within ±0.3% [1][2][3]. In this paper, we try to reconstruct realistic colored 3D surface model and 3D animation of the moving target from range images obtained by our 3D measurement system.

At first, we used ordinal CG techniques such as smoothing, shading, mapping and so on, but the result is not sufficiently realistic[4]. So, in this paper, we try to synthesize video images with range images obtained by our system.

To this aim, a video camera is fixed on our 3D measurement system and takes video images synchronizing with 3D measurement by it. Then, the measured 3D points are mapped onto the respective video images by means of the coordinate system transformation from coordinate system of 3D measurement system to that of video camera and perspective transformation. Thus, color, brightness and so on of the corresponding pixel are attributed to the mapped measured 3D point. Finally, the realistic colored 3D image and animation are reconstructed through the texture mapping technique.

1. Introduction

Recently, computer graphics(CG) is used in not only movie and TV commercial but also field of digital arts and so on, and has been widely applied for expression technique of information. But it is hard to deal with CG, because it requires much effort to input the 3D data by manual, and we needs expertise yet on making CG.

While, there is strong interest in obtaining 3D data at real time for the purpose of application of computer vision, engineering, medicine, apparel design and so on. In such situation, real-time 3D measurement system has greatly improved and become applicable.

In this regard, we developed a high-speed and continuous 3D measurement system which acquires 3D range data successively at video rates (30 scenes per second) with an error within ±0.3% [1][2][3]. If using this system as input device for 3D information of moving target, it may be possible to reconstruct realistic 3D CG and animation of existent objects briefly. From such viewpoint, we have been trying to make realistic 3D CG of existent human face from successive 3D range images obtained by our 3D measurement system. Although, our result is almost satisfactory, there remains somewhat problem in texture and color[4].

In this paper, we try to reconstruct realistic colored 3D surface model and 3D animation of the moving target from range images obtained by our system. To this aim, a video camera is fixed on our system and takes video images, synchronizing with 3D measurement by it. Then, we synthesize thus obtain 3D images and respective video images by coordinate system transformation and perspective transformation techniques. Finally, the realistic colored 3D image and animation are reconstructed.

2. Configuration of system

2.1. Outline of high-speed and continuous 3D measurement system

Schematic diagram of our 3D measurement system is illustrated in Figure 1. It is based on slit-ray projection method. The remarkable feature of it is mainly comes from its image plane constructed by PSD array which is horizontally non-divided and linear, where as vertically divided in numbers.as illustrated in Figure 2. Each PSD row element of the array is attached to the respective analog signal processors as shown in figure 2.

When the slit-ray is deflected to scan the field of interest by a rotating mirror, the resultant slit-like image passes across the image plane and each PSD row element outputs the analog position information of respective slit-like image

1051-4651/00 $10.00

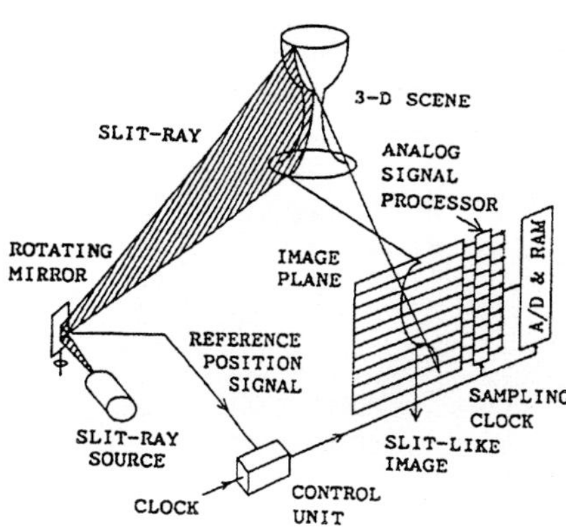

Figure 1. Schematic diagram of high-speed and continuous 3D measurement system

on the image plane in the form of current in real time. These analog signals are converted from current to voltage and amplified through the respective analog signal processors. Then, they are multiplexed and digitized at an appropriate sampling clock interval and stored in memory. Thus, we can acquire the positional information of the slit-like image on the image plane in real time without waiting for the one-frame interval as is required in most conventional methods with scanning image grabbers.

As the result, we can scan the slit-ray at a constant high angular velocity and calculate the deflection angle from the scanning time of the slit-ray. This scanning time is represented as the time elapse after the predetermined reference position signal(see figure 1). The elapsed time is measured by the same clock used for A/D conversion. Thus, the memory address gives the deflection angle of the slit-ray and stored data gives the position of the slit-like image on the image plane caused by that slit-ray. Thus, basic data for 3D measurement are acquired during only one scanning of the slit-ray at high-speed and continuously.

Our system makes us possible to obtain the successive 3D range image of 128 times 128 spatial resolution at video rates with an error within $\pm 0.3\%$.Details of our system is available elsewhere[1][2][3].

2.2. Configuration of system

In this paper, video camera V is fixed near the 3D measurement system M as shown in Figure 3. And they are located in such a manner that vertical axis of cameras are parallel to each other so that we can execute the system calibration easily.

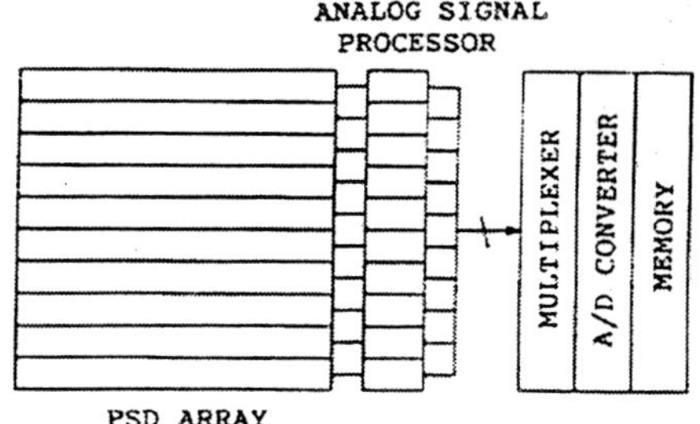

Figure 2. Configuration of the image plane(PSD array)

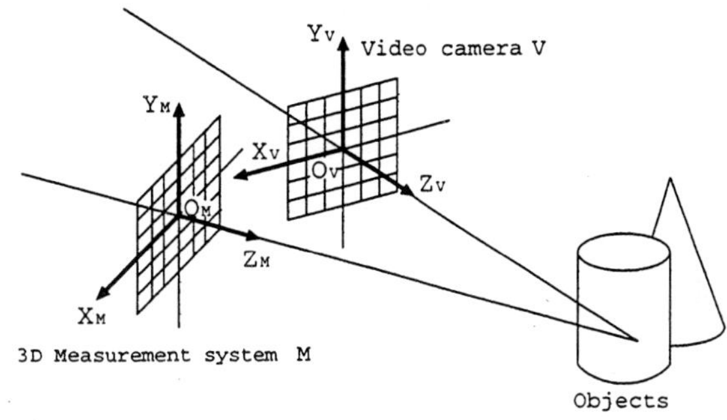

Figure 3. Configuration of system

Coordinate system of 3D measurement system $O_M - X_M Y_M Z_M$ and that of video camera $O_V - X_V Y_V Z_V$ are shown in Figure 3.

Now, in this paper, the coordinate of origin $O_V(V_X, V_Y, V_Z)$ expressed by coordinate system of 3D measurement system and angle θ between both cameras are predetermined.

Figure 4 shows configuration of the systems. In this paper, we suppose that the target is located among 550mm to 650mm from the origine O_M of the 3D measurement system, so we configure optical axis of video camera is toward R whose coordinate is $(0, 0, 600)$ in the coordinate system of 3D measurement system, as shown in Figure 4. Thus, visual field of both video camera and 3D measurement system are almost same and so information of most pixels in video image is available.

3. Synthesis of range image and video image

3.1. Technique of position matching

Position matching of video images and range images are executed as follow.

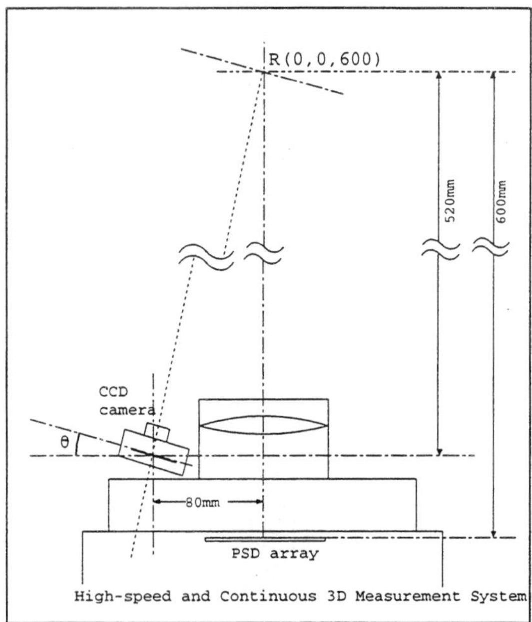

Figure 4. Configuration of measurement system and video camera

Process 1: Measured 3D points obtained by our system are transformed to coordinate system of video camera through the coordinate system transformation.
Process 2: Measured 3D points represented by coordinate system of video camera in preceding process are mapped onto respective video images by perspective transformation with parameters of video camera.

By carrying out above two processes for all measured 3D points, position matching of video and range images are completed. We can attribute the information(color, brightness and so on) of each pixel to the respective measured point. Above processes are formulated as follow.

Transformation from the coordinate system of measurement system to that of video camera is expressed by Equation (1).

$$(X_V, Y_V, Z_V, 1) = (X_M, Y_M, Z_M, 1)T_1T_2 \tag{1}$$

Where, (X_M, Y_M, Z_M) is the 3D coordinate of the measured point in the coordinate system of measurement system and (X_V, Y_V, Z_V) in that of video camera. T_1 and T_2 is the 4×4 transformation matrix which represents translation and rotation, respectively.

$$T_1 = \begin{bmatrix} 1 & 0 & 0 & 0 \\ 0 & 1 & 0 & 0 \\ 0 & 0 & 1 & 0 \\ -V_X & -V_Y & -V_Z & 1 \end{bmatrix} \tag{2}$$

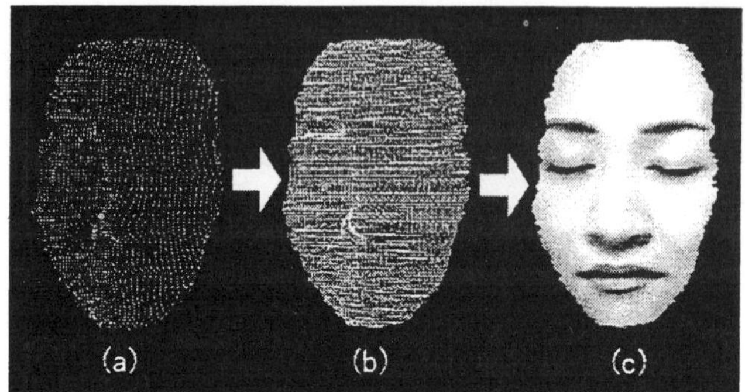

Figures 5. Process flow of rendering

$$T_2 = \begin{bmatrix} \cos\theta & 0 & \sin\theta & 0 \\ 0 & 1 & 0 & 0 \\ -\sin\theta & 0 & \cos\theta & 0 \\ 0 & 0 & 0 & 1 \end{bmatrix} \tag{3}$$

Equation for perspective transformation matrix, which represents perspective projection of 3D points onto image plane of video camera is given by Equation (4).

$$T_3 = \begin{bmatrix} 1 & 0 & 0 & 0 \\ 0 & 1 & 0 & 0 \\ 0 & 0 & 1 & 1/p \\ 0 & 0 & 0 & 1 \end{bmatrix} \tag{4}$$

Where p is perspective parameter to be calibrated.

By combining above four equation, the coordinate of mapped measured 3D point (Xp, Yp) is expressed by Equation (5) and (6).

$$Xp = \frac{p((X_M - V_X)\cos\theta - (Z_M - V_Z)\sin\theta)}{(X_M - V_X)\sin\theta + (Z_M - V_Z)\cos\theta + p} \tag{5}$$

$$Yp = \frac{p(Y_M - V_Y)}{(X_M - V_X)\sin\theta + (Z_M - V_Z)\cos\theta + p} \tag{6}$$

Therefore, the information of pixel at (Xp, Yp) is attributed to respective mapped measured 3D point. If (Xp, Yp) does not fall on exact location of pixel, we use the information of the nearest pixel to (Xp, Yp).

3.2. Synthesis of range image and video image

In general, range image obtained by 3D measurement system is discreetly sampled points (digital image) and so information between sampled points is lacked. We overcome this problem by texture mapping technique.

In general, texture images are distorted by 3D shapes. But spatial resolution of our system is so high that above mentioned distortion is little. In this connection, Figures 5 show (a) measured shape data as it is, (b) approximated result by triangles and (c) rendered result by texture mapping technique.

Figures 6 (a) show video image of existing human face, (b) front view of rendered result of it and (c) side view of rendered result of it. Figures 7 shows a series of 3D animation of speaking human face picked out from 32 scenes.

4. Conclusion

In this paper, we tried to synthesize video images and successive range images obtained by high-speed and continuous 3D measurement system, and to reconstruct realistic colored 3D surface model and animation.

In synthesizing, 3D points are mapped onto respective video images through simple coordinate system transformation and perspective transformation, and we can obtain realistic 3D surface model and animation through texture mapping technique briefly. In future, these method can be applied not only CG but also motion capture etc.

Acknowledgement

This work was partially supported by Kayamori Foundation of Information Science Advancement and Foundation of Chukyo University for Advanced Research.

References

[1] K. Araki, M. Sato, T. Noda, Y. Chiba, and M. Shimizu. High speed and continuous rangefinding system. *IEICE Trans. Special Issue on Computer Vision and Its Applications*, E74(10):3400–3406, 1991.

[2] K. Araki, M. Shimizu, T. Noda, Y. Chiba, Y. Tsuda, K. Ikegaya, K. Sannomiya, and M. Gomi. High speed and continuous 3-d measurement system. *11th IAPR International Conference on Pattern Recognition*, 4:62–65, 1992.

[3] K. Araki, M. Shimizu, T. Noda, Y. Chiba, Y. Tsuda, K. Ikegaya, K. Sannomiya, and M. Gomi. A high-speed and continuous 3d measurement system. *Machine Vision and Applications*, 8(2):79–84, 1995.

[4] K. Fujita, N. Katayama, T. Kawai, M. Shimizu, and K. Araki. Segmentation of 3d object and animation of an existent human face using high-speed and continuous 3d measurement system. *Trans. Institute of Image Electronics Engineers of Japan*, 24(5):567–575, 1995.

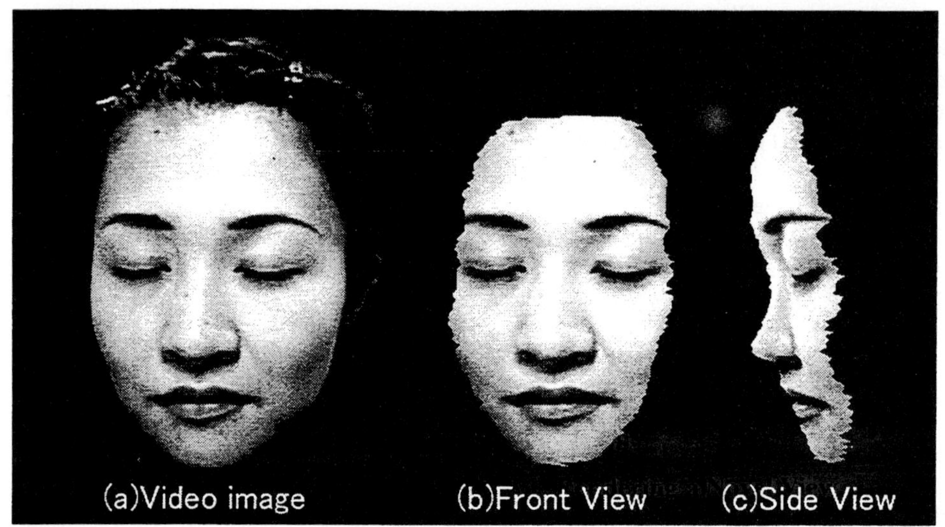

Figures 6. Result of colored 3D image

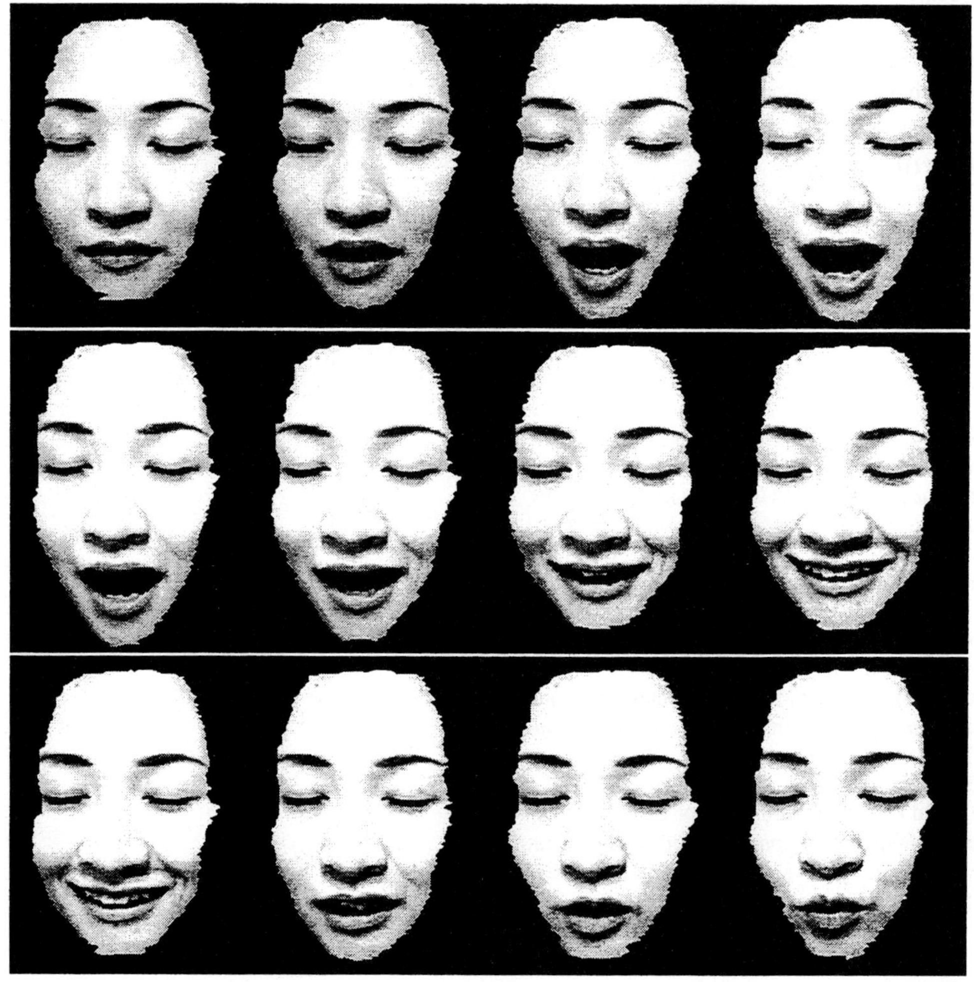

Figures 7. A series of 3D animation for a speaking human face, picked out from 32 scenes

Semi-automatic metric reconstruction of buildings from self-calibration: Preliminary results on the evaluation of a linear camera self-calibration method*

D. Q. Huynh† Y. S. Chou‡ H. T. Tsui‡

† School of Information Technology
Murdoch University
Perth WA 6150 Australia
d.huynh@murdoch.edu.au

‡ Department of Electronic Engineering
Chinese University of Hong Kong
Shatin, Hong Kong
{yschou,httsui}@ee.cuhk.edu.hk

Abstract

In this paper, we investigate the linear self-calibration method proposed by Newsam et al [7] for our project on 3D reconstruction of architectural buildings. This self-calibration method assumes that the principal point is known, the camera has square pixels and has no skew. It allows 3D shape to be reconstructed from two images while giving the camera the freedom to vary its focal length. Since the paper by Newsam et al reports only the theoretical work on camera self-calibration, in this paper, we evaluate the focal lengths obtained from their method with both synthetic data and real data. In real data where known 3D data are available, Tsai's calibration method is used for comparison. Our experimental results show that the focal lengths from the two methods differed by less than 5% and the reconstructed 3D shape was very good in that angles were well preserved. Future research will focus on improvement of 3D reconstruction in the presence of small image noise and further develop this method into a package for 3D reconstruction of buildings to be used by a layperson.

1. Introduction

It is now widely known that given a sufficient number of corresponding points the fundamental matrix F can be recovered from corresponding points alone. The 7 degrees of freedom property of F allows only 5 extrinsic parameters and 2 intrinsic parameters to be retrieved. To estimate more intrinsic camera parameters one must approach the problem by considering more images (of a static scene) while keeping the camera setting invariant [1] or assume that certain properties of the cameras are known (e.g. no skew, the pixels are square). In the latter approach, an additional assumption that the principal point is known has been incorporated [2, 7, 8]. This latter approach can be taken to be camera self-calibration for a partially calibrated camera whose focal length[1] is variable or camera self-calibration for two distinct partially-calibrated cameras.

The primary aim of our project is to reconstruct architectural buildings from partially calibrated images. The system to be built will be semi-automatic in that prominent image features will be automatically detected by a feature detector but a human operator will be involved to do some manual editing to the image correspondences, if necessary. More image feature correspondences will be automatically established, after the epipolar geometry is recovered, to achieve a dense reconstruction.

From a pair of images taken by a partially calibrated camera (We will not distinguish the case where two cameras are involved with the case where one camera which undergoes motion and whose focal length is variable. For a scene that contains an architectural building, the scene is static and the two cases above are identical) to the final metric reconstruction, a number of steps are involved: *(i)* partially calibrate the camera to estimate the principal point, *(ii)* estimate the epipolar geometry by optimally computing the fundamental matrix, *(iii)* retrieve the two unknown focal lengths of the images involved from the fundamental matrix, *(iv)* compute the extrinsic parameters or relative orientation between the two images for triangulation, *(v)* recover the 3D information of each pair of image corresponding points. To ensure that the final reconstruction in step *(v)* is optimal, the computation in all the precedent steps must be optimal. In this paper, we will present our preliminary results on the study of some of the aforementioned steps. In particular, we will use the linear self-calibration method proposed by Newsam et al [7] and will focus more

*This research was supported by the RGC grant CUHK4310/98E and in part supported by the Murdoch Special Research Grant MU.AMH.D.413.

[1] The term *focal length* here means the *effective focal length* for a pinhole camera model. This is different from the focal length of the lens in optics. Photogrammetrists use the term *principal distance* which may cause less confusion.

on step *(iii)* above. We chose to work on this method because the original paper [7] is a theoretical paper without experimental evaluation. More importantly, their method has a number of advantages as described below. First, it allows general camera motion which makes it possible for using a hand-held camera for 3D reconstruction; second, as it is an essentially linear algorithm, it is computationally efficient; third, it allows the focal length to vary so the camera can freely zoom in and out of the scene and has no restriction on its viewing distance and angle to the object(s) of interest. We hope to further develop this method into a package for 3D reconstruction of buildings used by a layperson. We will present our initial 3D reconstruction in the form of sparse 3D points at this stage. Development of a hybrid intensity-based and partial model-based stereo matching system is currently underway for dense 3D reconstructions.

2. Metric reconstruction from partially calibrated images

2.1. Estimating the camera principal point

The term *principal point* used in this paper describes the intersection point of the optical axis with the image plane. For images captured by a digital video camera, the assumption that the principal point is at the centre of the image frame has been used by many researchers, although for non-imaging process (e.g. digitised photographs) [11] the image centre is often unrelated to the principal point of the camera.

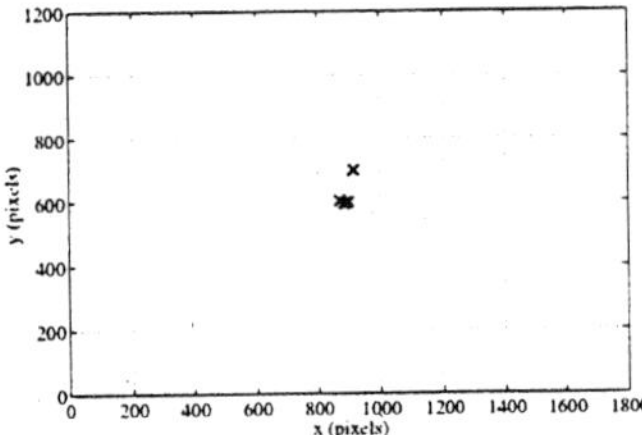

Figure 1. The estimated principal point coordinates from Tsai's calibration method.

We use a Fujitsu digital video camera with a zoom lens for our building reconstruction task. To estimate the location of the principal point of our camera, we conducted a number of experiments using Tsai's method [9] to calibrate the principal point that is required by Newsam et al's method [7]. Fig. 1 shows the estimated principal point coordinates for our digital camera whose image buffer is 1800×1200 pixels. Discarding the two principal points $(872.58, 604.06)$ and $(916.33, 698.64)$ that are slightly off the center of image frame, the average principal point was computed to be $(896.33, 598.64)$, which is very close to $(900, 600)$, the centre of the image buffer. In these experiments, the focal length varies from 995.72 to 4681.52 pixels due to zooming. Lavest et al [5] reported that the principal point was very stable under the change of the camera zoom. We would like to note that the principal point can move slightly when the camera changes its focus setting but for a good digital video camera this movement is fairly small. At the time of writing, we are conducting similar experiments with a Sony DCR-PC100 digital video camera. We hope to report further findings on the principal point of this camera in the future.

2.2. Optimal computation of F

The essential element of a good 3D reconstruction is an optimally computed fundamental matrix for the recovery of the epipolar geometry. Hartley [3] reports estimating the fundamental matrix using SVD with the image coordinates normalised. Since the linear method only minimises the algebraic error which has no meaningful geometric interpretation, nonlinear minimisation with a proper objective function must be sought. Luong and Faugeras [6] examine two minimisation criteria for the nonlinear method. These criteria, together with a few others, have been implemented by Zhang et al [12] in their `FMatrix` program. Thanks to Zhang for making the program available on the web. We were able to use it to conduct our experiments (see next section) on focal length recovery from synthetic and real data.

2.3. Linearly recovering two focal lengths from F

By assuming that the principal point is known (so the origin of the image coordinate system can be set at the principal point) and the camera contains square pixels, the camera matrices $\mathtt{A}$ and $\mathtt{A}'$ for the two viewing positions can be simplified to diagonal matrices. This allows the extrinsic parameters to be eliminated nicely from the 3×3 matrix $\mathtt{FF}^\top$ and leads to a linear self-calibration method for recovering two focal lengths. The full algorithm of this linear method and the proof of two classes of degenerate stereo configurations for self-calibration are reported in [7].

Experiments reported in this paper focus on focal length recovery using the linear self-calibration method described above. We carefully set up the experiments such that the degenerate stereo configurations (especially for class 1) mentioned in [7] were avoided (e.g. by enforcing a (small) tilt angle between the two camera orientation).

2.4. Essential matrix and triangulation

Having recovered the focal lengths, the essential matrix E can be estimated easily using the formula $\mathtt{E} = \mathtt{A}'^{-\top}\mathtt{F}\mathtt{A}^{-1}$ Our current version of triangulation for 3D reconstruction still has room for optimisation and is part of the on-going work of our project. Triangulation in the presence of image noise has been discussed by Weng et al [10] and recently by Hartley and Sturm [4]. We will conduct further investigation on this issue.

3. Experiments and discussion

For experiments with synthetic images where the true focal lengths were known, different levels of Gaussian noise of zero mean (the noise standard deviation, σ, varied from 0.1 to 1.0) were added to the true coordinates of the corresponding image points in both the left and right images. The perturbed image coordinates were passed to Zhang's `FMatrix` program for fundamental matrix computation and then focal length computation using Newsam et al's method. We had experimented the various minimisation criteria provided by `FMatrix`. We found that the criterion (`-ng`) that normalises (as mentioned in [3]) the corresponding point coordinates and minimises the gradient-weighted epipolar errors gave the best fundamental matrix, which in turn yielded the smallest focal length errors (Fig. 2(a)). The criterion (`-nnl`) that performs the normalisation and minimises the distances of corresponding points to the epipolar lines gave slightly larger focal length errors (Fig. 2(b)). The number of corresponding points used was 18. They were well distributed in the two simulated images of 1800×1200 pixels. The principal point was assumed to be known. The true focal lengths were 1720.40 and 1598.57 pixels. Each point in the plot is the average error of 50 simulations. Our experiments on synthetic data reveal that the fundamental matrix is susceptible to error in the presence of image noise. Furthermore, any perturbations to the image coordinates that are larger than 3 pixels may give an outlier effect to the fundamental matrix estimation. An outlier detection and elimination procedure is therefore essential if a fully automated building reconstruction system is desired.

(a) The `-ng` criterion (b) The `-nnl` criterion

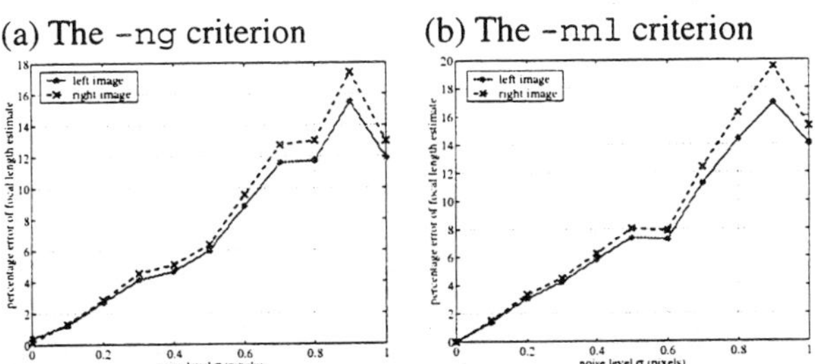

Figure 2. Percentage error of focal lengths against image noise.

Experiments on real images of indoor and outdoor scenes were also conducted. Images of indoor scenes were fully calibrated with a calibration target and the application of Tsai's method [9]. The idea was to compare the estimated focal lengths from Newsam et al [7] with those from Tsai [9] where true 3D data were available.

Fig. 3 shows a pair of images of a calibration target, with a number of corresponding points superimposed, in one of our indoor experiments. The calibration target has two orthogonal surfaces. The image on the left is frame 1 and the image on the right is frame 30 from an image sequence.

Figure 3. An image pair of a calibration target.

Feature points were detected and tracked by a corner detector with some manual editing as a post-process. Using the mean value of the estimated principal points reported in Section 2.1 for the linear algorithm [7], the estimated focal lengths for the two methods for nine different experiments are plotted in Fig. 4. The best fitted line to the computed

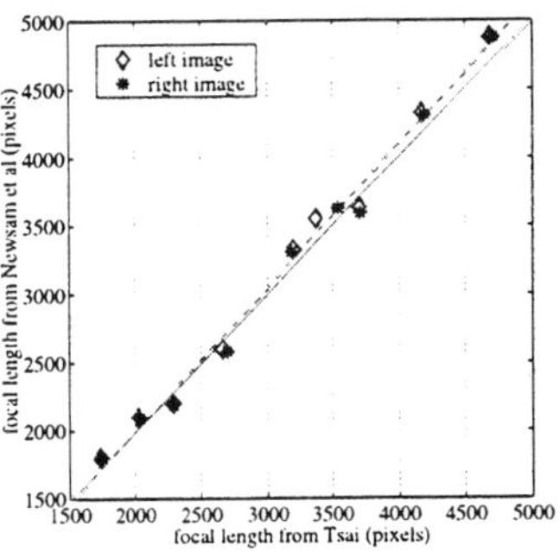

Figure 4. The estimated focal lengths from the two methods.

focal lengths is shown as a dashed line. Its slope was computed to be 0.95, which corresponds to an angle of inclination of 43.55°. The percentage error of the angle of inclination from the 45° line (solid diagonal line) is 3.23%. The vertical intercept of the fitted line is -113.33 pixels. One may argue that as we move outside the focal length interval $[1500, 5000]$ the two diagonal lines will be further apart (see Fig. 4). However, it is unlikely that the camera will have its focal length significantly below 1500 or above 5000 pixels as neither can the focal length of a camera vanish nor can it, for a perspective camera model, be infinite. Moreover, it is simply meaningless to extrapolate the errors in an error analysis this way. The results shown in Fig. 4 demonstrate that the linear algorithm [7] performs well in comparison with the calibration results from Tsai's method for a wide range of focal lengths.

The focal lengths estimated from the two methods for the nine experiments are tabulated in Table 4, in which each entry for the percentage error was computed as $\frac{f_N - f_T}{f_T}$, where f_T and f_N are the focal lengths from Tsai and Newsam et al respectively. The reconstruction of the sparse 3D points on the calibration target is shown in Fig 5. The angle between the two surfaces of the calibration target was estimated to be 88.10°, corresponding to an error of 2.11%. Since the true values of the focal lengths were not known in these real experiments and since Tsai's focal length estimates may contain small errors, the comparison above is only relative.

Left image			Right image		
Tsai	Newsam et al	%error	Tsai	Newsam et al	%error
4679.38	4877.61	4.24	4708.14	4876.17	3.57
4168.55	4325.65	3.77	4188.58	4310.44	2.91
3706.14	3632.60	−1.98	3712.18	3593.14	−3.21
3375.03	3549.70	5.18	3544.41	3628.50	2.37
3201.23	3323.73	3.83	3184.26	3307.75	3.88
2657.89	2598.74	−2.23	2697.37	2581.35	−4.30
2290.41	2201.54	−3.88	2287.37	2192.26	−4.16
2025.87	2097.49	3.54	2038.49	2093.15	2.68
1730.10	1803.67	4.25	1732.42	1802.12	4.02

Table 1. The computed focal lengths (in pixels) for the 9 image pairs.

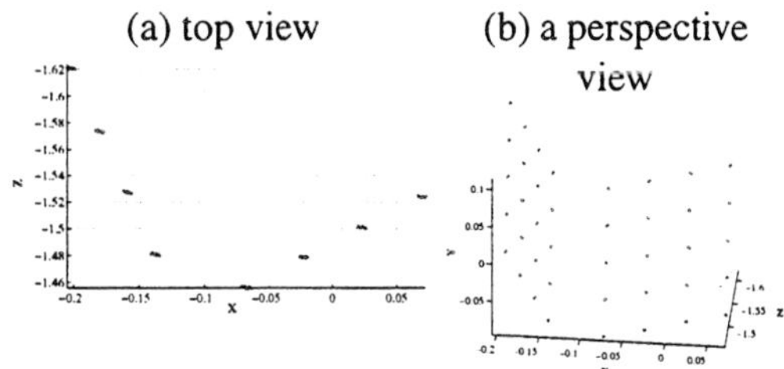

Figure 5. Metric reconstruction of the calibration target.

Fig. 6 shows a pair of images and the metric reconstruction of a building which has a large curved surface whose shape is a section of a cylinder. Using the self-calibration method, the focal lengths of the left and right images were computed to be 1804.30 and 1841.90 pixels. A good conic fitting program will be required to assess the reconstructed 3D shape in this experiment.

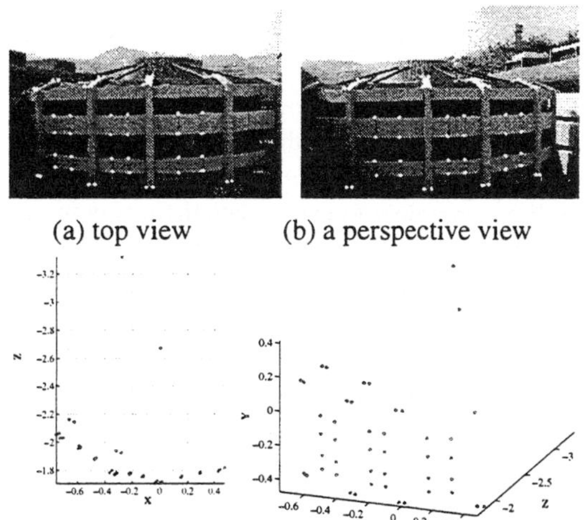

Figure 6. An image pair and the metric reconstruction of a building.

4. Conclusion

The linear method of Newsam et al [7] for recovering focal lengths in self-calibration has a number of advantages as discussed in the Introduction section of this paper. Our preliminary results show that the method gives good estimates of the focal lengths if the fundamental matrix has been accurately computed. We have also shown that using the computed focal lengths the 3D structure of a building can be achieved with a sufficiently good accuracy for visualisation. We believe that the reconstruction can be further improved if an optimal triangulation procedure is adopted. At the time of preparing this manuscript, we have not been able to achieve focal length estimation using other self-calibration methods, such as those of Hartley [2] and Pollefeys et al [8]. This will be part of our future research, in addition to the requirement to develop and enhance our method into an easy-to-use package for 3D reconstruction of buildings.

References

[1] O. D. Faugeras, Q. T. Luong, and S. J. Maybank. Camera Self-Calibration: Theory and Experiments. In *Proc. ECCV*, pages 321–334, May 1992.

[2] R. I. Hartley. Estimation of Relative Camera Positions for Uncalibrated Cameras. In *Proc. ECCV*, pages 579–587, May 1992.

[3] R. I. Hartley. In Defence of the 8-point Algorithm. In *Proc. ICCV*, pages 1064–1070, Jun 1995.

[4] R. I. Hartley and P. Sturm. Triangulation. In *ARPA*, 1994.

[5] J.-M. Lavest, G. Rives, and M. Dhome. Three-Dimensional Reconstruction by Zooming. *IEEE Trans. on Robotics and Automation*, 9(2):196–207, April 1993.

[6] Q. T. Luong and O. D. Faugeras. The Fundamental matrix: Theory, Algorithms, and Stability Analysis. *IJCV*, 17:43–75, 1996.

[7] G. N. Newsam, D. Q. Huynh, M. J. Brooks, and H.-P. Pan. Recovering Unknown Focal Lengths in Self-Calibration: An Essentially Linear Algorithm and Degenerate Configurations. In *International Archives of Photogrammetry and Remote Sensing*, volume XXXI, part B3, commission III, pages 575–580, Jul 1996.

[8] M. Pollefeys, R. Koch, and L. V. Gool. Self-Calibration and Metric Reconstruction in spite of Varying and Unknown Internal Camera Parameters. In *Proc. ICCV*, pages 90–95, Jan 1998.

[9] R. Y. Tsai. A Versatile Camera Calibration Technique For High-Accuracy 3D Machine Vision Metrology Using Off-The-Shelf TV Cameras And Lenses. *IEEE Journal of Robotics and Automation*, RA-3(4):323–344, Aug 1987.

[10] J. Weng, T. S. Huang, and N. Ahuja. *Motion and Structure from Image Sequences*. Springer-Verlag, 1993.

[11] R. G. Willson and S. A. Shafer. What is the Center of the Image? In *Proc. CVPR*, pages 670–671, 1993.

[12] Z. Zhang, R. Deriche, O. Faugeras, and Q.-T. Luong. A Robust Technique for Matching Two Uncalibrated Images through the Recovery of the Unknown Epipolar Geometry. *Artificial Intelligence*, 75(1-2):87–120, 1995.

Three-Dimensional Image Construction for Non-Destructive Testing Aided by Fuzzy Logic

Takashi MATSUMOTO[1)], Ken'ichi OHTA[1)], Yutaka HATA[1)], and Kazuhiko TANIGUCHI[2)]
[1)]*Department of Computer Engineering, Himeji Institute of Technology,* [2)]*Kinden Co., Ltd.*
matumoto@comp.eng.himeji-tech.ac.jp

Abstract

In this paper, we propose a fuzzy inference based method to visualize three-dimensional (3-D) structure of a tube buried in a concrete. The nondestructive testing (NDT) with pulse-radar, which makes it possible to non-destructively unmask tubes in a concrete, is one of the most remarkable techniques of NDT. However only expert can interpret the scanned data. In our work, we represent such expert's knowledge with fuzzy if-then rules. First, the method estimates candidate points of a tube on the scanned data. Second, 3-D links of the candidate points are constructed by inferring the continuousness of the tube. Thus, this method can extract the internal structure of the concrete. Our experimental result expressed the 3-D structure of tubes with high accuracy by comparing with the radiograph result.

1. Introduction

Breakage of a buried tube such as steel pipe, reinforcing bar and resin tube causes a serious problem in passing through the floor and wall for reinforcement or renewal. It is therefore required to view these internal structures. A nondestructive testing (NDT) has been used as a method for visualizing the internal structure. NDT with radiograph has been used in general method. However, it has a danger for treating the radiation. Moreover, the radiograph method is not only extensively time- consuming but also expensive. Therefore, NDT with pulse- radar [1]-[4] has been received considerable attention as one of the most effective techniques to nondestructively unmask tubes in a concrete structure. The expert knowledge is required to understand the raw scan data.

In this paper, we propose a method for visualizing three-dimensional (3-D) internal structure with fuzzy inference. The method is based on expert's knowledge of the pattern, the knowledge of intensity, and the knowledge of propagation delay on the scan data. We represent them with fuzzy if-then rules [5]-[7]. Our method consists of two steps. In the first step, the method extracts candidate of a tube on the scanned data with respect to the intensity pattern. In the second step, 3-D links of the candidate points can be constructed by inferring the continuous shape of the tube from 3-D scan data. Consequently, we can observe the internal structure of the concrete in this 3D visualization system. The experimental result could express the internal structure of the concrete with high accuracy by comparing with the radiograph result.

2. Scan Method

The raw scan data were obtained from a pulse-radar sensor (IRON SEEKER, KOMATSU CO., frequency approx. 1GHz,

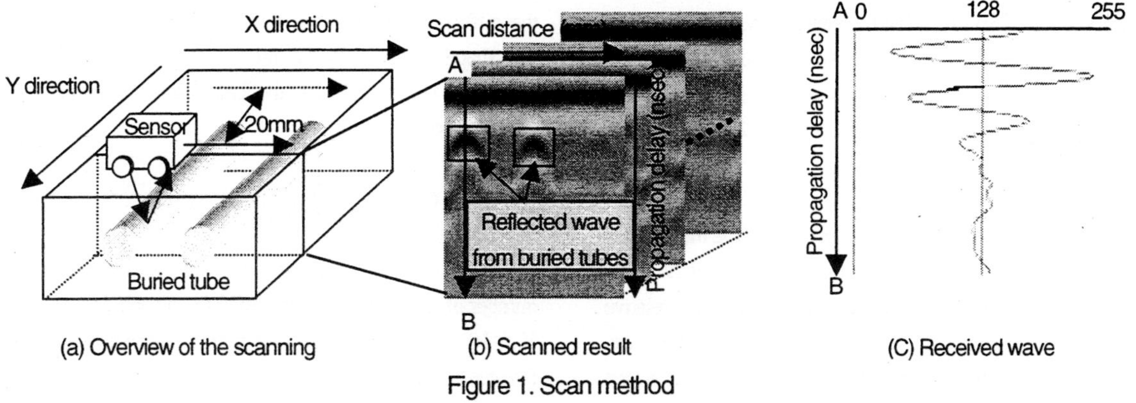

(a) Overview of the scanning (b) Scanned result (C) Received wave

Figure 1. Scan method

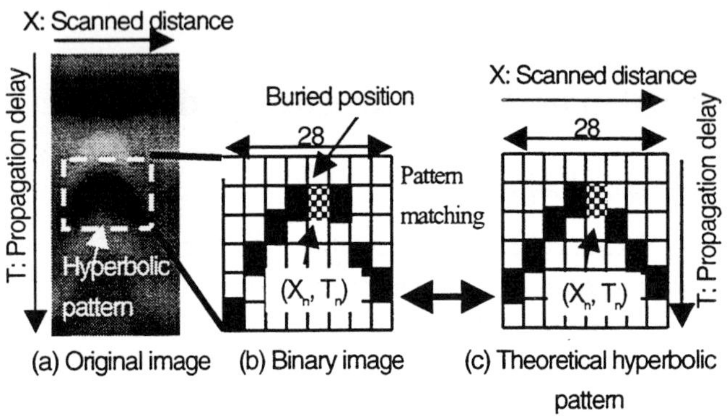

Figure 2. Knowledge of the hyperbolic pattern.

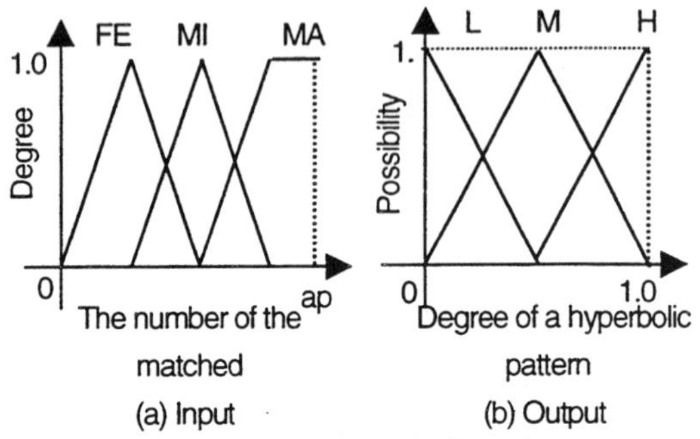

Figure 3. Membership function for the hyperbolic pattern.

pulse length=0.7ns, sampling at every 5mm) running on the surface of a material shown in Figure 1. The sensor independently moved along the axes, X and Y, at every 20mm in the scanning region. Amplitude of reflected wave appeared as intensity of an image and ranged between 0 and 255. Consequently, we obtained the cross section image data.

3. Estimation of the Buried Position

This section introduces expert's knowledge of the pulse-radar image to estimate the position of tubes in the image. They can be expressed by fuzzy inference [5]-[7]. We employ three types of knowledge: the hyperbolic pattern, intensity and propagation delay to do so.

3.1. Knowledge of the Hyperbolic Pattern

A tube in the image has a hyperbolical pattern as shown in Figure 2(a) [3],[4]. By replacing local minimum points of the intensity with "1" and replacing another points with "0" for each received wave the original image is binarized as shown in Figure 2(b). At the top of the hyperbolic pattern, a tube will be found. The recognition of the pattern is performed with matching the pattern with a theoretical hyperbolic pattern shown in Figure 2(c) [4]. The theoretical pattern in which the top of pattern is located at the point (X_n, T_n) is formed by,

$$\begin{cases} T = 2\times(\sqrt{(X-X_n)^2+(Y+D)^2}-D)/V \\ Y=(V\times T_n)/2, \quad V=C/\varepsilon_r \end{cases}$$

where notation T is the propagation delay at X, Y is the distance between the surface of a tube and one of a material, V is the propagation velocity, C is the velocity of light, ε_r is the relative permittivity of the material, and D is the radius of the tube. Let the number of matched points between the pattern on the binary image shown in Figure 2(b) and the theoretical pattern shown in Figure 2(c) be α. We define fuzzy if-then rules [5]-[7], to express the knowledge of the hyperbolic pattern,

Rule 1: If α is MA (Majority) then the μ_{HP} is H (High),
Rule 2: If α is MI (Middle) then the μ_{HP} is M (Middle),
Rule 3: If α is FE (Few) then the μ_{HP} is L (Low).

These membership functions such as MA, MI, FE, L, M, and H are shown in Figure 3. In this figure, ap is the number of the all point of the theoretical pattern. The inference result U_{HP} is obtained by a min-max inference,

$$U_{HP}(\alpha)=[\alpha\wedge MA\wedge H]\vee[\alpha\wedge MI\wedge M]\vee[\alpha\wedge FE\wedge L].$$

The center of gravity, μ_{GHP}, of the output fuzzy set is the degree for a tube with respect to the knowledge of the hyperbolic pattern.

3.2. Knowledge of The Intensity

A tube in the image has low intensity. The feature can be expressed by a cone, in which the top is the local minimum point of the intensity, as shown in Figure 4. We will find a tube at the local minimum point. The similar shape is often generated by the interference of reflected wave. We can find the difference between the tubes and the interference below. The shape produced by the interference is steeper than one by the tube. We can calculate the feature by the average gradient, $G_{ave.}$, at a point (X_0, Y_0) by,

$$G_{ave.}(X_0,Y_0)=\frac{1}{n}\left(\sum_{1=1}^{n}\frac{Z_1-Z_0}{\left((X_0-X_1)^2+(Y_0-Y_1)^2\right)^{1/2}}\right),$$

where Z_0 is the intensity at the point (X_0, Y_0), and n is the number of neighboring points satisfying a condition $|(X, Y)-(X_n, Y_n)|<10$. The following if-then rules are derived to express the features.

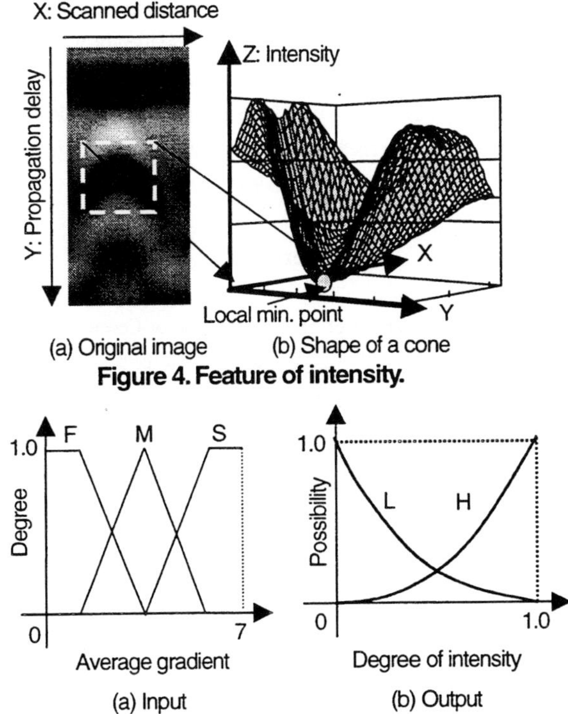

Figure 4. Feature of intensity.

Figure 5. Membership function for the intensity.

Rule 1: If $G_{ave.}$ is S (Steep) then the $\mu_{LMin.}$ is L (Low).
Rule 2: If $G_{ave.}$ is M (Middle) then the $\mu_{LMin.}$ is H (High).
Rule 3: If $G_{ave.}$ is F (Flat) then the $\mu_{LMin.}$ is L (Low).

Figure 5 shows the fuzzy membership functions. The inference result, $U_{LMin.}$ is obtain by a min-max inference,

$$U_{LMin}(G_{ave})=[G_{ave}\wedge S\wedge L]\vee[G_{ave}\wedge M\wedge H]\vee[G_{ave}\wedge F\wedge L]\ .$$

The center of gravity, $\mu_{GLMin.}$, of the output fuzzy sets is the degree for a tube with respect to the knowledge of the intensity.

3.3. Knowledge of the Propagation Delay

The above feature mentioned is also changed by the interfering of reflected waves. We show the relationship between features and the propagation delay as follows.

When the propagation delay is relatively short, the feature of the hyperbolic pattern appears clearly, and the feature of the intensity is unclear. When the propagation delay is relatively long, the feature of the hyperbolic pattern is unclear, and the feature of the intensity appears clearly. To express this fact, we combine the inference results of the degree for the feature of the hyperbolic pattern, μ_{GHP}, and for the feature of the intensity, μ_{GLMin} as follows,

$$\mu_{TD} = \min(1, wh\times\mu_{GHP} + wl\times\mu_{GLMin})$$

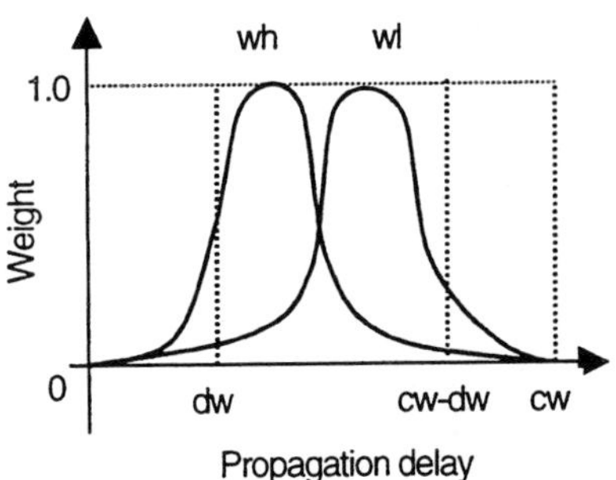

Figure 6. Determination of the weight for μ_{GHP} and μ_{GLMin}.

The weights wh and wl are defined in Figure 6. In this figure, cw and dw is the thickness of the material and the thickness of 'the cover' respectively. The cover is the region located from the surface to the closest reinforcing bar and consists of only concrete. In many case, the thickness of the material and the cover are preliminary known such as ultrasonic, electro-magnetic induction and so on, of course, the thickness can be measured when we scan the material. We thus obtain candidate points whose total degree, μ_{TD}, is higher than 0.5 to apply this process to input data.

4. 3-D Reconstruction of the Candidate Points

3-D links of the candidate points are found to visualize the 3-D continuous shapes of the tube. The method employs the knowledge of directivity of a tube. The tube runs straight or the bend rate is not large, and it reaches to the edges of the images. Thus, we calculate the cosine for expressing the directivity. According to the knowledge, the tube construction method is as follows.

Step 0: Set all candidate points in a 3-D space.

Step 1: Determine a point, $P_b(x, y, z)$, which is located near a boundary of scan region, as a base point. Set m=0, where m is the number of linked points.

Step 2: Search neighboring points, $PT_n(x_n, y_n, z_n)$, satisfying $|P_b - PT_n|<30$. They are regarded as target points. The notation n denotes the number of neighboring points.

Step 3: For neighboring points obtained in step 2, calculate the cosine, $\cos\theta_i$, the reference vector, **R**, with the direction vectors, $\mathbf{D}_i$. **R** and $\mathbf{D}_i$ are obtained as

$$\mathbf{R}=\begin{cases}\mathbf{P} & (m<3)\\ \bar{L}_m-\bar{L}_{m-2} & (m\geq 3)\end{cases},\quad \mathbf{D}_i=\vec{PT}_i-\vec{P}_b\ ,$$

where **P** is a perpendicular vector to the search direction, m is the number of linked points, i is the number of neighboring points ranged 1 and n, and L is linked point which satisfy $L_m=P_b$.

Step 4: Link the base point with the target point, If the $\cos\theta_i >$ 0.5 and $\cos\theta_i$ is the largest of all i ($1 \le i \le n$).

Step 5: If the target point was linked with the base point, the linked point is compiled into next base point and set $m \rightarrow m+1$, and go to step 2, otherwise go to step 1. If all set points are searched this process then stop.

The above steps can extract the links that almost reach to edge from another edge.

5. Experimental Result

Our method was applied to a material. Scan region was $400 \times 400mm^2$. Relative permittivity was 6.5, and the thickness of the concrete was 150mm (2.1nsec), and the thickness of the cover was 35mm (0.5nsec). The 3-D rendered image of the experimental results is shown in Figure 7(a). Our result is compared with the photo before concreted shown in Figure 7(b) and the radiograph shown in Figure 7(c) for evaluating the accuracy of our method. Our method can express the straight tube as a straight tube and the bent tube as a bent tube, for example tube "A" and tube "B". From the result of comparison, our method could visualize the internal structure with high accuracy. Our result also could express the depth information of tubes, which was difficult to understand in the radiograph. It required about 30 seconds to visualize the 3-D shape of the tube, running on personal computer (CPU 400MHz, 256MB Memory).

6. Conclusion and future work

In this paper, we proposed a method to visualize 3-D structure of tubes with fuzzy inference. Our method can estimate candidate points of a tube on scanned data represented by fuzzy rules. The candidate points are linked as a tube in 3-D space by evaluating the connectivity. Consequently, we obtain 3-D internal structure of tubes in the concrete. The obtained result can express the tube with high accuracy. It remains as a future work that our method will be applied to other structures to verify the accuracy and the robustness.

References

[1] P. Shaw, "Assessment of The Deterioration of Concrete in NPP –Causes, Effects and Investigate Methods," Proceedings of the joint EC OECD IAEA Specialists, 1997.

[2] A. L. Bartos, T. J. Gill, Jr. and T. Lyon, "Waveform Mapping of Piezoelectric Transducer Impulse Responses for Multi-Transducer Pattern Recognition –Based Ultrasonic NDE Systems," Materials Science Forum, vol. 210-213, pp. 863-870, 1996.

[3] T. Abe, Y. Kanemitsu, Y. Ichimura, A. Okamoto, "Underground Rader for Buried Object Investigation," Komatsugiho, vol.35, no.124, pp.130-137, 1989.

[4] Y. Nagashima, H. Yoshida, J. Masuda, K. Komatsu, "A Estimation of Buried Pipe Location by Using Zero-Crossed Synthetic Aperture," The Journal of The Institute of Electronic, Information, and Communication Engineers, vol. J76-B-II, no.7, pp.634-640, 1993.

[5] L. A. Zadeh, Fuzzy sets and applications, John Wiley and Sons, 1987.

[6] S. Kobashi, N. Kamiura , Y. Hata and M. Ishikawa, "Automatic robust threshold finding aided by fuzzy information granulation," Proc. of IEEE 1997 Int. Conf. on Image Processing, vol. 1, pp.711-714, Oct. 1997.

[7] Y. Hata, S. Kobashi, N. Kamiura and M. Ishikawa, "Fuzzy Logic Approach to 3D Magnetic Resonance Image Segmentation," Information Processing in Medical Imaging, Lecture Notes in Comp. Sci., Vol. 1230, pp. 387-392, Jun. 1997

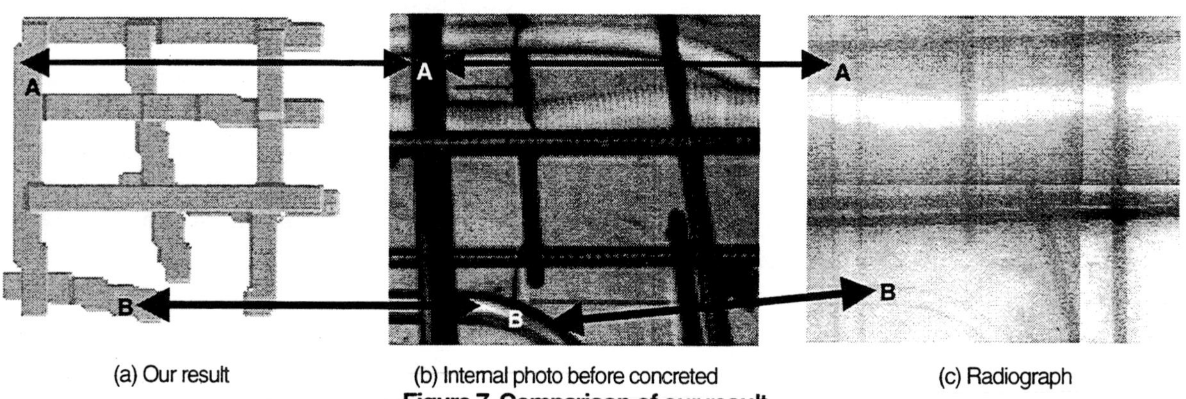

(a) Our result (b) Internal photo before concreted (c) Radiograph

Figure 7. Comparison of our result

Adaptive Human Motion Tracking using Non-synchronous Multiple Viewpoint Observations

Akira Utsumi Howard Yang Jun Ohya
ATR Media Integration & Communications Research Laboratories
2-2-2 Hikaridai Seikacho Sorakugun, Kyoto 619-0288, Japan
{utsumi,yhoward,ohya}@mic.atr.co.jp

Abstract

In this paper, we propose an adaptive human tracking system with non-synchronous multiple observations. Our system consists of three types of processes, discovering node for detecting newly appeared person, tracking node for tracking each target person, and observation node for processing one viewpoint (camera) images. We have multiple observation nodes and each node works fully independently. The tracking node integrates observed information based on reliability evaluation. Both observation conditions (number of cameras, relative distance between a human and cameras, extent of occlusion, etc.) and human motion states (walking, standing, sitting) are considered in the evaluation. Matching between tracking models and observed image features are performed in each observation node based on the position, size and color similarities of each 2D image. Due to the non-synchronous property, this system is highly scalable for increasing the detection area and number of observing nodes. Experimental results for some indoor scenes are also described.

1. Introduction

Detecting/understanding human behavior is a challenging research domain in computer vision. Many vision researchers have already proposed human motion detection/tracking methods [1, 2, 3, 4, 5, 6]. Most of these systems deal with the 3-D tracking of human movements. Dominant applications include man-machine interfaces using body movements, remote surveillance systems, and so on.

In vision-based human tracking, the most significant problem is occlusion. As a human body is a three dimensional articulated object, the appearance of a human body can drastically change according to view angle differences. In addition, when two or more persons are in the scene, one person can easily occlude other persons.

One powerful solution to avoid/reduce such occlusion problems is to employ a multiple-viewpoint approach. Some researchers have already proposed multiple camera based human tracking systems and shown the effects of this approach [7, 8, 9, 10]. However, most multiple-viewpoint systems assume simultaneous observations. In the synchronous systems, the total performance becomes worse with an increasing number of cameras, because the slowest image process determines the total throughput. Also, the redundancy among multiple observations increases with an increasing number of cameras.

In this paper, we propose a human tracking system with multiple-camera-based non-synchronous observation. In the system, each camera works fully independently. Using non-synchronous observation, our system can observe a target scene more densely in a time axis and have more scalability for the number of viewpoints. Multiple image features (position, size and color) help the integration process of multiple observations in the system.

2. System Overview

Figure 1 shows the configuration of our system. Here, each camera system (observation node) has its own processor and input images are processed independently. At each

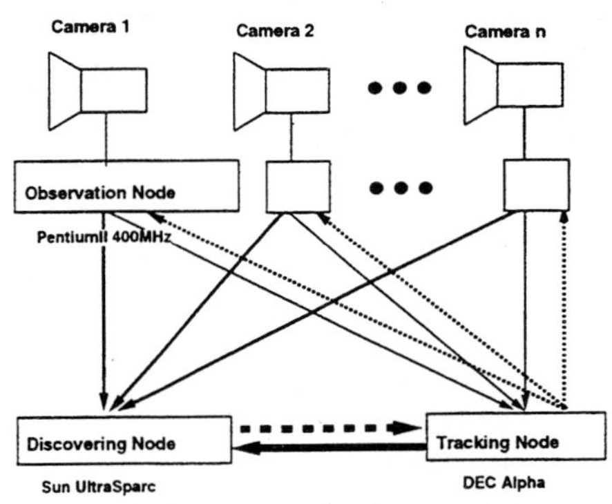

Figure 1. System Diagram

observation node, matchings between image features and tracking targets are determined based on the estimated 2-D positions, sizes and colors of the targets that are sent from the tracking node. After the matching process, the feature information corresponding to the targets is sent back to the tracking node to update the tracking. The remaining (unmatched) features are sent to a discovering node.

The discovering node detects people that newly appear in the scene based on the unmatched image features sent from the observation nodes. This information is sent to the tracking node to invoke a new tracking process.

The tracking node starts and updates each tracking with the information sent by the discovering node and observation nodes.

Following two sections give more details about the tracking and observation nodes.

3. Tracking Node

3.1. Observation model

First, we give a observation model for a target position. Figure 2 shows the observation model used in this system. The target object located at $\boldsymbol{X}$ in the world coordinates is projected on to the image plane of the camera at $\boldsymbol{C}$. θ is the angle between the target projection line $(C_i - X)$ and the $Y - Z$ plane. φ is the angle between the Z axis and the projection of the line $C_i - X$ to the $Y - Z$ plane. $\boldsymbol{R}_\varphi \boldsymbol{R}_\theta$ denotes the rotation matrix that rotates the line $C_i - X$ to parallel the Z axis. As a result, one observation can be expressed as follows.

$$\boldsymbol{H}_x \boldsymbol{R}_\varphi \boldsymbol{R}_\theta \boldsymbol{C}_i = \boldsymbol{H}_x \boldsymbol{R}_\varphi \boldsymbol{R}_\theta \boldsymbol{X} + \boldsymbol{e}_x. \tag{1}$$

$\boldsymbol{e}_x$ is the observation error (average 0, covariance matrix $\boldsymbol{V}_x$). In 3D,

$$\boldsymbol{H}_x = \begin{bmatrix} 1 & 0 & 0 \\ 0 & 1 & 0 \end{bmatrix}. \tag{2}$$

Furthermore, the target object is considered to have physical properties that can be observed as image features (especially, size (body height) and cloth color information in this case). Here, we express the properties as $\boldsymbol{S}$ ($\boldsymbol{S} = [C_h C_s C_v h]'$, average hue, saturation and intensity values of shirt region, a 3-D hight). $\boldsymbol{S}$ is observed as $\boldsymbol{s}$ in images, and the observation is expressed as follows.

$$\boldsymbol{s} = \boldsymbol{H}_s \boldsymbol{S} + \boldsymbol{e}_s, \tag{3}$$

where, $\boldsymbol{e}_s$ expresses the observation error like $\boldsymbol{e}_x$ in (1) (the covariance matrix is $\boldsymbol{V}_s$).

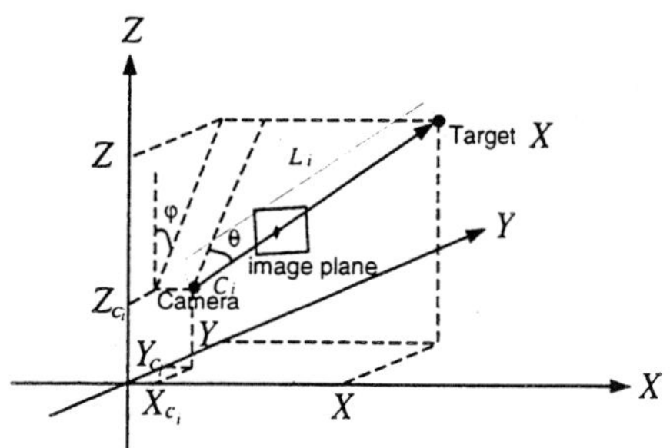

Figure 2. Observation Model

3.2. Transition (motion) model with state evaluation

Assuming a constant velocity for the target motion, the position and velocity of the target can be expressed as $[\ \boldsymbol{X}\ \ \dot{\boldsymbol{X}}\ ]'$. (Its covariance matrix is $\boldsymbol{P}_X$.) Here, $\dot{\boldsymbol{X}}$ expresses the target's velocity vector. Then, the position and velocity change in a small time difference can be described like this.

$$\begin{bmatrix} \boldsymbol{X}_{t_{n+1}} \\ \dot{\boldsymbol{X}}_{t_{n+1}} \end{bmatrix} = \boldsymbol{F}_X \begin{bmatrix} \boldsymbol{X}_{t_n} \\ \dot{\boldsymbol{X}}_{t_n} \end{bmatrix} + \boldsymbol{w}_{X,\Delta t}. \tag{4}$$

The transition matrix $\boldsymbol{F}_X$ is as follows in 3D.

$$\boldsymbol{F}_X = \begin{bmatrix} 1 & 0 & 0 & \Delta t & 0 & 0 \\ 0 & 1 & 0 & 0 & \Delta t & 0 \\ 0 & 0 & 1 & 0 & 0 & \Delta t \\ 0 & 0 & 0 & 1 & 0 & 0 \\ 0 & 0 & 0 & 0 & 1 & 0 \\ 0 & 0 & 0 & 0 & 0 & 1 \end{bmatrix}. \tag{5}$$

Here,

$$\Delta t = t_{n+1} - t_n. \tag{6}$$

$\boldsymbol{w}_{X,\Delta t}$ expresses the fluctuations of the velocity for time Δt.

Furthermore, we consider the transition of physical properties $\boldsymbol{S}$ in a time sequence as follows. (Its covariance matrix is $\boldsymbol{P}_S$.)

$$\boldsymbol{S}_{t_{n+1}} = \boldsymbol{I}_S \boldsymbol{S}_{t_n} + \boldsymbol{w}_{S,\Delta t}. \tag{7}$$

Here, $\boldsymbol{I}_S$ is a unit matrix having the same dimension as $\boldsymbol{S}$ (We assume the properties are constant). $\boldsymbol{w}_{S,\Delta t}$ denotes the transition fluctuations of the physical properties. The value $\boldsymbol{w}_X$ and $\boldsymbol{w}_S$ are controlled based on the estimated motion state of the target.

From the equation (1), (3), (4) and (7), each observation node can get the estimated 2-D feature values for the matching process.

3.3. Motion State Detection

The motion state detection process is simple in the current system. It is mainly based on human height observation. As mentioned before, the height of the body is tracked as a physical property in the tracking process. If the height becomes significantly small, it is decided as 'sitting'. Otherwise, the state is either 'standing' or 'walking'. These two states are separated based on the target motion. The detection should be based on primitive 2D image processing, but the current implementation simply utilizes motion vector $\dot{X}$ to distinguish these two states. If $\dot{X}$ is larger than a threshold value, it is decided as 'walking'.

Figure 3 shows a result of the state detection.

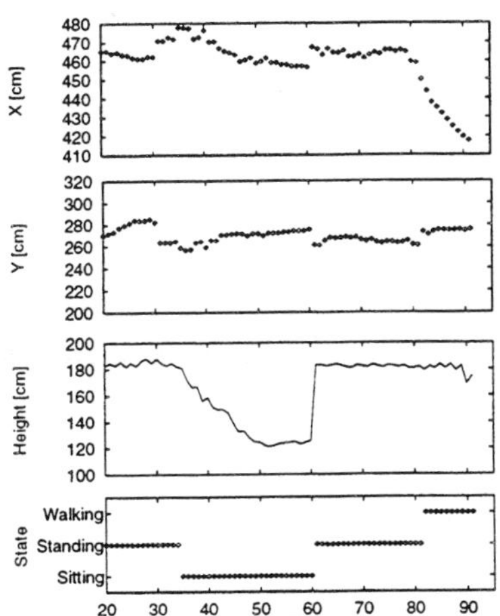

Figure 3. State Tracking Result (From the top: X position, Y position, human height and detected motion state for one person's motion.)

3.4. Tracking Algorithm

We introduce a Kalman filter based algorithm to integrate non-synchronized observations. The tracking models (X, $\dot{X}$, S) are updated using both the observation model and the transition model.

The size of the observation error becomes larger with increasing distance from the observing camera. We express the error size as follows.

$$V_t = \frac{\bar{L}}{l_i} V \simeq \frac{L}{l_i} V. \tag{8}$$

Here, L is the distance between the target and camera c; l_i is the focal length of the camera. We approximate the distance with $\bar{L}$ (the distance between C and $\overline{X}$) instead of L, because the actual distance L is not applicable.

Using the observation results (1) and the estimation (4), the position and velocity of the target $\begin{bmatrix} X & \dot{X} \end{bmatrix}$ can be estimated as follows.

$$\begin{bmatrix} \hat{X}_t \\ \hat{\dot{X}}_t \end{bmatrix} = \hat{P}_{X,t} \left(\overline{P}^{-1}_{X,t} \begin{bmatrix} \overline{X}_t \\ \dot{\overline{X}}_t \end{bmatrix} + \sum_i R_{\varphi,t} R_{\theta,t} H'_X \left(V^{-1}_{X,t} \right) H_X \left(R_{\varphi,t} R_{\theta,t} \right)' C \right). \tag{9}$$

Here,

$$\hat{P}^{-1}_{X,t} = \overline{P}^{-1}_{X,t} + R_{\varphi_t} R_{\theta_t} H'_X \left(V^{-1}_{X,t} \right) H_X \left(R_{\varphi_t} R_{\theta_t} \right)'. \tag{10}$$

Similarly, the physical properties S can be estimated.

The updating process is performed for every observation except for the occluded one.

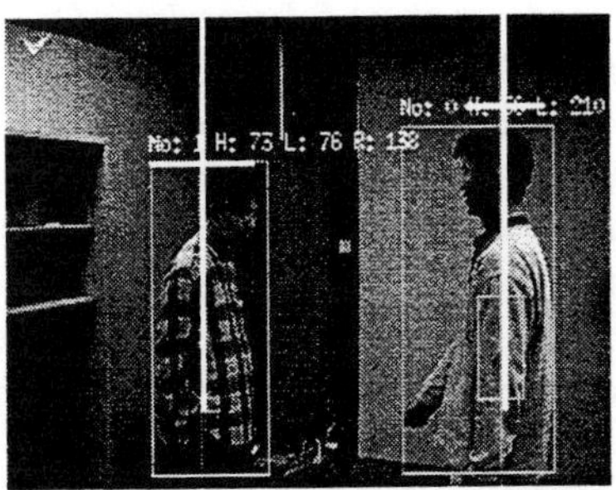

Figure 4. Feature Extraction (Larger rectangles are the areas including a human body. Cross signs are COGs detected. Smaller rectangles are regions used for average color calculation. Vertical and horizontal thick lines are the estimated 2-D positions and height respectively.)

4. Observation Node

4.1. Feature Extraction

This section describes the feature extraction process that takes place in each observation node.

We first perform region segmentation on the input images and separate the images into two regions (a human region and a background region). This segmentation is based on sequential image based adaptation [11]. After that, we apply distance transformation to the segmentation results. Consequently, each pixel has a certain distance from its nearest boundary pixel. We extract those pixels with the maximum value in the transformed image as COG (center of gravity).

Then, the average color values are calculated for a region neighboring the COG point.

4.2. Feature Matching at an Observation Node

As the tracking model for each human is a given as a Gaussian distribution (X and S. Section 3), the estimations of the observation positions are also given as Gaussian distributions (x, s). The matching between the image features and tracking models is based on the Mahalanobis distance between them.

If some unmatched COGs remain after the process, they must belong to a new object. Such data will be sent to the matching node.

5. Experiments

The following experiments were performed to evaluate our system.

Six observation nodes were placed around the scene. Each observation node include a camera and a PC (PentiumII, 400MHz). The speed of image processing in each observation model is about 5 frames/sec. One discovering node and one tracking node were connected through a network. All of the cameras were calibrated in advance.

In this experiment, two subjects are walking in the scene in different directions. Figure 5 shows the path the targets in the observation area and Figure 6 contains the data graphs of target's height, and HSV values during the experiment. As can be seen, each target was properly tracked based on the non-synchronous observations.

Also, our system stores the human activities into a database. Figure 7 shows an snapshot image of the database browser.

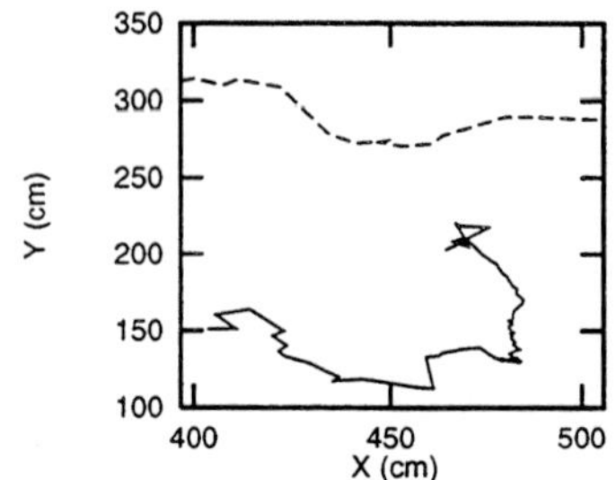

Figure 5. Tracking Result for Two Person

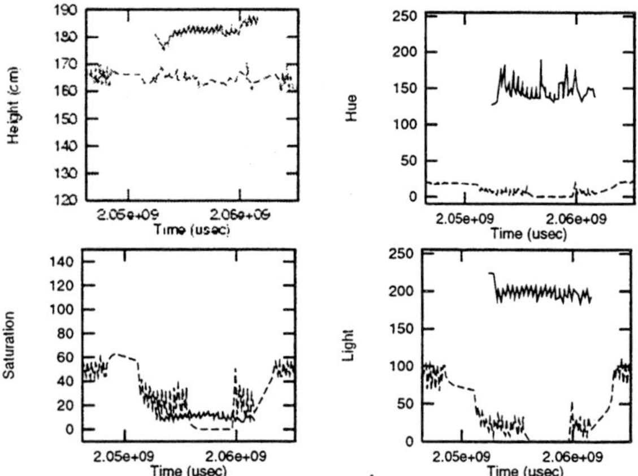

Figure 6. Detected Properties (HSV and Human Height for Fig. 4 Scene)

6. Conclusion

This paper has proposed an adaptive human tracking system with multiple camera based non-synchronous observations. Our system detects a human motion state from observed image features. Both the observation conditions and human motion states are considered in the tracking process by evaluating observation and motion reliabilities. Experiments show examples of tracking results.

In the future, we plan to develop a viewpoint switching mechanism using tracking reliability values for effective human identification and gesture recognition.

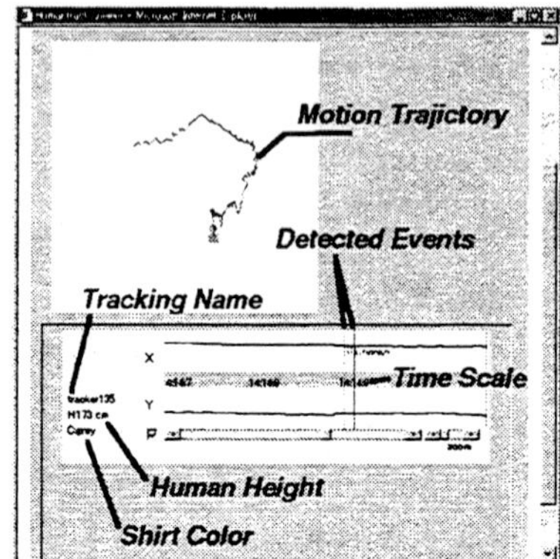

Figure 7. Database Browser (Snapshot)

References

[1] K. Rohr. Towards model-based recognition of human movements in image sequences. *CVGIP: Image Understanding*, 59(1):94–115, 1994.

[2] M. Yamamoto and K. Koshikawa. Human motion analysis based on a robot arm model. In *Proc. of CVPR*, pages 664–665, 1991.

[3] J. O'rourke and N. J. Badler. Model-based image analysis of human motion using constraint propagation. *IEEE Pattern Anal. Machine Intell.*, 2(6):522–536, 1980.

[4] Ali Azarbayejani and Alex Pentland. Real-time self-calibrating stereo person tracking using 3-d shape estimation from blob features. In *13th International Conference on Pattern Recognition*, pages 627–632, 1996.

[5] C. Wren, A. Azarbayejani, T. Darrell, and A. Pentland. Pfinder: Real-time tracking of the human body. In *SPIE proceeding vol. 2615*, pages 89–98, 1996.

[6] M. Patrick Johnson, P. Maes, and T. Darrell. Evolving visual routines. In *Proc. of Artificial Life IV*, pages 198–209, 1994.

[7] D. M. Gavrila and L. S. Davis. 3-d model-based tracking of humans in action: a multi-view approach. In *Proc. of CVPR*, pages 73–80, 1996.

[8] Q. Cai and J. K. Aggarwal. Tracking human motion using multiple cameras. In *Proc. of 13th International Conference on Pattern Recognition*, pages 68–72, 1996.

[9] Takeo Kanade, Peter Rander, and P. J. Narayanan. Virtualized reality: Constructing virtual worlds from real scenes. *IEEE MultiMedia*, 4(1):34–47, 1997.

[10] Akira Utsumi, Hiroki Mori, Jun Ohya, and Masahiko Yachida. Multiple-view-based tracking of multiple humans. In *Proc. of ICPR'98*, pages 597–601, 1998.

[11] Akira Utsumi and Jun Ohya. Hand image segmentation using sequential-image-based hierarchical adaptation. In *International Conference on Image Processing*, pages 208–211, 1997.

An Automatic Extraction and Display Method of Walking Persons' Trajectories

Shin-ichi Murakami and Akira Wada
Graduate School of Engineering, Tokyo Denki University, Japan
murakami@c.dendai.ac.jp, akira_w@ga2.so-net.ne.jp

Abstract

This paper describes an automatic extraction and display method of walking persons' trajectories which can be applied to video surveillance systems for a railway station, a convenience store and so on. We propose a method to transform 2D human images into 3D object images in real space, in order to get 3D positions of objects. The motion trajectories of walking persons are then displayed on a 2D display equipment in real time.

1. Introduction

In present days, a lot of video surveillance systems are installed in railway stations, assembly halls, convenience stores, etc. However, most of them are systems in which professional staffs recognize the motions of peoples by gazing at TV monitors. In such a system, staffs suffer much strain and furthermore, it requires high running costs.

To these kinds of systems, image recognition techniques can be effectively applied. Namely, a computer recognizes human positions and behaviors and issues alarm signals automatically in an emergency case. These techniques can alleviate the burdens of staffs and compress the running costs.

From this viewpoint, several kinds of systems, which utilize a pattern matching or an optical flow techniques have been studied [1], [2]. However, a pattern matching technique has some difficulties in its application to such an image sequence with many variations of human behaviors. An optical flow technique requires much processing time. Then, these techniques are not appropriate to a real time recognition system.

This paper proposes an automatic recognition and display system of walking persons' trajectories, which utilizes an image difference technique. Experimental results show that this technique can be applied to a system that contains several kinds of walking patterns such as crossing against-, kicking back-, and circulating patterns of people.

2. General flow of the recognition technique

Figure 1 shows the general flow diagram of our proposed method, where P_0, P_t, and P_{t-1} denote a background image frame, a present image frame and one clock past image frame, respectively.

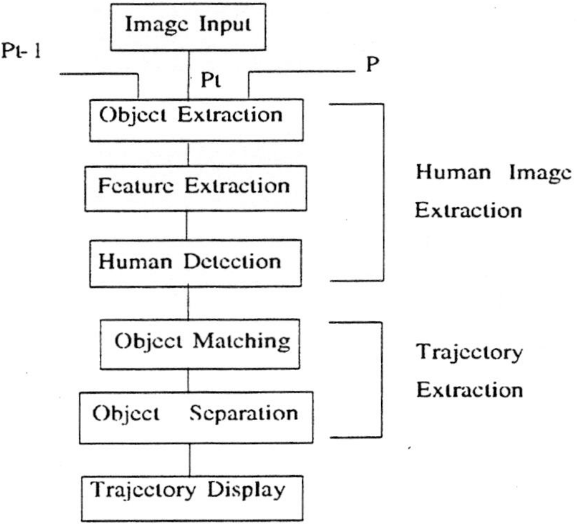

Figure 1. General flow of our proposed method

3. Extraction of human images

3.1 Extraction of moving and still objects

Surveillance images picked up by TV cameras generally contain both moving and still objects (walking and standing persons). The moving objects can be extracted by the following procedure.

Procedure 1:

(1) Generate an edge image E_b for a background frame.

(2) Generate an edge image E_t for a present frame.

(3) Calculate an edge difference image E_d between E_t and E_b.

(4) Generate an edge image E_{t-1} for a past frame.

(5) Calculate an edge difference image E'_d between E_t and E_{t-1}.

(6) Moving object can be obtained as E_d*E'_d, where "*" denotes the logical product of pixels between the two edge images.

The logical product in step (6) has effects to eliminate not only the shadows of persons in image frames but also the background portion emerged in the difference image. The still objects can be extracted by the following procedure.

Procedure 2:

(1) Calculate an edge difference image E_d between E_t and E_b.

(2) Generate the moving object image E_O by procedure 1 (6).

(3) Still object can be obtained as E_d-E_O, where "-" denotes the logical difference of pixels between the two edge images.

The logical difference in step (3) has an effect to eliminate the moving object from the difference image E_d.

(a) Background frame (b) t-1 frame

(c) Present frame (d) Extracted person image

Figure 2. Image frames containing a person

3.2 Transformation of object into a real space

In general, human images picked up by surveillance TV cameras are distorted because they are ordinary set at upper positions. Then the length of human bodies are often displayed shrunk.

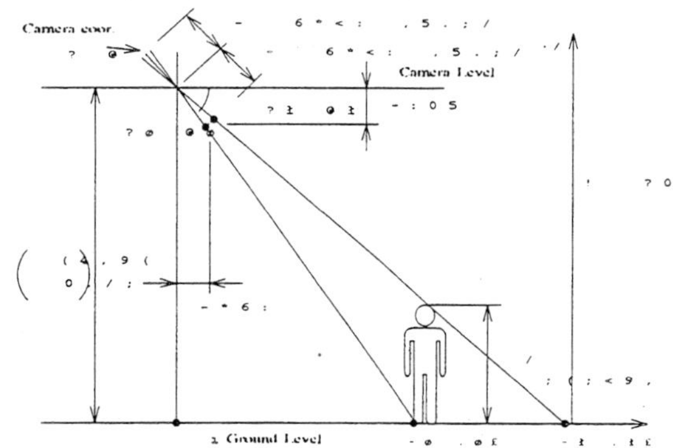

Figure 3. Camera configuration

However, the real length of human height can be retrieved by the following procedure.

Procedure 3(See Figure 3):

(1) The height h of human body can be calculated by equation (1).

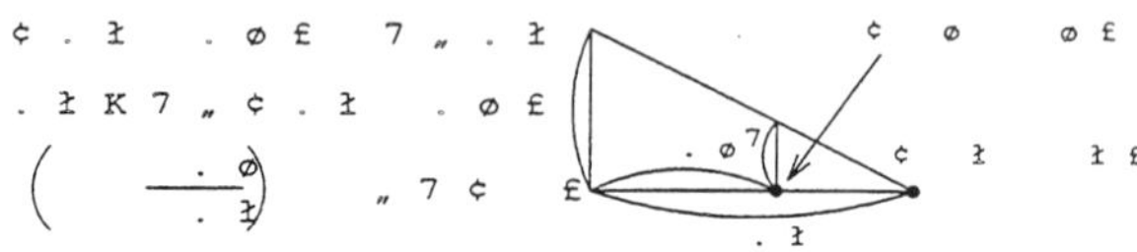

(2) The position in a real space can be represented by equation (2).

$$\left.\begin{aligned} X &= \frac{x}{f\sin\theta - y\cos\theta}H \\ Y &= \frac{f\cos\theta + y\sin\theta}{f\sin\theta - y\cos\theta}H \end{aligned}\right\}$$

Equation (1) shows that real sizes of persons can be calculated from a single shot of frame sequences.

By this procedure, we can get the real size of human height and his position in a real space. Then, the following features in a real space are defined as the attributes of every object.

Attributes of object:

(1) XY-position (standing position in a real space).

(2) Height (Length of the object)

(3) Height and width ratio of an object

(4) Symmetry degree of an object

3.3 Recognition of persons

To every extracted object image, the following recognition procedure of persons is applied.

Procedure 4:

(1) XY-position: Whether the extracted XY-position is within an allowable coordinates range in a real space or not?

(2) Height: Whether the extracted height is within an allowable height range of human body or not?

(3) Height and width ratio: Whether the extracted height and width ratio is within an allowable ratio range of human body or not?

(4) Symmetry degree: Whether the extracted symmetry degree is within an allowable symmetry degree range of human body or not?

If all these conditions are satisfied, the object is recognized as a human body. At the same time, we can discriminate whether the persons is an adult or a child.

4 Recognition of trajectories

4.1 Object matching

A trajectory of a walking person is extracted as a series of his positions in a frame sequence. However, a frame often contains several number of persons. Then, a matching process of individual persons in the consecutive frames is required. Namely, every person contained in a past frame has to be matched to a person image in a present frame.

The matching process is divided into two processes: one for moving objects and the other for still objects. For a moving object matching, motion prediction technique is effectively used.

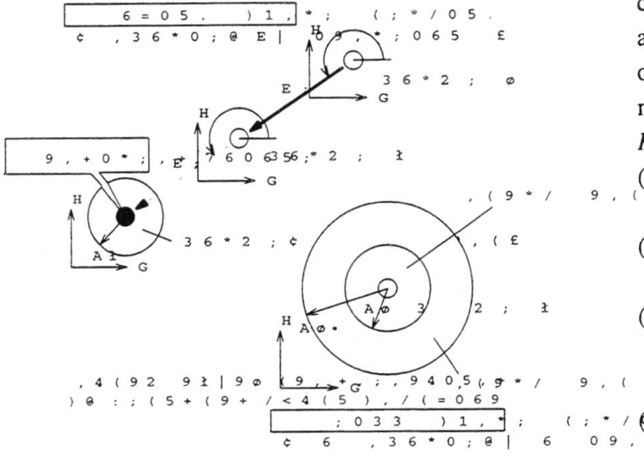

Figure 4 Prediction of object positions

Procedure 5(See Figure 4):

[A] Matching process for moving objects

(1) A motion vector (velocity and direction of object motion) is calculated as 2D vector connecting the object position in a present frame and that in a past frame.

(2) The predicted position range of an object in a future frame is set in a circle whose center is at the point extended from the present position by the motion vector obtained above and the radius is a proper value r_1.

(3) Within the predicted circle in a future frame, if there is an object with the same attributes of the object in the present frame, the object in the future frame is matched to the object in the present frame.

(4) The connecting line between the position of an object in a future frame and that in a present frame is extracted as a trajectory of the object.

[B] Matching process for still objects

(1) The predicted position range of an object in a future frame is set in a circle whose center is at the point of an object in the present frame and the radius is a proper value r_2.

(2) Within the predicted circle in the future frame, if there is an object with the same attributes of the object in the present frame, the object in the future frame is matched to the object in the present frame.

(3) The connecting line between the positions of the object in the future frame and that in the present frame is extracted as a trajectory of the object.

4.2 Merging of object regions

In the object matching method mentioned above, some object regions in a future frame often remain unmatched to any objects in the present frame. In general, a human body is composed of several parts such as a head, two hands, a trunk and two legs. If some of them are extracted separately, they often remain as unmatched objects. For this case, they can be merged by the following procedure.

Procedure 6:

(1) To every recognized human object in a present frame, a 3D object in real space is generated by Procedure 3.

(2) The future position of the generated object in real space is predicted by the motion vector mentioned in Procedure 5.

(3) The moving image in the future frame for the generated object in step (2) is generated by an inverse process of transformation technique in Procedure 3.

(4) The separate objects within the range of the generated image in step (3), are merged and matched to the moving object.

Figure 5 shows an example of merging process.

Figure 5 Merging of objects

4.3 Object identification

If a moving image contains a several number of persons walking cross each other, it is necessary to identify the persons individually. For this purpose, color-matching technique of human body is effective. This can be carried out by the following procedure.

Procedure 7(See Figure 6):

(1) An extracted person image is transformed into a human image in a real space by Procedure 3.

(2) The human image in real space is analyzed by a standard model of human body.

(3) Three points (head, chest and loin centers) are selected on the human image in a real space.

(4) The colors on these three points are added to the attributes

of the person.

(5) In case when several persons are crossing each other, the identification of each person can be carried out by this color attributes.

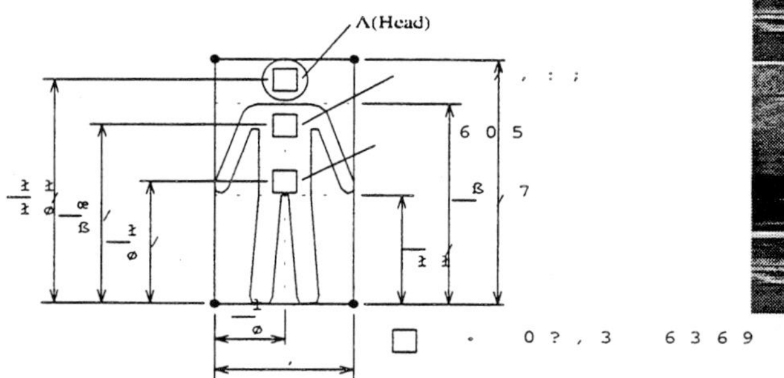

Figure 6 3-color points on human body

4.4 Display of walking persons' trajectories

The walking persons' trajectories are obtained as a series of extracted positions of persons in a real space. They are displayed on 2D display equipment. The attributes of every person such as his height, his class (child or adult) are displayed at the same time.

5 Experiments

5.1 Configuration of experiment

As a sample of video surveillance signals, image sequences of walking persons were picked up by a TV camera. The camera configurations are the same as shown in Figure 3. Three kinds of image signals shown in Table 1 are provided.

Table 1. Sample sequence

No.	No. of Persons	Modes	Durations
	2 adults	Crossing	4 seconds
	2 adults	Circulating	10 seconds
	2 adults	Kick back	8 seconds

5.2 Experimental results

Figure 7 shows the image frames for image sequence No.2. Figure 8 shows the recognition results of every person contained in image sequence No.2. Figure 9 shows the walking persons' trajectories. From these figures, it is cleared that the walking persons' trajectories can be correctly extracted.

6. Conclusion

Motion recognition and display method for walking persons' trajectories are described. The features of this method are summarized as follows:

(1) The position and attributes(heights and classes of persons) are recognized correctly.

(2) Recognition of walking persons and display of them can be obtained in a real time basis.

(3) It can be applied to a relatively complex image sequence which contains several number of walking persons and walking parttems.

Figure 7 Sample sequence No.2

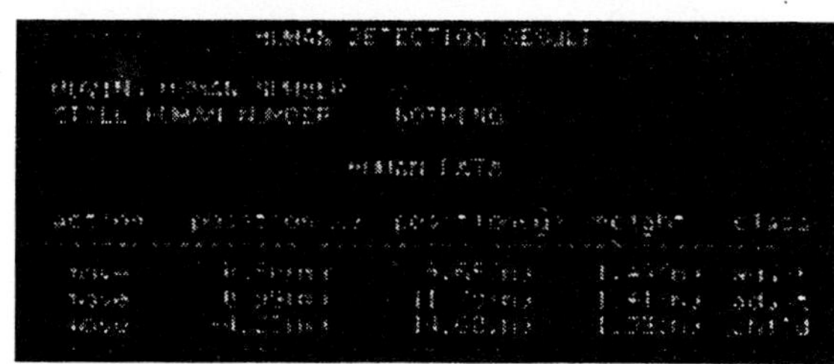

Figure 8 Recognition result for sequence No.2.

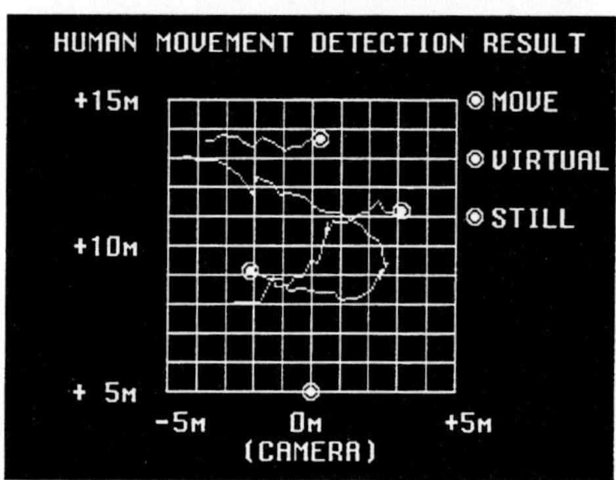

Figure 9 Extracted trajectories of walking persons

References

[1] PRMU96-178, pp.61-68, 1997 (in Japanese)

[2] IEEE Trans.Image Proc,Vol.7 No.5 pp.693 702 1998-03

[3] Proc. of 2nd Int. Conf. on Image Processing, pp.212-216, 1994

Blackboard Segmentation Using Video Image of Lecture and Its Applications

Masaki Onishi, Masao Izumi and Kunio Fukunaga
Department of Computer and Systems Sciences, College of Engineering,
Osaka Prefecture University, 1-1 Gakuen-cho, Sakai, Osaka, 599-8531 Japan
onishi@com.cs.osakafu-u.ac.jp, {izumi, fukunaga}@cs.osakafu-u.ac.jp

Abstract

We propose a method for segmentation of written regions on a blackboard in the lecture room using a video image. We firstly detect static edges of which locations on the image are stationary. And next, we extract several rectangular regions in which these static edges are located densely. Finally by use of fuzzy rules, extracted rectangles are merged as contextual regions, where letters and figures in each contextual region explain each context. And, we apply our method to automatic production of lecture video, and archives system of written regions on the blackboard in lecture rooms.

1. Introduction

Recently, universities and other kinds of schools begin to take an interest in a distance learning system, which can perform lectures at various locations far from lecturers at the same time [1]. State of the art low cost wide band communication system makes such systems realistic. On the other hand, usual lecture videos and lecture notes can be used for similar objective. And also lecture videos can be broadcasted at the learning system mentioned above. For that reason, automatic systems to make these contents have been applied to real lectures and technical talks in recent works [2, 3].

When you make lecture videos, it is important to take a shot as students are able to look at letters and figures on blackboard. Even if students want to take closer look only at the part of the blackboard, the conventional method tends to make video images which include the lecturer only or the whole blackboard. When we make lecture archives, we also record letters and figures on blackboard. Considering making lecture videos and archives automatically, it is necessary to divide blackboard into several written regions.

Here we propose a method of blackboard segmentation. And we propose a procedure for making lecture videos by use of proposed blackboard segmentation method. We confirm effectiveness of our method by experimental results. And we demonstrate to produce a lecture videos and WWW contents.

2. Separation of lecturer and characters

For understanding a lecture from lecture video images, there are two important objects in lecture video images, a lecturer and characters on blackboard written by the lecturer. (Here, we call letters and figures as 'characters'.) To separate them from video images, we use a method based on edge detection from spatiotemporal images of a video image sequence, because it is difficult to separate edges of lecturer and edges of written characters from an input image only. Since a lecturer is constantly moving around to explain and write characters on a blackboard, we detect edge images from a spatiotemporal image. The spatiotemporal image took advantage of several researches to detect camera operations [4], because edge direction of the spatiotemporal image shows moving flow of the camera. We use edge directions from several cross sections of the spatiotemporal image, in order to segment two kinds of edges, edges with moving objects (We call *dynamic edges*.) and edges with stationary objects (*static edges*).

A cross section perpendicular to the x axis of the spatiotemporal image $F(x, y, t)$ is called y-t cross section. And a cross section perpendicular to the y axis is called x-t cross section. The moving object such as a lecturer tends to make horizontal edges in x-t cross section and vertical edges in y-t cross section as shown in Figure 1. On the contrary, static objects such as characters on blackboard tends to make vertical edges in x-t cross section and horizontal edges in y-t cross section. Here we define intensity of *a dynamic edge* using Sobel operators.

$$| \nabla f^{\mathrm{d}}(x, y) |= \sqrt{f_t(x, t \mid y)^2 + f_t(y, t \mid x)^2}, \quad (1)$$

where $f(x, t \mid y)$ and $f(y, t \mid x)$ are x-t and y-t cross section respectively, and f_t is a differentiation of f. Similarly,

1051-4651/00 $10.00 © 2000 IEEE

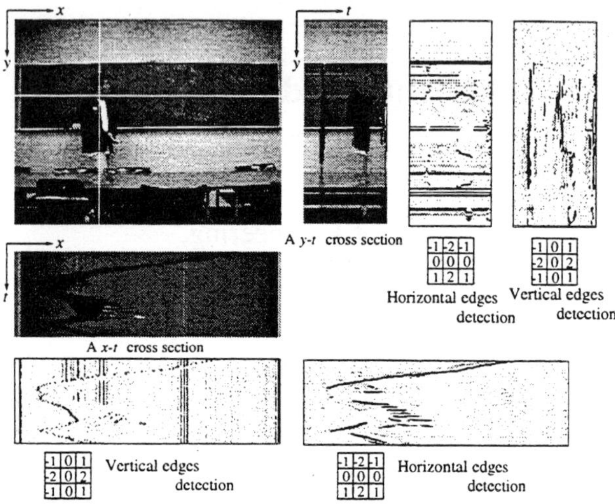

Figure 1. Edge detection of cross section.

intensity of *a static edge* is defined as follows:

$$| \nabla f^s(x,y) |= \sqrt{f_x(x,t \mid y)^2 + f_y(y,t \mid x)^2}. \quad (2)$$

However, there is also a case when a lecturer keeps standing without movement for a short period time. Then we assume that *static edges* keep static positions for several periods of time. The static edges are extracted as points which keep certain periods of time as edge points extracted by use of Sobel operators to both x-t and y-t cross sections of the spatiotemporal image.

Figure 2 shows an input image (a) and *a static and a dynamic edge* image (b). We can assure that characters on blackboard are extracted as *static edges*(gray level) and a lecturer is extracted as *dynamic edges*(black level) on usual lecture video images taken by fixed camera. This assumption can be confirmed in Figure 2 (b).

3. Blackboard segmentation

In this section, we extract *written blocks* by using *static edges*. Each *written block* is a unit area and holds letters and figures which, explain the same subject. *Written blocks* are characterized by the clock time when appeared on the video images, and ordered in time sequence. So ordered *written blocks* can be used as a resume of the lecture and so on. We assume that each *written block* consists of several *written rectangles*, which are formed by a following procedure.

A *written rectangle* is defined as a circumscribed rectangle of *static edges*, which are densely extracted by the method explained in the previous section. While *static edges* are being extracted in time consequently and densely, *written rectangle* is becoming larger. If dense *static edges*

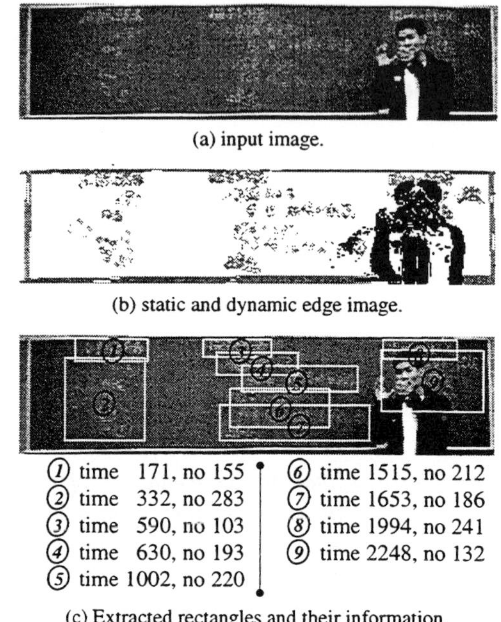

Figure 2. Example of processing result.

are not extracted during certain time period, and if a size and a location of already extracted *written rectangle* are not changed, the *written rectangle* is fixed and stored in terms of the time of being extracted, the location, the size, and the number of *static edges* which exist within the rectangle. The number of *static edges* in each *written rectangle* increases when a lecturer adds letters or figures in the rectangular area on the blackboard. And the number of *static edges* decreases when a lecturer erases some of letters or figures on the blackboard. If the number of *static edges* decreases rapidly and becomes close to zero, the *written rectangle* which holds such erased *static edges* is assumed as erased. Figure 2 (c) shows results of extract *written rectangles* on blackboard (white lines) and their appeared time and number of *static edges*.

In the next step, we try to extract *written blocks* by combining several *written rectangles* in considering time sequential and spatial situations of them. Usually lecturers draw letters and figures on the blackboard as a multi-column article. They tend to write letters from the top of the blackboard to the bottom to make another column on the blackboard. With this consideration, we assume next two rules that the blocking procedure must obey.

(1) If a presently considering *written rectangle* is located near the top of the blackboard and already extracted *written block* is located to the bottom of the blackboard, a considering *written rectangle* is not combined to the extracted *written block* and becomes a part of new *written block*.

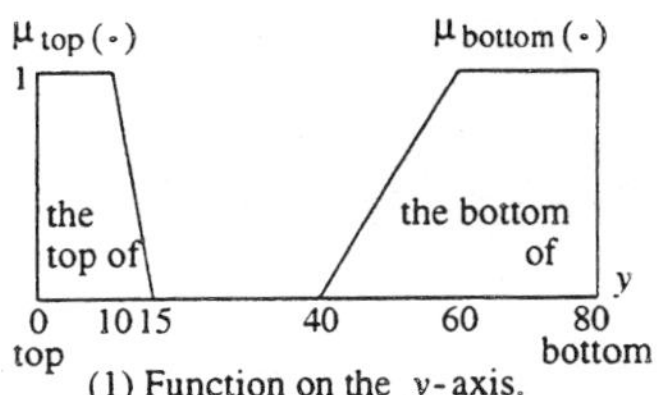

(1) Function on the y-axis.

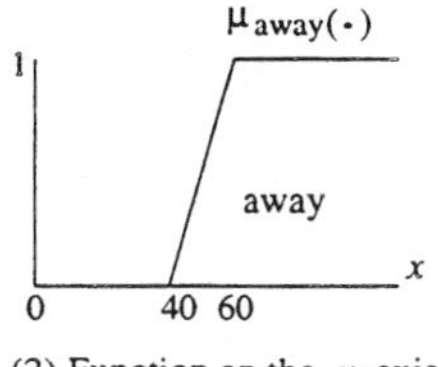

(2) Function on the x-axis.

Figure 3. Membership functions.

(2) If a presently considering *written rectangle* is located horizontally far from the already extracted *written block*, a considering *written block* becomes a part of new *written block*.

Fuzzy rules in Figure 3 are introduced to make above two rules apply a blocking procedure. The argument of function $\mu_{\text{top}}(\cdot)$ is y element of the location of presently considering *written rectangle*, the argument of $\mu_{\text{bottom}}(\cdot)$ should be y element of the location of the bottom of the extracted *written block*. And the argument of $\mu_{\text{away}}(\cdot)$ is the smallest distance between presently considering *written rectangle* and other rectangles. If $\mu_{\text{top}}(\cdot) \times \mu_{\text{bottom}}(\cdot) \geq$ threshold or $\mu_{\text{away}}(\cdot) \geq$ threshold, presently considering *written rectangle* should not be combined with already extracted *written block* and becomes a part of new *written block*.

4. Its Applications

We have proposed the method of blackboard segmentation. Next we demonstrate an example of applications using this method, such as an automatic production of lecture videos and lecture archives. Our systems use two cameras, the one is fixed and takes images for block extraction, and another one is for taking lecture video and can be panned, tilted and zoomed. We call the former *fixed camera*, and the latter *controlling camera*.

(i) Automatic production of lecture videos

Our system automatically decides the area should be viewed in a lecture video, on the location of extracted blocks and a lecturer. Students tend to look at a lecturer and written regions of blackboard during a lecture. The lecturer can be extracted as a region of *dynamic edges*, and written regions of blackboard are extracted some *written blocks*. So, in our system it is assumed that images in a video sequence should include a lecturer (*dynamic edges*) and some of written regions on the blackboard (*written blocks*). In the case that there are plural blocks on blackboard, we have to decide which the lecturer is using explaining or writing (we call *the current blocks*). The block, which includes a new *written rectangle*, is regarded as *a current block*, because it is supposed as an unfinished block. And the block, which

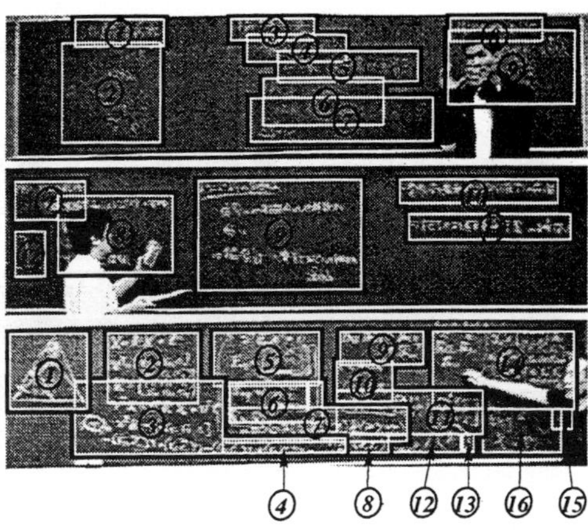

Figure 4. Experimental results of block extraction.

includes *dynamic edges*, is also regarded as *a current block*, because it is supposed to be used for explaining by a lecturer. *The controlling camera* changes a camera angle and zooming parameter to take a shot such that we can see a lecturer and *current blocks*.

Dynamic edges and *written blocks* are extracted from input image sequence taken by *the fixed camera*. Panning, tilting and zooming of *the controlling camera* are manipulated in order to produce lecture videos. In this experiment, we assume only one *controlling camera*, and the positions of *the controlling camera* and *the fixed camera* are known in advance.

(ii) Automatic production of lecture archives

Also our system can produce archives of the lecture as taking a note or a resume of the blackboard. Using results of *written blocks* extraction from fixed camera images, *the controlling camera* can take each *written block* as large as possible. When there is no *dynamic edge* in the *written block*, *the controlling camera* takes *a written block* on

Table 1. Rate of correct block extraction.

	Time	Rate	Error of Segmentation			
	(m's")	(%)	OS	OU	OE	NE
Mock	69'29"	94.8%	0.7%	3.0%	0.0%	1.6%
Real	170'53"	83.1%	1.9%	13.8%	1.2%	10.1%
Sum	240'22"	86.5%	1.5%	10.7%	0.8%	7.6%

	No	Rate	Error of Segmentation			
	(no)	(%)	OS	OU	OE	NE
Mock	87	96.6%	1.1%	2.3%	0.0%	—
Real	90	86.7%	3.3%	8.9%	1.1%	—
Sum	177	91.5%	2.3%	5.6%	0.6%	—

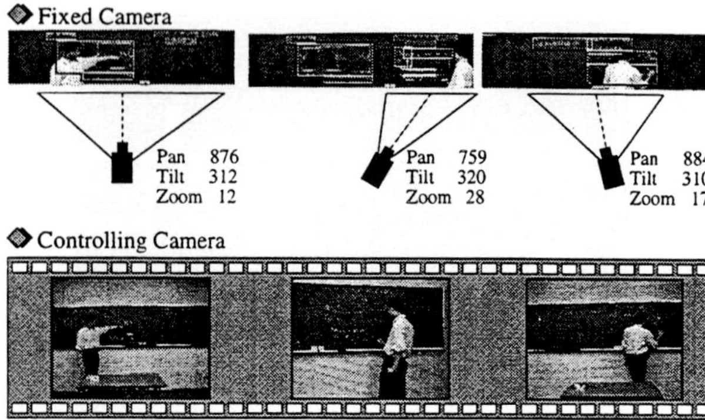

Figure 5. Example of demonstration of lecture video.

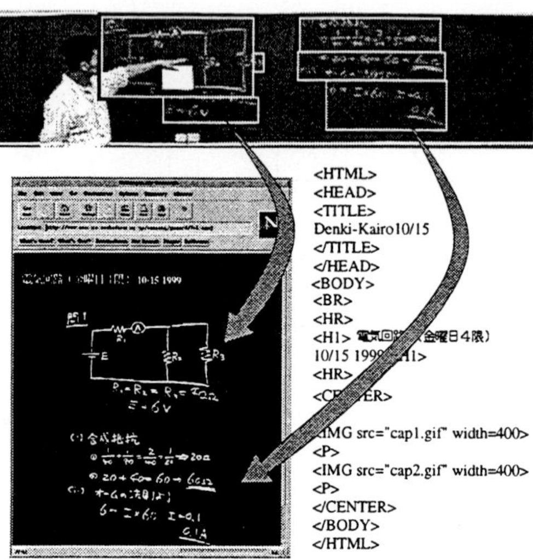

Figure 6. Example of demonstration on WWW.

blackboard. And in the case that a lecturer adds new letters in *a written block*, *the controlling camera* retakes the *written block* by detecting an increase of the number of *static edges*. These *written block* images can be used as wide accessible images for reviewing, such as Web pages demonstrated in a following section.

5. Experimental results

We test our algorithm of blackboard segmentation on 6 mock lectures (3 lecturers, total about 60 min.) and 3 real lectures (3 lecturers, total about 170 min.) image sequence. Figure 4 shows extracted *written rectangles* surrounded by white lines and *written blocks* by black lines [1]. *The written rectangles* are numbered in order of finishing to be written on time scale. And Table 1 shows the rate of correct *written block* extraction. From top to bottom are ratios in terms of whole lecture time, and ratios in terms of the number of rectangles. Error of segmentation can be classified into four categories: over segmentation (OS), over merging (OM), over extraction (OE) and no extraction (NE). OS is the case where the region of a single block is erroneously segmented into two or more regions, OM is the case where the regions of multiple blocks are merged into one region. And, OE is the case where others than characters are extracted erroneously, NE is the case where written characters can not be extracted.

Besides, Figure 5 shows a demonstration of lecture videos which is produced automatically. The upper row shows results of *written blocks* extraction, and parameters of 'Pan' ,'Tilt' and 'Zoom' are calculated from the coordinates of *dynamic edges* and *current rectangles*. The lower row shows produced lecture video from the controlling camera which is set parameters of 'Pan' ,'Tilt' and 'Zoom'. And Figure 6 shows a demonstration of lecture archives.

[1] See: http://www.com.cs.osakafu-u.ac.jp/~onishi/research-e.html

6. Conclusions

In this paper, we proposed a method to separate the written region on blackboard into dense segments using fuzzy rule. The edge detection from spatiotemporal image divides into moving objects and static objects. And the rectangles which enclosed edges of the static objects as written region on blackboard are separated into several blocks with regard to time sequential and spatial situations. As we have shown in experiments, the proposed method yields reliable blackboard segmentation on mock and real lectures. We assume that these results are quite useful to understand the circumstances of lectures. And as examples of its application, we demonstrated automatic production of lecture videos and lecture archives.

References

[1] S. C. Brofferio, "A University Distance Lesson System: Experiments, Services, and Future Developments," *IEEE Trans. on Education*, vol.41, no.1, pp.17–24, Feb. 1998.

[2] Y. Kameda, H. Miyazaki and M. Minoh, "A Live Video Imaging for Multiple Users," *Proc. of ICMCS'99*, vol.2, pp.897–902, July 1999.

[3] S.X.Ju, M.J.Black, S.Minneman, D.Kimber, "Summarization of Videotaped Presentations: Automatic Analysis of Motion and Gesture," *IEEE Trans. on Circuits and Systems for Video Technology*, vol.8, no.5, pp.686–696, Sep. 1998.

[4] F.M.Idris and S.Panchanathan, "Spatio-Temporal Indexing of Vector Quantized Video Sequences," *IEEE Trans. on Circuits and Systems for Video Technology*, vol.7, no.5, pp.728–740, Oct. 1997.

Comparison of Tracking Techniques Applied to Digital PIV

Dmitry Chetverikov, Marcell Nagy and Judit Verestóy
Computer and Automation Research Institute
Budapest, Kende u.13-17, H-1111 Hungary
csetverikov@sztaki.hu

Abstract

Digital Particle Image Velocimetry (DPIV) aims at flow visualisation and measurement of flow dynamics in numerous applications, including hydrodynamics, combustion processes and aeronautical phenomena. The fluid is seeded with particles that follow the flow and efficiently scatter light. Traditionally, FFT-based correlation techniques have been used to estimate the displacements of the particles in a digital PIV sequence. Recently, an optical flow estimation technique [8] developed in computer vision has been successfully applied to DPIV. In this paper we study the DPIV-efficiency of another group of tracking approaches, the feature tracking techniques. Velocity fields obtained by several methods are compared for synthetic and real PIV sequences. It is concluded that feature tracking algorithms applied to DPIV are a useful alternative to both the correlation and the optical flow algorithms.

1. Introduction

In this study we investigate the applicability and efficiency of feature based tracking algorithms in flow velocity measurement. Flow visualisation and measurement of flow dynamics are important for the analysis of combustion processes, hydrodynamic and aeronautical phenomena, flame propagation, heat exchange problems, construction of artificial heart pumps, and many other practical tasks [5].

In *particle image velocimetry* (PIV) applications, the fluid is seeded with particles that follow the flow and efficiently scatter light. Conventionally, multiple exposure cameras are used to capture images of the flow at different time instants. The images are recorded on photographic film. Optical correlation methods are then applied point-by-point to the entire negative, and the in-plane velocity of the particles between two consecutive images is determined.

Digital PIV, or DPIV, refers to the newly emerged technique of using high-performance CCD cameras and frame-grabbers to store and process the digitised PIV sequences directly by the computer. In DPIV, the conventional cross-correlation methods are implemented using the Fast Fourier Transform [9].

At the same time, estimation and tracking of motion in image sequences is a well-established branch of *computer vision* (CV). Here, real world scenes with large, rigid or deformable moving objects are usually considered. Two main classes of motion estimation methods are traditionally distinguished: the optical flow based [2] and the local feature based [4] techniques. Efficient algorithms are available in both classes. Applying them to particle flow image sequences may lead to essential improvement in visualisation and measurement results.

This opportunity has not been explored properly. Interaction between DPIV and CV has been limited to a few, although quite successful, attempts. The main reason might be the specifics of DPIV, where the basic assumptions and conditions differ from those typical for CV. In particular, very large numbers (thousands) of small and poorly visible particles are to be tracked. Individual particles may become invisible and temporarily disappear, re-appear again, leave the viewfield, or enter. Turbulent flows further complicate the task of velocity estimation, as the assumption of locally coherent motion does not hold in some areas.

Recently, Quénot et al. [8] presented an optical flow algorithm based on a dynamic programming (DP) technique and tested the algorithm with synthetic and real DPIV sequences, including complex flows. The results compare favourably to those obtained using the classical correlation-based DPIV methods. A substantial increase in both accuracy and spatial resolution of the velocity field has been achieved. Superior robustness to artificially generated noise has also been demonstrated.

Unfortunately, the algorithm [8] is very slow, with the execution time increasing drastically with image size. (Two of the proposed three versions run for hours.) Testing and applying the algorithm is problematic, at least for the time being. This motivates our search for reasonable alternatives to both the conventional and the DP techniques. Recently, we have made the first step in this direction by applying

1051-4651/00 $10.00

to DPIV our feature based tracking algorithm called IPAN Tracker [4]. (IPAN stands for Image and Pattern Analysis group.)

The results of this pilot attempt were presented in [10]. The tests compared the IPAN Tracker to the well-known KLT Tracker [3] and an early version of Quénot's algorithm, which are available on the Internet. Three standard synthetic DPIV sequences [1] were used. The sequences show simple, noise-free, wavy flows without vortices. Mean velocity magnitudes and standard deviations obtained by each algorithm were compared to their ground truth values. The results were similar, indicating that DPIV application of feature trackers is worth studying.

The initial tests [10] were encouraging, but their significance is limited. The overall mean velocity and variance are global indicators, which may hide numerous local errors that make the algorithm useless. The comparison should be done on the point-by-point basis. Also, to test the scope and the robustness of the alternative approaches, the database should contain both synthetic and real PIV sequences of varying complexity and degree of noise.

This is exactly what the current study does. The test results are now suitable for making specific and relevant conclusions concerning the DPIV-efficiency of feature based trackers.

The paper is organised as follows. In section 2 we give an overview of the algorithms used in our DPIV tests. Because of the lack of space, the discussion is short; the reader is referred to the original papers for all details. The main contribution of the paper are the experimental results, which are presented in section 3. Finally, conclusions are drawn and future plans discussed.

2. The compared approaches

In our tests, we run three different algorithms whose code was available: the initial version of Quénot's algorithm [6], the Kanade-Lucas-Tomasi (KLT) Tracker [3] and the IPAN Tracker [4] developed in our group. The last two are feature based tracking techniques whose performance was of primary interest. Moreover, we used the sequences and the numerical results presented in the recent paper [8], where 3 enhanced versions of Quénot's algorithm are compared to the conventional correlation-based techniques. (Unfortunately, the enhanced versions are not available for testing.) The correlation-based methods are discussed elsewhere [9, 8]. The other three approaches are sketched below.

Quénot's algorithm is an optical flow method based on dynamic programming (DP). DP was originally used for searching the optimal matching between two one-dimensional patterns. In this algorithm, it is extended to two dimensions. The global matching is searched that minimises a distance between two images. This is achieved by the Orthogonal Dynamic Programing (ODP) technique that slices each image into two orthogonal sets of parallel overlapping strips. The corresponding strips are then matched as one-dimensional signals. The number of operations required for an $N \times N$ image is $O(N^3 \log N)$.

In each pixel, the algorithm computes a velocity vector between any two images of a sequence, provided that the displacements are not too large. Results for both synthetic and real sequences, as well as the sequences themselves, can be downloaded from the ftp site [7].

The correlation methods and the method by Quénot do matching for the whole image, which can be very time consuming for large images. When individual particles can be detected, feature based techniques are also applicable and may provide a faster solution.

The feature based techniques extract local regions of interest (features) from the images and identify the corresponding features in each image of the sequence. The **KLT Tracker** selects features which are optimal for tracking, and keeps track of these features. A good feature is a textured patch with high intensity variation in both x and y directions, such as a corner. The algorithm defines a measure of dissimilarity that quantifies the change of appearance of a feature between the first and the current image frame, allowing for affine image changes. At the same time, a pure translation model of motion is used to track the selected features through the sequence. The number of operations depends on the image size N and the number of features N_f. The source code of the KLT Tracker can be downloaded from the web site [3].

The **IPAN Tracker** is a non-iterative, competitive feature point linking algorithm. It is based on a repetitive hypothesis testing procedure that switches between three consecutive image frames and maximises the smoothness of the evolving trajectories. In each new frame, the already established partial trajectories are extended. Feature points that appear or disappear can also be tracked. The number of operations is $O(N_f \cdot n_f^2)$, where n_f is the average number of features in the search area defined by the maximal possible displacement.

The IPAN Tracker is described in full detail in the recent paper [4] where a general, application-independent version of the algorithm is presented. Those parts of the approach that are specific to the PIV application are discussed in [10].

The feature trackers only measure velocity in the position of a feature. They do not provide uniform sampling of the flow velocity vector field needed for point-by-point comparison with other techniques. To make the comparison possible, we resample by interpolation the vector field to a regular grid.

3. Experimental results

The three algorithms, KLT, IPAN and the initial Quénot, were run on a number of standard synthetic and real sequences available on the Internet. In each case, velocity vectors were picked and compared in every eighth pixel. Following the standard DPIV practice adopted in [8], a velocity vector was represented by its magnitude (displacement) and orientation (angle). The comparison was done for the two components separately. The mean absolute deviation from the ground truth was calculated as the error. The variance of the absolute deviation was also obtained.

In the tables below, deviations from the ground truth are presented as the angle and the displacement errors. The angle is measured in degrees, the displacement in pixels. Typical (real, not CPU) times elapsed during execution are also shown, measured on a Pentium 333 MHz under Linux OS.

Tables 1 and 2 compare IPAN, KLT and the initial Quénot to an enhanced, very precise version of Quénot's algorithm [8]. The latter is taken as the ground truth. The input data are the **real** flow sequences ICEG1619 and ICEG4447 [7] visualised in figure 1. (The dots are the velocity vector origins.) The sequences show freezing in the lid cooled cavity, which is a relatively complex flow with vortices. The accuracy of the reference technique is estimated in [8] to be within 0.2 pixel/frame. Unfortunately, the CPU time of this algorithm is about 200 minutes.

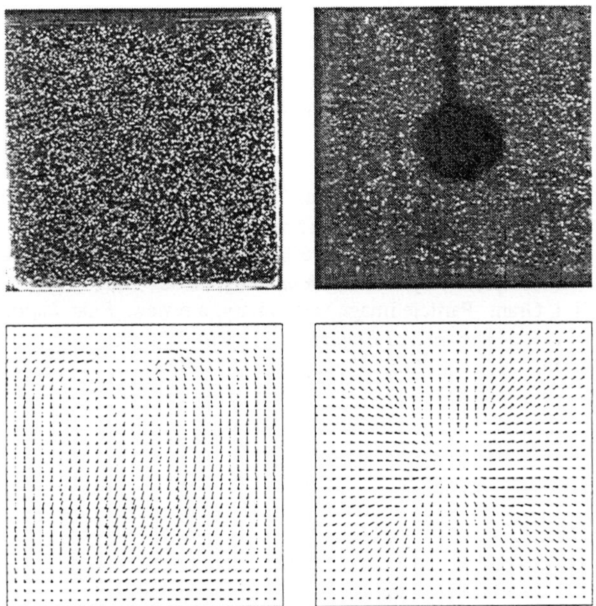

Figure 1. First frames and flow visualisation of sequences ICEG1619 and ICEG447 (KLT).

Tables 3 and 4 compare IPAN, KLT, Quénot's enhanced algorithm ODP2 and the conventional correlation-based method DPIV32 for the **synthetic** flow sequence CYLINDER [7]. N5, N10 and N20 are noisy versions of the original noise-free sequence N0 visualised in figure 2. The numbers indicate different degrees of noise varying from 5% to 20%. CYLINDER is a complex flow with mean displacement 7.6 pixel/frame. In this case, the ground truth is available. Experimental data for ODP2 and DPIV32 are reproduced from the study [8]. ODP2 is the fastest of the 3 enhanced versions discussed in this study. DPIV32 is a 32×32 window size correlator. (Note that for ODP2 and DPIV32 the CPU time is given.)

Table 1. Errors for ICEG1619

	IPAN	KLT	Quénot
Angle	6.86 ± 11.0	5.73 ± 8.3	5.58 ± 7.7
Displ.	0.60 ± 0.5	0.48 ± 0.4	0.51 ± 0.4
Time	20 sec	10 sec	130 sec

Table 2. Errors for ICEG4777

	IPAN	KLT	Quénot
Angle	9.70 ± 17.0	6.78 ± 10.8	13.0 ± 22.8
Displ.	0.72 ± 0.9	0.48 ± 0.5	0.79 ± 1.2
Time	10 sec	40 sec	170 sec

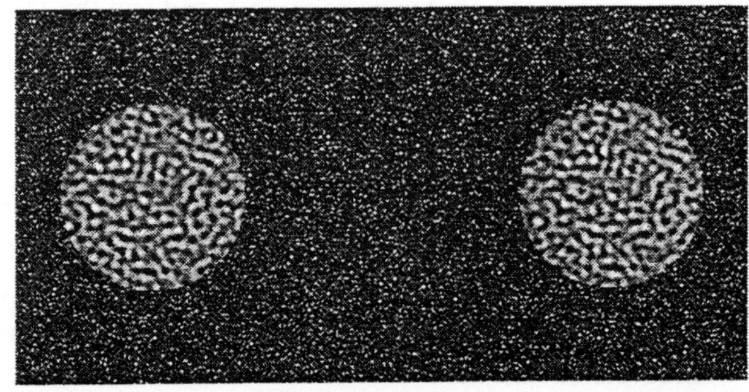

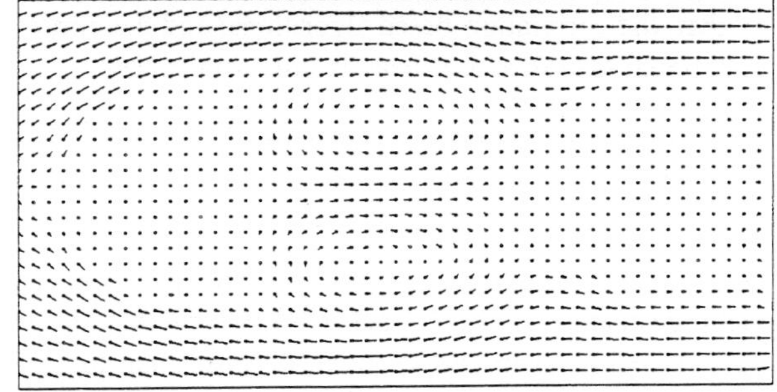

Figure 2. First frame and flow visualisation of sequence CYLINDER N0 (IPAN).

Table 3. Angle errors for CYLINDER

	IPAN	KLT	ODP2	DPIV32
N0	2.86 ± 5	2.55 ± 5	1.23 ± 2	5.95 ± 14
N5	3.58 ± 8	2.58 ± 5	1.83 ± 4	6.49 ± 15
N10	3.62 ± 6	2.57 ± 5	4.01 ± 11	8.75 ± 18
N20	6.48 ± 11	3.39 ± 6	6.70 ± 12	35.0 ± 36
Time	20 sec	15 sec	20 min*	10 min*

* CPU

Table 4. Displacement errors for CYLINDER

	IPAN	KLT	ODP2	DPIV32
N0	0.42 ± 0.5	0.36 ± 0.6	0.13 ± 0.1	0.55 ± 1.0
N5	0.50 ± 0.8	0.36 ± 0.6	0.21 ± 0.5	0.61 ± 1.2
N10	0.58 ± 0.8	0.35 ± 0.4	0.53 ± 1.4	0.77 ± 1.6
N20	0.91 ± 1.2	0.46 ± 0.7	0.88 ± 1.6	3.11 ± 4.1

4. Discussion

We have applied a number of motion tracking and estimation approaches developed in computer vision, to digital particle image velocimetry. Based on our experience, the following conclusions can be drawn from the presented experimental data.

Feature tracking algorithms should be considered as a useful alternative to both the correlation-based and the DP-based techniques. In particular:

- Feature trackers can provide flow velocity estimation accuracy competing with that of the conventional correlation-based techniques. At the same time, they are much faster.
- Although the accuracy of the trackers will hopefully be improved, we do not expect them to become as accurate as the most precise DP-based methods designed for DPIV. However, the latter are even slower than the correlation-based algorithms, and the computational load increases heavily with image size.
- The speed of the trackers can make them suitable for fast flow visualisation, qualitative estimation, and analysis of rapidly changing processes.

Due to its excellent, dynamic feature selection and matching scheme, the KLT Tracker is fast, scalable and robust. (Probably, even less sensitive to noise than the DP-based techniques.) As the speed does not depend drastically on image size, the KLT might be applicable to large images that cannot be processed by other techniques. The maximal number of tracked features and the maximal displacement allowed are still to be analysed.

The IPAN Tracker has a good trajectory optimisation procedure. It is more sensitive to noise than the KLT. An alternative feature extraction procedure (e.g., that of the KLT) can be considered. The speed depends on particles' density and maximum velocity rather than on their total number. The maximum velocity is a sensitive parameter that must be set carefully for proper operation.

The operation of the trackers is based on detection of features that are judged to be prominent and reliable. If no such features are found in a part of the flow, interpolation provides measurements in this part as well. This method may fail when relatively large areas of poor visibility (low contrast, blur, etc.) are present. The problem needs further research. Accuracy of flow estimation, as well as tractable flow complexity and speed are also to be addressed.

Online demonstration of the discussed algorithms is available on the Internet at the web site of the IPAN Research Group: `http://visual.ipan.sztaki.hu`. One can select an algorithm, set the parameters and run the algorithm on a short PIV sequence. The sequences used in our tests are provided. Alternatively, one can submit his/her own sequence.

Acknowledgement. This work is partially supported by OTKA under the grant T026592.

References

[1] Standard images for particle imaging velocimetry. `http://www.vsj.or.jp/piv/image-e.html`.

[2] J.L. Barron, D.J. Fleet, and S.S. Beauchemin. Performance of optical flow techniques. *International Journal of Computer Vision*, 12:1:43–77, 1994.

[3] Stan Birchfield. KLT: An Implementation of the Kanade-Lucas-Tomasi Feature Tracker. `http://vision.stanford.edu/~birch/klt/`.

[4] D. Chetverikov and J. Verestóy. Feature Point Tracking for Incomplete Trajectories. *Computing*, 62:321–338, 1999.

[5] I. Grant. Particle image velocimetry: a review. *Proc. Institution of Mechanical Engineers*, 211 Part C:55–76, 1997.

[6] J.L. Barron, D.J. Fleet, and S.S. Beauchemin. Test data for performance evaluation of optical flow techniques. `ftp://ftp.csd.uwo.ca/pub/vision`.

[7] G. Quénot. Data and procedures for development and testing of PIV applications. `ftp://ftp.limsi.fr/pub/quenot/opflow/`.

[8] G. Quénot, J. Pakleza, and T. Kowalewski. Particle image velocimetry with optical flow. *Experiments in Fluids*, 25, no.3:177–189, 1998.

[9] P.T. Tokumaru and P.E. Dimotakis. Image correlation velocimetry. *Experiments in Fluids*, 19:1–15, 1995.

[10] J. Verestóy. Digital PIV: a Challenge for Feature Based Tracking. In *Proc. 23rd Workshop of the Austrian Association for Pattern Recognition*, pages 165–174, 1999. (Extended version to appear in *Machine Graphics and Vision*, 2000.)

Coping with 3d Artifacts in Video Sequences

A. Griffin and J. Kittler
School of Electronic Engineering, Information Technology and Mathematics,
University of Surrey, Guildford, Surrey. GU2 7XH. U.K.
email {A.Griffin, J. Kittler}@ee.surrey.ac.uk

Abstract

Several video processing techniques with applications in video compression, shot-cut detection, mosaicing and so on are based around the mapping of the positions of feature points from video frame to video frame. This in turn is often based on the assumption that for the scene under observation a two dimensional approximation of the structure is adequate - both in terms of motion estimation and in the subsequent use of the feature correspondences obtained from the motion estimation process. This assumption is in general false. We propose a method for motion estimation based on an active mesh. In doing so we attempt to model the motion estimation not as an unconstrained motion of feature points moving independently, but as the estimation of a set of planar patches each undergoing a 3-d perspective motion. In doing so we note that our method allows us to fit to 3-d metrics with a high degree of accuracy.

1 Introduction

Video processing is currently enjoying a widespread proliferation, driving the recent growth of digital techniques in consumer electronics and of multimedia databases. Examples of video processing applications include video mosaicing (the synthesis of a panorama from individual frames), shot cut detection, object tracking and so on. These techniques all rely on some form of multi-frame image registration between frames whether it is image alignment (mosaicing) frame content comparison (shot cut detection) or object motion calculation (tracking).

The techniques traditionally employed for image registration share one common problem; they are based on a single two dimensional metric. This problem is minimised in the case where the entire scene being imaged is a relatively long distance away from the camera. In this case the scene approximates a plane and the projection via the camera to the 2d image plane has caused little loss of depth information. Between video frames feature correspondences are obtained by extracting motions of points. The mapping from frame to frame is then modelled by a single plane to plane perspective projection calculated as the best fit to a set of feature correspondences or less accurately an affine or translatory mapping.

Obviously the assumption that the scene approximates a plane is most likely false; video sequences are often based around a subject performing some actions. In a simple sequence the scene may consist of few objects and a distant background, a case that may be handled by modelling the background as approximately flat and extracting the objects with motion contrary to the model. More usually the scene is complex with many interacting objects and may often be based, for example, inside a room (where the assumption of a distant background does not apply). Consider a moving camera taking a video sequence of a 3-d scene comprised of a background with static objects in the foreground. Objects in the foreground will move with different 2-d motions to the background. If moving objects are contained within the scene, it would be the case that there would be several motions; the motion of the background (induced by the camera motion), the motions of the static objects (induced by the camera motion) and the motions of the non-stationary objects (induced both by object motions and the camera motion). This case is particularly ill suited to a single 2-d model.

To correctly represent that latter case we need to look at 3-d representations. Methods such as utilising the epipolar geometry [11] or the trifocal tensor [5] model the underlying geometry between the camera positions relating to two or three video frames and as such can be used to model the 3-d structure of the scene. The problem occurs when applying these 3-d metrics to video sequences. Firstly these methods often appear

1051-4651/00 $10.00 © 2000 IEEE

unstable in the presence of inaccurate feature data. Georgis [2] demonstrates the improvement obtained by utilising matches derived from high quality optic flow estimation versus feature corellation, but even then, the calculation of 3-d metrics may still be hampered by the presence of outliers and so on. Another problem occurs when attempting to calculate 3-d metrics from images for which the camera motion would lead to ambiguities in 3-d reconstruction [8]. One such case is for a purely translatory camera motion. Video sequences typically exhibit more lateral motion of the camera than rotation or zoom. Under this observation, the temporal closeness of adjacent video frames causes adjacent frames to exhibit negligible rotation and will approximate a translation. A solution appears to be the long tracking of features, with the assumption being that at some point during the sequence a valid camera configuration would occur and that a wide angular separation of the cameras would help induce stability.

2 Motion Estimation

Motion estimation between two images has a long research history [3],[1],[7],[10]. The fact that we are working with video sequences helps guarantee that we meet the rapid frame sampling constraint that should be satisfied for optic flow methods to succeed [3], but in doing so we need to constrain ourselves to using a purely translatory motion model. Between frames, the non-translatory components of motion such as shear, rotation and scaling are assumed to be negligible and considering them within a direct calculation can lead to the introduction of errors [7]. The translatory motion model is therefore employed and feature trajectories corroborated by checking the residual of each feature under a higher motion model after a certain number of frames. Traditionally this optic flow calculation is carried out within a small patch located around each feature [10]. This however is counterproductive. Features typically correspond not only to peaks of texture information within a single object, but more frequently are caused by some junction of objects and background within the image. Over time, the motion checking technique becomes less relevant; the 3-d motion of the camera causes a change in the composition of the patch, no motion model is able to compensate this.

Our solution is to approximate the scene by a set of planar patches with each patch defined by three corner features and the image of the triangular patches forming a mesh on the image plane. Each patch is then matched in subsequent images using a combination of gradient techniques [7] and weighted averaging to preserve mesh consistency. Under this scheme each patch corresponds to either a single object in which case the matching process is not hindered by the patch changing composition, or the patch spans for example a point on an object and two on the background. By examining the match residual we can detect these latter cases, and also situations where patches are being revealed or occluded by the effects of camera motion. After estimating the aggregate motions of the corner points of a triangular patch, we may then calculate an estimate of the 3-d plane-plane mapping of that patch from frame to frame. Rather than traditional motion estimation techniques where feature points are allowed unconstrained motions, we have attempted to guide the motion estimation based on the principle that we are looking at the constrained motion of planar patches under a 3-d motion of the camera.

3 Methodology

The first stage in our process is to locate features. We extract corners using the modified Harris Corner Detector as described in [11]. This is based on the following corner metric (defined for image window w and intensity gradients $\partial I/\partial x, \partial I/\partial y$)

$$R(x,y) = AB - C^2 - k(A+B)^2$$

$$\begin{aligned} A &= (\partial I/\partial x)^2 \otimes w \\ B &= (\partial I/\partial y)^2 \otimes w \\ C &= (\partial I/\partial x)(\partial I/\partial y) \otimes w \end{aligned}$$

Following [11] we take the value of k as 0.04 to help discriminate against step edges. R takes values that are positive in corner regions, negative in edge regions and small in flat regions. We extract our features by searching for local maxima of R that are greater than a given threshold.

Given a set of features we next group them into triangles. Whilst it may be possible to drive this process using image based metrics, for example locating triangle edges with object edges, we use an arbitrary grouping based upon a method for the Delauney Triangulation as described in [6]. This gives us a set of triangles that fit one of three basic forms, those that tessellate the background, those that tessellate objects and those that occupy the image regions between objects and background. At this stage we purge all patches with a small area and or a small minimum angle. Experience shows that these are tracked unreliably.

Between adjacent frames the triangular patches will undergo motion. There are many methods for the detection of motion between q frames; it is not necessary to go into detail here, for a full description of methods of motion detection the reader is directed to [1]. In brief, we assume that our triangular patch is of a single object and that the intensity and texture of that patch will remain constant between frames.

$$I(x,y,t) = I(\delta_1(x,y), \delta_2(x,y), t+\tau)$$

δ_1 and δ_2 define the motion field between frames. Since we assume a negligible perspective warping between frames [7] we use a translatory motion model as an approximation of the motion of a patch between adjacent frames. Following [10] We then minimise with respect to motion the residual.

$$\epsilon = \sum [I(\delta_1(x,y), \delta_2(x,y), t+\tau) - I(x,y,t)]^2$$

Taking the first-order Taylor expansion of $I(\mathbf{x}+\mathbf{d}, t+\tau)$ and taking derivatives with respect to $\mathbf{d}$ as zero, the following linear system is obtained.

$$G\mathbf{d} = \mathbf{e} = \sum_{\mathbf{w}} \begin{bmatrix} I_x^2 & I_x I_y \\ I_x I_y & I_y^2 \end{bmatrix} \begin{bmatrix} d_x \\ d_y \end{bmatrix} = \sum_{\mathbf{w}} \begin{bmatrix} I_t I_x \\ I_t I_y \end{bmatrix}$$

where $\mathbf{d} = [\mathbf{d_x}, \mathbf{d_y}]^{\mathbf{T}}$ specifies the motion parameters. The region $\mathbf{w}$ is defined by the triangular patch. $\mathbf{d}$ is then solved iteratively by taking $\mathbf{d_0} = [\mathbf{0}, \mathbf{0}]^{\mathbf{T}}$ and repeatedly predicting new frames via $\mathbf{d_i} = \mathbf{G}^{-1}\mathbf{e}_{(\mathbf{i-1})}$ until the motion estimate converges.

We desire as a part of the motion estimation that our mesh remains consistent with no holes. This is achieved by using the motion of each triangle to vote for the motion of each of its corners.

$$motion_{\triangle ABC} = motion_A = motion_B = motion_C$$

Each triangle has 3 corners, each of which is possibly a part of several triangles. Each triangle affects the motion estimate of its corners. We assume that a good estimation of the motion of a corner node is the weighted average of the motions of its triangles.

$$motion_A = \sum_i \frac{1}{w_i} motion_{\triangle AB_iC_i}$$

$$w_i = \frac{\epsilon}{\int_{R=\triangle AB_iC_i} dR}$$

Similar equations are derived for each feature. This formulation helps us overcome problems that occur when a triangular patch spans an object and the background, or when one patch occludes another. These problems are evidenced by a high residual. In the case when the patch consists of a moving object and part of the background the content of the triangle is constantly changing and offers less support to its corners than other triangles. When a triangular patch is being occluded, the residual will increase from frame to frame. When the occlusion (residual) increases above a certain level, the patch is removed from consideration. This also occurs when a patch moves out of the field of view.

After this averaging process, the motion of each individual triangle has imparted an aggregate motion to each of our features. The matrix G for each patch is calculated from one image, say the first, we then calculate our current motion estimate for each patch from this single image by inverse warping our aggregate motion estimates to our initial positions. At this point it is reasonable to employ a full plane-plane motion model which is readily solved for 3 point correspondences (x_i, y_i, z_i from our triangular patch). This models the estimated "3-d motion" of the planar patches. Similarly to other methods, we check the accuracy of this estimate by monitoring the residual of the patch. As the residual increases, both in absolute and relative terms, the influence of that patch is reduced. In this way if a patch is tracked badly, it has less influence on the aggregate motions of its corners.

4 Results

Space restrictions do not allow many pictorial results. Figure 1 shows the proposed method in action on a short video clip. Figure 1.1 shows the initial scene with the detected feature points marked and figure 1.2 the initial mesh. The motion of this seqence is relatively complex with the camera undergoing a complex 3-d motion and it is expected that the sequence will be rich in perspective effects. The mesh is adjusted at each frame in the sequence and several frames later the mesh has successfully adapted to fit the new scene viewpoint (figure 1.3).

We wish to quantify the benefits of this method. For this we consider the RMS distance of matches from the epipolar lines derived from the fundamental matrix calculated from a set of matches. We would hope that a 3-d estimation applied to our matches would yield a smaller overall error in fitting than other methods. We take the entire set of matches that correspond to rigid, stationary objects in the scene and fit firstly a least square approximation to the fundamental matrix and secondly a non-linear estimation [11]. Specifically, we calculate

$$RMSerror = \sqrt{\left(\frac{1}{N}\sum_{i=1}^{N} x_i'^T F x_i\right)^2}$$

Brief results are presented in table 1 for the first lab

Figure 1. The tracking method employed on the 'lab1' sequence

sequence, a second lab sequuence, and finally a short clip of taken from a movie; this is of two actors moving in front of a heavily structured 3-d background (as the actors are not part of the 3-d static scene, their matches were removed prior to the error calculation). These results show an overall improvement in the placement of features through our method versus a standard gradient based feature tracker.

Sequence	3-d Est. Method	Tracking Method	
		Mesh	Standard
Lab1	Linear FM	1.2	1.7
	Non-linear FM	1.1	1.4
Lab2	Linear FM	0.6	1.0
	Non-linear FM	0.4	0.7
Movie	Linear FM	0.6	1.0
	Non-linear FM	0.4	0.7

Table 1. RMS errors of 3-d Estimation "fit"

5 Conclusions

We have presented a method for finding feature correspondences throughout a series of video frames using an active mesh. The mesh is automatically derived from a single video frame based on image features. By considering the mesh as an image of planar patches each undergoing a plane-plane 3-d motion, we explicity take measures to avoid some of the inherent problems of tracking features through a sequence containing 3-d information and moving objects. This allows use to fit 3-d metrics to a high degree of accuracy.

6 Acknowledgements

The authors would like to acknowledge support from EPSRC grant GR/L61095. We would also like to acknowledge the use of Richard Shewchuk's triangle library [6].

References

[1] M. Bober. *General Motion Estimation and Segmentation from Image Sequences.* PhD. Thesis, University of Surrey (1994).

[2] M. Bober, N. Georgis, J. Kittler. *On Accurate and Robust Estimation of Fundamental Matrix* Computer Vision and Image Understanding, vol.72 p39-53 (1998).

[3] BKP. Horn, BG. Schunck. *Determining Optic Flow* Artificial Intelligence, vol.17, p185-203 (1981).

[4] D. Molloy, P.F. Whelan. *Tracking Using Self-Initialising Active Meshes.* 7th Int. Conf. Image Processing and its Applications, Manchester U.K., p701-705 (1999).

[5] A. Shashua, M. Werman *On the Trilinear Tensor of Three Perspective Views and its Underlying Geometry.* Proc. of the 1995 International Conference on Computer Vision, Boston MA (1995).

[6] R. Shewchuk. *Triangle: Engineering a 2D Quality Mesh Generator and Delaunay Triangulator.* ACM First Workshop on Applied Computational Geometry, Philadelphia, p124-133 (1996)

[7] J. Shi, C. Tomasi, *Good Features to Track.* IEEE Conf. CVPR 1994, Seattle, p593-600 (1994).

[8] P. Sturm *Critical motion sequences for monocular self-calibration and uncalibrated Euclidean reconstruction.* Proc. of the 1997 Conference on Computer Vision and Pattern Recognition, Puerto Rico, p1100-1105 (1997)

[9] PHS. Torr, A. Zisserman. *Robust Parametrization and computation of the trifocal tensor.* Image and Vision Computing, vol.15, p591-605 (1997).

[10] T. Tommasini, A. Fusiello, E. Trucco, V. Roberto *Making Good Features Track Better.* IEEE Conf. CVPR 1998, Santa Barbara, p178-183 (1998).

[11] Z. Zhang, R. Deriche, O. Faugeras, Q Luong *A Robust Technique for Matching Two Uncalibrated Images Through the Recovery of the Unknown Epipolar Geometry.* Technical Report nr 2273 INRIA. ISSN 0249-6399 (1994).

Detection and Location of People in Video Images Using Adaptive Fusion of Color and Edge Information

Sumer Jabri, Zoran Duric, Harry Wechsler
Department of Computer Science
George Mason University
Fairfax, VA 22030
{sjabri,zduric,wechsler}@cs.gmu.edu

Azriel Rosenfeld
Center for Automation Research
University of Maryland
College Park, MD 20742-3275
ar@cfar.umd.edu

Abstract

A new method of finding people in video images is presented. Detection is based on a novel background modeling and subtraction approach which uses both color and edge information. We introduce confidence maps—gray-scale images whose intensity is a function of our confidence that a pixel has changed—to fuse intermediate results and to represent the results of background subtraction. The latter is used to delineate a person's body by guiding contour collection to segment the person from the background. The method is tolerant to scene clutter, slow illumination changes, and camera noise, and runs in near real time on a standard platform.

1 Introduction

Many authors have developed methods of detecting people in images [1, 2, 3, 4, 6, 7]. Most of this work has been based on background subtraction using color or luminance information. The results usually suffer from false positives/negatives when conditions are not favorable. In this paper, we present a novel background subtraction method that utilizes both color and edge information to improve the quality and reliability of the results and overcome some of the difficulties faced by existing methods.

Our approach is divided into three main parts: (i) building and maintaining the background model, (ii) performing background subtraction, and (iii) delineating the foreground. We will illustrate our method using the images shown in Figure 1. These images were collected at the Keck Laboratory at the University of Maryland in College Park using a SONY progressive 3CCD digital camera; the images are RGB color, and the frame rate was sixty frames per second.

Figure 1. Frames 125 and 225 from a 300-frame sequence of a moving human.

2 Building the Background Model

The background is modeled in two distinct parts, the color model and the edge model. For each color channel, the color model is represented by two images which hold the mean and standard deviation of that color component in a video sequence of the static background scene. The mean image is computed at each pixel as a weighted mean

$$\mu_t = \alpha x_t + (1-\alpha)\mu_{t-1}$$

where μ_t is the mean computed up to frame t, α is the learning rate of the model, and x_t is the pixel value in frame t. In effect, this computes an exponentially weighted mean of all the previous values of the pixel. Subtracting incoming video frames from this mean will allow us to identify pixels that have changed color.

The standard deviation image σ_t is defined by

$$\sigma_t^2 = \alpha(x_t - \mu_t)^2 + (1-\alpha)\sigma_{t-1}^2.$$

It will be used in the confidence normalization phase during background subtraction.

The edge model is built by applying the Sobel edge operator to each color channel. This yields a horizontal difference image H and a vertical difference image V. Weighted means H_t and V_t and standard deviations are computed as in the color model. We maintain horizontal and vertical Sobel responses separately in order to preserve gradient direction information; whenever the gradient magnitude is needed, we compute it from these responses. This model will be used to locate changes in the structure of the scene as edges appear, disappear, or change direction.

Even in a static scene, frame to frame changes occur due to noise, camera jitter, and varying illumination. These factors are quite difficult to control. Therefore, to preserve the validity of our background model we update the mean images continuously. Figure 2 shows the images μ_{60}, H_{60}, and V_{60} computed from the green channel of the sequence illustrated in Figure 1.

Figure 2. Mean images for color, horizontal edges, and vertical edges (green channel shown) at the 60th frame of the sequence.

3 Background Subtraction

Background subtraction is performed by subtracting the color channels and edge channels separately and then combining the results.

3.1 Color-Based Subtraction

In the color subtraction phase, we subtract the current video frame from the stored mean image. This is done for each color channel, resulting in three difference images. Next, we perform a confidence normalization step for every channel using two thresholds, $m\sigma$ and $M\sigma$, derived from the standard deviation images. If the value of the difference is below $m\sigma$ the confidence is set to 0%, if it is above $M\sigma$ the confidence is set to 100%; for intermediate values of the difference, the confidence is scaled linearly:

$$C^c = \frac{D - m\sigma}{M\sigma - m\sigma} \times 100$$

where D is the difference value.

Since change in any color channel can be an indicator of a foreground region, we take the maximum of the three confidence images. The higher the value of this maximum at a pixel, the more confident we are that the pixel belongs to the foreground. Examples of these confidence maps for frames 125 and 225 in the sequence of Figure 1 are shown in Figure 3.

Figure 3. Color subtraction result for frames 125 and 225 of the sequence in Figure 1.

3.2 Edge-Based Subtraction

In the edge subtraction phase, we take into account the changes in both edge magnitude and edge direction. In this phase we also classify edges as foreground edges, occluded background edges, and background edges.

For each color channel, we subtract the current x and y difference images from the corresponding mean images:

$$\Delta H = |H - H_t|, \quad \Delta V = |V - V_t|$$

where H and V are the horizontal and vertical differences in the current frame and H_t and V_t are the mean horizontal and vertical differences. We then define the edge gradient as

$$\Delta G = \Delta H + \Delta V.$$

We now describe how we assign confidences to those Δ's. To illustrate this, suppose we have two background edges, one having magnitude 50 and the other 100. In the incoming video frame, suppose both edges change magnitude by the same amount, 10. The stronger edge has thus changed by 10%, whereas the weaker edge has changed by 20%—a much more significant change. The ratio of the difference to the strength of the edge can be used to express our confidence in the difference; we call it the edge reliability R. It is computed as follows: Let

$$G = |H| + |V|, \quad G_t = |H_t| + |V_t|, \quad G_t^* = \max\{G, G_t\}.$$

Then

$$R = \frac{\Delta G}{G_t^*}.$$

We use this R to weight the edge gradient difference: $R\Delta G$. The confidence that a pixel belongs to the foreground based on the edge strength in a color channel is then

$$C^e = \begin{cases} 0\% & R\Delta G < m\sigma \\ \frac{R\Delta G - m\sigma}{M\sigma - m\sigma} \times 100\% & m\sigma \leq R\Delta G \leq M\sigma \\ 100\% & R\Delta G > M\sigma \end{cases}$$

where σ is the sum of the standard deviations in the horizontal and vertical directions. The final confidence map is then built by taking a maximum of the three computed confidences; it is illustrated in Figure 4.

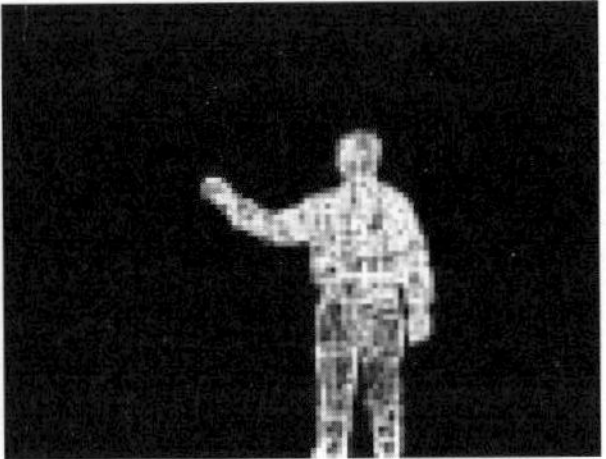

Figure 4. Edge subtraction result for frames 125 and 225 of the sequence in Figure 1.

This phase also classifies the edges using the following rules:

1. Occluding Edges: These are edges of objects that have entered the scene. They occur when there is a significant difference in some channel between the mean and current frames, and there is an edge in the current frame of significant strength, i.e. $G_t \geq m\sigma$.

2. Occluded Edges: These are background edges that have been occluded by objects. They occur when there is a significant difference between the mean and current edges, and there is no significant current edge.

3. Background Edges: These are mean edges that have not changed. They occur when there is no difference between the mean and current edges.

The edge subtraction phase produces two outputs: a confidence map of foreground edges, and an edge image in which edges have been classified as occluding, occluded, or background.

3.3 Combining the Color and Edge Subtraction Results

We combine the color and edge confidence maps by taking their maximum:

$$C = \max\{C^c, C^e\}$$

Figure 5 shows the result of this step for frames 125 and 225. It can be seen that the color and edge results complement one another to yield well-defined foreground objects.

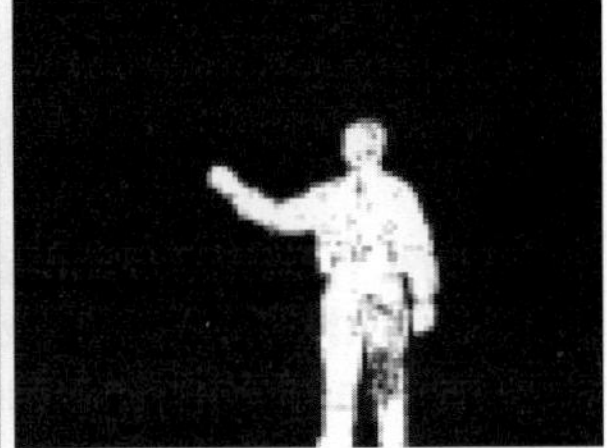

Figure 5. Combined subtractions for frames 125 and 225 of the sequence in Figure 1.

A single median filtering step is applied to the resulting confidence map to remove salt and pepper noise, i.e. to fill holes in regions of high confidence and remove isolated pixels in regions of low confidence. The final output of this step is a confidence map based on both color and edge subtraction results, as illustrated in Figure 6.

Figure 6. Combined subtraction results after median filtering for frames 125 and 225 of the sequence in Figure 1.

4 Locating and Delineating the Foreground

The foreground represents the objects that have entered the scene; it is defined by the gray level foreground confidence map, and by the contour that delineates the foreground objects from the background.

We use a connected components algorithm to label connected regions in the confidence map. A hysteresis thresholding step is then applied to remove false positives by eliminating all components that are not connected to a 100% confidence region. The resulting binary map, shown in Figure 7, contains the foreground regions detected by the our method; it is stored in our foreground model as the first representation.

Figure 7. Connected components after hysteresis thresholding for frames 125 and 225 of the sequence in Figure 1.

Finally, we extract the contours of these regions using a contour following algorithm. The resulting contours, shown in Figure 8, are stored in our foreground model as the second representation.

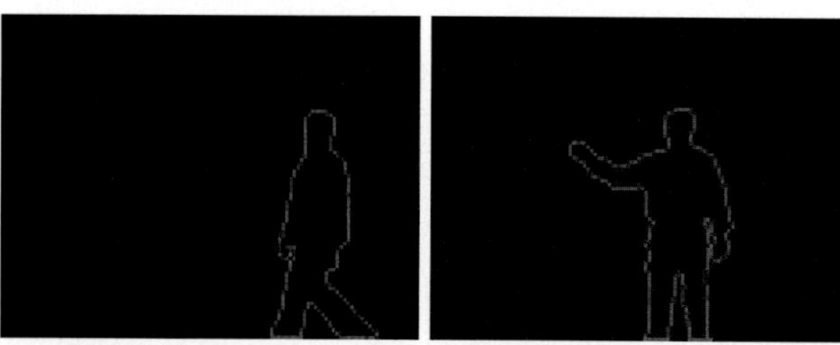

Figure 8. Collected contours for frames 125 and 225 of the sequence in Figure 1.

Figure 9 shows the segmented human with the contour overlaid in white to demonstrate the quality of segmentation and how well the delineating contour fits the human.

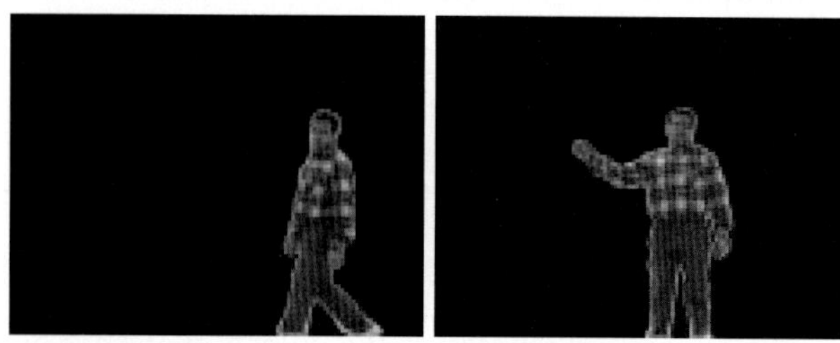

Figure 9. Segmented human for frames 125 and 225 of the sequence in Figure 1. The collected contours are overlaid in white over the image.

Our method was tested on 14 different video sequences, collected under various conditions [5]. These included 5 indoor sequences, using a SONY 3CCD progressive digital camera (Camera 1), with two kinds of illumination conditions: halogen and fluorescent. The remaining 9 sequences were outdoor sequences collected using a SONY CCD TR500 Handycam (Camera 2). The four system parameters were set to

$$\begin{array}{ll} m_c = 15 & m_e = 3 \\ M_c = 25 & M_e = 9 \end{array}$$

where m_c and M_c are the color thresholds, and m_e and M_e are the corresponding edge thresholds. These thresholds were not changed or tweaked for any of the sequences. Additional results can be viewed at *http://www.cs.gmu.edu/~sjabri/research/*.

5 Conclusions

The new method for detecting and locating people proved to be tolerant to camera noise and slight illumination changes. In addition, since edges are used in subtraction, this approach makes use of, and indeed favors, clutter in both the scene and the human (clothing, etc.). It could be used as a first step toward more task-specific research such as automated surveillance, augmented reality, human gesture recognition, human computer interaction, and very low bandwidth communication.

References

[1] J.W. Davis and A.F. Bobick. The representation and recognition of human movement using temporal templates. In *Proc. Computer Vision and Pattern Recognition*, pages 928–934, 1997.

[2] L.S. Davis, D. Harwood, and I. Haritoaglu. Ghost: A human body part labeling system using silhouettes. In *Proc. ARPA Image Understanding Workshop*, pages 229–235, 1998.

[3] D.M. Gavrila and L.S. Davis. 3D model-based tracking of humans in action: A multi-view approach. In *Proc. Computer Vision and Pattern Recognition*, pages 73–80, 1996.

[4] I. Haritaoglu, D. Harwood, and L. Davis. W4S: A real-time system for detecting and tracking people. In *Proc. Computer Vision and Pattern Recognition*, pages 962-968, 1998.

[5] S. Jabri. Detecting and delineating humans in video images. Master's thesis, Computer Science Department, George Mason University, Fairfax, Virginia, September 1999.

[6] S.X. Ju, M.J. Black, and Y. Yacoob. Cardboard people: A parameterized model of articulated image motion. In *Proc. International Workshop on Automatic Face and Gesture Recognition*, pages 38–44, 1996.

[7] C. R. Wren, A. Azarbayejani, T. Darrell, and A. Pentland. Pfinder: Real-time tracking of the human body. *IEEE PAMI*, 19:780–785, 1997.

Locating People in Indoor Scenes for Real Applications

Albert Pujol, Felipe Lumbreras, Xavier Varona, Juan José Villanueva
Computer Vision Center and Departament d'Informàtica
Edifici O, Universitat Autònoma de Barcelona
08193 Cerdanyola, Spain.
albert@cvc.uab.es

Abstract

A real person description application needs as first step a robust process of people location. Locating people supposes to find out the subject position and extent. This paper presents a robust architecture for solving this problem in static images. The work presented combines in a probabilistic manner, information from background, skin and shape models. This method is being tested in a large set of images for a real application.

1. Introduction

The framework of this application is a big project that tries to characterize people entering in a building. The goal of this project is to achieve a description of these people in a natural language. Nowadays skill persons do this task and we want to relegate this work to a computer vision system.

An application devoted to describe people in high level manner needs a previous step where each people in the image must be segmented. Only the interest subject should be analyzed and therefore the rest of people and background must be removed. This is usually referred as human body segmentation and it is the scope of the work described on this paper.

Some previous methods usually related to action and gait recognition [3] propose solutions for the human body segmentation problem. Some of them are based on motion information [5], human body texture [8], deformable shape models [6], and background modeling [4][7][9]. The method presented in this paper deals with a real application which restricts the usefulness of some of the previous methods, and present some advantages which can not be taken into account in a general purpose method. These restrictions are that of working with static indoor images, and that only the upper half of the human body appears in the images.

2. Overall application description

The security division of a casino has requested this application. The entrances to the casinos dispose of a set of register desks. Each of these desks disposes of a closed circuit camera. The images taken with these cameras are used to identify whomever person that could cause disturbances inside the casino. In these cases further entrance of this person can be banned.

The work presented in this paper shows the system that has been developed in order to make this process in a fast and automatic way. The process works as follow: 1) an image of the people placed in front of the desk is taken. 2) The acquired image is displayed on a screen on the desk. The silhouettes of each of the persons that appear in these images are marked in different colors. 3) The person in charge of the desk selects one of the persons of the image and introduces his name and identification number. 4) The image of that person is then recorded and used in order to obtain a brief high level description of the subject (hair color, height, cloth colors, and some face descriptors like presence of moustache, beard, ...)

The work described in this paper is related to the steps 1 to 3 of this architecture. So that, the process that we will describe here, receives as input an image (of an scene made up of one ore more subjects) and obtains as output the segmented image of the selected subject.

The method that we propose for segmenting people in crowded images works as follow: 1) The illumination of the image is corrected so that it resembles the illumination conditions of a background image model. 2) Pixels are classified as background, foreground, or skin. 3) The foreground pixels are grouped, so that pixels belonging to different persons have different labels. Each one of these steps will be described in the following sections.

3. Background subtraction

Detection of people implies to differentiate between background (strongly related to objects that not vary in the images) and foreground (related to people). Some previous works (Pfinder [9], W4 [4]) broach this problem in a statistical way. These methods usually take a set of background reference images. These images are used to estimate the probability density function (PDF) that an image pixel belongs to background. The PDF applied in these methods encompass in the same model the variations of the background pixels due to illumination changes and acquisition noise. The application of these methods to our problem produces an overrelaxed background model. Where changes on illumination produce the undesirable effect of increasing the number of possible foreground values being classified as background. We propose to restrict the background model dividing the problem of background subtraction into two steps: a) The illumination of the background of the image is corrected to resemble a reference background model. b) The PDF of the noise present in the background images is estimated. And the probability of belonging to the background is computed using this PDF.

3.1 Illumination correction

Despite that images are taken in an indoor environment, subtle changes in the global intensity contrast between images can be appreciated. Although the global contrast ratio between two images of the same background is near one, differences of 0.1 are typical, that means a difference of 25 gray levels in white regions. To minimize this trouble, images are adjusted in order to obtain similar global contrast values between the background of the images to be segmented and a reference background image.

Once a set of background images $\{B^1(x,y), B^2(x,y), \ldots, B^L(x,y)\}$has been acquired, the reference background image $M(x,y)=(M_R(x,y), M_G(x,y), M_B(x,y))$ is computed as its average. The effects of illumination changes are assumed to be isotropic and to act as an independent contrast factor for each color channel. That is to say, a background image $B^i(x,y)$ can be expressed as:

$$B^i(x,y) = M(x,y)\begin{pmatrix} k_R & 0 & 0 \\ 0 & k_G & 0 \\ 0 & 0 & k_B \end{pmatrix} + \varepsilon(x,y)$$

where $\varepsilon(x,y)=(\varepsilon_R(x,y), \varepsilon_G(x,y), \varepsilon_B(x,y))$ is a zero mean noise term, which will be explained in the next section, and k_R, k_G and k_B are the parameters that must be determined in order to correct the illumination. An estimation of the k factors (k_R, k_G and k_B) could be found by minimum squared errors, in a similar way as it is done in the eigenbackground model [7]. If it would be done, foreground objects could introduce a bias in the estimation of the contrast values. This estimation can be done in a more robust way by a voting process: the k factors between the image and the background reference image are calculated for each image location. The most voted k factor value will be taken as the global contrast term. To calculate these votes for an image pixel implies to perform a division of two values with a range form 0 to 255, presenting two drawbacks:

- The result of this division can go from 0 to infinity.
- The possible values of k are not evenly distributed. It means that not all the slopes in an integer grid have the same probability to occur due to the limitation of integer positions.

The first problem is solved using the arctangent of the division of these values. To avoid the second one, uniform random noise (±0.5) is added to each value before computing its arctangent. The differences between the voting distribution obtained with and without noise addition can be appreciated in Fig. 1.

3.2 Statistical Background Model

The noise error term can be seen as the belonging-to-background probability distribution. Some previous methods model this probability as a gaussian distribution. These methods estimate the variances of grays levels [4] or covariance matrixes of color values [9] of each image pixel. The method that we propose takes profit of the fact that it seems to be a correlation between the noise that appear in the images and the image pixel intensities. So that instead of computing a covariance matrix for each pixel, a unique covariance matrix is computed for all the pixels that present the same intensity level. This simplification has the advantage that covariance values can be robustly estimated with a more reduced number of background images. It can be expressed as:

$$\tilde{B}^i(x,y) = B^i(x,y) - M(x,y) = \left(\tilde{B}_R^{\,i}(x,y), \tilde{B}_G^{\,i}(x,y), \tilde{B}_B^{\,i}(x,y)\right)$$

$$\Sigma_l = \frac{1}{N \cdot L - 1}\sum_{i=1}^{L}\left(\tilde{B}^i(x,y)^T\, \tilde{B}^i(x,y)\right), \quad \forall (x,y) \,\big|\, \|M(x,y)\| = l$$

where Σ_l is the covariance matrix associated to the intensity level l, $\tilde{B}^i(x,y)$ is the illumination-corrected i-th background image, L is the number of background images and N is the number of pixels on the average background image with intensity equals to l.

Once the statistical noise model has been computed a log likelihood criteria is applied to the illumination-corrected images $I(x,y)$ in order to decide if a pixel corresponds to background or foreground, so that, a pixel will be considered as background if:

$$(I(x,y) - M(x,y))\Sigma^{-1}_{\|M(x,y)\|}(I(x,y) - M(x,y))^T < thr$$

where *thr* is a threshold of acceptance value.

2. Skin color detection

It is assumed that human skin color is an important image feature. Its chromatic values remain constant for more different imaging sources [2]. In our application, we model the color skin using a probabilistic approach. Usually skin color distributions are modeled using Mixtures of Gaussians. In our case this distribution has been modeled using a kernel regression method [1]. Direct comparison of the results obtained with these two models show that, given a big enough number of samples, kernel regression improves the results obtained using mixture of gaussians both in its discrimination capacity and speed.

The skin color distribution is easily estimated computing the frequencies of apparition of the different chrominance values for skin pixels. 4000 points from 40 different face images have been manually introduced in order to do so. For each one of these skin pixels its chrominance values (C_R and C_G) are computed as:

$$C_R = \frac{R}{R+G+B}, C_G = \frac{G}{R+G+B}$$

The resulting histogram is smoothed using a gaussian kernel. Its values are then normalized so that its sum is made equal to 1. Once this PDF has been estimated, we can compute the probability that an image pixel belongs to the skin class using the smoothed histogram as a look up table. This model presents some problems when background pixels have similar chromatic values than skin. To avoid them, skin and foreground probabilities are multiplied.

3. Foreground labeling

The aim of this process is to group the foreground pixels, so that different labels are assigned to the pixels belonging to each one of the subject (or furniture changes) of the scene. This process can be seen as: 1) obtaining a set of curves so that all the pixels of the subjects that appear into the scene are enclosed by a curve, and 2) all the pixels inside a closed curve belong to the same subject.

A first set of closed curves enclosing all the subjects of the scene are obtained. These curves are the contour points of the foreground mask obtained by the background subtraction process, we will call to these curves the Foreground Contour Curves set (**FCC**). And they are computed applying a morphological edge detector.

We will refer as $f_i(k)=(x,y)$ to the *i*-th curve of the **FCC** set. And $T(x)$ to a function that runs through the top of the **FCC** set of curves:

$$T(x) = \max_y \{f_i(t) | f_i(t) = (y, x)\}$$

In order to accomplish the second condition, new curves should be added to the **FCC** set so that each new curve must splits one of the regions defined by the previous curves into two regions. Each of these new regions must belong to different subjects.

It has to be noted that the function $T(x)$ of a head and also of a human torso, are convex functions. Thus, when non-convexities are detected in $T(x)$, they can be attributed to two sources: unions between head and torso or the joining points between two different subjects. Using this heuristic, convexity extreme of $T(x)$ are selected as candidate beginning of splitting curves. These curves must run down the image until the bottom of the image is reached.

For each one of the candidate starting points, a set of possible splitting curves are computed. A criterion function $J[f(t)]$ is determined in order to state the quality of each new curve. This function is the integral over $f(t)$ of the vertical derivatives absolute value of the image. In order to construct the splitting curves, a hill climbing methodology is used. So, the curve is made grow in the direction (considering a neighborhood) that maximizes the criterion function. Each time a new position is added to the curve the energy of this position is made equals to zero, avoiding the curve to go into loops and forcing to new splitting curves to run through paths different from the paths crossed by previous splitting curves. In order to force the curves to go down the image, downward directions are weighted higher than other directions.

Five possible curves are computed for each candidate splitting point. Beside these curves, those paths that can be constructed as combination of the previous curves are considered. The criterion function is evaluated then for each one of these candidates, and the one with highest value is taken.

Finally a set of correctly segmented human bodies will be selected from all the closed areas inside which a skin face-like blob has been previously detected.

4. Experimental Results and Validation

Fig. 2 shows some examples of the results obtained with the segmentation process. Some further work must be done in order to avoid some false splitting point candidates.

A major lack in background subtraction and human body segmentation works, is the process of qualitative assessment of the obtained results. In our case we have designed a simple test driven by our application requirements. In order to test the method the full process is actually being validated in the casino. Images are being annotated by hand, marking the contour points of the subject that is being registered. Two qualitative measures will be computed: 1) number of subjects that have been correctly detected. 2) Accuracy factor: for each subject, it is computed the maximum deviation between the measured and annotated contour. Preliminary test shown encouraging results.

7. Discussion and further work

An architecture for human body segmentation is presented. The described system has been designed for an application where images of persons are taken mean while they are in front of a register desk. This architecture can be easily extended to other surveillance applications.

Further work should be addressed in order take profit of human shape models, texture information and template matching.

Acknowledgements

This work has been partially funded by projects 2FD97-1800, TAP98-0618 and Casinos de Catalunya.

8. References

[1] C. M. Bishop, *Neural Networks for Pattern Recognition*, Oxford University Press , 1995.

[2] J. Cai and A. Goshtasby, "Detecting Human Faces in Color Images", in *Image and Vision Computing*, (**18**), pp. 63-75, 1999.

[3] D.M. Gavrilla, "The Visual Analysis of Human Movement: A Survey", in *Computer Vision and Image Understanding*, (**73**), 1, pp. 82-98, 1999.

[4] I. Haritaoglu, D. Harwood and L.S. Davis, "W4: Who? When? Where? What? A Real Time System for Detecting and Tracking People", in *Proceedings of Third International Conference on Automatic Face and Gesture Recognition*, pp. 222-227, Nara, Japan, 1998.

[5] S.X. Ju, M.J. Black and Y.Yacoob, "Cardboard People: A Parametrized Model of Articulated Image Motion", in *Proceedings of Second International Conference on Automatic Face and Gesture Recognition*, pp. 38-44, Killington, Vermont, 1996.

[6] J. McCormick and A. Blake, "A probabilistic exclusion principle for tracking multiple objects", in *Proceedings International Conference on Computer Vision (ICCV'99)*, Corfu, Greece, 1999.

[7] N. Oliver, B. Rosario and A. Pentland, "A Bayesian Computer Vision System for Modeling Human Interactions", in *Proceedings of Intl. Conference on Vision Systems (ICVS'99)*, Gran Canaria, Spain, 1999.

[8] M. Oren, C. Papageorgiou, P. Sinha, E. Osuna and T. Poggio, "Pedestrian Detection Using Wavelet Templates", in *Proceedings of IEEE Conference on Computer Vision and Pattern Recognition (CVPR'97)*, pp. 193-199, San Juan, Puerto Rico, 1997.

[9] C.R. Wren, A. Azarbayejani, T. Darrell and A.P. Pentland, "Pfinder: Real-Time Tracking of the Human Body", in *IEEE Trans. Pattern Analysis and Machine Intelligence*, (**19**), 7, pp. 780-785, 1997.

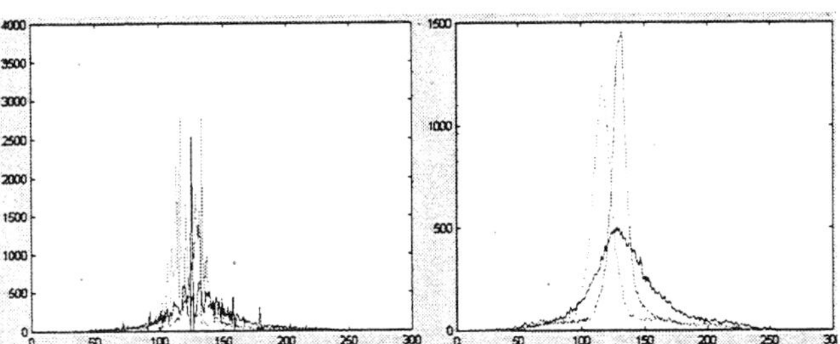

Figure 1. Contrast voting functions for red, green and blue channels, without (left) and with noise addition (right).

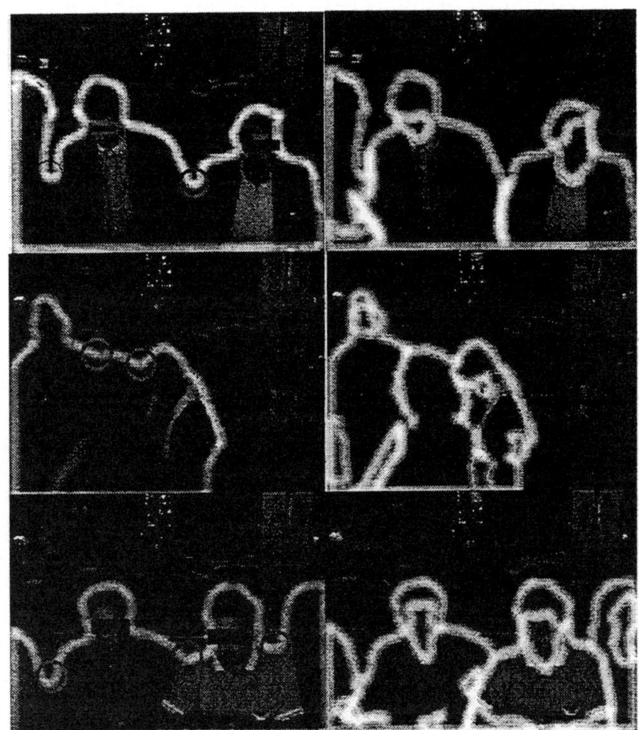

Figure 2. Left column shows contour of the mask obtained with background subtraction, circles have been drawn to show candidate splitting points. Right column shows an overlap display of all the splitting curves and the skin color area contours.

Monitoring Head/Eye Motion for Driver Alertness with One Camera

Paul Smith, Mubarak Shah, and N. da Vitoria Lobo
Computer Science, University of Central Florida, Orlando, FL 32816
{rps43158,shah,niels}@cs.ucf.edu

Abstract

We describe a system for analyzing human driver alertness. It relies on optical flow and color predicates to robustly track a person's head and facial features. Our system classifies rotation in all viewing directions, detects eye/mouth occlusion, detects eye blinking, and recovers the 3D gaze of the eyes. We show results and discuss how this system can be used for monitoring driver alertness.

1. Introduction

A system for classifying head movements would be useful in warning drivers when they fell asleep. Also, it could be used to gather statistics about a driver's gaze.

We describe a framework for analyzing movies of driving and determining when the driver is not paying adequate attention to the road. We use a single camera placed on the car dashboard. We focus on rotation of the head and blinking, two important cues for determining driver alertness.

Our head tracker consists of tracking the lip corners, eye centers, and sides of face. Automatic initialization of all features is achieved using color predicates[5] and connected component algorithms.

Occlusion of the eyes and mouth often occurs when the head rotates or the eyes close, so our system tracks through such occlusion and can automatically reinitialize when it mis-tracks. We implement blink detection and demonstrate that we can obtain 3-D direction of gaze from a single camera. These components allow us to classify rotation in all viewing directions and detect blinking, which, in turn, are necessary components for monitoring driver alertness.

First, we describe previous work and then describe our system in detail. We then present results, discuss driver alertness, and conclude.

1.1. Previous Work

Work on driver alertness [3] [4] [7] [8] [9] [10], to our knowledge, has not yet led to a system that works in a moving vehicle. The most recent of these [3], did not present any methods to acquire the driver's state. Further their method relies on LEDs, and uses multiple cameras to estimate facial orientation. A moving vehicle presents new challenges like variable lighting and changing backgrounds. The first step in analyzing driver alertness is to track the head. Several researchers have worked on head tracking [6] [2], and the various methods each have their pros and cons.

1.2. Input Data

The movies were acquired using a video camera placed on the car dashboard. The system runs on an UltraSparc using 320x240 size images with 30 fps video. Two drivers were tested under different daylight conditions ranging from broad daylight to parking garages. Some movies were taken in moving vehicles and others in stationary vehicles.

1.3. Parts Used from Other Research

A color predicate was originally developed by Kjeldsen *et al.* [5]. The idea, there, is to manually mark subsets of the RGB color space that the algorithm should recognize in future test images.

Anandan's optical flow algorithm [1] produces affine optical flow. It computes the global motion of a scene.

2. The Algorithm

Here is an overview of our algorithm.

1. Automatically initialize lips with color predicate and connected components
2. Automatically initialize eyes using color predicate and connected components
3. Track lip corners with dark line and color predicates
4. Track eyes with affine optical flow and color predicates
5. Construct a bounding box of head using color predicate
6. Determine rotation using distance between eye and lip feature points and sides of face
7. Determine blinking and eye disappearance using the number and intensity of pixels in eye region
8. Reconstruct 3D gaze using constant projection assumptions
9. Make inferences regarding driver's state using rotation and eye occlusion information
10. Decide, using rotation and distance constraints, if eye or lip tracking needs reinitialization
11. Repeat from step 3 for next frame

1051-4651/00 $10.00 © 2000 IEEE

2.1. Initializing Lip and Eye Feature Points

2.1.1. Automatic Lip Initialization

A color predicate was generated using 7 images of people's lips. A few of the training images together with their manually drawn lip regions and automatically selected lip colored pixels by the color predicate are shown in Fig 1.

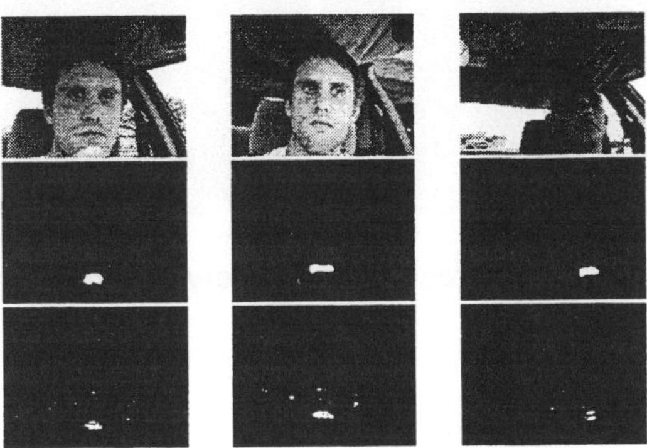

Figure 1. lip color predicate training.

The reason for the salt and pepper noise throughout the image is that backgrounds have lip-like colors in them. Also, parts of the faces were lip colored due to lighting conditions. Fig 2 shows the results of running the lip color predicate on non-training images. After obtaining this lip

Figure 2. color predicate non-trained images.

image, we apply a connected component algorithm to it, and the biggest lip colored region is identified as the mouth. We compute edges of this mouth region and declare these as the lip corners. The initialization does not need pinpoint accuracy as the lip tracker itself will overcome inaccuracies. Fig 3 shows the results of automatic lip initialization on the previously shown input images.

2.1.2. Automatic Eye Initialization

Automatic eye initialization uses skin color predicates as well, though in a different way. Fig 4 shows input images, manually selected skin regions, and the output of the color predicate program on training images.

Figure 3. Output of automatic lip initialization

Figure 4. skin color predicate training

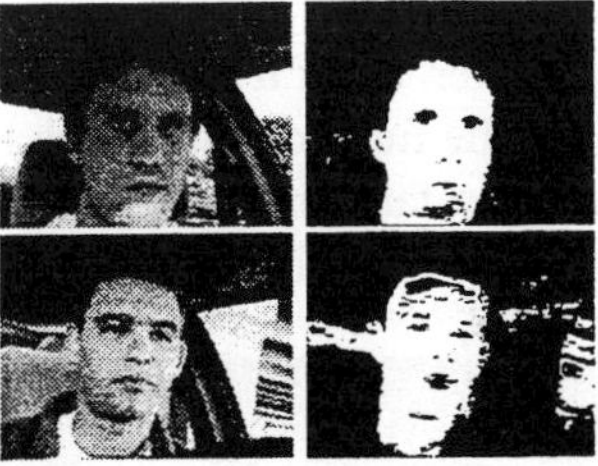

Figure 5. skin found in non-trained images

Fig 5 shows output of the skin color predicate on non-training images. Since eyes are not skin, they always show up as holes. Hence, we find connected components of non-skin pixels to find the eye holes. We find the two holes that are above the previously found lip region, and that satisfy the following size criteria for eyes. Since our dashboard camera is at a fixed distance from the face, we estimate the relative size of eyes to be between 15 and 800 pixels. For all images we tested(several hundred), we found these criteria to be reliable. Fig 6 shows results of automatic eye and lip initialization from various data sets.

2.2. Lip Tracking

We have a multi-stage lip tracker. The first stage is the most accurate but unstable. The second stage is not as accurate but more stable. The third stage is coarse but very stable. We use the first stage estimate, if it is correct. If not

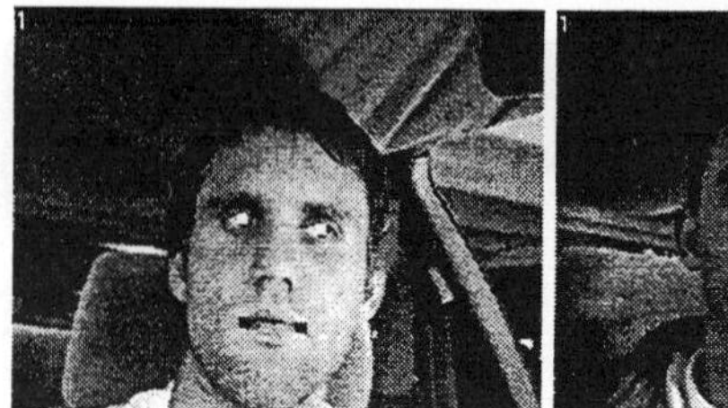

Figure 6. automatic eye and lip initialization

we take the second stage estimate. If both stages fail, we take the third stage estimate as the lip corners.

For the first stage, we automatically find the dark line between the lips, shown in Fig 7 as a white line. We compute this dark line as follows. We find the center of the lips from $\frac{PreviousCornerLeft+PreviousCornerRight}{2}$ and for each side of the mouth we start examining each pixel outward from the lip center. For each pixel, we consider a vertical line and find the darkest pixel, min $\frac{R+G+B}{3}$, on this vertical line. The darkest pixel will generally be a pixel on the dark line between the lips. We do this for 35 subsequent pixels, which is why the mouth line extends beyond the sides of the mouth. To determine where the lip corners are we obtain $f(x) = \frac{1}{DistanceFromClosestCorner} + \frac{1}{Brightness}$ for each pixel; this is because we want a pixel that is close to the previous lip corner, but if it is too bright, then it cannot be the lip corner. The function maximum is the lip corner. If this estimate is too far from the previous lip corner, we run the second stage of our algorithm, described next.

Figure 7. Examples of dark line between lips

Here we use a stricter color constraint. With the darkest line found, we select the pixel closest to the previous lip corner that has lip colored pixels above and below it.

If the second stage fails then we employ the third stage, which is simply reinitialization of the system, as described above in section 2.1.1, within the most recent lip region. In this way we have a method automatically able to correct itself when the tracking is lost due to occlusion. In subsequent frames the previous lip tracking steps will resume control and regain the exact position of the lip corners.

The reason for our hierarchical lip tracker is that large rotation, occlusion, or rapidly changing lighting breaks down the accurate(first) stage. The two other stages are more coarse, but they are more robust. Fig 8 shows the output of the lip tracker for a variety of images.

Figure 8. lip tracker for a variety of sequences

2.3. Eye Tracking

We have a multi-stage eye tracker with similar constraints to the multi-stage lip tracker. For the first stage, we go to the eye center in the previous frame and find the center of mass of the eye region pixels. Then we search a 5×5 window around the center of mass and look for the darkest pixel, which corresponds to the pupil. If this estimate produces a new eye center close to the previous eye center then we take this measurement.

If this stage fails, we run the second stage, where we search a window around the eyes and analyze the likelihood of each non-skin connected region being an eye. We limit the search space to a 7×20 window around the eye. We find the slant of the line between the lip corners. The eye centers we select are the centroids that have the closest slant to that of the lip corners. Still, this method by itself can get lost after occlusion. For simplicity in our description, we refer to these two stages together as the eye black hole tracker.

The third stage, which we call the affine tracker, runs in parallel with the first two stages. Since automatic initialization yields the eye centers, we construct windows around them, and then in subsequent frames, consider a second window centered around the same point. We compute the affine transformation between the windowed subimages and then, since we know the eye center in the previous frame, we warp the subimage of the current frame to find the new eye center. Thus, we have two estimates for the eye centers, one from the eye black hole tracker and one from the affine tracker. When there is rotation or occlusion or when the eye black hole tracker produces an estimate that is too far away from the previous frame, we use the affine tracker solely. In all other cases we take an average of the two trackers to be the eye center. Later, we discuss how we detect rotation.

We use Anandan's algorithm to compute the affine transformation. It is less likely to break down during heavy occlusion. The affine tracker is not as accurate as the eye black hole tracker, because of the interpolation in warping, which is why we don't use it exclusively unless as a last resort. Figs 9 and 10 show some results of the eye and mouth tracker in various images from the data sets.

Figure 9. whole head tracker

Figure 10. head tracker with eye occlusion

Sometimes, after occlusion, the eye tracker mis-tracks. To compensate, whenever the distance between the eyes gets to more than $\frac{1}{4}$M (where M is horizontal image size), we reinitialize the eyes. This criteria was adopted because we know both the location of the camera in the car and the approximate size of the head. We also reinitialize the eyes when the the lips reappear after complete occlusion, which we determine when the number of lip pixels in the lip region drops below five pixels and comes back. The reasoning being that if the lips are fully occluded, then the eyes will not be visible, so when they reappear we should reinitialize.

This eye tracker is very robust; it tracks successfully through occlusion and blinking in our experiments. Further, it is not affected by a moving background, and it has been verified to track continuously on sequences of 400 frames.

2.4. Bounding Box of Face

We can determine face rotation if we have the face's bounding box. To find this box, we start at the center of the head region, which is computed using the average of the eye centers and lip corners. We can do this because the center of the head is approximately located in between these four feature points. We could have found a more accurate centroid of the head, but only a rough estimate is needed here. Then for each side of the face, we start our search at a constant distance from the center of face and look inward finding the first consecutive five pixels that are all skin. Using five pixels, protects us from selecting the first spurious skin pixel. This approach gives an acceptable face contour. We show each side of the face as a straight line, produced from an average of all the positions for that (curved) side of the face in Fig 11, along with the tracked eyes and mouth.

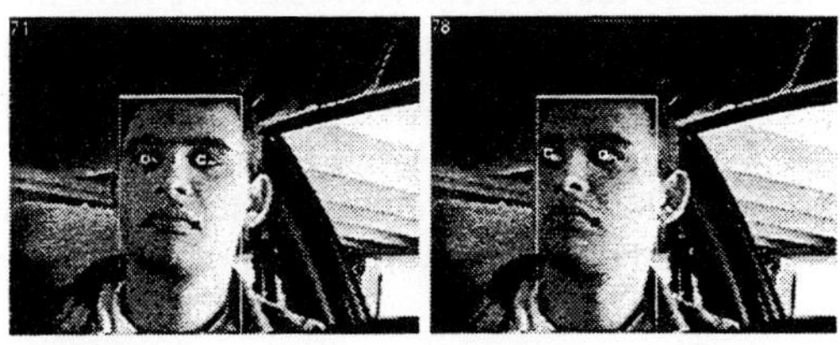

Figure 11. face trace with head tracker

2.5. Occlusion, Rotation, and Blinking

Often the driver blinks or rotates the head, so occlusion of the eyes or lips occurs, which we need to detect. To clarify: our tracker is able to track through most occlusion, but it does not recognize that occlusion (from rotation or blinking) occurred. For driver alertness, we need to develop algorithms to model occlusion so that we can identify these activities. Our occlusion model deals with rotation and blinking, important factors for driver alertness.

Because of foreshortening, when rotation occurs, depending on which direction rotation is occuring in, the distance between the feature points and sides of face will increase or decrease. So, in each frame we compute the distance from the sides and top of the face to the eye centers. We also compute the distance from the side of face from the mouth corners. We take the derivative of these measurements over time and when there is consistent decrease or increase in the distance, this indicates rotation. Formally, when more than half of the distances of a particular feature point indicate rotation in the same direction, then this feature point is assumed to be involved in head rotation. Fig 11 shows how the distance between the face sides and eye and mouth feature points increase and decrease during rotation.

Next, a voting system is constructed where each feature point predicts the direction of rotation. When half or more of the feature points detect rotation, then we declare rotation in this particular direction. Each feature point can be involved in rotation along combinations of directions, but some cases are mutually exclusive(e.g. simultaneous left and right rotation). We have verified that the system can detect rotation along combined directions (e.g. up and left). By considering the distance from the sides and top of head we can discriminate rotation from translation of the head.

Fig 12 shows the output of the whole head tracker including rotation analysis messages, automatically displayed by the system. Next, we present a method to determine when blinking occurs.

We have two methods to eye occlusion detection. The first method computes the likelihood of rotational occlusion of the eyes. To determine occlusion of the eyes we look for the number of skin pixels in the eye region, and when this increases to more than $\frac{4}{5}S$, where S is the size of the eye region, then we assume rotational occlusion is occuring. We know the size of the eye region because we have the non-skin region from the skin color predicate. The reason why we do not just announce rotational occlusion when rotation occurs is that rotation is not a sufficient condition to infer eye occlusion. During small rotation, both eyes will still be visible. Our method works well in rotational occlusion of the eyes.

The next method computes the likelihood of the eyes being closed (blinking). This method relies on the simple fact that the eyes contain eye whites. In each frame as long as there are eye-white pixels in the eye region then we assume that the eyes are open. If not, then we assume blinking in the particular eye is occuring. To determine what is considered eye-white color, in the first frame of each sequence we find the brightest pixel in the eye region. This allows the blink method to adapt to various lighting conditions.

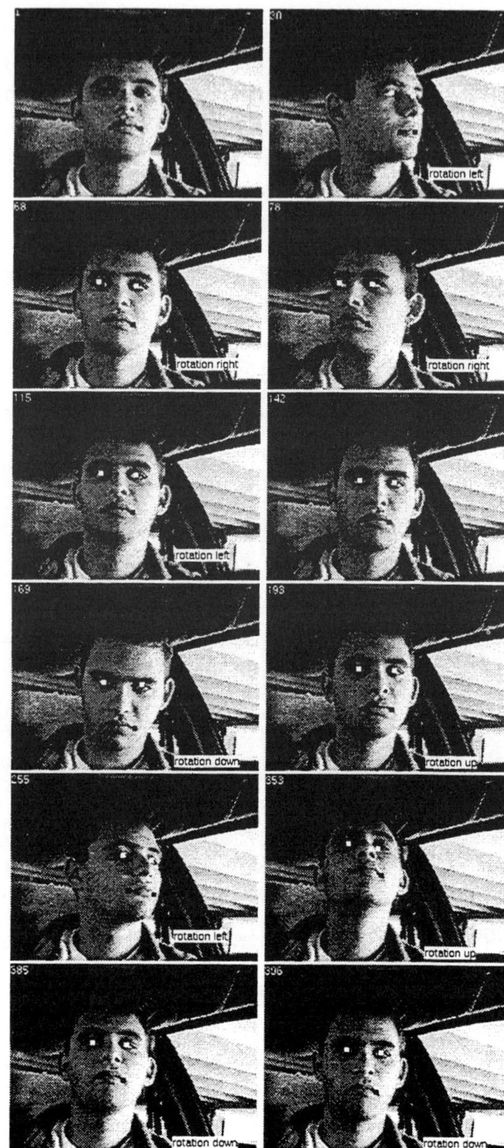

Figure 12. head tracker rotation messages

For the above eye occlusion detection, each eye is independent of the other. Now we are able to distinguish between rotational occlusion of eyes and the eyes closing(blinking). These methods give very good results. Fig 14 shows some of the results from blink detection for both short blinks and long eye closures.

2.6. Reconstructing 3D Gaze Direction

The problem of 3D reconstruction is a difficult one. Already, we have determined rotation information and now we provide a solution to 3D gaze tracking problem with a single camera. The reason we can do this is that we only need the direction of the gaze. For all practical purposes, the gaze could go on through the windshield. By making this assumption we eliminate the need to know the distance from the head to the camera. Also, if we assume that head size is relatively constant between people then we have all the information we need. Since we only want the direction of gaze, we need the x,y locations of the eyes and back of head. With this information, we can construct the line which passes through all the z coordinates. We know the eye locations, so if we can find the back of the head, then we can reconstruct the gaze. We have found through our experimentation that when rotation occurs, the back of the head can be approximated well by the average of the two eyes subtracted from its distance from the center of the head in the first frame. This assumption is valid because when rotation occurs, the average position of the two eyes moves in the opposite direction to the back of the head. When head translation occurs, we add the translation of the average position of the eyes to the original back of the head. This gives us the relative location of the back of the head(relative to the first frame). Since we have the x,y location of the eyes and the back of the head, we can draw lines in xyz space showing the direction of the gaze. This method allows us to derive the gaze direction.

Fig 13 shows some results from acquiring 3D gaze information. The first two pictures are the input pictures. The next two figures are the graphical 3D representation of the scene from the y,z plane (with the x axis coming out of the page). The lowest figure was just one of the pictures from the sequence which shows that the head moves up in this picture with no rotation. This is an important component of the system because now it is possible to generate statistics of where the driver's gaze is.

The system is not foolproof. Given a low-lighting picture the method of head tracking would break down. However, we have tested our program on twelve sequences ranging from 30-400 frames, and the system appears to be very robust and stable.

3. Driver Alertness

In this section we propose ideas about how to use our system to acquire the driver's state.

When the driver is looking away for too long, then we warn that the driver's alertness is too low. Similarly, when the driver's eyes are occluded (either from blinking or rotation occlusion), for too long we warn that the driver's alertness is too low. More of a rigorous analysis on the physiology of sleep behaviors is necessary before accurately determining when a driver has fallen asleep. For our system however, we are able to determine a basic set of criteria to determine driver vigilance. We can do the following. Since we know when the driver's eyes are closed we assume the driver has a low vigilance level if the eyes are closed for more than 40/60 frames. In each frame we always know the number of lip pixels in the image. So we can threshold this number, and whenever there are too few lip pixels we will assume that the head is heavily rotated. We can then print that the driver's vigilance level is too low. However, since it is natural for a driver to look left and right we will only print a driver inalertness message if the heavy lip occlusion occurs for more than 10/20 frames. Finally for general rotation that does not completely occlude the eyes, we will not give driver inalertness warnings unless the rotation is prolonged.

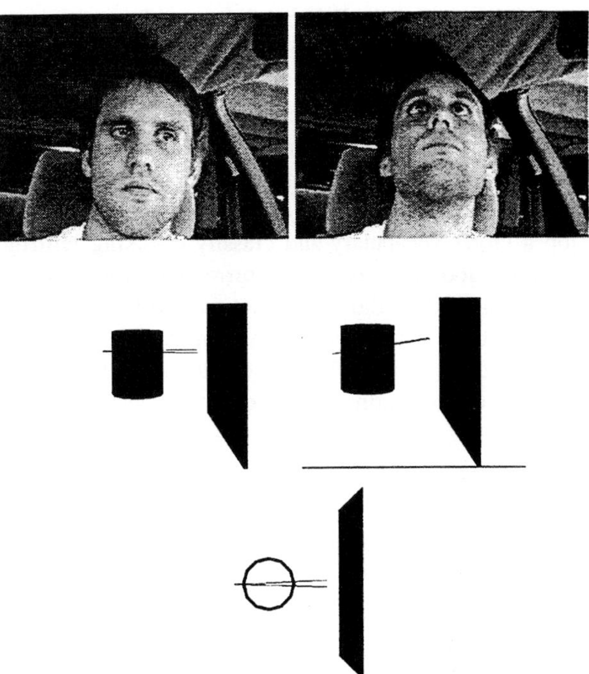

Figure 13. Acquiring 3D info

Again, it is not our intention to delve into the physiology of driver alertness at this time. We are merely demonstrating that with our framework, it is possible to collect driver information and begin to make inferences as to whether the driver is alert or not.

4. Summary and Future Directions

We presented a method to track the head, using color predicates to find the lips, eyes, and sides of the face. It was tested under varying daylight conditions with good success. We compute eye blinking, occlusion information, and rotation information to determine the driver's alertness level.

There are many future directions for driver alertness. For aircrafts and trains, the system could monitor head motions in general and track vehicle operator alertness.

As we can recognize all gaze directions, we could develop a larger vocabulary and classify checking left/right blind spots, looking at rear view mirror, checking side mirrors, looking at the radio/speedometer controls, and looking ahead. Also we could recognize yawning. Other improvements could be coping with hands occluding the face, drinking coffee, conversation, or eye wear.

References

[1] J.R. Bergen, P. Anandan, K. Hanna, R. Hingorani. "Hierarchical Model-Based Motion Estimation." Procs. ECCV, pp. 237-252, 1992.

[2] A.Gee and R. Cipolla. "Determining the Gaze of Faces in Images." Image and Vision Computing, 30:639-647, 1994.

[3] Qiang Ji and George Bebis "Visual Cues Extraction for Monitoring Driver's Vigilance." Procs. Honda Symposium, pp. 48-55, 1999.

[4] M.K. *et al.* "Development of a Drowsiness Warning System." 11th International Conference on Enhanced Safety of Vehicle, Munich, 1994.

[5] Rick Kjedlsen and John Kender "Finding Skin in Color Images." Face and Gesture Recognition, pp. 312-317, 1996.

[6] C. Morimoto, D. Koons, A. Amir, M. Flickner. "Realtime detection of eyes and faces." Workshop on Perceptual User Interfaces, pp. 117-120, 1998.

[7] R. Onken. "Daisy, an Adaptive Knowledge-Based Driver Monitoring and Warning System." Procs. Vehicle Navigation and Information Systems Conference, pp. 3-10, 1994.

[8] H. Ueno, M. Kaneda, and M. Tsukino. "Development of Drowsiness Detection System." Procs. Vehicle Navigation and Information Systems Conference, pp. 15-20, 1994.

[9] Wierville. "Overview of Research on Driver Drowsiness Definition and Driver Drowsiness Detection." 11th International Conference on Enhanced Safety of Vehicles, Munich 1994.

[10] K. Yammamoto and S. Higuchi. "Development of a Drowsiness Warning System." Journal of SAE Japan, 46(9), 1992.

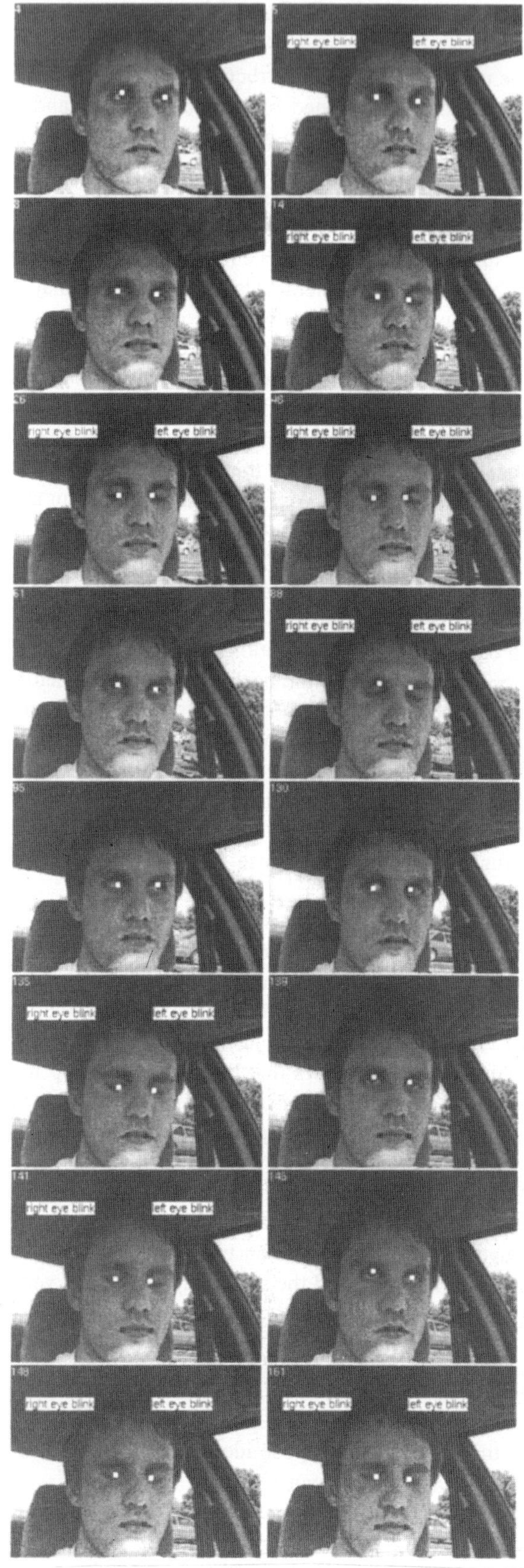

Figure 14. Blink detection with head tracker

Multiple People Tracking Using an Appearance Model Based on Temporal Color*

Hyungki Roh, Seonghoon Kang and Seong-Whan Lee
Center for Artificial Vision Research, Korea University
Anam-dong, Seongbuk-ku, Seoul 136-701, Korea
{hkroh, shkang, swlee}@image.korea.ac.kr

Abstract

We present a method for the detection and tracking of multiple people totally occluded or out of sight in a scene for some period of time in image sequences. Our approach is to use time weighted color information, i.e., the temporal color, for robust medium-term people tracking. It assures our system to continuously track people moving in a group with occlusion. Experimental results show that the temporal color is more stable than shape or intensity when used in various cases.

1. Introduction

A visual surveillance system is a common application of video processing research. Its goal is to detect and track people in a specific environment.

People tracking systems have many various properties from input camera type to detailed algorithm of body parts detection. Darrell *et al.* [1] used disparity and color information for individual person segmentation and tracking. Haritaoglu *et al.* introduced the W4 system [2] and the Hydra system [3] for detecting and tracking multiple people or the parts of their bodies. The KidsRoom system [4] is an application of *closed-world* tracking and utilizes of contextual information to simultaneously track multiple, complex, and non-rigid objects. The Pfinder system [5] used a multi-class statistical model of a person and the background for person tracking and gesture recognition.

The human tracking process is not so simple, in that it does more than merely predict the next position of the target person. The information for each person must be maintained although sometimes he/she is occluded by others or leaves the scene temporarily. To address this problem, each person has to be represented by an appearance model [3]. An appearance model is a set of features with which one person can be discerned from the others. The color, shape, texture or even face pattern can be one of the features of the appearance model.

In this paper, we propose a new people tracking method using an appearance model using the temporal color feature in the image sequences. The temporal color feature is a set of pairs of a color value and its associated weight. The weight is determined by the size, duration, frequency, and adjacency of a color object.

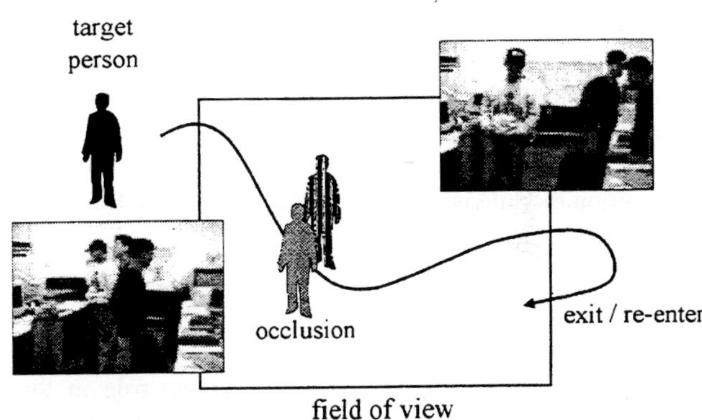

Figure 1. Difficulties in continous tracking of people

The basic motivation of the temporal color is that the color of the target person's clothes is relatively consistent. In traditional approaches, a temporal template is used for continuous tracking, but it is applicable only to the consecutive frame or a short time occlusion. Since the temporal color is a statistical color information with respect to time, it is not susceptible to shape change or noise. This advantage of the temporal color enables a continuous tracking of each person even when a lengthy occlusion occurs.

*This research was supported by Creative Research Initiatives of the Ministry of Science and Technology, Korea.

1051-4651/00 $10.00 © 2000 IEEE

2. Appearance model and temporal color

2.1. Tracking in various temporal scales

The person tracking process is a complex one, if there are multiple people in a scene, and even more so if they are interacting with one another. The tracking process can be classified into three types by the temporal scale, namely short-term, medium-term and long-term tracking [1].

The *short-term tracking* process is applied as long as the target stays in the scene. In this type of tracking, we use the second order motion estimation for the continuous tracking of the target person.

The *medium-term tracking* process is applied after the target person is occluded, either partially or totally, or if they re-enter the scene after a few minutes. Short-term tracking will fail in this case, since the position and size correspondences in the individual modules are unavailable. This type of tracking is very important because the meaningful activity of the tracked person may last for several minutes. The statistical appearance model is essential to accomplish medium-term tracking. The appearance model has many features for representing a person, such as shape, texture, intensity, color, and face pattern.

The *long-term tracking* process is the temporal extension of medium-term tracking. The temporal scale is extended to hours or days. Most of the features are unsuitable for this type of tracking, because they become unstable in such a large temporal scale. The only stable, and therefore useful, features are facial pattern and skin color. Since the face recognition module is not installed in our system, the long-term tracking cannot yet be supported.

2.2. Tracking with an appearance model

The appearance model plays an important role in the multiple people tracking system. Figure 2 shows the position of the appearance model within the tracking module.

The appearance model is used only for the multiple people tracking module because its main function is the proper segmentation and identification of the multiple people group. However, the appearance model can be used in short-term tracking to make it more robust with the positional information available from the model.

In multiple tracking module, the person segmentation process is required. For this purpose, the person segmentation method, which is introduced in [3], is used in our system.

Table 1 shows candidates for features which can be used in the appearance model. Each feature has its own characteristics. The discriminating power (DP) of a feature is its ability of identifying each person. The long-term, the mid-term, and the short-term stability (LS, MS, SS) of a feature

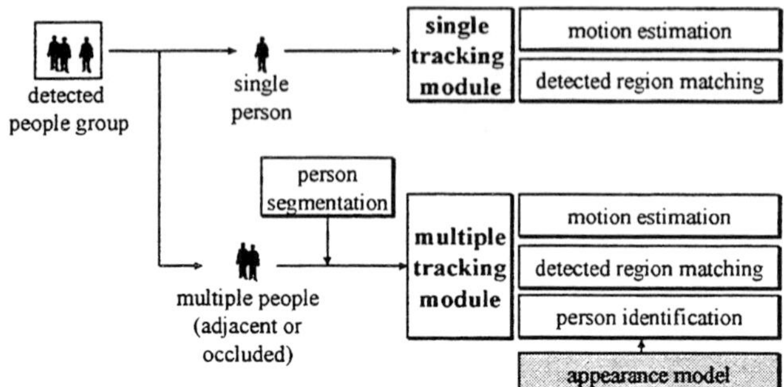

Figure 2. Appearance model in tracking

Table 1. Candidates for features

features	DP	LS	MS	SS	TC
body position	−	−	−	+	+ +
body shape	+	−	−	+	−
depth	−	−	−	+	− −
shirt color	+	−	+	+	+
texture	+	−	+	+	−
skin color	−	+	+	+	+
face pattern	+ +	+	+	+	− −

'+' means that the feature has benefit in the criterion and '−' means that the feature has difficulty in the criterion

indicate their reliability in the corresponding tracking. The time cost (TC) is the complexity of time that it takes in extracting feature information.

Since the color feature are most feasible for fast and robust medium-term tracking, we propose color-based features, namely, the temporal color feature.

2.3. Tracking with temporal color feature

The main idea of temporal color feature is to add shirt color information to the appearance model. The temporal color (F) is defined with the set of color values (C) and its temporal weights (w) as Equation (1).

$$F = \{(C_1, w_1), (C_2, w_2), ..., (C_n, w_n)\} \quad (1)$$

The variable n is determined by the number of color clusters. The first step for calculating the temporal color is the clustering of color space. For each person, a color histogram is constructed and the mean color value of each histogram bin is calculated. Avoiding the quantization error, two bins are merged if their color values are similar. In this way, two or three color clusters for each person can be obtained.

Temporal weight is determined by the size, duration, frequency of its associated color and the existence of adjacent

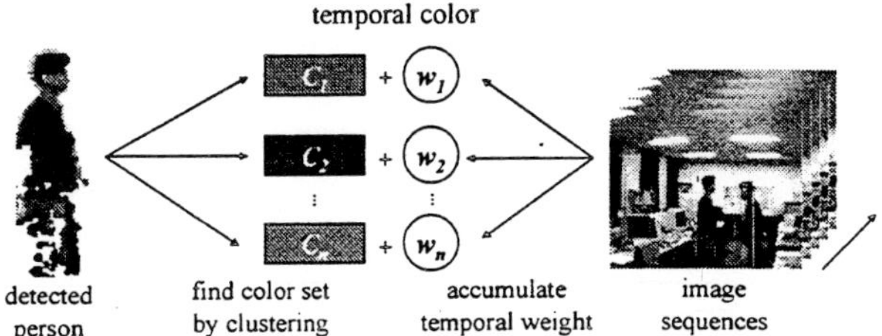

Figure 3. Temporal color

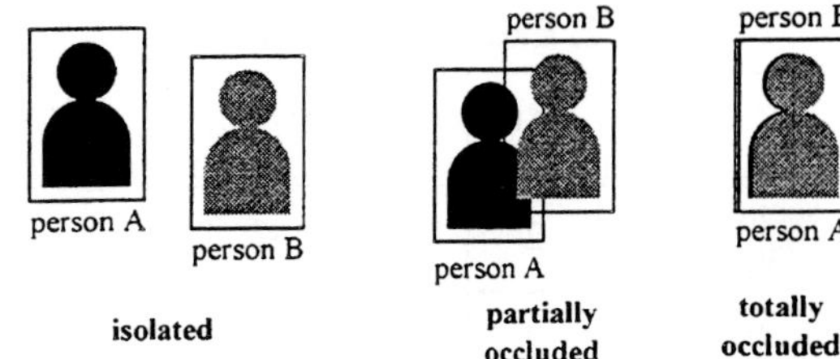

Figure 4. Cases which are considered in adjacency test

objects. The color information of a bigger size, longer duration, and with no adjacent object is more reliable. The relation between weight (w), size (S), duration and frequency (*TA*), and adjacency function (Γ) can be shown as:

$$w_n^t \propto \frac{S_n^t \cdot TA_n^t}{\Gamma(t)} \quad (2)$$

The higher the temporal weight, the more reliable its associated color value. The S is a constant value for each person and the *TA* (time accumulation variable) is increased when the same color is detected continuously.

To model the temporal weight in a computational system, it is simplified into a concrete form. The size and adjacency affect only the incremental degree of *TA*. *TA* represents the duration and frequency of the appearance of the pixel, the color of which is the same as *TA*'s associated color. The basic notion is to increase its weight when the color appears continuously in the frames, and to decrease its weight when the color disappears frequently or does not appear for long frames.

To simulate the effect of the shape size, the increasing and decreasing degrees of *TA* are adjusted to the size. The increasing degree (D_i) and decreasing degree (D_d) can be calculated by

$$D_i = \lfloor \frac{|S^t - S_m^{t-1}|}{S_m^{t-1}} \rfloor + 1 \text{ and } D_d = \lfloor \frac{S^{t-1}}{S_m^{t-1}} \rfloor + 1$$

$$\text{where } S_m^t = \frac{S_m^{t-1}(t-1) + S^t}{t} \quad (3)$$

In Equation (3), S^t is the shape size at time t and S_m^t is the average shape size until time t. When *TA* is increased, only D_i is employed, and when *TA* is decreased, only D_d is employed.

In addition, the adjacency function is simplified to the adjacency test described below:

- **isolated** : accumulate its color information
- **partially occluded** : accumulate its color information except for the emerging or vanishing color
- **totally occluded** : do not accumulate its color information for an occluded person, but accumulate its color information for an occluding person

The temporal weight calculation of the proposed method is summarized as follows:

- at $t = 0$, represent each color cluster by the temporal color value and its associated weight and the initial value is set to the base weight.
- at $t = n$, determine whether to increase the temporal weight or to decrease it, according to the result of the adjacency test.
- at $t = n$, increase each weight of the color feature by D_i, when there is a similar color feature at $t = n - 1$; otherwise, decrease it by D_d.

To identify each person after occlusion, the elements whose weight is over the base weight are only used for similarity computation.

3. Experimental results and analysis

Our tracking system was implemented and tested on a Pentium II – 333MHz PC, under the Windows 98 operating system. The test video data was acquired using SGI O_2 and a digital camera system. Two video data were collected that contained two or three moving persons in an indoor environment. The frame rate of the video data is varied from 10 Hz to 30 Hz and the size of the input image was 320 by 240 pixels.

Table 2 shows parameters and the number of errors for each experiment and Figure 5 shows an the tracking result for scene2 which contains three persons with very complex patterns of movements.

To confirm the robustness of the temporal color feature, the variance of the temporal color feature for each person is analyzed. If it is small, the temporal color could be considered as having a robust feature. We compare the color feature used in our system and the shape feature from the

Table 2. Experimental results

	NOP	FPS	SUM	DE	TE
scene one (30fps)	2	30	183	2	0
scene one (10fps)	2	10	61	4	0
scene two	3	10	158	14	2

NOP : number of persons, FPS : frame per second, SUM : sum of frames, DE : detection error, TE : tracking error

Figure 5. Experimental result (scene two)

temporal template used in [3, 4]. Because shape information includes local information, it is more sensitive to small changes. Therefore we use shape size for fair comparison.

Figure 6 shows that the color value of temporal weight is more stable than the shape information in an image sequence.

4. Conclusions and further research

In this paper, we proposed an appearance model based on temporal color for robust multiple people tracking in short- and mid-term tracking. Although the position, shape, and velocity are suitable features in tracking of consecutive frames, they cannot track the target continuously when the target disappears temporarily. Because the proposed temporal color is accumulated with its associated weight, the target can be continuously tracked when the target is occluded

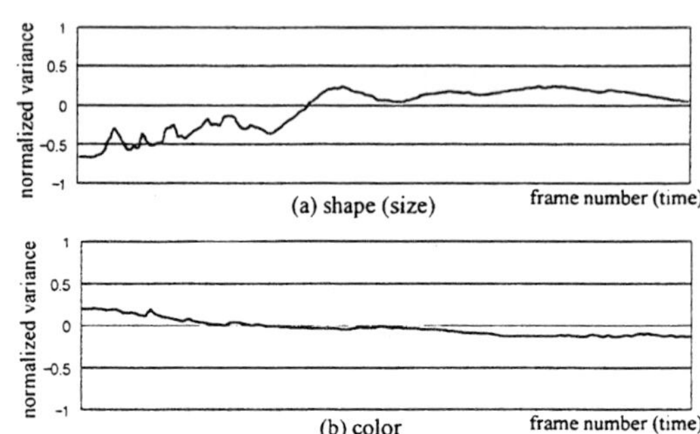

Figure 6. Comparison of stability of each feature with temporal information

or leaves the scene for a few seconds or minutes.

Our experimental results reveal the stability of the proposed method in the medium-term tracking. The proposed temporal feature can be generalized with any kind of features in the appearance model for person identification in the people tracking process.

Problems with temporal color only occur when people are in uniforms or clothes with similar color. To solve this problem, other features need to be used simultaneously for the tracked target, or face recognition of the target person is required.

Further research will be concentrated on the integration of the tracking system with face pattern recognition for long-term tracking.

References

[1] T. Darrell, G. Gordon, M. Harville, and J. Woodfill. Integrated person tracking using stereo, color, and pattern detection. *Proc. of IEEE Computer Society Conference on Computer Vision and Pattern Recognition, Santa Barbara, California*, pages 601–608, June 1998.

[2] I. Haritaoglu, D. Harwood, and L. S. Davis. W4: Who? when? where? what? a real time system for detecting and tracking people. *Proc. of International Conference on Face and Gesture Recognition, Nara, Japan*, pages 222–227, April 1998.

[3] I. Haritaoglu, D. Harwood, and L. S. Davis. Hydra: Multiple people detection and tracking using silhouettes. *Proc. of 2nd IEEE Workshop on Visual Surveillance, Fort Collins, Colorado*, pages 6–13, June 1999.

[4] S. S. Intille, J. W. Davis, and A. F. Bobick. Real-time closed-world tracking. *Proc. of IEEE Computer Society Conference on Computer Vision and Pattern Recognition, Puerto Rico*, pages 697–703, June 1997.

[5] C. Wren, A. Azarbayejani, T. Darrell, and A. Pentland. Pfinder: Real-time tracking of the human body. *IEEE Trans. on Pattern Analysis and Machine Intelligence*, 19(7):780–785, 1997.

Non-restrictive Visual Respiration Monitoring

Hiroaki Nakai,
Corp. R&D Center, Toshiba Corp.
1, Komukai-Toshiba-cho, Saiwai-ku
Kawasaki 212-8582, Japan
hiroaki.nakai@toshiba.co.jp

Ken Ishihara,
Medical Informatics, Ehime Univ. Hosp.
Shitsukawa, Shigenobu-cho, Onsen-gun
Ehime 791-0295, Japan
ken@m.ehime-u.ac.jp

Yoshio Miyake,
Grad. Sch. of Eng. Sci., Osaka Univ.
1-3, Machikaneyama-cho, Toyonaka-shi,
Osaka 560-8531, Japan
yoshio.miyake@nts.toshiba-eng.co.jp

Mutsumi Watanabe
Dept. of ICS, Fac. of Eng., Kagoshima Univ.
1-21-40, Korimoto
Kagoshima 890-0065, Japan
mutty@ics.kagoshima-u.ac.jp

Abstract

We have developed a novel visual sensing system that monitors respiration for 24 hours non-restrictively. The principle of the system is inter-image subtraction. Compared with conventional methods, the system has advantages which make it suitable for a long-term monitoring: 1) patients experience no physiological burden during sleep, 2) no manual operation is necessary since it has self-optimizing functions for image processing and 3) it judges patient's sleep condition adequately using statistical analysis. The system thus can be applied to predict abnormality of health conditions, and thus for example, alert care providers so that action can be taken with a view to preventing the sudden death of elderly people or, in case of children, to prevent occurrence of sudden infant death syndrome. It can be also applied to the detect clinically dangerous sleep apnea syndrome. Experimental results in a nursing home for the aged have shown the efficiency of the system.

1. Introduction

Monitoring of patients' respiration in hospitals and of elderly people's respiration in nursing homes for the aged are important tasks. By checking trends of respiration patterns, abnormality of patients' health conditions can be predicted so that action can be taken with a view to preventing the sudden death of elderly people or, in case of children, to prevent occurrence of sudden infant death syndrome. Monitoring of respiration patterns in real time also makes it possible to detect the clinically dangerous sleep apnea syndrome[2].

Conventionally, respiration has been monitored by restrictive methods, such as measuring temperature of a thermistor attached to a patient's nose or tension of a belt tightened around a patient's body[7]. These conventional methods, however, are unsuitable for a long respiration monitoring because they restrain the patient's body, i.e., patients cannot move freely and attached sensors detached due to the patients' movements. Several non-restrictive methods have been proposed. One method utilizes pressure-sensitive sensors set on a bed[1][5] and another utilizes image processing techniques[6]. The former uses a special bed, and therefore, subjects feel strange and that is inimical to natural sleep. The latter detects optical flow in accordance with respiratory body movements. Using an image processing method, respiration is measured noncontiguously, and therefore, patients do not experience the monitoring physically. However, optical flow imposes a huge computation cost, special image processing hardware is required for real-time monitoring, and a human operator is required for continuous monitoring and to set an image area optimal for manual measurement when a patient moves.

We have developed a visual respiration monitoring system based on inter-image subtraction[3]. To realize a real-time system consisting only of a PC and a camera, i.e., of equipment suitable for widespread use, we adopted an image subtraction for detecting a patient's respiration, which is the most CPU-intensive part of the system. We improved the accuracy of respiration measurement and the usability of the system to make it suitable for long-term monitoring, i.e., self-optimizing functions are implemented in the image processing parts of the system so that no manual operation is necessary in monitoring, and that also contributes

1051-4651/00 $10.00 © 2000 IEEE

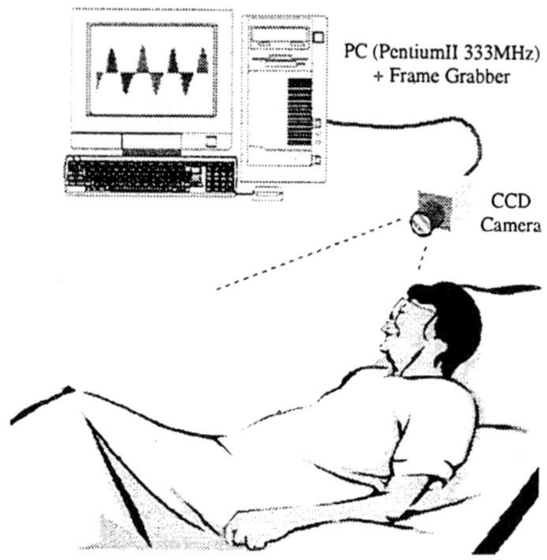

Figure 1. Overall view of the system.

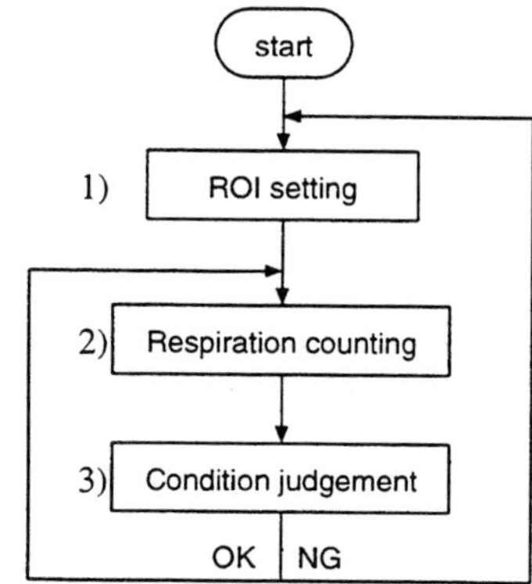

Figure 2. Flow of the system.

to improvement of S/N ratio of respiration patterns in poorly illuminated environments. We also implemented an automatic judgment function respecting the patients' sleep condition in order to check long-term trends of respiration instantly.

In this paper, we firstly describe the system in detail, and then report experimental results in a nursing home for the aged.

2. Visual respiration monitoring

Figure 1 shows the overall view of the respiration monitoring system. A CCD camera is set over a patient's head, and the angle of a camera is set so that the patient's chest can be seen at the center of a frame. Image frames taken by the camera are continuously sent to a PC via a frame grabber card.

Figure 2 shows the flow of image processing of the system, which is consists of three major modules: 1) ROI setting, 2) respiration counting and 3) condition judgment. At first, a region of interest (ROI) is automatically set at the optimal position to detect image change in accordance with patient's respiratory body movements. Next, image subtraction is executed between an ROI of a current frame and that of a previous frame to obtain respiration patterns in time domain. When the patient's respiration is judged to be normal at the condition judgment module, respiration counting continues. ROI will be reset when patient's respiration is not judged to be normal. We introduce parameter optimizing technique in the ROI setting module and the respiration counting module so as to improve the accuracy and the usability of the system. Each module is described in detail below.

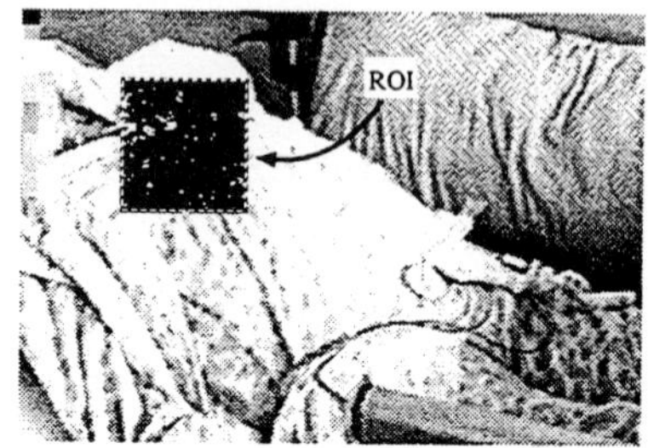

Figure 3. Example of a processed frame.

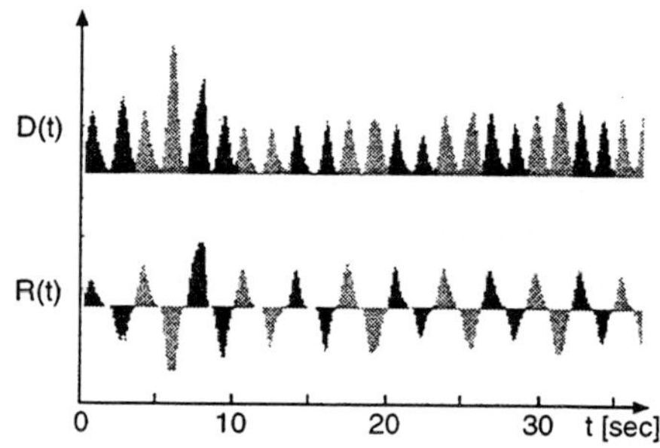

Figure 4. Example of a respiration pattern.

2.1. Respiration counting

We first describe the respiration counting module which performs the main function for monitoring respiration. We consider that effects of respiratory body movements are transferred to outer clothes or bedclothes that cover a body. Therefore, respiration must change gray scales of pixels at the chest area because the area must contain texture or shading. The primary aim of the system is to detect cessation of respiration or its characteristics in time domain, not to measure ventilation flow accurately, we adopted frame subtraction for quantifying amounts of image change in accordance with respiration. Figure 3 shows an example of an image processing result. A rectangular part is an ROI, where changes in gray scales are shown by white regions. The system subtracts the pixel values on an

ROI of a current frame from those of a previous one, and counts the number of pixels whose absolute difference values are larger than a preset threshold. The curves obtained by plotting these numbers with time-axis show pairs of positive peaks that represent one inhalation and one exhalation respectively, as shown in the Figure 4 $D(t)$. We reverse the second peak upside down against t-axis to emphasize changes in direction of respiratory body movements, as shown in Figure 4 $R(t)$ [1]. Respiration rate can be easily obtained by measuring time period between consecutive zero-crossing points from negative to positive of $R(t)$.

Many people find it difficult to sleep in a well-lighted room, and therefore, improvement in S/N ratio of respiration patterns is important in order to increase system robustness under noisy conditions for image processing, such as dark rooms. One method for achieving such an improvement is adaptive setting of the interval of frame subtraction. In preliminary experiments we found the optimal interval to be half the respiration period. The system changes the interval dynamically to the respiration period immediately preceding the current one. To avoid miss-counting of respiration caused by unexpected small image changes such as noise, adaptive thresholding is also implemented in the system, details of which have been described in a previous report[4].

2.2. ROI setting

The ROI setting module finds an effective ROI for respiration counting. When the subject makes only respiratory body movements, it can simply be assumed that the optimal position of ROI is where the largest image change occurs. Setting ROI at the largest changing area also improves S/N ratio in poorly illuminated environments as mentioned above. Therefore, changes in gray scales of pixels of the area being searched are accumulated, which is set over a bed, and then the ROI that containing the largest image change is found. Image change at each pixel is obtained by frame subtraction at a fixed interval and accumulated for a predefined period.

If respiration is judged to be abnormal at the condition judgment module, described in the next section, the system assumes that either respiration is clinically abnormal or changes in images are caused by non-respiratory body movements, such as the patient turning over in bed. In this case, the system changes ROI position dynamically according to the current accumulation status. When respiration is normal, ROI is fixed so as to continue respiration counting, and this prevents undesirable interruptions by external noise.

[1]The positive and negative peaks of $R(t)$ do not exactly correspond to inhalation and exhalation, respectively. Such miss-correspondence does not affect to the accuracy of respiration counting, and the turning over of the patterns makes it easy for users to recognize respiration patterns intuitively.

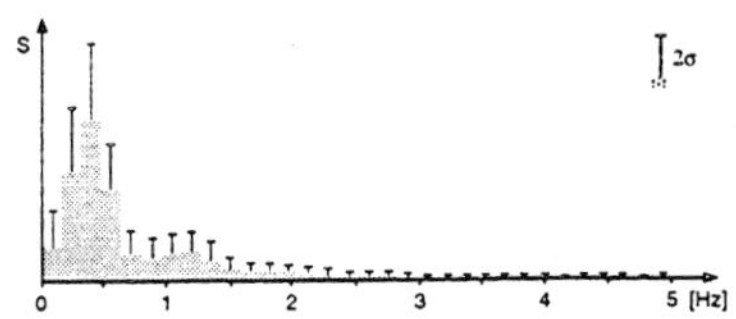

Figure 5. Average power spectrum.

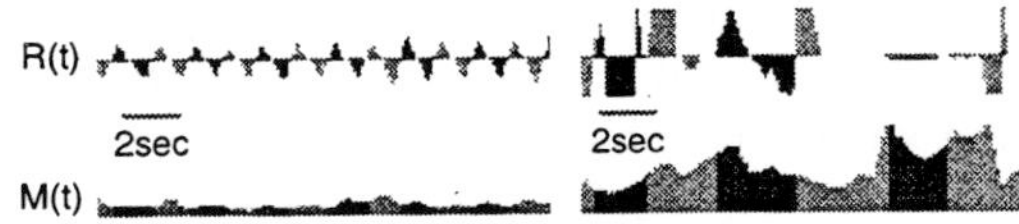

Figure 6. Example of Mahalanobis distance. Shown on the left is an example of M(t) when a subject's respiration is normal, and on the right one when the subject made non-respiratory movements (turned over in bed).

2.3. Condition judgment

To check if respiration rate is with in a normal range (for example > 5 *times/min.* and < 35 *times/min.*), is the simplest way to check if the respiration is clinically abnormal. However, even when the frequency of periodic movements is judged to be within a normal range, it cannot be determined whether the detected image change is caused by respiratory body movements or not. Therefore, methods for classifying body movements using respiration patterns or image changes are necessary. We implemented two statistical judgment methods for classifying. These methods can decrease arbitrary parameters of the system which have to be adjusted to various environments for adequate judgments.

Judgment using power spectrum of respiration

One method of differentiating the respiratory movements from non-respiratory ones is to compare frequency characteristics of periodic movements. We use power spectra to present the frequency characteristics. Power spectra can be obtained by applying fast Fourier transform to respiration patterns after convolving Hamming window function. In preliminary experiments we calculate the average power spectrum obtained when a patient's respiration is normal, as shown in Figure 5. We next compare the current power spectra by calculating Mahalanobis distance which is given by $M(t) = \{S(t)-\hat{S}\}\,\Sigma^{-1}\,\{S(t)-\hat{S}\}^T$ where S, $\hat{S}$ and Σ denote current power spectrum, average power spectrum and covariance matrix, respectively. Examples of obtained Mahalanobis distance are shown in Figure

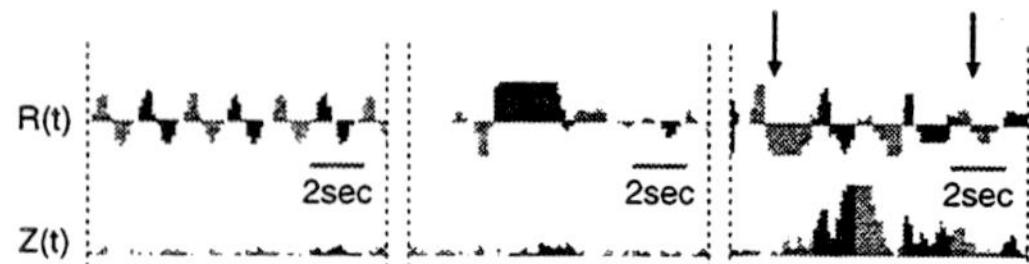

Figure 7. Example of histogram test. Shown on the left is an example of Z(t) when a subject's respiration is normal, in the middle is one when the subject turned over in bed, and on the right is one when the subject left the bed during the period indicated by the two arrows.

6, and it can be seen that $M(t)$ takes large value only when a subject made non-respiratory body movements. Non-respiratory movements are judged to have occured when $M(t)$ becomes greater than a preset threshold, since there is a significant difference in $M(t)$ when respiration is normal and when it is not.

Judgment using gray scale histogram

To prevent the system gives warnings that respiration has ceased when in fact the patient has left the bed, it is also important to check locality of body movements when the system detects large changes in images. We assume that large body movements that occur in a wide area over a bed, such as leaving the bed, cause changes in histogram of gray scales of pixels in a bed area. Relatively small body movements, such as turning over in bed and movements of legs or arms, will not cause changes in histogram since they occur inside the bed.

To determine whether there is a change in gray scale histogram or not, we utilized statistical hypothesis testing called *sign test*, which is a non-parametric test which can be applied in the case that no probability model can be assumed respecting data. We set two hypothesis, H_0 and H_1, to be "there are no differences between two histograms" and "there are differences between two histograms", respectively. We assume that H_0 is true and that the number of pixels that change in gray scale positively (x) is equal to the number of pixels that change negatively. Consequently, x constructs binomial distribution and because the number of pixels that change in gray scale (n) is sufficiently large ($n > 30$), binomial distribution can be approximated as normal distribution. We use the test statistic Z given by $Z = \frac{x-n/2}{\sqrt{n}/2} \sim N(0,1)$. Shown in Figure 7 are examples of obtained test statistic Z, and it can be seen that $Z(t)$ takes large value only when a subject makes large body movements, such as leaving the bed. When α denotes a significance level, and $Z_{\alpha/2}$ denotes a probability of $\alpha/2$ on a standard normal distribution, if $|Z|$ is greater than $Z_{\alpha/2}$, the system rejects the null hypothesis, meaning changes in images are caused by large body movements.

3. Experimental results

We used a PC with PentiumII 333MHz for CPU and Matrox's Meteor for frame grabber card. The Camera used was a Toshiba 1/2" CCD monochrome camera (IK-MF41D) with the minimum illuminance of 2 lux and mounting a f=6mm lens. The size of ROI is set to 80×80 pixels for the experiment. We used the system to monitor respiration of 10 patients aged from 68 to 94. The level of luminance around the patients' chest was set to 10 to 20 lux. For patients who strongly desired to sleep in complete darkness, we used infrared illumination (LEDs) and a CCD camera without an infrared filter. The patients' respiration was monitored for eight hours from 9 p.m. to 5 a.m. In this paper, we analyze the results for two patients.

Examples of experimental results are shown in Figure 8 and Figure 9 for 20 minutes each. Respiration patterns and status bar (results of condition judgment module) are shown in parallel. Figure 8 shows results for a patient suffering from subarachnoid hemorrhage and sleep apnea syndrome. Black sections on status bar indicate the time duration of no respiration that lasted for more than 10 seconds. We checked the accuracy of the results taken for 4 hours. By checking the video by sight, we found no respiration period 244 times against 251 times counted by the system. The system counted more mainly because there were small non-respiratory body movements during apnea and the system counted apneas before and after interruption as different, as shown in Figure 10. On the other hand, there is no miss-detection of apneas, and thus the system is efficient in detecting sleep apneas.

We next analyze the results for a different patient, as shown in Figure 9. This patient was a healthy person who frequently turned over in bed and left the bed. The system detected non-respiratory movements, including changes in gray scale histogram, several times just for one incident in the time period when the patient was leaving the bed and returning to it. Therefore, to check the accuracy of results, we avoided this period. Again, we checked the video by sight and noticed that a patient made relatively large non-respiratory body movements, i.e., turning over in bed, 97 times and relatively small ones, i.e., movements of arms and legs, 217 times. The system detected relatively large body movements 125 times. The main reason that the system detected more is that movements of arms in near distance from a camera were judged to be relatively large by the system.

Respiration of 10 patients was monitored. Among them sleep apnea syndrome had been diagnosed for

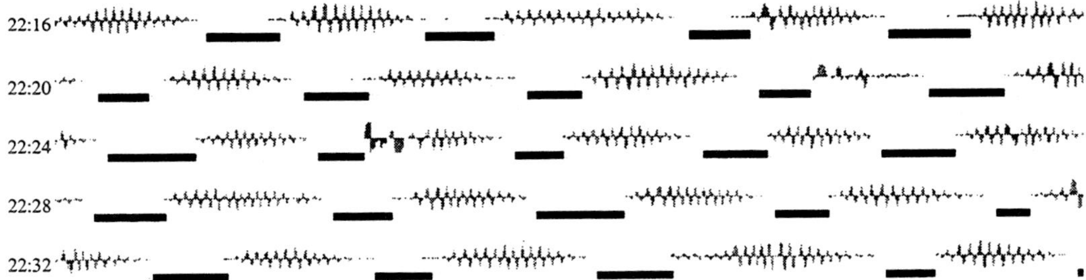

Figure 8. Example of respiration monitoring #1, Subject OM, a patient suffering from sleep apnea syndrome. Light gray periods and black periods on the status bar indicate periods when the patient's respiration is normal and apnea, respectively.

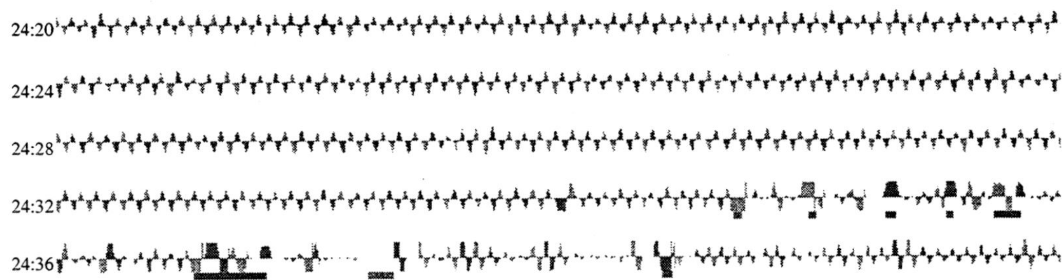

Figure 9. Example of respiration monitoring #2, Subject OU, a healthy person. Dark gray periods on the status bar indicate the patient's non-respiratory body movements. The subject turned over several times in bed (24:35 – 24:39).

only one patient prior to the experiment. In this experiment, however, we found four more patients who had apnea more often than 5 times per hour. Two patients among them died from arrhythmia possibly induced by sleep apnea. This proved the effectiveness of this system for screening sleep apnea syndrome and the predictability of abnormality of health condition.

Figure 10. Double detection case of a single apnea. (Sub. OM, 4:49 a.m.)

4. Conclusion

In this paper, we proposed a novel system for monitoring respiration. The system is sufficiently efficient for long time monitoring since it could count respiration accurately and could detect patients suffering from sleep apnea syndrome. A remote monitoring system can be easily constructed by sending condition data only, and we have already implemented emergency messaging and data transmission functions via the Internet. In future work, we intend to conduct extended experiments respecting practical long-term use in homes and hospitals, including remote monitoring.

References

[1] J. Alihanka et al. A new method for long-term monitoring of the ballistocardiogram, heart rate, and respiration. *American Journal of Physiology*, 240, 1981.

[2] C. Guilleminault et al. The sleep apnea syndromes. *Annual Review of Medicine*, 27:465, 1976.

[3] K. Ishihara. Development of visual sensing system for biomedical measurement using image processing technology on time series video image. In *Proc. of 32nd Conf. Japan Society of Medical Electronics and Biological Engineering*, volume 31, page 218, 1993.

[4] Y. Miyake et al. Improvement in accuracy of respiration pattern detection on visual senesing system. In *Proc. of IAPR Workshop on Machine Vision Applications, MVA'98*, pages 262–265, 1998.

[5] Y. Nishida et al. Monitoring patient respiration and posture using human symbiosis system. In *Proc. of Intr. Conf. on Intelligent Robots and Systems, IROS'97*, pages 632–639, 1997.

[6] Y. Nishida et al. Sleep apnea syndrome diagnosis based on image processing. *Journal of the Robotics Society of Japan*, 16(2):274–281, 1998. in Japanese.

[7] M. A. Sackner. Non-invasive respiratory monitoring. *Non-invasive Respiratory Monitoring, Inc.*, 1986.

Real-Time High Density People Counter using Morphological Tools

Antonio Albiol, Valery Naranjo
Departamento de Comunicaciones, Universidad Politécnica de Valencia
Camino de Vera s/n, 46022 Valencia, SPAIN
aalbiol,vnaranjo@dcom.upv.es

Inmaculada Mora
Departamento de Tecnologías de las Comunicaciones
EPS-Universidad Carlos III de Madrid
Avda. Universidad 30, 28911 Leganés (Madrid), SPAIN
inmoji@tsc.uc3m.es

Abstract

This paper deals with an application of image sequence analysis. In particular, it addresses the problem of determining the number of people who get into and out of a train carriage when it's crowded and background and/or illumination might change. The proposed system analyses image sequences and processes them using an algorithm based on the use of several morphological tools and optical flow motion estimation.

1 Introduction

The purpose of the work presented here was to provide a tool to the Spanish railway company capable of determining the number of people getting into and out of a train. Our system analyses images of a door, doing the surveillance from a zenital position above the train door. The camera is placed in the door mechanism box, and the acquired images are monochrome. The system described below requires neither special illumination nor markings to be deployed. An example of the camera view is depicted in figure 1. The placement of the camera above the door has the significant advantage that no occlusion occurs.

Varying conditions of illumination and background can be found at different stations, time of the day and weather conditions (there are underground and surface stations). This fact denies the use of background substraction techniques. Figure 1 shows sample frames of people passing with different densities.

Since a person usually takes more than one frame to cross the door, some form of time memory must be included in the algorithm. In order to reduce the memory storage requirements and to allow non-causal processing, the only thing that we perform each time we acquire a new frame is to store certain lines of the frame onto what we have called *stacks of lines*, which will be described with more detail in the next section. These stacks of lines contain all the required information to count the people and determine the direction of passing. The counting process actually starts after the doors are closed.

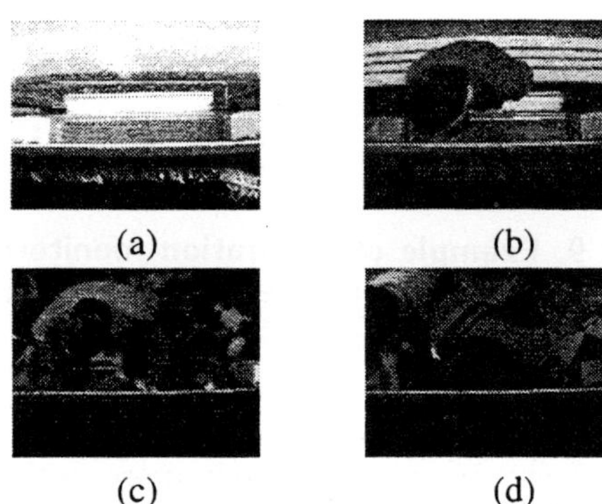

Figure 1. Example of full camera views. a): With nobody b) Isolated person. c) and d): Crowded situations.

Then, our algorithm can be at different states:

1. When doors are closed the camera lens is covered and the acquired image is completely black. We will assume that this is the initial state, that we have called *Closed-Doors State*. This state is abandoned when doors begin to open.

2. When the doors start to open, the storage of certain

lines of each frame starts. We call this, *Acquisition State*. We move to the next state when the doors end to close.

3. Right after doors have closed, we enter the *Counting State* and begin the actual counting. To do so, the stacks of lines are analysed in order to determine the number of people between at the last station. After finishing the counting we return to the first state.

The time required to process the stacks is considerably shorter than the time needed to acquire them, and much shorter too than the time needed for the train to reach the next station. In this sense we claim that our process is real-time. Strictly speaking we could say that it is a *delayed-real-time* algorithm.

The rest of the paper is organized as follows. In section 2 we describe how to build the stacks of lines. Section 3 gives an overview of the whole processing and is divided into three subsections corresponding to the main steps of the counting algorithm: people-background distinction, segmentation of individual persons and determination of direction. To conclude the paper we will give some results and conclusions.

2 Image Acquisition

During the acquisition state, three (horizontal) lines of every frame are stored image onto a separate stack each. These lines are shown in figure 2-b. We will call the first line (the topmost one in the figure) the *black line* and it corresponds to the platform-carriage gap[1]. The intermediate line, we will call it the *gradient line* and should coincide with the upper edge of the train step. The bottom line is located on the step and will be termed *white line*, because it is brighter than the *black* one.

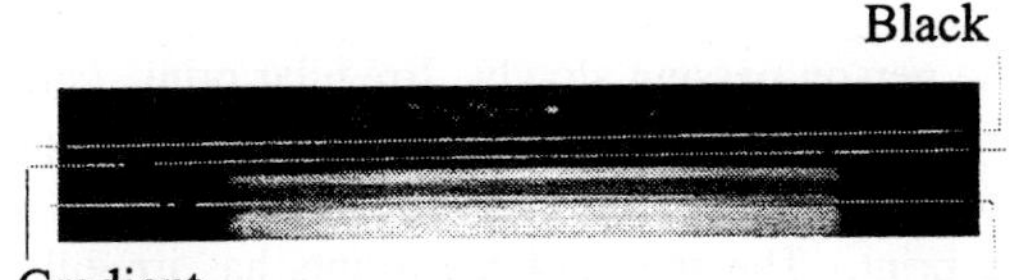

Figure 2. Detail of figure 1-a) to show the location of the black, gradient and white lines used to build the stacks.

Black and white lines simply contain the gray-level of the original image. For the gradient line, we compute the vertical gradient, and this is the value that we store. Each of these three lines is stacked on separate images where each row corresponds to a frame. At the end we will have three

[1]In surface stations it is not necessary black, but for convenience we will always call it this way.

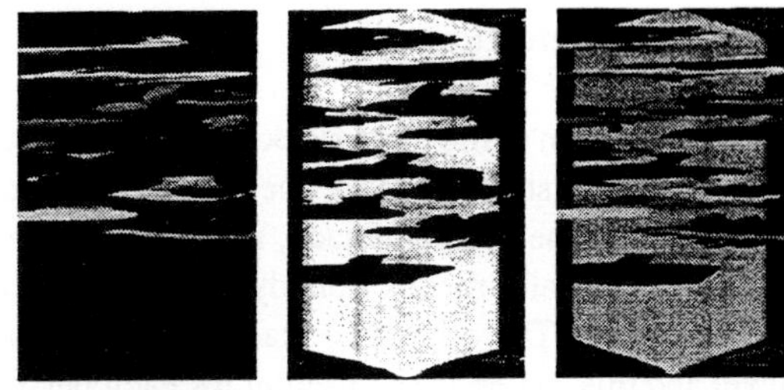

Figure 3. Example of stacks. From left to right: black, gradient and white stack.

stacks: one for black lines, one for gradient lines and one for white lines, which we will denote respectively as black, gradient and white stacks. In figure 3 we can see an example of stacks. The vertical axis corresponds to time (increasing downwards) while the horizontal axis is the horizontal dimension of the original images. Since the camera is fixed to the train, the position of the lines in the images does not change from station to station, and is configured (automatically) off-line during the installation.

Stacks like these will be the input to the actual processing algorithm. From the stacks it is quite obvious for a human observer (after a certain training) to see how many people have passed through the door. It suffices to count the number of blobs. At the top and bottom of the stacks a characteristic pattern due to opening and closing of doors can also be seen. In the following section we will explain how to do the counting from the stacks automatically.

3 Processing Algorithm

Once we have the stacks of lines, we must analyse them in order to find out how many people they contain. The processing is performed in three different stages:

1. Presence detection: The aim at this point is to create a binary image (with the same size as the stacks) that indicates when and where the *border line* is hidden by someone or something passing. The *border line* is the position of the frame that must be crossed in order to make a count and corresponds to the position of the gradient line.

2. Segmentation: its purpose is to segment the presence image into individual prints each one corresponding to a single person.

3. Direction estimation: After segmentation, we will have an *image* which will be null when nobody is passing and will contain a different label for each portion of the stacks corresponding to a different person. The objective is now to estimate the direction of passing at each of these *labels* of the stacks of lines.

3.1 Presence Detection

After examination of the three stacks of lines we decided to use the gradient stack to make the presence detection. This was because the gradient stack, unlike the other two stacks, bright normally means nobody and dark the presence of someone. The other two stacks show the actual gray-level and this can be very different for each person. In other words, we obtain a binary image, with the size same size of the stack, indicating the presence of a person at the border line.

The reason why gradient is low when someone is passing is because the lack of contrasted elements on a person image (see figure 1). However, the position of the gradient line was selected because it contains a high gradient. Nevertheless, a person may contain contrasted elements that may be at the gradient line position at some instant. See for instance the topmost blob of the gradient stack in figure 3. Fortunately when this happens, this situation lasts only for a few frames since people are moving. This property will be exploited to perform a prefiltering before thresholding.

The process for presence detection can be summarized as:

1. Pre-filtering: the purpose is to eliminate transients with too short duration that breaks the person print, given a high gradient value inside it. Morphological filter are very useful at this point because, unlike other filters like linear or median, they operate selectively on bright or dark elements of the image. However, the use of such filters in space-time images must be very careful, in order to obtain a meaningful filtering. In particular, we have used the morphological filter named opening by reconstruction [1]. We could enunciate, its action as 'remove all bright spots that do not have a minimum duration (height on the stacks) at any horizontal position'.

2. Determination of threshold: Due to illumination variations the needed threshold is different for each station. We find out the threshold by finding the rows of the stacks where we are sure that nobody is present.

3. Segmentation People/Background: Thresholding the filtered gradient stack yields a binary image indicating when and where was people passing.

   The result of the presence detection of the stacks in figure 3 is shown in figure 4

3.2 People segmentation

In order to count the people, we must segment the presence mask into individual prints due to a single person. The situation would be straightforward if no contact between persons could happen. Since this is not the case we have to design techniques for segmentation of the prints corresponding to each person. For explaining the separation techniques that we have used, we have prepared a synthetic image, shown in figure 5(a), to show how the different separation techniques work. That synthetic image contains the most important kind of problems encountered in our analysis. From top to bottom we can see the following prints:

Figure 4. Presence detection result of stacks in figure 3.

1. An isolated person, passing quickly. This can be noticed by the short vertical size of the print.

2. Two people passing side by side.

3. A single person passing exactly under the camera. The camera height is small, so wide angle lenses are used. In this case the print can be as wide as that of two people if the person happens to pass exactly under the camera.

4. Two people passing one immediately after the other, leaving no frame (row of the stack) of gap between them.

5. One person. Print with branches. This is a very common situation. Legs, arms, bags, etc. appear normally as narrow branches.

6. One person passing slowly. Irregular print. One person passing slowly takes many frames to completely cross the door. This causes a large vertical size of the print. The shape of real prints has irregularities as those shown.

The separation process is based on Width Function of the presence mask, which calculates an image of gray levels where each horizontal segment has a gray level indicating its width (see figure 5-b).

The separation process is divided into the following steps:

- Side contacts detection/separation: When a side contact happens a sudden increase in the width occurs. When a side contact finishes a sudden decrease of the width occurs. See figure 5-b, blob 2. Then, if we compute the vertical gradient of the width function an indication of side contacts can be easily got. Once a contact is detected, we proceed to separate the individual (side by side) prints by introducing artificial background points. Finally a shrinking of the resulting horizontal segments is performed to achieve complete separation (see figure 5-c, blob 2).

- Markers extraction: after side contact separation, only longitudinal separation remains. The information that we use to perform this separation is that the people prints have an *approximately* convex shape. That would suggest the use of the maxima of the width function as markers. In order to obtain only one marker for print we have computed the contrast of each maximum of the Width Function [2].The contrast of a maximum of the width function has the following meanings:
  - If there is a single maximum of width per blob, the contrast is the same as the width at the widest point.
  - If there are more than one maxima of width per blob (see figure 6), the contrast will coincide with the width for the highest maximum ($W1$ in figure 6) and will be the difference $W2 - W3$ for the other width maxima.
- Segmentation: If we were only interested in finding out the number of people, the process would have ended with the marker extraction. However in order to determine the direction in a robust manner, it is interesting to segment the presence image in order to integrate all the information concerning each person. We have used the watershed segmentation to the negative of the width function [3] using like markers the maxima of the Width Function with high Extinction Value. This splits the blob at the narrowest point between each pair of markers.

3.3 Direction Determination

We have used an algorithm based on optical flow [4] to estimate the direction of crossing the door. The speed obtained from the optical flow equation gives one value per pixel of the stack. For each label of the segmentation we compute the weighted average value of speed.

4 Summary and Conclusions

We have performed a large number of tests (149 train stops) corresponding to images taken at different times of different days in a railway line near Madrid. The test sequences include both indoor and outdoor stations. No parameter tuning has been made for the whole set of test sequences. The intensity of people passing varies from no one passing at certain stations, to an average intensity of more than one person per second. The results have an average of error of less than 2%.

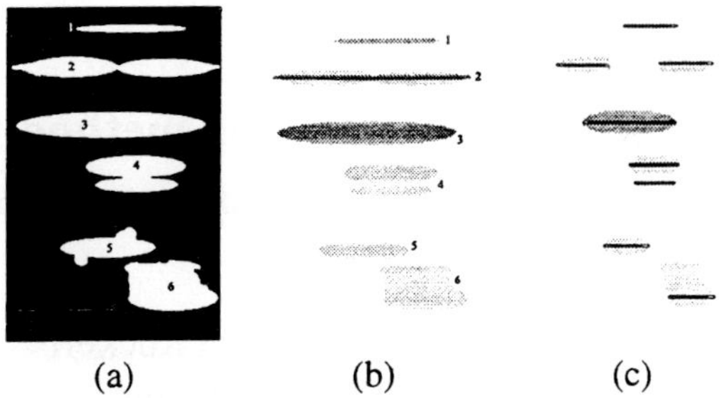

Figure 5. (a) Synthetic image used to explain the different separation techniques. (b) Markers (in black) and image to which we will apply the watershed. (c) Markers and input for watershed.

References

[1] P. Salembier and J. Serra, "Flat zones filtering, connected operators and filters by reconstruction," *IEEE Trans. on Image Processing*, vol. 3, pp. 1153–1160, august 1995.

[2] C. Vachier, *Extraction de caracteristiques, segmentation d'image et morphologie mathematique*. PhD thesis, Ecole Nationale Supériore des Mines, Paris, Décembre 1995.

[3] S. Beucher and F. Meyer, *Matehmatical Morphology in Image Processing*, ch. 12. The morphological Approach to Segmentation: The Watershed Transformation, pp. 433–481. Marcel Dekker Inc., 1993.

[4] A. M. Tekalp, *Digital Video Processing*, ch. 5. Optical Flow Methods, pp. 72–116. Prentice Hall, 1995.

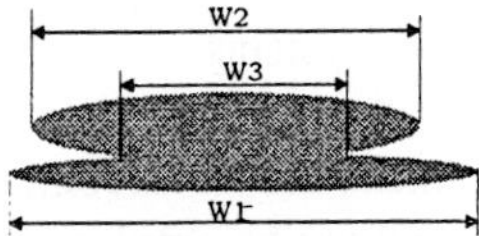

Figure 6. Widths involved in the contrast of the width function computation.

A bootstrapping method for autonomous and in site learning of generic navigation behaviour

Burkhard Iske, Ulrich Rückert
Heinz Nixdorf Institut
System and Circuit Technology
University of Paderborn
33102 Paderborn, Germany
iske@hni.upb.de, rueckert@hni.upb.de

Kurt Malmstrom[1], Joaquin Sitte[2]
School of Manufactural Engineering[1]
School of Computing Science[2]
Queensland University of Technology
Brisbane 4001, Australia
kmalmstrom@ieee.org, j.sitte@qut.edu.au

Abstract

To understand the behaviour of natural autonomous systems, research is carried out on artificial autonomous agents. This paper focuses on how simple behaviours can be learnt autonomously using a bootstrapping method. Firstly, a two dimensional Self-Organising Map is realised which provides the agent's sense of orientation. Once this relative positioning system has been established, the agent learns to navigate towards a target using the reinforcement learning technique of Q-Learning. Since only neural network processing is used, this technique emulates the distributed and adaptive information processing found in natural autonomous systems. Furthermore, due to its generality, the neural implementation developed is transferable to other artificial autonomous agents with different sensors and effector suites.

1. Introduction

Computer technology enables the execution of complex tasks and the automation of intricate processes. The main restriction is the requirement for an environment with constant and predictable conditions. However, the design of autonomous systems, which are capable of exploring and navigating through an unknown and dynamically changing environment, is still a challenging task. In particular research needs to be done in designing and programming their information processing systems.

In contrast, natural autonomous systems like animals, and particularly humans, have overcome this problem during the course of evolution by employing neural networks. So, it seems to be appropriate to take a natural autonomous system as a model for designing an artificial one. However, the behaviour of natural autonomous systems is not yet completely understood. This motivates research on designing behaviour and navigation of artificial autonomous systems, which will contribute further insight into the functioning of natural autonomous systems.

This work explores the question of how simple behaviour can be learned autonomously, independent of the system used, and without the help of simulations. While the methodology is independent of platform, the results presented have been accomplished on the new autonomous agent architecture introduced in Section 2. Section 3 describes the learning of the robot's sense of orientation. Section 4 presents learning of approaching a target. Section 5 relates this paper's navigation method to similar methods described in literature. Finally, Section 6 gives a conclusion of this work.

2. The robot

The agent used here is a self-developed, transputer based, cylindrical mini-robot with a diameter of 90mm and a height of just over 70mm [4]. It is equipped with two motors that enable differential steering and a faceted eye that consists of 8 infrared sensors. These sensors can detect intensity modulated infrared light at certain frequencies sent by one or several beacons in the agent's environment. Each beacon, and therefore frequency, can represent different meanings like obstacle or target.

Sensor signals are converted to 8-bit resolution. The processor on the robot does not have floating point support, integer math is therefor necessary in all methods described. In addition, the learning techniques implemented have been developed to be completed in a totally autonomous environment dictated by constraints such as battery life.

1051-4651/00 $10.00 © 2000 IEEE

3. The agent's sense of orientation

Since a bootstrapping method is desired to be implemented here, the agent has no prior knowledge of its environment and needs to learn a sense of orientation first. This sense of orientation should equip the agent with a relative positioning system (angle and distance of the beacon). This means that the 8 dimensional input space (resulting from the 8 sensors) has to be mapped to two dimensions: the relative angle and distance.

Self-Organising Maps (SOMs) [2] are well suited for solving a problem like this as the Kohonen algorithm is unsupervised and sensor characteristics are automatically adapted. This makes the method independent of the actual agent.

3.1. Training a SOM for the relative angle

In order to learn a SOM of relative angular information, numerous training vectors are required. These are acquired by allowing the agent to turn on the spot several times whilst reading and subsequently processing the training vectors. By processing the data immediately after reading, the implementation efficiency is increased because the training vectors do not have to be stored. The learning time required is also reduced because the duration of the computations of the Kohonen algorithm is equivalent to the delay between reading two training vectors. The sensor values read are normalised as no distance to beacon has been enforced.

The SOM consists of 33 neurones in a chain. Learning the relative angle showed, that just 200 training vectors and only one epoch were enough to achieve a good result. The initialisation weight values were 100 for all neurones. Equation 1 is used for calculating the weight changes, which is based on the standard Kohonen algorithm.

$$\Delta \vec{w}_{\vec{r}_i} = \left\lfloor \frac{\eta_{\text{num}} \times (\vec{x} - \vec{w}_{\vec{r}_i})}{\eta_{\text{denom}} \times 2^{\left\lfloor \frac{\|\vec{r}^* - \vec{r}_i\|^2}{\sigma} \right\rfloor}} \right\rfloor \quad \forall\, i \qquad (1)$$

The learning rate, η, was 0.3 and the neighbourhood width, σ, was decreasing from 20 to 1 during an epoch, which is not a standard method. Usually, several epochs would be used where the neighbourhood width would be decreasing over the epochs but kept constant during one epoch. Here a fast convergence rate is desired and experiments showed that the derivation introduced led to good results.

To find out how well the SOM had been learned, the beacon was moved around the robot at distances between 10cm and 70cm and the winning neurone for the different angles was determined.

Figure 1 illustrates the variance among the winning neurones. The plot contains the mean winner and the min-max error bars show the distance effects. The distance dependence is quite small because the signal characteristic is similar for both close and far distances. The error is relatively small, considering that the map was trained with only 200 training vectors and one epoch.

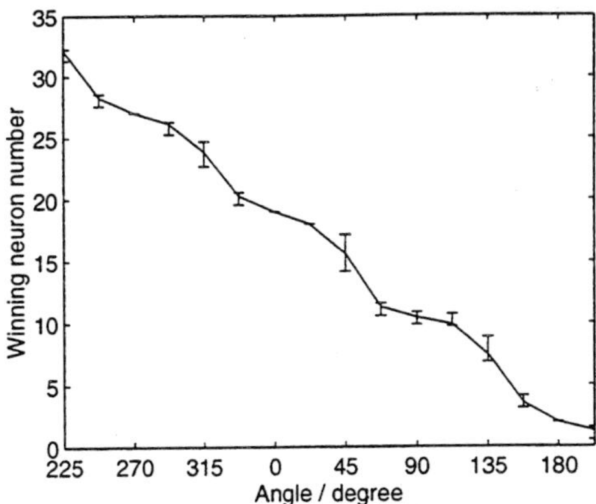

Figure 1. Winning neurones as the beacon is moved around the robot.

3.2. Training a SOM for angle and distance

The acquisition of the training vectors to form a map of both angle and distance is more complex because the robot should ideally meet all different orientations, at all different distances, equally often. Only this can ensure that neurones will be spread equally across the input space because the spatial position of the neurones represents the probability density function of the inputs.

A path that fulfils the conditions mentioned is a forward and backward motion with stops in between to turn on the spot. With the angular orientation sense established, the robot knows when it has made a full turn. To ensure that the robot goes straight to the beacon or straight away from it, the neurone that looks straight ahead needs to be found. This can easily be done if the index of the sensor that looks straight ahead is known.

The Self-Organising Map used consists of 9×9 neurones whereby each neurone has 4 direct neighbours except for those in the first and the last rows. These each have only 3 neighbours each. The neurones of the first column are connected to those of the last column as the angular information is also circular. The number of training vectors was chosen to be 1000 and two epochs were used. The learning rate, η, was linearly decreasing over the 2000 cycles from 0.2 to 0.05. The neighbourhood width, σ, was set to 1 at the beginning and then decreased linearly to 0.25. The way in which the parameters are set differs markedly from commonly used methods to ensure quick result achievement.

The initialisation plays a very important role on the

learning in this case. As a SOM for angular information has already been learned, this can be used for initialising the two dimensional map. There are two advantages. Firstly, training takes less time because the neurones are pre-trained. That is, the new generation of sense of orientation inherits information from the former one. Secondly, the initialisation influences the arrangement of the neurones among themselves.

By initialising the weight values of the neurones of the first row with the appropriate ones of the one dimensional SOM it can be achieved that these neurones will be active for different orientations close to the beacon. By subsequently initialising the following rows in the same manner but reducing the weight value magnitudes it can be achieved that the following rows will respond to different orientations at increasing distances.

To evaluate whether a result is acceptable a recorded data set is presented to the trained Kohonen map. The data set consists of sensor data recorded when the beacon was moved around the robot in steps of $22.5°$, at distances between 10cm and 90cm in steps of 10cm. At each position 10 sets of sensor data were recorded. To evaluate how well the SOM was learnt, the winning neurone was determined for each sensor data vector. The spatial position of the winning neurone is approximated to that of the recorded data vector. While this is not the exact position, it represents an approximation of the neurones' spatial arrangements. Figure 2 illustrates the result of the evaluation process. The solid line shows the connection between neurones whose index difference is ± 9 whereas the dashed line shows the connection of neurones whose index difference is ± 1. A perfect result would be a uniform grid with 9×9 points.

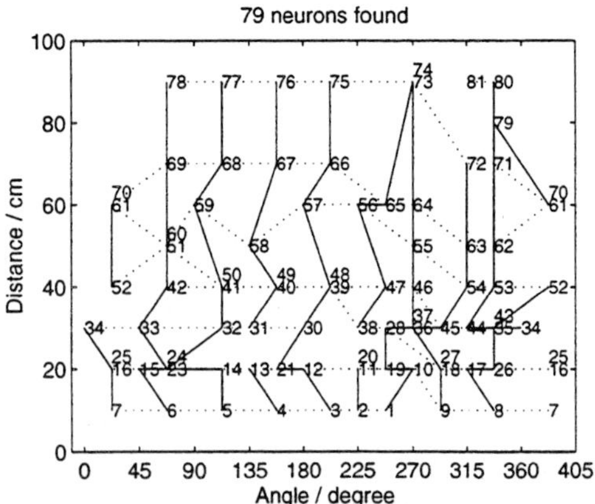

Figure 2. Spatial position of the neurones using the described evaluation method.

Since 10 sets of data were recorded for every position it is likely that different neurones were active at the same position, due to sensor noise. This method of evaluation cannot guarantee that each neurone will be found.

4. Incorporating SOMs with Q-Learning

The sensory-motor task to be learned by the agent is that of moving towards a beacon. Figure 3 shows how the Q-Learning method [8, 1] is incorporated with the SOM. The aim is to let each neurone of the learned SOM represent one distinct situation for reinforcement learning. In each of the situations (each neurone) there are several actions from which to choose. This leads to an association matrix (look-up table), where each row represents a situation and each column represents an action that can be taken. The entries in the association matrix are the Q-Values for each state-action pair.

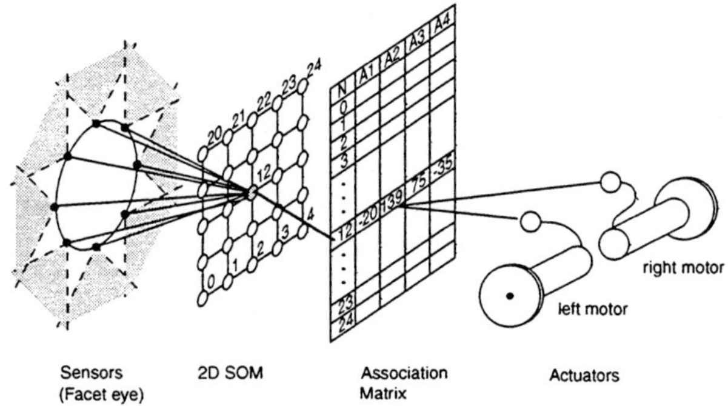

Figure 3. Incorporation of a SOM with Q-Learning

4.1. Learning to approach a beacon

The implementation of the Q-Learning is again driven by the real system's limited resources. As it is desirable to achieve a reasonable result quickly, it is advisable to use local reinforcement signals to speed up the learning. This means that not only is a reinforcement signal given if the agent reaches the target or moves out of range, but that there is also a reinforcement signal if the agent achieves or misses a subgoal by respectively approaching or retreating from the beacon.

While the subgoal can be easily defined, ascertaining whether the subgoal has been reached or not is problematic. It seems logical to use the agent's own sense of orientation to determine whether or not the subgoal has been achieved. Usually, the arrangement of the neurones of the SOM is not known. However, using the initialisation introduced in Section 3.2, it is possible to predict the spatial position of the neurones. Hence the success of the agent in achieving the subgoal can be determined simply by comparing the indices of the two most recently active neurones.

The policy chosen is an ϵ-greedy action selection [8], that is an undirected exploration (or random walk) of the action space. While other appropriate policies may exist, the main focus of this research is the influence of parameter variation on the speed of learning.

As the robot moves in its environment, each action taken is regarded as one training example. The learning is therefore incremental. Again all experiments are carried out in the real world and the training examples are not known beforehand.

Practical experience showed, that even 9×9 states (neurones) were too many causing a rather long learning time. The 9×9 SOM was therefore mapped to a 5×5 SOM increasing the robustness with respect to sensor noise but decreasing the positioning resolution. This opens the opportunity to map the coarse behaviour learnt using the 5×5 SOM back to the former map for fine-tuning.

After executing a large number of experiments using different parameter settings the most desirable behaviour emerged from a relatively high discount factor of $\gamma = 0.5$, a rather normal learning rate of $\eta = 0.1$ and a surprisingly high random action selection (exploration) of $\epsilon = 20\%$. Using 1000 training cycles seemed to be most appropriate. Due to the little number of training cycles a small negative reward after each training cycle did not lead to better results and was therefore discarded. The same holds for decreasing learning rates.

Having learnt to approach the beacon the opposite behaviour (fleeing from the beacon) can easily be learnt by simply inverting the rewards. Thus, complex behaviour can be generated by combining the two basic behaviours.

5. Discussion

This section presents similarities and differences between existing navigation methods and the navigation method described in this paper.

The way the agent's relative positioning system works is related to that from Sorouchyari [7]. Also Self-Organising Maps are used to extract the relative beacon position from the sensor data. The way the map is learned is also through exploration instead of recorded training vectors.

To see the whole problem from the agent's point of view instead of the designer's point of view helps to simplify not only the problem but also the computational expenditure. This is also proposed by Pfeifer et al. [6].

Neural reinforcement methods could successfully be implemented to solve the problem of learning goal directed navigation [3, 5]. The problem with these methods is that they run with simulations only, whereas Touzet [9] showed that they can also run on a real system. The navigation method used here is the analogical to Malmstrom et al. [3]. Moreover, it works with the real system and learns the navigation in a bootstrapping manner autonomously.

6. Conclusion

This work showed that it is possible to implement an agent independent bootstrapping learning method for simple navigation tasks. The results show that the parameter settings influence the performance of the navigation learnt dramatically.

This method was implemented and trained successfully on a real autonomous agent and even shows robustness to the ageing process of the agent's sensors. As the navigation and the positioning system are kept separately, the robot can keep adapting its sense of orientation (training the SOM) while performing navigation tasks.

Acknowledgments

Burkhard Iske was supported by the Weidmüller Stiftung during his Diploma thesis in Australia and is currently a scholarship holder of the DFG-Graduiertenkolleg "Parallele Rechnernetzwerke in der Produktionstechnik", GRK 124/2-96.

References

[1] L. P. Kaelbling, *Recent Advances in Reinforcement Learning*, Kluwer Academic Publishers, Boston, Dordrecht, London, 1996

[2] T. Kohonen, *Self-Organisation and Associative Memory*, second Edition, Springer-Verlag New York Berlin Heidelberg, 1988.

[3] K. Malmstrom, L. Munday, J. Sitte, *Learning of Sensory Motor Tasks by an Autonomous Agent*, Australian Journal of Intelligent Information Processing Systems, **4** No. 2, pp 129–141, Winter 1997

[4] K. Malmstrom, J. Sitte, Experimental Setup for Multiple Agent Interaction, *3rd IFAC Symposium on Intelligent Autonomous Vehicles*, pp. 37–42, March 1998.

[5] J. d. R. Millán, *Reinforcement learning of goal-directed obstacle-avoiding reaction strategies in an autonomous mobile robot*, Robotics and Autonomous Systems, **15**, pp 275–299, 1995

[6] R. Pfeifer, C. Scheier, *Sensory-motor coordination: The metaphor and beyond*, Robotics and Autonomous Systems, **20**, pp 157–178, 1997

[7] E. Sorouchyari, *Self-organizing Neural Network for Trajectory Control and Task Coordination of a Mobile Robot*, Connection Science, **2**(3), 1990

[8] R. S. Sutton, A. G. Barto, *Reinforcement Learning*, The MIT Press, Cambridge, Massachusetts, London, England, 1998.

[9] C. F. Touzet, *Neural reinforcement learning for behaviour synthesis*, Robotics and Autonomous Systems, **22**, pp 251–281, 1997

Commands Generation by Face Movements Applied to the Guidance of a Wheelchair for Handicapped People

L.M. Bergasa, M. Mazo, A. Gardel, R. Barea, L. Boquete
Departamento de Electrónica. Escuela Politécnica. Universidad de Alcalá
Campus Universitario s/n. 28805 Alcalá de Henares. MADRID. Spain
T:+34 91 885 6569-40 Fax: +34 91 885 6591
E-mail:bergasa@depeca.alcala.es http://www.depeca.alcala.es/users/bergasa/public

Abstract

This paper describes a vision-based commands generation system, by face movements, applied to the guidance of an electrical wheelchair for handicapped people with severe disabilities. Using a 2D color face tracker and a fuzzy detector the system computes face movements of the user and, depending on them, some commands are generated to drive the wheelchair. The system is non-intrusive and it allows visibility and freedom of head movements. It is able to learn the face movements of the user in an automatic initial setup, working even for people of different races. It is adaptive and, therefore, robust to light and background changes in inside environments. We report on some experimental results of this kind of guidance and some conclusions of its performance.

1. Introduction

Visual interfaces facilite natural and easy interfaces for human-robot interation. Nowadays there are many application that use them as: automatic focus in cameras [1], teleconferencing with improved visual sensation [2], face identification in security systems [3], gaze driven panorama image viewer for virtual reality systems [4], lips readers [5], assistance to the mobility of disabled people [6], etc.

Head movements and gestures can be a natural way to control an electrical wheelchair for handicapped people with severe disabilities that can't use a joystick.

The Electronics Department of University of Alcala has been working, for more than 6 years, on artificial means to assist the mobility of handicapped people. Nowadays, an electronic system is being developed, within SIAMO project (Integral System for Assisted Mobility) [7], in order to guide a multi-functional wheelchair for disabled or elderly people (Figure 1). This project adds to the control by joystick other alternatives guidance by: switches, voice, breath expulsion, eyes and face movements. At present, a wheelchair prototype is working using the guidance method by face movements. A 3D simulator has been designed as well, to help the users in adapting themselves to the system in a safer way.

The description of the global system architecture and the original skin segmentation method aplied was explained in the references [8][9]. Here, a brief explanation of the system architecture will be seen to understand the methodology followed in the design of the commands generation for controling the wheelchair by face movements. Some experimental results are given and finally some conclusions about its performance have been taken out.

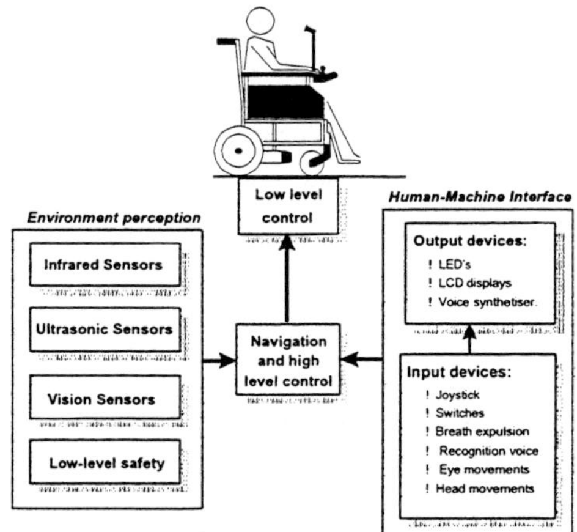

Figure 1. SIAMO Project

2. System architecture

Figure 2 shows the general system architecture. Through a CCD color micro camera, placed in front of the user, face images are acquired. These images are digitized by a frame-grabber and loaded in a PC Pentium II memory. To locate the head in the image, an original skin color segmentation algorithm has been used, called UASGM (Unsupervised and Adaptive Skin Gaussian Model) [9]. Then, a 2D face tracking is applied to the skin blob and, depending on its state vectors, a fuzzy detector of the head movements activates the transitions of a high control state machine that generates wheelchair's linear and angular speed (V_{cmd} ,Ω_{cmd}).

Applying the Kinematic model, linear and angular speed become angular speeds for every wheel ($\omega_{r,cmd}$ $\omega_{l,cmd}$) and they are sent to the low level control. In this level a PI controller has been designed to control the velocity of each wheel.

It can be clearly seen that there is a visual feedback loop, as the human user reacts according to the current circumstances.

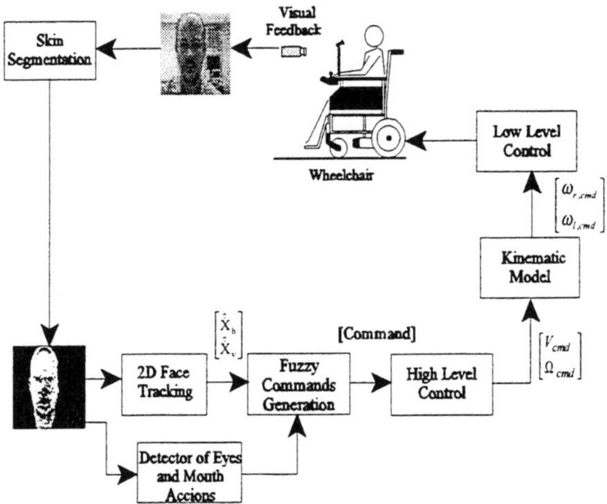

Figure 2. Architecture of the guidance by head movements

3. Fuzzy commands generation

The final goal is to guide a wheelchair using some commands that are activated by different facial movements. Applying the criteria of simplicity and robustness, taking into account the disabilities of the intended users, it has been estimated that the minimum number of commands necessary to guide a wheelchair are the following: on/off, forward/backward, turn left/right and increase/decrease speed.

To activate the speed commands, actions of head movements have been chosen and to activate the direction and on/off commands, eyes and mouth actions, as for example, hide the lips or wink an eye during certain time. This can be seen in figure 3.

Therefore, if user turns the head to the right the wheelchair will turn to the same direction. This happens as well if he turns his head to the left. Head rising involves the increment of wheelchair speed, and when the user bows it, this will decrease the speed.

Every time he winks an eye the wheelchair changes its state *on/off*; when lips are hidden it changes again for the command *forward/backward*. It is necessary to keep these special actions for, at least, two seconds just to let trigger the *direction* and *on/off* commands activation. Doing this, wrong commands are avoided as a consecuence of normal blinks. *On/off* commands allows to user activate or deactivate the system by themselves, so when it is in the off state, it can make any kind of movement being secure on the fact that no other command will be activated.

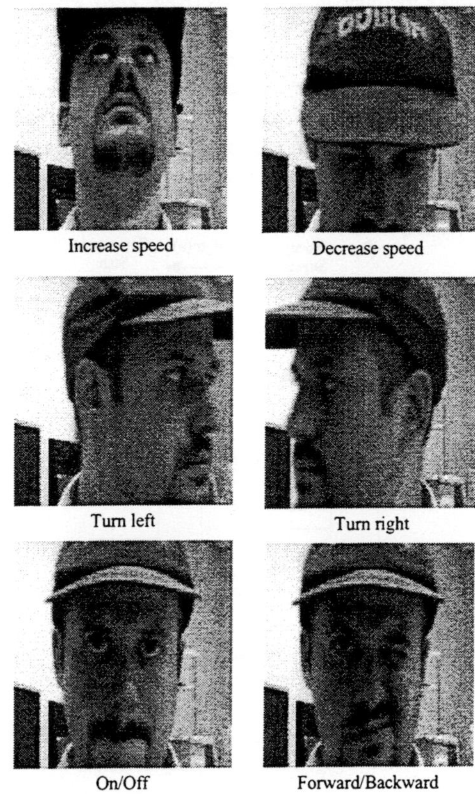

Figure 3. Facial actions that generate the commands

The speed commands are obtained as it is shown in schema of figure 4 (a). The 2D face tracker calculates the parameters center of gravity (x,y) , horizontal (h) and vertical (v) size of the face, on the skin blob, in order to obtain the face position and orientation. A zero-th order Kalman filter is used to estimate two independent state vectors: one of them for the horizontal variation (X_h =(x,h)) and the other one for the vertical variation (X_v =(y,v)). Two independent state vectors have been utilized because, in our application, users can do only horizontal and vertical head rotation movements. Of this manner computation time is reduced.

Derivatives of the estimated state vectors $(\hat{X}_h, \hat{X}_v)$ are the fuzzy inputs to a Sugeno detector with an output that will control the transitions of .the states machine responsible of generate the commands. The last transition (Spd_tr(n-1)) will be an extra input that controls which rules are used by the detector at each time.

The knowledge-base of the fuzzy system (figure 4(b)) is made up by an initial calibration process that normalises all the input variables to a range (-1,1). Each input variable has three membership funcitons (Neg, Zero, Pos). Zero is a triangular function while the others are trapezoidal. Said functions were adjusted in an experimental way. At last, fuzzy rules were chosen by direct observation according to the memberships shown in table 1. Positions with no membership are due to the fact that are dependent of the user and so are not generalizable.

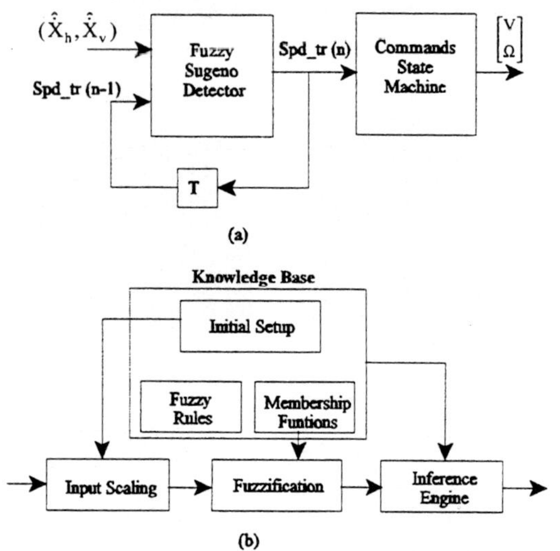

Figure 4. (a) Commands generation schema (b) Knowledge base of the fuzzy detector

As we work with the derivatives of the state vector, the actions speed are taken into account. It is not enough to do one action, but it must be executed with some speed. In this way some unvoluntary facial movements are eliminated.

In figure 5 it is shown a detection sequence of several head movements besides the temporal evolutions of the state variables derivatives used in the fuzzy detector.

The detection of eyes and mouth actions is based on the analisis of the holows on the skin blobs imposing some geometrical restrictions. Hollows appear in the blob because in the face there are some features like: eyes, mouth, eyebrowes, etc, that have different colors related with the skin. When the consecutive number of times that facial features (eyes or mouth) have not been detected is above a certain threshold, it is made a change in the direction or in the wheelchair state on/off, respectively.

Head Actions [Speed_tr]	Derivatives of the state vectors $\dot{h}_S$	$\dot{x}_{OS}$	$\dot{v}_S$	$\dot{y}_{OS}$
Still	Zero	Zero	Zero	Zero
Turn right starting	Pos	Neg		
Turn right ending	Neg	Pos		
Turn left starting	Pos	Pos		
Turn left ending	Neg	Neg		
Rise starting	Zero	Zero	Pos	
Rise ending	Zero	Zero	Neg	
Bow starting	Zero	Zero	Neg	Pos
Bow ending	Zero	Zero	Pos	Neg

Table 1. Fuzzy membership of the derivatives of the state vectors for the different head actions

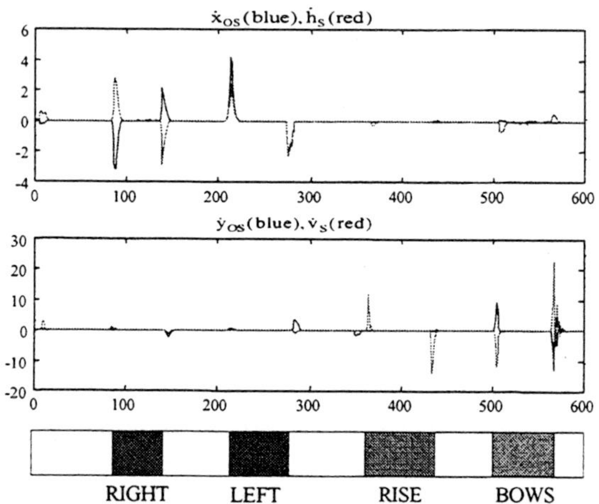

Figure 5. Examples of commands generation

Figure 6 shows the command generator state machine. This implements the high level control generating the linear and angular speed (V_{cmd}, Ω_{cmd}) as a function of time and the command activated. Turn commands modify angular speed in fix quantities each 100 ms and depending on the direction and on/off states. Acceleration and decceleration commands work of a similar way but with the linear speed. Speeds are saturated to a prearranged limits in order to improve the segurity of the guidance. The *direction* command change the movement between forward and backward and the on/off allows to stop the wheelchair and start the process.

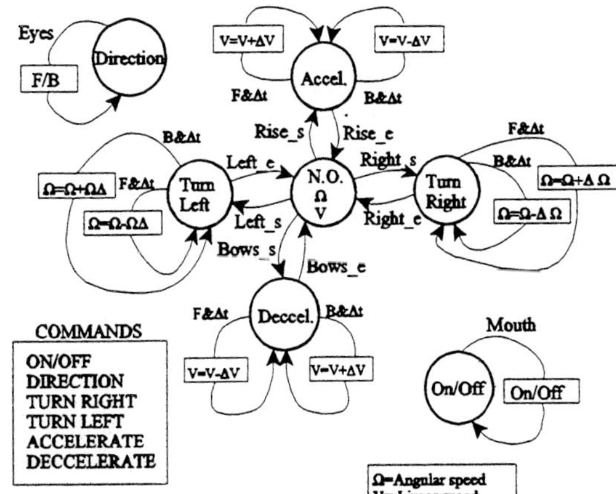

Figure 6. High level control state machine

4. Experimental results

The vision system is able to process up to 15 images per second, with a resolution of 128x128 pixels. During the testing stage it great robustness exhibited in the velocity commands. However, the winks detector introduced some mistakes with the movements of the wheelchair. In order to increase the system controllability this accion was sustituted by the lips hidding one, using a temporal threshold for diferentiate between the direction and the on/off. 10 commands per second are issued to the low level controller.The maximum wheelchair velocity was set to 1 m/s. The wheelchair prototype is provided with an ultrasonic ring and bumpers to increase safety during navigation. The system was tested for 5 different handicapped users in the Electronics Department labs and corridors, after some training on the simulator.

5. Conclusions

The conclusions obtained by the users after performing the test on the navigation system are presented bellow:

• It is non-intrusive, as it is passive, and there is no need for additional elements.
• Guidance complexity is decreased as more training is perfomed. We must also take into consideration that the camera is 80 cms in front of the user and, therefore, the system requires certain space for safe manoeubring.
• The simple commands set and the wheelchair response allow for easy controllability in environments with not too many obstacles. Command generation rate is one per second, allowing confortable maniovrability to some extent in narrow indoor enviroments.
• Audible feedback is included to ensure proper command acknowledgement.
• It works well in indoor environments, where suitable ilumination can be provided, decreasing the performance as light conditions get poorer. In outdoor environments there is no uniform ilumination (shadows, direct sun light, etc), decreasing also the system capabilities.

6. Acknowledgements

This work has been financed by the CICYT (Spanish Interministerial Science and Technology Commission) through the SIAMO project TER96-1957-C03-01.

7. References

[1] Test af Canon UC-X1Hi, HIFI electronik, 1995.

[2] De Silva, K. Aizawa, M. Hatori. "Detection and tracking of facial features by using edge pixel counting and deformable circular template matching. IEICE TRANS INF&SYST. VOL.E78-D, No 9, pp.1195-1207, September 1995.

[3] Kah-Kay Sun and Tomaso Poggio. "Example-based learning for view-based human face detection". IEEE Transactions on Pattern analisis and machine intelligence, Vol 220, nº1 , January 1998.

[4] Stiefelhagen, J. Yang and A. Waibel "A model based gaze tracking system". IEEE International Joint Symposia on Intelligence and Systems-Image, Speech&Natural Language Systems. 1997

[5] R. Meier, R. Stiefelhagen and J. Yang "Apreprocessing of visual speech under real word conditions".Proceedings of European Tutorial & Research Work Shop on Audio-Visual Speach Proccesing. 1997

[6] Heinzmann and A. Zelinsky, "Robust real-time face tracking and gesture recognition". Proceedings of IJCAI´97, International Joint Conference on Artificial Intelligence, August 1997.

[7] M. Mazo et al.,"Integral System for Assisted Mobility". 2nd International Workshop on Intelligent Control (IC´98)JCIS'98 Proceedings. Editor: Paul P. Wang. pp: 361-364. Durham (USA), 1998.

[8] L.M. Bergasa et al., " Guidance of a Wheelchair for Handicapped People by Head Movements". roceedings of the International Field and Service Robotics. FSR'99. pp:150-155. CMU. Pittsburgh. USA. August 99.

[9] LM. Bergasa et al., " Guidance of a Wheelchair for Handicapped People by Face Tracking". 7th IEEE International Conference on Emerging Technologies and Factory Automation. ETFA'99. Barcelona. October 1999.

Database Architecture for Autonomous Transportation Agents for On-scene Networked Incident Management (ATON)

*Mohan Trivedi, Shailendra Bhonsle, and Amarnath Gupta**
Department of Electrical and Computer Engineering,
*San Diego Supercomputing Center,
University of California, San Diego, USA.
Email: trivedi@ece.ucsd.edu

Abstract

A collection of distributed databases forms an important architectural component of the ATON project for networked incidence management of highway traffic. The database sub-architecture supports the architectural integration of many thematic areas of the ATON, and provides many high level abstractions that semantically correspond to traffic incidents. These databases are queried for the detection of local or distributed traffic incidents by many distributed control and analysis algorithms. The abstract database sub-architecture leads to many concrete databases of different types having different functions. The semantic event/activity database is one of them. The distributed multi-sensory sub-architecture detects atomic semantic events that occur in the environment. The event/activity database stores them and their temporal structures. An activity is a temporal composition of atomic events. A specialized query language is used to flexibly define and detect activities of interest. The query language embodies high level semantic pattern matching abstractions. Preliminary results of using the event/activity database are also presented in this paper.

1. Introduction

The eventual goal of the autonomous transportation agents for on-scene networked incident management (ATON) system is to automatically detect, verify, and manage traffic incidents. A traffic incident is defined as "an event that causes blockage of traffic lanes or any kind of restriction of the free movement of traffic" [5]. To achieve this goal, ATON uses clusters of video and acoustic sensors, mobile robotic agents and interactive multimedia workstations and interfaces, all connected using high-speed, high-bandwidth communication links. The project is divided into five thematic areas of robotics agents with coordinated behavior, distributed multi-sensory networks, ubiquitous tele-existence, distributed virtual environments, and distributed databases. Figure 1 shows a scenario for traffic incident detection, verification, and management. Many steps taken for incident management in this scenario are the automatic detection and reporting of incidents by sensor clusters, dispatch of a robotic *mothership* [6] or remote agent to the scene of the incident, dismounting of a team of little robotic agents [6] from the mothership to form a safe zone in a coordinated way, and assistance offered by the mother ship through tele-existence terminals.

This paper addresses the issues in the design of an integrated software architecture for coordination of many distributed control and analysis algorithms present in various thematic areas. The novel concept of using a set of distributed databases, having many different functions and types, is proposed for distributed coordination of these algorithms. This coordination paradigm using databases makes the whole architecture robust by providing means to efficiently manage current and past *states* of the *system* and the *monitored environment*. Such *states* are typically large in multi-sensory environments where some of the sensors could be as complex as omni-directional video sensors.

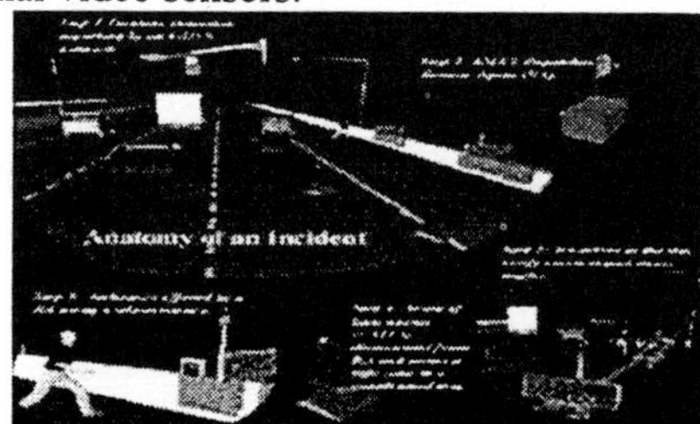

Figure 1. Scenario depicting steps associated with traffic incident management

Specialized databases are also used in ATON to provide high level semantic abstractions for flexible definition and detection of traffic incidents. These abstractions are those of semantic events [3, 4], activities [1, 2], and behaviors [2]. **Events** are atomic semantic units that are detected over a bounded temporal extent by fusion of multi-sensory information. **Activities**, which have much higher semantic content than events, are spatio-temporal compositions of events. A **behavior** is defined to be a set of activities. A traffic **incident** has an even higher level of semantic content, and is modeled using the abstractions of *events*, *activities*, and *behaviors*.

Apart from providing a direct semantic link to the notion of a traffic incident, high level semantic abstractions are also required by many distributed control

1051-4651/00 $10.00 © 2000 IEEE

algorithms to control robotic actuators in the real world. Computations of these abstractions from raw sensory data have prohibitive computational costs, and when the amount of sensory information produced is very large, it is best to delegate the role of these computations to a database.

In section 2, databases providing different functions are briefly described. The event/activity database is discussed in section 3, and preliminary results of using a semantic event/activity database are described in section 4.

2. Databases in the ATON architecture

Many functional classes of databases are required for the distributed decision making to detect and manage traffic incidents. In this subsection, we only concentrate on *world databases* or databases that deal with the *states* of the monitored environments. Figure 2 shows a few of these databases and functions that they provide. The distributed nature of these databases is not shown in this figure.

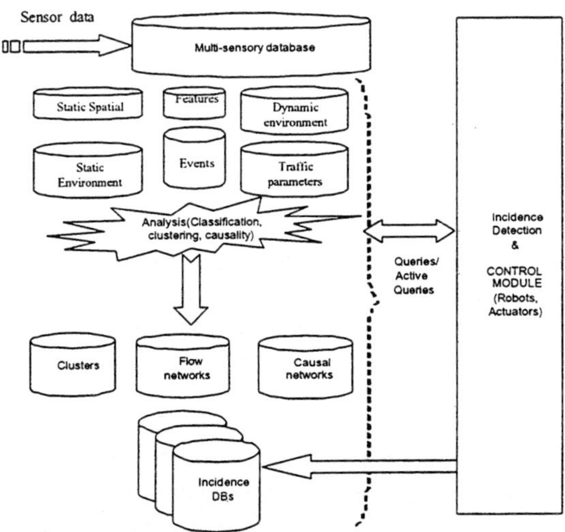

Figure 2. Many types of databases used in incidence detection and management

At the core representation level, the information gathered by sensors in a multi-sensory environment can be treated as a huge multi-sensory database. A part of this database may consist of the video of the segment of highway being monitored. Another part of this database may consist of just the average intensity of light at the monitored site sensed by an appropriate sensor. Using appropriate sensor fusion algorithms, many functional classes of information, stored in relevant databases, are derived from this raw multi-sensory database.

Spatial databases provide information about the spatial structure of the monitored environment like its division into regions corresponding to traffic lanes, curb, exit lane etc. The **environment** databases provide static or dynamic environmental conditions like fogginess, rain intensity, luminance etc. Spatial and environmental databases depend only on the environmental conditions at the monitored site, and these are independent of the actual traffic related facts. **Traffic parameter databases** provide a number of traffic related parameters like counters that indicate the rate of flow of traffic, parameters to indicate the *burstiness* of the traffic etc. These databases make use of spatial and environment databases for computations of these parameters.

There are two classes of databases that deal with high level, domain-dependent semantics of observations: the **feature** and the **event/activity** databases. The feature databases deal with features of either mobile objects or spatial regions of interest. For example, these features could relate to the color, size, centroid etc. of certain monitored mobile objects or to statistical properties of the backgroud region. Features are the basic domain-dependent semantic information associated with monitored mobile objects or spatial regions. Events usually represent the state-transition of observed mobile objects or spatial regions. They represent a form of atomic semantic units, and the monitored environment can be described as a collection of these events. In the next section, we describe a specific event database that stores events and their temporal structures.

A set of databases was listed above that provide basic information about the monitored objects and spatial regions. These databases are queried, and retrieved data is processed to provide information required by the ATON distributed decision making algorithms for incidence detection and management. For example, traffic flow analysis algorithms use these databases to produce flow networks. Many time-stamped versions of different types of such flow networks need to be kept in a separate database. Such specialized databases are our next level of databases providing a very high level semantic view of the physically distributed monitored environment.

The ***type*** of a database refers to its underlying data model. The range of database types that provide the required functions vary from the simplest and widely used ***relational model*** to data models that represent ***complex spatial and temporal structures***. In the following section, we describe one such complex database used in the ATON architecture.

3. Semantic event/activity database

Semantic activities are complex spatio-temporal compositions of semantic events. The event/activity database stores events and their spatio-temporal inter-relations. A transducer is used to detect events. The transducer uses raw sensor data, spatial information from a spatial database, and feature data of detected objects or regions of interest. The event/activity database query language provides high level semantic abstractions for specification of activities through its set of operations. These queries are executed against a database instance to detect activities. Also, there is provision for ***active queries***. These use query abstractions similar to those provided by the activity query language, but they execute in real-time and can notify different entities of the ATON architecture of occurrences of activities. Many components of such event/activity databases together with their interactions with the sensor processing elements and the event detection transducer are depicted in figure 3.

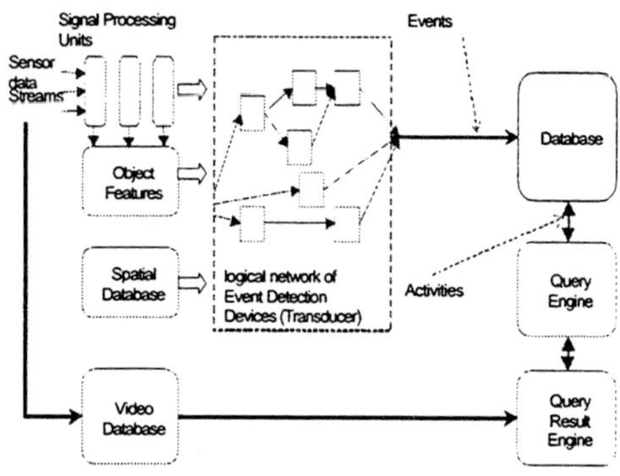

Figure 3. Detection and storage of semantic events and retrieval of semantic activities

Design of such semantic event/activity databases depends on many factors. Some of these factors are whether events represent states or state-transitions of objects, whether spatial, temporal, or spatio-temporal aspect is emphasized, how spatial and temporal *uncertainties* in event occurrences are represented, and whether the model of composition of activities from events is statistical or combinatorial. For our modeling purposes, we defined events to represent state-transitions of observed objects. These objects may be the mobile objects like moving cars in a highway segment, or spatial regions like a specified lane of the monitored highway.

We focused on the temporal composition of activities from events, and an important consideration was to take into account the ***temporal uncertainties*** in event occurrences. Assuming that such uncertainties for a given set of events are bounded by a constant, a model of composition of semantic activities from events is obtained that suitably represents the ***concurrent occurrences of events*** in the presence of such temporal uncertainties. The concurrency may be between events associated with ***multiple objects***, or between many events associated with a ***single agent***. Such concurrency in the presence of temporal uncertainties is *not modeled* by ubiquitous sequential temporal composition rules, or by its simple extensions [2].

The combinatorial structure obtained above corresponds to semiorders (a *proper* subclass of partial orders) under certain binary relation. The binary relation is *<precede,Δ>* such that *event x <precede, Δ> event y* if and only if the occurrence time of *y* is greater than the occurrence time of *x plus Δ*, where *Δ* is the fixed temporal uncertainty interval. Semiorders based temporal compositions represent a natural evolution of sequential composition rules. We designed a semiorder based data model and a corresponding query language that also embeds a semiorder pattern definition language. Many algorithmic and architectural issues associated with the design and implementation of this database is discussed in [2]. In the following section, we briefly describe a set of simple queries to illustrate our use of this database in the ATON architecture.

4. Preliminary results

A prototype of the semantic event/activity database was designed, developed, and used for detection of complex traffic related *activities*. A set of traffic related atomic events like *startLeftTurn*, *endLeftTurn*, *enterRegion*, *exitRegion* etc. were defined and the corresponding modules were inserted in the event detection transducer. Many atomic events are defined only with respect to the specific *spatial structure* of the monitored highway segment as described below. The spatial structure, depicted in figure 4, is stored in a surrogate spatial database. The highway segment is divided into many layers, where each layer consists of non-overlapping regions like *ExitLane*, *Lane1*, *Lane2*, *Curb*, etc. The event detection system queries this spatial database to appropriately detect atomic events like *LaneChange* by a car. The event/activity database stores the detected events and their spatial and temporal attributes.

Figure 4. Spatial structure of the highway segment being monitored

The dynamically changing monitored environment was represented in the event/activity database as a collection of occurred events, their temporal structure, and their parameters. Complex traffic activities were detected using queries defined using the activity query language.

Many complex temporal structures over a set of events were flexibly defined using *semiorder* patterns, which, in turn, were used by these queries. The execution of the query extracted the set of matching activities from the semiorder representation of the environment in the database. Although the prototype supports complex queries, for brevity, we only discuss a few simple representative queries. The Δ uncertainty bound was set to 100 ms in our experiments.

Query 1: (***Exit***) Find cars that entered *lane 1*, then entered the *exit lane*, and finally exited from the *exit lane*.

Query 2: (***Tailgate***) Find a set of cars that entered *lane 1* almost simultaneously.

Query 3: (***Simultaneous***) Find an object that *while* entering *lane 3* was also turning left.

The first query illustrates the sequential composition of an activity from atomic semantic events. An important fact is that *exponentially* many such *activities* can be defined on the same base set of *events*. Databases provide a tool to the user for ***flexible*** definition and detection of what is needed. This compares well to the currently used alternative of fixing a set of high level activities and then detecting them in an ad-hoc but efficient manner [7]. One of the results produced by this query is shown in figure 5.

Figure 5. Result of *Exit* query

The second query shows a semantic activity that is ***multi-agent*** and involves the specification of ***concurrency***. The third query involves ***multiple concurrent events*** associated with a ***single agent***. Some of the results produced by these queries are depicted in figure 6. Being able to handle the requirement of modeling concurrency of events in the presence of temporal uncertainties is an important strength of the semiorder database model.

These simple queries demonstrate the usefulness of the event/activity database model in the ATON architecture. Combinations of the essential elements of these queries specify semantic activities with very complex structures that the query language is able to deal with.

5. Conclusions

The role of databases in the integrated ATON architecture was described. It was pointed out that for detection and management of traffic incidents a number of databases having different *functions* and *types* are required. One of these many types of databases is the semantic event/activity database. These databases provide high level of abstraction for *flexible* definition and *detection* of semantic activities. These high level abstractions in turn help in the flexible definition and detection of *incidents* or *conditions* that lead to traffic incidents.

On the other hand, use of databases in such systems is a new paradigm for the integration of many distributed control and analysis algorithms that are present in many thematic areas. This is especially true in multi-sensory monitoring environments where the *global and local states* have large spatio-temporal extents and these states need to be made persistent for robust interactions amongst many distributed algorithms.

a. Tailgating

b. Simultaneous

Figure 6. Results of (a)*Tailgate* and (b) *Simultaneous* queries

6. References

[1] S. K. Bhonsle, et.al., "Complex visual activity recognition using a temporally ordered database", *3rd Int. Conf. Visual Information Management*, Amsterdam, June 1999.

[2] S. K. Bhonsle, "Semiorder Model for Temporal Composition of Activities from Events in Multi-Sensory Environments", *Ph.D. dissertation*, Dept. of Computer Science and Engineering, Univ. of Cal. San Diego, March 2000.

[3] W. I. Grosky, "Managing multimedia information in database systems", *Comm. ACM*, Vol. 40, No. 12, Dec. 1997.

[4] A. Gupta, S. Santini, and R. Jain, "In search of information in visual media", *Comm. ACM*, Vol. 40, No. 12, Dec. 1997.

[5] K. Ozbay and P. Kachroo, "Incident Management in Intelligent Transportation Systems", Artech House, 1999.

[6] M. M. Trivedi, K. C. Ng, N. Lassiter, and R. Capella, "New generation of multirobot systems", *IEEE Int. Conf. on Systems, Man, and Cybernatics*, San Diego, USA, Oct. 1998.

[7] R. Weil, J. Wootton and A Garcia-Ortiz, "Traffic Incident Detection: Sensors and Algorithms", *Math. Comput. Modelling* Vol 27, No. 9-11, pp. 257-291, 1998.

E.O.G. guidance of a wheelchair using neural networks

Rafael Barea, Luciano Boquete, Manuel Mazo, Elena López, L.M. Bergasa.
Electronics Department. University of Alcala.
Campus Universitario s/n. 28871Alcalá de Henares. Madrid. Spain.
T: +34 91 885 65 74 Fax: +34 91 885 65 91
e-mail: barea@depeca.alcala.es http://www.depeca.alcala.es/users/barea/public

Abstract

This paper presents a new method to control and guide mobile robots. In this case, to send different commands we have used electrooculography (EOG) techniques, so that, control is made by means of the ocular position (eye displacement into its orbit). A neural network is used to identify the inverse eye model, therefore the saccadic eye movements can be detected and know where user is looking. This control technique can be useful in multiple applications, but in this work it is used to guide a autonomous robot (wheelchair) as a system to help to people with severe disabilities. The system consists of a standard electric wheelchair with an on-board computer, sensors and graphical user interface running on a computer.

Keyword: Electrooculographic potential (EOG), neural networks, control system, handicapped people, wheelchair.

1. Introduction

Assistive robotics can improve the quality of life for disable people. Nowadays, there are many help systems to control and guide autonomous mobile robots. All this systems allow their users to travel more efficiently and with greater ease [1]. In the last years, the applications for developing help systems to people with several disabilities are increased, and therefore the traditional systems are not valid. In this new systems, we can see: videooculography systems (VOG) or infrared oculography (IROG) based on detect the eye position using a camera [2]; there are several techniques based in voice recognition for detecting basic commands to control some instruments or robots; the joystick (sometimes tactil screen) is the most popular technique used to control diferent applications by people with limited upper body mobility but it requires fine control that the person may be have difficulty to accomplish. All this techniques can be applied to different people according to their disability degree, using always the technique or techniques more efficiently for each person.

This paper reports initial work in the development of a robotic wheelchair system based in electrooculography [3]. Our system allows the users to tell the robot where to move in gross terms and will then carry out that navigational task using common sensical constraints, such as avoiding collision.

This wheelchair system is intented to be a general purpose navigational assistant in environments with accesible features such as ramps and doorways of sufficient width to allow a wheelchair to pass. This work is based on previous research in robot path planing and mobile robotics [4]; however, a robotic wheelchair must interact with its user, making the robotic system semiautonomous rather than completely autonomous.

This paper has been divided into the following sections: section 2 describes the electrooculography technique used to register the eye movement and the eye gaze, in section 3 you can see the method used to detect saccadic eye movement using neural network (RBF). In section 4, the visual control system is described. Section 5 shows some results and section 6 puts forward the main conclusions and lays down the main lines of work to be followed in the future.

2. Electrooculographic potential (EOG)

There are several methods to sense eye movement. In this work, the goal is to sense the electrooculographic potential (EOG). Our discrete electrooculographic control system (DECS) is based in record the polarization potential or corneal-retinal potential (CRP) [5]. This potential is commonly known as an electrooculogram. The EOG ranges from 0.05 to 3.5 mV in humans and is linearly proportional to eye displacement. The human eye is an electrical dipole with a negative pole at the fundus and a positive pole at the cornea.

This system may be used for increasing communication and/or control. The analog signal form the oculographic measurements has been turned into signal suitable for control purposes. The derivation of the EOG is achieved placing two electrodes on the outerside of the eyes to detect horizontal movement and another pair above and below the eye to detect vertical movement. A reference electrode is placed on the forehead. Figure 1 shows the electrode placement.

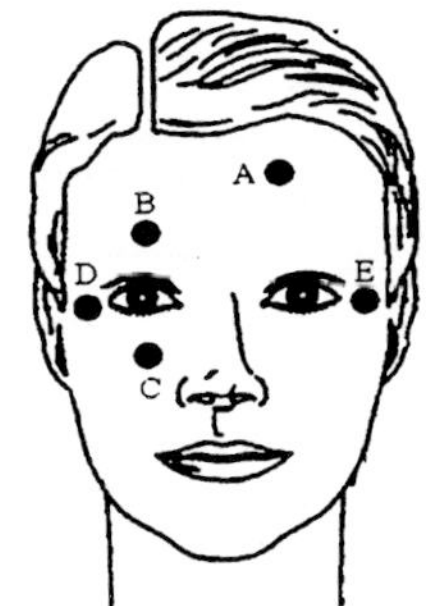

Fig 1.- Electrodes placement.

The EOG signal changes approximately 20 microvolts for each degree of eye movement. In our system, the signal are sampled 10 times per second.

The record of EOG signal have several problems [6]. Firstly, this signal seldom is deterministic, even for same person in different experiments.The EOG signal is a result of a number of factors, including eyeball rotation and movement, eyelid movement, different sources of artifact such as EEG, electrodes placement, head movements, influence of the luminance, etc.

For this reasons, it is neccesary to eliminate the shifting resting potential (mean value) because this value changes. To avoid this problem is necesary an ac diferential amplifier where a high pass filter with cutoff at 0.05 Hz and relatively long time constant is used. The amplifier used have programable gain ranging from 500,1000,2000 and 5000.

3. Detection of saccadic eye movement using neural network.

Saccadic eye movements are characterized by a rapid shift of gaze from one point of fixation to another. Generally, saccades are extremely variable, with wide variations in the latent period, time to peak velocity, peak velocity, and saccade duration. To detect this movements exist different techniques mainly based in detection of the derivation of the EOG signal.

In this paper, a technique to detect saccadic movements is presented, based in neural networks. Neural networks have been designed to perform complex functions in various fields of application including identification system and classification systems. Our aim is getting an inverse eye model (Figure 2) to detect where one person is looking as a function of detected EOG.

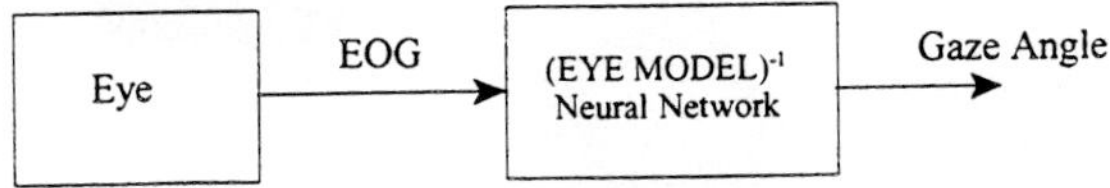

Figure 2. Eye model.

A Radial Basis Function Neural Network which only has one hidden layer is used and its ability as universal approximators of functions has been demonstrated [7].

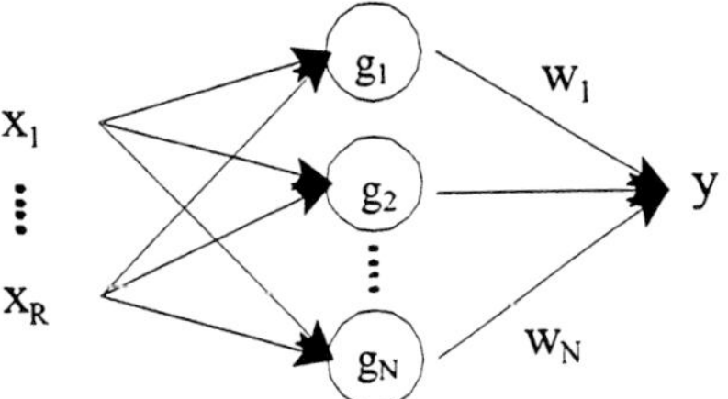

Figure 3. Model of radial basis function.

A non-lineal function g(**X**,**C**), where **X** is an R dimensional independent variable and **C** is a constant parameter of the same dimension, is said to be a radial basis function (RBF) when it depends solely on the distance between **X** and **C**: $\|\mathbf{X} - \mathbf{C}\|$. A function often used is an exponential one:

$$g_j(X,C_j) = e^{-\frac{(x_1-c_j)^2+(x_2-c_j)^2+..+(x_R-c_j)^2}{\sigma^2}} \quad (1)$$

If we consider a network of R inputs and one output (y) and defining the error to be minimized as:

$$E(k) = \frac{1}{2}\cdot[y(k) - y_d(k)]^2 = \frac{1}{2}\cdot[e(k)]^2 \quad (2)$$

The neural network output being:

$$y(k) = \sum_{j=1}^{N} w_j \cdot g_j(k) \quad (3)$$

and $y_d(k)$ the desired output at the moment k.

The equation for the adjustment of the weights is:

$$w_j(k+1) = w_j(k) - \alpha \cdot e(k) \cdot g_j(k) \quad (4)$$

Figure 4 shows the real EOG and the gaze angle desired for eye displacement between -40° and 40° with 10° increments during 5-second intervals with AC amplifier. The EOG signal is sampled each 0.2 s.

The network inputs are the present EOG signal and the last nine delayed because a RBF tapped delay network is used and the network output is the angle of the gaze desired. In our case, R=10 and N=20. To training the network is used MATLAB.

In figure 5, the result of the training is shown. It can be see that it is possible to detect de gaze angle detecting the saccadic movements using RBF neural network. Therefore, this inverse eye model allows us to know where a person is looking using EOG signal.

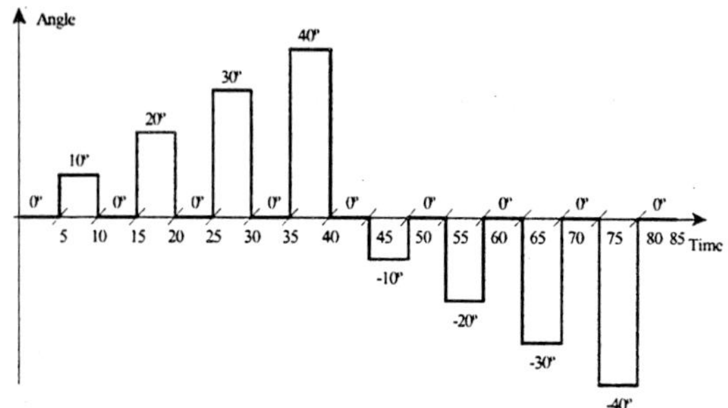

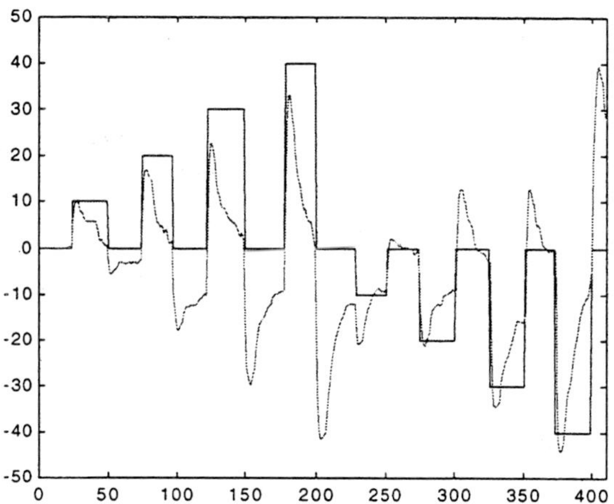

Figure 4. Eog signal and gaze angle desired.

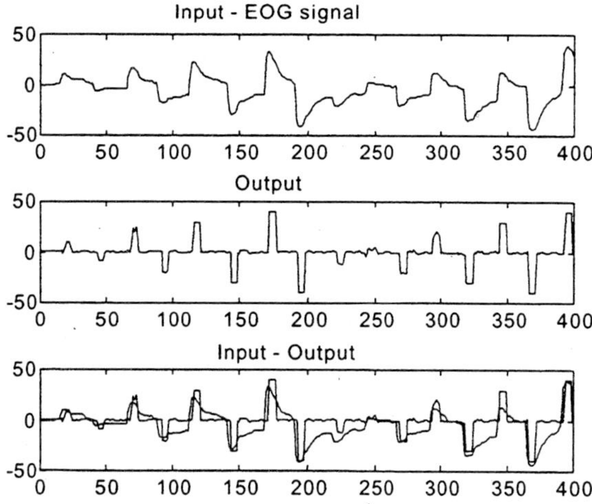

Figure 5.- Result using R.B.F.

4. Visual control system using electrooculography

The aim of this control system is to guide an autonomous mobile robot using the positioning of the eye into its orbit by means of EOG signal. In this case, the autonomous vehicle is a wheelchair for disable people. Figure 6 shows the scheme of the system.

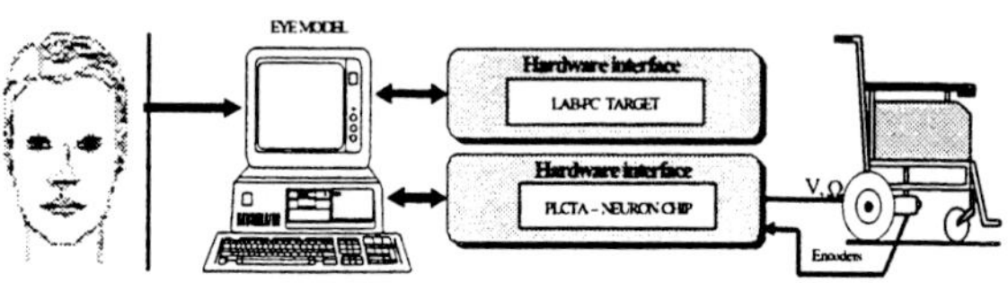

Figure 6. Wheelchair control system.

The EOG signal are processed in the computer and send the control command to the wheelchair. The command sent to the wheelchair are the separate linear speed for each wheel.

To control the robots movements multiple options can be used: interpretation of different commands generated by means of eye movements, generation of differents trajectories in functions of gaze points, etc. We are going to use the first option because it allows us to generate simple code for controlling the wheelchair using the eye position.

We need several alarm and stop commands for dangerous situations. This codes can be generated by means of the blink and alpha waves in EEG to detect when the eyelids are closed.

The robotic wheelchair system must be able to navigate indoor and outdoor environments and should switch automatically between navigations modes for these environment. Therefore, all this system can be apply different navigations modes in function of their disability degree, using always the techniques more efficiently for each people. It is necessary to use different support system to avoid collisions and the robotic system can switch automatically for controlling the system in an autonomous form. For example, if the user lost the control and the system is unstable, the wheelchair should switch and obtain the control system.

This work is included in a general purpose navigational assistant in environments with accesible features to allow a wheelchair to pass. This project is known as SIAMO project [1].

Figure 7 shows the user interface of the wheelchair.

Figure 7. User-wheelchair interface.

5. Results

In this section, several results for the wheelchair guidance are shown.

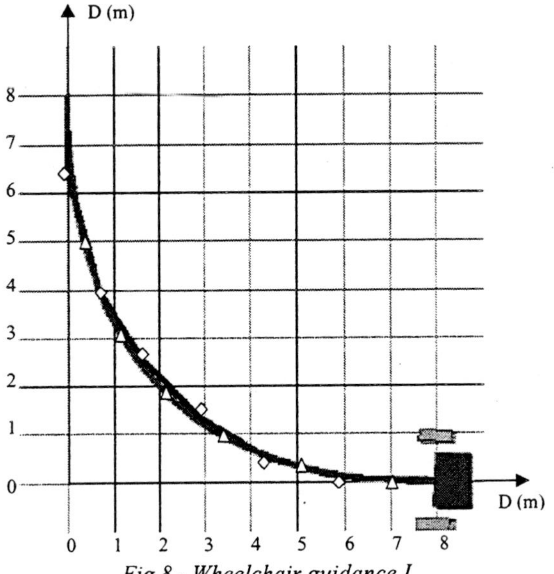

Fig 8.- Wheelchair guidance I.

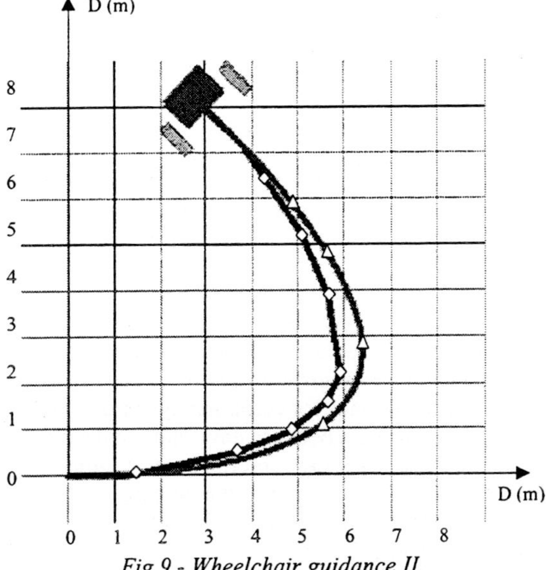

Fig 9.- Wheelchair guidance II.

In figures 8 and 9, the red line Δ represents a "3-spline curve-line" that we want to follow. This trajectory is obtained using a trajectory spline generator developed in SIAMO project. On the other hand, the blue line ◇ represents the trajectory obtained when the wheelchair is guided using EOG. Is possible to apreciate that the desired trajectory is followed with a small lateral error.

Nowadays, we are not try this control with persons with disabilities but we considerated that is not difficult to learn the control commands. Learning to use this system must be done in an acquired skill. Some studies have shown that disable persons usually requires about 15 minutes to learn to use this kind of systems [3].

6. Conclusions

This research project is aimed towards developed a usable, low-cost assistive robotic wheelchair system for disabled people. In this work, we presented a system that can be used as a means of control allowing the handicapped, especially those with only eye-motor coordination, to live more independient lives. Eye movements require minimum effort and allow direct selection techniques, and this increase the response time and the rate of information flow. Some of the previous wheelchair robotics research are restricted a particular location and in many areas of robotics, environmental assumptions can be made that simplify the navigation problem. However, a person using a wheelchair and EOG technique should not be limited by the device intended to assist them if the environment have accessible features.

7. Acknowledgments

The autors would like to express their gratitude to the "Comision Interministerial de Ciencia y Tecnología" (CICYT) for their support through the project TER96-1957-C03-01.

8. References

[1] SIAMO Project (CICYT). Electronics Department. University of Alcala. Madrid. Spain.

[2] Joseph A. Lahoud and Dixon Cleveland. "The Eyegaze Eyetracking System". LC Technologies, Inc. 4th Anual IEEE Dual-Use Technologies and Aplications Conference.

[3] James Gips, Philip DiMattia, Francis X. "EagleEyes Project". Curran and Peter Olivieri. Computer Science Department, Boston College. Mass. USA.

[4] R. Barea, L. Boquete, M. Mazo, E. López. "Guidance of a wheelchair using electrooculography". Proceeding of the 3rd IMACS International Multiconference on Circuits, Systems, Communications and Computers (CSCC'99). July 1999.

[5] M.C. Nicolau, J. Burcet, R.V. Rial. "Manual de técnicas de Electrofisiología clínica". University of Islas Baleares.

[6] Robert J.K. Jacob. "Eye Movement-Based Human-Computer Interaction Techniques: Toward Non-Command Interfaces". Human-Computer Interaction Lab. Naval Research Laboratory. Washington, D.C.

[7] J. Park and I.W. Sandberg. "Universal approximation using radial-basis-function network". Neural Comput. Vol 3, pp 246-257, 1991.

Intelligent Wheelchair Remotely Controlled by Interactive Gestures

Yoshinori Kuno[†,*], Teruhisa Murashima[†], Nobutaka Shimada[†] and Yoshiaki Shirai[†]
[†]Department of Computer-Controlled Mechanical Systems, Osaka University
2-1, Yamadaoka, Suita, Osaka 565-0871, Japan
kuno@mech.eng.osaka-u.ac.jp
[*]Department of Information and Computer Sciences, Saitama University
255, Shimo-okubo, Urawa, Saitama 338-8570, Japan

Abstract

We presented an intelligent wheelchair whose motion can be controlled by the user's face direction. In this paper, we propose to add intelligence to our wheelchair when the user is not riding. It can recognize the user's face and can move according to the gestures made by the user. Gesture is a good means to give commands because it can be used in noisy conditions and we would not like to speak loud in some public places. However, environments where wheelchairs are used cannot be controlled. This makes gesture recognition difficult. We propose an interactive way to solve this problem. When the wheelchair is not certain about the meaning of user's gesture, it guesses the meaning and moves a little accordingly to show its guess to the user. Then it observes the user's response, judging whether its guess is correct or not. This guess-action-observation cycle is repeated until the wheelchair can understand the user's intention.

1 Introduction

With the increase in the number of senior citizens, there is a growing demand for human-friendly wheelchairs as mobility aids. Recently, intelligent/robotic wheelchairs have been proposed to meet this need [1][2]. There have been two research issues with these wheelchairs: autonomous capabilities, such as avoiding obstacles, going to predesignated places, and passing through narrow or crowded areas using vision, ultrasonic, and other sensors; and human interfaces for easy operation. We also proposed an intelligent wheelchair considering the two issues [3]. The user can turn the wheelchair by moving his/her face in the desired direction. It can autonomously avoid obstacles and pass through narrow spaces using ultrasonic sensors.

All these wheelchairs, however, have intelligence only when the user is riding. In this paper, we propose to add an intelligent capability to our wheelchair when the user is not riding. In various occasions, people using wheelchairs have to get them off. They need to move their wheelchairs where they do not bother other people. Then, when they leave there, they want to make their wheelchairs come to them. It is convenient if we can do these operations by hand gestures, since hand gestures can be used in noisy conditions and we would not like to speak loud in some public places.

However, computer recognition of hand gestures is difficult in complex scenes. In our typical cases, many people are moving with their hands moving. Thus it is difficult to distinguish a coming-here or any other command gestures by the user from other movements in the scene. We propose to solve this problem by combining face recognition and gesture recognition. Our system first extracts face regions, detecting the user's face. Then it tracks the user's face and hands, recognizing hand gestures. Since the user's face has been located, a simple method can recognize hand gestures. It cannot be distracted by other movements in the scene.

Computer gesture recognition has another problem. Most conventional systems can recognize only gestures that are registered in advance either by dedicated programs or learning methods. Although we use such common predetermined-pattern gestures such as nodding for yes, many of our gestures are impromptu. Still we can usually make ourselves understood. In addition, even though we intend to make registered gestures, they may not be seen as the registered ones for computer systems. This often happens in actual cases, because environmental conditions such as background, viewing direction, and illumination are different from those in learning the gesture patterns. We propose to solve this problem by the interaction between the user and the wheelchair.

Suppose we are in a foreign country where we do not know the language spoken, and try to communicate with people there. Both use gestures, mainly impromptu ones to convey information. We may not understand their gestures. In this case, they may iterate the gestures or try to make another gesture. When we can guess the meaning of the gestures, we show our understanding by gestures or actual behaviors. If our understanding is appropriate, they may nod or make other actions showing yes. Otherwise, they may try to show our misunderstanding by gestures and will make another gesture. We can eventually understand each other through such interaction. We propose to use this interactive way to solve the unregistered gesture problem.

1051-4651/00 $10.00 © 2000 IEEE

2 Intelligent wheelchair system

This section briefly describes the total system of our intelligent wheelchair. Fig. 1 shows the configuration of the system. As a computing resource, it has a PC (Pentium II 266 MHz) with a real-time image processing board consisting of 256 processors developed by NEC [4]. It has sixteen ultrasonic sensors to see the environment and two video cameras. One camera is set up to see the environment, while the other to look at the user's face. The system can avoid obstacles and move along walls using the ultrasonic sensors. It can go straight autonomously using the environment-observing camera.

The system computes the face direction from images of the user-observing camera. We can pass our intentions to the system by turning our face. However, we may turn our face when we do not intend to turn. To discern turn-intended behaviors from others, the system uses data obtained from the ultrasonic sensors. It will not turn in the direction where it detects any objects close to it, because we do not want to turn toward the objects with which we are likely to collide.

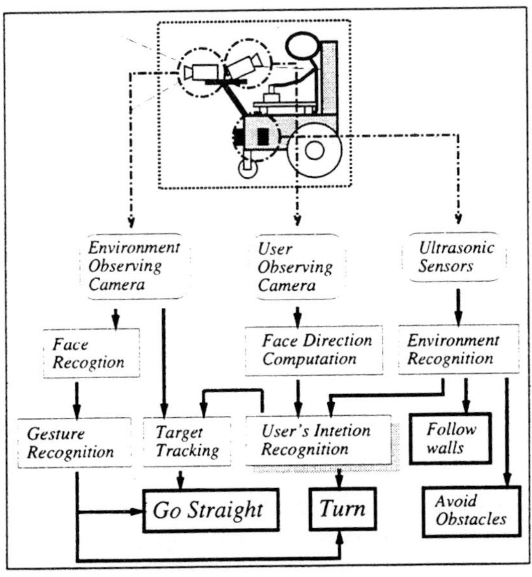

Figure 1. System configuration.

3 Gesture recognition through interaction

Using the environment-observing camera, the system recognizes gestures by the user when he/she is off the wheelchair. Our gesture recognition system consists of the following modules.

A. Face detection and recognition

In our system, we consider hand gestures and head motions, although mainly the former. Thus the system should first detect the hands by which gestures are made to the system. Many gesture recognition systems assume that the user is in their field of view. However, we cannot make this assumption in our intelligent wheelchair application. Many people around the wheelchair might move their hands. It is difficult to detect and recognize hand gestures among them.

We propose to combine face recognition with gesture recognition to solve this problem. We assume that only the user of the wheelchair can control it by gestures. Detecting human faces is relatively easy even in complex scenes because they are the skin color regions which several face features such as eyes, mouth, and nose exist. Then the system recognizes the user's face from the detected face regions. If it can locate the user's face, it can restrict the region where to search for the hands. The combination of face recognition and gesture recognition makes easier to recognize gestures in complex scenes. In addition, this makes the intelligent wheelchair listen only to its master. We use the eigenface method [5] for face recognition.

B. Hand detection and tracking

The system extracts two moving skin-color regions around the user's face as the hands, tracking them. The results of tracking are used for gesture recognition.

C. Registered-gesture recognition

The system needs a function to recognize registered gestures. Gestures whose meaning have been understood through interaction are registered and recognized thereafter by this function. We adopts the spotting recognition method [6] based on continuous dynamic programming for gesture recognition. We extract the following features for gesture recognition from the tracking result. For face gestures, we use the displacement of the face region between consecutive frames (motion vector) as shown in Fig. 2(a). For hand gestures, we use the positions of the hands with respect to the coordinate system whose origin is taken at the centroid of the face region as shown in Fig. 2(b). These features allow gesture recognition not to be affected by translational changes of the human position. In addition, the zoom-lens camera is adjusted automatically so that it can keep imaging the face region in the same predetermined size. This compensates the changes of distance between the human and the system.

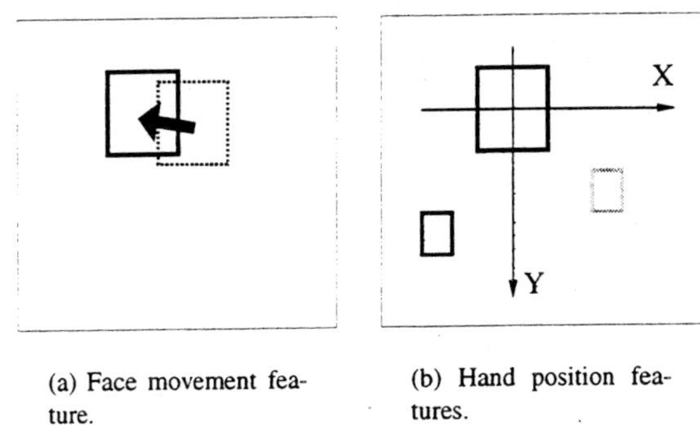

(a) Face movement feature.

(b) Hand position features.

Figure 2. Features for gesture recognition.

D. Unknown intentional gesture detection

Humans may make unregistered gestures. Or even though they intend to make registered gestures, they are not seen as the registered ones for the system. This often happens in actual cases, because environmental conditions such as background, viewing direction, and illumination are different from those in learning the gesture patterns.

To understand these unknown gestures, the system first needs to detect hand motions that humans make intentionally to convey some information. To do this, we use the following assumption. **Assumption 1**: Humans iterate the same gesture pattern if it does not seem to be understood. Based on this assumption, the system considers hand motions as intentional gestures if they are cyclic repetitive patterns.

The system detects such repetitive patterns as follows. It calculates the distance, $d(t)$ (t: time) from the center of the face region to the hand in the image. Fig. 3 shows $d(t)$ when a coming-here gesture by the left hand was repeated. Then it computes the autocorrelation of $d(t)$ by:

$$\kappa = \frac{\sum_t (d(t) - \overline{d})(d(t+\tau) - \overline{d})}{\sqrt{\sum_t (d(t) - \overline{d})^2 (d(t+\tau) - \overline{d})^2}} \quad (1)$$

From the result, the system obtains local maxima and minima. If several local minima are observed and the variance of the distances between neighboring minima is small, it determines that the hand movement shows a repetitive pattern, regarding the mean of the distances $\overline{\delta}$ as the cycle time of the gesture.

Then the system compares $d(t)$ and $d(t - \overline{\delta})$, choosing the point as the start point of the gesture from which the difference between the two curves becomes smaller than a predetermined threshold. In Fig. 3, the cross mark indicates the start point. From the start point, the time scale is segmented by the interval $\overline{\delta}$ as G1, G2, G3 and G4 in Fig. 3. The system extracts the hand motion data (tracking results) during each time segment. The average of all segment data is registered as the reference pattern for this gesture, whose meaning is unknown at this stage. After the system understands the meaning, it uses the pattern to recognize the gesture by the module C.

Although a left hand gesture is used as an example in the above explanation, the system can recognize gestures with both hands as well as those with either the left or right hand. Fig.4 shows the flow of the process. The system independently analyzes each hand motion. If it judges both hand motions to be repetitive patterns, it considers the hand motions as a gesture with both hands.

E. Intention guessing and action selection

The module D can tell that the human wants the system to do something. However, it cannot tell what the human wants. The system has the modules E and F to fill this gap.

The module E guesses the meaning of the gesture and selects an appropriate action for the system. In our wheelchair case, gestures are used for its motion commands. Thus the wheelchair's action is a small motion according to the guessed meaning.

Humans are good at this guessing using common knowledge among them. The current system, however, has a limited capability in this part. It relaxes the recognition conditions in the module C, choosing a registered pattern that

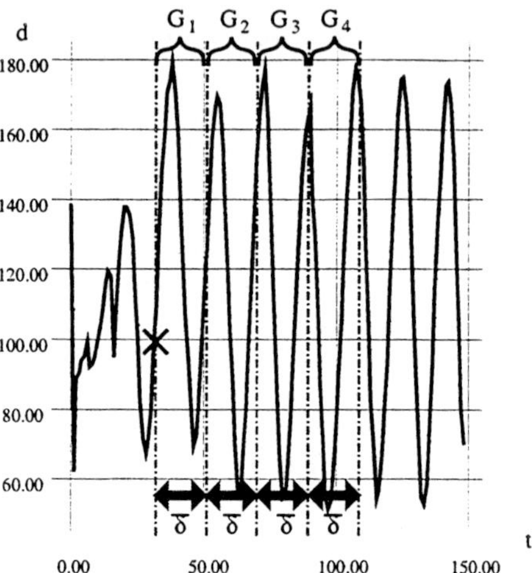

Figure 3. Segmentation.

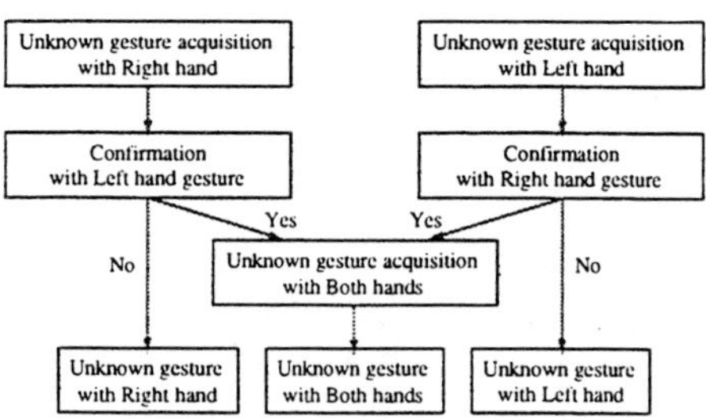

Figure 4. Flowchart of the method to detect unknown gestures.

matches partly with the current gesture pattern. If no pattern gives even partial match, it chooses an action among possible actions in the situation according to the predetermined order. In our wheelchair, the possible actions are only four: Come, Back, Right, and Left, which are arranged in this order.

F. Human reaction observation

The system observes the reaction of the human against the small motion to determine whether or not its guess is correct. If the reaction is one of the registered gestures such as nodding and the system can understand it by the module C, the decision is made according to the recognition result. Otherwise, the system uses a heuristic method based on the following assumption. **Assumption 2**: The guess is correct if the human continues the same gesture pattern or the same one in smaller degree. The latter suggests that the human wants the system to continue the same action a little more. If the human adopts different gestures, the guess is wrong. The module D starts working again.

4 Experiments

We performed the following experiments to prove the effectiveness of our approach.

Experiment 1

In the first experiment, the user made a coming-here gesture with both hands that was not registered in advance (Figs. 5 (a) and (b)). He repeated the gesture several times. The bold lines in Fig. 6 indicate the extracted gesture pattern by the module D. Since this gesture pattern did not match with any registered pattern even by the relaxed method, the system chose Come action in accordance with the predetermined order, moving slightly to the user (Fig. 5 (c)). Seeing this behavior, the user continued the same gesture. The system extracted the gesture pattern as indicate by the broken lines in Fig. 6. The gestures before and after the action were similar, and the second one was a little smaller than the first. Thus the system started the same action, coming to the user (Fig. 5 (d)). It was able to understand the user's intention through the above interaction.

Experiment 2

After the first experiment, the user made the same gesture. Since the gesture pattern had been registered then, the system came directly to the user.

(a) Feature racking.

(b) Initial position.

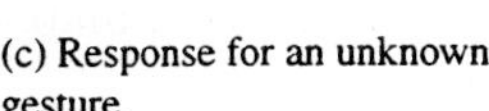

(c) Response for an unknown gesture.

(d) Action after understanding the user's intention.

Figure 5. Robot's action in the experiment 1.

Experiment 3

In the third experiment, the user made a gesture with his left hand by which he intended to order the wheelchair to turn right. The system extracted a gesture pattern from the repeated hand motions. Although this left-hand gesture had not been registered in advance, six right-hand gestures had been stored in the system. It compared the current pattern with those registered by the relaxed method, giving the similarity order to them. Since Turn-Right gesture with the right hand obtained the highest matching score, the wheelchair turned right a little. The user responded by the same gesture with a bit smaller scale to this action. The system recognized this. Then it completed the turn.

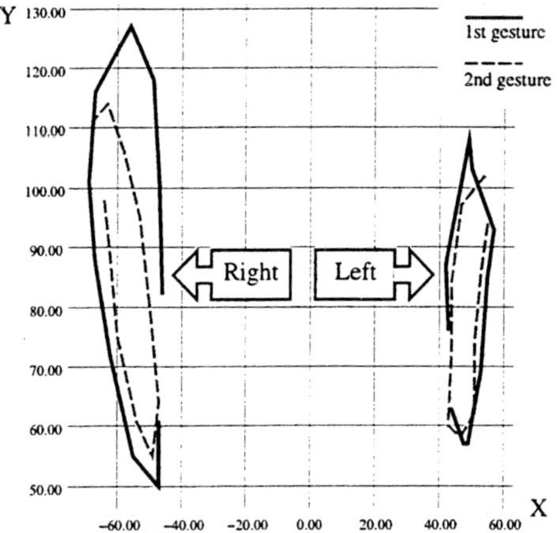

Figure 6. Obtained unknown gesture.

5 Conclusion

We have proposed a gesture-based interface for our intelligent wheelchair. It can understand even unregistered gestures through interaction with the user. The interaction is realized by the iteration of the guess-action-observation cycle. Experimental results confirm the usefulness of our approach.

References

[1] T. Gomi and A. Griffith, "Developing intelligent wheelchairs for the handicapped," *Lecture Notes in AI: Assistive Technology and Artificial Intelligence*, Springer, vol. 1458, pp. 150–178, 1998.

[2] R.C. Simpson and S.P. Levine, "Adaptive shared control of a smart wheelchair operated by voice control," *Proc. 1997 IEEE/RSJ International Conference on Intelligent Robots and Systems*, vol. 2, pp. 622–626, 1997.

[3] Y. Adachi, Y. Kuno, N. Shimada, and Y. Shirai, "Intelligent wheelchair using visual information on human faces," *1998 IEEE/RSJ International Conference on Intelligent Robots and Systems*, vol. 1 , pp. 354–359, 1998.

[4] S. Okazaki, Y. Fujita, and N. Yamashita, "A compact real-time vision system using integrated memory array processor architecture," *IEEE Trans. on Circuits and Systems for Video Technology*, vol. 5, no. 5, pp. 446–452, 1995.

[5] B. Moghaddam and A. Pentland, "Probabilistic visual learning for object representation," *IEEE Trans. on Pattern Analysis and Machine Intelligence*, vol. 19, no. 7, pp. 696–710, 1997.

[6] T. Nishimura, T. Mukai, and R. Oka, "Spotting recognition of gestures performed by people from a single time-varying image," *Proc. 1997 IEEE/RSJ International Conference on Intelligent Robots and Systems*, vol. 2, pp. 967–972, 1997.

Using Model-Based Localization with Active Navigation

Amit Adam
Dept. of Mathematics
amita@tx.technion.ac.il

Ehud Rivlin
Dept. of Computer Science
ehudr@cs.technion.ac.il

Ilan Shimshoni
Dept. of Industrial Engineering
ilans@ie.technion.ac.il

Technion – Israel Institute of Technology
Haifa 32000 – Israel

Abstract

Vision is an important sensor used for mobile robot navigation. One approach to localization which is based on vision is to compute camera egomotion with respect to base images. What characterizes this method of localization is that its performance varies greatly in different positions. Active navigation *is an approach to path and sensing planning which is designed to address varying performance of a sensor across the configuration space. In this paper we describe how to integrate a vision-based localization sensor with active navigation. We explain the localization process, how its performance varies across the configuration space, and the use of this variation by active navigation.*

1 Introduction

The ability to navigate from one point to another is a fundamental requirement for an autonomous mobile agent. For mobile robots, odometry is a basic navigation tool. However because odometry errors accumulate over time, it is common practice to augment the robot with external sensors which are used for navigation. Among these, vision is an important sensor. In this paper we present the use of a vision sensor within the *active navigation* paradigm.

One of the ways to use vision as a navigation sensor is to compute camera egomotion between images taken from the current configuration, and a base image taken from a fixed, known configuration. One advantage of this method is that it uses a small number of base images. However, for a fixed base image, at different positions of the robot we expect this positioning method to have different levels of success. In some positions with respect to base image the method might fail (because of occlusions for example), and in other positions it will work but with different levels of accuracy.

This characteristic of the localization sensor motivates us to use it in conjunction with active navigation. Active navigation [1] is an approach to navigation which takes into account the varying performance level of a positioning sensor across the configuration space. In this approach we consider the performance of the sensor together with two other important factors: the developing uncertainty in position, and the required level of localization. We use all these factors to plan sensing operations and actions which will enable the robot to navigate along its path.

In the next section we will motivate and describe the active navigation paradigm. We then describe our vision based localization method and how we estimate its different levels of performance at different configurations. Then we describe how we may optimally plan sensing operations along the path. The last section concludes the paper.

2 Active Navigation

2.1 Background and Motivation

In previous works [12, 6, 8, 10, 13, 11] it has been recognized that the accuracy of the localization obtained by invoking a sensor, will in general depend on the configuration the robot is in. In other words, the combination of sensor and environment defines some kind of map which describes the quality of localization obtained at each configuration by using the sensor. It is then natural to try and plan the sensing operations to occur while the robot is in areas in which the sensors work well: according to the above mentioned map, the localization quality in these areas is good.

Works which have considered this idea may be found in [12, 6, 8]. In these works the motion planning algorithm uses the sensor performance map to plan paths. In [10] a related notion is the information content of the environment at each configuration. Another similar idea motivated by visual servoing is described in [11].

The motion planning approach taken in previous works (for example [12, 10]) is to search for a path in free space by minimizing a function which takes into account both the length of the path and the sensory uncertainty along the path. (The sensor performance

1051-4651/00 $10.00 © 2000 IEEE

map has been termed Sensory Uncertainty Field (SUF) in [12]). This approach involves some arbitrary decision on how to trade off between sensory uncertainty and path length. These two different factors are usually combined into one objective function by introducing an arbitrary scale factor between the two.

We suggest an alternative approach. In our approach we first consider the "nominal path" the robot has planned by using a specific motion planning algorithm. Had there been no practical problems such as odometry errors and inaccurate prior information, this "nominal path" is the path the robot would have executed. We then consider the localization accuracy required along the path. This accuracy is determined by the special characteristics of the path and the motion planner which generated the path. This required localization accuracy, in addition to the sensory uncertainty field, affect our decisions on where the sensor should be invoked in order to update the position of the robot.

To summarize, we may say that previous approaches strive for the highest localization accuracy possible and compromise on this accuracy in order to account for the length of the path. In our approach we strive for localization accuracy which is at the level required by the nominal path which was generated by the motion planner. Actions are needed by the robot in order to ensure that at all times the localization accuracy which is achieved by the robot is in agreement with the required localization accuracy.

2.2 The Factors Involved

Let us assume a motion planning algorithm (see for example [9]) has planned a path between the source configuration and the target configuration. Our robot intends to execute this "nominal" path. With the environment and the path we associate three factors: the uncertainty in configuration, the accuracy required in the answer obtained after a position (or configuration) update, and the level of accuracy in localization which is obtainable by using the sensor in the current configuration. We now elaborate on each of these factors.

2.3 Uncertainty in Configuration

As the robot moves it keeps track of its current configuration. For various reasons (see for example [5]) uncertainty in the current configuration develops. We model this uncertainty as a probability distribution on the configuration space. Let $U(t)$ be the probability distribution representing the configuration of the robot at time t along the nominal path.

Different models have been suggested for the development of uncertainty in configuration. For example we may use the Gaussian probability distribution to

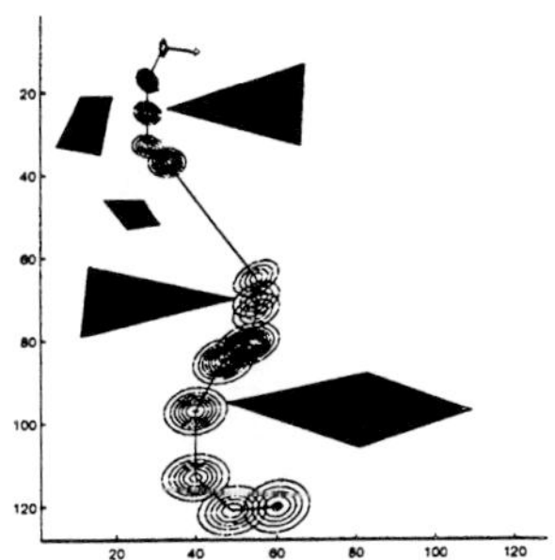

Figure 1: $U(t)$ - probability distribution of configuration at time t along the nominal path

model the position of the robot. The mean of the distribution is the nominal final position. The covariance matrix describes dispersion which is proportional to the length of the motion command. Its principal eigenvector is in the direction perpendicular to the heading direction, and the other eigenvector is in the heading direction. Fig. 1 shows an example of the development of uncertainty along the nominal path. A different model based on the triangular distribution may be found in [14].

2.4 Accuracy Requirement

We now consider the level of accuracy in position that is required from the sensor being used for position update. We consider the localization accuracy required *in the context of performing a nominal path planned by a motion planner.*

Let us view the nominal path as a sequence of straight line segments between "critical points". Critical points are defined as points in the configuration space that the nominal path passes through. The points are chosen in a way that guarantees that between the critical points the robot may move in simple, straight line segments. The choice of critical points is dependent on the motion planner. Each motion planning algorithm is based on a different idea which in turn defines different critical points.

We use two algorithms for motion planning to illustrate our definitions: the visibility graph algorithm and a cell decomposition algorithm [9]. In the visibility graph algorithm, the critical points are the vertices of the obstacles. It is guaranteed that from each vertex one may see the next vertex that is on the path. Hence motion between the critical points is indeed on simple, straight line segments.

In the cell decomposition algorithm, we define the critical points as the mid-boundary points between the adjacent cells the nominal path passes through. It is guaranteed that the line segment between one point to

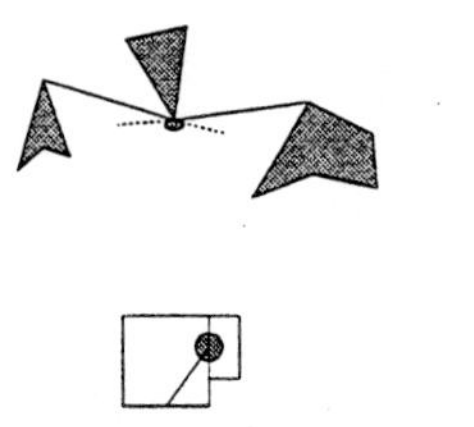

Figure 2: Critical regions in visibility graph and cell decomposition algorithms

the next is wholly contained in one cell. Hence it is guaranteed to be legal (i.e. not to collide with obstacles).

We now note the following observation. We may extend the critical points to critical regions which contain more points that satisfy the assumptions on which the motion planning algorithm is based. Hence, in the visibility graph algorithm, there are other points around the vertex from which both the previous and the next vertex are visible. In the cell decomposition algorithm, there are additional points near the mid-boundary point which satisfy the two "algorithmic" requirements. Firstly they will lead us from the current cell to the next cell, and secondly we may reach them from the current point by moving along a segment contained in the current cell. These extensions of critical points to critical regions is illustrated in Fig. 2.

The nominal path now clearly defines the accuracy requirements on localization, needed to guarantee completion of the path. Firstly, the robot should arrive with high probability in each of the critical regions. Secondly, in order to move between the critical regions, the robot should in principle just stick to the straight line segments connecting these regions. However, uncertainty in position may grow as long as the chances for collision with an obstacle stay low even with the uncertainty in position.

We stress the following point. The accuracy requirements are different in various regions of the configuration space, and for various nominal paths. For example, consider a path planned by a cell decomposition algorithm. In areas where the cells are large and have large boundaries between them, the critical regions are large. Hence the localization accuracy required is not very high. In other regions near obstacles, where cells are bound to be smaller, a higher localization accuracy may be required.

3 Varying Performance of Vision-Based Localization

We now turn to discuss the last factor involved - the performance of the sensor. In general the performance of the sensor varies across the configuration space and hence we can think of a map which associates with each configuration the accuracy of the localization result obtained by using the sensor at that configuration.

To illustrate this point, we will consider localization based on computation of camera motion based on several images. We assume that a camera is mounted on the robot. A base image is taken at a known configuration of the robot and camera. When localization is required, a second image is obtained. Point correspondences between the two images are found. From these correspondences the rotation and the direction of translation of the camera (w.r.t the base image configuration) may be found. In order to estimate the magnitude of translation, the robot has to make a small move and obtain a third image. Since the camera is mounted on the robot, and since the base image configuration of the robot and camera are known, the current configuration of the robot may now be deduced. Details of this localization algorithm may be found in [3].

In [2] we have shown how to predict the uncertainty in the direction of translation resulting from this localization method. In the case of pure translation motion it is well known that the segments created by connecting pairs of corresponding points between the two images all lay on lines which meet at the Focus of Expansion (FOE). Thus the direction of translation (or FOE) may be found in principle by computing this intersection point from the given set of corresponding pairs. However, when the measured correspondences are noised, the lines on which the segments lay will not meet at one point. In this case we minimize an objective function which approximates a Maximum Likelihood Estimate for the FOE. See [2] for details.

Let us now consider two different positions with respect to the base image. Fig. 3 shows the segments created by corresponding pairs between the base image and the images at the two different positions. The + marks the location of the FOE in each case. It is intuitively clear that if the segments in Fig. 3(a) are perturbed a little, the FOE will move more than if the segments in part (b) of the figure will be perturbed. Thus the FOE computation is less stable in the first configuration than in the second.

To obtain a quantitative measure of the dispersion of the FOE due to noise in the corresponding points, we used the linear approximation method presented in [7]. That work develops a method for computing the covariance of an estimator which is computed by minimizing

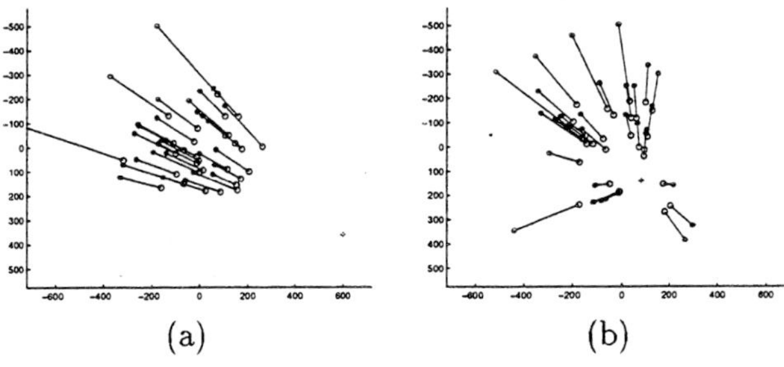

(a) (b)

Figure 3: An example of (a) unstable and (b) stable configurations

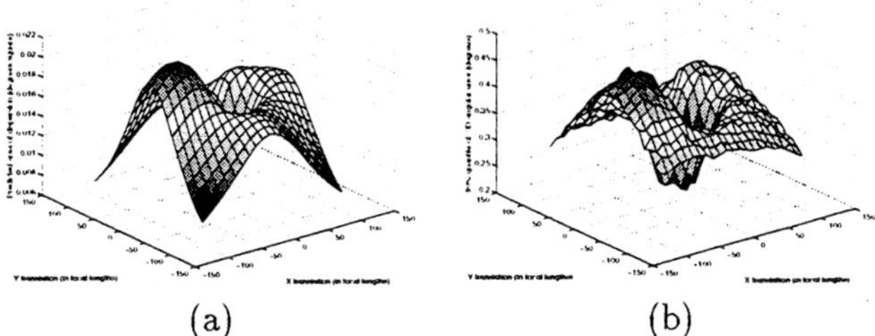

(a) (b)

Figure 4: Uncertainty in direction of translation, as a function of position with respect to the base image. (a) Predicted uncertainty. (b) Empirical measure of dispersion. The graph shows the 90'th percent quantile of the 3D angular error distribution at each configuration.

an objective function. We applied that method to the objective function we use for computing the FOE.

As an example we refer to Fig. 4. Here the base image was taken from position $(0,0)$. For each new position (X,Y), we have estimated the error in determining the direction of translation to the new position. The theoretical prediction is shown in the left figure. In the right figure we show the empirical results. The 90'th percent quantile of the angular error in direction, is plotted as a function of position with respect to the base image. Clearly we can see that the empirical results agree with the predicted map.

As another example, consider the images in Fig. 5 taken in our lab. Around 30 pairs of corresponding points were found. Based on these points, the FOE was computed and its dispersion predicted by our method. These predictions were then compared to the dispersion of FOE values obtained by minimizing the objective function on noised versions of the point correspondences. Figure 6 shows the actual dispersion of 50 FOE estimates, and the dispersions described by the predicted and empirical covariance matrices. The an-

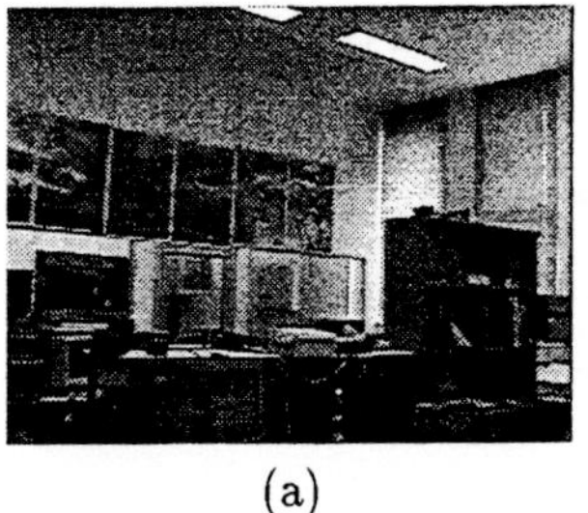

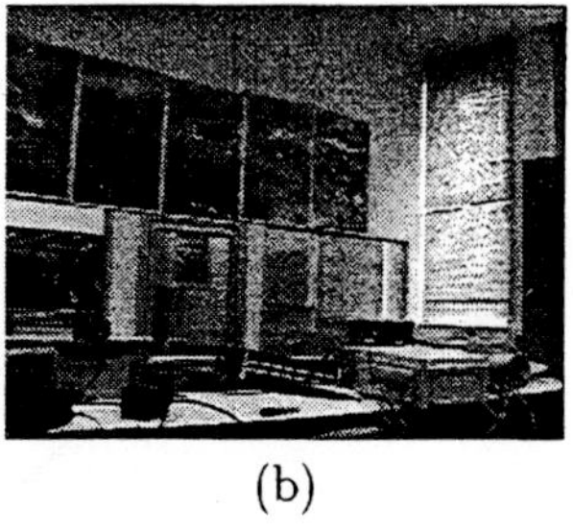

(a) (b)

Figure 5: Base image (a) and image after forward translation (b)

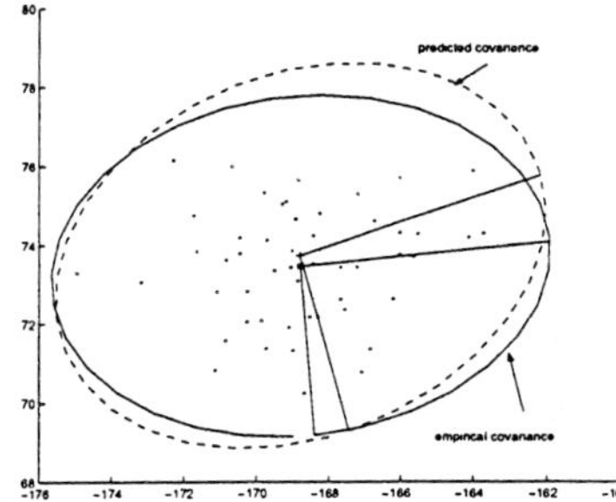

Figure 6: Predicted vs. empirical dispersion

gle between the principal axes of the two ellipses is 11.9 degrees. The ratios of the lengths of axes are 1.01 and 1.08. As is evident by these numbers and by looking at the figure, the prediction is quite accurate.

4 Planning Updates Along the Route

We will now describe an example of using the active navigation paradigm and the performance map derived above for the vision sensor. Our robot uses the visibility graph method to plan paths in the work space. The planned path in this method passes through the vertices of the obstacles. As described previously, the accuracy requirement in this case defines critical regions around these vertices.

Consider now the position uncertainty but only in the direction which is orthogonal to the heading direction. Let us assign a single number to measure this uncertainty - for example 3 standard deviations. This uncertainty grows linearly according to our model. The distance from obstacles and the size of the critical regions define its maximum allowed value. This maximum allowed value changes along the route and is actually a piecewise constant function. We now compute the uncertainty in direction of translation with respect to two given base images, by the method described above. This allows us to infer the maximal uncertainty in localization that will be obtained in the direction we are interested in. See Fig. 7.

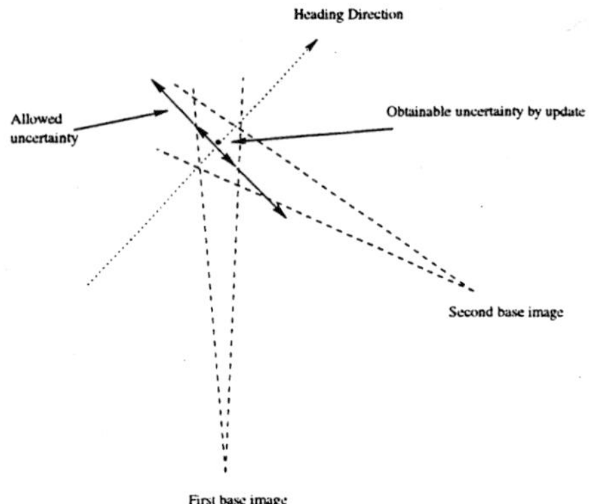

Figure 7: Allowed vs. obtainable uncertainty

We now let $U_n(t)$ denote the maximal uncertainty allowed, and $U_c(t)$ denote the uncertainty we will obtain by using the two base images. Let $U(t)$ denote the linearly growing uncertainty in position. At all times, the uncertainty $U(t)$ should be less than $U_n(t)$. Assume a position update at time t costs $C(t)$. The problem is to find times of update $t_1, t_2, \ldots$ which will ensure that

$$U(t) \leq U_n(t)$$

for $t = 1, 2, \ldots, T$, and this with minimal cost of update operations. Fig. 8 illustrates this problem. This

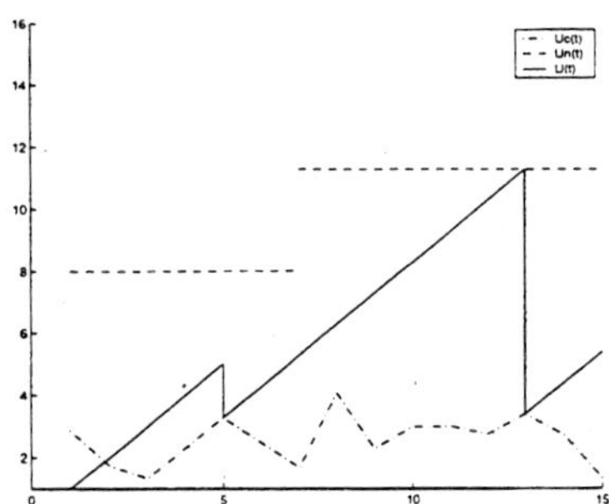

Figure 8: Find times for update actions which will ensure completion of the path with minimal cost (see text)

problem may be solved by the dynamic programming approach (see for example [4]). Let $f(u; i, j)$ denote the cost of reaching from $t = i$ to $t = j$ with initial uncertainty u at time $t = i$. Let the uncertainty $U(t)$ grow linearly with slope α. If

$$u + \alpha(t - i) \leq U_n(t)$$

for all $i \leq t \leq j$ then the no updates are necessary and $f(u; i, j) = 0$. Otherwise, $f(u; i, j)$ may be computed recursively as

$$f(u; i, j) = \min_{i+1 \leq t \leq j-1} \{f(u; i, t) + C(t) + f(U_c(t); t, j)\}$$

Using the method of dynamic programming an efficient computational scheme may be employed to find the optimal times at which updates should be made.

5 Discussion

When considering vision as a sensor for mobile robot localization, one cannot expect to obtain the same level of performance uniformly over the work space. The active navigation paradigm is an approach which is designed to address this rather common characteristic of localization sensors. In this paper we have shown how we may use a vision sensor and the active navigation approach to plan sensing along the route, in a way which will allow a robot to successfully navigate along the route, while keeping the sensing cost to a minimum.

So far we have addressed the uncertainty in the direction of translation. There are additional issues which affect vision-based localization performance. An important example of such an issue is the variance in ability to find corresponding points between the images. We plan to address this question in future work.

References

[1] Amit Adam, Ehud Rivlin, and Ilan Shimshoni. Active navigation, 1999. In preparation.

[2] Amit Adam, Ehud Rivlin, and Ilan Shimshoni. Computing the sensory uncertainty field of a vision based localization sensor. In *Proc. IEEE Int. Conf. on Robotics and Automation*, 2000. To appear.

[3] R. Basri, E. Rivlin, and I. Shimshoni. Visual homing: Surfing on the epipoles. *International Journal of Computer Vision*, 33(2), 1999.

[4] R. E. Bellman and S. E. Dreyfus. *Applied Dynamic Programming*. Princeton University Press, 1962.

[5] J. Borenstein, H.R. Everett, L. Feng, and D. Wehe. Mobile robot positioning: Sensors and techniques. *Journal of Robotic Systems*, 14(4):231–249, 1997.

[6] T. Fraichard and R. Mermond. Path planning with uncertainty for car-like robots. In *Proc. IEEE Int. Conf. on Robotics and Automation*, pages 27–32, 1998.

[7] R. M. Haralick. Propagating covariance in computer vision. In *Proc. of 12'th ICPR*, pages 493–498, 1994.

[8] A. Lambert and N. L. Fort-Piat. Safe actions and observation planning for mobile robots. In *Proc. IEEE Int. Conf. on Robotics and Automation*, pages 1341–1346, 1999.

[9] Jean-Claude Latombe. *Robot Motion Planning*. Kluwer Academic Publishers, 1991.

[10] N. Roy, W. Bugard, D. Fox, and S. Thrun. Coastal navigation - mobile robot navigation with uncertainty in dynamic environments. In *Proc. IEEE Int. Conf. on Robotics and Automation*, pages 35–40, 1999.

[11] R. Sharma and H. Sutanto. A framework for robot motion planning with sensor constraints. *IEEE Transactions on Robotics and Automation*, 13(1):61–73, February 1997.

[12] H. Takeda, C. Facchinetti, and J.C. Latombe. Planning the motions of a mobile robot in a sensory uncertainty field. *IEEE Transactions on Pattern Analysis and Machine Intelligence*, 16(10):1002–1017, October 1994.

[13] S. Thrun. Finding landmarks for mobile robot navigation. In *Proc. IEEE Int. Conf. on Robotics and Automation*, pages 958–963, 1998.

[14] S. Thrun, W. Bugard, and D. Fox. A probabilistic approach to concurrent mapping and localization for mobile robots. *Autonomous Robots*, 5:253–271, 1998.

Visual Memory Maps for Mobile Robots

Joaquín Salas*[†]
CICATA-IPN
José Siurob 10. Col. Alameda. CP 76040. Querétaro, Qro. México
E-mail: salas@mail.cicata.ipn.mx

Abstract

In this paper, we introduce the concept of Visual Memory Maps (VMM). A VMM is an ordered accumulation of visual information, classified to avoid redundancy and to provide fast retrieval through the comparison of newly acquired images with stored memories. We use VMM to give some low level visual capabilities to mobile robots. To do this, a mobile robot is guided through a path while it takes snapshots. The image stream is then converted into a VMM. Two problems that surge are both the representation of the image stream and the comparison of new frames with the VMM. In this research, we use Principal Component Analysis to have a compact representation and to index the image stream, and introduce a registration scheme to search for correspondence directly in the space of the principal components.

1. Introduction

Mobile robots can be used to transport things like food, papers, people or to perform surveillance tasks. But one way or another, mobile robots need to move. In order to move well, they rely on the correct processing of its sensory information and efficient use of their motion capabilities. In this paper, we investigate into the problem of visual perception for mobile robots in the realm of what is needed to help them to navigate and localize themselves in a certain environment. This problem has received considerable attention from the research community because it is fundamental if we are to succeed on producing truly autonomous entities[6]. The approaches followed include the reconstruction of sound three dimensional models, the engineering of the environment to enforce assumptions, and the construction of specialized visual systems. For instance, Sawhney et al.[8] use Kalman's filter to process sequences of images and eventually refine the measures of the objects. Nonetheless, many researchers have recognized that the reconstruction problem is a tough one[9]. Perhaps, this is the reason why engineering the environment has became appealing. One of the first approaches in this direction was the line following technique[4]. Here a line that specifies the path that the robot must follow is painted on the floor. Clearly, special care must be given to illumination conditions and crossways. Another approach is to place visual landmarks in the environment[1]. A visual landmark is like a beacon that once is detected may help the robot to localize, navigate and eventually finish its duties successfully. In general, modifying the environment makes it easier for the robot to operate. Perhaps, engineering the environment is a first step to understand the constraints that the workplace provides to build specialized vision systems. One example is the work of Nourbakhsh et al. [7]. They created a vision system for a mobile robot based on image focusing. The system has ample capabilities to avoid static and dynamic obstacles. Another example is Ian Horswill's work on stereo for mobile robots[3]. He uses the constraints of the environment as contextual cultural information that the robot employs to operate.

When we people move, we are more or less unconcerned about the surrounding physical objects. Indeed, we can recall places where we have been without having to stand on exactly the same position. All we need to do is to image a barely similar view. With the VMM concept, we intend to emulate the same functionality. A VMM is an ordered accumulation of visual information, compacted to avoid redundancy and classified to provide fast retrieval through the comparison of newly acquired images with stored memories. We use VMM

*This work was partially supported with grants from CONACYT under contract number 27725A, from SIGHO under contract number 19990205005 and from CEGEPI-IPN under contract number 990082.

[†]The author wants to thank to Prof. Carlo Tomasi whose guidance lead eventually to this work

to give some low level visual capabilities to mobile robots. To do this, a mobile robot is guided through a path while it takes snapshots. The image stream is then converted into a VMM. This requires much memory space. But under the current trends of price and technology development, the amount of memory becomes less and less an issue. For us, the prime problem is how to index these images for fast retrieval and processing.

In the rest of the paper, we define the concept of Visual Memory Maps and introduce tools for stream representation and efficient correspondence retrieval. In §2, we show that a possible way to have a compact representation and to index the image stream is through the use of Principal Component Analysis (PCA)[5]. As it is well known, a possible source of problems of performance for PCA may come from poor image registration. A possible registration scheme is introduced in §3. In this scheme, we search registration directly into the space of the principal components (that we later call Viewspace). This has the advantage that the image stream does not need to be stored. We show our experimental results in §4. Finally, we summarize and discuss possible research directions.

2. Compacting the Image Stream

In this section, we review PCA as a way to represent the image stream and to create a VMM. In this framework, we define some terminology. Consider the sequence of images $S = \{S_1, S_2, \ldots S_n\}$. Each image is stored into an $r \times c$ matrix. If we collect in $\mathbf{a}_k$ the entries of S_k in column-major order, using $\mathbf{a}_k = v(S_k)$, then we may construct the matrix $A_{rc \times n}$ as $A = [\mathbf{a}_1 - \bar{\mathbf{a}}, \mathbf{a}_2 - \bar{\mathbf{a}}, \ldots, \mathbf{a}_n - \bar{\mathbf{a}}]$, where $\bar{\mathbf{a}} = \frac{1}{n}\sum_{i=1}^{n} \mathbf{a}_i$. If the time between images is considerably short or general motion is slow, then subsequent images will look very similar. The objective of PCA is to find a basis for A such that the distance of its columns to the axes is minimized. It can be shown [5] that the axes of this basis are given by the set of eigenvectors of AA^T. Singular Value Decomposition (SVD) provides a technique to obtain the eigenvectors of AA^T ordered by the magnitude of its singular values[2]. That is, $A = U\Sigma V^T$, where $U_{rc \times rc}$ and $V_{n \times n}$ contain the eigenvectors of AA^T and A^TA respectively, and $\Sigma_{rc \times n}$ contains on its diagonal the nonzero singular values, of both AA^T and A^TA, in non increasing order. Under PCA, we construct $U_r = [\mathbf{u}_1, \mathbf{u}_2, \ldots, \mathbf{u}_r]$ with the r eigenvectors of AA^T, corresponding to the r largest singular values. It can be shown that this leads to the minimum error if the criterion used is the squared difference between the reconstructed and the original image. In our terminology, $\mathbf{u}_i$ is an Eigenview of the sequence, whereas U_r is called Viewspace. A possible way to choose r is using the ratio $\beta(r) = \sum_{i=1}^{r} \lambda_i / \sum_{i=1}^{n} \lambda_i$ and then use the decision rule $c(\alpha) = \min_r \{\beta(r) \leq \alpha\}$ for some predefined threshold $0 \leq \alpha \leq 1$. The projection of the images into Viewspace gives an r-index for each image in S as $T = U_r^T A$. We call Visual Memory Map to a projection like T.

3 Frame Registration

In this section, we introduce a registration scheme. Registration is sought directly in Viewspace instead of in the image space. This has the advantage that the image stream does not need to be stored. Consider a new frame $J_{h \times w}$. Our purpose is to register a sub image $S_{h_o \times w_o} \in J$ with respect to what already exits in the VMM. For our purposes, we want to find the displacement $\mathbf{d} = (d_x, d_y)^T$ of S in J and the affine transformation $B = I + D$, where I is the identity matrix and D is a deformation matrix given by $D = \begin{bmatrix} d_{11} & d_{12} \\ d_{21} & d_{22} \end{bmatrix}$, that make the projections in the VMM as similar as possible to a previous projection. That is,

$$\begin{aligned} e(D,\mathbf{d}) &= \min_{\mathbf{t}} \{f(D,\mathbf{d},\mathbf{t})\} \\ &= \min_{\mathbf{t}} \left\{(\mathbf{p}(D,\mathbf{d}) - \mathbf{t})^T(\mathbf{p}(D,\mathbf{d}) - \mathbf{t})\right\} \end{aligned} \tag{1}$$

Here, $\mathbf{t}$ is a column of T and represents a previous projection in Viewspace, and $\mathbf{p}(D,\mathbf{d})$ is given by $\mathbf{p}(D,\mathbf{d}) = U_r^T \mathbf{a}(D,\mathbf{d})$ The vector $\mathbf{a}$ is given by collecting the entries of S in column-major order. We obtain the minimum dissimilarity when we differentiate Eq.(1) with respect to both D and $\mathbf{d}$,

$$\begin{aligned} \partial f(D,\mathbf{d},\mathbf{t})/\partial D = \partial \mathbf{p}(D,\mathbf{d})/\partial D^T\,(\mathbf{p}(D,\mathbf{d}) - \mathbf{t}) = 0 \\ \partial f(D,\mathbf{d},\mathbf{t})/\partial \mathbf{d} = \partial \mathbf{p}(D,\mathbf{d})/\partial \mathbf{d}^T\,(\mathbf{p}(D,\mathbf{d}) - \mathbf{t}) = 0 \end{aligned} \tag{2}$$

The image $S(D\mathbf{x} + \mathbf{d})$ can be expressed in terms of the linear terms of its Taylor's series expansion as $S(D\mathbf{x} + \mathbf{d}) \approx S(\mathbf{x}) + \mathbf{g}^T(D\mathbf{x} + \mathbf{d})$, where $\mathbf{g} = \nabla S = [\partial S/\partial x, \partial S/\partial y]$ is the gradient of S. If we express $S(D\mathbf{x} + \mathbf{d})$ in column-major order and then use its projection into Visual Memory U_r, Eq. (2) can be expressed as the following linear system.

$$\begin{bmatrix} GG^T & G^T\mathbf{g}_v \\ \mathbf{g}_v^T G & \mathbf{g}_v^T\mathbf{g}_v \end{bmatrix} \begin{bmatrix} D_v \\ \mathbf{d} \end{bmatrix} = \begin{bmatrix} G^T(U_r\mathbf{t} - \mathbf{a}) \\ \mathbf{g}_v^T(U_r\mathbf{t} - \mathbf{a}) \end{bmatrix} \tag{3}$$

Here, $G = [G_1, G_2, \ldots, G_n]$ and G_i contains the entries of the Kronecker product[9] $\mathbf{x} \otimes \mathbf{g}^T$, for the range of the image, in column-major order; $\mathbf{g}_v$ contains the entries of the partial derivatives of the intensity $[v(\partial S/\partial x), v(\partial S/\partial y)]^T$; and $D_v = v(D)$ contains the entries of D also in column-major order. In order to find D_v and $\mathbf{d}$ the following iterative scheme can be used.

$$\begin{bmatrix} D_{v_{k+1}} \\ \mathbf{d}_{k+1} \end{bmatrix} = \begin{bmatrix} D_{v_k} \\ \mathbf{d}_k \end{bmatrix} + \begin{bmatrix} GG^T & G^T\mathbf{g}_v \\ \mathbf{g}_v^T G & \mathbf{g}_v^T \mathbf{g}_v \end{bmatrix}^{-1} \begin{bmatrix} G^T(U_r\mathbf{t} - \mathbf{a}) \\ \mathbf{g}_v^T(U_r\mathbf{t} - \mathbf{a}) \end{bmatrix} \quad (4)$$

Eq. (4) is used to compute registration in Viewspace. When a mobile robot actually captures an image, it search into its VMM for its previous projections until convergency is achieved or not matching is found.

4 Experimental Results

The previous scheme has been tested extensively with a mobile robot following routes that have been previously taught to it. When advancing straight ahead there is a lot of redundancy that permits large compaction of data. On the contrary, when the robot rotates some things appear and some others disappear in the new image with respect to the previous ones. In this section, we highlight the usefulness of the registration scheme when the mobile robot has to rotate. To do this, a mobile robot is placed in a position and then commanded to rotate on itself while grabbing snapshots of its surroundings. A few frames out of a 48 sequence are shown in Fig. 1. The VMM is built using the images in the sequence and the SVD decomposition to get the eigenvectors corresponding to the 17 largest singular values (in this particular case, it results in $\beta(17) \geq 0.8$). The VMM $T_{17\times 48}$ contains the projections of the images into Viewspace U_{17} (see Fig. 2).

The purpose of the VMM is to correlate a new image with what already exists. When the mobile robot moves to a different position and is commanded to inspect again its environment, it takes new snapshots. These new frames are projected into Viewspace and compared with the points in the VMM. To do this, a portion of the image is registered using the Viewspace and the projections in the VMM. Fig. 3 presents the results of searching for one snapshot. As D_v and $\mathbf{d}$ are computed the error function eventually decrease until convergence is achieved (in this case after 75 iterations). In the cases where convergence is not achieved, either because the starting point is not close enough to the minimum or because there was not conceivable registration, the error function starts growing fast.

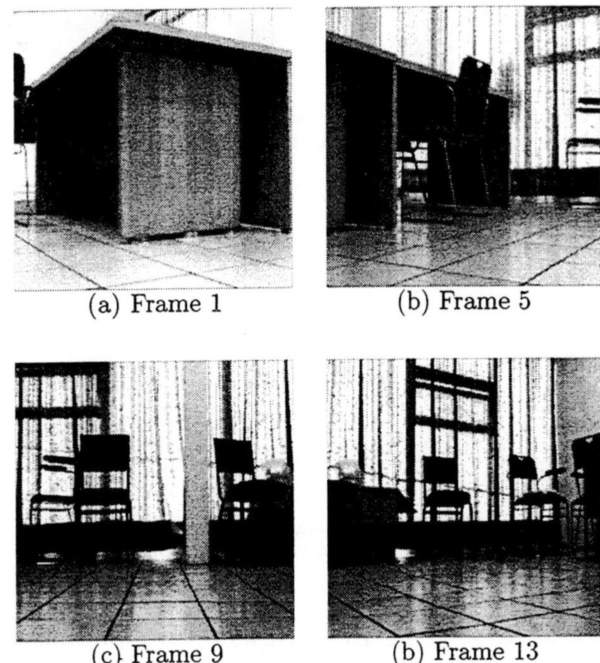

Figure 1. A few frames out of the 48 of the sequence. A mobile robot is placed in a position and then commanded to rotate on itself while grabbing snapshots of its surroundings.

Conclusion

In this document, we introduced the concept of Visual Memory Maps (VMM). VMM are ordered accumulation of visual information, classified to avoid redundancy, and to provide fast retrieval through the comparison of newly acquired images with stored memories. In this research, we use PCA to structure the image stream has a Visual Map. We also introduce a search scheme for image registration directly in Viewspace. We did experiments and the approach seems sound.

The parameters D and $\mathbf{d}$ can be further used for navigation and self localization as they provide information about the relative changes that has the present image frame with respect to the Visual Memory. Also, note that frame registration in VMM can be implemented in parallel, comparing independently each Eigenview with the projection of the newly acquired image.

As an aside, a popular approach to pattern recognition[10] uses PCA to obtain a set of indices to characterize a pattern. One of the problems with its use is precisely image registration. Our framework can

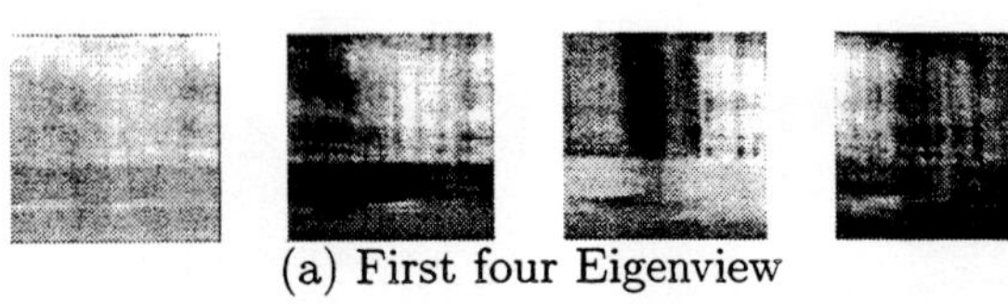

(a) First four Eigenview

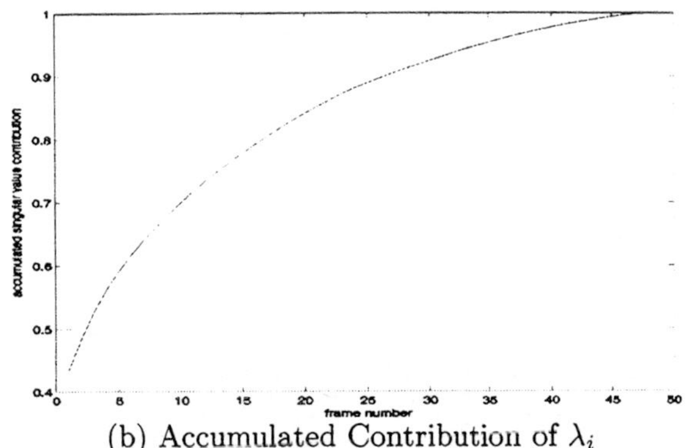

(b) Accumulated Contribution of λ_i

Figure 2. Some Eigenviews corresponding to the sequence described in §4.

complement such a method by combining registration with recognition directly.

References

[1] C. Becker, J. Salas, K. Tokusei, and J.-C. Latombe. Reliable Navigation using Landmarks. In IEEE International Conference on Robotics and Automation, pages 401–406, 1995.

[2] G. H. Golub and C. F. V. Loan. Matrix Computations. John Hopkins University Press, 1993.

[3] I. Horswill. Specialization of Perceptual Processes. PhD thesis, Massachusetts Institute of Technology, May 1993.

[4] S. Ishikawa, H. Kuwamoto, and S. Ozawa. Visual Navigation of an Autonomous Vehicle using White Line Recognition. IEEE Transactions on Pattern Analysis and Machine Intelligence, 10(5):743–749, 1988.

[5] M. Kirby and L. Sirovich. Application of the Karhunen-Loève Procedure for the Characterization of Human Faces. IEEE Transactions on Pattern Analysis and Machine Intelligence, 12(1):103–108, 1990.

[6] J.-C. Latombe. Robot Motion Planning. Kluwer Associate Publisher, 1991.

[7] I. Nourbakhsh, D. Andre, C. Tomasi, and M. Genesereth. Mobile Robot Obstacle Avoidance via Depth from Focus. Robotics and Autonomous Systems, 22:151–158, June 1997.

[8] H. S. Sawhney, R. Kumar, A. R. Hanson, and E. M. Riseman. Landmark-Based Navigation - Model Extension and Refinement. Technical Report COINS TR93-06, Department of Computer Science. University of Massachusetts at Amherst, 1993.

[9] J. Shi and C. Tomasi. Good Features to Track. In IEEE Conference on Computer Vision and Pattern Recognition, pages 593–600, 1994.

[10] M. Turk and A. P. Pentland. Face Recognition using Eigenfaces. In Proceedings of the International Conference on Pattern Recognition, pages 586–591, 1991.

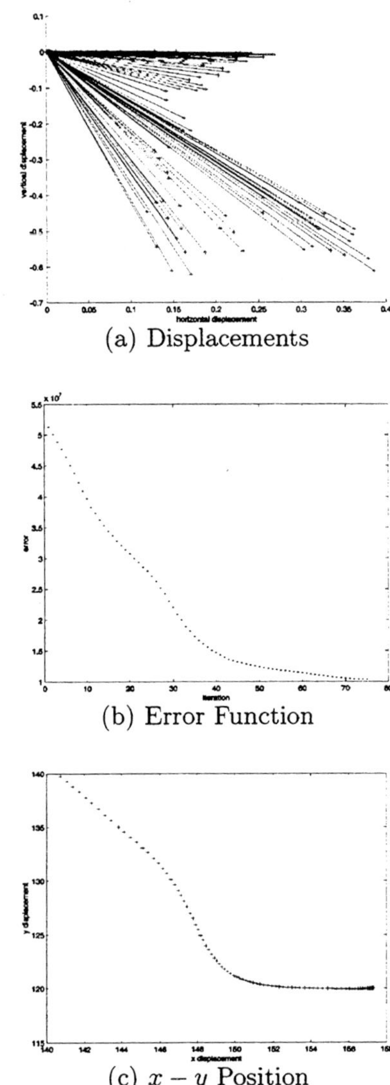

(a) Displacements

(b) Error Function

(c) $x - y$ Position

Figure 3. The model looks for the minimum value through a series of displacements(a) that eventually reduce the error function(b) in Eq. (1) as convergence is achieved(c).

Real-Time Ordnance Recognition in Color Imagery

Clark F. Olson

Jet Propulsion Laboratory, California Institute of Technology

4800 Oak Grove Drive, Mail Stop 125-209, Pasadena, CA 91109

http://robotics.jpl.nasa.gov/people/olson/homepage.html

Abstract

Military test ranges containing unexploded ordnance due to live-fire testing and training exercises are a significant safety problem in many locations. Automated cleanup of such sites is a challenging goal. Towards this end, this paper describes algorithms to detect a type of ordnance in current usage using color imagery. The techniques are designed to run in real-time using off-the-shelf hardware for use on an unmanned ground vehicle. Our methodology is to quickly detect candidate locations using color and stereo information. Additional processing is then applied to the candidate locations in order to eliminate false alarms. This technique has been tested on a set of imagery from a live-fire test range with outstanding results.

1 Introduction

The cleanup of unexploded ordnance in military test ranges is a dangerous task that is currently performed by human technicians walking through the range, visually detecting unexploded ordnance, and performing remediation. Automating this task will both reduce the cost of cleaning the test ranges and eliminate the danger to the technicians. We are working towards this goal through the use of computer vision to recognize the ordnance from an unmanned ground vehicle.

Our methododolgy has been designed to handle a scenario where the vehicle traverses a test range at approximately 5 mph. As the vehicle traverses, the ordnance recognition system examines the terrain in front of the vehicle looking for instances of ordnance. In this work, we have concentrated on a type of ordnance called BLU-97, which is in current usage in U.S. military test ranges (Fig. 1). The body of this type of ordnance is cylindrical and it is 20 centimeters long, with a 6 centimeter diameter. When new, the ordnance is bright yellow in color, but it is often weathered in practice on the test range.

We have designed algorithms for use in this scenario that can run in real-time (2-3 frames per second) using off-the-shelf hardware to ensure that the resulting system is timely and cost effective. In order to meet the constraints for real-time processing, it is crucial to use methods with low computational requirements. Our methodology is to first detect candidate locations very quickly using color and stereo data. Once the candidates have been detected, we can apply additional computation to reduce false alarms, since much of the image has been eliminated from consideration. Finally, evidential reasoning is used to combine the information for the hypothesis detection and verification modules in order to make a final decision on each candidate.

This technique has been evaluated using a test set collected at a live-fire test range near Nellis Air Force Base. The results indicate that the system is capable of a very high rate of detection and few false positives, while requiring low computational resources. We conclude with some lessons learned from this work.

2 Hypothesis detection

Our approach to detecting candidate locations of ordnance in the image is to first classify each pixel as ordnance-like or non-ordnance-like according to the color of the pixel. The candidates are then identified by locating blocks of connected ordnance-like pixels in the image. See Figure 2.

It has been shown that, under some simple assumptions about the scene, normalized color-space coordinates are independent of the scene geometry [2]:

$$(r, b, g) = \frac{(R, G, B)}{\sqrt{R^2 + G^2 + B^2}} \tag{1}$$

Thus, for scene points that are illuminated by the same spectral power distribution, the normalized image color is (largely) invariant to the orientation of the scene point, the orientation of the illumination, and the overall brightness of the illumination. If we approximate sunlight as having a constant color and disregard specularity and inter-reflection effects, then we meet this criteria, and the

Figure 1: Image of BLU-97 ordnance acquired at a Nellis Air Force Base test range.

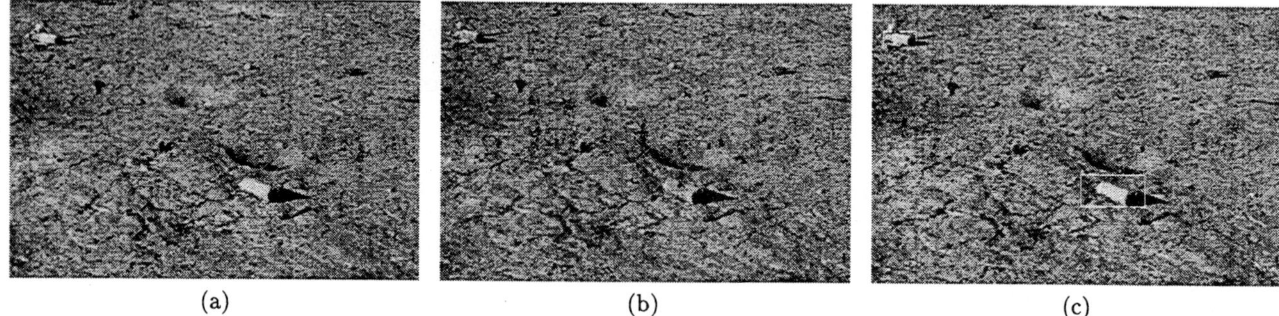

Figure 2: Hypothesis detection is performed by first classifying each pixel in the image as ordnance-like or non-ordnance-like according to its color. Hypothesis are then detected by finding large connected components using a threshold that varies with stereo range data. (a) Original image. (b) Classification results. The highlighted pixels were classified as ordnance-like. (c) Candidates located.

normalized ordnance color will be roughly constant. Of course, discoloration due to weathering and other effects, such as violations of the assumptions, will cause variation in the color. In our application, discoloration of the ordnance results in a greater variation in the image chromaticities than illumination effects. We have thus chosen not to use a complex illumination compensation method.

The technique that we use to classify pixels is to define a polyhedron in the normalized color space, corresponding to the colors that we define to be ordnance-like. The polyhedron we use is a rectangular solid defined by bounds on the normalized color coordinates:

$$t_r \geq r \geq T_r \tag{2}$$

$$t_g \geq g \geq T_g \tag{3}$$

$$t_b \geq b \geq T_b \tag{4}$$

This corresponds to a cone in the unnormalized color space with a six-sided, polygonal cross-section.

Now, we must determine the upper and lower bounds on these coordinates that will yield good classification of the ordnance-like pixels. We perform this through learning by example, using a method that approximates gradient descent search. At each iteration of the training, the number of errors that are made by the application of each of the inequalities is counted. Each threshold is then updated in the direction that would yield less overall errors. Training of the parameters has been performed on a dataset from the same site as the test set, but collected several months previously.

In practice, we compile the pixel classification yielded by the above method into a look-up table. Of course, this is a trade-off of time versus space. We have found very fast and accurate results can be obtained through the use of six bits to discretize each color. This incurs a storage requirement of 32K.

After classifying each of the pixels according to the above criterion, we detect the connected regions in the image that have been classified as ordnance-like. Detecting the connected components can be performed in linear time in the size of the image using a version of the union-find data structure [1]. This method uses a two-pass algorithm to detect the large, connected regions of ordnance-like pixels in the image. If the size of the region is larger than some threshold T (which we compute as a function of the range to the location), then the location is considered to be a candidate for further verification.

3 Verification

After detecting candidate ordnance locations, a variety of verification modules can be applied to the candidates in order to reduce the likelihood of detecting a false positive instance in the imagery. We can apply much more computation in these verification modules than in the initial hypothesis generation step since we have greatly reduced the area of the image in which we are interested.

3.1 Hypothesis resampling

A first step that is useful prior to applying the verification modules is to compute the dominant orientation in the image at the location of the hypothesis. We then resample the image, using the range and orientation information to transform a small area of the image around the candidate location such that the resampled image is at a canonical scale and orientation.

We detect the dominant orientation in the image by applying a simple gradient operator and then histogramming the gradient orientations found (weighted by the gradient magnitude) at each pixel. The histogram bin with the largest score is taken to be the dominant orientation of the hypothesis.

For each pixel in the resampled image, we then compute the corresponding location in the original image according to:

$$x = \frac{s_d}{s_h}(x_i - x_h)\cos\theta + \frac{s_d}{s_h}(y_i - y_h)\sin\theta \tag{5}$$

and

$$y = -\frac{s_d}{s_h}(x_i - x_h)\sin\theta + \frac{s_d}{s_h}(y_i - y_h)\cos\theta, \tag{6}$$

where θ is the dominant orientation, s_d is the desired scale, s_h is the scale of the hypothesis according to the range data, x_i and y_i and the coordinates in the resampled image, and x_h and y_h are the center position of the hypothesis in the original image.

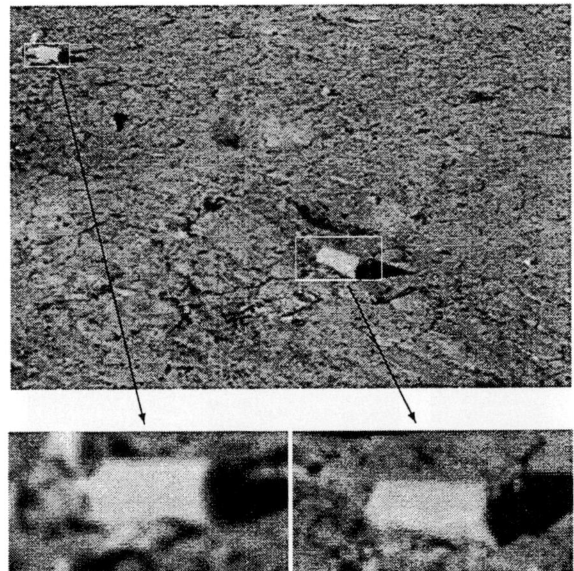

Figure 3: After candidates are located, they are resampled to a canonical size and orientation.

Figure 3 shows two examples of hypotheses that were resampled from an image.

3.2 Verification tests

Once the candidates have been resampled, we apply a series of tests to them, in order to determine which are actual instances of ordnance.

Gaussian filter. We apply a filter to the red band of the image consisting of the product of a Gaussian second derivative in the y-direction (across the cross-section of the ordnance) with a Gaussian in the x-direction (across the length of the ordnance). The filter is thus given by:

$$F(x,y) = \left(\frac{y^2 - \sigma_y^2}{2\pi\sigma_x\sigma_y^5}\right) e^{-\frac{x^2}{2\sigma_x^2} - \frac{y^2}{2\sigma_y^2}} \tag{7}$$

This yields high scores when the ordnance is present due to the yellow color of the ordnance in the center of the resampled candidates.

Parallel edge extraction. The gradients in the resampled candidate are histogrammed according to their orientation weighted by the gradient magnitude. If an orientation is found where the score is very high, this indicates either a single, very strong, straight edge is present, or a pair of strong parallel edges are present. Both of these cases are more likely if the candidate is an instance of the ordnance.

Height evaluation. Since we have stereo range data, it is sometimes possible to detect the difference in height of the terrain at the location of an ordnance instance. A simple technique that we use is to examine the range data corresponding to the pixels in each candidate and determine the minimum and maximum heights present. The difference in these values measures the amount of height variation in the candidate window.

Contrast evaluation. When the candidate is an instance of the ordnance, we expect a significant gradient between the ordnance and the background. While false positives might also yield such a high gradient, this will not always be the case, and we can thus use this information to help discriminate between true positive and false positives.

We generate a probabilistic score using each of these tests (in addition to the hypothesis generation state) that feed into an evidential reasoning process.

4 Evidential reasoning

Once the various verification modules have generated scores for each of the candidate ordnance locations, we must have some method for combining the scores into a single measure that can be used to evaluate each candidate. We use a linear opinion pool (see, for example, [3]), where the results of each measurement are combined according to some weighting factor that represents the confidence in the probability estimate that is generated.

Let H be the hypothesis that a certain candidate actually represents an ordnance instance. Each verification module v yields a probability value $P_v(H)$ that the hypothesis is correct and a weighting factor $W_v(H)$. We can combine the values from any two verification modules (for example v_1 and v_2) using the following relationships:

$$P_{v_1+v_2}(H) = \frac{W_{v_1}(H)P_{v_1}(H) + W_{v_2}(H)P_{v_2}(H)}{W_{v_1}(H) + W_{v_2}(H)} \tag{8}$$

$$W_{v_1+v_2}(H) = W_{v_1}(H) + W_{v_2}(H) \tag{9}$$

Since these equations are associative, it does not matter in which order the values are combined (the final result is the same). The candidate is finally accepted if, after combining all of the scores from the various verification modules, the probability value is above a pre-determined threshold.

5 Results

These techniques have been tested on a set of 350 images collected at a live-fire test range near Nellis Air Force Base that simulate the images that would be seen from an unmanned ground vehicle. The data set thus consists of sequences of images captured at short intervals along continuous paths. Training for the hypothesis detection stage was performed on a set of images collected at the same site collected one year earlier. Overall, 324 instances of 75 different bombs appear in the test set. We have evaluated the techniques with respect to both the detection performance using a ROC curve and the computational requirements of the techniques through benchmarking on a workstation.

After the application of the recognition techniques to the complete data set, the performance was evaluated versus a manual identification of the instances present. Each bomb was detected in at least one of the images containing the bomb. Several false negatives occurred for instances that appeared at a significant distance from the camera

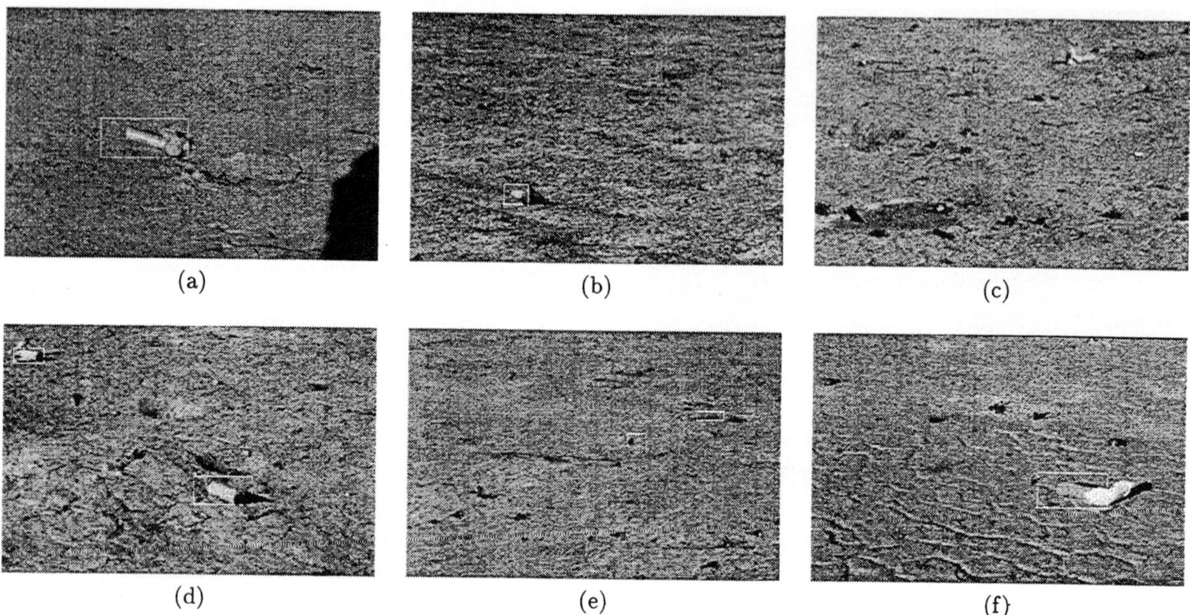

Figure 4: Results achieved on the Nellis Air Force Base data set. The boxes are detected ordnance locations.

and thus yielded small images of the bomb. In these cases, the bomb was always found when the camera traveled closer to it. In addition, 19 false positives are detected. Of the hypotheses reported, 92.6% were actually bombs.

Figure 4 shows results from this data set that include clutter and cases where the assumptions are violated by specularity, inter-reflection, and discolored ordnance. Despite the violation of various assumptions, the algorithm has little trouble discriminating between the ordnance and the background clutter.

In addition to the detection performance, we must consider the computation time required by the algorithms, since running in near real-time (2-3 frames per second) is necessary to accommodate a vehicle speed of of 5 MPH. The performance that we have observed on a workstation is 0.287 seconds per image to perform the stereo and hypothesis detection stages and 0.083 seconds per candidate to perform verification. A real-time system implementing these techniques with off-the-shelf hardware is likely to run slightly slower.

6 Concluding remarks

We have performed considerable work towards the generation of the real-time system to perform ordnance recognition. In addition to identifying algorithms that are successful in detecting instance of BLU-97 ordnance with a low rate of false positives, we have characterized the performance of these algorithms with respect to both the detection rate on a dataset from Nellis Air Force Base and the computation time required on a workstation.

In the course of this work, several lessons have become apparent. First, it is crucial for the initial hypothesis detection techniques to be extremely fast in order to accommodate real-time performance of the system. None of the more complex techniques that we experimented with were fast enough to support real-time operations. Next, stereo pre-processing yielded crucial information with respect to the scene depth. Without the depth information, the hypothesis threshold could not be set at a single value to yield a low rate of both false positives and false negatives. Finally, shape was not an adequate discriminator by itself. We initially believed that shape would be a more robust discriminator than color due to possible discoloration of the ordnance. However, in many cases the shape was not reliably detected, resulting in many false negatives. While the ordnance was sometimes discolored, the color still remained recognizable with respect to the background.

Acknowledgements

The research described in this paper was carried out by the Jet Propulsion Laboratory, California Institute of Technology, and was sponsored by the Air Force Research Laboratory at Tyndall Air Force Base, Panama City, Florida, through an agreement with the National Aeronautics and Space Administration.

References

[1] M. B. Dillencourt, H. Samet, and M. Tamminen. A general approach to connected-component labeling for arbitrary image representations. *Journal of the ACM*, 39(2):253–280, April 1992.

[2] G. Healey. Segmenting images using normalized color. *IEEE Transactions on Systems, Man, and Cybernetics*, 22(1):64–73, January/February 1992.

[3] F. Voorbraak. Combining evidence under partial ignorance. In *Proceedings of the First International Joint Conference on Qualitative and Quantitative Practical Reasoning*, pages 574–588, 1997.

REFLICS: Real-time Flow Imaging and Classification System

Sadahiro Iwamoto[1], Mohan M. Trivedi[1], and David M. Checkley[2]
[1]Electrical and Computer Engineering Department, University of California, San Diego
[2]Marine Life Research Group, Scripps Institution of Oceanography
siwamoto@ucsd.edu, trivedi@ece.ucsd.edu, dcheckley@ucsd.edu

Abstract

In this paper, we present Real-time Flow Imaging and Classification System (REFLICS), a real-time machine vision system for detecting and classifying pelagic fish eggs (e.g. sardine, anchovy) flowing through a shipboard pumping and filtering system. REFLICS images the dynamic flow with a progressive-scan area camera and a synchronized backlight strobe. Digitization and processing occur on a dual processor Pentium II PC and a pipeline image processing board. REFLICS uses a segmentation algorithm to locate fish egg-like objects in the image and then a classifier to determine fish egg, species, and development stage (age). We present an integrated system design of REFLICS and performance results. REFLICS can perform in 60Hz real-time, classify fish eggs with low false negative rates on data collected from real cruises, and work in harsh conditions aboard ships at sea. REFLICS allows more accurate and timely survey of fish stock in a cost-effective manner.

1. Introduction

Scientific research, resource management, and general understanding of life in the vast oceans depend on collecting data samples and analyzing them. Two important factors in such data collection and analysis are 1) spatial resolution and 2) temporal match. Higher spatial resolution data produces more accurate analysis. In a dynamic biological system like the ocean, data sampling is also time dependent. To determine the relationship between data and thus obtain accurate analysis requires the samplings to be performed in a short span of time as possible. These "rules" apply completely to the practice of fish stock estimation by conducting fish egg survey called Daily Egg Production Method (DEPM) [1]. Fishes like anchovy and sardine typically spawn eggs in patches less than 1km in diameter and last for only few days [2]. For time and cost reasons, egg samples are usually collected at 10 to 30 km intervals with several hours between samples. The area between is interpolated between the sampling point. Since the data is highly undersampled and not temporally matched, resource management agencies and scientists receive a very rough estimate of fish stock size.

Significant progress towards high resolution fish egg sampling was made when the Continuous Underway Fish Egg Sampler (CUFES) was developed [3]. CUFES, diagram shown in figure 1, consists of pumps and mesh filters to collect fish egg-size particles from the sea as the ship carrying it steams along. Theoretically, a continuous sampling of fish eggs could be performed with CUFES, but the sampling rate is still limited by human analysis speed. Since one trained person can analyze one sample bottle every 5 minutes and a ship usually travels at 10 knots, one sampling is still a cumulative count from a line 1.5km long.

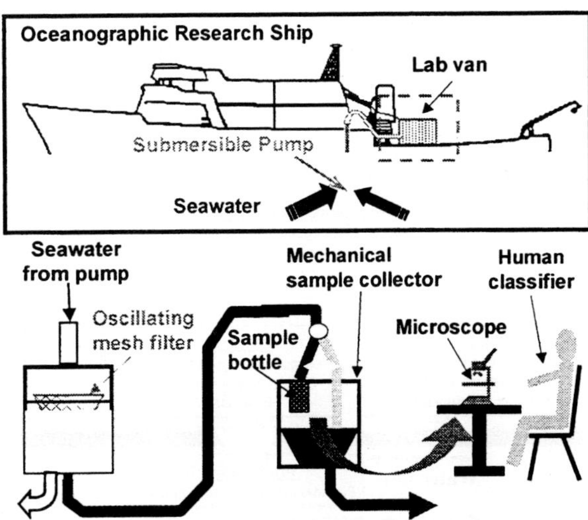

Figure 1. Diagram of CUFES system

Replacing the sample collection and human analysis with a machine vision system to count and classify fish eggs in the CUFES flow will allow continuous sampling of fish eggs. But there are several challenges to such a machine vision system. In CUFES, the water flows up to 15 liters per minute. Furthermore, water flow rate fluctuates due mainly to ship movement. To properly image the CUFES flow, REFLICS imaging must acquire and process images at high speed. Fish eggs appear in an ambient assemblage of similar size objects such as plankton and air bubbles. REFLICS must accurately distinguish fish eggs from other objects. Additionally, since fish eggs are rare events, REFLICS must have a low false negative rate. Finally, but not least, REFLICS must be rugged and reliable to operate in the harsh environments aboard ships at sea.

Two existing devices are similar to REFLICS in that they can image particles in a flow: the Video Plankton Recorder (VPR)[4][5] and the FlowCAM[6]. VPR images and classifies plankton *in situ* by towing an imaging system through the water. VPR's neural network-based classifier can determine the family of imaged plankton. VPR's dark field illumination imaging and Fourier shape descriptor feature are not suitable for translucent and rounds objects like fish eggs. FlowCAM is a shore-based system to image microplankton. Imaging is triggered by checking the fluorescence level of objects in the field of view. FlowCAM images a field of view too small for fish eggs and fish eggs do not fluoresce.

In the following section, we describe REFLICS's design concerning imaging, processing, and algorithms. In section 3, we present imaging, speed, and accuracy results from the current version of REFLICS. Finally, we describe future development work for REFLICS.

2. System Design

REFLICS is an integrated system consisting of number of modules working together. A block diagram of these modules and their interactions are shown below in figure 2.

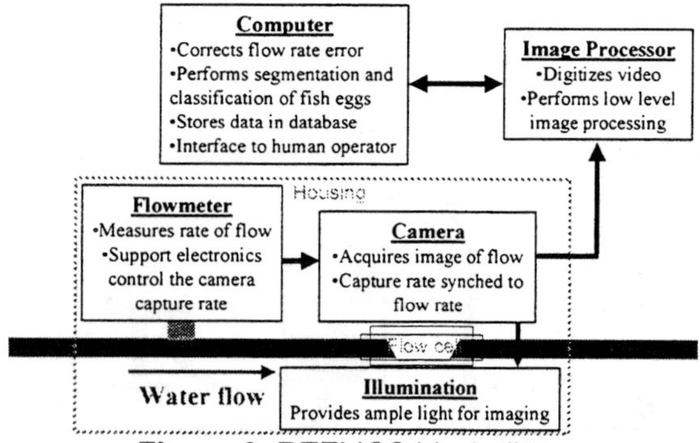

Figure 2. REFLICS block diagram

The synchronized strobe in backlight configuration allows the progressive-scan area camera to acquire a blur-free image of the flow. The image processor digitizes the video signal and performs low level image processing functions to clean and segment possible fish egg objects from the background. The image is transferred to the host processor to complete the segmentation, perform classification on the possible fish egg objects, and display the results to the user.

2.1. Flow Imaging Module

REFLICS uses a 60Hz progressive-scan area camera (Pulnix 6701AN) as its image sensor. To illuminate the flow without motion blur, a xenon flashlamp strobe synchronized to the video sync signal is used. Backlighting configuration is used to allow imaging of fish egg's translucent interior[7]. Custom designed glass flow imaging cell and a macro lens allows the camera to image the full flow field (20mm wide and deep) in focus with highest resolution possible.

To allow REFLICS to be used aboard ships at sea, the imaging system and support electronics are mounted in an aluminum and PVC housing. Interior of the rugged housing is compartmentalized to prevent any leaks from spreading. Cameras and illuminators are securely bolted down to prevent movement while in operation and the housing is mounted on shock absorbing material to dampen vibrations.

2.2. Video Processing Module

REFLICS must analyze every frame of video for fish eggs. To do so requires REFLICS to have considerable processing power to analyze the large amount of data produced by the imaging module. REFLICS uses a dual processor Pentium II 350MHz PC as its base system with a pipeline-based image processor card (Datacube MaxPCI) to handle video digitization and to perform low level image processing. Using a PC platform has several advantages. Current PCs have tremendous amount of processing power yet they are relatively low cost. Microsoft Windows NT operating system (OS) for the PC provides graphical user interface (GUI) environment, easy to use development tools, and support for multiple processors. And finally, PCs are easy to maintain because they use industry standard components. The MaxPCI incorporates a high speed image digitizer and performs image processing in a pipeline fashion. Pipelining allows low level image processing functions which does not require high level calculations but has high data rates to be performed in a real-time manner. REFLICS's high powered dual processor PC and MaxPCI is a powerful video processing module which provides the required performance while minimizing equipment, development, and maintenance costs.

2.3. Algorithms

The approach to detecting and classifying fish eggs is a two-step process:

1) Segment the image using background subtraction to find objects of interest, i.e. fish egg-sized objects.
2) Classify objects as fish eggs from the object image and extracted features. The classifier also determines the species and development stage of fish eggs.

The segmentation algorithm accepts images from the camera and finds regions of interest in the image which could be fish eggs. It does so by performing the following steps on each frame:

1) Absolute differencing with the background image (background subtraction) to show only moving objects
2) Thresholding to separate image into background and foreground
3) Morphological filtering to remove small noise pixels
4) Updating background image
5) Geometry preserving run length (GPRL) encoding to easily locate foreground pixels
6) Performing connectivity to label blobs

Background subtraction is a robust technique to isolate object pixels which works well when background is stationary. In ReFLICS, background varies very slowly over time so background subtraction is appropriate. Thresholding binarizes the image into foreground pixels and background pixels. Morphological filtering (erosion) removes very small object pixels that are usually noise. The background is updated to adjust to slight background changes over time. GPRL encoding occurs on the image processor and reduces processing time on the next operation, connectivity, by providing information whether a row contains foreground pixels or not [8]. Connectivity operation groups the individual foreground pixels into object blobs.

After obtaining segmented objects in the flow image, the classifier needs to determine whether or not the object is a fish egg. Furthermore, if the object is a fish egg, the classifier also needs to determine the species and the stage of development. REFLICS performs classification by following these steps:

1) Calculate area of objects and filter to eliminate objects too big or too small to be fish eggs
2) Extract moment, shape, and histogram features from remaining objects
3) Use nearest-neighbor classifier to determine whether object is a fish egg and species and age of the fish egg.

Use of the size filter is a simple and robust method to reduce the number of objects to classify and thus processing time. Fish eggs are round, translucent objects with a dark embryo whose size depends on the stage of development. Using moment, shape, and histogram features allow the nearest-neighbor classifier to distinguish fish eggs from other objects such as planktons and air bubbles.

2.4. Algorithm Implementation

The processing algorithms are coded to take maximum advantage of the camera rate processing of the pipeline image processor and of the PC's two processors. Data intensive calculations are mostly performed on the image processor and complex calculations (connectivity, blob analysis, classification) are performed on the two PC processors. The code is multithreaded to allow the two processors to work in parallel. Also, buffers are used between processing steps to maximize processor usage and to process continuously without dropping frames.

3. Results

REFLICS is an integration of several components. Individual modules as well as the integrated system were extensively tested in the lab as well as aboard ships.

REFLICS's imaging module was tested off the coast of California during Spring of 1999. Using a high capacity hard disk, we recorded several tens of thousands of CUFES flow image at 60 frames per second. Figure 3 shows a sardine egg imaged by REFLICS. Figure 4 shows an example of non-fish egg object, an euphasiid.

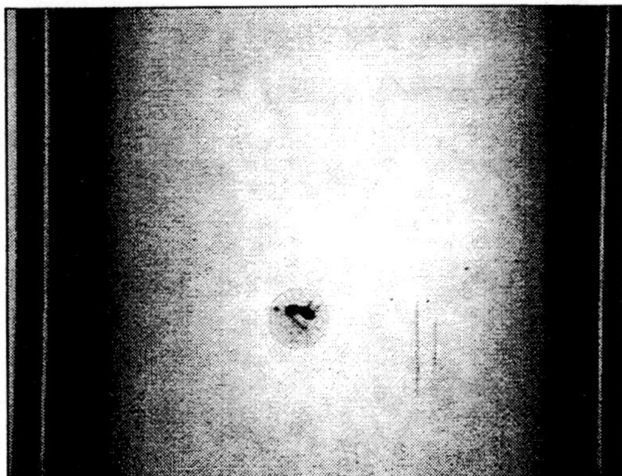

Figure 3. Image of a sardine egg

Figure 4. Image of an euphasiid

We tested REFLICS's segmenter performance in two ways. First, we imaged a moving test pattern to measure the segmentation speed in the lab. Using a pattern that resembles a typical flow condition, steady background with a varying number of 50x50 pixel fish egg-sized objects, the segmenter maintained a steady 60 fps processing speed until about 20 objects (table 1). A typical flow condition contains less than 10 fish egg-sized objects.

Number of moving objects	0	2	8	16	20	25
Speed (Frames per second)	60.0	60.0	60.0	60.0	59.6	59.1

Table 1. Segmentation speed

The segmentation was also tested aboard a Spring 2000 cruise. Segmentation results were saved while simultaneously CUFES samples were collected and counted for about 5 hours by a person. Counts between REFLICS's segmentation and human analysis shows very high correlation. The segmentation algorithm, multithreading, and multiprocessor/image processor lets REFLICS achieve real-time segmentation for CUFES flow.

Using 3600-frame segments (1 minute) containing sardine eggs and other objects captured during the April 1999 cruise, we tested the accuracy of the classification algorithm. The results from the five segments are shown in table 2. REFLICS's classification algorithm achieves the low false negative requirement while maintaining high true positive rate.

Test #	Eggs Imaged	True Positive	False Negative
1	14	14	0
2	16	16	0
3	13	11	2
4	19	16	3
5	12	12	0

Table 2. Classification results

4. Conclusions

We presented REFLICS, a real-time machine vision system to detect and classify fish eggs in flowing water. REFLICS images, segments, and classifies at required speed for CUFES flow. REFLICS is accurate enough to assist and eventually replace human analysis of CUFES samples. Finally, custom designed housing allows REFLICS to be used at its target environment at sea.

REFLICS can be improved in several ways. We are planning on implementing a neural network-based classifier. The classifier will use the original raw image of the object as well as the extracted features to classify. We are also planning on shifting the whole processing to the PC's CPUs. Instead of an image processor, the new REFLICS would use a framegrabber board in a fast multiprocessor PC. This configuration would further reduce the cost of REFLICS and be more attractive to its target users.

When deployed, REFLICS will be a cost-effective tool for resource managers and oceanographers to obtain more accurate, high resolution fish egg survey data in a timely manner.

Acknowledgements. This paper is funded by a grant from the National Sea Grant College Program, National Oceanic and Atmospheric Administration, U.S. Department of Commerce, under grant number NA66RG0477, project number 74-C-N through the California Sea Grant College System. The views expressed herein are those of the authors and do not necessarily reflect the views of NOAA or any of its sub-agencies. The U.S. Government is authorized to reproduce and distribute for governmental purposes.

5. References

[1] Lasker, R.H., "An egg production method for estimating spawning biomass of pelagic fish: Application to the northern anchovy", *NOAA Technical Report NMFS 36*, 1985.

[2] Dotson, R. Personal communication, April 1999.

[3] Checkley, D. M., Jr., P.B. Ortner, L.R. Settle, and S.R. Cummings, "A continuous, underway fish egg sampler", *Fish. Oceanogr.* 6:58-73, 1997.

[4] Davis, C.S., S.M. Gallagher, M.S. Berman, L.R. Haury, and J.R. Strickler, "The Video Plankton Recorder (VPR): design and initial results", *Arch. Hydrobiol./Beih. Ergebn. Limnol.* 36: 67-81, 1997.

[5] Tang, X., W.K. Stewart, L. Vincent, H. Huang, M. Marra, S.M. Gallagher, and C.S. Davis, "Automatic Plankton Image Recognition", *Artificial Intelligence Review*, 12:177-199, 1998.

[6] Sieracki, C.K., M.E. Sieracki, and C.S. Yentsch, "An imaging-in-flow system for automated analysis of marine microplankton", *Mar. Ecol. Prog. Ser.* 168: 285-296, 1998.

[7] Schroeder, H.E., "Practical Illumination Concept and Technique for Machine Vision Application", *Robots 8 Conference*, pp 14-43, 1984.

[8] *SILL Programmer's Manual*, Datacube Inc., pg. 4-17, 1994.

Remarks on a Real-Time 3D Human Body Posture Estimation Method using Trinocular Images

Kazuhiko Takahashi, Tatsumi Sakaguchi and Jun Ohya
ATR Media Integration and Communications Research Laboratories
2-2 Hikaridai Seika-cho Soraku-gun Kyoto 619-0288, Japan
{kylyn, tatsu, ohya}@mic.atr.co.jp

Abstract

This paper proposes a new real-time method of estimating human postures in 3D from trinocular images. The proposed method extracts feature points of the human body by applying a type of function analysis to contours of human silhouettes. To overcome self-occlusion problems, dynamic compensation is carried out using the Kalman filter and all feature points are tracked. The 3D coordinates of the feature points are reconstructed by considering the geometrical relationship between the three cameras. Experimental results confirm both the feasibility and the effectiveness of the proposed method, and an application example of the 3D human body posture estimation to a motion recognition system is presented.

1. Introduction

Recently, human motion analysis has become increasingly important for visual communications and virtual reality application, in recognizing and understanding non-verbal information such as a gestures and sign languages. Specifically, real-time 3D human posture estimation is important for many applications such as advanced human-machine interface systems and video game systems.

Approaches for measuring the posture or the motion parameters of a human body are classified into two categories: contact and non-contact types. Contact type devices, such as magnetic sensors, are easy to use and the acquired data is quite accurate, but they cause stress and are hard to handle since the person using them must wear them at all times. With non-contact type systems, in contrast, image analysis methods employed can lighten the burden on users. Accordingly, computer-vision-based technologies for estimating human postures in 3D in real-time are essential and several estimation methods have been studied [1, 2, 4, 5, 6, 7, 10, 11]; these methods do not achieve real-time performance, often lack robustness, and/or require a large computing power even if the method works in real-time. The authors have also proposed a real-time method [3] for estimating 3D human body postures. The advantages of the method are: (1) high-speed and robust processing, (2) no markers on the human body, and (3) little required computing power; the range of acceptable postures is limited because of the employed heuristic rules to obtain the feature points of the human body (e.g., the tip of the right foot exists in the lower and right side half of the body).

In this paper, we propose a new real-time method of estimating 3D human body postures from trinocular camera images. The proposed method extracts feature points of the human body by applying a type of function analysis to contours of the human silhouettes and tracks all feature points with an autoregressive model. The 3D coordinates of the feature points are reconstructed by using the results estimated from three images. Section 2 outlines our method and the estimation of feature points is explained in Section 3. Section 4 explains how to obtain the 3D coordinates of the feature points. Section 5 shows experimental results and section 6 presents an application example of the 3D human body posture estimation to a motion recognition system.

2. Outline of the 3D Estimation Method

To reconstruct human postures in 3D, we use three color CCD cameras [3], which observe a person from the top, front, and side as shown in Fig. 1. At each time instant, the person's posture is estimated in 3D by obtaining the 3D coordinates of feature points (i.e., top of the head, and tips of the hands and feet) taken from

1051-4651/00 $10.00 © 2000 IEEE

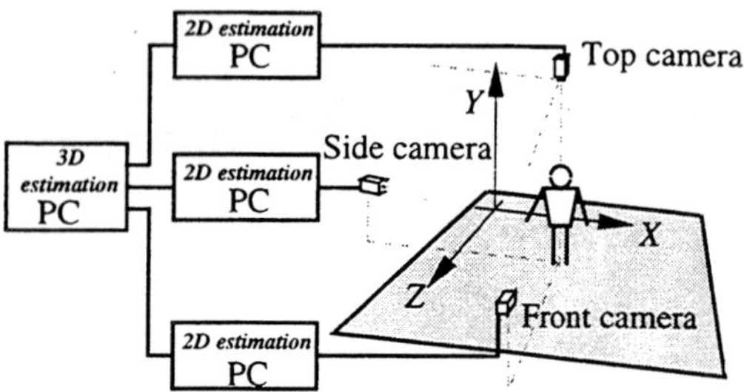

Figure 1. Trinocular camera systems.

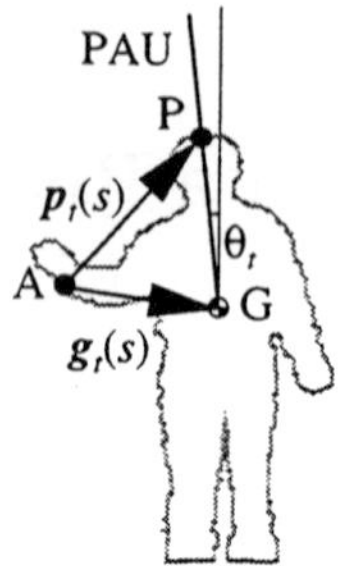

Figure 2. Definition of vectors.

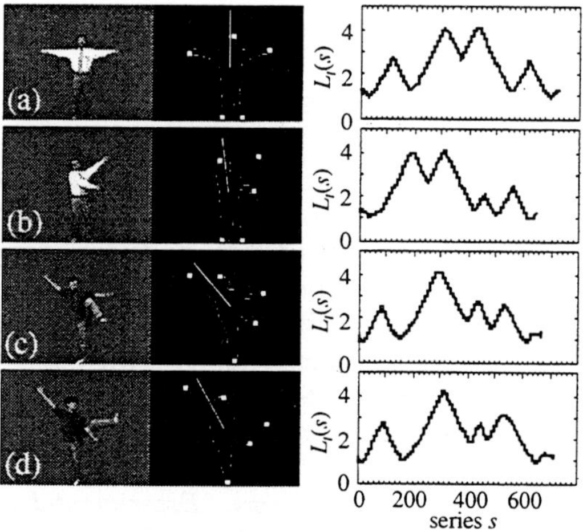

Figure 3. Examples of $L_t(s)$ curve analyses (left: camera/contour image, right: $L_t(s)$ curve).

the estimated 2D coordinates of corresponding points in the images captured by the three cameras.

In each image, feature points are extracted using a type of function analysis on contours of human silhouettes, when self-occlusions do not occur in the human silhouettes. A human silhouette is extracted by calculating the difference at each pixel between the background image and the input image and then thresholding the difference at that pixel. When self-occlusions occur, on the other hand, subtraction images each calculated between the present and previous frame images are used to detect feature points and then the time series for each feature point is approximated with the AR model to track the position of the feature point [9]. The parameters of the AR model are estimated by using the Kalman filter, whose input is the detected feature points in the present frame image. The extracting procedure is retried based on the prediction information one step ahead upon failure of the feature point detection using the subtraction image. If the detection fails again, the extracting procedure quits and goes back to the calibration mode. To reconstruct the 3D coordinates of the feature points, we combine the estimation results in 2D from the three views with considering the geometrical relationship between the three cameras.

3. Feature Points Extraction

First, the centroid of a human G, $[x_t^g\ y_t^g]$, where t denotes the frame number of an image, is located and the principal axis of the upper half of the body (PAU) is obtained as the inclination θ_t of the human silhouette's principal axis of inertia [3]. The contour image of the human silhouette is then obtained by a border tracking technique in the human silhouette. As shown in Fig. 2, a point P (which is the intersection of the PAU and the contour) is chosen and the point series $\{s\}$ (counted through the counter-clockwise direction from point P on the contour pixel) is considered, and then, a point A $[x_t(s)\ y_t(s)]$ is defined. By using the following function $L_t(s)$, we can define one-to-one mapping between the geometrical information of the contour image and the point series $\{s\}$.

$$L_t(s) = \sqrt{\boldsymbol{p}_t^2(s) + \boldsymbol{g}_t^2(s)} \tag{1}$$

where $\boldsymbol{p}_t(s) = \vec{AP}$ and $\boldsymbol{g}_t(s) = \vec{AG}$. Figure 3 shows examples of the function output (hereafter called an $L_t(s)$ curve) for several human body postures. By applying an $L_t(s)$ curve analysis to various human body postures, we could confirm that the local maximum points of the $L_t(s)$ curve correspond to feature points of the human body. Accordingly, the locations of the feature points can be obtained by the $L_t(s)$ curve analysis, but the analysis does not give any information on the following: which local maximum point is equivalent to which part of the human body. Therefore, by using an initial calibration posture (Fig. 3(a)) before starting the location procedure, we define the relationship between the local maximum points and feature points of the human body only once. Since all of the defined feature points are tracked in the following frame, we do not require *a priori* knowledge about the human body and heuristic rules to extract the feature points.

To track the feature points, we assume the AR model for every feature point as follows.

$$\Psi_t = \Gamma_t \Xi_t + \epsilon_t \tag{2}$$

where

$$\Psi_t = [\ \psi_t^{pT} \quad \psi_t^{hrT} \quad \psi_t^{hlT} \quad \psi_t^{frT} \quad \psi_t^{flT}\ ]^T,$$

$$\Xi_t = [\ \xi_t^{pT} \quad \xi_t^{hrT} \quad \xi_t^{hlT} \quad \xi_t^{frT} \quad \xi_t^{flT}\ ]^T,$$

$$\Gamma_t = diag\,[\ C_t^p \quad C_t^{hr} \quad C_t^{hl} \quad C_t^{fr} \quad C_t^{fl}\ ],$$

$$C_t^j = \begin{bmatrix} -x_{t-1}^j & -x_{t-2}^j \cdots -x_{t-\rho}^j & 0 & 0 & \cdots & 0 \\ 0 & 0 \quad \cdots \quad 0 & -y_{t-1}^j & -y_{t-2}^j & \cdots & -y_{t-\rho}^j \end{bmatrix},$$

$$\xi_t^{jT} = [a_1^j \quad a_2^j \quad \cdots \quad a_\rho^j \quad b_1^j \quad b_2^j \quad \cdots \quad b_\rho^j],$$

$\psi_t^{jT} = [x_t^j\ y_t^j]$, $j = p$ (top of the head), hl (tip of the left hand), hr (tip of the right hand), fl (tip of the left foot), and fr (tip of the right foot); ρ is the order of the model, a_i^j and b_i^j are the unknown parameters, and ϵ_t is the error vector modeled as a white noise process. The vector Ξ_t is estimated by using the Kalman filter as follows.

$$\hat{\Xi}_t = \hat{\Xi}_{t-1} + K_t(\Psi_t - \Gamma_t \Xi_{t-1}) \tag{3}$$

where $\hat{\Xi}_t$ is the estimated vector of the vector Ξ_t, and K_t is the Kalman gain matrix. The measurement vector Ψ_t is required for the calculation of the Kalman filter. The observation output ψ_t is obtained from the results of the $L_t(s)$ curve analysis or from those of the subtraction image processing [9]. After updating the Kalman filter, the optimal positions of the feature points can be estimated by using Eq. (2).

4. 3D Reconstruction

In the front image, all feature points are estimated by the proposed algorithm. Assuming a parallel projection, the 3D coordinates of the feature points, $[X_{Ft}^j\ Y_{Ft}^j\ Z_{Ft}^j]$, are calculated by using the 2D coordinates estimated from the front image, $[x_t^j\ y_t^j]$, as follows.

$$\begin{bmatrix} X_{Ft}^j \\ Y_{Ft}^j \\ Z_{Ft}^j \end{bmatrix} = \begin{bmatrix} 1 & 0 \\ 0 & 1 \\ 0 & 0 \end{bmatrix} \begin{bmatrix} x_t^j \\ y_t^j \end{bmatrix} \tag{4}$$

In the side image, we cannot define the relationship between the $L_t(s)$ curve and the feature points for the hands and feet using the calibration posture (Fig. 3(a)). Therefore, only the top of the head is estimated by the proposed algorithm in the side image, and the raw coordinates for the other feature points are obtained from the $L_t(s)$ curve analysis without information on the human body part. The relationship of the feature points is given by considering the validity with the results estimated from the other images. The 3D coordinates of the feature points, $[X_{St}^j\ Y_{St}^j\ Z_{St}^j]$, are calculated as follows.

$$\begin{bmatrix} X_{St}^j \\ Y_{St}^j \\ Z_{St}^j \end{bmatrix} = \begin{bmatrix} 0 & 0 \\ 0 & 1 \\ 1 & 0 \end{bmatrix} \begin{bmatrix} x_t^j \\ y_t^j \end{bmatrix} \tag{5}$$

In the top image, a rotation angle of the human body ϕ_t is defined by the PAU. The rotation angle is measured from the left hand orientation defined by the posture at the calibration. The origin of the $L_t(s)$ curve analysis, P, is the intersection of the contour pixels in the region of $[\ \phi_t,\ \pi + \phi_t]$ and the line that is perpendicular to the PAU and passes through the centroid. Using the calibration posture, we cannot define the relationship between the $L_t(s)$ curve and the feature points for the top of the head and feet. In the same way as for the side image processing, only the hands are estimated by the proposed algorithm in the top image and the relationship of the other feature points is given by considering the validity. The 3D coordinates of the feature points, $[X_{Tt}^j\ Y_{Tt}^j\ Z_{Tt}^j]$, are calculated as follows.

$$\begin{bmatrix} X_{Tt}^j \\ Y_{Tt}^j \\ Z_{Tt}^j \end{bmatrix} = \begin{bmatrix} 1 & 0 \\ 0 & 0 \\ 0 & -1 \end{bmatrix} \begin{bmatrix} x_t^j - x_t^g \\ y_t^j - y_t^g \end{bmatrix} + \begin{bmatrix} X_t^g \\ Y_t^g \\ Z_t^g \end{bmatrix} \tag{6}$$

Here, $[X_t^g\ Y_t^g\ Z_t^g]$ gives the 3D coordinates of the centroid estimated by the results obtained from both the front and side images.

With the geometrical relationship between the three cameras, we obtain the 3D coordinates of the feature points. Since some of the results obtained from the side and top images have no information between the coordinates and the human body part, we explain how to evaluate the validity and estimate the feature points by using these results. First, in the results obtained from the side image, those points whose coordinate Y_{St}^j is close to coordinate Y_{Ft}^j estimated from the front image are chosen as the feature point candidates of index j. Next, those points whose coordinate Z_{St}^j is close to coordinate Z_{Tt}^j obtained from among the top image are selected from the feature point candidates. Finally, the point whose coordinate X_{Tt}^j is closest to coordinate X_{Ft}^j estimated from the front image is defined as the feature point of index j. If more than one point remains in the final stage, the point whose distance to the feature point estimated from the front image is shortest, is selected as the feature point. Finally, the 3D coordinates of the feature points are calculated as follows.

$$\begin{bmatrix} X_t^j \\ Y_t^j \\ Z_t^j \end{bmatrix} = \begin{bmatrix} (X_{Ft}^j + X_{Tt}^j)/2 \\ (Y_{Ft}^j + Y_{St}^j)/2 \\ (Z_{St}^j + Z_{Tt}^j)/2 \end{bmatrix} \quad (7)$$

Note that the results from the front and side images are always used to locate the centroid and the top of the head.

5. Experimental Results

The proposed method was coded in the C++ language and implemented on a personal computer (Dual Pentium II 400MHz, Windows NT 4.0). To simplify the image processing, the backgrounds were green colored screens and chroma keyers were used to extract the human silhouettes. The images were digitized into the computer with a 320-by-240 pixel resolution. The order of the AR model was 3. The entire process for estimating human postures ran in real-time (17 frames/sec).

Figures 4 and 5 show examples of estimation results. The top of each figure shows the motion sequence from three directions and the bottom of the figure illustrates the 3D trajectories of the feature points estimated by the proposed method, in which the black squares and the white squares indicate the start and end positions of motions, respectively. The white lines in the figures each for the end of a motion sequence show the projections of the 3D trajectories to the directions of the individual views. As shown in these figure, locating the feature points is successful and accurate reconstruction takes place in 3D. In Fig. 4, body movements were observed during intervals when self-occlusion of the left hand occurred; the tip of the left hand could still be robustly tracked. In Fig. 5, the tip of the right foot was over the tip of the right hand and self-occlusion also occurred between the right hand and the right foot. Although these postures could not be estimated by using our conventional method based on heuristic rules [3], we could estimate the postures by using the proposed method. Overall, similar tracking results were obtained for the other motions and individuals. The proposed method can permit a rotation angle of the human body ϕ_t in the region of $[-\pi/4, \pi/4]$. The experimental results indicate the feasibility of our proposed method.

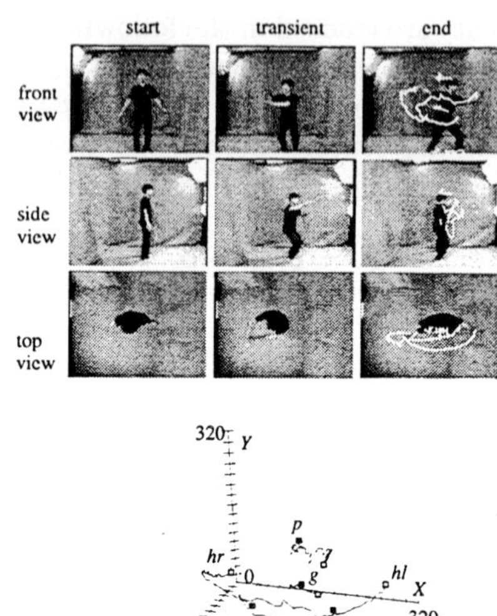

Figure 4. Estimation results of 3D human body posture: Tai Chi motion "single whip" (top: motion sequences, bottom: trajectories of feature points).

6. Example of Application

In this section, we present a motion recognition system using the 3D human body posture estimation. The time series data of the feature points' positions were input into the motion recognizer based on neural networks (NNs) [8]. The output of the NNs was: 1 or 0 depending on whether the classification of the motion type was correct or incorrect, respectively. To process the time-varying patterns, the input vector of the NNs, $\boldsymbol{U}_t$, is defined as follows.

$$\boldsymbol{U}_t = \begin{bmatrix} \boldsymbol{u}_t & \boldsymbol{u}_{t-1} & \boldsymbol{u}_{t-2} & \cdots & \boldsymbol{u}_{t-d} \end{bmatrix}^T, \quad (8)$$

where

$$\boldsymbol{u}_t = \begin{bmatrix} \boldsymbol{v}_t^{hr} & \boldsymbol{v}_t^{hl} & \boldsymbol{v}_t^{fr} & \boldsymbol{v}_t^{fl} \end{bmatrix},$$

$$\boldsymbol{v}_t^j = \begin{bmatrix} \frac{X_t^j - X_t^g}{X_c} & \frac{Y_t^j - Y_t^g}{Y_c} & \frac{Z_t^j - Z_t^g}{Z_c} \end{bmatrix}.$$

Here, X_c, Y_c, and Z_c are normalizing factors determined in the initial calibration. The NNs' learning is carried out according to the generalized δ-rule with the adaptive learning rate. Six different Tai Chi motions were used as the objective motions because the Tai Chi motions are common in the world. The Tai Chi motions were performed by the same individual, an expert in Chinese martial arts. Ten samples were collected for each motion. Forty-two of the samples (close data) were used for the NNs' training, and the remain-

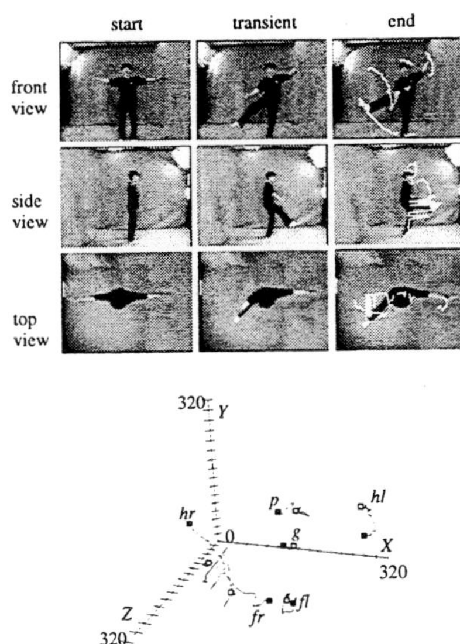

Figure 5. Estimation results of 3D human body posture: Long fist motion "right kick" (top: motion sequences, bottom: trajectories of feature points).

ing 18 samples (open data) were used for a recognition test. The start and end of each motion were manually segmented. The dead-time sampling number, d, in the input pattern vector $\boldsymbol{U}_t$ was 10 and the NNs was (120-40-12-6) network. After the learning converged, we obtained an average recognition rate of 99.7% to the closed data and a rate of 92.3% to the open data. We carried out an experiment using motion data performed by two individuals, not including the individual used in the learning process. The recognition rates were very low. Since it was the first time for the individuals to do Tai Chi motions, their motions were not smooth, with both the trajectories and the velocities of their motions very different from those of the expert individual. By using this system, the skills of beginners or nonprofessionals in objective motions can be evaluated. It can be considered that this has the possibility of achieving skillful motion training systems.

7. Summary and Conclusions

This paper has proposed a new real-time method able to estimate 3D human body postures from trinocular images. The proposed method extracts feature points of the human body by applying an $L_t(s)$ curve analysis to contours of human silhouettes extracted from the three images. The feature points are extracted by using the subtraction images when self-occlusions occur in the human silhouettes. Dynamic compensation is carried out by the tracking of all feature points using the AR model, whose parameters are estimated through on-line processing by the Kalman filter. The 3D coordinates of the feature points are reconstructed by using the results estimated from the three images while considering the geometrical relationship between the three cameras. The proposed method is implemented on a personal computer and runs in real-time (17 frames/sec). Experimental results confirm both the feasibility and the effectiveness of the proposed method. An application example of the 3D human body posture estimation to a motion recognition system is presented and its possibility is confirmed.

References

[1] D. M. Gavrila and L. S. Davis. 3-d model-based tracking of humans in action: a multi-view approach. In *Proc. of IEEE CVPR'96*, pages 73–80, 1996.

[2] I. Haritaoglu, D. Harwood, and L. S. Davis. W4: Who? when? where? what? a real time system for detecting and tracking people. In *Proc. of 3rd IEEE Int. Conf. on FG'98*, pages 222–227, 1998.

[3] S. Iwasawa, J. Ohya, K. Takahashi, T. Sakaguchi, S. Kawato, K. Ebihara, and S. Morishima. Real-time, 3d estimation of human body postures from trinocular images. In *Proc. on IEEE Int. Workshop on mPeople*, pages 3–10, 1999.

[4] I. A. Kakadiaris and D. D. Metaxas. Three-dimentional human body model acquisition from multiple views. *Int. J. of Computer Vision*, 30(3):191–218, 1998.

[5] Y. Kameda, M. Minoh, and K. Ikeda. Three dimensional pose estimation of an articulated object from its silhouette image. In *Proc. of ACCV'93*, pages 612–615, 1993.

[6] M. K. Leung and Y. H. Yang. First sight: A human body outline labeling system. *IEEE Trans. on PAMI*, 17(4):359–377, 1995.

[7] K. Rohr. Incremental recognition of pedestrians from image sequences. In *Proc. of IEEE CVPR'93*, pages 8–13, 1993.

[8] K. Takahashi and J. Ohya. Comparison of neural-network-based pattern classification methods with application to human motion recognition. In *Proc. on 5th Int. Conf. on EANN'99*, pages 63–68, 1999.

[9] K. Takahashi, T. Sakaguchi, and J. Ohya. Real-time estimation of human body postures using kalman filter. In *Proc. on 8th Int. Workshop on RO-MAN'99*, pages 189–194, 1999.

[10] C. Wren, A. Azarbayejani, T. Darrel, and A. Pentland. Pfinder: Real-time tracking of the human body. *IEEE Trans. on PAMI*, 19(7):780–785, 1997.

[11] M. Yamamoto, T. Kondo, T. Yamagiwa, and K. Yamanaka. Skill recognition. In *Proc. of 3rd IEEE Int. Conf. on FG'98*, pages 604–609, 1998.

Using Head Movement to Recognize Activity *

Anant Madabhushi and J. K. Aggarwal
Computer and Vision Research Center
Department of Electrical and Computer Engineering
The University of Texas at Austin
Austin, TX 78712, USA
aggarwaljk@mail.utexas.edu

Abstract

This paper presents a methodology for automatically identifying human actions in either the frontal or the lateral view. By tracking the movement of the head of the subject over successive frames of a monocular grayscale image sequence, we recognize 12 different actions. The head is segmented automatically in each frame, and the feature vectors extracted. Input sequences captured from a fixed CCD camera are matched against stored models of actions. The system uses the nearest neighbor classifier to identify the test action.

1 Introduction

Human actions are extremely diverse, and to build a system that can be used to successfully identify any type of action is a challenging problem. Aggarwal and Cai [1], in their work on human motion, discuss the different approaches used in the recognition of human activities. Ayers and Shah [2] have developed a system that makes context-based decisions about the actions of people in a room. In [3], Davis and Bobick computed motion energy and motion history images, which were employed for recognition using template matching. Some researchers have attempted the full three-dimensional reconstruction of the human form from image sequences, presuming that such information is necessary to understand the action taking place [10]. Polana and Nelson [9] used low-level non-parametric representation to represent repetitive activity.

An interesting fact about human activity is the inherent similarity in the way actions are carried out. That is, people sit, stand, walk, bend down and get up in a more or less similar fashion. An important part of human activity recognition has to do with the tracking of body parts [6]. We have found that the head of the subject is more distinctive in defining human action than any other body part. For instance, in the standing up action, the head moves forward initially and then backward, while moving upward continuously as well. In our system, we recognize 12 different types of actions by constructing a feature vector, which is the difference in the centroid of the head over successive frames. Based on the best match between the test sequence and the training models, the system classifies the test sequence as one of the training sequences. In a preliminary implementation [8], a Bayesian framework was used to classify actions based on manual segmentation. Our present implementation uses a nearest neighbor framework with automatic segmentation for recognition.

*This research was supported in part by the Army Research Office under contracts DAAH04-95-1-0494 and DAAG55-98-1-0230, and by the Texas Higher Education Coordinating Board, Advanced Research Project 97-ARP-275.

2 Modeling and Classification

In this section we describe the various steps in modeling our system and our procedure for identifying the test sequences.

2.1 Extracting feature vectors

By modeling the movement of the head for each action, we have means of recognizing that action. To do this, we estimate the centroid of the head in each frame. These are given as $[x_1, y_1] \dots [x_{n+1}, y_{n+1}]$. The difference in coordinates over successive frames is given by $[Dx_k, Dy_k]$.

$$Dx_k = x_{k+1} - x_k \tag{1}$$

$$Dy_k = y_{k+1} - y_k \tag{2}$$

The feature vectors in our case are the difference in the centroid of the head over successive frames.

$$X = [Dx_1, Dx_2, \dots, Dx_n] \tag{3}$$

$$Y = [Dy_1, Dy_2, \dots, Dy_n] \tag{4}$$

where X and Y are the feature vectors for the difference in x and y coordinates of the centroid of the head respectively. Dx_k, Dy_k are not absolute differences, since we would not be able to distinguish between similar pairs of actions like getting up-bending down, sitting down-standing up and rising-squatting. Each of these pairs of actions are almost identical as far as the movement of the head is concerned, except that they proceed in opposite directions. Standing up, for instance, is the reverse of the sitting down action. Using absolute differences would have confused the system as to whether the action was standing up or sitting down.

1051-4651/00 $10.00 © 2000 IEEE

2.2 Nearest neighbor formulation

The nearest neighbor classifier is a useful classification system when the number of training samples is small [4]. The nearest neighbor classifier assigns the feature vectors $\{X, Y\}$ to the same class Ω_ω (where $\omega \in \{1, 2, \ldots, 12\}$) as the training feature vectors nearest to it in the feature space. The test sequence is assigned to the training class that satisfies equation 5.

$$\min_{\omega}\{\sum_{u=1}^{n} |Dx_u - Dx_{\omega u}| + \sum_{u=1}^{n} |Dy_u - Dy_{\omega u}|\} \quad (5)$$

Thus we compute the absolute difference of the elements of the input test feature vectors $\{Dx_u, Dy_u\}$ and the elements of the training feature vectors $\{Dx_{\omega u}, Dy_{\omega u}\}$ and sum these differences over all the frames. The test sequence is assigned the label of the training class for which this sum is the least.

3 Detection and Segmentation

The detection and segmentation of the head is central to the recognition algorithm. We model our system by estimating the centroid of the head in each frame. Many human activity recognition algorithms depend on efficient tracking of a moving body part [5, 6]. Similarly, in our case the entire recognition algorithm is based on reliably tracking the centroid of the head. In [11] Sirohey used an upright ellipse to find the head in grayscale images. In [5] the head was found using the assumption that it is the highest point on the silhouette of the body. Our system recognizes action sequences in which the head is in various positions. Further, during some actions like the bending down action, the head is lower than the back. To overcome the above constraints we combine two motion-based segmentation techniques to find the head in each frame.

3.1 Frame Differencing

Motion is a strong cue that can aid segmentation [7]. We apply successive frame differencing to segment the head from the rest of the scene. By assuming that the background does not change over successive frames, we isolate only those objects that are moving.

$$\Delta I = |I_t - I_{t+1}| \quad (6)$$

where ΔI is the absolute difference of the t and the $t+1$ frames. Successive frame differencing allows us to exploit the fact that, for most actions, the head is the most mobile part of the body. In several action sequences, the head appears as the largest blob in the binarized difference image. After differencing, we perform connected component labelling and region removal to get rid of the smaller blobs. To identify the blobs belonging to the head, we use the important observation that the head is always at the extreme end of the body, if not at the highest point. Since there are no moving objects in the background, we can assume that the blob corresponding to the head contains pixels that are either at the top of the frame or at an extreme end of the frame. By retaining the blobs that contain pixels belonging to the leftmost column and the top row in the frame, we reduce the number of blobs that could be the head to two. The centroid of the blob is computed as the average of the position of all the pixels in it.

$$i_{fd} = \begin{bmatrix} i_{fd11} & i_{fd21} \\ \vdots & \vdots \\ i_{fd1n} & i_{fd2n} \end{bmatrix}; j_{fd} = \begin{bmatrix} j_{fd11} & j_{fd21} \\ \vdots & \vdots \\ j_{fd1n} & j_{fd2n} \end{bmatrix} \quad (7)$$

where i_{fd} and j_{fd} are the x and y coordinates of the centroids of the two blobs for all frames of an action sequence. The symbol fd refers to frame differencing. The first digit in the subscript refers to the blob number and the second refers to the frame number. Hence i_{fd13} refers to the x coordinate of the centroid of blob 1 in the third frame of the sequence. If there is only one blob in the third frame, then both i_{fd23} and j_{fd23} will be zero. Since we are differencing successive frames, both blobs may represent the head. In figure 1, (a) and (b) represent consecutive frames of the same sitting down sequence. The differenced image, after connected component labeling and region removal, contains two blobs. We see from 1(c) that both blobs, albeit unconnected, belong to the head. Sometimes, the two blobs may correspond to different body parts. We need to identify the blob belonging to the head. For frames that have two blobs, we compute the distance between their centroids and determine whether it is less than a threshold. This threshold is based on the average size of the blobs over all frames of the sequence. If the distance between the centroids of the two blobs is less than the threshold, the two blobs are regarded as being one, otherwise they are considered to be two separate blobs. However, if the two blobs are separate, we do not know which blob is the head. We use a background subtraction technique to identify the blob belonging to the head.

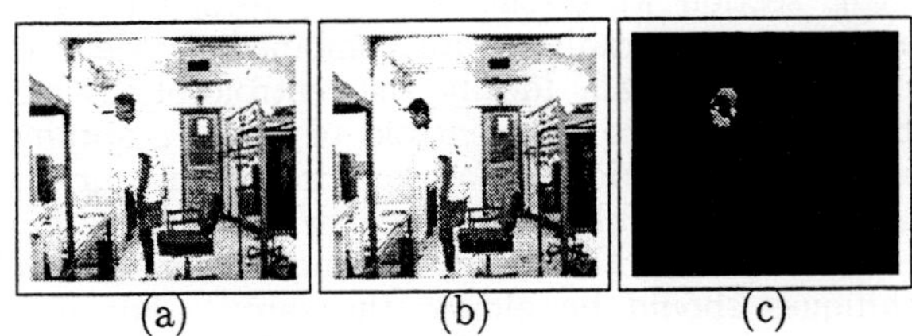

Figure 1: (a) First frame and (b) Second frame of action sequence (c) Filtered difference image.

3.2 Background subtraction

We use background subtraction to remove the slowly varying background gray levels in each frame, and median filtering to reconstruct the background [5]. We then subtract the background image from every frame in the sequence.

$$I_{sub} = |I_{bs} - I_{or}| \quad (8)$$

where I_{sub} is the background subtracted image, I_{bs} is the reconstructed background image and I_{or} is the original image from the action sequence. To the subtracted image, we apply the preprocessing techniques mentioned in section 3.1 to retain only one or two blobs. In figure 2 we see (a) the reconstructed background, (b) an individual frame in the sequence, and (c) the result of background subtraction. The centriods of the blobs are computed as in section 3.1 and given as:

$$i_{bs} = \begin{bmatrix} i_{bs11} & i_{bs21} \\ \vdots & \vdots \\ i_{bs1n} & i_{bs2n} \end{bmatrix} ; j_{bs} = \begin{bmatrix} j_{bs11} & j_{bs21} \\ \vdots & \vdots \\ j_{bs1n} & j_{bs2n} \end{bmatrix} \quad (9)$$

where i_{bs} and j_{bs} are the x and y coordinates of the centroids of the two blobs for all frames of an action sequence. The symbol bs refers to the background subtraction technique. The numbers in the subscripts have the same meaning as in section 3.1.

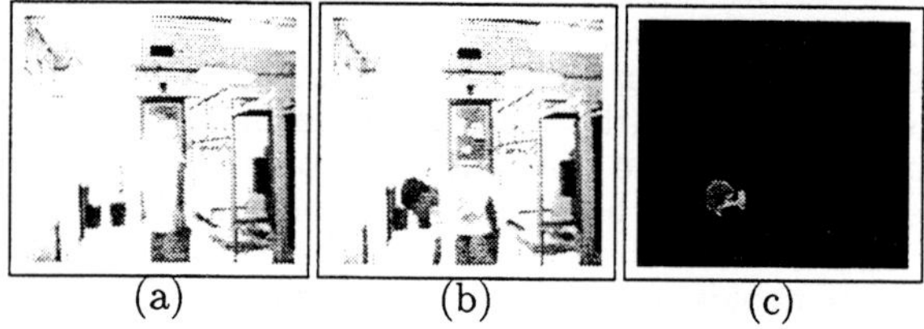

Figure 2: (a) Reconstructed background using median filtering (b) A frame of the action sequence (c) Segmented result of background subtraction.

3.3 Integrating the two paradigms

In this section we discuss how the results obtained from the two paradigms are combined to yield the centroid of the head. Ideally, the centroid of the head should be equal to the centroid of blob 1, obtained from the two techniques. For those frames in which the head was successfully segmented by both paradigms, the centroids of the head obtained from the two techniques should be almost the same. For every frame, we compute the difference of the x coordinate of the centroid of blob 1 for both paradigms. If this difference is less than a threshold (λ), the centroid of the head is the centroid of blob 1 of the background subtraction technique. If this is not so, we check to see if the second blob from the background differencing technique is present. If it is, we compute the difference between the x coordinate of the centroid of blob 1 obtained by frame differencing and the x coordinate of the centroid of blob 2 obtained by background subtraction. If this difference is greater than a threshold (α) or if the second blob in the background subtraction technique is absent, we compare the x coordinate of the centroid of blob 1 in the current frame with it's counterpart in the next frame for both paradigms. The centroid of the head is determined to be the centroid of blob 1 obtained from the technique that has a smaller difference. We observed that a variation in the x coordinate of the centroid of the blobs was accompanied by a similar variation in the y coordinate of the centroid. Hence we only considered i_{bs}, i_{fd} in our algorithm. The flowchart in figure 3 describes the algorithm we use to identify the blob that belongs to the head. Di_{bs1}, Di_{fd1} are the differences in x coordinates of the centroid of blob 1 over two successive frames, for the two paradigms. The subscripts 1 and 2 refer to the two blobs.

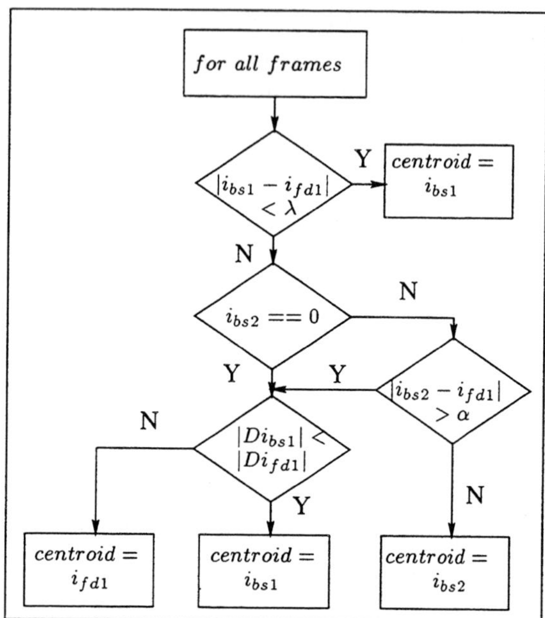

Figure 3: Algorithm used to resolve centroid of head.

4 System Implementation

A fixed CCD camera with a wide field of view working at 2 frames/sec was used to obtain the sequences. We used 36 training sequences, i.e. 3 training sequences for each class. People of diverse physical sizes were used to model the actions. The system detects the head of the subject in each frame and extracts the feature vectors. The test sequence is matched against stored models of different actions. The test sequence is identified as the training sequence to which it is closest. The subjects performed the actions at a comfortable pace. We assumed that each action was performed in roughly five seconds. We found that on average, ten frames were required to completely describe an action, i.e. n had the value 9. Most of the test sequences were performed at this frequency, although we also tested our model successfully on action sequences having 5, 6 and 7 frames. For an input sequence that has only five frames, we select alternate elements of the training feature vector.

5 Conclusion

In this paper, we have presented a system that can accurately recognize 12 actions using only the movement of the head. The system is robust for subjects of varying heights and weights. Unlike other head segmentation techniques, our approach does not make any assumptions about the position of the head in the frame [5, 11]. Further, the segmentation is robust to background clutter. Figure 4 shows five frames of the getting up sequence. Figures 5 and 6 show the results of background subtraction and frame differencing respectively. Of the 41 sequences that the system was tested on, 34 were correctly identified, giving us a classification rate of 83%. Table 1 gives the classification results of the individual action sequences. FV refers to the frontal view.

At this point, we have not been able to model and test all of the actions in [8] due to the problem of self occlusion for some actions in the frontal view. Further, the system is sensitive to the duration of the action and can only recognize sequences for frame rates in the vicinity of 2 frames/sec. This problem could be handled by increasing the dimensionality of the feature vectors. We also intend to normalize the feature vectors to make the system independent of the distance between the subject and the camera. Finally, the system can recognize only actions that involve head movement.

Type of Sequence	Total Number	Correctly Classified	Success Percent
Standing up	3	2	67
Sitting down	3	3	100
Bending down	4	3	75
Getting up	4	4	100
Walking	3	3	100
Rising (FV)	3	3	100
Rising	5	5	100
Squatting	3	2	67
Squatting (FV)	3	2	67
Side bend	3	2	67
Side bend (FV)	4	3	75
Hugging	3	2	67

Table 1: Classification of individual sequences

References

[1] J. K. Aggarwal and Qin Cai. Human motion analysis: A review. *Computer Vision and Image Understanding*, pages 428–440, 1998.

[2] Douglas Ayers and Mubarak Shah. Recognizing human action in a static room. *In Proceedings Computer Vision and Pattern Recognition*, pages 42–46, 1998.

[3] James Davis and Aaron Bobick. The representation and recognition of action using temporal plates. *In Proceedings Computer Vision and Pattern Recognition*, pages 928–934, 1997.

[4] R. O. Duda and P. E. Hart. *Pattern Classification and Scene Analysis*. New York Wiley, 1973.

[5] I. Haritaoglu, D. Harwood, and L.S Davis. Hydra: Multiple people detection and tracking using silhouettes. *IEEE Workshop on Visual Surveillance*, pages 6–13, 1999.

[6] Stephen S. Intille, James Davis, and Aaron Bobick. Real time closed world tracking. *In Proceedings IEEE International Conference on Computer Vision and Pattern Recognition*, pages 697–703, 1997.

[7] R. Jain, W.N. Martin, and J.K. Aggarwal. Segmentation through the detection of changes due to motion. *In Proceedings of Computer Graphics and Image Processing*, 11:13–34, 1979.

[8] Anant Madabhushi and J.K. Aggarwal. A Bayesian approach to human activity recognition. *IEEE Workshop on Visual Surveillance*, pages 25–32, 1999.

[9] R. Polana and R. Nelson. Detection and recognition of periodic, nonrigid motion. *International Journal of Computer Vision*, pages 261–282, 1997.

[10] J. Rehg and T. Kanade. Model based tracking of self-occluding articulated objects. *Proceedings of the 5th International Conference on Computer Vision*, pages 612–617, 1995.

[11] Saad Ahmed Sirohey. Human face segmentation and identification. Master's thesis, University of Maryland, 1993.

Figure 4: Frames of the getting up sequence

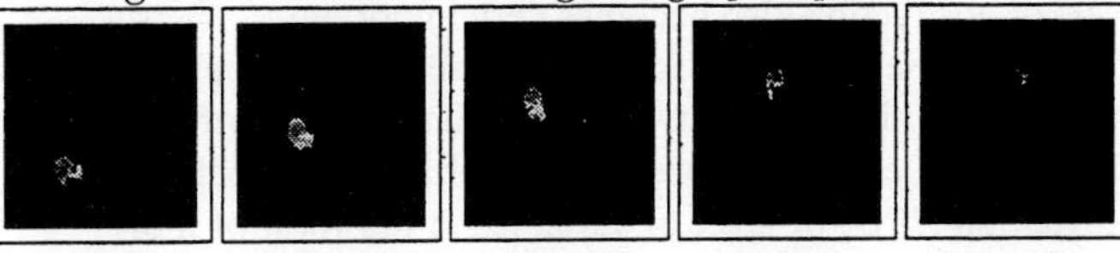

Figure 5: Frames after background subtraction

Figure 6: Frames after frame differencing

A Probabilistic Framework for Tracking in Wide-Area Environments

Hung H. Bui, Svetha Venkatesh and Geoff West
Department of Computer Science
Curtin University of Technology
Perth, WA 6001, Australia
{buihh, svetha, geoff}@cs.curtin.edu.au

Abstract

Surveillance in wide-area spatial environments is characterised by complex spatial layouts, large state space, and the use of multiple cameras/sensors. To solve this problem, there is a need for representing the dynamic and noisy data in the tracking tasks, and dealing with them at different levels of detail. This requirement is particularly suited to the Layered Dynamic Probabilistic Network (LDPN), a special type of Dynamic Probabilistic Network (DPN). In this paper, we propose the use of LDPN as the integrated framework for tracking in wide-area environments. We illustrate, with the help of a synthetic tracking scenario, how the parameters of the LDPN can be estimated from training data, and then used to draw predictions and answer queries about unseen tracks at various levels of detail.

1 Introduction

Surveillance in wide-area spatial environments is characterised by complex spatial layouts, large state space, and the use of multiple cameras/sensors. In dealing with a wide-area spatial environment, in addition to the ability to handle the dynamics and uncertainty of the environment, the ability to process information about the environment at various levels of abstraction also becomes very important.

Bayesian networks [7] is a well-established framework for dealing with uncertainty. A Bayesian network offers a graphical and compact representation of a joint probability distribution (JPD) of a set of variables in the form of a directed acyclic graph. The links from the parents to a particular node represent the causal dependency, and are parameterised by the conditional probability of the variable of the current node given the parent variables. For applications that need to deal with the temporal dynamics of the environment, the Dynamic Probabilistic Network (DPN) [4, 9] is a special Bayesian network architecture for representing the evolution of the domain variables over time. A DPN consists of a sequence of time-slices where each time-slice contains a set of variables representing the state of the environment at the current time, and the causal links from the current time-slice to the next represent the environment dynamics. A special case of the DPN where, in each time-slice, there is only a single state variable and an observation node, is the well-known hidden Markov model (HMM) [11]. Given the current set of observations, various inference techniques on the DPN can be used to make predictions about the future state variables (predicting), or about the unobserved variables in the past (smoothing) [8].

A number of applications of Bayesian networks in dealing with noisy data in spatio-temporal domains include monitoring and surveillance of traffic scenes [3, 6, 5], tracking human movement and group behaviours [10], recognising and classifying human gestures [1]. In all these applications, the domains are locally restricted, e.g. only a single room or a single ground space region is considered. Thus, the need for dealing with different levels of detail does not arise.

In this paper, we propose the use of the Layered Dynamic Probabilistic Network (LDPN) [2], a special type of the Dynamic Probabilistic Network, as an integrated probabilistic framework for tracking in wide-area environments. The LDPN can represent and handle uncertain spatial data at different levels of abstraction, thus is particularly suited for this task. We illustrate, with the help of a synthetic tracking scenario, how the parameters of the LDPN can be estimated from training data, and then used to draw predictions and answer queries about unseen tracks at various levels of detail.

2 The LDPN

The LDPN has a layered architecture (Fig. 1) that explicitly encodes the hierarchy of connected spatial locations in the environment. The layers in the LDPN correspond to paths through the environment at various levels of detail: the bottom layer represents the path at the coordinate level, and the intermediate layers represent a sequence of destinations (goals) that an agent is following at different levels of abstraction. For example, in a building environment, an agent's path can be examined at the coordinate level, at

1051-4651/00 $10.00

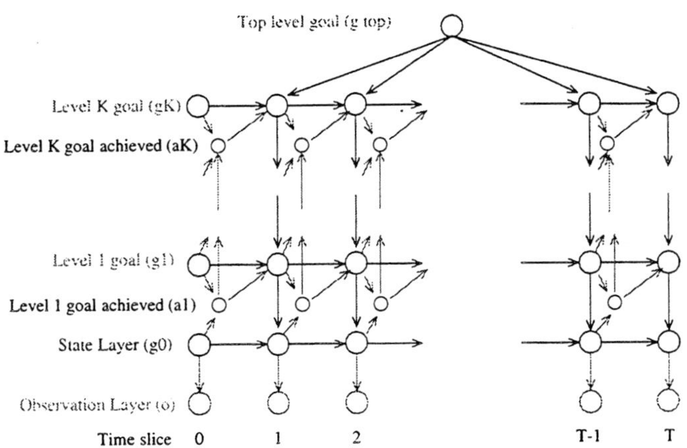

Figure 1. The LDPN model

the door-to-door level (sequence of doors that the agent is going through), or at the floor-to-floor level (sequence of staircases and lifts), etc.

A sequence of destinations can be viewed as a plan (sequence of sub-goals) that an agent is following. While the agent executes this plan, the current sub-goal determines how the sequence of sub-goals at the lower level would evolve. This type of *evolution influence* is encoded by the conditional transition probabilities from the previous sub-goal to the current sub-goal, given the value of the current goal at the layer above. The achievement of the current sub-goal also determines if the sub-goal at the higher level is also achieved. This type of *persistence influence* is encoded by the conditional probabilities that the sub-goal at the higher level is achieved given the current sub-goal is achieved.

The evolution transition matrix needs only be specified for the set of sub-goals in the vicinity of the current goal. For example, at the coordinate level, we only have to specify the evolution transition matrix within each room, assuming the room door(s) as the destination(s). At the door-to-door level, the transition matrix is specified between the set of doors in the same floor, assuming the floor exit(s) as the destinations. Thus, the partition of the environment into a hierarchy of smaller regions helps reduce the size of the evolution parameters, and makes the LDPN model scalable to large spatial environments.

Given a set of observations about the path at the coordinate level, the LDPN can be used to draw predictions of how the paths at different levels of detail would evolve in the future. In the next section, we illustrate the use of the LDPN model and its inference scheme described in [2] via a synthetic tracking problem in a complex spatial environment.

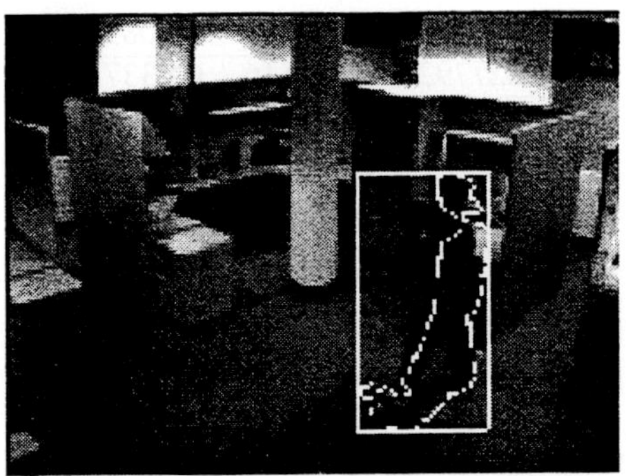

Figure 2. A typical room

3 Experiments and Results

The task involves tracking the movement of an object through a building consisting of 8 connected rooms (Fig. 4). Each room is modelled by a set of cells on a square grid. The four entrances to the building are labelled north (N), west (W), south (S) and east (E). In addition, the door in the center of the building (C) acts like an entrance between the building north wing and south wing.

The hierarchy of this spatial environment is constructed as follows. The state level (level 0) consists of the set of cells in all the rooms. Level 1 consists of the set of all doors and entrances. Level 2 consists of the set building entrances and the wing entrance (N, W, S, E, C). The top level (level 3) consists of only the four entrances to the building. Based on this hierarchy, a LDPN network is constructed that has four layers corresponding to the four levels of the hierarchy, together with an observation layer to handle the noisy observation data.

3.1 LDPN parameters acquisition

Before tracking can be carried out, the parameters of the LDPN needs to be specified.

The LDPN transition probabilities at the coordinate level and and observation model can be learned in each individual room separately using the standard method for HMM parameter re-estimation [11]. We assume that the all the rooms are identical, and perform this parameters re-estimation step with real data for the room shown in Fig. 2. A tracking module using background subtraction returns a noisy sequence of coordinates of the moving object (human). The object movement model and the camera observation (noise) model are then re-estimated using 20 such sequences. The resulting movement and observation model are shown in Fig. 3. The observation model contains the probability that the cell occupied by the agent will be observed as one of the cells in the 3×3 neighbourhood mask (Fig. 3(a)). Since the camera is looking at the room from the bottom left corner, we notice that the errors tend to spread

0.000000	0.004424	0.008549
0.027792	0.874516	0.033721
0.011796	0.039203	0.000000

(a) Observation model

0.000000	0.418944	0.000000
0.021860	0.538762	0.012991
0.000000	0.007443	0.000000

(b) Movement model

Figure 3. The movement and observation model

in the South-West to North-East direction. The movement model contains the probability that, given a destination in the front direction, the agent will move to the front, left, right, back cell, or stay in the same cell (Fig. 3(b) – note that the model in the figure has been oriented so that the front direction is pointing upward).

The parameters of the LDPN at the higher levels are simply the frequency that an object from one door, will move to one of the adjacent doors. In this experiment, for simplicity we specify these probabilities manually, but they can be easily recorded in a real scenario.

3.2 Tracking and predicting with LDPN

To simulate the tracking task, the structure and parameters of the LDPN are used to generate a random sequence of cells at the bottom level of the hierarchy to simulate the observation of an agent's path. Fig. 4 shows an example of a generated path (prior to being corrupted by noise from the observation model) entering the building via the West entrance and exiting the building via the East entrance. The number shown next to a position on the track represents the time when the agent is at that position.

With this set of generated observation points as input data, we run the LDPN inference algorithm to answer queries about the tracked object. At each time-slice, we look at three queries at different levels of abstraction: (1) which main entrance the object is heading to, (2) which room the object is currently in, and (3) which nearest door/entrance the agent is currently heading towards. The scope of the first query is the entire environment, whereas the scope of the other two queries is limited to the immediate surroundings of the current position of the tracked object. The answer to the first query is a probability distribution on the set of four building exits N, S, E, W; this is obtained by computing the conditional probability of the top-level goal node in the LDPN structure given the past sequence of observations. The answer to the second query is a probability distribution on the set of rooms $0, 1, \ldots, 7$; this is obtained by computing the conditional distribution of the current coordinate-level node in the LDPN. The answer to

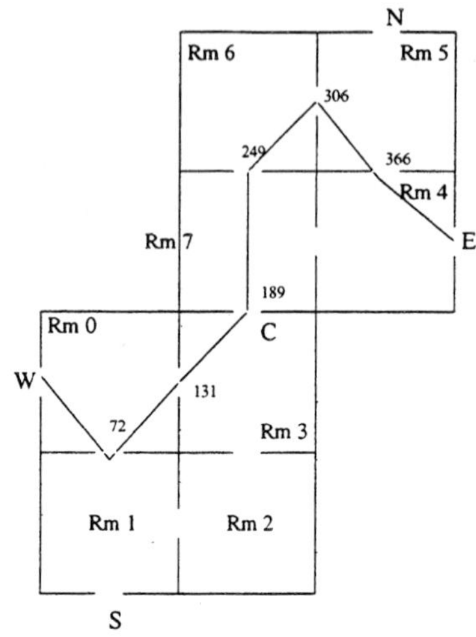

Figure 4. Synthetic track through the building

the third query is a probability distribution on the set of all doors and entrances; this is obtained from the conditional probability of the level-1 goal node.

The probabilities obtained for the first query are plotted in Fig. 5. The result shows the probabilities that the agent will exit the building via the three exits S, E, and N over time. Initially, the probabilities are the same. After the agent moves away from room 1 at time 72, $\Pr(S)$ starts to decrease. When the agent enters room 7 at time 189, $\Pr(S)$ drops to zero. At the same time, $\Pr(N)$ becomes greater than $\Pr(E)$. However, as the agent enters room 5 at time 306, $\Pr(E)$ becomes dominant as expected.

The results obtained from the second and third queries are plotted in Fig. 6 (a) and (b). Note that since there are many rooms and doors, we only plot the probabilities for room 0, 1 and 3 in Fig. 6(a), and the probabilities for the three doors exiting from room 0 (left, right, back) in Fig. 6(b).

Fig. 6(a) shows that from around time 70 to time 75, the object briefly enters room 1 from room 0, and then comes back to room 0. From around time 130, the object enters room 3 from room 0.

Fig. 6(b) shows the probabilities of the different doors that the object uses to exit from room 0. From time 0 to time 70, the object exits from room 0 via the back-door, and from time 70 to 130, the object exits from room 0 via the right-door.

4 Conclusion

In this paper, we have demonstrated the use of the LDPN for tracking object movement in a wide-area environment. We have shown that the LDPN can represent uncertain data in spatial domains and deal with them at different levels of detail.

By dividing the environment into regions corresponding to vicinities of the locations at the next higher level, the transition probabilities need only be specified at the vicinity surrounding each destination, thus making the size of the transition probability tables relatively constant and the LDPN model scalable to wide-area environments. Due to this hierarchal decomposition, the parameters of the LDPN can also be estimated separately for each region, simplifying the model acquisition step.

In our future work, we plan to deploy a system for tracking throughout an entire building area. Another possibility is to investigate coupled LDPNs for modelling group behaviours. Since the intermediate sub-goals are explicitly represented in the LDPN, a group behaviour can be specified by coupling some of these individual goals together.

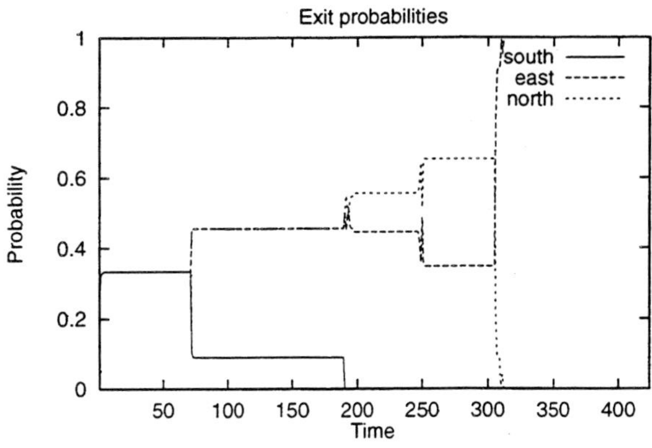

Figure 5. Result of the exit query

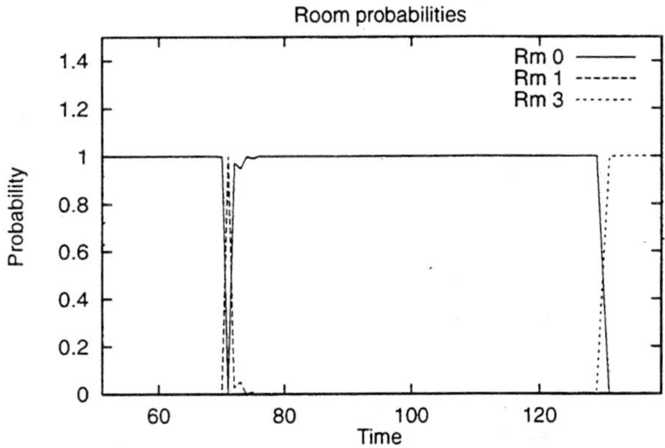

(a) Probabilities that the agent is at Room 0, 1, and 3

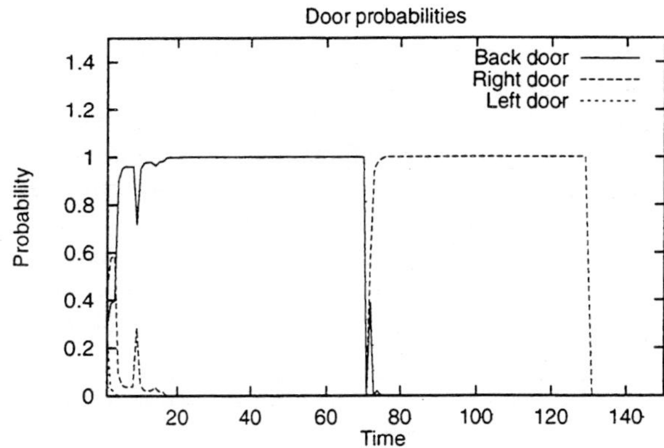

(b) Probabilities that the agent is exiting Room 0 via different doors

Figure 6. Results of the room and door queries

References

[1] M. Brand, N. Oliver, and A. Pentland. Coupled hidden Markov models for complex action recognition. In *IEEE Conference on Computer Vision and Pattern Recognition*, 1997.

[2] H. H. Bui, S. Venkatesh, and G. West. Layered dynamic Bayesian networks for spatio-temporal modelling. *Intelligent Data Analysis*, 3(5):339–361, 1999.

[3] H. Buxton and S. Gong. Advanced visual surveillance using Bayesian networks. In *Proceedings of the IEEE International Conference on Computer Vision*, 1995.

[4] T. Dean and K. Kanazawa. A model for reasoning about persistence and causation. *Computational Intelligence*, 5(3):142–150, 1989.

[5] R. Fraile and S. J. Maybank. Vehicle trajectory approximation and classification. In *Proceedings of the British Machine Vision Conference*, 1998.

[6] T. Huang, D. Koller, J. Malik, G. Ogasawara, B. Rao, S. Russell, and J. Weber. Automatic symbolic traffic scene analysis using belief networks. In *Proceedings of the National Conference on Artificial Intelligence (AAAI-94)*, 1994.

[7] F. Jensen. *An Introduction to Bayesian Networks*. Springer, 1996.

[8] U. Kjaerulff. A computational scheme for reasoning in dynamic probabilistic networks. In *Proceedings of the Eighth Annual Conference on Uncertainty in Artificial Intelligence*, pages 121–129, 1992.

[9] A. E. Nicholson and J. M. Brady. The data association problem when monitoring robot vehicles using dynamic belief networks. In *Proceedings of the Tenth European Conference on Artificial Intelligence*, pages 689–693, 1992.

[10] N. Oliver, B. Rosario, and A. Pentland. A Bayesian computer vision system for modeling human interactions. In *Proceedings ICVS-99*, 1999.

[11] L. R. Rabiner. A tutorial on Hidden Markov Models and selected applications in speech recognition. *Proceedings of the IEEE*, 77(2):257–286, 1989.

Active tracking based on Hausdorff matching

Victor Ayala-Ramirez * Carlos Parra † Michel Devy ‡
LAAS-CNRS
7, Av. du Col. Roche
31077 Toulouse Cedex 4, FRANCE
{ayala, michel}@laas.fr
cparra@venus.javeriana.edu.co

Abstract

We present an objet tracking system based on an edge model for the target characterization. The target position is estimated by looking for the model in the current image using a Hausdorff partial distance. Target is searched only in a sub-window of current edge image. Its boundaries are determined by a Kalman filter estimation that uses target dynamics to predict current position. We use a spiral searching strategy to find the actual position. The target model is updated in each iteration by using unidirectional partial distance from the image to the model. This model is refined by an enclosure operator in order to perform the target/ background discrimination. The parameters of our system can be modified in an active way along the tracking task. The system has shown to be robust to illumination changes and to pose variations. The system has been also embedded in a mobile robot for personal robotics applications and integrated in a real-time OS (3 Hz).

1. Introduction

This paper concerns a system approach for the design of an active tracking function. We aim to develop a general method which could integrate active perception [1, 3, 10]. Sensor and algorithm parameters are controlled in order to improve the performance of the target tracking task. Some recent works use Hausdorff matching [5, 9] for tracking but in a passive way. We present here a way to do active tracking using this same Hausdorff distance.

Our system is able to track an object in an image sequence in the case of a sensor motion or of an object motion. This system is based on the assumption that the 3D motion of the sensor or of the object can be characterized by using only a 2D representation. Figure 1 shows the block diagram of an active tracking system.

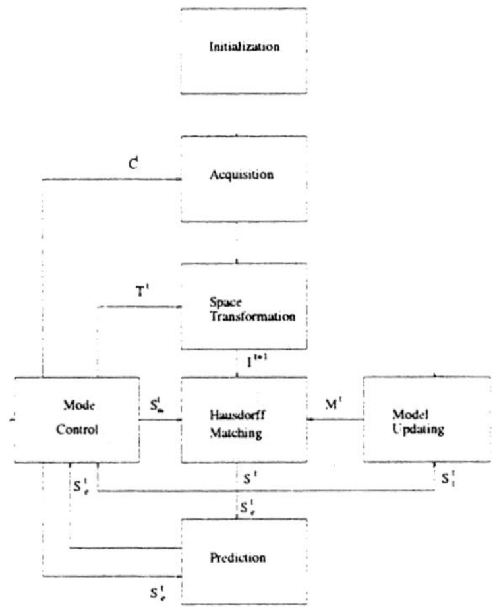

Figure 1. Block diagram of the tracking system.

The initialization process is executed only at the beginning or after the detection of a lack of consistency by a supervision in a higher level. The first step of the tracking process is the selection of a target to track. At this moment, the target is chosen in an interactive way at the start of the sequence. We do not have an *a priori* model of this target. It's characterized with its edge image as described below. We proceed then to search for it in the current image. This search is performed only in an image region the limits of which are given by the variance of a linear estimation process. Time to locate the target is also reduced by a spiral search strategy described below. Hausdorff matching is used to measure similarity between the model and the possible target instances in the current image. This matching is

*The work of V. Ayala-Ramirez is supported by a Mexico's CONACYT grant. His permanent address is: Universidad de Guanajuato (F.I.M.E.E.), Apdo. Postal 215-A, Salamanca, Mexico.

†The permanent address of C. Parra is: Universidad Javeriana, Carrera 7a. No. 40-62, Bogotá, Colombia.

‡This work has been partially supported by the ECOS-Nord action No. M99M01.

performed in the edge image space.

We update the model using the bidirectional partial Hausdorff distance to have a model that reflects current pose of the target. Position of the found target is input to a linear estimation process using a Kalman filter to guide the target localization in the next iteration of the tracking process. Prediction is also used to guide the space transformation to be performed in the next image in order to get the edge image necessary to Hausdorff matching. A mode controller is used to control the active behavior of the tracking process including sensor and algorithm parameter control. These controller actions will be detailed below.

2. Systems components

2.1. Hausdorff matching

The tracking is done using a comparison between an image and a model. The model and the image are binary elements extracted from a sequence of gray level images using an edge detector similar to [4].

A partial Hausdorff distance is used as a resemblance measurement between the target model and its presumed position in an image.

Given two sets of points P and Q, the Hausdorff distance is defined as [11]:

$$H(P,Q) = \max(h(P,Q), h(Q,P))$$

where

$$h(P,Q) = \max_{p\in P}\min_{q\in Q} \| p - q \|$$

and $\| \cdot \|$ is a given distance between two points p and q. The function $h(P,Q)$ (distance from set P to Q) is a measure of the degree in which each point in P is near to some point in Q. The Hausdorff distance is the maximum among $h(P,Q)$ and $h(Q,P)$.

By computing the Hausdorff distance in this way we obtain the most mismatched point between the two shapes compared; consequently, it is very sensitive to the presence of any outlying points. For that reason it is often appropriate to use a more general rank order measure, which replaces the maximization operation with a rank operation. This measure (partial distance) is defined as [6]:

$$h_k = K^{th}_{p\in P} \min_{q\in Q} \| p - q \|$$

where $K^{th}_{p\in P} f(p)$ denotes the K^{-th} ranked value of $f(p)$ over the set P.

2.2. Motion estimation for the target and the sensor

The first task to accomplish is to define the position of the model M^t in the next image I^{t+1} of the sequence. The search for the model in the image (or image's region) is done in some selected direction. The unidirectional partial distance is required from the model to the image to achieve this first step.

The minimum value of $h_k(M^t, I^{t+1})$ identifies the best "position" of M^t in I^{t+1}, under the action of some group of translations G. It is possible also to identify the set of translations of M^t such that $h_k(M^t, I^{t+1})$ is no larger than some value τ, in this case there may be multiple translations that have essentially the same quality [7].

However, rather than computing the single translation giving the minimum distance or the set of translations, such that its correspond h_k is no larger than τ, it is possible to find the first translation, such that its associated h_k is no larger than τ, for a given search direction.

Although the first translation which $h_k(M^t, I^{t+1})$ associated is less than τ it is not necessarily the best one, whether τ is small, the translation should be quite good. This is better than computing all the set of valuable translation, whereas the computing time is significantly minor.

2.3. Model refinement

Model refinement is used at every iteration to update the current model and to be able to track objects even if its pose changes. We use two mechanisms to refine the model: Firstly, we compute the unidirectional Hausdorff partial distance from the detected model in current image to the previous model.

Then we use the notion of enclosure [8] to affine more the model. This notion let us to separe more efficiently the target model from background edges that could be added in a parasitic way to it.

We apply an increasing size annular operator of unitary width relative to the center of the target model, and we look in a set of n orientation intervals θ_i with $\theta_i \in [\frac{2\pi i}{n}, \frac{2\pi(i+1)}{n})$ for edges parallel (within a tolerance) to the given annular sector. We compute then the angular extent $\alpha_i(r)$ of these edges, and we take the minimum enclosing radius r_i for every orientation θ_i as follows:

$$r_i = \min \{r_j | \alpha_i(r_j) > k\frac{2\pi}{n}\}$$

With $k \in [0,1]$, a fixed threshold. For each orientation θ_i, we keep the edges inside the minimum enclosing radius conserve r_i. This operation depends critically on the nature of the target and so, it can be spawn or not by the mode controller.

2.4. Target localization strategies

Target searching strategy is very important in order to reduce the searching time and to take advantage of the prediction of target position.

a) 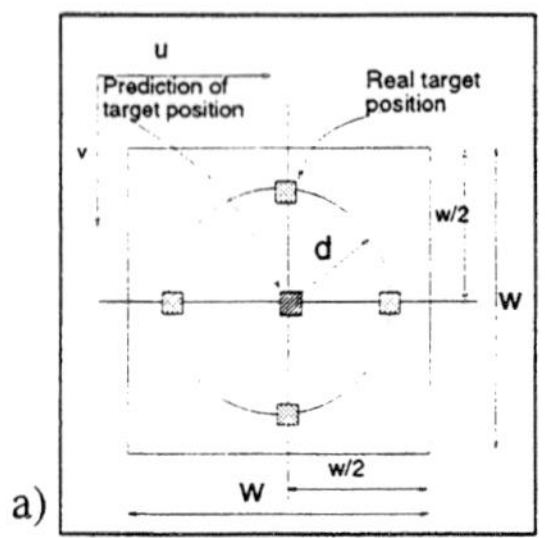

b) 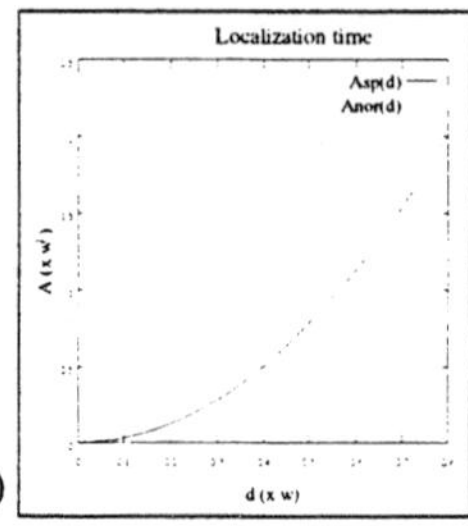

Figure 2. a) Target offset respect to the predicted position b)Target localization time by different search strategies.

The easier strategy used to search for the target is to do a top-down left-right search in a region of the current image. We propose a spiral search centered on the predicted position of the target. This strategy is more efficient than the top-down left-right strategy in most of cases. Execution time for a search window size for both strategies is shown in figure 2.

Spiral search locates target faster when the target has moved up to $\frac{1}{\sqrt{2\pi}}w$ with w being the size of the search window. Time to localization (A) is shown as a function of area swept before finding the target. $A_{sp}(d)$ represents the time used for the spiral search to find the target and $A_{nor}(d)$ the figure for the top-down left-right strategy

2.5. Mode control for sensor and algorithms

An active tracking formulation has to include the controllable parameters (sensor and algorithm parameters) of this process. We formulate our active tracking problem as follows:

In order to control our system in an active way, we need to have representations of sensor and algorithms states.

The sensor configuration at iteration i is denoted by C^i. C^i is a vector consisting of the different controllable parameter of the sensors, for example, tilt and pan position, gain, focus and zoom settings.

Given that we use a model representation distinct to the raw image acquired by our sensor, we can control also the way we extract the features from our acquired images. The parameters for this process are joined in a vector T^i.

Current state of the algorithm is defined by S^i. S^i is a composed structure of S^i_t, the target description parameters; S^i_c, the target estimation parameters; and S^i_m, the set of configurable parameters affecting the matching process.

At instant i, we want to locate the model M^{i-1} in an image I^i using a set of parameters representing current state of the tracking algorithm (i.e. S^{i-1}, C^{i-1} and T^{i-1}). Then we update the model (M^i) and the next state for the active controlled variables.

The mode controller has to control the active behavior of the tracking system including sensor and algorithm parameters (C^i, T^i and S^i_m). Some tasks performed by this module are:

- Control sensor gain in the acquisition stage to keep an appropiate number of edge points in an illumination changing environment.
- Modify sensor orientation to point always towards the target.
- Control of matching parameters in order to adapt to the nature of different tracked targets and to the nature of different environments where the target is going to evolve. For exemple, to adapt the threshold of the edge finding algorithms according to an outdoor/indoor environment.
- Update the linear estimation process according to changes in sensor configuration.

3. Results and Discussion

The tracking method was implemented in C on a real-time operating system (VxWorks) on board of a mobile robot, the computation running time is dependent on the region size examined to obtain the new target position. For sequences the code is capable of processing frames at a rate of about 3 Hz (with a model size of about 30x30 pixels and a search region of about 80x80 pixels) . In this case only a small region of the image is examined given that the new target position will lie within a vicinity of the previous one. Processing includes, edge detection, target localization, and model updating for a video image of (256x256 pixels).

Figures 3 shows an example of the tracking process. Figure 3 a) shows initial target selection, in this case the user specifies a rectangle in the frame that contains the target. In this sequence, our target corresponds to a poster that the robot tracks during its motion. An automatic target selection is possible by using other informations of the scene. In Figure 3 b),c) we show some frames of a processed sequence; we can see target localization and search region windows. Figure 3 d) shows the tracking of a poster through an image sequence. The poster chosen as target is marked in the figure with a boundary box. In these images the region being examined is estimated with a Kalman filter. Another larger boundary box is used to delineate the region of examination. The objective is to show the capacity of the method to identify a poster among the set of elements of the scene.

We have tested the robustness of our system with the following experimental set-up: We control a pan and tilt controllable camera to follow a circular path. We take a fixed object as our target. We can have a ground-truth estimation for image motion of the target in the image. We compare this ground-truth against the image motion computed by our system. Error in estimation is small as we can see in Figure 3 d).

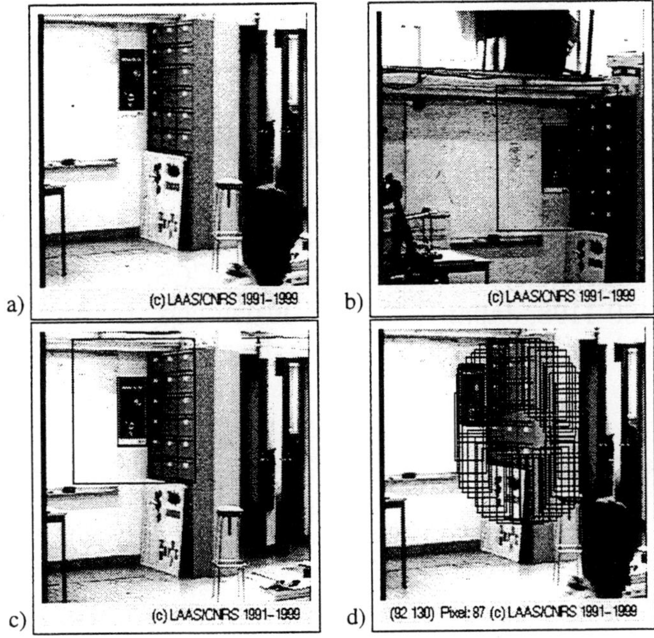

Figure 3. Tracking of a target with our tracking system implemented on an Hilare 2 bis robot. In a) the first image, in b) an intermediate frame, in c) the last frame of the test and in d) the target position along the test.

We have also used the system with images acquired in natural environments, that why we claim our system as a general one [9]. We do not show these images in the sake of space.

4. Conclusions and future work

We have shown the formalization of a general tracking system. Main characteristics of this system are: its active behavior for adaptation to changing environments and to different target characteristics. The system has also been implemented in a real time operating system.

We need to work more in the decoupling of sensor and algorithm modes, an inherent difficulty in active systems, to control more efficiently the tracking behavior.

The system has shown to be robust enough to be used in mobile robotics applications.

We will also work towards the integration with a 3-D relocalization method for mobile robots in indoor/outdoor applications[2].

References

[1] J. Aloimonos. Purposive and qualitative active vision. Technical report, University of Maryland Center for Automation Research, College Park, MD, 1990.

[2] V. Ayala-Ramirez, J. B. Hayet, F. Lerasle, and M. Devy. Visual localization of a mobile robot in indoor environments using planar landmarks. In *submitted to IROS-2000*. IEEE, 2000.

[3] R. Bajczy and M. Campos. Active and exploratory perception. *CVGIP: Image Understanding*, 56(1):31–40, July 1992.

[4] J. Canny. A computational approach to edge detection. *IEEE Transactions on Pattern Analysis and Machine Intelligence*, 8(6), 1986.

[5] C. Deutsch. Suivi et localisation d'une cible complexe connue par vision monoculaire. Technical Report RT-LVSN-97-04, Université Laval Computer Vision and Systems Laboratory, Sainte-Foy, Canada, 1997.

[6] D. Huttenlocher, A. Klanderman, and J. Rucklidge. Comparing images using the hausdorff distance. *IEEE Transactions on Pattern Analysis and Machine Intelligence*, 15(9), 1993.

[7] D. Huttenlocher, W. Rucklidge, and J. Noh. Tracking non-rigid objects in complex scenes. In *Fourth International Conference on Computer Vision*, 1993.

[8] M. F. Kelly and M. D. Levine. *Finding and Describing Objects in Complex Images*, pages 209–225. IEEE Computer Society Press, 1997.

[9] R. Murrieta-Cid, M. Briot, and N. Vandapel. Landmark identification and tracking in natural environment. In *Proceedings of the IEEE/RSJ IROS'98*, Victoria, Canada, 1998.

[10] H. H. Nagel. *Reflections on Active (Machine) Vision*, volume 83 of *NATO ASI Series*, pages 23–42. Springer Verlag, 1992.

[11] J. Serra. *Image analysis and mathematical morphology*. Academic Press, London, 1982.

An Interactive Facial Caricaturing System Based on the Gaze Direction of Gallery

Kazuhito Murakami
Aichi Prefectural University
Nagakute-cho, Aichi 480-1198, Japan
murakami@ist.aichi-pu.ac.jp

Masafumi Tominaga and Hiroyasu Koshimizu
SCCS, Chukyo University
Kaizu-cho, Toyota 470-0393, Japan
{tomy, hiroyasu}@koshi-lab.sccs.chukyo-u.ac.jp

Abstract

Facial caricaturing should be discussed from multiple viewpoints of three relations among the model, the caricaturist and the gallery. Furthermore, some kinds of interactive mechanism should be required between the caricaturist and the gallery. In this paper, we propose a dynamic and interactive caricaturing system. In our system, the utilization of in-betweening method realizes the generation mechanism from the caricaturist to the gallery, and on the contrary, the utilization of eye-camera vision realizes the feedback mechanism from the gallery to the caricaturist. The gallery mounts an eye-camera on the head, and the system reflects visual characteristics of the gallery directly onto the works of facial caricature. After observing the image of the model and analyzing the gaze direction and distribution, the system deforms some characteristic and impressive facial parts more strongly than other non-impressive facial parts, and generates the caricature which is suited especially for the gallery. In this paper, we demonstrate experimentally the effectivity of this method to integrate these kinds of viewpoints.

1. Introduction

From the viewpoint of computer vision, it is important to brush up the technique of drawing, and it is more important to clarify how the human vision extracts the feature points of the face and recognizes them in advance. In the conventional systems or researches concerning facial deformation or facial feature extraction [1], caricaturing has been discussed in the viewpoint of the relation only between the model and the caricaturist, and the flow of information also has been treated as one-way from the caricaturist to the gallery. As the caricature varies according to who draws the caricature, the evaluation varies who observes it [2]. From these analytical considerations, facial caricaturing should be discussed from multiple viewpoints of these three relations among the model, the caricaturist and the gallery. Furthermore, some kinds of interactive mechanism should be required between the caricaturist and the gallery.

In this paper, we propose an interactive caricaturing system. In our system, the utilization of in-betweening method realizes the generation mechanism from the caricaturist to the gallery, and on the contrary, the utilization of eye-camera vision realizes the feedback mechanism from the gallery to the caricaturist.

In section 2, the basic formalism and the system configuration of our proposed mechanism are described. In section 3, some experimental results of gaze distribution by using eye camera vision and some examples of caricatures are presented by using our interactive system.

2. System Configuration

2.1. Basic Formalism of Caricature Generation

Facial caricaturing should be discussed from all the view points of the model, the caricaturist and the gallery. The caricature generation is described as

$$Q = func_C(P, S_1, K) \tag{1}$$

$$K = func_G(P, S_2), \tag{2}$$

where, P is input face, S_1 and S_2 are reference, or standard, faces (afterward, mean face is used), K is visual interest parameter of a gallery, and Q is caricature of the person P. Subscripts C and G mean caricaturist and gallery, respectively.

1051-4651/00 $10.00 © 2000 IEEE

Suppose that Eq.(1) could be expanded and described in the following polynomial expression as

$$Q = func_C(P, S) + func_G(P, S) + func_C(func_G(P, S)) + ... \quad (3)$$

The second term in Eq.(3) is a feedback element from a gallery. The third term and its successors, the recursive feedback elements, are omitted hereafter in this paper, because these values are relatively not so serious.

Next, we assume that $func_C$ and $func_G$ could be characterized by the individuality feature and its weight. As one of the most simple expressions, let the individuality feature be the deviation $P - S$ and its weight be b, then caricature Q can be simply described as

$$Q = P + b_C(P - S) + b_G(P - S) \quad (4)$$

$$S = average(P_1, P_2, ..., P_M). \quad (5)$$

S is the mean face of the persons $P_1 \sim P_M$. This mean face is often used to extract individuality features. Of course, the above formalism is not a unique representation. Since the caricature depends on the caricaturist and the gallery, the functions or values b_C and b_G can be changed according to the principle of the system.

One of the main subjects is to introduce the gallery factor b_G. In our system, the degree of distributive interest for each facial feature point of the model P is measured by using eye camera, and this value is utilized as the factor of gallery b_G. So, in our system, caricature generation could be simply formalized as

$$Q = P + (b_C + b_G) \cdot (P - S). \quad (6)$$

2.2. Precise Description

In our system, facial features are represented by using N points of x and y coordinates of the facial contour as follows[1,2]:

$$x_i^{(Q)} = x_i^{(P)} + b_i \cdot (x_i^{(P)} - x_i^{(S)})$$
$$y_i^{(Q)} = y_i^{(P)} + b_i \cdot (y_i^{(P)} - y_i^{(S)}) \quad (7)$$
$$i = 1, 2, ..., N,$$

where, P is a primal input face, S is a reference face (mean face), Q is a deformed caricature and b is the degree of interest of the gallery. The mean face can be calculated by

$$x_i^{(S)} = \frac{1}{M}\sum_{j=1}^{M} x_i^{(P_j)}, \qquad y_i^{(S)} = \frac{1}{M}\sum_{j=1}^{M} y_i^{(P_j)} \quad (8)$$
$$i = 1, 2, ..., N,$$

where $x_i^{(P_j)}$ and $y_i^{(P_j)}$ are the x and y coordinates for the i-th feature point of the j-th normalized face data.

In our system, parameters $b_i (i = 1, 2, ..., N)$ could be calculated by T times gaze data $(x_{gaze}^{(t)}, y_{gaze}^{(t)})$ $(t = 1, 2, ..., T)$ as shown in the following methods.

- **method-1:**only caricaturist factor

  This is a simple in-betweening method. Assume that visual interests of a caricaturist for the model be distributed onto all of facial parts or feature points, and for example, let the values b_i be as follows.

$$b_i = 0.25 \quad (i = 1, 2, ..., N) \quad (9)$$

$$b_i = 1.00 \quad (i = 1, 2, ..., N) \quad (10)$$

- **method-2:**only gallery factor(1)

  The gaze distribution of a gallery decides the gallery factor. If a gallery looks at some facial parts, then assume that attractive facial features exist in them and the interest values become large in proportion to the length of gaze. The gaze distribution is calculated by the following steps; firstly divide an image into $n \times n$ sub-areas $a_{uv}(u, v = 1, 2, ..., n$; n is about 10), and count up the number (times) t_{uv} of gaze point $(x_{gaze}^{(t)}, y_{gaze}^{(t)})$ for $t = 1, 2, ..., T$, and finally calculate b_i as the ratio for the total T.

$$b_i = b_{max} \times \frac{t_{uv}}{T} \quad (i = 1, 2, ..., N)$$
$$here, (x_i, y_i) \subset a_{uv}. \quad (11)$$

- **method-3:**only gallery factor(2)

  Even though this is almost the same as **method-2**, not the length but the number of in/out times decides the gallery factor, that is, let b_i be in proportion to the number of saccade $s_{uv}(u, v = 1, 2, ..., n)$ into each sub-area.

$$b_i = b'_{max} \times \frac{s_{uv}}{\sum_{u,v} s_{uv}} \quad (i = 1, 2, ..., N)$$
$$here, (x_i, y_i) \subset a_{uv} \quad (12)$$

- **method-4:**only gallery factor(3)

  This is also almost the same as **method-2,-3**. The difference is that b is calculated in the unit of each facial part (not sub-area). The number of saccade into a rectangular area decides b. Transition matrix description from facial part to part expands a possibility to extract visual characteristics of a gallery.

- **method-5**:caricaturist factor + gallery factor

  The degree of interest $b_i (i = 1, 2, ..., N)$ could be determined by the combination of the caricaturist factor in **method-1** and the gallery factor in **method-2–4**. In this method, it is decided based on the distance between the gaze point $(x_{gaze}^{(t)}, y_{gaze}^{(t)})$ $(t = 1, 2, ..., T)$ and the feature point (x_i, y_i) $(i = 1, 2, ..., N)$, and this is defined as the integration for T times measured data. After normalization, the interest factor b_i for i-th feature point is defined as

$$b_i = b_{offset} + \beta \cdot (\frac{d_{min}}{d_i})^{\alpha} \quad (13)$$

$$d_{min} = minimum(d_i)(i = 1, 2, ..., N) \quad (14)$$

$$d_i = \frac{1}{T} \sum_{t=1}^{T} ((x_{gaze}^{(t)} - x_i)^2 + (y_{gaze}^{(t)} - y_i)^2)^{1/2}. \quad (15)$$

  here, b_{offset} is an offset value and decided experimentally. The value b_i of the most interested point becomes $b_{offset} + \beta$, and on the contrary, it becomes about b_{offset} around the uninterested points.

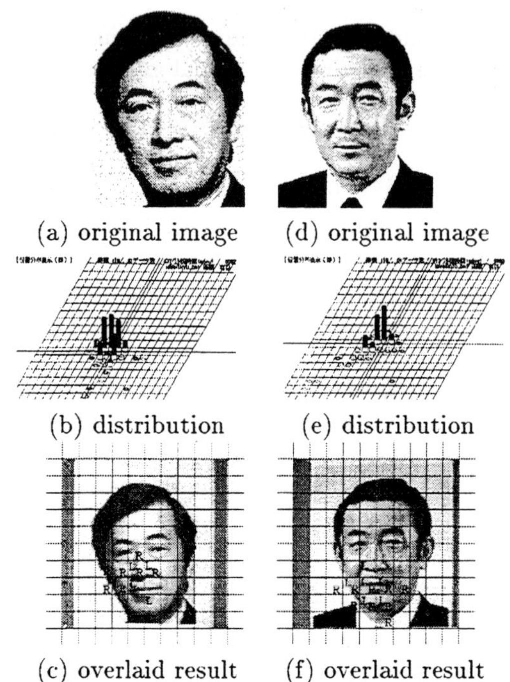

(a) original image (d) original image

(b) distribution (e) distribution

(c) overlaid result (f) overlaid result

Figure 1. Experimental results of the distribution of viewpoint (left: N.Kan, right: R.Hashimoto).

3. Caricature Generation Controlled by Gaze Direction

3.1. Gaze Detection by Eye Camera

The direction of the eye can be calculated by using the difference of the reflection-ratio of white part and colored-part (iris and pupil). Since the gray image is also inputted through small CCD camera attached on the eye-camera, the system can calibrate where the gallery looks at in the gray image[2].

Figure 1 shows an example of the examination. The models are Mr. Naoto Kan and Ryutaro Hashimoto, Japanese statesmen. Figure 1(a) is an original image, and the gaze distribution is shown in Fig.1(b). The horizontal and vertical axes show the location of the peak of the distribution. The result of distributions overlaid onto the original image with the marks L and R is shown in Fig.1(c). Although there is some differences between the left and right eye's distribution, it was clarified that the gallery looks mainly at the nose of this person. In the case of Fig.1(d)–(f), the gallery looks mainly at around the mouth and chin.

3.2. Examples of Caricatures

In order to realize the interactive caricaturing system, we introduced the deformation process by using an eye camera which is mounted on the head of the gallery. In this system, the facial parts which a gallery mainly focuses on are selectively deformed. It is expected that this system could directly reflect the visual characteristic information of the gallery onto the caricaturing process. Some works are shown in Fig.2–6.

Some caricatures by **method-1** are shown in Fig.2. In these figures, the feedback value $K = func_G(P, S)$ from the gallery to the system in Eq.'s(2),(3) is not considered (=0). If there is no feedback information from the gallery, the system (caricaturist) could not decide the proper values b_C, b_G in principle. So that, in these figures, some vague values, 0.00, 0.25, 0.50, 1.00, are given independently to the input face P. Consequently, some unexpected facial parts which are too much deformed or not too much deformed appeared in these caricatures.

Some caricatures by **method-2,3** are shown in Fig.3,4, respectively (image is Isabel of the Hapsburgs). In each case, there are some differences between testee A and B. Figure 5 is examples of the transition matrix in **method-4** (upper: testee A, lower: testee B).

Fig.6 shows the caricatures by **method-5**. Here, the values $b_i (i = 1, 2, ..., N)$ are determined based on the analysis of Eq.'s (13)–(15). Since the gallery looked mainly at the nose and cheek of this person, in Fig.6(a), coefficient b_i around the nose and cheeks became large, and for other facial parts it was decided that $b_{i(others)} = 0.4 \sim 0.6$. In the same way in Fig.6(b), since the gallery looked mainly at around the mouth and chin, it was decided that b_i around the mouth and chin became about $1.0 \sim 1.2$ and that $b_{i(others)} = 0.4 \sim 0.6$ for other facial parts by Eq.'s(13)–(15) ($\beta = 0.8, \alpha = 1.0, b_{offset} = 0.4$).

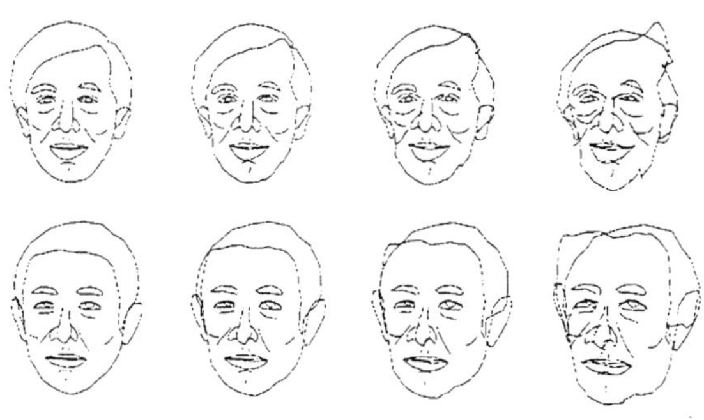

$b_i = 0.00$ $b_i = 0.25$ $b_i = 0.50$ $b_i = 1.00$

Figure 2. Examples of caricatures (N.Kan's :upper, R.Hashimoto's :lower) by **method-1**, the deformation weight $b_i(i = 1, 2, ..., N)$ is constant.

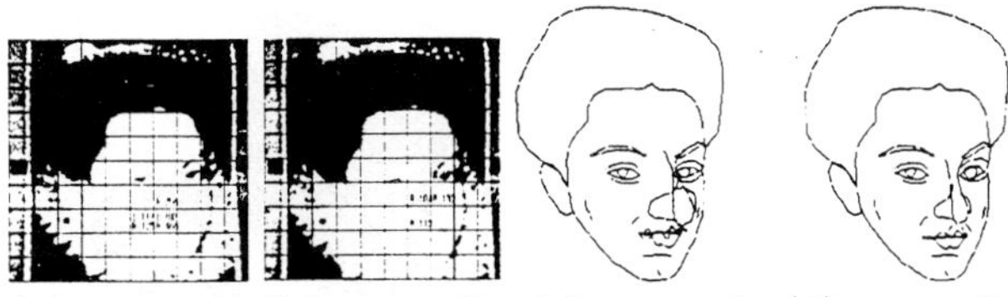

(a) testee A (b) testee B (c) testee A (d) testee B

Figure 3. Examples of gaze distributions and caricatures (Isabel) by **method-2**.

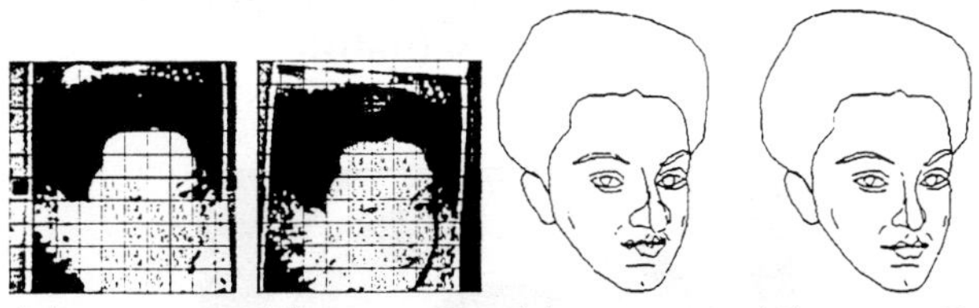

(a) testee A (b) testee B (c) testee A (d) testee B

Figure 4. Examples of gaze distributions and caricatures (Isabel) by **method-3**.

4. Conclusions

In this paper, (1) a mechanism to extract visual characteristics by using an eye camera, and (2) an interactive caricature generation mechanism controlled by the gaze distribution were proposed. And the effectivity of this method was experimentally demonstrated. It was experimentally known that the proposed method

	left eye braw	right eye braw	left eye	right eye	nose	mouth	other
left eye braw	0	0	0	0	0	0	1
right eye braw	0	0	0	0	0	0	0
left eye	0	0	0	0	8	0	10
right eye	0	0	2	0	5	0	1
nose	0	0	1	3	0	0	26
mouth	0	0	0	0	1	0	4
other	0	0	4	4	15	3	0

	left eye braw	right eye braw	left eye	right eye	nose	mouth	other
left eye braw	0	0	0	6	0	0	0
right eye braw	0	0	0	0	0	0	0
left eye	0	0	0	0	3	0	0
right eye	0	0	3	0	6	0	8
nose	6	0	0	7	0	0	0
mouth	0	0	3	0	0	0	2
other	6	0	6	4	3	0	0

Figure 5. Examples of transition matrix and caricatures by **method-4** (upper:testee A, lower:testee B).

(a) Naoto Kan (b) R. Hashimoto

Figure 6. The caricatures by **method-5**, the degree of interest $b_i(i = 1, 2, ..., N)$ are not constant.

improves the result compared with the conventional method where coefficients $b_i(i = 1, 2, ..., N)$ of all facial parts (points) are constant. This result shows (a)a possibility to extract facial features by using an eye camera, and (b)an effectivity to represent the gallery's visual characteristics onto facial caricaturing process.

In the experiment, although a static image is used for feature extraction, it is easily noticed and encouraging that it is better for the better facial extraction to utilize the continuous or motion images. To examine how to display these motion images to the gallery and how to analyze the gaze distribution are our future works.

Acknowledgments

This paper was partially supported by Grant-in-Aid for General Sci. Res., IMS HUTOP Res. Promotion, and High-Tech.Research Center Promotion.

References

[1] Brennan,S.E., "Degree of Master of Science in Vision Studies at MIT(Sep.1982).

[2] Murakami,K.,Tominaga,M. and Koshimizu,H.: "Dynamic Facial Caricaturing System Based on the Gaze Direction of Gallery", *Proc.of FG2000*, pp.136-141 (March 2000).

Application of Panoramic Annular Lens for Motion Analysis Tasks: Surveillance and Smoke Detection

Iván Kopilović[+] Balázs Vágvölgyi[+] Tamás Szirányi[+,++]

[+]*University of Veszprém, Dep. of Image Processing and Neurocomputing, H-8200 Veszprém, Egyetem u. 10, Hungary*

[++]*Analogical and Neural Computing Laboratory, Comp. & Aut. Inst., Hungarian Academy of Sciences, Kende u. 13-17, H-1111 Budapest, Hungary*

E-mail: kopi@silicon.terra.vein.hu, bvagvol@almos.vein.hu, sziranyi@sztaki.hu

Abstract

In this paper some applications of motion analysis are investigated for a compact panoramic optical system (Panoramic Annular Lens). Panoramic image acquisition makes multiple or mechanically controlled camera systems needless for many applications. Panoramic Annular Lens' main advantage to other omnidirectional monitoring systems is that it is a cheap, small, compact device with no external hyperboloidal, spherical, conical or paraboloidal reflecting surface as in other panoramic optical devices. By converting the annular image captured with an NTSC camera to a rectangular one, we get a low-resolution (cc. 2.8 pixels/degree horizontally and 3 pixels/degree vertically) image. We have developed algorithms, which can analyze this low-resolution image to yield motion information for surveillance and smoke detection.

1. Introduction

Surveillance with intelligent camera systems is becoming increasingly important in everyday life. It is widely used in traffic control, driving assistance and surgery. In these applications compactness is also essential.

It is well known that omnidirectional camera systems have many advantages compared to conventional optics. With large field of view we can avoid the use of multiple camera systems or mechanically controlled cameras. This is very useful in applications such as surveillance systems, intelligent vehicle control [2], endoscopic measurements [3], etc.

In our work we deal with a special lens called Panoramic Annular Lens (PAL) [1], which has different optical properties compared to other omnidirectional systems (Figure 1, 2). The main advantage of PAL is its small size, compactness, and sharp image mapping, although its vertical view angle is limited to about 50-70 degrees.

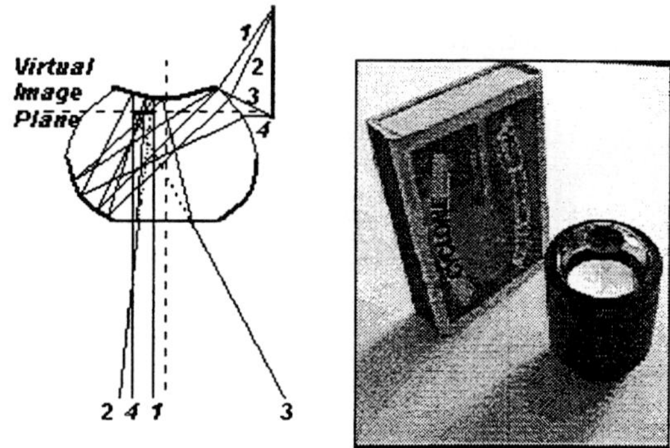

Figure 1. Image formation in PAL optics (left), and the PAL (right).

Figure 2. The annular image of the PAL.

1051-4651/00 $10.00 © 2000 IEEE

2. Motion analysis using the PAL optics

Surveillance systems employing omnidirectional optics have a lot of advantages against traditional systems that use pan-tilt-zoom (PTZ) cameras with conventional optics. Since they have full 360 degrees view, they are able to monitor the whole panorama around the camera and track any number of moving objects simultaneously without moving. These systems can substitute three or even more tracking PTZ cameras with only a single panoramic device.

Traditional controllable cameras are complex systems with several moving parts, thus they need heavy maintenance. On the other hand, omnidirectional optics are stationary devices. Furthermore, in case of moving or turning camera additional computations have to be carried out to identify the background in every camera position, and perspective distortion of the conventional optics has to be eliminated. Systems employing static omnidirectional devices do not have to deal with that difficulty. However, panoramic systems have special optical distortions that must be eliminated, and the annular input image must be transformed to a rectangular view before starting image processing. While systems with traditional optics project only a small portion of the panorama on the CCD array of the camera, omnidirectional optics projects the whole panorama on it. Thus, the resolution of objects is lower on the annular image than on the perspective image of the conventional optics. It is at most 2.8 pixels/degree horizontally and 3 pixels/degree vertically, with NTSC cameras.

In our system the PAL was used instead of omnidirectional optics equipped with hyperbolical mirrors.

2.1. Change detection

Our surveillance system uses statistical methods to find the background scene on the streaming video by extracting static regions from every frame and joining them together to the background image dynamically. Thereafter, foreground objects can be easily detected by simply subtracting the computed background from the actual image captured from the camera. A similar algorithm was developed at the University of Maryland [4] for mechanically controlled tracking cameras. In case of PAL this task is easier, because the background scene is a still image, so we do not have to deal with the always-changing distortion of the background.

In most cases, surveillance systems have to take care of the changing environment, especially when the system is installed outdoors. The method used for adaptation to the changing background is briefly described in Table 1.

Table 1. Adaptation to changing background.

• As a first step, a background image is maintained where the influences of illumination changes (e.g. shadows) are eliminated. See [5] for a similar illumination invariant method for background extraction. • The second step is the maintenance of the changing statistics of regions, and the suppression of the influences of recurrent disturbances (e.g. shaking of the trees). These routines can learn disturbances locally, and ignore them in the detection process (Figure 3). It is simple and does not need special image processing hardware unlike most recent surveillance systems.

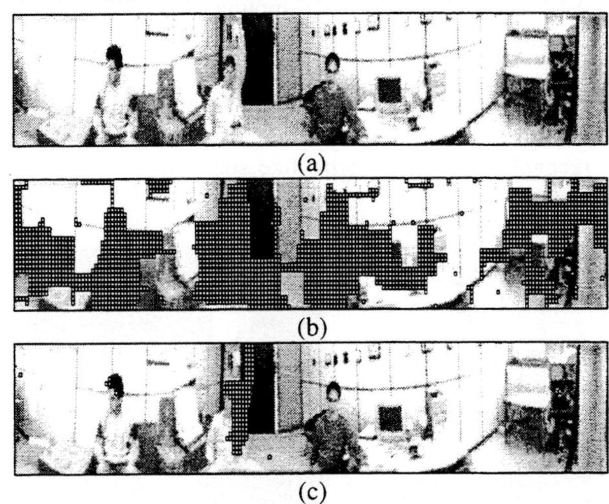

(a) (b) (c)

Figure 3. Motion detection: (a) noisy input (b) detection without filtering (c) detection with filtering out disturbances.

2.2. Tracking

The PAL makes tracking much easier in many cases. By the nature of the system it is possible to track any number of intruders simultaneously, without moving the camera. We developed two spatio-temporal estimation methods to track moving objects in the field of view of the PAL. The first method compares certain properties of found objects (e.g. size, shape, motion direction) on every two succeeding frames to find matching pairs of objects. In this way, real-time tracking (20-30 fps) with all preprocessing is possible even on a low cost PC.

2.3. Motion recognition

In intelligent surveillance applications it is important to recognize certain motion patterns or gestures, e.g. someone moves along a certain trajectory or sits down. We developed two kinds of motion recognition algorithms. One of them uses tracking information to find objects having special motion properties; the other computes the history of motion to find certain motion patterns. Finally, an advanced smoke recognition algorithm, detecting the special motion of smoke is presented in details.

2.3.1. Recognition based on tracking information. Using tracking information, several motion recognition tasks can be carried out. Our system uses them to filter out objects having certain properties, like certain size, shape, motion direction, relative velocity and trajectory.

2.3.2. Motion pattern recognition. History of the motion (Figure 4) is computed for every moving object with a method similar to [6]. The motion history image is obtained as a weighted time-average of the detected regions.

The motion history patterns are trained to a neural network. In the detection phase the neural network is able to recognize trained patterns, like someone sits down or lifts up his hand.

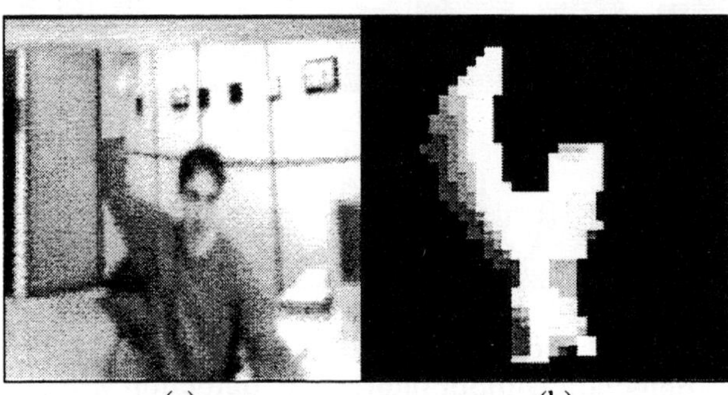

(a) (b)

Figure 4. Motion pattern recognition: (a) input sequence (b) motion history.

2.3.3. Smoke Motion Detection. Smoke detection is usually performed with chemical or optical sensors, but little is known about methods using digital image processing, although it may have advantages in situation where conventional sensors are less effective.

Difficulties arise with the discrimination of motion caused by non-smoke events (e.g. filter out human, vehicle or machine motion). We have developed a real-time smoke detection algorithm based on optical velocity field computation. The method detects irregularities in the optical velocity field due to smoke motion.

As a first step, we have give statistical characterisation of the computed velocity field. Two distinguished characteristics of velocity field were considered:

1. Non-self-similarity: motion of smoke tends to be non-self similar; in larger scales its motion is regular in smaller scales it is irregular.
2. Irregularities in motion due to non-rigidity: they are characterised through the statistics of the distribution of velocity vector orientations.

These assumptions were applied to analyse the optical velocity pattern. To account for non-self-similarity, a multiscale optical flow computation was applied with velocity warping [7]. The considerations above lead to the algorithm shown in Table 3.

The statistical analysis of irregularities in the motion field was performed as follows. In case of n orientations the interval $]0,\pi]$ is divided into n equal subintervals, and a distribution functions $f \in [0,1]^n$ is obtained. Some results obtained for smoke and non-smoke motions are shown in Figure 5(a) and 5(b). It is immediate that the distributions for smoke are more spread, and tend to be more uniform.

Since orientations 0 and π are identical, no mean and variance of the distribution exists. Therefore we tried to characterise distributions $f \in [0,1]^n$ by:

Entropy: $e_n(f) = -\frac{1}{\ln(n)} \sum_{i=1}^{n} f(i)\ln(f(i))$.

Variation: $v_n(f) = \left(\frac{1}{n} \sum_{i=1}^{n} \left(f(i) - \left(\frac{1}{n} \sum_{k=1}^{n} f(k) \right) \right)^2 \right)^{1/2}$.

Maximum-norm: $\|f\|_\infty = \max\{f(k) \mid k = 1,...n\}$.

Some of these values measured for test sequences are shown in Table 2. The entropy values separate quite well the two types of motion. The entropy distribution for a larger set of measurements is shown in Figure 5(c). Using these empirical data, we perform Bayesian threshold selection (t=0.68).

The system alarms if entropy exceeds the threshold. A detection example is shown in Figure 6.

Table 2 Statistics of orientation distributions.

$e_n(f)$		$v_n(f)$		$\|f\|_\infty$	
Smoke	Rigid	Smoke	Rigid	Smoke	Rigid
0.8993	0.7155	1.4982	1.7134	0.0191	0.0148
0.8276	0.2604	1.3461	1.9036	0.0041	0.0342
0.9522	0.3410	1.5380	1.2453	0.0221	0.0809

Table 3. The smoke detection algorithm.

1. Multiscale optical flow field computation.
2. Self-similarity test: Project back to the initial scale points that perform regular upward motion at the highest scale to obtain regions that contribute to that motion. Determine the local distribution of the velocity vector orientations for these regions.
3. Irregularity check: Compute irregularity measure (entropy) for the distributions.
4. Alarm if necessary: use a statistical (Bayesian) decision procedure.

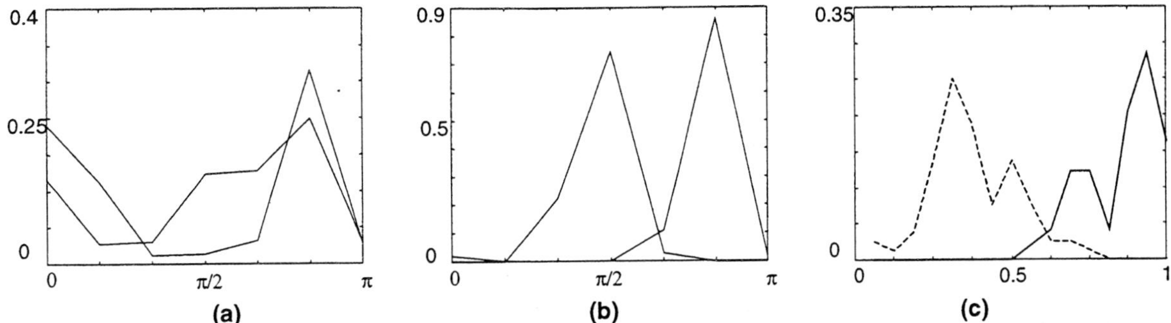

Figure 5 (a) Orientation distribution of the smoke motions. (b) Orientation distribution of non-smoke motions. (c) Entropy distribution: non-smoke (dashed line) and smoke motion (solid line).

Figure 6. Snapshot of the detection alarm. The non-smoke motion (arm) is not detected.

3. Conclusion

In this paper we have shown that a simple and cheap panoramic system can be well applied for surveillance systems for different (e.g. motion detection and smoke alarm) purposes using only this simple-to-mount device and our robust motion-analysis algorithms. For the smoke-detection further research includes the improvement of the algorithm by temporal filtering and more adaptive classification.

Acknowledgements

The help of László Czúni and Tamás Greguss are greatly acknowledged. This work has been supported by the Tateyama Co., Japan.

References

[1] P. Greguss. Exoscope – a New Omnidirectional Imaging and Holographic Device for Life Science Studies. *Optical Methods in Biomedical and Environmental Sciences*, Elsevier BV, 1994, pp. 309 – 312.

[2] Y. Yagi, Y. Nishizawa, M. Yachida. Map-Based Navigation for a Mobile Robot with Omnidirectional Image Sensor COPIS, *IEEE Transactions on Robotics and Automation, Vol. 11. No. 5.* October 1995.

[3] D. R. Matthys, J. A. Gilbert, P. Greguss. Endoscopic measurement using radial metrology with digital correlation, *Optical Engineering, Vol. 30, No.10,* October 1991, pp. 1455-1460.

[4] I. Haritaoglu, D. Harwood, L. S. Davis, Computer Vision Laboratory University of Maryland. Active Outdoor Surveillance. Proceedings of the *10th International Conference on Image Analysis and Processing*, Venice, September 1999, pp. 1096 – 1099.

[5] E. Durucan, J. Snoeckx, Y. Weilenmann. Illumination Invariant Background Extraction. Proceedings of the *10th International Conference on Image Analysis and Processing*, Venice, September 1999, pp. 1136 – 1139.

[6] J. W. Davis, A. F. Bobick. The Representation and Recognition of Action Using Temporal Templates. *IEEE Conference on Computer Vision and Pattern Recognition*, 1997.

[7] L. Barron, D.J. Fleet, S. Beauchemin. Performance of optical flow techniques, *International Journal of Computer Vision. 12(1)*, 1994, pp 43-77.

Extracting Actors, Actions and Events from Sports Video –A Fundamental Approach to Story Tracking–

Naoko Nitta, Noboru Babaguchi, Tadahiro Kitahashi
ISIR, Osaka University
8-1 Mihogaoka Ibaraki, Osaka 567-0047, Japan
{naoko, babaguchi, kitahashi}@am.sanken.osaka-u.ac.jp

Abstract

To effectively deal with the vast amount of videos, we need to construct a content-based representation for each video. As a step towards this goal, this paper proposes a method to automatically generate the semantical annotations for a sports video by integrating the text(closed-caption) and image stream. We first segment the text data and extract segments which are meaningful to grasp the story of the video, then extract the actors, the actions and the events of each scene which are useful for information retrieval by using the linguistic cues and the domain knowledge. We also segment the image stream so that each segment can associate with each text segment extracted above by using the image cues. Finally we can annotate the video by associating the text segments with the image segments. Some experimental results are presented and discussed in this paper.

1 Introduction

Continuous increase in the amount of multimedia data has strongly required the novel framework of simple but meaningful representation for its effective retrieval. One relevant representation for it could be the semantical structure, that is the story, of a multimedia product or a video, because people want to capture the story involved in it when viewing a video.

Video data consists of several multimodal information streams closely related one another: image, audio, text and so on. Obviously, each of the information streams gives us only limited amount of knowledge. However, by combining the results extracted from several information streams, we can get much more exact information about the story. Taking account of these issues, we integrate the text(Closed-Caption:CC) and the image stream, and try to extract information which should be important for the story from a sports video.

There has been much work related to this study [1-6]. S.Satoh et al. [1] have developed a system that identifies faces, by associating the faces extracted from image and names from text. I.Mani et al. [3], Q.Huang et al. [2] and Y.Nakamura et al. [4] each proposed a method to segment a news video into some meaningful parts and extract information about people/places from those segments using the text data.

Most of those studies focus on news videos, which assumingly needs the effective retrieval system considering its importance and vastness. Some recent work puts focus on sports videos to satisfy those needs to see some specific scenes or the highlight scenes etc. Since both the characteristics of the video and the information which should be extracted differ between news and sports, we find it difficult to use the system for news videos to sports videos as it is.

Now, we put focus on the structure of the sports game and try to extract information about each play which constructs a game. Taking account of the fact that the announcers are making a play-by-play commentary of the game, we will use linguistic data to extract information about those plays. We first segment the text data to extract the parts where the event may happen by utilizing key phrases which correspond to each event, and then get the main elements of the story of each game-progressing part such as the actors, the actions and the events. Then, paying attention to some image cues which are acquired with the knowledge of sports videos, we also try to extract those game-progressing parts and information about the event from the image stream to associate with the extracted text data. Finally, by matching those extracted parts with each other, we will obtain more accurate information than only from text data, and attach the obtained information to the exact matching part of the video.

2 Structure of a sports video

A TV program of a sports game is organized as Figure1. As you can see, a game is constructed as rep-

1051-4651/00 $10.00 © 2000 IEEE

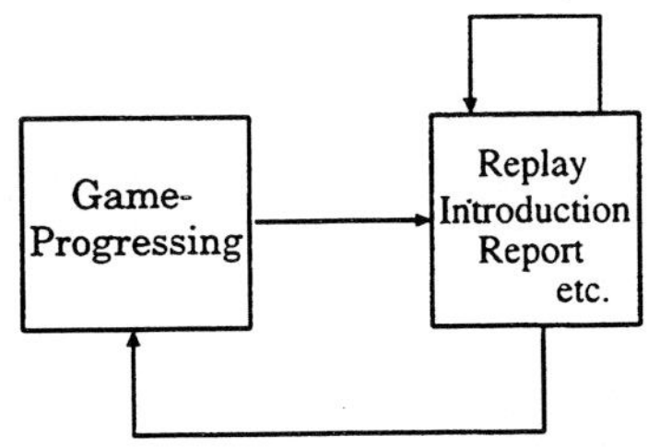

Figure 1. A program of sports game

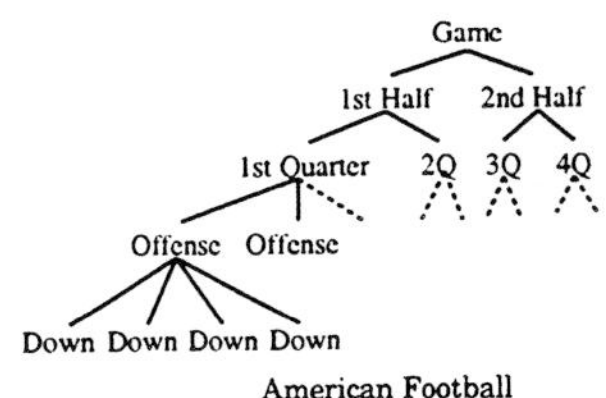

Figure 2. Structure of sports game

etitions of two parts: a game-progressing part in which a game is really progressing and a non-progressing part which consists of replays, reports, player introductions etc.

On the other hand, a sports game can be expressed as a tree, as shown in Figure2. A game is actually going on by repeating the fundamental element of the tree. In a sense, those fundamental elements can be viewed as basic logical units describing a sports game. Therefore, actors and plays in the unit will constitute the story of the game. Further, those units are closely related to the game-progressing parts. Note that such a tree-like structure is general to all kinds of sports.

There are several kinds of plays in every sports, run, throw, kick etc. as the basic actions, and touchdown, home run etc. as the events of the game. An "action" is independent of the kind of sports and has general meaning, while an "event" is a result of those actions and is specific to the kind of sports. We will extract those actions or events as well as actors who are doing the plays from each game-progressing parts to understand the story of the game. We use videos of American Football games as an example of the sports videos.

3 Extraction from Text Data

3.1 Extraction of Game-progressing Parts

Since the announcers talk about the situation of the game in a sports game program, we have a good chance to extract information about the game from linguistic data. In the game-progressing parts, the announcers use some characteristic phrases to specify the situation of the game. These phrases can be determined by the kind of the play. We use these phrases as key phrases and try to extract those game-progressing parts by

Table 1. Examples of the Key Phrases

actions/events	key phrases
RUN	UP TO 20-YARD LINE, GETS 5 YARDS, etc.
PASS	MAKES CATCH, THROWS TO PLAYER, etc.
TAKEN DOWN	TAKEN DOWN, STOPPED BY, etc.
KICK	PUNTER'S NAME, etc.
TOUCHDOWN	TOUCHDOWN
EXTRAPOINT	EXTRA POINT, etc.
FIELDGOAL	FIELD GOAL
RETURN	RETURN
PUNT	PUNT
KICKOFF	KICKOFF, etc.
INTERCEPT	INTERCEPTED, etc.
FUMBLE	FUMBLE, etc.

searching these key phrases. In addition, the information about the speaker is embedded in CC text. In sports videos, since an announcer always does a play-by-play commentary of the game, we can eliminate the parts in which every speaker except that announcer is speaking as non-progressing parts. Following these characteristics, we extract the game-progressing parts as follows:

1. Decide the key phrases by which they express the plays(actions/events) of American Football. The examples of these key phrases are shown in Table1.
2. Segment the CC text into its segments spoken by a single speaker, and identify the speaker of each segment.
3. Search the key phrases in each parts whose speaker is doing the running commentary, and if any key phrases are found, identify the part as a game-progressing part.

3.2 Actor, Action and Event Extraction

Now that we extracted the game-progressing parts from the close-caption text, we will identify the actors who are doing a play and the action they are taking. As indicated in the previous section, the outline of the play is given in the game-progressing parts. Considering this, we can get the information about the play from the extracted parts as follows:

action/event: Identify the action associated with the key phrases in Table1.

actor: Identify the actors as shown in Table2. In this table, "S" represents the name which appears before the key phrases, "BY" represents the name which appears after the word "by", "TO" represents the name which appears after the word "to" or "for", "O" represents the name which appears after the key phrases, and "–" means that it is impossible to determine the actor.

When there are more than one sentences which include the key phrases, however, we choose the sentence that appears earlier in the part, since they tend to talk about the play earlier than other topics in one part. Now we will summarize the method as follows:
For each extracted game-progressing part,

Table 2. How to determine the Actor

action/event	actor	how?	
RUN	who?		S
PASS	who?	active verbs meaning "THROW" →	S
		(passive) →	BY
		active verbs meaning "CATCH" →	–
		(passive) →	–
		(nouns) →	S
	whom?	active verbs meaning "THROW" →	TO
		(passive) →	TO
		active verbs meaning "CATCH" →	S
		(passive) →	BY
		(nouns) →	TO
TAKEN DOWN	who?	active verbs meaning "STOP" →	O
		(passive) →	S
	whom?	active verbs meaning "STOP" →	S
		(passive) →	BY
KICK	who?		S
	whom?		TO
TOUCHDOWN	who?		BY or S
EXTRAPOINT	who?		BY or S
FIELDGOAL	who?		BY or S
RETURN	who?		BY or S
PUNT	who?		BY or S
KICKOFF	who?		BY or S
INTERCEPT	who?	active verbs →	S
		(passive or noun) →	BY
FUMBLE	who?		BY or S

1. Check a sentence if it includes the key phrases determined as Table1.
2. If so, identify the actors and the actions/events as shown above. Otherwise, return to step 1 and check the next sentence.
3. If both the actors and the actions/events have been identified, determine them as the annotation for the game-progressing part. If either the actors or the actions/events have not been identified, return to step 1 and check the remaining sentences if the lacking information can be obtained.
4. If all of the sentences of the game-progressing part have been checked, determine the information obtained so far as the annotation for the game-progressing part is concerned.

4 Text-Image Association

The phrases in the CC text have "time-stamps" representing the time when they are spoken. Those stamps enable us to capture the time when the sentence is spoken on the video. Since a human CC translator types what is said just after he/she hears the utterance in sports videos, the data is supposed to delay appearing in the CC [1]. Moreover, the segmentation of the text data is too obscure to make the annotation to the exact matching part of the video.

To solve this problem, we now focus on the image stream. Based on the analysis of the actual American Football game videos, some cues can be found from the image stream. A game-progressing part always starts with some kinds of image. "Extra Point" and "Field Goal" start with the players lined up before the goal line and the scene is always taken horizontally to the lines(Figure3-(b)), and "Kick Off" and "Punt" start with the players lined up in the end of

[1]This is the characteristic of sports videos. The time difference between CC text and audio depends on the kind of videos.

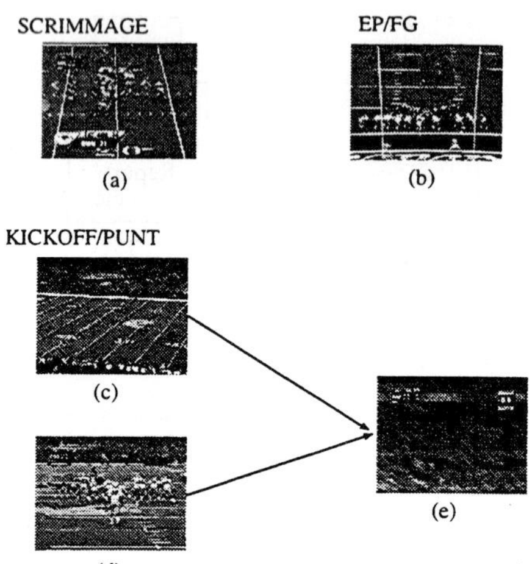

Figure 3. Examples of image cues

Table 3. Relationship between Action and Event

event	action
TOUCHDOWN	RUN, PASS, TAKEN DOWN, KICK
EXTRAPOINT	KICK
FIELDGOAL	KICK
RETURN	RUN, TAKEN DOWN
PUNT	KICK
KICKOFF	KICK
INTERCEPT	PASS, TAKEN DOWN
FUMBLE	RUN, PASS, TAKEN DOWN

the field (Figure3-(c),(d)) followed by the shot showing the ball flying (Figure3-(e)). Other plays always start with a formation called "scrimmage" in which players of each team line up face to face stationally for a while(Figure3-(a)). These frames have salient features compared to other frames and are considered to be relatively easy to discover. Since they use a single camera to take one play, every play ends with a shot change. Therefore, a shot change after those frames mentioned earlier should indicate the end of a game-progressing part. Taking advantage of these features, we associate the image stream with the CC text as follows:

1. Detect shot changes to segment the image stream.
2. Search the frames discussed above in the beginning parts of each shot (in the middle parts for the ball flying image), and if there is the frame, determine the shot as the game-progressing part.
3. If the image game-progressing segment exists just before the extracted CC segment, determine the segment as the corresponding video segment. Otherwise, discard the CC segment.
4. When we finish the association, check if the action represented by the initial frame (Figure 3) matches with the one extracted from CC.(See Table3 about the relationship between the event and the action.) If so, leave the action or the event as it is, otherwise, change the action or the event to the one obtained from image stream.

Table 4. Result of extraction from image stream

image	recall	precision
SCRIMMAGE	97%	89%
KICKOFF/PUNT	89%	89%
EP/FG	75%	75%

5 Experiments and Discussion

We first implemented the method of the extraction from CC text. We processed parts of 3 American Football videos(about 1 hour each). We were able to extract the game-progressing parts with the precision rate 87.3% and the recall rate 85.5% on average, then get information about plays from those extracted parts with the precision rate 80% and the recall rate 76% on average. After the inspection-based checking of the actual game-progressing parts in CC text, we considered we have extracted the game-progressing parts successfully if we could get the parts which had been checked. Moreover, when multiple actions are taking place in a game-progressing part, we say we extracted the information successfully if we could get one of those actions. The extracted information enables us to make such annotations as < RUN, MARTIN >, where RUN represents the action and MARTIN represents the actor. The result of this experiment tells us that

- Since the action tends to be referred earlier than the event, we tend to extract the action more frequently than the event. This verifies that an event is the consequence of actions. However, considering that the event is more important than the action for the story tracking, the event should take priority over the action.
- Since the actor is considered less important than the action and the event for the story, the announcer puts emphasis on the action and the event in explaining the play, and as a consequence, we find it relatively difficult to extract the actor.
- There are not always enough data in the CC text to extract the information about the plays. To cover the insufficiency, we need to consider the context and the structure of the sports game.

We next implemented the method of association of text and image stream and processed one of three American Football videos that were same as earlier. We extracted the game-progressing parts from the image stream with the precision rate 92% and the recall rate 98%. We present the details of the extraction result in Table4.
As a result of the association of results from CC and image stream, it was possible to extract the exact game-progressing parts in the video and get information about the play of each part with the precision rate 93% and the recall rate 89%. Due to the way of association, the extracted parts which can not find their associated parts may cancel each other, and as a consequence, the rate of excessive extraction drops, while the rate of insufficient extraction rises. Though the image cues do not play such a big role in extractiong information about plays, they may allow us to improve the annotation. For example, we often get "Run" as the action for "Kick Off" event from CC text since the "Run" action which always follows the "Kick Off" tends to be mentioned more often than the "Kick Off". The image cues help us to change it to "Kick Off & Return" which explains the situation more appropriately.

6 Conclusion

This paper proposed a method to extract actors, actions and events from a sports video by integrating the text and image stream. We implemented the method and were able to extract at least one piece of information about the play and attach the information to the exact matching game-progressing parts in the video with the precision rate 93% and recall rate 89%. As we discussed above, the rate of insufficient extraction rises as the result of integration. To prevent this, we should contrive some way of association by considering the context and the structure of the game. Though the use of the key phrases was really useful to extract information quickly and effectively, how to determine those key phrases automatically needs to be considered. We consider it possible to apply our method to other sports videos which can be structured likewise.

Acknowedgments – This work is partly supported by a Grant-in-Aid for scientific research from the Japan Society for the Promotion of Science.

References

[1] S.Satoh, Y.Nakamura and T.Kanade: "Name-It: Naming and Detecting Faces in News Videos", *IEEE Multimedia*.pp.22-35,1999.

[2] Q.Huang, Z.Liu, A.Rosenberg, D.Gibbon and B.Shahraray: "Automated Generation of News Content Hierarchy by Integrating Audio, Video, and Text Information", *Proc. ICASSP'99*.

[3] I.Mani, D.House, M.T.Maybury and M.Green: "Towards Content-Based Browsing of Broadcast" in Intelligent Multimedia Information retrieval, The MIT Press, pp.241-258, 1997.

[4] Y.Nakamura and T.Kanade: "Semantic Analysis for Video Contents Extraction – Spotting by Association in News Video.", *Proc. of The Fifth ACM International Multimedia Conference*, Nov 1997.

[5] A.G.Hauptmann and M.J.Witbrock: "Story Segmentation and Detection of Commercials In Broadcast News Video", *Proc. ADL-98*, April, 1998.

[6] N.Babaguchi, S.Sasamori, T.Kitahashi and R. Jain: "Detecting Events from Continuous Media by Intermodal Collaboration and Knowledge Use", *Proc. IEEE ICMCS'99*, Vol.1, pp.782-786, 1999.

Face Detection and Precise Eyes Location

Weimin Huang and Robert Mariani

RWCP* Multi-Modal Functions KRDL † Laboratory,
21 Heng Mui Keng Terrace, Singapore 119613
Email: {wmhuang,rmariani}@krdl.org.sg

Abstract

This paper presents a robust and precise scheme for face detection and precise facial feature location. Multiscale filters are used to obtain the pre-attentive features of objects, based on which different models are investigated to locate the face and facial features such as eyes, nose and mouth. The structural model is used to characterize the geometric pattern of facial components. The texture and feature models are used to verify the face candidates detected before. Since the eyeballs are the only features that are salient and have strong invariant property, the distance between them will be used to normalize faces for recognition. Motivated from this, with the face detected and the structural information extracted, a precise eyes location algorithm is applied using contour and region information. It detects, with a subpixellic precision, the center and the radius of the eyeballs of a person's eyes. The detected result can be used as an accurate normalization of images, which reduces greatly the number of possible scales used during the face recognition process.

1 Introduction

On-line face detection in a scene is the first step in Automatic human face recognition. It is still a problem considering the variation of illumination, skin tone, face scale and orientation and the complex background of the image. And obviously, the face pattern detection and normalization play critical roles since the errors of recognition are caused partially by the errors of the face detection and components detection.

Existing face detection methods include template-based[1], neural network-based[2, 3], model-based[4], color-based[5] and motion-based approaches[6].

In this paper we present the model-based approach to obtain the face location and facial components positions. Compared with the template-based methods, model-based approach is faster and more flexible.

Once we located the face and fixed the facial components area, further studies on the precise components detection can be carried out. The detected positions will be used for normalization or recognition directly. A salient and often used feature for normalization is the distance between eyes. Many ways including template matching[1], and feature searching[7, 8] are proposed up to now for eye detection. However, in order to improve the performance of recognition, the robust and accurate eyes detection should be a must.

With the precise detection of the eyeballs, we are able to reduce greatly the number of the scales under consideration during the recognition, and therefore to improve the performance and the speed of the recognition process. The algorithm detects the center and radius of the eyeballs at subpixellic accuracy.

2 Pre-attentive feature detection

In low resolution, the eye or eyebrow in the face image usually are dark bars which can be easily detected by the elongated second derivative Gaussian filter. In fact, the nose and mouth are also dark bars when face is in low resolution. So the response of the filtering is a peak or valley in the center of such a feature.

Given a filter, only the features in the same scale and same orientation could be detected. However, we found that even with a fixed scale filter the pre-attentive features in certain range can also be detected correctly. As an example, given the 2nd derivative Gaussian filter that is 13 taps in y-direction (25 taps in x-direction), a face's components can be detected as pre-attentive features when the distance between two eyes of the face is from 18 to 37 pixels in experiments.

*Real World Computing Partnership
†Kent Ridge Digital Labs

1051-4651/00 $10.00 © 2000 IEEE

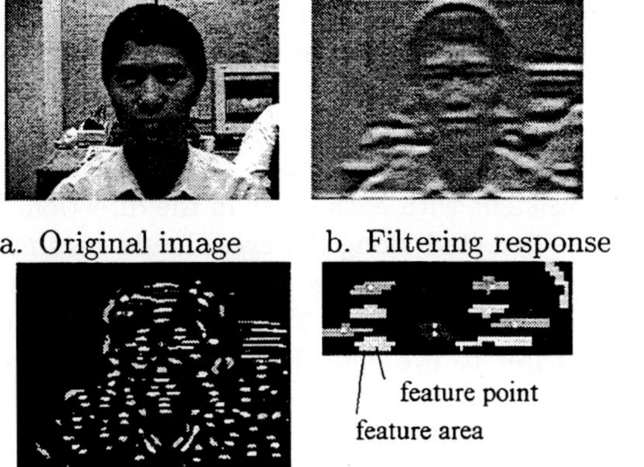

a. Original image b. Filtering response

c. Pre-attentive points d. Zoomed part

Figure 1. Pre-attentive feature detection

Of cause in order to detect features in different scales, multiscale filters in multiple orientations should be applied to the image. The face candidates screening is done from the smallest scale. If a face is detected, other scale space will not be searched. It can cover the scale range from 18 pixels to 74 (37×2) pixels and tilt range from -30 to +30 degree when detected in two discrete scales and three discrete orientations, which are enough for our system.

3 Facial image analysis

With the feature candidates obtained above, three models are investigated to search face pattern and facial components. The structure model is used to group feature points into face. It provides information on whether the area is face-like in structure. The texture model is used for similarity measurement with gray or color information for whether the pattern is face-like in texture. The feature model is used for feature measurement for whether a component is a facial feature.

3.1 Structure Model

The structure model groups the feature focusing points into face candidates using the geometric relationships defined in [4]. In this paper, a simplified version of face structure model is presented as follows.

For eyes area, two possible sub-structures are shown in Fig.2.a, two pairs of eye-eyebrow are shown, and Fig.2.b, one pair of eyes are shown. For mouth area, with the information of eye-pair, there is at least one local minimum feature point in the corresponding area. Considering the different expressions and other noise, there may be two or more local minima in the area. Shown in Fig.3, the mouth/nose will be one of the substructures.

All the relationships among the substructures should satisfy certain geometric conditions. In system, the sub-structures of eye-pair are detected first. With a sub-structure of eye-pair, the corresponding substructure of mouth-nose are searched. The *real world face* candidate is composed of the two sub-structures. Then the affine transformation are applied to the *face structure model* to fit the real world face structure.

a. Eye-eyebrows detected separately (left)
b. Eye-eyebrows detected as one maximum (right)

Figure 2. Eye area sub-structure, in the figure, gray area is the corresponding mouth area

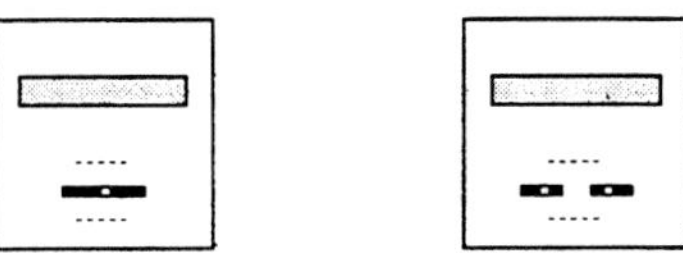

a. Mouth area, nose-mouth structure (left)
b. More maxima detected (right)

Figure 3. Mouth area sub-structure, in the figure, gray area is the corresponding eyes area

3.2 Texture Model

The texture model measures the gray or color similarities of a candidate with face model, including the variation between the facial regions (eyes, nose etc.), the symmetry of the face and the color/gray texture similarity between two regions of the face. Moreover, in the model, the symmetry of face in the filtered domain is enhanced because the related brightness is kept almost the same.

To measure the texture similarity, we use the two cheek areas, which are defined as the areas below eyes and at the side of nose. One example is shown in Fig.4.

The texture measurement is on two features. One is the gray level variance in the area:

$$V_l = \sqrt{\sum_{i,j}(I(i,j) - M)^2},$$

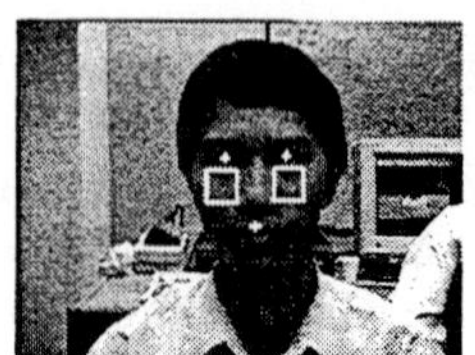
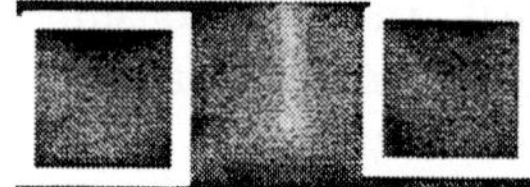

Figure 4. Cheek areas defined by the eye positions

where $I(i,j)$ is the intensity value at pixel (i,j) and M is the mean of the gray values in the area. The other kind of feature is gradient variance in the area.

$$V_G[n] = \sqrt{\sum_{i,j} G_I[n](i,j)^2},$$

where $G_I[n] = I * G[n]$, $G[n], n = 0,1,2,3$ are the 2D Sobel operators.

Let V_l^{left} be the V_l in the left cheek, V_l^{right} be the V_l in the right cheek, $V_G^{left}[n]$ be the $V_G[n]$ in left cheek and $V_G^{right}[n]$ be the $V_G[n]$ in the right cheek. The texture symmetry of the two cheek areas is then characterized by

$$R_l = \frac{|V_l^{left} - V_l^{right}|}{V_l^{left} + V_l^{right}},$$

$$R_G[n] = \frac{|V_G^{left}[n] - V_G^{right}[n]|}{V_G^{left}[n] + V_G^{right}[n]}, n = 0,1,2,3.$$

The ratio values are ideally 0. However in order to reduce the influence of spectacles and the variation of illumination and skin tone, we set

$$R_l < 0.30$$
$$R_G[n] < 0.33,\ n = 0,1,2,3$$

as the face texture model. The texture measurement itself can also be a feature of face. We believe that V_ls and V_Gs in all of the subregions that are below the eye region have the characteristics that can distinguish face pattern and many other non-face patterns.

3.3 Feature Model

The feature model compares the feature area to specific facial feature. Here we use the eigen-eyes method [9] combined with image feature analysis for eyes detection. Since the scale information has been obtained for each face candidate, via the structure model, the eigen-eye method can be applied here efficiently.

The normalized horizontal and vertical projections of the image of eye areas are the first kind of feature. The correlation of the projection with the template that is trained by samples is taken as a parameter of the similarity measurement.

Another important feature is the direction of the detected preattentive feature. Because the two eyes are consistent with each other in the direction, the directions detected along the eyes should be almost the same. The feature is used in combination with structure model (cf. section 3.1). More details of using image features to eye detection are presented in section 4.

3.4 Elimination of Conflicting Candidates

Let f_1 and f_2 the two conflicting face candidates, and $T^1 = (R_l^1, \{R_G^1[n], n = 0,1,2,3\})$ and $T^2 = (R_l^2, \{R_G^2[n], n = 0,1,2,3\})$ are respective texture measurement vectors (cf. section 3.2). Because the elements of the vector T^1 (resp. T^2), indicate the flatness of the cheek of f_1 (resp. f_2), we use the difference between the two vectors, denoted by D_{flat}, to indicate the similarity of flatness:

$$D_{flat} = \frac{1}{N}\sum_i (T_i^1 - T_i^2), N = 5.$$

The similarity in feature model is characterized by the eigen-eyes similarity. Let D_{DFFS}^1 and D_{DFFS}^2 the measurement of eigen-feature [9] similarity in the feature model for the eye pair 1 in face f_1 and the eye pair 2 in face f_2. We define

$$D_{eigen} = D_{DFFS}^1 - D_{DFFS}^2.$$

Using D_{flat} and D_{eigen}, we define the distance measure as

$$D(f_1, f_2) = \omega D_{flat} + (1-\omega) D_{eigen},$$

where ω=0.25. Notice that D_{flat} and D_{eigen} are already normalized, $0 \le D_{eigen}, D_{flat} \le 1$. The decision is

$$Detected\ face = \begin{cases} f_1, & if\ D(f_1,f_2) > \alpha \\ f_2, & if\ D(f_1,f_2) < -\alpha \end{cases}.$$

Empirically, the value of α is a very small positive number.

4 Precise Eye Location

Here, we propose a method to detect the center and the radius of the eyeballs with a subpixellic precision, considering the face recognition is done on face images that are normalized with the eyes position decided previously by the face model. We start from the initial eye position (x, y), and we look for the homogeneous circular regions as eyeballs centered at (x^*, y^*) and having a radius r^* in the subimage centered in (x, y) containing the eye. This research is reàlized in the zoomed image, and by the reverse coordinates transformation, we obtain the real coordinates with a precision of half a pixel.

We combine two complementary measures based on the edge information, namely the hough transform for the circle and the contour-correlation of circle model with the image, and we eliminate the invalid hypothesis using a measure of homogeneity associated to the image defined by the current disc. Finally, we use a robust method to select the best circle among all the possible circles.

4.1 Preprocessing

This preprocessing consists in three ordered steps. First, we construct a zoomed image of the eye, centered in (x, y), and we normalize it, in order to cancel the linear changes of contrast and brightness [10]. Then, we extract the edges from this normalized image, and finally, we improve the quality of the eyeball region, by reducing the quantity of light which is reflected within it.

The zoom factor applied to the face is determined, using the previous position of the two eyeballs, says (x_1, y_1) and (x_2, y_2), such that the final distance separating two eyes in the zoomed image is equal to 100 pixels. For the face recognition, we work with normalized images, such that the distance between two eyes is equal to 50 pixels. In these images, we noticed, before the proposed precise eyes detection, a position error of ± 3 pixels of the eyeball centers, crucial points for a good geometrical normalization and thus for a good recognition. Therefore, the precision obtained in the zoomed image is of half-pixel, in respect to the normalization for the recognition.

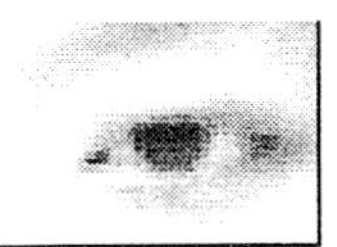

Figure 5. The Canny-deriche edge detection

4.2 Hypothesis Evaluation

A hypothesis $H(x, y, r)$ is a possible eyeball centered at (x, y) with radius r. To build the hypothesis set, we proceed in four steps: 1) using *a priori* knowledge, we select the set of likely hypothesis; 2) we compute the hough transform; 3) we compute the reciprocal operation using a contour correlation technique; 4) we keep only the homogeneous regions.

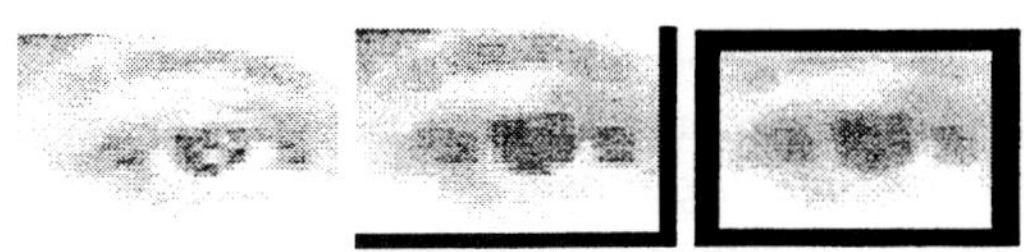

Figure 6. Cancelling the light reflected in the eye

original image (left); filtered image (middle); smoothed image (right)

Using an automatic thresholding method, we get the eyeball region by segmentation of the dark pixels, which is defined as the pixels having gray level less than a threshold τ, so that all the dark pixels occupy a small part, say 15%, of the eye area.

Finally, we obtain the set $H = \bigcup_{r=6}^{10} H(r)$ of the likely hypothesis, using the dilation (neighborhood of 2 pixels),

$$H(r) = \{(x, y, r) : \exists(i, j) : I(x + i, y + j) \leq \tau\}$$

where $-2 \leq i, j \leq 2$.

Figure 7. Automatic Thresholding Results

4.2.1 Circular Detection

Both the Hough transform and the contour correlation are used for finding discs on the contour image. The parameters are the disc center (x, y) and the radius r. Then, the hypothesis (x, y, r) is kept for subsequential analysis if

$$H = \{(x, y, r) \in H : acc(x, y, r) > M\}$$

where $acc(x, y, r)$ is the accumulator in Hough transform and $M = 3$.

The correlation of a hypothesis (x, y, r) with the digital circle $C(x, y, r)$ is computed as

$$cor(x, y, r) = \frac{1}{N} \sum_{(a,b) \in C(x,y,r)} \alpha(a, b)$$

where N is the number of pixels in the circle model,

$$\alpha(a, b) = \begin{cases} 0 & \textit{if } \beta(a, b) <= K \\ 1 & \textit{if } \beta(a, b) > K \end{cases}$$

$\beta(a,b)$ is the number of points having a nonzero edge magnitude in a 3x3 neighborhood of (a,b), which allows more robustness, against the variability of the shape of the observed circle, and against the possible breaks of the contour,

$$\beta(a,b) = \sum_{i=-1}^{1}\sum_{j=-1}^{1} contour(a+i, b+j).$$

Here $K = 3$.

The hypothesis are rejected by contour correlation, when the obtained score is too weak,

$$H = \{(x,y,r) \in H : cor(x,y,r) > th_{cor}\}.$$

with the threshold th_{cor} fixed to 0.6, which means that we accept an hypothesis only if at least 60% of the circle is present in the edge image.

4.2.2 Region Homogeneity

A hypothesis is an eyeball if 1) it is a homogeneous (monochromatic) region, 2) it is darker than the white region surrounding it. In order to compensate the presence of light within the eyeball, we use the grey level image, filtered in the preprocessing step.

A normalized standard deviation is used here as the homogeneity measure,

$$hom(x,y,r) = \frac{1}{255}\sigma\left(\frac{r_{min}}{r}\right)^2,$$

where σ is the standard deviation of the gray level in the region delimited by the digital disc $D(x,y,r)$ and r_{min} is the minimum radius allowed (here 6 pixels). The smaller the value of $hom(x,y,r)$, the better the homogeneity. With the intensity mean μ to measure the darkness of the region, we have

$$H = \{(x,y,r) \in H : \mu < \tau \wedge \mathrm{hom}(x,y,r) < th_\sigma\},$$

where τ has been fixed in the pre-selection step (4.2), and th_σ is defined for the disc of radius r_{min}

$$th_\sigma = \frac{5}{255} = 0.02.$$

It means that we tolerate a standard deviation of 5 grey levels around the mean value within 100 pixels.

4.3 Optimal Decision of the Location

We obtained three values for each valid hypothesis (x,y,r): 1) $acc(x,y,r)$; 2) $cor(x,y,r)$; 3) $hom(x,y,r)$. In order to get the best hypothesis of eyeball (x^*,y^*,r^*), we first select the best center (x^*,y^*) which minimizes a cost function, and secondly, we research the best radius.

4.3.1 Selecting the Best Center

The set V_r of the likely disc hypothesis is defined as the set of disc for which reasonable values of the contour correlation and the homogeneity values have been obtained

$$\begin{aligned} V_r &= \{(x,y,r) \in H : \\ & \quad cor(x,y,r) > \alpha \wedge hom(x,y,r) < \beta\}. \end{aligned}$$

for $\alpha = 0.6$ and $\beta = 0.015$. The potential centers set V is then given by

$$V = \{(x,y) : \exists(x,y,r) \in V_r\}$$

To select the best center in V, we define a cost function which combines the scores of Hough transform and contour correlation,

$$N(x,y) = \gamma\widehat{H}^2(x,y) + (1-\gamma)\widehat{C}^2(x,y)$$

where

$$\widehat{H}(x,y) = 1 - \frac{H(x,y)}{H_{max}}, \quad \widehat{C}(x,y) = 1 - \frac{C(x,y)}{C_{max}}$$

with

$$\begin{array}{ll} H(x,y) = \int_r acc(x,y,r) & H_{max} = \max_{(x,y)} H(x,y) \\ C(x,y) = \int_r cor(x,y,r) & C_{max} = \max_{(x,y)} C(x,y) \end{array}$$

Here $\gamma = 0.3$ weights the relative importance.

The values of N are normalized, and the optimal center position is then provided by the minimum value of $N(x,y)$, that is

$$(x^*,y^*) = \arg\min_{(x,y)} N(x,y).$$

4.3.2 Selecting the Best Circle

Let V_r^*, the set of the likely hypothesis centered in the neighborhood of (x^*,y^*), with $\epsilon_x = \epsilon_y = 1$,

$$V_r^* = \{(x,y,r) : |x-x^*| \le \epsilon_x \wedge |y-y^*| \le \epsilon_y\}.$$

The optimal hypothesis (x_c,y_c,r_c) is searched in V_r^*. For two hypothesis $h_1 = (x_1,y_1,r_1)$, $h_2 = (x_2,y_2,r_2)$, we define the order relation $h_1 >^* h_2$, if

$$cor(h_1) > cor(h_2) + \epsilon_{cor}$$

or

$$|cor(h_1) - cor(h_2)| < \epsilon_{cor} \wedge hom(h_1) < hom(h_2)$$

where $\epsilon_{cor} = 0.001$. We then obtain the optimal point $h_c = (x_c,y_c,r_c) \in V_r^*$ such that

$$h_c >^* h, \forall h \in (V_r^* - \{h_c\})$$

and the hypothesis is ultimately accepted if

$$\pi(h_c) > \pi, \ \textit{with}\ \pi(h_c) = cor(h_c) * (1 - hom(h_c)).$$

For the prefixed thresholds, namely α for the correlation and β for the homogeneity, the rejection threshold π has been fixed such that $\pi > \alpha(1-\beta)$. With $\alpha = 0.6$ and $\beta = 0.02$ (cf. 4.2.1,4.2.2), we can have $\pi = 0.6$.

5 Results and Discussion

We have proposed a scheme for face location and accurate eyes detection, which is based on multiple evidences, including facial components structure, texture similarity, component feature measurement and contour matching.

Applying the multiscale and multi-orientation filters bank to images, the proposed method can detect faces in the size from 18 pixel to 74 pixel and tilted from -30 degree to +30 degree.

The original image size is 384 × 288. For one image, it takes about 5.0 seconds to capture the eyes on Sun Ultra1 workstation, considering to search all the scale and orientation space. It can be faster if the color information is used to segment the image first. Upon the first face captured, the face tracking can be implemented for the on-line detection and human-machine interface. Total 852 images are captured, in which some persons provided several times for capturing their faces with different conditions, such as that of the illumination, background, with or without glasses, a little expressions etc.

Figure 8. Faces detected with eyes marked

There are 84 errors in face detection which are caused by tilt face (tilt angle larger than 30 degree), too much rotation in depth (so not front view), illumination unbalance including the bright reflection on the glasses, and model unfitting, the feature model in the current system can not fit too *dark* skin.

Based on the face detected, we also proposed a precise eye detection (half-pixel) combining contour and region information extracted from a zoomed image. The accuracy of the detection is defined by the difference between the one detected automatically and the one fixed manually. Here we have tested it against two databases. One is built from video images that contains more than 200 images. The other is a photo image database with more than 5000 frontal view faces.

Noticeable improvements have been realized, especially in the rotation and scale normalizations. In video image database, we got 100% eyes located accurately provided the face detected correctly before. On the photo database, only 2% failure is reported for either no eyes detected or wrong eyes position obtained, which are mainly caused by the poor quality of the images.

Another use of this algorithm is to evaluate, before the recognition, if a detected face is suitable for a good normalization or not, and therefore, for a successful recognition or not. To a specific hardware configuration, if the detected eyeballs are judged too small, too close or too far from each other, we expect that the normalization will be very unstable. Here the probability of confusion with another face is reduced, of cause with the increase of the rejection rate.

References

[1] S. Gutta et. al. Face recognition using ensembles of networks. In *Proc. of Int. Conf. on Pattern Recognition.* Vienna, Austria, Aug. 1996.

[2] H. A. Rowley, S. Baluja and T. Kanade. Human face detection in visual scenes. Technical Report CMU-CS-95-158, Dept of Computer Science, Carnegie Mellon University, July, 1995.

[3] S.-H. Lin, S.-Y. Kung and L.-J. Lin. Face recognition/detection by probabilistic decision-based neural network. *IEEE Trans. on Neural Networks*, 8(1):114–132, 1997.

[4] K. C. Yow and R. Cipolla. Feature-based human face detection. Technical Report CUED/F-INFENG/TR 249, Dept of Engineering, University of Cambridge, Cambridge, England, Aug, 1996.

[5] Q. Chen, H. Wu and M. Yachida. Face detection by fuzzy pattern matching. In *Proc. of 5th Int conf on Computer Vision*, pages 591–596. MIT, Boston, 1995.

[6] J. L. Crowley and J. Coutaz. Vision for man machine interaction. In *Proc. of Working Conference on Engineering for Human-Computer Interaction*, pages 187–217. (Grand Targhee Resort), 1995.

[7] J. Bala et. al. Visual routine for eye detection using hybrid genetic architectures. In *Proc. of Int. Conf. on Pattern Recognition.* Vienna, Austria, Aug. 1996.

[8] A. Yuille, D. Cohen and P. Hallinan. Feature extraction from faces using deformable templates. In *IEEE Computer Soc. Conf. on Computer Vision and Patt. Recog.*, pages 104–109, 1989.

[9] A. Pentland, B. Moghaddam and T. Starner. View-based and modular eigenspaces for face recognition. Technical Report No. 245, Perceptual Computing Section, Media Laboratory, MIT, 1994.

[10] T. H. Reiss. Recognizing planar objects using invariant image features. In *Lecture Notes in Computer Sciences, Springer Verlag, Vol. 676*, pages 14–15, 1993.

Generating Natural Language Description of Human Behavior from Video Images

Atsuhiro Kojima[†], Masao Izumi[‡], Takeshi Tamura[†], Kunio Fukunaga[‡]
[†]Library and Science Information Center, [‡]College of Engineering
Osaka Prefecture University
1-1, Gakuen-cho, Sakai City, Osaka, Japan
ark@center.osakafu-u.ac.jp

Abstract

In visual surveillance applications, it is becoming popular to perceive video images and to interpret them using natural language concepts. In this paper we propose a new approach to generate natural language description of human behavior appeared in real video images. First, a head region of a human, on behalf of the whole body, is extracted from each frames. Using a model based method, three dimensional pose and position of the head are estimated. Next, the trajectory of these parameters is divided into segments of monotonous motions. For each segment, we evaluate conceptual features such as degree of change of pose and position and that of relative distance to some objects in the surroundings, and so on. By calculating product of these feature values, a most suitable verb is selected and other syntactic elements are supplied. Finally natural language text is generated using technique of machine translation.

1. Introduction

Applying concepts of natural language to vision system is becoming popular. Traffic surveillance system, for instance, reports moving vehicles by series of motion verbs or short sentences rather than numerical expressions of the objects' location[4, 5]. In their method, fuzzy sets are used to associate trajectory segments and verbs by evaluating membership functions of trajectory attributes such as vehicle speed. Compared with vehicle movements, describing human behavior in image sequences is more complicated. In a visual surveillance system, human behavior is represented by scenarios, i.e. predefined sequences of events[9]. Similarly, in an automatic annotation system for sport scene, each formation of players is represented by belief networks based on visual evidence and temporal constraints[3]. These works focus on recognition of specific human behavior patterns, and natural language is used to express them simply. In natural language, however, there are various concepts about actions, events and states inherently, so that effective and adequate expression enough to convey the meanings of the scene is necessary.

To this end, contribution from artificial intelligence and natural language processing have been incorporated into some works. Herzog & Rohr[2] present three levels of representation from low-level geometrical description estimated from images to high-level linguistic description. Okada & Tamachi[8, 7] demonstrate explanation of behavior of entities in a series of linedrawings using simulated mind model.

In this paper, we propose a method to generate text in natural language which explains human behavior in real video images by extracting features of human motion and selecting verbs. We finally demonstrate linguistic surveillance system as an example of applications of our method.

2. Pose and position estimation of humans

To estimate human motions in video images, the pose and position of a human head are useful because they imply horizontal location of its whole body as well as direction of its face. Most of human actions have effects on other objects, and the objects can be determined by the direction of the human's eyes. Human head's pose and position estimation is made by model based method as described below.

2.1. Extraction of human head regions

First of all, we extract human region from each video frame. Here we use a stationary camera and assume that a scene background is almost out of motion. In this assumption, the background image can be stored previously, so human regions can be detected as regions which differ from

1051-4651/00 $10.00 © 2000 IEEE

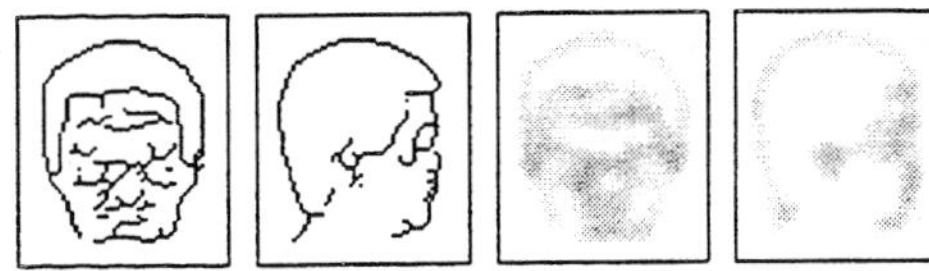

(a) edge image (b) dimmed edge image

Figure 1. Sample images of human head.

the background images. Out of the whole body region, we extract a head region of a human using chromaticity averages of previously calculated hair and facial skin colors.

2.2. Pose and position estimation using sample images

To estimate the pose of a head, we evaluate the similarity between input image and sample image. A set of sample images is prepared previously and the pose of each image is assumed to be known.

Edge extraction and thinning are applied to the head region. As for sample images, the same process is done previously as shown in Figure 1 (a). Since edge lines of input images and sample images are slightly different from each other, pose estimation fails if edge positions are compared directly. To avoid this problem, we apply dimming to them using Gaussian filter before comparison. Figure 1 (b) shows dimmed edge images of samples. Considering an image as a vector which consists of elements valued by each pixel grayscale, we define similarity as an inner product of two image vectors. The similarity becomes large when correlation of two images is high. So the pose of a head in the sample image which shows the largest similarity is supposed to be the estimated pose.

On the other hand, the position of a head can be calculated from size and position of the head in the image plain using projection transformation.

Applying these method into each video frames in which human behavior is taken, a trajectory of human head motion can be obtained. Figure 2 shows a part of the input video image in which a man (computer user) was entering the room, operating a computer (pc1) for a while, moving to another computer (ws2), operating it, and finally exiting the room. Figure 3 shows a trajectory of horizontal coordinates of the user on a map of the room. The arrangement of equipment in the room is assumed to be given previously.

3. Generation of behavioral expression

Since the trajectory of a man is merely a series of numerical data containing physical three dimensional coordinates of the human head, it is difficult to deduce events in natural language concepts directly from this trace. This section describes how to search the correspondence between physical

Figure 2. An example of input video image.

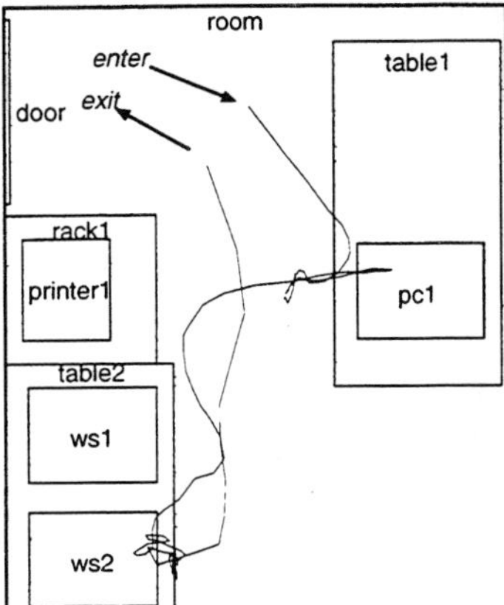

Figure 3. A trajectory of human in the room.

human head motion and verbs of natural language

3.1. Extraction of conceptual features of behavior

A series of motion of a man can be divided into some parts in which he/she dose a single act. In each part of a motion, changes of pose and position parameters supposed to be monotonic. So the trajectory of pose and position parameters is divided into segments by the following criteria.

1. Moving of the human head keeps almost the same direction.
2. The human head keeps around the same position.

By the way, concepts of events in natural language can be certified by conceptual features, such as motions of an agent itself, or changes of relative positions of the agent and an object influenced by the agent, and so on[8].

To indicate conceptual features of behavior in each motion segment, we use the feature values described in Table 1. A range of each feature value is $[0, 1]$, and the more apparent the feature is indicated, the closer to 1 the value is. For example, to evaluate the feature value of 'move_near', calculate d , the change of the distance of the agent to an object between at the beginning and at the end of the segment. Then the feature value is $f(d)$, where the sigmoid

Table 1. Values of conceptual features.

feature	range	meaning
features about motion		
time_elapse	real [0,1]	time elapsing or not
move	real [0,1]	object moves
move_near	real [0,1]	move toward object
move_apart	real [0,1]	move away from object
move_up	real [0,1]	move to up
move_down	real [0,1]	move to down
turn_toward	real [0,1]	turn to the direction of object
...	...	......
features about state		
face	real [0,1]	face to object
by	real [0,1]	locate near object
exist	integer 0/1	existing
...	...	......
features about characteristics		
prop_through	integer 0/1	able to be passed through
prop_operable	integer 0/1	able to be operated
...	...	......

function $f(x)$ is defined by the following equation of which the range is $[0, 1]$.

$$f(x) = \frac{1}{1 + Ae^{-Bx}} \tag{1}$$

where A and B are empirically selected constants.

3.2. Selection of verbs

Next, select the most suitable verb which explains the behavior in the considering segment by use of feature values calculated above. For instance, according to the analysis of concept of the verb 'to approach $\cdots$', its conceptual features are as follows.

1. Both an agent and an object are appearing in the scene during the behavior.
2. The distance between the agent and the object decreases as a result of the behavior.
3. In the beginning of the behavior, the agent faces the object.
4. At the end of the behavior, the agent is located near the object.

where 1 $\cdots$ 4 are corresponding to 'exist', 'move_near', 'face', 'by' in Table 1 respectively.

Table 2 shows examples of concepts of some verbs including *approach*. To clarify a difference in features of states between at the beginning and at the end of behavior,

Table 2. Construction of verbs from features.

verb	conceptual features
approach	exist$(a)^0$, exist$(a)^1$, exist$(o)^0$, exist$(o)^1$, face$(a, o)^0$, by$(a,o)^1$, move_near(a, o)
go away	exist$(a)^0$, exist$(a)^1$, exist$(o)^0$, exist$(o)^1$, by$(a, o)^0$, neg(by$(a, o)^1$), move_apart(a, o)
stand up	exist$(a)^0$, exist$(a)^1$, move_up(a)
sit down	exist$(a)^0$, exist$(a)^1$, move_down(a)
enter	neg(exist$(a)^0$), exist$(a)^1$, by$(a, o)^1$, prop_through(o)
exit	exist$(a)^0$, neg(exist$(a)^1$), by$(a, o)^0$, prop_through(o)
operate	exist$(a)^0$, exist$(a)^1$, time_elapse(a), face$(a, o)^0$, neg(move(a)), prop_operable(o)
...	......

a: agent, o: object, neg$(p) \equiv 1 - p$

let us denote 0 like exist$(a)^0$ as a value at the beginning of behavior, and 1 as a value at the end. In addition, as for transitive verbs such as *approach*, candidates of passive objects must be specified.

Since these conceptual features of verbs are evaluated numerically, define fitness for each combination of the verb and the object as a product of all these feature values about the verb. And after calculating fitness of candidates which are all the combinations of verbs and objects, the combination which shows the largest fitness is selected as a behavior which explains the considering segment.

Using this result, we define *behavioral expression* as a list of elements of *tag:value* format like follows with verbs, agents (actors) and objects.

[PRED:*verb*, AG:*agent*, OBJ:*object*, ..., SO-TIME:$time_1$, GO-TIME:$time_2$]

where PRED is a name of a verb, AG is an agent, OBJ is the objective, and there may be additional elements for some verbs, and where SO-TIME, GO-TIME are the time at the beginning of behavior and the time at the end, respectively.

3.3. Inference of higher level behavior

Since behavioral expression mentioned above is bound to the segment based on pose and position changes of human, granularity of behavioral expressions will be sometime unnecessarily fine.

So in this work, we infer higher level behavioral expression by applying production rules into consecutive several behavioral expressions. Next we show an example of a production rule as follows.

$$[\text{PRED:approach, AG:}a\text{, OBJ:}o\text{, SO-TIME:}t_1\text{, GO-TIME:}t_2]$$
$$\&\ [\text{PRED:sit-down, AG:}a\text{, SO-TIME:}t_2\text{, GO-TIME:}t_3]$$
$$\Rightarrow [\text{PRED:sit-down, AG:}a\text{, GO-LOC:}o\text{, SO-TIME:}t_1\text{, GO-TIME:}t_3]$$

This example shows a rule to produce 'to sit down at ···' from a combination of 'to approach ···' and 'to sit down'.

4. Generating text

We try to translate behavioral expression into natural language sentence by use of case structure transformation[6], one of machine translation technique based on the case grammar proposed by Fillmore[1]. Case structure representing the relationship between phrases in a sentence can be expressed by *case frame*, which have the same form as behavioral expression defined in 3.2.

Applying word dictionaries, case structure pattern of verbs, and syntax rules into behavioral expression, natural language text can be generated. Figure 4 shows the result of processing a series of behavioral expression and that of text.

5. Discussion

We clarified the way of transforming image data as geometrical and numerical information into conceptual and linguistic form base on analyses of conceptual features of verbs. In comparison with prior works, we regard the concepts of verbs in natural language as important and decompose them using *semantic primitives* mentioned in the field of natural language processing.

As a natural consequence of this, adequate verbs and passive objects can be selected in sophisticated and constructive way. Moreover, behavioral expression have the standard form of case frame, so that translation to natural language text can be performed by the standard machine translation technique.

6. Conclusion

In this work, we have proposed a method for generating natural language text explaining human behavior from video images.

To deal with more complex and various behavior of human, we are developping framework to cope with motion of hands and object grasping/releasing in future.

[PRED:enter, AG:man1, OBJ:door, SO-TIME:t1, GO-TIME:t2]
[PRED:go-away, AG:man1, OBJ:door, SO-TIME:t2, GO-TIME:t3]
[PRED:approach, AG:man1, OBJ:pc1, SO-TIME:t3, GO-TIME:t4]
[PRED:sit-down, AG:man1, SO-TIME:t4, GO-TIME:t5]
[PRED:operate, AG:man1, OBJ:pc1, SO-TIME:t5, GO-TIME:t6]
[PRED:stand-up, AG:man1, SO-TIME:t6, GO-TIME:t7]
⋮

(a) Behavioral expressions.

[PRED:enter, AG:man1, SO-LOC:door, SO-TIME:t1, GO-TIME:t3]
[PRED:sit-down, AG:man1, GO-LOC:pc1, SO-TIME:t3, GO-TIME:t5]
[PRED:operate, AG:man1, OBJ:pc1, SO-TIME:t5, GO-TIME:t6]
[PRED:stand-up, AG:man1, SO-TIME:t6, GO-TIME:t7]
⋮

(b) High-level behavioral expressions.

At the time t1, man1 entered from the door.
At the time t5, man1 sat down at PC-1.
From the time t5 to the time t6, man1 was operating PC-1.
At the time t6, man1 stood up.
At the time t10, man1 sat down at WS-2.
From the time t10 to the time t11, man1 was operating WS-2.
At the time t11, man1 stood up.
At the time t14, man1 exited from the door.

(c) Natural language text.

Figure 4. The result of text generation.

References

[1] C. J. Fillmore. The case for case. In E. Bach and R. Harms, editors, *Universals in linguistic theory*. Rinehart and Wiston, New York, 1968.

[2] G. Herzog and K. Rohr. Integrating vision and language: Towards automatic description of human movements. In *Proc. 19th Annual German Conf. on Artificial Intelligence*, pages 257–268, 1995.

[3] S. Intille and A. Bobick. Representation and visual recognition of complex, multi-agent actions using belief networks. Technical Report 454, M.I.T Media Lab. Perceptual Computing Section, 1998.

[4] H. Kollnig, H.-H. Nagel, and M. Otte. Association of motion verbs with vehicle movements extracted from dense optical flow fields. In *Proc. of 3rd European Conf. on Computer Vision '94*, pages 338–347, 1994.

[5] H.-H. Nagel. A vision of 'vision and language' comprises action: An example from road traffic. *Artifitial Intelligence Review*, 8:189–214, 1994.

[6] F. Nishida, S. Takamatsu, T. Tani, and T. Doi. Feedback of correcting information in postediting to a machine translation system. In *Proc. of COLING-88*, pages 476–481, 1988.

[7] N. Okada. Integrating vision, motion and language through mind. *Artifitial Intelligence Review*, 8:209–234, 1996.

[8] N. Okada and T. Tamachi. Interpretation of th meaning of moving pictures patterns and its description in natural language — semantic analysis —. *Trans. IEICE(D)*, J59-D(5):331–338, 1976. in Japanese.

[9] M. Thonnat and N. Rota. Image understanding for visual surveillance applications. In *Proc. of 3rd Int. Workshop on Cooperative Distributed Vision*, pages 51–82, 1999.

Model Predictive Control to Improve Visual Control of Motion: Applications in Active Tracking of Moving Targets

João P. Barreto, Jorge Batista, Helder Araújo
Institute of Systems and Robotics
Dept. of Electrical Engineering
University of Coimbra
3030 Coimbra - Portugal
jpbar@isr.uc.pt, batista@isr.uc.pt, helder@isr.uc.pt

Abstract

This paper deals with active tracking of 3D moving targets. Visual tracking is presented as a regulation control problem. The performance and robustness in visual control of motion depends both on the vision algorithms and the control structure. Delays and system latencies substantially affect the performance of visually guided systems. In this paper we discuss ways to cope with delays while improving system performance. Model predictive control strategies are proposed to compensate for the mechanical latency in visual control of motion.

1. Introduction

Visual control of motion is a major issue in active vision that involves complex topics of both visual processing and control [1]. This work discusses the problem of tracking moving targets using visual information to control camera motion. An architecture to achieve this goal is presented.

Visually guided systems are dynamic systems whose actions are derived directly from image information. Several strategies to extract visual information for motion control have been proposed [2, 3]. The visual processing must be fast, accurate and robust to achieve high performance behaviors. Mounting the camera on an active platform arises additional difficulties due to the self-induced image motion (egomotion). These problems are discussed and solutions are presented. Kalman filtering is used to estimate the target 3D parameters of motion and limit the effects of measurement errors in the image, allowing smooth tracking behaviors.

Delays in both feedforward and feedback paths of a dynamic system affect substantially the overall performance. This subject is exhaustively discussed in [4]. The latency

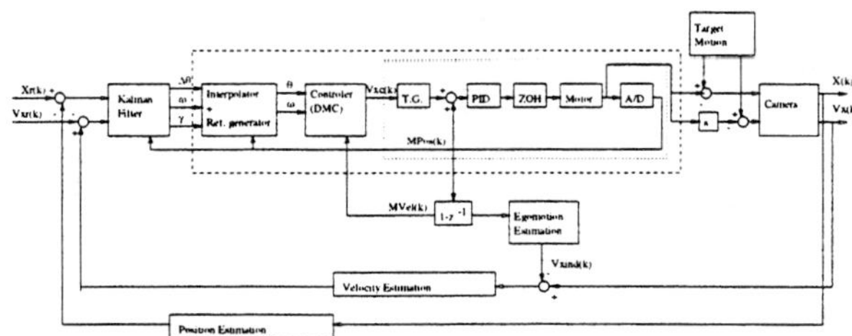

Figure 1. Smooth pursuit block diagram.

introduced by visual feedback is one of the reasons that make vision-based control so difficult. This paper focus on strategies to cope with delays in visual control of motion. The performance of our tracking system is increased by compensating the visual processing delays. Interpolation assuming a constant acceleration model of motion in 3D space is used. The plant to be controlled (in our case a robot head) also presents delays that affect the overall performance. Model predictive control techniques are proposed to cope with process delay in vision-based control. Plant models are obtained with standard system identification techniques and a dynamic matrix controller (DMC) is used in our tracking application. The performance of the DMC controller is discussed and compared with other possible control strategies.

2. System Architecture

In a monocular tracking application the camera has two independent rotational degrees of freedom: pan and tilt. The control of each of these degrees of freedom can be modeled by the schematic of Fig. 1. The system inputs (references) are the desired target position and velocity in the image, and the outputs are the actual target position and

1051-4651/00 $10.00 © 2000 IEEE

velocity in the image. This is typically a regulation control problem whose goal is to keep the moving target in a certain position in the image (usually its center).

In a real-time tracking systems we can identify three distinct concurrent processes: the vision processing of the images, the servo control of camera platform and the smooth pursuit controller (see 1). The visual feedback loop typically runs at 25Hz. A high gain, high sample rate local servocontroller is needed to ensure that close control over platform position and velocity is maintained with minimum error. Several dedicated servo control modules are commercially available. In our system, platform motion is generated by DC motors equipped with optical encoders for position feedback. Each axis is controlled by an independent module that implements a closed loop with a digital PID filter running at 1KHz. Each servo loop can be commanded in velocity by adding a profile generator that integrates the velocities sent by the user process. Communication is synchronous at a frequency of 166Hz. This means that user process can only send commands to the servo module and read the encoders in every 6ms time intervals. The smooth pursuit controller makes the interface between the high level visual loop and the low level servocontroller. It receives the result of visual processing and sends velocity commands to the servo loop. This middle level controller must run at the maximum communication rate (in our case 166Hz) to optimize global system performance.

3 The Visual Control Loop. Visual Processing Delays

Target motion acts as a perturbation that has to be compensated for. To implement high performance tracking certain issues, such as robustness to sudden changes of target trajectory and velocity, can not be neglected. Evaluation of both vision and control algorithms within a common framework is needed for the optimization of the global system performance [5]. This framework has been established in previous work [6]. To study and characterize the system regulation/control performance usual control test signals (step, ramp, parabola and sinusoid) must be applied.

Visual processing latency compromises the overall system performance. Computation time in extracting information from images must be minimized. A trade-off between efficiency, robustness and accuracy must be made when selecting the visual processing algorithms. Simultaneous position and velocity information are fundamental to achieve high performance smooth tracking behaviors. Thus both target position and velocity in image must be measured.

Image motion depends both on target motion and camera motion (egomotion). For visual control tasks we are only interested in the motion induced by targets, thus egomotion must be compensated for. Considering that the camera only

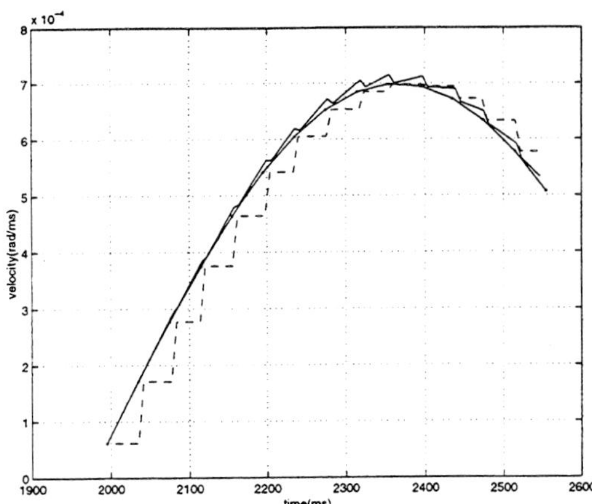

Figure 2. Target angular velocity (.-). Velocity command sent to actuator: initial implementation (–), using interpolation for visual delay compensation(-)

performs pure rotations and that there is no motion in the scene, two images are related by an homography. The homography is easily computed knowing the camera rotation measured using the motor encoders. Considering two consecutive frames, the difference image obtained after egomotion compensation contains the points where motion occurred. Position is estimated as the average location of the set of points with non-zero optical flow and non-zero brightness partial derivatives, with respect to X and Y, in the most recently grabbed image. It is assumed that all moving pixels in image have the same velocity. The velocity vector is estimated considering the flow constraint and applying a least-squares minimization. Gaussian pyramids are used to increase the range of image velocities that can be correctly estimated [6]. A Kalman filter is used to estimate the target angular parameters of motion (error in position $\Delta\theta$, velocity ω and acceleration γ) assuming a constant acceleration model between frames. This assumption is acceptable for frame acquisition rates of 25Hz and higher. The inputs to the Kalman (innovation) are the position and velocity measurements in the image and the output the state vector $\mathbf{x}$. The Kalman filter tuning has been performed with the help of our evaluation tools. Each grabbed image is processed (in a standard PC) and the parameters of motion of the target are available at the Kalman filter output 6ms after image acquisition. This is the visual latency. A structure with the estimated parameters, the image acquisition time and motor position at the acquisition time instant is sent by the high-level process (running at 25Hz) to the smooth pursuit controller (running at 166Hz). In our first control strategy the velocity command sent to the low-level loop is the sum of target velocity and tracking error in position multiplied by a gain K_p. The position component is fundamental to keep the regulation error small and to reduce the effects of occasional errors in velocity prediction. However the target motion information is sent to actuators with a delay of 6ms and kept constant until new visual information is received (see 2). This really compromises system performance. Interpolation assuming a constant acceleration model is used to compensate for the visual delay. Fig.2 compares the velocity command sent to the low-level loop with and without interpolation. Notice ripple at the top of the sinusoid, due to the highly non-linear variation of target velocity that is not described by the constant acceleration model used for interpolation.

4. Actuator/Plant Delay

Standard system identification techniques can be used to obtain the transfer function of the low-level control loop. The input considered is the velocity command sent to the profile generator (V_{xc}) and the output is the motor velocity (M_{vel}). Notice that the low-level loop runs at 1KHz and its output is being subsampled at 166Hz. Thus, the achievable model will not describe some high frequency behaviors. For our implementation the transfer function has a deadbeat of 2 sampling periods. It means that actuator/plant delay is nearly 12ms. This section discusses the use of model predictive controllers to cope with this delay.

$$J = \sum_{i=N_1}^{N_2} (y(n+i|n) - w(n+i))^2 + \sum_{j=N_1}^{N_2} \lambda \Delta u(n+j-1)^2 \tag{1}$$

There is a wide variety of MPC algorithms, but they always have three elements in common: a prediction model, an objective function and a minimization process to obtain the control law. The prediction model is used to estimate the system output $y(n+k|n)$ at future time instants knowing previous inputs and outputs. The general aim is to make future system outputs to converge for a desired reference $w(n)$. For that an objective function J is established. The general expression for such a function is given by equation 1. N_1 and N_2 bound the cost horizon, N_u is the control horizon, $u(n)$ is the control signal, $\Delta u(n)$ is the control increment ($\Delta u(n) = u(n) - u(n-1)$) and λ is relative weight used to achieve a more or less smooth control. In order to obtain present and future values of control law $u(n)$ the functional J is minimized.

The cost horizon is the future time interval where it is desirable for the output to follow the reference. Our process has a dead time of 2, thus we are going to consider $N_1 = 2$ (the output can not be forced before that). Assuming a frame rate of 25Hz, the middle level controller sends at most 7 velocity commands to the low-level loop without new visual information. Thus we are going to consider $N_2 = 8$.

Consider the step response $g(n)$ of a stable linear process without integrators. If $g(n) = 1$ for $n > N$ the system is completely described by the N first instants of $g(n)$. This is the cornerstone for a simple, robust and intuitive model predictive controller: the dynamic matrix control algorithm.

$$\mathbf{\Delta u} = (\mathbf{G}\mathbf{G^t} + \lambda \mathbf{I})^{-1}\mathbf{G^t}(\mathbf{w} - \mathbf{f}) \tag{2}$$

DMC uses the N first instants from the step response to predict the system output (in our case $N = 7$). It assumes a constant disturbance along the cost horizon. The disturbance is given by the difference between the actual system output and the predicted output ($d(n) = y(n) - y(n|n)$). The goal of our controller is to drive the output as close as possible to the reference in the least-squares sense. The control action for that is computed by equation 2. $\mathbf{G}$ is the dynamic matrix of the system, $\mathbf{\Delta u}$ is the control vector and $\mathbf{w}$ is the reference vector. $\mathbf{f}$ is called the free response vector because it does not depend on the future control actions. λ is the penalty for the control effort, by increasing this value the system becomes less responsive and smoother. Notice that only the first element of $\mathbf{\Delta u}$ is really sent to the motor. The vector is computed at each iteration to increase the robustness of the control to disturbances in the model. For more details on DMC controllers see [7].

Interpolation can be used, not only to compensate for the visual processing delay, but also to estimate target parameters of motion for future time instants. Visual information at the Kalman filter output is used to compute current and future target angular position and velocity assuming a constant acceleration model of motion. The goal of the DMC controller is to force the motor to have the same motion as the target in a near future. Considering that $\mathbf{w}$ is the desired motor velocity, it would be reasonable to use the predicted target velocity as reference for the DMC controller. The result of this control strategy can be observed in Fig.3(M)(D). Notice that by using only velocity information the system is not able to compensate for errors in position and the target is lost after a certain period. Despite that the motor successfully reaches target velocity.

$$\Delta_p = \frac{1}{6}\left(\frac{E_p}{T} - MV_o\right) - \frac{\Delta_v}{3}\left(\frac{M^2}{4} + 2\right) \tag{3}$$

Whenever a new image is grabbed, visual processing is used to compute target velocity and tracking position error. Perfect tracking is achieved if, at the next frame time instant, the system compensates for the error in position and moves at the estimated velocity. This is the goal considered to establish the reference $\mathbf{w}$ whose profile is depicted in Fig. 3(U). Consider P_o and V_o are the current motor position and velocity and $P_t(i)$ and $V_t(i)$ are the target position and

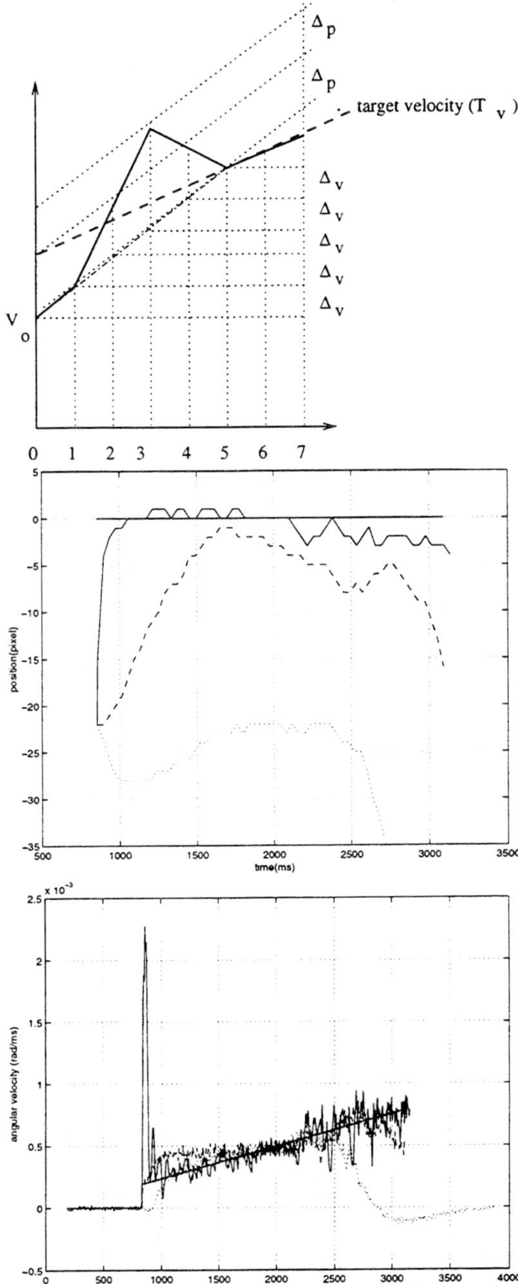

Figure 3. Top: Deriving the velocity reference trajectory: (–) is the target estimated velocity , and (-) is the reference velocity. Middle and Down: Tracking a target with a parabolic trajectory of motion: initial position 5deg, initial velocity 10deg/s, acceleration 15deg/s^2. Middle: Regulation performance. Target position in the image. Down: Regulation in angular velocity. Target (.-), First controller(–), DMC velocity controller (:), DMC velocity +position controller(-)

velocity at instant i. Then $\Delta_v = (V_t(M) - V_o)/M$ and Δ_p is computed by equation 3 where $E_p = P_t(M) - P_o$. M is the instant of convergence, making $M = 5$ motor velocity converge to target velocity in 5 samples (30ms). In this time interval the motor accelerates and then slightly decelerates to compensate for the position error. The velocity reference $\mathbf{w}$ is computed for each control iteration.

The increase in performance introduced by the DMC controller can be observed in Fig3. The error in position is immediately compensated and the target is kept in the center of the image along its parabolic motion. In the velocity regulation figure notice the initial peak that compensates for the position error. At the end the velocity regulation performance decreases for the three controllers. This is due to visual processing limitations. The velocity estimation algorithm is not able to measure velocities above a certain threshold. This has been discussed in previous work and Gaussian pyramids have been introduced to cope with this problem.

References

[1] S. Hutchinson, G. Hager, and P.I. Corke. A tutorial on visual servo control. *IEEE Trans. on Robotics and Automation*, 12(5):651–670, October 1996.

[2] K. Pahlavan, T. Uhlin, and J. Ekhlund. Integtaring primary ocular processes. *Proc. 2nd European Conf. on Computer Vision*, pages 526–541, 1992.

[3] E. D. Dickmanns, B. Mysliwetz, and T. Christians. An integrated spatio-temporal approach to automatic visual guidance of autonomous vehicles. *IEEE Trans. on Systems, Man and Cybernetics*, 20(6):1273–1284, November/December 1990.

[4] P. M. Sharkey and D. W. Murray. Delay versus performance of visually guided systems. *IEE Proc.-Control Theory Appl.*, 143(5):436–447, September 1996.

[5] P.I. Corke. Visual control of robot manipulators–a review. In K. Hashimoto, editor, *Visual Servoing*. World Scientific, New York, 1993.

[6] João P. Barreto, Paulo Peixoto, Jorge Batista, and Helder Araujo. Evaluation of the robustness of visual behaviors through performance characterization. In Markus Vincze and Gregory D. Hager, editors, *Robust Vision for Vision-Based Control of Motion*. IEEE Press, 1999.

[7] E. F. Camacho and C. Bordons. *Model Predictive Control*. Springer-Verlag, 1999.

Semi-Automatic Video-to-Site Registration for Aerial Monitoring*

C.Shekhar
Center for Automation Research
University of Maryland
College Park, MD 20742
Email: shekhar@cfar.umd.edu

Abstract

Aerial monitoring of ground sites using video cameras is playing an increasingly important role in autonomous surveillance applications. In such tasks it is important to be able to relate the activities detected in the video sequence to the 3D world, typically represented by a map, orthoimage or site model. Traditional image positioning approaches are generally not applicable to the real-time processing of (typically) low-resolution aerial video. This paper presents an approach to the automatic registration of aerial video to a site model. Low precision metadata are used to initialize the registration, and the resulting registration error is modeled as a simple translational shift. An operator-selected site feature is automatically tracked using frame stabilization parameters, and in each frame the registration error is corrected using the discrepancy between the metadata-predicted and tracked feature locations. This system runs on a PC in real time using less than 2% of the CPU. It has been demonstrated on real data obtained live during several flight experiments.

1 Introduction

The analysis of ground activities involving vehicles and humans is of interest in airborne surveillance applications. The high spatiotemporal resolution of a video camera makes it the sensor of choice for such applications. In the past, video sensors were not preferred, precisely because of the high volume of data generated, which had to be processed manually for the most part. Further, the moving platform gives rise to numerous false alarms.

Some recent developments in the vision field have mitigated these shortcomings. Firstly, the availability of reliable and fast image stabilization algorithms [3, 4, 1] have made it possible to compensate accurately for platform motion, and thus eliminate a prime source of false alarms. Secondly, the extensive use of contextual information made possible by the site model based image exploitation paradigm [2] have reduced the computational load of IU algorithms by orders of magnitude. Site models provide accurate topographic and geometric information about point sites, areas, and lines of communication, enabling the focusing of attention on portions of the image relevant to the activity being detected. A further benefit of using site models is a reduction in the number of false alarms, since much less data is processed, and many potential false alarms (due to trees, shadows, etc.) can be predicted and filtered out.

Site models are represented in 3D world coordinates. Essential to the use of site models is the real-time registration of the aerial video to the site, because the activities detected in the video have to be "geolocated" with respect to the site model. Registering an arbitrary aerial image to an arbitrary site model is an extremely difficult task, and virtually impossible in real-time with present technology. Fortunately, most aerial platforms used for video monitoring, such as the Twin Otter aircraft used in this work, are equipped with a variety of secondary sensors that provide "metadata" in the form of measurements of the position and orientation of the gimbal as well as the settings of the camera. Based on these measurements, it is possible to compute a 3x4 projection matrix mapping (in homogeneous coordinates) points in the 3D world to points in the image [6]. The reverse mapping is ill-posed in the general case, but if the scene consists of a flat plane, "geolocation" of points in the image can be accomplished using straightforward linear algebra [5].

The projection matrix computed using "raw" metadata is an approximate one. There are a number of different sources of error, but the ones that affect us the most are the errors in the gimbal azimuth and elevation. Typically, these inaccuracies result in geolocation errors of the order of 100m. This is unacceptably high for human activity monitoring, which typically requires a geolocation accuracy of about 5m. One obvious solution is to use the approximate projection matrix as an initial condition, and refine it using known site features

*Partially supported by the DARPA AVS Contract No. DAAB07-98-C-J019

1051-4651/00 $10.00 © 2000 IEEE

in the image. It would then be necessary to detect, identify and track these features in real time. While this is our ultimate objective, in the approach presented here we employ certain simplifications to make it more practical given the limited computing power and real-time requirements.

2 Metadata

The Twin Otter platform has a gimbal mounted on the underside, equipped with one or more cameras. The various sensors located on the gimbal and on the aircraft provide a number of different measurements, of which the following are of relevance to us:

- Platform/gimbal position: Latitude, longitude and altitude. These are converted to Cartesian world coordinates x_p, y_p, z_p (also referred to as UTM coordinates)
- Platform orientation: Roll , pitch, heading $(\theta_r, \theta_p, \theta_h)$
- Gimbal orientation: Azimuth, elevation, twist (ϕ_a, ϕ_e, ϕ_t)
- Camera internal parameters: Horizontal FOV, vertical FOV (F_h, F_v) and image size in pixels (n_c, n_r).

3 Projection Matrix Computation

The projection matrix M is a 3x4 matrix that maps points from the world to the image. It can be decomposed into a series of simpler transformations, from world (w) to platform (p) to gimbal (g) to camera (c) to image (i), as follows:

$$M = M_{c2i} M_{g2c} M_{p2g} M_{w2p} \tag{1}$$

The components are determined as follows:

$$M_{c2i} = \begin{bmatrix} f_x & 0 & t_x \\ 0 & f_y & t_y \\ 0 & 0 & 1 \end{bmatrix} \tag{2}$$

where $f_x = n_c/(2\tan^{-1}(F_x/2))$, and $f_y = n_r/(2\tan^{-1}(F_y/2))$ are the focal lengths in pixels. The terms t_x, t_y are the coordinates of the image center, or principal point. These are nominally set to zero, but are later used for refining the registration, as explained in Section 5.

$$M_{g2c} = R_x(\frac{\pi}{2} - \phi_e) R_z(\phi_a) \tag{3}$$

where the symbols $R_{x,y,z}(\alpha)$ represent rotations by an angle α about the x, y and z axes respectively.

M_{p2g} is determined by calibration. It is nominally set to the identity matrix.

$$M_{w2p} = M_{w2pR} M_{w2pT} \tag{4}$$

where

$$M_{w2pR} = R_y(-\theta_r) R_x(-\theta_p) R_z(\theta_h) \tag{5}$$

$$M_{w2pT} = \begin{bmatrix} 1 & 0 & 0 & -x_p \\ 0 & 1 & 0 & -y_p \\ 0 & 0 & 1 & -z_p \end{bmatrix} \tag{6}$$

4 Geolocation

Geolocating an image point is finding the corresponding point in the world. Each image pixel corresponds to a direction ray. If the topography of the scene is known (in the form of a digital terrain model, for example), this ray can be intersected with it to find the corresponding point in the 3D world. In particular, if the surface of the scene is planar, this inverse mapping takes a simple linear form [5].

Let $\mathbf{p}$ be an image point and $\mathbf{P}$ its corresponding scene point. Let M be the projection matrix. Let us assume that the surface of the scene can be approximated by a plane with normal $\mathbf{n}$. Then,

$$\mathbf{P} = \left[\left(I - \frac{\mathbf{m}\mathbf{n}^T}{\mathbf{m}^T\mathbf{n}} \right) M^- \right] \mathbf{p} \tag{7}$$

where M^- and $\mathbf{m}$ are, respectively, the pseudo-inverse and null vector of M, and I is the 4×4 identity matrix. Typically, we assume that the ground plane is of constant height z_0 above mean sea level, so $\mathbf{n} = (0, 0, -1, z_0)^T$. The matrix

$$\tilde{M} = \left(I - \frac{\mathbf{m}\mathbf{n}^T}{\mathbf{m}^T\mathbf{n}} \right) M^-$$

is the inverse projection matrix.

5 Registration Refinement

The camera matrix computed using "raw" metadata allows us to geolocate image points via Equation 7. For the Twin Otter platform, this results in geolocation errors of the order of 100m when the aircraft is flying at an altitude of 1500m. For many applications, this error is unacceptably high. Human activity monitoring typically requires the errors to be not greater than 5m. One obvious approach to reducing the error would be to use the raw geolocation as an initial condition, automatically find feature correspondences between the image and the world, and use the latter to refine the geolocation. Scene features are typically represented in the form of a site model. These should consist of features that can be easily identified in the video, such as road intersections, building corners, etc. A minimum of three point features is necessary to recalculate the projection matrix, and more will be required for a robust result.

There are some practical considerations to be taken into account here. Aerial video is often of lower resolution than ground video, so automatic feature detection and matching is highly non-trivial.The entire system is required to work in real-time, so expensive search mechanisms are to be avoided. Furthermore, some views may not have a sufficient number of visible features to perform a full projection matrix recomputation. Based on these considerations, we employ two simplifications in our present system.

The first simplification is to assume that the geolocation errors in any given image can be corrected by a pure translational shift. This assumption is valid if the camera is sufficiently far from the scene, and the camera roll is minimal. Both these conditions are are typically met in aerial surveillance imagery. Based on this simplification, we need only a single site feature correspondence to refine the registration. If a feature at (X, Y, Z) in the world maps to (x, y) in the image using the projection matrix M, whereas it is actually at (x_t, y_t) in the image, M is recalculated using

$$M_{c2i}^{\text{adjusted}} = \begin{bmatrix} f_x & 0 & t_x \\ 0 & f_y & t_y \\ 0 & 0 & 1 \end{bmatrix} \quad (8)$$

where $t_x = x_t - x$ and $t_y = y_t - y$. This essentially shifts the assumed principal point of the camera to align the predicted and actual feature locations in the image.

The second simplification is to permit the operator to interactively select a feature correspondence to initialize the semi-automatic registration. This is performed by using the mouse to click on a point in the live video. It would of course be impractical for the operator to do this for every frame, so we instead use frame stabilization parameters (FSP's) obtained as described in [1] to "track" the operator-selected site feature in the live video. When this tracked point drifts too far away from the true position in the video image, the operator re-locates the feature point by clicking on its true location. It is then tracked using FSP's. When a selected feature point leaves the field-of-view, the operator selects a new feature for tracking. Typically, the operator has to interact once a minute (or once every 1800 frames) to reposition a feature or to select a new feature. The geolocation accuracy thus obtained is of the order of 5m, which is acceptable for aerial monitoring.

6 Experimental Results

The system described in this paper has been implemented on a PC, and runs in real time using less than 2% of the CPU. It has been tested on real data obtained live during several flight experiments conducted at Fort AP Hill, VA. Sample results are shown in Fig. 1. The site model in this case consists of VRML objects representing the buildings, poles, fences, road boundaries and a number of salient points. Using the raw metadata, the site model is rendered on the video frame, as shown in Fig. 1(a). The errors in the metadata are so large that no site model objects are visible. The same frame is shown in Fig. 1(b), after the interactive feature location, and automatic tracking over 150 frames. Geolocation errors in this case were less than 5m for the site features of interest. The corresponding camera footprints are also shown in Figs. 1(c) and (d), superimposed on an orthoimage obtained from the US Geological Survey. Note that there are some differences between what is visible in the orthoimage, and what is actually present in the site, because the orthoimage was taken several years prior to the present effort.

7 Future Work

There are several ways in which the approach presented here can be improved. The major improvement we are currently working on is the automatic detection and tracking of site features. This would eliminate the need for operator intervention. Raw geolocation errors could be reduced by filtering the metadata based on stabilization parameters. The use of a detailed terrain model instead of the planar assumption will also lead to better geolocation accuracy.

Acknowledgments

I am grateful to Ross Cutler, Brian Burns, Rama Chellappa and Bob Bolles for helpful discussions. I thank Dave Scott for providing the site models, and Doug Ayers for suggesting improvements to this paper.

References

[1] P. Anandan, P. Burt, K. Dana, M. Hansen, and G. van der Wal. Real-time scene stabilization and mosaic construction. In *Proc. ARPA Image Understanding Workshop*, pages I:457–465, 1994.

[2] R. Chellappa, X. Zhang, P. Burlina, C. L. Lin, Q. Zheng, L. S. Davis, and A. Rosenfeld. An integrated system for site-model supported monitoring of transportation activities in aerial images. In *DARPA Image Understanding Workshop*, volume 1, pages 275–304, Palm Springs, CA, Feb. 1996.

[3] C. Morimoto and R. Chellappa. Evaluation of image stabilization algorithms. In *Proc. DARPA Image Understanding Workshop*, pages 295–302, 1997.

[4] S. Srinivasan and R. Chellappa. Image stabilization and mosaicking using the overlapped basis optical flow field. In *Proc. IEEE International Conference on Image Processing*, pages III:356–xx, 1997.

[5] R. Szeliski. Image mosaicing for tele-reality applications. In *Workshop on Applications of Computer Vision*, pages 44–53, 1994.

[6] L. Wixson, J. Eledath, M. Hansen, R. Mandelbaum, and D. Mishra. Image alignment for precise camera fixation and aim. In *Proc. IEEE Conference on Computer Vision and Pattern Recognition*, pages 708–715, 1998.

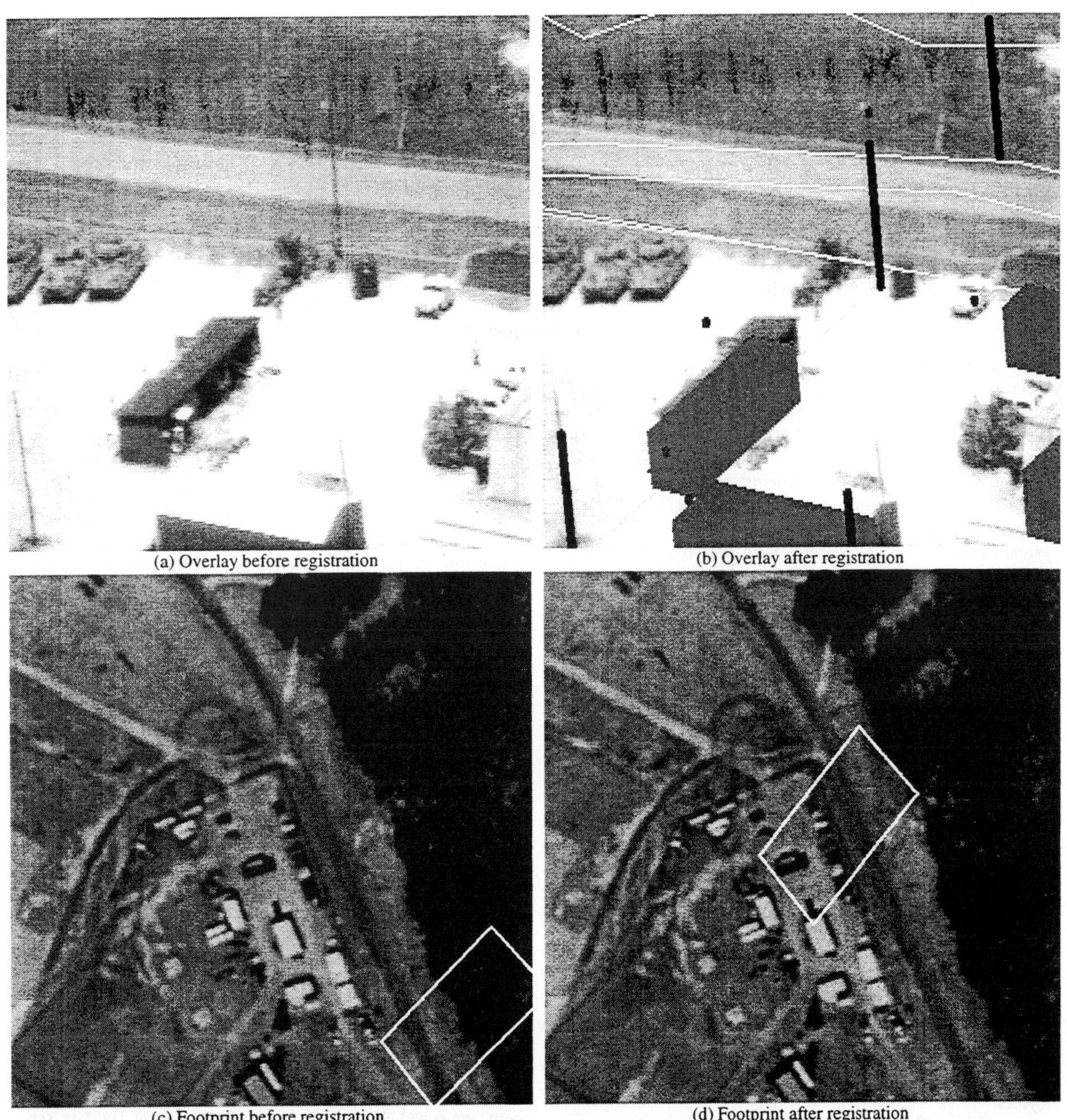

Figure 1. Results of the registration method are shown. The video image frame with the site model superimposed, before and after registration, are shown on the upper row. The site model is not visible in (a) because the error in the raw geolocation exceeds the field of view. The corresponding camera footprints are shown on the lower row, superimposed on an orthoimage of the site, obtained from USGS. (Parts of the orthoimage are outdated, so there are some discrepancies.)

A Flexible Laser Range Sensor Based on Spatial-temporal Analysis

Jiang Yu ZHENG

Kyushu Institute of Technology
Iizuka, Fukuoka 820-8500, Japan
Zheng@mse.kyutech.ac.jp

Abstract

This paper introduces a smart laser range sensor with many advantages over the current products. The device is portable for its lightness and possessing simplest components. The image data is recorded in digital videotape for late processing, which allows it to be used in wide areas and places just as shooting pictures by a camera. The measuring scope can be freely adjusted to cover various distances, which greatly saves manpower in measuring immovable objects or a site. The system employs a post-calibration so that it can be used easily onsite. Further, we obtain color of measured points, which has been realized so far only by complicated systems in constrained environments. All these functions are realized by spatial temporal analysis of the video images. This sensor system has been used in measuring unearthed relics at a world heritage site.

1. Introduction

The recent progresses in multimedia require use of 3D range data. Although various laser range sensors have been put on market, they have many inconveniences in measuring large scale, multi-type objects in limited spaces and general environments. Such devices are usually precisely mounted and have fixed sensing scope. This prevents them to be used in an unstable out-lab environment such as excavation site, museum, photo shop, etc. A device is very desired not to involve any heavy calibration so that a non-specialist can handle it. The sensing environment should not be limited to a dark room, but anywhere with reasonable ambient light. The device should be light enough to be moved frequently from position to position for sensing a large number of objects.

In order to facilitate the use of laser range finder in different areas, a revolutionary upgrade is demanded. We build a laser range sensor that is probably the simplest one for its simple structure and components, as well as its easy utilization. Nevertheless, it has many advanced properties:

(1) Camera direction and covering scope are adjustable.
(2) Neither pre-calibration nor onsite calibration of the system is needed. A post-calibration is carried out after images have been taken.
(3) It is portable for its lightness because it only consists of a finger-type laser projector and a small digital video camera that are driven on a rail [1-4].
(4) It catches not only depth but also color of surface points [3,4].

We can start with a casual camera directing towards objects of interest and then do laser scanning and taking video. Since image processing will be done later, measuring a large site is just recording video sequences continually from position to position.

The principle used in the image processing is the spatial temporal analysis. Based on the vanishing point principle of linear motion, a simple post-calibration method is designed. Colors of measured 3D points are obtained by looking at later images in the sequence according to the image velocities of the points. Every scanning yields an image sequence, which further results several intermediate images, i.e., two dynamic projection images [5], a depth map and a color map that contain all the 3D and color information. This compact and standard data set is effective for multimedia communication.

2. A Smart Laser Range Sensor

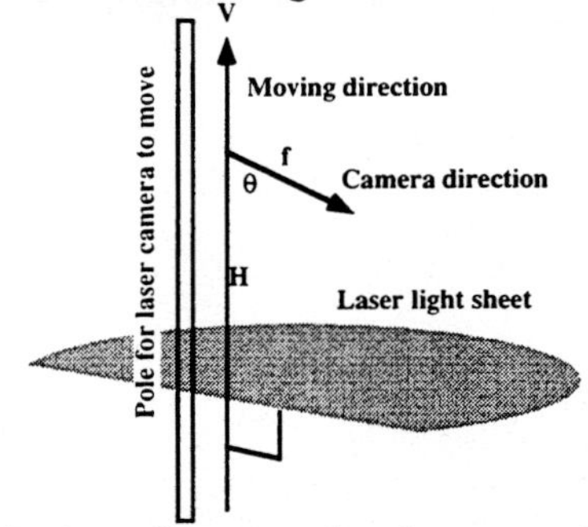

Fig. 1 Basic configuration of our laser range finder.

A laser-camera set is moved linearly in a selected constant speed (**V** in Fig. 1). A sheet of laser light is set orthogonal to the moving direction. The camera takes 30 images per second. The internal parameters of the camera such as focal length f, image center $\mathbf{o}(x_0, y_0)$ and frame distortion are known through a calibration.

After properly setting the camera towards a distance where targets may locate, the pitch θ is fixed. The image coordinate system may have a roll α with respect to the plane containing the motion direction and the camera axis (Fig. 2). The pan of camera is not important since the laser sheet is wide enough to keep the same system geometry under a slight change of pan. The camera exposure is set onsite at a level where the laser stripe on the surface will not be over-exposed and surface color is also taken in.

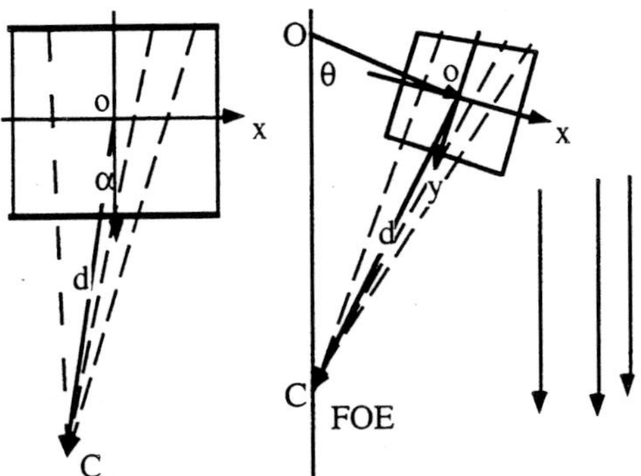

Fig. 2 The vanishing point in a linear motion.

If laser is on, there is a red stripe appearing on the object surface. It is taken into the camera. As the laser-camera set moves, the red stripe scans object surfaces. For each image coming in, our algorithm searches the laser stripe vertically, extracting edges and marking belts with a proper width between two edges. The hue and brightness are examined to verify the laser color. If several candidate belts are found, the best is always kept. After obtaining segments of laser stripes in an image, the algorithm extends segments from long ones to insure continuity and remove noise. The image position of the laser stripe in image t is registered as $L(x, y(x, t), t)$. For different t and x, we obtain a distribution $y(x, t)$ called *depth map*.

3. Spatial Temporal Analysis

As a camera moves along a line, all space points have a relative move opposite to the camera. It is well known that the projections of these parallel moves in the images approach to a *vanishing point* $C(x_c, y_c)$ (Fig. 2) or *FOE*. In most of our cases, the FOE is out of the camera frame. The approaching velocity of a point is constant for the fixed V and is dependent on the distance from the camera.

Further, we have a conclusion that the FOE on the image plane is also on the trace of camera focal point in the 3D space. In other word, FOE is also the projection of the motion vector of camera focal point on the image plane. This result can be easily proved.

If we pile the video images along the time axis, a spatial temporal volume is formed (Fig. 3). All points in the volume have their linear traces and finally reach a line that is parallel to time axis at the position of FOE. Most of the points will pass the top and bottom lines in the image (Fig. 2) if the camera moves over a long distance. In the spatial temporal volume, these points start from top plane and end at bottom plane.

In the spatial temporal volume, those red stripes form piece-wise smooth surface (Fig. 4) due to discontinuity in depth, occlusion by other surfaces and far background where the laser stripe exceeds the camera sight.

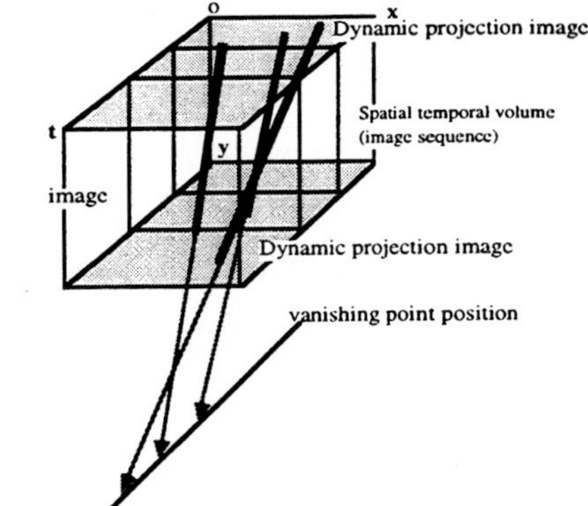

Fig3 Motion traces of points toward FOE.

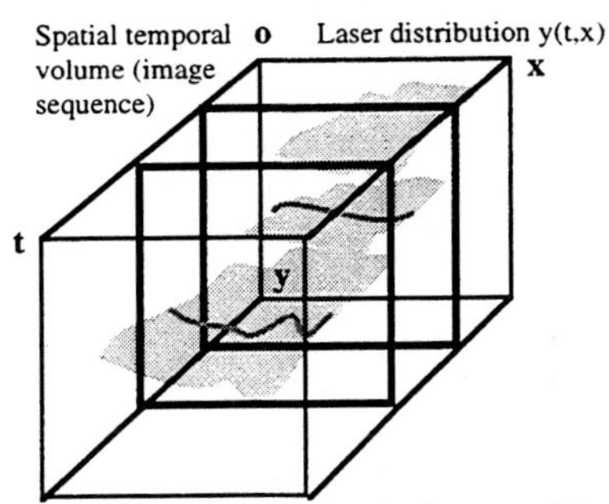

Fig. 4 Laser stripe distribution in the spatial temporal volume.

4. Post-calibration of the System

After a lot of video clips have been taken, we select those clips that the camera pose was first changed to compute θ and α, as well as distance H between the focus and laser plane. These system parameters will be used until the next clip where camera pose changes (Fig. 5).

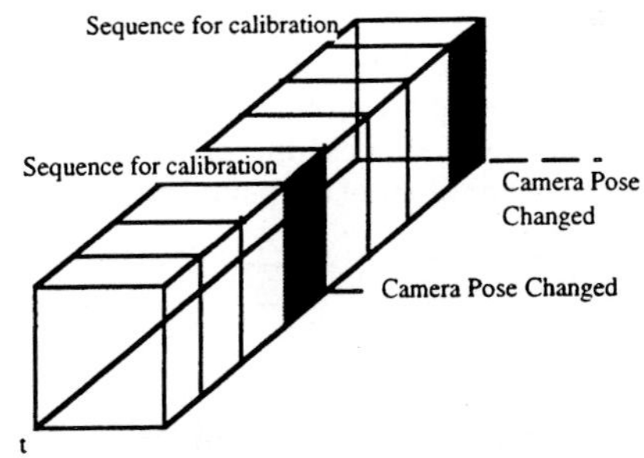

Fig. 5 Calibrating camera poses using video sequences.

For a video clip, we first compute the FOE from a set of motion vectors by locating distinguishable points. As described above, many image points in the top plane of the spatial temporal volume move to the bottom plane. If we collect both top and bottom plane images, we are able to find correspondences of those feature points, and further compute their image velocities. Suppose y_t and y_b are y coordinates of the top and bottom pixel lines, the top and bottom planes are two *Dynamic Projection Images* obtained from these two lines [5]. In these two dynamic projection images, we manually find a number of correspondences (x_i, t_i) and (x'_i, t'_i), $i=1,...n$. The FOE is the intersection of all the vectors (x'_i-x_i, y_b-y_t), where y_b-y_t is the image size. Therefore, $C(x_c, y_c)$ should be on all these vectors and satisfy their linear equations.

$$\frac{size_y}{x'_i - x_i} = \frac{y_c - y_t}{x_c - x_i}$$

We use the least squared error method to estimate (x_c, y_c).

After obtaining FOE, we find the distance and roll as

$$d = \sqrt{x_c^2 + y_c^2} \qquad \alpha = \tan^{-1}\frac{x_c}{y_c}$$

We therefore obtain each point (x, y) in a rectified coordinate system as (x_r, y_r) by applying a 2D rotation using obtained angle α. The angle θ is then

$$\theta = \tan^{-1}\frac{d}{f}$$

In order to obtain H, we need to take the laser stripe into consideration. If we select a pair of corresponding points (x_i, y_t, t_i) and (x'_i, y_b, t'_i) in dynamic projection images, which are the projections of the same 3D point, we can fully determine the linear trace of that point in the spatial temporal volume. If that point is at very front of the surface, it should be scanned by laser at a known time. Since the pixel trace of that point in the volume will become red somewhere. We therefore search along the point trace and find its intersecting position with a red laser surface. We can compute H from it by using image velocity equation that will be given in the next section.

5. 3D Measure of Surface Points

As we obtain a laser stripe in the image, we register the positions (x, y, t) in another image called *depth map* $(y=y(x, t))$. The intensity of the image is the y coordinates of laser points.

When we compute 3D positions of laser lit points, we first calculate their position in the rectified coordinate system without roll. Suppose the obtained coordinate is (x_r, y_r, t), the 3D position of the point becomes

$$X = \frac{Hx_r}{f\cos\theta + y_r\sin\theta} \qquad Y = t\frac{\partial Y}{\partial t} \qquad Z = H\frac{f\tan\theta - y_r}{f + y_r\tan\theta}$$

where $\partial Y/\partial t = |V|$.

6. Color Acquisition of 3D Points

Getting colors of surface points is necessary in many applications. Some laser range finder uses two cameras: one with a filter for laser detection and the other for color acquisition. It complicates the system. Some devices take images when laser is off, which requires synchronizing the laser and camera. There is another consideration to obtained color from projected white light, which may require a dark environment.

In our system, we get the exact colors of measured points after those points move out of the laser stripe. As laser points are extracted, their 3D positions become known. Since the camera move is controlled at a constant speed, the image velocities can be determined as

$$\frac{\partial x_r}{\partial t} = -\frac{x_r(f\cos\theta + y_r\sin\theta)}{Hf}\cos\theta\frac{\partial Y}{\partial t}$$

$$\frac{\partial y_r}{\partial t} = \frac{f}{H}\frac{\partial Y}{\partial t}\left(\cos\theta + \frac{y_r}{f}\sin\theta\right)\left(\sin\theta - \frac{y_r}{f}\cos\theta\right),$$

Because the image velocity of a surface point in y direction only depends on its y coordinate when it is lit by laser, a lookup table is enough to get its value from laser position. For each point on the laser stripe, we compute its image velocity and predict where it moves in the later images. Waiting for a time delay Δt, we pick up color at the predicted position where the laser has passed away. If such a position is still lit by laser because of a possible rapid change in depth, we can extend the delay further. The color of every point is registered in another image called *color map* $T(x,t)$, at the same position as in *depth map*. These data will be used in building 3D surface model. For a 3D model, points neighboring in *depth map* are connected to compose triangular patches. The surface model is covered with all these small patches.

7. Experiments

We have measured twenty statues at an archaeology excavation site — the Museum of Terra Cotta Warriors and Horses. The measure is done from different directions. Figure 6 is the dynamic projection images for post-calibration after the video sequence has been taken. Post-calibration is carried out for video sequences. Figure 7 gives a set of depth maps and Fig 8 is the measured 3D surface models.

The finest resolutions of the measured data are 0.3mm in Y direction, 0.5mm in X direction and 1mm in Z direction, covering a 3D space of 0.5m, 1m, 0.8m in X, Y, Z directions respectively. It can cover larger 3D region with a coarser resolution. Depending on a required resolution in Y direction (3mm~0.3mm), each scan takes 10~100 seconds.

In our analysis, we suppose two dynamic projection images are taken from top and bottom planes for the simplicity. In real case, there is no necessity to obey it. Directing the camera center at the average depth of objects to measure, laser stripes will frequently appear at the center part of images. Selecting two pixel lines away from center not only avoids red laser appearing in the dynamic projection images, but also increases the accuracy in the estimation of FOE. We can also select two pixel lines closer if the camera has a wide angle and objects are far away (object may not appear in both dynamic projection images due to limited length of linear move).

Our system use neither auxiliary equipment nor standard model in the calibration; the accuracy of a standard model itself is questionable sometimes. The only parameter our system relies on is the linear translation speed **V** guaranteed as accurate as 0.1mm at the speed of 10mm/sec. The final position error is from θ and H, caused by picking up corresponding points at dynamic projection images, which might have several pixels uncertainty. With the robust estimation, these errors can be reduced to minimum.

8. Conclusion

We built a flexible laser range finder that is probably the simplest one so far, not only because of its handy components but also because of its convenience in setting, measuring and carrying. Spatial temporal analysis is extensively used in image processing to simplify calibration and obtain color, which were two problems of using laser range finder in wide areas and for different applications.

Fig. 6 Two dynamic projection images for post calibration

9. References

[1] J. Y. Zheng, Z. L. Zhang, Virtual Recovery of Excavated Relics, IEEE Computer Graphics and Application, May-June, pp. 6-11, 1999.

[2] J. Y. Zheng, Z. L. Zhang, Digitizing and virtual recovering excavated relics in a world heritage site, International Conference on Virtual Systems and Multimedia 98, Vol. 2, pp. 654-660, 1998.

[3] J. Y. Zheng, Z. L. Zhang, Digital Archiving of an Archaeological Excavation Site for Multimedia Display, 14th International Conference on Pattern Recognition, Vol. 2, 1492-1496, 1998.

[4] J. Y. Zheng, Z. L. Zhang, N. Abe, Virtual Recovery of Excavated Archaeological Finds, IEEE Multimedia Systems Conference 98, pp. 348-357, 1998.

[5] J. Y. Zheng, S. Tsuji, Generating Dynamic Projection Images for Scene Representation and Understanding, Computer Vision and Image Understanding, Academic Press, Vol. 72, No. 3, December, pp. 237-256, 1998.

[6] P. Besl, Active, optical imaging sensors, Machine Vision and Application, 1988, pp. 127-152.

[7] J. Clark, E. Trucco, H-F. Cheung, Improving laser triangulation sensors using polarization. ICCV95, pp. 981-985, 1995.

Fig. 7 Depth maps of a measured statue from different directions.

Fig. 8 Measured 3D surface model of the statue in Fig. 7.

Screen projection camera for ranging far away objects

Michio Miwa, Masahiro Ishii, Yasuharu Koike, Makoto Sato
Tokyo Institute of Technology
4-5-15 Nagatsutacho Midori ku Yokohama, Kanagawa Japan
{mmiwa,ishii,koike,msato}@pi.titech.ac.jp

Abstract

This paper describes the principle and experimental results of a camera system that is composed of a commercially available CCD camera, a large-aperture lens, and an intermediate screen used to measure the distance between the camera and a far-away object by using Depth From Focus method.

1 Introduction

One of the most important problems of computer vision is how to measure the distance between the camera and an object by a passive method. The methods of Depth from Focus (DFF)[3, 4] and Depth from Defocus (DFD) [5, 1, 2] measure the distance based on the difference in blurring of images taken at different focal lengths. However, neither DFF nor DFD is valid for objects at a great distance, as the blurring of images differs little even when the images are taken at different focal lengths. When an image is taken by a CCD camera, the depth of field is proportional to the pitch between CCD elements and the square of the distance from the lens to the object, and inversely proportional to the lens aperture and focal length. It is difficult to manufacture large-aperture lenses or arrange CCD elements at fine pitches. Lenses of longer focal lengths reduce the depth of field, but also reduce the angle of field. To reduce the depth of field, therefore, we propose a screen-intermediate-type optical system, which is one of the shrinkage optical systems, composed of a large-aperture lens, ground glass screen, and CCD camera. The large-aperture lens used in the camera reduces the depth of field and the CCD camera takes an image of the object created on the screen.

2 Depth from focus

2.1 Camera mo del& the depth of eld

The distance v between the lens and the position of the focused image depends on the focal length f and the distance u between the lens and the object (Fig. 1). The relation between f, u, and v is given by the eq.(1).

$$\frac{1}{f} = \frac{1}{u} + \frac{1}{v} \tag{1}$$

When we want to get the distance of a object from the camera using the DFF method, we take many pictures as changing the v. And if we could know the picture on which the amount of defocus is smallest between these images, we could know the distance of the object from the camera by eq.(1). But if the amount of defocus is smaller than the pitch of the array of CCD element, we cannot distinguish the amount of blur. The distance which we can distinguish the movement of the object by the amount of defocus is known as the depth of field(eq.2). In this equation, Δ is the depth of field, ϵ is the pitch of the array of CCD elements, D is the diameter of the lens. The Δ becomes very large if the distance from the object to the lens is large. Usually we could not distinguish the amount of defocus if the distance of the object from the lens is more than 5 m.

$$\Delta = \frac{\epsilon u f D(u-f)}{f^2 D^2 - \epsilon^2 (u-f)^2} \tag{2}$$

3 Screen intermediate camera

To get the distance of the object far-away from the lens, we made a screen- intermediate-type camera(fig.2). Its depth of field is given by eq.(3), where is d_s is the diameter of a circle on the screen, and d is the diameter of ite image on the CCD. The

1051-4651/00 $10.00

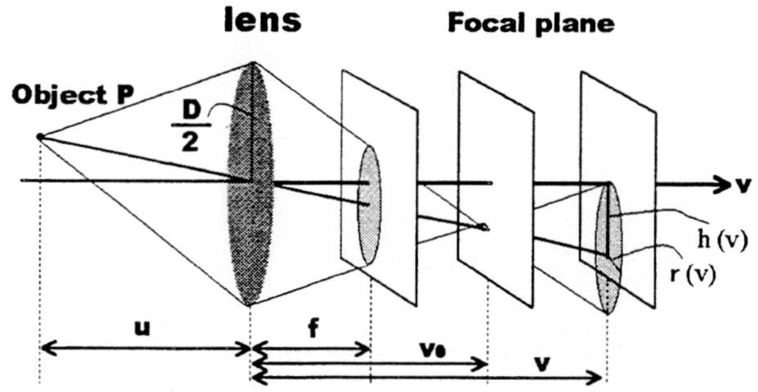

Figure 1. Camera model

depth of field (Δ_s) of the image taken by the camera is given by eq.(4), where D_s is the aperture and f_s is th focal length of the main lens.

$$\epsilon_s = \frac{d_s}{d}\epsilon \tag{3}$$

$$\Delta_s = \frac{\epsilon_s u_s f_s D_s (u_s - f_s)}{{f_s}^2 {D_s}^2 - {\epsilon_s}^2 (u_s - f_s)^2} \tag{4}$$

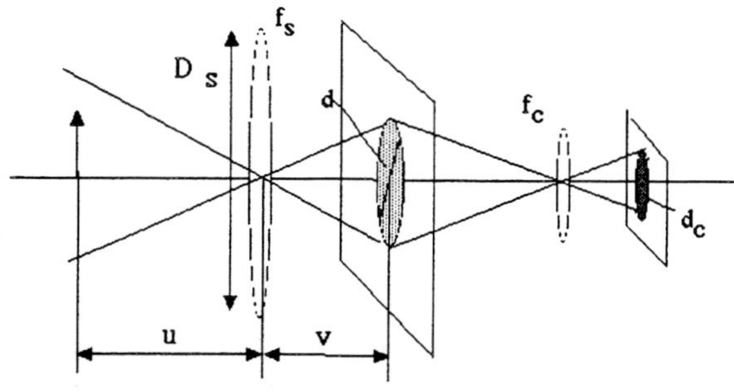

Figure 2. The area of a road mark in the detection window

Fig.3 shows the depth of field of the screen intermediate camera with conventional camera. In this case $d = 12.7mm$, $f = 30mm$, $\epsilon = 0.018mm$ as ordinary camera. And $d = 12.7mm$, $d_s = 126mm$, $f_s = 299.2mm$, $D_s = 53.4mm$ as the screen intermediate camera. The depth of field is about 2m when the object is 20m from the camera. So, we can get the distance of far-away objects.

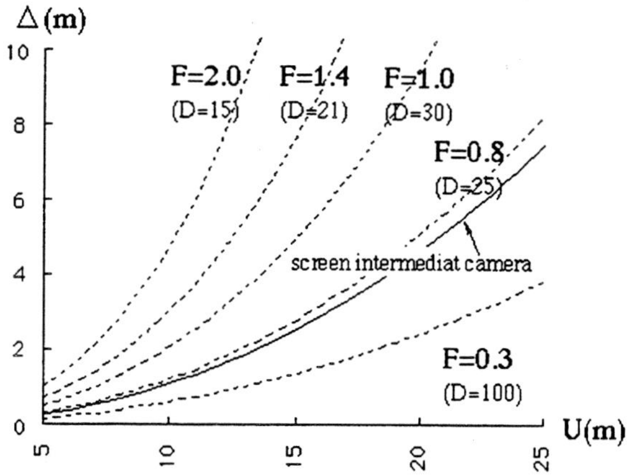

Figure 3. Depth of field by the screen intermediate camera

4 experiment

4.1 Experimentalsystem

Fig.?? shows the experimental system. In this system, the distance from the screen to the CCD camera is constant. And they are moved together. And the CCD camera is focused to the screen.

In this experimental system the distance from the screen to the CCD camera is L=178mm, the diameter of the area which is seen by the CCD camera is d=126mm, sight angle is $2\omega = 23.8$ degree.

4.2 Experiment ofrangingfarobjects

We used the system to take multi-focus images of panels set at distances of 10 m, 15 m, 20 m, and 25 m from the camera (in a corridor) at focal lengths of 10 m to 25 m. The test proved that the camera can distinguish different objects if the distance between them is larger than the depth of field, and that the depth of field must be made small in order to measure the distance between the camera and a far-away object. Although the proposed camera satisfactorily distinguished the objects used for the test, there were some measurement errors due to incorrect calibration. Because of the characteristic limitations of the DFF principle, the camera cannot be used to measure distances to floors, walls, ceilings, or other objects without textural patterns.

Fig.5 is layout of the panels. And fig.6 is one of the multi focus image. All images are gray scale 256 levels and the image size is 512 $\times$ 480 pixels.

Fig.7 shows the experimental system. When we got this ranging data, we used 4 images which is focused to each panels. We shrunk the images. And the center of shrinking is the point corresponding the focal axis. For comparing the amount of defocus, we used the dispersion of 5 × 5 around each pixels between these images. If the difference of the maximum and the minimum of these dispersion, we decide that we cannot get ranging data at this point. In fig.7, white dots means the point which is focused at the image. And the black dots means the point where we cannot get ranging data.

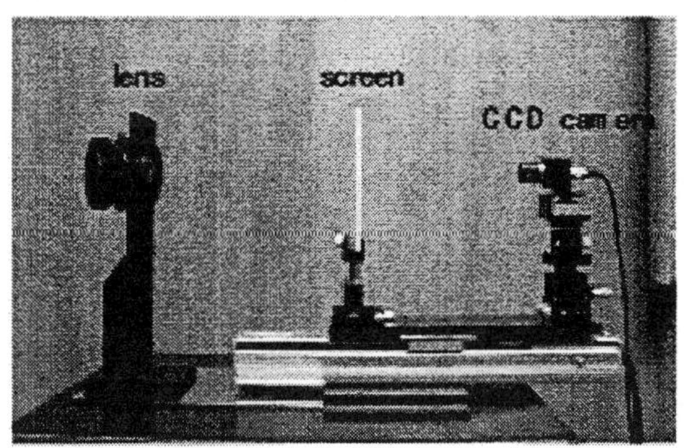

Figure 4. Experimenta system

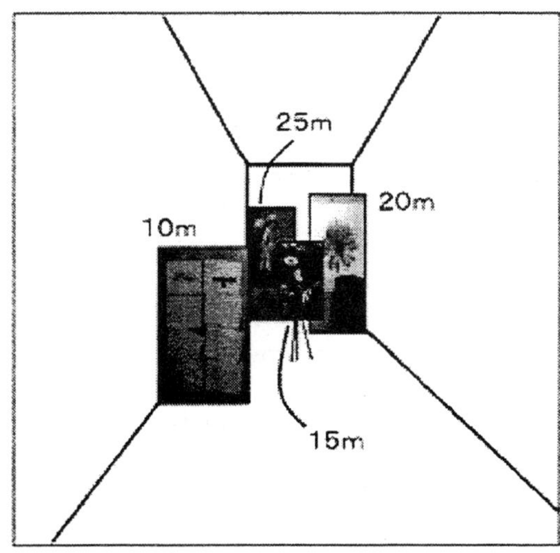

Figure 5. Target Objects

If each target is arranged as the distance of each poster is longer than the depth of field, we can distinguish each poster (fig.7). This result shows that we need shallow field of depth in far distance to range the far objects. And also it shows that our screen intermediate camera works well. Because of calibration error,

Figure 6. Multi focus image

there are some ranging error. Because of inability of DFF our system cannot range the place where there are no texture like floor or wall, ceiling. In the case of a luminous body like a fluorescent light or highlighted objects, it is impossible to range. Because in that case, the light from them is too strong. By adjusting the aperture of the CCD camera, we can adjust the light weak. But if the contrast of the light is too big, it is impossible to adjust the aperture to range all the objects in the sight.

4.3 Focusingon pixels

We can change the receiving plane size freely in the screen-intermediate type image observation system. When the focus (the distance to the object) changes, therefore, we can proportionally change the receiving plane size to take a picture of pixels of a multiple-focus image. When the screen moves from $v = v_1$ to $v = v_2$, for example, the image is magnified $\frac{m(v_2)}{m(v_1)} = M$ times according to the equation. If the receiving plane size d is also magnified M times in this situation, the image taken by the CCD camera is unchanged. Unlike the technique of using a telecentric optical system, this method enables us to freely select the field angle without compromising the advantages of the proposed observation system. We can use a zoom-lens camera as the CCD camera and use its zooming function to change the receiving plane size. In this paper, we adopt a model of a zoom-lens camera having a thin convex lens that moves while the focal length is changed. See Fig. 8. In this model, the receiving plane does not

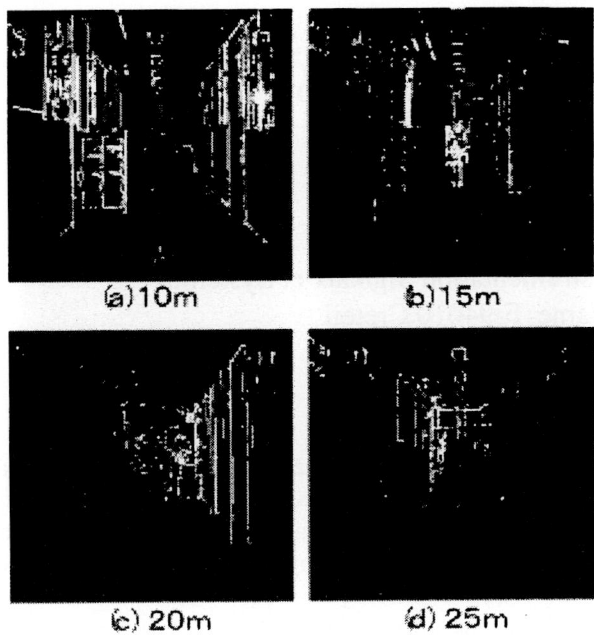

Figure 7. Experimental result

move, and therefore the distance L to the object is constant. When the lens moves, its focal length changes so that the lens always focuses on the receiving plane.

In Fig. 8, the image P_1, which is at a distance of h from the optical axis on the screen, creates an image through lens 1 on the receiving plane of the zoom-lens camera, which is a distance of L away from the image P_1. The created image is at a distance h_c from the optical axis. When the focal length of the zoom-lens camera is denoted by f_{c1}, the eq.5 holds. When the image P_1 is magnified M times, it becomes the image P_2, and the distance to the optical axis is also magnified M times. We can focus on the pixels, by changing the focal length from f_{c1} to f_{c2} and moving the lens from position 1 to position 2 so that the eq.6 holds. Based on the eq.5 and 6, f_{c2} is obtained from the eq.7. By zooming so as to satisfy the eq.7, we can focus on the pixels of the image taken at any field angle.

$$\frac{h}{L - f_{c1}} = \frac{h_c}{f_{c1}} \tag{5}$$

$$\frac{Mh}{L - f_{c2}} = \frac{h_c}{f_{c2}} \tag{6}$$

$$f_{c2} = \frac{Lf_{c1}}{ML - Mf_{c1} + f_{c1}} \tag{7}$$

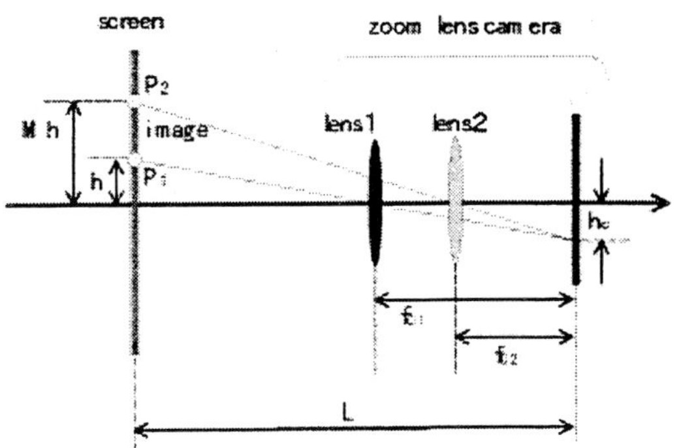

Figure 8. Zooming lens model

5 Conclusion

We made a optics using screen intermediate which can range the object at far distance. This camera is made up with a screen between a lens and a CCD camera. We made it sure that we can range the object in the distance from the camera 20m in the range of 5m.

References

[1] A.Pentland,"A New Sense for Depth of Field",IEEE Transaction on Pattern Analysis and Machine Intelligence, Vol.PAMI-9, No.4, July 1987

[2] A.Pentland,T.Darrell,"A Simple, Real-time Range Camera", Proceedings of the IEEE Computer Society Conference on Computer Vision and Pattern Recognition, San Diego, California, June 1989

[3] S. K. Nayer!$"Shape from Focus System!$" Proc. of IEEE Conf. Computer Vision and Pattern Recognition!$pp.302-308!$1992!%

[4] Murali Subbarao and Jenn-Kwei tyan:"Selecting the Optical Focus Measure for Autofocusing and Depth-From-Focus", IEEE Transactions On Pattern Analysis and Machine Intelligence, Vol.20,No.8, Aug 1998

[5] Murali Subbarao, Gopal Surya! "Depth from Defocus: A Spatial Domain Approach", , International Journal of Computer Vision, 13,3,271-294(1994))

A Fuzzy Logic Approach to Drusen Detection in Retinal Angiographic Images

A. Thaïbaoui , A. Raji, P. Bunel
Laboratoire d'Etude et de Recherche en Instrumentation Signaux et Systèmes
Université Paris 12 Val-de-Marne, F-94010 Créteil
taibaoui@univ-paris12.fr

Abstract

Drusen are yellow deposits at the level of the retinal pigment and are frequently associated with age-related macular degeneration (ARMD). Drusen often change in size, number and degree of confluence. A quantitative method to measure the development of drusen is needed for controlled studies of the natural history, prognosis, and treatment of ARMD. A novel method to detect drusen is presented. This method proceeds in two steps: an optimal partition followed by a fuzzy logic approach. The proposed method is used to quantify objectively drusen over time, it constitutes a diagnosis help tool to the long term follow-up of patients.

1. Introduction

Age-related macular degeneration (ARMD) is the commonest cause of registered blindness in Western society. Macular drusen, hard or soft, have often been observed at the early stages of age-related degeneration. Clinically, it has been shown that soft drusen and macular subretinal new vessels are associated in a statistically significative manner [1].

While drusen may not necessarily be accompanied by visual loss, they are prevalent in the elderly with features such as increasing number, size and degree of confluence. Fluorescein behavior are predictive of visual loss from macular degeneration. Although neither prevention nor treatment of drusen has been established, there is a need for accurate understanding of the natural history of this pathology.

To segment retinal angiographic images and especially drusen images, many methods have been studied and proposed [2][3]. Drusen images present many analysis difficulties : noise, low contrast, and often heterogeneity of regions. To overcome these problems, we introduce a new segmentation method which proceeds in two steps. The first step concerns an image optimal partition into three classes: the first class corresponds to the image background, the second class, called intermediate class, clustering all the ambiguous pixels is defined as a fuzzy region, the third one corresponds to drusen and is represented by the high gray levels. In the second step, the fuzzy logic is applied to the intermediate class by giving membership values for each gray level in the fuzzy region. Next, an iterative method, which includes the pixels spatial context, allows one to decide the pixels final belonging to the drusen class or to the background class.

The proposed segmentation method is used to quantify the area of macula affected by drusen objectively over time, and in an automatic fashion. The obtained results confirm the angiographic quantitative data.

2. Pre-segmentation

2.1 Optimal classification

The first step of the method is based on an optimal partitioning of the image gray-level into three classes $[Xi, Xi+1], i = 0, 1, 2$, obtained by minimization of the mean square error given by:

$$E = \sum_{i=0}^{2} \int_{X_i}^{X_{i+1}} (x - G_i)^2 p(x) dx \quad (1)$$

with respect to the probability density function $p(x)$ of the input gray-levels, where: $X_0 = X_{min}$, $X_3 = X_{max}$, and G_i is the representative level of the class $[Xi, Xi + 1[$. This leads to [4]:

$$X_i = (G_i + G_{i+1})/2 \qquad G_i = \frac{\int_{X_i}^{X_{i+1}} x\, p(x) dx}{\int_{X_i}^{X_{i+1}} p(x) dx} \quad (2)$$

2.2 Region homogenization

In order to improve the homogeneity of the obtained classes, a local parametric gray-level transformation of the

1051-4651/00 $10.00 © 2000 IEEE

form:

$$f(x) = ax^r + b \qquad x \geq 1 \qquad r \geq 1 \qquad (3)$$

is applied. The grey-levels of the class $[Xi, Xi+1]$ of centroid G_i are transformed into a new class $[Y_i, Y_{i+1}[$. We apply first the concave transformation $f(x)$ in the interval $[X_i, G_i[$. A convex transformation, which is symmetrical to $f(x)$ with respect to the inflexion point $(G_i, Y_{im} = \frac{Y_i+Y_{i+1}}{2})$, is then applied to the interval $[G_i, X_{i+1}[$. This transformation aims to concentrate the gray-levels of the obtained classes increasing hence their homogeneity [5] as illustrated in fig.1. The parameter r stands for an homogeneity coefficient.

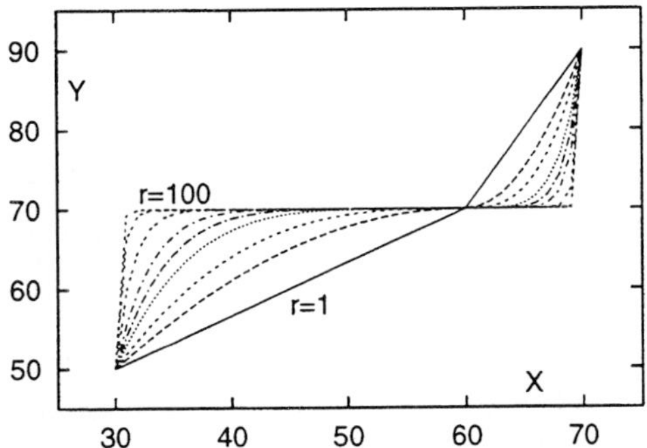

Figure 1. Transformation of the gray-levels $[X_i$=30,G_i=60,X_{i+1}=70] to [50,90]

3 Segmentation by fuzzy classification

In the fuzzy logic literature, an image X of size MxN with gray-levels ranging from L_{min} to L_{max} can be defined as an array of fuzzy singletons, each having a membership function value denoting its degree of brightness relative to some gray level l. Therefore, in fuzzy set notation we can write:

$$X = \{\mu_X(x_{mn}), m = 1, 2, ..., M; n = 1, 2, ..., N\} \quad (4)$$

where $\mu_X(x_{mn})$ denotes the grade of some brightness property possessed by the (m,n)th pixel.

As explained in the previous section, the drusen image is partitioned into three classes. The first class represents the image background, the second one the fuzzy region which contains the ambiguous pixels, and the third one represents the drusen which are brighter than the surrounding tissues and background. The fuzzy classification will be applied only in the second class representing the fuzzy region.

We use the following S-function to compute the membership $\mu_X(x_{mn})$ [6] in the fuzzy region defined in the interval $[a, c]$ by:

$$\mu_X(x) = S(x, a, b, c) = \begin{cases} 0 & x \leq a \\ \frac{(x-a)^2}{(b-a)(c-a)} & a \leq x \leq b \\ 1 - \frac{(x-c)^2}{(c-b)(c-a)} & b \leq x \leq c \\ 1 & x \geq c \end{cases} \quad (5)$$

where x is an independent variable and a, b and c are the parameters which determine the shape of the S-function. The parameter b can be any point between a and c. The question then is how to determine automatically the values of these parameters? The parameters a and c are determined by using the optimal partition which gives us the bounds of the interval $[a, c]$, and we use the local maximum fuzzy entropy criteria [7] to determine the value of b. The example of fig.2 illustrates a fuzzy region in the interval $[a, c]$. and the non fuzzy portions $[L_{min}, a]$ representing the background and $[c, L_{max}]$ corresponding to the drusen.

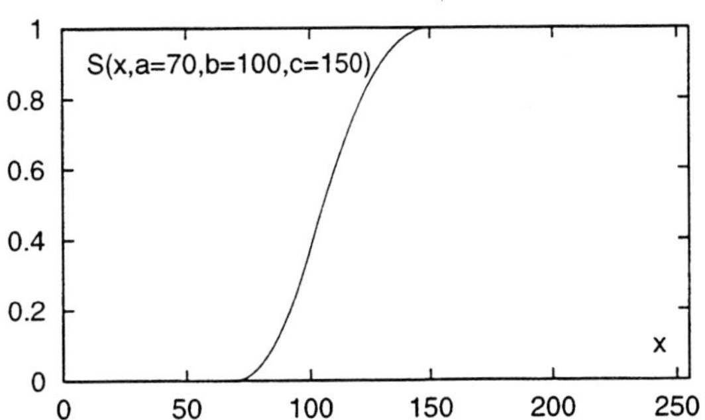

Figure 2. An example of the S function

In the last step, all the ambiguous pixels belonging to the fuzzy region will be classified in accordance with a spatial context based on their neighbourhood. The method we propose to classify those ambiguous pixels is an iterative process where the degree of belongingness μ_X of a pixel to the drusen in the interval [a,c] is compared to the mean

$$<\mu_X> = \frac{1}{K} \sum \mu_X$$

calculated in the pixel's neighbourhood of K pixels.
If $\mu_X \geq <\mu_X>$, then the value of μ_X is increased by ε, otherwise the value of μ_X is decreased by ε. The convergence is reached after some iterations. Then, the pixel is affected to the majority class.

The proposed algorithm can be summarized as follows:
Given an MxN image X with L different gray levels,

Step 1
Optimal partition of the image into three classes, the interval [a,c] is the fuzzy region.

Step 2
- Construct the "drusen" membership μ_X , which measures the fuzziness only on the fuzzy region. $\mu_X(x_i, a, b, c) = S(x_i, a, b, c)$ with $x_i \in [L_{min}, L_{max}]$ and $b \in [a, c]$
- Compute the image histogram $h(x), Lmin \leq x \leq Lmax$
- Compute the different fuzzy entropies $H(X)$ with different values of b ($a \leq b \leq c$) by:

$$H(X) = \frac{1}{MNLog2} \sum_{L_{min}}^{L_{max}} S_n(\mu_X(x, a, b, c))h(x)$$

where Sn(.) is the Shannon's function:

$$S_n(\mu_X(x_{mn})) = -\mu_X(x_{mn})log_2\mu_X(x_{mn})$$

$$-(1 - \mu_X(x_{mn}))log_2(1 - \mu_X(x_{mn}))$$

- Select b from $[a, c]$, corresponding to the maximum of H(X)

Step 3

Classification of the ambiguous pixels:
if $0 < \mu_X < 1$, then we compute $< \mu_X >= \frac{1}{K} \sum \mu_X$ in the neighbourhood.
if $\mu_X \leq < \mu_X >$, then $\mu_X = \mu_X + \varepsilon$
else $\mu_X = \mu_X - \varepsilon$
The convergence is reached when the majority of the values of the neighbourhood are equal to 1 or to 0, the pixel is affected to the majority class.

4 Experimental Results

The experiments have been performed on several digitized retinal angiographic images. In this application we follow-up patients to study the drusen's evolution over time. Fig.3 shows a 1024x1024x256 gray levels original soft drusen images of patient in 1983 and in 1988. We used a registration method to extract the region of interest (ROI) as two 256x256 images centered on the macula to study the evolution of drusen. The quantification's results obtained by our system confirm the clinical qualitative observations [9] that drusen change in number and size over time, increasing, decreasing and sometimes disappearing.

5 Conclusion

A novel approach using fuzzy logic to detect and quantify drusen in digitized retinal angiographic images is proposed. This approach consists of three major steps including image optimal partition, image enhancement, image fuzzification and segmentation. This automatic drusen detection proved useful in quantifying drusen area. This method is presented in the framework of medical applications as a diagnosis help tool to the pratician.

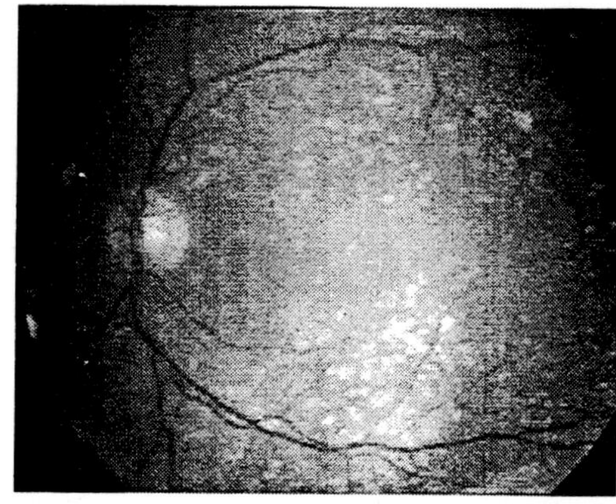

(a) in 1983

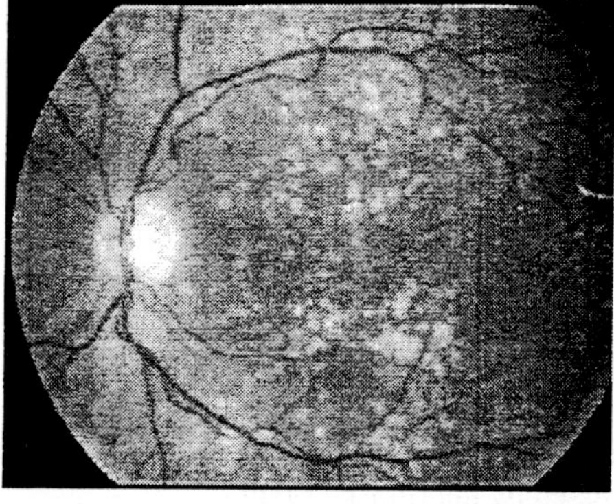

(b) in 1988

Figure 3. sequence of the 1024x1024 original soft drusen images in 1983 and 1988.

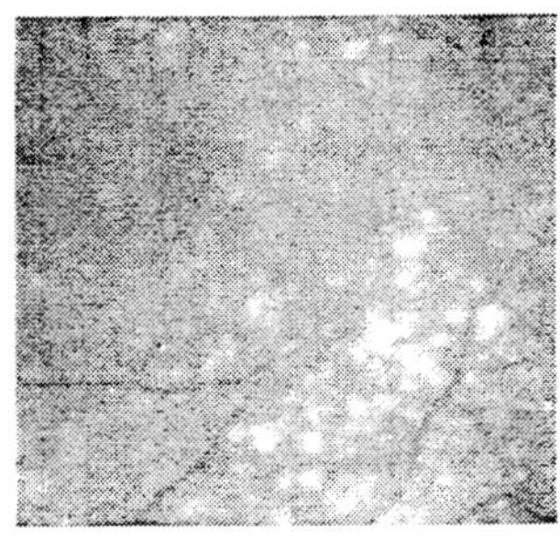
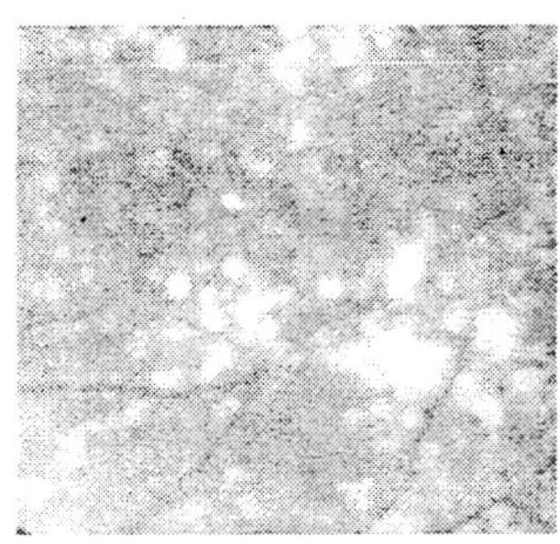

(a) 256x256 ROI of drusen images (in 1983 and 1988)

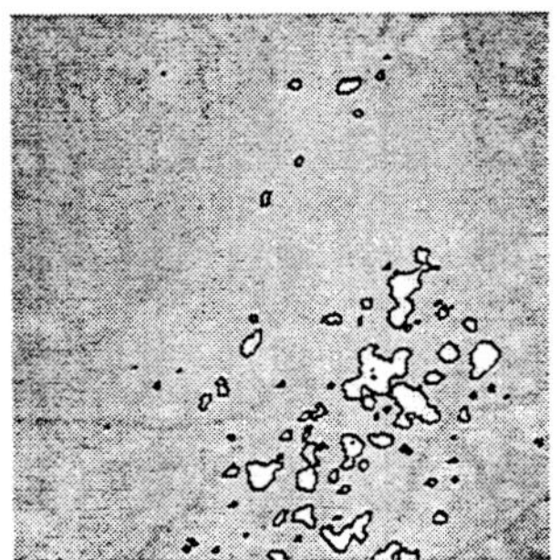
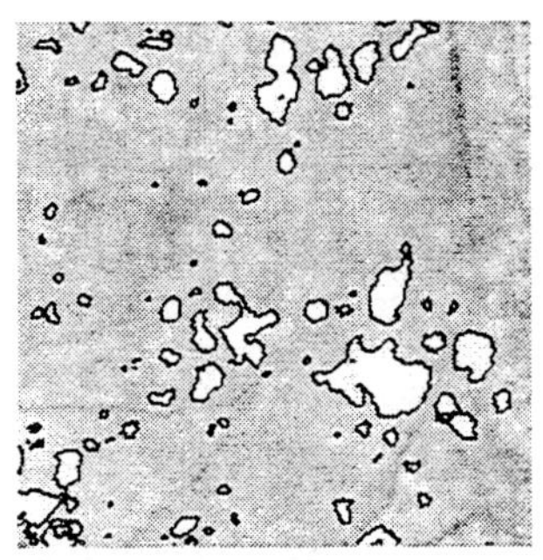

(b) results of segmentation

Figure 4. Drusen evolution from 1983 to 1988.

6 References

[1] G. Mimoun, G. Soubrane, G. Coscas, "Les drusen maculaires", J. Fr. Ophtalmol., 1990, Vol. 13, n 10, 511-530.
[2] E. Pelli, "Drusen measurement from fundus photographs using computer image analysis", Ophthalmol, 1986, Vol. 93, n 12, 1575-1580.
[3] Z. BenSbeh, L. D. Cohen, G. Mimoun, G. Coscas, G. Soubrane, "An adaptative contrast method for segmentation of drusen", In Proc. of I.C.I.P, Santa Barbara, Oct 1997.
[4] K. S. Shanmugan, K. S. Breipohl, "Random Signals, Detection, Estimation and Data Analysis", Wiley, New York, pp. 196-202.
[5] A. Raji, A. Thaïbaoui, E. Petit, P. Bunel, G. Mimoun, "A gray-level transformation-based method for image enhancement", Pattern Recognition Letters, Vol.19, n 13, pp 1207-1212, 1998.
[6] J. C. Brezdek and S. K. Pal, "Fuzzy models for pattern recognition", IEEE, New York, 1992.
[7] X. Q. Li, Z. W. Zhao, H. D. Cheng, C. M. Huang and R. W. Harris, "A fuzzy logic approach to image segmentation", In proceeding ICPR, pp. 337-341, 1994.
[8] T. Koné, P. Bunel, G. Mimoun, J. Kouakou, G. Coscas, "Analyse automatique d'images angiographiques rtiniennes: Application la dgnrescence maculaire lie l'âge", J. I.T.B.M., Vol 17, n3, pp.233-238, 1996.
[9] M. Sebag, E. Peli, M. Lahav, "Image analysis of changes in drusen area", ACTA Ophtalmologica, Vol 69, pp. 603-610, 1991.

A Machine Vision System for Inspecting Bearings

Joze Derganc, Franjo Pernus
University of Ljubljana
Faculty of Electrical Engineering
Trzaska cesta 25, 1000 Ljubljana, Slovenia
E-mail: joze.derganc@fe.uni-lj.si, franjo.pernus@fe.uni-lj.si

Abstract

In this paper we describe a machine vision system for inspecting bearings, which are an important part of electro-mechanical kWh meters. The system consists of a personal computer with a frame grabber, a black and white progressive scan CCD camera, and a mechanical device with a stepper motor controlled by a special controller connected to the RS232 port of the personal computer. The quality of a bearing depends on the eccentricity of the needle and the length of the needle that extends out of the cylinder. These two parameters are robustly and accurately defined by the Hough transform and the regression methods. The presented results show that the proposed machine vision system allows accurate, reproducible, and robust 100% inspection of bearings of electro-mechanical kWh meters and as such it may be a valuable tool for ensuring high-end-product quality.

1. Introduction

Visual inspection of parts and products by eye represents a high cost in the electronic, machine, pharmaceutical, food and other industries. Besides, such an inspection is time-consuming, tiring, inaccurate and subjective. Manufacturers therefore look for fast, accurate, reliable, and consistent automated visual inspection of their products to reduce manual involvement in the application of pass/fail criteria. During the last two decades, machine vision has been applied slowly but surely to a variety of manufacturing challenges, all with the goal of improving quality and productivity in the manufacturing process. Machine vision uses video cameras and computers to replace human vision in evaluation and inspection tasks. Features such as colour, size, and distance are used to evaluate parts and reject those with defects [1,2]. A machine vision inspection system introduces fast, precise, efficient and objective inspection. However, high speed, high quality and high resolution applications require innovative, customised solutions, outside the scope of standard "of the shelf" systems. In this paper we describe a machine vision system for inspecting bearings of electro-mechanical kWh meters.

2. Problem description

A vital part of an electro-mechanical kWh meter is the upper bearing, to which the main shaft with the aluminium plate that rotates under the electromagnetic effects produced by the current and voltage, is attached (Figure 1). The upper bearing is a hollow cylinder with a co-axial needle that is fixed to the bottom (Figure 2). The quality of the upper bearing depends on:

a) the eccentricity of the needle,
b) the length of the needle that extends out of the cylinder.

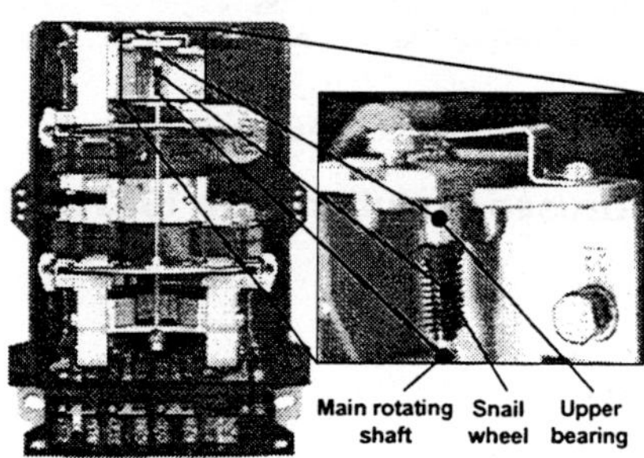

Figure 1. Position of the upper bearing in an electro-mechanical kWh meter.

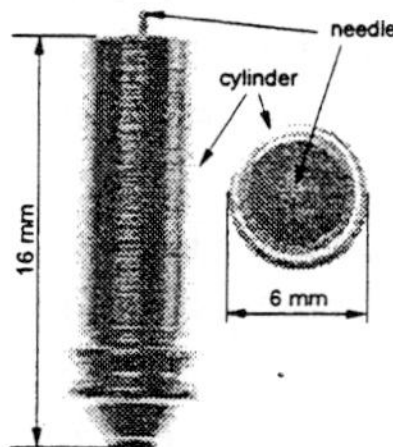

Figure 2. Upper bearing; side view (left), view from above (right).

The eccentricity, which may be visualised by rotating the bearing (Figure 3) may be determined from lines *ne* and *ref* i.e., the lines of symmetry of the needle and a cylinder, respectively (Figure 4). The median of a trapezoid, defined by the points PQRS, has been chosen to represent the eccentricity e in a certain position of the bearing. The eccentricity E is the largest median e of a number of trapeziods obtained during rotation. The mean height of the trapezoids represents the length d of the needle that extends out of the cylinder. The eccentricity E of a good bearing must be less than 0.1mm, while the length d of the needle must be 1.2mm ±0.1mm. The edges of a bearing are all straight lines, except at the top of the needle where edge points form a semiellipse. The parameters of the straight lines and the semiellipse, which are used to find the trapezoid PQRS, and thus the eccentricity and the length of a needle, have to be obtained fast, accurately, and robustly. Dust and other small particles on the bearing should not affect the measurements.

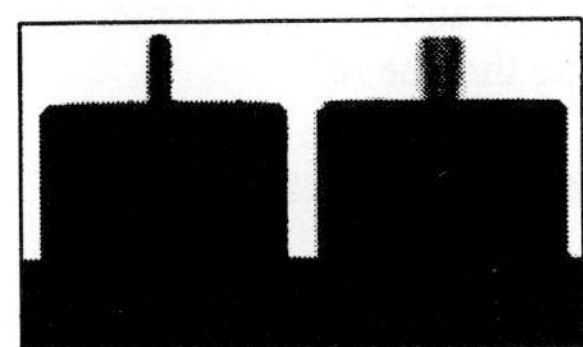

Figure 3. A straight (left) and an eccentric bearing (right) during rotation.

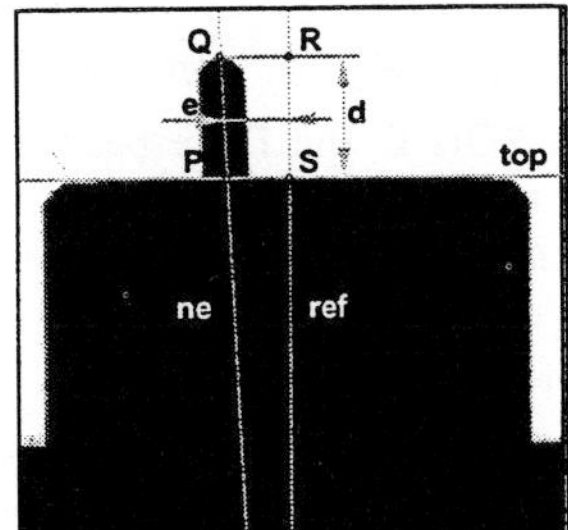

Figure 4. Eccentricity e of a bearing and the length d of the needle extending out of the cylinder.

3. The machine vision system

The machine vision system for measuring the eccentricity and the length of the needle consists of a personal computer (PC), a black and white progressive scan CCD camera, illumination, and a mechanical device with a stepper motor controlled by a special controller connected to the RS232 port of the PC (Figure 5). The system allows accurate non-contact measurements while the bearing is rotated.

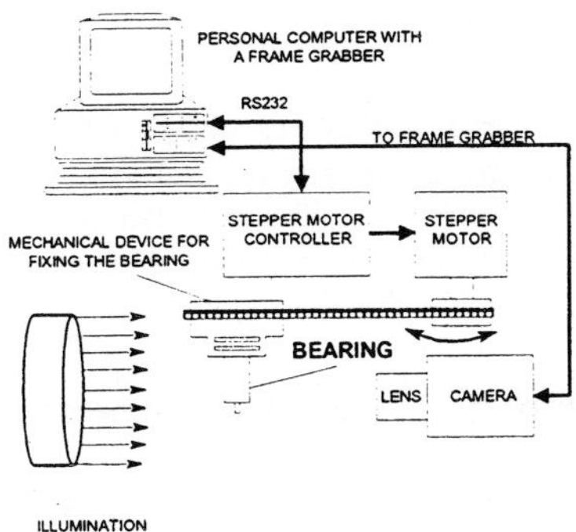

Figure 5. Outline of the machine vision system for inspecting bearings.

4. Methods of visual inspection

Figure 6 shows the flow chart of the bearing inspection procedure. After a bearing is set in its position in front of a camera, N images are taken during rotation for 360 degrees, each showing the bearing rotated for $k*360/N$, $k=0,1,2,\ldots,N-1$ degrees. In each image a differential edge operator is used to extract image points which have a high likelihood of being on or near the straight lines or the semiellipse.

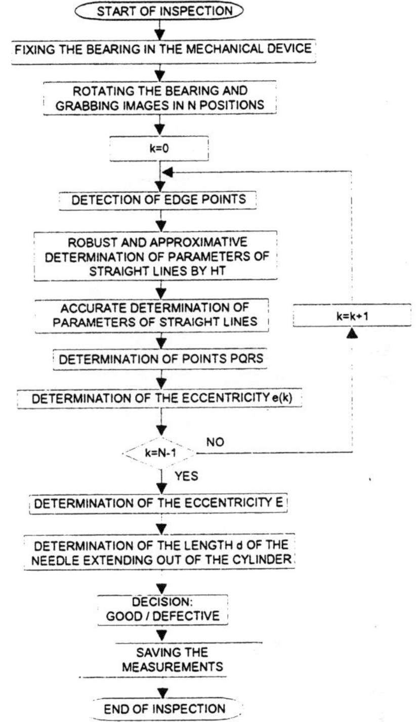

Figure 6. Flow chart of bearing inspection

The parameters of straight lines are obtained by Hough transform (HT), which is inherently robust against outliers and noise. Because the HT demands considerable computation, and lack of time is one of the major constraints on the inspection, accuracy is first sacrified to speed. The parameters of the straight lines are only approximately defined by HT but the accuracy is then improved by yet another step of processing. A line fitting procedure is added to refine the output of the HT procedure. In the following subsection a more detailed description of the algorithm is given.

4.1. Parametric description of edges

Because the system operates in a constrained and controlled environment, intensity profiles obtained along 7 predetermined lines (Figure 7 left) can be used to determine

6 regions of interest (ROIs) (Figure 7 right). In ROIs A-E the edges of a bearing are straight lines while in region F the edge forms a semiellipse. To define the parameters of the straight lines and the semiellipse, the Sobel operator [3] is first applied to derive the edge magnitude $G(x_i,y_i)$ at each pixel (x_i,y_i) of the image:

$$G(x_i,y_i)=\sqrt{g_x^2(x_i,y_i)+g_y^2(x_i,y_i)} \quad (1)$$

where g_x and g_y represent the partial gradients in the x and y direction, respectively. In each ROI only the pixels (x_i,y_i) for which:

$$G(x_i,y_i)> G_{max}/2 \quad (2)$$

where G_{max} is the highest gradient magnitude in a ROI, are kept. Second, a combination of the Hough transform and regression methods is used to determine the edges to sub-pixel accuracy.

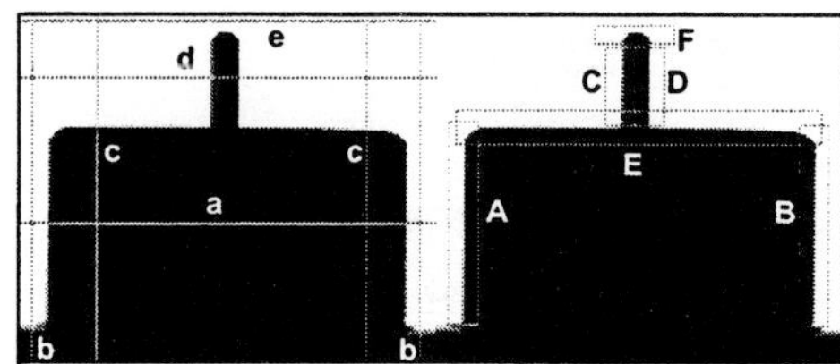

Figure 7. Lines a-e along which intensity profiles are determined (left). Regions of interest (A-E) in which we search for straight lines and region F in which a semiellipse is searched for (right).

Each vertical straight line in ROIs A-D may be parametrically described as:

$$x=\tilde{m}y+\tilde{c} \quad (3)$$

while the horizontal straight line in ROI E is defined as:

$$y=mx+c \quad (4)$$

In each ROI, coarse estimations of the parameters m, c and $\tilde{m}$, $\tilde{c}$ are obtained by the Hough transform [3]. The edge points (x_i,y_i), being consistent with a coarsely pre-defined straight line, i.e. the points for which:

$$\frac{|x_i-\tilde{m}y_i-\tilde{c}|}{\sqrt{1+\tilde{m}}}<d_{\max} \quad \text{or} \quad \frac{|y_i-mx_i-c|}{\sqrt{1+m}}<d_{\max} \quad (5)$$

where d_{max} is a predefined consistency threshold (d_{max}=3 pixels in our implementation), are further used to precisely define the parameters $\tilde{m}$ and $\tilde{c}$ by linear regression [4,5]:

$$\tilde{m}=\frac{\sum_{i=1}^{M}y_i^2\sum_{i=1}^{M}x_i-\sum_{i=1}^{M}y_i\sum_{i=1}^{M}x_iy_i}{M\sum_{i=1}^{M}y_i^2-\sum_{i=1}^{M}y_i\sum_{i=1}^{M}y_i} \quad (6)$$

$$\tilde{c}=\frac{M\sum_{i=1}^{M}x_iy_i-\sum_{i=1}^{M}x_i\sum_{i=1}^{M}y_i}{M\sum_{i=1}^{M}y_i^2-\sum_{i=1}^{M}y_i\sum_{i=1}^{M}y_i} \quad (7)$$

where M is the number of edge points which satisfy Eq. 5. Similar equations are used to accurately define the parameters m and c. The parameters ($\tilde{m}_A$, $\tilde{c}_A$) and ($\tilde{m}_B$, $\tilde{c}_B$) of the straight lines in ROIs A and B, respectively, representing the left and the right border of the cylinder, are used to determine the line *ref*:

$$x_{ref}=\frac{\tilde{m}_A+\tilde{m}_B}{2}y_{ref}+\frac{\tilde{c}_A+\tilde{c}_B}{2} \quad (8)$$

The line *ne* is defined as:

$$x_{ne}=\frac{\tilde{m}_C+\tilde{m}_D}{2}y_{ne}+\frac{\tilde{c}_C+\tilde{c}_D}{2} \quad (9)$$

where ($\tilde{m}_C$, $\tilde{c}_C$) and ($\tilde{m}_D$, $\tilde{c}_D$) are the parameters of the straight lines in ROIs C and D, respectively, representing the left and the right border of the needle. The line *top* in ROI E, representing the upper border of the cylinder is defined as:

$$y_{top}=m_Ex_{top}+c_E \quad (10)$$

The parameters of the semielliptic tip of a needle, lying in region F, are obtained by the regression method [5,6] using R points (x_i,y_i) which satisfy Eq. 2. The equation of an ellipse $Q(x,y)$ is:

$$Q(x,y)=a_1x^2+a_2xy+a_3y^2+a_4x+a_5y+1=0 \quad (11)$$

and

$$Q(x_i,y_i)=a_1x_i^2+a_2x_iy_i+a_3y_i^2+a_4x_i+a_5y_i+1 \quad (12)$$

is the algebraic distance of point (x_i,y_i) to the ellipse. The parameters of the ellipse, best fitting the R edge points, are obtained by minimising:

$$SE=\sum_{i=1}^{R}Q(x_i,y_i)^2 \quad (13)$$

Obtaining 5 partial derivatives of SE with respect to the parameters a_1, a_2, a_3, a_4 and a_5, and setting these partial derivatives to zero provides five simultaneous equations, the solution to which represents the parameters of the ellipse $Q(x,y)$ that minimises the error function SE.

4.2. Eccentricity and length of the needle

The equations of the straight lines i.e., *ne*, *ref*, and *top*, and the ellipse are used to define the trapezoid PQRS. The eccentricity $e(k)$, in each position k; $k=0,1,..N-1$, is determined as the median of the trapezoid:

$$e(k) = K_C \frac{\overline{PS} + \overline{QR}}{2} \quad (14)$$

where K_C is the calibration coefficient determined by analysing the image of a calibration bearing. Figure 8 shows how the eccentricities $e(k)$, $k=0,1,2,..,29$, change during the rotation of five bearings with the highest eccentricity 0.24, 0.17, 0,09, 0,05 and 0.02 mm, respectively. One can observe that the eccentricity values form discrete sine functions. The complex discrete spectrum $E^d(m)$ of such a function may be obtained by the Discrete Fourier Transform (DFT) [5] :

$$E^d(m) = \sum_{k=0}^{N-1} e(k) e^{-j\frac{2\pi}{N}mk} \quad m = 0..N-1 \quad k = 0..N-1 \quad (15)$$

The largest eccentricity E of a bearing is defined as:

$$E = \frac{2}{N} \left| E^d(1) \right| \quad (16)$$

The length $d(k)$ of the needle extending out of the cylinder in position k, $k=0,\dots,N-1$ is the distance between points R and S (Figure 4):

$$d(k) = K_C \overline{RS}(k) \quad (17)$$

The length of the needle d is obtained as a mean value of lengths $d(k)$:

$$d = \frac{1}{N} \sum_{k=0}^{N-1} K_C \overline{RS}(k) \quad (18)$$

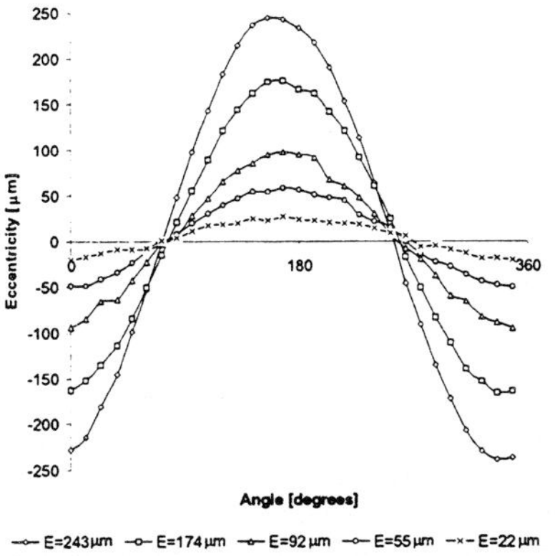

Figure 8. Eccentricities $e(k)$, $k=0,1,2,..,29$, of five bearings.

5 Results and conclusions

To test the influence of the number of images (N) taken per rotation on the value of the eccentricity E, this was determined from $N=3, 5, 10, 15, 20, 25$ and 30 views. At the same time for each N the reproducibility of the measurements was tested by starting the rotation of a bearing from 50 randomly selected positions. The results presented in the form of min, max, and median eccentricity values (Figure 9), indicate that the measurements are highly reproducible if the eccentricity is defined from $N \geq 10$ views of the bearing. Based on these results and because speed is a crucial factor, the machine vision system uses only 15 images to determine the eccentricity of a bearing.

In this paper a machine vision system for inspecting bearings of electro-mechanical kWh meters has been described. The obtained results show that the methods used to define the eccentricity of a bearing are fast and robust and that they give reproducible results. Such a machine vision system will be incorporated in the electro-mechanical kWh meters production line. It is expected that it will be a valuable tool for ensuring high-end-product quality.

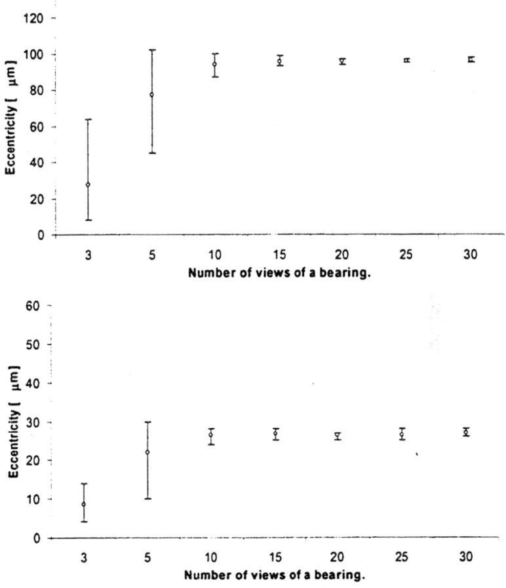

Figure 9. Reproducibility of the measured eccentricity for the bearing with $E=96\mu m$ (top) and $E=26\mu m$ (bottom).

References

[1] T.S. Newman, A.K. Jain, "*A survey of automated visual inspection*", Computer Vision and Image Understanding 61: 231-262, 1995

[2] J. Jarvis, "*Research directions in industrial machine vision*", A workshop summary, Computer 15: 55-61,1982

[3] M. Sonka, V. Hlavac, R. Boyle, *Image processing , Analysis and Machine Vison*, PWS Publishing, 1999

[4] E.R. Davies, *Machine vision: theory, algorithms, practicalities*, Academic Press, London 1990

[5] W.H. Press, S.A. Teulkolsky, W.T. Vetterling, B.P. Flannery, *Numerical recipies in C*, Cambridge university press, Cambridge, 1996

[6] P.L. Rosin, "*A note on the least squares fitting of ellipses*", Pattern Recognition Letters 14, 799-808, 1993

A Robust Algorithm for Segmenting Deformable Linear Objects from Video Image Sequences

Frank ABEGG, Dirk ENGEL, and Heinz WÖRN

Institute for Process Control and Robotics (IPR),
Computer Science Department, Universität Karlsruhe (TH), D-76128 Karlsruhe, Germany,
e-mail: [Abegg | dEngel | Woern]@ira.uka.de, http://wwwipr.ira.uka.de/~paro/

Abstract

A new algorithm for segmenting and tracking deformable (shape-changing) linear (thin and long with negligible diameter) objects in video images is presented. The core of algorithm is to detect the two boundary curves of a deformable linear object within adaptive tracking windows. The boundaries are found by analyzing the gray value gradients within the tracking windows. The algorithm allows moderate changes in the image brightness by introducing tolerance parameters to the algorithm. It also provides a robust tracking of the shape- and width-changing object by using a fuzzy estimation of the object's membership function at the tracked points. The result resulting describes the shape of the object and is used to define features for shape change detection.

1. Introduction

Although today robots can perform sensor-based operations on rigid objects very well, handling deformable objects with industrial robots is still a field where a lot of research has to be done. A new approach for handling deformable linear objects using the principle of contact state transitions was proposed by [1]. Investigations in the field of force/torque based robot operations using this approach showed the applicability of the new approach [2]. Since there are operations, of which we believe they can be performed better with machine vision sensors, we have built a basic image processing system for recognizing and tracking deformable linear objects. A description of the general approach combining contact state transitions of deformable linear objects with vision-based robot operations can be found in [3].

Many methods for realizing different tasks performed by a visually guided robotic system can be found in literature [4]. However, there are only few approaches concerning deformable objects, even though there are many industrial applications [5]. One example is cabling car door frames (Figure 1).

Regarding to the entire process of handling and assembly operations of deformable linear objects, we need to distinguish several modules, each responsible for one subtask of the process. We need a module for object recognition and tracking, a module for object analysis, and another module for controlling the robot.

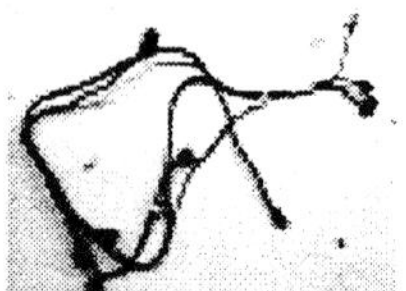

Figure 1: Example task for manipulating deformable linear objects: cabling of car door frames.

In this article, we investigate the module for object recognition and tracking. We formulate a general algorithm for the vision-based recognition and tracking of deformable linear objects (DLO) using a robot hand-mounted standard video camera. The output of the algorithm leads to the definition of a visual feature, being a robust indicator for change in the shape of the observed object.

Work concerning the automatic segmentation of general deformable objects is still a field of great interest in the image processing community. In the case of deformable objects, two main approaches can be found in the literature: model-based object segmentation and image-based object segmentation.

The approaches for model-based segmentation of deformable objects use active contours which are often called *snakes*. Active contours can be viewed as a kind of deformable template of an object. The model consists of energy-based model equations describing the behavior of non-rigid material by using constraint conditions for internal and external forces [6, 7]. In the case of recognizing a deformable linear object without a loop, active contours are not applicable due to the restrictions in their geometric flexibility [8]. Other methods extending the active contours to topologically adaptable snakes as the one of Lai are difficult to initialize.

Image-based approaches use the information provided by the pixels and their connections and can be found in every image processing book such as [9]. They can be classified into methods based on points, methods based on regions, and edge-based methods. Using these methods for recognizing deformable objects in front of a structured or textured background without any further information is hardly possible. This is because it seems to be improbable that a general function exists which uses only the pixel information for the decision whether a pixel belongs to the object of interest or not.

Additional knowledge like the geometric structure and geometric constraints of the object of interest is necessary in order to apply an image-based segmentation on cable-like deformable linear objects. For deformable linear objects, the curve describing the object shape and the width in pixels are very important parameters. The algorithm introduced in this paper extracts geometric and topological parameters from the image and uses them in the process of segmenting a deformable linear object. These parameters limit the list of possible object points and finally lead to a well-defined decision of the object membership function. The basic image analysis requires a gray-value-based and gradient-based pre-segmentation using only a few automatically computable thresholds. The base points describing the shape of the deformable objects are computed by taking the midpoint of two points lying each on one of the two found contours of the object, similar to the work of [9].

In the next section, a brief overview of our approach is given. The subsequent sections consider the questions: How does the algorithm for segmenting and tracking deformable linear objects work, and what are its input and output parameters (Section 3)? What are the results in using this approach (Section 4)? What are the conclusions and how should the work be continued (Section 5)?

2. Task Description and Solution

In the following, the observation of a deformable linear object (called *workpiece*) in a static environment (called *obstacle*) is considered. The observation is done with a monocular standard video camera mounted on the flange of an industrial robot (called *hand camera*). Comparisons between the observation with a stationary camera and the observation with a hand camera show that it is more robust to detect state changes with a hand camera, since it can be managed that the interesting parts of the workpiece always appears in the camera image. With a hand camera we have also less problems with light reflections and shadows by using an additional ring light mounted around the camera.

Now, it is supposed that there is an assembly task where the robot has to manipulate the workpiece in order to mount it onto a device. A typical workpieces can be a hose, an electric cable, or a piece of spring steal. The linear workpiece is gripped at one end and the robot gripper may perform arbitrary linear motions.During the assembly task, the workpiece is tracked with the vision system and its shape appearing in the camera image is analyzed in order to adapt the instructions given to the robot (Figure 2).Given this task, the vision system must be able to segment the shape of the workpiece, to track it, and to adapt the recognized shape when the workpiece is deformed by a contact with an obstacle. Since the contact detection is one of the basic requirements of our approach in handling deformable linear objects in assembly processes, the geometric image model of the workpiece shape derived from the vision system must provide the possibility to compute geometric features which give an indication of those shape changes. Furthermore, the recognition process must meet real time requirements when it is applied in an industrial process.

Figure 2: Setup of robot hand-mounted camera (left) and robot and hand camera in front of an obstacle (right)

In order to solve a mounting task like given above, we propose an image-based algorithm using additional knowledge about the used workpiece. As the algorithm is initialized by the user, the initial shape of the workpiece is detected. A tracking mechanism is able to adapt automatically the geometric image-model of the preceding workpiece shape with respect to the current workpiece shape. Image-geometric features derived from the workpiece model allow a further analysis of the workpiece shape. In the following section, the algorithm is described in detail.

3. Shape Recognition and Shape Tracking

The approach of the algorithm for segmenting DLOs of a camera image bases on edge detection. The idea is to follow the shape of the DLO represented by its contours whereby the width of the object may also change.

3.1 Recognition Process

In order to reduce the cost of the convolution operation carried out by the edge detection operator, a preprocessing of the image is performed. For this preprocessing, the user determines the average gray value of the DLO and its tolerance. For further computations only image subareas within this given gray value interval are regarded.

Within these subareas, rectangular regions of interest are processed in order to find corresponding borderline points of the DLO. Only within these segments the edges are computed. This strategy reduces computing costs and improves the liability to disturbance, because only relevant image areas are considered by the algorithm. As the initial rectangle segment is given by the user, further segments along the DLO are computed automatically.

For segmenting the DLO within the rectangle segments, more user given information is required. The sharpness threshold of the edges to detect and the object thickness must be adjusted. For further influence on the edge detection, the user has the choice between four implemented edge detection operators: Difference, Roberts, Sobel, or Laplacian-of-Gaussian operator. For our application, the Sobel-Operator has found to be the best suitable operator.

Another input parameter is the maximum allowed distance between two consecutive base points. By controlling this parameter, the user can increase the capability of bridging interruptions in the object shape.

After setting the parameters, the algorithm selects the base points within the rectangle segments based on the evaluation of a function using fuzzy logic. There are three criteria to be considered, forming our additional knowledge:

- the distance between the current point and the last segmented base point c_{point}
- the minimal distance between the current point and the tangent through the last segmented base point $c_{tangent}$
- the thickness of the DLO in current points $c_{thickness}$

All of these three criteria are normalized. An evaluation of one criterion with zero means a worst-suited point, an evaluation with one means a best-suited point.

These three criteria are combined to form one total evaluation criterion c_{total} :

$$c_{total} = c_{point} \cdot c_{tangent} \cdot c_{thickness}$$

If the borders of a rectangle segment are reached, a new segment has to be placed. New rectangle segments are placed next to the last rectangle segment and concentric to the intersection of the tangent at the last base point and the border of the last segment side (Figure 3).

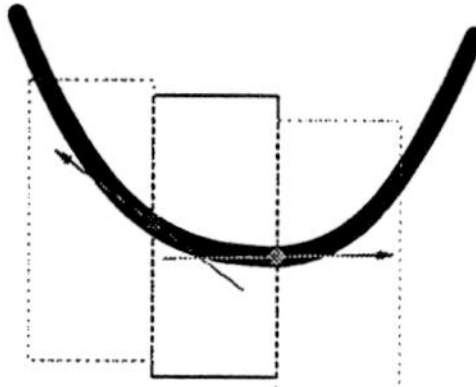

Figure 3: The placing of new rectangle segments

For a better adaptability to the property of a deformable object and its shape, the position of the rectangle segments is additionally shifted dependent from the slope of the tangent through the last base point (Figure 4).

The previously described algorithm and methods are solutions to segment DLO from a single image. The tracking of the DLO within an image sequence is realized by searching the DLO in each image frame within rectangle segments derived from a user-given number of base points computed in the image frame before.

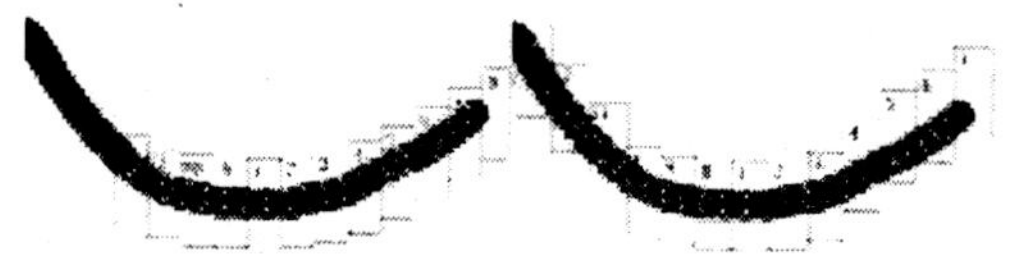

Figure 4: Adaptability to the object shape without considering the tangent slope (left) and with considering the tangent slope (right)

3.2 Feature Extraction

The base point list as a representation of the workpiece in the image space allows straightforward derivation of characteristic features like the length or the curvature of the workpiece in the image, which provide hints to contact state transitions of the workpiece when observed over time [3]. Since the data of these straightforward features are superimposed by noise, we developed a more robust feature.

A linear approximation of the workpiece shape is produced by computing the average base point coordinates and the average tangent angle of each base point. The resulting line and its intersection with the image borders enclose a trapezoidal surface (Figure 5). The size of this surface with respect to the size of the image surface carries only low noise and produces big peaks or rising curves when the workpiece shape changes. Evaluation results of this normalized feature (we name it F) are given in the next section.

Figure 5: Trapezoid given by the linear approximation of the shape a pneumatic wire (line through DLO together with dashed lines)

4. Experimental Results

The manipulation experiments were performed with a Kuka KR15 robot gripping a pneumatic polyurethane wire with outer diameter of 6 mm and a length of 300 mm. The robot controller executes motion commands sent from a Linux-PC with two 350 MHz Pentium II Processors. The PC also includes the image processing software with the presented algorithm and the frame grabber card (Eltec PC-Eye I). As hand camera, a standard video CCD-Camera with a remote sensor head is used (Teli CS 3710 C). The working environment providing the obstacles is either a car door frame which is mounted in a horizontal lying position or an artificial environment built of aluminum sheets mounted in different angles and with some holes of several different diameters (Figure 2).

Images of a tracking sequence, where the pneumatic wire is bent by moving it against an obstacle, show that our algorithm tracks well the changing contour of the wire (Figure 6).

Another experiment shows the stability of the segmented base points of the pneumatic wire (Figure 7). The average change of the endpoint angle w remains nearly constant when the robot is moved 30 steps without causing a change of the wire shape. The dashed line shows the average length change recorded during a movement causing a change of the wire shape. It can be seen that the maximum aberration is less than 5 pixels.

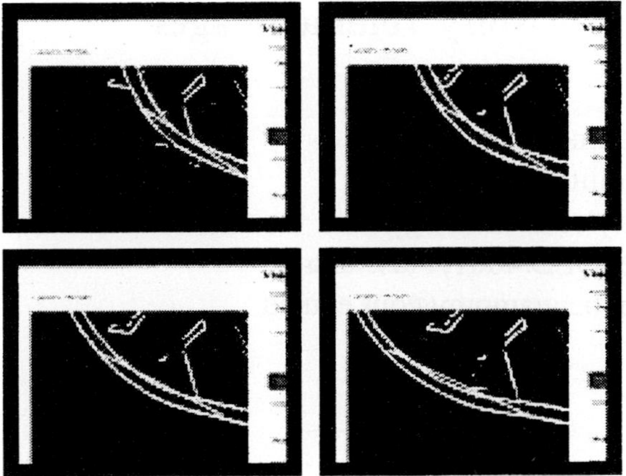

Figure 6: A bent pneumatic wire is tracked by the vision system. The circles indicate the computed base points

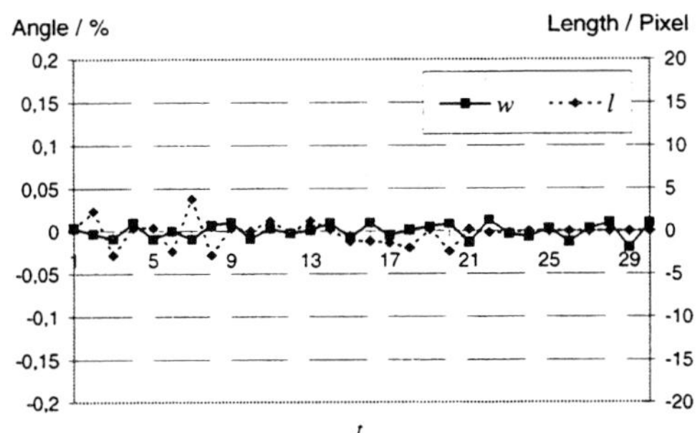

Figure 7: Diagram showing the stability of the segmented base points of a pneumatic wire

The diagram shown in Figure 8 was recorded during a point contact establishment operation with the robot and displays the feature of the linear approximation from Section 3.2. The sudden rise shows well the change of the extracted shape of the pneumatic wire. Further experiments confirmed the applicability of this feature for recognizing other state transitions of the wire.

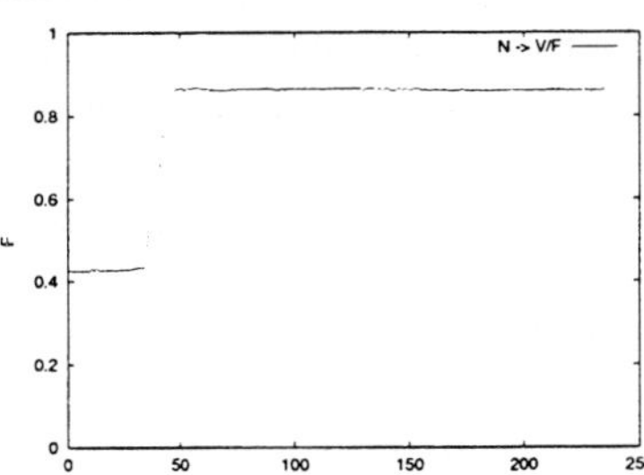

Figure 8: Course of the feature F of the linear approximation from Section 3.2 during a point contact establishment operation where n is the number of frames

5. Conclusions and Future Work

In this paper, a robust and fast algorithm for segmenting and tracking deformable linear objects with a standard video camera is proposed. The algorithm works well under daylight and artificial lighting conditions. The algorithm output can be used for computing indicators of object shape changes and enables a robot to manipulate deformable linear objects in order to solve an industrial-like task.

Future work will include the improvement of the algorithm and its implementation in stereo matching. Improvements for the user can be done by using yet more automatic threshold computations. For detecting changes in view direction, the feature analysis must be extended to a third cable dimension which can be the average of the width in every computed base point. Furthermore, we will investigate handling uncertainty and error estimation including an extensive stability analysis.

Acknowledgements

The work is funded by the European Commission in the framework of the BriteEuram-project HANDFLEX (Integrated modular solution for HANDling of FLEXible materials in industrial environments). We would like to thank the DaimlerChrysler AG, Germany, for supplying cables and cable forms.

References

[1] Henrich D., Ogasawara T., Wörn H. "Manipulating deformable linear objects – Contact states and point contacts". In: 1999 IEEE Int. Symp. on Assembly and Task Planning (ISATP'99), Porto, Portugal, July 21-24, 1999.

[2] Remde A., Wörn H.: "Manipulating deformable linear objects – Force based detection of contact state transitions –". Submitted to: 2000 IEEE/RSJ Int. Conf. on Intelligent Robots and Systems (IROS 2000), Takamatsu, Japan, October 2000.

[3] Abegg F., Henrich D., Wörn H.: "Manipulating deformable linear objects – Vision-based recognition of contact state transitions –". In Proc. Ninth Int. Conf. on Advanced Robotics (ICAR'99), pp. 135-140, Tokyo, Japan, October 27-29, 1999.

[4] Hutchinson S., Hager G.D., and Corke P.I.: "A tutorial on visual servo control". In: IEEE Trans. on Robotics and Automation, vol. 12, no. 5, October 1996.

[5] Byun J.-E., Nagata T.: "Determining the 3-D pose of a flexible object by stereo matching of curvature representations". In: Pattern Recognition, vol. 29 no. 8, pp. 1297-1308, 1996.

[6] Lai K. F., Chin R. T.: "Deformable Contours: Modeling and Extraction". In: IEEE Trans. on Pattern Analysis and Machine Intelligence, vol. 17, no. 11, November 1995.

[7] McInerney T., Terzopoulos D.: "Topologically Adaptable Snakes". In: Proc. of the Fifth Int. Conf. on Computer Vision (ICCV'95), Cambridge, MA, USA, June 1995.

[8] Jain R., Kasturi R., Schunck B.G.: "Machine Vision", McGraw-Hill, Inc., 1995.

[9] Han C.-C., Fan K.-C.: "Skeleton Generation of Engineering Drawings via Contour Matching". Pattern Recognition, vol 27, no. 2. pp. 261-275, 1994.

Accurate Localisation of Edges in Noisy Volume Images

Pi-chi Chou and Mohammed Bennamoun
Space Centre for Satellite Navigation
Queensland University of Technology
G.P.O. Box 2434, Brisbane, QLD 4001, Australia
E-mail: p.chou@qut.edu.au, m.bennamoun@qut.edu.au

Abstract

Advances in medical imaging modalities have made it possible to acquire volume images. One of the key steps used to split the raw volume image into meaningful sub-volumes is three-dimensional (3D) edge detection. This paper describes a new approach for 3D edge detection. It is based on the two-dimensional (2D) hybrid edge detector, which consists of a combination of the first and second order differential edge detectors. It was shown in the 2D case that the combination of the two differential edge detectors gave an accurate edge localisation whilst maintaining immunity to the noise in the image. Results using the 3D hybrid edge detector based on synthetic and real images are presented. They are also compared to the results using the 3D Gradient of the Gaussian (GoG) detector and the 3D Laplacian of the Gaussian (LoG) detector.

1 Introduction

Medical imaging modelity such as Magnetic Resonance Imagery (MRI) has made it possible to explore human anatomy without the need of making any incisions. Any of the existing modality has the ability to generate volume data [6], and this volume data can sometimes be seen as a series of 2D slices. One way of processing this data is to apply traditional 2D image processing techniques on each slice.

Deriche [5] have shown that with the same set of image data, the processing of a volumetric image is more robust and coherent than the processing of 2D cross-section images. In particular, 3D edge detection yields three advantages in comparison with 2D edge detection. 1) better immunity to noise; 2) better estimation of the gradient magnitude; and 3) computation of the 3D gradient.

Because of the capability of acquiring volume data and the superior performance of 3D image processing, volume image processing has become an important tool for medical image applications. To assist doctors and radiographers to make a diagnose using computer algorithms, meaningful anatomical structures and/or abnormal tissues must be segmented and identified. This can be accomplished using edge detection. This is usually followed by a post-processing stage consisting of linking the edges (edge linking and region merging).

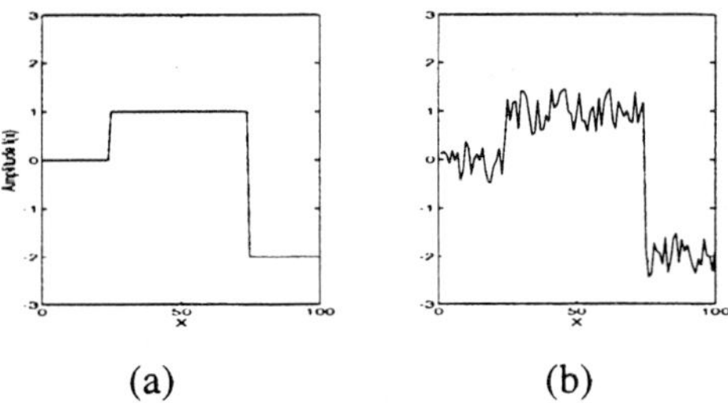

(a) (b)

Figure 1. (a) Ideal 1D step edge. (b) The ideal step edge corrupted by additive noise.

Edges are defined as points of transition between homogeneous regions. Many edge models exist, such as the step edge, the roof edge, and few other type of edges. The edge model that we use is an ideal step function corrupted by additive noise, see Figure 1.

A good edge detector should exhibit an accurate localisation of the edges and a good immunity to the noise in the image. In [4], Canny showed that there is a compromise between the above mentioned properties, due to the nature of the smoothing filter (uncertainty principle). Because of the properties of 3D edge detectors, many authors [7, 8, 9, 13] have extended existing 2D edge detectors to the 3D case. In this paper, we propose a new 3D Hybrid Edge Detector, which is an extension of the one previously proposed by the second author in the 2D case [2, 3]. This 3D Hybrid Detector has the ability to accurately localize the edges whilst maintaining immunity to the noise in the image.

The paper is organised as follows. Section 2 describes the process of Hybrid Edge Detection. Results based on MRI images are presented and compared in Section 3. Section 4 presents the conclusion and future directions.

1051-4651/00 $10.00 © 2000 IEEE

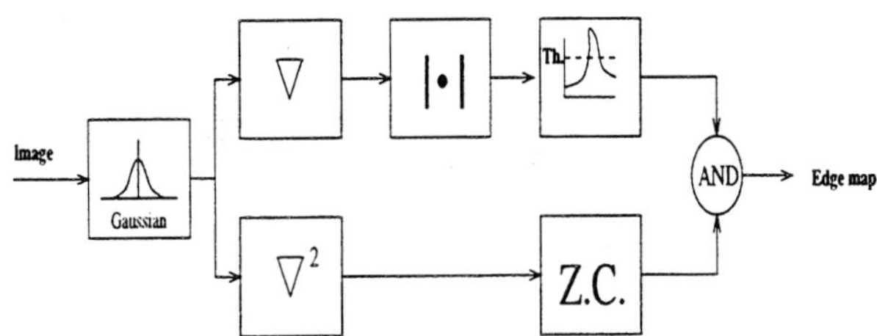

Figure 2. Block diagram of the Hybrid Edge Detector, where Z.C. stands for zero-crossing, $|\cdot|$ represents the magnitude and Th is the threshold.

2 The Hybrid Edge Detector

An edge can be detected computationally using differentiation [12]. The Hybrid Edge Detector is composed of two independent branches, which are the first and the second order differential edge detectors. In [12], Torre and Poggio showed that the detection of edges using differentiation is an ill-posed problem and therefore needs to be regularised [11].

The process of regularisation can be solved by a linear, low-pass filter. It was explained in [2], that the Gaussian filter is the most appropriate choice for such a task, since its properties best satisfy the conditions of minimal uncertainty [12]. In addition to other advantages of the Gaussian filter [10], the filter is chosen to be the smoothing filter of the Hybrid Edge Detector. The 3D Gaussian function has the following form:

$$G(x,y,z) = \frac{1}{2\pi\sigma^2}\exp\left(\frac{-(x^2+y^2+z^2)}{2\sigma^2}\right), \quad (1)$$

where σ is the scale of the Gaussian (smoothing parameter).

As for the second order derivative, the Laplacian operator is defined by:

$$\nabla^2 f = f_{xx} + f_{yy} + f_{zz}, \quad (2)$$

and the second order directional derivative in the direction $\vec{n}$ is defined by:

$$\begin{aligned}\frac{\partial^2 f}{\partial n^2} &= (f_x^2 f_{xx} + f_y^2 f_{yy} + f_z^2 f_{zz} + 2f_x f_y f_{xy} \\ &\quad +2f_y f_z f_{yz} + 2f_z f_x f_{zx})/(f_x^2 + f_y^2 + f_z^2) \quad (3)\end{aligned}$$

where f_x is the first order derivative with respect to x and f_{xx} is the second order derivative with respect to x. Both the Laplacian and the second order directional derivative operators perform similarly, however the Laplacian operator is a better choice for the following reasons: 1) The Laplacian is rotationally invariant while the directional derivative is dependent on the direction in which it is applied; 2) It is computationally more efficient; 3) The Laplacian is defined everywhere, whereas the directional derivative is undefined when the gradient of the function is zero [12]. Therefore the Laplacian operator is used in the Hybrid Edge Detector.

Based on the observations discussed above, the overall structure of the Hybrid Detector is as shown in Figure 2. The raw input image is first passed through a Gaussian filter. The smoothing effect of the filter depends only on the value of σ. The smoothed image is then passed through two independent branches, the upper branch is a first order differential operator, which in conjunction with the Gaussian filter forms the GoG edge detector. The lower branch is the second order differential operator and again combined with the Gaussian filter leads to the LoG edge detector.

The gradient of the smoothed image is first calculated at the GoG branch. Once the absolute value of the gradient is found, a global threshold is employed to determine the edge instead of finding the maxima and the minima of the gradient. The value of this threshold controls the thickness of the edge.

At the LoG branch, the smoothed image is initially passed through the Laplacian operator. The process then determines where the zero-crossings (ZCs) occur. The final decision of whether or not an edge is present is then made using a logical AND where the edges detected using the GoG and LoG branches are fused.

To accurately detect abnormal tissue inside the human

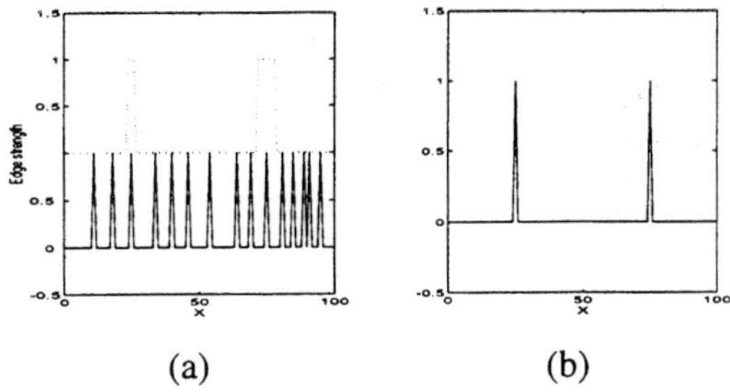

Figure 3. (a) Edges detected by GoG (top) and LoG (bottom) edge detectors using the signal in Figure 1 (b). (b) Result of the Hybrid Edge Detector.

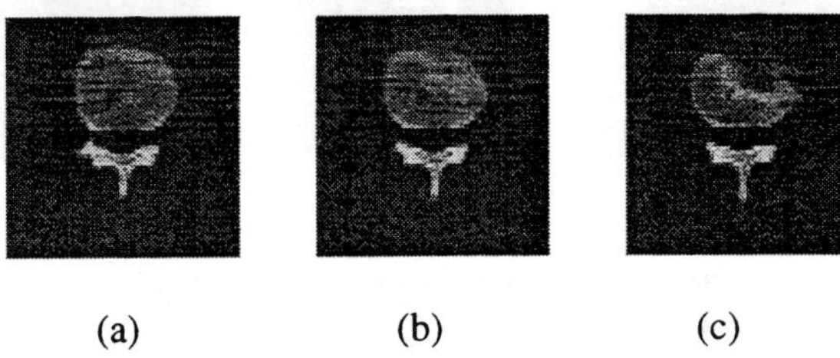

Figure 4. Three consecutive slices of brain MRI images

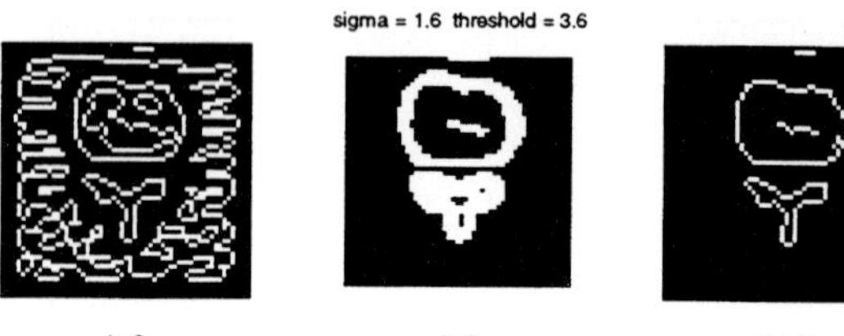

Figure 5. Results of edges detected using the 2D LoG, 2D GoG and 2D Hybrid Edge Detectors using Figure 4 (b) with $\sigma = 1$ and $Th = 3.6$

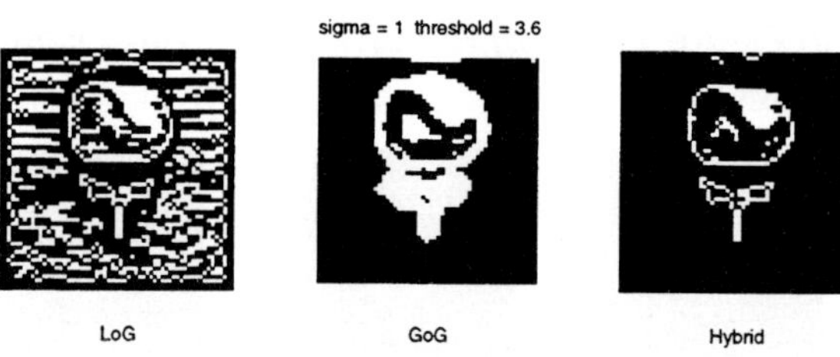

Figure 6. A slice of the volume edge generated using 3D LoG, 3D GoG and 3D Hybrid Edge Detectors with $\sigma = 1$ and $Th = 3.6$. This figure corresponds to the edges detected in slice (b) of Figure 4.

body, a good localisation of the edges is important when using any edge detector. On the other hand, it is commonly known that the LoG and GoG edge detectors are far from "good" when the image is distorted by noise. In general, the LoG detector is good in localising the edges through the use of ZCs, but its performance deteriorates with respect to the immunity to noise [2, 3]. Alternatively, the GoG is robust against noise, but its localisation is marked by large boundaries producing thick edges.

As shown in Figure 3 (a), the dashed line on the top of the figure represents the result of GoG detector and the solid line at the bottom is the result of LoG detector. It is clear from that figure that no false edges are detected by the GoG, however the detected edges are thick (poor localisation). The LoG detector acculately localised the true edge (good localisation) in addition to some false edges (poor immunity to noise). The result from the Hybrid Edge Detector is shown in Figure 3 (b). It is clear that the true edges are accurately localised by the Hybrid Edge Detector.

Since both the GoG and the LoG detector are easily extended to the 3D case and since the Hybrid Detector is the combination of these two detectors, it is also easily extendable to 3D. Results using the 3D Hybrid Edge Detector are presented in Section 3.

3 Results

This section discusses the effects of choosing different parameter values. All the results in this section are generated from the same volume image. The CT image volume is of size $60 \times 60 \times 75$ voxels. Figure 4 shows three selected consecutive slices. All the results presented in this section correspond to the slice of Figure 4 (b).

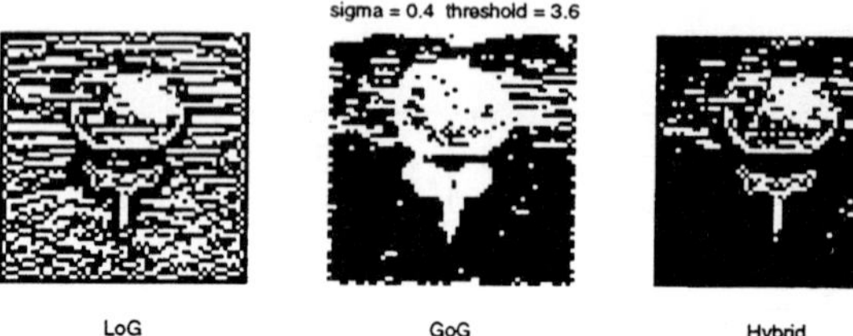

Figure 7. A slice of the volume edge generated using 3D LoG, 3D GoG and 3D Hybrid Edge Detectors with $\sigma = 0.4$ and $Th = 3.6$. This figure corresponds to the edges detected in slice (b) of Figure 4.

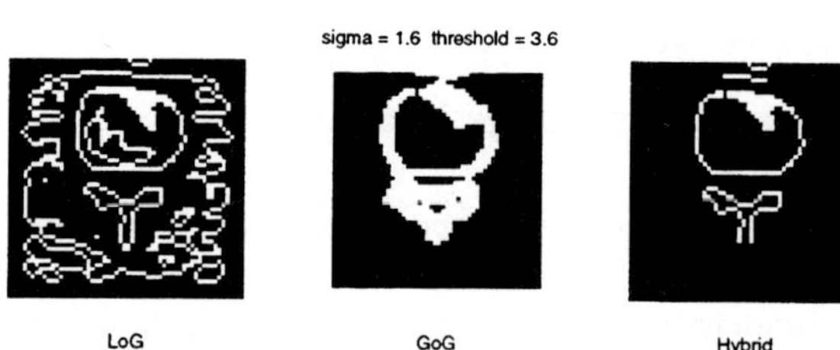

Figure 8. A slice of the volume edge generated using 3D LoG, 3D GoG and 3D Hybrid Edge Detectors with $\sigma = 1.6$ and $Th = 3.6$. This figure corresponds to the edges detected in slice (b) of Figure 4.

The results of 2D and 3D Hybrid Edge Detectors are compared in Section 3.1. The outcomes of the 3D Hybrid Edge Detector using different values of the parameters are presented in Section 3.2.

3.1 2D and 3D Hybrid Edge Detector

This section shows and compares the result generated using the 2D and the 3D Hybrid Edge Detectors. Results for both edge detectors are generated with the same parameter values. The slice shown in Figure 4 (b) is the input image to the 2D Hybrid Edge Detector. As shown in Figures 5 and 6, the edges detected using the 3D Hybrid Edge Detector are thicker in some areas. These are the edges parallel to the slice which corresponds to the area where there are significant changes between the consecutive slices as shown in Figure 4.

Besides these main disimilarities, another noticeable difference is the thickness of the edge when using the 2D and the 3D GoG. This is because the 3D GoG generates a 3D gradient. This is not a major problem, since the threshold controls the width of the edge.

sigma = 1 threshold = 1

LoG GoG Hybrid

Figure 9. A slice of the volume edge generated using 3D LoG, 3D GoG and 3D Hybrid Edge Detectors with $\sigma = 1$ and $Th = 1$. This figure corresponds to the edges detected in slice (b) of Figure 4.

sigma = 1 threshold = 9

LoG GoG Hybrid

Figure 10. A slice of the volume edge generated using 3D LoG, 3D GoG and 3D Hybrid Edge Detectors with $\sigma = 1$ and $Th = 9$. This figure corresponds to the edges detected in slice (b) of Figure 4.

3.2 Effects of Different Parameters

Results from the 3D Hybrid Edge Detector with different parameters are presented in this section.

Figures 7 and 8 display the effects of the smoothing parameter σ. This parameter affects the result of both the LoG and the GoG branches. A good selection of σ will aid the Gaussian filter to smooth the noise while maintaining the actual edges. If σ is too large, as shown in Figure 8 a number of actual edges will not be detected by both the LoG and the GoG branches. On the other hand, if σ is too small then many false edges (caused by noise) will be detected, as shown in (Figure 7).

Another parameter introduced in the GoG branch is the global threshold. The effect of the threshold value is shown in Figures 9 and 10. As demonstrated in Figure 10, if the threshold is too high, many edges with small gradient will be lost through the GoG branch. Otherwise, if the threshold value chosen is too low, the branch of GoG is not serving its purpose, as shown in Figure 9.

4 CONCLUSION

The results of both the 2D and 3D Hybrid Edge Detectors were presented. The effects on the selection of different parameter values were presented in Section 3. It was shown in Section 3.1 that the 3D Hybrid Edge detector yields better results than the 2D Hybrid Edge Detector, particularly in the z (direction orthogonal to MRI slice) dimension. The other important factor which affected the results was the selection of the parameters, which needs to be optimized.

One way of improving the results is to use different smoothing factors for each branch. However, this will increase the computation time significantly, depending on the σ and the window size of the Gaussian filter.

5 Acknowledgement

Thanks to Michael Schunk for his assistance in editing this manuscript.

References

[1] N. Ayache. Volume image processing - results and research challenges. Technical report, INRIA, Sophia-Antipolis, September 1993.

[2] M. Bennamoun and B. Boashash. Edge detection: Problems and solutions. In *IEEE International Conference on Systems, Man and Cybernetics*, Orlando, Florida, 1997.

[3] M. Bennamoun and B. Boashash. A probabilistic approach for automatic parameter selection for the hybrid edge detector. *IEICE transactions*, E80-A:1423–1429, August 1997.

[4] J. Canny. A computational approach to edge detection. *IEEE Transactions on Pattern Analysis and Machine Intelligence*, 8:679–698, 1986.

[5] R. Deriche. Using Canny's criteria to derive a recursively implemented optimal edge detector. *International Jounal of Computer Vision*, 1:167–187, 1987.

[6] G. Freiherr. 3D imaging in medicine: Synthesizing the third dimension. *Diagnostic Imaging*, 9:190–203, November 1987.

[7] H. K. Lui. Two and three dimensional boundary detection. *Cumput. Graphics Image Process.*, 6:123–134, 1977.

[8] O. Monga and R. Deriche. A new three dimensional boundary detection. In *International Conference on Pattern Recognition*, Paris, 1986.

[9] D. G. Morgenthaler and A. Rosenfeld. Multi-dimensional edge detection by hypersurface fitting. *IEEE Transactions on Pattern Analysis and Machine Intelligence*, 3:482–486, 1981.

[10] R. J. Schalkoff. *Digital Image Processing and Computer Vision*. John Wiley and Sons, 1989.

[11] A. Tikhonov and V. Arsenin. *Ill-Posed Problems*. Winston and Wiley, 1977.

[12] V. Torre and T. Poggio. On edge detection. *IEEE Transactions on Pattern Ananlysis and Machine Intelligence*, 8:147–163, 1986.

[13] S. W. Zucker and R. A. Hummel. A three dimensional edge operator. *IEEE Transactions on Pattern Analysis and Machine Intelligence*, 3:324–331, 1981.

Analysis of Wear Particles Using the Radon Transform

by V. F. LEAVERS
Manchester School of Engineering
Manchester University
Manchester M13 9PL
England
v.leavers@man.ac.uk

Abstract

An image processing technique is presented which automatically selects and characterises only those protrusions on the wear particle most likely to be active in the process of abrasion. The image data are not analyzed directly. Information concerning angularity is extracted from the distribution generated by the transformation of the binarized edge map. The method offers: an analytical definition of a corner and its apex; a quantitative estimate of angularity; robustness in the presence of missing boundary points; and, the potential to run automatically. The theory supporting the methodology is outlined and illustrated using simulated examples. The results of using the technique to process real image data are also presented.

1. MOTIVATION

It is generally assumed that the angularity of a wear particle has an influence on abrasive processes. However, to date, the determination of angularity remains one of the more difficult problems in both powder technology and wear particle analysis. Hawkins [1] presents an historical review of a range of quantitative methods available for determining angularity from particle outline and silhouettes. A more recent discussion of the problem is given by Verspui *et al* in [2]. They conclude that the theories described in the literature are either laborious or not suitable in image analysing systems. Their alternative methodology involves determining the angularity from curvature plots. However, in order to estimate the curvature of the contour it is necessary to take the second derivative of a position vector and this amplifies the effect of pixelation noise introduced by the digitisation process. The next stage in the algorithm is to determine the begin and end points of a corner. These are defined as points where the curvature is zero or passes through a positive minimum. The next stage of the algorithm is to calculate the tangents through the begin and end points. The angle of the corner is taken as the angle between the tangents. However, this says nothing about the roundness of the corner. Comparing the three shapes, A, B and C, shown in Fig. 1, using such a methodology would give excellent results in the case of the two shapes on the left; but, for the shape on the right, the apex angles will be underestimated giving values that are sharper than the corners or protrusions actually are. It is clear that this definition of a corner does not function well in the case of such rounded protrusions.

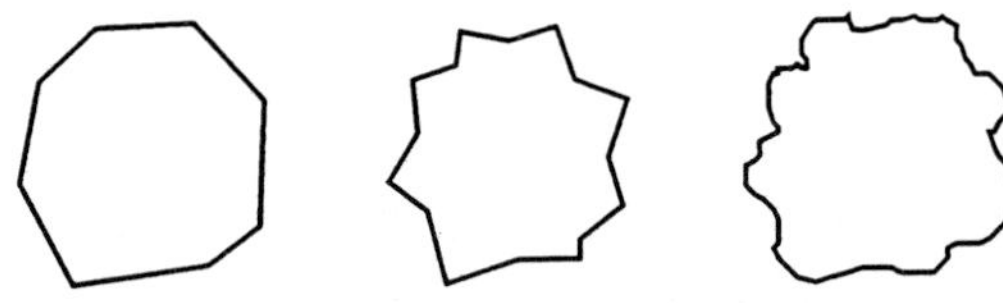

Fig. 1 From left to right: Shapes A, B and C

Other recent methods of determining angularity include the calculation of the fractal dimension of the particle boundary. For example see Kaye *et al* [3]. Stachowiak [4] gives an extensive review of the methods which use the calculation of the fractal dimension of the particle boundary and discusses their limitations. The technique most commonly employed to determine the complexity of a particle boundary is known as the structured walk, and also the Richardson method [4]. However, the results often exhibit bimodal characteristics associated with a distinction between structural and textural characteristics that are difficult to interpret with respect to abrasive properties.

Whereas calculation of the fractal dimension may give information about the complexity of the boundary of a shape, it says nothing about the arrangement of the boundary in space nor which specific parts of the boundary will contribute to the process of abrasion. For example: some protrusions will not become active in the abrasion process until the more prominent protrusions around them have been worn away. The same reasoning is valid for those methods which use the Fourier Transform to generate descriptions of shape. With respect to Fourier methods, the disadvantage of not knowing which parts of the boundary contribute to the process of abrasion is compounded by the fact that, in order to generate the descriptors associated with sharp corners requires an infinite number of coefficients [1] to be calculated and this is not computationally realistic.

The problem of deciding which parts of the boundary are active in the process of abrasion is a key point, which receives little attention in the current literature. Stachowiak [4] is one of the few authors to address this problem and introduces an angularity measure called the Spike Parameter Quadratic fit (SPQ). When calculating SPQ the particle boundary is approximated by a quadratic curve fit and a particle boundary centroid is located. The corners in the area outside the circle generated using this method are deemed to be of interest while those outside are not. The associated methodology for estimating the angularity is based on representing the particle boundary as a set of triangles constructed at different scales. This method suffers from the same disadvantage as that of Verspui *et al* [2] in that, while the geometric sharpness of a corner is well defined, it is not possible to simultaneously extract a measure for the roundness of a corner.

Thus, the aim of the current work is to develop an image processing technique which will automatically segment those protrusions most likely to take part in the process of abrasion and to parameterize the angularity of those protrusions in a manner that estimates not just the geometric sharpness of a corner but also its degree of roundness. In order to do this a novel use of the Radon Transform is proposed as detailed below.

2. USING THE RADON TRANSFORM TO DEFINE CORNERS AND ACTIVE ANGULARITY

The Radon transform may be written in the convenient form suggested by Gel'fand *et al.* [5]:

$$H(p, \xi) = \int_{-\infty}^{\infty} dx\, F(\mathbf{x})\delta(p-\xi \cdot \mathbf{x}) \qquad (1)$$

Where F(**x**) is a function defined on a domain D. In two dimensions, $\delta(p-\xi \cdot \mathbf{x})$, represents a delta function distribution situated along a line, L, with equation $p-\xi \cdot \mathbf{x} = 0$ where ξ is a unit vector in the direction of the normal to that line and p is the algebraic length of the normal.

Using the distribution generated by the transformation of the binarized edge map of the image it is possible to define the location of the apex of a corner as follows: as the tangents to a corner turn around the apex of that corner the value of p generated in the transform plane will increase, pass through a maximum value at the apex of the corner and then begin to decrease. That is, the point where the image point contributions to the corner change from one line defining the corner to the next. A point associated with a maximum value on the bounding curve will indicate the apex of a corner which is the radially outermost with respect to that particular angle. Thus, the current method analyses only the boundary curve of the transform space and has the important advantage of self-selecting only those corners or protrusions most likely to contribute to the process of abrasion. That is, only the apex of a radially outermost corner will generate an associated maximum on the bounding curve in transform space. It is these points which will make contact with any opposing surface and are thus the most likely to contribute to the process of abrasion.

Once a corner has been identified as contributing to the process of abrasion, a further piece of essential information is required: how spiky or rounded is the apex of the corner? The current method provides an estimate of this. Fig. 2 shows both the bounding curves (top curve in each plot) and the accumulated values along the bounding curves (bottom curve in each plot), from top to bottom, for the shapes A, B and C shown in Fig. 1. The values accumulated on the bounding curve are an expression of the degree of turning of the tangents to the corners of the shape. For example: the top graph, corresponding to the polygonal shape, has maxima in the accumulated values coincident with the minima on the bounding curve (see Fig. 2). At the apex of a corner the tangents will be turning most rapidly and at a rate determined by whether the corner is sharp or rounded. For a sharp corner, the tangents turn relatively quickly meaning that very few points will contribute to a particular tangent. For a rounded corner, many more points will contribute to a particular tangent as the tangents turn relatively slowly around the apex of the corner. The tangent associated with the apex of a corner is parameterized by the locus of a maximum value in the form of the bounding curve of the distribution in the transform space. The accumulated values around that point give information concerning the roundness or sharpness of the corner. Thus, an angularity factor, A, may be defined as a function of the average of the accumulated values on the bounding curve of the distribution at and around a maximum value. For a shape with many protrusions it is convenient to take the average value of the angularity factors of all of the protrusions as the Active Angularity Factor (AAF) for the whole shape.

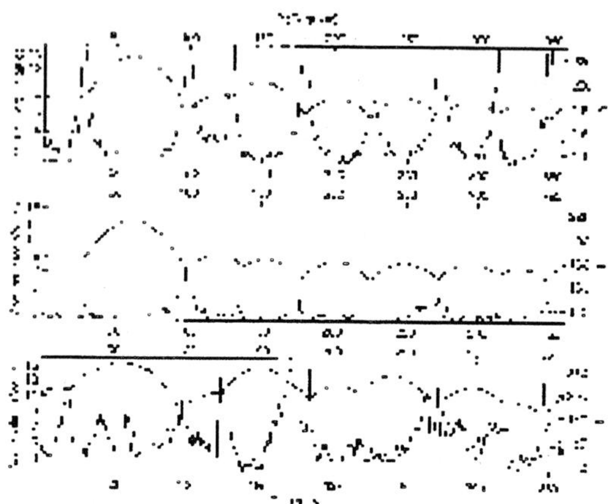

Fig. 2 Bounding curves and their corresponding accumulated values for, from top to bottom, shapes A, B and C

Fig. 2 shows that shape C has accumulated values, at and around the maxima in the bounding curve, which are greater than those generated by the first two shapes. Similarly, for the first two shapes, the smaller accumulated values, at and around the maxima, associated with the second shape indicate that the corners on that shape are indeed sharper than those on the first shape. The extracted values of the AAF show that the star shape has the highest value of active angularity (0.7), with the polygonal shape second (0.4), and the third, rounded shape, has the least value (0.2). A value for the AAF, which approaches 1, would indicate a needle-point. That is, the closer to 1 that the value of AAF becomes then the sharper the corners of the shape under detection.

Real image data were used to test the algorithm. These were chosen for the difficulties they pose. In particular, the technique was applied not only to the images of isolated particles but also to a group of particles, see Fig. 3. This is because abrasive particles may not be well separated but act in the form of agglomerations, see Fig. 3, shape 2.

  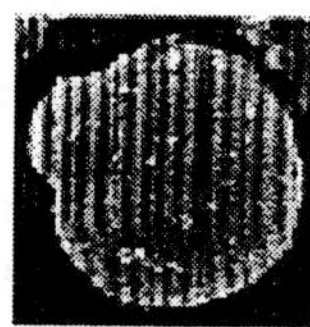

Fig. 3 From left to right: Shapes 1, 2 and 3

	Active Angularity Factor
Shape 1	**0.71 ± 0.29**
Shape 2	**0.49 ± 0.59**
Shape 3	**0.23 ± 0.15**

Shape 3 appears to the system to be a polygonal shape with many highly rounded protrusions or lobes (39). This effect is due to the digitized nature of the image. There is a relatively small value for the AAF, 0.23, indicating the rounded nature of the particle. The significant difference in the angularity of Shape 1, when compared to Shape 2, is expressed by a large percentage difference in the AAF's. Because the AAF is an average value, also shown is the standard deviation in that value. The standard deviation is a function both of the actual physical differences between the abrasive protrusions on a particular particle and the quality of the edge image from which the angularity values are derived.

3. CONCLUSION

When considering the abrasive properties of a particle, any measure of angularity is only meaningful if it is possible to identify those parts of the boundary which actually contribute to the process of abrasion. In order to define an Active Angularity Factor (AAF), a novel exploitation of the Radon Transform has been developed in which the bounding curve of the distribution in the Radon transform plane codes information concerning the angularity of the shape under detection in image space. The method has the advantage of being robust in the presence of missing boundary points. In summary, the current work offers: an analytical definition of a corner and its apex which is shown to function even when particles do not have conventional corners; a solution to the problem of determining which protrusions are active in the process of abrasion; and, the potential for automatic processing of image data.

REFERENCES

[1] Hawkins A.E., *The shape of powder-particle outlines*, John Wiley, New York, 1993.

[2] Verspui M.A., Van der Velden P. and Slikkerveer P.J., Angularity determination of abrasive particles. *Wear* Vol 199, pp 122-126, 1996.

[3] Kaye B.H., Clark G.G. and Liu Y., *Characterizing the structure of abrasive fine particles*

[4] Stachowiak G.W., Numerical characterisation of wear particle morphology and angularity of particles and surfaces. *Tribology* Vol 31, pp 139 - 157, 1998.

[5] Gel'fand I.M., Graev M.I. and Vilenkin N.Ya. *Generalized functions* Vol 5, Academic Press, New York, 1966.

Automatic Flaw Detection in Textiles Using a Neyman-Pearson Detector

George Mamic and Mohammed Bennamoun
Space Centre for Satellite Navigation
Queensland University of Technology
P.O. Box 2434, Brisbane, QLD 4001, Australia
E-mail: {g.mamic, m.bennamoun}@qut.edu.au

Abstract

A system for the automated visual inspection of textiles is discussed. The system consists of two main components, (1) the extraction of the texture features utilising the Karhunen-Loeve (KL), transform which provides optimal compression of the image data into a feature vector and (2) the detection of the flaw patterns using a Neyman-Pearson detector, which maximises the rate of detection for a specified false alarm rate. The performance of the system was evaluated on various fabrics and different types of textile flaws. The results indicate that the system can detect flaws which vary drastically in physical dimension and nature with a very low false alarm rate. Experimental results in the paper demonstrate the performance of the detector on some typical textile flaws.

1 Introduction

Quality control is an indispensable component of modern manufacturing, and the textile industry is no different to any other industry in this respect. The development of automated visual inspection (AVI) systems has been a response to the shortcomings which are exhibited by human inspectors. Their assessments of the severity of a flaw is based on experience and they generally have a maximum efficiency of about 80% [1]. In addition to this, AVIs can be incorporated into other automatic systems in the factory to produce a totally automated system for the processing and manufacture of textiles [10].

Some related texture analysis techniques and existing work in textile flaw detection will now be discussed:

Some of the earliest and most popular techniques for feature extraction used the spatial frequencies [13] of the texture and employed techniques based on the autocorrelation function and the discrete Fourier transform. Such concepts are extensively covered in many image processing textbooks [6, 8, 11].

The spatial gray level co-occurrence matrix (SGLC), which was introduced by Haralick et.al [7], is one of the most popular and widely used techniques in texture analysis. However, the technique does exhibit some limitations when applied to the characterisation of random textures with low contrast. Also it is often difficult to interpret the results of the SGLC and the technique is computationally expensive.

Model based texture analysis encompasses techniques such as autoregression, Markov random fields [3] and fractals, to name just a few. These techniques are based on a set of model parameters which may be used for texture restoration, synthesis and classification.

There have been a number of techniques which are specifically geared toward the detection of flaws in textiles. Bodnarova et.al. [1] used texture statistics based on the SGLC matrix and the χ^2 test. Cohen et. al [4] employed Gaussian Markov models, whilst Campbell and Murtagh [2] used a space dependent Fourier transform technique with a contextual decision fusion component to detect the flaws.

Section 2 of this paper provides a description of the types of flaws that are often encountered in textiles and the windowed KL transform that was employed in order to extract the feature vector. Section 3 describes the Neyman-Pearson test and Section 4 provides experimental results and discusses future directions for the work. Section 5 gives a summary of the paper.

2 Feature Extraction and Flaw Detection in Textiles

2.1 Flaw Types

Defects in textile materials are generally classified based upon their type, direction, appearance, size, location and repeating pattern. These defects occur due to problems which are encountered during the processes used in the production of the fabric.

Figures 1 and 2 show images of typical flaws which arise during the weaving process in the textile industry. Figure 1 displays an 'overshot' flaw about three-fifths of the way down the image. This type of flaw is the result of incorrect settings for the parts of the loom that influence the path and launch of the shuttle. Figure 2 contains a large oil-spot in the top left hand quadrant of the image [5]. These images illustrate the diversity in the size and nature of the flaws which are encountered in the textile industry. These range from distinct flaws such as the overshot flaw to the oil-spot, which provides no actual change in the flaw pattern but is easily discernible from the surrounding regions. These types of flaws and many others were successfully detected using the following method.

2.2 Feature Extraction

The extraction of good quality features is of paramount importance if one is to be able to successfully detect the flaws present in a textile sample. The technique employed for the feature extraction process in this case was the Karhunen-Loeve transform. Our choice was motivated by the fact that this transform provides an optimal compression of the normal texture pattern into a very small feature vector. The transform may be explained as follows [6]:
Given a population of random vectors corresponding to the pixel values in the image,

$$x = \begin{pmatrix} x_1 \\ x_2 \\ \vdots \\ x_m \end{pmatrix} \tag{1}$$

Then for n vector samples from a random population the mean vector $\boldsymbol{m_x}$ and the covariance matrix $\boldsymbol{C_x}$ may be calculated as follows.

$$\boldsymbol{m_x} = \frac{1}{n}\sum_{k=1}^{n} x_k \tag{2}$$

$$\boldsymbol{C_x} = \frac{1}{n}\sum_{k=1}^{n} x_k x_k^T - \boldsymbol{m_x}\boldsymbol{m_x}^T \tag{3}$$

Since we are dealing with images in this case the covariance matrix $\boldsymbol{C_x}$ is real and symmetric which means that a set of m orthonormal eigenvectors $\boldsymbol{e}_i$ and corresponding eigenvalues λ_i can always be found, where $i = 1 \dots m$. By rearranging the eigenvectors so that their corresponding eigenvalues are in descending order, the transformation matrix $\boldsymbol{\Psi}$ that maps the original population of vectors x into another set of vectors y is formed:

$$y = \boldsymbol{\Psi}(x - \boldsymbol{m_x}) \tag{4}$$

Equation (4) is referred to as the Karhunen-Loeve transform, with the mean $\boldsymbol{m_y}$ of the resulting y vectors being zero and the covariance $\boldsymbol{C_y}$ being a diagonal vector whose diagonal elements are the eigenvalues of $\boldsymbol{C_x}$[6]:

$$\boldsymbol{C_y} = \begin{pmatrix} \lambda_1 & & & 0 \\ & \lambda_2 & & \\ & & \ddots & \\ 0 & & & \lambda_m \end{pmatrix} \tag{5}$$

The significance of the above structure for $\boldsymbol{C_y}$ is that it shows that the elements of the transformed vector y are uncorrelated. In addition to this the eigenvalues of $\boldsymbol{C_x}$ and $\boldsymbol{C_y}$ are identical.

To apply this theory to the problem of textile flaw detection one must realise that in order to detect flaws they must at least be detected locally. Thus the KL transform must be performed within a window that is moved across the image. This windowed KL transform is then used to extract a feature vector for each part of the image. Since $\boldsymbol{m_y} = 0$, the mean of the transformed image cannot be used for the hypothesis testing stage. Instead, the eigenvalues of the covariance matrix $\boldsymbol{C_y}$ are used. These eigenvalues represent the variances of the extracted features and their distribution will be used as the discriminating feature in the classification process.

Thus the choice of the window function becomes a critical factor in the feature extraction. Very small window sizes, although they offer potentially good flaw localisation, often extract an insufficient number of features to reliably detect the flaws. On the other hand, if the window size is too large, smaller flaws do not change the feature vector significantly and hence are missed during the detection stage. Current testing has indicated that the size of the window should be approximately equal to the width of the flaw.

3 Neyman-Pearson Detection

The detection process adopted in this paper is the Neyman-Pearson test. Bayesian testing was rejected due to the difficulties which were foreseen in the gathering of training data for the range of flaws, which are present in the textile flaw detection problem. Another major difficulty with this form of hypothesis test is the estimation of the prior probabilities of the flaws. The hypothesis test has the following form:

$$\begin{aligned} \boldsymbol{H}: &\quad \text{There is no flaw present} \\ \boldsymbol{K}: &\quad \text{There is a flaw present,} \end{aligned} \tag{6}$$

where $\boldsymbol{H}$ denotes the null hypothesis and $\boldsymbol{K}$ the alternative hypothesis. The Neyman-Pearson test maximises the probability of detection for a given false alarm rate α , which is the probability of deciding that the alternative is true when in fact the null hypothesis is true [9]. In this case α would be a parameter determined by the specifications of the manufacturing process.

As mentioned in the previous section, the eigenvalues of the transformed image windows were chosen as the feature vector. Since these eigenvalues represent the variances of the transformed features, if the tested regions were significantly different then the distribution of the variances of the extracted features would also be quite different, hence providing a mechanism for the detection of flaws.

The feature vector was assumed to have the form of a multivariate Gaussian distribution,

$$p_F(\boldsymbol{f}) = \frac{1}{(2\pi)^{m/2}\|\Sigma\|^{1/2}} \times \exp\Big(-\frac{1}{2}(\boldsymbol{f}-\boldsymbol{\mu})^T\Sigma^{-1}(\boldsymbol{f}-\boldsymbol{\mu})\Big) \quad (7)$$

Where $\boldsymbol{f}$ is the extracted feature vector and m is the size of the feature vector $\boldsymbol{x}$, which in this case is equal to the window size chosen. The $\boldsymbol{\mu}$ and Σ are estimated using a large training sample, which is known to be defect free. Utilising the likelihood ratio approach for testing two means for a given covariance, the following test statistic may be derived [9, 12],

$$Z^2 = n(\overline{\boldsymbol{f}}-\boldsymbol{\mu})^T\Sigma^{-1}(\overline{\boldsymbol{f}}-\boldsymbol{\mu}) \quad (8)$$

For this case $n = 1$, hence $\overline{\boldsymbol{f}} = \boldsymbol{f}$. This form can be recognised as being the Mahalanobis distance between the feature vector and its mean. Under the null hypothesis the Z^2 statistic is distributed according to χ^2_m. Thus an appropriate threshold may be set according to the false alarm rate and the null hypothesis can be rejected or accepted accordingly.

4 Experimental Results and Discussion

As mentioned in Section 2 these techniques have been evaluated on a number of textile images with various flaws present. The detection experiments were carried out as follows:

1. Calculation of the parameters $\boldsymbol{\mu}$ and Σ. From a template image, which is free from flaws the eigenvalues of the covariance matrix of each window are extracted. The eigenvalues are sorted into descending order, thus the eigenvalues which represent the largest variation in the transformed plane are at the start of the feature vector. From the set of eigenvalues for each of the windows, the average feature vector $\boldsymbol{\mu}$ and the covariance matrix Σ can be extracted.

2. For each window in the potentially flawed sample the Z^2 statistic is calculated using the feature vector extracted and the $\boldsymbol{\mu}$ and Σ calculated from the flaw free sample. This is compared to the threshold that is determined using the significance level α when applied to the χ^2_m distribution and the appropriate decision made regarding whether or not a flaw is present.

Figure 1. The result of the algorithm as applied to the overshot flaw: Window Size = 4×4 (overlapped), $\alpha = 4 \times 10^{-12}$

As seen from Figures 1 and 2 the detection algorithm has successfully detected large portions of the flaws visible in the textiles. However, before any meaningful conclusions can be drawn, the results must be related back to the physical world. The images have a spatial sampling rate of 36 $pixels/mm^2$. In operation one could tolerate one 'falsely' detected window per $10,000\ m^2$. For a window size of 19×19 as is the case with the oilspot flaw, the minimum false alarm rate is 1×10^{-9}. As seen from the parameters, the algorithm can comfortably cope with such a requirement.

In order to detect very thin flaws, it was necessary to overlap the windows. This was due to the fact that for particular window sizes only a portion of the flaw was visible in any one window and hence could not be detected. This overlap technique was utilised in the detection of the overshot flaw with the false alarm rate of 4×10^{-12}. This is an order of magnitude lower than the 4.44×10^{-11} which is required for one window in error per $10,000\ m^2$ of fabric. Many other flaws were also tested and similar results were obtained.

The number of flops were examined to analyse the speed of execution of this code. The training of the sample and the detection of the oil-spot flaw required 9.5 million flops. The overshot flaw was considerably more expensive with 37 million flops due to the use of overlapping windows.

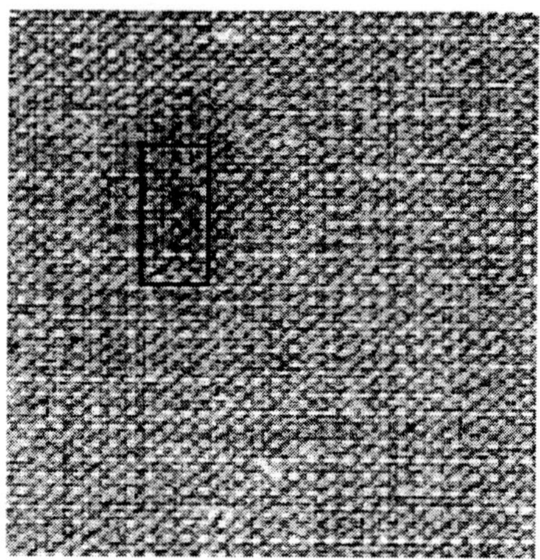

Figure 2. The result of the algorithm as applied to the oil-spot flaw: Window Size = 19×19, $\alpha = 1 \times 10^{-15}$

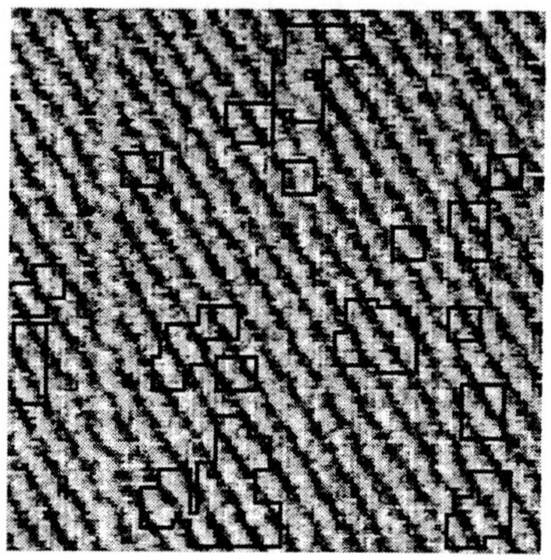

Figure 3. The result of the algorithm as applied to slack-ends: Window Size = 9×9, $\alpha = 1 \times 10^{-15}$

The algorithm was tested on a database of images with results comprable to those aforementioned being achieved, with the exception of cases where the textiles exhibited slack-ends and broken-pick flaws and this is an area of continuing research. An example of the failed detection is illustrated in Figure 3.

The development of a multi-resolution technique is also underway. The motivation behind this being the elimination of the requirement for the specification of the size of the window, thus making the system of textile flaw detection completely automatic.

5 Conclusions

We have described a technique for the detection of flaws from a wide range of textiles and flaws types. The problems of feature extraction and detection of flaws without *a-priori* knowledge about the flaw have been discussed. Experimental results on a range of flaws indicate the robustness of the presented technique as well as its applicability to the real world.

6 Acknowledgements

This work was conducted under the Strategic Partnership with Industry Research and Training scheme (SPIRT), of the Australian Research Council and Department of Education, Training and Youth Affairs.

References

[1] A. Bodnarova, M. Bennamoun, and K. Kubik. Suitability ananlysis of techniques for flaw detection in textiles using texture analysis. *Pattern Analysis and Applications*, to appear in August 2000.

[2] J. Campbell and F. Murtagh. Automatic visual inspection of woven textiles using a two-stage defect detector. *Optical Engineering*, 37(9):2536–2542, 1998.

[3] R. Chellapppa and S. Chatterjee. Classification of textures using Gaussian Markov random fields. *IEEE Trans. on Acoust. Speech and Signal Process.*, 33(4):959–963, 1985.

[4] F. Cohen, Z. Fan, and S. Attali. Automatic inspection of textile fabrics using textural models. *IEEE Trans. on Pattern Anal. Mach. Intell.*, 13(8):803–808, 1991.

[5] G. Company. Manual of standard fabric defects in the textile industry. Graniteville, South Carolina, 1975.

[6] R. Gonzalez and R. Woods. *Digital Image Processing*. Addison-Wesley Publishing Company, 1992.

[7] R. Haralick. Statistical and structural approaches to texture. *Proceedings of the IEEE*, 67(5):786–804, 1979.

[8] B. Jahne. *Practical Handbook on Image Processing for Scientific Applications*. CRC Press, 1997.

[9] W. Krzanowski. *Principles of Multivariate Analysis*. Oxford Science Publications, 1988.

[10] T. Newman and A. Jain. A survey of automated visual inspection. *Computer Vision and Image Understanding*, 61(2):231–262, 1995.

[11] R. Schalkoff. *Digital Image Processing and Computer Vision*. John Wiley and Sons, 1989.

[12] A. Whalen. *Detection of Signals in Noise*. Bell Telephone Laboratories, 1971.

[13] E. Wood. Applying Fourier and associated transforms to pattern characterisation in textiles. *Textile Research Journal*, pages 212–220, April 1990.

Color Classification of Archaeological Fragments *

Martin Kampel and Robert Sablatnig
Vienna University of Technology
Institute for Computer Aided Automation
Pattern Recognition and Image Processing Group
Favoritenstr.9/183-2, A-1040 Vienna, Austria
{kampel,sab}@prip.tuwien.ac.at

Abstract

We are developing an automated classification and reconstruction system for archaeological fragments. The goal is to relate different fragments belonging to the same vessel based on shape, material and color, thus the color information is important in the pre-classification process. In this work a color specification technique is proposed, which exploits the fact that the spectral reflectance of materials like archaeological fragments vary slowly in the visible. We explain how the acquisition system is calibrated in order to get accurate colorimetric information with respect to archaeological requirements. Experimental results are presented for archaeological objects and for a set of test color patches.

1 Introduction

Ceramics are one of the most widespread archaeological finds and are a short-lived material. This property helps researchers to document changes of style and ornaments. Especially ceramic vessels, where shape and decoration are exposed to constantly changing fashion, not only allow a basis for dating the archaeological strata, but also provide evidence of local production and trade relations of a community as well as the consumer behavior of the local population. The purpose of ceramic classification is to get a systematic view of the material found [2, 6] and is used to relate a fragment to existing parts in the archive.

Archaeologists determine the specific color of a fragment by matching it to the Munsell color patches [7]. Since this process is done "manually" by different archaeologists and under varying light conditions, results differ from each other. Archaeologists need digital color images of fragments for archivation purposes, thus the color information which is normally achieved with a color measurement instrument can be gained directly from the digital image for each pixel in the entire image.

We propose a solution to the color classification assuming that the spectral reflectance of archaeological fragments varies slowly in the visible spectrum. We present an approach for accurate colorimetric information on fragments, performed on digital images containing archaeological fragments under different illuminants. A characteristic vector analysis [9] of the reference reflectance leads to an algorithm that computes the colorimetrically accurate reflectance out of a video digitizing system.

The paper is organized as follows: In Section 2 we describe the theoretical background, in Section 3 we explain how we specify the colorimetric variables in order to calibrate the acquisition system with respect to archaeological requirements. Experimental results are described in Section 4 and we conclude with a summary and outline the future work.

2. Theory and Notation

Much of human color-vision research focuses on color constancy since it is the perceptual ability that permits us to discount spectral variation in the ambient light and assign stable colors: Maloney and Wandell [4] considered that both lighting and spectral reflectance are unknown, whereas Lee [3] simplified that problem by assuming that spectral illumination is known. Color and reflectance based object recognition was presented by [1, 8]. In order to provide a device-independent color specification we use reference colors from the MacBeth Color chart [5].

Our approach rests upon Lee's method assuming that spectral illumination is known and that the spectral re-

*This work was supported in part by the Austrian Science Foundation (FWF) under grant P13385-INF.

flectance of our material varies slowly in the visible spectrum. This means that small changes of RGB values should lead to small changes in reflectance. Prior knowledge about the illuminant leads to chromaticity and luminance information.

Each RGB pixel in a digitized image has a value proportional to weighted integral over the visible spectrum. This integral depends on three spectral variables. These are the *spectral irradiance* $E(\lambda)$, which describes the energy per second at each wavelength λ. The proportion of light of wavelenght λ reflected from an object is determined by the *surface spectral reflectance* $S(\lambda)$. We assume that there are k distinct channels in the digitizing system, we use $k = 3'$ for red, green and blue. We denote the *spectral response* of the kth channel as $R_k(\lambda)$ and a pixel value for the kth color channel as p_k.

$$p_k = \int S(\lambda)E(\lambda)R_k(\lambda)d(\lambda) \tag{1}$$

Eq 1 describes the relationship between pixel values and spectral quantities. We approximate the three integrals above as summations over wavelength, using values every $10nm$ in the visible spectrum from $400nm$ to $700nm$. If the proportionality factor in the $R_k(\lambda)$ is subsumed, one can construct the following matrix equation (Eq. 2). m denotes the steps to be taken in the spectrum.

$$p = SER \tag{2}$$

$p\ldots$ 1 by 3 row vector (RGB pixel)
$S\ldots$ 1 by m row vector,(surface reflectance)
$E\ldots m$ by m diagonal matrix, (spectral irradiance)
$R\ldots m$ by 3 matrix, (system spectral transfer function)

If we know elements of two of the arrays on the right side of Eq. 2 and the corresponding RGB pixel values on the left side, we can solve the unknown array. Since only an approximated knowledge of the system function R is assumed, the goal will be to:

- specify the system transfer function R more accurately by analyzing color samples with known reflectance of the MacBeth Color patches.
- use this new information to find the unknown spectral reflectance of other samples illuminated by the same light source.

The goal of the first step is to improve the transfer function R which leads to R_{new} (Eq. 3).

$$R_{new} = RR_1 \tag{3}$$

Therefore we digitize an image of the color chart, which is illuminated by the same light source that will be used when we evaluate unknown color samples. The digitization gives a q by 3-matrix P containing RGB values, where q denotes the number of patches of the color checker. Since we know the illumination E and the set of q reflectances S, we can form the q-by-3 matrix SER_{new}. This leads to Eq. 4. For the unknown R_1 a least square solution is used, which leads to an improved estimate of the system's spectral transfer function.

$$P = SERR_1 \tag{4}$$

The goal of the second step is to calculate the reflectances of unknown color samples. We use the RGB-values from the digitized color samples p, the improved transfer function R_{new} and the spectral irradience E in order to calculate spectral reflectances S (See Eq. 2).

Since $S(\lambda)$ varies smoothly for fragments we can accurately represent the spectral reflectance of a set of color standards with the first few components of a characteristic vector analysis [9]. In effect, this analysis allows us to reduce the dimensionality of S and leads to an algorithm that gives colorimetrically accurate spectral reflectance from red-green-blue output of the video digitizing system.

S_{mean} is defined as mean vector (1 by m) from the color checker reflectances at $m = 30$ equally-spaced wavelengths across the spectrum. S_{basis} (n by m matrix) denotes the characteristic vectors used. We use $n = 3$ characteristic vectors to represent the original data. A 1-by-n vector of basis weights (denoted B) is calculated when solving Eq. 5 by inserting the digitized RGB values into p.

$$B = (p - S_{mean}ER)(S_{basis}ER)^{-1} \tag{5}$$

When we multiply S_{basis} by the appropriate vector B and add the result to S_{mean}, we can reconstruct any spectral reflectance S in our set of colors (Eq. 6). For a more detailed description of the algorithm see [3].

$$S = S_{mean} + BS_{basis} \tag{6}$$

The technique used is a method for examining a number of sets of multivariate response data and determining linear transformations of the data to a smaller number of parameters which contains essentially all the information in the original data.

3 Color estimation process

First, the three spectral variables - irradiance of the lightsource $E(\lambda)$, camera transfer function $R_k(\lambda)$ and reflectance $S(\lambda)$ of the MacBeth reference chart - have to be initialized.

We use Tungsten Halogen Floodlamps 7700 (150W) and TL-light as lightsources. In order to recover colorimetric data from our samples under a variety of lightsources we use different types of lightsources. The spectral distribution was given by the manufacturer. Figure 1 shows the typical spectral distribution of TL-82 and TL-95 with slight differences between these two lamps.

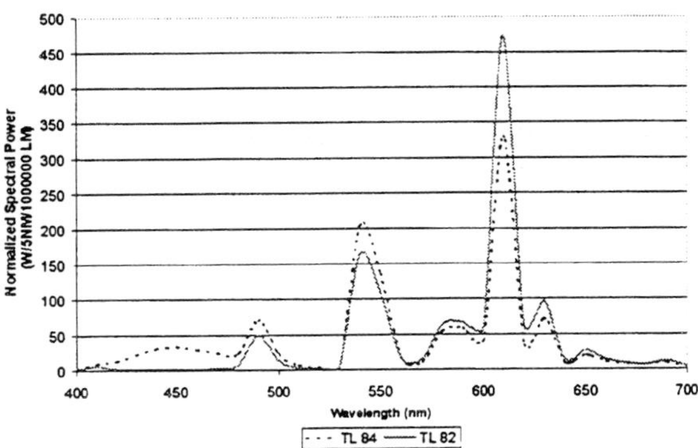

Figure 1. Spectral irradiance of TL-82 and TL-95

The video cameras used are a 3CCD DONPISHA XC-003P and a CCD-IKEGAMY ICD-700P. The Ikegamy camera is a single CCD-color CCTV camera, which is used to give out Y/C (chrominance/ luminance) separation signals. The Sony camera is a color video module, which uses a CCD for the pick-up device. It has an RGB signal output. Both cameras are one-chip-cameras. Figure 2 shows the spectral response curve of the DONPISHA camera. The data was provided by the manufacturer.

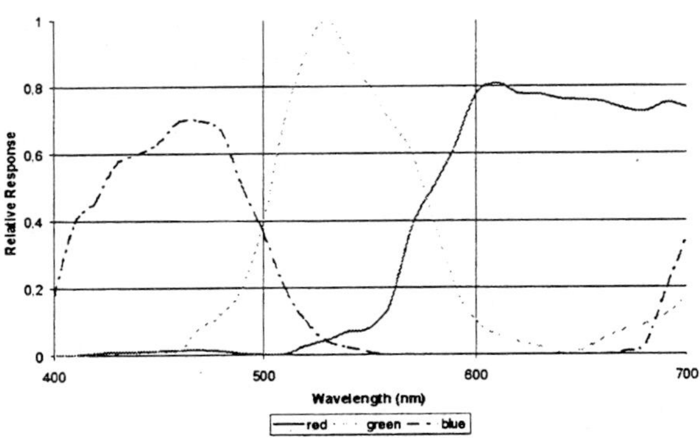

Figure 2. Typical spectral response of a Sony-camera

The spectral reflectance is scaled in equally-spaced wavelengths (every 10nm) across the spectrum. 12 colors of the MacBeth Color checker are used as a reference set and 12 are used for evaluation purposes. Their reflectance is measured using a spectroradiometer. For our reference set we choose colors which have a similar spectral distribution to the colors of our archaeological findings in order to maximize the achievable accuracy of the vector analysis.

In the next step we grab an image of an archaeological fragment, which leads to RGB values. Test regions are specified manually, and their RGB-Values are used to reconstruct the reflectance. Figure 3 shows two different test regions A and B.

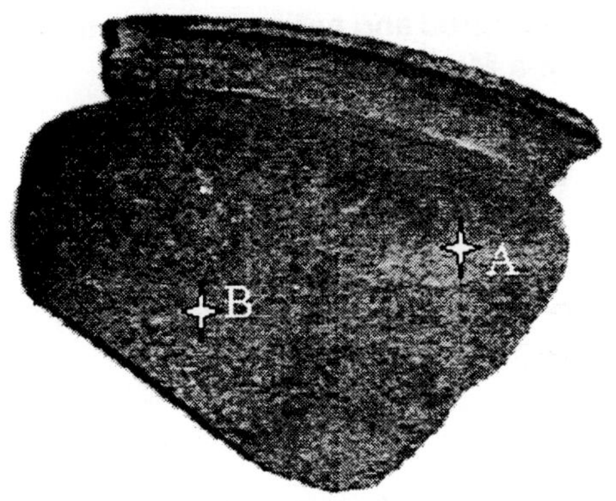

Figure 3. Test regions A and B

4 Results

Two experiments are presented: the first example with MacBeth Colors and the second with real fragments. In a first experiment we use the measured reflectance of 12 MacBeth color patches as reference and try to estimate the reflectance of the other 12 patches using the reference set. The resulting reflectance is compared to previous measured values.

Figure 4 shows the result for patch 1 (dark skin). In that case, the correlation equals $0,98$. The computed reflectances of the other 11 patches correlated between and $0,85$ and $0,98$ to their corresponding measured reflectances with an average correlation of $0,92$ (see Table 1). Lower correlation may be caused by the purely statistical representation of the underlying variables by the characteristic vector analysis.

In the second experiment we grab an image of a fragment and specify two test regions A and B (Figure 3). The reference set was chosen from the MacBeth color checker. The spectral reflectances of A and B are computed and visualized in Figure 5. For evaluation purposes we calculate CIE tristimulus values using a linear transformation and compare the achieved values with measured cromaticity coor-

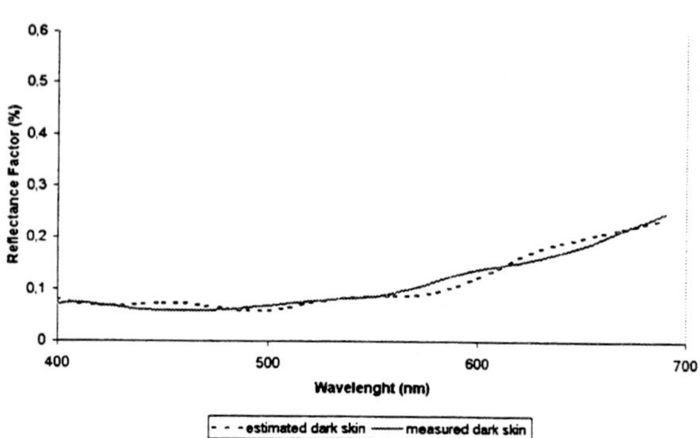

Figure 4. Measured and estimated spectral reflectance of a MacBeth Color Patch

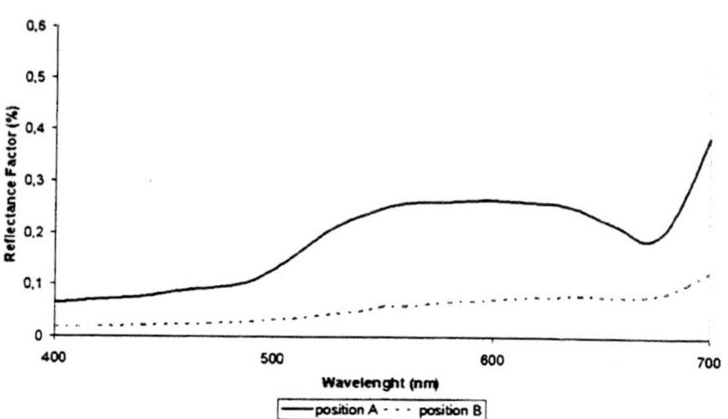

Figure 5. Calculated spectral reflectance of positions A and B

patchnr	corr	patchnr	corr
1	0.98	7	0.97
2	0.97	8	0.95
3	0.93	9	0.96
4	0.98	10	0.91
5	0.86	11	0.85
6	0.92	12	0.89

Table 1. Correlation between measured and calculated spectral reflectances of 12 Macbeth ColorChecker patches

dinates from a Chroma Meter CR-200b. Table 2 shows a comparison between measured and computed chromaticity coordinates. The final results are in the close neighborhood of the measured values. Since these results are influenced by the linear transformation we plan measurements using a spectroradiometer in order to allow direct comparison between measured and computed reflectances.

	Comp. A	Meas. A	Comp. B	Meas.B
x	0.48	0.33	0.49	0.40
y	0.39	0.34	0.41	0.37
Y	17.9	11.1	32.3	21.0

Table 2. Measured and computed cromaticity coordinates

5 Conclusion and Outlook

In this work we presented a technique for accurate color estimation, which plays an important role in the classification process for archaeological fragments. We proposed an application using a straightforward approach based on a linear color calibration technique. Since the color specification of a fragment is gained by different archaeologists and under varying lightning conditions the results differ from each other. The results obtained give a good initial estimate to the archaeologists. Future work goes towards color calibration without known illuminants in order to allow color estimation outside laboratory conditions.

References

[1] T. Gevers and W. M. Smeulders. Color-based Object Recognition. *Pattern Recognition*, 32(2):453–464, 1999.

[2] M. Kampel and R. Sablatnig. On 3d Modelling of Archaeological Sherds. In *Proc. of Int. Workshop on Synthetic-Natural Hybrid Coding and Three Dimensional Imaging*, pages 95–98, 1999.

[3] R. L. Lee. Colormetric calibration of a Video Digitizing System. *Colour Research and Application*, 13(3):180–186, 1988.

[4] L. T. Maloney and B. A. Wandell. Colour Constancy: a method for recovering surface spectral reflectance. *Journal of the Optical Society of America*, 3(1):29–33, 1986.

[5] C. S. McCamy, H. Marcus, and J. G. Davidson. A Colour-Rendition Chart. *Journal of Applied Photographic Engineering*, 2(3):95–99, 1976.

[6] C. Menard and R. Sablatnig. Computer based Acqusition of Archaeological Finds: The First Step towards Automatic Classification. In H. Kamermans and K. Fennema, editors, *Interfacing the Past, Computer Applications and Quantitative Methods in Archaeology*, number 28, pages 413–424, Leiden, March 1996. Analecta Praehistorica Leidensia.

[7] C. Menard and I. Tastl. Automated Color Determination for Archaeological Objects. In *Is&T 4th Color Imaging Conference*, pages 160–163, 1996.

[8] S. Nayar and R. Bolle. Reflectance Based Object Recogntion. *Int. Journal of Computer Vision*, 17(3):219–240, 1996.

[9] J. L. Simonds. Application of characteristic vector analysis to photographic and optical response data. *Journal of the Optical Society of America*, 53:968–974, 1963.

Dent Detection in Car Bodies

Tilo Lilienblum*, Peter Albrecht**, Roman Calow** and Bernd Michaelis*

**Otto von Guericke University, Institute for Electronics, Signal Processing and Communications PF 4120, 39016 Magdeburg, Germany lilie@iesk.et.uni-magdeburg.de*

***Institute for Neurosimulation and Image Technologies GmbH, Haus 65 (Zenit-Gebäude), Leipziger Str.44, 39120 Magdeburg, Germany*

Abstract

This paper describes a method for an automatic detection of small dents in car bodies which are not visible until the paintwork.

For an automatic error detection, two problems have to be solved: The accuracy of the measurement system has to be on a sufficient level and the errors have be detected in the 3-d measurement data.

The measuring of the surface shape can be done by an optical 3-d measurement system. This system consists of two cameras and one projector. The problem of error detection is solved by a method based on neural networks. The measurement data of one or more master workpieces is stored in the weights of a neural network. The calculation of the difference between the measurement data and the output of the neural network gives the resulting error surface.

In this paper, a combination of both technologies is described. This dent detection method is illustrated by an example.

1. Introduction

For an automatic detection of small dents in car bodies which normaly remain unnoticed before the body is painted, two problems have to be solved:

First problem: The accuracy of the measurement system has to be on a sufficient level. For 3-d measurement of surfaces a multitude of very different procedures exists. Examples for optical 3-d measurement methods are the photogrammetry [1], [8], [11] and the striped lighting method. A further development of the striped lighting method is the phase-shifting procedure [10].

Sufficient measurement accuracies are achieved with standard photogrammetrical methods featuring area correlation. However, it is difficult to measure strongly curved surfaces or steps in surfaces.

The striped lighting method is characterised by very high measurement frequency. However, the measurement accuracy is not sufficient and an accurate calibration of the system is not possible.

A photogrammetrical method with improved spatial resolution [2] is used for this application. This method is described in section 2.

Second problem: The automatic error detection. The quality check can be realised by calculation of the difference between the master and the measured workpiece which has to be checked (following called test workpiece).

The measurement of a master workpiece and substraction from the test workpiece is possible only in case of an exact adjustment. The requirements for the adjustment are very high if the errors to be detected of the test workpiece in relation to the workpiece size are very small. Often, such an exact adjustment is not possible. Mostly, the workpieces are not only shifted but bended and twisted because of torsion forces.

In this case, it is not possible to recognise errors automatically by difference calculation between the master and test workpiece.

The approximation of the test workpiece by polynoms or other functions is also a possible method. The approximation error should correspond with the error of the test workpiece. But this method can't be used for intricated workpieces (because the flexibility of the polynom is not sufficient in areas with strong curvature) and dents with a great area (because the flexibility of the polynom is to high).

To find the dents, a method based on a neural network is described (section 3). This method was described already in [6]. But, the new 3-d measurement method (section 2) produces better results. The neural network is normally used for the knowledge-based optical measurement technique applications [3], [4], [5], [7]. In section 4 the automatic dent detection is illustrated by an example, the measuring of a part of car doors.

2. The 3-d measurement system

The used 3-d measurement method is a photogrammetrical method with improved spatial resolution [2].
In Fig. 1 you can see a draft of the measurement system. The measurement method uses a number of grey-scale values from single pixels for calculations. These grey-scale values are generated by several images taken in succession. The principle of measurement consists in finding two pixels with approximately corresponding sequences of grey-scale values.

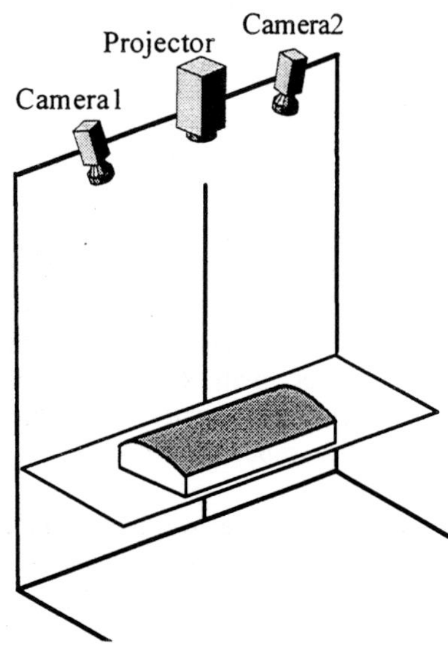

Fig. 1: Experimental set-up for the 3-d measurement

For the generation of the required images a number of different patterns has to be projected successively onto the surface of the measurement object.

At the University of Magdeburg, usually 12 stripe patterns with the same period but different phases have been used. Stripe patterns create high grey level gradients along the epipolar lines of the images. This is advantageous for the measurement process.

The standard deviation of the measurement values is 5 µm (cameras: 8 bit, analog; 752x572 pixel; measurement volume: 0.3x0.3x0.3 m²). If we used better cameras (for example 12 bit digital) or a smaller maeasurement volume, the standard deviation became smaller in accordance.

3. Use of associative memory for dent detection

The error can be detected by a neural network as follows (Fig. 2):
In the ***training phase***, several master workpieces in variable positions are measured. The measurement values of the surfaces of these master workpieces serve to train the weights of an artificial neural network. The whole spread of the possible different positions is considered by this method.
The measurement data of the master workpieces should be pre-processed for the training data generation to reduce the influence of possible errors on the weights to be calculated. New data sets can be produced without measuring by shifting some of the data sets. The number of the stored data can be increased in this way.
The calculation of the weights (training) of the neural network can then follow.
In the ***recall phase***, the test workpiece is measured. The measurement values are processed by the neural network. At the output, the shape of a master workpiece with the same position as the test workpiece appears. The calculation of the difference between the measuring values of test workpiece and the corresponding output values of the modified associative memory is the next step The result is the error of the test workpiece.
This result can be processed and analysed by standard methods of image processing and this way decided if the quality is sufficient.

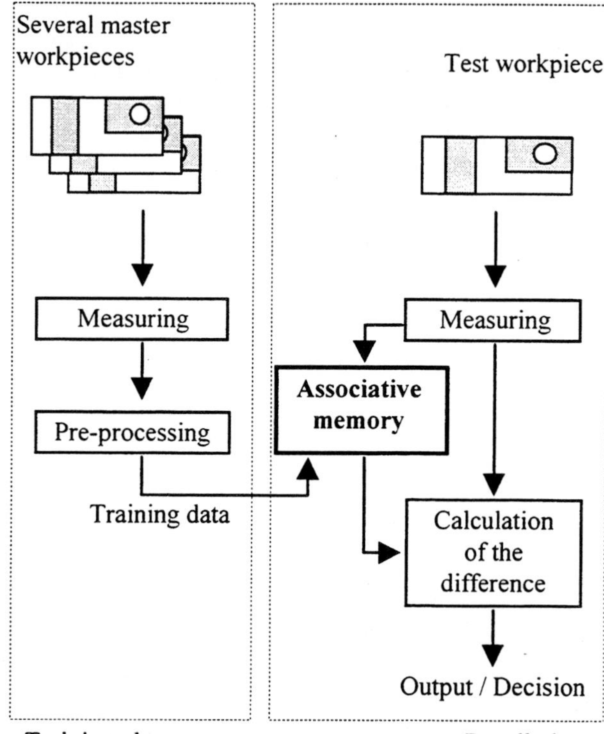

Fig. 2: Error detection by neural networks

The neural network is a modified associative memory. It was described already in several publications [4], [7].
The network is illustrated in Fig. 3. It has 2 active layers (hidden and output layer). The connections between the layers are linear. The z-coordinates of 3-d data are used

for the calculations. z_i is the vectorised Matrix of z-coordinates of the i-th measurement set of 3-d data. $Z = [z_1 \ldots z_n]$ is the matrix of all training data (n data sets).

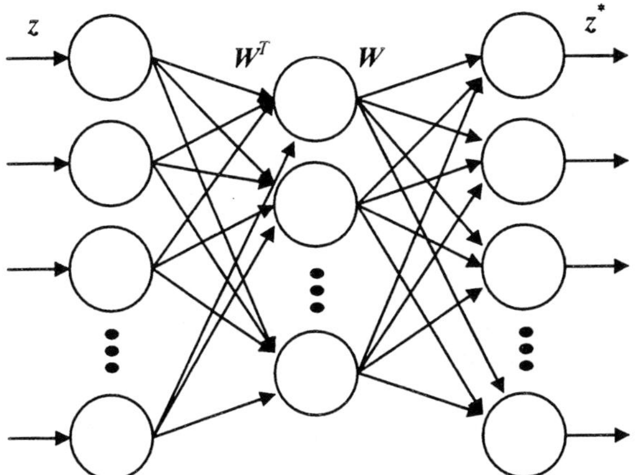

Fig. 3: Associative memory with 2 layers

The weights are calculated by the singular value decomposition

$$Z = USV.$$

S is a diagonal matrix with nonnegative diagonal elements (singular values of Z) in decreasing order. U contains the eigenvectors of the covariance matrix ZZ^T. The first m columns of U represent the weight matrix W of the neural network. m depends on the measurement object. In the example (in section 4), $m = 20$.
The processing by the neural network can be described by the equation

$$z_i^* = W(W^T z_i).$$

z_i is the vectorised matrix of the z-coordinates of the test workpiece.

4. Experimental results

To demonstrate the performance of the described method, an example of the measurement of several sheets metal of a car door out of a stamping factory is shown.
An area around the handle of the doors was measured. In this area the dent probability after the stamp process is very high and the detection of dents is complicated. However, such dents are visible after the paintwork. Fig. 4 show the measurment data of one sheet.
10 doors were measured. To simulate a dent one door was prepared. A piece of a film (with an area of 1 cm² and a thickness of 80 µm) was spliced at this door.
9 flawless sheets metal of the car door were measured and stored in the neural network. The 10th sheet was measured before and after the preparation. These both data sets represent the two test workpieces (one flawless and one faulty one). The dimensions of the measurement area were approximately 0.3m x 0.3m.

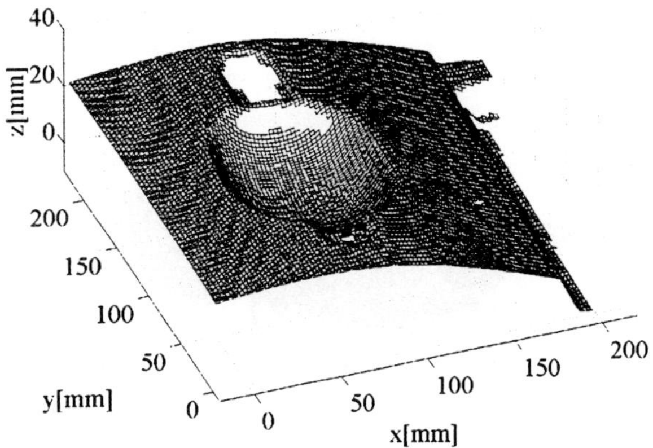

Fig. 4: 3-d data of the measurement area

To carry measurements the doors were fixed at three points to avoid torsion of the piece. Nevertheless, the lateral adjustment tolerance of the door was about 2 mm. Therefore, the detection of the error regions at the workpiece was not possible by a standard numerical method.
Data sets with 320 x 320 pixels were obtained with 3-d measurement system. 160 x 100 pixels were used in the figures.
From 9 masterpieces, 45 data sets were generated in different positions with lateral tolerance up to 2 mm (From every pieces, 5 data sets were generated). For presentation, regions which could not be measured were set to zero.
The associative memory was trained with these sets of data. The training time took approximatly 5 hours (calculated by a SGI Octane). This training is only necessary once for every measurement region.
A recall was made from the flawed test workpiece and the difference between the recall and the measurement data set was calculated. These calculation took about 1 s. Fig. 4 shows the result for the measurement regions. The flawed region is on the coordinate x = 5mm and y = 100 mm. The error region is evident.
A recall was also calculated from the flawless workpiece, which had not been used for training of the associative memory. The result of the difference calculation between the recall and the measurement is to be seen in Fig. 6. No error regions are detectable. The values are smaller (factor 10).
Comparing the results of the flawless masterpiece (Fig. 6) and the workpiece with error regions (Fig. 5) the distinction between OK- and NOT-OK-pieces was easy and also possible by numerical method with defined threshold within a few seconds.

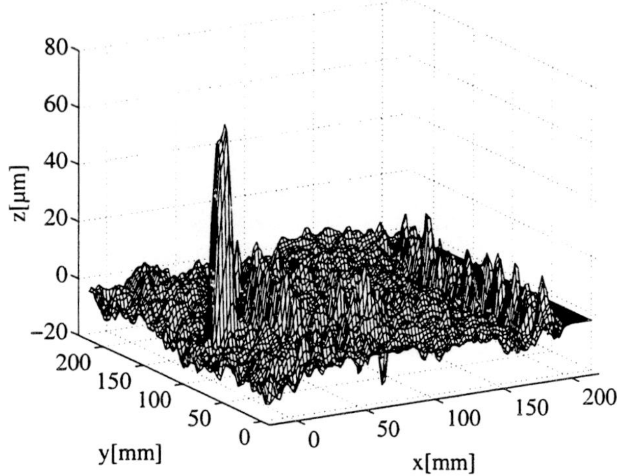

Fig. 5: Calculated difference for a flawed door

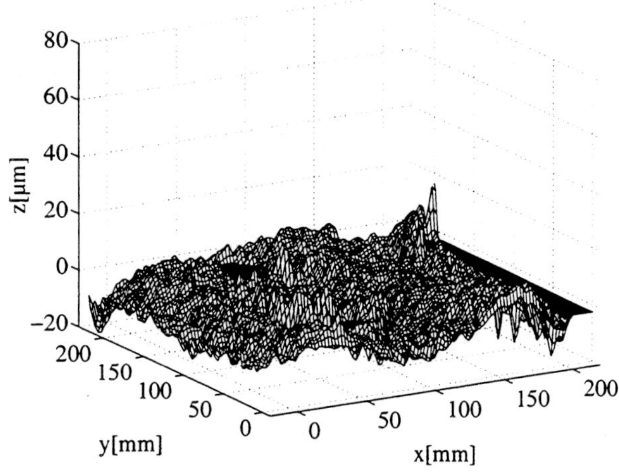

Fig. 6: Calculated difference for a flawless door

5. Conclusions

The given examples demonstrate the abilities of this method. The neural network stores the data of several master pieces and additional possible variations. Then, flawed workpieces are recognised automatically. The measurement results show, that an automatic detection of dents with a hight of 20 µm is possible.
Future work is necessary in the field of preprocessing the training data. In this way, a clear-cut detection of small and great dents will be possible.

In the presented example, an 8 bit analog CCD-camera was used. By using 12bit cameras with more pixels the measurement results can be improved essentially. That is our future work.

6. References

[1] Ackermann, F.: Digital Image Correlation: Performance and Potential Application in Photogrammetry. Contributions to the XVth ISPRS-Congress, Rio de Janeiro 1984, pp. 137-147

[2] Albrecht, P.; Michaelis, B.: Stereo Photogrammetry with Improved Spatial Resolution. The 14th International Conference on Pattern Recognition (ICPR '98), Brisbane, Queensland, Australia, 17.08-20.08.1998

[3] Krell, G.; Tizhoosh, H. R.; Lilienblum, T.; Moore, C. J., Michaelis, B.: Fuzzy Image Enhancement and Associative Feature Matching in Radiotherapy. Proceedings of the International Conference on Neural Networks (ICNN '97), Houston, Texas, 09.06.-12.06.1997, pp. 1490-1495

[4] Lilienblum, T.; Albrecht, P.; Michaelis, B.: Improvement of 3-D Data with Neural Networks. `Journal of Microelectronic Systems Integration`, Volume 5 (1997), No. 1, pp. 53-64

[5] Lilienblum, T.; Albrecht, P.; Michaelis, B.: 3D-Measurement of Geometrical Shapes by Photogrammetry and Neural Networks. 13th International Conference on Pattern Recognition (ICPR '96), Wien, pp. 330-334, 25.08.-30.08.1996.

[6] Lilienblum, T.; Günther, G.; Küchel, M.; Michaelis, B.: Error Detektion of the Surface Form by 3-D Measurement and Neural Networks. Proc. of the Tenth IMDSP Workshop '98, Alpbach, Austria, 12.7.-16.7.98, pp. 17-20

[7] Lilienblum, T.: Aufbereitung von 3D-Meßwerten unter Nutzung künstlicher neuronaler Netze. Dissertation. Shaker Verlag, 1999

[8] Loser, R.; Luhmann, T.: The Programmable Optical Measuring System POM - Applications and Performance. Comm. V, ISPRS Congress, Washington D.C., 1992

[9] Maack , Th.; Notni, G.; Schreiber, W,: Three-coordinate measurement of an object surface with a combined two-wavelength and two-source phase-shifting speckle interferometer. Elsevier Science B. V. 1995

[10] Strutz, T: Ein genaues aktives optisches Triangulations-verfahren zur Oberflächenvermessung. Dissertation, Otto-von-Guericke-Universität Magdeburg 1993

[11] Young, T. Y.: Handbook of Pattern Recognition and Image Processing: Computer Vision. Volume 2. Academic Press, San Diego 1994

High Precision 2-D Geometrical Inspection

Ville Kyrki, Heikki Kälviäinen
Lappeenranta University of Technology
Department of Information Technology
P.O. Box 20, FIN-53851 Lappeenranta, Finland
{ville.kyrki,heikki.kalviainen}@lut.fi

Abstract

Automated visual inspection has become important for modern industry mainly because production rates and the level of automation have continually increased. This paper presents a system for automated visual inspection of large two-dimensional parts. The system is capable of inspecting sheet metal parts using CAD data. The inspection is performed based on a CAD model. There are existing systems that perform this function but they are not particularly well suitable for in-place inspection. In the proposed system, the high precision inspection of individual features is performed by firstly estimating the global position of a part. Next, each local feature is measured using subpixel techniques. Finally, the measurements are compared with a CAD model. Experiments are presented to evaluate the precision of system components. According to the results, the calibration procedure seems to be the factor that has the greatest effect on the final precision. Last, a comparison to similar systems is made and some suggestions are given how the precision could be further improved.

1. Introduction

The level of automation in industry is continually increasing. Although quality control techniques have generally improved, inspection of products is still required to guarantee the high quality of products [1]. Machine vision is one of the means to improve inspection efficiency. Automated visual inspection has attracted a substantial amount of interest in the research community [8]. The task is to visually determine, whether a product is correct or not according to a set of specifications. This task is seldom an easy one since many inspections require considerable visual and reasoning abilities. Flexibility and adaptivity is sometimes also required. However, visual inspection applications are typically highly specialized. Newman and Jain [8] declare that almost all inspection systems have been designed to perform the inspection on an object whose position is highly constrained. Nevertheless, inspection systems should be integrated to the manufacturing environment to allow autonomous inspection without losing production efficiency.

In sheet metal production, water jet and laser cutting machines together with punch presses are used to cut the relatively thin metal sheets to almost any geometrical shape. Optical measurement of such large two-dimensional parts has been studied by Stanke et al. [9]. They state the following requirements: handling of large parts, complete contour measurement, fast image acquisition, precision ranging to 0.2 mm, conversion of the result in a CAD-like format, and low cost implementation. However, their objective is to produce a CAD-like file, and no comparison between the results and some predetermined measures has been described. In addition, the inspection is performed on a back lighted measurement table, which requires the parts to be moved to the table and back. A more optimal solution for production efficiency would be to inspect the parts on a conveyor belt immediately after processing. Ionescu and Sasarman [4] present another automated optical inspection system which includes also the comparison of the measurements and some tolerances. However, the system must be programmed individually for each part and each dimensional measurement must be separately specified. Thus, integration of the system to a production line seems to be very inefficient, if the number of different parts is high.

The requirements of an automated inspection system for punch press quality assurance are precision, efficient integration, low cost implementation, and speed. The geometrical precision requirement is 0.1 mm which is very high. Thus, the resolution range of video cameras is not sufficient and subpixel methods have to be used [2]. A large portion of the research on subpixel techniques concentrates on the theoretical aspects, e.g., [7]. Thus, the practical applicability of these techniques should be measured considering the precision globally, i.e., taking into account the calibration.

In this study a prototype system for two-dimensional optical measurement is presented. The objective of the system is to measure two-dimensional geometrical shapes based on CAD data without special arrangements. The measurements can be performed as in-place measurements, e.g., on a conveyor belt. The results are compared with measures specified in a CAD file. The system is capable to measure positions of edges and circles. Measurement methods and inspection algorithms are presented in Sec. 2. Precision of the system has been determined with experiments shown in Sec. 3. More details of the study can be found in [6].

2. Methods

The inspection process is divided into two phases, training and inspection. Before any inspection can be performed, each model must be trained in the system using CAD data, which consist of geometrical dimensions of an object (see Fig. 1). The model training is presented in the following algorithm:

Algorithm 1 *Model training.*

1. Convert a CAD file into a list of features.
2. Produce a template based on the features.
3. Determine the center of mass of the template.
4. Determine optimal registration parameters and store them for registration.

Each object is inspected using the following algorithm:

Algorithm 2 *Object inspection.*

1. Determine the center of mass of the part.
2. Determine the orientation of the part.
3. Measure each individual feature.
4. Analyze the results to determine the exact location of the part.
5. Compare the results with CAD features.

There are four parts of the system that are especially interesting for the accurate measurement of large sheet metal parts: calibration, registration, subpixel measurement methods, and comparison with the model.

2.1. Calibration

Before inspection can be performed, the system must be calibrated to take into account the physical setup. Calibration determines a mapping between an image and a physical world. Thus, the mapping relates every point in the image with certain physical coordinates and vice versa. The calibration is performed using an intermediate object plane which is a distortion free ideal two-dimensional pixel space. This means that the physical coordinates are first transformed into the object plane using a standard rigid body transform [5, p. 353]. Then, these intermediate coordinates are transformed into the image plane using a non-linear mapping. The parameters for the transforms are obtained by imaging a specially prepared calibration plate that contains known features in known positions. The non-linear transform is performed using a linear interpolation between certain measured points.

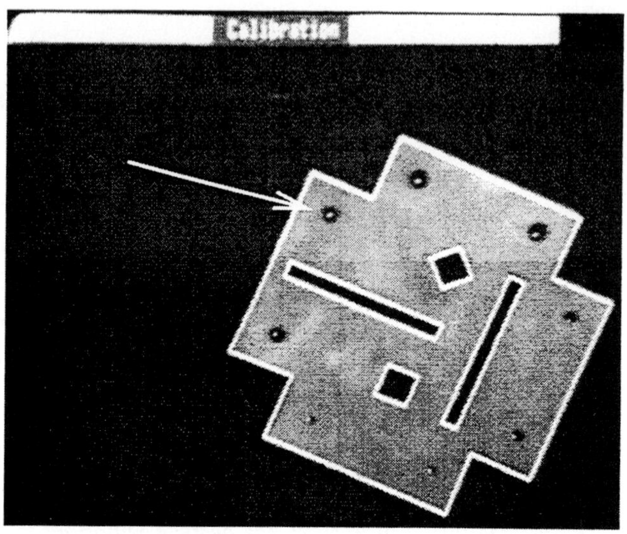

Figure 1. Part registration.

2.2. Registration

In the registration subsystem an estimate for the location and orientation of a part is determined. Registration is performed in two phases. First, the center of mass is determined. Then, the orientation is estimated.

The center of mass (c_x, c_y) of an object is determined as the first moment using

$$c_x = \frac{\sum_i g_i x_i}{\sum_i g_i} \quad c_y = \frac{\sum_i g_i y_i}{\sum_i g_i} \tag{1}$$

where x_i and y_i are the coordinates of pixel i, and g_i are mapped pixel gray values as shown in Fig. 2. Background pixels are mapped to value 0, foreground pixels (object pixels) to value 1. Pixels that have gray values between these two levels are mapped on the interval from 0 to 1 using linear interpolation. Mapping parameters are determined using the gray-level histogram of the image.

After the center of mass has been fixed, the orientation of a part is determined using the polar transform. A ring centered to the center of mass is transformed to the polar domain. The transformation is shown in Fig. 3. Transformation parameters, i.e., the radius and width of the ring,

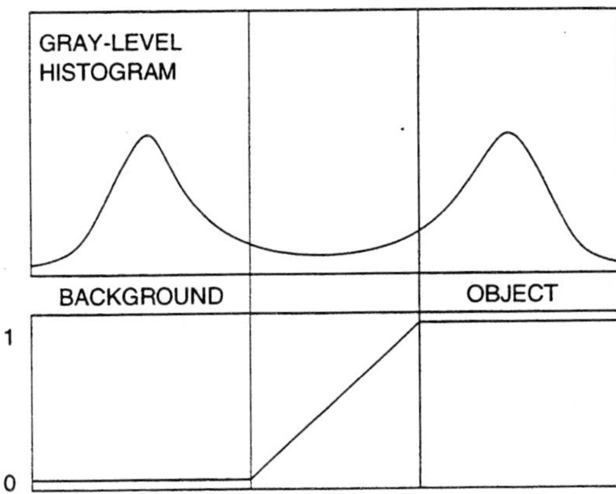

Figure 2. Mapping of gray levels.

and the dimensions of the polar coordinate space, are determined when the model is trained by selecting automatically the values that minimize possible confusion. That is, such parameter values are selected that result in the lowest probability of determining the rotation incorrectly. For example, the ring parameters are determined so that the features defining the rotation most accurately lie inside the ring [6]. The estimation of the rotation is reduced in the polar domain into one-dimensional search for maximum normalized correlation between the polar images of the model and the inspected part [6]. By using the normalized correlation the effect of changing illumination is reduced.

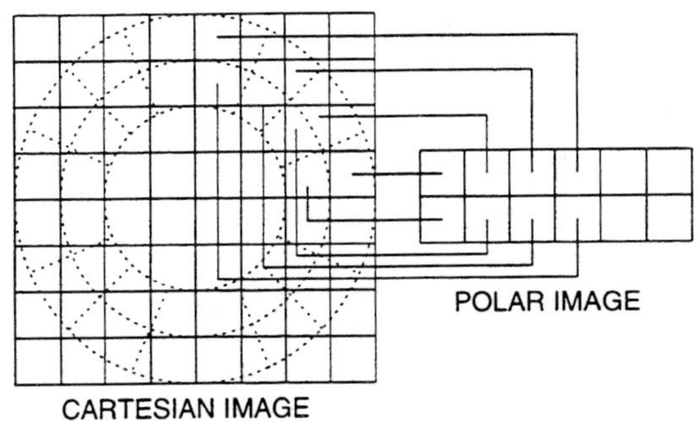

Figure 3. Transform from Cartesian to polar coordinates.

2.3. Subpixel measurement methods

Features are measured according to the estimate of object location determined in the registration phase, i.e., each individual feature is measured with a feature extractor placed to the estimated location of the feature. Two methods are used for individual feature measurements. Firstly, the center of mass for a circle is measured using connected blob analysis. This means that the centroid is determined using Eq. 1 taking into account only connected non-zero pixels. Connectivity is defined as 8-connectivity [5, p. 40].

Secondly, locations of individual edges are measured using calipers [4]. In this method, each edge segment is first projected onto a one-dimensional image as shown in Fig. 4. Next, the one-dimensional image is processed with a finite difference edge detection filter. The filter is of form $y[i] = x[i+2] + x[i+1] - x[i-1] - x[i-2]$. Finally, the maximum of the edge filter output is located by computing the center of mass for the filtered 1-D image. The location of the maximum is the edge location in respect to the position of the caliper.

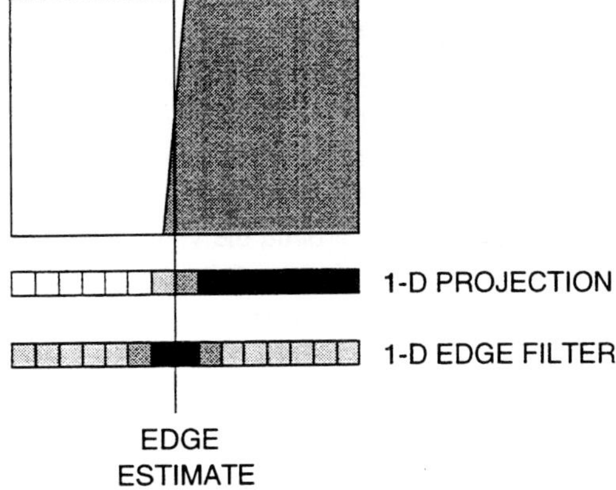

Figure 4. Measuring an edge with a caliper.

2.4. Comparison with specifications

After the individual features have been measured, a more precise estimate for the object location is derived. This is performed using an estimation technique presented by Cox et al. in [3]. After the more precise estimate has been determined, each feature location is compared to the corresponding location defined by the CAD model. If any comparison fails, i.e., if the distance between the measurement and the model is greater than some given threshold, the part is classified as incorrect. Otherwise, if every measurement fits to the specified tolerances, the part is classified as correct.

3. Experiments and results

Experiments were performed to assess the geometrical precision of the system. A part shown in Fig. 1 was used in the measurements. As the final precision is affected by several factors, each of the factors was separately experimentally evaluated. Firstly, the precision of blob centroid measurements was evaluated. The circular hole marked with an arrow in Fig. 1 was used as a feature to measure. The standard deviation of the location was 1.6 % of the pixel size for a stable object. The standard deviation of the area of the hole was 16 %, i.e., 0.16 pixels. The precision of blob centroid measurements was further evaluated by measuring the distance between two similar circular holes. Before each measurement, the part was randomly displaced by a small amount. The standard deviation of the distance was 0.05 pixels.

Caliper precision was estimated by measuring the distance between two parallel lines. Before each measurement, the part was randomly displaced. For a caliper with a width of 13 pixels, the standard deviation of the distance was 0.19 pixels. For a 129 pixel wide caliper, the standard deviation was 0.15 pixels.

To estimate the precision of the calibration procedure, another set of blob distance measurements was performed. The physical world distance between two circular holes was measured. This means that the coordinates of the blob centroids were transformed into physical domain before calculating the distance between them. In addition, the part was measured in several places around the view in various orientations. The standard deviation of the distance was 0.13 mm which corresponds to 0.35 pixels.

4. Discussion

The standard deviation of 0.35 pixels was achieved for physical distance measurements. However, if the distribution of measurements is Gaussian, the standard deviation of a single location measurement is 0.24 pixels. This result is derived from $\sigma^2 = \sigma_1^2 + \sigma_2^2$, where σ is the total standard deviation and σ_i are the component deviations. Thus, the variance of the distance is the sum of the variances of the location. This result seems to indicate an accuracy of one fourth of the pixel size. Stanke et al. present that the camera precision can be exceeded by 5 to 10 times using a back lighted measuring table and line-scan cameras. However, using their approach, the processing time of a part is supposed to be clearly more than the processing time with measurements performed on a conveyor belt. In addition, no comparison scheme to compare CAD images with the measurements has been presented. Ionescu and Sasarman present that the precision can be augmented fifty times by subpixel techniques. However, in their system each caliper has over 200 variable parameters that have to be fine tuned by the user.

An important restriction to note about the system presented in this paper is that the thickness of objects is not taken into account. When the ratio between the object size and camera distance increases, some kind of a thickness correction mechanism must be used. However, Stanke et al. present a simple algorithmic correction mechanism that could be used [9].

Considering the setup, i.e., using one stationary camera with no special lighting, the results are encouraging. However, for very large sheet metal parts (e.g., 2000 mm) the approach seems inapplicable. For example, to attain a resolution of 0.1 mm for a 2000 mm object requires the camera resolution to be 5000 pixels with one fourth of a pixel accuracy. For smaller objects the approach seems applicable, e.g., for a 600 mm object the camera resolution needs to be 1500 pixels using the restrictions presented.

There seem to be a few options to further improve the precision. An obvious approach is to increase camera resolution. Quite often this is possible, as currently the size of CCD arrays can be up to 4000 $\times$ 4000 pixels for area sensors and 10 000 pixels for line-scan cameras. Considering the results presented in Sec. 3 it seems that the calibration procedure is the most prominent error source in the system.

Acknowledgements

This research was supported by Intelligent Industrial Systems Laboratory (IISt-Lab) of Lappeenranta University of Technology (LUT), Finland. The authors would like to thank Mr. Jari Selesvuo from Department of Mechanical Engineering of LUT.

References

[1] G. A. H. Al-Kindi, R. M. Baul, and K. F. Gill. Vision-controlled cnc machines. *Computing & Control Engineering Journal*, 4(2):92–96, April 1993.

[2] D. Braggins. Achieving sub-pixel precision. *Sensor Review*, 10(4):174–177, 1990.

[3] I. J. Cox, J. B. Kruskal, and D. A. Wallach. Predicting and estimating the accuracy of a subpixel registration algorithm. *IEEE Transactions on Pattern Analysis and Machine Intelligence*, 12(8):721–734, August 1990.

[4] D. Ionescu and M. Sasarman. Automated optical inspection of geometrical shapes. In *IMTC/98 Conference Proceedings*, volume 1, pages 14–17, 1998.

[5] R. Jain, R. Kasturi, and B. G. Schunck. *Machine Vision*. McGraw-Hill, Inc., 1995.

[6] V. Kyrki. Punch press quality assurance using machine vision. Master's thesis, Lappeenranta University of Technology, Department of Information Technology, Finland, 1999.

[7] E. P. Lyvers, O. R. Mitchell, M. L. Akey, and A. P. Reeves. Subpixel measurements using a moment-based edge operator. *IEEE Transactions on Pattern Analysis and Machine Intelligence*, 11(12):1293–1308, 1989.

[8] T. S. Newman and A. K. Jain. A survey of automated visual inspection. *Computer Vision and Image Understanding*, 61(2):231–262, 1995.

[9] G. Stanke, L. Zedler, A. Zorn, F. Weckend, and H.-G. Weide. Sub-pixel accuracy by optical measurement of large automobile components. In *Proceedings of the 24th Annual Conference of the IEEE Industrial Electronics Society*, volume 4, pages 2431–2433, 1998.

Knowledge Based Fingerprint Image Enhancement

Xiping Luo, Jie Tian
AILAB, Institute of Automation, The Chinese Academy of Sciences, Beijing,100080
e_mail: luoxiping@yahoo.com, tian@readchina.com

Abstract

Fingerprint enhancement is a critical step in fingerprint identification. Most of the existing enhancement algorithms are based on local ridge direction. The main drawback of these methods lies in the fact that false estimate of local ridge direction will lead to poor enhancement. But the estimate of local ridge directions is unreliable in the areas corrupted by noise where enhancement is most needed. In this paper, we proposed a rule-based method to do fingerprint enhancement. We introduced human knowledge about fingerprints into the enhancement process in the form of rules and simulate what an expert will do to enhance a fingerprint image. In our method, the skeleton image is used to give ridge connection information for the enhancement of the binary image. Experiments show our algorithm is fast and has excellent performance.

1.Introduction

Most of the existing enhancement algorithms are based on the local ridge direction. Like the direction oriented ridge enhancement algorithm of Douglas Hung[1] and the algorithm of Lin Hong et.al [2][4] which uses Gabor filters. The main drawback of these methods lie in the fact that false estimate of local ridge direction will lead to poor enhancement. But the estimate of local ridge directions is unreliable in the areas corrupted by noise where enhancement is most needed

Unlike other images, fingerprint image has its own characteristics. It is valuable to introduce human knowledge into the processing of fingerprint images and simulate what an expert will do to enhance a fingerprint image. In this paper, we used human knowledge about fingerprint in the form of rules to guide the enhancement process and proposed a rule-based method to do fingerprint enhancement by the joint consideration of the binary image and the skeleton image of ridges and valleys.

Section 2 gives a brief description of our enhancement system and explains the algorithm we used. Details of the algorithm are introduced in section 3. Section 4 gives the experimental results. We conclude in section 5.

Supported by The Chinese National Science Fundation

2.System description

Steps of our enhancement system are shown in figure 1. The input gray-level fingerprint image is binarized to get the binary image. Then the binary image is thinned to get the skeleton image. Finally, we use the ridge connection information contained in the skeleton image to enhance the binary image.

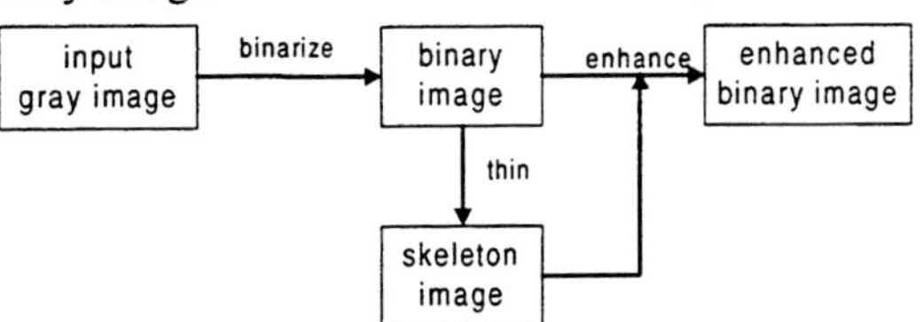

Figure 1. Framework of the enhancement algorithm

The general step of fingerprint identification in most previous works is as follows: First gets the binary image and the skeleton image and then uses the skeleton image to extract minutiae and do post processing on the skeleton image to purify minutiae[3][5]. Here we will give the reasons why we didn't follow the general step and use the skeleton image to extract minutiae directly. One reason is that the enhanced binary image can have other usage such as the estimation of orientation field in fingerprint classification. Another reason is that Some complex ridge structures cannot be easily recovered from the skeleton image alone, they can only be recovered by enhance the binary image and thin the enhanced image again.

3 Details of the algorithm

In our enhancement algorithm, we will consider the skeleton of ridges and valleys simultaneously and the same rules are used in both sets of skeletons. In the skeleton image, pixels in the skeleton of ridges have gray value 0, pixels in the skeleton of valleys have gray value 128, all the other pixels have gray value 255.

Before introducing the rules used in the enhancement process, we first give some definitions. A point in the skeleton image is called an end point if its gray value is 128 or 0 and has only one point of the same gray value 8-connected with it. While a bifurcation point has 3 point

1051-4651/00 $10.00 © 2000 IEEE

of the same gray value 8-connected with it, and a cross point has 4 point of the same gray value 8-connected with it. All these three kind of points are called vertices. The skeleton of ridges or valleys connecting two vertices is called edge. We call vertices and edges of the ridges type 1, those of the valleys type 0. The length of an edge is the number of pixels in this edge. By these definitions, an end point is a point connected with only one edge, a bifurcation point is a point connected with 3 edges, a cross point is a point connected with 4 edges. See Figure 2, we say a bifurcation point A satisfy strict bridge condition if angle $\angle BAD>165$ and $75<\angle BAC<105$ and $75<\angle CAD<105$. We say a bifurcation point A satisfy loose bridge condition if angle $\angle BAD>135$ and $45<\angle BAC<135$ and $45<\angle CAD<135$.

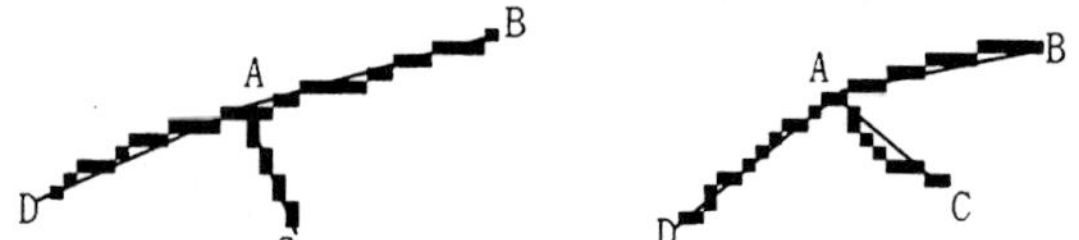

Figure 2. Strict and loose bridge condition

Rule 1: process bridge

See figure 3

Condition: Two bifurcation points A and B connected by an edge shorter than a predefined threshold. Both points satisfy the loose bridge condition.

Action: Connect related end points C and D of the other type in the binary image. Delete A and B from the set of bifurcation points. Delete C and D from the set of end points.

Figure 3. Demonstration of rule 1

Rule 2: process breaks

See figure 4

Condition: Two end points A and B of the same type faces each other. Their distance is within a predefined threshold. The line connecting A and B will not cross any edge of the same type as A.

We say end point A and end point B faces each other if angle $\angle BAA_1>165$ and $\angle ABB_1>165$.

Action: Connect A and B in the binary image. Delete A and B from the set of end points. Delete the related bifurcation C and D of the other type from the set of bifurcation points. C and D may not satisfy the loose bridge condition and can not be taken as bridge.

Figure 4.Demonstration of rule 2

Rule 3: process complex connection

The existence of cross point is due to the complex connection of edges. Three main cases of complex connections will be processed by this rule.

Case 3.1: See figure 5.

Condition: A is a cross point. One of the edges connect with A also connects with a bifurcation point B which satisfies strict bridge condition. The edge connecting A and B is shorter than a predefined threshold as in rule 1.

Action: Take A and B as a bridge, do the same as in rule 1. Then set A as a bifurcation point.

Figure 5. Demonstration of rule 3, case 3.1

Case 3.2: See figure 6.

Condition: A is a cross point. The condition of case 3.1 is not satisfied. Angle $\angle A_1AA_2<60$ and $\angle A_3AA_4<60$.

Action: Connect related end points B and C of the other type in the binary image. Delete A from the set of cross points. Delete B, C from the set of end points.

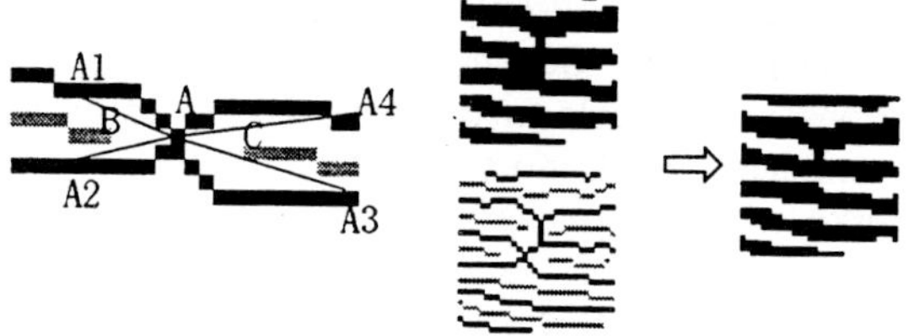

Figure 6. Demonstration of rule 3, case 3.2

Case 3.3: See figure 7.

Condition: A is a cross point. The conditions of case 3.1 and case 3.2 are not satisfied. In addition, one of the edges connects with A also connects with a bifurcation point B which satisfies loose bridge condition. The edge connecting A and B is shorter than a predefined threshold as in rule 1.

Action: Take A and B as a bridge, do the same as in rule 1. Then set A as a bifurcation point.

Figure 7. Demonstration of rule 3, case 3.3

Rule 4: Process blur

See figure 8.

Condition: Two bifurcation points A and B are connected by an edge shorter than a predefined threshold. Angle $\angle A_1AA_2<60$ and $\angle B_1BB_2<60$.

Action: Connect the related end points C and D of the other type in the binary image. Delete A and B from the set of bifurcation points. Delete C and D from the set of end points

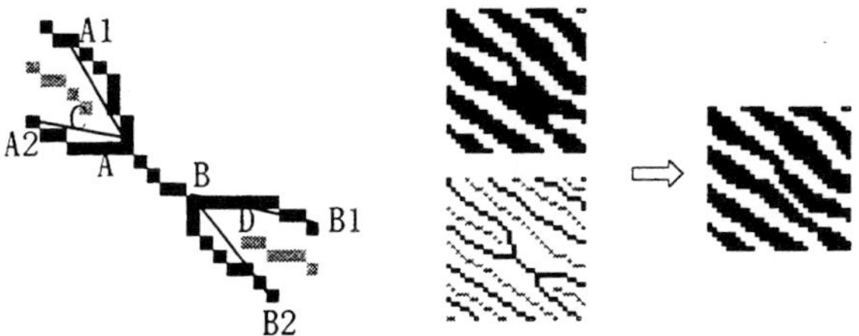

Figure 8. Demonstration of rule 4

Rule 5: Process scar

Peeling of finger epidermis will cause scar in fingerprint image. One kind of scar is the break of ridges in a local area, such a case can be handled by rule 2. Two major other cases of scar will be handled by this rule.

Case 5.1: See figure 9.

Condition: A bifurcation point A satisfies strict bridge condition. Two of the edges having the largest between-edge angle among the three edges connect with point A also connects with point B and C respectively. B and C are bifurcation point or turning point. Both edges are shorter than a predefined threshold. In addition, there have three end points D, E and F faces A, B and C respectively.

B is called a turning point if angle $\angle ABB_1<105$. We say point D faces point A, if angle $\angle DAA_1>165$.

Action: Connect A and D, B and E, C and F in the binary image. Break the connection of A and B, A and C. Delete A, B, C, D, E and F from the corresponding point sets.

Figure 9. Demonstration of rule 5, case 5.1

Case 5.2: See figure 10.

Condition: A bifurcation point A satisfies strict bridge condition. Two of the edges having the largest between-edge angle among the three edges connect with point A also connects with point B and C respectively. B and C are bifurcation point or turning point. Both edges are shorter than a predefined threshold. In addition, there has a bifurcation point D faces A and satisfies the same condition as A. B and E, C and F faces each other respectively.

Action: Connect A and D, B and E, C and F in the binary image. Break the connection of A and B, A and C, D and E, D and F. Delete A, B, C, D, E and F from the corresponding point sets.

Figure 10. Demonstration of rule 5, case 5.2

Rule 6: Process False connection

This rule handles two major cases of false connection of ridges.

Case 6.1: See figure 11.

Condition: A bifurcation point A and an end point B of the same type face each other. Their distance is within a predefined threshold. The line connecting A and B will not cross any edge of the same type as A.

We say end point B and bifurcation point A faces each other if angle $\angle BAD<90$ and $\angle ABB_1>90$

Action: Connect B and C in the binary image. Break the connection between A and C. Where C is a point in the edge connect with point A, B and C are on the same side of line AD. Delete A and B from the set of Bifurcation points and the set of end points respectively.

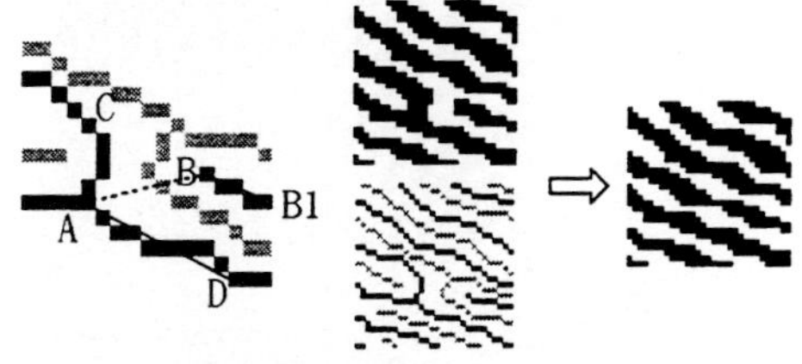

Figure 11. Demonstration of rule 6, case 6.1

Case 6.2 See figure 12.

Condition: Two bifurcation points A and B of the same type face each other. Their distance is within a predefined threshold. The line connecting A and B will not cross any edge of the same type as A

We say bifurcation point A and bifurcation point B faces each other if angle $\angle A_1AB<90$ and $\angle B_1BA<90$.

Action: Connect C and D in the binary image. Break the connection between A and C, B and D. Where C is a point in the edge connect with point A. D is a point in the edge connect with point B. C and D are on the same side of line AA_1 and line BB_1. Delete A and B from the set of bifurcation points.

Figure 12. Demonstration of rule 6, case 6.2

4. Experimental results

The images we used for experiment were captured using a fingerprint scanner. The size of the image is 320×320. All the experiments were done in PII 350 MHz PC. The total time needed to enhance a gray level image is only about 0.342 seconds. Table I gives the distribution of the computational time. Figure.13 gives an example of the results of the enhancement steps. Figure.13 (a) is the original gray level image, (b) is the final enhanced binary image.

Table I. Computation time in PII 350 MHz PC

Threshold	Post process	Thin	Enhance	Total
0.122s	0.09s	0.066s	0.064s	0.342s

5.Conclusion and discussion

Fingerprint image is a special kind of image and has its own characteristics. Most of the known techniques for fingerprint image enhancement are direction-oriented and rely heavily on the correct estimate of local ridge direction. But the estimate of local ridge directions is unreliable in the areas corrupted by noise where enhancement is most needed. In this paper, we proposed a rule-based method to do fingerprint enhancement. This method tried to simulate what an expert will do to enhance a fingerprint image. The skeleton image is used to give information of the connect relation of ridges for the enhancement of the binary image.

In the rule based enhancement process, the handling of complex ridge connections is a difficult problem and needs to be further investigated.

Reference

[1] D.C.Douglas Hung, Enhancement and Feature Purification of Fingerprint Images. Pattern Recognition, Vol.26, No.11, pp.1661-1671,1993

[2] Lin Hong, Yifei Wan, and Anil Jain, Fingerprint image Enhancement:Algorithm and Performance Evaluation, IEEE Trans on Pattern Analysis and Machine Intelligence, vol.20, No.8. pp777-789, 1998

[3] Alessandro Farina, Zsolt M.Kovacs-Vajna, Alberto Leone, fingerprint minutiae extraction from skeletonized binary images, Pattern Recognition, Vol.32, pp.877-889,1999

[4] Anil Jain, Lin Hong and Ruud Bolle, On-Line Fingerprint Verification, IEEE Trans on Pattern Analysis and Machine Intelligence, vol.19, No.4. pp302-313, 1997

[5] Qinghan Xiao and H. Raafat, Fingerprint Image Postprocessing: A Combined Statistical and Structural Approach, *Pattern Recognition*,Vol 24, No.10, pp.985-992,1991.

(a)

(b)

Figure 13 example of enhancement (a).original image (b) enhanced binary image

Object Recognition and Detection by a Combination of Support Vector Machine and Rotation Invariant Phase Only Correlation

Chikahito Nakajima Norihiko Itoh
Central Research Institute of Electric Power Industry, Tokyo 201-8511 JAPAN

Massimiliano Pontil Tomaso Poggio
Massachusetts Institute of Technology
45 Carleton, Cambridge, MA 02142 USA

Abstract

This paper proposes an object recognition and detection method by a combination of Support Vector Machine Classifier (SVM) and Rotation Invariant Phase Only Correlation (RIPOC). SVM is a learning technique that is well founded in statistical learning theory. RIPOC is a position and rotation invariant pattern matching technique. We combined these two techniques to develop an augmented reality system. This system can recognize and detect objects from image sequences without special image marks or sensors and show information about the objects through a head-mounted display. Performance is real time.

1 Introduction

We are developing a support system for maintenance training of electric power facilities using object recognition and detection techniques. To assist in the training, we are evaluating the use of augmented reality through a head mounted display, small cameras, and image processing.

Many systems in augmented reality have been developed in a variety of applications such as maintenance, repair, assistance of surgery, and guidance of navigation [1, 2]. They typically use special marks or sensors on the target objects to facilitate detection and classification of objects and determination of their poses. In this system, we intend to recognize and detect objects without special marks or sensors. This paper proposes an object recognition and detection method by a combination of Support Vector Machine (SVM) classifiers [3] and Rotation Invariant Phase Only Correlation (RIPOC) [4].

SVM is a technique for learning from examples that is well-founded in statistical learning theory. SVM has recently received a great deal of attention and has been applied to areas such as handwritten character recognition, 3D object recognition, text categorization and object detection [3]. If a large amount of sample data of the target objects is available, SVM is a very useful tool for summarizing the data in terms of the support vectors. A drawback of "pure" learning techniques from examples, like SVM, is that they need large data sets for effective training. Moreover object detection or recognition has to be performed at many locations and scales in a given image [6].

RIPOC is a pattern matching technique which measures rotation and translation between two images. RIPOC computes the correlation between the two images by means of the Fast Fourier Transformation (FFT). It uses the FFT amplitude for measuring the rotation and the FFT phase for measuring the translation. When applied to object recognition, RIPOC has to compute the correspondences among all the object templates and all the images in the sequence. This method is not sufficient to perform moving object recognition by its own because of its lack of robustness against changes in the background.

This paper describes a new method for object recognition and detection from image sequences. The system uses a hierarchy of SVMs for object recognition and RIPOC for pose detection. Our preliminary experimental results indicate the advantage of a combination of the two techniques and open the possibility of applying the system to maintenance training in an industrial domain. The paper is organized as follows. Section 2 presents a description of the system outline. Section 3 describes the results of the system. Section 4 summarizes our work and presents our future research.

2. System Outline

The system consists of three parts: Image I/O, Recognition and Detection. Figure 1 shows an outline of the system. Each image from a camera is distributed to the Recognition module and the Detection module through the Image I/O module. The results of recognition and detection are displayed on a Head Mounted Display (HMD). Each part is working independently on different computers.

1051-4651/00 $10.00 © 2000 IEEE

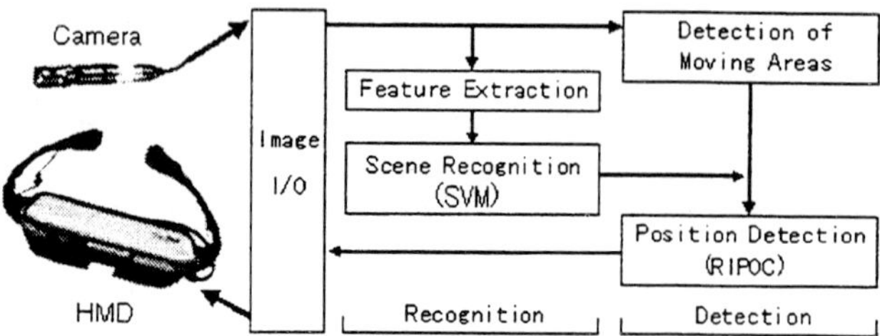

Figure 1. Outline of the system.

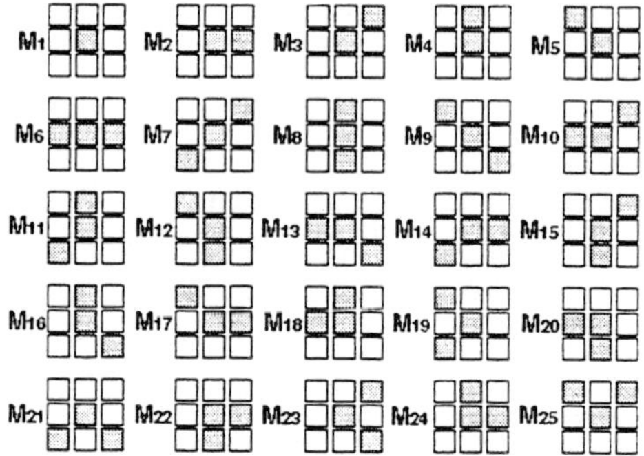

Figure 2. Mask patterns.

2.1 Recognition Module

The Recognition module has two processes: a feature extraction process and a scene recognition process.

2.1.1 Feature Extraction

The system uses a set of features which are obtained by convolving the local mask patterns shown in Figure 2 with a given image. These masks have been introduced in [7] for position invariant object detection. Let M^i, $i = 1, \ldots, 25$, be the mask pattern in Figure 2 and V_k the 3×3 patch at pixel k in an image. In our system, the *i-th* feature, F_i, is given by $\sum_k M^i \cdot V_k$, where the sum is on the image pixels. We have used not only the simple convolution but also a non-linear convolution, $F_i = \sum_k C_{(k,i)}$ where

$$C_{(k,i)} = \begin{cases} V_k \cdot M^i & : \; if\; V_k \cdot M^i = \max_j (V_k \cdot M^j) \\ 0 & : \; otherwise. \end{cases}$$

The system uses the simple convolution from the mask 1 to 5 and the non-linear convolution from the mask 6 to 25. The non-linear convolution works mainly on edge areas in an image. The non-linear operation has been inspired by recent work in [8] and has shown good performance for people recognition in our previous work [9].

To detect color, the human visual system uses responses of three types of the receptors, known as red, green and blue, and combines them in the retina. This paper uses a simple combination model, such as "R+G-B", "R-G" and "R+G", suggested by physiological study [10]. The system extracts 75 (25×3) features from the three types of the above RGB combinations.

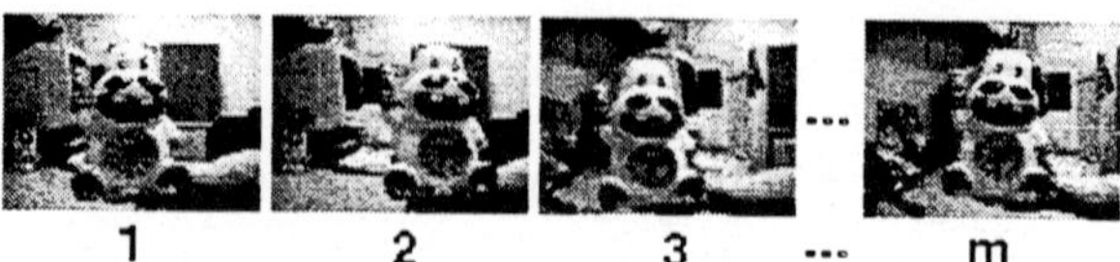

Figure 3. An example of a training data set for SVM.

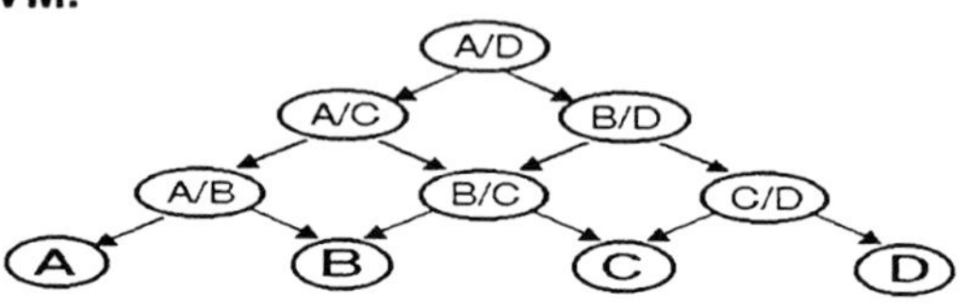

Figure 4. A decision graph of SVM.

2.1.2 Recognition of a Scene

Figure 3 shows an example of training images for one class. The m in Figure 3 is the number of training images for the class and is set to 60 in this experiment. Each class is represented by a set of m vectors, each vector consists of the 75 features extracted above. The system uses a linear SVM [3, 5] that determines the hyperplane $\mathbf{w} \cdot \mathbf{x} + b$ which best separates two classes. The $\mathbf{w}$ is the weight vector, the $\mathbf{x}$ is the vector of features, and b is a constant. This hyperplane is the one which maximizes the distance or *margin* between the two classes. The margin, equal to $2\|\mathbf{w}\|^{-1}$, is an important geometrical quantity because it provides an estimator of the similarity of the two classes.

The SVM is computed for each pair of n classes. Recognition of the object in a new image is based on the decision graph of SVMs [11]. The graph for four classes (A, B, C, D) is shown in Figure 4. Each node in the graph is associated with a pair of classes. Classification of an input vector starts from the root node (A/D) of the graph. Notice that the classification result depends on the initial position of each class in the graph. A possible heuristic to improve classification performance consists of selecting the SVMs with the largest margin in the top node (A/D) of the graph; we use this strategy. A similar method based on a binary decision graph of SVMs is also discussed in [5]. In both cases, classification of an input vector requires the evaluation of $n - 1$ SVMs.

2.2 Detection Module

The object detection module has two parts: detection of moving areas and position detection of the object. In the position detection part, the system selects a template image from a set of object templates by using the result of the Recognition module.

a. b.

Figure 5. An example of moving area extraction.

2.2.1 Detection of Moving Area

In this system, we are using two filters to detect moving areas from images. One is the extraction of differences between the new input image and the average image. The average image is automatically calculated over k frames without moving edge extraction. In this experiment k is 3. Generally, the result of this filter has a lot of noise. To reduce the noise, the system uses another filter which extracts moving edges from the image sequence and fills the interior of the edges with the original pixel values. Figure 5-a is an image in the image sequences and Figure 5-b is the combination of the two filters. In Figure 5-b, the moving area is extracted.

2.2.2 Position Detection

Let $f_1(m, n)$ be a template image, and $f_2(m, n)$ an image in the image sequence. Both image sizes are $M \times N$ pixels, $m = 0, ..., M-1$, $n = 0, ..., N-1$. The discrete Fourier transformation for f_1 and f_2 are $F_1(u, v) = A(u, v)e^{j\theta(u,v)}$ and $F_2(u, v) = B(u, v)e^{j\phi(u,v)}$, $u = 0, ..., M-1$, $v = 0, ..., N-1$. $A(u, v)$ and $B(u, v)$ are amplitude spectral functions, θ and ϕ are phase spectral functions. Now we define new discrete Fourier images $F_1'(u, v) = e^{j\theta(u,v)}$ and $F_2'(u, v) = e^{j\phi(u,v)}$ where the amplitude spectral functions A and B are set to 1. The correlation of F_1' and F_2' is $H_{12}(u, v) = e^{j(\theta-\phi)}$. The inverse Fourier transform of H_{12} is :

$$G_{12}(r, s) = \frac{1}{MN} \sum_{u=0}^{M-1} \sum_{v=0}^{N-1} e^{j(\theta-\phi)} e^{j2\pi(\frac{ur}{M} + \frac{vs}{N})}$$

where $r = 0, ..., M-1$, $s = 0, ..., N-1$. The transform value is calculated by G_{12}.

If the image f_2 is translated along the horizontal direction by τ, $f_3(m, n) = f_2(m + \tau, n)$, the inverse Fourier transform becomes $G_{13}(r, s) = G_{12}(r + \tau, s)$. The peak of G_{12} moves in the same direction by τ. It is possible to detect image translation (direction and distance) from the peak shift. This method is called Phase Only Correlation (POC) [12]. However POC is not adequate for image rotation.

To treat image rotation, the system uses Rotation Invariant Phase Only Correlation (RIPOC) [4]. At first, it considers only the amplitude spectral functions A and B of F_1, F_2. The A and B are transformed to polar-space. Next it extracts the shift transformation value on the polar-space by using the above POC. This shift value indicates the rotation of the two images. Then the input image is rotated based on the measured rotation result. Finally, it measures the transformation from the template image to the input image by POC. Thus RIPOC is able to measure rotation and transformation of the images.

3 Experimentation

In this experiment, we used four classes for the system. Sixty images for each class, taken under a moving camera as in Figure 3, were used for training the SVM. One template image, as in Figure 5-b, for each class was provided to the RIPOC. This system runs in real time by distributing processing on three computers.

Figure 6 shows one result from the system. The lower left corner of each image shows the result of the SVM classification and the upper left corner shows the result of the RIPOC for each frame. The center cross in each image is the average position of RIPOC results over 5 frames. Figure 7 shows the SVM results for the image sequence in Figure 6 which contains 170 frames. The misclassifications in Figure 7 were caused by blurred images which occurred in the sequence from time to time.

Figure 8 shows the results for a rotated object and a object sitting on a table. The rotated object as in Figure 8-a was recognized and detected by the system. The object sitting on a table was recognized by the SVM, as in the lower left corner of Figure 8-b, but the object area wasn't detected, because moving areas weren't included on the image. Figure 9 shows the result when the camera moves from Figure 9-a to Figure 9-b. The detection result of moving areas, as in the upper left corner of Figure 9-b, included not only the moving object but also a part of background. However it found the correct position by the RIPOC, because the system used the true template which was selected by the SVM.

Figure 10-c,d are results where we replaced the object detection point with images of a brain, which are selected automatically, by the result of the SVM.

4 Conclusion

This paper presents an object recognition and detection method by a combination of SVM and RIPOC to develop an augmented reality system. The system can recognize and detect objects in real time from image sequences without special image marks or sensors and can show information about the objects through a head-mounted display.

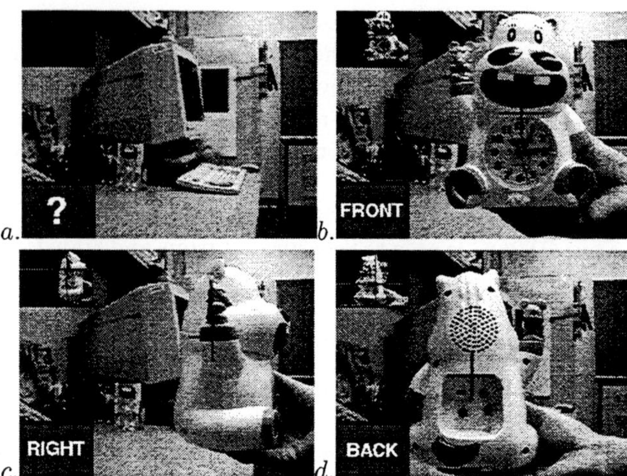

Figure 6. Results for four classes.

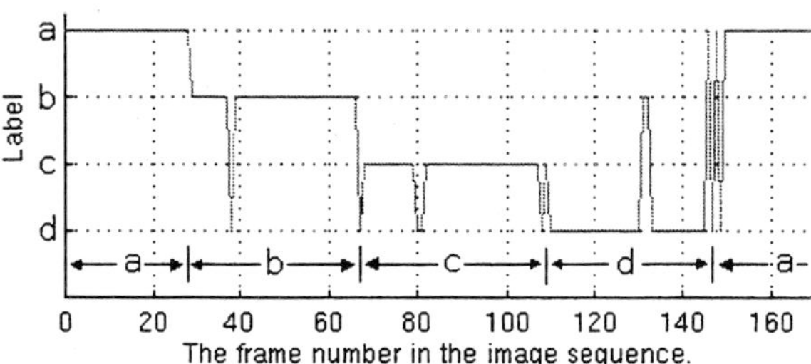

Figure 7. Recognition results for the image sequence. The bottom labels (a, b, c and d) show the true classes. The spikes in the graph are misclassifications.

This system is one part of the augmented reality system that we have been developing. We are now planning to combine the system and an image retrieval system to introduce the augmented reality system into maintenance training of electric power facilities.

Figure 8. Results for a rotated object and a object sitting on a table.

Figure 9. Results for a moving camera.

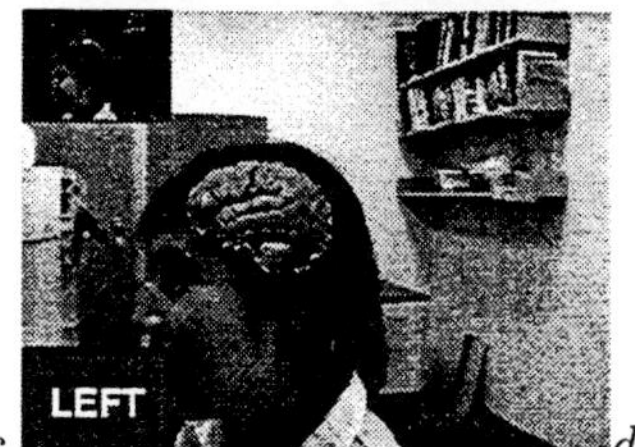

Figure 10. Results for four classes and overlaid pictures.

References

[1] J. Rekimoto and K. Nagao. The world through the computer: Computer augmented interaction with real world environments. *Proc. of UIST*, 1995.

[2] S. Feiner, B. MacIntyre, T. Hollerer, and A. Webster. A touring machine: prototyping 3d mobile augmented reality system for exploring the urban environment. *Proc. of ISWC*, 1997.

[3] V. Vapnik. Statistical learning theory. *John Wiley & Sons inc.*, 1998.

[4] G. X. Ritter and J. N. Wilson. Pattern matching and shape detection. *Computer Vision Algorithms in Image Algebra*,CRC Press,1996.

[5] M. Pontil and A. Verri. Support vector machines for 3-D object recognition. *IEEE Trans. PAMI*, 1998.

[6] C. Papageorgiou and T. Poggio. Pattern classification approach to dynamical object detection. *Proc. of ICCV*, 1999.

[7] T. Kurita, K. Hotta, and T. Mishima. Scale and rotation invariant recognition method using higher-order local autocorrelation features of log-polar image. *Proc. of ACCV*, 1998.

[8] M. Riesenhuber and T. Poggio. Hierarchical models of object recognition in cortex. *Nature Neuroscience*, 2(11), 1999.

[9] C. Nakajima, M. Pontil and T. Poggio. People recognition and pose estimation in image sequences. *Proc. of IJCNN*, 2000.

[10] K. Uchikawa. Mechanisnm of color perception. *Asakura syoten*, (Japanese), 1998.

[11] J. Platt, N. Cristianini, and J. Shawe-Taylor. Large margin DAGs for multiclass classification. *Advances in Neural Information Processing Systems*, 2000 (to appear).

[12] K. Kobayashi, H. Nakajima, T. Aoki, K. Kawamata and T. Higuchi. Filtering on phase only correlation domain and its applications. *ITE Technical Report*, 21(42),1997.

On-line system setup in a cellar of a flotation plant

W. X. Wang , O. Stephansson and S.C. Wang
Division of Engineering Geology, Royal Institute of Technology, S-100 44, Stockholm
E_mail: weixing.wang@imenco.se , ove@aom.kth.se, scwang@aom.kth.se

Abstract

This paper describes an online system for froth images of a flotation cellar in mineral processing. The aim of the system setup is to obtain optical information of froth images. Information will then be used for optimization of mineral flotation procedures. In this study, we have designed an illumination system for gabbing froth image with a constant illumination, studied image quality evaluation and classification algorithms. They are used for selecting right types of images for further processing. Special segmentation algorithms for bubbles, and about 40 parameters for froth image analysis are presented. Both Dos software and Windows software have been developed and tested in the laboratory and filed.

1. Introduction

With the rapid development of computer imaging techniques, several on-line systems have been studied and set up for evaluating and controlling mineral froth in real time. The project ChaCo (The Characterization of Flotation Froth Structure and Color by Machine Vision) is a project within the 4th EU - program. The aim of the project is to develop an on-line optical system for monitoring mineral froth variation and making optimization for mineral processing production. The system consists of three parts: (1) Illumination system for grabbing high quality froth images; (2) Image processing and analysis of the visual information; and (3) Froth modeling for controlling mineral processing. This paper presents the on-line system at Garpenberg mine of Boliden mineral in Sweden, the system does not include the part of froth modeling.

2. System configuration and work sequence

A system for froth analysis was set up in a mineral processing plant. The image acquisition system includes two cameras with protecting tubes, a lamp, a protecting box against to dust and variable lighting. A CCD camera grabs froth images from a froth cellar (Figure 1), and transfers the pictures to a frame grabber that is connected to a PC computer. The software first detects the image to judge if the image quality is good enough for further processing, and if not, it ignores that image. This procedure we called "automatic selection of froth images". For any selected image, the global image processing algorithms are applied to extract global features of froth image, such as color, texture. Then the image is classified into different classes based on a rough estimation of bubble size distribution. After image classification, a bubble delineation algorithm is used for image segmentation-delineation of each individual bubble. Finally algorithms for image analysis are applied for calculating about 32 parameters for each individual bubble, such as moments, different kinds of sizes, shapes and textures.

The system hardware configuration is shown in Fig. 2, and the software working sequence is shown in Fig.3. The system has been tested in a laboratory for several months, and field for two short periods. The testing results show that the system works well for auto-image grabbing, image preprocessing, image classification, image segmentation and image analysis of froth bubble images.

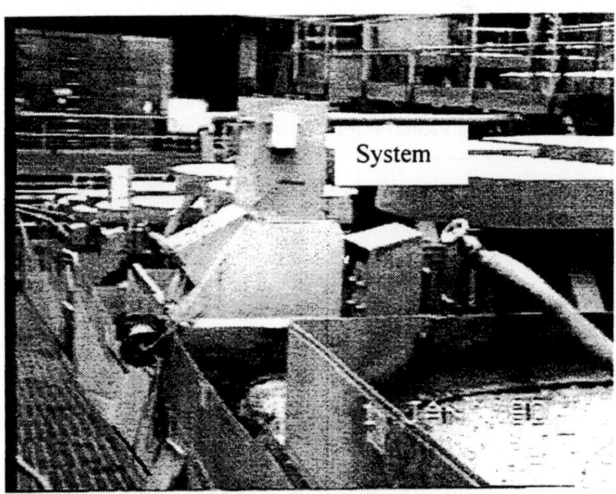

Fig. 1 Flotation plant and image system.

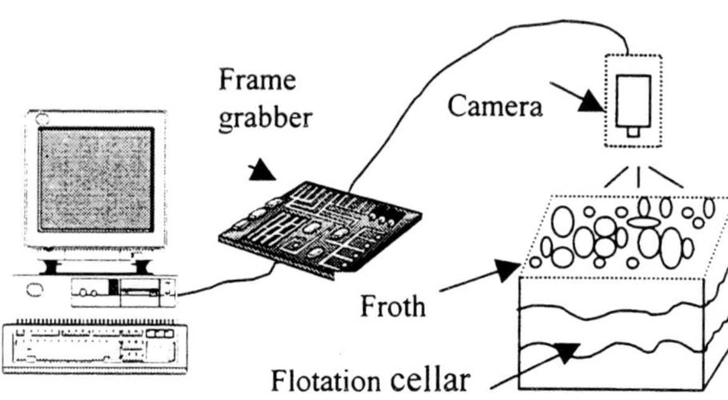
Frame
grabber
Camera
Froth
Flotation cellar

Fig. 2 On-line image system for the flotation bubbles in mineral processing.

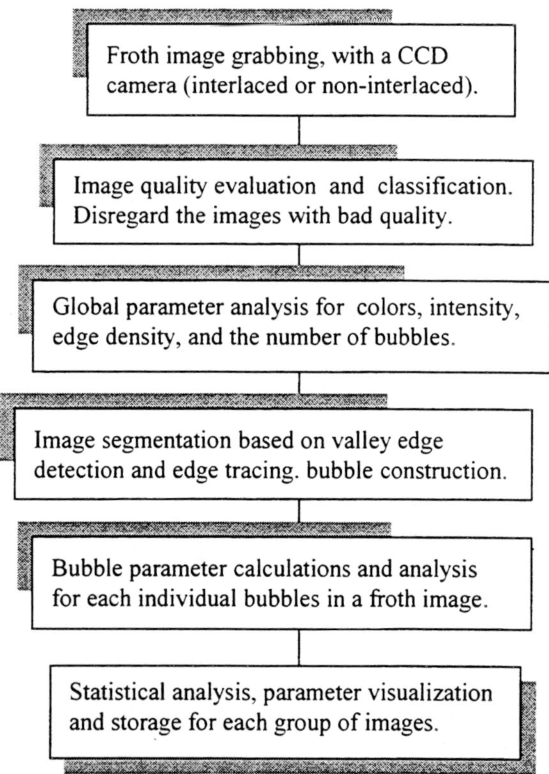
Froth image grabbing, with a CCD camera (interlaced or non-interlaced).
Image quality evaluation and classification. Disregard the images with bad quality.
Global parameter analysis for colors, intensity, edge density, and the number of bubbles.
Image segmentation based on valley edge detection and edge tracing. bubble construction.
Bubble parameter calculations and analysis for each individual bubbles in a froth image.
Statistical analysis, parameter visualization and storage for each group of images.

Fig. 3 Software work sequence for froth images.

3. Image evaluation and characterization

An image evaluation algorithm was developed for image segmentation. The algorithm evaluates image quality and outputs the information for the usage of image segmentation and classification. The output information includes global information of image color, intensity and texture, and local information such as object size, shape, surface smoothness, strength of gradient magnitude of the boundary of objects etc. The number of output parameters is almost up to 50. For the froth images, the evaluation results show that image color, intensity and texture vary on camera illumination system and type of minerals and slurry concentration. The bubble shape is convex, its surface is rough, and the gradient magnitude is low. The good aspect is that each of bubbles includes one white spot where gray value is much higher than other part of the bubble. Most of boundaries of bubbles are valley edges, which are important cues for froth image segmentation. For images taken from the same cellar over a time period, where illumination and mineral concentration are the same, the white spots can be used for image classification.

In order to detect the white spots, the algorithm applies the dynamic-optimal thresholding technique over the whole image to obtain the thresholding values for different regions. The size of the region is auto-decided by the algorithm based on the quality and resolution of the image. When the thresholding values are obtained, the thresholding value for each pixel of image is re-calculated. Finally, the gray level image is binarised and white spots distribution is obtained for the froth image classification. For most situations, larger white spots give large bubbles. From this, the algorithm calculates the size distribution of white spots, and from the size distribution of white spots, the average size of bubbles and the property of bubble size distribution are estimated. This algorithm can quickly detect the number of bubbles, average size of bubbles (weighted by area) and the property of bubble size distribution.

4. Image segmentation

The size, shape, texture and color of bubbles in a froth image is very important information for optimizing flotation. To determine these parameters, the bubbles in a froth image have to be delineated first. We have tested different existing segmentation algorithms, none of them works for the froth images, because of the special optical properties of bubbles. Due to the special characteristics of froth images and a large variation of froth image patterns and quality, it is difficult to use classical segmentation algorithms. Therefore, a new segmentation algorithm was developed to delineate every individual bubble in a froth image. All the functions or subroutines for image preprocessing and classification were developed based on the requirements of the developed froth image segmentation algorithm.

A new segmentation algorithm based on valley-edge detection and edge tracing has been developed. In order to detect bubble edges and omit the edges of the white spots, the algorithm just detects valley-edges between bubbles in the first step. It detects each image pixel to find if it is the lowest valley point in a certain direction. If it is, the pixel is marked as an edge candidate. Before this procedure, to alleviate noise, an image enhancement procedure was added for filter out the noise pixels.

After valley-edge detection, the majority of edges are marked at one time, but some small gaps between edges, and noise still exist in the image. To reduce the noise, a clean up procedure was developed. To fill the gaps, an edge tracing algorithm was applied, in which, edges are smoothed into one pixel width. Endpoints and their directions are detected, and edge tracing starts from the detected endpoints. When a new valley-edge pixel is found, the algorithm uses it as a new endpoint, and the valley-edge tracing procedure continues until a contour of a bubble is closed, examples of image segmentation are shown in Fig. 4.

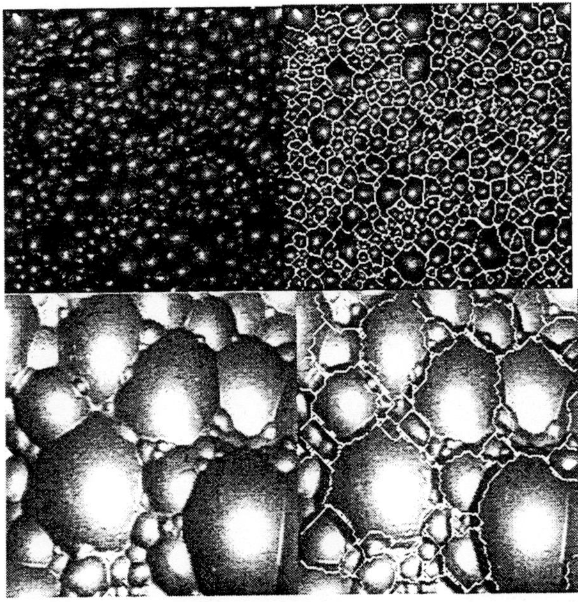

Fig.4 Image segmentation of froth images with small, and large bubbles.

5. Bubble analysis

After image segmentation based on boundary tracing segmentation algorithm, we need to analyze each bubble in a froth image. Based on the discussion with our partners, we have calculated 32 parameters for each bubble. Some of the parameters are listed in Table 1.

Table 1. List of 28 parameters for online system of bubbles

No.	Description
1	Area of bubble (unit: pixel)
2	X-center coordinate of bubble
3	Y-center coordinate of bubble
4	(Bubble area /its surrounding scanning box) * 100
5	The most left point on X scanning direction
6	The most top point on Y scanning direction
7	The most right point on X scanning direction
8	The most bottom point on Y scanning direction
9	Box width in X direction
10	Box height in Y direction
11	Box area
12	The ratio of a bubble area to its scanning box area
13	The second moment in X direction
14	The second moment for X and Y
15	The second moment in Y direction
16	The orientation of a bubble: Angle
17	The equivalent ellipse width
18	The equivalent ellipse length
19	Elongation of ellipse
20	Equivalent circle diameter
21	Width of minimum Ferret box
22	Length of minimum Ferret box
23	Elongation of Ferret box
24	Rectangularity of Ferret box
25	The perimeter of bubble
26	The maximum radii of bubble
27	The minimum radii of bubble
28	Roundness

In addition to the above parameters, we have also made subroutines or functions to calculate global parameters for each froth image, some of them are shown in Table 2.

Table 2. Global parameters for each froth image

No.	Description
1	Average intensity of a bubble
2	Standard deviation of intensity of a bubble
3	Average red color of a bubble
4	Standard deviation of red color of a bubble
5	Average green color of a bubble
6	Standard deviation of green color of a bubble
7	Average blue color of a bubble
8	Standard deviation of blue color of a bubble
9	Average edge intensity of a bubble
10	Standard deviation of edge intensity of a bubble
11	Average intensity on a bubble's boundary
12	Standard deviation of edge intensity of a bubble
13	The ratio: Red/ Blue
14	The ratio: Red / Green
15	The ratio: Green / Blue

6. Conclusions

In this study, an online system for froth images has been setup and tested in the field, and special algorithms for image processing and segmentation have been developed for froth images. The system works in real production. Additional work is needed for froth modeling which is of important for production control in mineral processing.

Acknowledgment

This paper is part of the EU project, Esprit LTR Project No. 24931, ChaCo at KTH, supported financially by the EU 4th Program. Thanks go to our project partners Boliden Mineral Company, Helsinki University of Technology and University of ROM for providing valuable help in system setup and testing of algorithms for image processing and analysis of froth images.

References

1. N. Sadr-Kazemi and J. J. Cilliers, 1997, An image processing algorithm for measurement of flotation froth bubble size and shape distributions, Mineral Engineering, Vol. 10, No. 10, pp. 1075-1083.
2. Symonds, P. J. And De Jager, G., 1992, A technique for automatically segmenting images of the surface froth structures that are prevalent in flotation cells. Proceedings of the 1992 South African Symposium on Communications and Signal Processing. University of Cape Town, Rondebosch, South Africa, 11 September, pp. 111-115.
3. Guarini, M., Cipriano, A., Soto, A. & Cuesalaga, A., 1995, Using image processing techniques to evaluate the quality of mineral flotation process. In Proceedings of the 6th International Conference on Signal Processing, Applications and Technology, Boston, October 24-25, pp. 1227-1231.
4. A. Cipriano, M. Guarini, R. Vidal, A. Soto etc., 1998, A real time visual sensor for supervision of flotation cells, Mineral Engineering, Vol. 11, No. 6, pp. 489-499.
5. W.X. Wang & O. Stephansson, 1999, A Robust Bubble Delineation Algorithm for Froth Images, The second International Conference on Intelligent Processing and Manufacturing of Materials, Hawaii July 10-15, pp. 471-476.
6. W.X. Wang & O. Stephansson, 1996, Automatic Selection of Fragment Images from A Moving Conveyor Belt, *Mining Engineering,* Vol. 48, No. 8, 83-88.

Shape Measurement and Sketching Systems for Porcelain Using Image Technology

Kazuhiko Shiranita* Kenichiro Hayashi* Akifumi Otsubo* and Ryuzo Takiyama**
**Industrial Technology Center of Saga Prefecture **Kyushu Institute of Design*
E-mail:shiranita@saga-itc.go.jp

Abstract

We developed a system for automatically sketching patterns on the surface of porcelain. The system consists of two parts – measurement for the three-dimensional (3-D) porcelain piece using slit lighting and automatic pattern sketching. Since we classified porcelain pieces into two types by shape, two 3-D measurements were developed. We propose calculating of 3-D coordinates simply and quickly. Sketching uses numerical control. Numerical control data for sketching patterns onto porcelain were generated using results measured by the measurement and CAD systems. Experimental results verified the system's effectiveness.

1. Introduction

Mechanization in the machinery and electronics industries has progressed rapidly, but lagged in industries such as porcelain, which remain dependent on manual labor and are strongly valued as traditional and industrial arts with high added value. The shortage of young skilled professionals in the porcelain industry now presents serious problems, however, calling for manufacturing techniques ensuring improved quality. Automated porcelain manufactures, especially techniques for sketching and painting patterns on porcelain, have long been awaited. To date, Morita and Watanabe[1] proposed sketching patterns on porcelain surface and sketch pen, using optical distance sensors. This is used to sketch on convex porcelain but not in cavities.

We propose a numerical control (NC) system for automatically sketching patterns on porcelain. Generally, NC data are generated by computer-aided design (CAD). In sketching, NC data is done using CAD as follows:

To obtain NC data, data on the shape of the porcelain sample must be input into CAD, requiring a yet unavailable system for measuring sample shapes. Section 2 proposes measuring porcelain sample shapes using 3-D slit lighting [2][3][4]. We propose highly accurate, fast measurement and dealing with dead angles.

NC data used to sketch patterns is effectively generated by CAD. Section 3 describes generating NC data using measurement results using the method in Section 2 and CAD and sketching driven by NC data. Section 4 generates NC data for sketching actual patterns and describes an experiment sketching on porcelain using NC data. Experimental results verify the system's effectiveness.

2. 3-D measurement

2.1. System configuration

Porcelain has different shapes broadly classified into two rotational such as vases and pots and flat such as plates and dishes. We propose two 3-D measurements for porcelain (Figs.1 and 2) – "rotational" and "flat". These measurements consist of a slit-light projector, two cameras, an image digitizer, a personal computer (PC), a rotation table and a X-Y table; measurement is as follows:

In rotational, the porcelain sample is set on the rotation table and slit light from the projector is projected to precisely overlap the rotation table axis. To measure the entire shape, the table is rotated. In flat, the porcelain sample is set under the X-Y table, and slit light from the projector fixed on the X-Y table Y-axis is projected onto the porcelain sample parallel to the Y-axis (Fig.2). To measure the entire sample in flat, the Y-axis of the table shifts along the X-axis.

Thus, in both systems, while fixing the relative position between two cameras and the projector, measurement is by scanning the set of two cameras and projector, or by rotating the porcelain sample. The rotation angle of the rotation table and the distance moved on the X-axis at a time are given by the PC.

For each rotational rotation and flat displacement, the corresponding image of the slit line is captured by the two cameras and fed to the PC as images quantified in 256×256 pixels with 64 gray levels using the image digitizer. If each rotational angle is 6° in rotational, 60 images are captured by each camera. As stated, an image consists of 256×256 pixels. The slit-line position in each of 256 horizontal scanning lines in rotational image and in each

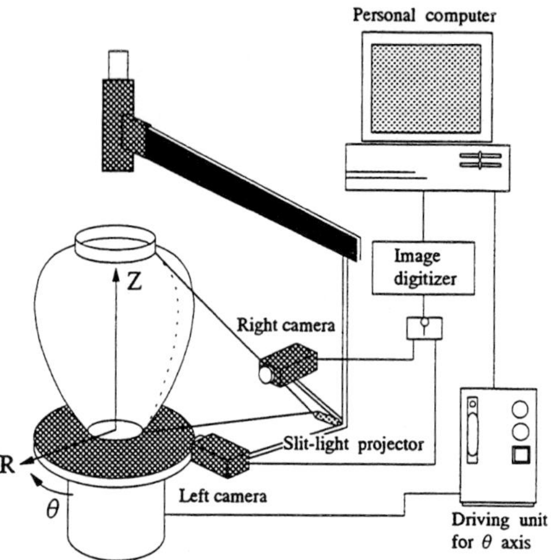

Fig.1. 3-D measurement (rotational).

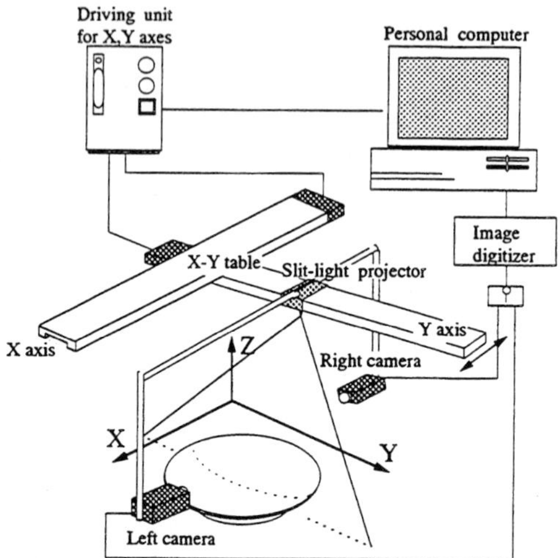

Fig.2. 3-D measurement (flat).

of 256 vertical scanning lines in the flat image are based on our calculated 3-D coordinates proposed below.

2.2. Calculation of 3-D coordinates

We calculated 3-D coordinates for rotational and flat (Figs.1 and 2) expressed in cylindrical coordinates (θ,R,Z) and in the rectangular coordinates (X,Y,Z) (Figs.3 and 4). 2-D coordinates of photographed planes are expressed as (U_L,V_L) and (U_R,V_R).

These measurements have a relatively constant position between the projector and cameras, with slit light projected parallel to the R-Z plane in rotational and parallel to the Y-Z plane in flat, and rotation angle θ and displacement along the X-axis timed by the PC.

Using these parameters, we propose simple, useful calculation of 3-D coordinates and equations representing the relation between camera coordinates (U,V) and 3-D coordinates (θ,R,Z), and the relation between (U,V) and 3-D coordinates (U,V,Z)

$$\left.\begin{array}{l}\Delta\theta = \text{constant} \\ R = f1(U,V) \\ Z = f2(U,V)\end{array}\right\} \quad (1)$$

$$\left.\begin{array}{l}\Delta X = \text{constant} \\ Y = f3(U,V) \\ Z = f4(U,V)\end{array}\right\} \quad (2)$$

In Eqs.(1) and (2), θ and X are calculated by the PC. R and Z in Eq.(1) and Y and Z in Eq.(2) are obtained from functions *f1*, *f2*, *f3* and *f4*. Since the lens actually is quite distorted, these functions must be revised based on the amount of distortion.

3-D coordinates are obtained as follows: a 10×10 (mm) grid pattern is set on the R-Z plane in rotational and the Y-Z plane in flat so origins coincide and photographed. We studied positions where known (R,Z) and (Y,Z) on the

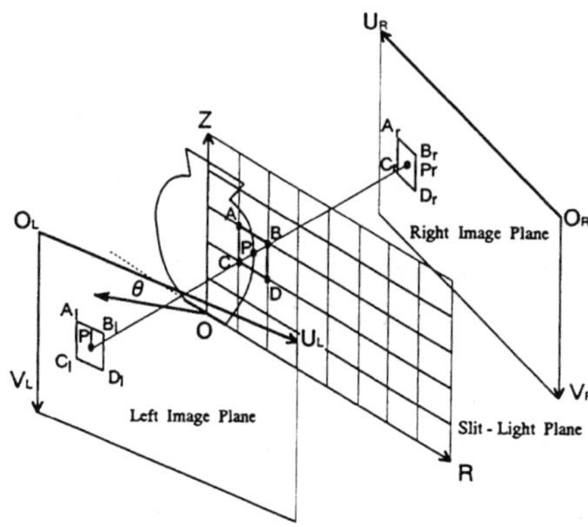

Fig.3. Relation between cylindrical coordinates (θ, R, Z) and camera coordinates (U,V).

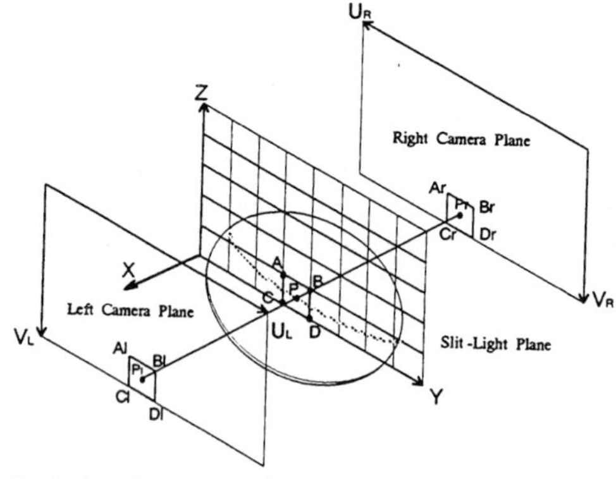

Fig.4. Relation between rectangular coordinates (X, Y, Z) and camera coordinates (U,V).

grid pattern are mapped on the (U,V) coordinates captured by cameras. We tabulate the relation between (U,V) and (R,Z) coordinates and (U,V) and (Y,Z) coordinates. With this table, we calculate (R,Z) of point P on the slit line (Fig.3): Point P is mapped to point P_l on the left camera plane (Fig.5). Point P_l is surrounded by grid points A_l, B_l, C_l and D_l. Vectors from camera origin O to points P_l, A_l,

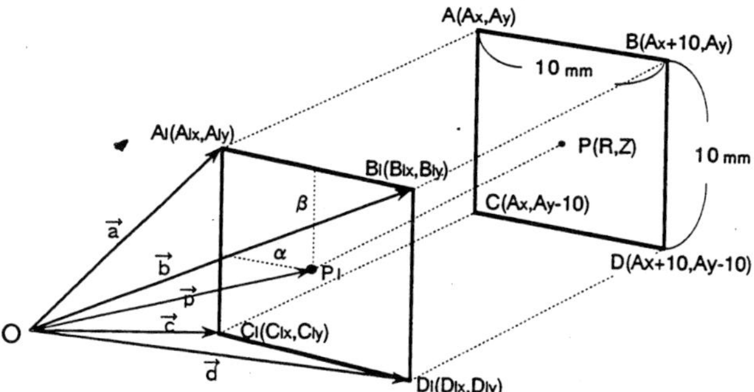

Fig.5. Vector expression of 2-D coordinates in left camera plane.

B_l, C_l, D_l are shown (Fig.5) and vector p defined as follows.

$$\vec{p} = (1-\alpha)(1-\beta)\vec{a} + \alpha(1-\beta)\vec{b} + (1-\alpha)\beta\vec{c} + \alpha\beta\vec{d}$$
$$(0 \le \alpha, \beta \le 1) \qquad (3)$$

α and β are obtained by solving Eq.(3) and R and Z expressed by Eqs.(4) and (5), using α and β.

$$R = A_x + 10\alpha \qquad (4)$$
$$Z = A_y - 10\beta \qquad (5)$$

3-D coordinates in rotational are calculated simply and quickly and, in flat, calculated similarly.

2.3. Dead angles

This section describes dealing with dead angles. We consider the case of point P on the slit line (Figs.3 and 4), captured by both cameras. Left camera results are used as 3-D coordinates of point P. If point P is captured only by the right camera, results camera are used.

We dealt with dead angles using an example in flat (Table 1) where they are represented with "?". We search from u_l=0 to u_l=255 to determine at which of u_l dead angles occur. When dead angles occur – "?" are found – we calculate 3-D coordinates of Y_l and Z_l at u_l and v_l, just before and after "?". In the table, just before Y_l is 99.3 and before Z_l is 22.2 as shown in ①, and just after Y_l is 104.8 and after Z_l is 19.1 as shown in ②. We search for Y_r and Z_r in the right camera with minimum Euclidean distances to ① and ②. In the table, these equal ③ and ④. Y_r and Z_r represented by "?" in the left camera are replaced by 3-D coordinates of Y_r and Z_r between ③ and ④, taking care of dead angles in the left camera.

In rotational, dead angles are dealt with as described above.

3. Sketching

This section describes sketching (Fig.6), consisting of 3-D CAD [5], a sketching machine with four axes (X, Y, Z, and θ axes), a NC program [6], a sketch pen fitted along the Z-axis, and a PC. Patterns are sketched on porcelain by NC. To generate NC data for sketching (Fig.7), the surface of the porcelain sample is measured as described above and results input to CAD. In CAD, using the measured results, 3-D spline curves are constructed by regarding points on slit lines as control points of 3-D spline curves. A curved surface of porcelain is constructed by regarding 3-D spline curves as control curves of a curved surface. Sketched patterns are input in advance to CAD and projected onto the 3-D constructed porcelain. The loci of these projected patterns are NC data. The sketching machine is driven by NC data, and patterns are sketched on the porcelain surface. NC data output by CAD are transformed to correspond to sketching machine coordinates. To sketch on a curved porcelain surface, X, Y, Z and θ axes are driven and to sketch on a flat porcelain surface, X, Y and Z axes are driven.

Table 1. Example dealing with dead angles in flat.

u_l	v_l	Y_l	Z_l (mm)	Y_r	Z_r (mm)	u_r	v_r
0	105.4	22.8	0.2	20,4	0.3	255	100.4
1	105.4	23.4	0.1	21.2	0.2	254	100.4
.	.	.	.	.	.	.	.
104	133.7	① 99.3	22.2	③ 99.4	22.0	151	128.6
105	?	?	?	100.2	22.0	150	128.6
106	?	?	?	101.0	22.0	149	128.5
107	?	?	?	101.7	22.0	148	128.5
108	?	?	?	102.5	21.7	147	128.2
109	?	?	?	103.2	20.5	146	126.7
110	?	?	?	104.0	19.9	145	125.9
111	130.0	②104.8	19.1	④104.9	19.0	144	124.9
.	.	.	.	.	.	.	.
254	105.3	199.8	0.3	198.4	0.4	1	100.3
255	105.3	200.9	0.4	199.2	0.2	0	100.3

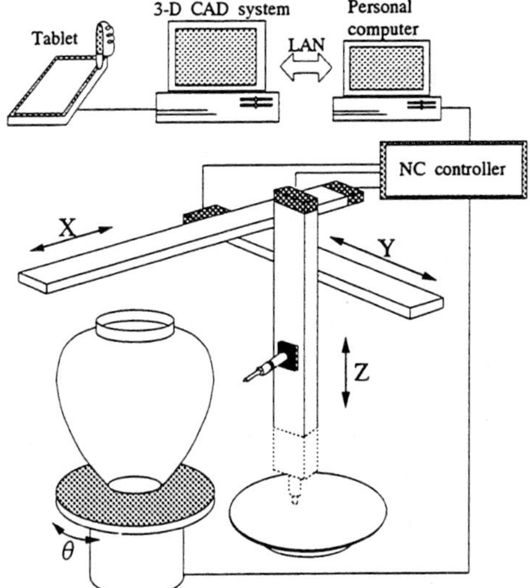

Fig.6. Sketching configuration.

4. Experimental results

4.1. Measurement accuracy

To determine measurement accuracy, we measured diameters of 6 different cylinders using rotational and flat (Table 2). In a visual field of 300 $\times$ 300 mm^2, measurement error was 0.6 mm in both measurements.

Table 2. Measurement results.

Source	Rotational		Flat	
	Result	Error	Result	Error
140.0	139.5	0.5	140.3	0.3
138.3	138.8	0.5	138.2	-0.1
137.6	137.5	-0.1	137.3	-0.3
136.7	137.2	0.5	136.9	0.2
135.2	135.6	0.4	135.8	0.6

4.2. Sketching

The sketching experiment used the sketching system we developed (Fig.6). Porcelain vase and plate shapes to be sketched were measured using rotational and flat described above. Comparison (Fig.8 and actual vase and plate) confirmed that shapes were measured accurately. Measurement time – from start measurement to display of results on the CRT – was about 10 seconds, mostly slit light projection. Time required for computing 3-D coordinates was 0.3s – extremely practical.

Measured data was input to CAD. NC data for sketching patterns on the porcelain vase and plate were generated, then sketching was done (Fig.9). Results confirm sketching of patterns on porcelain is equivalent to that of a skilled professional, with satisfactory measurement accuracy.

5. Conclusions

We proposed a system for automatically sketching patterns on porcelain. To implement sketching, we proposed sketching using NC data output by CAD. The system consisted of measurement and sketching. For measurement, we proposed measuring different sample shapes within a practical time frame using slit lighting. For sketching, we proposed sketching using NC. Experimental results showed the system sketched patterns in the same manner as a skilled professional. Thus, results verified the system's usefulness for sketching patterns on porcelain.

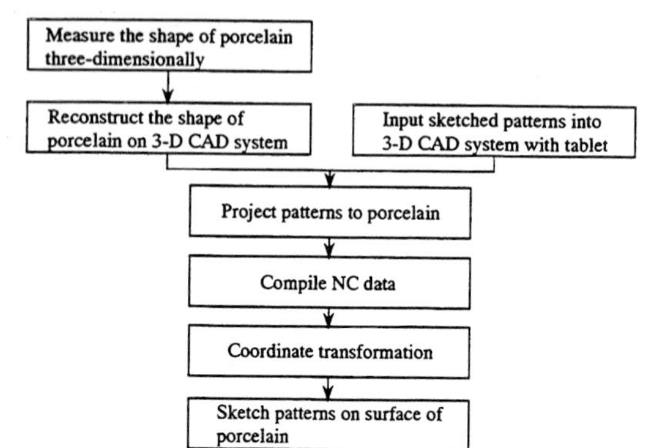

Fig.7. Process for sketching patterns on porcelain.

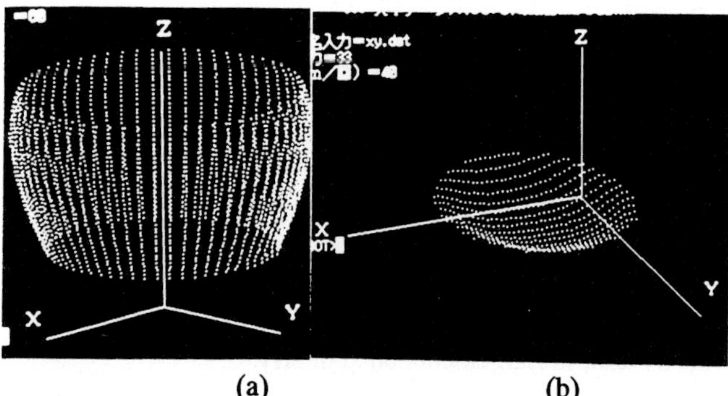

(a) (b)

Fig.8. Examples of the display of measured results: (a) vase and (b) plate.

Fig.9. Resultant sketches on the vase and plate.

6. References

[1] H. Morita and Y. Watanabe, "Sketching machine for porcelain", *Patent report of Japan*, 1989-313380, 1989, pp. 465-469.

[2] M. Gomi, T. Kawahara, K. Iketani, Y. Tsuda, and K.Sannomiya, "A 3-D scanner system for CAD", *Technical report of IEICE Japan*, PRU91-87, 1991, pp. 71-78.

[3] T. Ishimatsu, N. Taguchi, T. Ochiai, and T. Oohata, "Fast 3-D measuring technique using a look-up table", *Journal of JSME*, 57-538(c), 1991, pp. 179-183.

[4] S. Inokuchi, and K. Sato, *Three dimensional image measurement*, Shoukoudo, 1990.

[5] Toshiba Inc., *ANVIL-5000 users manual*, 1987.

[6] Karatsu Iron Inc., *NC-MATE-4 users manual*, 1990.

Textile Flaw Detection Using Optimal Gabor Filters

A. Bodnarova, M. Bennamoun and S. J. Latham

Space Centre for Satellite Navigation
Queensland University of Technology
GPO Box 2434, Brisbane 4001, QLD Australia
E-mail: a.bodnarova@student.qut.edu.au

Abstract

This study presents a new automatic and fast approach to design optimised Gabor filters for textile flaw detection applications. The defect detection problem is solved by using a semi-supervised approach. The aim is to automatically discriminate between "known" nondefective background textures and "unknown" defective textures. The parameters of the optimal 2-D Gabor filters are derived by constrained minimisation of a Fisher cost function. Such optimised Gabor filters are capable of detecting both, structural and tonal defects. This adaptable approach can detect a large variety of flaw types, while at the same time, accounting for their changing appearance in different texture backgrounds. When applied to a large database of textile fabrics, accurate detection with a low false alarm rate was achieved.

1. Introduction

In this work, we aim to design optimal 2-D Gabor filters for detecting defects in homogeneously textured woven fabrics. The 2-D Gabor filters have been successfully used in a large number of image analysis and computer vision applications. They are one of the most suitable and frequently used tools for texture boundary detection, texture image segmentation/discrimination and texture classification/recognition [2, 3, 6, 8, 10, 11] and have recently been applied to textile flaw detection [1, 4, 5].

The textile flaw detection problem, as viewed in this paper, has a *semi-supervised* nature. The *supervised* part implies that the background texture of the textile fabric is known a-priori. The detection part is *unsupervised*, because the types of defects that can be encountered in the process are not known. Consequently, the aim is to automatically discriminate between "known" non-defective background textures and "unknown" defective textures. By implicitly expecting certain shapes and orientations of defects, as addressed in the introduction of constraints in Section 2.4, many of the unanticipated defects can be detected. The optimisation process used for each of the constraints is outlined in Figure 1.

Optimised 2-D Gabor Algorithm

Optimal Gabor filters for the textile flaw detection task are designed by minimising a cost function using the mean and standard deviation of the filtered feature images, as detailed in Section 2. The cost function is based on the *Fisher criterion* (Section 2.3),

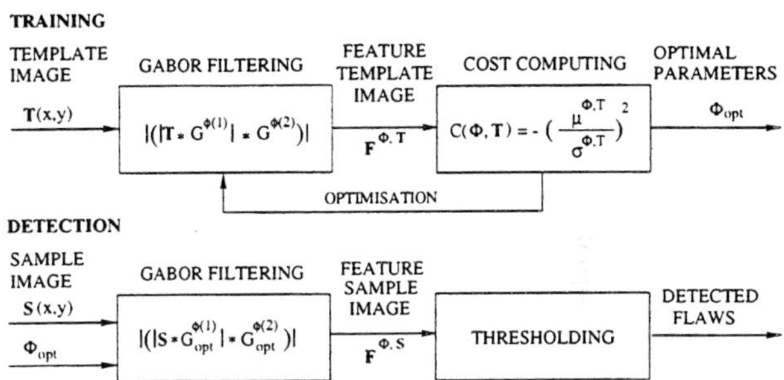

Figure 1. Optimised 2-D Gabor algorithm for each constraint.

which is frequently used in the pattern recognition literature [7] and has also been applied in supervised texture segmentation problems [9].

The Fisher cost function used in our textile flaw detection application optimises the Gabor filter parameters to detect a certain type of flaw as it appears in a particular texture background. For a given set of Gabor filters, this function is a measure of how well a particular filter maximises the mean energy of an image while at the same time having a good discriminatory behaviour. Parameters of each filter are minimised as a number of paired sets of 2-D Gabor filters, one effectively tuned to the background texture and the other used for smoothing, are applied to the unflawed template image. Statistical properties of the filtered template image are used to discriminate regions of flawed pixels in a defective sample image, as described in Section 3. Since the change in tonal properties of some classes of defects causes a shift of the feature image histogram mean intensity value, the median intensity value of the feature image is used for thresholding. Using this thresholding function optimised Gabor filters capable of detecting the *structural* and *tonal* defects are effectively designed. Thresholded results from each of the sets of optimal Gabor filters are combined to produce the final classification results. These results are presented in Section 4 followed by conclusions in Section 5.

2. Optimal Gabor Filters for Textile Flaw Detection

This section formulates a constrained minimisation problem, whose solution yields "optimal" defect detecting Gabor filters. Here, the word "optimal" refers to the notion that the flaw detecting Gabor filter parameters minimise a specific cost function as defined in Section 2.3.

2.1. Gabor Filtering of Images

The application of a Gabor Transform in image analysis is in the construction of a bank of Gabor filters. The impulse response of each of these filters in the spatial domain is a sinusoidal plane wave of a certain frequency and orientation modulated by a Gaussian envelope.

Filtering the image function $V(x,y)$ with the Gabor function $\mathcal{G}(x,y)$ is defined by the following convolution

$$\begin{aligned} H(x,y) &= V(x,y) * \mathcal{G}(x,y) \\ &= \int_{-\infty}^{\infty}\int_{-\infty}^{\infty} V(\alpha,\beta)\mathcal{G}(x-\alpha,y-\beta)\,d\alpha\,d\beta\,. \end{aligned}$$

A 2-D Gabor function centered at the (x,y) spatial coordinates can be expressed as

$$\begin{aligned} \mathcal{G}^{\phi}(x,y) &= \mathcal{G}(x,y,\sigma_x,\sigma_y,f_x,f_y,\theta) \\ &= e^{-\left(\left(\frac{X(x,y,\theta)}{\sigma_x}\right)^2+\left(\frac{Y(x,y,\theta)}{\sigma_y}\right)^2\right)} e^{i(f_x x+f_y y)}, \end{aligned} \tag{1}$$

where $\boldsymbol{\Phi} = (\sigma_x,\sigma_y,f_x,f_y,\theta)$ is the vector form of the five Gabor parameters and (X,Y) are the rotated (x,y) coordinates

$$\begin{aligned} X(x,y,\theta) &= x\cos(\theta) + y\sin(\theta), \\ Y(x,y,\theta) &= -x\sin(\theta) + y\cos(\theta). \end{aligned}$$

This Gabor function consists of a Gaussian envelope with spatial extent and bandwidth (σ_x,σ_y) and the major axes rotated by an angle θ about the z-axis, multiplied by a complex sinusoid centered at the 2-D frequency (f_x,f_y) and orientation $\gamma = \tan^{-1}(f_y/f_x)$. These parameter values control the orientation, radial frequency bandwidth and the centre frequency of the Gabor function. By varying the Gabor parameters, filters of different shapes, orientations and frequency characteristics can be designed, which aid in the detection of a wide variety of textile defects.

2.2. Feature Extraction

Textile images are filtered using Gabor filters so that instead of considering the intensity of an image pixel or its neighborhood, the local frequency response/energy is used to discriminate between a defective and a nondefective pixel. To determine the frequency response for each pixel in an image V, the image is convolved with Gabor filters in a two step process (see Figure 1). The symbols T and S in this figure denote the template and sample images respectively.

The first step is to convolve the image V with the real and imaginary parts of the Gabor filter and to take the absolute value of the resulting complex image elements to produce an intermediate feature matrix. This feature matrix characterises the frequency response, or energy, associated with the image V. Since the noise present in this image causes large variance in the element samples (we are interested in the mean frequency response for a particular texture), a second filtering step is performed in order to smooth the image. A second convolution uses another Gabor filter, which is a low pass/smoothing filter. The optimised Gabor filters tend to give a high response for unflawed textures, whereas their response for defective texture is usually low.

The feature matrix/image $F^{\Phi,V}$ associated with the image V and the parameters of two Gabor filters $\boldsymbol{\Phi} = \left(\phi^{(1)},\phi^{(2)}\right)$ are defined as

$$\boldsymbol{\Phi} = \left(f_x^{(1)},f_y^{(1)},\sigma_x^{(1)},\sigma_y^{(1)},\theta^{(1)},f_x^{(2)},f_y^{(2)},\sigma_x^{(2)},\sigma_y^{(2)},\theta^{(2)}\right),$$

$$F^{\Phi,V} = \left|\left(\left|V * \mathcal{G}^{\phi^{(1)}}\right| * \mathcal{G}^{\phi^{(2)}}\right)\right| \tag{2}$$

where the matrix norm $|\cdot|$ of a convolved image W is defined element by element as

$$|W|(x,y) = \sqrt{\mathcal{R}(W(x,y))^2 + \mathcal{I}(W(x,y))^2}.$$

Here, $\mathcal{R}(W)$ is the real part of W and $\mathcal{I}(W)$ is the imaginary part of W.

2.3. The Fisher discrimination cost function

The design of the optimal 2-D Gabor filters for textile flaw detection is here solved by constrained minimisation based on the *Fisher criterion*. This criterion has been frequently used in the two-texture supervised segmentation problems where the aim is to automatically discriminate between two "known" textures [9]. Given two texture samples $\mathcal{T}^{(1)}(x,y)$ and $\mathcal{T}^{(2)}(x,y)$, the following is computed to find φ which maximises the *Fisher function*:

$$F(\varphi) = \frac{\left(\mu_{\mathcal{T}^{(1)}} - \mu_{\mathcal{T}^{(2)}}\right)^2}{\sigma^2_{\mathcal{T}^{(1)}} + \sigma^2_{\mathcal{T}^{(2)}}}, \tag{3}$$

where $\mu_{\mathcal{T}^{(1)}}$ and $\mu_{\mathcal{T}^{(2)}}$ are the feature means and $\sigma^2_{\mathcal{T}^{(1)}}$ and $\sigma^2_{\mathcal{T}^{(2)}}$ are the feature variances of these two textures. The Fisher criterion for the two texture segmentation case measures the difference of two means normalised by the averaged variance [7]. This segmentation problem resembles the defect detection task based on the discrimination of "unknown" defective textures from a "known" non-defective texture background.

Given an $M \times N$ template textile image T, the *cost* associated with the parameters of our two Gabor filters, is defined as

$$C(\boldsymbol{\Phi},T) = -\left(\frac{\mu^{\Phi,T}}{\sigma^{\Phi,T}}\right)^2, \tag{4}$$

where the mean $\mu^{\Phi,T}$ and standard deviation $\sigma^{\Phi,T}$ are defined in terms of the $P \times Q$ feature matrix $F^{\Phi,T} = \left[f_{i,j}^{\Phi,T}\right]$ (defined in equation (2)),

$$\begin{aligned} \mu^{\Phi,T} &= \frac{1}{PQ}\sum_{i=1}^{P}\sum_{j=1}^{Q} f_{i,j}^{\Phi,T}, \\ \left(\sigma^{\Phi,T}\right)^2 &= \frac{1}{PQ-1}\sum_{i=1}^{P}\sum_{j=1}^{Q}\left(f_{i,j}^{\Phi,T} - \mu^{\Phi,T}\right)^2. \end{aligned}$$

For a given set of Gabor filter parameters, the cost function $C(\boldsymbol{\Phi},T)$ is a measure of how well a particular filter maximises the mean energy of an image ($\mu^{\Phi,T}$ of the feature pixels), while having good discriminatory behaviour as expressed in terms of a small variance $\sigma^{\Phi,T}$ of the feature pixels.

2.4. Constraints for detecting different flaw types

Our flaw detecting Gabor filters are optimal in that they detect both, the *structural* and *tonal* defects. *Structural* anomalies in the weaving patterns are caused by weaving errors or dirt, oil and colour contamination woven into the textural structure of the textile. When this pollution or a change of colour effects a large area of the woven textile, the tonal rather than structural properties of the background texture are altered and such defects are recognised as *tonal*.

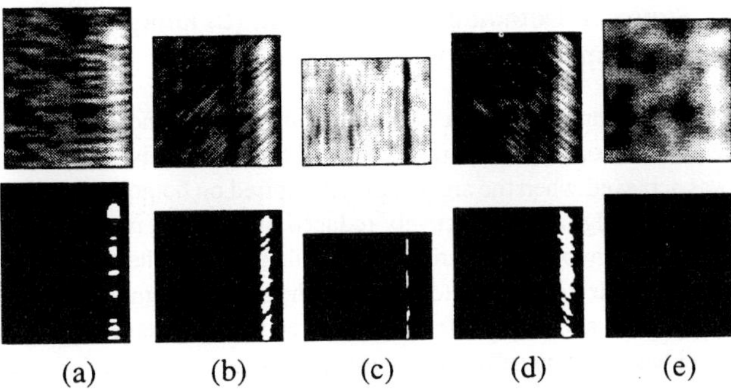

(a) (b) (c) (d) (e)

Figure 2. Warp float flaw filtered sample (top row) and detection (bottom row) images for each set of constraints.

By constraining some of the Gabor filter parameters to specific values, the filter is designed to detect flaws with known geometrical properties as they appear in a particular textile background. To account for the majority of flaw types, the optimal parameters for multiple sets of constraints are computed. Figure 1 shows the optimisation process used for each of these constraints.

The set of constraints consists of preset values for one orientation θ and one spatial extent σ_y parameter.

1. Orientation θ (see Figure 2) – as the majority of textile flaws appear in horizontal (a), vertical (c) and diagonal directions (b) and (d), only four θ values were considered.
2. Spatial extent σ_y – this parameter determines the "thickness" of the filter. In the first four Gabor filters (Figure 2 (a) - (d)), we preset the value of $\sigma_y = 1.5$ pixels for each of the four orientations, aiming to identify flaws which are 9 pixels thick (looking at the 3 σ_y each way from the median). The fifth Gabor filter (Figure 2 (e)) accounts for larger area or spot defects and is tuned to horizontal direction with the σ_y parameter equal to 4 pixels.

The minimisation of the cost function is performed with respect to the following six Gabor filter parameters: $f_x^{(1)}, f_y^{(1)}, \sigma_x^{(1)}, f_x^{(2)}, f_y^{(2)}, \sigma_x^{(2)}$ for each of the five sets of constraints. The optimal filter outputs for each set of equality constraints used for discriminating warp float defect (see Figure 5(a)) is presented in Figure 2.

3. Classification of Filtered Feature Images

The optimal 2-D Gabor filters derived by the algorithm are specifically geared towards the detection of flaws in woven textiles. Mean and standard deviation statistics of the template feature images, which were used to determine the parameters of the optimal filters, are also used to classify/threshold pixels from a sample

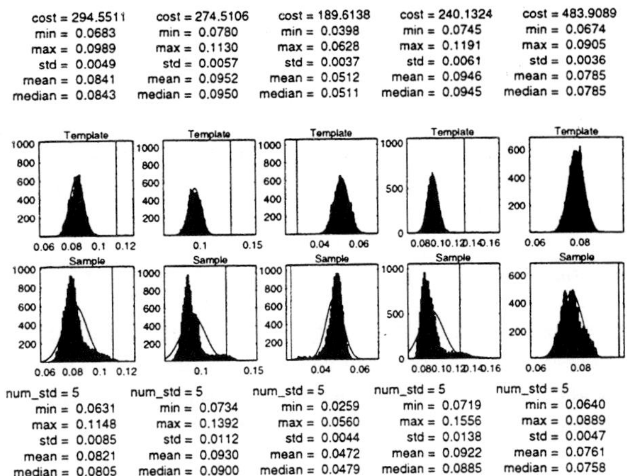

Figure 3. "Warp float" flaw histogram statistics.

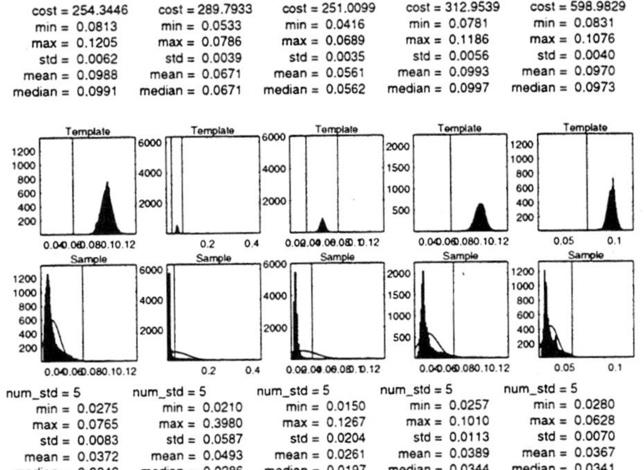

Figure 4. "Soiled end" flaw histogram statistics.

image. Each feature image contains information for discriminating a certain "type" of flaw using the pairs of optimised filters (i.e., one feature image per constraint set) . Since the change in tonal properties of some classes of defects causes the shift of the feature image histogram mean intensity value, the median intensity value of the feature image is used for thresholding. The discrimination/detection results from each of the different sets of optimal filters are combined using the union operator to produce a final classification result as can be seen in Figure 5.

Thresholding

The sample image is first filtered with the optimal Gabor filters, after which a thresholding based on the standard deviation of the template image is performed. A "distance to median" threshold is used to detect flaws in a sample image. Standard deviation $\sigma^{\Phi,T}$, number of standard deviations n_i (derived in Equation 5) and the confidence intervals of the means and standard deviation estimates are used to threshold away from the median intensity of the filtered image. The number of standard deviations is determined from the histogram "width" as follows:

$$n_i = \frac{\max_{i,j}\left(F_{i,j}^{\Phi,T}\right) - \min_{i,j}\left(F_{i,j}^{\Phi,T}\right)}{2\sigma_i^{\Phi,T}} + 1, \qquad (5)$$

where $max_{i,j}\left(F_{i,j}^{\Phi,T}\right)$ and $min_{i,j}\left(F_{i,j}^{\Phi,T}\right)$ are respectively the maximum and minimum intensity values of the template filtered feature image. This number of standard deviations on either side of the median intensity, considering the interval of confidence for the mean value $[med_{min} - med_{max}]$, is then used for the thresholding of the filtered sample image. The returned binary image is equal to 0 if

$$med_{min} - n_i\sigma^{\Phi,T} \leq F^{\Phi,T}(i,j) \leq med_{max} - n_i\sigma^{\Phi,T},$$

otherwise it is equal to 1. This thresholding function returns the classification of pixels in the image as defective (1) or non-defective (0). The thresholding based on Equation 5 results in a minimum of $n = 4$ standard deviations. Anything outside this range is most likely to be an outlier, which in the flaw detection case indicates a flawed texture. In order to eliminate some false alarms, the term "+1" was added to the n_i result.

Figures 3 and 4 provide the statistics of the filtered template (top half of the figures) and sample (bottom half of the figures) feature image histograms for each of the five sets of Gabor filters. In Figure 3 these filters were optimised to detect the warp float defect of Figure 5(c). The threshold is shown by the vertical line inside the sample and template images. To emphasise the importance of using the histogram median value, the sample feature image histograms for the soiled end defect, the example of which is shown in Figure 5(d), are provided in Figure 4. The soil end flaw is an example of a *tonal* defect, which can be effectively detectable only when the median value of these histograms is used. From examining the thresholding of the sample images it can be seen that the defective pixels appear five standard deviations from the median value of each distribution, or rather in the tail of these distributions.

4. Detection Results

The proposed optimised 2-D Gabor algorithm was evaluated using a database of homogeneous textile images. This database consisted of two sets of 25 woven textile images each. The non-defective template images comprised the first part of the set. Flawed samples with structural (Figure 5(a), (b)) and tonal (Figure 5(c), (d)) defects in the corresponding template backgrounds formed part of the second set. All images were of size 150x150 pixels (8 bit grey level range), acquired by scanning at 150 dots per inch resolution. The criteria of correct detection, good localisation and unique response to a single defect were used to assess the performance of the algorithm. The defects were correctly detected and localised in all 25 images. In four of these the detection was accompanied with a small false alarm rate (see Figure 5(c)). These false detections however, were always smaller than the detected defects and could easily be eliminated by an appropriate postprocessing (such as morphological operations). The results proved that our optimised 2-D Gabor filter selection delivers high detection rates and low false alarm rates.

5. Conclusions

This study has successfully solved the textile flaw detection problem by designing optimal 2-D Gabor filters. This solution is automatic and adaptable to the detection of a large variety of textile flaw types (both structural and tonal), while accounting for their

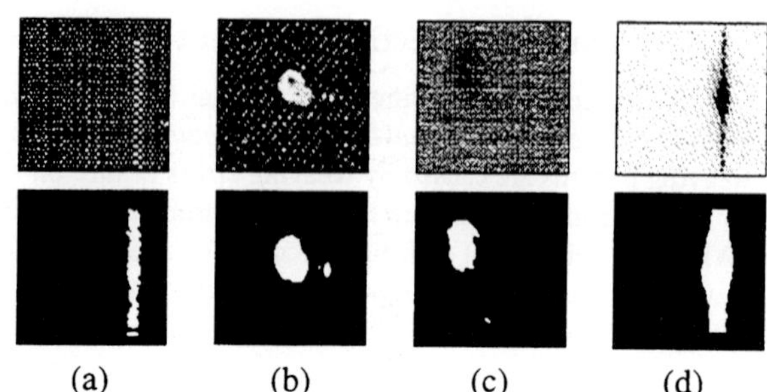

(a) (b) (c) (d)

Figure 5. Detected (a) warp float, (b) kinky filling, (c) oil spot and (d) soiled end defects.

changing appearance in different texture backgrounds. The detection rate of 100% accompanied with a very low false alarm rate was achieved when the algorithm was applied on homogenous textiles. The algorithm effectively reduced undesirable noise caused by the system or due to variation in textile designs. The constraints used in its design helped to eliminate the need for template image comparison and hence offered major practical advantages over the pixel based comparison techniques.

Acknowledgements

This study has been supported under the Strategic Partnerships with Industry Research and Training Scheme, of the Australian Research Council and the Department of Education, Training and Youth Affairs.

References

[1] A. Bodnarova, M. Bennamoun, and S. Latham. Flaw detection in jacquard fabrics using Gabor filters. In *SPIE Int. Symp.*, Boston, MA, USA, Sept. 1999.

[2] A. Bovik, M. Clark, and W. Geisler. Multichannel texture analysis using localised spatial filters. *IEEE Trans. on PAMI*, 12(1):55–72, January 1990.

[3] D. Dunn and E. Higgins. Optimal Gabor filters for texture segmenation. In *IEEE Transactions on Image Processing*, volume 4, pages 947–964, July 1995.

[4] J. Escofet, R. Navarro, M. Millán, and J. Pladellorens. Detection of local defects in textile webs using Gabor filters. *SPIE*, 2785:163–170, 1996.

[5] J. Escofet, R. Navarro, M. Millán, and J. Pladellorens. Detection of local defects in textile webs using Gabor filters. *Opt. Eng.*, 37(8):2297–2307, Aug. 1998.

[6] I. Fogel and D. Sagi. Gabor filters as texture discriminator. *Biological Cybernetics*, 61:103–113, 1989.

[7] K. Fukunaga. *Statistical Pattern Recognition.* Academic, New York, 2nd edition, 1990.

[8] A. Jain and F. Farrokhnia. Unsupervised texture segmentation using Gabor filters. *Pattern Recognition*, 24(12):1167–1186, 1991.

[9] T. Randen and J. Husøy. Texture segmentation using filters with optimized energy separation. *IEEE Transactions on Image Processing*, 8(4):571–582, 1999.

[10] A. Teuner, O. Pichler, and B. Hosticka. Unsupervised texture segmentation of images using tuned matched Gabor filters. *IEEE Trans. on Image Processing*, 4(6):863–870, June 1995.

[11] T. Weldon, W. Higgins, and D. Dunn. Efficient Gabor filter desing for texture segmenation. *Pattern Recognition*, 29(12):2005–2015, 1996.

A Two Stage Defect Recognition Method for Parquet Slab Grading

Hannu Kauppinen
Machine Vision and Media Processing Unit
Infotech Oulu, Department of Electrical Engineering
P.O.Box 4500, FIN-90014 University of Oulu
hannu.kauppinen@ee.oulu.fi

Abstract

This paper demonstrates the use of a simple but effective color-based inspection method in parquet slab grading. The approach is to divide the image to small rectangular regions and calculate color percentile features from these areas. Classification is performed in two stages: defect detection and recognition. The recognition results are further used in determining the final grade for the parquet slabs. Comparative results are also presented.

1. Introduction

In parquet slab grading, the grade of a slab is determined by measuring the sizes and the number of the defects, and the slab is assigned the best grade requirements it fulfills. The grading is performed on several grades depending on the parquet type, for example to the grades: classic, harmony, variation and fire wood, or prime, standard, flamy, extra flamy and fire wood.

However, human made grading seldom follows strict numerical rules, but is mostly based on observing the general visual appearance of the slabs. Important is also the ability to notice certain very small defects, like cracks or spots. Observation of the general visual appeareance is composed of defect shape and color observations and surface color and grain formation observation. Therefore, an approach not measuring the dimensions and locations of the defects, but rather creating an overview of the surface could be sufficient to this application.

A partner of the ESPRIT - P21023 (CATIE) project, Junckers Industrier A/S, Denmark, was interested in testing the wood inspection methods developed by University of Oulu (called the *UO method*) for the parquet slab defect recognition. They were developing a new slab grading line having automated grading based on color machine vision. Earlier, they have been using grey-level machine vision in collaboration with DTU, the Technical University of Denmark [1]. DTU was also participating the CATIE project, developing further their methods. From the comparisons of the methods of DTU and UO, Junckers established important information on the attainable defect recognition rates and grading accuracy, and also of the implementation complexity.

The requirements by Junckers Industrier A/S for the machine vision system are grading of 3 slabs (70 mm x 625 mm) per second, about 0.08 mm (transversal) x 0.36 mm (longitudinal) imaging resolution, and a grading accuracy better than 85%.

2. The inspection method

The UO method is a two-stage *non-segmenting* method using color histogram percentile features and *k*-NN classifiers, originally proposed in [2]. For more details of the method, see [3]. The non-segmenting method means 'segmentation' which does not try to decompose the image into meaningful regions, but makes the partitioning regardless of the contents of the image. In this experiment, the partitioning is made to non-overlapping rectangular regions of size 32x32 pixels. Features are calculated from each region and they are classified to relevant classes. Non-overlapping regions have been used by many researchers in wood surface inspection, for example, in [4], [5] and [6].

The first stage of the non-segmenting method performs defect detection and the second stage defect recognition. The defect detection stage classifies the rectangles into two classes: *good* and *suspicious* rectangles. The defect recognition classifies further the suspicious rectangles to the various defect categories.

The features used are RGB color histogram percentile features, described in details in [3]. The percentiles are calculated from a cumulative histogram $C_k(x)$, which is defined as a sum of the normalised histogram $P_k(x)$ of color channel k of all the values that are smaller than x or equal to x. Finding a value for a percentile feature is finding the x, when $C_k(x)$ is known, requiring an inverse function of $C_k(x)$. Let us denote the percentile feature value with $F_k(y)$, we get the relation

$$F_k(y) = C_k^{-1}(y) = x, \tag{1}$$

where y is a value of the cumulative histogram in the range [0%, 100%].

The feature vectors used in the classification are composed of selected sets of plain percentile features and differences of two percentile values either from the same color channel or from two different color channels.

3. Test setup

The method testing requires large amounts of manually labelled images. Color images were taken with line-scan cameras with several imaging arrangements during the project. One of the first imaging arrangements for demonstrating the achievable image quality with a 12-bit color line-scan camera is shown in Fig. 1.

Fig. 1. An experimental setup for taking high quality color images from parquet slabs (printed with permission from Junckers Industrier A/S).

The image set used consists of 150 images of beech wood slabs used for training and 360 images used for the grading test. The training areas were marked by creating *painted images*, where the pixels belonging to the selected training class are marked with colors by hand.

To evaluate the defect detection and recognition accuracy, rectangular samples were collected from the training areas marked in the painted images. The number of rectangular samples obtained from the training images was 26855, and their distribution to different classes can be seen from the *all samples* column in Table 1.

A set of 117 color percentile features was calculated for the training samples. A feature selection algorithm was used to find the best features for defect detection and recognition. To carry out feature selection, subsets of the training samples were taken in order to obtain a roughly equal number of samples for the classes to be separated. The number of samples for the subsets for defect detection and defect recognition best feature selection are shown in Table 1.

Table 1. The number of parquet training samples totally and in the subsets for best feature selection.

class	The number of samples		
	all samples	defect detection subset	defect recognition subset
Good_wood	16027	763	100
Sknot (sound knot)	430	47	107
Bknot (black knot)	102	51	102
Rpith (red pith)	788	49	112
Bpith (black pith)	380	47	95
Bark_pocket	392	49	98
Grain	1129	51	102
Streak	12	12	12
Crack	1009	50	100
Split	73	73	73
Lhydrolysis (light hydrolysis)	1542	51	102
Dhydrolysis (dark hydrolysis)	1632	49	102
Discoloration	1737	51	102
Lglucose (light glucose spot)	215	53	107
Dglucose (dark glucose spot)	574	52	95
Water_stain	813	50	101
TOTAL	26855	1498	1510

3.1. Defect detection

For the defect detection feature selection, the training subset contains roughly equal numbers of samples of *good wood* and of the group formed by all the defects together, as shown in Table 1.

The classification result of a defect detection test is shown in Fig. 2 in the form of a confusion matrix.

```
Training set samples 1498
Test set samples 26855
kNN classifier, k=3, 13 features

Total error is 3.53 %

            G
            o
            o
            d
            _    O
            w    T
            o    H
            o    E
            d    R    Error

Good_wood 15713   314    2.0 %
    OTHER   633 10195    5.8 %

UNKNOWN          -> Good_wood     0 of     0 samples (  0.00%)
Good_wood        -> Good_wood 15713 of 16027 samples ( 98.04%)
Sknot            -> Good_wood    77 of   430 samples ( 17.91%)
Bknot            -> Good_wood     0 of   102 samples (  0.00%)
Rpith            -> Good_wood     0 of   788 samples (  0.00%)
Bpith            -> Good_wood     0 of   380 samples (  0.00%)
Bark_pocket      -> Good_wood     0 of   392 samples (  0.00%)
Grain            -> Good_wood   343 of  1129 samples ( 30.38%)
Streak           -> Good_wood     0 of    12 samples (  0.00%)
Crack            -> Good_wood     4 of  1009 samples (  0.40%)
Split            -> Good_wood     0 of    73 samples (  0.00%)
Lhydrolysis      -> Good_wood    63 of  1542 samples (  4.09%)
Dhydrolysis      -> Good_wood     0 of  1632 samples (  0.00%)
Discoloration    -> Good_wood     2 of  1737 samples (  0.12%)
Lglucose         -> Good_wood    69 of   215 samples ( 32.09%)
Dglucose         -> Good_wood    72 of   574 samples ( 12.54%)
Water_stain      -> Good_wood     3 of   813 samples (  0.37%)
```

Fig. 2. Results of defect detection tests for the training material. A confusion matrix of good-defect classification, and a detailed listing of defects classified to *good wood.*

The classification was made as a two-class classification, *good wood* versus *all defects*, denoted with the class name *other*. The listing below the confusion matrix shows the number of misclassifications of each defect class to the *good wood* class, i.e., the error escapes.

In the classification, the defect detection subset was used as a training set, and *all samples* were used for testing. Because the training set is a subset of the test set, during the classification it has to be assured that the samples from the same image are never used at the same time in the training and test sets. This was achieved by removing the training samples originating from the same parquet slab image than the tested sample during classification of each sample. After classification, the removed training samples are returned to the training set, and the same check is performed for the next test sample to be classified.

The confusion matrix indicates that the false alarm rate, classification from good wood to other, is only 2.0 %. The error escape rate is larger, almost 6 %. However, more than half of the error escapes consists of areas manually labeled to the class *grain*, since *grain* is very close to the *good wood* color and properties. It is important, that the *cracks* and *splits* are very well detected.

3.2. Defect recognition

The subset of training samples for defect recognition best feature selection consists of roughly an equal number of samples from each defect class, as the last column of Table 1 shows. *Good wood* is also included in the training set to be able to classify some of the false alarms back to *good wood*.

The classification result of the 10509 (=314+10195) samples detected as defects at the previous stage is shown as a confusion matrix in Fig. 3.

Training set samples 1510
Test set samples 10509
kNN classifier, k=3, 15 features

Total error is 20.06 %

	UNKNOWN	Good_wood	Sknot	Bknot	Rpith	Bpith	Bark_pocket	Grain	Streak	Crack	Split	Lhydrolysis	Dhydrolysis	Discoloration	Lglucose	Dglucose	Water_stain	
UNKNOWN	.	.	.	.	.	.	.	.	.	.	.	.	.	.	.	.	.	0.0 %
Good_wood	.	35	41	.	2	.	.	112	.	.	.	4	.	.	83	35	2	88.9 %
Sknot	.	3	225	.	37	2	6	21	.	40	5	.	.	4	2	4	4	36.3 %
Bknot	.	.	.	69	.	2	26	1	.	2	.	.	2	.	.	.	.	32.4 %
Rpith	.	.	22	1	692	2	3	2	.	4	4	13	.	20	.	15	10	12.2 %
Bpith	.	1	.	2	1	272	20	.	5	13	31	14	2	15	4	.	.	28.4 %
Bark_pocket	.	.	1	77	.	54	242	2	.	7	1	.	2	6	.	.	.	38.3 %
Grain	.	9	59	.	11	8	.	601	2	7	4	13	.	24	33	15	.	23.5 %
Streak	.	.	.	.	.	2	.	3	6	1	.	.	.	.	.	.	.	50.0 %
Crack	.	.	31	22	10	30	5	13	3	772	41	22	27	11	6	4	8	23.2 %
Split	.	.	.	.	1	2	.	.	.	4	65	1	.	.	.	.	.	11.0 %
Lhydrolysis	.	1	.	.	27	3	.	14	.	1	.	1396	2	17	.	18	.	5.6 %
Dhydrolysis	.	.	.	17	5	7	33	.	.	7	1	45	1452	65	.	.	.	11.0 %
Discoloration	.	.	11	2	127	71	15	47	2	5	15	40	10	1375	2	8	5	20.7 %
Lglucose	.	1	.	.	.	.	.	.	.	.	.	.	.	.	115	30	.	21.2 %
Dglucose	.	.	.	.	9	.	.	1	.	1	.	.	.	.	89	393	9	21.7 %
Water_stain	.	.	10	3	13	.	.	1	1	9	.	2	.	2	19	59	691	14.7 %

Fig. 3. Results of defect recognition tests for the training material.

The confusion matrix shows that the overall correct recognition rate was about 80%. The worst cases are the remaining *good wood* samples, which are mostly confused with class *grain* and *glucose*. Not too many error escapes are caused at this stage. *Streak* has a relatively high error percentage, which is probably due to the small number of samples of this defect type. On the other hand, *splits* are well classified although their number is small too. Light and dark glucose spots (*lglucose* and *dglucose*) are mostly confused to each other.

Some recognition results are illustrated in Fig. 4. It can be seen, that there are some clearly correct recognitions, but also cases that are not. Because the purpose is to have an overview of the board for grading, it is possible that a very accurate recognition is not necessary.

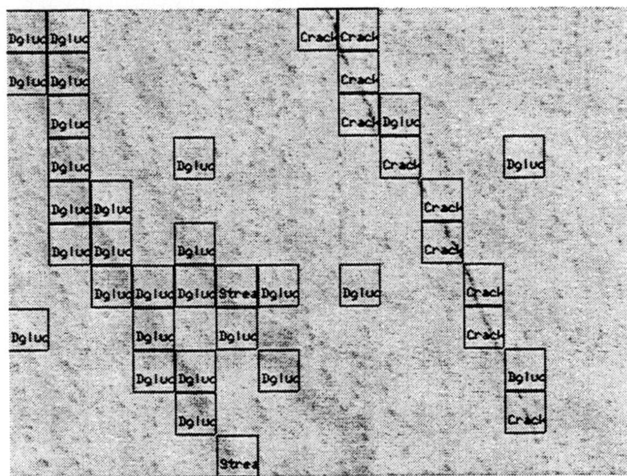

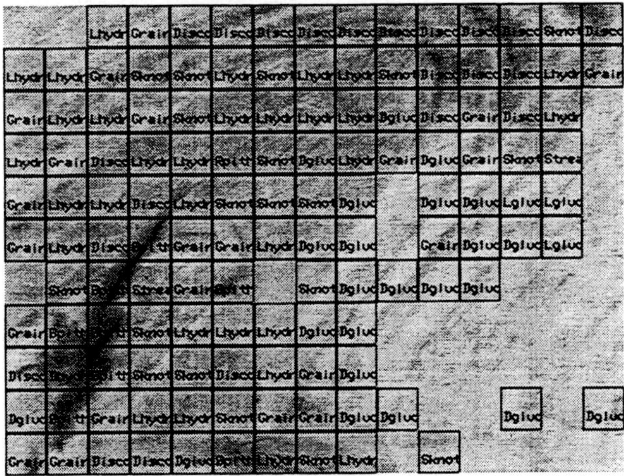

Fig. 4. Examples of the detected and recognized defects with the non-segmenting method.

However, on this level it is very difficult to evaluate how good grading accuracy can be achieved. It is very difficult to also compare the recognition results to the DTU method because of different approaches for recognition. Implementing a higher level grading algorithm that can accept the recognition results from both methods was necessary.

3.3. Parquet grading results

For the grading test, 360 images consisting 120 images from each of the three different grades, *classic*, *harmony* and *variation*, were used as the test material. Examples of the grades are illustrated in Fig. 5.

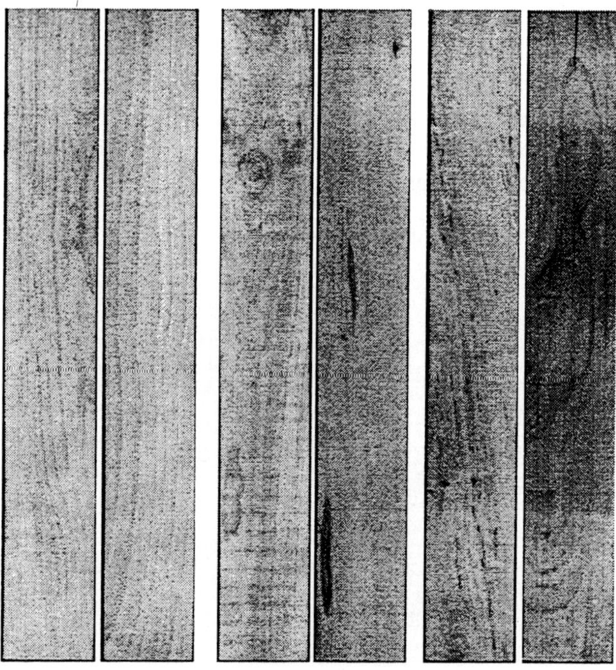

Fig. 5. Examples of parquet slab grades. The slab pairs from left to right: classic, harmony and variation.

The grading of the slabs is performed by a grading algorithm implemented by DTU. The grading tests for the recognition results of both the UO and DTU methods were performed by Junckers and DTU. The grading algorithm calculates the distribution of the different recognized defect classes on a parquet slab, and judges the grade using a CART (classification and regression tree) classifier. The grading results are presented as confusion matrices in Tables 2 and 3.

Table 2. Grading result with the DTU method.

		grade		
		classic	harmony	variation
grade	classic	87.0 %	11.0 %	2.0 %
	harmony	33.0 %	51.0 %	16.0 %
	variation	3.0 %	19.0 %	79.0 %

Table 3. Grading result with the UO method.

		grade		
		classic	harmony	variation
grade	classic	78.0 %	20.0 %	2.0 %
	harmony	22.0 %	58.0 %	20.0 %
	variation	0.0 %	22.0 %	78.0 %

There are only small differences between the results. The DTU method is better with the classic grade and the UO method with harmony grade. For further analysis, the effect of the misgradings to the value of each grade should be known.

4. Conclusions

This experiment shows the results of the non-segmenting method for parquet grading. Further, comparative results with a method from DTU were presented. The non-segmenting method was suitable for parquet defect recognition, because the locations of the defects are not very important in parquet sorting. The general appearance of a parquet slab is depicted by the distribution of the defects on which the slab grading is based on.

The performance level in the final grading was quite similar for the UO and DTU methods. Because of close collaboration between DTU and Junckers, the DTU method was selected to be implemented in the inspection system.

The images used in the experiments were of preliminary quality and much better results were obtained by DTU and Junckers in later tests with the final quality images.

5. Acknowledgments

The support of EU ESPRIT programme is gratefully acknowledged. Mr. Niels Schmidt from Junckers Industrier A/S and Mr. Johan Doré from Technical University of Denmark are thanked for providing the test material and comparative results.

6. References

[1] B.K. Ersbøll and K. Conradsen, "Automated grading of wood slabs: The development of a prototype system", *Industrial Metrology 2*, 1992, pp. 219-236.

[2] O. Silvén and H. Kauppinen, "Color vision based methodology for grading lumber", The 12th International Conference on Pattern Recognition, Jerusalem, Israel, 1994, pp. 787-790.

[3] H. Kauppinen, *Development of a color machine vision method for wood surface inspection*, dissertation, Oulu University Press, Oulu, 1999. Available in electronic format: http://herkules.oulu.fi/isbn9514254244

[4] R.W. Conners, C.W. McMillin, and R.E. Vasquez-Espinosa, "A prototype software system for locating and identifying surface defects in wood", 7th International Conference on Pattern Recognition, Montreal, Canada, 1984, pp. 416-419.

[5] P.J. Sobey and E.C. Semple, "Detection and sizing visual features in wood using tonal measures and a classification algorithm", *Pattern Recognition 22*, 1989, pp. 367-380.

[6] I. Yläkoski and A. Visa, "A two-stage classifier for wooden boards", 8th Scandinavian Conference on Image Analysis, Tromsø, Norway, 1993, pp. 637-641.

A Parallel Algorithm for Tracking of Segments in Noisy Edge Images

P.E. López-de-Teruel
Dpto. Ingeniería y Tecnología de Computadores

A. Ruiz
Dpto. Informática y Sistemas

J.M. García
Dpto. Ingeniería y Tecnología de Computadores

Universidad de Murcia, Campus de Espinardo, s/n
30080 Murcia (Spain)
E-mail: {pedroe,jmgarcia}@ditec.um.es, aruiz@dif.um.es

Abstract

We present a parallel implementation of a probabilistic algorithm for real time tracking of segments in noisy edge images. Given an initial solution –a set of segments that reasonably describe the input binary edge image–, the algorithm efficiently updates the parameters of these segments to track the movements of objects in the image in successive image frames. The proposed method is based on the EM algorithm –a technique for parameter estimation of statistical distributions in presence of incomplete data–, used here to estimate the parameters of a mixture density. The algorithm is highly susceptible of parallelization, because of the uncoupled nature of the computations needed on its main data structures. This property is exploited in order to make an efficient version for parallel distributed memory environments, under the message passing paradigm. We carefully describe the details of the implementation, and finally, we show an evaluation of the algorithm in a NOW (Network Of Workstations), using the standard Message Passing Interface (MPI) library. Our evaluation shows that the reached speedup is very close to the ideal optimum.

1. Introduction

Describing an edge image in terms of straight segments is a standard medium level processing technique in computer vision systems. Its main goal is to find some kind of elemental structure in the previously segmented image, as an intermediate step where further high level processing is needed, such as object recognition or extraction of 3D information.

Although finding segments is a basic problem treated in almost all generic machine vision references [2][5], most of the available methods are based in just two different approaches, namely, the *feature space transformation* methods, and the *aggregational* methods. *Feature space* techniques are based on the well-known Hough transform [4], where lines are expressed in some convenient parametric form, and a single transformation is applied to all the input edge points, each of them *voting* for an unique or a set of line candidates in the transformed parameter space. *Aggregational methods*, on the other side, try to group edge elements into extended boundaries by looking for contour lines, that are processed later to be piecewise approximated by segments [10]. In principle, both kind of techniques are thought for static images. So, to be applied in moving scenes, they have to start from scratch in each new frame.

In this paper we adopt a completely different approach to the task of segment finding, reformulating it as an statistical parameter estimation problem. The key idea is to deal with the binary input image (previously segmented in order to find edges of objects with any standard filtering technique) as a random sample of points in a bidimensional space, drawn from a probability density function that is modeled like a mixture of 'segment-like' elemental densities. Figure 1 shows the idea: The problem of segment detection is transformed into the problem of estimating the parameters of the mixture that most likely generated the corresponding input edge image. The EM algorithm [8] will be used for this task.

Our approach has several advantages over the traditional methods: First, the *dynamics of the model*: the algorithm is specially useful in the tracking of moving segments in a temporal sequence of images, using the previously obtained solution and the current input to obtain the new set of segments. Second, the ability to cope with *low-quality input edge images*, as noise points are, as we will see, explicitly contained in the probabilistic model. And finally, the susceptibility for massive *parallelization*, because of the regular nature of the computations performed by the algorithm.

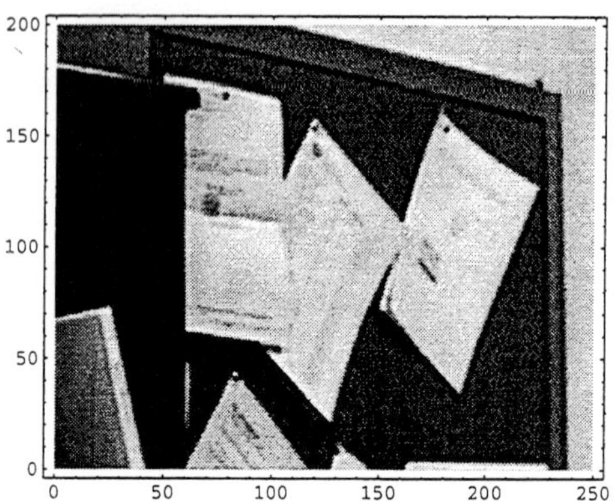

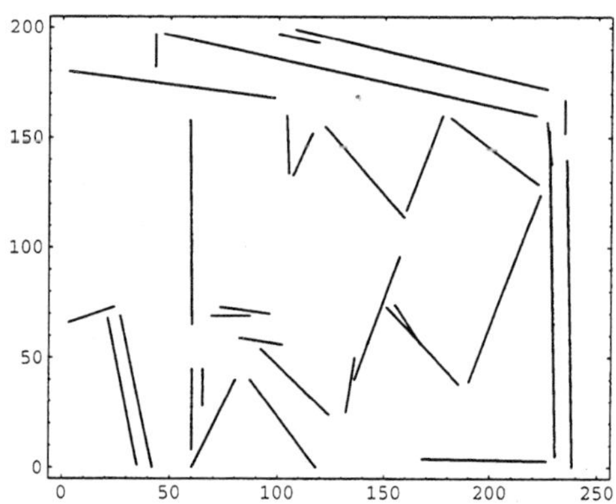

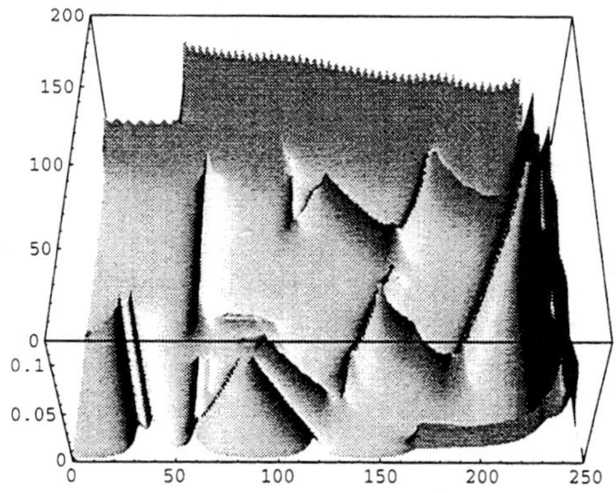

Figure 1. A sample image, a set of segments describing its edge points, and the corresponding mixture *pdf*.

2. Theoretical Foundations

As we have already stated, we use a probabilistic approach to estimate the parameters of the segments in a new image, given a prior solution and a new set of input points. The aim is to exploit the ability of EM of finding structure in data: Each point has influence in the calculation of each segment, but progressively, it is taken into account just for computing the component that most likely generated it, losing its influence on the calculus of the rest of components. In this section we describe the mathematical details of the adaptation of the EM algorithm to efficiently cope with segment tracking in noisy environments.

2.1. First Step: Weighted Assignation of Points to Segments

First of all, we need an elemental component of the mixture to model individual segments. To define the probability density function (*pdf*) of each component, we use a previous and straightforward definition of $d((x,y),S)$, the distance from a point (x,y) to a segment S: it will be the distance of the point to the nearest extreme of the segment, if the projection of (x,y) along the direction of S falls out of the segment, and simply the perpendicular distance of (x,y) to S otherwise. Using this previous definition, the following equation defines a proper *pdf* in the XY plane domain:

$$p\{(x,y)|S\} = \frac{1}{(d((x,y),S)+1)^3(\pi + L)} \tag{1}$$

where L is the length of S. It can be shown that the above function is defined over the whole domain $\Re^2$, it integrates to one, and it is inversely proportional in each point (x,y) to the distance of the point to the segment S.

Given the previous definition, we can compute the *a posteriori* probability q_{ie} that an input point (x_e, y_e) has been generated by a segment S_i. This is analogous to the E-step (*expectation step*) of the classic EM algorithm:

$$\begin{gathered} q_{ie}^{(t+1)} = p\{S_i^{(t)}|(x_e,y_e)^{(t+1)}\} = \\ \frac{P_i^{(t)} p\{(x_e,y_e)^{(t+1)}|S_i^{(t)}\}}{\sum_{j=1}^{N} P_j^{(t)} p\{(x_e,y_e)^{(t+1)}|S_j^{(t)}\}}, \\ \forall i \in \{1,\ldots,N\}, e \in \{1,\ldots,M^{(t+1)}\} \end{gathered} \tag{2}$$

Here, N is the number of segments, M is the number of points, and P_i is the *a priori* probability of each segment S_i. Values with superscript (t) correspond to the tth image in the sequence. Note that, here, N is fixed, but $M^{(t+1)}$, the number of input points, could change in time.

2.2. Second Step: The Adjustment of Segments

Now we can recompute the new extreme points of each segment S_i using all the input points (x_e, y_e), weighted by their probabilities q_{ie} of being part of such segment. In order to do it, we first compute the new *a priori* probability P_i, mean (row) vector $\vec{\mu}_i$, and covariance 2×2 matrix Σ_i

of each component. This is analogous to the M-step (*maximization step*) of the classic EM algorithm:

$$P_i^{(t+1)} = \frac{1}{M^{(t+1)}} \sum_{e=1}^{M^{(t+1)}} q_{ie}^{(t+1)} \quad (3)$$

$$\vec{\mu}_i^{(t+1)} = \frac{1}{M^{(t+1)} P_i^{(t+1)}} \sum_{e=1}^{M^{(t+1)}} q_{ie}^{(t+1)} (x_e, y_e) \quad (4)$$

$$\Sigma_i^{(t+1)} = \frac{1}{M^{(t+1)} P_i^{(t+1)}} \cdot$$

$$\sum_{e=1}^{M^{(t+1)}} q_{ie}^{(t+1)} ((x_e, y_e) - \vec{\mu}_i^{(t+1)})^T \cdot ((x_e, y_e) - \vec{\mu}_i^{(t+1)}) \quad (5)$$

$$\forall i \in \{1, \ldots, N\}$$

Now we can assume that the points in each segment present a strong correlation between x and y, as they should be straight segments. Then, we can calculate the main (i.e., major) eigenvalue, λ_{i1}, and the corresponding eigenvector $\vec{v}_{i1}$, of each covariance matrix Σ_i:

$$\lambda_{i1} = \max\{(\sigma_{11})_i + (\sigma_{22})_i \pm \sqrt{((\sigma_{11})_i + (\sigma_{22})_i)^2 - 4((\sigma_{11})_i(\sigma_{22})_i - (\sigma_{12})_i^2)}\} \quad (6)$$

$$\vec{v}_{i1} = (\frac{\lambda_{i1} - 2(\sigma_{22})_i}{2(\sigma_{12})_i}, 1) \quad (7)$$

These give us the direction of the segments. The minor eigenvalue in each component, λ_{i2}, corresponding to the other eigenvector $\vec{v}_{i2}$ (orthogonal to $\vec{v}_{i1}$), should be much smaller, and can be rejected (in fact, it would be zero in a perfect segment). Using the values of λ_{i1} and $\vec{v}_{i1}$, it is easy to compute the extreme points (x_{i1}, y_{i1}) and (x_{i2}, y_{i2}) for the segment S_i:

$$\{(x_{i1}, y_{i1}), (x_{i2}, y_{i2})\} = \mu_i \pm \sqrt{3\lambda_{i1}} \frac{\vec{v}_{i1}}{|\vec{v}_{i1}|} \quad (8)$$

In the above formulae, we assume that the projection of points into their corresponding segment are uniformly distributed along its direction $\vec{v}_{i1}$, and obviously centered in $\vec{\mu}_i$. Given that the eigenvalue λ_{i1} is exactly the variance of the sample points projected along that direction, and that the variance of an unidimensional uniform distribution in an interval of length L is $\frac{L^2}{12}$, it is straightforward to see that the length of the segment S_i is exactly $L = \sqrt{12\lambda_{i1}}$. Thus, we multiply $\frac{L}{2} = \sqrt{3\lambda_{i1}}$ by the normalized eigenvector $\frac{\vec{v}_{i1}}{|\vec{v}_{i1}|}$, and respectively subtract and add it to $\vec{\mu}_i$ in order to obtain the extremes of the segment.

2.3. Noise Treatment

Noise points are a problem in our approach. In most edge images, many spurious points appear, caused by noise in the sensor, textures, reflects, limitations of the filtering technique, and so on. If these points are not treated in a special way, they could drastically disturb the solutions, moving the segments away from their correct locations. To solve this problem, we introduce in the mixture an additional uniform bidimensional component to capture these noise points. That is, the mixture is not constituted only by the N elemental segment-like components, but also has an additional uniform component across the XY plane, with the same limits than the whole image frame. This component gives a constant *a priori* probability $p\{(x,y)|Noise\} = \alpha$ to each input point of having been produced by noise. The constant α can be modified in order to cope with different amounts of noise. The algorithm remains the same, except that now we have to compute a new $q_{N+1\,e}$ value for each point, the *a posteriori* probability that it has been generated by the uniform component. Empirical tests confirmed that the solution is satisfactory, with noise points being captured by the uniform component during the EM algorithm iteration, while aligned points were adequately tracked by the rest of segment-like components.

3. Improving the Performance: Parallelization of the Algorithm

In this section, we show how we take advantage of the symmetry in the involved computations in the EM algorithm for mixtures [7]. The first clear data parallelism can be found in the E-step: We can distribute the processing of the $p\{(x_e, y_e)|S_i\}$ and the subsequent q_{ie} values (eqs. (1) and (2)) matrix by input points, indexed by e. This distribution avoids the need for communications among processors in the normalizations needed by eq. (2). This solves the E-Step of the algorithm in an efficient way, at a minimal communication cost (only the segment parameters must be sent to all the processors; the input points can be partitioned among them).

A second source of parallelism can be exploited in the M-Step, when parameters of the mixture are recomputed using the q_{ie} matrix: Once that we have the q_{ie} values calculated, but distributed among the processors, we can compute the *intermediate parameters* P_{ip}, $\vec{\mu}_{ip}$ and Σ_{ip} for each component i on each processor p, but taking into account only the points assigned to the corresponding processor, using the eqs. (3), (4) and (5), conveniently modified as follows:

$$Parameter_{ip}^{(t+1)} = \frac{1}{\frac{M^{(t+1)}}{P} P_i^{(t+1)}} \sum_{e=(p-1)\frac{M^{(t+1)}}{P}+1}^{p\frac{M^{(t+1)}}{P}} \cdots, \quad (9)$$

$$\forall p \in \{1, \ldots, P\}$$

where p indexes the processors, from 1 to P (total number of available processors). Note that these computations can still be performed under the initial data distribution, without the need for additional communications. But, of course, what we need are the final values of P_i, $\vec{\mu}_i$ and (σ_i). So, to complete the M-Step, we have to gather the intermediate values obtained in (9) in all the processors, and using them, compute the final values. This is the second communication point of the algorithm, after the initial distribution:

$$P_i^{(t+1)} = \frac{1}{P} \sum_{p=1}^{P} P_{ip}^{(t+1)} \tag{10}$$

$$\vec{\mu}_i^{(t+1)} = \frac{1}{PP_i^{(t+1)}} \sum_{p=1}^{P} P_{ip}^{(t+1)} \vec{\mu}_{ip}^{(t+1)} \tag{11}$$

$$\Sigma_i^{(t+1)} = \frac{1}{PP_i^{(t+1)}} \sum_{p=1}^{P} P_{ip}^{(t+1)} (\Sigma_{ip}^{(t+1)} + \vec{\mu}_{ip}^{(t+1)T} \cdot \vec{\mu}_{ip}^{(t+1)}) \tag{12}$$

$$\forall i \in \{1, \ldots, N\}$$

Eqs. (10) and (11) are fairly straightforward, while eq. (12) uses the well known property that the total covariance of a set of subsamples is the mean of the covariances plus the covariance of the means of the subsamples.

For the sake of simplicity, we have supposed that $M^{(t+1)}$ is a multiple of P. But if this condition does not hold, the only change that must be made is to weight each intermediate value with its corresponding proportion of points assigned to that processor, i.e. $\frac{M_p^{(t+1)}}{M^{(t+1)}}$, instead of the value $\frac{1}{P}$, that appears in eqs. (10), (11) and (12), and $M_p^{(t+1)}$ instead of $\frac{M^{(t+1)}}{P}$ in eq. (9)[1].

In (10), (11) and (12), a new data partition can be done to take advantage of parallelism, in this case by segments, indexed by i. Each processor is assigned a subset of segments $i = (p-1)\frac{N}{P}, \ldots p\frac{N}{P}$. We can also compute this way the extremes of the segments, using eqs. (6), (7), and (8). The final results have to be broadcasted again to all the processors, to begin with the next iteration. This is the third and last communication point of the parallel algorithm.

Figure 2 shows in pseudo-code the *message-passing* program for segment detection and tracking, in which the three communication points are emphasized. In fact, we have centered the discussion in the inner loop, corresponding to EM iteration (tracking of segments). If the noise component grows too much, then perhaps there are new objects in the scene, or some old ones have disappeared, and the current number of segments may have became inadequate. In this case, we have to reinitialize the solution with the external detection algorithm.

Input: *(Array of changing M sample points)*
(x_e, y_e), for $e = 1, \ldots, M$.
Output: *(Array of changing N segments)*
$((x_{i1}, y_{i1}), (x_{i2}, y_{i2}))$, for $i = 1, \ldots, N$.

Main Iteration: *(Infinite Loop)*
Repeat
Input: *(From Lower Levels of the Vision System)*
·Read current list of edge points (x_e, y_e), for $e = 1, \ldots, M$.
Initialization: *(Segment Detection)*
·Compute an initial solution $((x_{i1}, y_{i1}), (x_{i2}, y_{i2}))$, for $i = 1, \ldots, N$, with some standard (possibly parallel) algorithm (i.e. Hough).
·Assign $P_i := \frac{1}{N+1}$, for $i = 1, \ldots, N+1$.
EM Iteration: *(Segment Tracking)*
Repeat
Process 0:
Input: *(From Lower Levels of the Vision System)*
·Read current list of edge points (x_e, y_e), for $e = 1, \ldots, M$.
Data Distribution: *(First Communication Point)*
·Send points (x_e, y_e), $e = ((p-1)\frac{M}{P} + 1, \ldots, p\frac{M}{P})$ to respective processors p, for $p = 1, \ldots, P$
·Broadcast $((x_{i1}, y_{i1}), (x_{i2}, y_{i2}))$, for $i = 1, \ldots, N$, and P_i, for $i = 1, \ldots, N+1$, to all P processors.
For all processes $p = 1, \ldots, P$**:**
E step: *(Q Matrix Computation)*
·Compute $p\{(x_e, y_e)|S_i\}$, for $i = 1, \ldots, N+1$, and $e = ((p-1)\frac{M}{P} + 1, \ldots, p\frac{M}{P})$, using eqs. (1) and $p\{(x_e, y_e)|S_i\} = \alpha$ (for $i = N+1$).
·Compute q_{ie}, for $i = 1, \ldots, N+1$, and $e = ((p-1)\frac{M}{P} + 1, \ldots, p\frac{M}{P})$, using eq. (2).
M1 step: *(Intermediate Parameters Computation)*
·Compute P_{ip}, $\vec{\mu}_{ip}$, and Σ_{ip}, for $i = 1, \ldots, N$, using eqs. (3), (4) and (5), but adapted to the corresponding subset of points by eq. (9).
Intermediate Gathering: *(Second Communication Point)*
·Gather $P_{ip'}$, $\vec{\mu}_{ip'}$, and $\Sigma_{ip'}$ from the rest of processes $p' = 1, \ldots, P, p' \neq p$.
M2 step: *(Final Parameters Computation)*
·Compute P_i, $\vec{\mu}_i$, and Σ_i, for $i = (p-1)\frac{N}{P} + 1, \ldots, (p)\frac{N}{P}$, using eqs. (10), (11) and (12).
·Compute $((x_{i1}, y_{i1}), (x_{i2}, y_{i2}))$, for $i = (p-1)\frac{N}{P} + 1, \ldots, p\frac{N}{P}$, for $i = 1, \ldots, N$, using eqs. (6), (7), and (8).
Process 0:
Segments Gathering: *(Third Communication Point)*
·Gather $((x_{i1}, y_{i1}), (x_{i2}, y_{i2}))$, for $i = 1, \ldots, N$ and P_i $\forall i = 1, \ldots, N+1$.
Output: *(To Upper Levels of the Vision System)*
(... Use output in higher levels...)
Until $P_{N+1} > Threshold$.
Until FALSE

Figure 2. Parallel message passing algorithm for segment tracking (pseudo-code).

4. Evaluation

We conclude with some performance results obtained executing an MPI implementation [7] of our proposed parallel algorithm in a cluster of workstations [1]. The cluster had the following technical characteristics: Pentium MMX 200 MHz, 256 KB cache, 64 MB RAM nodes, communicated by a Fast Ethernet 3Com 100 Mbps, and MPICH 1.0.13 for Linux as the MPI library [3] implementation.

Figure 3 shows the processing times *vs* the number of processors for several problem sizes $M \times N$, after 100

[1]Of course, $M_p^{(t+1)}$ is the number of input points assigned to processor p, usually $\lfloor \frac{M^{(t+1)}}{P} \rfloor + 1$ for processors $p = 1, \ldots, M^{(t+1)} \bmod P$ and $\lfloor \frac{M^{(t+1)}}{P} \rfloor$ for processor $p = M^{(t+1)} \bmod P + 1, \ldots, P$. This is the assignation of points that presents a better load balancing, assumed that the P processors are identical.

iterations of E and M steps. The reduction in execution time as we increment the number of workstations participating in the computation (P) is very promising: The reached speedups are not very far from the ideal optimum P. The implementation, therefore, shows to be highly scalable, mainly due to the reductions performed in the size of communications, and the symmetric distribution of the computations (good *load balancing*). Using the 7 processors simultaneously, up to 5 frames per second were processed for images with $M = 2000$ edge points and $N = 50$ segments, typical values for usual image sizes. Of course, the higher the values of M and N, the less the frames per second that the system was capable to process, but, also, the better the reached *speedup*. This is mainly due to the fact that, as we increase the size of the problem, the increment in the quantity of parallel computations is more important than the increment in the size of communications, the traditional bottleneck in NOWs.

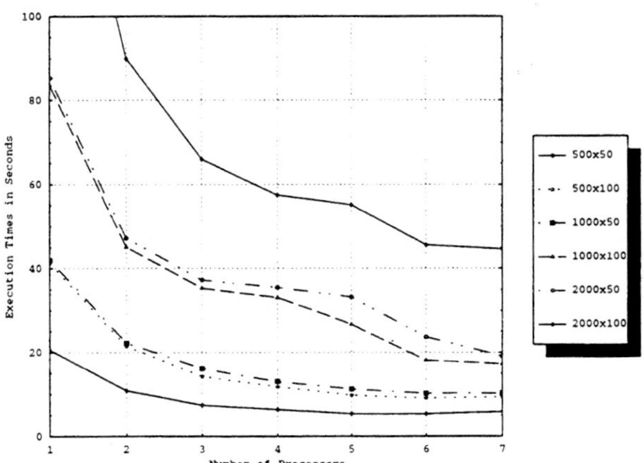

Figure 3. Performance measures for 100 EM iterations on several (N, M) input values.

5. Conclusions

In this paper, we have presented an innovative parallel algorithm to track segments in real time computer vision environments, using a probabilistic technique. We have also shown how it can be efficiently implemented in distributed memory parallel machines. The algorithm shows very good results in both speedup and scalability, as it takes advantage of a careful load balancing and minimization of communications. As a result, for small/medium image sizes, the number of frames per seconds that can be processed allows for real time application in tracking of moving scenes.

The technique is specially appropriate for clusters of PCs, where the shared communication medium does not suppose a severe bottleneck [9]. In these clusters, very good performance/cost ratios can be achieved if the parallel algorithms are specifically designed for those distributed memory environments [6]. This suggests the interesting possibility of using this kind of parallel machines in computer vision, with standard PCI image acquisition cards. In this way, we can significantly improve the overall processing speed of our computer vision system, obtaining an interesting performance/cost ratio, and real-time processing of moving scenes.

6. Acknowledgements

This work has been partially supported by the Spanish CICYT under grants TIC97-0897-C04-02 and TIC98-0559.

References

[1] T. Anderson, D. Culler, and D. Patterson. A case for NOW. *IEEE Micro*, 15(1):55–64, 1999.

[2] E. Davids. *Machine Vision, 2nd Edition*. McGraw-Hill, 1997.

[3] W. Gropp, E. Lusk, and A. Skjellum. *Using MPI: Portable Parallel Programming with the Message Passing Interface*. MIT Press, 1994.

[4] P. Hough. Methods and means for recognising complex patterns. *U.S. Patent 3 069 654*, 1962.

[5] R. Jain, R. Kasturi, and B. Schunk. *Machine Vision*. McGraw-Hill, 1995.

[6] B. Lester. *The Art of Parallel Programming*. Prentice Hall, 1993.

[7] P. López-de-Teruel, J. García, and M. Acacio. The parallel EM algorithm and its applications in computer vision. *Proceedings of the PDPTA'99, CSREA Press*, 1999.

[8] G. McLachlan and T. Krishnan. *The EM Algorithm and Extensions*. John Wiley and Sons, 1997.

[9] J. Piernas, A. Flores, and J. García. Analyzing the performance of MPI in a cluster of workstations based on fast ethernet. 4th *European PVM/MPI Users' Group Meeting. Lecture Notes in Computer Science*, 1332:17–24, 1997.

[10] P. Rosin. Techniques for assesing polygonal approximation of curves. *IEEE Transactions on Pattern Analysis and Machine Intelligence*, 19:659–666, 1997.

A Weighted Distance Approach to Relevance Feedback

Selim Aksoy, Robert M. Haralick
Intelligent Systems Laboratory
University of Washington
Seattle, WA 98195-2500 USA

Faouzi A. Cheikh, Moncef Gabbouj
Signal Processing Laboratory
Tampere University of Technology
P.O. Box 553, FIN-33101 Tampere, Finland

Abstract

Content-based image retrieval systems use low-level features like color and texture for image representation. Given these representations as feature vectors, similarity between images is measured by computing distances in the feature space. Unfortunately, these low-level features cannot always capture the high-level concept of similarity in human perception. Relevance feedback tries to improve the performance by allowing iterative retrievals where the feedback information from the user is incorporated into the database search. We present a weighted distance approach where the weights are the ratios of standard deviations of the feature values both for the whole database and also among the images selected as relevant by the user. The feedback is used for both independent and incremental updating of the weights and these weights are used to iteratively refine the effects of different features in the database search. Retrieval performance is evaluated using average precision *and* progress *that are computed on a database of approximately 10,000 images and an average performance improvement of 19% is obtained after the first iteration.*

1. Introduction

Image retrieval has received significant attention in recent years. Initial work on content-based retrieval focused on using low-level features like color and texture for image representation. After each image is associated with a feature vector, similarity between images is measured by computing distances between feature vectors in the feature space. It is generally assumed that the features are able to locate visually similar images close to each other in the feature space so that non-parametric approaches, like the k-nearest neighbor search, can be used for retrieval.

Unfortunately, none of the existing feature extraction algorithms can always map visually similar images to nearby locations. A common observation in retrieval results is that sometimes images that are quite irrelevant to the query image are also retrieved simply because they are close to it in the feature space. Therefore, post-processing methods [2] are usually required to improve the results.

The high-level concept of similarity and subjectivity in human perception cannot always be captured by the low-level features. To make the user have more control on the search criteria, some systems allowed the user to weight the features [9, 3]. This is not generally applicable because the ordinary user does not usually have a detailed understanding of the low-level features designed by an expert.

Recently, relevance feedback has been the most commonly applied post-processing technique. The main idea is to include the human user in the retrieval loop. An initial search is done in the database using the original query image input by the user. Upon being presented the results of this search, the user labels some of the these images as relevant and irrelevant according to his/her information needs. The goal is to incorporate this feedback information into the database search in terms of iterative retrievals.

A common approach for relevance feedback in image databases has been to use the ideas that were developed in the information retrieval literature [12]. A commonly used technique has been the vector space model where a new query feature vector is generated as a weighted linear combination of the original feature vector and the feature vectors of the images that were labeled as relevant or irrelevant by the user [12, 6]. Other approaches include using keywords [8], creating a probabilistic user model [7], modifying the distance measure [4], reorganizing the retrieval results [5], feature density estimation [10], and iterative weight updating [13, 11].

Retrieval algorithms depend on features directly computed from images. We want to use only the information fed back by the user instead of using artificial keywords or heuristic assumptions. We also cannot assume anything about the user's information need, neither can we assume any distributions for the relevancy and irrelevancy he/she is looking for. Therefore, we decided to weight the automatically computed features in the k-nearest neighbor search according to user's responses. The ratios of standard deviations of the feature values both for the whole database and also among the images selected as relevant by the user are used in both independent and incremental updating of the weights.

Experiments were done on a database of approximately 10,000 images and the retrieval performance was evaluated using average *precision* computed for a manually groundtruthed data set. We also defined a new measure called *progress* to measure the performance. The following section describes the motivation and details of our weighted distance approach. Section 3 presents the experiments and discusses the results. Conclusions are given in Section 4.

2. The Weighted Distance Approach

2.1. Definitions

First, we present some definitions that will be used in the following sections.

K: Number of iterative searches.

Q: Number of features in a feature vector.

R^k= {retrieval set after the k'th search}, $k = 0, \ldots, K$, while R^0 being the whole database.

R^k_{rel}= {set of images in R^k that are marked as relevant}.

F^k_j= {values of the j'th feature components of the images in R^k}.

$F^k_{\text{rel},j}$= {values of the j'th feature components of the images in R^k_{rel}}.

In our retrieval scenario, similarity between images is measured by computing distances between feature vectors in the feature space. Given two feature vectors x and y and the weight vector w, we use the weighted L_1 distance

$$\rho(x, y; w) = \sum_{j=1}^{Q} |w_j(x_j - y_j)| \tag{1}$$

and the weighted L_2 distance

$$\rho(x, y; w) = \left(\sum_{j=1}^{Q} |w_j(x_j - y_j)|^2 \right)^{1/2} . \tag{2}$$

2.2. Motivation

From the pattern recognition point of view, for a feature to be good, its variance among all the images in the database should be large but its variance among the relevant images should be small. Any one of these is not enough alone but characterizes a good feature when combined with the other.

Given these observations, we decided to use $w^k_j = \sigma^0_j / \sigma^k_{\text{rel},j}$, where $\sigma^0_j = \text{std}(F^0_j)$ and $\sigma^k_{\text{rel},j} = \text{std}(F^k_{\text{rel},j})$, as the weight for the j'th feature in the $k+1$'st iteration. For a given image, there is a small set of relevant images in the database; on the other hand, the rest of the images can be categorized as irrelevant. We preferred using only the relevant images because the small set of feedback images that are selected by the user for both relevancy and irrelevancy will probably provide a better estimate for the former case.

Depending on σ^0_j and $\sigma^k_{\text{rel},j}$, four different situations can arise as shown in Table 1:

Table 1: Motivation for the weight selection. Moving upwards in the table represents a situation that is closer to ideal.

σ^0_j	$\sigma^k_{\text{rel},j}$	$w^k_j = \sigma^0_j / \sigma^k_{\text{rel},j}$
large	small	large
large	large	~ 1
small	small	~ 1
small	large	small

- When σ^0_j is large and $\sigma^k_{\text{rel},j}$ is small, w^k_j becomes large. This means that the feature has a diverse set of values in the database but its values for relevant images are similar. This is a desired situation and shows that this feature is very effective in distinguishing this specific relevant image set so a large weight assigns more importance to this feature.
- When both σ^0_j and $\sigma^k_{\text{rel},j}$ are large, w^k_j is close to 1. This means that the feature may have good discrimination characteristics in the database but is not effective for this specific relevant image group. The resulting weight does not give any particular importance to this feature.
- When both σ^0_j and $\sigma^k_{\text{rel},j}$ are small, w^k_j is again close to 1. This is a similar but slightly worse situation than the previous one. The feature is not generally effective in the database and is not effective for this relevant set either. No importance is given to this feature.
- When σ^0_j is small and $\sigma^k_{\text{rel},j}$ is large, w^k_j becomes small. This is the worst case among all the possibilities. The feature is not generally effective and even causes the distance between relevant images to increase. A small weight forces the distance measure to ignore the effect of this feature.

All of the resulting weights in these four cases are consistent with the desired situations in an ideal retrieval.

2.3. Iterative retrieval

The retrieval algorithm can be described as follows:

1. Initialize all weights uniformly as $w^0_j = 1/Q$, $j = 1, \ldots, Q$. Compute σ^0_j, $j = 1, \ldots, Q$.
2. For $k = 1, \ldots, K$,
   (a) Search the database using w^{k-1}_j and obtain R^k.
   (b) Get feedback from the user as R^k_{rel}.
   (c) Compute $\sigma^k_{\text{rel},j}$, $j = 1, \ldots, Q$.
   (d) Compute

$$w^k_j = \frac{\sigma^0_j}{\sigma^k_{\text{rel},j}}, j = 1, \ldots, Q \tag{3}$$

and normalize as $w_j^k = w_j^k / \sum_{j=1}^{Q} w_j^k$.

3. Do the final search using $w_j^K, j = 1, \ldots, Q$.

To compute $\sigma_{\text{rel},j}^k$ in 2c, we use two methods:

- Independent update: Standard deviations are estimated independently in every iteration using only that iteration's retrieval sets, i.e.

$$(\sigma_{\text{rel},j}^k)^2 = E((F_{\text{rel},j}^k)^2) - E(F_{\text{rel},j}^k)^2, j = 1, \ldots, Q$$

where $E(F_{\text{rel},j}^k)$ and $E((F_{\text{rel},j}^k)^2)$ are the first and second moments of the sample $F_{\text{rel},j}^k$ respectively.

- Incremental update: We assume that user's notion of similarity does not change as the iterations progress and he/she is consistent in consecutive iterations. Therefore, standard deviations are incrementally updated in every iteration, i.e.

$$(\sigma_{\text{rel},j}^k)^2 = \left(\frac{|R_{\text{rel}}^{k-1}| E((F_{\text{rel},j}^{k-1})^2) + |R_{\text{rel}}^k| E((F_{\text{rel},j}^k)^2)}{|R_{\text{rel}}^{k-1}| + |R_{\text{rel}}^k|} \right) - \left(\frac{|R_{\text{rel}}^{k-1}| E(F_{\text{rel},j}^{k-1}) + |R_{\text{rel}}^k| E(F_{\text{rel},j}^k)}{|R_{\text{rel}}^{k-1}| + |R_{\text{rel}}^k|} \right)^2,$$

j=1,...,Q, where the retrieval sets are updated as $R^k = R^k \cup R^{k-1}$ and $R_{\text{rel}}^k = R_{\text{rel}}^k \cup R_{\text{rel}}^{k-1}$ after every iteration.

When all the values in $F_{\text{rel},j}^k$ are the same, i.e. all images have the same value for that feature, we assign a large constant value to w_j^k.

3. Experiments and Results

3.1. Database population

Our database contains 10,410 256 × 256 images that include aerial images (Fort Hood Data of the RADIUS Project) and remote sensing images (LANDSAT). For performance evaluation, we randomly selected 340 images and formed a groundtruth of 7 categories; parking lots, roads, residential areas, landscapes, LANDSAT USA, DMSP North Pole and LANDSAT Chernobyl. Textural features described in [1] were used for image representation. The first set of features are the line-angle-ratio statistics that use spatial relationships and properties of lines, and the second set of features are the variances of co-occurrence statistics of pixels in particular spatial relationships.

3.2. Retrieval performance

We measure the retrieval performance by *precision* which is defined as the percentage of retrieved images that are actually relevant. Retrieval results in terms of precision averaged over the groundtruth images are given in Figure 1. The search engine performs a new search in the database and retrieves 12 images in every iteration. Independent updating was used for both L_1 and L_2 distances. The results

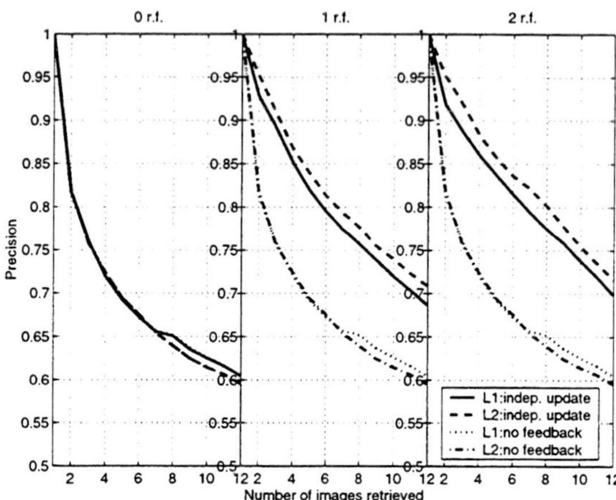

Figure 1: Average *precision* for the first two iterations.

Table 2: Average *precision* when 12 images are retrieved. Improvements for each iteration over the previous iteration are given in paranthesis.

Distance	0 rf	1 rf	2 rf
L_1	0.60	0.69 (13.53%)	0.70 (1.71%)
L_2	0.60	0.71 (19.03%)	0.72 (1.06%)

are summarized in Table 2. We can see that slightly better results could be obtained on the average when the L_2 distance was used. We tried up to five iterations and the largest average improvement was obtained as 19% after the first iteration. This is a desirable situation that shows a fast convergence.

When the whole database is searched in every iteration, the improvement is usually a few additional relevant images and this can also be achieved by showing a new set of images from the retrieval set of the original query instead of waiting for the computation of getting feedback and doing one more search. Another way of investigating how well the relevance feedback performs is to compare the performance of iterative retrieval with that of the original search in terms of the *progress* made towards retrieving a specific number of images. After obtaining the feedback, the search engine performs a new search in the database but ignores all the images that were retrieved in previous iterations. Therefore, a new set of 12 images are retrieved in every iteration. This performance is compared with the case where the next set of 12 images from the retrieval set of the original search are presented to the user (showing the next page in the user interface). Given n as a specific number of images retrieved, we define *progress* as the ratio of two precisions,

$$Progress = \frac{|\text{relevant images among } n \text{ after } \lceil n/12 \rceil \text{ iterations}|}{|\text{relevant images among } n \text{ retrieved without feedback}|}. \tag{4}$$

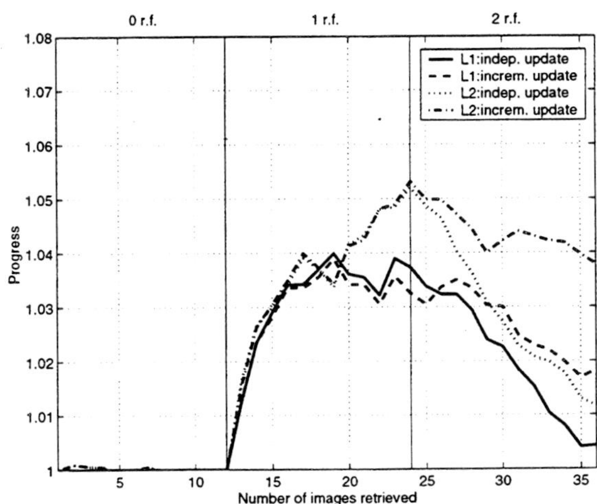

Figure 2: Average *progress* for the first two iterations.

Table 3: Average *progress* when 12, 24 and 36 images are retrieved.

Distance	0 rf	1 rf	2 rf
L_1:Indep. update	1	1.037	1.004
L_1:Increm. update	1	1.033	1.018
L_2:Indep. update	1	1.052	1.012
L_2:Increm. update	1	1.053	1.038

When progress is greater than 1, it means the feedback algorithm is effective and converges faster. Average progress is given in Figure 2. The results are summarized in Table 3. We can see that incremental updating performed better than independent updating. The largest improvement was obtained as 5.3% greater progress over the no feedback case.

4. Conclusions and Future Work

We presented a weighted distance approach where the weights were the ratios of standard deviations of the feature values both for the whole database and also among the images selected as relevant by the user. We discussed the effects of independent weight updating where the weights were estimated independently in every iteration using only the feedback information in that iteration, and incremental weight updating where the weights were incrementally updated in every iteration using the feedback information in that iteration as well as the previous iterations.

Retrieval performance was evaluated in terms of average *precision* and *progress* for a groundtruth database and an average performance improvement of 19% was obtained after the first iteration, which shows a fast convergence.

One issue to be addressed further is to investigate other functions of the standard deviations as weight updating methods. The results may also be improved if the feedback for irrelevant images is also incorporated into the database search.

References

[1] S. Aksoy and R. M. Haralick. Textural features for image database retrieval. In *Proceedings of IEEE Workshop on Content-Based Access of Image and Video Libraries, in conjunction with CVPR'98*, pages 45–49, Santa Barbara, CA, June 1998.

[2] S. Aksoy and R. M. Haralick. Graph–theoretic clustering for image grouping and retrieval. In *Proceedings of IEEE Conference on Computer Vision and Pattern Recognition*, volume 1, pages 63–68, Colorado, June 1999.

[3] J. R. Bach, C. Fuller, A. Gupta, A. Hampapur, B. Horowitz, R. Humphrey, R. Jain, and C.-F. Shu. The virage search engine: An open framework for image management. In *SPIE Storage and Retrieval of Image and Video Databases*, February 1996.

[4] J.-Y. Chen, C. Bouman, and J. Dalton. Active browsing using similarity pyramids. In *Proceedings of the VII IS&T/SPIE Conference on Storage and Retrieval for Image and Video Databases*, volume 3656, pages 144–154, San Jose, CA,, January 1999.

[5] J.-Y. Chen, C. Taskiran, E. Delp, and C. Bouman. Vibe: A new paradigm for video database browsing and search. In *Proceedings of IEEE Workshop on Content-Based Access of Image and Video Libraries*, pages 96 –100, 1998.

[6] T.-S. Chua, W.-C. Low, and C.-X. Chu. Relevance feedback techniques for color-based image retrieval. In *Proceedings of Multimedia Modeling*, pages 24–31, 1998.

[7] I. Cox, M. Miller, S. Omohundro, and P. Yianilos. Pichunter: Bayesian relevance feedback for image retrieval. In *Proceedings of the 13th IAPR International Conference on Pattern Recognition*, volume 3, pages 361–369, 1996.

[8] I. Cox, T. Papathomas, J. Ghosn, P. Yianilos, and M. Miller. Hidden annotation in content based image retrieval. In *Proceedings of IEEE Workshop on Content-Based Access of Image and Video Libraries*, pages 76–81, 1997.

[9] M. Flickner, H. Sawhney, W. Niblack, J. Ashley, Q. Huang, B. Dom, M. Gorkani, J. Hafner, D. Lee, D. Petkovic, D. Steele, and P. Yanker. The QBIC project: Querying images by content using color, texture and shape. In *SPIE Storage and Retrieval of Image and Video Databases*, pages 173–181, 1993.

[10] C. Nastar, M. Mitschke, and C. Meilhac. Efficient query refinement for image retrieval. In *Proceedings of IEEE Conference on Computer Vision and Pattern Recognition*, pages 547–552, June 1998.

[11] J. Peng, B. Bhanu, and S. Qing. Probabilistic feature relevance learning for content-based image retrieval. *Computer Vision and Image Understanding, Special Issue on Content-Vased Access of Image and Video Libraries*, 75(1/2):150–164, July/August 1999.

[12] Y. Rui, T. Huang, and S. Mehrotra. Content-based image retrieval with relevance feedback in MARS. In *Proceedings of IEEE International Conference on Image Processing*, 1997.

[13] Y. Rui, T. Huang, M. Ortega, and S. Mehrotra. Relevance feedback: A power tool for interactive content-based image retrieval. *IEEE Transactions on Circuits and Systems for Video Technology*, 8:644–655, September 1998.

Obtaining Genericity for Image Processing and Pattern Recognition Algorithms

Thierry Géraud, Yoann Fabre, Alexandre Duret-Lutz
EPITA Research and Development Laboratory
14-16 rue Voltaire, F-94276 Le Kremlin-Bicêtre cedex, France
thierry.geraud@lrde.epita.fr

Dimitri Papadopoulos-Orfanos, Jean-François Mangin
Service Hospitalier Frédéric Joliot, CEA
4 place du Général Leclerc, F-91401 Orsay cedex, France
papadopo@shfj.cea.fr

Abstract

Algorithm libraries dedicated to image processing and pattern recognition are not reusable; to run an algorithm on particular data, one usually has either to rewrite the algorithm or to manually "copy, paste, and modify". This is due to the lack of genericity of the programming paradigm used to implement the libraries. In this paper, we present a recent paradigm that allows algorithms to be written once and for all and to accept input of various types. Moreover, this total reusability can be obtained with a very comprehensive writing and without significant cost at execution, compared to a dedicated algorithm. This new paradigm is called "generic programming" and is fully supported by the C^{++} language. We show how this paradigm can be applied to image processing and pattern recognition routines. The perspective of our work is the creation of a generic library.

1. Introduction

Great effort has gone into building image processing and pattern recognition libraries that can be used and augmented by different research centers. However, the main difficulty that is systematically encountered and that remains unsolved is how to manage the large number of input types used in this domain. An algorithm developed for a particular input can rarely be reused. As a consequence, no one library has succeeded in being unanimously adopted by the scientific community.

An ideal library should be generic, i.e. supply generic algorithms. A generic image processing algorithm is written once, and indistinctly accepts 2D and 3D images (isotropic or not), regions, region adjacency graphs, image and graph pyramids, sequences, collections and so forth; the types of data contained in these structures is scalar (Boolean, integer or float), complex, composed (e.g. RGB). Existing libraries are usually dedicated to a particular data structure (mostly 2D images) and their algorithms are restricted to few data types (mostly unsigned 8 bit integers). Ideal pattern recognition algorithms also have this problem: for instance, a given primitive such as a contour can have different representations.

Most algorithm data can have different forms (i.e., different types) and should be used as the input of algorithms in a transparent way. In this paper, we show that recent advances in C^{++} programming allow this genericity with a very comprehensive syntax and without leading to a significant extra cost of execution time as compared to dedicated algorithms. This new paradigm is called "generic programming". We have successfully applied it both to low level image processing routines and to high level pattern recognition algorithms in a library that we are currently developing.

In section 2, we present the generic programming paradigm and its benefits compared to usual paradigms. Then, in section 3, we explain how to design a generic algorithm and we show with a simple example algorithm how this paradigm can be applied to the field of image processing, and how we can obtain maximal genericity. Lastly, in section 4, we conclude and give future perspectives of our work.

2. The generic programming paradigm

To emphasize the benefits of generic programming applied to image processing and computer vision, we will first point out some drawbacks of existing libraries.

1051-4651/00 $10.00 © 2000 IEEE

2.1. Current libraries

In current C libraries, an algorithm has to be written as many times as there are input types [1]; see figure 1. For instance, a simple addition of a constant to image elements leads to four routines if we want this algorithm to deal with 2D and 3D images with Boolean or floating elements. Since the combination "algorithms $\times$ structure types $\times$ data types" can be enormous, many libraries limit the number of structure types and data types handled by each algorithm. The C-like programming paradigm has two main drawbacks: the capabilities of such libraries are limited, and introducing a new structure type or data type is a tedious task.

Some object languages such as C^{++} offer genericity, which means that classes and procedures can be parametrized. A common use of genericity is to parameterize the definitions of data structures and routines by the data type of their elements. As a consequence, reusability is enhanced but, although some libraries use genericity in this way [6, 5], the reusability is far from being total: routines still have to be written for each structure type. In fact, existing libraries do not rely on the generic programming paradigm presented below.

The limits of reusability of image processing algorithms induced by different programming paradigms are explained with further details in [3].

2.2. The novelty

Generic programming is a new paradigm to write fully generic algorithms without leading to significant overheads at run-time as compared to dedicated code. This paradigm is very attractive for scientific numerical programming and is used in some recent libraries: CGAL [2] and Blitz++ [7], respectively dedicated to geometric and algebraic calculi.

The generic programming paradigm is based on two key ideas:

- an algorithm is parametrized by its input types (in contrast to data parameterization, see section 2.1),
- the tools, helper objects needed by the algorithm, are deduced from its input (like the iterators presented in section 3.2).

When an algorithm is used, the compiler generates the appropriate machine code for the particular input types; see figure 2. Moreover, each method call in this code can be replaced by its implementation, so the cost of method calls is avoided. Therefore, the executable code is similar to that of a routine written for the particular input types and generic procedures are roughly as fast as dedicated procedures. Generic programming makes the compiler do the work that the programmer has to do in usual programming.

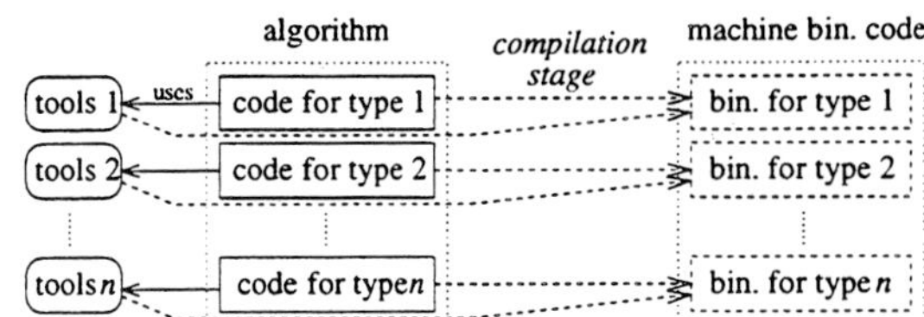

Figure 1. Usual mechanism in *C*.

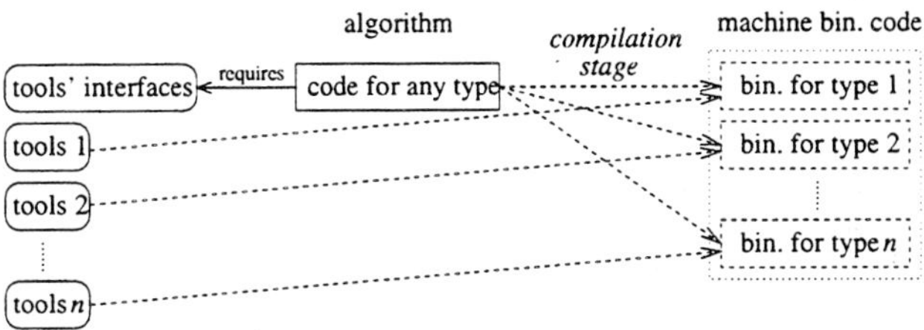

Figure 2. Generic mechanism in C^{++}.

C^{++} is a language that offers a good compromise between efficiency and generic capabilities [4], so all existing generic libraries are implemented in C^{++}. In the next section, we present the syntactic bases which are of prime importance to understand the generic programming paradigm.

2.3. Syntax

The sample code below gives a part of the definition of a generic 2D image class in C^{++}:

```
template< typename T >  // parameterization
class Image2D {
  public:
    typedef T value_type;    // a type alias
    size_t size() const;     // a method
    //...
};
```

This code contains two main syntactical elements.

Firstly, the class definition is parametrized (keyword `template`) and a single parameter is defined, `T`, whose nature is a type (keyword `typename`). This parameter represents the type of the image elements. For instance, the programmer can then use the type `Image2D<float>` to manipulate 2D images containing floating values. The parameterization thus allows the definition of only one class per structure type in the library whatever the data type.

Lastly, one can define a type alias (keyword `typedef`) within a class; for instance, the parametric class `Image2D` contains the alias `value_type`, which gives the element type, `T`. Such an alias is used as follows:

```
typename class_name::alias_name
```

Let us consider a procedure that is parametrized by the type `I` of an input aggregate; this aggregate is the argument input of the procedure. In the procedure body, the programmer can use type aliases such as I::value_type, and methods of I such as in input.size(); see for instance proc in the code below:

```
template< typename I >  // parametrization
void proc( I& input ) {
  size_t  a_size = input.size();
  typename I::value_type  a_value;
  //...
}

int main() {
  Image2D<float>  ima;
  proc( ima );
}
```

When proc is called, the type I is known, and the dedicated procedure is compiled (if it has not already been compiled). The compiler then checks that the type effectively contains a method size() and an alias value_type (these two points represent a required interface). Since it is the case for the type Image2D<float>, in main(), the variable value is of type float in the compiled routine.

3. Generic algorithm design

The generic programming paradigm being quite recent, algorithm design does not follow a standard process. So, we first present the method that we have established.

3.1. Design method

The design method is sequential and composed of several steps.

1. Express the algorithm in mathematical language while paying attention to remaining as general as possible. This step ensures that we will not provide an algorithm that depends upon particular considerations (for instance, an algorithm linked to a given data structure).
2. Identify the objects that are involved in the expression obtained at the previous step and describe their role and their required behavior.
3. Point out each algorithm option that should be set by the user, and give each option a default value if it is pertinent. If needed, return to step 2 to take into account these options.
4. Analyze the dependencies between the types of the objects used in the algorithm, and deduce its parameters.
5. Finally, write the generic algorithm.

3.2. A simple example

To illustrate how to obtain the highest genericity for an image processing or pattern recognition algorithm, let us study a very simple example: the addition of a constant to the elements of an aggregate.

Step 1 For the sake of genericity, let us first generalize this example and consider that the algorithm has to be designed for any operator similar to val += cst. We can then formulate this algorithm as follows : "for each element of an input aggregate, apply the operator to the element value". Please note that this description conceals all implementation details related to the particular types of the objects that could be involved in the algorithm.

Step 2 The objects involved in the algorithm are: an input aggregate (argument input), an iterator (internal variable iter), a constant value (argument cst).

To translate this description into a generic algorithm, the introduction of an object which iterates over the elements of an aggregate is required; such an object, called an *iterator*, is a common tool in software design. One iterator class is defined per structure type and all iterators provide the same interface (i.e., the same subset of methods and aliases) in order to be uniformly manipulated. In this way, iterating over graph vertices leads to the same syntax as iterating over image points.

Step 3 The options of the algorithm are:

- an operator (for instance, a saturated addition),
- a predicate to restrict the addition to certain elements of the aggregate (by default, the predicate returns always true),
- an accessor to specify, if the element type is structured, which field is concerned by the addition (by default, the accessor is the identity; its name is get_value<>),

Each option is translated into one extra object in the algorithm.

Step 4 Let us denote by I the type of the input aggregate, by C the type of the constant value, by O the type of the operator, by P the type of the predicate, by get_A the type of the accessor (when accessing field A of I), and by T the type of the iterator. Then, we have the following statements:

- C is given by get_A::output_type,
- T is given by I::iterator_type,
- get_A<>::input_type is given by I::value_type and get_A<>::output_type is given by I::value_type::A_type,
- O::args_type is given by get_A::output_type.

The parameters of the algorithm are: `I`, `O`, `P`, and `get_A`. The first parameter is known when the algorithm is called and the last two parameters have default values. The only parameter that the user has to set is `O`.

Step 5 The core of the algorithm is transformed into the following description. Define `iter` on `input`; then, for each iteration handled by `iter`, conditioned by `pred`, apply `oper` with `cst` on the value given by `iter` through `access`. Finally, this algorithm is ready to be translated into the generic C^{++} code[1]:

```
template< typename O,
          template< class U > class get_A = get_value,
          typename P = Pred_true >
struct op
{
   template< typename I > static
   void on( I& input,
            const get_A< I::value_type >::output_type& cst,
            P pred = P() )
   {
      O oper;     get_A< I::value_type > access;
      I::iterator_type  iter( input );
      for ( iter.first(); ! iter.isDone(); iter.next() )
         if ( pred( access( iter() ) ) )
            oper( access( iter() ), cst );
   }
};
```

This algorithm accepts various structure and data types. Moreover, the user can parameterize its behavior (for instance, the user can subtract a constant value from the red component of some elements of a 3D image). Since the user is not required to set all parameters, the simplest call of the algorithm (arithmetical plus) is:

```
op<plus>::on( input, cst );
```

4. Conclusion

In this paper, we have presented the generic programming paradigm that enables the implementation of generic algorithms. Then, we have demonstrated with an example how to apply this paradigm to the field of image processing and pattern recognition and how to obtain the highest genericity.

The main difficulty of building a generic library lies in correct designing of algorithms and tools. For that, the closer the code is to the theory, the better the genericity is. Although the example given in this paper is very simple, the design process is rigorously equivalent for high-level routines.

This paradigm has five major advantages that we set out below.

Reusability Since algorithms are generic, their reusability is maximal. Each algorithm is programmed only once and accepts data of various types. When one wants to introduce a new data type in the library, one only has to conform to few requirements in order to benefit from the existing algorithms.

Functionalities From the viewpoint of the user, such a library is no more complicated than current libraries. Algorithms can be called very simply because they define their own default settings, while it remains possible for the user to be more specific.

Development The development cost of a generic algorithm is dramatically reduced as compared to that of current libraries (see figures 1 and 2). Consequently, maintenance and reliability are significantly improved.

Efficiency Generic algorithms are roughly as fast as dedicated algorithms (the compiler expands generic code and makes it similar to dedicated code).

Federative A generic library is able to federate tools and algorithms developed by different research centers. We believe that this point is of prime importance for the community because such a library enhances the capitalization of knowledge.

We are currently developing such a library whose first version will be soon freely available. We do not aim at providing a wide range of algorithms and tools but the most usual ones to facilitate algorithm programming.

[1]The full implementation of the example is available at the URL `http://www.lrde.epita.fr/download/`

References

[1] M. Dobie and P. Lewis. Data structures for image processing in C. *Pattern Recognition Letters*, 12(8):457–466, 1991.

[2] A. Fabri, G. Giezeman, L. Kettner, S. Schirra, and S. Schönherr. On the design of CGAL, the computational geometry algorithms library. Technical Report 3407, INRIA, 1998.

[3] T. Géraud, Y. Fabre, D. Papadopoulos-Orfanos, and J.-F. Mangin. Vers une réutilisabilité totale des algorithmes de traitement d'images. In *17th Symposium on Signal and Image Processing (GRETSI'99)*, volume 2, pages 331–334, Vannes, France, September 1999. In French; available in English as a technical report at `http://www.lrde.epita.fr/publications`

[4] S. Haney and J. Crotinger. How templates enable high-performance scientific computing in C++. *IEEE Computing in Science and Engineering*, 1(4), 1999.

[5] C. Kohl and J. Mundy. The development of the Image Understanding Environment. In *Proceedings of the International Conference on Computer Vision and Pattern Recognition*, pages 443–447, 1994.

[6] G. Ritter, J. Wilson, and J. Davidson. Image Algebra: an overview. *Computer Vision, Graphics, and Image Processing*, 49(3):297–331, 1990.

[7] T. Veldhuizen. Arrays in Blitz++. In *Proc. of the 2nd Intl. Conf. in Object-Oriented Parallel Environments (ISCOPE'98)*, number 1505 in Lectures Notes in Computer Science, pages 223–230. Springer Verlag, 1998.

Spatio-Temporal Segmentation with Edge Relaxation and Optimization Using Fully Parallel Methods

Tamás Sziranyi[+] László Czúni
Department of Image Processing and Neurocomputing,
University of Veszprém, Egyetem u. 10, H-8200 Veszprém, Hungary

[+] *also with: Analogical and Neural Computing Laboratory, Comp. & Aut. Inst., Hungarian Academy of Sciences, Kende u. 13-17, H-1111 Budapest, Hungary*
E-mail: sziranyi@sztaki.hu, czuni@almos.vein.hu

Abstract

In this paper we outline a fully parallel and locally connected computation model for the spatio-temporal segmentation of motion events in video sequences. We are searching for a new algorithm, which can be easily implemented in one-pixel/one-processor cell-array VLSI architectures at high-speed. Our proposed algorithm starts from an oversegmented image, then the segments are merged by applying the information coming from the spatial and temporal auxiliary data: motion fields and motion history, which is calculated from consecutive image frames. This grouping process is defined through a similarity measure of neighboring segments, which is based on the values of intensity, speed and the time-depth of motion history. As for checking the merging process there is a feedback implemented, by that we can accept or refuse the cancellation of a segment-border. Our parallel approach is independent of the number of segments and objects, since instead of graph representation and serial processing of these components, image features are defined on the pixel-level. We use simple functions, easily realizable in VLSI, like arithmetic and logical operators, local memory transfers and convolution.

1. Introduction

Our efforts are aimed at finding solutions to the spatio-temporal segmentation problem that need almost low-level, simple functions that can be implemented on special parallel VLSI architectures with superior speed. Then the output of these low-level operations can be forwarded to a high-level processor responsible for controlling the whole operation and for final interpretation. Since most of the work would be done on a parallel processor array, significant speed-up could be achieved compared to other processor architectures as shown in [9].

One simple example is Mitsubishi's so called "Artificial Retina" [11] or other smart pixel arrays in optical computing. These digital architectures' functionality is very limited but similar systems can forecast a more intelligent class of smart cameras of the future.

The typical example for the higher cell-complexity of cellular processor arrays is the family of the Cellular Nonlinear Network (CNN) chips [2,4]. CNN can process images locally on the pixel-level with small neighborhood connectivity. It can perform convolution, nonlinear (sigmoid) dynamics in a feed-forward/feed-back operation mode with many additional features like those that conventional computers have: local and global memories, pixel-level logical and arithmetic functions, digital memories, all in one single chip.

Some results have been achieved for the segmentation of moving image parts by using optical-flow estimation and Markov Random Field (MRF) based computations in the CNN architecture using fully parallel and local functions [9]. Now, our goal is to develop a spatio-temporal object-segmentation method using edge relaxation.

2. Main Building Blocks and Cell Functions of the Method

This section lists those image processing functions that are used as the building blocks of the whole processing cycle. These sub-tasks, such as finding edges, filtering noise, estimating motion parameters, etc. can be considered as subroutines that are executed in fully parallel on the cell-array platform. The following main components are used in our model:

- Nonlinear [8] (or anisotropic [6]) diffusion to get better segmentation of the intensity image, or to run external-edge controlled smoothing inside a region.
- Estimation of optical flow can be done by using fully parallel methods [9].
- Motion history: It is a map containing the value of motion-duration for each motion-compensated point. The longer is the time since the pixel has been moving from its preceding places, the greater is its motion

history value (MH), which is saturated ($|MH| \le MH_{\max}$). The history-map gives a time-support for the segmentation.

- Morphology operators implemented in parallel [12].
- Removal of disocclusion effects in parallel [9].

An important limit of physical realization is the radius of local connectivity. We use only first (4 neighbors are connected) or second order (8 neighbors are connected) neighborhood relations, higher order would make hardware realization troublesome.

Necessary cell functions and components:

- Comparison of neighboring pixels.
- Convolution (a basic function already realized in VLSI chips [2]).
- Arithmetic and logical functions, relations.
- Analog or logical (binary) cell memories (the number of memory per pixel is also limited by hardware considerations).
- Non-linear functions: absolute value, gradient, etc.

3. Edge Optimization for Spatio-Temporal Segmentation

Our algorithm is mainly based on three inputs: the oversegmented image (based on gray-scale information), the estimated/segmented optical flow and the motion history information. We found that in many cases the joint utilization of intensity values and the current motion information (motion estimated between two consecutive frames) was not enough to satisfactorily define the contours of objects. On the other hand, the probability that two neighboring image blobs belong to the same object is the higher the more of the following three requirements are satisfied:

1. The two blobs have similar color (or gray-scale intensity value). In case of textured areas, texture filters [7] can be applied to label these regions.
2. The two blobs have similar velocity.
3. The two blobs had similar motion in the recent past.

In our spatio-temporal segmentation process we apply a split & merge algorithm to find coherent image areas based on these three features of neighboring regions.

As for the pre-segmentation of the 2D motion vector field MRF-based techniques can be applied with a restriction that random elements are chosen from a close neighborhood to ensure fast convergence of the method. To reduce the dimensionality of the whole spatio-temporal segmentation problem it is possible to replace motion vectors with scalars by a clustering method. In our experiments we simply dropped one component, the segmentation algorithm seemed to be quite robust and gave satisfactory results when we considered only the magnitude of velocity vectors.

The Segmentation Process

We introduce an optimization algorithm where contours are responsible to get an optimal spatio-temporal segmentation of video sequences.

Three edge maps are generated during the algorithm: edges separating areas of different intensity values ($\boldsymbol{E_{in}}$), edges separating different motion fields ($\boldsymbol{E_m}$) and edges separating fields of different motion history values ($\boldsymbol{E_{mh}}$). Edge-fragments of these three maps are different subsets of the spatio-temporal binary edge map $\boldsymbol{E_{segm}}$, which is a subset of the edge map of the oversegmented image ($\boldsymbol{E_{os}}$). The three edge maps ($\boldsymbol{E_{in}}$, $\boldsymbol{E_m}$, $\boldsymbol{E_{mh}}$) are weighted and then added to form a unified edge map ($\boldsymbol{E_u}$) that is thresholded and used to modify the actual $\boldsymbol{E_{segm}}$. Then the intensity, motion and motion history fields are updated by diffusion inside the contours of the new $\boldsymbol{E_{segm}}$. If the difference between the new state of the three feature fields and their previous state is too large, some edges may be restored. Then at the next iteration the three different edge maps are measured again and a new unified map is formed, etc.

The optimization is based on the following implicit model: When the three edge maps are added to form a new unified edge map, the applied threshold criterion is analogous to evaluating a *Dam-potential* between the neighboring segments S_i and S_j:

$$D(S_i, S_j) = \sum_{k=1}^{3} w_k \left| L_k(S_i) - L_k(S_j) \right| \tag{1}$$

where L_1 = intensity, L_2 = motion (magnitude of the segmented motion field), L_3 = motion history, while w_k is a weighting coefficient. If $D(S_i, S_j)$ is above a threshold, then the edge is kept, otherwise deleted at that location. The reconstruction of edges is a necessary part of the algorithm, because the merging of similar neighboring regions *in one step* can result in the merging of distant areas that have very different values (see Fig. 1). Hence we use the following expressions to measure the effects of edge removal. First, we define the new average feature values over a segment:

$$L_k(S_M) = \sum_{S_i \subseteq S_M} \frac{A_i L_k(S_i)}{A_M} \tag{2}$$

is the kth feature value of the unified region S_M obtained by merging regions S_i, corresponding segment-areas are denoted by A_M and A_i. The change due to the formation of a new region S_M is expressed for each S_i ($S_i \subseteq S_M$) by the difference of the old and the new levels:

$$Q(S_M, S_i) = \sum_{k=1}^{2} \left| L_k(S_M) - L_k(S_i) \right|. \tag{3}$$

If $Q(S_M, S_i)$ is above a predefined value, then the previously eliminated but stored edge-fragments around S_i are reconstructed (see Fig. 1). Notice that no intensity is considered in the edge reconstruction process. It means that regions with different intensity can be merged more easily than with different motion information. Averaging over an area, defined by eq. (2), is implemented by a diffusion process inside the edge-defined borders.

The individual steps of the proposed algorithm are the following. (Figs. 2 and 3 show some examples illustrating the results.)

1. ***Segment the input image***, based on intensity observations, possibly to a large number of segments of characteristic closed regions. The resulted segmented image is called oversegmentation, and it gives the finest partitioning that could be achieved in the whole spatio-temporal segmentation process.

2. ***Produce the edge map of the oversegmented intensity field (E_{os}) by an edge-detector*** [12]. E_{os} is a binary map showing the more-or-less closed segment-borders of the oversegmented image parts. In the segmentation process the state variable is the actual edge map, the binary E_{segm}.

- Starting condition: $E_{segm} = E_{os}$.

3. ***Diffuse intensity, motion and motion history fields*** inside the regions defined by E_{segm} with the help of external edge controlled diffusion. We finish this smoothing procedure with a morphological equalization to get the same value for all the pixels inside the regions defined by the contours. It ensures that the Dam-potential is equal along a given edge-fragment. Then make the gray-scale edge maps of these fields, namely E_{in}, E_m and E_{mh} respectively. These non-binary (gray-scale) maps contain the edge-strength values between the different diffused areas in the same points where the oversegmented binary edge-segments are in E_{segm}.

4. ***Weight and add together the three maps E_{in}, E_m and E_{mh} to form a unified map E_u***. In our experiments we applied the next weights (w):

$$w(E_{in}) : w(E_m) : w(E_{mh}) = 0.2 : 1.2 : 1.2.$$

5. ***Threshold the superimposed edge-map E_u*** and reduce the edges in E_{segm}. $E_{segm} := E_{segm} \setminus E_u^{(thresholded)}$. Edges of E_{segm} below a threshold in E_u are neglected.

6. ***Approximate the average motion and motion history feature*** fields by external edge controlled diffusion inside the contours of the modified E_{segm}. This diffusion is just similar to the diffusion of step 3.

7. ***Correct E_{segm} with reconstruction (E_{rec})***. Naturally, an optimal segmentation algorithm would need some feedback [5]. Although, in the cell array framework no graph based optimization or higher-level understanding is available, feedback is still possible. In every cycle, the change between the current motion fields and previously segmented motion fields is measured. Over those areas, where the difference (given by eq. (3)) is greater than a predefined value, a mask is generated *(E_{rec})*. Then with the help of this mask we can reconstruct edges from the stored edge map of the previous iteration cycle: $E_{segm} := E_{segm} \cup E_{rec}$. Fig. 1 illustrates a typical situation.

8. Cycle controlling

- ***Decrease edge weights.*** In our experiments we decreased edge weights by 0-20%. If this relaxation-factor is small, then edge destruction is slow; otherwise the different regions merge into each other faster.
- ***Go to step 3.***

According to our test results, approximately 10-15 iterations were sufficient to get stable edge contours. Morphology operators may then be used to get thin lines as a final result.

A very important issue is the execution-time of the above algorithm. Considering parameters of a VLSI 64x64 cell-array processor chip [4] (save/load of 64x64 image: 90μsec, arithmetic operation 0.5μsec, logical operation: 0.1μsec, convolution: 2μsec) we can achieve *12msec* total processing time, including several preprocessing steps of [8,9]. The cited experimental processor's technology (0.5μm, 10MHz clock) is far from the available technological limits – but it still achieves high algorithmic speed at low power consumption of 1.2W.

4. Summary

The resulted map (E_{segm}) contains the contours of the spatio-temporal objects. This map can be forwarded to a vector based DSP process for further analysis, such as MPEG-4 video transmission or motion analysis applications.

In this work we have shown that spatio-temporal segmentation can be done by using only parallel steps operating in a small neighborhood. The proposed steps can be easily implemented in a cell-array processor containing very simple VLSI instructions on the cell-level. The above algorithm can be run in real-time for greater images, and the processing time is *independent* of the number of objects or the complexity of the image information.

5. References

[1] P. Bouthemy and E. Francois, "Motion Segmentation and Qualitative Dynamic Scene Analysis from an Image Sequence", *Int. J. Comp. Vision*, Vol.10:2, 1993, pp. 157-182.

[2] R. Domínguez-Castro et al., "A 0.8μm CMOS Two-Dimensional Programmable Mixed-Signal Focal-Plane Array Processor with On-Chip Binary Imaging and Instructions Storage", *IEEE Journal of Solid-State Circuits*, Vol.32, No.7, 1997, pp. 1013-1026.

[3] M. Gelgon, P. Bouthemy, "A Region-Level Graph Labeling Approach to Motion-Based Segmentation", Technical Report, INRIA, 1996.

[4] G. Linan, S. Espejo, R. Dominguez-Castro, E. Roca, "A. Rodríguez-Vázquez: A Mixed Signal 64x64 CNN Universal Machine Chip", *Proc. of MicroNeuro'99*, IEEE, Granada, Spain, 1999, pp. 61-68.

[5] F. Moscheni, S. Bhattacharjee, M. Kunt, "Spatiotemporal Segmentation Based on Region Merging", *IEEE Transactions on PAMI*, Vol.20, No.9, 1998, pp. 897-915.

[6] P. Perona, T. Shiota, J. Malik, "Anisotropic Diffusion, Geometry Driven Diffusion In Computer Vision", *Kluwer Academic Publishers*, 1992 pp. 73-92.

[7] T. Szirányi, M. Csapodi, "Texture Classification and Segmentation by Cellular Neural Network using Genetic Learning", *Computer Vision and Image Understanding*, Vol.71, No.3, 1998, pp. 255-270.

[8] T. Szirányi, I. Kopilovic, B. P. Tóth, "Anisotropic Diffusion as a Preprocessing Step for Efficient Image Compression", *Proc. of the 14th ICPR*, Brisbane, *IAPR&IEEE*, Australia, 1998, pp. 1565-1567.

[9] T. Szirányi, K. László, L. Czúni, F. Ziliani, "Object oriented motion-segmentation for video-compression in the CNN-UM", *Journal of VLSI Signal Processing*, Vol.23, No.2-3, 1999, pp. 479-496.

[10] T. Szirányi, J. Zerubia, "Markov Random Field Image Segmentation using Cellular Neural Network", *IEEE Circuits and System I*, Vol.44, 1997, pp. 86-89.

[11] T. Toyoda, Y. Nitta, E. Funatsu, Y. Miyake, W. Freeman, J. Ohta, and K. Kyuma, "Artificial retina chips as image input interfaces for multimedia systems", *Proc. of the* OECC'96, Chiba, Japan, July, 1996.

[12] Á. Zarándy, et al., "Implementation of Binary and Gray-Scale Mathematical Morphology", *IEEE Circuits and Systems I*, Vol.45. No.2, 1998, pp. 163-168.

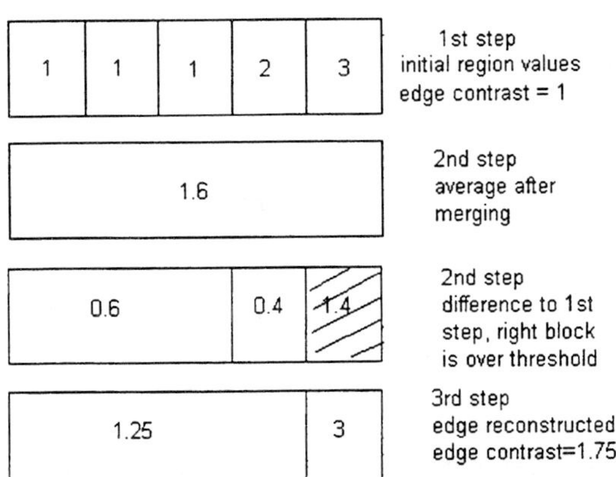

Figure 1. Edge reconstruction in the edge based optimization model. In the first step all five regions are merged but then at the next step the one on the right is separated. The difference between its value and the average of the five blocks was over a threshold of 1.0.

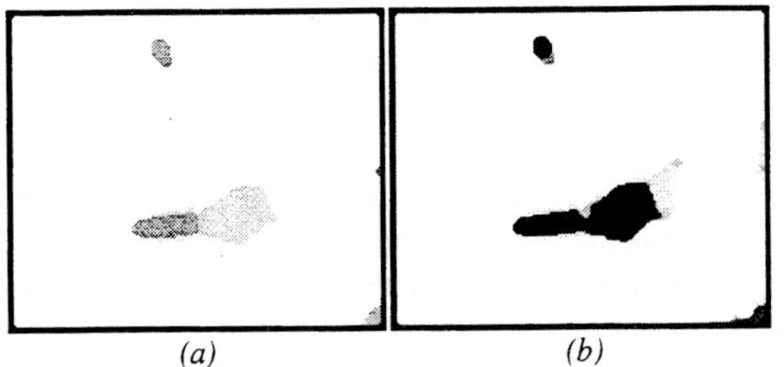

(a) *(b)*

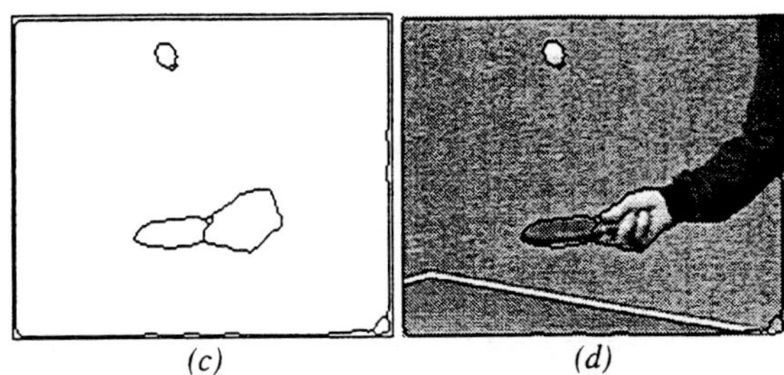

(c) *(d)*

Figure 2. Spatio-temporal segmentation of the sequence "Table Tennis". (a) magnitude of velocity, (b) motion history after the 10th iteration; (c) final contours after the 10th iteration, (d) final contours projected onto the input image.

(a) *(b)* *(c)* *(d)* *(e)* *(f)* *(g)*

Figure 3. Edge optimization for the spatio-temporal segmentation of "Mother and Daughter". Oversegmented input frame, (b) motion of the current frame, edges of the (c) 1st, (d) 3rd, (e) 5th, (f) 9th, iterations, (g) final edge map (10th iteration) projected onto the input image.

Transparent Parallel Image Processing by way of a Familiar Sequential API

F.J. Seinstra and D. Koelma
Intelligent Sensory Information Systems
Faculty of Science, University of Amsterdam
Kruislaan 403, 1098 SJ Amsterdam, The Netherlands
(fjseins, koelma)@science.uva.nl

Abstract

This paper describes an infrastructure that enables transparent development of image processing software for parallel computers. The infrastructure's main component is an image processing library containing operations capable of running on distributed memory MIMD-style parallel hardware. Since the library has a programming interface identical to that of a familiar sequential image processing library, the parallelism is completely hidden from the user. All library functions are based on an abstract parallel image processing machine (APIPM), introduced in this paper. To guide the process of automatic parallelization and optimization, a performance model is defined for operations implemented using APIPM instructions. Experiments show that for realistic image operations performance predictions are highly accurate. These results suggest that the infrastructure's core forms a powerful basis for automatic parallelization and optimization of complete applications.

1. Introduction

For many years it has been recognized that the application of parallelism in low level image processing can be highly beneficial. Consequently, references to optimal parallel algorithms [9] and dedicated parallel architectures [3] abound in the literature. In spite of this, the gap between the areas of image processing and high performance computing has remained large. This is mainly due to the fact that image processing researchers consider most parallel solutions 'too cumbersome' to apply. Rather than blaming the image processing community, researchers in high performance computing should provide tools that allow the development of software in a way that is highly familiar to image processing researchers. In addition, such tools should be applicable to commonly available general purpose parallel computers.

The ideal solution is a fully automatic parallelizing compiler. Unfortunately, the fundamental problem of automatic and optimal *partitioning* remains unsolved. Another possibility is the design of a parallel programming language, either general purpose [14] or aimed at image processing specifically [1]. However, in accordance with the remarks made in [6], we feel that a parallel language is not the preferred solution. Even a few simple language annotations are often considered cumbersome, and thus should be avoided.

In this research we aim at the creation of a *software library* containing a set of abstract data types and associated pixel level operations executing in (data) parallel fashion. All parallelization and optimization is to be hidden from the user by a programming interface identical to that of a familiar *sequential* image processing library. The routines in the library should be capable of running on general purpose distributed memory MIMD-style parallel hardware.

In this paper we describe a software infrastructure that, apart from the library itself, consists of several components dealing with the aspects of automatic parallelization, portability, optimizations across sequences of library calls, etcetera. We focus on the definition of an abstract parallel image processing machine (APIPM), and the modeling of the performance of routines implemented using APIPM instructions. Experiments show that the instruction set, and the performance models based on it, together form a solid basis for automatic parallelization and optimization.

In related work [12] the need for parallel libraries for low level image processing is stressed as well. However, performance models for optimization across library calls are often not incorporated [4]. Also, definition of an abstract parallel image processing machine has been considered rarely. The only references found (see [2] and later work by the same authors) describe the successful implementation of a portable parallel abstract machine. This machine, however, is defined at a lower level of abstraction than our APIPM.

This paper is organized as follows. Section 2 gives an infrastructure overview. Section 3 introduces the APIPM and its instruction set. In Section 4 a performance model is defined for routines implemented using APIPM instructions only. In Section 5 model predictions are compared with re-

1051-4651/00 $10.00 © 2000 IEEE

sults obtained on a real machine that fits within the APIPM model. Concluding remarks are given in Section 6.

2. Infrastructure

The complete infrastructure consists of six logical components (see Figure 1). The first component (C1) is a sequential library that contains several classes of low level image processing routines typically used by image processing researchers. Currently we have adopted an existing library (Horus, see [5]), but in principle the results of this research should be applicable to comparable libraries as well.

The sequential library is extended with several routines that introduce the parallelism into the system (C2). The routines (for the scattering, gathering, broadcasting, and redistribution of image data in a parallel system) are 'kernel' routines, not available in the programming interface. In the resulting extended library all sequential image processing operations are *fully separated* from the additional parallel routines. As separate image data distribution operations are an integrated part of the library, the creation of parallel versions of sequential image processing routines becomes a manageable task. This strategy may result in a loss of efficiency (albeit marginal), but programmability is greatly enhanced.

Each class of operations in the library is annotated with a performance model (C3) for execution time prediction. The models are essential for the process of automatic parallelization and optimization of complete applications. In addition, the models are useful as an indication to users or image library creators as well.

Components C1-C3 constitute a complete library with sequential and parallel capabilities. The components are sufficient for writing parallel image processing applications by hand. To fully hide the parallelism from the image processing application programmer, whilst ensuring efficiency of execution, three additional components are required.

First, a benchmarking tool (C4) is needed to obtain values for the model parameters. The process of benchmarking is guided by the operations that form the APIPM instruction set.

For a complete program the system needs to know what library routines are being applied, and the order of application. This information is available from the program code. Rather than implementing a complete parser, a simple tool is implemented to allow users to specify their algorithms (C5).

Once the performance models, the benchmarking results, and the algorithm specification are available a scheduler (C6) is required to find an optimal parallel solution for the application at hand. Whether the scheduling results are static or generated and updated dynamically is still an important future research issue.

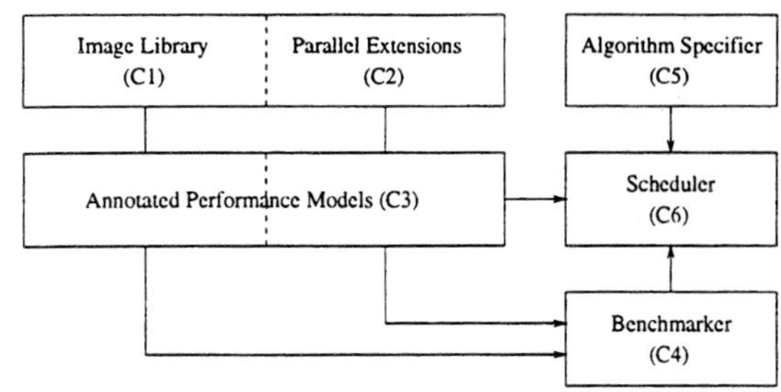

Figure 1. Infrastructure overview.

3. Abstract Parallel Image Processing Machine

In this research, all library implementations and performance models are based on the definition of an abstract parallel image processing machine (or APIPM, see Figure 2). An APIPM consists of one or more abstract sequential image processing machines (ASIPMs), each consisting of four related components: (1) a *sequential image processing unit*, capable of executing APIPM instructions, one at a time, (2) a *memory unit*, capable of storing (image) data, (3) an *I/O unit*, for transporting data from the memory unit to external sensing or storage devices, and (4) *data channels*, the means by which data is transported between the ASIPM units and external devices. In a complete APIPM the memory unit of each ASIPM is connected with those of all other ASIPMs.

Note that this definition of the APIPM reflects a state-of-the-art distributed memory MIMD-style parallel machine. It only differs from a general purpose machine in that each sequential unit is designed for image processing related tasks only. Although a fully connected communication network is often not present, we still have included one in our APIPM. This is because in most multicomputer systems communication is based on circuit-switched message routing, which makes a network *virtually* fully connected.

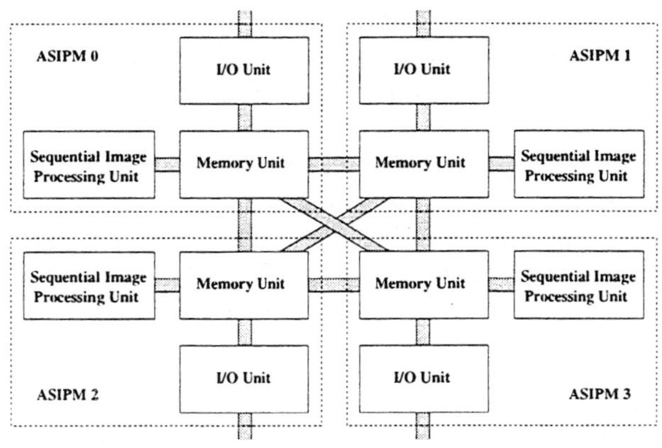

Figure 2. APIPM comprising of 4 ASIPMs.

opcode	memory instructions
CREATE	allocate data block in memory unit
MEMCOPY	copy data in memory unit
DELETE	free up data block in memory unit
opcode	**image processing instructions**
UPOP	unary pixel operation (no argument)
UPOPC	unary pixel operation (constant value as argument)
UPOPI	unary pixel operation (complete image as argument)
BPOPC	binary pixel operation (constant value as argument)
BPOPI	binary pixel operation (complete image as argument)
REDUCOP	global reduce operation
NEIGHOP	generalized neighborhood operation
TEMPLOP	generalized template operation
GEOMAT	geometric transformation (matrix as argument)
GEOROI	geometric transformation (region of interest)
opcode	**I/O instructions**
IMPORT	import data from external device
EXPORT	export data to external device
opcode	**communication instructions**
SEND	send data to other ASIPM
RECV	receive data from other ASIPM

Figure 3. Simplified APIPM instruction set.

The APIPM instruction set (see Figure 3) consists of three classes of sequential operations: (1) memory operations, for example for the creation of scratch images, or the copying of border data, (2) *fundamental* image operations, for the processing of image data without (internal) creation of additional data structures, and (3) I/O routines, for transporting data to external devices, and vice versa. The parallelism is introduced by an additional class of routines containing *communication* operations. These routines enable the exchange of data among ASIPM units. For reasons of simplicity, in the overview of Figure 3 the operands for each opcode have been left out.

A substantial part of all sequential and parallel low level image processing operations can be implemented using operations from the APIPM instruction set only. These include all image processing operations that can be written as a non-recursive neighborhood operation, or as a geometric transformation (for more information, see [7]). In the (near) future we expect the APIPM instruction set to be extended to incorporate other operations as well. In addition, it is important to note that the programming interface for each parallel image processing operation in our library (that has been implemented using APIPM instructions) has remained identical to its sequential counterpart.

4. Annotated Performance Models

To achieve automatic parallelization and optimization of complete image processing applications, the modeling of the performance of library operations is an essential part of our infrastructure. Based on the APIPM, we have designed a performance model that is *simple*, *accurate*, and *portable* to machines that fit within the APIPM model. In our model we assume that the performance of each library operation can be partitioned into *independent* time intervals, each corresponding to the execution time of a single APIPM instruction. The overall performance of a library operation is obtained by simply adding the execution times of all internal APIPM instructions.

This is formalized as follows. Let $\mathbf{I} = \{I_1, I_2, \cdots, I_n\}$ be the APIPM instruction set. Let $\mathbf{P} = \{P_{I_1}, P_{I_2}, \cdots, P_{I_n}\}$ be the set of performance values for all instructions in $\mathbf{I}$. We assume that, for any system capable of running APIPM instructions, and for each instruction in $\mathbf{I}$, P_{I_i} can be obtained by benchmarking. Also, let $\mathbf{L} = \{\mathbf{L}_1, \mathbf{L}_2, \cdots, \mathbf{L}_m\}$ be the set of all m routines implemented using instructions in $\mathbf{I}$ only. For all library operations $\mathbf{L}_x$ ($x \in \{1, \cdots, m\}$) we define $\mathbf{L}_x = \{I_1, I_2, \cdots, I_n\}$, in combination with the number of occurrences (or *count*) of each APIPM instruction in $\mathbf{L}_x$: $\mathbf{C}_x = \{C_{I_1,x}, C_{I_2,x}, \cdots, C_{I_n,x}\}$. The count of each instruction can have any value in $\mathbb{N}$ (including 0). The expected total execution time of operation $\mathbf{L}_x$ is obtained by

$$T_{\mathbf{L}_x} = \sum_{i=1}^{n} C_{I_i,x} P_{I_i} \tag{1}$$

A similar model was defined in [8], but used for rather different purposes: general machine characterization based on an Abstract Fortran Machine.

A problem with the simplistic model formalized above is that most APIPM instructions (and related performance values) are not single static entities. This is because the execution of an instruction is often dependent on its operands. Therefore, a static entity for each possible operand combination must be incorporated in our model. To avoid an explosion of static entities we allow each instruction I_i and each value P_{I_i} to be *parameterized*. For example, a 'datatype' parameter is incorporated in almost all instructions (e.g. giving $I_i('int')$ and $I_i('float')$). Also, a 'data-input-size' parameter is required for most performance values in $\mathbf{P}$ (e.g. giving $P_{I_i(datatype)}(size)$).

As it is our goal to include no knowledge of underlying hardware, no assumptions can be made about performance growth rates in relation to data input size. To avoid benchmarking for each possible input size, we assume a linear growth rate in the region around each measured size. For each measured input size a 'per data item' value can be obtained by dividing the measured value by the input size. The performance of an operation, for each size s_{in} within the region around the measured size s_m, is then given by

$$P_{I_i(datatype)}(s_{in}) = s_{in} \frac{P_{I_i(datatype)}(s_m)}{s_m}$$

For all communication operations we have created more sophisticated models, based on the 'three paths of commu-

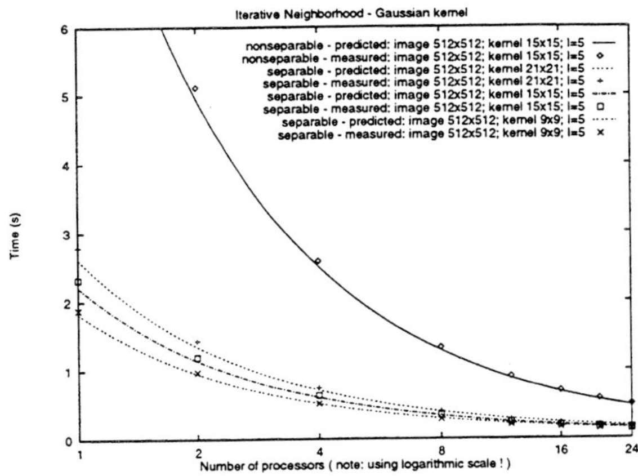

Figure 4. Measured and predicted times for an iterative (5x) Gaussian kernel operation (separable & non-separable) on a 512^2 image.

nication' defined in this project. Discussion, however, is beyond the scope of this paper (see also [10, 11]).

5. Performance Measurements and Validation

To validate the performance models a number of experiments were performed on the 24-node Distributed ASCI Supercomputer (DAS [13]) located at the University of Amsterdam. All nodes contain a 200 Mhz Pentium Pro with 64 Mbyte of DRAM and are connected by a 1.2 Gbit/sec full-duplex Myrinet SAN network. At time of measurement, the clusters ran RedHat Linux 2.0.36.

By running simple benchmarking operations we have obtained values for the performance parameters in our models. Based on these values we have estimated the execution times of many library operations. Unfortunately, space limits the discussion to only one operation: the differential structure of images. In the measurements presented here we have limited ourselves to the first and second order derivatives in the x- and y-direction (five in total).

As is well known, there are many reasons to compute a derivative using convolution with a Gaussian kernel. To avoid round-off errors, the size of the convolution mask should depend on the scale σ and the order of the derivative. A conservative estimate for the average kernel size using only first and second order derivatives is 15x15 pixels. Performance values, obtained by computing the five derivatives in sequence on a 512x512 image, using both separated and nonseparated kernels of various sizes, are depicted in Figure 4. The results are presented only for a row-wise distribution of the image data. As can be seen, on any number of processors, the predicted execution times for all experiments are highly accurate.

6. Conclusions

In this paper we have described an infrastructure that allows an image processing researcher to develop parallel applications transparently. This is made possible by a parallel image processing library, with a programming interface identical to that of a sequential library, that completely hides the parallelism from the user. We have discussed the abstract parallel image processing machine (APIPM), and the performance models based on it. Experiments performed on a machine that fits within the APIPM model show that our performance models are highly accurate. These results strongly suggest that the core of our infrastructure forms a powerful basis for automatic parallelization and optimization of complete image processing applications.

References

[1] J. Brown and D. Crookes. A High Level Language for Parallel Image Processing. *Image and Vision Computing*, 12(2):67–79, Mar. 1994.

[2] D. Crookes and P. Morrow. Design Considerations for a Portable Parallel Abstract Machine for Low Level Image Processing. In *BCS Workshop on Abstract Machine Models for Highly Parallel Computers*, pages 107–110, Mar. 1991.

[3] D. Hammerstrom and D. Lulich. Image Processing Using One-Dimensional Processor Arrays. *Proceedings of IEEE*, 84(7):1005–1018, 1996.

[4] L. Jamieson et al. A Software Environment for Parallel Computer Vision. *IEEE Computer*, 25(2):73–75, Feb. 1992.

[5] D. Koelma, E. Poll, and F. Seinstra. Horus (Release 0.9.2). Technical report, University of Amsterdam, Feb. 2000.

[6] C. Pancake and D. Bergmark. Do Parallel Languages Respond to the Needs of Scientific Programmers. *IEEE Computer*, 23(12):13–23, Dec. 1990.

[7] G. Ritter and J. Wilson. *Handbook of Computer Vision Algorithms in Image Algebra*. CRC Press, Inc, 1996.

[8] R. Saavedra-Barrera et al. Machine Characterization Based on an Abstract High-Level Language Machine. *IEEE Transactions on Computers*, 38(12):1659–1679, Dec. 1989.

[9] A. Saoudi and M. Nivat. Optimal Parallel Algorithms for Multidimensional Template Matching and Pattern Matching. In *Proceedings ICPIA'92*, pages 240–246, Dec. 1992.

[10] F. Seinstra and D. Koelma. Modeling Performance of Low Level Image Processing Routines on MIMD Computers. In *Proceedings of ASCI'99*, pages 307–314, June 1999.

[11] F. Seinstra and D. Koelma. Accurate Performance Models of Parallel Low Level Image Processing Operations Based On a Simple Abstract Machine. Technical report, University of Amsterdam, Apr. 2000.

[12] R. Taniguchi et al. Software Platform for Parallel Image Processing and Computer Vision. In *Parallel and Distr. Methods for Image Processing*, volume 3166, pages 2–10, 1997.

[13] The Distributed ASCI Supercomputer. Information available at: http://www.cs.vu.nl/das/.

[14] G. Wilson and P. Lu. *Parallel Programming Using C++*. Scientific and Engineering Comp. Series. MIT Press, 1996.

3-D Shape Measurement Using a Focused-Section Method

Akira Ishii
Department of Robotics
Ritsumeikan University
aishii@se.ritsumei.ac.jp

Abstract

This paper presents a method for measuring a 3-D shape based on a scheme of shape-from-focus. The method includes the practical object-scanning mechanism of a light-section (or light stripe sectioning) method and the versatility of a conventional shape-from-focus method. A focused plane is inclined typically at 45° to an optical axis of an image-taking lens in order to sweep an object in the same way that a fan-shaped light does in the light-section method. The focused-section method (FSM) processes a focused section image in order to detect an object contour which is an intersection curve of a focused section and an object surface. The contour was obtained by calculating a centroid of a spatial distribution for focus measure on each video raster. A ridge with a height of 200 μm could be measured by the FSM at a precision of 20 μm using a 1/3 "CCD camera with a 60- mm f/2.8 macro lens. A linearity of 3 mm high x 2 mm wide x 2 mm depth was experimentally confirmed.

1. Introduction

A light-section method (LSM), which is also called a triangulation method, that uses a fan-shaped light, is typical means of an on-line measurement for products that are of 3-D shape [1]. Even though this scheme accurately measures and quickly measures the shape of an object that is on a conveyer or in a seam-tracking for arc-welding, it needs a structured light. Also, the use of a laser produces a speckled pattern that obstructs the rough surface measurement. Stereo vision is versatile in principle but is often not reliable in binocular-image processing for detecting disparities. So, applications of stereo vision are restricted to the measurement of simple shapes and structures [2]. A shape-from-focus method (SFFM) is simple, reliable in image processing and versatile, but needs to have an object stopped to take a sequence of defocused images [3]. This requirement is a significant barrier in applying the SFFM to on-line measurement of 3-D shape in a production line.

To establish a simple, versatile, and practical method of measuring 3-D shape in a production line, a new SFFM was studied. In the new method, a focused plane is inclined to an optical axis of the lens. So, the inclined-focused plane can sweep a laterally moving object in the same way as a fan-shaped light in the LSM and can produce contours of the object using a focus analysis without specially structured illumination and without stopping the object for measurement. Formulation for contour detection is presented and experimental results are given to show the performance and precision of the focused-section method (FSM).

2. Measurement principle of FSM

The focused-section method is performed in an optical system shown in Fig. 1. A focused plane, a-b, is inclined at angle θ to an optical axis of an imaging lens with focal length f and is imaged on a CCD image sensor, a'-b', which is inclined at angle φ to the optical axis. This is the Scheimpflug condition [4] and is formulated by the following equation.

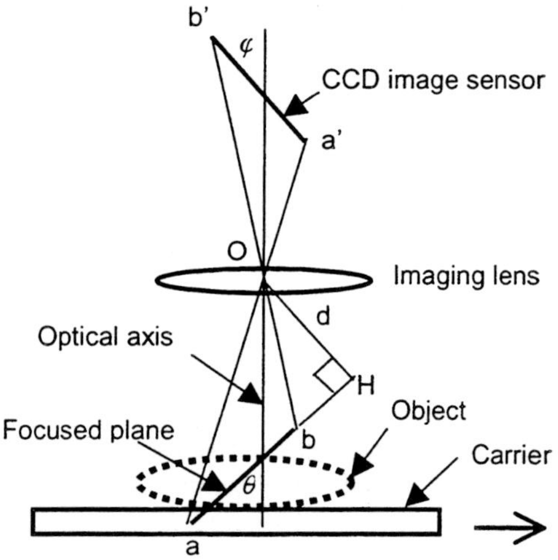

Fig. 1. Optical system for FSM.

$$d = f \cos\theta(\tan\theta - \tan\varphi), \quad (1)$$

where d is length of the vertical line from the center of the lens, O, to the foot, H, on the focused plane, a-b, and f is the focal length of the lens. Typically, when $\theta = \varphi = 45°$, $d = 2^{1/2}$ f and the imaging magnification is 1 at the optical axis.

When a focused plane and an object surface intersect, the contour of the object section is defined at each position of a carrier conveying the object (Fig. 2). The focused section is analogous to a fan-shaped light in a conventional light-section method. Each contour can be obtained by detecting focused points in an image of the focused section using a specific focus-measure [5]. This process of detecting 3-D positions is different from that in a conventional shape-from-focus method [3], where a sequence of defocused images of an object are taken at equal distances while moving the object on a carrier along an optical axis and where a just-focused position of the carrier is detected as the depth coordinates z for each pixel (x, y) of the object image (Fig. 3).

3. Detection of contours

Various focus-measures [5] can be used to detect the contour of a focused section. But the Laplacian measure, which is based on second difference, was found to perform better than the intensity-gradient measures. The intensity-gradient operator [6] is sensitive to defocused edges and their output components disturb to detect a true focus point. Since the original Laplacian operator is unstable, a modified Laplacian operator Lm(i, j) [3] was adopted to define the focus measure Fcs(i, j) at a pixel (i, j) of the focused section image as shown below:

$$Fcs(i,j) = \sum_{n=-N}^{N} Lm(i+n, j), \quad (2)$$

$$\begin{aligned} Lm(i,j) &= |I(i+sp,j) - 2I(i,j) + I(i-sp,j)| \\ &+ |I(i,j+sp) - 2I(i,j) + I(i,j-sp)| \\ &\geq T, \end{aligned} \quad (3)$$

where I(i, j) is the brightness at a pixel (i, j), (2N+1) is the focus estimation width, sp is the difference calculation spacing, and T is the threshold value.

Thus, a contour line, G(i), is computed for an image size of 512 x 440 as follows.

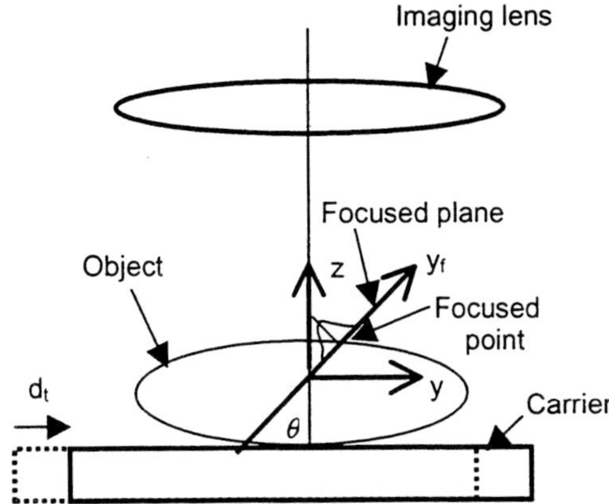

Fig. 2. Shape measurement by FSM. The x-axis is perpendicular to the figure.

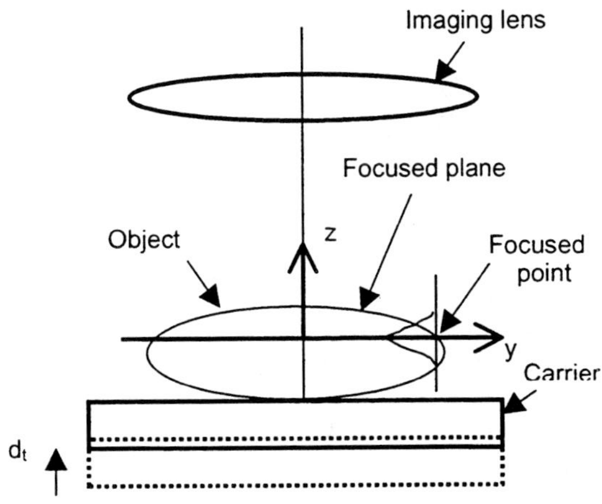

Fig. 3. Shape measurement by SFFM. The x-axis is perpendicular to the figure.

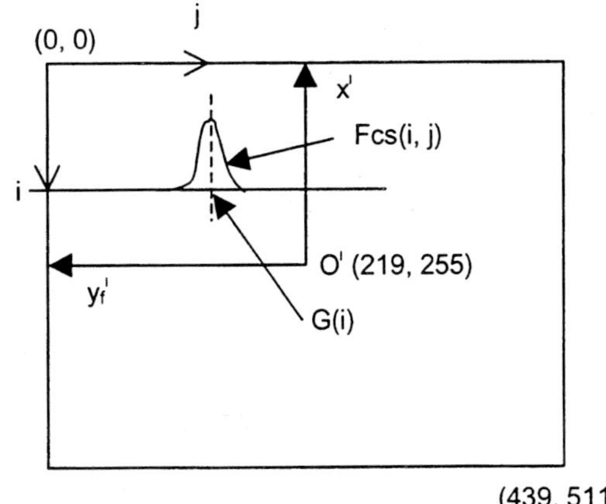

Fig. 4. Coordinate system of the focused plane Image.

$$G(i) = \frac{\sum_{j=sp}^{511-sp} jFcs(i,j)}{\sum_{j=sp}^{511-sp} Fcs(i,j)}, \qquad (i = 0,1,\cdots,439) \quad (4)$$

A 3-D coordinate system, (x, y, z), is set in the object space so that the z-axis coincides with the optical axis (Fig. 2). A y_f-axis is a projection of the y-axis on the focused plane. The conjugate coordinate system, (x^i, y^i, z^i), which is not shown in Fig. 2, is set in the image space. On the focused-plane image, a y_f^i-axis is set to be the conjugate axis with the y_f-axis (Fig. 4). 3-D coordinates, x^i, y^i, z^i, for the focused point (i, G(i)) are described using the system parameters as shown below.

$$\begin{aligned} x^i &= \Delta(219-i), \\ y^i &= y_f{}^i \sin\varphi \\ &= \Delta(255 - G(i))\sin\varphi, \\ z^i &= y_f{}^i \cos\varphi \\ &= \Delta(255 - G(i))\cos\varphi, \end{aligned} \qquad (5)$$

where Δ is the pixel pitch of a CCD image sensor.

In the object space, the coordinates of a contour point, x, y, z, are given as follows.

$$\begin{aligned} x &= M(z/z^i)x^i, \\ y &= M(z/z^i)y^i, \\ z &= \left(\frac{fM^{-1}}{z^i + fM}\right)z^i, \end{aligned} \qquad (6)$$

where M is the magnification for the conjugates origins of the coordinates systems; M = $\tan\theta / \tan\varphi$.

4. Experiments

4.1. Linearity and precision evaluation

The height of a contour line, where a horizontally moving 45°-wedge and a focused plane intersect at a right angle, was measured at each carrier distance d_t in order to evaluate the FSMs linearity and precision (Fig. 5). The wedge was made of an aluminum alloy and was given a rough surface by chemical processing. Specifications of an experimental measurement system are given in Table 1. An outline of an experimental setup is shown in Fig. 6. A mean value z_a and variance c^2 of z-coordinates of points

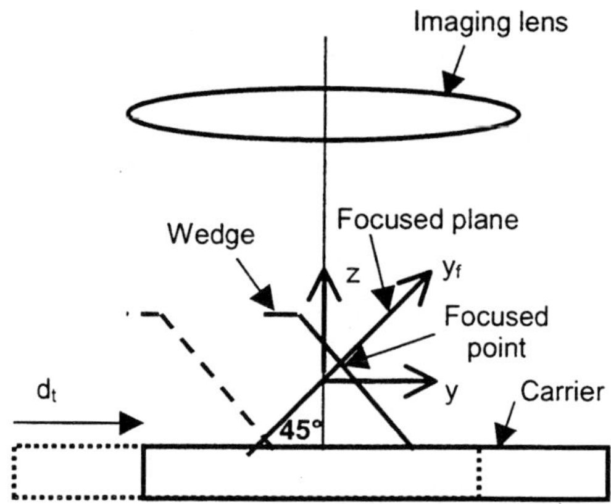

Fig. 5. Measurement of a 45° wedge.

Table 1. System specifications

Image size	512 x 440 pixels
Pixel pitch Δ	7.3 μm
Image sensor angle φ	45°
Focused plane angle θ	45°
Imaging lens	Micro-Nikkor 60mm f / 2.8
Illumination	diffused illumination of a Halogen-lamp (100 W) with a green filter
Carrier	a single-axis table driven by a stepping motor

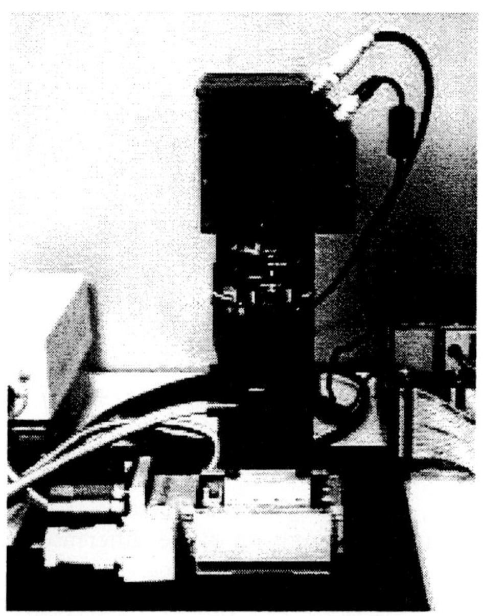

Fig. 6. Outline of an FSM experimental setup.

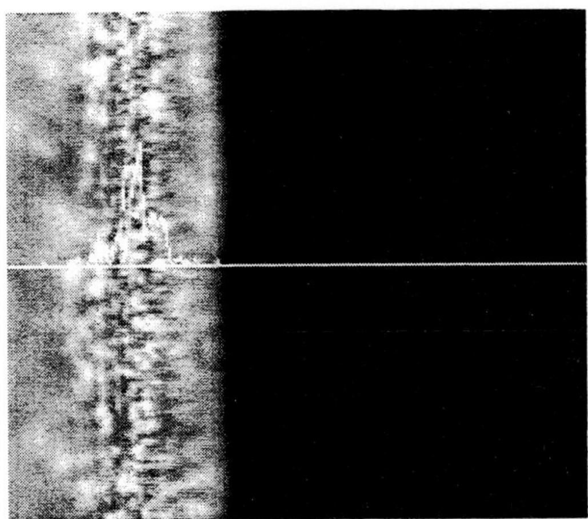

Fig. 7. Focus measure distribution on the intersection area of the wedge and focused plane.

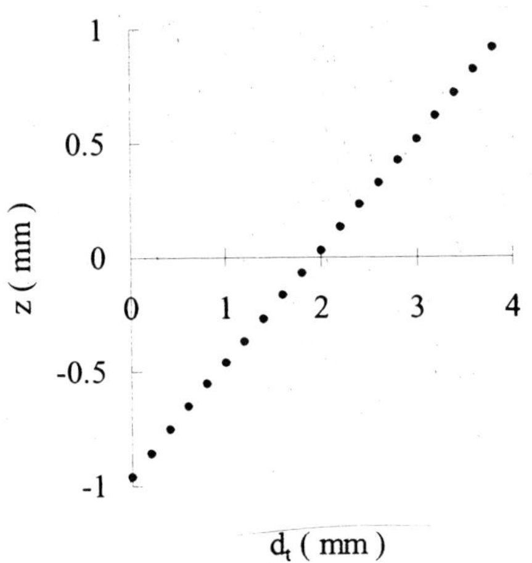

Fig. 9. Linearity evaluation by measuring wedge height. Standard deviation from a regressive straight line: 0.004 mm.

on each contour line of the wedge were calculated for evaluating the linearity of mean values to moving distances of the carrier and measurement precision 2σ .

A mean value, z_a, at a carrier distance d_t was calculated from Eq. (6) as follows.

$$z_a = \left(\frac{f}{z_a^i + f} \right) z_a^i ,$$

$$z_a^i = \Delta(255 - G_a)\cos 45° ,$$

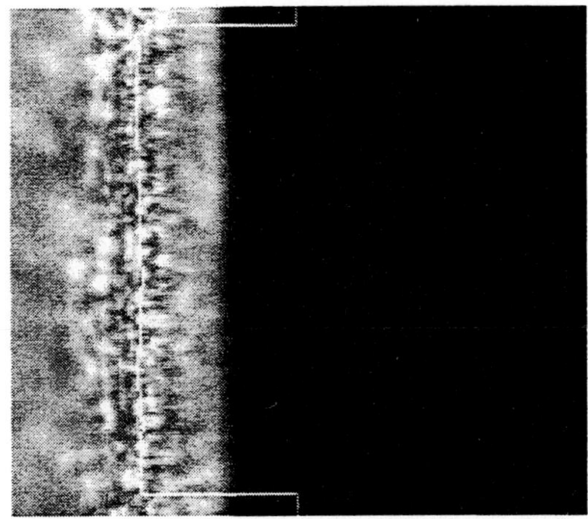

Fig. 8. Detection of a contour on the wedge.

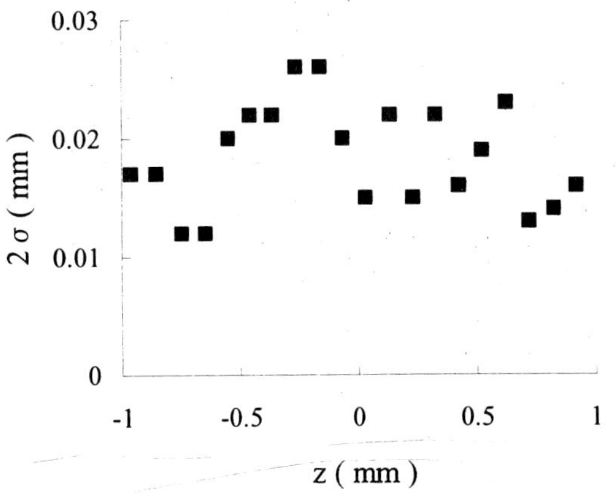

Fig. 10. Measurement precision (2σ) of z-coordinates; σ is the standard deviation.

$$G_a = \frac{\sum_{i=N+sp}^{439-N-sp} G(i)}{440 - 2N - 2sp} . \tag{7}$$

Variance was estimated by the following equation (8).

$$\sigma^2 = \frac{\sum_{i=N+sp}^{439-N-sp} (G(i) - G_a)^2}{439 - 2N - 2sp} . \tag{8}$$

Constants, N, sp, T, in equations (2) and (3), were chosen as follows.

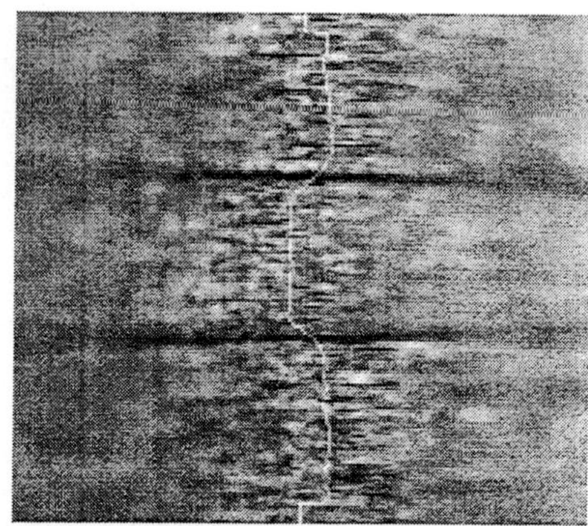

Fig. 11. Detection of a contour crossing of a ridge that is 200 μm high and 1 mm wide.

$$N = 15, \quad sp = 2, \quad T = 30. \tag{9}$$

Figure 7 shows the focus measure distribution, Fcs(i, j), on the wedge. Figure 8 shows the obtained contour, {G(i), i = N + sp, N + sp + 1, ..., 439 – N – sp }.

For each carrier distance, d_t, Fig. 9 shows a mean contour height, z_a, which was obtained by averaging the z-coordinates of a contour along the x-axis (Eq. (7)). The standard deviation of z_a from a regressive straight line fitted by the least-square method was 0.004 mm and sufficient linearity in the measurement was confirmed. Figure 10 shows the measurement precision $2c$, which was calculated from the standard deviation of z-coordinates along the x-axis using Eq. (8), and which was distributed around 0.02 mm for a measurement space of 2 mm deep. The standard deviation of a focus measures distribution, Fcs(i, j), which means the thickness of the focused section, ranged from 0.12 to 0.17 mm. This depends on the F-number and the resolving power of the imaging lens.

4.2. Measurement of a minute ridge

To see real use of the FSM, a minute ridge with a height of 200 μm (nominal) was measured. The ridge was chemically processed in the same way as the wedge. Fig. 11 shows a detected contour crossing the ridge. Fig. 12 shows its measured profile. Peak-to-peak fluctuation was 20 μm. This shows that the resolution is sufficient for measuring a depth of 200 μm or more. A 10-to-90% rise section, which means lateral resolution, was 0.2 mm.

5. Summary and conclusions

Contour lines of an object were obtained by detecting the intersection lines of a focused plane and an object surface based on focus measure. Contour points were defined as a centroid of a focus measure distribution on each row of pixels of a section image. Linearity of measurement was confirmed in a measurement space of 3 mm high x 2 mm wide x 2 mm depth. The measurement precision was 0.02 mm in depth. The measurement of a minute ridge with a height of 200 μm and a width of 1mm successfully demonstrated a depth resolution of 0.02 mm and a lateral resolution of 0.2 mm.

The results were obtained using a 1/3"-CCD image sensor and an F2.8 macro lens. Cutting-edge digital camera technologies and a smaller F-number lens with high resolution are sure to increase measurement space in proportion to a sensor size, and to improve precision in the inverse proportion to F-number. It is natural that a lower precision design with smaller magnification gives a larger measurement space.

Because the FSM has the advantage of having a lateral object-scanning capability that is over a conventional shape-from-focus method, it can measure large and long products flowing on a production line. Also, since the FSM has the advantages of having flexibility in lighting and insensitivity to object surface property over the LSM, the FSM is expected to be widely used in the machine and electronics industry as well as in the foods and apparel industry.

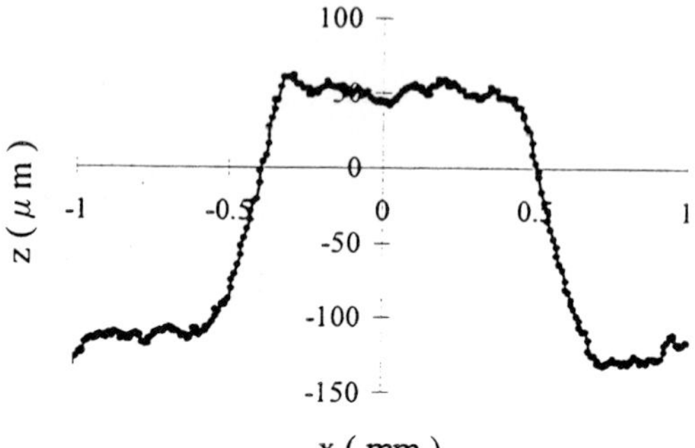

Fig. 12. A measured profile of the ridge.

References

[1] B. G. Batchelor and P. F. Whelan, Intelligent Vision Systems for Industry, Springer-Verlag, London, 1997, p. 360.

[2] L. F. Holeva, Applications of AI, Machine Vision and Robotics, Chapman & Hall, London, 1997, p.1273.

[3] S. K. Nayar and Y. Nakagawa, "Shape from Focus,"IEEE Trans. Pattern Analysis and Machine Intell., Vol. 16, No. 8, pp. 824-831, 1994.

[4] E. Krotkov, "Focusing," International Journal of Computer Vision, Vol. 1, pp. 223-237, 1987.

[5] M. Bass, editor in chief, Handbook of optics, Vol. 2, 2nd ed., McGraw-Hill, New York, 1995, p. 1.7.

[6] R. A. Jarvis, "Focus optimization criteria for computer image processing," Microscope, Vol. 24, No. 2, pp. 163-180, 1976.

A Minutia Matching Algorithm in Fingerprint Verification

Xiping Luo, Jie Tian and Yan Wu
AILAB, Institute of Automation, The Chinese Academy of Sciences, Beijing,100080
e_mail: luoxiping@yahoo.com, tian@readchina.com

Abstract

Fingerprint matching is one of the most important problem in AFIS. In general, we use minutiae such as ridge endings and ridge bifurcation to represent a fingerprint and do fingerprint matching through minutiae matching. In this paper, we proposed a minutia matching algorithm which modified Jain et al.'s algorithm. Our algorithm can better distinguish two images from different fingers and is more robust to nonlinear deformation. Experiments done on a set of fingerprint images captured with an inkless scanner shows that our algorithm is fast and has high accuracy.

1.Introduction

Fingerprint verification determines whether two fingerprints are from the same finger or not. Many fingerprint verification methods have appeared in literature over the years[1]-[4]. In general, the two most prominent features used in fingerprint matching are ridge ending and ridge bifurcation called minutiae.

The algorithm proposed in this paper is originated from the algorithm of Anil Jain et al.[5], but our method differs in three points. Firstly, the alignment method we used is different. Secondly, we introduce ridge information into the following matching process. Thirdly, the method of [5] uses a fixed sized bounding box during the matching process, while we replace it with a bounding box whose size is changeable and is more robust to nonlinear deformations between the fingerprint images.

Section 2 introduced our minutiae matching method in detail. Section 3 gives the experimental results. We conclude in section 4.

2.Minutia matching

For each detected minutia, the following parameters are recorded:

1) x and y coordinate of the minutia point
2) orientation which is defined as the local ridge orientation of the associated ridge
3) The type of the minutia point, that is whether the minutia is ridge ending or ridge bifurcation.
4) The associated ridge.

The associated ridge is represented by points sampled at the average inter-ridge distance along the ridge linked with the corresponding minutiae point.

Minutia matching in the polar coordinate has several advantages as observed in [5]. we will do minutia matching in the polar coordinate.

2.1 Alignment of minutiae set

Let $P=\left((x_1^P, y_1^P, \theta_1^P)^T, \ldots, (x_M^P, y_M^P, \theta_M^P)^T\right)$

denote the set of M minutiae in the template image and

$$Q=\left((x_1^Q, y_1^Q, \theta_1^Q)^T, \ldots, (x_N^Q, y_N^Q, \theta_N^Q)^T\right)$$

denote the set of N minutiae in the input image.

For every minutia P_i ($1 \leq i \leq M$) and Q_j ($1 \leq j \leq N$) in the template and input minutiae set, denote *rotate[i][j]* as the rotation angle between the input and template image if we take P_i and Q_j as the reference point of the corresponding image. If P_i and Q_j can be taken as a corresponding minutia pair, that is the associate ridges of P_i and Q_j are similar to each other to a certain degree *rotate[i][j]* will assume a value between 0 and 360, otherwise we set *rotate[i][j]* as 400 to represent the fact that P_i and Q_j are not corresponding minutia pair.

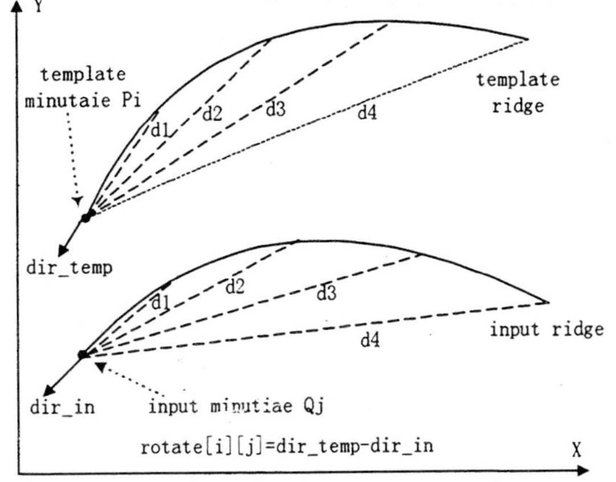

Figure.1 Alignment of the input ridge and the template ridge

Supported by The Chinese National Science Fundation

1051-4651/00 $10.00 © 2000 IEEE

If P_i and Q_j are not the same type, set *rotate[i][j]* as 400. Otherwise let R and r represent the associated ridge of minutia P_i and Q_j. Match R against r to get the difference of these two ridge according to the following formula:

$$Diff\_dist = \frac{1}{L}\sum_{i=0}^{L}|R(d_i) - r(d_i)|$$
$$Diff\_ang = \frac{1}{L}\sum_{i=0}^{L}|R(\alpha_i) - r(\alpha_i)| \qquad (1)$$

Where L is the number of points recorded. $R(d_i)$ is the distance from point i on ridge R to minutia P_i. $R(\alpha_i)$ is the angle between the line connecting point i on ridge R to minutia P_i and the orientation of minutia P_i. $r(d_i)$ and $r(\alpha_i)$ have similar means. See Figure 1.

If *Diff_dis* is larger than T_d or *diff_ang* is larger than T_α, we set *rotate[i][j]* as 400. Otherwise calculate *rotate[i][j]* as:

$$rotate[i][j] = dir\_temp\text{-}dir\_in \qquad (2)$$

Where *dir_temp* is the orientation of P_i and *dir_in* is the orientation of Q_j.

To align the input minutiae set with the template minutiae set in the polar coordinate, all that needs to be done is to translate the input minutiae and the template minutiae to polar coordinate with respect to the reference minutiae P_i and Q_j, and then add the angle *rotate[i][j]* to the radial angle of the polar coordinate of every input minutia. That is, for any minutiae $(x_i, y_i, \theta_i)^T$, apply the following formula:

$$\begin{pmatrix} r_i \\ e_i \\ \theta_i \end{pmatrix} = \begin{pmatrix} \sqrt{(x_i - x^r)^2 + (y_i - y^r)^2} \\ \tan^{-1}\left(\frac{y_i - y^r}{x_i - x^r}\right) + rotate[i][j] \\ \theta_i - \theta^r \end{pmatrix} \qquad (3)$$

Where $(x^r, y^r, \theta^r)^T$ is the coordinate of the reference minutia, and $(r_i, e_i, \theta_i)^T$ is the representation of the minutia in the polar coordinate system (r_i represents the radial distance, e_i represents the radial angle, and θ_i represents the orientation of the minutia with respect to the reference minutia).

2.2 Aligned minutia matching

The steps of our minutia matching algorithm are given below:

1) For i $(1 \leq i \leq M)$ and j $(1 \leq j \leq N)$,. if *rotate[i][j]*=400, then repeat this step and choose another P_i and Q_j, else go to step 2). If all possible minutia pairs have been considered, go to step 5).
2) Take P_i and Q_j as reference minutia. Convert each minutia point in the template minutia set and the input minutiae set to the polar coordinate system with respect to the corresponding reference minutia using the method introduced in the end of section 2.1.
3) Represent the template and the input minutiae in the polar coordinate system as symbolic strings by concatenating each minutia in the increasing order of radial angles:

$$P_i^s = \left((r_1^P, e_1^P, \theta_1^P)^T, \ldots, (r_M^P, e_M^P, \theta_M^P)^T \right) \qquad (4)$$

$$Q_j^s = \left((r_1^Q, e_1^Q, \theta_1^Q)^T, \ldots, (r_N^Q, e_N^Q, \theta_N^Q)^T \right) \qquad (5)$$

4) Match the resulting strings P_i^s and Q_j^s with the process which will be introduced below to find the matching score of P_i^s and Q_j^s. Record it as *m_score[i][j]*. Then go to step 1).
5) Find the maximum value of *m_score[i][j]* and use it as the matching score of the input and template minutiae set. If the matching score is higher than a threshold value, then the input image is considered to come from the same finger as the template image, else we would consider these two images as coming from different fingers.

Before describing the process matching the strings P_i^s and Q_j^s, we will introduce the bounding box and its size.

A bounding box is a box placed around the template minutia, see fig.2. Two sides of the bounding box have constant radial angle, while the other two have constant radius. We use *angle_size* to represent the angle difference between the two sides that have constant radius and *radius_size* to represent the radius difference between the two sides that have constant angle, that is:

angle_size=angle_high-angle_low.

radius_size=radius_high-radius_low.

The size of a bounding box is represented by *angle_size* and *radius_size*.

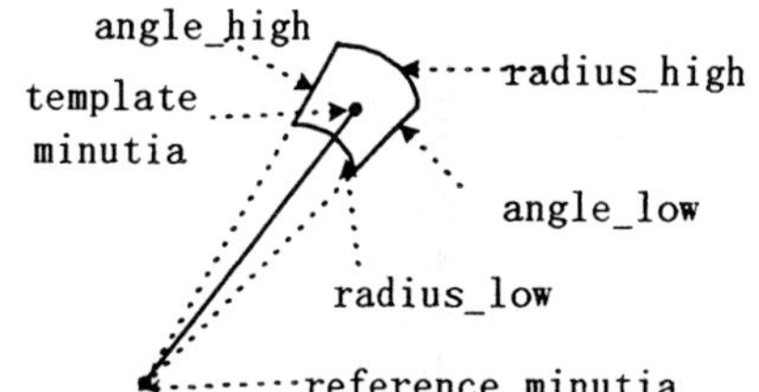

Figure.2 Bounding box

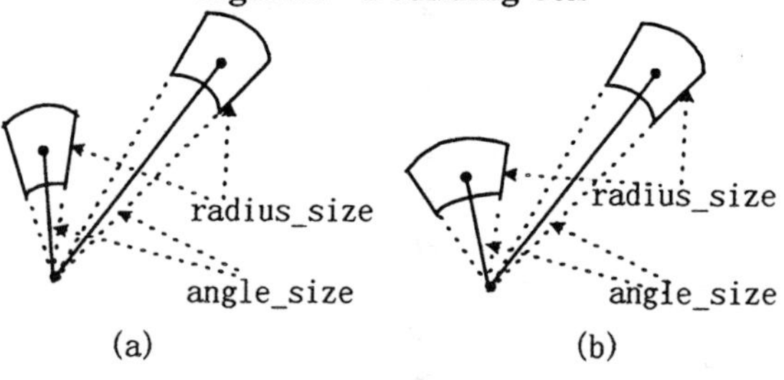

Figure.3 (a).Fixed sized bounding box
(b).Changeable sized bounding box

. We will use a changeable sized bounding box in our algorithm. The value of *angle_size* and *radius_size* of the bounding box in every minutia is changed according to the radius of the minutia. If the radius of the template minutia is larger, then its bounding box will have a larger *radius_size* and a smaller *angle_size*. The difference between the fixed sized bounding box and changeable sized bounding box can be seen in fig.3. The following formula is used to get the *radius_size* and *angle_size* of the bounding box attched to a template minutia with a radius of r:

$$radius\_size = \begin{cases} r\_small & \text{if } r\_size < r\_small \\ r\_size & \text{if } r\_small < r\_size < r\_large \\ r\_large & \text{if } r\_size > r\_large \end{cases} \quad (6)$$

$$r\_size = \frac{r}{\alpha} \quad (7)$$

$$angle\_size = \begin{cases} a\_small & \text{if } a\_size < a\_small \\ a\_size & \text{if } a\_small < a\_size < a\_large \\ a\_large & \text{if } a\_size > a\_large \end{cases} \quad (8)$$

$$a\_size = \frac{\beta}{r^2} \quad (9)$$

Where *r_small, r_large, a_small, a_large* are the lower and upper bound of the *radius_size* and *angle_size* respectively. α and β are predefined constants.

The purpose for using a changeable sized bounding box instead of a fixed size one is to deal with nonlinear deformation more robustly. When the radius of the minutia is small, a small deformation will mean a large change of the radial angle while the change of radius remains small. Hence in this case the *angle_size* of the bounding box should be larger and the *radius_size* of the bounding box should be smaller. On the other hand, when the radius of the minutia is large, a small change in radial angle will cause a large change in the position of the minutia. While the radius can have larger deformation as it is the accumulation of deformation from all the regions between this minutia and the reference minutia. Hence in this case the *angle_size* of the bounding box should be larger and the *radius_size* of the bounding box should be smaller.

Let *input_point[l]* denote the l th point in the input string Q_j^s and *template_point[k]* denote the k th point in the template string P_i^s. Let *angle_size[k]* and *radius_size[k]* denote the size of the bounding box of the k th minutia of the template string. *angle_high[k], angle_low[k], radius_high[k], radius_low[k]* denote the value of the four sides of the bounding box of the k th minutia in the template string. The process matching the strings P_i^s and Q_j^s is described below:

1).Decide the size of the bounding box for each minutia in the template minutia set using (6),(7),(8) and (9) and set *m_score[i][j]*=0.

2). While $1 \leqslant k \leqslant M$ do

While $1 \leqslant L \leqslant N$ and $e_L^P <$ *angle_high[k]* do

If *template_point[k]* and *input_point[L]* satisfy *condition1*, then

m_score[i][j]= m_score[i][j]+1;

Adjust bounding box;

end if

Increase L;

End while

Increase k;

End while

In the above process, *condition1* is defined as:

$$condition1 = \begin{cases} true & \text{if } \begin{cases} radius\_low[k] < (r_l^P - r_k^Q) < radius\_high[k] \\ angle\_low[k] < \Delta e < angle\_high[k] \\ \Delta\theta < \varepsilon \\ rotate[k][l] < 400 \end{cases} \\ false & \text{otherwise} \end{cases} \quad (10)$$

$$\Delta e = \begin{cases} a & \text{if } (a = (e_L^P - e_k^Q + 360) \bmod 360) < 180 \\ a - 180 & \text{otherwise} \end{cases} \quad (11)$$

$$\Delta\theta = \begin{cases} a & \text{if } (a = (\theta_L^P - \theta_k^Q + 360) \bmod 360) < 180 \\ a - 180 & \text{otherwise} \end{cases} \quad (12)$$

The advantage of introducing ridge information (embodied in *rotate[i][j]*) into the matching process lies in two aspects. Firstly, how to choose a reliable reference point pair is a very difficult problem in fingerprint matching. If we consider all possible point pairs and then choose the pair that gives the largest matching score, the computational burden will be too heavy. By the introduction of ridge information, we can greatly reduce the number of point pairs that can be used as reference point pair. P_i and Q_j can be used as reference point pair only when *rotate[i][j]<400.* That is to say, when the associate ridges of P_i and Q_j are similar to each other in a certain degree. In this way, we solved the problem of reference point pair choosing with low computational cost. Secondly, by introducing the ridge information into the matching process, our algorithm can better distinguish two images from different fingers while has little influence on the matching of two images from the same finger. It is because if two fingerprint images come from the same finger, the associate ridges of their corresponding point pairs should similar to each other in a certain degree. That is to say, when we are matching two fingerprint images come from the same finger, if P_k and Q_l are corresponding point pair, it is likely *rotate[k][l]<400.* But when we are matching two fingerprint images come from different fingers, it is very likely P_k and Q_l satisfy all the other conditions of being a corresponding point pair but *rotate[k][l]=400*.

3 Experimental results

The fingerprint image database we used contains 1000 fingerprint images captured from 100 different fingers, 10 images for each finger.

Two images are considered to match well if the matching score is higher than a certain threshold.

In fingerprint verification, we consider the 10 images coming from the same finger as a template. A total of 100 templates were contained in the database. Every image in the database is matched with its own template containing the other nine images of the same finger, and with the other 99 templates. If an image can match well with one of the images in a template, we say it matches well with the template. If an image matches well with the template containing the images coming from the same finger as itself, then a correct verification is established. If an image can not match well with the template containing the images coming from the same finger as itself, it is rejected. If an image matches well with a template contains the images from different fingers, then a false verification is established.

Denote *reject_num* as the number of rejected images, *correct_num* as the number of correct verifications, *false_num* as the number of false verifications, then is verification rate and reject rate is calculated as below:

$$verification\ rate = \frac{correct\_num}{correct\_num + false\_num} \times 100\%$$

$$reject\ rate = \frac{reject\_num}{1000} \times 100\%$$

In fingerprint recognition, each image k (k=1, 2, ..., 1000) is matched against the other 999 images in the database, the top n (n=1, 2, ..., 10) matching score of image k matched with the other images is recorded. If at least one of the correct fingerprint images (the images from the same finger as image k) present among the best n(n=1, 2, ..., 10) matches, then increase *match_num[n]* by 1. *match_num[n]* is denoted as the total number of the correct best n matches. The matching rate of the top n matches is calculated as below:

$$matching\ rate = \frac{match\_num[n]}{1000} \times 100\%$$

Table II gives the matching rate in our experiment.

Table I: the verification rate and Reject rate

Verification rate	Reject rate
100%	13.3%
99.885%	12.8%
99.659%	12.1%
99.554%	10.7%
98.908	9.4%

Table II. Top 10 matching rate

Number of best matches	Matching rate
1	98.3%
2	98.9%
3	99.1%
4	99.1%
5	99.1%
6	99.2%
7	99.3%
8	99.4%
9	99.4%
10	99.4%

The experiment is done on PC computer with PII 350 CPU. The average time for matching two minutiae sets is only 0.018 seconds. Anil Jain et.al reported an average time of 2.55 seconds on a SPARC 20 workstation. We can't compare our algorithm with the one proposed in [5] for two reasons. Firstly, the database we used is different from theirs. Secondly, the formula used to calculate the verification rate, reject rate, and matching rate is not given in [5], they are obvious not the one we used because the data reported in [5] is impossible if our formula are used.

4 Conclusion and Discussion

This paper introduced an algorithm to deal with the problem of minutia matching in fingerprint verification. We used a method that is simple and effective to do fingerprint image alignment. In addition, we introduced ridge information into the process of matching and used a changeable sized box in the matching process, all the above makes our algorithm more able to distinguish images from different fingers and can deal with the nonlinear deformation more robustly.

How to introduce more ridge information into the matching process in a simple way is a problem that needs to be further investigated.

Reference

[1] D.K.Isenor and S.G.Zaky, Fingerprint Identification using graph matching, Pattern Recognition, Vol.19, No.2, pp.113-122,1986

[2] Andrew.K.Hrechak and James A.Mchugh, Automated fingerprint recognition using structural matching. Pattern Recognition, Vol.23, No.8, pp.893-904,1990

[3] Sanjay Ranade and Azriel Rosenfeld, Point Pattern Matching by Relaxation, Pattern Recognition, Vol.12, pp.269-275, 1980

[4] Shih-hsu Chang, Fang-Hsuan Cheng, Wen-hsing Hsu and Guo-zua Wu, Fast algorithm for point pattern matching: invariant to translations, rotations and scale changes. *Pattern Recognition*, Vol.29, pp.311-316,1997

[5] Anil Jain, Lin Hong and Ruud Bolle, On-Line Fingerprint Verification, IEEE Trans on Pattern Analysis and Machine Intelligence, vol.19, No.4. pp302-313, 1997

An Optical Music Recognition System for the Notation of the Orthodox Hellenic Byzantine Music

Velissarios G. Gezerlis
University of Athens, Dept. of Informatics,
Div. of Communication and Signal Processing,
Panepistimioupolis, TYPA Buildings,
157 84, Athens, Greece.
e-mail: gbelis@di.uoa.gr

Sergios Theodoridis
University of Athens, Dept. of Informatics,
Div. of Communication and Signal Processing,
Panepistimioupolis, TYPA Buildings,
157 84, Athens, Greece.
e-mail: stheodor@di.uoa.gr

Abstract

In this paper we present, for the first time, the development of a new system for the off-line optical recognition of the characters of the Orthodox Hellenic Byzantine Music Notation, that has been established since 1814. We describe the structure of the new system, and propose algorithms for the recognition of the 71 distinct character classes, based on Wavelets, 4-projections and other structural and statistical features. Using a simple Nearest Neighbor classifier and a tree-structured classification schema, the accuracy of 99.3 % was achieved, in a database of about 18,000 Byzantine music character patterns. The development of such a system is of great importance to musicologists, especially in our days, which are marked by an increased interest, world wide, for the study and understanding of Eastern type musical forms.

1. Introduction

Byzantine Music originates from the Ancient Hellenic music and is the type of music that was developed, formed and cultured, in the area of the Hellenic Orthodox Christian Church, flourished mainly in the Byzantine era, continued its course in the afterwards metabyzantine years and evolved, throughout the years, to the form which is known today, serving always the worship needs of the Orthodox Church [1].

A lot of research effort has been invested over the last forty years, for the development of systems that are able to understand and optical recognize the western music notes [2]. However, it is the first time that an OCR system is developed for the Byzantine Music (BM).

The goal of this work is to develop a new optical recognition system for the ***Notation of the Hellenic Orthodox Byzantine Music***. The Byzantine Music Notation (BMN), i.e., the way of writing a *psalm*, is of particular interest, not only for the great variety of the used symbols, but also for the way of combination of the symbols, making *semantic musical groups* of different meanings.

The OBMR (Optical Byzantine Music Recognition) system is an off-line optical recognition system and consists of three different and independent stages: a) the ***Segmentation*** stage, b) the ***Recognition*** stage, and c) the ***Semantic Musical Group Recognition*** stage. This paper is focused on the Recognition stage. Towards this goal, various feature generation techniques were developed, such as features based on wavelet transform, 4-projections and other structural and statistical features that have been derived from the contour processing. The classification system evolves around an hierarchical tree-structured pre-classification schema and a Nearest Neighbor Classifier.

2. Byzantine Music Notation

Byzantine Music is a special type of phonetic music, having its own Notation and its own way of performance. An example of the morph and the structure of a *psalm* of the BM is given in fig. 1. As we can notice in this figure, each line of the psalm consists of two parts (or one pair). The first one is the Byzantine music Notation (BMN), called *chant*. Chants are composed by 71 distinct symbols-characters (see table 1), which are combined to form groups of symbols, each one having its own semantic musical meaning and its own musical performance. In the BM more than 2,500 groups of such symbols exist. The second part of each line, corresponding to the singing part of the psalm, consists of the spoken words and syllables written in the Hellenic alphabet. This kind of Notation, which is called *«Analytical Script»* of BM, is the newest one completed and established for use into the Orthodox Church in 1814, e.g., [1].

2.1 The Main Characteristics of the BMN

- The BMN is written from left to right.
- The characters of the notation are not distinguished in caps or lower case ones (see table 1).

1051-4651/00 $10.00

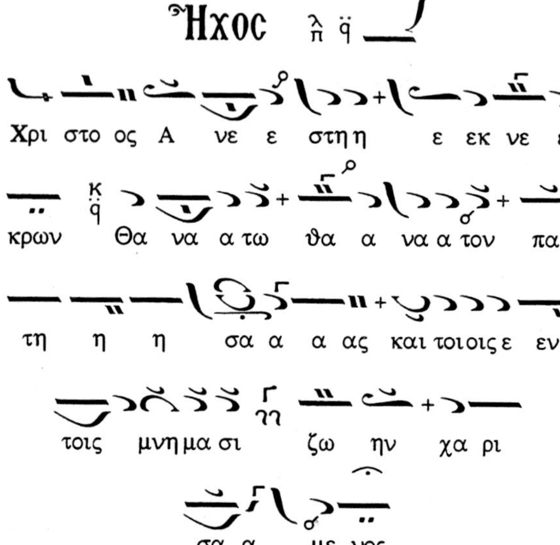

Figure 1. A psalm of the Byzantine Music which is called «Christ is Risen».

- The BMN characters do not touch each other in a musical text and are always separated (see fig. 1).
- The BMN characters are combined so that to be in left or right, above or below and left or right diagonal position. (fig. 1).
- Many characters of the BMN are identical with others, and are distinguished only by their relative rotation of 45^0, 90^0, 135^0, or 180^0 (e.g., the symbols «petasti» and «elafro» differ by 180^0 rotation).
- Moreover, fig. 1 and table 1, show that there are characters (e.g., «clasma» and «oligon») with a substantial difference in size.
- Finally, each one of the resulting semantic musical groups consists of 2 - 10 and even more characters, and corresponds to a different note, or is performed by a *chanter* with a special musical way. This characteristic led us to the conclusion that the OBMR system should extract and recognize semantic musical groups of characters.

Table 1. The 71 distinct symbols of the BMN.

1	isson		37	fthora of Zo	
2	oligon		38	fthora of Ni*	
3	petasti		39	fthora of Di*	
4	kentima		40	fthora of Ni**	
5	ipsili		41	fthora of Pa*	
6	apostroph.		42	fthora of Di**	
7	iporoi		43	fthora of Zo*	
8	elafro		44	diarkis diesi	
9	hamili		45	diarkis ifesi	
10	clasma		46	diesi	
11	apli	•	47	monogrami diesi	
12	varia		48	digrami diesi	
13	stavros	+	49	trigrami diesi	
14	komma	,	50	tetragrami diesi	
15	korona		51	ifesi	
16	ifen		52	monogrami ifesi	
17	gorgo		53	digrami ifesi	
18	digorgo		54	trigrami ifesi	
19	trigorgo		55	tetragrami ifesi	
20	argo		56	di	
21	imiolio		57	ke	
22	diargo		58	zo	
23	psifisto		59	ni	
24	omalo		60	pa	
25	syndesmos		61	vu	
26	antikenoma		62	ga	
27	endofono		63	delta	
28	zigos		64	imifi	
29	kliton		65	lamda	
30	spathi		66	martiria Ga	
31	fthora of Ni		67	martiria Zo	
32	fthora of Pa		68	martiria Pa	
33	fthora of Vu		69	tonos	
34	fthora of Ga		70	hi	x
35	fthora of Di		71	stigmi	.
36	fthora of Ke				

* used for distinguishing the similar names

3. The OBMR System Description

The overall structure of the OBMR system (see fig. 3), is divided into the following three stages: a) The ***Segmentation Stage***, which is divided into three tasks: i) to segment the whole page into line pairs, ii) to separate the chant from the Hellenic script below it and iii) to extract the individual characters from the chant. b) The ***Recognition Stage***, which takes as input bitmaps of the characters of BMN, and consists of three main steps: i) the *preprocessing*, ii) the *feature generation*, and iii) the *classification*, which will be discussed in detail into the next section. c) The ***Semantic Musical Group Recognition Stage***, which takes as input the character identification numbers (cids), as well as information from the segmentation stage related to the topological relationship of the characters [7]. Based on this information, we construct the semantic musical groups and recognize them using a data base that works as a grammar and contains all the possible groups of the BMN. Finally, the final ***post processing*** step, takes as input the group identification numbers and gives as output the final result, which may be the conversion to a true type font, or the performance of the BM.

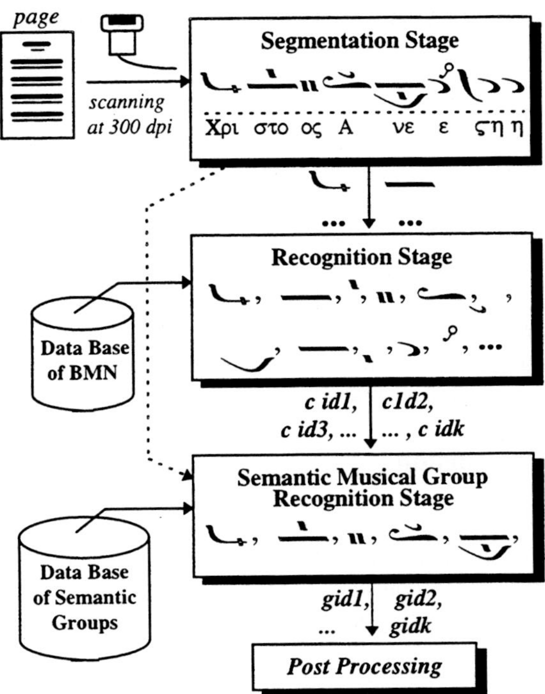

Figure 3. The structure of the OBMR system.

3.1 Description of the Data Base of the BMN

The data base of the BMN developed for our needs consists of approximately 18,000 symbols in the form of 256 gray scale window bitmap files. We have created 250 different patterns for each one of the 71 classes. These 250 pattern characters consist of: i) real scanned characters from Byzantine music books ii) printed characters using a new software for writing the BMN called Byzwriter 1.0 (developed by the author) and iii) carefully painted by hand characters so as to resemble to the printed ones. So, the developed data set is semi-printed and semi-handwritten (see fig. 3.1).

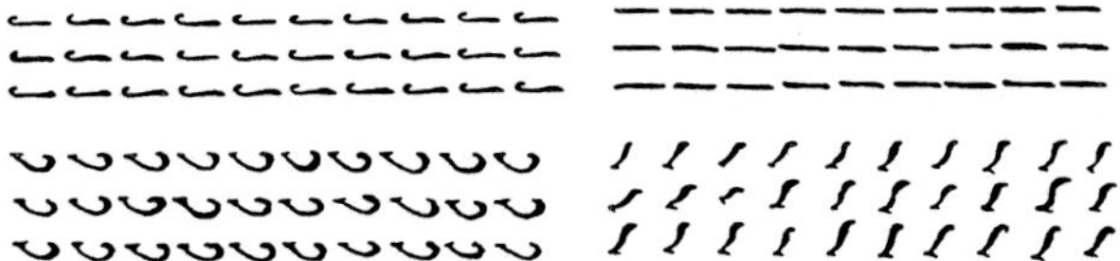

Figure 3.1. Samples of the BMN data base.

4. The Recognition Stage

The three main steps of the recognition stage are:

4.1 Preprocessing

Preprocessing aims to make the characters invariant to translation and scaling. However, the rotation invariance is not desirable for this system, since there are distinct characters which are identical, but rotated. The preprocessing algorithms employed for the image characters are:

- *Binarization* into black and white bi-level image.
- *Edge smoothing* for the border of the image character and for the filling of one pixel holes.
- *Size normalization* of the image character, fixing the image size to 72x72 pixels, e.g., [3].

4.2 Feature Generation

Both structural and statistical features are generated, e.g., [3], [6]:

4.2.1 Structural features. i) The *Euler number* (E_N) of the character is computed. This feature separates the set of 71 classes into three smaller subsets, depending on the number of internal holes. ii) The *Principal Axis Direction* (PA) of the character is computed, and iii) the *Ratio of the Horizontal Bounding Rectangle* (Ratio_of_HBR) of the character is derived. These three structural features separate the original set of 71 classes of table 1 into 20 smaller subsets with an average of 10 characters per subset. This constitutes an hierarchical preclassification schema, making the classification simpler, faster and more efficient, and it exploits the specific characteristics of the BMN.

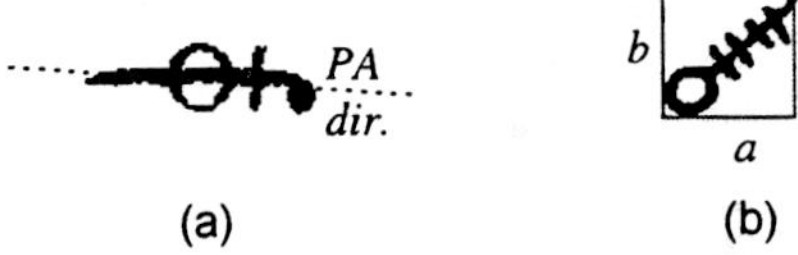

Figure 4.2.1. a) Principal axis direction, and b) Ratio of HBR (=b/a).

4.2.2. Statistical features. The statistical features that have been adopted are a) the Discrete Wavelet Transform (DWT), e.g. [4], [8], of the contour function of the character and b) the DWT of the 4-projections of the image character.

a) First, we compute the contour of the character. For reducing the variation of the contour function, we introduce the idea of an *adaptive starting point*, based on the value of Euler number. We use the *Left Diagonal starting point*, if $E_N = 1$, which is the first pixel detected, scanning the image left diagonally and the *Right Diagonally starting point*, if $E_N = 0, -1$ *or* -2, scanning the image right diagonally. Moreover, using the approximation method of the *Bezier Splines* we can fix, approximately, the length L of the contour function to be a power of 2 (e.g., $2^7 = 128$) points (see fig. 4.2.2). This, not only smoothes the contour function but also is useful for the application of the DWT, which requires the periodic function to have a period equal to a power of 2, e.g., [4], [8]. So, the contour can be represented as a closed parametric curve c in the complex

plane C, i.e.,

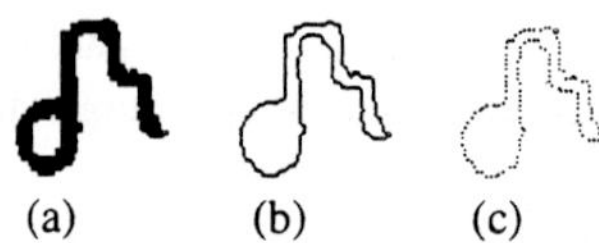

Figure 4.2.2. a) The binarized character «delta». b) The contour of length L. c) The approximated smoothed version using the Bezier splines having dimension 128 = 2^7.

$$c(i)= x(i)+ jy(i), \qquad i=0...L-1$$

where L is equal to *128* points and j denotes the imaginary unit. We can consider that the function c is periodic with period L. Then the DWT of c would be:

$$DWT(c(i))= DWT(x(i))+ jDWT(y(i))$$

b) We compute the 4-projections of an image character i.e., horizontal, vertical, left-diagonal, right-diagonal (see fig. 4.2.3). A vector $P(i)$, $i=0...447$, is generated, that contains the values of the 4 projections. In the sequel, the DWT is applied on this vector.

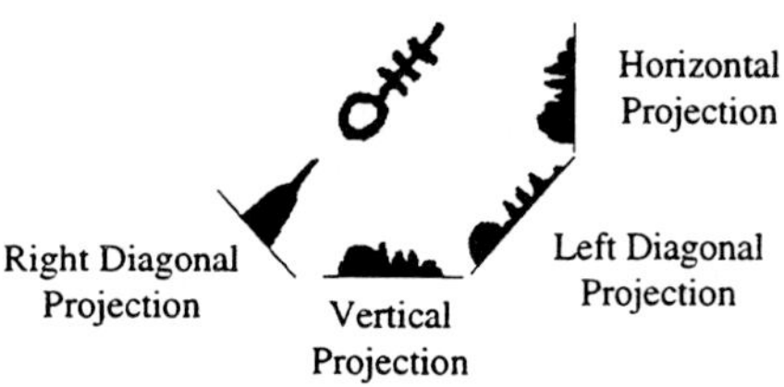

Figure 4.2.3. The character «tetragrami diesi» and its 4-projections.

For the computation of the DWT the low and high pass «db2» (Daubechies 2) filters are used. The Discrete wavelet decomposition is applied onto the $x(i)$ and $y(i)$, $i=0...127$, vectors of the contour function and onto the $P(i)$, $i=0...447$, vector of the projection and a final feature vector F of dimension 60 is obtained. This consists of the *16 + 16 = 32* lowest wavelet descriptors of the x and y decomposition plus the *28* lowest wavelet descriptors of the P decomposition. To the best of our knowledge, such a feature vector has never been used before. We use this feature vector for the final classification of the characters using a Nearest Neighbor Classifier (NNC) together with the preclassification schema described above, which is trained and tested using the developed database of the BMN.

5. Experimental Results

After extensive experimentation, together with other off-the self techniques, we concluded that the above combination of features serves the needs of our problem best and gave the best results. The application of described features with the NNC classifier and the structural pre-classification schema resulted in an average accuracy of 96,17 %. However, it was observed that certain classes of characters were mutually confused during classification. Thus, a post-classification stage was developed that solved all the confusions [5]. For the final evaluation of the system the *Leave-ten-method* (LTM) was adopted and tested on the developed data base, and resulted in an overall final accuracy of 99,3%. Finally, the described method was applied on various real scanned pages of BMN and the recognition accuracy ranged from 96% to 100%.

6. Conclusion

In this paper, we presented an off-line OBMR system for the optical recognition of the BMN, for the first time. For the recognition stage of the system both structural and statistical features were generated, such as the Euler number, the Principal axis direction, the Ratio of HBR, the DWT on the approximated version of the contour function and the DWT on the 4-projection vector of the image character. For the classification a tree-structured hierarchical scheme was adopted followed by a NNC classifier.

7. References

[1] D.G.Panagiotopoulos «Theory and Practice of the Church Byzantine Music», 1991.

[2] D. Bainbridge and N. Carter «Automatic Reading of Music Notation», *Handbook of Character Recognition and Document Image Analysis,* pp. 583-603. 1997.

[3] S. Mori, H. Nishida, H. Yamada, «Optical Character Recognition», *Wiley Series* 1999.

[4] S. Theodoridis, K. Koutroumbas «Pattern Recognition», *Academic Press* 1998.

[5] V.G.Gezerlis, S. Theodoridis «A Post-Classification Scheme for an OCR System for the Notation of the Orthodox Hellenic Byzantine Music», *Submitted to Eusipco-2000 conference, Finland,* Oct. 1999.

[6] Øivind D. Trier, A. K. Jain, T. Taxt, «Feature Extraction Methods for Character Recognition-A Survey», *Pattern Recognition, Vol. 29, no 4,* pp. 641-662, 1996.

[7] S.W.Lu, Y. Ren, C.Y. Suen, «Hierarchical Attributed Graph Representation and Recognition of Handwritten Chinese Characters», *Pattern Recognition, vol. 24, no 7,* pp. 617-632, 1991.

[8] G.C.-H.Chuang, C.-C. Jay Kuo, «Wavelet Descriptors of Planar Curves: Theory and Applications», *IEEE Trans. on Image Processing, vol. 5, no 1,* pp. 56-70, Jan. 1996.

Comparison of Some Multiple Expert Strategies: An Investigation of Resource Prerequisites and Achievable Performance

A. F. R. Rahman and M. C. Fairhurst
University of Kent, Canterbury, UK

Abstract

Implementation of various multiple expert decision combination approaches for recognition of machine printed characters involves costs in terms of number of processing elements and the overall layout of the decision fusion hierarchy. This paper investigates the relationship between the implementation cost and the performance achieved by these approaches. Seven different multiple expert decision combination approaches have been investigated in terms of this cost versus performance profile.

1. Introduction

Multiple expert decision combination approaches have become very attractive choices as practical solutions to the task of character recognition, as they have been shown to enhance the overall recognition performance of a typical single classifier (expert). Various such approaches have been proposed, ranging from relatively simple to very sophisticated methods (Suen *et al.*[9], Rahman and Fairhurst[8], Ho *et al.*[2], Kittler *et al.*[5] etc.). In most cases, these approaches enhance the overall recognition performance of the system, but this enhancement is often achieved at the price of additional structural and implementation complexity. This arises because of the introduction of additional logic and increased processing requirements.

An interesting problem arises when it is required to select a particular multiple expert decision combination approach to solve a specific character recognition task. It is realised that adoption of any multiple expert approach results in additional structural complexity, thereby increasing the implementation cost, but an important question to ask is whether selecting an approach with higher implementation cost automatically ensures a higher recognition performance compared to another approach having lower implementation cost. This is a question that deserves some investigation, because in most practical cases, implementation cost and recognition performance are both parameters of importance for selecting a particular solution and therefore the relationship between these two parameters needs to be assessed in order to select the most appropriate decision combination approach.

In this paper, the relationship between the implementation cost and the attainable overall performance is investigated. A general analysis of the problem is presented, along with comparative analysis of seven selected multiple expert decision combination approaches within a typical illustrative task domain.

2. Selected Multiple Expert Decision Combination Methods

A range of multiple expert decision combination methods have been selected for comparison in terms of resource prerequisites and achievable performance as applied to the task of character recognition. These methods include the following:

- The Aggregation Method (AM) (Ho *et al.*[2]),
- The Ranking Method (RM) (Mazurov *et al.*[6]),
- The Behaviour Knowledge Space Method (BKSM) (Huang and Suen[3]),
- The Majority Voting Scheme (MVS) (Kittler and Hatel[4]).
- Serial Combination Method (SCM) (Rahman and Fairhurst[8]),
- Confidence Based Combination Method (CBCM) (Rahman and Fairhurst[7]) and,
- Hybrid Combination Method (HCM) (Rahman and Fairhurst[1]).

3. Selected Independent Experts

To compare the performances of different multiple expert configurations, a pool of experts is selected, as follows:

- *Binary Weighted Scheme(BWS):* This employs a technique based on *n-tuple* sampling (Rahman and Fairhurst[8]).
- *Frequency Weighted Scheme(FWS):* This employs an *n-tuple* based technique where the memory elements calculate the relative probability distribution of the group of *n-tuples* (Rahman and Fairhurst[8]).
- *Multi-layer Perceptron Network(MLP):* This is the standard multilayer perceptron neural network structure, employing the standard error backpropagation algorithm (Rahman and Fairhurst[8]).
- *Moment-based Pattern Classifiers(MPC):* These statistical algorithms make use of the nth order mathematical moments derived from the binarised patterns. Discrimination is derived from a maximum likelihood classifier (Rahman and Fairhurst[8].

4. Selected Database

The database chosen for all the experiments presented in this paper contains samples of machine printed characters (0..9, A..Z, with no distinction made between the characters '1/I' and '0/O') (Rahman and Fairhurst[1]).

5. Resource Prerequisite: An Analysis

Before adopting a particular multiple expert approach, it is very important to analyse the cost of its implementation. This is an issue often neglected in the comparison of various such approaches, since in most cases the principal emphasis is given to performance analysis in terms of absolute recognition rates. Here, some prerequisites of successful implementation of multiple expert decision combination approaches are discussed.

5.1. Number of Processing Elements

Processing elements are the computational and controlling backbone of multiple expert decision combination approaches. There are two types of processing elements, active and passive elements. The active processing elements are the elements (classifiers) which specifically perform recognition-oriented computations. On the other hand, the passive elements perform the tasks of data re-routing and establishing physical pathways among the different active elements in the configuration.

5.2. Structure of the Decision Combination Framework

The number of processing elements in a multiple expert decision fusion technique is an important consideration in defining the implementation cost of such approaches. More important still, however, is the framework in which these processing elements are placed relative to each other which primarily defines the structural configuration of the complete system. There are three different ways in which the structural layout can be defined (Rahman and Fairhurst[8]). These are:

- ***Vertical Layout***: In this case, the processing elements are arranged in a sequential fashion.
- ***Horizontal Layout***: In this case, the processing elements are arranged in a parallel fashion, so that they function concurrently and independently.
- ***Hybrid Layout***: In this case, the processing elements are arranged in a fashion which is a hybridisation of the first two configurations.

Type of Algorithm	Number of Processing Elements					
	Digits			Digit+Upp. Case		
	Act.	Pas.	Tot.	Act.	Pas.	Tot.
AM	5	0	5	5	0	5
RM	4	1	5	4	1	5
BKSM	4	1	5	4	1	5
MVS	4	1	5	4	1	5
SCM	4	0	4	4	0	4
CBCM	4	2	6	4	2	6
HCM	4	1	5	6	1	7

Table 1. Comparison among different configurations: Processing elements

6. Comparison of Approaches

6.1. Number of Processing Elements

Since the number of elements is directly dependent on the number of experts in the configuration, comparison should be made among various configurations having the same number of experts. Table 1 presents a comparison of the combined configurations consisting of four cooperating experts when applied to the recognition of numeral classes based on the number of processing elements in the overall configuration. It is observed that the SCM is the simplest, having the same number of processing elements as the number of experts. The RM, BKSM, MVS and the HCM have four active elements and a single passive element. The AM, on the other hand, has five active elements and no passive element. The CBCM employs four active elements and two passive elements.

Type of Algorithm	Type of Layout
AM	Hybrid
RM	Horizontal
BKSM	Horizontal
MVS	Horizontal
SCM	Vertical
CBCM	Horizontal
HCM	Hybrid

Table 2. Comparison among different configurations: Processing elements

6.2. Structure of the Decision Combination Framework

Table 2 presents a comparison of the various combination methods in terms of the structural layout. The SCM has a vertical decision combination layout. In the CBCM, RM, BKSM and the MVS, the active experts are placed in the hierarchy in such a way that there is no direct connection or data transfer channel between them. Because of these particular connectivity characteristics, the decisions delivered by the experts in such a framework are not influenced in any way by any other expert, and only a single passive expert combines their respective decisions. Finally, in the HCM and AM, the experts are connected using a combination of vertical and horizontal layout.

Type of Algorithm	Ranking	
	Digits	Digit+Upp. Case
AM	2	2
RM	1	1
BKSM	1	1
MVS	1	1
SCM	0	0
CBCM	4	3
HCM	3	4

Table 3. Comparison among different configurations: Ranking

6.3. Comments on Implementation Cost

From the discussion presented so far, it is now possible to rank the various various multiple expert decision combination approaches in terms of implementation cost (Table 3). For the sake of simplicity, the ranking is made on a linear scale between 0 to 4 (where 0 is the least and 4 is the most expensive). The SCM has been found to be the least and the CBCM to be the most expensive. Other approaches have intermediate costs associated with their implementation.

Type of Expert	Optimum Recognition Rate	
	Digit Classes %	Digit + Upper Case Letters %
BWS	98.24	95.70
FWS	98.48	97.25
MPC	96.80	94.08
MLP	98.34	96.25

Table 4. Performance comparison of the different experts

Type of Algorithm	Overall Performances	
	Digit Classes	Digits Plus Upper Case
AM	98.66	97.53
RM	98.73	97.92
BKSM	98.81	98.01
MVS	98.71	97.75
SCM	98.99	98.21
CBCM	98.98	97.98
HCM	99.14	98.61

Table 5. Comparison among different configurations

6.4. Relative Overall Performance

Table 4 presents the performance of the various experts when working independently. Table 5 presents the comparative performances of the various decision combination approaches. It is seen from these results that the HCM performs best, followed by the BKSM and the CBCM. The AM, the RM and the MVS produced comparable performance on the selected databases. The SCM was moderately successful compared to other approaches.

Type of Algorithm	Approach Number	Overall Performances	
		Digit Classes	Digits Plus Upper Case
AM	1	0	0
RM	2	2	2
BKSM	3	3	4
MVS	4	1	1
SCM	5	5	5
CBCM	6	4	3
HCM	7	6	6

Table 6. Ranking the various approaches in terms of recognition performance

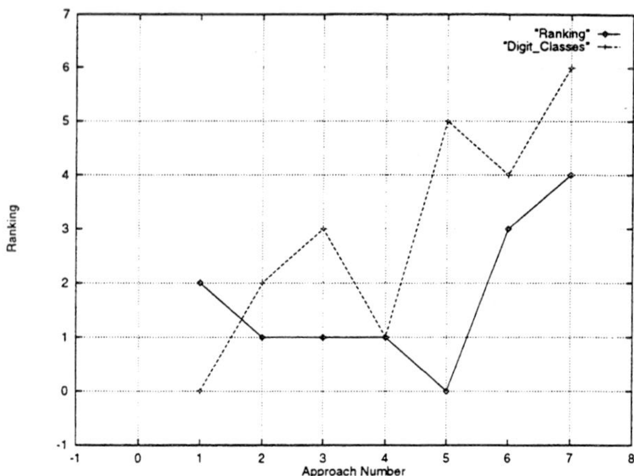

Figure 1. Comparison of the rank versus performance

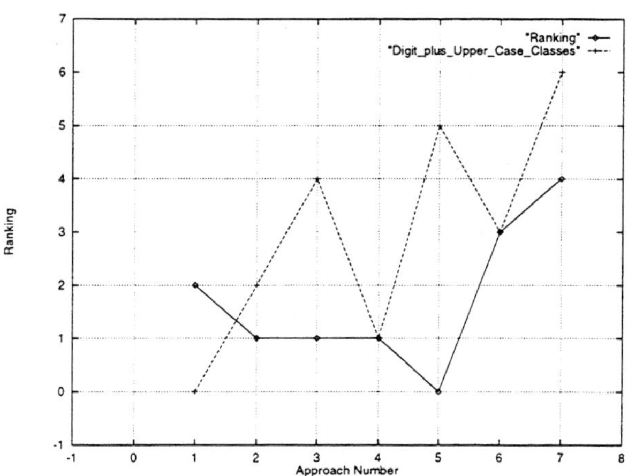

Figure 2. Comparison of the rank versus performance

6.5. Cost Versus Performance Profile

It is now possible to rank the various multiple expert approaches in terms of the overall performance achieved for the two specific tasks, the recognition of digit classes and the recognition of digit plus upper case letter classes. Table 6 presents these rankings. For the sake of simplicity, the ranking is made on a linear scale between 0 to 6 (where 0 is the least successful and 6 is the most successful). Figures 1 and 2 present such cost versus performance profiles for the cases of digits and digits plus upper case letters respectively. The parameters used in the X and Y axes are already assigned in Table 6.

A very interesting observation can be made from these cost-performance profiles. It is noted that there is no direct functional relationship between the cost and the achievable performance, which means that additional computational complexity does not automatically lead to higher performance. This also demonstrates that it is entirely possible to design very powerful multiple expert decision combination approaches without a corresponding increase in the implemental complexity.

7. Summary and Conclusions

This paper has investigated the relationship between the implementation cost and the attainable overall performance of various multiple expert decision combination approaches for the recognition of machine printed characters. It has been demonstrated that there is no direct functional relationship between the implementation cost and achievable performance, which indicates that before selecting a particular approach all the parameters of interest, including the implementation cost and attainable performance, need to be assessed before a selection is made. It is also demonstrated that it is perfectly possible to design very powerful multiple expert decision combination approaches without proportionally increasing the implemental complexity.

References

[1] M. C. Fairhurst and A. F. R. Rahman. A generalised approach to the recognition of structurally similar handwritten characters. *IEE Proc. on Vision, Image and Signal Processing*, 144(1):15–22, 1997.

[2] T. K. Ho, J. J. Hull, and S. N. Srihari. Decision combination in multiple classifier systems. *IEEE Trans. Pattern Analysis and Machine Intelligence*, 16(1):66–75, Jan. 1994.

[3] Y. S. Huang and C. Suen. A method of combining multiple experts for the recognition of unconstrained handwritten numerals. *IEEE Trans. Pattern Analysis and Machine Intelligence*, 17(1):90–94, Jan. 1995.

[4] J. Kittler and M. Hatef. Improving recognition rates by classifier combination. In *Proc. 5th Int. Workshop on Frontiers of Handwriting Recognition*, pages 81–102, 1996.

[5] J. Kittler, A. Hojjatoleslami, and T. Windeatt. Weighting factors in multiple expert fusion. In *Proc. British Machine Vision Conference*, pages 41–50, 1997.

[6] V. D. Mazurov, A. I. Krivonogov, and V. L. Kazantsev. Solving of optimisation and identification problems by the committee methods. *Pattern Recognition*, 20(4):371–378, 1987.

[7] A. F. R. Rahman and M. C. Fairhurst. Exploiting second order information to design a novel multiple expert decision combination platform for pattern classification. *Electronics Letters*, 33(6):476–477, 1997.

[8] A. F. R. Rahman and M. C. Fairhurst. An evaluation of multi-expert configurations for recognition of handwritten numerals. *Pattern Recognition*, 31(9):1255–1273, 1998.

[9] C. Y. Suen, C. Nadal, R. Legault, T. A. Mai, and L. Lam. Computer recognition of unconstrained handwritten numerals. *Proceedings of the IEEE*, 80(7):1162–1180, 1992.

Object Recognition using Appearance Models Accumulated into Environment

Yasushi MAE, Tomohiro UMETANI, Tatsuo ARAI and Kenji INOUE
Department of Systems and Human Science
Graduate School of Engineering Science, Osaka University
1-3 Machikaneyama, Toyonaka, Osaka 560-8531, JAPAN
mae@sys.es.osaka-u.ac.jp

Abstract

This paper proposes a new method of object recognition using appearance models accumulated into RFID(Radio Frequency IDentification) tag attached to environment. Robots recognize the object using appearance models accumulated in the tag on the object. If the robot fails recognition, the robot acquires a model of the object and accumulates it to the tag. Since robots in the environment observe the object from different points of view at different time, various appearance models are accumulated as time passes. In order to accumulate many models, eigenspace analysis is applied. The eigenspace is reconstructed every time robots acquire the model. Experimental result of object recognition shows effectiveness of the proposed method.

1. Introduction

Object recognition is one of the basic tasks for robots in order to achieve more complex tasks given by human beings in office, home, and so on. Several appearance-based model matching methods have been proposed[1, 2, 3]. Appearance model is suitable for modeling objects autonomously by robots, since robots can acquire the appearance of objects without prior knowledge about the object. If the acquired models can be accumulated into the object, robots can recognize the object without observation.

Several methods storing information into environment have been proposed[4, 5, 6]. A drawback of methods using visual marks[4, 5] is that robots cannot overwrite visual marks. A RFID system, which includes reader/writer and RFID tags, is one of the solutions for sharing information between robots. A special device called IDC(Intelligent Data Carrier), which is a kind of RFID tag with large amount of memory and CPU, has also been developed[6]. A robot with a reader/writer can share the models acquired by other robots through these tags attached to objects.

In this paper, we propose a new method of object recognition using appearance object models accumulated into RFID tags attached to objects. The robot recognizes the object using the accumulated models in the tag. If no matching models are in the tag, the robot observes the object and accumulates the acquired model into the tag as shown in **Fig.1**(a). The robots come to recognize the object without sensing as shown in Fig.1(b) as time passes, since robots acquire the models from different view point and accumulate them to the tag. Eigenspace analysis is applied to accumulate many models. The eigenspace is reconstructed every time robots acquire the model. Since the accumulated models in the tag can be shared by every robot in the environment, the method is effective for cooperative and multiple robots system.

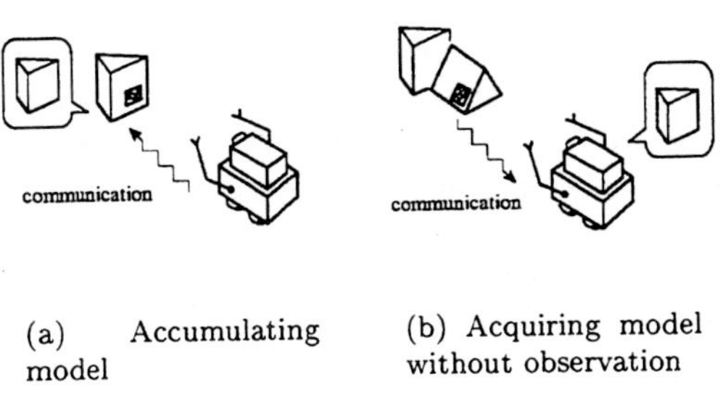

(a) Accumulating model (b) Acquiring model without observation

Figure 1. Basic Idea of Our Method

2. Overview of Our Method

We assume a robot is given an appearance model of a target object from a point of view for object recognition. The outline of the object recognition is as follows.

(1) The robot searches the environment for the target objects. If the robot finds an object, go to (2). Otherwise go to (1). (2) If an accumulated model in the tag on the object matches the given model, the robot recognizes the object as a target object without sensing. Otherwise go to (3). (3) The robot acquires the object model by sensing. (4) The robot accumulates the acquired model to the tag. (5) If the acquired model matches the given model, the robot recognizes the object as a target object. Otherwise go to (1).

We use euclidean distance as a matching measure. If the distance between the models are small enough, these models are matched. If the number of models is large, the eigenspace analysis is used for accumulating many models. In this case, the distance of models is measured on the eigenspace.

3. Acquisition of Object Model

The appearance edges of an object are used as an appearance model of an object. The edges belonging to an object are approximated by straight segments. We call a set of these segments edge segments.

3.1. Extraction of Object Region

In a scene like **Fig.2**(a), it is difficult to extract edges belonging to an object from an image, because other edges belonging to the background are also observed in the image (see Fig.2(b)). If a robot can move an object a little, the robot can extract an object region by thresholding the differentiated images.

A robot can move its arm a little even the robot knows nothing about the environment. When the arm touches an object and moves it a little, the edges belonging to the same object may be moved at the same time. Figure 2(c) shows the region with motion when the robot moves the object a little. The region corresponds to an object region. The edges are searched for the neighborhood of the region and extracted. Figure 2(d) shows the extracted edges. We can see the edges almost correspond to the edges of an object.

3.2. Construction of Object Model

We use Hough transform for extracting the edge segments. If the object edges are near an extracted line, the corresponding parts of the line is extracted as an edge segment. If the edge segments are adjacent, the adjacent end points are replaced by the intersection of the adjacent edge segments. **Figure 3**(a) shows edge segments constructed from the object edges of Fig.2(d). The squares in the figure indicate the end points of the segments. Figure 3(b) shows an acquired model after normalizing the size to 16×16.

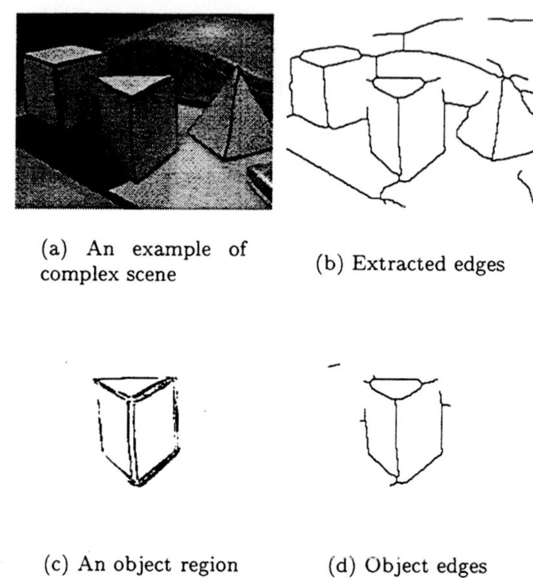

(a) An example of complex scene (b) Extracted edges

(c) An object region (d) Object edges

Figure 2. Extraction of object edges

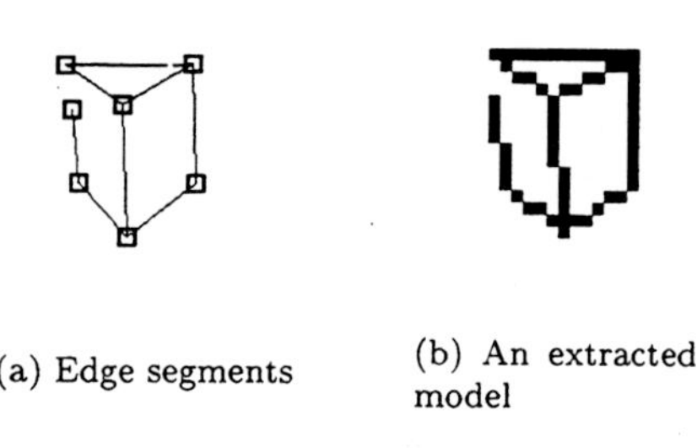

(a) Edge segments (b) An extracted model

Figure 3. Appearance edge model

4. Accumulation of Object Models

4.1. Reconstruction of Eigen Space

The eigenspace is reconstructed every time robots observe the object and acquire the model. The number of times of the observation by robots is denoted by t. Every time robots acquire a model, t is incremented by 1. The number of the accumulated models in a tag is denoted by N. The dimension of the eigenspace is denoted by m.

If $N < m+1$, the eigenspace cannot be constructed. If the memory space is not full, the appearance model is accumulated into a tag as it is. If the memory space is full, the accumulating models must be selected.

If $N \geq m+1$, the eigenspace can be constructed from the N models. The projected coordinates on the eigenspace are stored instead of the appearance models. When N and t become $m+1$, the initial eigenspace is constructed from the first N models. An appearance model is denoted by $\boldsymbol{X}$. The dimension of $\boldsymbol{X}$ is denoted by n. A mean vector of $\boldsymbol{X}$ is denoted by $\boldsymbol{m}$. The feature vectors are derived from

$$\mathrm{x} = \boldsymbol{X} - \boldsymbol{m}. \tag{1}$$

The $n \times n$ covariance matrix S is derived from

$$S = E\{(\boldsymbol{X} - \boldsymbol{m})(\boldsymbol{X} - \boldsymbol{m})^T\}. \tag{2}$$

The normalized eigenvectors $\boldsymbol{a}_i, i, \cdots, n$, correspond to the eigenvalues λ_i, respectively. We select m eigenvectors correspond to the largest m eigenvalues in order to construct m-dimensional eigenspace, By using the $m \times n$ projection matrix A, n-dimensional feature vector x is projected to m-dimensional vector $\boldsymbol{y}$ on the eigenspace,

$$\boldsymbol{y} = A\boldsymbol{x}, \tag{3}$$

where,

$$A = \begin{bmatrix} \boldsymbol{a}_1{}^T \\ \vdots \\ \boldsymbol{a}_m{}^T \end{bmatrix}, \boldsymbol{y} = \begin{bmatrix} y_1{}^T \\ \vdots \\ y_m{}^T \end{bmatrix}. \tag{4}$$

If $t > N$, the eigenspace is reconstructed using the N reconstructed appearance models and a newly acquired appearance model.

A reconstructed appearance model is denoted by $\boldsymbol{X}'(= \boldsymbol{x}' + \boldsymbol{m})$, where $\boldsymbol{x}'$ denotes a projected vector of $\boldsymbol{y}$ to the original appearance model space and $\boldsymbol{m}$ is a mean vector of $\boldsymbol{X}$ at $t-1$. The projected vector $\boldsymbol{x}'$ is derived from

$$\boldsymbol{x}' = A^T \boldsymbol{y}. \tag{5}$$

4.2. Selection of Accumulating Models

The various kind of appearance of the object should be accumulated on the eigenspace. We divide the eigenspace to hyper-cubic cells. Each cell can include a model at most. When every cell includes a model, the accumulated models are distributed uniformly on the eigenspace. The size of the cell relates the resolution of recognition. If the size is large, the range of the appearance of the object projected to the same cell becomes large. The number of the cells are determined by the maximum number of the models. If multiple models are in the same cell, we remove the models except one nearest to the center of the cell in the experiment. In this method, similar appearance models are removed and the memory space for storing models are saved.

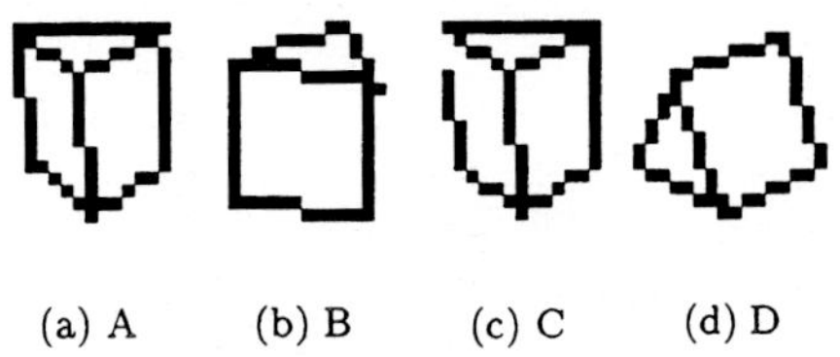

(a) A (b) B (c) C (d) D

Figure 4. Acquired models

Table 1. The sum of the distances between 3 models

ABC	ABD	ACD	BCD
0.77	0.99	0.71	0.96

5. Experiments

First, we show the experiment in a current RFID system which can store 3 appearance models in a tag. If the volume of the memory is full, one of the models must be removed so that the various appearance models could be stored. The pair of the models whose distance is the minimum are selected as candidates. One of them is removed so that the sum of the distances between the models in a tag becomes the maximum. **Figure 4**(a),(b),(c),(d) show a set of models. **Table 1** shows the sum of the distances between the 3 models except one. The distance is normalized by the dimension of the model n. A model C is removed from a set of models. We can see the combination of ABD with a wide variety of the appearances has the maximum sum of the distances.

Figure 5(a) shows a scene where the model A is acquired. The model A matches to the given model. Figure 5(b) shows a scene that the robot cannot recognize the target object from the current point of view, since the object posture is changed. Even in this case, the robot can recognize the object using accumulated model A.

Next, we show the validity of reconstructing the eigenspace for appearance-based object recognition. We use a set of appearance edge models of cube. We use 18 models of a cube whose angle of the point of view changes from 0 to 85 degree by every 5 degree. We select a model at random from a set of the models one by one, and reconstruct the eigenspace successively. **Figure 6** shows a reconstructed eigenspace at $t = 30$. The black points indicate the projected coordinates of the appearance models on the eigenspace. The lattice indicates the boundary of the cells whose size is

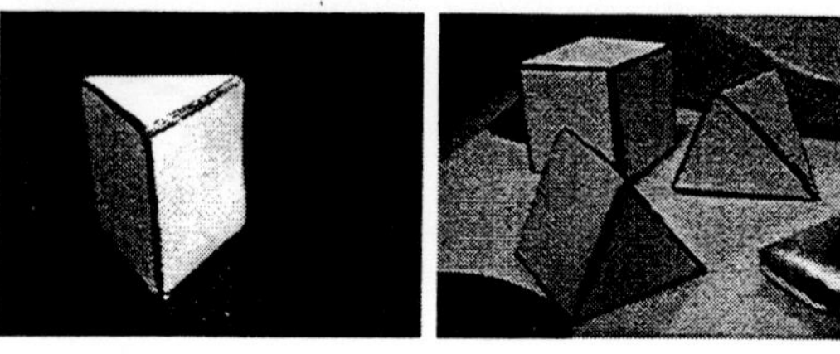

(a) Object in a simple environment

(b) Object with different appearance

Figure 5. Object in different environments

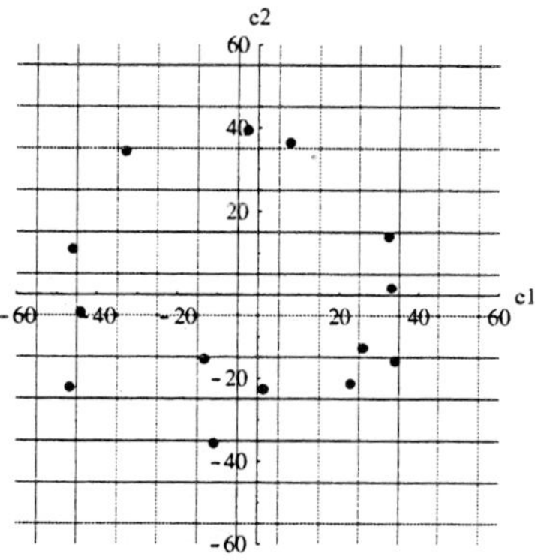

Figure 6. Accumulated models on an eigenspace

10×10. We can see the 14 models are scattered on the eigenspace and each of them is in a cell. We can see the various appearances are accumulated on the eigenspace.

We compare the eigenspace reconstructed successively and the eigenspace constructed at a time. **Figure 7**(a) shows projected points of 18 appearance models of a cube to the eigenspace at $t = 30$. Figure 7(b) shows projected points of the same models to the eigenspace constructed at a time using the corresponding models which are accumulated at $t = 30$. The consecutive projected points are connected by line. We can see the projected patterns are similar and the neighboring appearance models are projected consecutively on both eigenspaces. Thus we can say that the successive reconstructed eigenspace is used to measure the distance between the appearance models.

6. Conclusion

We proposed a new method of object recognition using appearance models accumulated into RFID tag

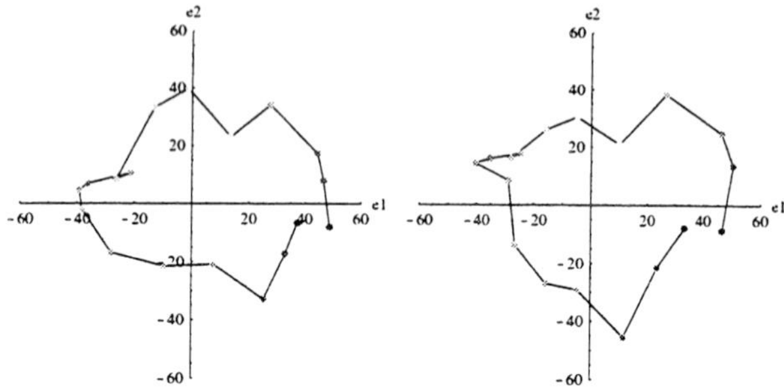

(a) eigenspace reconstructed successively

(b) eigenspace constructed at a time

Figure 7. Reconstructed eigenspace

attached to environment. Robots recognize the object using accumulated appearance models of the object. The eigenspace is reconstructed every time robots observe the object and acquire a model. The robots can recognize the object using accumulated models, even if the current appearance of the object is different from the given appearance model.

This work was supported by Grant-In-Aid for Scientific Research under Grant No.11750207 from Japan Society for Promotion of Science.

References

[1] A.Pentland,B.Moghaddam, and T.Starner, "View-based and modular eigenspace for face recognition," *IEEE Conf. on CVPR*,pp.84-91,1994.

[2] H.Murase, and S.K.Nayer, "Visual learning and recognition of 3-D objects from appearance," *International Journal of Computer Vision*,Vol.14,pp.5-24,1995.

[3] B.J.A.Kruse and R.Bunschoten, "Probabilistic localization by appearance models and active vision ," *Proc. of IEEE ICRA*,pp.2255-2260,1999.

[4] J.Ota, et al., "Environmental Support Method for Mobile Manipulators Using Visual Marks with Memory Storage," *Journal of the Robotics Society of Japan*,Vol.17,No.5,pp.670-676,1999.

[5] L.M.Soh, et al., "Recognition Using Labelled Objects," Proc. of 14th International Conference on Pattern Recognition,Vol.2, pp.1336-1338,1998.

[6] T.Fujii, et al., "Knowledge Sharing among Multiple Autonomous Mobile Robots through Indirect Communication using Intelligent Data Carrier," *Proc. of IEEE/RSJ Int. Conf. on IROS*,pp.1466-1471,1996.

Recognition of Local Features for Camera-based Sign Language Recognition System

Kazuyuki Imagawa, Hideaki Matsuo
Kyushu Multimedia System Laboratory,
Matsushita Electric Industrial Co., LTD.,
693-47, Kawazu, Iizuka, Fukuoka,
820-0067, JAPAN,
E-mail:{imagawa,matsuo}@qrl.mei.co.jp.

Rin-ichiro Taniguchi, Daisaku Arita
Department of Intelligent Systems,
Kyushu University,
6-1, Kasuga-Koen, Kasuga, Fukuoka,
816-8580, JAPAN
E-mail:{rin,arita}@is.kyushu-u.ac.jp.

Shan Lu, Seiji Igi
Intelligent Communications Division,
Communications Research Laboratory
4-2-1, Nukui-Kitamachi, Koganei, Tokyo, 184-8795, JAPAN
E-mail:{lu,igi}@crl.go.jp.

Abstract

A sign language recognition system is required to use information from both global features, such as hand movement and location, and local features, such as hand shape and orientation. In this paper, we present an adequate local feature recognizer for a sign language recognition system. Our basic approach is to represent the hand images extracted from sign-language images as symbols which correspond to clusters by a clustering technique. The clusters are created from a training set of extracted hand images so that a similar appearance can be classified into the same cluster on an eigenspace. The experimental results indicate that our system can recognize a sign language word even in two-handed and hand-to-hand contact cases.

1. Introduction

The recognition of hand gestures is important technology for the human-machine interface. One of the most structured sets of gestures is evident in sign language. Sign language is known to be composed of gesture components, which consist of global features, such as hand movements and locations, and local features, such as hand shapes and orientations [1]. Therefore, a sign language recognition system is required to analyze information from both of these features.

To date, there have been several systems designed for sign-language recognition using the vision-based approach. These systems are divided into two categories: one is a motion-based system [2]; the other is a posture-based system [3]. The motion-based systems only handle global features. They track the location of hands and only recognize their motions. The other is a posture-based system which recognizes a hand posture at a static hand location. Both of these systems require the static appearance of a hand. However, for sign language recognition, both hand posture and hand motion should be recognized.

Meanwhile, appearance-based approaches have been used for gesture recognition [4, 5]. They use 2D hand image sequences as gesture templates. The images are projected on a feature space, such as an eigenspace or a set of templates, and then a trajectory derived from the images are recognized so that they can achieve temporal invariance. However, these methods are not considered for the wide variability of hand appearances caused by involuntary changes in hand orientation or finger bending. In addition, these methods do not address the issue of two-handed gestures or unsegmented hand images such as a hand in front of a face, which are inevitable in sign language.

In this paper, we present an adequate local feature recognizer for a sign language recognition system. Our system first selects possible words from a dictionary using detected global features, and then narrows the words down to one by using detected local features. Building on a successful local feature recognizer, the hand images that are extracted from sign-language images are represented as symbols which correspond to clusters by a clustering technique. The clusters were created from a training set of extracted hand images so that a similar appearance can be classified into the same cluster on an eigenspace.

2. System Architecture

The goal of our system is to create a vision-based system that recognizes sign language from both global features and local features. The system segments hand regions from sign language images. We have already presented a method which recognizes a sign langauge word by global features[6]. It detects 3-D hand positions for global features, and acquires hand images for local features, Then, the system recognizes sign language by detecting both the global and local features.

Our system architecture is based on the knowledge of sign language studies. Generally, sign language is mainly recognized from global features. The local features are used for verification or for the selection of candidates previously derived from the global features. Therefore, our system initially segments sign language into a set of words, and selects word candidates by the detected global features. Then, it narrows them down to one by using the detected local features.

Local features are represented as a hand shape and by orientation at the beginning and the end of a sign language word in the field of sign-language phonology [1]. Therefore, local features are also computed from hand images of the whole body or just the upper body at the beginning and end of a word.

3. Local Feature Recognition

In local feature recognition, the hand images extracted from sign-language images are represented as symbols which correspond to clusters, by the use of a clustering technique, in order to deal with the wide variability of hand appearances. First, the low-resolution hand images extracted from the sign-language images from the whole or upper body are acquired. These images are then divided into one-hand and hand-to-hand contact image sets. Next, an eigenspace on each set is computed, and similar appearances of hand images in each set are classified into the same cluster by the clustering technique. According to the clustering results, the hand images at the beginning and ath the end of a word are assigned symbols, $\{S_b, S_e\}$. The system learns and recognizes the symbol sequence.

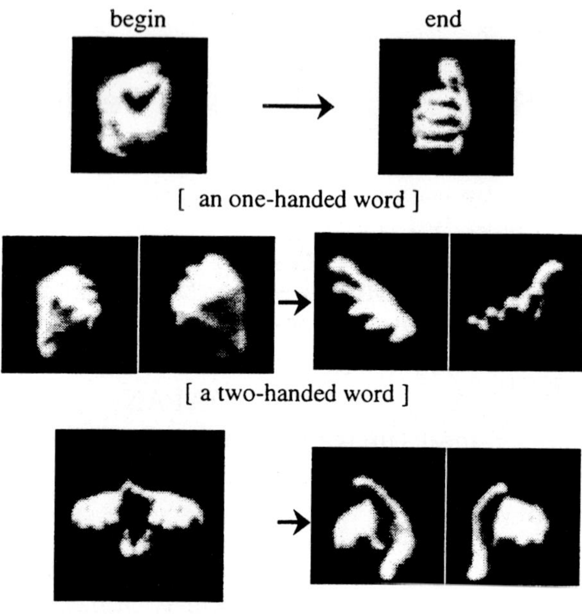

Figure 1. The examples of hand images at the beginning and end of a word.

In order to design the classifier, we acquired hand images extracted from the image sequences of sign-language words from multiple subjects. Each subject repeats each word approximately a dozen times, in order to acquire various appearances of the hand by involuntary changes in hand orientation or finger bending. In each sequence, skin regions are tracked, and hand regions are determined by our hand tracker [7]. Hand images are extracted at the beginning and end of each sequence. In order to choose the images at the beginning and end of a word, the tracker detects the times when the hands are stopped and when they make contact. Then, a system regards the time of the first detection as the beginning point, and the last time as the ending point.

The background region is removed by a skin-region mask in each hand image, and then each image is normalized with respect to size and illumination. Figure 1 shows the examples of hand images. Since sign language is often performed by two hands, extracted hand images include images in which hands are in contact with each other. Therefore, two sets of hand images, one-hand images and hand-to-hand contact images, are obtained.

The k eigenvectors with the largest eigenvalues were computed by the Karhunen-Loeve Transform (seen in [8]) from each image set, treating each frame as a column of pixel values. Then, the k-dimensional subspace spanned by the eigenvectors is defined as a feature space, which is called an *eigenspace*. The feature vector of the image is obtained by projecting it onto the eigenspace.

Next, the feature vectors are divided into clusters by an unsupervised clustering algorithm, so that a similar appearance can be classified into the same cluster. Since the training set lacks *a priori* information such as the number of clusters, we used the Carman method, a variant of the ISODATA algorithm [9].

ISODATA is a nearest-centroid non-hierarchical clustering algorithm. It is based on a k-means clustering, and it examines the k-means results and conditionally changes the current number of clusters, k, by splitting or merging clusters. Carman et al. presented this method which controls splitting or merging with a rule that searches for the minimum value of an Akaike's information criterion (AIC).

The AIC and the distance measure are defined as follows. Given a training set $U = (\boldsymbol{u}_j), j = 1, \ldots, N$, and a partition of clusters(h_i),$(1 \leq i \leq c)$, a distance measured D between $\boldsymbol{u}_j$ and h_i is defined as a log-likelihood discriminating function obtained from a maximum likelihood estimation such as,

$$D(\boldsymbol{u}_j, h_j) = -1\frac{1}{2}\ln|\boldsymbol{\Sigma}_i| - \frac{1}{2}\chi^2(\boldsymbol{u}_j; \boldsymbol{\mu}_i, \boldsymbol{\Sigma}_i), \tag{1}$$

where $\boldsymbol{\Sigma}_i$ is a covariance matrix in cluster i, $\boldsymbol{\mu}_i$ is a mean vector of the cluster i, and $\chi^2(\cdot)$ is a Mahalanobis distance. The AIC criterion is defined as,

$$AIC = -2\ln(L[\hat{\Theta}_c]) + 2m(c), \tag{2}$$

where Θ is a set of parameters of a cluster. $L[\hat{\Theta}_c]$ is the likelihood function evaluated at the maximum likelihood estimate of the distribution parameters for c clusters, and $m(c)$ is the number of estimated parameters for c clusters. Consequently, the training sets for both one-hand images and hand-to-hand contact images are classified by this method, and the codebook of each set is designed by each clustering result.

When a sign-language image sequence is given in symbols, each hand image at the beginning and at the end of a sign-language word is projected onto the eigenspace, and a cluster is then determined by a maximum likilihood algorithm by using Equation 1. Then, hand images at the beginning and end of the word are assigned symbols, $\{S_b, S_e\}$. In a one-handed image, a symbol which corresponds to a codeword in the codebook is solely assigned. In two-handed images, symbols $i, j (i \leq j)$ by the right and left hands are combined into a symbol such as $i * c_h + j$, where c_h is the number of

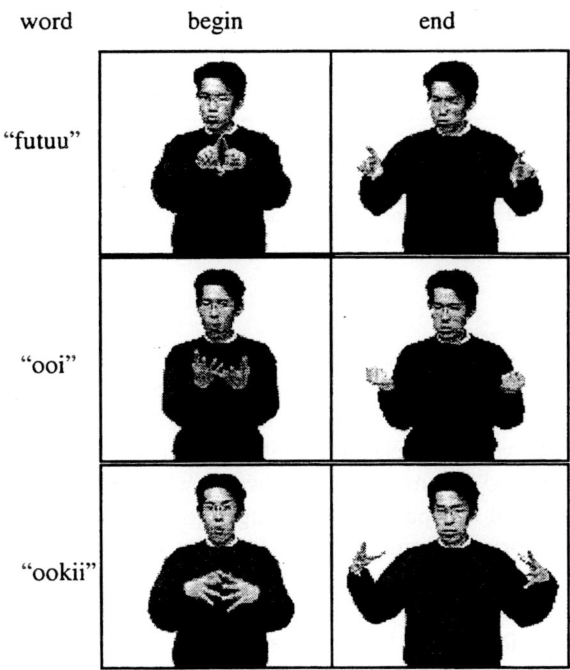

Figure 2. The examples of the words which have the same global features.

clusters for the one-handed set. In hand-to-hand contact cases, an offset value $O, (O \geq 2c_h)$ is added to the symbol value.

The local feature recognizer learns and recognizes the symbol sequence $\{S_b, S_e\}$. Since the length of the sequence is only two, the temporal invariance in recognition is not necessary. Therefore, we used a k-nearest neighbor classification rule for recognition.

When a hand is placed in front of a face, the hand and face regions cannot be segmented by the mask of a skin region alone. A m-by-n observation window is slid within the scope of the hand and face regions, and the cluster and the corresponding likelihoods are then computed at each location. The selection of the location and the cluster corresponds to the highest likelihood.

4. Experiment

4.1. Experimentation

We carried out experiments to evaluate the local feature recognizer. Sign language words used in the experiments were selected from approximately 160 words which are usually used in dialogues at a post office counter, because we expect that the system will be used

Table 1. Selected categories used in the experiment.

Category	description	Num. of words
CR0	One-handed, move forward	13
CR1	Two-handed, move bottom	8
CR2	Hand-to-hand contact, move to open	12

as public service counters such as a post office. The performance of the local feature recognizer was examined according to the estimation of a word recognition result from words which have the same global features. We observed the images of these words which had been prepared in a Japanese-Sign-Language database [10], and categorized them by global features, such as *the number of acting hands*, *hand-to-hand contact*, *hand movement*, and *hand location*. Consequently, 18 categories were found in the analysis. These categories could be classified into three groups, "*one-handed words*", "*two-handed and non-contact words*", and "*hand-to-hand contact words*". In each group, we selected a category which has the greatest number of words in the group, as shown in Table 1. Figure 2 shows the examples of the JSL words which have the same global features. These words were categorized into the same category. They cannot be divided by global features alone.

In each sign-language word, we prepared approximately 60 samples taken from six subjects under natural fluorescent lights. In CR0, there were five words in which a hand overlaps the face. For these words, the subject wore a black mask and performed them. In order to segment a sign-language word easily from whole movement, the subjects stopped their hands at the beginning and end of the word. From each sample, hand images at the beginning and end of a word were extracted and normalized to 64 × 64 pixels in a one-handed image or 80 × 80 in a hand-to-hand contact image. Then, these images were divided between one-handed and hand-to-hand contact images.

In order to evaluate the system, two types of experiments were performed. The first experiment was designed to examine the performance of word recognition in the system. Hand images were divided into halves. One was used for learning, and the other was used for recognition. They were exchanged and repeated. We also tested simple template image matching to compare it with our method. For the templates, the average of learning images at the beginning or end of the same word is computed.

The second experiment was designed to estimate the ability of the system to locate and recognize hands when a hand is overlapping a face. The five hand-overlapping words were acquired by the subjects removing their black masks. The system had learned by the samples of the first experiment, and it then located the position of the hand and recognized these images.

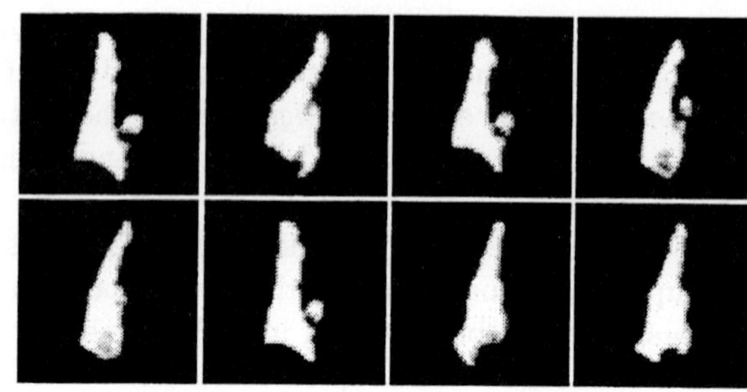

Figure 3. The examples of acquired hand images at the beginning of a word

Table 2. Recognition rates in the first experiment.

category	Our method	Template matching
CR0	94%	90%
CR1	93%	87%
CR2	94%	83%

4.2. Experimental results

Table 2 shows the results of the first experiment. In all categories, we have achieved greater than 93 % correct recognition rates. Therefore, these indicate that our system can classify the words which have the same global features by local features, because the words in each category have the same global features. Especially, CR1 and CR2, which are the categories, "two-handed and non-contacted words" and "hand-to-hand contact words". These results indicate that our system could recognize a sign language word even in two-handed and hand-to-hand contact cases.

On the other hand, we obtained from 83 % to 90 % correct recognition rates in the template image matching. These results are approximately 5 % less than those of our method. For example, Figure 3 shows images at the beginning of the same word. These images include a variation of hand appearance by a thumb position. Therefore, some images are misclassified in the simple template image matching. Thus, this indicates that our method can deal with the wide variations of

Table 3. Recognition and correct location rates in the second experiment.

Category	Recognition	Correct location
CR0	72%	85%

(a)

(b)

(c)

Figure 4. Typical location results when a hand overlaps a face.

hand appearances by observing these cases.

In the first experiment, the system was tested under the various dimensions of the eigenspace. Consequently, we obtained 90 % at 5 dimensions and 94 % at 10 dimensions. There was no rise over 10 dimensions. Therefore, we determined that the dimension of the eigenspace was 10. This result indicates that our method efficiently compresses the features for hand recognition. Our method can recognize local features in real time.

Table 3 shows the second experimental results when a hand overlaps a face. We obtained 72 % for correct recognition rate, and 85 % for correct location rate. This indicates that our method is also valid for locating the hand in front of a face. Figure 4 shows the detected hand location by our method. Figure 4 (a) and (b) are the success cases of both recognition and location. On the other hand, Fig. 4 (c) is the incorrect case. In this case, the system mistook both the location and the recognition because of the shade of a hand. Dealing with the situations of two-hands and hands over a face was not tested in the experiment. Further developments and experiments will be needed with these situations.

5. Conclusion and Future Work

In this paper, we have presented a local feature recognizer for the sign language recognition system, which first selects candidates by detecting global features, then narrowing the choices to one by using local features. The local feature recognizer recognizes sign language by the low-resolution hand images extracted from the images of a whole body or just the upper body. The experimental results indicate that our system could recognize a sign language word even in two-handed and hand-to-hand contact cases.

References

[1] W. Stokoe, D. C. Casterline, and C. G. Groneberg, *A Dictionary of American Sign Language on Linguistic Principles*, Linstok Press, London, 1976.

[2] T. Starner, J. Weaver, and A. Pentland, "Real-Time American Sign Language Recognition Using Desk and Wearable Computer Based Video", *IEEE Trans. Pattern Anal. & Mach. Intell.*, Vol.20, No.12, pp.1371-1375, 1998

[3] C. Uras, and A. Verri, "On the Recognition of the alphabet of the sign language through size functions", *Proc. 12th IAPR Int. Conf. on Pattern Recognition*, Vol.2, pp. 334-338, 1994.

[4] T. Darrell, and A. Pentland, "Space-Time Gestures", *Proc. IEEE Conference on Computer Vision and Pattern Recognition*, pp.335-340, 1993

[5] A. F. Bobick, and A. D. Wilson, "A State-Based Approach to the Representation and Recognition of Gesture", *IEEE Trans. Pattern Anal. & Mach. Intell.*, Vol. 19, No. 12, pp.1325-1337, 1997.

[6] H. Matsuo, S. Igi, S. Lu, Y. Nagashima, Y. Takata, and T. Teshima: "Recognition Algorithm with Non-contact for Japanese Sign-Language using Morphological Analysis", Gesture Workshop, Bielefeld, German, pp.273-284 (1997).

[7] K. Imagawa, "Color-based Hands Tracking System for Sign Language Recognition", *Proc. of IEEE Conf. on Automatic Face and Gesture Recognition*, pp.462-467, April, 1998.

[8] M. A. Turk, and A. P. Pentland, "Face recognition using eigenfaces", *Proc. of IEEE Conference on COmputer Vision and Pattern Recognition*, pp.586-591, June, 1991.

[9] C. Carman, and M. Merickel, "Supervising ISODATA with an Information Theoretic Stopping Rule", Pattern Recognition, Vol.23, No.12, pp. 185-197, (1990).

[10] Communications Research Laboratory, "Japanese Sign-language Video Database", http://jsl-db.crl.go.jp.

Visual State Recognition for a Target-Reaching Task

G. Cicirelli & T. D'Orazio & A. Distante
Istituto Elaborazione Segnali ed Immagini - C.N.R.
Via Amendola, 166/5 - 70126 Bari (Italy)
(cicirelli/dorazio/distante)@iesi.ba.cnr.it

Abstract

In this paper we present a learning algorithm that realizes a simple goal-reaching task for an autonomous vehicle when only visual information about the goal is provided. The robot has to reach a door from every position of the environment. The state of the system is based on visual information received by a TV-camera placed on the mobile robot. The vision algorithm is able to determine the relative position between the vehicle and the door according to the slopes of the contour lines of the door. A learning phase is carried out in simulation to obtain the optimal state-action rules. The learned knowledge is then transferred on the real robot for the testing phase. Experimental results show the generality of the knowledge learned as the real robot is always able to execute its paths towards the door in different environments.

1. Introduction

Studies regarding intelligent robots have received a great attention in the scientific community in the last years both for the biological aspects involved, and for the robots' physical structure required. Behavior-based systems [2] have shown that some kind of intelligence is able to emerge by reacting to what can be perceived in the environment. These systems use behaviors as a way of decomposing the control policy needed to accomplish a task and are very useful for making robots adaptable to the dynamics of the real world environment. However, the behaviors, in these systems, are usually organized in a fixed and pre-defined manner, causing a loss of flexibility when new goals and situations must be faced. For this reason, the need for robots that learn robust behaviors in a real environment has increased. In these contexts the use of visual information has been limited in literature because of the difficulties and the cost of processing visual data [8, 7]. Actually sonar sensor, odometry and proximity sensors have been used to solve elementary behaviors limited only to local tasks. Visual sensors, instead, can be more useful since they are able to detect distant goals and permit the acquisition of suitable behaviors for more global goal-directed tasks [1, 6].

In our work we have considered a target-reaching task by using a vision-based learning algorithm. The robot has to move towards the door from every point in the environment until it is located adjacent to the door. The recognition of the door is a difficult task to solve with vision approaches when no constraints are imposed. The use of a sparse set of 3D-segments in [4] obtained with a trinocular stereo approach, with some constraints on orientation, height range and shape does not guarantee the recognition of a door among other objects of the same type (like cupboards or bookcase). In our work the color information has been used to make recognition easier. The color camera placed on the vehicle captures always images of the door which are color coded. A simple threshold process generates a binary image according to the red points of the environment. Then the contour of the door is extracted. The particular setting of the contour lines of the door is used to define the state of the system. The state involves information about the vehicle position with respect to the door: (Near, Medium, Far) for the distance and (Front, Left, Right) for the relative orientation. In simulation the robot learns the proper action to reach the door from each of these states (learning phase). After the learning phase a testing phase has been carried out in the real environment. In this phase the learning is turned off and the robot is always forced to choose the optimal action in each state. During the testing phase the robot performs some paths from different starting positions towards the door using the knowledge learned in simulation.

The paper is organized as follows. In Section 2 we describe how the system state is recognized. Successively in Section 3 the experiments, realized with both simulated and real robot, are shown.

2. Task Description

In this paper we present a method of vision-based reinforcement learning for a door-reaching behavior in a closed and free environment. The only source of information is the image of the door captured by the on-board camera of the robot. The considered task also involves the ability of searching and recognizing the red door of our laboratory. For this purpose we have used a neural network trained using the quickprop algorithm [5]. The original RGB image (see Fig. 1) is transformed into HSI values. Therefore, by using a threshold process, a binary image is obtained (see Fig. 2). The input to the network is the black and white sub-sampled image. The output of the net is a binary label predicting the presence of the door in the image. Even if different red objects are located in the environment the neural network is able to detect the door as the red pixels identifying the door have a particular spatial disposition. The search and the detection of the door is activated at the beginning of the task, whereas, during navigation, the door is always in the current image as a tracking module for keeping the door centered in the image is applied.

Figure 1: One of the input colored images of the door taken by the camera from the (Left, Medium) region.

2.1. Visual State Recognition

The state of the system is defined according to the distance and the orientation of the door with respect to the vehicle. Three regions for the distance (Near, Medium, Far) and three for the orientation (Left, Front, Right) are considered. The combinations of these two sets of regions represent the possible states of the vehicle. The couple (Front, Near) is the goal state as the robot is located near the door, therefore the navigation stops. Each image captured by the camera placed on the robot is processed as follows. Once the black and white image (Fig. 2) is obtained from the original colored one as described above, the contour of the white region is detected. The three lines, one horizontal and two vertical, that delimit the red door are extracted (see Fig. 3).

Figure 2: The black and white image obtained applying the threshold process on the image of Fig.1.

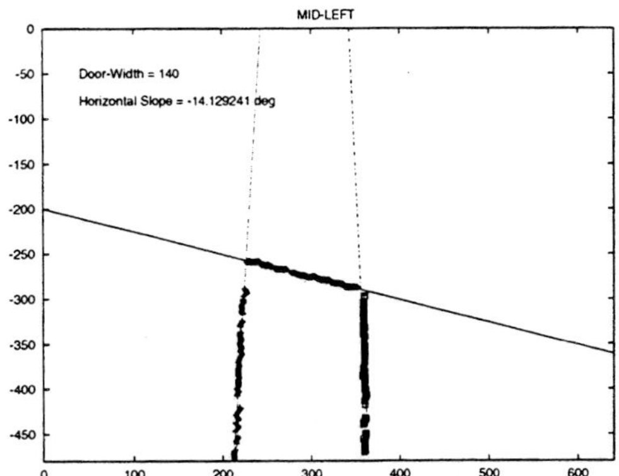

Figure 3: The extracted contour of the door.

The slope of the horizontal line and the distance between the two vertical lines (door width) are used to identify the region of the environment from which the image was taken or equivalently the region in which the vehicle is. In fact if the door slopes to the right the observer is on the left side, if the door is upright the observer is in front of it, and finally if the door slopes to the left the observer is on the right side. The door width in the image plane gives the information about the distance between the vehicle and the door. The slope of the horizontal line, instead, gives the information about the relative orientation between the vehicle and the door. In order to represent the state of the system in terms of slope and width variations of the door, at a first stage different snapshots of the door have been taken from those positions in the environment that delimit the considered regions. Then these images have been processed to fix the ranges of variations of both the slope and width of the door. Figs. 4 a) and b) show respectively these ranges for both the distance and the relative orientation between the vehicle and the door.

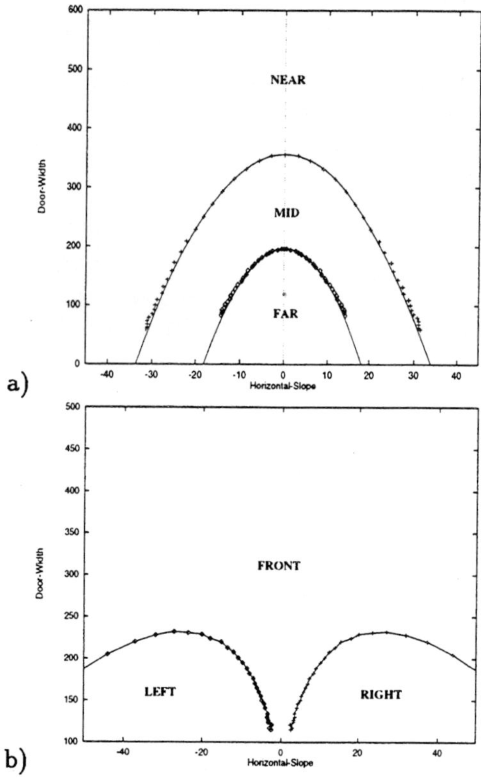

Figure 4: Ranges of variation of the door width and slope to determine the a) Near, Mid and Far region; and b) the Left, Front and Right region.

2.2. The Learning Algorithm

The algorithm used to find the optimal state-action rules is the well known Q-learning algorithm [9]. Once the current system state s_t relative to the door has been evaluated an action a_t is selected by using an action selection function. The action space is discrete and contains eight actions corresponding to the absolute orientations that the agent can take in each state: $\mathcal{A} = \{0, 45, 90, ..., 315\}$ (*degrees*). Performing one action means that the vehicle rotates until it is oriented towards the selected direction and translates until the current state changes. The robot is rewarded only when it reaches the goal state, whereas it is penalized when it bumps into the surrounding walls (*delayed reward*). For major details see [3].

3. The Experiment

A number of experiments have been performed to test the visual goal-reaching behavior described in the previous sections. A simulation phase and a testing phase have been considered. In the simulation phase the state-action mapping is completely learned, while in the testing phase the optimality of the acquired behavior is evaluated in the real environment.

3.1. The Simulation Phase

The described learning procedure has been initially investigated using the Nomad200 simulator provided by the Nomadic Inc. The simulated environment has been drawn according to the real environment setting in order to make possible the successive transfer of the learned policy from the simulated to the real test-bed. The environment is 240 *inches* wide and 140 *inches* long, the door is 31.5 *inches* wide and 82.7 *inches* high and is positioned in the (Front, Near) region. At each time step the robot observes its current state then selects and performs an action entering in a new state and updating the control policy. To learn the optimal policy a number of trials has been executed. A trial is the execution of a specified number of paths from different starting positions fixed in the environment. Each path terminates with a success if the goal-state is achieved or with a failure if a collision occurs. After 10 trials, we have verified that the Q-values reached their quasi-stable values then we stopped the learning phase. Fig. 5 shows the optimal actions obtained after the learning phase.

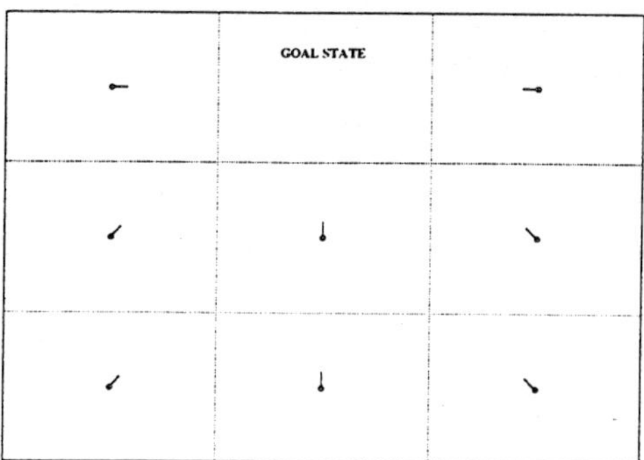

Figure 5: Optimal actions obtained after the learning phase in simulation.

3.2. The Testing Phase

During the testing phase the learning algorithm is switched off and a number of paths are performed by the agent in the real environment. In each state the agent performs an action that is evaluated as weighted average of the optimal actions of the current and adjacent states. We decided to do this because of the limited state space and the error in the state estimation due to the peculiarity of the visual information. As a consequence the paths performed have smooth trajectories as shown in Figs. 6, 7 and 8.

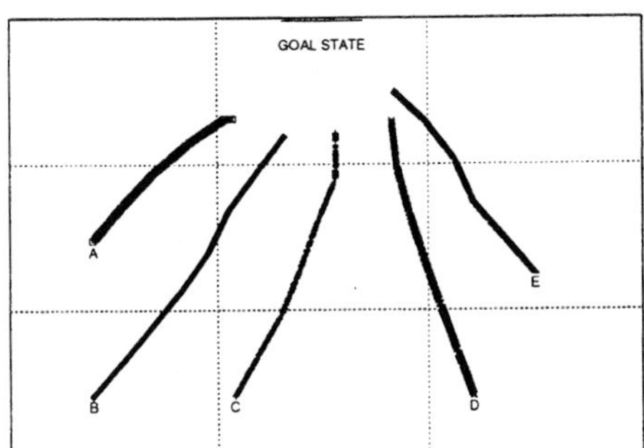

Figure 6: Real paths executed in our laboratory. The "A", "B", "C", "D" and "E" labels indicate the start position of each path.

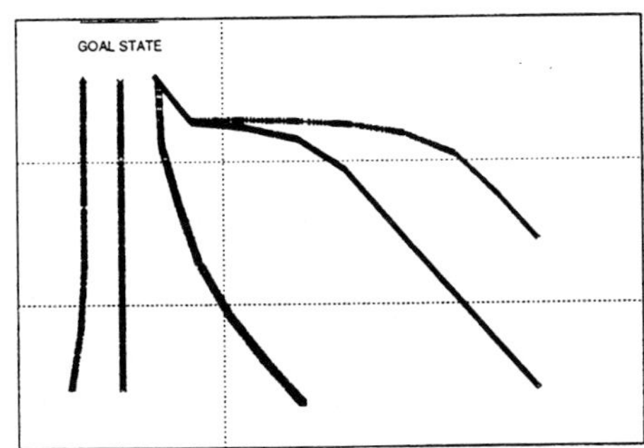

Figure 7: Real paths in a different environment. The door is on the left.

We have also tested the learned policy in other environments where the door is in different locations. This means that the goal position has changed. In figures 7 and 8 two different rooms of our building are depicted. Note that in figure 8 the door is on the right side of the longer wall of the room, and in figure 7 the door is on the left. The robot is always able to reach the door in every rooms. It behaves successfully in each environment by using the same learned policy. Learning a new policy is not needed because of the considered definition of the state of the system. In fact it is defined with respect to the goal and not to the environment. This permits to use the same policy in different environments producing successful performances. The definition of the system state independently of the absolute goal position is an important property for developing general behaviors.

4 Conclusions

In this work a method of vision-based reinforcement learning for a goal-reaching behavior has been considered. The optimal policy has been learned in simulation than it is transferred to the real robot. The state of the system has been defined by using visual information obtained by the camera placed on the robot. Also the state definition is general since it relates to the goal. The generalization capability of the learned behavior has emerged when the vehicle had to reach different goal positions by using its own experience without any re-learning rule.

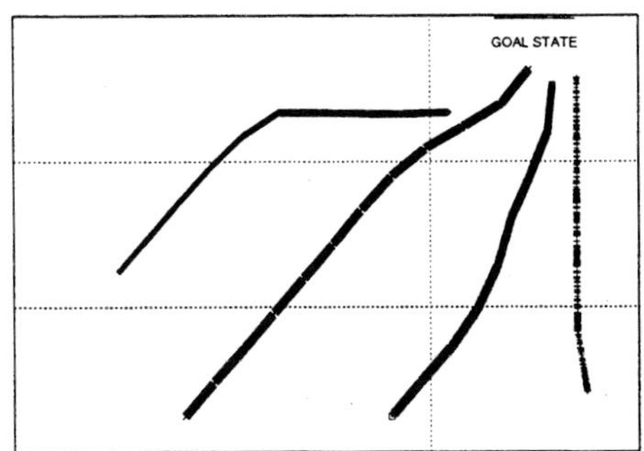

Figure 8: Real paths in a different environment. The door is on the right.

References

[1] M. Asada, S. Noda, S. Tawaratsumida, and K. Hosoda. Purposive behavior acquisition for a real robot by vision-based reinforcement learning. *Machine Learning*, page 279, May/June 1996.

[2] R. Brooks. Intelligence without reason. Technical report, Massachusetts Institute of Technology, 1991. A.I.Memo 1293.

[3] G. Cicirelli, T.D'Orazio, and C. Distante. A vision-based approach for learning a goal-reaching behavior. In *IEEE International Conference on Intelligent Vehicles, Germany*, 1998.

[4] D.Kim and R. Nevatia. A methos for recognition and localization of generic objects for indoor navigation. *IEEE IUW*, 1994.

[5] S. E. Fahlman. An empirical study of learning speed in back-propagation networks. In *CMU-CS-88-162*, 1988.

[6] S. Mahadevan, G. Theochaous, and N. Khaleeli. Rapid concept learning for mobile robots. *Machine Learning*, 1998. in press.

[7] S. Nayar and T. Poggio. *Early Visual Learning*. Oxford University Press, 1996.

[8] M. V. Srinivasan and S. Venkatesh. *From living Eyes to Seeing Machines*. Oxford University Press, 1997.

[9] C. J. Watkins and P. Dayan. Technical note - q-learning. *Machine Learning*, 8(3/4):323–339, 1992.

Comparison of face verification results on the XM2VTS database

J. Matas[1,2], M. Hamouz[1], K. Jonsson[1], J. Kittler[1], Y. Li[1], C. Kotropoulos[3], A. Tefas[3], I. Pitas[3], Teewoon Tan[5], Hong Yan[5], F. Smeraldi[7], J. Bigun[4], N. Capdevielle[7], W. Gerstner[7], S. Ben-Yacoub[8], Y. Abdeljaoued[7], E. Mayoraz[6]

[1]Centre for Vision Speech and Signal Processing
University of Surrey, Guildford, GU2 7XH, UK
{g.matas, m.hamouz, k. jonsson, j.kittler, y.li}@eim.surrey.ac.uk

[2]Center for Machine Perception
CTU Prague, Karlovo nám. 13, 121 35
Czech Republic

[3]Department of Informatics
Aristotle University of Thessaloniki
Box 451, Thessaloniki 540 06, Greece
{costas, tefas, pitas}@zeus.csd.auth.gr

[4]Halmstadt University
Box 823, S-30115 Halmstad, Sweden
josef.bigun@ide.hh.se

[5]University of Sydney
NSW 2006 Australia
{teewoon,yan}@ee.usyd.edu.au

[6]Motorola Inc.
Eddy.Mayoraz@lexicus.mot.com

[7]Swiss Federal Institute of Technology
DI, 1015 Lausanne, Switzerland
{nathalie.capdevielle, wulfram.gerstner, yousri.abdeljaoued}@epfl.ch

[8]Swisscom AG
Souheil.BenYacoub@swisscom.com

Abstract

The paper presents results of the face verification contest that was organized in conjunction with International Conference on Pattern Recognition 2000 [14]. Participants had to use identical data sets from a large, publicly available multimodal database XM2VTSDB. Training and evaluation was carried out according to an a priori known protocol ([7]). Verification results of all tested algorithms have been collected and made public on the XM2VTSDB website [15], facilitating large scale experiments on classifier combination and fusion. Tested methods included, among others, representatives of the most common approaches to face verification – elastic graph matching, Fisher's linear discriminant and Support vector machines.

1 Introduction

Hundreds of papers have been published on the face verification and recognition problem [11, 2]. Direct comparison of the reported methods is typically rather difficult, because tests are performed on different data, with large variations in test and model database sizes, viewing conditions, background etc. Standard face databases are publicly available, e.g. Yale [21], Harvard [16] , Olivetti [19], M2VTS [18] to name a few commonly used (see the face recognition homepage [17] for a longer list. Even if the same database is used, it may be split differently into test and training sets. Moreover, results are often evaluated using different methodologies.

For face recognition, the FERET test [10, 9] provided a comparison of a number of algorithms. However, a similar test was missing for the *face verification* (or authentication) task. Verification and recognition differ in at least three fundamental aspects. Firstly, a client – an authorized user of a personal identification system – is assumed to be cooperative and makes an identity claim. Computationally this means that it is not necessary to consult the complete set of models (reference images in our case) in order to verify a claim. A test image is thus compared to a small number of reference images of the person whose identity is claimed and not, as in the recognition scenario, with every image (or some descriptor of an image) in a potentially large database. Secondly, an automatic authentication system must operate in near-real time to be acceptable to users. And finally, in recognition experiments only images of people from the training database are presented to the system, whereas the case of an impostor (most likely a previously unseen person) is of utmost importance for authentication.

In order to collect face verification results on an identical, publicly available, data set using a standard performance assessment methodology a contest was organized in conjunction with the ICPR 2000. Besides assessing the quality of various face verification methods, the contest's secondary objective was to make the results of different methods on particular algorithms available to the research community. Placing the results, in a predefined format, on a publicly accessible web site [15] enables large scale experiments on classifier combination and fusion as well as the study of dependencies of errors of a wide range of face verification methods.

The results published are based completely on self-assessment of the research groups providing the error rates. In the original call for participation [14], a second part of the test on sequestered data was mentioned, but we were not able to carry it out in time to meet the publication deadline. Unlike in the FERET test, where each research group obtained a different subset of the database, all research groups have identical data sets and therefore can assess their performance at any time. We believe that this open approach, trusting the published results, will increase in the long term the number of algorithms that will be tested on the XM2VTSDB subset.

The rest of the paper is structured as follows. In section 2, the image dataset and the evaluation protocol is described. In section 3 results evaluated according to the Lausanne protocol are presented. Section 4 introduces other results, that are not exactly according to the Lausanne protocol.

2 XM2VTS database and Lausanne protocol

The XM2VTS database [8] is a multimodal database consisting of face images, video sequences and speech recordings taken of 295 subjects at one month intervals. This database is available at the cost of distribution from the University of Surrey (see [20] for details). The database is primarily intended for research and development of personal identity verification systems where it is reasonable to assume that the client will be cooperative. Since the data acquisition was distributed over a long period of time, significant variability of appearance of clients, e.g. changes of hair style, facial hair, shape and presence or absence of glasses, is present in the recordings - see figure 1.

The subjects were volunteers, mainly employees and PhD students at the University of Surrey of both sexes and many ethnical origins. The XM2VTS database contains 4 sessions. During each session two head rotation and "speaking" shots were taken. From the "speaking" shot, where subjects are looking just below the camera while reading a phonetically balanced sentence, a single image with a closed mouth was chosen. Two shots at each session, with and without glasses, were acquired for people regularly wearing glasses.

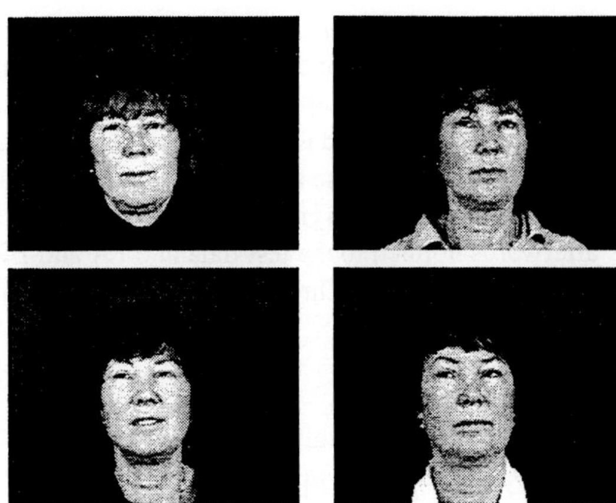

Figure 1. Sample images from XM2VTS database

For the task of personal verification, a standard protocol for performance assessment has been defined. The so called Lausanne protocol splits randomly all subjects into a client and impostor groups. The client group contains 200 subjects, the impostor group is divided into 25 evaluation impostors and 70 test impostors. Eight images from 4 sessions are used.

From these sets consisting of face images, training set, evaluation set and test set is built. There exist two configurations that differ by a selection of particular shots of people into the training, evaluation and test set. The training set is used to construct client models. The evaluation set is selected to produce client and impostor access scores, which are used to find a threshold that determines if a person is accepted or not (it can be a client-specific threshold or global threshold). According to the Lausanne protocol the threshold is set to satisfy certain performance levels (error rates) on the evaluation set. Finally the test set is selected to simulate realistic authentication tests where impostor's identity is unknown to the system. The evaluation set is also used in fusion experiments (classifier combination) for training, but this is not relevant in the context of this paper.

The performance measures of a verification system are the False Acceptance rate (FA) and the False Rejection rate (FR). False acceptance is the case where an impostor, claiming the identity of a client, is accepted. False rejection is the case where a client, claiming his true identity, is rejected. FA and FR are given by:

$$FA = EI/I * 100\% \qquad FR = EC/C * 100\% \quad (1)$$

where EC is the number of impostor acceptances, I is

the number of impostor claims, EC the number of client rejections, and C the number of client claims. Both FA and an FR are influenced by an acceptance threshold. To simulate real application the threshold is set on the data from evaluation set to obtain certain false acceptance on the evaluation set (FAE) and false rejection error (FRE). The same threshold is afterwards applied to the test data and FA and FR on the test set are computed. Three thresholds are defined on the evaluation set:

$$\begin{aligned} T_{FAE=0} &= \arg\min_T(FRE|FAE=0) \\ T_{FAE=FRE} &= (T|FAE=FRE) \\ T_{FRE=0} &= \arg\min_T(FAE|FRE=0) \end{aligned} \quad (2)$$

Consequently, performance on the test set is characterised by six error rates:

$$\begin{array}{ll} FA_{FAE=0} & FR_{FAE=0} \\ FA_{FAE=FRE} & FR_{FAE=FRE} \\ FA_{FRE=0} & FR_{FRE=0} \end{array} \quad (3)$$

3 Results on XM2VTS database evaluated according to the Lausanne protocol

This section describes results of face verification methods that either participated in the contest or had been tested according to the Lausanne protocol. In all cases, files storing verification results have been made public.

3.1 Dalle Molle Institute for Perceptual Artificial Intelligence (IDIAP)

The Elastic Graph Matching introduces a specific face representation. Each face is represented by a set of feature vectors positioned on nodes of a coarse, rectangular grid placed on the image. Moduli of complex Gabor responses from filters with 6 orientations and 3 resolutions are used as features. The matching consists of two consecutive steps: rigid matching and deformable matching. Advantages of the elastic graph matching are the robustness against variation in face position, and expression. This owes to the Gabor features, the rigid matching stage, and the deformable matching stage [1]. Results can be found in tables 1 and 2.

3.2 Aristotle University of Thessaloniki

The approach of C. Kotropoulos, A. Tefas and I. Pitas [5] also falls into the Elastic Graph Matching category. However, novel features based on multiscale dilation and erosion operations are computed at each node of the grid. Verification score is a function of the matching energy which in turn is a complex function of the grid deformation and the difference of response of the morphological operators obtained at node locations. Results of the method are labelled **AUT** in tables 1 and 2.

3.3 University of Surrey

University of Surrey provided several results (see tables 1 and 2).

In [6] the problem of face verification using linear discriminant analysis was addressed and the issue of matching score investigated. The improved understanding about the role of metric led to a novel way of measuring the distance between probe image and a model. The effect of various photometric normalizations on the matching scores was also investigated. In tables 1 and 2 the group of results are referred to as **UniS–X–X–NC** which stands for normalized correlation used as distance measure and as **UniS–X–X–SM** which stands for the novel proposed metric. The experiments were conducted using both types of thresholding - a client-specific thresholds and global thresholds. Also both types of registration were used — fully-automatic registration (based on robust correlation described in [4] — see next paragraph) and semi-automatic registration, where the eyes of people were located manually. Results with the automatic registration are available only in Configuration I.

Another verification approach is based on the use of robust correlation and Support vector machines [4]. The problem of the registration was treated as an optimization task via estimating the optimal transformation parameters by maximizing a similarity function. The influence of signal noise, occluding objects and suboptimalities in the transformation models were reduced by applying robust estimation techniques. The classification of face patterns was carried out by using a support vector machine. The registered and photometrically normalized images were projected into a subspace optimized for representation or discrimination. The client–specific thresholding was used. The results are referred to as **UniS–SVM** and are available only for configuration I.

3.4 University of Sydney

Fractal image coding was applied to the task of face verification. Two subsystems constituted this face verification system, namely the face detection and the face verification components. Central to both systems is the notion of the Fractal Neighbor Distance (FND). The detection system firstly performed a rough location of the head, based on the assumption of a blue background. A search was then performed in the reduced region. This involved the use of a generic face template, the fractal code of which had been generated. Afterwards the Fractal Neighbor Distances between localized head images and the images stored in the database were computed. The minimal FND was taken as a score [13]. See tables 1 and 2 for results.

4 Other results

In this section results that have not been obtained according to the protocol are presented.

4.1 Swiss Federal Institute of Technology (EPFL)

In the approach of Smeraldi et al. [12] a concept of Retinal vision was introduced. The raw visual input was analyzed by means of a log-polar retinotopic sensor, whose receptive fields consisted of a vector of modified Gabor filters designed in the log-polar frequency plane. The Gabor responses extracted by placing the sensor over the corresponding facial regions were then used to perform authentication. The implementation of knowledge representation using Support vector machine classifier was used. Since the training and test sets were used exactly according to the Lausanne protocol (although evaluation set was not used at all), it is still possible to compare the results. The aposteriori equal error rate on the test set was about 0.50%.

5 Conclusion and Future Work

This paper presents a comparison of face verification algorithms that was organized in conjunction with International Conference on Pattern Recognition 2000. Fourteen face verification methods were tested using identical data sets from a large, publicly available multimodal database XM2VTSDB. Training and evaluation was carried out according to an a priori known protocol. Verification results of all tested algorithms have been collected and made public on the internet [15], facilitating large scale experiments on classifier combination and fusion.

References

[1] S. Ben-Yacoub, Y. Abdeljaoued, and E. Mayoraz. Fusion of face and speech data for person identity verification. *IEEE Transactions on Neural Networks*, 10(05):1065–1074, 1999.

[2] R. Chellappa, C. L. Wilson, and S. Sirohey. Human and machine recognition of faces: A survey. *Proceedings of the IEEE*, 83(5):704–740, May 1995.

[3] K. Jonsson. *Robust Correlation and Support Vector Machines for Face Identification.* PhD thesis, University of Surrey, 2000.

[4] K. Jonsson, J. Kittler, Y. P. Li, and J. Matas. Support Vector Machines for Face Authentication. In T. Pridmore and D. Elliman, editors, *British Machine Vision Conference*, pages 543–553, 1999.

[5] C. Koutropoulos, A. Tefas, and I. Pitas. Morphological elastic graph matching applied to frontal face authentication under well-controlled and real conditions. Technical report, Aristotle university of Thessaloniki, 1999.

[6] Y. Li, J. Kittler, and J. Matas. On Matching Scores of LDA-based Face Verification. In T. Pridmore and D. Elliman, editors, *Proc British Machine Vision Conference BMVC2000*, page submitted, London, UK, September 2000. University of Bristol, British Machine Vision Association.

[7] J. Luettin and G. Maître. Evaluation Protocol for the extended M2VTS Database (XM2VTSDB). IDIAP-COM 05, IDIAP, 1998.

[8] K. Messer, J. Matas, J. Kittler, J. Luettin, and G. Maitre. XM2VTSDB: The Extended M2VTS Database. In *Second International Conference on Audio and Video-based Biometric Person Authentication*, March 1999.

[9] P. Phillips, H. Wechsler, J.Huang, and P. Rauss. The FERET database and evaluation procedure for face-recognition algorithm. *Image and Vision Computing*, 16:295–306, 1998.

[10] P. J. Phillips, H. Moon, P. Rauss, and S. A. Rizvi. The FERET evaluation methodology for face-recognition algorithms. In *Proceedings of CVPR97*, pages 137–143, 1997.

[11] A. Samal and P. Iyengar. Automatic Recognition and Analysis of Human Faces and Facial Expressions: A Survey . *Pattern Recognition*, 25:65–77, 1992.

[12] F. Smeraldi, N. Capdevielle, and J. Bigun. Face Authentication by retinotopic sampling of the Gabor decomposition and Support Vector Machines. In *Proceedings of the 2nd International Conference on Audio and Video Based Biometric Person Authentication (AVBPA'99), Washington DC (USA)*, 1999.

[13] T. Tan and H. Yan. Face recognition by fractal transformations. In *Proc. IEEE ICASSP*, pages 3537–3540, 1999.

[14] http://xm2vtsdb.ee.surrey.ac.uk/face-icpr2000/index.html.

[15] http://xm2vtsdb.ee.surrey.ac.uk/results/face/verification_LP/.

[16] ftp://hrl.harvard.edu/pub/faces.

[17] http://www.cs.rug.nl/~peterkr/FACE/face.html.

[18] http://ns1.tele.ucl.ac.be/M2VTS/.

[19] http://www.cam-orl.co.uk/facedatabase.html.

[20] http://xm2vtsdb.ee.surrey.ac.uk/.

[21] http://cvc.yale.edu/projects/yalefaces/yalefaces.html.

EXPERIMENT	Configuration I								
	Evaluation set			Test set					
	[1]FAE = [2]FRE	FAE (FRE=0)	FRE (FAE=0)	FAE=FRE		FRE=0		FAE=0	
				FA	FR	FA	FR	FA	FR
[3]**AUT**	8.1	48.4	19.0	8.2	6.0	46.6	0.8	0.5	20.0
[4]**IDIAP**	8.0	54.9	16.0	8.1	8.5	54.5	0.5	0.5	20.5
[5]**Sydney**	12.9	94.4	70.5	13.6	12.3	94.0	0.0	0.0	81.3
[6]**UniS–A–G–NC**	5.7	96.4	26.7	7.6	6.8	96.5	0.3	0.0	27.5
[7]**UniS–A–S–NC**	5.3	99.3	25.3	7.4	6.8	99.4	0.0	0.0	24.3
[8]**UniS–S–G–NC**	3.5	81.1	16.2	3.5	2.8	81.2	0.0	0.0	14.5
[9]**UniS–S–S–NC**	3.3	92.9	15.7	3.3	3.0	93.5	0.0	0.0	14.0
[10]**UniS–A–G–SM**	10.0	99.8	93.8	9.8	8.8	100.0	0.0	0.0	97.3
[11]**UniS–A–S–SM**	7.0	97.3	63.7	5.8	7.3	99.6	0.0	0.0	58.5
[12]**UniS–S–G–SM**	6.5	93.9	40.0	6.5	5.3	94.1	0.0	0.0	37.5
[13]**UniS–S–S–SM**	2.5	84.2	25.7	2.3	2.5	85.0	0.3	0.0	24.3
[14]**UniS–SVM**	6.9	—	—	7.7	6.3	—	—	—	—

Table 1. Error rates according to the Lausanne protocol for configuration I

[1]**FAE** stands for false acceptance error rate on evaluation set
[2]**FRE** stands for false rejection error rate on evaluation set
[3]**AUT** Aristotle University of Thessaloniki
[4]**IDIAP** Dalle Molle Institute for Perceptual Artificial Intelligence
[5]**Sydney** University of Sydney
[6]**UniS–A–G–NC** University of Surrey, full automatic registration, global threshold, normalized correlation
[7]**UniS–A–S–NC** University of Surrey, full automatic registration, client-specific threshold, normalized correlation
[8]**UniS–S–G–NC** University of Surrey, semi-automatic registration, global threshold, normalized correlation
[9]**UniS–S–S–NC** University of Surrey, semi-automatic registration, client-specific threshold, normalized correlation
[10]**UniS–A–G–SM** University of Surrey, full automatic registration, global threshold, special metric
[11]**UniS–A–S–SM** University of Surrey, full automatic registration, client-specific threshold, special metric
[12]**UniS–S–G–SM** University of Surrey, semi-automatic registration, global threshold, special metric
[13]**UniS–S–S–SM** University of Surrey, semi-automatic registration, client-specific threshold, special metric
[14]**UniS–SVM** University of Surrey, fully-automatic registration, Support vector machine

EXPERIMENT	Configuration II								
	Evaluation set			Test set					
	[1]FAE = [2]FRE	FAE (FRE=0)	FRE (FAE=0)	FAE=FRE		FRE=0		FAE=0	
				FA	FR	FA	FR	FA	FR
[3]**AUT**	6.5	36.9	18.8	6.2	3.5	34.7	0.8	0.5	16.3
[4]**IDIAP**	7.0	59.4	19.8	7.7	7.3	0.3	54.2	1.0	18.0
[5]**Sydney**	14.1	98.4	80.8	13.0	12.3	98.1	0.0	0.0	84.8
[6]**UniS–S–G–NC**	1.3	43.5	9.3	1.3	1.8	44.2	0.3	0.0	9.0
[7]**UniS–S–S–NC**	1.3	55.4	8.5	1.2	1.5	55.6	0.3	0.0	8.5
[8]**UniS–S–G–SM**	3.5	42.0	18.8	3.5	3.8	42.1	0.5	0.0	19.5
[9]**UniS–S–S–SM**	1.3	23.1	18.8	1.2	1.0	22.6	0.3	0.0	20.5

Table 2. Error rates according to the Lausanne protocol for configuration II

[1]**FAE** stands for false acceptance error rate in evaluation set
[2]**FRE** stands for false rejection error rate in evaluation set
[3]**AUT** Aristotle University of Thessaloniki
[4]**IDIAP** Dalle Molle Institute for Perceptual Artificial Intelligence
[5]**Sydney** University of Sydney
[6]**UniS–S–G–NC** University of Surrey, semi-automatic registration, global threshold, normalized correlation
[7]**UniS–S–S–NC** University of Surrey, semi-automatic registration, client-specific threshold, normalized correlation
[8]**UniS–S–G–SM** University of Surrey, semi-automatic registration, global threshold, special metric
[9]**UniS–S–S–SM** University of Surrey, semi-automatic registration, client-specific threshold, special metric

Performance Evaluation of Line Drawing Recognition Systems

Atul K. Chhabra
Bell Atlantic Network Systems
Advanced Technology
White Plains, NY 10604, USA
atul@basit.com

Ihsin T. Phillips
Computer Science/Software Engineering Dept.
Seattle University
Seattle, WA 98122, USA
yun@seattleu.edu

Abstract

This paper presents the results of the third international graphics recognition contest. We evaluated the performance of four different vectorization systems on scanned images of CAD drawings. The EditCost Index *was used for comparative evaluation of the systems. The performance curves of the systems on the test images are presented in this paper.*

1. Introduction

The problem of automatic interpretation of engineering drawing images, or graphics recognition, has been studied for a long time. In recent years, several new vectorization methods have been proposed [6, 15, 11] and many commercial vectorization systems have been developed. There is need for frequent comparative evaluation in this field in order to measure the progress made over time. Without performance evaluation contests or benchmarks, future progress in the field is not possible or, at least, not measurable.

Performance evaluation of graphics recognition system is relatively a young field. The contest described here was preceded by a dashed line detection contest [12] and a raster to vector conversion contest [9, 14]. Both of these past contests used only synthetic images of engineering drawings. Here, we report the methods used to generate realistic test images and the results of the graphics recognition contest.

The performance metric used here is identical to the one we presented earlier in [13] and [10]. What is different here is the systematic methodology for generating real test data.

2. The data set

The major shortcoming of the previous graphics recognition contest was the lack of real data. The past contest used only synthetic images, i.e., images generated on a computer and lacking any scanning artifacts such as image noise and global & local geometric distortions. In order to address this problem, we set up a procedure for acquiring real scanned images along with the respective ground truth.

We started by seeking access to large databases of technical CAD files on the internet. Of the drawing archives we discovered, two organizations [2, 1] agreed to let us use their drawings for the contest. The online drawing archives of these two institutions contain numerous real and complex CAD drawings. Since it was very time consuming to convert the scanned images into usable testing data for the graphics recognition contest, we were limited to using a small set of the test files.

Although we tested the participating systems on only ten images of engineering drawings, we plan to grow the data set over time and conduct a more comprehensive contest in the future. For this contest, a majority of the effort was consumed in setting up the procedure for acquiring scanned images of engineering drawings and aligning the scanned images to the ground truth data. In addition, a lot of time was devoted to cleaning up the idiosyncrasies of the engineering drawings that would have made the performance evaluation very difficult. For example, in the CAD files, many straight lines were duplicated, many other lines were fragmented (in the CAD form), there were hatched regions and arrow heads that our current evaluation methodology is not built to handle.

After cleanup, the CAD files (in AutoCAD's DXF file format) were converted into the simple VEC format [8] using the *dxf2vec* PERL script developed for the earlier contest. The VEC files were then rendered into TIFF Group 4 compressed bi-level images using the vector to image rendering C program, *vec2tiff* [8] also developed for the previous contest. *Vec2tiff* allows you to introduce controlled perturbation at the vector level. The TIFF images were then printed at 200 dots per inch onto ANSI E-size paper using an HP DesignJet 650 printer. Next, the prints were scanned at 200 dots per inch using a roller-feed scanner (Contex

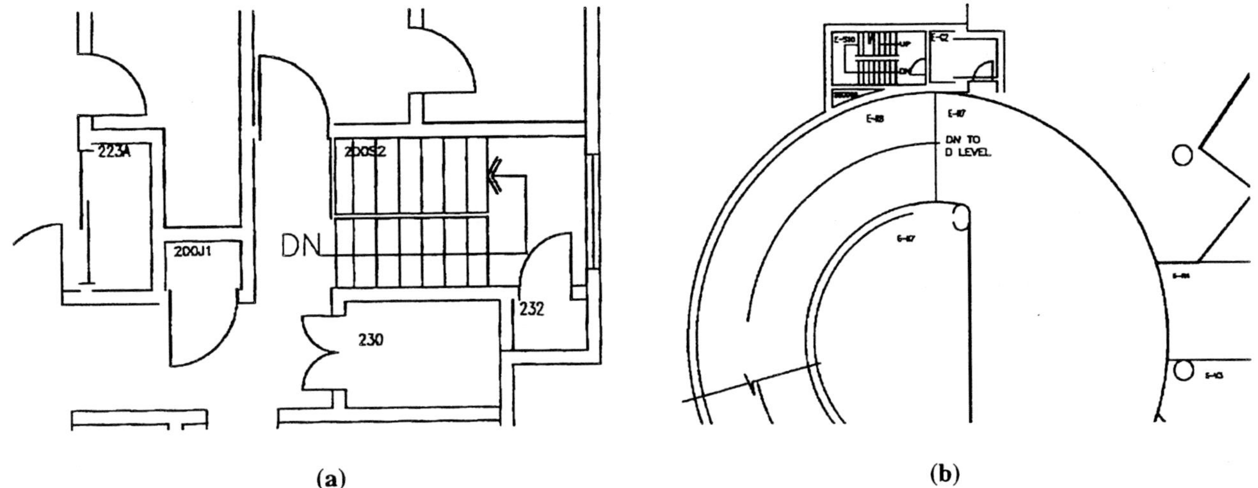

(a) (b)

Figure 1. Sections of test images of architectural drawings: (a) 2032_02.tif and (b) 2212_e.tif.

FSS-8000 scanner). Of course, during the scanning process, in addition to the pixel level distortion or noise, significant geometric distortions were introduced. The simplest form of such distortions is translation or skew. But often, there is more complex distortion that cannot be corrected by affine transforms. We needed to use four control points, ideally, the four corners of the drawing frame, for aligning the scanned image with the ground truth. The most general transformation that uses four point correspondences and maps straight lines to straight lines (but not necessarily preserving parallelism between parallel lines) is the planar projective transformation [17]. This transformation can be expressed as follows, where H is a homogeneous matrix.

$$\begin{bmatrix} ax' \\ ay' \\ a \end{bmatrix} = \begin{bmatrix} h_{11} & h_{12} & h_{13} \\ h_{21} & h_{22} & h_{23} \\ h_{31} & h_{32} & h_{33} \end{bmatrix} \begin{bmatrix} x \\ y \\ 1 \end{bmatrix}$$

For each point correspondence, we get two linear equations for h_{ij}'s.

$$\begin{aligned} x'(h_{31}x + h_{32}y + h_{33}) &= h_{11}x + h_{12}y + h_{13} \\ y'(h_{31}x + h_{32}y + h_{33}) &= h_{21}x + h_{22}y + h_{23} \end{aligned}$$

With four point correspondences, we get eight linear equations. We set h_{33} to 1, and then solve for the rest of the eight h coefficients. In practice, we apply the inverse of this process. For every pixel (x', y') in the transformed image, we compute the corresponding point (x, y) in the input image and copy the pixel value of the input point to the transformed point. When we apply this inverse transformation, the resulting x and y values are real numbers. We round them to the nearest integers.

We applied the above methodology to collect a total of ten large and complex scanned line drawing images. Of these, five were architectural drawings and five were mechanical drawings. All the scanned images were aligned with the ground truth. Small sections of a few test drawing are shown in Figures 1 and 2. The participating vectorization systems were tested using the procedure described below.

Although ten images appears to be a small dataset, we wish to point out that each of these images contains an average of 600 graphical entities. Despite using just ten images of engineering drawings, we were able to get more or less consistent trends in the performance of the participating systems. As we stated earlier, we will work on enlarging this data set.

A few sample scanned images were placed on the web site for the contest and the participants were asked to tweak their systems for the two classes of images (architectural and mechanical). To be fair to all participants, it must be stated that not all participants used these sample images (training images) to fine tune their system. Most participants just handed us their systems and asked us to evaluate them. We did our best to be fair in not giving any undue advantage to one system over the other. But it is possible that we did not know all the performance enhancing tricks available to expert users of these systems.

Since some of the participating systems are unable to interpret dashed lines (they recognize them as several disjointed straight line segments), we decided to limit the test images to continuous lines, arcs, and circles, in addition to text regions.

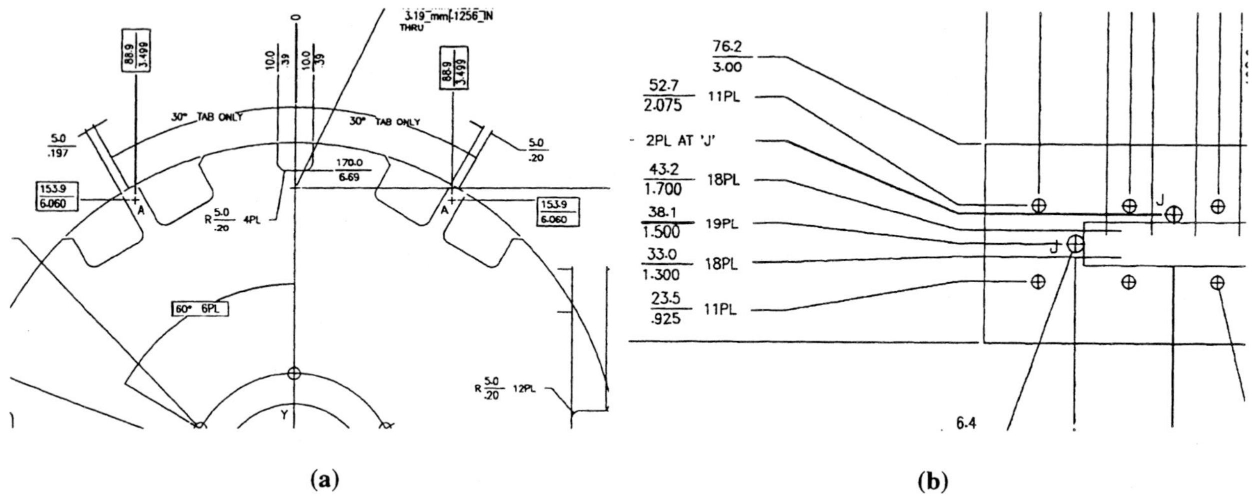

(a) (b)

Figure 2. Sections of test images of mechanical drawings: (a) pal151.tif and (b) pal343.tif.

3. Performance Evaluation

The following vectorization systems were evaluated in this contest: Scan2CAD [3], TracTrix 2000 [4], Vectory [5], and VrLiu [16].

The performance metrics used for this contest were identical to the ones used earlier [13, 10]. Essentially, we ran automated scripts to find the goodness of match between every recognized entity and ground truth entity. Based on the acceptance threshold, a potential match can be accepted or rejected. If a detected entity is not accepted as matching with any ground truth entity, then it becomes false alarm. If a ground truth entity is not matched with any detected entity, it is considered as a miss. Of course, the most obvious kind of match is a one-to-one match. But, in complex line drawings, one will always find one-to-many and many-to-one types of matches (e.g., due to fragmentation of lines). In [13], we proposed a measure called the *EditCost Index* that covers all the types of matches and mis-matches and gives you a single measure of how expensive it would be for a person to correct the mistakes made by the recognition system. For each system and each test drawing, we obtained curves for the *EditCost Index* by varying the acceptance threshold on the goodness of a low level match between a pair of graphical entities. For the ten test images used in this contest, the *EditCost Index* curves are plotted in Figure 3.

Before we could start the performance evaluation, we had to deal with data clean up issues. The commercial vectorization systems report the vectorization results in the AutoCAD DXF format [7]. We used our *dxf2vec* script to convert the DXF files into VEC files that our performance evaluation routines could understand. At this point, we discovered that the TracTrix 2000 software reported wrong x and y extents in the DXF output. Also, it returned the vectors in inches or mm's and not in pixel units. So we had to massage the results of this software to line up in the right area of the image. Once we aligned the vectorization results of TracTrix 2000 with the ground truth data, the rest of the performance evaluation was done automatically. There was no manual processing required for any other software.

4. Results

From Figure 3, we observe that the vectorization systems show a consistent trend, relative to each other, over all the test drawings. From the figure, it is apparent that Vectory and Scan2CAD have the lowest *EditCost Index* values, with Vectory having a slight edge over Scan2CAD. With the exception of one drawing, the next best performer is the TracTrix 2000 system. VrLiu has a consistent higher *EditCost Index* than Vectory, Scan2CAD, and TracTrix. Unfortunately, two of the three systems from the last contest could be tested in this contest. VPStudio did not participate. And the MDUS system could not be tested because we did not have an SGI machine handy (MDUS runs on the SGI Irix operating system). All the systems tested here run in the Windows 95 or 98 environment. We tested these systems on personal computers with Windows 95.

While this analysis is valuable in determining the usefulness of a vectorization system, it does not show the complete picture. In practical applications, it makes a big difference if you have to adjust just one operating parameter of a system or if you have to struggle with a dozen parameters. In future contests, we need to also incorporate the sensitivity analysis of the systems to their operating parameters.

5. Conclusions

The last graphics recognition contest [9, 13, 10] helped us develop the metrics for evaluating the performance of graphics recognition systems. In this contest, we concentrated on the methodology for collecting real data with ground truth. We hope that in future runs of this contest, we will have lot more real data at our disposal. Also, we hope to test the sensitivity of a system's performance to its internal operating parameters.

By comparing the reports of the last contest held in 1997 and this current contest, one can see visible progress in the field. Our hope is that this testing will become a regular part of research and development in this field and will contribute to further improvement in vectorization algorithms and systems.

6. Acknowledgements

The authors with to thank the Facilities Management department of the University of California, San Francisco, CA, and the BaBar Silicon Vertex Tracker (SVT) project of the Lawrence Berkeley National Laboratory, Berkeley, CA, for permitting the use of their drawings for this study. Thanks are also due to the participants who provided us with their vectorization software and documentation.

References

[1] Drawing archive for the BaBar Silicon Vertex Tracker (SVT) particle detector. Lawrence Berkeley National Laboratory (LBNL), Berkeley, CA. http://www-eng.lbl.gov/~luft/babar/.

[2] Facilities management floor plan archive. University of California, San Francisco. http://www.fm.ucsf.edu/.

[3] Scan2CAD version 5.1d(32) vectorization software, Softcover International Limited, London, UK. http://www.softcover.com.

[4] TracTrix 2000 version 3.0.11.0 vectorization software, Trix Systems AB, Vegby Sweden, and Trix Systems, Inc., Chelmsford, MA, USA. http://www.trixsystems.se or http://www.trixsystems.com.

[5] Vectory version 4.00-021 vectorization software, Graphikon GmbH, Berlin, Germany. http://www.graphikon.de.

[6] *Proceedings of Third IAPR International Workshop on Graphics Recognition*, Jaipur, India, September 1999. Revised versions of selected papers to appear in a LNCS volume, 2000.

[7] Autodesk, Inc. *AutoCAD Release 13 Customization Guide*. 1995.

[8] A. Chhabra and I. Phillips. A benchmark for graphics recognition systems. In *Proceedings of the IEEE Computer Society Workshop on Empirical Evaluation Methods in Computer Vision*, Santa Barbara, CA, June 1998.

[9] A. Chhabra and I. Phillips. The second international graphics recognition contest – raster to vector conversion: A report. In K. Tombre and A. Chhabra, editors, *Graphics Recognition: Algorithms and Systems, Second International Workshop, Nancy, France, August 1997, Selected Papers*, volume 1389 of *Lecture Notes in Computer Science*, pages 390–410. Springer Verlag, 1998.

[10] A. Chhabra and I. Phillips. Edit cost index as a measure of performance of graphics recognition systems. In *Proceedings of the IAPR International Workshop on Graphics Recognition (GREC'99)*, pages 331–334, Jaipur, India, September 1999.

[11] R. Kasturi and K. Tombre, editors. *Graphics Recognition: Methods and Applications*, volume 1072 of *Lecture Notes in Computer Science*. Springer Verlag, 1996. Selected papers from GREC'95.

[12] B. Kong, I. Phillips, R. Haralick, A. Prasad, and R. Kasturi. A benchmark: Performance evaluation of dashed line detection algorithms. In R. Kasturi and K. Tombre, editors, *Graphics Recognition: Methods and Applications, First International Workshop, University Park, PA, USA, August 1995, Selected Papers*, volume 1072 of *Lecture Notes in Computer Science*, pages 270–285. Springer, Berlin, 1996.

[13] I. Phillips and A. Chhabra. Empirical evaluation of graphics recognition systems. *IEEE Trans. Pattern Analysis and Machine Intelligence*, 21(9), September 1999.

[14] I. Phillips, J. Liang, A. Chhabra, and R. Haralick. A performance evaluation protocol for graphics recognition systems. In K. Tombre and A. Chhabra, editors, *Graphics Recognition: Algorithms and Systems, Second International Workshop, Nancy, France, August 1997, Selected Papers*, volume 1389 of *Lecture Notes in Computer Science*, pages 372–389. Springer Verlag, 1998.

[15] K. Tombre and A. Chhabra, editors. *Graphics Recognition: Algorithms and Systems*, volume 1389 of *Lecture Notes in Computer Science*. Springer Verlag, 1998. Selected papers from GREC'97.

[16] L. Wenyin. VrLiu version 0.99 vectorization software.

[17] A. Zisserman. Four points define a planar projective transformation. Available: http://www.dai.ed.ac.uk/CVonline/LOCAL_COPIES/EPSRC_SSAZ/epsrc_ssaz.html. In R. Fisher, editor, *CVonline: On-Line Compendium of Computer Vision [Online]*. Available: http://www.dai.ed.ac.uk/CVonline/. May 16, 2000.

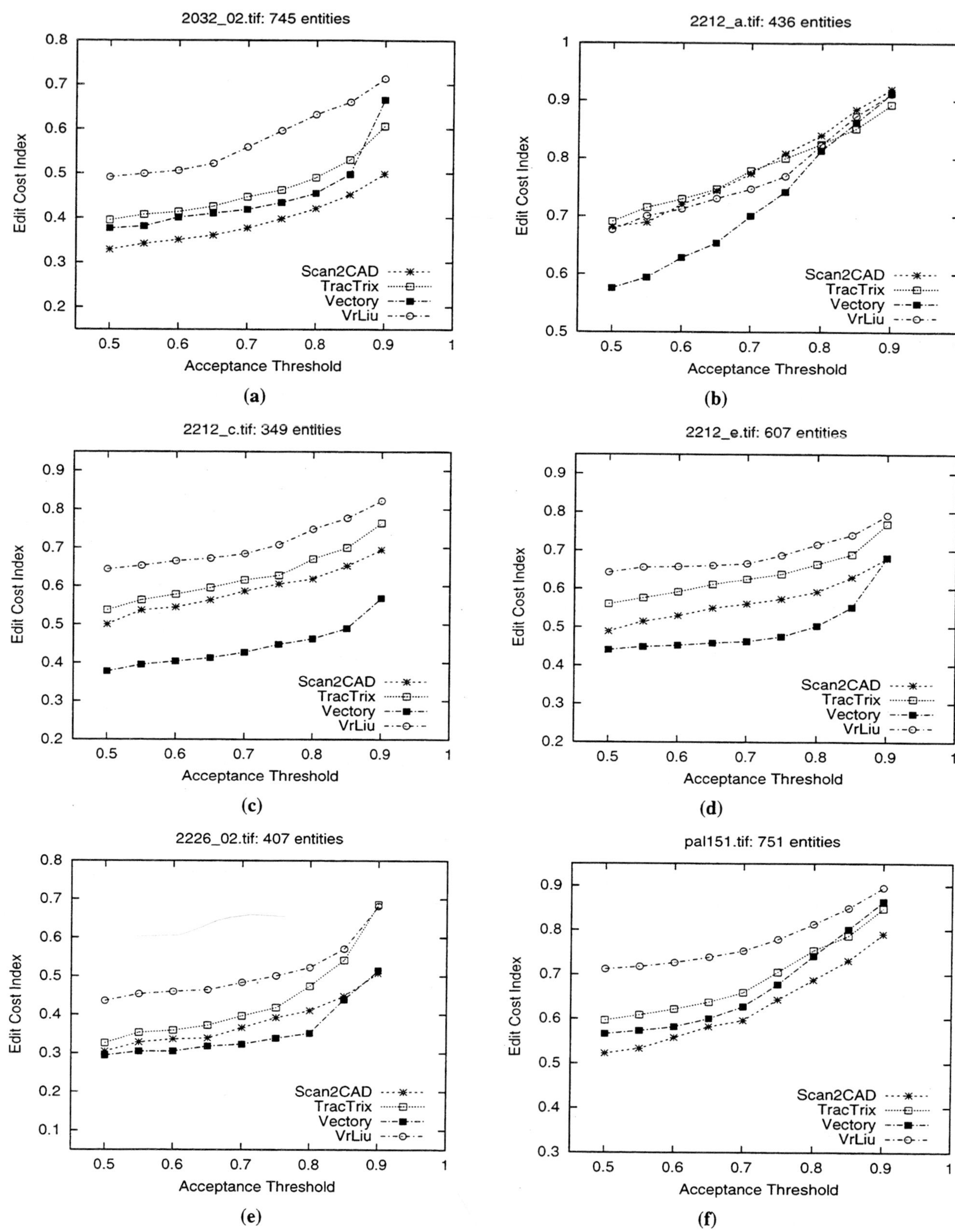

Figure 3. The *EditCost Index* curves for the four vectorization systems on five architectural drawings (a-e) and five mechanical drawings (f-j).

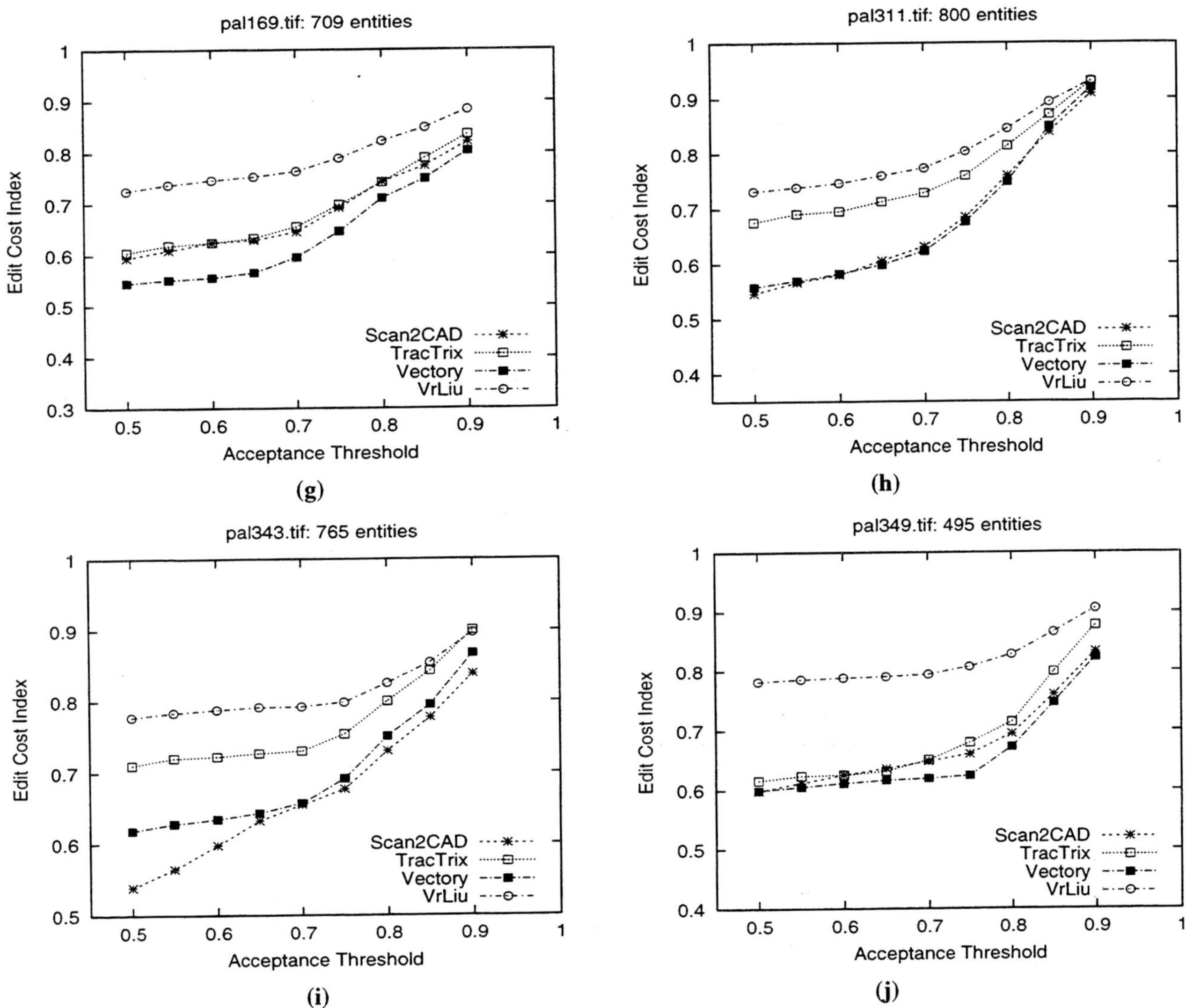

Figure 3. The *EditCost Index* curves for the four vectorization systems on five architectural drawings (a-e) and five mechanical drawings (f-j).

Algorithm Performance Contest

Selim Aksoy, Ming Ye, Michael L. Schauf, Mingzhou Song, Yalin Wang, Robert M. Haralick
Intelligent Systems Laboratory, University of Washington, Seattle, WA, 98195-2500, USA

Jim R. Parker, Juraj Pivovarov, Dominik Royko
University of Calgary, Dept. of Computer Science, Calgary, Canada

Changming Sun
CSIRO Mathematical and Information Sciences, Locked Bag 17, North Ryde, NSW 1670, Australia

Gunnar Farnebäck
Computer Vision Lab., Dept. of Electrical Eng., Linköping University, SE-581 83 Linköping, Sweden

Abstract

This contest involved the running and evaluation of computer vision and pattern recognition techniques on different data sets with known groundtruth. The contest included three areas; binary shape recognition, symbol recognition and image flow estimation. A package was made available for each area. Each package contained either real images with manual groundtruth or programs to generate data sets of ideal as well as noisy images with known groundtruth. They also contained programs to evaluate the results of an algorithm according to the given groundtruth. These evaluation criteria included the generation of confusion matrices, computation of the misdetection and false alarm rates and other performance measures suitable for the problems. This paper summarizes the data generation for each area and experimental results for a total of six participating algorithms.

1. Introduction

The contest home page and the packages are available at http://isl.ee.washington.edu/IAPR/ICPR00. All the software was written in C and developed in the Unix environment. The participants were allowed to use any set of parameters to generate test images for algorithm development. A specific set of parameters were supplied to generate data for the final experiments. The experiments were run by the participants themselves and the final results that were the output of the evaluation algorithms were submitted to the contest organizers.

The following sections describe the data generation and experimental results for the binary shape recognition, symbol recognition and image flow estimation areas.

2. Binary Shape Recognition

2.1. Data Generation

This package was prepared by Michael L. Schauf and Selim Aksoy. It was intended to provide a test data set with known groundtruth to evaluate binary shape recognition algorithms. It included code for generation of primitives and shape prototypes as the groundtruth model set, and perturbed images containing translated and scaled prototypes as the test data set.

The program started with the generation of shape models. A shape model was composed of a set of primitives. Each primitive was mildly constrained so that its digital image bore a reasonable resemblance to the ideal continuous primitive. The primitives for this data set were lines, circles, triangles, sectors, and quadrilaterals. Each primitive had some restriction on its free parameters in order to retain its general properties. The different primitives were randomly selected, generated and combined to form the different shape models. Each shape model was constrained so that each primitive slightly overlapped another.

Once the shape models were generated, they were randomly selected to be placed in an image. Each selected shape model was placed in the image at a random location with a random scale with the only constraint that its bounding box did not overlap with any other shape model's bounding box that was already in the image. Since we knew the locations and scales of the models in all images, we had the complete groundtruth.

Testing the robustness of recognition algorithms also requires the design of images containing varying levels of noise. For the addition of noise, the Document Degradation Model by Kanungo [4] was used. This model added pepper noise in such a way that pixels around the borders of the shape models had a higher probability of switching to opposite values than those pixels farther away from the border. Additional noise was added by generating non-relevant shape models and scaling them smaller than the smallest scale of the relevant models. Some example noisy images are given in Figure 1. Model and image sizes, overlap between primitives in a model, range for the number of primitives in a model, range for the number of models in an image, range for the scales of models in an image, and noise level were some of the parameters that were allowed to be changed in the code.

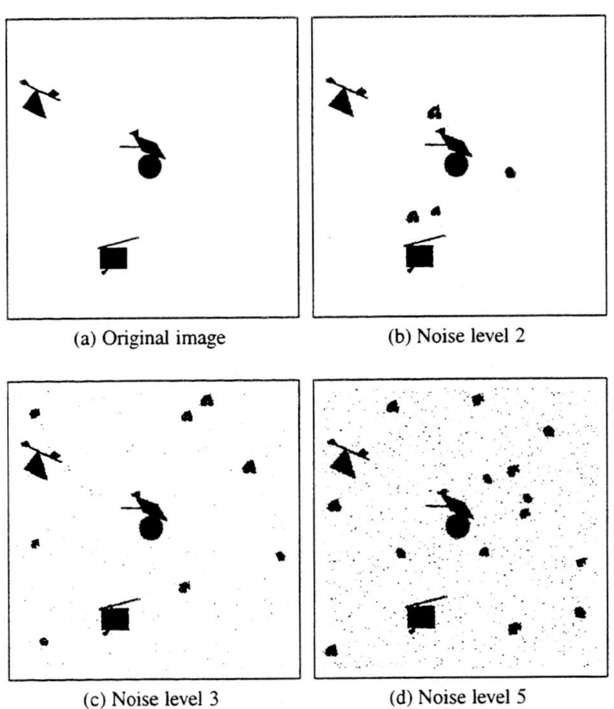

Figure 1: Example shape images.

The package also included a program for performance evaluation on a database of images with their groundtruth and recognition algorithm results. The output of the program was a confusion matrix and a success score for the recognition algorithm. The program read the groundtruth information for each image and compared it with the recognition results. The success value was a linear combination of the correct detection rate, incorrect detection rate, misdetection rate, false alarm rate, and the accuracy of the detected location and scale.

2.2. Experiments

2.2.1. Schauf, Aksoy and Haralick Algorithm

The only result available for this package is the results of the binary shape recognition algorithm by Michael L. Schauf, Selim Aksoy and Robert M. Haralick from the Intelligent Systems Laboratory, University of Washington, USA. The algorithm [6] introduces a size invariant method to recognize complex two-dimensional shapes using multiple generalized recursive erosion transforms. The method accomplishes the same kind of recognition that templates of each shape at multiple scales would do, but the method takes constant time per pixel regardless of the scale of the prototype. The method workes on noisy images without requiring noise removal as preprocessing.

Experiments were run on 100 noisy images having a total of 254 randomly translated and scaled models plus a number of extraneous small shapes that might appear like a model. The algorithm had 5 misdetections and 13 false alarms. The confusion matrix is given in Table 1.

3. Symbol Recognition

3.1. Data Generation

This package was prepared by Ming Ye, Mingzhou Song, Yalin Wang and Selim Aksoy. It was intended to provide a test data set with known groundtruth to evaluate binary symbol recognition algorithms. The symbol library consisted of electrical symbols as the model set and noisy versions of randomly translated and scaled symbols as the test data set. The symbol library contained 25 electrical symbols where each ideal symbol image was 512x512 pixels. The symbols were all line drawings with a 30 pixel line width.

An instantiation of a symbol was obtained by scaling the symbol image down to a certain size between 40 and 160 pixels. Because of the high resolution of the library symbols, the observed symbol had a thick enough line width so that it was very unlikely that broken lines existed after denoising. The observed symbols might also have a small rotation angle.

In order to generate test data, an empty image was first partitioned into square patches, each of which had the same size. A randomly selected symbol was randomly scaled and put into each of the patches, with the centroid of the symbol lying at the patch center. No symbol occluded others. Since we knew the locations and scales of the symbols in all images, we had the complete groundtruth. It is worth mentioning that such symbol arrangement was just for synthesis convenience, but not for the ease of recognition.

There were three major types of noise perturbing the observations: quantization error, replacement noise, and salt-and-pepper noise. Quantization error came from scaling the library symbol, because the scaling factor could be any real value while the pixel positions had to be integers. Salt-and-pepper noise flipped the pixel values by a certain probability. Replacement noise flipped the pixel values as to a more complex probability model. The chance of a pixel being flipped increased as the pixel was closer to areas of the opposite value and as such areas increased. Replacement noise was common to documents which have been manipulated quite a few times by facsimiling, copying and so on. Some noisy images are given in Figure 2.

Table 1: Confusion matrix for Schauf *et al.*'s binary shape recognition algorithm. Rows represent correct models and columns represent detected models. Performance measures include misdetection (MD), average location error (ALE), average scale error (ASE) and false alarm (FA).

	Assigned Models										MD	ALE	ASE
Original Models	32	0	0	0	0	0	0	0	0	0	0	2.6939	0.0109
	0	28	0	0	0	0	0	0	0	0	0	2.2733	0.0081
	0	0	30	0	0	0	0	0	0	0	3	3.3781	0.0124
	0	0	0	30	0	0	0	0	0	0	0	3.1621	0.0120
	0	0	0	0	16	0	0	0	0	0	0	4.1056	0.0191
	0	0	0	0	0	22	0	0	0	0	0	2.7724	0.0111
	0	0	0	0	0	0	20	0	0	0	0	2.1297	0.0117
	0	0	0	0	0	0	0	21	0	0	0	1.4366	0.0054
	0	0	0	0	0	0	0	0	27	0	1	1.9564	0.0073
	0	0	0	0	0	0	0	0	0	28	1	2.5694	0.0119
FA	0	0	0	0	0	11	2	0	0	0			

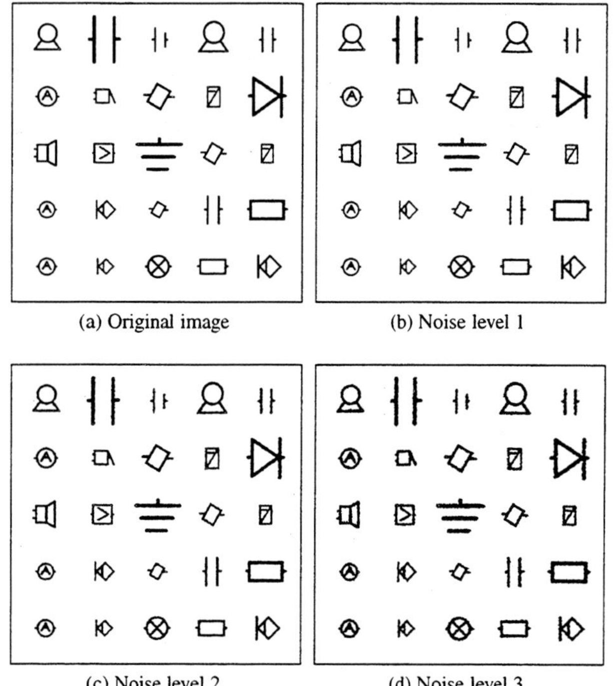

(a) Original image (b) Noise level 1

(c) Noise level 2 (d) Noise level 3

Figure 2: Example symbol images.

The package also included a program for performance evaluation. The program read the groundtruth information for each image, compared it with the recognition results and output a confusion matrix. For convenience of comparison, we summarized the confusion matrices of all sizes and noise levels by the number of wrong assignments, misdetections, false alarms, average location errors and average scale errors.

3.2. Experiments

First, 50 images that contain 25 symbols with sizes "all 75x75", "all 50x50" and "all random" were generated. This made up 150 images with 25 symbols in each image. Then each image was perturbed with three levels of noise separately. This made up an additional of 450 images.

3.2.1. Ye and Haralick Algorithm

Two algorithms were submitted to this contest. The first one is by Ming Ye and Robert M. Haralick from the Intelligent Systems Laboratory, University of Washington, USA. This is a segmentation-free symbol recognition algorithm [8] purely using mathematical morphology. Given a page of symbols, the algorithm simultaneously determines the positions and scaling factors of all the symbols which come from the given symbol library. Each symbol has a feature set composed of the relative maxima of the recursive erosion transforms from a few structural elements. The feature set has the property that the distance between any two features within the set is proportional to their scales. Given an observed feature, the algorithm decides whether it has come from a hypothesized symbol by examining if it establishes a similar proportional relationship with its neighboring observations to that of the symbol. For a given image, the algorithm starts from the feature observation with the largest value and works till all feature points are assigned to certain symbols. Before extracting feature points from the image, morphological closing and opening operations are conducted to reduce noise impact.

A very simple version of this recognition system was implemented. The overall confusion matrix is given in Table 2. The errors are mainly due to two reasons. First, as mathematical morphology operations are fragile to holes, this system breaks down when the noise level is high. Second, because only three features are used for each symbol, this system is not discriminative enough. The first problem can be alleviated by using non-morphological denoising methods and the second can be improved by developing more

Table 2: Confusion matrix for Ye and Haralick's symbol recognition algorithm when the results for all noisy images are combined. Rows represent correct models and columns represent detected models. Performance measures include misdetection (MD), average location error (ALE), average scale error (ASE), false alarm (FA) and wrong scale detection (WSD).

	Assigned Models																									MD	ALE	ASE
	230	0	37	0	0	0	0	0	0	0	0	0	19	14	0	8	64	0	0	0	0	13	0	0	29	66	7.4208	2.0471
	5	202	134	0	0	0	0	0	0	0	0	38	93	0	0	0	9	0	0	0	0	4	0	0	1	129	1.8423	1.0724
	1	0	334	0	0	0	0	0	0	0	0	0	25	0	0	0	0	0	0	0	0	0	0	0	0	129	3.1368	1.3732
	0	0	0	8	0	0	0	0	0	0	0	0	56	0	0	0	0	0	0	24	0	0	0	0	5	126	0.0358	0.0882
	18	0	56	0	1	0	0	0	0	0	0	0	46	0	0	5	7	15	0	0	42	9	0	0	9	245	0.1633	0.0267
	14	0	105	0	0	45	0	0	5	0	0	0	5	0	0	2	0	0	0	0	0	1	0	0	10	206	0.9131	0.2900
	0	0	0	1	5	0	44	5	0	0	0	0	133	0	0	0	0	0	0	6	0	0	0	0	0	259	0.3733	0.2990
	35	0	8	0	0	0	0	66	0	0	0	0	0	0	0	0	15	0	0	0	0	0	0	0	0	371	0.7509	0.3584
	10	0	153	0	0	0	0	0	133	0	0	0	17	0	0	0	11	0	0	0	0	0	0	0	0	150	0.9366	0.4326
	72	0	34	0	0	0	0	1	0	112	0	0	23	2	5	10	5	0	0	0	0	2	0	0	0	175	1.5702	0.8116
	2	0	18	0	0	0	0	0	0	41	57	0	106	0	0	0	3	0	0	0	0	0	0	0	4	72	0.9324	0.1622
	89	0	14	0	0	0	0	0	0	0	0	184	25	2	0	0	24	0	0	0	0	0	0	0	4	216	2.2608	0.8462
	6	0	28	0	0	0	0	0	0	0	0	0	238	0	0	19	15	0	0	0	0	102	0	0	0	276	2.8707	1.3403
	5	0	7	0	0	0	0	0	0	0	0	0	0	102	1	0	0	0	0	0	0	0	0	0	0	71	4.2794	1.1383
	0	0	21	0	0	0	0	0	0	0	0	0	0	0	85	0	0	0	0	0	0	0	0	0	0	158	4.0596	1.6531
	47	0	26	0	0	0	0	0	0	0	0	0	16	3	0	73	35	0	0	0	0	77	0	0	4	142	4.0397	1.5101
	162	0	36	0	0	0	0	5	0	0	0	0	36	5	0	0	183	0	0	0	0	13	0	0	96	19	7.1570	2.7056
	33	0	59	0	0	9	0	0	0	0	5	0	22	5	0	15	10	48	0	0	3	3	0	0	33	244	2.4146	0.7739
	7	0	24	0	0	14	0	1	6	15	4	0	6	0	0	0	8	0	42	0	0	8	0	20	0	145	0.7890	0.2737
	14	0	64	0	0	0	0	5	0	0	0	0	76	0	0	0	14	0	0	237	0	16	0	0	5	160	2.1797	1.1420
	8	0	14	0	0	0	0	0	0	0	0	0	41	0	0	0	0	0	0	0	60	0	0	0	4	59	0.8312	0.2647
	55	4	30	0	0	0	0	0	0	0	0	0	0	0	0	0	63	0	0	0	0	37	0	0	30	255	0.4408	0.0913
	6	2	190	0	0	0	0	0	87	5	5	0	13	0	0	0	9	0	0	0	0	0	166	0	6	243	1.8791	1.1622
	26	0	33	0	0	0	0	3	0	0	0	0	102	0	0	18	55	4	0	0	0	10	0	160	17	199	1.9390	0.8208
	111	0	19	0	0	0	0	0	0	0	0	0	22	0	0	12	60	0	0	0	0	17	0	0	39	86	1.9237	0.4960
FA	0	0	0	0	0	0	0	0	0	0	0	0	0	0	0	0	0	0	0	0	0	0	0	0	0			
WSD	20	0	0	0	0	0	0	0	0	0	0	0	2	0	0	0	14	0	0	3	0	0	0	0	0			

refined features.

3.2.2. Parker, Pivovarov and Royko Algorithm

The second submission is by J. R. Parker, J. Pivovarov and D. Royko from the Department of Computer Science, University of Calgary, Canada. The algorithm [5] first extracts the unknown symbol into a bilevel image which is called image A. Then a scaled vector template is plotted into a blank image with the same size bounding box as the unknown image, which is called image B. Thick lines are plotted in this image, based on the measured "estimated pen width" of image A. Next, the algorithm iterates through all pixels of A and measures how far the nearest matching pixel is in B, i.e. if $A(i,j)$ is a foreground pixel, finds the 8-distance to the nearest foreground pixel in B, if $A(i,j)$ is a background pixel, finds the 8-distance to the nearest background pixel in B. This gives a distance map, $M = \text{map}(A,B)$ where $M(i,j)$ is the distance from pixel $A(i,j)$ to the nearest matching pixel in B. Then, the squares of all the entries in $\text{map}(A,B)$ and $\text{map}(B,A)$ are summed. This is the measure of goodness-of-fit of the particular orientation of the template plotted in image B to the object in image A. A small set of orientations, $-3°, \ldots, +3°$, are used and the one with minimum distance is found. This is stored as the distance from A to that particular template. This can be implemented efficiently through the use of dynamic programming, and requires a constant (small) number of image passes. Two passes of noise removal consisting of an averaging filter followed by an edge-cleaning filter are performed. A final smoothing is performed along the bounding boxes of each extracted symbol.

This algorithm achieved a recognition rate of 100% on all test data with an unoptimized execution time of approximately 5 symbols per second on an Intel Celeron 400MHz PC. The confusion matrix is given in Table 3.

4. Image Flow Estimation

4.1. Data Generation

This package included synthetic and real image sequences and their optic flow groundtruth generation for performance evaluation in terms of false alarm rate, misdetection rate and average error vector magnitude. The two synthetic image sequences were rot and div. They were generated using a ray-tracing method which traced each ray passing through the camera and an image pixel, and found out if it touched the surface of the 3D object. If it did, the surface intensity was recorded for that pixel, otherwise a background value was recorded. For accuracy of the inten-

Table 3: Confusion matrix for Parker *et al.*'s symbol recognition algorithm when the results for all noisy images are combined.

	Assigned Models																									MD	ALE	ASE
	480	0	0	0	0	0	0	0	0	0	0	0	0	0	0	0	0	0	0	0	0	0	0	0	0	0	0.7248	0.7846
	0	615	0	0	0	0	0	0	0	0	0	0	0	0	0	0	0	0	0	0	0	0	0	0	0	0	1.0456	1.3737
	0	0	489	0	0	0	0	0	0	0	0	0	0	0	0	0	0	0	0	0	0	0	0	0	0	0	0.9917	0.6351
	0	0	0	219	0	0	0	0	0	0	0	0	0	0	0	0	0	0	0	0	0	0	0	0	0	0	0.8746	2.1794
	0	0	0	0	453	0	0	0	0	0	0	0	0	0	0	0	0	0	0	0	0	0	0	0	0	0	0.9401	2.0193
	0	0	0	0	0	393	0	0	0	0	0	0	0	0	0	0	0	0	0	0	0	0	0	0	0	0	0.9213	3.0666
	0	0	0	0	0	0	453	0	0	0	0	0	0	0	0	0	0	0	0	0	0	0	0	0	0	0	0.8852	2.5840
	0	0	0	0	0	0	0	495	0	0	0	0	0	0	0	0	0	0	0	0	0	0	0	0	0	0	1.0261	0.9972
	0	0	0	0	0	0	0	0	474	0	0	0	0	0	0	0	0	0	0	0	0	0	0	0	0	0	0.9627	1.5840
	0	0	0	0	0	0	0	0	0	441	0	0	0	0	0	0	0	0	0	0	0	0	0	0	0	0	1.0177	1.6244
	0	0	0	0	0	0	0	0	0	0	303	0	0	0	0	0	0	0	0	0	0	0	0	0	0	0	0.8461	1.1549
	0	0	0	0	0	0	0	0	0	0	0	558	0	0	0	0	0	0	0	0	0	0	0	0	0	0	0.8632	1.2364
	0	0	0	0	0	0	0	0	0	0	0	0	684	0	0	0	0	0	0	0	0	0	0	0	0	0	0.8734	0.7166
	0	0	0	0	0	0	0	0	0	0	0	0	0	186	0	0	0	0	0	0	0	0	0	0	0	0	0.8547	3.3598
	0	0	0	0	0	0	0	0	0	0	0	0	0	0	264	0	0	0	0	0	0	0	0	0	0	0	0.7557	2.4719
	0	0	0	0	0	0	0	0	0	0	0	0	0	0	0	423	0	0	0	0	0	0	0	0	0	0	1.2268	0.2076
	0	0	0	0	0	0	0	0	0	0	0	0	0	0	0	0	555	0	0	0	0	0	0	0	0	0	0.6594	0.9158
	0	0	0	0	0	0	0	0	0	0	0	0	1	0	0	0	0	488	0	0	0	0	0	0	0	0	1.3944	0.6332
	0	0	0	0	0	0	0	0	0	0	0	0	0	0	0	0	0	0	300	0	0	0	0	0	0	0	1.1690	0.4996
	0	0	0	0	0	0	0	0	0	0	0	0	0	0	0	0	0	0	0	591	0	0	0	0	0	0	0.8583	0.4768
	0	0	0	0	0	0	0	0	0	0	0	0	0	0	0	0	0	0	0	0	186	0	0	0	0	0	1.3291	0.3490
	0	0	0	0	0	0	0	0	0	0	0	0	0	0	0	0	0	0	0	0	0	474	0	0	0	0	1.0470	3.6406
	0	0	0	0	0	0	0	0	0	0	0	0	0	0	0	0	0	0	0	0	0	0	732	0	0	0	0.9582	0.7132
	0	0	0	0	0	0	0	0	0	0	0	0	0	0	0	0	0	0	0	0	0	0	0	627	0	0	0.8403	0.6434
	0	0	0	0	0	0	0	0	0	0	0	0	0	0	0	0	0	0	0	0	0	0	0	0	366	0	0.7517	0.4322
FA	0	0	0	0	0	0	0	0	0	0	0	0	0	0	0	0	0	0	0	0	0	0	0	0	0			
WSD	0	0	0	0	0	0	0	0	0	0	0	0	0	0	0	0	0	0	0	0	0	0	0	0	0			

sity values, a sinusoidal function was used as the 3D surface pattern. Example frames and flow field groundtruth for the synthetic image sequences are given in Figure 3. Three real image sequences, Taxi, Rubik and SRI were obtained from Barron *et al.* [1]. Examples are given in Figure 4.

4.2. Experiments

4.2.1. Ye and Haralick Algorithm

Three algorithms were submitted to this contest. The first one is by Ming Ye and Robert M. Haralick from the Intelligent Systems Laboratory, University of Washington, USA. The algorithm [9] forms a set of constraint equations from the first and second order derivatives for each pixel, and solves a combined set of equations from a neighborhood for the image flow at the central pixel by assuming a constant local motion model. The derivatives are estimated from a 3D cubic facet model. This image flow estimation scheme has shown generally good results. Besides it provides a covariance matrix with each estimate as a reliable error measurement, which can help subsequent applications make judicious use of the image flow estimates. The covariance matrix is obtained from propagating image noise through the facet model and the image flow constraint equation, considering the correlation of the constraints. Its effectiveness has been verified by a successful χ^2 hypothesis testing based selection scheme.

The false alarm rate, misdetection rate and the average absolute error vector magnitude for the synthetic image sequences are given in Table 4. The optical flow fields for the real image sequences are given in Figure 4.

4.2.2. Sun Algorithm

The second submission is by Changming Sun from CSIRO Mathematical and Information Sciences, Australia. The algorithm [7] uses fast area cross correlation and 3D shortest-path techniques to obtain a dense optical flow field. Fast correlation is achieved by using the box filtering technique which is invariant to the size of the correlation window. The motion for each scan line of the input image is obtained from the correlation coefficient volume by finding the best 3D path using dynamic programming techniques rather than simply choosing the position that gives the maximum cross correlation coefficient. Sub-pixel accuracy is achieved by fitting the local correlation coefficients to a quadratic surface. Currently only two images are used for the optical flow estimation. Typical running time for a 256x256 image is in the order of a few seconds.

The correlation window sizes were in the range of 15x15 and 19x19. The matching search range was from -3 to +3 pixels in both the x and the y directions. The algorithm only used two frames in an image sequence for the flow estimation (the middle ones were used, usually frames 9 and 10). The running time of the algorithm was 14.35s for an image of size 316x252 on a 85MHz SUN SPARCserver1000. The false alarm rate, misdetection rate and the average absolute error vector magnitude for the synthetic image sequences are given in Table 4. The optical flow fields obtained for the real image sequences are given in Figure 4.

4.2.3. Farnebäck Algorithm

The third submission is by Gunnar Farnebäck from the Computer Vision Laboratory, Linköping University, Sweden. The algorithm [2, 3] starts by computing 3D spatiotemporal orientation tensors from the image sequence. This is done by a method based on carefully weighted least squares approximations of signal neighborhoods by quadratic polynomials. Then the orientation tensors are combined under the constraints of a parametric motion model, in this case just a translation, to produce velocity estimates. This is done locally in each neighborhood, without regard to possible discontinuities in the velocity field, but with a Gaussian weighting of the points in the neighborhood. Computationally the weighted least squares approximations are most demanding, but since these can be computed efficiently by a hierarchical scheme of separable convolutions, the algorithm is very fast.

The algorithm used filters of effective size 9x9x9 and the tensors were combined over local neighborhoods of size 15x15. On a Sun Ultra 30, this took 2 seconds for each sequence (velocities were computed only for the frame where we had groundtruth). The algorithm was implemented as Matlab m-files, except for the convolutions which were computed by a Matlab mex-file implemented in C. The false alarm rate, misdetection rate and the average absolute error vector magnitude for the synthetic image sequences are given in Table 4. The optical flow fields obtained for the real image sequences are given in Figure 4.

5. Conclusions

Because it takes a considerable amount of effort to prepare ground truthed data sets and evaluation software for pattern recognition processing algorithms, it was hoped that there would be many researchers who would participate in the contests. Unfortunately, this was not the case. We will keep the data sets and evaluation software out on the web so that by next ICPR more researchers will have tried their hand at these tasks and a more comprehensive discussion and comparison of techniques can be made.

References

[1] J. L. Barron, S. S. Beauchemin, and D. J. Fleet. Performance of optical flow techniques. *International Journal of Computer Vision*, 12(1):43–77, 1994. ftp://csd.uwo.ca/pub/vision/TESTDATA/.

[2] G. Farnebäck. Spatial Domain Methods for Orientation and Velocity Estimation. Lic. Thesis LiU-Tek-Lic-1999:13, Dept. EE, Linköping University, SE-581 83 Linköping, Sweden, March 1999. Thesis No. 755, ISBN 91-7219-441-3, ftp://ftp.isy.liu.se/pub/bb/Theses/LicTheses/G_Farneback_lic.ps.gz.

[3] G. Farnebäck. Fast and accurate motion estimation using orientation tensors and parametric motion models. In *Proceedings of 15th IAPR International Conference on Pattern Recognition*, Barcelona, Spain, September 2000.

[4] T. Kanungo, R. M. Haralick, and H. S. Baird. Power functions and their use in selecting distance functions for document degradation model validation. In *Proceedings of the Third International Conference on Document Analysis and Recognition*, volume 2, pages 734–739, 1995.

[5] J. R. Parker. Vector templates and handprinted symbol recognition. Technical Report 95/559/11, University of Calgary, Department of Computer Science, Calgary, Canada, 1995.

[6] M. Schauf, S. Aksoy, and R. M. Haralick. Model-based shape recognition using recursive mathematical morphology. In *Proceedings of 14th IAPR International Conference on Pattern Recognition*, volume 1, pages 202–204, Brisbane, Australia, August 16–20 1998.

[7] C. Sun. Fast optical flow using cross correlation and shortest-path techniques. In *Proceedings of Digital Image Computing: Techniques and Applications*, pages 143–148, Perth, Australia, December 7–8 1999. http://extra.cmis.csiro.au/IA/changs/doc/motion_dicta99.ps.gz.

[8] M. Ye and R. M. Haralick. Recognizing symbols using mathematical morphology. Technical report, Intelligent Systems Laboratory, 1998.

[9] M. Ye and R. M. Haralick. Image flow estimation using facet model and covariance propagation. In M. Cheriet and Y. H. Yang, editors, *Vision Interface: Real World Applications of Computer Vision*, volume 35 of *MPAI*, pages 209–241. World Scientific Pub Co., 2000.

Table 4: Image flow quantitative comparison on div and rot sequences. The false alarm rate (FA), misdetection rate (MD) and the average absolute error vector magnitude (AEVM) are given for each algorithm.

	Div			Rot		
	FA	MD	AEVM	FA	MD	AEVM
Ye	4.76	1.26	0.0388	3.39	0.67	0.0931
Sun	40.6	0	0.0784	31.12	0	0.1254
Farnebäck	50.66	0	0.0270	40.45	0	0.0481

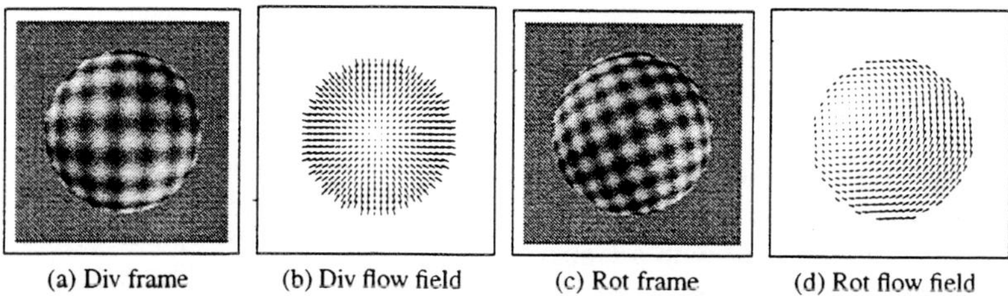

(a) Div frame (b) Div flow field (c) Rot frame (d) Rot flow field

Figure 3: Central frames of both div and rot sequences, and their true flow fields.

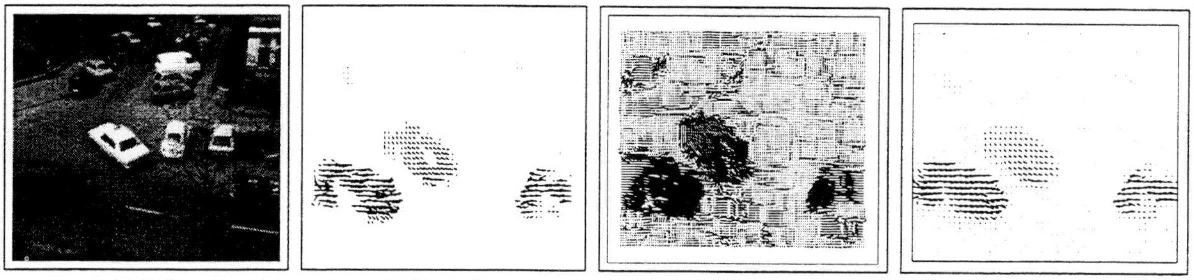

(a) Taxi (b) Taxi – Ye (c) Taxi – Sun (d) Taxi – Farnebäck

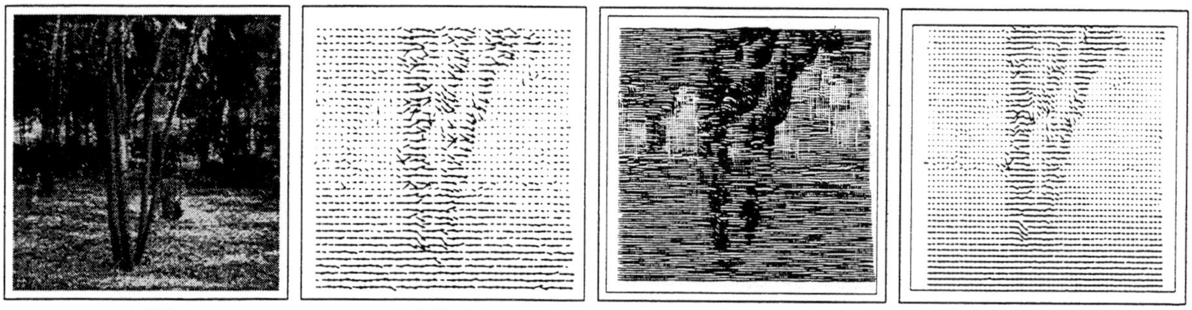

(e) SRI (f) SRI – Ye (g) SRI – Sun (h) SRI – Farnebäck

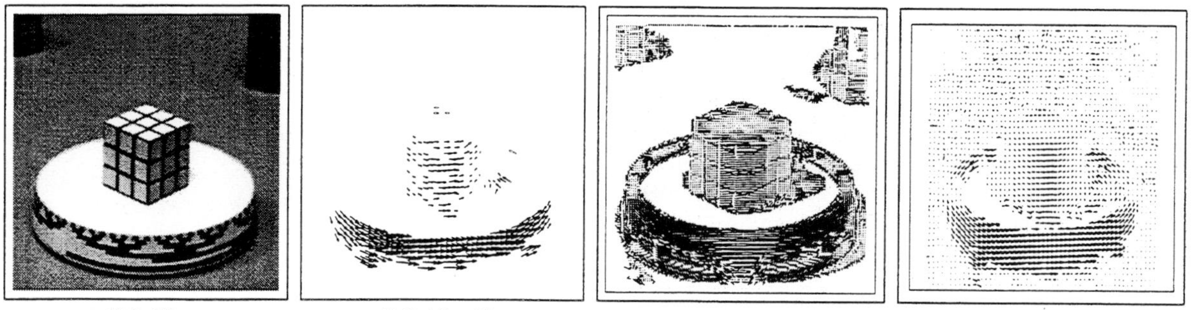

(i) Rubik (j) Rubik – Ye (k) Rubik – Sun (l) Rubik – Farnebäck

Figure 4: Image flow test sequences and flow field results.

Some Further Results of Experimental Comparison of Range Image Segmentation Algorithms

X. Jiang[1], K. Bowyer[2]
Y. Morioka[3], S. Hiura[3], K. Sato[3], S. Inokuchi[3]
M. Bock[4], C. Guerra[5,6]
R.E. Loke[7], J.M.H. du Buf[7]
[1]Department of Computer Science, University of Bern, Switzerland
[2]Department of Computer Science & Engineering, University of South Florida, Tampa, USA
[3]Department of Systems and Human Science, Osaka University, Japan
[4]Department of Statistics, Purdue University, West-Lafayette, USA
[5]Dipartimento di Elettronica e Informatica, Universita' di Padova, Padova, Italy
[6]Department of Computer Sciences, Purdue University, West-Lafayette, USA
[7]Vision Laboratory, University of Algarve, Faro, Portugal

Abstract

A range image segmentation contest was organized in conjunction with ICPR'2000. The goal is to continue the effort of experimentally evaluating range image segmentation algorithms initiated in [3, 4]. This paper summarizes the results of the contest.

1 Introduction

Typically, published range image segmentation methods are not evaluated using pixel-level ground truth in real images. Also, a direct comparison to other approaches is not a usual practice. This obvious problem motivated the recent development of a rigorous methodology for experimentally evaluating range image segmentation algorithms [3, 4]. It involves a large number of real range images with manually specified ground truth and a set of defined performance metrics. So far, six segmentation methods have been evaluated within this comparative framework.

In order to continue this effort, K. Bowyer and X. Jiang organized a range image segmentation contest in conjunction with ICPR'2000. The contest is based on the methodology developed in [3, 4] and therefore extends the set of segmentation algorithms that has already been evaluated there.

This paper summarizes the results of the contest. First, we briefly discuss the comparative framework. Then, the involved segmentation algorithms are described. Finally, the evaluation results and some discussions conclude the paper.

2 Comparative framework

The comparative framework consists of sets of real range images and performance metrics; for full details see [3, 4] or http://marathon.csee.usf.edu/seg-comp/SegComp.html. By considering and reasonably exploring the dimensions of the range image segmentation problem, three image sets were acquired: 40 images (512×512 8-bit pixels) using an ABW structured light scanner, 40 images (512×512 12-bit pixels) using a Perceptron laser range finder, and 60 images (480×640 8-bit pixels) using a K2T model GRF-2 structured light scanner. Although numerous methods to acquire range data have been demonstrated, these two types of sensors (structured light and time-of-flight) predominate. The ABW and Perceptron image set only contain planar surfaces, while curved surfaces are also included in the K2T image set[1]. All images of the three sets have region ground truth that was created manually.

Given a machine segmentation and the ground truth of a range image, five performance metrics are defined: number of correct detections, over-segmentations, under-segmentations, missed regions, and noise regions. In deciding region classifications a threshold $T, 0.5 < T \leq 1.0$, is needed to reflect the strictness of the decisions.

Each image set is disjointly divided into a set of training images and a set of test images. The number of training images is 10 (ABW), 10 (Perceptron), and 20 (K2T), respectively. The training images are used to find the optimal

[1]The K2T data contains an objectionable level of artifact, and is being replaced with data from a Cyberware scanner.

parameters of a segmentation algorithm. Using these optimal parameters, the segmentation algorithm is run on all test images. The performance metrics are computed based upon the segmentation results of the test images and serve as the basis for a comparison of different algorithms.

3 Experimental methods

In the range image segmentation contest we experienced phenomena similar to that reported in earlier studies [3, 4] and the JISCT stereo evaluation [1], in which only three of five research groups completed the testing of their algorithms. Initially, more than twenty groups have shown their potential interest in the contest. Finally, only three groups provided results. At least one other group actively looked at participating, but did not complete the evaluation for some reason. Also, only results on the ABW image set are currently available from the three final groups.

Compared to the four segmentation methods evaluated in [3], the three algorithms here represent substantially different design choices. These algorithms and their parameter selection are briefly described in this section.

3.1 Segmentation algorithms

3.1.1 OU segmentation algorithm

The segmentation algorithm OU (developed at Osaka University) is based on the analysis of intersection of the scene by arbitrary planes. At first, the range image is divided into two hemi-spaces by an imaginary plane, then we binarize each pixel on the range image. If the scene consists of polyhedra, the binarized image can be represented by the set of polygons. On that image, the issue of plane detection is turned into edge detection on the binary image. We can use various 2-D image analysis techniques such as edge-point tracking or Hough transform for that task. We applied Hough transform for derivative image to do it, because test images contain much noise. We can also use the topological information in the binary image for end-point determination and grouping detected line segments.

The imaginary plane is translated step by step and we obtain the set of line segments. To accelerate this algorithm, we limit the voting space for Hough transform using information of prior line detection. Then we make planes by grouping line segments: If two lines share a plane, the lines are parallel to each other and have a close distance. Therefore we classify all line segments into several groups using gradient, distance and arrangement of end-points of the lines. We can also exploit the topological cue of binary image. For example, if we cope with a tetrahedron, triangle or quadrangle is observed on each binary image and one polygon is entirely included in another polygon.

Finally the range image is filled by polygons which are generated from two neighboring lines. Against the case of fragmentation of polygons (usually concave polygons cause that problem), we evaluate the normal vectors of each planar surface and unify them if the difference of normal vectors of neighboring planar surfaces is small enough.

3.1.2 PPU segmentation algorithm

The PPU segmentation algorithm (developed at Purdue University and Padova University) combines several strategies for generating a master list of different planes and their associated sets of range image elements that combine to make up the description of the image. The three main procedures are all based on random sampling to reduce the computational complexity of the search. Each procedure has a distinct method for generating a candidate plane and a distinct objective function for evaluating the candidate and selecting the "best" plane among the candidates. (The number of candidate planes generated by a procedure is set by a parameter that changes as the size of the master list increases.) Each plane on the master list has an associated distinct set of range image elements labeled for the plane.

The first two procedures *CoplanarLines* and *LinePoint* depend on the image only through its edge points which are generated by an edge detector in a preprocessing phase. The parameters of candidate planes are found by randomly selecting a pair of proper subsets of the edge points: two coplanar lines, either parallel or not, for CoplanarLines, and a line and a point not belonging to the line, for LinePoint. In both cases, the objective function for a candidate plane is the number of edge points that belong to the plane, i.e. are within ϵ distance from the plane, where ϵ is a small constant set to 1 in the current implementation.

The third procedure *AlternativeStrategy* generates a candidate plane that fits a small window of range points unlabeled by previously selected planes in the master list. It uses as objective function the total number of unlabeled range points that are within ϵ distance from the candidate plane. This procedure tends to be computationally intensive due to the lengthy computation of the objective function. Thus, it is invoked only when the other two procedures produce "best" planes that are not significant, as described below.

At each iteration, to detect a new plane for the master list the three main procedures are invoked sequentially in a given order; the next one executed only when the previous ones do not detect a significant plane. The significance of a plane selected as "best" by a procedure is expressed as the percentage (among the currently unlabeled range points) of range points that are within a given distance of the plane. When this percentage is above a certain threshold S, the detected plane is accepted for the master list and a set associated with the new plane is assigned its new label; otherwise, the plane is discarded. The threshold S is updated dynamically during the processing.

Once the parameters of the new plane for the master list are found at a given iteration, the tentative set of range points associated with the new plane becomes all the points in the image which are within a given distance of the plane. Thus the plane is expanded over the entire image and all the fragments of the same surface in the image are labeled as belonging to the same plane. The fragments are generally due to occlusion but may also correspond to different faces of the same concave object or of different objects. Labeling conflicts may arise because some points in the tentative set may be close to another plane on the master list and may also occur in the set of points labeled for the other plane. A conflict at a range point in the tentative set is resolved in favor of the label with the highest number of occurrences in a small window centered at the point.

It is important to note that the labeling scheme here is unlike most existing segmentation algorithms that assign different labels to unconnected fragments of the same plane. The ground truth images used in the experiments for this contest follow the common scheme of having different labels for the fragments. As a consequence, the comparison of the outputs produced by the PPU segmentation algorithm with the ground truth images available in these experiments may not be meaningful for some images.

3.1.3 UA segmentation algorithm

The segmentation algorithm UA (developed at University of Algarve) performs a fast hierarchical processing in a multiresolution pyramid, or quadtree, based on [5, 6]. It must be noted that the method has only very recently been adapted for range images. Its current disadvantage is the information loss which is caused by linearly combining the components of the surface normal vector. This is needed because this method presumes a one-dimensional feature space. Of course this is a topic for future research. The method consists of the following 6 steps.

First, a quadtree of L levels is built with at the base (level 0) the original range image on a regular grid. Low-resolution depth data at each higher level are determined by a lowpass filtering of depths at the lower level in non-overlapping blocks of size 2×2. This reduces the noise, allowing the estimation of accurate normal vectors at the highest level $L-1$.

Second, each pixel in the tree is set to $W_x n_x + W_y n_y + W_z n_z$, where W_x, W_y and W_z are weights and $[n_x\ n_y\ n_z]^T$ is the pixel's normal vector. The normal vector is computed from the orientation of a plane spanned by the Cartesian coordinates of the pixel and 2 of its 4-connected neighbours, such that the 3 pixels form a small triangle. From all combinations the triangle with the smallest maximum depth between its pixels is used in order to avoid the use of data from multiple surface patches.

Third, a new filter technique is applied in order to increase the homogeneity of the data and to reduce the noise. It consists of an adjustment and a smoothing, which are performed at each level, starting at level $L-1$ and ending at level 0. In the adjustment, data at a lower resolution are used to determine those at the higher resolution. Pixels are set to $\Delta(d_l - \mu) + f_{l+1}$, with d_l being the value of a pixel at the lower level l $(0 \leq l < L-1)$, f_{l+1} the value of its parent pixel at level $l+1$, μ the mean of the pixel values in a $S_p \times S_p$ neighbourhood of the pixel and Δ a scaling factor controlling the contrast. In the smoothing, N_f iterations of an edge-preserving homogeneity filter are performed using 8 different configurations.

Fourth, at level $L-1$, data clusters are determined using the local-centroid algorithm [6], with a mask size S_c. Thereafter, the segmentation at level $L-1$ is obtained by setting each pixel to the label of its nearest cluster.

Fifth, starting at level $L-1$ and ending at level 1, the segmentation at each lower level is obtained by refining the boundary. For each boundary pixel a refinement is performed which consists of calculations at 2 adjacent levels l and $l-1$: At level l, the orientation of the vector orthogonal to the boundary is determined. Then, at level $l-1$, the data in the neighbourhood of each child of the boundary voxel are convolved with a one-dimensional filter of size S_f, which is positioned according to this orientation. The label which is allocated to each child is determined using a nearest-cluster criterion between its filter response and the clusters.

Sixth, at level 0, a component labelling is performed, because the segmentation may contain regions which have the same label, but which are not spatially connected. All regions smaller than a minimum region size S_r are disregarded.

In future research we plan to apply a multi-dimensional clustering together with an adaptation of the filter techniques used in the tree.

3.2 Selected parameters

3.2.1 Parameters for the OU algorithm

We use five parameters. T0 is the translation step of imaginary plane. We set the imaginary plane perpendicular to the optical axis, and set T0 = 1.0 because the value of each pixel on range image is integer. Parameter T1 is used for Hough transform. If the peak value of voting space exceeds T1, we detect the line. To detect short line segment, initially we use T1 = 150[pixel] then decrease to 10. T2 and T3 are used for grouping line segments. T2 is the threshold of direction of the line segment and T3 distance. We use

T2=5.0[degree] and T3=20 [pixel]. T4 is the threshold of unifying fragmented surfaces, T4=3.0[degree].

3.2.2 Parameters for the PPU algorithm

Several parameters are used in the program. A number of them deal with the random sampling paradigm and are used to specify the number of trials required to obtain a reasonable estimate of a parametric shape.

A few of the parameters are described here. The procedure CoplanarLines uses the parameter *nl* as an upper bound for the number of lines extracted from the set of edge points and used to recover a plane. *nl* is set to 20 in the program. Each such line is the best line found in the set of edge points. After it is detected, the edge points close to it are removed from the list and the line detection procedure is repeated. To determine the best line in a set of n edge points, n out of the $(n \times (n-1))/2$ possible lines through pairs of edge points are randomly selected and examined. Other parameters are used to evaluate the goodness of the planar fit.

3.2.3 Parameters for the UA algorithm

There are 10 parameters for this segmentation algorithm which can be divided into 2 groups of importance: L, W_x, W_y, W_z, S_c and Δ, S_p, N_f, S_f, S_r. For the ABW imagery, different parameter combinations were run on all 10 training images. First, in order to determine L, W_x, W_y, W_z and S_c, all 1920 combinations of $L = [1,2,3]$, $W_a = W_b = W_c = [0,1,2,4]$ and $S_c = [59,69,79,89,99,109,119,129,139,149]$ were used with $\Delta = 2$, $S_p = 3$, $N_f = 1$, $S_f = 7$ and $S_r = 160$. Second, all 144 combinations of $\Delta = [1,2,4,8]$, $S_p = [3,5,7]$, $N_f = [1,2,3]$ and $S_f = [3,7,11,15]$ with L, W_x, W_y, W_z and S_c set to the determined values and S_r set to 160. For each parameter set average metrics were created by running the compare tool on the training images using the comparison thresholds [0.51,0.6,0.7,0.75,0.8,0.9,0.95]. The results which scored the highest average measure in correct detections were selected. The associated parameters were $L=2$, $W_x=1$, $W_y=4$, $W_z=1$, $S_c=79$, $\Delta=2$, $S_p=3$, $N_f=2$, $S_f=11$ and $S_r=160$.

4 Experimental results

Figure 1 shows the scores of the five performance metrics for the three segmentation algorithms, graphed against the compare tool tolerance T. The scores at a moderate tolerance $T = 0.8$ are tabulated in Table 1. At the weakest tolerance ($T = 0.51$) the segmentation algorithms scored between 39% and 80% correct detections on the ABW imagery. At $T = 0.8$ the best score for correct detection was 65%.

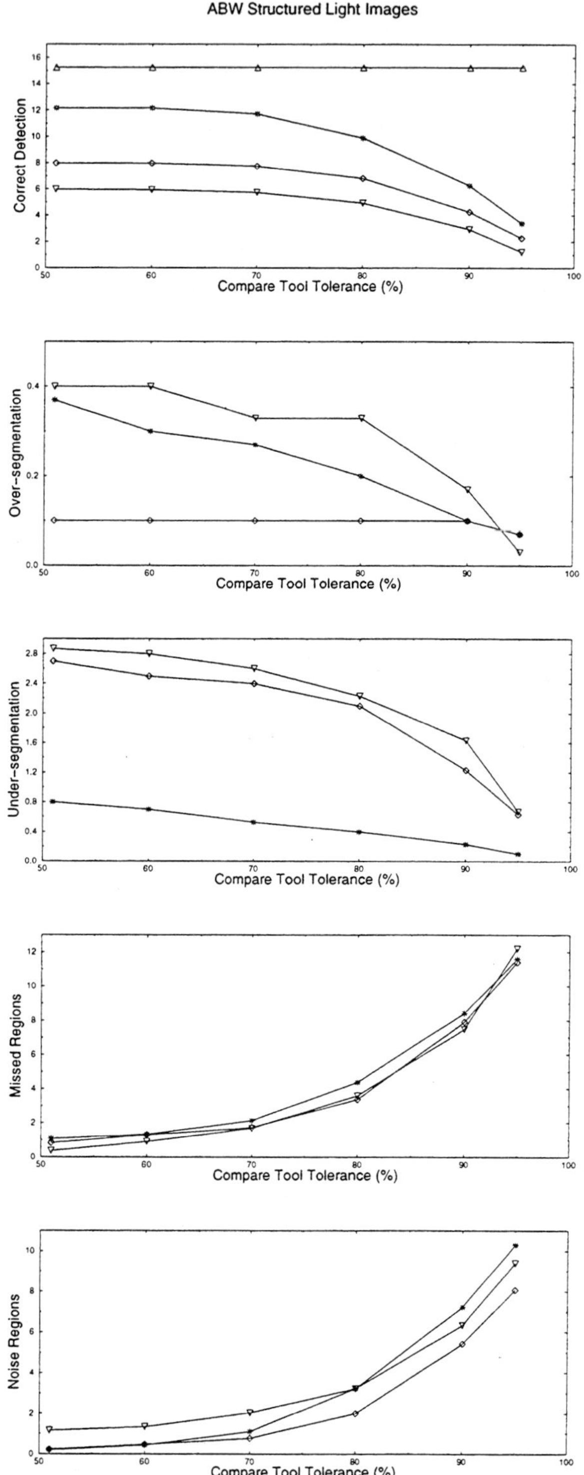

Figure 1. Performance metrics for 30 ABW test images. Symbols: △ = average number of regions per image (maximum number of correct detections), ∗ = OU, ◇ = PPU, ▽ = UA.

Table 1. Average results of all three segmentation algorithms on 30 ABW test images at $T = 0.8$.

algorithm	GT regions	correct detection	over-segmentation	under-segmentation	missed	noise
OU	15.2	9.8	0.2	0.4	4.4	3.2
PPU	15.2	6.8	0.1	2.1	3.4	2.0
UA	15.2	4.9	0.3	2.2	3.6	3.2

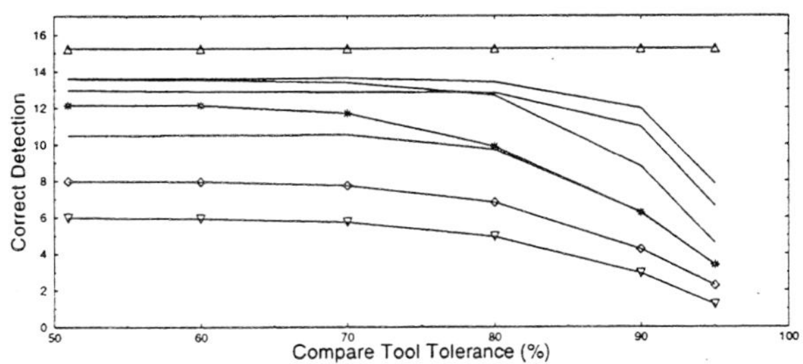

Figure 2. Performance metrics for 30 ABW test images. The four unlabeled curves correspond to the four segmentation algorithms evaluated in [3].

Substantial high under-segmentation scores can be observed for PPU and UA. For PPU the reason is that, at least in its current implementation, disconnected parallel/coplanar surface patches are labeled as a single region (this problem may be solved by a postprocessing step). For UA the high under-segmentation scores result from the mentioned information loss which is caused by linearly combining the components of the surface normal vector.

Compared to the results from the earlier study [3], no real improvement could be achieved, as illustrated in Figure 2, where the correct detection scores for the four segmentation algorithms evaluated there are drawn. Partly, this is caused by the under-segmentation problem discussed above.

The average processing times for the algorithms on ABW data, per image, were 6 hours (OU) on a Pentium-III 500MHz computer with 256 MB memory, 4 minutes (PPU) on a Sun Ultra 5, and 28.9 seconds (UA) on an SGI Origin 200QC server using only 1 of the 4 available CPUs.

5 Discussion

The effort of experimentally evaluating range image segmentation algorithms, as initiated in [3], is continued by a contest in conjunction with ICPR'2000. Three research groups provided results on the ABW image set. The number of evaluated segmentation algorithms on this set is increased from four to seven now. Although no real improvement compared to earlier results could be achieved, these new algorithms are based on design choices that are substantially different from those from [3]. It would certainly be interesting to make a new comparison after some obvious enhancement is done. In particular, a significant improvement of the UA algorithm is expected when the one-dimensional clustering would be replaced by a multi-dimensional one. Also, the issue of disconnected GT regions on the same surface should be accounted for.

Acknowledgements

Professor Bowyer's work is supported by National Science Foundation grant IIS-9731821.

References

[1] R.C. Bolles *et al.*, The JISCT stereo evaluation. *Proc. of Image Understanding Workshop*, Washington, D.C., 263–274, 1993.

[2] M. A. Fischler and R. C. Bolles, Random sample consensus: a paradigm for model fitting with applications to image analysis and automated cartography, *CACM*, 24: 381–395, 1981.

[3] A. Hoover *et al.*, An experimental comparison of range image segmentation algorithms, *IEEE Transactions on PAMI*, 18(7): 673–689, 1996.

[4] M.W. Powell *et al.*, Comparing curved-surface range image segmenters, *Proc. of the 6th ICCV*, Bombay, India, 286–291, 1998.

[5] R.E. Loke and J.M.H. du Buf, Hierarchical 3D data segmentation by shape-based boundary refinement in an octree using orientation-adaptive filtering, *Tech. Report UALG-ISACS-TR03*, March 1998, in prep. for publication.

[6] R. Wilson and M. Spann, *Image Segmentation and Uncertainty*, Research Studies Press Ltd., Letchworth, 1988.

— Notes —

Index of Authors – Track 4

— Notes —

Press Activities Board

Revised 9 November 1999